Chain Saw

SERVICE MANUAL ■ 10TH EDITION

Intertec Publishing
P.O. Box 12901 ■ Overland Park, KS 66282-2901
Phone: 800-262-1954 Fax: 800-633-6219

Library of Congress Catalog Card Number 99-62953

This book can be recycled. Please remove cover.

Cover photo courtesy of Stihl Inc.
536 Viking Drive
Virginia Beach, VA 23452

Chain Saw

SERVICE MANUAL ■ 10TH EDITION

Chain Saw Manufacturers:

- Allis-Chalmers
- Alpina
- Castor
- Clinton
- Danarm
- John Deere
- Dolmar
- Echo
- Frontier
- Green Machine
- Homelite
- Husqvarna
- Jonsered
- Lombard
- Makita
- Massey-Ferguson
- McCulloch
- Olympyk
- Partner
- Pioneer
- Pioneer/Partner
- Poulan
- ProKut
- RedMax
- Remington
- Roper
- Shindaiwa
- Solo
- Stihl
- Tanaka

Intertec Book Division

President Raymond E. Maloney
Vice President, Book Division Ted Marcus

EDITORIAL

Director
Randy Stephens

Senior Editor
Mark Jacobs

Editors
Mike Hall
Tom Fournier
Frank Craven
Paul Wyatt

Associate Editor
Robert Sokol

Technical Writers
Ron Wright
Ed Scott
George Parise
Mark Rolling
Michael Morlan

Warehouse and Production Manager
Terry Distin

Editorial Production Manager
Shirley Renicker

Senior Editorial Production Coordinator
Dylan Goodwin

Editorial Production Coordinator
Melissa Carle

Editorial Production Assistants
Renee Colley
Greg Araujo
Dennis Conrow
Shara Pierceall
Susan Hartington

Advertising Coordinator
Jodi Donohoe

Advertising Production Specialist
Kim Sawalich

Technical Illustrators
Steve Amos
Robert Caldwell
Mitzi McCarthy
Michael St. Clair

MARKETING/SALES AND ADMINISTRATION

Product Development Manager
Michael Yim

Marketing Assistant
Melissa Abbott

Art Director
Al Terwelp

Associate Art Director
Chris Paxton

Sales Manager/Marine
Dutch Sadler

Sales Manager/Manuals
Ted Metzger

Sales Manager/Motorcycles
Matt Tusken

Sales Coordinator
Paul Cormaci

Telephone Sales Supervisor
Terri Cannon

Telemarketing Sales Representatives
Susan Kay
Joelle Stephens

Customer Service/Fulfillment Manager
Caryn Bair

Fulfillment Coordinator
Susan Kohlmeyer

Customer Service Supervisor
Mildred Cofield

Customer Service Representative
Angela Stephens

The following books and guides are published by Intertec Publishing.

CLYMER SHOP MANUALS
Boat Motors and Drives
Motorcycles and ATVs
Snowmobiles
Personal Watercraft

ABOS/INTERTEC/CLYMER BLUE BOOKS AND TRADE-IN GUIDES
Recreational Vehicles
Outdoor Power Equipment
Agricultural Tractors
Lawn and Garden Tractors
Motorcycles and ATVs
Snowmobiles and Personal Watercraft
Boats and Motors

AIRCRAFT BLUEBOOK-PRICE DIGEST
Airplanes
Helicopters

AC-U-KWIK DIRECTORIES
The Corporate Pilot's Airport/FBO Directory
International Manager's Edition
Jet Book

I&T SHOP SERVICE MANUALS
Tractors

CONTENTS

SAW CHAIN, BAR, SPROCKET AND CLUTCH SERVICE

CARBURETOR SERVICE

ENGINE SERVICE

CHAIN SAW SECTIONS

ROPER

SHINDAIWA

SOLO

STIHL

TANAKA

DUAL DIMENSIONS

This service manual provides specifications in both the U.S. Customary and Metric (SI) systems of measurement. The first specification is given in the measuring system perceived by us to be the preferred system when servicing a particular component, while the second specification (given in parenthesis) is the converted measurement. For instance, a specification of "0.011 inch (0.28 mm)" would indicate that we feel the preferred measurement, in this instance, is the U.S. system of measurement and the metric equivalent of 0.011 inch is 0.28 mm.

Saw Chain, Guide Bars and Sprockets

SAW CHAIN

CHAIN NOMENCLATURE

Note component parts of chain shown in Fig. CM1 exploded view. The cutters remove material being sawed while saw chain is driven by engagement of drive links with engine sprocket. Side links connect drive links and ride against bar. Special chain types such as anti-kickback or ripping chain may use components designed as a safety feature or for specialized cutting.

CHAIN SIZE

Saw chain size is determined by chain pitch and gage. Pitch is the distance between alternate chain rivets divided by half as shown in Fig. CM2. Common pitch sizes are 1/4, 3/8, 0.404, 7/16 and 1/2 inch. Gage is the drive link thickness measured at the tang as shown in Fig. CM3. Common gage sizes are 0.050, 0.058 and 0.063 inch.

Chain size must be matched with engine drive sprocket and bar sprocket, if so equipped. Mismatching chain and sprocket will result in damage to both components as well as possible damage to engine should chain break.

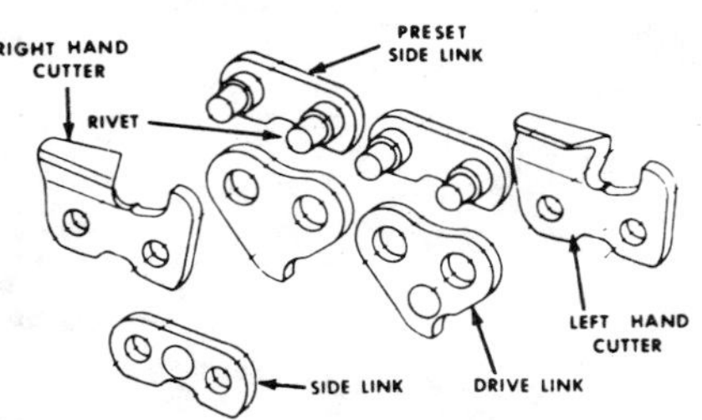

Fig. CM1—Exploded view of typical section of saw chain.

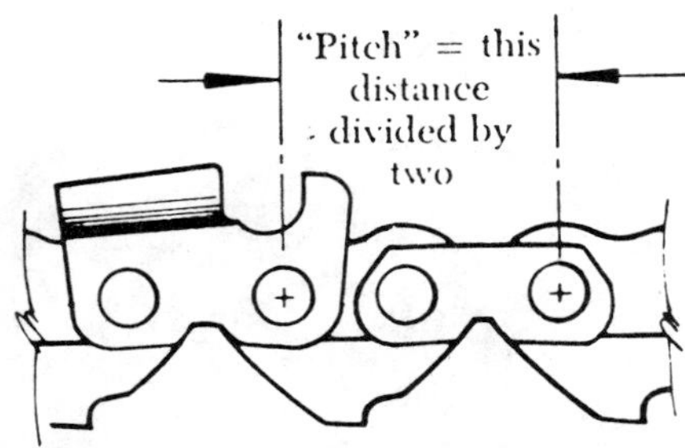

Fig. CM2—Chain pitch is measured between rivet pins as shown above.

CHAIN TYPES

The two common types of chain cutters are chipper and chisel. Note in Fig. CM4 that cutting edge of chipper cutter is round while cutting edge of chisel cutter is square. Different configurations of chisel and chipper cutters may be used to meet specific cutting requirements. Refer to subsequent CHAIN SHARPENING section for procedures and tools used when sharpening chipper and chisel chain types.

Anti-kickback saw chain uses drive links or side links which extend as they travel around tip of bar thereby preventing contact between cutter link and wood. Refer to Fig. CM5. Possibility of saw kickback is lessened if cutter contact is prevented as chain travels around bar nose.

CHAIN BREAK IN, TENSION AND LUBRICATION

BREAKING IN A NEW CHAIN. As with any machine or accessory containing moving parts, the first hour or so of operation can make a great difference to the length of life. Careful attention to the instructions for breaking in and making tension adjustments can greatly add to the life of the chain.

The following instructions are important and will add to the life of saw chain:

1. If possible, soak chain in oil bath before use and between uses.
2. Install chain properly with recommended chain tension.
3. Run chain at slow speed for about 5 minutes, giving it plenty of oil.
4. Stop engine and readjust chain tension.
5. Recheck tension until chain is fully broken in.
6. Keep chain well lubricated when in use.
7. Keep chain sharp.
8. Correct chain tension, especially on bar lengths of 32 inches and over, is important to prevent the chain jumping the bar and causing damage to the equipment and loss of time to the operator.

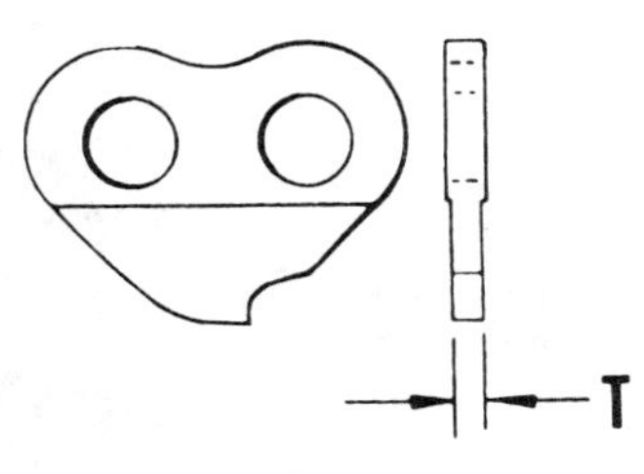

Fig. CM3—Saw chain gage size is thickness of drive link tang (T).

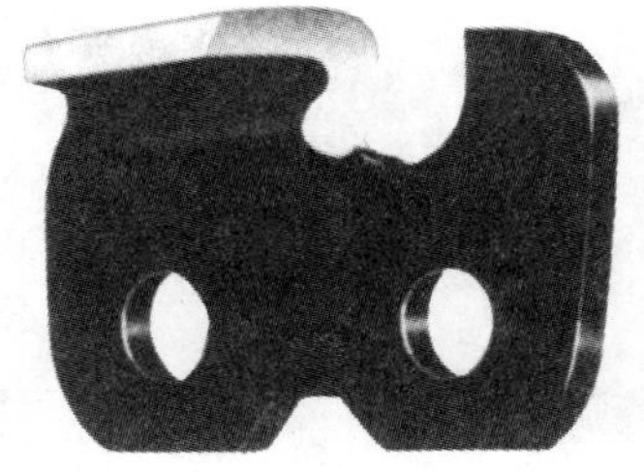

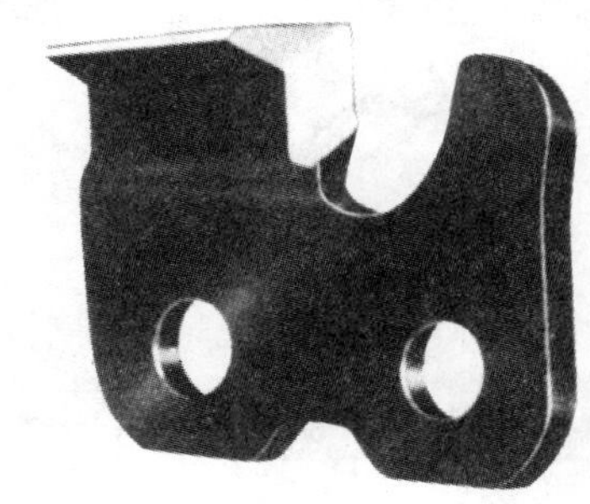

Fig. CM4—View of chipper and chisel cutters.

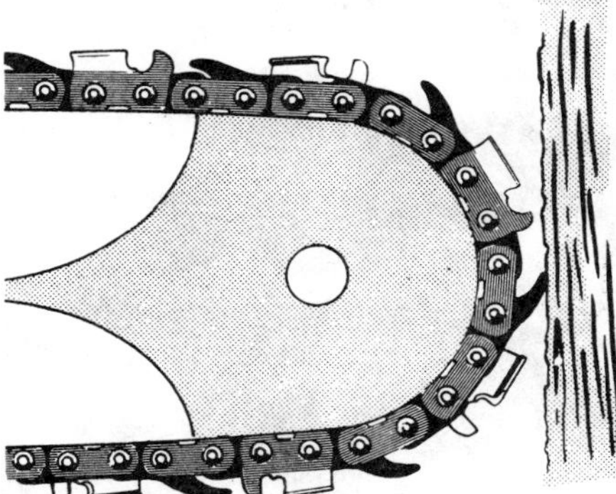

Fig. CM5—Protruding drive links of anti-kickback chain prevent cutter contact with wood as cutters travel around bar nose.

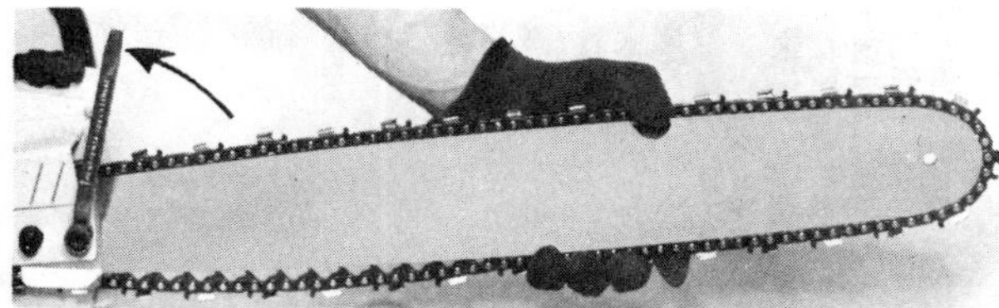

Fig. CM6—Loosen bar retaining nuts prior to chain adjustment.

CHAIN TENSION ADJUSTMENTS. Correct tension is very important. It will increase the life of the saw and chain. Loose tension is a major cause of saw chain problems; it ruins chain, bar and sprocket. Check chain tension often, but make adjustments only when the attachments have cooled off. To insure correct tension follow steps shown in Figs. CM6, CM7, CM8, CM9, CM10 and CM11.

It is well known that over-tension, or a tight chain, will lead to excessive wear on both the guide bar and the side links of the chain, thus shortening the life of the bar and chain. The chain can also damage the guide bar if it is too loose. The chain will damage the guide bar immediately behind the stellite tip by a pounding operation. Further damage at the tail end of the bar can be caused by excessive pounding as the chain arcs off the sprocket. These pounding forces will cause stress in the chain components, which may eventually break, or the pounding may cause the chain to have stiff links. A loose chain may jump off of the bar, damaging the drive links, or wear the rails of the guide bar itself.

LUBRICATION. The importance of proper lubrication of the chain and guide bar cannot be over-stressed. Each rivet in the chain should be considered as a bearing and must be lubricated. This is particularly important in direct drive or high speed chains. The same applies to bearing surface between the chain and the guide bar.

Clean chain in solvent before and after filing, then give chain an oil bath for proper lubrication. DO NOT leave it all to the oil pump. Be sure to use the correct weight of clean oil (not reclaimed crankcase oil) to allow maximum chain lubrication under all cutting conditions and varying temperatures. Good quality chain oil winter or summer grade is recommended. A good grade SAE 10 to SAE 40 motor oil may also be used, depending upon prevailing temperature.

Adequate lubrication is essential to assure the maximum life of the chain. Be generous with the application of oil to the bar and chain. Thin the oil with kerosene or fuel oil in cold weather.

CHAIN MAINTENANCE

The chain saw engine may be perfectly maintained, but, if the chain does not function properly, it is impossible to obtain satisfactory results. The power head exists merely as a convenient method of moving a saw chain in

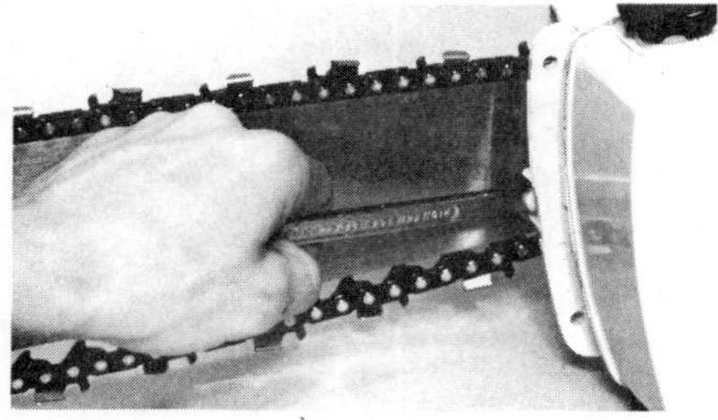

Fig. CM7—Tighten chain adjusting screw.

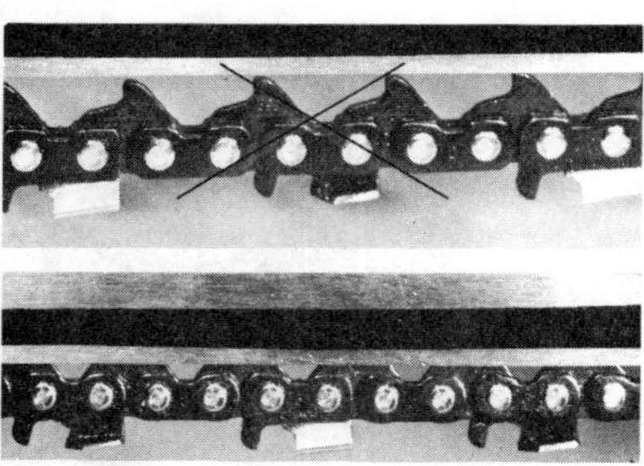

Fig. CM8—For correct tension tighten chain adjusting screw until chain just touches bottom bar rails. Chain on roller and sprocket nose bars must be tighter.

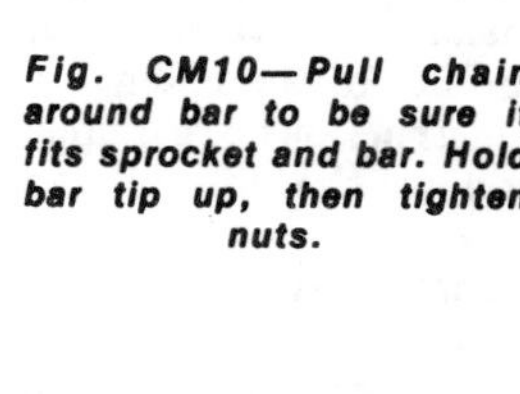

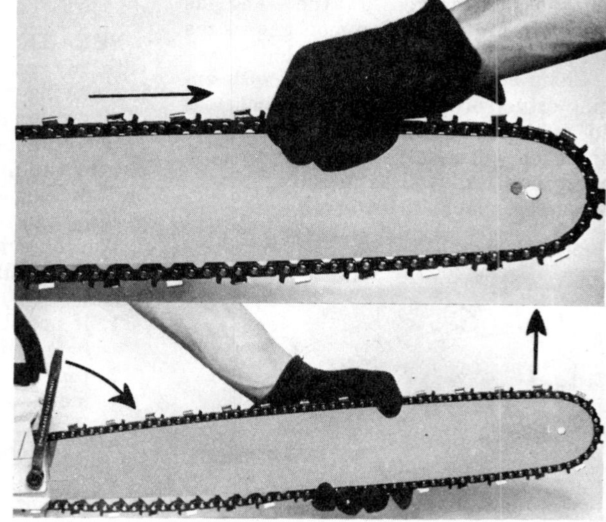

Fig. CM10—Pull chain around bar to be sure it fits sprocket and bar. Hold bar tip up, then tighten nuts.

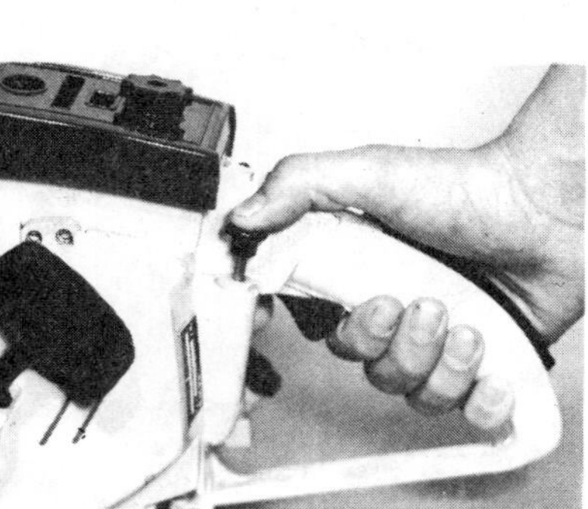

Fig. CM9—Make sure chain is always properly lubricated.

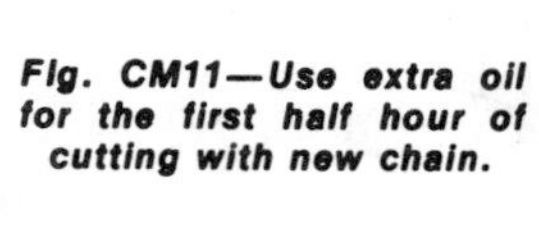

Fig. CM11—Use extra oil for the first half hour of cutting with new chain.

order to cut wood. Correct maintenance and operating conditions are essential to insure the proper functioning of your chain and hence the chain saw.

CHAIN SHARPENING

CHIPPER CHAIN. A full round file (not a rat tail) is used to sharpen the chipper-type chains. For good results, the procedures shown in Figs. CM12, CM13. CM14 and CM15 should be adopted.

For average sawing, maintain the filing angles shown in Figs. CM16 and CM17 by holding the file in the position shown in Figs. CM12 through CM15. Do not allow the file to drag on the backstroke, and rotate the file occasionally to increase file life. Approximately 1/10th of the file diameter should be above the cutting edge of the cutter. If the distance is less than this, the cutting edge will be too blunt; if distance is greater, a rapidly wearing feather edge will result. For convenience, file alternate (either all right hand or left hand) cutters; then reverse the chain in the vise or turn the saw around and file the remaining cutters. All cutters must be filed alike and the same amount to keep the cutting edges at the same height. Check this by laying a file or straightedge across the tops of the cutters. Continue filing high cutters in normal manner until all cutters are same height.

Suggested file sizes for standard (chipper-type) chain:

Chain Pitch	Round File Size
1/4"	1/8"
3/8"	3/16"
.404"	7/32"
7/16", 1/2"	1/4"

Different size and design chain will require different file sizes. If manufacturer's recommendations are not available, refer to the above chart.

After filing the cutting edges, check the depth gages, or riders as they are sometimes called, for correct distance below the cutting edges (Fig. CM18). Depth gages are generally checked with a tool that is pre-set for the desired distance, as the one shown in Figs. CM19 and CM20, or a tool with an adjustable setting.

Average depth gage (joint) setting for standard chain:

Chain Pitch	Depth Gage Setting
1/4"	.020"
3/8"	.020"
.404"	.030"
7/16"	.030"
1/2"	.030"-.040"

The normal top plate filing angle of 35° and the depth gage distances for different pitch chain have been determined to be the most satisfactory for general sawing. However, the woodsman may, through trial and error, find the most suitable depth gage distance for a particular condition. No specific figures can be given due to the variety of sawing conditions, but the following

Fig. CM12—File from inside to outside of cutter.

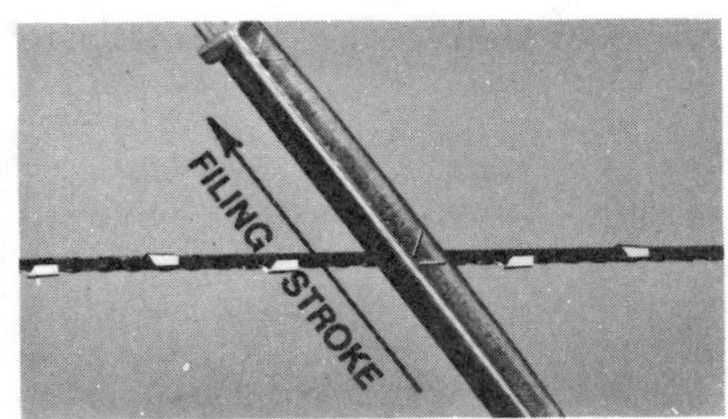

Fig. CM13—Place file holder on cutter; keep mark on holder parallel with chain.

Fig. CM14—Hold file level. Press against cutter and make 2 or 3 light strokes forward.

Fig. CM15—Sharpen all cutters on one side of chain. Move to other side and file all cutters on opposite side of chain.

CORRECT

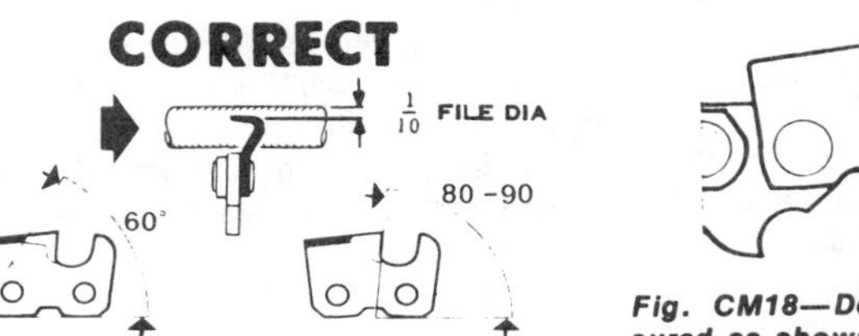

WRONG

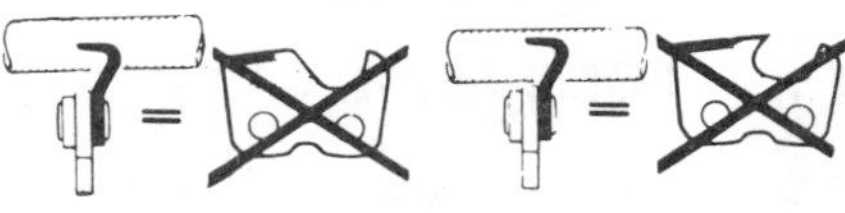

Fig. CM16—Correct shape of cutter will help chain to cut faster and remain sharp longer. Back slope is caused by file held too high. Hooked edge is caused by file held too low.

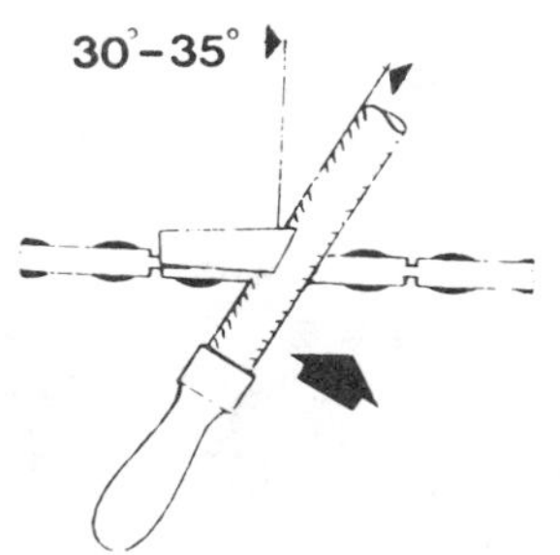

Fig. CM17—Angle of cutting face should be 35 degrees as shown. Insufficient top angle causes chain to cut roughly and dull very quickly. Excessive top angle causes side thrust and wear on sides of drive lugs.

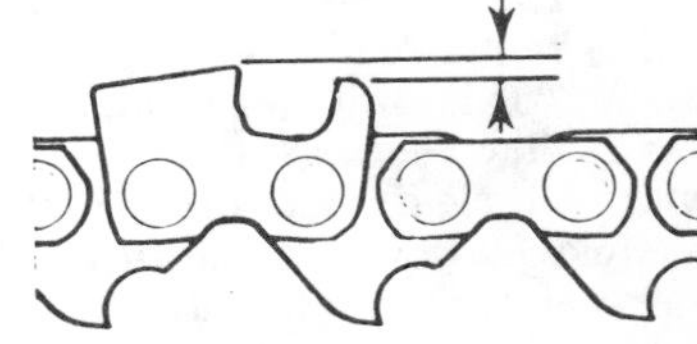

Fig. CM18—Depth gage clearance is measured as shown. This is also known as joint clearance.

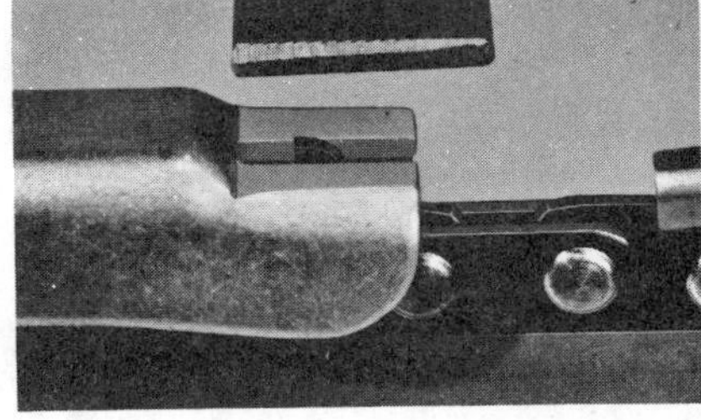

Fig. CM19—If depth gage projects above tool, file depth gage level with tool.

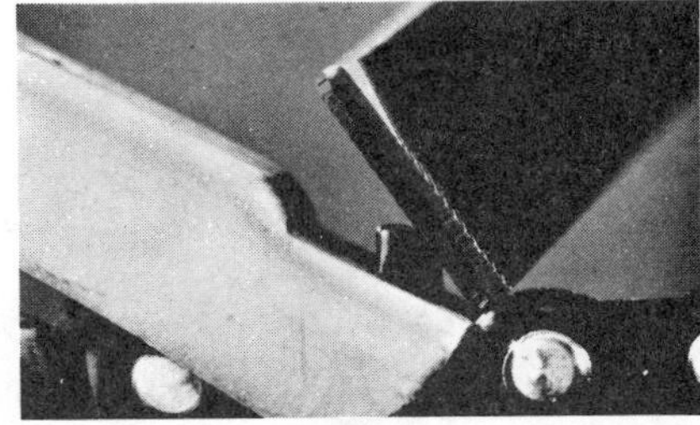

Fig. CM20—Round off front corner of depth gage. Tilt tool to protect top of cutter.

information can be used as a guide.

A. On larger horsepower saws and saws with slow chain speeds, the depth gage distance may be increased, which will allow the cutter to take a larger chip. The depth gage distance should be decreased on small saws and direct drive saws.

B. When cutting continually in soft woods, the depth gage distance can be increased somewhat.

C. When cutting hard woods, frozen or resin timber, the depth gage distance should be decreased.

When sharpening the cutting edges on the saw chain, the drive link tangs should also be sharpened to keep the guide groove clean, and any burrs on the sides of the drive link tangs should be removed.

CHISEL. Refer to Fig. CM4 for view of chisel type saw chain. To sharpen chisel chain a bevel or round file is used, depending on manufacturer. Hold file at a 10° angle as shown in View B of Fig. CM21. Note top and side plate angles in Fig. CM22. Refer to CHIPPER CHAIN section for depth gage settings.

GULLETS. The gullet is the open area between the depth gage and the side plate. The gullet should be cleaned out with a round file before every fifth sharpening. This will keep the gullet open and allow better chip clearance and more efficient side plate cutting action. Hold file level as shown in Fig. CM23 and at a 20° angle with cutter.

REPAIRS

Saw chain repairs are accomplished by removing damaged links and installing new links which requires disconnecting chain (chain breaking). Use of a chain breaker is the preferred method of removing chain rivets when disconnecting a chain. When a chain breaker is not available, such as at the work site, file off the rivet head and drive out the rivet using a sharp punch. A small chisel or screwdriver may be used to spread side links if rivet is not completely cleared.

Rivet spinning tools are available to install rivets when assembling chain links. If a spinner is not available, then a ball peen hammer may be used if special care is taken. DO NOT strike the rivet head too hard. This can cause a fracture in the rivet drum. The rivet can be peened over on the outside circumference with light taps of the hammer. The rivet should not have a flat appearance caused by pounding the rivet and making it spread from the center. Rivets that are pounded flat will not have enough strength around the circumference. See Figs. CM24 and CM25.

CHAIN TROUBLE DIAGNOSIS

If the chain is not performing satisfactorily:

1. Remove chain from bar.
2. Clean with solvent to remove pitch and resin.
3. Compare chain with the illustrations and list shown in accompanying table.
4. Repair as indicated.

GUIDE BARS

SOLID NOSE BARS

Guide rails are sometimes split from the bar being pinched while the saw is hung up in a cut. Splits of two inches long or less can be repaired by using ordinary welding methods on bars with non-hardened rails. Repairing splits on bars with hardened rails requires special equipment for re-hardening the rails.

Small kinks or bends in guide bars can be removed by laying the bar on the large true anvil or other similar work surface and using light hammer blows to bring the bar back into shape. See Fig. CM26. Technique is very similar to straightening other flat metal pieces.

Use a file to funnel the entrance to the guide rail groove of the bar as

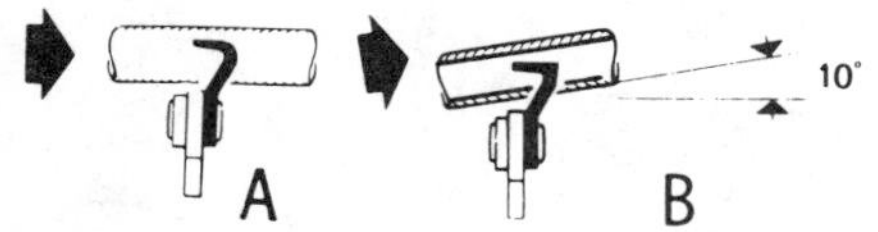

Fig. CM21—Hold file level for chipper chain as shown in View A. File must be held at 10 degrees for chisel chain as shown in View B.

Fig. CM23—Before every fifth sharpening, clean out gullets with round file. Hold file level and at 20 degree angle to cutter.

Fig. CM24—Rivets can be installed using a ball peen if carefully done.

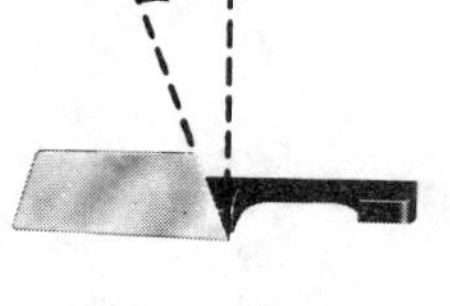

Top Plate Filing Angle 20°. Gradually increase angle as cutter is filed back.

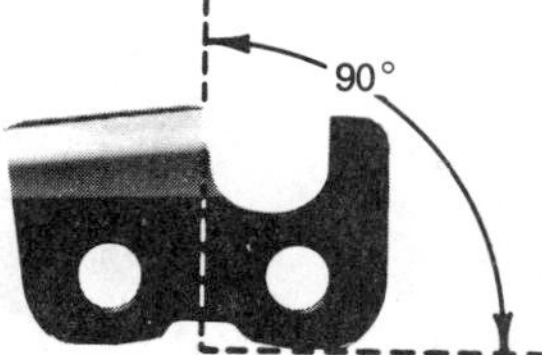

Side Plate Angle 90°.

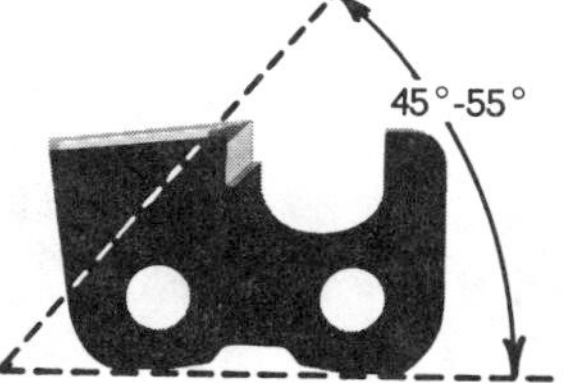

Top Plate Cutting Angle 45°-55°.

Fig. CM22—View of top and side plate specifications for chisel chain.

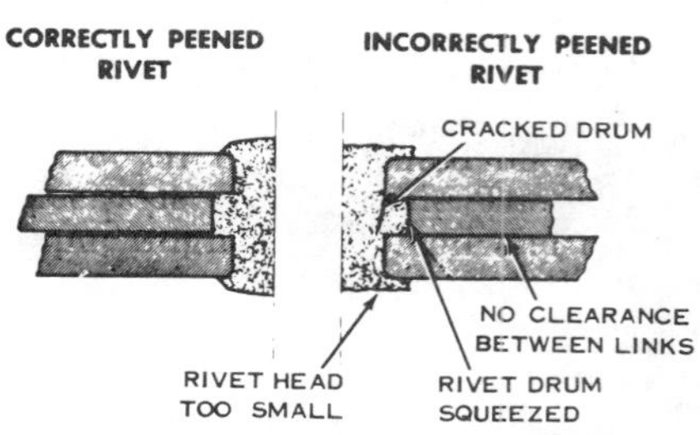

Fig. CM25—Views showing correctly installed rivet and rivet damaged by incorrect installation.

common problems found with CUTTERS and LINKS

	FAILURE	CAUSE	REMEDY		FAILURE	CAUSE	REMEDY
	Concave side link and cutter bottoms.	Chain run too tight. Insufficient lubrication. Cutters dull.	Decrease chain tension. Check oiler, file cutters.	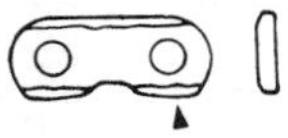	Side wear.	Abrasive cutting condition.	Check for grit in timber being cut. Lubricate well.
	Heel wear on cutters and side links.	Chain run too loose. Too much joint. Cutters dull.	Increase chain tension. Maintain basic .025" joint. File cutters.		Back nicked.	Chain run too loose.	Increase tension.
	Slight heel wear cutters and side links.	Back slope on cutters—chain slightly tight. Cutters dull.	Remove back slope. Decrease chain tension. File cutters.		Back rounded to bottom.	Worn sprocket. Chain run too loose.	Increase tension. Renew sprocket.
	Excessive bottom wear on cutters and side links.	Insufficient joint—chain run tight, filing blunt—no undercut, cutters dull.	Increase joint to .025". Decrease tension—refer to filing instr. File cutters.		Back and front of link peened.	Worn or wrong pitch sprocket.	Renew sprocket. Increase tension.
	Severe side wear and abrasive damage.	Caused by striking stone or nails, etc. Cutters dull.	All visible abrasion must be removed by filing cutters back. File cutters.		Back peened.	Worn sprocket. Dull cutters.	Renew sprocket. File cutters.
	Crack under rear rivet.	Cutters dull or hooked.	Refer to filing instructions.		Bottom peened and worn.	Link riding on bottom of bar groove. Bar rails worn. Dull cutters.	Renew bar. File cutters.
	Crack under front rivet.	Insufficient joint.	Increase joint to basic .025".		Bottom point rolled up.	Link bottoming in worn sprocket. Dull cutters.	Renew sprocket. File cutters.
	Cracks under both rivets.	Chain run dull and tight—insufficient joint.	Refer to filing instr. Increase joint to basic .025".		Bottom rough and broken off.	Chain run too tight causes stretch and climbs up on sprocket teeth.	Renew worn chain or sprocket. Run chain with less tension.
	Bottom peened and burred.	Hooked cutters—dull—no undercut causes chain to pound on rails.	Eliminate hook. Refer to filing instructions.		Drive lugs worn on sides.	Excessive face angle of cutters causes side thrust.	Refer to filing instructions.
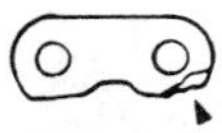	Front peened.	Chain run too slack—crowds at bar entry.	Increase tension.		Drive lugs worn on one side.	Excessive face angle of cutters on one side.	Cutters must have equal face angles.
	Clearance notch peened.	Sprocket teeth worn.	Renew sprocket.	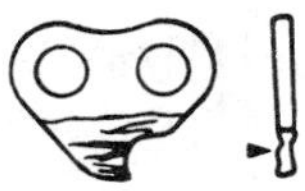	Chain jumps out of bar groove.	Uneven filing. Chain run too loose.	Increase chain tension. Refer to filing instructions.

shown in the "right" view in Fig. CM27. If the guide rails are as in the "wrong" view in this illustration, damage to the chain can occur as the chain enters the groove.

Check the fit of the chain to the guide bar as shown in Fig. CM28. If the tangs of the drive links touch the bottom of the guide rail groove, poor cutting and damage to the chain will result. The side links of the chain should ride on the rails and the tangs should clear the bottom of the guide groove. When replacing a chain or a guide bar, the length of the tang and the guide bar groove depth should be checked.

If the guide rails are worn or rough, they can be ground smooth and the groove deepened on a special bar grinding machine.

ROLLER AND SPROCKET NOSE BARS

LUBRICATION. The precision bearings in the roller and sprocket nose bar must be lubricated regularly for efficient operation and long life. Grease nose bearing every time saw is refueled. Always grease the bearing after a day's use. Grease bearing by cleaning oil hole and inserting grease with any good type hand grease gun with a needle nozzle. Insert nozzle into hole in center of roller as shown in Fig. CM29 and pump gun until grease flows from rim of roller or sprocket. A lighter grease may be necessary for winter operation.

ROLLER SIDE PLATE CARE. Refer to Fig. CM30. Remove burrs that form on side plate of roller with a flat file. Pump bearing full of grease before filing. File away from slot so filings will not get into bearing. Wipe filings from inside and outside of roller before mounting chain.

ROLLER AND SPROCKET RENEWAL. Roller and sprocket may be removed by drilling or punching out retaining rivets in end of guide bar. Remove roller or sprocket and install new roller or sprocket with new retaining rivets. Care should be taken not to damage rivets or mounting holes when peening or driving out rivets.

NOTE: Be sure sprocket size is matched to chain size. Mismatched sprocket and chain will cause excessive wear.

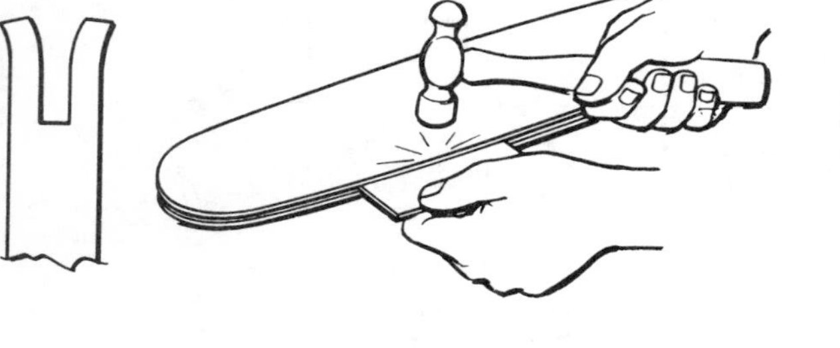

Fig. CM26—Use steel shim 0.004 inch thicker than drive link tangs to close spread bar rails.

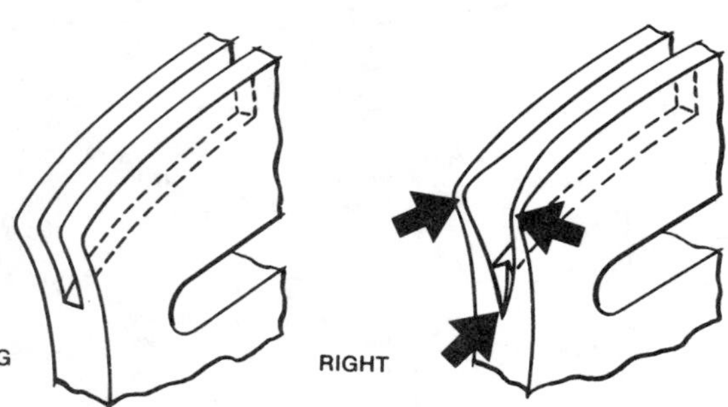

Fig. CM27—Cut funnel shaped opening to guide groove with file.

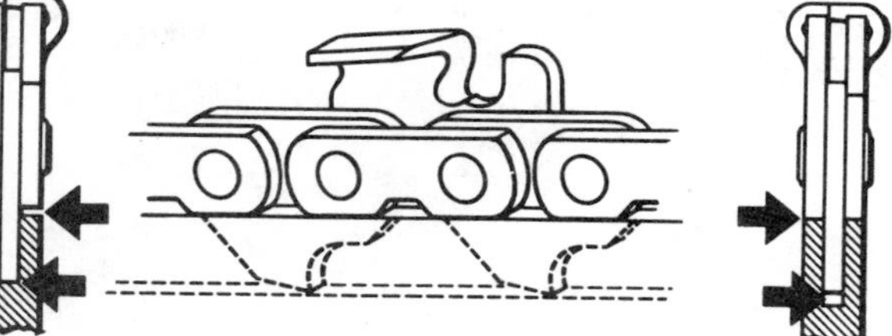

Fig. CM28—Guide groove too shallow in cross section view of left. Tang must clear bottom of groove as in cross section view at right.

SPROCKETS AND CLUTCHES

SPROCKETS

Two types of chain drive sprockets are used: The integral star and the self-aligning rim sprocket shown in Fig. CM31. The integral star sprocket is permanently attached to the clutch drum. The self-aligning rim sprocket assembly shown in Fig. CM32 consists of a splined hub fastened to the clutch drum and the rim sprocket is located over the splined hub. The sprocket is permitted to float on the splined hub and automatically align with groove in the guide bar. Sprockets for gear drive saws fit on the output shaft instead of a hub on the clutch drum.

FAILURES AND CAUSES. Drive sprockets are, like any moving part subject to extreme friction, subject to wear. A worn sprocket can quickly damage the bar and the chain. The illustrations in Fig. CM31 are typical examples of worn sprockets which should be renewed to keep from damaging the bar and chain. Wear on the sprocket teeth can be caused by any of the following:

1. Wrong pitch chain.
2. Insufficient chain lubrication.
3. Excessive chain tension.
4. Improper chain filing and jointing.
5. A badly worn and possibly stretched chain has a slight varia-

Fig. CM29—Lubricate roller or sprocket nose bar.

Fig. CM30—Remove burrs from roller side plates.

tion in pitch which will contribute to rapid wear of sprocket teeth.

6. A badly worn bar will contribute to rapid wear of the chain which will cause the sprocket to wear. Rapid deterioration and wear on chain drive lugs, side links and cutters will result from installing a new chain. Never install a new chain on a worn sprocket or bar.

Fig. CM31—View of self-aligning sprocket (left) and worn integral star sprocket (right).

CLUTCH

CLUTCH BEARING. The clutch drum and sprocket can rotate freely (or stop) when the clutch is disengaged. A caged needle roller bearing is located between the clutch drum hub and the shaft. The bearing on most models uses the shaft as the inner race and the clutch drum hub as the outer race and can be removed by hand without any special tools.

Clutch needle bearing failure is often caused by storing the saw after operating under extremely wet conditions. The water will penetrate the needle bearing, form rust and cause the needles to become locked. It is recommended that the clutch drum be removed periodically (depending on local conditions) and the bearing repacked with a good grade of water-resistant grease (not water pump grease).

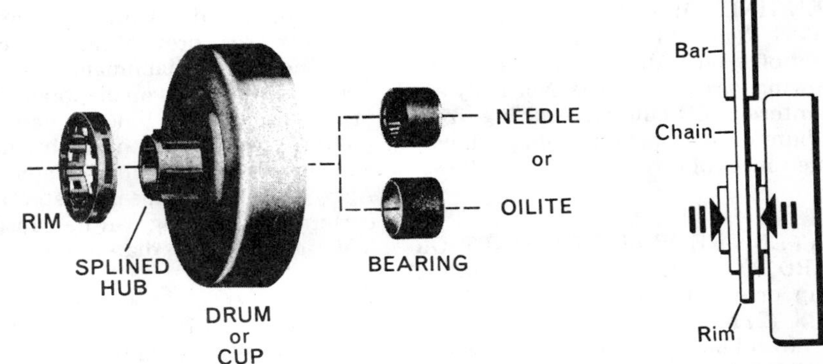

Fig. CM32—View of typical self-aligning sprocket and clutch assembly. Note that sprocket can float on splined hub to align with bar groove.

CLUTCH DRUM AND SHOES. Rapid clutch drum wear, shoe glazing or grooving may be caused by any of the following:

1. Improper filing. Hooked cutters and excessive joint will especially cause the clutch to slip.
2. Chain pinched in cut causing clutch to slip. Throttle should be released immediately when chain becomes pinched.
3. Oil soaked or worn clutch shoes. Clutch shoes should be inspected periodically. Glazing can be removed by wire brushing or other similar method.

OFF-SEASON STORAGE

When storing a chain saw for periods longer than 30 days, the following storage instructions should be followed: Drain all fuel from the fuel tank. Start and run the engine until it stops to remove fuel from carburetor. Drain oil from oil tank. Remove guide bar and chain and clean them thoroughly. Store the chain in a small container with engine oil covering the chain. Apply light coat of oil to guide bar and wrap it in paper. Clean exterior of the saw. Remove the spark plug and pour one teaspoon of two-cycle engine oil or a rust inhibitor product into the combustion chamber. Install spark plug and pull starter rope slowly several times to distribute the oil over the cylinder. Store the saw in a dry, well-ventilated place away from corrosive agents such as garden chemicals and fertilizer.

To remove saw from storage, remove spark plug and pull starter rope several times to clear cylinder of excess oil. Clean and gap spark plug or install a new spark plug. Install guide bar and chain and adjust chain to proper tension. Fill fuel tank with fresh fuel/oil mixture. Do not use old fuel that has been stored more than 90 days. Fill chain oil tank with clean chain oil.

CARBURETOR SERVICE

GENERAL CARBURETOR SERVICE

TROUBLESHOOTING

ENGINE OPERATIONAL SYMPTOMS. Refer to Fig. TR1 for schematic view of typical diaphragm carburetor showing location of parts. Normally encountered difficulties resulting from carburetor malfunction, along with possible causes of difficulty, are as follows:

A. ENGINE WILL NOT START OR HARD TO START. Could be caused by: (1) incorrect idle mixture screw adjustment, (2) restricted or plugged fuel filter or fuel line, (3) throttle shaft worn, (4) choke shaft worn or not functioning properly, (5) inlet needle valve stuck closed, (6) metering lever worn, bent, binding, or set too low, (7) metering diaphragm cover vent hole restricted or plugged, (8) metering diaphragm, gasket or cover leaking, (9) low speed fuel passages restricted or plugged.

B. CARBURETOR FLOODS. Could be caused by: (1) dirt or foreign particles preventing inlet fuel needle from seating, (2) damaged or worn fuel inlet needle and/or seat preventing proper seating of needle, (3) diaphragm lever spring not seated correctly on diaphragm lever, (4) metering lever binding or set too high, (5) hole in pump diaphragm, (6) Welch plug in fuel chamber is loose. Also, when fuel tank is located above carburetor, flooding can be caused by leaking fuel pump diaphragm.

C. ENGINE RUNS LEAN. Could be caused by: (1) fuel tank vent plugged, (2) restricted fuel filter or fuel line, (3) high speed fuel passages restricted, (4) hole in fuel metering diaphragm, (5) metering lever worn, binding, distorted or set too low, (6) high speed mixture screw incorrectly adjusted, (7) leak in pulse passage, (8) leaky gaskets between carburetor and cylinder intake port. Also, check for leaking crankshaft seals, porous or cracked crankcase or other cause for air leak into crankcase.

D. ENGINE WILL NOT ACCELERATE SMOOTHLY. Could be caused by: (1) idle or main fuel mixture screws set too lean on models without accelerating pump, (2) inoperative accelerating pump, on carburetor so equipped, due to plugged channel, leaking diaphragm, stuck piston, etc., (3) restricted low speed fuel passage, (4) restricted tank vent, fuel filter or fuel line, (5) plugged air filter, (6) restricted vent hole in metering cover, (7) restricted pulse channel, (8) defective pump diaphragm, (9) metering lever set too low, (10) defective manifold or carburetor mounting gaskets.

E. ENGINE STOPS WHEN DECELERATING. Could be caused by: (1)

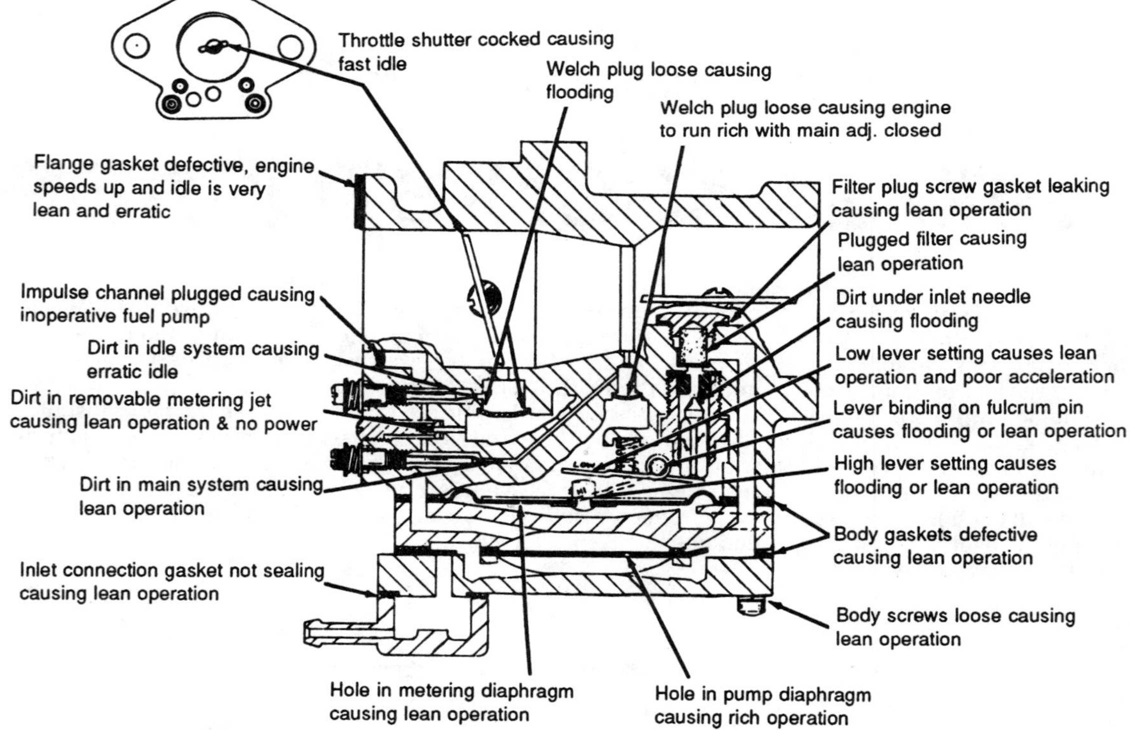

Fig. TR1—Schematic cross-sectional view of a diaphragm type carburetor illustrating possible causes of malfunction.

idle speed, idle mixture or high speed mixture screws incorrectly adjusted, (2) defective pump diaphragm, (3) pulse passage leaking or restricted, (4) air leaks between carburetor and crankcase, (5) throttle shaft worn, (6) metering lever set too high, (7) fuel inlet needle binding.

F. ENGINE WILL NOT IDLE. Could be caused by: (1) incorrect adjustment of idle fuel and/or idle speed screws, (2) idle discharge or air mixture ports plugged, (3) fuel channel plugged, (4) fuel tank vent, filter or fuel line restricted, (5) leaky gaskets between carburetor and cylinder intake ports.

G. ENGINE IDLES WITH LOW SPEED NEEDLE CLOSED. Could be caused by: (1) metering lever set too high or stuck, (2) fuel inlet needle not seating due to wear or damage, (3) Welch plug covering idle ports not sealing properly.

H. ENGINE RUNS RICH. Could be caused by: (1) plugged air filter, (2) low speed or high speed mixture screws incorrectly adjusted or damaged, (3) metering lever worn, binding, distorted or set too high, (4) fuel pump diaphragm defective, (5) fuel inlet needle valve leaking, (6) Welch plug leaking, (7) faulty governor valve (if so equipped).

I. ENGINE HAS LOW POWER UNDER LOAD. Could be caused by: (1) main mixture screw incorrectly adjusted, (2) plugged fuel tank vent, filter or fuel line, (3) pulse channel leaking or restricted, (4) defective pump diaphragm, (5) plugged air filter, (6) air leaks between carburetor and crankcase, (7) metering lever distorted or set too low, (8) hole in metering diaphragm or gasket leaking, (9) faulty nozzle check valve.

PRESSURE TESTING

A hand pump and pressure gauge may be used to test fuel system for leakage when diagnosing problems with diaphragm carburetors. With engine stopped and cooled, first adjust carburetor low-speed and high-speed mixture screws to chain saw manufacturer's recommended initial settings. Remove fuel tank cap and withdraw fuel line out fuel tank opening. Remove strainer on end of fuel line and connect a suitable pressure tester as shown in Fig. CS1. Pressurize system until 7 psi (48 kPa) is read on pressure gauge. Pressure reading must remain constant. If not, remove components as needed and connect pressure tester directly to carburetor inlet fitting as shown in Fig. CS2. Pressurize carburetor until 7 psi (48 kPa) is read on pressure gauge. If pressure reading now remains constant, the fuel line is defective. If pressure reading decreases, then carburetor must be removed for further testing.

Connect pressure tester directly to carburetor inlet fitting and submerge carburetor assembly into a suitable container filled with a nonflammable solution or water as shown in Fig. CS3. Pressurize carburetor until 7 psi (48 kPa) is read on pressure gage. Observe carburetor and note location of leaking air bubbles. If air bubbles escape from around jet needles or venturi, then inlet needle or metering mechanism is defective. If air bubbles escape at impulse opening, then pump diaphragm is defective. If air bubbles escape from around fuel pump cover, then cover gasket or pump diaphragm is defective.

Fig. CS2—View showing connection of pressure tester directly to carburetor inlet fitting. Refer to text.

To check inlet needle and metering mechanism, first rotate low and high speed mixture screws inward until lightly seated. Pressurize system until 7 psi (48 kPa) is read on pressure gage. If pressure reading does not remain constant, inlet needle is leaking. If pressure remains constant, depress metering diaphragm with a suitable length and thickness of wire through the vent hole in metering diaphragm cover. This will lift inlet needle off its seat and pressurize the metering chamber. A slight drop in pressure reading should be noted as metering chamber becomes pressurized. If no drop in pressure reading is noted, the inlet needle is sticking. If pressure does not hold after a slight drop, a defective metering mechanism or leaking high or low speed Welch plugs are indicated. To determine which component is leaking, submerge carburetor as previously outlined. Pressurize carburetor until 7 psi (48 kPa) is read on pressure gage, then depress metering diaphragm as previously outlined. If bubbles escape from hole in metering diaphragm cover, metering diaphragm is defective. If bubbles escape from within venturi, determine which discharge port the air bubbles are escaping from to determine which Welch plug is leaking.

If low or high speed running problems are noted, the passage beneath the respective Welch plug may be restricted. To test idle circuit, adjust low speed mixture screw to recommended initial setting and rotate high speed mixture screw inward until lightly seated. Pressurize carburetor until 7 psi (48 kPa) is read on pressure gage. Depress meter-

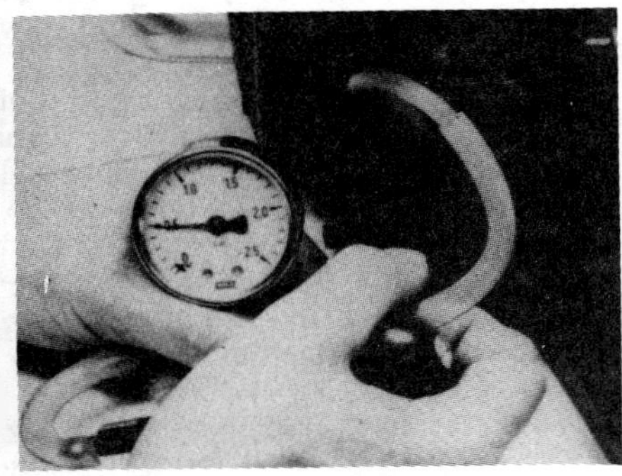

Fig. CS1—View showing connection of pressure tester to fuel tank fuel line. Refer to text.

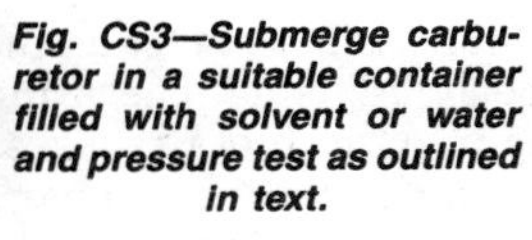

Fig. CS3—Submerge carburetor in a suitable container filled with solvent or water and pressure test as outlined in text.

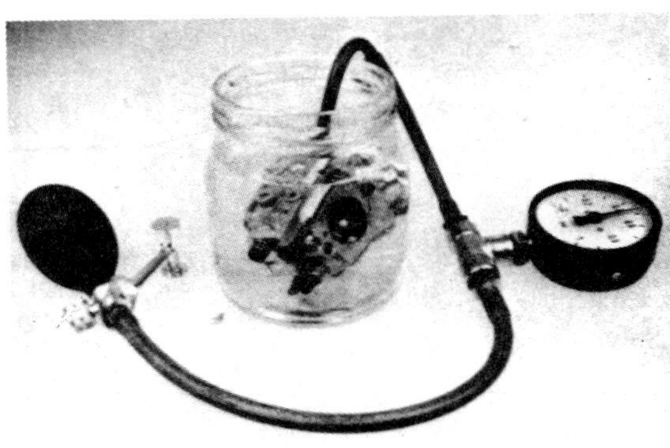

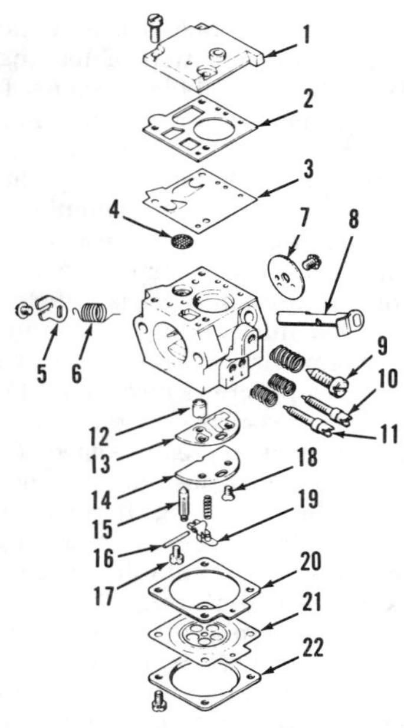

Fig. CS5—Exploded view of Bing 48 series carburetor.

1. Pump cover
2. Gasket
3. Pump diaphragm
4. Screen
5. Retainer
6. Return spring
7. Throttle plate
8. Throttle shaft
9. Idle speed screw
10. High speed adjusting screw
11. Low speed adjusting screw
12. Main jet
13. Gasket
14. Circuit plate
15. Needle valve
16. Pin
17. Screw
18. Screw
19. Metering lever
20. Gasket
21. Metering diaphragm
22. Cover

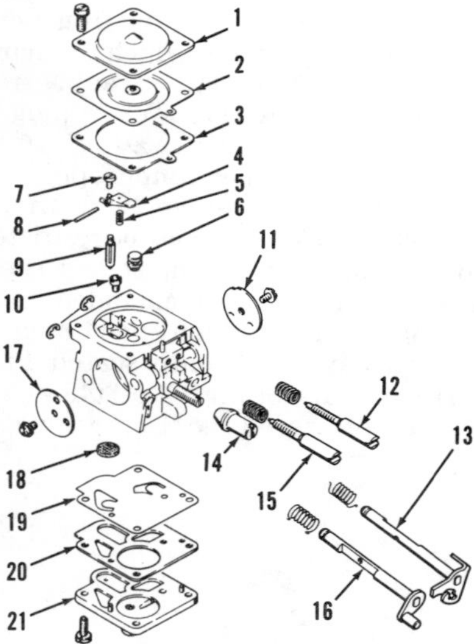

Fig. CS6—Exploded view of Bing 49 series carburetor.

1. Cover
2. Metering diaphragm
3. Gasket
4. Metering lever
5. Spring
6. Main jet
7. Screw
8. Pin
9. Needle valve
10. Fixed jet
11. Throttle plate
12. Low speed mixture screw
13. Throttle shaft
14. Idle speed screw
15. High speed mixture screw
16. Choke shaft
17. Choke plate
18. Screen
19. Pump diaphragm
20. Gasket
21. Pump cover

ing diaphragm as previously outlined. If pressure reading does not drop off or drops off very slowly, a restriction is indicated. To test high speed circuit, adjust high speed mixture screw to recommended initial setting and turn low speed mixture screw inward until lightly seated. Pressurize carburetor and depress metering diaphragm as previously outlined and note pressure gage. If pressure reading does not drop off or drops off very slowly, a restriction is indicated.

Refer to specific carburetor service section and repair defect or renew defective component as needed.

ADJUSTMENT

Initial setting for the mixture adjusting needles is listed in the specific saw MAINTENANCE section of this manual. Make final carburetor adjustment with engine warm and running. Make certain that engine air filter is clean before performing final adjustment, as a restricted air intake will affect the carburetor settings.

Adjust idle speed screw so that engine is idling at just below clutch engagement speed; do not try to make engine idle any slower than this. Adjust idle fuel needle for best engine idle performance, keeping the mixture as rich as possible (turn needle out to enrich mixture). If necessary, readjust idle speed screw. To adjust main fuel needle, operate engine at wide-open throttle and find the rich and lean drop-off points, and set the mixture between them. Main fuel needle may also be adjusted while engine is under cutting load to obtain optimum performance without excessive smoke. Do not operate saw with high speed mixture set too lean as engine damage may occur due to lack of lubrication and overheating.

If idle mixture is too lean and cannot be properly adjusted, consider the possibility of plugged idle fuel passages, expansion plug for main fuel check valve loose or missing, main fuel check valve not seating, improperly adjusted inlet control lever, leaking metering diaphragm or malfunctioning fuel pump.

If idle mixture is too rich, check idle mixture screw and its seat in carburetor body for damage. Check causes for carburetor flooding.

If high speed mixture is too lean and cannot be properly adjusted, check for dirt or plugging in main fuel passages, improperly adjusted metering lever, malfunctioning metering diaphragm or main fuel check valve. Also check for damaged or missing packing for high speed mixture screw and for malfunctioning fuel pump.

If high speed mixture is too rich check high speed mixture screw and its seat for damage. Check for improperly adjusted metering lever or faulty fuel inlet needle valve. Check for faulty governor valve if carburetor is so equipped.

Setting or adjusting the metering control lever (metering diaphragm lever height) necessitates disassembly of the carburetor. Refer to the following carburetor sections for adjusting the lever height.

BING

Models 48 And 49

These carburetors are diaphragm type carburetors with integral fuel pumps.

OPERATION. Operation of Bing carburetors is typical of other diaphragm type carburetors. Pressure and vacuum impulses from engine crankcase actuate the fuel pump diaphragm. Movement of the diaphragm draws fuel out of the tank to the carburetor fuel pump chamber. A metering diaphragm regulates the amount of fuel that is delivered to the engine. Engine suction is transmitted through the fuel ports in the carburetor air passage to the fuel side of the metering chamber. Atmospheric pressure on the dry side of metering diaphragm then pushes the diaphragm toward the fuel metering lever, which opens the fuel inlet needle valve. Fuel from the fuel pump flows past the needle valve into the metering chamber. The fuel in the metering chamber is then drawn through the idle or high speed adjusting orifices and out the idle discharge holes or main nozzle in carburetor air passage by engine suction.

OVERHAUL. Clean carburetor externally prior to disassembly. Refer to Fig. CS5 and CS6 and disassemble carburetor. Clean and inspect all components. Sharp objects should not be used to clean orifices or passages as fuel flow may be altered.

Check metering diaphragm and fuel pump diaphragm for punctures or tears that may affect operation. Examine fuel inlet valve and seat for wear or damage. Fuel mixture screws must be renewed if grooved or broken. Inspect mixture needle seats in carburetor body and renew body if seats are damaged or excessively worn.

When reassembling carburetor, renew all gaskets. Diaphragm lever (19—Fig. CS5) should be flush with circuit plate (14) on 48 series carburetors.

DELL'ORTO

Model FTR-16-12

Dell'Orto carburetor Model FTR-16-12 is a diaphragm type carburetor with an integral fuel pump.

OPERATION. Operation of Dell'Orto carburetor Model FTR-16-12 is typical of other diaphragm type carburetors. Inlet needle valve (14–Fig. CS7), low and high speed mixture screws (5 and 6) and metering diaphragm (2) are incorporated into metering block (4) which can be separated from carburetor body (10).

OVERHAUL. Clean carburetor externally prior to disassembly. Refer to Fig. CS7 and disassemble carburetor. Clean and inspect all components. Inspect metering diaphragm (2) and fuel pump diaphragm (23) for punctures or tears which may affect operation. Examine fuel inlet valve (14) and seat. Inlet valve is renewable, but metering block (4) must be renewed if needle seat is excessively worn or damaged. Sharp objects should not be used to clean orifices or passages as fuel flow may be altered. Fuel mixture screws (5 and 6) must be renewed if grooved or broken. Inspect mixture needle seats in metering block (4) and renew metering block if seats are damaged or excessively worn.

To reassemble carburetor, reverse order of disassembly. Renew gaskets (3, 7 and 25). Diaphragm lever (11) should be flush with chamber floor.

TILLOTSON

Models HC, HJ And HL

Tillotson Model HC, HJ and HL carburetors are diaphragm type carburetors with Model HL having an integral diaphragm fuel pump. Operation and servicing of these carburetors is similar and covered in the following paragraphs.

OPERATION. Operation of Model HL carburetor is outlined in the following paragraphs. Operation of HC and HJ carburetors is similar to HL but they are not equipped with a diaphragm fuel pump.

A cross-sectional schematic view of a typical Tillotson Series HL diaphragm type carburetor with integral fuel pump is shown in Fig. CS9. The top of the pump diaphragm is vented to the engine crankcase through the channel (8). As the diaphragm pulsates, fuel is drawn into the carburetor through inlet (1), screen (28) and pump inlet valve (3A). The fuel is then pumped through outlet valve (3B) into supply channel (17). Engine suction through main jet (15) and idle jets (10) is transmitted to the top of the carburetor diaphragm (25) and atmospheric pressure through vent (23) pushes upward on the diaphragm (25) overcoming spring (20) pressure and unseating inlet needle (18) allowing fuel to flow into diaphragm chamber (6).

When starting an engine, closing choke disc (16) increases the vacuum in the carburetor throat so the carburetor will function at the low cranking rpm.

When the engine is idling, the throttle disc is almost completely closed and there is not enough air passing through venturi (14) to create any vacuum on main jet (15). A vacuum is created at primary idle jet (10A), however, and the fuel necessary for running the engine is drawn through that jet.

As the throttle disc is opened, enough vacuum is created on secondary idle jet port (10B) so fuel is drawn through that port also. At a certain point, the throttle disc is open far enough so the velocity of air passing through the venturi is sufficient to lower the pressure at main fuel discharge port (15) so fuel will flow through this port also. Opening the throttle disc farther results in, higher air velocities and lower venturi pressures

Fig. CS7—Exploded view of Dell'Orto Model FTR-16-12 carburetor.

1. Cover
2. Metering diaphragm
3. Gasket
4. Metering block
5. Low speed mixture screw
6. High speed mixture screw
7. Gasket
8. Screen
9. High speed valve
10. Body
11. Diaphragm lever
12. Pin
13. Spring
14. Fuel inlet valve
15. Throttle plate
16. Throttle shaft
17. Bushing
18. Return spring
19. Bushing
20. Retainer
21. Fuel inlet fitting
22. Screen
23. Fuel pump diaphragm & check valves
24. Idle speed screw
25. Gasket
26. Fuel pump cover
27. Plate

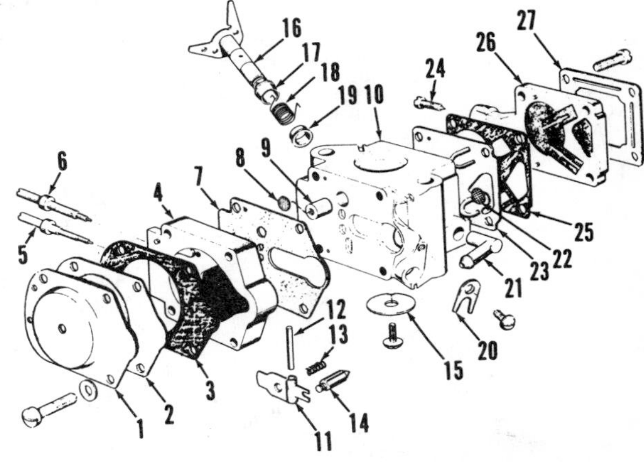

1. Fuel inlet
2. Pump body
3. Pump diaphragm
3A & B. Pump valves
4. Gasket
5. Gasket
6. Metering chamber
7. Idle needle
8. Impulse channel
9. Idle fuel orifice
10. Idle ports
11. Throttle shutter
12. Main fuel orifice
13. Body
14. Venturi
15. Main fuel port
16. Choke shutter
17. Inlet channel
18. Inlet valve
19. Main needle
20. Spring
21. Diaphragm lever
22. Fulcrum pin
23. Vent hole
24. Cover
25. Diaphragm
26. Atmospheric chamber
27. Gasket
28. Screen
29. Screw
30. Fuel chamber
31. Pulse chamber
32. Strainer cover

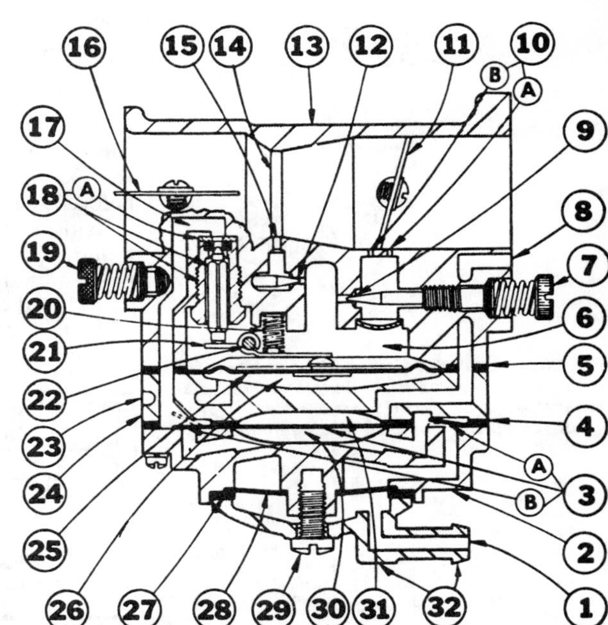

Fig. CS9—Cross-sectional schematic view of Tillotson Series HL diaphragm carburetor. Some models of this type carburetor are equipped with an accelerator pump.

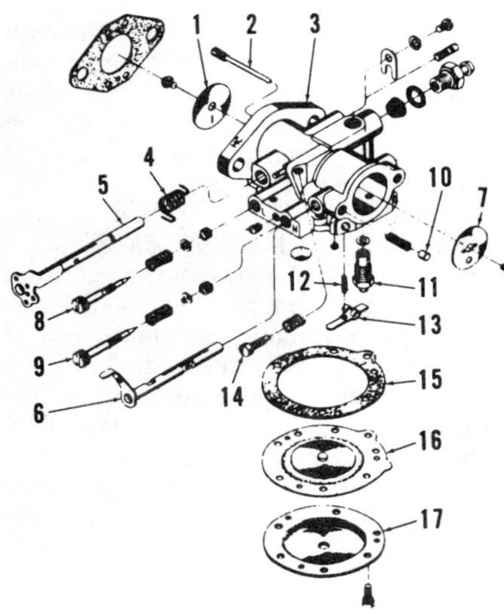

Fig. CS10—Exploded view of Tillotson Model HC carburetor. Model HJ is similar.

1. Throttle plate
2. Lever pin
3. Body
4. Return spring
5. Throttle shaft
6. Choke shaft
7. Choke plate
8. Idle mixture screw
9. High speed mixture screw
10. Choke friction pin
11. Fuel inlet valve assy.
12. Spring
13. Diaphragm lever
14. Idle speed screw
15. Gasket
16. Metering diaphragm
17. Cover

Fig. CS11—Exploded view of Tillotson Model HL carburetor. On some HL carburetors, pump diaphragm (19) and valves (20) are one-piece. Governor valve (25) is not used on all carburetors.

1. Throttle plate
2. Lever pin
3. Body
4. Throttle return spring
5. Idle mixture screw
6. Drain plug
7. High speed mixture screw
8. Choke detent
9. Gasket
10. Fuel inlet valve assy.
11. Spring
12. Diaphragm lever
13. Idle speed screw
14. Choke plate
15. Gasket
16. Metering diaphragm
17. Diaphragm cover
18. Gasket
19. Fuel pump diaphragm
20. Fuel pump valves
21. Pump body
22. Screen
23. Gasket
24. Fuel inlet
25. Governor valve
26. Diaphragm lever pin

that increase the flow of fuel out of the discharge ports.

Any vacuum created at idle discharge ports (10) or main fuel discharge port (15) is transferred through metering chamber (6) to diaphragm (25). Air pressure entering through atmospheric vent hole (23) pushes against the diaphragm because of the vacuum and overcomes pressure applied by spring (20) through control lever (21). This releases inlet needle valve (18) and allows fuel to enter the metering chamber in a direct relationship to the vacuum created at the fuel discharge ports. The higher the vacuum, the greater the movement of the diaphragm and the larger the opening of the needle valve. Thus, fuel is metered into the carburetor to meet the needs of the engine.

Some HL carburetors are equipped with governor valve (25–Fig. CS11) which enrichens the fuel mixture at the governed speed and prevents engine overspeeding. Original governor assembly is tuned for each engine and cannot be renewed. A disc may be installed in place of governor assembly.

OVERHAUL. Since the Model HL carburetor is the most widely used carburetor, overhaul procedures for the Model HL will be covered. Overhaul of Models HC and HJ is similar to the HL carburetor with the exception of the fuel pump. Refer to Figs. CS10 and CS11.

DISASSEMBLY. Clean carburetor and inspect for signs of external damage. Remove idle speed screw and inspect screw, washer and spring. Inspect threads in carburetor body for damage and repair with a Heli-Coil insert, if necessary.

Remove the filter cover, cover gasket, and filter screen. Clean filter screen by flushing with solvent and dry with compressed air. The cover gasket should be renewed whenever filter screen is serviced. Clean all dirt from plastic cover before assembly.

Remove the six body screws, fuel pump cover casting, fuel pump diaphragm and gasket. Diaphragm should be flat and free from holes. The gasket

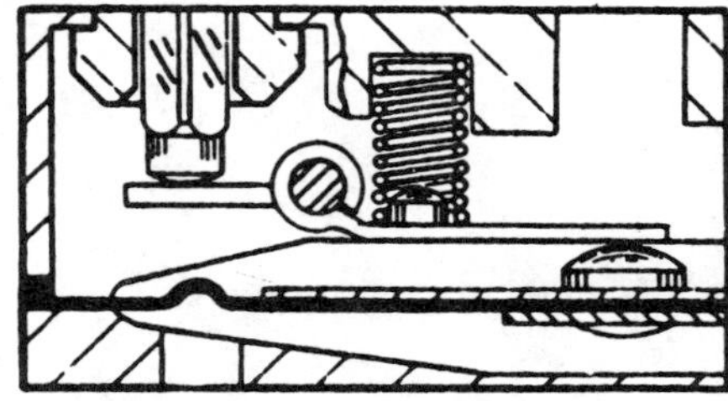

Fig. CS12—Diaphragm lever should be flush with diaphragm chamber floor.

should be renewed if there are holes or creases in the sealing surface.

Remove the diaphragm cover casting, metering diaphragm and diaphragm gasket. Inspect the diaphragm for holes, tears and other imperfections.

Remove the fulcrum pin, inlet control lever and inlet tension spring. Care must be used while removing parts due to spring pressure on inlet control lever. The spring must be handled carefully to prevent stretching or compressing. Any alteration to the spring will cause improper carburetor operation. If in doubt as to its condition, renew it.

Remove inlet needle. Remove inlet seat assembly using a 5/16 inch thin wall socket. Remove the inlet seat gasket.

Inlet needles and seats are in matched sets and should not be interchanged. Needle and seat assembly must be clean for proper performance. Use a new gasket when installing the insert cage. Do not force cage as threads may be stripped or the cage distorted. Use a torque wrench and tighten cage to 25-30 in.-lbs. (2.8-3.4 N•m).

Remove both high speed and idle mixture screws and inspect points. Notice the idle mixture screw point has the step design to minimize point and casting damage. The mixture screws may be damaged from being forced into the casting seat or possibly broken off in the casting. They may be bent. If damage is present be sure to inspect condition of casting. If adjustment seats are damaged, a new body casting is required.

ASSEMBLY. Install the main nozzle ball check valve if this part was found to be defective. Do not overtighten as distortion will result. Install new Welch plugs if they were removed. Place the new Welch plugs into the casting counterbore with convex side up and flatten it to a tight fit using a 5/16 inch flat end punch. If the installed Welch plug is concave, it may be loose and cause an uncontrolled fuel leak. The correctly installed Welch plug is flat.

Install inlet seat and tighten to 25-30 in.-lbs. (2.8-3.4 N•m). Install inlet needle. Install inlet tension spring, inlet control lever, fulcrum pin and fulcrum pin retaining screw. The inlet control lever must rotate freely on the fulcrum pin. Adjust inlet control lever so the center of the lever that contacts the metering diaphragm is flush to the metering chamber floor as shown in Fig. CS12.

Place metering diaphragm gasket on the body casting. Install metering diaphragm next to gasket. Reinstall diaphragm cover casting over metering diaphragm and gasket. Install pump gasket on diaphragm cover first, then the fuel pump diaphragm should be assembled next to the gasket and the flap valve member next to the fuel pump diaphragm so that the flap valves will seat against the fuel pump cover. Reinstall fuel pump cover and attach with six body screws. The above parts must be assembled in the proper order or the carburetor will not function properly.

Install filter screen on fuel pump cover. Install gasket on filter screen and replace filter cover over filter screen and gasket and attach with center screw.

Install high speed and idle mixture screws in their respective holes being careful not to damage points.

Welch plugs seal the idle bypass ports and main nozzle ball check valve from the metering chamber. Removal of these plugs is seldom necessary because of lack of wear in these sections and any dirt that may accumulate can usually be blown out with compressed air through the mixture screw holes. If removal of the Welch plugs is necessary, drill through the Welch plug using a 1/8-inch drill bit. Allow the drill bit to just break through the Welch plug. If the drill bit travels too deep into the cavity, the casting may be ruined. Pry the Welch plug out of its seat using a small punch.

Inspect the idle bypass holes to ensure they are not plugged. Do not push drill bits or wires into the metering holes. This may damage the flow characteristics of the holes and upset carburetor performance. Blow out plugged holes with compressed air. Remove main nozzle ball check assembly with a screwdriver of correct blade width. If ball check is defective, engine idling will be hampered unless high speed mixture screw is shut off or there will be poor high speed performance with high speed mixture screw adjusted at 1¼ turns open. Replace the ball check if defective.

Removing choke and throttle plates before cleaning the body is not necessary if there is no evidence of wear. Indication of wear will require the removal of plates to check the casting. To remove the plates, first mark the position of the plates on their respective shafts to assure correct reassembly. The plates are tapered for exact fit in the carburetor bore. Remove two screws and pull the plate out of the carburetor body. Remove the throttle shaft clip and pull the shaft out of the casting. Examine both the shaft and body bearing areas for wear. Should either part show wear then either the shaft or the body or both will have to be renewed. Remove the choke shaft from the body carefully so the friction ball and spring will not fly out of the casting. Inspect the shaft and bushings for wear.

Model HK

Tillotson Model HK carburetor is a diaphragm type with an integral diaphragm type fuel pump.

OPERATION. Operation of Tillotson Model HK is basically similar to that described for the Tillotson HL carburetor in preceding section, the main difference being that the Series HK carburetor is a compactly designed unit usually used on lightweight, small displacement engines.

OVERHAUL. Carburetor may be disassembled after inspecting unit and referral to exploded view in Fig. CS13. Clean components using a suitable solvent and compressed air. Do not attempt to clean metered passages with drill bits or wire as carburetor performance may be affected.

Inspect inlet lever spring (20) and renew if stretched or damaged. Inspect diaphragms for tears, cracks or other damage. Renew idle and high speed adjusting needles if needle points are grooved or broken. Carburetor body must be renewed if needle seats are damaged. Fuel inlet needle has a rubber tip and seats directly on a machined orifice in circuit block (19). Inlet needle or circuit block should be renewed if excessively worn.

With circuit block components installed, note height of long end of diaphragm lever (21). Lever end should be flush with chamber floor in circuit block. Bend lever adjacent to spring to obtain correct lever height.

Models HS, HT And HU

Tillotson Models HS, HT and HU carburetors are diaphragm type with integral diaphragm type fuel pumps. Operation and servicing of HS, HT and HU carburetors are similar and covered in the following paragraphs.

OPERATION. A cross-sectional schematic view of a Tillotson Series HS carburetor is shown in Fig. CS14. Operation of Models HS, HT and HU carburetors is basically similar to that described for the Tillotson HL carburetor in OPERATION section of Models HC, HJ and HL section. Some Model HS carburetors are equipped with a governor valve (26—Fig. CS15), consisting of a check ball and spring. The governor valve resonates at a desired engine speed that allows excess fuel to bypass the check ball and enter directly into carburetor bore. The rich fuel mixture causes the engine to lose power and slow down, thereby preventing overspeeding.

OVERHAUL. Refer to appropriate exploded view of carburetor shown in Fig. CS15, CS15A or CS16. Thoroughly clean outside of carburetor prior to disassem-

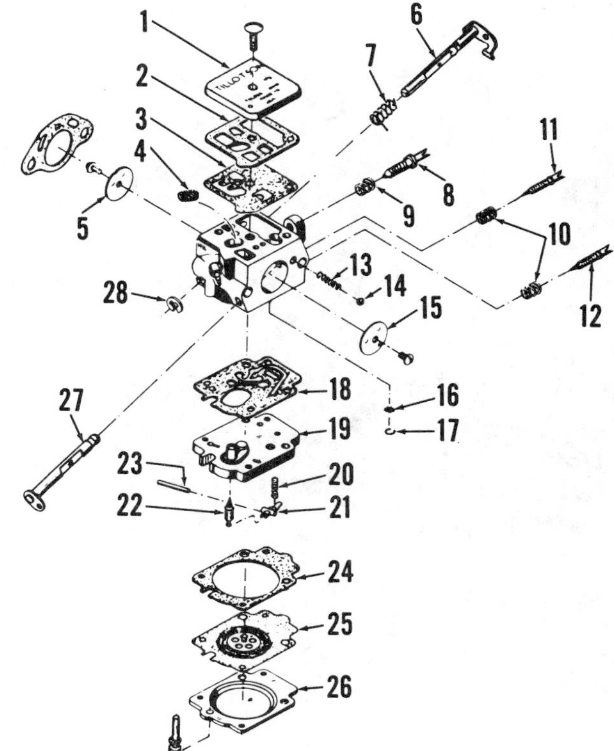

Fig. CS13—Exploded view of Tillotson Model HK carburetor.

1. Pump cover
2. Gasket
3. Fuel pump diaphragm & valves
4. Screen
5. Throttle plate
6. Throttle shaft
7. Throttle return spring
8. Idle speed screw
9. Spring
10. Spring
11. Idle mixture screw
12. High speed mixture screw
13. Spring
14. Detent ball
15. Choke plate
16. Screen
17. Retainer
18. Gasket
19. Circuit block
20. Spring
21. Diaphragm lever
22. Fuel inlet needle
23. Lever pin
24. Gasket
25. Metering diaphragm
26. Cover
27. Choke shaft
28. "E" ring

bly. Remove pump cover and metering chamber cover for access to internal components. Clean filter screen (4—Fig. CS17). Welch plugs may be removed by prying out with a sharp punch as shown in Fig. CS19. Use care not to damage carburetor casting when removing Welch plugs. Clean components using solvent and compressed air. Do not attempt to clean passages with drill bits or wire as carburetor calibration may be affected if passages are enlarged.

Inspect metering lever spring and renew if stretched or damaged. Check diaphragms for tears, cracks or other damage. Renew idle and high speed adjusting needles if needle points are grooved or broken. Carburetor body must be renewed if needle seats are damaged. Fuel inlet needle has a rubber tip and seats directly on a machined orifice in carburetor body. Carburetor body should be renewed if seat for inlet needle is damaged.

Carburetor may be reassembled by reversing disassembly procedure. Adjust position of metering lever so lever is flush with diaphragm chamber floor as shown in Fig. CS20. Bend lever adjacent to spring to obtain correct lever position. Note that on some HS carburetors the metering diaphragm is hooked to the metering lever.

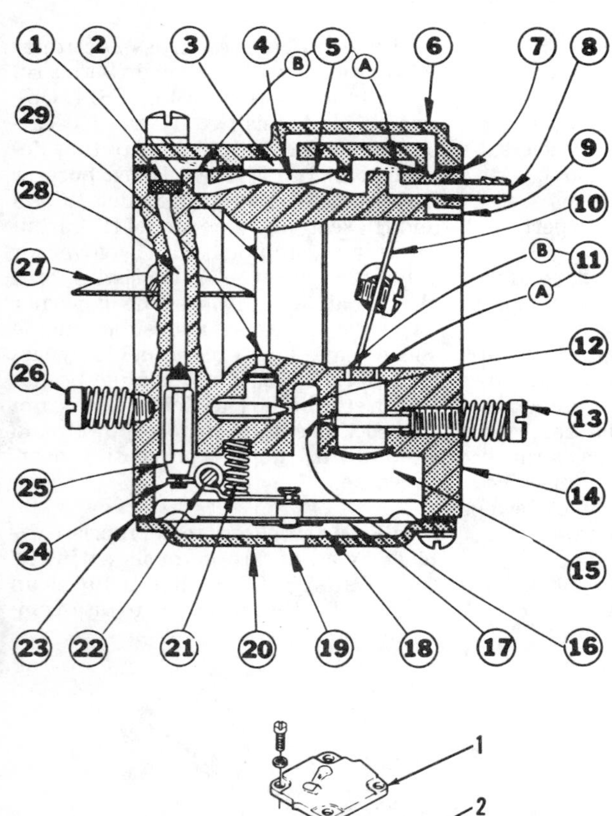

Fig. CS14—Cross-sectional view of typical Series HS Tillotson diaphragm-type carburetor.

1. Filter screen
2. Venturi
3. Pulse chamber
4. Fuel chamber
5. Pump diaphragm
5A. Inlet valve
5B. Outlet valve
6. Pump body
7. Gasket
8. Inlet fitting
9. Impulse channel
10. Throttle plate
11. Primary (A) & secondary (B) idle ports
12. Main fuel orifice
13. Idle fuel needle
14. Carburetor body
15. Metering chamber
16. Idle fuel orifice
17. Metering diaphragm
18. Atmospheric chamber
19. Vent hole
20. Diaphragm cover
21. Spring
22. Fulcrum pin
23. Gasket
24. Diaphragm lever
25. Inlet valve
26. Main fuel needle
27. Choke disc
28. Inlet channel
29. Main fuel port

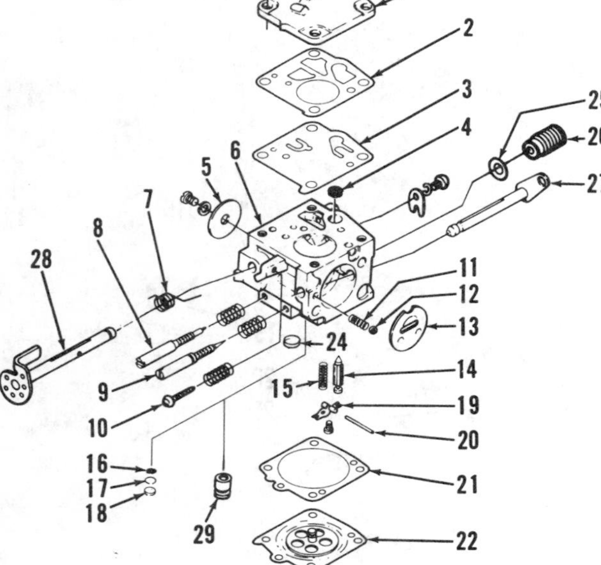

Fig. CS15—Exploded view of Tillotson Model HS carburetor.

1. Pump cover
2. Gasket
3. Fuel pump diaphragm & valves
4. Screen
5. Throttle plate
6. Body
7. Throttle return spring
8. Idle mixture screw
9. High speed mixture screw
10. Idle speed screw
11. Spring
12. Choke friction ball
13. Choke plate
14. Fuel inlet valve
15. Spring
16. Screen
17. Screen retainer
18. Welch plug
19. Diaphragm lever
20. Lever pin
21. Gasket
22. Metering diaphragm
23. Cover
24. Welch plug
25. Gasket
26. Governor
27. Choke shaft
28. Throttle shaft
29. Check valve

WALBRO

Models HD, HDA, HDB, HDC And SDC

Walbro carburetor Models HD, HDA, HDB, HDC and SDC are diaphragm type carburetors with integral diaphragm type fuel pumps. Some carburetors are also equipped with an accelerator pump. Model number on Model HD, HDA, HDB or HDC carburetor is found on side of carburetor adjacent to fuel mixture adjusting screws. Model number on Model SDC carburetors is stamped on bottom of carburetor.

OPERATION. In Fig. CS21, a cross-sectional schematic view of a Walbro

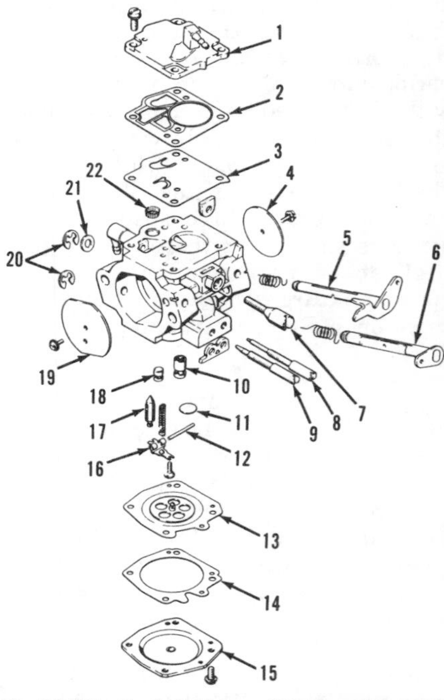

Fig. CS15A—Exploded view of Tillotson Model HT carburetor.

1. Fuel pump cover
2. Gasket
3. Pump diaphragm
4. Throttle plate
5. Throttle shaft
6. Choke shaft
7. Idle speed screw
8. Low speed mixture needle
9. High speed mixture needle
10. Valve jet
11. Cup plug
12. Pin
13. Metering diaphragm
14. Gasket
15. Cover
16. Metering lever
17. Fuel inlet needle
18. Main jet
19. Choke plate
20. "E" rings
21. Washer
22. Filter

Series SDC carburetor is shown. Operation of Models HD, HDA, HDB and HDC is similar to Model SDC and discussion will also apply to Models HD, HDA, HDB and HDC except for explanation of Model HDC accelerator pump.

Except for some models, Model SDC carburetor is equipped with an accelerator pump. When throttle is open, indexing hole in throttle shaft (25 – Fig. CS21) opens pulse passage (4) to accelerator pump passage (8). Pressure against pump diaphragm (9) compresses spring (10) and pressurizes fuel passage (11), ejecting excess fuel from main nozzle (27). When throttle is closed, or partially closed, indexing hole closes pulse passage and accelerator pump spring returns diaphragm to original position, drawing fuel back up passage (11) to recharge accelerator pump.

At idle speed, air is drawn into carburetor through air bleed hole (13) and mixed with fuel from idle fuel passage in what is called the "emulsion channel." More air enters idle fuel cavity through the two idle holes (24) nearest venturi and the fuel:air mixture is ejected from the third idle hole. Air cannot enter the main fuel nozzle (27) as the check valve (15) closes against its seat when engine is idling. Note that idle fuel supply must first pass main (high speed) metering needle (14) before it reaches idle fuel needle (22).

Model HDC carburetors with accelerator pump, except HDC 70, have a pulse passage (P – Fig. CS22) in carburetor body which allows crankcase pulsations to enter idle fuel circuit. The pulse passage is opened and closed by throttle

Fig. CS17 – Be sure to clean filter screen (4 – Fig. CS15 or CS16) when servicing carburetor.

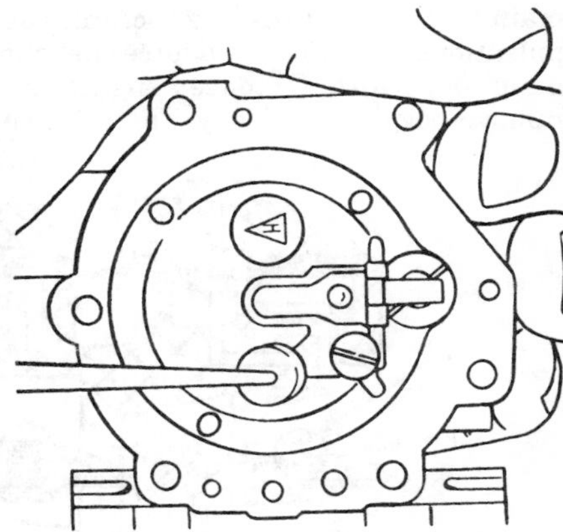

Fig. CS19 – A punch can be used to remove Welch plugs as shown.

Fig. CS18 – View showing location of Welch plugs (18 & 24 – Fig. CS15).

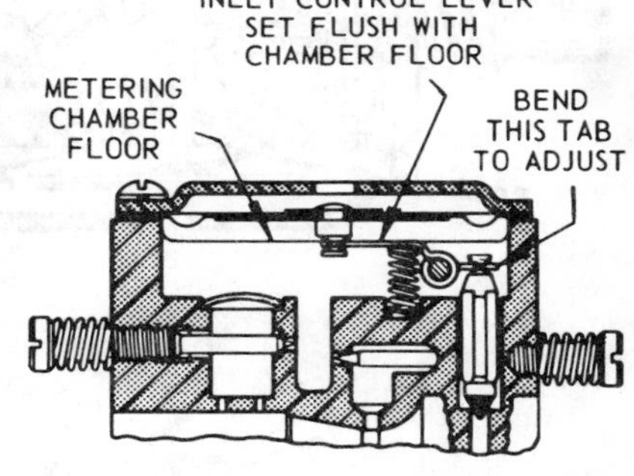

Fig. CS20—Diaphragm lever on Tillotson Models HS, HT and HU should be flush with diaphragm chamber floor as shown above.

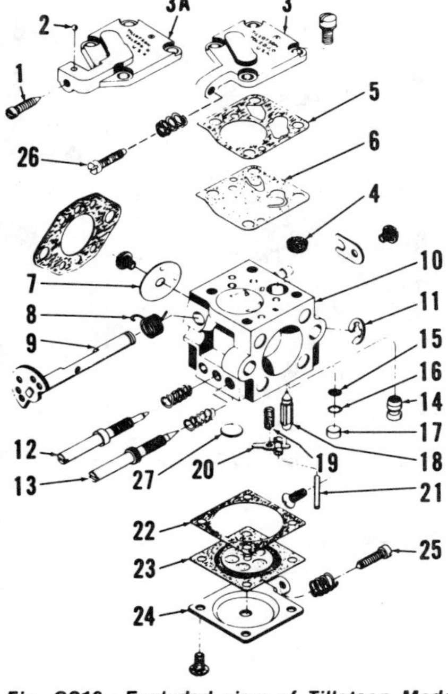

Fig. CS16 – Exploded view of Tillotson Model HU carburetor. Note difference in idle speed screw location used on fuel pump covers (3 and 3A) of some carburetors. Idle speed screw (25) may be located in cover (24).

1. Idle speed screw
2. Friction ball
3. & 3A. Fuel pump cover
4. Screen
5. Gasket
6. Fuel pump diaphragm & valves
7. Throttle plate
8. Return spring
9. Throttle shaft
10. Body
11. "E" ring
12. Idle mixture screw
13. High speed mixture screw
14. Nozzle check valve
15. Screen
16. Retainer
17. Cup plug
18. Fuel inlet valve
19. Spring
20. Diaphragm lever
21. Lever pin
22. Gasket
23. Metering diaphragm
24. Cover
25. Idle speed screw
26. Idle speed screw
27. Welch plug

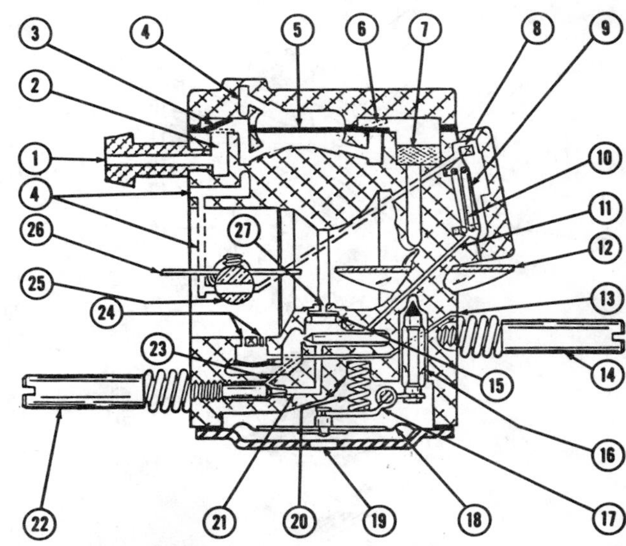

1. Fuel inlet
2. Surge chamber
3. Inlet check valve
4. Crankcase pulse channel
5. Fuel pump diaphragm
6. Outlet check valve
7. Fuel filter
8. Accelerator pulse channel
9. Accelerator diaphgram
10. Accelerator spring
11. Accelerator fuel channel
12. Choke disc
13. Idle air bleed channel
14. Main (high speed) fuel needle
15. Main orifice check valve
16. Inlet needle
17. Metering lever
18. Metering diaphragm
19. Atmospheric vent
20. Metering diaphragm spring
21. Idle fuel channel
22. Idle fuel needle
23. Idle fuel passage
24. Idle air and fuel holes
25. Throttle shaft
26. Throttle disc
27. Main fuel orifice

Fig. CS21 – Cross-sectional schematic view of Walbro Series SDC carburetor with accelerator pump. Some models are not equipped with accelerator pump and passages (8 and 11) are plugged. Fuel cavity above metering diaphragm extends to cavity shown at tip of main fuel needle (14).

shaft (S). Passage is closed when throttle is closed and open when throttle is open. When pulse passage is open, crankcase pulsations pass by idle fuel needle (IN) and act directly on fuel in main fuel circuit (MF). If throttle is opened rapidly, engine will tend to "bog" because vacuum in carburetor bore is insufficient to pull fuel from main fuel orifice. Pressure of crankcase pulsations is sufficient to force fuel out main fuel orifice (O) to feed engine and remove bogging tendency. The relative strength of the crankcase pulsations is such that they will affect engine operation only when there is a low vacuum condition such as previously described.

The accelerator pump of Model HDC 70 uses a rubber bladder that accumulates fuel. Fuel in the bladder is ejected through the main fuel orifice when low vacuum occurs in the carburetor bore. Operation is similar to SDC carburetor previously described.

Model HDC circuit plate (CP – Fig. CS22) may have a hole (MJ) to serve as main jet. High speed adjustment needle on these models is used only to enrichen high speed mixture. Main fuel supply is fully adjustable with high speed adjustment needle on all other models as hole (MJ) is nonexistent.

OVERHAUL. Thoroughly clean the carburetor prior to disassembly. Refer to appropriate exploded view of carburetor (Figs. CS23, CS24, CS25 or CS26). Remove fuel pump cover and metering chamber cover for access to internal components. It is not necessary to remove the throttle shaft or choke shaft unless they need to be replaced. Care should be taken not to lose the detent ball and spring that will be released when choke shaft is removed. Removal of Welch plugs (if used) from carburetor body is recommended in order to thoroughly clean all internal pas-

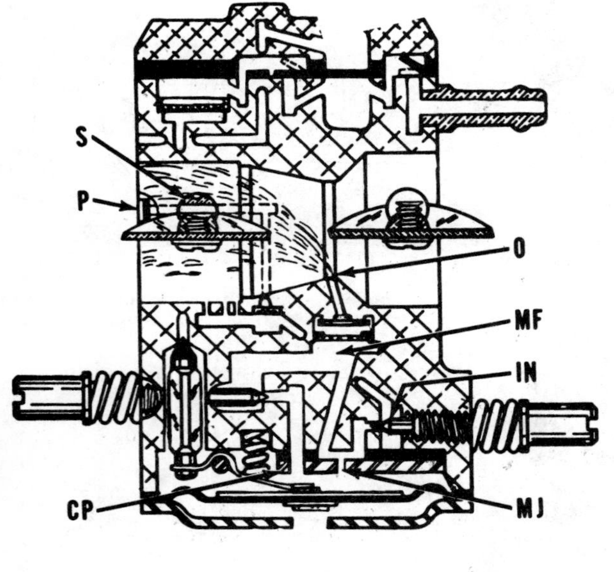

Fig. CS22–Cross-sectional view of Walbro Model HDC carburetor showing accelerator pump pulse passage (P). Refer to text for operation.

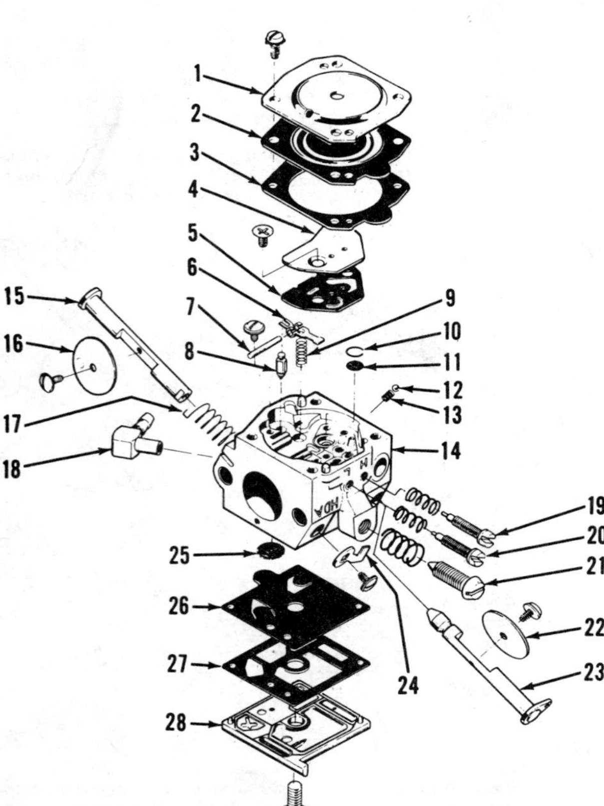

Fig. CS23–Exploded view of Walbro Model HD and Model HDA carburetor.

1. Cover
2. Metering diaphragm
3. Gasket
4. Circuit plate
5. Gasket
5. Diaphragm lever
7. Pin
8. Fuel inlet valve
9. Spring
10. Retainer
11. Check valve screen
12. Choke friction ball
13. Spring
14. Body
15. Throttle shaft
16. Throttle plate
17. Return spring
18. Fuel inlet
19. High speed mixture screw
20. Low speed mixture screw
21. Idle speed screw
22. Choke plate
23. Choke shaft
24. Throttle stop
25. Fuel inlet screen
26. Fuel pump diaphragm & valves
27. Gasket
28. Pump cover

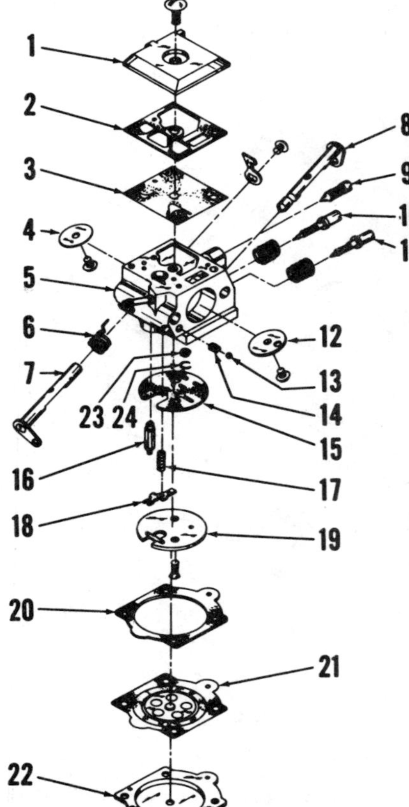

Fig. CS24–Exploded view of Walbro Model JDB and HDC carburetors.

1. Pump cover
2. Gasket
3. Fuel pump diaphragm & valves
4. Throttle plate
5. Body
6. Return spring
7. Throttle shaft
8. Choke shaft
9. Idle speed screw
10. Idle mixture screw
11. Higp speed mixture screw
12. Choke plate
13. Choke friction ball
14. Spring
15. Gasket
16. Fuel inlet valve
17. Spring
18. Diaphragm lever
19. Circuit plate
20. Gasket
21. Metering diaphragm
22. Cover
23. Check valve screen
24. Retainer

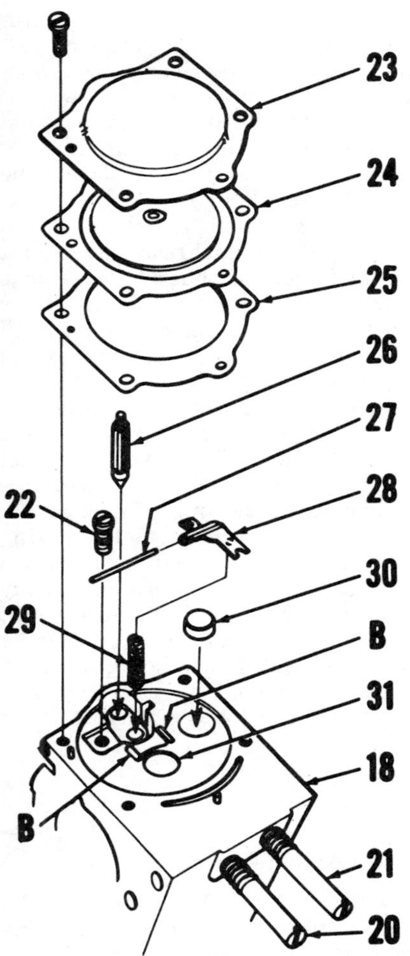

Fig. CS25–Exploded view of metering diaphragm assembly used on Walbro Model SDC. Refer to Fig. CS26 for other carburetor components.

B. Bosses
18. Body
20. High speed mixture screw
21. Idle mixture screw
22. Lever pin screw
23. Cover
24. Diaphragm
25. Gasket
26. Fuel inlet valve
27. Lever pin
28. Diaphragm lever
29. Spring
30. Idle passage plug
31. Main channel plug

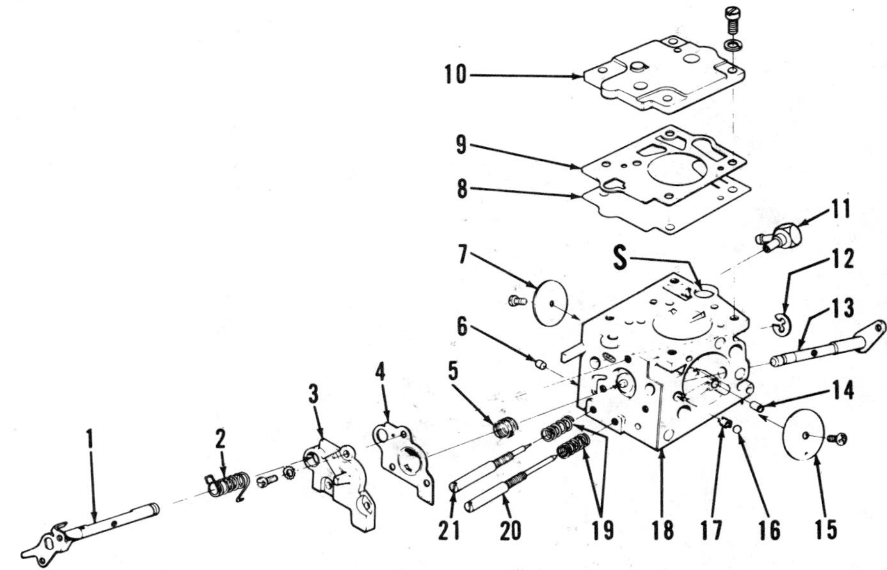

Fig. CS26–Exploded view of Walbro Model SDC carburetor with accelerator pump assembly. Refer to Fig. CS25 for metering diaphragm assembly.

S. Fuel screen
1. Throttle shaft
2. Return spring
3. Pump cover
4. Accelerator
5. Spring
6. Limiting plug
7. Throttle plate
8. Fuel pump diaphragm
9. Gasket
10. Pump cover
11. Elbow fitting
12. "E" ring
13. Choke shaft
14. Idle air jet
15. Choke plate
16. Detent ball
17. Spring
18. Body
19. Springs
20. High speed mixture screw
21. Idle mixture screw

sages. Welch plugs can be removed using a small sharp pointed punch as shown in Fig. CS27. Be careful not to damage the casting below the Welch plug when removing the plug.

Clean all components in suitable solvent. The manufacturer recommends using a spray type carburetor cleaner rather than a commercial dip tank type of cleaner. Sharp objects should not be used to clean orifices or passages as fuel flow may be altered. Compressed air should not be used to clean main nozzle as check valve may be damaged. A check valve repair kit is available to renew a damaged valve.

Inspect parts for wear or damage and replace as needed. Torn, frayed or porous diaphragms must be replaced. Examine fuel inlet needle and seat for wear. If a wear groove is evident on the needle, it should be replaced. If the seat is worn or damaged, the carburetor must be renewed. Inspect tips of mixture needles for wear or damage. Mixture needles must be renewed if grooved or broken, but carburetor must be replaced if needle seats are worn or damaged. Fuel screens should be cleaned or renewed.

When reassembling carburetor, apply a thin coat of fuel resistant sealant such as fingernail polish to outer edge of Welch plug. Use a suitable size driver to tap on domed part of Welch plug until it becomes flat. Wipe off any excess sealant. Fuel metering lever should be flush with a straightedge laid across carburetor body of Model HDA, HDB or HDC as shown in Fig. CS28. On Model SDC, the metering lever should be flush with bosses on chamber floor as shown in Fig. CS29. Be sure that lever spring correctly contacts locating dimple on lever before measuring lever height. Bend lever to obtain correct lever height.

Models WA, WB, WG, WJ, WS And WT

Walbro carburetor Models WA, WB, WG, WJ, WS and WT are diaphragm type carburetors with integral fuel pumps.

OPERATION. Operation of WA, WB, WG, WJ, WS or WT carburetors is similar to Walbro SDC carburetor discussed in preceding section. Some carburetors are equipped with a governor valve (8—Fig. CS33, 13—Fig. CS34 and 7—Fig. CS35) consisting of a check ball and spring. The governor valve is designed to resonate when the engine exceeds its governed speed. This allows

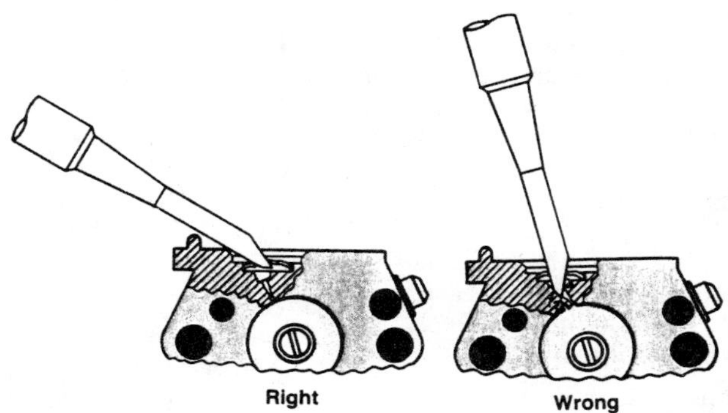

Fig. CS27—Welch plug may be removed using a sharp pointed punch. Be careful not to damage casting below the plug.

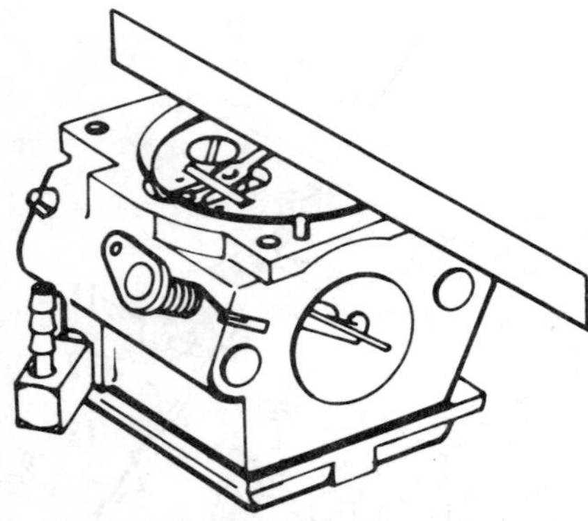
Fig. CS28—Metering lever on Models HDA, HDB or HDC should just touch a straightedge laid on carburetor body as shown.

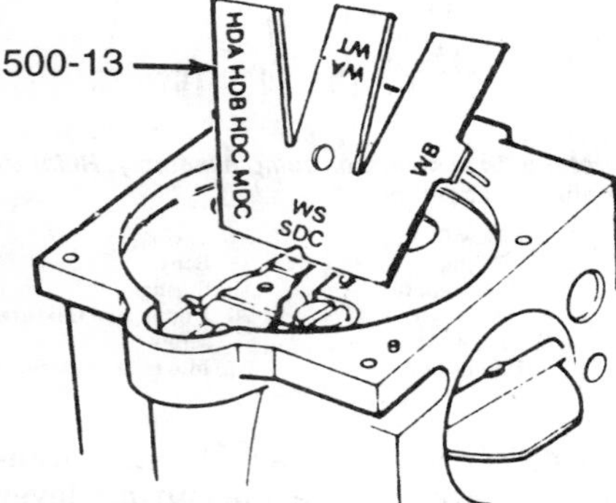

Fig. CS29—Metering lever on Model SDC should just touch Walbro tool 500-13 placed on bosses adjacent to the lever. Bend lever arm to adjust.

excess fuel to bypass the check ball and flow directly into the carburetor bore. The resulting excessively rich fuel:air mixture causes the engine to lose power and slow down. The governor valve is designed for specific engines and should not be altered.

OVERHAUL. Thoroughly clean carburetor prior to disassembly. Refer to appropriate exploded view of carburetor (Figs. CS30, CS31, CS32, CS33, CS34 or CS35). Remove fuel pump cover and metering chamber cover for access to internal components. It is not necessary to remove the throttle shaft or choke shaft unless excessive wear or damage is evident, and the renewal of parts is necessary. Care should be taken not to lose detent ball and spring, which will be released when choke shaft is removed. In order to thoroughly clean internal fuel channels, removal of Welch plugs from carburetor body is recommended. Welch plugs can be removed using a small sharp pointed punch as shown in Fig. CS27. Be careful not to damage casting below Welch plugs when removing plugs.

Clean all components in suitable solvent. The manufacturer recommends using a spray type carburetor cleaner

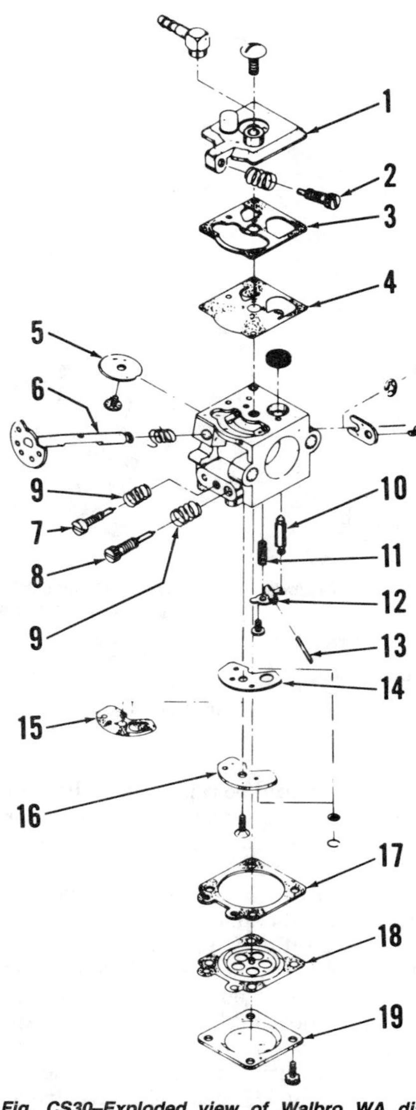

Fig. CS30–Exploded view of Walbro WA diaphragm carburetor.

1. Fuel pump cover
2. Idle speed screw
3. Gasket
4. Fuel pump diaphragm
5. Throttle plate
6. Throttle shaft
7. Idle mixture screw
8. High speed mixture screw
9. Springs
10. Fuel inlet valve
11. Spring
12. Diaphragm lever
13. Pin
14. Gasket
15. Circuit plate diaphragm
16. Circuit plate
17. Gasket
18. Metering diaphragm
19. Cover

rather than a commercial dip tank type of cleaner. Sharp objects should not be used to clean orifices or passages as fuel flow may be altered. On WG, WS and WT models, do not direct compressed air through main nozzle (18—Figs. CS32 and CS34) or (25—Fig. CS35) as check valve may be damaged.

Inspect parts for wear or damage and replace as needed. Torn, frayed or porous diaphragms must be replaced. Examine fuel inlet needle and seat for wear. If a wear groove is evident on the needle, it should be replaced. If the seat is worn or damaged, the carburetor must be renewed. Inspect tips of mixture needles for wear or damage. Mixture needles must be renewed if grooved or broken, but carburetor must be replaced if needle seats are worn or damaged. Fuel screens should be cleaned or renewed.

When reassembling carburetor, apply a thin coat of fuel resistant sealant such as fingernail polish to outer edge of Welch plug. Use a suitable size driver to tap on domed part of Welch plug until it becomes flat. Wipe off any excess sealant.

Use Walbro tool 500-13 or a straightedge to set metering lever height. On Models WA and WS carburetors, fuel metering lever should be flush with metering plate as shown in Fig. CS36. On Model WB carburetor, fuel metering lever should be 3/64-1/16 inch (1.2-1.6 mm) below surface of carburetor body as shown in Fig. CS37. On Models WG, WJ and WT carburetors, metering lever should just touch the leg of setting gauge as shown in Fig. CS38. Bend metering lever to obtain correct lever height.

Model MDC

Walbro carburetor Model MDC is a diaphragm type carburetor with an integral fuel pump.

OPERATION. Operation of Model MDC carburetor is typical of other Walbro diaphragm type carburetors described elsewhere in this section.

OVERHAUL. Clean carburetor externally prior to disassembly. Refer to Fig. CS39 for exploded view of carburetor. Unbolt and remove cover (26) for access to internal components. It is not necessary to remove the throttle shaft or choke shaft unless excessive wear or damage is evident, and the renewal of parts is necessary. In order to thoroughly clean all internal passage, removal of Welch plugs from carburetor body is recommended. Welch plugs can be removed using a small sharp pointed punch as shown in Fig. CS27. Be careful not to damage casting below Welch plugs when removing plugs.

Clean all components in suitable solvent. The manufacturer recommends using a spray type carburetor cleaner rather than a commercial dip tank type of cleaner. Sharp objects should not be used to clean orifices or passages as fuel flow may be altered.

Inspect metering diaphragm (22) and fuel pump diaphragm (25) for punctures or tears and renew if needed. Examine fuel inlet valve (19) and seat. Inlet valve is renewable, but carburetor body must be renewed if valve seat is

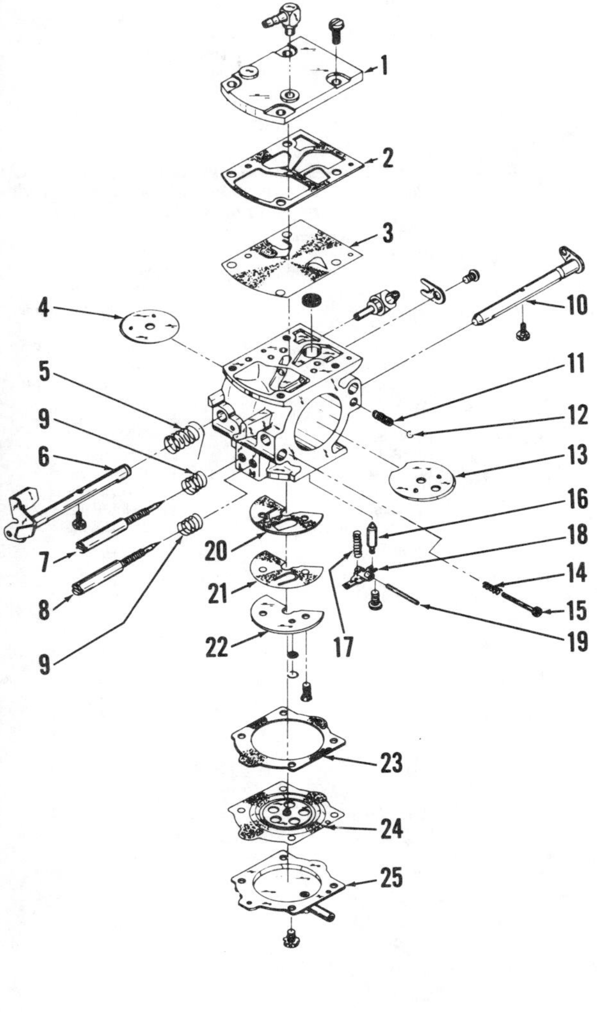

Fig. CS31–Exploded view of Walbro WB diaphragm carburetor.

1. Fuel pump cover
2. Gasket
3. Diaphragm
4. Throttle plate
5. Spring
6. Throttle shaft
7. Idle mixture screw
8. High speed mixture screw
9. Springs
10. Choke shaft
11. Spring
12. Choke friction ball
13. Choke plate
14. Spring
15. Idle speed screw
16. Fuel inlet valve
17. Spring
18. Diaphragm lever
19. Pin
20. Gasket
21. Circuit plate valve
22. Circuit plate
23. Gasket
24. Metering diaphragm
25. Cover

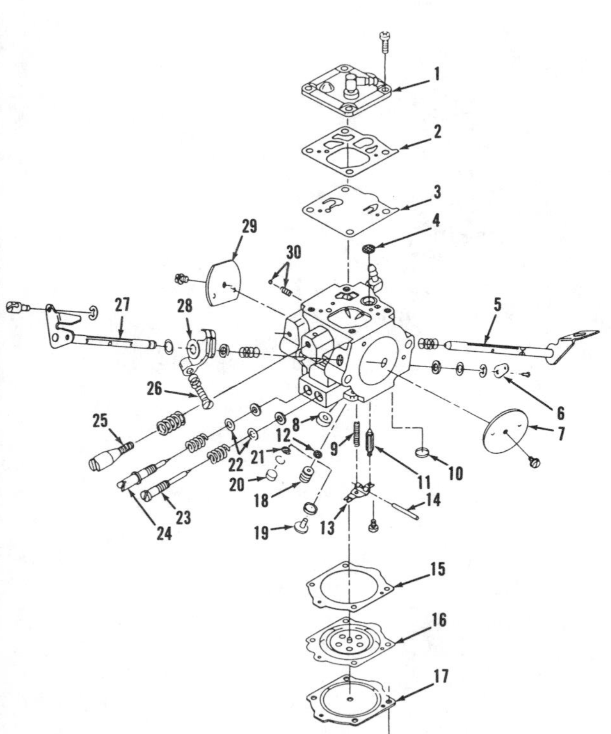

Fig. CS32–Exploded view of Walbro WG diaphragm carburetor. High speed mixture needle (23) is not used on some carburetors.

1. Fuel pump cover
2. Gasket
3. Fuel pump diaphragm
4. Screen
5. Choke shaft
6. Throttle lever
7. Throttle plate
8. Nozzle
9. Spring
10. Welch plug
11. Fuel inlet needle
12. Screen
13. Metering lever
14. Pin
15. Gasket
16. Metering diaphragm
17. Cover
18. Nozzle jet
19. Jet kit
20. Cup plug
21. Screen
22. Washers
23. High speed needle
24. Low speed needle
25. Idle speed screw
26. Lever tension screw
27. Throttle shaft
28. Throttle lever
29. Choke plate
30. Detent ball & spring

excessively worn or damaged. Fuel mixture screws (3 and 4) must be renewed if tips are grooved or broken. Carburetor body must be renewed if mixture screw seats are damaged or worn. Fuel screen (29) should be inspected and cleaned.

When reassembling carburetor, note that choke and throttle plate must be installed as shown in Fig. 40. Dimple (D) must be in position on inner side of plate. Fuel metering lever (17—Fig. CS39) should be flush with surface of metering chamber.

Models WY, WYK, WYJ And WYM

Walbro Series WY carburetors are diaphragm type carburetors that use a barrel type throttle rather than a throttle plate.

OPERATION. Pressure and vacuum impulses from the engine crankcase actuate the fuel pump diaphragm (4—Fig. CS41). Movement of the diaphragm draws fuel out of the tank, through the inlet screen (10) to the fuel pump chamber. Low pressure in front of the throttle barrel (12) causes the metering diaphragm (6) to raise, opening the needle valve (9) and allowing the correct amount of fuel to enter the metering chamber. Rotation of the throttle lever (1) opens the throttle barrel (12), increasing the volume of air flow. As the throttle lever rotates, ramp (2) forces the metering needle (3) off its seat to allow a specific amount of fuel to flow from the fuel discharge nozzle (11) to match the increase in air flow. The fuel flow is controlled by the position of the metering needle up to approximately 3/4 throttle, at which time fuel flow is limited by the fixed main jet (7).

OVERHAUL. Thoroughly clean carburetor prior to disassembly. To disassemble, remove screws securing diaphragm cover plate (1—Fig. CS42) and separate fuel metering components from carburetor body. Unbolt and remove bracket (19) and withdraw throttle barrel (21). Throttle barrel is available only as an assembly and should not be disassembled.

Clean all channels using compressed air and solvent. Do not use wires or drills to clean orifices as calibration of carburetor may be affected. Inspect metering diaphragm (2) and fuel pump diaphragm (12) for tears, pin holes or other damage and renew as needed. Check fuel metering valve (7) and seat and renew if wear or damage is evident. Fuel pump body (8) must be renewed if inlet seat is worn or damaged.

When reassembling, place a straightedge across pump body as shown in Fig.

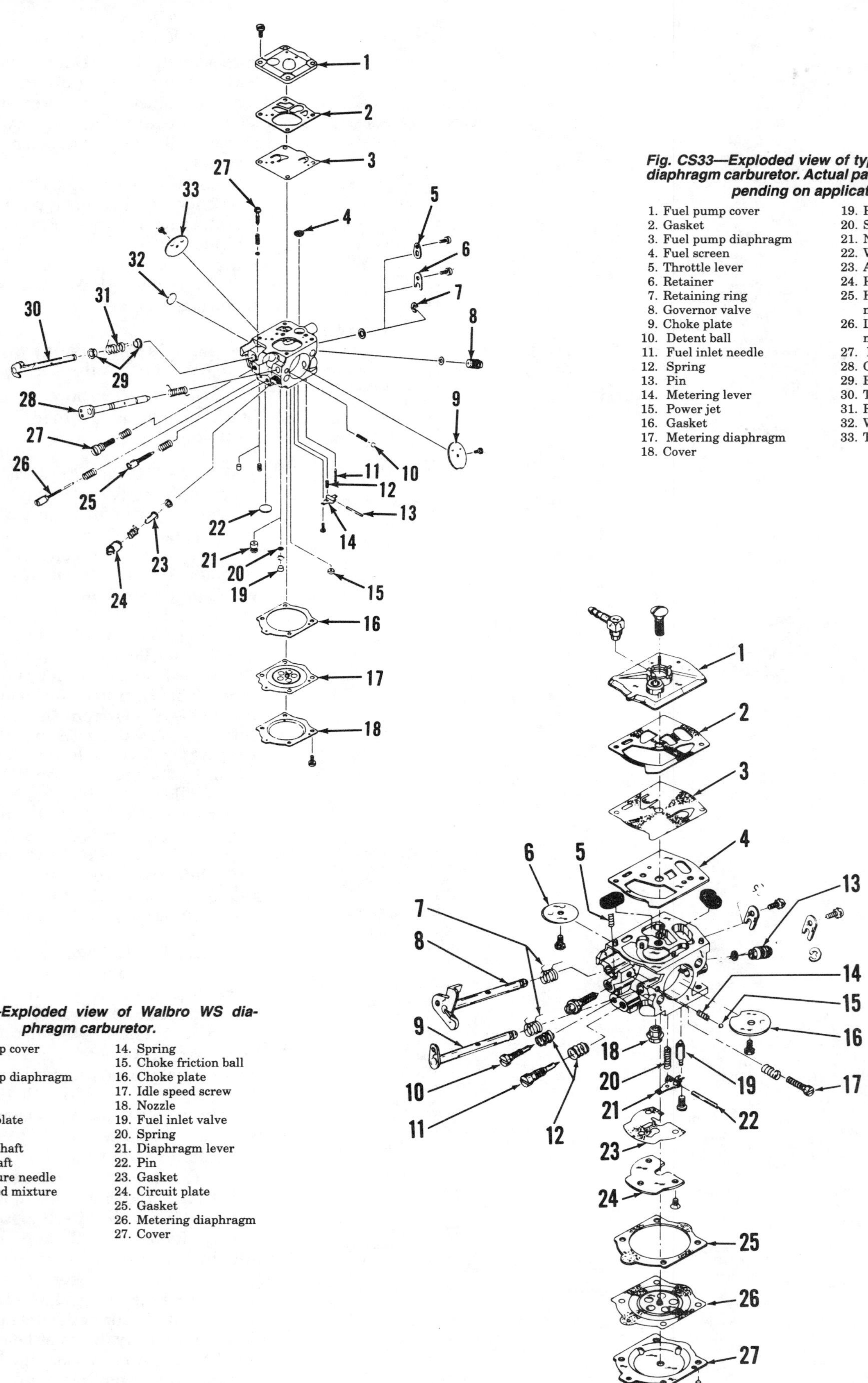

Fig. CS33—Exploded view of typical Walbro WJ diaphragm carburetor. Actual parts may vary, depending on application.

1. Fuel pump cover
2. Gasket
3. Fuel pump diaphragm
4. Fuel screen
5. Throttle lever
6. Retainer
7. Retaining ring
8. Governor valve
9. Choke plate
10. Detent ball
11. Fuel inlet needle
12. Spring
13. Pin
14. Metering lever
15. Power jet
16. Gasket
17. Metering diaphragm
18. Cover
19. Plug
20. Screen
21. Nozzle seat
22. Welch plug
23. Accelerator pump
24. Plug
25. High-speed mixture needle
26. Low-speed mixture needle
27. Idle speed screw
28. Choke shaft
29. Bushings
30. Throttle shaft
31. Return spring
32. Welch plug
33. Throttle plate

Fig. CS34–Exploded view of Walbro WS diaphragm carburetor.

1. Fuel pump cover
2. Gasket
3. Fuel pump diaphragm
4. Plate
5. Spring
6. Throttle plate
7. Springs
8. Throttle shaft
9. Choke shaft
10. Idle mixture needle
11. High speed mixture needle
12. Springs
13. Governor
14. Spring
15. Choke friction ball
16. Choke plate
17. Idle speed screw
18. Nozzle
19. Fuel inlet valve
20. Spring
21. Diaphragm lever
22. Pin
23. Gasket
24. Circuit plate
25. Gasket
26. Metering diaphragm
27. Cover

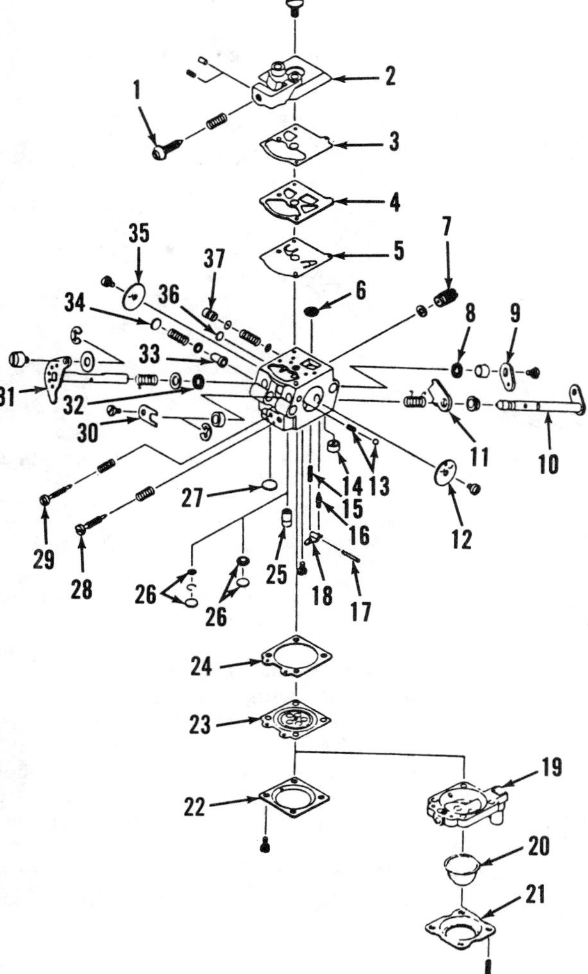

Fig. CS35—Exploded view of typical Walbro WT diaphragm carburetor. Actual parts may vary, depending on the application.

1. Idle speed screw
2. Cover
3. Surge diaphragm
4. Gasket
5. Fuel pump diaphragm
6. Fuel screen
7. Governor valve
8. Seal
9. Throttle lever
10. Choke shaft
11. Fast idle lever
12. Choke plate
13. Detent ball & spring
14. Check valve seat
15. Spring
16. Fuel inlet needle
17. Pin
18. Metering lever
19. Primer body
20. Primer bulb
21. Retainer plate
22. Retainer plate
23. Metering diaphragm
24. Gasket
25. Check valve
26. Valve seat & plug
27. Welch plug
28. High-speed screw
29. Low-speed screw
30. Retainer clip
31. Throttle shaft
32. Seal
33. Accelerator diaphragm
34. Plug
35. Throttle plate
36. Welch plug
37. Accelerator piston

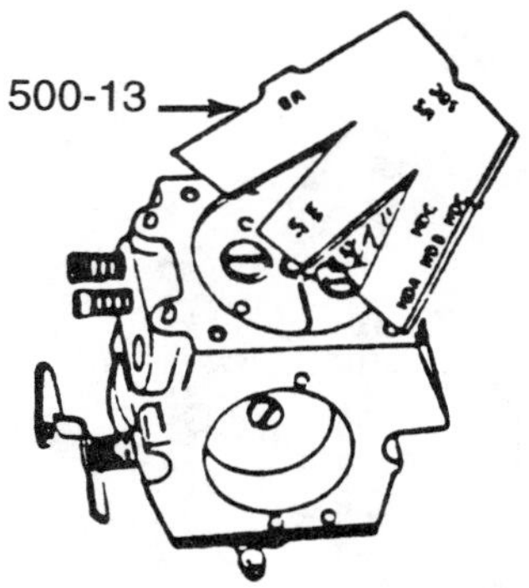

Fig. CS38—On Walbro WG, WJ and WT carburetors, metering lever should just touch the leg of setting gauge as shown.

CS43 to check metering lever height. Distance (D) between metering lever and carburetor body surface should be 0.060 inch (1.5 mm). If necessary, bend the metering lever to obtain specified height. Refer to Fig. CS42 for assembly order of gaskets, pump diaphragm (12), pump plate (11), pump base (8) and metering diaphragm (2).

Metering needle (3—Fig. CS41) has been calibrated at the factory for proper low-speed mixture setting and should not be disturbed. If needle requires adjustment, start and run engine until normal operating temperature is obtained. Adjust needle to obtain highest idle engine rpm, then turn needle 1/8 turn counterclockwise. High speed mixture is controlled by the fixed main jet (14—Fig. CS42) and is not adjustable.

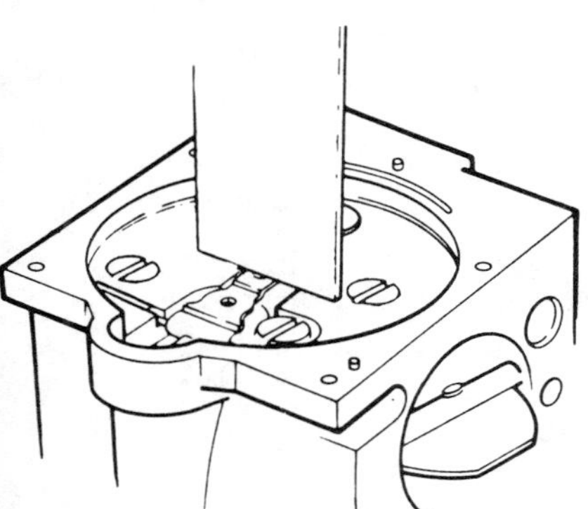

Fig. CS36—Diaphragm lever on Walbro WA and WS carburetors should be flush with circuit plate.

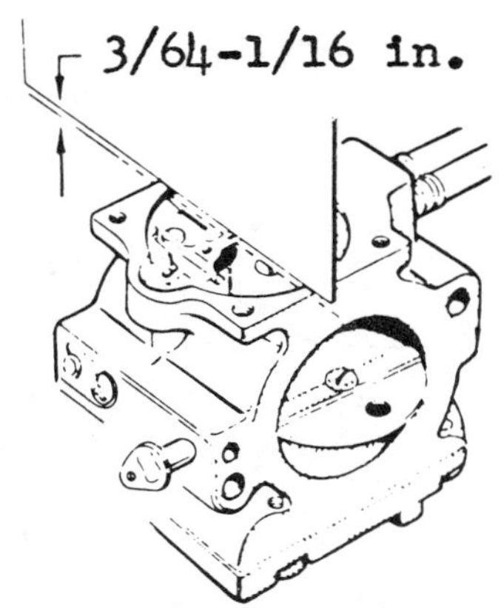

Fig. CS37—Diaphragm lever on Walbro WB carburetors should be 3/64 to 1/16 in. (1.2-1.6 mm) from machined surface to carburetor body.

ZAMA

Models C1, C1S, C1Q, C1U, C2, C2S, C3A, LA, LB, M1, Z1, And Z1A

These Zama carburetors are diaphragm type carburetors with integral fuel pumps.

OPERATION. Pressure and vacuum impulses from the engine crankcase actuate the fuel pump diaphragm (Fig. CS44). Movement of the diaphragm draws fuel out of the tank to the fuel pump chamber.

A metering diaphragm regulates the amount of fuel that is delivered to the engine. Engine suction is transmitted through the fuel ports to the fuel side of the metering chamber. Atmospheric pressure on the dry side of the metering diaphragm then pushes the diaphragm toward the fuel metering lever, which moves the fuel inlet needle valve off its seat. Pressurized fuel from the fuel pump flows past the needle valve into the metering chamber. The fuel in the metering chamber is then drawn through the idle adjusting orifice and out the idle discharge hole in the carburetor air passage by engine suction.

As the throttle valve opening increases, the secondary and third idle ports are exposed to engine vacuum, which increases the vacuum applied to the fuel side of the metering diaphragm. The diaphragm is pushed farther toward the metering lever, increasing the needle valve opening so more fuel will flow through the carburetor.

As the throttle valve progressively opens from part throttle to wide-open position, increased air flow through the carburetor venturi creates a vacuum at the main nozzle. When pressure at the main nozzle is less than the pressure in the metering chamber, fuel flows past the main mixture adjusting needle and out the main nozzle to the carburetor air passage.

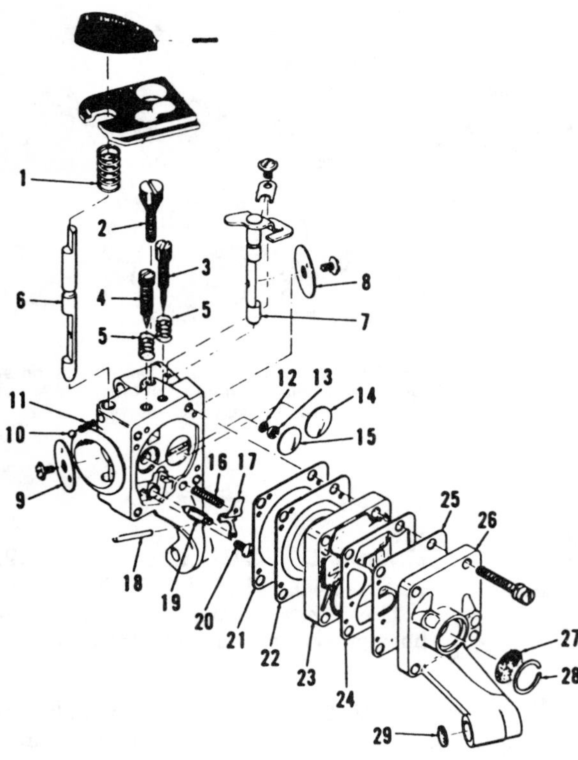

Fig. CS39–Exploded view of Walbro MDC diaphragm carburetor.

1. Spring
2. Idle speed screw
3. Idle mixture screw
4. High speed mixture screw
5. Spring
6. Choke shaft
7. Throttle shaft
8. Throttle plate
9. Choke plate
10. Choke detent ball
11. Spring
12. Valve
13. Seat
14. Plug
15. Plug
16. Spring
17. Fuel inlet lever
18. Lever pin
19. Inlet needle valve
20. Screw
21. Gasket
22. Diaphragm
23. Fuel pump body
24. Gasket
25. Diaphragm
26. Cover
27. Vent screen
28. Retainer
29. Inlet screen

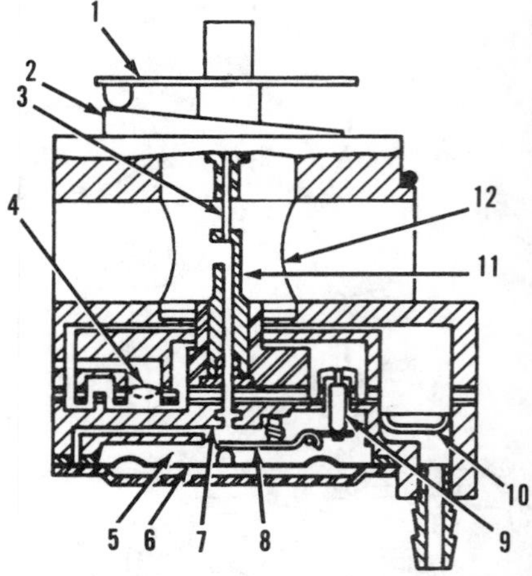

Fig. CS41–Cross-sectional view of Walbro Model WYM carburetor.

1. Throttle plate
2. Ramp
3. Metering needle
4. Pump diaphragm
5. Metering chamber
6. Metering diaphragm
7. Main jet
8. Metering lever
9. Needle valve
10. Screen
11. Discharge nozzle
12. Throttle barrel

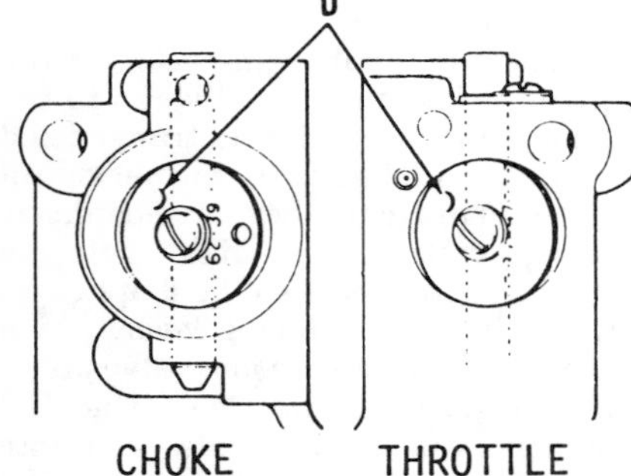

Fig. CS40–On Walbro MDC carburetor, choke and throttle plates must be installed on shafts as shown above. Dimples (D) must be on inside of plate.

OVERHAUL. Clean the carburetor externally prior to disassembly. Refer to appropriate exploded view (Fig. CS45, CS46, CS47, CS48, CS49, CS50, CS51, CS52 or CS53). Remove fuel pump cover and metering chamber cover for access to internal components. Remove diaphragms, gaskets, metering lever, fuel inlet needle valve, fuel mixture adjusting screws and fuel screen.

If the main nozzle check valve does not seat properly, the result is an unstable or erratic idle. Wide open throttle performance normally remains unaffected. To test for faulty main nozzle, blow air by mouth through the high-speed needle feed hole with a small hose. With the needle open two turns, air should flow through, but you should not be able to suck air back. If the nozzle is a pressed in assembly, do not remove it unless there is evidence that the nozzle is faulty.

It may not be necessary to remove the Welch plug. To check for plugged fuel passage, spray carburetor cleaner into the low speed needle hole. If cleaner sprays out the progression holes in the throttle bore, passage is open and there is no reason to remove the Welch plug.

If Welch plug removal is required, use a small diameter sharp-pointed

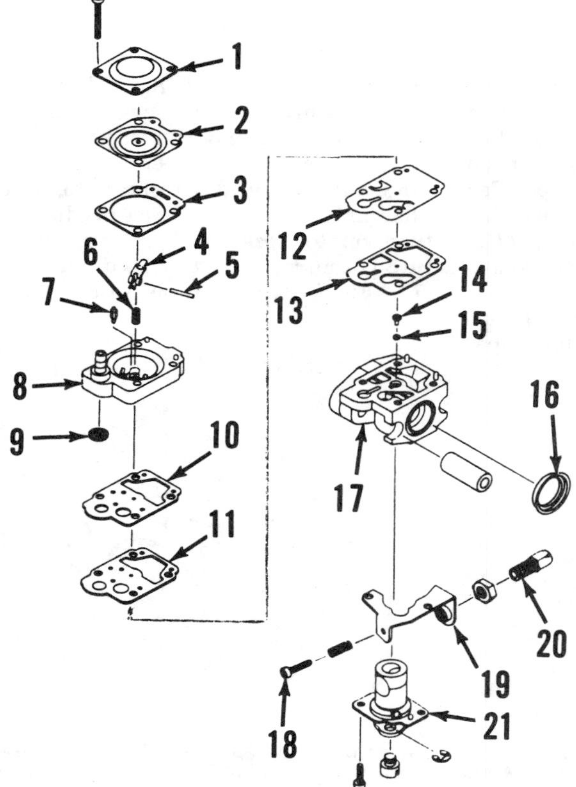

Fig. CS42—Exploded view of typical WY series carburetor. Some parts may differ, depending on application.

1. Cover
2. Metering diaphragm
3. Gasket
4. Metering lever
5. Pin
6. Spring
7. Fuel inlet needle
8. Fuel pump body
9. Fuel screen
10. Gasket
11. Pump plate
12. Pump diaphragm
13. Gasket
14. Main jet
15. Seal ring
16. Seal
17. Carburetor body
18. Idle speed screw
19. Bracket
20. Cable screw
21. Throttle barrel

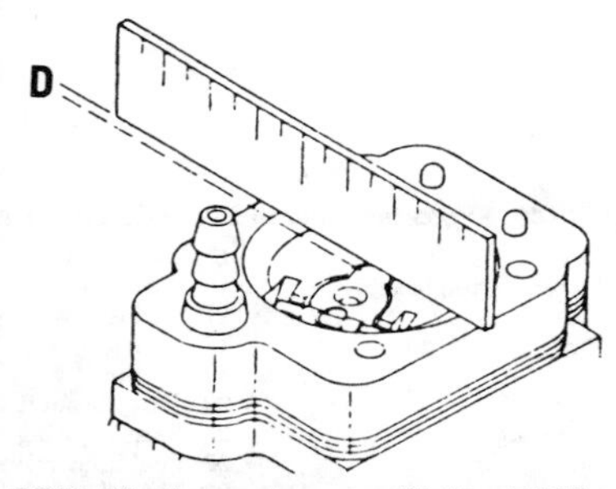

Fig. CS43–Diaphragm lever on Walbro WYM carburetor should be 0.060 inch (1.5 mm) below machined surface of carburetor body (dimension D).

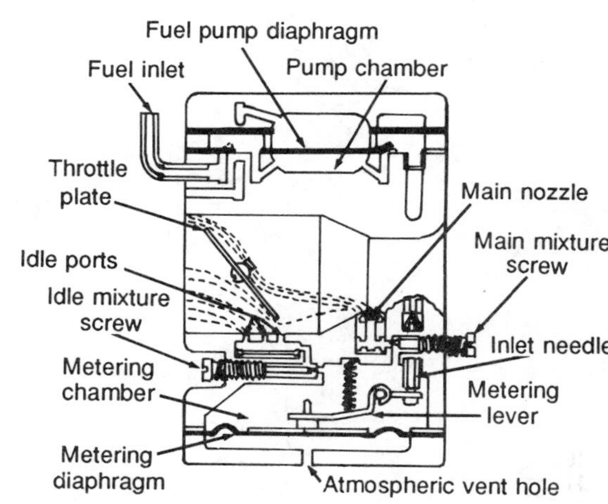

Fig. CS44–Cross-sectional view of typical Zama diaphragm type carburetor.

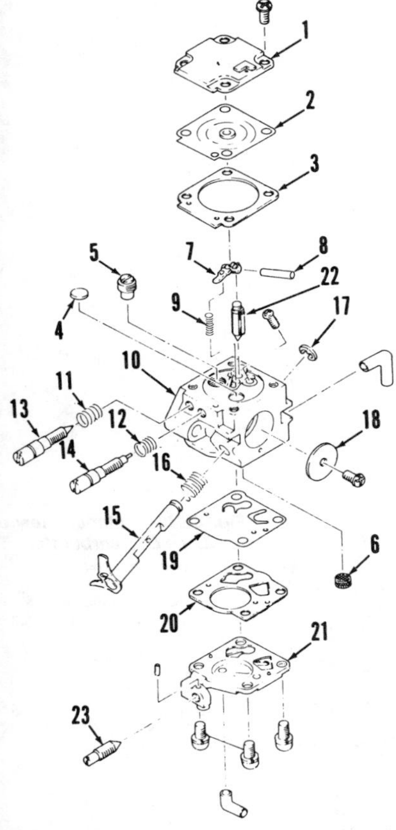

Fig. CS45–Exploded view of Zama C1 carburetor.

1. Cover
2. Metering diaphragm
3. Gasket
4. Welch plug
5. Check valve nozzle
6. Screen
7. Metering lever
8. Pin
9. Spring
10. Body
11. Spring
12. Spring
13. High speed mixture screw
14. Low speed mixture screw
15. Throttle shaft
16. Return spring
17. "E" clip
18. Throttle plate
19. Fuel pump diaphragm & check valves
20. Gasket
21. Fuel pump
22. Fuel inlet valve
23. Idle speed screw

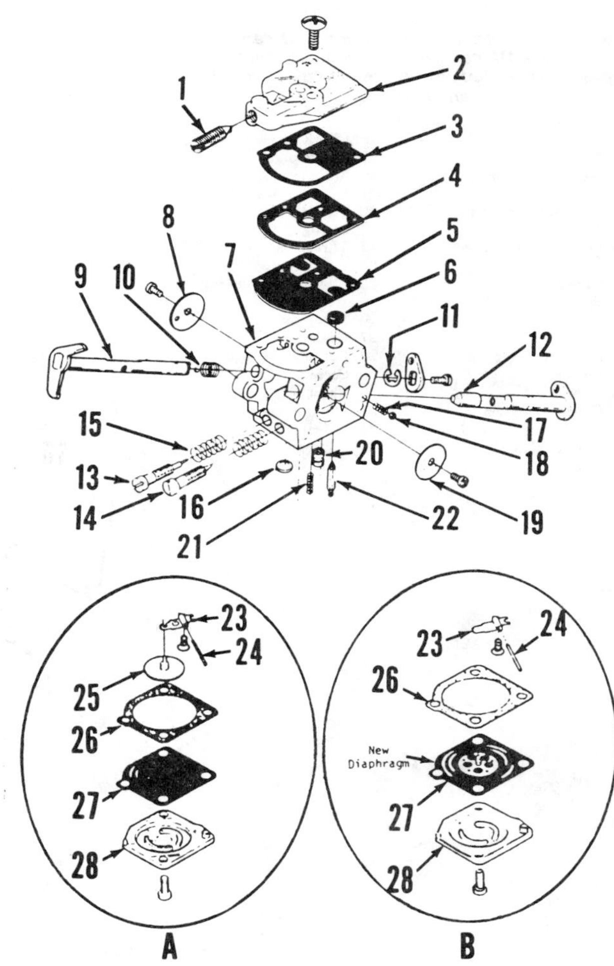

Fig. CS46–Exploded view of Zama C1S carburetor. Note differences in diaphragm assembly. "A" shows the old type diaphragm assembly and "B" shows the new type diaphragm assembly.

1. Idle speed screw
2. Fuel pump cover
3. Gasket
4. Plate
5. Fuel pump diaphragm
6. Screen
7. Carburetor body
8. Throttle plate
9. Throttle shaft
10. Spring
11. "E" clip
12. Choke shaft
13. Idle mixture screw
14. High speed mixture screw
15. Spring
16. Plug
17. Spring
18. Detent ball
19. Choke plate
20. Check valve
21. Spring
22. Fuel inlet valve
23. Metering lever
24. Pin
25. Metering disc
26. Gasket
27. Metering diaphragm
28. Cover

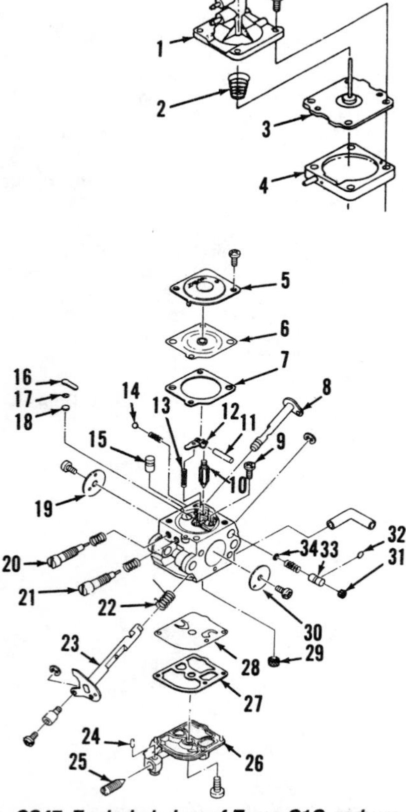

Fig. CS47–Exploded view of Zama C1Q carburetor. Zama C1U carburetor is similar. Items (1 through 4) are used on carburetors equipped with an oil pump.

1. Oil pump body
2. Plunger spring
3. Plunger assy.
4. Metering chamber cover
5. Metering chamber cover
6. Metering diaphragm
7. Gasket
8. Choke shaft
9. Screw
10. Needle valve
11. Pin
12. Metering lever
13. Spring
14. Check ball
15. Check valve nozzle
16. Welch plug
17. Check valve retainer
18. Check valve
19. Choke plate
20. Main mixture screw
21. Idle mixture screw
22. Throttle return spring
23. Throttle shaft
24. Friction pin
25. Idle speed adjusting screw
26. Pump cover
27. Gasket
28. Pump diaphragm
29. Screen
30. Throttle plate
31. Strainer
32. "O" ring
33. Plunger
34. Strainer

Fig. CS48–Exploded view of Zama C2 carburetor.

1. Cover
2. Metering diaphragm
3. Gasket
4. Pin
5. Screw
6. Screen
7. Metering lever
8. Spring
9. Check valve nozzle
10. Choke shaft
11. Welch plug
12. "E" clip
13. High speed mixture screw
14. Low speed mixture screw
15. Choke plate
16. Ball
17. Spring
18. Spring
19. Spring
20. Throttle shaft
21. Return spring
22. Fuel inlet valve
23. Throttle plate
24. Fuel pump diaphragm & check valves
25. Plate
26. Gasket
27. Fuel pump cover
28. Body

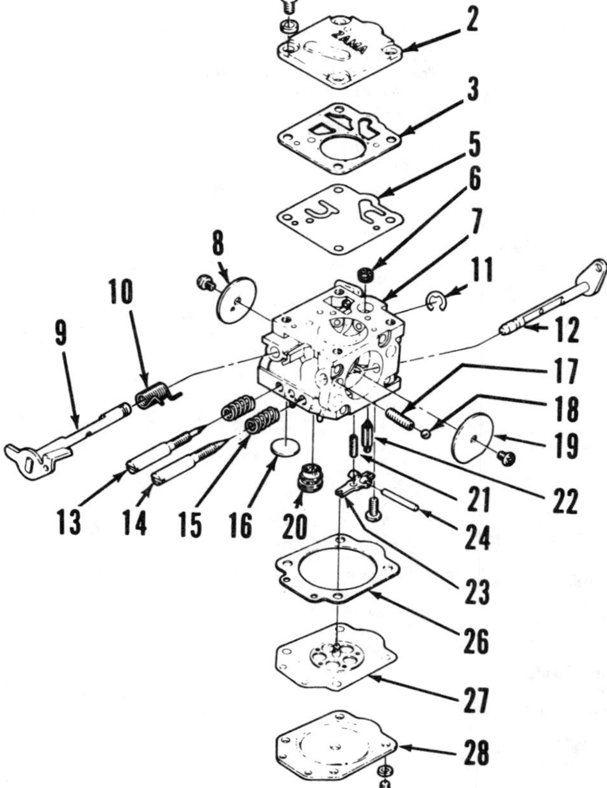

Fig. CS49–Exploded view of Zama C2S carburetor.

2. Fuel pump cover
3. Gasket
5. Fuel pump diaphragm & check valves
6. Screen
7. Carburetor body
8. Throttle plate
9. Throttle shaft
10. Spring
11. "E" clip
12. Choke shaft
13. Low speed mixture screw
14. High speed mixture screw
15. Spring
16. Plug
17. Spring
18. Check ball
19. Choke plate
20. Check valve nozzle
21. Spring
22. Fuel inlet needle valve
23. Metering lever
24. Pin
26. Gasket
27. Metering diaphragm
28. Cover

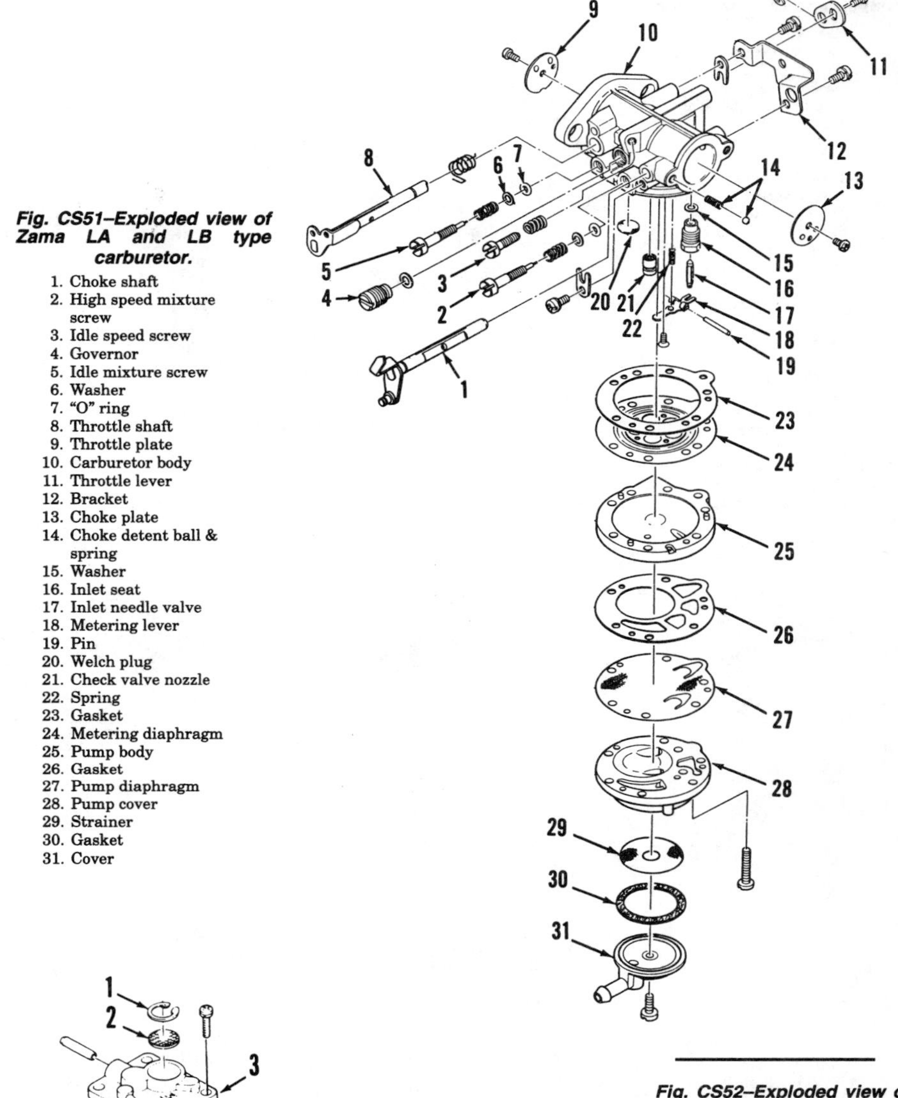

Fig. CS51–Exploded view of Zama LA and LB type carburetor.

1. Choke shaft
2. High speed mixture screw
3. Idle speed screw
4. Governor
5. Idle mixture screw
6. Washer
7. "O" ring
8. Throttle shaft
9. Throttle plate
10. Carburetor body
11. Throttle lever
12. Bracket
13. Choke plate
14. Choke detent ball & spring
15. Washer
16. Inlet seat
17. Inlet needle valve
18. Metering lever
19. Pin
20. Welch plug
21. Check valve nozzle
22. Spring
23. Gasket
24. Metering diaphragm
25. Pump body
26. Gasket
27. Pump diaphragm
28. Pump cover
29. Strainer
30. Gasket
31. Cover

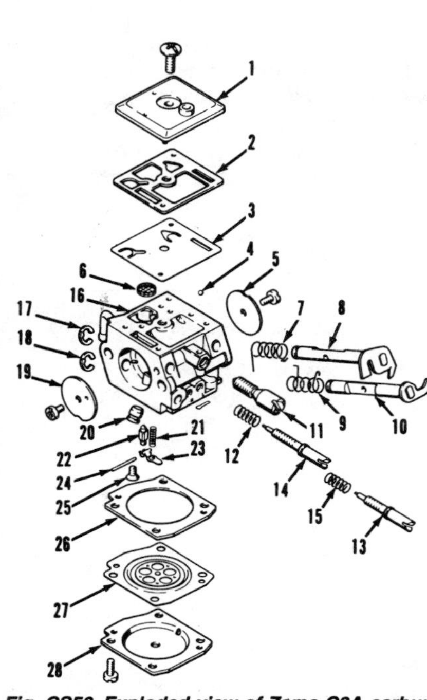

Fig. CS50–Exploded view of Zama C3A carburetor. Model C3M carburetor is similar except that fuel mixture screws are located on opposite side of carburetor body.

1. Fuel pump cover
2. Gasket
3. Fuel pump diaphragm & check valves
4. Ball
5. Throttle plate
6. Screen
7. Return spring
8. Throttle shaft
9. Return spring
10. Choke shaft
11. Idle speed screw
12. Spring
13. High speed mixture screw
14. Low speed mixture screw
15. Spring
16. Carburetor body
17. "E" clip
18. "E" clip
19. Choke plate
20. Check valve nozzle
21. Spring
22. Fuel inlet needle valve
23. Metering lever
24. Pin
25. Screw
26. Gasket
27. Metering diaphragm
28. Cover

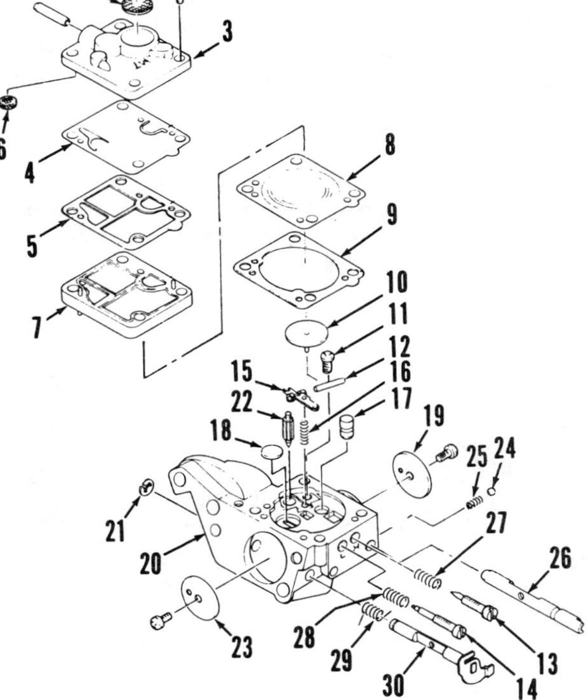

Fig. CS52–Exploded view of Zama M1 carburetor.

1. Snap ring
2. Screen
3. Fuel pump cover
4. Fuel pump diaphragm & check valves
5. Gasket
6. Screen
7. Metering block
8. Metering diaphragm
9. Gasket
10. Disc
11. Screw
12. Pin
13. High speed mixture screw
14. Low speed mixture screw
15. Metering lever
16. Spring
17. Check valve nozzle
18. Welch plug
19. Choke plate
20. Carburetor body
21. "E" clip
22. Fuel inlet needle valve
23. Throttle plate
24. Ball
25. Spring
26. Choke shaft
27. Spring
28. Spring
29. Return spring
30. Throttle shaft

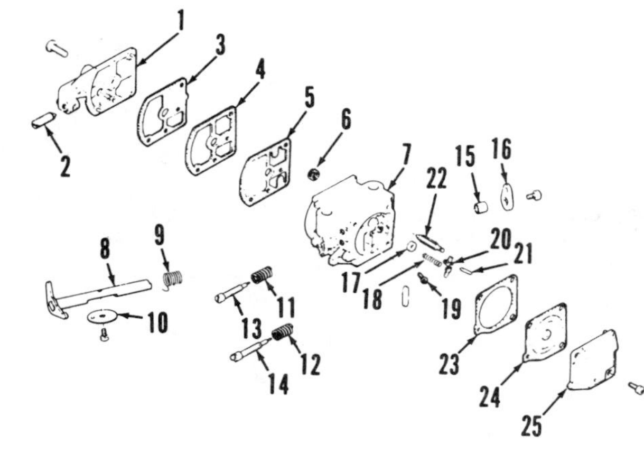

Fig. CS53–Exploded view of Zama Z1 and Z1A carburetor.

1. Fuel pump cover
2. Idle speed screw
3. Plate
4. Gasket
5. Fuel pump diaphragm & check valves
6. Screen
7. Body
8. Throttle shaft
9. Return spring
10. Throttle plate
11. Spring
12. Spring
13. High speed mixture screw
14. Low speed mixture screw
15. Collar
16. Retainer
17. Welch plug
18. Spring
19. Screw
20. Metering lever
21. Pin
22. Fuel inlet valve
23. Gasket
24. Metering diaphragm
25. Cover

early model carburetors, note the new design diaphragm assembly (B—Fig. CS46). Always install the new style diaphragm assembly when servicing old style carburetors.

Examine the fuel inlet needle valve and seat. On some carburetors, the inlet valve and seat are renewable. On other models, inlet valve is renewable, but carburetor body must be renewed if valve seat is damaged or excessively worn.

Fuel mixture screws must be renewed if tip is grooved or broken. Inspect mixture screw seats in carburetor body. The carburetor body must be renewed if screw seats are damaged or excessively worn.

When reassembling carburetor, note the following: If nozzle is pressed in

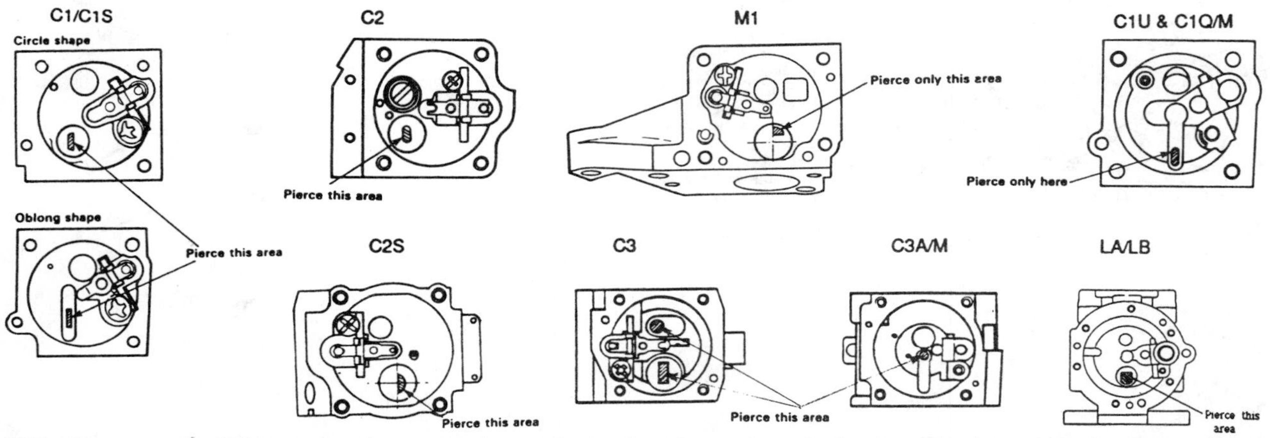

Fig. CS54—When removing Welch plug on Zama carburetors, note the shaded area shown in the above drawings where the plug may be pierced.

punch to pierce the Welch plug. Let the punch just pierce the plug, then pry the plug out of the casting. Pierce the Welch plug in the shaded area shown in Fig. CS54. Be careful not to damage the body casting below the plug.

Clean and inspect all components. Manufacturer recommends cleaning fuel channels by blowing spray type carburetor cleaner through the idle and main adjusting orifices. Manufacturer DOES NOT recommend the use of dip tank type cleaner. Sharp objects should not be used to clean orifices or passages as fuel flow may be altered.

Check metering diaphragm and fuel pump diaphragm for punctures or tears that will affect operation. On some type, apply a light film of oil to the outside of nozzle. Carefully press the nozzle assembly into carburetor body until it is flush with the metering chamber floor. Apply a thin coat of fuel-resistant sealant around the outer edge of new Welch plug prior to installing. Press the Welch plug firmly into its cavity. Wipe off excess sealant.

Note the two types of metering levers shown in Fig. CS55. If metering lever is the type shown in left view, adjust clearance "A" to 0-0.012 in. (0-0.3 mm). Straight type metering lever shown in right view should be flush with the metering chamber floor. Carefully bend the metering lever to obtain the correct setting.

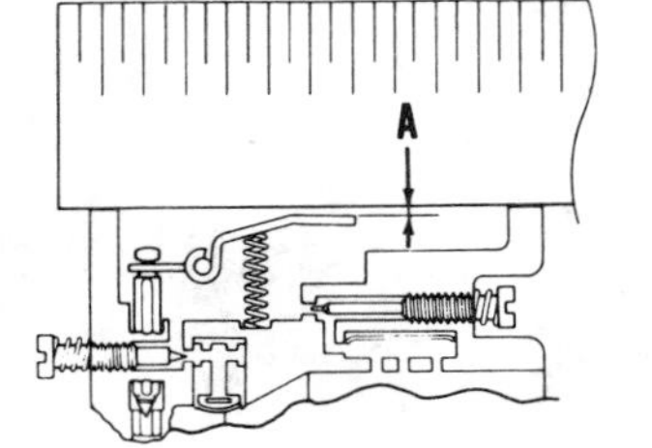

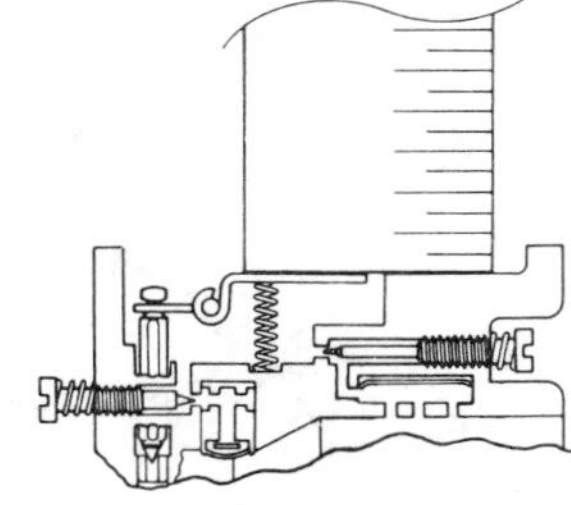

Fig. CS55–Note position of metering lever in the different carburetor castings. Metering lever in right view must be flush as shown. Adjust metering lever in left view so distance "A" is 0-0.012 inch (0-0.3 mm).

ENGINE SERVICE

GENERAL ENGINE SERVICE

TROUBLESHOOTING

ENGINE OPERATIONAL SYMPTOMS. An engine must develop compression, have an ignition spark and receive the proper fuel:air mixture to run. To check engine for compression, turn crankshaft slowly. As engine piston is coming up on the compression stroke, a definite resistance to turning should be felt. This resistance should be noted on every crankshaft revolution on a two-stroke engine. Compression gages are also available and may be used to check compression pressure. Where available from the engine manufacturer, specifications will be given for engine compression pressure in the engine service sections of this manual.

To check for ignition spark, the use of a special test plug is recommended. If test plug is not available, disconnect spark plug wire from spark plug and position wire terminal about 1/8 inch (3 mm) from cylinder. While cranking engine, a bright blue spark should snap across the gap. If spark is weak or no spark appears, ignition system is faulty.

An engine loss of power complaint may be caused by a dull saw chain, a chain that is adjusted too tightly or a chain brake that is dragging.

Always check and make any necessary adjustments or repairs to the ignition system, air filter, fuel supply, carburetor, saw chain and chain brake system before looking for faults on the engine. When troubleshooting the engine for malfunction, always inspect the most obvious and easily checked items first. Some normally encountered difficulties resulting from engine malfunction and the possible causes of difficulty are as follows:

A. ENGINE IS HARD TO START, IDLES ROUGHLY OR STALLS AT IDLE SPEED, BUT OPERATES NORMALLY AT FULL THROTTLE. This condition is normally caused by an air leak in the intake system. Check for (1) crankcase seals leaking, (2) intake manifold leaking, (3) crankcase damaged or mating surfaces not properly sealed.

B. ENGINE OVERHEATING. Check for (1) insufficient air circulation caused by air inlet in fan housing blocked or cylinder fins plugged, (2) plugged exhaust port or muffler, (3) air leak in crankcase or intake system resulting in lean fuel:air mixture, (4) intake air preheater (if so equipped) being used at too high ambient temperature.

C. ENGINE DOES NOT DELIVER FULL POWER. Check for (1) exhaust port or muffler plugged, (2) piston rings leaking or broken.

Fig. 100—To pressure test crankcase, a hand pump (1) and pressure gage (2) may be connected to engine intake port using adapter plate (3) in place of carburetor. Refer to text.

CRANKCASE PRESSURE TEST. Pressure testing the crankcase is an important part of troubleshooting and repair of two-cycle engines that is often overlooked. An improperly sealed crankcase allows supplementary air to enter the engine and upsets the fuel:air mixture. This can cause the engine to be hard to start, run rough, have low power and overheat.

To test crankcase for leakage, a suitable hand pump and pressure gage must be connected to the crankcase. Remove muffler and carburetor. Fabricate a seal using gasket paper to cover the exhaust port, then reinstall muffler. Use either of the following methods to connect a hand pump and pressure gage to crankcase. Fabricate an adapter plate and install in place of the carburetor to cover and seal the intake manifold port. The adapter plate must have a nipple to connect pressure hose of tester as shown in Fig. 100. An alternate method of testing is as follows: Fabricate a seal using gasket paper to cover the intake port and reinstall carburetor. Connect a suitable hand pump and pressure gage to carburetor pulse line, or plug carburetor end of pulse line and install pressure tester in spark plug hole. If testing leakage through spark plug hole, position piston at bottom dead center. If testing leakage through intake manifold or pulse line, position piston at top dead center. Apply pressure until gage reads 7 psi (48 kPa) and close pump vent screw. Pressure should remain constant. If pressure drops more than 2 psi (14 kPa) in 30 seconds, leak must be located.

Crankcase seals may also be tested for a vacuum leak using a vacuum pump in place of pressure pump as outlined above. Actuate vacuum pump until gage indicates vacuum of 7 psi (48 kPa). If vacuum reading remains constant or decreases no more than 2 psi (14 kPa), crankcase seals are in good condition. If seals fail to hold a vacuum, even if no pressure leak was indicated, they should be renewed.

If crankcase leakage is indicated, use a soap and water solution to check gaskets, crankcase seals, pulse line and castings for leakage.

ALLIS-CHALMERS

Model	Bore mm (in.)	Stroke mm (in.)	Displacement cc (cu. in.)	Drive Type
85	45.41 (1.788)	36.49 (1.437)	59 (3.6)	Gear*
95, 195, 295	45.41 (1.788)	36.49 (1.437)	59 (3.6)	Direct

* Reciprocating blade.

MAINTENANCE

SPARK PLUG. Recommended spark plug is Champion CJ8. Spark plug electrode gap should be 0.025 inch (0.63 mm).

CARBURETOR. All models are equipped with a Tillotson Model HS diaphragm carburetor. Initial idle and high speed mixture settings are one turn open. Adjust idle speed screw so that engine idles at engine speed just below clutch engagement speed. Adjust idle mixture screw so that engine will accelerate without lagging or faltering. Adjust high speed mixture screw to give optimum performance under cutting load. It may be necessary to readjust idle mixture screw after adjusting high speed screw. Be sure mixture settings are not too lean as engine damage may result.

Refer to Tillotson section of CARBURETOR SERVICE section for carburetor operation and overhaul.

MAGNETO AND TIMING. A flywheel magneto is used on all models. Breaker point gap should be 0.015 inch (0.38 mm) for Model 95 and 0.017 inch (0.43 mm) for all other models. Ignition timing is fixed but incorrect breaker point gap will affect timing. Magneto air gap should be 0.012 inch (0.30 mm).

LUBRICATION. All engines are lubricated by mixing oil with fuel. Fuel:oil ratio is 16:1. Oil should be a good quality SAE 30 oil designed for chain saw or air-cooled two-stroke engines.

All models are equipped with a manual chain oiler except Model 85 which is equipped with a blade in place of the chain. Models 195 and 295 are also equipped with an automatic chain oiler. Fill oil reservoir with a good quality SAE 30 Service MS oil if ambient temperature is above 40°F (4°C) or SAE 10W if temperature is below 40°F (4°C).

CARBON. Carbon deposits should be removed from muffler and exhaust ports at regular intervals. When scraping carbon, be careful not to damage engine cylinder. Do not allow loosened carbon to enter cylinder.

REPAIRS

CYLINDER. All models are equipped with a chrome plated cylinder. Renew

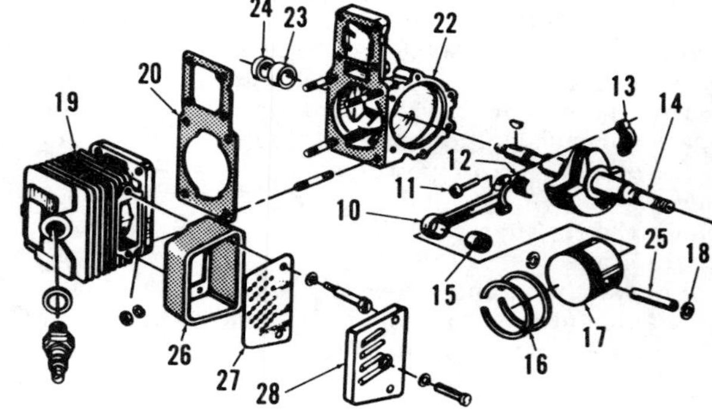

Fig. A1—Exploded view of Model 95 engine. Refer to Fig. A2 for parts identification except: 26. Muffler; 27. Muffler Baffle; 28. Cover.

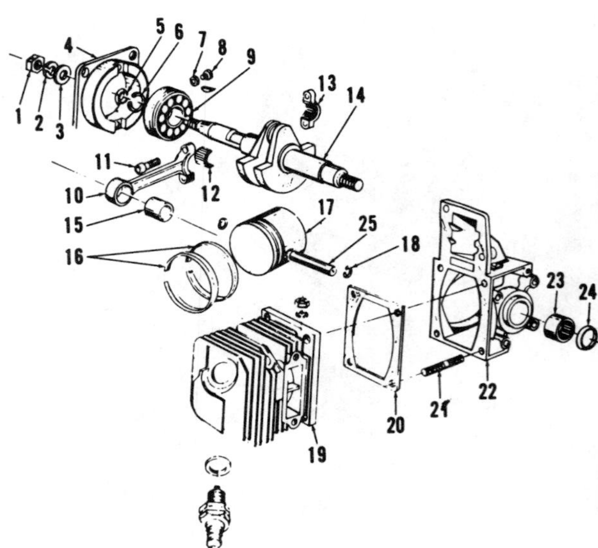

Fig. A2—Exploded view of engine used on Models 85, 195 and 295. Carrier (4) is a partial view of rear of bearing carrier (15—Fig. A6).

1. Nut
2. Lockwasher
3. Washer
4. Bearing carrier
5. Seal
6. Snap ring
7. Washer
8. Cap screw
9. Bearing
10. Connecting rod
11. Socket head screw
12. Bearing rollers (25)
13. Rod cap
14. Crankshaft
15. Bearing
16. Piston rings
17. Piston
18. Snap ring
19. Cylinder
20. Gasket
21. Stud
22. Crankcase
23. Bearing
24. Seal
25. Piston pin

cylinder if cylinder is scored, cracked or excessively worn. Only standard size piston and rings are available.

PISTON, PIN AND RINGS. All models are equipped with two piston rings. Piston rings are retained by pins in ring grooves and must be aligned with pins when cylinder is installed. Install piston so ring locating pins are on magneto side of engine. Piston wrist pin has one closed end, which must be towards exhaust port. Heat piston to about 200°F (93°C) to aid in pin installation. Piston pin snap rings should be installed so sharp edge is out.

Pistons and rings are available in standard size only. Manufacturer does not specify piston or piston ring clearances.

CONNECTING ROD. Connecting rod may be removed after removing cylinder and piston. Unscrew connecting rod screws and remove rod and cap being careful not to lose loose bearing rollers. There are 25 bearing rollers in Model 85, 95, 195 and 295 connecting rod. Connecting rod small end bearing must be pressed out of rod. Be sure rod is properly supported when removing or installing bearing.

Use heavy grease to hold roller bearings in rod and cap. Match marks on sides of rod and cap must be aligned during installation.

CRANKSHAFT AND CRANKCASE. Crankshaft is supported in antifriction bearings at both ends. Flywheel end of crankshaft on Model 95 is supported by a needle roller bearing (23 – Fig. A1) in the crankcase while a ball bearing (9 – Fig. A2) contained in bearing carrier (4) is used to support flywheel end of crankshaft on all other models. Clutch end of crankshaft on Model 95 is supported by a ball bearing (3 – Fig. A3) in bearing carrier (7) while a needle roller bearing (23 – Fig. A2) in crankcase (22) supports clutch end of crankshaft on all other models.

Fuel, oil, ignition, starter and clutch assemblies must be removed from engine to remove crankshaft. Remove cylinder piston and connecting rod. On Models 85, 195 and 295, remove bearing carrier (4 – Fig. A2), bearing (9) and crankshaft (14) from crankcase. Unscrew retaining cap screws (8) and separate bearing (9) and crankshaft from carrier (4). Remove snap ring (6) and pull bearing (9) off crankshaft. To remove crankshaft on Model 95, unscrew bearing carrier (7 – Fig. A3) screws and remove bearing carrier and crankshaft from crankcase. Remove crankshaft from bearing (3). Unscrew two retaining screws (1) and separate bearing from carrier (7). To reassemble, reverse disassembly procedure. Install ball bearing with groove in outer race adjacent to crankshaft counterweight. Bearing holder (4 – Fig. A2) and bearing carrier (7 – Fig. A3) must be heated to 200°F (93°C) before installing bearing.

CLUTCH. Clutch hub is equipped with left hand threads. Clutch hub bearing is available for all models. Refer to Figs. A3, A4 or A7 for exploded view of clutch.

REED VALVE. All models are equipped with reed valve induction with four reed petals on a pyramid reed cage. Inspect reed valve for nicks, chips or burrs. Be sure reed petal lays flat against seat.

AUTOMATIC CHAIN OILER. Models 195 and 295 are equipped with an automatic chain oiler. Oil pump is driven by cam (18 – Fig. A4) on engine crankshaft. Inspect bronze gear (19) and renew if gear teeth are broken or ex-

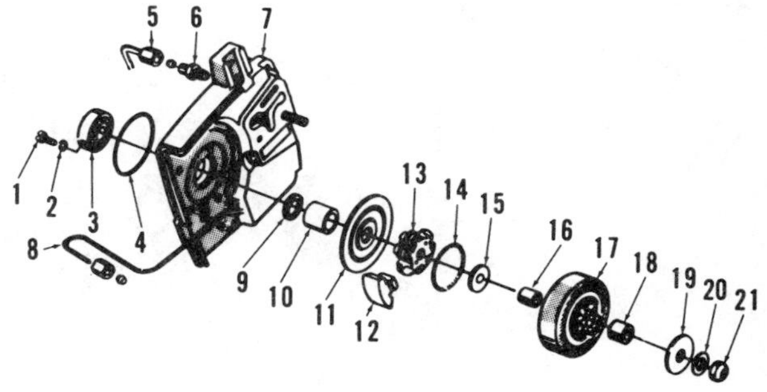

Fig. A3 — Exploded view of clutch and bearing housing carrier used on Model 95.

1. Cap screw
2. Washer
3. Bearing
4. "O" ring
5. Oil line
6. Oil fitting
7. Bearing housing carrier
8. Oil line
9. Seal
10. Sleeve
11. Clutch cover
12. Clutch shoe
13. Clutch hub
14. Spring
15. Thrust washer
16. Bearing race
17. Clutch drum
18. Bearing
19. Washer
20. Washer
21. Nut

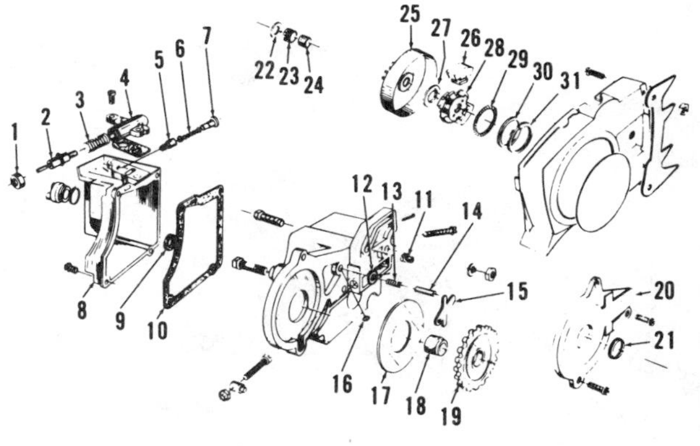

Fig. A4 — Exploded view of Model 195 and Model 295 manual and automatic oil pump and clutch assemblies.

1. Plunger
2. Plunger rod
3. Spring
4. Manual oil pump housing
5. Intake valve
6. Spring
7. Oil pump button
8. Oil tank
9. Gasket
10. Gasket
11. Oil outlet valve
12. Washer
13. Spring
14. Piston
15. Lever
16. Quad ring
17. Disc
18. Cam
19. Gear
20. Automatic oil pump cover
21. Seal
22. Thrust washer
23. Bearing
24. Bearing race
25. Clutch drum
26. Clutch shoe
27. Thrust washer
28. Clutch hub
29. Clutch spring
30. Retaining ring
31. Spirolox

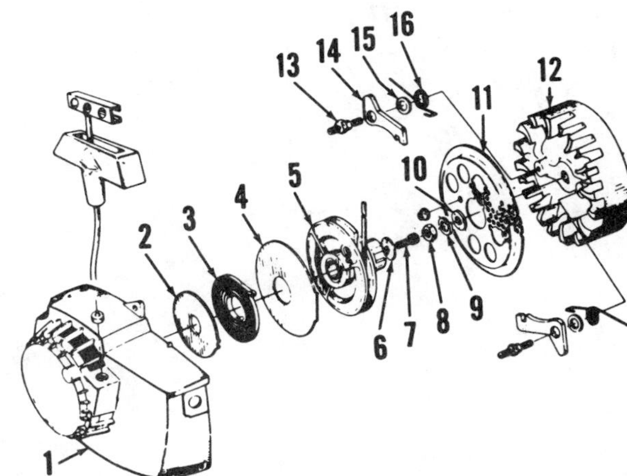

Fig. A5 — Exploded view of Model 95 rewind starter.

1. Starter housing
2. Spring plate
3. Rewind spring
4. Spring cover
5. Rope pulley
6. Washer
7. Screw
8. Flywheel nut
9. Lockwasher
10. Washer
11. Flywheel cover
12. Flywheel
13. Stud
14. Starter dog
15. Washer
16. Spring

cessively worn. If button on lever (15) is worn, renew lever. Pack oil pump cavity with a suitable grease before reassembly. Install seal (21) in cover and carefully install cam (18) in seal with step of cam towards seal until seal seats against shoulder of cam. Be careful not to damage seal. Install pump lever (15) in cover and gear (19) on cam (18). Place thrust washer (12), spring (13), piston (14) and quad ring (16). Install cover (20) and pump components in cover on crankshaft.

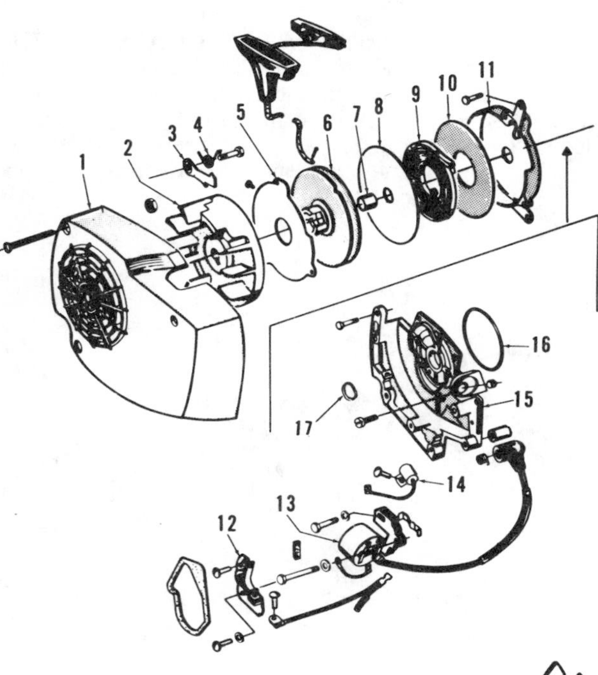

Fig. A6—Exploded view of recoil starter and ignition assembly used on Models 85, 195 and 295.

1. Fan housing
2. Flywheel
3. Starter dog
4. Spring
5. Plate
6. Rope pulley
7. Bearing
8. Spring plate
9. Rewind spring
10. Spring plate
11. Starter housing
12. Breaker-points
13. Coil & armature
14. Condenser
15. Side cover
16. "O" ring
17. Seal

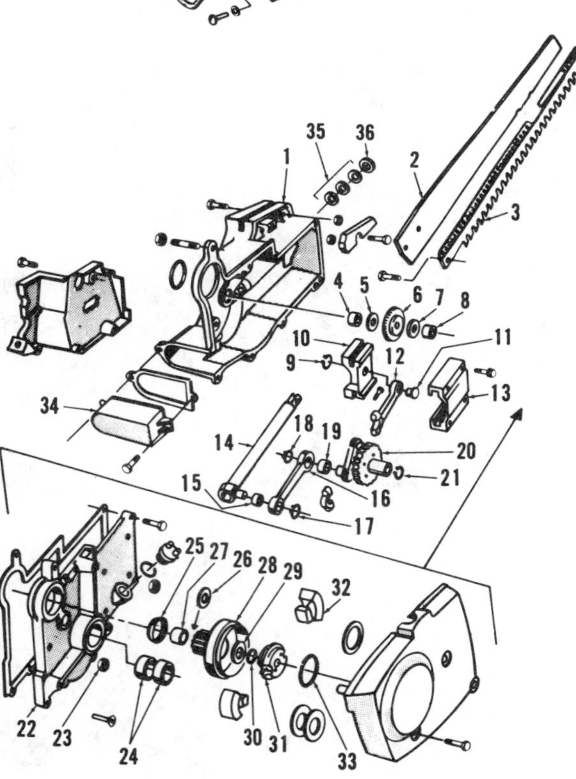

Fig. A7—Exploded view of gear drive assembly used on Model 85. Later models use interlocking seals and a metal back seal in place of seals (35) and retainer (36) shown. Refer to text.

1. Housing
2. Bar
3. Blade
4. Bearing
5. Washer
6. Idler gear
7. Washer
8. Bearing
9. Snap ring
10. Counterweight
11. Pin
12. Counterweight rod
13. Retaining guide
14. Plunger
15. Bearing
16. Connecting rod
17. Snap ring
18. Snap ring
19. Bearing
20. Driven gear
21. Snap ring
22. Cover
23. Nut
24. Bearings
25. Seal
26. Washer
27. Bearing
28. Clutch drum
29. Washer
28. Clutch drum
29. Washer
30. Seal
31. Clutch hub
32. Clutch shoe
33. Clutch spring
34. Cap
35. Seals
36. Retainer

REWIND STARTER. Refer to Figs. A5 and A6 for exploded views of rewind starters. Rewind spring on Model 95 should be wound in clockwise direction when viewed installed in housing. Rewind spring should be wound in counterclockwise direction on Models 85, 195 and 295. Starter rope on Model 95 should be wound on a rope pulley in clockwise direction when viewed installed in starter housing. Starter rope should be wound in counterclockwise direction on Models 85, 195 and 295. Turn rope pulley sufficient turns to place tension on rewind spring before passing rope through outlet so rope will rewind into housing.

TRANSMISSION. Model 85 is equipped with a transmission to drive the saw blade. To disassemble transmission, remove blade, clutch cover and clutch. Remove snap ring (21–Fig. A7) and unscrew transmission cover (22) screws. Remove cover and inspect bearings (24), bearing (27) and seal (25) for wear or damage. Remove snap ring (17). If plunger (14) is to be removed, remove cap (34) and withdraw plunger. Remove screws retaining guide (13) and withdraw transmission assembly. Disassembly of remainder of transmission is self-evident.

Inspect components for wear or damage. Counterweight (10) and counterweight rod (12) are available only as a unit assembly. To reassemble, reverse disassembly procedure and note the following:

Forty needle rollers are used between counterweight rod (12) and driven gear (20). Hold rollers in place with heavy grease. Recess on counterweight rod (12) should be adjacent to gear (20). Note difference in seal (35 and 36) assembly between early and late models. Earlier models used three seals (35) and a metal retainer (36). Later models use two interlocking type seals and a metal back seal. Interlocking seals should have lips inward while metal back seal should have lip out. Install metal back seal so it stands out from housing about 1/16 inch (1.58 mm). Early models should have later seal assembly installed. Install seal (25) so metal back stands out 1/32 inch (0.79 mm) from outside of housing.

ALPINA

Model	Bore mm (in.)	Stroke mm (in.)	Displacement cc (cu. in.)	Drive Type
330, A330, A432	36.5 (1.44)	30.4 (1.2)	32 (1.9)	Direct
380, A380, 438, A438	39.7 (1.56)	30.4 (1.2)	38 (2.3)	Direct

MAINTENANCE

SPARK PLUG. Recommended spark plug is Champion CJ7Y for all models. Spark plug electrode gap should be 0.5 mm (0.020 in.).

CARBURETOR. Models A330 and A380 are equipped with a Walbro WA diaphragm type carburetor. Models A432 and A438 are equipped with a Dell'Orto diaphragm type carburetor. Refer to Walbro and Dell'Orto sections of CARBURETOR SERVICE section for service procedures and exploded views.

High speed mixture is not adjustable on Models A330 and A380. Initial setting of low speed mixture screw is 1⅜ turns open on Model A330 and 1½ turns open on Model A380. Initial setting on Models A432 and A438 is 1¾ turns open for low speed mixture screw and 1½ turns open for high speed mixture screw.

Final adjustment should be made with engine running at operating temperature. Adjust engine idle speed to just below clutch engagement speed. Adjust low-speed mixture so engine will accelerate cleanly without hesitation. Adjust high-speed mixture to obtain maximum no-load speed of 11,200 rpm on Model A432 and 11,700 rpm on Model A438.

IGNITION. All models are equipped with a breakerless electronic ignition system. Ignition coil and all electronic circuitry are contained in a one-piece ignition module. Ignition timing is not adjustable. Air gap between ignition module legs and flywheel magnets should be 0.35 mm (0.014 in.). Loosen ignition module mounting screws and move module to adjust air gap. Use a suitable thread locking solution on module screws to prevent screws from vibrating loose. If flywheel requires removal, use Alpina tool 3630260 or a suitable equivalent to withdraw flywheel. Tighten flywheel nut to 34.3 N•m (26 ft.-lbs.).

LUBRICATION. The engine is lubricated by mixing oil with the fuel. Use a good quality oil designed for use in air-cooled two-stroke engines. Fuel:oil ratio is 16:1 for all models. Use a separate container when mixing fuel and oil.

Models A330 and A380 are equipped with an automatic oil pump which utilizes crankcase pulsations to pressurize oil tank. Pump output is adjustable. Models A432 and A438 are equipped with an automatic plunger type oil pump driven by a worm gear on engine crankshaft. Pump output is not adjustable. Refer to OIL PUMP under REPAIRS section for service procedures and exploded views.

Use clean automotive oil for saw chain lubrication. On Models A330 and A380, oil viscosity must be chosen according to ambient temperature. For example, use SAE 30 for warm weather operation and SAE 15 for cold weather operation.

REPAIRS

CYLINDER, PISTON PIN AND RINGS. Cylinder is chrome plated and should be renewed if cracking, scoring or other damage is noted in cylinder bore.

NOTE: Piston aligns connecting rod on rod bearing rollers (25—Fig. AP1). Excessive piston movement during or after cylinder removal may allow rod bearing rollers to fall into crankcase.

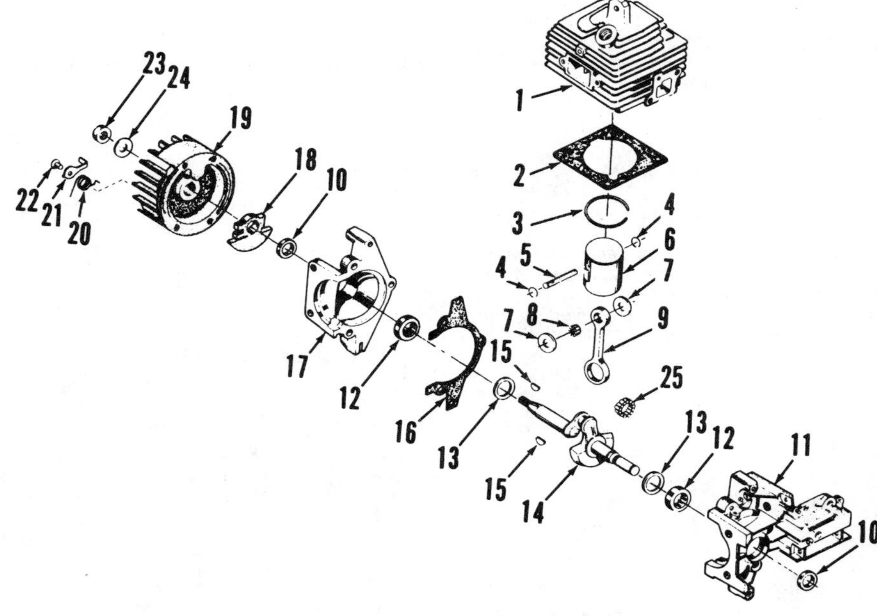

Fig. AP1—Exploded view of engine assembly typical of all models noting counterweight (18) is absent on Models A432 and A438. Two pawl assemblies (20, 21 and 22) are used.

1. Cylinder
2. Gasket
3. Piston ring
4. Snap ring
5. Piston pin
6. Piston
7. Thrust washer
8. Bearing rollers
9. Connecting rod
10. Seal
11. Right crankcase half
12. Main bearing
13. Thrust washer
14. Crankshaft
15. Key
16. Gasket
17. Left crankcase half
18. Counterweight
19. Flywheel
20. Spring
21. Pawl
22. Pin
23. Nut
24. Washer
25. Bearing rollers

Piston and cylinder are matched during production to get desired piston-to-cylinder clearance of 0.02 mm (0.0008 in.). Original piston and cylinder are marked "A." Factory renewal piston and cylinder assemblies are marked "B." Piston or cylinder marked "C" is 0.127 mm (0.005 in.) oversize while piston or cylinder marked "D" is 0.127 mm (0.005 in.) undersize. Piston and cylinder markings should match, however, a new piston marked "B" can be installed in a used cylinder marked "A."

NOTE: Do not install a new piston marked "B" or "C" into a new cylinder marked "A."

Piston is equipped with one piston ring. A locating pin is present in ring groove to prevent ring rotation. Maximum allowable piston ring end gap is 1.0 mm (0.039 in.). Piston pin (5 – Fig. AP1) rides on 18 loose bearing rollers (8). Use Alpina tool 4180010 or a suitable equivalent with proper size drivers to remove and install piston pin. Hold bearing rollers (8) in place with heavy grease and place thrust washer (7) on each side of rod before installing piston. Install piston with arrow on piston crown facing toward exhaust side of cylinder. Make certain piston ring end gap is properly positioned around locating pin in ring groove before installing cylinder. Tighten cylinder screws to 8.8 N•m (78 in.-lbs.).

CRANKSHAFT, CONNECTING ROD AND CRANKCASE. Crankshaft (14 – Fig. AP1) is supported at both ends with caged roller bearings (12). Bearings (12) locate in crankcase halves (11 and 17). To split crankcase halves, first remove cylinder and crankcase halves mounting screws. Insert a screwdriver or similar tool between crankcase and crankshaft counterweight. Carefully pry crankcase halves apart being careful not to damage crankcase mating surfaces.

NOTE: Crankshaft runout can be checked before disassembly of engine. To check runout, remove clutch and flywheel. Mount a dial indicator on both ends of crankshaft as close as possible to bearings (12). Check runout while rotating crankshaft. Runout should not exceed 0.07 mm (0.0027 in.).

Connecting rod rides on 12 loose bearing rollers (25). Connecting rod can be removed from crankshaft after crankcase halves are separated. Hold bearing rollers on crankpin with heavy grease when installing connecting rod. Note location of thrust washers (13). Counterweight (18) is used on Models A330 and A380 only. Do not use gasket sealing compounds on crankcase gasket (16). Tighten crankcase screws using a crisscross pattern to 6.9 N•m (61 in.-lbs.).

CLUTCH. Models A432, A438 and later Models A330 and A380 are equipped with the centrifugal clutch shown in Fig. AP2. Early Models A330 and A380 are equipped with the centrifugal clutch shown in Fig. AP3. Complete clutch assemblies are interchangeable, although, individual components are not. Clutch hubs (2 – Figs. AP2 and AP3) have left-hand threads. Inspect shoes, hub, drum and needle bearing for excessive wear or damage due to overheating. Clutch shoes are available only as a complete set. Tighten clutch hub to 18.6 N•m (14 ft.-lbs.).

OIL PUMP. Models A330 and A380 are equipped with the pressure-type chain oiling system shown in Fig. AP4. Impulse hose (3) connects to crankcase. Crankcase pulsations pressurize oil tank (1). Check valve (4) prevents chain oil from entering crankcase. Pump output is regulated by rotating screw (8). Clockwise rotation decreases output. Shut-off valve (10) is linked to throttle trigger, preventing oil flow at idle speed.

Oil tank (1) must hold pressure for proper operation of system. Pressurize oil tank to 34.5 kPa (5.0 psi) to check for leakage in tank or leak-back of check

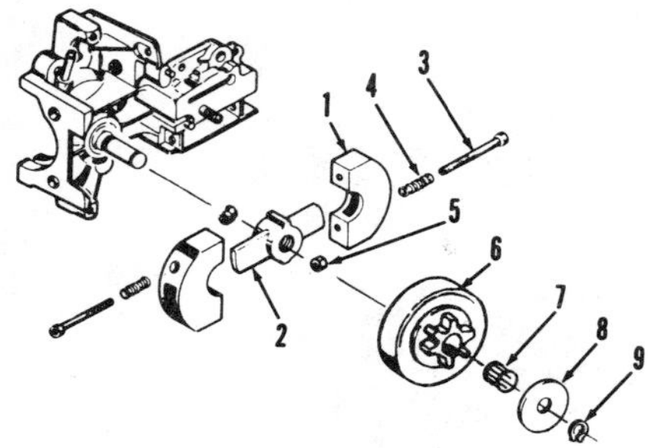

Fig. AP2 – Exploded view of centrifugal clutch assembly used on Models A432, A438 and later Models A330 and A380. Refer to Fig. AP3 for exploded view of clutch assembly used on early Models A330 and A380.

1. Shoe
2. Hub
3. Screw
4. Spring
5. Nut
6. Drum
7. Needle bearing
8. Washer
9. Snap ring

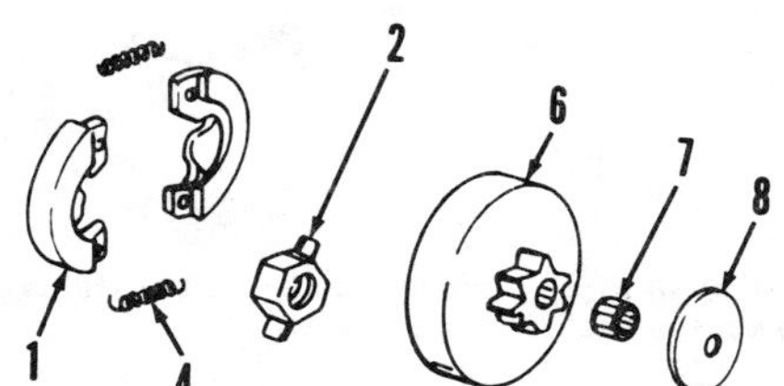

Fig. AP3 – Exploded view of centrifugal clutch assembly used on early Models A330 and A380. Refer to legend in Fig. AP2 for component identification.

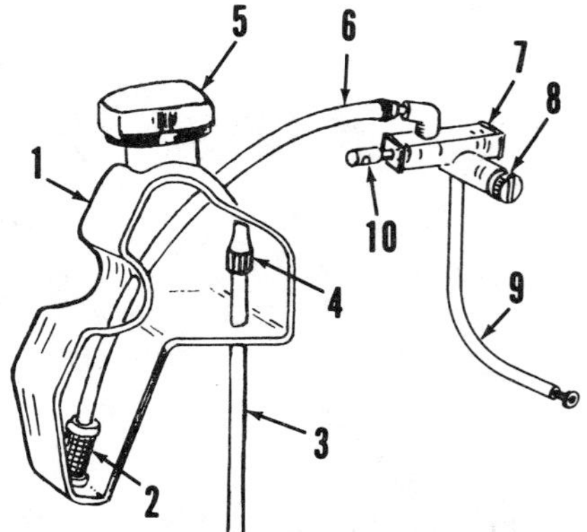

Fig. AP4 – View showing automatic oiling system used on Models A330 and A380.

1. Oil tank
2. Oil filter
3. Impulse hose
4. Check valve
5. Cap
6. Hose
7. Metering valve assy.
8. Adjusting screw
9. Discharge hose
10. Shut-off valve

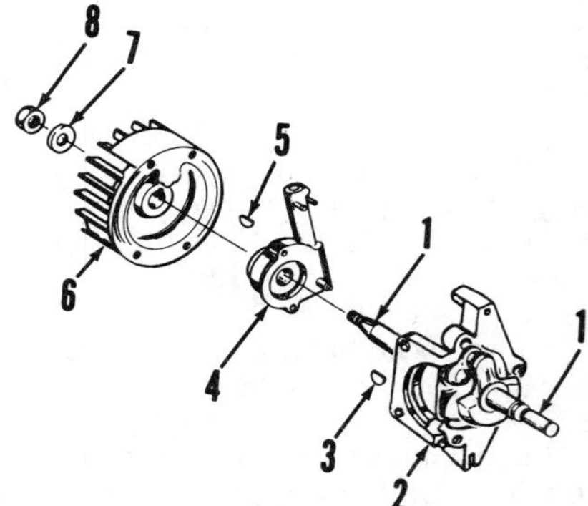

Fig. AP5 – View showing location of automatic oil pump used on Models A432 and A438. Refer to Fig. AP6 for exploded view of oil pump assembly (4).

1. Crankshaft
2. Left crankcase half
3. Oil pump key
4. Oil pump assy.
5. Flywheel key
6. Flywheel
7. Washer
8. Nut

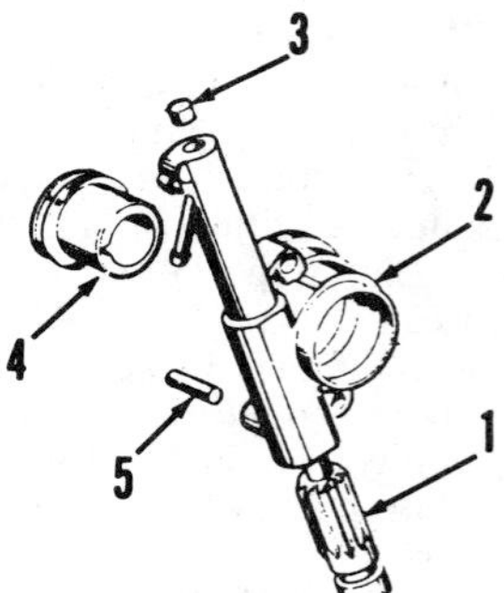

Fig. AP6 – Exploded view of automatic oil pump assembly used on Models A432 and A438.

1. Plunger
2. Pump body
3. Plug
4. Worm gear
5. Cam pin

valve (4). Malfunctions are often due to check valve (4) stuck closed preventing crankcase pulsations from entering oil tank.

Models A432 and A438 are equipped with the automatic oil pump shown in Figs. AP5 and AP6. Pump output is not adjustable. Plunger (1–Fig. AP6) is rotated by worm gear (4) on engine crankshaft. Oil is pumped by plunger (1) as plunger reciprocates in pump body (2) due to cam pin (5) riding in oblique groove in plunger.

Remove flywheel (6—Fig. AP5) to gain access to oil pump. Withdraw cam pin (5—Fig. AP6) to remove plunger (1). Inspect all components for excessive wear or damage and renew if needed. Tighten flywheel nut (8–Fig. AP5) to 34.3 N•m (26 ft.-lbs.).

REWIND STARTER. Models A330 and A380 are equipped with the rewind starter shown in Fig. AP7. Models A432 and A438 are equipped with the rewind starter shown in Fig. AP8.

On all models, remove starter housing (7–Figs. AP7 and AP8) to disassemble starter. Withdraw housing (7) sufficiently to disconnect ignition switch wires then remove housing. Remove rope handle and allow rope to slowly wind into starter housing to relieve tension on rewind spring. Remove screw (1) and carefully remove rope pulley (4). If rewind spring (6) must be removed, care should be taken to prevent personal injury due to uncontrolled uncoiling of spring.

Install rewind spring (6) into housing (7) in a clockwise direction starting with outer coil end. Wrap starter rope around rope pulley in a clockwise direction as viewed from flywheel side of pulley. To preload rewind spring, pull out a loop of rope from notch in rope pulley and rotate pulley ½ turn clockwise. Rope handle should be snug against housing with rope retracted. With rope fully extended, rope pulley should be able to rotate an additional ½ turn to prevent rewind spring breakage.

On all models, starter pawls (21–Fig. AP1) are secured on flywheel with pins (22). Drive pins out from inside of flywheel to remove pawls. Use Alpina tool 3630260 or a suitable equivalent to remove flywheel. Use a suitable thread locking solution on pins (22) when reassembling pawls. Tighten flywheel nut to 34.3 N•m (26 ft.-lbs.).

CHAIN BRAKE. Some models are equipped with the chain brake system shown in Fig. AP9. Chain brake is actuated when operator's hand strikes hand guard (15). Forward movement of actuator (13) trips latch (11) allowing spring (4) to pull brake band (2) tight around clutch drum (6). Pull back hand guard (15) to reset chain brake.

To adjust chain brake, disengage brake by pulling hand guard (15) to rearmost position (toward engine). Install guide bar and saw chain and properly adjust chain tension. Rotate brake tension adjustment screw (between brake arm mounting studs at front of actuator) clockwise, while pulling saw chain around guide bar, until chain movement becomes difficult. Back off adjustment screw (counterclockwise) until chain moves freely around guide bar. Make certain brake band does not contact clutch drum with brake in the disengaged position.

Fig. AP7—Exploded view of rewind starter used on Models A330 and A380.

1. Screw
2. Washer
3. Rope
4. Rope pulley
5. Spring cover
6. Rewind spring
7. Housing
8. Rope handle
9. Eyelet

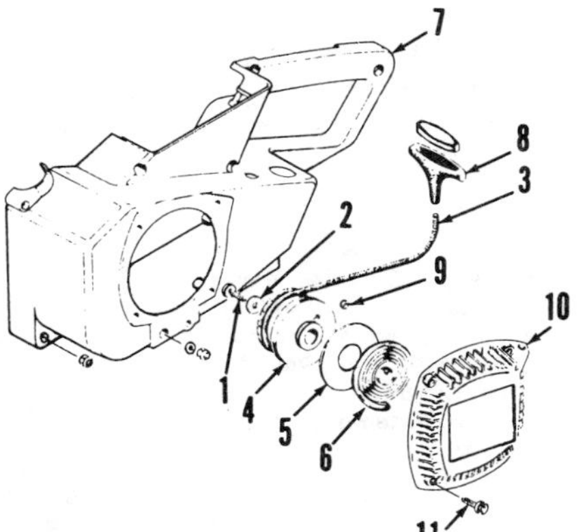

Fig. AP8—Exploded view of rewind starter used on Models A432 and A438. Refer to Fig. AP7 for component identification except cover (10) and screw (11).

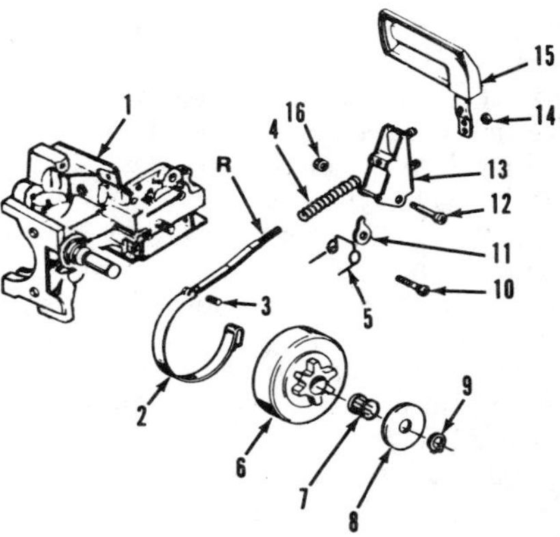

Fig. AP9—Exploded view of chain brake system used on some models. Brake tension screw (not shown) is located at front of actuator (13) between hand guard (15) mounting studs.

1. Right crankcase half
2. Brake band
3. Pin
4. Spring
5. Spring
6. Drum
7. Needle bearing
8. Washer
9. Snap ring
10. Screw
11. Latch
12. Shoulder screw
13. Actuator
14. Nut
15. Hand guard
16. Nut
R. Rod

ALPINA

Model	Bore mm (in.)	Stroke mm (in.)	Displ. cc (cu. in.)	Drive Type
A40, A40E, Pro 40	40 (1.57)	31.5 (1.24)	40 (2.44)	Direct
P41, Pro 41	40 (1.57)	31.5 (1.24)	40 (2.44)	Direct
P45, Pro 45, Pro 45E	41 (1.61)	33.8 (1.33)	45 (2.74)	Direct

MAINTENANCE

SPARK PLUG. Recommended spark plug for all models is Champion CJ7Y. Electrode gap should be 0.5 mm (0.020 in.).

CARBURETOR. Models A40, A40E, Pro 40 and early Pro 45 and Pro 45E models are equipped with a Tillotson HU diaphragm carburetor. All other models are equipped with a Dell'Orto C16.12 diaphragm carburetor. Refer to Tillotson and Dell'Orto sections of CARBURETOR SERVICE section for service procedures and exploded views.

Initial adjustment on Models A40, A40E and Pro 40 is 1¼ turns open for low speed mixture screw and ¾ turn open for high speed mixture screw. Initial adjustment on Model Pro 41 is 2⅛ turns open for low speed mixture screw and ¾ turn open for high speed mixture screw. Initial adjustment on Models Pro 45 and Pro 45E is 1¾ turns open for low speed mixture screw and 1¼ turns open for high speed mixture screw.

Final adjustment should be made with engine running at operating temperature. Adjust idle speed to just below clutch engagement speed. Adjust low speed mixture screw so engine will accelerate cleanly without hesitation. Adjust high speed mixture screw to obtain maximum no-load speed of 11,700 rpm on Models A40, A40E and Pro 40, 12,000 rpm on Model Pro 41 and 12,400 rpm on Models Pro 45 and Pro 45E.

IGNITION. Models A40 and Pro 45 manufactured prior to 1981 are equipped with a breaker-point ignition system. Refer to Fig. AP15. Breaker-point gap should be 0.45-0.50 mm (0.018-0.020 in.). Air gap between ignition coil and flywheel magnets should be 0.45 mm (0.018 in.). Ignition timing is not adjustable, however, breaker-point gap will affect timing. Be certain point gap is adjusted correctly as a gap too wide will advance timing and a gap too close will retard timing.

All other models, including Models A40 and Pro 45 manufactured after 1980, are equipped with a breakerless electronic ignition system. Refer to Fig. AP16. Ignition coil and all electronic circuitry are contained in a one-piece ignition module (8). Ignition timing is not adjustable. Air gap between ignition module and flywheel magnets should be 0.35 mm (0.014 in.).

On all models, use Alpina tool 4180100 or a suitable equivalent bolt-type puller to remove flywheel. Remove starter pawl bolts (4) to accommodate puller bolts. Use a suitable thread locking solution on pawl bolts during reassembly. Tighten flywheel nut to 28.4 N·m (21 ft.-lbs.). Use a suitable thread-locking solution on ignition coil/module attaching screws if air gap is adjusted.

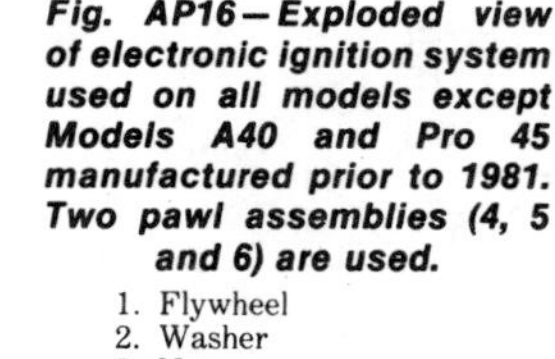

Fig. AP16 — Exploded view of electronic ignition system used on all models except Models A40 and Pro 45 manufactured prior to 1981. Two pawl assemblies (4, 5 and 6) are used.

1. Flywheel
2. Washer
3. Nut
4. Bolt
5. Pawl
6. Spring
7. Clamp
8. Ingition module
9. Primary lead
10. Ignition switch
11. High tension lead
12. Screw

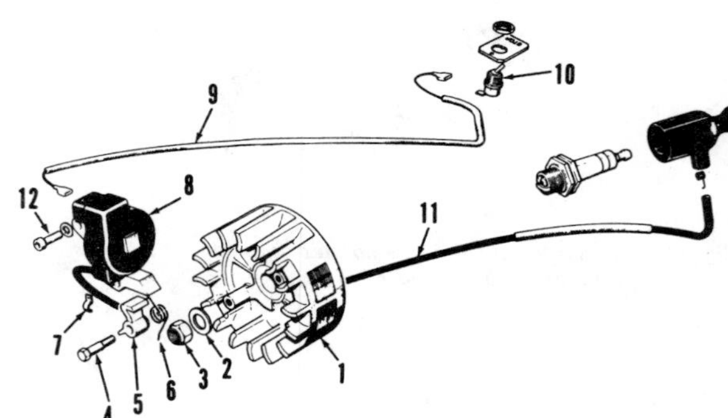

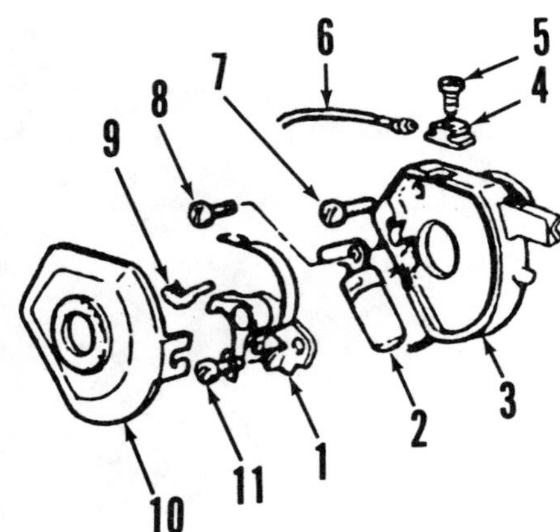

Fig. AP15 — Exploded view of breaker-point ignition system used on Models A40 and Pro 45 manufactured prior to 1981.

1. Breaker points
2. Condenser
3. Breaker box
4. Insulator
5. Screw
6. Primary lead
7. Screw
8. Screw
9. Felt wick
10. Cover
11. Screw

Fig. AP17 — Exploded view of engine assembly used on all models.

1. Cylinder
2. Gasket
3. Piston rings
4. Piston
5. Piston pin
6. Snap ring
7. Needle bearing
8. Crankshaft & connecting rod assy.
9. Main bearings
10. Seal
11. Seal
12. Key
13. Gasket

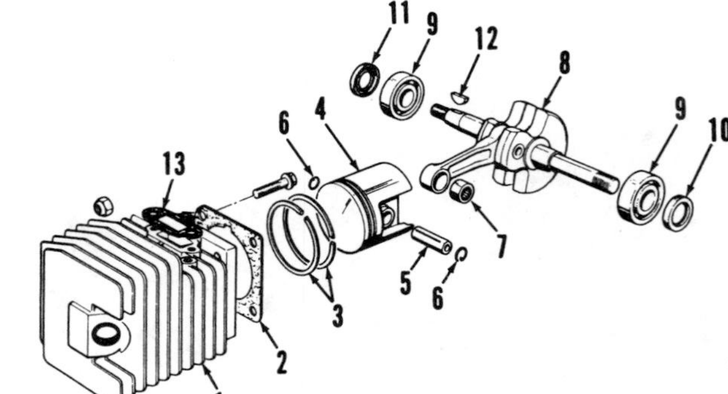

LUBRICATION. The engine is lubricated by mixing oil with the fuel. Use a good quality oil designed for use in air-cooled two-stroke engines. Fuel:oil mixture should be a 16:1 ratio. Use a separate container when mixing fuel and oil.

All models are equipped with the automatic oil pump shown in Fig. AP23. Pump output is not adjustable. Use clean automotive oil for saw chain lubrication.

REPAIRS

CYLINDER, PISTON, PIN AND RINGS. Cylinder bore is chrome plated and should be renewed if cracking, scoring or other damage is noted in cylinder bore.

Piston and cylinder are matched during production to get desired piston-to-cylinder clearance of 0.02 mm (0.0008 in.). Original equipment piston and cylinder are marked "A." Factory renewal piston and cylinder assemblies are marked "B." Piston or cylinder marked "C" is 0.127 mm (0.005 in.) oversize. Piston or cylinder marked "D" is 0.127 mm (0.005) undersize. Piston and cylinder markings should match, however a new piston marked "B" can be installed into a used cylinder marked "A."

NOTE: Do not install a new piston marked "B" or "C" into a new cylinder marked "A."

Piston is equipped with two piston rings. Piston ring end gap should not exceed 1.0 mm (0.039 in.). Locating pins are present in ring grooves to prevent ring rotation. Make certain ring end gaps are properly postioned around locating pins when installing cylinder.

Piston pin (5–Fig. AP17) rides in needle bearing (7) and is retained with two snap rings (6). Use Alpina tool 4180010 or a suitable equivalent to press out pin. Piston may be heated to approximately 110°-120° C (230°-248° F) to ease installation of piston pin.

NOTE: Use electric oven or hot oil bath to heat piston. Do not use an open flame.

Install piston into cylinder with arrow on piston crown facing toward exhaust port.

CRANKSHAFT, CONNECTING ROD AND CRANKCASE. Crankshaft and connecting rod are available as a unit assembly only. Check rotation of connecting rod around crankpin and renew crankshaft assembly if roughness, excessive play or other damage is noted. Check crankshaft runout by supporting crankshaft assembly between two counter points – such as a lathe. Make certain no damage exists to centering holes at each end of crankshaft. Maximum allowable runout is 0.08 mm (0.0031 in.).

NOTE: Crankshaft runout can be checked while still assembled in crankcase. Remove clutch and flywheel and mount dial indicators on both sides of crankshaft as close to main bearings as possible. Measure runout while rotating crankshaft. Renew crankshaft assembly if runout exceeds 0.07 mm (0.0027 in.), when measured in this manner.

Crankshaft is supported at both ends by ball-type main bearings (9–Fig. AP17) that locate in crankcase halves (2 and 3–Figs. AP18, AP19 and AP20). Use the proper drivers to re-

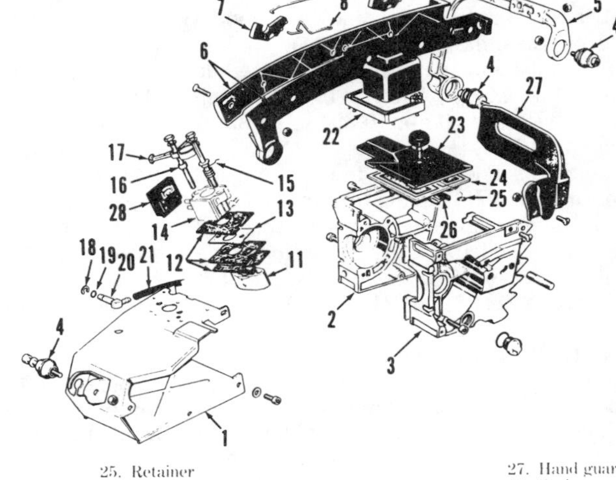

Fig. AP18—Exploded view of crankcase, handle assemblies, carburetor and related components used on A40, A40E and Pro 40 models.

1. Cylinder cover
2. Left crankcase half
3. Right crankcase half
4. Vibration isolator
5. Front handle
6. Rear grip assy.
7. Throttle trigger
8. Throttle rod
9. Throttle rod
10. Throttle trigger
11. Intake spacer
12. Gaskets
13. Heat shield
14. Carburetor
15. Spring
16. Spacer
17. Choke valve
18. "E" ring
19. "O" ring
20. Fitting
21. Fuel hose
22. Seal
23. Cover
24. Air filter
25. Retainer
26. Air filter support
27. Hand guard
28. Seal

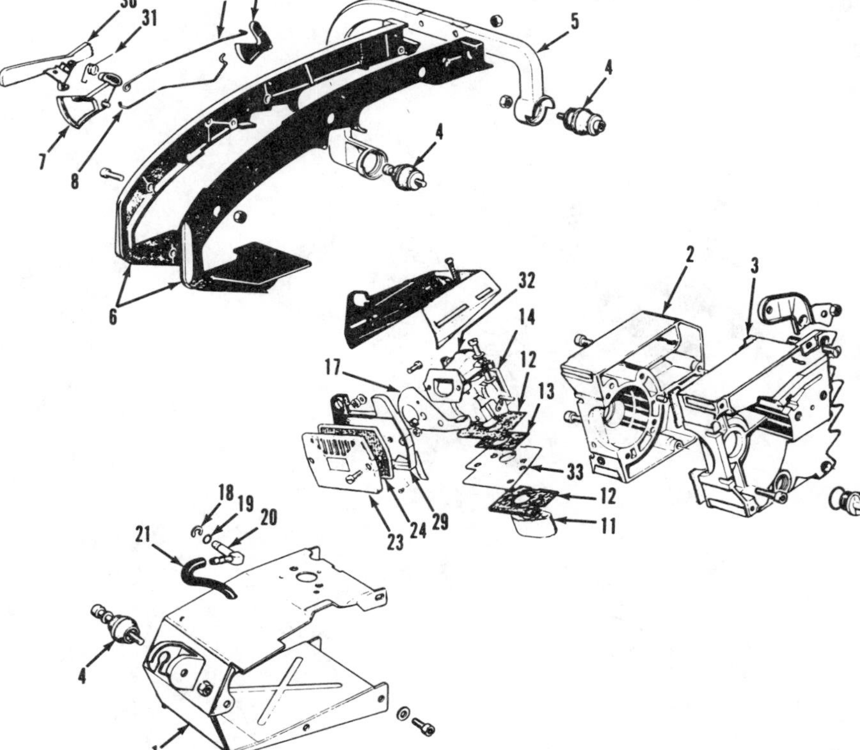

Fig. AP19—Exploded view of crankcase, handle assemblies, carburetor and related components used on Model Pro 41. Refer to legend in Fig. AP18 for component identification except for air filter base (29), safety lever (30), spring (31), air intake (32) and gasket (33).

move and install main bearings. Use Alpina tool 4180900 to install crankshaft assembly into main bearing. Refer to Fig. AP21. Do not use gasket sealer on crankcase gasket. On Models A40, A40E and Pro 40, make certain air filter support (26–Fig. AP18) is in position before assembling crankcase halves. Tighten crankcase screws using a crisscross pattern to 6.9 N·m (61 in.-lbs.).

CLUTCH. All models are equipped with the centrifugal clutch assembly shown in Fig. AP22. Clutch hub (1) has left-hand threads. On some early model clutch assemblies, hub (1) has 9 mm (0.354 in.) mounting threads while all later model (after 1978) clutch assemblies use 10 mm (0.394 in.) mounting threads.

Inspect shoes (2), drum (7), needle bearing (6) and bushing (5) for excessive wear or damage due to overheating and renew if needed. Shoes (2) are available only as a complete set. Tighten clutch hub (1) to 28.4 N·m (21 ft.-lbs.).

OIL PUMP. All models are equipped with the automatic oil pump assembly shown in Fig. AP23. Pump output is not adjustable. Oil is pumped by plunger (2) which is driven by worm gear (3) on end of engine crankshaft. Pump plunger (2) reciprocates in pump body (1) due to cam bolt (14) riding in oblique groove in plunger. Plunger can be removed from housing after removing cam bolt (14) and bushing (4). Inspect worm gear (3), plunger (2) and pump body (1) for excessive wear or damage. Always renew seal (12) and washers (18) during reassembly of pump.

REWIND STARTER. Refer to Fig. AP24 for exploded view of rewind starter used on all models.

To disassemble starter, remove starter housing (1) from saw. Remove rope handle (3) and carefully allow rope to wind into housing (1). Remove nut (6) and washer (5). Rope pulley (4) and rewind spring and case assembly (2) can now be removed from housing.

Install rewind spring (2) into housing (1) with open side of case facing housing (1). Wind rope onto rope pulley (4) in a clockwise direction as viewed from flywheel side of pulley. Lubricate shaft (S) with a suitable low temperature grease. Rotate rope pulley ½ turn clockwise before passing rope through rope guide (G) to preload rewind spring. Rope handle should be snug against housing with rope retracted. If not, lift a loop of rope from pulley and place into notch (N) in pulley. While holding rope in notch, rotate pulley clockwise to increase rewind spring tension. With rope fully extended, rope pulley should be able to rotate ½ turn further. If not, repeat above procedure, only rotate pulley counterclockwise to decrease rewind spring tension.

Refer to Fig. AP16 for exploded view of starter pawl assemblies. Use a suitable thread locking solution on pawl bolts (4). Tighten flywheel nut to 28.4 N·m (21 ft.-lbs.).

CHAIN BRAKE. Some Pro 41, Pro 45 and Pro 45E models are equipped with a chain brake system designed to quickly stop chain movement should kickback occur. Refer to Fig. AP25 for exploded view of chain brake system used. Chain brake is activated when operator's hand strikes chain brake lever (1), disengaging latch (7) and allowing spring (14) to pull brake band (10) tight around clutch drum. Pull back chain brake lever to reset mechanism.

Disassembly for repair or component renewal is evident after inspection of unit and referral to Fig. AP25. No adjustment of chain brake system is required.

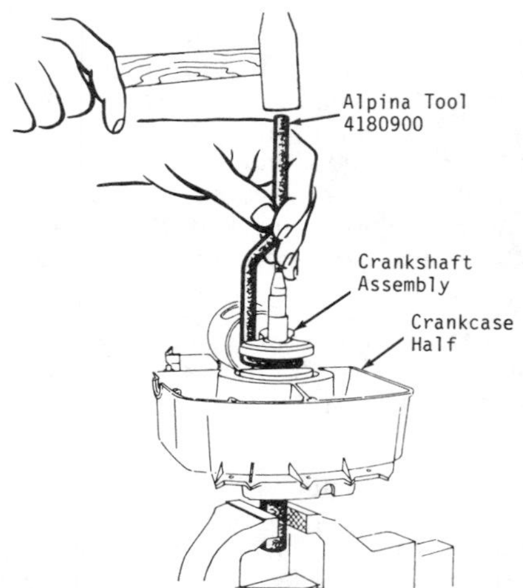

Fig. AP21 – View showing installation procedure of crankshaft and connecting rod assembly into crankcase using Alpina tool 4180900. Main bearing (9 – Fig. AP17) is pressed into crankcase half prior to installation of crankshaft assembly.

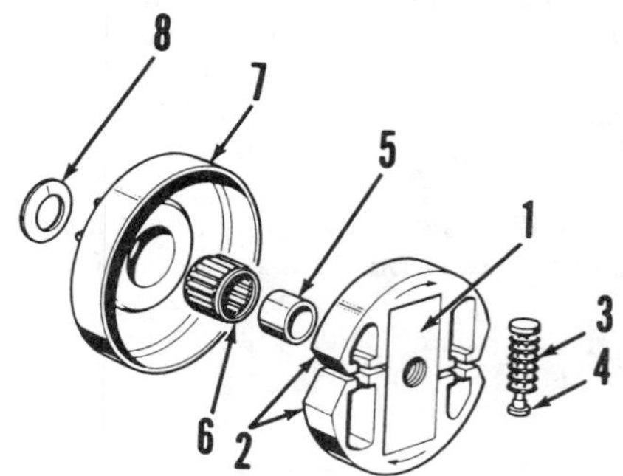

Fig. AP22 – Exploded view of clutch assembly used on all models manufactured after 1978. Early model clutch assembly is similar except hub (1) has 9 mm (0.354 in.) mounting threads. Late model hub has 10 mm (0.394 in.) mounting threads.

1. Hub
2. Shoes
3. Spring
4. Spring guide
5. Bushing
6. Needle bearing
7. Drum
8. Washer

Fig. AP20 – Exploded view of crankcase, handle assemblies, carburetor and related components used on Models Pro 45 and Pro 45E. Refer to legend in Fig. AP18 for component identification except for safety lever (30), spring (31), air intake (32) and gasket (33).

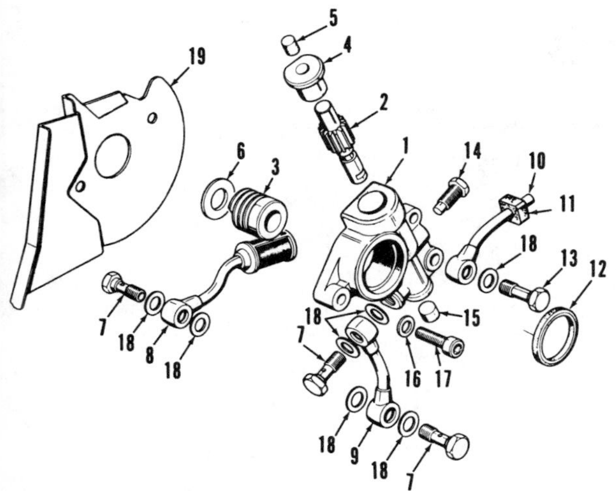

Fig. AP23—Exploded view of automatic oil pump used on all models.

1. Pump body
2. Plunger
3. Worm gear
4. Bushing
5. Felt plug
6. Thrust washer
7. Banjo bolt
8. Pickup & filter assy.
9. Suction line
10. Oil line
11. Seal
12. Seal
13. Banjo bolt
14. Cam bolt
15. Plug
16. Washer
17. Screw
18. Washers
19. Plate

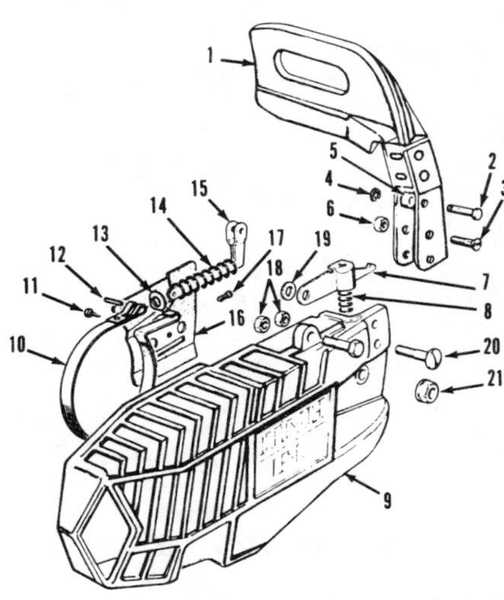

Fig. AP25—Exploded view of chain brake assembly used on so equipped Pro 41, Pro 45 and Pro 45E models.

1. Chain brake lever
2. Pin
3. Screw
4. "E" ring
5. Spacer
6. Nut
7. Latch
8. Spring
9. Housing
10. Brake band
11. Screw
12. Pin
13. Washer
14. Spring
15. Arm
16. Guide plate
17. Screw
18. Nuts
19. Washer
20. Screw
21. Nut

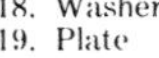

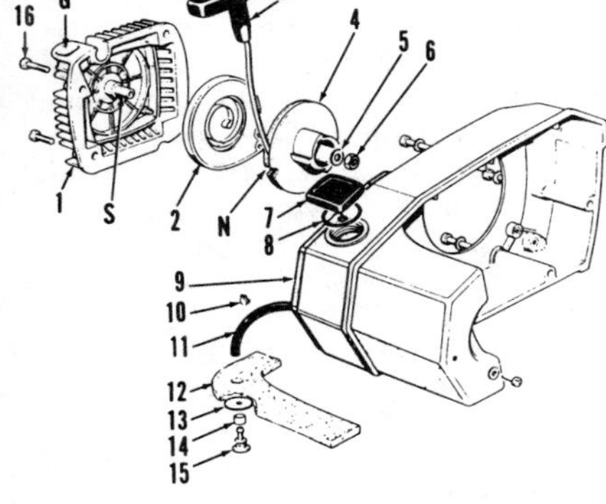

Fig. AP24—Exploded view of rewind starter, left engine cover and fuel tank assembly and related components. Refer to Fig. AP16 for view of flywheel and starter pawls.

G. Rope guide
N. Notch
S. Shaft
1. Starter housing
2. Rewind spring & case assy.
3. Rope handle
4. Rope pulley
5. Washer
6. Nut
7. Fuel cap
8. Seal
9. Left engine cover & fuel tank assy.
10. Clamp
11. Fuel hose
12. Felt
13. Washer
14. Fuel screen
15. Fuel pickup

ALPINA

Model	Bore mm (in.)	Stroke mm (in.)	Displacement cc (cu. in.)	Drive Type
P55, Pro 55, Pro 55E, Pro 56	44 (1.73)	36 1.42)	55 (3.4)	Direct
P65, Pro 65, Pro 65E, Pro 66	47 (1.85)	37.3 (1.47)	65 (4.0)	Direct

MAINTENANCE

SPARK PLUG. Recommended spark plug for all models is Champion CJ7Y. Electrode gap should be 0.5 mm (0.020 in.).

CARBURETOR. All models are equipped with a Tillotson HK diaphragm carburetor. Refer to Tillotson section of CARBURETOR SERVICE section for service procedure and exploded view.

Initial adjustment of low speed mixture screw is 1½ turns open on Models Pro 55, Pro 55E and Pro 56 and 1⅜ turns open on Models Pro 65, Pro 65E and Pro 66. Initial adjustment of high speed mixture screw is ¾ turn open for all models.

Final adjustment should be made with engine running at operating temperature. Adjust idle speed to just below clutch engagement speed. Adjust low speed mixture screw so engine will accelerate cleanly without hesitation. Adjust high speed mixture screw to obtain maximum no-load speed of 12,000 rpm for Models Pro 55, Pro 55E and Pro 56 and 11,600 rpm for Models Pro 65, Pro 65E and Pro 66.

IGNITION. Model Pro 55 manufactured prior to 1985 and Model Pro 65 manufactured prior to 1984 are equipped with a breaker-point ignition system. Breaker-point gap should be 0.45-0.50 mm (0.018-0.020 in.). Air gap between ignition coil legs and flywheel magnets should be 0.45 mm (0.018 in.). Loosen coil attaching screws and move coil to adjust air gap. Use a suitable thread locking solution on coil attaching screws. Ignition timing is not adjustable, however, breaker-point gap will affect timing. Be sure breaker-point gap is adjusted correctly as a gap too wide will advance timing and a gap too close will retard timing.

Models Pro 55E, Pro 65E, Pro 56, Pro 66 and Model Pro 55 manufactured after 1984 and Model Pro 65 manufactured after 1983 are equipped with a breakerless electronic ignition system. Some models are equipped with a standard ignition coil with an electronic module located behind flywheel. On other models, ignition coil and all electronic circuitry are contained in a one-piece ignition module/coil (2–Fig. AP35). Air gap between ignition module/coil and flywheel magnets should be 0.35-0.40 mm (0.014-0.016 in.). Use a suitable thread locking solution on module/coil attaching screws.

On all models, use Alpina tool 4180140 to remove flywheel. If Alpina tool 4180140 is not available, remove starter pawl assemblies (6, 7, 8 and 9) to accomodate a bolt-type puller. Use a suitable thread locking solution on pawl bolts (6) during reassembly. Tighten flywheel nut (10) to 34.8 N·m (26 ft.-lbs.).

LUBRICATION. The engine is lubricated by mixing oil with the fuel. Use a

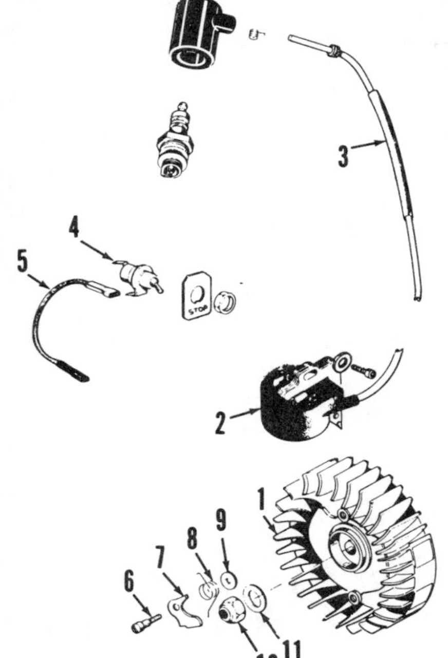

Fig. AP35—Exploded view of breakerless electronic ignition system used on Models Pro 56 and Pro 66. Other models are similar. Refer to text.

1. Flywheel
2. Ignition module/coil
3. High tension lead
4. Ignition switch
5. Primary lead
6. Pawl bolt
7. Pawl
8. Spring
9. Washer
10. Nut
11. Washer

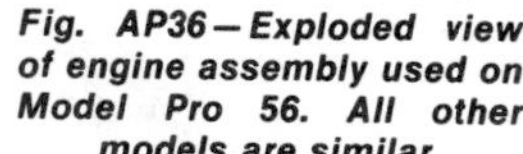

Fig. AP36—Exploded view of engine assembly used on Model Pro 56. All other models are similar.

1. Cylinder
2. Gasket
3. Piston rings
4. Piston
5. Retainer
6. Needle bearing
7. Piston pin
8. Crankshaft & connecting rod assy.
9. Right main bearing
10. Woodruff key
11. Left main bearing
12. Seal
13. Left crankcase half
14. Seal
15. Oil cap
16. Vibration isolator
17. Gasket
18. Right crankcase half

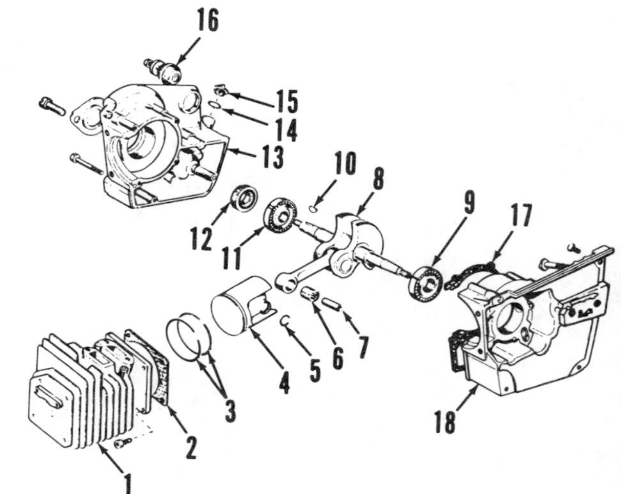

good quality oil designed for use in air-cooled two-stroke engines. Fuel:oil mixture should be a 16:1 ratio. Use a separate container when mixing fuel and oil.

All models are equipped with an automatic chain oil pump. Oil pump is driven by a worm gear coupled to clutch drum. Pump output is not adjustable. Refer to OIL PUMP under REPAIRS section for service and exploded view. Use clean automotive oil for saw chain lubrication.

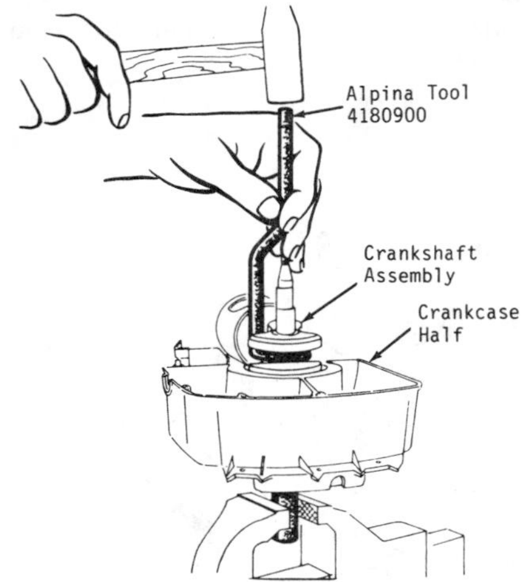

Fig. AP37—View showing installation of crankshaft and connecting rod assembly into crankcase using Alpina tool 4180900. Main bearing (9—Fig. AP36) is pressed into crankcase half prior to installation of crankshaft assembly.

REPAIRS

CYLINDER, PISTON, PIN AND RINGS. Cylinder bore is chrome plated and should be renewed if cracking, scoring or other damage is noted in cylinder bore.

Piston and cylinder are matched during production to get desired piston-to-cylinder clearance of 0.02 mm (0.0008 in.). Original equipment piston and cylinder are marked "A." Factory renewal piston and cylinder assemblies are marked "B." Piston or cylinder marked "C" is 0.127 mm (0.005 in.) oversize. Piston or cylinder marked "D" is 0.127 mm (0.005 in.) undersize. Piston and cylinder markings should match, however, a new piston marked "B" can be installed into a used cylinder marked "A."

NOTE: Do not install a new piston marked "B" or "C" into a new cylinder marked "A."

Piston is equipped with two piston rings. Piston ring end gap should not exceed 1.0 mm (0.039 in.). Locating pins are present in ring grooves to prevent ring rotation. Make certain ring end gaps are properly positioned around locating pins when installing cylinder.

Piston pin (7–Fig. AP36) rides in needle bearing (6) and is retained with two snap-rings (5). Use Alpina tool 4180010 or a suitable equivalent to press out pin. Piston may be heated to approximately 110°-120° C (230°-248° F) to ease piston pin installation.

NOTE: Use electric oven or hot oil bath to heat piston. Do not use an open flame.

Install piston into cylinder with arrow on piston crown facing toward exhaust port.

CRANKSHAFT, CONNECTING ROD AND CRANKCASE. Crankcase and connecting rod (8–Fig. AP36) are available as a unit assembly only. Check rotation of connecting rod around crankpin and renew crankshaft assembly if roughness, excessive play or other damage is noted. Check crank-

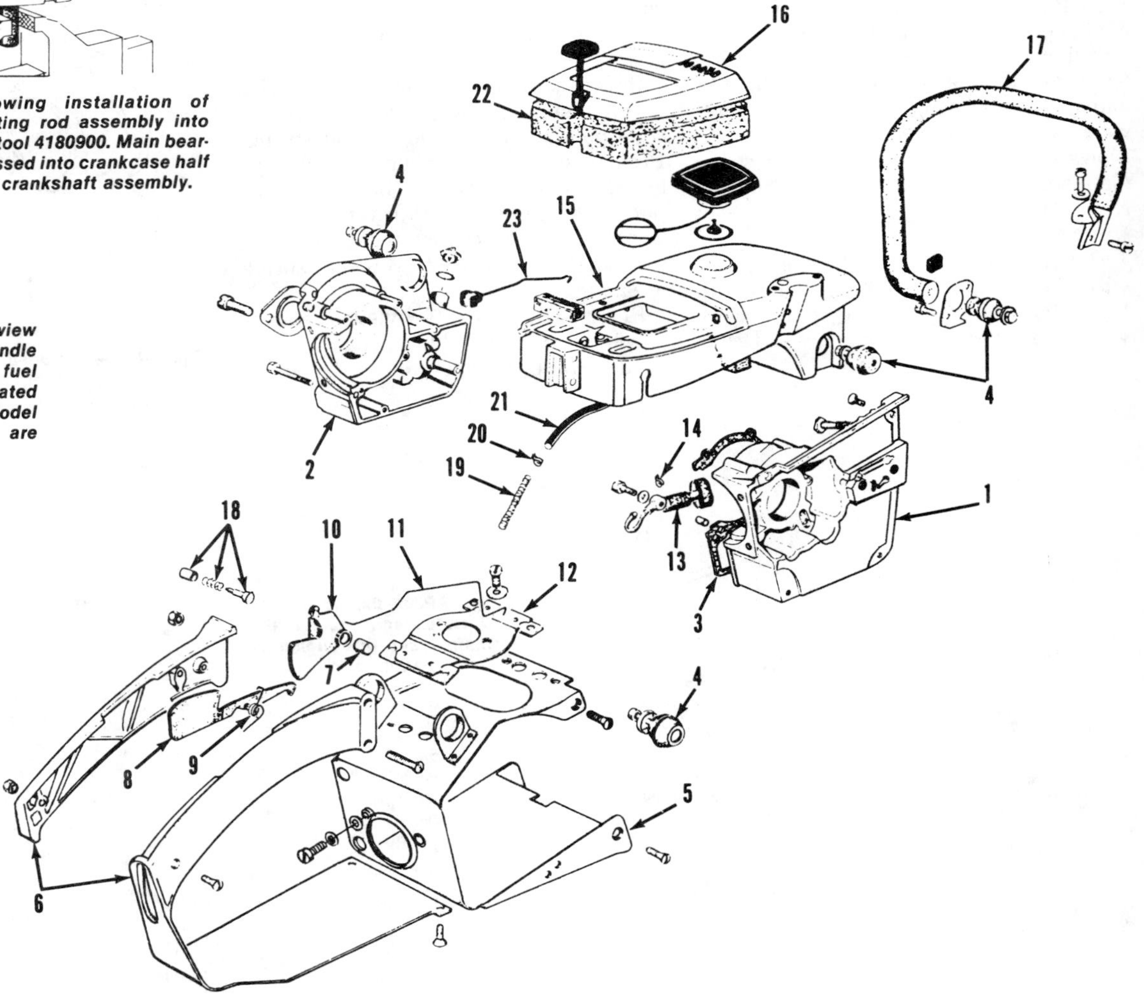

Fig. AP38—Exploded view of rear grip and front handle assemblies, crankcase, fuel tank assembly and related components used on Model Pro 56. Other models are similar.

1. Right crankcase half
2. Left crankcase half
3. Gasket
4. Vibration isolator
5. Cylinder cover
6. Rear grip assy.
7. Bushing
8. Safety lever
9. Spring
10. Trigger
11. Throttle rod
12. Carburetor support
13. Oil pickup assy.
14. Clamp
15. Fuel tank assy.
16. Air filter cover
17. Front handle assy.
18. Trigger lock assy.
19. Spring
20. Clamp
21. Fuel hose
22. Air filter
23. Choke rod

shaft runout by supporting crankshaft assembly between two counter points such as a lathe. Make certain no damage exists to centering holes at each end of crankshaft. Maximum allowable runout is 0.08 mm (0.0031 in.).

NOTE: Crankshaft runout can be checked while still assembled in crankcase. Remove clutch and flywheel and mount dial indicators on both sides of crankshaft as close to main bearings as possible. Measure runout while rotating crankshaft. Renew crankshaft assembly if runout exceeds 0.07 mm (0.0027 in.) when measured in this manner.

Crankshaft is supported at both ends with ball-type main bearings (9 and 11). Main bearings are located in crankcase halves (13 and 18). Use the proper size drivers to remove and install main bearings. Use Alpina tool 4180900 to install crankshaft assembly into main bearing. Refer to Fig. AP37. Do not use gasket sealer on crankcase gasket (17–Fig. AP36). Tighten crankcase screws using a crisscross pattern to 6.4 N·m (57 in.-lbs.).

CLUTCH. Refer to Fig. AP39 for an exploded view of clutch assembly used on all models. Clutch hub (4) has left hand threads. Inspect shoes (5), drum (3) and needle bearing (2) for excessive wear or damage due to overheating. Shoes (5) are available only as a complete set. Tighten clutch hub (4) to 41.2 N·m (31 ft.-lbs.).

OIL PUMP. All models are equipped with the automatic oil pump shown in Fig. AP40. Oil is pumped by plunger (6) which is rotated by worm gear (1). Drive lugs (L) on worm gear (1) engage clutch drum, therefore oil is pumped only when saw chain is rotating.

To disassemble pump, remove cam bolt (5), plug (8) and bushing (7). Plunger (6) can now be removed for inspection or renewal. Carefully inspect seal (2) and seal surface on worm gear (1). Note that slight wear on seal or worm gear may allow pump to draw air causing pump malfunction. It is recommended to renew seal (2) any time pump is disassembled.

REWIND STARTER. All models are equipped with the rewind starter shown in Fig. AP41. To disassemble starter, remove starter housing (5) from saw. Remove rope handle (4) and carefully allow rope to wind into starter, relieving tension on rewind spring (2). Starter drive (6) is a press fit in rope pulley (3). Remove rope and tap drive (6) out of pulley (3) toward flywheel side of housing (5) using a proper size punch and hammer.

Rewind spring (2) is retained in a plastic case. Install spring with open side of case toward starter cover (1). Install starter drive (6) with hole in drive aligned with hole in rope pulley. Wind rope onto rope pulley in a clockwise direction as viewed from flywheel side of pulley.

Rotate starter cover (1) clockwise before installing cover screws to engage rope pulley and preload rewind spring. Preload spring only enough to pull rope handle snug against housing. Rope pulley should be able to rotate an additional 1/2 turn clockwise with rope fully extended to prevent rewind spring breakage.

Refer to Fig. AP35 for view of starter pawls. Use a suitable thread locking solution on pawl bolts (6).

CHAIN BRAKE. Some models are equipped with a chain brake system designed to stop chain movement should kickback occur. Chain brake is activated when operator's hand strikes hand guard (12–Fig. AP39), tripping lever (16) and allowing spring (15) to draw brake band (14) tight around clutch drum (3). Pull back hand guard to reset mechanism.

Disassembly is evident after inspection of unit and referral to exploded view. Renew any component excessively worn or damaged. Chain brake should be clean and free of sawdust and dirt accumulation. No adjustment of chain brake is required.

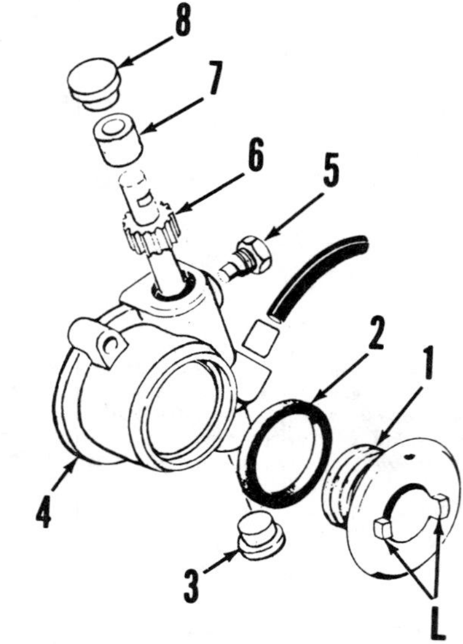

Fig. AP40—Exploded view of automatic oil pump assembly.

1. Worm gear
2. Seal
3. Plug
4. Housing
5. Cam bolt
6. Plunger
7. Bushing
8. Plug
L. Drive lugs

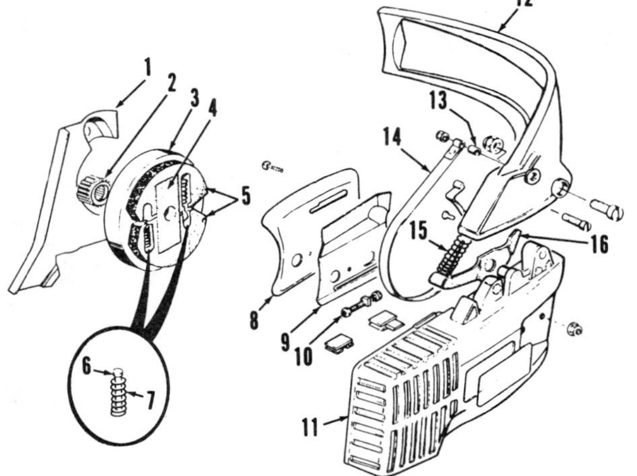

Fig. AP39—Exploded view of clutch and chain brake. Chain brake is optional on all models.

1. Plate
2. Needle bearing
3. Drum
4. Hub
5. Shoes
6. Spring guide
7. Spring
8. Inner guide plate
9. Outer guide plate
10. Bar adjusting screw
11. Cover
12. Hand guard
13. Spacer
14. Brake band
15. Spring
16. Lever

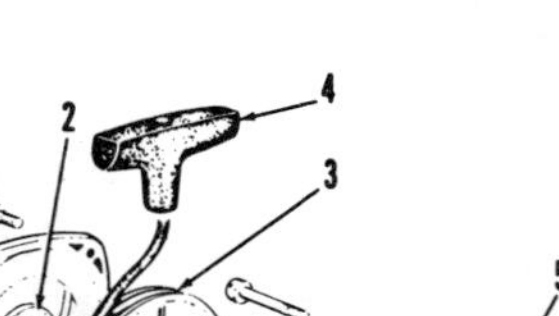

Fig. AP41—Exploded view of rewind starter assembly.

1. Starter cover
2. Rewind spring
3. Rope pulley
4. Rope handle
5. Housing
6. Starter drive
7. Baffle
8. Bushing

ALPINA

Model	Bore mm (in.)	Stroke mm (in.)	Displacement cc (cu. in.)	Drive Type
070, 070S, A70, Pro 70, Super Pro 70S	51 (2.0)	34.5 (1.36)	70 (4.3)	Direct
P90, Pro 90, Super Pro 90	54 (2.13)	39.1 (1.54)	90 (5.5)	Direct
P120, Pro 120, Super Pro 120	58 (2.28)	45.5 (1.79)	120 (7.3)	Direct

MAINTENANCE

SPARK PLUG. Recommended spark plug for all models is Champion CJ7Y. Electrode gap should be 0.5 mm (0.020 in.).

CARBURETOR. All models are equipped with a Tillotson HS diaphragm carburetor. Refer to Tillotson section of CARBURETOR SERVICE section for service and exploded views.

Initial adjustment of low speed mixture screw is 1⅞ turns open on Super Pro 120, 2 turns open on Super Pro 90 and 1¾ turns open on all other models. Initial adjustment of high speed mixture screw is ⅞ turn open on Super Pro 120 and ¾ turn open on all other models. Final adjustment should be made with engine running at operating temperature. Adjust idle speed to just below clutch engagement speed. Adjust low speed mixture screw so engine will accelerate cleanly without hesitation. Adjust high speed mixture screw to obtain maximum speed of 10,300 rpm on Super Pro 120, 9,700 rpm on Super Pro 90 and 10,500 rpm on all other models.

IGNITION. Models 070 and 070S manufactured prior to 1984 are equipped with a breaker-point ignition system. All other models, including Models 070 and 070S manufactured after 1983, are equipped with a breakerless electronic ignition system.

Breaker-Point Ignition. Breaker-point gap should be 0.45-0.50 mm (0.018-0.020 in.). Air gap between ignition coil lamination and flywheel magnets should be 0.45 mm (0.018 in.). Use a suitable thread locking solution on coil attaching screws. Ignition timing is not adjustable, however, breaker-point gap will affect timing. Be sure breaker-point gap is adjusted correctly.

Electronic Ignition. Refer to Fig. AP51 for exploded view of electronic ignition system used on Models A70, Super Pro 70 and so equipped Models 070 and 070S. Note that coil (8) is located outside of flywheel (1) while ignition module (13) is located behind flywheel (1). Super Pro 90 and Super Pro 120 models are equipped with electronic ignition system shown in Fig. AP52. Ignition coil and all electronic circuitry are contained in one-piece ignition module (13).

Except for faulty wiring or wiring connections, repair of ignition system malfunctions is accomplished by component renewal.

On Super Pro 90 and Super Pro 120 models, air gap between ignition module and flywheel magnets should be 0.65 mm (0.026 in.). Air gap between ignition coil and flywheel magnets on all other models should be 0.40 mm (0.016 in.). Use a suitable thread locking solution on module (or coil) attaching screws. Ignition timing is not adjustable on all models.

Starter pawl assemblies (2, 3, 4 and 7–Fig. AP51) can be removed to accomodate a suitable bolt-type puller to remove flywheel on all models. Use a suitable thread locking solution on bolts (2) when reassembling pawls. Tighten flywheel nut to 39.2 N·m (29 ft.-lbs.) on Super Pro 90 and Super Pro 120 models and 28.4 N·m (21 ft.-lbs.) on all other models.

LUBRICATION. The engine is lubricated by mixing oil with the fuel. Use a good quality oil designed for use in air-cooled two-stroke engines. Fuel:oil mixture should be a 16:1 ratio. Use a separate container when mixing fuel and oil.

Models 070S and Super Pro 70 are equipped with a manual and automatic chain oil pump. All other models are only equipped with an automatic chain oil

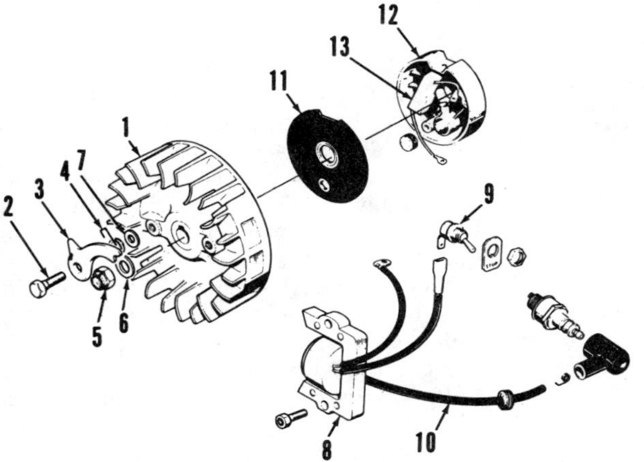

Fig. AP51—Exploded view of electronic ignition system used on Models A70, Super Pro 70, and Models 070 and 070S manufactured after 1983. Two pawl assemblies (2,3, 4 and 7) are used.

1. Flywheel
2. Bolt
3. Pawl
4. Spring
5. Nut
6. Washer
7. Washer
8. Ignition coil
9. Ignition switch
10. High tension lead
11. Cover
12. Module case
13. Module

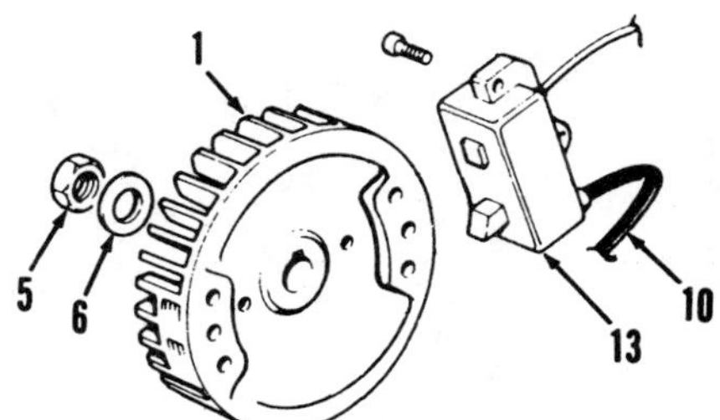

Fig. AP52—Exploded view of electronic ignition system used on Super Pro 90 and Super Pro 120 models. Refer to Fig. AP51 for component identification.

pump. Automatic oil pump output is only adjustable on Super Pro 90 and Super Pro 120 models. Refer to OIL PUMP under REPAIRS for service and exploded views of manual and automatic oil pump assemblies. Use clean automotive oil for saw chain lubrication.

REPAIRS

CYLINDER, PISTON, PIN AND RINGS. Cylinder bore is chrome plated and should be renewed if cracking, scoring or other damage is noted in cylinder bore. Note that cylinder used on Super Pro 90 and Super Pro 120 models is equipped with decompression valve (28–Fig. AP54) to ease starting.

Piston and cylinder are matched during production to get desired piston-to-cylinder clearance of 0.02 mm (0.0008 in.). Original equipment piston and cylinder are marked "A." Factory renewal piston and cylinder assemblies are marked "B." Piston or cylinder marked "C" is 0.127 mm (0.005 in.) oversize. Piston or cylinder marked "D" is 0.127 mm (0.005 in.) undersize. Piston and cylinder markings should match, however, a new piston marked "B" can be installed into a used cylinder marked "A."

NOTE: Do not install a new piston marked "B" or "C" into a new cylinder marked "A."

Piston is equipped with two piston rings. Piston should be inspected and renewed if cracking or scoring is noted. Maximum allowable piston ring end gap is 1.0 mm (0.039 in.). Locating pins are present in ring grooves to prevent ring rotation. Be certain ring end gaps are properly positioned around locating pins when installing cylinder. Tighten cylinder screws to 11.8 N·m (9 ft.-lbs.) on all models.

On Models 070, 070S, A70 and Super Pro 70, piston pin (8–Fig. AP53) is a press fit in connecting rod small end. Piston rides in needle bearings (7) installed in each side of piston. Piston pin is retained with two snap rings (9). Use Alpina tool 4180020 or a suitable equivalent press to remove and install piston pin. Be sure piston is properly supported to prevent damage to piston.

On all other models, piston pin (8–Fig. AP54) is a press fit in piston and rides in one needle bearing (7) installed in connecting rod small end. Piston pin is retained with two wire clips (9). Use Alpina tool 4180010 or a suitable equivalent to remove and install piston pin. Piston may be heated to approximately 110°-120° C (230°-248° F) to ease installation of piston pin.

NOTE: Use electric oven or hot oil bath to heat piston. Do not use an open flame.

On all models, install piston into cylinder with arrow on piston crown facing toward exhaust port.

CRANKSHAFT, CONNECTING ROD AND CRANKCASE. Crankshaft and connecting rod are available as a unit assembly only. Check rotation of connecting rod around crankpin and renew crankshaft assembly if roughness, excessive play or other damage is noted. Check crankshaft runout by supporting crankshaft between two counter points such as a lathe. Make certain no damage is present in centering holes at each end of crankshaft. Renew crankshaft assembly if runout exceeds 0.08 mm (0.0031 in.).

NOTE: Crankshaft runout can be checked while still assembled in crankcase. Remove clutch and flywheel and mount dial indicators on each side of crankshaft as close to main bearings as possible. Measure runout while rotating crankshaft. Renew crankshaft assembly if runout exceeds 0.07 mm (0.0027 in.) when measured in this manner.

Crankshaft is supported with ball-type main bearings (12–Fig. AP53) or (24 and 25–Fig. AP54) at both ends. Main bearings are a press fit into crankcase halves. Use the proper size drivers to remove and install main bearings. Use Alpina tool 4180900 or a suitable equivalent to install crankshaft assembly into crankcase. Refer to Fig. AP57. Do not use gasket sealer on crankcase gasket. Tighten crankcase screws using a crisscross pattern to 7.8 N·m (69 in.-lbs.) on Super Pro 90 and Super Pro 120 models and 7.3 N·m (69 in.-lbs.) on Super Pro 90 and Super Pro 120 models and 7.3 N·m (65 in.-lbs.) on all other models.

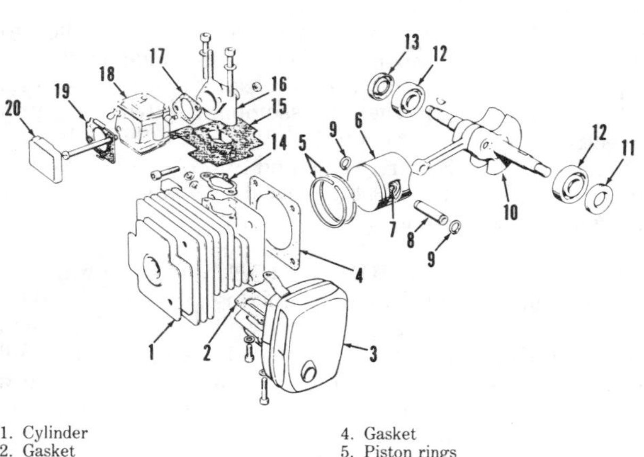

Fig. AP53—Exploded view of engine assembly, carburetor and related components used on all models except Super Pro 90 and Super Pro 120. Two needle bearings (7) are used. Refer to text.

1. Cylinder
2. Gasket
3. Muffler
4. Gasket
5. Piston rings
6. Piston
7. Needle bearing
8. Piston pin
9. Snap ring
10. Crankshaft & connecting rod assy.
11. Seal
12. Main bearing
13. Seal
14. Gasket
15. Gasket
16. Intake manifold
17. Gasket
18. Carburetor
19. Plate
20. Screen

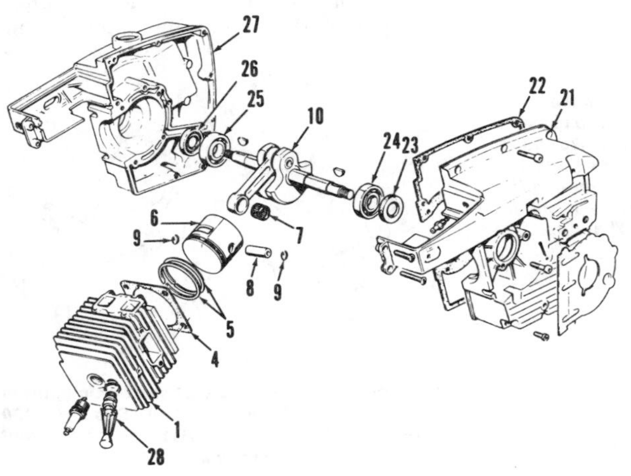

Fig. AP54—Exploded view of engine assembly used on Super Pro 90 and Super Pro 120 models.

1. Cylinder
4. Gasket
5. Piston rings
6. Piston
7. Needle bearing
8. Piston pin
9. Wire clip
10. Crankshaft & connecting rod assy.
21. Right crankcase half
22. Gasket
23. Seal
24. Main bearing
25. Main bearing
26. Seal
27. Left crankcase half
28. Decompression valve

CLUTCH. Late Models 070, 070S, A70 and Super Pro 70 are equipped with the clutch assembly shown in Fig. AP58. Late Models Super Pro 90 and Super Pro 120 are equipped with the clutch assembly shown in Fig. AP60. Refer to Fig. AP59 for view of shoes (4), hub (5) and spring (3) used on all early models. Note that hub (5–Figs. AP58, AP59 and AP60) is keyed to crankshaft on all models. Inspect shoes (4–Fig. AP58 or Fig. AP60), drum (7) and needle bearing (9) for excessive wear or damage due to overheating. Use Alpina tool 4180110 or a suitable bolt-type puller to remove clutch. Nut (12) has right-hand threads. Clutch shoes (4) are available only as a complete set. Tighten nut (12) to 45.1 N•m (33 ft.-lbs.) on Super Pro 90 and Super Pro 120 models and 35.3 N•m (26 ft.-lbs.) on all other models.

OIL PUMP. Refer to Fig. AP61 for exploded view of manual chain oil pump used on Models 070S and Super Pro 70. Disassembly for repair or component renewal is evident after inspection of unit and referral to Fig. AP61. Hoses (4) must be renewed if pump is disassembled. Be sure clamps (3) are tight and properly installed to prevent leakage.

Refer to Fig. AP62 for exploded view of automatic oil pump used on Models 070, 070S, A70 and Super Pro 70. Oil is pumped by piston (5) which is rotated by drive plate (10). Drive plate is cycled up and down by plunger (15) which rides on cam of engine crankshaft. Piston (5) rotates one notch with each down stroke of drive plate (10). Spring (12) forces piston brake (13) against piston (5), preventing piston (5) from backing up during drive plate (10) return stroke.

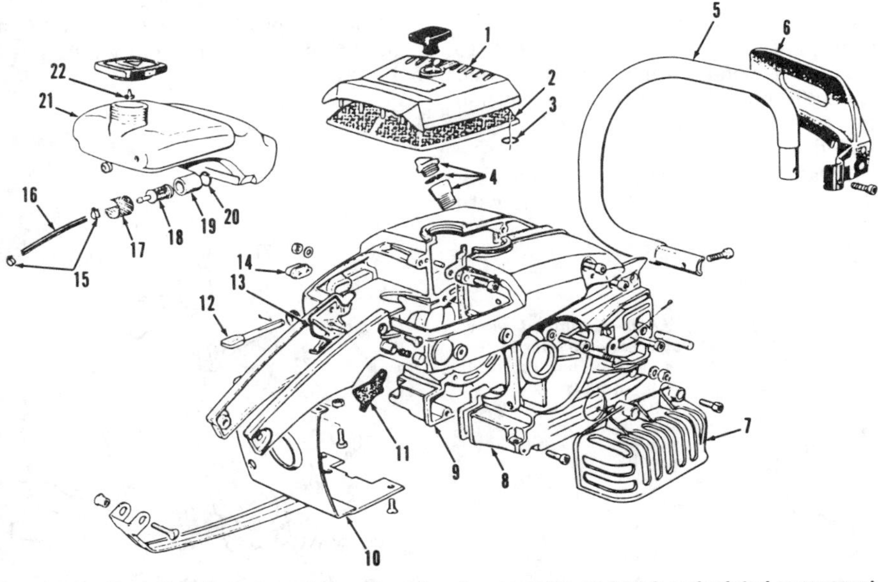

Fig. AP55—Exploded view of crankcase, front handle assembly, fuel tank and related components used on Models 070, 070S and A70.

1. Cover
2. Air filter
3. Snap ring
4. Oil tank cap assy.
5. Front handle
6. Hand guard
7. Muffler cover
8. Right crankcase half
9. Left crankcase half
10. Cylinder cover
11. Trigger
12. Choke lever
13. Throttle rod
14. Grommet
15. Clamp
16. Fuel hose
17. Screen
18. Fuel pickup
19. Filter
20. "O" ring
21. Fuel tank
22. Vent valve

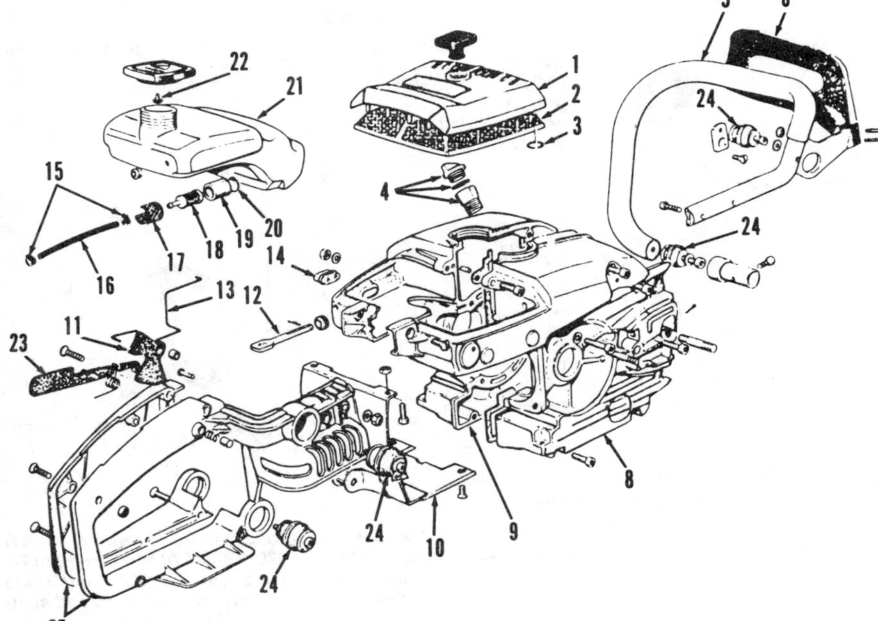

Fig. AP56—Exploded view of crankcase, front handle assembly, rear grip assembly, fuel tank and related components used on Model Super Pro 70. Refer to legend in Fig. AP55 for component identification except, safety lever (23), vibration isolator (24) and rear grip assembly (25). Super Pro 90 and Super Pro 120 models are similar.

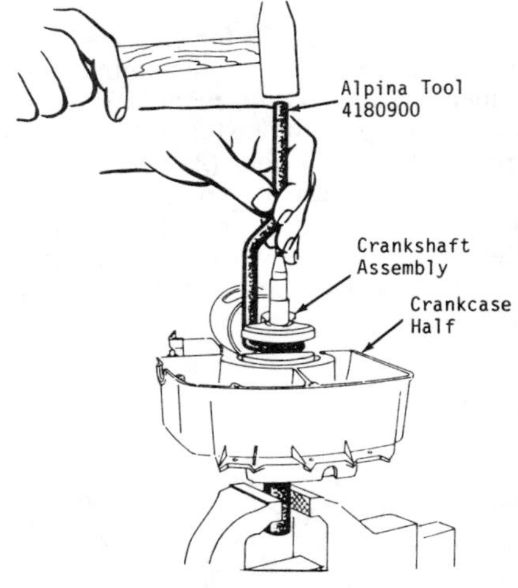
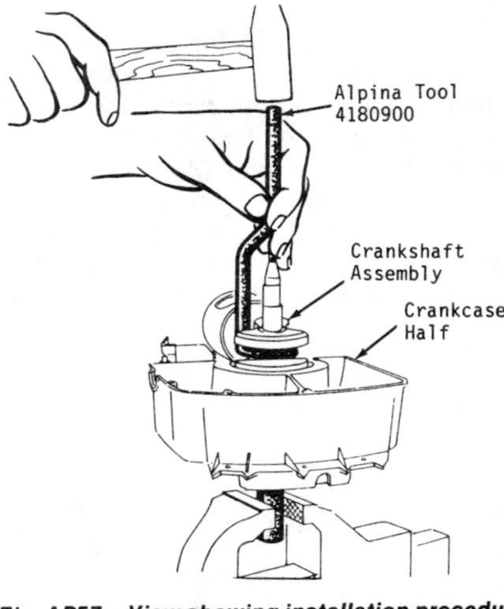

Fig. AP57—View showing installation procedure of crankshaft and connecting rod assembly into crankcase half using Alpina tool 4180900. Main bearing is pressed into crankcase half prior to installation of crankshaft assembly.

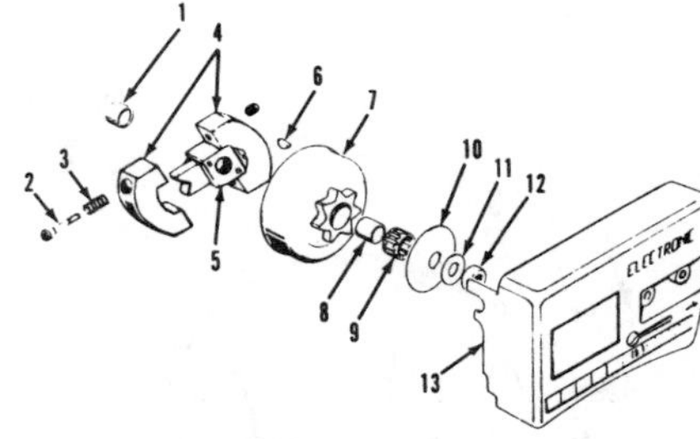

Fig. AP58—Exploded view of new design clutch used on late 070, 070S, A70 and Super Pro 70 models.

1. Bushing
2. Screw
3. Spring
4. Shoes
5. Hub
6. Woodruff key
7. Drum
8. Bushing
9. Needle bearing
10. Washer
11. Washer
12. Nut
13. Cover

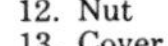

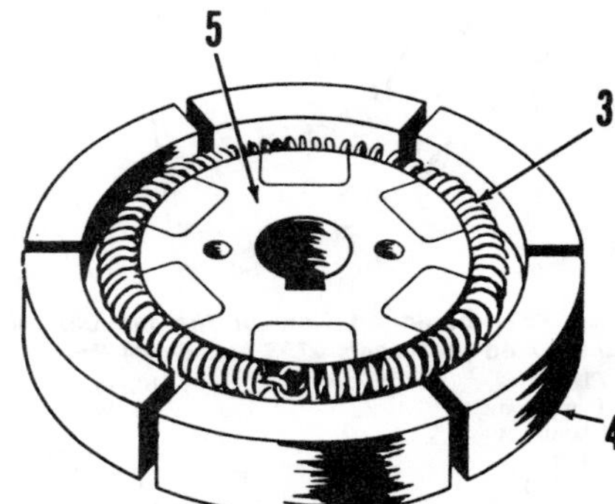

Fig. AP59—View showing clutch shoes (4), hub (5) and spring (3) used on all early models.

Plunger (15) is 31 mm (1.22 in.) long when new. Renew plunger if worn shorter than 30.3 mm (1.193 in.). Renew drive plate (10) if wear at piston contact area exceeds 1.5 mm (0.059 in.) when compared with a new drive plate. Reservoir (R) should be filled with high temperature lithium base grease and capped with felt plug (20). Pump output is not adjustable.

Refer to Fig. AP63 for exploded view of adjustable automatic oil pump used on Super Pro 90 and Super Pro 120 models. Oil is pumped by piston (5) which is rotated by worm gear (23) mounted on engine crankshaft. Pump output is regulated by turning adjusting lever (28). Renew piston and worm gear if excessive wear or damage is noted. Closely inspect seal (30) and seal surface on worm gear (23). Note that slight wear on seal or worm gear may allow pump to draw air causing pump malfunction. It is recommended to renew seal (30) any time pump is disassembled.

REWIND STARTER. To disassemble starter, remove rope handle (10 – Fig. AP64) and carefully allow rope to wind into housing, relieving tension on rewind spring (5). Remove screw (9) and rope pulley (6) using caution not to dislodge rewind spring (5). If rewind spring (5) must be removed, use caution not to allow spring to uncoil uncontrolled.

Install rewind spring (5) into housing (2) in a clockwise direction starting with outer coil. Install rope onto rope pulley (6) in a clockwise direction as viewed from flywheel side of pulley. Rotate pulley (6) clockwise to apply tension on rewind spring. Apply only enough tension on rewind spring (5) to pull rope handle snug against housing. Rope pulley should be able to rotate an additional ½ turn with rope completely extended.

Refer to Fig. AP51 for exploded view of starter pawl assemblies. Use a suitable thread locking solution on pawl bolts (2).

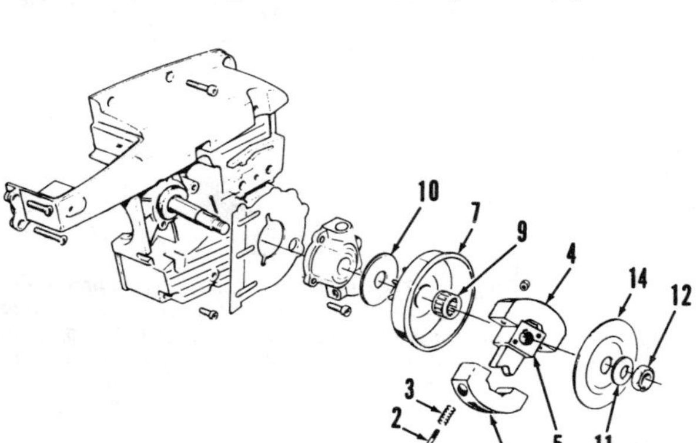

Fig. AP60 – Exploded view of clutch used on later Super Pro 90 and Super Pro 120 models.

2. Screw
3. Spring
4. Shoes
5. Hub
7. Drum
9. Needle bearing
10. Washer
11. Washer
12. Nut
14. Washer

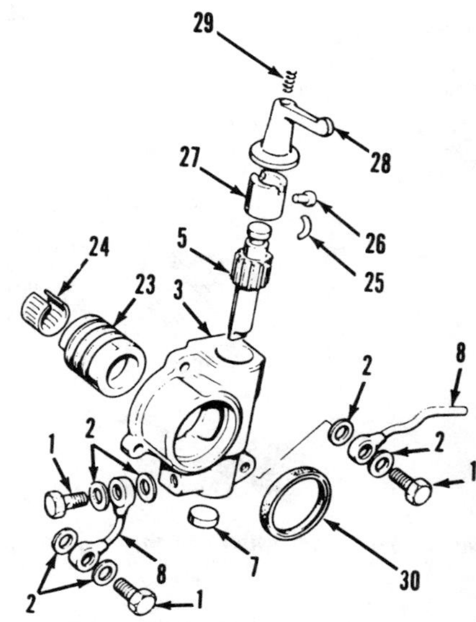

Fig. AP63 – Exploded view of adjustable automatic oil pump used on Super Pro 90 and Super Pro 120 models.

1. Banjo bolt
2. Washers
3. Pump body
5. Piston
7. Plug
8. Tube
23. Worm gear
24. Collar
25. Pin
26. Pin
27. Bushing
28. Adjusting lever
29. Spring
30. Seal

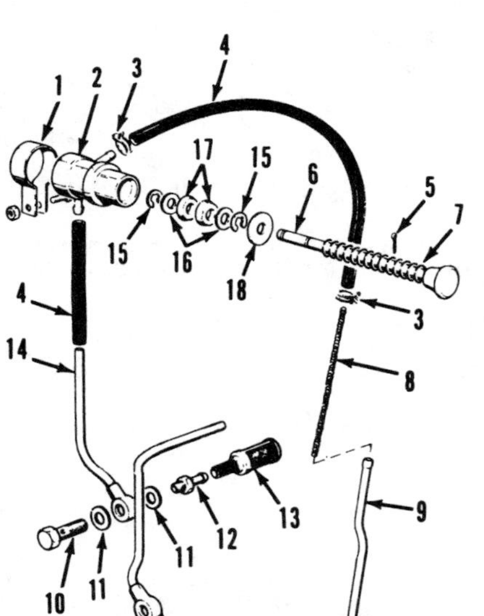

Fig. AP61 – Exploded view of the manual oil pump used on Models 070S and Super Pro 70.

1. Clamp
2. Pump body
3. Clamp
4. Hose
5. Cotter pin
6. Piston
7. Spring
8. Spring
9. Tube
10. Bolt
11. Washer
12. Fitting
13. Oil pickup
14. Tube
15. "E" ring
16. Washers
17. Seals
18. Washer

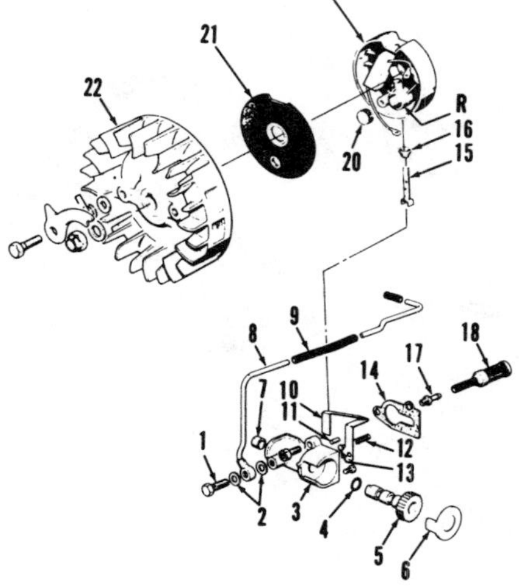

Fig. AP62 – Exploded view of automatic oil pump used on Models 070, 070S, A70 and Super Pro 70.

1. Banjo bolt
2. Washers
3. Pump body
4. "O" ring
5. Piston
6. Cover
7. Plug
8. Tube
9. Hose
10. Drive plate
11. Pin
12. Spring
13. Piston brake
14. Gasket
15. Plunger
16. Seal
17. Fitting
18. Oil pickup
19. Module case
20. Felt plug
21. Cover
22. Flywheel
R. Reservoir

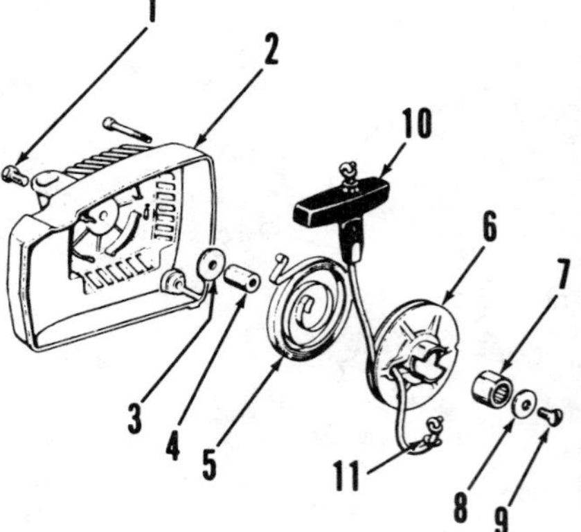

Fig. AP64 – Exploded view of rewind starter used on Models 070, 070S, A70 and Super Pro 70. Super Pro 90 and Super Pro 120 models are similar except, washer (11) is not used and shaft (4) is part of housing (2).

1. Bolt
2. Housing
3. Washer
4. Shaft
5. Rewind spring
6. Rope pulley
7. Needle bearing
8. Washer
9. Screw
10. Rope handle
11. Washer

CASTOR

Model	Bore mm (in.)	Stroke mm (in.)	Displacement cc (cu. in.)	Drive Type
330, C330, 432	36.5 (1.44)	30.4 (1.2)	32 (1.9)	Direct
380, 438, C438	39.7 (1.56)	30.4 (1.2)	38 (2.3)	Direct

MAINTENANCE

SPARK PLUG. Recommended spark plug is Champion CJ7Y for all models. Spark plug electrode gap should be 0.5 mm (0.020 in.).

CARBURETOR. Models 330 and 380 are equipped with a Walbro WA diaphragm type carburetor. Models 432 and 438 are equipped with a Dell'Orto diaphragm type carburetor. Refer to Walbro and Dell'Orto sections of CARBURETOR SERVICE section for service procedures and exploded views.

High speed mixture is not adjustable on Models 330 and 380. Initial setting of low speed mixture screw is 1⅜ turns open on Model 330 and 1½ turns open on Model 380. Initial setting on Models 432 and 438 is 1¾ turns open for low speed mixture screw and 1½ turns open for high speed mixture screw.

Final adjustment should be made with engine running at operating temperature. Adjust engine idle speed to just below clutch engagement speed. Adjust low speed mixture so engine will accelerate cleanly without hesitation. Adjust high speed mixture to obtain maximum no-load speed of 11,200 rpm on Model 432 and 11,700 rpm on Model 438.

IGNITION. All models are equipped with a breakerless electronic ignition system. Ignition coil and all electronic circuitry are contained in a one-piece ignition module. Ignition timing is not adjustable. Air gap between ignition module legs and flywheel magnets should be 0.35 mm (0.014 in.). Loosen ignition module mounting screws and move module to adjust air gap. Use a suitable thread locking solution on module screws to prevent screws from vibrating loose. If flywheel requires removal, use Castor tool 3630260 or a suitable equivalent to withdraw flywheel. Tighten flywheel nut to 34.3 N·m (26 ft.-lbs.).

LUBRICATION. The engine is lubricated by mixing oil with the fuel. Use a good quality oil designed for use in air-cooled two-stroke engines. Fuel:oil ratio is 16:1 for all models. Use a separate container when mixing fuel and oil.

Models 330 and 380 are equipped with an automatic oil pump which utilizes crankcase pulsations to pressurize oil tank. Pump output is adjustable. Models 432 and 438 are equipped with an automatic plunger type oil pump driven by a worm gear on engine crankshaft. Pump output is not adjustable. Refer to OIL PUMP under REPAIRS section for service procedures and exploded views.

Use clean automotive oil for saw chain lubrication. On Models 330 and 380, oil viscosity must be chosen according to ambient temperature. For example, use SAE 30 for warm weather operation and SAE 15 for cold weather operation.

REPAIRS

CYLINDER, PISTON, PIN AND RINGS. Cylinder is chrome plated and should be renewed if cracking, scoring or other damage is noted in cylinder bore.

NOTE: Piston aligns connecting rod on rod bearing rollers (25 – Fig. CR1). Excessive piston movement during or after cylinder removal may allow rod bearing rollers to fall into crankcase.

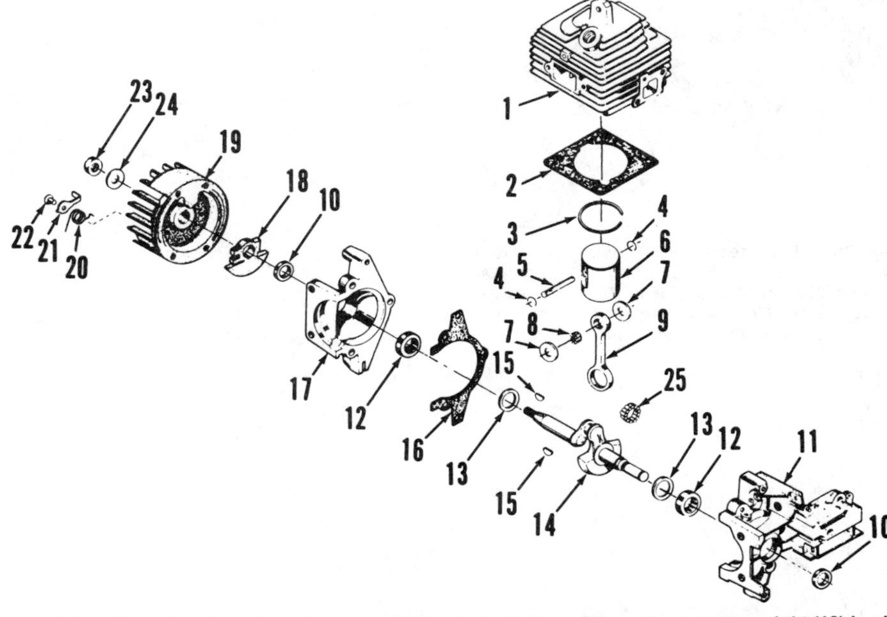

Fig. CR1 – Exploded view of engine assembly typical of all models noting counterweight (18) is absent on Models 432 and 438. Two pawl assemblies (20, 21 and 22) are used.

1. Cylinder
2. Gasket
3. Piston ring
4. Snap ring
5. Piston pin
6. Piston
7. Thrust washer
8. Bearing rollers
9. Connecting rod
10. Seal
11. Right crankcase half
12. Main bearing
13. Thrust washer
14. Crankshaft
15. Key
16. Gasket
17. Left crankcase half
18. Counterweight
19. Flywheel
20. Spring
21. Pawl
22. Pin
23. Nut
24. Washer
25. Bearing rollers

Piston and cylinder are matched during production to get desired piston-to-cylinder clearance of 0.02 mm (0.0008 in.). Original piston and cylinder are marked "A." Factory renewal piston and cylinder assemblies are marked "B." Piston or cylinder marked "C" is 0.127 mm (0.005 in.) oversize while piston or cylinder marked "D" is 0.127 mm (0.005 in.) undersize. Piston and cylinder markings should match, however, a new piston marked "B" can be installed in a used cylinder marked "A."

NOTE: Do not install a new piston marked "B" or "C" into a new cylinder marked "A."

Piston is equipped with one piston ring. A locating pin is present in ring groove to prevent ring rotation. Maximum allowable piston ring end gap is 1.0 mm (0.039 in.). Piston pin (5 – Fig. CR1) rides on 18 loose bearing rollers (8). Use Castor tool 4180010 or a suitable equivalent with proper size drivers to remove and install piston pin. Hold bearing rollers (8) in place with heavy grease and place thrust washer (7) on each side of rod before installing piston. Install piston with arrow on piston crown facing toward exhaust side of cylinder. Make certain piston ring end gap is properly positioned around locating pin in ring groove before installing cylinder. Tighten cylinder screws to 8.8 N·m (78 in.-lbs.)

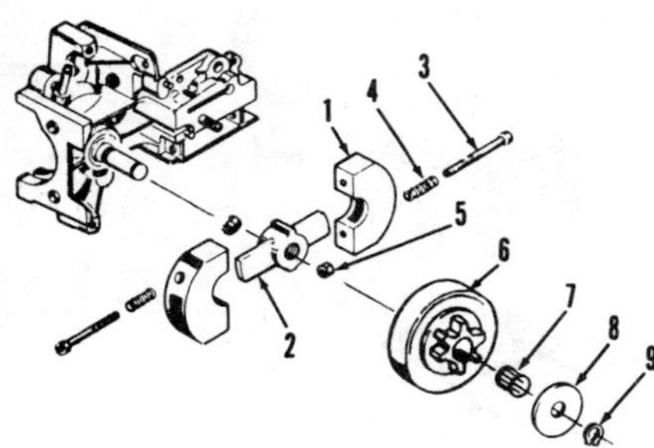

Fig. CR2 – Exploded view of centrifugal clutch assembly used on Models 432, 438 and later Models 330 and 380. Refer to Fig. CR3 for exploded view of clutch assembly used on early Models 330 and 380.

1. Shoe
2. Hub
3. Screw
4. Spring
5. Nut
6. Drum
7. Needle bearing
8. Washer
9. Snap ring

Fig. CR3 – Exploded view of centrifugal clutch assembly used on early Models 330 and 380. Refer to legend in Fig. CR2 for component identification.

CRANKSHAFT, CONNECTING ROD AND CRANKCASE. Crankshaft (14 – Fig. CR1) is supported at both ends with caged roller bearings (12). Bearings (12) are located in crankcase halves (11 and 17). To split crankcase halves, first remove cylinder and crankcase halves mounting screws. Insert a screwdriver or similar tool between crankcase and crankshaft counterweight. Carefully pry crankcase halves apart being careful not to damage crankcase mating surfaces.

NOTE: Crankshaft runout can be checked before disassembly of engine. To check runout, remove clutch and flywheel. Mount a dial indicator on both ends of crankshaft as close as possible to bearings (12). Check runout while rotating crankshaft. Runout should not exceed 0.07 mm (0.0027 in.).

Connecting rod rides on 12 loose bearing rollers (25). Connecting rod can be removed from crankshaft after crankcase halves are separated. Hold bearing rollers on crankpin with heavy grease when installing connecting rod. Note location of thrust washers (13). Counterweight (18) is used on Models 330 and 380 only. Do not use gasket sealing compounds on crankcase gasket (16). Tighten crankcase screws using a crisscross pattern to 6.9 N·m (61 in.-lbs.).

CLUTCH. Models 432, 438 and later Models 330 and 380 are equipped with the centrifugal clutch shown in Fig. CR2. Early Models 330 and 380 are equipped with the centrifugal clutch shown in Fig. CR3. Complete clutch assemblies are interchangeable, although, individual components are not. Clutch hubs (2 – Figs. CR2 and CR3) have left-hand threads. Inspect shoes, hub, drum and needle bearing for excessive wear or damage due to overheating. Clutch shoes are available only as a complete set. Tighten clutch hub to 18.6 N·m (14 ft.-lbs.).

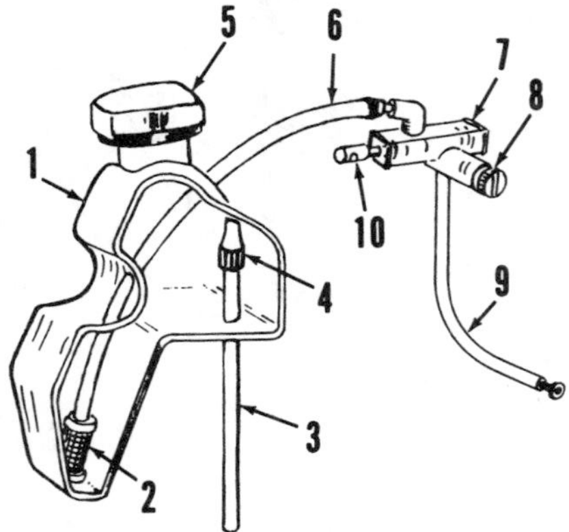

Fig. CR4 – View showing automatic oiling system used on Models 330 and 380.

1. Oil tank
2. Oil filter
3. Impulse hose
4. Check valve
5. Cap
6. Hose
7. Metering valve assy.
8. Adjusting screw
9. Discharge hose
10. Shut-off valve

OIL PUMP. Models 330 and 380 are equipped with the pressure-type chain oiling system shown in Fig. CR4. Impulse hose (3) connects to crankcase. Crankcase pulsations pressurize oil tank (1). Check valve (4) prevents chain oil from entering crankcase. Pump output is regulated by rotating screw (8). Clockwise rotation decreases output. Shut-off valve (10) is linked to throttle trigger, preventing oil flow at idle speed.

Oil tank (1) must hold pressure for proper operation of system. Pressurize oil tank to 34.5 kPa (5.0 psi) to check for leakage in tank or leak-back of check valve (4). Malfunctions are often due to check valve (4) stuck closed preventing crankcase pulsations from entering oil tank.

Fig. CR5 – View showing location of automatic oil pump used on Models 432 and 438. Refer to Fig. CR6 for exploded view of oil pump assembly (4).

1. Crankshaft
2. Left crankcase half
3. Oil pump key
4. Oil pump assy.
5. Flywheel key
6. Flywheel
7. Washer
8. Nut

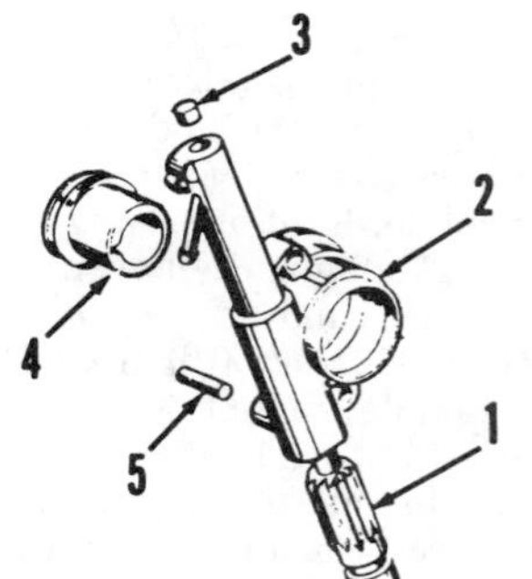

Fig. CR6 – Exploded view of automatic oil pump assembly used on Models 432 and 438.

1. Plunger
2. Pump body
3. Plug
4. Worm gear
5. Cam pin

Models 432 and 438 are equipped with the automatic oil pump shown in Figs. CR5 and CR6. Pump output is not adjustable. Plunger (1–Fig. CR6) is rotated by worm gear (4) on engine crankshaft. Oil is pumped by plunger (1) as plunger reciprocates in pump body (2) due to cam pin (5) riding in oblique groove in plunger.

Remove flywheel (6–Fig. CR5) to gain access to oil pump. Withdraw cam pin (5–Fig. CR6) to remove plunger (1). Inspect all components for excessive wear or damage and renew if needed. Tighten flywheel nut (8–Fig. CR5) to 34.3 N•m (26 ft.-lbs.).

REWIND STARTER. Models 330 and 380 are equipped with the rewind starter shown in Fig. CR7. Models A432 and A438 are equipped with the rewind starter shown in Fig. CR8.

On all models, remove starter housing (7–Figs. CR7 and CR8) to disassemble starter. Withdraw housing (7) sufficiently to disconnect ignition switch wires then remove housing. Remove rope handle and allow rope to slowly wind into starter housing to relieve tension on rewind spring. Remove screw (1) and carefully remove rope pulley (4). If rewind spring (6) must be removed, care should be taken to prevent personal injury due to uncontrolled uncoiling of spring.

Install rewind spring (6) into housing in a clockwise direction starting with outer coil end. Wrap starter rope around rope pulley in a clockwise direction as viewed from flywheel side of pulley. To preload rewind spring, pull out a loop of rope from notch in rope pulley and rotate pulley ½ turn clockwise. Rope handle should be snug against housing with rope retracted. With rope fully extended, rope pulley should be able to rotate an additional ½ turn to prevent rewind spring breakage.

On all models, starter pawls (21–Fig. CR1) are secured on flywheel with pins (22). Drive pins out from inside of flywheel to remove pawls. Use Castor tool 3630260 or a suitable equivalent to remove flywheel. Use a suitable thread locking solution on pins (22) when reassembling pawls. Tighten flywheel nut to 34.3 N•m (26 ft.-lbs.).

CHAIN BRAKE. Some models are equipped with the chain brake system shown in Fig. CR9. Chain brake is actuated when operator's hand strikes hand guard (15). Forward movement of actuator (13) trips latch (11) allowing spring (4) to pull brake band (2) tight around clutch drum (6). Pull back hand guard (15) to reset chain brake.

To adjust chain brake, disengage brake by pulling hand guard (15) to rearmost position (toward engine). Install guide bar and saw chain and properly adjust chain tension. Rotate brake tension adjustment screw (between brake arm mounting studs at front of actuator) clockwise, while pulling saw chain around guide bar, until chain movement becomes difficult. Back off adjustment screw (counterclockwise) until chain moves freely around guide bar. Make certain brake band does not contact clutch drum with brake in the disengaged position.

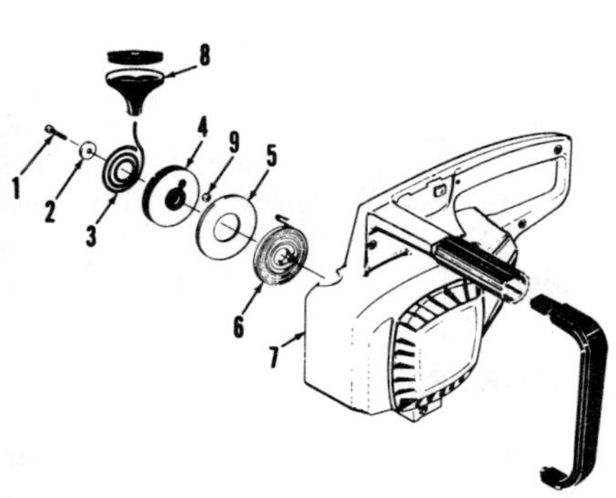

Fig. CR7—Exploded view of rewind starter used on Models 330 and 380.

1. Screw
2. Washer
3. Rope
4. Rope pulley
5. Spring cover
6. Rewind spring
7. Housing
8. Rope handle
9. Eyelet

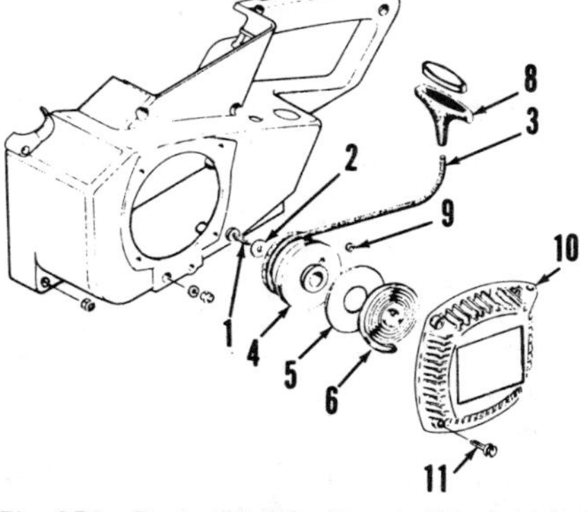

Fig. CR8—Exploded view of rewind starter used on Models 432 and 438. Refer to Fig. CR7 for component identification except cover (10) and screw (11).

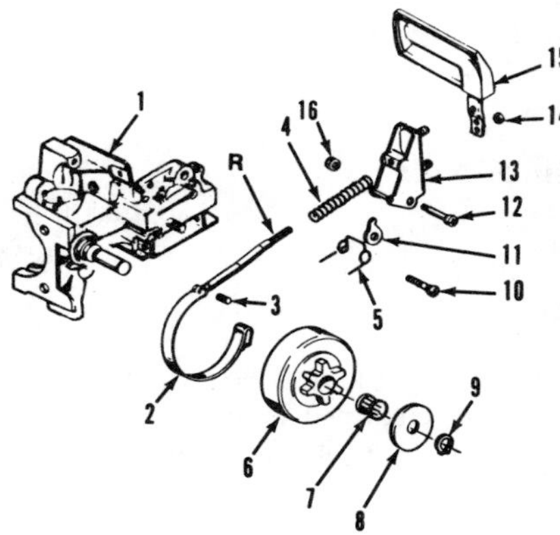

Fig. CR9—Exploded view of chain brake system used on some models. Brake tension screw (not shown) is located at front of actuator (13) between hand guard (15) mounting studs.

1. Right crankcase half
2. Brake band
3. Pin
4. Spring
5. Spring
6. Drum
7. Needle bearing
8. Washer
9. Snap ring
10. Screw
11. Latch
12. Shoulder screw
13. Actuator
14. Nut
15. Hand guard
16. Nut
R. Rod

CLINTON

Model	Bore mm (in.)	Stroke mm (in.)	Displacement cc (cu. in.)	Drive Type
D-25	47.6 (1.875)	41.3 (1.625)	78.4* (4.48)	Direct
D-35	53.9 (2.125)	41.3 (1.625)	94.7 (5.78)	Direct

* Some D-25 may have the same bore and displacement as D-35.

MAINTENANCE

SPARK PLUG. Spark plug electrode gap should be 0.025-0.028 inch (0.63-0.71 mm) on all models. Use Champion spark plug type number, or equivalent, as outlined in following chart:

Model No.	Champion Type No.
D-25	TJ-8J, CJ-8*
D-35, type A	H-10J
All other types	J-8J

*With special connector.

CARBURETOR. Models D-25 and D-35 are equipped with a Tillotson HC-11A diaphragm carburetor and a separate fuel pump as shown in Fig. CL2.

For initial adjustment on all models, open main jet adjustment screw 1¼ turns and idle jet adjustment screw ¾ turn. Turn idle speed adjustment screw one full turn after contact is made with throttle stop.

Final adjustment is made with engine running and warmed up. Set idle speed adjustment screw to give an idle speed of 1800 to 2200 rpm. (Clutch should stay disengaged at proper idle speed.) Adjust idle jet screw to obtain smoothest engine operation; then open jet a very slight amount over this setting. With saw under cutting load, adjust main jet adjustment screw to obtain even engine speed. This setting will vary from 1 to 1½ turns open.

Refer to Tillotson carburetor section in CARBURETOR SERVICE section for exploded view and carburetor overhaul on Tillotson carburetors.

MAGNETO AND TIMING. Flywheel type Clinton magneto is used. Set breaker contact gap to 0.020 inch (0.51 mm). Spark timing is fixed at 33 to 35 degrees and is nonadjustable. Armature air gap is 0.005 to 0.007 inch (0.13-0.18 mm). Edge gap (distance between trailing edge of flywheel magnet and edge of coil lamination core after magnet has passed coil lamination core) is ⅛ to ¼ inch (3.18-6.35 mm). Condenser capacity is 0.13 to 0.14 mfd. Spark should jump ⅛ inch (3.18 mm) gap at cranking speed and a 3/16-inch (4.76 mm) gap at engine operating speed.

CAUTION: Check gap at running speed for a brief instant only, to avoid damage to coil.

LUBRICATION. Recommended fuel: oil mixture for Model D-25 is ¾ pint (0.35 L) oil mixed with one gallon (3.78 L) of regular gasoline. SAE 30 oil for chain saw engines should be used. On Model D-35, this mixture should be used for the engine break-in period and then reduced to ½ pint (0.24 L) of oil mixed with 1 gal. (3.78 L) of regular gasoline.

Fill chain oiler tank with new SAE 30 motor oil. Press plunger several times to be sure oiler pump is working. Dilute chain oil with 50 percent kerosene in cold weather, or when cutting wood with high pitch, sap or resin content.

REPAIRS

CLEANING CARBON. To clean the exhaust valve ports, remove muffler and turn engine so that piston is below ports. Clean the exhaust ports by scraping with a blunt tool. Take care not to score the top of the piston.

TIGHTENING TORQUES. Graphite should be applied to threads of all screws which thread into die cast parts.

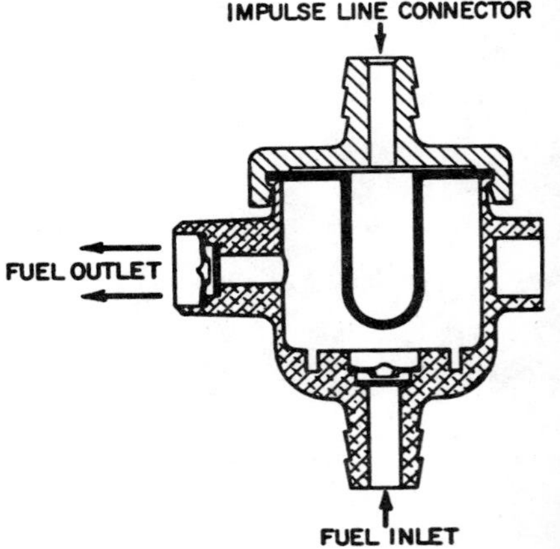

Fig. CL2—Cross-sectional view of fuel pump used with Tillotson carburetor. Renew fuel pump assembly if inoperative; component parts are not serviceable.

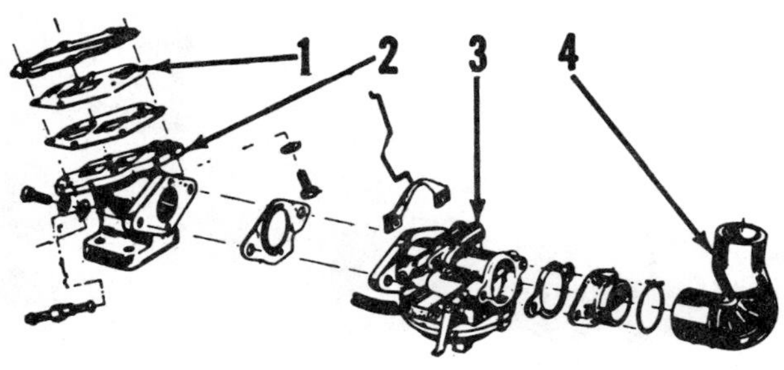

Fig. CL1—Induction system of Clinton chain saw engine.

1. Reed plate
2. Induction bracket
3. Carburetor
4. Carburetor to air cleaner hose

Fastener Location	Torque Value
Guide bar mounting studs	125-175 in.-lbs. (14.1-19.8 N•m)
Sprocket nut	33-37 ft.-lbs. (44.9-50.3 N•m)
Reduction housing to block	150-175 in.-lbs. (16.9-19.8 N•m)
Clutch to crankshaft (1st nut)	110-120 in.-lbs. (12.4-13.6 N•m)
(2nd nut, where used)	190-210 in.-lbs. (21.5-23.7 N•m)
Induction bracket to block	30-50 in.-lbs. (3.4-5.6 N•m)
Carburetor to induction bracket	30-50 in.-lbs. (3.4-5.6 N•m)
Bearing plate to block	80-90 in.-lbs. (9.0-10.2 N•m)
Flywheel nut	31-35 ft.-lbs. (42.2-47.6 N•m)
Stator plate to bearing plate	50-60 in.-lbs. (5.6-6.8 N•m)
Blower housing to bearing plate	80-90 in.-lbs. (10.0-10.2 N•m)
Spark plug	230-270 in.-lbs. (26.0-30.5 N•m)
Cap to connecting rod	*
Muffler body to block	60-70 in.-lbs. (6.8-7.9 N•m)
Air deflectors to cylinder block	15-20 in.-lbs. (1.7-2.2 N•m)
Tubular handle	60-80 in.-lbs. (6.8-9.0 N•m)
Starter to blower housing	30-40 in.-lbs. (3.4-4.5 N•m)
Reed plate to induction bracket	20-25 in.-lbs. (2.2-2.8 N•m)
Condenser	10-15 in.-lbs. (1.1-1.7 N•m)
Tank strap to block	20-25 in.-lbs. (2.2-2.8 N•m)
Cover to transmission casting	20-25 in.-lbs. (2.2-2.8 N•m)
Spike to casting	120-130 in.-lbs. (13.6-14.7 N•m)

*See CONNECTING ROD paragraph.

BEARING PLATE. Because of the pressure and vacuum pulsations in crankcase, bearing plate and gasket must form an air-tight seal when installed. Make sure gasket surfaces are not cracked, nicked or warped, that oil passages in crankcase, gasket and plate are aligned and that correct number and thickness of thrust washers are used. Also check to be sure the right cap screws are installed when engine is reassembled.

CAUTION: Cap screws (1 – Fig. CL5) may bottom in threaded holes (2) if incorrect screws are used. When long screws are tightened, damage to cylinder walls can result.

CONNECTING ROD. Piston and connecting rod assembly are removed from bottom of the crankcase after first removing the crankshaft. The long sloping side of the piston is the exhaust side; place this side of piston to exhaust port when installing piston and connecting rod assembly.

On Model D-25, an aluminum connecting rod, with a cast-in bronze insert is used. Crankpin diameter is 0.7788-0.7795 inch (19.781-19.799 mm). Desired clearance between crankpin and connecting rod is 0.0021-0.0037 inch (0.053-0.094 mm). Renew connecting rod and/or crankshaft if clearance exceeds 0.005 inch (0.13 mm).

On Model D-35, crankpin bearing consists of 25 uncaged needle bearings. Either a steel connecting rod or a forged aluminum connecting rod with renewable steel bearing liner is used. The aluminum rod and bearing liner are interchangeable with the steel rod. Renew crankshaft, steel rod or bearing liner if bearing surfaces show signs of wear or are scored. When installing connecting rod to crankpin, place 13 needle rollers between crankpin and rod. Apply low temperature grease to rod cap and stick the remaining 12 rollers to cap.

On all models, place cap on connecting rod with mating marks aligned and torque rod cap screws to proper torque value as follows:

Model D-25	55-65 in.-lbs. (6.2-7.3 N•m)
Model D-35:	
Aluminum rod	80-90 in.-lbs. (9.0-10.2 N•m)
Steel rod	100-110 in.-lbs. (11.3-12.4 N•m)

PISTON, PIN AND RINGS. On Model D-25, piston is fitted with two pinned piston rings. On Model D-35, the

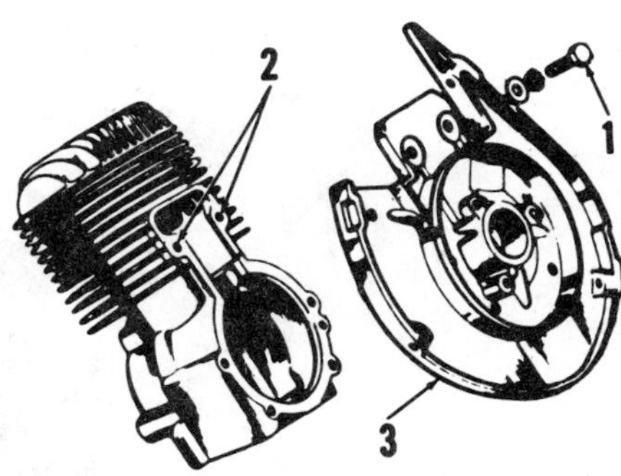
Fig. CL5 – If cap screws (1) which thread into holes (2) are too long, they may bottom and damage cylinder walls.

Fig. CL3 – Exploded view of Clinton magneto and related parts.

1. Stator cover & gasket
2. Condenser
3. Magneto cam
4. Breaker-points
5. Stator plate, coil & armature
6. Crankshaft seal
7. Crankcase side plate
8. Main needle bearing
9. Starter housing
10. Rewind spring
11. Rope pulley
12. Pawl
13. Pawl spring
14. Actuator spring
15. Actuator
16. Retaining ring
17. Blower cover
18. Starter cup
19. Flywheel

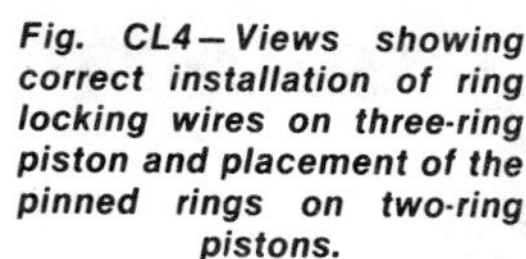
Fig. CL4 – Views showing correct installation of ring locking wires on three-ring piston and placement of the pinned rings on two-ring pistons.

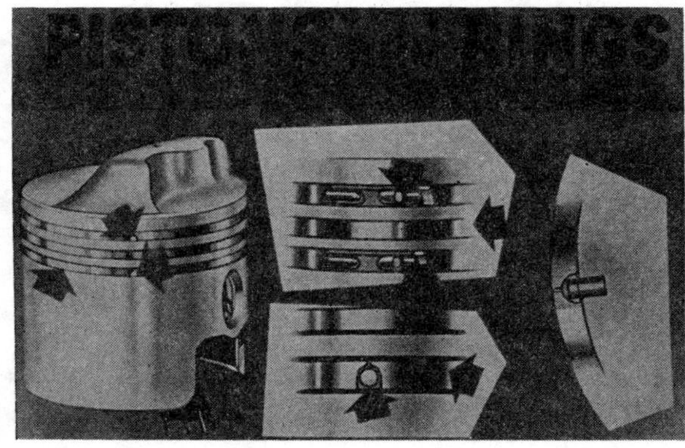

aluminum alloy piston is fitted with three compression rings. A ring lock wire is placed in a small groove at the bottom of each ring groove to prevent rings from moving into the port holes. To install lock wires refer to Fig. CL4 and proceed as follows: Hold piston with intake side facing right. (The sharp contoured side of the piston is the intake side.) Place the three lock wires over the piston with the lock ring tab to the right of the locating hole on top and bottom ring, and to the left of locating hole on center ring. When placing rings on the piston, be sure that recess in ring gap is placed over lock wire ring tab, so ring gap can close when piston is inserted in the cylinder. Use piston ring compressor when installing piston.

Ring end gap should be 0.007 inch (0.18 mm) with wear limit to 0.017 inch (0.43 mm). Ring side clearance should not be more than 0.002 inch (0.05 mm). Pistons and rings are available in 0.010 inch (0.25 mm) and 0.020 inch (0.51 mm) oversizes as well as in standard size.

The piston pin must be installed with closed end inserted into intake side of piston. The piston pin is available in one size only and should be renewed when the connecting rod is renewed.

CYLINDER. Cylinder block is die cast with integral cast iron cylinder liner. Clearance between piston skirt and cylinder wall measured at right angle to piston pin and below ports should be 0.0045 to 0.0050 inch (0.114-0.127 mm) with wear limit of 0.007 inch (0.178 mm). If worn beyond the 0.007 inch (0.178 mm) wear limit when checked with a new piston, hone to the next oversize and leave the cross-hatch pattern in the cylinder wall to provide piston lubrication. Do not polish cylinder wall.

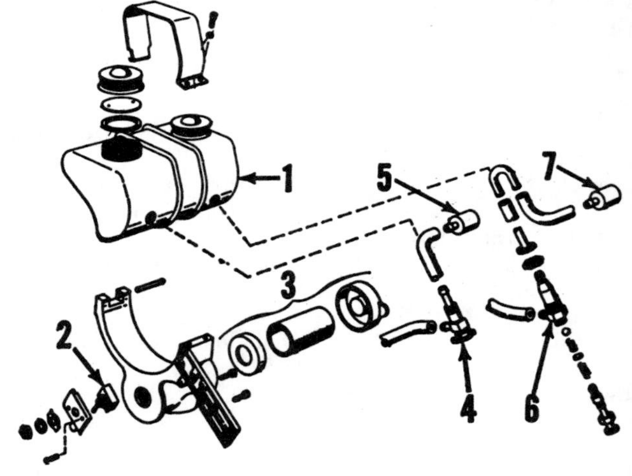

Fig. CL7—View identifies fuel-chain oil tank assembly and related components, air cleaner assembly and magneto grounding switch.
1. Fuel-chain oil tank
2. Magneto grounding switch
3. Air cleaner
4. Fuel shut-off valve
5. Fuel pickup
6. Oiler pump
7. Oil pickup

CRANKSHAFT. On Model D-25, the flywheel end of the crankshaft is supported in a sleeve type bushing. Desired bushing to crankshaft main journal clearance is 0.0013-0.0030 inch (0.033-0.076 mm), maximum allowable clearance is 0.0040 inch (0.102 mm). Crankshaft journal diameter (new) is 0.7495-0.7502 inch (19.037-19.055 mm); renew crankshaft if journal is worn to a diameter of 0.7475 inch (18.986 mm) or less. Bushing is renewable in bearing plate; ream bushing to a diameter of 0.7515-0.7525 inch (19.088-19.113 mm) after installation.

On Model D-35, flywheel end of crankshaft is supported in a needle bearing. Renew the crankshaft if bearing surface shows signs of wear or is scored. Renew the needle bearing if any roller has flat spots or if any two rollers can be separated the width of one roller. Install needle bearing by pressing on lettered end of bearing cage only.

Drive end of crankshaft is supported in a ball bearing on all models. Crankshaft end play is controlled by the ball bearing which is a snug fit in crankcase and on crankshaft. The ball bearing (12–Fig. CL6) is held in place in the crankcase with two snap rings (15 and 16) and on the crankshaft with a snap ring (13). On early production models, shims were used between the bearing and outer snap ring (15) to remove any side play of the bearing outer race between the snap rings. Shims are not required on late production units.

To remove the crankshaft, proceed as follows: Remove the carburetor adapter (23) and reed plate (20); then, remove the connecting rod cap (27) and needle bearing rollers (on models so equipped). Push the piston and connecting rod unit to top of cylinder. Remove bearing plate (33). Then, remove oil seal (14) from pto end of crankshaft to allow removal of snap ring (13). Turn crankshaft so that throw will clear connecting rod and push crankshaft from crankcase. Reinstall by reversing removal procedures.

Fig. CL6—View of typical Clinton chain saw engine.
1. Flywheel key
2. Connecting rod
3. Piston
4. Snap rings
5. Piston pin
6. Ring lock wires (3)
7. Piston rings (3)
8. Spark plug
9. Cylinder
10. Baffle
11. Exhaust
12. Ball bearing
13. Snap ring
14. Crankshaft seal
15 & 16. Snap rings
17. Gasket
18. Reed stop
19. Valve reed
20. Reed plate
21. Gasket
22. Fuel line
23. Carburetor adapter
24. Gasket
25. Needle rollers
26. Bearing liners
27. Rod cap
28. Fitting
29. Impulse line
30. Gasket
31. Needle bearing
32. Crankshaft seal
33. Bearing plate

CRANKSHAFT SEALS. Seals must be maintained in good condition because of leakage through seals would cause loss of power. It is important therefore to carefully inspect the seals and to exercise extreme care when renewing seals to prevent their being damaged. Use seal protector over ends of crankshaft or tape shaft to prevent seal damage.

REED VALVE. The reed valve unit can be inspected after removing carburetor and induction bracket as a single unit. Renew reed plate if petal is broken, cracked, warped or rusted, or if seat for petal is not smooth. Reed petal and plate are available only as an assembly.

CLUTCH A roller type clutch is used. There is no adjustment to the clutch, but if it does not engage and disengage properly, it should be inspected for worn or broken parts or for incorrect assembly. The clutch is shown in Fig. CL8. Rollers, clutch hub, and band asembly are available as individual replacement parts or as an assembly. Refer to Fig. CL8 for correct assembly of clutch.

The clutch drum (2–Fig. CL8) on Model D-25 is fitted with a renewable bushing that rides on the engine crankshaft. Desired clearance of bushing to crankshaft is 0.0010-0.0035 inch (0.025-0.089 mm); renew bushing if clearance exceeds 0.004 inch (0.102 mm). On Model D-35, the clutch drum is equipped with a renewable needle bearing.

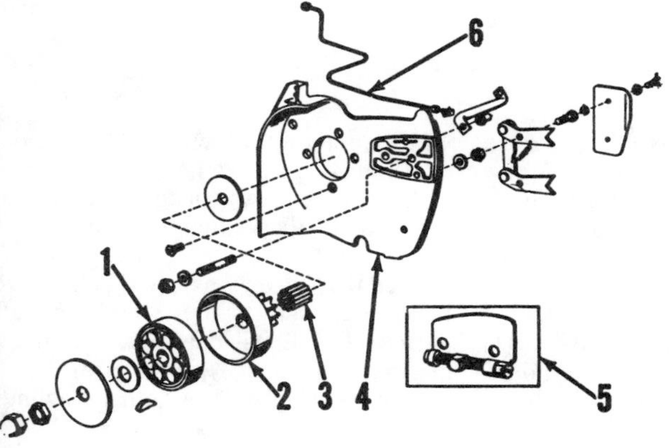

Fig. CL8–Exploded view of drive clutch and bar mounting plate on direct drive models. Item (3) is a bushing on Model D-35.

1. Clutch assy.
2. Clutch drum & chain sprocket
3. Clutch drum needle bearing
4. Bar mounting plate
5. Bar adjusting plate
6. Chain oiler tube

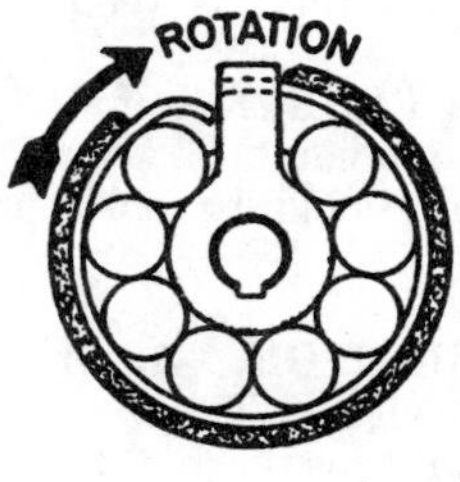

Fig. CL9–Showing assembly of clutch.

DANARM

Model	Bore mm (in.)	Stroke mm (in.)	Displacement cc (cu. in.)	Drive Type
1-36, 36AV, 1-36 MkII	36.5 (1.4375)	32.5 (1.28)	34.4 (2.1)	Direct

MAINTENANCE

SPARK PLUG. Recommended spark plug is Champion CJ6. Spark plug electrode gap should be 0.025 inch (0.63 mm).

CARBURETOR. All models are equipped with a Tillotson Model HU diaphragm type carburetor. Refer to Tillotson section of CARBURETOR SERVICE section for service procedures and exploded views.

Initial adjustment of idle mixture screw and high speed mixture screw is 1 turn open.

Final adjustment of high speed mixture screw should be made with engine warm and engine under cutting load. High speed mixture must not be adjusted too lean as engine may be damaged.

MAGNETO AND TIMING. All models are equipped with a conventional flywheel magneto ignition system. Refer to Fig. DA3 for exploded view of ignition assembly.

Breaker point gap for all models should be 0.015 inch (0.38 mm). Ignition timing is fixed but breaker point gap will affect ignition timing and should be set correctly.

LUBRICATION. Engine is lubricated by mixing oil with fuel. Recommended fuel:oil ratio is 16:1. A good quality SAE 30 oil designed for chain saw engines should be used.

Fill chain oil tank with SAE 30 moto oil. Chain oil may be diluted up to 50 per cent for winter usage by addin kerosene or diesel fuel to chain oil.

CARBON. Carbon should be remove from exhaust system and cylinde periodically. Loose carbon should not b allowed to enter cylinder and car should be taken not to damage cylinde or piston.

REPAIRS

CYLINDER, PISTON, PIN AN RINGS. Cylinder (16 – Fig. DA1) is als upper crankcase half. Crankshaft i loose in crankcase when cylinder is re moved. Care must be taken not to nic or scratch crankcase mating surface during disassembly.

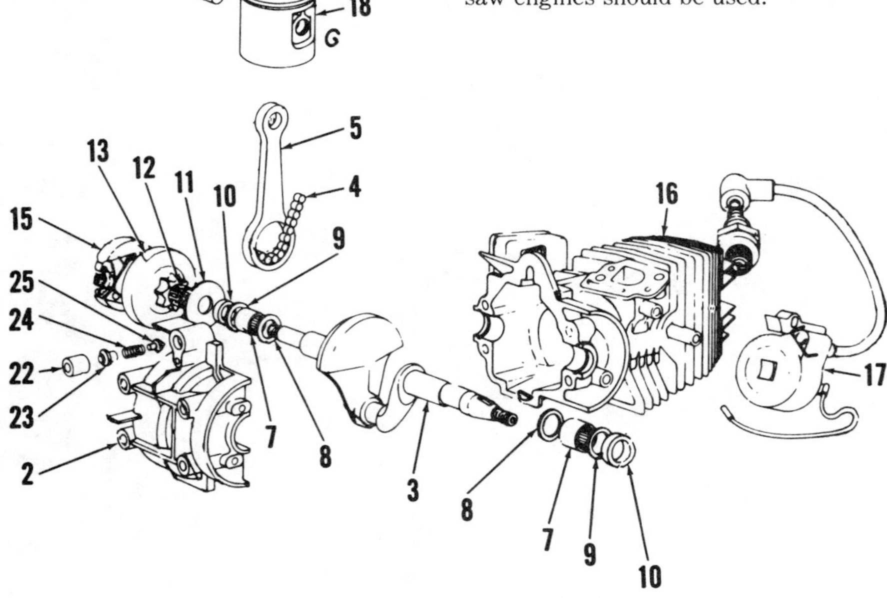

Fig. DA1 – Exploded view of engine.

2. Crankcase
3. Crankshaft
4. Roller bearings
5. Connecting rod
7. Needle bearing
8. Washer
9. Retaining ring
10. Seal
11. Thrust washer
12. Bearing
13. Clutch drum
15. Clutch assy.
16. Cylinder
17. Ignition coil
18. Piston
19. Piston ring
20. Piston pin
21. Pin retainer
22. Spacer
23. Spring seat
24. Spring
25. Pulse valve

Fig. DA2 – Exploded view of manual oil pun and front housing.

1. Piston
2. "O" ring
3. Spring
4. Spring seat
5. Ball
6. Pump body
7. Screen
8. Front housing
9. Fuel hose
10. Filter
11. Front cove
12. Spring
13. Spring
14. Oil outlet va
15. Nut

Cylinder head is integral with cylinder and cylinder must be removed to remove piston. Piston is equipped with a single piston ring and a floating type piston pin (20). It may be necessary to heat piston to remove or install piston pin. Piston, pin and ring are available in standard size only. Cylinder bore is chrome and should be inspected to determine if chrome is scored, peeling or excessively worn. Renew cylinder and piston if damaged or excessively worn.

Refer to CRANKSHAFT section for proper assembly of crankcase and cylinder.

CONNECTING ROD. To remove connecting rod, remove cylinder (16–Fig. DA1). Note that cylinder is also upper crankcase half and crankshaft assembly is loose when cylinder is removed. Connecting rod (5) is one-piece and supported on crankpin by 11 loose bearing rollers (4). Be careful not to lose loose rollers that may fall out during disassembly. Rollers can be removed by sliding rod off rollers. To install rod bearing, hold rollers in place with heavy grease or petroleum jelly and position rod over rollers. Be sure rollers do not fall out during assembly of crankcase.

NOTE: Early and late model piston and connecting rod are not individually interchangeable. Later model piston and rod are available only as a unit assembly and may be installed in early model saws. Early piston and rod are no longer available.

CRANKSHAFT AND SEALS. Crankshaft is supported by needle roller bearings (7–Fig. DA1) at both ends. Crankshaft assembly may be removed after removing stator plate, clutch and cylinder assemblies. Care should be taken when removing cylinder as crankshaft will be loose in crankcase and connecting rod may slide off bearing rollers allowing them to fall into crankcase.

Before reassembling crankcases, apply a light coat of nonhardening sealant to crankcase mating surface. Be sure mating surfaces are not damaged during assembly. Retaining rings (9) must fit in ring grooves of crankcase and cylinder.

CLUTCH. A two-shoe centrifugal type clutch is used on all models. Clutch hub has left hand thread. Clutch bearing (12–Fig. DA1) should be inspected for excessive wear or damage. Inspect clutch shoes and drum for signs of excessive heat.

OIL PUMP. All models are equipped with a manual oil pump and automatic oiling system. Refer to Fig. DA2 for exploded view of manual oil pump. Automatic oiling is accomplished by crankcase pulsations which pressurize oil tank and force oil to bar. A one-way valve (25–Fig. DA1) prevents oil from entering crankcase.

NOTE: Later models are equipped with a duckbill type valve in place of valve components (22, 23, 24 and 25).

RECOIL STARTER. Refer to Fig. DA3 for exploded view of pawl type starter used on all models. Care should be taken if necessary to remove rewind spring (12) to prevent spring from uncoiling uncontrolled.

Rewind spring (12) should be wound in clockwise direction in housing. Wind starter rope in clockwise direction around rope pulley (11) as viewed in starter housing (4).

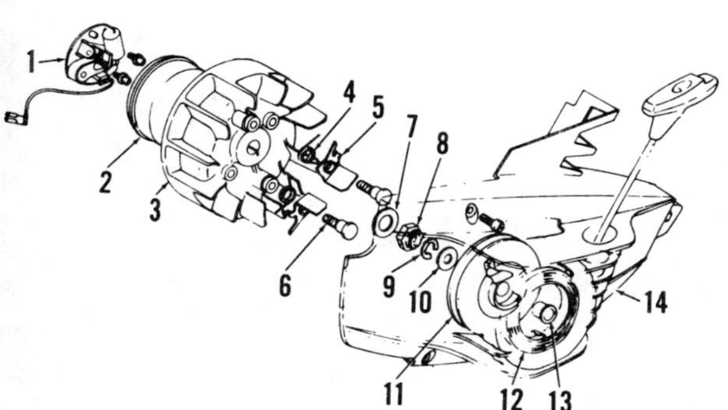

Fig. DA3—Exploded view of ignition and rewind starter.

1. Stator plate
2. Cover
3. Flywheel
4. Spring
5. Pawl
6. Pivot pin
7. Washer
8. Nut
9. Snap ring
10. Thrust washer
11. Rope pulley
12. Rewind spring
13. Bushing
14. Starter housing

JOHN DEERE

Model	Bore mm (in.)	Stroke mm (in.)	Displacement cc (cu. in.)	Drive Type
18	46 (1.81)	35 (1.38)	59 (3.6)	Direct
19	48.5 (1.91)	35 (1.38)	65.5 (4.0)	Direct
23	52.3 (2.06)	38.1 (1.5)	82 (5.0)	Direct
61, 81*, 91	38.1 (1.5)	30.5 (1.2)	34.4 (2.1)	Direct

* Includes electric start 81 model.

MAINTENANCE

SPARK PLUG. Recommended spark plug is Champion CJ6 or AC CS-42. Spark plug electrode gap should be 0.025 (0.63 mm).

CARBURETOR. All models are equipped with a Model HS or HU Tillotson diaphragm carburetor. Initial adjustment of high and low speed mixture screws is one turn open from a lightly seated position. Final adjustment should be made with engine running at operating temperature. Adjust low speed mixture so engine will accelerate cleanly without hesitation.

NOTE: High speed mixture on Models 61, 81, 81 Electric Start and 91 is preset at factory.

Adjust high speed mixture on Models 18, 19 and 23 to obtain optimum full throttle performance under cutting load. Do not adjust high speed mixture too lean as overheating and engine damage could result. Adjust idle speed to just below clutch engagement speed.

Refer to Tillotson section of CARBURETOR SERVICE section for carburetor operation and overhaul.

MAGNETO AND TIMING. A flywheel magneto is used on all models. Breaker-point gap should be 0.015 inch (0.38 mm). Ignition timing is fixed. Be sure breaker-point gap is correct as incorrect gap setting will affect ignition timing. Breaker-points are located under flywheel. Flywheel may be removed using a suitable flywheel puller.

Magneto air gap should be 0.010 inch (0.25 mm). Adjust air gap by loosening coil mounting screws and installing 0.010 inch (0.25 mm) shim stock between coil legs and flywheel. Move coil legs against shim stock and tighten coil mounting screws. Remove shim stock.

LUBRICATION. Engine is lubricated by mixing oil with the fuel. Recommended fuel:oil ratio is 16:1. Type of oil should be a good quality SAE 30 oil designed for chain saw or air-cooled two-stroke engines.

A manual chain oil pump is used on all models. Models 18, 19, 23, 81, 81 Electric Start and 91 are also equipped with an automatic chain oiler. Oil in oil tank is pressurized by engine crankcase pulsations to force chain oil to the chain. Oil output on Models 23, 81, 81 Electric Start and 91 is adjusted by turning adjusting screw located near trigger on rear grip. Oil output on Models 18 and 19 is adjusted by turning metering screw located at the base of front handle on the right hand side. John Deere Bar and Chain Lubricant is recommended by manufacturer for chain saw oil.

CARBON. Carbon deposits should be removed from muffler and exhaust ports at regular intervals. Do not allow loose carbon to enter cylinder. Be careful not to damage piston or cylinder.

REPAIRS

TIGHTENING TORQUES. Recommended tightening torques are listed in the following table.

Models 18, 19 and 23

Connecting rod screws	55 in.-lbs. (6.2 N·m)
Cylinder base nuts	70 in.-lbs. (8.0 N·m)
Starter cup nut	175 in.-lbs. (19.8 N·m)
Clutch nut	160 in.-lbs. (18.1 N·m)
Carburetor mounting screws	50 in.-lbs. (5.6 N·m)
Muffler screws	100 in.-lbs. (11.3 N·m)

Models 61, 81, 81 Electric Start and 91

Connecting rod screws	35 in.-lbs. (4.0 N·m)
Cylinder base screws	60 in.-lbs. (6.8 N·m)
Starter cup nut	150 in.-lbs. (17.0 N·m)
Clutch nut	150 in.-lbs. (17.0 N·m)
Carburetor mounting screws	45 in.-lbs. (5.1 N·m)
Muffler screws	60 in.-lbs. (6.8 N·m)

CYLINDER, PISTON, PIN AND RINGS. To remove cylinder on Models 18, 19 and 23, remove starter housing, clutch, flywheel and stator. Remove carburetor and disconnect oil lines. Disconnect impulse line on Models 18 and 19. Detach rear handle cover and remove compression release rod on Models 19 and 23. Remove rear handle assembly. Detach right crankcase cover (19 – Fig. JD5), unscrew cylinder base nuts and remove cylinder.

To remove cylinder on Models 61, 81, 81 Electric Start and 91, remove chain guard, starter housing and carburetor cover. Disconnect choke linkage and ignition switch wire. Disconnect throttle linkage and fuel line and remove carburetor. Remove rear handle assembly while pulling linkage through grommets. Unscrew coil mount screw in cylinder head. Unscrew cylinder base screws and remove cylinder.

Cylinder on all models is chrome plated and oversize pistons and rings are not available. Inspect cylinder for excessive wear, cracking, scoring or flaking of chrome bore. Install piston rings with bevel edge on ring toward top of piston. Install piston so "EXH" marking on piston crown is toward exhaust port of cylinder. Be sure piston ring end gap is correctly positioned around piston ring locating pin when installing cylinder.

CONNECTING ROD. Remove cylinder and piston to detach connecting rod from crankshaft. Unscrew connecting rod screws and remove connecting rod and cap being careful not to lose loose bearing rollers (14–Fig. JD4 or JD5). Twenty-eight bearing rollers are used on Models 18 and 19. All other models are equipped with twenty-four bearing rollers. Manufacturer recommends renewing rollers whenever connecting rod is removed. Connecting rod is fractured and has match marks on one side of rod and cap. Be sure rod and cap are correctly meshed and match marks are aligned during assembly.

CRANKSHAFT AND CRANKCASE. Crankshaft removal on Models 61, 81, 81 Electric Start and 91 requires removing clutch, starter housing and flywheel assemblies. Clutch has left hand threads. Remove cylinder, piston and connecting rod as previously outlined. Remove front handle, detach crankcase cover (1–Fig. JD4) and remove crankshaft.

Crankshaft is supported by roller bearings (3) in crankcase cover (1) and crankcase (8). Press seals (2) and roller bearings (3) out of crankcase cover and crankcase and inspect for damage and excessive wear. Check crankshaft for damaged bearing surfaces or discoloration.

Crankshaft roller bearings must be installed so numbered side of bearing will be toward connecting rod. Press on numbered side of bearing until bearing is 0.010 inch (0.25 mm) below surface of casting. Press seals into cover (1) or crankcase (8) until flush with surface. Crankshaft end play should be 0.008-0.022 inch (0.20-0.56 mm).

To remove crankshaft on Models 18, 19 and 23, remove cylinder, piston and connecting rod as previously outlined. Crankshaft can not be removed from crankcase. Crankcase can be separated from fuel tank on Models 18, 19 and 23.

Inspect bearings and seals for damage or excessive wear. Crankshaft bearings should be installed so numbered side of bearing is inward. Press on inward side of bearing so bearing is 0.010 inch (0.25 mm) below surface of casting. Seals should be flush with surface. Crankshaft end play should be 0.005-0.015 inch (0.13-0.38 mm).

AUTOMATIC CHAIN OILER. All models are equipped with an automatic chain oiling system. Crankcase pulsations are directed through check valve (C–Fig. JD6) to oil tank. Oil in tank is pressurized and metered to chain by adjusting screw. Check valve (C) is renewable and should be inspected if spark plug is fouling due to excessive oil or engine exhaust smoke indicates excessive oil burning. Defective check valve may allow pressurized oil in oil tank to flow through crankcase impulse passage into crankcase.

Models 18, 19 and 23 are equipped with an oil shut-off valve which is actuated by a link connected to the throttle trigger which shuts off oil output when engine is idling.

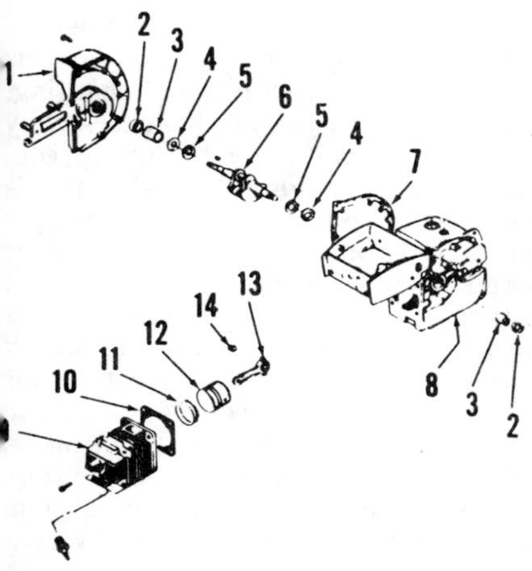

Fig. JD4—Exploded view of engine used on Models 61, 81, 81 Electric Start and 91. Some models use a bushing in place of bearing (5).

1. Crankcase cover
2. Seal
3. Bearing
4. Thrust washer
5. Thrust bearing
6. Crankshaft
7. Gasket
8. Crankcase
9. Cylinder
10. Gasket
11. Piston rings
12. Piston
13. Connecting rod & cap
14. Bearing

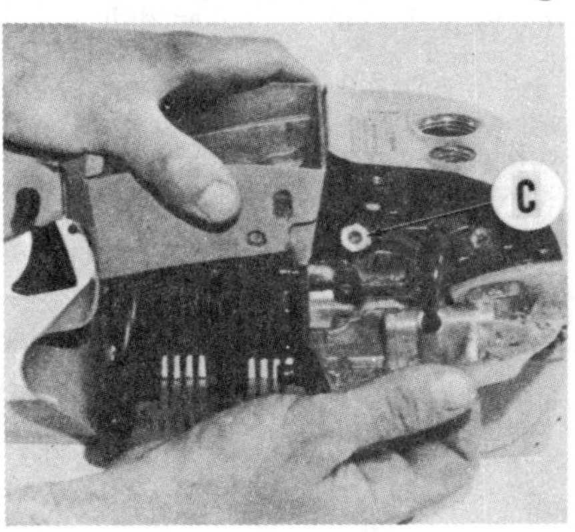

Fig. JD6—View showing location of check valve (C) in oil tank on Models 18 and 19. Model 23 is similar except check valve is located on right side of oil tank. On all other models equipped with automatic oil pump, check valve is located in impulse line fitting at oil tank.

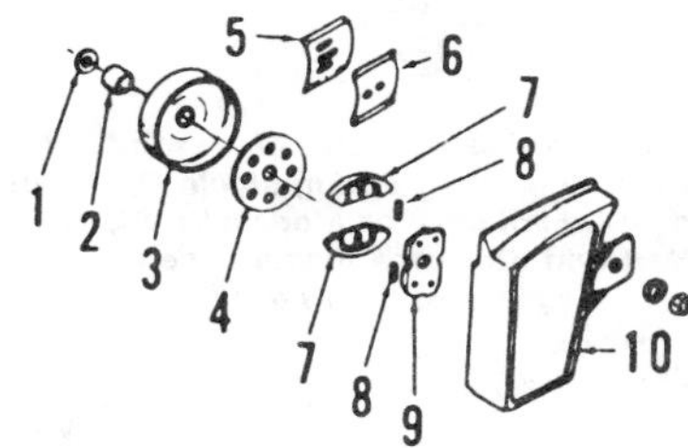

Fig. JD7—Exploded view of clutch assembly used on Models 61, 81, 81 Electric Start and 91.

1. Thrust washer
2. Bearing
3. Clutch drum
4. Cover
5. Inner bar guide
6. Outer bar guide
7. Clutch shoe
8. Spring
9. Clutch hub
10. Cover

Fig. JD5—Exploded view of engine used on Models 18, 19 and 23. Refer to Fig. JD4 for component identification except, bearing (15), piston pin (16), retainer (17), "O" ring (18) and right crankcase cover (19).

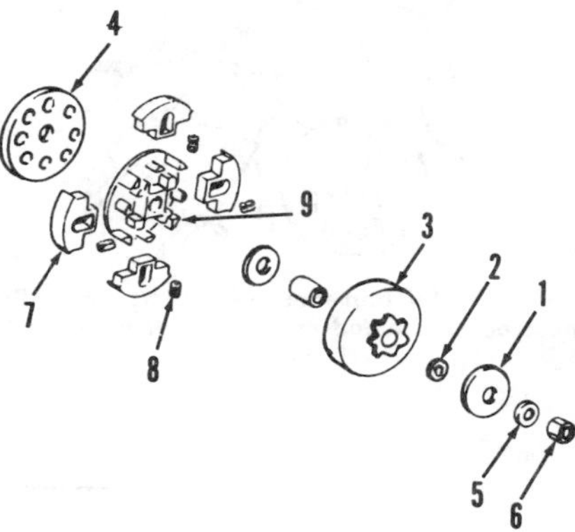

Fig. JD8—Exploded view of clutch assembly used on Models 18, 19 and 23.

1. Washer
2. Bearing
3. Clutch drum
4. Cover
5. Washer
6. Nut
7. Clutch shoe
8. Spring
9. Clutch hub

MANUAL CHAIN OIL PUMP. All models are equipped with a manual plunger type oil pump. Pump assembly on 61, 81, 81 Electric Start and 91 models is mounted on inside of oil tank cover which must be removed for access to pump assembly. Pump assembly is mounted in rear handle grip on Models 18, 19 and 23. Inspect oil pump components wear or damage which may cause leakage or decreased oil output.

CLUTCH. Refer to Fig. JD7 for exploded view of centrifugal clutch used on Models 61, 81, 81 Electric Start and 91. Refer to Fig. JD8 for exploded view of centrifugal clutch used on Models 18, 19 and 23. Clutch hub (9) is screwed on crankshaft with left-hand threads. Inspect clutch and renew any components found to be excessively worn or damaged.

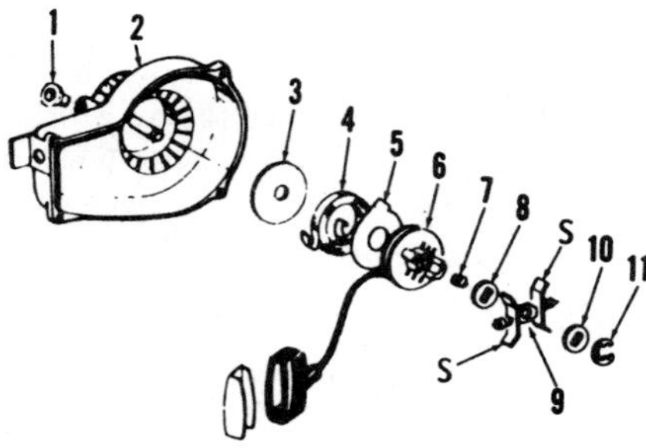

Fig JD9—Exploded view of rewind starter typical of all models. Spring shield (3) and dust shield (5) are not used on Models 61, 81, 81 Electric Start and 91. Some models use a screw in place of "E" ring (11).

1. Rope bushing
2. Starter housing
3. Spring shield
4. Rewind spring
5. Dust shield
6. Rope pulley
7. Brake spring
8. Fiber washer
9. Friction shoe assy.
10. Fiber washer
11. "E" ring

REED VALVE. A reed valve induction system is used on 18, 19 and 23 models with the reed valve assembly located between rear handle and air box assembly and crankcase. Inspect reed petal for cracks or chips and reed valve seat for damage which may prevent satisfactory reed valve operation.

REWIND STARTER. Refer to Fig. JD9 for exploded view of rewind starter. To disassemble starter, remove starter housing from saw. Detach rope handle and allow rope to rewind into starter. Unscrew retaining screw or pry off "E" clip (11), if so equipped, and remove friction shoe assembly. Remove rope pulley (6) being careful not to disturb rewind spring. Be careful not to allow spring to uncoil uncontrolled.

To reassemble starter, reverse disassembly procedure. Install rewind spring so coils are in clockwise direction starting with outer coil. Grease pulley post in housing (2) lightly. Wrap rope around pulley (6) in clockwise direction as viewed with pulley in housing. Be sure inner hook of rewind spring (4) engages pulley. Place tension on rewind spring by turning pulley three turns clockwise before passing rope through hole in housing. Components in friction shoe assembly (9) are not available individually. Friction shoe components must be assembled as shown in Fig. JD10. One edge of each friction shoe must be sharp to properly engage starter cup. Note in Fig. JD9 the location of sharp edges (S) for correct starter assembly. Renew fiber washers (8 and 10) if glazed or oil soaked.

ELECTRIC STARTER. Model 81 Electric Start is equipped with an electric motor to start engine. The electric motor is driven by an external 12 volt battery which may be recharged. Starter mechanism is gear driven by electric motor as shown in Fig. JD11.

Wires for electric starter should be connected as follows: One white lead of battery connector (6) should be connected to rear pole of switch (4) while other white lead should be connected to positive "+" terminal of starter motor. A black wire should be connected between negative "−" terminal of starter motor and middle pole of switch (4). A green wire should be connected to middle poles of switch (4) and grounded to starter housing (5). A blue wire should be connected to front pole of switch (4) and the ignition coil primary wire.

Battery should be discarded if minimum voltage level of 12.8 volts is not attained after 48 hours of charging. The battery charger may be checked by connecting a voltmeter to battery connector if charger-exposed pin is negative. With battery charger plugged into a 110 volt circuit, battery charger output should be in excess of 7.5 volts. If battery and charger operate satisfactorily, remove starter cover and note if starter motor will turn freely. If starter motor is not binding, connect battery to starter housing plug and using a voltmeter and appropriate voltage checks, determine if starter switch, starter motor or wiring is defective.

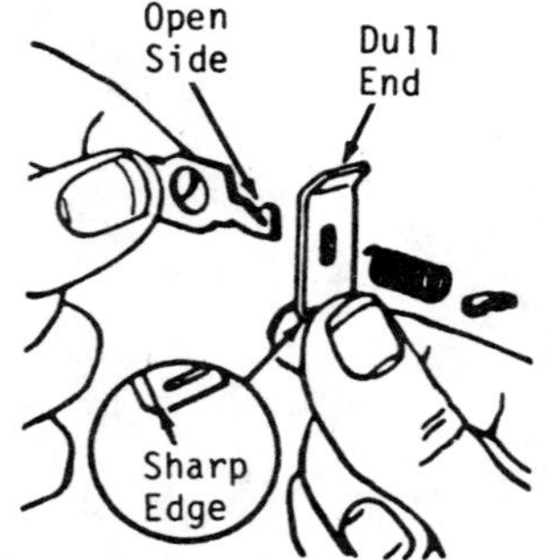

Fig. JD10—Friction shoe assembly (9—Fig. JD9) must be assembled as shown above. Refer to text.

Fig. JD11—Exploded view of electric starter used on Model 81 Electric Start. Note position of sharp edges (S) of friction shoes.

1. Cover
2. Starter motor
3. Pinion gear
4. Starter switch
5. Starter housing
6. Battery connector
7. Idler gear
8. Starter gear
9. Drive washer
10. Spring
11. Fiber washer
12. Friction shoe assy.
13. Fiber washer
14. Washer
15. SEMS screw

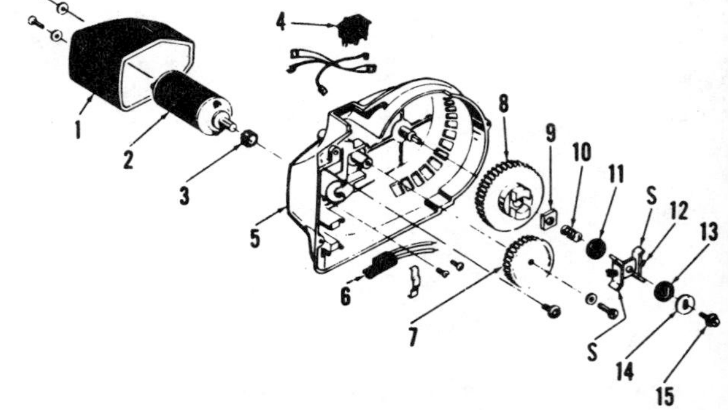

JOHN DEERE

Model	Bore mm (in.)	Stroke mm (in.)	Displacement cc (cu. in.)	Drive Type
28, 30	37 (1.457)	28 (1.102)	30.1 (1.83)	Direct
40V	40 (1.575)	28 (1.102)	35.2 (2.15)	Direct
50V	42 (1.65)	32 (1.26)	44.3 (2.7)	Direct
55V	42 (1.65)	36 (1.42)	49.9 (3.04)	Direct
60V	46 (1.81)	36 (1.42)	59.8 (3.65)	Direct
70V	50 (1.97)	36 (1.42)	70.7 (4.31)	Direct
80EV	52 (2.05)	37 (1.46)	78.6 (4.8)	Direct

MAINTENANCE

SPARK PLUG. Recommended spark plug is Champion CJ8 or NGK BM-6A for Models 28, 30, 40V, 50V and 55V. Recommended spark plug for all other models is Champion CJ7Y or NGK BPM-7A. On all models, spark plug electrode gap should be 0.025 inch (0.63 mm).

CARBURETOR. Models 28, 30 and 40V are equipped with a Walbro WA diaphragm type carburetor. A Tillotson HU carburetor is used on 50V models prior to serial number 017521 while a Walbro WA carburetor is used after serial number 017520. A Walbro HDB carburetor is used on 55V models while Models 60V and 70V are equipped with a Tillotson HS carburetor and Model 80EV is equipped with a Walbro SDC carburetor. Refer to Tillotson or Walbro section of CARBURETOR SERVICE section for carburetor overhaul and exploded views.

Initial setting of idle and high-speed mixture screws is one turn open from a lightly seated position. Make final carburetor adjustments with engine running at operating temperature. Adjust idle mixture screw so engine will accelerate without stumbling. Adjust high-speed mixture screw to obtain optimum performance with saw under cutting load. Adjust idle speed screw so engine idles just under clutch engagement speed.

IGNITION. Model 80EV is equipped with a breakerless capacitor discharge ignition system. Repair of ignition system malfunction except for faulty wiring connections is accomplished by renewal of ignition system components. Ignition timing is not adjustable.

All other models are equipped with a conventional flywheel magneto ignition system having breaker points located under the flywheel. Breaker-point gap should be 0.014 inch (0.35 mm). Magneto air gap should be 0.016 inch (0.40 mm) on all models.

Correct ignition timing is 30 degrees BTDC. Reference marks are located on flywheel and crankcase to set ignition timing. With flywheel turning counterclockwise, first mark "F" on flywheel periphery indicates ignition point when aligned with crankcase mark while second mark "T" indicates top dead center. Ignition timing on Models 28, 30, 40V, 50V and 55V is adjusted by altering breaker-point gap while timing on Models 60V and 70V is adjusted by rotating stator plate. Tighten flywheel nut on Models 28, 30, 40V, 50V and 55V to 14.5-17 ft.-lbs. (19.7-23.1 N·m) and on Models 60V and 70V to 24-26 ft.-lbs. (32.6-35.4 N·m).

LUBRICATION. The engine is lubricated by mixing oil with the fuel. Fuel:oil ratio is 40:1 when using John Deere

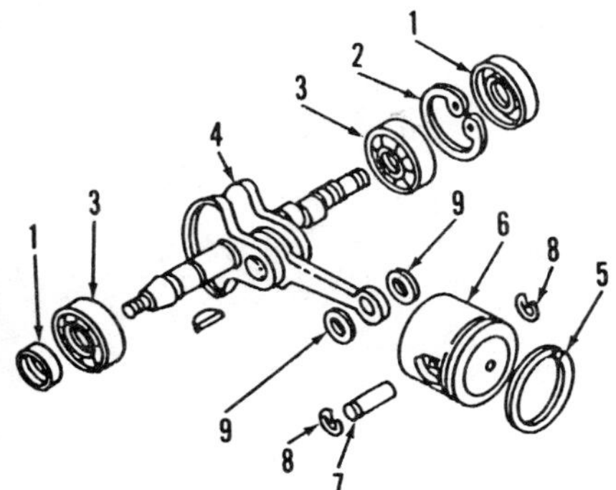

Fig. JD20 — Exploded view of engine assembly used on Model 28.

1. Seal
2. Snap ring
3. Ball bearing
4. Crankshaft & rod assy.
5. Piston ring
6. Piston
7. Piston pin
8. Pin retainer
9. Spacers

Fig. JD21 — Exploded view of engine assembly typical of all models except Model 28. Flywheel side snap ring (11) is absent on 55V models.

1. Seal
2. Clutch side snap ring
3. Ball bearing
4. Crankshaft & rod assy.
5. Piston rings
6. Piston
7. Piston pin
8. Pin retainer
10. Needle bearing
11. Flywheel side snap ring

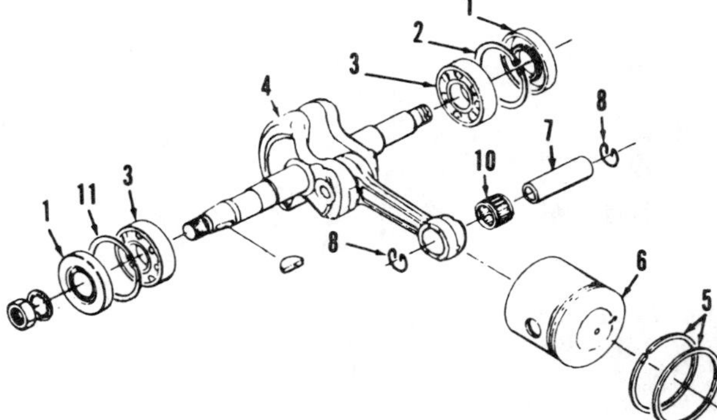

2-Cycle Engine Oil. If John Deere 2-Cycle Engine oil is not available, a good quality oil designed for two-stroke air-cooled engines may be used when mixed at a 32:1 ratio. Use a separate container when mixing the oil and gas.

Clean SAE 10 or SAE 30 automotive oil may be used to lubricate chain and bar. Cut oil with up to 33 percent kerosene during cold weather to aid lubrication.

REPAIRS

CYLINDER, PISTON, PIN AND RINGS. Cylinder bore is chrome plated on all models and oversize pistons and rings are not available. Inspect cylinder bore for scoring, flaking or other damage to chrome surface.

Install piston with arrow on piston crown toward exhaust port. Install piston pin with closed end toward exhaust port. Piston rings are pinned in ring grooves to prevent rotation. Be sure piston ring end gaps are properly positioned around piston ring locating pins when installing cylinder. On 55V models, tighten cylinder base nuts to 75-85 in.-lbs. (8.5-9.6 N•m). On all other models, tighten cylinder base nuts to 65-75 in.-lbs. (7.3-8.5 N•m).

CRANKSHAFT, CONNECTING ROD AND CRANKCASE. All models are equipped with a crankshaft and connecting rod unit assembly which is supported in the crankcase by ball bearings at both ends. Crankshaft and connecting rod are not available separately.

Check crankshaft runout by supporting crankshaft at points (A – Fig. JD22) and measure at points (B). Maximum allowable runout is 0.002 inch (0.05 mm). Side clearance between rod big end and crankshaft should be 0.0098-0.0118 inch (0.25-0.30 mm).

Crankshaft main bearings are located in crankcase by snap rings (2 and 11 – Fig. JD21) on all models except 28 and 55V models. The clutch side main bearing of 28 and 55V models is located by a snap ring but flywheel side main bearing is located by a shoulder in the crankcase. Install oil seals with open side toward inside of crankcase.

A needle bearing (10 – Fig. JD21) is used in connecting rod small end of all models except Model 28 which supports piston pin directly in rod. Note spacers (9 – Fig. JD20) used on Model 28.

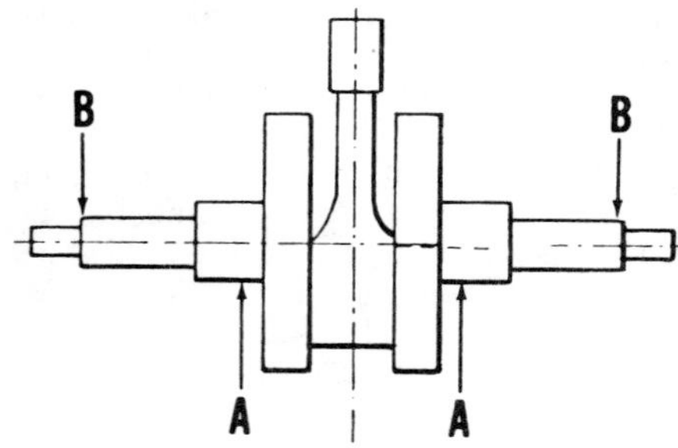

Fig. JD22 – Measure crankshaft by supporting crankshaft at points (A). Maximum runout measured at points (B) should not exceed 0.002 inch (0.05 mm).

CLUTCH. Note that clutch nut and clutch hub have left-hand threads on all models.

Refer to Fig. JD23 for view of clutch used on Models 28, 30 and 40V. Clutch hub and shoes (1) are available only as a unit assembly. Be sure washer (2) is installed between clutch hub and drum.

Models 50V, 55V and 60V are equipped with the three-shoe clutch shown in Fig. JD25 while Models 70V and 80EV are equipped with the six-shoe clutch shown in Fig. JD24. The clutch drum on all models rides on a renewable needle roller bearing. Be sure washer (W – Fig. JD25) on Model 60V is installed between clutch hub and drum.

OIL PUMP. All models are equipped with an automatic oil pump. Refer to Fig. JD26. The pump is operated by a cam on the crankshaft which actuates plunger (6).

When installing oil pump, proceed as follows: If removed, install dowel (8) on Models 30 and 50V. On all models, screw oil pump assembly (3) into crankcase until lightly seated. Remove bar and chain so oil port is exposed then start and run saw at half throttle. Turn oil pump counterclockwise so maximum oil flow is obtained then continue counterclockwise rotation until oil flow is small but not stopped. Install spring washer (7) over dowel (8) on Models 30 and 50V.

Install dial (2) when applicable, so dial can only be turned clockwise and install screw (1).

A manual oil pump is used on Models 50V, 60V, 70V and 80EV. The manual oil pump consists of pump mechanism and two check valves. Check valves are located just above clutch drum and must function freely for proper pump operation.

REWIND STARTER. To disassemble rewind starter, remove starter housing, remove rope handle and allow rope

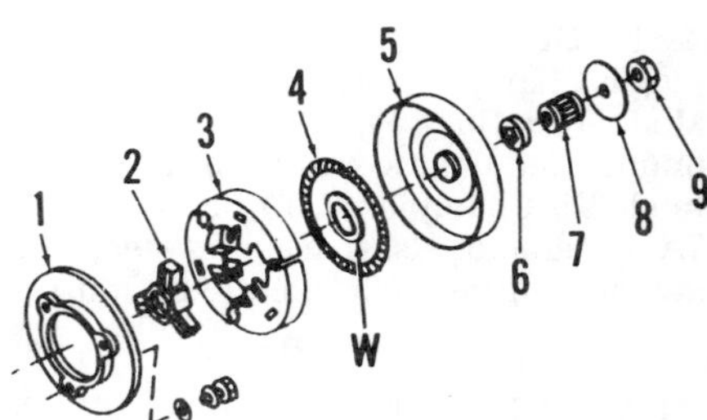

Fig. JD25 – Exploded view of clutch used on Models 50V, 55V and 60V. Washer (W) is used only on Model 60V.

1. Dust seal
2. Clutch hub
3. Clutch shoes
4. Garter spring
5. Clutch drum
6. Sprocket
7. Needle bearing
8. Washer
9. Nut

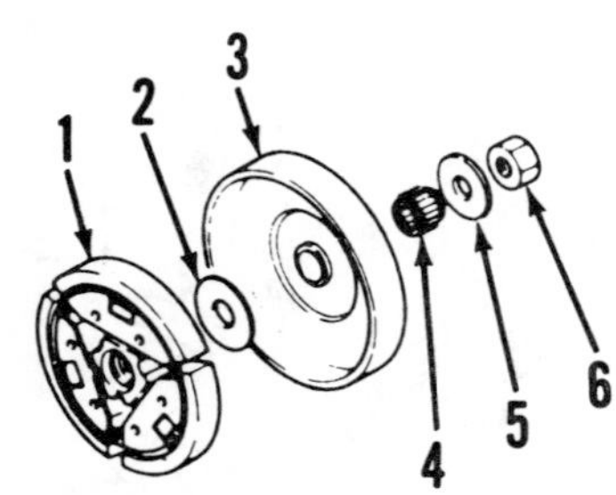

Fig. JD23 – Exploded view of clutch used on Models 28, 30 and 40V.

1. Hub & shoe assy.
2. Washer
3. Clutch drum
4. Needle bearing
5. Washer
6. Nut

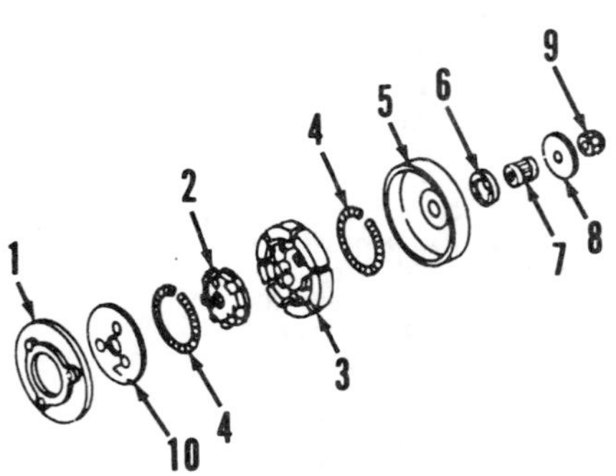

Fig. JD24 – Exploded view of clutch used on Models 70V and 80EV.

1. Dust seal
2. Clutch hub
3. Clutch shoes
4. Garter spring
5. Clutch drum
6. Sprocket
7. Needle bearing
8. Washer
9. Nut
10. Washer

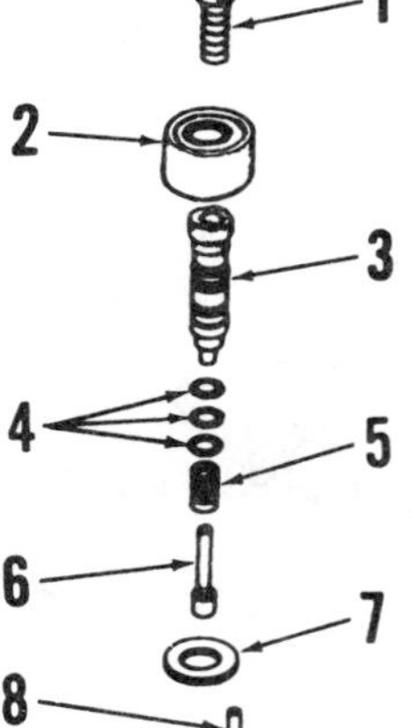

Fig. JD26 – Exploded view of automatic oil pump typical of all models. Spring washer (7) and dowel (8) are used only on Models 30 and 50V.

1. Set screw
2. Adjusting dial
3. Pump body
4. "O" rings
5. Spring
6. Plunger
7. Spring washer
8. Dowel

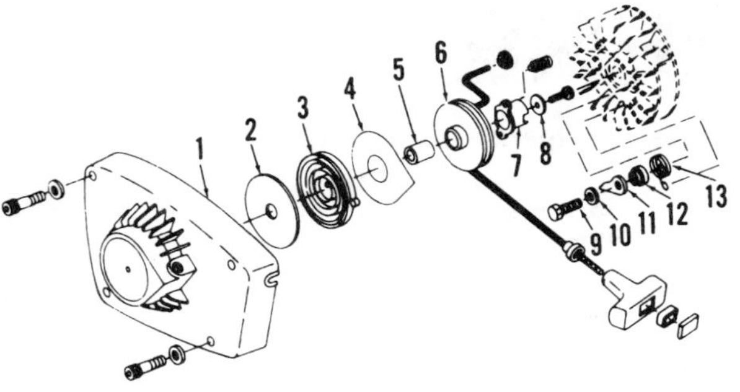

Fig. JD27 — Exploded view of rewind starter used on Models 30 and 50V. Models 40, 55V, 60V, 70V and 80EV are similar.

1. Starter housing
2. Plate
3. Rewind spring
4. Plate
5. Bushing
6. Rope pulley
7. Starter cup
8. Washer
9. Screw
10. Washer
11. Pawl
12. Spacer
13. Spring

to rewind into housing. Unscrew rope pulley screw and carefully remove rope pulley (6 – Fig. JD27 or Fig. JD28), being careful not to dislodge rewind spring (3). If necessary to remove rewind spring, care should be used not to allow spring to uncoil uncontrolled.

Install rewind spring (3) into starter housing (1) with coils wrapped in a clockwise direction from outer end of spring. Wind rope around pulley in a clockwise direction as viewed from flywheel side of pulley. Turn pulley three or four turns clockwise before passing rope through outlet. Check starter operation. It should be possible to pull rope to its full extension and still turn rope pulley approximately ½ turn clockwise. If rewind spring binds before rope is fully extended, reduce pre-tension on rope by pulling rope up into notch in rope pulley and allowing pulley to rotate one turn counterclockwise. Recheck starter operation.

COMPRESSION RELEASE VALVE. Models 60V, 70V and 80EV are equipped with a compression release valve which is located adjacent to exhaust port in cylinder. When servicing valve, clean all components of carbon being sure hole in valve body (4 – Fig. JD29) is clean. After assembling valve, stake nut (1) to valve (6).

CHAIN BRAKE. Some models are equipped with an optional chain brake system designed to stop chain movement should kickback occur. The chain brake system available for Models 30, 40, 50V, 60V and 70V uses a spring-loaded set of brake shoes located inside clutch/brake drum to stop the chain when the operator's hand strikes the chain brake lever. Pull back chain brake lever to reset mechanism. No adjustment of brake mechanism is required.

The optional chain brake system for Model 55V is activated when the operator's hand strikes chain brake lever (1 – Fig. JD30) thereby forcing actuating cam (4) to release spring (3). Spring (3) then draws brake band tight around clutch drum to stop chain. Chain brake operation is similar on 80EV models. On 55V and 80EV models, brake band is adjusted by rotating adjuster (9 – Fig. JD30 or 17 – Fig. JD31) as required. Brake band should not contact clutch drum when chain brake is disengaged.

On all models, disassembly for repair or renewal of individual components is evident after inspection of unit and on Models 55V and 80EV, referral to the appropriate exploded view.

Fig. JD28 — Exploded view of rewind starter used on Model 28.

1. Starter housing
2. Rewind spring case
3. Rewind spring
6. Rope pulley
8. Washer
9. Spacer
11. Spring
12. Pawl
13. Flywheel
15. Screw

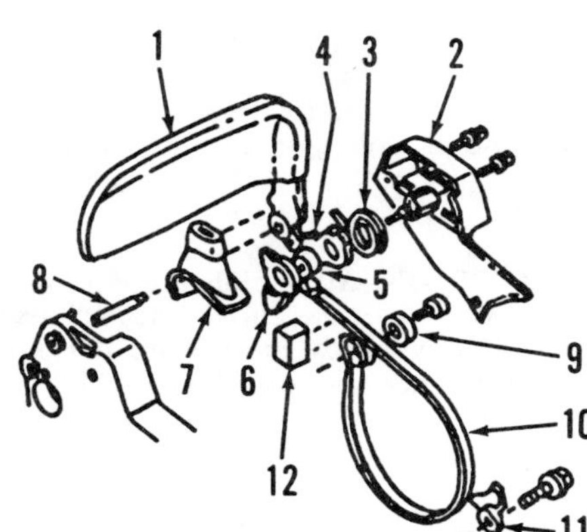

Fig. JD30 — Exploded view of chain brake system used on some 55V models.

1. Chain brake lever
2. Shield
3. Spring
4. Actuating cam
5. Spacer
6. Brake band lever
7. Dust cover
8. Pivot pin
9. Brake band adjuster
10. Brake band
11. Brake band retainer
12. Dust seal

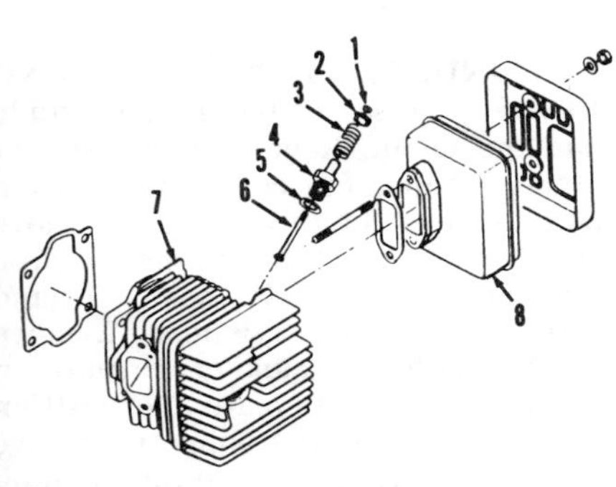

JD29 — Exploded view of compression release valve used on Models 60V, 70V and 80EV.

1. Nut
2. Washer
3. Spring
4. Valve body
5. Seal
6. Valve
7. Cylinder
8. Muffler

Fig. JD31 — Exploded view of chain brake system used on some 80EV models.

1. Hand guard
2. Chain brake lever
3. Dust cover
4. Nut
5. Spring
6. Washer
7. Spacer
8. Actuating lever
9. Washer
10. Shield
11. Dust seal
12. Brake band lever
13. Washer
14. Spring
15. Sleeve
16. Brake band
17. Brake band adjuster

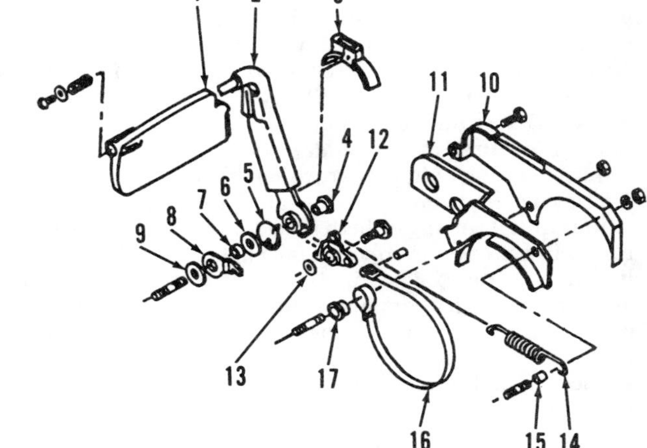

JOHN DEERE

Model	Bore mm (in.)	Stroke mm (in.)	Displacement cc (cu. in.)	Drive Type
35EV	39 (1.535)	28 (1.102)	33.4 (2.04)	Direct
45EV	40 (1.575)	32 (1.26)	40.2 (2.45)	Direct
46EV	42 (1.65)	32 (1.26)	44.3 (2.7)	Direct
51SV	42 (1.65)	36 (1.42)	49.9 (3.04)	Direct
55EV	42 (1.65)	36 (1.42)	49.9 (3.04)	Direct
55SV	44 (1.732)	36 (1.42)	54.7 (3.34)	Direct
65EV, 65SV	47 (1.85)	37 (1.46)	64.2 (3.86)	Direct

MAINTENANCE

SPARK PLUG. Recommended spark plug for Model 35EV is John Deere TY6089. Recommended spark plug for Model 45EV is NGK BPM6A or BPMR6A. Recommended spark plug for Model 46EV is John Deere AM54611. Recommended spark plug for Models 51SV, 55SV and 65SV is John Deere TY6072. Recommended spark plug for Model 55EV is Champion CJ8 or NGK BM6A. Recommended spark plug for Model 65EV is Champion CJ7Y or NGK BPM7A.

On all models, spark plug gap should be 0.635 mm (0.025 in.).

CARBURETOR. A Zama CIS-K3A diaphragm type carburetor is used on Model 35EV. Model 45EV is equipped with a Walbro WA-93 diaphragm type carburetor and Model 46EV is equipped with a Walbro WA-133 diaphragm type carburetor. A Walbro HDA carburetor is used on Models 51SV and 55SV. A Walbro HDB carburetor is used on Models 55EV, 65EV and 65SV. Refer to Walbro or Zama section of CARBURETOR SERVICE section for carburetor overhaul procedures and exploded views.

Initial setting of idle mixture screw is 1¼ turns open from a lightly seated position. Initial setting of high speed mixture screw is one turn open from a lightly seated position. Make final carburetor adjustments with engine running at operating temperature. Adjust idle mixture screw so engine will accelerate without stumbling. Adjust high speed mixture screw until a four-cycling sound is heard at full throttle (no-load). Do not operate saw with high speed mixture set too lean as engine damage may occur due to lack of lubrication and overheating. Adjust idle speed screw so engine idles just under clutch engagement speed.

IGNITION. All models are equipped with a breakerless capacitor discharge ignition system. There is no periodic maintenance required for the ignition system. Ignition timing is not adjustable.

LUBRICATION. The engine is lubricated by mixing oil with the fuel. Recommended fuel:oil ratio is 40:1 when using John Deere 2-Cycle Engine Oil. If John Deere 2-Cycle Engine Oil is not available, a good quality oil designed for two-stroke air-cooled engines may be used when mixed at a 32:1 ratio. Always mix fuel and oil in a separate container. Never mix fuel and oil directly in fuel tank. Regular leaded or unleaded gasoline is recommended. The use of premium gasoline, gasohol or other alcohol blended fuels is not recommended.

John Deere Bar and Chain Lubricant is recommended to lubricate chain and bar. This oil is prediluted to operate properly in a wide range of temperatures.

Clean SAE 10 or SAE 30 automotive oil may also be used to lubricate chain and bar. SAE 30 oil is recommended for use when temperature is above 4°C (40°F), SAE 10 oil is recommended when temperature is between -18°C (0°F) and 4°C (40°F). At temperatures below -18°C (0°F), cut oil with up to 33 percent kerosene to aid lubrication.

REPAIRS

COMPRESSION TEST. Engine should be cold when checking compression pressure. Remove spark plug and install compression test gage. Pull recoil rope and note pressure gage reading. Compression pressure should be minimum of 585 kPa (85 psi) for Models 35EV and 45EV, 930 kPa (135 psi) for Model 46EV, 690 kPa (100 psi) for Model 55EV, 620 kPa (90 psi) for Model 65EV and 1000 kPa (145 psi) for Models 51SV, 55SV and 65SV.

CRANKCASE PRESSURE. An improperly sealed crankcase can cause the engine to be hard to start, run rough, have low power and overheat. Refer to ENGINE SERVICE section of this manual for crankcase pressure test procedure. If crankcase leakage is indicated, pressurize crankcase and use a soap and water solution to check gaskets, seals, pulse line and castings for leakage.

CYLINDER, PISTON, PIN AND RINGS. To disassemble, remove guide bar and chain. Remove recoil starter housing, inner fan cover and ignition module. Hold the flywheel and remove clutch case and clutch assembly. Note that clutch assembly has left-hand threads. Remove flywheel. Remove front handle, air cleaner, carburetor, carburetor adapter plate and muffler. Remove anti-vibration support. Remove rear handle, fuel tank, oil tank and oil pump. Remove cylinder cover. Remove cylinder mounting screws and pull cylinder off piston. Support piston with a towel to prevent damage to piston skirt.

Remove rings from piston ring grooves. Remove piston pin retainers and push piston pin out of piston and connecting rod. If piston pin is a tight fit in piston, use a suitable piston pin tool such as JDZ-23 to remove pin as shown in Fig. JD51.

Cylinder bore is chrome plated on all models and oversize piston and rings are not available. Inspect cylinder for scoring, flaking, excessive wear or other damage to chrome surface. Check piston ring groove wear by inserting new ring in ring groove and measure side clearance with a feeler gage as shown in Fig. JD52. Renew piston if side clearance is excessive. Measure piston skirt diameter at bottom of skirt 90 degrees from pin bore. Measure piston pin bore and piston pin outside diameter.

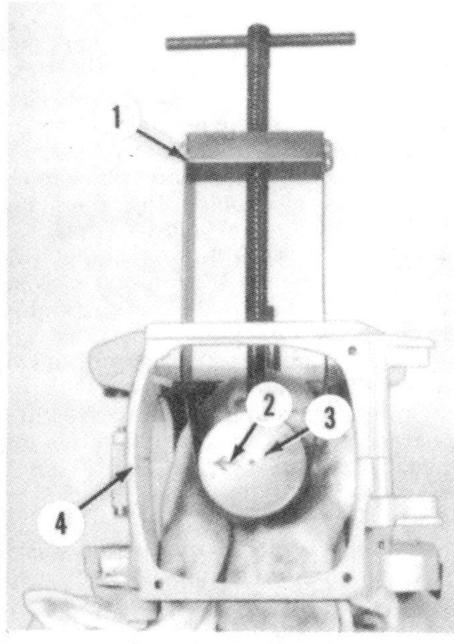

Fig. JD51—When installing piston (3), make certain that arrow (2) on piston crown points toward exhaust side of crankcase (4).

1. Piston pin tool
2. Arrow
3. Piston
4. Crankcase

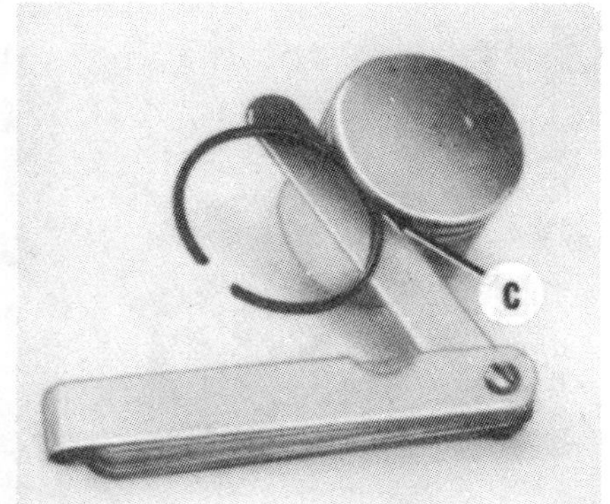

Fig. JD52—To check piston ring groove wear, insert new ring in groove and use a feeler gage to measure side clearance (C). Refer to text.

Refer to following chart for wear limits.

Model 35EV

Piston skirt diameter . . . . . .38.88 mm (1.531 in.)
Ring side clearance . . . . .0.01 mm (0.004 in.)
Piston pin bore . . . . .9.027 mm (0.3554 in.)
Piston pin diameter . . . . .8.98 mm (0.3535 in.)

Model 45EV

Piston skirt diameter . . . . . .30.89 mm (1.5705 in.)
Ring side clearance . . . . .0.01 mm (0.004 in.)
Piston pin bore . . . . .10.03 mm (0.395 in.)
Piston pin diameter . . . . .9.98 mm (0.393 in.)

Models 46EV, 51SV, 55EV

Piston skirt diameter . . . . . .41.89 mm (1.649 in.)
Ring side clearance . . . . .0.01 mm (0.004 in.)
Piston pin bore . . . . .10.03 mm (0.395 in.)
Piston pin diameter . . . . .9.98 mm (0.393 in.)

Model 55SV

Piston skirt diameter . . . . . .43.90 mm (1.728 in.)
Ring side clearance . . . . .0.01 mm (0.004 in.)
Piston pin bore . . . . .10.03 mm (0.395 in.)
Piston pin diameter . . . . .9.98 mm (0.393 in.)

Models 65EV, 65SV

Piston skirt diameter . . . . . .46.89mm (1.846 in.)
Ring side clearance . . . . .0.01 mm (0.004 in.)
Piston pin bore . . . . .12.03 mm (0.4736 in.)
Piston pin diameter . . . . . . .11.98 mm (0.4717 in.)

To reassemble, install piston with arrow on piston crown toward exhaust port side of crankcase as shown in Fig. JD51. Heating piston in hot water or oil will ease installation of piston pin. If piston pin cannot be installed by hand, use a piston pin tool (1) to push pin into piston. Note that piston rings must not be installed on piston when using piston pin tool. Install piston pin with closed end toward exhaust port. Install new retainer rings (11—Fig. JD53) after pin is installed. Piston rings are pinned in ring grooves to prevent rotation. Be sure piston ring end gaps are properly positioned around locating pins before installing cylinder. Lubricate piston and cylinder with oil, then slide cylinder

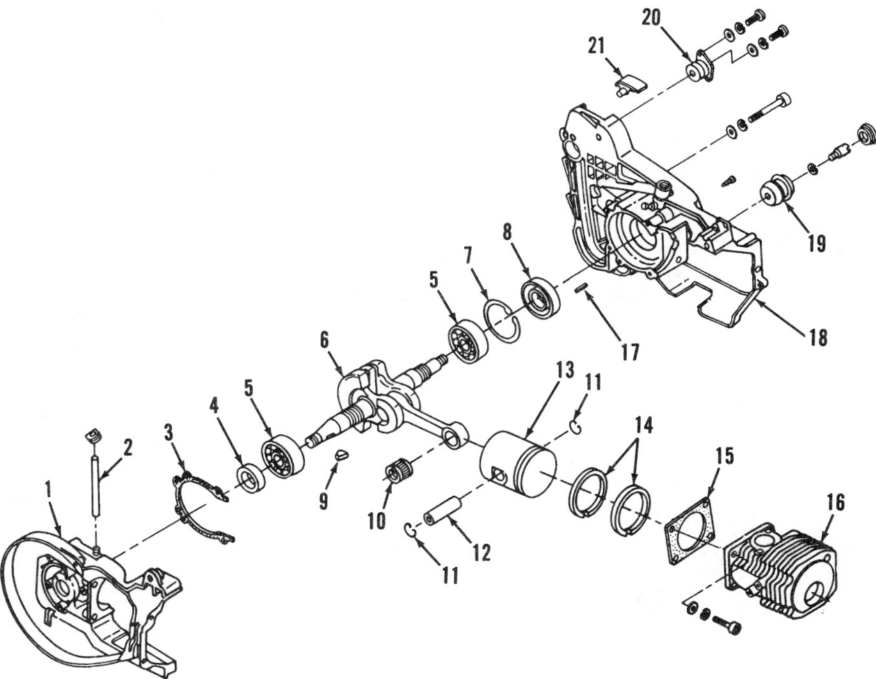

Fig. JD53—Exploded view of typical chain saw engine. Some models are equipped with thrust washers on either side of connecting rod needle bearing (10).

1. Crankcase half
2. Pipe
3. Gasket
4. Seal
5. Bearings
6. Crankshaft & connecting rod assy.
7. Snap ring
8. Seal
9. Key
10. Needle bearing
11. Retaining rings
12. Piston pin
13. Piston
14. Piston rings
15. Gasket
16. Cylinder
17. Dowel pin
18. Crankcase half
19. Vibration damper
20. Vibration damper
21. Cover

over piston. Do not rotate cylinder during installation as ring end gap may misalign and damage cylinder. Tighten cylinder mounting screws alternately to 14.7-16.9 N·m (130-150 in.-lbs.) on Model 35EV. On all other models, tighten cylinder screws to 8-9 N·m (70-80 in.-lbs.).

CRANKSHAFT, CONNECTING ROD AND CRANKCASE. All models are equipped with a crankshaft and connecting rod assembly which is supported in the crankcase by ball bearings at both ends. Crankshaft and connecting rod are not available separately.

To remove crankshaft assembly, first remove cylinder and piston as previously outlined. Remove crankcase screws. Hold one side of crankcase and tap other end of crankshaft with a plastic mallet to separate crankcase halves. Hold other side of crankcase and tap crankshaft out of crankcase. If main bearings (5—Fig. JD53) remain on crankshaft, use suitable puller to remove bearings. If main bearings stay in crankcase, heat crankcase halves using a heat lamp or blow dryer to aid in removal of bearings. Always renew bearings whenever they are removed. A needle bearing (10) is used in connecting rod small end on all models. On some models, spacers are located on either side of the needle bearing.

Check crankshaft runout by supporting crankshaft at the main bearing journals and use a dial indicator to measure runout at outer end of crankshaft. Maximum allowable runout is 0.05 mm (0.002 in.). Replace crankshaft assembly if discolored from excessive heat.

When reasssembling do not use any type of sealant between outer race of main bearings and crankcase bores. Bearings are designed to allow outer race to creep during operation. Heat crankcase prior to installing bearings. Install oil seals (4 and 8) with open side toward inside of crankcase. Tighten crankshaft screws evenly to 1.9-2.5 N·m (17-22 in.-lbs.) on Model 35EV. On all other models, tighten crankcase screws to 8.0-9.0 N·m (70-80 in.-lbs.). On all models, tap end of crankshaft with a plastic mallet, then retorque crankcase screws. Make certain that crankshaft rotates freely. Complete reassembly by reversing disassembly procedure.

Fig. JD54—Exploded view of bar and chain lubricating oil pump assembly.

1. Screw
2. Stop washer
3. Pump body
4. "O" rings
5. Spring
6. Piston

IGNITION. Repair of ignition system malfunction, except for faulty wiring connections, is accomplished by renewal of ignition system components.

To test ignition system, disconnect spark plug cable and connect cable to suitable spark tester such as D-05351ST. Set tester gap to 4 mm (0.160 in.).

NOTE: Do not set tester gap greater than 4 mm (0.160 in.) as ignition components may be damaged if spark is not able to jump the tester gap.

Position ignition switch in start position. Pull recoil starter rope and observe tester for spark. If there is no spark or a weak spark, ignition system is faulty. Perform the following tests to determine which component is at fault.

To test ignition switch, remove starter housing/fan cover. Disconnect ignition switch leads from ignition module and ground. Connect a continuity tester to stop switch leads. Continuity should be indicated when switch is in "Stop" position, and no continuity should be indicated when switch is in "On" position. Renew switch if it fails this test.

Air gap between ignition module coil lamination and flywheel magnet should be 0.3-0.4 mm (0.012-0.016 in.). To adjust, remove module mounting screws and coat threads with suitable thread locker. Install screws loosely and place a proper thickness feeler gage between coil lamination and flywheel magnet. Allow the magnet to pull module against the feeler gage, then tighten mounting screws.

Test flywheel magnets for loss of magnetism. Magnets should be able to attract a metal object from 25 mm (1 in.) away. If not, renew flywheel. Check flywheel for worn keyway or key that may result in incorrect ignition timing and poor engine performance. Renew key and/or flywheel as necessary.

Test resistance of ignition coil using an ohmmeter as follows: Disconnect coil primary lead and spark plug lead. Set ohmmeter on RX1 scale and connect meter leads to primary lead and ground to measure primary resistance. Meter reading should be 0.7-1.0 ohms on Models 45EV and 65EV, 0.0-0.5 ohms on Models 51SV and 55SV and 0.0-0.2 ohms on all other models. Set ohmmeter on RX1000 scale and connect meter leads to primary lead and spark plug cable end. Meter reading should be 7000-10,000 ohms on Models 45EV and 65EV, 500-1500 ohms on Model 65SV and 1500-3000 ohms on all other models. If meter readings are within 10 percent of specifications, coil may be considered satisfactory.

Test ignition module by substituting a known good module. Renew module assembly if faulty.

OIL PUMP. All models are equipped with an automatic oil pump that provides lubrication to chain and bar. Refer to Fig. JD54. The pump is located in crankcase and is operated by a cam on the crankshaft that actuates plunger (6).

Pump is accessible after removing rear handle and gas and oil tanks. Remove screw (1) and stop washer (2). Turn pump body (3) counterclockwise until loose, then pull pump assembly from crankcase.

When installing oil pump, proceed as follows: Lubricate "O" rings (4) with oil, then thread pump into crankcase until seated lightly. If original pump is being installed, unscrew pump until index mark (1—Fig. JD55) is aligned with stop fin (2) on crankcase. This is point of maximum oil flow. Position stop washer (2) on pump so pump can be turned counterclockwise only from this point.

If a new pump is being installed, thread pump into crankcase until seated lightly. Remove bar and chain so oil port is exposed. Start and run engine at medium speed. Turn pump counterclockwise until maximum oil flow is ob-

Fig. JD55—Index mark (1) on oil pump should be aligned with fin (2) on crankcase at point of maximum oil output.

tained. Stop engine and place a punch mark on top of pump in line with stop fin on crankcase for future reference. Install stop washer so pump can be turned counterclockwise only from this point.

REWIND STARTER. Refer to appropriate Fig. JD56, JD57 or JD58 for exploded view of rewind starter assembly. To disassemble rewind starter, remove starter housing (1) from engine. Remove rope handle (3) and allow rope to rewind into housing. Unscrew rope pulley mounting screw (10) and remove rope pulley (8), being careful not to dislodge rewind spring (5). If necessary to remove rewind spring, care should be used not to allow spring to uncoil uncontrolled.

Apply a light coat of multipurpose grease to both sides of rewind spring. Install rewind spring in starter housing with coils wrapped in clockwise direction from outer end of spring. Wind rope around pulley in a clockwise direction as viewed from flywheel side of pulley. Turn pulley three or four turns clockwise before passing rope through starter housing. Check starter operation. It should be possible to pull rope to its full extension and still turn rope pulley approximately ½ turn clockwise. If rewind spring binds before rope is fully extended, reduce spring tension by pulling rope up into notch in rope pulley and allowing pulley to rotate one turn counterclockwise. Recheck starter operation.

CLUTCH. To remove clutch assembly, unbolt and remove guide bar and chain. Remove chain brake assembly if so equipped. Remove spark plug and install a piston stop tool in spark plug hole, or remove starter housing, inner fan cover and ignition module and hold flywheel with a filter wrench. Note that clutch nut (8—Fig. JD59) and clutch hub (2) have left-hand threads. Remove retaining nut (8), clutch drum (5), clutch shoes (3) and hub (2).

Inspect all parts for excessive wear and renew as necessary. Renew chain sprocket (Fig. JD60) if teeth are worn in excess of 1 mm (0.040 in.). If sprocket is worn excessively, check chain drive links for wear also. Do not install a new chain over a worn sprocket.

To install clutch, reverse removal procedure. Be sure that ends of spring (4—Fig. JD59) are positioned away from interference with joints of clutch shoes (3). On Model 35EV, tighten clutch hub to 27.7-31.6 N·m (245-280 in-lbs.) and tighten clutch retaining nut to 9.0-10.7 N·m (80-95 in.-lbs.). On all other models, tighten clutch hub and clutch retaining nut to 19.8-23.7 N·m (175-210 in.-lbs.).

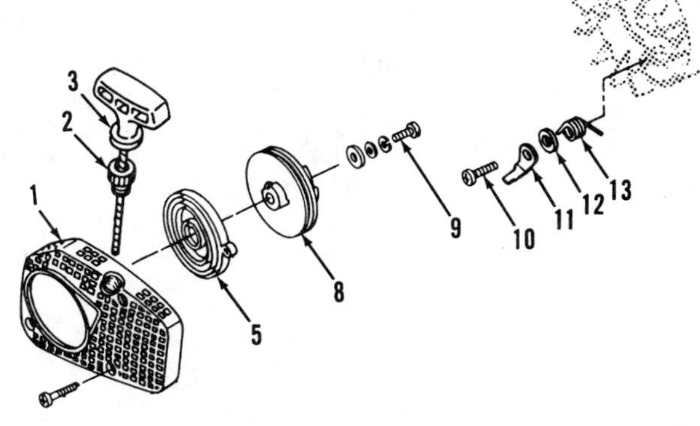

Fig. JD56—Exploded view of rewind starter used on Model 35EV.

1. Starter housing
2. Guide
3. Rope handle
5. Rewind spring
8. Pulley
9. Screw
10. Screw
11. Ratchet
12. Spacer
13. Spring

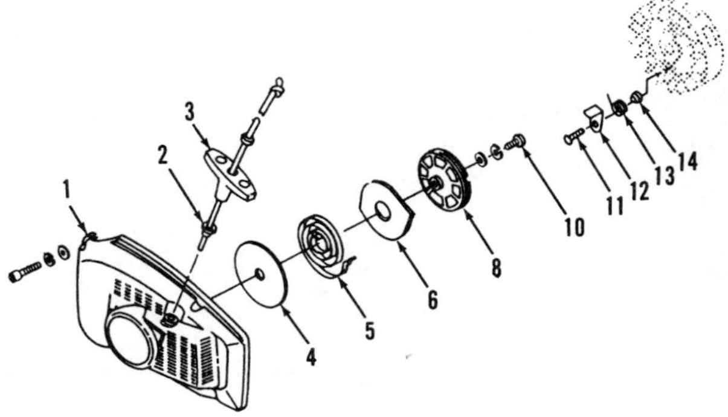

Fig. JD57—Exploded view of rewind starter used on Models 45EV and 46EV.

1. Starter housing
2. Guide
3. Rope handle
4. Plate
5. Rewind spring
6. Plate
8. Pulley
10. Screw
11. Screw
12. Pawl
13. Spacer
14. Spring

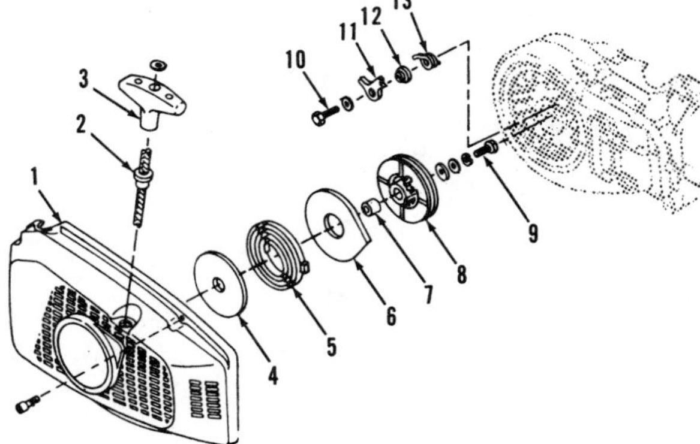

Fig. JD58—Exploded view of rewind starter used on Models 65EV and 65SV. Models 51SV, 55EV and 55SV are similar.

1. Starter housing
2. Guide
3. Rope handle
4. Plate
5. Rewind spring
6. Plate
7. Bushing
8. Pulley
9. Screw
10. Screw
11. Ratchet
12. Spacer
13. Spring

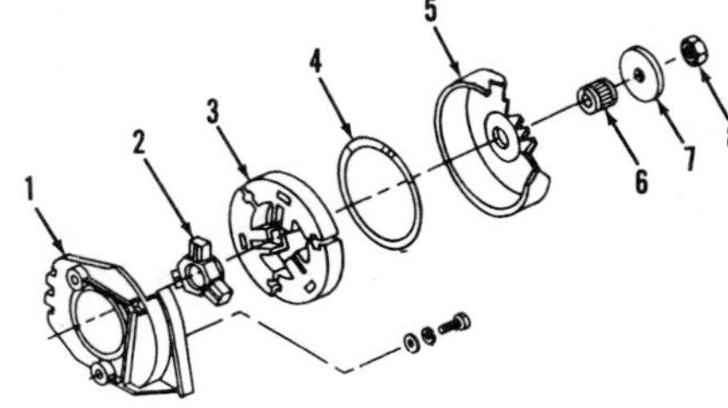

Fig. JD59—Exploded view of clutch assembly typical of all models. Note that nut (8) and hub (2) have left-hand threads.

1. Plate
2. Clutch hub
3. Clutch shoes
4. Spring
5. Clutch drum
6. Needle bearing
7. Washer
8. Nut

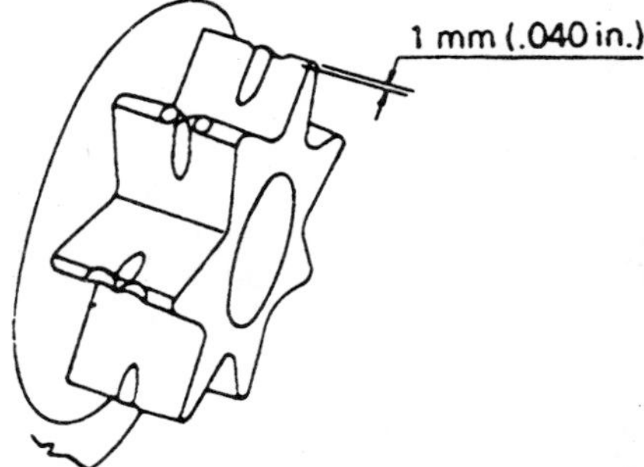

Fig. JD60—Renew clutch drum if sprocket teeth are worn in excess of 1 mm (0.040 in.).

CHAIN BRAKE. Some models are equipped with a chain brake system designed to stop chain movement should saw kickback occur. The chain brake system is activated when the operator's hand strikes the chain brake lever (1—Fig. JD61), thereby forcing actuating cam (13) to release the spring (14). Spring pressure then draws brake band (6) tight around clutch drum to stop chain.

There are three positions of chain brake handle: When brake handle (1) is fully forward, brake is engaged; when handle is in center position, brake is disengaged; when handle is fully rearward, brake is in refueling position. To check chain brake operation, push handle fully forward to engage brake. Try to pull chain forward by hand. If chain is not held securely by brake when brake is engaged, adjust as follows:

Remove guide bar, chain and brake cover (10—Fig. JD61). Loosen screw (9) and turn band adjuster (8) while intermittently engaging handle until desired brake tension is obtained. Be sure that clutch drum turns freely when brake lever is in disengaged position. Tighten adjuster screw to 6.8-7.9 N·m (60-70 in.-lbs.).

To remove chain brake assembly, remove guide bar cover, guide bar and chain. Remove brake cover (10—Fig. JD61). Remove brake band retainer (5), pivot bolt (14) and brake band anchor bolt (9). Remove chain brake components and inspect for wear or damage.

When reassembling, tighten pivot bolt (15) to 5.6 N·m (50 in.-lbs.). If handle pivot pin (3) was removed, apply thread locking compound to plain end of pin, then install plain end of pin into hole in casting until flush with back of casting. Tighten brake band retainer screw to 6.8-7.9 N·m (60-70 in.-lbs.). Adjust brake as previously outlined.

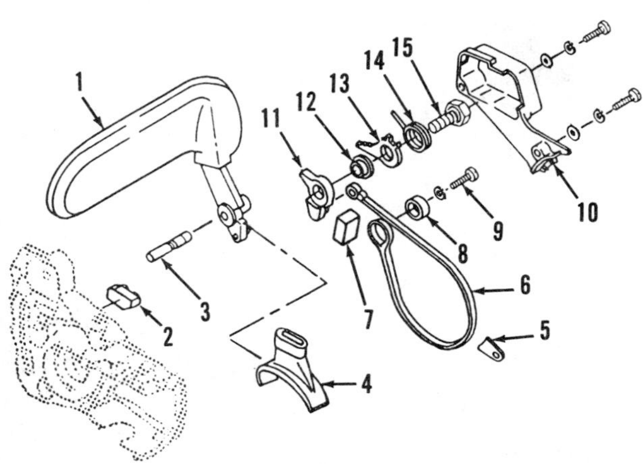

Fig. JD61—Exploded view of chain brake assembly used on some models.

1. Handle
2. Reset rubber
3. Pin
4. Cover
5. Brake band retainer
6. Brake band
7. Seal
8. Brake band adjuster
9. Screw
10. Cover
11. Brake band lever
12. Spacer
13. Actuating cam
14. Spring
15. Pivot bolt

JOHN DEERE

Model	Bore mm (in.)	Stroke mm (in.)	Displacement cc (cu. in.)	Drive Type
450V	43 (1.69)	31 (1.22)	45 (2.75)	Direct
800V	52 (2.05)	38 (1.5)	80.7 (4.9)	Direct

MAINTENANCE

SPARK PLUG. Recommended spark plug is John Deere AM 54611 or equivalent. Spark plug electrode gap should be 0.6-0.7 mm (0.012-0.016 in.).

CARBURETOR. A Walbro HDA series diaphragm type carburetor is used on all models. Refer to Walbro section of CARBURETOR SERVICE section for carburetor overhaul procedure and exploded view of carburetor.

On Model 450V, initial setting of idle mixture screw (2—Fig. JD71) and high speed screw (1) is 1 turn out from lightly seated position. On Model 800V, initial setting of idle mixture screw is 1¼ turns out from lightly seated position and initial setting of high speed screw is 1 turn out from lightly seated position. Make final carburetor adjustments with engine running at operating temperature. Adjust idle mixture screw to obtain fastest idle speed and so engine will accelerate without stumbling. Adjust idle speed screw (3) so engine idles just under clutch engagement speed. Adjust high speed screw so maximum engine speed at full throttle with no load is obtained and four-cycling sound stops, then turn screw out (counterclockwise) until a four-cycling sound just returns at full throttle (no-load). Do not operate saw with high speed mixture too lean as engine damage may occur due to lack of lubrication and overheating.

IGNITION. All models are equipped with a breakerless capacitor discharge ignition system. There is no periodic maintenance required for the ignition system. Ignition timing is not adjustable.

LUBRICATION. The engine is lubricated by mixing oil with the fuel. Recommended fuel:oil ratio is 50:1 when using John Deere 2-Cycle Engine Oil. If John Deere 2-Cycle Engine Oil is not available, a good quality oil designed for two-stroke air-cooled engines may be used when mixed at a 32:1 ratio. Always mix fuel and oil in a separate container. Never mix fuel and oil directly in fuel tank. Regular leaded or unleaded gasoline is recommended. The use of premium gasoline, gasohol or other alcohol blended fuels is not recommended.

John Deere Bar and Chain Lubricant is recommended to lubricate chain and bar. This oil is prediluted to operate properly in a wide range of temperatures.

Clean SAE 10W-40 automotive oil may also be used to lubricate chain and bar. At temperatures below -10°C (15°F), oil may be cut with up to 33 percent kerosene to aid lubrication.

REPAIRS

COMPRESSION TEST. Engine should be cold when checking compression pressure. Remove spark plug and install compression test gage. Pull recoil rope and note pressure gage reading. Compression pressure should be minimum of 1000 kPa (145 psi) for Model 450V and 924 kPa (134 psi) for Model 800V.

CRANKCASE PRESSURE TEST. An improperly sealed crankcase can cause the engine to be hard to start, run rough, have low power and overheat. Refer to ENGINE SERVICE section of this manual for crankcase pressure test procedure. If crankcase leakage is indicated, pressurize crankcase and use a soap and water solution to check gaskets, seals, pulse line and castings for leakage.

CYLINDER, PISTON, PIN AND RINGS. To disassemble, remove guide bar and chain. Remove air cleaner cover and filter element, recoil starter housing, front handle and cylinder cover. Remove muffler, carburetor, air cleaner housing, heat shield and intake boot. Remove cylinder mounting screws and pull cylinder off piston. Support piston with a towel to prevent damage to piston skirt. Remove rings from piston ring grooves. Remove piston pin retainers and use suitable piston pin tool, such as JDZ-23, to push piston pin out of piston and connecting rod.

Cylinder bore is chrome plated on all models and oversize piston and rings are not available. Inspect cylinder for scoring, flaking, excessive wear or other damage to chrome surface. Check piston ring groove wear by inserting new ring in ring groove and measure side clearance with a feeler gage as shown in Fig. JD72. Renew piston if side clearance exceeds 0.1 mm (0.004 in.). Measure piston skirt diameter at bottom of skirt 90 degrees from pin bore. Renew piston if skirt diameter is less than 42.95 mm (1.691 in.) on Model 450V and 51.95 mm (2.045 in.) on Model 800V. Measure piston pin bore and piston pin outside diameter. Wear limit for pin bore is 10.03

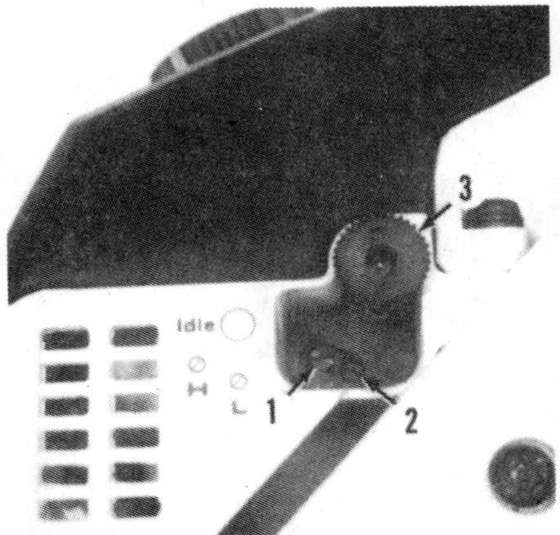

Fig. JD71—View of carburetor adjustment points. Refer to text.

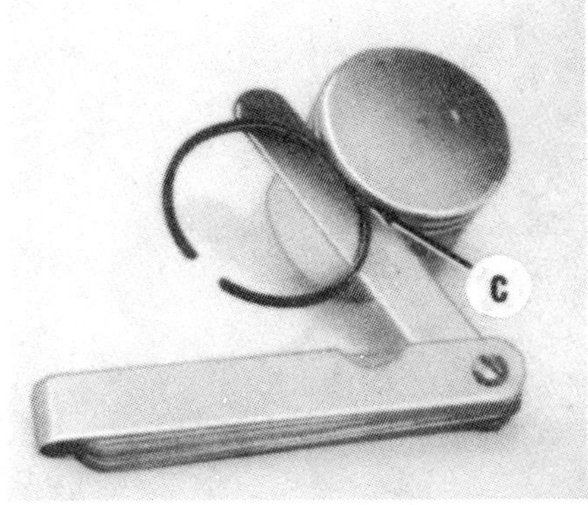

Fig. JD72—To check piston ring groove wear, insert new ring in groove and use a feeler gage to measure side clearance (C). Refer to text.

mm (0.395 in.) for Model 450V and 13.027 mm (0.513 in.) for Model 800V. Wear limit for pin outside diameter is 9.98 mm (0.393 in.) for Model 450V and 12.98 mm (0.511 in.) for Model 800V.

To reassemble, install piston with arrow on piston crown pointing toward exhaust port side of crankcase. Heating piston in hot water or oil will ease installation of piston pin. Install one new piston pin retaining ring (7—Fig. JD73), then use a piston pin tool to push pin (6) into piston. Note that piston rings must not be installed on piston when using piston pin tool. Install the other new retainer ring (7) after pin is installed. Piston rings (4) are pinned in ring grooves to prevent rotation. Be sure piston ring end gaps are properly positioned around locating pins before installing cylinder. Lubricate piston and cylinder with oil, then slide cylinder over piston. Do not rotate cylinder during installation as ring end gap may misalign from locating pins and damage rings and cylinder. Tighten cylinder mounting screws alternately to 7.9 N·m (70 in.-lbs.) on Model 450V and 13.6 N·m (120 in.-lbs.) on Model 800V.

CRANKSHAFT, CONNECTING ROD AND CRANKCASE. All models are equipped with a crankshaft and connecting rod unit assembly (10—Fig. JD73) that is supported by ball bearings (9) at both ends. Crankshaft and connecting rod are not available separately.

To remove crankshaft assembly, remove guide bar and chain. Remove air cleaner cover and filter element, recoil starter housing, front handle, inner fan cover, ignition module and cylinder cover. Remove muffler, carburetor, air cleaner housing, heat shield and intake boot. Remove spark plug and install piston stop or end of a rope in spark plug hole to lock piston and crankshaft. Remove clutch assembly, noting that unit has left-hand threads. Remove fan retaining nut and starter pawls. Use a suitable puller to remove flywheel from crankshaft. Remove rear handle and fuel tank. Unscrew oil pump worm gear (2—Fig. JD74) and remove oil pump cover plate (1). Disconnect oil lines (6 and 15) and remove oil pump (4) and spacer (3). Remove cylinder mounting screws and pull cylinder off piston. Support piston with a towel to prevent damage to piston skirt. Remove rings from piston ring grooves. Remove piston pin retainers and use suitable piston pin tool, such as JDZ-23, to push piston pin out of piston and connecting rod. Remove screws from crankcase halves. Attach a puller to flywheel side of crankcase and tighten puller screw against end of crankshaft. Tap crankcase halves with a soft hammer while alternately tightening puller until crankcase halves are separated. Press crankshaft out of clutch side of crankcase half. If main bearings remain on crankshaft, use a suitable puller to remove bearings. Bearings usually stay in crankcase. Press bearings and seals out of crankcase.

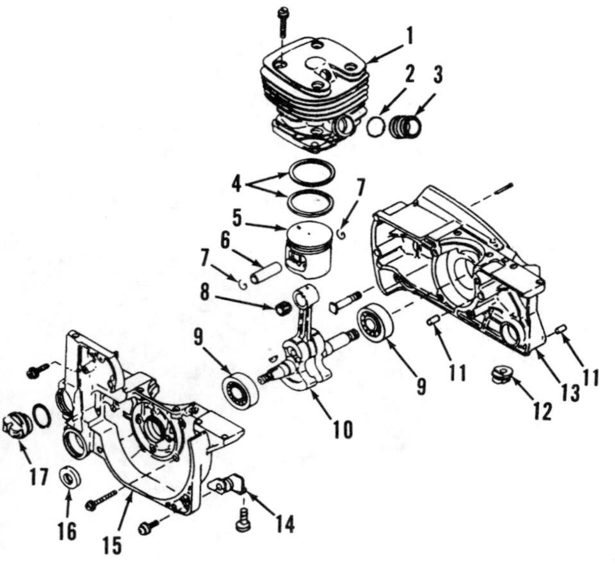

Fig. JD73—Exploded view of engine used on Model 800V saw. Model 450V is similar.

1. Cylinder
2. Band
3. Intake boot
4. Piston rings
5. Piston
6. Piston pin
7. Retaining rings
8. Needle bearing
9. Bearings
10. Crankshaft & connecting rod assy.
11. Dowel
12. Insulator cushion
13. Crankcase half
14. Insulator cushion
15. Crankcase half
16. Seal
17. Cap

Fig. JD74—Exploded view of chain oiler system.

1. Cover
2. Worm gear
3. Spacer
4. Automatic oil pump
5. "O" ring
6. Oil line
7. Filter
8. Adjuster knob
9. Spring
10. "O" ring
11. Retainer
12. Oil seal
13. Connector
14. Pipe
15. Oil line
16. Nipple
17. Gasket
18. Check ball
19. Spring
20. Retainer
21. Plug
22. Screw
23. Pin
24. Spring
24. Manual oil pump housing
25. Spring
26. "O" ring
27. Pump piston

Inspect crankshaft for discoloration caused by excessive heat. Renew assembly if discolored. Renew main bearings (9—Fig. JD73) if they do not rotate smoothly. Needle bearing (8) in small end of connecting rod should be renewed if scratched or discolored. Note that crankshaft is marked with red, blue or white paint, and replacement needle bearing must be matched to paint color.

To reassemble, place crankshaft in a freezer to cool it. Heat bearings to maximum of 150°C (300°F), then assemble hot bearings on cool crankshaft. Do not apply any type of sealant to outer diameter of bearings as they are designed to creep during operation. Heat crankcase halves to maximum of 150°C (300°F). Apply thin coat of plastic gasket to mating surface of one crankcase half, then assemble crankshaft, bearings and crankcase halves. Tighten crankcase screws in diagonal pattern to 7.9 N·m (70 in.-lbs.). Lubricate main bearings with 2-cycle oil and make certain that crankshaft turns freely. Lubricate lip of seals with high temperature grease and install in crankcase. Seals must be installed flush with machined surface of crankcase. Install oil pump spacer (3—Fig. JD74) so chamfered side is facing crankshaft seal. Refer to OIL PUMP section for detailed pump installation instructions. Complete reassembly by reversing disassembly procedure.

OIL PUMP. All models are equipped with an automatic oil pump to provide lubrication for guide bar and chain. A piston type manual oil pump is also used on all models. The automatic pump is operated by the clutch sprocket which turns a worm gear in the oil pump to actuate a spring-loaded plunger.

To remove automatic oil pump, unbolt and remove guide bar and chain. Remove spark plug and install piston stop tool or end of a rope in spark plug hole. Remove clutch assembly, noting that clutch has left-hand threads. Unscrew worm gear (2—Fig. JD74) and remove pump cover plate (1). Disconnect oil lines (6 and 15) and remove oil pump assembly.

Oil pump may be disassembled for inspection, but individual parts are not available. Complete pump must be renewed if any part is worn or damaged. To disassemble, remove plug (6—Fig. JD75). Rotate plunger (5) until hole in plunger is visible in opening in pump housing (1). Push plunger in to relieve spring tension on cam (2) and withdraw cam. Pull plunger from housing bore. To reassemble, reverse disassembly procedure.

When installing automatic oil pump, use grease to hold "O" ring (5—Fig. JD74) in place on rear of pump. Install spacer (3) so chamfered side is facing crankshaft oil seal. The cam (1—Fig. JD76) has a groove in top that is offset to one side. Position cam so narrow half-moon section of top of cam is toward front of saw. Rotate oiler control shaft (5) so blade in shaft engages groove in cam. Install oil pump plate and tighten screws 4 N·m (35 in.-lbs.).

To check operation of automatic oiler, hold saw over a clean surface and run engine at half throttle. Oil should spray off end of guide bar. If not, make sure that oil outlet hole is clean and check adjustment of oiler control knob. If these items are satisfactory, renew oil pump.

To remove manual oil pump, remove starter housing and inner fan cover. Remove screws retaining insulator cushion and manual oiler. Pull out pump and disconnect oil line.

To disassemble manual oil pump, drive out pin (23—Fig. JD74) and withdraw piston (27). Remove nipple (16) and plug (21) carefully to remove check balls (18) and springs (19). To reassemble, reverse disassembly procedure. Be sure that check balls (18) and springs (19) are installed in sequence shown in Fig. JD74.

To check operation of manual oiler, connect hose to pump inlet nipple and place other end of the hose in container of oil. Actuate piston by hand until oil flows from outlet port. If air bubbles are mixed with oil or if no oil is pumped, pump is faulty.

IGNITION. Repair of ignition system malfunction, except for faulty wiring connections, is accomplished by renewal of ignition system components.

To test ignition system, disconnect spark plug cable and connect cable to suitable spark tester such as D-05351ST. Set tester gap to 4 mm (0.160 in.).

NOTE: Do not set tester gap greater than 4 mm (0.160 in.) as ignition components may be damaged if spark is not able to jump the tester gap.

Position ignition switch in start position. Pull recoil starter rope and observe tester for spark. If there is no spark or a weak spark, ignition system is faulty. Perform the following tests to determine which component is at fault.

To test ignition switch, remove starter housing/fan cover. Disconnect ignition switch lead from ignition module. Connect a continuity tester to stop switch lead and to ground. Continuity should be indicated when switch is in "Stop" position, and no continuity should be indicated when switch is in "On" position. Renew switch if it fails this test.

Air gap between ignition module coil laminations and flywheel magnet should be 0.3-0.4 mm (0.012-0.016 in.). To adjust, remove module mounting screws and coat threads with suitable thread locker. Install screws loosely and place a proper thickness feeler gage between coil laminations and flywheel magnet. Allow the magnet to pull module against the feeler gage, then tighten mounting screws.

Test flywheel magnets for loss of magnetism. Magnets should be able to attract a metal object from 25 mm (1 in.) away. If not, renew flywheel. Check flywheel for worn keyway or key which may result in incorrect ignition timing and poor engine performance. Renew key and/or flywheel as necessary.

Test resistance of ignition coil using an ohmmeter as follows: On Model 450V, disconnect coil primary lead and spark plug lead. Set ohmmeter on RX1 scale and connect meter leads to primary lead of coil and ground to measure primary resistance. Meter reading should be 0.1-0.5 ohms. Model 800V has unitized coil and module and no test of primary coil is possible. On all models, set ohmmeter on RX1000 scale and connect meter leads to module lead and spark plug cable end to check secondary resistance. Meter reading should be 2000-2500 ohms on Models 450V and 100-1500 ohms on Model 800V. If meter readings are within 10 percent of specifications, coil may be considered satisfactory.

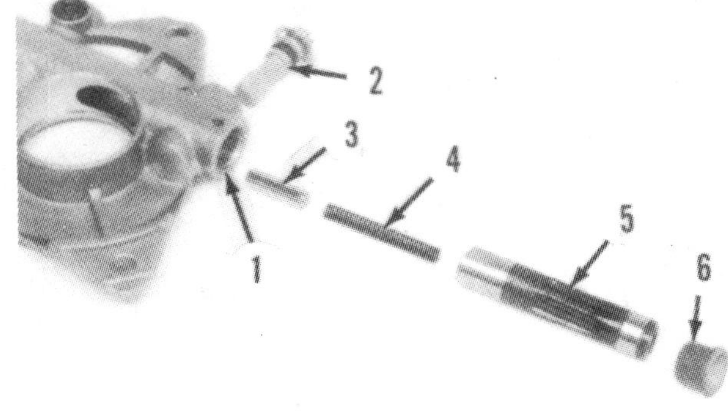

Fig. JD75—Exploded view of automatic oil pump.
1. Pump housing
2. Cam
3. Piston
4. Spring
5. Pump plunger
6. Plug

Fig. JD76—View of automatic oiler mounted on engine.
1. Cam
2. Spacer
3. Oil lines
4. Pump housing
5. Control shaft

Test ignition module by substituting a known good module. Renew module assembly if faulty.

REWIND STARTER. Refer to Fig. JD77 for exploded view of rewind starter assembly. To disassemble rewind starter, remove starter housing (1) from engine. Remove rope handle (3) and allow rope to rewind into housing. Unscrew rope pulley mounting screw (9) and remove rope pulley (8), being careful not to dislodge rewind spring (5).

IMPORTANT: If necessary to remove rewind spring, care should be used not to allow spring to uncoil uncontrolled. Spring is not held in place by a retainer and will uncoil when removed.

New rope should be 850 mm (33.5 in.) long for Model 450V and 900 mm (35.4 in.) long for Model 800V. Apply a light coat of multipurpose grease to both sides of rewind spring. Install rewind spring in starter housing with coils wrapped in clockwise direction from outer end of spring. Fully unwind rope and hold in notch of pulley. Install pulley in housing, apply thread locking compound to screw (9) and tighten screw securely. Thread rope through housing guide (2) and handle. Tie a knot in end of rope. While holding rope in notch of pulley, turn pulley clockwise against spring pressure four revolutions. Disengage rope from notch in pulley and allow rope to wind onto pulley. Check starter operation. It should be possible to pull rope to its full extension and still turn rope pulley approximately ½ turn clockwise. If rewind spring binds before rope is fully extended, reduce spring tension by pulling rope up into notch in rope pulley and allowing pulley to rotate one turn counterclockwise. Recheck starter operation.

CLUTCH. To remove clutch assembly, unbolt and remove guide bar and chain. Remove chain brake assembly if so equipped. Remove spark plug and install a piston stop tool or the end of a rope in spark plug hole to lock piston and crankshaft. Unscrew clutch assembly (left-hand threads) from crankshaft using JDM-99 clutch tool or other suitable tool. Remove screws retaining clutch plates (9—Fig. JD78) to clutch shoes (5). Pry out spring (6) and separate shoes from hub (7).

Inspect all parts for excessive wear and renew as necessary. Renew chain sprocket (1) if teeth are worn in excess of 1 mm (0.040 in.). If sprocket is worn excessively, check chain drive links for wear also. Do not install a new chain over a worn sprocket.

To install clutch, reverse removal procedure. Chamfered side of clutch hub (7) must be on opposite side from spring (6) and plates (9). Be sure that ends of spring are positioned away from interference with joints of clutch shoes (5). On Model 800V, end of spring should be aligned with nylon cushion (8) in plate. Tighten plate retaining screws (4) to 4.0 N·m (35 in.-lbs.). Lubricate needle bearing (3) with high temperature grease, then install clutch drum (2) and sprocket (1) making sure that drum splines mate with oil pump worm gear. Tighten clutch hub to 21.5 N·m (188 in.-lbs.) on Model 450V and 30 N·m (265 in.-lbs.) on Model 800V.

CHAIN BRAKE. Some models are equipped with a chain brake system designed to stop chain movement should saw kickback occur. The chain brake system is activated when the chain brake lever (1—Fig. JD79) is moved forward, which actuates the brake and draws brake band (11) tight around clutch drum to stop the chain.

There are two positions of chain brake handle: When brake handle (1) is pushed fully forward, brake is engaged; when handle is pulled rearward, brake is disengaged. Brake must engage when 1.5-2.0 kg (3.3-4.4 lbs.) force is applied to handle. To adjust chain brake handle tension, remove guide bar cover and brake cartridge. Turn handle set screw (2—Fig. JD79) clockwise to increase force required to engage brake, or turn screw counterclockwise to decrease force required.

To check chain brake operation, push handle fully forward to engage brake. Try to pull chain forward by hand. If chain is not held securely by brake when brake is engaged, adjust as follows: Remove guide bar cover and outer guide bar plate (800V only). Remove chain brake cartridge (11—Fig. JD79) from cover. Turn adjusting nut (12) clockwise to tighten brake band or counterclockwise to loosen brake band. Initial adjustment of adjusting nut is two turns counterclockwise from lightly seated position. Reinstall chain brake cartridge and guide bar cover and check brake operation. Repeat adjustment procedure as necessary. Be sure that clutch drum turns freely when brake lever is in disengaged position. If brake cannot be adjusted properly, disassemble and check for damaged components.

To remove chain brake assembly, remove guide bar cover (14—Fig. JD79). Remove chain brake cartridge mounting screws and remove cartridge from cover. Remove handle pivot bolt (9) and handle assembly. Remove tension screw (10), adjusting nut (12) and cover from brake cartridge. Inspect spring, cam and lever in cartridge for wear or damage.

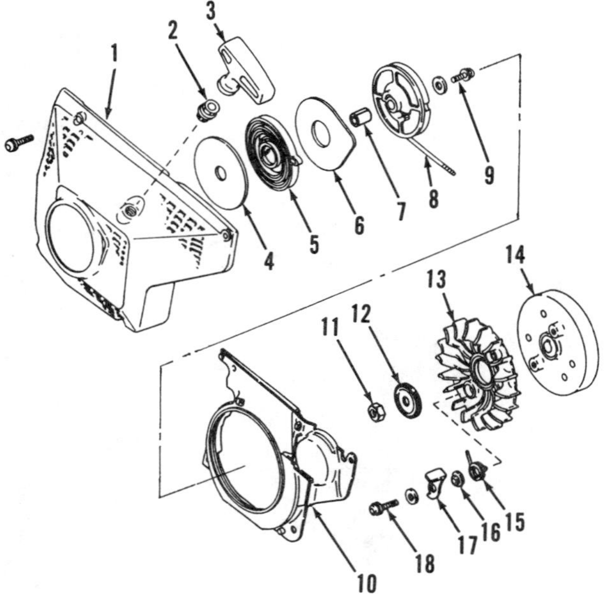

Fig. JD77—Exploded view of rewind starter assembly. Bushing (7) is not used on Model 450V.

1. Starter housing
2. Rope guide
3. Rope handle
4. Plate
5. Rewind spring
6. Plate
7. Bushing
8. Pulley
9. Screw
10. Fan cover
11. Nut
12. Washer
13. Fan
14. Flywheel
15. Spring
16. Spacer
17. Ratchet
18. Screw

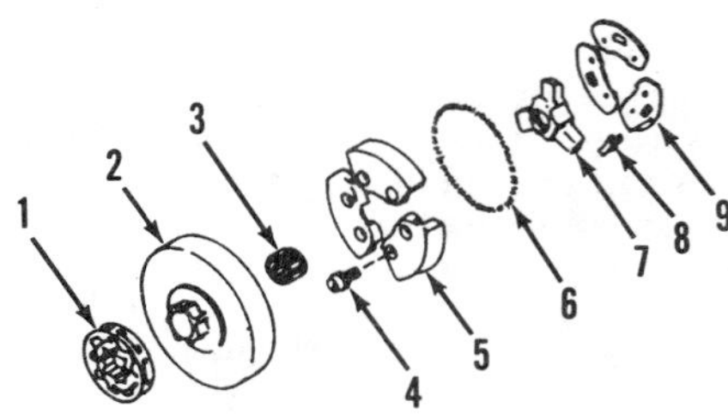

Fig. JD78—Exploded view of clutch assembly. Nylon cushion (8) is not used on Model 450V.

1. Sprocket
2. Clutch drum
3. Bearing
4. Screw
5. Clutch shoes
6. Spring
7. Clutch hub
8. Nylon cushion
9. Clutch plates

Brake cartridge and band must be renewed as an assembly.

To reassemble, reverse disassembly procedure. Initial setting of brake cartridge adjusting nut (12) is two turns counterclockwise from lightly seated position. Initial setting of handle set screw (2) is three turns counterclockwise from lightly seated position. Tighten guide bar cover screws to 21.5 N·m (188 in.-lbs.). Adjust brake as outlined previously.

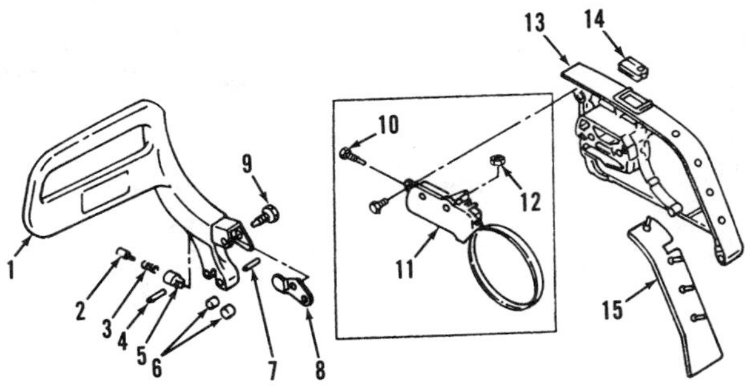

Fig. JD79—Exploded view of chain brake assembly.

1. Handle
2. Set screw
3. Spring
4. Pin
5. Connector
6. Spacers
7. Pin
8. Stop lever
9. Pivot bolt
10. Tension screw
11. Chain brake cartridge
12. Adjusting nut
13. Cover
14. Guide bar cover
15. Shield

JOHN DEERE

Model	Bore mm (in.)	Stroke mm (in.)	Displacement cc (cu. in.)	Drive Type
66SV (Twin Cyl.)	36 (1.42)	30 (1.18)	61 (3.7)	Direct

MAINTENANCE

SPARK PLUG. Recommended spark plug is John Deere AM54611 or Champion CJ-6Y. Spark plug electrode gap should be 0.6-0.7 mm (0.024-0.028 in.).

CARBURETOR. A Walbro HDA diaphragm type carburetor is used. Refer to Walbro section of CARBURETOR SERVICE section for carburetor overhaul procedure and exploded view of carburetor.

Initial setting of idle mixture screw and high speed mixture screw is 1$^1/_8$ to 1$^1/_4$ turns out from a lightly seated position.

Make final carburetor adjustments with engine running at operating temperature. Adjust idle mixture screw to obtain fastest idle speed and smooth acceleration. Adjust idle speed screw so engine idles just under clutch engagement speed. Operate saw at full throttle with no load and adjust high speed mixture screw until maximum engine speed is obtained and "four-cycling" sound stops, then back adjustment screw out until four-cycling sound just returns. Do not operate saw with high speed mixture too lean as engine damage may occur due to lack of lubrication and overheating.

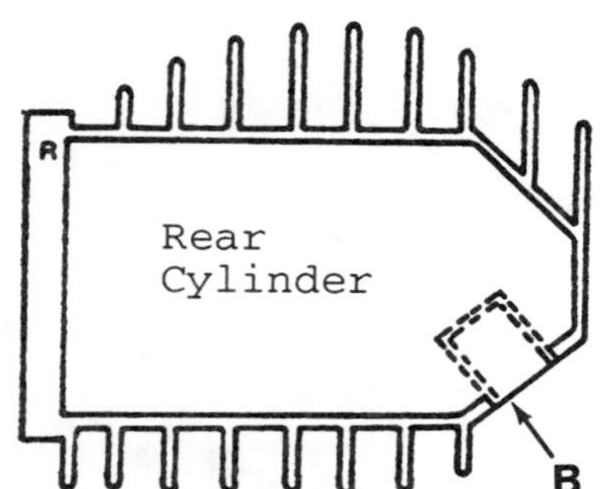

Fig. JD90—Front cylinder is marked with letter "F" at magneto side of cylinder flange and spark plug hole (A) faces upward. Rear cylinder is marked with letter "R" at pto side of flange and spark plug hole faces downward.

IGNITION. A breakerless capacitor discharge ignition system is used. No periodic maintenance is required for the ignition system. Ignition timing is not adjustable.

LUBRICATION. The engine is lubricated by mixing oil with the fuel. Recommended fuel:oil ratio is 50:1 when using John Deere 2-Cycle Engine Oil. If John Deere 2-Cycle Engine Oil is not available, a good quality oil designed for two-stroke air-cooled engines may be used when mixed at a 32:1 ratio. Always mix fuel and oil in a separate container. Never mix fuel and oil directly in fuel tank. Regular leaded or unleaded gasoline is recommended. The use of premium gasoline, gasohol or other alcohol blended fuels is not recommended.

John Deere Bar and Chain Lubricant is recommended to lubricate chain and bar. This oil is prediluted to operate properly in a wide range of temperatures.

Clean SAE 10W-40 automotive oil may also be used to lubricate chain and bar. At temperatures below -10°C (15°F), oil may be cut with up to 33 percent kerosene to aid lubrication.

REPAIRS

COMPRESSION TEST. Engine should be cold when checking compression pressure. Remove both spark plugs and install compression test gage in one spark plug hole. Pull recoil rope and note pressure gage reading. Compression pressure should be minimum of 758 kPa (110 psi). Repeat compression test for other cylinder.

CRANKCASE PRESSURE TEST. An improperly sealed crankcase can cause the engine to be hard to start, run rough, have low power and overheat. Refer to ENGINE SERVICE section of this manual for crankcase pressure test procedure. If crankcase leakage is indicated, pressurize crankcase and use a soap and water solution to check gaskets, seals, pulse line and castings for leakage.

CYLINDER, PISTON, PIN AND RINGS. Model 66SV is equipped with an opposed twin-cylinder engine. Cylinder bores are chrome plated and oversize pistons and rings are not available.

To remove pistons, remove guide bar and chain, starter housing, front handle and chain brake if so equipped. Remove spark plug covers, air cleaner assembly, carburetor, manual oil pump and automatic oil pump. Remove base plate, muffler, rear handle and fuel tank, carburetor adapter and reed valve and cylinder covers. It is not necessary to mark cylinders prior to removal as front cylinder is marked with letter "F" at magneto side of cylinder base flange (Fig. JD90) and rear cylinder is marked with letter "R" at pto side of cylinder flange. Remove cylinder mounting screws and withdraw cylinders from crankcase. Mark the pistons so they can be installed in their original positions if reused. Remove piston rings and piston pin retainers, then use a suitable piston pin tool, such as JDZ-23, to push piston pins out of pistons. Remove piston and needle bearing from each connecting rod.

Inspect cylinders for scoring, flaking, excessive wear or other damage to chrome surface and renew as necessary. Check piston ring groove wear by inserting new ring in ring groove and measure side clearance with a feeler gage as shown in Fig. JD91. Renew piston if side clearance exceeds 0.1 mm (0.004 in.). Measure piston skirt diameter at bottom of skirt 90 degrees from pin bore. Renew piston if skirt diameter is less than 35.88 mm (1.4125 in.). Measure piston pin bore and piston pin outside diameter. Wear limit for pin bore is 9.03 mm (0.3555 in.) and wear limit for pin outside diameter is 8.98 mm (0.3535 in.).

To assemble, install pistons with arrows on piston crown facing toward exhaust port. Heating piston in hot water or oil will ease installation of piston pin (10—Fig. JD92). Install one new piston pin retaining ring (9), then push piston pin into place. If necessary, use a piston pin tool to push pin into piston. Note that piston rings must not be installed on piston when using piston pin tool. Install the other new retainer ring (9) after pin is installed. Pins are located in piston ring grooves to prevent ring rotation. Be sure piston ring end gaps are properly positioned around locating pins before installing cylinder. Lubricate piston and cylinder with oil, then slide cylinder over piston. Do not rotate cylinder during installation as ring end gap may misalign from locating pins and damage rings and cylinder. Note that front cylinder is identified with letter "F" on base flange (Fig. JD90) and spark plug hole (A) faces upward. Rear cylinder is identified with letter "R" on base flange and spark plug hole (B) faces downward. Tighten cylinder mounting screws alternately to 8-9 N·m (70-80 in.-lbs.). Complete installation by reversing removal procedure.

CRANKSHAFT, CONNECTING ROD AND CRANKCASE. Crankshaft (16—Fig. JD92) is supported in crankcase by ball bearings at both ends. Crankshaft and connecting rods are not available separately.

To remove crankshaft assembly, remove guide bar and chain, chain brake, starter housing and front handle. Remove spark plugs and install a piston stop tool or the end of a rope in one of the spark plug holes to lock piston and crankshaft. Unscrew clutch drum nut (left-hand threads) and remove clutch drum. Unscrew clutch hub (left-hand threads) using JDM-99 clutch tool or other suitable tool. Remove flywheel nut, then use suitable puller to remove flywheel. Remove cylinders and pistons as outlined above. Remove crankcase mounting screws. Hold clutch side crankcase half (21) and tap on clutch end of crankshaft with plastic mallet to separate crankcase halves. Hold flywheel side crankcase half (2) and tap end of crankshaft to separate crankshaft from crankcase. If bearings (12) remain on crankshaft, use suitable puller to remove bearings from shaft. Bearings usually stay in crankcase halves. Pry out oil seals (1 and 24) and remove snap ring (18). Heat crankcase halves with heat lamp, then press bearings out of crankcase halves.

Renew needle bearings (11) if rollers are scratched or discolored. Maximum inside diameter of connecting rod small end bore is 12.025 mm (0.4734 in.). Renew crankshaft assembly if small ends of connecting rods are discolored. Measure side clearance between big end of connecting rods and crankshaft flange. Renew crankshaft assembly if clearance exceeds 0.4 mm (0.016 in.).

When assembling, heat crankcase halves with heat lamp before installing bearings. Do not apply any sealant to outer diameter of bearings (12) as they are designed to creep in crankcase bore during operation. Install new oil seals (1 and 24) until flush with outer surface of crankcase. Apply plastic gasket to mating surface of crankcase halves, assemble crankshaft and crankcase halves and tighten crankcase screws diagonally to 8-9 N·m (70-80 in.-lbs.). Tap ends of crankshaft with plastic hammer, then retorque crankshaft screws. Make sure that crankshaft turns freely. Complete assembly by reversing disassembly procedure.

IGNITION. Repair of ignition system malfunction, except for faulty wiring connections, is accomplished by renewal of ignition system components.

To test ignition system, disconnect spark plug cable and connect cable to suitable spark tester such as D-05351ST. Set tester gap to 4 mm (0.160 in.).

NOTE: Do not set tester gap greater than 4 mm (0.160 in.) as ignition components may be damaged if spark is not able to jump the tester gap.

Position ignition switch in start position. Pull recoil starter rope and observe tester for spark. If there is no spark or a weak spark, ignition system is faulty. Perform the following tests to determine which component is at fault.

To test ignition switch, remove starter housing/fan cover. Disconnect igni-

Fig. JD91—To check piston ring groove wear, install new ring in groove and use feeler gage to measure side clearance (C). Refer to text.

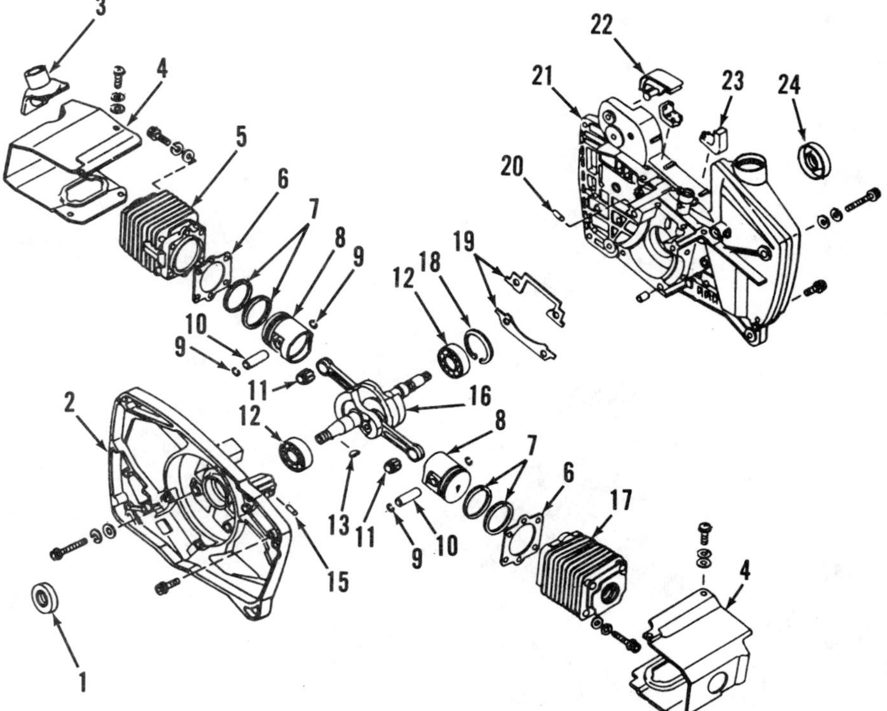

Fig. JD92—Exploded view of Model 66SV engine.

1. Oil seal
2. Crankcase half
3. Spark plug cover
4. Cylinder cover
5. Front cylinder
6. Gasket
7. Piston rings
8. Piston
9. Retaining rings
10. Piston pin
11. Needle bearing
12. Ball bearing
13. Key
15. Dowel pin
16. Crankshaft assy
17. Rear cylinder
18. Snap ring
19. Gasket
20. Dowel pin
21. Crankcase half
22. Cover
23. Cushion
24. Oil seal

tion switch leads from ignition module and ground. Connect a continuity tester to stop switch leads. Continuity should be indicated when switch is in "Stop" position, and no continuity should be indicated when switch is in "On" position. Renew switch if it fails this test.

Air gap between ignition module coil laminations and flywheel magnet should be 0.3-0.4 mm (0.012-0.016 in.). To adjust, remove module mounting screws and coat threads with suitable thread locker. Install screws loosely and place a proper thickness feeler gage between coil laminations and flywheel magnet. Allow the magnet to pull module against the feeler gage, then tighten mounting screws.

Test flywheel magnets for loss of magnetism. Magnets should be able to attract a metal object from 25 mm (1 in.) away. If not, renew flywheel. Check flywheel for worn keyway or key which may result in incorrect ignition timing and poor engine performance. Renew key and/or flywheel as necessary.

Test resistance of ignition coils using an ohmmeter as follows: Remove starter housing and disconnect coil to CDI module lead. Set ohmmeter on RX1 scale and connect meter leads to primary lead and ground to measure primary resistance. Meter reading should be 0.0-0.2 ohms. Set ohmmeter on RX1000 scale, disconnect spark plug lead and connect meter leads to spark plug cable end and ground. Meter reading should be 1000-1500 ohms. Repeat test for other coil. If meter readings are within 10 percent of specifications, coil may be considered satisfactory.

To test CD ignition module excitor coil, disconnect coil to module lead. Connect ohmmeter leads to stop switch lead and module laminations. Resistance should measure 130-200 ohms. Renew module assembly if faulty.

OIL PUMP. All models are equipped with an automatic oil pump which provides lubrication to chain and bar. A manual oil pump is used to provide additional oil when necessary. Refer to Fig. JD93. The automatic pump is located in crankcase and is operated by a cam on the crankshaft which actuates plunger (7).

To remove automatic pump, remove screw (1—Fig. JD93), adjuster knob (2) and grommet (3). Turn pump body (4) counterclockwise until loose, then pull pump assembly from crankcase.

When installing oil pump, proceed as follows: Lubricate "O" rings (5) with oil, then thread pump into crankcase until seated lightly. If original pump is being installed, unscrew pump until index mark (M—Fig. JD94) is aligned with stop fin (S) on crankcase. This is point of maximum oil flow. Install grommet (3) and knob so pump can be turned counterclockwise only from this point.

If a new pump is being installed, thread pump into crankcase until seated lightly. Remove bar and chain so oil port is exposed. Start and run engine at medium speed. Turn pump counterclockwise until maximum oil flow is obtained. Stop engine and place a punch mark on top of pump (4—Fig. JD94) in line with stop fin on crankcase for future reference. Install grommet and adjuster knob so pump can be turned counterclockwise only from this point.

To remove manual oil pump, remove air filter cover and filter element. Unscrew nut (16—Fig. JD93), disconnect oil lines (25 and 26) and remove pump assembly.

Withdraw piston (17) and spring (19) from pump body (20). Remove fittings (24), springs (21) and check balls (22). Inspect all parts for wear or damage and renew as necessary. Install new "O" ring (18) on piston. When reassembling, be sure to note correct installation sequence of check balls (22) and springs (21).

REWIND STARTER. Refer to Fig. JD95 for exploded view of rewind starter assembly. To disassemble rewind starter, remove starter housing (1) from engine. Remove rope handle (3) and allow rope to rewind into housing. Unscrew rope pulley mounting screw (12) and remove rope pulley (8), being careful not to dislodge rewind spring (5). If necessary to remove rewind spring, care should be used not to allow spring to uncoil uncontrolled.

New starter rope length should be 915 mm (35.4 in.). Apply a light coat of multipurpose grease to both sides of rewind spring. Install rewind spring in starter housing with coils wrapped in clockwise direction from outer end of spring. With rope fully unwound from pulley, feed

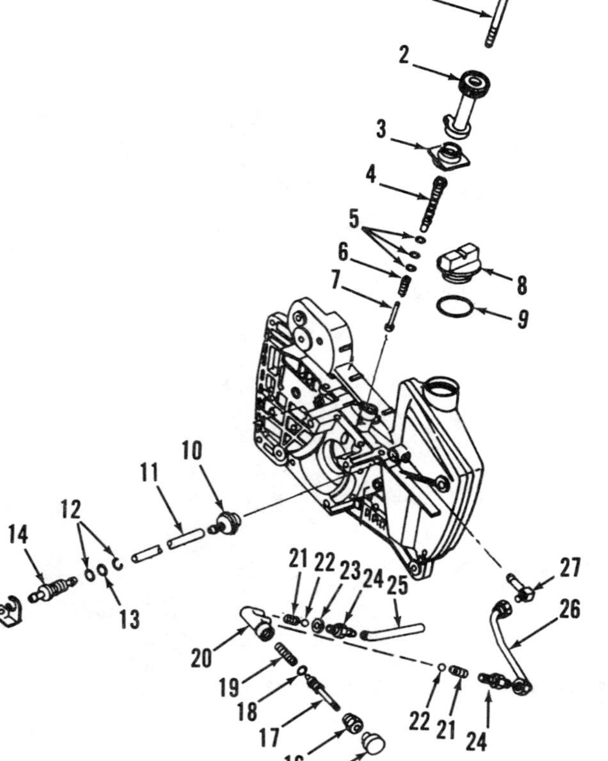

Fig. JD93—Exploded view of chain oiler system.

1. Screw
2. Adjuster knob
3. Grommet
4. Automatic oil pump body
5. "O" rings
6. Spring
7. Piston
8. Cap
9. "O" ring
10. Oil filter
11. Tube
12. Clips
13. "O" ring
14. Connector
15. Knob
16. Nut
17. Piston
18. "O" ring
19. Spring
20. Manual oil pump body
21. Springs
22. Check balls
23. Gasket
24. Nipple
25. Oil inlet line
26. Oil discharge line
27. Connector

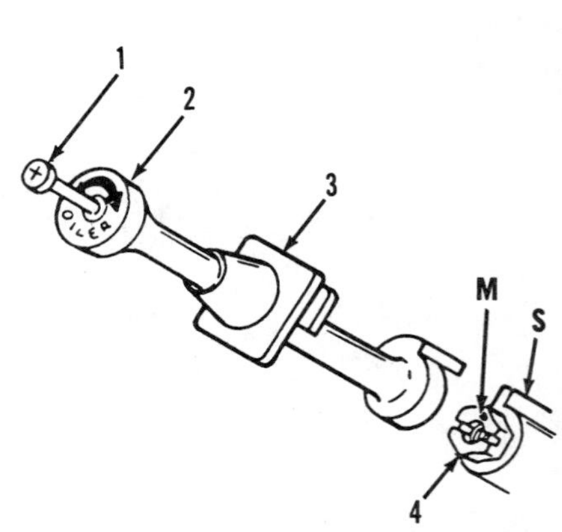

Fig. JD94—Index mark (M) on automatic oil pump (4) should be aligned with stop fin (S) at point of maximum oil discharge.

1. Screw
2. Adjuster knob
3. Grommet
4. Pump body

end of rope through guide and attach handle. Position rope in slot in pulley so it will not wind onto pulley, then turn pulley four turns clockwise. Release rope from pulley notch and allow rope to wind around pulley as pulley is slowly released. Check starter operation. It should be possible to pull rope to its full extension and still turn rope pulley approximately ½ turn clockwise. If rewind spring binds before rope is fully extended, reduce spring tension by pulling rope up into notch in rope pulley and allowing pulley to rotate one turn counterclockwise. Recheck starter operation.

CLUTCH. To remove clutch assembly, unbolt and remove guide bar and chain. Remove chain brake assembly if so equipped. Remove spark plug and install a piston stop tool or end of a rope in spark plug hole to lock piston and crankshaft. Note that clutch nut (10—Fig. JD96) and clutch hub (3) have left-hand threads. Remove retaining nut (10) and clutch drum (7). Use JDM-99 clutch tool or other suitable tool to unscrew clutch hub (3) from crankshaft. Remove clutch plate mounting screws (6), spring (4) and shoes (5).

Inspect all parts for excessive wear and renew as necessary. Renew chain sprocket if teeth are worn in excess of 1 mm (0.040 in.). If sprocket is worn excessively, check chain drive links for wear also. Do not install a new chain over a worn sprocket.

To install clutch, reverse removal procedure. Be sure that ends of spring (4—Fig. JD96) are positioned away from interference with joints of clutch shoes (5). Tighten clutch hub and clutch drum retaining nut to 20-24 N·m (175-210 in-lbs.).

CHAIN BRAKE. Some saws are equipped with a chain brake system designed to stop chain movement should saw kickback occur. The chain brake system is activated when the operator's hand strikes the chain brake handle (3—Fig. JD97), thereby forcing actuating cam (5) to release the spring (14). Spring pressure then draws brake band (7) tight around clutch drum to stop chain.

There are three positions of chain brake handle: When brake handle (3) is fully forward, brake is engaged; when handle is in center position, brake is disengaged; when handle is fully rearward, brake is in service position. To check chain brake operation, push handle fully forward to engage brake. Try to pull chain forward by hand. If chain is not held securely by brake when brake is engaged, adjust as follows:

Remove guide bar, chain and brake cover (16—Fig. JD97). Loosen screw (11) and turn band adjuster (9) while intermittently engaging handle until desired brake tension is obtained. Be sure that clutch drum turns freely when brake lever is in disengaged position. Tighten adjuster screw to 6.8-7.9 N·m (60-70 in.-lbs.).

To remove chain brake assembly, remove guide bar cover, guide bar and chain. Remove brake cover (16—Fig. JD97). Remove brake band retainer (8), pivot bolt (15) and brake band anchor bolt (11). Remove chain brake components and inspect for wear or damage.

When reassembling, tighten pivot bolt (15) to 5.6 N·m (50 in.-lbs.). If handle pivot pin (1) was removed, apply thread locking compound to plain end of pin, then install plain end of pin into hole in casting until flush with back of casting. Be sure cam on handle (3) is positioned under lobe on connector lever (5). Tighten brake band retainer screw to 6.8-7.9 N·m (60-70 in.-lbs.). Adjust brake as previously outlined.

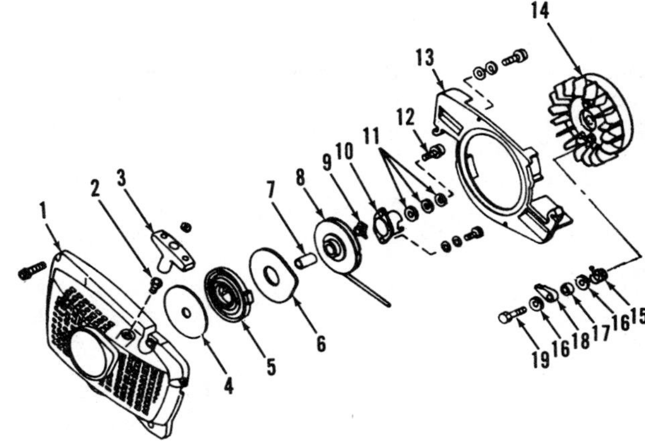

Fig. JD95—Exploded view of rewind starter assembly.

1. Starter housing
2. Rope guide
3. Rope handle
4. Plate
5. Rewind spring
6. Plate
7. Bushing
8. Pulley
9. Clip
10. Pawl catch
11. Washers
12. Screw
13. Plate
14. Flywheel
15. Spring
16. Washers
17. Spacer
18. Pawl
19. Screw

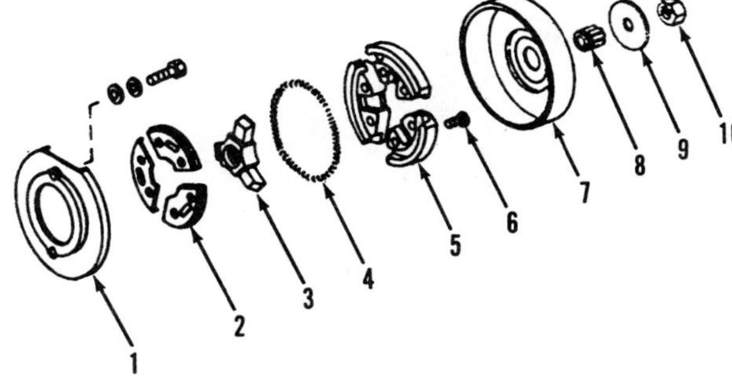

Fig. JD96—Exploded view of clutch assembly.

1. Plate
2. Clutch plates
3. Clutch hub
4. Spring
5. Clutch shoes
6. Screw
7. Clutch drum
8. Bearing
9. Washer
10. Nut

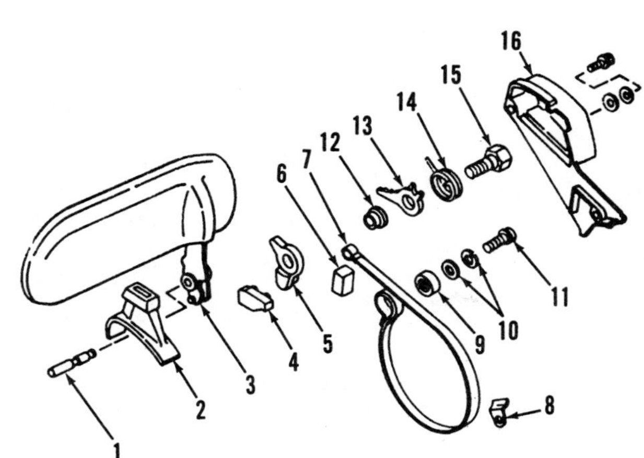

Fig. JD97—Exploded view of chain brake assembly.

1. Pivot pin
2. Cover
3. Handle
4. Rubber cushion
5. Actuating lever
6. Seal
7. Brake band
8. Band retainer
9. Adjuster
10. Washers
11. Screw
12. Spacer
13. Stop lever
14. Spring
15. Pivot bolt
16. Cover

JOHN DEERE

Model	Bore mm (in.)	Stroke mm (in.)	Displacement cc (cu. in.)	Drive Type
25EV	35 (1.38)	29 (1.14)	27.9 (1.7)	Direct

MAINTENANCE

SPARK PLUG. Recommended spark plug for all models is Champion CJ8Y. Spark plug electrode gap should be 0.6-0.7 mm (0.024-0.028 in.).

CARBURETOR. A Zama C1S diaphragm type carburetor (5—Fig. JD100) is used on Model 25EV. Refer to Zama section of CARBURETOR SERVICE section for service procedures and exploded view of carburetor.

Initial adjustment of low and high speed mixture screws is $1^1/_8$ turns open from a lightly seated position. Make final adjustment with engine warm and running. Adjust low speed mixture screw so engine idles smoothly and will accelerate cleanly without hesitation. Adjust idle speed screw so engine idles just below clutch engagement speed. Adjust high speed screw until maximum engine speed at full throttle with no load is obtained and four-cycling sound stops, then turn screw out (counterclockwise) until a four-cycling sound just returns at full throttle (no-load). Do not operate saw with high speed mixture too lean as engine damage may occur due to lack of lubrication and overheating.

Fig. JD100—Exploded view of fuel tank and related components.

1. Screw
2. Choke knob
3. Choke shutter
4. Spacer
5. Carburetor
6. Gasket
7. Reed valve assy.
8. Gasket
9. Fuel tank
10. Tank vent
11. Cushion
12. Fuel filter
13. Washer
14. Fuel hose

IGNITION. All models are equipped with a capacitor discharge ignition system. Refer to Fig. JD101. Ignition timing is fixed at 30 degrees BTDC and is not adjustable. Air gap between flywheel magnets and ignition module core should be 0.3-0.4 mm (0.012-0.016 in.).

LUBRICATION. Engine is lubricated by mixing engine oil with fuel. Regular grade automotive gasoline is recommended. Recommended oil is John Deere 2-Cycle Engine Oil mixed with the fuel at a 50:1 ratio. If John Deere 2-Cycle Engine Oil is not available, a good quality oil designed for air-cooled two-stroke engines may be used when mixed with fuel at a 32:1 ratio. Use a separate container when mixing the oil and gas.

All models are equipped with an automatic chain oil pump. John Deere Bar and Chain Lubricant is recommended to lubricate the chain and bar. This oil is prediluted to operate properly in a wide range of temperatures.

Clean SAE 10W-40 automotive oil may also be used to lubricate chain and bar. At temperatures below -10°C (15°F), oil may be cut with up to 33 percent kerosene to aid lubrication.

REPAIRS

CYLINDER, PISTON, PIN AND RINGS. Cylinder bore is chrome plated on all models and oversize pistons and rings are not available. Renew cylinder if scoring, flaking, wear or other damage to chrome surface of cylinder is evident.

Piston (4—Fig. JD102) has a single piston ring (3). Maximum allowable ring end gap is 0.5 mm (0.020 in.). Insert a new ring in piston ring groove and use a feeler gage to measure ring side clearance. Maximum allowable ring side

Fig. JD101—View of capacitor discharge ignition components.

1. Flywheel
2. Ignition module
3. Stop switch
4. Ignition coil
5. Spark plug

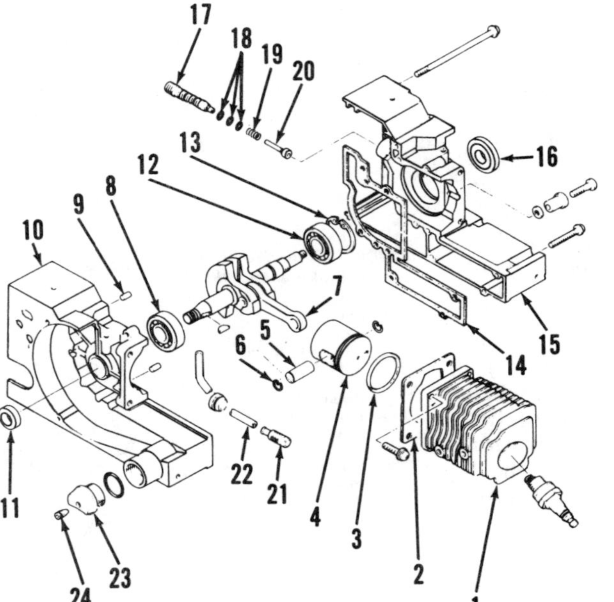

Fig. JD102—Exploded view of engine and automatic oil pump.

1. Cylinder
2. Gasket
3. Piston ring
4. Piston
5. Piston pin
6. Wire retainer
7. Crankshaft & connecting rod assy.
8. Main bearing
9. Dowel
10. Left crankcase half
11. Seal
12. Main bearing
13. Snap ring
14. Gasket
15. Right crankcase half
16. Seal
17. Oil pump housing
18. "O" ring
19. Spring
20. Pump plunger
21. Oil filter
22. Oil hose
23. Oil filler cap
24. Oil tank vent

clearance in piston ring groove is 0.1 mm (0.004 in.). Renew piston if side clearance is excessive. A locating pin is present in piston ring groove to prevent piston ring rotation. Be sure ring end gap is indexed with locating pin when installing cylinder. Tighten cylinder retaining screws evenly to 3.5-4.0 N·m (30-35 in.-lbs.).

The floating type piston pin (5) is retained by wire retainers (6) and rides directly in the small end of connecting rod. Be sure piston is properly supported when removing or installing piston pin to prevent damage to piston or connecting rod. Arrow on piston crown must point toward exhaust port when installing piston.

CRANKSHAFT, CONNECTING ROD AND CRANKCASE. The crankshaft and connecting rod unit assembly (7—Fig. JD102) is supported in the crankcase by ball bearings at both ends. Crankshaft and connecting rod are not available separately. Crankcase halves (10 and 15) must be split to remove crankshaft assembly.

Check crankshaft runout by supporting crankshaft at points (A—Fig. JD103) and measuring at points (B). Maximum allowable runout is 0.05 mm (0.002 in.). Check main bearings (8 and 12—Fig. JD102) for smooth operation and renew as necessary. Check rotation of connecting rod around crankpin and renew assembly if roughness or other damage is found.

Flywheel side main bearing (8—Fig. JD102) is held in position by a shoulder in crankcase half (10), while a snap ring (13) retains clutch side main bearing (12). Snap ring (13) should be installed in crankcase so open end of ring is around oil hole and snap ring does not obstruct lubrication passage. Preheating crankcase halves with a hair dryer or heat lamp will ease installation of main bearings. Install crankshaft seals (11 and 16), open side toward each other, flush with outer face of crankcase. Tighten crankcase screws evenly to final torque of 2.0-2.5 N·m (17-22 in.-lbs.). Tighten flywheel nut to 17.5-21.5 N·m (155-190 in.-lbs.).

REED VALVE. Reed valve (7—Fig. JD100) should be inspected whenever carburetor is removed. Reed petal (P—Fig. JD104) should seat very lightly against insulator block (B) throughout its entire length with the least possible tension. Tip of reed petal must not stand open more than 0.3 mm (0.012 in.). Reed stop (S) opening should be 6 mm (0.24 in.). Individual reed valve components are not available.

CLUTCH. Refer to Fig. JD105 for exploded view of three-shoe centrifugal clutch used on all models. Clutch hub (1) and nut (8) have left-hand threads (turn clockwise to remove). Clutch drum (5) rides on a needle roller bearing (6). Needle roller bearing should be inspected for damage or discoloration and lubricated with a suitable high temperature grease. Inspect clutch shoes and drum for damage due to overheating. Clutch hub (1), shoes (2) and spring (3) are available as a unit assembly only.

When installing clutch, clutch hub should be positioned with chamfered thread opening side towards crankshaft. Tighten clutch hub (1) to 28-31 N·m (20-23 ft.-lbs.) and nut (8) to 13-15 N·m (9-11 ft.-lbs.).

OIL PUMP. All models are equipped with an automatic, plunger type chain oil pump. Plunger (20—Fig. JD102) is actuated by a cam on the crankshaft. Oil pump output is adjusted by rotating the pump housing (17). Oil pump may be removed for cleaning and inspection after removing the air filter and unscrewing oil pump assembly from crankcase.

To check oil pump operation, apply oil drops to oil inlet hole of pump cylinder and make sure oil is discharged from outlet holes while operating pump plunger manually. Oil pump, other than "O" rings (18), is serviced as an assembly. When installing pump, screw the housing (17) in until lightly seated. Run saw at medium speed and unscrew pump housing approximately one turn until maximum oil output is obtained. Pump housing location should be marked for future reference. Rotate pump housing counterclockwise from maximum output position to decrease oil output.

REWIND STARTER. To disassemble rewind starter, remove starter housing (14—Fig. JD106), remove rope handle and allow rope to rewind into housing. Unscrew rope pulley screw (10) and remove rope pulley (12), being careful not to dislodge rewind spring. If necessary to remove rewind spring, care should be used not to allow spring to uncoil uncontrolled.

Install rewind spring in starter housing with coils wrapped in a clockwise direction from outer end of spring. Wind rope around pulley in a clockwise direction as viewed from flywheel side of pulley. Turn pulley three turns clockwise before passing rope through outlet. Check starter operation. It should be possible to pull rope to its full exten-

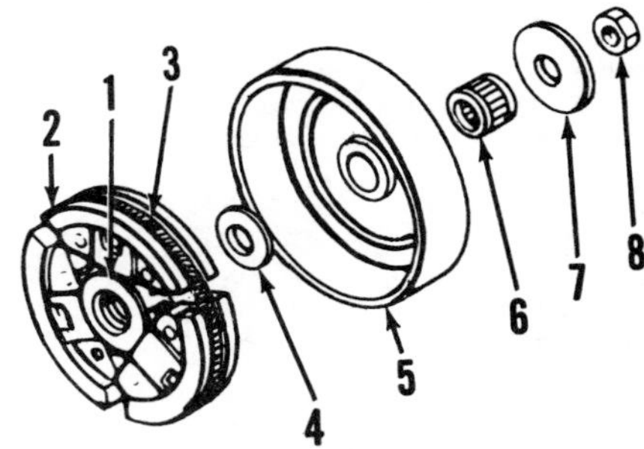

Fig. JD105—Exploded view of clutch assembly.

1. Hub
2. Shoe
3. Spring
4. Washer
5. Drum
6. Needle bearing
7. Washer
8. Nut

Fig. JD103—Measure crankshaft runout by supporting crankshaft at points (A). Maximum runout measured at points (B) should not exceed 0.05 mm (0.002 in.).

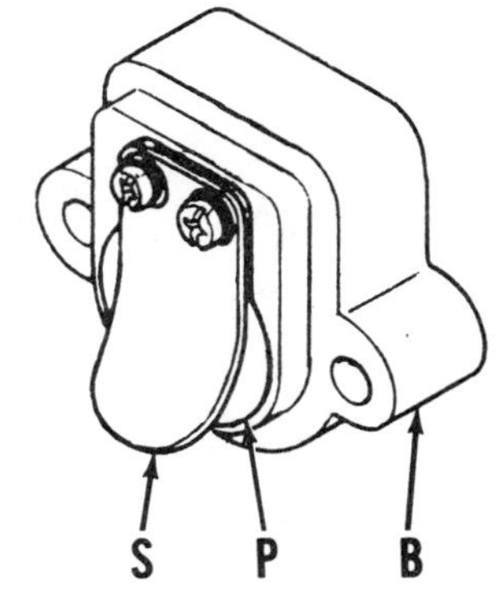

Fig. JD104—View of reed valve unit assembly. Refer to text for service information.

Fig. JD106—Exploded view of rewind starter assembly.

1. Flywheel
2. Lockwasher
3. Spring washer
4. Nut
5. Pawl spring
6. Washer
7. Pawl
8. Spacer
9. Screw
10. Screw
11. Washer
12. Rope pulley
13. Rewind spring
14. Starter housing
15. Rope guide
16. Rope handle

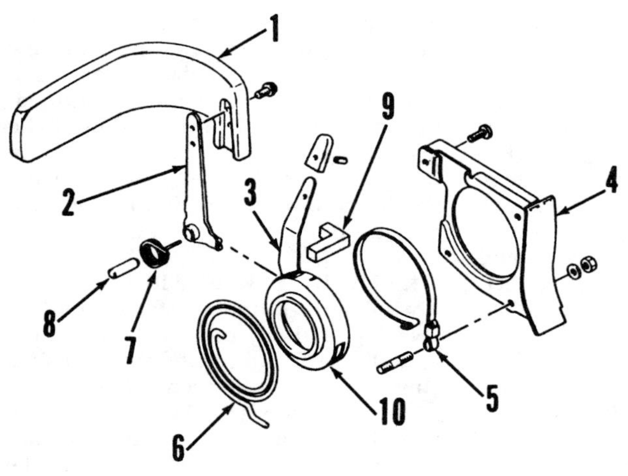

Fig. JD107—Exploded view of chain brake system used on some saws.

1. Hand guard
2. Brake lever
3. Reset lever
4. Brake cover
5. Brake band
6. Brake spring
7. Spring
8. Shaft
9. Seal
10. Brake band case

sion and still turn rope pulley approximately 1/2 turn clockwise. If rewind spring coil binds before rope is fully extended, reduce tension on spring by pulling rope up into notch in rope pulley and allowing pulley to rotate one turn counterclockwise. Recheck starter operation.

CHAIN BRAKE. Some saws are equipped with a chain brake system designed to stop chain movement should kickback occur. Chain brake is activated when operator's hand strikes hand guard (1—Fig. JD107), tripping brake lever (2) and releasing brake band case (10) which allows brake spring (6) to draw brake band (5) tight around clutch drum.

Brake band (5), brake band case (10) and brake spring (6) are removed and renewed as an assembly. No adjustment of chain brake system is required. Make certain clutch drum turns freely with chain brake in off position after reassembly of chain brake system.

SACHS-DOLMAR

Model	Bore	Stroke	Displ.	Drive Type
CT	56 mm (2.20 in.)	48 mm (1.89 in.)	118 cc (7.2 cu. in.)	Direct

MAINTENANCE

SPARK PLUG. Recommended spark plug is Bosch WSR6F. Spark plug electrode gap should be 0.51 mm (0.020 in.).

CARBURETOR. Model CT is equipped with a Tillotson HL diaphragm carburetor. Initial setting of idle and high speed mixture screws is 1¼ turns open from a lightly seated position. Adjust low speed mixture so engine will accelerate cleanly without hesitation. The high speed screw should be adjusted to give optimum performance under load. Adjust idle speed to just below clutch engagement speed.

The carburetor used on Model CT is equipped with a ball valve type governor which enrichens the fuel mixture at the governed speed and prevents engine overspeeding. Original governor assembly is tuned for each engine and cannot be renewed. If damaged, a fiber disk must be used in place of the governor spring and ball valve.

Refer to Tillotson section of CARBURETOR SERVICE section for carburetor operation and overhaul.

IGNITION TIMING. Early models were equipped with a breaker-point ignition system while later models are equipped with a breakerless electronic ignition system. Breaker-point gap on models so equipped should be 0.4 mm (0.016 in.)

Ignition timing on models equipped with breaker points should be 3.4 mm (0.134 in.) BTDC. Timing on models with electronic ignition should be 2.6 mm (0.102 in.) BTDC.

Ignition timing on electronic ignition is correct if marks on flywheel, crankcase and ignition base plate are aligned. Refer to Fig. D1. If flywheel, crankcase or ignition base plate has been renewed or altered, use the following procedure to time engine: Position piston at ignition firing position using a dial indicator assembly protruding into spark plug hole. Make a mark on crankcase which is aligned with mark on flywheel. Remove flywheel and loosen ignition base plate screws. Align mark on ignition base plate with mark on crankcase and tighten base plate screws.

Air gap between poles of ignition coil and flywheel and trigger coil and flywheel should be 0.25-0.39 mm (0.010-0.015 in.).

TROUBLE-SHOOTING ELECTRONIC IGNITION. If spark plug will not fire and spark plug and wiring are not faulty, proceed as follows: Remove flywheel and check for loose, corroded or damaged connections and wires. Discharge condenser by shorting to ground.

Fig. D1—Electronic ignition is correctly timed when marks on crankcase and ignition base plate are aligned.

To check ignition coil, disconnect ignition coil leads. Connect ohmmeter leads to primary wire of coil and to ground. Resistance should be 1 ohm. Connect ohmmeter leads to high tension wire and to ground. Resistance should be 1,000-3,000 ohms. Renew coil if shorted or open windings are found or ohmmeter readings do not agree with specifications.

To check charging coil, disconnect coil leads. Some charging coils have a diode connected to coil. Connect ohmmeter leads to coil leads and read resistance. If coil does not have a diode connected to coil, resistance should be 500-1600 ohms. If coil has a diode connected, connect ohmmeter leads to coil leads, take reading, then reverse ohmmeter leads and take another reading. Second reading should be ten times greater or smaller than first reading. Renew coil if any readings are incorrect.

Capacitance of storage condenser should be 0.6-0.9 mfd. Condenser is mounted integrally with base plate and must be renewed as a unit.

Trigger coil may be checked by substituting a new or good coil in place of original coil. Ignition timing must be checked and readjusted if necessary when trigger coil or ignition coil is renewed.

Fig. D4—Exploded view of Model CT engine.

1. Cylinder
2. Piston ring
3. Piston
4. Snap ring
5. Piston pin
6. Gasket
7. Bearing
8. Washer
9. Clutch drum
10. Bearing race
11. Bearing
12. Retainer plate
13. Clutch springs
14. Clutch hub
15. Retainer plate
16. Clutch shoe
17. Bearing
18. Nut
19. Crankshaft & rod assy.
20. Washer
21. Slotted nut
22. Bearing

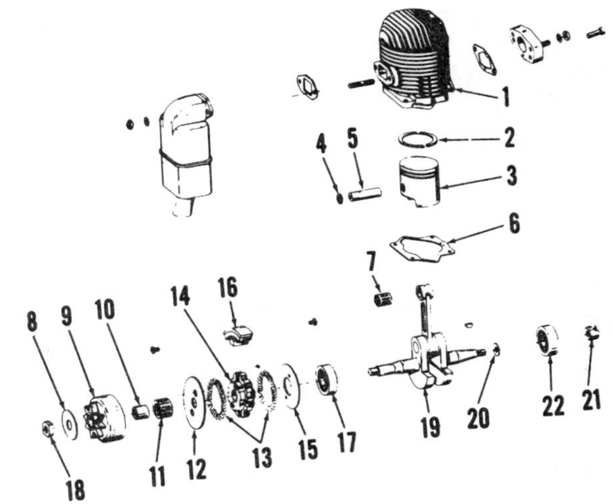

Illustrations courtesy Dolmar U.S.A., Inc.

LUBRICATION. The engine is lubricated by mixing oil with the fuel. Recommended oil is Sachs-Dolmar two-stroke engine oil. Fuel mixture should be a 40:1 ratio when using recommended oil. During break-in period (first the hours of operation), mix oil and fuel at a 30:1 ratio. If Sachs-Dolmar two-stroke engine oil in not available, a good quality oil designed for use in air-cooled two-stroke engines may be used when mixed at a 25:1 ratio after break-in period or 20:1 ratio during break-in period. Use a separate container when mixing fuel and oil.

Model CT is equipped with an automatic chain oil pump. Oil pump is driven by worm gear on engine crankshaft. Oil pump output may be varied by turning adjusting screw (16 – Fig. D6). Turning screw clockwise will decrease oil output while turning screw counterclockwise will increase oil output.

CARBON. Carbon deposits should be removed from muffler and exhaust ports at regular intervals. When scraping carbon, be careful not to damage cylinder or piston. Do not allow loosened carbon into cylinder.

REPAIRS

PISTON, PIN, RINGS AND CYLINDER. To remove cylinder on Model CT, remove front handle and carburetor cover. Disconnect oil lines and remove starter housing assembly. Remove carburetor and muffler. Remove cylinder.

CONNECTING ROD, CRANKSHAFT AND CRANKCASE. The crankcase must be split to remove connecting rod and crankshaft assembly. To disassemble crankcase, remove chain, clutch, handle assembly, rewind starter, ignition assembly, cylinder and piston. Remove any other components which prevent disassembling crankcase. Remove clutch side crankcase half first from crankshaft. Separate crankshaft and remaining crankcase.

Connecting rod and crankshaft are a pressed together assembly which should be disassembled only by a shop with the tools and experience necessary to assemble and realign crankshaft. Connecting rod and bearing are available. Crankshaft runout should not exceed 0.015 mm (0.0006 in.). Heat crankcase before installing crankshaft and bearings.

CLUTCH. Refer to Fig. D4 for exploded view of clutch. Clutch nut has left-hand threads. A puller should be used to remove hub (14 – Fig. D4). Clutch springs should be renewed in pairs. Tighten clutch nut to 39.4 N·m (29 ft.-lbs.)

CHAIN OILER. Model CT is equipped with an automatic chain oiler driven by a worm gear.

The pump shaft and worm gear (4 – Fig. D6) is driven by a notch in flywheel retaining nut (21 – Fig. D4). Oil pump may be disassembled by removing starter housing and referring to Fig. D4.

REWIND STARTER. Refer to Fig. D6 for exploded view of rewind starter. When disassembling starter, be sure rewind spring is not allowed to uncoil uncontrolled as spring may cause personal injury. Heat starter housing to remove and install pivot pin (26). Install pin so snap ring groove stands above pin bore shoulder 18.1 mm (0.713 in.) Rewind spring should be installed with windings in clockwise direction as viewed with spring in housing. Rope should be wound on pulley in clockwise direction as viewed with pulley installed in starter housing.

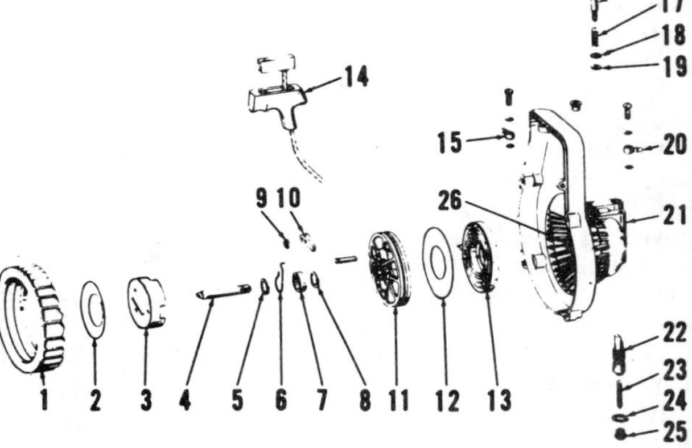

Fig. D6 – Exploded view of rewind starter and oil pump. Turn adjusting screw (16) to regulate oil pump flow.

1. Flywheel
2. Plate
3. Starter cup
4. Oil pump shaft
5. Snap ring
6. Pawl spring
7. Spacer
8. Snap ring
9. "E" ring
10. Starter pawl
11. Rope pulley
12. Plate
13. Rewind spring
14. Rope handle
15. Oil fitting
16. Oil pump adjusting screw
17. Spring
18. Shim (0.5 mm)
19. Washer
20. Oil fitting
21. Starter housing
22. Oil pump gear & shaft
23. Spring
24. Washer
25. Plug
26. Pivot pin

SACHS-DOLMAR

Model	Bore	Stroke	Displ.	Drive Type
122 Super, 123	47 mm (1.850 in.)	40 mm (1.575 in.)	70 cc (4.2 cu. in.)	Direct
133, 133 Super	52 mm (2.047 in.)	40 mm (1.575 in.)	85 cc (5.2 cu. in.)	Direct
143MX	55 mm (2.165 in.)	40 mm (1.575 in.)	95 cc (5.8 cu. in.)	Direct
152, 153	55 mm (2.165 in.)	42 mm (1.654 in.)	100 cc (6.1 cu. in.)	Direct

MAINTENANCE

SPARK PLUG. Recomended spark plug for Model 122 Super is Bosch HS5E. Recommended spark plug for all other models is Bosch WSR6F. Spark plug electrode gap should be 0.51 mm (0.020 in.).

CARBURETOR. All models are equipped with a Tillotson HS diaphragm carburetor. Refer to Tillotson section of CARBURETOR SERVICE section for overhaul and exploded view of carburetor.

Initial setting of idle and high speed mixture screws is approximately one turn open from a lightly seated position. Final adjustment should be made with engine running at operating temperature. Adjust low speed mixture so engine will accelerate cleanly without hesitation. Adjust high speed mixture to obtain optimum performance under a cutting load. Adjust idle speed screw so engine idles just below clutch engagement speed.

IGNITION. Early 122 Super, 152 and 153 models are equipped with a conventional flywheel magneto ignition system. Breaker-point gap on models so equipped should be 0.3-0.4 mm (0.012-0.016 in.). Later 122 Super, 152 and 153 models, and all 133, 133 Super and 143 MX models are equipped with a breakerless ignition system. Ignition timing should be 2.1-2.5 mm (0.083-0.098 in.) BTDC on Models 152 and 153, and 2.2 mm (0.086 in.) BTDC on all other models.

Individual components of the breakerless ignition system used on some models are not available separately.

Ignition timing on Model 122 Super is set using Dolmar tool 956 007 000 as shown in Fig. D9. With right side of timing tool resting against base of stator plate, left side of timing tool should be aligned with mark on stator plate. If mark and edge of timing tool are not aligned, loosen stator plate screws and rotate stator plate until mark is aligned with tool.

To check timing on all other models, position engine at recommended ignition point using a dial indicator assembly protruding into spark plug hole. Make reference marks on flywheel and starter housing. Check timing with a power timing light at 8,000 rpm. If reference marks are not aligned at 8,000 rpm, rotate stator plate to adjust.

LUBRICATION. The engine is lubricated by mixing oil with regular grade gasoline. Recommended oil is Sachs-Dolmar two-stroke engine oil.

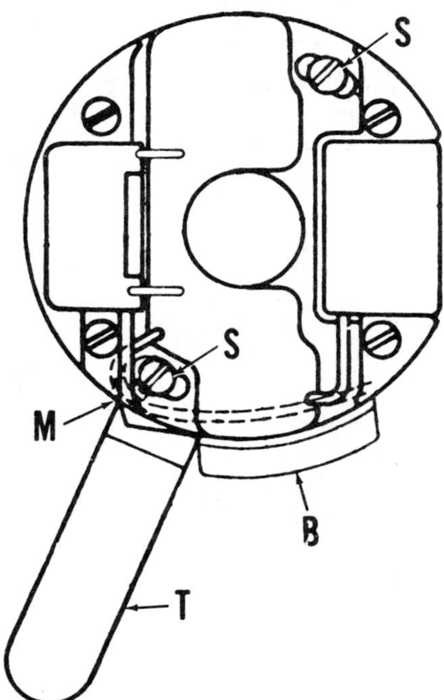

Fig. D9 — View showing location of timing gage (T) when setting ignition timing on Model 122 Super. Mark (M) on stator plate should align with left edge of gage (T) when right edge of gage is against stator plate base (B). Loosen stator plate screws (S) and rotate stator plate if mark (M) and gage are not aligned.

Fuel and oil mixture should be a 40:1 ratio when using recommended oil. During break-in period (first ten hours of operation), mix fuel and oil at a 30:1 ratio. If Sachs-Dolmar two-stroke engine oil is not available, a good quality oil designed for use in air-cooled two-stroke engines may be used when mixed at a 25:1 ratio after break-in period or 20:1 ratio during break-in period. Use a separate container when mixing oil and fuel.

All models are equipped with an automatic chain oil pump. Oil pump is driven by a worm gear on engine crankshaft. Oil pump output is varied by turning adjusting screw adjacent to clutch on Models 123 and 153 or adjacent to chain bar spike on all other models. Turning screw clockwise will decrease oil output while turning screw counterclockwise will increase oil output.

REPAIRS

PISTON, PIN, RINGS AND CYLINDER. The cylinder may be removed after removal of airbox cover, air cleaner, carburetor, cylinder shroud and muffler. The cylinder is chrome plated and should be inspected for excessive wear or damage to chrome plating.

Piston pin is retained by wire retainers and rides in roller bearing in the small end of the connecting rod. The piston is equipped with two piston rings which are retained in position by locating pins in the ring grooves. The piston must be installed with the arrow on the piston crown pointing toward the exhaust port. Some pistons have a letter "A" stamped near the arrow which must not be confused with letter stamped on piston crown to indicate piston size.

Cylinder and piston are marked "A," "B" or "C" during production to obtain desired piston-to-cylinder clearance. Cylinder and piston must have same letter marking to obtain proper clearance. Cylinders are stamped on top of cylinder or on cylinder frame. Pistons are stamped on piston crown but letter indicating piston size should not be confused with letter "A" which is stamped on some piston crowns to indicate which side of piston must be installed adjacent to exhaust port. Tighten cylinder screws to 10 N·m (88 in.-lbs.).

CONNECTING ROD, CRANKSHAFT AND CRANKCASE. Crankcase halves must be split on all models to remove crankshaft assembly. The crankshaft is supported at both ends by ball bearings. Connecting rod and crankshaft are a pressed together assembly which should be disassembled only be a shop with the tools and experience necessary to assemble and realign crankshaft. Connecting rod, bearing and crankpin are available as a unit assembly.

Heat crankcase to ease installation of main bearings. Heat main bearing inner races to install crankshaft. Tighten crankcase screws to 7 N·m (62 in.-lbs.).

On Models 122 Super and 152, the automatic oil pump is driven by worm (2–Fig. D11) located between main bearing and oil seal. On these models, worm must be pressed on crankshaft prior to installing crankshaft assembly in crankcase.

CLUTCH. Three, four and six-shoe clutches have been used. The clutch on all models is retained by a nut with left-hand threads. A puller should be used to remove clutch hub from crankshaft. Models 122 Super and early 152 are equipped with two springs (15–Fig. D11) which should be renewed in pairs.

Tighten clutch nut to 26 N·m (19 ft.-lbs.) on all models.

CHAIN OIL PUMP. All models are equipped with an automatic chain oil pump. The oil pump on Models 123, 133, 133 Super, 143 MX and 153 is contained in a removable oil pump housing (10–Fig. D11A) with plunger (9) driven by worm gear (2) located outside the right crankcase oil seal. The oil pump on 122 Super and 152 models is contained in the right crankcase half as shown in Fig. D11. Plunger (5) is driven by worm gear (2) which is located between main bearing and oil seal (11).

Worm gear (2–Fig. D11 or D11A) may be extracted without removing crankshaft by using special Sachs-Dolmar tool 957 434 00. Use a thrust cap over crankshaft to prevent damage to crankshaft or threads. Mark worm gear location on Models 122 Super and 152 prior to removal. Heat worm gear approximately 104° C (220° F) prior to installation. Install Model 152 worm so smooth end abuts main bearing. Install Model 123 worm so outer edge is 11.8-12.4 mm (0.465-0.488 in.) from pump mounting surface on crankcase.

On Models 122 Super and 152, be sure cam screw (9–Fig. D11) is correctly meshed with groove in plunger (5) during assembly. Install seal (11–Fig. D11A) on Models 123, 133, 133 Super, 143 MX and 153 with seal lip facing toward clutch.

REWIND STARTER. Refer to Fig. D12 or D13 for exploded views of rewind starters. To disassemble starter, remove starter housing from saw, remove rope handle and allow rope to wind into starter. Remove snap ring(s) and withdraw rope pulley, being careful not to dislodge rewind spring, precautions should be taken to prevent spring from uncoiling uncontrolled.

Install rewind spring in starter housing in clockwise direction from outer end. Starter rope length is 100 cm (39.4 in.) for Models 122 Super, 123, 133, 133

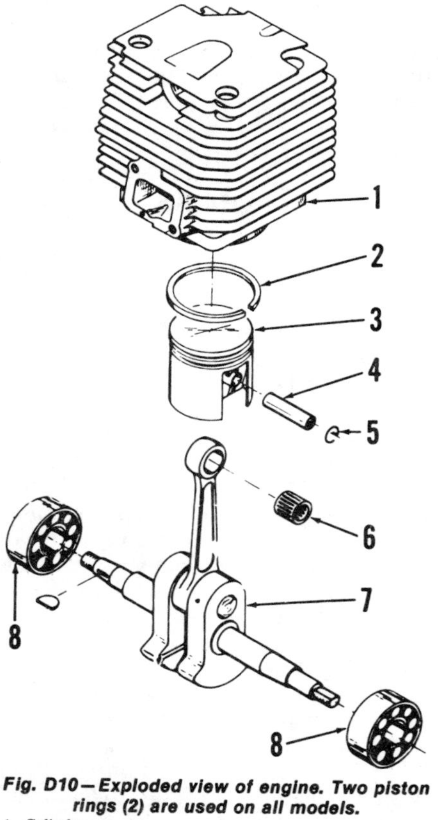

Fig. D10—Exploded view of engine. Two piston rings (2) are used on all models.

1. Cylinder
2. Piston rings
3. Piston
4. Piston pin
5. Pin retainer
6. Needle bearing
7. Crankshaft & rod assy.
8. Ball bearing

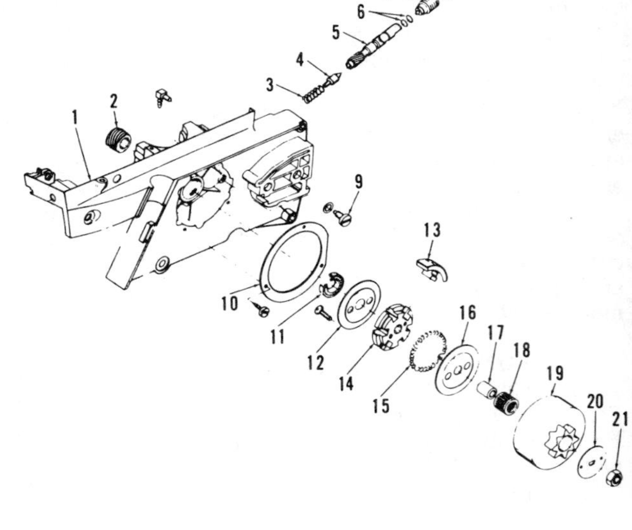

Fig. D11—Exploded view of Model 152 oil pump and clutch assemblies. Model 122 Super is similar. Two garter springs (15) are used. Oil pump worm gear (2) is pressed on crankshaft.

1. Right crankcase half
2. Oil pump worm gear
3. Spring
4. Thrust pin
5. Oil pump plunger
6. "O" rings
7. Adjusting screw
8. Snap ring
9. Cam screw
10. Cover plate
11. Seal
12. Guide plate
13. Clutch shoe
14. Clutch hub
15. Garter spring
16. Guide plate
17. Inner bearing race
18. Needle bearing
19. Clutch drum
20. Washer
21. Nut

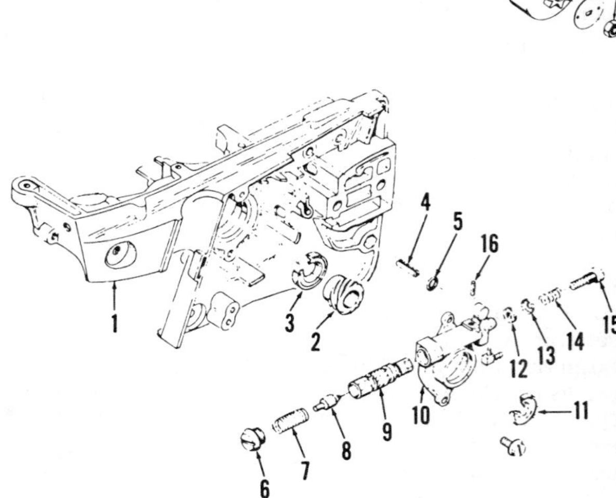

Fig. D11A—Exploded view of oil pump used on Models 123, 133, 133 Super, 143 MX and 153.

1. Right crankcase half
2. Worm gear
3. Oil seal
4. Pin
5. "O" ring
6. Plug
7. Spring
8. Thrust pin
9. Plunger
10. Pump housing
11. Seal
12. Rubber washer
13. Spring seat
14. Spring
15. Adjusting screw
16. Pin

Super and 143 MX, and 115 cm (45¼ in.) for Models 152 and 153. Wind rope around rope pulley in clockwise direction as viewed with pulley in starter housing. Pawl springs (8–Fig. D13) on Models 152 and 153 must be positioned against spring spacer (7) as shown in Fig. D14. To place tension on starter rope, rotate rope pulley clockwise 4½ turns on Models 122 Super, 123, 133, 133 Super and 143 MX and 5 turns on Models 152 and 153 before passing rope through outlet. Check operation of rewind starter. Rope handle should rest snugly against starter housing with rope released. It should be possible to turn rope pulley clockwise at least ¼ turn with rope fully extended. Readjust spring tension if rope handle is loose against starter housing or rewind spring is coil bound with rope fully extended.

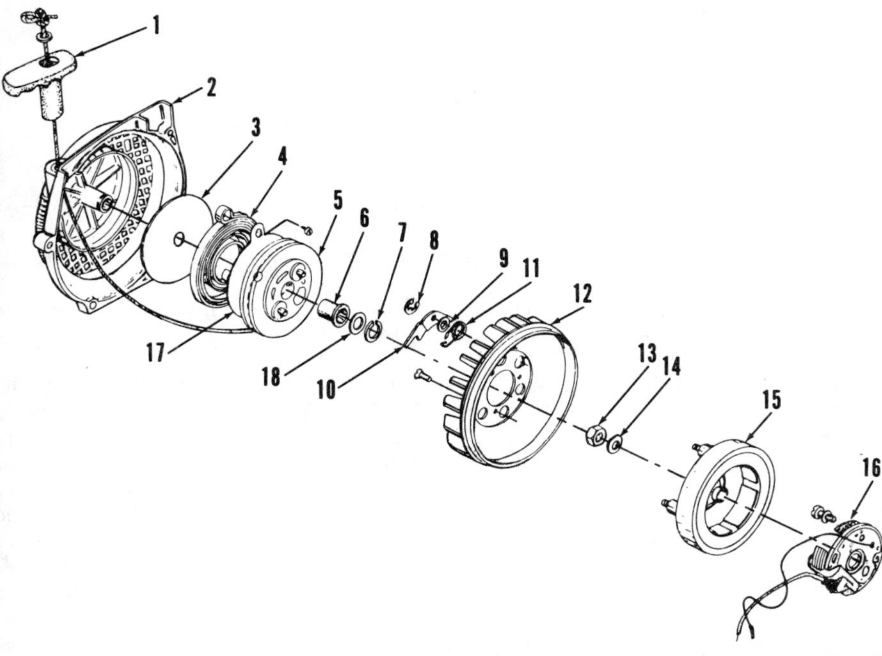

Fig. D12—Exploded view of rewind starter and ignition assemblies used on Models 123, 133, 133 Super and 143MX. Model 122 Super is similar.

1. Rope handle
2. Starter housing
3. Spacer plate
4. Rewind spring
5. Rope pulley
6. Bushing
7. Snap ring
8. "E" ring
9. Washer
10. Pawl
11. Spring
12. Fan
13. Nut
14. Spring washer
15. Flywheel
16. Stator plate & ignition assy.
17. Spacer plate
18. Washer

CHAIN BRAKE. Some models are equipped with a chain brake system designed to stop chain movement should kickback occur. Chain brake is activated when operator's hand strikes hand guard (1–Fig. D15) causing chain brake lever (2) to disengage brake band and lever assembly (6) allowing spring (8) to draw brake band tight around clutch drum (9). Pull back hand guard to reset mechanism.

Disassembly for repair or component renewal is evident after referral to exploded view and inspection of unit. No adjustment of chain brake system is required.

Fig. D14—View showing installation of spring spacer (7), pawl springs (8) and pawls (9).

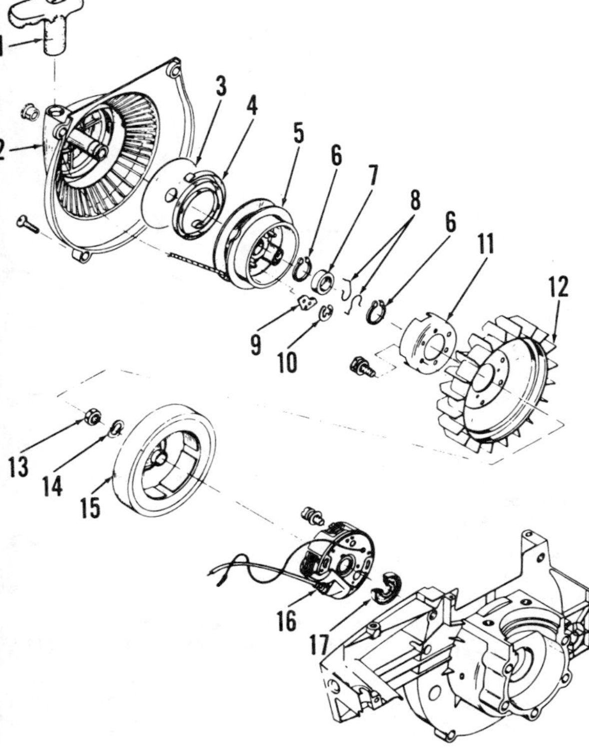

Fig. D13—Exploded view of rewind starter and ignition assemblies used on Model 152. Model 153 is similar. Refer to Fig. D14 for installation of pawl springs (8).

1. Rope handle
2. Starter housing
3. Spacer
4. Rewind spring
5. Rope pulley
6. Snap ring
7. Spacer
8. Pawl springs
9. Pawl
10. "E" ring
11. Starter cup
12. Fan
13. Nut
14. Spring washer
15. Flywheel
16. Stator plate & ignition assy.
17. Seal

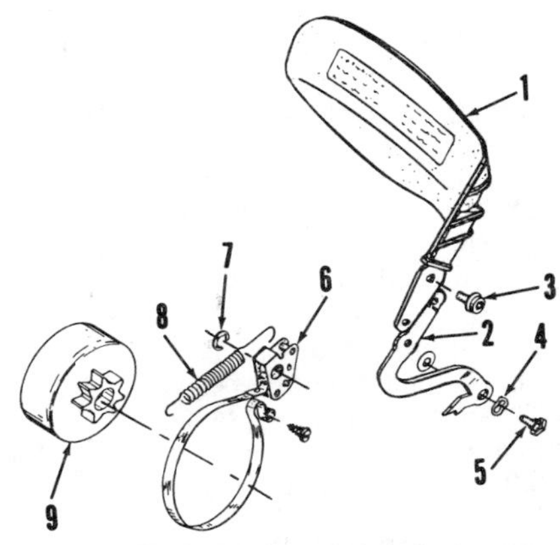

Fig. D15—Exploded view of chain brake system typical of type used on all models.

1. Hand guard
2. Brake lever
3. Screw
4. Wave washer
5. Shoulder bolt
6. Brake band & lever assy.
7. "E" ring
8. Spring
9. Clutch drum

Illustrations courtesy Dolmar U.S.A., Inc.

SACHS-DOLMAR

Model	Bore	Stroke	Displ.	Drive Type
112, 113, 114	45 mm (1.77 in.)	32 mm (1.26 in.)	51 cc (3.1 cu. in.)	Direct
116	45 mm (1.77 in.)	35 mm (1.38 in.)	56 cc (3.4 cu. in.)	Direct
117, 119, 120	47 mm (1.85 in.)	35 mm (1.38 in.)	61 cc (3.7 cu. in.)	Direct
120 Super	49 mm (1.93 in.)	36 mm (1.42 in.)	68 cc (4.1 cu. in.)	Direct

MAINTENANCE

SPARK PLUG. Recommended spark plug is Bosch WSR6F. Electrode gap should be 0.51 mm (0.020 in.).

CARBURETOR. Bing 48B102, Tillotson HK and HS and Walbro HD and HDA diaphragm type carburetors have been used. Refer to appropriate sections of CARBURETOR SERVICE section for service procedures and exploded views.

Initial setting of low speed mixture screw and high speed mixture screw is one turn open on Models 114, 117 and 119. Initial adjustment on all other models is 1½ turns open for low speed mixture and one turn open for high speed mixture. Final adjustment should be made with engine running at operating temperature. Adjust low speed mixture screw so engine will accelerate cleanly without hesitation. Adjust high speed mixture screw to obtain optimum performance with saw under cutting load. Do not adjust high speed mixture too lean as overheating and engine damage could result. Adjust idle speed to just below clutch engagement speed.

IGNITION. Models 112 and 117 are equipped with a breaker-point flywheel magneto ignition system. Breaker-point gap should be 0.3-0.4 mm (0.012-0.016 in.). Special Sachs-Dolmar tool 956 009 000 or a cutaway flywheel must be used to set breaker-point gap. Ignition timing is 1.8 mm (0.071 in.) BTDC for Model 112 and 2.2 mm (0.087 in.) for Model 117. Rotate stator plate to adjust ignition timing. Air gap between ignition coil laminations and flywheel should be 0.3 mm (0.012 in.) on Model 117 and 0.20-0.30 mm (0.008-0.012 in.) on Model 112.

Models 113, 114, 116, 119, 120 and 120 Super are equipped with a breakerless solid-state ignition system. Ignition timing is 1.8 mm (0.071 in.) BTDC for Model 114 and 2.2 mm (0.087 in.) for Model 119. Rotate stator plate to adjust ignition timing. Timing is fixed on all other models and not adjustable. Air gap between ignition coil laminations and flywheel should be 0.20-0.30 mm (0.008-0.012 in.). Flywheel nut on all models should be tightened to 30 N·m (22 ft.-lbs.).

LUBRICATION. The engine is lubricated by mixing oil with the fuel. Recommended oil is Sachs-Dolmar two-stroke engine oil. Fuel mixture should be a 40:1 ratio when using recommended oil. During break-in period (first ten hours of operation), mix oil and fuel at a 30:1 ratio. If Sachs-Dolmar two-stroke engine oil is not available, a good quality oil designed for use in air-cooled two-stroke engines may be used when mixed at a 25:1 ratio after break-in period or 20:1 ratio during break-in period. Use a separate container when mixing oil and fuel.

All models are equipped with an automatic chain oil pump. The oil pump is driven by a worm gear on engine crankshaft. Oil pump output is varied by turning adjusting screw on saw underside. Turning screw clockwise decreases oil flow while turning screw counterclockwise increases oil flow.

REPAIRS

PISTON, PIN, RINGS AND CYLINDER. The piston pin is retained by wire retainers and rides in a roller bearing in connecting rod small end. Two piston rings are used on Models 117, 119, 120 and 120 Super while a single piston ring is used on all other models.

Cylinder is chrome plated and cannot be bored oversize. Cylinder and piston are marked "A," "B," or "C" during production to obtain desired piston-to-cylinder clearance. Cylinder and piston must have same letter marking to obtain proper clearance. Cylinder is stamped near spark plug hole while piston is stamped on crown. Install piston so arrow on piston crown points toward exhaust port. Tighten cylinder screws to 10 N·m (88 in.-lbs.).

CONNECTING ROD, CRANKSHAFT AND CRANKCASE. Crankcase must be split on all models to remove crankshaft. The crankshaft is supported on both ends by a ball type main bearing. Connecting rod and crankshaft are a unit assembly and are not available separately on all models except Model 119. Crankshaft on Model 119 should be disassembled only by personnel with equipment and skills necessary to assemble and realign crankshaft assembly.

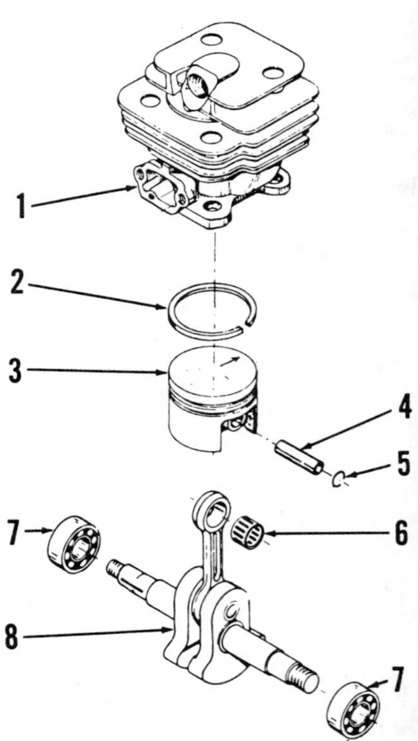

Fig. D20—Exploded view of engine. Two piston rings (2) are used on Models 117 and 119.

1. Cylinder
2. Piston ring
3. Piston
4. Piston pin
5. Pin retainer
6. Needle bearing
7. Ball bearing
8. Crankshaft & rod assy.

Illustrations courtesy Dolmar U.S.A., Inc.

Crankcase should be heated to 99°-121° C (210°-250° F) to install main bearings. Clutch side main bearing inner race should be heated to approximately 104° C (220° F) to ease installation of bearing onto crankshaft. Flywheel side main bearing is a sliding fit on crankshaft. Install crankcase seals with open side facing inward and outer diameter flush with outer surface of crankcase.

Upon reassembly, tighten crankcase screws to 5 N·m (44 in.-lbs.). Install cylinder and retighten crankcase screws to 7 N·m (62 in.-lbs.).

CLUTCH. Clutch hub on all models has left-hand threads. Clutch on Models 112, 113, 114, 116, 120 and 120 Super has two shoes while three clutch shoes are used on Models 117 and 119. Tighten clutch hub to 55 N·m (40 ft.-lbs.) on Models 112, 113, 114, 116, 120 and 120 Super or to 48 N·m (35 ft.-lbs.) on Models 117 and 119.

CHAIN OIL PUMP. All models are equipped with the chain oil pump shown in Fig. D22. Plunger (8) is driven by worm gear (4) mounted on crankshaft. On early models, crankcase oil seal lip seals against a shoulder on worm while on later models shoulder on worm gear is absent and oil seal lip rides against crankshaft. Be sure correct worm gear and oil seal are used. Worm gear may be extracted without removing crankshaft. Use Sachs-Dolmar special tool 957 430 000 when removing or installing worm with a shoulder. Shoulder of worm gear should contact with main bearing. On models equipped with shoulderless worm gear, use Sachs-Dolmar special tool 957 433 000 to remove and install worm gear. When removing worm gear, be sure to use a protective cap over crankshaft to prevent damage to crankshaft. Worm gear should be heated to approximately 104° C (220° F) prior to installation. Install seal (15) so seal lip is toward clutch.

REWIND STARTER. Refer to Fig. D21 for exploded view of rewind starter. To disassemble starter, remove starter housing from saw, remove rope handle and allow rope to rewind into starter. Detach snap ring (6) and remove rope pulley being careful not to dislodge rewind spring. If rewind spring must be removed, caution should be taken not to allow spring to uncoil uncontrolled.

Install rewind spring in starter housing in clockwise direction from outer spring end. Starter rope length should be 100 cm (39½ inches). Wind rope around rope pulley in clockwise direction as viewed with pulley in starter housing. Place sufficient tension on rope by turning rope pulley approximately four turns before passing rope through outlet so handle will rest snugly against starter housing with rope released. It should be possible to turn rope pulley clockwise with rope fully extended. Readjust spring tension if rope handle is loose against starter housing or rewind

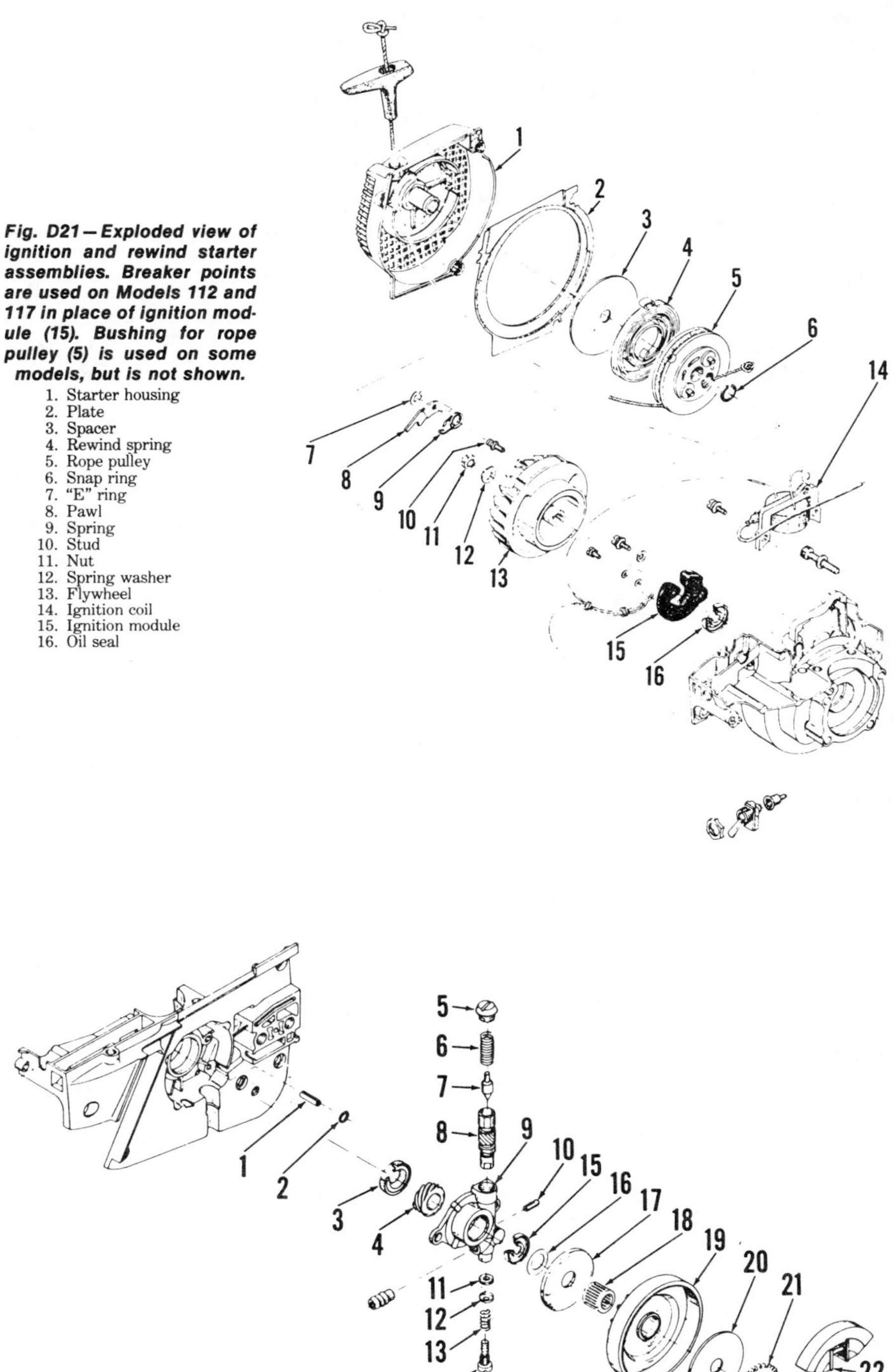

Fig. D21—Exploded view of ignition and rewind starter assemblies. Breaker points are used on Models 112 and 117 in place of ignition module (15). Bushing for rope pulley (5) is used on some models, but is not shown.

1. Starter housing
2. Plate
3. Spacer
4. Rewind spring
5. Rope pulley
6. Snap ring
7. "E" ring
8. Pawl
9. Spring
10. Stud
11. Nut
12. Spring washer
13. Flywheel
14. Ignition coil
15. Ignition module
16. Oil seal

Fig. D22—Exploded view of oil pump and clutch assemblies.

1. Pin
2. "O" ring
3. Oil seal
4. Worm gear
5. Plug
6. Spring
7. Thrust pin
8. Plunger
9. Pump housing
10. Pin
11. Rubber washer
12. Spring seat
13. Spring
14. Adjusting screw
15. Seal
16. Thrust washer
17. Washer
18. Bearing
19. Clutch drum
20. Washer
21. Spring
22. Clutch shoe
23. Clutch hub

Illustrations courtesy Dolmar U.S.A., Inc.

spring is coil bound with rope fully extended.

CHAIN BRAKE. Some models are equipped with a chain brake system designed to stop chain movement should kickback occur. Chain brake is activated when operator's hand strikes hand guard (1 – Fig. D23) causing chain brake lever (2) to disengage brake band and lever assembly (8) allowing spring (6) to draw brake band tight around clutch drum. Pull back hand guard to reset mechanism.

Disassembly for repair and component renewal is evident after inspection of unit and referral to exploded view Fig. D23. No adjustment of chain brake system is required.

HEATED HANDLES. Some models are equipped with an electric handle heating system. A generator located behind the flywheel supplies an electrical current to heating elements in front handle and rear grip.

Test generator and heating elements with an ohmmeter. A zero reading indicates a short circuit in component being tested. Check for possible damaged insulation which may be repairable. An infinity reading indicates an open circuit and component being tested is faulty and should be renewed. Front handle and heating element are a unit assembly and are not available separately.

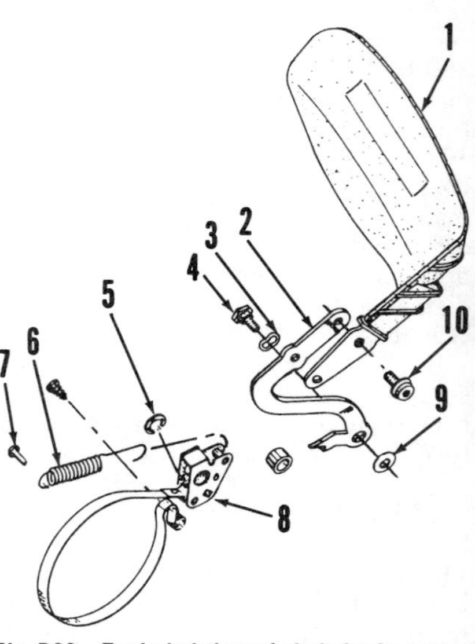

1. Hand guard
2. Lever
3. Wave washer
4. Shoulder bolt
5. "E" ring
6. Spring
7. Pin
8. Brake band & lever assy.
9. Washer
10. Screw

Fig. D23 — Exploded view of chain brake system

Illustrations courtesy Dolmar U.S.A., Inc.

SACHS-DOLMAR

Model	Bore	Stroke	Displ.	Drive Type
100, 100 Super	37 mm (1.46 in.)	31 mm (1.22 in.)	33 cc (2.0 cu. in.)	Direct
102	40 mm (1.57 in.)	31 mm (1.22 in.)	39 cc (2.38 cu. in.)	Direct
103, 105, 108	42 mm (1.65 in.)	29 mm (1.14 in.)	40 cc (2.44 cu. in.)	Direct

MAINTENANCE

SPARK PLUG. Recommended spark plug for Models 100, 100 Super and 102 is Champion RDJ7Y. Recommended spark plug for Models 103, 105 and 108 is Champion RCJ8. Electrode gap on Models 100 and 100 Super should be 0.6 mm (0.024 in.). Electrode gap on all other models should be 0.51 mm (0.020 in.).

CARBURETOR. Models 100, 100 Super and 102 are equipped with a Walbro WT diaphragm carburetor. Models 103, 105 and 108 are equipped with a Walbro WA diaphragm carburetor. Refer to Walbro section of CARBURETOR SERVICE section for exploded views and service procedures.

Initial adjustment on Model 100 is 1¼ turns open for high speed mixture screw and 1⅛ turns open for low speed mixture screw. Initial adjustment for Model 100 Super is ¾ turn open for high speed mixture screw and 1½ turns open for low speed mixture screw. On all other models, initial adjustment is one turn open for both high and low speed mixture screws.

Final adjustment should be made with engine running at operating temperature. Adjust low speed mixture so engine will accelerate cleanly without hesitation. Adjust high speed mixture to obtain optimum full throttle performance under cutting load. Do not adjust high speed mixture too lean as overheating and engine damage could result. Adjust idle speed to just below clutch engagement speed.

IGNITION. All models are equipped with a breakerless electronic ignition system. All electronic circuitry is contained in a one-piece ignition module assembly (6–Figs. D35 and D36). Air gap between ignition module lamination and flywheel (3) should be 0.2-0.3 mm (0.008-0.012 in.) on all models. Ignition timing is fixed and not adjustable.

LUBRICATION. The engine is lubricated by mixing oil with the fuel. Recommended oil is Sachs-Dolmar two-stroke engine oil. Fuel mixture should be a 40:1 ratio when using the recommended oil. During break-in period (first ten hours of operation), mix fuel and oil at a 30:1 ratio. If Sachs-Dolmar two-stroke engine oil is not available, a good quality oil designed for use in air-cooled two-stroke engines may be used when mixed at a 25:1 ratio after break-in period or 20:1 ratio during break-in period. Use a separate container when mixing fuel and oil.

All models are equipped with an automatic chain oil pump. Oil pump is driven by a worm gear on engine crankshaft. Oil pump output is adjustable on all models except Model 100. Refer to OIL PUMP in REPAIRS section for service, adjustment procedures and exploded views.

Manufacturer recommends using Sachs-Dolmar saw chain oil. If Sachs-Dolmar saw chain is not available, use a good quality oil designed specifically for saw chain lubrication.

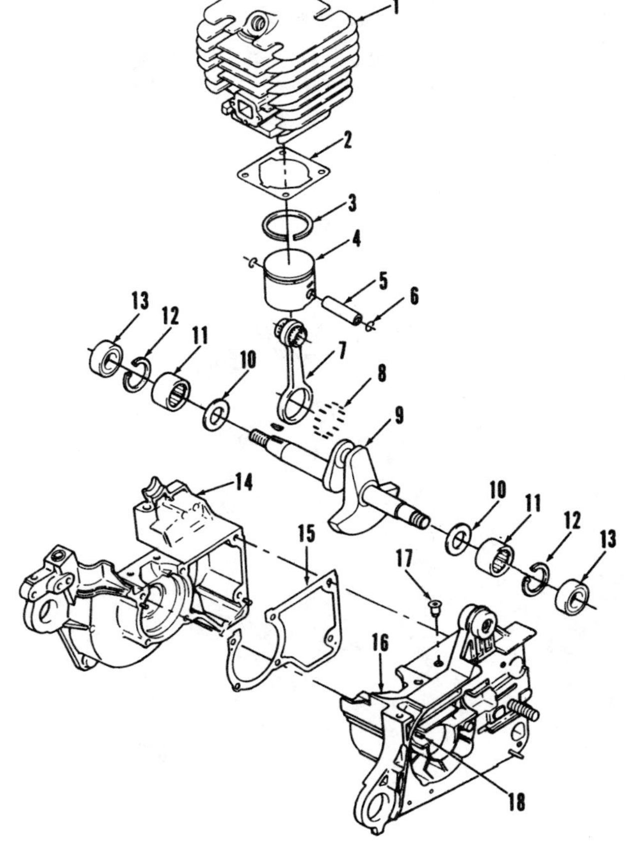

Fig. D33—Exploded view of engine assembly used on Models 100, 100 Super and 102.

1. Cylinder
2. Gasket
3. Piston ring
4. Piston
5. Piston pin
6. Pin retainer
7. Connecting rod
8. Bearing rollers
9. Crankshaft
10. Thrust washer
11. Main bearing
12. Snap ring
13. Seal
14. Left crankcase half
15. Gasket
16. Right crankcase half
17. Oil tank vent
18. Guide pin

Illustrations courtesy Dolmar U.S.A., Inc.

REPAIRS

PISTON, PIN, RING AND CYLINDER. Piston is equipped with one piston ring on all models. The piston pin rides in a needle roller bearing in rod small end and is held in place with two wire retainers. Cylinder has a Nikasil impregnated bore and should be renewed if excessively worn or damaged. Piston, ring and cylinder are available in standard size only on Models 100, 100 Super and 102. Piston and cylinder on Models 103, 105 and 108 are marked "A," "B" or "C" during production to obtain desired piston-to-cylinder clearance. Cylinder and piston must have like markings to maintain proper clearance. Cylinders are marked on top of cylinder or on cylinder frame. Pistons are marked on piston crown. Install piston with arrow on piston crown toward exhaust port.

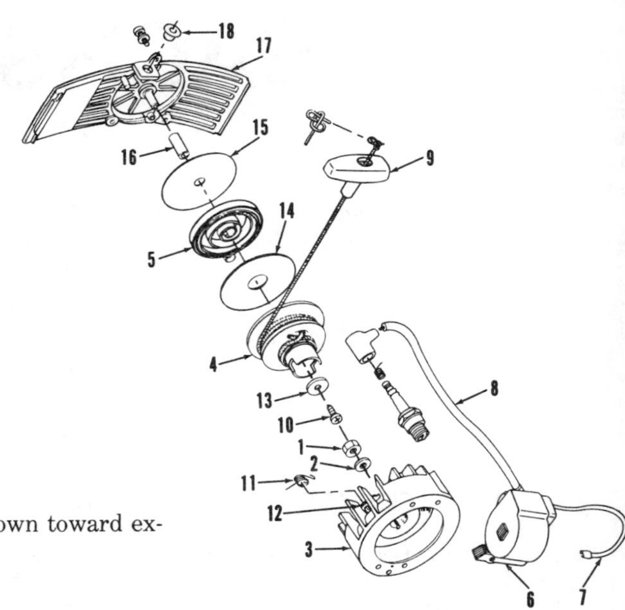

Fig. D36—Exploded view if ignition and rewind starter assemblies used on Models 103, 105 and 108.

1. Nut
2. Washer
3. Flywheel
4. Rope pulley
5. Rewind spring
6. Ignition module
7. Short circuit wire
8. High tension lead
9. Rope handle
10. Screw
11. Pawl spring
12. Pawl
13. Washer
14. Plate
15. Plate
16. Sleeve
17. Starter housing
18. Rope guide

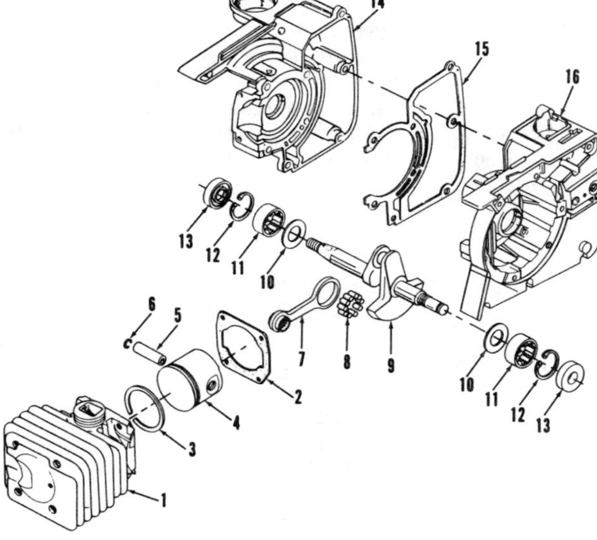

Fig. D34—Exploded view of engine assembly used on Models 103, 105 and 108. Refer to Fig. D33 for component identification.

NOTE: Use care when handling piston and rod assembly to prevent rod from slipping off bearing rollers as rollers are loose and may fall into crankcase.

Tighten cylinder screws to 6-8 N·m (53-71 in.-lbs.).

CONNECTING ROD, CRANKSHAFT AND CRANKCASE. On early models, connecting rod (7–Figs. D33 and D34) is separate from crankshaft (9) and rides in 12 loose bearing rollers (8). Connecting rod and needle bearing in rod small end are a unit assembly. Loose bearing rollers (8) at crankpin can be removed after rod is slipped off rollers. Bearing rollers may be held in place with a heavy grease during rod installation.

The crankshaft is supported at both ends with caged needle roller main bearings (11). Main bearings locate against snap rings (12). Note location of thrust washers (10) at both ends of crankshaft. On some later models, crankshaft, connecting rod and crankpin bearing are a unit assembly.

Heat may be applied to crankcase halves (14 and 16) to ease installation of main bearings. On Models 103, 105 and 108, manufacturer recommends using Loctite 242 or a suitable equivalent on outer diameter of crankcase seals (13) before installing seals.

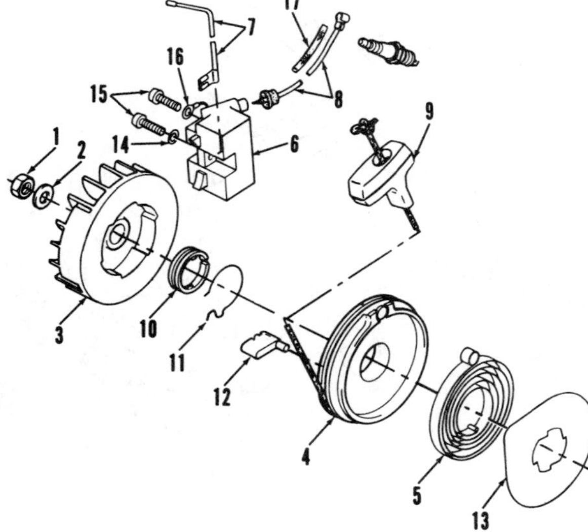

Fig. D35—Exploded view of ignition and rewind starter assemblies used on Models 100, 100 Super and 102.

1. Nut
2. Washer
3. Flywheel
4. Rope pulley
5. Rewind spring
6. Ignition module
7. Short circuit wire
8. High tension lead
9. Rope handle
10. Retainer ring
11. Brake spring
12. Pawl
13. Plate

CLUTCH. Refer to Fig. D37 for exploded view of clutch assembly used on Models 100, 100 Super and 102. Refer to Fig. D38 for exploded view of clutch used on Models 103, 105 and 108. Clutch assembly (1–Fig. D37 and Fig. D38) has left-hand threads on all models. Clutch drum (2–Fig. D37) on Models 100, 100 Super and 102 is available only with a

Illustrations courtesy Dolmar U.S.A., Inc.

fitted needle bearing. Shim (3) is used on Model 100 Super only. Clutch shoes and hub are available only as a complete assembly. Manufacturer recommends using special Sachs-Dolmar tool 950 500 020 to remove and install clutch assembly.

Clutch drum (2–Fig. D38) is separate from needle bearing (4) on Models 103, 105 and 108. Note location of spacers (3 and 5). Install thin spacer (3) between engine and clutch assembly (1) and thick spacer (5) between clutch drum (2) and snap ring (6). Manufacturer recommends using special Sachs-Dolmar tool 950 500 020 to remove and install clutch assembly.

OIL PUMP. All models are equipped with automatic chain oil pumps. Pump output is adjustable on all models except Model 100.

Pump plunger (11–Fig. D37) on Models 100, 100 Super and 102 is driven by worm gear (5) on crankshaft. Use special Sachs-Dolmar tool 950 500 010 to remove and install worm gear on crankshaft. After oil pump has been removed, suction line (6) can be removed for inspection or renewal. Pump plunger (11) and body (7) should be renewed only as a complete unit.

When installing pump assembly, be certain guide bore (G) in pump body properly engages guide pin (18–Fig. D33) in right crankcase half (16).

Adjust oil pump output on late 100 Super and 102 models by rotating adjusting screw (14–Fig. D37) located under saw. On early 100 Super and 102 models, adjust oil pump output by pulling down adjustment pin with a hooked wire or other suitable tool and sliding adjusting bushing forward or rearward. Forward position is maximum output. Refer to Fig. D39 for view of adjustment procedure.

Refer to Fig. D38 for exploded view of automatic oil pump used on Models 103, 105 and 108. Oil is pumped by plunger (16), driven by worm gear (15) which is rotated by drive spring (7). When installing pump, make certain drive spring (7) properly engages clutch drum (2) and worm gear (15). Pump output is adjusted by rotating adjusting screw (9) located at top right of saw.

REWIND STARTER. Flywheel must be removed to gain access to starter on Models 100, 100 Super and 102. To relieve tension on rewind spring, remove rope handle (9–Fig. D35) and carefully allow rope pulley (4) to unwind relieving tension on spring. To disassemble starter, pry off brake spring (11) and remove retainer ring (10). Lift off rope pulley (4) being careful not to dislodge rewind spring.

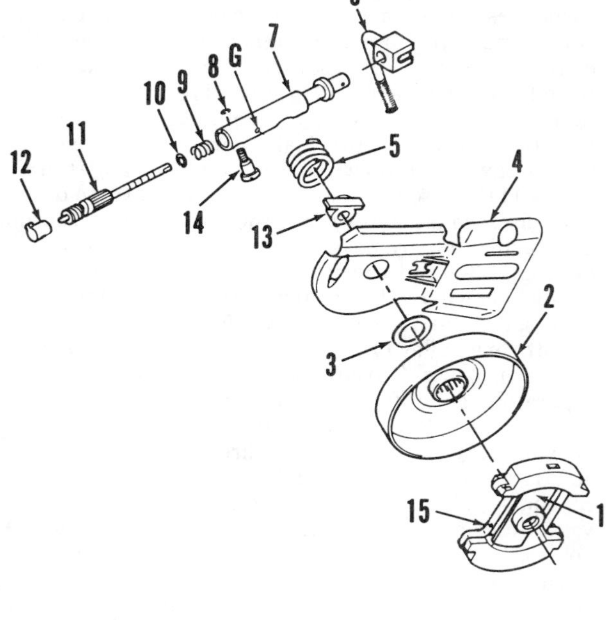

Fig. D37—Exploded view of clutch assembly used on Models 100, 100 Super and 102 and chain oil pump assembly used on Models 100 Super and 102. Oil pump shown is used on later models. Refer to Fig. D39 for adjustment procedure on early model pumps. Nonadjustable pump used on Model 100 is similar. Shim (3) is used on Model 100 Super only.

G. Guide bore
1. Clutch assy.
2. Clutch drum
3. Shim
4. Plate
5. Worm gear
6. Suction line assy.
7. Pump body
8. "O" ring
9. Spring
10. Washer
11. Plunger
12. Plug
13. Seal
14. Adjusting screw
15. Clutch spring

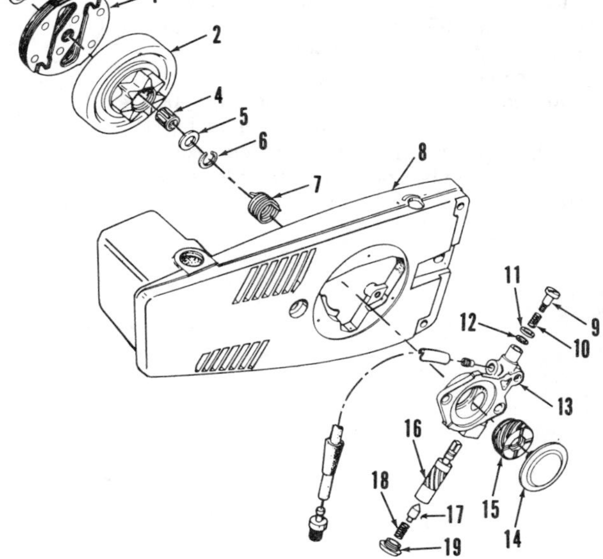

Fig. D38—Exploded view of clutch assembly and chain oil pump assembly used on Models 103, 105 and 108.

1. Clutch assy.
2. Clutch drum
3. Spacer
4. Needle bearing
5. Spacer
6. Snap ring
7. Drive spring
8. Chain guard & oil tank assy.
9. Adjusting screw
10. Spring
11. Washer
12. "O" ring
13. Pump body
14. Cap & shaft assy.
15. Worm gear
16. Plunger
17. Thrust pin
18. Spring
19. Plug

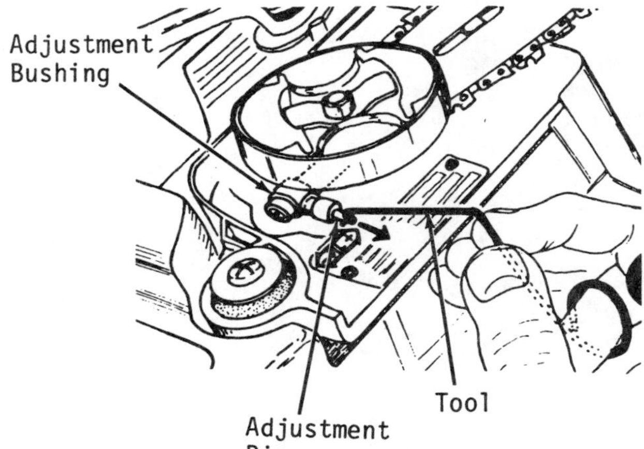

Fig. D39—View showing oil pump output adjustment procedure on early Models 100 Super and 102. Refer to text.

Rewind spring (5) should be wound in a clockwise direction starting with outer coil. Wind rope onto rope pulley in a counterclockwise direction as viewed from flywheel side of pulley. Install retainer ring (10) with end gap pointing toward ignition coil (6). Make certain starter pawl (12) properly engages brake spring (11). Refer to Fig. D40.

To disassemble starter on Models 103, 105 and 108, remove rope handle (9–Fig. D36) and carefully allow rope pulley to unwind, relieving tension on rewind spring (5). Remove screw (10) and lift off rope pulley (4).

Starter pawls (12) are not available separately from flywheel (3). Rewind spring (5) should be wound into starter housing (17) in a clockwise direction starting with outer coil. Wind rope onto rope pulley (4) in a clockwise direction as viewed from flywheel side of starter housing.

To preload rewind spring on all models, wind rope completely onto rope pulley. Rotate rope pulley two turns counterclockwise on Models 100, 100 Super and 102 and two turns clockwise on Models 103, 105 and 108. Hold rope pulley tightly to prevent unwinding. Pass rope through rope guide and install rope handle. With rope retracted, rope handle should be snug against housing. With rope completely extended, rope pulley should be able to rotate at least 1/4 turn further.

CHAIN BRAKE. Some models are equipped with a chain brake system designed to stop chain movement should kickback occur. Chain brake is activated when operator's hand strikes chain brake lever (1–Fig. D41). Forward movement of chain brake lever disengages brake latch (4) and allows spring (8) to draw brake band (10) tight around clutch drum stopping chain movement. Pull back chain brake lever to reset mechanism.

Disassembly for repair or component renewal is evident after inspection of unit and referral to Fig. D41. No adjustment of chain brake system is required.

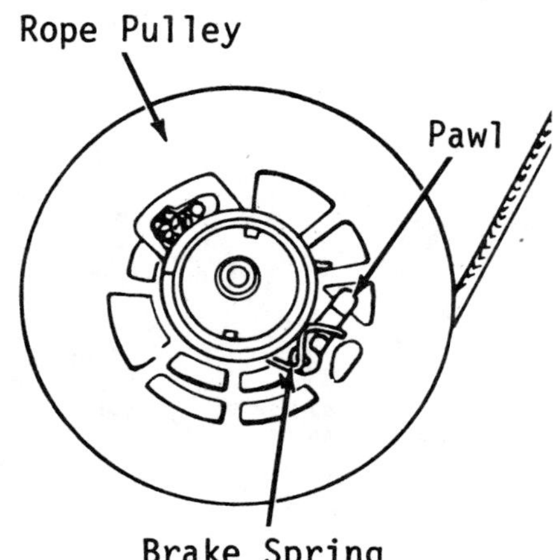

Fig. D40—View showing proper engagement of starter pawl and brake spring.

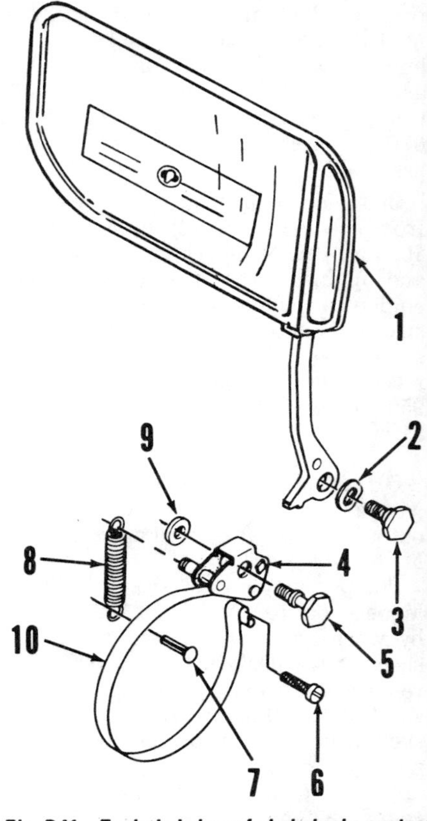

Fig. D41—Exploded view of chain brake system used on models so equipped.

1. Chain brake lever
2. Wave washer
3. Shoulder bolt
4. Latch
5. Shoulder bolt
6. Screw
7. Pin
8. Spring
9. Spacer
10. Brake band

DOLMAR

Model	Bore mm (in.)	Stroke mm (in.)	Displacement cc (cu. in.)	Drive Type
109	40 (1.57)	34 (1.34)	43 (2.62)	Direct
110, 110i, 110 Extra	40 (1.57)	34 (1.34)	43 (2.62)	Direct
111, 111i	44 (1.73)	34 (1.34)	52 (3.17)	Direct
115, 115i, 115 Extra	44 (1.73)	34 (1.34)	52 (3.17)	Direct

MAINTENANCE

SPARK PLUG. Recommended spark plug is Bosch WSR-6F or NGK BPMR-7A. Electrode gap should be 0.5 mm (0.020 in.) for all models. The spark plug should be tightened to the torque listed in the TIGHTENING TORQUE paragraph.

CARBURETOR. Walbro WT 76 carburetor is used on 109 and 111 models; Tillotson HU 83C or HU 83D carburetor is used on 110 and 115 models. Refer to the appropriate Tillotson or Walbro section of the CARBURETOR SERVICE section in this manual for service and exploded views. Refer to Fig. D101 for the location of carburetor fuel mixture adjusting needles. Initial setting of the low-speed mixture needle (L) for all models is 1 turn open from lightly seated. Initial setting of the high-speed mixture needle (H) for 109 and 111 models is 1 turn open from lightly seated. Initial setting for 110 and 115 models is 1-1/8 turns open from lightly seated.

To adjust the mixture needles, first remove and clean the air filter, then reinstall it. Start the engine and allow it to run until it reaches normal operating temperature. If necessary, turn each of the mixture needles clockwise until seated lightly, then back the needles out (counterclockwise) to the initial setting so the engine can be started. Turn the idle speed stop screw so the engine idles at about 2,500 rpm.

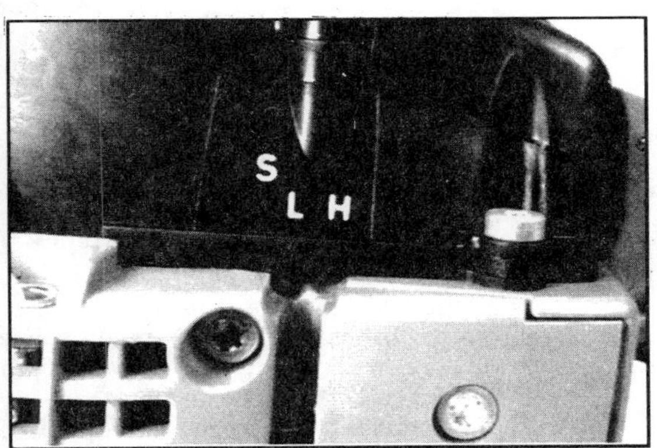

Fig. D101—View showing location of the carburetor adjustment screws. The idle speed stop screw is located at "S," low-speed mixture needle at "L" and high-speed mixture needle at "H."

Fig. D102—The chain oil adjustment screw is located as shown. The chain and guide bar are removed for clarity. Turn the screw clockwise to reduce the amount of oil or counterclockwise to increase the amount of oil.

Adjust the low-speed mixture needle so the engine idles smoothly and accelerates without hesitation. Adjust the idle speed screw so clutch does not engage when engine is idling, then recheck low-speed mixture adjustment.

Adjust the high-speed mixture needle to provide the best performance while operating at maximum speed under load. The high-speed mixture needle may be set slightly rich to improve performance under load. The engine may be damaged if the high-speed mixture is set too lean.

Final adjustment of the mixture needles should be within 1/4 turn of the initial settings. Large differences may indicate air leaks, plugged passages or other problems.

To remove carburetor, first remove filter cover and air filter. Disconnect fuel line from the carburetor. Remove carburetor mounting screws. Lift out carburetor and disconnect choke lever and throttle linkage. When installing carburetor, tighten the carburetor attaching screws to the torque listed in the TIGHTENING TORQUE paragraph.

IGNITION. All models are equipped with a breakerless electronic ignition system. All electronic circuitry is contained in a one-piece ignition module/coil located outside the flywheel. Ignition timing is fixed and not adjustable. The flywheel attaching nut should be tightened to the torque listed in TIGHTENING TORQUE paragraph.

Illustrations courtesy Dolmar U.S.A., Inc.

Fig. D103—Exploded view of a typical engine assembly.

1. Cylinder
2. Piston ring
3. Piston
4. Piston pin
5. Retainer ring
6. Gasket
7. Crankshaft & connecting rod assy.
8. Main bearings
9. Crankshaft right seal
10. Oil tank vent
11. Right crankcase half
12. Gasket
13. Left crankcase half
14. Crankshaft left seal
15. Needle bearing
16. Key

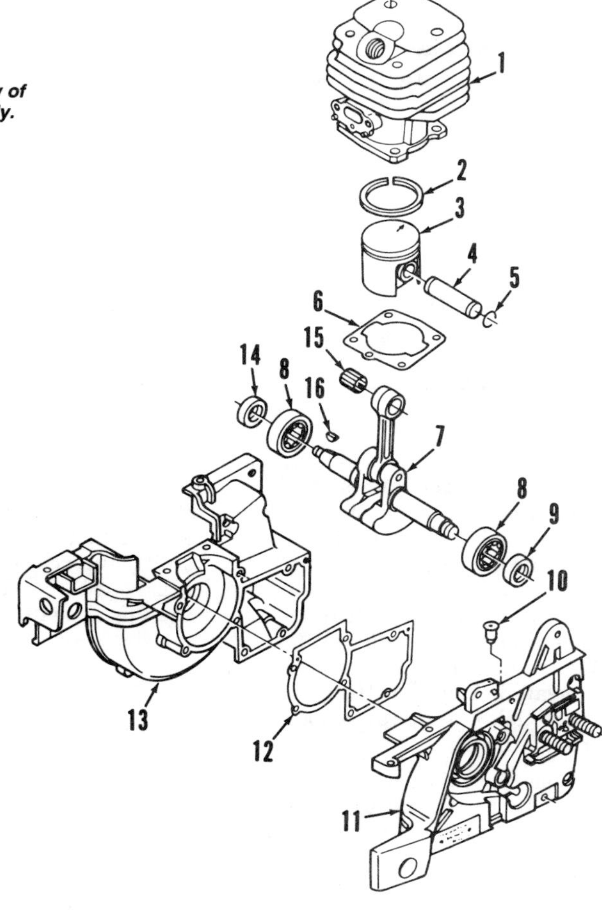

Air gap between the legs of the module/coil and the flywheel magnets should be 0.2-0.3 mm (0.008-0.012 in.). When installing, set the air gap between the flywheel magnets and the legs of the ignition module as follows.

Install the ignition module, but tighten the two screws only enough to hold it in place away from the flywheel. Insert setting gauge (part No. 944 500 890) or brass/plastic shim stock of the proper thickness between the legs of the ignition module and the flywheel, then turn the flywheel until the flywheel magnets are near the module legs. Loosen the screws attaching the ignition module and press legs of the ignition module against the setting gauge. Tighten the two attaching screws to the torque listed in the TIGHTENING TORQUE paragraph.

Remove the setting gauge, then turn the flywheel and check that flywheel does not hit the legs of the coil.

LUBRICATION. The engine is lubricated by mixing oil with the gasoline. The manufacturer recommends mixing DOLMAR two-stroke oil with regular grade gasoline at a ratio of 40:1 after break-in. When using regular two-stroke engine oil, mix at a ratio of 25:1. During the initial break-in, the fuel:oil ratio should be 30:1 when using DOLMAR oil or 20:1 when using other approved oil.

Use a separate container to mix gasoline and oil before filling the fuel tank. The manufacturer recommends not using fuel containing alcohol.

The saw is equipped with an automatic chain oiler system. The manufacturer recommends using DOLMAR Saw Chain oil or other good quality oil designed for lubricating saw chain. Make sure the oil reservoir is filled at all times.

The volume of oil delivered by the pump is adjustable by turning screw (Fig. D102). The screw is located under the saw on the right side.

REPAIRS

TIGHTENING TORQUE. Recommended tightening torque values are as follows.

Carburetor attaching screws . . . . 5.0-5.5 N•m (44-49 in.-lb.)
Clutch hub . . . . 35.0-35.5 N•m (310-314 in.-lb.)
Crankcase . 10-11 N•m (88.5-97 in.-lb.)
Cylinder . . . 10-11 N•m (88.5-97 in.-lb.)
Flywheel . . 25-30 N•m (221-265 in.-lb.)
Ignition module/coil . . . . 6-7 N•m (53-62 in.-lb.)
Muffler . . . . 8.5-9.0 N•m (75-80 in.-lb.)
Spark plug . . . . 20-30 N•m (177-265 in.-lb.)
Tubular handle . . . . 2.7-3.0 N•m (23.9-26.5 in.-lb.)
Vibration isolator . . . . 1.8-2.2 N•m (15.9-19.5 in.-lb.)

PISTON, PIN, RINGS AND CYLINDER. Refer to Fig. D103 for exploded view of typical engine. Transfer ports and passages of the cylinder for 110 and 115 models are machined, while the ports and passages are die cast for 109 and 111 models.

Models 109 and 111 are equipped with one piston ring and models 110 and 115 are equipped with two piston rings. Rings are pinned in the groove(s) of all models to prevent movement.

The piston pin rides in a needle bearing (15) located in the upper end of the connecting rod. The piston pin is retained in the piston by retainer rings (5) located in the piston at each end of the pin. Always install new retainer rings if they are removed, and position the open end of retainers toward the bottom of the piston.

Inspect the cylinder bore for excessive wear or damage. Oversize parts are not available and the cylinder is available only with a matching piston. Piston may be available separately, but the cylinder and piston are available as a matched set. Tops of the cylinder and piston for 110 and 115 models are marked with "A, B," or "C" and both should have the same letter.

When installing the piston, make sure the arrow on the top of the piston is visible and pointing toward the exhaust (muffler) side of the cylinder. Tighten the cylinder retaining screws to the torque listed in TIGHTENING TORQUE paragraph.

CRANKSHAFT, CONNECTING ROD AND CRANKCASE. The clutch, oil pump, pump drive worm, flywheel, cylinder, and piston must be removed before separating the crankcase halves. Rotate the crankshaft in the crankcase main bearings and check for roughness before removing the crankshaft assembly. Tap the crankcase as necessary with a soft faced hammer to separate the halves.

Illustrations courtesy Dolmar U.S.A., Inc.

The roller type main bearings (8—Fig. D103) and shaft seals (9 and 14) are located in the case halves. Main bearings and shaft seals should be removed only if new parts will be installed in the case halves.

Rotate the connecting rod around the crankpin while checking for roughness, excessive play or other damage. The crankshaft and connecting rod are a unit assembly and not available separately.

Do not remove the main bearings (8) from the crankcase unless it is necessary to install new bearings. Heat the case halves to approximately 100 degrees C (212 degrees F) before pressing the bearings from or into the case bores.

When assembling, lubricate the shaft seals and bearings with clean engine oil. Insert the crankshaft in the clutch side crankcase half, position a new gasket against the case, and then assemble the other case half. Tighten the screws attaching the crankcase halves to the torque listed in TIGHTENING TORQUE paragraph.

CLUTCH. A two-shoe centrifugal clutch is used on all models. The clutch used on 109, 110 and 111 models uses two leaf springs (7—Fig. D104). The clutch used on 115 models uses a coil type garter spring (7—Fig. D105).

On all models, the clutch hub is attached to the right end of the engine crankshaft with left-hand threads (rotate clockwise to remove). Special tool (part No. 944 500 680 for 115 models or No. 944 500 690 for 109, 110 and 111 models) should be used to grip the clutch hub while turning. Keep the crankshaft from turning by using an appropriate piston stopper. The clutch drum can be withdrawn after the hub and shoes are removed.

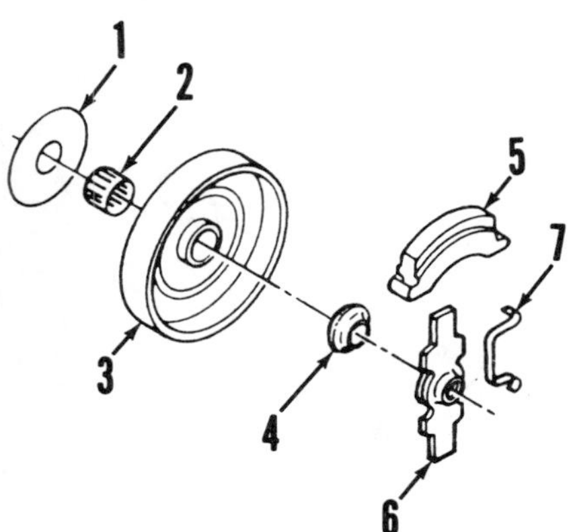

Fig. D104—Exploded view of clutch typical of type used on 109, 110 and 111 models.

1. Stop disc
2. Needle bearing
3. Clutch drum
4. Special spacer
5. Clutch shoe
6. Clutch hub
7. Spring (2 used)

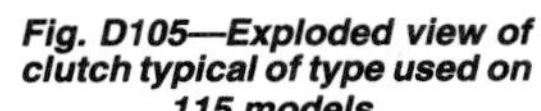

Fig. D105—Exploded view of clutch typical of type used on 115 models.

1. Stop disc
2. Needle bearing
3. Clutch drum
4. Special spacer
5. Clutch shoe
6. Clutch hub
7. Spring
8. Floating sprocket

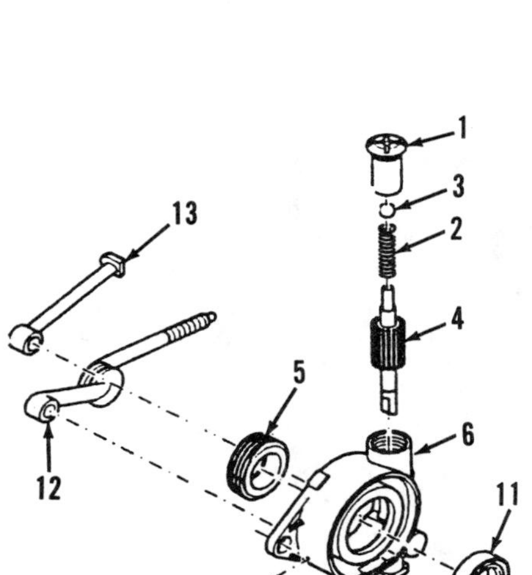

Fig. D106—Exploded view of the automatic chain oil pump, typical of all models.

1. Plug
2. Spring
3. Ball
4. Plunger
5. Worm gear
6. Housing
7. "O" ring
8. Washer
9. Spring
10. Adjusting screw
11. Seal
12. Suction line to pump
13. Pressure line

The original chain drive sprocket of 109 and 111 models is integral with the clutch drum (3—Fig. D104). The clutch drum with separate floating sprocket (8—Fig. D105) is originally installed on 110 and 115 models, but may be installed on other models.

Lightly lubricate the needle bearing located in the clutch drum before assembling. Tighten the clutch hub to the torque listed in TIGHTENING TORQUE paragraph.

OIL PUMP. All models are equipped with an automatic chain oil pump typical of the type shown in Fig. D106. Oil is pumped by plunger (4), which is turned by worm gear (5). Pump output is adjusted by turning screw (10).

The oil pump can be unbolted and pulled from the engine after removing the clutch assembly. Oil suction and pressure lines can be inspected after the oil pump is removed. Install new hoses if cracked or leaking. Use suitable sealer on suction hose to prevent leakage. Special tool (part No. 957 433 000) should be used to pull the worm drive gear (5) from the crankshaft.

Inspect plunger (4), worm gear (5) and bore in pump housing (6) for wear or damage. If wear or damage is excessive, it is suggested that a new pump assembly and worm drive gear be installed.

To install the worm gear, screw the worm gear onto special tool (part No. 957 433 000), then heat the worm gear to approximately 100 degrees C (212 degrees F). Position the worm gear on the crankshaft until the tool is bottomed, allow the worm gear to cool, then remove the special tool leaving the worm on the crankshaft.

REWIND STARTER. Refer to Fig. D107 for exploded view typical of the starter used. The starter assembly can be unbolted and removed from the engine. If the spring is under pressure, remove the assembly from the engine, pull the rope out about 20 cm (8 in.), hold the pulley (5), unwind the rope from the pulley, then allow the pulley to slowly unwind. Remove clip (7) and washer (6), then slide pulley (5) from the shaft. Make sure spring is completely unwound before removing the pulley.

If rope is broken, new rope should be 98 cm (38 in.) long and 3.5 mm (1/8 in.) in diameter. Attach new rope to pulley, making sure that knot in end of rope is properly nested in the pulley.

If not damaged, the rewind spring (3) should remain in spring case (4) after the case is detached from the housing. Inspect the spring to make sure that both ends are in good condition and the spring is not broken.

If the spring is removed from the spring case, it should be wound into the case in a counterclockwise direction starting with the outer coil. New spring and case are available as an assembly with the spring installed in the case.

Illustrations courtesy Dolmar U.S.A., Inc.

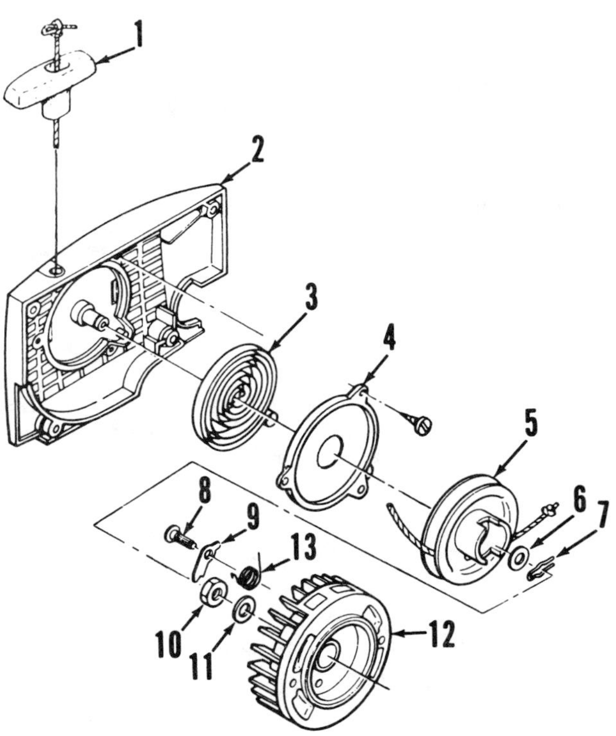

Fig. D107—Exploded view of the rewind starter assembly.

1. Handle
2. Starter housing
3. Rewind spring
4. Spring case
5. Rope pulley
6. Washer
7. Clip
8. Pawl stud
9. Pawl
10. Flywheel nut
11. Washer
12. Flywheel
13. Pawl spring

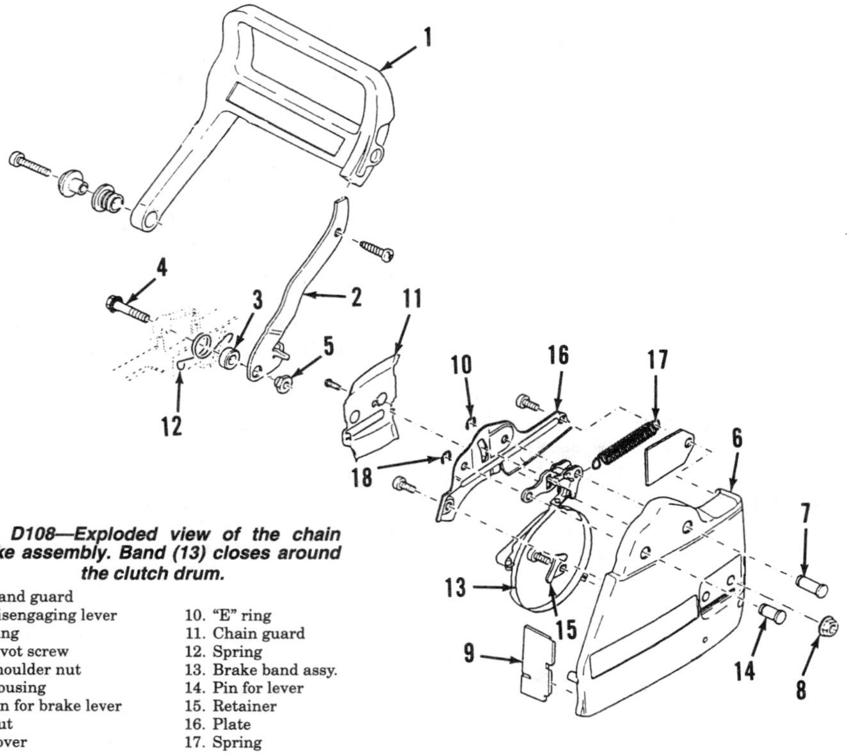

Fig. D108—Exploded view of the chain brake assembly. Band (13) closes around the clutch drum.

1. Hand guard
2. Disengaging lever
3. Ring
4. Pivot screw
5. Shoulder nut
6. Housing
7. Pin for brake lever
8. Nut
9. Cover
10. "E" ring
11. Chain guard
12. Spring
13. Brake band assy.
14. Pin for lever
15. Retainer
16. Plate
17. Spring

Attach the spring case to the housing with the spring installed.

Install the pulley (5) with rope attached. The pulley should engage the inner end of the spring (3). Install washer (6) and clip (7). Wind rope onto the pulley, preload the pulley approximately 2 turns, insert the end of the rope through guide in the housing then attach the handle (1).

Pull the rope out fully and check that pulley can be turned an additional 1/2 turn without causing the spring to bind. Allow the rope to rewind and make sure the handle is pulled against the housing. If the spring binds, remove some spring preload and recheck. If the handle is not pulled against the housing, increase the preload and recheck.

Inspect the condition of the pawl (9) and spring (13), then replace parts as necessary. The stud should be pressed into the flywheel after coating the surface of the stud and bore with locking agent (part No. 980 009 000 or equivalent).

CHAIN BRAKE. The chain brake assembly is designed to stop the chain quickly should saw kickback occur. The chain brake is activated when the operator's hand strikes the hand guard (1—Fig. D108). When the brake system is activated, spring (17) draws the brake band (13) tight around the clutch drum. To release, pull the hand guard back until the mechanism is reset.

The chain brake must be released before the housing (6) can be removed. To disassemble, insert a screwdriver through slot in cover plate (16—Fig. D108) and release chain brake. Remove retaining rings (10 and 18) and screws attaching cover plate to housing (6). Unhook brake spring (17) and withdraw brake band assembly (13).

Inspect and renew components as necessary. Lubricate all of the pivot points with suitable low temperature grease when assembling. No adjustment of the mechanism is required.

HEATED HANDLES. Some models are equipped with electrically heated handles. A generator (9—Fig. D109), lo-

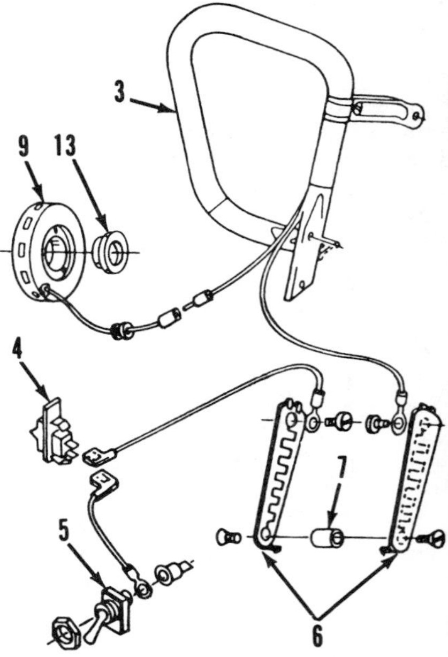

Fig. D109—Exploded view of the electric handle heating system available on some models. Generator coil (9) is located behind the flywheel.

3. Front handle & heating attachment
4. Heater switch
5. Ignition switch
6. Rear grip heater elements
7. Connector
9. Generator

Illustrations courtesy Dolmar U.S.A., Inc.

cated behind the flywheel, supplies electrical current to the heating elements (6). Switch (4) completes the circuit to ground, allowing the current to heat the handle (3) and elements (6).

Heating elements and wiring can be checked for continuity with an ohmmeter. Front element is not available separately from the handle. Be sure generator mounting surfaces are clean and mounting screws are tight to insure a proper ground connection. Renew generator if no other component is found faulty.

SACHS-DOLMAR

Model	Bore	Stroke	Displ.	Drive Type
166	56 mm (2.20 in.)	48 mm (1.89 in.)	118 cc (7.2 cu. in.)	Direct

MAINTENANCE

SPARK PLUG. Recommended spark plug is Bosch WSR6F. Electrode gap should be 0.5 mm (0.020 in.).

CARBURETOR. A Walbro WB diaphragm type carburtor is used. Refer to Walbro section of CARBURETOR SERVICE for service and exploded view.

Initial adjustment is 1¼ turns open for low speed mixture screw and 1½ turns open for high speed mixture screw. Final adjustment should be made with engine running at operating temperature. Adjust low speed mixture so engine will accelerate cleanly without hesitation. Adjust high speed mixture to obtain optimum full throttle performance under cutting load. Adjust idle speed to approximately 2,800 rpm or just below clutch engagement speed.

IGNITION. A breakerless electronic ignition system is used. Ignition coil and all electronic circuitry are contained in a one-piece ignition module located outside flywheel. Ignition timing is fixed at 3.0 mm (0.12 in.) BTDC and not adjustable. Air gap between flywheel magnets and ignition module lamination should be 0.2-0.3 mm (0.008-0.12 in.).

LUBRICATION. The engine is lubricated by mixing oil with the fuel. Recommended oil is Sachs-Dolmar two-stroke engine oil. Fuel and oil mixture should be a 40:1 ratio when using the recommended oil. During break-in period (first ten hours of operation), mix fuel and oil at a 30:1 ratio. If Sachs-Dolmar two-stroke engine oil is not available, a good quality oil designed for use in air-cooled two-stroke engines may be used when mixed at a 25:1 ratio after break-in period or 20:1 ratio during break-in period. Use a separate container when mixing fuel and oil.

Manual and automatic chain oil pumps are used. Automatic oil pump output is adjustable. Refer to OIL PUMP section for service and adjustment procedure. Manufacturer recommends using Sachs-Dolmar saw chain oil. If Sachs-Dolmar saw chain oil is not available, use a good quality oil designed specifically for saw chain lubrication.

REPAIRS

CYLINDER, PISTON, PIN AND RINGS. Cylinder (2–Fig. D67) may be equipped with a decompression valve (1) to ease engine starting. Cylinder bore should be inspected for excessive wear or damage. Oversize piston and rings are not available. Piston (4) is equipped with two piston rings (3). Piston rings are pinned in ring grooves to prevent ring rotation. Make certain ring end gaps are properly positioned around locating pins when installing cylinder. Piston pin (5) rides in needle bearing (8) in connecting rod small end and is held in position with two wire retainers (6). Install piston with arrow on piston crown toward exhaust port.

CRANKSHAFT, CONNECTING ROD AND CRANKCASE. Crankcase halves (11 and 16—Fig. D67) must be split to remove crankshaft assembly (9). Crankshaft is supported at both ends with ball bearings (13 and 15). Crankshaft and connecting rod are a unit assembly and are not available separately. Rotate connecting rod around crankpin and renew assembly if roughness, excessive play or other damage is noted. Heat crankcase halves to ease installation of ball bearings.

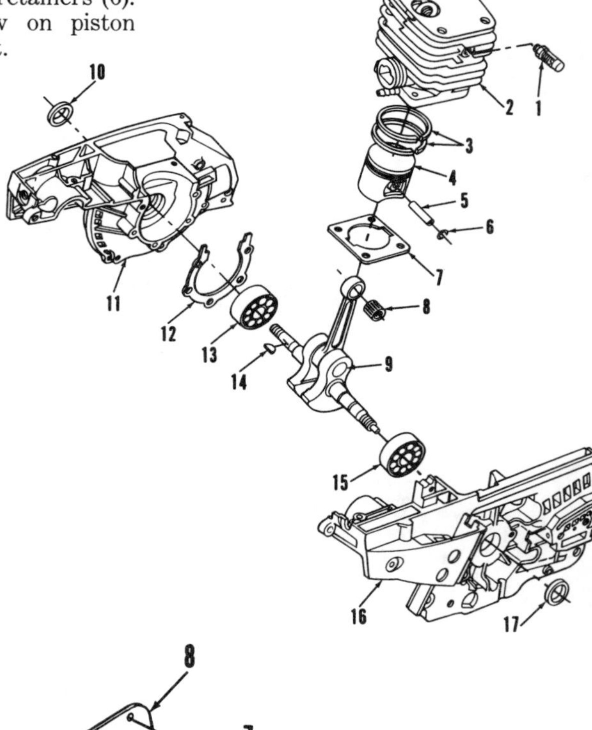

Fig. D67—Exploded view of engine assembly.

1. Decompression valve
2. Cylinder
3. Piston rings
4. Piston
5. Piston pin
6. Retainer
7. Gasket
8. Needle bearing
9. Crankshaft & connecting rod assy.
10. Seal
11. Left crankcase half
12. Gasket
13. Ball bearing
14. Key
15. Ball bearing
16. Right crankcase half
17. Seal

Fig. D68—Exploded view of clutch assembly.

1. Hub
2. Shoe
3. Spring
4. Plate
5. Drum
6. Needle bearing
7. Thrust washer
8. Plate

Illustrations courtesy Dolmar U.S.A., Inc.

CLUTCH. Refer to Fig. D68 for exploded view of the four shoe centrifugal clutch used. Clutch hub (1) has left-hand threads. Manufacturer recommends using Sachs-Dolmar tool 944 500 670 to remove and install clutch hub. Always renew shoes (2) as a complete set.

OIL PUMP. Refer to Fig. D69 for exploded view of manual and automatic oil pump assemblies. Worm gear (18) on engine crankshaft drives pump plunger (4). Automatic oil pump output is adjusted by rotating adjusting screw (10) located on bottom of saw on clutch side. Turn screw clockwise to decrease output. Use Sachs-Dolmar tool 957 434 000 to remove and install worm gear. Be sure to use protective cap 950 228 010 or a suitable equivalent over stub of crankshaft when pulling off worm to prevent damaging crankshaft. Install seal (6) with seal lip toward clutch.

REWIND STARTER. Refer to Fig. D70 for exploded view of rewind starter. To disassemble starter, remove rope handle (3) and allow rope to rewind into rope pulley (9). Remove snap ring (15), brake springs (14), compression ring (11) and snap ring (10). Do not interchange snap rings (10 and 15). Remove rope pulley (9) being careful not to dislodge rewind spring (7). If rewind spring must be removed, use caution not to allow spring to uncoil uncontrolled.

Install rewind spring into starter housing in a clockwise direction starting from outer coil. Starter rope should be 100 cm (39.5 in.) in length and 4 mm (5/32 in.) in diameter. Wind rope around rope pulley in a clockwise direction as viewed from flywheel side of starter housing. With rewind starter reassembled, preload rewind spring as follows:

Wind as much rope as possible around rope pulley. Pull out rope handle approximately 50 cm (20 in.) and secure rope pulley from turning. Rewind slack rope back onto pulley and release pulley allowing rewind spring tension to retract remainder of rope. Rope handle should be snug against housing with rope fully retracted.

CHAIN BRAKE. Some models are equipped with a chain brake system designed to quickly stop chain movement should kickback occur. Chain brake is activated when operator's hand strikes hand guard (1 – Fig. D71) causing brake lever (2) to disengage lever assembly (15) allowing spring (14) to draw brake band (8) tight around clutch drum. Pull back hand guard to reset mechanism.

Disassembly for repair or inspection is evident after referral to exploded view and inspection of unit. Lightly lubricate all pivot points. No adjustment of chain brake system is required.

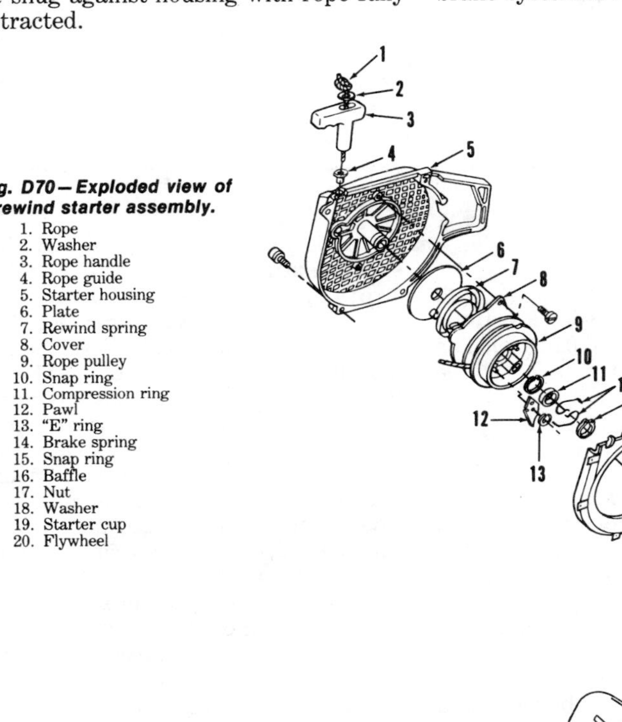

Fig. D70 — Exploded view of rewind starter assembly.

1. Rope
2. Washer
3. Rope handle
4. Rope guide
5. Starter housing
6. Plate
7. Rewind spring
8. Cover
9. Rope pulley
10. Snap ring
11. Compression ring
12. Pawl
13. "E" ring
14. Brake spring
15. Snap ring
16. Baffle
17. Nut
18. Washer
19. Starter cup
20. Flywheel

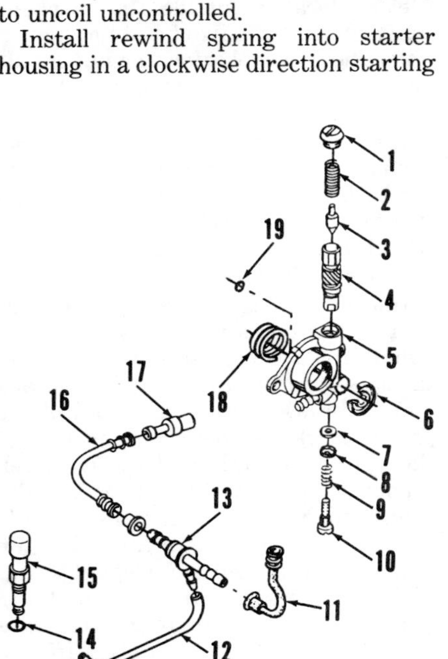

Fig. D69 — Exploded view of automatic and manual oil pump assemblies.

1. Plug
2. Spring
3. Thrust pin
4. Plunger
5. Pump body
6. Seal
7. Seal
8. Washer
9. Spring
10. Adjusting screw
11. Suction hose
12. Oil hose
13. "T" fitting
14. "O" ring
15. Manual pump assy.
16. Oil hose
17. Oil pickup
18. Worm gear
19. "O" ring

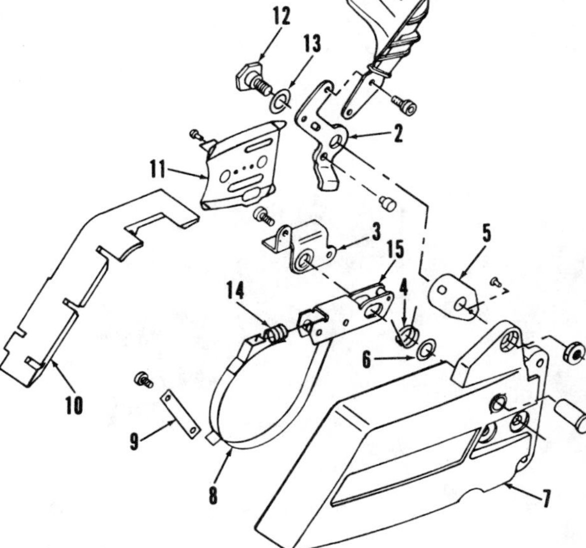

Fig. D71 — Exploded view of chain brake system.

1. Hand guard
2. Brake lever
3. Bracket
4. Spring
5. Lock plate
6. Spacer
7. Cover
8. Brake band
9. Brake band retainer
10. Cover
11. Guide plate
12. Shoulder bolt
13. Wave washer
14. Spring
15. Lever assy.

Illustrations courtesy Dolmar U.S.A., Inc.

DOLMAR

Model	Bore mm (in.)	Stroke mm (in.)	Displacement cc (cu. in.)	Drive Type
116	45 (1.77)	35 (1.38)	56 (3.4)	Direct
116 Super	47 (1.85)	35 (1.38)	61 (3.7)	Direct
116si	46 (1.81)	36 (1.42)	60 (3.66)	Direct
120	47 (1.85)	35 (1.38)	61 (3.7)	Direct
120 Super	49 (1.93)	36 (1.42)	68 (4.15)	Direct
120si	49 (1.93)	36 (1.42)	68 (4.15)	Direct

MAINTENANCE

SPARK PLUG. Recommended spark plug is Bosch WSR-5F. Electrode gap should be 0.5 mm (0.020 in.). The spark plug should be tightened to the torque listed in the TIGHTENING TORQUE paragraph.

CARBURETOR. Tillotson HS or HU carburetor is used on all models. Verify carburetor model, then refer to the appropriate Tillotson section of the CARBURETOR SERVICE section for service and exploded views.

To remove carburetor, remove air filter cover and filter element. Disconnect fuel line. Remove carburetor mounting screws and withdraw carburetor and intake elbow. Disconnect choke lever and throttle linkage.

Tighten the screws attaching the intermediate flange and screws attaching the carburetor to the torque listed in the TIGHTENING TORQUE paragraph.

Refer to Fig. D111 for the location of carburetor adjustment screws. Initial setting of both the low-speed and high-speed mixture needles for all models is 1 turn open from lightly seated.

To adjust the mixture needles, first remove and clean the air filter, then reinstall it. Start the engine and allow it to run until it reaches normal operating temperature. If necessary, turn each of the mixture needles clockwise until seated lightly, then back the needles out (counterclockwise) to the initial setting so the engine can be started. Turn the idle speed stop screw so the engine idles at about 2,400 rpm.

Adjust the low-speed mixture needle (L) so the engine idles smoothly and accelerates without hesitation. Adjust the idle speed screw (S) so clutch does not engage when engine is idling, then recheck low-speed mixture adjustment.

Adjust the high-speed mixture needle (H) to provide the best performance while operating at maximum speed under load. The high-speed mixture needle may be set slightly rich to improve performance under load. The engine may be damaged if the high-speed mixture is set too lean.

Fig. D111—View showing location of the carburetor adjustment screws. The idle speed stop screw is located at "S," low-speed mixture needle at "L" and high-speed mixture needle at "H."

Final adjustment of the mixture needles should be within 1/4 turn of the initial settings. Large differences may indicate air leaks, plugged passages or other problems.

IGNITION. All models are equipped with a breakerless electronic ignition system. All electronic circuitry is contained in a one-piece ignition module/coil located outside the flywheel. Ignition timing is fixed and not adjustable. The flywheel attaching nut should be tightened to the torque listed in TIGHTENING TORQUE paragraph.

Air gap between the legs of the module/coil and the flywheel magnets should be 0.15 mm (0.006 in.). When installing, set the air gap between the flywheel magnets and the legs of the ignition module as follows.

Install the ignition module, but tighten the two screws only enough to hold it in place away from the flywheel. Insert setting gauge (part No. 944 500 890) or brass/plastic shim stock of the proper thickness between the legs of the ignition module and the flywheel, then turn the flywheel until the flywheel magnets are near the module legs. Loosen the screws attaching the ignition module and press legs of the ignition module against the setting gauge. Tighten the two attaching screws to the torque listed in the TIGHTENING TORQUE paragraph. Remove the setting gauge, then turn the flywheel and check that flywheel does not hit the legs of the coil.

LUBRICATION. The engine is lubricated by mixing oil with the gasoline fuel. The manufacturer recommends mixing DOLMAR two-stroke oil with

Illustrations courtesy Dolmar U.S.A., Inc.

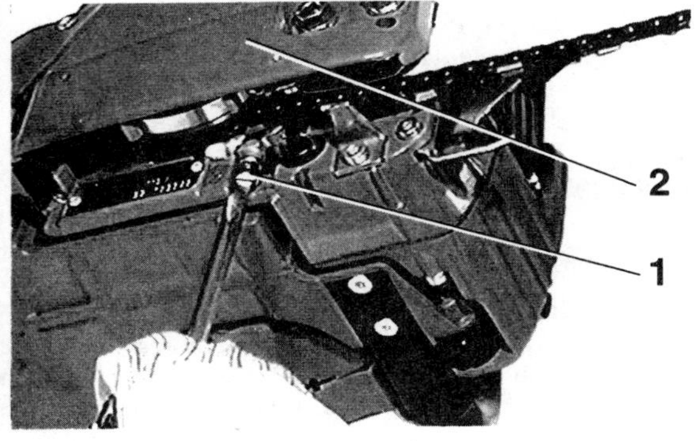

Fig. D112—The chain oil adjustment screw is located as shown. The chain and guide bar are removed for clarity. Turn the screw clockwise to reduce the amount of oil or counterclockwise to increase the amount of oil.

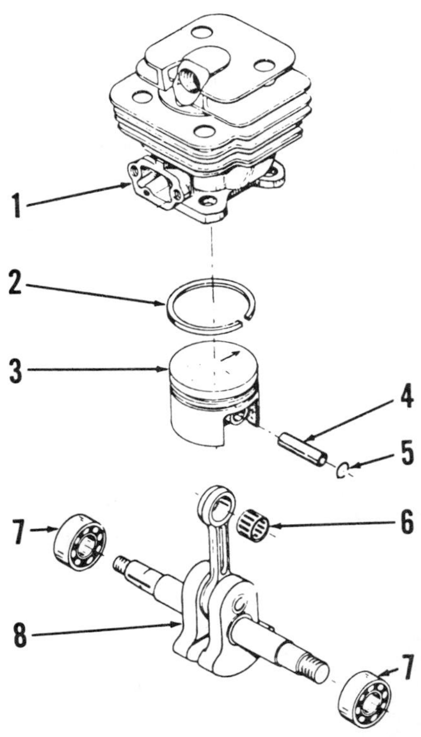

Fig. D113—Exploded view of the cylinder, piston, cylinder and crankshaft assembly typical of all models.

1. Cylinder
2. Piston rings
3. Piston
4. Piston pin
5. Retaining rings
6. Needle bearing
7. Main bearings
8. Crankshaft and connecting rod assy.

regular grade gasoline at a ratio of 40:1 after break-in. When using regular two-stroke engine oil, mix at a ratio of 25:1. During the initial break-in (first 10 hours) the fuel to oil ratio should be 30:1 when using DOLMAR oil or 20:1 when using other approved oil.

Use a separate container to mix gasoline and oil before filling the fuel tank. The manufacturer recommends not using fuel containing alcohol.

The saw chain is lubricated by oil contained in the oil reservoir by the automatic chain oil pump. The manufacturer recommends using DOLMAR Saw Chain oil or other good quality oil designed for lubricating saw chain. Make sure the reservoir is filled at all times.

The volume of oil delivered by the pump is adjustable by turning screw (Fig. D112) located under the saw on the right side. The engine must be stopped before turning the adjusting screw. Turn the screw clockwise to reduce the amount of oil or counterclockwise to increase the amount of oil.

REPAIRS

TIGHTENING TORQUE. Recommended tightening torque values are as follows.

Carburetor attaching screws.... 5.0-7.0 N•m (44-62 in.-lb.)
Clutch hub........... 52.5-57.5 N•m (39-42 ft.-lb.)
Crankcase . 10-11 N•m (88.5-97 in.-lb.)
Cylinder............. 11.5-12.5 N•m (102-110 in.-lb.)
Flywheel .... 27.5-30.0 N•m (243-265 in.-lb.)
Ignition module/coil..... 3.0-4.0 N•m 26.6-35 in.-lb.)
Intermediate flange (intake) .... 5.5-6.5 N•m (48.5-57.5 in.-lb.)
Muffler... 8.0-9.0 N•m (71-79.7 in.-lb.)
Spark plug.............. 20-30 N•m (177-265 in.-lb.)
Tubular handle .... 4.5-5.5 N•m (40-48.7 in.-lb.)
Vibration isolator .... 7.0-8.0 N•m (62-70.8 in.-lb.)

POWER HEAD. The following disassembly procedure can generally be used when removing the power head. Remove sprocket guard and chain brake assembly. Remove chain and bar, muffler, clutch assembly, oil pump, starter housing, ignition module, flywheel, carburetor and intake manifold. Unbolt and remove top handle. Remove screws attaching power head to fuel tank and withdraw power head.

PISTON, PIN, RINGS AND CYLINDER. Refer to Fig. D113 for exploded view of typical piston and cylinder. To remove cylinder, remove four retaining screws and lift cylinder off the piston.

Two piston rings are used and are pinned in the grooves to prevent movement. The piston pin rides in a needle bearing (6) located in the upper end of the connecting rod. The piston pin is retained in the piston by retainer rings (5) located in the piston at each end of the pin.

Always install new retainer rings if they are removed and position the ring ends toward the bottom of the piston. When assembling, make sure the arrow on the piston crown is visible and pointing toward the exhaust (muffler) side of the cylinder.

Inspect the cylinder bore for excessive wear or damage. Oversize parts are not available and the cylinder is available only with a matching piston. Pistons may be available separately. Tops of the cylinder and piston are marked with "A, B," or "C" and both should have the same letter. Tighten the cylinder retaining screws to the torque listed in TIGHTENING TORQUE paragraph.

CRANKSHAFT, CONNECTING ROD AND CRANKCASE. The clutch, oil pump, pump drive worm, flywheel, cylinder, and piston must be removed before separating the crankcase halves. Rotate the crankshaft in the crankcase main bearings and check for roughness before removing the crankshaft assembly.

Tap the crankcase as necessary with a soft faced hammer to separate the halves. The ball type main bearings (7—Fig. D113) and shaft seals are located in the case halves. Main bearings and shaft seals should be removed only if new parts will be installed in the case halves.

Rotate the connecting rod around the crankpin while checking for roughness, excessive play or other damage. The crankshaft and connecting rod are a unit assembly and not available separately.

If main bearings (7) are to be removed from the crankcase, heat the case halves to approximately 100 degrees C (212 degrees F) before pressing the bearings from or into the case bores.

When assembling, lubricate the shaft seals and bearings with clean engine oil. Insert the crankshaft in the clutch (right) side crankcase half, position a new gasket against the case then assemble the other case half. Tighten the screws attaching the crankcase halves to the torque listed in TIGHTENING TORQUE paragraph.

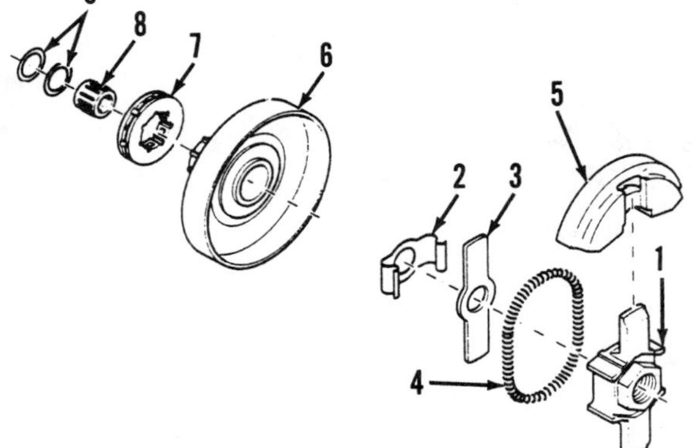

Fig. D114—Exploded view of typical clutch assembly.

1. Clutch hub
2. Clamp
3. Guide piece
4. Spring
5. Shoes
6. Clutch drum
7. Sprocket
8. Needle bearing
9. Spacer washers

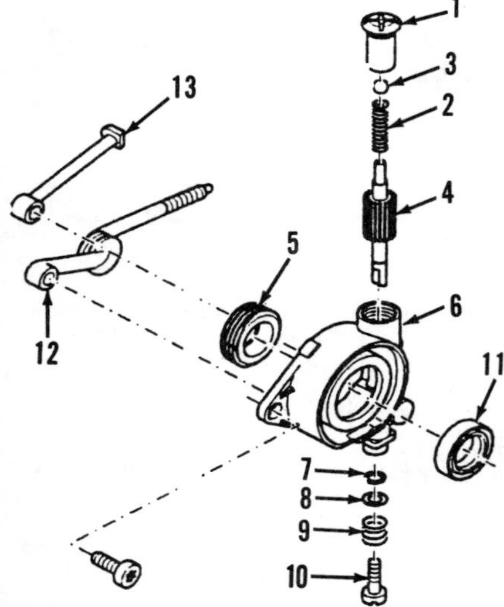

Fig. D115—Exploded view of the automatic chain oil pump, typical of all models.

1. Plug
2. Spring
3. Ball
4. Plunger
5. Worm gear
6. Housing
7. "O" ring
8. Washer
9. Spring
10. Adjusting screw
11. Seal
12. Suction line to pump
13. Pressure line

CLUTCH. A two shoe centrifugal clutch with a coil type garter spring (4—Fig. 114) is used. The clutch hub is attached to the right end of the engine crankshaft with left-hand threads. Keep the crankshaft from turning by using an appropriate piston stopper. The clutch hub can be turned using a 17 mm socket wrench. Note that clutch hub has left-hand threads (turn clockwise to remove). The clutch drum can be withdrawn after the hub and shoes are removed. The floating chain drive sprocket is splined to the clutch drum.

When assembling, install the smaller spacer (9) next to the oil pump, with the larger spacer (9) next to the clutch drum. Grease the needle bearing (8) lightly before assembling the bearing and drum. Assemble the clutch shoes (5), and spring (4) on the hub (1), making sure the connection of the spring is centered in one of the shoes. Assemble thrust plate (3) and clamp (2). Install the clutch assembly, tightening the hub to the torque listed in TIGHTENING TORQUE paragraph.

OIL PUMP. All models are equipped with an automatic chain oil pump typical of the type shown in Fig. D115. Oil is pumped by plunger (4), which is turned by worm gear (5). Pump output is adjusted by turning screw (10).

The oil pump can be unbolted and pulled from the engine after removing the clutch assembly. Oil suction and pressure lines can be inspected after the oil pump is removed. Install new hoses if cracked or leaking. Use suitable sealer on suction hose to prevent leakage. Special tool (part No. 957 433 000) should be used to pull the worm drive gear (5) from the crankshaft.

Inspect plunger (4), worm gear (5) and bore in pump housing (6) for wear of damage. If wear or damage is excessive, it is suggested that a new pump assembly and worm drive gear be installed. To install the worm gear, screw the worm gear onto special tool (part No. 957 433 000), then heat the worm gear to approximately 100 degrees C (212 degrees F). Position the worm gear on the crankshaft until the tool is bottomed, allow the worm gear to cool, then remove the special tool leaving the worm on the crankshaft.

REWIND STARTER. Refer to Fig. D116 for exploded view of the rewind starter. The starter assembly can be unbolted and removed from the engine. If the recoil spring is under pressure, remove the assembly from the engine, pull the rope out about 20 cm (8 in.), hold the pulley (5), unwind the rope from the pulley, then allow the pulley to slowly unwind. Remove clip (6) and washer (7), then slide pulley (5) from the shaft. Make sure spring is completely unwound before removing the pulley.

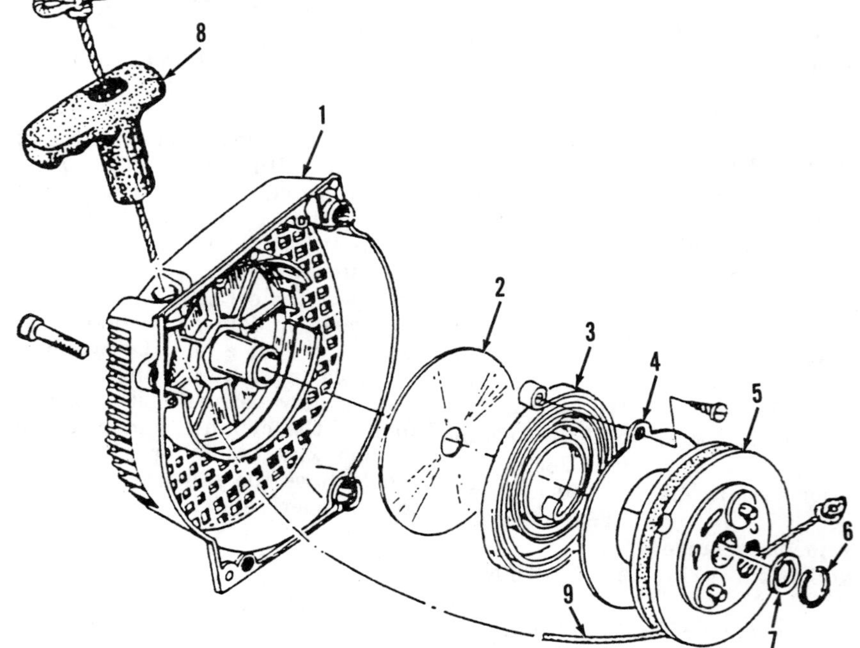

Fig. D116—Exploded view of the rewind starter typical of models 116 and 120.

1. Starter housing
2. Spacer
3. Recoil spring
4. Plate
5. Pulley
6. Snap ring
7. Washer
8. Handle
9. Rope

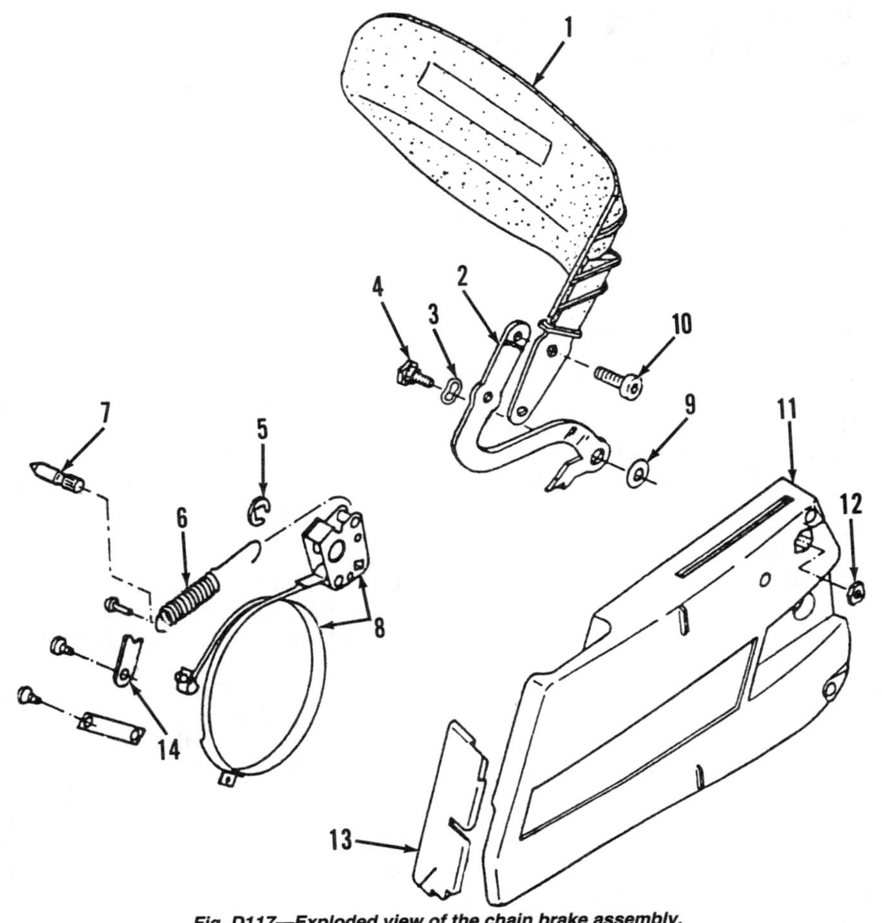

Fig. D117—Exploded view of the chain brake assembly.

1. Hand guard
2. Lever
3. Wave washer
4. Shoulder bolt
5. "E" ring
6. Brake spring
7. Pin
8. Brake band & lever assy.
9. Washer
10. Screw
11. Housing
12. Nut
13. Cover
14. Retainer

New starter rope is 100 cm (40 in.) long and 4 mm in diameter. Attach rope to the pulley, making sure that the knot is properly nested in the pulley.

If not damaged, the rewind spring (3) can remain in the housing. Inspect the spring to make sure that both ends are in good condition and the spring is not broken. If the spring is removed, it should be wound into the housing in a clockwise direction starting with the outer coil. Attach the spring case (4) to the housing after the spring is installed.

Install the pulley (5) with rope attached. The pulley should engage the inner end of the spring (3). Install washer (7) and clip (6). Wind rope onto the pulley, preload the pulley approximately 2 turns, insert the end of the rope through guide in the housing then attach the handle (8). Pull the rope out fully and check that pulley can be turned an additional 1/2 turn without causing the spring to bind. Allow the rope to rewind and make sure the handle is pulled against the housing. If the spring binds, remove some spring preload and recheck. If the handle is not wound against the housing, increase the preload and recheck.

Inspect the condition of the pawl and spring attached to the flywheel. The pawl stud should be pressed into the flywheel after coating the surface of the stud and bore with locking agent (part No. 980 009 000 or equivalent).

CHAIN BRAKE. The chain brake assembly is designed to stop the chain quickly should kickback occur. The chain brake is activated when the operator's hand strikes the hand guard (1—Fig. D117). When the brake system is activated, spring (6) draws the brake band (8) tight around the clutch drum. To release the brake, pull the hand guard back until the mechanism is reset.

The chain brake must be released before the housing (11) can be removed. To disassemble, push brake lever (2—Fig. D117) forward to relieve spring tension. Unscrew shoulder bolt (4) and remove lever (2). Unhook spring (6) and remove from housing. Disengage "E" ring (5) and withdraw brake band (8).

Lubricate all of the pivot points with suitable low temperature grease when assembling. No adjustment of the mechanism is required.

DOLMAR

Model	Bore mm (in.)	Stroke mm (in.)	Displacement cc (cu. in.)	Drive Type
309	47 (1.85)	40 (1.57)	70 (4.27)	Belt
343	55 (2.16)	40 (1.57)	95 (5.8)	Belt

MAINTENANCE

SPARK PLUG. Recommended spark plug is Bosch WSR-6F. Electrode gap should be 0.5 mm (0.020 in.). The spark plug should be tightened to the torque listed in the TIGHTENING TORQUE paragraph.

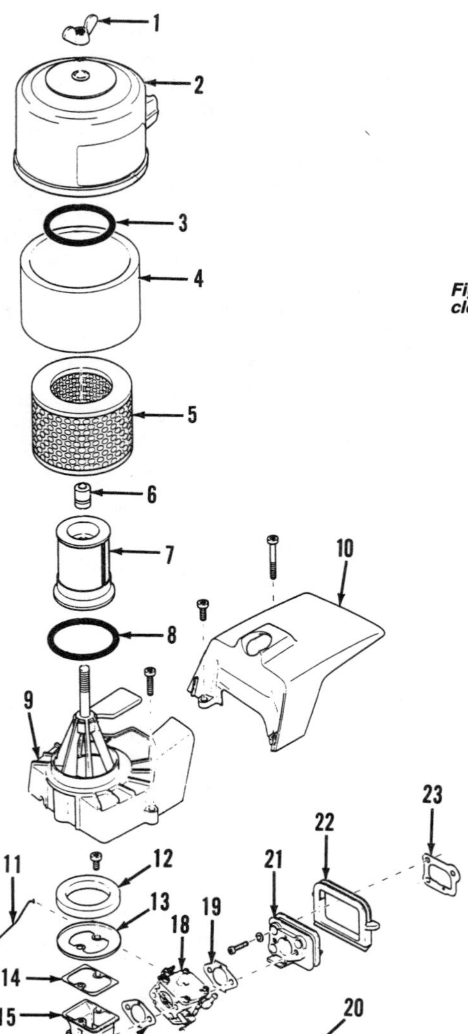

CARBURETOR. Tillotson HS-239B or HS-239C carburetor is used. Refer to the appropriate Tillotson section of the CARBURETOR SERVICE section for service and exploded views.

To remove carburetor, first remove air filter and cover assembly (18—Fig. D131). Remove carburetor mounting screws. Disconnect fuel line, choke and throttle, and withdraw carburetor from engine. Tighten the carburetor attaching screws to the torque listed in the TIGHTENING TORQUE paragraph.

Fig. D131—Exploded view of the air cleaner, carburetor and associated parts.

1. Wing nut
2. Cover
3. "O" ring (57x7 mm)
4. Prefilter
5. Filter element
6. Rubber spacer
7. Inner filter
8. "O" ring (57x7 mm)
9. Cover
10. Cover
11. Throttle link
12. Gasket
13. Plate
14. Gasket
15. Connecting sleeve
16. Gasket
17. Choke shaft
18. Carburetor
19. Gasket
20. Foam cover plate
21. Intermediate flange
22. Gasket
23. Gasket

To adjust carburetor, remove air filter and filter cover (9—Fig. D131) for access to fuel mixture needles. Initial setting of the low-speed and high-speed mixture needles is 1 turn open from lightly seated.

To adjust the mixture needles, start the engine and allow it to run until it reaches normal operating temperature. If necessary, turn each of the mixture needles clockwise until seated lightly, then back the needles out (counterclockwise) to the initial setting so the engine can be started. Turn the idle speed stop screw so the engine idles at about 2,300 rpm.

Adjust the low-speed mixture needle so the engine idles smoothly and accelerates without hesitation. Adjust the idle speed to just slower than clutch engagement speed, then recheck low-speed mixture adjustment.

Adjust the high-speed mixture needle to provide the best performance while operating at maximum speed under load. The high-speed mixture needle may be set slightly rich to improve performance under load. The engine may be damaged if the high-speed mixture is set too lean.

Final adjustment of the mixture needles should be within 1/4 turn of the initial settings. Large differences may indicate air leaks, plugged passages or other problems.

IGNITION. All models are equipped with a breakerless electronic ignition system with a one-piece ignition module/coil located under the flywheel. Ignition timing is fixed and not adjustable. Use a puller (part No. 957 427 010 or equivalent) to remove the flywheel from the tapered end of the crankshaft.

Tighten the two screws attaching the ignition coil/module to 4.0-5.0 N•m (35-44 in.-lb.) when assembling.

Tighten the flywheel attaching nut to 25-30 N•m (220-265 in.-lb.).

LUBRICATION. The engine is lubricated by mixing oil with the gasoline fuel. The manufacturer recommends mixing DOLMAR two-stroke oil with regular grade gasoline at a ratio of 40:1 after break-in. When using regular two-stroke engine oil, mix at a ratio of 25:1. During the initial break-in (first 10 hours) the fuel to oil ratio should be 30:1 when using DOLMAR oil or 20:1 when using other approved oil.

Always use a separate container to mix gasoline and oil before filling the fuel tank. The manufacturer recommends not using fuel containing alcohol.

REPAIRS

TIGHTENING TORQUE. Recommended tightening torque values are as follows.

Carburetor attaching screws . . . . 5.0-7.0 N•m (44-62 in.-lb.)
Clutch hub. . . . . 23.5-28.5 N•m (208-252 in.-lb.)
Crankcase . . . . 10-11 N•m (88.5-97 in.-lb.)
Cylinder. . . . . 10.5-12.5 N•m (93-110.6 in.-lb.)
Flywheel . . . . 25-30 N•m (221-265 in.-lb.)
Ignition module/coil . . . . . 4.0-5.0 N•m (35-44 in.-lb.)
Intermediate flange (inlet) 6.0-7.0 N•m (53-62 in.-lb.)
Muffler. . . . . 12-16 N•m (106-141.6 in.-lb.)
Spark plug. . . . . 20-30 N•m (177-265 in.-lb.)
Tubular handle . . . . 14-15 N•m (124-133 in.-lb.)
Vibration isolator . . . . 10-11 N•m (88.5-97 in.-lb.)

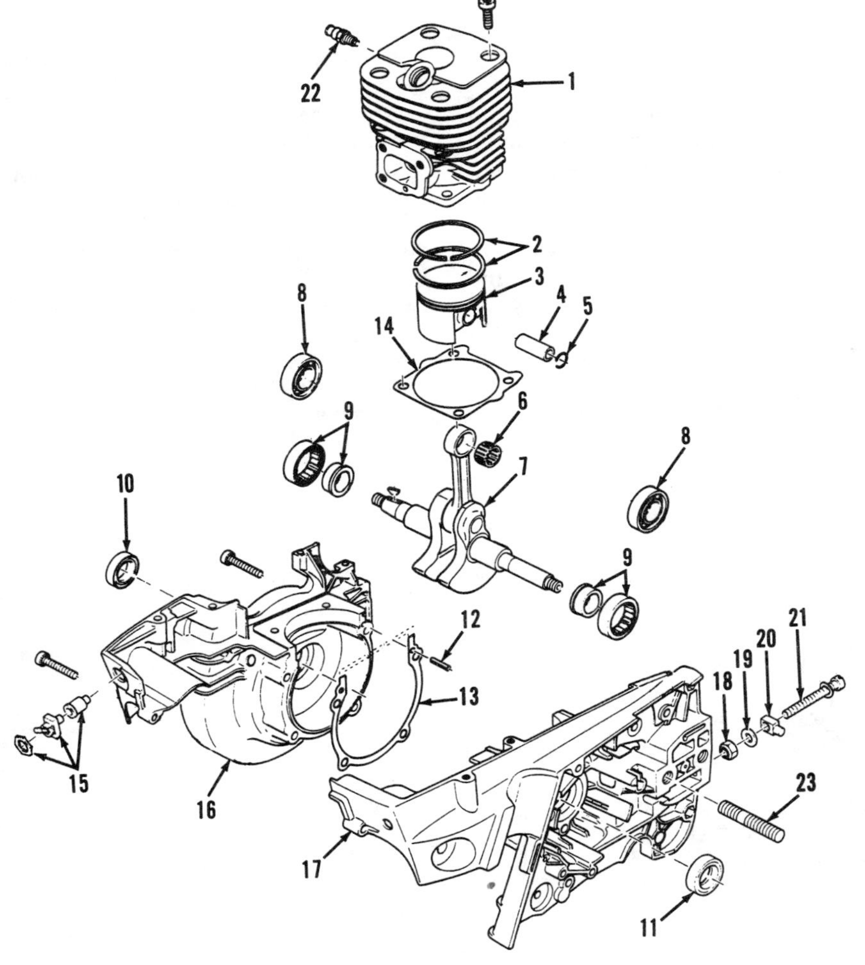

Fig. D132—Exploded view of the cylinder, crankshaft, crankcase and associated parts. Main bearings are ball type (8) for 309 models and roller type (9) for 343 models.

1. Cylinder
2. Piston rings
3. Piston
4. Piston pin
5. Retaining rings
6. Needle bearing
7. Crankshaft & connecting rod
8. Ball bearings (309 models)
9. Roller bearings (343 models)
10. Left side seal
11. Right side seal
12. Dowel
13. Gasket
14. Gasket
15. Engine stop switch
16. Crankcase left half
17. Crankcase right half
18. Self-locking nut
19. Washer
20. Nut with pin
21. Adjuster screw
22. Decompression valve
23. Stud

PISTON, PIN, RINGS AND CYLINDER. The cylinder can be removed after removal of the airbox cover, air cleaner, carburetor (Fig. D131), cylinder cover and muffler. The piston pin (4—Fig. D132) is retained by wire retainer rings (5). The pin operates in a needle bearing (6) at the upper end of the connecting rod. The piston is equipped with two piston rings (2) which are prevented from rotating in their grooves by locating pins.

The decompression valve (22) installed in the cylinder of some models can be removed for cleaning, inspection and replacement. Inspect the cylinder bore for excessive wear or damage. Oversize parts are not available. The piston is available separately, but the cylinder is only available with the proper piston.

When assembling, make sure the arrow on the piston crown is visible and pointing toward the exhaust (muffler) side of the cylinder. If removed, always install new piston pin retainer rings (5). Make certain that retaining ring is seated in the groove and position the ring ends toward the bottom of the piston. Tighten the cylinder retaining screws to the torque listed in TIGHTENING TORQUE paragraph.

CRANKSHAFT, CONNECTING ROD AND CRANKCASE. On 309 models, the crankshaft is supported in two ball type main bearings (8—Fig. D132). On 343 models, the crankshaft is supported in two roller type main bearings (9) with inner races that are separate from the crankshaft. The connecting rod and crankshaft are a pressed together assembly, available only as a unit.

To remove the crankshaft and connecting rod assembly, remove the flywheel and ignition coil/module from the left side; carburetor, cylinder and piston from the top; and the cutting assembly and clutch from the right side. Remove the attaching screws and tap the crankcase as necessary with a soft faced hammer to separate the halves.

Use appropriate pullers to remove the main bearings only if new units are

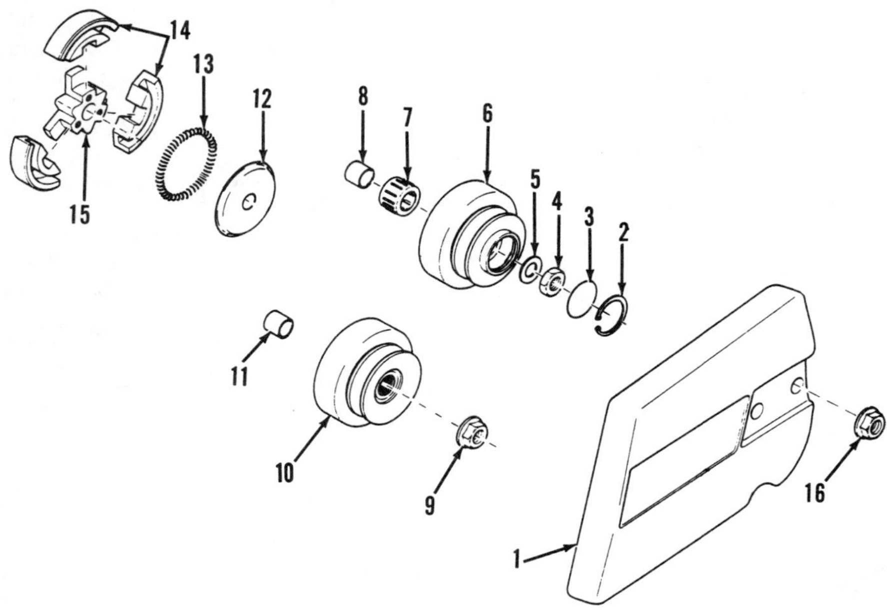

Fig. D133—Exploded view of the clutch and drive pulley. The clutch drum of some models is equipped with cover (3) and snap ring (2), while other models may be as shown in the lower view (9, 10 & 11).

1. Cover
2. Snap ring
3. Cover
4. Nut
5. Washer
6. Drum & pulley
7. Needle bearing
8. Inner ring
9. Nut
10. Drum & pulley
11. Inner ring
12. Guide washer
13. Clutch spring
14. Clutch shoes
15. Clutch hub
16. Clamping nut

being installed. Heating the crankcase will make removal and installation of the main bearings easier.

CLUTCH. To remove the clutch, first remove the disk cutter attachment. Two different types of clutch drums have been used. If so equipped, remove the snap ring (2—Fig. D133) and cover (3). On all models, nut (4 or 9) has left-hand thread (turn clockwise to remove). Remove the nut, then withdraw the clutch drum from the crankshaft. Remove the washer (12), then use puller (part No. 957 432 000 or equivalent) to pull the clutch hub from the crankshaft.

Inspect the clutch drum (6 or 10), shoes (14), spring (13) and drive hub (15). Replace parts as necessary. Always install clutch shoes (14) as a complete set of three. Be sure to clean the crankshaft and matching bore of the clutch hub thoroughly before installing the clutch hub. Install the washer (12), spacer (8 or 11) and clutch drum (6 or 11). Install the washer (5) if so equipped and nut (4 or 9), tightening the nut to the torque listed in TIGHTENING TORQUE paragraph. On models equipped with cover (3), fill the space under the cover with grease before installing cover and snap ring (2).

REWIND STARTER. Refer to Fig. D134 for exploded view of typical starter. The starter can be removed as a unit by unbolting the housing (2).

To disassemble the starter, remove the handle (1) and allow the rope to wind into the housing. Remove snap ring (7) and lift the rope pulley (6) from the housing. Be careful to prevent injury in case the spring (4) unwinds suddenly.

Clean and inspect parts for damage. The 4 mm diameter starter rope should be 100 cm long. Lubricate the recoil

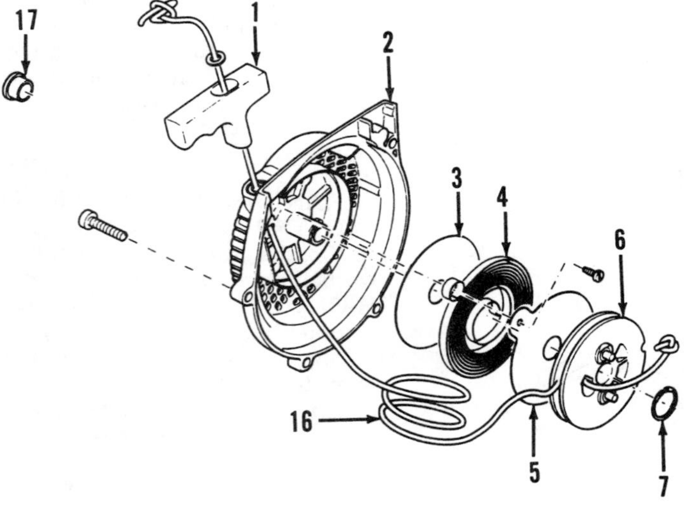

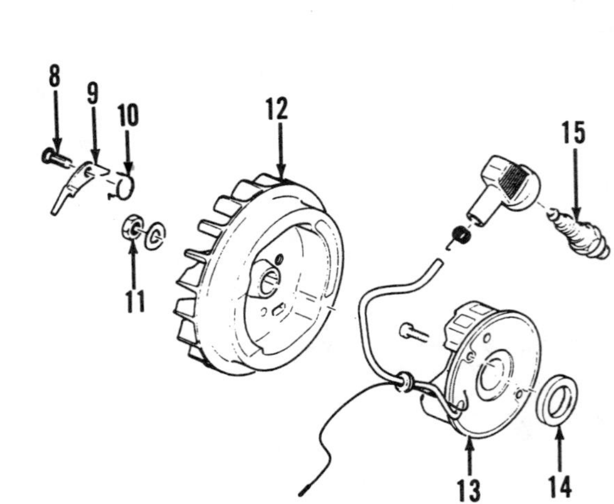

Fig. D134—Exploded view of the recoil starter, flywheel and ignition unit typical of all models.

1. Handle
2. Housing
3. Spacer plate
4. Spring
5. Plate
6. Pulley
7. Snap ring
8. Pivot pin
9. Pawl
10. Spring
11. Nut
12. Flywheel
13. Ignition coil/module
14. Felt washer
15. Spark plug
16. Rope
17. Plug

Illustrations courtesy Dolmar U.S.A., Inc.

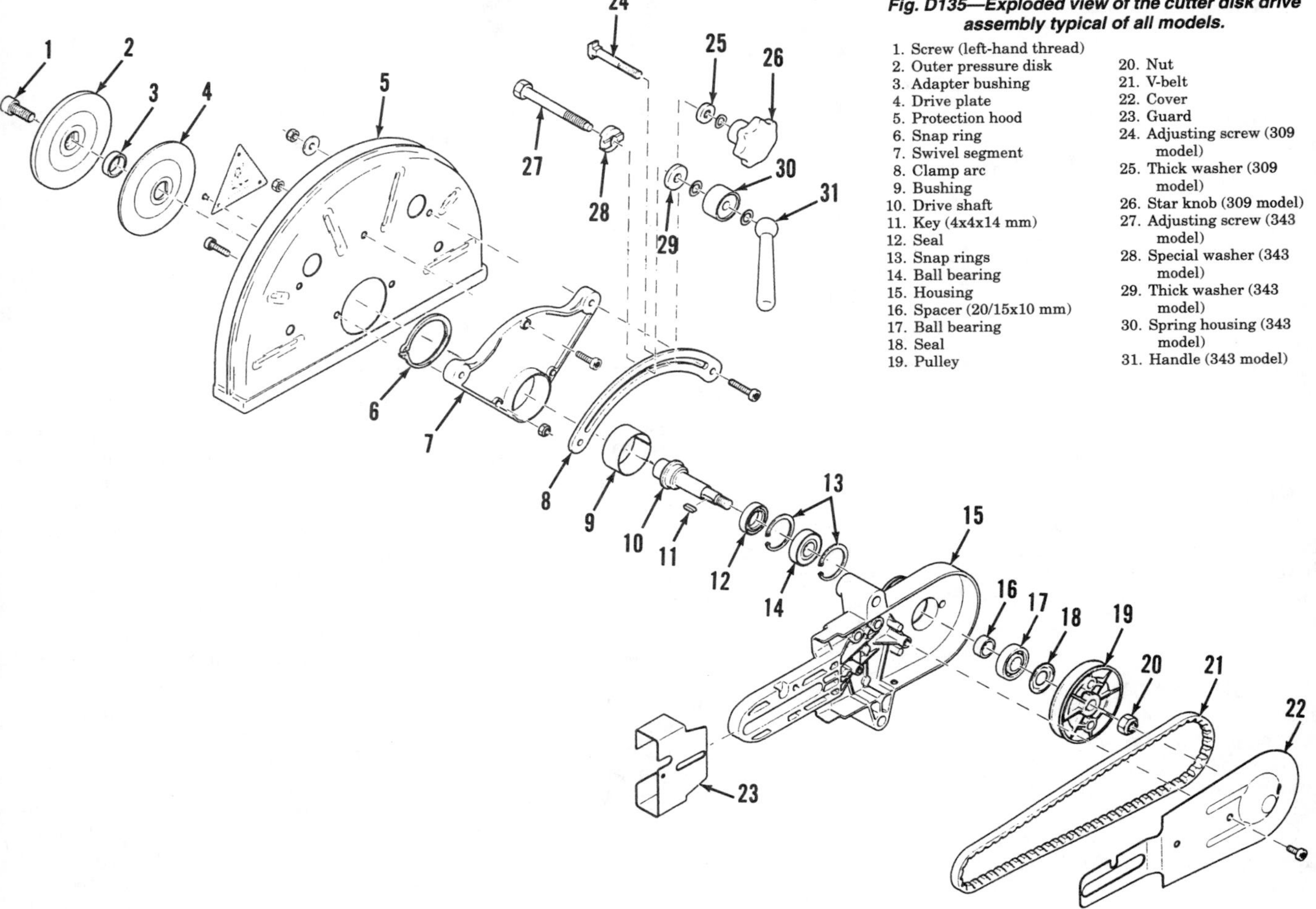

Fig. D135—Exploded view of the cutter disk drive assembly typical of all models.

1. Screw (left-hand thread)
2. Outer pressure disk
3. Adapter bushing
4. Drive plate
5. Protection hood
6. Snap ring
7. Swivel segment
8. Clamp arc
9. Bushing
10. Drive shaft
11. Key (4x4x14 mm)
12. Seal
13. Snap rings
14. Ball bearing
15. Housing
16. Spacer (20/15x10 mm)
17. Ball bearing
18. Seal
19. Pulley
20. Nut
21. V-belt
22. Cover
23. Guard
24. Adjusting screw (309 model)
25. Thick washer (309 model)
26. Star knob (309 model)
27. Adjusting screw (343 model)
28. Special washer (343 model)
29. Thick washer (343 model)
30. Spring housing (343 model)
31. Handle (343 model)

spring, position spacer plate (3) in the housing cavity, then wind the spring (4) into the housing in a clockwise direction beginning with the outside coil. Install the spacer plate (5) and secure with screw.

Wind the rope onto the pulley (6) in a clockwise direction as viewed from the flywheel side of pulley, then install over the post in housing. Preload the recoil spring by turning the pulley about 4 turns clockwise before passing the rope through the opening in the housing (2) and attaching the handle. Install snap ring (7) and check spring preload as follows.

Pull the rope out fully and check that pulley can be turned an additional 1/2 turn without causing the spring to bind. Allow the rope to rewind and make sure the handle is pulled against the housing. If the spring binds, remove some spring preload and recheck. If the handle is not wound against the housing, increase the preload and recheck.

Inspect the condition of the pawl and spring attached to the flywheel. The pawl stud should be pressed into the flywheel after coating the surface of the stud and bore with locking agent (part No. 980 009 000 or equivalent). Install a new flywheel if damaged.

DISK CUTTER ATTACHMENT. Refer to Fig. D135. The unit can be assembled to position the cutter blade toward the center or toward the outside. The guard (5) must be relocated on the housing (15) and the housing (15) must be separated from the power head and turned over to reposition the cutter blade. The cutting disk for 309 models is 300 mm diameter and 350 mm diameter for 343 models. Other differences will be noticed between the units for 309 and 343 models. Either unit can be mounted on a guide trolley.

To remove the unit, loosen clamping nuts (16—Fig. D133), then loosen adjusting screw (21—Fig. D132). Remove clamping nuts and cover (1—Fig. D133). Withdraw the cutter attachment from the mounting studs. Installation procedure is the reverse of removal. Make sure the pin of nut (20—Fig. D132) is aligned with the hole in the housing (15—Fig. D135). Adjust belt tension while assembling.

The belt can be removed and replaced after removing the cover (22—Fig. D135). The drive belt for 309 models is FO-Z XPZ 750. The drive belt for 343 models is FO-Z XPZ 867. The unit must be installed and assembled loosely to adjust the tension. Turn adjusting screw (21—Fig. D132) until the belt tension is correct. A special belt tension measuring tool (part No. 950 100 500) is available. Tighten the clamping nuts (16—Fig. D133) when tension is correct.

To disassemble, separate the unit from the power head. Remove the cutting disk and drive disk (4). Remove the protective cover (22) and drive belt. Insert a punch through the hole in pulley (19—Fig. D135) and into hole in housing (15) to prevent pulley from turning. Remove nut (20) and withdraw the pulley from the shaft. Reinstall nut (20) on the shaft temporarily, then bump the shaft from the bearings. Do not remove seals (12 and 18) or bearings (14 and 17) unless new parts are available. A snap ring (13) is located between the seal (12 and bearing (14). Heat the housing around bearings (14 and 17) before removing or installing the bearings.

DOLMAR

Model	Bore mm (in.)	Stroke mm (in.)	Displacement cc (cu. in.)	Drive Type
PS-33, PS-340, PS-341	37 (1.45)	31 (1.22)	33 (2.01)	Direct
PS-400, PS-401, PS-410, PS-411	40 (1.57)	31 (1.22)	39 (2.38)	Direct

MAINTENANCE

SPARK PLUG. Recommended spark plug is Champion RDJ-7Y or NGK BPMR-6F. Electrode gap should be 0.5 mm (0.020 in.). The spark plug should be tightened to the torque listed in the TIGHTENING TORQUE paragraph.

CARBURETOR. Walbro WT 174 carburetor is used on all models. Refer to the appropriate Walbro section of the CARBURETOR SERVICE section in this manual for service and exploded views.

To remove carburetor, remove air cleaner cover and air filter element. Unscrew carburetor mounting nuts. Disconnect throttle linkage, choke lever, fuel line and impulse tube. Withdraw carburetor from intake manifold. When reinstalling, tighten the carburetor attaching nuts to the torque listed in the TIGHTENING TORQUE paragraph.

Initial setting of the low-speed mixture needle (1—Fig. D141) and high-speed mixture needle (2) is 1 turn open from lightly seated. To adjust the mixture needles, first remove and clean the air filter, then reinstall it. Start the engine and allow it to run until it reaches normal operating temperature. If necessary, turn each of the mixture needles clockwise until seated lightly, then back the needles out (counterclockwise) to the initial setting so the engine can be started. Turn the idle speed stop screw so the engine idles at about 2,600 rpm.

Adjust the low-speed mixture needle so the engine idles smoothly and accelerates without hesitation. Adjust the idle speed to just slower than clutch engagement speed then recheck low-speed mixture adjustment.

It is recommended that a tachometer be used to obtain an accurate high-speed mixture setting. Maximum allowable speed with bar and chain installed is 11,500 rpm for PS-33, PS-340/341 models or 12,000 rpm for PS-400/410 models. The high-speed mixture needle may be set slightly rich to improve performance under load. The engine may be damaged if the high-speed mixture is set too lean.

Final adjustment of the mixture needles should be within 1/4 turn of the initial settings. Large differences may indicate air leaks, plugged passages or other problems.

Fig. D141—View showing location of the carburetor adjustment screws. The idle speed stop screw is located at "Speed," low-speed mixture needle at "L" and high-speed mixture needle at "H."

IGNITION. All models are equipped with a breakerless electronic ignition system. All electronic circuitry is contained in a one-piece ignition module/coil located outside the flywheel. Ignition timing is fixed and not adjustable. The flywheel attaching nut should be tightened to the torque listed in TIGHTENING TORQUE paragraph.

Air gap between the legs of the module/coil and the flywheel magnets should be 0.2 mm (0.008 in.). When installing, set the air gap between the flywheel magnets and the legs of the ignition module as follows.

Install the ignition module, but tighten the two screws only enough to hold it in place away from the flywheel. Insert setting gauge (part No. 944 500 890) or brass/plastic shim stock of the proper thickness between the legs of the ignition module and the flywheel, then turn the flywheel until the flywheel magnets are near the module legs. Loosen the screws attaching the ignition module and press legs of the ignition module against the setting gauge.

Tighten the two attaching screws to the torque listed in the TIGHTENING TORQUE paragraph. Remove the setting gauge, then turn the flywheel and check that flywheel does not hit the legs of the coil.

LUBRICATION. The engine is lubricated by mixing oil with the gasoline fuel. The manufacturer recommends mixing DOLMAR two-stroke oil with regular grade gasoline at a ratio of 40:1 after break-in. When using regular two-stroke engine oil, mix at a ratio of 25:1. During the initial break-in (first 10 hours) the fuel to oil ratio should be 30:1 when using DOLMAR oil or 20:1 when using other approved oil.

Always use a separate container to mix gasoline and oil before filling the fuel tank. The manufacturer recommends not using fuel containing alcohol.

The saw is equipped with an automatic chain oiling system. The manufacturer recommends using DOLMAR Saw Chain oil or other good quality oil

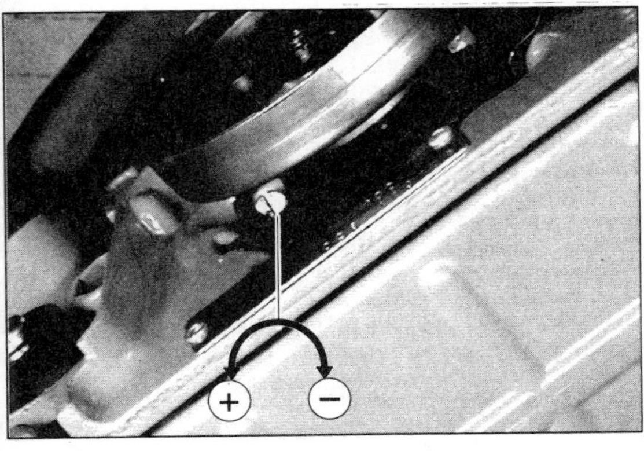

Fig. D142—The chain oil adjustment screw is located as shown. Turn the screw clockwise to reduce the amount of oil or counterclockwise to increase the amount of oil.

designed for lubricating saw chain. Make sure the reservoir is filled at all times.

The volume of oil delivered by the pump is adjustable by turning the adjustment screw located under the saw on the right side (Fig. D142). The type of wood being cut and the type of chain determines the correct amount of oil that should be delivered to the chain.

REPAIRS

TIGHTENING TORQUE. Recommended tightening torque values are as follows.

Carburetor attaching screws . . . . 2.5-2.7 N·m (22-24 in.-lb.)
Clutch hub . . . . 22.5-27.5 N·m (199-243 in.-lb.)
Crankcase . . . . 10-11 N·m (88.5-97 in.-lb.)
Cylinder . . . . 5.5-6.5 N·m (48.6-57.5 in.-lb.)
Decompression valve (341 & 401) . . . . 8 N·m (71 in.-lb.)
Flywheel . . . . 17.5-20 N·m (155-177 in.-lb.)
Ignition module/coil . . . . 3-4 N·m (26.6-35.4 in.-lb.)
Intermediate flange (intake) . . . 6-6.5 N·m (53-57.5 in.-lb.)
Muffler . . . . 8-9 N·m (71-80 in.-lb.)
Spark plug . . . . 14-16 N·m (124-141.6 in.-lb.)
Tubular handle . . . . 2-3 N·m (17.7-26.5 in.-lb.)
Vibration isolator . . . . 2-3 N·m (17.7-26.5 in.-lb.)

PISTON, PIN, RINGS AND CYLINDER. The cylinder can be removed after removal of air filter cover, cylinder cover, muffler, carburetor and intake manifold. Remove four screws attaching cylinder to crankcase and withdraw cylinder from the piston.

Refer to Fig. D143 for exploded view of typical piston and cylinder. One piston ring is used and is pinned in the groove to prevent movement.

NOTE: Be careful when moving the connecting rod with the cylinder removed. It is possible to dislodge the loose needle rollers located at the crankshaft end of the connecting rod.

The piston pin rides in a needle bearing permanently located in the upper end of the connecting rod. The piston pin is retained in the piston by rings (6) located in the piston at each end of the pin. Always install new retainer rings if they are removed, and position the open end of the rings toward the bottom of the piston.

Inspect the cylinder bore for excessive wear or damage. Oversize parts are not available. The piston and cylinder are available separately. The decompression valve installed in the cylinder of 341 and 401 models can be removed for cleaning, inspection and replacement.

When assembling, make sure the arrow on the piston crown is visible and pointing toward the exhaust (muffler) side of the cylinder. A fork tool can be positioned between the bottom of the piston skirt and the crankcase to prevent movement of the piston when installing the cylinder.

Use a suitable ring compressor to compress the piston ring, making certain that the ring ends surround the locating pin. Lubricate cylinder with engine oil, then slide cylinder over the piston. Tighten the cylinder retaining screws to the torque listed in TIGHTENING TORQUE paragraph.

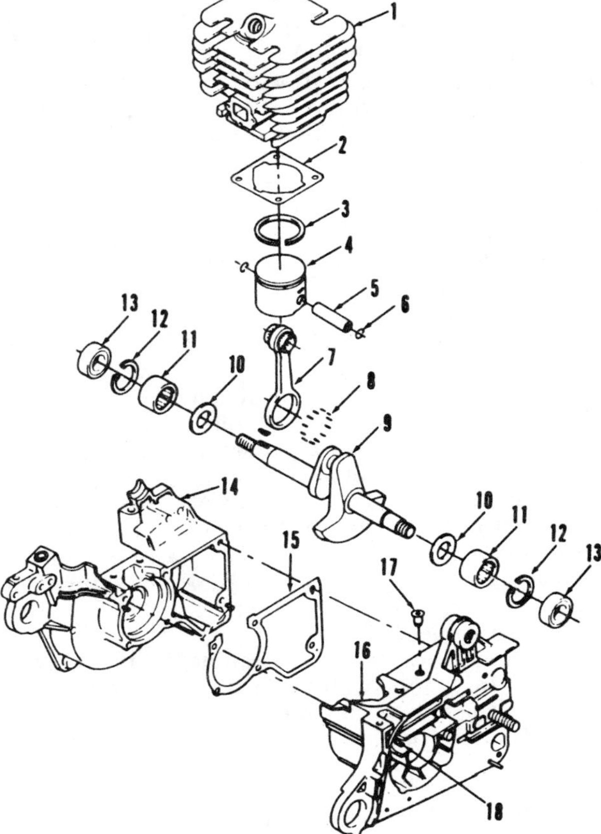

Fig. D143—Exploded view of the cylinder, crankcase, crankshaft and associated parts typical of all models.

1. Cylinder
2. Gasket
3. Piston ring
4. Piston
5. Piston pin
6. Pin retainer rings
7. Connecting rod
8. Bearing rollers (12 used)
9. Crankshaft
10. Thrust washers
11. Main bearings
12. Snap rings
13. Seals
14. Crankcase left half
15. Gasket
16. Crankcase right half
17. Oil tank vent
18. Guide pin

CRANKSHAFT, CONNECTING ROD AND CRANKCASE. Crankshaft is supported by main bearings (11—Fig. D143) located in a split crankcase (14 and 16). Power head must be separated from the fuel tank/handle as-

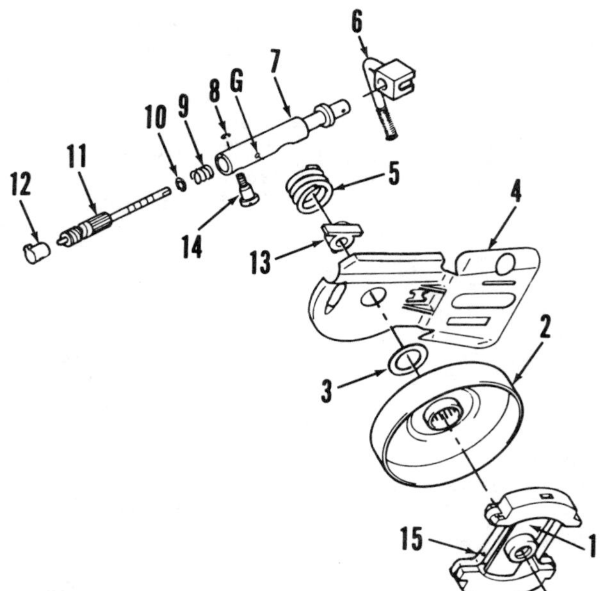

Fig. D144—Exploded view of clutch and chain oil pump assembly.

G. Alignment hole
1. Clutch assy.
2. Clutch drum
3. Shim
4. Plate
5. Worm gear
6. Suction line assy.
7. Pump body
8. "O" ring
9. Spring
10. Washer
11. Plunger
12. Plug
13. Seal
14. Adjusting screw
15. Clutch spring

sembly in order to service the crankshaft and connecting rod.

The clutch, oil pump, pump drive worm, flywheel, cylinder, and piston must be removed before separating the crankcase halves. Remove the attaching screws and tap the crankcase as necessary with a soft faced hammer to separate the halves. DO NOT insert any type of pry bar between the crankcase halves as damage to the crankcase sealing surfaces could result.

Twelve loose needle rollers (8—Fig. D143) are located between the connecting rod and the crankshaft crankpin. The loose rollers can be removed after slipping the rod (7) from the bearing rollers. Make sure that all rollers are removed and installed when servicing the bearing. Use grease to hold the rollers in place while assembling the connecting rod.

Do not attempt to remove the needle bearing from piston pin end of connecting rod. The bearing is not available except as a unit with the connecting rod.

The crankshaft is supported at both ends by caged needle roller bearings (11). The main bearings must be seated against the snap rings (12). Do not damage or lose thrust washers (10). Do not remove the main bearings or crankcase seals (13) unless new parts will be installed. Seals can be removed and new seals installed using an appropriate seal puller (part No. 944 500 870 or equivalent) without separating the crankcase halves.

If main bearings were removed from crankcase bores, install snap rings (12) and press the main bearings into bores against the snap rings. Assemble the connecting rod (7) and twelve bearing rollers (8) using grease to hold the rollers in position. Install thrust washer (10) on each end of the crankshaft. Install the oil pump suction hose and position the crankcase gasket over the dowel studs of the right crankcase half.

Install the crankshaft into the right crankcase half, then install the left case half. Tighten the screws attaching the crankcase halves to the torque listed in TIGHTENING TORQUE paragraph. Install the piston and cylinder.

CLUTCH. Refer to Fig. D144. The clutch hub (1) is attached to the right end of the engine crankshaft with left-hand threads (turn clockwise to remove). To remove clutch, first remove sprocket guard and chain brake assembly. Prevent the crankshaft from turning by using an appropriate piston stopper. The clutch hub can be removed using the special tool (part No. 944 500 690) or equivalent wrench (turn clockwise). The clutch drum (2) can be withdrawn after the hub and shoes are removed.

The drum and bearing are available only as an assembly. Inspect the clutch drum and chain drive sprocket, then replace parts as necessary. The clutch shoes and hub (1) are available only as an assembly, but springs (15) are available separately.

When assembling, install the smaller shim (3) before installing the clutch drum. Grease the needle bearing in the clutch drum lightly before installing the drum. Install the clutch assembly, tightening the hub to the torque listed in TIGHTENING TORQUE paragraph.

OIL PUMP. All models are equipped with an automatic chain oil pump typical of the type shown in Fig. D144. Oil is pumped by plunger (11), which is turned by worm gear (5). Pump output is adjusted by turning screw (14).

The oil pump can be removed from the engine after removing the clutch assembly and plate (4). Pull pump from the suction line (6). The suction line can be pulled from the crankcase if required. Special tool (part No. 950 500 011) should be used to pull the worm drive gear (5) from the crankshaft.

Inspect plunger (11), worm gear (5) and bore in pump housing (7) for wear or damage. If wear or damage is excessive, it is suggested that a new pump assembly and worm drive gear be installed. Grease the pump plunger (11) liberally with silicone grease before assembling the pump.

To install the worm gear, screw the worm gear onto special tool (part No. 950 500 011), then heat the worm gear to approximately 100 degrees C (212 degrees F). Position the worm gear on the crankshaft until the tool is bottomed, allow the worm gear to cool, then remove the special tool leaving the worm on the crankshaft.

Install the filter at the end of suction line (6) and lubricate the line with silicone grease before installing in the crankcase. Insert the pump body into the suction line and move it into position. Make sure the hole in the pump housing engages the pin on the side of the crankcase near the crankshaft.

REWIND STARTER. Remove the flywheel to gain access to the recoil starter (Fig. D145). Remove the handle (10) and carefully allow the rope pulley (7) to unwind and relieve tension on spring (8).

To disassemble, remove the brake spring (5) and retainer ring (4), then lift the rope pulley from the engine. Remove the cover (9) and spring (8) if necessary, being careful to prevent injury when spring unwinds.

Clean and inspect parts for damage. The 3 mm diameter starter rope should be 90 cm long. Lubricate the recoil spring, then wind the spring into the pulley in a clockwise direction beginning with the outside coil. Wind the rope onto the pulley in a counterclockwise direction as viewed from the flywheel side of pulley.

Assemble cover (9), spring (8) and pulley (7) and install the retainer ring (4) with the end gap toward the ignition coil (11). Make sure starter pawl (6) properly engages the brake spring (5) as shown in Fig. D146.

Wind the rope completely onto the rope pulley. To preload the rewind spring, hold the rope tight into the

Illustrations courtesy Dolmar U.S.A., Inc.

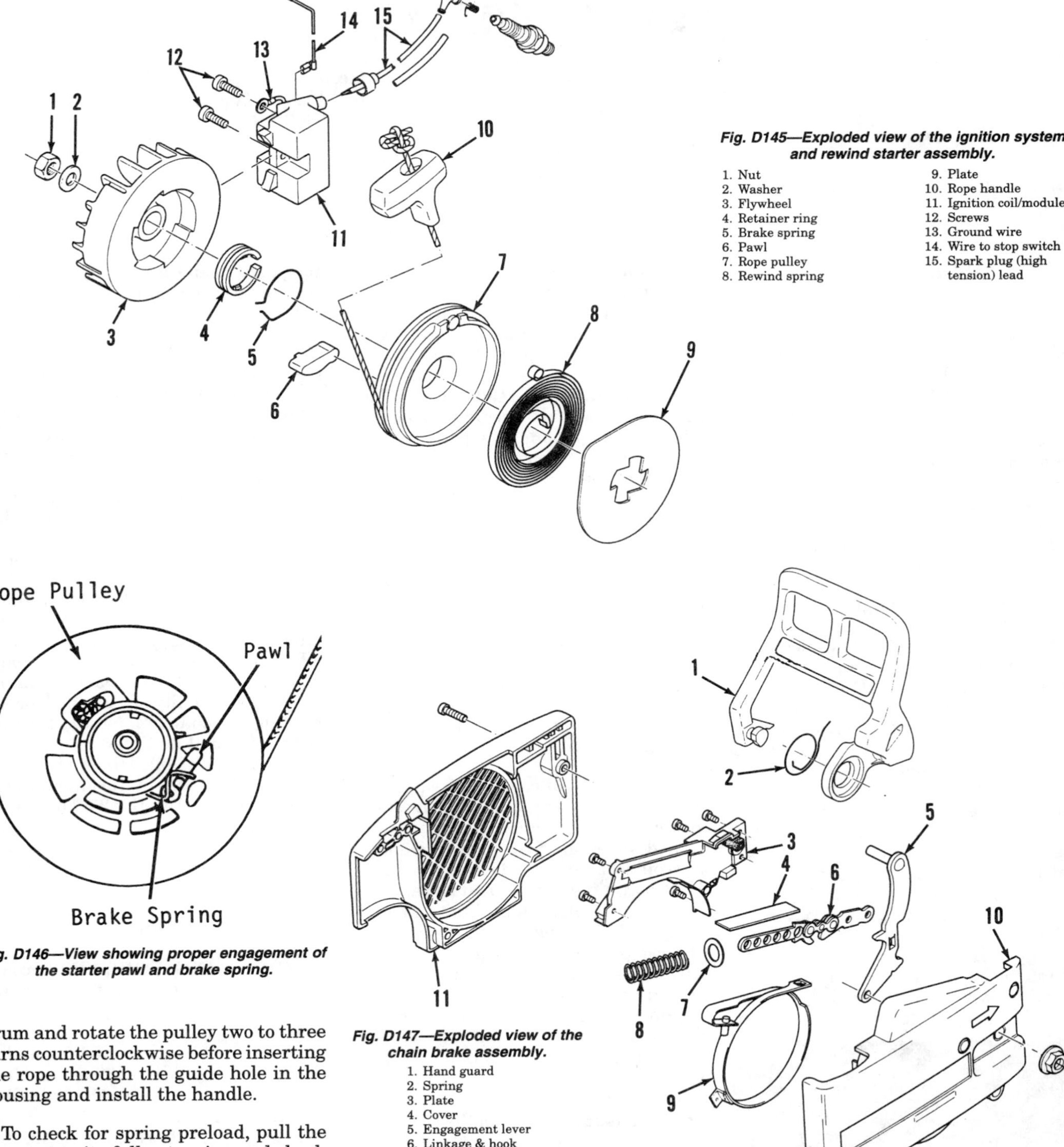

Fig. D145—Exploded view of the ignition system and rewind starter assembly.

1. Nut
2. Washer
3. Flywheel
4. Retainer ring
5. Brake spring
6. Pawl
7. Rope pulley
8. Rewind spring
9. Plate
10. Rope handle
11. Ignition coil/module
12. Screws
13. Ground wire
14. Wire to stop switch
15. Spark plug (high tension) lead

Fig. D146—View showing proper engagement of the starter pawl and brake spring.

Fig. D147—Exploded view of the chain brake assembly.

1. Hand guard
2. Spring
3. Plate
4. Cover
5. Engagement lever
6. Linkage & hook
7. Washer
8. Spring
9. Brake band
10. Cover

drum and rotate the pulley two to three turns counterclockwise before inserting the rope through the guide hole in the housing and install the handle.

To check for spring preload, pull the rope out to its full extension and check that pulley can be turned an additional 1/2 turn without causing the spring to bind. Allow the rope to rewind and make sure the handle is pulled against the housing. If the spring binds, remove some spring preload and recheck. If the handle is not wound against the housing, increase the preload and recheck.

CHAIN BRAKE. The chain brake assembly is designed to stop the chain quickly should kickback occur. The chain brake is activated when the operator's hand strikes the hand guard (1—Fig. D147). When the brake system is activated, spring (8) tightens the brake band (9) around the clutch drum. To release, pull the hand guard back until the mechanism is reset.

The chain brake must be released before the housing (10) can be removed. To disassemble, remove cover plate (3). Lift out brake band (9), spring (8), linkage (6) and lever (5). Lubricate all of the pivot points with suitable low temperature grease when assembling. No adjustment of the mechanism is required.

DOLMAR

Model	Bore mm (in.)	Stroke mm (in.)	Displacement cc (cu. in.)	Drive Type
PS-9000	52 (2.05)	42 (1.65)	90 (5.5)	Direct

MAINTENANCE

SPARK PLUG. Recommended spark plug is Bosch WSR-6F or NGK BPMR-7A. Electrode gap should be 0.5 mm (0.020 in.). The spark plug should be tightened to the torque listed in the TIGHTENING TORQUE paragraph.

CARBURETOR. Bing 49-B carburetor is used. Refer to the appropriate Bing section of the CARBURETOR SERVICE section in this manual for service and exploded views.

Initial setting of the low-speed and high-speed mixture needles is 1 turn open from lightly seated. Note that the outer face of adjusting guide is marked with the letters "L", "H" and "S" to indicate the location of the low-speed and high-speed mixture needles and idle speed stop screw (Fig. D150).

To adjust the mixture needles, first remove and clean the air filter, then reinstall it. Start the engine and allow it to run until it reaches normal operating temperature. If necessary, turn each of the mixture needles (L and H) clockwise until seated lightly, then back the needles out (counterclockwise) to the initial setting so the engine can be started. Turn the idle speed stop screw (S) so the engine idles at about 2,200 rpm.

Adjust the low-speed mixture needle (L) so the engine idles smoothly and accelerates without hesitation. Adjust the idle speed to just slower than clutch engagement speed, then recheck low-speed mixture adjustment.

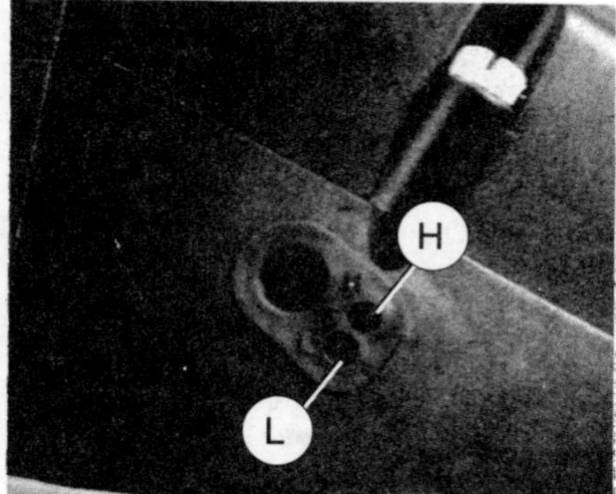

Fig. D150—Carburetor adjustment guide is marked with letters "L", "H" and "S" to indicate location of low-speed and high-speed mixture screws and idle speed stop screw.

It is recommended that a tachometer be used to obtain an accurate high-speed mixture setting. Maximum allowable no-load speed (with bar and chain installed) is 11,800 rpm. The high-speed mixture needle may be set slightly rich to improve performance under load. The engine may be damaged if the high-speed mixture is set too lean.

Final adjustment of the mixture needles should be within 1/4 turn of the initial settings. Large differences may indicate air leaks, plugged passages or other problems.

Carburetor (7—Fig. D151) can be removed after removal of air cleaner cover (1), filter element (3), cover (5) and bracket (6). Disconnect fuel line, vent line (8), choke lever (14) and throttle cable. Withdraw carburetor from bottom cover (9).

IGNITION. All models are equipped with a breakerless electronic ignition system. All electronic circuitry is contained in a one-piece ignition module/coil located outside the flywheel. Ignition timing is fixed and not adjustable. The ignition unit limits engine speed to 11,800 rpm.

Air gap between the legs of the module/coil and the flywheel magnets should be 0.2 mm (0.008 in.). When installing, set the air gap between the flywheel magnets and the legs of the ignition module as follows.

Install the ignition module, but tighten the two screws only enough to hold it in place away from the flywheel. Insert setting gauge (part No. 944 500 890) or brass/plastic shim stock of the proper thickness between the legs of the ignition module and the flywheel, then turn the flywheel until the flywheel magnets are near the module legs. Loosen the screws attaching the ignition module and press legs of the ignition module against the setting gauge.

Tighten the two attaching screws to the torque listed in the TIGHTENING TORQUE paragraph. Remove the setting gauge, then turn the flywheel and check to be sure that the flywheel does not hit the legs of the coil.

LUBRICATION. The engine is lubricated by mixing oil with the gasoline fuel. The manufacturer recommends mixing DOLMAR two-stroke oil with regular grade gasoline at a ratio of 50:1. When using regular two-stroke engine oil, mix at a ratio of 40:1.

Always use a separate container to mix gasoline and oil before filling the fuel tank. The manufacturer recommends not using fuel containing alcohol.

The saw is equipped with an automatic chain oiling system. An automatic oil pump supplies oil to the bar and chain. The manufacturer recommends using DOLMAR Saw Chain oil or other good quality oil designed for lubricating saw chain. Make sure the reservoir is filled at all times.

The volume of oil delivered by the pump is adjustable by turning adjustment screw (1—Fig. D152). The screw is located under the saw on the right side. Turn screw counterclockwise to increase oil output or clockwise to decrease oil delivery.

REPAIRS

TIGHTENING TORQUE. Recommended tightening torque values are as follows.

Carburetor . . . . 6-7 N•m (53-62 in.-lb.)
Clutch hub . . . . 52.5-57.5 N•m (465-509 in.-lb.)
Crankcase . 10-11 N•m (88.5-97 in.-lb.)
Cylinder . . . . . 9-11 N•m (80-97 in.-lb.)
Flywheel . . . . 27.5-32.5 N•m (243-288 in.-lb.)
Ignition module/coil . . . . 6-7 N•m (53-62 in.-lb.)
Intermediate flange (intake) . . . . 5.5-6.5 N•m (48.7-57.5 in.-lb.)
Muffler . . . . . 8-12 N•m (71-106 in.-lb.)
Spark plug . . . . 24.5-25.5 N•m (217-226 in.-lb.)
Tubular handle . . . . 7-8 N•m (62-71 in.-lb.)

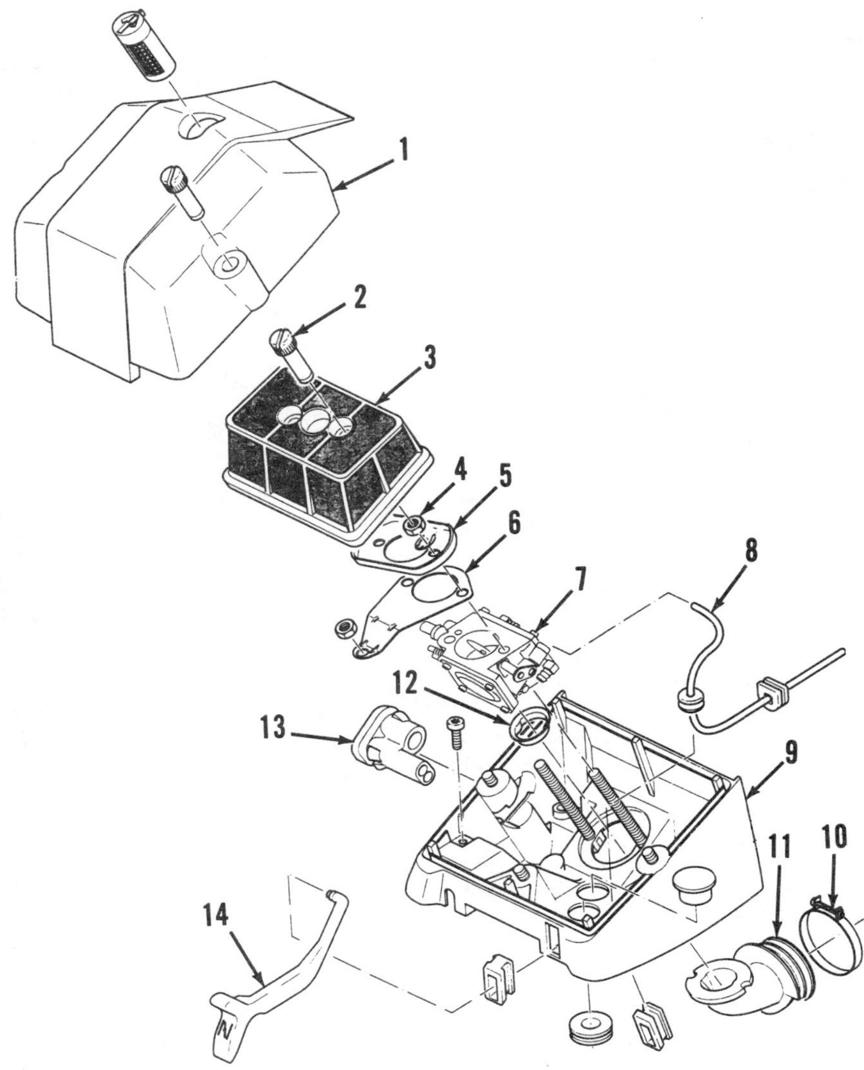

Fig. D151—Exploded view of air cleaner and intake system.

1. Cover
2. Nut
3. Air filter
4. Nut
5. Filter holder
6. Bracket
7. Carburetor
8. Vent tube
9. Bottom cover
10. Clamp
11. Intake tube
12. Gasket
13. Adjusting guide
14. Choke lever

Fig. D152—The chain oil adjustment screw (1) is located underneath the saw. Turn the screw clockwise to reduce the amount of oil or counterclockwise to increase the amount of oil.

Vibration isolator . . . . 5-6 N•m (44-53 in.-lb.)

PISTON, PIN, RINGS AND CYLINDER. Refer to Fig. D153. The cylinder can be removed after removal of the airbox cover (1—Fig. D151), air cleaner (3), carburetor (7), bottom cover (9), cylinder cover, muffler, starter housing and sprocket guard. Remove four screws attaching cylinder to crankcase and withdraw cylinder from the piston.

The piston pin is retained by wire retainer rings (9—Fig. D153). Remove retaining rings and push pin (10) out of piston. Remove piston and needle bearing (8) from connecting rod. The piston is equipped with two piston rings (12), which are prevented from rotating in their grooves by locating pins.

The cylinder may be equipped with a decompression valve (13) to ease starting. The decompression valve can be removed for cleaning, inspection and replacement.

Inspect the cylinder bore for excessive wear or damage. Oversize parts are not available. The piston is available separately, but the cylinder is only available with a matching piston. Tops of the cylinder and piston are marked with "A, B," or "C" and both should have the same letter.

When assembling, make sure the arrow on the piston crown is visible and pointing toward the exhaust (muffler) side of the cylinder. If removed, always install new piston pin retainer rings (9). Make certain that retaining rings are seated in the groove and position the ring ends toward the bottom of the piston.

Slide a fork tool or a piece of wood between the bottom of the piston skirt and the crankcase to hold the piston up while installing the cylinder. Use a suitable ring compressor to compress the piston rings, making certain that the ring end gaps are aligned with the locating pins. Lubricate cylinder with engine oil and slide cylinder over the piston. Tighten the cylinder retaining screws to the torque listed in TIGHTENING TORQUE paragraph.

CRANKSHAFT, CONNECTING ROD AND CRANKCASE. The powerhead must be separated from the fuel tank/handle assembly (24—Fig. D154) in order to service the crankshaft and connecting rod. The clutch, oil pump, pump drive worm, flywheel, cylinder, and piston must be removed before separating the crankcase halves.

Remove screws attaching crankcase halves together, then tap the crankcase as necessary with a soft faced hammer to separate the halves. DO NOT insert any type of pry bar between the crankcase halves as damage to the crankcase sealing surfaces could result.

The ball type main bearings (6—Fig. D153) and shaft seals (2 and 21) are located in the case halves. Main bearings and shaft seals should be removed only if new parts will be installed in the case halves. Rotate the connecting rod

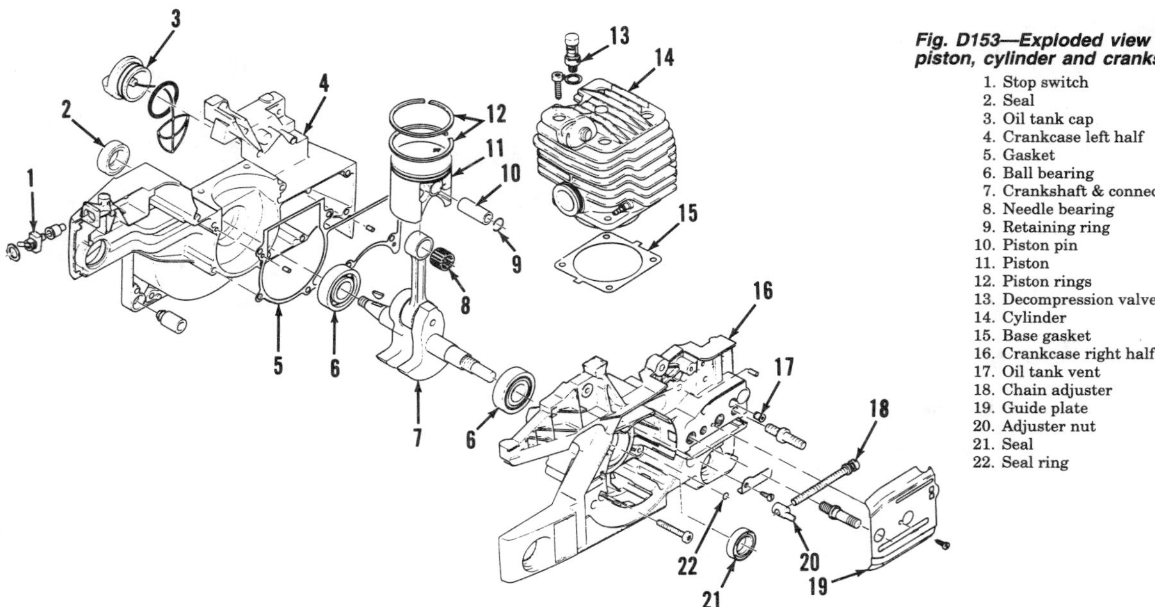

Fig. D153—Exploded view of the cylinder, piston, cylinder and crankshaft assembly.

1. Stop switch
2. Seal
3. Oil tank cap
4. Crankcase left half
5. Gasket
6. Ball bearing
7. Crankshaft & connecting rod
8. Needle bearing
9. Retaining ring
10. Piston pin
11. Piston
12. Piston rings
13. Decompression valve
14. Cylinder
15. Base gasket
16. Crankcase right half
17. Oil tank vent
18. Chain adjuster
19. Guide plate
20. Adjuster nut
21. Seal
22. Seal ring

around the crankpin while checking for roughness, excessive play or other damage. The crankshaft and connecting rod are a unit assembly and not available separately.

Do not remove the main bearings from the crankcase unless it is necessary to install new bearings. Heat the case halves to approximately 100 degrees C (212 degrees F) before pressing the bearings from or into the case bores. Install the main bearings before installing the seals. Special tools (part No. 944 603 360, 944 603 370 and 944 603 410 or equivalent) are required for installing new crankshaft seals.

When assembling, lubricate the shaft seals and bearings with clean engine oil. Insert the crankshaft in the clutch side crankcase half, position a new gasket against the case, and then assemble the other case half. Tighten the screws attaching the crankcase halves to the torque listed in TIGHTENING TORQUE paragraph.

CLUTCH. The three shoe centrifugal clutch is shown in Fig. D155. The floating sprocket (9) and clutch drum (11) can be withdrawn after the removing the "E" ring (6) and washers (7 and 8). The needle bearing (10) located in the clutch drum should be lubricated lightly before assembling.

The clutch hub is attached to the right end of the engine crankshaft with left-hand threads (turn clockwise to remove). Special tool (part No. 944 603 420) should be used to grip the clutch hub while turning. Prevent the crankshaft from turning by using an appropriate piston stopper. Clutch springs are available, but the shoes and hub are not available except as a complete clutch assembly. Tighten the clutch hub to the torque listed in TIGHTENING TORQUE paragraph.

OIL PUMP. An automatic chain oil pump is shown in Fig. D155. Oil is pumped by plunger (32), which is turned by worm gear (23). Pump output is adjusted by turning screw (27).

The oil pump can be unbolted and pulled from the engine after removing the clutch and chain brake assemblies. Failure of the oil tank vent (17—Fig. D153) or sealing ring (22) may cause oiling problems.

The vent is removed by pushing it into oil tank using a 4 mm diameter punch, then a 6 mm punch is used to

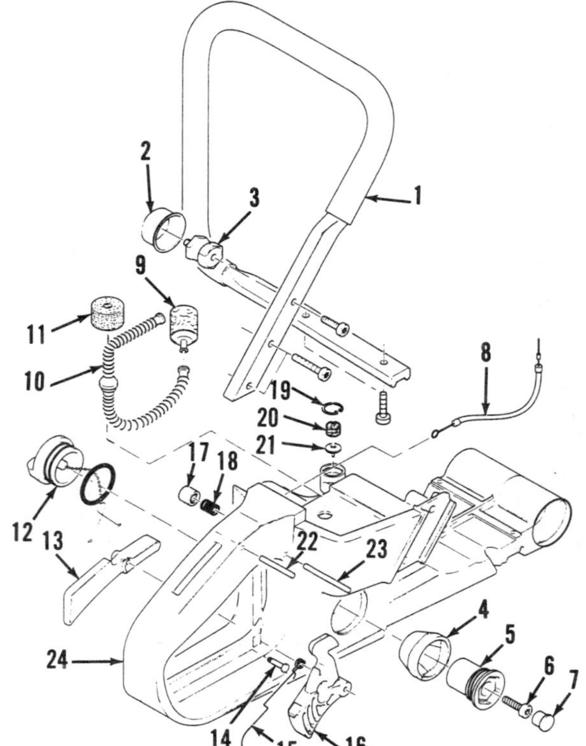

Fig. D154—Exploded view of the fuel tank, handles and associated parts.

1. Tubular handle
2. Cup
3. Vibration isolator
4. Spacer (4 used)
5. Vibration isolator (4 used)
6. Screw
7. Plug
8. Throttle cable
9. Fuel filter
10. Fuel line
11. Seal
12. Cap
13. Throttle interlock
14. Pin
15. Return spring
16. Throttle trigger
17. Button
18. Spring
19. Snap ring
20. Filter
21. Air valve
22. Pin (3x28 mm)
23. Pin (3x45 mm)
24. Fuel tank & handle

Illustrations courtesy Dolmar U.S.A., Inc.

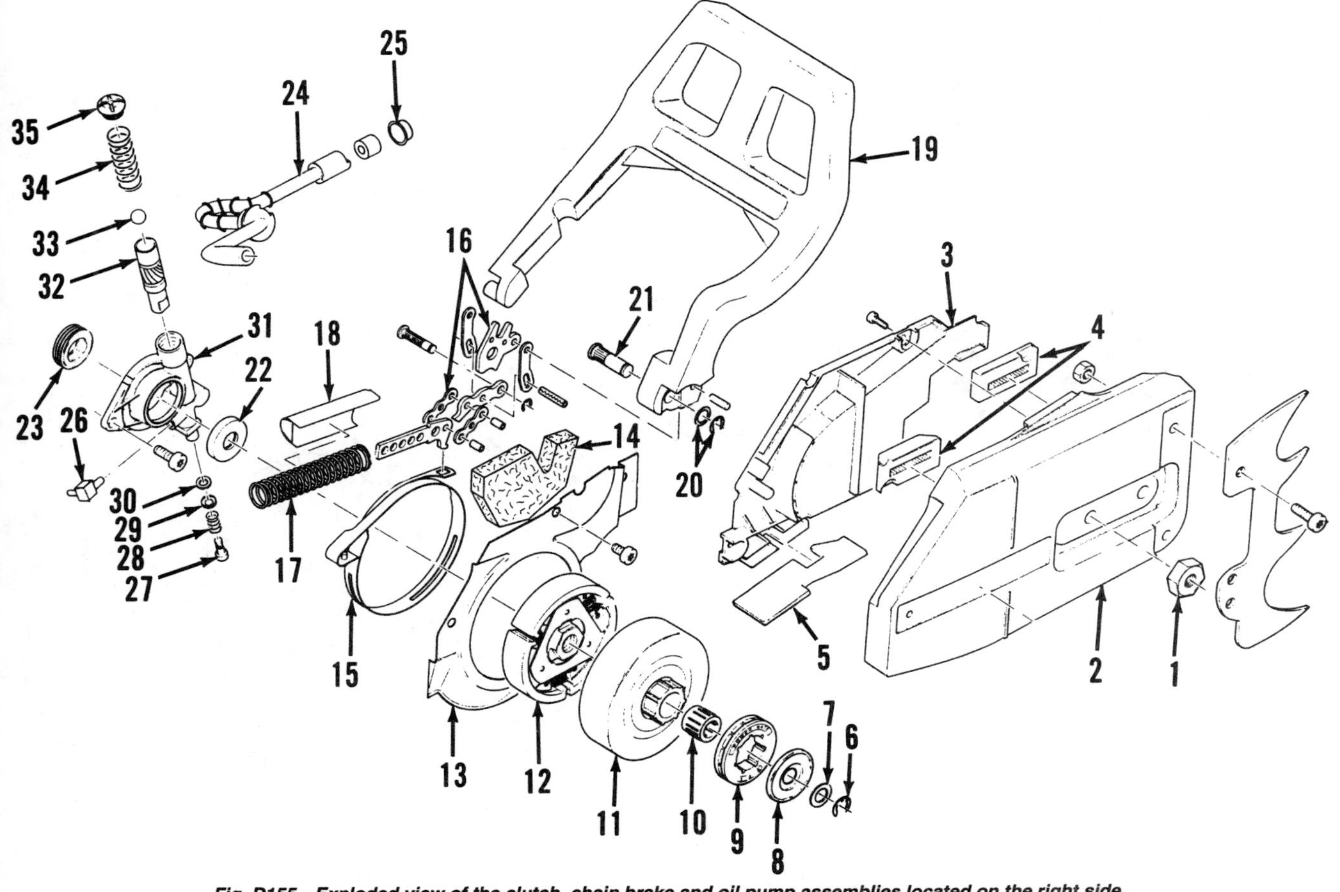

Fig. D155—Exploded view of the clutch, chain brake and oil pump assemblies located on the right side.

1. Clamp nuts
2. Cover
3. Chip guide
4. Chain guide
5. Rubber plate
6. "E" ring
7. Washer
8. Washer
9. Sprocket
10. Needle bearing
11. Clutch drum
12. Clutch assembly
13. Plate
14. Foam
15. Brake band
16. Brake linkage
17. Brake spring
18. Spring guide
19. Hand guard
20. "E" ring & washer
21. Pin
22. Seal
23. Pump drive worm
24. Suction line
25. Filter screen
26. Elbow
27. Adjusting screw
28. Spring
29. Washer
30. Seal
31. Housing
32. Pump body
33. Ball
34. Spring
35. Plug

press the new vent into position. Lip of seal (22—Fig. D155) should be toward clutch.

Use special tool (part No. 957 434 000 or equivalent) to remove and install the drive worm (23). To install the worm gear, screw the worm gear onto special tool, then heat the worm gear to approximately 100 degrees C (212 degrees F). Position the worm gear on the crankshaft until the tool is bottomed, allow the worm gear to cool, then remove the special tool leaving the worm on the crankshaft.

CHAIN BRAKE. The chain brake assembly is designed to stop the chain quickly should kickback occur. The chain brake is activated when the operator's hand strikes the hand guard (19—Fig. D155). When the brake system is activated, spring (17) tightens the brake band (15) around the clutch drum (11). To release, pull the hand guard back until the mechanism is reset.

To remove the brake band (15), first remove the clutch drum (11) and clutch assembly (12). Engage the chain brake by pushing hand guard (19) forward. Engaging the brake after removing the clutch drum relaxes the spring (17) enough to remove the band.

Install cover (part No. 944 603 390) over the spring to hold it in position, then unhook the ends of the chain brake and lift it out. The spring (17) can be removed using pointed pliers after removing the temporarily installed cover.

The brake linkage (16) can be disassembled and removed after removing "E" rings and pins. Installation of the brake spring is easier using needle nose pliers (part No. 944 603 080 or equivalent) to compress the spring.

Install the brake band by hooking the ends of the band over the mounting points. Install cover (part No. 944 603 390 or equivalent) before compressing the brake spring (releasing the brake band). The chain brake must be released before the clutch can be removed. No adjustment of the mechanism is required.

REWIND STARTER. Refer to Fig. D156 for exploded view of the rewind starter. The starter assembly can be unbolted and removed from the engine.

If the recoil spring is under pressure, remove the starter from the engine. Pull the rope out about 20 cm (8 in.) and hold the pulley (5). Unwind the rope from the pulley, then allow the pulley to slowly unwind. Remove screw (7) and axle (6), then slide pulley (5) from the shaft. Make sure spring is completely unwound before removing the pulley.

If starter cord is damaged, replace with 100 cm of new 4 mm diameter rope. Tie a knot in end of rope and attach rope to pulley. Be sure that the knot is properly nested in the pulley.

If not damaged, the rewind spring (3) can remain in spring case (4). Inspect the spring to make sure that both ends are in good condition and the spring is not broken. If the spring is removed, it

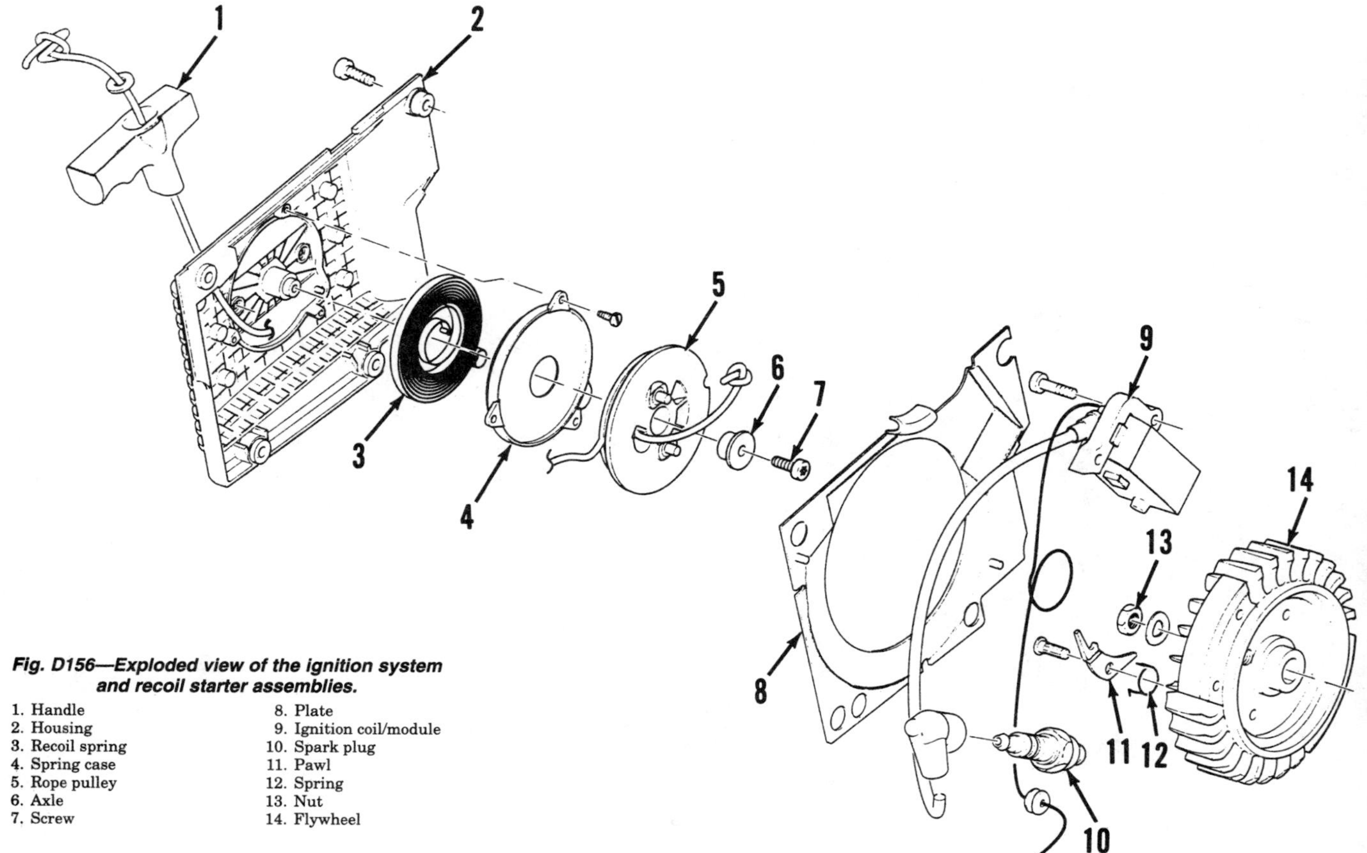

Fig. D156—Exploded view of the ignition system and recoil starter assemblies.

1. Handle
2. Housing
3. Recoil spring
4. Spring case
5. Rope pulley
6. Axle
7. Screw
8. Plate
9. Ignition coil/module
10. Spark plug
11. Pawl
12. Spring
13. Nut
14. Flywheel

should be wound into the case (4) in a counterclockwise direction starting with the outer coil. Attach the spring case (4) to the housing after the spring is installed.

Install the pulley (5) with rope attached. The pulley should engage the inner end of the spring (3). Install axle (6) and screw (7). Wind rope onto the pulley in clockwise direction. Preload the pulley approximately 2 turns clockwise, insert the end of the rope through guide in the housing, and attach the handle (1).

Pull the rope out fully and check that pulley can be turned an additional 1/2 turn without causing the spring to bind. Allow the rope to rewind and make sure the handle is pulled against the housing. If the spring binds, remove some spring preload and recheck. If the handle is not wound against the housing, increase the preload and recheck.

Inspect the condition of the pawl (11) and spring (12) attached to the flywheel. The pawl stud should be pressed into the flywheel after coating the surface of the stud and bore with locking agent (part No. 980 009 000 or equivalent).

Illustrations courtesy Dolmar U.S.A., Inc.

DOLMAR

Model	Bore mm (in.)	Stroke mm (in.)	Displacement cc (cu. in.)	Drive Type
PS-6000	46 (1.81)	36 (1.41)	60 (3.6)	Direct
PS-6800	49 (1.92)	36 (1.41)	68 (4.1)	Direct

MAINTENANCE

SPARK PLUG. Recommended spark plug is Bosch WSR-6F. Electrode gap should be 0.5 mm (0.020 in.). The spark plug should be tightened to the torque listed in the TIGHTENING TORQUE paragraph.

CARBURETOR. Tillotson HS-236 carburetor is used. Refer to the appropriate Tillotson section of the CARBURETOR SERVICE section in this manual for service and exploded views.

To remove carburetor, first remove air filter cover (1—Fig. D160) and filter element (2). Remove carburetor mounting screws. Disconnect fuel line and throttle link (13), and withdraw carburetor from engine.

Carburetor adjusting screws are located on the left side of the saw (Fig. D161). Initial setting of the low-speed mixture needle (L) and high-speed mixture needle (H) is 1 turn open from lightly seated. It is recommended that a tachometer be used to achieve correct adjustment of the carburetor.

To adjust the mixture needles, start the engine and allow it to run until it reaches normal operating temperature. If necessary, turn each of the mixture needles clockwise until seated lightly, then back the needles out (counterclockwise) to the initial setting so the engine can be started. Turn the idle speed stop screw (S) so the engine idles at about 2,400 rpm.

Adjust the low-speed mixture needle (L) so the engine idles smoothly and accelerates without hesitation. Adjust the idle speed so that engine idles at 2,400 rpm (clutch must not engage), then recheck low-speed mixture adjustment.

It is recommended that a tachometer be used to obtain an accurate high-speed mixture setting. Adjust high-speed mixture needle (H) to obtain the following maximum speed with bar and chain installed: 13,000 rpm for PS-6000 models or 12,500 rpm for PS-6800 models. The high-speed mixture needle may be set slightly rich to improve performance under load. The engine may be damaged if the high-speed mixture is set too lean.

Final adjustment of the mixture needles should be within 1/4 turn of the initial settings. Large differences may indicate air leaks, plugged passages or other problems. Make certain that hot air shutter (4—Fig. D160) is closed during warm weather operation.

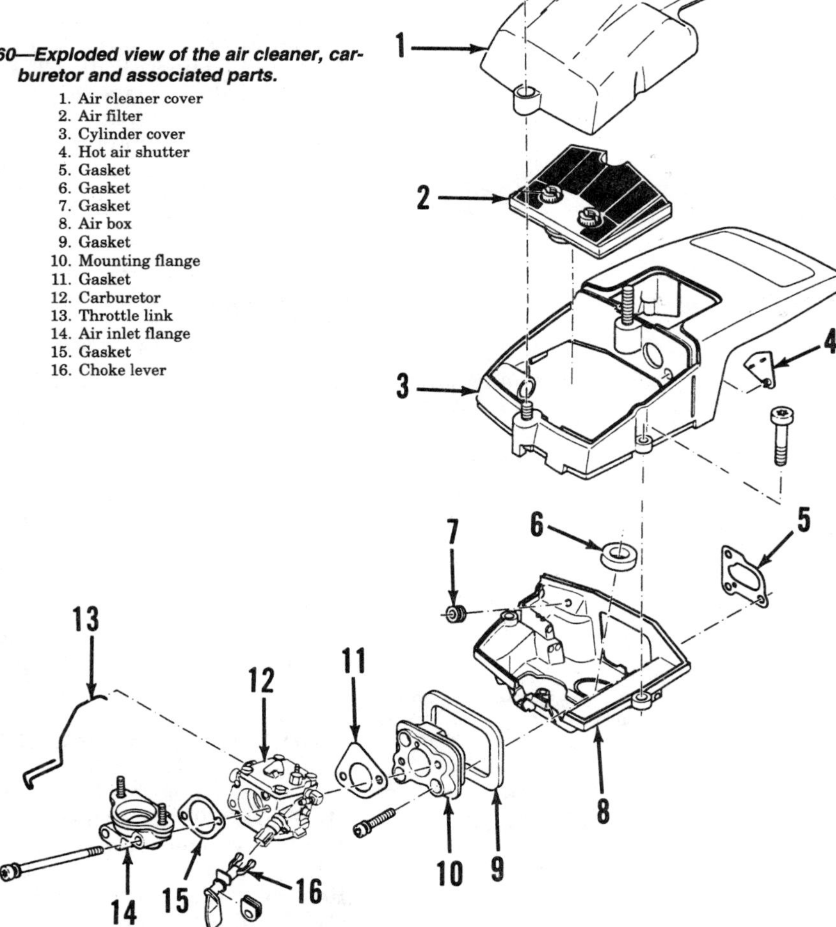

Fig. D160—Exploded view of the air cleaner, carburetor and associated parts.

1. Air cleaner cover
2. Air filter
3. Cylinder cover
4. Hot air shutter
5. Gasket
6. Gasket
7. Gasket
8. Air box
9. Gasket
10. Mounting flange
11. Gasket
12. Carburetor
13. Throttle link
14. Air inlet flange
15. Gasket
16. Choke lever

IGNITION. All models are equipped with a breakerless electronic ignition system with a one-piece ignition module/coil. Ignition timing is fixed and not adjustable.

LUBRICATION. The engine is lubricated by mixing oil with the gasoline fuel. The manufacturer recommends mixing DOLMAR two-stroke oil with regular grade gasoline at a ratio of 50:1 after break-in. When using regular

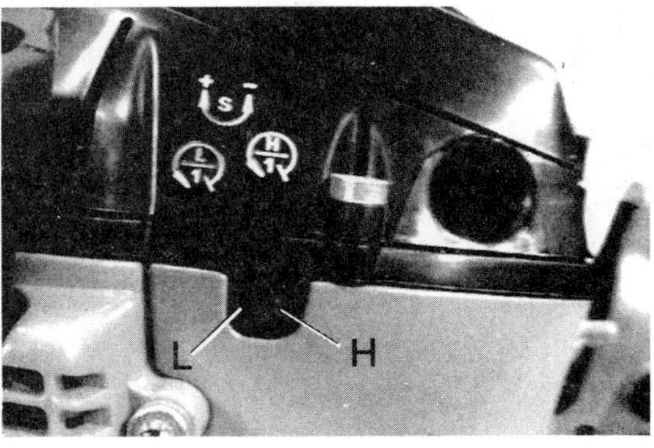

Fig. D161—Carburetor adjustment screws are accessible on left side of saw. Low speed mixture screw is located at "L", high-speed mixture screw is at "H" and idle speed screw is at "S".

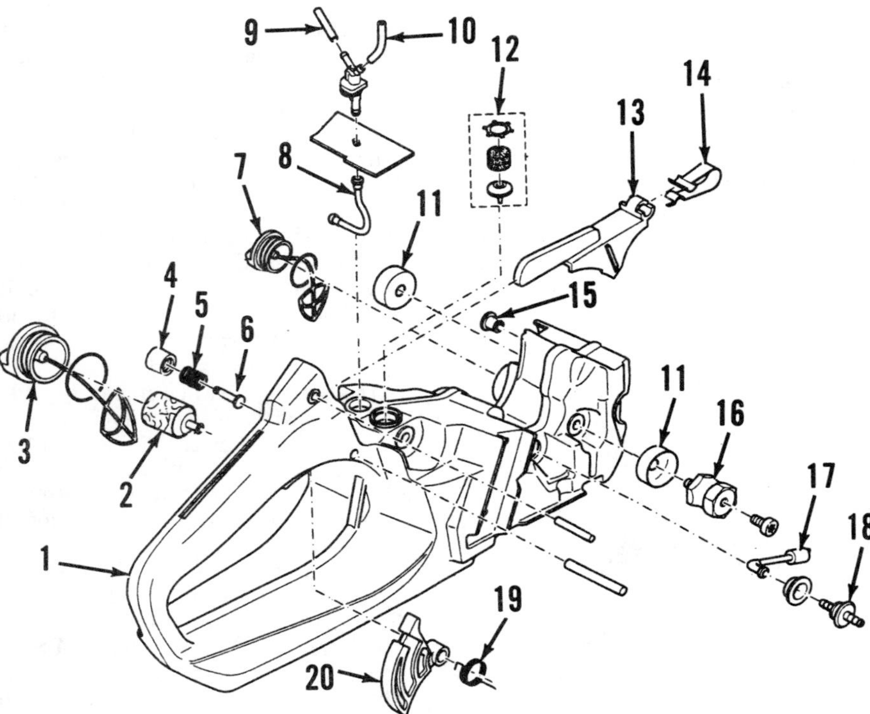

Fig. D162—Fuel and oil tank are located in handle housing. A fuel filter (2) is located in the fuel tank.

1. Handle
2. Fuel filter
3. Fuel cap
4. Half-throttle lock button
5. Spring
6. Plunger
7. Oil cap
8. Fuel suction line
9. Vent line
10. Fuel line
11. Cup
12. Vent valve
13. Lock lever
14. Spring
15. Vent valve
16. Vibration damper
17. Oil suction line
18. Oil nipple
19. Spring
20. Throttle lever

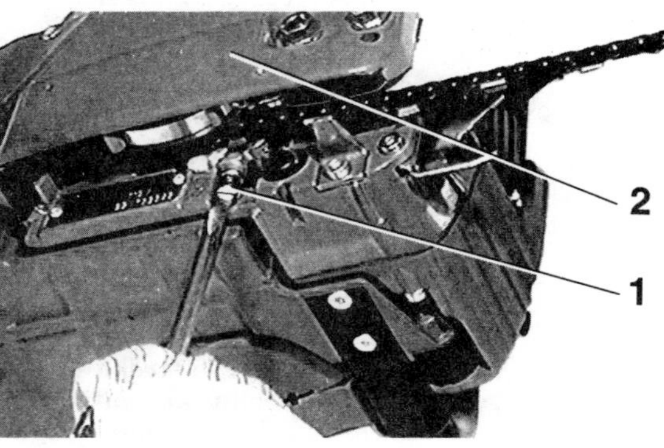

Fig. D163—The chain oil adjustment screw (1) is located in the housing underneath the sprocket guard (2). Turn the screw clockwise to reduce the amount of oil or counterclockwise to increase the amount of oil.

two-stroke engine oil, mix at a ratio of 40:1. The manufacturer recommends not using fuel containing alcohol.

Always use a separate container to mix gasoline and oil before filling the fuel tank. A fuel filter (2—Fig. D162) is located in the fuel tank. Filter should be inspected periodically for contamination and replaced as necessary. Filter can be pulled out through tank filler opening using a piece of wire bent at one end to form a hook.

The saw is equipped with an automatic chain oiling system. The manufacturer recommends using DOLMAR Saw Chain oil or other good quality oil designed for lubricating saw chain. Make sure the reservoir is filled at all times.

The volume of oil delivered by the pump is adjustable by turning the adjusting screw located in the housing underneath the sprocket guard (Fig. D163). The screw is accessible from below. The engine must be stopped before turning the adjusting screw.

REPAIRS

CRANKCASE PRESSURE TEST. An improperly sealed crankcase can cause the engine to be hard to start, run rough, have low power and overheat. Refer to ENGINE SERVICE section of this manual for crankcase pressure test procedure. If crankcase leakage is indicated, pressurize the crankcase and use a solution of soap and water to check gasket, seals, pulse line and castings for leakage.

TIGHTENING TORQUE. Recommended tightening torque values are as follows.

Carburetor attaching
screws . . . . 5.0-7.0 N·m
(44-62 in.-lb.)
Crankcase . . . . 10-11 N·m
(88.5-97 in.-lb.)
Cylinder. . . . . 10.5-12.5 N·m
(93-110.6 in.-lb.)
Flywheel . . . . 25-30 N·m
(221-265 in.-lb.)
Muffler. . . . . 12-16 N·m
(106-141.6 in.-lb.)
Spark plug. . . . . 20-30 N·m
(177-265 in.-lb.)

PISTON, PIN, RINGS AND CYLINDER. The cylinder can be removed after removal of the airbox cover (1—Fig. D160), air cleaner (2), carburetor (12), cylinder cover (3), intake manifold (10), air box (8) and muffler. Remove four screws attaching cylinder (1—Fig. D164) to crankcase and withdraw cylinder from piston.

Illustrations courtesy Dolmar U.S.A., Inc.

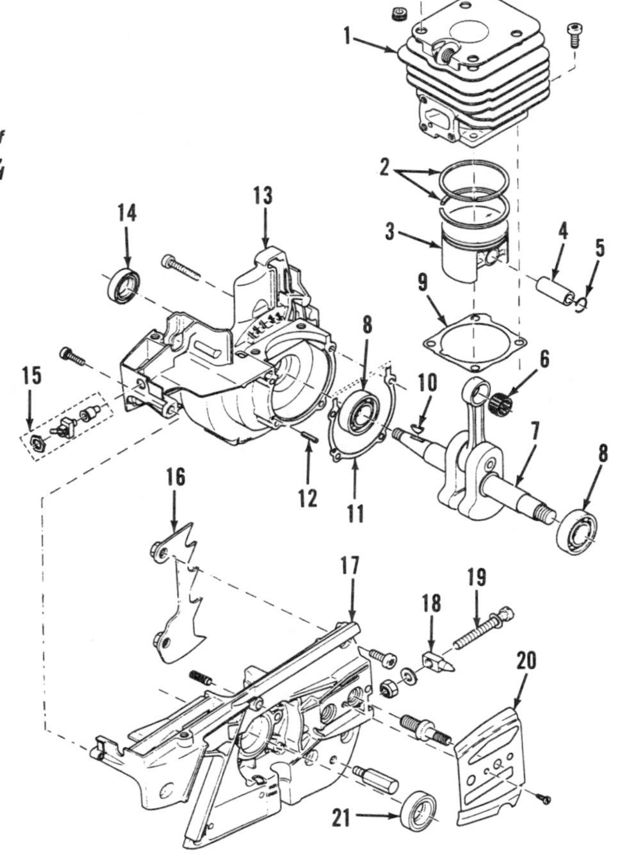

Fig. D164—Exploded view of the cylinder, crankshaft, crankcase and associated parts.

1. Cylinder
2. Piston rings
3. Piston
4. Piston pin
5. Retaining ring
6. Needle bearing
7. Crankshaft & connecting rod
8. Ball bearings
9. Gasket
10. Wooodruff key
11. Gasket
12. Dowel
13. Crankcase left half
14. Seal
15. Engine stop switch
16. Spike bar
17. Crankcase right half
18. Nut w/pin
19. Chain adjusting screw
20. Guide plate
21. Seal

The piston pin (4—Fig. D164) is retained by wire retainer rings (5). The pin operates in a needle bearing (6) at the upper end of the connecting rod. Remove retaining ring and push pin from piston to separate piston from connecting rod. The piston is equipped with two piston rings (2) that are prevented from rotating in their grooves by locating pins.

Inspect the cylinder bore for excessive wear or damage. Oversize parts are not available. The piston is available separately, but the cylinder is only available with a matching piston as a set.

When assembling, make sure that the arrow on the piston crown is visible and pointing toward the exhaust (muffler) side of the cylinder. If removed, always install new piston pin retainer rings (5). Make certain that retaining ring is seated in the groove and position the ring ends toward the bottom of the piston.

Slide a fork tool or a piece of wood between the bottom of the piston skirt and the crankcase to hold the piston up while installing the cylinder. Use a suitable ring compressor to compress the piston rings, making certain that the ring ends surround the locating pins. Lubricate cylinder with engine oil and slide cylinder over the piston. Tighten the cylinder retaining screws to the torque listed in TIGHTENING TORQUE paragraph.

CRANKSHAFT, CONNECTING ROD AND CRANKCASE. The crankshaft (7—Fig. D164) is supported in two ball type main bearings (8). The connecting rod and crankshaft are a pressed together assembly, available only as a unit.

To remove the crankshaft and connecting rod assembly, remove the starter housing, flywheel and ignition coil/module from the left side. Remove the cylinder cover, carburetor, air box, cylinder and piston from the top. Remove bar and chain, chain brake assembly, clutch assembly and oil pump assembly from the right side. Remove fuel tank/rear handle (1—Fig. D162) from crankcase.

Remove the attaching screws and tap the crankcase as necessary with a soft faced hammer to separate the halves. Be careful not to damage sealing surfaces of the crankcase halves.

Use appropriate pullers to remove the main bearings (8—Fig. D164) only if new units are being installed. Heating the crankcase to approximately 100 degrees C (212 degrees F) will make removal and installation of the main bearings easier.

When assembling, lubricate the shaft seals and bearings with clean engine oil. Insert the crankshaft in the clutch (right) side crankcase half, position a new gasket (11) against the case, and assemble the other case half. Tighten the screws attaching the crankcase halves to the torque listed in TIGHTENING TORQUE paragraph.

CLUTCH. A two-shoe centrifugal clutch with a coil type garter spring is used. The clutch hub (1—Fig. D165) is attached to the right end of the engine crankshaft with left-hand threads (turn clockwise to remove).

To remove clutch, first remove sprocket guard and chain brake assembly. Remove bar and chain. Remove spark plug and install a suitable piston stop tool or length of rope in spark plug hole to prevent the crankshaft from turning. The clutch hub can be turned using a 17 mm socket wrench. The clutch drum (6) can be withdrawn after the hub and shoes are removed. The chain drive floating sprocket (7) is splined to the clutch drum.

When assembling, install the smaller spacer (10) next to the oil pump, with the larger spacer (9) next to the clutch drum. Grease the needle bearing (8) lightly before assembling the bearing and drum. Assemble the clutch shoes (5), and spring (4) on the hub (1), making sure that the connection of the spring is centered in one of the shoes. Assemble thrust plate (3) and clamp (4). Install the clutch assembly, tightening the hub to the torque listed in TIGHTENING TORQUE paragraph.

OIL PUMP. All models are equipped with an automatic chain oil pump typical of the type shown in Fig. D165. Oil is pumped by plunger (14), which is turned by worm gear (11). Pump output is adjusted by turning screw (19).

The oil pump can be unbolted and pulled from the engine after removing the clutch assembly. Oil suction and pressure lines can be inspected after the oil pump is removed. Install new hoses if cracked or leaking.

Inspect plunger (14), worm gear (11) and bore in pump housing (17) for wear or damage. If wear or damage is excessive, it is suggested that a new pump assembly and worm drive gear be installed.

CHAIN BRAKE. The chain brake assembly is designed to stop the chain quickly should kickback occur. The

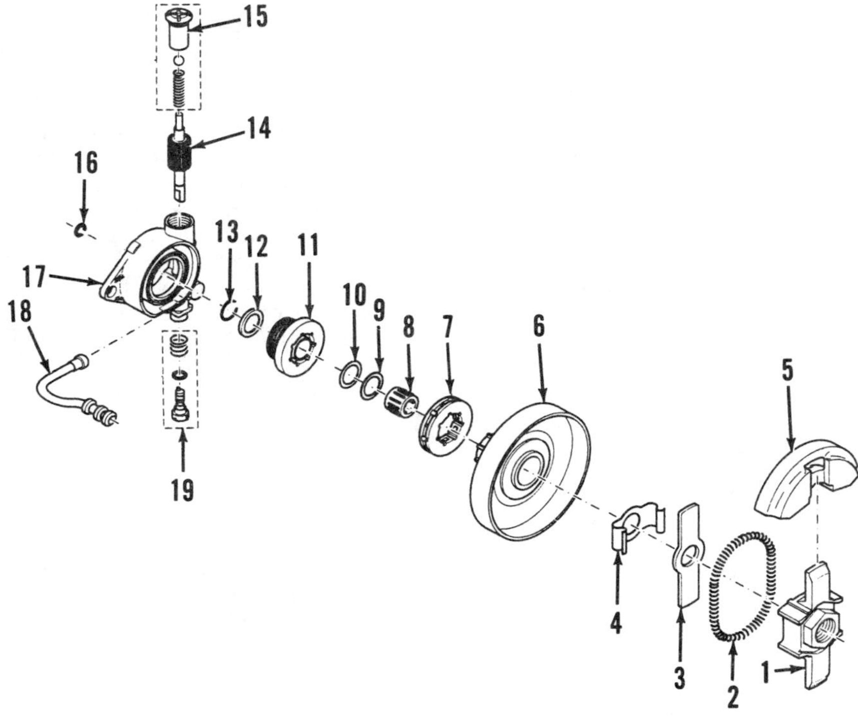

Fig. D165—Exploded view of the clutch assembly and oil pump.

1. Clutch hub
2. Spring
3. Guide
4. Clamp
5. Clutch shoe (2 used)
6. Clutch drum
7. Chain sprocket
8. Roller bearing
9. Thrust washer
10. Washer
11. Oil pump worm
12. Thrust washer
13. Snap ring
14. Oil pump plunger
15. Guide bushing
16. "O" ring
17. Oil pump housing
18. Oil suction line
19. Pump adjusting screw

chain brake is activated when the operator's hand strikes the hand guard (4—Fig. D166). When the brake system is activated, spring (11) tightens the brake band (9) around the clutch drum. To release, pull the hand guard back until the mechanism is reset.

To remove the brake assembly, unbolt and remove sprocket guard (7) with chain brake components from the saw.

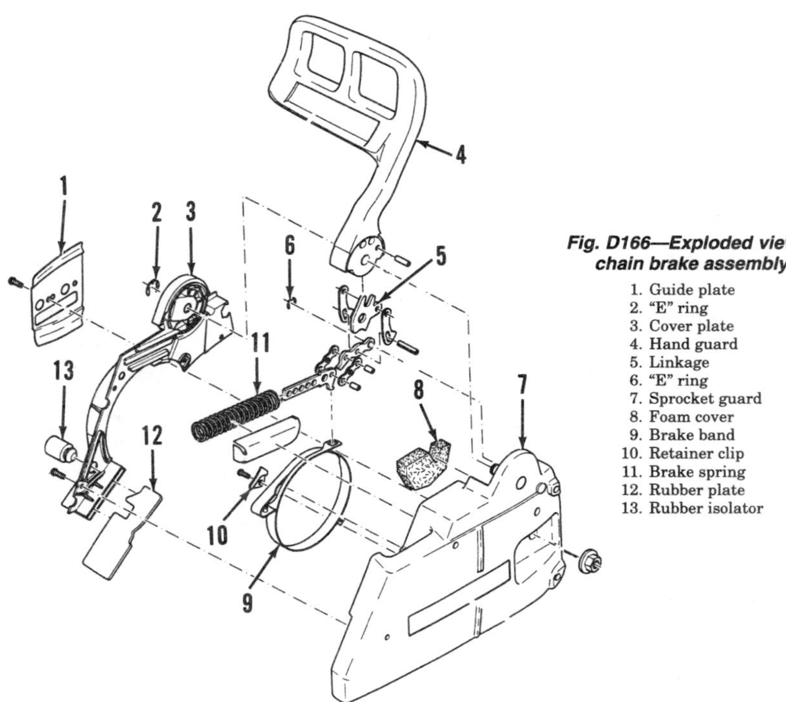

Fig. D166—Exploded view of chain brake assembly.

1. Guide plate
2. "E" ring
3. Cover plate
4. Hand guard
5. Linkage
6. "E" ring
7. Sprocket guard
8. Foam cover
9. Brake band
10. Retainer clip
11. Brake spring
12. Rubber plate
13. Rubber isolator

Engage the chain brake by pushing hand guard (19) forward. Engaging the brake relaxes the spring (11). Remove cover plate (3). Separate handle with linkage, spring (11) and brake band (9) from sprocket guard.

Inspect parts and replace as necessary. No adjustment of the mechanism is required.

REWIND STARTER. Refer to Fig. D167 for exploded view of typical starter. The starter can be removed as a unit by unbolting the housing (1).

To disassemble the starter, remove the rope handle and allow the rope to wind into the housing. Remove snap ring (7) and lift the rope pulley (6) from the housing. Be careful to prevent injury in case the spring (3) unwinds suddenly.

Clean and inspect parts for damage. The 4 mm diameter starter rope (5) should be 100 cm long. Replacement rewind spring (3) comes under tension in a wire retaining ring. Do not remove the retaining ring. Lightly lubricate the spring with grease.

To assemble, position spacer plate (2) in the housing cavity. If installing new rewind spring (3), push the spring with wire retainer into the housing. The wire retainer will slide off the spring as the spring is pushed into the housing. If installing original rewind spring, wind the spring into the housing in a clockwise direction beginning with the outside coil. Install the spacer plate (4) and secure with screw.

Wind the rope onto the pulley (6) in a clockwise direction as viewed from the flywheel side of pulley, then install over the post in housing. Preload the recoil spring by turning the pulley about 4 turns clockwise before passing the rope through the opening in the housing (1) and attaching the handle. Install snap ring (7) and check spring preload as follows.

Pull the rope out fully and check that pulley can be turned an additional 1/2 turn without causing the spring to bind. Allow the rope to rewind and make sure the handle is pulled against the housing. If the spring binds, remove some spring preload and recheck. If the handle is not wound against the housing, increase the preload and recheck.

Inspect the condition of the pawl (8—Fig. D167) and spring (9) attached to the flywheel (10). The pawl stud should be pressed into the flywheel after coating the surface of the stud and bore with locking agent (part No. 980 009 000 or equivalent). Install a new flywheel if damaged.

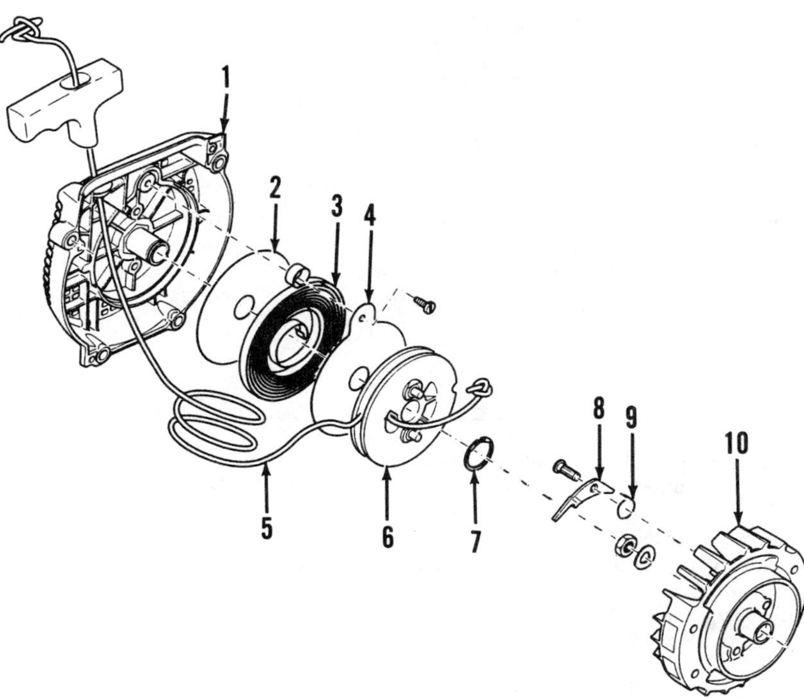

Fig. D167—Exploded view of the recoil starter and flywheel typical of all models.

1. Starter housing
2. Spacer plate
3. Rewind spring
4. Plate
5. Rope & handle
6. Pulley
7. Snap ring
8. Starter pawl
9. Spring
10. Flywheel

Illustrations courtesy Dolmar U.S.A., Inc.

ECHO

Model	Bore mm (in.)	Stroke mm (in.)	Displacement cc (cu. in.)	Drive Type
CS-60S	48 (1.89)	34 (1.34)	61.5 (3.75)	Direct
CS-100	57 (2.24)	40 (1.57)	102 (6.23)	Direct

MAINTENANCE

SPARK PLUG. Recommended spark plug for Model CS-60S is NGK BM-6A. Recommended spark plug for Model CS-100 is NGK B-7S. Electrode gap for both models should be 0.024-0.028 inch (0.61-0.71 mm).

CARBURETOR. Model CS-60S is equipped with a Tillotson Model HS diaphragm carburetor while Model CS-100 is equipped with a Tillotson Model HL diaphragm carburetor. Refer to Tillotson section of CARBURETOR SERVICE section for an exploded view and service information on carburetors.

Initial setting of idle mixture screw is one turn open and high speed mixture screw is ¾ turn open. Make final adjustments with engine warm and running. Adjust idle speed screw so engine idles just below clutch engagement speed. Adjust idle mixture screw so engine will accelerate without stumbling. Adjust high speed mixture screw to obtain optimum performance with saw under a cutting load. Do not adjust mixture screws too lean as engine damage may result.

IGNITION. Both models are equipped with a flywheel magneto ignition system. Breaker point gap should be 0.012-0.016 inch (0.30-0.40 mm). Correct ignition timing for Model CS-60S is 25 degrees BTDC. Correct ignition timing for Model CS-100 is 30 degrees BTDC. Reference marks are provided on cylinder and flywheel to set ignition timing. With flywheel turning counterclockwise, first mark on flywheel periphery indicates ignition point when aligned with mark on cylinder. Second mark indicates Top Dead Center when aligned with mark on cylinder. Adjust ignition timing by rotating stator plate. When reinstalling flywheel, tighten nut to 330-365 in.-lbs. (37.3-41.2 N•m).

LUBRICATION. The engine is lubricated by oil mixed with fuel. Regular grade automotive gasoline is recommended. Recommended oil is Echo air-cooled two-stroke engine oil mixed with fuel at a 50:1 ratio. If Echo air-cooled two-stroke engine oil is not available, use a good quality oil designed for use in air-cooled two-stroke engines mixed with fuel at a 32:1 ratio.

Clean SAE 20 or SAE 30 automotive oil may be used to lubricate chain and bar. Dilute oil with up to 50 percent kerosene during cold weather to aid lubrication.

REPAIRS

CYLINDER HEAD. Model CS-100 is equipped with a removeable cylinder head. Do not damage cylinder head or cylinder mating surfaces. Inspect cylinder head surface for warpage. Tighten cylinder head screws to 95-130 in.-lbs. (10.8-14.7 N•m).

CYLINDER, PISTON, RINGS AND PIN. Cylinder head on Model CS-100 is removeable as indicated in previous paragraph while cylinder head on Model CS-60S is integral with cylinder. Cylinder bore is chrome plated on both models and oversize piston and rings are not available. Maximum piston ring end gap is 0.02 inch (0.5 mm), and maximum

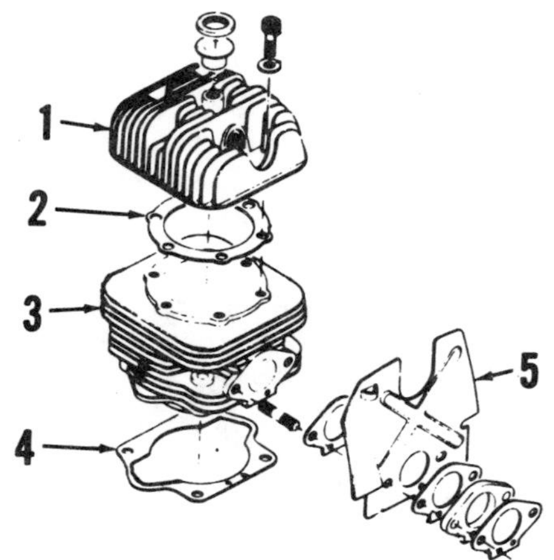

Fig. E1—Exploded view of cylinder assembly used on Model CS-100. Model CS-60S is similar but does not have a removeable cylinder head.

1. Cylinder head
2. Gasket
3. Cylinder
4. Gasket
5. Shroud

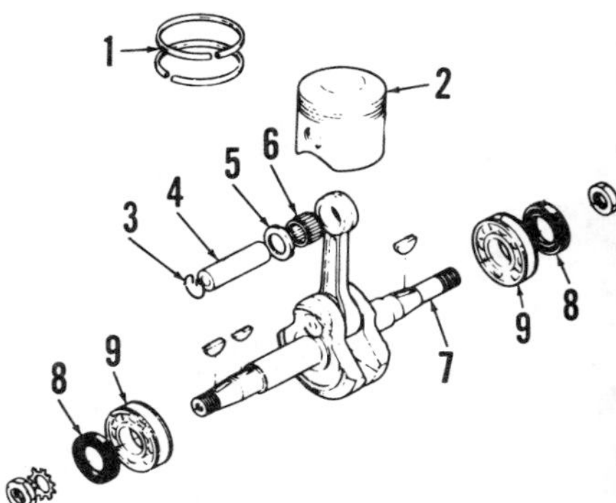

Fig. E2—Exploded view of Model CS-60S crankshaft, rod and piston assembly.

1. Piston rings
2. Piston
3. Pin retainer
4. Piston pin
5. Spacer (2)
6. Bearing
7. Crankshaft & rod assy.
8. Seal
9. Ball bearing

Fig. E3—Exploded view of Model CS-100 crankshaft, rod and piston assembly.

1. Piston rings
2. Piston
3. Pin retainer
4. Piston pin
5. Spacer
6. Bearing
7. Connecting rod
8. Roller bearing
9. Seal
10. Washer
11. Ball bearing
12. Rod cap
13. Crankshaft

Illustrations courtesy Echo Inc.

ring side clearance is 0.004 inch (0.10 mm).

Inspect cylinder bore for scoring, flaking or other damage to the chrome surface. Install piston so arrow on piston crown is toward exhaust port. Piston rings are pinned to prevent rotation. Be sure piston ring end gaps are properly positioned around piston ring locating pins when installing cylinder.

CRANKSHAFT CONNECTING ROD AND CRANKCASE. Crankshaft is supported at both ends by ball bearings. Connecting rod and crankshaft on Model CS-60S are available only as a unit assembly. Connecting rod and crankshaft on Model CS-100 are available separately. Connecting rod rides on a caged roller bearing (6–Fig. E2 or E3). Inspect connecting rod, bearing and crankpin for excessive wear or damage.

Check crankshaft runout by supporting crankshaft at points (A–Fig. E4) and measure at points (B). Maximum allowable runout is 0.002 inch (0.05 mm).

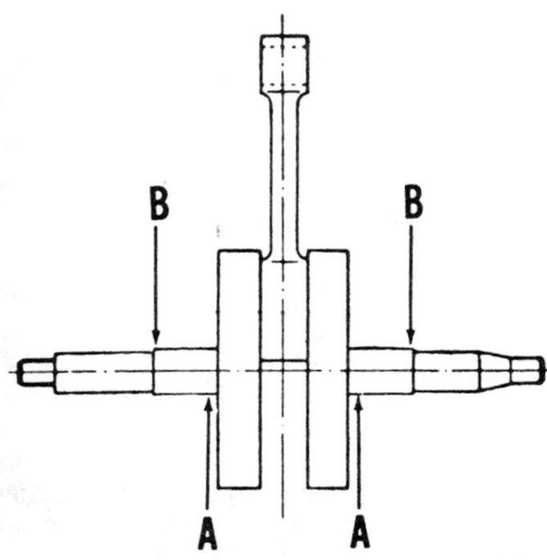

Fig. E4–Support crankshaft at points (A) and measure runout at points (B). Runout must not exceed 0.002 inch (0.05 mm).

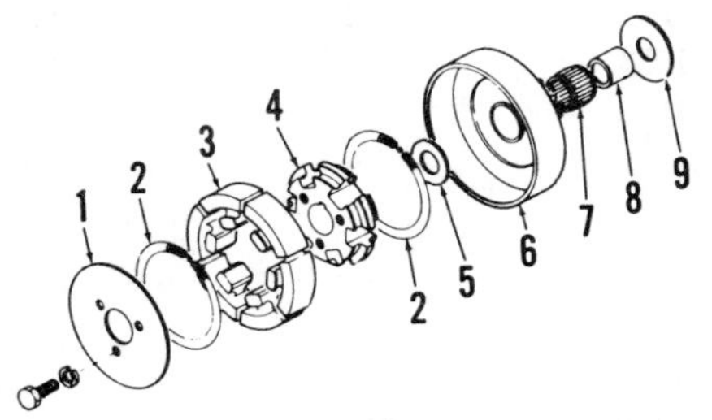

Fig. E5–Exploded view of Model CS-60S clutch.

1. Cover
2. Garter spring
3. Clutch shoes
4. Clutch hub
5. Washer
6. Clutch drum
7. Bearing
8. Inner race
9. Washer

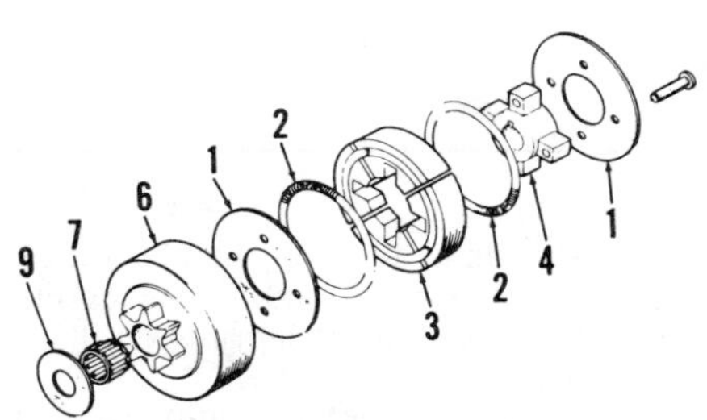

Fig. E6–Exploded view of Model CS-100 clutch. Refer to Fig. E5 for parts identification.

CLUTCH. Model CS-60S is equipped with the six-shoe centrifugal clutch shown in Fig. E5, while Model CS-100 is equipped with the four-shoe centrifugal clutch shown in Fig. E6. The clutch drum on both models rides on a caged needle roller bearing. Inspect clutch drum and shoes for excessive wear or damage due to overheating.

REWIND STARTER. Refer to Fig. E7 for an exploded view of rewind starter. To disassemble starter, remove rope handle and allow rope to wind into starter housing. Care should be used when disassembling starter to prevent rewind spring from uncoiling uncontrolled.

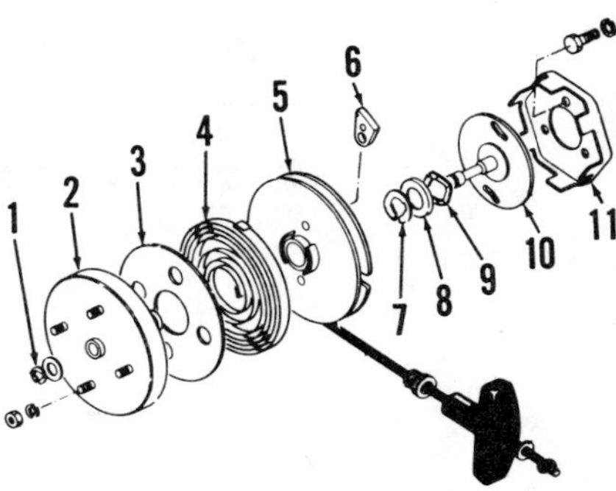

Fig. E7–Exploded view of rewind starter used on Models CS-60S and CS-100.

1. "E" ring
2. Spring housing
3. Plate
4. Rewind spring
5. Rope pulley
6. Pawl
7. "E" ring
8. Washer
9. Spring washer
10. Spindle
11. Starter cup

Illustrations courtesy Echo Inc.

ECHO

Model	Bore mm (in.)	Stroke mm (in.)	Displacement cc (cu. in.)	Drive Type
CS-302, 315	37 (1.46)	28 (1.1)	30.1 (1.83)	Direct
CS-302S	39 (1.53)	28 (1.1)	33.4 (2.04)	Direct
CS-351, 351VL	40 (1.57)	28 (1.1)	35.2 (2.14)	Direct
CS-451, 451VL, 452, 452VL, 452VLP	42 (1.65)	32 (1.26)	44.3 (2.69)	Direct
CS-601, CS-602, 602VL	46 (1.81)	36 (1.42)	59.8 (3.65)	Direct
CS-701, 702, 702VL, 702EVL	50 (1.97)	36 (1.42)	70.7 (4.32)	Direct
CS-750, 750VL, 750EVL, 750EVLP	52 (2.03)	37 (1.46)	78.6 (4.8)	Direct

MAINTENANCE

SPARK PLUG. Recommended spark plug is NGK BPM−7A for Models CS-602, CS-602VL, CS-702, CS-702VL, CS-702EVL, CS-750, CS-750VL and CS-750EVL. Recommended spark plug for all other models is NGK BM-6A. Electrode gap should be 0.024-0.028 inch (0.61-0.71 mm).

CARBURETOR. Models CS-750, CS-750VL and CS-750EVL are equipped with a Walbro SDC carburetor. All other models are equipped with either a Walbro WA, Tillotson HU or Tillotson HS carburetor. Refer to CARBURETOR SERVICE section for carburetor overhaul.

Initial setting of idle and high speed mixture screws is one turn open. Make final carburetor adjustments with engine at operating temperature. Adjust idle mixture screw so engine will accelerate without stumbling. Adjust high speed mixture screw to obtain optimum performance with saw under cutting load. Adjust idle speed screw so engine idles just under clutch engagement speed.

IGNITION. Models CS-702EVL and CS-750EVL are equipped with a breakerless capacitor discharge ignition system. Repair of ignition system malfunction except for faulty wiring connections is accomplished by renewal of ignition system components. Ignition timing is fixed at 30 degrees BTDC and is not adjustable.

All other models are equipped with a flywheel magneto ignition system using breaker points. Breaker point gap should be 0.012-0.016 inch (0.30-0.40 mm). Correct ignition timing is 30 degrees BTDC. Reference marks are provided on crankcase and flywheel to set ignition timing. With flywheel turning counterclockwise, first mark on flywheel periphery indicates ignition point when aligned with mark on crankcase. On some models the flywheel mark is lettered "M" or "F." A second flywheel mark when aligned with the crankcase mark indicates piston is at TDC. Adjust ignition timing by rotating stator plate on Models CS-601, CS-602, CS-602VL, CS-701, CS-702, CS-702VL, CS-750 and CS-750VL. On all other breaker-point models, adjust timing by increasing or decreasing breaker-point gap.

On all models, air gap between flywheel magnets and ignition module or magneto core legs should be 0.012-0.016 inch (0.30-0.40 mm).

LUBRICATION. The engine is lubricated by mixing oil with fuel. Regular grade automotive gasoline is recommended. Recommended oil is Echo air-cooled two-stroke engine oil mixed with fuel at a 50:1 ratio. If Echo air-cooled two-stroke engine oil is not available, use a good quality oil designed for use in air-cooled two-stroke engines mixed with fuel at a 32:1 ratio.

Clean SAE 20 or SAE 30 automotive oil may be used to lubricate chain and bar. Dilute oil with up to 50 percent kerosene during cold weather to aid lubrication. Automatic oil pump output is adjusted by turning knob located on top side of saw near front handle.

REPAIRS

CYLINDER, PISTON, PIN AND RINGS. Cylinder bore is chrome plated on all models and oversize pistons and rings are not available. Inspect cylinder bore for scoring, flaking or other damage to chrome surface.

Piston ring end gap should be 0.004-0.012 inch (0.10-0.30 mm); maximum allowable ring end gap is 0.020 inch (0.51 mm). Piston ring side clearance should be 0.002 inch (0.05 mm) with a maximum allowable side clearance of 0.004 inch (0.10 mm).

Install piston with arrow on piston crown toward exhaust port. On Models CS-602, CS-602VL, CS-702, CS-702VL, CS-750, CS-750VL and CS-750EVL, install piston pin with closed end toward exhaust port. Piston rings are pinned in ring grooves to prevent rotation. Be sure piston end gaps are properly positioned around piston ring locating pins

Illustrations courtesy Echo Inc.

when installing cylinder. Tighten cylinder base nuts to 70-80 in.-lbs. (7.9-9.0 N•m) on Models CS-302 and CS-302S. Tighten cylinder base nuts to 30-35 in.-lbs. (3.4-3.9 N•m) on Model CS-315, 45-50 in.-lbs. (5.1-5.6 N•m) on Models CS-451, CS-451VL, CS-452 and CS-452VL and 65-75 in.-lbs. (7.4-8.4 N•m) on all other models.

CRANKSHAFT CONNECTING ROD AND CRANKCASE. All models are equipped with a crankshaft and connecting rod unit assembly which is supported in the crankcase by ball bearings at both ends. Crankshaft and connecting rod are not available separately.

Check crankshaft runout by supporting crankshaft at points (A – Fig. E12) and measure at points (B). Maximum allowable runout is 0.002 inch (0.05 mm).

Crankshaft main bearings are located in crankcase by snap rings (2 – Fig. E11) on all models except CS-315. The clutch side main bearing of Model CS-315 is located by a snap ring but flywheel side main bearing is located by a shoulder in the crankcase. Some models may be equipped with a lubrication passage designed to lubricate oil pump cam and plunger. Make certain snap ring (2 – Fig. E11 or Fig. E11A) does not obstruct passage when installed (snap ring gap should surround oil passage hole). Install crankshaft seals, open sides toward each other, flush with outer face of crankcase.

A needle bearing is used in connecting rod small end of all models except Model CS-315 which supports piston pin directly in rod. Note spacers (10 – Fig. E11A) used on Model CS-315.

CLUTCH. Models CS-302, CS-302S, CS-315, CS-351 and CS-351VL are equipped with the clutch assembly shown in Fig. E13. Rivets (R) must be removed to separate clutch shoes and hub. Refer to Fig. E14 for exploded view of clutch used on Models CS-701, CS-702, CS-702VL, CS-702EVL, CS-750, CS-750VL and CS-750EVL. Clutch used on all other models is shown in Fig. E13A.

Clutch nut and hub have left-hand threads. Clutch drum on Model CS-315 is retained by a snap ring. On all models, the clutch drum rides on a roller bearing. Bearing should be periodically inspected and lubricated with a suitable

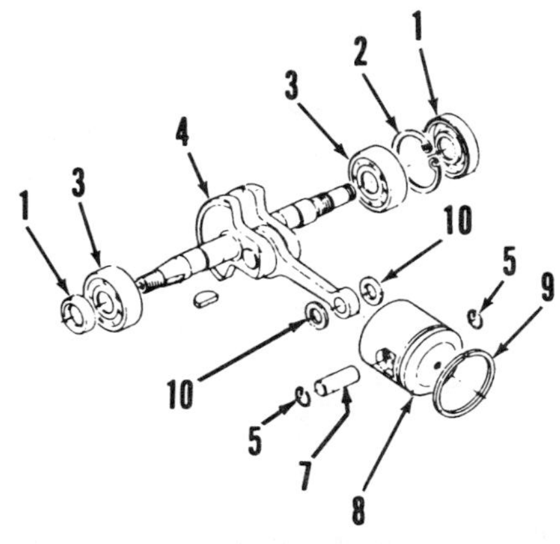

Fig. E11A — Exploded view of crankshaft assembly used on Model CS-315. Refer to Fig. E11 for parts identification except for: 10. Spacers.

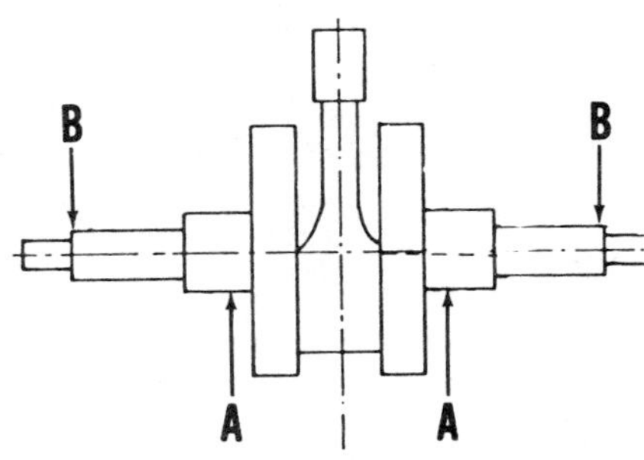

Fig. E12 — Measure crankshaft by supporting crankshaft at points (A). Maximum runout measured at points (B) should not exceed 0.002 inch (0.05 mm).

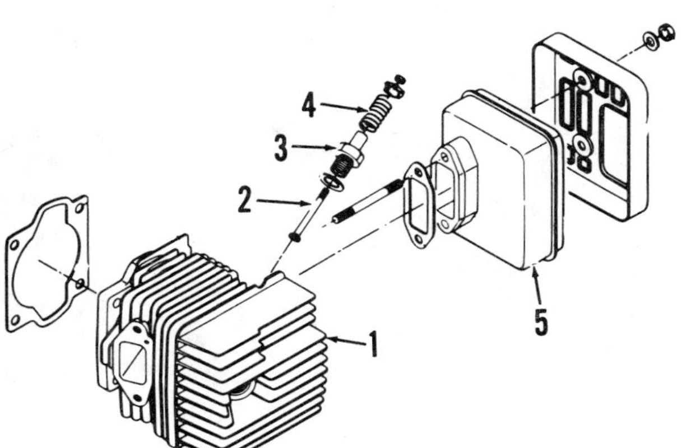

Fig. E10 — Exploded view of cylinder and compression release valve on Models CS-601, CS-602, CS-602VL, CS-701, CS-702, CS-702VL, CS-702EVL, CS-750, CS-750VL and CS-750EVL.

1. Cylinder
2. Compression release valve
3. Valve seat
4. Spring
5. Muffler

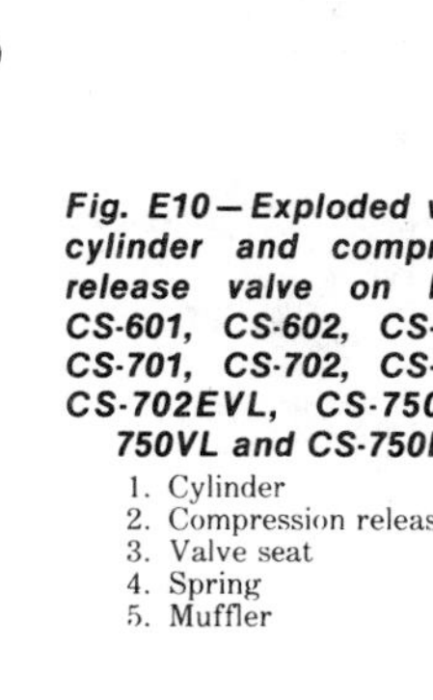

Fig. E13 — Exploded view of clutch used on Models CS-302, CS-302S, CS-315, CS-351 and CS-351VL. Remove rivets (R) to separate clutch shoe components. Refer to Fig. 13A for parts identification.

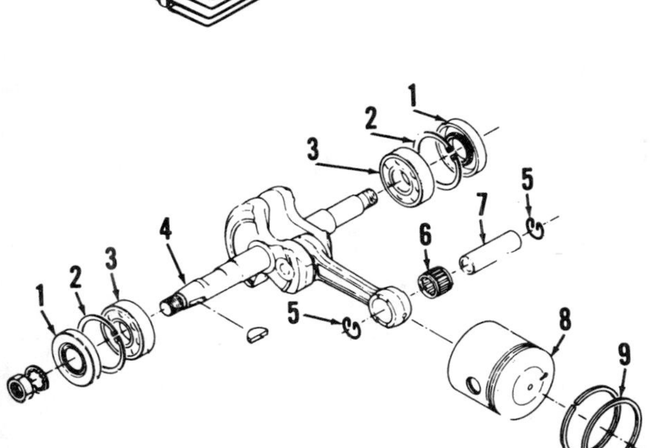

Fig. E11 — Exploded view of crankshaft assembly used on all models except CS-315.

1. Seal
2. Snap ring
3. Ball bearing
4. Crankshaft & rod assy.
5. Pin retainer
6. Needle roller bearing
7. Piston pin
8. Piston
9. Piston rings

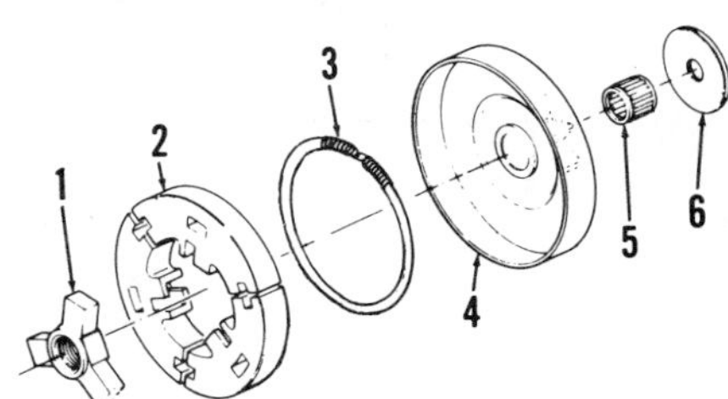

Fig. E13A — Exploded view of clutch used on Models CS451, CS451VL, CS-452, CS-452VL and CS-601. Clutch used on Models CS-602 and CS-602VL is similar.

1. Clutch hub
2. Clutch shoes
3. Garter spring
4. Clutch drum
5. Needle roller bearing
6. Washer

Illustrations courtesy Echo Inc.

high temperature grease. Inspect clutch shoes and drum for damage due to overheating. Renew excessively worn or damaged components.

OIL PUMP. All models are equipped with an automatic plunger type chain oil pump. The plunger on all models except CS-601 and CS-701 is actuated by a cam on the crankshaft as shown in Fig. E15. The plunger on Models CS-601 and CS-701 is actuated by cam follower (16–Fig. E16) which rides on a cam attached to the clutch drum. Refer to Fig. E17 or E18 for an exploded view of the automatic oil pump.

When installing pump body, screw body in until lightly seated then run saw at medium speed and unscrew pump body approximately ½ to 1 turn until maximum oil output is obtained. Mark pump body for future reference then install adjusting knob so it is against stop for maximum oil output and must be turned counterclockwise to decrease oil output.

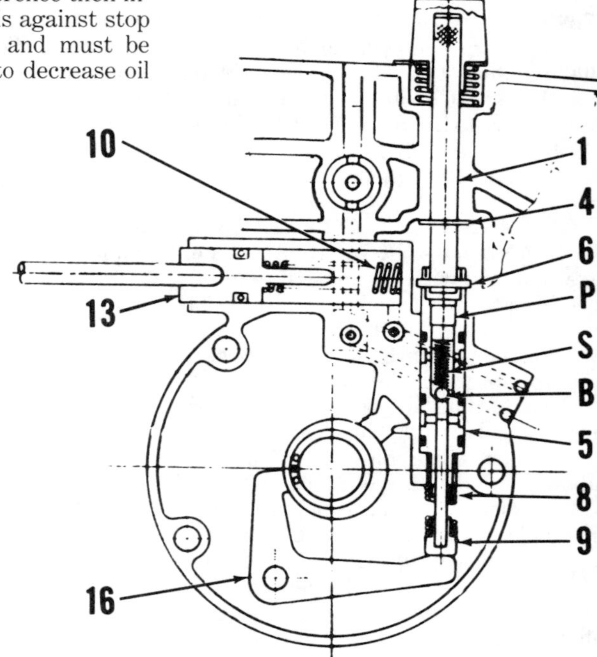

Fig. E16—Cross-sectional view of manual and automatic oil pumps used on Models CS-601 and CS-701. Note location of plunger (P), spring (S) and ball (B) in pump body (5—Fig. E18). Refer to Fig. E18 for parts identification.

Fig. E14—Exploded view of clutch used on Models CS-701, CS-702, CS-702VL, CS-702EVL, LCS-750, CS-750VL and CS-750EVL.

1. Washer
2. Needle roller bearing
3. Snap ring
4. Clutch drum
5. Garter spring
6. Clutch shoes
7. Clutch hub
8. Washer

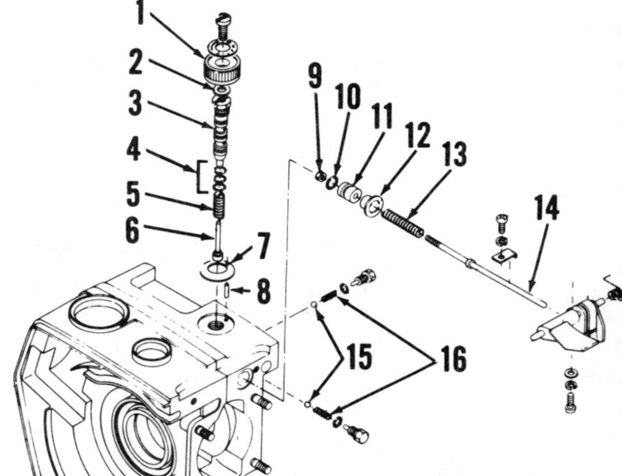

Fig. E17—Exploded view of typical automatic and manual oil pumps used on all models except CS-601 and CS-701. Manual pump is not used on Models CS-302, CS-302S, CS-315, CS-351 and CS-351VL.

1. Adjusting knob
2. Washer
3. Pump body
4. "O" rings
5. Spring
6. Piston
7. Spring disc
8. Pin
9. Nut
10. "O" ring
11. Manual pump piston
12. Spring seat
13. Spring
14. Rod
15. Check ball
16. Spring

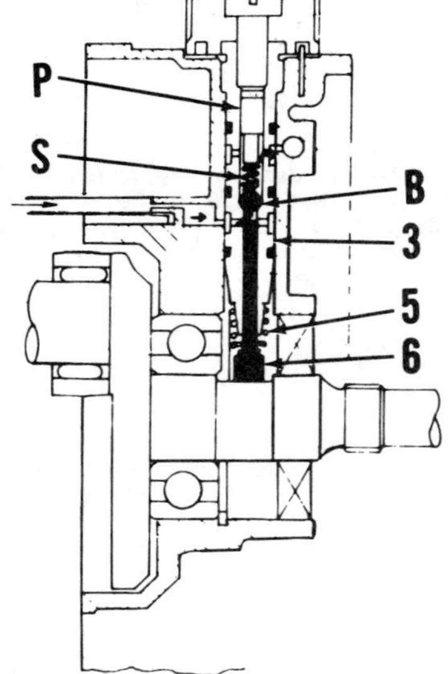

Fig. E15—Typical cross-sectional view of automatic oil pump used on all models except CS-601 and CS-701. Note location of plunger (P), spring (S) and ball (B) in pump body (3—Fig. E17). Refer to Fig. E17 for identification of components (3, 5 and 6).

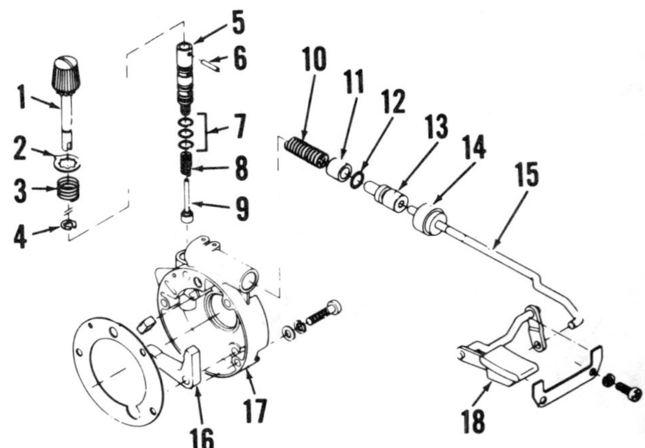

Fig. E18—Exploded view of automatic and manual oil pumps used on Models CS-601 and CS-701.

1. Adjuster
2. Spring disc
3. Spring
4. "E" ring
5. Pump body
6. Pin
7. "O" rings
8. Spring
9. Automatic pump piston
10. Spring
11. Spring seat
12. "O" ring
13. Manual pump piston
14. Rod cap
15. Rod
16. Cam follower
17. Pump housing
18. Manual pump actuator

REWIND STARTER. To disassemble rewind starter, remove starter housing, remove rope handle and allow rope to rewind into housing. Unscrew rope pulley screw and carefully remove rope pulley being careful not to dislodge rewind spring. If necessary to remove rewind spring, care should be used not to allow spring to uncoil uncontrolled.

Install rewind spring in starter housing or spring case with coils wrapped in a clockwise direction from outer end of spring. Wind rope around pulley in a clockwise direction as viewed from flywheel side of pulley. Turn pulley three or four turns clockwise before passing rope through outlet. Check starter operation. It should be possible to pull rope to its full extension and still turn rope pulley approximately ½ turn clockwise. If rewind spring coil binds before rope is fully extended, reduce pretension on rope by pulling rope up into notch in rope pulley and allowing pulley to rotate one turn counterclockwise. Recheck starter operation.

CHAIN BRAKE. Some models may be equipped with a chain brake system designed to stop chain movement should kickback occur. Chain brake is activated when operator's hand strikes chain brake lever and hand guard assembly (1–Fig. E21) tripping dog (10), releasing latch (7) and allowing spring (5) to pull brake band (4) tight around clutch drum. Pull back chain brake hand guard and lever assembly (1) to reset mechanism. Rotate adjusting cam (6) to adjust brake band (4). Brake band should not contact clutch drum after adjustment. Disassembly and component renewal is evident after inspection of unit and referral to Fig. E21.

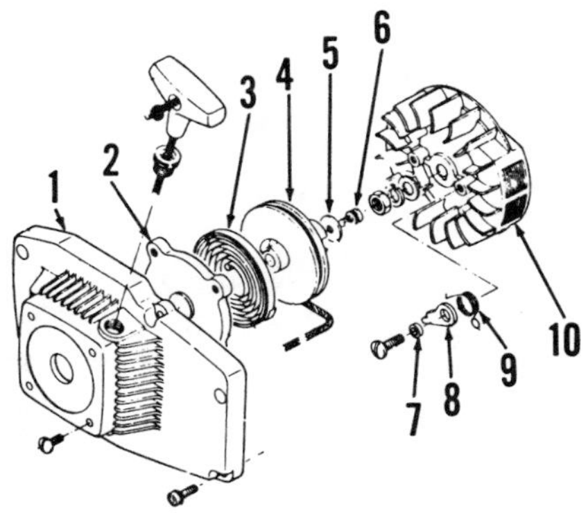

Fig. E20—Exploded view of rewind starter used on Model CS-315.

1. Starter housing
2. Spring case
3. Rewind spring
4. Rope pulley
5. Washer
6. Screw
7. Spacer
8. Starter pawl
9. Spring
10. Flywheel

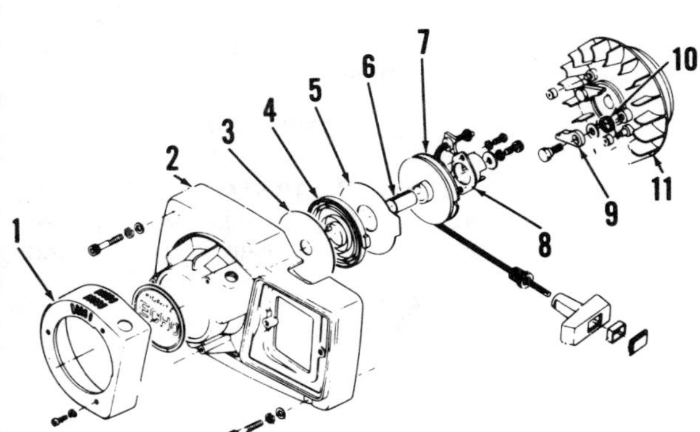

Fig. E19—Exploded view of typical rewind starter used on all models except Model CS-315.

1. Cover
2. Starter housing
3. Washer
4. Rewind spring
5. Washer
6. Bushing
7. Rope pulley
8. Starter cup
9. Pawl
10. Spring
11. Flywheel

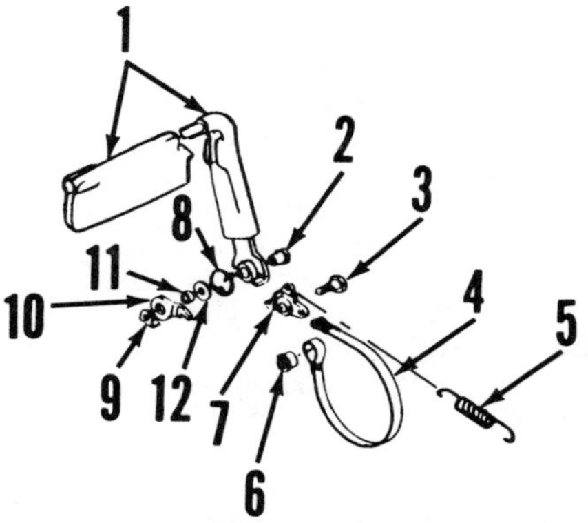

Fig. E21—Exploded view of chain brake system used on so equipped models.

1. Hand guard & lever assy.
2. Nut
3. Pivot screw
4. Brake band
5. Spring
6. Adjusting cam
7. Latch
8. Spring
9. Stop
10. Dog
11. Spacer
12. Washer

Illustrations courtesy Echo Inc.

ECHO

Model	Bore mm (in.)	Stroke mm (in.)	Displacement cc (cu. in.)	Drive Type
CS-280E, 280EP, 290EVL, 290EVLP	35 (1.378)	29 (1.142)	27.9 (1.703)	Direct

MAINTENANCE

SPARK PLUG. Recommended spark plug for all models is Champion CJ8Y. Spark plug electrode gap should be 0.6-0.7 mm (0.024-0.028 in.).

CARBURETOR. A Zama C1S-K1, C1S-K1A or C1S-K1B diaphragm type carburetor type carburetor is used on all models. Refer to Zama section of CARBURETOR SERVICE section for service and exploded views.

Initial adjustment of low and high speed mixture screws is 1⅛ turns open from a lightly seated position. Make final adjustment with engine warm and running. Adjust idle speed screw so engine idles just below clutch engagement speed. Adjust low speed mixture screw so engine will accelerate cleanly without hesitation. Adjust high speed mixture screw to obtain optimum performance under cutting load.

IGNITION. All models are equipped with a capacitor discharge ignition system. Refer to Fig. E24. Ignition timing is fixed at 30 degrees BTDC and is not adjustable. Air gap between flywheel magnets and ignition module core should be 0.3-0.4 mm (0.012-0.016 in.).

LUBRICATION. Engine is lubricated by mixing engine oil with fuel.

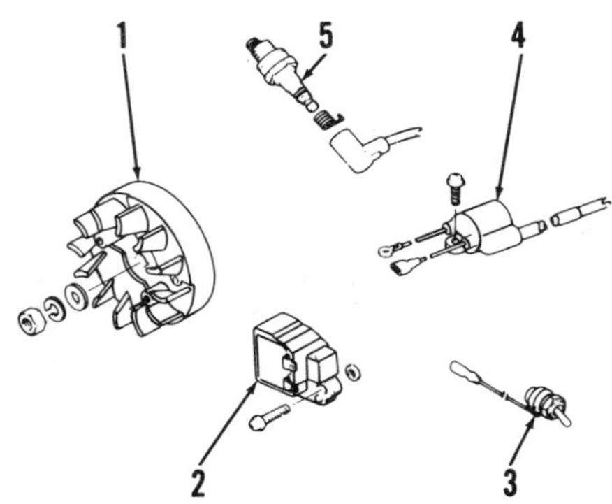

Fig. E24 — View of Models CS-290EVL and CS-290EVLP ignition components. Models CS-280E and CS-280EP are similar.

1. Flywheel
2. Ignition module
3. Stop switch
4. Ignition coil
5. Spark plug

Regular grade automotive gasoline is recommended. Recommended oil is Echo air-cooled two-stroke oil mixed with fuel at a 50:1 ratio. If Echo oil is not available, a good quality oil designed for air-cooled two-stroke engines may be used when mixed with fuel at a 32:1 ratio. Use a separate container when mixing the oil and gas.

All models are equipped with an automatic chain oil pump. Clean automotive oil may be used. Oil viscosity should be chosen according to ambient temperature. Oil pump output is adjustable. Refer to OIL PUMP section for service and adjustment procedures.

REPAIRS

CYLINDER, PISTON, PIN AND RINGS. Cylinder bore is chrome plated on all models and oversize pistons and

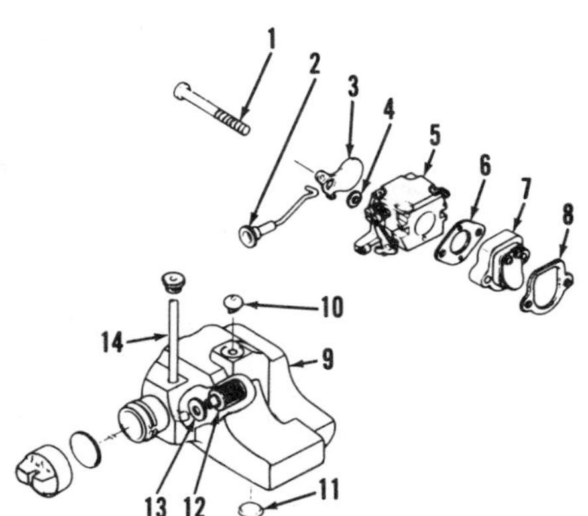

Fig. E23 — Exploded view of fuel tank and related components.

1. Screw
2. Choke knob
3. Choke shutter
4. Spacer
5. Carburetor
6. Gasket
7. Reed valve assy.
8. Gasket
9. Fuel tank
10. Tank vent
11. Cushion
12. Fuel filter
13. Washer
14. Fuel hose

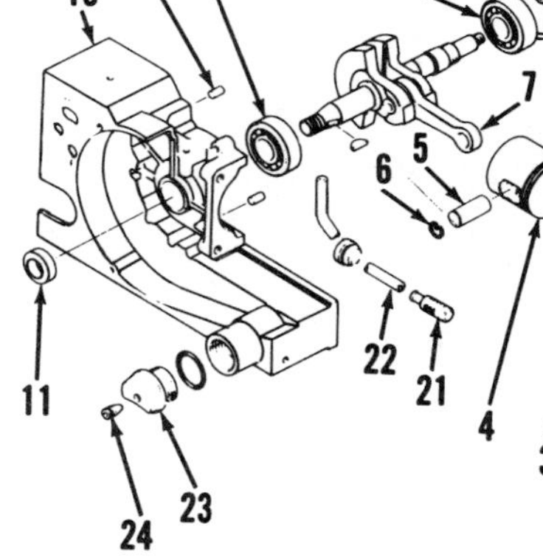

Fig. E25 — Exploded view of engine and automatic oil pump.

1. Cylinder
2. Gasket
3. Piston ring
4. Piston
5. Piston pin
6. Wire retainer
7. Crankshaft & rod assy.
8. Main bearing
9. Dowel
10. Left crankcase half
11. Seal
12. Main bearing
13. Snap ring
14. Gasket
15. Right crankcase half
16. Seal
17. Oil pump housing
18. "O" ring
19. Spring
20. Pump plunger
21. Oil filter
22. Oil hose
23. Oil filler cap
24. Oil tank vent

Illustrations courtesy Echo Inc.

rings are not available. Inspect cylinder bore for scoring, flaking or other damage to chrome surface.

Piston has a single piston ring. Maximum allowable ring end gap is 0.5 mm (0.020 in.). Maximum allowable piston ring in ring groove side clearance is 0.1 mm (0.004 in.). A locating pin is present in piston ring groove to prevent piston ring rotation. Be sure ring end gap is around locating pin when installing cylinder.

The floating type piston pin is retained by wire retainers and rides directly in the small end of connecting rod. Be sure piston is properly supported when removing or installing piston pin to prevent damage. Arrow on piston crown must point toward exhaust port when installing piston.

CRANKSHAFT, CONNECTING ROD AND CRANKCASE. All models are equipped with a crankshaft and connecting rod unit assembly which is supported in the crankcase by ball bearings at both ends. Crankshaft and connecting rod are not available separately.

Check crankshaft runout by supporting crankshaft at points (A – Fig. E26) and measuring at points (B). Maximum allowable runout is 0.05 mm (0.002 in).

Flywheel side main bearing (8 – Fig. E25) is held in position by a shoulder in crankcase half (10) while a snap ring (13) retains clutch side main bearing (12). Snap ring (13) should be installed in crankcase so open end of ring is around oil hole and snap ring does not obstruct lubrication passage. Install crankshaft seals (11 and 16), open sides toward each other, flush with outer face of crankcase.

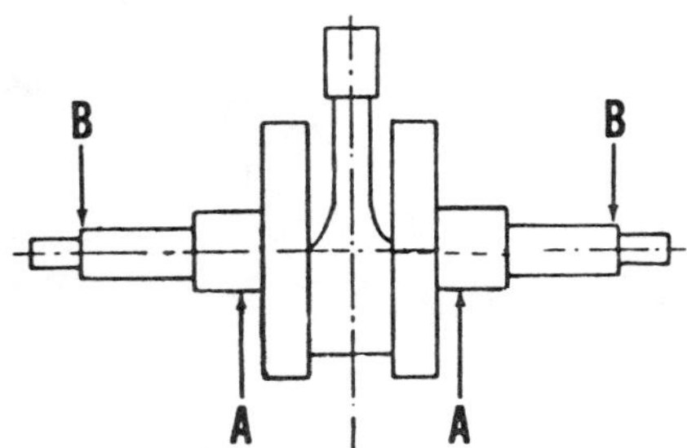

Fig. E26 – Measure crankshaft by supporting crankshaft at points (A). Maximum runout measured at points (B) should not exceed 0.05 mm (0.002 in.).

REED VALVE. Reed valve (7 – Fig. E23) should be inspected whenever carburetor is removed. Reed petal (P – Fig. E28) should seat very lightly against insulator block (B) throughout its entire length with the least possible tension. Tip of reed petal must not stand open more than 0.3 mm (0.012 in.). Reed stop (S) opening should be 6 mm (0.24 in.). Individual reed valve components are not available.

CLUTCH. Refer to Fig. E29 for exploded view of three-shoe centrifugal clutch used on all models. Clutch hub (1) and nut (8) have left-hand threads. Clutch drum (5) rides on a needle roller bearing (6). Needle roller bearing should be inspected for damage or discoloration and lubricated with a suitable high temperature grease. Inspect clutch shoes and drum for damage due to overheating. Clutch hub (1), shoes (2) and spring (3) are available as a unit assembly only. When installing clutch, clutch hub should be positioned with chamfered thread opening side towards crankshaft. Tighten clutch hub (1) to 27.6-31.6 N•m (20-23 ft.-lbs.) and nut (8) to 13-15 N•m (9-11 ft.-lbs.).

OIL PUMP. All models are equipped with an automatic, plunger type chain oil pump. Plunger (20 – Fig. E25) is actuated by a cam on the crankshaft. Oil pump output is adjusted by rotating the pump housing (17). Oil pump may be disassembled for cleaning or renewal of individual components after removing the air filter and withdrawing oil pump assembly from crankcase.

When installing pump, screw housing (17) in until lightly seated. Run saw at medium speed and unscrew pump housing approximately one turn until maximum oil output is obtained. Pump housing location should be marked when at maximum output for future reference. Rotate pump housing counterclockwise from maximum output position to decrease oil output.

REWIND STARTER. To disassemble rewind starter, remove starter housing (14 – Fig. E30), remove rope handle and allow rope to rewind into housing. Unscrew rope pulley screw (10) and carefully remove rope pulley (12) being careful not to dislodge rewind spring. If necessary to remove rewind spring, care should be used not to allow spring to uncoil uncontrolled.

Install rewind spring in starter housing with coils wrapped in a clockwise direction from outer end of spring. Wind rope around pulley in a clockwise direction as viewed from flywheel side of pulley. Turn pulley three turns clockwise before passing rope through outlet. Check starter operation. It should be possible to pull rope to its full extension and still turn rope pulley approximately ½ turn clockwise. If rewind spring coil binds before rope is fully extended, reduce pre-tension on rope by pulling rope up into notch in rope pulley and allowing pulley to rotate one turn counterclockwise. Recheck starter operation.

CHAIN BRAKE. Models CS-280EP and CS-290EVLP are equipped with a

Fig. E28 – View of reed valve unit assembly. Refer to text for service information.

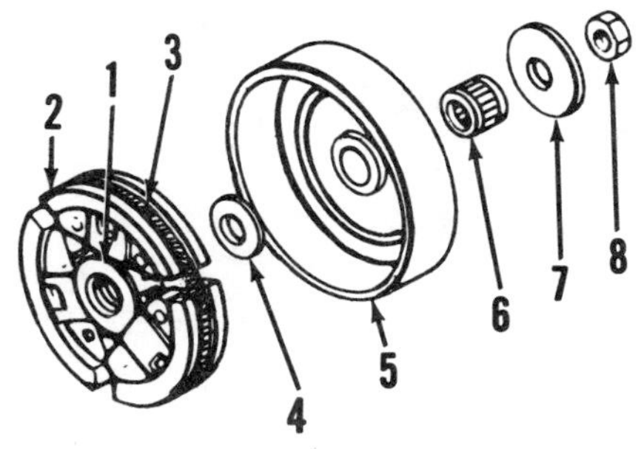

Fig. E29 – Exploded view of clutch assembly.

1. Hub
2. Shoe
3. Spring
4. Washer
5. Drum
6. Needle bearing
7. Washer
8. Nut

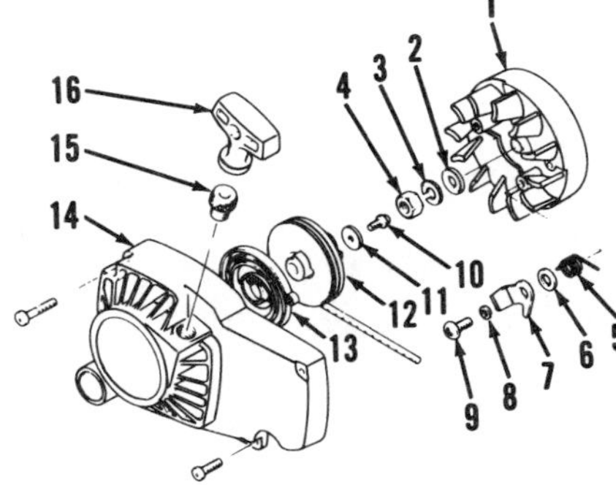

Fig. E30 – Exploded view of typical rewind starter assembly.

1. Flywheel
2. Lockwasher
3. Spring washer
4. Nut
5. Pawl spring
6. Washer
7. Pawl
8. Spacer
9. Screw
10. Screw
11. Washer
12. Rope pulley
13. Rewind spring
14. Starter housing
15. Rope guide
16. Rope handle

chain brake system designed to stop chain movement should kickback occur. Chain brake is activated when operator's hand strikes hand guard (1–Fig. E31) tripping brake lever (2), releasing brake band case (10) and allowing brake spring (6) to draw brake band (5) tight around clutch drum. Brake band (5), brake band case (10) and brake spring (6) are removed and renewed as an assembly. If brake spring (6) is removed or renewed, Echo special tool 566834 can be used to hold brake spring (6) in position on brake band case (10) while reassembling unit. No adjustments of chain brake system is required. Make certain clutch drum turns freely with chain brake in off position after reassembly of chain brake system.

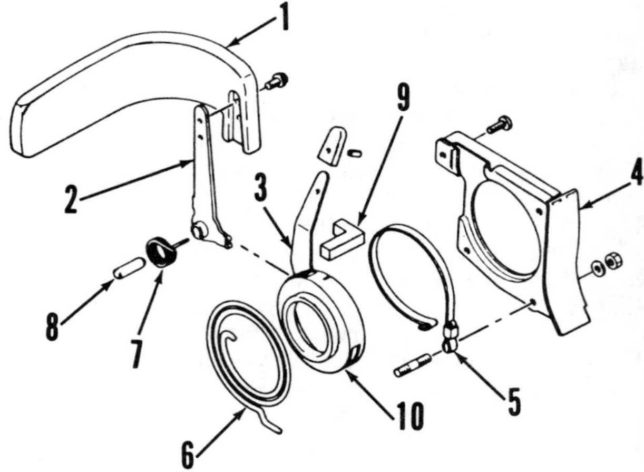

Fig. E31—Exploded view of chain brake system used on Models CS-280EP and CS-290EVLP.

1. Hand guard
2. Brake lever
3. Reset lever
4. Brake cover
5. Brake band
6. Brake spring
7. Spring
8. Shaft
9. Seal
10. Brake band case

Illustrations courtesy Echo Inc.

ECHO

Model	Bore mm (in.)	Stroke mm (in.)	Displacement cc (cu. in.)	Drive Type
CS-330EVL, 330EVLP	39 (1.53)	28 (1.1)	33.4 (2.04)	Direct
CS-400EVL, 400EVLP	40 (1.57)	32 (1.26)	40.2 (2.45)	Direct
CS-440EVL, 440EVLP	42 (1.65)	32 (1.26)	44.3 (2.7)	Direct
CS-500VL, 500VLP, 500EVL, 500EVLP, 510EVL, 510EVLP	42 (1.65)	36 (1.42)	49.9 (3.04)	Direct
CS-550EVL, 550EVLP	44 (1.73)	36 (1.42)	54.7 (3.34)	Direct
CS-650EVL, 650EVLP, 660EVL, 660EVLP	47 (1.85)	37 (1.46)	64.2 (3.92)	Direct

MAINTENANCE

SPARK PLUG. Recommended spark plug is Champion CJ8 or equivalent for Models CS-330EVL and CS-330EVLP and Champion CJ8Y for Models CS-400EVL, CS-400EVLP, CS-500VL, CS-500VLP, CS-500EVL and CS-500EVLP. Recommended spark plug for all other models is Champion CJ7Y or equivalent. Spark plug electrode gap should be 0.6-0.7 mm (0.024-0.028 in.) on all models.

CARBURETOR. Models CS-330EVL and CS-330EVLP are equipped with a Zama C1S type carburetor. Models CS-400EVL, CS-400EVLP, CS-440EVL and CS-440EVLP are equipped with a Walbro WA type carburetor. Models CS-510EVL, CS-510EVLP, CS-550EVL and CS-550EVLP are equipped with a Walbro HDA type carburetor. All other models are equipped with a Walbro HDB carburetor. Refer to Zama or Walbro section of CARBURETOR SERVICE section for carburetor overhaul procedures and exploded views.

Initial setting of both low and high speed mixture screws on CS-330EVL models is 1¼ turns open from a lightly seated position. Initial setting for Models CS-400EVL, CS-400EVLP, CS-440EVL and CS-440EVLP is ¾-1¼ turns open for high speed mixture screw and one turn open for low speed mixture screw. On Models CS-500VL, CS-500VLP, CS-500EVL and CS-500EVLP, initially adjust high speed mixture screw to ¼-1 turn open and low speed mixture screw to 1-1¼ turns open. On all other models except CS-650EVL and CS-650EVLP, adjust high speed mixture screw to ¾ turn open and low speed mixture screw to 1⅛ turns open.

On CS-650EVL models, initial adjustment of low speed mixture screw is 1⅛ turns open. Initial high speed mixture needle adjustment may be ½ or 1¼ turns open due to carburetor design differences. Check carburetor setting decal located externally on saw for proper initial adjustment. Should decal be absent, set high speed mixture needle one turn open and observe performance. Reset to approximately ¼ turn open if required. Do not adjust high speed mixture needle too lean as engine may be damaged.

On all models, perform final carburetor adjustments with engine at operating temperature and running. Adjust idle speed screw just below clutch engagement speed. Adjust low speed mixture screw so engine will accelerate cleanly without hesitation. Adjust high speed mixture screw to obtain optimum performance under cutting load.

IGNITION. Models CS-500VL and CS-500VLP are equipped with a conventional flywheel magneto ignition system using breaker-points while all other models are equipped with a breakerless electronic ignition system.

On CS-500VL and CS-500VLP models, breaker-point gap should be 0.3-0.4 mm (0.012-0.016 in.). Correct ignition timing is 30 degrees BTDC. A reference mark is provided on flywheel to set ignition timing. With flywheel turning counterclockwise, first mark (F–Fig. E33) on flywheel periphery indicates ig-

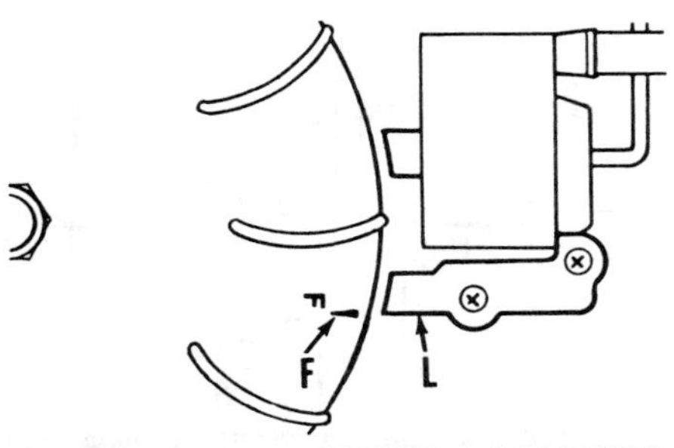

Fig. E33—Ignition on CS-500VL and CS-500VLP models should occur when flywheel mark (F) is aligned with leading pole outer edge (L).

Illustrations courtesy Echo Inc.

nition point when aligned with outer edge of leading magneto core pole (L). Adjust ignition timing by varying breaker-point gap. Air gap between flywheel magnets and magneto coil legs should be 0.4 mm (0.016 in.). Loosen magneto mounting screws and move magneto to adjust air gap.

On all other models, ignition timing is not adjustable. Air gap between flywheel magnets and ignition module or coil core should be 0.4 mm (0.016 in.). Repair of electronic ignition system malfunction is accomplished by renewal of ignition components. Be sure wiring is properly connected.

LUBRICATION. Engine is lubricated by mixing engine oil with fuel. Regular grade automotive gasoline is recommended. Recommended oil is Echo air-cooled two-stroke oil mixed with fuel at a 50:1 ratio. If Echo oil is not available, a good quality oil designed for air-cooled two-stroke engines may be used when mixed with fuel at a 32:1 ratio. Use a separate container when mixing the oil and gas.

All models are equipped with an automatic chain oil pump. Clean automotive oil may be used. Oil viscosity should be chosen according to ambient temperature. Oil pump output is adjustable. Refer to OIL PUMP section for service and adjustment procedures.

REPAIRS

CYLINDER, PISTON, PIN AND RINGS. Cylinder bore is chrome plated on all models and oversize pistons and rings are not available. Inspect cylinder bore for scoring, flaking or other damage to chrome surface.

The piston is equipped with two piston rings. Maximum allowable ring end gap is 0.5 mm (0.020 in.). Maximum allowable piston ring in ring groove side clearance is 0.1 mm (0.004 in.). Renew rings, piston or cylinder as required when service limits are exceeded. A locating pin is present in piston ring grooves to prevent piston ring rotation. Be sure ring end gap is around locating pin when installing cylinder.

The piston pin is retained by wire retainers and rides in needle roller bearing in small end of connecting rod. Be sure piston is properly supported when removing or installing piston pin to prevent damage to connecting rod. Arrow on piston crown must point toward exhaust port when installing piston.

CRANKSHAFT, CONNECTING ROD AND CRANKCASE. All models are equipped with a crankshaft and connecting rod unit assembly which is supported in the crankcase by ball bearings at both ends. Crankshaft and connecting rod are not available separately.

Check crankshaft runout by supporting crankshaft at points (A – Fig. E35) and measure at points (B). Maximum allowable runout is 0.05 mm (0.002 in.).

Flywheel side main bearing (11 – Fig. E34) is held in position by a shoulder in crankcase half (14) while snap ring (16) retains clutch side main bearing (15). Some models may be equipped with a lubrication passage designed to lubricate oil pump cam and plunger. Make certain snap ring (16) does not obstruct passage when installed (snap ring gap should surround oil passage hole). Install crankshaft seals (13 and 17), open sides toward each other, flush with outer face of crankcase.

OIL PUMP. All models are equipped with an automatic plunger type chain oil pump. The plunger (25 – Fig. E34) is actuated by a cam on the crankshaft. Oil pump output is adjusted by rotating knob (21) which is secured to pump housing (22) by screw (20). Oil pump may be disassembled for cleaning or renewal of individual components after removing output adjustment knob (21) and unscrewing pump housing (22) from crankcase.

When installing pump housing, screw housing in until lightly seated. Run saw at medium speed and unscrew pump housing approximately ½ to 1 turn until maximum oil output is obtained. Mark pump housing for future reference then install adjusting knob so it is against

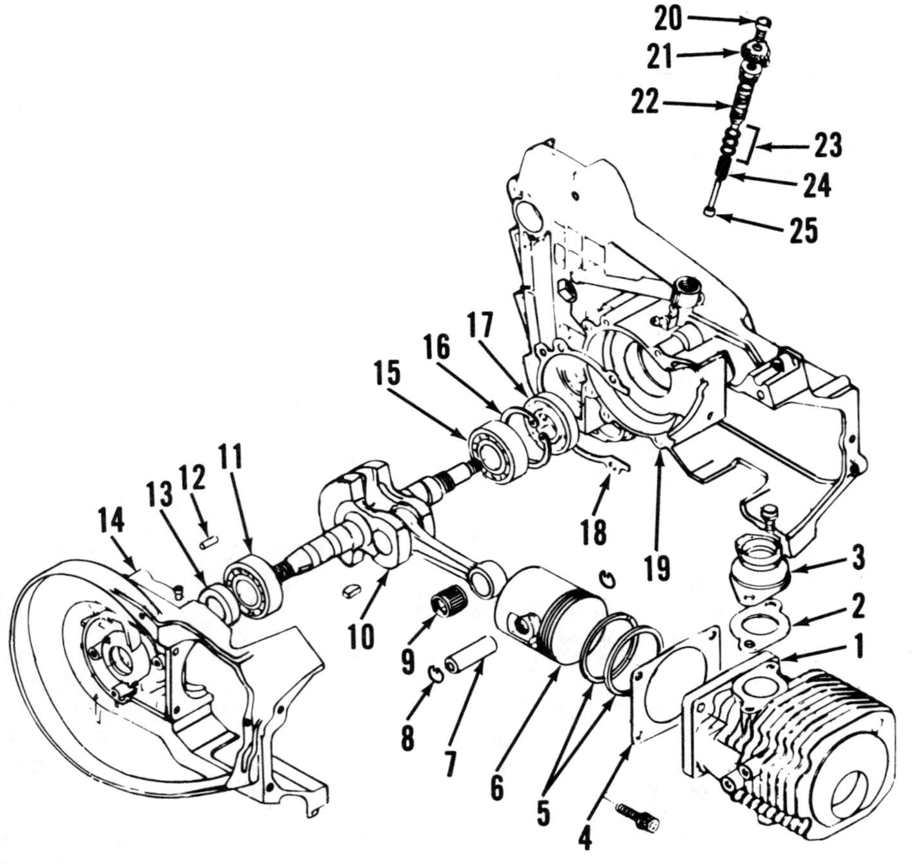

Fig. E34 – Exploded view of Model CS-500EVL engine assembly. Other models are similar.

1. Cylinder
2. Gasket
3. Intake manifold
4. Gasket
5. Piston rings
6. Piston
7. Piston pin
8. Pin retainer
9. Needle bearing
10. Crankshaft & rod assy.
11. Bearing
12. Guide pin
13. Seal
14. Left crankcase half
15. Bearing
16. Snap ring
17. Seal
18. Gasket
19. Right crankcase half
20. Screw
21. Knob
22. Oil pump housing
23. "O" ring
24. Spring
25. Oil pump plunger

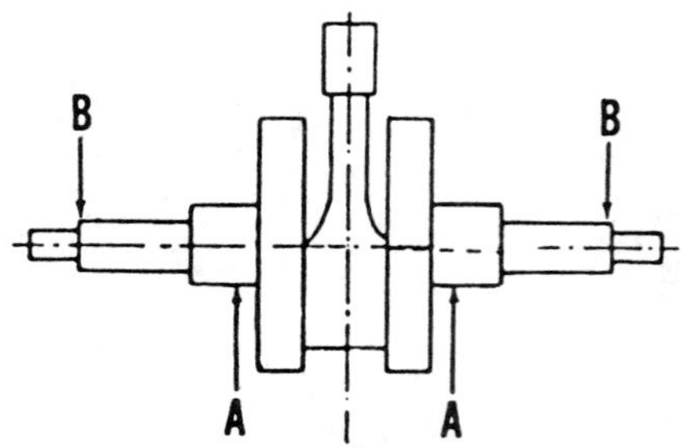

Fig. E35 – Measure crankshaft by supporting crankshaft at points (A). Maximum runout measured at points (B) should not exceed 0.05 mm (0.002 in.).

stop for maximum oil output and must be turned counterclockwise to decrease oil output.

CLUTCH. Some models are equipped with the clutch assembly shown in Fig. E37. Clutch hub, shoes and garter spring (1) are a unit assembly and are not available separately on early model saws. Individual clutch components are available on late model saws. Refer to Fig. E38 for exploded view of clutch used on all other models. Individual clutch components are available.

On all models, clutch nut and hub have left-hand threads. Clutch drum rides on a needle roller bearing. Inspect clutch shoes and drum for damage due to overheating. Renew excessively worn or damaged components. Clutch hub and nut should be tightened to 20.2-23.7 N•m (14.9-17.5 ft.-lbs.).

REWIND STARTER. To disassemble rewind starter, remove starter housing, remove rope handle and allow rope to rewind into housing. Unscrew rope pulley screw and carefully remove rope pulley, being careful not to dislodge rewind spring. If necessary to remove rewind spring, care should be used not to allow spring to uncoil uncontrolled.

Install rewind spring in starter housing with coils wrapped in a clockwise direction from outer end of spring. Wind rope around pulley in a clockwise direction as viewed from flywheel side of pulley. Turn pulley three turns clockwise before passing rope through outlet. Check starter operation. It should be possible to pull rope to its full extension and still turn rope pulley approximately ½ turn clockwise. If rewind spring coil binds before rope is fully extended, reduce pretension on rope by pulling rope up into notch in rope pulley and allowing pulley to rotate one turn counterclockwise. Recheck starter operation.

CHAIN BRAKE. Some models are equipped with a chain brake system designed to stop chain movement should kickback occur. Chain brake is activated when operator's hand strikes chain brake lever (1–Fig. E40) tripping actuating cam (4), allowing spring (5) to draw brake band (11) tight around clutch drum. Pull back chain brake lever (1) to reset mechanism.

Disassembly for repair and component renewal is evident after referral to Fig. E40 and inspection of unit. Chain brake system should be periodically cleaned and inspected for excessive wear or other damage to clutch drum, brake band or linkage.

To adjust chain brake, loosen screw (8) and rotate adjusting cam (9). Make certain clutch drum turns freely and chain brake band does not contact clutch drum when chain brake is disengaged.

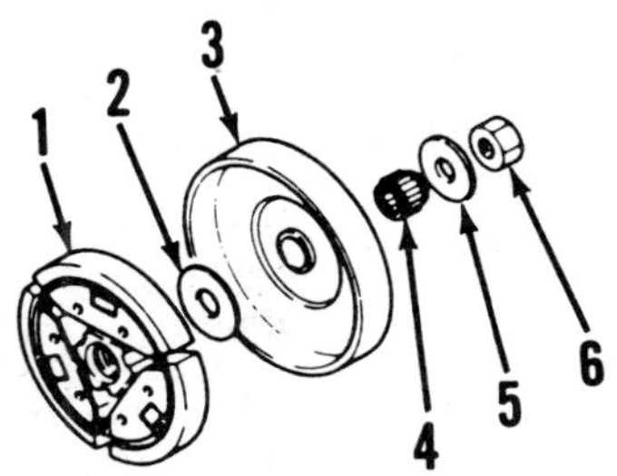

Fig. E37—Exploded view of typical clutch assembly used on all models except CS-500VL, CS-500VLP, CS-500EVL, CS-500EVLP, CS-650EVL and CS-650EVLP models. Only Models CS-330EVL and CS-330EVLP use washer (2).

1. Hub & shoe assy.
2. Washer
3. Drum
4. Needle bearing
5. Washer
6. Clutch nut

Fig. E39—Exploded view of typical rewind starter assembly used on all models. Washer (5) is not used on CS-330EVL and CS-330EVLP models.

1. Starter housing
2. Washer
3. Rope handle
4. Rope guide
5. Washer
6. Rewind spring
7. Washer
8. Rope pulley
9. Washer
10. Screw
11. Cap screw
12. Washer
13. Pawl
14. Spacer
15. Spring
16. Nut
17. Flywheel

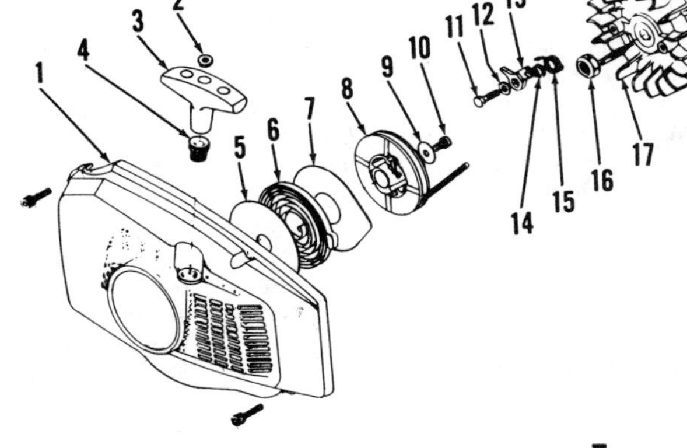

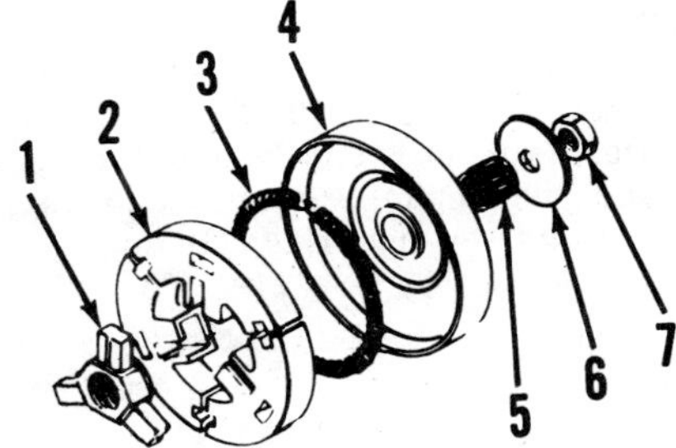

Fig. E38—Exploded view of clutch assembly used on Models CS-500VL, CS-500VLP, CS-500EVL, CS-500EVLP, CS-650EVL and CS-650EVLP.

1. Hub
2. Clutch shoes
3. Garter spring
4. Clutch drum
5. Needle roller bearing
6. Washer
7. Clutch nut

Fig. E40—Exploded view of chain brake system used on so equipped models.

1. Chain brake lever
2. Brake band lever
3. Spacer
4. Actuating cam
5. Spring
6. Pivot screw
7. Cover
8. Screw
9. Adjusting cam
10. Brake band retainer
11. Brake band
12. Dust seal
13. Rubber bumper
14. Pin

ECHO

Model	Bore mm (in.)	Stroke mm (in.)	Displacement cc (cu. in.)	Drive Type
CS-900EVL, 900EVLP	54 (2.126)	40 (1.575)	91.6 (5.59)	Direct

MAINTENANCE

SPARK PLUG. Recommended spark plug is NGK BPM7A or equivalent. Spark plug electrode gap should be 0.6-0.7 mm (0.024-0.028 in.).

CARBURETOR. A Walbro SDC diaphragm type carburetor is used. Refer to Walbro section of CARBURETOR SERVICE section for carburetor overhaul and exploded views.

Initial adjustment for both low speed and high speed mixture screws is one turn open from a lightly seated position. Make final adjustment with engine warm and running. Adjust idle speed screw so engine idles just below clutch engagement speed. Adjust low speed mixture screw so engine will accelerate cleanly without hesitation. Adjust high speed mixture screw to obtain optimum performance under cutting load. Do not adjust high speed mixture too lean as engine may be damaged.

IGNITION. Both models are equipped with a two-piece breakerless capacitor discharge ignition system. Refer to Fig. E41. Repair of ignition system malfunction except for faulty wiring connections, is accomplished by renewal of ignition system components. Ignition timing is not adjustable but should be checked periodically to ensure correct ignition module operation.

To check ignition timing, first remove the spark plug and starter housing from saw. Locate ignition timing reference marks provided on crankcase and flywheel periphery (Fig. E42). Insert a dial indicator into spark plug opening, then position piston at exactly TDC. Crankcase stationary mark (M) and flywheel mark "T" (TDC) should be aligned. If marks do not align, remove flywheel and renew flywheel key as required. Reinstall flywheel, then rotate flywheel counterclockwise until first mark "F" (30 degrees BTDC) is aligned with stationary mark (M). Ensure marks are aligned, then paint similar marks on ignition module and flywheel fin. Marks must be visible when starter housing is installed. Install starter housing and connect a suitable power timing light. Start and run saw at idle speed and observe timing marks. If marks do not align, renew ignition module and retest.

Air gap between flywheel magnets and ignition module core should be 0.3-0.4 mm (0.012-0.016 in.). Tighten flywheel nut to 32.3-36.2 N·m (23.8-26.7 ft.-lbs.).

LUBRICATION. Engine is lubricated by mixing engine oil with fuel. Regular grade automotive gasoline is recommended. Recommended oil is Echo air-cooled two-stroke oil mixed with fuel at a 50:1 ratio. If Echo oil is not available, a good quality oil designed for air-cooled two-stroke engines may be used when mixed with fuel at a 32:1 ratio. Use a separate container when mixing the oil and gas.

A manual and automatic chain oil pump is used. Clean automotive oil may be used. Oil viscosity should be chosen according to ambient temperature. Oil pump output is adjustable. Refer to OIL PUMP section for service and adjustment procedures.

REPAIRS

CYLINDER, PISTON, PIN AND RINGS. The vertical cylinder has a chrome plated bore and oversize piston and rings are not available. Inspect cylinder bore for scoring, flaking or other damage to chrome surface.

The piston is equipped with two piston rings. Maximum allowable ring end gap is 0.5 mm (0.020 in.). Maximum allowable piston ring in ring groove side clearance is 0.1 mm (0.004 in.). Renew rings, piston or cylinder as required when service limits are exceeded. A locating pin is present in piston ring grooves to prevent piston ring rotation. Be sure ring end gap is around locating pin when installing cylinder.

The piston pin is retained by wire retainers and rides in needle roller bearing in small end of connecting rod. Be sure piston is properly supported when removing or installing piston pin to prevent damage. Arrow on piston crown must point toward exhaust port when installing piston.

CRANKSHAFT, CONNECTING ROD AND CRANKCASE. The crankshaft, crankpin and connecting rod are pressed together and are available only as a complete assembly. Crankshaft assembly is supported in the crankcase by ball bearings at both ends.

Check crankshaft runout by supporting crankshaft at points (A – Fig. E44) and measuring at points (B). Maximum allowable runout is 0.05 mm (0.002 in.).

Crankshaft main bearings are located in crankcase by snap rings (10 and 15 –

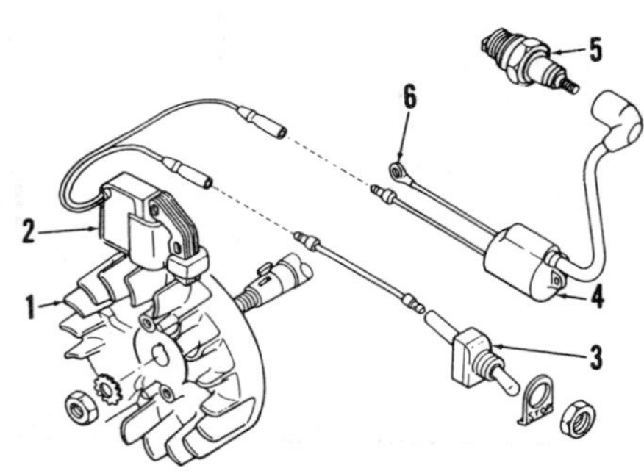

Fig. E41 – Illustrated view of ignition components.

1. Flywheel
2. Ignition module
3. Stop switch
4. Ignition coil
5. Spark plug

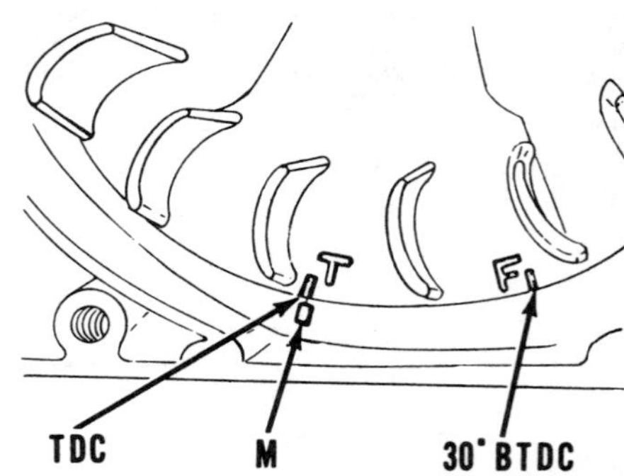

Fig. E42 – View of ignition timing reference marks. Refer to text.

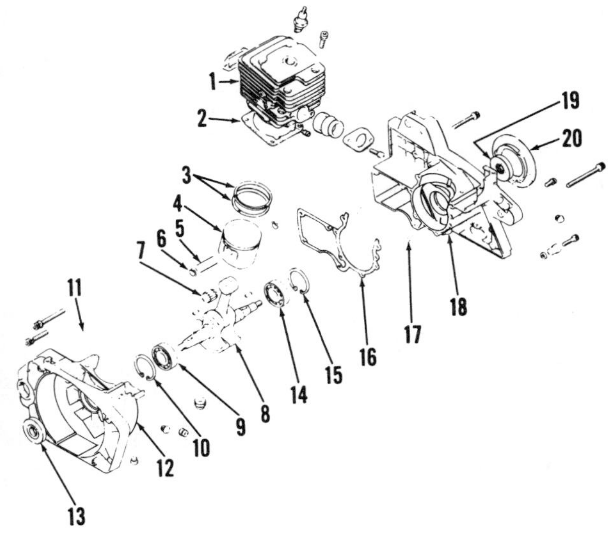

Fig. E43—Exploded view of engine assembly.

1. Cylinder
2. Gasket
3. Piston rings
4. Piston
5. Piston pin
6. Pin retainer
7. Needle bearing
8. Crankshaft & rod assy.
9. Bearing
10. Snap ring
11. Guide pin
12. Left crankcase half
13. Seal
14. Bearing
15. Snap ring
16. Gasket
17. Guide pin
18. Right crankcase half
19. Seal
20. Seal retainer

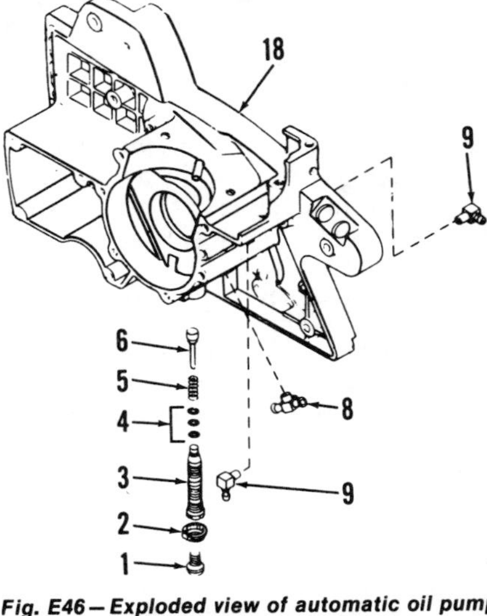

Fig. E46—Exploded view of automatic oil pump assembly. Connector (8) and elbow connectors (9) are also shown in Fig. E45.

1. Adjusting screw
2. Adjusting stop
3. Oil pump housing
4. "O" ring
5. Spring
6. Pump plunger
8. Connector
9. Elbow connector
18. Right crankcase half

Fig. E43). Right crankcase half (18) has a lubrication passage designed to lubricate oil pump cam and plunger. Make certain snap ring (15) does not obstruct passage when installed (snap ring gap should surround oil passage hole). Install crankshaft seals (13 and 19), open sides toward each other, flush with outer face of crankcase half (12) and seal retainer (20).

OIL PUMP. Both models are equipped with manual and automatic chain oiler pumps. Refer to Fig. E45 for exploded view if manual oil pump and related components. Check balls (10) must move freely for proper pump operation. Renew "O" ring (4) and hoses as required when signs of hardening or cracking are evident.

Refer to Fig. E46 for exploded view of automatic oil pump. The plunger (6) is actuated by a cam on the crankshaft. Oil pump output is adjusted by rotating screw (1) located underneath saw. Oil pump may be disassembled for cleaning or renewal of individual components after removing pump cover plate, adjusting screw (1), adjustment stop (2) and unscrewing pump housing (3) from crankcase.

When installing pump housing, screw housing in until lightly seated. Remove saw chain, guide bar and side plates so oil pump output may be observed. Run saw at medium speed and unscrew pump housing approximately ½ to 1 turn until maximum oil output is obtained. Mark pump housing for future reference, then install adjustment stop (2) so it is against stop for maximum oil output and must be turned counterclockwise to decrease oil output.

CLUTCH. Both models are equipped with the four-shoe centrifugal clutch shown in Fig. E48. Clutch nut (14) has left hand threads. Clutch hub (4) is a snug fit on crankshaft. A Woodruff key prevents independent rotation of hub and crankshaft. It may be necessary to use a puller to withdraw clutch hub and shoe assembly. Individual clutch components are available.

Clutch drum rides on a caged needle roller bearing. Inspect clutch drum and shoes for excessive wear or damage due to overheating. Renew excessively worn or damaged components. Clutch nut should be tightened to 19.9-23.7 N·m (15.17 ft.-lbs.).

REWIND STARTER. To disassemble rewind starter (Fig. E49), remove starter housing and rope handle then allow rope to rewind into housing. Unscrew rope pulley screw and carefully

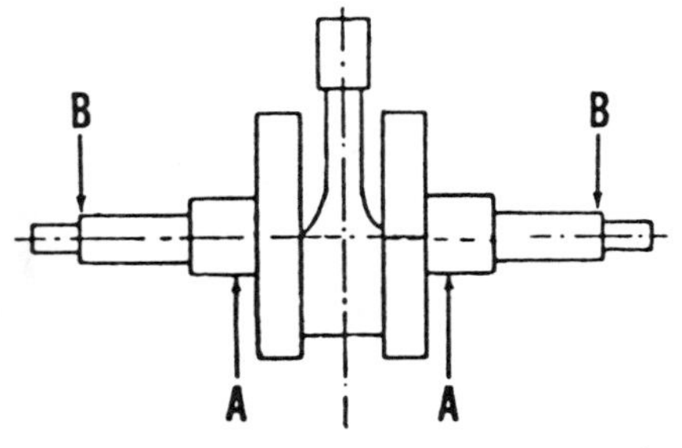

Fig. E44—Measure crankshaft by supporting crankshaft at points (A). Maximum runout measured at points (B) should not exceed 0.05 mm (0.002 in.).

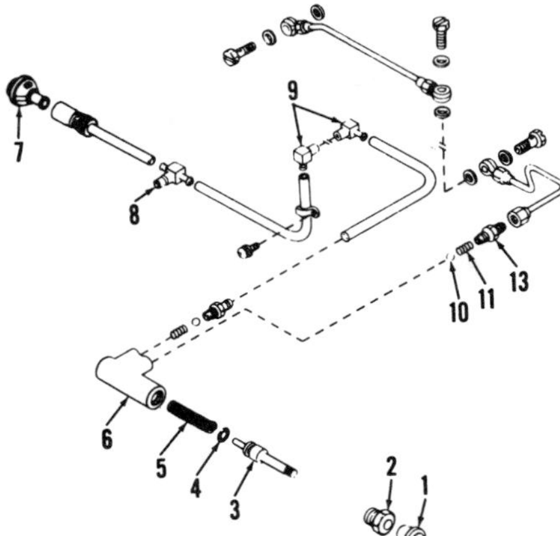

Fig. E45—Exploded view of manual chain oiler pump and related components.

1. Button
2. Bushing
3. Plunger
4. "O" ring
5. Spring
6. Housing
7. Oil pickup
8. Connector
9. Elbow connector
10. Check ball
11. Spring
13. Oil outlet fitting

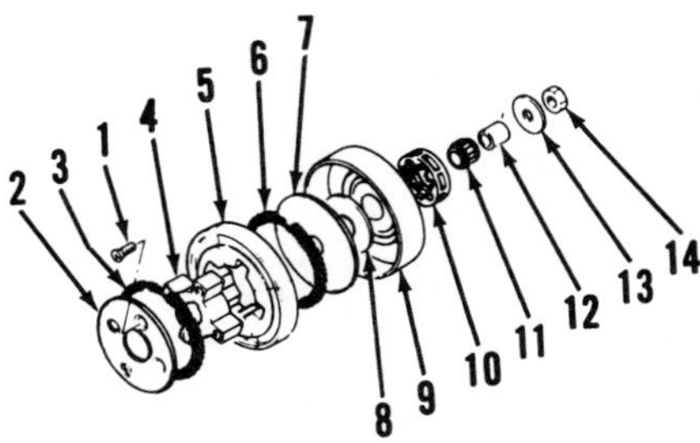

Fig. E48—Exploded view of clutch assembly.

1. Screw
2. Washer
3. Garter spring
4. Clutch hub
5. Clutch shoes
6. Garter spring
7. Washer
8. Washer
9. Clutch
10. Sprocket
11. Needle bearing
12. Spacer
13. Washer
14. Nut

remove rope pulley being careful not to dislodge rewind spring. If necessary to remove rewind spring, care should be used not to allow spring to uncoil uncontrolled.

Install rewind spring in starter housing with coils wrapped in a clockwise direction from outer end of spring. Wind rope around pulley in a clockwise direction as viewed from flywheel side of pulley. Turn pulley three turns clockwise before passing rope through outlet. Check starter operation. It should be possible to pull rope to its full extension and still turn rope pulley approximately ½ turn clockwise. If rewind spring coil binds before rope is fully extended, reduce pre-tension on rope by pulling rope up into notch in rope pulley and allowing pulley to rotate one turn counterclockwise. Recheck starter operation.

CHAIN BRAKE. Model CS-900EVLP is equipped with a chain brake system designed to stop chain movement should kickback occur. The chain brake system is activated when the operator's hand strikes the chain brake lever (1 – Fig. E50) thereby forcing actuating cam (8) to release spring (9). Brake band is adjusted by rotating adjuster (12). Brake band should not contact clutch drum when chain brake is disengaged.

Disassembly for repair or renewal of individual components is evident after inspection of unit and referral to the exploded view.

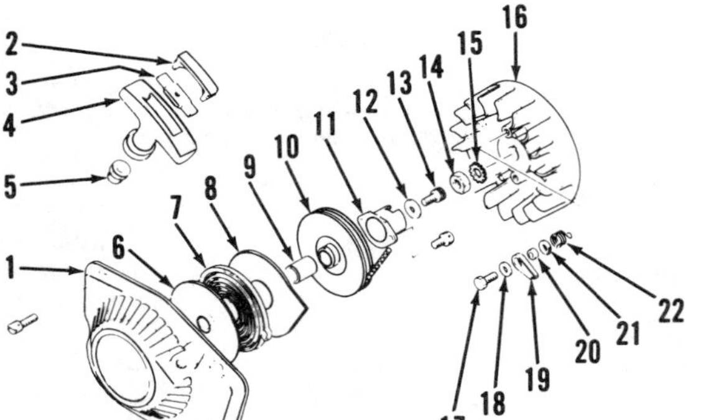

Fig. E49 – Exploded view of rewind starter assembly.

1. Starter housing
2. Cover
3. Insert
4. Rope handle
5. Rope guide
6. Washer
7. Rewind spring
8. Washer
9. Bushing
10. Rope pulley
11. Starter cup
12. Washer
13. Screw
14. Nut
15. Washer
16. Flywheel
17. Cap screw
18. Washer
19. Pawl
20. Spacer
21. Washer
22. Spring

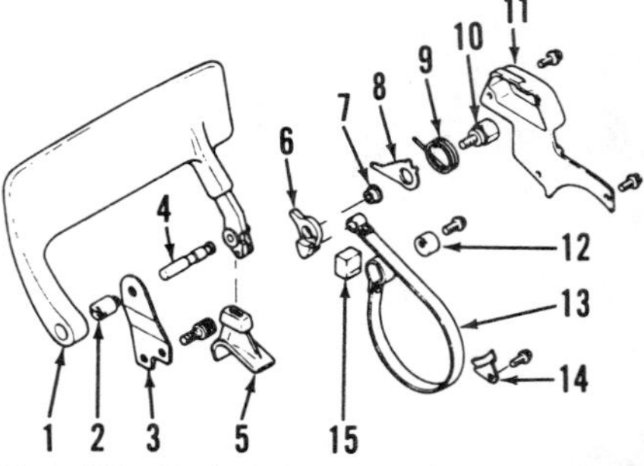

Fig. E50 – Exploded view of chain brake assembly used on Model CS-900EVLP.

1. Chain brake lever
2. Pivot pin
3. Support
4. Pivot pin
5. Dust cover
6. Brake band lever
7. Spacer
8. Actuating cam
9. Spring
10. Cap screw
11. Shield
12. Brake band adjuster
13. Brake band
14. Brake band retainer
15. Dust seal

ECHO

Model	Bore mm (in.)	Stroke mm (in.)	Displacement cc (cu. in.)	Drive Type
CS-4000, 4100	40 (1.575)	31 (1.22)	39 (2.38)	Direct
CS-4500, 4600	43 (1.693)	31 (1.22)	45 (2.75)	Direct
CS-5500	46 (1.811)	33 (1.299)	54.8 (3.35)	Direct
CS-6700	50 (1.969)	34 (1.339)	66.8 (4.07)	Direct
CS-8000	52 (2.047)	38 (1.496)	80.7 (4.925)	Direct

MAINTENANCE

SPARK PLUG. Recommended spark plug for all models is Champion CJ6Y or equivalent. Spark plug electrode gap for all models should be 0.6-0.7 mm (0.024-0.028 in.).

CARBURETOR. All models are equipped with a Walbro HDA diaphragm type carburetor. Refer to Walbro section of CARBURETOR SERVICE section for overhaul and exploded view.

Initial adjustment of both low and high speed mixture screws is 1¼ turns open from a lightly seated position. Make final adjustment with engine running at operating temperature.

Adjust idle speed screw so engine idles just under clutch engagement speed. Adjust low speed mixture screw to obtain maximum idle speed, then turn adjusting screw counterclockwise ⅛ turn. Readjust idle speed screw so saw chain does not move when engine is idling. Adjust high speed mixture screw so engine speed reaches 12,000 to 13,000 rpm at full throttle. If tachometer is not available, adjust high speed mixture screw to obtain maximum engine speed at full throttle, then turn screw counterclockwise ⅛ turn. Do not adjust high speed mixture screw too lean as overheating and engine damage could occur.

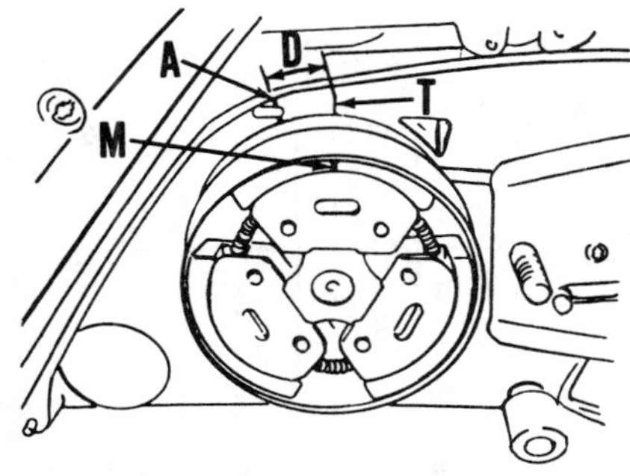

Fig. E57—View of ignition timing reference marks. Refer to text.

IGNITION. All models are equipped with an electronic capacitor discharge ignition system. Model CS-8000 is equipped with a one-piece ignition coil and module assembly, while all other models are equipped with a separate ignition coil and module. Ignition timing is not adjustable, but may be checked using the following procedure:

Remove sprocket cover, chain, guide bar and spark plug. Position piston at top dead center (TDC), then scribe a mark (M—Fig. E57) on clutch shoe and an adjacent mark (T) on engine body. On Models CS-4000, CS-4100, CS-4500 and CS-4600, scribe another mark (A) on engine body a distance of 18 mm (0.70 in.) counterclockwise of TDC mark (T). On Models CS-5500 and CS-6700, mark (A) should be 19 mm (0.75 in.) from TDC mark (T). On Model CS-8000, mark (A) should be 20 mm (0.79 in.) from TDC mark (T). Install spark plug and connect a suitable timing light. Operate engine above 5000 rpm and observe timing marks. Marks (M) and (A) should be aligned if ignition timing is operating properly. If marks (M) and (A) do not align, check for sheared or damaged flywheel key or damaged flywheel keyway. If no damage to key or keyway is noted, renew ignition module and recheck ignition timing.

Air gap between ignition module and flywheel magnets should be 0.35 mm (0.014 in.).

LUBRICATION. Engine is lubricated by mixing engine oil with fuel. Regular grade automotive gasoline is recommended. Recommended oil is Echo air-cooled two-stroke engine oil mixed with fuel at a 50:1 ratio. If Echo air-cooled, two-stroke oil is not available, use a good quality oil designed for use in air-cooled two-stroke engines mixed with fuel at a 32:1 ratio. Use a separate container when mixing the oil and gas.

All models are equipped with an automatic chain oil pump. Some models are equipped with an optional manual oil pump. Oil designed for bar and chain lubrication is recommended, but clean automotive oil may also be used. Oil viscosity should be chosen according to the ambient temperature. Refer to OIL PUMP section for service and adjustment procedures.

REPAIRS

CRANKCASE PRESSURE TEST. An improperly sealed crankcase can cause the engine to be hard to start, run rough, have low power and overheat. Refer to ENGINE SERVICE section of this manual for crankcase pressure test procedure. If crankcase leakage is indicated, pressurize crankcase and use a soap and water solution to check gaskets, seals, pulse line and castings for leakage.

TIGHTENING TORQUES. Tightening torque values are as follows:

Clutch hub
- CS4000, CS-4100, CS-4500
- CS4600, CS-5500 . . . . . 19.8-22.6 N·m (175-200 in.-lbs.)
- CS-6700, CS-8000 . . . . 44.1-46.9 N·m (390-415 in.-lbs.)

Clutch plate . . . . 3.4-4.5 N·m (30-40 in.-lbs.)

Crankcase . . . . 7.4-8.4 N·m (65-75 in.-lbs.)
Cylinder
CS-8000 . . . . 13.0-14.7 N·m (115-130 in.-lbs.)
All other models . . . . 7.4-8.4 N·m (65-75 in.-lbs.)
Flywheel . . . . 19.8-24.3 N·m (175-215 in.-lbs.)
Ignition coil . . . . 3.4-4.5 N·m (30-40 in.-lbs.)
CDI module . . . . 3.4-4.5 N·m (30-40 in.-lbs.)
Spark plug . . . . 14.7-16.9 N·m (130-150 in.-lbs.)
Muffler
CS-4000, CS-4500 . . . . . . 4.5-5.6 N·m (40-50 in.-lbs.)
CS4100, CS-4600, CS-5500, CS-6700 . . . . . . 7.4-8.4 N·m (65-75 in.-lbs.)
CS-8000 . . . . 13.0-14.7 N·m (115-130 in.-lbs.)
Oil pump . . . . 3.4-4.5 N·m (30-40 in.-lbs.)
Guide bar . . . . 19.8-22.6 N·m (175-200 in.-lbs.)

CYLINDER, PISTON, PIN AND RINGS. To remove cylinder and piston, remove air cleaner cover, air filter and cylinder cover. Disconnect throttle link and fuel line from carburetor. Remove carburetor from engine. Remove cap screw retaining muffler bracket to crankcase. Remove cylinder mounting screws and withdraw cylinder from crankcase. Note that cylinder base has been coated with liquid gasket and may be hard to remove. If necessary, gently tap cylinder with plastic hammer to loosen gasket compound. Remove piston rings from piston. Remove piston pin retaining rings (5—Fig. E58) and push piston pin (4) out of piston. Echo piston holder 897719-02830 and piston pin tool 897702-30131 should be used to ease piston pin removal and installation.

The cylinder has a chrome plated bore and oversize piston and rings are not available. Cylinder should be renewed if scoring, flaking or other damage is noted in cylinder bore.

The piston is equipped with two piston rings. Use a feeler gage to measure ring side clearance in piston ring groove. Maximum allowable ring side clearance is 0.1 mm (0.004 in.) for all models. Renew piston if side clearance is excessive. Maximum piston ring end gap is 0.05 mm (0.002 in.) for all models. Maximum allowable piston pin bore diameter is 10.027 mm (0.395 in.) for Models CS-4000, CS-4100, CS-4500 and CS-4600; 11.027 mm (0.434 in.) for Model CS-5500; 12.027 mm (0.474 in.) for Model CS-6700; 13.027 mm (0.513 in.) for Model CS-8000. Minimum piston pin outer diameter is 9.98 mm (0.393 in.) for Models CS-4000, CS-4100, CS-4500 and CS-4600; 10.98 mm (0.432 in.) for Model CS-5500; 11.98 mm (0.472 in.) for Model CS-6700; 12.98 mm (0.511 in.) for Model CS-8000.

Lubricate needle bearing in connecting rod prior to installing piston. Position piston so arrow mark on piston crown points toward exhaust port side of engine. Use piston pin tool to install piston pin. Install new pin retaining rings. Locating pins are present in piston ring grooves to prevent ring rotation. Make certain piston ring end gap is positioned around locating pin when installing cylinder. Lubricate piston and cylinder wall with oil and apply Loctite 515 liquid gasket to cylinder-to-crankcase mating surface. Do not rotate cylinder when installing over piston as rings may be damaged. Tighten cylinder mounting screws to 7.4-8.4 N·m (65-75 in.-lbs.) on all models except CS-8000. On Model CS-8000, tighten cylinder mounting screws to 13.0-14.7 N·m (115-130 in.-lbs.).

CRANKSHAFT, CONNECTING ROD AND CRANKCASE. To remove crankshaft, first remove air cleaner cover and spark plug. Install piston stop tool in spark plug hole to lock piston. Remove sprocket guard, guide bar and chain. Unscrew clutch assembly (left-hand threads) from crankshaft. Unbolt and remove oil pump assembly. Remove starter housing and remove flywheel nut (right-hand threads) and starter pawls. Remove fan and install puller on flywheel. Pull flywheel off crankshaft. Remove ignition module and coil assembly. Remove cylinder and piston as previously outlined. Separate front and rear handles from crankcase. Remove screws securing crankcase halves, then use Echo puller 897502-19830 or suitable equivalent to separate crankcase halves (9 and 10—Fig. E58). Use care not to damage crankcase mating surfaces. Heat crankcase halves to 150°C (300°F) and press bearings (8) out of crankcase halves. Crankshaft and connecting rod are a unit assembly (7) and are not available separately.

Check crankshaft for runout by supporting crankshaft at points (A—Fig. E59) and measure at points (B). Maximum allowable runout is 0.05 mm (0.002 in.). Connecting rod small end bore diameter should not exceed 13.025 mm (0.513 in.) on Models CS-4000, CS-4100, CS-4500 and CS-4600; 15.025 mm (0.592 in.) on Model CS-5500; 16.025 mm (0.631 in.) on Model CS-6700; 17.025 mm (0.670 in.) on Model CS-8000.

Crankcase halves should be heated before installing ball bearings. Do not use an open flame and do not exceed 150°C (300°F) when heating crankcase halves. After bearings are installed in crankcase halves, heat bearing races to ease installation of crankshaft. Apply Loctite 515 to mating surfaces of crankcase. Make certain crankshaft is centered in crankcase and turns freely.

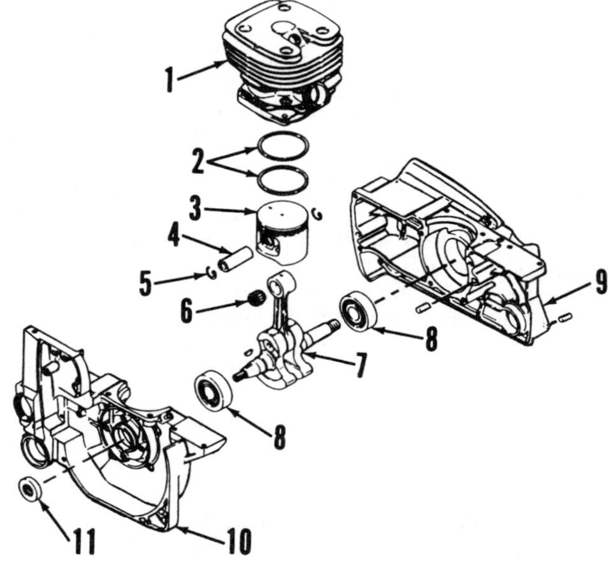

Fig. E58—Exploded view of engine assembly.

1. Cylinder
2. Piston rings
3. Piston
4. Piston pin
5. Piston pin retainer
6. Needle roller bearing
7. Crankshaft & connecting rod assy.
8. Ball bearings
9. Right crankcase half
10. Left crankcase half
11. Crankcase seal

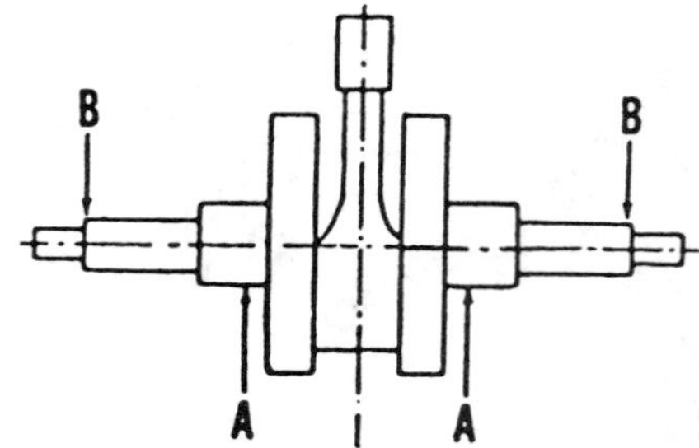

Fig. E59—Measure crankshaft runout by supporting at points (A). Maximum runout measured at points (B) should not exceed 0.05 mm (0.002 in.).

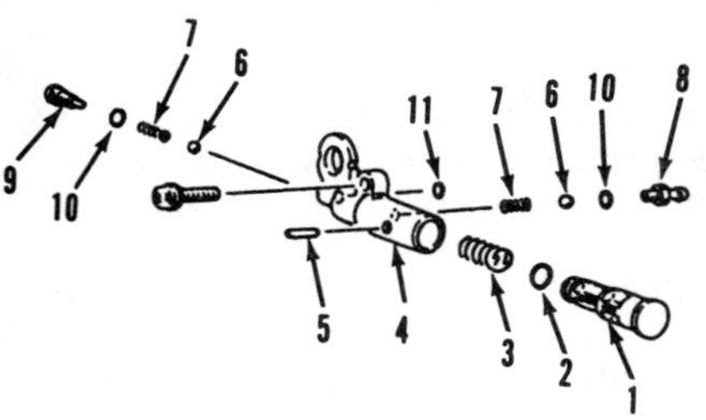

Fig. E60—Exploded view of manual chain oil pump used on some models.

1. Plunger
2. "O" ring
3. Plunger spring
4. Pump body
5. Roll pin
6. Check ball
7. Spring
8. Inlet fitting
9. Plug
10. "O" ring
11. "O" ring

Tighten crankcase screws to 7.4-8.4 N·m (65-75 in.-lbs.).

OIL PUMP. All models are equipped with an automatic chain oil pump. Some models are equipped with an optional manual oil pump. Refer to Fig. E60 for exploded view of manual oil pump. Check balls (6) must move freely for proper operation.

If oil does not reach guide bar and chain, check the following: Remove oil strainer from oil tank and check for being plugged. Clean or renew as necessary. Check for plugged oil tank air vent. Remove guide bar and side plate to clean vent. Make certain oil tubes and passages are clean and there are no pin hole leaks. If these items are satisfactory, remove and inspect oil pump assembly.

All models except Model CS-8000 are equipped with the automatic oil pump shown in Fig. E61. Model CS-8000 is equipped with automatic oil pump shown in Fig. E62. On all models, pump plunger is driven by worm gear (1) and pump output is adjusted by rotating knob (9).

For access to oil pump, remove clutch cover, guide bar, chain and clutch assembly. Unbolt and remove oil pump from crankcase.

Note that late style automatic oil pump plunger has fewer teeth than early style plunger. If an early style plunger is found to be excessively worn or damaged, it is recommended that plunger and worm gear be renewed as a set using late style components.

When reassembling oil pump, be sure "V" ring seal is positioned correctly on pump plunger as shown in Fig. E63. Lubricate all parts with grease during assembly.

When installing oil pump, make certain slot in control pin is aligned with adjuster knob. Be sure washer (2—Fig. E61) is installed with beveled side facing the crankcase. Be careful not to pinch the oil line when installing oil pump to crankcase. Tighten oil pump mounting screws to 3.4-4.5 N·m (30-40 in.-lbs.).

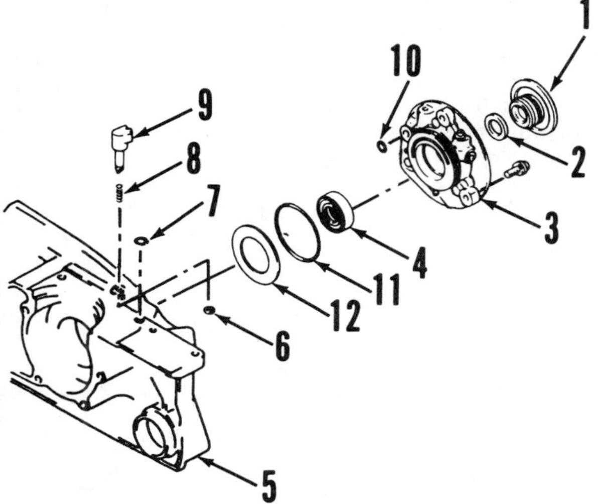

Fig. E61—Exploded view of automatic chain oil pump typical of all models except Model CS-8000.

1. Worm gear
2. Washer
3. Oil pump assy.
4. Crankcase seal
5. Right crankshaft half
6. "E" clip
7. "O" ring
8. Spring
9. Adjusting knob
10. "O" ring
11. "O" ring
12. Plate

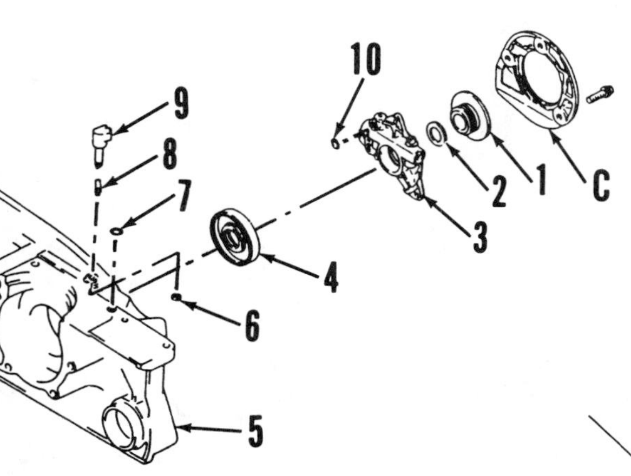

Fig. E62—Exploded view of automatic chain oil pump used on Model CS-8000. Refer to Fig. E61 for component identification except for cover (C).

CLUTCH. All models are equipped with the three-shoe centrifugal clutch shown in Fig. E64. Clutch hub (3) has left-hand threads. Use Echo special tool 897505-16130 or a suitable equivalent to remove clutch hub. Clutch drum (7) rides on needle roller bearing (6). Bearing, clutch shoes (5) and drum (7) should be inspected for wear, damage or discoloration due to overheating and renewed as necessary.

When reassembling, lubricate needle bearing with high temperature grease. Make certain shoe side plates (2) are fac-

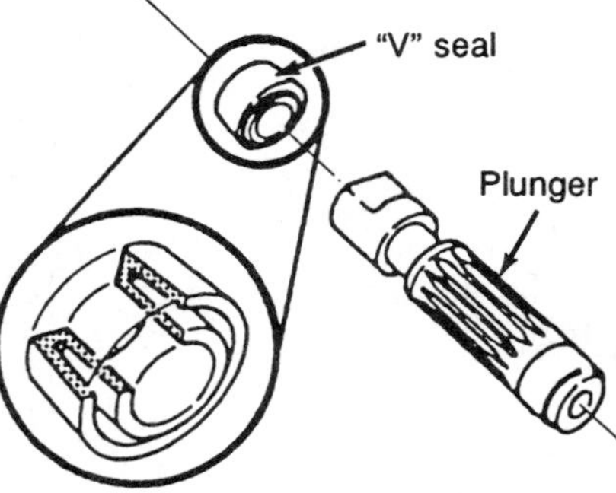

Fig. E63—When installing "V" seal on oil pump plunger, make certain open side of seal is positioned as shown in above drawing.

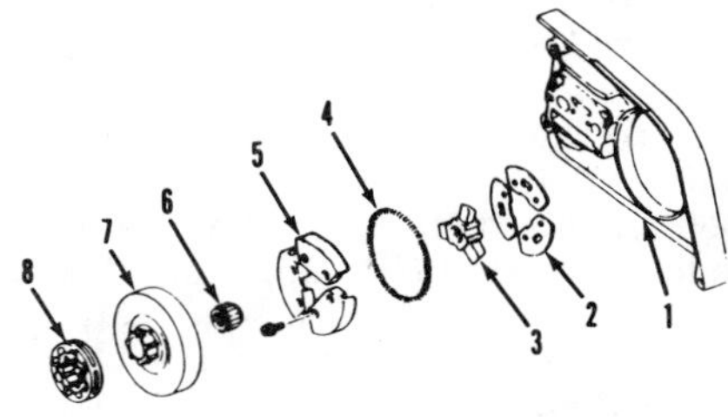

Fig. E64—Exploded view of clutch assembly.

1. Cover
2. Side plate
3. Hub
4. Garter spring
5. Clutch shoes
6. Needle roller bearing
7. Drum
8. Sprocket

Illustrations courtesy Echo Inc.

ing inward. Tighten clutch hub to 44.1-46.9 N·m (390-415 in.-lbs.).

REWIND STARTER. To disassemble rewind starter, remove starter housing (1—Fig. E65) from engine. Pull out rope until notch in rope pulley (8) aligns with rope guide (2). Place rope into notch in pulley and allow pulley to slowly unwind, releasing tension on rewind spring. Remove screw (10) and lift out rope pulley. Use caution not to allow rewind spring (5) to unwind uncontrolled.

If rewind spring is removed, wind into starter housing in a clockwise direction starting with outer coil. Wind rope onto pulley in a clockwise direction as viewed from inside starter housing. Install pulley in housing making certain pulley engages inner end of rewind spring.

To apply tension on rewind spring, hook rope in notch in rope pulley. While holding rope in notch, turn pulley approximately two turns clockwise. Remove rope from notch in pulley and allow pulley to rewind. Rope handle should be snug against starter housing. If not, repeat procedure, turning pulley one additional turn clockwise.

When installing starter assembly on saw, slowly pull rope to engage pawls (14) on flywheel.

CHAIN BRAKE. Some saws are equipped with a chain brake system designed to stop chain movement should kickback occur. Chain brake is activated when operator's hand strikes chain brake lever (1—Fig. E66), drawing brake band (15) tight around clutch drum.

To disassemble chain brake, remove sprocket guard (19) and separate brake assembly from sprocket guard. Remove adjusting nut (18) and tension screw (8). Separate spring (12), stopper (13), brake lever (14), spring (17), clevis (16) and brake band (15). Renew parts as necessary.

To reassemble, reverse disassembly procedure. Lubricate contact surfaces of stopper and brake lever with grease. Tighten tension screw (8) until seated. Move brake lever (14) to disengaged position, tighten adjusting nut (18) until seated, then turn nut out (counterclockwise) to the following initial settings: Models CS-4000, CS-4100, CS-4500, CS-4600 and CS-8000—2.5 to 3 turns out; Model CS-5500—1 to 1.5 turns out; Model CS-6700—1.5 to 2 turns out.

If saw chain does not stop when brake is activated, adjust as follows: Remove sprocket guard and turn adjusting nut (18) clockwise to tighten brake band. Install chain brake and sprocket guard and test for proper operation.

IGNITION SYSTEM. Except for faulty wiring and connections, repair of ignition system malfunctions is accomplished by component renewal.

To check for faulty ignition switch, remove fan cover and disconnect ignition switch wire. Connect ohmmeter or continuity tester leads to ignition switch wire and to good engine ground. There should not be continuity when switch is in RUN position. There should be continuity when switch is in OFF position.

To test ignition coil, remove air cleaner cover and fan cover. On all models except Model CS-8000, disconnect spark plug terminal and connect ohmmeter probes to test points "R1" as shown in Fig. E67 to test primary coil reistance and to test points "R2" to test secondary coil resistance. Primary coil resistance should be 0.1-0.5 ohm and secondary coil resistance should be 2.0-2.5 ohms. On Model CS-8000, disconnect spark plug wire and connect ohmmeter probes to points "R3" as shown in Fig. E68. Secondary coil resistance should be 1.0-1.5 ohms.

There is no practical way to test ignition module other than replacing unit with a known good unit and checking for spark. If ignition system then operates satisfactorily, module is faulty.

HEATED HANDLES. Some models are equipped with a front and rear handle heating system. A generator coil located under flywheel supplies electrical current to heating coils in front and rear handles.

To test handle heating coils, disconnect heating coil lead wires and connect an ohmmeter to coil wires. Meter should read 3.5-4.5 ohms for front handle and 0.85-1.05 ohms for rear handle. Heating coils and handles must be renewed as a unit assembly.

To test generator coil, connect one ohmmeter probe to generator coil lead and remaining ohmmeter probe to a good engine ground. Meter should read 1.0-1.8 ohms. To gain access to generator coil, fan housing and flywheel must first be removed.

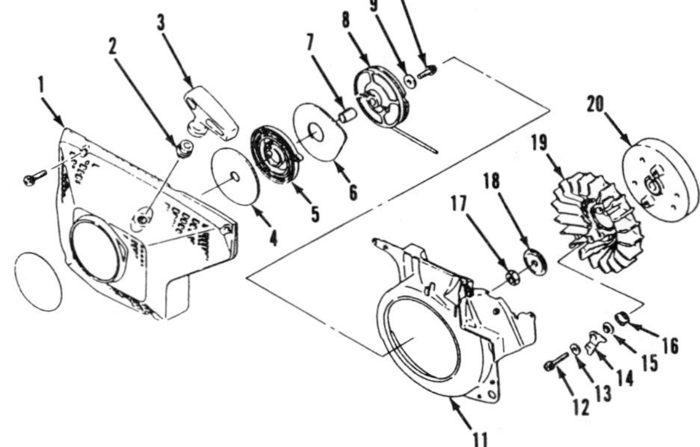

Fig. E65—Exploded view of rewind starter assembly.

1. Housing
2. Rope guide
3. Rope handle
4. Washer
5. Rewind spring
6. Washer
7. Bushing
8. Rope pulley
9. Washer
10. Screw
11. Fan cover
12. Screw
13. Washer
14. Pawl
15. Spacer
16. Pawl spring
17. Nut
18. Washer
19. Fan
20. Flywheel

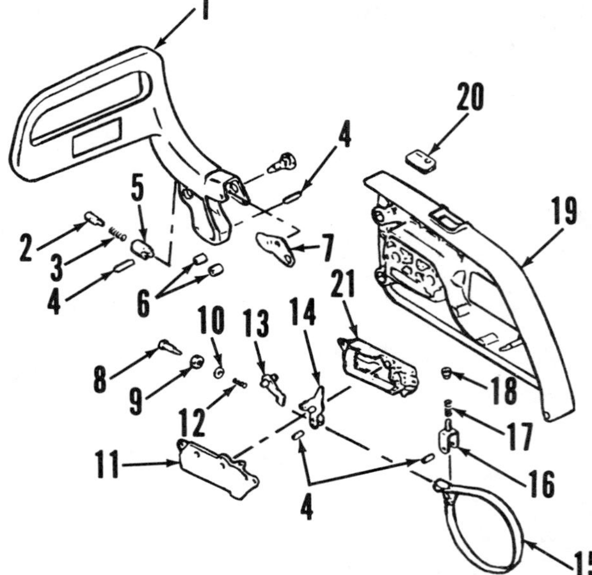

Fig. E66—Exploded view of typical chain brake system used on some models.

1. Chain brake lever
2. Stopper
3. Spring
4. Pin
5. Holder
6. Spacers
7. Lever
8. Screw
9. Nut
10. Washer
11. Cover
12. Spring
13. Stopper
14. Lever
15. Brake band
16. Clevis
17. Spring
18. Nut
19. Sprocket guard
20. Cover
21. Brake cover

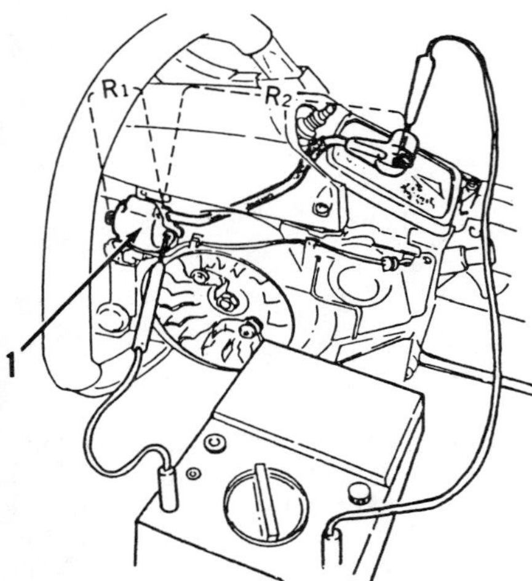

Fig. E67—Drawing showing ignition coil test points for primary coil resistance "R1" and secondary coil resistance "R2" for all models except Model CS-8000.

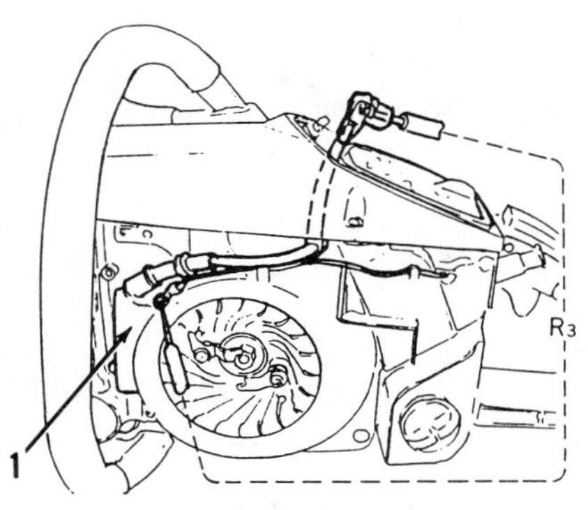

Fig. E68—Drawing showing ignition coil test points for secondary coil resistance "R3" for Model CS-8000.

ECHO

Model	Bore mm (in.)	Stroke mm (in.)	Displacement cc (cu. in.)	Drive Type
CST-610EVL, 610EVLP	36 (1.417)	30 (1.181)	61 (3.72)	Direct

MAINTENANCE

SPARK PLUG. Recommended spark plug is NGK BPM7A or Champion CJ6Y. Recommended electrode gap is 0.55-0.65 mm (0.022-0.026 in.).

CARBURETOR. A Walbro HDA diaphragm type carburetor is used. Refer to Walbro section of CARBURETOR SERVICE for service and exploded views.

Initial adjustment for both high and low speed mixture screws is 1⅛ to 1¼ turns open from a lightly seated position. Make final adjustment with engine running at operating temperature. Adjust low speed mixture so engine will accelerate cleanly without hesitation. Adjust high speed mixture to obtain optimum full throttle performance under a cutting load. Do not adjust high speed mixture too lean as overheating and engine damage could result.

IGNITION. An electronic capacitor discharge ignition system is used. Refer to Fig. E75. Note two separate ignition coils (4) which fire both cylinders simultaneously. Ignition module (5) contains a built in electronic ignition timing advance system. Except for faulty wiring and connections, repair of ignition system malfunctions is accomplished by renewal of ignition system components. Ignition timing is not adjustable but should be checked periodically to ensure proper operation of ignition module.

To check ignition timing it will be necessary to first lock clutch drum (5–Fig. E79) to crankshaft. Remove spark plug leads and properly ground. Remove chain guard, saw chain, guide bar, nut (8) and washer (7).

NOTE: Nut (8) has left-hand threads.

Install Echo special washer tool 900600-00010 (W–Fig. E76) or equivalent washer with a 10 mm (0.393 in.) inner diameter, 22 mm (0.866 in.) outer diameter and 1.5 mm (0.059 in.) thickness on crankshaft end and tighten nut (8–Fig. E79) to 19.8-23.7 N·m (175-210 in.-lbs.). Remove starter housing. Rotate flywheel to align "F" mark on flywheel with mark on crankcase. Scribe reference marks (M–Fig. E76) on clutch drum and chain brake cover. Install starter housing, reattach spark plug leads and connect a suitable power timing light. Start engine and allow to warm-up to normal operating temperature. Operate engine at 7,000 rpm and observe timing marks. Reference marks (M) should be aligned. If reference marks (M) do not align, check for sheared or damaged flywheel key or damaged flywheel keyway. If no damage to key or keyway is noted, renew ignition module and recheck ignition timing. Remove clutch drum locking washer and reassemble components. Tighten nut (8–Fig. E79) to 19.8-23.7 N·m (175-210 in.-lbs.).

Air gap between ignition module (5–Fig. E75) and flywheel magnets (1) should be 0.3 mm (0.012 in.). Incorrect adjustment will affect ignition timing.

Fig. E75—Exploded view of electronic ignition system.

1. Flywheel
2. Ignition switch
3. Spark plug
4. Ignition coil
5. Ignition module

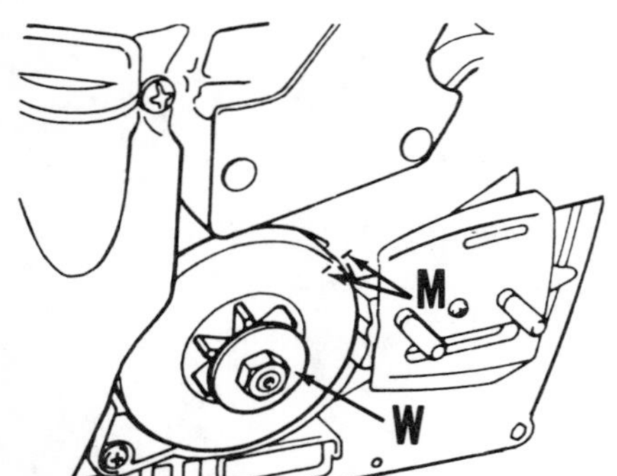

Fig. E76—View showing positioning of timing reference marks (M) and Echo special washer tool 900600-00010. Refer to text.

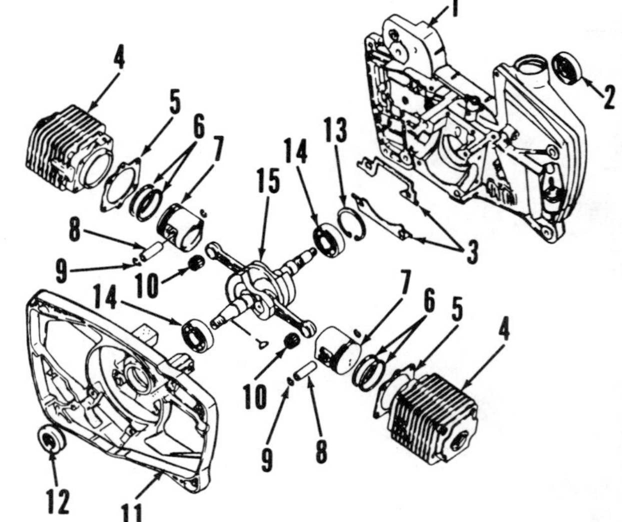

Fig. E77—Exploded view of two-cylinder engine assembly.

1. Right crankcase half
2. Crankcase seal
3. Gaskets
4. Cylinder
5. Cylinder gasket
6. Piston rings
7. Piston
8. Piston pin
9. Piston pin retainer
10. Needle roller bearing
11. Left crankcase half
12. Crankcase seal
13. Snap ring
14. Ball bearing
15. Crankshaft & connecting rods assy.

Illustrations courtesy Echo Inc.

LUBRICATION. Engine is lubricated by mixing engine oil with fuel. Regular grade automotive gasoline is recommended. Recommended oil is Echo air-cooled two-stroke engine oil mixed with fuel at a 50:1 ratio. If Echo air-cooled two-stroke engine oil is not available, use a good quality oil designed for use in air-cooled two-stroke engines mixed with fuel at a 32:1 ratio. Use a separate container when mixing the oil and gas.

Both models are equipped with automatic and manual chain oil pumps. Clean automotive oil may be used. Oil viscosity should be chosen according to ambient temperatures. Automatic oil pump output is adjustable. Refer to OIL PUMP section for service and adjustment procedures.

REPAIRS

CYLINDERS, PISTONS, PINS AND RINGS. Cylinder bores are chrome plated and oversize pistons and rings are not available. Inspect cylinder bore for scoring, flaking or other damage to chrome surface.

Pistons are equipped with two piston rings. Maximum allowable ring end gap is 0.5 mm (0.020 in.). Maximum allowable piston ring in ring groove side clearance is 0.1 mm (0.004 in.). Renew cylinders, pistons and piston rings as required if service limits are exceeded. When installing piston rings, install semi-keystone ring in top piston ring groove and rectangular piston ring in second ring groove. Locating pins are present in ring grooves to prevent piston ring rotation. Make certain ring end gaps are around locating pins when installing cylinders.

Piston pin (8 – Fig. E77) rides in needle roller bearing (10) and is held in place by two wire retainers (9). To remove piston pin, remove wire retainers, properly support piston then carefully tap out piston pin using a suitable driver. Echo special tool 8977102-04320 should be used to remove and install piston pins.

When installing pistons, make certain triangular mark on piston crown faces downward toward cylinder exhaust port.

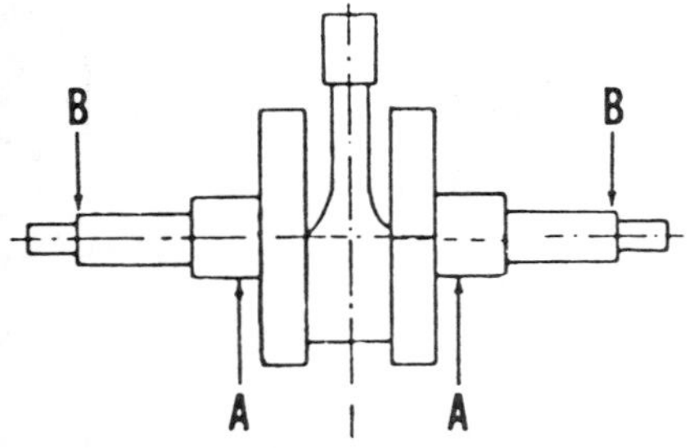

Fig. E78 — Measure crankshaft runout by supporting crankshaft at points (A). Maximum runout measured at points (B) should not exceed 0.05 mm (0.002 in.).

CRANKSHAFT, CONNECTING RODS AND CRANKCASE. Crankshaft and connecting rods (15 – Fig. E77) are a unit assembly and are not available separately. Crankshaft is supported by two ball bearings (14). Clutch side ball bearing is retained in position by snap ring (13) while flywheel side ball bearing is held in position by a shoulder in crankcase half.

Check crankshaft runout by supporting crankshaft at points (A – Fig. E78) and measuring at points (B). Maximum allowable runout is 0.05 mm (0.002 in.).

Crankcase ball bearing bores should be heated with a heat gun or heat lamp to ease reassembly. Do not use an open flame. Make certain crankshaft turns freely before final tightening of crankcase cap screws. Tighten crankcase cap screws to 7.9-9.0 N•m (70-80 in.-lbs.).

REED VALVE. The reed valve assembly should be inspected whenever the carburetor is removed. Reed petals should seat lightly against insulator block. Renew reed valve assembly if reed petals are cracked, warped or damaged.

CLUTCH. Refer to Fig. E79 for an exploded view of three-shoe centrifugal clutch used. Clutch hub (2) and nut (8) have left-hand threads. Clutch drum (5) rides on needle roller bearing (6). Inspect clutch shoes (4) and drum (5) for excessive wear or damage due to overheating. Inspect needle roller bearing for damage or discoloration. Install clutch with side plates (1) facing inward. Tighten clutch hub to 19.8-23.7 N•m (175-210 in.-lbs.). Tighten clutch nut to 22.6-27.1 N•m (200-240 in.-lbs.).

OIL PUMP. All models are equipped with automatic and manual chain oil pumps. Refer to Fig. E80 for exploded view of manual oil pump. Check balls (8) must move freely for proper pump operation. Renew "O" ring (4) and hoses as required when signs of hardening and cracking are found.

Refer to Fig. E81 for cross-sectional view of automatic oil pump. Plunger (4) is actuated by cam (5) on crankshaft. Pump output is adjusted by rotating valve (1). Oil pump is removed for cleaning and inspection by unscrewing valve (1) from housing.

After reassembling automatic oil pump assembly, screw in valve (1) until lightly seated. Remove saw chain and

Fig. E79 — Exploded view of clutch assembly.

1. Side plates
2. Hub
3. Garter spring
4. Shoes
5. Drum
6. Needle roller bearing
7. Washer
8. Nut

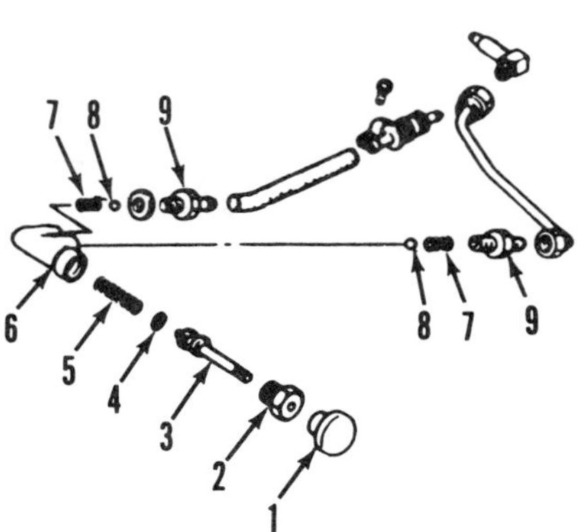

Fig. E80 — Exploded view of manual oil pump.

1. Button
2. End cap
3. Plunger
4. "O" ring
5. Spring
6. Housing
7. Spring
8. Check ball
9. Fitting

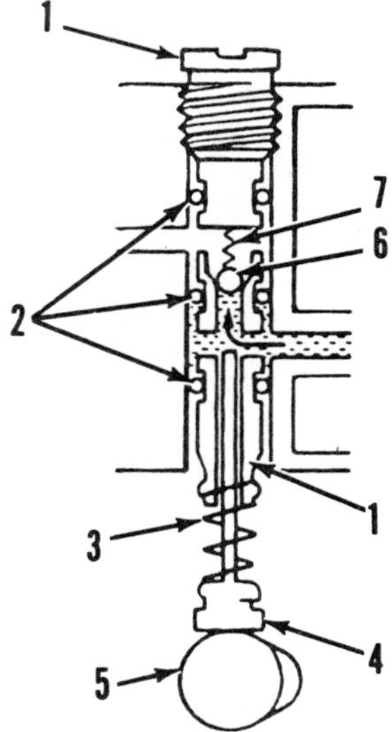

Fig. E81 — Cross-sectional view of automatic oil pump.

1. Valve
2. "O" rings
3. Spring
4. Plunger
5. Cam
6. Check ball
7. Spring

Illustrations courtesy Echo Inc.

guide bar and run engine at half throttle. Rotate valve (1) counterclockwise until maximum oil output is obtained (approx. ¾ turn). Mark top of valve (1) adjacent to housing stop tab for future reference, then install oiler adjustment knob assembly so valve (1) can only be turned counterclockwise to decrease oil pump output.

REWIND STARTER. To disassemble rewind starter, remove rope handle (3–Fig. E82) and allow rope to slowly rewind into starter housing (1). Remove screw (12) and carefully lift out rope pulley (8) noting how rope pulley engages rewind spring (5). If necessary to remove rewind spring, care must be taken not to allow spring to uncoil uncontrolled.

Install rewind spring into starter housing in a clockwise direction starting with outer coil. Wind rope on rope pulley in a clockwise direction as viewed from flywheel side of pulley. Install rope pulley into starter housing making sure pulley properly engages rewind spring. Rotate pulley four turns clockwise before passing rope through rope guide (2) and installing rope handle (3). Tension on rewind spring is correct when rope handle is tight against starter housing and rope pulley can be rotated ½ turn clockwise when rope is fully extended.

CHAIN BRAKE. Model CST-610EVLP is equipped with a chain brake system designed to stop chain movement should kickback occur. Chain brake is activated when operator's hand strikes chain brake lever (1–Fig. E83), tripping latch (11) and allowing spring (12) to draw brake band (6) tight around clutch drum. Pull back chain brake lever to reset mechanism. Disassembly for service and component renewal is evident after referral to exploded view and inspection of unit. To adjust brake band, loosen screw (9) and rotate adjusting cam (8). Adjust brake band so saw chain will not move with chain brake engaged. Brake band should not contact clutch drum with chain brake disengaged.

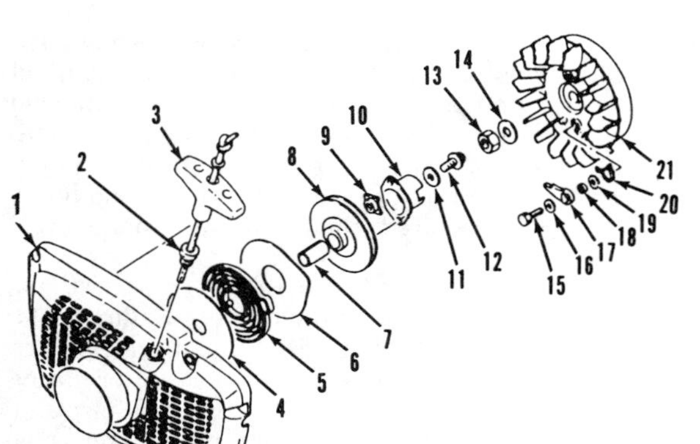

Fig. E82—Exploded view of rewind starter assembly.

1. Starter housing
2. Rope guide
3. Rope handle
4. Washer
5. Rewind spring
6. Washer
7. Bushing
8. Rope pulley
9. Clip
10. Starter cup
11. Washer
12. Screw
13. Nut
14. Washer
15. Cap screw
16. Washer
17. Pawl
18. Spacer
19. Washer
20. Pawl spring
21. Flywheel

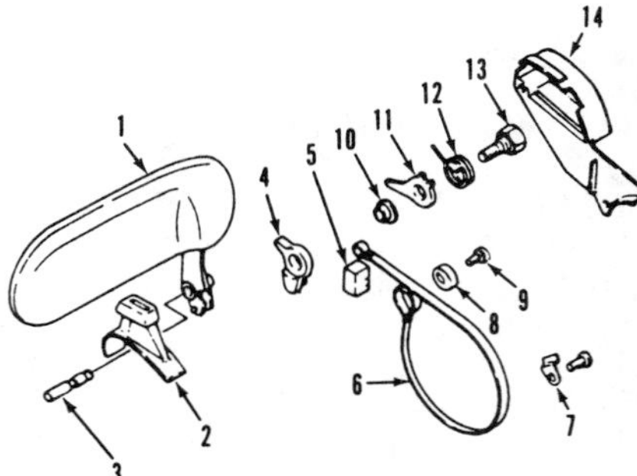

Fig. E83—Exploded view of chain brake system used on Model CST-610EVLP.

1. Chain brake lever
2. Dust cover
3. Pivot pin
4. Brake band lever
5. Dust seal
6. Brake band
7. Brake band retainer
8. Adjusting cam
9. Screw
10. Spacer
11. Latch
12. Spring
13. Cap screw
14. Shield

Illustrations courtesy Echo Inc.

ECHO

Model	Bore mm (in.)	Stroke mm (in.)	Displacement cc (cu. in.)	Drive Type
CS-3000, 3050	37.0 (1.457)	28.0 (1.102)	30.1 (1.836)	Direct
CS-3400, 3450	39.0 (1.535)	28.0 (1.102)	33.4 (2.037)	Direct

MAINTENANCE

SPARK PLUG. Recommended spark plug is Champion CJ-7Y or NGK BPM7A. Electrode gap should be 0.6-0.7 mm (0.024-0.028 in.). The spark plug should be tightened to the torque listed in the TIGHTENING TORQUE paragraph.

CARBURETOR. Walbro WT-385A and WT-402A carburetors are used. Refer to the appropriate Walbro section of the CARBURETOR SERVICE section for service and exploded views.

To remove carburetor (8—Fig. E100), remove air cleaner cover (1) and filter element (3). Remove screws attaching carburetor to insulator manifold (11). Disconnect fuel line, throttle linkage, and choke link from carburetor. Remove the carburetor. Tighten the carburetor attaching screws to the torque listed in the TIGHTENING TORQUE paragraph.

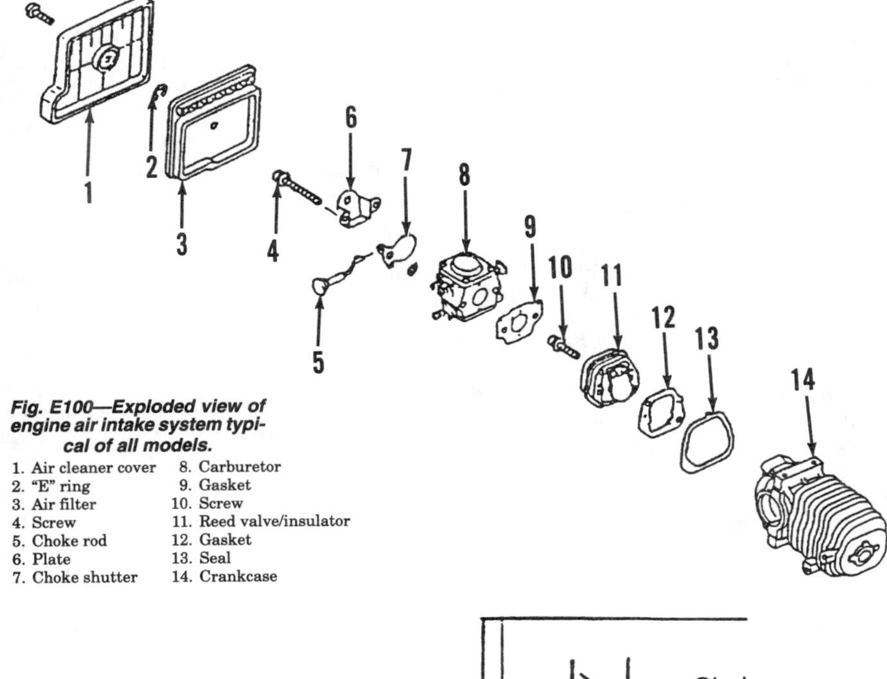

Fig. E100—Exploded view of engine air intake system typical of all models.

1. Air cleaner cover
2. "E" ring
3. Air filter
4. Screw
5. Choke rod
6. Plate
7. Choke shutter
8. Carburetor
9. Gasket
10. Screw
11. Reed valve/insulator
12. Gasket
13. Seal
14. Crankcase

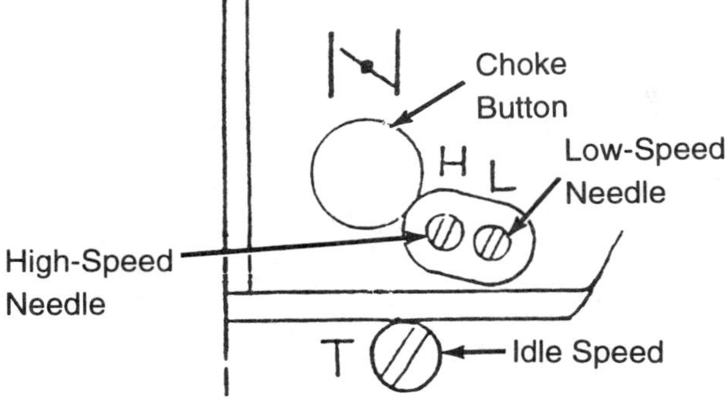

Fig. E101—Carburetor adjustment screws are located on left front side of the saw.

Initial setting for both low-speed and high-speed mixture needles (Fig. E101) of CS-3000 and CS-3050 models is 1-1/4 turns open from lightly seated. Initial setting for both low-speed and high-speed mixtures needles of CS-3400 and CS-3450 models is 1-1/8 turns open from lightly seated.

To adjust the mixture screws, first remove and clean the air filter, then reinstall it. Start the engine and allow it to run until it reaches normal operating temperature. If necessary, turn each of the mixture needles clockwise until seated lightly, then back the needles out (counterclockwise) to the initial setting so the engine can be started. Turn the idle speed stop screw (T—Fig. E101) so the engine idles at about 2,700-3,300 rpm.

Adjust the low-speed mixture needle (L) so the engine idles smoothly and accelerates without hesitation. Adjust the idle speed to just slower than clutch engagement speed, then recheck low-speed mixture adjustment.

Adjust the high-speed mixture needle (H) to provide the best performance while operating at maximum speed under load. It is recommended that a tachometer be used when adjusting the high-speed needle. Maximum no-load speed with bar and chain installed is 11,000 to 12,000 rpm. The high-speed mixture screw may be set slightly rich to improve performance under load. The engine may be damaged if the high-speed screw is set too lean.

Final adjustment of the mixture needles should usually be within 1/4 turn of the initial settings. Large differences may indicate air leaks, plugged passages or other problems.

IGNITION. All models are equipped with a breakerless, electronic, capacitor discharge (CDI) ignition system. All electronic circuitry is contained in a one-piece ignition module/coil located outside the flywheel. Ignition timing is fixed and not adjustable. The flywheel attaching nut should be tightened to

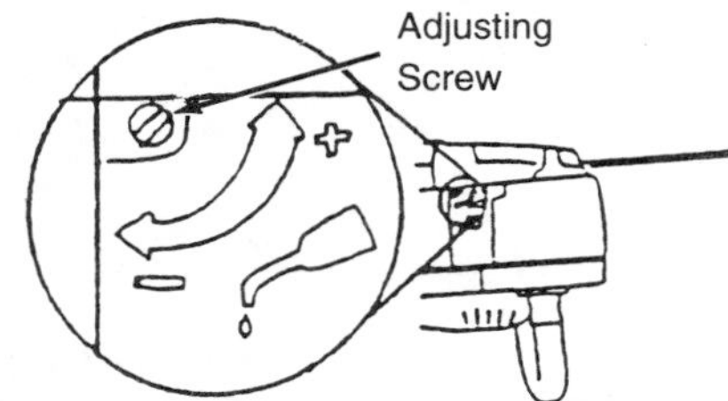

Fig. E102—The volume of oil delivered by chain oiler pump can be changed by turning adjuster located under the saw. Turning adjuster clockwise reduces the amount of oil.

the torque listed in TIGHTENING TORQUE paragraph.

Air gap between the legs of the module/coil and the flywheel magnets should be 0.3 mm (0.012 in.). When installing, set the air gap between the flywheel magnets and the legs of the ignition module as follows.

Install the ignition module, but tighten the two screws only enough to hold it in place away from the flywheel. Insert brass/plastic shim stock of the proper thickness between the legs of the ignition module and the flywheel, then turn the flywheel until the flywheel magnets are near the module legs. Loosen the screws attaching the ignition module and press legs of the ignition module against the shim stock. Tighten the two attaching screws to the torque listed in the TIGHTENING TORQUE paragraph.

Remove the setting gauge, then turn the flywheel to be sure the flywheel does not hit the legs of the coil. Threads of the screws attaching the coil/module should be coated with Loctite #222, Loctite #242 or equivalent to prevent loosening.

LUBRICATION. The engine is lubricated by mixing oil with the gasoline fuel. The manufacturer recommends mixing ECHO two-stroke oil with regular grade (89 octane) gasoline at a ratio of 50:1 after break-in. When using regular two-stroke engine oil, mix at a ratio of 32:1. During the initial break-in (first 10 hours) the fuel to oil ratio may also be increased to improve initial lubrication.

Always use a separate container to mix gasoline and oil before filling the fuel tank. The manufacturer recommends not using fuel containing methyl alcohol, more than 10% ethyl alcohol or more than 15% MTBE.

All saws are equipped with an automatic chain oiling system. An oil pump supplies oil to the chain when the saw is operating. The manufacturer recommends using ECHO Saw Chain oil or other good quality oil designed for lubricating saw chain. Make sure the reservoir is filled at all times.

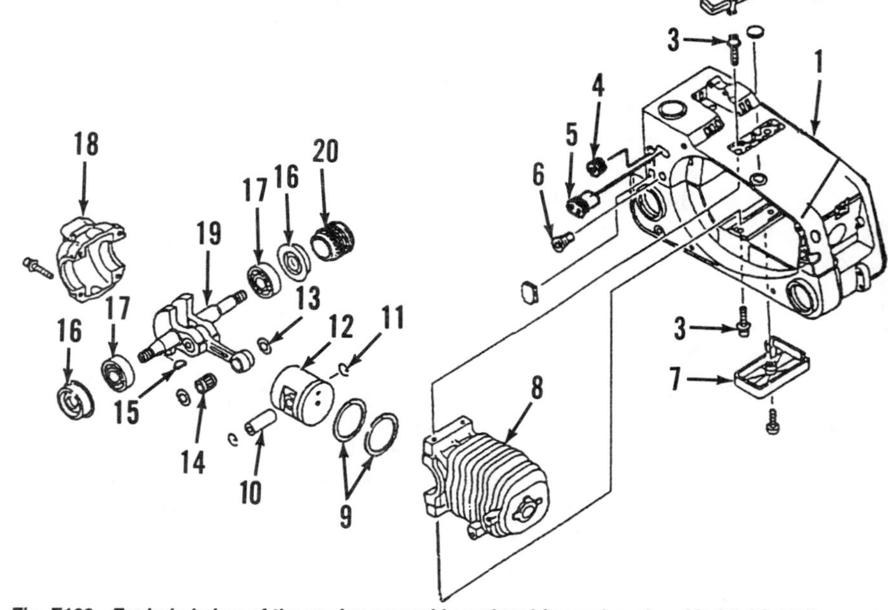

Fig. E103—Exploded view of the engine assembly and tank/cover housing. Model CS-3450 uses two piston rings (9). All other models are equipped with a single piston ring.

1. Tank/cover housing
2. Top cover
3. Screws
4. Choke grommet
5. Mixture needle grommet
6. Idle speed grommet
7. Bottom cover
8. Cylinder
9. Piston rings
10. Piston pin
11. Retaining rings
12. Piston
13. Washers
14. Needle bearing
15. Woodruff key
16. Seals
17. Main bearings
18. Crankcase half
19. Crankshaft & connecting rod
20. Worm gear

The volume of oil delivered by the pump is adjustable by turning adjuster (Fig. E102). The adjuster is located under the saw on the right side.

REPAIRS

CRANKCASE PRESSURE TEST. An improperly sealed crankcase can cause the engine to be hard to start, run rough, have low power and overheat. Refer to ENGINE SERVICE section of this manual for crankcase pressure test procedure. The engine should be tested at pressures between 21 kPa (3 psi) and 48 kPa (7 psi). If crankcase leakage is indicated, pressurize the crankcase and use a solution of soap and water to check gasket, seals, pulse line and castings for leakage.

TIGHTENING TORQUES. Recommended tightening torque values are as follows.

Brake lever (hand guard) . . . . 3-4 N•m (25-35 in.-lb.)
Carburetor
Attaching screws . . . . 35-45 N•m (30-40 in.-lb.)
Clutch hub . . . . 20-23 N•m (175-200 in.-lb.)
Crankcase . . . . . 3-4 N•m (25-35 in.-lb.)
Engine mounting screws . . . . 8-9 N•m (70-80 in.-lb.)
Flywheel . . 12-14 N•m (105-120 in.-lb.)
Front handle . . 3-4 N•m (25-35 in.-lb.)
Guide bar . . . . 20-23 N•m (175-200 in.-lb.)
Ignition
module/coil . . . 3-4 N•m (25-35 in.-lb.)
Muffler . . . . 6-7 N•m (50-60 in.-lb.)
Oil pump . . . . . . 3-4 N•m (25-35 in.-lb.)
Reed valve . . 0.8-1.2 N•m (7-10 in.-lb.)
Reed valve block (insulator) . . 4-5 N•m (35-45 in.-lb.)
Spark plug . . . . 15-17 N•m (130-150 in.-lb.)
Starter
Housing . . 2.5-3.5 N•m (20-30 in.-lb.)
Pawl . . . . 3-4 N•m (25-30 in.-lb.)
Throttle latch . 0.6-0.8 N•m (5-7 in.-lb.)
Vibration isolator
Front . . . . 2-3 N•m (17-25 in.-lb.)
Rear (M4) . . . . 2.5-3.5 N•m (20-30 in.-lb.)
Rear (M5) . . . . 3.5-4.5 N•m (30-40 in.-lb.)
Other bolt, nut & screw
M3 . . . . 0.6-0.8 N•m (5-7 in.-lb.)
M4 . . . . 1.3-1.8 N•m (11-16 in.-lb.)
M5 . . . . 2.7-3.2 N•m (23-28 in.-lb.)
M6 . . . . 4.5-6.5 N•m (40-55 in.-lb.)
M8 . . . . 11-15 N•m (95-130 in.-lb.)

REMOVE AND INSTALL ENGINE ASSEMBLY. Service to the engine will often require removal of the engine (powerhead) from the tank/cover housing (1—Fig. E103). If the engine is to be disassembled, remove the ignition coil/module, flywheel and oil pump worm gear. These parts do not need to

Illustrations courtesy Echo, Inc.

be removed if the crankcase halves will not be separated. Remove the guide bar cover, muffler, clutch assembly, oil pump assembly, carburetor, reed valve/insulator assembly and ignition switch. Remove covers (2 and 7), then remove the four screws (3) located beneath the covers. Withdraw the engine from the tank/cover housing.

Tighten the engine mounting screws to the torque listed in the TIGHTENING TORQUES paragraph when assembling.

PISTON, PIN, RINGS AND CYLINDER. Remove the engine as described in REMOVE AND INSTALL ENGINE ASSEMBLY paragraph. Remove the four screws attaching the crankcase halves (8 and 18—Fig. E103) together. Tap the ends of the crankshaft gently with a soft mallet to separate the crankcase halves. Hold the crankshaft in the lower crankcase half while withdrawing the piston from the cylinder and upper crankcase half.

Inspect the cylinder, rings and piston for damage. The chrome plating inside the cylinder bore should not show any wear or scratches. The piston ring should not be broken or stuck in the piston groove. Side clearance of the ring in the groove should not exceed 0.15 mm (0.006 in.) for models with 37 mm cylinder bore; 0.10 mm (0.004 in.) for models with 39 mm cylinder bore. The piston should move freely around the piston pin on the connecting rod with no noticeable play.

If necessary to remove the piston from the connecting rod, remove snap rings (11—Fig. E103) from each side of the piston. If the piston pin does not remove easily, heat the piston and use a suitable piston pin removal tool to press the pin (10) from the piston. Be sure to catch the bearing (14) and washers (13) as the piston is removed.

Install new parts if bearing rollers are discolored by heat or if the condition of the roller bearing is in any way questionable.

Be sure the ends of the piston ring fit properly around the locating pin in the piston groove. When installing the piston, the arrow on top of piston must point toward the exhaust (muffler) side of the engine. Lubricate the piston pin (10), bearing (14), washers (13) and connecting rod bore with engine oil before assembling.

New retaining rings (11) should be installed each time they are removed. When assembled, gaps in the piston pin retaining rings should be toward the top (spark plug) end of the piston.

Refer to CRANKSHAFT, CONNECTING ROD AND CRANKCASE paragraph for removal and inspection of the crankshaft and connecting rod assembly. Also, refer to this paragraph for assembly of the crankcase.

CRANKSHAFT, CONNECTING ROD AND CRANKCASE. Refer to the PISTON, PIN, RINGS AND CYLINDER paragraph for separation of the crankcase and removal of the piston from the cylinder. If necessary, tap the crankcase gently to remove the crankcase from the main bearings and seals.

Clean the crankcase thoroughly and inspect for any nick, burrs, cracks or other damage. Be sure all sealer is removed if the crankcase is to be reassembled.

Inspect the cylinder bore in the upper half as described in the PISTON, PIN, RINGS AND CYLINDER paragraph. Upper and lower crankcase halves are available only as a set. The crankshaft and connecting rod are available only as an assembly. The new crankshaft/rod assembly should also include new main bearings and seals.

Do not remove the ball type main bearings from the crankshaft unless replacement is required. The main bearings can be removed using a suitable wedge (knife) type puller. Support the crankshaft and heat the bearing while pressing new bearings onto the crankshaft main journals.

Refer to PISTON, PIN, RINGS AND CYLINDER paragraph and assemble the piston, connecting rod and crankshaft in the upper crankcase half. Lubricate the crankshaft seals with engine oil and install on the crankshaft with the lips toward the inside.

Immediately before installing the lower half of the crankcase, apply Loctite #515, Loctite #518 or equivalent to the crankcase mating surfaces of the lower half and Loctite #675 or equivalent to the bearing bore surfaces of the lower crankcase half. Install the lower crankcase half with the threaded hole for the oil pump aligned with similar hole in the upper half.

Make sure the main bearings and seals fit properly in the case bores and tighten the four screws attaching the case halves. Rotate the crankshaft while tightening to make sure the bearings do not bind. Tighten the crankcase screws to the torque listed in the TIGHTENING TORQUES paragraph when assembling.

Check the crankcase for leaks as described in CRANKCASE PRESSURE TEST paragraph before installing the engine. The muffler attaching screws should be retightened to the torque listed in the TIGHTENING TORQUES paragraph after the engine has been run and allowed to cool.

CLUTCH. To remove the clutch, first remove the sprocket guard (20—Fig. E104), chain and guide bar (19). If the starter is installed, pull the rope out about 20 cm (8 in.) and make a temporary knot at the rope guide to prevent

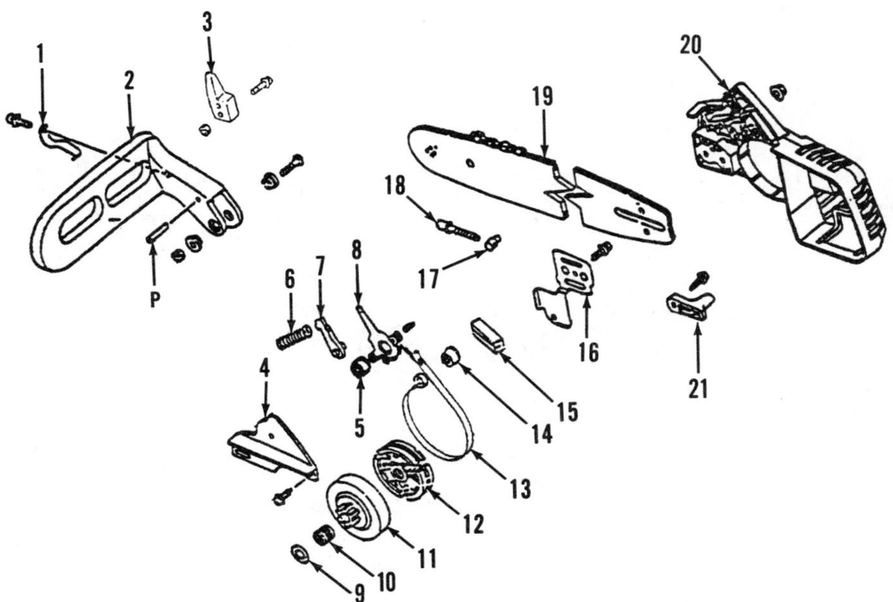

Fig. E104—Exploded view of the clutch and chain brake assemblies.

1. Spring
2. Hand guard
3. Brake weight
4. Brake cover
5. Spacer
6. Spring
7. Brake stopper
8. Brake lever
9. Washer
10. Bearing
11. Clutch drum
12. Clutch hub
13. Brake band
14. Brake adjuster
15. Seal cover
16. Guide plate
17. Chain adjuster
18. Adjuster screw
19. Bar & chain
20. Sprocket guard

damage to the starter when reinstalling clutch.

Prevent the flywheel from turning by removing the spark plug, then installing a piston stop tool (or a loop of rope) in the spark plug hole. Note that clutch hub (12) has left-hand threads. Use a suitable tool (part No. 897505-16131 or equivalent) to turn the clutch hub (12) in a **clockwise direction** as indicated by the arrow to unscrew the clutch hub from the engine crankshaft. Do not use power tools to remove the clutch. Remove the sprocket and clutch drum (11) and needle bearing (10).

Inspect all parts of the clutch for wear, evidence of overheating or other damage and replace parts as necessary. New clutch shoes should be installed if worn to less than 1 mm (0.040 in.) thickness. The clutch hub, shoes and return springs are available only as an assembly. Install a new drum if worn larger than 61.0 mm (2.40 in.) or otherwise damaged.

Lubricate the needle bearing with all-purpose lithium-based grease before installing the bearing and clutch drum. Install the clutch hub and shoes with the chamfer at the threaded center toward the engine. Turn clutch hub counterclockwise to install and tighten to the torque listed in TIGHTENING TORQUE paragraph using the special tool. Do not use any power tool to install the clutch hub. Complete assembly by reversing disassembly procedure.

OIL PUMP. An automatic oiling system lubricates the guide bar and chain. The oil is supplied by the oil pump shown in Fig. E105. The pump plunger (16) is driven by a worm gear located on the engine crankshaft.

To remove oil pump, first remove the sprocket guard (20—Fig. E104) and chain brake assembly. Remove chain, guide bar (19) and chain guide plate (16). Remove clutch assembly. Unbolt the oil pump housing (13—Fig. E105) and pull the pump assembly from the engine. If necessary, use a suitable puller (part No. 897708-19831) to pull the oil pump drive worm from the crankshaft.

To disassemble the removed pump, remove plug (17) and retaining ring (12). Remove the adjuster (19). Bump the housing on a soft surface if necessary to jar the plunger (16), spring (15) and V-ring (14) from the housing bore.

Clean and inspect parts for wear or damage. Parts should move freely in housing bores without excessive clearance. Install a new pump assembly if parts are worn. Some individual parts may be available separately if only that part is damaged.

A small wire (paper clip) can be used to remove and install the V-ring (14—Fig. E106). If necessary to remove the V-ring, a new V-ring should be installed. Open side of "V" should be toward gear on pump shaft.

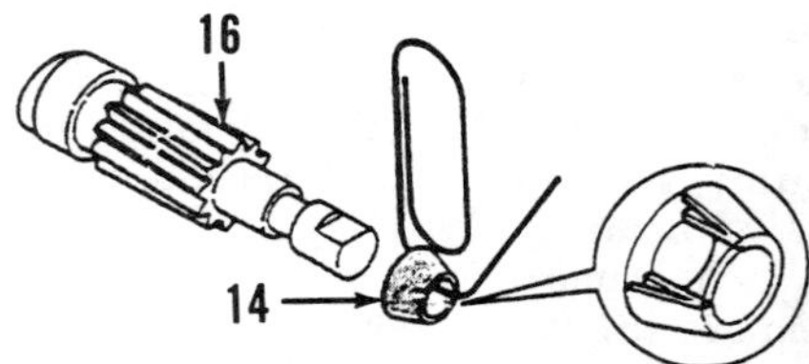

Fig. E106—Install V-ring seal (14) with lips facing plunger gear (16).

Insert spring (15—Fig. E105) in housing bore, coat plunger (16) and seal (14) with grease and insert it into the housing bore. Push the plunger into the housing bore to compress the spring (15) and hold the plunger IN while installing the adjuster (19). Hold the plunger by exerting thumb pressure against the gear located on the plunger. Install the spring (18), washer and adjuster (19) with the flat on the side of the adjuster facing the pump housing wall. It will be necessary to compress spring by pressing on adjuster (19) to install retaining ring (12).

Lubricate the cam of the adjuster with grease, then install plug (17). If removed, use special tool (part No. 897708-37530) to install new drive worm on the crankshaft. Drive worm should be bottomed against the crankshaft.

Connect oil lines to the pump body and attach the pump body to the engine. Complete assembly by reversing disassembly procedure. The oil pump should discharge 1.5-13 cc (0.05-0.44 fl. oz.) of oil per minute when the engine is operating at 7,000 rpm. Refer to the LUBRICATION paragraph in the Maintenance section for adjustment.

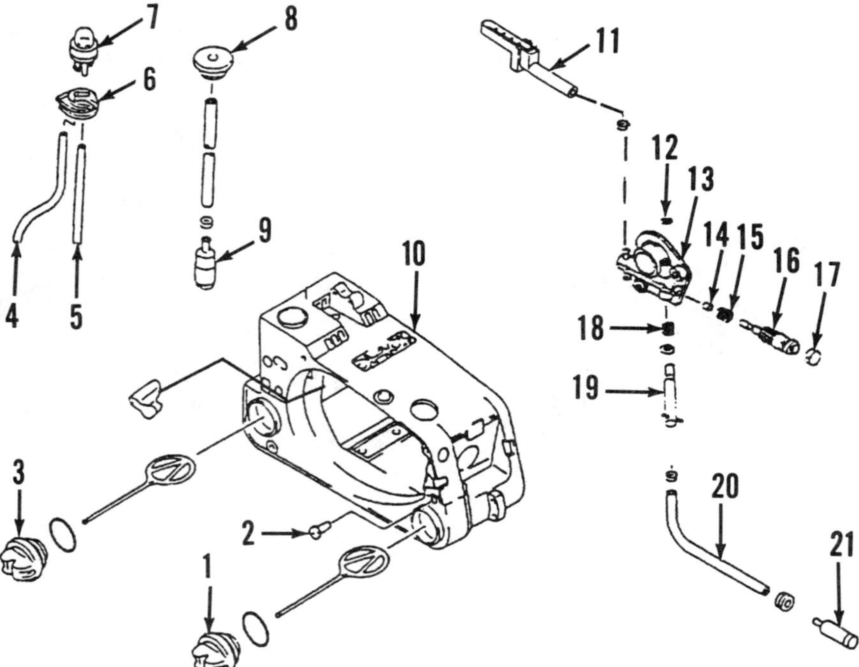

Fig. E105—Exploded view of the oil pump.

1. Oil tank cap
2. Oil tank check valve
3. Fuel tank cap
4. Fuel line
5. Return line
6. Bracket
7. Fuel primer bulb
8. Grommet
9. Fuel filter
10. Fuel/oil tank housing
11. Oil delivery pipe
12. Retaining ring
13. Oil pump housing
14. V-ring seal
15. Spring
16. Plunger
17. Cap
18. Spring
19. Adjusting screw
20. Oil pick-up tube
21. Oil strainer

REWIND STARTER. Refer to Fig. E107 for exploded view of the starter assembly. To disassemble starter, first unbolt and remove starter housing (1) from saw. Pull starter rope out about 20 cm (8 in.) and make a temporary knot at the rope guide to prevent the rope from rewinding into the starter. Remove handle (3), then untie the temporary knot. Hold the pulley (6) while allowing the rope to slowly wind into the starter housing. Unbolt and remove guide plate (8). Remove screw (7), washer, pulley (6) and rope.

If the rope is to be replaced, remove all of the old rope, then install 85 cm (33.5 in.) of new 3.0 mm (0.12 in.) diameter rope.

The rewind spring (4) may remain contained in housing (5). If required, rewind spring may now be removed. Use

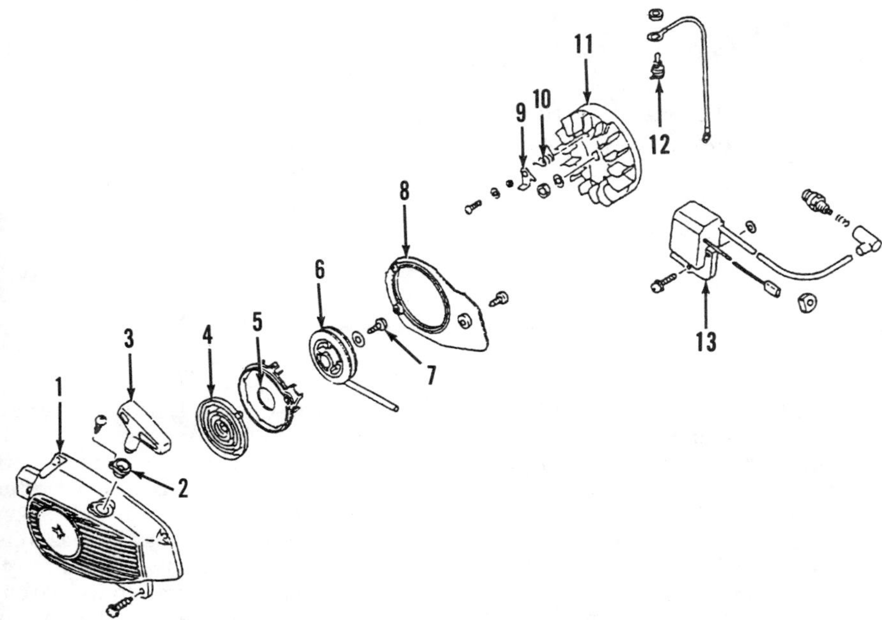

Fig. E107—Exploded view of the rewind starter assembly. Ignition coil/module is shown at (13).

1. Starter housing
2. Rope grommet
3. Handle
4. Rewind spring
5. Starter plate
6. Pulley
7. Screw
8. Guide plate
9. Starter pawl
10. Spring
11. Flywheel
12. Ignition stop switch
13. Ignition coil/module

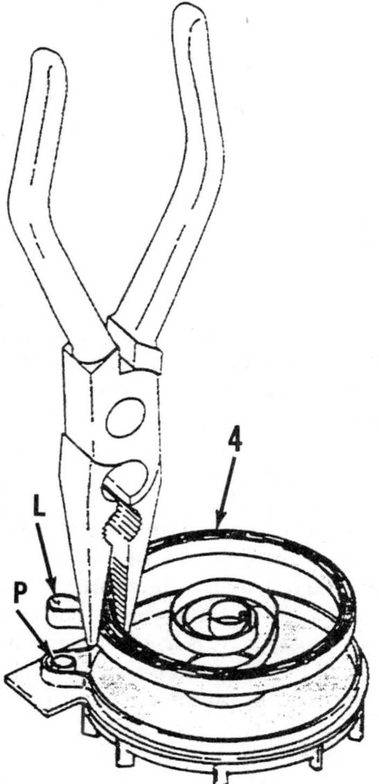

Fig. E108—Installing rewind spring (4). Spring loop (L) goes over spring holder pin (P).

caution not to allow spring to unwind uncontrolled.

Reassemble starter components by reversing disassembly procedure while noting the following: Install rewind spring into spring housing so that outer loop of spring (L—Fig. E108) goes over pin (P) of spring holder. Wind the rewind spring counterclockwise into housing. Lubricate rewind spring with a small amount of all-purpose grease.

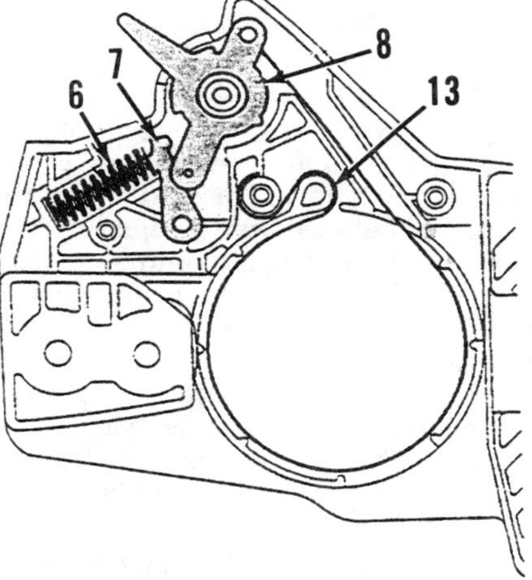

Fig. E109—Drawing showing installation of chain brake parts.

6. Brake spring
7. Stop
8. Brake lever
13. Brake band

Wind rope fully on pulley in clockwise direction as viewed with pulley in the starter housing. Install rope pulley against the spring housing (5—Fig. E107) with the pulley engaging the inner end of the spring. Install the spring, spring housing, pulley and rope in the starter housing (1) and secure with screw (7).

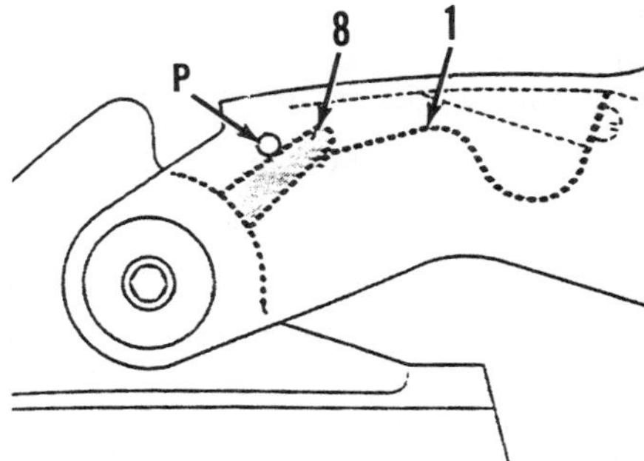

Fig. E110—Drawing showing relative position of the spring (1), brake lever (8) and pin (P).

Guide the end of the rope through the starter housing and guide (2), then install the handle (3). Pull a loop of rope between the inside of the starter housing and the pulley and place rope in notch in pulley. Turn the rope pulley (6) several turns clockwise to place tension on rewind spring. Release pulley and check starter operation. With rope fully extended, it should be possible to rotate rope pulley a minimum of 1/2 turn clockwise before rewind spring bottoms. Do not place more tension on rewind spring than is necessary to draw rope handle against housing.

CHAIN BRAKE. The chain brake is designed to stop the chain if kickback should occur. The chain brake is activated when the operator's hand strikes the hand guard (2—Fig. E104) or if the tip of the guide bar strikes an object with sufficient force to trip the brake mechanism. When the brake is engaged, a spring (6) tightens the band (13) around the clutch drum (11) to stop the drum, sprocket and chain. Pull the hand guard (2) back to reset the mechanism.

Unbolt and remove the sprocket guard (20), which contains the brake assembly. Push the hand guard (2) forward to the engaged position. Remove the hand guard pivot bolt and the two spacers, then remove hand guard.

Remove the cover (4) and check operation and condition of the brake parts. Install new parts as necessary.

Assemble brake lever (8) with brake band (13), brake stopper (7) and spring (6) to sprocket guard as shown in Fig E109. Install sprocket guard and brake assembly. Position brake lever (8) between pin (P) and spring (1) in hand guard as shown in Fig. E110. Move hand guard to disengaged position (forward) when installing sprocket guard on saw.

ECHO

Model	Bore mm (in.)	Stroke mm (in.)	Displacement cc (cu. in.)	Drive Type
CS-3600	39.0 (1.535)	30.0 (1.181)	35.8 (2.187)	Direct
CS-3900	41.0 (1.614)	30.0 (1.181)	39.6 2.417)	Direct

MAINTENANCE

SPARK PLUG. Recommended spark plug for CS-3600 models is Champion CJ-7Y, Champion (resistor) RCJ-7Y or NGK BMP7A. Recommended spark plug for CS-3900 models is Champion CJ-6Y or Champion (resistor) RCJ-7Y. Electrode gap should be 0.6-0.7 mm (0.024-0.028 in.). The spark plug should be tightened to the torque listed in the TIGHTENING TORQUE paragraph.

CARBURETOR. Walbro WT-88 or WT-88A carburetor is used on CS-3600 models; Walbro WT-188, WT-188A or WT-188B carburetor is used on CS-3900 models. Refer to the appropriate Walbro section of the CARBURETOR SERVICE section for service and exploded views. Initial setting for the low-speed mixture needle (Fig. E190) of CS-3600 model is 7/8 to 1 turn open from lightly seated. Initial setting for the low-speed mixture needle of CS-3900 model is 1 to 1-1/4 turns open from lightly seated.

Initial setting for the high-speed mixture needle (Fig. E190) of CS-3600 model is 1-1/8 to 1-1/4 turns open from lightly seated. Initial setting for the high-speed mixture needle of CS-3900 model is 1-1/4 turns open from lightly seated.

To adjust the mixture screws, first remove and clean the air filter, then reinstall it. Start the engine and allow it to run until it reaches normal operating temperature. If necessary, turn each of the mixture needles clockwise until seated lightly, then back the needles out (counterclockwise) to the initial setting so the engine can be started. Turn the idle speed stop screw so the engine idles at about 2800-3000 rpm.

Adjust the low-speed mixture needle so the engine idles smoothly and accelerates without hesitation. Adjust the idle speed to just slower than clutch engagement speed, then recheck low-speed mixture adjustment. The idle speed after final adjustment should be 3000 rpm for CS-3600 models; 2800 rpm for CS-3900 models.

Adjust the high-speed mixture needle to provide the best performance while operating at maximum speed under load. It is recommended that a tachometer be used when adjusting the high-speed needle. Maximum no-load speed with bar and chain installed is 12,000-13,000 rpm for Model CS-3600 or 13,000-14,000 rpm for Model CS-3900. The high-speed mixture screw may be set slightly rich to improve performance under load. The engine may be damaged if the high-speed screw is set too lean.

Final adjustment of the mixture needles should usually be within 1/4 turn of the initial settings. Large differences may indicate air leaks, plugged passages or other problems.

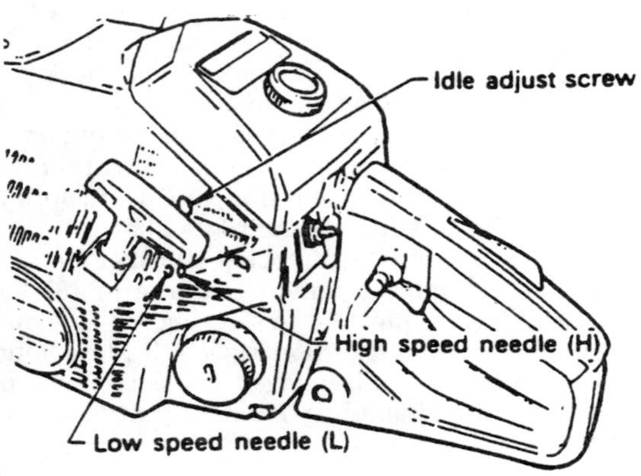

Fig. E190—Carburetor adjustment points.

To remove carburetor, remove air cleaner cover (9—Fig. E191), air filter (11), seal (12) and air cleaner bracket (16). Disconnect fuel line, pulse line and throttle rod. Remove the carburetor. When installing, tighten the carburetor attaching screws to the torque listed in the TIGHTENING TORQUE paragraph.

IGNITION. All models are equipped with a breakerless, electronic, capacitor discharge (CDI) ignition system. All electronic circuitry is contained in a one-piece ignition module/coil located outside the flywheel. Ignition timing is fixed and not adjustable. The nut attaching the flywheel should be tightened to the torque listed in TIGHTENING TORQUE paragraph.

Air gap between the legs of the module/coil and the flywheel magnets should be 0.3-0.4 mm (0.012-0.016 in.) for CS-3600 models; 0.25-0.3 mm (0.010-0.012 in.) for CS-3900 models. When installing, set the air gap between the flywheel magnets and the legs of the ignition module as follows.

Install the ignition module, but tighten the two screws only enough to hold it in place away from the flywheel. Insert brass/plastic shim stock of the proper thickness between the legs of the ignition module and the flywheel, then turn the flywheel until the flywheel magnets are near the module legs. Loosen the screws attaching the ignition module and press legs of the ignition module against the shim stock. Tighten the two attaching screws to the torque listed in the TIGHTENING TORQUE paragraph. Remove the setting gauge, then turn the flywheel to be sure the flywheel does not hit the legs of the coil.

LUBRICATION. The engine is lubricated by mixing oil with the gasoline fuel. The manufacturer recommends mixing ECHO two-stroke oil with regular grade (87 octane) gasoline at a ratio

Illustrations courtesy Echo, Inc.

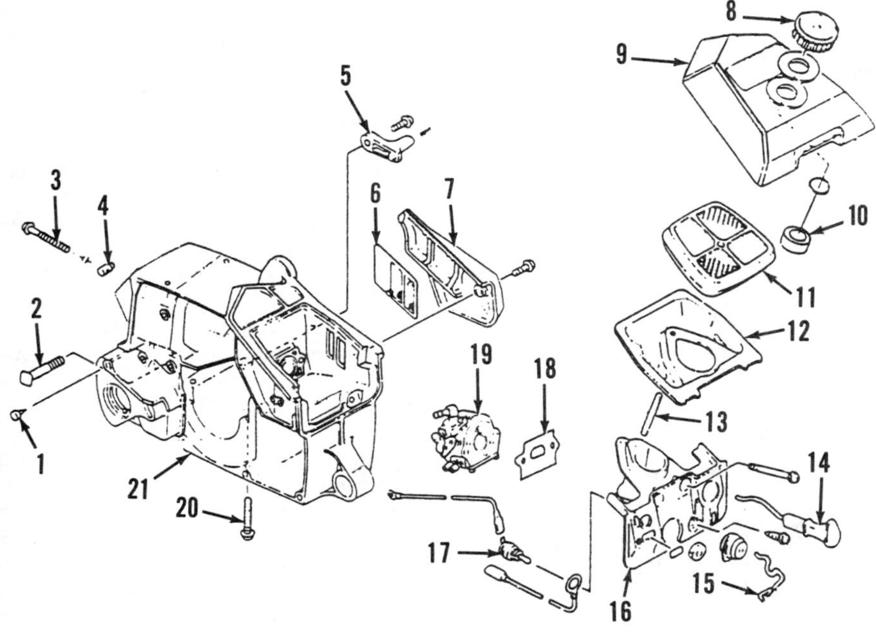

Fig. E191—Exploded view of engine covers and air cleaner assembly.

1. Check valve
2. Guide bar stud
3. Chain tension screw
4. Chain adjuster nut
5. Chain catcher
6. Dust screen
7. Side cover
8. Knob
9. Air cleaner cover
10. Seal
11. Air filter
12. Seal
13. Stud
14. Choke lever
15. Throttle rod
16. Air cleaner bracket
17. On/off switch
18. Gasket
19. Carburetor
20. Engine mounting screw
21. Engine cover

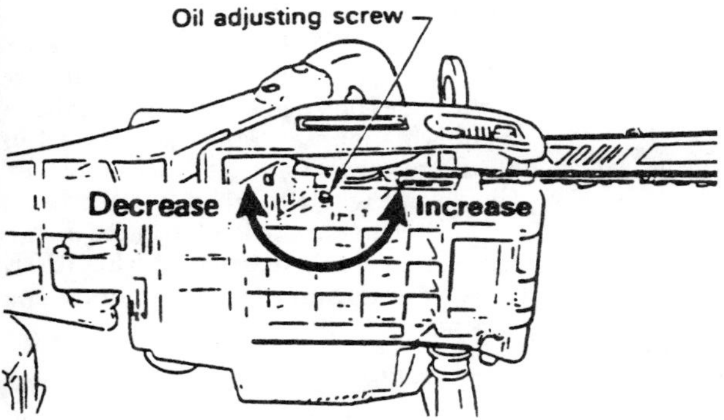

Fig. E192— The volume of oil delivered by chain oiler pump can be changed by turning adjuster located under the saw. Turning adjuster clockwise reduces the amount of oil.

of 50:1 after break-in. When using regular two-stroke engine oil, mix at a ratio of 32:1. During the initial break-in (first 10 hours) the fuel to oil ratio may also be increased to improve initial lubrication.

Always use a separate container to mix gasoline and oil before filling the fuel tank. The manufacturer recommends not using fuel containing methyl alcohol, more than 10% ethyl alcohol or more than 15% MTBE.

All saws are equipped with an automatic chain oiling system. The manufacturer recommends using ECHO Saw Chain oil or other good quality oil designed for lubricating saw chain. Make sure the reservoir is filled at all times.

The volume of oil delivered by the oil pump is adjustable by turning adjuster (Fig. E192). The adjuster is located under the saw on the right side. The correct amount of oil that should be delivered to the chain depends upon the type of chain and wood being cut.

REPAIRS

CRANKCASE PRESSURE TEST. An improperly sealed crankcase can cause the engine to be hard to start, run rough, have low power and overheat. Refer to ENGINE SERVICE section of this manual for crankcase pressure test procedure. The engine should be tested at pressures between 21 kPa (3 psi) and 48 kPa (7 psi). If crankcase leakage is indicated, pressurize the crankcase and use a solution of soap and water to check gasket, seals, pulse line and castings for leakage.

TIGHTENING TORQUE. Recommended tightening torque values are as follows.

Air cleaner stud. . . . . 1.3-1.8 N•m (11-16 in.-lb.)
Brake lever (hand guard) . 1.3-1.8 N•m (11-16 in.-lb.)
Carburetor
  Attaching screws. . . . . 4-5 N•m (35-45 in.-lb.)
Clutch hub. . . . . 15-17 N•m (130-150 in.-lb.)
Clutch plate. . 2-2.5 N•m (17-22 in.-lb.)
Crankcase. . 7.5-8.5 N•m (65-75 in.-lb.)
Engine mounting screws . 7.5-8.5 N•m (65-75 in.-lb.)
Fan cover . . 3.5-4.5 N•m (30-40 in.-lb.)
Flywheel. . 12-14 N•m (105-120 in.-lb.)
Front handle . . 3-4 N•m (25-35 in.-lb.)
Guide bar . 20-23 N•m (175-200 in.-lb.)
Ignition
  Module/coil . 3-3.5 N•m (25-30 in.-lb.)
Muffler . . . . 7.5-8.5 N•m (65-75 in.-lb.)
Oil pump. . . 3.5-4.5 N•m (30-40 in.-lb.)
Rear handle
  Bottom . . . 1.5-2.5 N•m (13-22 in.-lb.)
  Top . . . . 3-4 N•m (25-35 in.-lb.)
Spark plug. . . . . 15-17 N•m (130-150 in.-lb.)
Starter
  Housing . . 2.5-3.5 N•m (20-30 in.-lb.)
  Pawl . . . . . 7.5-8.5 N•m (65-75 in.-lb.)
Throttle latch . 0.6-0.8 N•m (5-7 in.-lb.)
Vibration isolator
  M4 . . . . 2.5-3 N•m (22-26 in.-lb.)
  M5. . . . . . . 3.5-4.5 N•m (30-40 in.-lb.)
Other bolt, nut & screw
  M3. . . . . 0.6-0.8 N•m (5-7 in.-lb.)
  M4. . . . . . . 1.3-1.8 N•m (11-16 in.-lb.)
  M5. . . . . . . 2.7-3.2 N•m (23-28 in.-lb.)
  M6. . . . . . . 4.5-6.5 N•m (40-55 in.-lb.)

REMOVE AND INSTALL ENGINE ASSEMBLY. Service to the engine may require removal of the engine (powerhead) from the tank/cover housing (21—Fig. E191). Remove starter housing, muffler, flywheel and ignition coil/module. On late models, remove the two nuts (B—Fig. E193) attaching the engine ground plate. On all models, remove the guide bar cover,

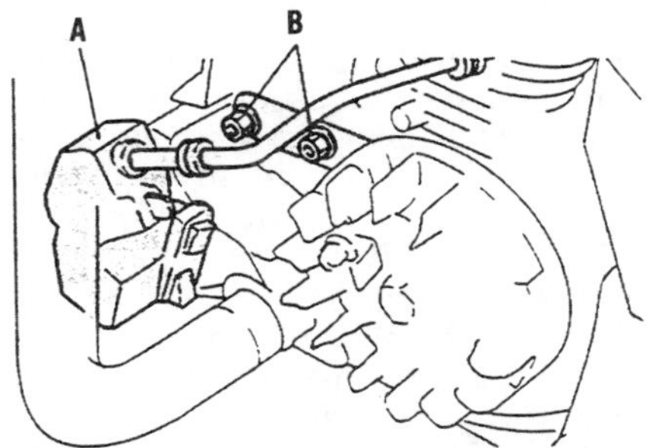

Fig. E193—The ignition coil module (A) must be removed for access to ground plate mounting nuts (B).

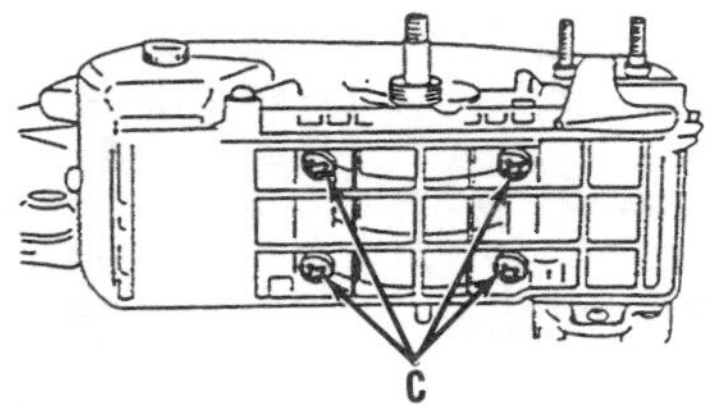

Fig. E194—The engine is attached to the tank/cover housing with four screws (C).

clutch assembly, oil pump assembly and carburetor. Remove four screws (C—Fig. E194) at bottom of engine, then withdraw the engine from the tank/cover housing.

Coat the threads of the engine mounting screws (Fig. E194) with Loctite #222 or equivalent before installing. Tighten the engine mounting screws to the torque listed in the TIGHTENING TORQUE paragraph when assembling. The muffler attaching screws should be retightened to the torque listed in the TIGHTENING TORQUE paragraph after the engine has been run and allowed to cool.

PISTON, PIN, RINGS AND CYLINDER. Remove the engine as described in REMOVE AND INSTALL ENGINE ASSEMBLY paragraph. Remove the four screws attaching the crankcase halves together (1 and 10—Fig. E195). Tap the ends of the crankshaft gently with a soft mallet to separate the crankcase halves. Hold the crankshaft in the lower crankcase half while withdrawing the piston from the cylinder and upper crankcase half.

Inspect the cylinder, rings and piston for damage. The chrome plating inside the cylinder bore should not show any wear or scratches. The piston ring should not be broken or stuck in the piston groove. The piston should move freely around the piston pin on the connecting rod with no noticeable play.

If necessary to remove the piston, from the connecting rod, remove snap rings (6) from each side of the piston. If the piston pin (5) does not remove easily, heat the piston and use a suitable piston pin removal tool to press the pin from the piston. Be sure to catch the bearing (7) as the piston is removed. Install new parts if bearing rollers are discolored by heat or if the condition of the roller bearing is in any way questionable.

Be sure the ends of the piston ring fit properly around the locating pin in the piston groove. When installing the piston, the arrow on top of piston must point toward the exhaust (muffler) side of the engine.

Lubricate the piston pin (5), bearing (7) and connecting rod bore with engine

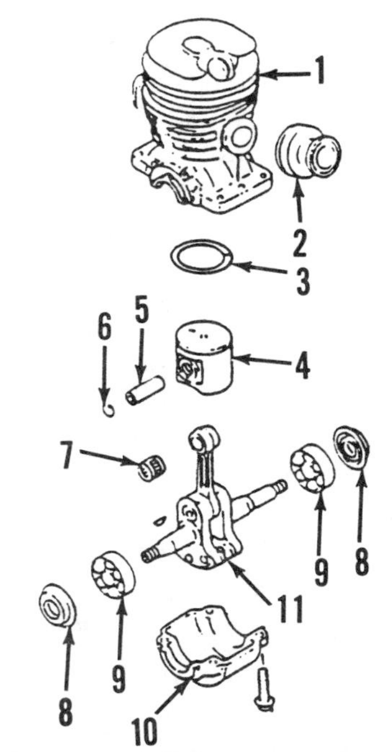

Fig. E195—Exploded view of the engine assembly.

1. Cylinder/upper crankcase
2. Intake adapter
3. Piston ring
4. Piston
5. Piston pin
6. Retaining ring
7. Needle bearing
8. Seals
9. Main bearings
10. Crankcase lower half
11. Crankshaft & connecting rod assy.

oil before assembling. New piston pin retaining rings (6) should be installed each time they are removed. When assembled, gaps in the retaining rings should be toward the top (spark plug) end of the piston.

Refer to CRANKSHAFT, CONNECTING ROD AND CRANKCASE paragraph for removal and inspection of the crankshaft and connecting rod assembly. Also, refer to this paragraph for assembly of the crankcase.

CRANKSHAFT, CONNECTING ROD AND CRANKCASE. Refer to the PISTON, PIN, RINGS AND CYLINDER paragraph for separation of the crankcase and removal of the piston from the cylinder. If necessary, tap the crankshaft gently to separate the crankcase halves from the main bearings and seals.

Clean the crankcase thoroughly and inspect for any nick, burrs, cracks or other damage. Be sure all sealer is removed if the crankcase is to be reassembled.

Inspect the cylinder bore in the upper half as described in the PISTON, PIN, RINGS AND CYLINDER paragraph. Upper and lower crankcase halves are available only as a set. The crankshaft and connecting rod are available only as an assembly. The new crankshaft/rod assembly should also include new main bearings and seals.

Do not remove the ball type main bearings (9—Fig. E195) from the crankshaft unless replacement is required. The main bearings can be removed using a suitable wedge (knife) type puller. Support the crankshaft and heat the bearing while pressing new bearings onto the crankshaft main journals.

Refer to PISTON, PIN, RINGS AND CYLINDER paragraph and assemble the piston, connecting rod and crankshaft in the upper crankcase half. Lubricate the crankshaft seals (8) with engine oil and install on the crankshaft with the lips toward the inside.

Immediately before installing the lower half of the crankcase, apply Loctite 515 or equivalent to the crankcase mating surfaces of the lower half (S—Fig. E196). Assemble lower crankcase half to upper half as shown in Fig. E196. Make sure the main bearings and seals fit properly in the case bores. Install the four screws attaching the case halves. Rotate the crankshaft while tightening the screws to make sure the bearings do not bind. Tighten the crankcase screws to the torque listed in the TIGHTENING TORQUE paragraph.

Prior to installing the carburetor adapter (Fig. E196), apply a liquid gasket maker such as Loctite 515 to groove inside the adapter. Make sure that tab of the carburetor adapter faces down as shown in Fig. E196 when installed.

Check the crankcase for leaks as described in CRANKCASE PRESSURE TEST paragraph before installing the engine.

CLUTCH. To remove the clutch, first remove the sprocket guard, chain and guide bar. If the starter is installed, pull the rope out about 20 cm (8 in.) and make a temporary knot at the rope guide to prevent damage to the starter.

Prevent the flywheel from turning by removing the spark plug and installing a piston stop tool (or a loop of rope) in the spark plug hole. The clutch hub (7—Fig. E197) have left-hand threads. Use a suitable tool (part No. 897505-16131 or equivalent) to turn the hub in a clockwise direction as indicated by the arrow to unscrew the clutch hub from the engine crankshaft. Do not use power tools to remove the clutch. Remove the sprocket (2) and clutch drum (3) and needle bearing.

Remove screws attaching three clutch plates (8—Fig. E197) to clutch shoes (5) to disassemble clutch. Inspect all parts of the clutch for wear, evidence of overheating or other damage and replace parts as necessary. New clutch

Illustrations courtesy Echo, Inc.

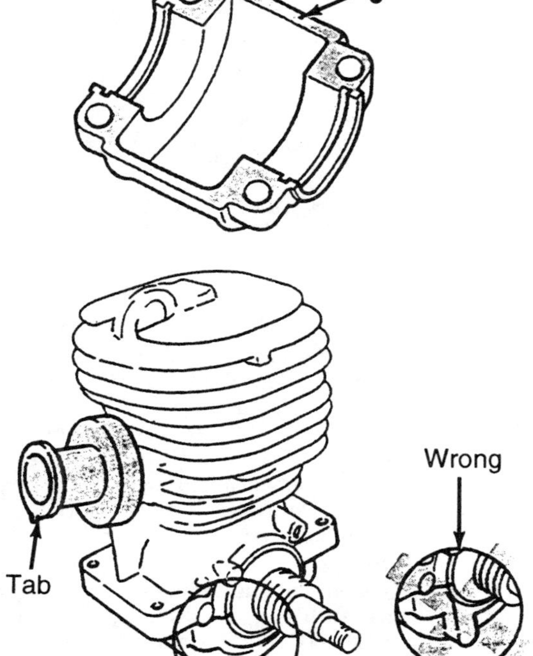

Fig. E196—When assembling engine, apply liquid gasket maker on seam (S) of crankcase lower half. Note correct installation of crankcase halves.

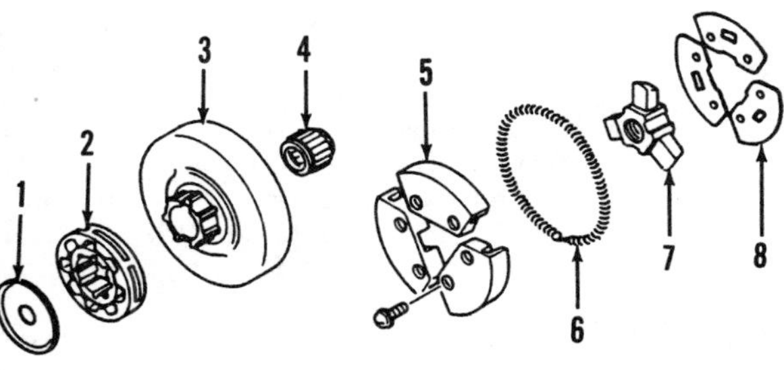

Fig. E197—Exploded view of the clutch assembly.

1. Washer
2. Sprocket
3. Clutch drum
4. Bearing
5. Clutch shoes
6. Spring
7. Clutch hub
8. Clutch plates

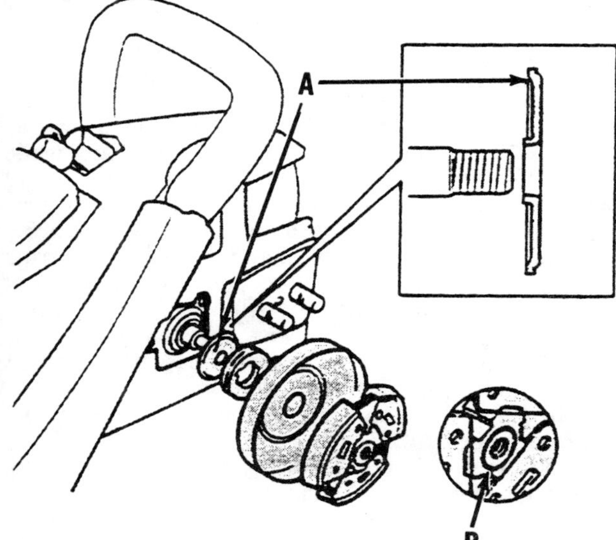

Fig. E198—Note correct position of washer (A) and clutch hub (B) when installing clutch.

shoes should be installed if worn excessively. The clutch hub (7), shoes (5) and spring (6) are available as an assembly, but individual service parts may be available. Install a new clutch drum if deformed, worn or otherwise damaged.

Lubricate the needle bearing (4—Fig. E197) with all-purpose lithium-based grease before installing the bearing and clutch drum. Note the following special instructions when assembling the clutch. Hook both ends of spring (6) together, and position the ends in the center of one of the shoes (5). Install clutch plates (8) so that side of plates with rounded edge faces the clutch spring. Assemble clutch hub (7) to shoes with beveled edge of the hub "arms" facing the clutch plates (8).

When installing clutch, be sure that washer (A—Fig. E198) is installed in correct direction. Install the clutch hub and shoes so that side of hub with circular protrusion (B) faces outward. Turn clutch hub counterclockwise to install. Tighten the clutch hub to the torque listed in TIGHTENING TORQUE paragraph using the special tool. Do not use any power tool to install the clutch hub.

OIL PUMP. All saws are equipped with an automatic guide bar and chain oiling system. The oil pump shown in Fig. E199 supplies oil. The pump plunger is driven by the worm gear (3), which is located on the engine crankshaft.

Remove the chain clutch assembly, chain, guide bar and chain guide plate. Unbolt the oil pump housing (2—Fig. E199) and pull the pump assembly from the engine. If necessary, use a suitable puller (part No. 897708-19831) to pull the oil pump drive worm (3) from the crankshaft.

To disassemble the removed pump, depress tab (A—Fig. E200) while pulling plug (B) from the housing. If equipped with a steel control pin (C), remove retaining ring from the pin. If equipped with a plastic control pin (D), compress the split end of the pin with pliers and push the pin into pump body. Withdraw adjuster (4—Fig. E201) from pump body. Bump the housing on a soft surface if necessary to jar the pump plunger (3) and spring (1) from the housing bore.

Clean and inspect parts for wear or damage. Parts should move freely in housing bores without excessive clearance. Install a new pump assembly if parts are worn. Some individual parts may be available separately if only that part is damaged.

A small wire (paper clip) can be used to remove and install the V-ring

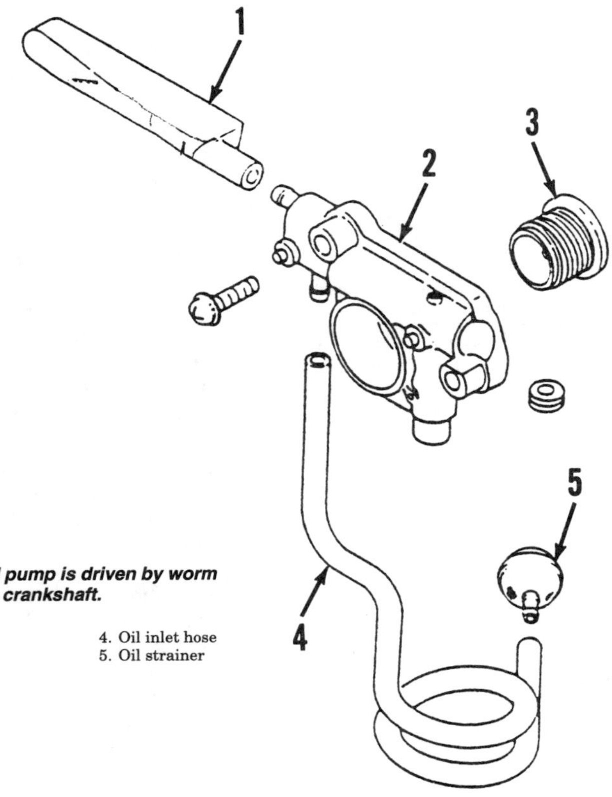

Fig. E199—The chain oil pump is driven by worm gear (3) on crankshaft.

1. Discharge pipe
2. Oil pump assy.
3. Worm gear
4. Oil inlet hose
5. Oil strainer

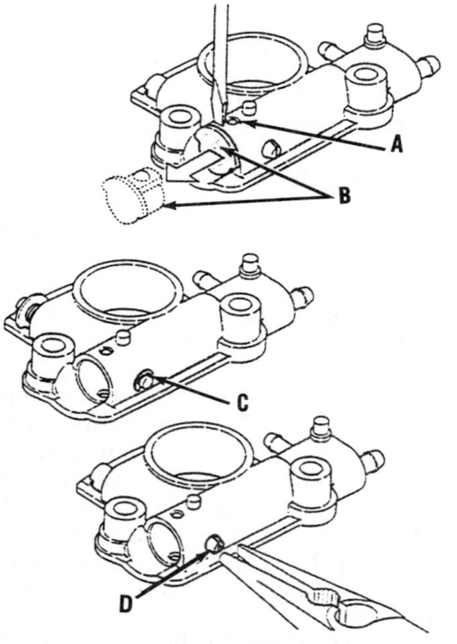

Fig. E200—Views showing disassembly of the oil pump. Refer to text.

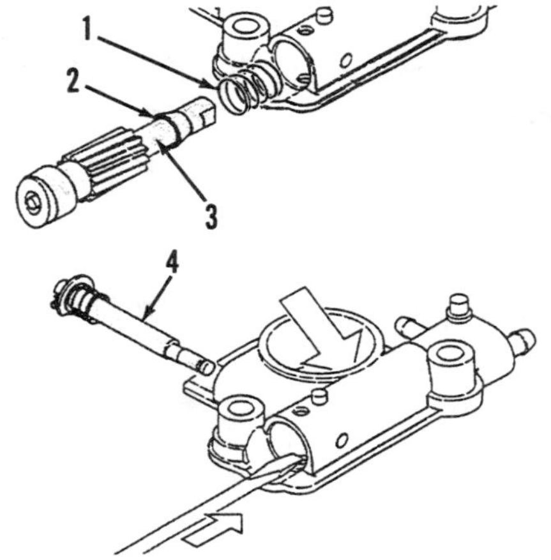

Fig. E201—Views showing removal and installation of oil pump plunger (3) and adjuster (4). Refer to text.

(2—Fig. E201). If necessary to remove the V-ring, a new V-ring should be installed. Open side of "V" should be toward gear on pump plunger.

Insert the pump spring in housing bore, coat plunger and V-ring with grease and insert it into the housing bore. Push the plunger into the housing bore to compress the spring and hold the plunger IN while installing the adjuster as shown in Fig. E201. Hold the plunger by exerting thumb pressure against the gear located on the plunger.

Note that protrusion (P—Fig. E202) on head of plastic type control pin or punch marks (S) on head of steel type control pin should face wall of pump body as shown in Fig. E202. It will be necessary to compress spring by pressing on adjuster to install retaining ring (C—Fig. E200) if equipped with a steel adjuster. If equipped with a plastic adjuster, push end through until it catches (D).

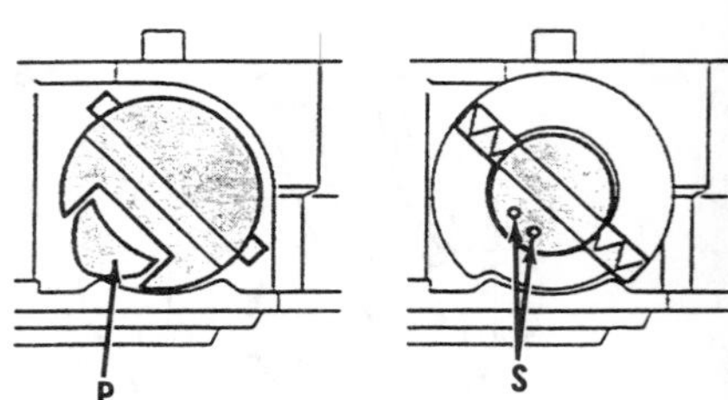

Fig. E202—Views showing correct installation of the oil pump control pin (adjuster). Type shown at (P) is plastic; type shown at (S) is steel.

Grease the cam of the adjuster with multipurpose grease, then install the end plug (B—Fig. E200). If removed, use special tool (part No. 897708-37530) to install the drive worm on the crankshaft. Drive gear should be bottomed against the crankshaft. Connect oil lines to the pump body and attach the pump body to the engine.

Complete assembly by reversing disassembly procedure. Refer to the LUBRICATION paragraph in the Maintenance section for adjustment.

REWIND STARTER. Refer to Fig. E203 for exploded view of the starter assembly. To disassemble starter, first unbolt and remove starter housing (1) from saw. Pull starter rope out about 20 cm (8 in.) and make a temporary knot at the rope guide to prevent the rope from rewinding into the starter. Remove handle (3), then untie the temporary knot. Hold the pulley (6) while allowing the rope to slowly wind into the starter housing.

Remove screw (8), pulley (6) and rope (7). If the rope is to be replaced, remove all of the old rope, then install 85 cm (33.5 in.) of new 3.0 mm (0.12 in.) diameter rope.

The rewind spring (4) may remain contained in housing (5). If required, rewind spring (4) can now be removed. Use caution not to allow spring to unwind uncontrolled.

Reassemble starter components by reversing disassembly procedure while noting the following: New rewind spring is contained in a temporary retainer. Install rewind spring into spring housing so that outer loop of spring (L—Fig. E204) goes over pin (P) of spring holder. Wind the rewind spring counterclockwise into housing. Lubricate rewind spring with a small amount of all-purpose grease.

Wind rope on pulley (6—Fig. E203) three or four turns in clockwise direction. Assemble pulley against the spring housing (5) with the pulley cog engaging the inner end of the spring. Install the spring, spring housing, pul-

Illustrations courtesy Echo, Inc.

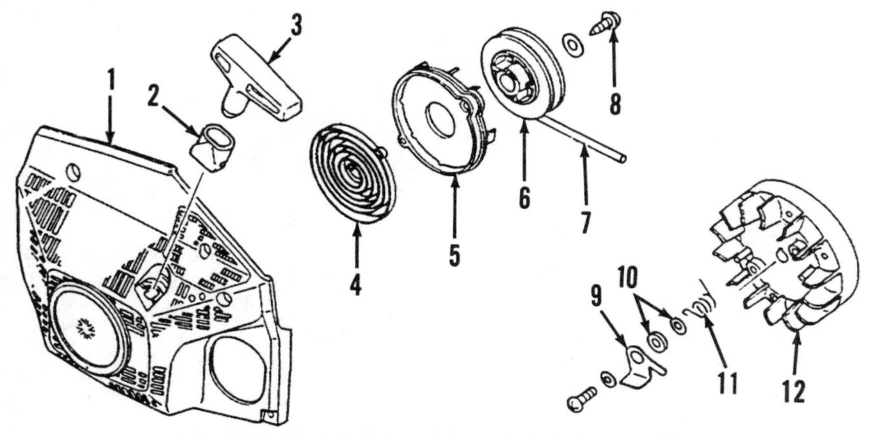

Fig. E203—Exploded view of the rewind starter assembly.

1. Starter housing
2. Rope grommet
3. Handle
4. Rewind spring
5. Starter plate
6. Pulley
7. Rope (3 mm x 85 cm)
8. Screw
9. Starter pawl
10. Spacers
11. Spring
12. Flywheel

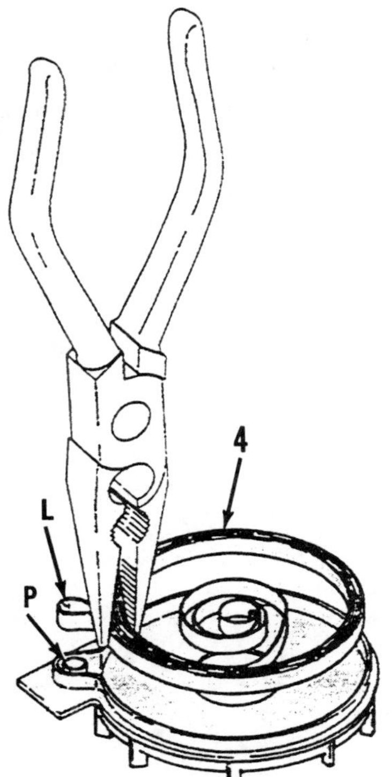

Fig. E204—Installing rewind spring (4). Spring loop (L) goes over spring holder pin (P).

Fig. E205—Exploded view of chain brake assembly.

1. Spring
2. Hand guard
3. Spacer
4. Brake lever
5. Sprocket guard
6. Adjuster
7. Brake band
8. Cover
9. Brake stop
10. Brake spring
11. Pins

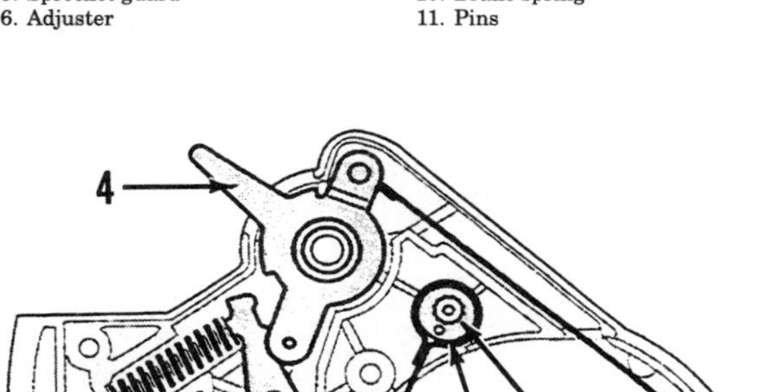

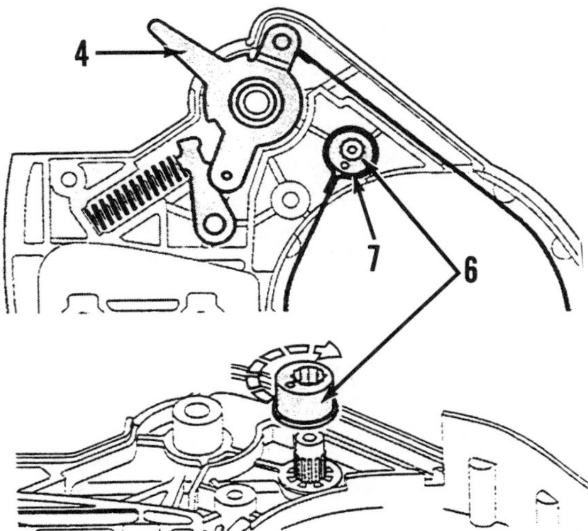

Fig. E206—Views showing correct assembly of chain brake and location of brake adjuster.

ley and rope in the starter housing (1) and install the washer and screw (8). Guide the end of the rope through the starter housing and guide (2), then install the handle (3).

Pull a loop of rope between the inside of the starter housing and the pulley and place rope in notch in pulley. Turn the rope pulley (6) several turns clockwise to place tension on rewind spring. Release the rope from notch in pulley and allow pulley to rewind slowly.

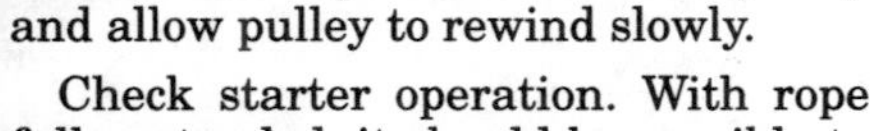

Check starter operation. With rope fully extended, it should be possible to

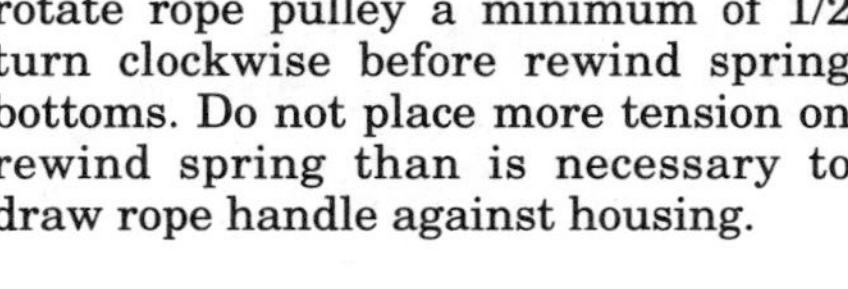

rotate rope pulley a minimum of 1/2 turn clockwise before rewind spring bottoms. Do not place more tension on rewind spring than is necessary to draw rope handle against housing.

CHAIN BRAKE. The chain brake is designed to stop the chain if kickback should occur. The chain brake is activated when the operator's hand strikes the hand guard (2—Fig. E205) or if the tip of the guide bar strikes an object with sufficient force to trip the brake mechanism.

When the brake is engaged, a spring (10) tightens the band (7) around the clutch drum to stop the drum, sprocket and chain. Pull the hand guard (2) back to reset the mechanism.

Unbolt and remove the sprocket guard (5), which contains the brake assembly. Push the hand guard (2) forward to the engaged position. Remove hand guard pivot bolt and withdraw the hand guard.

Remove the cover (8) and check operation and condition of the brake parts. Carefully disengage spring (10) from sprocket guard (5) and remove remaining brake parts from sprocket guard.

Install new parts as necessary. Refer to Fig. E205 and Fig. E206 when assembling. Be sure that brake lever (4) is positioned between spring (1) and pin (11) as shown in Fig. E207. Move hand guard to disengaged position when installing sprocket guard to saw.

Clutch drum must turn freely when brake is in disengaged (cutting) position. Clutch drum should not rotate when brake is in engaged position. The brake can be adjusted by removing the sprocket guard and turning the adjuster (6—Fig. E206).

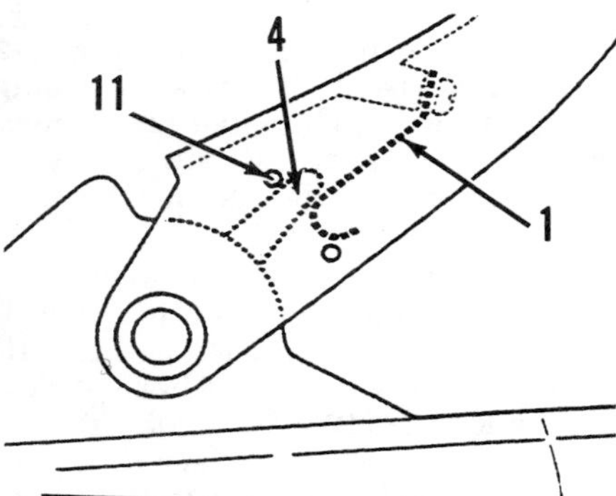

Fig. E207—View showing correct assembly of brake hand guard. Refer to text.

HANDLES AND VIBRATION ISOLATORS The front and rear handles are equipped with vibration isolators (Fig. E208). Unbolt and remove handles to inspect and/or replace the isolators.

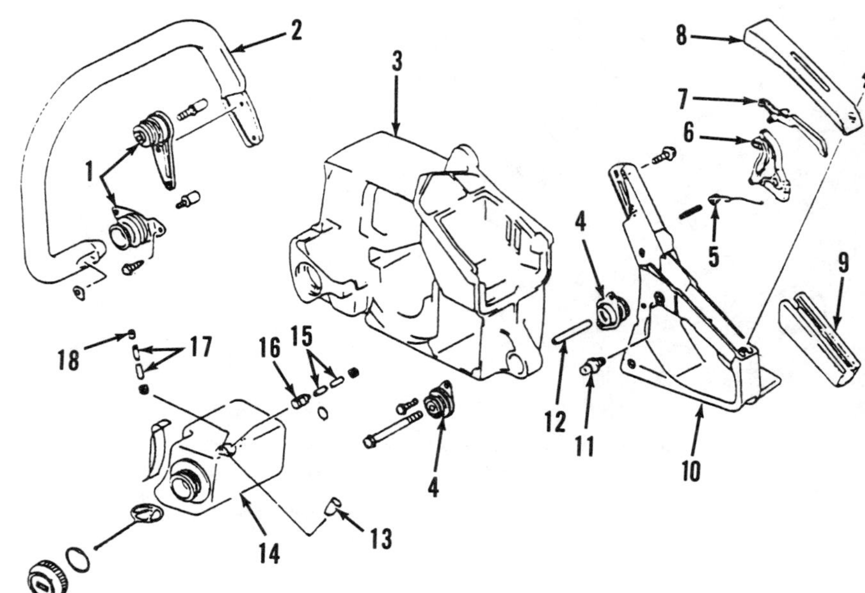

Fig. E208—Drawing showing relative position of the handles and vibration isolators.

1. Isolators
2. Front handle
3. Engine/tank cover
4. Isolators
5. Return spring
6. Throttle control
7. Throttle lockout
8. Handle cover
9. Handle grip
10. Rear handle
11. Throttle latch
12. Collar
13. Plug
14. Fuel tank
15. Fuel line
16. Fuel strainer
17. Pulse line
18. Check valve

Illustrations courtesy Echo, Inc.

FRONTIER

Model	Bore mm (in.)	Stroke mm (in.)	Displacement cc (cu. in.)	Drive Type
Mark I, Mark V.I.P., 35, 35 VIP, F-35, F-35 VIP, FB-35, FB-35 VIP	36.5 (1.4375)	32.5 (1.28)	34.4 (2.1)	Direct

MAINTENANCE

SPARK PLUG. Recommended spark plug is Champion CJ6. Spark plug electrode gap should be 0.025 inch (0.63 mm).

CARBURETOR. A Tillotson Model HU diaphragm carburetor or a Walbro Model WA diaphragm carburetor may be used. Refer to Tillotson or Walbro section of CARBURETOR SERVICE section for service procedures and exploded view.

Initial adjustment of idle mixture screws is 1½ turns open while initial adjustment of high speed mixture screw is 1⅛ turns open.

Final adjustment of high speed mixture screw should be made with engine warm and engine under cutting load. High speed mixture must not be adjusted too lean as engine may be damaged.

IGNITION. Early models are equipped with a breaker-point type flywheel magneto ignition system while later models use a breakerless electronic ignition system. Refer to Fig. FR3 for an exploded view of breaker-point ignition system used on early models.

On models with breaker-point ignition, breaker-point gap should be 0.018 inch (0.45 mm) for new points and 0.015 inch (0.38 mm) for used points. Ignition timing is fixed but breaker-point gap will affect ignition timing and should be set correctly. On models with electronic ignition, ignition timing is fixed and nonadjustable.

On all models, tighten flywheel nut to 15 ft.-lbs. (20.4 N·m).

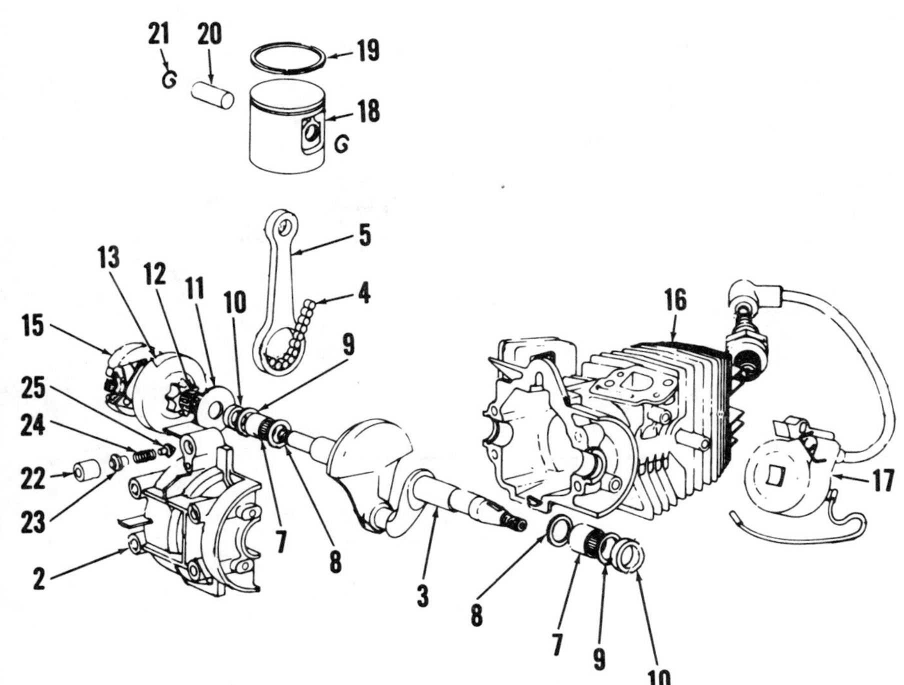

Fig. FR1 — Exploded view of engine used on all models.

2. Crankcase
3. Crankshaft
4. Roller bearing
5. Connecting rod
7. Needle bearing
8. Washer
9. Retaining ring
10. Seal
11. Thrust washer
12. Bearing
13. Clutch drum
15. Clutch assy.
16. Cylinder
17. Ignition oil
18. Piston
19. Piston ring
20. Piston pin
21. Pin retainer
22. Spacer
23. Spring seat
24. Spring
25. Pulse valve

LUBRICATION. The engine is lubricated by mixing oil with the fuel. Recommended fuel:oil ratio is 16:1. A good quality oil designed for chain saw engines should be used.

Fill chain oil tank with SAE 30 motor oil. Chain oil may be diluted up to 50 percent for winter usage by adding kerosene or diesel fuel to chain oil.

CARBON. Carbon should be removed from exhaust system and cylinder periodically. Loose carbon should not be allowed to enter cylinder and care should be taken not to damage cylinder or piston.

REPAIRS

CYLINDER, PISTON, PIN AND RINGS. Cylinder (16–Fig. FR1) on all models is also upper crankcase half. Crankshaft is loose in crankcase when cylinder is removed. Care must be taken not to nick or scratch crankcase mating surfaces during disassembly.

Cylinder head is integral with cylinder and cylinder must be removed to remove piston. Piston is equipped with a single piston ring and a floating type piston pin (20). Piston, pin and ring are available in standard size only. Cylinder bore is chrome and should be inspected to determine if chrome is scored, peeling or excessively worn. Renew cylinder and piston if damaged or excessively worn.

Refer to CRANKSHAFT section for proper assembly of crankcase and cylinder. Tighten cylinder retaining screws to 50-55 in.-lbs. (5.6-6.2 N·m)

CONNECTING ROD. To remove connecting rod, remove cylinder (16–Fig. FR1). Note that cylinder is also upper crankcase half and crankshaft assembly is loose when cylinder is removed. Connecting rod (5) is one-piece and supported on crankpin by 11 loose bearing rollers (4). Be careful not to lose loose rollers that may fall out during disassembly. Rollers can be removed by sliding rod off rollers. To install rod bearing, hold rollers in place with heavy grease or petroleum jelly and position rod over rollers. Be sure rollers do not fall out during assembly of crankcase.

CRANKSHAFT AND SEALS. Crankshaft is supported by needle roller bearings (7–Fig. FR1) at both ends. Crankshaft assembly may be removed after removing stator plate, clutch and cylinder assemblies. Care should be taken when removing cylinder as crankshaft will be loose in crankcase and connecting rod may slide off bearing rollers allowing them to fall into crankcase.

Before reassembling crankcases, apply a light coat of nonhardening silicone sealant to crankcase mating surface. Be sure mating surfaces are not damaged during assembly. Retaining rings (9) must fit in ring grooves of crankcase and cylinder.

CLUTCH. A two-shoe centrifugal type clutch is used on all models. Clutch hub has left-hand threads. Clutch bearing (12–Fig. FR1) should be inspected for excessive wear or damage. Inspect clutch shoes and drum for signs of excessive heat.

OIL PUMP. All early models are equipped with a manual oil pump and automatic oiling system. Refer to Fig. FR2 for an exploded view of manual oil pump. Automatic oiling is accomplished by crankcase pulsations which pressurize oil tank and force oil to bar. A one-way valve (25–Fig. FR1) prevents oil from entering crankcase.

NOTE: Later models equipped with manual oil pump and automatic oiling system are equipped with a duckbill type valve in place of valve components (22, 23, 24 and 25).

Later model saws are equipped with a positive displacement oil pump assembly located behind flywheel. Oil pump assembly is driven by a worm gear on crankshaft. Remove oil pump plunger retaining roll pin and withdraw plunger, gear and spring to service. Use suitable tools to pry worm gear off crankshaft. Renew any component that is excessively worn or damaged. Plunger is available only with complete oil pump assembly.

REWIND STARTER. Refer to Fig. FR3 for an exploded view of pawl type starter used on all models. Care should be taken while removing rewind spring to prevent spring from uncoiling uncontrolled.

Rewind spring (12) should be wound in clockwise direction in housing. Wind starter rope in clockwise direction around pulley (11) as viewed in starter housing (14). Place tension on rope by turning rope pulley three turns clockwise before passing rope end through rope outlet.

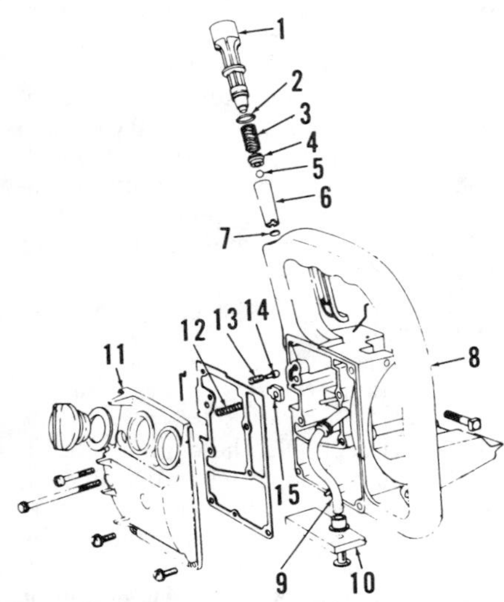

Fig. FR2—Exploded view of manual oil pump and front housing.

1. Piston
2. "O" ring
3. Spring
4. Spring seat
5. Ball
6. Pump body
7. Screen
8. Front housing
9. Fuel hose
10. Filter
11. Front cover
12. Spring
13. Spring
14. Oil outlet valve
15. Nut

Fig. FR3—Exploded view of rewind starter used on all models. Breaker-point ignition (1) is used on early models.

1. Stator plate
2. Cover
3. Flywheel
4. Spring
5. Pawl
6. Pivot pin
7. Washer
8. Nut
9. Snap ring
10. Thrust washer
11. Rope pulley
12. Rewind spring
13. Bushing
14. Starter housing

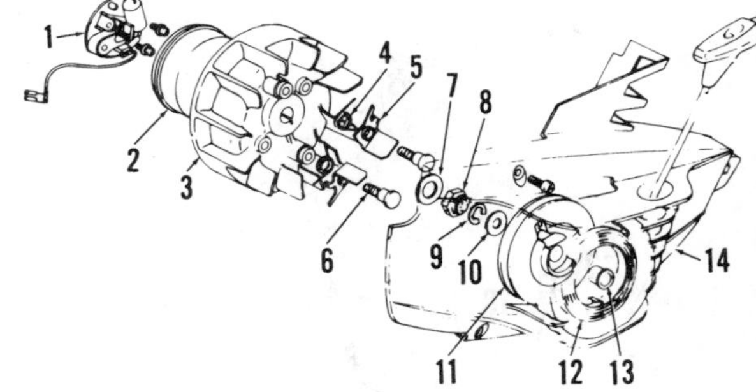

GREEN MACHINE BY JOHN DEERE

Model	Bore mm (in.)	Stroke mm (in.)	Displacement cc (cu. in.)	Drive Type
20	...	...	30	Direct

MAINTENANCE

SPARK PLUG. Recommended spark plug is Champion DJ7Y. Spark plug electrode gap should be 0.025 inch (0.6 mm) for all models.

CARBURETOR. All models are equipped with a Walbro HDC or Zama diaphragm type carburetor. Refer to CARBURETOR SERVICE section in this manual for carburetor overhaul procedures and exploded views.

Both the low-speed and high-speed mixture needles have stops that limit the amount of adjustment to 1/2 turn. Turn both mixture needles counterclockwise until they stop. Start and run the engine until it reaches operating temperature.

Turn low-speed mixture needle as necessary until maximum idle speed is reached then turn needle 1/8 turn counterclockwise to enrich the mixture slightly. The engine should accelerate cleanly without hesitation. If engine stumbles or seems sluggish when accelerating, adjust the idle mixture until engine accelerates without hesitation. Adjust idle speed stop screw so engine idles without stalling and chain does not rotate.

Adjust high-speed mixture needle with saw running at wide-open throttle. Adjust the high-speed mixture needle to obtain maximum speed, then turn needle 1/8 turn counterclockwise to enrich the mixture slightly. Do not operate saw with high-speed mixture too lean because engine damage may result from lack of lubrication and overheating.

IGNITION. The breakerless solid-state ignition system is serviced by renewing the spark plug and/or ignition module. Remove recoil starter housing for access to ignition module.

There is no periodic maintenance required, however, air gap between ignition module and flywheel is adjustable.

Adjust air gap by loosening the screws attaching the module retaining screws, then place a 0.015 inch (0.38 mm) shim stock between flywheel and the legs of the ignition module. Turn the flywheel if necessary to locate the flywheel magnets near the ignition module. Press the ignition module against the flywheel so that the legs of the ignition module are firmly against the shim stock, then tighten the attaching screws to the torque listed in the TIGHTENING TORQUE paragraph. Remove the setting gauge, then turn the flywheel and check that flywheel does not hit the legs of the coil.

LUBRICATION. The engine is lubricated by mixing oil with gasoline. Recommended oil is GREEN MACHINE 32:1 or GREEN MACHINE Premium Exact Mix oil mixed at ratio as designated on oil container. If GREEN MACHINE oil is not available, good quality oil designed for air-cooled 2-cycle engines may be used but must be mixed at 32:1 ratio. Oils formulated for use at less than 32:1 ratio, oils designed for outboard (water-cooled) engines or automotive (4-stroke) oils should not be used. Always mix oil and gasoline in a separate container.

GREEN MACHINE Premium Exact Mix oils contain an antioxidant fuel stabilizer and mixed fuel should stay fresh for up to 30 days.

Saw chain is lubricated by oil from an automatic oil pump. Recommended chain oil is GREEN MACHINE Bar and Chain Oil or clean SAE 30 oil. The rate of oil flow depends on engine speed and is not adjustable.

REPAIRS

CRANKCASE PRESSURE TEST. An improperly sealed crankcase can cause the engine to be hard to start, run rough, have low power and overheat. Refer to ENGINE SERVICE section of this manual for crankcase pressure test procedure. If crankcase leakage is indicated, pressurize crankcase and use a soap and water solution to check gaskets, seals, pulse line and castings for leakage.

TIGHTENING TORQUE VALUES. Tightening torque values are listed in the following table.

Carburetor mounting screws	35-45 in.-lbs. (4.0-5.9 N·m)
Clutch drum nut	100-125 in.-lbs. (11.3-14.0 N·m)
Clutch hub	100-150 in.-lbs. (11.3-14.0 N·m)
Crankcase screws	55-65 in.-lbs.* (6.2-7.3 N·m)
Flywheel	100-150 in.-lbs. (11.3-14.0 N·m)
Ignition module screws	30-40 in.-lbs.* (3.4-4.5 N·m)
Intake manifold mounting screws	35-45 in.-lbs.* (4.0-5.0 N·m)
Muffler mounting screws	40-50 in.-lbs.* (4.5-5.6 N·m)
Reed mounting screws	10-15 in.-lbs. (1.1-1.7 N·m)
Spark plug	120-180 in.-lbs. (13.6-20.0 N·m)

*Apply thread locking compound to screw threads.

CRANKSHAFT, CYLINDER, PISTON, PIN AND RINGS. To disassemble, remove guide bar and chain, starter housing and front handle. Remove stop switch (6—Fig. GM101) from engine housing and disconnect electrical leads. Remove chain brake assembly. Remove air cleaner cover, muffler guard and muffler. Remove primer bulb and disconnect throttle rod (10). Remove engine housing mounting screws and separate engine (11) from engine housing (1).

Remove oil tank and fuel tank. Remove air filter (15—Fig. GM102), carburetor (14) and intake manifold (12).

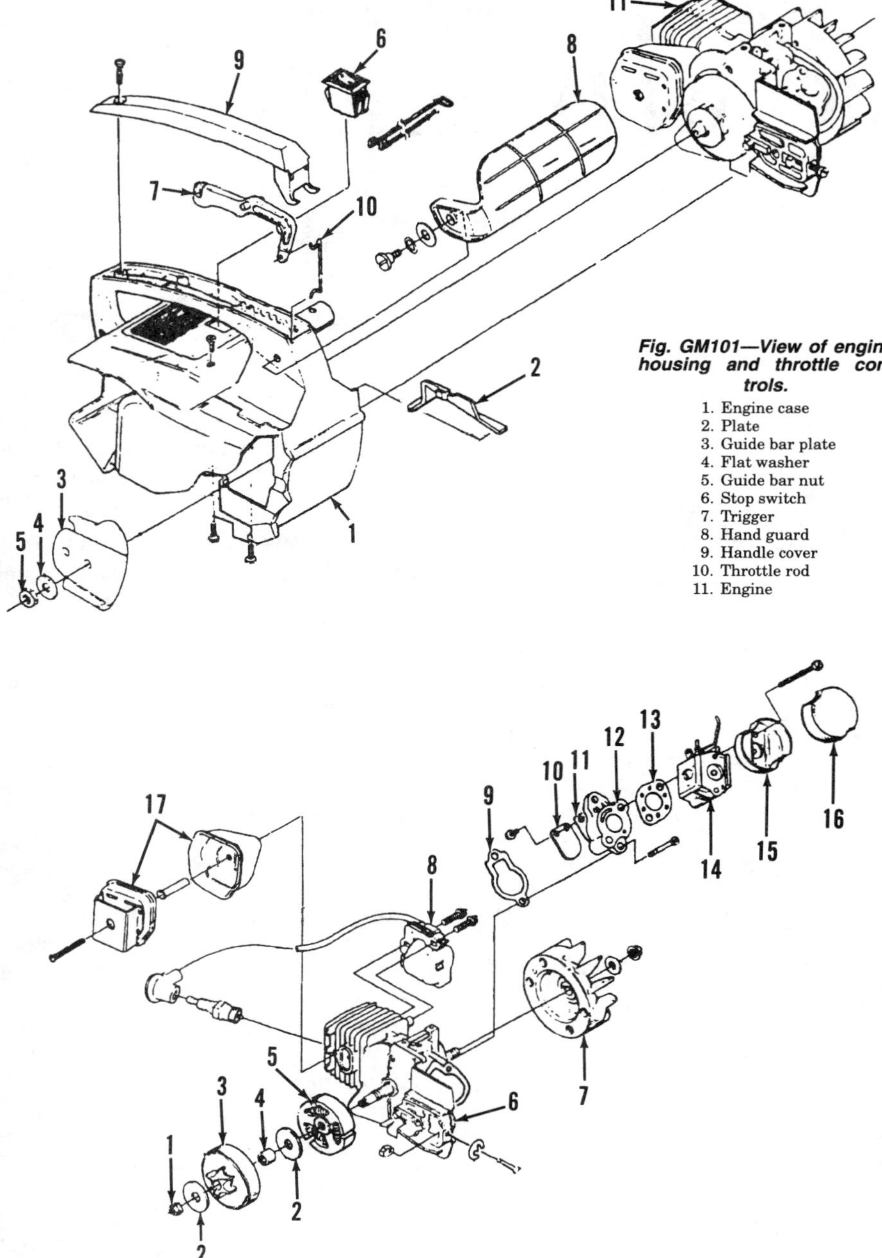

Fig. GM101—View of engine housing and throttle controls.

1. Engine case
2. Plate
3. Guide bar plate
4. Flat washer
5. Guide bar nut
6. Stop switch
7. Trigger
8. Hand guard
9. Handle cover
10. Throttle rod
11. Engine

Fig. GM102—Exploded view of clutch, muffler and intake components typical of late models. Chain oil pump is mounted on fuel metering side of carburetor.

1. Nut
2. Washers
3. Clutch drum
4. Needle bearing
5. Clutch hub & shoes
6. Power head
7. Flywheel
8. Ignition unit
9. Gasket
10. Reed stop
11. Reed
12. Intake manifold
13. Gasket
14. Carburetor
15. Air filter housing
16. Filter element
17. Muffler

Remove ignition module/coil assembly (8).

Remove spark plug and insert end of a rope in the cylinder to act as a piston stop. Unscrew clutch drum mounting nut (1—Fig. GM102) and remove clutch drum (3). Use suitable tool to unscrew clutch hub (5) from crankshaft. Note that clutch hub has left-hand threads (rotate clockwise to remove). Remove flywheel mounting nut (right-hand threads) and use a suitable puller to remove flywheel from crankshaft.

Remove crankcase mounting screws and separate crankcase (14—Fig. GM103) from cylinder (1). Withdraw crankshaft, connecting rod and piston from cylinder. Care should be taken not to scratch or nick mating surfaces of cylinder and crankcase. Remove piston ring (2) from piston. Remove retainer clips (3) and push piston pin (5) out of piston. Separate piston and needle bearing (7) from connecting rod.

Crankshaft needle bearings (10) are held loosely in their cages. Before removing needle bearings from crankshaft, coat the crankshaft with multipurpose grease. Then, slide the bearings through the grease and off the crankshaft. The grease will retain the needle bearings in the cage.

To reassemble, reverse the disassembly procedure while noting the following special instructions: Install piston on connecting rod so locating pin in ring groove is facing flywheel (keyed) side of crankshaft. Install thrust washers (11—Fig. GM103) with grooved side facing crankshaft counterweights. Use multipurpose grease to retain needle rollers in main bearing cages (10). Install main bearings with lettered side facing outward. Install spacers (9) with open side toward cylinder. Lubricate lip of seals (8) with grease before installation.

Make certain that piston ring end gap indexes with locating pin in piston ring groove. Lubricate piston and cylinder bore with oil, compress the piston ring and slide piston into cylinder.

Flat side of thrust washers (11) must face the crankcase (14). Apply light coat of RTV silicone sealant to crankcase mating surface then assemble crankcase to cylinder. Be sure crankshaft seals (8) are flush with outer surface of cylinder and crankcase. Gently tap on both ends of crankshaft to center all components, then tighten crankcase screws to specified torque.

CLUTCH. To remove clutch assembly, first separate engine from engine housing as outlined in CRANKSHAFT, CYLINDER, PISTON, PIN AND RINGS section.

Remove spark plug and insert end of a rope in cylinder to act as a piston stop. Unscrew nut (1—Fig. GM102) and remove clutch drum (3), washers (2) and bearing (4). Use suitable clutch tool to remove clutch hub (5) and shoes. Note that clutch hub has left-hand threads (rotate clockwise to remove). Disconnect springs and separate clutch shoes from hub.

Inspect clutch components for wear or damage and renew as necessary. To reinstall, reverse removal procedure.

AUTOMATIC CHAIN OILER SYSTEM. A pressurized oil tank system automatically lubricates the bar and chain when the saw is operating. Crankcase pulses are used to pressur-

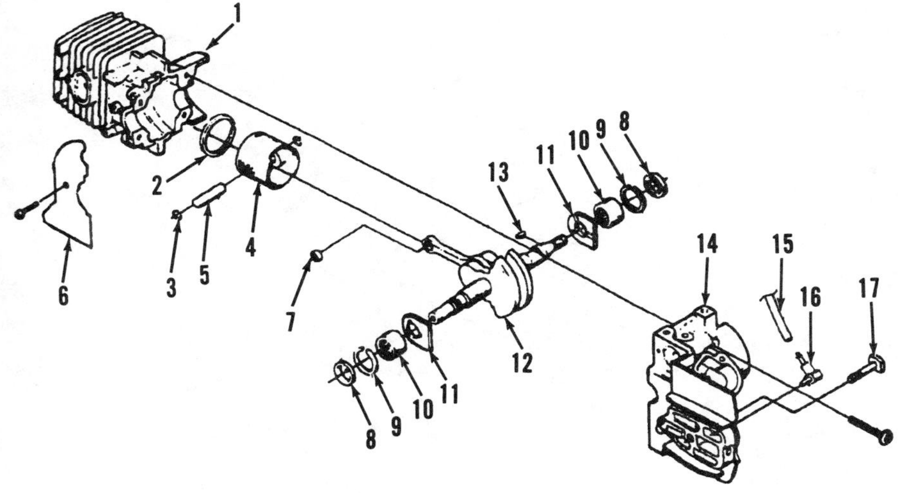

Fig. GM103—Exploded view of typical engine.

1. Cylinder
2. Piston ring
3. Retaining clip
4. Piston
5. Piston pin
6. Dust shield
7. Needle bearing
8. Oil seal
9. Spacer
10. Needle bearing
11. Thrust washer
12. Crankshaft & connecting rod assy.
13. Key
14. Crankcase
15. Oil line
16. Check valve
17. Guide bar bolt

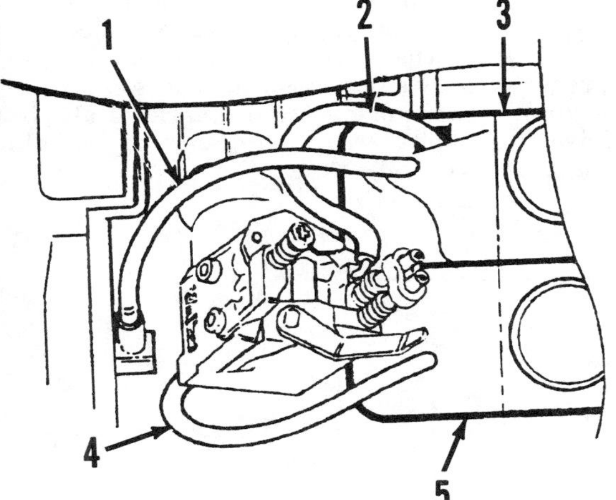

Fig. GM104—Drawing showing correct routing of chain oiler system hoses and fuel system hoses. Hoses should be the correct length for proper operation.

1. Oil pick-up line
2. Pressure pulse line
3. Oil tank
4. Fuel line
5. Fuel tank

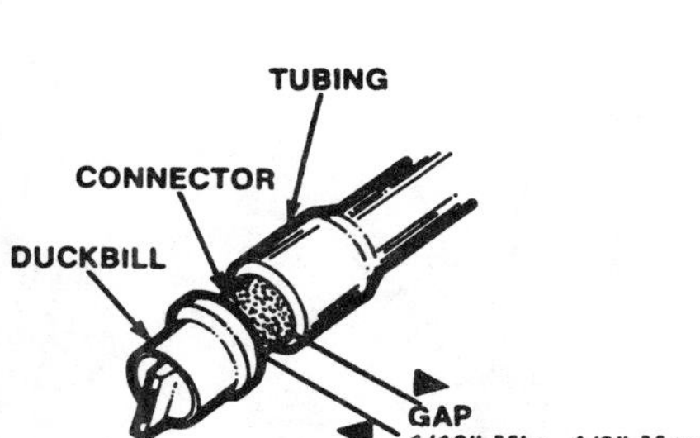

Fig. GM105—Gap between "duckbill" check valve and tubing end must be 1/16-1/8 inch (1.6-3.1 mm).

ize the oil tank, forcing oil directly from the oil tank to the guide bar oil outlet. In temperatures below 32 degrees F (0 degrees C), it may be necessary to dilute chain oil with one part of kerosene to four parts of oil to allow system operation.

If chain oil flow is inadequate or has stopped completely, proceed as follows: Check condition of oil tank cap. Cap must seal tank opening to allow oil tank to pressurize. Make sure that oil level is not above the "duckbill" check valve and that oil pick-up is at bottom of tank.

Check the condition of the oil filter on pick-up line and clean or renew as required. Check diameter of oil metering orifice located in oil pick-up line above oil filter. Diameter of orifice should not be less than 0.046 inch (1.18 mm).

Oil pick-up line (1—Fig. GM104) should be 8 inches (203 mm) long with 3-3/4 inches (99.25 mm) out of the oil tank (3). The oil tank pressure pulse line (2) should be 2-3/4 inches (69.85 mm) long. The fuel line (4) is 5-1/2 inches (139.7 mm) long with 1-3/4 inches (44.45 mm) out of the fuel tank (5). Refer to Fig. GM104.

Connect a suitable pressure tester to oil tank using a test cap (cap having a fitting for a hose). Pressurize tank to 4-5 psi (28-34 kPa) and check for free flowing oil at guide bar.

If there is no oil flow, check for pinched or restricted oil lines. With pressure tester still installed, start and run saw at wide-open throttle for about 10 seconds. Tank should pressurize to 2.5 to 6 psi (17-41 kPa). While engine idles or is shut off, pressure should drop to zero after approximately 5 seconds.

If tank fails to pressurize, check the condition of crankcase pulse line by submerging the "duckbill" check valve (shown in Fig. GM105) in oil while the saw is running. Constant bubbles should emit from the check valve with slight bubbling from the porous connector located between the check valve and line. A connector that is too porous will not maintain the required 2.5 psi (17 kPa) minimum for proper oiling.

If oil flow is excessive or continues to flow after saw is shut off, proceed as follows: Excessive oil flow may be caused by incorrect installation of "duckbill" check valve (Fig. GM105). There should be a gap of 1/16-1/8 inch (1.6-3.1 mm) between check valve and end of pulse line thereby allowing porous connector to bleed off pressure while engine idles or is shut off. A good connector will bleed off pressure in approximately 5 seconds.

REWIND STARTER. To service rewind starter, remove starter housing (11—Fig. GM106) from saw. Pull starter rope and hold rope pulley with notch in pulley adjacent to rope outlet. Pull rope back through outlet so it engages notch in pulley and allow pulley to completely unwind.

Unscrew pulley retaining screw (7) and remove rope pulley being careful not to dislodge rewind spring in housing. Care must be taken if rewind spring is removed to prevent injury if spring is allowed to uncoil uncontrolled.

Rewind spring is wound in clockwise direction in starter housing. Rope is wound on rope pulley in clockwise direction as viewed with pulley in housing.

To place tension on rewind spring, pass rope though rope outlet in housing and install rope handle. Pull rope out and hold rope pulley so notch on pulley is adjacent to rope outlet. Pull rope back through outlet between notch in pulley and housing. Turn rope pulley clockwise to place tension on spring. Release pulley and check starter action. Do not place more tension on rewind spring than is necessary to draw rope handle up against housing.

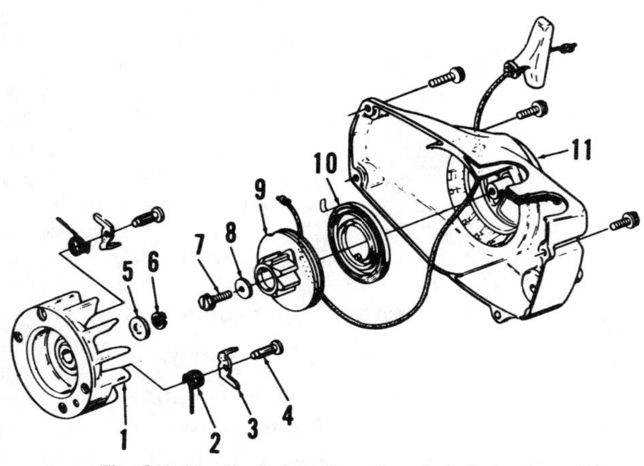

Fig. GM106—Exploded view of rewind starter assembly.

1. Flywheel
2. Spring
3. Starter pawl
4. Pawl pin
5. Washer
6. Nut
7. Cap screw
8. Washer
9. Rope pulley
10. Rewind spring
11. Housing

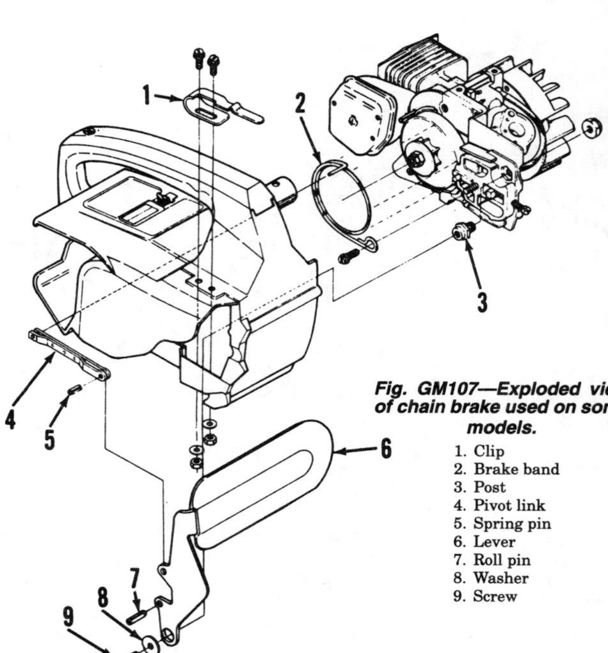

Fig. GM107—Exploded view of chain brake used on some models.

1. Clip
2. Brake band
3. Post
4. Pivot link
5. Spring pin
6. Lever
7. Roll pin
8. Washer
9. Screw

CHAIN BRAKE. The chain brake system is designed to stop chain movement should kickback occur. Chain brake is activated when operator's hand strikes chain brake handle (6—Fig. GM107), thereby drawing brake band (2) around clutch drum.

To disassemble chain brake, remove guide bar and chain. Remove the brake mounting screws. Use screwdriver to pry brake band off clutch drum, then lift brake band and handle assembly out over guide bar pad. No adjustment of chain brake system is required. Renew any component that is excessively worn or damaged. Lubricate all pivot points with Molykote or suitable equivalent.

GREEN MACHINE BY JOHN DEERE

Model	Bore mm (in.)	Stroke mm (in.)	Displacement cc (cu. in.)	Drive Type
30	43.4 (1.71)	32.5 (1.28)	49.2 (3.0)	Direct

MAINTENANCE SPARK PLUG. Recommended spark plug is Champion CJ6Y or RCJ6Y. Specified electrode gap is 0.025 inch (0.6 mm). The spark plug should be tightened to the torque listed in the TIGHTENING TORQUE paragraph.

CARBURETOR. Either a Walbro or Zama diaphragm type carburetor is used. Refer to CARBURETOR SERVICE section for overhaul procedures and exploded views. Tighten the carburetor attaching screws to the torque listed in the TIGHTENING TORQUE paragraph.

Both the low-speed and high-speed mixture needles (Fig. GM200) have stops that limit the amount of adjustment to 1/2 turn. Turn both mixture needles counterclockwise until they stop. Start and run the engine until it reaches operating temperature.

Turn low-speed mixture needle as necessary until maximum idle speed is reached then turn needle 1/8 turn counterclockwise to enrich the mixture slightly. The engine should accelerate cleanly without hesitation. If engine stumbles or seems sluggish when accelerating, adjust the idle mixture until engine accelerates without hesitation. Adjust idle speed stop screw so engine idles without stalling and chain does not rotate.

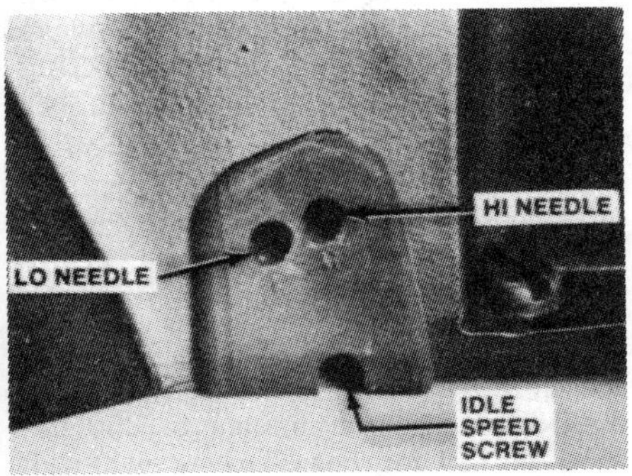

Fig. GM200—View of carburetor adjustment points. Refer to text for adjustment procedure.

Adjust high-speed mixture needle with saw running at wide-open throttle. Adjust the high-speed mixture needle to obtain maximum speed, then turn needle 1/8 turn counterclockwise to enrich the mixture slightly. Do not operate saw with high-speed mixture too lean because engine damage may result from lack of lubrication and overheating.

IGNITION. A breakerless, solid state electronic ignition system is used. Electronic components are contained in a one-piece ignition module/coil located outside the flywheel. Ignition timing is fixed and not adjustable. The flywheel attaching nut should be tightened to the torque listed in TIGHTENING TORQUE paragraph.

Air gap between the legs of the module/coil and the flywheel magnets should be 0.3 mm (0.012 in.). When installing, set the air gap between the flywheel magnets and the legs of the ignition module as follows.

Install the ignition module, but tighten the two screws only enough to hold it in place away from the flywheel. Insert brass/plastic shim stock of the proper thickness between the legs of the ignition module and the flywheel, then turn the flywheel until the flywheel magnets are near the module legs. Loosen the screws attaching the ignition module and press legs of the ignition module against the shim stock. Apply thread locking compound to the two screws before tightening to the torque listed in the TIGHTENING TORQUE paragraph. Remove the setting gauge, then turn the flywheel and check that flywheel does not hit the legs of the coil.

Solid state ignition modules will not produce a spark unless flywheel is turned briskly by starter operation. Solid state modules produce an orange colored spark. Ignition system may be considered satisfactory if it can produce a spark across a 0.125 inch (3.2 mm) gap.

If ignition fails to produce a spark, first inspect for loose or broken wires or faulty ignition switch and repair as necessary. Also, check air gap between flywheel magnets and legs of the ignition coil/module. If condition is still questioned, substitute a known good module and check for spark.

LUBRICATION. The engine is lubricated by mixing oil with gasoline. Recommended oil is "GREEN MACHINE 32:1" or GREEN MACHINE Premium Exact Mix. Mix the oil with unleaded gasoline at the ratio designated on the oil container. Oils formulated at less than 32:1 ratio or non 2-cycle oils should not be used. Always mix oil and gasoline in a separate container. The manufacturer does not recommend using fuel containing alcohol.

Saw chain is lubricated by oil from an automatic oil pump. The rate of oil flow depends upon engine speed and is not adjustable. Recommended chain oil is GREEN MACHINE Bar and Chain Oil or new SAE 30 oil. Make sure the reservoir is filled at all times.

REPAIRS

CRANKCASE PRESSURE TEST. An improperly sealed crankcase can cause the engine to be hard to start, run rough, have low power and overheat. Refer to ENGINE SERVICE section of this manual for crankcase pressure test procedure. If crankcase leakage is indicated, pressurize the crankcase and use a solution of soap and water to check gasket, seals, pulse line and castings for leakage.

TIGHTENING TORQUE. Recommended tightening torque values are as follows.

Carburetor attaching
screws . . . . 3.4-4.5 N•m (30-40 in.-lb.)

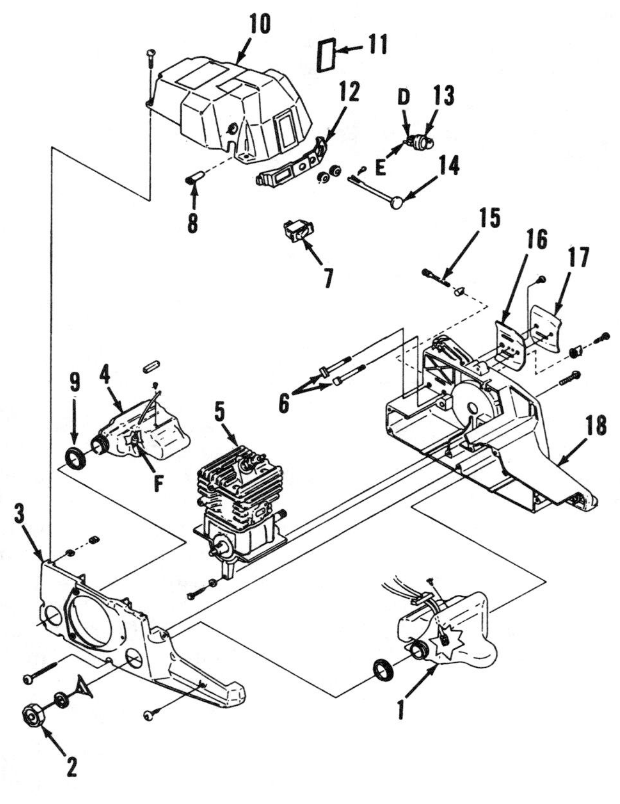

Fig. GM201—Exploded view of engine covers, fuel tank and oil tank.

1. Fuel tank
2. Tank cap
3. Engine side cover
4. Oil tank
5. Power head
6. Guide bar bolts
7. Ignition switch
8. Carburetor grommet
9. Tank dust seals
10. Cylinder cover
11. Air inlet screen
12. Control panel
13. Fuel primer bulb
14. Choke rod
15. Chain adjusting screw
16. Guide bar plate
17. Guide bar plate
18. Engine housing

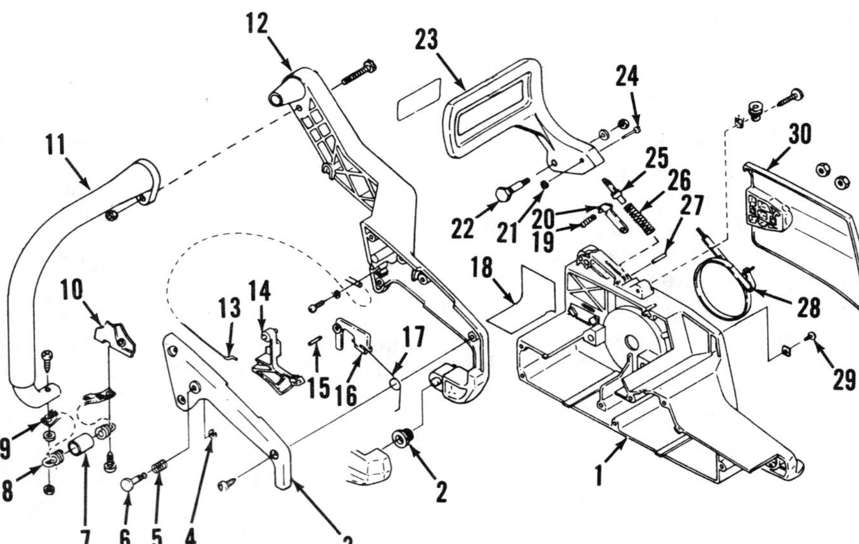

Fig. GM202—Exploded view of handle assembly and chain brake assembly.

1. Engine housing
2. Isolator
3. Handle cover
4. Retaining ring
5. Spring
6. Throttle lock pin
7. Sleeve
8. Spring
9. Spring retainer
10. Bracket
11. Handlebar
12. Handle
13. Throttle cable
14. Throttle trigger
15. Pin
16. Throttle lock
17. Throttle spring
18. Heat deflector
19. Spring
20. Brake latch
21. Retaining ring
22. Shoulder bolt
23. Chain brake lever
24. Pin
25. Brake adjuster
26. Compression spring
27. Pin
28. Brake band
29. Retaining screw
30. Drive case cover

Clutch drum nut . . . . 17-23 N•m (150-200 in.-lb.)
Clutch hub . . . . 17-23 N•m (150-200 in.-lb.)
Crankcase* . . . . 8-9 N•m (70-80 in.-lb.)
Flywheel . . 23-28 N•m (200-350 in.-lb.)
Ignition module/coil* . . . . . 5.4-6.6 N•m (45-55 in.-lb.)
Spark plug . . . . 14.4-22 N•m (120-180 in.-lb.)

* Apply thread locking compound to screw threads.

CRANKSHAFT, CONNECTING ROD AND CRANKCASE. To disassemble, remove guide bar and chain. Remove air filter assembly and detach the throttle cable from carburetor. Unbolt and remove handlebar assembly (11—Fig. GM202) and engine side cover (3—Fig. GM201).

Remove spark plug and install a piston stop tool or the end of a rope in spark plug hole to lock piston and prevent the crankshaft from turning. Unscrew clutch retaining nut (32—Fig. GM203), then remove drum (27). Use a suitable tool to unscrew the clutch hub (23) and remove the clutch assembly (23, 24 and 25). Both the nut (32) and clutch hub (23) have left-hand thread (turn clockwise to remove). Remove flywheel attaching nut (12) then use suitable puller to remove flywheel. The flywheel nut has right-hand threads.

Remove chain brake band retaining screw (29—Fig. GM202). Push brake lever (23) forward and remove engagement pin (24) from handle. Use a screwdriver to twist and release brake adjuster (25) and compression spring (26) from brake latch (20). Unscrew brake adjuster from brake band and remove brake band.

Remove engine housing mounting screws, disconnect oil line from automatic oil pump and separate engine housing (1) from engine. Remove fuel tank (1—Fig. GM201) and oil tank (4). Unbolt and remove oil pump (15—Fig. GM203) and worm gear (22). Remove ignition module, carburetor and muffler.

Remove crankcase mounting screws and tap crankcase with a plastic mallet to separate crankcase assembly. Remove crankshaft, connecting rod and piston assembly. Remove piston pin retaining ring (37) and push piston pin (36) out of piston (35).

Remove crankshaft seals (16 and 21). Check ball bearings (18) for roughness or binding and renew as necessary. Inspect crankshaft and connecting rod (20) for scoring or for discoloration caused by overheating and renew as necessary. Crankshaft and connecting rod are available only as an assembly.

When reassembling, install piston on connecting rod so piston ring locating pin is facing intake port. Make certain that piston pin retaining rings (37—Fig. GM203) fit tightly in groove in piston boss.

When installing new bearings on crankshaft, heat bearings to 350 degrees F (180 degrees C) using either an oil bath or a heat gun (do not use an open flame). Lubricate lip of seals (16

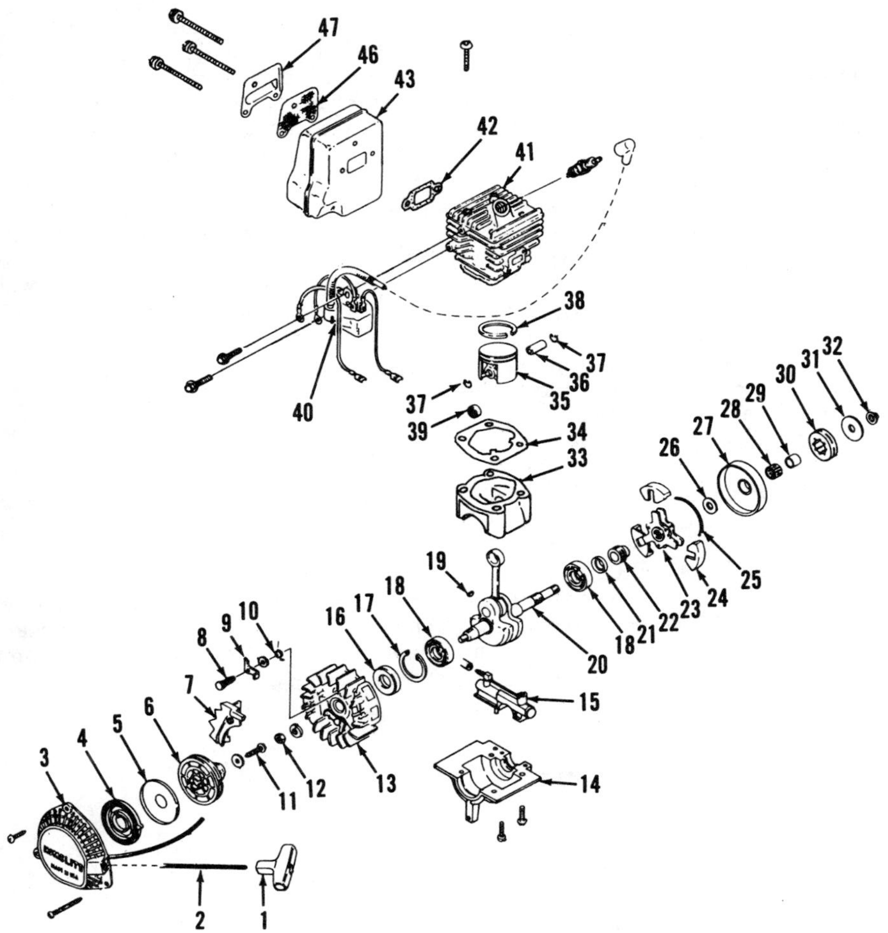

Fig. GM203—Exploded view of the engine, clutch and rewind starter.

1. Rope handle
2. Rope
3. Starter housing
4. Rewind spring
5. Spring cup
6. Pulley
7. Side housing
8. Shoulder bolt
9. Starter pawl
10. Spring
11. Screw
12. Nut
13. Flywheel
14. Crankcase
15. Oil pump
16. Seal
17. Snap ring
18. Bearings
19. Key
20. Crankshaft & connecting rod assy.
21. Seal
22. Worm gear
23. Clutch hub
24. Clutch shoe
25. Spring
26. Thrust washer
27. Clutch drum & sprocket
28. Needle bearing
29. Bearing inner race
30. Sprocket
31. Washer
32. Nut
33. Crankcase half
34. Gasket
35. Piston
36. Piston pin
37. Retaining rings
38. Piston ring
39. Roller bearing
40. Ignition module
41. Cylinder
42. Gasket
43. Muffler body
46. Spark arrestor screen
47. Cover

and 21) with oil before installing on crankshaft.

Apply light film of oil to cylinder and piston. Apply light coat of sealer to the mating surface of crankcase and outer edge of bearing bore on clutch side of crankcase. Do not apply any oil or sealer to outer diameter of large oil seal (16) on ignition side of crankshaft. Insert piston into cylinder, making sure that piston ring end gap is positioned around locating pin in piston ring groove and facing the intake port.

Be sure that bearing retaining ring (17) is positioned in groove in crankcase and that tapered side of crankshaft is on same side as ignition module mounting bosses on cylinder. Outer surface of large oil seal (16) should be flush with outer surface of crankcase. Apply thread locking compound to the crankcase screws before tightening to the torque listed in the TIGHTENING TORQUE paragraph. Complete engine assembly by reversing disassembly procedure.

PISTON, PIN, RINGS AND CYLINDER. The cylinder (41—Fig. GM203) is attached to crankcase by four screws. Refer to CONNECTING ROD, CRANKSHAFT AND CRANKCASE section for disassembly procedure. After removing cylinder, inspect cylinder bore for excessive wear, scoring or other damage and renew as necessary.

The piston pin (36) is retained by clips (37) at both ends of pin. A renewable type needle bearing (39) that is located in connecting rod supports the piston pin. Renew piston pin and/or needle bearing if worn or damaged.

A single piston ring (38) is used. A locating pin is located in piston ring groove to prevent piston ring from rotating in the groove. When assembling piston on connecting rod, be sure locating pin is positioned on intake port side (away from the exhaust side of engine). Make certain that piston ring end gap fits around its locating pin when installing piston in cylinder.

CLUTCH. To remove clutch assembly, first remove spark plug and install piston stop tool or insert end of a rope in cylinder to act as a piston stop. Remove the drive case cover (30—Fig. GM202), guide bar and chain.

The clutch drum nut (32—Fig. GM203) and clutch hub (23) both have left-hand threads and are removed by turning clockwise. Remove clutch drum nut (32), washer (31), needle bearing (28 and 29), clutch drum (27) and thrust washer (26). Use clutch tool to unscrew clutch hub (23) from crankshaft.

If disassembly is required, disconnect spring (25) and separate clutch shoes (24) from hub. The hub and shoes are available as an assembly including the spring.

Inspect clutch components for wear or damage and renew as necessary. When assembling clutch, position spring ends in open area between two of the clutch shoes. Install clutch assembly with open side facing outward. Lubricate needle bearing with all-temperature multipurpose grease. Tighten clutch hub and clutch retaining nut to the torque listed in the TIGHTENING TORQUE paragraph.

CHAIN OILER PUMP. Saw is equipped with an automatic chain oiler system. The oil pump (15—Fig. GM203) is mounted on the crankcase and driven by worm gear (22). To remove oil pump, it is necessary to separate power head (5—Fig. GM201) from engine side cover (3) and housing (18).

Inspect pump for wear or damage. Rotate pump plunger gear and make sure plunger moves back and forth in pump body. The pump is serviced only as a complete assembly.

A filter (F—Fig. GM201) is located on end of oil pickup line. Make sure filter is clean and oil line is not damaged. A "duckbill" check valve that is pressed into oil tank wall vents the oil tank (4). Be sure that check valve opens properly.

REWIND STARTER. To service rewind starter, remove starter housing (3—Fig. GM203) from engine cover. Pull starter rope and hold rope pulley with notch in pulley adjacent to rope outlet. Pull rope back through outlet so it engages notch in pulley and allow pulley to slowly unwind to relieve spring tension.

Unscrew pulley retaining screw (11) and remove rope pulley being careful not to dislodge rewind spring (4) in housing. Care must be taken if rewind spring is removed to prevent injury if spring is allowed to uncoil uncontrolled.

Rope length is 46 inches (117 cm). Rope is wound on rope pulley in clockwise direction as viewed with pulley in housing. To place tension on rewind spring, pass rope though rope outlet in housing and install rope handle. Pull rope out and hold rope pulley so notch on pulley is adjacent to rope outlet. Pull rope back through outlet between notch in pulley and housing. Turn rope pulley in clockwise direction two turns to place tension on spring. Release pulley and check starter action.

Do not place more tension on rewind spring than is necessary to draw rope handle up against housing. After starter is assembled, pull rope all the way out, then try to rotate pulley clockwise by hand. If pulley will not rotate, spring is bottomed out and pulley should be turned in counterclockwise direction one turn to relieve tension from spring.

CHAIN BRAKE. The chain brake system designed to stop chain movement should kickback occur. The chain brake is activated when operator's hand strikes chain brake lever (23—Fig. GM202). When activated (engaged), the brake band (28) is drawn around clutch drum by spring (26).

To disassemble chain brake, remove guide bar and chain. Remove brake band retaining screw (29). Push lever (23) forward, remove retaining ring (21) and drive engagement pin (24) out of lever. Place a screwdriver between brake band adjuster (25) and brake latch (20) and twist screwdriver to release the adjuster from the latch. Unscrew adjuster from brake band (28) and remove brake band. Drive dowel pin out of engine housing to remove brake latch (20) and spring (19).

Renew any component found that is excessively worn or damaged. Lubricate all pivot points with Molykote or suitable equivalent.

When reassembling, thread adjuster (25) on brake band (28) until clutch drum cannot be turned by hand then loosen adjuster until drum just turns freely. The chain brake should stop saw chain instantly when engaged. Brake band should not contact clutch drum when disengaged.

HOMELITE

Model	Bore mm (in.)	Stroke mm (in.)	Displacement cc (cu. in.)	Drive Type
EZ	36.5 (1.4375)	33 (1.3)	34.4 (2.1)	Direct
Super EZ, Super EZ AO	39.7 (1.5625)	33.3 (1.3125)	40.9 (2.5)	Direct

MAINTENANCE

SPARK PLUG. A Champion DJ-6J spark plug with tapered seat is used; no gasket is required. Adjust electrode gap to 0.025 inch (0.63 mm).

CARBURETOR. A Walbro Model HDC diaphragm type carburetor is used on all models. Refer to Walbro section of CARBURETOR SERVICE section for overhaul and exploded view of carburetor.

For initial carburetor adjustment, back idle speed adjusting screw out until throttle valve will completely close, then turn screw back in until it contacts idle stop plus ½ turn additional. Turn both fuel adjusting needles in until lightly seated, then back main fuel needle (located to left and marked "HI" on grommet when viewing adjustment needle side of throttle handle) out about one turn and back idle ("LO") needle out about ¾ turn. Start engine, readjust idle speed and fuel needles so engine idles at just below clutch engagement speed. With engine running at full throttle under load, readjust main fuel needle so engine will run at highest obtainable speed without excessive smoke.

To adjust starting speed (speed at which engine will run with throttle latch engaged), stop engine and remove chain, guide bar, air filter cover and air filter. Open trigger adjusting screw ⅛ turn clockwise. With trigger latched, start engine and run at half throttle (not at high speed) for 30-50 seconds to warm it up. Release throttle trigger, then latch it while engine is running. If engine stops, restart it. With throttle trigger latched, gently hold trigger down and slowly back trigger adjusting screw out counterclockwise until engine falters, then turn screw back in 1/16 turn clockwise. Squeeze and release trigger to idle engine, then shut engine off with stop switch. Try to restart engine; if hard to start, open screw another 1/16 turn at a time until enough for consistent starting. When starting speed is satisfactorily adjusted, stop engine and reinstall guide bar, chain, air filter and filter cover. If engine will start readily and saw chain does not turn or only turns slowly, adjustment is correct. If chain turns rapidly with throttle latched, repeat adjustment procedure to set starting speed slower.

MAGNETO AND TIMING. A conventional flywheel type magneto ignition system is used on early models while later Super EZ Automatic models are equipped with solid-state ignition. The solid-state ignition system is serviced by renewing the spark plug and/or ignition module. Air gap between ignition module and flywheel is adjustable. Adjust air gap by loosening module retaining screws and place a 0.015 inch (0.38 mm) shim stock between flywheel and module. Remove shim stock.

Note the following on breaker point equipped models: Breaker points are contained in a breaker-box under the flywheel. Ignition timing is not adjustable. Breaker point gap should be 0.015 inch (0.38 mm) and must be correct or ignition timing will be affected. Condenser capacity should be approximately 0.2 mfd. Air gap between flywheel and coil should be 0.015 inch (0.38 mm).

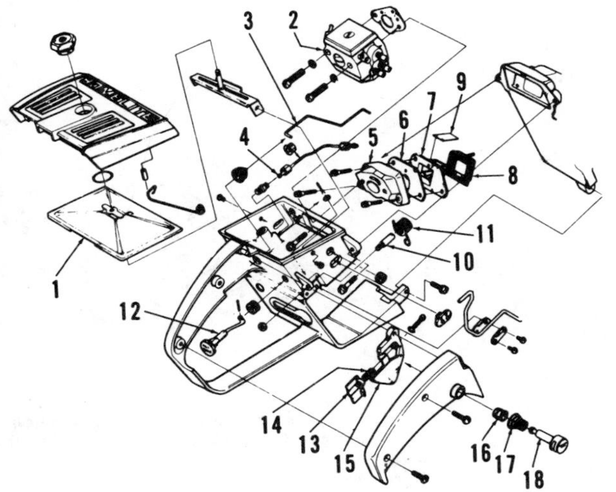

Fig. HL1—Exploded view of handle assembly and related assemblies.

1. Air filter
2. Carburetor
3. Throttle rod
4. Oil line
5. Spacer
6. Gasket
7. Reed valve seat
8. Reed retainer
9. Reed petals
10. Spring post
11. Spring
12. Choke rod
13. Throttle stop
14. Spring
15. Trigger
16. Bushing
17. Spring
18. Throttle latch

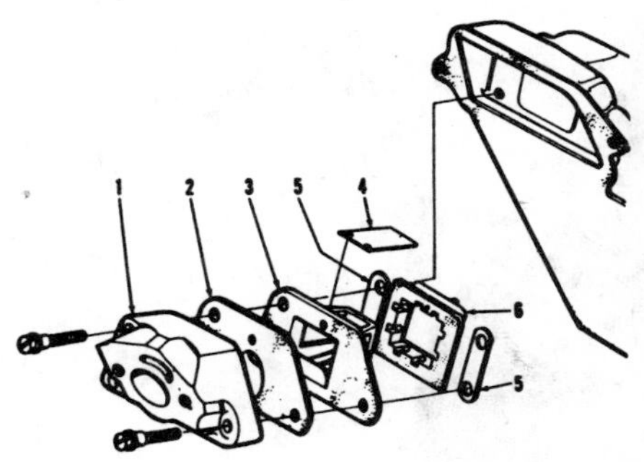

Fig. HL2—View showing reed valve and spacer used prior to assembly shown in Fig. HL1.

1. Reed spacer
2. Gasket
3. Reed seat
4. Valve reeds
5. Spacers
6. Reed retainer

CARBON. Carbon deposits should be removed from muffler and exhaust ports at regular intervals. When scraping carbon, be careful not to damage chamfered edges of exhaust ports or scratch piston. A wooden scraper should be used. Turn engine so piston is at top dead center to prevent carbon from falling into cylinder. Do not attempt to run engine with muffler removed.

LUBRICATION. The engine is lubricated by mixing oil with unleaded gasoline. Recommended oil is Homelite two-stroke oil mixed at ratio as designated on oil container. If Homelite oil is not available, a good quality oil designed for two-stroke engines may be used when mixed at a 16:1 ratio, however, an antioxidant fuel stabilizer (such as Sta-Bil) should be added to fuel mix. Antioxidant fuel stabilizer is not required with Homelite® oils as they contain fuel stabilizer so the fuel mix will stay fresh up to one year.

Fill chain oiler reservoir with Homelite® Bar and Chain oil or with light weight motor oil (not over SAE 30). In cold weather, thin oil with kerosene until it will flow freely.

The clutch needle roller bearing should be cleaned and relubricated after each 100 hours of use. A high temperature grease such as Homelite® ALL-TEMP Multipurpose Grease or equivalent should be used.

REPAIRS

TIGHTENING TORQUES. Recommended tightening torques are listed in the following table.

Fastener	Torque
4/40 Flange bearing	5-6 in.-lbs. (0.6-0.7 N•m)
6/32 Compression release clamp	20-24 in.-lbs. (2.3-2.7 N•m)
6/32 Compression release post nut	20-24 in.-lbs. (2.3-2.7 N•m)
6/32 Breaker-box	20-24 in.-lbs. (2.3-2.7 N•m)
6/32 Breaker-point adjustable arm	20-24 in.-lbs. (2.3-2.7 N•m)
6/32 Condenser	20-24 in.-lbs. (2.3-2.7 N•m)
8/32 Air filter bracket	25-30 in.-lbs. (2.8-3.4 N•m)
8/32 Connecting rod	55-66 in.-lbs. (6.2-7.5 N•m)
8/32 Throttle handle cover	35-42 in.-lbs. (3.9-4.7 N•m)
8/32 Rewind spring cover	35-42 in.-lbs. (3.9-4.7 N•m)
8/32 Intake manifold (reed spacer)	20-24 in.-lbs. (2.3-2.7 N•m)
8/32 Coil assembly	20-24 in.-lbs. (2.3-2.7 N•m)
8/32 Automatic oiler pump	35-42 in.-lbs. (3.9-4.7 N•m)
8/32 Fuel tank	35-42 in.-lbs. (3.9-4.7 N•m)
10/32 Main bearing retainer screws	50-60 in.-lbs. (5.6-6.8 N•m)
10/32 Stack muffler	50-60 in.-lbs. (5.6-6.8 N•m)
10/32 Muffler body	50-60 in.-lbs. (5.6-6.8 N•m)
10/32 Muffler cap	35-42 in.-lbs. (3.9-4.7 N•m)
10/32 Starter housing	50-60 in.-lbs. (5.6-6.8 N•m)
10/32 Carburetor	20-24 in.-lbs. (2.3-2.7 N•m)
10/32 Starter pawl studs	50-60 in.-lbs. (5.6-6.8 N•m)
10/32 Handle bar	50-60 in.-lbs. (5.6-6.8 N•m)
12/24 Throttle handle	80-96 in.-lbs. (9.0-10.8 N•m)
12/24 Fuel tank to crankcase	75-90 in.-lbs. (8.5-10.2 N•m)
12/24 Drivecase	75-90 in.-lbs. (8.5-10.2 N•m)
1/4-28 Cylinder nuts	100-120 in.-lbs. (11.3-13.6 N•m)
5/16-24 Rotor (flywheel) nut	100-120 in.-lbs. (11.3-13.6 N•m)
14 mm Spark plug	120-144 in.-lbs. (11.3-16.3 N•m)
Clutch	180-216 in.-lbs. (20.3-24.4 N•m)

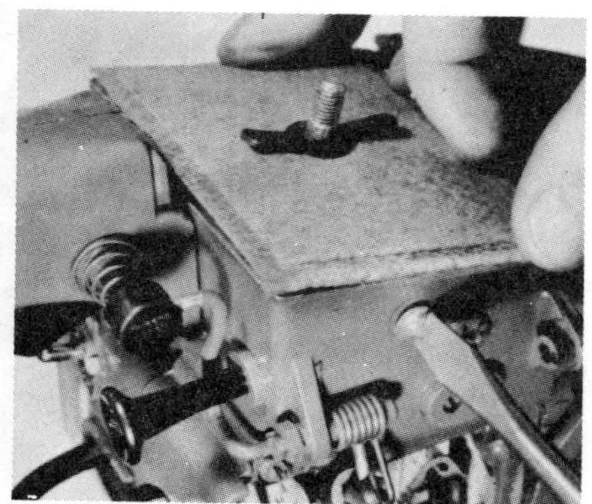

Fig. HL3 – Before tightening screws retaining air filter bracket in throttle handle, place air filter element on bracket stud and align filter with edges of air box.

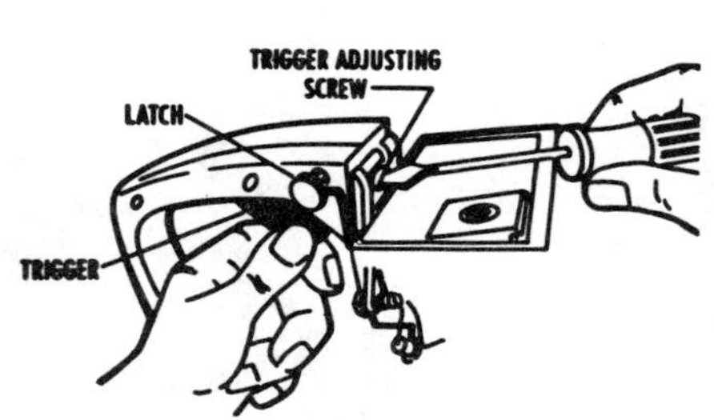

Fig. HL4 – Refer to text for procedures to adjust starting speed.

SPECIAL SERVICE TOOLS. Special service tools which may be required are listed as follows:

Tool No. Description & Model Usage

24299 – Anvil, crankshaft installation.
24300 – Sleeve, crankshaft bearing.
24294 – Plug, needle bearing assembly.
24292 – Plug, seal removal.
24298 – Plug, bearing and seal.
24320 – #3 Pozidriv screwdriver bit.
24982-1 – Torx driver bit.
A-24290 – Bracket, rotor remover.
A-24060 – Wrench, clutch spanner.
A-24309 – Jackscrew, crankshaft and bearing.
23136-1 – Body for A-24309.
24295 – Bearing collar for A-24309.
24291 – Sleeve, drivecase seal.

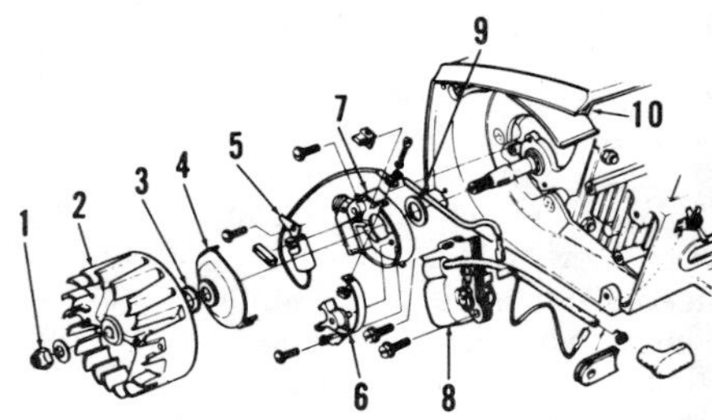

Fig. HL5 – Exploded view of ignition assembly. Felt seal (3) is cemented to breaker-box cover (4).

1. Nut
2. Flywheel
3. Felt seal
4. Box cover
5. Condenser
6. Breaker-points
7. Breaker-box
8. Ignition coil
9. Felt seal
10. Fuel tank

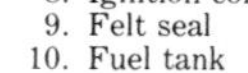

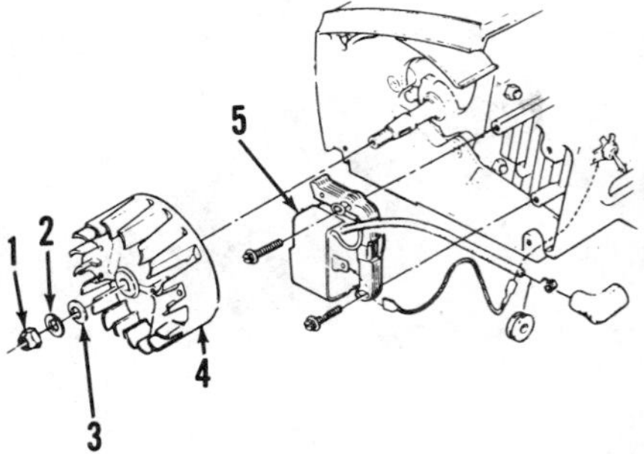

Fig. HL6 – Exploded view of solid-state ignition used on later Super EZ Automatic models.

1. Nut
2. Lockwasher
3. Washer
4. Flywheel
5. Ignition module

24297 – Sleeve, crankcase seal.
JA-31316-4 – Test spark plug.
17789 – Carburetor repair tool kit.
A-93791 – Wrench, "S" clutch.
94197 – Carburetor tester.
94194 – Compression gage.

COMPRESSION PRESSURE. For optimum performance of Model Super EZ Automatic, cylinder compression pressure should be 155-185 psi (1069-1275 kPa) with engine at normal operating temperature. Engine should be inspected and repaired when compression pressure is 90 psi (620 kPa) or below.

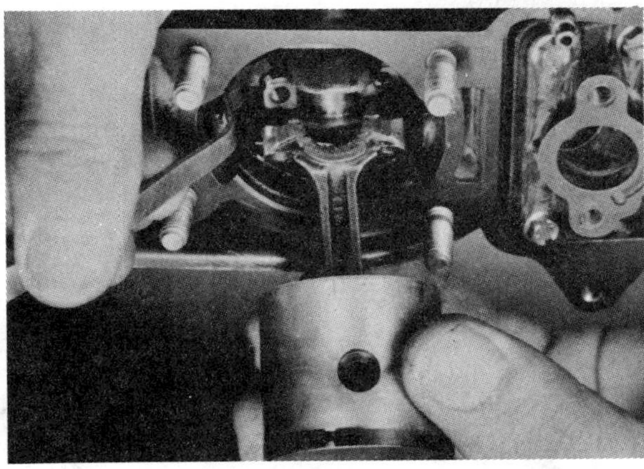

Fig. HL8 – Installing piston and connecting rod assembly using locally made tool to hold rod cap in position. Tool can be made from flat strip of metal. Using grease, stick 14 rollers in cap and 14 rollers in rod; make sure that match marks on rod and cap are aligned.

CONNECTING ROD. Connecting rod and piston assembly can be detached from crankshaft after removing cylinder; refer to Fig. HL8. Be careful to remove all of the 28 loose needle bearing rollers.

Renew connecting rod if bent, twisted or if crankpin bearing surface shows visible wear or is scored. The needle roller bearing for piston pin should be renewed if any roller shows flat spots or if worn so that any two rollers can be separated the width equal to thickness of one roller and if rod is otherwise serviceable. Press on lettered side of bearing cage only when removing and installing bearing.

The crankpin needle rollers should be renewed at each overhaul. To install connecting rod, refer to Fig. HL8. Stick 14 rollers in cap with grease. Support rod cap in crankcase, then place rod over crankpin and to cap with match marks aligned and install new retaining cap screws.

PISTON, PIN AND RINGS. The piston has two pinned piston rings. The rings should be renewed whenever engine is disassembled for service.

Piston pin is retained in piston by "Rulon" plastic plugs. Insert a plug at each end of pin in piston bore and be sure piston pin and plugs are centered in piston.

Assemble piston to connecting rod so piston ring locating pin is toward intake side (away from exhaust port).

CYLINDER. The cylinder can be unbolted and removed from crankcase after removing starter housing and throttle handle. Be careful not to let piston strike crankcase as cylinder is removed.

The cylinder bore is chrome plated and cylinder should be renewed if the chrome plating has worn through exposing the softer base metal. Also inspect for cracks and damage to compression release valve bore.

CRANKSHAFT, BEARINGS AND SEALS. Crankshaft is supported by a roller bearing (19 – Fig. HL7) mounted in crankcase bore and by a ball bearing (23) mounted in drivecase (18).

To remove crankshaft, first remove clutch assembly, automatic oil pump on models so equipped, starter housing, magneto rotor, throttle handle, cylinder, piston and connecting rod assembly and the fuel/oil tank assembly. Remove retaining screws and separate drivecase and crankshaft from crankcase.

NOTE: Use "Pozidriv" or "Torx" screwdriver bit, according to type of screw head, only when removing drivecase to fuel tank cover screw (25).

Remove the two main bearing retaining screws (21) and bearing retainers (22), then push crankshaft and ball bearing (23) from drivecase. Remove snap ring (24) and press crankshaft from ball bearing.

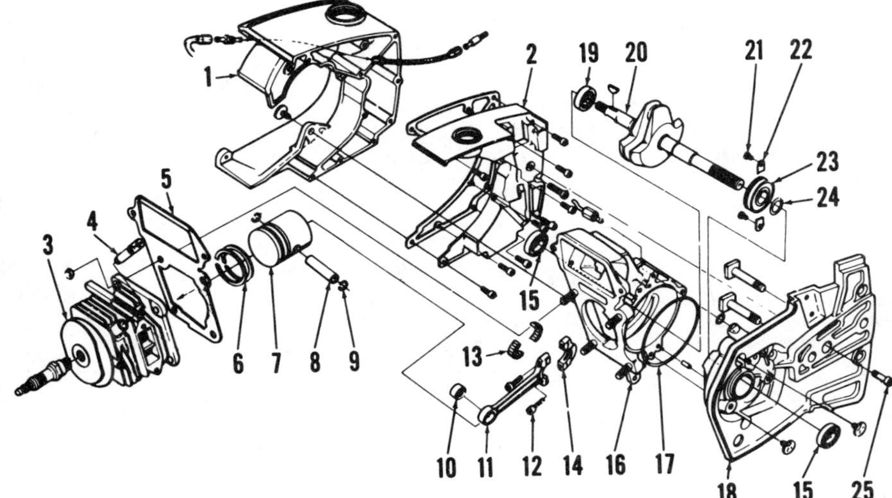

Fig. HL7 – Exploded view of typical engine assembly.

1. Fuel tank
2. Oil tank
3. Cylinder
4. Compression release valve
5. Gasket
6. Piston rings
7. Piston
8. Piston pin
9. Pin retainer
10. Needle bearing
11. Connecting rod
12. Cap screw
13. Bearing rollers (28)
14. Connecting rod cap
15. Seal
16. Crankcase
17. "O" ring
18. Drivecase
19. Roller bearing
20. Crankshaft
21. Screw
22. Bearing retainer
23. Ball bearing
24. Snap ring
25. Screw

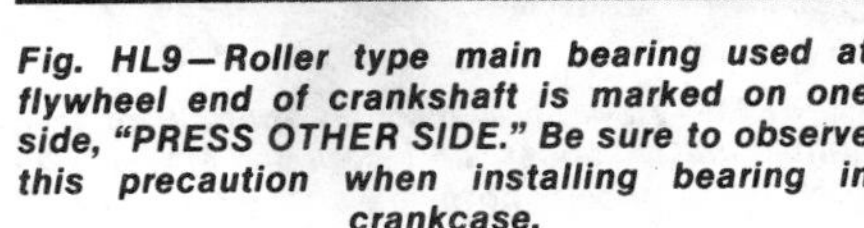

Fig. HL9 – Roller type main bearing used at flywheel end of crankshaft is marked on one side, "PRESS OTHER SIDE." Be sure to observe this precaution when installing bearing in crankcase.

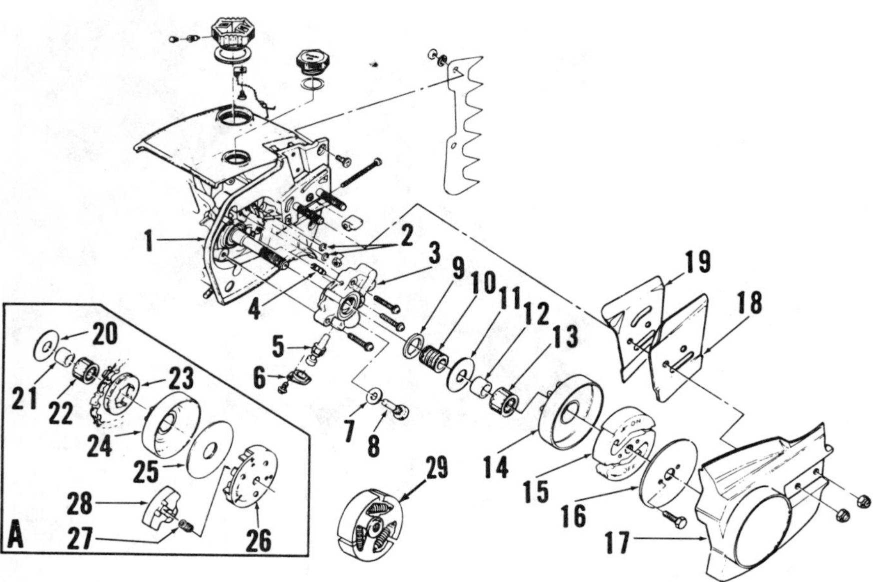

Fig. HL10—Exploded view of automatic oil pump and clutch assemblies. Inset A shows three-shoe type clutch. Sprocket (23) and clutch drum (24) are integral on some models. Clutch assembly (29) is later three-shoe type.

1. Drivecase
2. "O" rings
3. Oil pump body
4. Tube
5. Gear
6. Cap
7. Gasket
8. Cam screw
9. Seal
10. Worm gear
11. Thrust washer
12. Inner race
13. Bearing
14. Clutch drum
15. Hub
16. Cover
17. Drivecase cover
18. Outer guide plate
19. Inner guide plate
20. Thrust washer
21. Inner race
22. Bearing
23. Sprocket
24. Clutch drum
25. Thrust washer
26. Clutch hub
27. Spring
28. Clutch shoe
29. Clutch assy.

Fig. HL10A—View of correct installation of "S" type clutch hub in drum.

When reassembling, be sure groove in outer race of ball bearing is towards crankpin and that retaining snap ring is seated in groove on crankshaft. Install new seals (15) with lip of seal inward. Using protector sleeve to prevent damage to seal, press the crankshaft and ball bearing into drivecase and install new retaining screws and washers. Assemble crankcase to crankshaft and drivecase using new "O" ring (17) and protector sleeve to prevent damage to crankcase seal. Be sure bar studs are in place before installing fuel tank.

COMPRESSION RELEASE. When throttle lock is pushed in, a lever connected to throttle lock lifts away from compression release valve (4–Fig. HL7). When engine is cranked, compression forces valve open and compression is partly relieved through port in cylinder. Squeezing throttle trigger after engine is running releases throttle lock, allowing spring (11–Fig. HL1) to snap lever against release valve, closing the valve.

Service of compression release valve usually consists of cleaning valve seat and port in cylinder as carbon may gradually fill the port.

When overhauling engine, cylinder should be inspected for any damage to compression release port.

PYRAMID REED VALVE. A "Delrin" plastic pyramid type reed intake valve seat and four reeds are used. Reeds are retained on pins projecting from the reed seat by a moulded retainer. Inspect reed seat, retainer and reeds for any distortion, excessive wear or other damage.

To reinstall, use a drop of oil to stick each reed to the plastic seat, then push reed retainer down over the seat and reeds. Then install the assembly in crankcase; never install retainer, then attempt to install reed seat and reeds.

AUTOMATIC CHAIN OILER PUMP. Refer to Fig. HL10 for exploded view showing automatic chain oiler pump installation. After removing clutch, the pump can be removed from crankshaft and drivecase. The pump body, flange and plunger are available as a complete pump assembly, less worm gear, only. Check valve parts, cam screw and worm gear are available separately. If pump body and/or plunger are scored or excessively worn, it will be necessary to install a new pump.

CLUTCH. Refer to Fig. HL10 for exploded view of types of clutches used. Early models were equipped with three-shoe clutch shown in Inset A. "S" type clutch (15) was used next and later

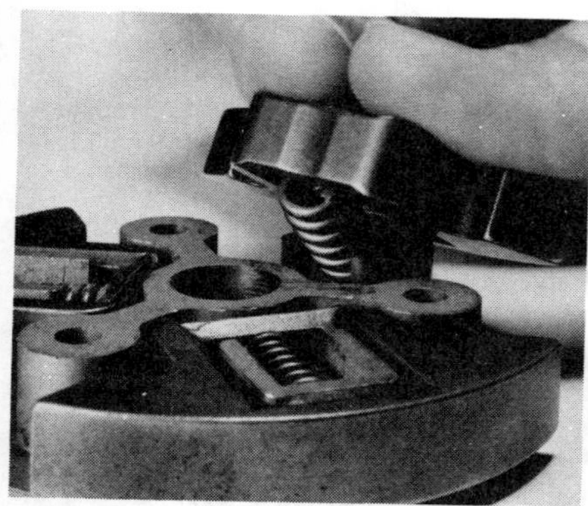

Fig. HL11—View showing easy method of installing clutch shoes and springs. Model EZ clutch is not shown; however, method is same.

Fig. HL12—Exploded view of rewind starter used on early models.

1. Stud
2. Spring
3. Pawl
4. Washer
5. Nut
6. Flywheel
7. Cover
8. Spring shield
9. Spring lock
10. Rewind spring
11. Spring shield
12. Snap ring
13. Rope pulley
14. Washer
15. Bushing
16. Screen
17. Starter housing
18. Rope handle

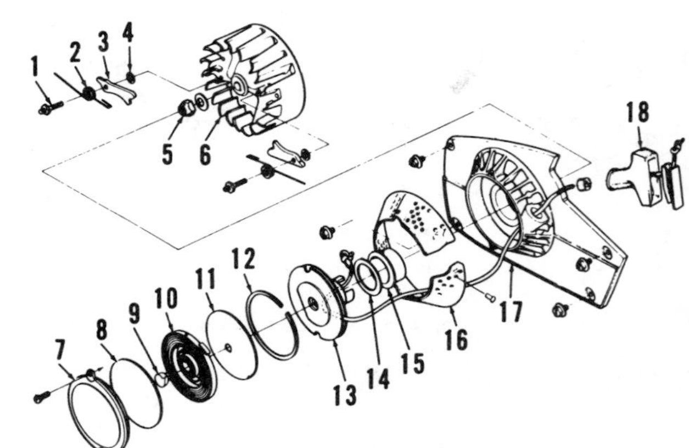

models are equipped with three-shoe clutch (29).

The clutch hub on all types has left hand threads. Special tool A-93791 may be used when removing or installing "S" type clutch while tool A-24060 may be used when removing or installing three-shoe type clutch.

Clean and inspect clutch hub, drum and bearing for damage or excessive wear. Inspect crankshaft for wear or damage caused by a defective clutch bearing. Refer to Fig. HL10A for correct installation of "S" type clutch. Tighten "S" clutch hub to 100 in.-lbs. (11.3 N·m).

Install clutch shoes on early three-shoe clutch as shown in Fig. HL11. Install either three-shoe clutch so "OFF" on hub faces out. Tighten early three-shoe clutch hub (26 – Fig. HL10) to 180 in.-lbs. (20.3 N·m). Tighten later clutch hub (29) to 250-300 in.-lbs. (28.2-33.9 N·m).

REWIND STARTER. Exploded view of early production rewind starter is shown in Fig. HL12 and late production rewind starter is shown in Fig. HL13. Starter can be removed as a complete unit by removing housing retaining screws.

To disassemble starter on early models, hold cover (7 – Fig. HL12) while removing retaining screws, then allow cover to turn slowly until spring tension is released. Remainder of disassembly is evident from inspection of unit and with reference to exploded view.

To disassemble starter on late models, pull starter rope fully out, hold starter pulley (8 – Fig. HL13) from turning, pull all slack in rope out inner side of fan housing and allow pulley to unwind slowly until spring tension is relieved. Remainder of disassembly is evident from inspection of unit and with reference to exploded view.

Fig. HL14 shows correct installation of starter dogs on flywheel for early models, late models will be similar. When installing a new starter rope, knot rope ends and coat with Duxseal, then trim excess rope next to knot. Rewind spring is wound in clockwise direction in cover (7 – Fig. HL12) or housing (11 – Fig. HL13).

Set rewind spring tension as follows: On early models, turn cover (7 – Fig. HL12) in a clockwise direction to pull rope handle against starter housing, then continue turning cover three more times.

On late models, hook rope in notch on flywheel side of pulley (8 – Fig. 13), then pull up loop of cord between notch and housing (11). Turn pulley in a clockwise direction three turns and hold. Pull rope handle, removing all slack in rope and disengage rope from notch. Release rope handle. If handle is not snug against starter housing, repeat tensioning procedure turning pulley only one turn at a time.

MUFFLER. Some later Super EZ Automatic models may experience vapor lock due to exhaust gas directed toward drivecase cover. The air filter and carburetor may be discolored due to heat. Muffler #A96580 with deflector (D – Fig. HL15) may be installed to prevent hot exhaust gas from reaching drivecase cover.

Fig. HL14 – View showing proper installation of pawl springs.

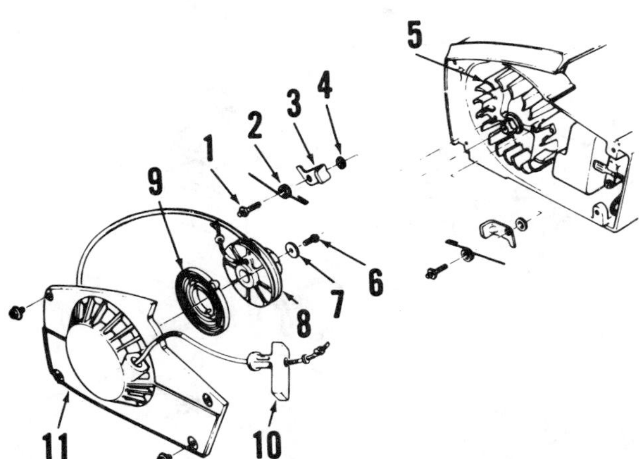

Fig. HL13 – Exploded view of rewind starter used on late models.

1. Stud
2. Spring
3. Pawl
4. Washer
5. Flywheel
6. Screw
7. Washer
8. Rope pulley
9. Rewind spring
10. Rope handle
11. Starter housing

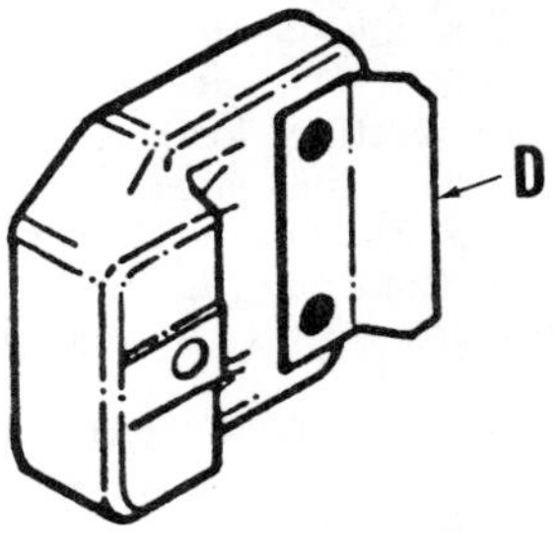

Fig. HL15 – View of Super EZ Automatic muffler #A96580 with exhaust gas deflector (D).

HOMELITE

Model	Bore mm (in.)	Stroke mm (in.)	Displacement cc (cu. in.)	Drive Type
XL-12	44.4 (1.75)	34.9 (1.375)	54.1 (3.3)	Direct
Super XL, Super XL-AO, SXL-AO, Old Blue, Big Red	46.0 (1.8125)	34.9 (1.375)	58.2 (3.55)	Direct

MAINTENANCE

SPARK PLUG. Model XL-12 is equipped with a Champion CJ8 spark plug while Model Super XL Automatic uses a CJ6. For heavy duty service, a Champion UTJ11P gold-paladium tip spark plug can be used.

For all models, set spark plug electrode gap to 0.025 inch (0.63 mm).

CARBURETOR. A Tillotson HS, Walbro SDC or Zama diaphragm carburetor is used. Refer to CARBURETOR SERVICE section for service procedures and exploded views.

Initial adjustment of idle mixture screw is 1¾ turns open and for high speed mixture screw is 1¼ turns open. Adjust idle mixture screw and idle speed screw so engine idles just below clutch engagement speed. Make high speed mixture adjustment with engine warm and under cutting load. It may be necessary to readjust one mixture screw after adjusting the other mixture screw as the functions of the idle and high speed mixture screws are related.

MAGNETO AND TIMING. A Wico or Phelon flywheel type magneto with external armature is used on early models while late models are equipped with solid state ignition. The solid state ignition system is serviced by renewing the spark plug and/or ignition module. Air gap between ignition module and flywheel is adjustable. Adjust air gap by loosening module retaining screws and place a 0.015 inch (0.38 mm) shim stock between flywheel and module. Remove shim stock.

Note the following on breaker-point equipped models: Units equipped with Phelon magneto will have a letter "P" stamped after the serial number. The Wico and Phelon magnetos are similarly constructed, so care should be taken to properly identify magneto before ordering service parts. Breaker-points and condenser are located behind flywheel.

Armature core and stator plate are riveted together and are serviced only as a unit. Stator plate fits firmly on shoulder of crankcase; hence, armature air gap is nonadjustable.

Late production Wico magneto stator plates are built to retain a felt seal (5–Fig. HL33); the seal cannot be used with early production Wico stator plates. All Phelon stator plates are built to retain the felt seal (5).

Magneto stator plate has slotted mounting holes, and should be rotated as far clockwise as possible before tightening mounting screws to obtain correct ignition timing of 30 degrees BTDC. Set breaker point gap to 0.015 inch (0.38 mm). Condenser capacity should test 0.16-0.20 mfd.

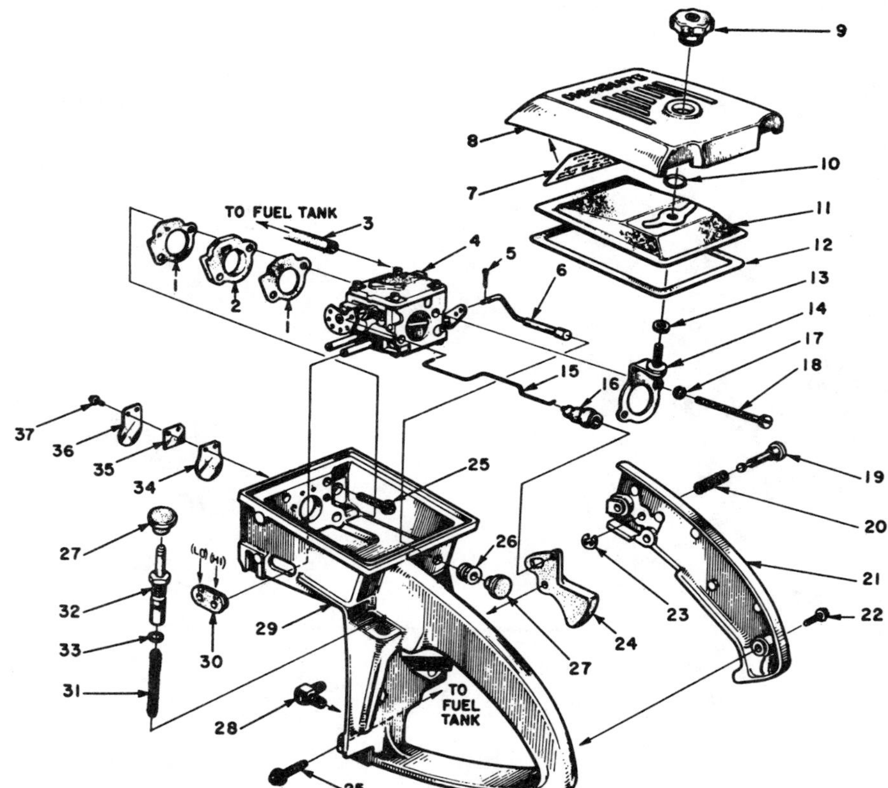

Fig. HL30—Exploded view of air box (throttle handle) and related parts on models with flat reed intake valve (34). Refer to Fig. HL31 for models equipped with pyramid reed valve.

1. Gasket
2. Insulator
3. Fuel line
4. Carburetor
5. Cotter pin
6. Choke rod
8. Filter cover
9. Nut
10. Snap ring
11. Filter element
12. Gasket
13. Gasket
14. Bracket
15. Throttle rod
16. Boot
19. Throttle latch pin
20. Spring
23. Snap ring
24. Throttle trigger
26. Grommet
27. Choke button
28. Check valve
29. Air box
30. Grommet
31. Spring
32. Pump plunger
33. "O" ring
34. Reed valve
35. Reed back-up
36. Reed stop

CAUTION: Be careful when installing breaker-points not to bend tension spring any more than necessary; if spring is bent excessively, spring tension may be reduced causing improper breaker-point operation. Late Wico units have a retaining clip and flat washer to secure breaker arm on pivot post.

LUBRICATION. The engine is lubricated mixing oil with unleaded gasoline. Recommended oil is Homelite® two-stroke oil mixed at ratio as designated on oil container. If Homelite® oil is not available, a good quality oil designed for two-stroke engines may be used when mixed at a 16:1 ratio, however, an antioxidant fuel stabilizer (such as Sta-Bil) should be added to fuel mix. Antioxidant fuel stabilizer is not required with Homelite® oils as they contain fuel stabilizer so the fuel mix will stay fresh up to one year.

Fill chain oiler reservoir with Homelite® Bar and Chain oil or a light weight oil (no heavier than SAE 30). In cold weather, chain oil can be diluted with kerosene to allow easier flow of oil through pump and lines.

CARBON. Muffler and cylinder exhaust ports should be cleaned periodically to prevent loss of power due to carbon build up. Remove muffler and scrape free of carbon. With muffler removed, turn engine so that piston is at top dead center and carefully remove carbon from exhaust ports with a wooden scraper. Be careful not to damage chamfered edges of exhaust ports or to scratch piston. **Do not** run engine with muffler removed.

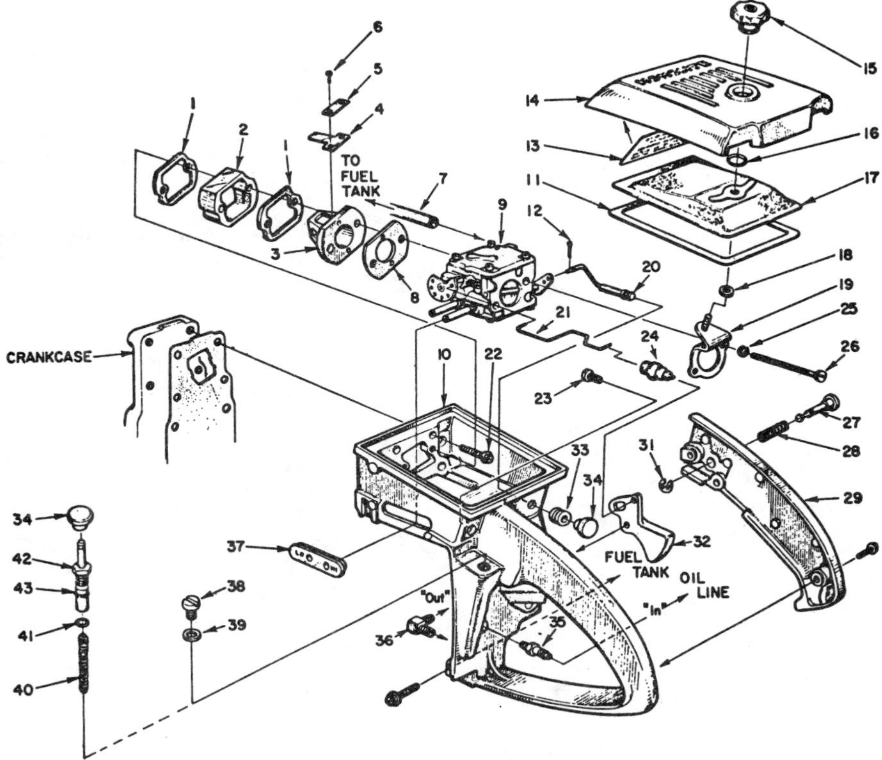

Fig. HL31 — Exploded view of air box and throttle handle assembly for models equipped with pyramid reed type intake valve. Idle speed adjusting screw (23) on some models, is located in air box instead of on carburetor body; remove idle speed adjusting screw and spring from new service carburetor before installing carburetor on these models. Early type aluminum reed seat is shown; refer to Fig. HL32 for late type plastic (Delrin) seat and moulded reed retainer.

1. Gaskets
2. Spacer
3. Reed seat
4. Valve reeds (4)
5. Retaining plates
7. Fuel line
8. Gasket
9. Carburetor
10. Air box
11. Gasket
14. Cover
17. Filter
18. Gasket
19. Bracket
20. Choke rod
21. Throttle rod
23. Idle speed screw
24. Boot
27. Throttle latch pin
28. Spring
29. Handle cover
31. Snap ring
32. Throttle trigger
33. Grommet
35. "In" check valve
36. "Out" check valve
37. Grommet
38. Plug (AO models)
39. Gasket
40. Spring (manual oiler)
41. "O" ring
43. Manual pump plunger
43. "O" ring

REPAIRS

TIGHTENING TORQUE VALUES. Tightening torque values are as follows:

4/40 Reed & stop to chamber . . . . 5-6 in.-lbs. (0.6-0.7 N·m)
4/20 Oil line plate or shield to tank . . . . 5-6 in.-lbs. (0.6-0.7 N·m)
8/32 Throttle handle cover . . . . 40-48 in.-lbs. (4.5-5.4 N·m)
8/36 Connecting rod . . . . . . 55-66 in.-lbs. (6.2-7.5 N·m)
10/32 Muffler cap . . . . 50-60 in.-lbs. (5.6-6.8 N·m)
10/32 Bearing retainer . . . . 55-66 in.-lbs. (6.2-7.5 N·m)
10/32 Screen to rotor . . . . . 50-60 in.-lbs. (5.6-6.8 N·m)
10/32 Drivecase cover . . . . . 55-66 in.-lbs. (6.2-7.5 N·m)

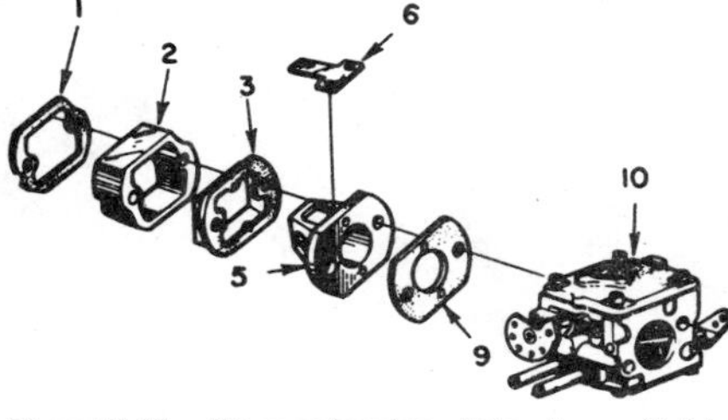

Fig. HL32 — View showing late type Delrin plastic reed seat (5) and moulded reed retainer (3). Reeds (6) are held on pins protruding from seat by the retainer. Refer to text for assembly instructions.

1. Gasket
2. Spacer
3. Reed retainer
5. Reed seat
6. Reeds (4)
9. Gasket
10. Carburetor

Fig. HL33 — Exploded view of Wico magneto used on some models. Phelon magneto used on other models is similar. Felt seal (5) is not used on early models.

1. Flywheel
2. Cover
3. Gasket
4. Breaker-points
5. Felt seal
6. Gasket
7. Condenser
8. Ignition coil
9. Coil clip
10. Armature core
11. Stator plate

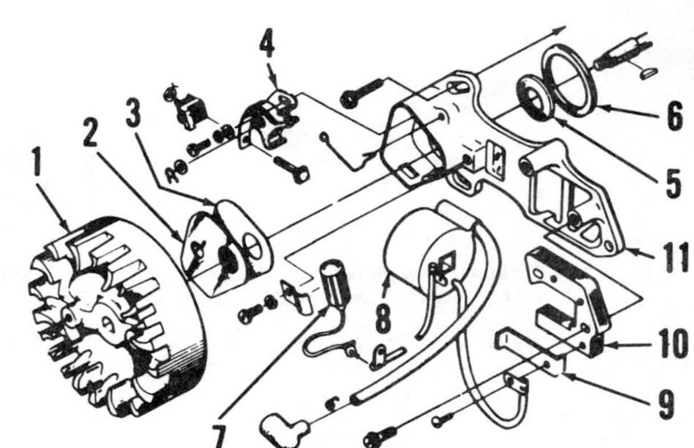

10/32 Pulley to fan housing . . . . 50-60 in.-lbs. (5.6-6.8 N·m)
10/32 Flanged inner race for pulley . . . . 55-66 in.-lbs. (6.2-7.5 N·m)
10/32 Carburetor to chamber . . . . 50-60 in.-lbs. (5.6-6.8 N·m)
12/24 Handle bar to fuel tank . . . . 80-96 in.-lbs. (9.0-10.8 N·m)
12/24 Bracket to drivecase . . . . 80-96 in.-lbs. (9.0-10.8 N·m)
12/24 Stator to crankcase and cylinder . . . . 80-96 in.-lbs. (9.0-10.8 N·m)
12/24 Drivecase to crankcase . . . . 80-96 in.-lbs. (9.0-10.8 N·m)
12/24 Carburetor chamber to fuel tank . . . . 80-96 in.-lbs. (9.0-10.8 N·m)
12/24 Muffler to cylinder . . 80-96 in.-lbs. (9.0-10.8 N·m)
1/4-20 Fuel tank to crankcase . . . . 80-96 in.-lbs. (9.0-10.8 N·m)
12/24 Fan housing to fuel tank . . . . 80-96 in.-lbs. (9.0-10.8 N·m)
1/4-28 Cylinder nuts . . . . 100-120 in.-lbs. (11.3-13.6 N·m)
12/24 Pawl studs to rotor . . . . 80-96 in.-lbs. (9.0-10.8 N·m)
1/4-20 Handle bar to bracket . . . . 100-120 in.-lbs. (11.3-13.6 N·m)
1/4-20 Bumper screws . . . . 80-96 in.-lbs. (9.0-10.8 N·m)
3/8-24 Clutch nut . . . . 150-180 in.-lbs. (16.9-20.3 N·m)
5/8-32 Clutch . . . . 150-180 in.-lbs. (16.9-20.3 N·m)
5/16-24 Rotor nut . . . . . . 150-180 in.-lbs. (16.9-20.3 N·m)
1/2-20 Clutch to crankshaft . . . . 150-180 in.-lbs. (16.9-20.3 N·m)
14 mm Spark plug . . . . . . 250-300 in.-lbs. (28.2-33.9 N·m)
Clutch spider . . . . 180-216 in.-lbs. (20.3-24.4 N·m)

HOMELITE SERVICE TOOLS. Listed below are Homelite tool numbers, tool description and model application of tools for servicing.

Tool No. Description & Model Usage
04197 – Carburetor tester
17789 – Carburetor repair tool kit.
22820-1 – Bearing collar for A-23137.
23136 – Body for A-23137.
23756 – Plug, connecting rod bearing removal and installation, all models.
23757 – Plug, needle roller type main bearing installation, all models.
23758 – Plug, crankcase seal installation, all models; drivecase seal installation, Model XL-12.
23759 – Sleeve, crankcase seal protector, all models; drivecase seal protector, Model XL-12.

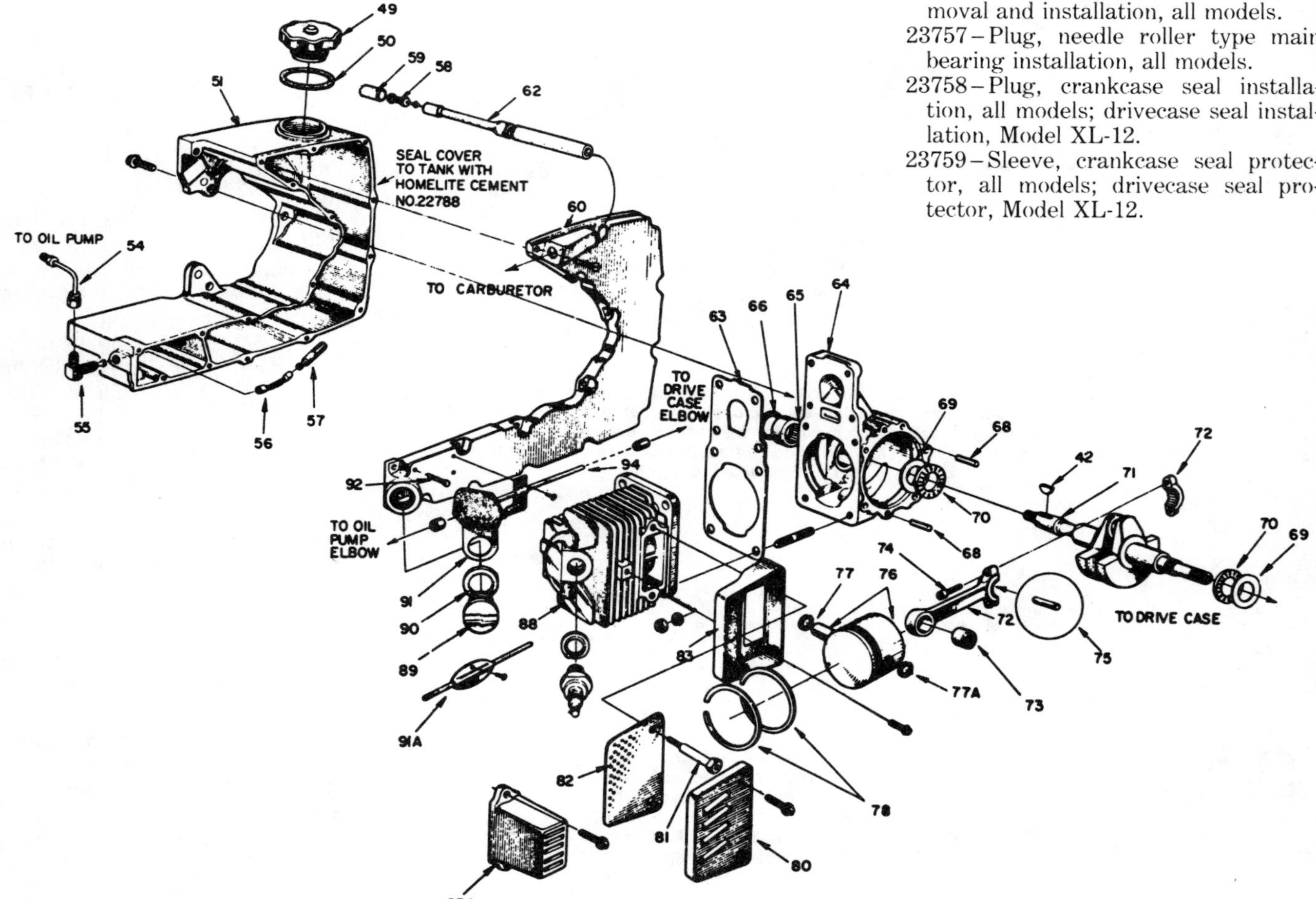

Fig. HL34 – Exploded view showing power head and fuel tank construction of Model XL-12; refer to Fig. HL35 for Model Super XL Automatic. Dowel pin (68) are used on later models. Refer to text. Single or two-piece muffler may be used. Shield (91) is not used on later models.

42. Woodruff key
49. Fuel tank cap
50. Gasket
51. Fuel tank
54. Oil line
55. Check valve
56. Oil line
57. Oil filter
58. Fuel pickup
59. Fuel filter
60. Tank cover (late)
62. Flexible fuel line
63. Gasket
64. Crankcase
65. Needle bearing
66. Crankshaft seal
68. Dowel pins
69. Thrust washers
70. Thrust bearings
71. Crankshaft
72. Connecting rod & cap
80. Muffler cap
81. Special studs
82. Baffle
83. Muffler body
83A. Muffler
88. Cylinder
89. Oil cap
73. Needle bearing
74. Rod cap screws
75. Needle rollers
76. Piston & pin
77. Snap ring
77A. Snap ring
78. Piston rings
90. Gasket
91. Shield
91A. Plate
92. Cotter pin (breather)
94. Oil line

23800 – Sleeve, crankcase seal installation, all models; drivecase seal installation. Model XL-12.
23819 – Plug, clutch drum needle bearing installation, all direct drive models.
23843 – Sleeve, drive seal installation, Model Super XL Automatic.
23844 – Sleeve, drive seal protector, Model Super XL Automatic.
23845 – Plug, drivecase seal installation, Model Super XL Automatic.
23846 – Anvil, crankshaft installation, Model Super XL Automatic.
23884 – Sleeve, bearing and shaft, Model Super XL Automatic.
94194 – Compression gage.
A-23137 – Jackscrew, crankshaft assembly and installation, all models except XL-12.
A-23841-A – Wrench, guide bar stud insert, Model Super XL Automatic.
A-23934 – Wrench, clutch plate removal and installation, all late production.
A-23949 – Remover, piston pin with Spirol pin at exhaust side of piston.
A-23960 – Remover and locking bracket, rotor (flywheel), all models.
JA-31316-4 – Test spark plug.

COMPRESSION PRESSURE. For optimum performance on all models, cylinder compression pressure should be 130-155 psi (896-1069 kPa) with engine at normal operating temperature. Engine should be inspected and repaired when compression pressure is 90 psi (620 kPa) or below.

CONNECTING ROD. Connecting rod and piston assembly can be removed after removing cylinder from crankcase. Refer to Fig. HL39. Be careful to remove all of the loose needle rollers when detaching rod from crankpin. Early models have 28 loose needle rollers; starting with serial number 207-1277, 31 needle rollers are used.

NOTE: A different crankshaft and connecting rod are used on late models with 31 needle rollers.

Renew connecting rod if bent or twisted, or if crankpin bearing surface is scored, burned or excessively worn. The caged needle roller piston pin bearing can be renewed by pressing old bearing out and pressing new bearing in with Homelite tool 23756. Press on lettered end of bearing cage only.

It is recommended that the crankpin needle rollers be renewed as a set whenever engine is disassembled for service. On early models with 28 needle rollers, stick 14 needle rollers in the rod and remaining 14 needle rollers in rod cap with light grease or beeswax. On late models with 31 needle rollers, stick 16 rollers in rod and 15 rollers in rod cap. Assemble rod to cap with match marks aligned, and with open end of piston pin towards flywheel side of engine. Wiggle the rod as cap retaining screws are being tightened to align the fractured mating surfaces of rod and cap.

PISTON, PIN AND RINGS. The piston is fitted with two pinned compression rings. Renew piston if scored, cracked or excessively worn, or if ring side clearance in top ring groove exceeds 0.0035 inch (0.089 mm).

Recommended piston ring end gap is 0.070-0.080 inch (1.78-2.03 mm); maximum allowable ring end gap is 0.085 inch (2.16 mm). Desired ring side clearance in groove is 0.002-0.003 inch (0.05-0.08 mm).

Piston, pin and rings are available in standard size only. Piston and pin are available in a matched set, and are not available separately.

Piston pin has one open and one closed end and may be retained in piston with snap rings or a Spirol pin. A wire retaining ring is used on exhaust side of piston on some models and should be removed.

To remove piston pin on all models, remove the snap ring at intake side of piston. On piston with Spirol pin at exhaust side, drive pin from piston rod with slotted driver (Homelite tool A-23949). On all other models, insert a 3/16 inch (4.76 mm) pin through snap

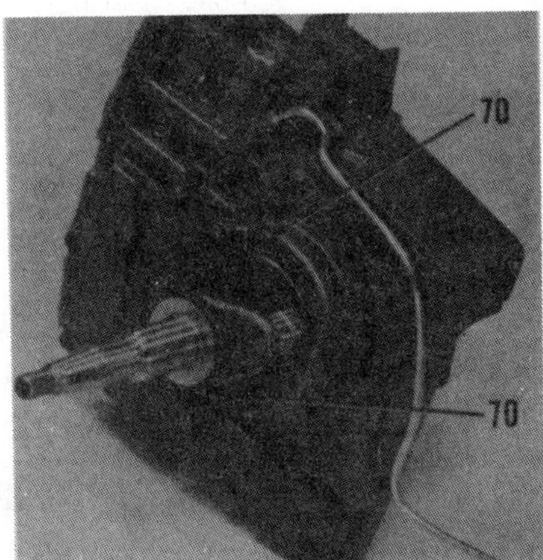

Fig. HL36 – View showing crankcase removed from drivecase and crankshaft on models equipped with ball bearing at drive end of crankshaft. To remove crankshaft from drivecase, bearing retaining screws (70) must first be removed.

Fig. HL35 – Exploded view showing latest type fuel tank and later construction of power head; refer to Fig. HL34 for early units. Ball bearing (72) is retained on crankshaft by snap ring (73) and in drivecase by two screws (70) and special washers (71); refer to Fig. HL36. Latest models have 31 loose needle rollers (75) at crankpin; earlier models have 28 rollers. Tank cover (58) is sealed to tank (53) with cement (Homelite part 22788) and is retained with 16 screws (59). Later tanks are permanently bonded.

42. Woodruff key
49. Fuel tank cap
50. Gasket
53. Fuel tank
54. Pipe plug
55. Fuel filter
56. Pick-up head
57. Grommet
58. Fuel tank cover
59. Screws (16)
63. Gasket
64. Crankcase
65. Needle bearing
66. Crankshaft seal
69. Crankshaft
70. Bearing screws
71. Special washers
72. Ball bearing
73. Snap ring
74. Connecting rod
75. Needle rollers
76. Needle bearing
77. Rod cap screws
78. Piston & pin
79. Snap ring
79A. Snap ring
81. Piston rings
83. Muffler cap
84. Special studs
85. Baffle
86. Muffler body
91. Cylinder
92. Plate
93. Spark arrestor

Fig. HL38 – Be sure the steel thrust washers (26) are to outside of thrust bearings (27) when installing crankshaft on Model XL-12. Model Super XL Automatic does not use thrust washers or thrust bearings.

ring at exhaust side and drive piston pin out as shown in Fig. HL40.

When reassembling piston to connecting rod, be sure to install closed end of piston pin towards exhaust side of piston (away from piston ring locating pin). Fit the Waldes Truarc snap ring in groove of pin bore with sharp edge out and turn ring gap towards closed end of piston.

CRANKSHAFT AND BEARINGS. On Model XL-12 the crankshaft is supported in two caged needle roller bearings and crankshaft end play is controlled by a roller bearing and hardened steel thrust washer on each end of the shaft. Refer to Fig. HL38. On Model Super XL Automatic, flywheel end of crankshaft is supported in a needle bearing in crankcase and drive end is supported in a ball bearing located in drivecase; end play is controlled by the ball bearing.

Maximum allowable crankshaft end play on models with thrust bearings (Fig. HL38) is 0.020 inch (0.51 mm); renew thrust bearings if end play is excessive. Normal end play is approximately 0.010 inch (0.25 mm).

Renew the crankshaft if any of the main bearing, crankpin bearing or thrust bearing surfaces or sealing surfaces are scored, burned or excessively worn. Renew the drivecase ball bearing if excessively loose or rough. Also, reject crankshaft if flywheel keyway is beat out or if threads are badly damaged.

CYLINDER. The cylinder bore is chrome plated. Renew the cylinder if chrome plating is worn away exposing the softer base metal.

CRANKCASE, DRIVECASE AND SEALS. On all models, crankshaft seals can be renewed without disassembling crankcase, drivecase and crankshaft unit. With magneto armature and core assembly removed, pry seal from crankcase. Install new seal over crankshaft with lip of seal inward, then using driver sleeve, drive seal into crankcase. Seal in drivecase can be pried out after removing clutch assembly and, on models so equipped, the automatic chain oiler pump. Install seal with lip inward and drive into position with sleeve.

NOTE: Use of seal protectors is recommended; if protectors are not available, wrap threads on crankshaft with thin plastic tape to prevent damage to seal lips.

Crankcase can be removed from crankshaft and drivecase after removing cylinder, piston and connecting rod and removing retaining screws. On Model XL-12, crankshaft can be withdrawn from drivecase. On Model Super XL Automatic, remove the two bearing retaining screws (70–Fig. HL35) special washers (71), then press crankshaft and ball bearing (72) from drivecase. Remove snap ring (73), then press crankshaft out of the ball bearing.

Inspect the needle roller bearing in crankcase, and on Model XL-12, the needle roller bearing in drivecase. Bearings should be renewed if any needle roller has flat spots or is otherwise damaged, or if rollers are worn so any two rollers can be separated a width equal to thickness of one roller. Always press against lettered end of bearing cage when removing and installing needle roller bearings. Needle roller bearings should be installed using appropriate installation plug.

Install new ball bearing on crankshaft using jackscrew or by supporting crankshaft at crank throw and installing bearing in a press. Groove in outer race of bearing must be toward crankpin.

Renew crankshaft seals before assembling crankshaft, crankcase and drivecase. Using installation plug, press seal into position with lip to inside of crankcase. On Model XL-12, install thrust bearings on crankshaft next to crankpin throw, then install the hardened steel rust washers at outer side of each thrust bearing. On Model Super XL Automatic, first assemble crankshaft and drivecase by placing seal protector on crankshaft, then pulling crankshaft and ball bearing into drivecase with jackscrew and adapters. Install two NEW bearing retaining screws and lockwashers. On Model XL-12, place seal protector on crankshaft and insert crankshaft in crankcase. Then, on all models, assemble crankcase to drivecase using new gasket.

NOTE: On early production, crankcase was sealed to drivecase with an "O" ring; however, use of "O" ring has been discontinued and a gasket, rather than an "O" ring, should be used on all models.

On all late production models, crankcase is fitted with dowel pins to provide a more positive alignment of crankcase and drivecase. Service crankcases are drilled for dowel pins, but dowel pins are not installed so crankcase can be used with early type drivecase not drilled for dowels. If renewing late type crankcase fitted with dowel pins, two new dowel pins must be obtained and installed in new crankcase; install dowel pins so they protrude 0.165-0.180 inch (4.19-4.57 mm) from crankcase.

PYRAMID REED VALVE. All models are equipped with a pyramid reed type intake valve with four reeds. Early production reed seat was made of

Fig. HL39 — Piston and connecting rod assembly can be removed from crankpin after removing cylinder from crankcase. Note piston ring locating pin on intake side of piston.

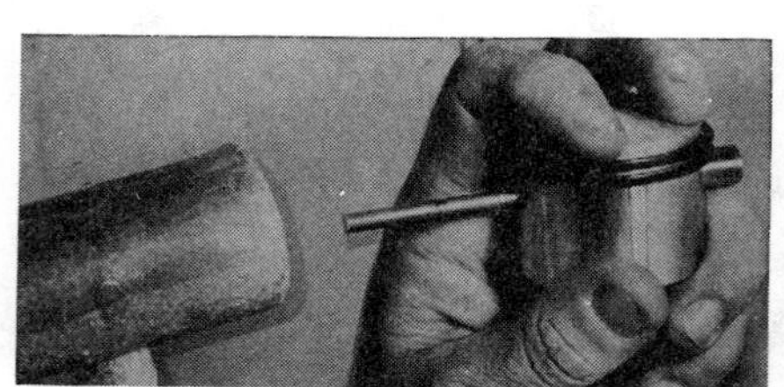

Fig. HL40 — After removing snap rings the piston pin can be tapped out using a 3/16 inch (4.76 mm) rod as shown or, on pistons with Spirol pin at exhaust side, by driving piston pin out with slotted driver (Homelite tool A23949).

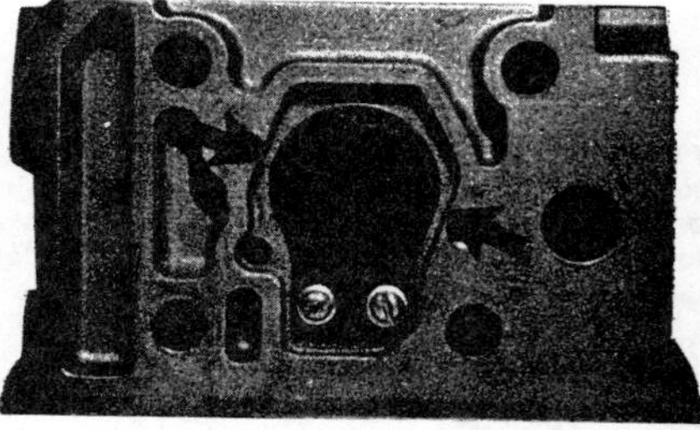

Fig. HL41 — When installing reed valve on air box (models with flat reed intake valve only), be sure reed is centered between the two points indicated by arrows.

aluminum and reeds were retained to seat by spring plates and screws.

Late production reed seat (see Fig. HL32) is made of Delrin plastic. The reeds fit onto pins protruding from the plastic seat and are held in place by a molded retainer, eliminating the retaining spring plates and screws.

Reeds, spring plates and retaining screws are available for servicing the early type aluminum reed seat. However, if the seat is worn or damaged beyond further use, the Delrin seat and molded retainer is used as replacement.

When assembling reeds to aluminum seat, apply Loctite to retaining screws to keep them from working loose. Renew the spacer gaskets and carburetor gasket and install the spacer, reed seal assembly and carburetor as in Fig. HL31.

To assemble and install Delrin reed seat and reeds, proceed as follows: Fit reed retainer (3 – Fig. HL32) into spacer (2) so the pin on retainer clears cut-out in spacer. Using a drop of oil under each reed, stick the reeds to pyramid seat so holes in reeds fit over the pins molded into seat. Place the retainer and spacer over the reeds and seat so all parts are locked together, then install the valve assembly and carburetor with new gaskets (1 and 8).

CLUTCH. Refer to Fig. HL42 for exploded view of typical clutch assembly. Illustration shows late type clutch assembly using three compression springs (11) to hold shoes retracted in plate (10) and in insets at lower left corner, the early type clutch using garter type springs (11A) to hold shoes to spider (10A). The early type clutch (inset) and late type clutch are interchangeable as an assembly. Clutch plate (10) or spider (10A) is threaded to crankshaft.

If clutch will not disengage (chain continues to turn) with engine at idle speed, check for broken, weak or improperly installed clutch springs. If clutch slips under load and engine continues to run at high speed, excessive wear of clutch shoes is indicated.

On early production Model XL-12, clutch drum was equipped with an Oilite bushing. All later clutch drums, including service clutch drum for early XL-12, are fitted with caged needle roller bearings. When renewing early bushing type clutch drum, a new needle bearing inner race must also be installed.

Renew needle roller bearing inner race if wear marks are visible. Renew bearing in clutch drum if any roller has flat spots or is damaged, or if worn to extent that any two rollers can be separated the width equal to the thickness of one roller. Using installer

1. Handle bar
4. Bumper spike
7. Bracket
8. Clutch cover (late)
8A. Clutch cover (early)
9. Clutch shoe (late)
9A. Clutch shoe (early)
10. Clutch plate (late)
10A. Clutch spider (early)
11. Clutch spring (late)
11A. Clutch spring (early)
12. Inner guide bar plate
12A. Guide bar spring
13. Outer guide bar plate
15. Drivecase cover
16. Crankshaft nut
17. Flat washer
18. Thrust washer
19. Clutch drum & sprocket
20. Needle bearing
21. Bearing inner race
22. Thrust washer

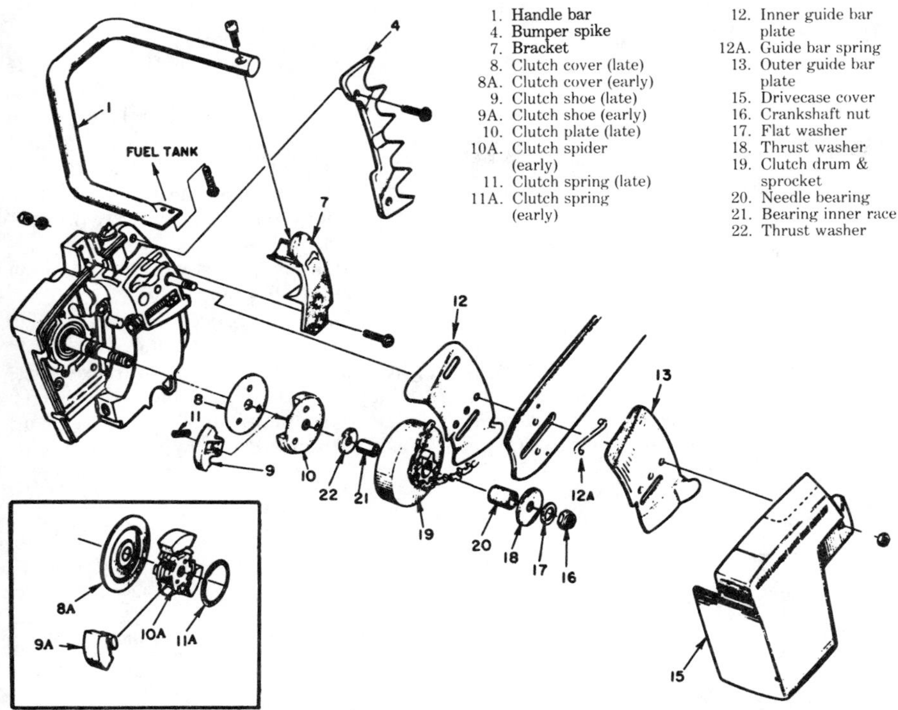

Fig. HL42 – Exploded view of typical direct drive clutch assembly. Late type clutch assembly (items 8, 9, 10 & 11) is interchangeable as a unit with early production clutch shown in inset at lower left corner.

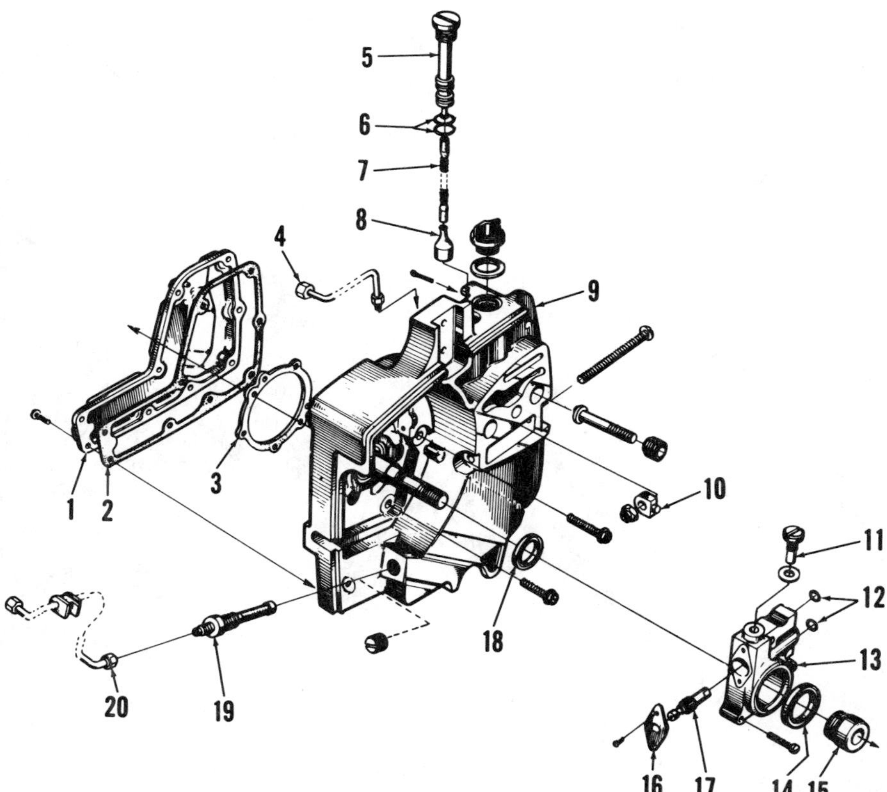

Fig. HL43 – Exploded view of automatic chain oil pump on models so equipped.

1. Oil reservoir cover
2. Gasket
3. Gasket
4. Oil line
5. Oil line tube
6. "O" rings
7. Oil line
8. Oil filter
9. Drivecase
10. Bar adjusting pin
11. Cam screw
12. "O" rings
13. Pump body
14. Felt seal
15. Worm gear
16. Flange
17. Plunger
18. Crankshaft seal

plug, press against lettered side of needle bearing cage when installing bearing.

Refer to Fig. HL47 for assembly of late type clutch.

AUTOMATIC CHAIN OILER PUMP. Refer to Fig. HL43 for exploded view of typical automatic oiler pump installation, and to Fig. HL44 for schematic view showing pump operation.

The automatic oiler pump pump is accessible after removing the clutch assembly from crankshaft and disconnecting oil lines. Pump plunger (17–Fig. HL43) and body (13) are available as a complete assembly only which includes flange (16), cam screw (11), gasket, "O" rings (12), sealing felt (14) and flange retaining screws; however, all parts except plunger and body are available separately.

Inspect tip of cam screw (11) and cam groove on plunger (17) for wear and plunger bore in body and piston portion of plunger for scoring or wear. Renew pump assembly if body and/or piston is worn or damaged beyond further use.

REWIND STARTER. Refer to Fig. HL49 or HL50 for an exploded view of early or late rewind starter. There were some models equipped with the early starter that used some of the components shown on the later starter. Service procedures for all of these starters are the same.

To disassemble starter, pull starter rope fully out, hold starter pulley from turning, pull all slack in rope out inner side of fan housing and allow pulley to unwind slowly until spring tension is relieved. Remove the slotted hex head screw retaining pulley to post and remove starter pulley and cup with flat retaining washer. Remove the rewind spring and, if so equipped, the spring shields, from fan housing. Remove rope from pulley and handle.

Starter pulley post in fan housing is not renewable; a new fan housing must be installed if post is broken loose, or on mid-range production models without starter post bushing, if post is worn so that pulley is not held in proper position. Renew flanged bushing on early production models if bushing is worn excessively and fan housing is serviceable. Renew rope bushing if worn.

To reassemble, proceed as follows: Do not lubricate starter spring, but apply light oil sparingly to starter post, bushing (if used) and bore of starter pulley. Place outer shield (if used) in fan housing, then install rewind spring with

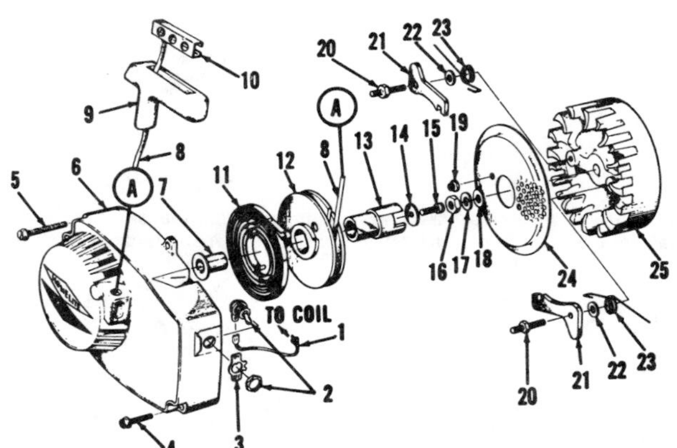

1. Ground wire
2. Ignition switch
6. Blower (fan) housing
7. Bushing
8. Starter rope
9. Hand grip
10. Insert
11. Rewind spring
12. Rope pulley
13. Starter cup
14. Washer
15. Socket head screw
16. Flywheel nut
17. Lockwasher
18. Flat washer
20. Pawl studs
21. Pawls
22. Washers
23. Pawl springs
24. Rotating screen
25. Flywheel

Fig. HL49—Exploded view of early rewind starter components and related parts. Starter unit is mounted on shaft (starter post) which is an integral part of the blower housing.

Fig. HL44—Automatic oil pump worm gear (W) driven by crankshaft turns plunger (P) at 1/20 engine speed. As plunger turns, cam on end of plunger engages cam screw (C) causing the plunger to go back and forth. Flat end of plunger acts as inlet and outlet valve.

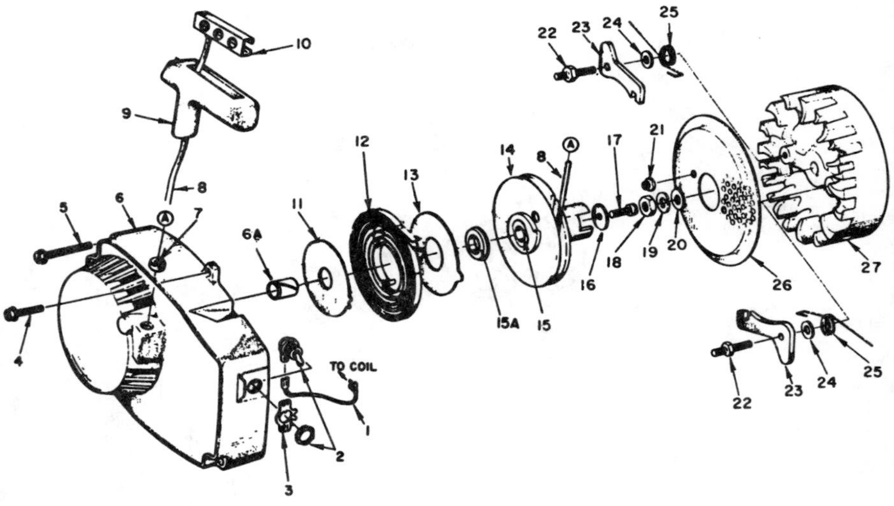

Fig. HL50—Exploded view of later production rewind starter.

1. Ground lead
2. "ON-OFF" switch
3. Switch plate
6. Fan housing
6A. Bushing
7. Rope bushing
8. Starter rope
9. Starter handle
10. Insert
11. Inner spring shield
12. Rewind spring
13. Outer spring shield
14. Starter pulley
15. Spring lock
15A. Spring lock bushing
16. Retaining washer
17. Hex head screw
18. Crankshaft nut
19. Lockwasher
20. Flat washer
21. Screen retaining nuts
22. Pawl studs
23. Starter pawls
24. Washers
25. Pawl springs
26. Air screen
27. Rotor (flywheel)

Fig. HL47—View showing easy method for installing late type clutch shoes and springs on clutch plate.

Fig. HL51 – When installing starter pawls (21), be sure pawl return springs (23) are located in flywheel vanes so they are parallel to the pawls as shown.

loop in outer end over spring post in fan housing and install inner spring shield (if used). Attach starter cord to pulley, insert rope through rope bore or bushing in fan housing and attach handle and insert to outer end of rope. Wind rope onto starter pulley. Place pulley and starter cup (with spring lock and spring lock bushing if integral pulley and lock are used) on starter post and be sure spring lock or pulley is properly engaged with rewind spring. Install retaining washer and hex head screw and tighten screw to 50 in.-lbs. (5.6 N•m). Pull rope out about two feet and hold pulley from turning. Locate notch in pulley at cord insert in housing and pull up loop of cord between notch and housing. Holding onto pulley, wind cord three more turns onto pulley by turning pulley, then let spring rewind pulley until handle is pulled against fan housing.

HOMELITE

Model	Bore mm (in.)	Stroke mm (in.)	Displacement cc (cu. in.)	Drive Type
XL-923	52.4 (2.06)	38.1 (1.5)	82.1 (5.01)	Direct
Super XL925, SLX-925, SLX-955	52.4 (2.06)	38.1 (1.5)	80.1 (5.01)	Direct
VI-944, VI-955	52.4 (2.06)	38.1 {1.5)	82.1 (5.01)	Direct

MAINTENANCE

SPARK PLUG. Models so equipped with a solid-state, one-piece ignition module (above lot number C246) use a Champion DJ6Y spark plug. Early models (below lot number C246) use Champion CJ6, or Champion UJ11G for heavy duty operation. It will be necessary to pull the plug wire further out of the retaining clip in the air box when using UJ11G spark plug. Set electrode gap to 0.025 inch (0.63 mm) on all models.

CARBURETOR. All models are equipped with a Tillotson Model HS diaphragm carburetor. Refer to Tillotson section of CARBURETOR SERVICE section for carburetor overhaul and exploded views.

Initial setting of idle speed mixture screw and high speed mixture screw shown in Fig. HL76 is one turn open (later Model SXL-925 is not equipped with a high speed mixture screw). Make final adjustments with engine warm. Adjust idle mixture screw so that engine idles smoothly and will accelerate cleanly. Adjust high speed mixture screw, on models so equipped, to obtain optimum performance with saw under cutting load. Do not adjust high speed screw too lean as engine may be damaged.

On models with Simplex starting system (decompression valve and adjustable starting speed), speed at which engine runs with throttle latch engaged can be adjusted by turning eccentric throttle trigger pivot pin (28–Fig. HL79).

MAGNETO. Three types of magnetos are used. Models XL-923 and VI-944 are equipped with a conventional flywheel type magneto. Models VI-955 and early SXL-925 are equipped with a capacitor discharge (CD) magneto. Later SXL-925 models are equipped with a one-piece solid-state ignition. Refer to appropriate following paragraph for service information on each type magneto.

CONVENTIONAL (BREAKER POINT) MAGNETO. Refer to Fig. HL81 for exploded view of magneto. Breaker-points and condenser are accessible after removing starter housing, flywheel and breaker-box cover. Adjust breaker-point gap to 0.015 inch (0.38 mm). Condenser capacity should test 0.18-0.22 mfd. After reinstalling flywheel, check armature air gap which should be 0.005-0.007 inch (0.13-0.18 mm). To adjust air gap loosen core retaining screws, turn flywheel so magnets are below legs of armature core and place plastic shim (Homelite® part 23987) between armature and magnets. Push flywheel toward core legs and tighten armature retaining screws, then remove shim.

CAPACITOR DISCHARGE (CD) MAGNETO. Refer to Fig. HL84 for exploded view of the capacitor discharge (CD) magneto used on all early and some later SXL-925 and VI-955 models.

The capacitor discharge magneto can be considered OK if spark will jump a 3/8 inch (9.5 mm) gap when turning engine at cranking speed. If magneto fails to

Fig. HL76—Drawing showing locations of fuel mixture adjustment needles, idle speed needle and throttle stop lever.

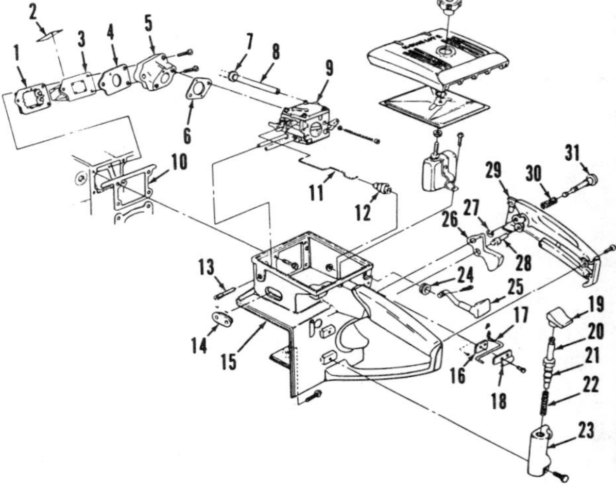

Fig. HL79—Typical exploded view of air box and manual oil pump assemblies used on Models XL-923 and SXL-925.

1. Reed retainer
2. Reed petal
3. Reed valve seat
4. Gasket
5. Intake manifold
6. Gasket
7. Grommet
8. Fuel line
9. Carburetor
10. Gasket
11. Throttle rod
12. Boot
13. Idle speed screw
14. Grommet
15. Air box
16. Plate
17. Compression release lever
18. Clamp
19. Manual oiler button
20. Oil pump plunger
21. "O" rings (2)
22. Spring
23. Oil pump body
24. Grommet
25. Choke rod
26. Throttle trigger
27. "E" ring
28. Eccentric pin
29. Handle cover
30. Spring
31. Throttle latch pin

produce spark, service consists of locating and renewing inoperative unit; no maintenance is necessary.

To check magneto with volt-ohmmeter, proceed as follows: Remove starter housing and disconnect wire from ignition switch. Check to be sure there is no continuity through switch when in "ON" position to be sure a grounded switch is not cause of trouble and inspect wiring to be sure it is not shorted.

CAUTION: Be sure storage capacitor is discharged before touching connections; flip ignition switch to "OFF" position or ground switch lead (S).

Resistance through secondary (high tension) winding of transformer coil should be 2400 to 2900 ohms and resistance through primary winding should be 0.2-0.4 ohms. Connect ohmmeter leads between high tension (spark plug wire and ground, then between input terminal and ground. If transformer coil does not test within specifications, renew coil and recheck for spark at cranking speed. If magneto still does not produce spark, check generator as follows:

Remove rotor (flywheel) and disconnect lead from generator to generator (G) terminal on module (3) and switch lead (S) at ignition switch. Connect negative lead of ohmmeter to ground wire from generator and the positive lead of ohmmeter to generator (G) wire. The ohmmeter should register showing continuity through generator. Reverse leads from ohmmeter; ohmmeter should then show no continuity (infinite resistance) through generator. Renew generator if continuity is noted with ohmmeter leads connected in both directions. A further check can be made using voltmeter if continuity checked correctly. Remove spark plug and reinstall rotor leaving wire (G) from generator disconnected. Connect positive (red) lead from voltmeter to wire (G) from generator and negative (black) lead of voltmeter to magneto back plate; wires must be routed so starter can be reinstalled. A firm pull on starter rope

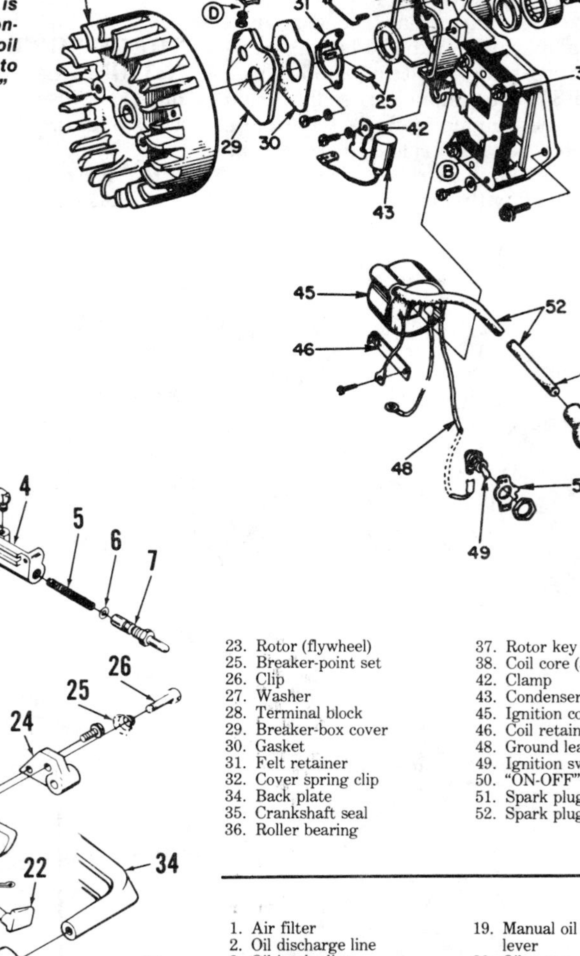

Fig. HL81—Exploded view of conventional flywheel type magneto. Coil clip retaining screw location is shown by letter "B." Condenser lead and ignition coil primary lead are attached to terminal block (28) at "D."

23. Rotor (flywheel)
25. Breaker-point set
26. Clip
27. Washer
28. Terminal block
29. Breaker-box cover
30. Gasket
31. Felt retainer
32. Cover spring clip
34. Back plate
35. Crankshaft seal
36. Roller bearing
37. Rotor key
38. Coil core (armature)
42. Clamp
43. Condenser
45. Ignition coil
46. Coil retaining clip
48. Ground lead
49. Ignition switch
50. "ON-OFF" plate
51. Spark plug terminal
52. Spark plug wire

Fig. HL80—Exploded view of Models VI-944 and VI-955. Note vibration isolating bushings (30).

1. Air filter
2. Oil discharge line
3. Oil intake line
4. Manual oil pump
5. Spring
6. "O" ring
7. Oil pump plunger
8. Gasket
9. Reed retainer
10. Reed petal
11. Reed valve seat
12. Gasket
13. Intake manifold
14. Gasket
15. Carburetor
16. Throttle rod
17. Frame
18. Idle speed stop screw
19. Manual oil pump lever
20. Oiler arm
21. Compression release lever
22. Choke rod
23. Trigger
24. Trigger cover
25. Spring
26. Throttle latch
27. Snap ring
28. Washer
29. Shaft
30. Vibration bushing
31. Handle
32. Washer
33. Snap ring
34. Mounting arm

should spin engine at about 500 rpm and voltmeter should show minimum reading of 4 volts. If both generator and transformer coil tested OK, a faulty ignition module (3) should be suspected.

A partial check of ignition module can be made using ohmmeter. With ohmmeter set to R X 1000 scale, connect positive (red) lead of ohmmeter to module terminal marked "Gen." and negative ohmmeter lead to module ground connection (see Fig. HL85). An instant deflection of ohmmeter needle should be noted; if not, reverse ohmmeter leads and observe needle. If no deflection of needle is noted with ohmmeter leads connected in either direction, module is faulty and should be renewed. If needle deflection is observed, select R X 1 (direct reading) scale of ohmmeter and connect positive (red) lead to module terminal marked "Gen." and place negative (black) lead against terminal marked "Trans." Place a screwdriver across the two trigger poles (see Fig. HL85); the ohmmeter needle should deflect and remain deflected until the ohmmeter lead is released from the module terminal. If the desired results are obtained with ohmmeter checks, the module is probably OK; however, as this is not a complete check and other magneto components and wiring check OK, renew module if no ignition spark can be obtained.

SOLID-STATE IGNITION. Later SXL-925 models are equipped with a one-piece solid-state ignition module (27–Fig. HL86). The solid-state ignition system is serviced by renewing the spark plug or ignition module, however, be sure all wires are connected properly and the ignition switch functions correctly before renewing ignition module. Air gap between ignition module and flywheel is adjustable. Loosen module retaining screws and place a 0.015 inch (0.38 mm) shim between flywheel and module. Hold module against shim, tighten module retaining screws and remove shim.

THREE-PIECE SOLID-STATE IGNITION. The three-piece solid-state ignition is used on some later Model VI-955 and SXL-925 engines.

NOTE: The tester shown in Figs. HL88 and HL89 can be fabricated from 70-500 V neon tester (Radio Shack number 272-201) and two leads with alligator clips.

Refer to Fig. HL87 and test for spark as shown. If weak spark or no spark is observed, refer to Fig. HL88 and test coil as follows: Remove spark plug and fan housing. Disconnect primary ignition wire from coil table "A." Connect one tester lead to the switch terminal and connect the other test lead to a good ground on the engine block. Temporarily reinstall the starter and fan housing. Move the switch to "ON" or "RUN" and spin the engine with the starter. A good coil will light the tester with a bright, pulsing glow. Replace the coil if other results are observed.

To test the trigger module, refer to Fig. HL89 and connect one of the tester leads to the disconnected coil primary wire and other tester lead to a good ground on the engine block. Reinstall the starter and fan housing. Move the switch to "ON" or "RUN" and spin the engine with the starter. If the tester glows brightly, the trigger circuit is functioning. Remove the flywheel and replace the trigger module if other results are oserved.

When reinstalling the flywheel, torque the flywheel nut to 150 in.-lbs. (17 N•m). Adjust coil-to-flywheel air gap to 0.015 inch (0.38 mm) using the black plastic feeler gage (part 24306). Tighten coil holddown screws to 20 in.-lbs. (2.25 N•m).

LUBRICATION. The engine is lubricated by mixing oil and unleaded gasoline. Recommended oil is Homelite®

Fig. HL84—Exploded view of Phelon capacitor discharge type magneto used on Models SXL-925 and VI-955.

G. Connector to "Gen." terminal
S. Connector to "ON-OFF"
1. Magneto rotor (flywheel)
2. Dust cap
3. Ignition module
4. Back plate
5. High tension wire & terminal
6. Transformer coil
7. Generator coil & armature

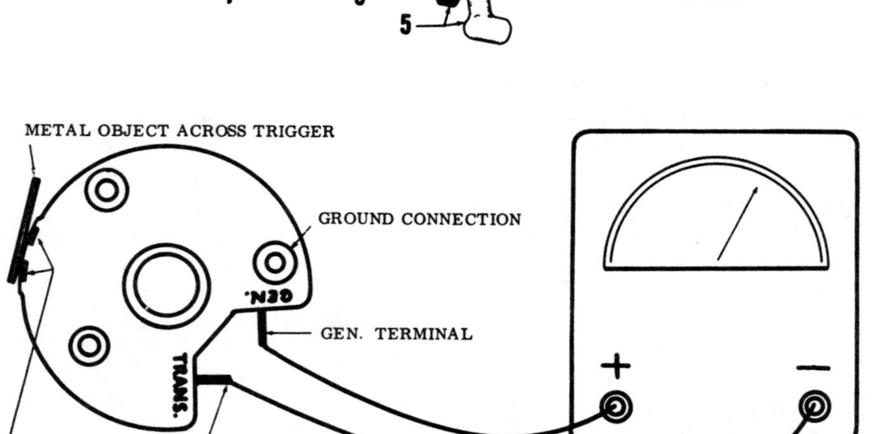

Fig. HL85—Drawing showing volt-ohmmeter to ignition module (3—Fig. HL84) for checking module. It should be noted that this is not a conclusive test and module should be renewed in event of spark failure when other magneto components test OK.

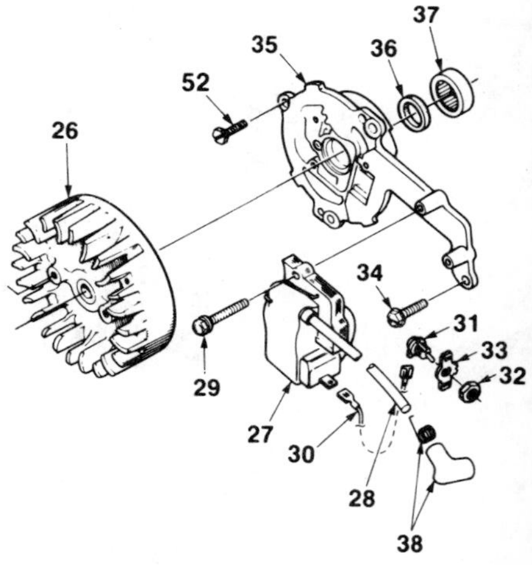

Fig. HL86—View of one-piece solid-state ignition used on later SXL-925 models.

26. Flywheel
27. Ignition module
28. High tension wire
29. Sems screws
30. Ground lead
31. Ignition switch
32. Nut
33. Indicating plate
34. Screw
35. Back plate
36. Crankshaft seal
37. Roller bearing
38. Spark plug terminal
52. Screw

two-stroke oil mixed at ratio as designated on the oil container. If Homelite® oil is not available, a good quality oil designed for two-stroke engines may be used when mixed at a 16:1 ratio, however, and antioxidant fuel stabilizer (such as Sta-Bil) should be added to fuel mix. Antioxidant fuel stabilizer is not required with Homelite® oils as they contain fuel stabilizer so the fuel mix will stay fresh up to one year.

Fill chain oiler reservoir with Homelite® Bar and Chain oil or a light oil (no heavier than SAE 30). In cold weather, chain oil can be diluted with kerosene to allow easier flow of oil through pump and lines.

The clutch drum and sprocket should be removed and the needle roller bearing and inner race be cleaned and greased occasionally.

CARBON. Muffler and cylinder exhaust ports should be cleaned periodically to prevent loss of power due to carbon build up. Remove muffler cover and baffle plate and scrape muffler free of carbon. With muffler cover removed, turn engine so piston is at top dead center and carefully remove carbon from exhaust ports with wooden scraper. Be careful not to damage the edges of exhaust ports or to scratch piston. Do not attempt to run engine with muffler baffle plate or cover removed.

REPAIRS

TIGHTENING TORQUE VALUES. Tightening torque values are as follows:

8/32 Connecting rod	55-66 in.-lbs. (6.2-7.5 N•m)
3/8-24 Clutch nut	150-180 in.-lbs. (16.9-20.3 N•m)
3/8-24 Rotor nut	150-180 in.-lbs. (16.9-20.3 N•m)
1/4-28 Cylinder nuts	100-120 in.-lbs. (11.3-13.6 N•m)
14 mm Spark plug	150-180 in.-lbs. (16.9-20.3 N•m)

RECOMMENDED SERVICE TOOLS. Special tools which will aid servicing are as follows:

Tool No. Description & Model Usage

23987 – Shim, magneto air gap, all models except with capacitor magneto.
24306 – Shim, capacitor discharge magneto air gap.
23955 or 23955-I – Plug, connecting rod bearing installation, all models.
A-23965 – Jackscrew, crankshaft and bearing.
23136-1 – Jackscrew body.
22820-4 – Collar, main bearing installation.
23971 – Sleeve, crankcase seal protector.
23972 – Sleeve, crankcase seal installation, all models.
23957 – Plug, crankshaft seal installation, all models.
A-23696-A – Wrench, clutch spider, all models with 6-shoe spring type clutch.
A-17146 – Wrench, clutch plate, all models with 3-shoe type clutch.
A-23960 – Puller, flywheel (magneto rotor) all models.
23420 – Plug, sprocket bearing, all models.
23956 – Plug, back plate bearing and seal, Model XL-923.
A23962 – Jackscrew, back plate bearing, all models.
23846-2 – Anvil, back plate bearing, all models.
A-23951 – Remover, piston pin, piston with Spirol pin.
22828 – Pliers, piston pin snap ring, all models except with Rulon plastic pin retaining plugs.
23846-1 – Anvil, crankshaft installation, all models.
23846-2 – Anvil, back plate bearing, all models.
24006-1 – Aligning plate, crankshaft installation, all models.
24304 – "Pozidriv" screwdriver bit.
24230 – "Pozidriv" hand screwdriver.
24982-01 – "Torx" bit, ¼ in. shank.
24982-02 – "Torx" bit, 5/16 in. shank.
24302 – Plug, backplate seal, models SXL-925, VI-944 and VI-955.
23528 – Wrench, connecting rod, all models.
JA-31316-4 – Test spark plug.
17789 – Carburetor tool kit.
14197 – Carburetor tester.
94194 – Compression gage.

COMPRESSION PRESSURE. For optimum performance of Model SXL-925, cylinder compression pressure should be 155-185 psi (1069-1275 kPa) with engine at normal operating temperature. Engine should be inspected and repaired when compression pressure is 90 psi (620 kPa) or below.

Fig. HL87 — Test for proper spark with a test plug as shown for models with three-piece solid-state ignition.

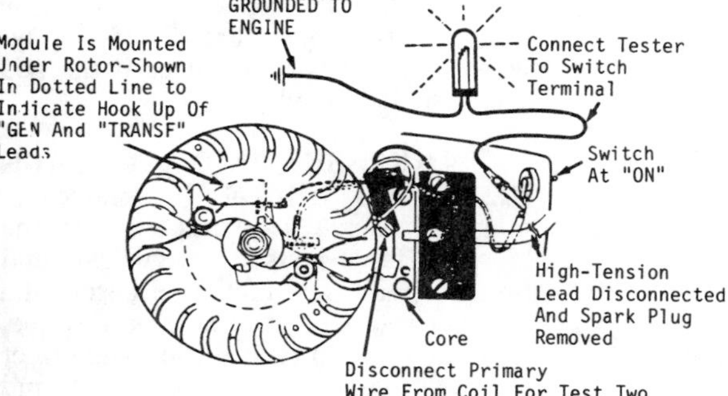

Fig. HL88 — Test coil with a neon tester connected as shown for models with three-piece solid-state ignition.

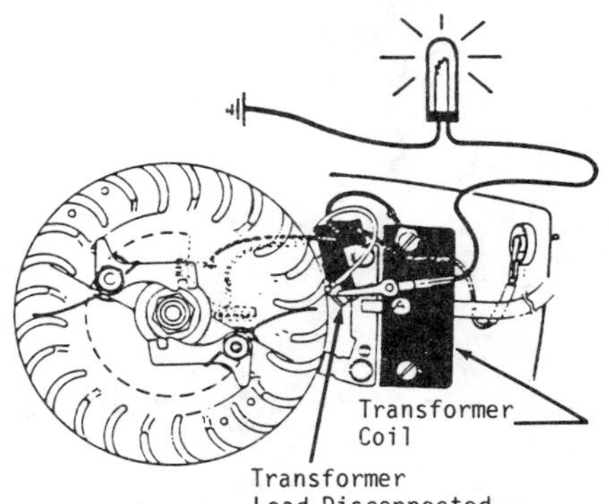

Fig. HL89 — Test trigger module (under flywheel) with a neon tester as shown for models with three-piece solid-state ignition.

COMPRESSION RELIEF VALVE. Models XL-923 and VI-944 are equipped with a compression relief (decompression) valve. The poppet type relief valve is mounted in a port adjacent to exhaust port as shown in Fig. HL90. The valve is opened as throttle lock plunger is depressed to lock position. If valve fails to close when throttle lock plunger is released, either remove valve and clean using a carbon solvent or renew the valve assembly. Copper sealing washer is available separately.

CYLINDER. The cylinder bore is chrome plated. Renew cylinder if chrome plating is worn away exposing the softer base metal.

To remove cylinder, first remove the blower (fan) housing, carburetor and air box (handle) assemblies and remove the screw retaining magneto back plate to flywheel side of cylinder. The cylinder can then be unbolted from crankcase and removed from the piston.

PISTON, PIN AND RINGS. All models are equipped with piston fitted with two pinned compression rings. Desired ring side clearance in groove is 0.002-0.003 inch (0.05-0.08 mm), renew the piston if side clearance in top groove with new ring is 0.0035 inch (0.089 mm) or more. Recommended piston ring end gap is 0.070-0.080 inch (1.78-2.03 mm); maximum allowable ring end gap is 0.085 inch (2.16 mm). Piston, pin and rings are available in standard size only. Pin and piston are available as a fitted set only.

When installing piston pin, be sure closed end is toward exhaust side of piston (away from piston ring locating pin). Insert piston pin snap rings using special pliers; sharp edge of snap ring must be out and locate end gap towards closed end of piston.

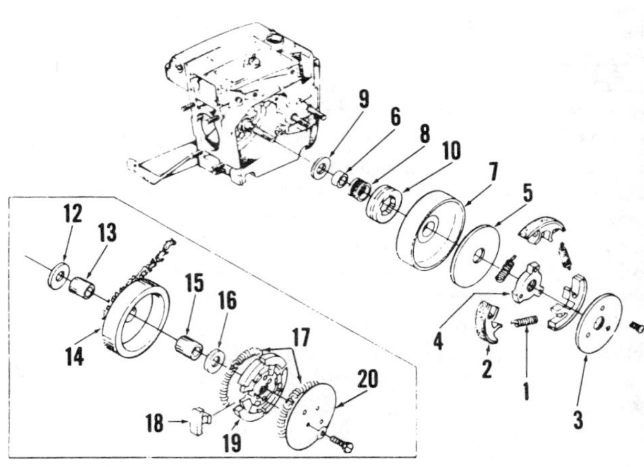

Fig. HL91—Models may be equipped with clutch components (1 through 10) or clutch components (12 through 20).

1. Spring
2. Clutch shoe
3. Cover
4. Hub
5. Thrust washer
6. Inner race
7. Drum
8. Bearing
9. Thrust washer
10. Sprocket
12. Thrust washer
13. Inner race
14. Drum
15. Bearing
16. Thrust washer
17. Spring
18. Clutch shoe
19. Hub
20. Cover

CONNECTING ROD. Connecting rod and piston assembly can be removed after removing cylinder from crankcase. Be careful to remove all of the 28 loose needle rollers when detaching rod from crankpin.

Renew connecting rod if bent or twisted, or if crankpin bearing surface is scored, burned or excessively worn. The caged needle roller piston pin bearing can be renewed by pressing old bearing out and pressing new bearing in with Homelite® tool 23955 or 23955-1. Press on lettered end of bearing cage only.

It is recommended that crankpin needle rollers be renewed as a set whenever engine is disassembled for service. Stick 14 needle rollers in rod and the remaining 14 needle rollers in rod cap with light grease or beeswax. Assemble rod to cap with match marks aligned and with open end of piston pin toward flywheel side of engine. Wiggle the rod as cap retaining screws are being tightened to align the fractured surfaces of rod and cap.

CRANKSHAFT. Flywheel end of crankshaft is supported in a roller bearing in magneto back plate and drive end is supported in a ball bearing located in crankcase. End play is controlled by the ball bearing.

Renew the crankshaft if the flywheel end main bearing or crankpin bearing surface or sealing surfaces are scored, burned or excessively worn. Renew the ball bearing if excessively loose or rough. Also, reject crankshaft if flywheel keyway is beat out or if threads are badly damaged.

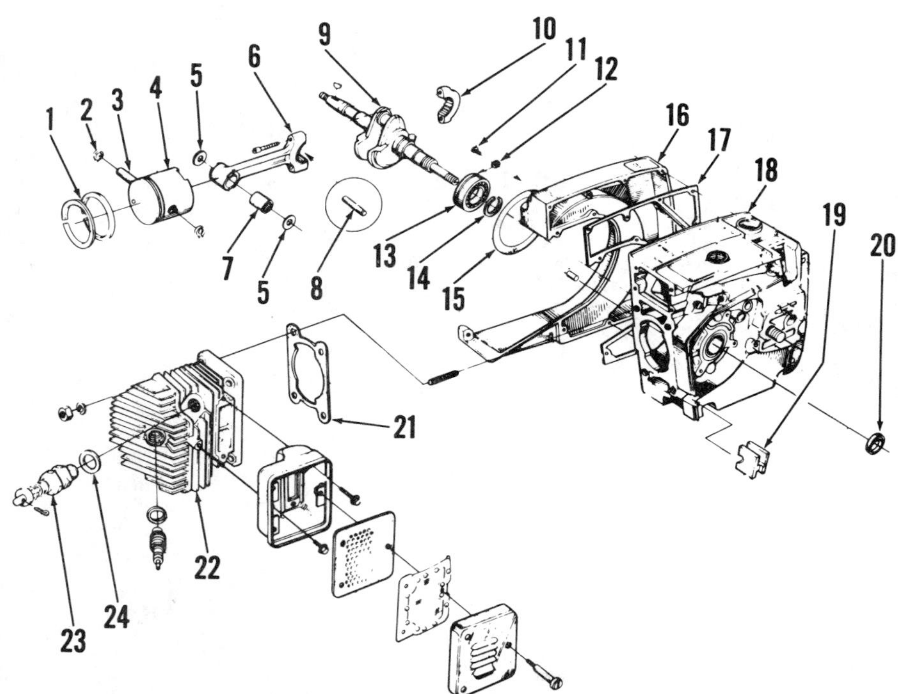

Fig. HL90—Exploded view of engine assembly. Compression relief valve is used on Models XL-923 and VI-944.

1. Piston rings
2. Snap ring
3. Piston pin
4. Piston
5. Thrust washer
6. Connecting rod
7. Needle bearing
8. Bearing rollers (28)
9. Crankshaft
10. Rod cap
11. Screw
12. Bearing retainer
13. Bearing
14. Snap ring
15. "O" ring
16. Fuel tank
17. Gasket
18. Crankcase
19. Grommet
20. Seal
21. Gasket
22. Cylinder
23. Compression relief valve
24. Washer

CRANKCASE MAGNETO BACK PLATE AND SEALS. To remove the magneto back plate, first remove the blower (fan) housing, flywheel and breaker-point assemblies. Loosen the cylinder retaining stud nuts on flywheel side of engine to reduce clamping effect on back plate boss, then unbolt and remove the back plate assembly from crankcase.

To remove crankshaft from crankcase, first remove the cylinder, connecting rod and piston assembly and the magneto backplate as previously outlined. Remove the drive clutch assembly and, on models so equipped, the automatic chain oiler drive worm and pump from drive end of crankcase and shaft. Then, remove the two ball bearing retaining screws (11–Fig. HL90) from inside of crankcase and remove the crankshaft and ball bearing assembly from crankcase. Remove snap ring (14) and press crankshaft from bearing if necessary.

REED VALVES. All models are equipped with pyramid reed valves. The pyramid seat is of "Delrin" plastic and the 0.004 inch (0.10 mm) thick reeds are located by pins molded in the seat. The reeds are held in place by a molded retainer that also serves as a gasket between reed seat and crankcase. When installing intake elbow and "Delrin" seat assembly, insert reed retainer into crankcase first. Stick reeds to seat with oil, then insert seat with reeds.

CLUTCH. Model SXL-925 is equipped with either a three- or six-shoe clutch while all other models are equipped with a six-shoe clutch. See Fig. HL91.

To remove clutch, first remove screws retaining clutch cover to clutch hub and remove cover. Torx screws are used on three-shoe clutch and may be removed with tools 24982-01 or 24982-02. Unscrew clutch hub (L.H. thread) from crankshaft using a spanner wrench (Homelite® tool A-17146) for three-shoe clutch or tool A-23696-A for six-shoe clutch). The clutch drum, bearing and inner race can then be removed from crankshaft.

Clutch shoes and springs on all models should be renewed as a set. When reassembling six-shoe clutch, be sure the identifying marks on the shoes are all to same side of the assembly. Inspect bearing and lubricate with Homelite ALL-TEMP Multipurpose Grease (# 24551) or a lithium base grease.

CHAIN OILER. Saws may be equipped with manual chain oiler pump only or with both a manual pump and an automatic chain oiler pump.

The manual oiler pump is installed as shown in Fig. HL79 or Fig. HL80; these illustrations show exploded view of the pump assembly. Usually, service of the manual pump consists of renewing the plunger and shaft "O" rings.

To service the automatic chain oiler pump, the clutch drum and spider must first be removed from the crankshaft as outlined in a preceding paragraph. Refer to Fig. HL93 for operational diagram of pump and to Fig. HL92 for exploded view of pump assembly.

REWIND STARTER. Refer to Fig. HL94 for exploded view of rewind starter. To disassemble starter after removing fan housing and starter assembly from saw, proceed as follows:

On models with slotted rope pulley, pull rope fully out, hold pulley from turning and pry knot end of rope from pulley. Allow pulley to rewind slowly.

On models without slot in pulley, pull rope outward a short distance, hold rope, pry retainer from starter handle and untie knot in outer end of rope. Allow pulley to rewind slowly.

Then, on all models, remove the socket head screw, flat washer cup and rope pulley.

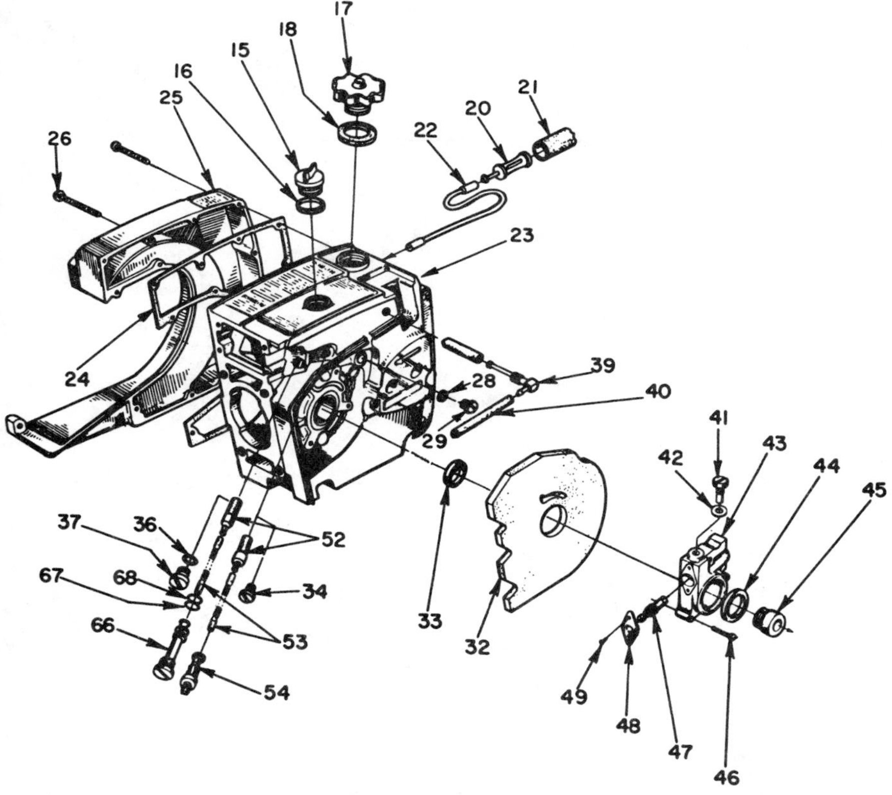

Fig. HL92 — Exploded view showing automatic chain oiler pump, manual and automatic oil pick-ups, crankcase and oil reservoir and fuel tank. Automatic oil pump plunger (47) and pump body (43) are available as a matched set only. Plug (34) is used to seal opening when saw is not equipped with manual chain oiler; plug (37) and washer (36) are used on models not equipped with automatic chain oiler.

15. Chain oil cap
16. Gasket
17. Fuel tank cap
18. Gasket
20. Pickup head
21. Fuel filter
22. Flexible line
23. Crankcase
24. Gasket
25. Fuel tank
26. Tank cover screws
28. Gasket
29. Cap
32. Saw dust shield
33. Crankshaft seal
34. Plug
36. Sealing washer
37. Plug
39. Elbow
40. Fuel line
41. Oil pump cam
42. Gasket
43. Oil pump body
44. Felt seal
45. Worm gear
46. Pump retaining screws
47. Pump gear/plunger
48. Flanged bearing
49. Screws
52. Oil pickups
53. Flexible oil lines
54. Connector
66. Oil line tube
67. Gasket
68. "O" ring

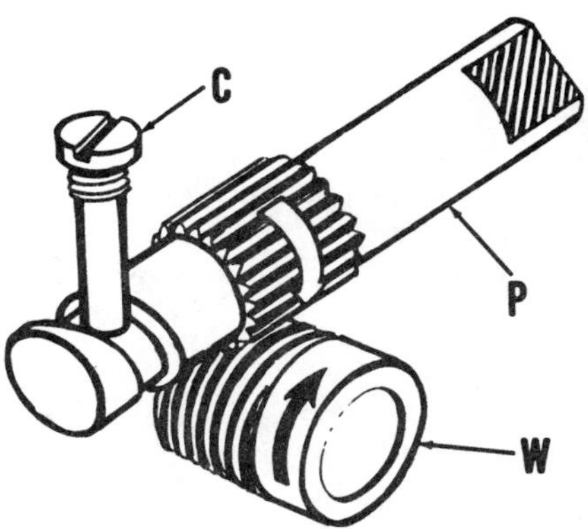

Fig. HL93 — Schematic diagram of automatic chain oiler pump operation. Worm gear (W) on crankshaft drives (rotates) pump plunger (P). Cam cut in plunger rides against cam screw (C) causing plunger to move back and forth as it rotates. Flat on plunger acts as a valve as it opens intake port on downward stroke and outlet port on upward stroke.

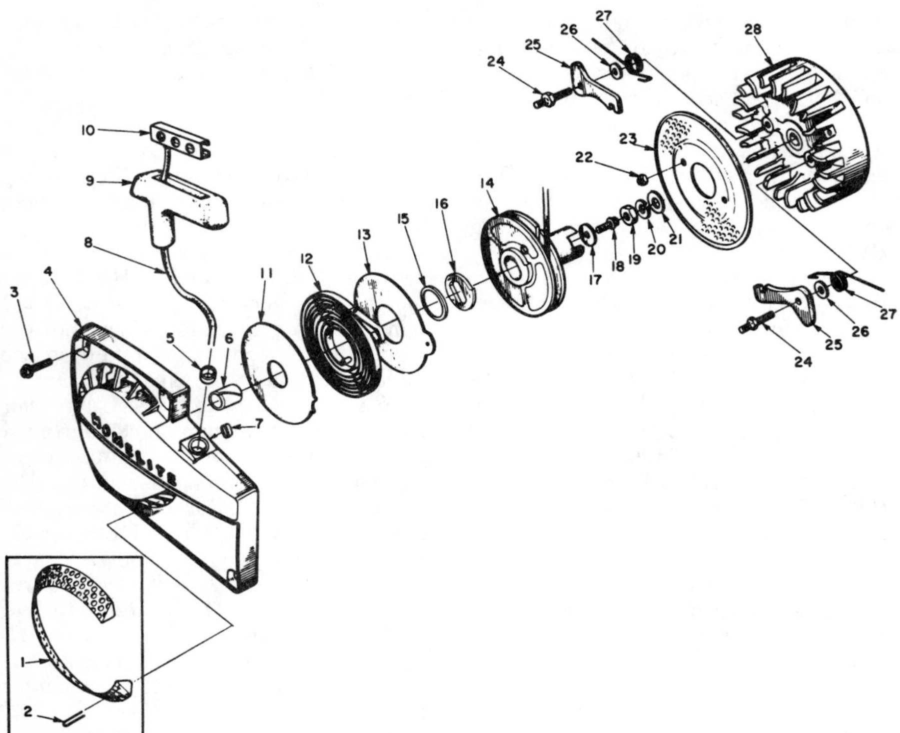

Fig. HL94 – Exploded view of starter. An air flow ring is used in place of screen (23) on some models.

1. Screen
2. Fastener clips
3. Hex head screws
4. Fan housing
5. Rope bushing
6. Starter post bushing
7. Rewind spring bushing
8. Starter rope
9. Handle
10. Rope retainer
11. Inner spring shield
12. Rewind spring
13. Outer spring shield
14. Starter pulley
15. Spring lock bushing
16. Spring lock
17. Retaining washer
18. Hex head screw
19. Flywheel (rotor) nut
20. Lockwasher
21. Flat washer
22. Lock nuts
23. Rotating screen
24. Pawl studs
25. Starter pawls
26. Washers
27. Pawl springs
28. Flywheel (rotor)

CAUTION: Rewind spring may be dislodged and can cause injury if allowed to uncoil uncontrolled. Rope bushing, starter post bushing, and/or rewind spring bushing in housing should be renewed if worn.

When reassembling starter, lubricate starter post lightly and install spring dry except for a small amount of lithium base grease on edges of spring.

Reassemble starter using exploded view in Fig. HL94 as a guide. Prewind spring about 2-4 turns.

HOMELITE

Model	Bore mm (in.)	Stroke mm (in.)	Displacement cc (cu. in.)	Drive Type
Super WIZ 55	50.8 (2.0)	34.9 (1.375)	70.8 (4.32)	Gear
Super WIZ 66	50.8 (2.0)	38.1 (1.5)	77.0 (4.7)	Gear
Super WIZ 80	55.6 (2.1875)	39.3 (1.547)	95.0 (5.8)	Gear

MAINTENANCE

SPARK PLUG. Recommended spark plug is Champion J6J for Super WIZ 55 and Super WIZ 66 and Champion UJ11G for Super WIZ 80. Electrode gap should be 0.025 inch (0.63 mm). In high temperatures or for heavy duty operation, use UJ7G plug in place of J6J or UJ11G. In extremely cold weather, a UJ12 plug may be used to avoid cold fouling and improve starting.

CARBURETOR. All models are equipped with a Tillotson Model HL diaphragm type carburetor. Carburetor model number is stamped on carburetor mouting flange. Refer to Tillotson section of CARBURETOR SERVICE section for carburetor overhaul and exploded views.

For initial starting equipment, close both fuel mixture needles lightly (turn clockwise), then open idle fuel needle ¾ turn counterclockwise and main fuel needle one to 1¼ turns counterclockwise. Back idle speed stop screw out until throttle disc will fully close, then turn screw back in until it contacts throttle shaft arm plus one additional turn.

Make final adjustment with engine warm and running. Adjust idle speed screw so that engine will run at just below clutch engagement speed, then adjust idle fuel mixture needle so engine runs smoothly. Readjust idle speed stop screw if necessary. With engine running at full throttle under load (stall chain in cut), adjust main fuel needle so engine runs at highest obtainable speed without excessive smoke. Idle fuel needle is left, main fuel needle is to right.

THROTTLE CONNECTIONS. The throttle trigger is not directly connected with the carburetor throttle shaft arm. When throttle trigger is released, the throttle shaft arm should be held against the idle speed stop screw. Squeezing throttle trigger moves the throttle rod or lever away from carburetor shaft arm allowing the throttle opening spring (nongoverned models) or governor spring to move throttle to wide open

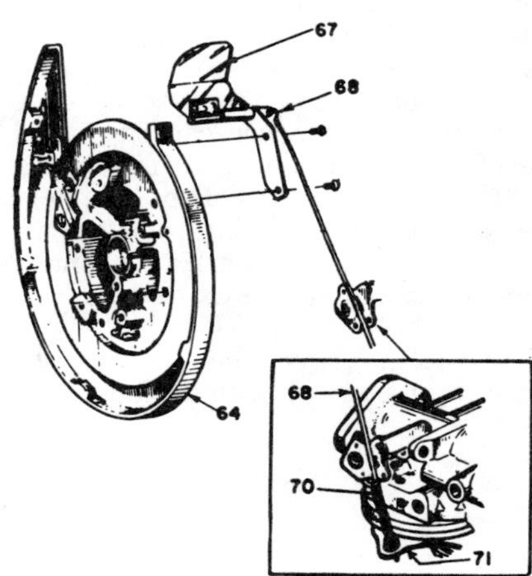

Fig. HL211—View showing governor hookup used on Super WIZ 66 and Super WIZ 80. Refer to Fig. HL215; throttle rod is connected at hole numbered (3). Governor spring (70) is compressed between bracket (71) and shoulder on governor rod.

64. Back plate
67. Governor assy.
68. Governor rod
70. Governor spring
71. Spring bracket

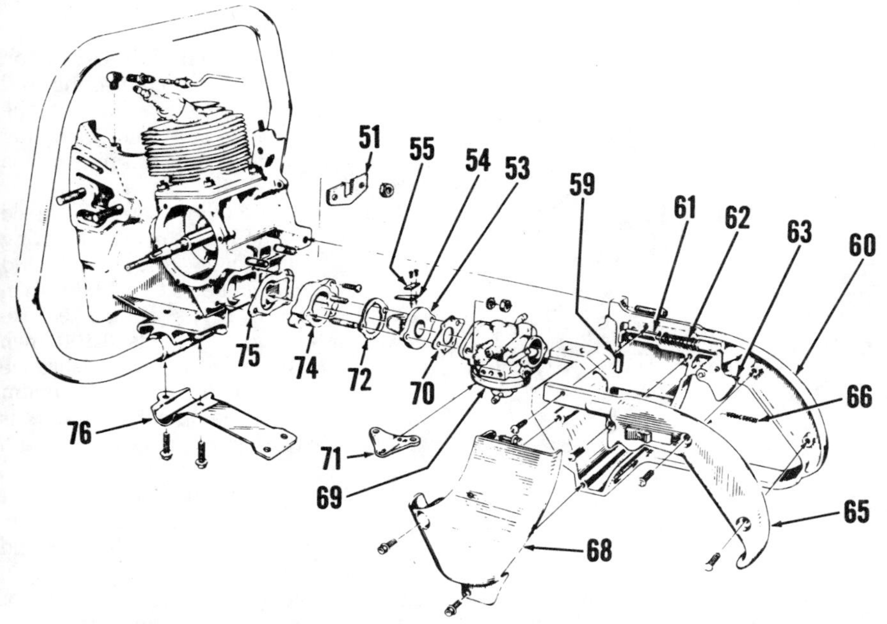

Fig. HL202—Exploded view showing typical throttle controls and carburetor mounting.

51. Fuel tank strap
53. Pyramid reed seat
54. Inlet reeds
55. Reed clamps
59. Throttle rod sleeve
60. Throttle handle
61. Throttle rod
62. Throttle spring
63. Throttle trigger
65. Handle cover
66. Throttle latch spring
68. Carburetor shield
69. Carburetor
70. Gasket
71. Spring bracket
72. Gasket
74. Pyramid reed spacer
75. Gasket
76. Brace

Fig. HL215—View showing throttle shaft arm typical of all carburetors. It is important that throttle opening or governor spring and/or link be hooked into proper hole. Refer also to Fig. HL211.

position. Check action of throttle linkage, carburetor throttle shaft and throttle opening or governor spring with engine stopped.

GOVERNOR. All models except Super WIZ 55 are equipped with an air vane type governor to prevent overspeeding of engine when saw is out of cut. Maximum no-load engine speed should be 7500 rpm; engine peak horsepower is obtained at about 6000 rpm.

With engine not running, check to see that governor spring will fully open throttle when throttle trigger is squeezed to wide open position. With engine warm and running at no load, governor should limit engine speed to about 7500 rpm by closing carburetor throttle. Check governor air vane and linkage for free operation and renew governor if worn or damaged.

MAGNETO. Refer to Fig. HL217 for exploded view of typical REPCO magneto. Breaker points, coil and condenser are accessible after removing flywheel. Homelite® rotor removing tool AA-22560 should be used.

Adjust breaker-point gap to 0.015 inch (0.38 mm). Condenser capacity should test 0.18-0.22 mfd. A new cam wiper felt (53) should be installed whenever breaker-points are being renewed. Adjust position of felt so it lightly contacts cam surface of engine crankshaft.

LUBRICATION. The engine is lubricated by mixing oil with unleaded gasoline. Recommended oil is Homelite® two-stroke oil mixed at ratio as designated on oil container. If Homelite® oil is not available, a good quality oil designed for two-stroke engines may be used when mixed at a 16:1 ratio, however, an anti-oxidant fuel stabilizer (such as Sta-Bil) should be added to fuel mix. Anti-oxidant fuel stabilizer is not required with Homelite® oils as they contain fuel stabilizer so the fuel mix will stay fresh up to one year.

Maintain oil level in gearcase to arrow on inspection window using Homelite® Gear Oil or SAE 90 gear lubricant. Check oil level with saw setting on level surface. Do not overfill.

Chain oiler tank should be filled with Homelite® Bar and Chain Oil or SAE 30 motor oil. In low temperatures, dilute chain oil with one part of kerosene to four parts of oil.

CARBON REMOVAL. Carbon deposits shoud be removed from exhaust ports and muffler at regular intervals. Use a wood scraper and be careful not to damage edges of exhaust ports. Piston should be at top dead center when removing carbon. Do not attempt to start engine with muffler removed.

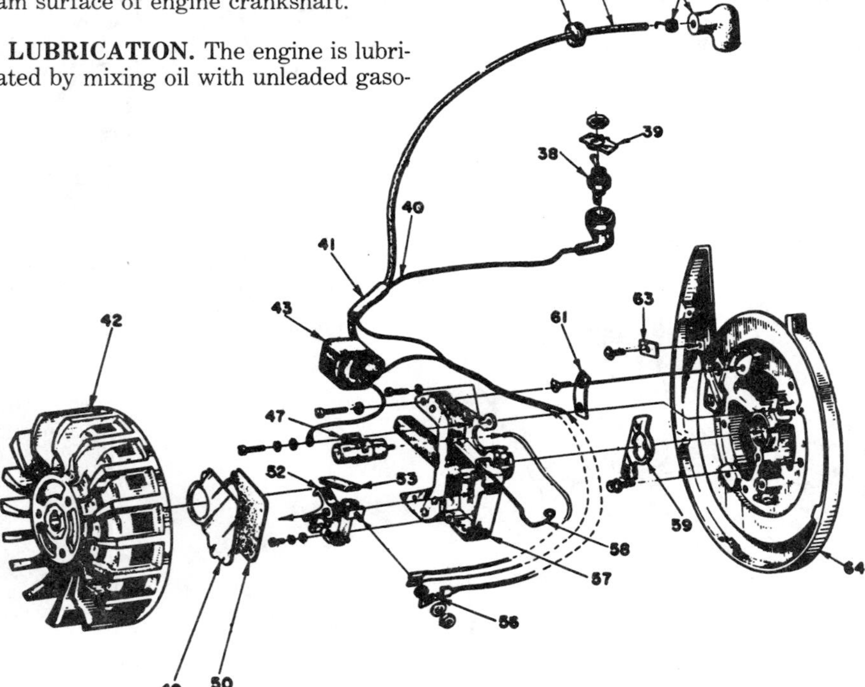

Fig. HL217 — Exploded view of typical REPCO magneto used on all models. Rotor (flywheel) has three tapped holes for installation of remover (Homelite® tool AA-22560). Magneto back plate (64) supports crankshaft seal and needle bearing.

35. Plug terminal
36. High tension wire
37. Grommet
38. "ON-OFF" switch
39. Switch plate
40. Ground wire
41. Sleeve
42. Rotor
43. Ignition coil
47. Condenser
49. Breaker cover
50. Gasket
52. Breaker points
53. Cam wiper felt
56. Ground wire tab
57. Armature core
58. Cover clip
59. Sealing felt
61. Wire clamp, inner
63. Wire clamp, outer

REPAIRS

CONNECTING ROD. Connecting rod and piston assembly can be removed after removing cylinder from crankcase. Be careful to remove all of the loose needle rollers when detaching rod from crankpin. Models Super WIZ 55 and Super WIZ 66 and 27 needle rollers while Super WIZ 80 has 31 loose needle rollers.

Renew connecting rod if bent or twisted, or if crankpin bearing surface is scored, burned or excessively worn or if Formica thrust washers are deeply grooved or are not completely bonded to rod. The caged needle roller piston pin bearing can be renewed by pressing old bearing out and new bearing in using Homelite® tool A-23809. Press on lettered end of bearing cage only.

Homelite recommends renewing the crankpin needle rollers at each overhaul. New needle rollers are supplied in a wax strip; wrap the strip around crankpin, then assemble connecting rod cap on the crankpin. When reassembling engine after inspection, use light grease or beeswax to stick 16 rollers to rod and cap. Install piston and connecting rod assembly so pinned ends of piston rings are away from exhaust port (muffler) side of engine.

On Models Super WIZ 55 and Super WIZ 66, tighten the connecting rod cap screws to 55-60 in.-lbs. (6.2-6.8 N·m). On Model Super WIZ 80, tighten rod cap screws to a torque of 70-80 in.-lbs. (7.9-9.0 N·m). Wiggle rod and cap as the screws are tightened to align fracture mating surfaces.

PISTON, PIN AND RINGS. Piston can be removed from connecting rod after removing cylinder. Support the piston while removing and installing piston pin. Pin is retained in piston by a snap ring at each end of pin.

The aluminum alloy piston is fitted with two pinned piston rings. Ring width is 0.037 inch (0.94 mm) and end gap should be 0.070-0.080 inch (1.78-2.03 mm). Rings should be renewed if end gap exceeds 0.100 inch (2.54 mm). Minimum ring side clearance is 0.0025 inch (0.063 mm); maximum ring side clearance in ring groove is 0.004 inch (0.10 mm). Piston, pin and rings are available in standard size only.

Renew piston and pin, which are not available separately, if any of the following defects are noted: Visible up and down play of pin in piston bore, cracks in piston or hole in piston dome, scoring of piston accompanied by aluminum deposits in cylinder bore, piston ring locating pin worn to half of original thickness, or if side clearance of new ring exceeds 0.004 inch (0.10 mm). Refer to CYLIN-

DER paragraph for information from cylinder bore.

Assemble piston to connecting rod or install piston and rod assembly so piston ring locating pin side of piston is toward intake side of cylinder (away from exhaust ports). Always use new piston pin retaining snap rings.

CYLINDER. Cylinder bore is chrome plated; plating is light gray in color and does not have appearance of polished chrome. Because cylinder is honed after plating, the chrome bore looks much like the base metal of the aluminum cylinder. If plating has been penetrated by scoring or other causes, the aluminum exposed will appear as a bright area. These bright areas are usually, but not always, located at edges of cylinder ports. If further checking, as outlined in following paragraph, shows that chrome has been penetrated, the cylinder should be renewed.

In some instances, particles of metal from scored piston are deposited on the cylinder bore. This condition is indicated by a rough appearance and deposits can be removed using a rubber impregnated grinding wheel mounted in a ¼ inch electric drill. If a screwdriver will scratch the cleaned surface, chrome plating has been worn away and the cylinder should be renewed. Also, renew the cylinder if cracked or if more than three critical cooling fins are broken off.

When installing both a new piston and a new cylinder, clean and oil both parts and place piston in cylinder bore without rings or connecting rod. The piston should fall freely when cylinder is turned up. If not, select a new piston or a new cylinder that will give this desired fit.

CRANKSHAFT, BEARINGS AND SEALS. The drive end of the crankshaft is supported in a ball bearing (24–Fig. HL219) which is retained in crankcase by two screws (26) and special washers (25) which engage groove in ball bearing outer race. Crankshaft is held in position by a snap ring (23) at outer side of bearing. The flywheel end crankshaft journal rotates in a caged needle roller bearing supported in magneto back plate (64–Fig. HL217).

To remove crankshaft, first remove cylinder, piston and connecting rod assembly, clutch spider and drum, flywheel (magneto rotor) and magneto back plate.

NOTE: On models with governor, be sure to disconnect governor linkage before attempting to remove back plate.

Remove the two bearing retaining screws (26–Fig. HL219) and washers (25), then bump or push crankshaft and bearing from crankcase. To remove ball bearing, remove snap ring (23) and press crankshaft from bearing.

Renew magneto end needle bearing if any roller shows visible wear or flat spot, or if rollers can be separated more than width of one roller. Renew drive end ball bearing if bearing is rough or has perceptible wear. Inspect crankshaft magneto end and crankpin journals and renew crankshaft if wear marks are visible. Also, renew crankshaft if tapered end fits loosely in magneto rotor or if keyway is enlarged. Crankshaft runout should not exceed 0.003 inch (0.08 mm).

New crankshaft seals and sealing gasket should always be installed when reassembling engine. Install new seal in crankcase with lip of seal inward (toward main bearing position). Install ball bearing on crankshaft with retaining groove in outer race toward crankshaft throw, then install retaining snap ring. Soak new gasket in oil, then position gasket in crankcase. Install crankshaft and bearing using seal protector sleeve and jackscrew, then secure bearing in position using new special washers and screws. Install new seal in back plate with new gasket.

Homelite® special tools for installing bearings, crankshaft seals and crankshaft are as follows:

A-23137–Jackscrew, crankshaft and bearing.
23136–Jackscrew body.
22820-1–Collar, crankshaft and bearing.
22812-1–Plate, shaft aligning.
23233–Plug, back plate & crankcase seal.
23232–Sleeve, crankshaft seal.
23391-1–Plug, back plate bearing.

CRANKCASE. With crankshaft and bearing removed, check bearing bore. A lapped appearance indicates that the bearing outer race has been turning in the bore. If bearing fits loose in bore, renew the crankcase and/or bearing as necessary to obtain a tight fit. New ball bearing special retaining washers and screws should always be used when reassembling.

REED VALVE. The reed valve should be inspected whenever carburetor is removed. All models are equipped with a pyramid reed type valve which has renewable reeds. Refer to Fig. HL221.

CLUTCH. A shoe type clutch is used on all models and clutch hub is threaded to engine crankshaft. All models have right hand threads. Refer to Fig. HL225 for exploded view.

On Models Super WIZ 55 and Super WIZ 66, standard clutch shoes are ⅝ inch (15.8 mm) wide; optional heavy duty clutch shoes are ¾ inch (19.0 mm) wide. Standard and heavy duty clutch components are not individually

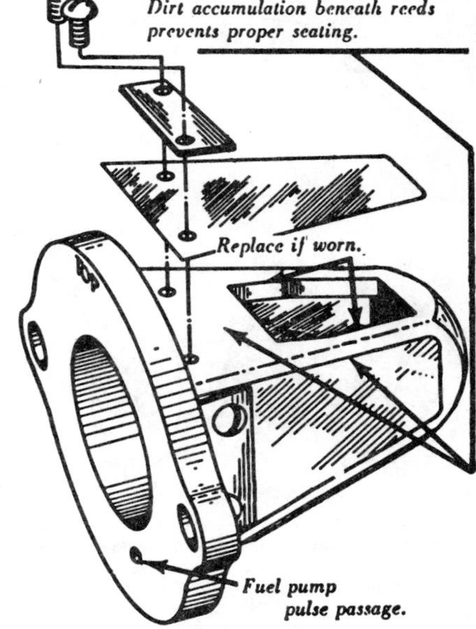

Fig. HL221–Inspection points for pyramid reed seat and reeds.

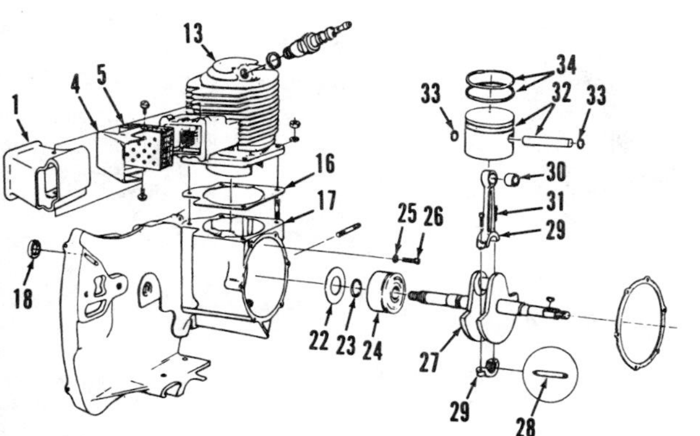

Fig. HL219–Exploded view of typical engine.

1. Heat damper
4. Exhaust cap
5. Muffler element
13. Cylinder
16. Gasket
17. Crankcase
18. Crankshaft seal
22. Gasket
23. Snap ring
24. Ball bearing
25. Special washers
26. Special screws
27. Crankshaft
28. Needle rollers
29. Connecting rod & cap
30. Needle bearing
31. Connecting rod screws
32. Piston & pin
33. Snap rings
34. Piston rings

interchangeable; also, a different gear case cover is required with heavy duty clutch. Clutch drum bushing is renewable on all models.

Homelite® tool A-23696 can be used with wrench to remove clutch spider. When assembling clutch, be sure end loops of springs are closed and are located at the center of a clutch shoe. If installing new clutch drum, wash off protective coating with petroleum solvent.

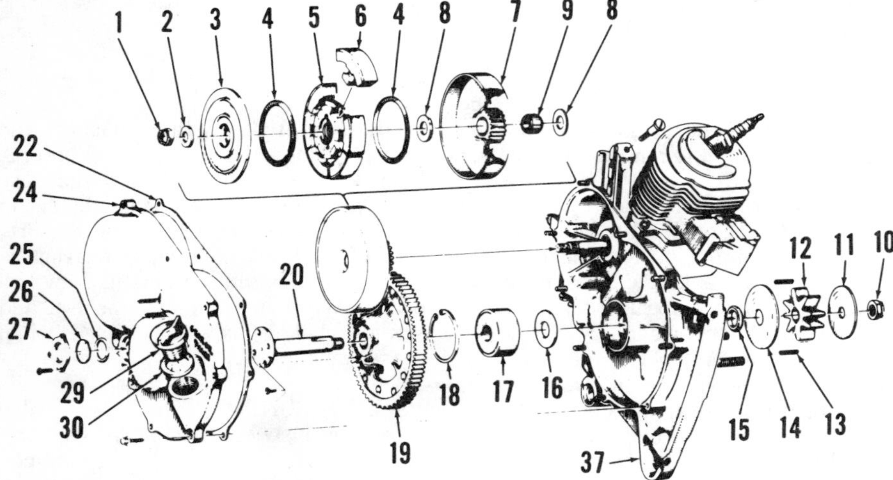

Fig. HL225 – Exploded view of transmission. One standard and two optional gear ratios are available. Standard gear ratio of 3.57:1 is provided by output gear with 75 teeth and clutch drum with 21 teeth. Optional 2.84:1 ratio requires output (driven) gear with 71 teeth and clutch drum gear with 25 teeth. On 2:1 optional gear ratio, output gear has 64 teeth and clutch drum gear has 32 teeth.

1. Crankshaft nut
2. Flat washer
3. Clutch cover
4. Clutch springs
5. Clutch spider
6. Clutch shoes
7. Clutch drum & gear
8. Thrust washer
9. Bronze bushing
10. Sprocket shaft nut
11. Sprocket washer
12. Chain sprocket
13. Sprocket keys
14. Sprocket washer
15. Sprocket spacer
16. Formica seal
17. Ball bearing
18. Snap ring
19. Driven (output) gear
20. Sprocket shaft
22. Gasket
24. Transmission cover
25. "O" ring
26. Window
27. Window plate
29. Filler cap
30. Gasket
37. Crankcase & gear case

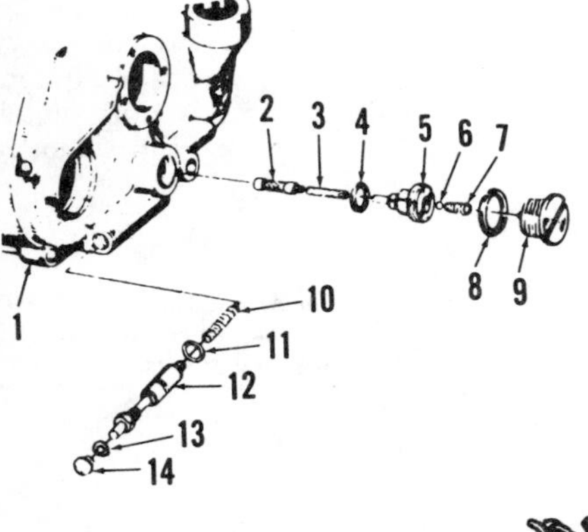

Fig. HL226 – Exploded view of typical manual oil pump assembly.

1. Fuel tank
2. Oil filter
3. Oil line
4. Gasket
5. Valve seat
6. Check ball
7. Check valve spring
8. Gasket
9. Plug
10. Spring
11. "O" ring
12. Pump plunger
13. "O" ring
14. Button

TRANSMISSION. All models have a two-gear transmission as shown in Fig. HL225.

To service transmission, first drain oil from transmission case, then remove the screws retaining cover to case. Tap cover lightly, if necessary, to loosen gasket seal and remove the cover.

To disassemble transmission, remove nut (1 – Fig. HL225) from crankshaft, remove washer and clutch cover (3) and using Homelite® special tool A-23696, turn clutch hub counterclockwise while holding engine from turning to remove the spider and shoe assembly. Remove clutch drum (7) and thrust washers (8) from crankshaft. Remove sprocket nut (10), sprocket (12) and related parts, then using soft mallet, bump sprocket shaft (20) and gear from case. Remove snap ring (18), then press bearing from case using Homelite® special tool 23228. Renew the Formica seal (16) before installing new bearing. Remove retaining screws, then remove output gear (19) from sprocket shaft. Reverse disassembly procedure and use Fig. HL225 as a guide to reassemble. Reinstall cover with new gasket and fill transmission to proper level with lubricant.

REWIND STARTER. Refer to Fig. HL228 for exploded view of starter. When installing rewind spring, pulley and rope, spring should be pretensioned so pulley will rewind all rope and pull rope handle lightly against starter housing. If spring is tensioned too tightly, or if starter rope is too long, spring can be damaged by being wound too tightly when starter rope is pulled out. Friction shoe assembly (8) is available as a unit assembly only. If friction shoes have been disassembled, they must be reassembled as shown in Fig. 229. Be sure that starter is properly placed on starter pulley so sharp edges of clutch shoes are pointing in direction shown in Fig. HL228.

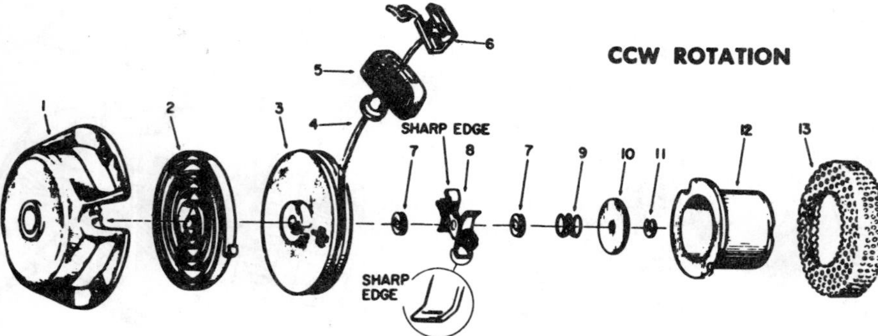

Fig. HL228 – Exploded view of Fairbanks-Morse starter. Fig. HL229 shows proper method of assembling friction shoe assembly if it has been disassembled for some reason; individual parts of friction shoe assembly are not available. Note direction for shaft edges of shoes when reassembling starter.

1. Cover
2. Rewind spring
3. Rope pulley
4. Starter rope
5. Handle grip
6. Grip insert
7. Brake washers
8. Friction shoe assy.
9. Brake spring
10. Retaining washer
11. Retaining ring
12. Starter cup
13. Starter screen

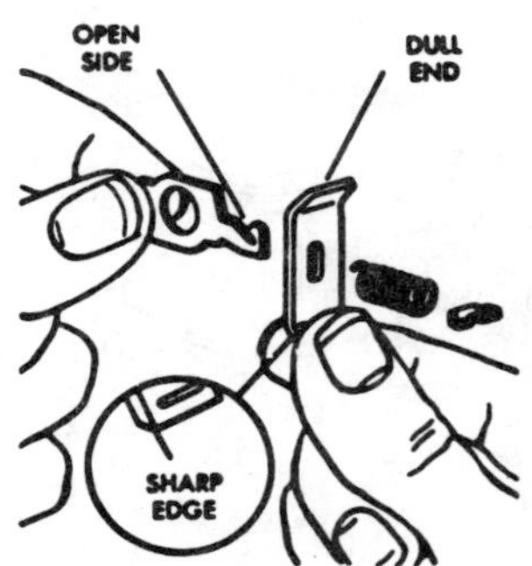

Fig. HL229 – If Fairbanks-Morse starter friction shoe assembly is disassembled, be sure to reassemble as shown.

HOMELITE

Model	Bore mm (in.)	Stroke mm (in.)	Displacement cc (cu. in.)	Drive Type
Little Red XL	...	...	30	Direct
LX-30 Bandit	...	...	30	Direct
XL, XL 2	33.34 (1.3125)	30.16 (1.1875)	26.2 (1.6)	Direct
Super 2, VI Super 2, 2-2SL	36.51 (1.4375)	30.16 (1.1875)	31.2 (1.9)	Direct
180, 180-16	...	...	30	Direct
192, 200	...	...	33	Direct

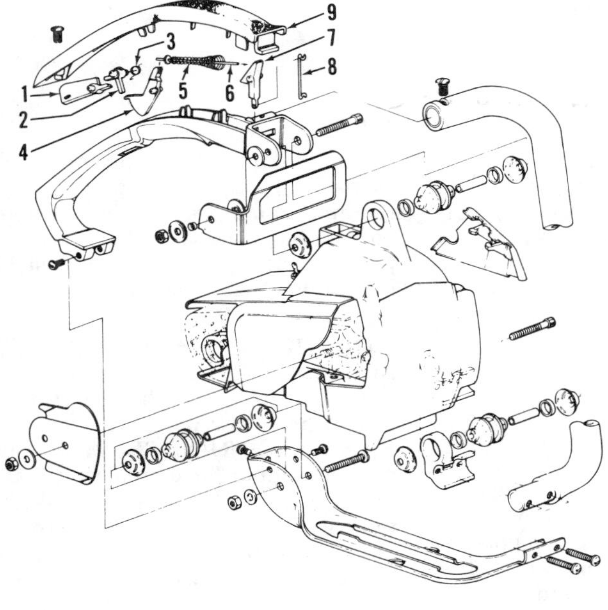

Fig. HL240—Exploded view of throttle trigger mechanism and associated parts used on VI Super models.

1. Throttle safety lever
2. Throttle safety stop
3. Spring
4. Trigger
5. Spring
6. Trigger rod
7. Throttle lever
8. Throttle rod
9. Handle cover

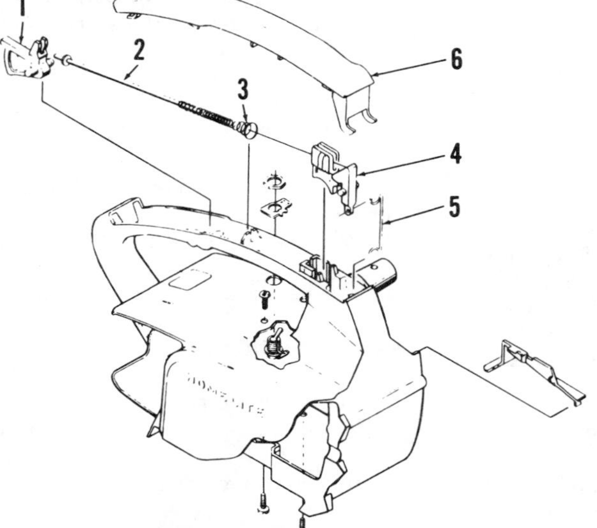

Fig. HL241—View showing dual trigger mechanism of some models.

1. Rear trigger
2. Trigger rod
3. Spring
4. Front trigger
5. Throttle rod
6. Handle cover

MAINTENANCE

SPARK PLUG. Recommended spark plug is Champion RDJ7Y for VI Super-2SL model saw. Recommended spark plug for all other models is Champion DJ7Y. Spark plug electrode gap should be 0.025 inch (0.6 mm) for all models.

CARBURETOR. Some Super-2 and Super-2SL models may be equipped with a Walbro HDC diaphragm carburetor. Other models may be equipped with a Tillotson HK, Walbro HDC, Zama C1Q or Zama C2S diaphragm type carburetor. Refer to CARBURETOR SERVICE section in the front of this manual for carburetor overhaul procedures and exploded views. Refer to Fig. HL240, HL241 and HL242 for exploded views of throttle controls.

Initial adjustment of low-speed and high-speed mixture needles on early models is one turn open from a lightly seated position. On late models, the mixture needles have adjustment limiters that limit the amount of adjustment to 1/2 turn. On these models, turn the mixture needles counterclockwise until they stop.

On all models, start engine and run until operating temperature is reached. Turn low-speed mixture needle until maximum idle speed is reached, then turn needle 1/8 turn counterclockwise. Engine should accelerate cleanly without hesitation. If engine stumbles or seems sluggish when accelerating, adjust low-speed mixture screw until engine accelerates without hesitation. Adjust idle speed screw so engine idles without stalling and chain does not rotate.

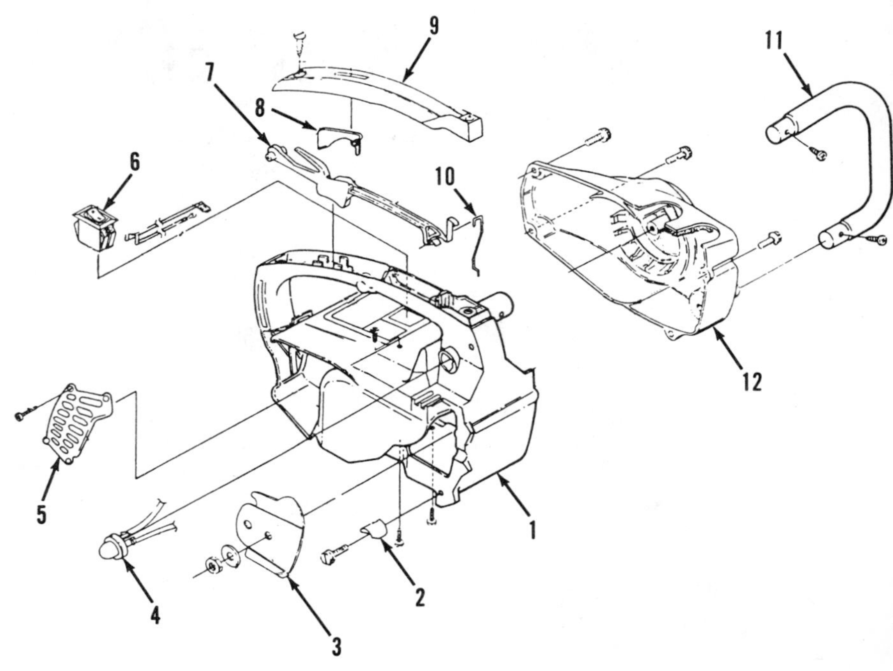

Fig. HL242—View typical of late model case assembly.

1. Engine case
2. Chain stop
3. Guide bar plate
4. Fuel primer bulb
5. Muffler shield
6. Stop switch
7. Trigger
8. Trigger lock
9. Handle cover
10. Throttle rod
11. Front handle
12. Starter housing

Adjust high-speed mixture needle with saw running at wide open throttle. Adjust needle to obtain maximum speed, then turn needle 1/8 turn counterclockwise. Do not operate saw with high speed mixture too lean as engine damage may result from lack of lubrication and overheating.

IGNITION. All models use a conventional magneto ignition system. Early models are equipped with a breaker point-type ignition, while later models are equipped with a breakerless solid-state ignition.

The solid-state ignition system is serviced by renewing the spark plug and/or ignition module. There is no periodic maintenance required, however, air gap between ignition module and flywheel is adjustable.

Adjust air gap by loosening the screws attaching the module retaining screws then place a 0.015 inch (0.38 mm) shim stock between flywheel and the legs of the ignition module. Turn the flywheel if necessary to locate the flywheel magnets near the ignition module. Press the ignition module against the flywheel magnets until the legs of the ignition module are firmly against the shim stock then tighten the attaching screws to the torque listed in the TIGHTENING TORQUE paragraph. Remove the setting gauge, then turn the flywheel and check that flywheel does not hit the legs of the coil.

Note the following on breaker-point equipped models. Breaker-point gap should be 0.015 inch (0.38 mm). Air gap between magneto unit and flywheel magnet should be 0.015 inch (0.38 mm) and may be set using shim stock.

Ignition timing is fixed and cannot be adjusted, however, breaker-point gap must be correct, because it will affect ignition timing. Improper breaker point gap may also affect ignition operation, preventing the engine from operating properly.

LUBRICATION. The engine is lubricated by mixing oil with gasoline. Recommended oil is Homelite 2-cycle engine oil mixed at ratio as designated on oil container. If Homelite oil is not available, good quality oil designed for air-cooled 2-cycle engines at 40:1 or 50:1 ratios may be used but must be mixed at 32:1 ratio. Oils formulated at less than 32:1 ratio or non 2-cycle (automotive) oils should not be used.

Manufacturer recommends that an antioxidant fuel stabilizer, such as STA-BIL, should be added to the fuel mix if Homelite oil is not used. Antioxidant fuel stabilizer is not required when using Homelite oils as they contain fuel stabilizer. Always mix oil and gasoline in a separate container.

Saw chain is lubricated by oil from an automatic oil pump. Recommended chain oil is Homelite Bar and Chain Oil or equivalent oil designed for bar and chain lubrication. The rate of oil flow depends on engine speed and is not adjustable.

REPAIRS

COMPRESSION TEST. Engine should be hot when checking compression pressure. Remove spark plug and install compression test gage. Pull starter rope and note pressure gage reading. Compression pressure should be 115-145 psi (800-1000 kPa). Compression pressure below 90 psi (620 kPa) indicates an engine problem.

CRANKCASE PRESSURE TEST. An improperly sealed crankcase can cause the engine to be hard to start, run rough, have low power and overheat. Refer to the ENGINE SERVICE section of this manual for crankcase pressure test procedure. If crankcase leakage is indicated, pressurize crankcase and use a soap and water solution to check gaskets, seals, pulse line and castings for leakage.

TIGHTENING TORQUE VALUE. Tightening torque values are listed in the following table.

Flywheel. . . . . 100-150 in.-lbs. (11.3-14.0 N·m)
Clutch drum nut . . . . . 100-125 in.-lbs. (11.3-14.0 N·m)
Clutch hub . . . . 100-150 in.-lbs. (11.3-14.0 N·m)
Spark plug . . . . 120-180 in.-lbs. (13.6-20.0 N·m)
Crankcase screws . . . . . .55-65 in.-lbs.* (6.2-7.3 N·m)
Reed mounting screws . . 10-15 in.-lbs. (1.1-1.7 N·m)
Intake manifold mounting screws. . . . . 35-45 in.-lbs.* (4.0-5.0 N·m)
Carburetor mounting screws. . . . . 35-45 in.-lbs. (4.0-5.9 N·m)

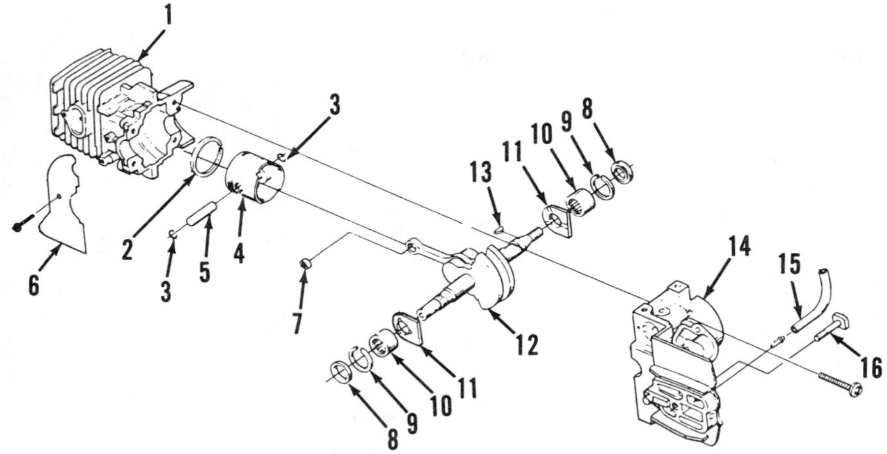

Fig. HL243—Exploded view of engine typical of all models.

1. Cylinder
2. Piston ring
3. Retaining clip
4. Piston
5. Piston pin
6. Dust shield
7. Needle bearing
8. Oil seal
9. Spacer
10. Needle bearing
11. Thrust washer
12. Crankshaft & connecting rod assy.
13. Key
14. Crankcase
15. Oil line
16. Guide bar bolt

Muffler mounting screws . . . . 40-50 in.-lbs.* (4.5-5.6 N•m)
Ignition module screws . . . . 30-40 in.-lbs.* (3.4-4.5 N•m)
*Apply thread locking compound to screw threads.

COMPRESSION PRESSURE. For optimum performance of all models, cylinder compression pressure should be 115-145 psi (795-1000 kPa) with engine at normal operating temperature. Engine should be inspected and repaired when compression pressure is 90 psi (620 kPa) or below.

CRANKSHAFT, CYLINDER, PISTON, PIN AND RINGS. To disassemble, remove guide bar and chain, starter housing and front handle. Remove stop switch from engine housing and disconnect electrical leads. Remove chain brake assembly on models so equipped. Remove air cleaner cover, muffler guard and muffler. Remove primer bulb and disconnect throttle rod. Remove engine housing mounting screws and separate engine from engine housing. Remove oil tank and fuel tank. Remove air filter, carburetor and intake manifold. Remove ignition module/coil assembly.

Remove spark plug and insert end of a rope in the cylinder to act as a piston stop. Unscrew clutch drum mounting nut. Use clutch removal tool (Homelite tool A-24060) or equivalent to remove clutch hub from crankshaft. Note that clutch hub has left-hand threads (turn clockwise to remove). Remove flywheel mounting nut (right-hand threads) and use a suitable puller to remove flywheel from crankshaft.

Remove crankcase mounting screws and separate crankcase (14—Fig. HL243) from cylinder (1). Withdraw crankshaft, connecting rod and piston from cylinder. Care should be taken not to scratch or nick mating surfaces of cylinder and crankcase. Remove piston ring (2) from piston. Remove retainer clips (3) and push piston pin (5) out of piston. Separate piston and needle bearing (7) from connecting rod.

Crankshaft needle bearings (10) are held loosely in their cages. Before removing needle bearings from crankshaft, coat the crankshaft with multipurpose grease. Then, slide the bearings through the grease and off the crankshaft. The grease will retain the needle bearings in the cage.

To reassemble, reverse the disassembly procedure while noting the following special instructions: Install piston on connecting rod so locating pin in ring groove is facing flywheel (keyed) side of crankshaft. Install thrust washers (11—Fig. HL243) with grooved side facing crankshaft counterweights. Use multipurpose grease to retain needle rollers in main bearing cages (10). Install main bearings with lettered side facing outward. Install spacers (9) with open side toward cylinder. Lubricate lip of seals (8) with grease before installation.

Make certain that piston ring end gap indexes with locating pin in piston ring groove. Lubricate piston and cylinder bore with oil, compress the piston ring and slide piston into cylinder. Flat side of thrust washers (11) must face the crankcase (14).

Apply light coat of RTV silicone sealant to crankcase mating surface, then assemble crankcase to cylinder. Be sure crankshaft seals (8) are flush with outer surface of cylinder and crankcase. Gently tap on both ends of crankshaft to center all components, then tighten crankcase screws to specified torque.

CLUTCH To remove clutch assembly, first separate engine from engine housing as outlined in CRANKSHAFT, CYLINDER, PISTON, PIN AND RINGS section. Remove spark plug and insert end of a rope in cylinder to act as a piston stop.

Note that clutch drum nut (1—Fig. HL244) and clutch hub (6) have left-hand threads (turn clockwise to remove). Remove clutch drum nut (3), needle bearing (4) and washers (2). Use clutch tool (Homelite part number A-24060) or other suitable tool to remove clutch hub (6). Disconnect springs (5) and separate clutch shoes (7) from hub.

Inspect clutch components for wear or damage and renew as necessary. To reinstall, reverse removal procedure.

AUTOMATIC CHAIN OILER SYSTEM. All models are equipped with an automatic chain oiler system. Some models are equipped with a crankcase pulse actuated automatic chain oil pump. On early models, the oil pump assembly is mounted on the crankcase (Fig. HL245). On later models, the pulse driven diaphragm type pump is mounted on the fuel metering side of the carburetor (14—Fig. HL244). Some models are equipped with a pressurized oil tank system. Refer to the appropriate following paragraphs to service automatic chain oiler systems.

Diaphragm Type Pump (Early). A defective oil pump may cause excessive smoke during operation, hydraulic lock preventing starting of engine or oil leaking from guide bar pad while engine idles or is shut off. If any of these conditions exist and excessive smoke is not due to improperly mixed fuel, proceed as follows:

Attach a suitable pressure gauge and hand pump to oil pickup line as shown in Fig. HL246 and pressurize system to 5-8 psi (34-55 kPa). If system does not hold pressure, then oil is leaking past pump body (6—Fig. HL245) and crankcase (25). Renew pump body.

To remove pump body, remove pump cover (2), spring (3) and diaphragm and plunger. Seal off the pressure and pulse passages in crankcase and insert a small wad of paper in pump body bore.

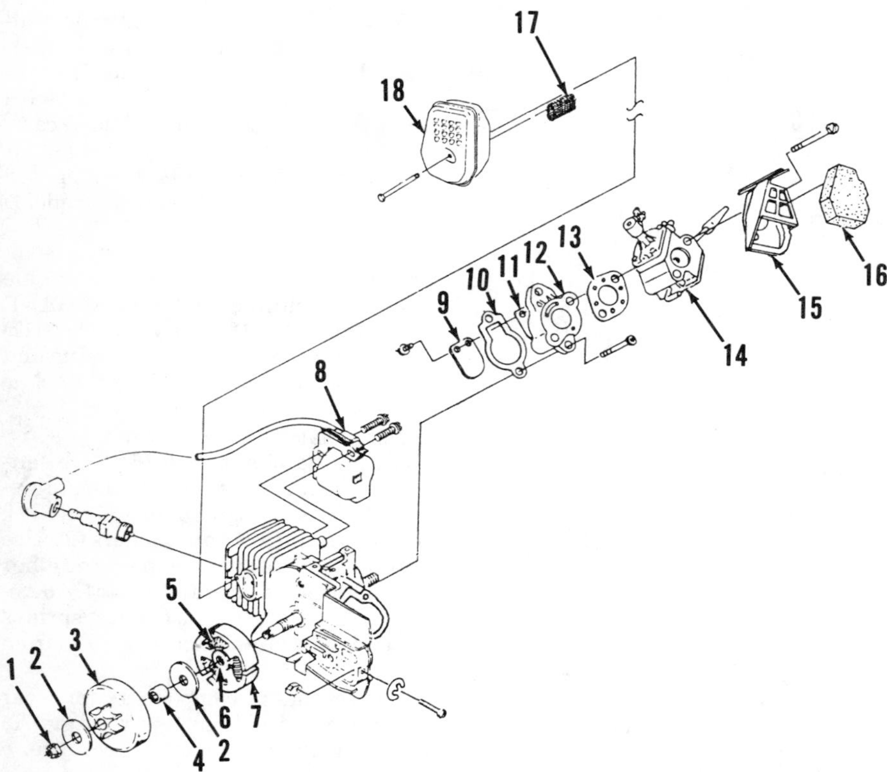

Fig. HL244—Exploded view of clutch, muffler and intake components typical of late models. Chain oil pump is mounted on fuel metering side of carburetor.

1. Nut
2. Washers
3. Clutch drum
4. Needle bearing
5. Spring
6. Clutch hub
7. Clutch shoe
8. Ignition unit
9. Reed stop
10. Gasket
11. Reed
12. Intake manifold
13. Gasket
14. Carburetor & oil pump assy.
15. Air filter housing
16. Filter element
17. Spark arrestor
18. Muffler

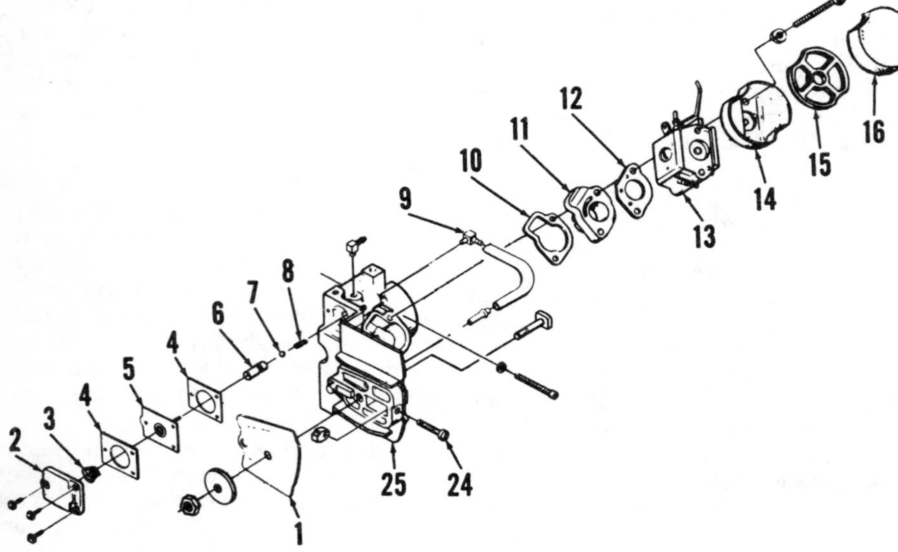

Fig. HL245—Exploded view of early crankcase, intake components and automatic chain oil pump assembly.

1. Guide bar plate
2. Pump cover
3. Spring
4. Gasket
5. Diaphragm & plunger
6. Oil pump cylinder
7. Check ball
8. Spring
9. Oil line
10. Gasket
11. Intake manifold
12. Gasket
13. Carburetor
14. Filter housing
15. Retainer
16. Air filter
24. Chain tension adjusting screw
25. Crankcase

Two methods of detaching pump body are recommended. One method is to drill into pump body bore with a 7/64 inch drill bit approximately 1/2 inch (12.7 mm), then tap a #2 "easy out" into bore. Twist and pull pump body from crankcase. The other method is to drill and tap pump body bore with a 10-32 thread then use a suitable puller to withdraw pump body from crankcase. Make certain that check ball (7) and spring (8) are not lost when pump body is removed.

Thoroughly clean all parts and pump bore in crankcase. Measure length of new pump body and related bore in crankcase, then install required number of Homelite 0.015 inch thick gaskets 69596 to position diaphragm end of pump body 0.0-0.015 inch (0.0-0.38 mm) above diaphragm chamber floor as shown at (A—Fig HL246).

Insert spring (8—Fig. HL245) and check ball (7) into crankcase. Check ball may also be placed in ball seat end of pump body using a small amount of grease to hold ball in position. Using a suitable arbor press, insert pump body halfway into crankcase. Apply a bead of RTV silastic sealer around upper third of body, then continue pressing body into crankcase until it seats in bore. Wipe off excess sealer. Insert diaphragm and plunger and work it against check ball several times making sure it operates freely. Allow RTV sealer to dry.

Pressure test pump as previously outlined to check repair. If system does not hold pressure, then pump bore in crankcase is damaged or defective and renewal of crankcase assembly is required. If system holds pressure, reassemble remaining components and fill oil tank.

With bar and chain removed, start and run saw at wide open throttle in 15 second intervals. Oil pump should deliver 12-17 cc/minute during test and 5-12 cc/minute under actual operating conditions. Shut off engine and check for leaks.

Diaphragm Type Pump (Late) In this system, crankcase pressure pulses pressurize the oil tank. Oil in the tank is then pressure fed to a pulse driven, positive displacement diaphragm type oil pump mounted on the carburetor which pumps the oil to guide bar outlet. See Fig. HL247 for drawing of automatic oiler and fuel system hose connections.

To pressure test automatic oiler system, install a test cap (oil cap with a hose connector fitting) on oil tank and connect hand pressure tester with a pressure gauge as shown in Fig.

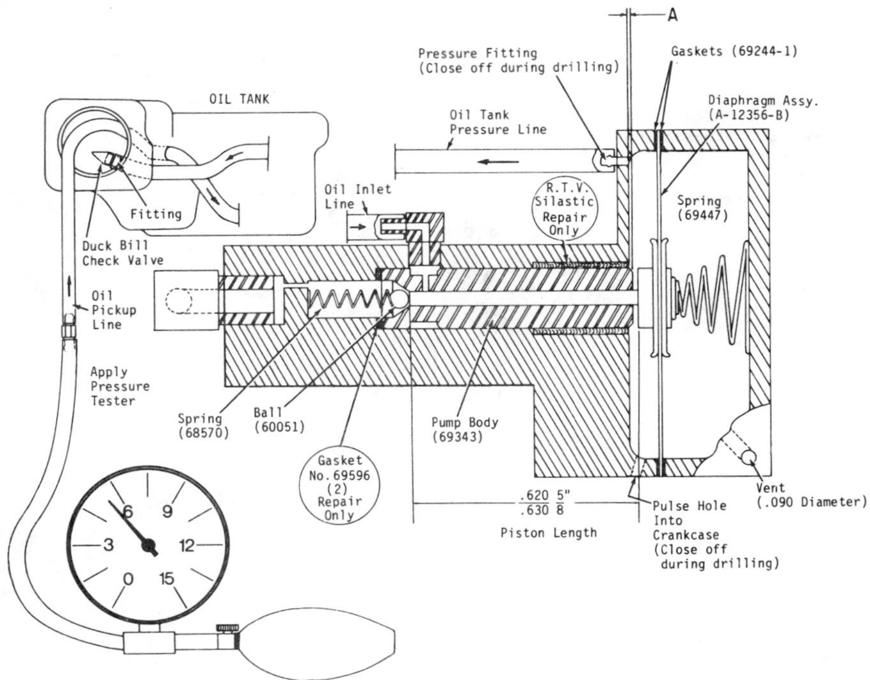

Fig. HL246—Diagram showing pressure tester hook-up and diaphragm oil pump components used on some models.

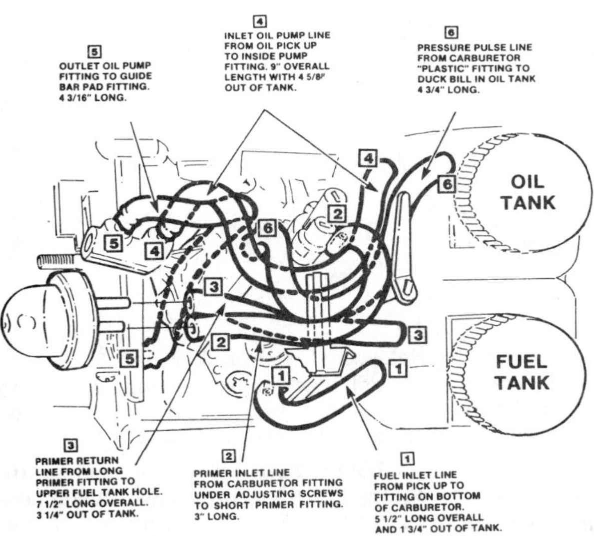

Fig. HL247—Drawing showing correct routing of chain oiler system hoses and fuel system hoses for models equipped with a pressurized oil tank and a diaphragm type oil pump.

Fig. HL248—To pressure test chain oiler system, install a test cap (oil cap with a hose fitting) on oil tank and connect pressure tester to fitting as shown.

HL248. Run saw until it is at operating temperature. Then, run engine at wide-open throttle for five to ten seconds while noting pressure gauge reading. Pressure gauge should read at least 2-3 psi (14-20 kPa).

If automatic oiler now works, renew oil cap and/or gasket. If oil tank does not pressurize with engine running, actuate hand pump to pressurize tank. If oil is now pumped to guide bar outlet, pressure pulse line is faulty.

To test pressure line, install a plastic line over "duckbill" check valve at oil tank end of pressure line and use pressure tester to apply 3-4 psi (21-27 kPa) to check valve. Renew check valve if it will not hold pressure.

If pressure line is satisfactory, clamp two oil tank lines and pressurize tank with 5-6 psi (35-41 kPa). If tank does not hold pressure, examine for location of leak. If tank pressurizes when running but there is no oil output, remove oil pick-up tube from tank and check for plugged oil filter or a pin hole in pick-up tube.

If oil pick-up line is satisfactory, apply 7-10 psi (48-69 kPa) pressure to pick-up line. The oil pump check valve should unseat at this pressure, causing a rapid drop in pressure gauge reading. If check valve does not unseat, disassemble oil pump and inspect unit. Oil pump diaphragm plunger length should measure between 0.620-0.630 inch (15.75-16.0 mm). Renew parts as necessary.

Oil pump can be pressure tested for leaks with carburetor removed from engine. Connect pressure tester to oil pump inlet fitting and pressurize to 5-6 psi (35-41 kPa). If necessary, submerge carburetor and oil pump assembly in solvent to locate leak.

Pressurized Oil Tank System. Some saws use crankcase pulses to pressurize the oil tank, forcing oil directly from the oil tank to the guide bar oil outlet. In temperatures below 32 degrees F (0 degrees C), it is necessary to dilute chain oil with one part of kerosene to four parts of oil to allow system operation.

If chain oil flow is inadequate or has stopped completely, proceed as follows: Check condition of oil tank cap. Cap must seal tank opening to allow oil tank to pressurize. Make sure that oil level is not above the "duckbill" check valve and that oil pick-up is at bottom of tank.

Check the condition of the oil filter on pick-up line and clean or renew as required. Check diameter of oil metering orifice located in oil pick-up line above oil filter. Diameter of orifice should not

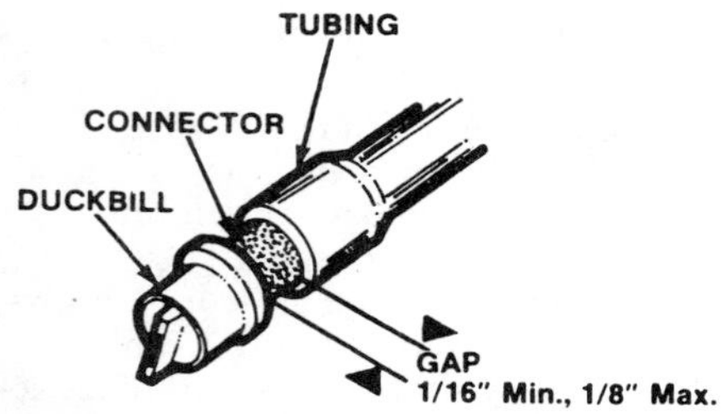

Fig. HL249—Gap between "duckbill" check valve and tubing end must be 1/16-1/8 inch (1.6-3.1 mm).

Fig. HL250—Exploded view of rewind starter assembly.

1. Flywheel
2. Spring
3. Starter pawl
4. Pawl pin
5. Washer
6. Nut
7. Cap screw
8. Washer
9. Rope pulley
10. Rewind spring
11. Housing

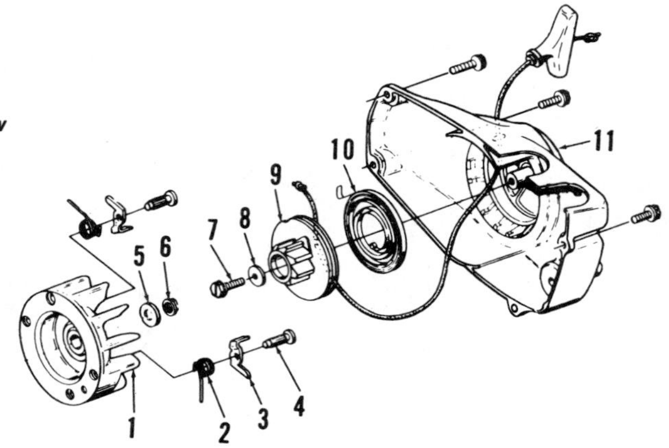

Fig. HL251—Exploded view of chain brake used on some models.

1. Clip
2. Brake band
3. Post
4. Pivot ling
5. Spring pin
6. Lever
7. Roll pin
8. Washer
9. Screw

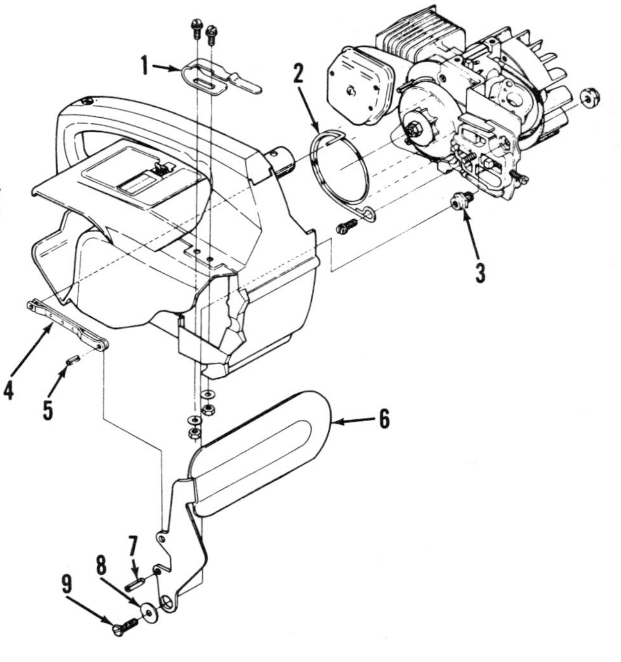

be less than 0.046 inch (1.18 mm). Oil pick-up line should be 4 to 4-1/8 inches (102-105 mm) long on outside of tank and positioned under the carburetor throttle stop.

Connect a suitable pressure tester to oil tank using a test cap (cap having a fitting for a hose). Pressurize tank to 4-5 psi (28-34 kPa) and check for free flowing oil at guide bar. If there is no oil flow, check for pinched or restricted oil lines.

With pressure tester still installed, start and run saw at wide-open throttle for about 10 seconds. Tank should pressurize to 2.5 to 6 psi (17-41 kPa). While engine idles or is shut off, pressure should drop to zero after approximately 5 seconds.

If tank fails to pressurize, check the condition of crankcase pulse line by submerging the "duckbill" check valve (shown in Fig. HL249) in oil while the saw is running. Constant bubbles should emit from check valve with slight bubbling from porous connector located between check valve and line. A connector that is too porous will not maintain the required 2.5 psi (17 kPa) minimum for proper oiling.

If oil flow is excessive or continues to flow after saw is shut off, proceed as follows: Excessive oil flow may be caused by incorrect installation of "duckbill" check valve (Fig. HL249). There should be a gap of 1/16-1/8 inch (1.6-3.1 mm) between check valve and end of pulse line thereby allowing porous connector to bleed off pressure while engine idles or is shut off. A good connector will bleed off pressure in approximately 5 seconds.

Oil may also be siphoning from tank to outlet after engine is shut off and can be corrected by installing Homelite Oil Filter A-78889 which contains a check valve that shuts off oil flow when tank pressure drops below 2 psi (14 kPa).

REWIND STARTER. To service rewind starter, remove starter housing (11—Fig. HL250) from saw. Pull starter rope and hold rope pulley with notch in pulley adjacent to rope outlet. Pull rope back through outlet so it engages notch in pulley and allow pulley to completely unwind.

Unscrew pulley retaining screw (7) and remove rope pulley being careful not to dislodge rewind spring in housing. Care must be taken if rewind spring is removed to prevent injury if spring is allowed to uncoil uncontrolled.

Rewind spring is wound in clockwise direction in starter housing. Rope is wound on rope pulley in clockwise direction as viewed with pulley in housing.

To place tension on rewind spring, pass rope though rope outlet in housing and install rope handle. Pull rope out and hold rope pulley so notch on pulley is adjacent to rope outlet. Pull rope back through outlet between notch in pulley and housing. Turn rope pulley clockwise to place tension on spring. Release pulley and check starter action. Do not place more tension on rewind spring than is necessary to draw rope handle up against housing.

CHAIN BRAKE. Some models are equipped with a chain brake system designed to stop chain movement should kickback occur. Chain brake is activated when operator's hand strikes chain brake handle (6—Fig. HL251), thereby drawing brake band (2) around clutch drum.

To disassemble chain brake, remove guide bar and chain. Remove the brake mounting screws. Use screwdriver to pry brake band off clutch drum, then lift brake band and handle assembly out over guide bar pad.

No adjustment of chain brake system is required. Renew any component that is excessively worn or damaged. Lubricate all pivot points with Molykote or suitable equivalent.

HOMELITE

Model	Bore mm (in.)	Stroke mm (in.)	Displacement cc (cu. in.)	Drive Type
350, 350 B, 350 HG, 350 SL Automatic	44.4 (1.75)	36.6 (1.44)	57.0 (3.5)	Direct
360, 360 HG, 360 SL, 360 W Automatic	44.4 (1.75)	36.6 (1.44)	57.0 (3.5)	Direct
35SL	44.4 (1.75)	36.6 (1.44)	57.0 (3.5)	Direct

MAINTENANCE

SPARK PLUG. Recommended spark plug is Champion DJ6J. Electrode gap should be 0.025 in. (0.63 mm). Tighten spark plug to 16.9 N·m (150 in.-lb.) torque.

CARBURETOR. A Walbro Model HDC-16, HDC-21 or HDC-23 diaphragm carburetor is used on 350 series saws while a Walbro HDC-39 or HDC-39A carburetor is used on 360 and 35SL series saws. Refer to the appropriate Walbro section of the CARBURETOR SERVICE section for service and exploded views. Tighten the carburetor attaching screws to the torque listed in the TIGHTENING TORQUE paragraph.

Correct carburetor adjustment procedure is determined by which type of high-speed fuel delivery system is used in the carburetor. Model HDC-16 carburetors were originally designed with a 0.037 inch main jet in the circuit plate and the high speed adjustment needle was used to enrich the high speed fuel mixture. Later Model 350 saws are equipped with Model HDC-21 carburetors which have a 0.033 inch main jet circuit plate. Some HDC-16 or HDC-21 carburetors may have been modified.

Fig. HL260—View of the carburetor idle speed stop screw (I), high-speed mixture needle (H) and low-speed (idle) mixture needle (L) typical of all models.

Note the location of the carburetor adjusting screws in Fig. HL260 and refer to the following paragraphs for carburetor adjustment.

Model HDC-16 and HDC-21 carburetors with fixed main jets are adjusted as follows. First remove and clean the air filter, then reinstall it. Set the initial adjustment of the high-speed mixture needle by turning it clockwise until it is lightly seated (closed). Turn the low-speed (idle) mixture needle clockwise until lightly seated (closed), then turn the needle counterclockwise 1 turn. Start the engine and allow it to run until it reaches normal operating temperature.

Turn the idle speed stop screw so the engine idles as slowly as possible, but continues to run. Turn the low-speed needle slowly clockwise until the engine speed begins to fall (slow) and note the position of the needle. Turn the low-speed needle counterclockwise to enrich the mixture until the engine speed again begins to fall and notice the location. Set the mixture needle halfway between the two points. Adjust the idle speed to just slower than clutch engagement speed, then recheck low-speed mixture adjustment.

The normal setting of the high-speed mixture needle is closed (lightly seated). To determine the best setting for the high-speed mixture needle, run the saw at idle speed and open (counterclockwise) the high-speed needle 1 turn. Close the needle slowly 1/8 turn at a time while noting the engine speed. The ideal setting is where the engine runs the fastest and has the most power. The best setting of high-speed needle should be closed or nearly closed.

To adjust Model HDC-23 carburetor, or HDC-16 or HDC-21 carburetors that have been modified to provide full adjustment, proceed as follows. Remove and clean the air filter, then reinstall it. Properly tension and lubricate the chain. Make sure all components including covers are installed.

NOTE: The engine must not be placed under any load during carburetor adjustment. The chain must be free to move and nothing must contact the chain during the adjustment.

Set initial adjustment of the low-speed mixture needle 1 3/16 turns open (counterclockwise) from lightly seated and high-speed mixture needle 1 1/4 turns open (counterclockwise) from lightly seated. Start the engine and allow it to run until it reaches normal operating temperature.

Turn the idle speed stop screw so the engine idles as slowly as possible, but continues to run. Accelerate the engine momentarily, then return the engine to slow (idle) speed. Turn the low-speed mixture needle slowly clockwise to find the position where the engine runs at the fastest idle. Squeeze throttle trigger quickly to check for smooth acceleration. If the engine stumbles or hesitates, open the low-speed needle slightly, but not more than the initial setting. The engine should idle smoothly at the lowest possible speed (approximately 2,500-2,800 rpm) and speed should not fluctuate when the attitude of the saw is changed.

Adjust high-speed mixture screw to obtain optimum engine performance while under cutting load. The high-speed mixture screw may be set slightly rich to improve performance under load. The engine may be damaged if the high-speed screw is set too lean.

To adjust Walbro Model HDC-39 or HDC-39A carburetor, proceed as follows. First remove and clean the air filter, then reinstall it. Set initial

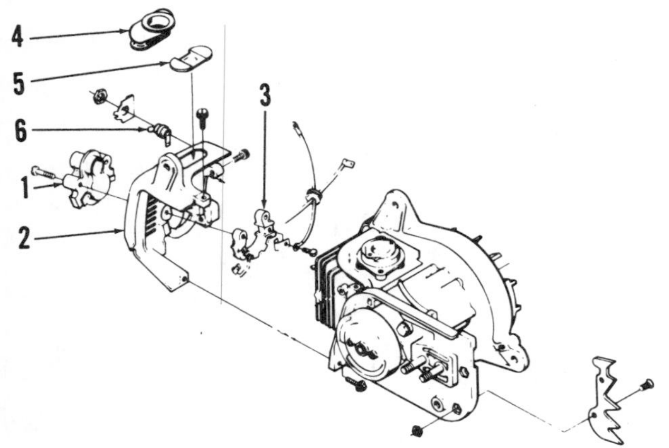

Fig. HL261—Exploded view of cylinder shield assembly typical of 350 and 360 series. Heat exchanger (4) is used in place of plug (5) in cold weather to warm the carburetor air box.

1. Transformer
2. Cylinder shield
3. Transformer receptacle
4. Heat exchanger
5. Plug
6. Ignition switch

adjustment of the low- and high-speed mixture needles 1-1/4 turns open (counterclockwise) from lightly seated. Start the engine and allow it to run until it reaches normal operating temperature.

Turn the idle speed stop screw so the engine idles as slowly as possible, but continues to run. Adjust the low-speed mixture needle so the engine idles smoothly and accelerates without hesitation. Adjust the idle speed to just slower than clutch engagement speed, then recheck low-speed mixture adjustment.

Adjust the high-speed mixture needle to provide the best performance while operating at maximum speed under load. The high-speed mixture screw may be set slightly rich to improve performance under load. The engine may be damaged if the high-speed screw is set too lean.

Final adjustment of the mixture needles should be within 1/4 turn of the initial settings. Large differences may indicate air leaks, plugged passages or other problems.

The maximum no-load speed of saws equipped with fully adjustable carburetors is 12,500 rpm. They should be adjusted to operate in a no-load range of 11,000-12,500 rpm. A tachometer is necessary to accurately adjust the high-speed needle. If the no-load speed at full throttle is below 11,000 rpm, turn the high-speed mixture needle clockwise.

NOTE: The final position of the high-speed mixture needle should not be less than 7/8 turn open when the saw is operated at altitudes below 5,000 feet.

MAGNETO AND TIMING. All models are equipped with a breakerless electronic ignition system. On 350 and 360 series, the ignition module is mounted adjacent to the flywheel. The high tension transformer is mounted on the cylinder shield as shown in Fig. HL261 and covers the spark plug. The transformer must be removed for access to the spark plug.

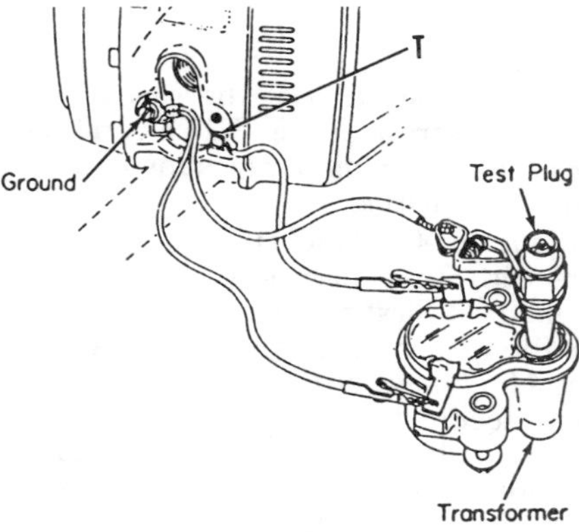

Fig. HL262—A test plug may be used to determine if the ignition system is operating properly. Refer to text for attaching wires to the ignition system of 350 or 360 series saws shown.

On 35SL models, all of the electronic circuitry is contained in a one-piece ignition module/coil located outside the flywheel. Ignition timing is fixed and not adjustable. On all models, tighten the flywheel attaching nut to the torque listed in the TIGHTENING TORQUE paragraph.

On 350 and 360 series, the ignition system is serviced by replacing the spark plug, ignition module, high tension transformer or wires with new components. The ignition system can be checked using a test plug or spark plug with the side electrode removed as follows. Remove the high tension transformer and install the test plug as shown in Fig. HL262. Test wire should be inserted behind receptacle tab (T). Push the ignition switch to run position and operate the starter briskly.

If the test plug sparks, the ignition is operating satisfactorily and the spark plug should be replaced. If no spark is present at the test plug, then another transformer should be installed and operation should be checked as before. If a known good transformer does not correct the problem, the ignition module, ignition switch or connecting wires should be suspected.

Air gap between the legs of the module/coil and the flywheel magnets should be 0.015 inch (0.38 mm). When installing, set the air gap between the flywheel and the legs of the ignition module as follows. Install the ignition module, but tighten the two screws only enough to hold it in place away from the flywheel. Insert brass/plastic shim stock of the proper thickness between the legs of the ignition module and the flywheel as shown in Fig. HL263. Turn the flywheel until the flywheel magnets are near the module legs, loosen the attaching screws (S), press legs of the ignition module against the shim stock, then tighten the two screws to the torque listed in the TIGHTENING TORQUE paragraph. Remove the setting gauge, then turn the flywheel and check that flywheel does not hit the legs of the module.

On 35SL models, the condition of the ignition system can be checked using a test plug attached to the high tension

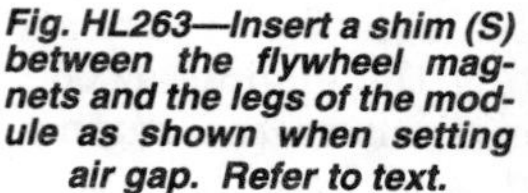

Fig. HL263—Insert a shim (S) between the flywheel magnets and the legs of the module as shown when setting air gap. Refer to text.

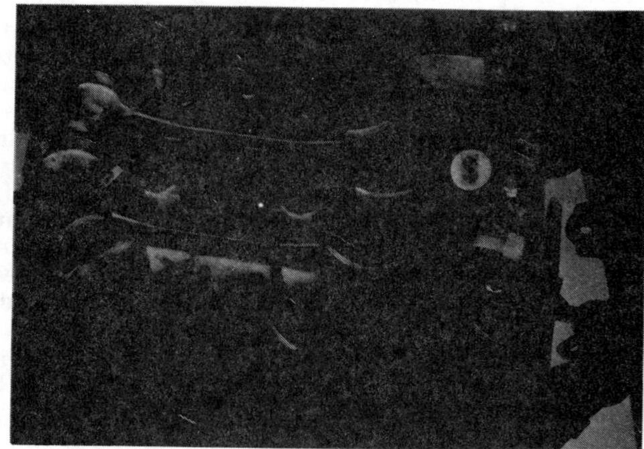

lead in place of the spark plug. Operate the starter and check for spark at the test plug. All electronic circuitry except the ignition switch and connecting wires are contained in a one-piece ignition module/coil located outside the flywheel.

Ignition timing is fixed and not adjustable. Air gap between the legs of the module/coil and the flywheel magnets should be 0.008-0.012 inch (0.2-0.3 mm.). When installing, set the air gap between the flywheel magnets and the legs of the ignition module as follows.

Install the ignition module, but tighten the two screws only enough to hold it in place away from the flywheel. Insert brass/plastic shim stock of the proper thickness between the legs of the ignition module and the flywheel, then turn the flywheel until the flywheel magnets are near the module legs. Loosen the screws attaching the ignition module and press legs of the ignition module against the shim stock. Tighten the two attaching screws to the torque listed in the TIGHTENING TORQUE paragraph. Remove the setting gauge, then turn the flywheel and check that flywheel does not hit the legs of the coil.

LUBRICATION. The engine is lubricated by mixing oil with the gasoline fuel. The manufacturer recommends mixing Homelite two-stroke oil with regular grade gasoline at a ratio designated on the oil container.

If Homelite oil is not available, use good quality oil designed for two-stroke engines at a ratio of 16:1. If Homelite oil is not used, the manufacturer suggests mixing an anti-oxidant fuel stabilizer (such as Sta-Bil) with the fuel and oil mixture. Homelite oil contains a fuel stabilizer and should stay fresh up to one year.

Always use a separate container to mix gasoline and oil before filling the fuel tank. The manufacturer recommends not using fuel containing alcohol.

All saws are equipped with an automatic chain oiling system. The manufacturer recommends using Homelite Bar and Chain oil or equivalent. Make sure the oil reservoir is filled at all times.

A sprocket nose bar is used and should be lubricated periodically each working day by removing the chain and forcing a good quality grease such as Homelite ALL-TEMP Multi-Purpose Grease through the lube hole in the nose of the bar. Bar should be warm before greasing. Force grease into the nose of bar until dirty grease is forced out and clean fresh grease is evident. Remove excess grease, then install the saw chain.

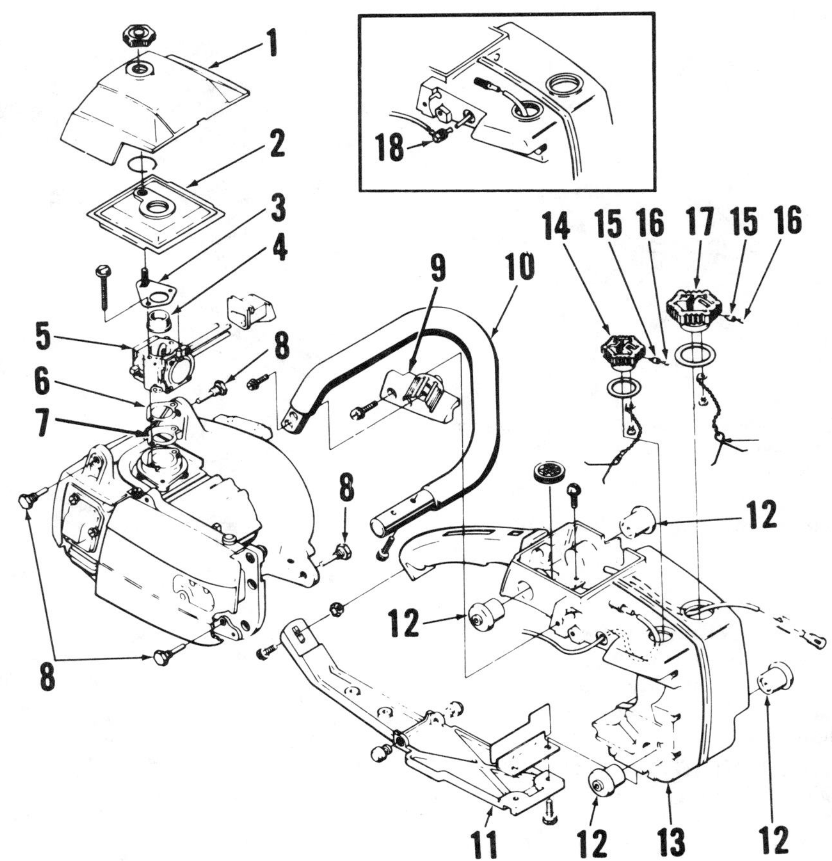

Fig. HL264—Exploded view of the engine housing assembly. Some housings will have a threaded elbow fitting (18) on the oil pickup tube as shown in the inset.

1. Filter cover
2. Air filter
3. Spring plate
4. Flange bushing
5. Carburetor
6. Gasket
7. Flange bushing
8. Isolator pins
9. Handle bar bracket
10. Handle bar
11. Handle brace
12. Vibration isolators
13. Engine housing
14. Oil cap
15. Duckbill (check) valve
16. Bronze filter
17. Fuel cap
18. Elbow fitting

Lubricate the clutch needle bearing after each 100 hours of operation with Homelite ALL-TEMP Multi-Purpose Grease.

MUFFLER. The muffler should be removed, disassembled and cleaned periodically. Carbon should be removed from the muffler and exhaust port to prevent excessive build-up and power loss. Do not allow loose carbon to enter the cylinder while cleaning.

VIBRATION ISOLATORS. All models are equipped with cushion type vibration isolators (12—Fig. HL264) between the power head and housing assembly (13). Isolators can be renewed as follows.

Remove the air filter cover, filter, drive case cover and guide bar. Remove the handle brace (11). Unscrew the two screws attaching the carburetor and disconnect the pulse line at rear of carburetor. Lift and angle carburetor and grommet on carburetor adjustment screws to gain access to two screws in the floor of air box, then remove these two screws.

Remove isolator pins (8) and lift upward on throttle grip (1—Fig. 265) and gently slide engine housing (13—Fig. 264) free of power head until it is possible to remove the rear isolators. Disconnect chain oil line and slide housing further off power head for access to the front isolators.

Reverse isolator removal procedure to reassemble the saw. Apply a thin coat of gasket sealant to both sides of intake gasket (6—Fig. HL264). Carburetor pulse line should be routed around rear of air box and over carburetor control rods before connecting pulse line to carburetor. Tighten the carburetor mounting screws, handle brace attaching screws and isolator pins to the torque listed in TIGHTENING TORQUE paragraph.

REPAIRS

CRANKCASE PRESSURE TEST. An improperly sealed crankcase can cause the engine to be hard to start, run rough, have low power and overheat. Refer to ENGINE SERVICE section of this manual for crankcase pressure test

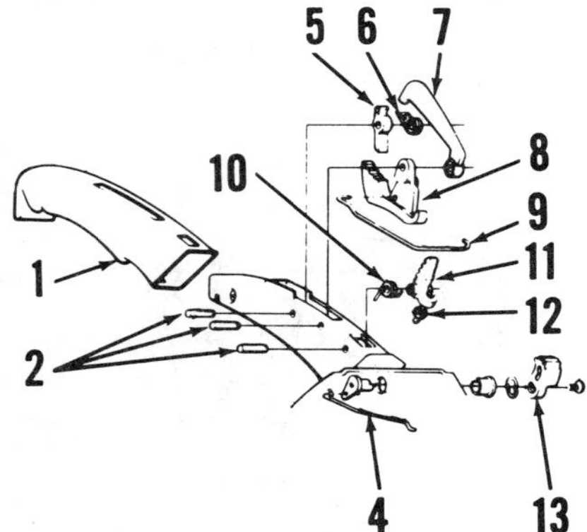

Fig. 265—Exploded view of throttle trigger assembly typical of most models.

1. Handle grip
2. Dowel pin
4. Choke rod
5. Trigger lock lever
6. Spring
7. Trigger lock
8. Trigger
9. Throttle rod
10. Spring
11. Trigger latch
12. Screw
13. Choke knob

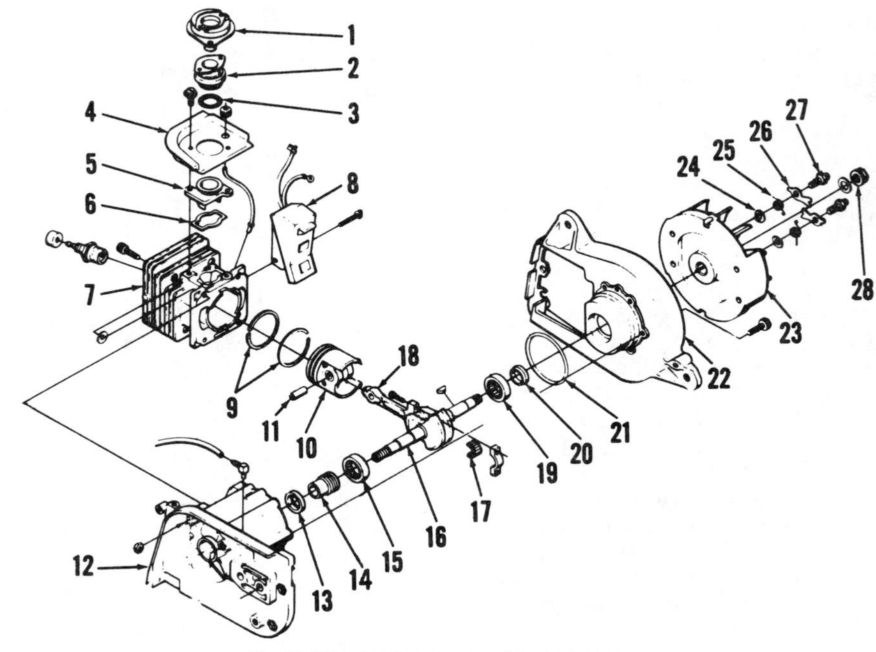

Fig. HL266—Exploded view of typical engine.

1. Carburetor flange
2. Connector
3. Garter spring
4. Air deflector
5. Intake manifold
6. Gasket
7. Cylinder
8. Ignition module
9. Piston rings
10. Piston & bearings
11. Piston pin
12. Crankcase
13. Seal
14. Oil pump worm gear
15. Roller bearing
16. Crankshaft
17. Needle bearing
18. Connecting rod
19. Roller bearing
20. Seal
21. "O" ring
22. Back plate
23. Flywheel
24. Lockwasher
25. Spring
26. Starter pawl
27. Stud
28. Nut

procedure. If crankcase leakage is indicated, pressurize the crankcase and use a solution of soap and water to check gasket, seals, pulse line and castings for leakage.

TIGHTENING TORQUE. Recommended tightening torque values are as follows.

Air box to carburetor screws. . 5.1 N•m (45 in.-lb.)
Air deflector screws. . . . . 5.1 N•m (45 in.-lb.)
Back plate screws . . . . 5.1 N•m (45 in.-lb.)
Carburetor mounting screws . 5.1 N•m (45 in.-lb.)
Clutch
  Plate "S" clutch . . . . 39.5 N•m (350 in.-lb.)
  Hub . . . . N•m (in.-lb.)
Connecting rod screws . . . . . . 6.8 N•m (60 in.-lb.)
Cylinder . . . . 9 N•m (80 in.-lb.)
Flywheel . . . . 28.2-33.9 N•m (250-300 in.-lb.)
Handle brace screws . . . . 5.1 N•m (45 in.-lb.)
Ignition
  350/360 Module . . . . 3.9 N•m (35 in.-lb.)
  35SL Module/coil . . . . 3.9 N•m (35 in.-lb.)
  350/360 Transformer coil . . . . . 3 N•m (27 in.-lb.)
Muffler . . . . 5.1 N•m (45 in.-lb.)
Spark plug . . . . . 16.9 N•m (150 in.-lb.)
Starter
  Housing . . . . 5.1 N•m (45 in.-lb.)
  Pawl studs . . . . 6.8-7.9 N•m (60-70 in.-lb.)
Vibration isolator . . . 9 N•m (80 in.-lb.)

HOMELITE SERVICE TOOLS. Listed below are Homelite tool numbers and descriptions.

Tool number	Description	(Model Usage)
A-17146	Clutch wrench	(3-shoe 360 series)
A-23696-A	Clutch wrench	("S" clutch models)
A-23934	Clutch wrench	(3-shoe 350 series)
A-24290	Flywheel puller	
A-24871	Piston pin removal & installation	
23136-6	Crankcase seal removal	
23759	Crankcase seal installation	
23846-1	Crankcase bearing removal	
23846-2	Backplate bearing & seal removal	
24826	Seal installation plug	
24827	Bearing & seal removal & installation	
14868	Oil pump alignment plug	
A-24994	Ignition tester	
JA-31316-4	Test spark plug	
17789	Carburetor repair tool kit	
94197	Carburetor tester	
94112	Compression gauge	

COMPRESSION PRESSURE. For optimum performance, cylinder compression pressure should be 140-170 psi (966-1,173 kPa) with the engine at normal operating temperature. The engine should be inspected if compression is 90 psi (620 kPa) or less.

PISTON, PIN, RINGS AND CYLINDER. The cylinder can be removed using the following procedure. Remove handle bar and chain guide bar. Use the procedure in VIBRATION ISOLATORS paragraphs to remove the housing assembly (13—Fig. HL264) from the power head. Remove the starter housing.

On 350 and 360 series, disconnect wires from ignition module, then unbolt and remove module and transformer (1—Fig. HL261). On 35SL models, detach wires from the module/coil, then unbolt and remove the unit.

On all models, unbolt and remove the cylinder shield (2). Detach the muffler from the power head and remove the intake manifold (5—Fig. HL266). Remove the socket head screws attaching the cylinder (7) to crankcase, then withdraw the cylinder straight away from the piston. If the cylinder is twisted while removing it, piston rings may catch in the cylinder ports and break, causing damage to the cylinder, piston and/or rings.

The cylinder has a hard chrome bore, which should be inspected for excessive wear of damage. The piston is equipped with two rings and is available in standard size only. The piston pin (11—Fig.

Fig. HL267—Alignment marks (M) on connecting rod must match when installing the connecting rod cap. Arrow adjacent to "EXH" on piston must point toward the exhaust port side of engine (down) when installing the piston and connecting rod on the crankshaft.

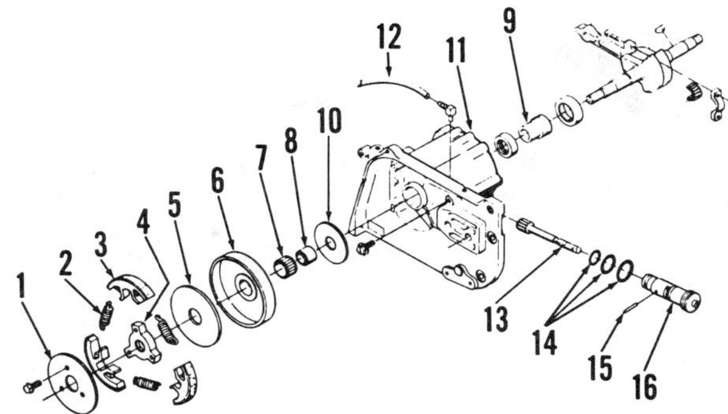

Fig. HL269—Exploded view of the clutch and oil pump typical of late 360 series and 35SL saws.

1. Cover
2. Spring
3. Shoe
4. Hub
5. Washer
6. Clutch drum
7. Bearing
8. Inner race
9. Worm gear
10. Washer
11. Crankcase
12. Oil line
13. Oil pump plunger
14. "O" rings
15. Pin
16. Pump body

Fig. HL268—Prevent the flywheel from turning when removing the flywheel nut or clutch hub by inserting a 1/4 inch (6.35 mm) diameter rod through the hole in back plate and into the notch in the flywheel as shown.

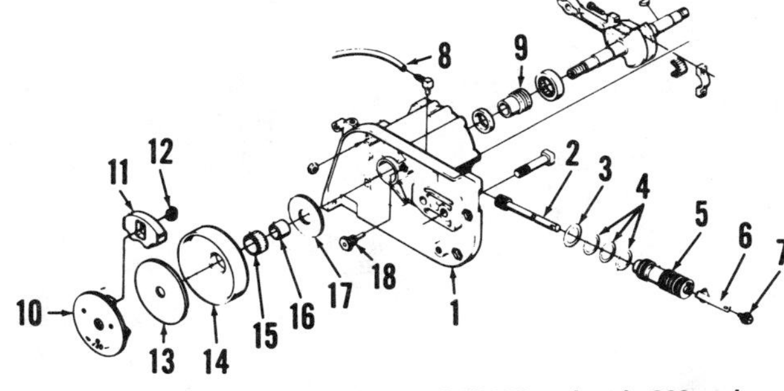

Fig. HL270—Exploded view of the oil pump typical of all 350 and early 360 series saws. The clutch shown is typical of the type used on later 350 and early 360 series saws.

1. Crankcase
2. Oil pump plunger
3. "O" rings
4. "O" rings
5. Pump body
6. Adjusting lever
7. Screw
8. Oil line
9. Oil pump worm gear
10. Clutch hub
11. Clutch shoe
12. Spring
13. Washer
14. Clutch drum
15. Bearing
16. Bearing race
17. Washer
18. Cam screw

HL266) is pressed into the connecting rod and rides in two needle bearings in the piston. Piston and bearings are available only as a unit. The piston must be installed with the side of piston indicated by the arrow on the piston boss marked "EXH" pointing down, toward the exhaust port. Refer to Fig. HL267.

CONNECTING ROD. The connecting rod can be removed after removing the cylinder as outlined in the preceding PISTON, PIN, RINGS AND CYLINDER paragraphs. The connecting rod is of the "fractured" type and two socket head screws secure its cap. The connecting rod operates on 25 loose needle bearings around the crankshaft crankpin.

Marks (M—Fig. HL267) at the big end must be aligned and the cap and rod carefully aligned during assembly. While assembling the connecting rod and cap, the 25 loose bearing needles may be held in place around the crankpin with suitable grease.

CRANKSHAFT, CRANKCASE AND SEALS. To disassemble the crankcase, first remove the clutch as outlined in the appropriate CLUTCH paragraphs. Unbolt and remove the starter housing and the flywheel (Fig. HL268). Remove the cylinder as described in the PISTON, PIN, RINGS AND CYLINDER paragraphs and the connecting rod as in the preceding CONNECTING ROD paragraph.

Remove the screw attaching the back plate (22—Fig. HL266) to the crankcase (12). If necessary, bearings and seals may be pressed from the back plate and crankcase using appropriate tools. Refer to the HOMELITE SERVICE TOOLS paragraph.

Inspect the crankshaft bearings, seals and "O" ring (21) for damage or excessive wear. Do not attempt to remove bearings (15 and 19) or seals (13 and 20) unless new parts will be installed. When assembling the crankcase, be sure "O" ring (21) is properly seated.

CLUTCH. Some models may be equipped with a three-shoe clutch shown in Fig. HL269, Fig. HL270 or Fig. HL271. Other models are equipped with a one-piece "S" type clutch shown in Fig. HL272.

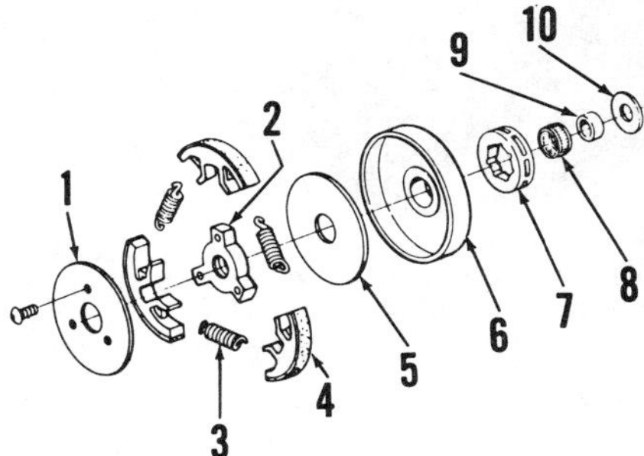

Fig. HL271—Exploded view of clutch assembly typical of late 360 series and 35SL saws.

1. Cover plate
2. Hub
3. Spring
4. Shoe
5. Washer
6. Clutch drum
7. Sprocket
8. Bearing
9. Inner race
10. Washer

The procedure for removal of all clutches is similar. Hold the flywheel, preventing it from turning using a 1/4 inch (6.35 mm) rod as shown in Fig. HL268. Turn the clutch hub (4—Fig. HL269, 10—Fig. HL270, 2—Fig. HL271 or 3—Fig. HL272) in a clockwise direction as indicated by the arrow on the hub. See Fig. HL273.

CHAIN OIL PUMP. All models are equipped with a plunger type auto-

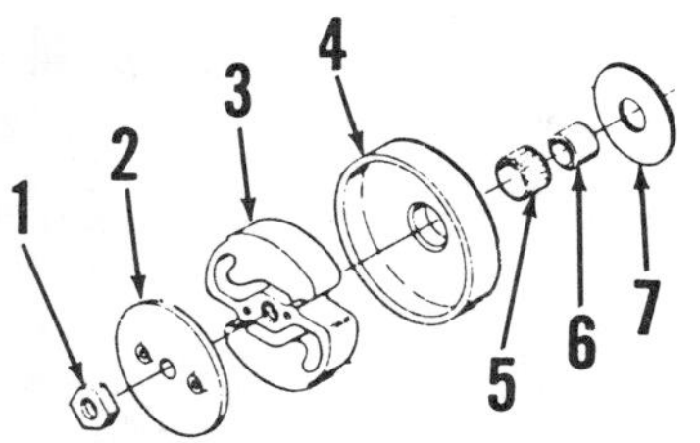

Fig. HL272—View of "S" clutch used on some models. Cover (2) is threaded on some models and nut (1) is not used. Note the correct installation of hub (3) in the upper view.

1. Nut
2. Cover
3. Hub
4. Clutch drum
5. Bearing
6. Inner race
7. Washer

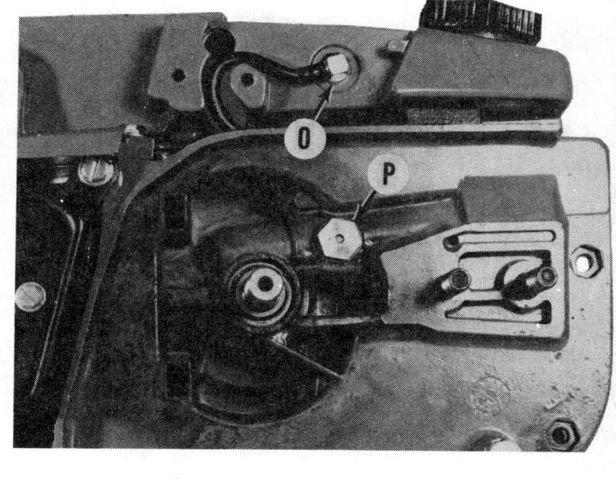

Fig. HL275—Oil line fitting (O) must point toward the 8 o'clock position and the oil line must be routed as shown. Cam screw (P) must be installed carefully on models so equipped so it will mesh properly with the cam in oil pump plunger (2-Fig. HL270).

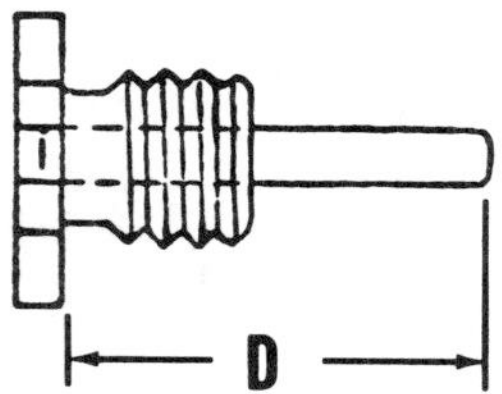

Fig. HL276—Length (D) of cam screw pin must be 0.553-0.557 inch (14.05-14.18 mm) when measured as shown above. Adjust length (D) by driving pin in or out of the cam screw as necessary.

Fig. HL273—The clutch is removed by unscrewing in a clockwise direction as indicated by the arrow on hub. Refer to Fig. HL264 for preventing the crankshaft from turning.

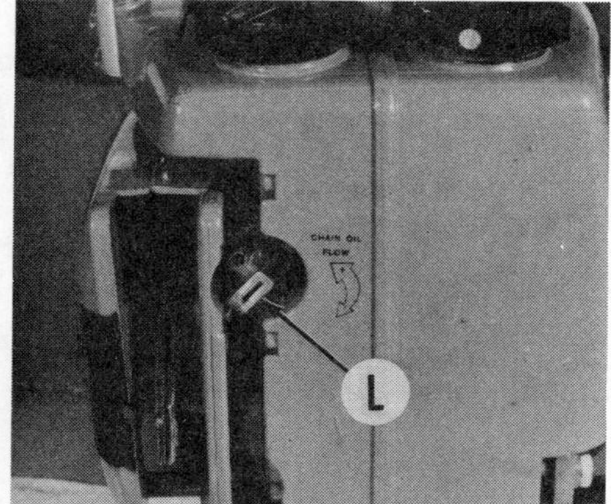

Fig. HL274—The output of oil pump on all 350 series and early 360 series saws can be adjusted by turning the lever (L). Turning the lever counterclockwise will increase the flow of oil and turning clockwise will reduce the amount of oil.

matic chain oil pump as shown in Fig. HL269 or Fig. HL270. The pump is driven by worm gear (9) on the engine crankshaft.

All 350 and early 360 series saws are equipped with the oil pump shown in Fig. HL270. The crankcase can be identified by "12061-A" stamped in the crankcase. Oil output is adjusted by turning the lever shown in Fig. HL274.

Oil pump assembly can be withdrawn after unscrewing the cam screw (P—Fig. HL275). Measure depth of the cam screw pin as shown in Fig. HL276. The depth should be 0.553-0.557 inch (14.05-14.18 mm) and can be adjusted by driving the pin in or out of the adjusting screw. The pin will not engage the slot in the plunger correctly if the pin does not have the correct dimension (D).

Measure the depth (D—Fig. HL277) of plug (P) in the pump bore. The plug should be 2.011-2.018 inches (51.08-51.21 mm) from the end of the pump. Lubricate the pump components before assembly.

Align the cam groove in plunger with the slot in pump body using tool 24868. Carefully install the pump body in the housing to prevent the plunger from moving out of alignment with pump body slot. Screw the cam screw (P—Fig. HL275) into the housing being sure the cam screw pin properly engages the slot in pump body (5—Fig. HL270) and cam groove in plunger (2). Do not tighten the cam screw with a wrench until the final turns to be sure parts are aligned correctly.

Late 360 series and all 35SL saws are equipped with the automatic chain oil pump shown in Fig. HL269. Oil pump output is not adjustable.

On all models, the oil tank cap has a bronze filter and a one-way valve to admit air into the oil tank. If the filter is dirty or valve is defective, oil in the tank will not flow to the pump properly. Valve and filter in the oil tank cap can be checked by operating the saw, first with the cap tight then with the cap loose. If oil output is increased with the cap loose, the filter and valve should be inspected.

Oil output fitting on the oil tank should point at 8 o'clock position as shown in Fig. HL275 to properly route the oil tube. Reduced oil output can also be caused by a clogged oil strainer at the end of the oil tube in the oil tank or by leaking, flattened or clogged lines.

REWIND STARTER. Refer to Fig. HL278 for an exploded view of the starter typical of type used on all models. The starter can be disassembled without removing the housing (1) except to remove and install the bushing (2).

To disassemble the starter, remove screws attaching cover (8) and allow the cover to rotate until tension is re-

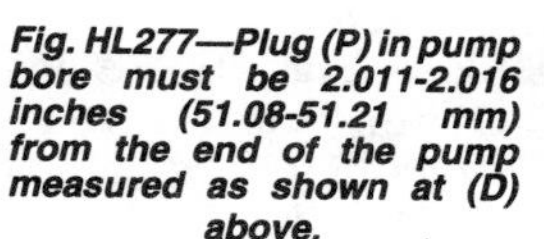

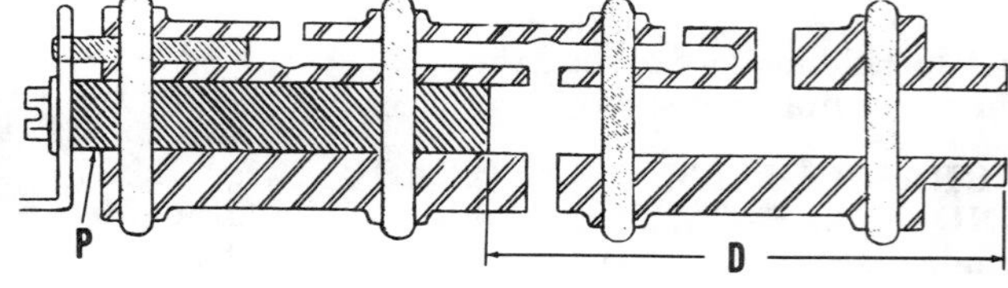

Fig. HL277—Plug (P) in pump bore must be 2.011-2.016 inches (51.08-51.21 mm) from the end of the pump measured as shown at (D) above.

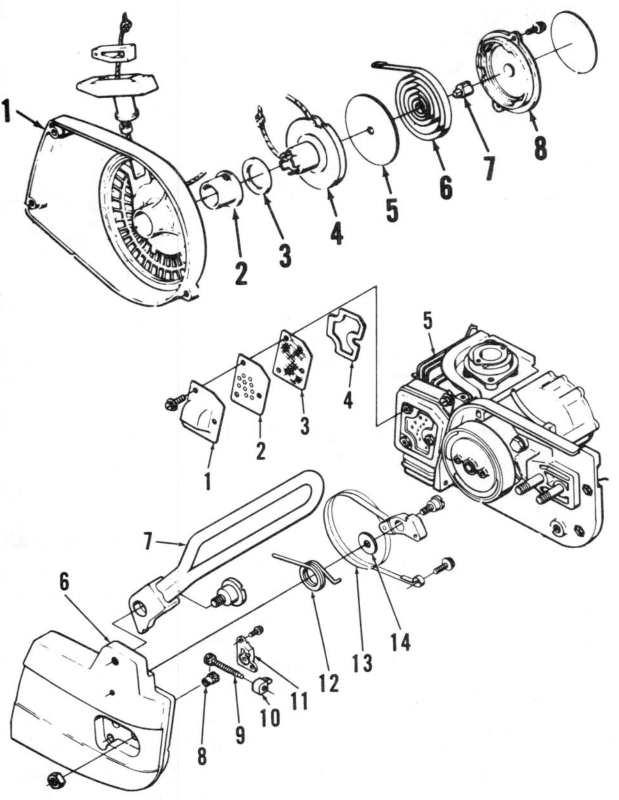

Fig. HL278—Exploded view of the rewind starter. Make sure concave (dished) side of washer (3) is toward pulley (4) when assembling.

1. Starter housing
2. Bushing
3. Spring washer
4. Rope pulley
5. Washer
6. Rewind spring
7. Spring post
8. Cover

Fig. HL279—Exploded view of the chain brake and muffler for Model 350 SL.

1. Exhaust plate
2. Baffle
3. Spark arrestor
4. Gasket
5. Power head
6. Drive cover
7. Brake lever
8. Guide bar adjuster
9. Chain tension adjusting screw
10. Pin
11. Gear cover
12. Spring
13. Chain brake band
14. Washer

Fig. HL280—Exploded view of chain brake mechanism typical of that used on 360 series and 35SL saws.

1. "E" ring
2. Roller
3. Sleeve
4. Actuating lever
5. Washer
6. Spring
7. Washer
8. Latch
9. Shoulder bolt
10. "E" ring
11. Brake band
12. Dowel pin
13. Screw
14. Washer
15. Spring
16. Sleeve
17. Cover

moved from spring (6). Remove the cover with the spring, shield (5) and post (7). Untie knot in the end of rope then remove the rope handle, pulley (4) and rope. Inspect bushing (2) and remove housing (1) if necessary to remove the bushing. Bushing is a press fit in housing.

Do not remove the old bushing if it is to be reused, but lubricate the bushing with oil before assembling. Note the direction that spring (6) is wound in Fig. HL278. A new spring should be lightly lubricated on its edges with Homelite ALL-TEMP Multi-Purpose Grease or suitable lithium base grease before installing spring in the cover. Do not over-lubricate the spring.

Place the spring post (7) in the center of spring and snap shield (5) into cover (8). Install the rope end through the pulley and housing then install the rope handle. Turn the pulley clockwise until the rope is wound on pulley. Install spring washer (3) with the cupped (concave) side toward the pulley (4). Install spring and cover assembly on housing, but do not install the cover attaching screws. Be sure that the spring post (7) engages hole in pulley (4).

To place tension on the rewind spring, turn cover (8) clockwise until the rope handle is held against the housing (1). Do not turn the cover too much or the spring may break when the rope is pulled to its full length. Install the screws attaching the cover then check for starter operation. The spring may tighten and bind before the rope is fully extended if the spring is wound too tight. The rope will not retract fully against the housing if the spring is not wound tightly enough.

CHAIN BRAKE. Models 35SL, 350SL and 360SL are equipped with a chain brake mechanism to stop the saw chain quickly in case of an emergency. In the event of kickback, the operator's left hand will be forced forward against the brake lever (7-Fig. HL279 or 4-Fig. HL280). Forward movement of the brake lever will release the mechanism causing the brake band to wrap around the clutch drum. Normal rotation of the clutch drum will then help tighten the band stopping the drum and saw chain.

Check the chain brake for proper operation by pushing the brake lever forward while the engine is running fast enough to engage the clutch and saw chain. The chain should stop instantly. If the chain brake does not operate properly, the outer surface of the clutch drum may be glazed. Remove glaze with emery cloth then clean the drum and surrounding area. The clutch drum and brake band must not be bent or nicked. On Models 35SL and 360SL, dowel pin (12—Fig. HL280) must be driven into crankcase bore until 0.375 inch (9.52 mm) of the pin is left extending from the crankcase.

HOMELITE

Model	Bore mm (in.)	Stroke mm (in.)	Displacement cc (cu. in.)	Drive Type
650	54.0 (2.125)	43.7 (1.72)	100 (6.1)	Direct
750, 750E	57.2 (2.25)	43.7 (1.72)	112 (6.8)	Direct

MAINTENANCE

SPARK PLUG. Recommended spark plug is Champion CJ4 for Model 650 and CJ3 for Model 750. Spark plug electrode gap should be 0.025 inch (0.63 mm).

CARBURETOR. All models are equipped with a Walbro WB diaphragm carburetor. Refer to CARBURETOR SERVICE section for carburetor service.

Initial adjustment of idle and high speed mixture screws is one turn open. Adjust idle speed screw so that engine idles at approximately 2400-2600 rpm.

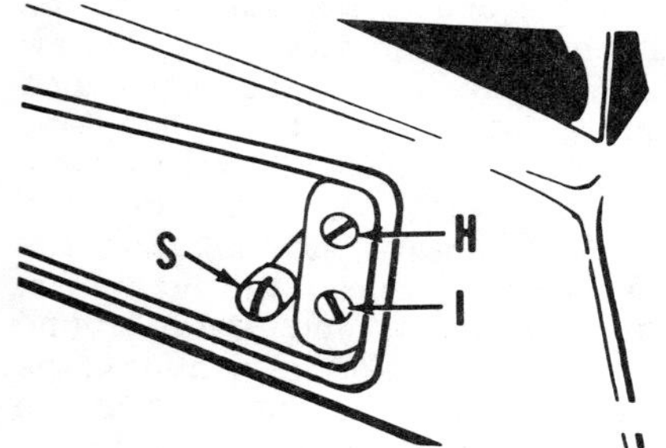

Fig. HL290—View showing location of carburetor high speed mixture screw (H), idle mixture screw (I) and idle speed screw (S).

Adjust idle mixture screw to obtain maximum engine speed at idle. If necessary, readjust idle speed screw to obtain engine idle speed of approximately 2400-2600 rpm.

To adjust high speed mixture screw, proceed as follows: Run saw at idle until engine reaches operating temperature. Turn high speed mixture needle counterclockwise approximately 1/8-1/4 turn. Check performance of saw. Engine should accelerate without hesitation and should not exceed 12,000 rpm at full throttle under no load. When high speed no-load rpm has been adjusted within the correct range, maximum power should occur at desired cutting speed.

Models 650 and 750E are equipped with a trigger latch mechanism coupled to a compression release valve to aid engine starting. Starting speed is adjusted by turning slotted head adjustment screw (13–Fig. HL292) at top and front of saw handle. Turning screw clockwise raises starting speed while turning screw counterclockwise lowers starting speed. Adjust starting speed by latching trigger in start position, start engine and turn screw until desired engine speed is obtained. Stop engine and restart to check starting speed.

MAGNETO AND TIMING. A solid state ignition is used on all models. The ignition module is mounted adjacent to the flywheel while the high tension transformer covers the spark plug and is mounted on the cylinder shield. The high tension transformer must be removed for access to spark plug.

The ignition system is serviced by replacing the spark plug, ignition module, high tension transformer or wires with new components. The ignition system can be checked using a test plug or spark plug with the side electrode removed as follows: Remove the high tension transformer and install the test plug and connect test wires as shown in Fig. HL291. Test wire should be inserted behind receptacle tab (T). Push ignition switch to run position and briskly operate starter. If test plug sparks then ignition system is operating satisfactorily and the spark plug should be checked. If no spark is seen at test plug then another transformer should be checked. If no spark is seen when another transformer is checked, then suspect a faulty ignition module, faulty ignition switch or loose connections.

High tension transformer and leads may be checked by disconnecting wires

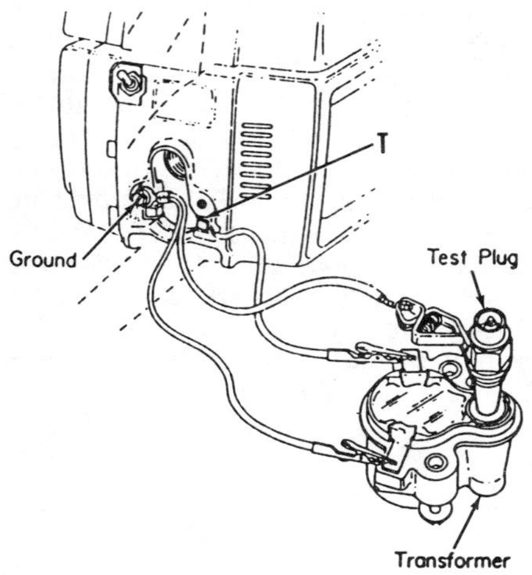

Fig. HL291—A test plug may be used to determine if ignition system is operating correctly. Refer to text.

Fig. HL292—Exploded view of handle components. Inset shows trigger lock mechanism used on Model 750E to aid in cold starting.

1. Throttle trigger
2. Throttle rod
3. Cover
4. Spring
5. Compression release cam
6. Pivot pin
7. Snap ring
8. Trigger pin
9. Spring
10. Choke lever
11. Choke rod
12. Pivot pin
13. Set screw
14. Spring
15. Compression release arm
16. Shoulder screw
17. Compression release valve
18. Spring

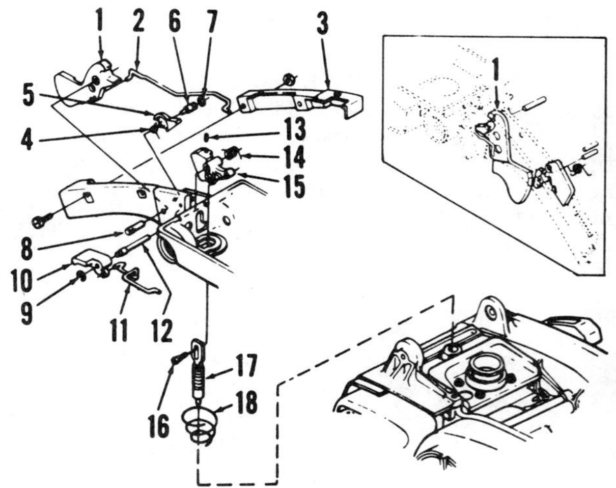

at ignition module which lead from ignition module to transformer receptacle and connecting an ohmmeter to end of wires. There should be continuity between wire ends. If continuity does not exist, disassemble rear of saw until access is possible to two transformer receptacle leads and disconnect leads. Check continuity of each wire and terminal.

To check ignition switch and lead, connect one probe of ohmmeter to switch terminal and ground other probe to ignition module core. Check continuity of ignition switch and lead with switch in "RUN" and "STOP" positions. If continuity exists when switch is in "RUN" position, switch or lead is shorted and must be replaced. Continuity should exist with switch in "STOP" position. If continuity is not present in "STOP" position, check connection of switch lead and replace lead and switch if necessary.

Air gap between ignition module and flywheel is adjustable. Adjust air gap by loosening module retaining screws and place 0.015 inch (pink) (0.38 mm) shim stock between flywheel and module.

If the flywheel is removed using Homelite® tool A-17106-B, which attaches to starter pawl studs, the starter pawl studs must be retightened to 70-90 in.-lbs. (7.9-10.2 N·m) to restore any possible torque loss.

LUBRICATION. The engine is lubricated by mixing oil with unleaded gasoline. Recommended oil is Homelite® two-stroke oil mixed at ratio as designated on oil container. If Homelite® oil is not available, a good quality oil designed for two-stroke engines may be used when mixed at a 16:1 ratio, however, an antioxidant fuel stabilizer (such as Sta-Bil) should be added to fuel mix. Antioxidant fuel stabilizer is not required with Homelite® oils as they contain fuel stabilizer so the fuel mix will stay fresh up to one year.

Saw chain is lubricated by oil from an automatic or manual chain oil pump. Recommended saw chain oil is Homelite® Bar and Chain Oil. Clean automotive oil may also be used if the former is not available. SAE 30 oil should be used in warm temperatures above 40°F (4°C) and cut with 20 percent kerosene in cold temperatures. A light weight oil such as SAE 10 or SAE 5 may also be used in cold temperatures.

Automatic chain oil pump is designed to leave approximately 3 ounces (88.7 mL) of oil in oil tank when one tankful of fuel is consumed after oil and fuel tanks had been full.

A sprocket nose bar is used and should be lubricated periodically by removing chain and forcing a good quality grease such as Homelite® ALL-TEMP Multipurpose Grease through lube hole in nose of bar. Bar should be warm before applying grease. Force grease into nose of bar until dirty grease is forced out and fresh grease is evident.

VIBRATION ISOLATORS. All models are equipped with vibration isolators between engine and engine housing. Use the following procedure to remove vibration isolators:

Remove drivecase cover chain and bar, and bumper spikes. Remove throttle handle brace (15–Fig. HL293) and handle bar. Remove air filter cover and filter and disconnect choke rod from choke lever. Unscrew carburetor mounting screws and remove air intake tube (5). Lift metal shield (6) off air box and pull carburetor free of adjustment needle grommet. Disconnect pulse line and fuel line from carburetor. Disconnect manual oil pump lines at pump end. Unscrew four screws in front wall of air box which secure front and rear assemblies together. Disconnect manual oil line from fitting at automatic oil pump housing.

Unscrew two front vibration isolators screws (16) and with a screwdriver, work isolators (17) clear of their sockets in drivecase wall and back plate. Remove fuel and oil tanks and disconnect oil line from oil tank. Unscrew vibration isolators (17) from tank.

NOTE: Do not continue twisting isolator if it will not unscrew easily. It may be necessary to use a small pin punch or screwdriver placed against the rubber-to-metal bond and tapped with a hammer to unscrew isolator.

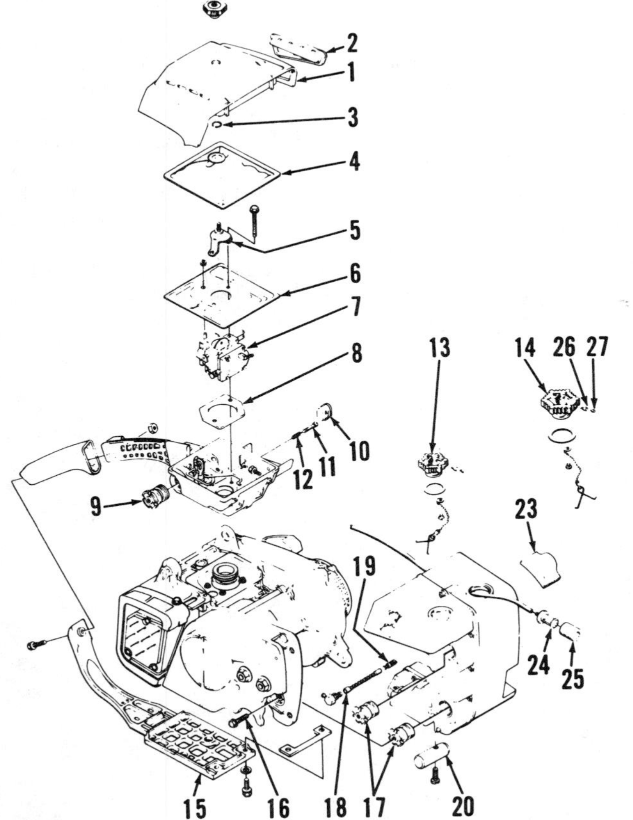

Fig. HL293—View of induction, fuel and oil assemblies.

1. Air filter cover
2. Air intake
3. Retaining ring
4. Air filter
5. Bracket
6. Air box shield
7. Carburetor
8. Spacer plate
9. Rear vibration isolator
10. Grommet
11. Idle speed screw
12. Spring
13. Oil tank cap
14. Fuel tank cap
15. Handle brace
16. Vibration isolator screw
17. Front vibration isolator
18. Oil line
19. Oil pickup
20. Chain stop
23. Fuel tank bumper
24. Fuel pickup
25. Fuel filter
26. Check valve
27. Filter

Remove shoulder screw (16–Fig. HL292) and disconnect compression release valve (17) and arm (15). Remove heat insulating spacer. Push rubber carburetor flange through floor of air box and using technique previously described, remove two rear vibration isolators.

Vibration isolators are retained by threaded inserts pressed into castings. Threads of inserts and isolator should be sprayed with "LPS" prior to installation of a new or used isolator. If insert is loose or damaged, screw an isolator into insert and pull isolator and insert out as a unit. Both the insert recess in casting and the insert must be cleaned with Locquic Grade N Primer before installing insert. Apply Loctite Grade AA Sealant to outer surface of insert and press insert into casting.

REPAIRS

TIGHTENING TORQUES. Tightening torque values are as follows:

Spark plug .... 150 in.-lbs. (16.9 N•m)
Clutch plate .... 180 in.-lbs. (20.3 N•m)
Clutch cover screws .... 35 in.-lbs. (3.9 N•m)
Flywheel nut .... 250-300 in.-lbs. (28.2-33.9 N•m)
Back plate screws .... 45 in.-lbs. (5.1 N•m)
Cylinder screws .... 80 in.-lbs. (9.0 N•m)
Connecting rod screws .... 70-80 in.-lbs. (7.9-9.0 N•m)
Starter housing screws ...... 35 in.-lbs. (3.9 N•m)

COMPRESSION PRESSURE. For optimum performance, cylinder compression pressure at normal engine operating temperature should be 155-185 psi (1069-1275 kPa) on 650 models and 135-165 psi (931-1138 kPa) on 750 and 750E models. Engine should be inspected and repaired when compression pressure is 90 psi (620 kPa) or below.

CYLINDER, PISTON, PIN AND RINGS. Cylinder has chrome bore which should be inspected for wear or damage. Piston and rings are available in standard sizes only. Piston pin is pressed in rod and rides in two needle roller bearings in piston. Homelite® tool A-24871 may be used to remove or install piston pin. Piston and bearings are available as a unit assembly only.

Note that one piston pin boss is marked with an arrow and "EXH." Install piston with side indicated by arrow toward exhaust port.

CONNECTING ROD. Connecting rod is fractured type secured by two socket head screws. Connecting rod rides on a split caged needle bearing at big end. Marks at big end of rod must be aligned and cap and rod properly mated during reassembly. Needle bearings may be held around crankpin with a suitable grease to aid in assembly.

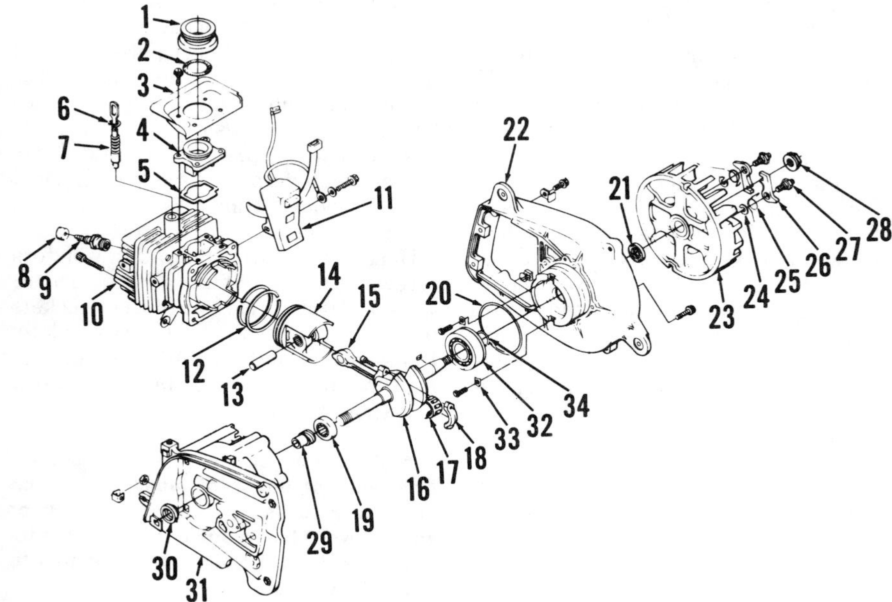

Fig. HL294 — Exploded view of Models 750 and 750E engine. Model 650 is similar except second roller bearing (19) is used in place of components (32, 33 and 34).

1. Rubber carburetor flange
2. Garter spring
3. Air deflector
4. Intake manifold
5. Gasket
6. Snap ring
7. Compression relief valve
8. Grommet
9. Spark plug
10. Cylinder
11. Ignition module
12. Piston rings
13. Piston pin
14. Piston
15. Connecting rod
16. Crankshaft
17. Split cage bearing
18. Rod cap
19. Roller bearing
20. "O" ring
21. Seal
22. Back plate
23. Flywheel
24. Lockwasher
25. Spring
26. Starter pawl
27. Pawl stud
28. Roller bearing
29. Oil pump worm
30. Seal
31. Crankcase
32. Ball bearing
33. Bearing retainer
34. Snap ring

CRANKSHAFT, CRANKCASE AND SEALS. Crankshaft on 750 and 750E models is supported by roller bearing (19 – Fig. HL294) and ball bearing (32). Crankshaft on 650 models is supported by roller bearings (19) in the back plate and crankcase. Crankcase on 650 models may be removed after unscrewing crankcase screws. To remove crankcase on 750 models, unscrew crankcase screws and remove crankcase (31). Remove bearing retainers (33), heat back plate (no more than 300°F [149°C]) and remove crankshaft with bearing (32). Wrap tape around crankshaft end to protect crankshaft and remove snap ring (34). Press bearing (32) off crankshaft.

On all models, roller bearings and seals may be pressed out of crankcase and back plate using Homelite® or other suitable tools. When removing crankcase seal (30), force oil pump worm (29) and seal (30) to outside of crankcase by inserting driver from inside of crankcase. Force bearing (19) to inside of crankcase for removal.

Inspect bearings, seals and "O" ring (20) for damage or excessive wear. When reassembling crankcase, be sure

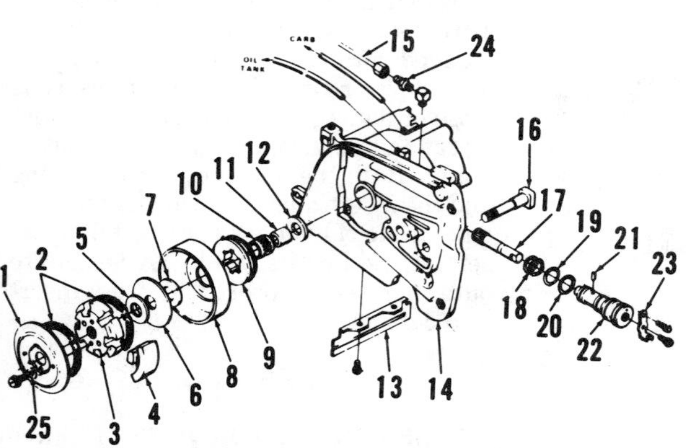

Fig. HL295 — Exploded view of clutch and oil pump assemblies.

1. Cover
2. Clutch spring
3. Clutch hub
4. Clutch shoe
5. Thrust washer (1 in.)
6. Thrust washer (2 in.)
7. Thrust washer (1⅛ in.)
8. Clutch drum
9. Sprocket
10. Bearing
11. Bearing race
12. Thrust washer (1⅛ in.)
13. Heat shield
14. Crankcase
15. Manual discharge line
16. Guide bar stud
17. Oil pump plunger
18. "O" rings
19. "O" ring
20. "O" ring
21. Cam pin
22. Oil pump body
23. Bracket
24. Fitting
25. Belleville washer

Fig. HL295A — Exploded view of late model clutch assembly.

1. Cover
2. Clutch spring
3. Clutch hub
4. Clutch shoe
6. Thrust washer
7. Thrust washer
8. Clutch drum
9. Sprocket
10. Bearing
11. Bearing race
12. Thrust washer

"O" ring (20) is properly seated. Install bearings so unstamped side is toward inside of crankcase and back plate.

CLUTCH. Refer to Fig. HL295 or HL295A for exploded view of clutch assembly. To remove clutch, prevent flywheel rotation by inserting 3/16 inch rod through hole located in bottom of back plate into notch in flywheel. Using a Homelite® clutch spanner or a suitable tool, unscrew clutch hub (3) in clockwise direction as shown by arrow on hub.

Inspect bearing and lubricate with Homelite® ALL-TEMP Multipurpose Grease (#24551) or a lithium base grease. Clutch shoes (4) should be renewed as a complete set.

AUTOMATIC CHAIN OIL PUMP. All models are equipped with an automatic oil pump driven by worm (29–Fig. HL294) on crankshaft. Oil is pumped by plunger (17–Fig. HL296) as it reciprocates due to cam pin (21) located in cam groove (G). Oil enters pump through port (A) and passes around pump body (22) to enter plunger bore through port (B). Oil exists through ports (C, D and E) to saw chain. Oil may be pumped through port (F) and fitting (24) to manual oil pump. Oil is also routed through ports (H and J) to cam groove to reduce back pressure on oil plunger.

To disassemble automatic oil pump, unscrew oil pump bracket screw and gently withdraw oil pump body (22–Fig. HL295). Do not lose cam pin (21) which is loose in pump body. Remove pin (21) and slide pump plunger out of pump body. Inspect pump plunger, body and "O" rings for excessive wear or damage. An excessively loose fit between pump plunger and pump body will cause low pump output. Oil "O" rings before installation in grooves of pump body. "O" rings must be straight in grooves and not twisted. Oil "O" rings before inserting pump body and plunger assembly into pump housing.

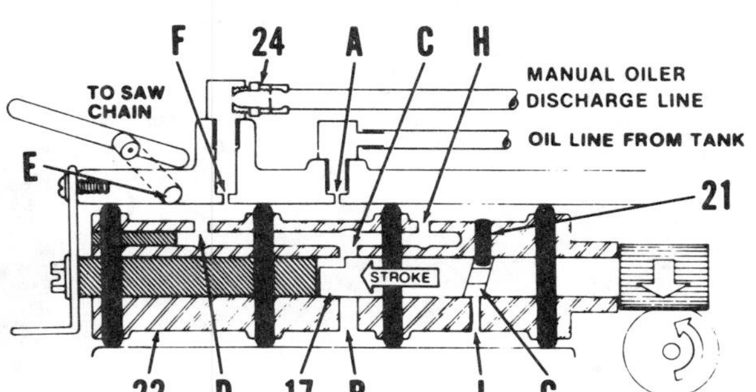

Fig. HL296—Cross-section of oil pump. Refer to text for operation.

If oil pump operates correctly but oil output is insufficient, disconnect and clean oil lines and fittings (Fig. HL295). Install outlet elbow in oil tank wall to provide an angle of as close to 90 degrees as shown in Fig. HL298 without pinching line. Elbow threads should be coated with thread sealant.

REWIND STARTER. Refer to Fig. 301 for an exploded view of starter assembly. Starter pawl components attached to flywheel are shown in Fig. HL294.

To disassemble starter, hold cover (14–Fig. HL301) and unscrew retaining screws. Allow cover to turn until spring tension is relieved and remove cover.

NOTE: If outer hook of spring catches on starter housing, pull cover away from housing until cover is allowed to turn.

Remove screw (4) to separate rope pulley (7) from cover. Remove snap ring (8) for access to rewind spring. If starter pawl assemblies must be removed, unscrew housing screws and remove starter housing (2). Threaded inserts are available if stud holes are damaged in flywheel.

Clean and inspect components. Lubricate sides of rewind spring with a small amount of Homelite® ALL-TEMP Multipurpose grease or a lithium base grease. Do not oil spring. Install inner spring shield (11), rewind spring (10) and spring lock (12) in cover with spring wound as shown in Fig. HL302. Install outer spring shield (9–Fig. HL301) and snap ring (8). Insert bushings (6 and 13) in rope pulley (7) being sure knobs on bushings align with notches in pulley.

90°

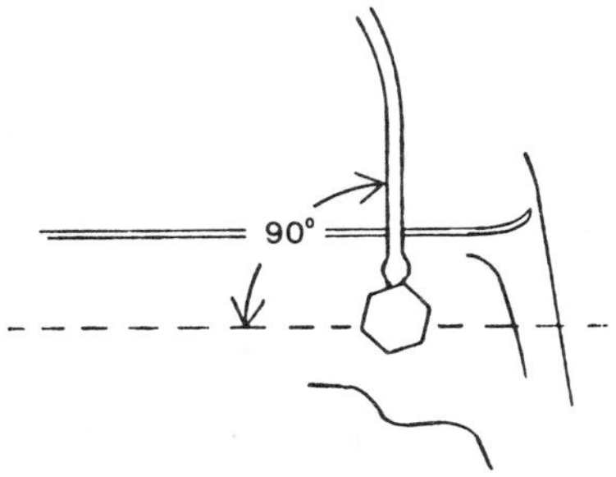

Fig. HL298—Oil line and fitting in oil tank must be angled close to 90 degrees as shown above.

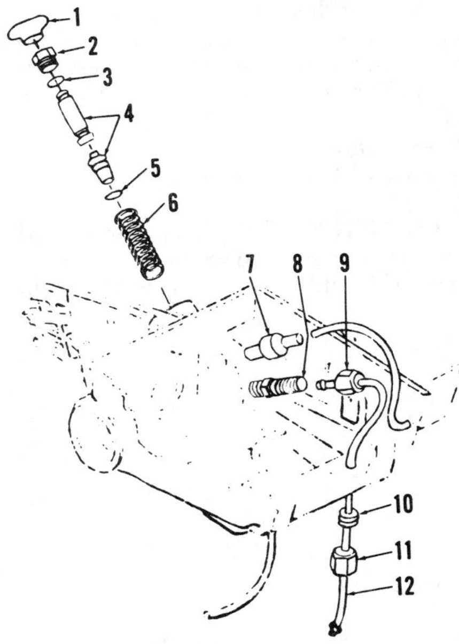

Fig. HL299—Exploded view of manual oil pump. End of oil line (12) is connected to fitting (24–Fig. HL296). Oil line (12) must be disconnected from fitting and pulled into air box for removal.

1. Button
2. Plunger nut
3. "O" ring
4. Plunger assy.
5. "O" ring
6. Spring
7. Check valve
8. Check valve
9. Compression nut
10. Grommet
11. Compression nut

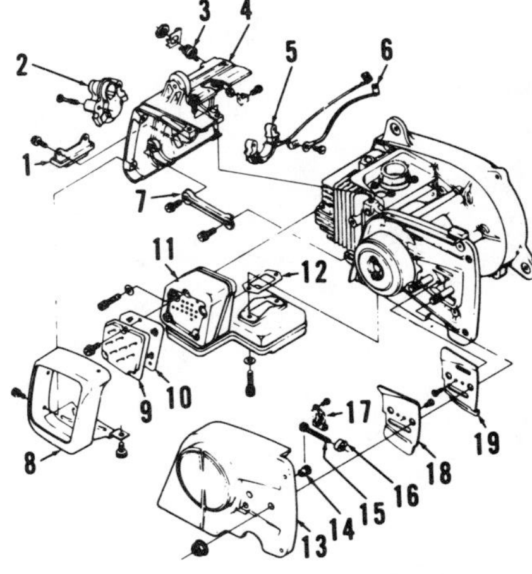

Fig. HL300—Exploded view of exhaust and chain tensioning assemblies.

1. Rear snubber
2. High tension coil
3. Ignition switch
4. Cylinder shield
5. Coil receptacle
6. Ground lead
7. Brace
8. Muffler shield
9. Muffler cap
10. Spark arrestor
11. Muffler
12. Gasket
13. Cover
14. Guide bar adjuster gear
15. Chain tension adjuster screw
16. Pin
17. Gear cover
18. Outer guide bar plate
19. Inner guide bar plate

Slide pulley onto post in cover and check to be sure splines on pulley engage splines in spring lock. Install and tighten cap screw (4) to 45 in.-lbs. (5.1 N•m). Wind rope around pulley in clockwise direction as viewed from screw end of pulley. Set cover in housing. Pull rope handle and then allow rope to rewind so starter pawls will be forced open and pulley hub can slide between them into place. Turn cover clockwise 2 or 3 turns to preload rewind spring, snap plastic screen into place and install cover screws. Check starter operation.

COMPRESSION RELEASE. All models are equipped with a compression release to aid starting. A leaking compression release valve may be repaired by cleaning valve seat with Homelite® tool A-24884. This tool is designed to remove carbon without removing metal from valve seat. Piston must be at TDC and engine positioned with valve side down to prevent debris from entering cylinder.

Inspect valve stem for wear which may not allow valve to seat properly and renew valve if valve stem is excessively worn. Examine pin connecting valve link to stem and renew assembly if pin is worn or loose.

Install compression release valve with sharp side of snap ring (6 – Fig. HL294) out. Push compression release valve and snap ring down into valve bore making sure snap ring fully engages snap ring groove. Homelite® tool A-24876 may be used to seat snap ring in groove.

Later Model 750 is equipped with a cylinder having a smaller compression release hole and a matching compression release valve. Later compression release valve is identified by a groove located as shown in Fig. HL303. Early and late cylinders and compression release valves are not interchangeable.

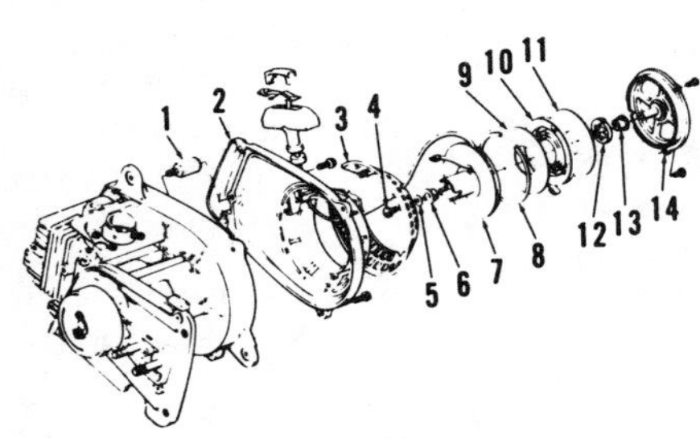

Fig. HL301 – Exploded view of rewind starter.

1. Spacer
2. Starter housing
3. Screen
4. Capscrew
5. Lockwasher
6. Bushing
7. Rope pulley
8. Snap ring
9. Outer spring shield
10. Rewind spring
11. Inner spring shield
12. Spring lock
13. Bushing
14. Cover

Fig. HL302 – View of rewind spring installation in starter cover. Hook outer loop (A) of spring in notch as shown. Inner loop (B) of spring must be curved inward to engage notch of spring lock.

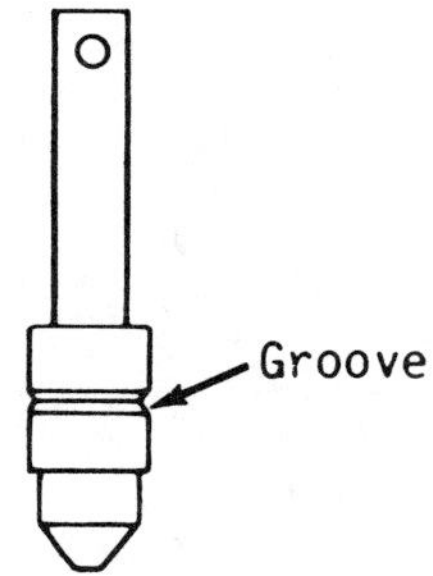

Fig. HL303 – The compression release valve on later Model 750 is identified by the groove shown above.

HOMELITE

Model	Bore mm (in.)	Stroke mm (in.)	Displacement cc (cu. in.)	Drive Type
450, 450 HG, 450 SL, 450 W	47.6 (1.875)	41.3 (1.625)	74.0 (4.5)	Direct
550, 550 SL, 550 W	51.0 (2.0)	41.3 (1.625)	84.0 (5.1)	Direct

MAINTENANCE

SPARK PLUG. Recommended spark plug is Champion DJ6J for all models. Spark plug electrode gap should be 0.025 inch (0.63 mm).

CARBURETOR. All models are equipped with a Walbro SDC diaphragm carburetor. Refer to Walbro section of CARBURETOR SERVICE section for carburetor service.

Initial adjustment of idle and high speed mixture screws is one turn open except on 450, 450W, 450HG and 450SL which has a fixed high speed jet and high speed mixture is not adjustable. Adjust idle speed screw so engine idles at approximately 2400-2600 rpm. Adjust idle mixture screw so engine will accelerate cleanly without bogging. If necessary, readjust idle speed screw to obtain engine idle speed of approximately 2400-2600 rpm.

To adjust high speed mixture screw on 550, 550W and 550SL, proceed as follows: Run saw at idle until engine reaches operating temperature. Turn high speed mixture needle to obtain optimum performance with saw under cutting load.

Starting speed is adjusted by turning slotted head adjustment screw in fast idle latch. See Fig. HL311. Turning screw clockwise raises starting speed while turning screw counterclockwise lowers starting speed. Adjust starting speed by latching trigger in start position, start engine and turn screw until desired engine speed is obtained. Stop engine and restart to check starting speed.

MAGNETO AND TIMING. A solid state ignition is used on all models. The ignition module is mounted adjacent to the flywheel while the high tension transformer covers the spark plug and is mounted on the cylinder shield. The high tension transformer must be removed for access to spark plug. The ignition module on 450, 450W, 450HG and 450SL uses an electronic governor to prevent overspeeding of engine.

The ignition system is serviced by replacing the spark plug, ignition module, high tension transformer or wires with new components. The ignition system can be checked using a test plug or spark plug with the side electrode removed as follows: Remove the high tension transformer and install the test plug and connect test wires as shown in Fig. HL312. Test wire should be inserted behind receptacle tab (T). Push ignition switch to run position and briskly operate starter. If test plug sparks then ignition system is operating satisfactorily and the spark plug should be checked. If no spark is seen at test plug then another transformer should be checked. If no spark is seen when another transformer is checked, then suspect a faulty ignition module, faulty ignition switch or loose connections.

High tension transformer and leads may be checked by disconnecting wires at ignition module which lead from ignition module to transformer receptacle

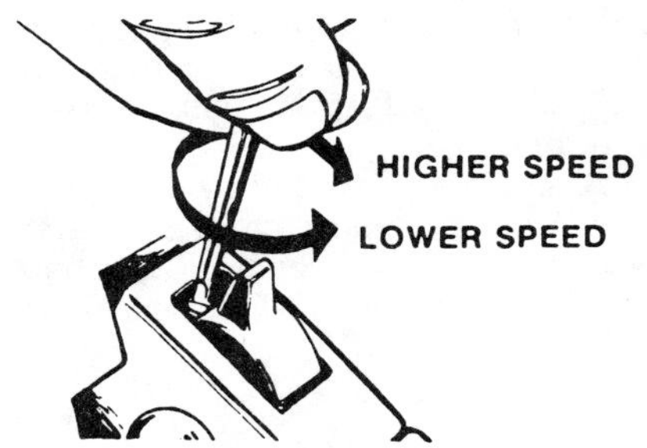

Fig. HL311—View showing location of fast idle screw.

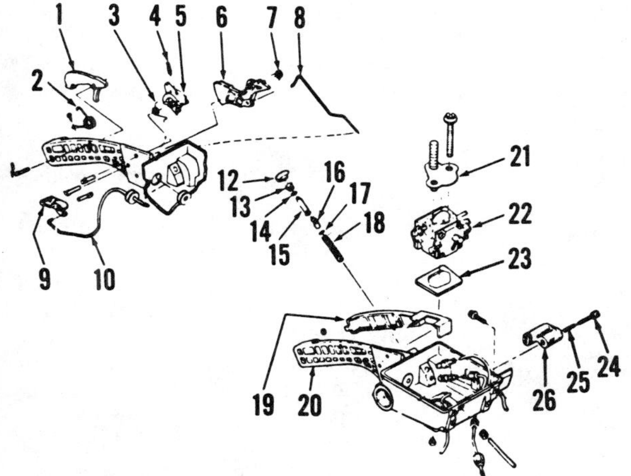

Fig. HL310—Exploded view of handle, air box and manual oil pump assemblies.

1. Lockout
2. Spring
3. Spring
4. Fast idle screw
5. Throttle latch
6. Throttle trigger
7. Spring
8. Throttle rod
9. Choke lever
10. Choke rod
12. Oil pump button
13. Nut
14. "O" ring
15. Rod
16. Plunger
17. "O" ring
18. Spring
19. Handle cover
20. Handle & air box
21. Bracket
22. Carburetor
23. Spacer
24. Idle speed screw
25. Spring
26. Grommet

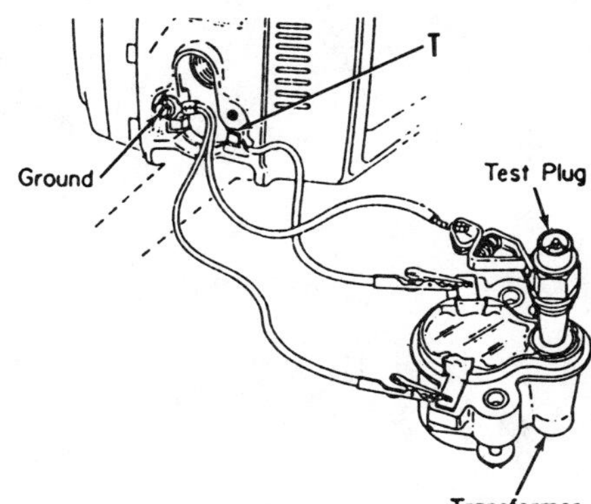

Fig. HL312—A test plug may be used to determine if ignition system is operating correctly. Refer to text.

and connecting an ohmmeter to end of wires. There should be continuity between wire ends. If continuity does not exist, disassemble rear of saw until access is possible to two transformer receptacle leads and disconnect leads. Check continuity of each wire and terminal.

To check ignition switch and lead, connect one probe of ohmmeter to switch terminal and ground other probe to ignition module core. Check continuity of ignition switch and lead with switch in "RUN" and "STOP" positions. If continuity exists when switch is in "RUN" position, switch or lead is shorted and must be replaced. Continuity should exist with switch in "STOP" position. If continuity is not present in "STOP" position, check connection of switch lead and replace lead and switch if necessary.

Air gap between ignition module and flywheel is adjustable. Adjust air gap by loosening module retaining screws and place 0.015 inch (0.38 mm) (pink) shim stock between flywheel and module.

LUBRICATION. The engine is lubricated by mixing oil with unleaded gasoline. Recommended oil is Homelite® two-stroke oil mixed at ratio as designated on oil container. If Homelite® oil is not available, a good quality oil designed for two-stroke engines may be used when mixed at a 16:1 ratio, however, an antioxidant fuel stabilizer (such as Sta-Bil) should be added to fuel mix. Antioxidant fuel stabilizer is not required with Homelite® oils as they contain fuel stabilizer so the fuel mix will stay fresh up to one year.

Saw chain is lubricated by oil from an automatic or manual chain oil pump. Recommended saw chain oil is Homelite® Bar and Chain Oil. Clean automotive oil may be used if the former is not available. SAE 30 oil should be used in warm temperatures above 40°F (4°C) and cut with 20 percent kerosene in cold temperatures. A light weight oil such as SAE 10 or SAE 5 may also be used in cold temperatures.

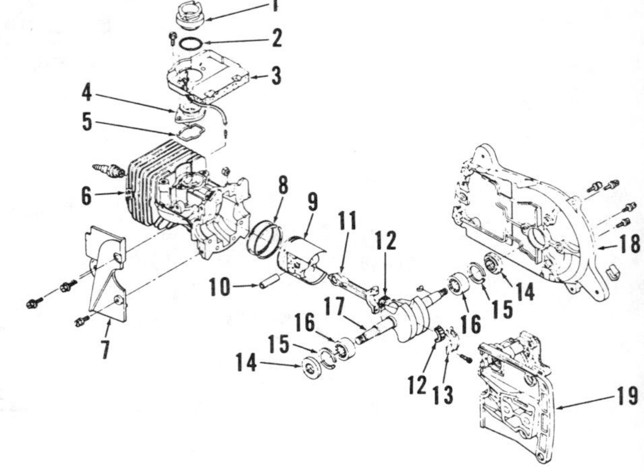

Fig. HL314 – Exploded view of engine.

1. Connector
2. Garter spring
3. Air deflector & seal
4. Intake manifold
5. Gasket
6. Cylinder
7. Shield
8. Piston rings
9. Piston
10. Piston pin
11. Connecting rod
12. Bearing
13. Rod cap
14. Seal
15. Snap ring
16. Bearing
17. Crankshaft
18. Back plate
19. Crankcase

REPAIRS

TIGHTENING TORQUE VALUES. Tightening torque values are as follows:

Connecting rod .... 65-78 in.-lbs. (7.3-8.8 N·m)
Crankcase retaining screws .... 60-72 in.-lbs. (6.8-8.2 N·m)
Starter housing .... 45-54 in.-lbs. (5.1-6.1 N·m)

COMPRESSION PRESSURE. For optimum performance, cylinder compression pressure at normal operating temperature should be 160-190 psi (1104-1311 kPa) on 450, 450W, 450HG and 450SL models and 125-155 psi (863-1069 kPa) on 550, 550W and 550SL models. Engine should be inspected and repaired when compression pressure is 90 psi (620 kPa) or below.

CYLINDER, PISTON, PIN AND RINGS. The cylinder may be separated from crankcase after removing screws securing cylinder to crankcase. Care should be used when separating cylinder and crankcase as crankshaft may be dislodged from crankcase. Inspect cylinder bore and discard cylinder if excessively worn or damaged. Cylinder may not be bored for oversize pistons and oversize cylinders are not available. Refer to CONNECTING ROD, CRANKSHAFT AND CRANKCASE. section when installing cylinder.

The piston is equipped with two piston rings. Oversize pistons and rings are not available. The piston pin rides in nonrenewable needle bearings in piston. Piston and bearings are available only as a unit assembly.

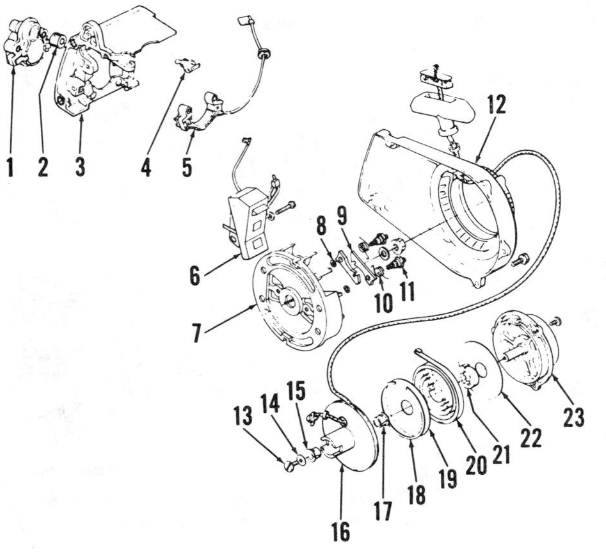

Fig. HL313 – Exploded view of ignition system and rewind starter.

1. Transformer
2. Grommet
3. Shield
4. Ignition switch
5. Transformer receptacle
6. Ignition module
7. Flywheel
8. Lockwasher
9. Starter pawl
10. Spring
11. Stud
12. Starter housing
13. Screw
14. Washer
15. Bushing
16. Rope pulley
17. Bushing
18. Snap ring
19. Outer spring shield
20. Rewind spring
21. Spring lock
22. Inner spring shield
23. Cover

CONNECTING ROD, CRANKSHAFT AND CRANKCASE. Refer to preceding section and remove cylinder. Separate crankshaft assembly from crankcase and disassemble as required. Inspect components and renew any which are damaged.

Connecting rod (11 – Fig. HL314) rides on twelve caged bearing rollers (12). The crankshaft is supported by roller bearings (16) which are installed so lettered end is toward snap rings (15).

Tighten connecting rod screws to 65-75 in.-lbs. (7.3-8.4 N·m). When assembling crankcase and cylinder, use a suitable sealant on mating surfaces. Be sure components are properly assembled and snap rings (15) engage grooves in cylinder and crankcase. Before final tightening of crankcase screws, lightly tap both ends of crankshaft to obtain proper crankshaft end play. Tighten crankcase retaining screws to 60-70 in.-lbs. (6.8-7.9 N·m).

AUTOMATIC OIL PUMP. All models are equipped with an automatic oil pump. Refer to Fig. HL315 for an exploded view of oil pump. Check ball must move freely for proper pump operation. Oil pump output is not adjustable. Note the following troubleshooting procedure:

Automatic oil pump fails but manual oiler functions: Check automatic oil pump pickup for blockage. Connect a vacuum gage to pickup line and run saw at wide-open throttle under no load or while cutting and note vacuum gage reading. A good pump will develop 25-28 inches of vacuum (Mercury). Remove oil pump cover (1–Fig. HL315) and check for cracks, and on early models, be sure lead shot plug in cover is sealing properly, otherwise, the pump cover must be renewed. Lightly push on plunger (2) and note if plunger is lifting ball check valve (6) off its seat. Also check for binding of plunger in bore and for a defective diaphragm. Plunger must not turn in diaphragm. There must be sufficient oil film in pump body (4) so "O" ring on plunger of later models does not drag. Pulse and vent holes must be open. Blow air through system from strainer end of pickup; air should exit through plunger bore of pump body (4). With plunger inserted in pump body, pressurize pickup line at strainer end and check for leaks in line or between pump body (4) and plunger. Pressurize delivery side of automatic oil pump at manual oil pump fitting so air exits from guide bar pad, then plug guide bar pad hole. Check that check ball (6) is seating and pump body "O" rings (5) do not leak. Using a suitable tool (an old plunger may be reduced in diameter by 0.020 in.), lift check ball (6) off its seat to check for free flow through delivery end of pump body. With check ball lifted off its seat, blow air into strainer end of pickup line; air should exit from guide bar pad.

Manual oiler fails but automatic oil pump functions: Check manual oil pump pickup for blockage. Disconnect outlet line fitting from manual oil pump then blow air into outlet line; air should exit from guide bar pad. DO NOT USE EXCESSIVE AIR PRESSURE AS SEAL AT CRANKCASE MAY BE DAMAGED. If air does not exit from bar pad then blockage exists in line, crankcase fitting or in crankcase passage prior to joining common delivery passage with auto oil pump. This test will also reveal leaks in line and fittings. Pressurize pickup line at strainer end and check for leaks in line, fittings and around pump plunger "O" rings (14 and 17–Fig. HL310). Remove manual oil pump and inspect components and be sure all parts operate freely. Be sure spring returns pump to full up/intake position.

Automatic and manual oil pumps malfunction: Be sure oil tank is filled with proper oil. Operate manual oil pump. If manual oil pump operates freely, check for blocked oil pickup strainers and improperly positioned pickup lines. Reinstall oil tank cap, but do not tighten. Operate both oil pumps. If pumps work satisfactorily, then renew oil tank cap as it is not venting properly.

If manual oil pump builds pressure when operated so plunger will not depress, then there is blockage at some point in output passage. Disconnect manual oil pump outlet line from manual pump fitting and operate both pumps. Manual pump should force oil from outlet fitting while auto pump should force oil from loose end of outlet line. Remove automatic oil pump body (4–Fig. HL315) and disconnect manual pump outlet line from crankcase fitting. Blow air into guide bar pad oil outlet to possibly blow blocking material through pump body or through manual pump delivery passage. If blockage will not blow free, then crankcase must be removed to clean passages in engine.

CLUTCH. Models 550, 550W and 550SL are equipped with clutch shown in Fig. HL317 while Models 450, 450W, 450HG and 450SL may be equipped with either clutch shown in Fig. HL318. Clutch hub on all models has left hand threads. Clutch shoes should be renewed only as a set. Inspect bearing and lubricate with Homelite®ALL-TEMP Multipurpose Grease (#24551) or a lithium base grease.

REWIND STARTER. Refer to Fig. HL313 for an exploded view of starter assembly.

To disassemble starter, hold cover (23) and unscrew retaining screws. Allow cover to turn until spring tension is relieved and remove cover.

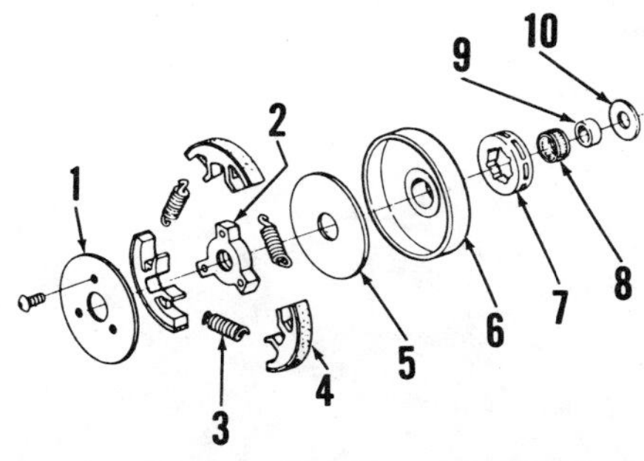

Fig. HL317—View of Model 550, 550W and 550SL clutch.

1. Cover plate
2. Hub
3. Spring
4. Shoe
5. Washer
6. Clutch drum
7. Sprocket
8. Bearing
9. Inner race
10. Washer

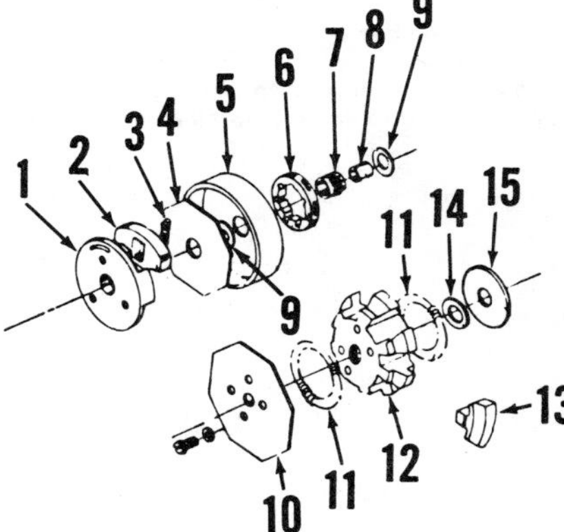

Fig. HL318—Exploded view of two clutches which may be used on Models 450, 450W, 450HG and 450SL.

1. Hub
2. Shoe
3. Spring
4. Plate
5. Clutch drum
6. Sprocket
7. Bearing
8. Inner race
9. Washer
10. Cover
11. Garter spring
12. Hub
13. Shoe
14. Washer
15. Washer

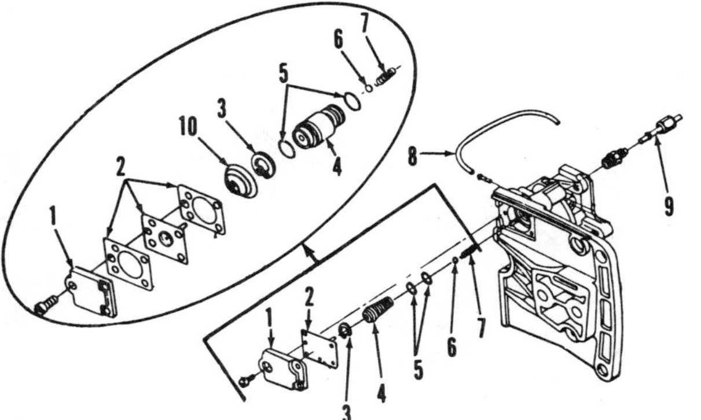

Fig. HL315—Exploded view of automatic oil pump. Components in upper view are used on 550 series saws while components in lower view are used on 450 series saws.

1. Oil pump cover
2. Plunger & diaphragm
3. Snap ring
4. Pump body
5. "O" rings
6. Check ball
7. Spring
8. Oil line
9. Oil line
10. Spring

NOTE: If outer hook of spring catches on starter housing, pull cover away from housing until cover is allowed to turn.

Unscrew screw (13) to separate rope pulley (16) from cover. Remove snap ring (18) for access to rewind spring. If starter pawl assemblies must be removed, unscrew housing screws and remove starter housing (12). Threaded inserts are available if stud holes are damaged in flywheel.

Clean and inspect components. Lubricate sides of rewind spring with a small amount of Homelite® ALL-TEMP Multipurpose grease or a lithium base grease. Do not oil spring. Install inner spring shield (22), rewind spring (20) and spring lock (21) in cover with spring wound as shown in Fig. HL319. Install outer spring shield (19–Fig. HL313) and snap ring (18). Insert bushings (15 and 17) in rope pulley (16) being sure knobs on bushings align with notches in pulley. Slide pulley onto post in cover and check to be sure splines on pulley engage splines in spring lock. Install and tighten cap screw (13) to 45 in.-lbs. (5.1 N·m). Wind rope around pulley in clockwise direction as viewed from screw end of pulley. Set cover in housing. Pull rope handle and then allow rope to rewind so starter pawls will be forced open and pulley hub can slide between them into place. Turn cover clockwise 2 or 3 turns to preload rewind spring, snap plastic screen into place and install cover screws. Check starter operation.

CHAIN BRAKE. Model 450SL and 550SL are equipped with a chain brake mechanism (Fig. HL320 or HL321) to stop saw chain motion in the event of kickback. In the event of kickback, the operator's left hand will force brake actuating lever forward and brake band will wrap around the clutch drum to stop clutch drum rotation. Chain brake effectiveness may be checked by running chain saw with chain turning but not cutting. Push chain brake actuating lever forward. Chain brake should stop chain instantly. If chain brake does not operate correctly, outer surface of clutch drum may be glazed. Remove glaze with emery cloth being sure to clean drum afterwards. Clutch drum and brake band must not be bent or nicked.

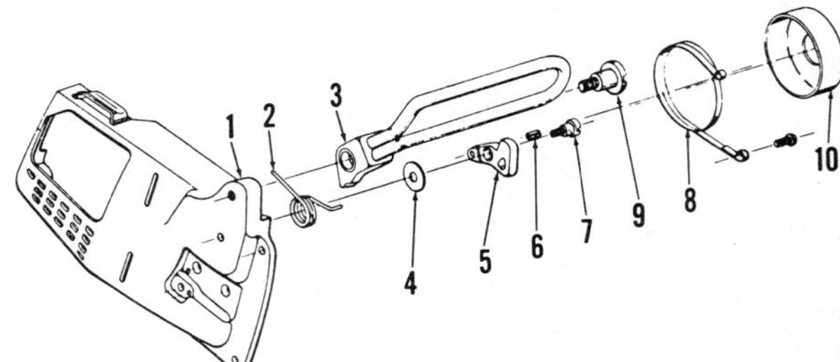

Fig. HL320—Exploded view of chain brake used on Model 450SL.

1. Cover
2. Spring
3. Actuating lever
4. Washer
5. Latch
6. Roll pin
7. Shoulder screw
8. Brake band
9. Shoulder screw
10. Drum

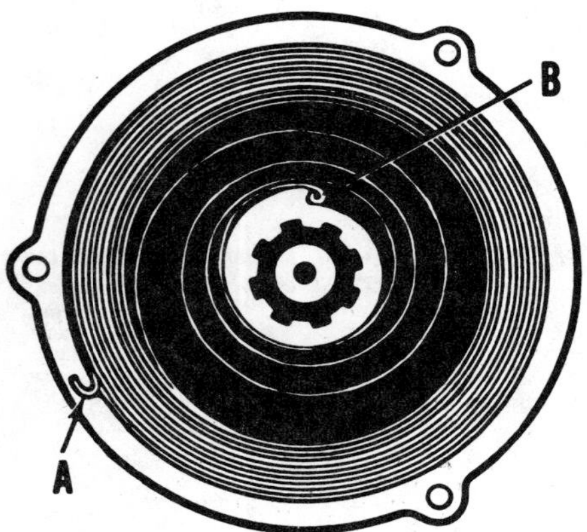

Fig. HL319—View of rewind spring installation in starter cover. Hook outer loop (A) of spring in notch as shown. Inner loop (B) of spring must be curved inward to engage notch of spring lock.

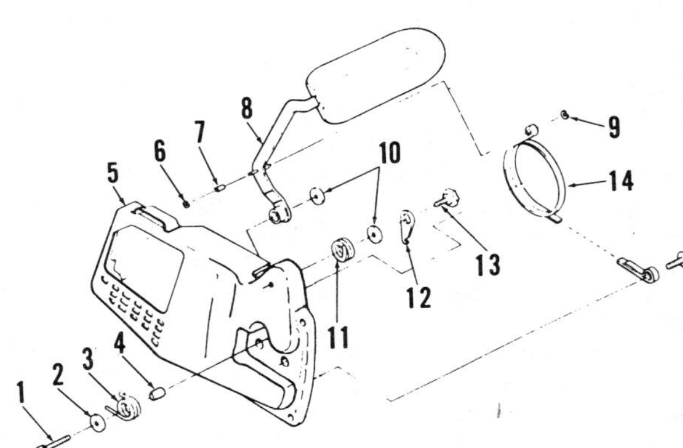

Fig. HL321—Exploded view of chain brake used on Model 550SL.

1. Screw
2. Washer
3. Spring
4. Sleeve
5. Cover
6. "E" ring
7. Roller
8. Actuating lever
9. "E" ring
10. Washers
11. Spring
12. Latch
13. Shoulder screw
14. Brake band

HOMELITE

Model	Bore mm (in.)	Stroke mm (in.)	Displacement cc (cu. in.)	Drive Type
240, 240 HG, 240 SL, 245 HG, 245 SL	40.0 (1.563)	32.0 (1.25)	40.0 (2.4)	Direct

MAINTENANCE

SPARK PLUG. Recommended spark plug is Champion DJ7Y for all models. Spark plug electrode gap should be 0.025 inch (0.63 mm).

CARBURETOR. A Zama C1S-H4 diaphragm carburetor is used on 240HG and 240SL models while 245HG and 245SL models may be equipped with either a Walbro WT-19 or Zama C1S-H8 diaphragm carburetor. Refer to CARBURETOR SERVICE section for service procedures and exploded views.

As noted in the Zama service section, the metering diaphragm and metering disc are a one-piece assembly on later models. All Model 245 saws are equipped with the late type metering diaphragm. Service carburetor A-96352-A is also equipped with the later type metering diaphragm. When servicing early carburetors with the separate metering disc and diaphragm, the later one-piece diaphragm assembly (available in repair kit 96646-A) should be installed.

Initial adjustment of idle and high speed mixture screws is one turn open. Adjust idle speed screw so engine idles just below clutch engagement speed. Adjust idle mixture screw so engine accelerates smoothly. If necessary, readjust idle speed screw.

To adjust high speed mixture screw, proceed as follows. Run saw at idle until engine reaches operating temperature. Turn high speed mixture needle to obtain optimum performance with saw under cutting load.

MAGNETO AND TIMING. A solid state ignition is used on all models. The solid-state ignition system is serviced by renewing the spark plug and/or ignition module. Air gap between ignition module and flywheel is adjustable. Adjust air gap by loosening module retaining screws and place a 0.015 inch (0.4 mm) shim stock between flywheel and module.

LUBRICATION. The engine is lubricated by mixing oil with unleaded gasoline. Recommended oil is Homelite® two-stroke oil mixed at ratio as designated on oil container. If Homelite® oil is not available, a good quality oil designed for air-cooled two-stroke engines may be used when mixed at a 16:1 ratio, however, an antioxidant fuel stabilizer (such as Sta-Bil) should be added to fuel mix. Antioxidant fuel stabilizer is not required with Homelite® oils as they contain fuel stabilizer so the fuel mix will stay fresh up to one year.

Chain oil tank should be filled with Homelite® Bar and Chain Oil or a good quality SAE 30 oil. It may be necessary to use SAE 10 oil or oil mixed with kerosene if temperature is below 40°F (4°C).

Clutch needle bearing should be cleaned and lubricated periodically with Homelite® ALL-TEMP Multipurpose Grease.

MUFFLER. Outer screen of muffler should be cleaned of debris every week or after each 50 hours of use. Carbon should be removed from muffler and engine ports to prevent excessive car-

Fig. HL325—View of trigger assembly used on 240HG and 240SL models.

1. Handle cover
2. Interlock
3. Spring
4. Throttle trigger
5. Throttle rod
6. Filter chamber

Fig. HL325S—View of trigger assembly and manual oil pump used on 245HG and 245SL models.

1. Handle cover
2. Interlock
3. Spring
4. Throttle trigger
5. Throttle cable
6. Filter chamber
7. Throttle lock pin
8. Spring
9. "E" ring
10. Button
11. Nut
12. Manual oil pump

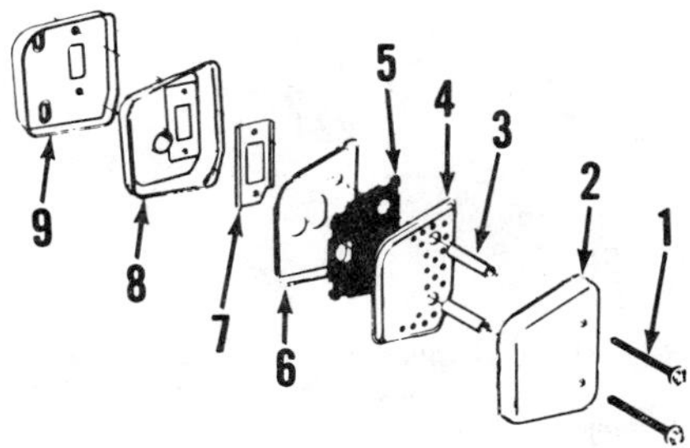

Fig. HL326—Exploded view of muffler.

1. Screw
2. Cap
3. Spacer
4. Outer baffle
5. Screen
6. Inner baffle
7. Support
8. Body
9. Deflector

bon build-up and power loss. Do not allow loose carbon to enter cylinder and be careful not to damage exhaust port or piston. Refer to Fig. HL326 when reassembling muffler.

REPAIRS

TIGHTENING TORQUE VALUES. Tightening torque values are listed in following table.

Carburetor retaining screws	18-33 in.-lbs. (2.0-3.7 N•m)
Chain brake band	27-44 in.-lbs. (3.1-5.0 N•m)
Chain brake lever	36-55 in.-lbs. (4.1-6.2 N•m)
Clutch hub	90-165 in.-lbs. (10.2-18.6 N•m)
Clutch nut	68-110 in.-lbs. (7.7-12.4 N•m)
Crankcase screws	54-82 in.-lbs. (6.1-9.3 N•m)
Flywheel	90-165 in.-lbs. (10.2-18.6 N•m)
Ignition module	27-44 in.-lbs. (3.1-5.0 N•m)
Muffler	63-88 in.-lbs. (7.1-9.9 N•m)
Spark plug	140-160 in.-lbs. (15.8-18.1 N•m)
Starter pulley screw	36-55 in.-lbs. (4.1-6.2 N•m)
Vibration isolator	36-55 in.-lbs. (4.1-6.2 N•m)

COMPRESSION PRESSURE. For optimum performance of all models, cylinder compression pressure should be 130-160 psi (897-1104 kPa) with engine at normal operating temperature. Engine should be inspected and repaired when compression pressure is 90 psi (620 kPa) or below.

CYLINDER, PISTON, PIN AND RINGS. Cylinder may be removed after unscrewing socket head cap screws in bottom of crankcase (13–Fig. H327). Be careful when removing cylinder as crankshaft assembly will be loose in crankcase. Care should be taken not to scratch or nick mating surfaces of cylinder and crankcase.

Inspect crankshaft bearings and renew if scored or worn. Thrust washers (9) should be installed with shoulder to inside. Bearings (10) should be installed with lettered end towards crankshaft. Crankshaft seals are installed with seal lip to inside. Cylinder and crankcase mating surfaces should be cleaned then coated with room temperature vulcanizing (RTV) silicone sealer before assembly.

Early model cylinders are equipped with an open exhaust port while a bridged exhaust port is used on later model cylinders. Early model pistons are equipped with piston ring locating pins in ring groove. Later model pistons do not have piston ring locating pins and top piston ring should be installed so end gap is opposite exhaust port. End gap of bottom piston ring should be 90 degrees from top ring end gap. Piston ring end gap should be 0.003-0.017 inch (0.08-0.43 mm).

Bearings, seals and thrust washers must be positioned correctly on crankshaft before final assembly. Use the following procedure for crankshaft installation: With piston assembly installed on rod, insert piston in cylinder being sure piston rings are properly located. Install thrust washers (9), bearings (10), retaining rings (11) and seals (12) on crankshaft. Place 0.015 inch

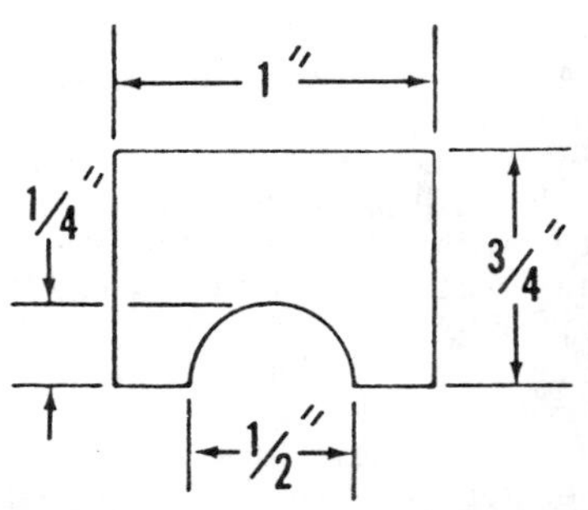

Fig. HL328—Shims used in crankshaft assembly may be made by putting 0.015 inch thick plastic, metal, or other suitable material in the outline shown above. Refer to Fig. HL329 and text.

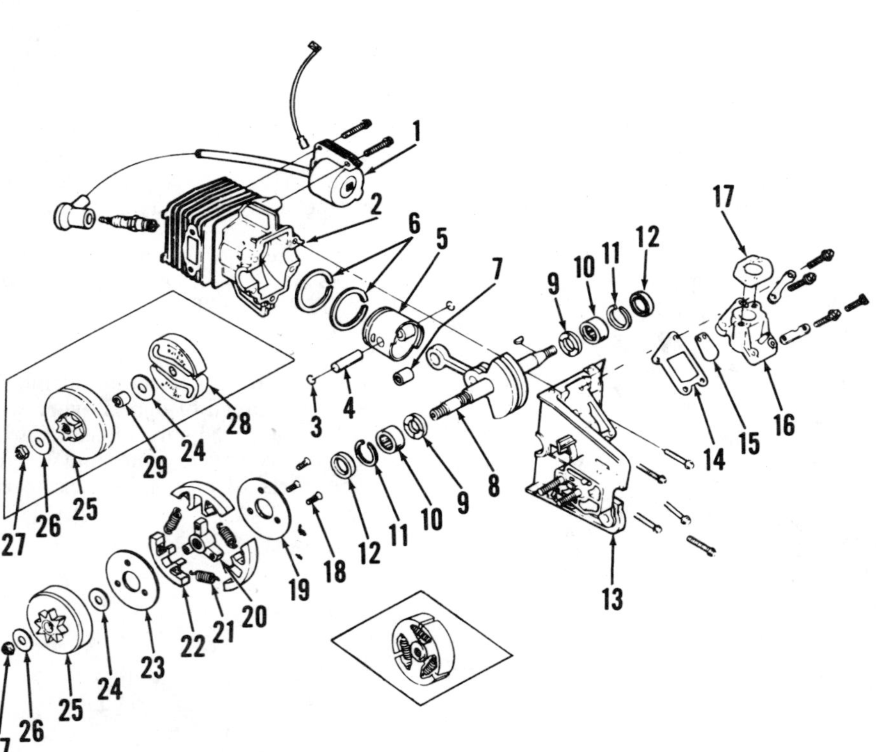

Fig. HL327—Exploded view of engine and clutch assemblies. Models 245HG and 245SL are equipped with three-shoe clutch. Models 240HG and 240SL are equipped with "S" clutch (inset).

1. Ignition module
2. Cylinder
3. Retainer
4. Piston pin
5. Piston
6. Piston rings
7. Needle bearing
8. Crankshaft
9. Thrust washer
10. Needle bearing
11. Retaining ring
12. Seal
13. Crankcase
14. Gasket
15. Reed petal
16. Intake manifold
17. Gasket
18. Screw
19. Cover plate
20. Clutch hub
21. Clutch spring
22. Clutch shoe
23. Cover plate
24. Thrust washer
25. Clutch drum/bearing
26. Thrust washer
27. Nut
28. "S" clutch/hub
29. Needle bearing

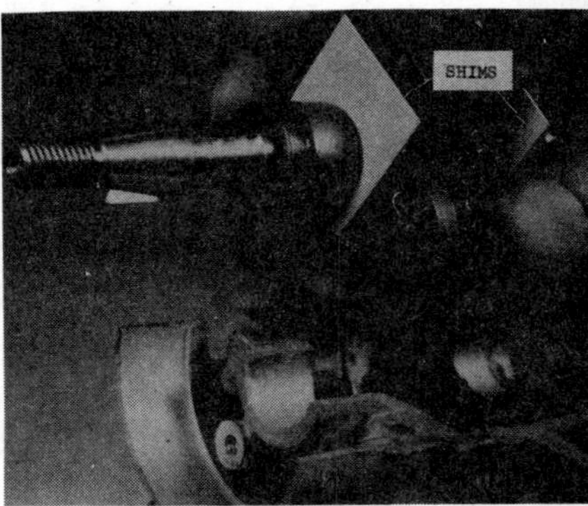

Fig. HL329—View showing placement of shims (Fig. HL328) between thrust washers (9—Fig. HL327) and bearings (10) for correct crankshaft assembly. Refer to text.

thick shims shown in Fig. HL328 between thrust washers and bearings as shown in Fig. HL329. Gently push seals toward crankshaft counterweights until assemblies are snug. Remove shims and complete assembly being careful not to disturb position of thrust washers, bearings and seals. Before final tightening of crankcase screws, lightly tap both ends of crankshaft to obtain proper crankshaft end play, then tighten crankcase screws.

CLUTCH. Refer to Fig. HL327 for exploded view of clutch assemblies used. Models 240HG and 240SL are equipped with the "S" type centrifugal clutch (28) shown in inset while Models 245HG and 245SL are equipped with the three-shoe type clutch (20, 21 and 22). On both types, clutch nut (27) and hub (20 or 28) have left-hand threads

NOTE: "OUTSIDE" marked on side of hub of "S" type clutch.

Clean and inspect clutch hub, drum and bearing for damage or excessive wear. Inspect crankshaft for wear or damage caused by defective clutch bearing. Clutch bearing contains 21 needle rollers which will fall out when bearing is removed if the following procedure is not followed. Roll a tube of paper approximately the size of the crankshaft and slide the clutch drum and bearing off the crankshaft and on to the rolled paper. The roll of paper will prevent the bearing needle rollers from falling out and the drum and bearing can be installed by reversing the procedure. If bearing is removed without using the above procedure, the needle bearings will fall out and a new bearing must be installed as needle rollers are too small.

NOTE: Be sure all 21 needle rollers are present in bearing race.

New bearings can be installed without using above procedure since wear has not yet loosened rollers.

CHAIN OIL PUMP. All models are equipped with a crankcase pulse actuated automatic chain oiler pump. Crankcase pulses actuate diaphragm and plunger (3 – Fig. HL330) to force oil out oil outlet (O). Inspect diaphragm (3) and "O" ring (2) for leaks.

Models 245HG and 245SL are also equipped with a manual oil pump (12 – Fig. HL325A) to supply additional lubrication when required. Individual manual oil pump components are not available and pump must be renewed as a unit assembly.

VIBRATION ISOLATORS. All models are equipped with vibration isolators between engine and engine housing. Vibration isolators may be renewed after removing handle bar (3 – Fig. HL331), starter housing (2) and air box (1). Use Fig. HL331 as a guide to reassemble vibration isolator components.

REWIND STARTER. To service recoil starter, remove starter housing from saw. Pull starter rope and hold rope pulley with notch in pulley adjacent to rope outlet. Pull rope back through outlet so it engages notch in pulley and allow pulley to completely unwind. Unscrew pulley retaining screw (8 – Fig. HL332) and remove rope pulley being careful not to dislodge rewind spring in housing. Care must be taken if rewind

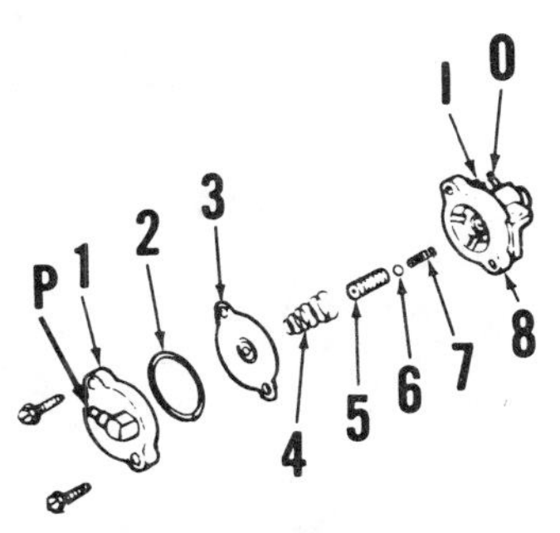

Fig. HL330 — Exploded view of automatic oil pump. Oil enters pump through inlet tube (I) and exits through tube (E). Diaphragm (3) is actuated by crankcase pulsations through pulse fitting (P).

1. Cover
2. "O" ring
3. Diaphragm & plunger
4. Spring
5. Stud
6. Check ball
7. Spring
8. Body

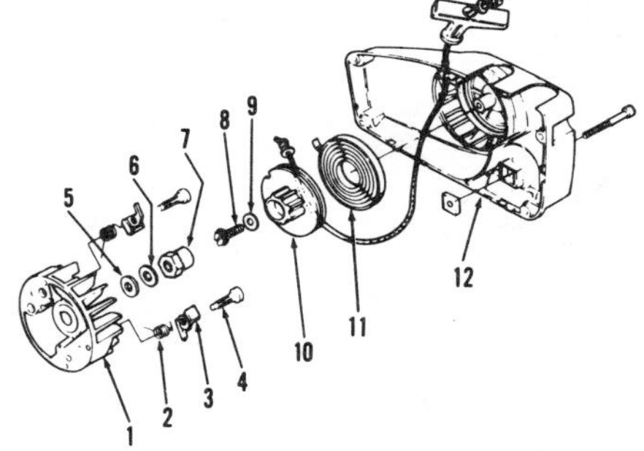

Fig. HL332 — Exploded view of rewind starter.

1. Flywheel
2. Spring
3. Pawl
4. Pawl pin
5. Washer
6. Lockwasher
7. Nut
8. Screw
9. Washer
10. Rope pulley
11. Rewind starter
12. Starter housing

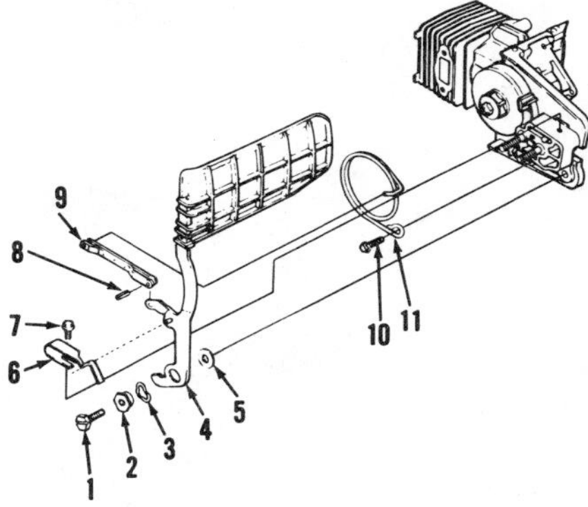

Fig. HL333 — Exploded view of chain brake used on Models 240SL and 245SL.

1. Screw
2. Cam
3. Curved washer
4. Brake lever
5. Thrust washer
6. Clip
7. Screw
8. Roll pin
9. Pivot link
10. Screw
11. Brake band

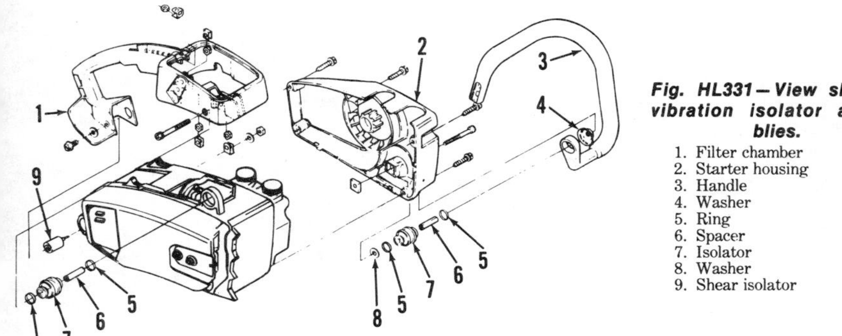

Fig. HL331 — View showing vibration isolator assemblies.

1. Filter chamber
2. Starter housing
3. Handle
4. Washer
5. Ring
6. Spacer
7. Isolator
8. Washer
9. Shear isolator

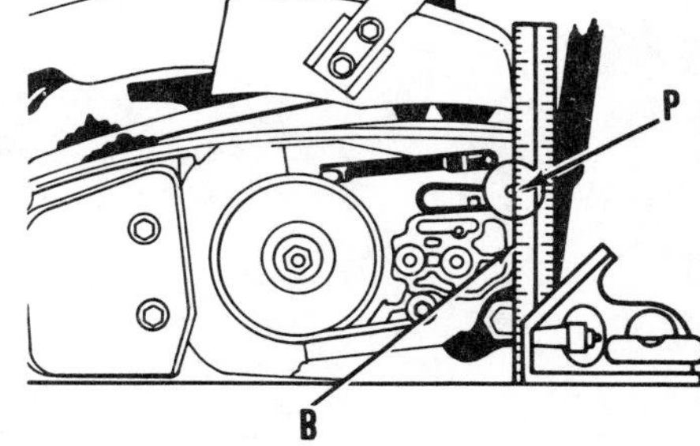

Fig. HL334 — Brake lever pin (P) is normally in line with front edge of guide bar pad (B). Refer to text for adjustment.

spring is removed to prevent injury if spring is allowed to uncoil uncontrolled.

Rewind spring is wound in clockwise direction in starter housing. Rope is wound on rope pulley in clockwise direction as viewed with pulley in housing. To place tension on rewind spring, pass rope through rope outlet in housing and install rope handle. Pull rope out and hold rope pulley so notch on pulley is adjacent to rope outlet. Pull rope back through outlet between notch in pulley and housing. Turn rope pulley clockwise to place tension on spring. Release pulley and check starter action. Do not place more tension on rewind spring than is necessary to draw rope handle up against housing.

CHAIN BRAKE. Models 240SL and 245SL are equipped with a chain brake mechanism to stop saw chain motion in the event of kickback. In the event of kickback, the operator's left hand will force brake lever (4 – Fig. HL333) forward and brake band (11) will wrap around the clutch drum to stop clutch drum rotation. Chain brake should stop chain instantly. If chain brake does not operate correctly, outer surface of clutch drum may be glazed. Remove glaze with emery cloth being sure to clean drum afterwards. Clutch drum and brake band must not be bent or nicked.

The force needed to actuate brake lever (4) is adjustable by rotating cam (2). Maximum force needed to actuate brake lever is obtained with cam down. Cam rotation will also alter position of brake lever. If brake lever must be repositioned after rotating cam, loosen retaining screw and relocate clip (6). The location of clip also determines the clearance between brake band (11) and clutch drum. Normal position for lever pin (P – Fig. HL334) is in line with front edge of guide bar pan (B).

HOMELITE

Model	Bore mm (in.)	Stroke mm (in.)	Displacement cc (cu. in.)	Drive Type
330, 330 SL, 330 W	43.0 (1.687)	37.0 (1.464)	53.6 (3.27)	Direct

MAINTENANCE

SPARK PLUG. Recommended spark plug is Champion DJ7Y for all models. Spark plug electrode gap should be 0.025 inch (0.63 mm).

CARBURETOR. All models may be equipped with a Walbro WT or Zama diaphragm type carburetor. Refer to CARBURETOR SERVICE section for carburetor service and exploded views.

Initial adjustment of low speed mixture screw (L – Fig. HL340) and high speed mixture screw (H) is one turn open. Adjust idle speed screw so engine idles just below clutch engagement speed. Adjust low mixture screw to obtain maximum engine speed at idle and smooth acceleration. If necessary readjust idle speed screw.

To adjust high speed mixture screw, proceed as follows: Run saw at idle until engine reaches operating temperature. Turn high speed mixture needle to obtain optimum performance with saw under cutting load.

MAGNETO AND TIMING. A solid state ignition is used on all models. The solid-state ignition system is serviced by renewing the spark plug and/or ignition module. Air gap between ignition module and flywheel is adjustable. Adjust air gap by loosening module retaining screws and place a 0.015 inch (0.38 mm) shim stock between flywheel and module.

Although ignition system malfunctions are usually caused by spark plug and/or ignition module failure, erratic engine operation, especially under load, may be due to ignition switch lead wire grounding on the cylinder or muffler. Make certain switch lead wire is routed and secured as shown in Fig. HL342 and wire connections at ignition switch are properly positioned to prevent contact with cylinder or muffler. Ignition switch ground wire should be secured to saw at a 45 degree angle from saw centerline (not straight back).

LUBRICATION. The engine is lubricated by mixing oil with unleaded gasoline. Recommended oil is Homelite® two-stroke oil mixed at ratio as designated on oil container. If Homelite® oil is not available, a good quality oil designed for air-cooled two-stroke engines may be used when mixed at a 16:1 ratio, however, an antioxidant fuel stabilizer (such as Sta-Bil) should be added to fuel mix. Antioxidant fuel stabilizer is not required with Homelite® oils as they contain fuel stabilizer so the fuel mix will stay fresh up to one year.

Chain oil tank should be filled with Homelite® Bar and Chain Oil or a good quality SAE 30 oil. It may be necessary to use SAE 10 oil or oil mixed with kerosene if temperature is below 40°F (4°C).

Clutch needle bearing should be removed, cleaned and lubricated periodically with Homelite® ALL-TEMP Multipurpose Grease.

MUFFLER. Muffler should be disassembled, cleaned of debris and inspected every week or as required. Renew muffler components that are cracked or worn excessively. Carbon should be removed from muffler and engine ports to prevent excessive carbon build-up and power loss. Do not allow loose carbon to enter cylinder and be careful not to damage exhaust port or piston. Refer to Fig. HL343 when reassembling muffler.

REPAIRS

TIGHTENING TORQUE VALUES. Tightening torque values are listed in following table.

Carburetor retaining screws .... 20-30 in.-lbs. (2.3-3.4 N·m)
Chain brake band .... 70-80 in.-lbs. (7.9-9.0 N·m)
Chain brake shield .... 40 in.-lbs. (4.5 N·m)

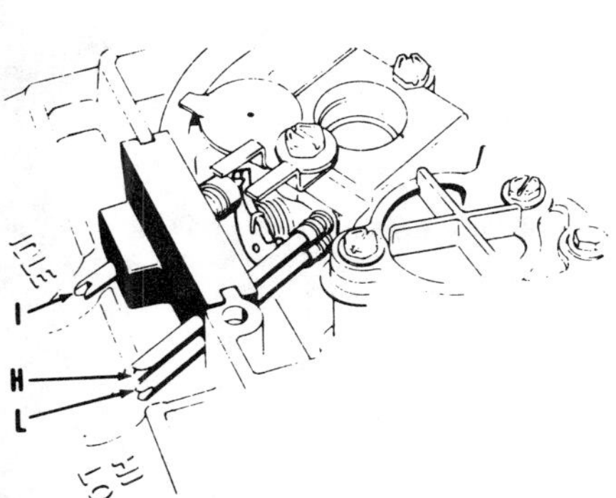

Fig. HL340 – View showing location of idle speed screw (I), low speed mixture screw (L) and high speed mixture screw (H).

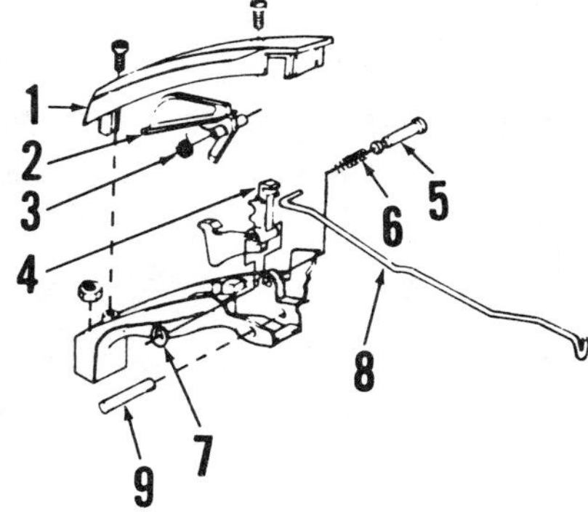

Fig. HL341 – View of trigger assembly.

1. Handle cover
2. Interlock
3. Spring
4. Throttle trigger
5. Throttle lock pin
6. Spring
7. "E" ring
8. Throttle rod
9. Groove pin

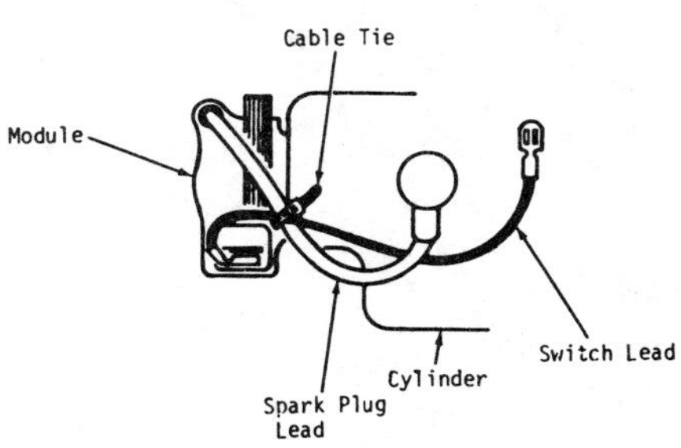

Fig. HL342 – Route and secure ignition switch lead as shown to prevent "shorting out" of ignition systems. Refer to text.

Chain stop	30-40 in.-lbs. (3.4-4.5 N•m)
Clutch nut	100-120 in.-lbs. (11.3-13.6 N•m)
Crankcase screws	60-70 in.-lbs. (6.8-7.9 N•m)
Flywheel	250-300 in.-lbs. (28.2-33.9 N•m)
Ignition module	70-80 in.-lbs. (7.9-9.0 N•m)
Muffler	60-70 in.-lbs. (6.8-7.9 N•m)
Spark plug	120-180 in.-lbs. (13.6-20.3 N•m)
Starter pulley	40-50 in.-lbs. (4.5-5.6 N•m)
Vibration isolator	40-50 in.-lbs. (4.5-5.6 N•m)

COMPRESSION PRESSURE. For optimum performance of all models, cylinder compression pressure should be 130-160 psi (897-1104 kPa) with engine at normal operating temperature. Engine should be inspected and repaired when compression pressure is 90 psi (620 kPa) or below.

CYLINDER, PISTON, PIN AND RINGS. Cylinder may be removed after unscrewing socket head cap screws in bottom of crankcase (13 – Fig. H344). Be careful when removing cylinder as crankshaft assembly will be loose in crankcase. Care should be taken not to scratch or nick mating surfaces of cylinder and crankcase.

Inspect crankshaft bearings (10) and renew if scored or worn. Crankshaft seals are installed with seal lip to inside. Cylinder and crankcase mating surfaces should be flat and free of nicks and scratches. Mating surfaces should be cleaned then coated with room temperature vulcanizing (RTV) silicone sealer before assembly.

Bearings, seals and thrust washers must be positioned correctly on crankshaft before final assembly. Use the following procedure for crankshaft installation: With piston assembly installed on rod, insert piston in cylinder being sure piston rings are aligned on locating pins. Install thrust washers (9), bearings (10), retaining rings (11) and seals (12) on crankshaft. Place 0.015 inch thick shims shown in Fig. HL345 between thrust washers and bearings as shown in Fig. HL346.

Gently push seals toward crankshaft counterweights until assemblies are

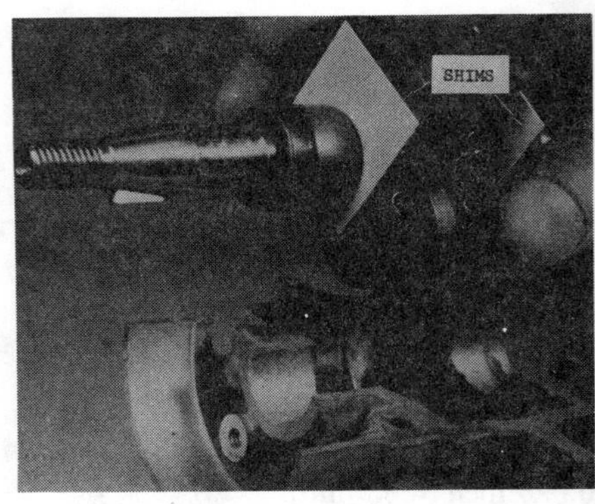

Fig. HL346 – View showing placement of shims (Fig. HL345) between thrust washers (9 – Fig. HL344) and bearings (10) for correct crankshaft assembly. Refer to text.

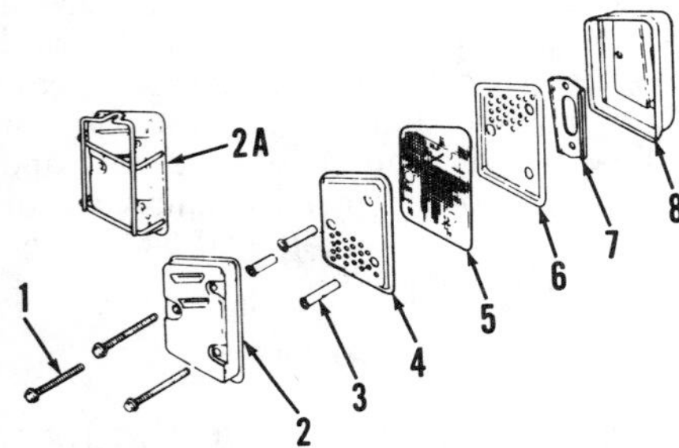

Fig. HL343 – Exploded view of muffler. Cap (2A) is used on Model 330W.

1. Screw
2. Cap
3. Spacer
4. Outer baffle
5. Screen
6. Inner baffle
7. Plate
8. Body

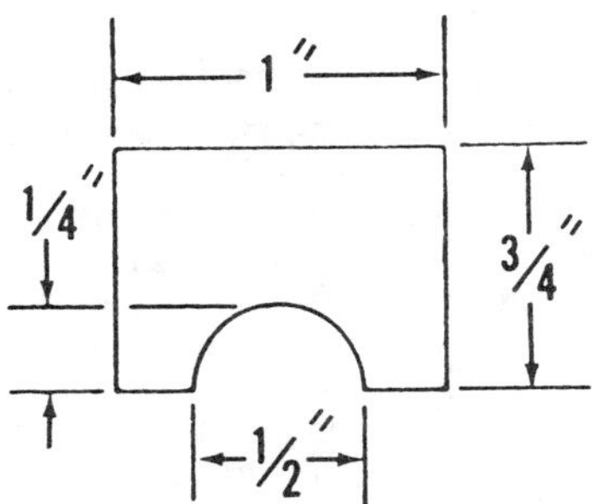

Fig. HL345 – Shims used in crankshaft assembly may be made by cutting 0.015 inch thick plastic, metal or other suitable material in the outline shown above. Refer to Fig. HL346 and text.

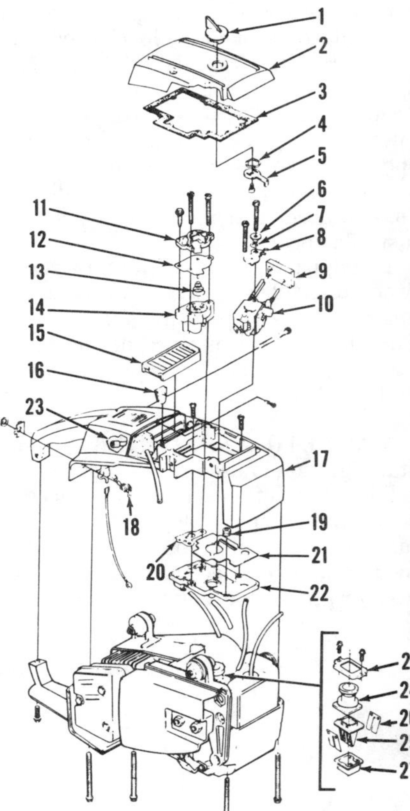

Fig. HL347 – Exploded view of oil pump and air box assemblies.

1. Choke knob
2. Cover
3. Gasket
4. Wave washer
5. Choke lever
6. Spacer
7. Wave washer
8. Choke plate
9. Grommet
10. Carburetor
11. Oil pump cover
12. Diaphragm & plunger
13. Spring
14. Oil pump body
15. Air filter
16. Grommet
17. Top engine housing
18. Ignition switch
19. Grommet
20. Gasket
21. Gasket
22. Plate
23. Retainer
24. Boot
25. Reed seat
26. Reed valve
27. Reed retainer

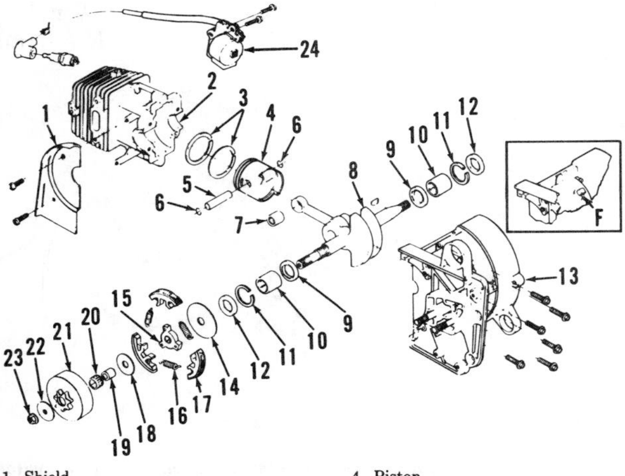

Fig. HL344 – Exploded view of engine and clutch assemblies. Pulse fitting (F) is connected to oil pump pulse hose.

1. Shield
2. Cylinder
3. Piston rings
4. Piston
5. Piston pin
6. Retainer
7. Needle bearing
8. Crankshaft
9. Thrust washer
10. Needle bearing
11. Retainer ring
12. Seal
13. Crankcase
14. Thrust washer
15. Hub
16. Spring
17. Shoe
18. Thrust washer
19. Inner race
20. Roller bearing
21. Clutch drum
22. Thrust washer
23. Nut
24. Ignition module

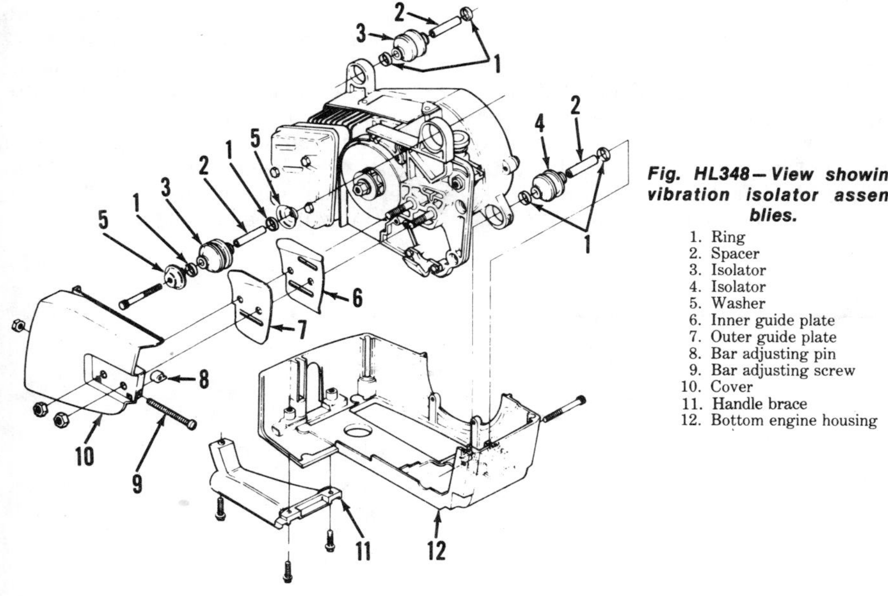

Fig. HL348—View showing vibration isolator assemblies.

1. Ring
2. Spacer
3. Isolator
4. Isolator
5. Washer
6. Inner guide plate
7. Outer guide plate
8. Bar adjusting pin
9. Bar adjusting screw
10. Cover
11. Handle brace
12. Bottom engine housing

snug. Remove shims and complete assembly being careful not to disturb position of thrust washers, bearings and seals. Before final tightening of crankcase screws, lightly tap both ends of crankshaft to obtain proper crankshaft end play, then tighten crankcase screws.

CLUTCH. Refer to Fig. HL344 for exploded view of shoe type clutch used on all models. Clutch hub (15) has left-hand threads and is removed by unscrewing clockwise.

Needle roller bearing (20) should be removed, cleaned and lubricated after each 100 hours of operation. A high temperature grease such as Homelite® ALL-TEMP Multipurpose Grease should be used. Inspect crankshaft for wear or damage caused by defective clutch bearing.

If clutch slips with engine running at high speed under load, check the clutch shoes for excessive wear. If chain continues to turn with engine running at idle speed (below normal clutch engagement speed), check for broken, weak or distorted clutch springs.

PYRAMID REED VALVE. A pyramid type reed intake valve seat (25–Fig. HL347) and four reeds (26) are used. Reeds are retained on pins projecting from the reed seat by retainer (27). Inspect reed seat, retainer and reeds for any distortion, excessive wear or other damage.

To reinstall, use a drop of oil to stick each reed to the seat, then push reed retainer down over the seat and reeds. Then install the assembly in crankcase; never install retainer, then attempt to install reed seat and reeds.

AUTOMATIC CHAIN OILER PUMP. All models are equipped with a crankcase pulse actuated automatic chain oiler pump (11 through 14–Fig. HL347). Crankcase pulses actuate diaphragm and plunger (12) to force oil out oil outlet. Check oil pump assembly for leaks. Carefully inspect cover (11) and diaphragm (12). If oil pump is defective due to warpage of cover (11), sand cover until flat or renew cover.

VIBRATION ISOLATORS. All models are equipped with vibration isolators between engine and engine housing. Vibration isolators may be renewed after removing top engine housing (17–Fig. HL347) and bottom engine housing (12–Fig. HL348). Use Fig. HL348 as a guide to reassemble vibration isolator components.

REWIND STARTER. To service rewind starter, unscrew mounting screws and remove starter housing (11–Fig. HL349). Rotate ratchet (6) until it stops at end of shaft on pulley (8), then slide ratchet lever (7) off ratchet. Pull starter rope and hold rope pulley with notch in pulley adjacent to rope outlet. Pull rope back through outlet so it engages notch in pulley and allow pulley to completely unwind. Unscrew pulley retaining screw (4) and disengage ratchet (6) from pulley shaft. Detach rope handle, then remove pulley from starter housing while being careful not to dislodge rewind spring in housing.

When assembling starter, wind rope around rope pulley in a clockwise direction as viewed with pulley in housing. Pass rope through rope outlet in housing and install rope handle. Place pulley in housing. Reinstall ratchet (6) on pulley shaft and secure assembly with flat washer (5) and screw (4). To place tension on rewind spring, pull rope out and hold rope pulley so notch on pulley is adjacent to rope outlet. Pull rope back through outlet between notch in pulley

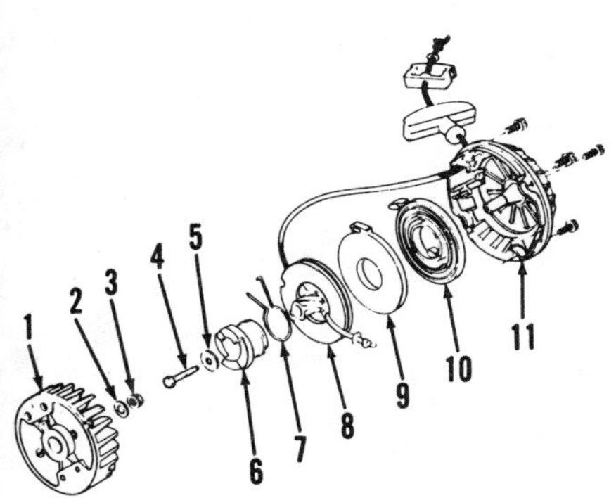

Fig. HL349—Exploded view of rewind starter.

1. Flywheel
2. Washer
3. Nut
4. Screw
5. Washer
6. Ratchet
7. Ratchet lever
8. Rope pulley
9. Spring case
10. Rewind spring
11. Starter housing

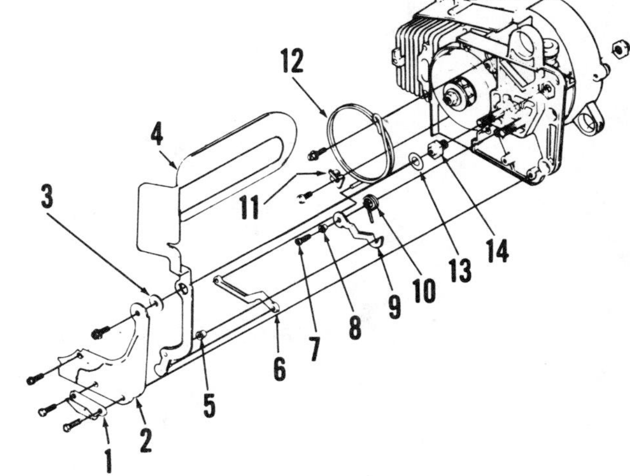

Fig. HL350—Exploded view of chain brake used on Model 330SL.

1. Chain stop
2. Shield
3. Washer
4. Brake lever
5. Bushing
6. Link
7. Screw
8. Spacer
9. Detent
10. Spring
11. Bracket
12. Brake band
13. Spring washer
14. Insert

and housing. Turn rope pulley clockwise to place tension on spring. Release pulley and check starter action. Do not place more tension on rewind spring than is necessary to draw rope handle up against housing. Slide ratchet lever (7) with hooked end up, on ratchet while guiding hooked end between posts of starter housing. Check operation of starter assembly before installing on saw.

CHAIN BRAKE. Model 330SL is equipped with a chain brake mechanism to stop saw chain motion in the event of kickback. In the event of kickback, the operator's left hand will force brake lever (4–Fig. HL350) forward and brake band (12) will wrap around the clutch drum to stop clutch drum rotation. Chain brake should stop chain instantly. If chain brake does not operate correctly, outer surface of clutch drum may be glazed. Remove glaze with emery cloth being sure to clean drum afterwards. Clutch drum and brake band must not be bent or nicked.

HOMELITE

Model	Bore mm (in.)	Stroke mm (in.)	Displacement cc (cu. in.)	Drive Type
410, 410 SL, 410 SLF	49.0 (1.937)	35.0 (1.375)	67.0 (4.1)	Direct

MAINTENANCE

SPARK PLUG. Recommended spark plug is Champion DJ7Y for all models. Spark plug electrode gap should be 0.025 inch (0.63 mm).

CARBURETOR. Model 410 is equipped with a Walbro WS diaphragm carburetor. Refer to Walbro section of CARBURETOR SERVICE section for carburetor overhaul and exploded view.

Remove carburetor cover to perform initial carburetor adjustments. Initial adjustment of idle speed screw (I – Fig. HL355) is 1/2-3/4 turn clockwise after lobe on idle speed screw just contacts throttle stop lever (T). Initial adjustment of low speed mixture screw (L) is 1-1 3/4 turns open and high speed mixture screw (H) is 1-1 1/4 turns open. Install carburetor cover and start saw.

Adjust low mixture screw to obtain maximum engine speed at idle and smooth acceleration, then adjust idle speed screw so engine idles just below clutch engagement speed.

To adjust high speed mixture screw, proceed as follows: Run saw at idle until engine reaches operating temperature. Turn high speed mixture needle to obtain optimum performance with saw under cutting load.

Note check valve (20 – Fig. HL356) and filter (19) which are used to vent fuel tank. Filter must be clean and valve must operate properly for required fuel flow to carburetor.

Fig. HL355 – View of carburetor adjustment screws. Refer to text for adjustment.

MAGNETO AND TIMING. Model 410 is equipped with a solid-state ignition. The solid-state ignition system is serviced by renewing the spark plug and/or ignition module. Air gap between ignition module and flywheel is adjustable. Adjust air gap by loosening module retaining screws and place a 0.015 inch (0.38 mm) shim stock between flywheel and module.

LUBRICATION. The engine is lubricated by mixing oil with unleaded gasoline. Recommended oil is Homelite® two-stroke oil mixed at ratio as designated on oil container. If Homelite® oil is not available, a good quality oil designed for two-stroke engines may be used when mixed at a 16:1 ratio, however, an antioxidant fuel stabilizer (such as Sta-Bil) should be added to fuel mix. Antioxidant fuel stabilizer is not required with Homelite® oils as they contain fuel stabilizer so the fuel mix will stay fresh up to one year.

Chain oil tank should be filled with Homelite® Bar and Chain Oil or a good quality SAE 30 oil. It may be necessary to use SAE 10 oil or oil mixed with kerosene if temperature is below 40°F (4°C).

Clutch needle bearing should be removed, cleaned and lubricated periodically with Homelite® ALL-TEMP Multipurpose Grease.

MUFFLER. Muffler should be disassembled and periodically cleaned. Renew muffler components that are cracked or worn excessively. Check engine exhaust port and remove excessive carbon build-up as required. Do not allow loose carbon to enter cylinder

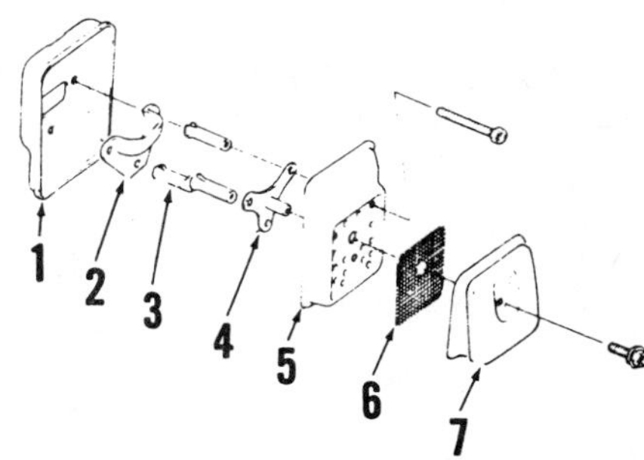

Fig. HL357 – Exploded view of muffler.

1. Body
2. Plate
3. Spacer
4. Spacer plate
5. Cover
6. Screen
7. Cap

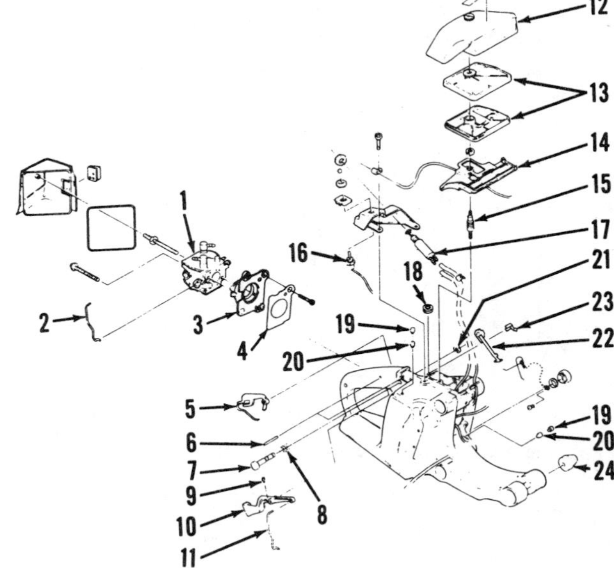

Fig. HL356 – Exploded view of handle assembly.

1. Carburetor
2. Throttle rod
3. Plate
4. Spacer
5. Trigger lock
6. Pin
7. Throttle lock pin
8. Spring
9. Set screw
10. Trigger
11. Throttle rod
12. Cover
13. Air filter
14. Support
15. Stud
16. Ignition switch
17. Manual oil pump
18. Boot
19. Filter
20. Check valve
21. "E" ring
22. Choke rod
23. Retainer
24. Vibration isolator

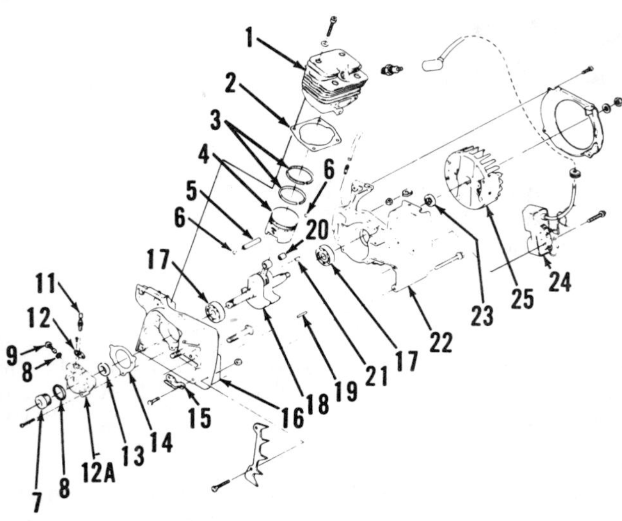

Fig. HL358—Exploded view of engine and oil pump.

1. Cylinder
2. Gasket
3. Piston rings
4. Piston
5. Piston pin
6. Retainer
7. Worm
8. Felt seal
9. Cam screw
10. Gasket
11. Plunger & gear
12. Retainer
12A. Automatic oil pump body
13. Seal
14. Gasket
15. Chain stop
16. Crankcase half
17. Ball bearing
18. Crankshaft
19. Dowel pin (2)
20. Needle bearing
21. Key
22. Crankcase half
23. Seal
24. Ignition module
25. Flywheel

and be careful not to damage exhaust port on piston. Refer to Fig. HL357 when reassembling muffler.

REPAIRS

TIGHTENING TORQUE VALUES. Tightening torque values are listed in following table.

Auto oil pump	40-50 in.-lbs. (4.5-5.6 N•m)
Auto oil pump cam screw	50-60 in.-lbs. (5.6-6.8 N•m)
Carburetor adapter	30-40 in.-lbs. (3.4-4.5 N•m)
Carburetor retaining screws	40-50 in.-lbs. (4.5-5.6 N•m)
Chain stop	30-40 in.-lbs. (3.4-4.5 N•m)
Clutch cover	40-50 in.-lbs. (4.5-5.6 N•m)
Clutch hub	350-450 in.-lbs. (39.5-50.8 N•m)
Crankcase screws	80-90 in.-lbs. (9.0-10.2 N•m)
Flywheel	250-300 in.-lbs. (28.2-33.9 N•m)
Ignition module	50-60 in.-lbs. (5.6-6.8 N•m)
Muffler	80-90 in.-lbs. (9.0-10.2 N•m)
Muffler exhaust cap	40-50 in.-lbs. (4.5-5.6 N•m)
Spark plug	120-180 in.-lbs. (13.6-20.3 N•m)
Starter pulley	10-20 in.-lbs. (1.1-2.2 N•m)
Vibration isolator	60-70 in.-lbs. (6.8-7.9 N•m)

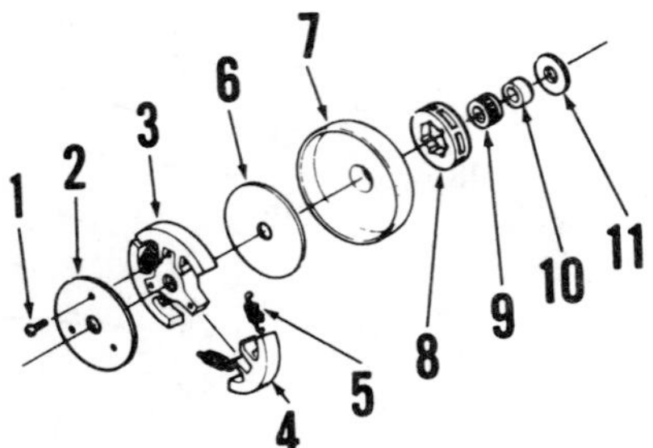

Fig. HL359—Exploded view of clutch.

1. Torx screw
2. Plate
3. Clutch hub
4. Clutch shoe
5. Spring
6. Thrust washer
7. Clutch drum
8. Sprocket
9. Roller bearing
10. Inner race
11. Thrust washer

COMPRESSION PRESSURE. For optimum performance of all models, cylinder compression pressure should be 140-170 psi (966-1173 kPa) with engine at normal operating temperature. Engine should be inspected and repaired when compression pressure is 90 psi (620 kPa) or below.

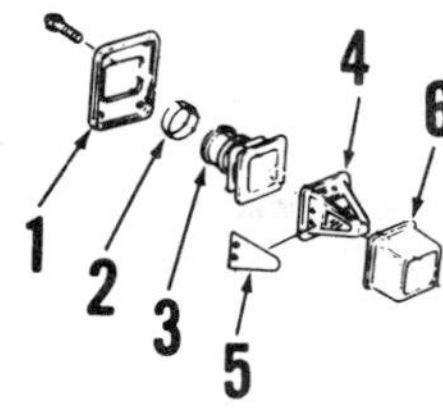

Fig. HL360—Exploded view of reed valve assembly.

1. Retainer
2. Stiffener
3. Connector
4. Seal
5. Reed
6. Retainer

PISTON, PIN, RINGS AND CYLINDER. The cylinder is secured to crankcase by four socket head screws. After removing cylinder, inspect cylinder bore for damage and excessive wear.

The piston pin is retained by clips at both ends of pin. The piston pin is supported by a renewable needle bearing in the connecting rod. Renew piston pin if worn or damaged.

The piston is equipped with two piston rings. Piston and cylinder are graded at factory according to size. Piston and cylinder are available only as a matched set.

Late models are equipped with a longer piston pin bearing (20–Fig. HL358) than early models. Piston pin bosses on late model pistons are wider apart to accept the wider bearing. Long bearing cannot be installed in an early piston and short bearing must not be installed in a late piston as excessive side play will result in engine failure. Early bearing width is 0.506-0.512 inch (12.9-13.0 mm) while late bearing width is 0.568-0.574 inch (14.4-14.6 mm).

CONNECTING ROD, CRANKSHAFT AND CRANKCASE. Crankcase halves must be split for access to crankshaft. The crankshaft is supported by ball bearings at both ends of shaft. Connecting rod, crankpin and crankshaft are a pressed together assembly and separate components are not available. Rod and crankshaft must be serviced as a unit assembly.

CLUTCH. Refer to Fig. HL359 for an exploded view of clutch. Cover plate (2) is retained by Torx head screws (1). Clutch hub (3) has left-hand threads. Clutch shoes and springs should be renewed only as sets. Inspect bearing (9) and lubricate with Homelite® ALL-TEMP Multipurpose Grease.

REED VALVE. A pyramid type reed valve as shown in Fig. HL360 is used. Reeds are retained on pins projecting

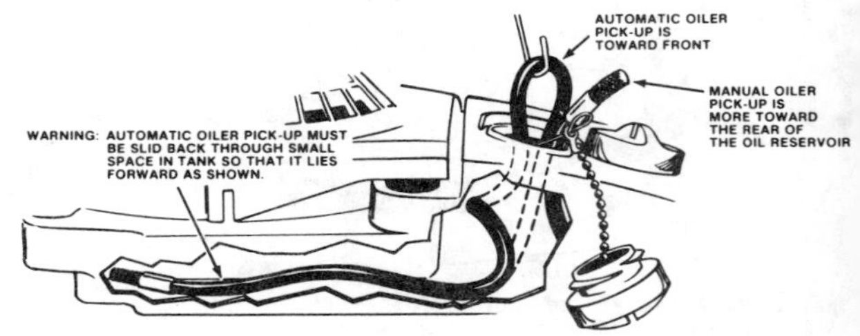

Fig. HL361—View showing installation of oil pickup lines.

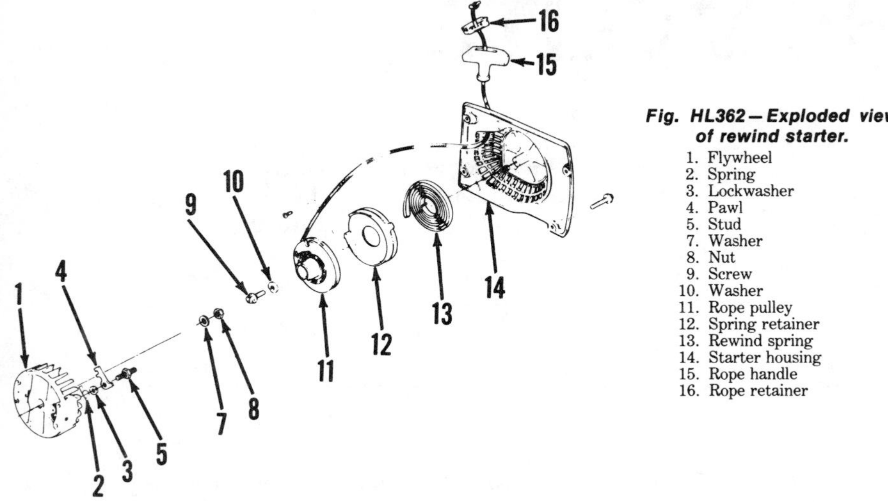

Fig. HL362—Exploded view of rewind starter.

1. Flywheel
2. Spring
3. Lockwasher
4. Pawl
5. Stud
7. Washer
8. Nut
9. Screw
10. Washer
11. Rope pulley
12. Spring retainer
13. Rewind spring
14. Starter housing
15. Rope handle
16. Rope retainer

from the reed seat by a molded retainer (6). Inspect reed seat, retainer and reeds for any distortion, excessive wear or other damage.

To reinstall reed valve, use a drop of oil to stick each reed to the plastic seat, then push reed retainer down over the seat and reeds. Then install the assembly in the crankcase; never install retainer, then attempt to install reed seat and reeds.

AUTOMATIC CHAIN OILER PUMP. The automatic chain oiler pump used is shown in Fig. HL358. The pump can be removed after removing the clutch. Inspect all pump components and renew any part which is damaged or excessively worn. Oil pump output is not adjustable.

Note check valve (20–Fig. HL356) and filter (19) which are used to vent oil tank. Filter must be clean and valve must operate properly for oil to enter oil pumps. Refer to Fig. HL361 for view of correct installation of oil pickup lines.

VIBRATION ISOLATORS. The engine assembly is supported in the handle assembly by six vibration isolators (24–Fig. HL356). The vibration isolators are held in place with Torx head threaded pins. Renew split or otherwise damaged vibration isolators.

REWIND STARTER. To disassemble starter, remove starter from saw then detach rope handle and allow rope to wind into starter. Unscrew pulley retaining screw (9–Fig. HL362) and remove rope pulley while being careful not to dislodge rewind spring. If rewind spring must be removed, unscrew spring retainer screw and lift out retainer and spring. Care should be used not to allow spring to unwind uncontrolled.

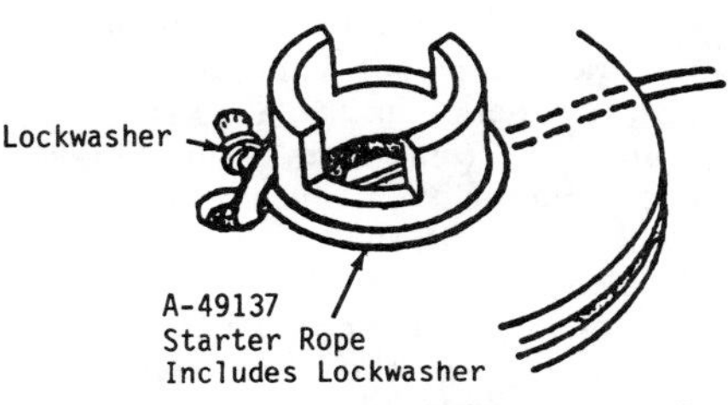

Fig. HL363—Insert rope through rope pulley hole and the rope around pulley hub as shown.

Rope length should be 45 inches (114 cm). Apply heat or cement to end of rope and insert rope end through hole in rope pulley and tie a hitch around pulley hub as shown in Fig. HL363. Wind rope around pulley in clockwise direction as viewed from hub side of pulley. Insert rope end through rope outlet of starter housing (14–Fig. HL362) and attach rope handle. Install washer (10) and screw (9). Pull rope back through rope outlet and engage rope in pulley notch. Turn rope pulley clockwise to apply tension to rewind spring. Two complete revolutions of the pulley should provide sufficient tension. Check starter operation, then install on engine.

CHAIN BRAKE. Refer to Fig. HL364 for an exploded view of chain brake. The chain brake will be triggered when the operator's hand forces brake lever (9) forward. The chain brake should stop saw chain instantly. If chain brake does not operate correctly, outer surface of clutch drum may be glazed. Remove glaze using emery cloth being sure to clean drum afterward. Clutch drum and brake band must not be bent or nicked.

Fig. HL364—Exploded view of chain brake.

1. Cover
2. Clip
3. Bushing
4. Spacer
5. Pivot link
6. Rivet
7. Brake band
8. Spring
9. Brake lever
10. Washer
11. Spring
12. Shoulder screw
13. Dowel pin
14. Retainer
15. Outer guide bar plate
16. Inner guide bar plate
17. Shield
18. Pin

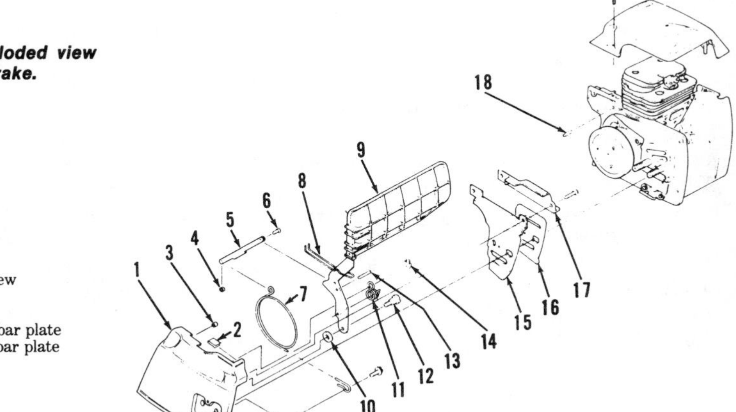

HOMELITE

Model	Bore mm (in.)	Stroke mm (in.)	Displacement cc (cu. in.)	Drive Type
290	42.0 (1.65)	34.0 (1.34)	47.5 (2.9)	Direct
340	45.0 (1.77)	34.0 (1.34)	54.1 (3.3)	Direct

MAINTENANCE

SPARK PLUG. Recommended spark plug is Champion RCJ6Y, CJ6Y or equivalent. Specified electrode gap is 0.025 inch (0.63 mm) for CJ6Y plugs and 0.020 inch (0.51 mm) for RCJ6Y plugs.

CARBURETOR. A Tillotson HU diaphragm type carburetor is used. Refer to CARBURETOR SERVICE section for overhaul procedures and exploded view.

A view of the carburetor mixture screws is shown in Fig. HL370. Initial adjustment of the idle speed screw is 3/4 to 1 turn clockwise after contacting the throttle stop lever. Initial adjustment of the idle speed mixture screw is 1½ turns counterclockwise from the seated position on Model 340 and 7/8 turn counterclockwise from the seated position on Model 290. Initial adjustment of the high speed mixture screw is 1 turn counterclockwise from the seated position on both models. Make final adjustments with engine warm and running. Adjust idle speed screw so engine idles just below clutch engagement speed. Adjust low speed mixture screw so engine will accelerate cleanly without hesitation. Adjust high speed mixture screw to obtain optimum performance under cutting load.

A view of the carburetor linkage is shown in Fig. HL371.

MAGNETO AND TIMING. A solid-state ignition system is used. Timing is fixed and set at 29 degrees BTDC. The solid-state ignition system is serviced by renewing the spark plug, ignition module (1 – Fig. HL375) or coil (3).

Two types of ignition systems have been used. Some early production units used a SEMS ignition system (blue module and black coil) while later and current production units use a Prufrex ignition system (blue module and blue coil). Components from one system are not compatible with the other. Service parts will only supply the Prufrex system. If an ignition system component fails on a SEMS system, the entire system will have to be replaced. The Prufrex module is part 98365 and the Prufrex coil is part 98366. Adjust rotor (flywheel)-to-module air gap to 0.008-0.012 inch (0.2-0.3 mm).

LUBRICATION. The engine is lubricated by mixing oil with unleaded gasoline. Recommended oil is Homelite® two-stroke oil mixed at the ratio designated on the oil container. If Homelite® oil is not available, a good quality oil designated for two-stroke engines may be used when mixed at a 16:1 ratio; however, an antioxidant fuel stabilizer (such as Sta-Bil) should be added to the fuel mix. Antioxidant fuel stabilizer is not required with Homelite® oils, as they contain fuel stabilizer so the fuel mix will stay fresh up to one year. Fuel tank capacity is 25.3 ounces (748 mL).

The chain oil tank should be filled with Homelite® Bar and Chain Oil or a good quality SAE 30 oil. Tank capacity is 16 ounces (473 mL). It may be necessary to use SAE 10 oil or oil mixed with kerosene if temperature is below 40°F (4°C).

REPAIRS

TIGHTENING TORQUE VALUES. Tightening torque values are listed in the following table:

Guide bar to crankcase	89 in.-lbs. (10.1 N•m)
Transfer port	27 in.-lbs. (3.1 N•m)
Engine to housing	62 in.-lbs. (7 N•m)
Spark plug	120-180 in.-lbs. (13.6-20.3 N•m)
Cylinder to crankcase	53 in.-lbs. (6 N•m)
Clutch to crankshaft	204 in.-lbs. (23 N•m)
Flywheel to crankshaft	168 in.-lbs. (19 N•m)
Module to cylinder	44 in.-lbs. (5 N•m)

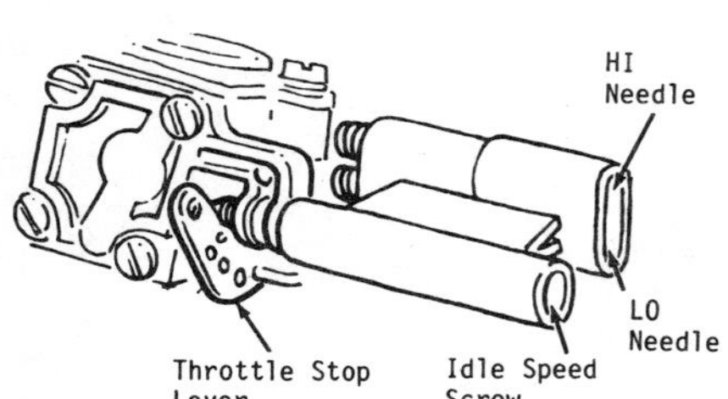

Fig. HL370—View of carburetor adjustment screws.

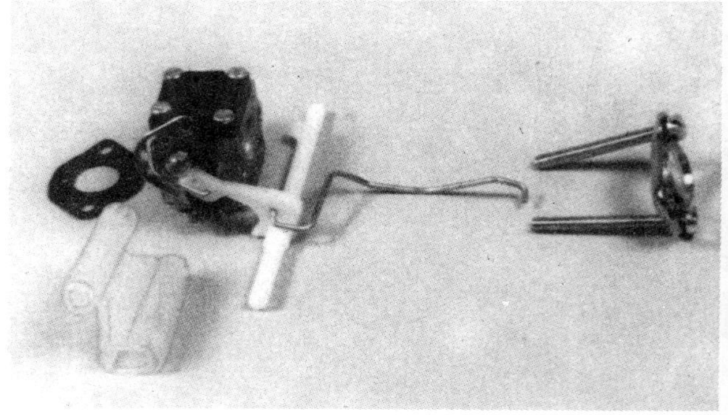

Fig. HL371—View of correct throttle linkage assembly.

Starter cover . . . . 10 in.-lbs. (1.1 N·m)
Oil pump to engine . . . . 10 in.-lbs. (1.1 N·m)

COMPRESSION PRESSURE. For optimum performance, cylinder compression pressure should be 140-170 psi (966-1173 kPa) with engine at normal operating temperature. Engine should be inspected and repaired when compression pressure is 90 psi (620 kPa) or below.

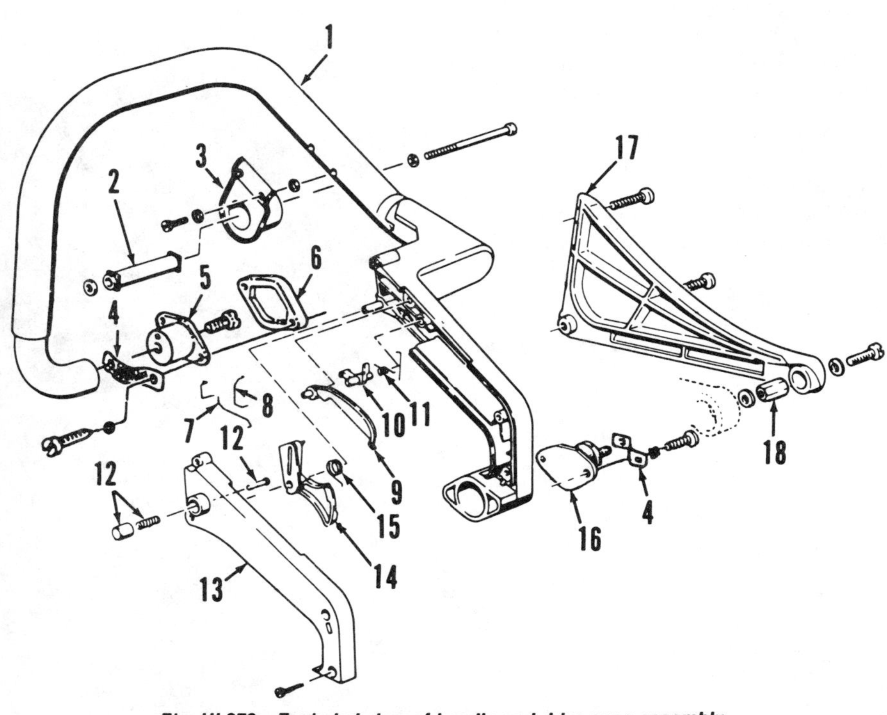

Fig. HL373—Exploded view of handle and drive case assembly.

1. Handle
2. Spacer
3. Isolator
4. Strap
5. Isolator
6. Spacer
7. Link
8. Link
9. Lock
10. Lever
11. Spring
12. Lock assy.
13. Cover
14. Trigger
15. Spring
16. Isolator
17. Guard
18. Nut

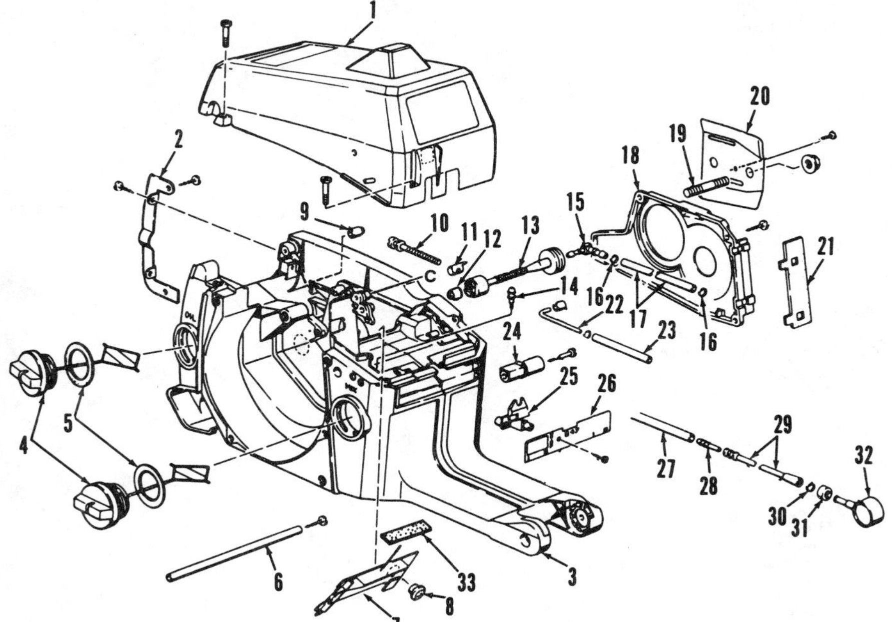

Fig. HL374—Exploded view of engine housing.

1. Cover
2. Bumper plate
3. Housing
4. Caps
5. Gaskets
6. Tube
7. Baffle
8. Plug
9. Check valve
10. Chain adjusting screw
11. Pin
12. Strainer
13. Oil tube
14. Fitting
15. Elbow fitting
16. Clamp
17. Rubber tubing
18. Oil pump cover
19. Stud
20. Plate
21. Protector
22. Tube
23. Rubber tubing
24. Chain stop
25. Support
26. Switch plate
27. Rubber tubing
28. Fitting
29. Fuel line
30. Clamp
31. Weight
32. Filter

CONNECTING ROD, CRANKSHAFT AND CRANKCASE. Crankcase halves (1 and 16–Fig. HL377) must be split for access to crankshaft. The crankshaft (12) is supported by ball bearings (13) at both ends. Connecting rod, crankpin and crankshaft are pressed-together assembly and separate components are not available. Rod and crankshaft must be serviced as a unit assembly.

When installing bearings onto crankshaft, heat the bearing(s) to a temperature of 350°F (177°C) in hot oil. The bearing retaining rings should align with the grooves in the bearing bore of the crankcase. Note that the tapered (rotor) end of the crankshaft should be on the same side of the cylinder as the port cover with the module mounting boss.

When assembling the lower crankcase half onto the cylinder, apply a light coat of sealant to the mating surface and outer edge of the bearing bore. Note that the two large mounting ears on the crankcase lower half should be on the clutch side. The outer surfaces of the seals should be flush with the outside edge of the bearing bores.

When installing the shortblock assembly into the engine housing, loosely install the two screws on the rotor side, then install the five screws on the clutch side. Tighten all shortblock mounting screws evenly.

PISTON AND RINGS. Model 290 uses two piston rings and Model 340 uses one piston ring. Specified ring end gap is 0.006-0.014 inch (0.15-0.35 mm) for Model 290 and 0.008-0.016 inch (0.2-0.4 mm) for Model 340.

Install piston with arrow pointing toward exhaust side of cylinder as shown in Fig. HL378.

A matched cylinder and crankcase assembly is used. The piston for Model 290 is serviced separately, while the piston for Model 340 is only available as an assembly along with the cylinder and the crankcase.

CLUTCH. Refer to Fig. HL379 for an exploded view of shoe type clutch used on both models. Clutch hub (9) has left-hand threads. Turn clockwise to remove from crankshaft. The clutch shoes should only be replaced in sets of three.

Needle roller bearing (4) should be removed, cleaned and lubricated periodically. A high temperature grease such as Homelite® ALL-TEMP Multipurpose Grease should be used. Inspect crankshaft for wear or damage caused by a defective clutch bearing.

If clutch slips with engine running at high speed under load, check clutch shoes (8) for excessive wear. If chain continues to turn with engine running at idle speed (below normal clutch engagement speed), check for broken, weak or distorted clutch springs.

When reassembling clutch, hook spring ends together between any two of the clutch shoes.

AUTOMATIC CHAIN OILER PUMP. The gear driven, automatic chain oiler pump used on Models 290 and 340 is shown in Fig. HL379. Oil pump output is adjustable with five positions from 0.27-0.68 ounce (8-20 mL). A recessed screw is located at the bottom of the engine housing. Press screw inward with a flat screwdriver and rotate screw clockwise to increase flow and counterclockwise to reduce flow.

The oil pump may be removed after removing the clutch. When disassembling the pump, press spring-loaded plunger in while removing cam pin from pump housing as shown in Fig. HL380. Inspect all pump components. Renew any

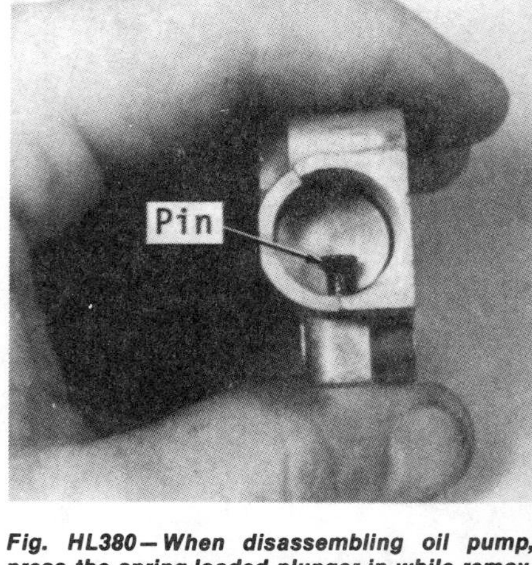

Fig. HL380—When disassembling oil pump, press the spring-loaded plunger in while removing the cam pin from the pump housing.

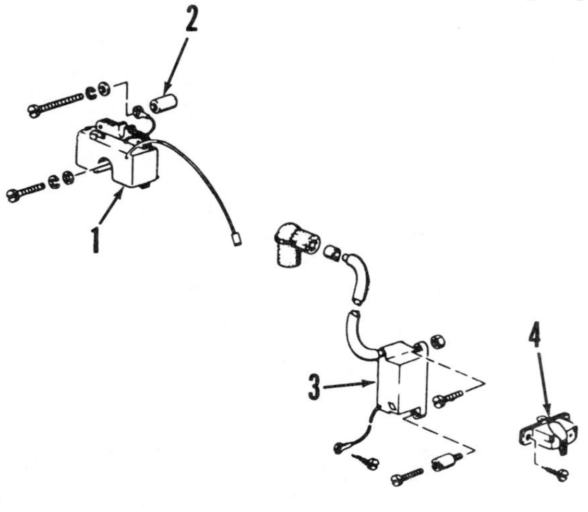

Fig. HL375—View of ignition components.

1. Module
2. Spacer
3. Coil
4. Switch

Fig. HL378—Install piston onto connecting rod with arrow pointing toward exhaust port.

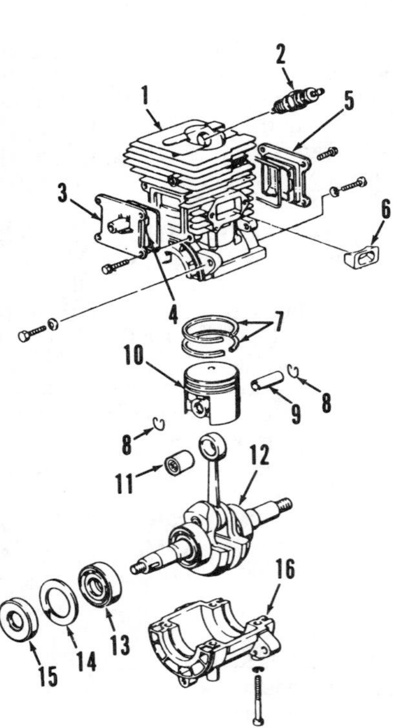

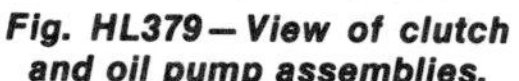

Fig. HL377—Exploded view of engine. Install intake port insert (6) so notched corners face up.

1. Crankcase & cylinder
2. Spark plug
3. Cover
4. "O" ring
5. Insert
6. Insert
7. Piston ring(s)
8. Retainer clip
9. Piston pin
10. Piston
11. Bearing
12. Crankshaft assy.
13. Bearing
14. Retainer
15. Seal
16. Lower crankcase

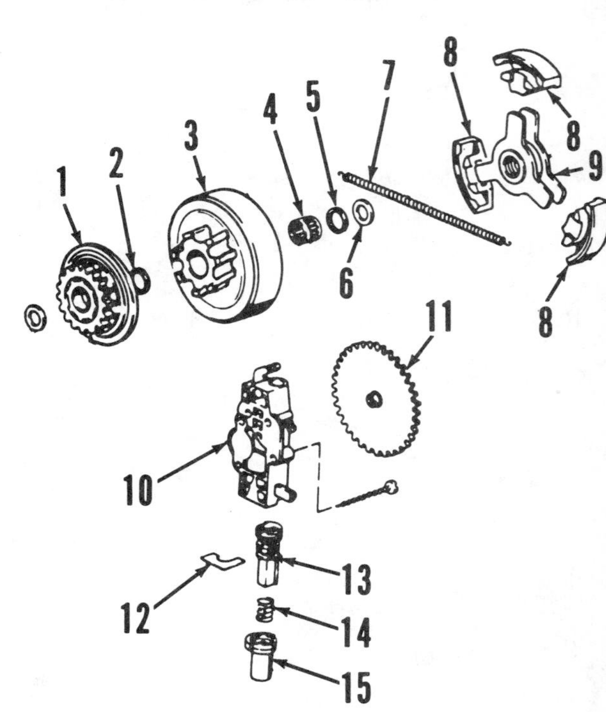

Fig. HL379—View of clutch and oil pump assemblies.

1. Hub
2. Felt seal
3. Drum
4. Bearing
5. Felt seal
6. Thrust washer
7. Spring
8. Shoe
9. Hub
10. Housing
11. Gear
12. Plate
13. Plunger
14. Spring
15. Plug

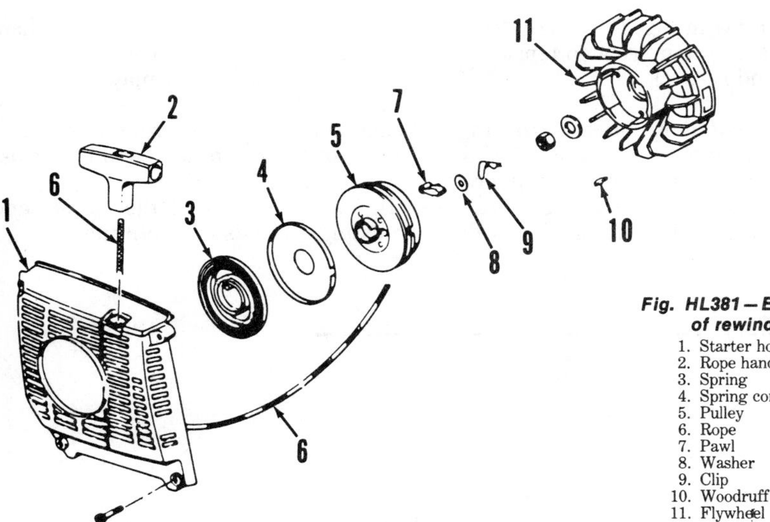

Fig. HL381—Exploded view of rewind starter.

1. Starter housing
2. Rope handle
3. Spring
4. Spring container
5. Pulley
6. Rope
7. Pawl
8. Washer
9. Clip
10. Woodruff key
11. Flywheel

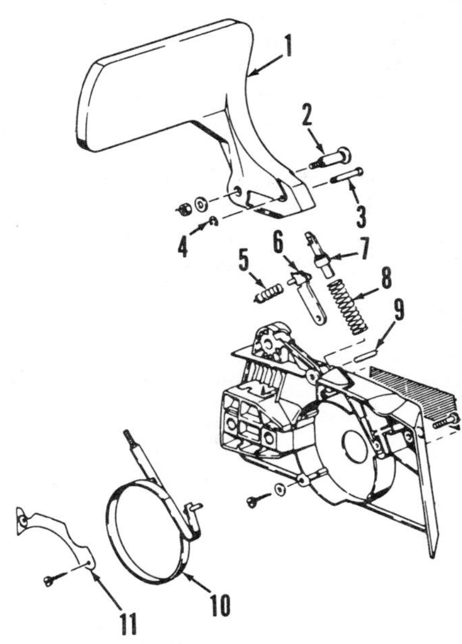

Fig. HL385—Exploded view of chain brake assembly.

1. Lever
2. Shoulder bolt
3. Pin
4. "E" ring
5. Spring
6. Latch
7. Adjuster
8. Spring
9. Pin
10. Brake band
11. Cover

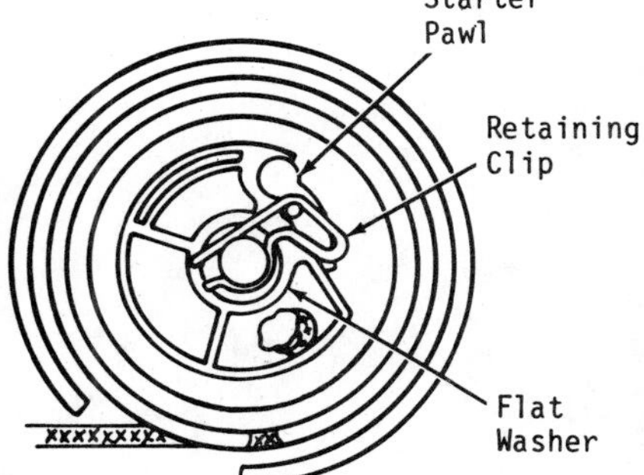

Fig. HL382—Pin on starter pawl must engage loop of retaining clip as shown.

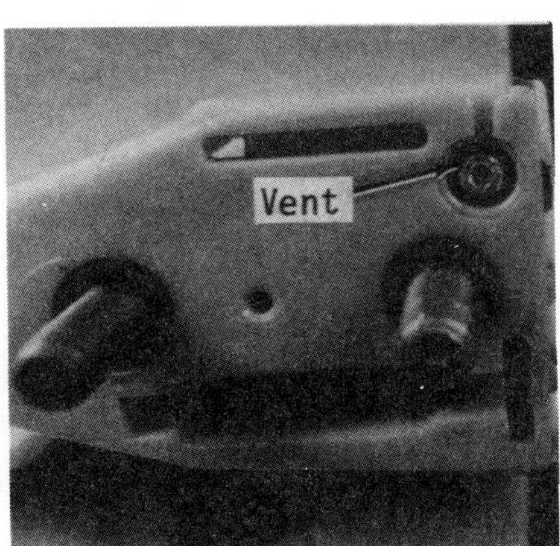

Fig. HL384—View of the guide bar pad showing location of the oil tank vent. Keep vent clear of sawdust.

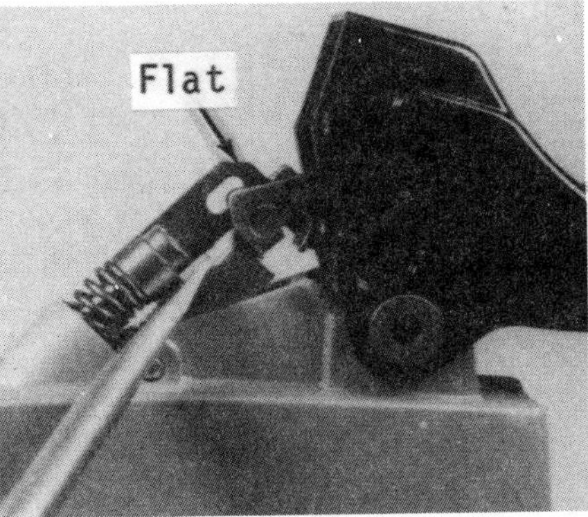

Fig. HL386—View of chain brake mechanism. Insert a screwdriver as shown, then turn screwdriver to release adjuster from latch. When assembling components, position adjuster so flat is up as shown.

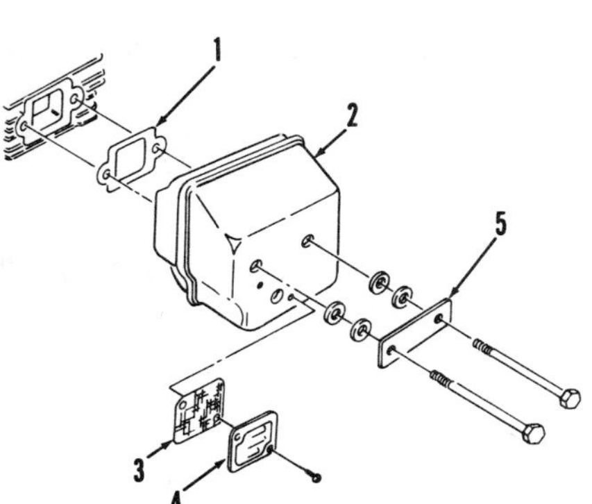

Fig. HL383 Exploded view of muffler.

1. Gasket
2. Muffler
3. Spark arrestor
4. Cover plate
5. Lockplate

part which is damaged or excessively worn.

Refer to Fig. HL374 for an exploded view of oil pump tubing and filter screen. Be sure vent shown in Fig. HL384 is free from sawdust.

MUFFLER. The muffler should be disassembled and periodically cleaned. Renew muffler components that are cracked or worn excessively. Check engine exhaust port and remove excessive carbon buildup as required. Do not allow loose carbon to enter cylinder, and be careful not to damage exhaust port or piston. Refer to Fig. HL383 for an exploded view of the muffler.

REWIND STARTER. Refer to Fig. HL381 for an exploded view of the rewind starter. To disassemble starter, remove starter from saw, then detach rope handle and allow rope to wind into starter housing. Remove clip (9) from starter post and remove pulley (5). If rewind spring (3) must be removed, lift out retainer and spring while being careful not to dislodge spring. Take care not to allow spring to unwind uncontrolled when separating spring from container.

When reassembling starter, note the following: Rewind spring must be installed in spring container (4) so spring is coiled in a counterclockwise direction from outer spring end. Rope length should be 35 inches (89.7 cm). Apply cement to rope end or fuse end with heat before installing rope. Insert rope into rope pulley and tie a knot at pulley end. Wrap rope around pulley in a clockwise direction as viewed from pawl side of pulley. Leave approximately 10 inches (25.4 cm) of rope unwrapped. Apply a light coat of grease to starter housing pulley post. Assemble starter, insert rope through rope outlet and install rope handle. See Fig. HL382 for proper installation of retaining clip. To prewind spring, position rope in notch in outside edge of rope pulley. While holding rope in notch, rotate rope pulley two turns clockwise, then remove rope from notch, release pulley and allow rope to wind onto pulley.

Before installing starter, check starter operation. Be sure spring is not bottomed out when starter rope is fully extended. It must be possible to rotate pulley clockwise with rope fully extended; if not, decrease spring prewind tension by one turn and recheck.

CHAIN BRAKE. Refer to Fig. HL385 for an exploded view of the chain brake. The chain brake will be triggered when the operator's hand forces brake lever (1) forward. The chain brake should stop the chain instantly. If chain brake does not operate correctly, outer surface of clutch drum may be glazed. Remove glaze using an emery cloth, being sure to clean drum afterward. Clutch drum and brake band (10) must not be bent or nicked.

Initial adjustment of the brake band adjusting screw is in 7 to 9 full turns.

HOMELITE

Model	Bore mm (in.)	Stroke mm (in.)	Displacement cc (cu. in.)	Drive Type
250, 252	39.6 (1.56)	32.5 (1.28)	41 (2.5)	Direct
CS40, CS4018	39.6 (1.56)	32.5 (1.28)	41 (2.5)	Direct
300	43.4 (1.71)	32.5 (1.28)	49.2 (3.0)	Direct
CS50, CS5020	43.4 (1.71)	32.5 (1.28)	49.2 (3.0)	Direct

MAINTENANCE

SPARK PLUG. Recommended spark plug is Champion CJ6Y or resistor type RCJ6Y or RDJ7Y for all models. Specified electrode gap is 0.025 inch (0.6 mm). The spark plug should be tightened to the torque listed in the TIGHTENING TORQUE paragraph.

CARBURETOR. Walbro HD, Walbro WT, Zama C1Q and Zama C3A diaphragm type carburetors have been used. Refer to the installed carburetor for type used then to the specific CARBURETOR SERVICE section in this manual for overhaul procedures and exploded views.

Initial adjustment of carburetor low-speed mixture needle (Fig. HL400) and high-speed mixture needle is 1 to 1-1/8 turns counterclockwise from a lightly seated position. Make final adjustment with engine at operating temperature and running. Be sure air filter is clean and in place before making final carburetor adjustment.

To adjust the mixture needles, first remove and clean the air filter, then reinstall it. Start the engine and allow it to run until it reaches normal operating temperature. If necessary, turn each of the mixture needles clockwise until seated lightly, then back the needles out (counterclockwise) to the initial setting so the engine can be started.

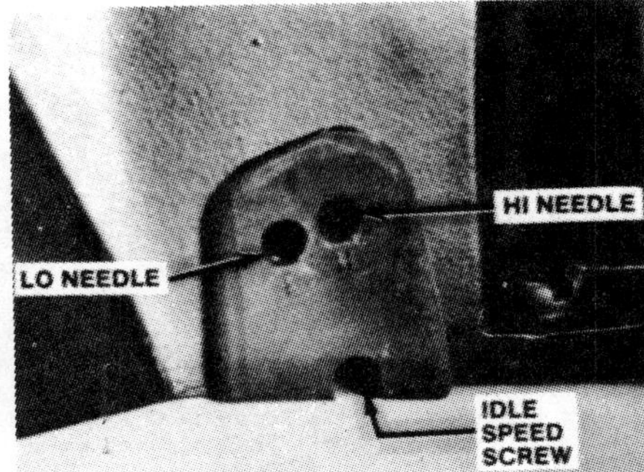

Fig. HL400—View of carburetor adjustment points. Refer to text for adjustment procedure.

Turn the idle speed stop screw so the engine idles at about 2,500 rpm. Adjust the low-speed mixture needle so the engine idles smoothly and accelerates without hesitation. Adjust the idle speed to just slower than clutch engagement speed then recheck low-speed mixture adjustment.

Adjust the high-speed mixture needle to provide the best performance while operating at maximum speed under load. The high-speed mixture screw may be set slightly rich to improve performance under load. The engine may be damaged if the high-speed mixture is set too lean.

Final adjustment of the mixture needles should be within 1/4 turn of the initial settings. Large differences may indicate air leaks, plugged passages or other problems.

IGNITION. A breakerless, solid-state electronic ignition system is used. Electronic components are contained in a one-piece ignition module/coil located outside the flywheel. Ignition timing is fixed and not adjustable. The flywheel attaching nut should be tightened to the torque listed in TIGHTENING TORQUE paragraph.

There is no periodic maintenance required, however, air gap between ignition module and flywheel is adjustable. Air gap between the legs of the module/coil and the flywheel magnets should be 0.3 mm (0.012 in.).

When installing, set the air gap between the flywheel magnets and the legs of the ignition module as follows. Install the ignition module, but tighten the two screws only enough to hold it in place away from the flywheel. Insert brass/plastic shim stock of the proper thickness between the legs of the ignition module and the flywheel, then turn the flywheel until the flywheel magnets are near the module legs. Loosen the screws attaching the ignition module and press legs of the ignition module against the shim stock. Apply thread locking compound to the two screws before tightening to the torque listed in the TIGHTENING TORQUE paragraph. Remove the setting gauge, then turn the flywheel and check that flywheel does not hit the legs of the coil.

Solid-state ignition modules will not produce a spark unless flywheel is turned briskly by starter operation. Solid-state modules produce an orange colored spark. Ignition system may be considered satisfactory if it can produce a spark across a 0.125 inch (3.2 mm) gap.

If ignition fails to produce a spark, first inspect for loose or broken wires or faulty ignition switch and repair as necessary. Also, check air gap between flywheel magnets and legs of the ignition coil/module. If condition is still questioned, substitute a known good module and check for spark.

LUBRICATION. The engine is lubricated by mixing oil with gasoline. Recommended oil is "HOMELITE 32:1" or HOMELITE Premium Exact Mix. Mix the oil with unleaded gasoline at the ratio designated on the oil container. Oils formulated at less than 32:1 ratio or non 2-cycle oils should not be used. Always mix oil and gasoline in a separate container. The manufacturer recommends not using fuel containing alcohol.

Saw chain is lubricated by oil from an automatic oil pump. The rate of oil flow depends upon engine speed and is not adjustable. Recommended chain oil is HOMELITE Bar and Chain Oil or equivalent. Make sure the reservoir is filled at all times.

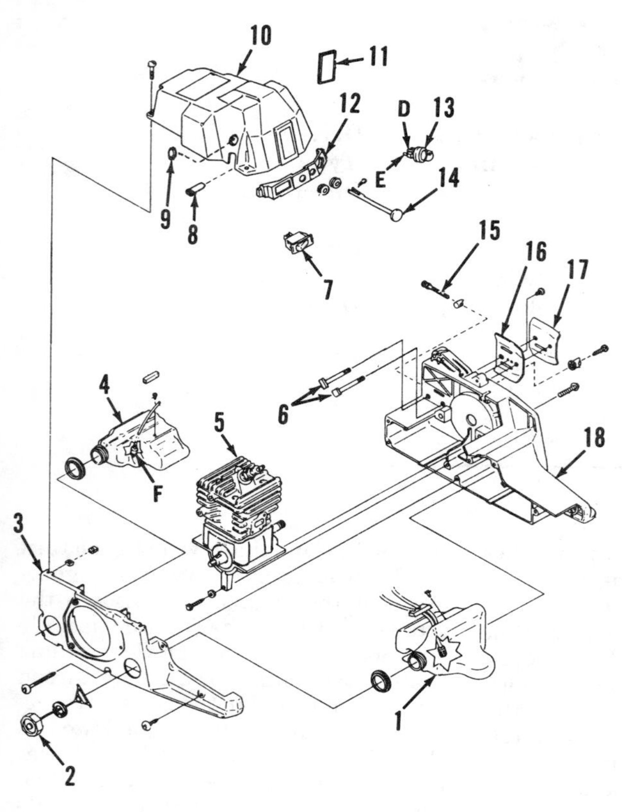

Fig. HL401—Exploded view of engine covers, fuel tank and oil tank.

1. Fuel tank
2. Tank cap
3. Engine side cover
4. Oil tank
5. Power head
6. Guide bar bolts
7. Ignition switch
8. Carburetor grommet
9. Idle speed plug (some models)
10. Cylinder cover
11. Air inlet screen
12. Control panel
13. Fuel primer bulb
14. Choke rod
15. Chain adjusting screw
16. Guide bar plate
17. Guide bar plate
18. Engine housing

REPAIRS

CRANKCASE PRESSURE TEST. An improperly sealed crankcase can cause the engine to be hard to start, run rough, have low power and overheat. Refer to ENGINE SERVICE section of this manual for crankcase pressure test procedure. If crankcase leakage is indicated, pressurize the crankcase and use a solution of soap and water to check gasket, seals, pulse line and castings for leakage.

TIGHTENING TORQUE. Recommended tightening torque values are as follows.

Carburetor attaching screws . . . 3.4-4.5 N•m (30-40 in.-lb.)
Clutch drum nut. . . . . 17-23 N•m (150-200 in.-lb.)
Clutch hub . . . . 17-23 N•m (150-200 in.-lb.)
Crankcase* . . . 8-9 N•m (70-80 in.-lb.)
Flywheel . 23-28 N•m (200-350 in.-lb.)
Ignition module/coil* . . . . 5.4-6.6 N•m (45-55 in.-lb.)
Spark plug. . . . . 14.4-22 N•m (120-180 in.-lb.)

* Apply thread locking compound to screw threads.

CONNECTING ROD, CRANKSHAFT AND CRANKCASE. To disassemble, remove guide bar and chain. Remove air filter assembly and disconnect throttle cable from carburetor. Unbolt and remove handlebar assembly (11—Fig. HL402) and engine side cover (3—Fig. HL401).

Remove spark plug and install a piston stop tool or the end of a rope in spark plug hole to lock piston and prevent the crankshaft from turning. Unscrew clutch retaining nut (32—Fig. HL403 or Fig. HL404) and remove the drum (27). Use clutch tool (Homelite part number A-01182) or other suitable tool to unscrew the clutch hub from the crankshaft. Note that clutch hub has left-hand threads (turn clockwise to remove). Remove the clutch assembly (23, 24 and 25). Remove flywheel attaching nut (12) then use suitable puller to remove flywheel. The flywheel nut has right-hand threads.

Remove chain brake band retaining screw (29—Fig. HL402). Push brake lever (23) forward and remove engagement pin (24) from handle. Use a screwdriver to twist and release brake adjuster (25) and compression spring (26) from brake latch (20). Unscrew brake adjuster from brake band and remove brake band.

Remove engine housing mounting screws, disconnect oil line from automatic oil pump and separate engine housing (1) from engine. Remove fuel tank (1—Fig. HL401) and oil tank (4). Unbolt and remove oil pump (15—Fig. HL403 or Fig. HL404) and worm gear (22).

Remove ignition module, carburetor and muffler. Remove crankcase mounting screws and tap crankcase with a plastic mallet to separate crankcase assembly. Remove crankshaft, connecting rod and piston assembly. Remove pis-

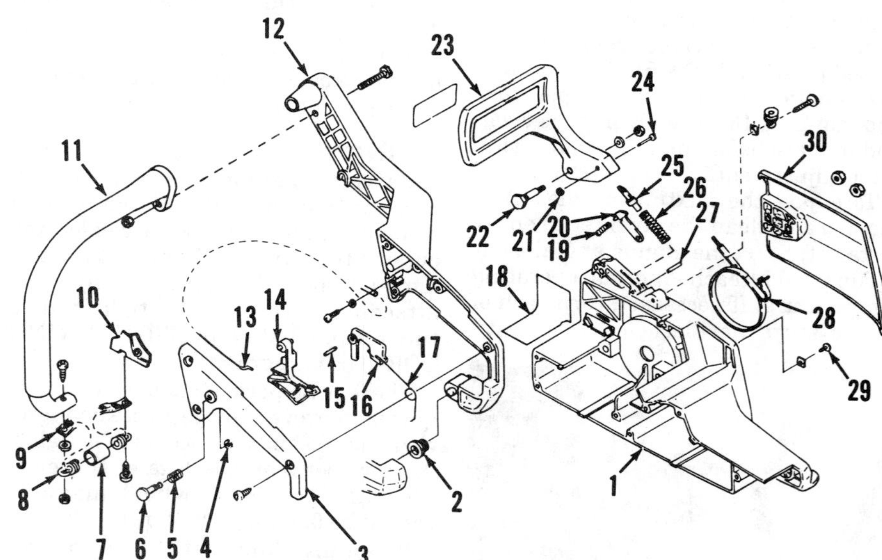

Fig. HL402—Exploded view of handle assembly and chain brake assembly.

1. Engine housing
2. Isolator
3. Handle cover
4. Retaining ring
5. Spring
6. Throttle lock pin
7. Sleeve
8. Spring
9. Spring retainer
10. Bracket
11. Handlebar
12. Handle
13. Throttle cable
14. Throttle trigger
15. Pin
16. Throttle lock
17. Throttle spring
18. Heat deflector
19. Spring
20. Brake latch
21. Retaining ring
22. Shoulder bolt
23. Chain brake lever
24. Pin
25. Brake adjuster
26. Compression spring
27. Pin
28. Brake band
29. Retaining screw
30. Drive case cover

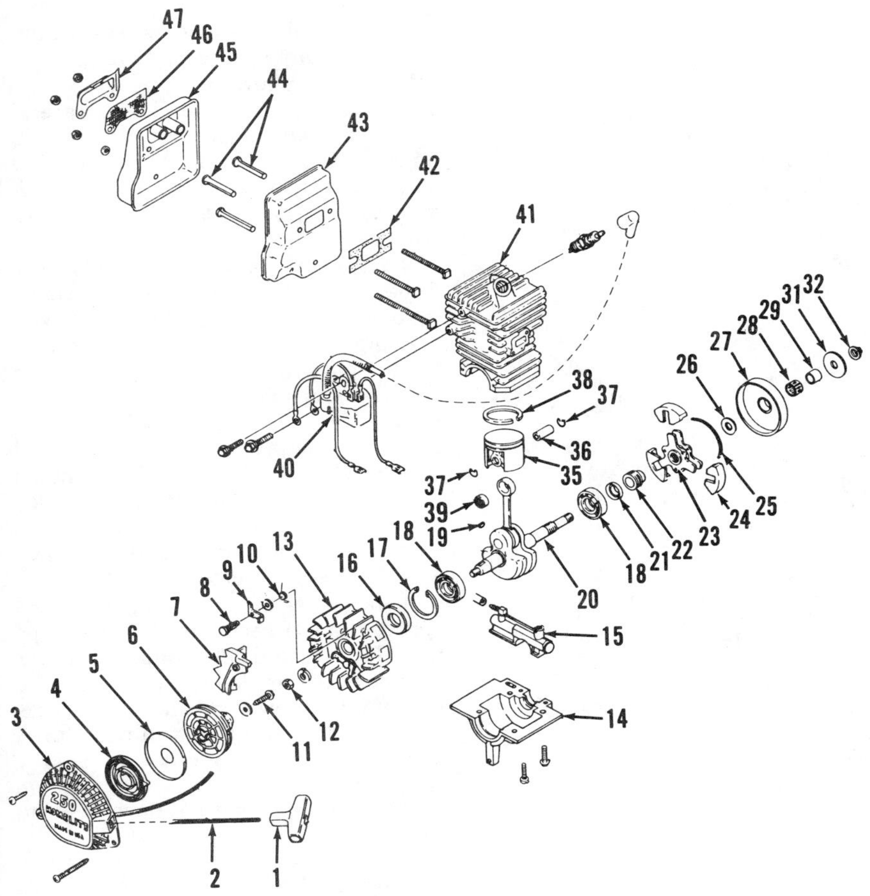

Fig. HL403—Exploded view typical of 41 cc engines.

1. Rope handle
2. Rope
3. Starter housing
4. Rewind spring
5. Spring cup
6. Pulley
7. Side housing
8. Shoulder bolt
9. Starter pawl
10. Spring
11. Screw
12. Nut
13. Flywheel
14. Crankcase
15. Oil pump
16. Seal
17. Snap ring
18. Bearings
19. Key
20. Crankshaft & connecting rod assy.
21. Seal
22. Worm gear
23. Clutch hub
24. Clutch shoe
25. Spring
26. Thrust washer
27. Clutch drum & sprocket
28. Needle bearing
29. Bearing inner race
31. Washer
32. Nut
35. Piston
36. Piston pin
37. Retaining rings
38. Piston ring
39. Roller bearing
40. Ignition module
41. Cylinder
42. Gasket
43. Muffler body
44. Spacers
45. Muffler cover
46. Spark arrestor screen
47. Cover

ton pin retaining ring (37) and push piston pin (36) out of piston (35).

Remove crankshaft seals (16 and 21). Check ball bearings (18) for roughness or binding and renew as necessary. Inspect crankshaft and connecting rod (20) for scoring or for discoloration caused by overheating and renew as necessary. Crankshaft and connecting rod are available only as an assembly.

When reassembling, install piston on connecting rod so piston ring locating pin is facing intake port. Make certain that piston pin retaining rings (37—Fig. HL403 or Fig. HL404) fit tightly in groove in piston boss.

When installing new bearings on crankshaft, heat bearings to 350 degrees F (180 degrees C) using either an oil bath or a heat gun (do not use an open flame). Lubricate lip of seals (16 and 21) with oil before installing on crankshaft.

Apply light film of oil to cylinder and piston. Apply light coat of silastic sealer to mating surface of crankcase and outer edge of bearing bore on clutch side of crankcase. Do not apply any oil or sealer to outer diameter of large oil seal (16) on ignition side of crankshaft. Insert piston into cylinder, making sure that piston ring end gap is positioned around locating pin in piston ring groove and facing the intake port. Be sure that bearing retaining ring (17) is positioned in groove in crankcase and that tapered side of crankshaft is on same side as ignition module mounting bosses on cylinder.

Outer surface of large oil seal (16) should be flush with outer surface of crankcase. Apply thread locking compound to the crankcase screws before tightening to the torque listed in the TIGHTENING TORQUE paragraph. Complete engine assembly by reversing disassembly procedure.

PISTON, PIN, RING AND CYLINDER. The cylinder (41—Fig. HL403 or Fig. HL404) is attached to the crankcase by four screws. Refer to CONNECTING ROD, CRANKSHAFT AND CRANKCASE section for disassembly procedure. After removing cylinder, inspect cylinder bore for excessive wear, scoring or other damage and renew as necessary.

The piston pin (36) is retained by clips (37) at both ends of pin. A renewable needle bearing (39) that is located in connecting rod supports the piston pin. Renew piston pin and/or needle bearing if worn or damaged.

A single piston ring (38) is used on all models. A locating pin is located in piston ring groove to prevent piston ring from rotating in the groove. When assembling piston on connecting rod, be sure locating pin is positioned on intake port side (away from the exhaust side of engine). Make certain that piston ring end gap fits correctly around its locating pin when installing piston in cylinder.

CLUTCH. To remove clutch assembly, first remove spark plug and install piston stop tool or insert end of a rope in cylinder to act as a piston stop. Remove the drive case cover, guide bar and chain. Remove clutch drum nut (32—Fig. HL403 or Fig. HL404), washer (31), needle bearing (28 and 29), clutch drum (27) and thrust washer (26). Use clutch tool (Homelite part number A-01182) or other suitable tool to unscrew clutch hub (23) from crankshaft. Note that clutch hub has left-hand threads (turn clockwise to remove).

If disassembly is required, disconnect spring (25) and separate clutch shoes (24) from hub. The hub and shoes are available as an assembly including the spring.

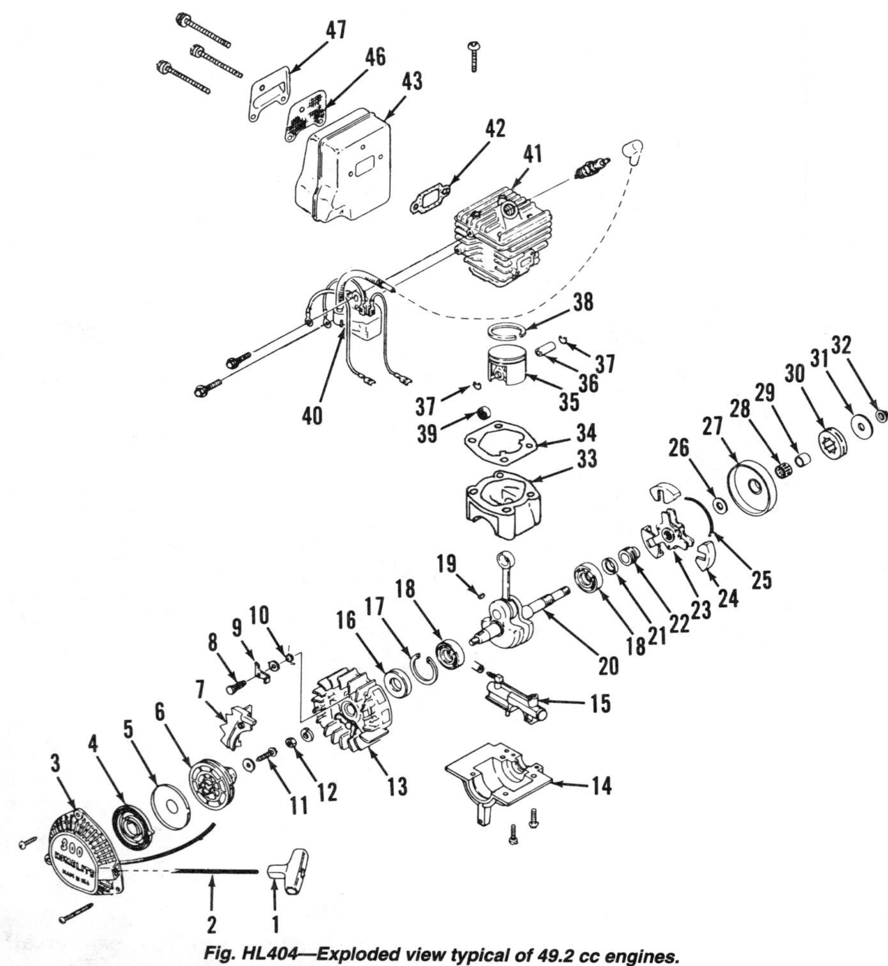

Fig. HL404—Exploded view typical of 49.2 cc engines.

1. Rope handle
2. Rope
3. Starter housing
4. Rewind spring
5. Spring cup
6. Pulley
7. Side housing
8. Shoulder bolt
9. Starter pawl
10. Spring
11. Screw
12. Nut
13. Flywheel
14. Crankcase half
15. Oil pump
16. Seal
17. Snap ring
18. Bearings
19. Key
20. Crankshaft & connecting rod assy.
21. Seal
22. Worm gear
23. Clutch hub
24. Clutch shoe
25. Spring
26. Thrust washer
27. Clutch drum
28. Needle bearing
29. Bearing inner race
30. Sprocket
31. Washer
32. Nut
33. Crankcase half
34. Gasket
35. Piston
36. Piston pin
37. Retaining rings
38. Piston ring
39. Roller bearing
40. Ignition module
41. Cylinder
42. Gasket
43. Muffler
46. Spark arrestor screen
47. Cover

Inspect clutch components for wear or damage and renew as necessary. When assembling clutch, position spring ends in open area between two of the clutch shoes. Install clutch assembly with open side facing outward. Lubricate needle bearing with all-temperature multipurpose grease. Tighten clutch hub and clutch retaining nut to the torque listed in the TIGHTENING TORQUE paragraph.

CHAIN OILER SYSTEM. All models are equipped with an automatic chain oiler system. The oil pump (15—Fig. HL403 or Fig. HL404) is mounted on the crankcase and driven by worm gear (22). To remove oil pump, it is necessary to separate power head (5—Fig. HL401) from engine side cover (3) and housing (18).

Inspect pump for wear or damage. Rotate pump plunger gear and make sure plunger moves back and forth in pump body. Pump is serviced as a complete assembly.

A filter (F—Fig. HL401) is located on end of oil pickup line. Make sure filter is clean and oil line is not damaged. A "duckbill" check valve that is pressed into oil tank wall vents the oil tank (4). Be sure check valve opens properly.

REWIND STARTER. To service rewind starter, remove starter housing (3—Fig. HL403 or Fig. HL404) from engine cover. Pull starter rope and hold rope pulley with notch in pulley adjacent to rope outlet. Pull rope back through outlet so it engages notch in pulley and allow pulley to slowly unwind to relieve spring tension.

Unscrew pulley retaining screw (11) and remove rope pulley being careful not to dislodge rewind spring (4) in housing. Care must be taken if rewind spring is removed to prevent injury if spring is allowed to uncoil uncontrolled.

Rope length is 46 inches (117 cm). Rope is wound on rope pulley in clockwise direction as viewed with pulley in housing. To place tension on rewind spring, pass rope though rope outlet in housing and install rope handle. Pull rope out and hold rope pulley so notch on pulley is adjacent to rope outlet. Pull rope back through outlet between notch in pulley and housing. Turn rope pulley in clockwise direction two turns to place tension on spring. Release pulley and check starter action.

Do not place more tension on rewind spring than is necessary to draw rope handle up against housing. After starter is assembled, pull rope all the way out, then try to rotate pulley clockwise by hand. If pulley will not rotate, spring is bottomed out and pulley should be turned in counterclockwise direction one turn to relieve tension from spring.

CHAIN BRAKE. All models are equipped with a chain brake system designed to stop chain movement should kickback occur. The chain brake is activated when operator's hand strikes chain brake lever (23—Fig. HL402). When activated (engaged), the brake band (28) is drawn around clutch drum by spring (26).

To disassemble chain brake, remove guide bar and chain. Remove brake band retaining screw (29). Push lever (23) forward, remove retaining ring (21) and drive engagement pin (24) out of lever. Place a screwdriver between brake band adjuster (25) and brake latch (20) and twist screwdriver to release the adjuster from the latch. Unscrew adjuster from brake band (28) and remove brake band. Drive dowel pin out of engine housing to remove brake latch (20) and spring (19).

Renew any component found to be excessively worn or damaged. Lubricate all pivot points with Molykote or suitable equivalent.

When reassembling, thread adjuster (25) on brake band (28) until clutch drum cannot be turned by hand, then loosen adjuster until drum just turns freely. The chain brake should stop saw chain instantly when engaged. Brake band should not contact clutch drum when disengaged.

HOMELITE

Model	Bore mm (in.)	Stroke mm (in.)	Displacement cc (cu. in.)	Drive Type
540, 8800	54.0 (2.125)	38.8 (1.53)	88.5 (5.4)	Direct

MAINTENANCE

SPARK PLUG. Recommended spark plug is Champion CJ6Y or equivalent. Specified electrode gap is 0.020 inch (0.5 mm).

CARBURETOR. A Walbro WJ diaphragm type carburetor is used on all models. Refer to the appropriate Walbro section of the CARBURETOR SERVICE section for overhaul procedures and exploded views.

Initial adjustment of carburetor low-speed mixture needle (Fig. HL500) is one turn open from a lightly seated position. Initial adjustment of high-speed mixture needle is 1-1/4 to 1-3/8 turns open from a lightly seated position. Make final adjustment with engine at operating temperature and running. Be sure air filter is clean and in place before making final carburetor adjustment.

Adjust low-speed mixture needle to obtain maximum idle speed, then turn needle counterclockwise 1/8 turn. Engine should accelerate cleanly without hesitation. If engine stumbles or seems sluggish when accelerating, adjust low-speed mixture needle until engine accelerates without hesitation. Adjust idle speed stop screw so engine idles without stalling and chain does not rotate.

Adjust high-speed mixture needle with saw running at wide open throttle. Adjust needle to obtain maximum speed, then turn needle 1/8 turn counterclockwise. Do not operate saw with high-speed mixture too lean as engine damage may result from lack of lubrication and overheating. Engine "no-load" speed with a properly tensioned chain must not exceed 12,000 rpm.

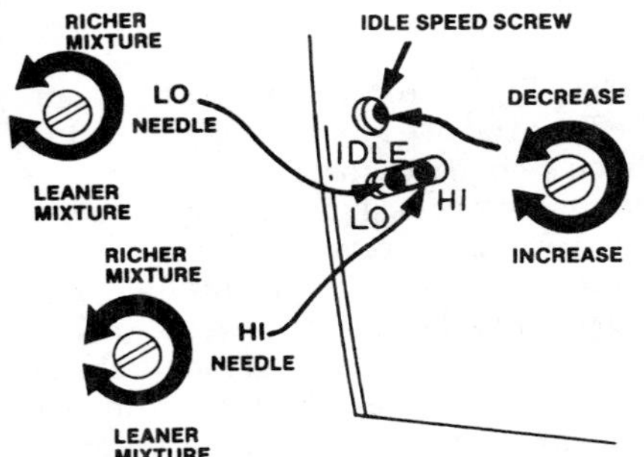

Fig. HL500—View of carburetor adjustment points. Refer to text for adjustment procedure.

IGNITION. A breakerless solid-state ignition system is used on all models. The solid-state ignition system is serviced by renewing the spark plug and/or ignition module.

There is no periodic maintenance required, however, air gap between ignition module and flywheel is adjustable. Air gap between the legs of the module/coil and the flywheel magnets should be 0.012 inch (0.30 mm). When installing, set the air gap between the flywheel magnets and the legs of the ignition module as follows.

Install the ignition module, but tighten the two screws only enough to hold it in place away from the flywheel. Insert brass/plastic shim stock of the proper thickness between the legs of the ignition module and the flywheel, then turn the flywheel until the flywheel magnets are near the module legs. Loosen the screws attaching the ignition module and press legs of the ignition module against the shim stock. Apply thread locking compound to the two screws before tightening to the torque listed in the TIGHTENING TORQUE paragraph. Remove the setting gauge, then turn the flywheel and check that flywheel does not hit the legs of the coil.

LUBRICATION. The engine is lubricated by mixing oil with unleaded gasoline. The use of fuel containing alcohol "gasohol" is not recommended. Recommended oil is Homelite 32:1 2-cycle engine oil mixed at ratio of 32:1 as designated on the oil container. If Homelite oil is not available, a good quality oil designated for air-cooled, 2-cycle engines at 40:1 or 50:1 ratios may be used at the Homelite specified 32:1 ratio. Oils formulated at less than 32:1 ratio or non 2-cycle oils should not be used.

Manufacturer recommends that an antioxidant fuel stabilizer, such as STA-BIL, should be added to the fuel mix if Homelite oil is not used. Antioxidant fuel stabilizer is not required when using Homelite oils as they contain fuel stabilizer. Always mix oil and gasoline in a separate container.

Saw chain is lubricated by oil from an automatic oil pump. Recommended chain oil is Homelite Bar and Chain Oil or equivalent. Make sure the reservoir is filled at all times.

The rate of oil flow is adjustable. Oiler adjustment screw is located on right side of saw between the crankcase and clutch drum. Adjustment screw has three positions: Low, Medium and High.

NOTE: Do not attempt to adjust oiler screw when engine is running.

REPAIRS

CRANKCASE PRESSURE TEST. An improperly sealed crankcase can cause the engine to be hard to start, run rough, have low power and overheat. Refer to ENGINE SERVICE section of this manual for crankcase pressure test procedure. If crankcase leakage is indicated, pressurize crankcase and use a soap and water solution to check gaskets, seals, pulse line and castings for leakage.

IGNITION MODULE. Solid-state ignition modules will not produce a spark unless flywheel is turned briskly by starter operation. Solid-state modules produce an orange colored spark. Ignition system may be considered satisfactory if it can produce a spark across a 0.125 inch (3.2 mm) gap.

If ignition fails to produce a spark, first check for loose connection, broken wire or faulty ignition switch. Check air gap between flywheel magnets and module. Specified gap is 0.012 inch (0.3 mm). Air gap is adjusted by loosening module mounting screws and relocating module.

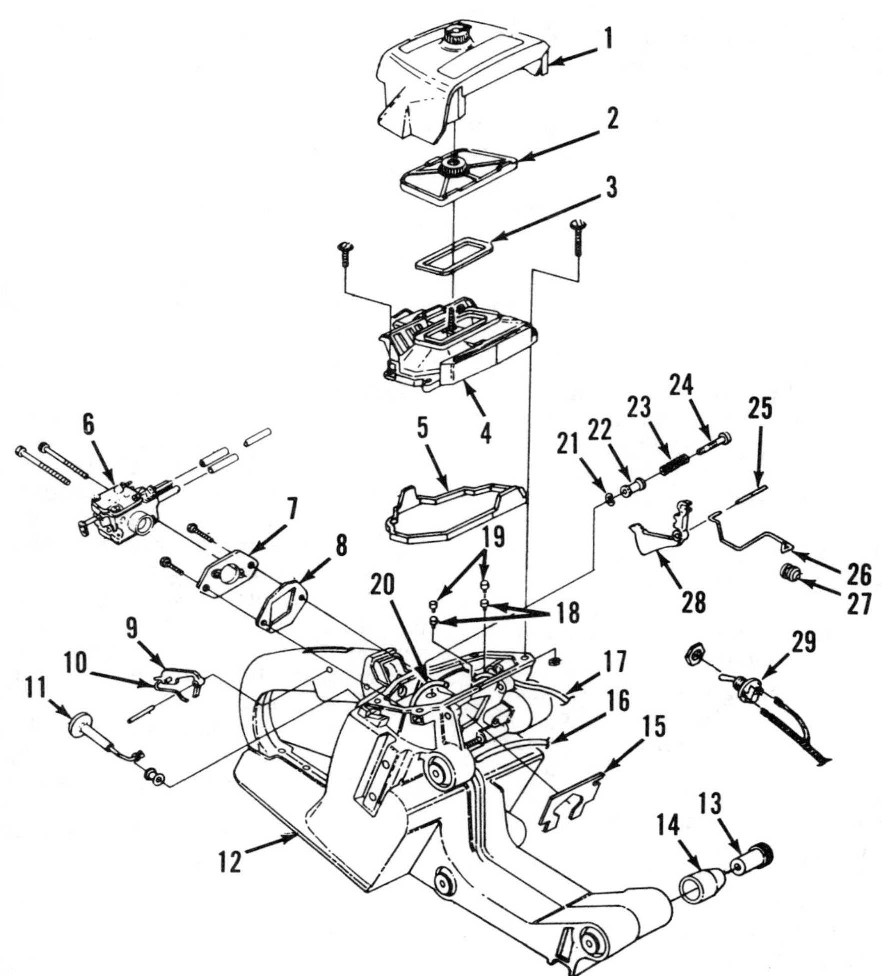

Fig. HL501—Exploded view of rear handle, carburetor chamber assembly and control linkage.

1. Air filter cover
2. Air filter
3. Gasket
4. Carburetor chamber cover
5. Gasket
6. Carburetor
7. Carburetor adapter
8. Gasket
9. Trigger lock
10. Spring
11. Choke rod
12. Rear handle assy.
13. Sleeve
14. Vibration isolator
15. Bracket
16. Oil line
17. Pulse line
18. Duckbill check valves
19. Filters
20. Fuel line
21. "E" ring
22. Flanged bushing
23. Spring
24. Throttle lock pin
25. Trigger pin
26. Throttle rod
27. Boot
28. Throttle trigger
29. Ignition switch

To determine if module unit is faulty, substitute a known good module and check for spark.

PISTON, PIN, RING AND CYLINDER. To disassemble, remove cylinder cover, air filter cover (1—Fig. HL501), air filter (2), carburetor chamber cover (4) and carburetor (6). Unbolt and remove muffler assembly.

Remove screws attaching cylinder to crankcase and withdraw cylinder (1—Fig. HL502). Remove cylinder baffle and intake adapter from cylinder. Remove piston pin retaining rings (4) and press piston pin (5) out of piston (6). Separate piston and needle bearing (7) from connecting rod.

After removing cylinder, inspect cylinder bore for excessive wear, scoring or other damage and renew as necessary. A renewable needle bearing (7) located in connecting rod supports the piston pin. Renew piston pin and/or needle bearing if worn or damaged.

Piston is fitted with two piston rings (3). A locating pin is located in piston ring grooves to prevent piston ring rotation. When assembling piston on connecting rod, be sure locating pin is positioned on intake port side.

Make certain that piston rings are positioned with end gaps around locating pins when installing piston in cylinder. Apply light film of oil to piston rings and cylinder bore prior to assembling piston and cylinder.

CONNECTING ROD, CRANKSHAFT AND CRANKCASE. To disassemble, remove guide bar and chain. Remove cylinder cover, air filter assembly and carburetor. Unbolt and remove handlebar assembly and starter housing.

Remove spark plug and install a piston stop tool or the end of a rope in spark plug hole to lock piston and crankshaft. Unscrew clutch hub (left-hand threads) and remove clutch assembly from crankshaft. Unbolt and remove oil pump (22—Fig. HL502). Remove the flywheel attaching nut (right-hand threads), then use suitable puller to remove flywheel.

Disconnect wiring and remove ignition module (17). Disconnect oil line and pulse line. Remove the vibration isolator pins (19) then separate power head from rear handle assembly.

Remove screws attaching cylinder to crankcase, then separate cylinder from crankcase. Remove piston from connecting rod. Remove crankcase mounting screws and tap crankcase with a plastic mallet to separate crankcase halves (11 and 18). Remove crankshaft and connecting rod assembly (9).

Remove crankshaft seals (12 and 21). Check ball bearings (8) for roughness or binding and renew as necessary. Inspect crankshaft and connecting rod for scoring or discoloration caused by overheating and renew as necessary. Crankshaft and connecting rod are available only as an assembly.

When reassembling, install piston on connecting rod so piston ring locating pins are facing intake port. Make certain that piston pin retaining rings (4) fit tightly in groove in piston boss.

When installing new bearings on crankshaft, heat bearings to 350 degrees F (180 degrees C) using either an oil bath or a heat gun (do not use an open flame). Lubricate lip of seals (12 and 21) with oil before installing on crankshaft.

Apply light film of oil to cylinder and piston. Apply light coat of Silastic sealer to mating surface of crankcase. Be sure crankshaft is installed with tapered end on same side as ignition module (17). Apply thread locking compound to crankcase screws and tighten evenly. Complete engine assembly by reversing disassembly procedure.

CLUTCH. To remove clutch assembly, first remove spark plug and install piston stop tool or insert end of a rope in cylinder to act as a piston stop. Remove the drive case cover, guide bar and chain. Note that clutch hub (30—Fig. HL502) has left-hand threads (rotate clockwise to remove). Remove clutch hub with shoes (31), clutch drum (28) and sprocket (27). Disconnect spring (29) and separate clutch shoes from hub.

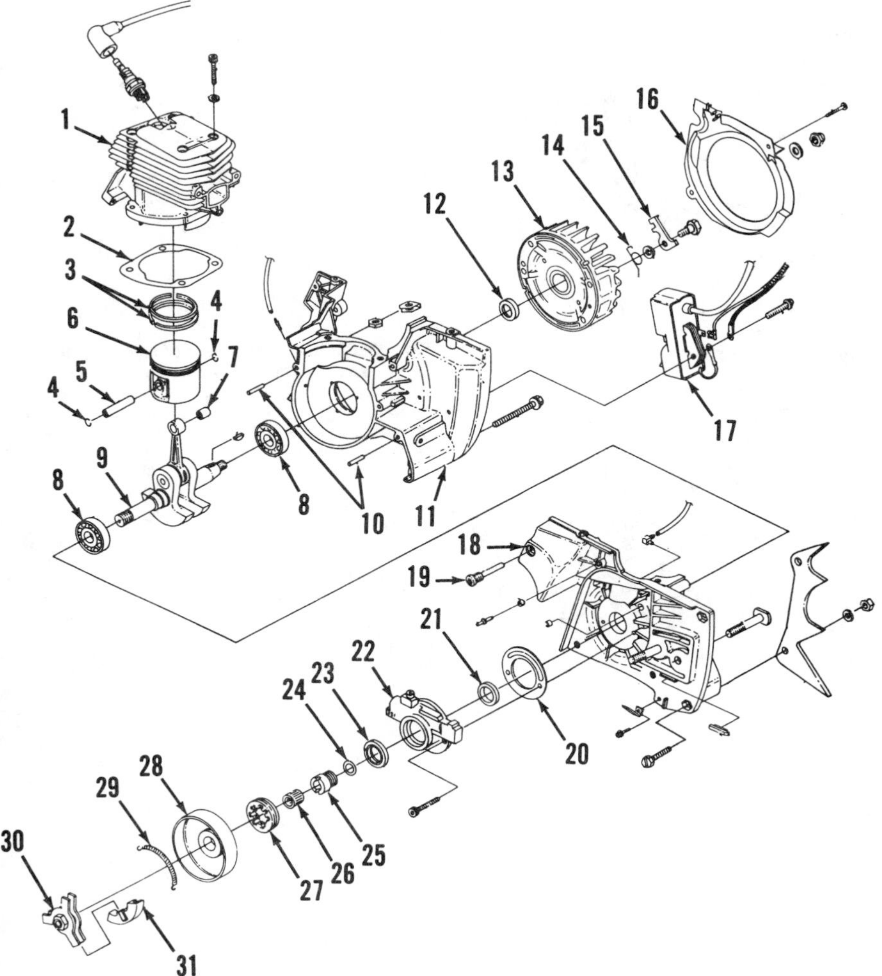

Fig. HL502—Exploded view of engine assembly.

1. Cylinder
2. Gasket
3. Piston rings
4. Retaining rings
5. Piston pin
6. Piston
7. Needle bearing
8. Ball bearings
9. Crankshaft & connecting rod assy.
10. Dowel pins
11. Crankcase half
12. Oil seal
13. Flywheel
14. Spring
15. Pawl
16. Air deflector
17. Ignition module
18. Crankcase half
19. Isolator pin
20. Gasket
21. Oil seal
22. Oil pump assy.
23. Felt seal
24. Thrust washer
25. Worm gear
26. Needle bearing
27. Sprocket
28. Clutch drum
29. Spring
30. Clutch hub
31. Clutch shoe

Inspect clutch components for wear or damage and renew as necessary. When assembling clutch, position spring ends in open area between two of the clutch shoes. Lubricate needle bearing (26) with all-temperature multipurpose grease.

CHAIN OILER SYSTEM. All models are equipped with an automatic chain oiler system. The oil pump (22—Fig. HL502) is mounted on the crankcase and driven by worm gear (25). To remove oil pump, it is necessary to remove drive case cover, guide bar and chain, and clutch assembly. Remove the pump attaching screws then withdraw pump from crankcase.

Inspect pump for wear or damage. Pump is serviced as a complete assembly. A filter screen is located on end of oil pickup line. Make sure screen is clean and oil line is not damaged. A "duckbill" check valve (18—Fig. HL501) vents the oil tank. Be sure the check valve opens properly.

REWIND STARTER. To service rewind starter, remove starter housing (3—Fig. HL503) from engine. Pull starter rope and hold rope pulley with notch in pulley adjacent to rope outlet. While holding pulley (6), pull the rope back through outlet so it engages the notch in pulley then allow pulley to slowly unwind to relieve spring tension.

Unscrew pulley retaining screw (8) and remove rope pulley being careful not to dislodge rewind spring (4) in housing. Care must be taken if rewind spring is removed to prevent injury if spring is allowed to uncoil uncontrolled.

Rope is wound on rope pulley in clockwise direction as viewed with pulley in housing. To place tension on rewind spring, pass rope though rope outlet in housing and install rope handle. Pull rope out and hold rope pulley so notch on pulley is adjacent to rope outlet. Pull rope back through outlet between notch in pulley and housing. Turn rope pulley in clockwise direction two turns to place tension on spring. Release pulley and check starter action.

Do not place more tension on rewind spring than is necessary to draw rope handle up against housing. After starter is assembled, pull rope all the way out, then try to rotate pulley clockwise by hand. If pulley will not rotate, spring is bottomed out and pulley should be turned in counterclockwise direction one turn to relieve tension from spring.

CHAIN BRAKE. All models are equipped with a chain brake system designed to stop chain movement should kickback occur. Chain brake is activated when operator's hand strikes chain brake lever (20—Fig. HL503), thereby drawing brake band (23) around clutch drum.

To disassemble chain brake, remove drive case cover (26). Remove brake band cover (21). Push the brake lever (20) forward, remove retaining ring and push the engagement pin (31) out of

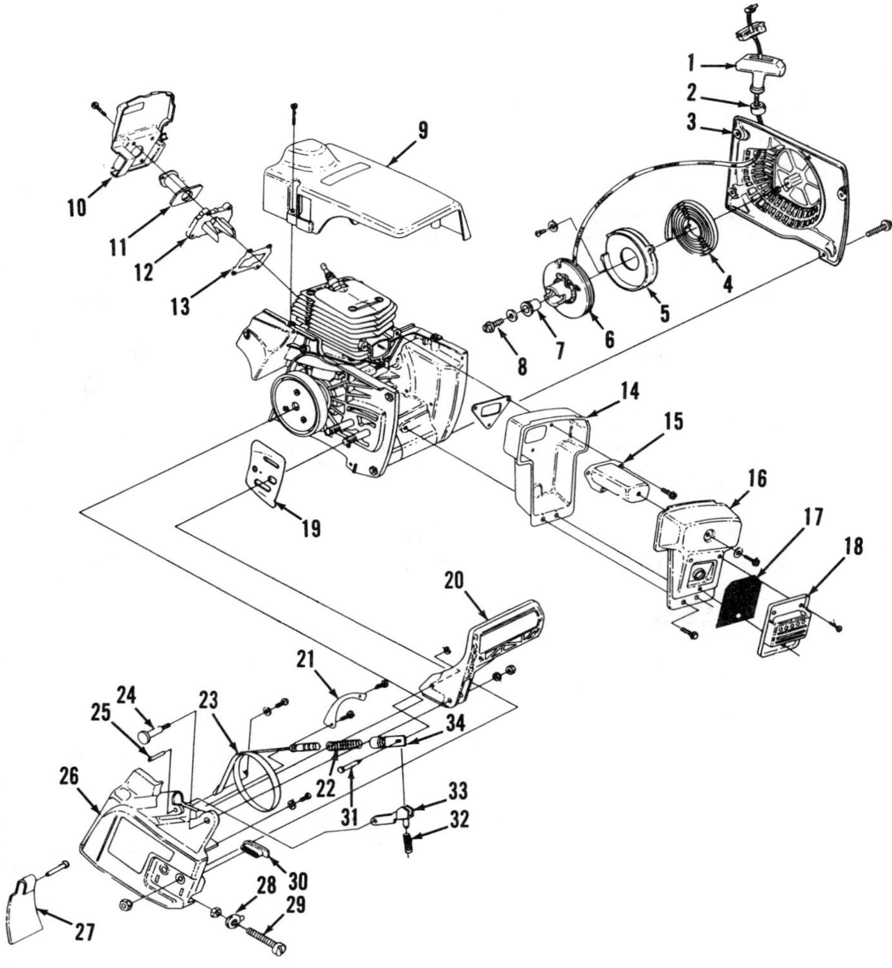

Fig. HL503—Exploded view of rewind starter assembly and chain brake assembly.

1. Rope handle
2. Rope guide
3. Starter housing
4. Rewind spring
5. Spring holder
6. Rope pulley
7. Bushing
8. Screw
9. Cylinder cover
10. Cylinder baffle
11. Intake boot
12. Intake adapter
13. Gasket
14. Muffler body
15. Muffler
16. Muffler cover
17. Spark arrestor screen
18. Cover
19. Guide bar plate
20. Brake lever
21. Brake cover
22. Brake spring
23. Brake band
24. Shoulder bolt
25. Pin
26. Drive case cover
27. Sawdust shield
28. Bar adjusting pin
29. Adjusting screw
30. Chain guide
31. Pin
32. Spring
33. Brake latch
34. Adjuster

brake lever. Place a screwdriver between brake band adjuster (34) and brake latch (33) and twist screwdriver to release the adjuster and brake spring (22) from the latch. Remove adjuster from brake band (23), remove brake band retaining screw and withdraw brake band. Drive dowel pin (25) out of housing to remove brake latch (33) and spring (32).

Renew any component that is excessively worn or damaged. Lubricate all pivot points with Molykote or suitable equivalent.

When reassembling, thread adjuster (34) on brake band (23) until clutch drum cannot be turned by hand, then loosen adjuster until drum just turns freely. The chain brake should stop saw chain instantly when engaged. Brake band should not contact clutch drum when disengaged.

HUSQVARNA

Model	Bore mm (in.)	Stroke mm (in.)	Displacement cc (cu. in.)	Drive Type
33, 35, 35 VR, 35 VRA, 35 VRCB, 37, H37	36.5 (1.4375)	32.5 (1.28)	34.0 (2.1)	Direct

MAINTENANCE

SPARK PLUG. Recommended spark plug is Champion CJ6. Spark plug electrode gap should be 0.025 inch (0.63 mm).

CARBURETOR. A Walbro WA diaphragm type carburetor is used on Models 35, 35VR, 35VRA and 37 and a Walbro WT diaphragm type carburetor is used on Model 33. Refer to CARBURETOR SERVICE section for service on Walbro carburetor.

Initial setting of both high and low speed mixture screws is 1⅛ turns open from a lightly seated position. Make final adjustment with engine warm and running. Adjust idle speed screw so engine idles just below clutch engagement speed. Adjust low speed mixture screw so engine will accelerate cleanly without hesitation. Adjust high speed mixture screw to obtain optimum performance under cutting load.

Note location of throttle link for Models 35, 35VR, 35VRA and 37 shown in Fig. H1.

Fig. H1—On Models 35, 35VR, 35VRA and 37, throttle link (L) must be installed as shown when assembling handle.

IGNITION. Early models are equipped with a breaker-point type flywheel magneto ignition system while later models use a breakerless electronic ignition system.

Breaker-point gap should be 0.015 inch (0.38 mm) on models so equipped. Ignition timing is fixed on all models but breaker-point gap on applicable models should be set correctly or timing will be affected. On all models, air gap between flywheel magnets and ignition coil legs should be 0.016 inch (0.41 mm).

LUBRICATION. Engine is lubricated by mixing oil with fuel. Recommended fuel:oil ratio is 50:1 when using Husquvarna Two-Stroke Oil. If Husqvarna Two-Stroke Oil is not available, fuel:oil ratio should be 25:1 using a good quality SAE 30 oil designed for chain saw engines.

Fill chain oil tank with SAE 30 motor oil. Chain oil may be diluted up to 50 percent for winter usage by adding kerosene or diesel fuel to chain oil.

CARBON. Carbon should be removed from exhaust system and cylinder peri-

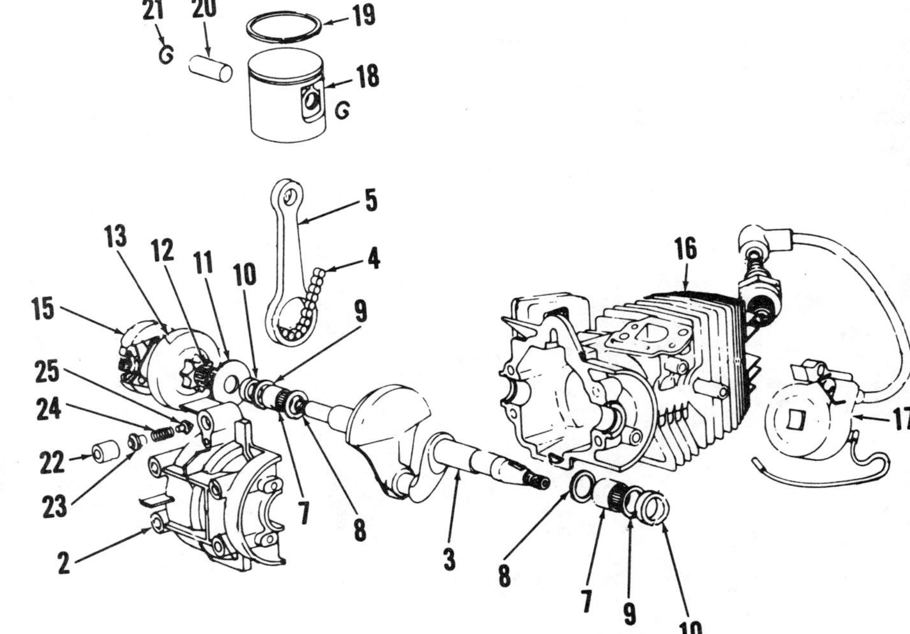

Fig. H2—Exploded view of early model engine. Later models are similar.

2. Crankcase
3. Crankshaft
4. Roller bearing
5. Connecting rod
7. Needle bearing
8. Washer
9. Retaining ring
10. Seal
11. Thrust washer
12. Bearing
13. Clutch drum
15. Clutch assembly
16. Cylinder
17. Ignition coil
18. Piston
19. Piston ring
20. Piston pin
21. Pin retainer
22. Spacer
23. Spring seat
24. Spring
25. Crankcase pressure valve

Illustrations courtesy Husqvarna Forest & Garden Co.

odically. Loose carbon should not be allowed to enter cylinder and care should be taken not to damage cylinder or piston.

REPAIRS

CYLINDER, PISTON, PIN AND RINGS. Cylinder (16–Fig. H2) is also upper crankcase half. Crankshaft is loose in crankcase when cylinder is removed. Care must be taken not to nick or scratch crankcase mating surfaces during disassembly.

Cylinder head is integral with cylinder and cylinder must be removed to remove piston. Piston is equipped with a single piston ring and floating type piston pin (20). Later models are equipped with needle bearings in connecting rod small end. On later models, piston and connecting rod are available as a unit assembly only. On all models, piston and ring are available in standard size only. Cylinder bore is chrome and should be inspected to determine if chrome is scored, peeling or excessively worn. Renew cylinder and piston if damaged or excessively worn.

Refer to CRANKSHAFT section for proper assembly of crankcase and cylinder.

CONNECTING ROD. To remove connecting rod, remove cylinder (16–Fig. H2). Note that cylinder is also upper crankcase half and crankshaft assembly is loose when cylinder is removed. Connecting rod (5) is one-piece and supported on crankpin by 11 loose bearing rollers (4). Be careful not to lose loose rollers that may fall out during disassembly. Rollers can be removed by sliding rod off rollers. To install rod bearing, hold rollers in place with heavy grease or petroleum jelly and position rod over rollers. Be sure rollers do not fall out during assembly of crankcase.

CRANKSHAFT AND SEALS. Crankshaft is supported by needle roller bearings (7–Fig. H2) at both ends. Crankshaft assembly may be removed after removing stator plate, clutch and cylinder assemblies. Care should be taken when removing cylinder as crankshaft will be loose in crankcase and connecting rod may slide off bearing rollers allowing them to fall into crankcase.

Before reassembling crankcases, apply a light coat of nonhardening sealant to crankcase mating surface. Be sure mating surfaces are not damaged during assembly. Retaining rings (9) must fit in ring grooves (G–Fig. H3) of crankcase and cylinder.

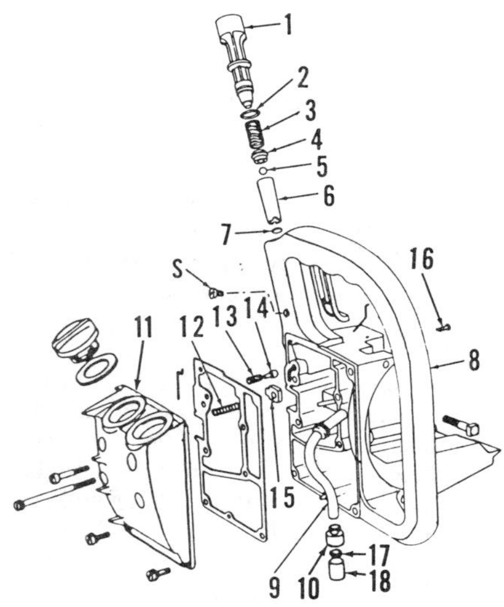

Fig. H4—Exploded view of manual oil pump and front housing used on later models equipped with pulsation type automatic oiling system. Duckbill type valve (16) is used instead of early model valve components (22, 23, 24 & 25) shown in Fig. H2.

1. Piston
2. "O" ring
3. Spring
4. Spring seat
5. Ball
6. Pump body
7. Screen
8. Front housing
9. Fuel hose
10. Fuel pickup
11. Front cover
12. Spring
13. Spring
14. Oil outlet valve
15. Nut
16. Duckbill check valve
17. Secondary filter
18. Fuel filter

CLUTCH. A two-shoe centrifugal type clutch is used on all models. Clutch hub has left hand thread. Clutch bearing (12–Fig. H2) should be inspected for excessive wear or damage. Inspect clutch shoes and drum for signs of excessive heat.

OIL PUMP. All early models are equipped with a manual oil pump and automatic oiling system. Refer to Fig. H4 for exploded view of manual oil pump. Automatic oiling is accomplished by crankcase pulsations which pressurize oil tank and force oil to bar. A one-way valve (25–Fig. H2 on early models or 16–Fig. H4 on later models) prevents oil from entering crankcase.

NOTE: Early and late crankcases (2–Fig. H2) may not be interchanged unless valve type is also changed.

Later model saws are equipped with a positive displacement oil pump assembly located behind flywheel. Oil pump

Fig. H3—Be sure retaining rings (R) are seated in grooves (G) of crankcase and cylinder.

Fig. H6—On manual oil pump models, oil exhaust valve (14) and spring (13) are installed in hole (H) in tank.

Illustrations courtesy Husqvarna Forest & Garden Co.

assembly is driven by a worm gear on crankshaft. Remove oil pump plunger retaining roll pin and withdraw plunger, gear and spring to service. Use suitable tools to pry worm gear off crankshaft. Renew any component that is excessively worn or damaged. Plunger is available only with complete oil pump assembly.

REWIND STARTER. Refer to Fig. H7 for exploded view of pawl type starter typical of the type used on all models. Care should be taken when removing to remove rewind spring (12) to prevent spring from uncoiling uncontrolled.

Rewind spring (12) should be wound in clockwise direction in housing. Wind starter rope in clockwise direction around rope pulley (11) as viewed in starter housing (14).

CHAIN BRAKE. Model 33, 35, 35VRA and 37 are equipped with a chain brake designed to stop the saw chain quickly should kick-back occur. It is necessary to unlock the brake before removing or installing the clutch cover (1–Fig. H8 or Fig. H9). Depending on cutting operation, dust shield should be occasionally removed so sawdust and debris can be cleaned from the brake mechanism.

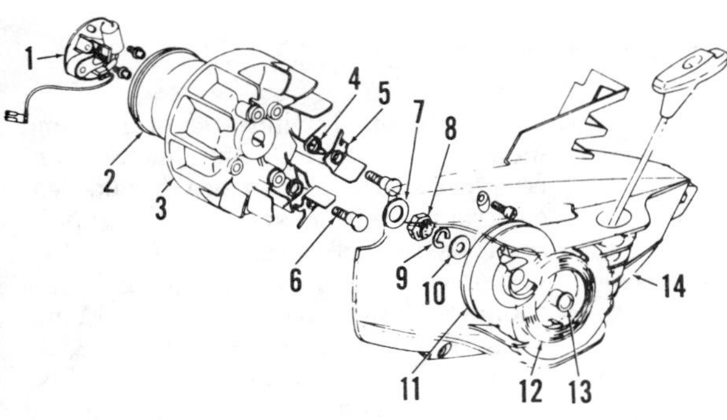

Fig. H7—Exploded view of ignition and rewind starter used on early models. Rewind starter used on later models is similar.

1. Stator plate
2. Cover
3. Flywheel
4. Spring
5. Pawl
6. Pivot pin
7. Washer
8. Nut
9. Snap ring
10. Thrust washer
11. Rope pulley
12. Rewind spring
13. Bushing
14. Starter housing

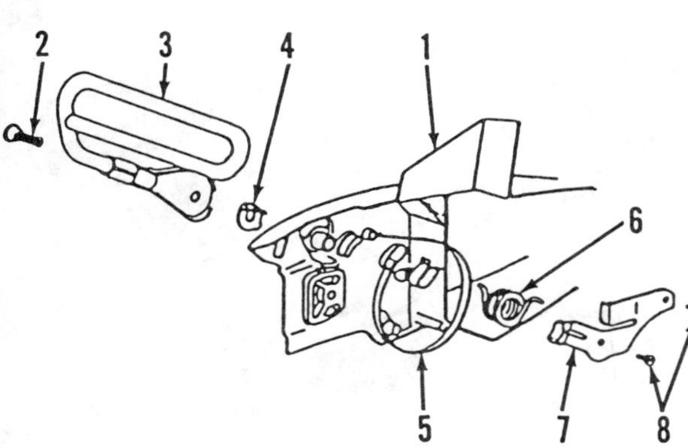

Fig. H8—Exploded view of chain brake assembly typical of type used on 35, 35VRA and 37 models.

1. Clutch cover
2. Pivot pin
3. Trip lever
4. Stop plate
5. Brake band
6. Spring
7. Detent cover
8. Cap screw

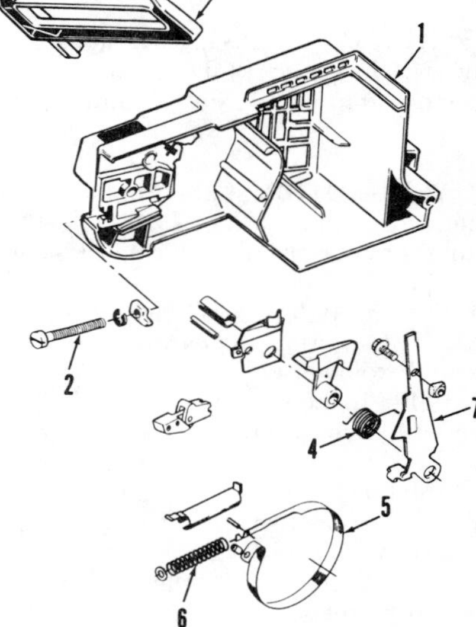

Fig. H9—Exploded view of chain brake assembly used on Model 33.

1. Clutch cover
2. Adjusting bolt
3. Guard
4. Spring
5. Brake band
6. Spring
7. Lever

Illustrations courtesy Husqvarna Forest & Garden Co.

HUSQVARNA

Model	Bore mm (in.)	Stroke mm (in.)	Displacement cc (cu. in.)	Drive Type
40 Rancher, 140S, 240 S, 240 SE, 240 SG, 340 SE, 340 SG	40.0 (1.575)	32.0 (1.26)	40.0 (2.4)	Direct
44, 44 CB, 44 Rancher, 444 CB, 444 SE, 444 SG	42 (1.654)	32 (1.26)	44 (2.7)	Direct

MAINTENANCE

SPARK PLUG. Recommended spark plug is Champion RCJ7Y. Spark plug electrode gap should be 0.5 mm (0.020 in.).

CARBURETOR. Late Model 44 is equipped with a Walbro Model HDA diaphragm carburetor. All other models are equipped with a Walbro Model HDC carburetor. Refer to CARBURETOR SERVICE section for carburetor service and exploded view.

On 140S models equipped with Walbro HDC 10 carburetors, initial setting of low speed mixture screw is 3/4 turn open while initial setting of high speed mixture screw is 1/2 turn open. Initial setting for late Model 44 with Walbro Model HDA carburetor is 1 1/4 turns open for low and high speed mixture screws. Initial setting for all other models is one turn open for low speed and high speed mixture screws.

On all models, make final adjustment with engine warm and running. Adjust idle speed screw so engine idles just below clutch engagement speed. Adjust low speed mixture screw so engine will accelerate cleanly without hesitation. Adjust high speed mixture screw to obtain optimum performance under cutting load.

Note that intake manifold must be installed with oval opening next to cylinder and round opening next to carburetor.

IGNITION. Models 40 Rancher, 140S and 240S are equipped with a breaker-point type flywheel magneto ignition system. Air gap between flywheel and coil legs should be 0.30-0.35 mm (0.012-0.014 in.). Breaker-point gap should be 0.3-0.4 mm (0.012-0.016 in.). Breaker-points should begin to open when mark on flywheel is 2.5 mm (0.1 in.) from upper edge of lower coil leg as shown in Fig. H10. Use a suitable test light or continuity meter to check breaker-point opening.

Models 240SE, 240SG, 340SE and 340SG are equipped with a two-piece breakerless electronic ignition system. An ignition module (6–Fig. H11) is located in the rewind starter housing. Models 44, 444SE and 444SG are equipped with a one-piece breakerless electronic ignition system. Air gap on both types of breakerless ignition systems, between flywheel and coil legs, should be 0.30-0.35 mm (0.012-0.014 in.).

On all models, flywheel may have two crankshaft key grooves. Key groove marked "P" is used on models equipped with Prufrex ignition systems while the

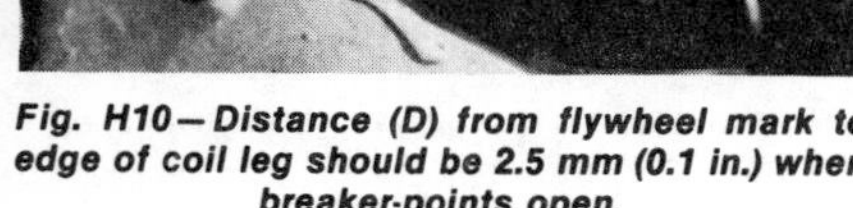

Fig. H10—Distance (D) from flywheel mark to edge of coil leg should be 2.5 mm (0.1 in.) when breaker-points open.

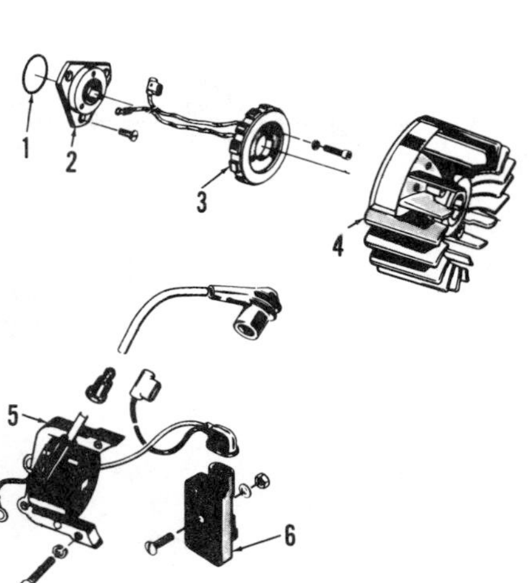

Fig. H11—Exploded view of electronic ignition system used on Models 240SE, 240SG, 340SE and 340SG. Generating coil (3) is used on Models 240SG and 340SG with heated handles.

1. "O" ring
2. Seal retainer
3. Generating coil
4. Flywheel
5. Ignition coil
6. Ignition module

Fig. H12—Exploded view of engine. Oil pump drive gear (8) is used on Models 140S, 240S, 240SE and 240SG. Note oil pump gear in Fig. H17 used on all other models.

1. Air baffle
2. Intake manifold
3. Cylinder
4. Piston ring
5. Piston & pin
6. Pin retainer
7. Bearing
8. Oil pump drive gear
9. Bearing
10. Crankshaft & rod assy.

Illustrations courtesy Husqvarna Forest & Garden Co.

other key groove is used on models equipped with Bosch and breaker-point ignition systems. Tighten flywheel nut to 23.5-28.4 N·m (17-21 ft.lbs.).

LUBRICATION. Recommended fuel:oil ratio for engine lubrication is 50:1 when using Husqvarna Two-Stroke Oil. If Husqvarna Two-Stroke Oil is not available, fuel:oil ratio should be 25:1 using a good quality oil designed for use in two-stroke air-cooled engines.

The chain is lubricated by oil from an automatic chain oil pump. Clean automotive oil may be used. Oil viscosity should be chosen according to ambient temperature. Oil may be cut with up to 50 percent kerosene in extremely cold weather.

Oil pump output on 140S, 240S, 240SE and 240SG is not adjustable. Oil pump output on all other models is adjusted by exchanging cam screw (2–Fig. H17). Cam screw is available from the manufacturer in three color-coded sizes. A white cam screw indicates minimum oil output, a plain cam screw indicates standard oil output while a green cam screw indicates maximum oil output. Refer to OIL PUMP section for replacement procedure.

REPAIRS

CYLINDER, PISTON, PIN AND RINGS. Cylinder has a chrome bore which should be inspected for flaking, cracking or other damage to chromed surface. Some pistons are equipped with one piston ring while others are equipped with two piston rings. Piston ring groove has a locating pin to prevent piston ring rotation. Arrow on piston crown must point toward exhaust port when installing piston.

Piston and cylinder are graded according to size to provide correct piston-to-cylinder clearance. Piston and cylinder bore sizes are indicated by a letter stamped on the piston crown or on the top of the cylinder. See Fig. H13. If cylinder is new or has very little use, piston and cylinder grade should be the same. If cylinder is used but not excessively worn, a piston with the same grade or a piston with the next largest grade may be installed. For instance, pistons with grade letters "B"or "C" may be installed in a used cylinder with grade letter "B." Grade letter "A" denotes smallest cylinder or piston while grade letter "E" denotes largest cylinder or piston. Tighten cylinder base screws to 8.8-9.8 N·m (78-87 in.-lbs.)

CRANKSHAFT, CONNECTING ROD AND CRANKCASE. Crankshaft and connecting rod are a unit assembly. It will be necessary to heat crankcase halves to remove or install crankshaft and main bearings. Care should be taken not to damage mating surfaces of crankcase halves. Check rotation of connecting rod around crankpin and renew crankshaft unit if roughness or other damage is found.

When reassembling crankshaft and crankcase halves, install main bearings allowing for installation of oil pump on drive side and crankshaft seal housing on flywheel side. A special tool is available from the manufacturer to properly position main bearings and crankshaft in crankcase. Tighten crankcase screws to 7-8 N·m (61-69 in.-lbs.). Make certain crankshaft is centered in crankcase and will rotate freely.

CLUTCH. All models are equipped with the two-shoe centrifugal clutch shown in Fig. H14. Clutch hub (1) has left hand threads. Inspect clutch shoes and drum for excessive wear or damage due to overheating. Clean and inspect clutch hub, drum and bearing for damage or excessive wear. Inspect clutch bearing lubrication hole in crankshaft end and clutch bearing contact surface on crankshaft for wear or damage.

AUTOMATIC OIL PUMP. Models 140S, 240S, 240SE and 240SG are equipped with the automatic oil pump shown in Fig. H15 and Fig. H16. Oil pump output is not adjustable. Access to oil pump components is obtained after removing guide bar plate (8–Fig. H15). Withdraw pin (14), unscrew plug (12) and withdraw plunger (15). Oil pump is

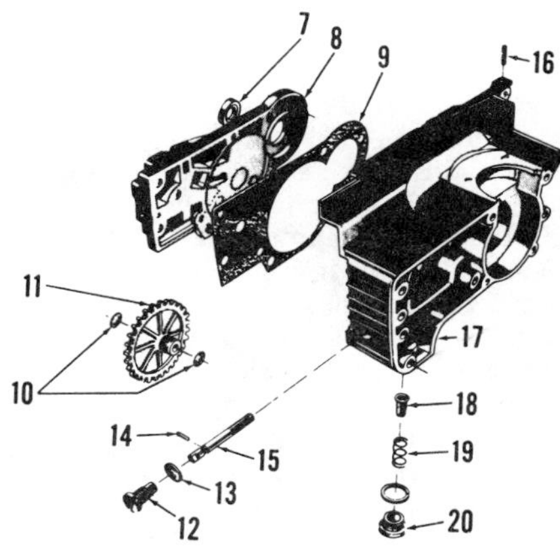

Fig. H15—Exploded view of early oil pump assembly.

7. Oil seal
8. Bar plate
9. Gasket
10. Washers
11. Oil pump gear
12. Plug
13. Washer
14. Pin
15. Plunger
16. Dowel pin
17. Right crankcase half
18. Screen
19. Spring
20. Plug

Fig. H13—View showing location of cylinder and piston grade letters. Grade "D" is shown.

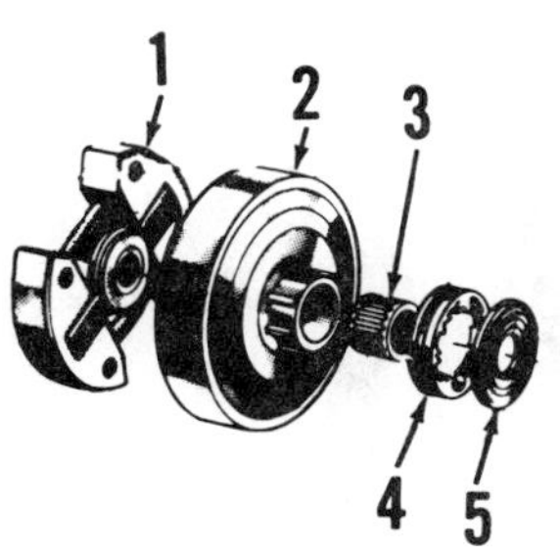

Fig. H14—Exploded view of clutch.

1. Clutch hub & shoes
2. Clutch drum
3. Bearing
4. Sprocket
5. Washer

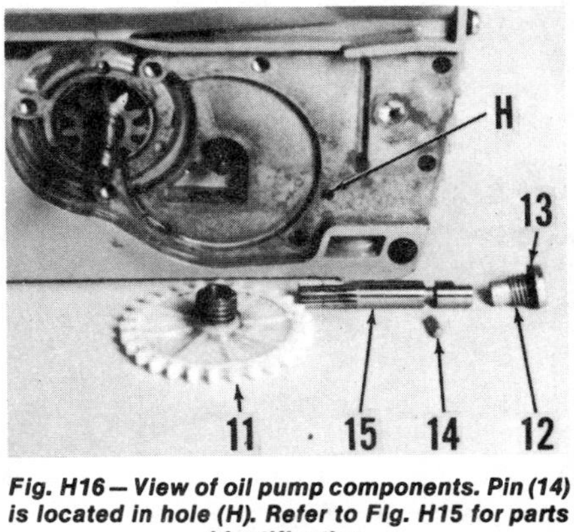

Fig. H16—View of oil pump components. Pin (14) is located in hole (H). Refer to Fig. H15 for parts identification.

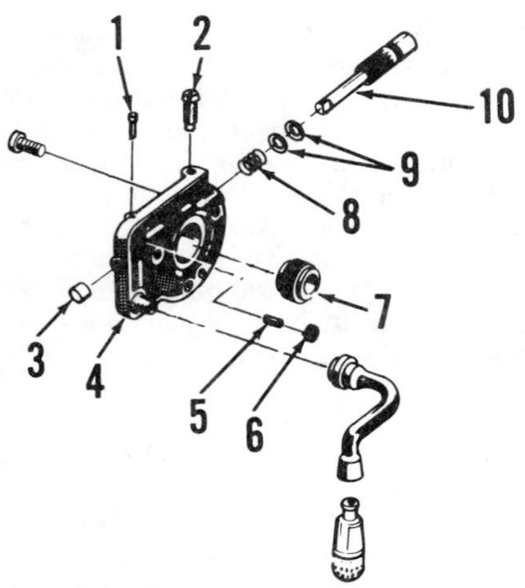

Fig. H17—Exploded view of oil pump used on Models 40 Rancher, 44, 340SE, 340SG, 444SE and 444SG.

1. Plug
2. Cam screw
3. Plug
4. Pump body
5. Tube
6. Seal
7. Drive gear
8. Spring
9. Washers
10. Plunger

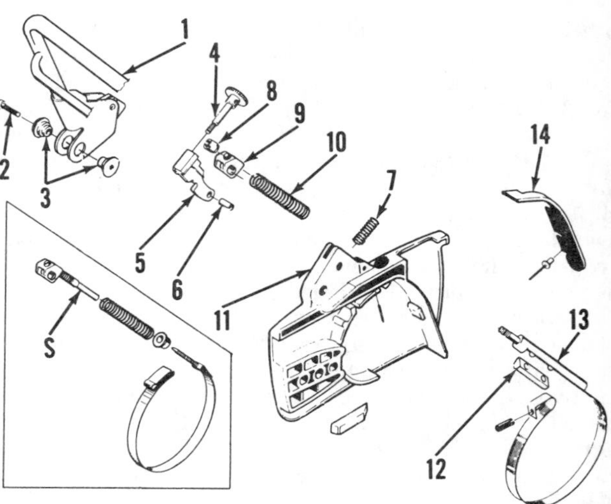

Fig. H19A—Exploded view of typical chain brake used on later models. Some models may have adjustable type brake band shown in inset.

1. Hand guard
2. Cap screw
3. Trunnion
4. Trigger button
5. Trigger lever
6. Pin
7. Spring
8. Nut
9. Latch
10. Spring
11. Housing
12. Guide
13. Brake band
14. Chain guard

driven by gear (8–Fig. H12) on crankshaft. A special tool is available from the manufacturer so gear can be removed without removing crankshaft.

Automatic oil pump used on all other models is shown in Fig. H17. Oil pump output is adjusted by exchanging cam screw (2–Fig. H17). Cam screw is available from the manufacturer in three color-coded sizes. A white cam screw indicates minimum oil output, a plain cam screw indicates standard oil output while a green cam screw indicates maximum oil output. Remove clutch for access to oil pump. Unscrew cam screw (2) before withdrawing pump plunger (10). Pump plunger (10) is driven by worm gear (7) on crankshaft. A special tool is available from the manufacturer for worm gear removal. Collar on worm gear must be toward oil pump when installed.

REWIND STARTER. To disassemble rewind starter on all models, first remove starter housing from saw. Pull starter rope and hold rope pulley with notch in pulley adjacent to rope outlet. Pull rope back through outlet so it engages notch in pulley and allow pulley to completely unwind. Unscrew pulley retaining screw (6–Fig. H18) and carefully remove rope pulley. If rewind spring must be removed, care should be taken not to allow spring to uncoil uncontrolled.

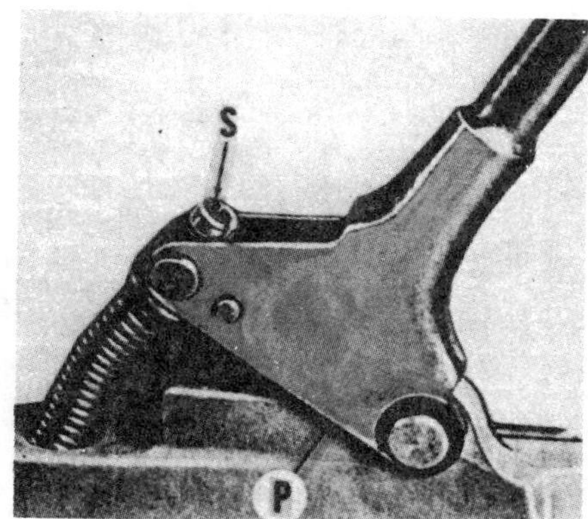

Fig. H19—Turn screw (S) to adjust chain brake on early models. Refer to text.

Install rewind spring in starter housing with spring coiled in clockwise direction from outer spring end. Wrap starter rope around rope pulley in a clockwise direction as viewed with pulley in starter housing. Turn rope pulley two turns clockwise before passing rope through rope outlet to place tension on rewind spring. Spring tension is correct if rope pulley can be rotated at least ½ turn further when rope is pulled completely out.

When installing starter assembly on saw, make sure starter pulley properly engages pawls on flywheel before tightening retaining cap screws.

CHAIN BRAKE. Some models may be equipped with a chain brake system designed to stop chain movement should kickback occur. Several types of chain brake systems have been used.

The chain brake on early models is activated when the operator's hand strikes the hand guard. To adjust chain brake on early models, pull back hand guard and be sure mechanism is cocked. Turn adjusting screw (S–Fig. H19) in until chain cannot be pulled around bar then turn screw out three or four turns. If screw has a square head, be sure screw head does not rest on side plates (P).

The chain brake on later models is activated either by the operator's hand striking the hand guard (1–Fig. H19A) or by sufficient force being applied to the guide bar tip during kickback to cause the front handle to contact the trigger button (4) resulting in automatic

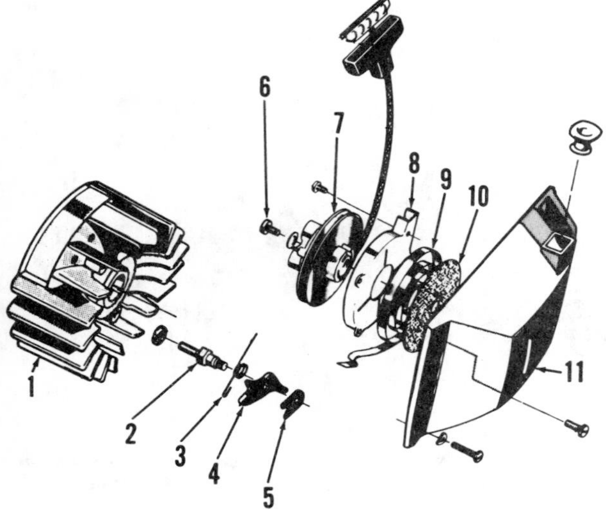

Fig. H18—Exploded view of Models 40 Rancher and 44 rewind starter. Other models are similar.

1. Flywheel
2. Pawl stud
3. Spring
4. Pawl
5. Clip
6. Screw
7. Rope pulley
8. Rope guide
9. Rewind spring
10. Washer
11. Starter housing

Illustrations courtesy Husqvarna Forest & Garden Co.

activation of brake mechanism. To adjust chain brake on later models, first pull back hand guard and be sure mechanism is cocked then determine if brake system has an adjustable brake band as shown in inset of Fig. H19A. If brake band is adjustable, turn adjusting screw (S) in until chain cannot be pulled around bar then turn screw out three or four turns. Chain should rotate freely around bar. Check brake band tension adjustment by starting saw and running at wide open throttle, then manually engage chain brake. Chain should stop rotating immediately. On models without adjustable brake band, be sure spring retaining nut (8) is tight against its seat. On all models, gap between trigger button (4) and front handle should be adjusted so chain brake will automatically activate when a 6.2-9.8 N (1.4-2.2 lbs.) force is applied on guide bar tip. A suitable spring balance should be used for testing and adjustment.

HUSQVARNA

Model	Bore mm (in.)	Stroke mm (in.)	Displacement cc (cu. in.)	Drive Type
163 S, 263 CD	47.0 (1.85)	36.0 (1.42)	63.0 (3.8)	Direct
65, L65	48.0 (1.89)	36.0 (1.42)	65.0 (4.0)	Direct
77, L77, 280S, 380 CD, 380 S, 480 CB, 480 CD	52.0 (2.05)	36.0 (1.42)	77.0 (4.7)	Direct
285 CB, 285 CD	52 (2.05)	40 (1.57)	85 (5.2)	Direct
298 XP, 1100 CD, 2100, 2100 CD, 2100 XP	56 (2.2)	40 (1.57)	99 (6.0)	Direct

MAINTENANCE

SPARK PLUG. Recommended spark plug is Champion CJ6 for Models 285CD, 1100CD and 2100CD or Champion RCJ7Y for all other models. Electrode gap should be 0.5 mm (0.020 in.).

CARBURETOR. A Tillotson Model HS diaphragm carburetor is used on all models. Refer to CARBURETOR SERVICE section for service and exploded view of carburetor.

Initial adjustment of high speed mixture screw is one turn open for Models 285CS, 298XP, 2100CD and 2101XP and 3/4 turn open for all other models. Initial adjustment of low speed mixture screw is one turn open on 65, 77 and 285CD models; 1¼ turns open on 298XP, 480CD, 2100CD and 2101XP models and 3/4 turn open on all other models.

On all models, make final adjustment with engine warm and running. Adjust idle speed screw so engine idles just below clutch engagement speed. Adjust low speed mixture screw so engine will accelerate cleanly without hesitation. Adjust high speed mixture screw to obtain optimum performance under cutting load.

IGNITION. Models 77, 263CD, 285CD, 298XP, 380CD, 480CD, 1100CD, 2100CD, 2101XP and late L77 are equipped with breakerless capacitor discharge ignition systems while all other models are equipped with breaker point flywheel magneto ignition systems.

Ignition timing on Models 77, 263CD, 285CD, 298XP, 380CD, 480CD, 1100CD, 2100CD, 2101XP and late L77 is correct when mark on stator plate is aligned with mark on crankcase. Refer to Fig. H20 or H21. On 1100CD models, ignition timing may be checked with a power timing light by running engine at 8000 rpm. Mark on flywheel should align with mark on cylinder or crankcase.

Models equipped with breaker-points should have breaker-point gap of 0.3-0.4 mm (0.012-0.016 in.). Ignition timing is adjusted by loosening stator plate mounting screws and rotating stator plate. Ignition timing is adjusted as follows: Remove flywheel and attach Husqvarna timing tool 50 25 059-01 to end of crankshaft. Turn tool until pointer is aligned with mark (A – Fig. H22) on crankcase as shown in Fig. H22. Loosen stator plate mounting screws and rotate stator plate until coil leg contacts tang (B) on timing tool. Retighten stator plate mounting screws. Using a suitable continuity tester, adjust breaker-points to just open when timing tool pointer is aligned with mark on crankcase. Air gap between ignition coil legs and flywheel should be 0.2-0.3 mm (0.008-0.012 in.). To check air gap, affix tape to coil legs until thickness equals

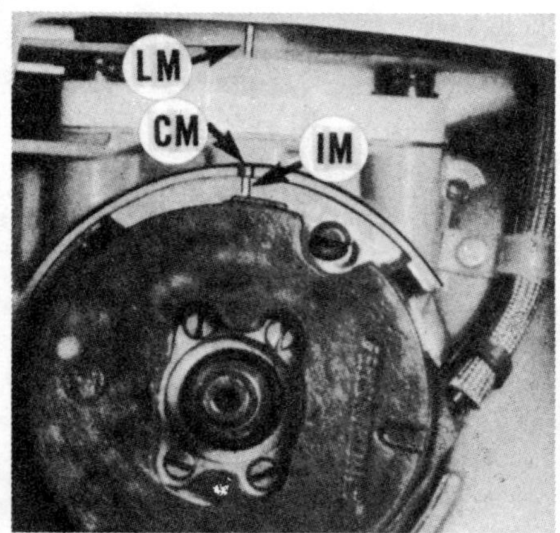

Fig. H20 — View of stator plate on early 1100CD models. Ignition timing is correct when mark (IM) on stator plate is aligned with mark (CM) on crankcase. Timing mark LM) on cylinder should align with mark on flywheel at 8000 rpm if timing is checked with timing light.

Fig. H21 — View of stator plate on 77, 263CD, 298XP, 380CD, 480CD, 2100CD, 2101XP and later L77 and 1100CD models with SEM ignition. Ignition timing is correct when mark (M) on stator is aligned with crankcase mark (arrow). Ignition timing procedure is the same for 263CD, 285CD and 380CD models with Bosch ignition system.

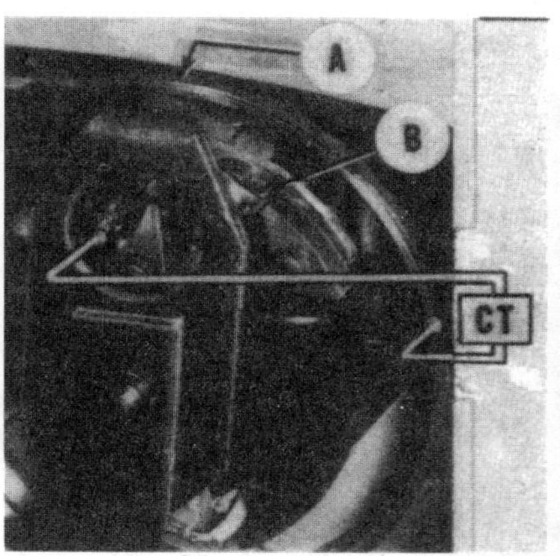

Fig. H22 — View showing installation of timing tool 50 25 059-01 and connection of continuity tester (CT) on models with breaker-point ignition system. Refer to text for timing procedure.

Illustrations courtesy Husqvarna Forest & Garden Co.

desired air gap. Loosen coil mounting screws and push coil outward. Install flywheel and rotate slowly while noting if tape drags against flywheel. Remove flywheel and if tape dragged against flywheel, tighten coil screws to 4.0-4.5 N•m (35-40 in.-lbs.). If tape did not drag against flywheel, elongate coil mounting holes and repeat procedure.

Fig. H23 — View showing location of oil pump adjusting screw on models so equipped.

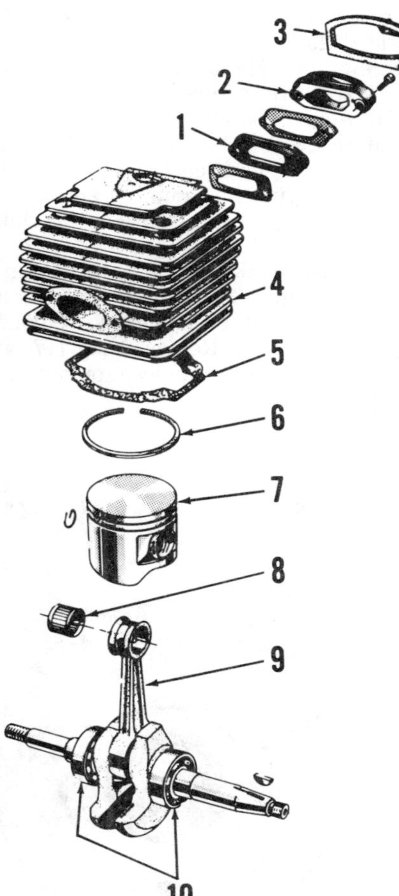

Fig. H24 — Exploded view of engine.

1. Insulator
2. Intake manifold
3. Baffle
4. Cylinder
5. Gasket
6. Piston rings (2)
7. Piston
8. Roller bearing
9. Crankshaft & rod assy.
10. Bearings

LUBRICATION. The engine is lubricated by mixing oil with the fuel. Recommended fuel:oil ratio is 50:1 when using Husqvarna Two-Stroke Oil. If Husqvarna Two-Stroke Oil is not available, fuel:oil ratio should be 25:1 using a good quality oil designed for use in air-cooled two-stroke engines.

All models are equipped with an automatic oil pump. On 65, L65, 77 and L77 models, oil pump output is determined by the stroke of plunger (17 – Fig. H27). Plunger is available from the manufacturer in two sizes, 1.2 mm and 1.4 mm. Refer to OIL PUMP section for identification and replacement procedure.

On all other models, oil pump output is determined either by turning an adjusting screw (S – Fig. H23) or by changing position of cam screw (CS – Fig. H29). On models equipped with adjusting screw (S – Fig. H23), number "1" indicates minimum oil output while number "4" provides maximum oil output. If oil pump does not have adjusting screw (S), then oil output is adjusted using cam screw (CS – Fig. H29) located on rear of pump. Refer to OIL PUMP section.

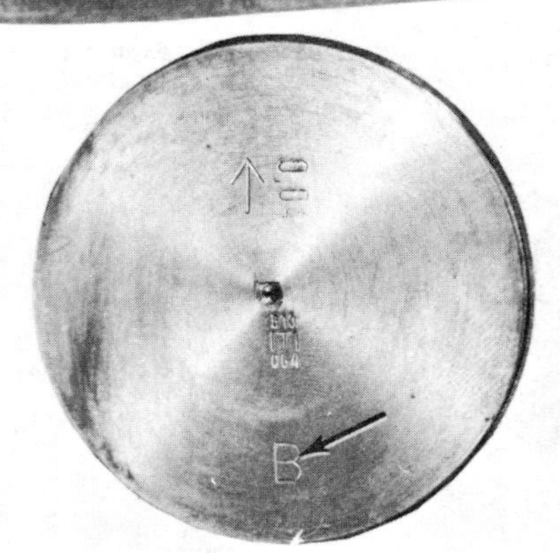

Fig. H25 — Arrows show location of piston and cylinder letter grades. Be sure arrow stamped in piston crown points toward exhaust port when installing piston. Grade "B" is shown.

REPAIRS

TIGHTENING TORQUES. Refer to the following table when tightening fasteners:

Fastener Diameter	
4 mm	4.5-5.5 N•m (40-50 in.-lbs.)
5 mm	5.5-6.8 N•m (50-60 in.-lbs.)
6 mm	10-11.8 N•m (90-105 in.-lbs.)
8 mm	28.2-32.8 N•m (250-290 in.-lbs.)
10 mm	36.7-42.4 N•m (325-375 in.-lbs.)

PISTON, PIN, RINGS AND CYLINDER. Cylinder bore is chrome plated and should be inspected for excessive wear and damage to chrome surface. Inspect piston and discard if excessive wear or damage is evident.

On Models 298XP, 2101XP and late 2100CD, new cylinders are available only with fitted pistons. On all other models and early 2100CD models, piston and cylinder are graded with a letter according to size. Piston is marked on piston crown while cylinder is marked on top as shown in Fig. H25. Letter sizes range from "A" to "C" on Models 285CD, 1100CD and 2100CD and from "A" to "E" on all other models, with "A" being smallest size. Piston and cylinder grades should match although one size larger piston may be installed in a used cylinder. For instance, a piston graded "C" may be used in a cylinder graded "B."

Piston must be installed with arrow on piston crown pointing toward exhaust port. Refer to Fig. H25. Piston is equipped with two piston rings. Locating pins are present in piston ring

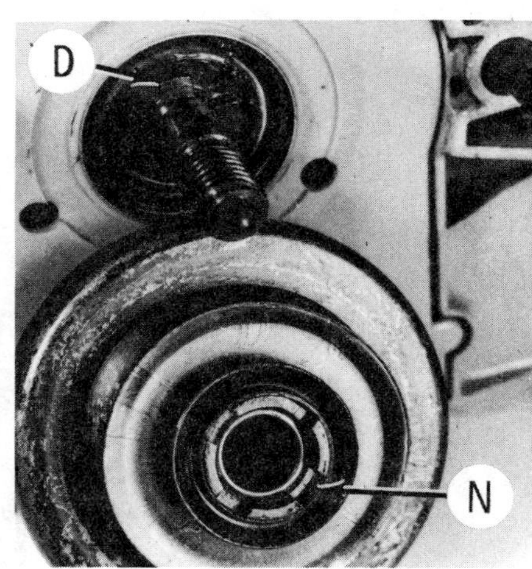

Fig. H26 — Dogs (D) on oil pump drive gear must mesh with notches (N) on clutch drum.

Illustrations courtesy Husqvarna Forest & Garden Co.

grooves to prevent piston ring rotation. Be sure ring end gaps are around locating pins when installing cylinder.

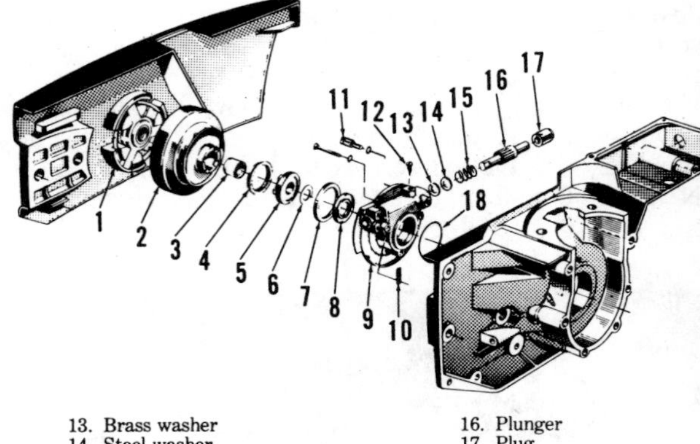

Fig. H28—Exploded view of oil pump and clutch assemblies used on all models except L65 and L77. Refer to Fig. H29 for view of non-adjustable oil pump used on some models.

1. Clutch shoes & hub
2. Clutch drum
3. Needle bearing
4. Seal
5. Oil pump drive gear
6. Washer
7. Seal
8. Seal
9. Oil pump housing
10. Gasket
11. Adjuster screw
12. Cam screw
13. Brass washer
14. Steel washer
15. Spring
16. Plunger
17. Plug
18. "O" ring

CRANKSHAFT, CONNECTING ROD AND CRANKCASE. Crankshaft and connecting rod are a unit assembly. It will be necessary to heat crankcase halves to remove or install crankshaft and main bearings. Care should be taken not to damage mating surfaces of crankcase halves. Check rotation of connecting rod around crankpin and renew crankshaft unit if roughness or other damage is noted.

Reassemble crankshaft and crankcase halves as follows: Place a main bearing over flywheel end of crankshaft then press bearing inner race flush against bearing seat. Heat bearing seat area in corresponding crankcase half and install crankshaft. Make sure main bearing outer race seats fully in crankcase. Heat bearing seat area in drive half of crankcase and install drive side main bearing allowing for installation of oil pump. A special tool is available from the manufacturer to properly position drive side main bearing in crankcase. After assembling crankcase halves together, make certain crankshaft is centered in crankcase and will rotate freely.

CLUTCH. All models are equipped with a three-shoe centrifugal clutch. Clutch hub has left hand threads. Inspect clutch shoes and drum for excessive wear or damage due to overheating. Clean and inspect clutch hub, drum and bearing for damage or excessive wear. Inspect clutch bearing lubrication hole in crankshaft end and clutch bearing contact surface on crankshaft for wear or damage.

The oil pump is driven by clutch drum. Be sure notches on rear of clutch drum mesh with dogs (D–Fig. H26) of oil pump drive gear when installing clutch assembly.

OIL PUMP (Models 65, L65, 77 And L77.) All models are equipped with an automatic oil pump which is driven by the clutch drum. Notches on the back of the clutch drum engage dogs on oil pump drive gear (7–Fig. H27) which rides on the crankshaft. Plunger (17) is driven by worm gear (14), through driven gear (12) from drive gear (7). Pin (19) rides in cam groove of plunger (17) resulting in reciprocating motion of plunger. Oil pump output is determined by the stroke of plunger (17). Two plungers are available from the manufacturer to vary oil pump output and are marked for output identification. Maximum oil output is obtained if plunger marked 1.4 mm is installed while minimum oil output results if plunger marked 1.2 mm is installed.

Access to oil pump on 65, L65, 77 and L77 models is gained by removing oil pump cover plate (6). Remove pin (19), plug (16), then withdraw plunger (17 and remove worm gear (14).

(All other models). Refer to Fig. H28 for exploded view of typical oil pump used. Two variations of pump have been produced and are identified by oil adjustment method. Oil pump shown in Fig H28 is adjusted by turning screw (11) as shown in Fig. H23. Oil pump shown in Fig. H29 is adjusted by relocating cam screw (CS). Maximum oil output is obtained if cam screw is installed in hole "II" while minimum oil output results if cam screw is installed in hole "I." Screw (S) must be installed in remaining hole On both types of pump, oil pump drive gear (5–Fig. H28) is driven by clutch drum (2).

To disassemble pump with adjusting screw (Fig. H28), unscrew adjusting screw (11) and, on models so equipped cam screw (12). Remove plug (17) and plunger (16) by carefully tapping pump

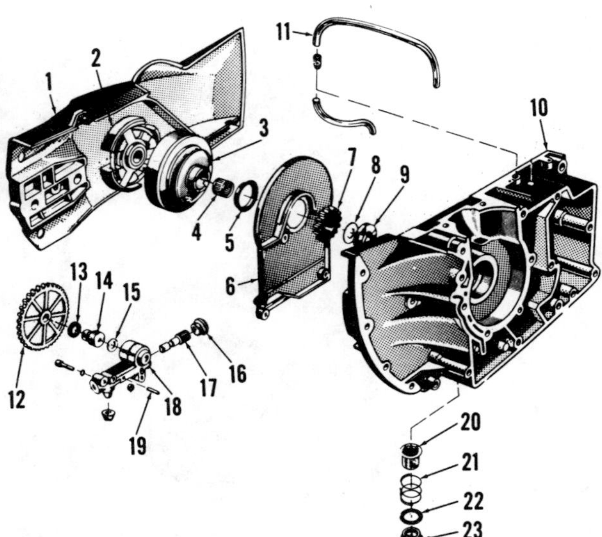

Fig. H27—Exploded view of oil pump and clutch assemblies used on Models 65, 77, L65 and 77.

1. Side cover
2. Clutch shoes & hub
3. Clutch drum
4. Needle bearing
5. Seal
6. Oil pump cover
7. Oil pump drive gear
8. Washer
9. Seal
10. Right crankcase half
11. Vent hose
12. Oil pump driven gear
13. Washer
14. Worm gear
15. Washer
16. Plug
17. Plunger
18. Oil pump housing
19. Cam pin
20. Screen
21. Spring
22. Gasket
23. Plug

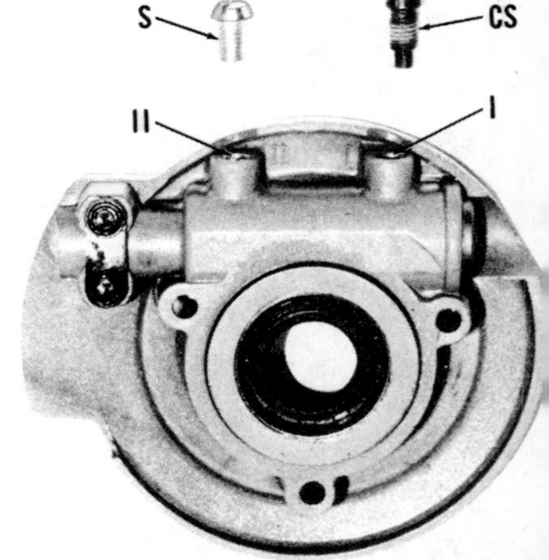

Fig. H29—View of oil pump used on some models. Oil pump output is determined by installation of cam screw (CS) in hole (I) or hole (II). Refer to text.

Illustrations courtesy Husqvarna Forest & Garden Co

housing against a solid object. Withdraw remaining components from housing.

To disassemble pump with cam screw (CS–Fig. H29), remove cam screw (CS) and screw (S) then use the same procedure as previously outlined to withdraw plug and plunger.

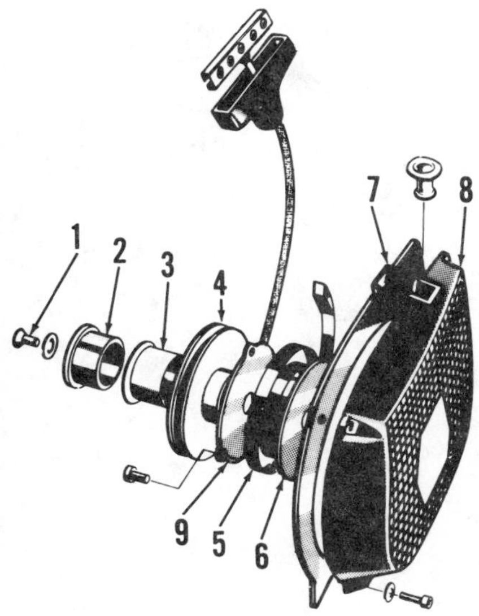

Fig. H30—Exploded view of rewind starter used on all models except 280S, 298XP, 1100CD, 2100CD and 2101XP. Plate (9) is not used on all models.

1. Screw
2. Pivot
3. Bushing
4. Rope pulley
5. Rewind spring
6. Washer
7. Plate
8. Starter housing
9. Plate

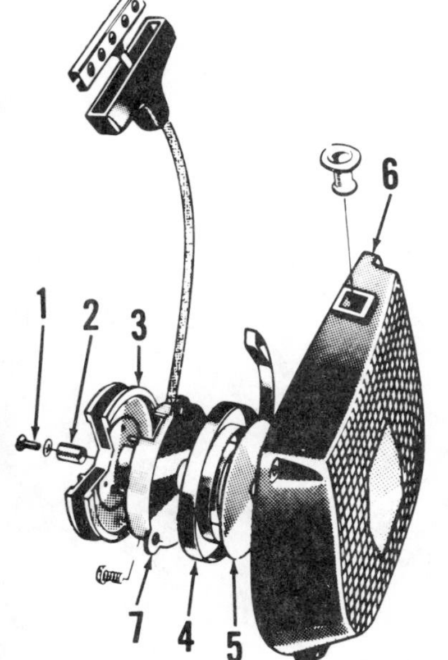

Fig. H31—Exploded view of starter used on Models 280S, 298XP, 1100CD, 2100CD and 2101XP. Rope guide (7) is not used on Models 280S or 1100CD.

1. Screw
2. Bushing
3. Rope pulley
4. Rewind spring
5. Washer
6. Starter housing
7. Rope guide

On both types of pump, be sure crankshaft seal (8–Fig. H28) and "O" ring (18) are not damaged or debris will enter main bearing.

REWIND STARTER. Refer to Fig. H30 or H31 for an exploded view of rewind starter. Note that starter used on 163S, 263CD, 285CD, 380CD, 380S and 480CD models has an intermediate plate (7–Fig. H30) which retains rope handle. Rope handle may be knocked from notch in starter housing if plate is not held against housing during removal from saw.

To disassemble rewind starter on all models, first remove starter housing from saw. Pull starter rope and hold rope pulley with notch in pulley adjacent to rope outlet. Pull rope back through outlet so it engages notch in pulley and allow pulley to completely unwind. Unscrew pulley retaining screw and carefully remove rope pulley. If rewind spring must be removed, care should be taken not to allow spring to uncoil uncontrolled.

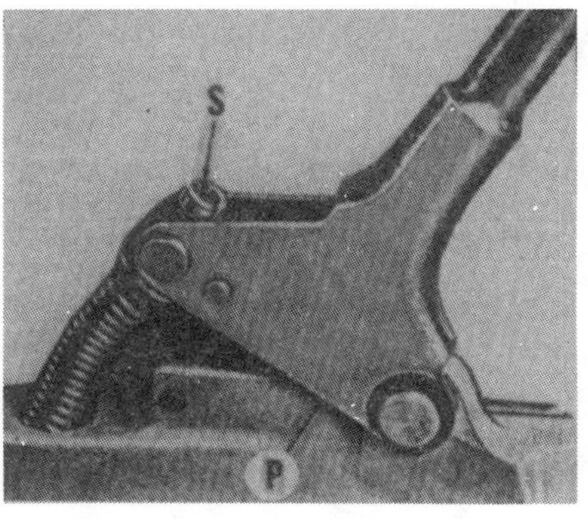

Fig. H32—Turn screw (S) to adjust chain brake on early models. Refer to text.

Install rewind spring in starter housing with spring coiled in clockwise direction from outer spring end. Wrap starter rope around rope pulley in a clockwise direction as viewed with pulley in starter housing. Turn rope pulley two turns clockwise before passing rope through rope outlet to place tension on rewind spring. Spring tension is correct if rope pulley can be rotated approximately ½ turn further when rope is pulled completely out.

When installing starter assembly on saw, make sure starter pulley properly engages pawls on flywheel before tightening retaining cap screws.

CHAIN BRAKE. Some models may be equipped with a chain brake system designed to stop chain movement should kickback occur. Several types of chain brake systems have been used.

The chain brake is activated either by the operator's hand striking the brake lever (1–Fig. H33 or Fig. H34) or by sufficient force being applied to the guide bar tip during kickback to cause the front handle to contact trigger lever (6–Fig H33) on so equipped models or trigger button (2–Fig. H34) on 298XP

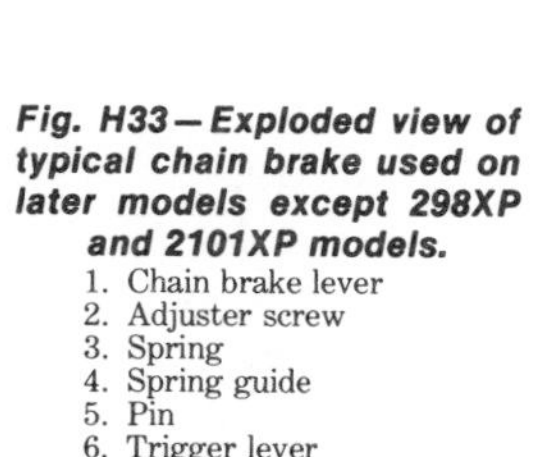

Fig. H33—Exploded view of typical chain brake used on later models except 298XP and 2101XP models.

1. Chain brake lever
2. Adjuster screw
3. Spring
4. Spring guide
5. Pin
6. Trigger lever
7. Side plates
8. Spring
9. Pin
10. Side cover
11. Spring
12. Brake rod & band
13. Trigger arm
14. Front handle

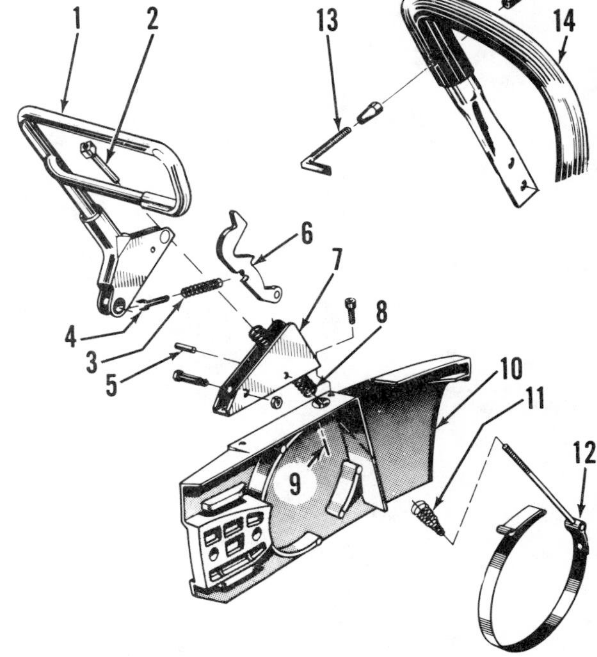

and 2101XP models resulting in automatic activation of brake mechanism.

To adjust chain brake shown in Fig. H33, pull back brake lever and be sure mechanism is cocked. Turn adjusting screw (2) in until chain cannot be pulled around bar then turn screw out approximately four turns. If screw has a square head, be sure screw head does not rest on brake lever side plates. Chain should rotate freely around bar. Check brake band tension adjustment by starting saw and running at wide open throttle, then manually engage chain brake. Chain should stop rotating immediately. Adjust gap between trigger lever (6) and trigger arm (13) so chain brake will automatically activate when a 12.4 N (2.8-3.4 lbs.) force is applied on guide bar tip. A suitable spring balance should be used for testing and adjustment.

On Models 298XP and 2101XP, be sure spring retaining nut (4–Fig. H34) is tight against its seat. Gap between trigger button (2) and front handle should be adjusted so chain brake will automatically activate when a 12.4-15.1 N (2.8-3.4 lbs.) force is applied on guide bar tip. A suitable spring balance should be used for testing and adjustment.

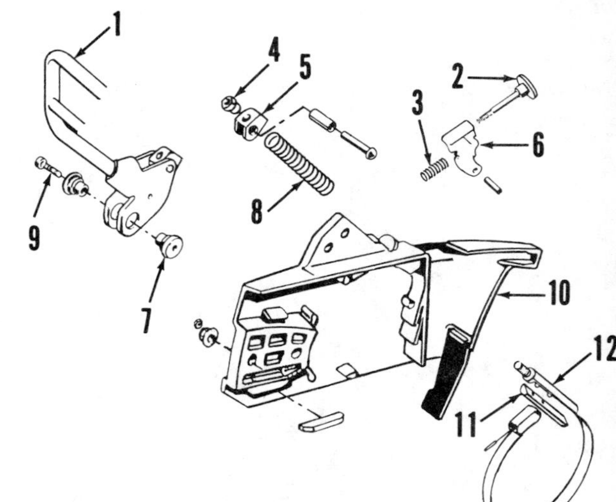

Fig. H34—Exploded view of chain brake assembly used on Models 298XP and 2101XP.

1. Chain brake lever
2. Trigger button
3. Spring
4. Nut
5. Latch
6. Trigger lever
7. Trunnion
8. Spring
9. Allen screw
10. Housing
11. Guide
12. Brake band

HUSQVARNA

Model	Bore mm (in.)	Stroke mm (in.)	Displacement cc (cu. in.)	Drive Type
61, 61 CB, 61 Rancher, 162 SE, 162 SG	48.0 (1.89)	34.0 (1.34)	61.5 (3.75)	Direct
66, 266, 266 CB, 266 SG, 266 XP, 268, 268 XP	50.0 (1.97)	34.0 (1.34)	66.7 (4.1)	Direct
272 XP, 272 XPG	52 (2.05)	34.0 (1.34)	72 (4.4)	Direct

MAINTENANCE

SPARK PLUG. Recommended spark plug is Bosch WS7F or Champion RCJ7Y. Electrode gap should be 0.5 mm (0.020 in.).

CARBURETOR. A Tillotson Model HS diaphragm carburetor is used on all models except Model 61, which may be equipped with a Tillotson HS or a Walbro WS carburetor. Refer to Tillotson or Walbro section of CARBURETOR SERVICE section for carburetor overhaul and exploded views.

On 268XP and 272XP models, initial adjustment of low- and high-speed mixture needles is one turn open. On all other models, initial adjustment of low-speed mixture needle is one turn open and high-speed mixture needle is 3/4 turn open. On all models, make final adjustment with engine warm and running.

Turn low-speed mixture needle (L-Fig. H40) clockwise to obtain highest idle speed, then turn screw 1/4 turn counterclockwise. Engine should accelerate cleanly without hesitation. If engine stumbles or seems sluggish when accelerating, adjust idle mixture screw until engine accelerates without hesitation.

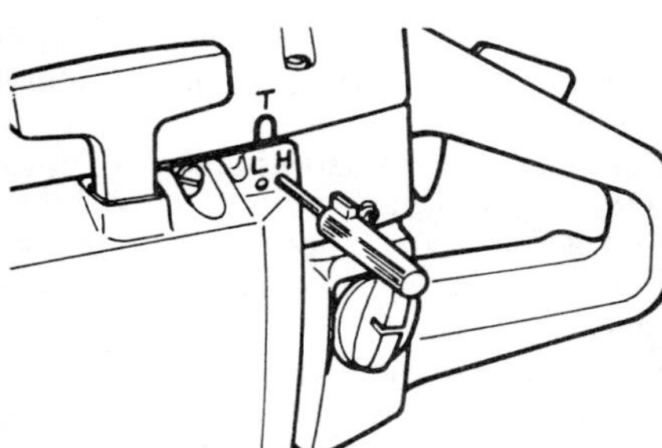

Fig. H40—View showing location of carburetor adjusting points typical of all models. Idle speed screw is at (T), idle mixture screw is at (L) and high speed mixture screw is at (H).

Adjust high-speed mixture needle (H) to obtain optimum performance under cutting load. Make certain engine no-load speed (bar and chain installed) does not exceed 12,000 rpm on Models 61, 66 and 162, or 12,500 rpm on Models 266, 268 and 272.

Do not operate saw with high-speed mixture too lean because engine damage may result from lack of lubrication and overheating.

Adjust idle speed stop screw (T) so engine idles just below clutch engagement speed.

IGNITION. All models are equipped with an electronic breakerless ignition system. Ignition timing is not adjustable and no periodic maintenance is required. Air gap between ignition coil and flywheel should be 0.30 mm (0.012 in.).

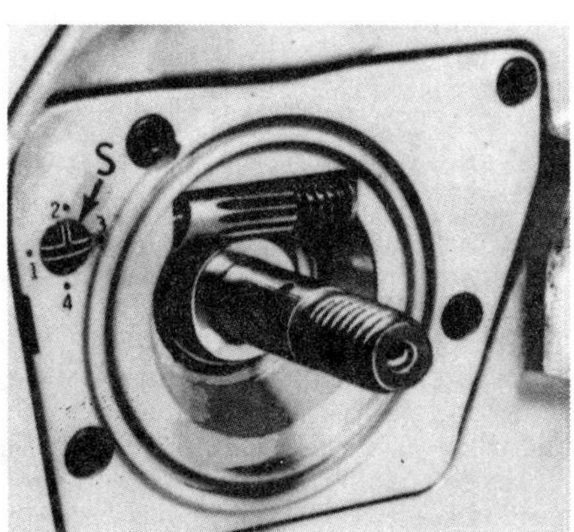

Fig. H41—View showing location of oil pump adjusting screw (S). Adjusting screw shown is set at position 2.

LUBRICATION. The engine is lubricated by mixing oil with the fuel. Recommended fuel:oil ratio is 50:1 when using Husqvarna Two-Stroke Oil. If Husqvarna Two-Stroke Oil is not available, use good quality oil designed for use in air-cooled two-stroke engines mixed at 25:1 ratio.

All models are equipped with an adjustable automatic chain oil pump. Adjustment is possible after clutch removal. Turn adjusting screw (S-Fig. H41) for desired oil output; position number "1" is minimum output, position number "4" is maximum output.

REPAIRS

CRANKCASE PRESSURE TEST. An improperly sealed crankcase can cause the engine to be hard to start, run rough, have low power and overheat. Refer to ENGINE SERVICE section of this manual for crankcase pressure test procedure. If crankcase leakage is indicated, pressurize crankcase and use a soap and water solution to check gaskets, seals, pulse line and castings for leakage.

TIGHTENING TORQUE. Refer to the following table when tightening fasteners.

Carburetor-
61, 66, 162 . . . . 4-6 N·m (35-53 in.-lbs.)
266, 268, 272 . . . . 2-3 N·m (18-26 in.-lbs.)
Crankcase screws . . . . 7-9 N·m (62-79 in.-lbs.)
Cylinder screws . . . . 8-10 N·m (71-88 in.-lbs.)
Clutch hub . . . . 30-40 N·m (22-29 ft.-lbs.)
Flywheel nut . . . . 30-40 N·m (22-29 ft.-lbs.)

Muffler . . . . .7-8 N•m (62-70 in.-lbs.)
Oil pump. . . . . .3-4 N•m (26-35 in.-lbs.)
Spark plug . . . . 20 N•m (15 ft.-lbs.)
4 mm screw . . . . 4.5-5.5 N•m (40-50 in.-lbs.)
5 mm screw . . . . 5.5-6.8 N•m (50-60 in.-lbs.)
6 mm screw. . . . . 10-11.8 N•m (90-105 in.-lbs.)
8 mm screw . . . . 28.2-32.8 N•m (250-290 in.-lbs.)
10 mm screw . . . . 36.7-42.4 N•m (325-375 in.-lbs.)

PISTON, PIN, RINGS AND CYLINDER. To disassemble, remove cylinder cover and air filter assembly. Disconnect carburetor linkage and fuel line. Remove screws attaching muffler bracket to crankcase. Remove cylinder mounting screws and lift cylinder with muffler and carburetor from crankcase. Remove piston pin retaining rings (5-Fig. H42) and push piston pin out of piston. Remove carburetor and muffler from cylinder.

Clean carbon from cylinder ports and piston. Inspect cylinder and piston for excessive wear or damage. Slight scuffing of piston and cylinder wall may be polished out using fine emery cloth.

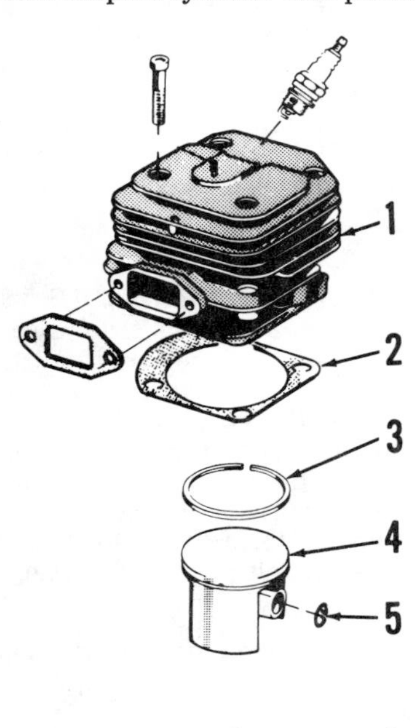

Fig. H42—Exploded view of engine components typical of all models.

1. Cylinder
2. Gasket
3. Piston ring
4. Piston
5. Pin retainer
6. Bearing
7. Crankshaft & connecting rod assy.
8. Roller bearing

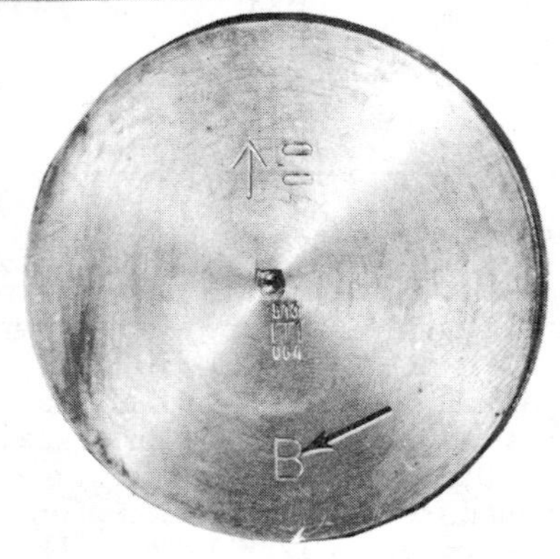

Fig. H43—Arrows showing location of piston and cylinder letter grades. Be sure arrow stamped in piston crown points toward exhaust port when installing piston. Grade "B" is shown.

On Models 266XP, 268XP and 272XP, new cylinder is available only with a fitted piston, but new piston is available separately for installation in used cylinder. On all other models, piston and cylinder are graded with a letter according to size. Piston is marked on piston crown while cylinder is marked on top as shown in Fig. H43. Letter sizes range from "A" to "C," with "A" being the smallest size. Piston cylinder grades should match, although one size larger piston may be installed in a used cylinder. For instance, a piston graded "C" may be used in a cylinder graded "B."

Piston must be installed with arrow on piston crown pointing toward exhaust port. Refer to Fig. H43. A locating pin is present in piston ring groove to prevent piston ring rotation. Be sure ring end gap is positioned around the locating pin when installing cylinder. Lubricate roller bearing (8-Fig. H42) and piston with oil before installing cylinder. Tighten cylinder mounting screws evenly to 8-10 N•m (71-88 in.-lbs.).

CRANKSHAFT, CONNECTING ROD AND CRANKCASE. To disassemble, remove chain and guide bar, cylinder cover, air filter assembly, starter assembly and air baffle. Remove spark plug and install a piston stop in spark plug hole. Remove flywheel mounting nut (right-hand threads) and starter pawls. Use suitable puller to remove flywheel.

Remove ignition module and generator coil if so equipped. Remove clutch assembly (left-hand threads) and oil pump. Remove cylinder mounting screws and pull cylinder off piston. Separate piston from connecting rod. Separate tank and handle assembly from crankcase.

Remove crankcase mounting screws and use Husqvarna tool 502 51 61-01, or other suitable puller tool, to separate crankcase halves and press crankshaft out of main bearings. It will be necessary to heat crankcase halves to remove and install main bearings. Care should be taken not to damage mating surfaces of crankcase halves.

Crankshaft and connecting rod are a unit assembly. Check rotation of connecting rod around crankpin and renew crankshaft unit if roughness or other damage is found. The connecting rod should not have any radial clearance (up and down play) on the crankpin.

To reassemble, reverse the disassembly procedure. Heat crankcase halves and position tool 502 50 30-04 against outside face of crankcase half, then press main bearing in from inside crankcase until bearing bottoms against tool. Be sure crankshaft is snug against the main bearings and centered in crankcase. Tighten crankcase screws evenly, starting with screws closest to crankshaft, to 7-9 N•m (62-79 in.-lbs.).

CLUTCH. All models are equipped with a three-shoe centrifugal clutch (Fig. H44), which is accessible after removing chain brake assembly and chain guide bar. Clutch hub has left-hand threads (turn clockwise to remove).

Inspect clutch shoes (1), drum (2) and bearing (3) for excessive wear or damage due to overheating. Renew clutch shoes if there is less than 1 mm (0.039 in.) of clutch material remaining at the most worn section. Shoes must be renewed as a set. Inspect chain sprocket teeth for excessive wear and renew as necessary.

Lubricate the needle bearing with grease. Tighten clutch hub to 30-40 N•m (22-29 ft.-lbs.).

OIL PUMP. All models are equipped with an automatic oil pump, which is

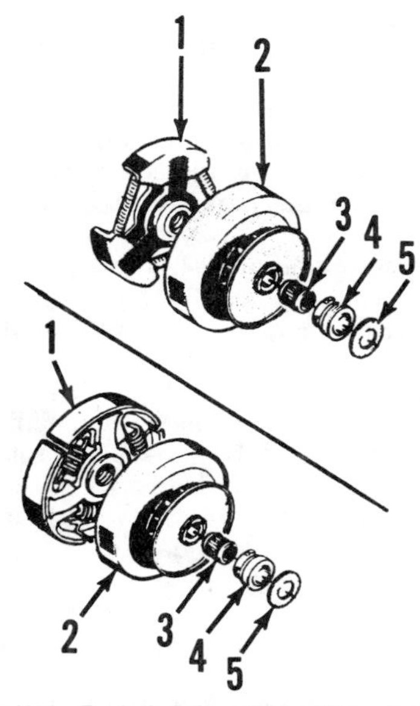

Fig. H44—Exploded view of two different styles of clutch assemblies. Notches on back of clutch drum (2) engage dogs on oil pump drive gear (4).

1. Hub & shoes
2. Clutch drum
3. Bearing
4. Oil pump drive gear
5. Washer

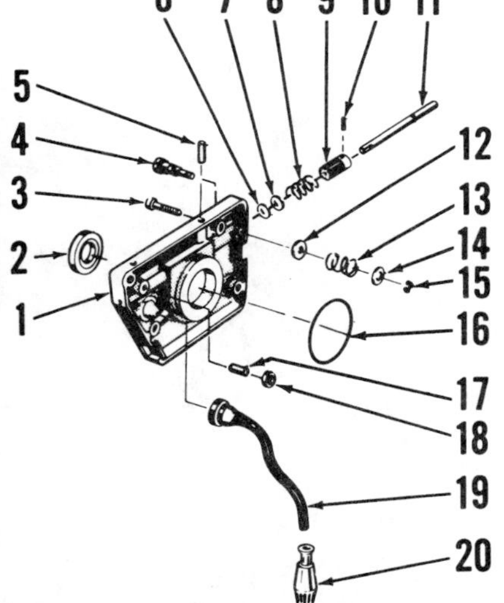

Fig. H45—Exploded view of automatic oil pump. When assembling, note location of brass and steel washers (6 and 7).

1. Pump housing
2. Oil seal
3. Screw
4. Adjusting screw
5. Pin
6. Brass washer
7. Steel washer
8. Spring
9. Driven gear
10. Screw
11. Plunger
12. Washer
13. Spring
14. Washer
15. "E" ring
16. "O" ring
17. Oil tube
18. Seal
19. Oil hose
20. Oil pickup

driven by the clutch drum. Notches on the back of the clutch drum engage dogs on oil pump drive gear (4—Fig. H44) which rides on the crankshaft. The oil pump drive gear engages driven gear (9–Fig. H45) which is secured to plunger (11) by set screw (10). Oil pump output is adjusted by turning screw (4).

To remove oil pump, first remove guide bar, clutch and oil pump mounting screws. Using two screwdrivers, insert blade tips into notches provided in pump housing and carefully withdraw oil pump.

To disassemble for cleaning and inspection, remove "E" ring (15), washers (12 and 14) and spring (13). Remove adjusting screw (4). Remove set screw (10) and withdraw plunger (11), driven gear (9), spring (8) and washers (6 and 7).

Lubricate parts with oil during assembly. Be sure steel washer (7) is closest to spring (8). Install new oil seal (2) and "O" ring (16).

To reinstall, it is recommended that sleeve, tool number 50 25 053-01, be placed over crankshaft end to prevent damage to oil seal (2). Tighten pump mounting screws to 3-4 N•m (27-35 in.-lbs.).

Fig. H46—Exploded view of rewind starter.

1. Spring
2. Washer
3. Pawl
4. Pin
5. Rope pulley
6. Rope guide
7. Rewind spring
8. Starter housing
9. Screw

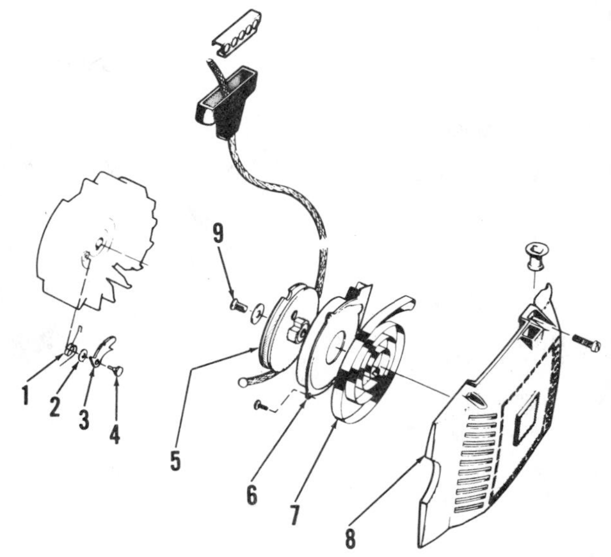

REWIND STARTER. To disassemble rewind starter, remove starter housing from saw. Pull starter rope and hold rope pulley (5–Fig. H46) with notch in pulley adjacent to rope outlet. Pull rope back through outlet so it engages notch in pulley and allow pulley to slowly unwind. Unscrew pulley retaining screw (9) and carefully remove rope pulley. If rewind spring (7) must be removed, care should be taken not to allow spring to uncoil uncontrolled.

Install rewind spring in starter housing with spring coiled in clockwise direction from outer spring end. Wrap starter rope around rope pulley in a clockwise direction as viewed with pulley in starter housing. Turn rope pulley two turns clockwise before passing rope through rope outlet to place tension on rewind spring. Spring tension is correct if rope pulley can be rotated approximately 1/4 turn further when rope is at its greatest length.

When installing starter assembly on saw, make sure starter pulley properly engages pawls on flywheel before tightening retaining cap screws.

CHAIN BRAKE. Some models may be equipped with a chain brake system designed to stop chain movement should kickback occur. Several types of chain brake systems have been used. Refer to Fig. H47, Fig. H48 and Fig. H48A for exploded views of different styles of brake mechanisms used.

The chain brake is activated either by the operator's hand striking the hand guard (1) or by sufficient force being applied to the guide bar tip during kickback to cause the front handle to contact trigger lever (6–Fig. H47) on early models, trigger button (9–Fig. H48) or trigger assembly (4–Fig. H48A) on later models, resulting in automatic activation of brake mechanism.

To adjust chain brake on early models, pull back brake lever and be sure mechanism is cocked. Turn adjusting screw (2–Fig. H47) in until chain cannot be pulled around bar, then turn screw out approximately four turns. If screw has a square head, be sure screw head does not rest on hand guard side plates. Chain should rotate freely around bar.

Check brake band tension adjustment by starting saw running at wide open throttle, then manually engage chain brake. Chain should stop rotating immediately.

Adjust gap between trigger lever (6–Fig. H47) and trigger arm (10) so chain brake will automatically activate when a 6.2-9.8 N (1.4-2.2 lbs.) force is applied on guide bar tip. A suitable

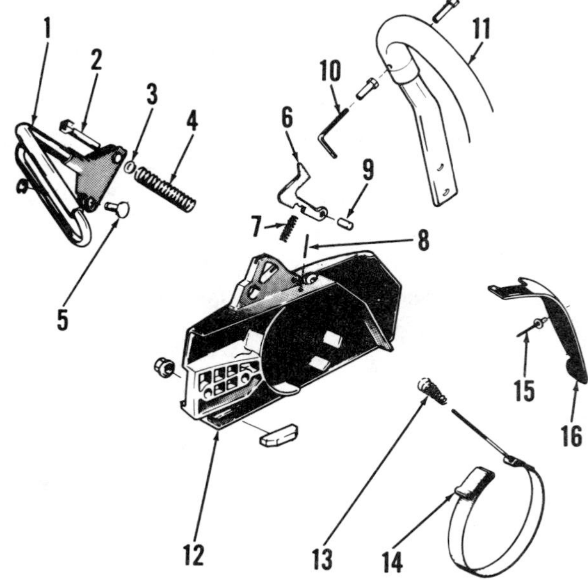

Fig. H47—Exploded view of early model chain brake.

1. Chain brake lever
2. Adjusting screw
3. Washer
4. Spring
5. Pin
6. Trigger lever
7. Spring
8. Pin
9. Pin
10. Trigger arm
11. Front handle
12. Side cover
13. Spring
14. Brake rod & band
15. Rivet
16. Chain guard

spring balance should be used for testing and adjustment.

To adjust chain brake on later models equipped with brake mechanism shown in Fig. H48, first pull back hand guard and be sure mechanism is cocked, then determine if brake system has an adjustable brake band as shown in inset of Fig. H48.

If brake band is adjustable, follow early model brake band adjustment procedures as outlined in previous paragraph. On models without adjustable brake band, be sure spring retaining nut (4) is tight against its seat.

On all models, gap between trigger button (9) and front handle should be adjusted so chain brake will automatically activate when a 6.2-9.8 N (1.4-2.2 lbs.) force is applied on guide bar tip. A suitable spring balance should be used for testing and adjustment.

No adjustment is required for chain brake shown in Fig. H48A.

HANDLE HEATER. Models 162SG, 266SG and 272XPG are equipped with a front and rear handle heating system. A generator coil (4-Fig. H49) located

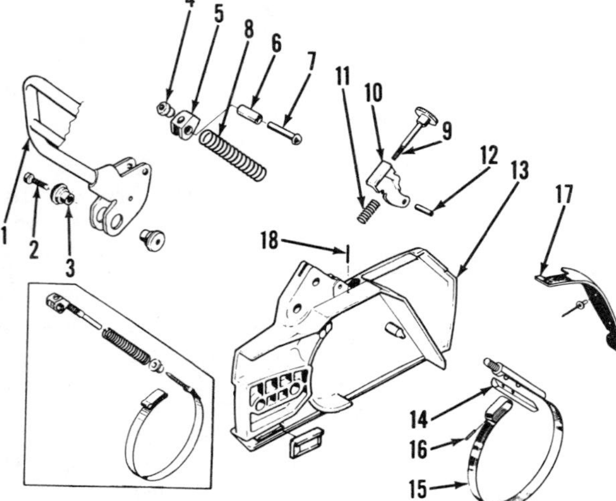

Fig. H48—Exploded view of late style chain brake used on some models. Some models may have adjustable type brake band as shown in inset.

1. Hand guard
2. Cap screw
3. Trunnion
4. Nut
5. Latch
6. Bushing
7. Rivet
8. Spring
9. Trigger button
10. Trigger lever
11. Spring
12. Pin
13. Housing
14. Guide
15. Brake band
16. Pin
17. Chain guard
18. Pin

Fig. H48A—Exploded view of latest style chain brake mechanism used on some models.

1. Hand guard
2. Retainer
3. Pin
4. Trigger assy.
5. Brake spring
6. Brake band
7. Pin
8. Pin
9. Spring
10. Pivot sleeves
11. Sawdust guard
12. Brake housing
13. Chain tension adjusting bolt
14. Brake cover

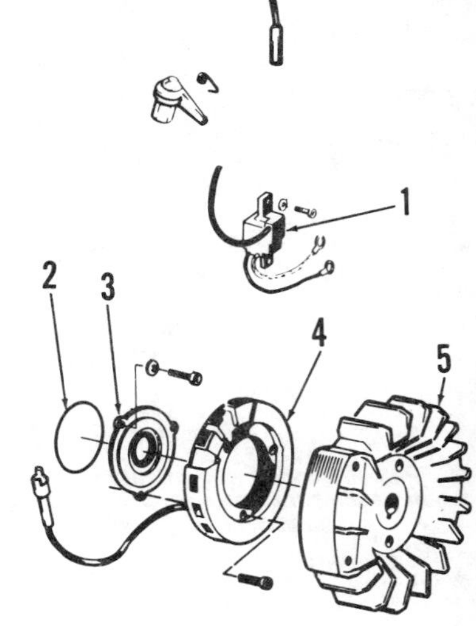

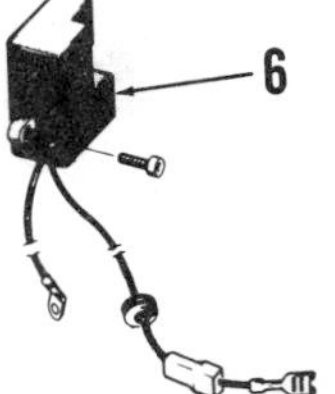

Fig. H49—Exploded view of ignition system. Generator coil (4) for heated handles is used on Models 162SG and 266SG.

1. Ignition coil
2. "O" ring
3. Seal & retainer
4. Generator coil
5. Flywheel
6. Ignition module

Illustrations courtesy Husqvarna Forest & Garden Co.

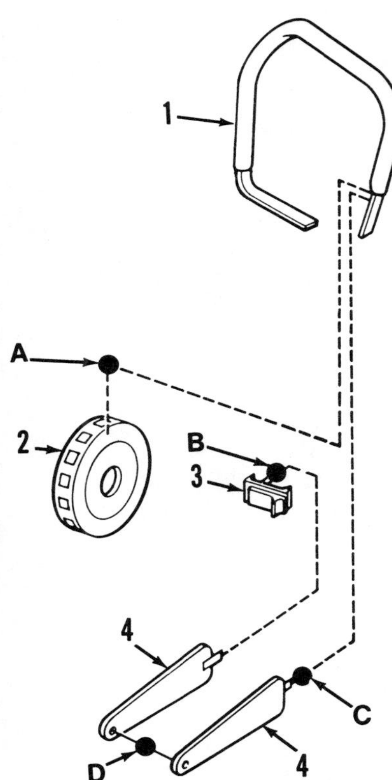

Fig. H50—Schematic drawing of handle heating system used on some models. Refer to text for testing procedures.

1. Front handle element
2. Generator
3. Switch
4. Rear handle elements

underneath the flywheel produces approximately 20 volts at 8500 rpm to provide an electrical current to heating coils in front and rear handles.

On some models, a thermostat that closes at approximately 10 degrees C (50 degrees F) regulates the heating system. On other models, a switch located next to the rear handle controls the heating system.

An ohmmeter may be used to check resistance of heating elements. To test rear handle elements (4-Fig. H50), connect ohmmeter test leads between points "D" and "B," and "D" and "C." Meter reading should be 0.7-0.9 ohms for each element.

To test both rear and front handle elements, connect ohmmeter test leads between points "A" and "B." Meter reading should be 5.1-5.7 ohms. If readings are significantly higher or lower, check for corroded connections or broken wires.

To check generator output, connect voltmeter between point "A" and crankcase (ground). With heater switch turned "ON" and saw running at about 10,000 rpm, meter reading should be about 20 volts. If there is low or no voltage, check generator windings for open or short circuit, loss of magnetism or faulty wiring.

HUSQVARNA

Model	Bore mm (in.)	Stroke mm (in.)	Displacement cc (cu. in.)	Drive Type
133 CB, 133 SE, 133 SG	38.0 (1.49)	30.0 (1.18)	34.0 (2.1)	Direct
238 SE, 238 SG	40.0 (1.575)	30.0 (1.18)	37.4 (2.3)	Direct
42, 242, 242 G, 242 XP, 242 XPG	42.0 (1.65)	30.0 (1.18)	42.0 (2.5)	Direct
246	44.0 (1.73)	30.0 (1.18)	46.0 (2.8)	Direct
181, 181 SE, 181 SG, 281 XP, 281 XPG	52.0 (2.05)	38.0 (1.49)	80.7 (4.9)	Direct
288 XP, 288 XPG	54.0 (2.12)	38.0 (1.49)	88.0 (5.3)	Direct

MAINTENANCE

SPARK PLUG. Recommended spark plug for Models 42, 133SE, 133SG, 181SE, 181SG, 238SE, 238SG and 246 is Champion CJ7Y or resistor type Champion RCJ7Y. Recommended spark plug for all other models is Champion CJ8Y. Spark plug electrode gap should be 0.5 mm (0.020 in.) on all models.

CARBURETOR. Models 181SE, 281XP, 281XPG, 288XP and 288XPG are equipped with a Tillotson HS diaphragm type carburetor. All other models are equipped with a Walbro HDA carburetor. Refer to CARBURETOR SERVICE section for overhaul information and exploded views of Tillotson HS and Walbro HDA carburetors.

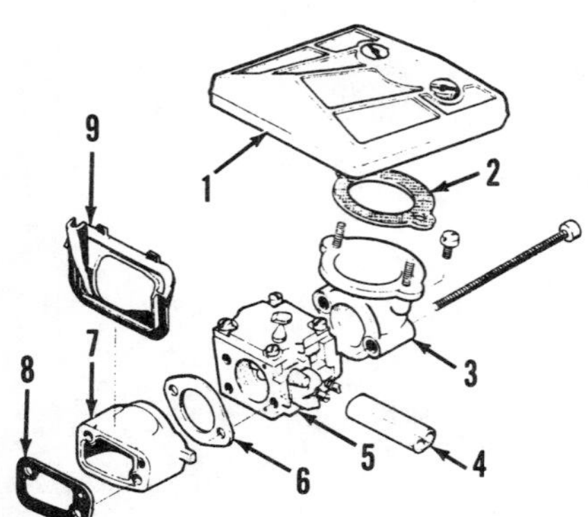

Fig. H51—Exploded view of air intake components typical of all models.

1. Air filter
2. Gasket
3. Intake elbow
4. Adjustment guide
5. Carburetor
6. Gasket
7. Intake adapter
8. Gasket
9. Plate

Refer to Fig. H51 for exploded view of air intake components typical of all models. Exploded view of fuel tank and throttle control is shown in Fig. H52.

On all models, initial adjustment of both low-speed and high-speed mixture needles is one turn open from a lightly seated position. Make final adjustment with engine warm and running.

Adjust the low-speed mixture needle to obtain highest idle speed, then turn screw 1/4 turn counterclockwise. Engine should accelerate cleanly without hesitation. If engine stumbles or seems sluggish when accelerating, adjust low-speed mixture needle until engine accelerates without hesitation.

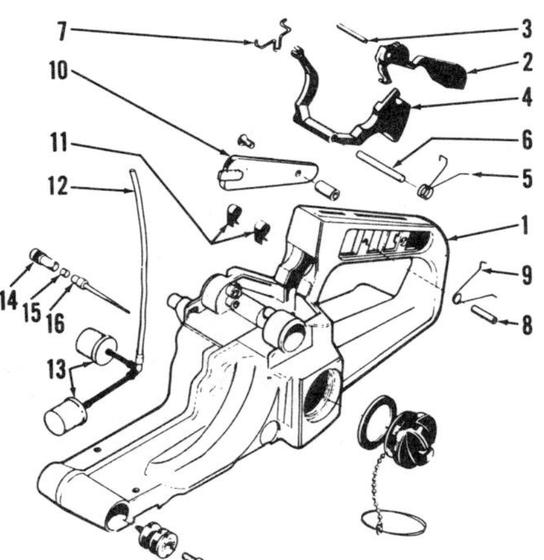

Fig. H52—Exploded view of fuel tank/rear handle assembly used on 133SE models. Other models are similar.

1. Fuel tank/rear handle
2. Throttle trigger lock
3. Pin
4. Throttle trigger
5. Spring
6. Pin
7. Throttle rod
8. Pin
9. Spring
10. Cover
11. Retainer
12. Hose
13. Fuel filter
14. Vent retainer
15. Filter
16. Vent orifice

Adjust high-speed mixture needle to obtain optimum performance under cutting load. Maximum no-load speed (with bar and chain installed) is 12,500 rpm for 181, 281 and 288 models; 14,500 rpm for 42 model; 15,500 for 242 models; 15,000 rpm for other models.

Do not adjust high-speed mixture too lean because the engine may be damaged due to lack of lubrication and overheating.

Adjust idle speed stop screw so engine idles just below clutch engagement speed.

IGNITION. All models are equipped with a breakerless electronic ignition system. Ignition timing is not adjustable. Air gap between ignition module core (2-Fig. H53) and flywheel magnets should be 0.3 mm (0.012 in.). Adjust air gap by loosening ignition module attaching screws, setting correct clearance then tightening the attaching screws.

LUBRICATION. The engine is lubricated by mixing oil with the fuel. Recommended oil is Husqvarna Two-Stroke Oil mixed at a ratio of 50:1. If Husqvarna Two-Stroke Oil is not available, good quality oil designed for two-stroke engines may be used when mixed at a 25:1 ratio. Use a separate container when mixing the oil and gas.

Illustrations courtesy Husqvarna Forest & Garden Co.

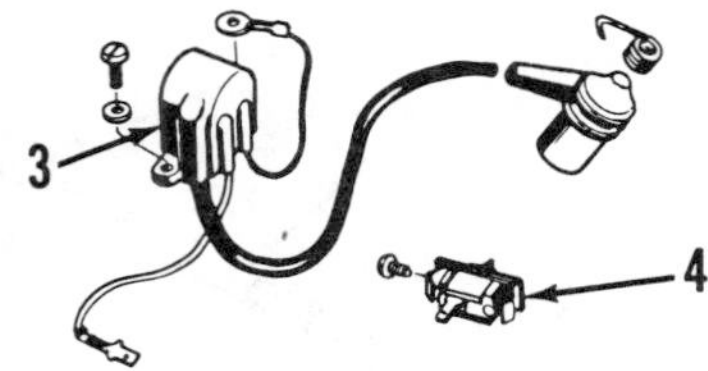

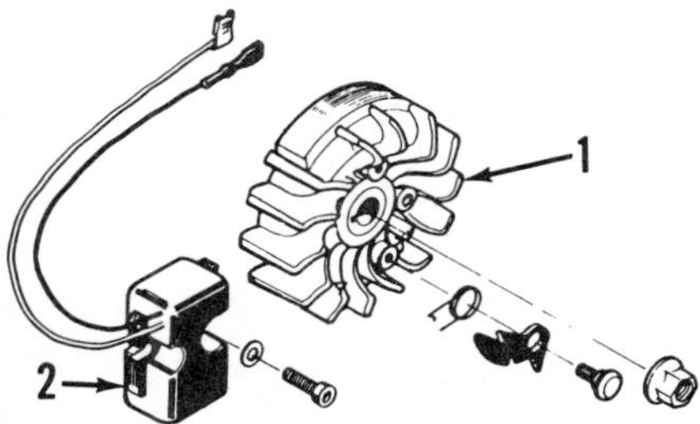

Fig. H53—Exploded view of ignition system typical of all models.

1. Flywheel
2. Module
3. Coil
4. Ignition switch

Fig. H55—Exploded view of 133SE and 133SG engine assembly. Other models are similar.

1. Cylinder
2. Gasket
3. Piston ring
4. Piston
5. Piston pin retainer
6. Crankshaft & connecting rod assy.
7. Needle bearing
8. Ball bearing
9. Left crankcase half
10. Seal
11. Pin
12. Ball bearing
13. Seal
14. Gasket
15. Guide dowel
16. Right crankcase half

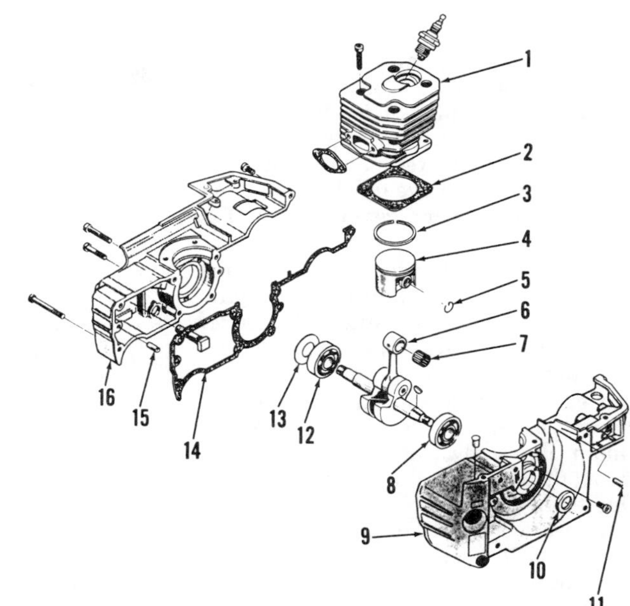

Fig. H54—View showing oil pump adjusting screw (11) on 181SE, 181SG, 281XP, 281XPG, 288XP and 288XPG models.

Fig. H56—Arrows show location of letter grades on a typical piston and cylinder. Be sure arrow stamped in piston crown points toward exhaust port when installing piston.

All models are equipped with an automatic chain oiling system. Good quality chain oil is recommended, although clean automotive oil may also be used. If automotive type oil is used, oil viscosity should be chosen according to ambient temperature.

Oil pump output on 181SE, 181SG, 281XP, 281XPG, 288XP and 288XPG models is adjustable; remove clutch to obtain access to adjusting screw. Adjust oil output by turning screw (11-Fig. H54). Position "1" is minimum and position "4" is maximum. Oil pump output on all other models is not adjustable.

REPAIRS

CRANKCASE PRESSURE TEST. An improperly sealed crankcase can cause the engine to be hard to start, run rough, have low power and overheat. Refer to ENGINE SERVICE section of this manual for crankcase pressure test procedure. If crankcase leakage is indicated, pressurize crankcase and use a soap and water solution to check gaskets, seals, pulse line and castings for leakage.

CYLINDER, PISTON, RINGS AND PIN. To disassemble, remove cylinder cover and air filter assembly. Disconnect carburetor linkage and fuel line. Remove screws attaching muffler bracket to crankcase. Remove cylinder mounting screws and lift cylinder with muffler and carburetor from crankcase.

Remove piston pin retaining ring (5-Fig. H55) and push piston pin out of piston. Remove carburetor and muffler from cylinder.

Cylinder has a chrome bore that should be inspected for flaking, cracking or other damage to chrome surface. Inspect piston and discard if excessive wear or damage is evident. New cylinder is available only with fitted piston, however, a new piston is available for installation in a used cylinder.

On some models, piston and cylinder are graded with a letter according to size. Piston is marked on piston crown and cylinder is marked on top as shown in Fig. H56. On Models 133SE, 133SG, 181SE and 181SG, letter sizes range from "A" to "C" with "A" being the smallest size. On early Models 281XP, 281XPG, 288XP and 288XPG, letter sizes range from "A" to "B" with "A" being the smallest size. On later models, piston and cylinder are available in one class size. The early class "A" and "B" pistons are interchangeable with the single class late cylinder.

A locating pin is present in piston ring groove to prevent piston ring rotation. Be sure ring end gap is positioned around locating pin when installing cylinder. Arrow on piston crown (Fig. H56) must point toward exhaust port when installing piston. Be sure the piston pin retainers are seated snugly in piston boss.

CRANKSHAFT, CONNECTING ROD AND CRANKCASE. To disassemble, remove chain and guide bar, cylinder cover, air filter assembly, starter assembly and air baffle. Remove spark plug and install a piston stop in spark plug hole. Remove flywheel mounting nut (right-hand threads) and starter pawls. Use suitable puller to remove flywheel. Remove ignition module and generator coil if so equipped.

Remove clutch assembly (left-hand threads) and oil pump. Remove cylinder mounting screws and pull cylinder off piston. Separate piston from connecting rod.

Separate tank and handle assembly from crankcase. Remove crankcase mounting screws and use Husqvarna tool 502 51 61-01, or other suitable puller tool, to separate crankcase halves and press crankshaft out of main bearings. It will be necessary to heat crankcase halves to remove and install main bearings. Care should be taken not to damage mating surfaces of crankcase halves.

Crankshaft and connecting rod are a unit assembly. Check rotation of connecting rod around crankpin and renew crankshaft unit if roughness or other damage is found. The connecting rod should not have any radial clearance (up and down play) on the crankpin.

To reassemble, reverse the disassembly procedure. Heat crankcase halves and position tool 502 50 30-04 against outside face of crankcase half, then press main bearing in from inside crankcase until bearing bottoms against tool. Be sure crankshaft is snug against the main bearings and centered in crankcase. Tighten crankcase screws evenly, starting with screws closest to crankshaft.

CLUTCH. Models 133SE, 133SG, 238SE, 238SG, early 42, 242, 242G and early 242XP and 242XPG are equipped with the two-shoe centrifugal clutch shown in Fig. H57. Models late 42, 181SE, 181SG, 281XP, 281XPG, 288XP, 288XPG and late 242XP, 242XPG and 246 are equipped with the three-shoe centrifugal clutch shown in Fig. H58. On all models, clutch hub (1) has left-hand threads (turn clockwise to remove). Inspect clutch shoes and drum for excessive wear or damage due to overheating. Inspect clutch drum bearing and crankshaft for wear or damage.

On 181SE, 181SG, 281XP, 281XPG and 288XP models, the oil pump is driven by the clutch drum. Be sure notches on rear of clutch drum mesh with dogs of oil pump drive gear when installing clutch assembly.

OIL PUMP. Models 133SE, 238SE, 238SG, 42, 242, 242G, 242XP, 242XPG

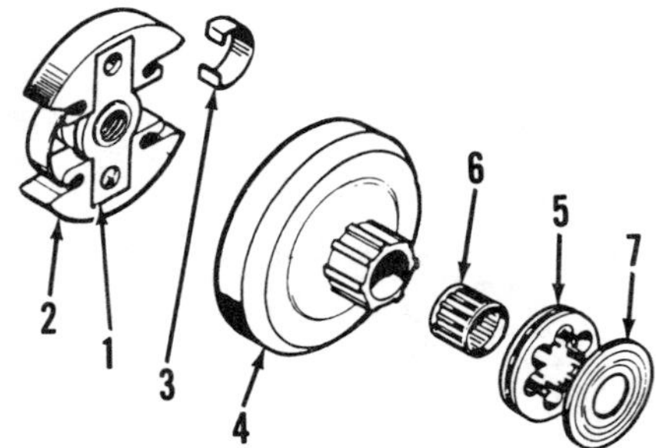

Fig. H57—Exploded view of two-shoe clutch assembly used on 133SE, 133SG, 238SE, 238SG, early 42, 242, 242G, early 242XP and early 242XPG models.

1. Hub
2. Shoe
3. Spring
4. Drum
5. Sprocket
6. Needle bearing
7. Washer

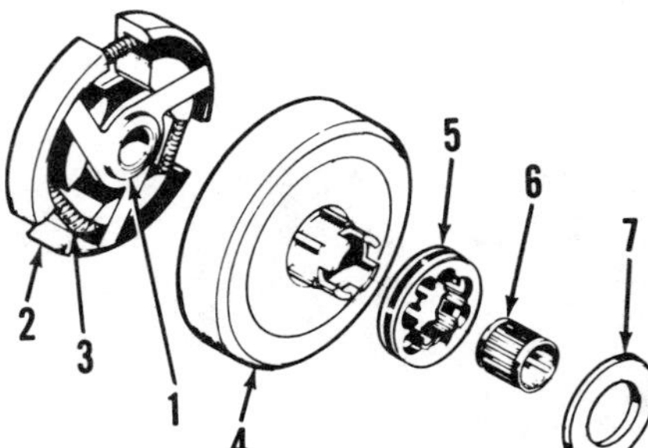

Fig. H58—Exploded view of three-shoe clutch assembly used on late 42, 181SE, 181SG, 281XP, 281XPG, 288XP, 288XPG, late 242XP, late 242XPG and 246 models.

1. Hub
2. Shoe
3. Spring
4. Drum
5. Sprocket
6. Needle bearing
7. Washer

and 246 are equipped with the nonadjustable automatic oil pump shown in Fig. H59. On these models, the oil pump is driven by worm gear (8) on crankshaft. Oil is then pumped by the rotating plunger (3) as it reciprocates due to the end of the cam screw (16) riding in operating groove of plunger.

Oil filter screen (17) is accessible after removing oil pump assembly. Oil pump may be disassembled for cleaning or renewal of individual components after removing cam screw (16) and withdrawing plunger (3). Make certain end of cam screw (16) properly engages groove in plunger (3) when reassembling pump.

Models 181SE, 181SG, 281XP, 281XPG, 288XP and 288XPG are equipped with the adjustable automatic oil pump shown in Fig. H60.

On these models, oil pump is driven by clutch drum. Notches on back of clutch drum engage dogs on oil pump drive gear (8-Fig. H60) which rides on the crankshaft. Oil is then pumped as

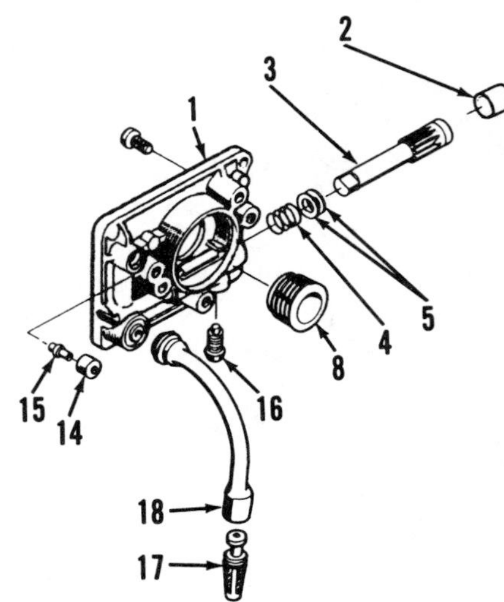

Fig. H59—Exploded view of automatic chain oiler pump used on 133SE, 133SG, 238SE, 238SG, 42, 242, 242G, 242XP, 242XPG and 246 models.

1. Pump housing
2. Plug
3. Plunger
4. Spring
5. Washers
8. Worm gear
14. Seal
15. Tube
16. Cam screw
17. Filter screen
18. Inlet hose

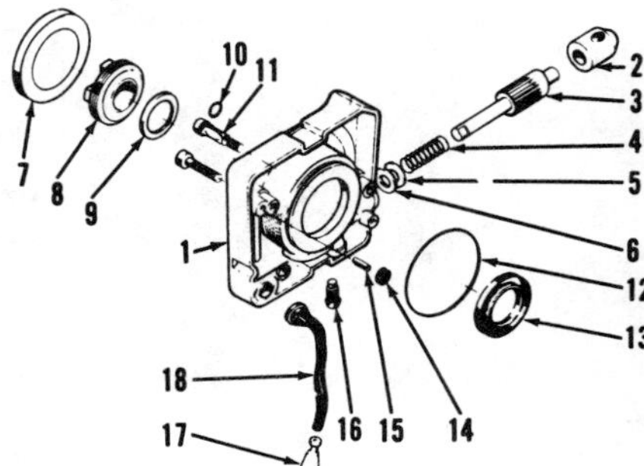

Fig. H60—Exploded view of adjustable oil pump used on 181SE, 181SG, 281XP, 281XPG, 288XP and 288XPG models.

1. Pump housing
2. Plug
3. Plunger
4. Spring
5. Steel washer
6. Brass washer
7. Sleeve
8. Drive gear
9. Washer
10. "O" ring
11. Adjusting screw
12. "O" ring
13. Seal
14. Seal
15. Tube
16. Cam screw
17. Filter screen
18. Inlet hose

drive gear rotates the plunger (3). Oil pump output is adjusted by turning screw (11). Adjustment is possible after clutch is removed. Turn adjusting screw for desired output; position "1" is minimum and position "4" is maximum.

Oil filter screen (17) is accessible after removing oil pump assembly and withdrawing hose (18) from crankcase. Oil pump may be disassembled for cleaning or renewal of individual components after removing cam screw (16), adjusting screw (11) and withdrawing plunger (3).

When reassembling pump, make certain steel washer (5) and brass washer

Illustrations courtesy Husqvarna Forest & Garden Co.

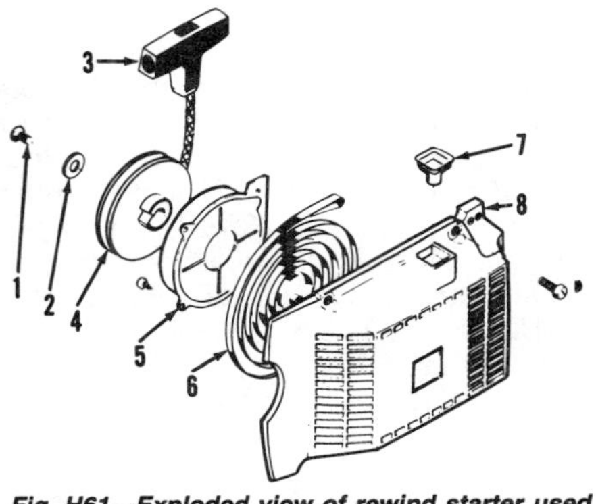

Fig. H61—Exploded view of rewind starter used on 181SE, 181SG, 281XP, 281XPG, 288XP and 288XPG models. Other models are similar.

1. Screw
2. Washer
3. Rope handle
4. Rope pulley
5. Spring retainer
6. Rewind spring
7. Rope guide
8. Starter housing

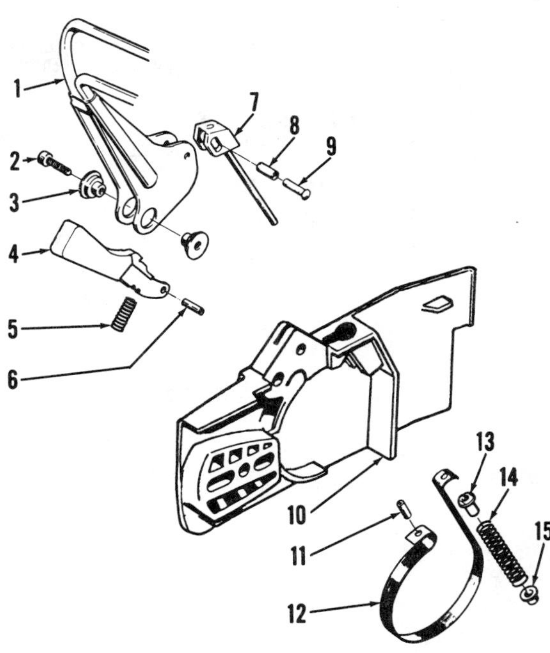

Fig. H62—Exploded view of chain brake assembly used on 133SE and 133SG models.

1. Chain brake lever
2. Allen screw
3. Trunnion
4. Trigger lever
5. Spring
6. Pin
7. Latch
8. Sleeve
9. Rivet
10. Brake housing
11. Pin
12. Brake band
13. Spring guide
14. Brake spring
15. Spring seat

(6) are installed as shown in exploded view. Sleeve (7) must be installed with concave side out. Outer edge of sleeve (7) should be flush with oil pump housing surface.

REWIND STARTER. To disassemble rewind starter, remove starter housing from saw. Pull starter rope and hold rope pulley (4-Fig. H61) with notch in pulley adjacent to rope outlet. Pull rope back through outlet so it engages notch in pulley and allow pulley to completely unwind.

Unscrew pulley retaining screw (1) and carefully remove rope pulley. If rewind spring (6) must be removed, care should be taken not to allow spring to uncoil uncontrolled.

Install rewind spring in starter housing with spring coiled in clockwise direction from outer spring end. Wrap starter rope around rope pulley in a clockwise direction as viewed with pulley in starter housing. Turn rope pulley two turns clockwise before passing rope through rope outlet to place tension on rewind spring. Spring tension is correct if rope pulley can be rotated approximately 1/4 turn further when rope is at its greatest length.

When installing starter assembly on saw, make sure starter pulley properly engages pawls on flywheel before tightening retaining cap screws.

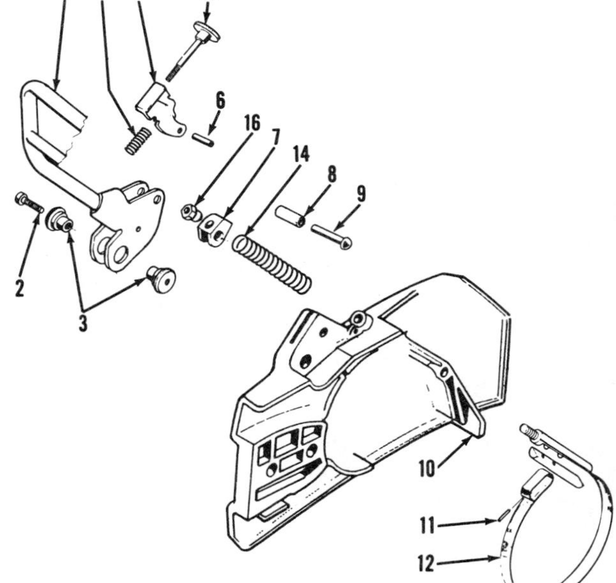

Fig. H63—Exploded view of chain brake assembly used on 181SE, 181SG, and some 281XP and 281XPG models.

1. Brake lever
2. Screw
3. Trunnion
4. Trigger lever
5. Spring
6. Pin
7. Latch
8. Sleeve
9. Rivet
10. Brake housing
11. Pin
12. Brake band
14. Brake spring
16. Nut
17. Trigger button

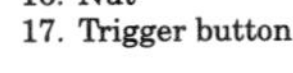

CHAIN BRAKE. All models are equipped with a chain brake system designed to stop chain movement should kickback occur.

Refer to Fig. H62 for chain brake system used on 133SE and 133SG models. Refer to Fig. H63 for chain brake system used on 181SE, 181SG, and some 281XP and 281XPG models. Refer to Fig. H64 for chain brake system used on Models 238SE, 238SG, 42, 242, 242G, 242XP, 242XPG, 246, 288XP, 288XPG, some 281XP and some 281XPG models.

On all models, chain brake is activated either by the operator's hand striking the chain brake lever (1) or by sufficient force being applied to the guide bar tip during kickback. Pull chain brake lever rearward to reset brake mechanism.

On 181SE, 181SG and some 281XP and 281XPG models, gap between trigger button (17-Fig. H63) and front handle should be adjusted so chain brake will automatically activate when a 7.6-11.1 N (1.7-2.5 lbs.) force is applied on guide bar tip. A suitable spring balance should be used for testing and adjustment. Turning the trigger button (17) counterclockwise reduces force required to activate brake.

On all other models, adjustment of brake mechanism is not required.

Illustrations courtesy Husqvarna Forest & Garden Co.

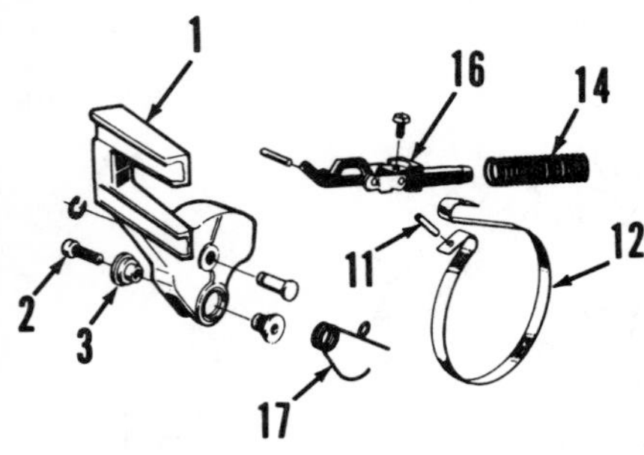

Fig. H64—Exploded view of chain brake assembly used on 238SE, 238SG, 42, 242, 242G, 242XP, 242XPG, 246, 288XP, 288XPG, some 281XP and some 281XPG models.

1. Brake lever
2. Screw
3. Trunnion
11. Pin
12. Brake band
14. Spring
16. Trigger assy.

HANDLE HEATER. Some models are equipped with a front and rear handle heating system. A generating coil located underneath the flywheel produces approximately 20 volts at 8500 rpm to provide an electrical current to heating coils in front and rear handles. A switch located to the right of the rear handle on 133SG, 238SG and 242G models controls the electric current. The heating system of 181SG and 281XPG models is regulated by a thermostat that closes at approximately 10 degrees C (50 degrees F).

Illustrations courtesy Husqvarna Forest & Garden Co.

HUSQVARNA

Model	Bore mm (in.)	Stroke mm (in.)	Displacement cc (cu. in.)	Drive Type
50, 50 CB, 50 Rancher	44.0 (1.732)	32.0 (1.26)	49.0 (3.0)	Direct
50 Special, 51	45.0 (1.77)	32.0 (1.26)	51.0 (3.1)	Direct
55	46.0 (1.81)	32.0 (1.26)	53.0 (3.2)	Direct

MAINTENANCE

SPARK PLUG. Recommended spark plug is Champion RCJ7Y. Spark plug electrode gap should be 0.5 mm (0.020 in.).

CARBURETOR. A Walbro WA-82 diaphragm type carburetor is used on Models 50 and 50 Rancher. A Walbro WT-170 diaphragm type carburetor is used on Models 51 and 55. Refer to Walbro section of CARBURETOR SERVICE section for service procedures and exploded views of carburetors.

On all models, initial adjustment of low and high speed mixture screws is 1¼ turns open from a lightly seated position. Make final adjustment with engine warm and running.

Turn low mixture screw clockwise to obtain highest idle speed, then turn screw ¼ turn counterclockwise. Engine should accelerate cleanly without hesitation. If engine stumbles or seems sluggish when accelerating, adjust idle mixture screw until engine accelerates without hesitation. Adjust high speed mixture screw to obtain optimum performance under cutting load. Do not operate saw with high speed mixture too lean as engine damage may result from lack of lubrication and overheating. Adjust idle speed screw so engine idles just below clutch engagement speed.

IGNITION. All models are equipped with a one-piece breakerless electronic ignition system. Two types of ignition systems have been used and are interchangeable. The color of the ignition module (2—Fig. H66) designates the manufacturer. Prufrex ignition modules are yellow and Electrolux ignition modules are black. On both types of ignition systems, air gap between ignition module core and flywheel magnets should be 0.3 mm (0.012 in.). Ignition timing is not adjustable.

LUBRICATION. Engine is lubricated by mixing oil with the fuel. Recommended oil is Husqvarna Two-Stroke Oil mixed at a ratio of 50:1. If Husqvarna Two-Stroke Oil is not available, a good quality oil designed for two-stroke air-cooled engines may be used when mixed at a 25:1 ratio. Use a separate container when mixing the oil and gas.

All models are equipped with an automatic chain oil pump. Clean automotive oil may be used. Oil viscosity should be chosen according to ambient temperature. Oil pump output is not adjustable.

REPAIRS

CYLINDER, PISTON, RINGS AND PIN. Cylinder has a chrome bore which should be inspected for flaking, cracking or other damage to chromed surface. Inspect piston and discard if excessive wear or damage is evident. New cylinders are available only with fitted pistons but new pistons are available for installation in used cylinders.

The piston (4—Fig. H67) is fitted with a single piston ring (3). A locating pin is present in piston ring groove to prevent piston ring rotation. Oversize pistons and rings are not available. Be sure ring end gap is positioned around locating pin when installing cylinder.

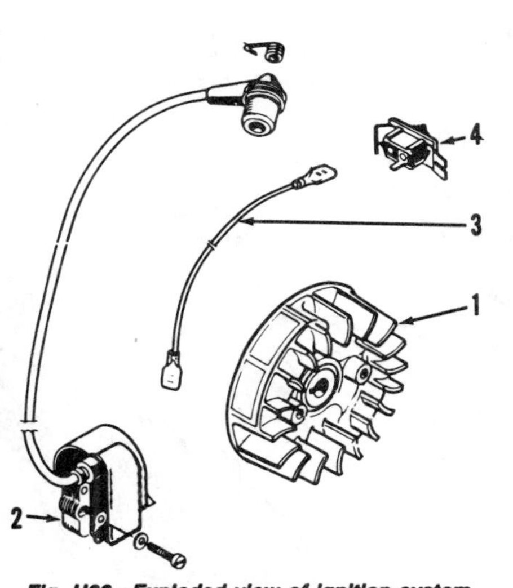

Fig. H66—Exploded view of ignition system.

1. Flywheel
2. Ignition module
3. Ground lead
4. Ignition switch

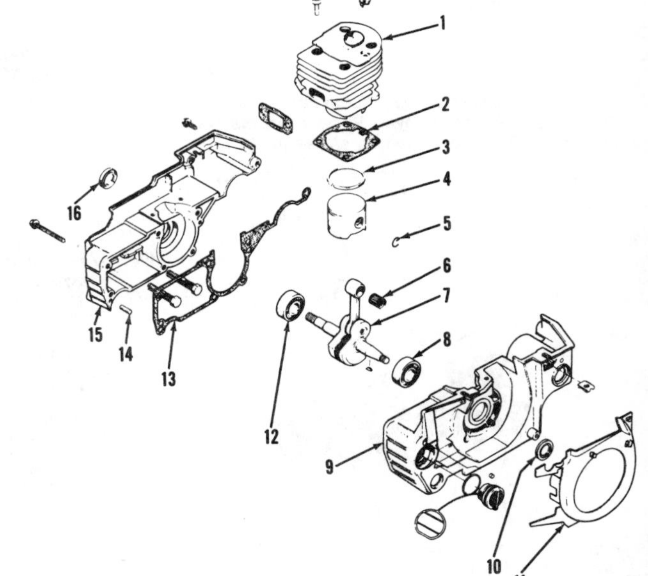

Fig. H67—Exploded view of engine assembly.

1. Cylinder
2. Gasket
3. Piston ring
4. Piston
5. Piston pin retainer
6. Needle bearing
7. Crankshaft & rod assy.
8. Ball bearing
9. Left crankcase half
10. Seal
11. Fan cover
12. Ball bearing
13. Gasket
14. Guide dowel
15. Right crankcase half
16. Seal

Illustrations courtesy Husqvarna Forest & Garden Co.

The piston pin is retained by wire retainers and rides in needle roller bearing in small end of connecting rod. Be sure piston is properly supported when removing piston pin to prevent damage. Arrow on piston crown must point toward exhaust port when installing piston.

CRANKSHAFT, CONNECTING ROD AND CRANKCASE. Crankshaft and connecting rod are a unit assembly. It will be necessary to heat crankcase halves to remove or install crankshaft and main bearings. Care should be taken not to damage mating surfaces of crankcase halves. Check rotation of connecting rod around crankpin and renew crankshaft unit if roughness or other damage is found.

When reassembling crankshaft and crankcase halves, be sure main bearing outer races are bottomed against their seats in crankcase. A special tool is available from the manufacturer to properly position main bearings and crankshaft in crankcase. Make certain crankshaft is centered in crankcase and will rotate freely. Clutch side crankshaft seal should be installed 1.58 mm (1/16 in.) below flush of crankcase face.

CLUTCH. Two types of two-shoe centrifugal clutches have been used on 50 Rancher models. Refer to Fig. H68 or Fig. H69 for exploded view of clutch assemblies. Refer to Fig. H70 for exploded view of two-shoe centrifugal clutch assembly used on Models 50, 51 and 55. On all types of clutches, clutch hub (1) has left hand threads (turn clockwise to remove).

Inspect clutch shoes (2) and drum (5) for excessive wear or damage due to overheating. Inspect bearing (6) and crankshaft for wear or damage. Renew components as necessary.

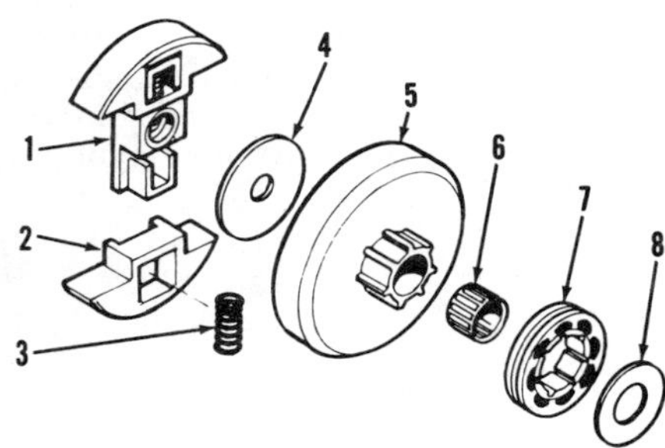

Fig. H68—Exploded view of clutch assembly used on some 50 Rancher saws. Some saws may be equipped with clutch assembly shown in Fig. H69.

1. Hub
2. Shoe
3. Spring
4. Washer
5. Drum
6. Needle bearing
7. Floating sprocket
8. Washer

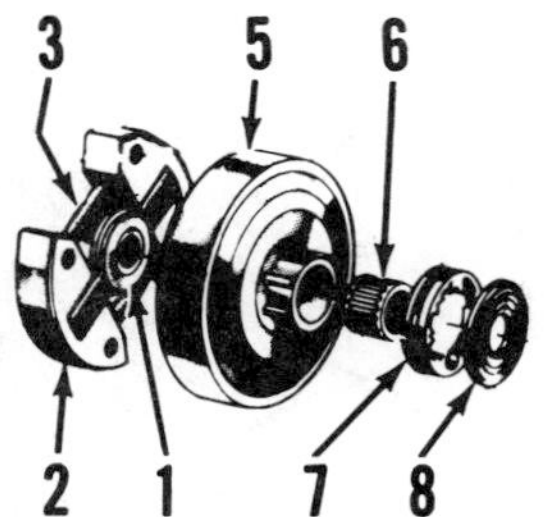

Fig. H69—Exploded view of clutch assembly used on some 50 Rancher saws. Refer to Fig. H68 for parts identification.

OIL PUMP. All models are equipped with an automatic chain oiler pump which is driven by worm gear (11—Fig. H71) on crankshaft. Oil pump output is not adjustable.

Access to oil pump components is obtained after removing chain, guide bar, clutch and oil pump cover plate (2). Oil pump pickup hose (9) and filter spring (10) may be withdrawn from oil tank using a suitable screwdriver. When reassembling observe the following: Spring (10) must be completely installed on hose (9). After installing oil pickup assembly in oil tank, make certain spring (10) is perpendicular to oil tank bottom as shown in Fig. H72. Oil pickup assembly may be inspected through oil filler opening. "O" ring (6—Fig. H71) should be installed on gear end of housing (7) 10-12 mm (7/16 in.) from housing end. Notch in housing should engage locating lug in crankcase.

REWIND STARTER. To disassemble rewind starter, remove starter housing from saw. Pull starter rope and hold rope pulley (10—Fig. H73) with notch in pulley adjacent to rope outlet. Pull rope back through outlet so it engages notch in pulley and allow pulley to com-

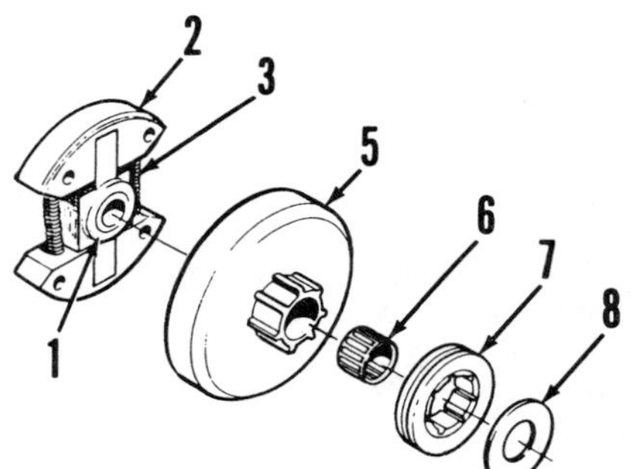

Fig. H70—Exploded view of clutch assembly used on Models 50, 51 and 55. Refer to legend in Fig. H68 for parts identification.

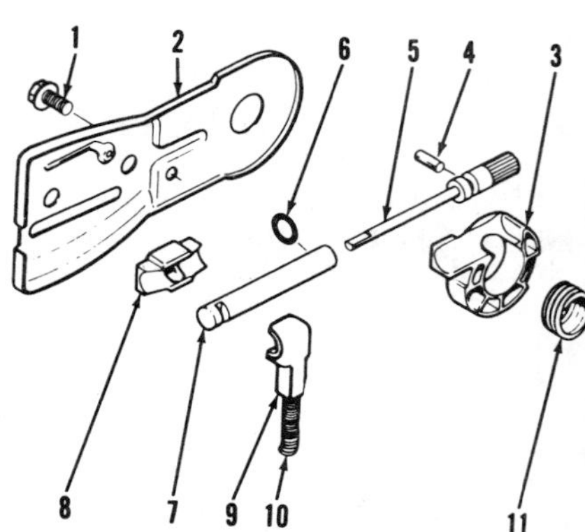

Fig. H71—Exploded view of oil pump assembly.

1. Cap screw
2. Cover plate
3. Gear protector
4. Pin
5. Plunger
6. "O" ring
7. Pump housing
8. Outlet tube
9. Inlet hose
10. Spring
11. Drive gear

Fig. H72—View of oil tank with left crankcase removed to show proper installation of oil pickup components (9 and 10).

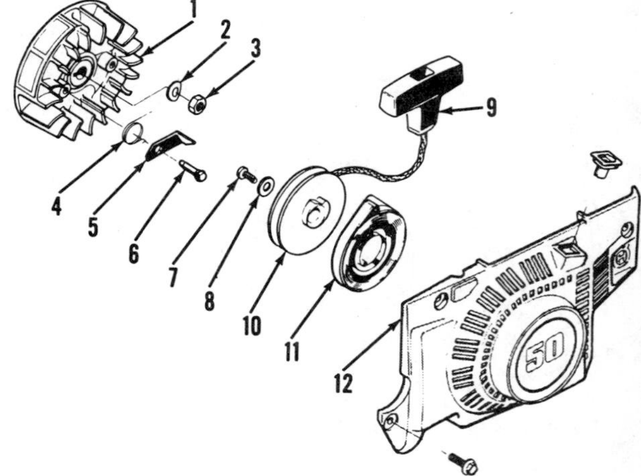

Fig. H73—Exploded view of rewind starter.

1. Flywheel
2. Washer
3. Nut
4. Spring
5. Pawl
6. Retainer
7. Cap screw
8. Washer
9. Rope handle
10. Rope pulley
11. Rewind spring
12. Starter housing

Illustrations courtesy Husqvarna Forest & Garden Co.

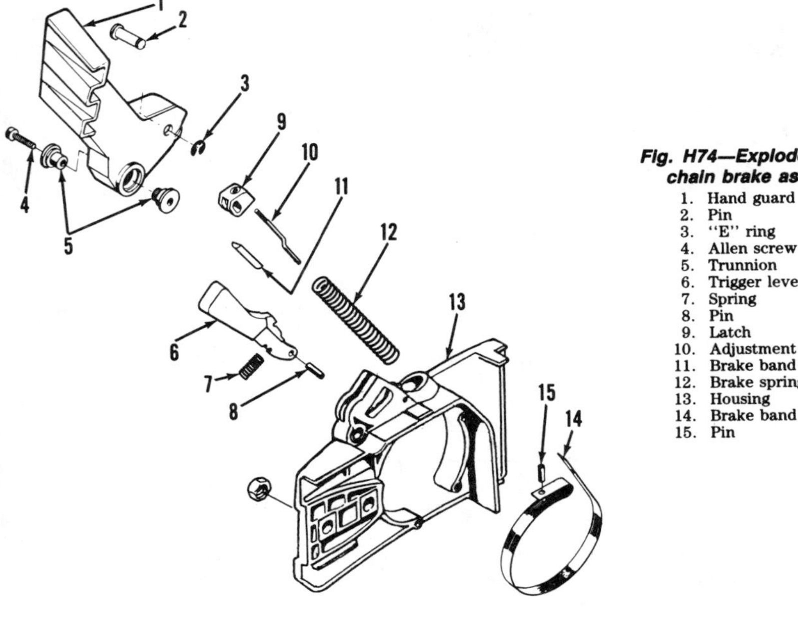

Fig. H74—Exploded view of chain brake assembly.

1. Hand guard
2. Pin
3. "E" ring
4. Allen screw
5. Trunnion
6. Trigger lever
7. Spring
8. Pin
9. Latch
10. Adjustment rod
11. Brake band retainer
12. Brake spring
13. Housing
14. Brake band
15. Pin

pletely unwind. Unscrew pulley retaining cap screw (7) and remove rope pulley. If rewind spring requires removal, care should be taken not to allow spring to uncoil from retainer.

Reassembly is the reverse of disassembly while noting the following: Wrap starter rope around rope pulley in a clockwise direction as viewed with pulley in starter housing. Turn rope pulley two turns clockwise before passing rope through rope outlet to place tension on rewind spring or reverse the procedure used to relieve spring tension outlined in the previous paragraph. Spring tension is correct if rope pulley can be rotated approximately ½ turn further when rope is at its greatest length.

When installing starter assembly on saw, make sure starter pulley properly engages pawls on flywheel before tightening retaining cap screws.

CHAIN BRAKE. Refer to Fig. H74 or Fig. H75 for exploded view of chain brake assembly. The chain brake assembly is designed to stop chain movement should kickback occur. Chain brake is activated either by the operator's hand striking the hand guard (1) or by sufficient force being applied to the guide bar tip during kickback to dislodge the trigger lever (6) and release brake spring (12) thereby pulling brake band (14) tight around clutch drum to stop the chain. Pull hand guard rearward to reset brake mechanism.

Disassembly of chain brake for repair or renewal of individual components is evident after removing brake housing (13) from saw. No adjustment of late style chain brake (Fig. H75) is required. On early style brake (Fig. H74), brake band adjustment should be checked after reassembly and installation of chain brake on saw. The distance between disengaged position (A—Fig. H76) and engaged position (B) of hand guard, as measured at point (P), should be 4 mm (0.157 in.). When brake mechanism is in the engaged position, gently pull back hand guard until resistance is felt before meauring. Adjustment is accomplished by varying the length of rod (10—Fig. H74).

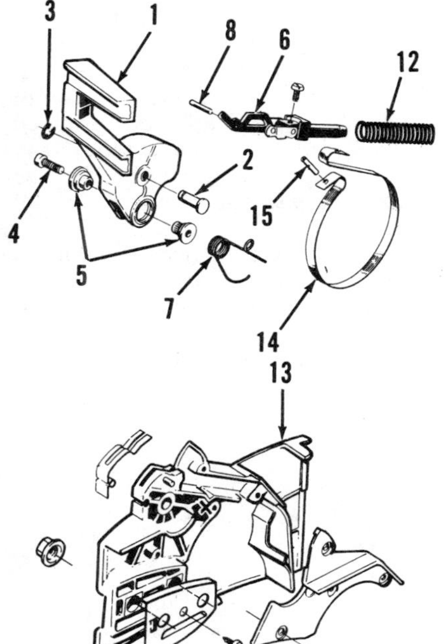

Fig. H75—Exploded view of late style chain brake assembly. Refer to Fig. H74 for identification of parts.

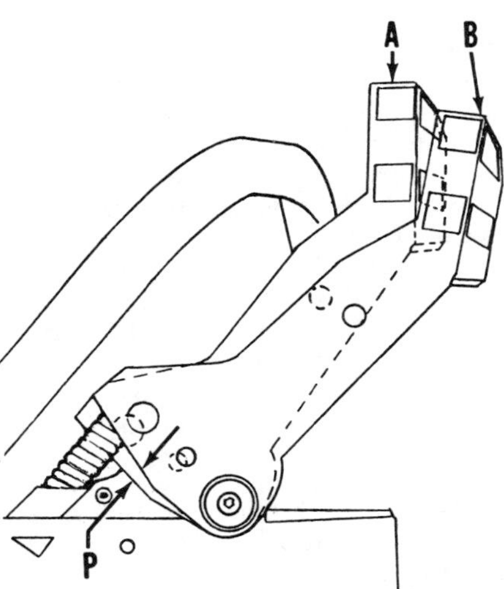

Fig. H76—Properly adjusted, hand guard travel between chain brake disengaged position (A) and engaged position (B) should be 4 mm (0.157 in.) when measured at point (P). Refer to text.

Illustrations courtesy Husqvarna Forest & Garden Co.

HUSQVARNA

Model	Bore mm (in.)	Stroke mm (in.)	Displacement cc (cu. in.)	Drive Type
154, 154 SE, 154 SG, 254, 254 XP, 254 XPG	45.0 (1.77)	34.0 (1.34)	54.0 (3.3)	Direct
257	46.0 (1.81)	34.0 (1.34)	57 (3.5)	Direct
262 XP, 262 XPG	48.0 (1.89)	34.0 (1.34)	62 (3.8)	Direct

MAINTENANCE

SPARK PLUG. Recommended spark plug for all models is Champion RCJ7Y. Recommended electrode gap for all models is 0.5 mm (0.020 in.).

CARBURETOR. A Walbro HDA carburetor is used on all models. Refer to Walbro section of CARBURETOR SERVICE for service procedures and exploded view of carburetor. Refer to Fig. H185 for exploded view of fuel tank and intake components.

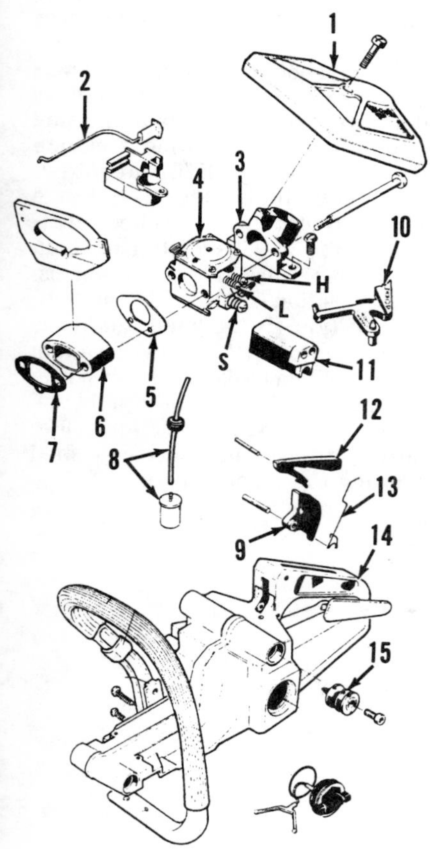

For 254 models, initial adjustment for carburetor mixture screws is 1 ¼ turns open for low-speed mixture screw (L—Fig. H185) and 1 ½ turns open for high-speed mixture screw (H). For all other models, initial adjustment for both the low-speed and high-speed mixture screws is one turn open from a lightly seated position. Make final adjustment with engine warm and running.

Adjust idle speed screw (S) so engine idles just below clutch engagement speed. Adjust low-speed mixture screw so engine idles smoothly and accelerates cleanly without hesitation.

Adjust high-speed mixture screw to obtain optimum performance under cutting load. Maximum no-load speed (with bar and chain installed) is 13,800 rpm for 254XP model and 13,500 rpm for all other models. Do not adjust high-speed mixture screw too lean as overheating and engine damage could result.

IGNITION. All models are equipped with breakerless ignition system shown in Fig. H186. Ignition timing is not adjustable.

Air gap between ignition module core and flywheel magnets should be 0.3 mm (0.012 in.). Adjust air gap by loosening ignition module retaining screws and repositioning module.

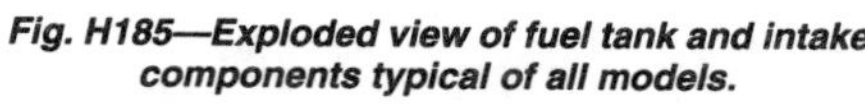

Fig. H185—Exploded view of fuel tank and intake components typical of all models.

- L. Low-speed mixture screw
- H. High-speed mixture screw
- S. Idle speed screw
- 1. Air cleaner
- 2. Choke linkage
- 3. Air inlet elbow
- 4. Carburetor
- 5. Gasket
- 6. Intake adapter
- 7. Gasket
- 8. Fuel line & strainer
- 9. Throttle trigger
- 10. Throttle linkage
- 11. Adjustment guide
- 12. Throttle lock
- 13. Throttle link
- 14. Fuel tank/handle assy.
- 15. Vibration isolator

LUBRICATION. Engine is lubricated by mixing oil with the fuel. Recommended oil is Husqvarna Two-Stroke Oil mixed at a ratio of 50:1. If Husqvarna Two-Stroke Oil is not available, a good quality oil designed for two-stroke air-cooled engines may be used when mixed at a 25:1 ratio. Use a separate container when mixing oil and gasoline.

All models are equipped with an automatic bar and chain oiling system. Oil designed for bar and chain lubrication is recommended, although automotive type oil can be used. Oil viscosity should be chosen according to ambient temperature.

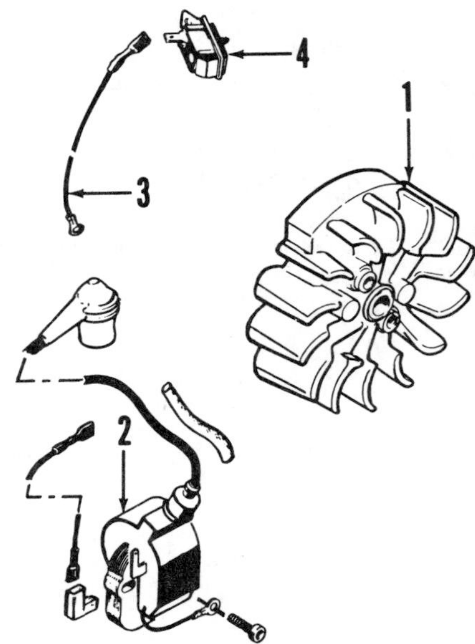

Fig. H186—Exploded view of ignition system.

1. Flywheel
2. Ignition module
3. Ground lead
4. Ignition switch

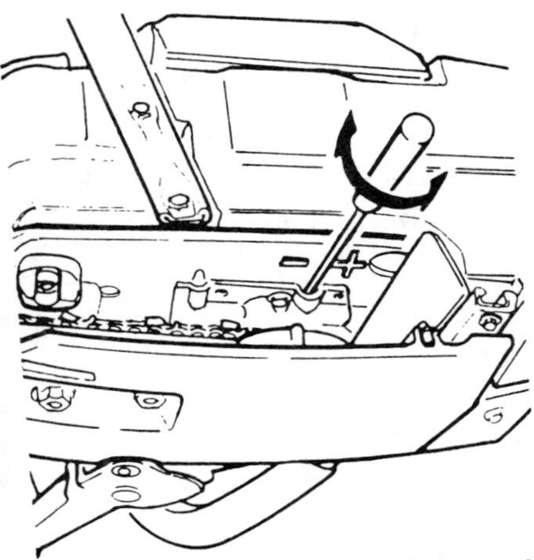

Fig. H187—Insert a screwdriver as shown to adjust chain oil pump output.

The output of the oil pump is adjustable. DO NOT adjust oil pump with engine running. To adjust pump output, insert screwdriver into adjustment slot at bottom of saw as shown in Fig. H187. Rotate adjusting screw clockwise to decrease oil pump output or counterclockwise to increase output.

Recommended adjustment is one turn out from a lightly seated position on saws equipped with a 33-38 cm (13-15 in.) guide bar and two to three turns out from a lightly seated position on saws equipped with a 38-45 cm (15-18 in.) guide bar.

CYLINDER, PISTON AND RING. To disassemble, remove cylinder cover and air filter assembly. Disconnect carburetor linkage and fuel line. Remove carburetor and muffler. Remove cylinder mounting screws and lift cylinder (1—Fig. H188) from crankcase. Remove piston pin retaining ring and push piston pin out of piston (4).

Cylinder has a chrome bore which should be inspected for flaking, cracking or other damage to chromed surface. Inspect piston and discard if excessive wear or damage is evident.

New cylinder is available only with a fitted piston. Piston is renewable only in standard size and as an assembly with piston ring, piston pin, needle roller bearing and retaining clips.

The piston is fitted with a single piston ring. On 254 and 254G models, a 1.0 mm (0.04 in.) and a 1.5 mm (0.06 in.) thickness ring have been used. Make sure correct size piston ring is used when renewing piston ring on a used piston.

On all models, a locating pin is present in piston ring groove to prevent piston ring rotation. Be sure that ring end gap is around locating pin when installing cylinder.

The piston pin is retained in the piston by wire retainers. Install retainers with open end toward piston crown. The pin rides in a needle roller bearing in small end of connecting rod. Be sure that piston is properly supported when removing and installing pin to prevent damage. Arrow on piston crown must point toward exhaust port when installing piston.

CRANKSHAFT, CONNECTING ROD AND CRANKCASE. To disassemble, remove sprocket guard, guide bar and chain, and rewind starter housing. Remove spark plug and install a piston stop in spark plug hole (a length of rope can be inserted into spark plug hole). Remove flywheel nut (right-hand threads) and clutch assembly (left-hand threads). Remove oil pump assembly. Remove carburetor, muffler, cylinder, and fuel tank/handle assembly.

It will be necessary to heat crankcase halves (9 and 17—Fig. H188) to remove or install crankshaft and main bearings. Care should be taken not to damage mating surfaces of crankcase halves.

Check rotation of connecting rod around crankpin and renew crankshaft unit if roughness or other damage is noted.

When reassembling crankshaft and crankcase halves, be sure that main bearing outer races are properly positioned in crankcase halves. Crankcase must be centered in crankcase halves and rotate freely.

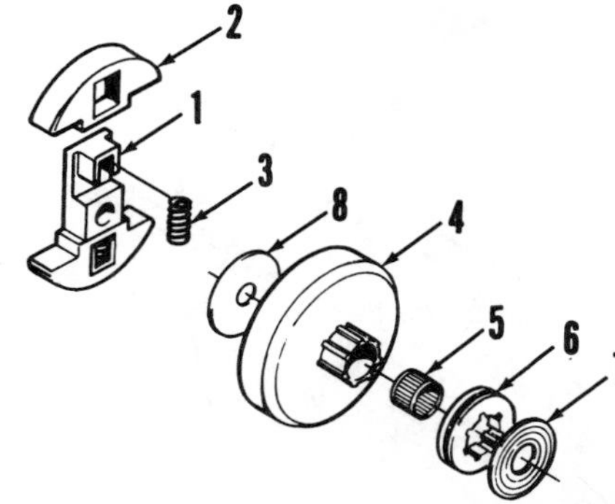

Fig. H189—Exploded view of two-shoe clutch assembly used on Models 154SE, 154SG, 254, 254G and 257.

1. Hub
2. Clutch shoe
3. Spring
4. Drum
5. Needle bearing
6. Sprocket
7. Washer
8. Washer

CLUTCH. Models 154SE, 154SG, 254, 254G and 257 are equipped with two-shoe centrifugal clutch shown in Fig. H189. Models 262XP and 262XPG are equipped with a three-shoe centrifugal clutch shown in Fig. H190.

To remove clutch assembly, remove sprocket guard, bar and chain. On all models, clutch hub (1) has left-hand threads (rotate clockwise to remove).

Inspect clutch shoes (2) and clutch drum (4) for excessive wear or damage due to overheating. Inspect clutch drum, needle bearing (5) and crankshaft end for damage. Clutch hub (1)

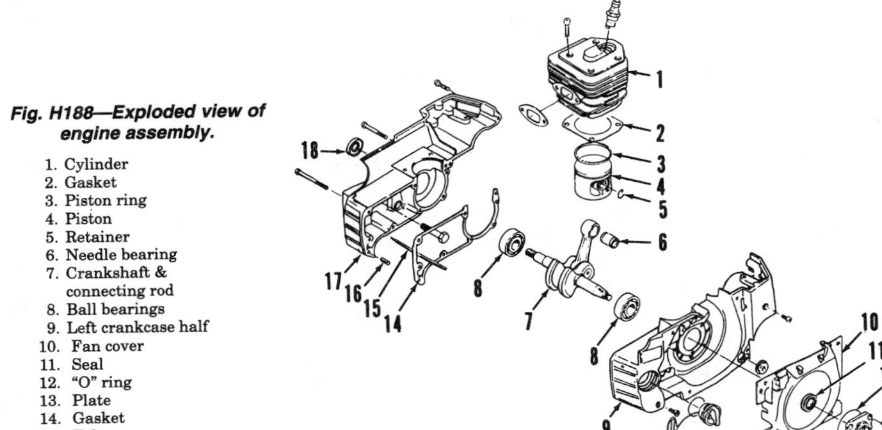

Fig. H188—Exploded view of engine assembly.

1. Cylinder
2. Gasket
3. Piston ring
4. Piston
5. Retainer
6. Needle bearing
7. Crankshaft & connecting rod
8. Ball bearings
9. Left crankcase half
10. Fan cover
11. Seal
12. "O" ring
13. Plate
14. Gasket
15. Tube
16. Guide dowel
17. Right crankcase half
18. Seal

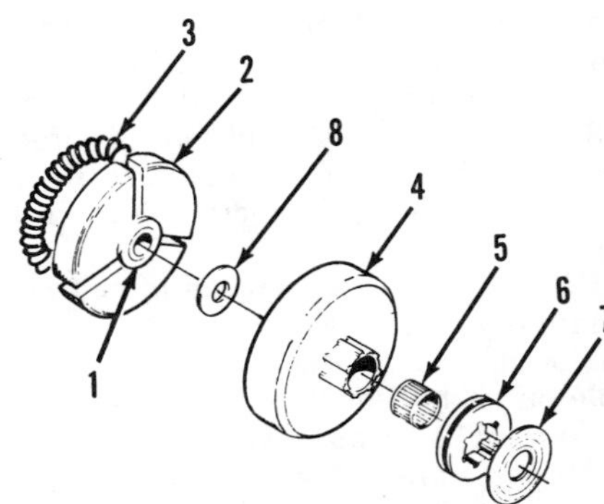

Fig. H190—Exploded view of three-shoe clutch assembly used on Models 262XP and 262XPG.

1. Clutch hub
2. Clutch shoes
3. Spring
4. Clutch drum
5. Needle bearing
6. Sprocket
7. Washer
8. Washer

Illustrations courtesy Husqvarna Forest & Garden Co.

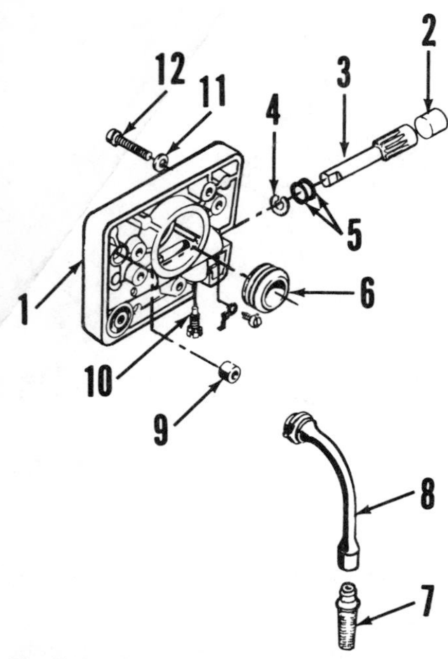

Fig. H191—Exploded view of adjustable, automatic chain oil pump.

1. Pump housing
2. Plug
3. Plunger
4. Washer
5. Washers
6. Worm drive gear
7. Oil screen
8. Suction hose
9. Seal
10. Adjusting screw
11. Washer
12. Screw

and clutch shoes (2) are available as an assembly. Clutch drum (4) is available with bearing (5), sprocket (6) and washer (7). Spring (3), needle bearing (5), sprocket (6) and washer (7) are available separately.

OIL PUMP. All models are equipped with the adjustable, automatic chain oil pump shown in Fig. H191. Do not adjust oil pump output with engine running.

To adjust oil pump output, insert screwdriver into adjustment slot as shown in Fig. H187. Rotate adjusting screw clockwise to decrease oil pump output or counterclockwise to increase oil flow.

Recommended adjustment is one turn out from a lightly seated position on saws equipped with a 33-38 cm (13-15 in.) guide bar and two to three turns out from a lightly seated position on saws with a 38-45 cm (15-18 in.) guide bar.

Oil pump can be removed after first removing sprocket guard, bar and chain, and clutch assembly. Use a suitable puller to remove worm drive gear (6—Fig. H191) from crankshaft.

All parts are renewable individually except for oil pump housing (1), which is renewable only as a complete oil pump assembly.

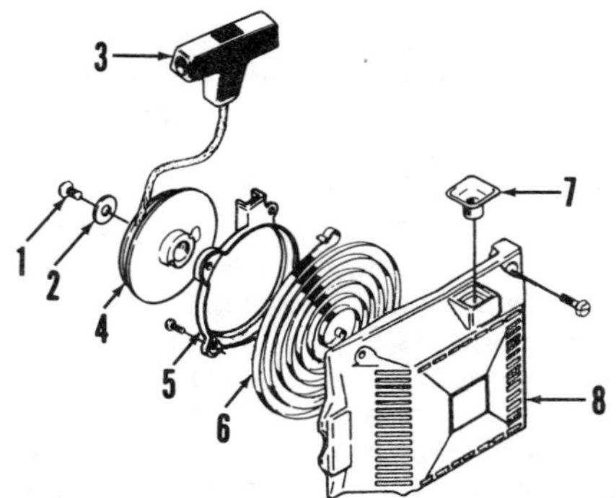

Fig. H192—Exploded view of rewind starter typical of all models.

1. Screw
2. Washer
3. Rope handle
4. Rope pulley
5. Spring retainer
6. Rewind spring
7. Rope guide
8. Starter housing

REWIND STARTER. To disassemble starter, remove starter housing from saw. Pull starter rope and remove rope handle (3—Fig. H192). Allow starter pulley to slowly unwind until spring tension is completely relieved.

Remove pulley retaining screw (1) and remove rope pulley (4). If rewind spring (6) must be removed, care should be taken not to allow spring to uncoil uncontrolled. Wear gloves and eye protection when removing the rewind spring. Remove spring retainer (5) and carefully remove the spring.

Install rewind spring in starter housing with spring coiled in a clockwise direction from outer spring end. Wrap starter rope around pulley in a clockwise direction as viewed with pulley in starter housing. Insert rope through rope guide in starter housing and attach handle.

To place tension on rewind spring, turn rope pulley until notch in pulley is adjacent to rope outlet. Pull rope between the notch between the notch in pulley and the housing. Rotate pulley in clockwise direction two turns. Release the rope from the notch in pulley and allow rope to wind onto pulley.

Do not place more tension on rewind spring than is necessary to draw rope handle up against housing. To check starter operation, pull rope all the way out. Spring tension is correct if rope pulley can be rotated approximately ½ turn further when rope is pulled to its maximum length.

When installing starter assembly, make sure that starter pulley properly engages pawls on flywheel before tightening retaining screws.

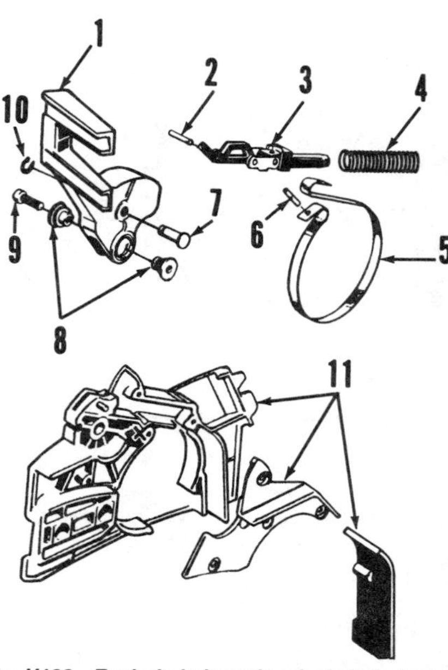

Fig. H193—Exploded view of typical chain brake assembly.

1. Brake lever
2. Pin
3. Trigger assy.
4. Spring
5. Brake band
6. Band retainer
7. Pin
8. Trunnions
9. Allen screw
10. Retainer
11. Side housing assy.

CHAIN BRAKE. All models are equipped with a chain brake system designed to stop movement of chain should saw kickback occur. Refer to Fig. H193) for exploded view of chain brake system used.

On all models, chain brake is activated either by the operator's hand striking the hand guard (1) or by sufficient force being applied to bar tip during kickback to dislodge trigger assembly (3) and release the brake spring (4). The spring tightens the brake band (5) against the clutch drum to stop chain movement. Pull hand guard back to reset brake mechanism.

Remove sprocket guard (11—Fig. H193) to inspect brake mechanism. No adjustment of the brake is required.

HANDLE HEATER. All models are equipped with front and rear handle heating system. A generating coil located under the flywheel produces approximately 20 bolts at 8500 rpm to provide an electrical current to heating coils in handles. A switch located to the right of the rear handle controls the current.

HUSQVARNA

Model	Bore mm (in.)	Stroke mm (in.)	Displacement cc (cu. in.)	Drive Type
40	40.0 (1.575)	32 (1.26)	40.0 (2.4)	Direct
45	42.0 (1.654)	32.0 (1.26)	44.0 (2.7)	Direct

MAINTENANCE

SPARK PLUG. Recommended spark plug for all models is Champion RCJ7Y. Spark plug electrode gap should be 0.5 mm (0.020 in.).

CARBURETOR. A Walbro WT or Zama C1Q diaphragm type carburetor is used on Models 40 and 45. Refer to Walbro or Zama section of CARBURETOR SERVICE for service procedures and exploded views of carburetors.

Initial adjustment of low and high speed mixture screws is one turn open from a lightly seated position. Make final adjustment with engine warm and running.

Adjust low speed mixture screw to obtain highest idle speed, then turn screw 1/4 turn counterclockwise. Engine should accelerate cleanly without hesitation. If engine stumbles or seems sluggish when accelerating, adjust low speed mixture screw until engine accelerates without hesitation. Adjust high speed mixture screw to obtain optimum performance under cutting load. Do not operate saw with high speed mixture too lean as engine damage may result from lack of lubrication and overheating. Adjust idle speed screw so engine idles just below clutch engagement speed.

IGNITION. All models are equipped with a breakerless electronic ignition system. Ignition timing is not adjustable. Air gap between ignition module core (2—Fig. H94) and flywheel magnets should be 0.3 mm (0.012 in.). Adjust by loosening ignition module retaining screws and repositioning module.

LUBRICATION. Engine is lubricated by mixing oil with the fuel. Recommended oil is Husqvarna Two-Stroke Oil mixed at a ratio of 50:1. If Husqvarna Two-Stroke Oil is not available, a good quality oil designed for two-stroke air-cooled engines may be used when mixed at a 25:1 ratio. Use a separate container when mixing oil and gasoline.

All models are equipped with an automatic chain oil pump. A good quality chain oil is recommended, although clean automotive oil may also be used. If automotive type oil is used, oil viscosity should be chosen according to ambient temperature. Oil pump output is not adjustable.

REPAIRS

CRANKCASE PRESSURE TEST. An improperly sealed crankcase can cause the engine to be hard to start, run rough, have low power and overheat. Refer to ENGINE SERVICE section of this manual for crankcase pressure test procedure. If crankcase leakage is indicated, pressurize crankcase and use a soap and water solution to check gaskets, seals, pulse line and castings for leakage.

CYLINDER, PISTON, RINGS AND PIN. The piston pin (5—Fig. H95) is re-

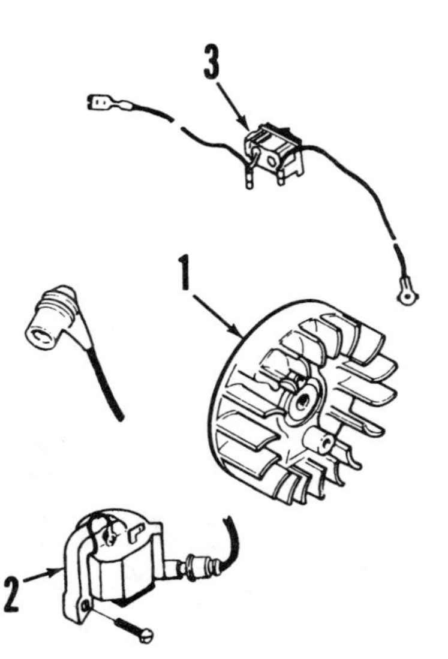

Fig. H94—Exploded view of ignition system.
1. Flywheel
2. Ignition module
3. Ignition switch

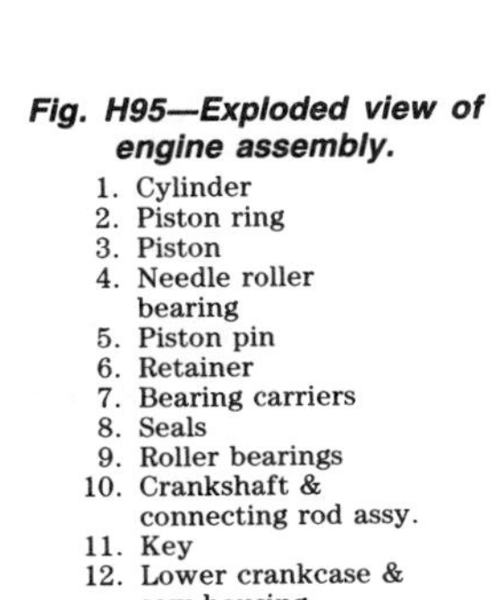

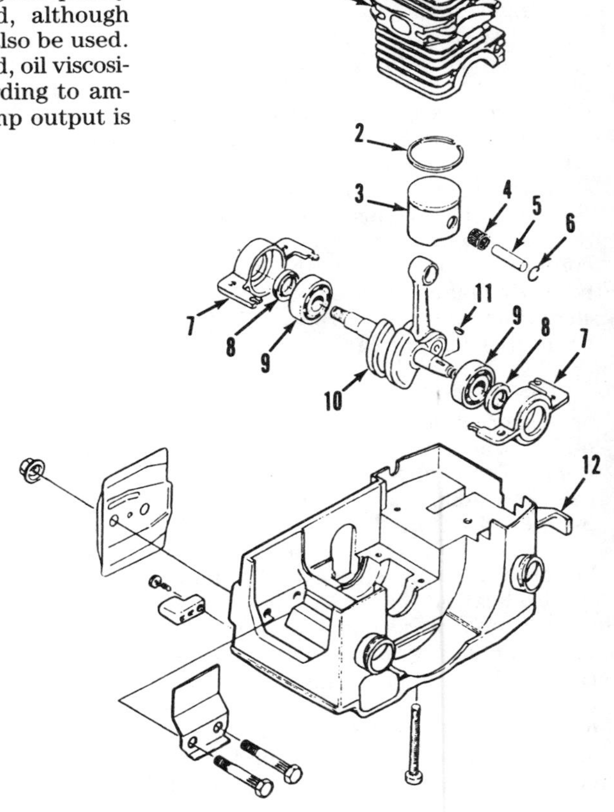

Fig. H95—Exploded view of engine assembly.
1. Cylinder
2. Piston ring
3. Piston
4. Needle roller bearing
5. Piston pin
6. Retainer
7. Bearing carriers
8. Seals
9. Roller bearings
10. Crankshaft & connecting rod assy.
11. Key
12. Lower crankcase & saw housing

Illustrations courtesy Husqvarna Forest & Garden Co.

tained by wire retainers (6) and rides in a needle roller bearing (4) in small end of connecting rod. Be sure piston is properly supported when removing piston pin to prevent damage to connecting rod.

Cylinder has a chrome bore which should be inspected for flaking, cracking or other damage to chromed surface. Inspect piston and discard if excessive wear or damage is evident. New cylinder is available only with fitted piston, however, a new piston is available for installation in a used cylinder.

The piston is fitted with a single piston ring (2—Fig. H95). A locating pin is present in piston ring groove to prevent piston ring rotation. Be sure ring end gap is positioned around locating pin when installing cylinder. Arrow on piston crown must point toward exhaust port when installing piston. Be sure the piston pin retainers are seated snugly in piston boss.

CRANKSHAFT, CONNECTING ROD AND CRANKCASE. Crankshaft and connecting rod are a unit assembly. Crankshaft main bearings (9—Fig. H95) are supported in interlocking bearing carriers (7).

To disassemble, remove chain and guide bar, cylinder cover, air filter assembly and starter housing. Remove muffler, carburetor and intake manifold. Remove spark plug and install a piston stop in spark plug hole to lock crankshaft. Remove flywheel mounting nut (right-hand threads) and starter pawls. Use suitable puller to remove flywheel. Remove ignition module and air baffle plate. Remove clutch assembly (left-hand threads) and oil pump. Remove power head mounting screws and withdraw cylinder, piston and crankshaft as an assembly from lower crankcase (12). Remove piston pin retainers (6), piston pin (5) and piston (3) from connecting rod. Use suitable puller to remove oil pump worm gear from crankshaft. Remove main bearing carriers (7), seals (8) and bearings (9) from crankshaft.

Check rotation of connecting rod around crankpin and renew crankshaft unit if roughness or other damage is found. The connecting rod should not have any radial clearance (up and down play) on the crankpin.

To reassemble, reverse the disassembly procedure. Install seals (8) so lip is toward bearings (9). Make sure mating surfaces of bearing carriers, crankcase and cylinder are clean and dry. Place a thin bead of suitable form-in-place gasket compound onto sealing areas of lower crankcase (12) and cylinder (1). Assemble crankshaft and cylinder in crankcase and tighten mounting screws in a criss-cross pattern to 11 N·m (97 in.-lbs.). Make certain crankshaft rotates freely.

CLUTCH. Both models are equipped with three-shoe centrifugal clutch shown in Fig. H96, which is accessible after removing chain brake assembly and chain guide bar. Clutch hub has left-hand threads (turn clockwise to remove).

Inspect clutch shoes (2), drum (4) and bearing (5) for excessive wear or damage due to overheating. Clutch shoes and hub are available as an assembly. Inspect chain sprocket teeth for excessive wear and renew as necessary. Lubricate needle bearing with grease.

OIL PUMP. All models are equipped with an automatic oil pump that is driven by a worm gear (5—Fig. H97) on the crankshaft. Oil pump output is not adjustable.

To remove oil pump, first remove guide bar, clutch assembly. Remove worm gear using suitable puller. Remove oil pump mounting screws and withdraw pump assembly. Oil pump suction pipe (6) and strainer (7) may be removed from oil tank using a screwdriver.

Inspect pump plunger assembly (2) for wear or damage and renew as necessary. Lubricate parts with oil during assembly.

REWIND STARTER. To disassemble rewind starter, remove starter housing from saw. Pull starter rope and hold rope pulley (8—Fig. H98) with notch in pulley adjacent to rope outlet. Pull rope back through outlet so it engages notch in pulley, then allow pulley to slowly unwind. Unscrew pulley retaining screw and carefully remove rope pulley. If rewind spring (9) must be removed, care should be taken not to allow spring to uncoil uncontrolled.

Install rewind spring in starter housing with spring coiled in clockwise direction as viewed from flywheel side. Wrap starter rope around rope pulley in a clockwise direction as viewed with pulley in starter housing. Turn rope pulley two turns clockwise before passing rope through rope outlet to place ten-

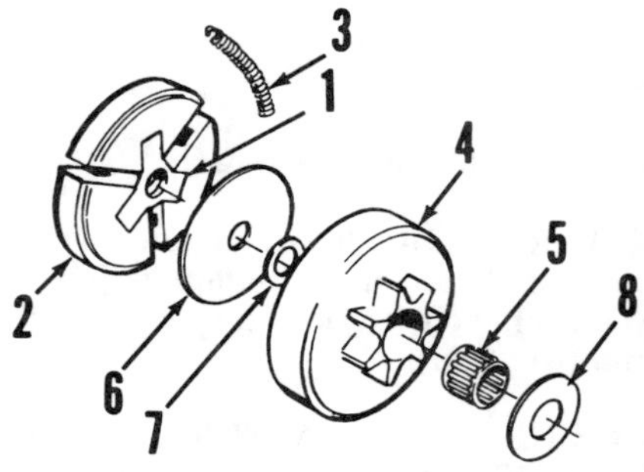

Fig. H96—Exploded view of clutch assembly.

1. Hub
2. Shoe
3. Spring
4. Clutch drum
5. Needle bearing
6. Washer
7. Washer
8. Washer

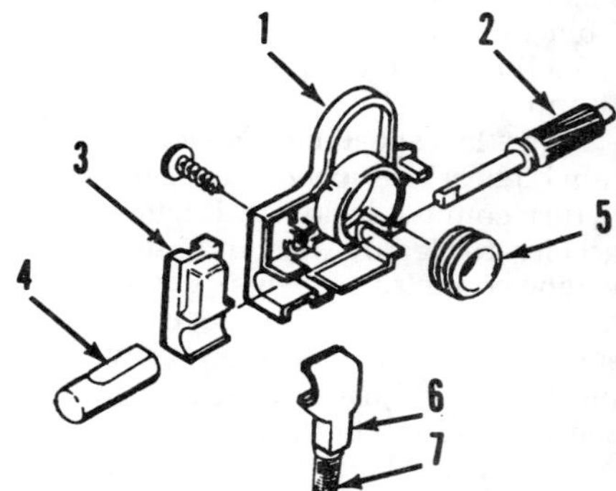

Fig. H97—Exploded view of automatic oil pump assembly.

1. Pump housing
2. Plunger
3. Pressure pipe
4. Plunger housing
5. Worm gear
6. Suction pipe
7. Strainer

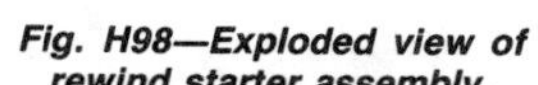

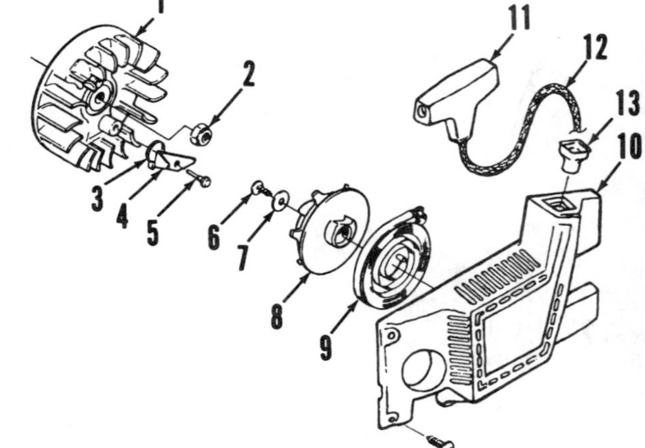

Fig. H98—Exploded view of rewind starter assembly.

1. Flywheel
2. Nut
3. Spring
4. Pawl
5. Retainer
6. Screw
7. Washer
8. Rope pulley
9. Rewind spring
10. Starter housing
11. Handle
12. Starter rope
13. Rope guide

Illustrations courtesy Husqvarna Forest & Garden Co.

sion on rewind spring. Spring tension is correct if rope pulley can be rotated approximately $^1/_4$ turn further when rope is at its greatest length.

When installing starter assembly on saw, make sure starter pulley properly engages pawls on flywheel before tightening retaining cap screws.

CHAIN BRAKE. All models are equipped with a chain brake system designed to stop chain movement should kickback occur. The chain brake is activated either by the operator's hand striking the hand guard (1—Fig. H99) or by sufficient force being applied to the guide bar tip during kickback to cause the front handle to contact trigger lever (3), resulting in automatic activation of brake mechanism.

To disassemble, remove brake housing (11) from saw. Remove trunnion retaining screw (9), tap trunnions (8) out of hand guard and remove hand guard from housing. Remove brake cover plate and carefully pry brake spring (4) from housing. Drive out pin (2) and withdraw brake trigger (3) and brake band (5).

Inspect all parts for wear or damage. Renew brake band if band thickness is less than 0.75 mm (0.030 in.). To reassemble, reverse the disassembly procedure. No adjustment of brake mechanism is necessary.

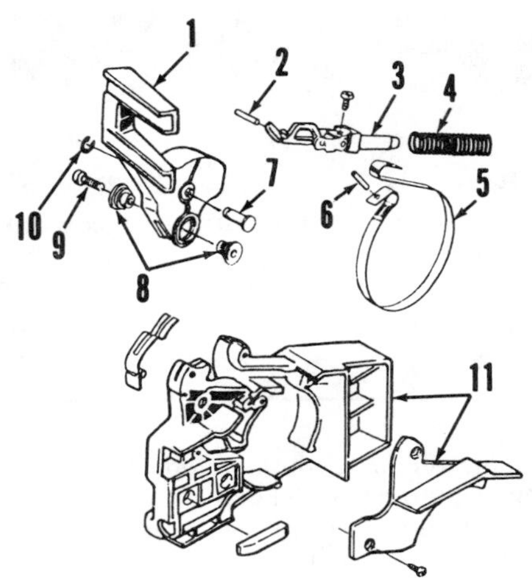

Fig. H99—Exploded view of chain brake mechanism.

1. Hand guard
2. Pin
3. Trigger assy.
4. Brake spring
5. Brake band
6. Band retainer
7. Pin
8. Trunnion
9. Allen screw
10. Retainer
11. Side housing assy.

HUSQVARNA

Model	Bore mm (in.)	Stroke mm (in.)	Displacement cc (cu. in.)	Drive Type
36	38.0 (1.5)	32.0 (1.26)	36.0 (2.2)	Direct
41	40.0 (1.575)	32 (1.26)	40.0 (2.4)	Direct

MAINTENANCE

SPARK PLUG. Recommended spark plug for all models is Champion RCJ7Y. Spark plug electrode gap should be 0.5 mm (0.020 in.).

CARBURETOR. A Walbro WT diaphragm type carburetor is used on Models 36 and 41. Refer to Walbro section of CARBURETOR SERVICE for service procedures and exploded view of carburetor.

Initial adjustment of low and high speed mixture screws is 1¼ turns open from a lightly seated position. Make final adjustment with engine warm and running.

Turn low speed mixture screw clockwise to obtain highest idle speed, then turn screw ¼ turn counterclockwise. Engine should accelerate cleanly without hesitation. If engine stumbles or seems sluggish when accelerating, adjust low speed mixture screw until engine accelerates without hesitation. Adjust high speed mixture screw to obtain optimum performance under cutting load. Do not operate saw with high speed mixture too lean as engine damage may result from lack of lubrication and overheating. Adjust idle speed screw so engine idles just below clutch engagement speed.

IGNITION. All models are equipped with a breakerless electronic ignition system. Ignition timing is not adjustable. Air gap between ignition module core and flywheel magnets should be 0.3 mm (0.012 in.). Adjust by loosening ignition module retaining screws and repositioning module.

LUBRICATION. Engine is lubricated by mixing oil with the fuel. Recommended oil is Husqvarna Two-Stroke Oil mixed at a ratio of 50:1. If Husqvarna Two-Stroke Oil is not available, a good quality oil designed for two-stroke air-cooled engines may be used when mixed at a 25:1 ratio. Use a separate container when mixing oil and gasoline.

All models are equipped with an automatic chain oil pump. A good quality chain oil is recommended, although clean automotive oil may be used. If automotive type oil is used, oil viscosity should be chosen according to ambient temperature. Oil pump output is not adjustable.

REPAIRS

CRANKCASE PRESSURE TEST. An improperly sealed crankcase can cause the engine to be hard to start, run rough, have low power and overheat. Refer to ENGINE SERVICE section of this manual for crankcase pressure test procedure. If crankcase leakage is indicated, pressurize crankcase and use a soap and water solution to check gaskets, seals, pulse line and castings for leakage.

CYLINDER, PISTON, RINGS AND PIN. To disassemble, the power head must first be removed from saw housing as follows: Remove cylinder cover, starter housing, clutch cover, chain and bar. Remove spark plug and install piston stop tool or end of a rope in spark plug hole to lock crankshaft. Remove flywheel, clutch assembly and oil pump. Remove ignition module and air baffle. Remove air cleaner assembly and disconnect fuel line and carburetor linkage. Remove carburetor and muffler. Remove anti-vibration insulators (1—Fig. H101) and separate handle and fuel tank assembly (3) from saw housing (11—Fig. H102). Remove cap screws (12)

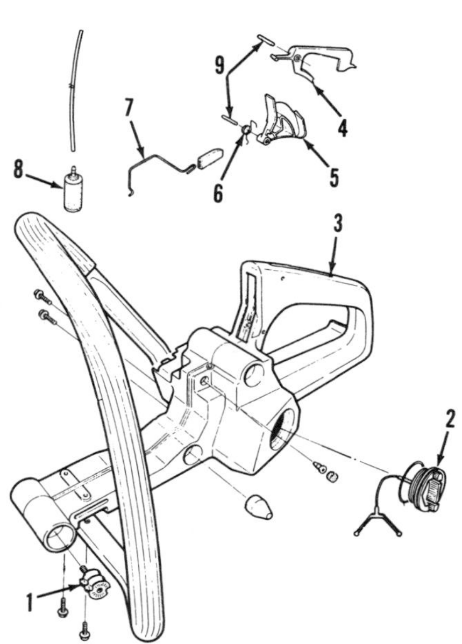

Fig. H101—Exploded view of throttle linkage and handle assembly.

1. Anti-vibration sleeve
2. Fuel tank cap
3. Handle & fuel tank assy.
4. Throttle trigger lock
5. Throttle trigger
6. Return spring
7. Throttle rod
8. Fuel filter
9. Pins

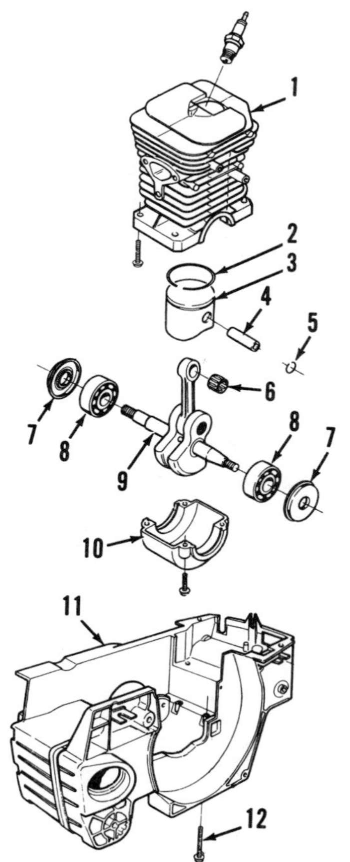

Fig. H102—Exploded view of power head.

1. Cylinder head
2. Piston ring
3. Piston
4. Piston pin
5. Retainer ring
6. Needle bearing
7. Seals
8. Bearings
9. Crankshaft & connecting rod assy.
10. Crankcase
11. Saw housing
12. Cap screw

Illustrations courtesy Husqvarna Forest & Garden Co.

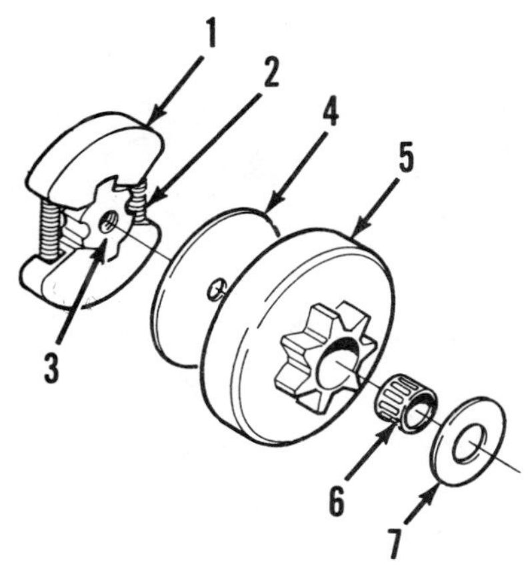

Fig. H103—Exploded view of two-shoe centrifugal clutch used on all models.

1. Clutch shoe
2. Spring
3. Hub
4. Washer
5. Clutch drum
6. Needle bearing
7. Washer

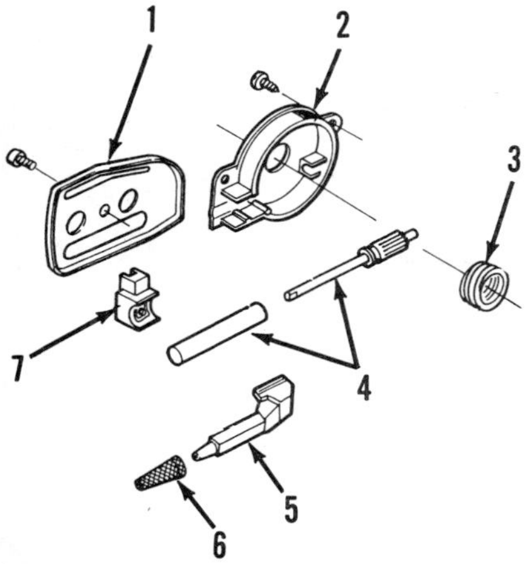

Fig. H104—Exploded view of automatic oil pump assembly.

1. Cover
2. Pump housing
3. Worm gear
4. Pump plunger
5. Oil suction tube
6. Oil screen
7. Bracket

attaching power head to saw housing and remove power head. Remove crankcase mounting screws and separate crankcase (10), crankshaft (9) and cylinder (1). Remove piston pin retaining ring (5) and push piston pin (4) out of piston.

Cylinder should be inspected for flaking, cracking or other damage. Inspect piston and discard if excessive wear or damage is evident. Cylinder and crankcase are available only as an assembly.

A locating pin is present in piston ring groove to prevent piston ring rotation. Be sure ring end gap is positioned around locating pin when installing cylinder. Arrow on piston crown must point toward exhaust port when installing piston. Be sure the piston pin retainers are seated snugly in piston boss. Lubricate piston and cylinder with engine oil prior to reassembly. Apply bead of RTV silicone sealer to mating surface of cylinder and crankcase. Tighten crankcase mounting screws evenly. Complete assembly in reverse of disassembly procedure.

CRANKSHAFT AND CONNECTING ROD. Refer to CYLINDER, PISTON, RINGS AND PIN paragraph for removal of crankshaft and connecting rod assembly (9—Fig. H102). Use suitable pullers to remove oil pump worm gear and main bearings from crankshaft.

Crankshaft and connecting rod are a unit assembly. Check rotation of connecting rod around crankpin and renew crankshaft unit if roughness or other damage is found. The connecting rod should not have any radial clearance (up and down play) on the crankpin.

When assembling engine, install seals (7) so lip is toward bearings (8). Apply small bead of RTV silicone sealant to mating surface of cylinder and crankcase and tighten crankcase mounting screws evenly. Make certain crankshaft rotates freely.

CLUTCH. All models are equipped with a two-shoe centrifugal clutch (Fig. H103), which is accessible after removing chain brake assembly and chain guide bar. Clutch hub has left-hand threads (turn clockwise to remove).

Inspect clutch shoes (1), drum (5) and bearing (6) for excessive wear or damage due to overheating. Clutch shoes must be renewed as a set. Inspect chain sprocket teeth for excessive wear and renew as necessary. Lubricate needle bearing with grease.

OIL PUMP. All models are equipped with an automatic oil pump that is driven by a worm gear (3—Fig. H104) on the crankshaft. Oil pump output is not adjustable.

To remove oil pump, first remove chain brake housing, guide bar and clutch assembly. Remove worm gear using suitable puller. Remove oil pump mounting screws and withdraw pump assembly. Oil pump suction pipe (5) and strainer (6) may be removed from oil tank using a screwdriver.

Inspect pump plunger assembly (4) for wear or damage and renew as necessary. Lubricate parts with oil during assembly.

REWIND STARTER. To disassemble rewind starter, remove starter housing from saw. Pull starter rope and hold rope pulley (5—Fig. H105) with notch in pulley adjacent to rope outlet. Pull rope back through outlet so it engages notch in pulley, then allow pulley to slowly unwind. Unscrew pulley retaining screw and carefully remove rope pulley. If rewind spring (6) must be removed, care should be taken not to allow spring to uncoil uncontrolled.

Install rewind spring in starter housing with spring coiled in clockwise direction as viewed from flywheel side. Wrap starter rope around rope pulley in a clockwise direction as viewed with

Illustrations courtesy Husqvarna Forest & Garden Co.

pulley in starter housing. Turn rope pulley two turns clockwise before passing rope through rope outlet to place tension on rewind spring. Spring tension is correct if rope pulley can be rotated approximately 1/4 turn further when rope is fully extended.

When installing starter assembly on saw, make sure starter pulley properly engages pawls on flywheel before tightening retaining cap screws.

CHAIN BRAKE. All models are equipped with a chain brake system designed to stop chain movement should kickback occur. The chain brake is activated either by the operator's hand striking the hand guard (2—Fig. H106) or by sufficient force being applied to the guide bar tip during kickback to cause the front handle to contact trigger lever (4), resulting in automatic activation of brake mechanism.

To disassemble, remove brake housing (12) from saw. Remove pivot sleeve retaining screw, tap sleeves (10) out of hand guard and remove hand guard from housing. Remove brake cover plate (14) and carefully pry brake spring (5) from housing. Drive out pin (3) and withdraw brake trigger (4) and brake band (6).

Inspect all parts for wear or damage. Renew brake band if band thickness is less than 0.75 mm (0.030 in.). To reassemble, reverse the disassembly procedure. No adjustment of brake mechanism is necessary.

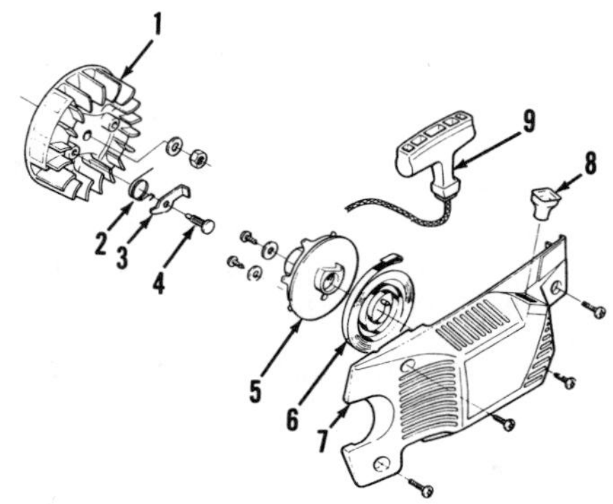

Fig. H105—Exploded view of rewind starter assembly.

1. Flywheel
2. Spring
3. Pawl
4. Retainer
5. Rope pulley
6. Rewind spring
7. Starter housing
8. Rope guide
9. Rope handle

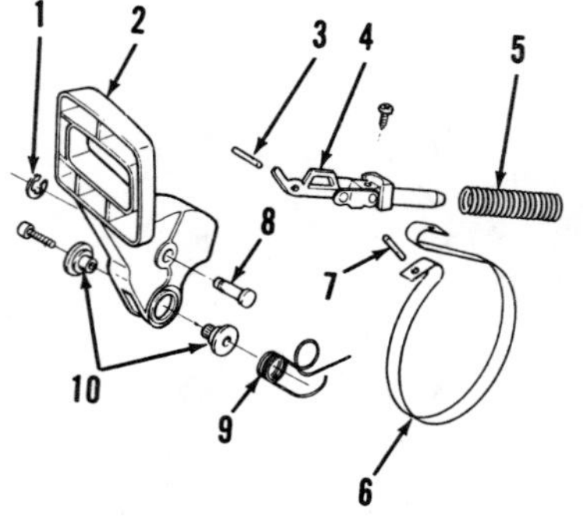

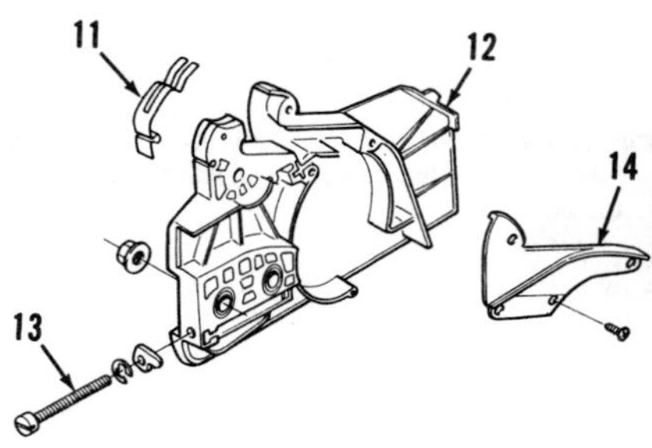

Fig. H106—Exploded view of chain brake mechanism.

1. Hand guard
2. Retainer
3. Pin
4. Trigger assy.
5. Brake spring
6. Brake band
7. Pin
8. Pin
9. Spring
10. Pivot sleeves
11. Spring
12. Brake housing
13. Chain tension adjusting bolt
14. Brake cover

Illustrations courtesy Husqvarna Forest & Garden Co.

HUSQVARNA

Model	Bore mm (in.)	Stroke mm (in.)	Displacement cc (cu. in.)	Drive Type
394 XP, 394 XPG	...	...	94 (5.7)	Direct

MAINTENANCE

SPARK PLUG. Recommended spark plug is Champion CJ8Y. Spark plug electrode gap should be 0.5 mm (0.020 in.).

CARBURETOR. All models are equipped with a Walbro WJ diaphragm type carburetor. Refer to CARBURETOR SERVICE section for overhaul information and exploded view of Walbro WJ carburetor.

Initial adjustment of both low and high speed mixture screws is $1^1/_2$ turns open from a lightly seated position. Make final adjustment with engine warm and running. Adjust low speed mixture screw to obtain highest idle speed, then turn screw $^1/_4$ turn counterclockwise. Engine should accelerate cleanly without hesitation. If engine stumbles or seems sluggish when accelerating, adjust low speed mixture screw until engine accelerates without hesitation. Adjust high speed mixture screw to obtain optimum performance under cutting load. Do not adjust high speed mixture needle too lean as engine may be damaged due to lack of lubrication and overheating. Adjust idle speed screw so engine idles just below clutch engagement speed.

IGNITION. All models are equipped with a breakerless electronic ignition system. Ignition timing is not adjustable. Air gap between ignition module core and flywheel magnets should be 0.4 mm (0.015 in.). Adjust air gap by loosening ignition module retaining screws.

LUBRICATION. The engine is lubricated by mixing oil with the fuel. Recommended oil is Husqvarna Two-Stroke Oil mixed at a ratio of 50:1. If Husqvarna Two-Stroke Oil is not available, a good quality oil designed for two-stroke engines may be used when mixed at a 25:1 ratio. Use a separate container when mixing the oil and gas.

All models are equipped with an automatic chain oil pump. A good quality chain oil is recommended, although clean automotive oil may also be used. If automotive type oil is used, oil viscosity should be chosen according to ambient temperature.

Oil pump output is adjustable; pump adjusting screw is accessible on underside of saw. Do not adjust oil pump output with engine running. Rotate adjusting screw clockwise to decrease oil pump output and counterclockwise to increase pump output.

REPAIRS

CRANKCASE PRESSURE TEST. An improperly sealed crankcase can cause the engine to be hard to start, run rough, have low power and overheat. Refer to ENGINE SERVICE section of this manual for crankcase pressure test procedure. If crankcase leakage is indicated, pressurize crankcase and use a soap and water solution to check gaskets, seals, pulse line and castings for leakage.

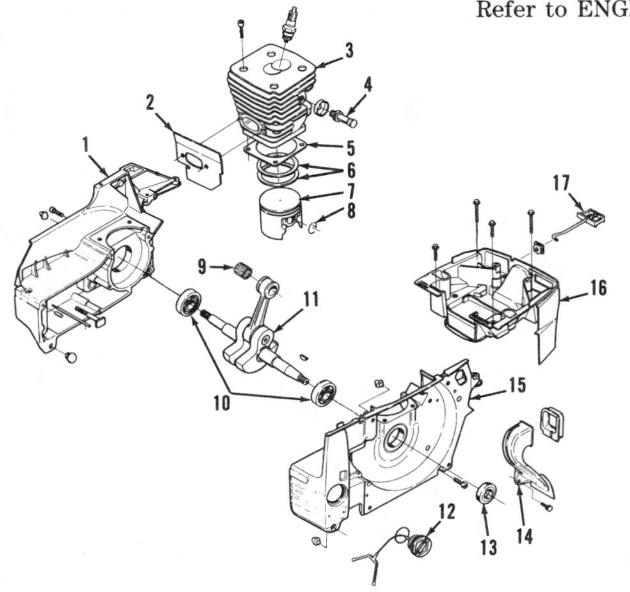

Fig. H110—Exploded view of engine assembly.

1. Crankcase half
2. Heat shield
3. Cylinder
4. Compression release mechanism
5. Gasket
6. Piston rings
7. Piston
8. Retaining ring
9. Needle bearing
10. Main bearings
11. Crankshaft & connecting rod assy.
12. Oil tank cap
13. Seal
14. Intake air duct
15. Crankcase half
16. Air cleaner housing
17. Choke rod

CYLINDER, PISTON, RINGS AND PIN. To disassemble, remove air cleaner cover, air filter and cylinder cover. Disconnect carburetor linkage and fuel line. Remove screws attaching muffler bracket to crankcase. Remove cylinder mounting screws and lift cylinder with carburetor and muffler from crankcase. Remove piston pin retaining ring (8—Fig. H110) and push piston pin out of piston. Remove carburetor and muffler from cylinder.

Cylinder has a chrome bore which should be inspected for flaking, cracking or other damage to chromed surface. Inspect piston and discard if excessive wear or damage is evident. New cylinder is available only with fitted piston, however, a new piston is available for installation in a used cylinder.

Arrow on piston crown must point toward exhaust port when installing piston. Be sure the piston pin retainers are seated snugly in piston boss. A locating pin is present in piston ring groove to prevent piston ring rotation. Be sure ring end gap is positioned around locating pin when installing cylinder.

CRANKSHAFT, CONNECTING ROD AND CRANKCASE. To disassemble, remove chain and guide bar, cylinder cover, air filter assembly, starter housing and air baffle. Remove spark plug and install a piston stop in spark plug hole. Remove flywheel mounting nut (right-hand threads) and starter pawls. Use suitable puller to remove flywheel. Remove ignition module and generator coil if so equipped. Remove clutch assembly (left-hand threads) and oil pump. Remove cylinder mounting screws and pull cylinder off piston. Separate piston from connecting rod. Remove air filter housing (16—Fig H110). Separate fuel tank and handle assembly from crankcase. Remove crankcase mounting screws and use suitable puller tool to separate crankcase halves (1 and 15) and press crankshaft (11) out of main bearings (10). Care should be taken not to damage mating surfaces of crankcase halves.

Crankshaft and connecting rod are a unit assembly. Check rotation of connecting rod around crankpin and renew crankshaft unit if roughness or other damage is found. The connecting rod should not have any radial clearance (up and down play) on the crankpin.

To reassemble, reverse the disassembly procedure. Heat crankcase halves to ease installation of main bearings. Be sure crankshaft is snug against the main bearings and centered in crankcase. Tighten crankcase screws evenly, starting with screws closest to crankshaft.

CLUTCH. All models are equipped with the three-shoe centrifugal clutch shown in Fig. H111. Remove clutch cover, guide bar and chain. Clutch hub (1) has left-hand threads (turn clockwise to remove). Inspect clutch shoes (2) and drum (4) for excessive wear or damage due to overheating. Check chain sprocket (5) and splines on clutch drum for wear and damage. Inspect clutch drum bearing (6) and crankshaft for wear or damage. When reassembling, lubricate needle bearing with high-temperature grease.

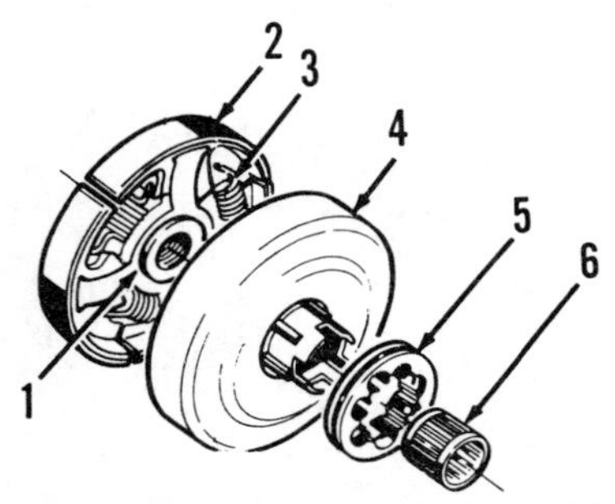

Fig. H111—Exploded view of clutch assembly.

1. Clutch hub
2. Clutch shoe
3. Spring
4. Clutch drum
5. Sprocket
6. Needle bearing

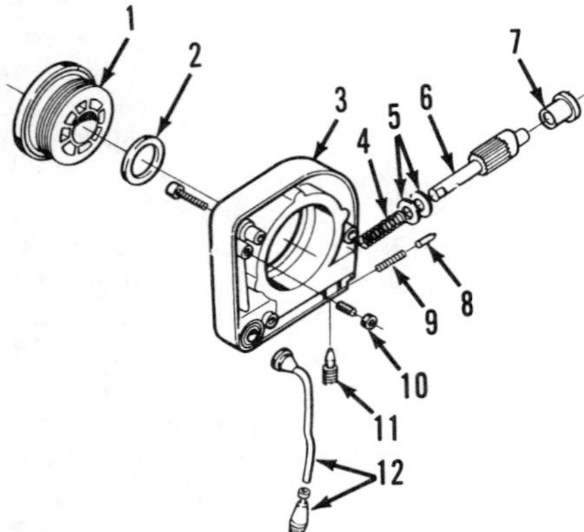

Fig. H112—Exploded view of automatic oil pump assembly.

1. Drive gear
2. Seal
3. Pump housing
4. Spring
5. Washers
6. Plunger
7. Plug
8. Pin
9. Spring
10. Seal
11. Adjusting screw
12. Oil pickup tube & screen

OIL PUMP. All models are equipped with the adjustable automatic oil pump shown in Fig. H112. Oil pump output is adjusted by turning screw (11).

Drain oil tank and remove clutch cover, guide bar, chain and clutch assembly for access to oil pump. Oil filter screen (12) is accessible after removing oil pump assembly. Oil pump may be disassembled for cleaning and inspection after removing plug (7) and withdrawing plunger (6). When reassembling pump, make certain steel washer (5) is next to spring (4).

REWIND STARTER. To disassemble rewind starter, remove starter housing (8—Fig. H113) from saw. Pull starter rope and hold rope pulley (10) with notch in pulley adjacent to rope outlet. Pull rope back through outlet so it engages notch in pulley and allow pulley to completely unwind. Unscrew pulley retaining screw (4) and carefully remove rope pulley. If rewind spring (9) must be removed, care should be taken not to allow spring to uncoil uncontrolled.

Install rewind spring in starter housing with spring coiled in clockwise direction from outer spring end. Wrap starter rope around rope pulley in a clockwise direction as viewed with pulley in starter housing. Turn rope pulley two turns clockwise before passing rope through rope outlet to place tension on rewind spring. Spring tension is correct if rope pulley can be rotated approximately ½ turn further when rope is fully extended.

When installing starter assembly on saw, make sure starter pulley properly engages pawls on flywheel before tightening retaining cap screws.

CHAIN BRAKE. All models are equipped with a chain brake system designed to stop chain movement should kickback occur. The chain brake is activated by the operator's hand striking the hand guard (5—Fig. H114) that actuates trigger mechanism (8), allowing brake spring (9) to force brake band (10) tight around clutch drum to stop chain movement. Pull back hand guard to reset mechanism.

To disassemble, remove brake housing (11) from saw. Remove pivot sleeve retaining screw (2), tap sleeves (3) out of hand guard and remove hand guard from housing. Remove brake cover plate (12) and carefully pry brake spring (9) from housing. Drive out retaining pin and withdraw brake trigger (8) and brake band (10).

Inspect all parts for wear or damage. Renew brake band if band thickness is less than 0.75 mm (0.030 in.). To reassemble, reverse the disassembly procedure. No adjustment of brake mechanism is necessary.

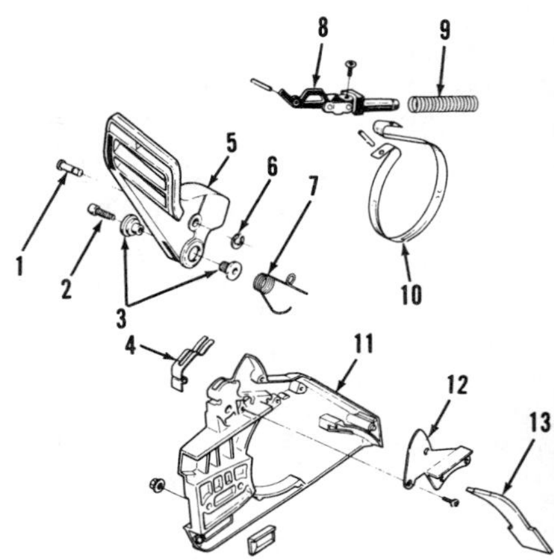

Fig. H114—Exploded view of chain brake mechanism.

1. Pin
2. Screw
3. Sleeves
4. Spring
5. Hand guard
6. "E" ring
7. Spring
8. Trigger mechanism
9. Brake spring
10. Brake band
11. Brake housing
12. Cover
13. Sawdust guard

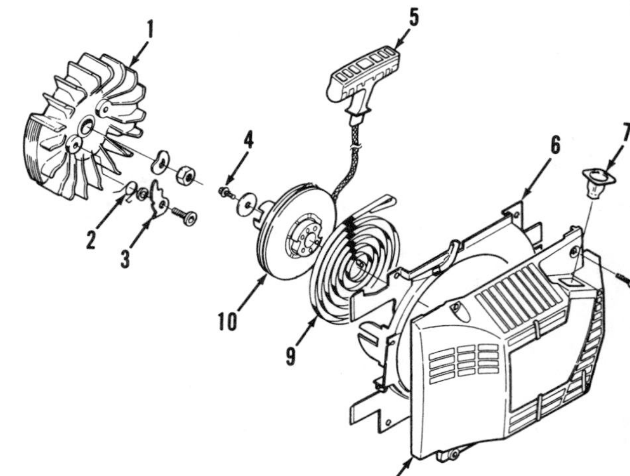

Fig. H113—Exploded view of rewind starter assembly.

1. Flywheel
2. Spring
3. Pawl
4. Screw
5. Rope handle
6. Air baffle
7. Rope guide
8. Starter housing
9. Rewind spring
10. Rope pulley

Illustrations courtesy Husqvarna Forest & Garden Co.

HUSQVARNA

Model	Bore mm (in.)	Stroke mm (in.)	Displacement cc (cu. in.)	Drive Type
3120 XP	60 (2.36)	42 (1.654)	118.7 (7.2)	Direct

MAINTENANCE

SPARK PLUG. Recommended spark plug is Champion CJ8Y. Spark plug electrode gap should be 0.5 mm (0.020 in.).

CARBURETOR. All saws are equipped with a Walbro WG diaphragm type carburetor. Refer to CARBURETOR SERVICE section for overhaul information and exploded view of Walbro WG carburetor.

Initial adjustment of low speed mixture screw is 1¼ turns open from a lightly seated position. Make final adjustment with engine warm and running. Adjust low speed mixture screw to obtain highest idle speed, then turn screw ¼ turn counterclockwise. Engine should accelerate cleanly without hesitation. If engine stumbles or seems sluggish when accelerating, adjust low speed mixture screw until engine accelerates without hesitation. Adjust idle speed screw so engine idles just below clutch engagement speed. A fixed main jet is used and no adjustment of high speed mixture is required.

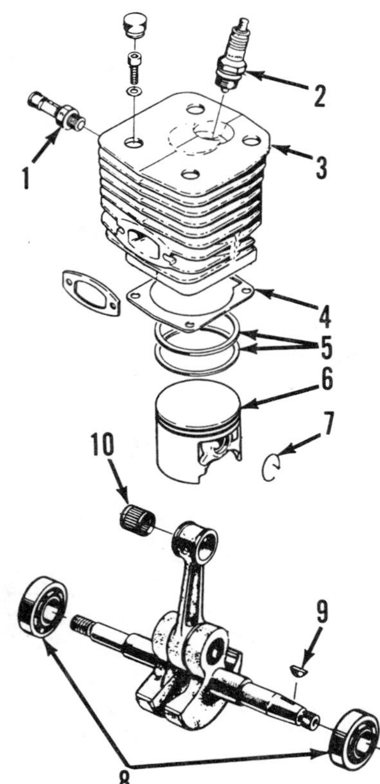

Fig. H120—Exploded view of crankshaft and piston.

1. Compression release valve
2. Spark plug
3. Cylinder
4. Gasket
5. Piston rings
6. Piston
7. Retaining ring
8. Main bearings
9. Crankshaft & connecting rod assy.
10. Needle bearing

IGNITION. All saws are equipped with a breakerless electronic ignition system. Ignition timing is not adjustable. Air gap between ignition module core and flywheel magnets should be 0.4 mm (0.015 in.). Adjust air gap by loosening ignition module retaining screws.

LUBRICATION. The engine is lubricated by mixing oil with the fuel. Recommended oil is Husqvarna Two-Stroke Oil mixed at a ratio of 50:1. If Husqvarna Two-Stroke Oil is not available, a good quality oil designed for two-stroke engines may be used when mixed at a 25:1 ratio. Use a separate container when mixing the oil and gas.

All saws are equipped with an automatic chain oil pump. A good quality chain oil is recommended, although clean automotive oil may also be used. If automotive type oil is used, oil viscosity should be chosen according to ambient temperature.

REPAIRS

CRANKCASE PRESSURE TEST. An improperly sealed crankcase can cause the engine to be hard to start, run rough, have low power and overheat. Refer to ENGINE SERVICE section of this manual for crankcase pressure test procedure. If crankcase leakage is indicated, pressurize crankcase and use a soap and water solution to check gaskets, seals, pulse line and castings for leakage.

CYLINDER, PISTON, RINGS AND PIN. To disassemble, remove air cleaner cover, cylinder cover, air filter, air filter housing and carburetor. Remove screws attaching muffler bracket to crankcase. Remove cylinder mounting screws and lift cylinder (3—Fig. H120) with muffler from crankcase. Remove piston pin retaining ring (7), push piston pin out of piston (6) and separate piston and needle bearing (10) from connecting rod. Remove muffler from cylinder.

Cylinder has a chrome bore that should be inspected for flaking, cracking or other damage to chromed surface. Inspect piston and discard if excessive wear or damage is evident. New cylinder is available only with fitted piston. However, a new piston is available for installation in a used cylinder.

Arrow on piston crown must point toward exhaust port when installing piston. Be sure the piston pin retainers are seated snugly in piston boss. A locating pin is present in piston ring grooves to prevent piston ring rotation. Be sure ring end gap is positioned around locating pin when installing cylinder. Lubricate cylinder bore and piston rings with engine oil prior to assembly.

CRANKSHAFT, CONNECTING ROD AND CRANKCASE. To disassemble, remove chain and guide bar, cylinder cover, air filter assembly, starter housing and air baffle. Remove spark plug and install a piston stop in spark plug hole. Remove flywheel mounting nut (right-hand threads) and starter pawls. Use suitable puller to remove flywheel. Disconnect ignition wiring and remove ignition module. Remove clutch assembly (left-hand threads) and oil pump assembly. Remove cylinder mounting screws and pull cylinder off piston. Separate piston from connecting rod. Remove screws securing vibration isolators (11—Fig. H121) and springs (7) and separate fuel tank and handle assembly (6) from crankcase. Remove crankcase mounting screws and use suitable puller tool to separate crankcase halves (14 and 19) and press crankshaft (9—Fig. H120) out of main bearings (8). Care should be taken not to damage mating surfaces of crankcase halves.

Crankshaft and connecting rod are a unit assembly. Check rotation of connecting rod around crankpin and renew crankshaft unit if roughness or other damage is found. The connecting rod should not have any radial clearance (up and down play) on the crankpin.

To reassemble, reverse the disassembly procedure. Heat crankcase halves to ease installation of main bearings. Be sure crankshaft is snug against the main bearings and centered in crankcase. Tighten crankcase screws evenly, starting with screws closest to crankshaft.

CLUTCH. All saws are equipped with the three-shoe centrifugal clutch shown in Fig. H122. Saws may be equipped with clutch drum (2) with integral chain sprocket or with separate clutch drum (2A) and sprocket (2B).

Remove clutch cover, guide bar and chain for access to clutch. Clutch hub (1) has left-hand threads (turn clockwise to remove). Inspect clutch shoes and drum for excessive wear or damage due to overheating. Check chain sprocket and splines on clutch drum for wear and damage. Inspect clutch drum bearing (3) and crankshaft for wear or damage. When reassembling, lubricate needle bearing with high-temperature grease.

OIL PUMP. All saws are equipped with the adjustable automatic oil pump shown in Fig. H123. Oil pump output is adjusted by turning screw (8). The adjusting screw has four positions—minimum oil flow is obtained when screw is turned fully clockwise and maximum pump output is obtained when screw is turned fully counterclockwise. Output of oil pump may also be controlled by a manual override system. Manual override lever (12—Fig. H121) is connected to pump output control arm (10—Fig. H123) by cable (16). Rotation of override control lever moves the pump control arm (10) to maximum output position, overriding the setting of pump adjusting screw. Note that if adjusting screw is set to maximum output position, overrride system will not provide any additional oil output.

Drain oil tank and remove clutch cover, guide bar, chain and clutch assembly for access to oil pump. Oil pickup tube and filter screen (16—Fig. H121) is accessible after removing oil pump assembly.

Oil pump may be disassembled for cleaning and inspection after removing plunger bracket (9—Fig. H123) and withdrawing pump plunger (14).

Inspect all parts for wear and renew as necessary. Renew oil seal (6) and "O" rings (5 and 7). Lubricate parts with oil when reassembling. Oil seal (6) should installed so that it protrudes 0.2-0.4 mm (0.008-0.016 in.) beyond outer surface of pump housing (4).

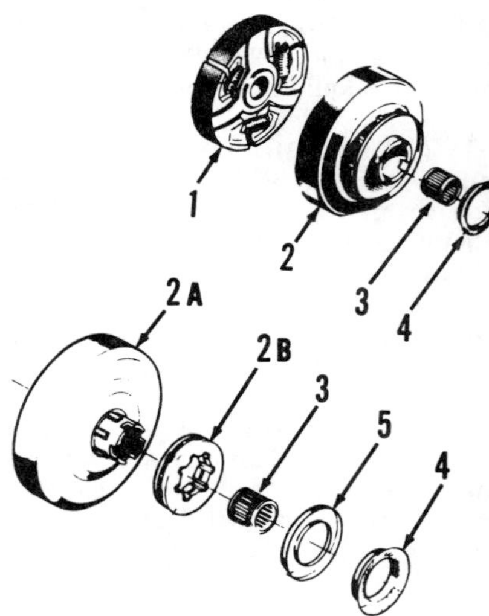

Fig. H122—Exploded view of clutch assembly. Chain sprocket may be integral with clutch drum or separate on some models.

1. Clutch assy.
2. Clutch drum & sprocket
2A. Clutch drum
2B. Chain sprocket
3. Needle bearing
4. Seal
5. Washer

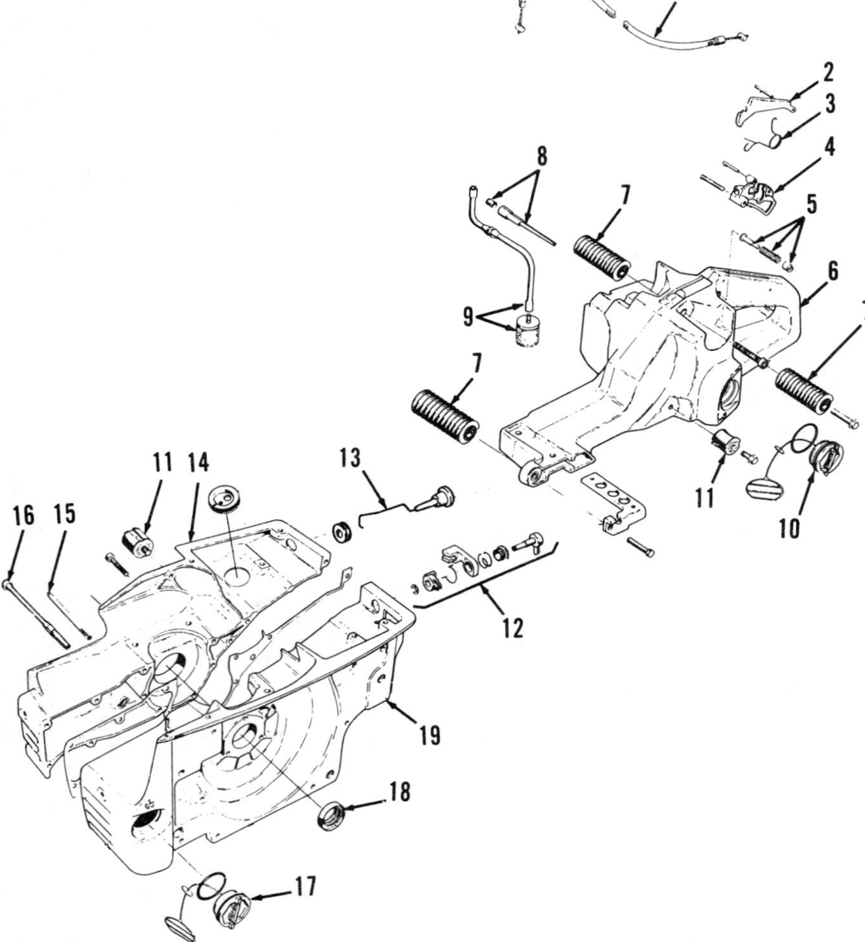

Fig. H121—Exploded view of crankcase and rear handle.

1. Throttle cable
2. Throttle trigger lock
3. Spring
4. Throttle trigger
5. Lock pin
6. Rear handle
7. Springs
8. Fuel tank vent
9. Fuel line & filter
10. Fuel tank cap
11. Vibration isolator mount
12. Oil pump override lever assy.
13. Choke rod
14. Crankcase half
15. Oil line
16. Oil pickup tube
17. Oil tank cap
18. Seal
19. Crankcase half

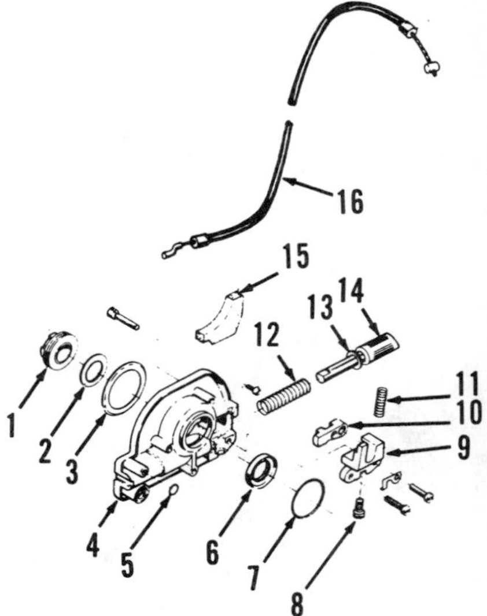

Fig. H123—Exploded view of automatic oil pump.

1. Worm gear
2. Washer
3. Sleeve
4. Pump housing
5. "O" ring
6. Seal
7. "O" ring
8. Adjusting screw
9. Plunger bracket
10. Pump output control arm
11. Spring
12. Spring
13. Washer
14. Pump plunger
15. Seal
16. Override cable

Illustrations courtesy Husqvarna Forest & Garden Co.

REWIND STARTER. To disassemble rewind starter, remove starter housing (10—Fig. H124) from saw. Pull starter rope and hold rope pulley (8) with notch in pulley adjacent to rope outlet. Pull rope back through outlet so it engages notch in pulley and allow pulley to completely unwind. Unscrew pulley retaining screw (6) and carefully remove rope pulley. If rewind spring (9) must be removed, care should be taken not to allow spring to uncoil uncontrolled.

Install rewind spring in starter housing with spring coiled in clockwise direction from outer spring end. Wrap starter rope around rope pulley in a clockwise direction as viewed with pulley in starter housing. Turn rope pulley two turns clockwise before passing rope through rope outlet to place tension on rewind spring. Spring tension is correct if rope pulley can be rotated approximately $^1/_2$ turn further when rope is fully extended.

When installing starter assembly on saw, make sure starter pulley properly engages pawls on flywheel before tightening retaining cap screws.

CHAIN BRAKE. All models are equipped with a chain brake system designed to stop chain movement should kickback occur. The chain brake is activated by the operator's hand striking the hand guard (1—Fig. H125) which actuates trigger mechanism (10), allowing brake spring (7) to force brake band (9) tight around clutch drum to stop chain movement. Pull back hand guard to reset mechanism.

To disassemble, remove brake housing (15) from saw. Remove pivot sleeve retaining screw (2) and tap sleeves (3) out of hand guard. Remove hand guard pin (5) and remove hand guard from housing. Place unit in a vise and place tension against brake rod (6) and spring (7). Drive pin (13) out of housing and carefully release spring tension. Remove band retaining screw (14). Unscrew brake rod from brake band (12) and withdraw brake band from housing.

Inspect all parts for wear or damage. Renew brake band if band thickness is less than 0.75 mm (0.030 in.).

To reassemble, position brake band in brake housing. Install plastic guide (8), then thread brake rod onto band until it is bottomed (recess in end of rod should be facing down). Install brake trigger and use vise to place tension on brake spring. Push brake trigger (10) into locked position, then install pin (13). Install hand guard (1). No adjustment of brake mechanism is necessary.

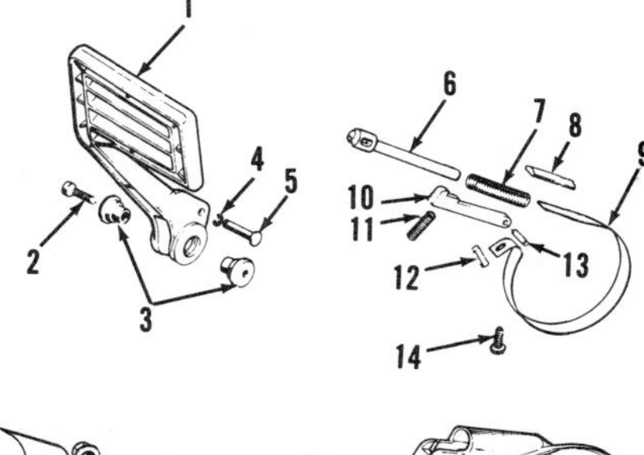

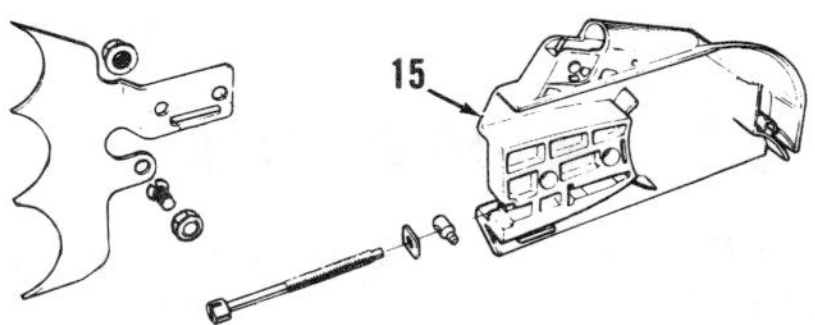

Fig. H125—Exploded view of chain brake mechanism.

1. Hand guard
2. Screw
3. Sleeves
4. "E" ring
5. Pin
6. Brake rod
7. Brake spring
8. Plastic guide
9. Brake band
10. Trigger lever
11. Spring
12. Pin
13. Pin
14. Screw
15. Brake housing

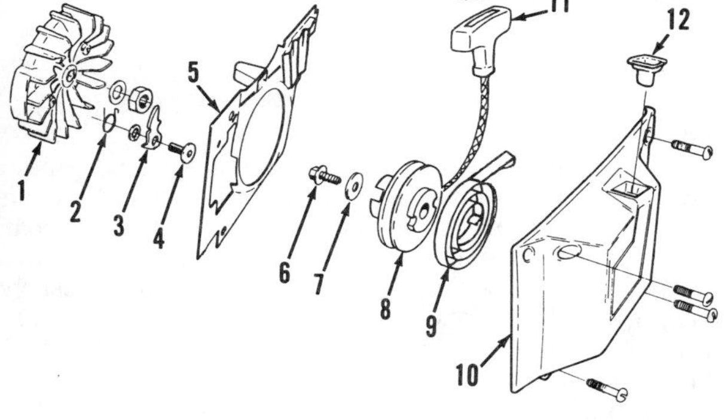

Fig. H124—Exploded view of rewind starter assembly.

1. Flywheel
2. Spring
3. Pawl
4. Pin
5. Air baffle
6. Screw
7. Washer
8. Rope pulley
9. Rewind spring
10. Starter housing
11. Rope handle
12. Rope guide

Illustrations courtesy Husqvarna Forest & Garden Co.

JONSERED

Model	Bore mm (in.)	Stroke mm (in.)	Displacement cc (cu. in.)	Drive Type
49SP, 50, 51, 52, 52E	44 (1.732)	32 (1.26)	49 (3.0)	Direct
60, 62	45 (1.77)	35 (1.378)	56 (3.4)	Direct
70E	50 (1.968)	35 (1.378)	69 (4.2)	Direct
75	50 (1.968)	38 (1.496)	75 (4.6)	Direct
111, 111 S	56 (2.2)	45 (1.77)	110 (6.7)	Direct
451E, 451EV	42 (1.654)	32 (1.26)	44.3 (2.7)	Direct
521 EV	44 (1.732)	32 (1.26)	49 (3.0)	Direct
601, 621	45 (1.77)	35 (1.378)	56 (3.4)	Direct
751	50 (1.968)	38 (1.496)	75 (4.6)	Direct
801	52 (2.047)	38 (1.496)	80 (4.9)	Direct

MAINTENANCE

SPARK PLUG. Recommended spark plug is Bosch WS7F for Models 50, 51, 52E, 521EV and 111 and Champion CJ7Y for all other models. Recommended spark plug electrode gap is 0.5 mm (0.020 in.).

CARBURETOR. All models are equipped with a Tillotson diaphragm carburetor. Refer to Tillotson section of CARBURETOR SERVICE section for exploded view and overhaul of carburetor.

Initial carburetor adjustment is one turn open from a lightly seated position for both low and high speed mixture screws. Make final adjustment with engine warm and running. Adjust idle speed screw so engine idles just below clutch engagement speed. Adjust low speed mixture screw so engine will accelerate cleanly without hesitation. Adjust high speed mixture screw to obtain optimum performance under cutting load.

Fig. J1—Exploded view of ignition assembly used on Models 50, 51 and 52.

1. Cover
2. Ignition coil
3. Movable ignition breaker-point
4. Fixed ignition breaker-point
5. Condenser
6. Stator plate
7. Seal

IGNITION. Models 451E, 451EV, 52E, 521EV and 70E are equipped with a breakerless capacitor discharge ignition system. All other models are equipped with a flywheel magneto ignition system with breaker-points located under the flywheel.

On all breaker-point models, point gap should be 0.4 mm (0.016 in.). Ignition timing for all breaker-point models is listed in the following table. Ignition timing is adjusted by loosening stator plate retaining screws and rotating stator plate. Rotate stator plate clockwise to advance timing and counterclockwise to retard timing.

Model	Ignition Timing BTDC
49SP	2.0 mm (0.079 in.)
50, 51, 52	2.0 mm (0.079 in.)
60, 601	3.2 mm (0.126 in.)
62, 621	2.7 mm (0.106 in.)
75, 751	2.5 mm (0.098 in.)
801	2.7 mm (0.106 in.)
111	3.8 mm (0.150 in.)

On electronic ignition models, ignition timing is fixed. Individual electronic ignition components are available separately on 451E, 451EV and 70E models while electronic components must be serviced as a unit assembly on 52E and

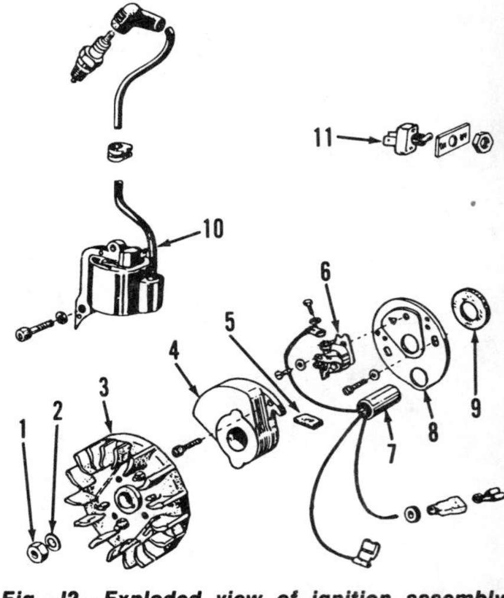

Fig. J2—Exploded view of ignition assembly used on 49SP models.

1. Nut
2. Washer
3. Flywheel
4. Cover
5. Oil wick
6. Fixed ignition breaker-point
7. Condenser
8. Stator plate
9. Seal
10. Ignition coil
11. Stop switch

Illustrations courtesy Jonsered Power Products AB

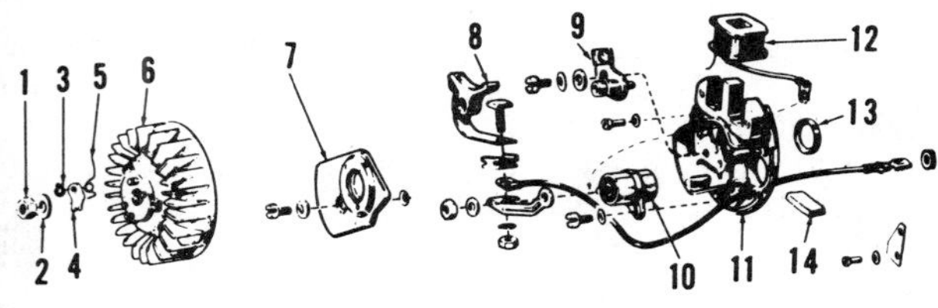

Fig. J3—Exploded view of ignition and flywheel assemblies used on Models 60, 601, 62, 621, 75, 751 and 801.

1. Nut
2. Washer
3. Snap ring
4. Starter dog
5. Spring
6. Flywheel
7. Cover
8. Movable ignition breaker-point
9. Fixed ignition breaker-point
10. Condenser
11. Stator plate
12. Ignition coil
13. Seal
14. Oil wick

521EV models. Air gap between flywheel magnets and ignition coil legs should be 0.3 mm (0.012 in.).

LUBRICATION. The engine is lubricated by mixing oil with the fuel. Recommend oil is Jonsered engine oil or a BIA certified air-cooled two-stroke engine oil approved for 40:1 fuel mixtures. Recommend fuel mixture ratio is 40:1 when using an approved engine oil. If a recommended oil is not available, a good quality oil designed for air-cooled two-stroke engines may be used when mixed with the fuel at a 20:1 ratio. Use a separate container when mixing the oil and gas.

All models are equipped with an automatic chain oiler. A good quality chain oil should be used according to ambient temperature. Automatic oil pump discharge on all models except Models 50 and 51 is adjusted by turning adjusting screw shown in Fig. J4 or Fig. J5. Initial setting is 1½ turns open. Turning screw clockwise decreases oil flow. Automatic oil pump on Models 50 and 51 is not adjustable.

CARBON. Carbon deposits should be removed from muffler and exhaust ports at regular intervals. When scraping carbon, be careful not to damage engine cylinder. Do not allow loosened carbon into cylinder.

REPAIRS

CYLINDER, PISTON, PIN AND RINGS. Cylinder is chrome plated and oversize pistons are not available. Cylinders and pistons on all early models are graded during production according to manufacturing tolerances. Pistons and cylinders may be graded "A, B, C, D, E, F and G." "A" pistons and cylinders are largest. Piston and cylinder should be of same grade. Later models do not have graded cylinders or pistons.

Cylinder should be checked for scoring, cracking or peeling of chrome surface. Install piston on all models so arrow on piston crown (Fig. J10) is pointing toward exhaust port. Care should be taken when installing cylinder on all models so piston rings are positioned correctly around piston ring locating pins. On some models, thrust washers are installed adjacent to the connecting rod small end bearing.

CONNECTING ROD, CRANKSHAFT AND CRANKCASE. Connecting rod is equipped with a needle bearing in small end. Some models also have thrust washers on both sides of small end bearing. Connecting rod and crankshaft are a unit assembly on all models. Automatic oil pump should be removed prior to crankcase separation. Connecting rod, crankshaft and bearing should not be disassembled except by a shop equipped to realign crankshaft. Main bearings on Model 50 are roller type and are a press fit in crankcases. Bearings are installed with lettering on bearing

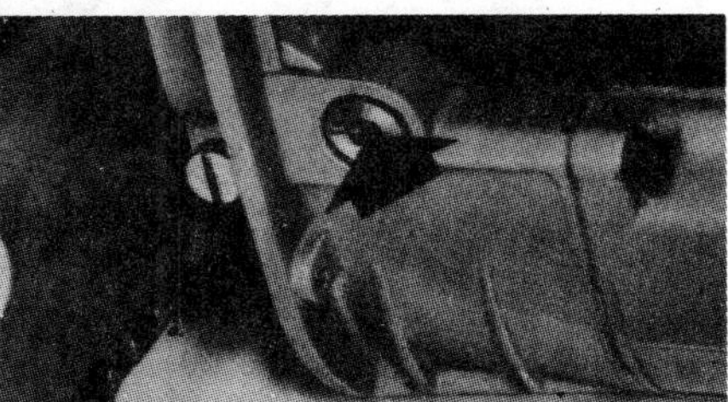

Fig. J4—View of oil pump adjusting screw on Models 60, 601, 62, 621, 75, 751 and 801.

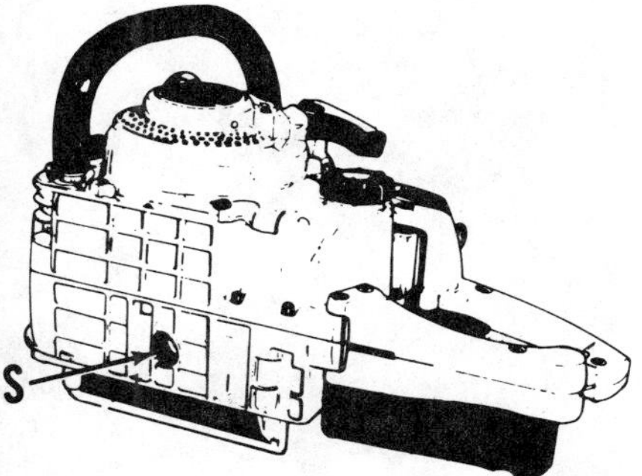

Fig. J5—View showing location of oil pump adjusting screw on Models 451E, 451EV, 495P, 52, 52E, 521EV, 70E and 111.

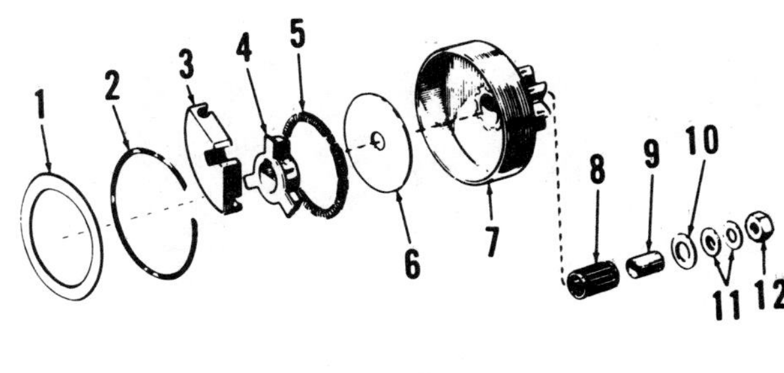

Fig. J6—Exploded view of clutch used on Models 75 and 751. Other models are similar.

1. Washer
2. Snap ring
3. Clutch shoe
4. Clutch hub
5. Spring
6. Washer
7. Clutch drum
8. Bearing
9. Bearing race
10. Washer
11. Washer
12. Nut

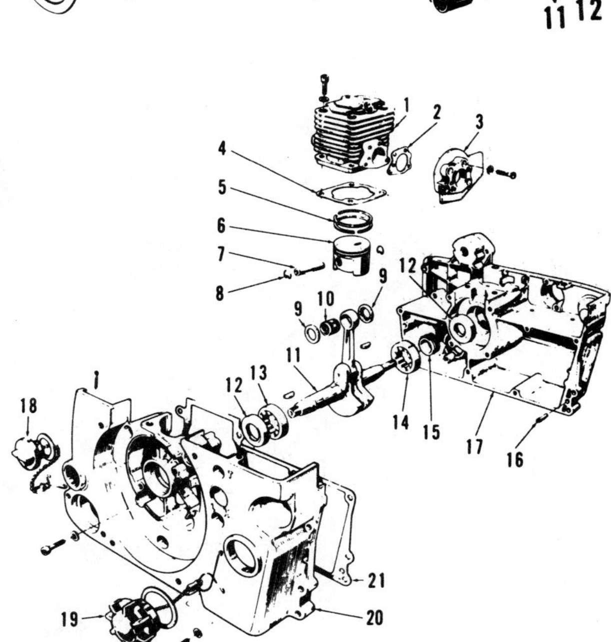

Fig. J8—Exploded view of engine used on Models 50, 51, 52, 52E and 521 EV. Models 451E, 451EV, 49SP and 70E are similar.

1. Cylinder
2. Gasket
3. Spacer
4. Gasket
5. Piston rings
6. Piston
7. Piston pin
8. Retainer
9. Washer
10. Bearing
11. Crankshaft & rod assy.
12. Seal
13. Bearing
14. Bearing
15. Oil pump drive gear
16. Dowel pin
17. Crankcase half
18. Oil cap
19. Fuel cap
20. Crankcase half
21. Gasket

Illustrations courtesy Jonsered Power Products AB

toward outside of crankcase. Bearings on all other models are pressed on crankshaft. Oil pump cam on Models 60, 75, 601, 621, 751 and 801 should be installed as shown in Fig. J11 with highest point of cam pointing toward crankpin.

Unthreaded end of oil pump worm gear (15 – Fig. J8) used on Models 49SP, 52, 52E and 521EV must be installed against inner race of main bearing (14).

CLUTCH. Clutch on all models is retained by a nut. Clutch retaining nut has left hand threads. Refer to Fig. J6 for exploded view of clutch.

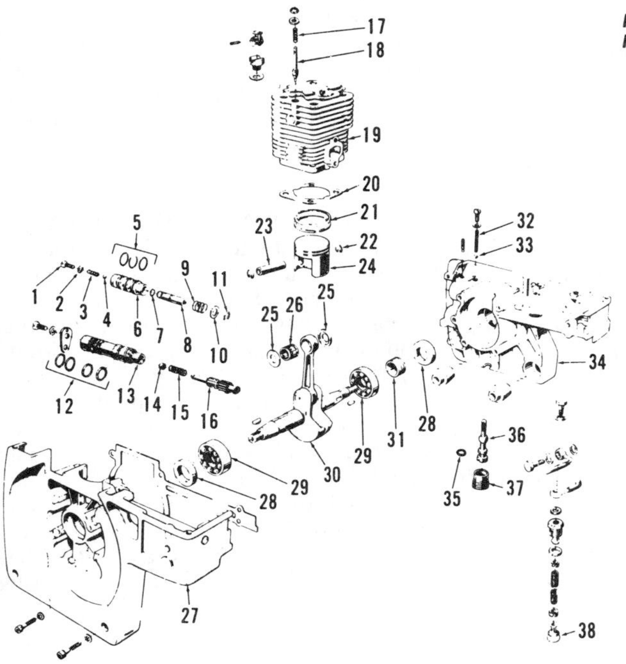

Fig. J8A — Exploded view of Model 111 engine assembly.

1. Screw
2. Washer
3. Spring
4. Ball
5. "O" rings
6. Manual oil pump housing
7. "O" ring
8. Piston
9. Spring
10. Washer
11. Snap ring
12. "O" rings
13. Automatic oil pump housing
14. Bushing
15. Spring
16. Piston
17. Spring
18. Compression release valve
19. Cylinder
20. Gasket
21. Piston rings
22. Pin retainer
23. Piston pin
24. Piston
25. Washer
26. Bearing
27. Left crankcase half
28. Seal
29. Bearing
30. Crankshaft & rod assy.
31. Oil pump worm gear
32. Spring
33. Ball
34. Right crankcase half
35. "O" ring
36. Oil pump adjusting screw
37. Retainer
38. Oil pickup

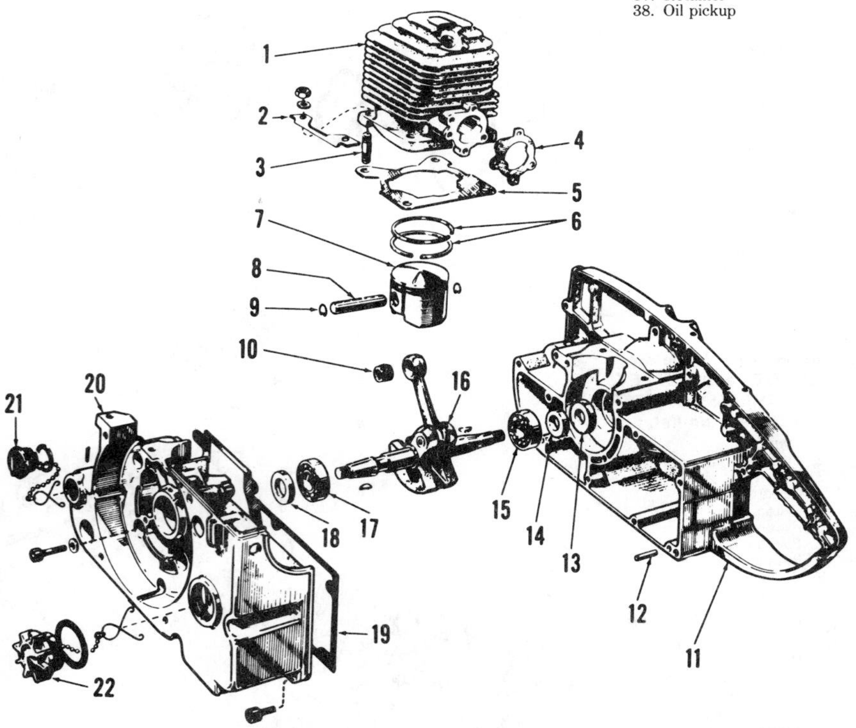

Fig. J9 — Exploded view of typical engine on Models 60, 601, 62, 621, 75, 751 and 801.

1. Cylinder
2. Lockplate
3. Stud
4. Gasket
5. Gasket
6. Piston rings
7. Piston
8. Piston pin
9. Retainer
10. Bearing
11. Crankcase half
12. Dowel pin
13. Seal
14. Oil pump cam
15. Bearing
16. Crankshaft & rod assy.
17. Bearing
18. Seal
19. Gasket
20. Crankcase half
21. Oil cap
22. Fuel cap

AUTOMATIC OIL PUMP. All models are equipped with a crankshaft driven automatic oil pump. Oil pump on Models 49SP, 50, 51, 52, 52E, 70E and 111 is worm driven while all other models are driven by a cam. Refer to Figs. J8A, J12, J13, J14 or J15 for exploded or cross-sectional view of oil pump.

Guide pin (4 – Fig. J12) on Models 50 and 51 rides in a cam groove in piston (7) and must be removed before piston is withdrawn from housing (3). Worm gear (15 – Fig. J8) and cam (14 – Fig. J9) are pressed on crankshaft. Install cam so highest part is pointing toward crankpin as shown in Fig. J11. Unthreaded end of oil pump worm gear (15 – Fig. J8) used on Models 49SP, 52, 52E, 70E and 521EV must be installed against inner race of main bearing (14).

REWIND STARTER. Refer to Fig. J17 for exploded view of rewind starter used on Models 60, 601, 75 and 751. To disassemble starter, remove rope handle and allow rope to rewind into starter. Remove starter housing (1) and starter assembly. Lift rope pulley and rope out of housing being careful not to disturb rewind spring (3). Outer end of rewind spring is retained by two slots in starter housing and is wound in clockwise direction. Inspect rope pulley bearing for wear or damage. Rope is wound on pulley in clockwise direction as viewed with pulley installed in housing. After

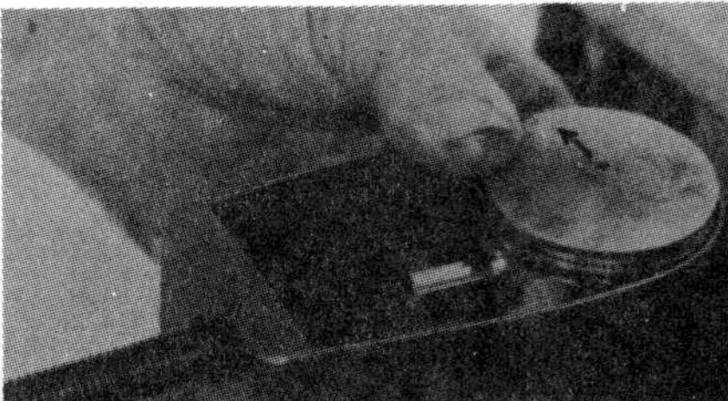

Fig. J10 — Install piston so arrow on piston crown on all models will point toward exhaust port.

Fig. J11 — Oil pump cam is installed on Models 60, 62, 75, 601, 621, 751 and 801 with high point of cam (arrow) toward crankpin.

Illustrations courtesy Jonsered Power Products AB

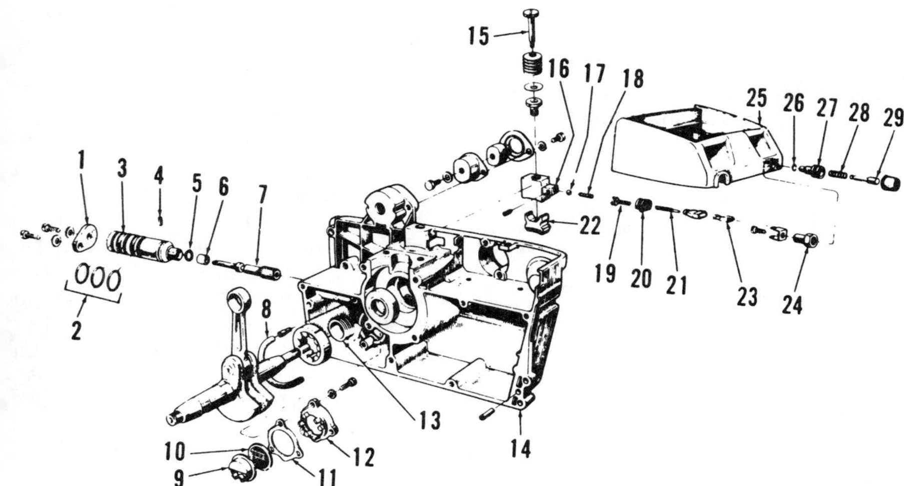

Fig. J12—Exploded view of automatic oil pump and kickback mechanism used on Models 50 and 51.

1. Plate
2. "O" rings
3. Housing
4. Guide pin
5. "O" ring
6. Bushing
7. Piston
8. Oil line
9. Adapter
10. Screen
11. Gasket
12. Cover
13. Oil pump drive gear
14. Crankcase half
15. Kickback plunger
16. Housing
17. Hall
18. Spring
19. Ground wire
20. Grommet
21. Ground wire
22. Brake shoe
23. Terminal
24. Fitting
25. Air filter
26. Clip
27. Fitting
28. Spring
29. Kill button

starter assembly is fitted to fan housing and rope handle is installed, turn starter housing (1) until rope handle is pulled against rope outlet and turn starter housing (1) one complete turn and install housing retaining screws. This will place tension on the rewind spring so rope will rewind correctly.

Models 49SP, 50, 51, 52, 52E, 521EV, 62, 70E, 111, 621 and 801 are equipped with the rewind starter shown in Fig. J18. Starter assembly used on Models 451E and 451EV is similar. To disassemble starter, remove starter housing from engine. On Models 50 and 51 the ignition wire and spark plug lead to the high tension coil in the starter housing must be disconnected. Remove rope handle and allow rope to rewind in housing. Unscrew rope pulley retaining screw (15) and remove rope pulley (7). Rewind spring may be removed after removing cover (6). Care should be taken when removing spring as injury could result from uncontrolled spring removal.

Rewind spring is wound in clockwise direction. Install rope so it is wound in clockwise direction when rope pulley is installed in housing. To preload rewind spring, reassemble starter assembly in housing. Pull rope handle until there is approximately 30 cm (12 in.) of rope beyond rope outlet and notch in pulley is adjacent to outlet. Hold pulley and pull rope back through outlet. Insert rope in notch and rotate pulley one turn clockwise to preload spring. Pull rope handle and check starter operation.

KICKBACK MECHANISM. Models 451E, 451EV, 50, 51, 52E, 521EV and 70E are equipped with a kickback mechanism to stop the chain should the saw kickback while cutting. Mechanism is activated when operator's hand

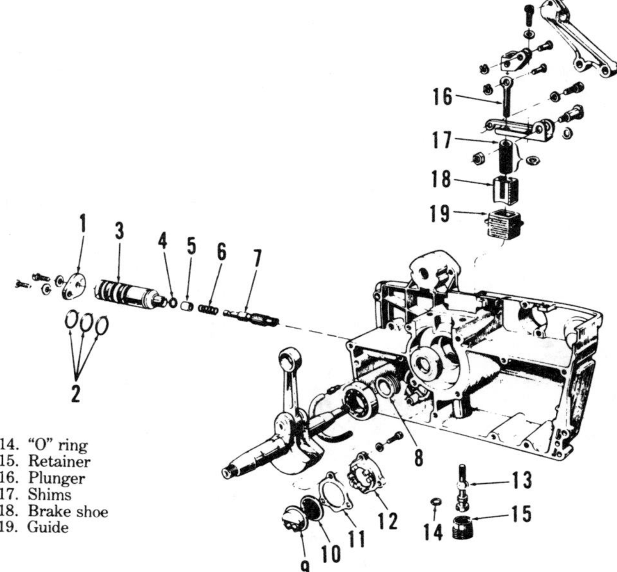

Fig. J13—Exploded view of automatic oil pump and chain brake used on 44 cc (2.7 cu. in.), 49 cc (3.0 cu. in.) and 69 cc (4.2 cu. in.) displacement models, except Models 50 and 51. Later model oil pump is equipped with four "O" rings (2) and bushing (5) is absent. Oil strainer (10) on 44 cc (2.7 cu. in.) models is located in bottom oil tank plug.

1. Retainer
2. "O" rings
3. Housing
4. "O" ring
5. Bushing
6. Spring
7. Piston
8. Oil pump worm gear
9. Adapter
10. Oil strainer
11. Gasket
12. Cover
13. Oil pump adjusting screw
14. "O" ring
15. Retainer
16. Plunger
17. Shims
18. Brake shoe
19. Guide

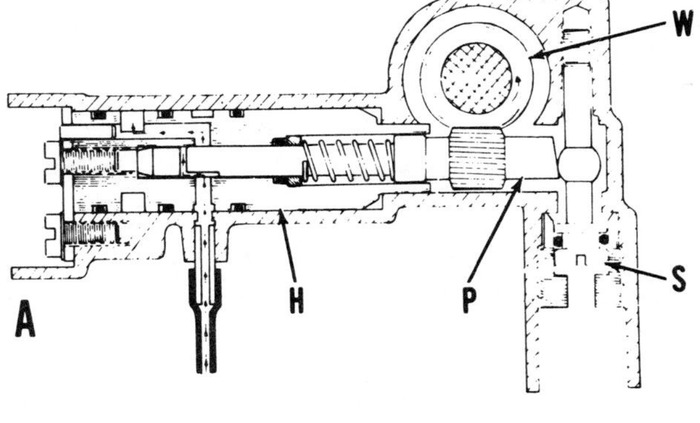

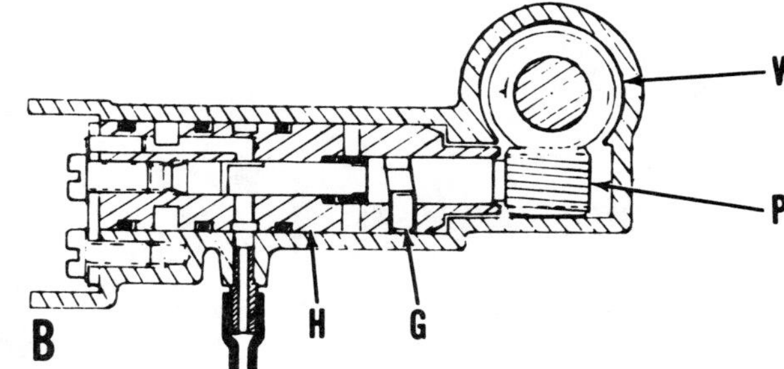

Fig. J14—Cross-sectional view of worm gear driven automatic oil pumps. Adjustable pump (View A) is used on 44 cc (2.7 cu. in.), 49 cc (3.0 cu. in.), 69 cc (4.2 cu. in.) and 110 cc (6.7 cu. in.) displacement models except for Models 50 and 51 which use nonadjustable pump shown in (View B).

G. Guide pin
H. Housing
P. Piston
S. Adjusting screw
W. Worm gear

Illustrations courtesy Jonsered Power Products AB

strikes kickback bar. Brake shoe (22–Fig. J12 or 18–Fig. J13) is forced against the clutch drum to stop chain. The ignition on Models 50 and 51 is also grounded to stop the engine.

On all models except Models 50 and 51, there should be 0.5-1.0 mm (0.020-0.040 in.) between brake shoe and clutch drum with kickback lever in rest position. Add additional shims to shim pack (17–Fig. J13) until desired gap is obtained.

HANDLE HEATER. Models 451EV and 521EV are equipped with handles which are heated by electric current. The electric current is generated by a series of coils surrounding the flywheel. The heater is controlled by a toggle switch on the left side of the saw. On 521EV models, the heater is off when the switch is in the middle position, on low heat when the switch is forward or in the "1" position and on high heat when the switch is rearward or in the "2" position. On 451EV models, heater is either on or off.

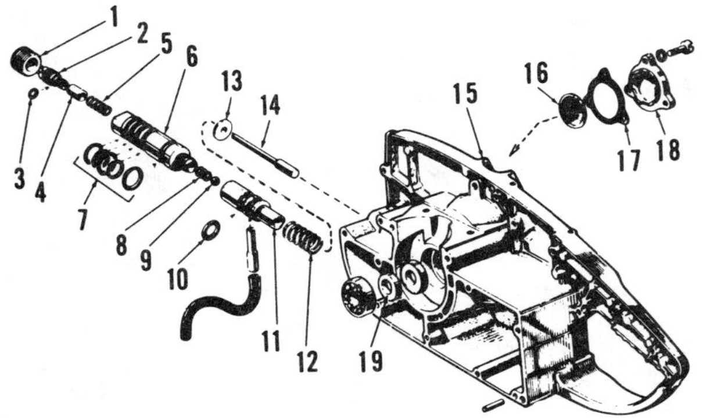
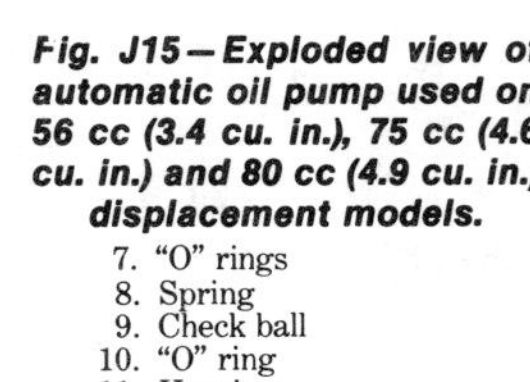

Fig. J15—Exploded view of automatic oil pump used on 56 cc (3.4 cu. in.), 75 cc (4.6 cu. in.) and 80 cc (4.9 cu. in.) displacement models.

1. Plug
2. Adjuster
3. "O" ring
4. Valve
5. Spring
6. Housing
7. "O" rings
8. Spring
9. Check ball
10. "O" ring
11. Housing
12. Spring
13. Spring retainer
14. Piston
15. Crankcase half
16. Screen
17. Gasket
18. Cover
19. Pump drive cam

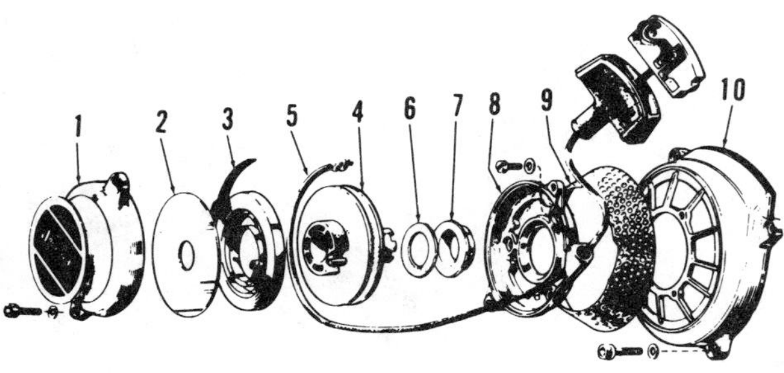

Fig. J17—Exploded view of rewind starter used on Models 60, 75, 601 and 751.

1. Starter housing
2. Washer
3. Rewind spring
4. Rope pulley
5. Rope
6. Washer
7. Bearing
8. Base plate
9. Dirt guard
10. Fan housing

Fig. J18—Exploded view of typical rewind starter assembly used on all models except Models 60, 601, 75 and 751.

1. High tension coil
2. Dirt guard
3. Starter housing
4. Washer
5. Rewind spring
6. Cover
7. Rope pulley
8. Bushing
9. Washer
10. Snap ring
11. Starter dog
12. Spring
13. Fan
14. Flywheel
15. Screw

Illustrations courtesy Jonsered Power Products AB

JONSERED

Model	Bore mm (in.)	Stroke mm (in.)	Displacement cc (cu. in.)	Drive Type
361, 361 AV, 365, 370	36.5 (1.44)	32.5 (1.28)	34.4 (2.1)	Direct

MAINTENANCE

SPARK PLUG. Recommended spark plug for Model 370 is Champion RCJ7Y. Recommended spark plug for all other models is Champion CJ6. Electrode gap for all models is 0.50 mm (0.020 in.).

CARBURETOR. A Tillotson HU or Walbro WA diaphragm type carburetor has been used on Models 361 and 361AV. Models 365 and 370 are equipped with a Walbro diaphragm type carburetor. Refer to CARBURETOR SERVICE section for service on Tillotson or Walbro carburetor.

Initial setting of both high and low speed mixture screws is 1⅛ turns open from a lightly seated position. Make final adjustment with engine warm and running. Adjust idle speed screw so engine idles just below clutch engagement speed. Adjust low speed mixture screw so engine will accelerate cleanly without hesistation. Adjust high speed mixture screw to obtain optimum performance under cutting load.

On 361AV models, throttle trigger (9–Fig. J19) may occasionally become restricted by air filter connector (3). Should this occur, remove the air filter connector and trim off the required amount of material from the connector to allow free throttle trigger movement.

On all models, air leakage sometimes develops between heat shield (7) and cylinder making carburetor adjustment very difficult. If air leakage is suspected, remove carburetor and related components, then measure the thickness of gasket (8). If gasket (8) is 0.30-0.38 mm (0.012-0.015 in.) thick, then two gaskets of this thickness are required to stop air leakage. Current production models are equipped with on 0.63-0.72 mm (0.025-0.028 in.) thick gasket.

IGNITION. Early models are equipped with a breaker-point type flywheel magneto ignition system while later models use a breakerless electronic ignition system.

Breaker-point gap should be 0.38 mm (0.015 in.) on models so equipped. Ignition timing is fixed on all models but breaker-point gap on applicable models should be set correctly or timing will be affected. On all models, air gap between flywheel magnets and ignition coil legs should be 0.38 mm (0.015 in.).

LUBRICATION. The engine is lubricated by mixing oil with gasoline. Recommended oil is Jonsered engine oil or a BIA certified air-cooled two-stroke engine oil approved for 40:1 fuel mixtures. Recommended fuel mixture ratio is 40:1 when using an approved engine oil. If a recommended oil is not available,

Fig. J19—Exploded view of vibration isolated handles and air intake components used on 361AV models.

1. Choke retainer
2. Choke
3. Air filter connector
4. Connector guide
5. Carburetor
6. Gasket
7. Heat shield
8. Gasket
9. Throttle trigger
10. Throttle lock
11. Contact spring

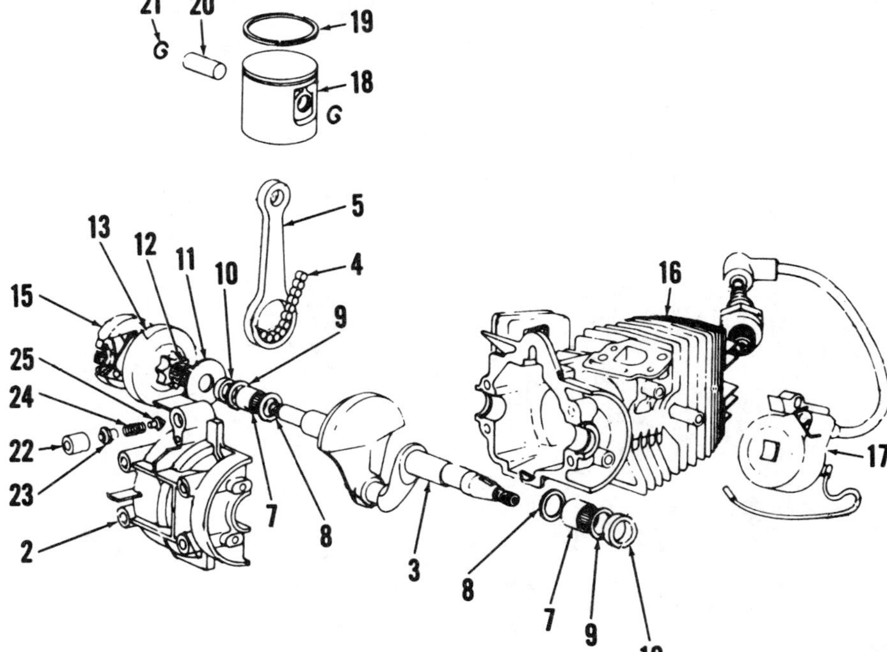

Fig. J20—Exploded view of early model engine assembly. Spacer (22), spring seat (23), spring (24) and pulse valve (25) are absent on Models 365 and 370. Washers (8) are absent on Model 370.

2. Crankcase
3. Crankshaft
4. Roller bearing
5. Connecting rod
7. Needle bearing
8. Washer
9. Retaining ring
10. Seal
11. Thrust washer
12. Bearing
13. Clutch drum
15. Clutch assy.
16. Cylinder
17. Ignition coil
18. Piston
19. Piston pin
20. Piston pin
21. Pin retainer
22. Spacer
23. Spring seat
24. Spring
25. Pulse valve

a good quality oil designed for air-cooled two-stroke engines may be used when mixed with the fuel at a 20:1 ratio.

Models 361 and 361AV are equipped with automatic and manual chain oil pumps. Models 365 and 370 are equipped with an automatic chain oil pump only. A good quality chain oil should be used with viscosity chosen according to ambient temperature. Automatic oil pump output is not adjustable.

CARBON. Carbon should be removed from exhaust system and cylinder periodically. Loose carbon should not be allowed to enter cylinder and care should be taken not to damage cylinder or piston.

REPAIRS

CYLINDER, PISTON, PIN AND RINGS. Cylinder (16–Fig. J20) on all models is also upper crankcase half. Crankshaft is loose in crankcase when cylinder is removed. Care must be taken not to nick or scratch crankcase mating surfaces during disassembly.

Cylinder head is integral with cylinder and cylinder must be removed to remove piston. Piston is equipped with a single piston ring and floating type piston pin (20). Later models are equipped with a needle bearing in connecting rod small end. On later models, piston and connecting rod are available as a unit assembly only. On all models, piston and ring are available in standard size only. Cylinder bore is chrome and should be inspected to determine if chrome is scored, peeling or excessively worn. Renew cylinder and piston if damaged or excessively worn.

Refer to CRANKSHAFT section for proper assembly of crankcase and cylinder.

CONNECTING ROD. To remove connecting rod, remove cylinder (16–Fig. J20). Note that cylinder is also upper crankcase half and crankshaft assembly is loose when cylinder is removed. Connecting rod (5) is one-piece and supported on crankpin by 11 loose bearing rollers (4). Be careful not to lose loose rollers that may fall out during disassembly. Rollers can be removed by sliding rod off rollers. To install rod, hold rollers in place with heavy grease or petroleum jelly and position rod over rollers. Be sure rollers do not fall out during assembly of crankcase.

CRANKSHAFT AND SEALS. Crankshaft is supported by needle roller bearings (7–Fig. J20) at both ends. Crankshaft assembly may be removed after removing stator plate, clutch and cylinder assemblies. Care should be taken when removing cylinder as crankshaft will be loose in crankcase and connecting rod may slide off bearing rollers allowing them to fall into crankcase.

Before reassembling crankcases, apply a light coat of nonhardening sealant to crankcase mating surface. Be sure mating surfaces are not damaged during assembly. Retaining rings (9) must fit in ring grooves of crankcase and cylinder.

CLUTCH. A two-shoe centrifugal type clutch is used on all models. Clutch hub has left hand thread. Clutch bearing (12–Fig. J20) should be inspected for excessive wear or damage. Inspect clutch shoes and drum for signs of excessive wear or damage due to overheating.

OIL PUMP. Models 361 and 361AV are equipped with a manual oil pump and automatic oiling system. Refer to Fig. J21 for exploded view of manual oil

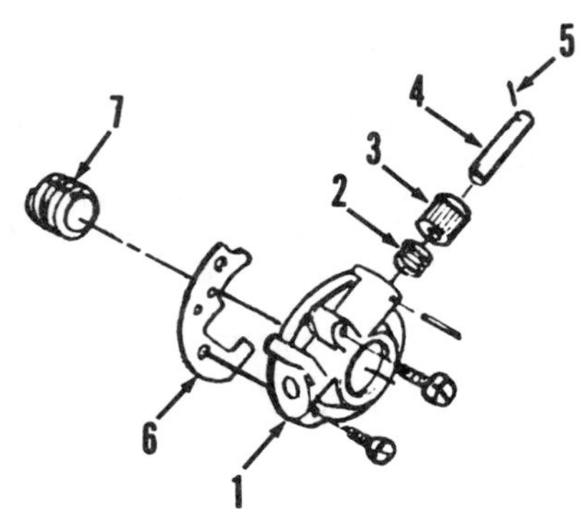

Fig. J22—Exploded view of automatic oil pump used on Models 365 and 370.

1. Housing
2. Spring
3. Driven gear
4. Plunger
5. Pin
6. Gasket
7. Worm gear

Fig. J21—Exploded view of manual oil pump and front housing used on later Models 361 and 361AV. Duckbill type valve (16) is used instead of early model valve components (22, 23, 24 and 25) shown in Fig. J20.

1. Piston
2. "O" ring
3. Spring
4. Spring seat
5. Ball
6. Pump body
7. Screen
8. Front housing
9. Fuel hose
10. Fuel pickup
11. Front cover
12. Spring
13. Spring
14. Oil outlet valve
15. Nut
16. Pressure check valve
17. Secondary filter
18. Fuel filter

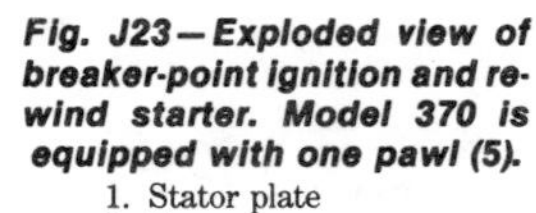

Fig. J23—Exploded view of breaker-point ignition and rewind starter. Model 370 is equipped with one pawl (5).

1. Stator plate
2. Cover
3. Flywheel
4. Spring
5. Pawl
6. Pivot pin
7. Washer
8. Nut
9. Snap ring
10. Thrust washer
11. Rope pulley
12. Rewind spring
13. Bushing
14. Starter housing

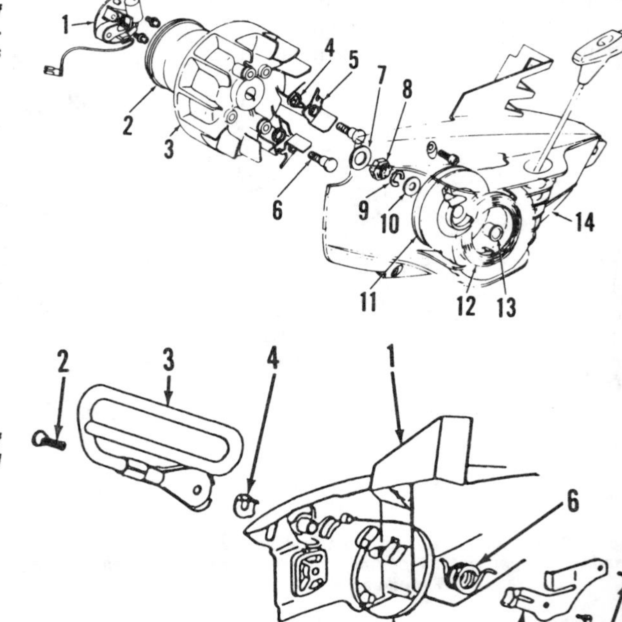

Fig. J24—Exploded view of chain brake assembly used on all models except 370.

1. Clutch cover
2. Pivot pin
3. Trip lever
4. Stop plate
5. Brake band
6. Spring
7. Detent cover
8. Cap screws

Illustrations courtesy Jonsered Power Products AB

pump. Models 365 and 370 are equipped with an automatic oil pump only. Automatic oiling on Models 361 and 361AV is accomplished by crankcase pulsations which pressurize oil tank and force oil to bar. A one-way valve (25–Fig. J20 on early Models 361 and 361AV or 16–Fig. J21 on later models) prevents oil from entering crankcase.

NOTE: Early and late crankcase (2–Fig. J20) may not be interchanged unless valve type is also changed.

Models 365 and 370 are equipped with an automatic oil pump driven by worm gear (7–Fig. J22) on flywheel side of crankshaft. Oil pump output is not adjustable.

REWIND STARTER. Refer to Fig. J23 for exploded view of pawl type starter used on all models except 370. Model 370 is similar. Care should be taken if necessary to remove rewind spring (12) to prevent spring from uncoiling uncontrolled. Rewind spring (12) should be wound in clockwise direction in housing. On later models, rewind spring is contained in a cassette making it unnecessary to uncoil spring during removal or installation. Wind starter rope in clockwise direction around rope pulley (11) as viewed in starter housing (14).

Check clearance between starter pawls (5) and head on pivot pin (6). Clearance should not exceed 0.5 mm (0.02 in.). Excessive clearance may cause premature wear of pawl engagement areas on rope pulley and unsatifactory operation during engine starting. Tighten pawls by carefully tapping pivot pins into the flywheel.

CHAIN BRAKE. A chain brake which can stop the saw chain quickly is available as an option on all models. It is necessary to unlock the brake before removing or installing clutch cover (1–Fig. J24 or 5–Fig. J24A). Sawdust and debris should be cleaned from around the brake mechanism as needed to ensure proper operation of chain brake.

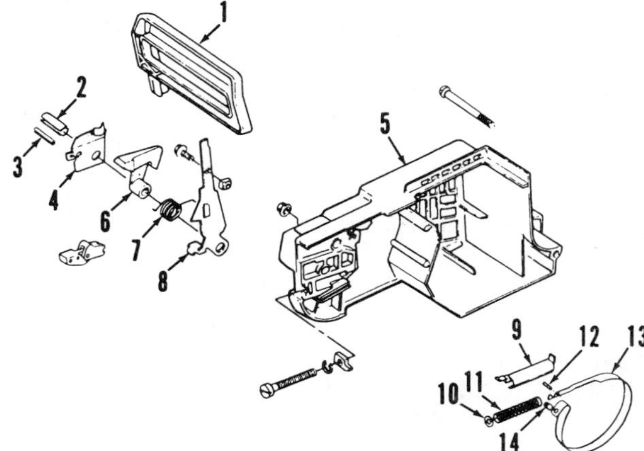

Fig. J24A—Exploded view of chain brake assembly used on Model 370.

1. Guard
2. Roll pin
3. Roll pin
4. Detent cover
5. Clutch cover
6. Inertia weight
7. Spring
8. Lever
9. Cover
10. Washer
11. Spring
12. Roll pin
13. Brake band
14. Pin

JONSERED

Model	Bore mm (in.)	Stroke mm (in.)	Displacement cc (cu. in.)	Drive Type
455	42 (1.65)	32 (1.26)	44.3 (2.7)	Direct
510 SP, 520 SP	44 (1.732)	32 (1.26)	49 (3.0)	Direct
535	45 (1.77)	32 (1.26)	50.9 (3.1)	Direct

MAINTENANCE

SPARK PLUG. Recommended spark plug is Bosch WS7F for all models. Recommended spark plug electrode gap is 0.5 mm (0.020 in.).

CARBURETOR. Models 510SP and 520SP are equipped with a Tillotson HK diaphragm carburetor. Models 455 and 535 are equipped with a Walbro HDA diaphragm carburetor. Refer to Tillotson or Walbro section of CARBURETOR SERVICE section for exploded views and overhaul of carburetor.

Carburetors used on later 510SP models and all 520SP models are equipped with an additional jet (J–Fig. J25) located in the main fuel discharge port (P). The extra jet provides a more efficient fuel:air mixture through the carburetor venturi and stabilizes engine idle speed. Jet is available from the manufacturer and can be installed in early production 510SP model carburetors as follows: Remove carburetor from saw, then refer to exploded view of Tillotson HK type carburetor in CARBURETOR SERVICE section for parts identification. Invert carburetor and remove diaphragm cover plate and related components. Remove clip (C) from main fuel discharge port (P) and withdraw screen (S). Press jet into main fuel discharge port then reinstall screen and clip. The remainder of reassembly is the reverse of disassembly.

On all models, fuel tank vent hose and carburetor hoses should be routed as shown in Fig. J26. If hoses require renewal, they should be cut to the proper length to avoid kinked and pinched hoses. Recommended lengths are: fuel hose (F–Fig. J26) 120 mm (4.7 in.); pulse hose (P) 105 mm (4.1 in.); vent hose (V) 190 mm (7.5 in.).

Initial carburetor adjustment of both high and low speed mixture screws is one turn open from a lightly seated position. Make final adjustment with engine warm and running. Adjust idle speed screw so engine idles just below clutch engagement speed. Adjust low speed mixture screw so engine will accelerate cleanly without hesitation. Adjust high speed mixture screw to obtain optimum performance under cutting load.

IGNITION. A breakerless capacitor discharge ignition system is used on all models. Ignition timing is fixed. Individual electronic components are not available separately and must be serviced as a unit assembly. Air gap between flywheel magnets and ignition module core should be 0.30-0.40 mm (0.012-0.016 in.).

LUBRICATION. The engine is lubricated by mixing oil with the fuel. Recommended oil is Jonsered engine oil or a BIA certified air-cooled two-stroke engine oil approved for 40:1 fuel mixtures. Recommended fuel mixture ratio is 40:1 when using an approved engine oil. If a recommended engine oil is not available, a good quality oil designed for air-cooled two-stroke engines may be used when mixed with the fuel at a 20:1 ratio. Use a separate container when mixing the oil and gas.

The chain is lubricated by oil from an automatic chain oil pump. Oil pump output on Models 510SP and 535SP is not adjustable. Oil pump output on Models 455 and 535 is adjustable by rotating screw (35–Fig. J29) located on bottom

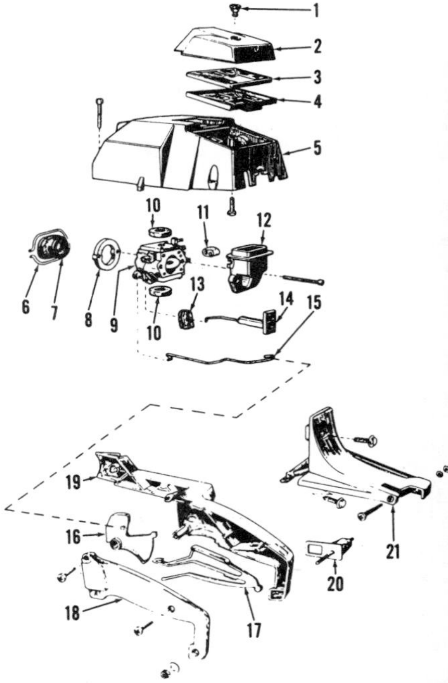

Fig. J27—Exploded view of air box and throttle control assembly used on 520SP models. Air box components used on 510SP, 455 and 535 models are similar.

1. Nut
2. Filter cover
3. Upper air filter half
4. Lower air filter half
5. Engine cover
6. Clamp
7. Intake manifold
8. Mounting flange
9. Carburetor
10. Carburetor support
11. Mixture screw cover
12. Air filter connector
13. Grommet
14. Choke knob & link
15. Throttle link
16. Trigger
17. Trigger lock
18. Handle cover
19. Handle
20. Vibration isolator
21. Rear handle support

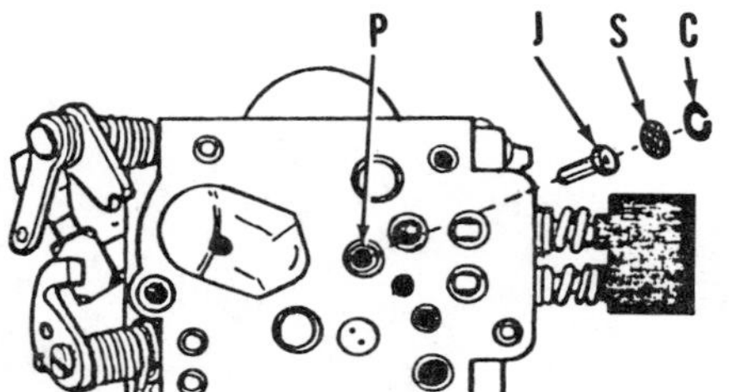

Fig. J25—View of carburetor body showing location of jet (J) used on later 510SP model and all 520 SP model carburetors.

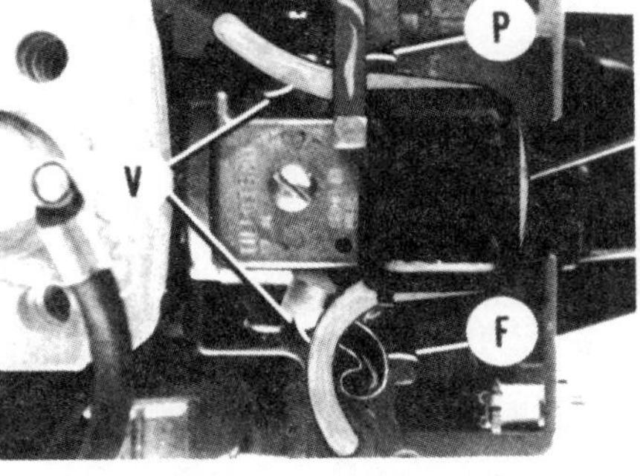

Fig. J26—Fuel tank vent hose (V), pulse hose (P) and fuel supply hose (F) should be routed as illustrated.

Illustrations courtesy Johsered Power Products AB

of saw. Clean automotive oil may be used. Oil viscosity should be chosen according to ambient temperature.

Refer to OIL PUMP section for service information.

CARBON. Carbon deposits should be removed from muffler and exhaust ports at regular intervals. When scraping carbon, be careful not to damage engine cylinder. Do not allow loosened carbon into cylinder.

REPAIRS

CYLINDER, PISTON, PIN AND RINGS. The piston is accessible after removing the cylinder assembly. Piston is fitted with one piston ring. A locating pin is present in piston ring groove to prevent piston ring rotation. Oversize pistons and rings are not available. Piston, piston pin and cylinder are renewable as matched sets only. All models have needle type piston pin bearings. Install piston so arrow on piston crown points toward exhaust port.

On later 510SP models, the base flange on cylinder (2–Fig. J28) has been increased in thickness from 8 mm (0.315 in.) to 17.5 mm (0.689 in.) and the cylinder retaining bolts (1) lengthened from 60 mm (2.36 in.) to 70 mm (2.75 in.). Whenever cylinder assembly is renewed, measure cylinder base flange thickness to ensure proper retaining bolt length.

CONNECTING ROD, CRANKSHAFT AND CRANKCASE. Connecting rod is equipped with a needle bearing in small end. A roller bearing supports the connecting rod on the crankpin while the crankshaft rides in two ball bearings. Connecting rod and crankshaft are not available separately and must be serviced as a unit assembly.

To remove the crankshaft assembly, first remove the cylinder and piston assembly, then carefully pry upper crankcase half (8–Fig. J28 or Fig. J29) loose from lower crankcase half (18). Invert upper crankcase half to disconnect oil pressure hose (28–Fig. J28). On some early models, oil supply line (22) is connected directly to upper crankcase half and requires removal of oil pickup (23) so line may be pulled through opening in lower crankcase half. On all models, withdraw crankcase assembly from lower crankcase half.

Oil pump drive gear (13–Fig. J28 or Fig. J29) should be removed using special tool 504915505. Main bearings (14 and 15) may be removed with a suitable puller. Check rotation of connecting rod around crankpin and renew crankshaft unit if roughness or other damage is found. Carefully clean and inspect crankcase half mating surfaces, removing any burrs or nicks that may prevent an airtight seal.

Press main bearings on crankshaft until bottomed against bearing seats. Install oil pump drive gear on flywheel side of crankshaft using special tool 504905602. Apply a suitable high temperature grease on lips of crankshaft seals (12 and 17), then install locating washer (16) and crankshaft seals on crankshaft. Open side of seals should be facing each other. Place assembled crankshaft into lower crankcase half. Apply a thin coat of room temperature vulcanizing (RTV) silicone sealer on lower crankcase half, then install upper crankcase half. Position new cylinder base gasket (3) on crankcase. Base gas-

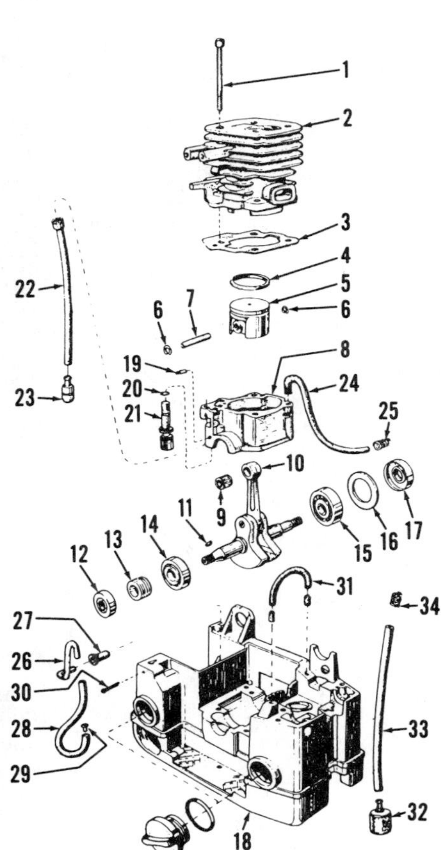

Fig. J28—Exploded view of typical engine assembly used on 510SP and 520SP models.

1. Bolt
2. Cylinder
3. Gasket
4. Piston ring
5. Piston
6. Retainer
7. Piston pin
8. Upper crankcase half
9. Bearing
10. Crankshaft & rod assy.
11. Key
12. Seal
13. Oil pump drive gear
14. Main bearing
15. Main bearing
16. Locating washer
17. Seal
18. Lower crankcase half
19. Pin
20. "O" ring
21. Oil pump plunger
22. Oil supply hose
23. Oil pickup
24. Crankcase pulse hose
25. Clamp
26. Oil pressure line
27. Grommet
28. Oil pressure hose
29. Fitting
30. Oil tank vent
31. Fuel tank vent hose
32. Fuel pickup
33. Fuel hose
34. Clamp

Fig. J29—Exploded view of engine assembly used on Models 455 and 535.

1. Bolt
2. Cylinder
3. Gasket
4. Piston ring
5. Piston & pin assy.
6. Retainer
7. Bearing
8. Upper crankcase half
9. Bearing
10. Crankshaft & connecting rod assy.
11. Key
12. Seal
13. Oil pump drive gear
14. Main bearing
15. Main bearing
16. Locating washer
17. Seal
18. Lower crankcase half
19. Washer
20. "O" rings
21. Oil pump plunger
22. Oil supply hose
23. Oil pickup
24. Crankcase pulse hose
25. Clamp
26. Oil pressure line
27. Grommet
28. Fuel cap
29. Fitting
30. Oil tank vent
31. Fuel tank vent hose
32. Fuel pickup
33. Fuel hose
34. Clamp
35. Oil pump adjuster
36. Oil pump retainer
37. Spring

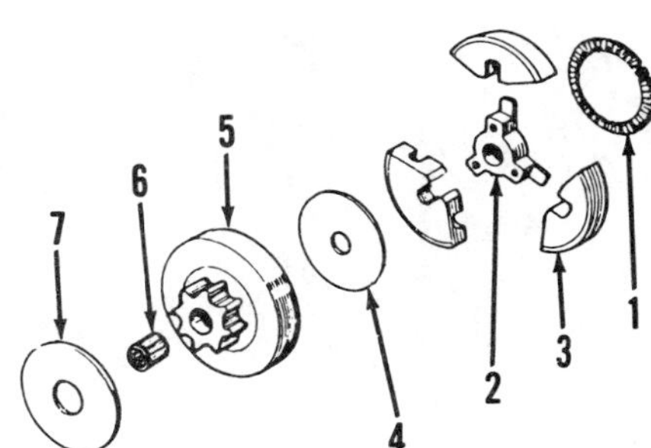

Fig. J30—Exploded view of clutch assembly used on all models.

1. Spring
2. Hub
3. Shoe
4. Washer
5. Clutch drum
6. Bearing
7. Washer

Illustrations courtesy Johsered Power Products AB

ket should be installed without sealer. Remainder of reassembly is the reverse of disassembly.

CLUTCH. Refer to Fig. J30 for exploded view of clutch assembly. To remove clutch, prevent flywheel rotation by removing the spark plug and inserting a loop of rope into the cylinder. Unscrew clutch hub (2) in clockwise direction as shown by arrow on hub.

Inspect clutch shoes (3) and drum (5) for signs of excessive heat. Clutch shoes should be renewed only as a set. Clutch bearing (6) should be inspected for excessive wear or damage. Lubricate clutch bearing with a lithium base grease prior to reassembly.

OIL PUMP. All models are equipped with an automatic oil pump driven by gear (13–Fig. J28 or Fig. J29) on crankshaft. Oil is pumped by plunger (21) as it rotates in pump bore. Oil pump output is not adjustable on Models 510SP and 520SP.

To obtain access to oil pump components on Models 510SP and 520SP, upper crankcase half (8–Fig. J28) must be removed as outlined in CONNECTING ROD, CRANKSHAFT AND CRANKCASE section. Remove pin (19) to withdraw plunger (21) from upper gearcase half.

On later models, pin (19) has been replaced with a cap screw and "O" ring seal. Early models can be changed to accept plunger retaining cap screw part 504020035 and "O" ring seal part 740420200 as follows: With pin and plunger removed from upper crankcase half, enlarge pin bore using a 4.3 mm diameter drill bit, then thread a 5 mm tap into hole. Thoroughly clean upper crankcase half ensuring all metal particles have been removed before reassembly.

During reassembly make certain oil pressure hose (28) does not become pinched which can restrict oil delivery. Oil pressure hose length should be 85 mm (3.35 in.).

Models 455 and 535 are equipped with an adjustable automatic chain oil pump. Pump output is adjusted by rotating adjuster (35–Fig. J29) located on bottom of saw. Oil is pumped by plunger (21) which is driven by gear (13).

To disassemble pump, remove oil pump retainer (36). Using a suitable tool with a hooked end, withdraw adjuster (35), plunger (21), washer (19) and spring (37). Inspect "O" rings (20) for cracking or hardening. Inspect adjuster and plunger for excessive wear or other damage. Renew components as needed.

REWIND STARTER. Refer to Fig. J31 for an exploded view of starter assembly. To disassemble starter, first remove starter housing from saw. Pull starter rope and hold rope pulley with notch in pulley adjacent to rope outlet. Pull rope back through outlet so it engages notch in pulley and allow pulley to completely unwind. Unscrew pulley retaining screw and carefully withdraw rope pulley. If required, rewind spring and spring cassette (10 and 11) may now be renewed.

Reassemble starter components by reversing disassembly procedure while noting the following: Rope is wound on rope pulley in clockwise direction as viewed with pulley in housing. To place tension on rewind spring, pass rope through rope outlet in housing and install rope handle. Pull rope out and hold rope pulley so notch on pulley is adjacent to rope outlet. Pull rope back through outlet between notch in pulley and housing. Turn rope pulley clockwise to place tension on spring. Release pulley and check starter action. It should be possible to rotate rope pulley ½-turn clockwise with rope fully extended. Do not place more tension on rewind spring than is necessary to draw rope handle against housing.

CHAIN BRAKE. Some models may be equipped with a chain brake system designed to stop chain movement should kickback occur. The chain brake is activated when the operator's hand strikes the chain brake lever (1–Fig. J32) moving trigger (2) thereby forcing actuating lever (6) to release spring (10). Spring then draws brake band (11) tight around clutch drum to stop chain. Pull back chain brake lever to reset mechanism. Lightly lubricate actuating lever (6), inner cover plate (7) and trigger (2) with Molykote or equivalent grease when reassembling. No adjustment of brake mechanism is required.

Disassembly for repair or renewal of individual components is evident after inspection of unit and referral to Fig. J32.

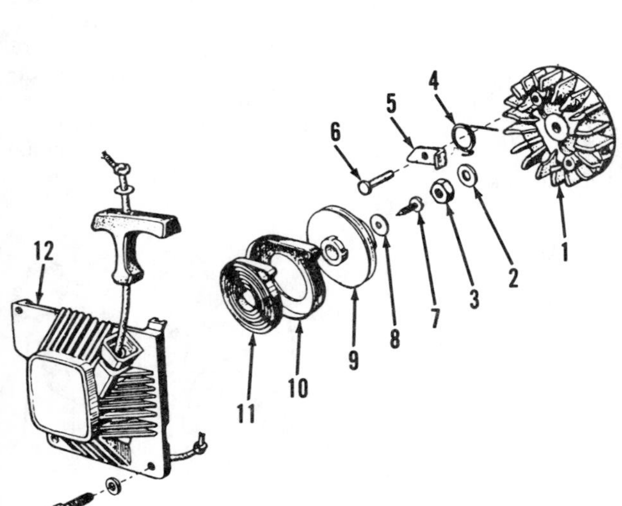

Fig. J31—Exploded view of rewind starter assembly used on all models.

1. Flywheel
2. Washer
3. Flywheel nut
4. Spring
5. Pawl
6. Pin
7. Screw
8. Washer
9. Rope pulley
10. Rewind spring cassette
11. Rewind spring
12. Starter housing

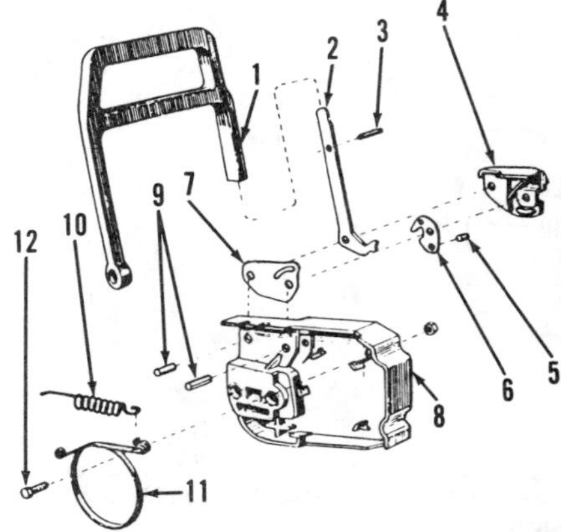

Fig. J32—Exploded view of chain brake assembly used on some models.

1. Chain brake lever
2. Trigger
3. Roll pin
4. Outer cover plate
5. Pin
6. Actuating lever
7. Inner cover plate
8. Housing
9. Roll pin
10. Spring
11. Brake band
12. Cap screw

JONSERED

Model	Bore mm (in.)	Stroke mm (in.)	Displacement cc (cu. in.)	Drive Type
625, 625 II, 630, 630 Super	48 (1.89)	34 (1.34)	61.5 (3.75)	Direct
670, 670 Champ, 670 Super, 670 Super II	50 (1.968)	34 (1.34)	66.8 (4.1)	Direct

MAINTENANCE

SPARK PLUG. Recommended spark plug is Bosch WS7F. Recommended spark plug electrode gap is 0.5 mm (0.020 in.).

CARBURETOR. A Tillotson HS diaphragm type carburetor is used. Refer to Tillotson section of CARBURETOR SERVICE section for exploded views and overhaul of carburetor.

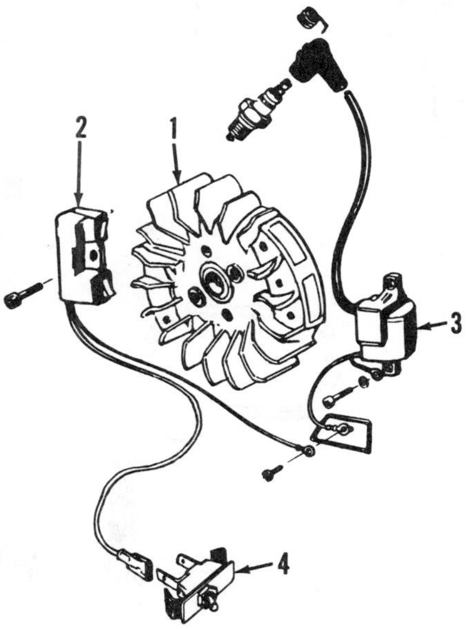

Fig. J34—Exploded view of electronic ignition components.

1. Flywheel
2. Trigger module
3. Ignition coil
4. Stop switch

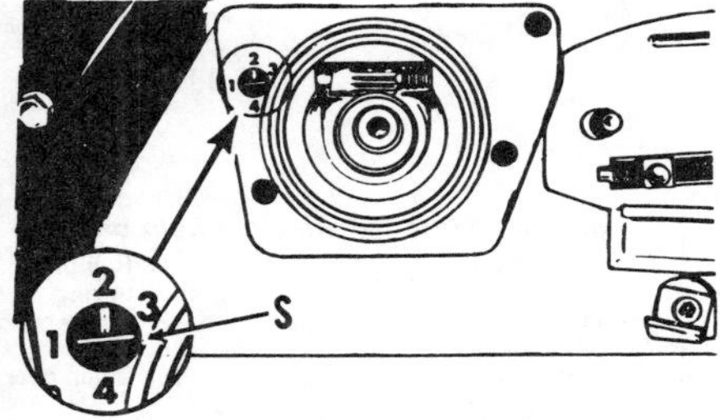

Fig. J35—View of oil pump with clutch removed. Oil pump adjusting screw (S) is set at position "2."

Initial carburetor adjustment is 1¼ turn open from a lightly seated position for both low and high speed mixture screws. Make final adjustment with engine warm and running. Adjust idle speed screw so engine idles just below clutch engagement speed. Adjust low speed mixture screw so engine will accelerate cleanly without hesitation. Adjust high speed mixture screw to obtain optimum performance under cutting load.

IGNITION. All models are equipped with an electronic breakerless ignition system. Ignition timing is not adjustable. Air gap between trigger module (2–Fig. J34) and flywheel magnets should be 0.3-0.4 mm (0.012-0.016 in.).

LUBRICATION. The engine is lubricated by mixing oil with the fuel. Recommended oil is Jonsered engine oil or a BIA certified air-cooled two-stroke engine oil approved for 40:1 fuel mixtures. Recommended fuel mixture is 40:1 when using an approved engine oil. If a recommended engine oil is not available, a good quality oil designed for air-cooled two-stroke engines may be used when mixed with the fuel at a 20:1 ratio. Use a separate container when mixing the oil and gas.

All models are equipped with an adjustable automatic chain oil pump. Adjustment is possible without clutch removal. Turn screw (S–Fig. J35) for desired oil output–position "1" is minimum, position "4" is maximum.

REPAIRS

PISTON, PIN, RINGS AND CYLINDER. Cylinder bore is chrome plated and should be inspected for excessive wear and damage to bore surface. Inspect piston and discard if excessive wear or damage is evident. Oversize pistons are not available.

Piston must be installed with arrow on piston crown pointing toward exhaust port. Piston on Model 630 is equipped with two piston rings. Piston on Models 625 and 670 is equipped with one piston ring. A locating pin is present in piston ring grooves to prevent piston ring rotation. Be sure ring end gap is around locating pin when installing cylinder.

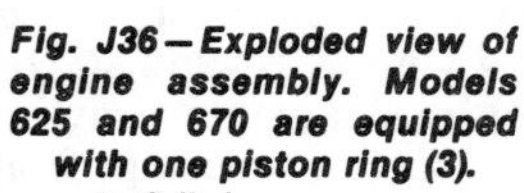

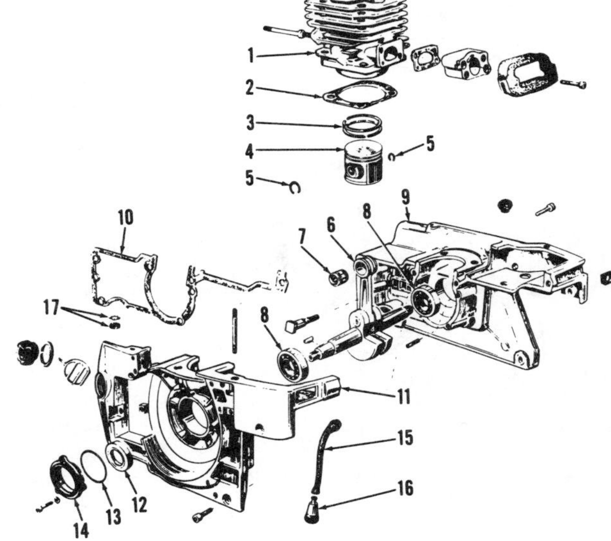

Fig. J36—Exploded view of engine assembly. Models 625 and 670 are equipped with one piston ring (3).

1. Cylinder
2. Gasket
3. Piston rings
4. Piston & pin assy.
5. Piston pin retainer
6. Crankshaft assy.
7. Needle bearings
8. Ball bearing
9. Right crankcase half
10. Gasket
11. Left crankcase half
12. Seal
13. "O" ring
14. Seal housing
15. Hose
16. Oil strainer
17. Oil tank vent

CONNECTING ROD, CRANKSHAFT AND CRANKCASE. Connecting rod is equipped with a needle bearing in small end. Crankshaft and connecting rod are a unit assembly. It will be necessary to heat crankcase halves to remove or install crankshaft and main bearings. Care should be taken not to damage mating surfaces of crankcase halves. Check rotation of connecting rod around crankpin and renew crankshaft unit if roughness or other damage is found.

When reassembling crankshaft and crankcase halves, install main bearings allowing for installation of oil pump on drive side and crankshaft seal housing on flywheel side. A special tool is available from the manufacturer to properly position main bearings and crankshaft in crankcase. Tighten crankcase screws to 7-8 N·m (61-69 in.-lbs.). Make certain crankshaft is centered in crankcase and will rotate freely.

CLUTCH. A three-shoe centrifugal clutch is used. Clutch hub has left-hand threads. Inspect clutch shoes and drum for excessive wear or damage due to overheating. Clean and inspect clutch hub, drum and bearing for damage or excessive wear. Inspect clutch bearing lubrication hole in crankshaft end and clutch bearing contact surface on crankshaft for wear or damage.

The oil pump is driven by the clutch drum. Be sure notches on rear of clutch drum mesh with dogs of oil pump drive gear when installing clutch assembly.

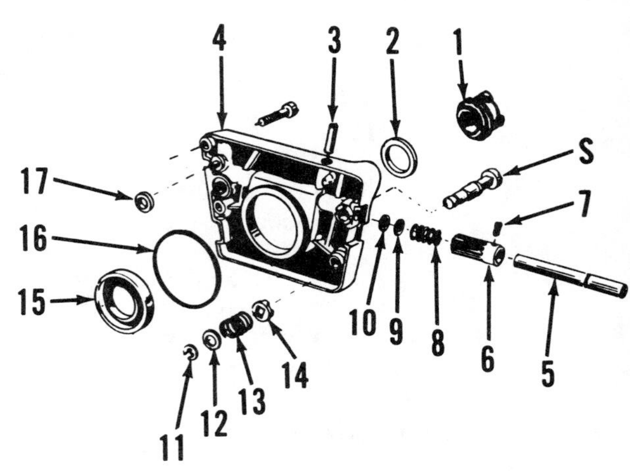

Fig. J38—Exploded view of automatic oil pump.

S. Adjusting screw
1. Drive gear
2. Washer
3. Pin
4. Pump housing
5. Plunger
6. Driven gear
7. Set screw
8. Spring
9. Steel washer
10. Brass washer
11. "E" ring
12. Washer
13. Spring
14. Washer
15. Seal
16. "O" ring
17. Seal

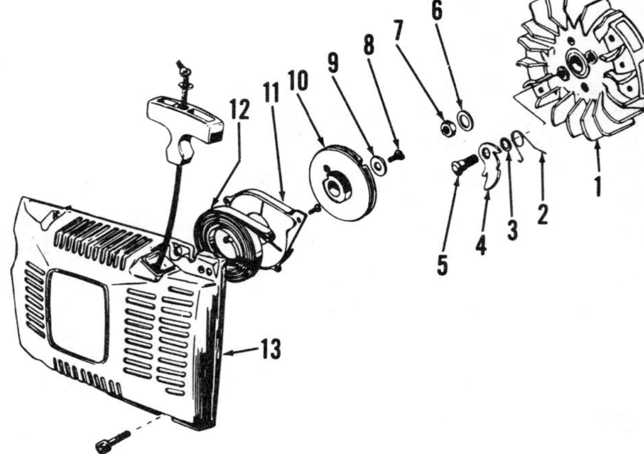

Fig. J40—Exploded view of rewind starter assembly.

1. Flywheel
2. Pawl spring
3. Washer
4. Pawl
5. Pivot pin
6. Washer
7. Nut
8. Screw
9. Washer
10. Rope pulley
11. Spring cover
12. Rewind spring
13. Starter housing

AUTOMATIC OIL PUMP. All models are equipped with an automatic oil pump which is driven by the clutch drum. Notches on the back of the clutch drum engage dogs on oil pump drive gear (1–Fig. J38) which rides on the crankshaft. The oil pump drive gear engages driven gear (6) which is secured to plunger (5) by set screw (7). Oil pump output is adjusted by turning screw (S).

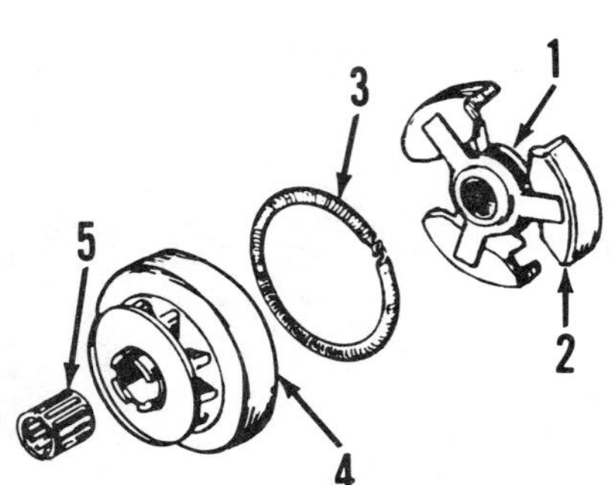

Fig. J37—Exploded view of clutch assembly.

1. Hub
2. Shoe
3. Spring
4. Drum
5. Bearing

To remove oil pump, first remove the clutch, chain, guide bar and oil pump retaining cap screws. Using two suitable screwdrivers, insert blade tips into notches provided in pump housing and carefully withdraw oil pump. To reinstall, manufacturer recommends placing special tool 502 50 53 01 over crankshaft end to prevent damage to oil seal (15).

REWIND STARTER. Refer to Fig. J40 for exploded view of rewind starter assembly. To disassemble rewind starter, remove starter housing from saw. Pull starter rope and hold rope pulley (10) with notch in pulley adjacent to rope outlet. Pull rope back through outlet so it engages notch in pulley and allow pulley to completely unwind. Unscrew pulley retaining screw (8) and carefully remove rope pulley. If rewind spring must be removed, care should be taken not to allow spring to uncoil uncontrolled.

Install rewind spring in starter housing with spring coiled in clockwise direction from outer spring end. Wrap starter rope around rope pulley in a clockwise direction as viewed with

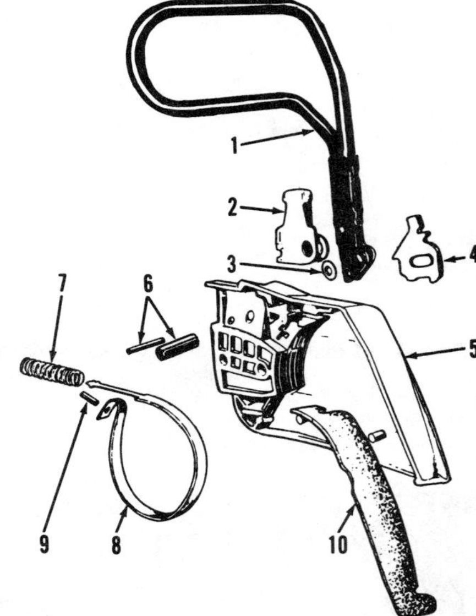

Fig. J41—Exploded view of chain brake.

1. Chain brake lever
2. Sleeve
3. Washer
4. Actuating plate
5. Housing
6. Roll pin
7. Spring
8. Brake band
9. Pin
10. Chain guard

pulley in starter housing. Turn rope pulley two turns clockwise before pass-

Illustrations courtesy Jonsered Power Products AB

ing rope through rope outlet to place tension on rewind spring. Spring tension is correct if rope pulley can be rotated approximately ½ turn further when rope is pulled completely out.

When installing starter assembly on saw, make sure starter pulley properly engages pawls on flywheel before tightening retaining cap screws.

CHAIN BRAKE. All models are equipped with a chain brake system designed to stop chain movement should kickback occur. Chain brake is activated when the operator's hand strikes the chain brake lever thereby forcing actuating plate (4 – Fig. J41) off of pin in housing releasing spring (7). Spring then draws brake band tight around clutch drum to stop chain. Pull back chain brake lever to reset mechanism. No adjustment of brake mechanism is required.

If brake requires disassembly for repair or renewal of individual components, it is recommended that a clutch drum be inserted in brake band and brake engaged, to facilitate removal of brake lever. When reassembling, make certain spring (7) is screwed completely on brake band and roll pins (6) are installed with split side toward front of saw.

HANDLE HEATER. Some models may be equipped with the handle heating system shown in Fig. J42. A generating coil (1) located under the flywheel produces an electric current which flows in series to the front handle (2), rear handle halves (3 and 5), heater control switch (6) and then grounded at the ignition stop switch (7) to complete the circuit.

The heating system may be tested using a suitable ohmmeter. Separate the wire connection from heater control switch (6) to ignition stop switch (7) and attach a tester lead to the wire. Ground other tester lead to the saw. Heating system may be considered satisfactory if tester reads 5-6 ohms resistance.

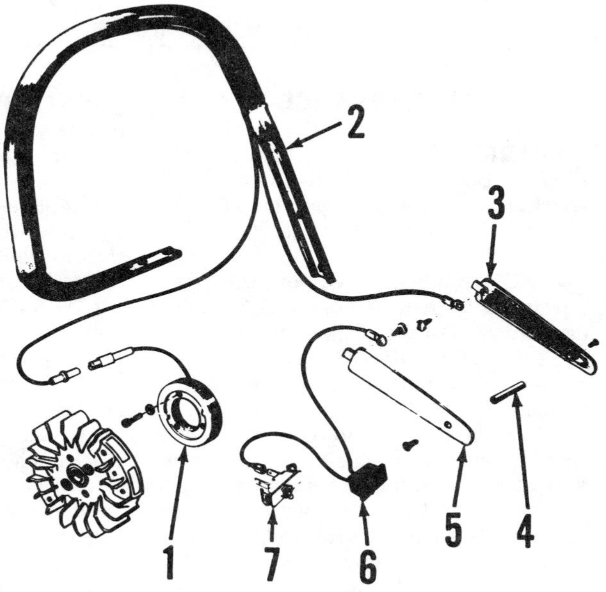

Fig. J42 — Exploded view of handle heating system used on some models.

1. Generating coil
2. Front handle
3. Right handle half
4. Connector
5. Left handle half
6. Heater control switch
7. Ignition stop switch

JONSERED

Model	Bore mm (in.)	Stroke mm (in.)	Displacement cc (cu. in.)	Drive Type
820, 830, 830 Dlx	52 (2.047)	38 (1.496)	80.7 (4.9)	Direct
910 D, 910 E, 910 EV, 920, 920 Super, 930 Super, 930 Dlx	54 (2.126)	38 (1.496)	87 (5.3)	Direct

MAINTENANCE

SPARK PLUG. Recommended spark plug is Bosch WS7F. Recommended spark plug electrode gap is 0.5 mm (0.020 in.).

CARBURETOR. All models are equipped with a Tillotson diaphragm carburetor. Refer to Tillotson section of CARBURETOR SERVICE section for exploded view and overhaul of carburetor.

Initial carburetor adjustment is 1¼ turns open for low speed mixture screw and 1 turn open for high speed mixture screw. Make final carburetor adjustment with engine warm and running. Adjust idle speed screw so engine idles just below clutch engagement speed. Adjust low speed mixture screw so engine will accelerate cleanly without hesitation. Adjust high speed mixture screw to obtain optimum performance under cutting load.

IGNITION. A breakerless capacitor discharge ignition system is used on all models. Ignition timing is fixed. Individual electronic components are available separately. Air gap between flywheel magnets and trigger module should be 0.3 mm (0.012 in.).

LUBRICATION. The engine is lubricated by mixing oil with the fuel. Recommended oil is Jonsered engine oil or a BIA certified air-cooled two-stroke engine oil approved for 40:1 fuel mixtures. Recommended fuel mixture ratio is 40:1 when using an approved engine oil. If a recommended oil is not available, a good quality oil designed for air-cooled two-stroke engines may be used when mixed with the fuel at a 20:1 ratio. Use a separate container when mixing the oil and gas.

All models are equipped with an automatic chain oiler. A good quality chain oil should be used. Viscosity should be chosen according to ambient temperature. Automatic oil pump discharge is adjusted by turning adjusting screw through opening on bottom side of saw. Initial setting is 1½ turns open. Turning screw clockwise decreases oil flow. Models 830 and 930 Super may be equipped with an optional manual chain oil pump.

CARBON. Carbon deposits should be removed from muffler and exhaust ports at regular intervals. When scraping carbon, be careful not to damage engine cylinder. Do not allow loosened carbon into cylinder.

REPAIRS

CYLINDER, PISTON, PIN AND RINGS. Refer to Fig. J44 for exploded view of engine. Cylinder bore is chrome plated and should be inspected for excessive wear and damage to bore surface. Inspect piston and discard if excessive wear or damage is evident. Oversize pistons and rings are not available. Piston and cylinder are renewable as matched sets only. All models have needle type piston pin bearings. Models 910E and 910EV are also equipped with thrust washers on

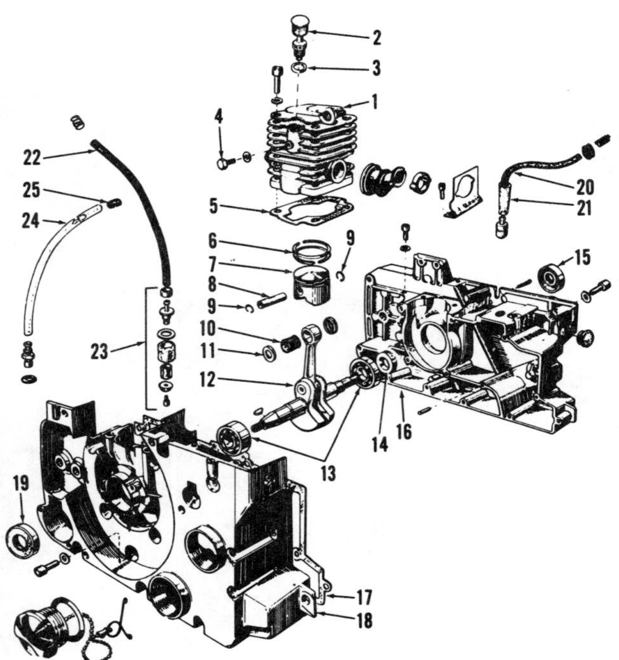

Fig. J44—Exploded view of engine assembly used on 910E and 910EV models. Models 820, 830, 920 and 930 Super are similar.

1. Cylinder
2. Decompression valve
3. Washer
4. Cap screw
5. Gasket
6. Piston rings
7. Piston
8. Piston pin
9. Piston pin retainer
10. Needle bearing
11. Thrust washer
12. Crankshaft assy
13. Ball bearing
14. Oil pump drive gear
15. Seal
16. Right crankcase half
17. Gasket
18. Left crankcase half
19. Seal
20. Oil hose
21. Oil strainer
22. Fuel hose
23. Fuel filter assy
24. Vent hose
25. Fitting

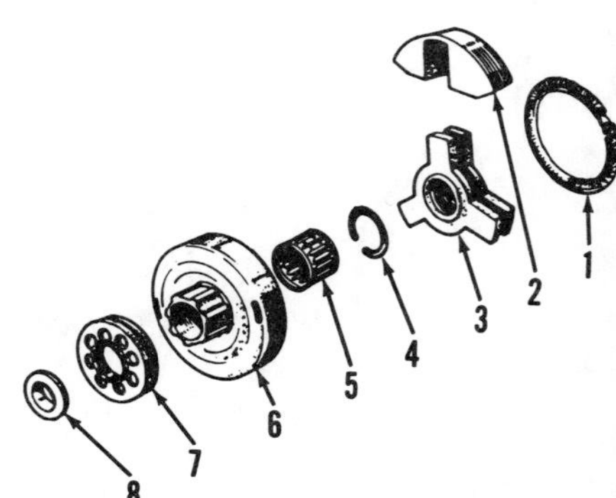

Fig. J45—Exploded view of typical clutch assembly. Ring (4) is not used on 820, 830, 920 and 930 Super models.

1. Spring
2. Shoe
3. Hub
4. Ring
5. Bearing
6. Drum
7. Sprocket
8. Washer

Illustrations courtesy Jonsered Power Products AB

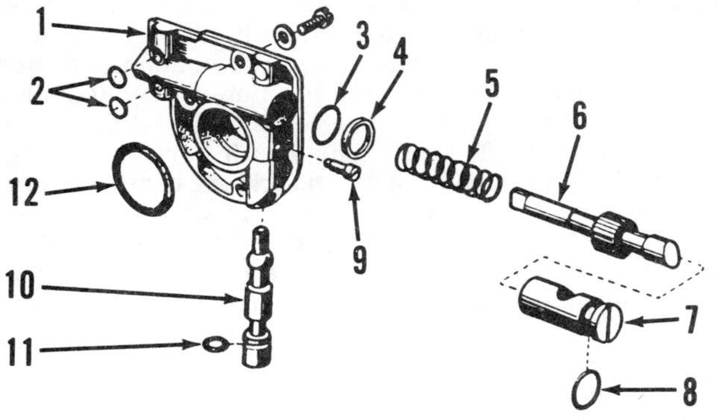

Fig. J47—Exploded view of automatic oil pump assembly used on all models.

1. Pump body
2. "O" rings
3. "O" ring
4. Washer
5. Spring
6. Plunger
7. Plug
8. "O" ring
9. Screw
10. Adjusting screw
11. "O" ring
12. Seal ring

both sides of connecting rod small end. On all models, install piston so arrow on piston crown points toward exhaust port.

Piston is equipped with two piston rings. A locating pin is present in piston ring grooves to prevent piston ring rotation. Be sure ring end gap is around locating pin when installing cylinder.

CYLINDER ROD, CRANKSHAFT AND CRANKCASE. Connecting rod is equipped with a needle bearing in small end. Crankshaft and connecting rod are a unit assembly. It will be necessary to heat crankcase halves to remove or install crankshaft and main bearings. Care should be taken not to damage mating surfaces of crankcase halves. Check rotation of connecting rod around crankpin and renew crankshaft unit if roughness or other damage is found.

CLUTCH. A three-shoe centrifugal type clutch is used on all models. Refer to Fig. J45 for exploded view of clutch assembly used on 910E and 910EV models. Models 820, 830, 920 and 930 Super clutch is similar. Inspect clutch shoes and drum for excessive wear or damage due to overheating. Inspect clutch drum, bearing and crankshaft for damage. On 910E and 910EV models, a ring (4) has been installed between the crankshaft and hub (3) to prevent possible crankshaft breakage. Renew ring (4) everytime clutch hub is removed.

AUTOMATIC OIL PUMP. All models are equipped with a crankshaft driven automatic oil pump. Refer to Fig. J47 for exploded view of oil pump.

Oil pump operation is accomplished when plunger (6) is rotated by a worm gear installed on crankshaft. While rotating, the plunger reciprocates as the oblique end of plunger bears against adjuster (10) ball thereby pumping oil. Oil output is changed in turning adjuster (10). The oil pump assembly is accessible after clutch removal.

REWIND STARTER. Refer to Fig. J48 for exploded view of rewind starter assembly. To disassemble rewind starter, remove starter housing from saw. Pull starter rope and hold rope pulley (10) with notch in pulley adjacent to rope outlet. Pull rope back through outlet so it engages notch in pulley and allow pulley to completely unwind. Unscrew pulley retaining screw (7) and carefully remove rope pulley. If required, rewind spring and cassette (11 and 12) may now be renewed.

Reassemble starter components by reversing disassembly procedure while noting the following: Rope is wound on rope pulley in clockwise direction as viewed with pulley in housing. To place tension on rewind spring, pass rope through rope outlet in housing and install rope handle. Pull rope out and hold rope pulley so notch on pulley is adjacent to rope outlet. Pull rope back through outlet between notch in pulley and housing. Turn rope pulley clockwise to place tension on spring. Release pulley and check starter action. Do not place more tension on rewind spring than is necessary to draw rope handle up against housing. With rope completely extended, it should be possible to rotate rope pulley an additional ½ turn if spring tension is correct.

CHAIN BRAKE. All models are equipped with a chain brake system designed to stop chain movement should kickback occur. Chain brake is

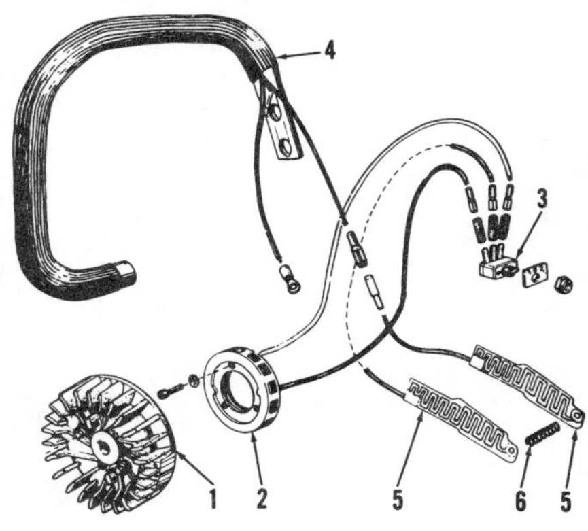

Fig. J50—Exploded view of handle heating system used on all 910EV models and some 820, 830, 920 and 930 Super models.

1. Flywheel
2. Generating coil
3. Heater control switch
4. Front handle
5. Rear handle heating elements
6. Spring connector

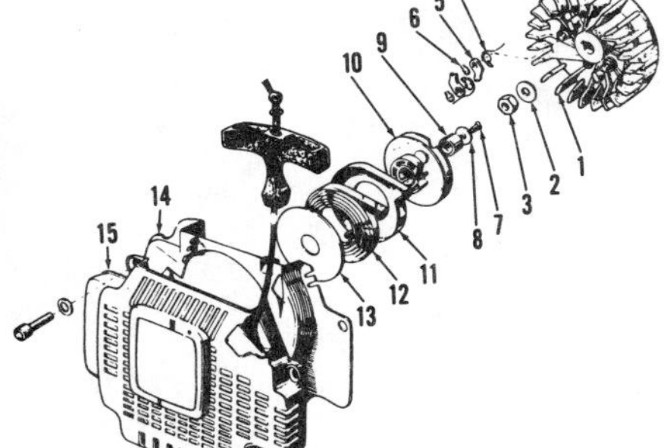

Fig. J48—Exploded view of rewind starter assembly used on all models.

1. Flywheel
2. Washer
3. Nut
4. Spring
5. Pawl
6. Snap ring
7. Screw
8. Washer
9. Bushing
10. Rope pulley
11. Spring cassette
12. Rewind spring
13. Washer
14. Shield
15. Starter housing

Fig. J49—Exploded view of chain brake.

1. Housing
2. Chain tensioner
3. Pin
4. Adjusting pin
5. Washer
6. Chain brake lever
7. Sleeve
8. Plate
9. Bushing
10. Washer
11. Socket head screw
12. Actuating plate
13. Spring
14. Brake band
15. Cover plate

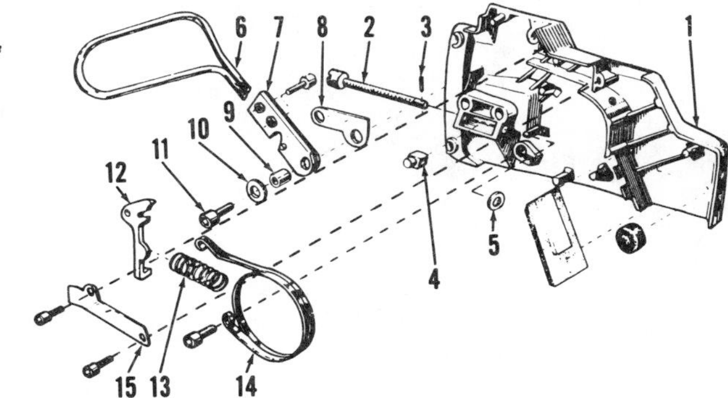

Illustrations courtesy Jonsered Power Products AB

activated when the operator's hand strikes the chain brake lever thereby forcing actuating plate (12—Fig. J49) off a pin in sleeve (7) releasing spring (13). Spring then draws brake band (14) tight around clutch drum to stop chain. Pull back chain brake lever to reset mechanism. No adjustment of brake mechanism is required.

Disassembly for repair or renewal of individual components is evident after inspection of unit and referral to the exploded view.

HANDLE HEATER. All 910EV models and some 820, 830, 920 and 930 Super models are equipped with the handle heating system shown in Fig. J50. A generating coil (2) located behind the flywheel (1) produces an electric current which flows through control switch and then to heating elements in the rear and front handles. The heater is off when the switch is in the middle position, on low heat when the switch is in the "1" position and on high heat when the switch is in the "2" position. To test handle heating system, disconnect the ground and the center connector at heater control switch (3). Connect ohmmeter probes to disconnected wires. Handle heating system is acceptable if resistance is 5-6 ohms.

Illustrations courtesy Jonsered Power Products AB

JONSERED

Model	Bore mm (in.)	Stroke mm (in.)	Displacement cc (cu. in.)	Drive Type
490, 590	45 (1.77)	32 (1.26)	50.8 (3.1)	Direct

MAINTENANCE

SPARK PLUG. Recommended spark plug is Bosch WS7F. Recommended electrode gap is 0.5 mm (0.020 in.).

CARBURETOR. All models are equipped with a Walbro WA diaphragm type carburetor. Refer to Walbro section of CARBURETOR SERVICE section for service and exploded views.

Initial adjustment for both high and low speed mixture screws is 1-1/8 turns open from a lightly seated position. Make final adjustment with engine running at operating temperature. Adjust idle speed to just below clutch engagement speed. Adjust low speed mixture so engine will accelerate cleanly without hesitation. Adjust high speed mixture to obtain optimum full throttle performance under cutting load. Do not adjust high speed mixture too lean as overheating and engine damage could result.

IGNITION. A breakerless capacitor discharge ignition system is used on all models. Ignition timing is fixed. All electronic circuitry is contained in a one piece ignition module. Except for faulty wiring connections, repair of ignition system malfunctions is accomplished by component renewal. Air gap between ignition module and flywheel magnets should be 0.30-0.40 mm (0.012-0.016 in.).

LUBRICATION. The engine is lubricated by mixing oil with the fuel. The recommended oil is Jonsered engine oil or a BIA certified air-cooled two-stroke engine oil approved for 40:1 fuel mixtures. Recommended fuel mixture ratio is 40:1 when using an approved oil. If a recommended oil is not available, a good quality oil designed for air-cooled two-stroke engine may be used when mixed with the fuel at a 20:1 ratio.

All models are equipped with an adjustable automatic chain oil pump. A good quality chain oil should be used and viscosity chosen according to ambient temperature. Refer to AUTOMATIC OIL PUMP section for service and adjustment procedures.

CARBON. Carbon deposits should be removed from muffler and exhaust ports at regular intervals. When removing carbon use caution not to damage piston or cylinder. Position piston to block exhaust ports to prevent loosened carbon from entering cylinder.

REPAIRS

CYLINDER, PISTON, PIN AND RINGS. Cylinder bore is chrome plated and should be inspected for cracking, flaking or other damage. Oversize pistons and rings are not available.

Piston must be installed on connecting rod with arrow on piston crown pointing toward exhaust ports. The piston pin rides in a needle roller bearing and is held in place by two wire retainers. Refer to Fig. J55 for exploded view of engine assembly.

The piston is fitted with a locating pin in piston ring groove to prevent ring rotation. Make certain ring end gap is around locating pin when installing cylinder. Tighten cylinder bolts to 9 N·m (80 in.-lbs.).

CONNECTING ROD, CRANKSHAFT AND CRANKCASE. Crankshaft and connecting rod (10—Fig. J55) are a unit assembly and are not available separately. Check rotation of connect-

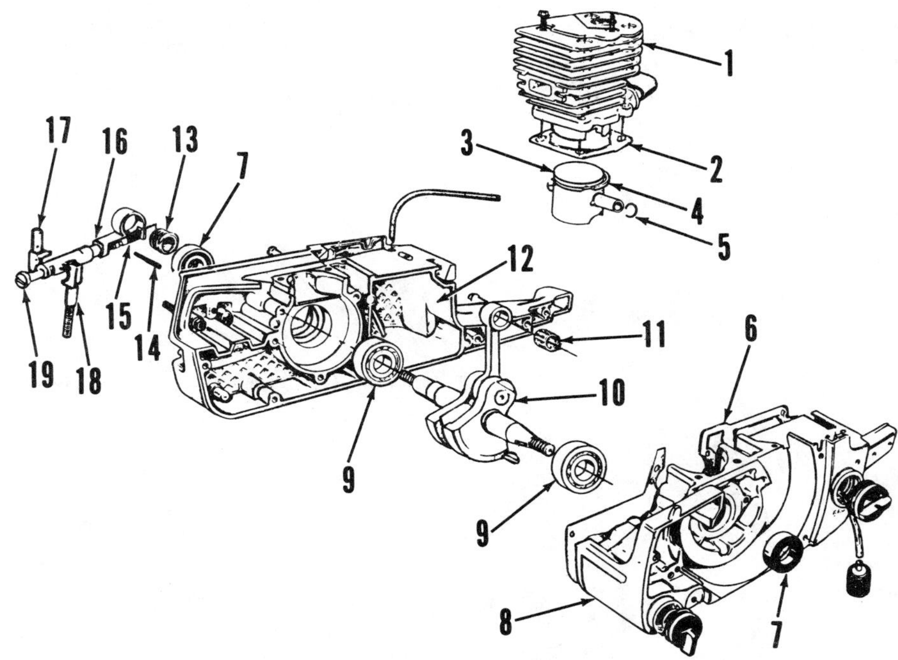

Fig. J55—Exploded view of engine assembly and automatic oil pump.

1. Cylinder
2. Cylinder gasket
3. Piston & pin assy.
4. Piston ring
5. Retainer
6. Gasket
7. Crankcase seal
8. Left crankcase half
9. Main bearing
10. Crankshaft & connecting rod assy.
11. Needle roller bearing
12. Right crankcase half
13. Worm gear
14. Cam pin
15. Plunger
16. Housing
17. Oil discharge hose
18. Oil suction hose
19. Adjusting screw

ing rod around crankpin and renew if roughness, excessive play or other damage is found.

The oil pump worm gear (13) must be removed before crankcase can be separated. The manufacturer recommends using special tool 50538187 (right-hand threads) to remove worm gears on early saws and special tool 502540102 (left-hand threads) to remove worm gears on late model saws. The manufacturer recommends using special tool 502516101 to separate crankcase halves (8 and 12).

To reassemble crankcase, press main bearings (9) onto crankshaft. Heat area around main bearing bore of flywheel side crankcase half (8) and install crankshaft assembly into crankcase half. Heat main bearing bore of clutch side crankcase half and assemble crankcase halves together. Tighten crankcase cap screws to 9 N·m (80 in.-lbs.). Make certain crankshaft turns freely in crankcase. Install crankcase seals flush with crankcase.

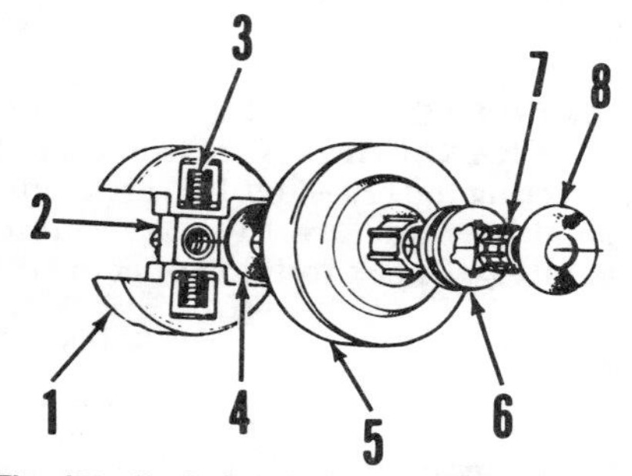

Fig. J56—Exploded view of clutch assembly.

1. Shoe
2. Hub
3. Spring
4. Washer
5. Drum
6. Sprocket
7. Needle roller bearing
8. Washer

CLUTCH. A two-shoe centrifugal clutch is used. Clutch hub (2—Fig. J56) has left-hand threads. Clutch shoes (1) and drum (5) should be inspected for excessive wear or damage due to overheating. Needle roller bearing (7) should be inspected for damage or discoloration and lubricated with Molykote or equivalent high temperature grease. Tighten clutch hub to 35 N·m (25 ft.-lbs.).

AUTOMATIC OIL PUMP. All models are equipped with an adjustable automatic chain oil pump driven by worm gear (13—Fig. J55). Oil is pumped by plunger (15) as it reciprocates due to cam pin (14) riding in operating groove of plunger. Pump output is adjusted by rotating adjusting screw (19).

Inspect discharge (17) and suction (18) hoses for cracking or hardening. Inspect plunger (15), worm gear (13) and cam pin for excessive wear. When installing oil pump, make certain notch in pump housing engages boss in crankcase casting.

REWIND STARTER. All models are equipped with the starter assembly shown in Fig. J57. To disassemble starter, pull out approximately 30 cm (12 in.) of rope and align notch in rope pulley (8) with rope guide (11). Insert rope into notch in pulley and carefully allow pulley to unwind, releasing tension on rewind spring (9). Remove screw (5) and washer (6) and carefully remove pulley. If rewind spring must be removed, depress tabs which secure rewind spring cover to starter housing (10) with a screwdriver or suitable tool.

To reassemble starter, lightly oil rewind spring and install into starter housing. Wind approximately five revolutions of rope onto rope pulley in a clockwise direction as viewed from flywheel side of pulley. Install rope pulley into starter housing and tighten screw (5) to 2.0 N·m (15 in.-lbs.). Pull out length of rope and position rope into notch of pulley. Turn rope pulley clockwise to preload rewind spring. Rope pulley should be able to rotate an additional ½ turn with rope fully extended. Do not place more tension on rewind spring than is necessary to draw rope handle up against housing.

CHAIN BRAKE. Some models are equipped with a chain brake system designed to stop chain movement should kickback occur. The chain brake is activated when operator's hand strikes chain brake lever (1—Fig. J58) tripping actuating plate (4) and allowing spring (7) to draw brake band (8) tight around clutch drum. Pull back chain brake lever to reset mechanism.

Disassembly for repair and component renewal is evident after referral to exploded view and inspection of unit.

When reassembling, make certain spring (7) is screwed completely onto brake band (8) and roll pins (3 and 5) are installed with split sides facing forward.

HANDLE HEATER. Some models are equipped with optional handle

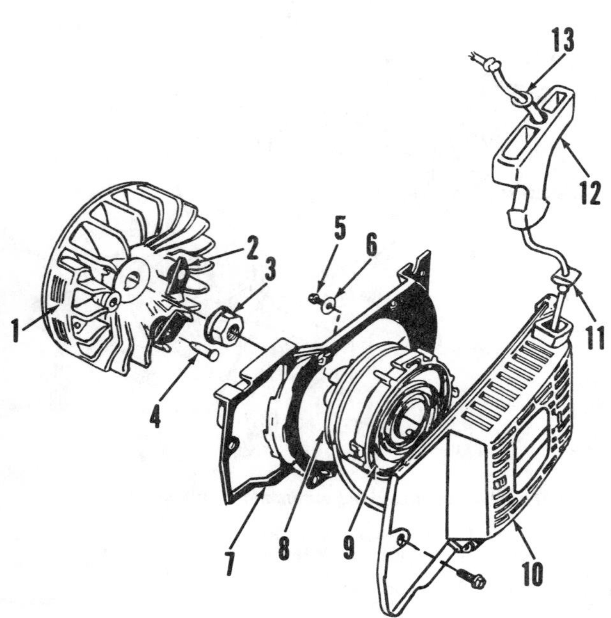

Fig. J57—Exploded view of rewind starter assembly.

1. Flywheel
2. Pawl
3. Nut
4. Pin
5. Screw
6. Washer
7. Shield
8. Rope pulley
9. Rewind spring & cover assy.
10. Housing
11. Rope guide
12. Rope handle
13. Washer

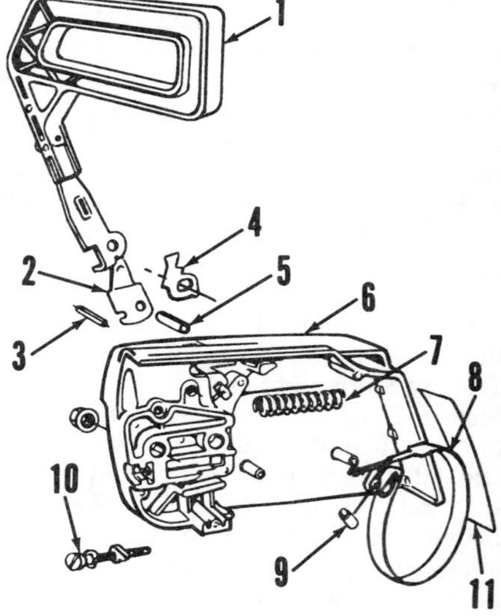

Fig. J58—Exploded view of chain brake system used on some models.

1. Chain brake lever
2. Sleeve
3. Roll pin
4. Actuating plate
5. Roll pin
6. Brake housing
7. Spring
8. Brake band
9. Pin
10. Chain adjuster assy.
11. Chain guard

Illustrations courtesy Jonsered Power Products AB

heating system shown in Fig. J59. Handle heating system utilizes exhaust heat from muffler and directs heat to front and rear handles through heat tubes (5). Front handle temperature is controlled by adjusting screw (9) while rear handle temperature is controlled by adjusting screw (10). Turning adjusting screws completely in shuts off heat.

To service system, remove muffler and disassemble. Clean carbon deposits and soot from muffler (1) and valve assembly (6). Clean heat tubes with manufacturer's special tool 505382908 or equivalent long flexible probe. Inspect heat tubes for cracking or other damage and renew as necessary. Make certain heat tubes are not pinched or rubbing against sharp edges upon reassembly.

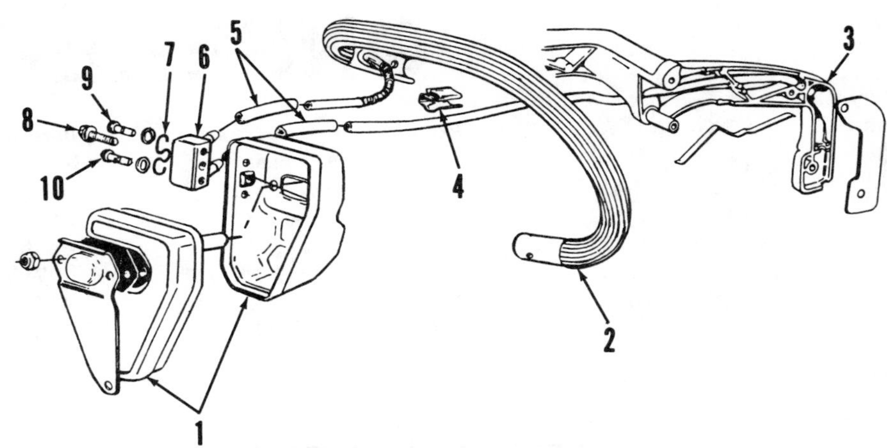

Fig. J59—Exploded view of handle heating system used on some models.

1. Muffler assy.
2. Front handle
3. Rear handle
4. Clip
5. Heat tubes
6. Valve assy.
7. Wire bail
8. Cap screw
9. Adjuster screw
10. Adjuster screw

Illustrations courtesy Jonsered Power Products AB

JONSERED

Model	Bore mm (in.)	Stroke mm (in.)	Displacement cc (cu. in.)	Drive Type
2041, 2041 Turbo	40 (1.57)	32 (1.26)	40.2 (2.5)	Direct
2045, 2045 Turbo	42 (1.65)	32 (1.26)	44.3 (2.7)	Direct
2050, 2050 Turbo	44 (1.732)	32 (1.26)	48.7 (3.0)	Direct

Saws identified as Turbo models use the centrifugal force of the cooling air moved by the fan to separate some of the foreign matter from air delivered to the carburetor intake. Larger wood chips and other impurities in air circulated by the cooling fan are thrown to the outside by centrifugal force, while cleaner air nearer the fan is collected by a nozzle and directed toward the carburetor intake. Finer impurities are captured by the air filter.

MAINTENANCE

SPARK PLUG. Recommended spark plug is Champion RCJ7Y or NGK BPMR 7A. Electrode gap should be 0.5-0.7 mm (0.020-0.027 in.). The spark plug should be tightened to the torque listed in the TIGHTENING TORQUE paragraph.

CARBURETOR. A Zama C1Q diaphragm carburetor is used. Refer to the appropriate Zama section of the CARBURETOR SERVICE section for service and exploded views.

Initial setting of the low- and high-speed mixture needles (Fig. J70) is 1 turn open from lightly seated. To adjust the mixture screws, first remove and clean the air filter, then reinstall it. On Turbo models, check the fan cooling passage and the Turbo duct to the carburetor. Make sure the Turbo duct is clean and properly sealed. On all models, start the engine and allow it to run until it reaches normal operating temperature. If necessary, turn each mixture needle clockwise until seated lightly, then back the needle out (counterclockwise) to the initial setting so the engine can be started.

Fig. J70—View of the carburetor adjustment locations. Low-speed mixture needle is located at (L), high-speed mixture needle is at (H) and idle speed stop screw is located at (T).

Turn the idle speed stop screw (T—Fig. J70) so the engine idles at just below clutch engagement rpm. Adjust the low-speed mixture needle (L) so the engine idles smoothly and accelerates without hesitation. If necessary, readjust the idle speed to just slower than clutch engagement speed, then recheck low-speed mixture adjustment.

Adjust the high-speed mixture needle (H) to provide the best performance while operating at maximum speed under load. Maximum no-load speed (bar and chain installed) is 12.500 rpm for all models. The high-speed mixture screw may be set slightly rich to improve performance under load. The engine may be damaged if the high-speed screw is set too lean.

Final adjustment of the mixture needles should be within 1/4 turn of the initial settings. Large differences may indicate air leaks, plugged passages or other problems.

To remove carburetor, remove cylinder cover and air cleaner (1—Fig. J71). Remove handlebar mounting screws and fold handlebar out of the way. Unbolt and remove air cleaner support (2). Disconnect throttle wire and fuel line from carburetor. Remove the carburetor (3).

When installing carburetor, tighten the carburetor attaching screws to the torque listed in the TIGHTENING TORQUE paragraph.

IGNITION. All models are equipped with a breakerless electronic ignition system. All electronic circuitry is contained in a one-piece ignition module/coil located outside the flywheel. Ignition timing is fixed and not adjustable. The flywheel attaching nut should be tightened to the torque listed in TIGHTENING TORQUE paragraph.

Air gap between the legs of the module/coil and the flywheel magnets should be 0.3 mm (0.012 in.). When installing, set the air gap between the flywheel magnets and the legs of the ignition module as follows.

Install the ignition module, but tighten the two screws only enough to

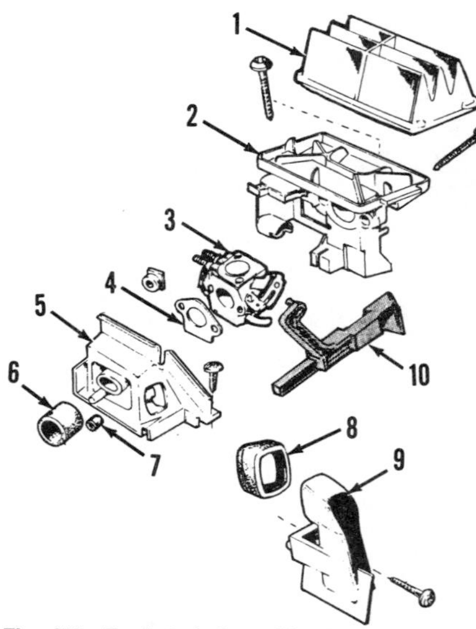

Fig. J71—Exploded view of intake components. Air duct (9) and boot (8) are used on Turbo models.

1. Air filter
2. Air cleaner support
3. Carburetor
4. Gasket
5. Insulator
6. Intake manifold
7. Impulse tube
8. Boot
9. Air duct
10. Choke lever

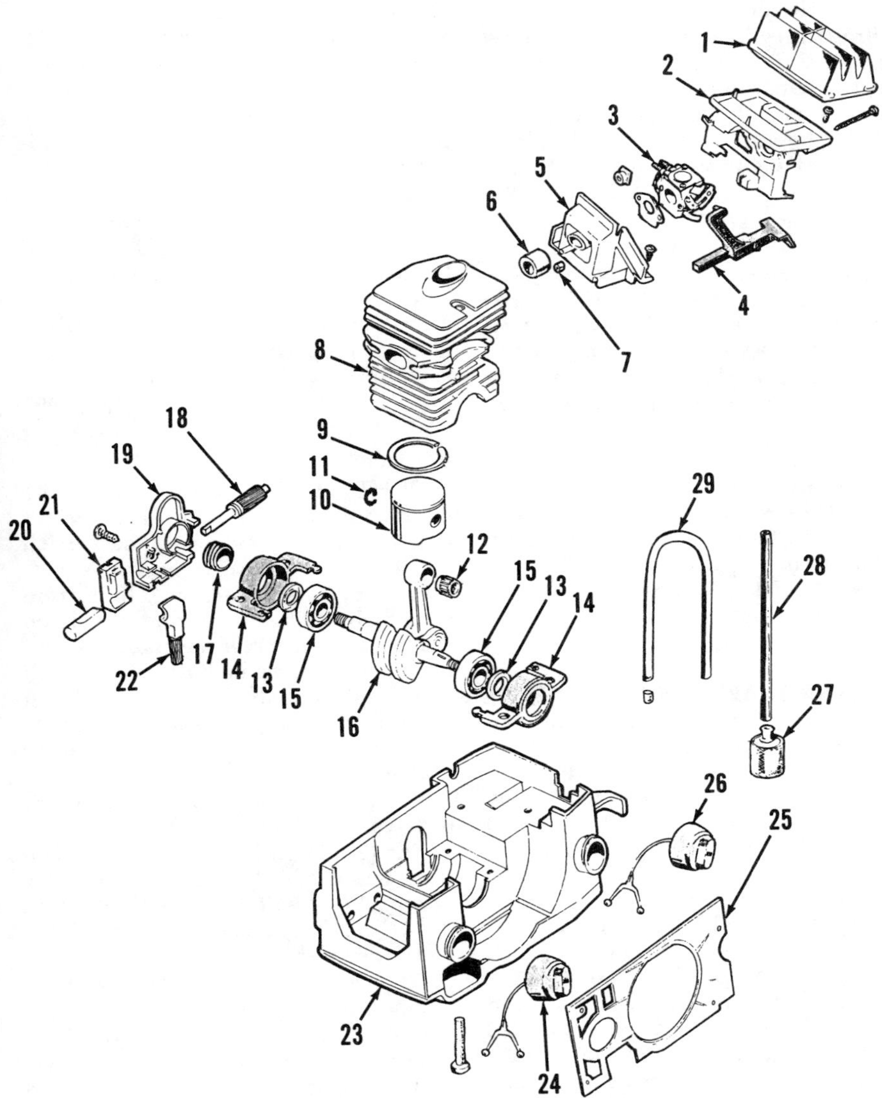

Fig. J72—Exploded view of typical engine components.

1. Air filter
2. Filter housing
3. Carburetor
4. Choke lever
5. Insulator
6. Intake connector
7. Impulse tube
8. Cylinder
9. Piston ring
10. Piston
11. Retaining ring
12. Needle bearing
13. Seal rings
14. Crankshaft seats
15. Ball bearings
16. Crankshaft & connecting rod
17. Worm gear
18. Pump plunger
19. Oil pump housing
20. Pump cylinder
21. Pressure pipe
22. Suction pipe & filter
23. Crankcase
24. Oil tank cap
25. Air baffle
26. Fuel tank cap
27. Filter screen
28. Fuel hose
29. Fuel tank vent hose

hold it in place away from the flywheel. Insert setting gauge (part No. 502 51 34-05) or brass/plastic shim stock of the proper thickness between the legs of the ignition module and the flywheel, then turn the flywheel until the flywheel magnets are near the module legs. Loosen the screws attaching the ignition module and press legs of the ignition module against the shim stock. Tighten the two attaching screws securely. Remove the setting gauge, then turn the flywheel and check to be sure the flywheel does not hit the legs of the coil.

LUBRICATION. The engine is lubricated by mixing oil with the gasoline fuel. The manufacturer recommends mixing Jonsered two-stroke engine oil with regular grade gasoline at a ratio of 50:1. When using regular two-stroke engine oil, mix at a ratio of 25:1.

Always use a separate container to mix gasoline and oil before filling the fuel tank. The manufacturer recommends not using fuel containing alcohol.

All saws are equipped with an automatic bar and chain oiling system. The manufacturer recommends using good quality oil designed for lubricating saw chain. Automotive engine oil may also be used. Select oil viscosity according to the ambient temperature.

Make sure the reservoir is filled at all times and the small oil passages do not become blocked. The volume of oil delivered by the pump is not adjustable

REPAIRS

CRANKCASE PRESSURE TEST. An improperly sealed crankcase can cause the engine to be hard to start, run rough, have low power and overheat. Refer to ENGINE SERVICE section of this manual for crankcase pressure test procedure. If crankcase leakage is indicated, pressurize the crankcase and use a solution of soap and water to check gasket, seals, pulse line and castings for leakage.

TIGHTENING TORQUE. Recommended tightening torque values are as follows.

Carburetor	3-4 N•m (26.5-35 in.-lb.)
Clutch hub	30-35 N•m (265-310 in.-lb.)
Cylinder	10-12 N•m (88.5-106 in.-lb.)
Flywheel	25-30 N•m (221-265 in.-lb.)
Muffler	7-8 N•m (62-71 in.-lb.)
Spark plug	20-22 N•m (177-195 in.-lb.)
Starter	2-3 N•m (18-26.5 in.-lb.)

PISTON, PIN, RING AND CYLINDER. To disassemble, remove cylinder cover, air filter, starter housing, flywheel, saw chain, guide bar, clutch assembly and oil pump. Remove stop switch and fuel tank vent tube (29—Fig. J72). Remove muffler. Disconnect throttle cable and fuel line (28) and remove carburetor (3) and air filter holder (2). Remove screws attaching carburetor heat shield (5) to crankcase.

Remove four screws from the bottom of the crankcase (23) that attach the cylinder (8) to the crankcase. Lift cylinder from the piston (10) and lower crankcase (23).

If necessary to remove the crankshaft, main bearings and seals (13, 14, 15 and 16), refer to CRANKSHAFT AND CONNECTING ROD paragraph.

Illustrations courtesy Jonsered Power Products AB

Fig. J73—Attach the piston to the connecting rod so arrow on piston crown points toward the exhaust side (port) of engine.

Remove retaining rings (11) and push pin from the piston. Remove needle bearing (12) from the bore in connecting rod small end.

Inspect the cylinder for any damage and install new parts as necessary. If the chrome plating is worn from the cylinder, a new cylinder should be installed. The piston, ring and cylinder are available in standard size only. The piston and cylinder are available for service only as a matched set and the cylinder should not be bored oversize. Check the intake connector (6) for cracking or other damage.

Lubricate needle bearing (12) with engine oil before assembling. Position the piston over the connecting rod and needle bearing with the arrow on piston crown toward the exhaust side of engine (Fig. J73). Install retaining rings (11—Fig. J72) with the opening toward the top or bottom of the piston. Install the piston ring into the piston groove so that ends of the ring correctly engage the locating pin in the groove. The locating pin prevents the ring from rotating and the ends of the piston ring must fit around this pin.

Lubricate the connecting rod lower bearing, cylinder bore, piston and ring. Make sure the ends of the piston ring surround the pin located in ring groove, then gently compress the ring while installing the cylinder straight down over the piston. If the cylinder is twisted, the ring can catch in a port and break the end of the ring. Install screws attaching cylinder to crankcase (23) and tighten in a crossing pattern evenly to the torque listed in TIGHTENING TORQUE paragraph.

NOTE: Sealer is not used between the cylinder (8—Fig. J72) and crankcase lower half (23). The cylinder attaching screws should be retightened after assembly is complete, engine has run for 2-3 minutes, then allowed to cool.

When assembling, be sure impulse channel (7—Fig. J72)) is in place in cylinder. Install a new impulse channel if lost or damaged. Slide the intake connector (6), onto the cylinder, then install the carburetor and air cleaner housing.

CRANKSHAFT AND CONNECTING ROD. The crankshaft and connecting rod are available only as an assembly (16—Fig. J72); individual components are not available. A shop experienced in servicing built-up crankshaft assemblies can align the shaft.

To remove the crankshaft and connecting rod assembly, remove the cylinder and piston as described in PISTON, PIN, RING AND CYLINDER paragraphs. Remove the oil pump (18 through 22) as described in the OIL PUMP paragraph. Lift the crankshaft, connecting rod, main bearings, seals, retainers and oil pump drive worm (13 through 17) as an assembly from the crankcase.

The crankshaft should turn smoothly inside main bearings with no perceptible play or ratcheting. Refer to the OIL PUMP paragraph for removal of the worm gear (17). The main bearings (15) and seals (13) fit inside retainer halves (14). Twist retainers to separate the interlocking ends. A screwdriver or similar tool can be used to pull the retainers from the main bearings.

Use suitable tools to remove and install new main bearings and seals. Lubricate lips of seals with engine oil before installing over the crankshaft. Make sure that tabs of retainer halves (14) are properly interlocked while assembling.

Refer to PISTON, PIN, RING AND CYLINDER paragraphs for installing these parts.

CLUTCH. Refer to Fig. J74. The clutch hub (16) is attached to the right end of the engine crankshaft with left-hand threads (turn clockwise to remove). Prevent the crankshaft from turning by using an appropriate piston stopper and unscrew the clutch assembly from the crankshaft. The clutch drum and chain drive sprocket (19) can be withdrawn after the hub and shoes are removed. Do not lose needle bearing (20) or washer (21).

The clutch shoes (15) and hub (16) are available only as an assembly, but spring (17) is available separately. The thickness of the shoes to the groove for spring (17) should be more than 1 mm (0.04 in.). The inside diameter of the clutch drum should not exceed 64.4 mm (2.534 in.). Inspect all parts for wear or damage and replace as necessary.

If shoes are removed from the hub, assemble the spring and three shoes. Install two of the shoes on the hub and clamp the hub and shoes in a vice, then use a screwdriver to carefully install the third shoe. When assembled, the coupling for spring (17) should be in the middle of one of the shoes.

Grease the needle bearing in the clutch drum lightly before installing the drum. Install the clutch assembly, tightening the hub to the torque listed in TIGHTENING TORQUE paragraph.

OIL PUMP. The automatic oil pump is driven by worm gear (17—Fig. J72) on the crankshaft. Oil is pumped by plunger (18) as it rotates in the pump cylinder (20). Pump output is not adjustable for these models.

To remove the oil pump, first remove the clutch cover (13—Fig. J74) and chain brake. Remove the guide bar, chain and clutch assembly. Unbolt and remove the chain guide plate and the oil pump housing (19—Fig. J72). Lift the pump (18 and 20) and pressure pipe (21) from the housing. Use special tool

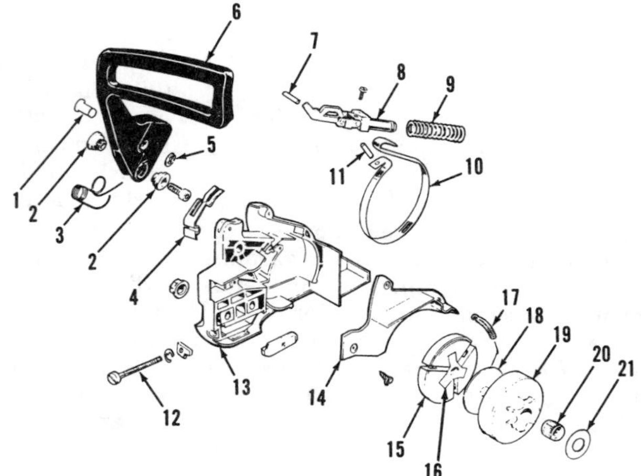

Fig. J74—Exploded view of the chain brake and clutch assemblies.

1. Pin
2. Pivot sleeves
3. Spring
4. Spring
5. "E" ring
6. Hand guard
7. Pin
8. Brake trigger mechanism
9. Brake actuating spring
10. Brake band
11. Pin
12. Chain adjusting screw
13. Clutch cover and brake housing
14. Brake cover
15. Clutch shoes
16. Clutch hub
17. Spring
18. Washer
19. Clutch drum
20. Needle bearing
21. Washer

Illustrations courtesy Jonsered Power Products AB

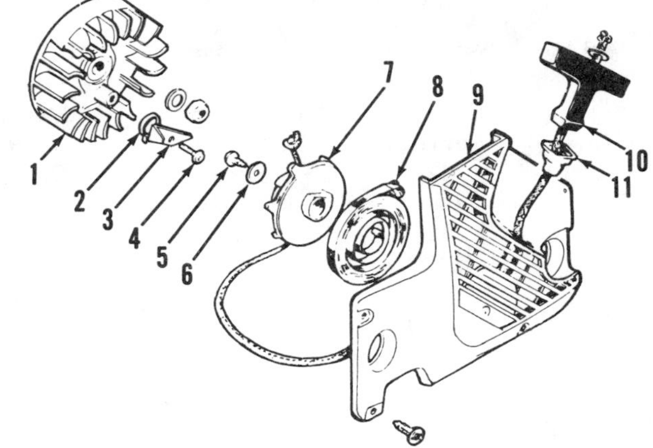

Fig. J75—Exploded view of the rewind starter assembly.

1. Flywheel
2. Spring
3. Starter pawl
4. Screw
5. Screw
6. Washer
7. Rope pulley
8. Rewind spring
9. Starter housing
10. Rope handle
11. Rope guide

(part No. 505 38 18-17) to remove the drive worm (17). If necessary, pull the oil suction pipe and filter (22) from the oil tank.

Clean and inspect all parts, then replace any that are damaged. Use the worm gear special tool to install the worm gear (17) on the crankshaft. Lubricate the oil suction pipe before inserting, then make sure the pipe is completely seated in the housing.

CHAIN BRAKE. The chain brake is designed to stop the saw chain quickly should kickback occur. The chain brake is activated when the operator's hand strikes the hand guard (6—Fig. J74). Forward movement of the guard disengages the trigger assembly (8) allowing the spring (9) to tighten the band (10) around the clutch drum. The brake is released and the mechanism is reset by pulling back on the guard. Keep the chain brake clean and free of sawdust and dirt accumulation.

To disassemble, remove cover (13—Fig. J74) with brake assembly. Disengage brake, then remove hand guard (6). Remove brake cover (14). Carefully disengage brake spring (9) from cover (13). Remove brake band (10) and linkage from cover.

Inspect all parts carefully and install new parts as necessary. Install a new brake band if any part of the band is worn to less than 0.8 mm (0.032 in.) thickness.

Lubricate all pivot points lightly when assembling. Do not allow any lubricant to get on gripping surfaces of the clutch drum or brake band. No adjustment of chain brake system is required.

REWIND STARTER. Refer to Fig. J75. The starter housing (9) can be unbolted and the assembly removed from the saw. Pull the starter rope out about 20 cm (8 in.) and hold the pulley (7) to keep the rope from rewinding. Pull a loop of rope from between the housing (9) and the pulley (7) into one of the notches molded into the edge of the pulley. Hold the loop and allow the pulley to turn slowly until the spring is completely unwound. Remove the retaining screw (5) and washer (6), then lift the pulley (7). The rewind spring (8) can be removed if necessary, but be careful to control the spring as it is removed to prevent injury.

Clean and inspect parts for damage. Lubricate the recoil spring, then wind spring (8) into the housing cavity in a clockwise direction beginning with the outside coil.

If detached, attach the rope to the pulley and make sure the knot is securely nested in the pulley. Insert the end of the rope through the housing (9) and guide (11), then attach handle (10). Wind as much of the rope onto the pulley (7) as possible. Position the pulley over the post in housing with a loop in the rope between the housing and pulley, then preload the recoil spring by turning the pulley about 4 turns clockwise before releasing the rope loop. Install washer (6) and screw (5).

Check for proper spring preload as follows. Pull the rope out fully and check to be sure the pulley can be turned an additional 1/2 turn without causing the spring to bind. Allow the rope to rewind and make sure the handle is pulled against the housing. If the spring binds, pull a loop in the rope between the housing and the pulley, release some spring preload (about 1 turn), then recheck. If the handle is not wound against the housing, increase the preload and recheck.

Inspect the condition of the pawl (3) and spring (2) attached to the flywheel. On some models, the pawl assembly may be part of a plate attached by the flywheel retaining nut.

HEATED HANDLES. The saw may be equipped with heated handles. A generating coil located under the flywheel provides current that can flow in series through a control switch, to the front handle heater element, to heated hand plates in the rear handle, then to ground. The heating system may be tested using an ohmmeter. Normal resistance should be 5-6 ohms. Service is limited to replacement of parts necessary to complete the circuit.

JONSERED

Model	Bore mm (in.)	Stroke mm (in.)	Displacement cc (cu. in.)	Drive Type
2051, 2051 Turbo	45 (1.77)	32 (1.26)	50.8 (3.1)	Direct
2054 Turbo	46 (1.81)	32 (1.26)	53.2 (3.2)	Direct
2055 Turbo	46 (1.81)	32 (1.26)	53.2 (3.2)	Direct

Saws identified as Turbo models use the centrifugal force of the cooling air moved by the fan to separate some of the foreign matter from air delivered to the carburetor intake. Larger wood chips and other impurities in air circulated by the cooling fan are thrown to the outside by centrifugal force, while cleaner air nearer the fan is collected by a nozzle and directed toward the carburetor intake. Finer impurities are captured by the air filter.

MAINTENANCE

SPARK PLUG. Recommended spark plug is Champion RCJ7Y or NGK BPMR 7A. Electrode gap should be 0.5-0.7 mm (0.020-0.027 in.). The spark plug should be tightened to the torque listed in the TIGHTENING TORQUE paragraph.

CARBURETOR. A Walbro HDA diaphragm carburetor is used. Refer to the appropriate Walbro section of the CARBURETOR SERVICE section for service and exploded views. Initial setting of the low-speed mixture needle is 1 turn open from lightly seated. Initial setting of the high-speed mixture needle is 1 turn open for 2051 model or 1 1/4 turn open from lightly seated for 2054 and 2055 models.

To adjust the mixture screws, first remove and clean the air filter, then reinstall it. On Turbo models, check the fan cooling passage and the Turbo duct to the carburetor. Make sure the Turbo duct is clean and properly sealed. On all models, start the engine and allow it to run until it reaches normal operating temperature. If necessary, turn each of the mixture needles clockwise until seated lightly, then back the needles out (counterclockwise) to the initial setting so the engine can be started.

Turn the idle speed stop screw (T—Fig. J80) so the engine idles at about 2,400 rpm. Adjust the low-speed mixture needle (L) so the engine idles smoothly and accelerates without hesitation. Adjust the idle speed to just slower than clutch engagement speed, then recheck low-speed mixture adjustment.

Adjust the high-speed mixture needle (H) to provide the best performance while operating at maximum speed under load. The high-speed mixture screw may be set slightly rich to improve performance under load. The engine may be damaged if the high-speed screw is set too lean.

Final adjustment of the mixture needles should be within 1/4 turn of the initial settings. Large differences may indicate air leaks, plugged passages or other problems.

Refer to Fig. J81 for an exploded view of air intake system and throttle controls. To remove carburetor (11), remove cylinder cover (1) and air filter (2). Remove carburetor mounting screws. Lift carburetor and disconnect vent pipe, choke lever (17), throttle cable (16), fuel line and impulse line (7). Remove the carburetor.

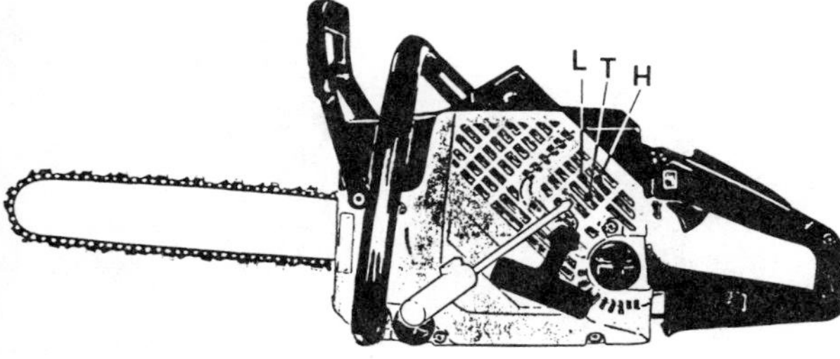

Fig. J80—Carburetor idle speed adjusting screw is located at (T), low-speed mixture needle at (L) and high-speed mixture needle at (H).

When installing carburetor, note the following special instructions. Throttle wire should be connected to throttle lever from inside to out. Vent pipe should be positioned under the fuel line. Tighten the carburetor attaching screws to the torque listed in the TIGHTENING TORQUE paragraph.

IGNITION. All models are equipped with a breakerless electronic ignition system and the ignition timing is fixed and not adjustable. The flywheel attaching nut should be tightened to the torque listed in TIGHTENING TORQUE paragraph.

The ignition system of early models may include the ignition module (12—Fig. J82), microprocessor (6), engine stop switch and connecting wires. The electronic circuitry of later models is contained in a one-piece ignition module/coil located outside the flywheel and the engine stop switch.

When testing all models, if there is no spark first check the condition of the engine stop switch. To test the switch, detach wires from the switch and attach a continuity meter (or ohmmeter) to the switch leads. With the stop switch in OFF position, the meter should indicate continuity. With the switch in ON position, the meter should indicate an open circuit. Install a new switch if it fails either test.

Air gap between the legs of the coil/module and the flywheel magnets should be 0.3-0.4 mm (0.012-0.16 in.) for early models with microprocessor. Air gap for later models with one piece ignition coil/module should be 0.3 mm (0.012 in.). When assembling, set the air gap between the flywheel magnets and the legs of the ignition coil as follows.

Illustrations courtesy Jonsered Power Products AB

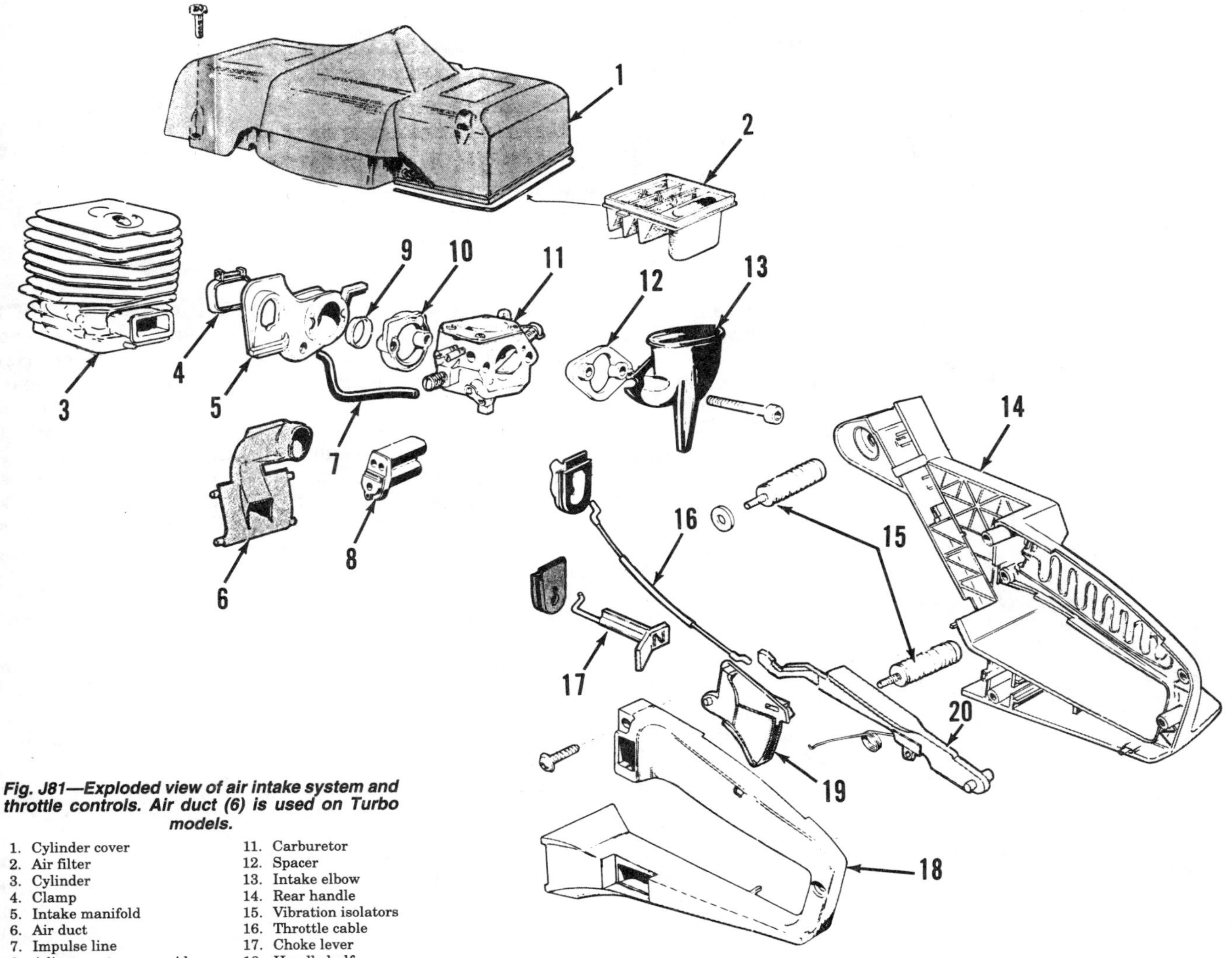

Fig. J81—Exploded view of air intake system and throttle controls. Air duct (6) is used on Turbo models.

1. Cylinder cover
2. Air filter
3. Cylinder
4. Clamp
5. Intake manifold
6. Air duct
7. Impulse line
8. Adjustment screw guide
9. Seal
10. Insulator
11. Carburetor
12. Spacer
13. Intake elbow
14. Rear handle
15. Vibration isolators
16. Throttle cable
17. Choke lever
18. Handle half
19. Throttle trigger
20. Throttle latch

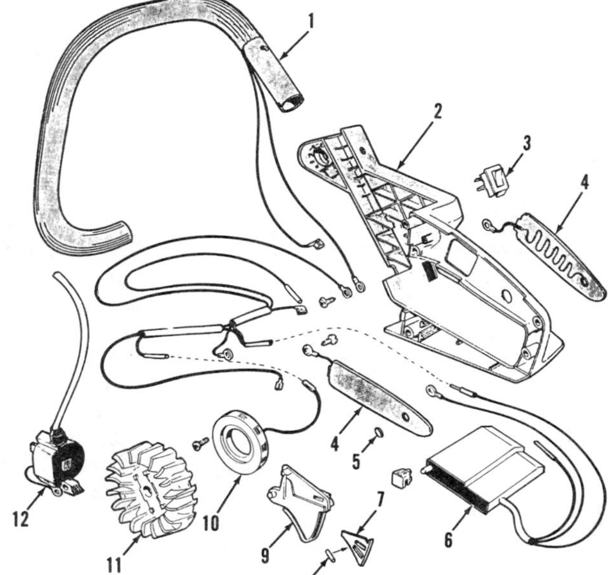

Fig. J82—Exploded view of the handle heating system and ignition coil/module (12) typical of early 2051 models.

1. Front tubular handle
2. Rear handle
3. Heater switch
4. Rear handle heater plates
5. Plug
6. Microprocessor
7. Magnet case
8. Magnet
9. Housing
10. Generator coil
11. Flywheel
12. Ignition coil/module

Install the ignition coil, but tighten the two screws only enough to hold it in place away from the flywheel. Insert setting gauge (part No. 502 51 34-05) or brass/plastic shim stock of the proper thickness between the legs of the ignition coil and the flywheel, then turn the flywheel until the flywheel magnets are near the coil legs. Loosen the screws attaching the ignition coil and press legs against the shim stock. Tighten the two attaching screws securely. Remove the setting gauge, then turn the flywheel and check to be sure the flywheel does not hit the legs of the coil.

A special tester (part No. 506 18 65 01 or equivalent) is required to test the microprocessor (6) used on early models. The tester requires a 12-volt power supply. Attach the wires from the microprocessor to the tester and observe the indicator lights. The green light should be lit when 12-volts is supplied the

Illustrations courtesy Jonsered Power Products AB

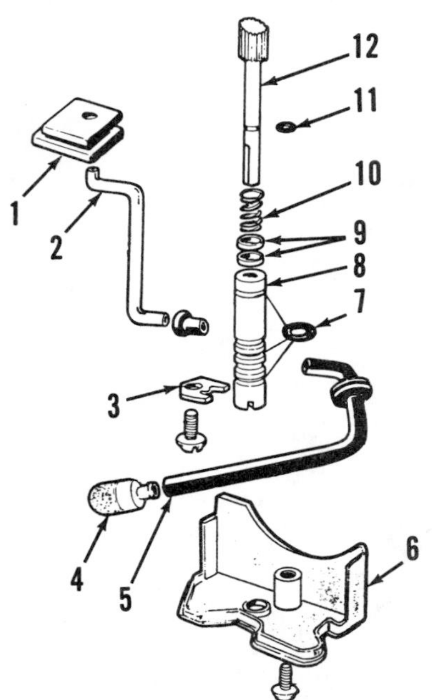

Fig. J83—Exploded view of the automatic chain oil pump. Oil pump output volume is adjusted by turning pump body (8).

1. Plate
2. Oil pressure tube
3. Retainer bracket
4. Oil strainer
5. Oil suction tube
6. Cover
7. "O" ring
8. Cylinder
9. Washers
10. Spring
11. "O" ring
12. Plunger

tester. The red lamp should light when the microprocessor is producing spark.

Set the tester speed check knob to zero, then turn the knob clockwise slowly to increase speed while observing the tester lights. The indicator lights should indicate the microprocessor is producing sparks when set between 2,400-2,700 rpm. Spark should NOT occur when rpm is above 14,800.

To remove the microprocessor (6) from early models, remove plug (5) from the rear handle and remove the screw located behind the plug. Remove the three Torx screws, then lift off the left half of the handle. Remove the screw from the rear anti-vibration mount and remove the microprocessor. Remove the magnet case (7) and magnets (8) from the throttle control.

To assemble, reverse the removal procedure. Two magnets (8) should be positioned in case (7) with the poles facing the same direction.

LUBRICATION. The engine is lubricated by mixing oil with the gasoline fuel. The manufacturer recommends mixing Jonsered two-stroke engine oil with regular grade gasoline at a ratio of 50:1. When using regular two-stroke engine oil, mix at a ratio of 25:1.

Always use a separate container to mix gasoline and oil before filling the fuel tank. The manufacturer recommends not using fuel containing alcohol.

All saws are equipped with an automatic bar and chain oiling system. Oil is delivered to the guide bar by the automatic chain oil pump whenever the engine is running.

The manufacturer recommends using good quality oil designed for lubricating saw chain. Automotive engine oil may also be used. Make sure the reservoir is filled at all times and the small oil passages do not become blocked. Select oil viscosity according to the ambient temperature.

The volume of oil delivered by the pump can be adjusted by turning the slot in the bottom of the pump body (8—Fig. J83) with a screwdriver. Turn the pump body clockwise to increase the amount of oil or counterclockwise to decrease oil.

REPAIRS

CRANKCASE PRESSURE TEST. An improperly sealed crankcase can cause the engine to be hard to start, run rough, have low power and overheat. Refer to ENGINE SERVICE section of this manual for crankcase pressure test procedure. If crankcase leakage is indicated, pressurize the crankcase and use a solution of soap and water to check gasket, seals, pulse line and castings for leakage.

TIGHTENING TORQUE. Recommended tightening torque values are as follows.

Carburetor	3-4 N·m (26.5-35 in.-lb.)
Clutch hub	30-35 N·m (265-310 in.-lb.)
Cylinder	10-12 N·m (88.5-106 in.-lb.)
Flywheel	25-30 N·m (221-265 in.-lb.)
Muffler	7-8 N·m (62-71 in.-lb.)
Spark plug	20-22 N·m (177-195 in.-lb.)
Starter	2-3 N·m (18-26.5 in.-lb.)

PISTON, PIN, RING AND CYLINDER. To disassemble, remove cylinder cover, air filter and starter housing. Disconnect the fuel line, vent line, impulse line, choke lever and throttle cable, then remove the carburetor. Unbolt and remove the muffler. Remove screw from the right front vibration damper. Remove four screws from bottom of crankcase (17—Fig. J84) that attach the cylinder (1) to the crankcase, then lift the cylinder straight up. Remove retaining rings (4) and push pin from the piston. Remove needle bearing (6) from the bore in connecting rod small end.

If necessary to remove the crankshaft, connecting rod and main bearings, refer to CRANKSHAFT, CONNECTING ROD AND CRANKCASE paragraphs.

Inspect the cylinder for any damage and install new parts as necessary. If the chrome plating is worn from the cylinder, a new cylinder should be installed. The piston, ring and cylinder

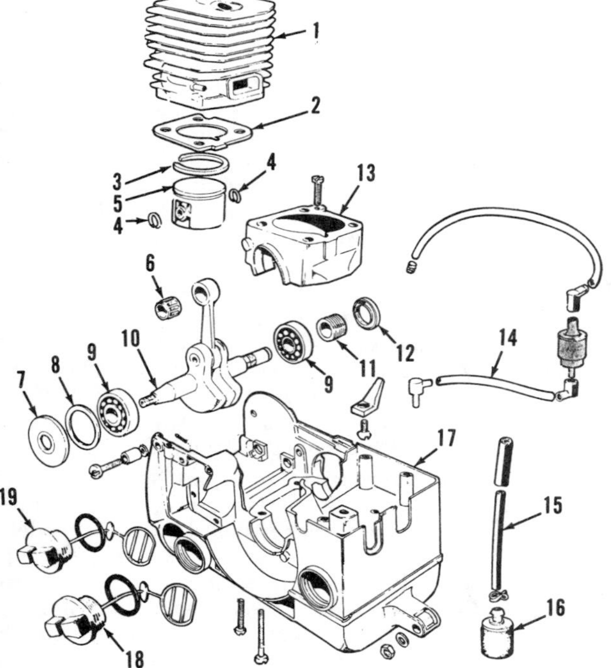

Fig. J84—Exploded view of the engine components.

1. Cylinder
2. Gasket
3. Piston ring
4. Retaining rings
5. Piston
6. Needle bearing
7. Seal
8. Locating washer
9. Ball bearings
10. Crankshaft & connecting rod
11. Worm gear
12. Seal
13. Upper crankcase half
14. Fuel tank vent hose
15. Fuel line
16. Fuel filter
17. Lower crankcase half
18. Fuel tank cap
19. Oil tank cap

are available in standard size only. The piston and cylinder are available for service only as a matched set and the cylinder should not be bored oversize.

Lubricate needle bearing (6) with engine oil before assembling. Position the piston over the connecting rod and needle bearing with the arrow on piston crown toward the exhaust side of engine. Install retaining rings (4) with the opening toward the top or bottom of the piston.

Install the piston ring into the piston groove so that ends of the ring correctly engage the locating pin in the groove. The locating pin prevents the ring from rotating and the ends of the piston ring must fit around this pin.

Lubricate the connecting rod lower bearing, cylinder bore, piston and ring. Make sure the ends of the piston ring surround the pin located in ring groove, then gently compress the ring while installing the cylinder straight down over the piston. If the cylinder is twisted, the ring can catch in a port and break the end of the ring.

Install the cylinder attaching screws from under the crankcase and tighten in a crossing pattern evenly to the torque listed in TIGHTENING TORQUE paragraph.

CRANKSHAFT, CONNECTING ROD AND CRANKCASE. The crankshaft and connecting rod are available only as an assembly (10—Fig. J84); individual components are not available. A shop experienced in servicing built-up crankshaft assemblies can align the shaft.

To remove the crankshaft and connecting rod assembly, remove the oil pump as described in the OIL PUMP paragraph. Remove the cylinder and piston as described in PISTON, PIN, RING AND CYLINDER paragraphs, then lift the crankcase upper half away from the lower half and crankshaft.

Screw in the crankcase upper half (13) operates against the oil pump. Install a new screw if damaged. Lift the crankshaft, connecting rod, main bearings, seals, retainers and oil pump drive worm (7 through 12) as an assembly from the crankcase lower half.

The crankshaft should turn smoothly inside main bearings with no perceptible play or ratcheting. Refer to the OIL PUMP paragraph for removal of the worm gear (11). Use suitable tools to remove and install new main bearings and seals. Remove main ball bearings from crankshaft using suitable puller and press new bearings onto the crankshaft until seated against the shaft shoulder. Refer to OIL PUMP paragraph when installing the worm gear

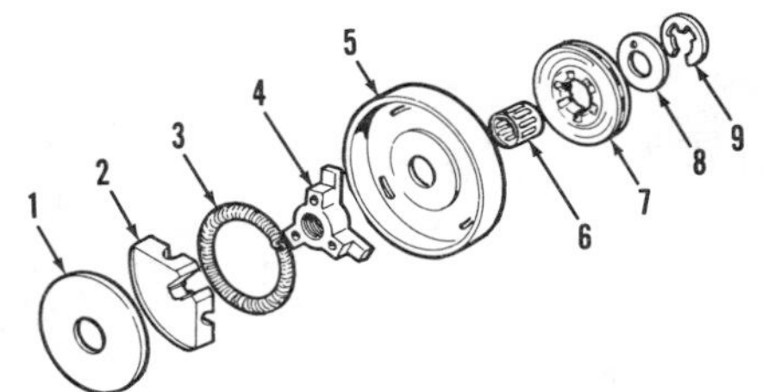

Fig. J85—Exploded view of the clutch assembly.

1. Washer
2. Clutch shoe
3. Spring
4. Clutch hub
5. Clutch drum
6. Needle bearing
7. Sprocket
8. Washer
9. "E" ring

(11). Lubricate lips of seals with engine oil before installing over the crankshaft.

Clean and inspect the mating surfaces of the crankcase halves (13 and 17) for nicks or burrs that might prevent an air tight seal. Slight imperfections may be removed by lapping the surfaces lightly.

Position the crankshaft, bearings and seals (7 through 12) in the lower crankcase half (17). Apply a thin bead of sealer (part No. 503 26 70 01 or equivalent) to the mating surface of lower half (17), over the main bearings and seals. Install the upper half (13), then refer to PISTON, PIN, RING AND CYLINDER paragraphs for installing these parts.

CLUTCH. Refer to Fig. J85. To remove the sprocket, remove the cover, guide bar and chain from the right side. Remove "E" ring (9) and washer (8), then slide the sprocket (7) from the clutch drum (5). The drum and needle bearing (6) can be removed if necessary.

The clutch hub (4) is attached to the right end of the engine crankshaft with left-hand threads (turn clockwise to remove). First remove the clutch drum as described above. Keep the crankshaft from turning by using an appropriate piston stopper and unscrew the clutch assembly from the crankshaft.

The clutch shoes (2), spring (3) and hub (4) are available as an assembly, but spring (3) is available separately. The thickness of the shoes to the groove for spring (3) should be more than 1 mm (0.04 in.). The inside diameter of the clutch drum should not exceed 79.8 mm (3.142 in.). Inspect all parts for wear or damage and replace as necessary.

If shoes are removed from the hub, assemble the spring and three shoes. Install two of the shoes on the hub, then use special tool (502 50 49-01 or equivalent) to carefully install the third shoe. When assembled, the coupling for spring (3) should be in the middle of one of the shoes.

Install the clutch assembly, tightening the hub to the torque listed in TIGHTENING TORQUE paragraph. Grease the needle bearing in the clutch drum lightly before installing the drum.

OIL PUMP. An automatic oiling system supplies lubricating oil to the guide bar and chain. Oil is delivered by the pump (Fig. J83) which is driven by worm gear (11—Fig. J84). The oil pump plunger (12—Fig. J83) rotates in cylinder (8) to pump the oil. The volume of oil can be adjusted by turning the cylinder as described in the LUBRICATION paragraph in the Maintenance section.

To remove the oil pump, first remove the cover and chain brake from the right side. Remove the chain and guide bar. Remove the screw attaching the small cover (6), then remove the cover. Clean the saw, especially the area around the oil pump to prevent the entrance of wood chips into the lubrication system. Remove the screw and clamp (3), then pull the pump from its bore. If necessary, the pump inlet hose and strainer (4 and 5) can be removed and cleaned.

Check the outlet tube and plate (1 and 2) for damage or obstruction. Clearances and passages of the lubrication system are small and even small impurities can prevent proper oiling. Always install new "O" rings when assembling.

REWIND STARTER. Refer to Fig. J86. The starter housing (1) can be unbolted and the assembly removed from the saw. Pull the starter rope out about 20 cm (8 in.) and hold the pulley (6) to keep the rope from rewinding. Pull a loop of rope from between the housing (1) and the pulley (6) into one of the notches molded into the edge of the pulley. Hold the loop and allow the pulley to turn slowly until the spring is completely unwound.

Remove the retaining screw (7) and washer, then lift the pulley (6) from the shaft. The spring case (5) and rewind spring (4) can be removed if necessary. Spring should remain in case, but be careful to control the spring as it is removed to prevent injury.

Clean and inspect parts for damage. Inspect the condition of the pawls and springs (8). On some models, parts of the pawl assemblies may be installed on two pivot screws attached to the flywheel.

Lubricate the recoil spring, then wind spring (4) into the case (5) cavity in a counterclockwise direction beginning with the outside coil. Install the

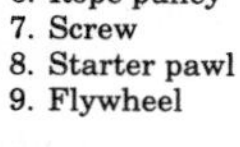

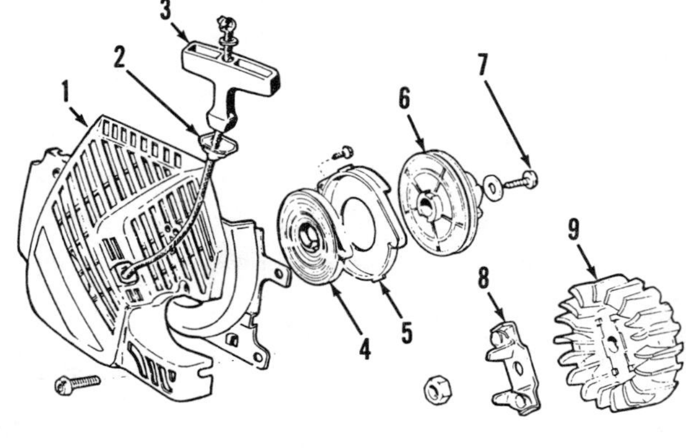

Fig. J86—Exploded view of the rewind starter assembly.

1. Starter housing
2. Rope guide
3. Handle
4. Rewind spring
5. Spring case
6. Rope pulley
7. Screw
8. Starter pawl
9. Flywheel

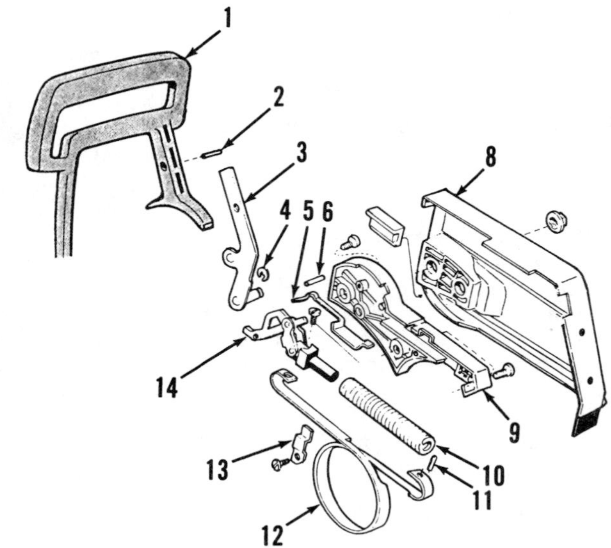

Fig. J87—Exploded view of the chain brake assembly.

1. Hand guard
2. Pin
3. Lever
4. "E" ring
5. Spring
6. Pin
8. Clutch cover
9. Brake housing
10. Tension spring
11. Pin
12. Brake band
13. Retaining bracket
14. Trigger assy.

spring and spring case and tighten the retaining screw securely.

If detached, attach the rope to the pulley and make sure the knot is securely nested in the pulley. Insert the end of the rope through the housing (1) and guide (2), then attach handle (3). Wind as much of the rope onto the pulley (6) as possible. Position the pulley over the post in housing with a loop in the rope between the housing and pulley, then preload the recoil spring by turning the pulley about 4 turns clockwise before releasing the rope loop. Install washer and screw (7).

Check for proper spring preload as follows. Pull the rope out fully and check to be sure the pulley can be turned an additional 1/2 turn without causing the spring to bind. Allow the rope to rewind and make sure the handle is pulled against the housing. If the spring binds, pull a loop in the rope between the housing and the pulley, release some spring preload (about 1 turn), then recheck. If the handle is not wound against the housing, increase the preload and recheck.

CHAIN BRAKE. The chain brake is designed to stop the saw chain quickly should kickback occur. The chain brake is activated when the operator's hand strikes the hand guard (1—Fig. J87). Forward movement of the guard disengages the trigger assembly (14) allowing the spring (10) to tighten the band (12) around the clutch drum. The brake is released and the mechanism is reset by pulling back on the guard.

To disassemble the brake, first remove screw securing hand guard to starter side of saw. Remove clutch cover (8—Fig. J87), bar and chain. Unbolt and remove brake housing (9). Remove spring retainer bracket (13), then carefully remove brake spring (10). Remove "E" ring (4) and withdraw brake band (12) and linkage.

Inspect all parts carefully and install new parts as necessary. Install a new brake band if any part of the band is worn to less than 0.8 mm (0.032 in.) thickness.

Lubricate all pivot points lightly when assembling. Do not allow any lubricant to get on gripping surfaces of the clutch drum or brake band. No adjustment of chain brake system is required.

HEATED HANDLES. The saw may be equipped with heated handles. A generating coil (10—Fig. J82) located behind the flywheel provides current that flows in series through a control switch (3), to the front handle heater element (1), to heated hand plates (4) in the rear handle, then to ground. The heating system may be tested using an ohmmeter. Normal resistance should be 5-6 ohms. Service is limited to replacement of parts necessary to complete the circuit.

JONSERED

Model	Bore mm (in.)	Stroke mm (in.)	Displacement cc (cu. in.)	Drive Type
2094, 2094 Turbo	56 (2.2)	38 (1.496)	93.6 (5.7)	Direct
2095 Turbo	56 (2.2)	38 (1.496)	93.6 (5.7)	Direct

Saws identified as Turbo models use the centrifugal force of the cooling air moved by the fan to separate some of the foreign matter from air delivered to the carburetor intake. Larger wood chips and other impurities in air circulated by the cooling fan are thrown to the outside by centrifugal force, while cleaner air nearer the fan is collected by a nozzle and directed toward the carburetor intake. Finer impurities are captured by the air filter.

MAINTENANCE

SPARK PLUG. Recommended spark plug is Champion RCJ7Y or NGK BPMR 7A. Electrode gap should be 0.5-0.7 mm (0.020-0.027 in.). The spark plug should be tightened to the torque listed in the TIGHTENING TORQUE paragraph.

CARBURETOR. Tillotson HS 238B carburetor is used on 2094 models; Tillotson HS 265A carburetor is used on 2995 models. Refer to the appropriate Tillotson section of the CARBURETOR SERVICE section for service and exploded views. Initial setting of the low-speed and high-speed mixture needles is 1-1/4 turn open from lightly seated for all models.

To adjust the mixture screws, first remove and clean the air filter, then reinstall it. Start the engine and allow it to run until it reaches normal operating temperature. If necessary, turn each of the mixture needles clockwise until seated lightly, then back the needles out (counterclockwise) to the initial setting so the engine can be started.

Turn the idle speed stop screw (T—Fig. J90) so the engine idles at about 2,400 rpm. Adjust the low-speed mixture needle (L) so the engine idles smoothly and accelerates without hesitation. Adjust the idle speed to just slower than clutch engagement speed, then recheck low-speed mixture adjustment.

Adjust the high-speed mixture needle (H) to provide the best performance while operating at maximum speed under load. Maximum no-load speed (with bar and chain installed) is 13,000 rpm. The high-speed mixture screw may be set slightly rich to improve performance under load. The engine may be damaged if the high-speed screw is set too lean.

Final adjustment of the mixture needles should be within 1/4 turn of the initial settings. Large differences may indicate air leaks, plugged passages or other problems.

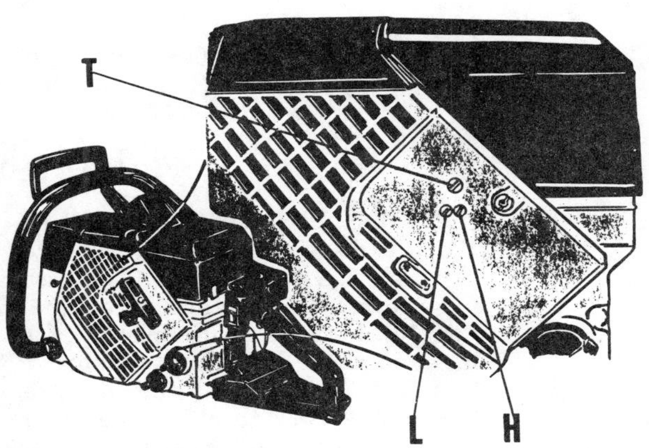

Fig. J90—View of saw showing location of carburetor adjustment screws. Idle speed screw is located at (T), low-speed mixture needle is located at (L) and high-speed mixture needle is located at (H).

To remove carburetor, first remove cylinder cover (1—Fig. J92), air cleaner cover (2) and air filter (3). Disconnect impulse tube (4), fuel line (24) and choke lever. Remove carburetor mounting screws. Tilt and lift carburetor so that throttle cable can be disconnected. Disconnect vent tube and remove carburetor. Tighten the carburetor attaching screws to the torque listed in the TIGHTENING TORQUE paragraph.

IGNITION. All models are equipped with a breakerless electronic ignition system. All electronic circuitry is contained in a one-piece ignition module/coil located outside the flywheel. Ignition timing is fixed and not adjustable. The flywheel attaching nut should be tightened to the torque listed in TIGHTENING TORQUE paragraph.

Air gap between the legs of the module/coil and the flywheel magnets should be 0.3 mm (0.012 in.). When installing, set the air gap between the flywheel magnets and the legs of the ignition module as follows.

Install the ignition module, but tighten the two screws only enough to hold it in place away from the flywheel. Insert setting gauge (part No. 502 51 34-05) or brass/plastic shim stock of the proper thickness between the legs of the ignition module and the flywheel, then turn the flywheel until the flywheel magnets are near the module legs. Loosen the screws attaching the ignition module and press legs of the ignition module against the setting gauge. Tighten the two attaching screws to the torque listed in the TIGHTENING TORQUE paragraph. Remove the setting gauge, then turn the flywheel and check to be sure the flywheel does not hit the legs of the coil.

LUBRICATION. The engine is lubricated by mixing oil with the gasoline fuel. The manufacturer recommends mixing Jonsered two-stroke engine oil with regular grade gasoline at a ratio of

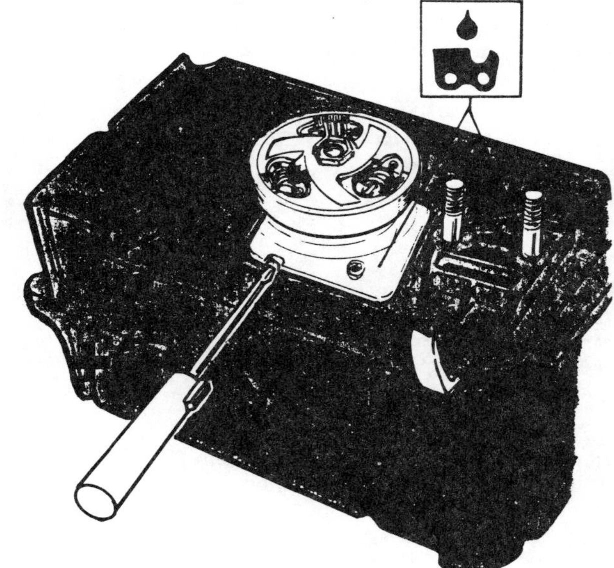

Fig. J91—Bar and chain oil pump adjusting screw is accessible at bottom of saw. It is not necessary to remove the bar and chain to adjust the oil pump.

50:1. When using regular two-stroke engine oil, mix at a ratio of 25:1.

Always use a separate container to mix gasoline and oil before filling the fuel tank. The manufacturer recommends not using fuel containing alcohol.

All saws are equipped with an automatic bar and chain oiling system. Oil is delivered to the guide bar by the automatic chain oil pump. The manufacturer recommends using good quality oil designed for lubricating saw chain. Automotive engine oil may also be used. Select oil viscosity according to the ambient temperature. Make sure the reservoir is filled at all times and the small oil passages do not become blocked.

NOTE: DO NOT adjust the oil pump with the engine running.

The volume of oil delivered by the pump can be adjusted by turning the adjusting screw (Fig. J91) with a screwdriver. The screw is located in the bottom of the pump body. Turn the screw clockwise to increase the amount of oil or counterclockwise to decrease oil. It is not necessary to remove the bar and chain to adjust the oil pump.

REPAIRS

CRANKCASE PRESSURE TEST. An improperly sealed crankcase can cause the engine to be hard to start, run rough, have low power and overheat. Refer to ENGINE SERVICE section of this manual for crankcase pressure test procedure. If crankcase leakage is indicated, pressurize the crankcase and use a solution of soap and water to check gasket, seals, pulse line and castings for leakage.

TIGHTENING TORQUE. Recommended tightening torque values are as follows.

Carburetor	5-6 N•m (44-53 in.-lb.)
Clutch hub	30-40 N•m (265-354 in.-lb.)
Cylinder	10-12 N•m (88.5-106 in.-lb.)
Crankcase	7-9 N•m (62-80 in.-lb.)
Decompression valve	12-14 N•m (106-124 in.-lb.)
Flywheel	30-40 N•m (265-354 in.-lb.)
Muffler	10-12 N•m (88.5-106 in.-lb.)
Spark plug	20-22 N•m (177-195 in.-lb.)
Starter	2.5-4 N•m (22-35 in.-lb.)

PISTON, PIN, RING AND CYLINDER. To disassemble, remove air filter cover (2—Fig. J92), air filter (3) and cylinder cover (1). Unbolt and remove muffler (15). Detach impulse hose (4), fuel line and choke lever from carburetor. Remove carburetor (5) and air filter holder (6). Detach throttle cable as carburetor is removed. Remove cylinder

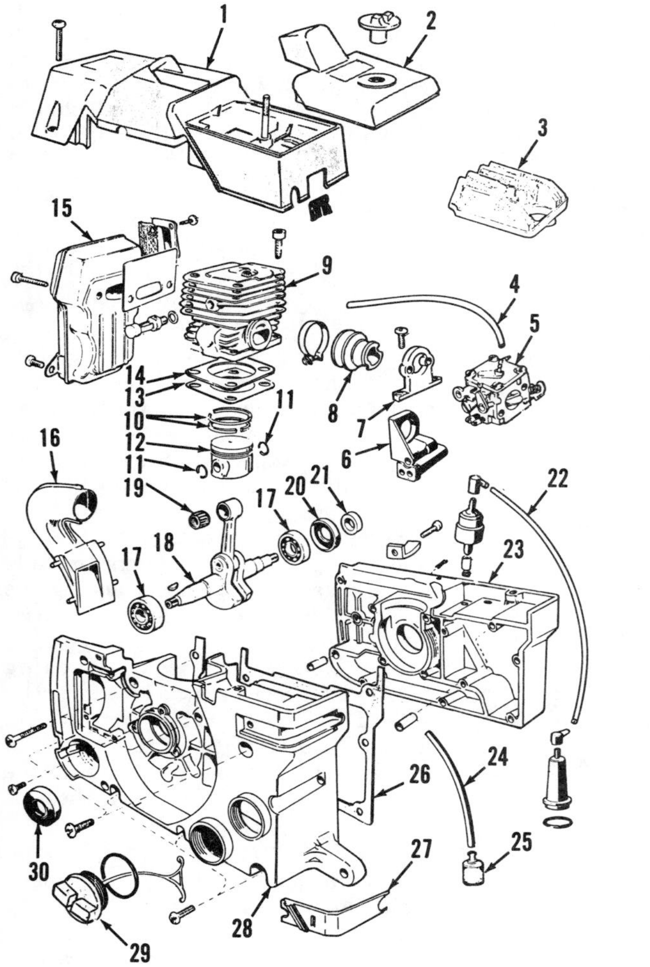

Fig. J92—Exploded view of the engine assembly typical of all models.

1. Cylinder cover
2. Air filter cover
3. Air filter
4. Impulse tube
5. Carburetor
6. Air filter holder
7. Bracket
8. Intake tube
9. Cylinder
10. Piston ring(s)
11. Retaining rings
12. Piston
13. Base gasket
14. Insulator plate
15. Muffler
16. Air intake nozzle
17. Ball bearings
18. Crankshaft & connecting rod assy.
19. Needle bearing
20. Seal
21. Worm gear
22. Vent tube
23. Crankcase half
24. Fuel line
25. Fuel filter
26. Gasket
27. Cover
28. Crankcase half
29. Fuel tank cap
30. Seal

attaching screws, then lift cylinder (9) away from the crankcase. To remove piston (12), remove piston pin retaining rings (11) and push pin from piston.

Inspect the cylinder bore and piston for scuffing, scoring or excessive wear. Cylinder, piston, ring, piston pin and needle bearing are available as a matched set.

Lubricate the connecting rod bore, bearing (19), piston pin, piston, ring and cylinder with clean engine oil before assembling. Attach piston to connecting rod so that the arrow on piston crown points toward the exhaust side of engine.

Install new cylinder base gasket (13) and insulator (14), if used, with round edges up toward the cylinder. Tighten the cylinder attaching screws in a crossing pattern to the torque listed in TIGHTENING TORQUE paragraph. Complete assembly by reversing disassembly procedure.

CONNECTING ROD, CRANKSHAFT AND CRANKCASE. The connecting rod is equipped with a needle bearing at the small end for the piston pin. A roller bearing located in the lower end of the connecting rod operates on the crankshaft crankpin. The ends of the crankshaft are supported in ball bearings. The crankshaft is made up of parts that are pressed together trapping the connecting rod and its lower bearing. The crankshaft/connecting rod is available only as a complete assembly.

To remove the crankshaft (18—Fig. J92), remove the guide bar, chain, chain brake assembly, clutch assembly and the oil pump. Remove the starter housing, flywheel, generator, carburetor and ignition coil/module. Remove the rear handle and fuel pump assembly.

Remove the muffler, cylinder and piston. Use a suitable puller (part No. 502 71 35 01) to pull the oil pump drive worm (3—Fig. J94) from the crankshaft. Remove the screws attaching the crankcase halves together, then carefully separate the halves (23 and 28—Fig. J92) using a tool (part No. 502 51 61-01) to push the end of the crankshaft from the case bore.

Check the crankshaft main ball bearings (17) for roughness or other damage, then install new bearings if required. Do not remove main bearings (17) unless renewal is required.

Check the rotation of the connecting rod around the crankpin and install a new connecting rod and crankshaft assembly if rough, loose or any other damage is noticed. Carefully clean and inspect the crankcase and cylinder sealing surfaces for any nicks, burrs, cracks or other damage that would prevent an air tight seal.

Observe the following procedure when assembling. If main bearings are not installed in the bores of the crankcase halves, heat the case halves to assist during the assembly. If the main bearings did not remain installed on the crankshaft assembly, press the main bearings into the heated bores of the crankcase halves. If the main bearings are to be reinstalled and were not removed from the crankshaft, be sure the crankcase halves are heated sufficiently to permit assembly without distorting the crankcase. Use the correct special puller to pull the crankshaft into the clutch side crankcase half.

Make sure the connecting rod is properly positioned and does not bind while assembling. Make sure the gasket (26) is properly positioned and all holes are aligned, then install the flywheel side crankcase half using the same special puller and procedure. Install and tighten the screws attaching the crankcase halves together, while checking the crankshaft for binding.

If the crankshaft binds while assembling the case halves, determine the cause and correct before continuing with the assembly. Tighten the crankcase screws to the torque listed in TIGHTENING TORQUE paragraph. Use seal protectors and lubricate the seal lips when installing crankshaft seals. Complete assembly by reversing disassembly procedure.

CLUTCH. To remove the clutch, first remove the clutch cover, chain brake assembly, chain and guide bar. Remove the sprocket (1—Fig. J93), clutch drum (2) and needle bearing (3). Prevent the flywheel from turning by removing the spark plug and installing a piston stop tool (or a loop of rope) in the spark plug hole. Turn the clutch hub (left-hand threads) in a clockwise direction as indicated by the arrow to unscrew the hub from the engine crankshaft. Use a suitable tool (part No. 502 54 04-01 for 2077 models) to turn the hub.

Inspect all parts of the clutch for wear, evidence of overheating or other damage and replace parts as necessary. New clutch shoes should be installed if worn to less than 1 mm (0.040 in.) thickness. The clutch hub (4), shoes (6) and return springs (5) are available only as an assembly. Install a new drum if worn or otherwise damaged.

When assembling, tighten the clutch hub to the torque listed in TIGHTENING TORQUE paragraph. Lubricate the needle bearing with grease before installing the bearing and clutch drum. Complete assembly by reversing disassembly procedure.

OIL PUMP. The guide bar and chain are lubricated by oil supplied by the oil pump shown in Fig. J94. The pump plunger (11) is driven by the worm gear (3). The worm gear (3) is located under the pump housing and is pressed onto the crankshaft. Use a suitable puller (part No. 502 54 09-01) to pull the oil pump drive worm (3) from the crankshaft.

To disassemble the removed pump, remove the adjusting screw (6), then bump the housing on a soft surface if necessary to jar the locking pin (8) and

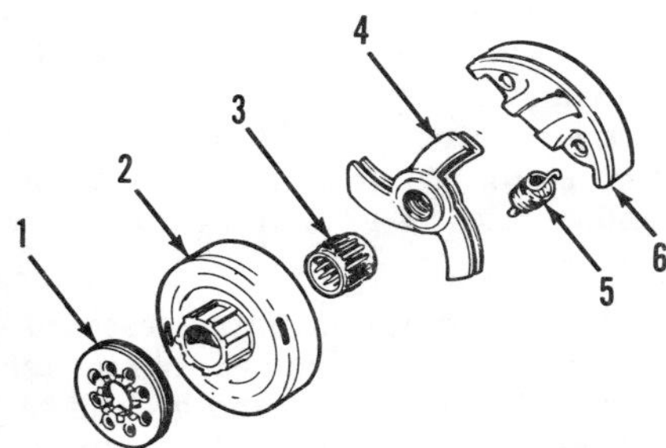

Fig. J93—Exploded view of late style clutch assembly. Early style clutch is similar except a single spring is used to retain the clutch shoes.

1. Sprocket
2. Clutch drum
3. Needle bearing
4. Clutch hub
5. Spring (3 used)
6. Clutch shoe (3 used)

Fig. J94—Exploded view of the oil pump and related parts.

1. Oil pump housing
2. Seal
3. Worm gear
4. Oil suction tube
5. Oil strainer
6. Adjusting screw
7. Spring
8. Locking pin
9. Spring
10. Washers
11. Plunger
12. Sleeve

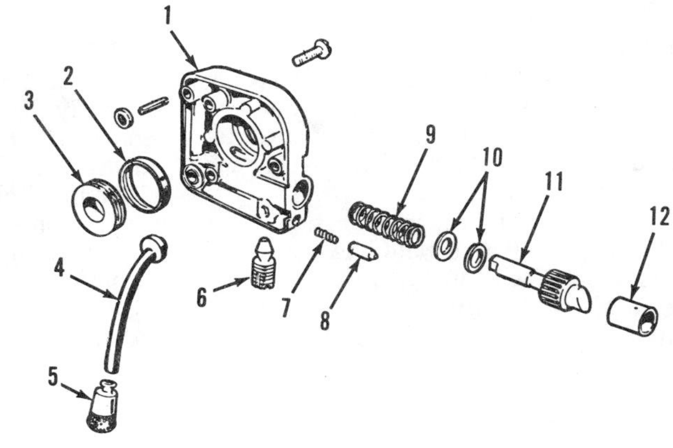

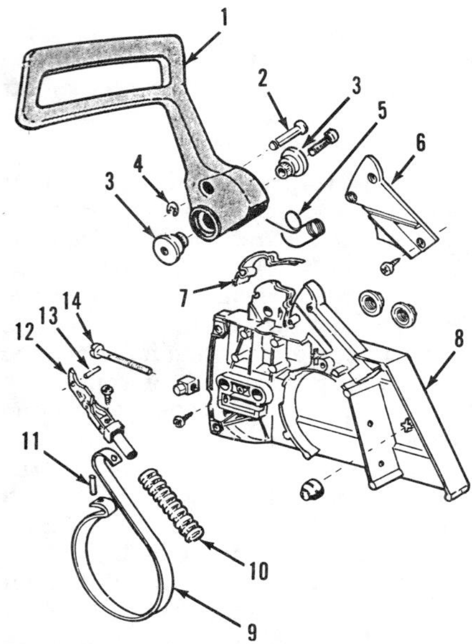

Fig. J95—Exploded view of typical chain brake assembly.

1. Brake lever
2. Pin
3. Swivel nuts
4. "E" ring
5. Spring
6. Cover
7. Spring
8. Housing
9. Brake band
10. Spring
11. Pin
12. Brake lever
13. Pin
14. Chain adjusting screw

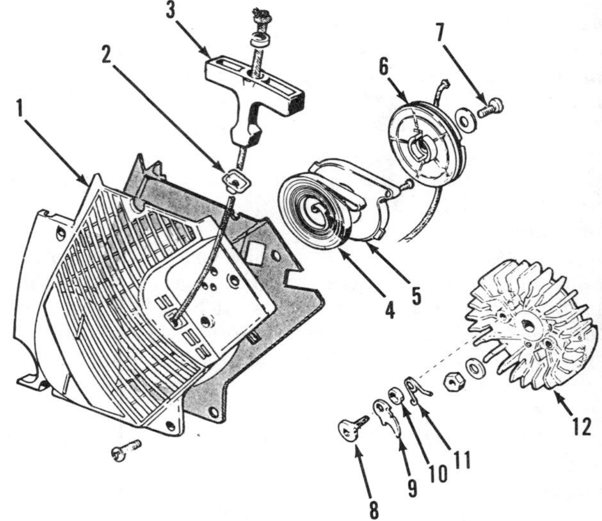

Fig. J96—Exploded view of rewind starter assembly.

1. Starter housing
2. Rope guide
3. Rope handle
4. Rewind spring
5. Spring case
6. Rope pulley
7. Screw
8. Screw
9. Starter pawl
10. Spacer
11. Spring
12. Flywheel

spring (7) from the housing bore. Remove the plastic plug/sleeve (12) from the plunger bore if necessary to remove the plunger (11), washers (10) and spring (9).

Clean and inspect parts for wear or damage. Parts should move freely in housing bores without excessive clearance. Install a new pump assembly if parts are worn. Some individual parts may be available separately if only that part is damaged.

Assemble the pump and install on the crankcase. Complete assembly by reversing disassembly procedure.

CHAIN BRAKE. The chain brake is designed to stop the chain if kickback should occur. The chain brake is activated when the operator's hand strikes the hand guard (1—Fig. J95) or if the tip of the guide bar strikes an object with sufficient force to trip the brake mechanism.

When the brake is engaged, a spring (10) tightens the band (9) around the clutch drum to stop the drum, sprocket and chain. Pull the hand guard (1) back to reset the mechanism.

To check for proper operation, shut the engine off and hold the tip of the guide bar about 30 cm (12 in.) above a tree trunk or other firm wood object. Release the front handle and allow the saw to rotate around the rear handle until the tip of the guide bar strikes the tree trunk. The brake should activate. Reset the brake and start the engine. Run the engine at full (wide open) throttle, then move the brake lever (1) to activate the brake. The saw chain should stop immediately. If the chain brake fails to perform correctly, disassemble and inspect parts for wear or damage. The chain brake is not adjustable.

To disassemble, remove the brake housing (8). Remove swivel nuts (3) and hand guard (1). Unbolt and remove brake spring cover (6). Carefully remove the brake spring (10) from the housing. Remove the split pin (13) and brake band retaining screw, then remove brake mechanism from the housing.

A new brake band should be installed if the thickness of the old band is less than 0.75 mm (0.030 in.). To assemble, reverse the disassembly procedure. When installing brake lever (1), be sure the forward nose of the steel link (12) is positioned behind the pin (2) and spring (5) inside the brake lever. Lubricate brake linkage contact surfaces with light oil.

REWIND STARTER. Refer to Fig. J96 for an exploded view of the starter assembly. To disassemble starter, first remove starter housing (1) from saw. Pull starter rope out about 30 cm (12 in.). While holding rope pulley (6), pull loop of rope back through outlet and place rope in notch in pulley. Then, allow pulley to slowly unwind.

Unscrew pulley retaining screw (7) and carefully withdraw rope pulley. If required, rewind spring (4) may now be removed. Use caution not to allow spring to unwind uncontrolled.

Reassemble starter components by reversing disassembly procedure while noting the following: Lubricate pulley pivot pin with small amount of grease. Lubricate rewind spring with a few drops of light oil.

Wind rope fully on pulley in clockwise direction as viewed with pulley in housing. Install rope pulley in housing, then pull rope handle out about 30 cm (12 in.) and pull loop of rope back through outlet as in removal procedure. Turn rope pulley two additional turns clockwise to place tension on rewind spring. Release pulley and check starter operation.

With rope fully extended, it should be possible to rotate rope pulley a minimum of 1/2 turn clockwise before rewind spring bottoms. Do not place more tension on rewind spring than is necessary to draw rope handle against housing.

HANDLE HEATER. Saws may be equipped with electrically heated handles. A generator coil (6—Fig. J97) located under the flywheel produces an electric current which flows in series to a switch (3), the front handle (1), rear handle plates (4) and then grounded to saw body.

The heating system may be tested using an ohmmeter. Connect ohmmeter between heater switch and ground cable. Resistance should be approximately 5-6 ohms.

Illustrations courtesy Jonsered Power Products AB

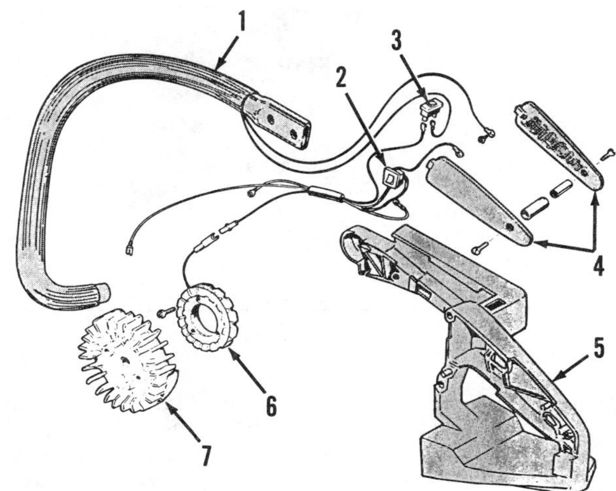

Fig. J97—Exploded view of electric handle heating system.

1. Front handle
2. Stop switch
3. Heater switch
4. Rear handle heating plate
5. Rear handle
6. Generator
7. Flywheel

JONSERED

Model	Bore mm (in.)	Stroke mm (in.)	Displacement cc (cu. in.)	Drive Type
Pro 35	38 (1.5)	30 (1.18)	34 (2.1)	Direct

MAINTENANCE

SPARK PLUG. Recommended spark plug is Bosch WS7F or Champion CJ7Y. Electrode gap should be 0.5 mm (0.020 in.). The spark plug should be tightened to the torque listed in the TIGHTENING TORQUE paragraph.

CARBURETOR. Walbro WT66 carburetor is used. Refer to the appropriate Walbro section of the CARBURETOR SERVICE section for service and exploded views. Initial setting of the low- and high-speed mixture needles is 1-1/4 turns open from lightly seated.

To adjust the mixture screws, first remove and clean the air filter, then reinstall it. Start the engine and allow it to run until it reaches normal operating temperature. If necessary, turn each of the mixture needles (H and L—Fig. J101) clockwise until seated lightly, then back the needles out (counterclockwise) to the initial setting so the engine can be started.

Turn the idle speed stop screw (T) so the engine idles at just below the clutch engagement rpm. Adjust the low-speed mixture needle (L) so the engine idles smoothly and accelerates without hesitation. Adjust the idle speed to just slower than clutch engagement speed, then recheck low-speed mixture adjustment.

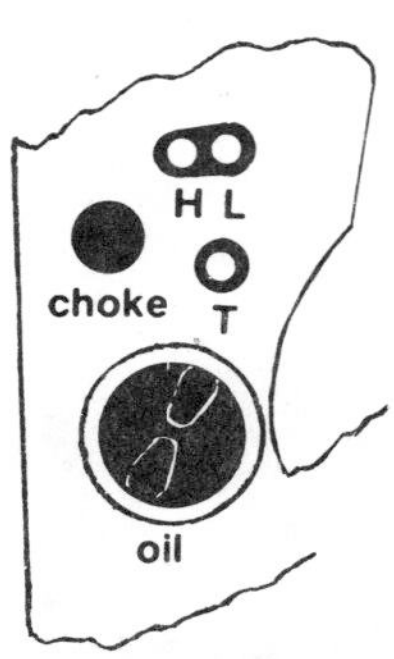

Fig. J101—Drawing showing the location of carburetor idle speed stop screw (T), low-speed mixture needle (L) and high-speed mixture needle (H).

Adjust the high-speed mixture needle (H) to provide the best performance while operating at maximum speed under load. Maximum no-load speed (with bar and chain installed) is 11,500 rpm. The high-speed mixture needle may be set slightly rich to improve performance under load. The engine may be damaged if the high-speed mixture is set too lean.

Final adjustment of the mixture needles should be within 1/4 turn of the initial settings. Large differences may indicate air leaks, plugged passages or other problems.

To remove carburetor, first remove filter cover, air filter, adjustment guide and fuel hose. Remove carburetor mounting screws. Disconnect throttle lever and lift out carburetor and reed plate. Tighten the carburetor attaching screws to the torque listed in the TIGHTENING TORQUE paragraph.

IGNITION. All models are equipped with a breakerless electronic ignition system. All electronic circuitry is contained in a one-piece ignition module/coil located outside the flywheel. Ignition timing is fixed and not adjustable, but should occur at 28 degrees BTDC. The flywheel attaching nut should be tightened to the torque listed in TIGHTENING TORQUE paragraph.

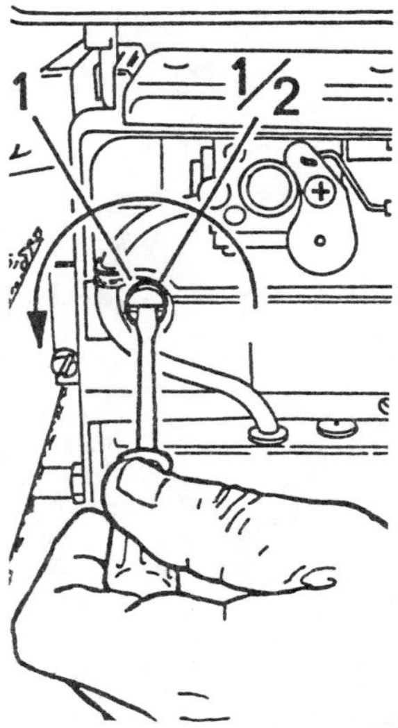

Fig. J102—The chain oil pump is adjusted as shown after removing the air filter cover.

Air gap between the legs of the module/coil and the flywheel magnets should be 0.3 mm (0.012 in.). When installing, set the air gap between the flywheel magnets and the legs of the ignition module as follows.

Install the ignition module, but tighten the two screws only enough to hold it in place away from the flywheel. Insert setting gauge or brass/plastic shim stock of the proper thickness between the legs of the ignition module and the flywheel, then turn the flywheel until the flywheel magnets are near the module legs. Loosen the screws attaching the ignition module and press legs of the ignition module against the setting gauge. Tighten the two attaching screws to the torque listed in the TIGHTENING TORQUE paragraph. Remove the setting gauge, then turn the flywheel and check that the flywheel does not hit the legs of the coil.

LUBRICATION. The engine is lubricated by oil mixed with the gasoline fuel. Use only high quality oil certified for two-stroke air-cooled engines. Mix oil with regular grade gasoline at a ratio of 40:1 after break-in. Always use a separate container to mix gasoline and oil before filling the fuel tank.

The saw is equipped with an automatic bar and chain oiling system. Lubricating oil is supplied by the automatic chain oil pump. Keep the reservoir filled with a good quality oil designed for lubricating saw chain. Automotive engine oil may also be used. Select oil viscosity according to the ambient temperature.

The volume of oil delivered by the pump is adjustable by turning the pump body (Fig. J102). Remove the air filter cover (36—Fig. J103) for access to oil pump body. Initial setting is accomplished by turning the body in until lightly seated, then backing out (turn-

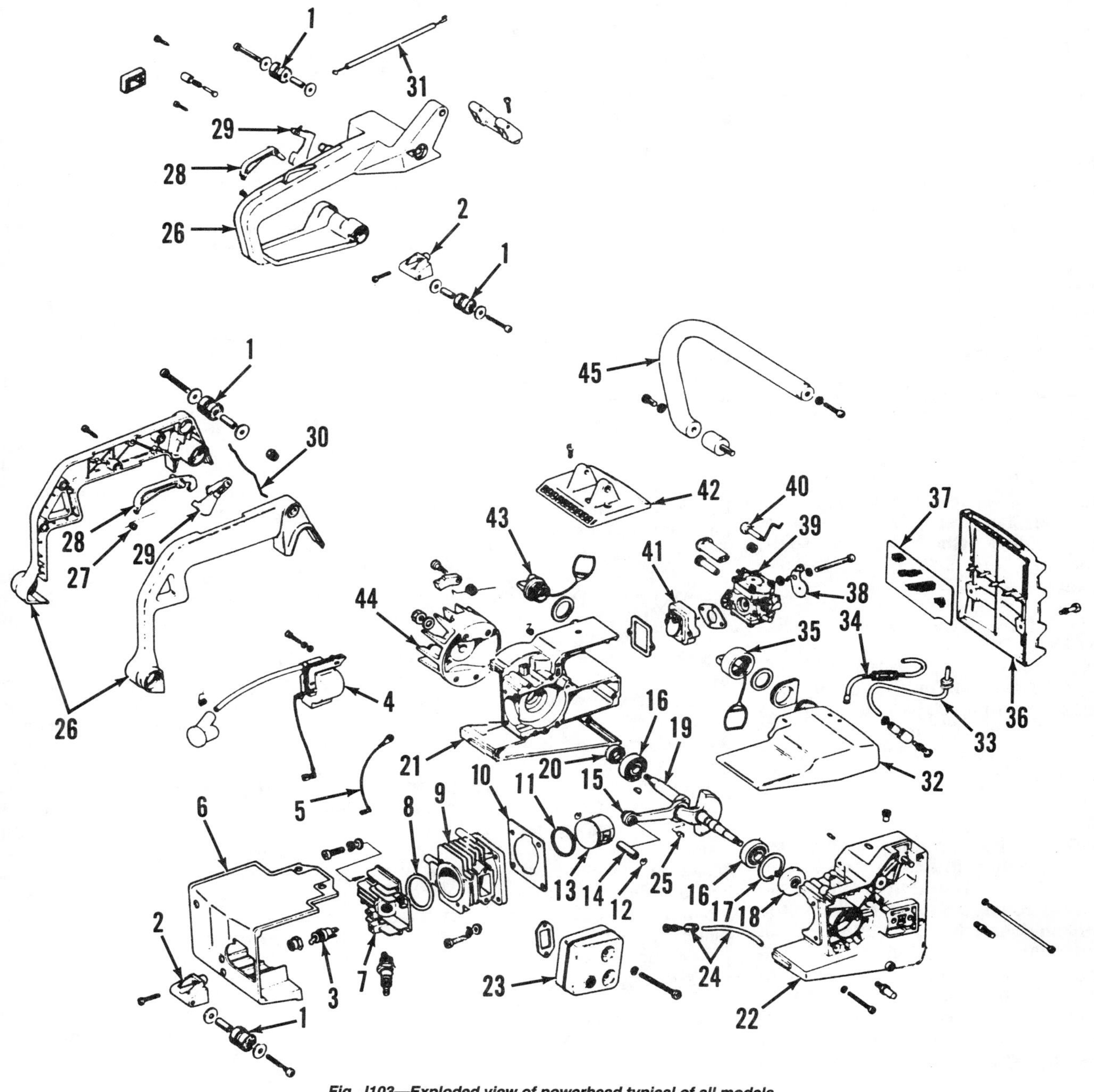

Fig. J103—Exploded view of powerhead typical of all models.

1. Rubber mount
2. Rear handle mounting bracket
3. Engine stop switch
4. Ignition coil/module
5. Stop switch wire
6. Cylinder cover
7. Cylinder head
8. Head gasket
9. Cylinder
10. Cylinder base gasket
11. Piston ring
12. Retaining rings
13. Piston
14. Piston pin
15. Needle bearing & connecting rod
16. Main bearings
17. Snap ring
18. Seal
19. Crankshaft
20. Seal
21. Crankcase left half
22. Crankcase right half
23. Muffler
24. Oil pickup tube & screen
25. Bearing rollers
26. Rear handle
27. Spring
28. Interlock
29. Throttle lever
30. Throttle link
31. Throttle cable
32. Fuel tank
33. Fuel line and pickup
34. Vent tube
35. Furl tank cap
36. Air filter cover
37. Air filter
38. Choke plate
39. Carburetor
40. Choke knob
41. Reed valve assy.
42. Handle top mounting plate
43. Oil tank cap
44. Flywheel
45. Tubular handle

ing counterclockwise) between 1/2 turn to 1 turn.

REPAIRS

TIGHTENING TORQUE. Recommended tightening torque values are as follows.

Bar clamp studs & nuts . . . . . . 10 N•m (88.5 in.-lb.)

Blade brake

Brake anchor . . . . . . 4 N•m (35 in.-lb.)

Hand guard attachment . . . . . 1.5 N•m (13.3 in.-lb.)

Hand guard pivot . . . . 5 N•mm (44 in.-lb.)

Carburetor attaching screws . . . 5 N•m (44 in.-lb.)

Clutch

Drum nut . . . . 6 N•m (53 in.-lb.)

Hub . . . . 19.5 N•m (172.5 in.-lb.)

Crankcase . . . . 3 N•m (26.5 in.-lb.)

Cylinder

Base. . . . . 6 N•m (53 in.-lb.)

Head . . . . 6 N•m (53 in.-lb.)

Flywheel . . . . . 19.5 N•m (172.5 in.-lb.)
Front cover. . . . . . . 2 N•m (17.7 in.-lb.)
Ignition module/coil . . . . 2 N•m (17.7 in.-lb.)
Muffler . . . . 4 N•m (35 in.-lb.)
Spark plug . . . . . 27.5 N•m (243 in.-lb.)
Starter
Housing. . . . . 1.5 N•m (13.3 in.-lb.)
Pulley retainer. . . . 2 N•m (17.7 in.-lb.)
Tubular handle
Top . . . . 2 N•m (17.7 in.-lb.)
Bottom . . . . 4 N•m (35 in.-lb.)
Vibration isolator . 3 N•m (26.5 in.-lb.)
Vibration isolator (rear handle). . . . . . 4 N•m (35 in.-lb.)

CRANKCASE PRESSURE TEST. An improperly sealed crankcase can cause the engine to be hard to start, run rough, have low power and overheat. Refer to the ENGINE SERVICE section of this manual for crankcase pressure test procedure. If crankcase leakage is indicated, pressurize the crankcase and use a solution of soap and water to locate the leak. Check gaskets, seals, pulse line and castings for possible leakage.

PISTON, PIN, RINGS AND CYLINDER. To disassemble, remove the starter housing, ignition coil/module (4—Fig. J103), muffler cover, muffler (23), rear handle assembly (26) and cylinder cover (6). Remove screws from the cylinder base and lift the cylinder (9) and head (7) from the crankcase and piston (13).

NOTE: When cylinder is removed, the connecting rod can move toward the flywheel end enough to release the bearing rollers located between the crankshaft and the connecting rod. Be extremely careful during and after cylinder removal to prevent movement of the connecting rod from releasing the rollers. Special plastic clip (part No. 10.00091) or other suitable retainer clip can be located on the crankshaft to help locate the connecting rod. Refer to Fig. J104. Remove this locating tool after the cylinder is located over the piston, just before moving the cylinder against the crankcase and installing the cylinder base screws.

Remove piston ring (11—Fig. J103) and piston pin retainer rings (12). Use a suitable pin removal tool to press the pin (14) from the piston.

The cylinder bore is chrome plated and should be renewed if cracked, worn or if plating is worn through. Inspect the piston skirt for scuffing, scratches or excessive wear. Install new piston and cylinder as necessary. It is recommended that new piston ring (11) and pin retainer rings (12) be installed each time they are removed from the piston.

Check the fit of the piston pin (14) in the piston and install new pin and piston as necessary. Inspect the needle bearing (15) in the small end of the connecting rod for excessive wear or discoloration due to overheating.

Attach the piston to the connecting rod with the arrow on the top of piston pointing toward the exhaust port (muffler). It is recommended that a dummy pin be used to align the piston with the needle bearing (15) during assembly. Be sure the pin retaining rings (12) fully engage the grooves in the piston and opening of ring is toward the crankshaft.

Position the base gasket (10) and install the piston ring in the piston groove. A locating pin in the piston groove prevents the ring from rotating. Make certain that ring end gap is properly positioned around the locating pin when installing the cylinder. Lubricate piston ring and cylinder bore with engine oil before assembling over the piston and ring.

CRANKSHAFT, CONNECTING ROD AND CRANKCASE. The crankcase halves must be separated to remove the crankshaft, but the shaft seals can be removed without splitting using special tools (part No. 10.00040 and 10.00089 or equivalent).

To separate the case halves, remove the starter assembly and ignition coil/module from the left side. Remove spark plug and install piston stop tool or a loop of rope in spark plug hole. Remove flywheel nut. Tap on flywheel counterweights (not on magnets) with a soft hammer to release flywheel from crankshaft.

Remove the air filter (36 and 37—Fig. J103), carburetor (39) and reed valve assembly (41). Remove the saw chain (5—Fig. J105), guide bar (4), clutch (7 through 16), chain brake (17 through 24), oil pump (25 through 28) and muffler from the right side. Remove the handles (26 and 45—Fig. J103), cylinder cover (6) and handle mounting plate (42). Remove the cylinder (9) and head (7).

NOTE: When cylinder is removed, the connecting rod can move toward the flywheel end enough to release the bearing rollers (25) located between the crankshaft and the connecting rod. Be extremely careful not to lose the bearing rollers or to damage the connecting rod or crankshaft while removing the cylinder or while the cylinder is removed. Special plastic clip (part No. 10.00091) can be located on the crankshaft to help locate the connecting rod. Refer to Fig. J104. Remove this special tool during assembly after the cylinder is located over the piston, just before moving the cylinder against the crankcase and installing the cylinder base screws.

Remove the screws attaching the case halves together and bump the crankcase with a soft faced hammer as necessary to separate the halves. Use caution not to damage the mating surfaces of the cases or the crankshaft.

Main bearings should not be removed unless new bearings are to be installed. If bearing remains in case bore, the crankcase can be heated to help remove main bearing. If the main bearing remains on the crankshaft, use appropriate puller to remove main bearing.

Make sure all of the connecting rod bearing rollers are installed. Grease can be used to hold rollers in place while assembling. A special tool (part No. 10.00091) can be attached to the smaller side of the crankshaft (Fig. J104) while assembling to prevent the connecting rod from moving enough to release the bearings.

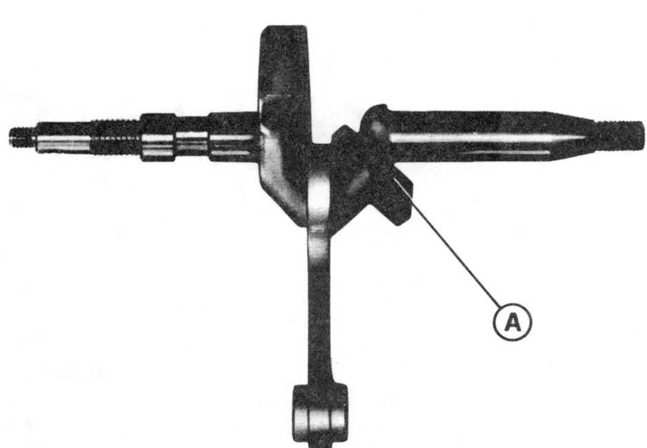

Fig. J104—View of plastic clip (part No. 10.00091) attached to the crankshaft to prevent the connecting rod from moving and releasing bearing rollers.

Illustrations courtesy Jonsered Power Products AB

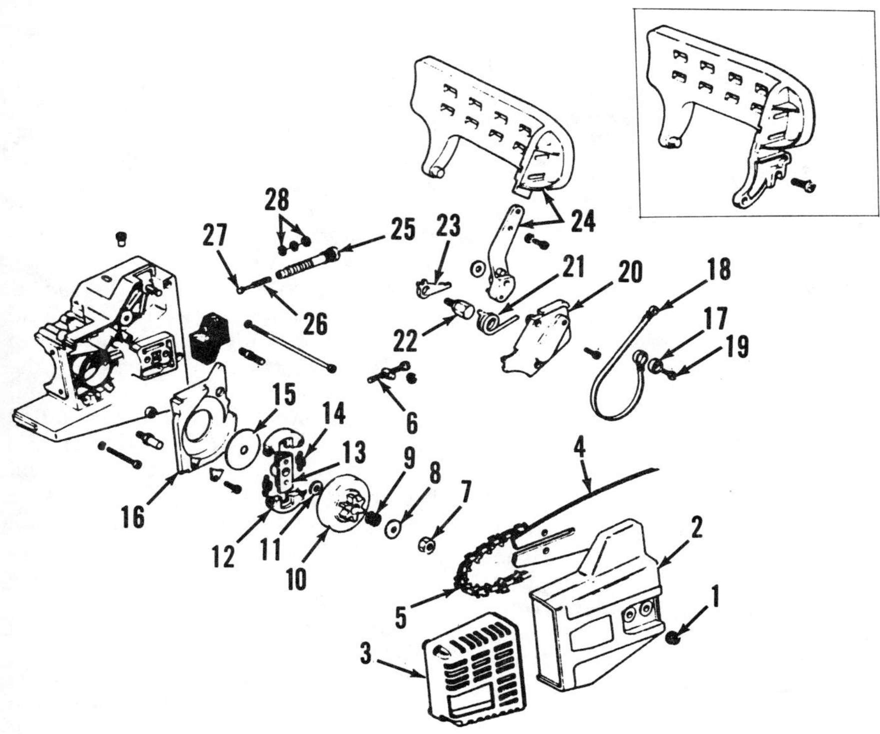

Fig. J105—Exploded view of the chain brake, clutch and oil pump assemblies. The hand guard may be slightly different than either type shown.

1. Clamping nut
2. Clutch cover
3. Muffler cover
4. Guide bar
5. Saw chain
6. Chain adjusting screw & nut
7. Nut
8. Washer
9. Needle bearing
10. Clutch drum
11. Washer
12. Clutch shoe
13. Clutch hub
14. Clutch spring
15. Washer
16. Plate
17. Bushing
18. Brake band
19. Anchor screw
20. Cover
21. Spring
22. Pivot
23. Release arm
24. Hand guard
25. Oil pump body
26. Spring
27. Plunger
28. Sealing rings

If assembling with new main bearings, press the main bearings onto the crankshaft until seated against shoulder. Position the clutch (right) crankcase half (22—Fig. J103) on work bench. Heat the case around the main bearing bore and insert the crankshaft until the main bearing is seated in the case bore. With the crankshaft vertical, the small side of the crankshaft should be up. Coat the mating surfaces of the crankcase halves with sealer before joining the halves.

Heat the flywheel (left) crankcase half (21) around the main bearing bore and assemble over the crankshaft, main bearing and other case half. The case halves should fit together before installing the attaching screws and the operation should be completed before the sealer hardens. Tighten the case screws in a crossing pattern to the torque listed in the TIGHTENING TORQUE paragraph.

Carefully turn the crankshaft to make sure the shaft is not binding after the case screws are tightened, but be careful not to release the connecting rod bearing rollers. Be sure that crankshaft is free before continuing. Lubricate ends of crankshaft before pressing new seals (18 and 20) in position.

Install the piston, cylinder and cylinder head, then pressure test the engine. Correct any problems before continuing assembly. Complete assembly by reversing disassembly procedure.

CLUTCH. The two shoe centrifugal clutch is shown in Fig. J105. The clutch retaining nut (7) has left-hand threads and must be turned clockwise to remove. The chain brake must be released to remove the clutch drum (10).

Withdraw the clutch drum from the crankshaft and inspect the condition of the needle bearing (9) and drum and sprocket (10). The clutch shoes (12), springs (14) and hub (13) can be inspected at this time. A special pin wrench that engages the two holes in the clutch hub must be used to remove the clutch hub. Use an appropriate piston stop to prevent the crankshaft from turning and turn the clutch hub clockwise to remove the hub.

Inspect all parts carefully and install new parts as required. It is important to install shoes and springs in sets of two. The sprocket attached to the clutch drum should usually be replaced after installing 2 new chains, but excessive wear may indicate earlier replacement is necessary.

Grease the needle bearing (9) lightly before assembling. Refer to TIGHTENING TORQUE paragraph when assembling.

OIL PUMP. The adjustable, automatic chain oil pump is located under the air cleaner cover (36—Fig. J103). The pump is shown in Fig. J105. Remove the pump (25) by turning its body counterclockwise (Fig. J102) until the pump is removed.

Inspect all parts and replace as necessary. Lubricate the sealing rings (28—Fig. J105) generously when assembling the pump. Refer to the adjustment procedure in the LUBRICATION paragraph in the Maintenance section.

CHAIN BRAKE. The chain brake is designed to stop the saw chain quickly should kickback occur. The chain brake is activated when the operator's hand strikes the hand guard (24—Fig. J105). Forward movement of the hand guard disengages the release arm (23) allowing the spring (21) to tighten the band (18) around the clutch drum. The brake is released and the mechanism is reset by pulling back on the hand guard.

Procedure for disassembly is evident after removing the cover (2), saw chain (5) and guide bar (4). The chain brake should be engaged when removing the spring (21). Inspect all parts carefully and install new parts as necessary.

Lubricate all pivot points lightly when assembling. Do not allow any lubricant to get on gripping surfaces of the clutch drum or brake band. No adjustment of chain brake system is required.

REWIND STARTER. The starter can be removed as a unit by unbolting the housing (2—Fig. J106). To relieve tension on the spring, pull the handle about 30 cm from the housing and hold the rope pulley. Pull a loop in the rope between the housing and pulley with

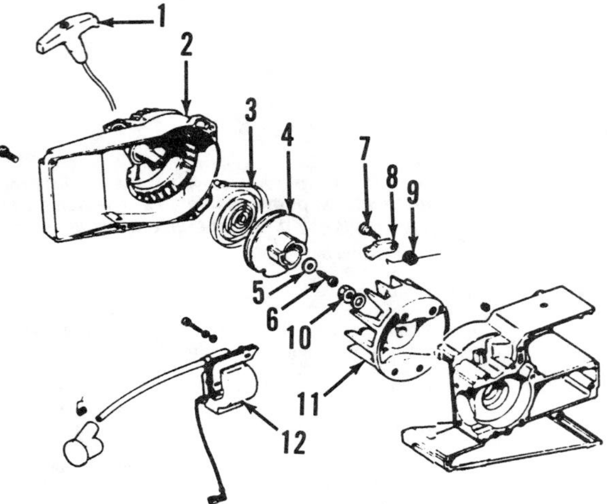

Fig. J106—Exploded view of the recoil starter and ignition system.

1. Handle
2. Starter housing
3. Recoil spring
4. Rope pulley
5. Washer
6. Screw
7. Stud
8. Pawl
9. Spring
10. Nut
11. Flywheel

the rope entering the notch in the pulley. Allow the pulley to unwind slowly until the spring is completely unwound.

Remove screw (6) and lift the rope pulley (4) from the housing. Be careful to prevent injury in case the spring (3) unwinds suddenly.

Clean and inspect parts for damage. The 3.5 mm diameter starter rope should be 89 cm long. Lubricate the recoil spring, then wind spring (3) into the housing cavity in a clockwise direction beginning with the outside coil. If detached, attach the rope to the pulley and make sure the knot is securely nested in the pulley.

Insert the end of the rope through the housing (2) and attach the handle (1). Wind as much of the rope onto the pulley (4) in a clockwise direction (viewed from the flywheel side of pulley) as possible. Position the pulley over the post in housing with a loop in the rope between the housing and pulley, then preload the recoil spring by turning the pulley about 5 turns clockwise before releasing the rope loop. Install washer (5) and screw (6).

Check for proper spring preload as follows. Pull the rope out fully and check that the pulley can be turned an additional 1/2 turn without causing the spring to bind. Allow the rope to rewind and make sure the handle is pulled against the housing. If the spring binds, pull a loop in the rope between the housing and the pulley, release some spring preload (about 1 turn), then recheck. If the handle is not wound against the housing, increase the preload and recheck.

Inspect the condition of the pawl and spring attached to the flywheel. The pawl stud should be pressed into the flywheel after coating the surface of the stud and bore with locking agent. Install a new flywheel if damaged.

JONSERED

Model	Bore mm (in.)	Stroke mm (in.)	Displacement cc (cu. in.)	Drive Type
2036 Turbo	38 (1.5)	32 (1.26)	36.3 (2.2)	Direct
2040 Turbo	40 (1.57)	32 (1.26)	40.2 (2.5)	Direct

Saws identified as Turbo models use the centrifugal force of the cooling air moved by the fan to separate some of the foreign matter from air delivered to the carburetor intake. Larger wood chips and other impurities in air circulated by the cooling fan are thrown to the outside by centrifugal force, while cleaner air nearer the fan is collected by a nozzle and directed toward the carburetor intake. Finer impurities are captured by the air filter.

MAINTENANCE

SPARK PLUG. Recommended spark plug is Champion RCJ7Y or NGK BPMR 7A. Electrode gap should be 0.5 mm (0.020 in.). The spark plug should be tightened to the torque listed in the TIGHTENING TORQUE paragraph.

CARBURETOR. Walbro WT 289 carburetor is used. Refer to the appropriate Walbro section of the CARBURETOR SERVICE section for service and exploded views.

Initial setting of the low-speed and high-speed mixture needles is 1-1/4 turns open from lightly seated. Refer to Fig. J111.

To adjust the mixture screws, first remove and clean the air filter, then reinstall it. Start the engine and allow it to run until it reaches normal operating temperature. If necessary, turn each of the mixture needles clockwise until seated lightly, then back the needles out (counterclockwise) to the initial setting so the engine can be started.

Turn the idle speed stop screw (T) so the engine idles at about 3,000 rpm. Adjust the low-speed mixture needle (L) so the engine idles smoothly and accelerates without hesitation. Adjust the idle speed to just slower than clutch engagement speed, then recheck low-speed mixture adjustment.

Adjust the high-speed mixture needle (H) to provide the best performance while operating at maximum speed under load. Maximum no-load speed (with bar and chain installed) is 13,000 rpm. The high-speed mixture screw may be set slightly rich to improve performance under load. The engine may be damaged if the high-speed screw is set too lean.

Final adjustment of the mixture needles should be within 1/4 turn of the initial settings. Large differences may indicate air leaks, plugged passages or other problems.

To remove carburetor (3—Fig. J112), first remove cylinder cover and clean the area around the carburetor. Remove air filter (1) and filter holder (2). Disconnect fuel line, throttle cable and choke lever. Remove the carburetor.

When installing carburetor, be sure that throttle cable is inserted through guide in air filter holder (2). Tighten the carburetor attaching screws to the torque listed in the TIGHTENING TORQUE paragraph.

IGNITION. All models are equipped with a breakerless electronic ignition system. All electronic circuitry is contained in a one-piece ignition module/coil (2—Fig. J113) located outside the flywheel. Ignition timing is fixed and not adjustable. The flywheel attaching nut should be tightened to the torque listed in TIGHTENING TORQUE paragraph.

Air gap between the legs of the module/coil and the flywheel magnets should be 0.3 mm (0.012 in.). When installing, set the air gap between the flywheel magnets and the legs of the ignition module as follows.

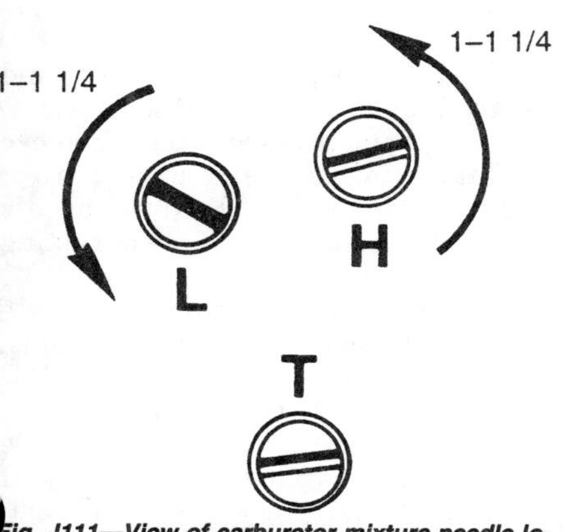

Fig. J111—View of carburetor mixture needle locations. Low-speed mixture needle is located at (L), high-speed mixture needle is at (H) and idle speed stop screw is located at (T).

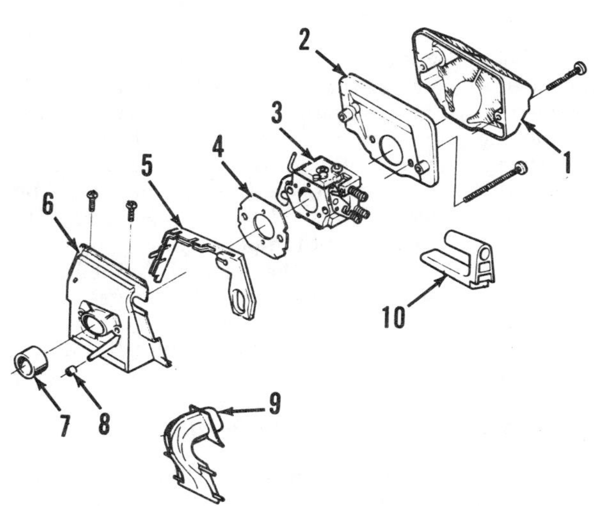

Fig. J112—Exploded view of engine intake system.

1. Air cleaner
2. Filter base
3. Carburetor
4. Gasket
5. Filter bracket
6. Insulator
7. Intake manifold
8. Impulse tube
9. Air intake nozzle
10. Adjustment guide

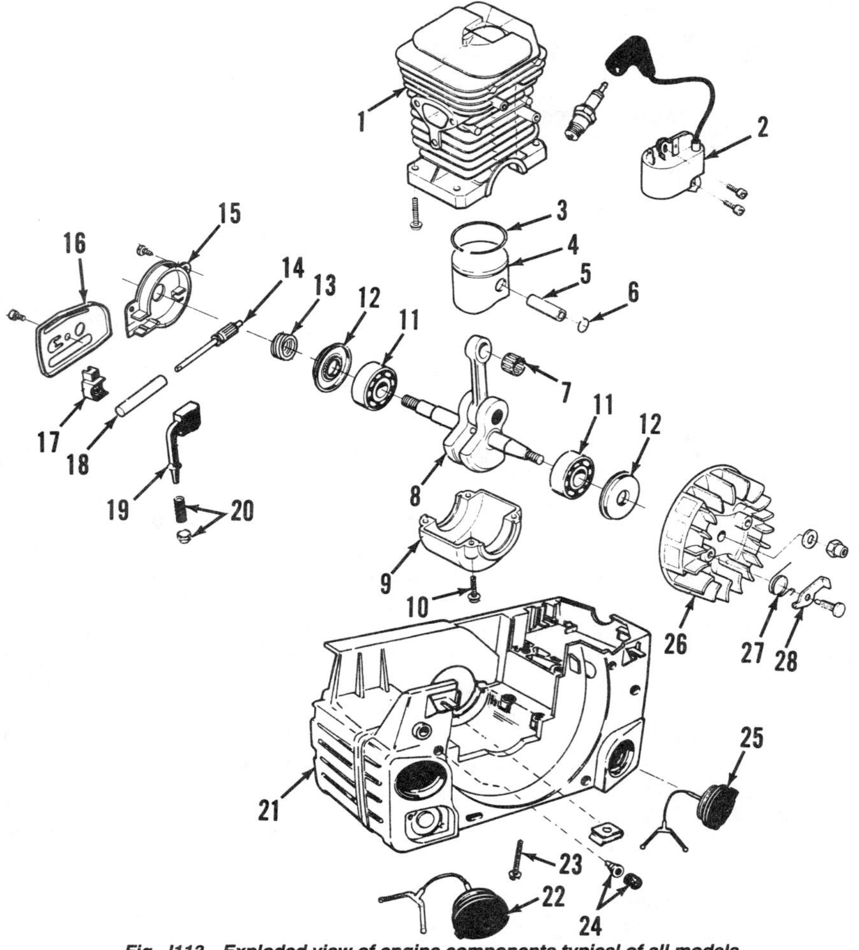

Fig. J113—Exploded view of engine components typical of all models.

1. Cylinder
2. Ignition module/coil
3. Piston ring
4. Piston
5. Piston pin
6. Retaining ring
7. Needle bearing
8. Crankshaft/connecting rod assy.
9. Crankcase lower half
10. Screw
11. Ball bearings
12. Seals
13. Worm gear
14. Pump plunger
15. Oil pump housing
16. Guard plate
17. Rubber connector
18. Pump cylinder
19. Suction pipe
20. Filter screen
21. Engine/tank housing
22. Oil tank cap
23. Screw
24. Vent
25. Fuel tank cap
26. Flywheel
27. Spring
28. Starter pawl

Install the ignition module, but tighten the two screws only enough to hold it in place away from the flywheel. Insert setting gauge (part No. 502 51 34-05) or brass/plastic shim stock of the proper thickness between the legs of the ignition module and the flywheel, then turn the flywheel until the flywheel magnets are near the module legs. Loosen the screws attaching the ignition module and press legs of the ignition module against the setting gauge. Tighten the two attaching screws securely. Remove the setting gauge, then turn the flywheel and check to be sure the flywheel does not hit the legs of the coil.

LUBRICATION. The engine is lubricated by mixing oil with the gasoline fuel. The manufacturer recommends mixing Jonsered two-stroke engine oil with regular grade gasoline at a ratio of 50:1. When using regular two-stroke engine oil, mix at a ratio of 25:1. Always use a separate container to mix gasoline and oil before filling the fuel tank. The manufacturer recommends not using fuel containing alcohol.

The saw is equipped with an automatic chain oiling system. Oil is delivered to the guide bar by the automatic chain oil pump. The manufacturer recommends using good quality oil designed for lubricating saw chain. Automotive engine oil may also be used. Select oil viscosity according to the ambient temperature.

Make sure the reservoir is filled at all times and the small oil passages do not become blocked. The volume of oil delivered by the pump is not adjustable.

REPAIRS

CRANKCASE PRESSURE TEST. An improperly sealed crankcase can cause the engine to be hard to start, run rough, have low power and overheat. Refer to ENGINE SERVICE section of this manual for crankcase pressure test procedure. If crankcase leakage is indicated, pressurize the crankcase and use a solution of soap and water to check gasket, seals, pulse line and castings for leakage.

TIGHTENING TORQUE. Recommended tightening torque values are as follows.

Carburetor	3-4 N·m (26.5-35.4 in.-lb.)
Clutch hub	30-35 N·m (265-310 in.-lb.)
Crankcase/Cylinder	10-12 N·m (88.5-106 in.-lb.)
Flywheel	25-30 N·m (221-265 in.-lb.)
Lower housing to engine	10-12 N·m (88.5-106 in.-lb.)
Muffler	7-8 N·m (62-71 in.-lb.)
Spark plug	20-22 N·m (177-195 in.-lb.)
Starter	2-3 N·m (18-26.5 in.-lb.)

PISTON, PIN, RING AND CYLINDER. To disassemble, remove cylinder cover, air filter, starter housing, flywheel, muffler, saw chain, guide bar, clutch assembly and oil pump. Remove the screw that attaches handlebar to cylinder. Unbolt and remove the carburetor, adapter housing and turbo nozzle.

Remove the four screws (23—Fig. J113) attaching the engine crankcase to the lower housing (21). Lift the engine assembly from the lower housing. Remove the four screws (10) attaching lower crankcase half (9) to cylinder/crankcase (1). Tap lower crankcase half with a plastic hammer to separate the crankcase halves. DO NOT use a screwdriver to pry the halves apart as the crankcase sealing surfaces are easily damaged.

Withdraw the piston, crankshaft and connecting rod assembly from the cylinder and upper crankcase half. Remove retaining rings (6) and push pin (5) from the piston (4). Remove needle bearing (7) from the bore in connecting rod small end.

If necessary to disassemble the crankshaft, main bearings and seals, refer to CRANKSHAFT AND CONNECTING ROD paragraph.

Inspect the cylinder for any damage and install new parts as necessary. If the chrome plating is worn from the cylinder, a new cylinder should be installed. The piston, ring and cylinder are available in standard size only. The

Illustrations courtesy Jonsered Power Products AB

piston and cylinder are available for service only as a matched set and the cylinder should not be bored oversize.

Lubricate the needle bearing (7—Fig. J113) with engine oil before assembling. Position the piston over the connecting rod and needle bearing with the arrow on piston crown toward the exhaust side of engine. Install retaining rings (6) with the opening toward the top or bottom of the piston.

Install the piston ring into the piston groove so ends of the ring correctly engage the locating pin in the groove. The locating pin prevents the ring from rotating and the ends of the piston ring must fit around this pin.

Lubricate the connecting rod lower bearing, cylinder bore, piston and ring. Make sure the ends of the piston ring surround the pin located in ring groove, then gently compress the ring while installing the cylinder straight over the piston. If the cylinder is twisted, the ring can catch in a port and break the end of the ring.

Make sure both main bearings (11—Fig. J113) and seals (12) are properly seated in the upper crankcase. Clean the mating surfaces of the crankcase halves, then apply a thin even coat of sealer to the mating surfaces. Install the lower crankcase half (9). The machined surface at the side of the lower crankcase half, near the seal, must be toward the flywheel side of engine. Tighten crankcase screws (S) in a crossing pattern evenly to the torque listed in TIGHTENING TORQUE paragraph.

Attach the engine to the lower housing (21) and tighten the screws (23) in a crossing pattern to the torque listed in the TIGHTENING TORQUE paragraph.

When assembling, be sure impulse channel (8—Fig. J112) is in place in cylinder. Install a new impulse tube if the old tube is lost or damaged. Slide the intake connector (7) onto the cylinder, then install the carburetor and air cleaner housing. Install muffler so that exhaust outlet is turned upwards and away from the cylinder.

After assembly is completed, the manufacturer recommends that the bar and chain be installed and the engine run 2-3 minutes. Stop the engine and allow to cool, then tighten cylinder screws (10—Fig. J113) again to the correct torque.

CRANKSHAFT AND CONNECTING ROD. The crankshaft and connecting rod are available only as an assembly (8—Fig. J113); individual components are not available. A shop experienced in servicing built-up crankshaft assemblies can align the shaft.

Remove the crankshaft and connecting rod assembly as described in PISTON, PIN, RING AND CYLINDER paragraphs. The crankshaft should turn smoothly inside main bearings (11) with no perceptible play or ratcheting.

Refer to the OIL PUMP paragraph for removal of the worm gear (13). The main bearings (11) and seals (12) fit bores in the crankcase halves (1 and 9). Use suitable tools to remove and install new main bearings and seals. Lubricate lips of seals with engine oil before installing over the crankshaft. Make sure that mating surfaces of the crankcase halves are properly cleaned before assembling.

Refer to PISTON, PIN, RING AND CYLINDER paragraphs for installing these parts. Make sure both main bearings (11—Fig. J113) and seals (12) are properly seated in the upper crankcase before installing the lower half (10).

CLUTCH. Refer to Fig. J114. To remove clutch, first remove clutch cover (8), bar and chain. The clutch hub (14) is attached to the right end of the engine crankshaft with left-hand threads (turn clockwise to remove). Prevent the crankshaft from turning by using an appropriate piston stopper. Unscrew the clutch assembly from the crankshaft. Special tool (part No. 530 03 11-12) is available from the manufacturer to unscrew the clutch hub from the crankshaft. The clutch drum (16) and chain drive sprocket can be withdrawn after the hub and shoes are removed. Do not lose needle bearing (17) or washer (15).

The clutch shoes (12) and hub (14) are available only as an assembly, but spring (13) is available separately. Renew clutch shoes if thickness of the shoes is less than 1 mm (0.040 in.) at the most worn part. The inside diameter of the clutch drum must not exceed 64.4 mm (2.534 in.). Inspect all parts for wear or damage and replace as necessary.

If shoes are removed from the hub, assemble the spring and one of the shoes on the hub. Clamp the hub, the one installed shoe and spring in a vise, position the second shoe on the hub, then use a screwdriver to carefully pry the spring in position over the second shoe. When assembled, the coupling for spring (13) should be in the middle of one of the shoes.

Grease the needle bearing in the clutch drum lightly before installing the drum. Install the clutch assembly, tightening the hub to the torque listed in TIGHTENING TORQUE paragraph.

OIL PUMP. The automatic oil pump is driven by worm gear (13—Fig. J113) on the crankshaft. Oil is pumped by plunger (14) as it rotates in the pump cylinder (18). Pump output is not adjustable for these models.

To remove the oil pump, first remove the clutch cover and chain brake (Fig. J114). Remove the guide bar, chain and clutch assembly. Unbolt and remove the chain guide plate (16—Fig. J113) and the oil pump housing (15). Lift the pump (14 and 18) and rubber connector (17) from the housing. Use special tool (part No. 530 03 11-36) to remove the drive worm (13). If necessary, pull the oil suction pipe (19) and filter (20) from the oil tank.

Clean and inspect all parts, then replace any that are damaged. Use the worm gear special tool to install the worm gear (13) on the crankshaft. Lubricate the oil suction pipe (19) before inserting in oil tank. Make sure that the suction pipe is completely seated in the tank housing.

CHAIN BRAKE. The chain brake is designed to stop the saw chain quickly should kickback occur. The chain brake is activated when the operator's hand strikes the hand guard (3—Fig. J114). Forward movement of the hand guard disengages the trigger assembly (5) allowing the spring (6) to tighten the band (7) around the clutch drum (16). The brake is released and the mechanism is reset by pulling back on the guard. Keep the chain brake clean and free of sawdust and dirt accumulation.

Remove the clutch cover (8) to inspect and service the brake assembly. To disassemble, push hand guard (3) forward to release the brake. Remove hand guard mounting screw and drive out pivot sleeves (1). Separate hand guard from clutch cover. Remove cover plate (9). Carefully pry spring (6) out of cover. Drive out pin (4) and remove trigger assembly (5) and brake band (7).

Inspect all parts carefully and install new parts as necessary. Install a new brake band if any part of the band is worn to less than 0.8 mm (0.032 in.) thickness.

Lubricate all pivot points lightly when assembling. Do not allow any lubricant to get on gripping surfaces of the clutch drum or brake band. No adjustment of chain brake system is required.

REWIND STARTER. Refer to Fig. J115. The starter housing (4) can be unbolted and the assembly removed from

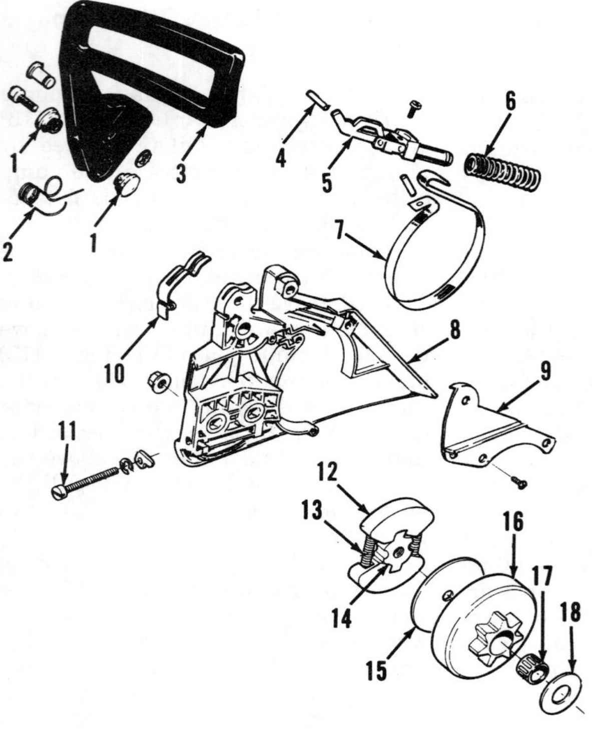

Fig. J114—Exploded view of the chain brake and clutch assemblies.

1. Pivot sleeves
2. Spring
3. Hand guard
4. Pin
5. Brake trigger mechanism
6. Brake spring
7. Brake band
8. Clutch cover/brake housing
9. Brake cover
10. Spring
11. Chain adjusting screw
12. Clutch shoes
13. Clutch spring
14. Clutch hub
15. Plate
16. Clutch drum
17. Needle bearing
18. Washer

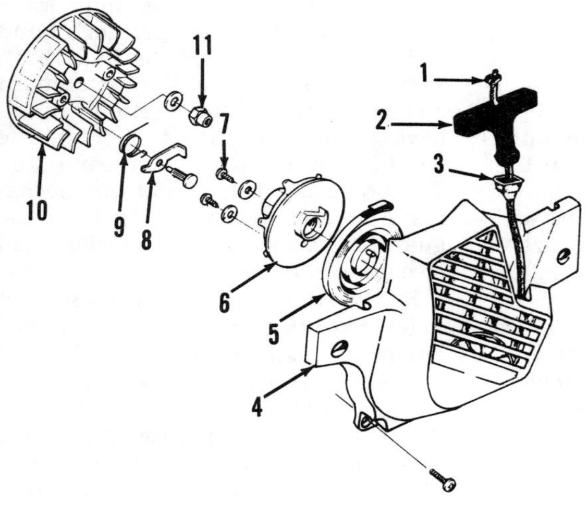

Fig. J115—Exploded view of the rewind starter assembly.

1. Starter rope
2. Handle
3. Rope guide
4. Starter housing
5. Rewind spring
6. Rope pulley
7. Screw
8. Starter pawl
9. Spring
10. Flywheel
11. Nut

the saw. Pull the starter rope out about 20 cm (8 in.) and hold the pulley (6) to keep the rope from rewinding. Pull a loop of rope from between the housing (4) and the pulley (6) into one of the notches molded into the edge of the pulley. Hold the loop and allow the pulley to turn slowly until the spring is completely unwound.

Remove the retaining screw (7) and washer, then lift the pulley (6) from housing. The rewind spring (5) can be removed if necessary, but be careful to control the spring as it is removed to prevent injury.

Clean and inspect parts for damage. Lubricate the recoil spring, then wind spring (5) into the housing cavity in a clockwise direction beginning with the outside coil. If detached, attach the rope to the pulley and make sure the knot is securely nested in the pulley. Insert the end of the rope through the housing (4) and guide (3), then attach handle (2). Wind the rope clockwise onto the pulley (6).

Position the pulley over the post in housing with a loop in the rope between the housing and pulley, then preload the recoil spring by turning the pulley about 4 turns clockwise before releasing the rope loop. Install washer and screw (7).

Check for proper spring preload as follows. With rope fully extended, it should be possible to rotate the pulley an additional 1/2 turn without causing the spring to bind. Allow the rope to rewind and make sure the handle is pulled against the housing. If the spring binds, pull a loop in the rope between the housing and the pulley, release some spring preload (about 1 turn), then recheck. If the handle is not wound against the housing, increase the preload and recheck.

Inspect the condition of the pawl (8) and spring (9) attached to the flywheel. On some models, the pawl assembly may be part of a plate attached by the flywheel retaining nut.

JONSERED

Model	Bore mm (in.)	Stroke mm (in.)	Displacement cc (cu. in.)	Drive Type
2077	52 (2.05)	36 (1.42)	76.5 (4.7)	Direct
2083 Turbo	54 (2.13)	36 (1.42)	82.4 (5.0)	Direct

Saws identified as Turbo models use the centrifugal force of the cooling air moved by the fan to separate some of the foreign matter from air delivered to the carburetor intake. Larger wood chips and other impurities in air circulated by the cooling fan are thrown to the outside by centrifugal force, while cleaner air nearer the fan is collected by a nozzle and directed toward the carburetor intake. Finer impurities are captured by the air filter.

MAINTENANCE

SPARK PLUG. Recommended spark plug for 2077 is Champion RCJ7Y or NGK BPMR7A. Recommended spark plug for 2083 is Champion RCJ6Y or NGK BPMR7A. Electrode gap should be 0.7 mm (0.028 in.) for both models. The spark plug should be tightened to the torque listed in the TIGHTENING TORQUE paragraph.

CARBURETOR. Walbro WJ28B carburetor is used on all models. Refer to the appropriate Walbro section of the CARBURETOR SERVICE section for service and exploded views. Tighten the carburetor attaching screws to the torque listed in the TIGHTENING TORQUE paragraph.

Fig. J120—Illustration showing location of carburetor adjustment screws. Idle speed screw is located at (T), idle mixture needle is located at (L) and high speed mixture needle is located at (H).

Initial setting of the low-speed and high-speed mixture needles (Fig. J120) is 1 ¼ turns open from lightly seated. To adjust the mixture screws, first remove and clean the air filter, then reinstall it. Start the engine and allow it to run until it reaches normal operating temperature. If necessary, turn each of the mixture needles clockwise until seated lightly, then back the needles out (counterclockwise) to the initial setting so the engine can be started.

Turn the idle speed stop screw (T—Fig. J120) so the engine idles at about 3,500 rpm. Adjust the low-speed mixture needle (L) so the engine idles smoothly and accelerates without hesitation. Adjust the idle speed to just slower than clutch engagement speed, then recheck low-speed mixture adjustment.

Adjust the high-speed mixture needle (H) to provide the best performance while operating at maximum speed under load. Maximum no-load speed (with bar and chain installed) is 13,500 rpm. The high-speed mixture screw may be set slightly rich to improve performance under load. The engine may be damaged if the high-speed screw is set too lean.

Final adjustment of the mixture needles should be within 1/4 turn of the initial settings. Large differences may indicate air leaks, plugged passages or other problems.

IGNITION. A breakerless electronic ignition system is used and electronic circuitry is contained in a one-piece ignition module/coil located outside the flywheel. Ignition timing is fixed and not adjustable. The flywheel attaching nut should be tightened to the torque listed in TIGHTENING TORQUE paragraph.

Air gap between the legs of the module/coil and the flywheel magnets should be 0.3 mm (0.012 in.). When installing, set the air gap between the flywheel magnets and the legs of the ignition module as follows.

Install the ignition module, but tighten the two screws only enough to hold it in place away from the flywheel. Insert setting gauge (part No. 502 51 34-05 or brass/plastic shim stock of the proper thickness) between the legs of the ignition module and the flywheel, then turn the flywheel until the flywheel magnets are near the module legs. Loosen the screws attaching the ignition module and press legs of the ignition module against the setting gauge. Tighten the two attaching screws securely. Remove the setting gauge, then turn the flywheel and check to be sure that the flywheel does not hit the legs of the coil.

LUBRICATION. The engine is lubricated by mixing oil with the gasoline fuel. The manufacturer recommends mixing Jonsered two-stroke engine oil with regular grade gasoline at a ratio of 50:1. When using regular two-stroke engine oil, mix at a ratio of 25:1. Always use a separate container to mix gasoline and oil before filling the fuel tank. The manufacturer recommends not using fuel containing alcohol.

An automatic oil pump provides lubrication for the bar and chain. The manufacturer recommends using good quality oil designed for lubricating saw chain. Automotive engine oil may also be used. Select oil viscosity according to the ambient temperature.

Make sure the reservoir is filled at all times and the small oil passages do not become blocked. The volume of oil delivered by the pump is adjustable by turning the screw (Fig. J121). Initial setting is with the adjustment screw turned in until lightly seated then turned out 3 full turns. The screw is accessible from under the saw.

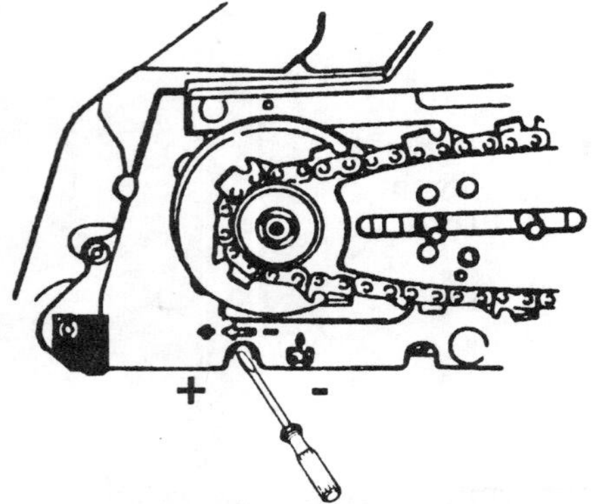

Fig. J121—Illustration showing adjustment of chain oil pump adjustment screw.

REPAIRS

CRANKCASE PRESSURE TEST. An improperly sealed crankcase can cause the engine to be hard to start, run rough, have low power and overheat. Refer to ENGINE SERVICE section of this manual for crankcase pressure test procedure. If crankcase leakage is indicated, pressurize the crankcase and use a solution of soap and water to check gasket, seals, pulse line and castings for leakage.

TIGHTENING TORQUE. Recommended tightening torque values are as follows.

Carburetor	1.5 N•m (13 in.-lb.)
Clutch hub	20-22 N•m (177-194 in.-lb.)
Crankcase halves	7-9 N•m (62-80 in.-lb.)
Cylinder to Crankcase	8-10 N•m (71-88.5 in.-lb.)
Decompression valve (2083)	12-14 N•m (106-124 in.-lb.)
Flywheel	30-35 N•m (265-310 in.-lb.)
Muffler	13-15 N•m (115-133 in.-lb.)
Spark plug	20-22 N•m (177-194 in.-lb.)
Starter	2-3 N•m (18-26.5 in.-lb.)

PISTON, PIN, RING AND CYLINDER. To disassemble, remove cylinder cover (1—Fig. J122), air filter cover (2) and air filter (3). Unbolt and remove muffler. Detach impulse hose, fuel line and choke lever from carburetor. Remove carburetor (5) and air filter holder (4). Detach throttle cable as carburetor is removed. Remove cylinder attaching screws, then lift cylinder (9) away from the crankcase. Remove piston pin retaining rings (15), push pin (12) from piston, and remove the piston (14) and needle bearing (16).

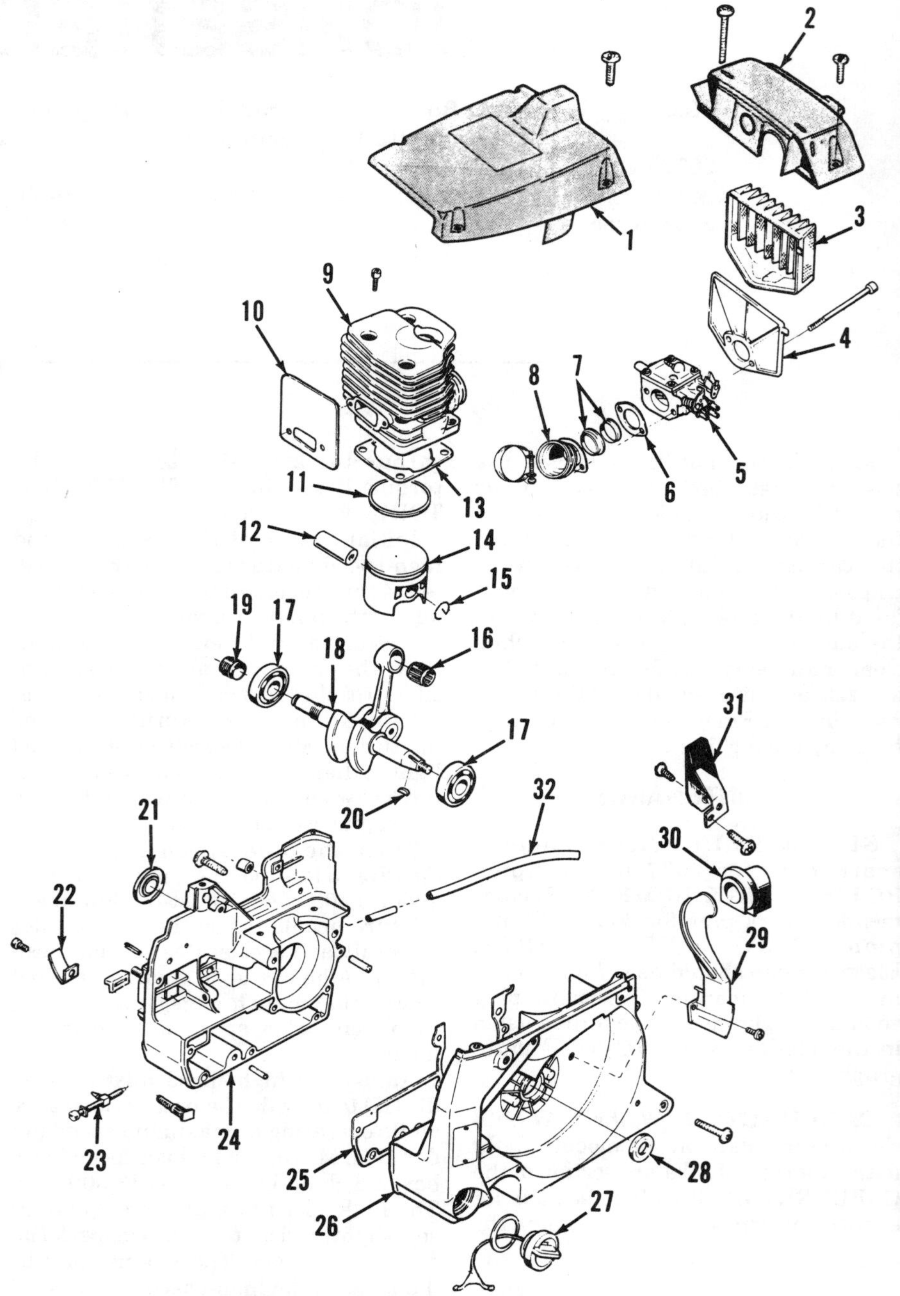

Fig. J122—Exploded view of engine assembly.

1. Cylinder cover
2. Air filter cover
3. Air filter
4. Air filter holder
5. Carburetor
6. Gasket
7. Seal
8. Intake tube
9. Cylinder
10. Insulator plate
11. Piston ring
12. Piston pin
13. Base gasket
14. Piston
15. Retaining ring
16. Needle bearing
17. Ball bearing
18. Crankshaft/connecting rod assy.
19. Worm gear (2077)
20. Woodruff key
21. Seal
22. Case protector
23. Chain adjuster
24. Crankcase half
25. Gasket
26. Crankcase half
27. Oil tank cap
28. Seal
29. Air intake nozzle
30. Connector
31. Deflector
32. Impulse tube

Inspect the cylinder bore and piston for scuffing, scoring or excessive wear. Cylinder, piston, ring, piston pin and needle bearing are available as a matched set.

Lubricate the connecting rod bore, bearing (16), piston pin (12), piston (14), ring (11) and cylinder with clean engine oil before assembling. Attach the piston with the arrow on top pointing toward the exhaust side of engine. Install new cylinder base gasket (13) with round edges up toward the cylinder. Make certain that ends of piston ring (11) are positioned at the locating pin in piston ring groove.

Compress the piston ring and slide the cylinder over the piston. Do not

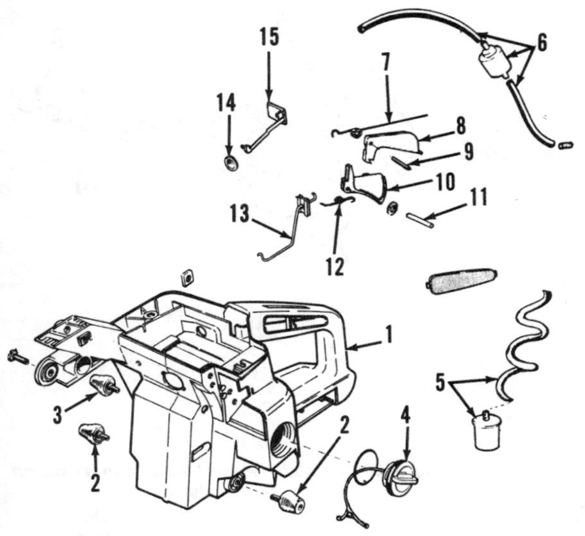

Fig. J123—Exploded view of rear handle and fuel tank assembly. The assembly is attached to the engine assembly with vibration isolators (2 and 3).

1. Rear handle & fuel tank
2. Vibration isolators
3. Vibration isolator
4. Fuel tank cap
5. Fuel filter & tube
6. Fuel tank vent & non-return valve
7. Spring
8. Throttle interlock
9. Pin
10. Throttle trigger
11. Pin
12. Spring
13. Throttle link
14. Guide washer
15. Choke rod

twist the cylinder during installation as the piston ring could become disengaged from the locating pin and damage the cylinder. Tighten the cylinder attaching screws in a crossing pattern to the torque listed in TIGHTENING TORQUE paragraph. Complete assembly by reversing disassembly procedure.

CONNECTING ROD, CRANKSHAFT AND CRANKCASE. The connecting rod is equipped with a needle bearing (16—Fig. J122) at the piston pin end and a roller bearing at the crankpin end. The crankshaft is supported in ball bearings (17).

The crankshaft is made up of parts that are pressed together, trapping the connecting rod and its lower bearing. DO NOT disassemble. The crankshaft/connecting rod is available only as a complete assembly.

To remove the crankshaft (18—Fig. J122), remove the guide bar, chain, chain brake assembly, clutch assembly and the oil pump. Remove the starter housing, flywheel, generator, carburetor and ignition coil/module. Remove the rear handle and fuel tank assembly (1—Fig. J123).

Remove the muffler, cylinder and piston. Use a suitable puller (part No. 502 54 09-01) to pull the oil pump drive worm (19—Fig. J122) from the crankshaft of 2077 models. Remove the screws attaching the crankcase halves together, then carefully separate the halves (24 and 26—Fig. 122) using a tool (part No. 502 51 61-01) to push the end of the crankshaft from the case bore.

Check the crankshaft main ball bearings (17) for roughness or other damage, then install new bearings if required. Do not remove main bearings (17) unless renewal is required. Check the rotation of the connecting rod around the crankpin. Install a new connecting rod and crankshaft assembly if rough, loose or any other damage is noticed. Carefully clean and inspect the crankcase and cylinder sealing surfaces for any nicks, burrs, cracks or other damage that would prevent an air tight seal.

Observe the following procedure when assembling. If main bearings are not installed in the bores of the crankcase halves, heat the case halves to assist during the assembly. If the main bearings did not remain installed on the crankshaft assembly, press the main bearings into the heated bores of the crankcase halves. If the main bearings are to be reinstalled and were not removed from the crankshaft, be sure the crankcase halves are heated sufficiently to permit assembly without distorting the crankcase.

Use the correct special puller (for 2077 models, use tool part No. 502 50 30-13; for 2083 models, use tool part No. 502 50 30-14) to pull the crankshaft into the clutch side crankcase half. Make sure the connecting rod is properly positioned and does not bind while assembling. Make sure the gasket (25) is properly positioned and all holes are aligned, then install the flywheel side crankcase half using the same special puller and procedure.

Install and tighten the screws attaching the crankcase halves together, while checking the crankshaft for binding. If the crankshaft binds while assembling the case halves, determine the cause and correct before continuing with the assembly. Tighten the crankcase screws to the torque listed in TIGHTENING TORQUE paragraph.

Use seal protectors and lubricate the seal lips when installing crankshaft seals (21 and 28—Fig. J122). Complete assembly by reversing disassembly procedure.

CLUTCH. To remove the clutch, first remove the clutch cover, chain brake assembly, chain and guide bar. Remove the sprocket (3—Fig. J124), clutch drum (2) and needle bearing (4). Prevent the flywheel from turning by removing the spark plug and installing a piston stop tool (or a loop of rope) in the spark plug hole. Turn the clutch hub (1) in a clockwise direction (left-hand threads) as indicated by the arrow to unscrew the clutch hub from the engine crankshaft. Use a suitable tool (part No. 502 54 04-01 for 2077 models) to turn the hub.

Inspect all parts of the clutch for wear, evidence of overheating or other damage and replace parts as necessary. New clutch shoes should be installed if worn to less than 1 mm (0.040 in.) thickness. The clutch hub, shoes and return springs are available only as an assembly. Install a new drum if worn or otherwise damaged.

When assembling, tighten the clutch hub to the torque listed in TIGHTENING TORQUE paragraph. Lubricate the needle bearing with grease before installing the bearing and clutch drum. Complete assembly by reversing disassembly procedure.

CHAIN BRAKE. The chain brake is designed to stop the chain if kickback should occur. The chain brake is activated when the operator's hand strikes the hand guard (13—Fig. J124) or if the tip of the guide bar strikes an object with sufficient force to trip the brake mechanism. When the brake is engaged, a spring (8) tightens the band (7) around the clutch drum (2) to stop the drum, sprocket and chain. Pull the hand guard (13) back to reset the mechanism.

To check for proper operation, shut the engine off and hold the tip of the guide bar a specific test distance above a tree trunk or other firm wood object. The test distance is 45 cm (14 in.) for saws with 11-16 in. guide bars; 55 cm (22 in.) for saws with 18-22 in. guide bars; 65 cm (26 in.) for saws with 24-28 in. guide bars; 80 cm (32 in.) for saws with 30-36 in. guide bars. Release the front handle and allow the saw to rotate around the rear handle until the tip of the guide bar strikes the tree trunk. The brake should activate.

Reset the brake and start the engine. Run the engine at full (wide open) throttle, then move the hand guard (13) to activate the brake. The saw chain should stop immediately. If the chain brake fails to perform correctly, disas-

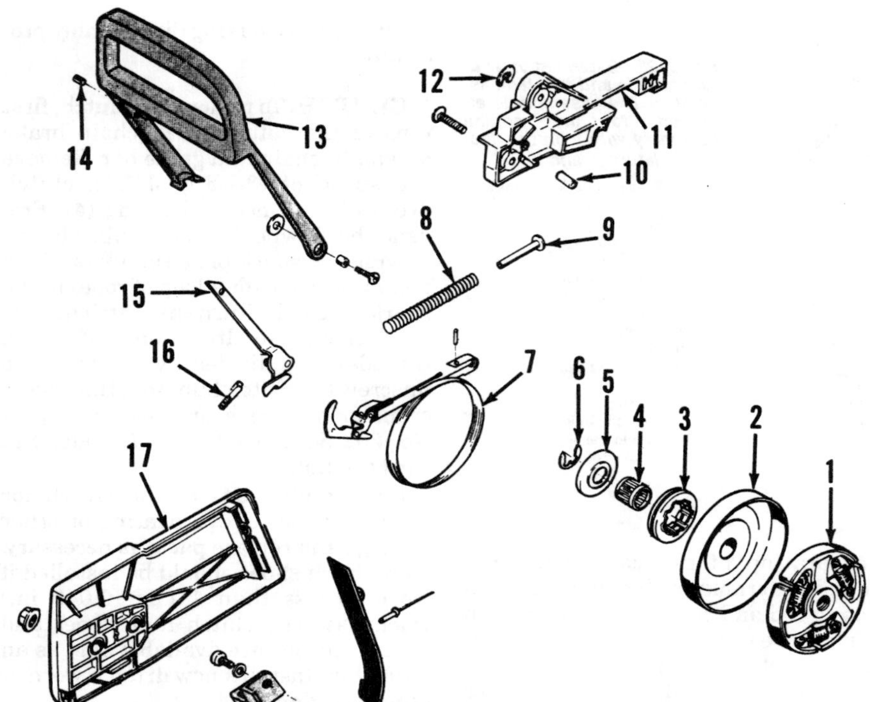

Fig. J124—Exploded view of clutch and chain brake assemblies typical of all models.

1. Clutch hub & shoes
2. Clutch drum
3. Sprocket
4. Needle bearing
5. Retainer
6. "E" ring
7. Brake band
8. Brake spring
9. Plunger
10. Pin
11. Brake housing
12. "E" ring
13. Hand guard
14. Pin
15. Brake lever
16. Pawl & spring
17. Cover

semble and inspect parts for wear or damage. The chain brake is not adjustable.

To disassemble, remove the pivot bolt from the flywheel side of the hand guard (13). Unbolt and remove the cover (17), saw chain and guide bar. Clean around the brake band and housing. Remove the three screws attaching brake housing (11) to the cover, then remove the brake assembly.

Lift the toggle joint of the band assembly (7) carefully with a screwdriver and remove the band and spring assembly from the housing. Brake lever (15) can be removed after removing snap ring (12). Lever (15) is retained in hand guard (13) with pin (14).

A new brake band should be installed if the thickness of the old band is less than 0.8 mm (0.0315 in.). To assemble, reverse the disassembly procedure.

The longer side of pawl (16) must be toward housing (11). Hold the pawl against pressure of the spring with a screwdriver while installing lever (15). Install brake band (7) with the toggle joint over the pin (10) located in the housing. Install the brake spring (8) and pin (9) in the brake band and compress the spring enough to install the spring, pin and band in the housing. Lubricate brake linkage contact surfaces with light oil.

OIL PUMP. The guide bar and chain are lubricated by oil supplied by the automatic oil pump shown in Fig. J125 or Fig. J126. The pump plunger (8) is driven by the worm gear (4).

On 2077 models, the worm gear (4—Fig. J125) is located under the pump housing and is pressed onto the crankshaft. Use a suitable puller (part No. 502 54 09-01) to pull the oil pump drive worm from the crankshaft of 2077 models.

On 2083 models, the worm gear (4—Fig. J126) is located outside the pump housing and is driven by the clutch hub.

To disassemble the removed pump, remove the adjusting screw (12—Fig. J125 or Fig. J126). Bump the housing on a soft surface if necessary to jar the locking pin (10) and spring (11) from the housing bore. Remove the plastic plug (9) from the plunger bore if necessary to remove the plunger (8), washers (7) and spring (6).

Clean and inspect parts for wear or damage. Parts should move freely in housing bores without excessive clearance. Install a new pump assembly if parts are worn. Some individual parts may be available separately if only that part is damaged.

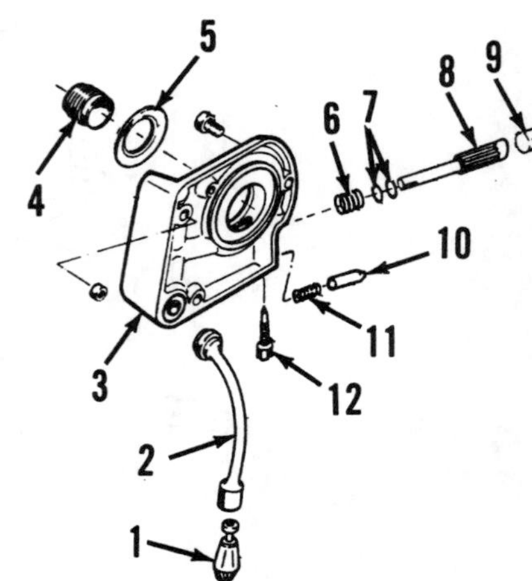

Fig. J125—Exploded view of the oil pump used on 2077 models.

1. Oil strainer
2. Suction tube
3. Oil pump housing
4. Worm gear
5. Washer
6. Spring
7. Washers
8. Plunger
9. Sleeve
10. Locking pin
11. Spring
12. Adjusting screw

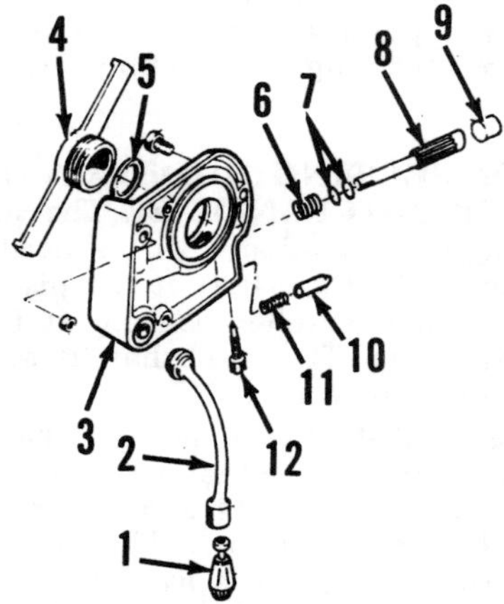

Fig. J126—Exploded view of the oil pump used on 2083 models.

1. Oil strainer
2. Suction tube
3. Oil pump housing
4. Worm gear
5. Seal
6. Spring
7. Washers
8. Plunger
9. Sleeve
10. Locking pin
11. Spring
12. Adjusting screw

Assemble the pump and install on the crankcase. Washer (5) should be installed with the concave (cupped) side toward the outside. Complete assembly by reversing disassembly procedure.

REWIND STARTER. Refer to Fig. J127 for an exploded view of the starter assembly. To disassemble starter, first unbolt and remove starter housing (1) from saw. Pull starter rope out about 30 cm (12 in.). While holding rope pulley (7), pull loop of rope back through outlet

Illustrations courtesy Jonsered Power Products AB

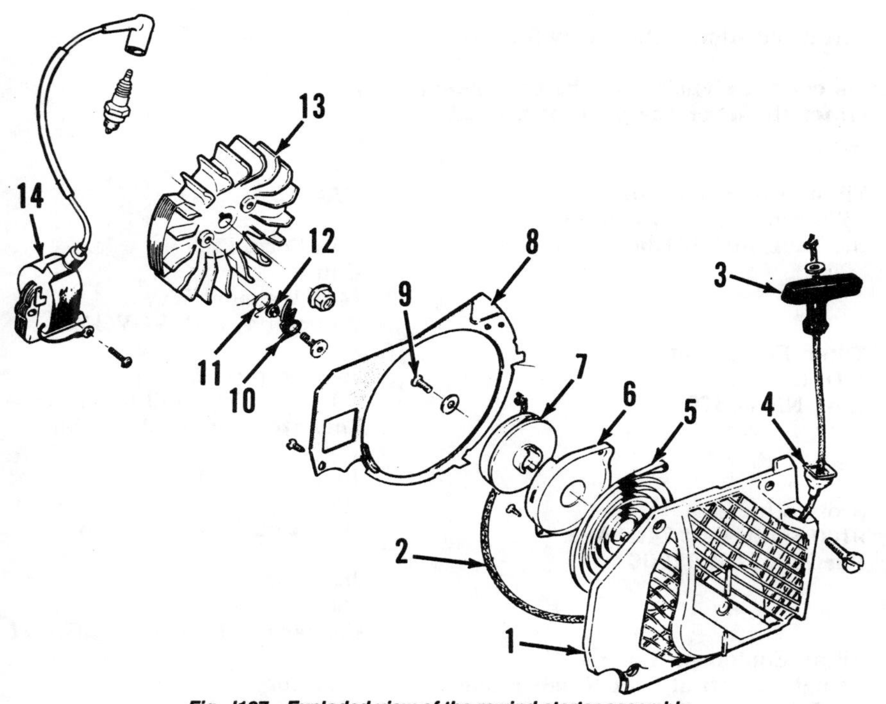

Fig. J127—Exploded view of the rewind starter assembly.

1. Starter housing
2. Rope
3. Handle
4. Rope guide
5. Rewind spring
6. Spring case
7. Pulley
8. Plate
9. Screw
10. Starter pawl
11. Spring
12. Spacer
13. Flywheel
14. Ignition module/coil

and place rope in notch in pulley. Then, allow pulley to slowly unwind.

Unscrew pulley retaining screw (9) and carefully withdraw rope pulley. If required, rewind spring (5) may now be removed. Use caution not to allow spring to unwind uncontrolled.

Reassemble starter components by reversing disassembly procedure while noting the following: Lubricate pulley pivot pin with small amount of grease. Lubricate rewind spring with a few drops of light oil. Wind rope fully on pulley in clockwise direction as viewed with pulley in housing.

Install rope pulley in housing, then pull rope handle out about 30 cm (12 in.) and pull loop of rope back through outlet as in removal procedure. Turn rope pulley two additional turns clockwise to place tension on rewind spring. Release pulley and check starter operation.

With rope fully extended, it should be possible to rotate rope pulley a minimum of 1/2 turn clockwise before rewind spring bottoms. Do not place more tension on rewind spring than is necessary to draw rope handle against housing.

JONSERED DISTRIBUTORS

(Arranged Alphabetically by States)

These firms carry extensive stocks of repair parts. Contact them for the parts you need.

Tilton Equipment Co.
6202 Sears Ave.
Little Rock, AR 72209

Scotsco Inc.
2601 Del Monte
West Sacramento, CA 95691

Scotsco Inc.
6767 East 50th
Commerce City, CO 80022

Tilton Equipment Co.
P.O. Box 1008
1295 Old Alpharetta Road
Alpharetta, GA 30201

Tilton Equipment Co.
1379 Jamike Ave.
Erlanger, KY 41018

Tilton Equipment Co.
4575 North Chatsworth Street
St. Paul, MN 55126

Tilton Equipment Co.
P.O. Box 68
Rye, NH 03870

Scotsco Inc.
9160 South East 74th Ave.
Portland, OR 97206

Tilton Equipment Co.
Lehigh Industrial Park Number One
2147 Ave. C
Bethlehem, PA 18017

CANADA

Josa Corp. Ltd.
Unit 3
1411 Walmont Way
Richmond, B.C. VGV 1Y3

Josa Corp. Ltd.
C.P./Box 5500, 180 Hamford
Lachute, Quebec J8H 4B5

Josa Corp. Ltd.
290 Baig Blvd.
Moncton, N.B. E1E 1C8

Josa Corp. Ltd.
630 Broadway
Cornerbrook, NFLD A2H 4O7

Josa Corp. Ltd.
1151 Russel Street
Thunder Bay, Ontario P7B 5M6

LOMBARD

Model	Bore mm (in.)	Stroke mm (in.)	Displacement cc (cu. in.)	Drive Type
AP42, AP42AV, AP42D, AP42DAV, AP42SE	47.5 (1.87)	38.1 (1.5)	68.8 (4.2)	Direct
Comango, Super Comango, Lightning II, Lightning III	47.5 (1.87)	38.1 (1.5)	68.8 (4.2)	Direct

MAINTENANCE

SPARK PLUG. Recommended spark plug is Champion CJ7Y for all the AP prefix models and CJ6 for all other models. Electrode gap should be 0.025 inch (0.63 mm).

CARBURETOR. Refer to CARBURETOR SERVICE section for servicing of Tillotson HS carburetor.

Initial adjustment of carburetor is as follows: Back out throttle stop screw until it no longer contacts throttle shaft lever, then turn stop screw in until it contacts throttle shaft lever and give it an additional 3/4 turn. Turn idle and high speed mixture screws in until they seat lightly, then back out idle mixture screw 7/8-1 turn and the high speed mixture screw 1-1 1/8 turns.

To make final adjustments, start engine and bring to operating temperature, adjust idle mixture screw until engine idles smoothly, then if necessary, adjust throttle stop screw until engine is operating at 2200-2500 rpm (just below clutch engagement). Following these adjustments, richen the idle mixture slightly (1/16-1/8 turn).

To adjust high speed mixture, load saw (make a cut) and adjust high speed mixture needle until saw operates smoothly, then richen mixture slightly by backing out high speed mixture screw about 1/8-turn.

IGNITION. Early models are equipped with a breaker-point type flywheel magneto ignition system while later models use a breakerless electronic ignition system.

Breaker-Point Models. Ignition timing for Lightning II and III models should be 30 degrees BTDC while ignition timing is fixed on all other models. Breaker-point gap on all models should be 0.015 inch (0.38 mm). Tighten flywheel nut to 190-200 in.-lbs. (21.5-22.6 N·m) torque.

Breakerless Models. Ignition timing is fixed on all models. Air gap between flywheel and ignition module should be 0.015 inch (0.38 mm). Tighten flywheel nut to 190-200 in.-lbs. (21.5-22.6 N·m) torque. Two types of ignition modules are used on later models and are not interchangeable. The module may be identified by its color and if required, must be renewed with the same color module.

LUBRICATION. Engine is lubricated by mixing lubricating oil with gasoline. Use a separate container when mixing the fuel and oil. Mix 1/2 pint (118 mL) of Lombard two-stroke engine oil (No. 1-1840) or SAE 30 motor oil with each gallon (3.7853 L) of regular gasoline.

Fill chain oil reservoir with SAE 30 motor oil. During cold weather, use lighter oil or dilute the SAE 30 oil up to 50 percent with kerosene as necessary.

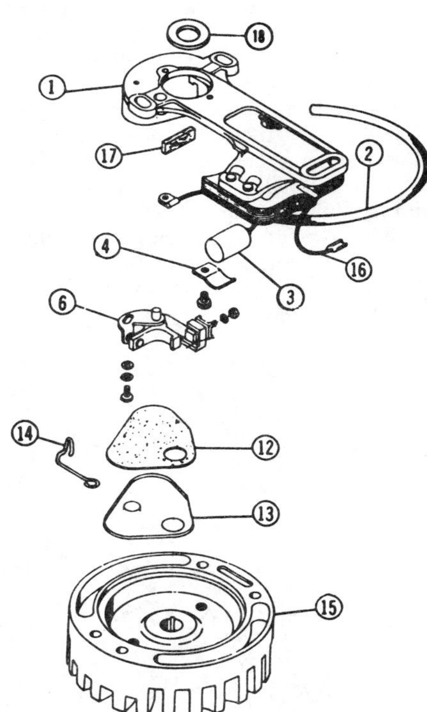

Fig. LO6—Exploded view showing component parts of breaker-point type magneto used on models with adjustable ignition timing. Models with fixed timing are similar. See text.

1. Stator assy.
2. Coil & leadwire
3. Condenser
4. Clamp
6. Breaker-points
12. Gasket
13. Cover
14. Cover spring
15. Flywheel
16. Switch lead
17. Lubricating felt
18. Crankshaft seal

Clutch drum should be removed after every eight or ten cutting hours and a few drops of SAE 30 oil placed on drum bearing.

CARBON. Muffler and exhaust ports should be cleaned of carbon every thirty hours or less. To clean, remove muffler and turn engine until piston is at bottom of stroke. Use a blunt instrument, or wood scraper and remove all carbon from exhaust ports and surrounding chamber being careful not to damage exhaust ports. Remove spark plug. Shake out loosened particles and crank engine several times to blow out any remaining carbon. Clean muffler, then reinstall the muffler and spark plug.

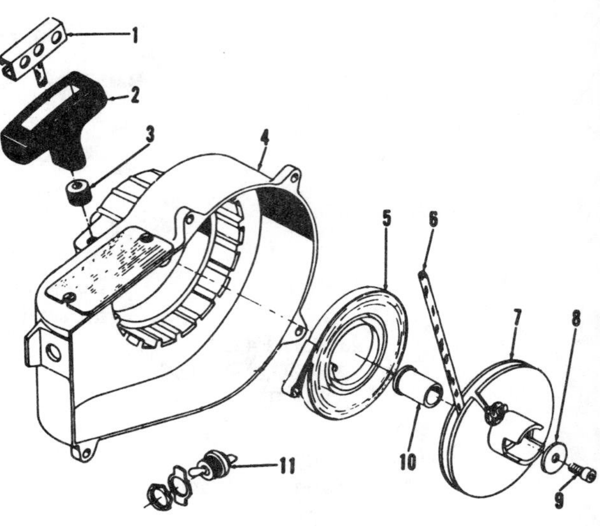

Fig. LO8—Exploded view showing component parts of starter assembly. Starter is mounted on a starter post (shaft) which is an integral part of blower housing.
1. Insert
2. Handle
3. Cushion
4. Blower (starter) housing
5. Rewind spring
6. Cord (rope)
7. Pulley
8. Washer
9. Socket head screw
10. Flange bushing
11. Switch

REPAIRS

PISTON, PIN AND RINGS. All models are fitted with two pinned rings. Standard sizes only are available for all models. Renew piston if clearance between piston skirt and cylinder exceeds 0.008 inch (0.20 mm), measured at right angle to piston pin, or if side clearance of new ring in top ring groove exceeds 0.010 inch (0.25 mm). Also inspect piston for cracks, scoring or loose fit of piston in piston bores. Piston and pin are available as a matched assembly only. Desired clearance between pin and pin bore in piston is 0.0001-0.0002 inch (0.0025-0.0051 mm).

Desired piston ring end gap is 0.008-0.018 inch (0.203-0.457 mm). Desired ring side clearance in piston groove is 0.005-0.008 inch (0.127-0.203 mm). Renew rings if end gap is excessive or side clearance exceeds 0.010 inch (0.25 mm) in new piston.

Piston, pin and rings are available in standard size only.

CYLINDER. Cylinder bore is chrome plated and must not be rebored. Renew cylinder if chrome plating is worn through to expose the softer base metal. Tighten cylinder retaining nuts to 73-83 in.-lbs. (8.2-9.4 N•m) torque.

CONNECTING ROD. Early models are equipped with a removable connecting rod. Late models are equipped with a connecting rod/crankshaft unit assembly which should not be disassembled.

On early models, connecting rod rides on 24 loose bearing rollers which must be renewed as a set. Use grease to hold rollers in place during assembly and place 12 rollers in cap and 12 rollers in rod. Assemble rod to cap with match marks aligned. Be sure surfaces of rod and cap mate properly and tighten rod screws to 60-65 in.-lbs. (6.8-7.3 N•m) torque.

On all models, piston pin is supported in connecting rod by a needle bearing. Bearing should not be removed as bearing and rod are available only as a unit assembly.

CRANKSHAFT. On all models, crankshaft is supported in two caged needle roller bearings except some earlier models which use a ball bearing and a needle roller bearing. Crankshaft end play is controlled by needle roller type thrust bearings. Crankshaft end play should be not less than 0.006 inch (0.15 mm) nor more than 0.027 inch (0.68 mm).

Renew the needle roller main bearings if any needle has flat spots or if rollers can be separated the width of one roller. Press only on lettered end of bearing during installation. If equipped with a ball bearing, inspect ball bearing for wear, pitting or scoring.

Renew crankshaft if any of the bearing surfaces are worn, scored or burned. Also check keyways and threads for signs of wear or damage.

CRANKSHAFT OIL SEALS. It is important that crankcase seals be maintained in good condition or loss of crankcase pressure and engine power will result.

Use extreme caution to prevent damage to seals during installation. If a sleeve installation tool is not available, use tape to cover any splines, shoulders or threads which the seals must pass over.

REED VALVE. The reed valve assembly can be removed after removing carburetor and air box. A flat reed valve assembly and a pyramid reed valve assembly have been used. Renew reeds if cracked or worn and be sure reeds are centered over openings of reed plate. Use all new gaskets during installation.

CLUTCH. The two-shoe centrifugal clutch (30–Fig. LO9) is threaded to

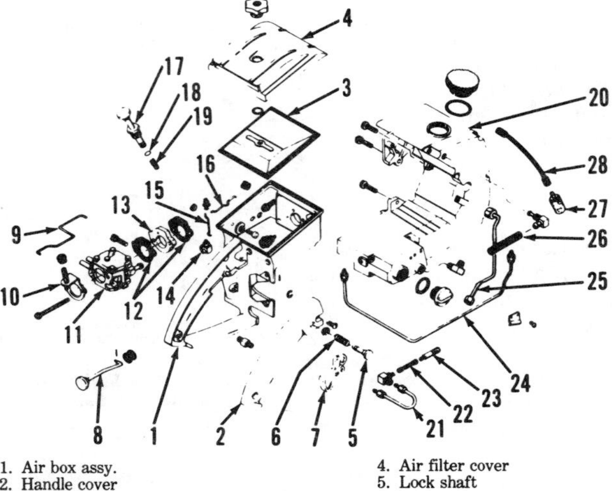

Fig. LO7—View showing typical air box and throttle handle assembly.
1. Air box assy.
2. Handle cover
3. Air filter element
4. Air filter cover
5. Lock shaft
6. Lock spring
7. Throttle trigger
8. Choke lever
9. Throttle link
10. Cover bracket
11. Carburetor
12. Gasket
13. Spacer
14. Oil valve
15. Pull link
16. Push link
17. Oil pump assy.
18. "O" ring
19. Spring
20. Fuel & oil tank
21. Oil inlet line
22. Oil pickup tube
23. Oil pickup
24. Oil outlet line
25. Oil line
26. Fuel line
27. Fuel pickup
28. Fuel pickup tube

crankshaft and is removed by locking crankshaft and turning clutch assembly in a clockwise direction.

If clutch slips under load at engine high speed, check for excessive wear of clutch shoes. If clutch will not disengage (chain creeps) at engine idle speed, check for broken, weak or distorted clutch springs.

Sprocket (drum) bushing is renewable and the drum should be removed after every eight or ten cutting hours and a few drops of SAE 30 oil placed on the bushing. Do not overlubricate bushing as excess oil could result in the clutch slipping.

STARTER. To disassemble starter, remove blower housing, then refer to Fig. LO8 and proceed as follows: Pull starter rope out fully, hold pulley and pry rope knot from pulley, then let pulley rewind slowly. Hold pulley and remove screw (9). Lift pulley and bushing (10) from starter post. Spring (5) can now be removed from housing but use caution as the rapidly uncoiling spring could cause injury.

Install spring in blower housing with loop in outer end over pin in blower housing and be sure spring is coiled in direction shown. Install bushing and spring and turn pulley clockwise until it engages spring. Insert new rope through handle and hole in blower housing. Knot both ends of rope and harden the knots with heat or cement. Turn pulley eight turns clockwise and slide knot into slot of pulley and let pulley rewind slowly.

Starter pawls can be removed from flywheel after blower housing and starter assembly is removed and procedure is obvious.

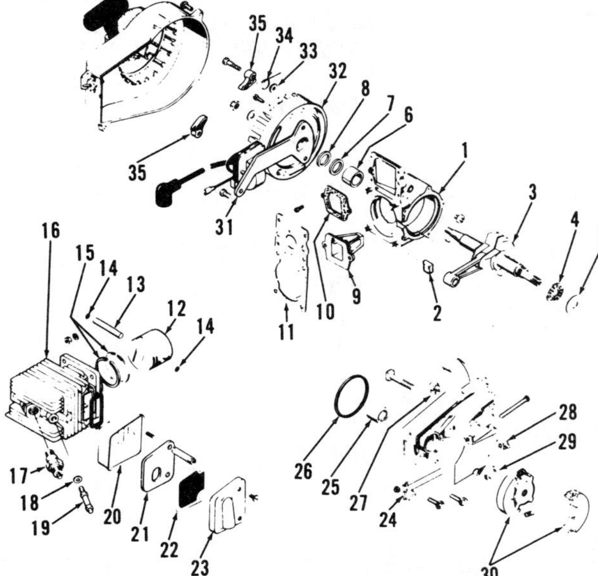

Fig. LO9—Exploded view showing typical power head used on late models. Other models are similar.

1. Crankcase
2. Crankcase plug
3. Crankshaft & rod assy.
4. Thrust bearing
5. Bearing race
6. Main bearing
7. Oil seal
8. Felt seal
9. Reed valve assy.
10. Gasket
11. Gasket
12. Piston
13. Piston pin
14. Retaining ring
15. Piston rings
16. Cylinder
17. Spark plug
18. Washer
19. Decompression valve
20. Muffler body
21. Baffle plate
22. Screen
23. Muffler cover
24. Crankcase cover
25. Main bearing
26. "O" ring
27. Metering valve
28. Tensioner block
29. Oil seal
30. Clutch assy.
31. Stator assy.
32. Flywheel
33. Washer
34. Pawl spring
35. Starter pawl

LOMBARD

Model	Bore mm (in.)	Stroke mm (in.)	Displacement cc (cu. in.)	Drive Type
AP 22, AP-22-1, AP22D, AP22D-1	38.1 (1.5)	31.7 (1.25)	36.1 (2.2)	Direct
AP24, AP24D, AP24SE	39.7 (1.562)	31.7 (1.25)	39.3 (2.4)	Direct
Little Lightning	38.1 (1.5)	31.7 (1.25)	36.1 (2.2)	Direct
Little Lightning Super	39.7 (1.562)	31.7 (1.25)	39.3 (2.4)	Direct

MAINTENANCE

SPARK PLUG. Recommended spark plug is Champion CJ7Y. Electrode gap should be 0.025 inch (0.63 mm).

CARBURETOR. A Tillotson Model HU or Walbro WA diaphragm carburetor has been used. Refer to CARBURETOR SERVICE section for an exploded view of carburetor and carburetor service.

Initial adjustment of idle and high speed mixture screws is 1 turn open. Make final adjustments with engine warm and running. Adjust idle mixture screw so engine will accelerate cleanly without stumbling. Adjust high speed mixture screw to obtain optimum performance with saw under cutting load. Adjust idle speed screw so engine idles just below clutch engagement speed.

IGNITION. Early models are equipped with a breaker-point type flywheel magneto ignition system while later models use a breakerless electronic ignition system.

Breaker-point gap should be 0.015 inch (0.38 mm) on models so equipped. Ignition timing is fixed on all models but breaker-point gap on applicable models should be set correctly or timing will be affected. Flywheel nut tightening torque is 100-125 in.-lbs. (11.3-14.1 N·m).

LUBRICATION. The engine is lubricated by mixing oil with the fuel. Recommended fuel:oil ratio is 16:1. Oil should be a good quality SAE 20 or SAE 30 oil designed for two-stroke air-cooled engines.

Clean SAE 20 or SAE 30 oil may be used for chain lubrication in warm weather. Dilute chain oil up to 50 percent with kerosene during cold weather operation.

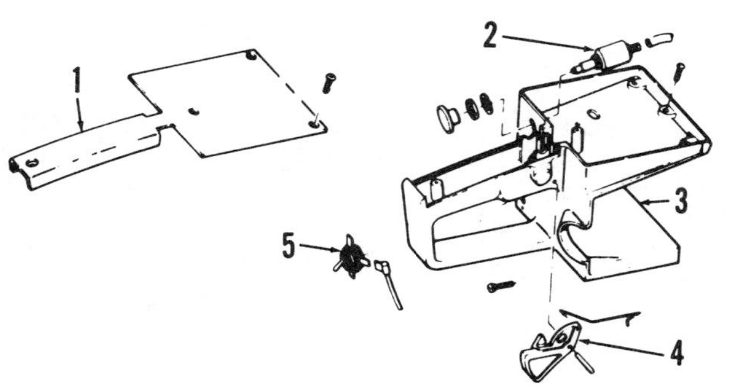

Fig. LO10—Exploded view of rear handle assembly.
1. Cover
2. Manual oil pump
3. Rear handle
4. Throttle trigger
5. Ignition switch

REPAIRS

CYLINDER, PISTON, PIN AND RINGS. Cylinder is also upper crankcase half. Oil and fuel tank cover (34–Fig. LO11) must be removed for access to cylinder screws. Crankshaft assembly will be loose when cylinder is separated from crankcase (24). Be careful not to nick or damage crankcase mating surfaces.

The piston is equipped with two piston rings. Piston pin (6) rides in caged needle roller bearing (8) in small end of connecting rod. Cylinder (3) has a chrome bore and oversize pistons and rings are not available. Inspect cylinder bore for excessive wear or damage to chrome surface. Tighten cylinder screws to 60-80 in.-lbs. (6.8-9.0 N·m). Refer to following paragraph for proper assembly of crankcase and cylinder.

CONNECTING ROD, CRANKSHAFT AND CRANKCASE. Cylinder (3–Fig. LO11) must be removed for access to crankshaft assembly. Refer to previous section for cylinder removal.

Connecting rod and crankshaft are a unit assembly and must be serviced as such. Apply a light coat of nonhardening sealant to crankcase mating surfaces before assembly. Be sure retaining rings

(12) fit properly in grooves of crankcase and cylinder. Tighten cylinder-to-crankcase screws to 60-80 in.-lbs. (6.8-9.0 N•m).

CLUTCH. Saw may be equipped with a two-shoe or three-shoe centrifugal clutch. Clutch hub has left-hand threads. Clutch shoes and hub are available as a unit only. Inspect clutch components for excessive wear or damage.

REWIND STARTER. Refer to Fig. LO12 for an exploded view of rewind starter. To disassemble starter, remove rope handle and allow rope to wind into starter housing. Unscrew housing screws and detach starter housing (1) from left side cover (10). Remove "E" ring (8) and remove rope pulley. If necessary, remove wire retainer (6) and dislodge rewind spring from starter housing. Caution should be used to prevent spring from uncoiling uncontrolled.

Install rewind spring in starter housing with spring wound in clockwise direction from outer end. Wind rope around pulley in clockwise direction as viewed with rope pulley installed in housing. Pass end of rope through rope outlet in side cover (10) and install starter assembly on side cover without screws. Turn housing (1) clockwise until rope handle rests snugly against rope outlet. Install housing screws and check starter operation.

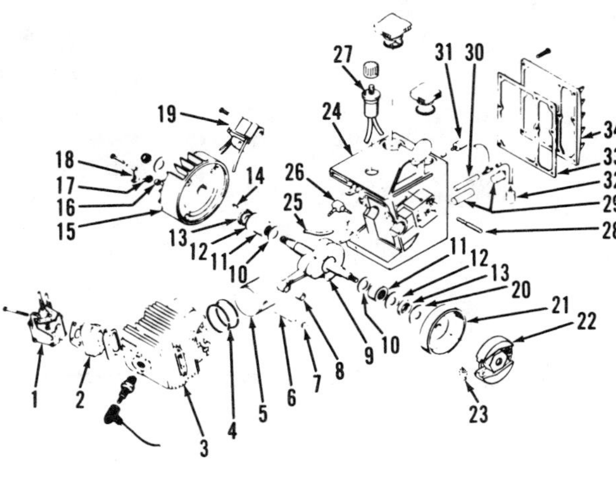

Fig. LO11—Exploded view of engine.

1. Carburetor
2. Spacer
3. Cylinder
4. Piston rings
5. Piston
6. Piston pin
7. Pin retainer
8. Bearing
9. Crankshaft & rod assy.
10. Thrust washer
11. Main bearing
12. Retainer
13. Seal
14. Key
15. Flywheel
16. Spacer
17. Pawl spring
18. Starter pawl
19. Ignition module
20. Washer
21. Clutch drum
22. Clutch hub & shoes
23. Clutch spring
24. Crankcase
25. Fuel line
26. Fitting
27. Oil regulator
28. Lubrication orifice
29. Valve & tube assy.
30. Oil line
31. Fuel pickup
32. Oil pickup
33. Gasket
34. Cover

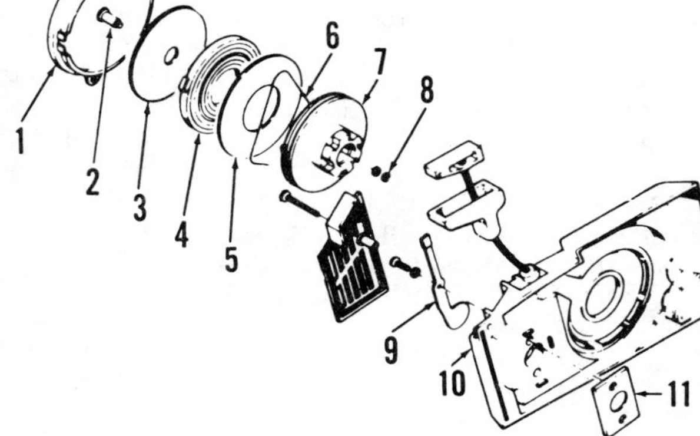

Fig. LO12—Exploded view of rewind starter.

1. Housing
2. Spindle
3. Plate
4. Rewind spring
5. Plate
6. Wire retainer
7. Rope pulley
8. "E" ring
9. Choke plate
10. Side cover
11. Gasket

MAKITA

Model	Bore mm (in.)	Stroke mm (in.)	Displacement cc (cu. in.)	Drive Type
DS330, DS-330S	37 (1.45)	31 (1.22)	33 (2.01)	Direct
DS-390	40 (1.57)	31 (1.22)	39 (2.38)	Direct

MAINTENANCE

SPARK PLUG. Recommended spark plug is Champion RDJ-7Y or NGK BPMR-6F. Electrode gap should be 0.5 mm (0.020 in.). The spark plug should be tightened to the torque listed in the TIGHTENING TORQUE paragraph.

CARBURETOR. Walbro WT 174 carburetor is used on all models. Refer to the appropriate Walbro section of the CARBURETOR SERVICE section for service and exploded views. Initial setting of the low-speed mixture needle (1—Fig. MK11) and high-speed mixture needle (2) is 1 turn open from lightly seated. To adjust the mixture needles, first remove and clean the air filter, then reinstall it. Start the engine and allow it to run until it reaches normal operating temperature. If necessary, turn each of the mixture needles clockwise until seated lightly, then back the needles out (counterclockwise) to the initial setting so the engine can be started.

Turn the idle speed stop screw so the engine idles at about 2,600 rpm. Adjust the low-speed mixture needle so the engine idles smoothly and accelerates without hesitation. Adjust the idle speed to just slower than clutch engagement speed, then recheck low-speed mixture adjustment.

Adjust the high-speed mixture needle to provide the best performance while operating at maximum speed under load. Maximum no-load speed (with bar and chain installed) is 11,500 rpm for DCS 330 or 12,000 rpm for DCS390. The high-speed mixture needle may be set slightly rich to improve performance under load. The engine may be damaged if the high-speed mixture is set too lean.

Final adjustment of the mixture needles should be within 1/4 turn of the initial settings. Large differences may indicate air leaks, plugged passages or other problems.

To remove carburetor, first remove air filter cover. Remove carburetor mounting nuts. Disconnect throttle link, choke link, fuel line and impulse tube. Withdraw carburetor from intake manifold. When reinstalling, tighten the carburetor attaching nuts to the torque listed in the TIGHTENING TORQUE paragraph.

IGNITION. All models are equipped with a breakerless electronic ignition system. All electronic circuitry is contained in a one-piece ignition module/coil located outside the flywheel. Ignition timing is fixed and not adjustable. The flywheel attaching nut should be tightened to the torque listed in TIGHTENING TORQUE paragraph.

Air gap between the legs of the module/coil and the flywheel magnets should be 0.2 mm (0.008 in.). When installing, set the air gap between the flywheel magnets and the legs of the ignition module as follows.

Install the ignition module, but tighten the two screws only enough to hold it in place away from the flywheel. Insert setting gauge (part No. 944 500 890) or brass/plastic shim stock of the proper thickness between the legs of the ignition module and the flywheel, then turn the flywheel until the flywheel magnets are near the module legs. Loosen the screws attaching the ignition module and press legs of the ignition module against the shim stock. Tighten the two attaching screws to the torque listed in the TIGHTENING TORQUE paragraph.

Remove the shim stock, then turn the flywheel and check that flywheel does not hit the legs of the coil.

LUBRICATION. The engine is lubricated by mixing oil with the gasoline fuel. The manufacturer recommends mixing MAKITA two-stroke oil with regular grade gasoline at a ratio of 40:1 after break-in. When using regular two-stroke engine oil, mix at a ratio of 25:1. During the initial break-in (first 10 hours) the fuel to oil ratio should be 30:1 when using MAKITA oil or 20:1 when using other approved oil.

Always use a separate container to mix gasoline and oil before filling the fuel tank. The manufacturer recommends not using fuel containing alcohol.

The saw chain is equipped with an automatic chain oiling system. The manufacturer recommends using MAKITA Saw Chain oil or other good quality oil designed for lubricating saw chain. Make sure the reservoir is filled at all times.

Fig. MK11—View showing location of the carburetor adjustment screws. The idle speed stop screw is located at "Speed," low-speed mixture needle at "L" and high-speed mixture needle at "H."

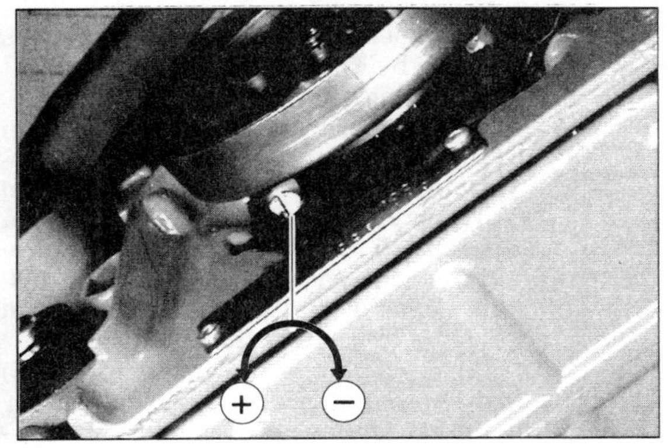

Fig. MK12—The chain oil adjustment screw is located as shown. Turn the screw clockwise to reduce the amount of oil or counterclockwise to increase the amount of oil.

The volume of oil delivered by the pump is adjustable by turning screw (Fig. MK12). The screw is located under the saw on the right side.

REPAIRS

TIGHTENING TORQUE. Recommended tightening torque values are as follows.

Carburetor
 Attaching screws . . . . 2.5-2.7 N•m (22-24 in.-lb.)
Clutch hub . . . . 22.5-27.5 N•m (199-243 in.-lb.)
Crankcase . . . . 10-11 N•m (88.5-97 in.-lb.)
Cylinder . . . . 5.5-6.5 N•m (49-57.5 in.-lb.)
Decompression valve . . . . 8 N•m (71 in.-lb.)
Flywheel . . . . 17.5-20.0 N•m (155-177 in.-lb.)
Ignition
 Module/coil . . . . 3.0-4.0 N•m (26.5-35 in.-lb.)
Intermediate flange . . . . . 6.0-6.5 N•m (53-57.5 in.-lb.)
Muffler . . . . 8.0-9.0 N•m (71-80 in.-lb.)
Spark plug . . . . 14.0-16.0 N•m (124-142 in.-lb.)
Tubular handle . . . . 2.0-3.0 N•m (18-26.5 in.-lb.)
Vibration isolator . . . . 2.0-3.0 N•m (18-26.5 in.-lb.)

PISTON, PIN, RINGS AND CYLINDER. The cylinder can be removed after removal of air filter cover, cylinder cover, muffler, carburetor and intake manifold. Remove four screws attaching cylinder to crankcase and withdraw cylinder from piston.

Refer to Fig. MK13 for exploded view of typical piston and cylinder. One piston ring is used and is pinned in the groove to prevent movement.

NOTE: Be careful when moving the connecting rod with the cylinder removed. It is possible to dislodge the loose needle rollers located at the crankshaft end of the connecting rod.

The piston pin rides in a needle bearing permanently located in the upper end of the connecting rod. The piston pin is retained in the piston by rings (6) located in the piston at each end of the pin. Always install new retainer rings if they are removed and position the opening toward the bottom of the piston.

Inspect the cylinder bore for excessive wear or damage. Oversize parts are not available. The piston and cylinder are available separately.

When assembling, make sure the arrow on the piston crown is visible and pointing toward the exhaust (muffler) side of the cylinder. A fork tool can be positioned between the bottom of the piston skirt and the crankcase to prevent movement of the piston when installing the cylinder.

Use a suitable ring compressor to compress the piston ring, making certain that the ring end gap is aligned with the locating pin. Lubricate cylinder with engine oil, then slide cylinder over the piston. Tighten the cylinder retaining screws to the torque listed in TIGHTENING TORQUE paragraph.

CRANKSHAFT, CONNECTING ROD AND CRANKCASE. The crankshaft is supported by main bearings (11—Fig. MK13) located in a split crankcase (14 and 16). Power head must be separated from the fuel tank/handle assembly in order to service the crankshaft and connecting rod. The clutch, oil pump, pump drive worm, flywheel, cylinder, and piston

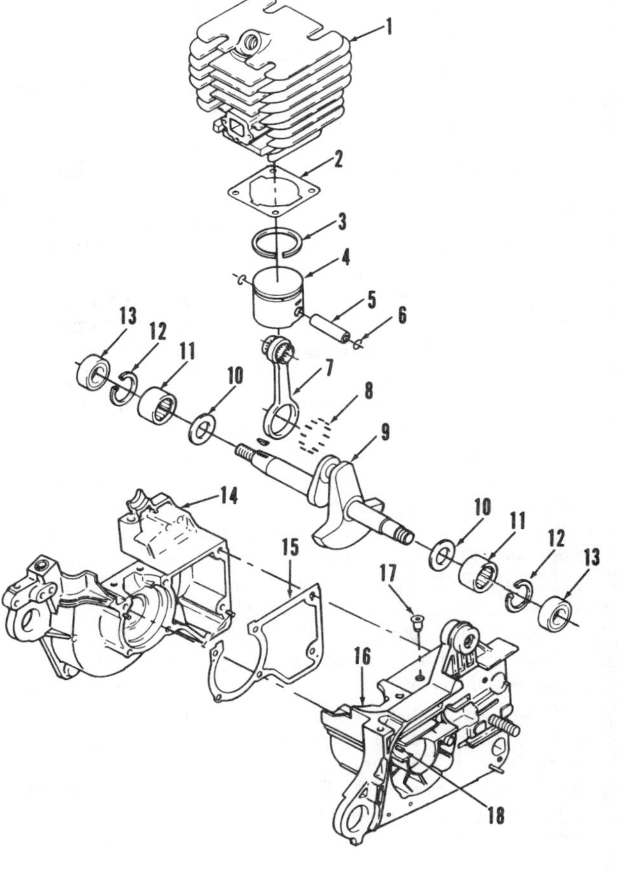

Fig. MK13—Exploded view of the cylinder, crankcase, crankshaft and associated parts typical of all models.

1. Cylinder
2. Gasket
3. Piston ring
4. Piston
5. Piston pin
6. Pin retainer rings
7. Connecting rod
8. Bearing rollers (12 used)
9. Crankshaft
10. Thrust washers
11. Main bearings
12. Snap rings
13. Seals
14. Crankcase left half
15. Gasket
16. Crankcase right half
17. Oil tank vent
18. Guide pin

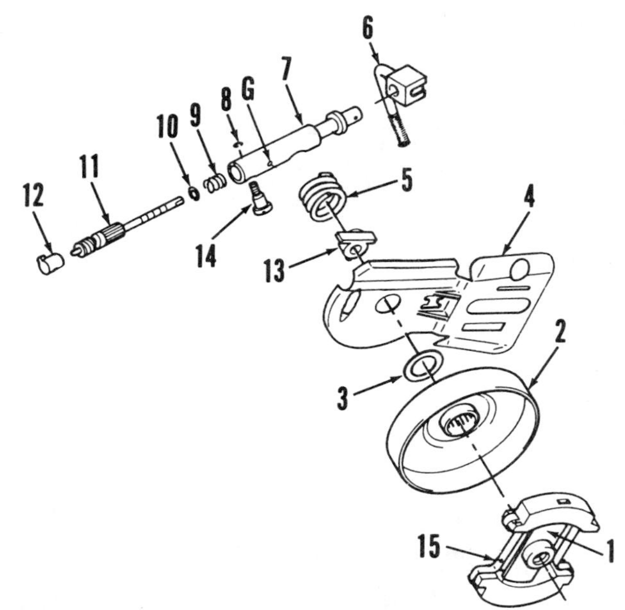

Fig. MK14—Exploded view of clutch and chain oil pump components.

G. Alignment hole
1. Clutch assy.
2. Clutch drum
3. Shim
4. Plate
5. Worm gear
6. Suction line assy.
7. Pump body
8. "O" ring
9. Spring
10. Washer
11. Plunger
12. Plug
13. Seal
14. Adjusting screw
15. Clutch spring

must be removed before separating the crankcase halves.

Remove the attaching screws and tap the crankcase as necessary with a soft faced hammer to separate the halves. DO NOT insert any type of pry bar between the crankcase halves as damage to the crankcase sealing surfaces could result.

Twelve loose needle rollers (8—Fig. MK13) are located between the connecting rod and the crankshaft crankpin. The loose rollers can be removed after slipping the rod (7) from the bearing rollers. Make sure that all rollers are removed and installed when servicing the bearing. Use grease to hold the rollers in place while assembling the connecting rod.

Do not attempt to remove the needle bearing that supports the piston pin from the top of connecting rod. The bearing is not available except as a unit with the connecting rod.

The crankshaft is supported at both ends by caged needle roller bearings (11). The main bearings must be seated against the snap rings (12). Do not damage or lose thrust washers (10). Do not remove the main bearings or crankcase seals (13) unless new parts will be installed. Seals can be removed and new seals installed using an appropriate seal puller (part No. 944 500 870 or equivalent) without separating the crankcase halves.

Install snap rings (12) and press the main bearings into bores against the snap rings, if removed from the crankcase bores. Assemble the connecting rod (7) and twelve bearing rollers (8) using grease to hold the rollers in position. Install thrust washer (10) on each end of the crankshaft. Install the oil pump suction hose and position the crankcase gasket over the dowel studs of the right crankcase half.

Install the crankshaft into the right crankcase half, then install the left case half. Tighten the screws attaching the crankcase halves to the torque listed in TIGHTENING TORQUE paragraph. Install the piston and cylinder.

CLUTCH. Refer to Fig. MK14. The clutch hub (1) is attached to the right end of the engine crankshaft with left-hand threads (turn clockwise to remove). Prevent the crankshaft from turning by using an appropriate piston stopper. The clutch hub can be turned using the special tool (part No. 944 500 690) or equivalent wrench. The clutch drum (2) can be withdrawn after the hub and shoes are removed.

The drum and bearing are available only as an assembly. Inspect the clutch drum and chain drive sprocket, then replace parts as necessary. The clutch shoes and hub (1) are available only as an assembly, but springs (15) are available separately.

When assembling, install the smaller shim (3) before installing the clutch drum. Grease the needle bearing in the clutch drum lightly before installing the drum. Install the clutch assembly, tightening the hub to the torque listed in TIGHTENING TORQUE paragraph.

OIL PUMP. All models are equipped with an automatic chain oil pump typical of the type shown in Fig. MK14. Oil is pumped by plunger (11), which is turned by worm gear (5). Pump output is adjusted by turning screw (14).

The oil pump can be removed from the engine after removing the clutch assembly and plate (4). Pull pump from the suction line (6). The suction line can be pulled from the crankcase if required. Special tool (part No. 950 500 011) should be used to pull the worm drive gear (5) from the crankshaft.

Inspect plunger (11), worm gear (5) and bore in pump housing (7) for wear of damage. If wear or damage is excessive, it is suggested that a new pump assembly and worm drive gear be installed. Grease the pump plunger (11) liberally with silicone grease before assembling the pump.

To install the worm gear, screw the worm gear onto special tool (part No. 950 500 011), then heat the worm gear to approximately 100 degrees C (212 degrees F). Position the worm gear on the crankshaft until the tool is bottomed, allow the worm gear to cool, then remove the special tool leaving the worm on the crankshaft.

Install the filter at the end of suction line (6) and lubricate the line with silicone grease before installing in the crankcase. Insert the pump body into the suction line and move it into position. Make sure the hole in the pump housing engages the pin on the side of the crankcase near the crankshaft.

REWIND STARTER. Remove the flywheel to gain access to the recoil starter (Fig. MK15). Remove the handle (10) and carefully allow the rope pulley (7) to unwind and relieve tension on spring (8).

To disassemble, remove the brake spring (5) and retainer ring (4), then lift the rope pulley from the engine. Remove the cover (9) and spring (8) if necessary, being careful to prevent injury when spring unwinds.

Clean and inspect parts for damage. The 3 mm diameter starter rope should be 90 cm long. Lubricate the recoil spring, then wind the spring into the pulley in a clockwise direction beginning with the outside coil. Wind the rope onto the pulley in a counterclockwise direction as viewed from the flywheel side of pulley.

Assemble cover (9), spring (8) and pulley (7) and install the retainer ring (4) with the end gap toward the ignition coil (11). Make sure starter pawl (6) properly engages the brake spring (5) as shown in Fig. MK16.

Wind the rope completely onto the rope pulley. To preload the rewind spring, hold the rope tight into the drum and rotate the pulley two to three

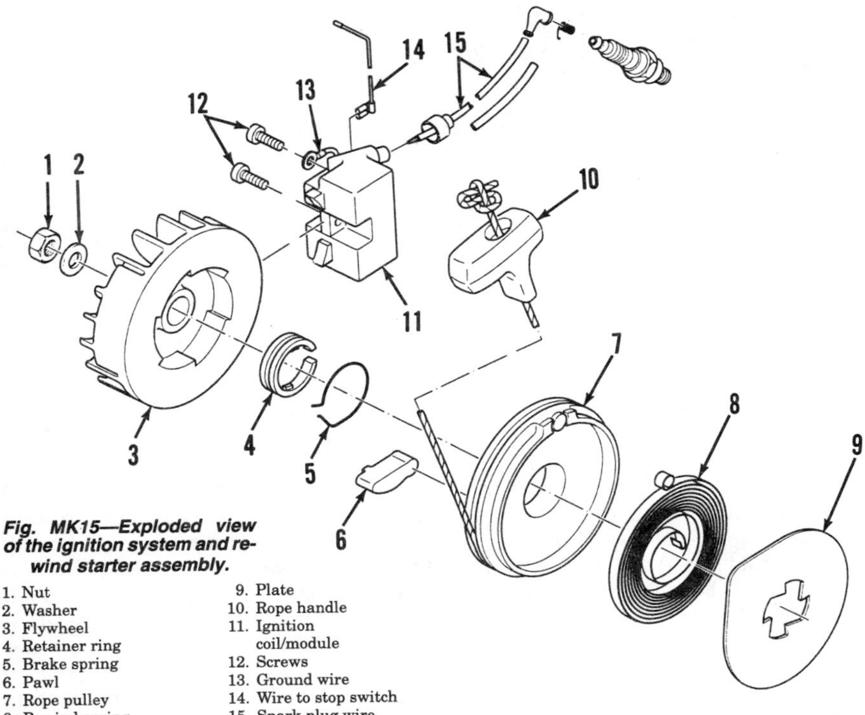

Fig. MK15—Exploded view of the ignition system and rewind starter assembly.

1. Nut
2. Washer
3. Flywheel
4. Retainer ring
5. Brake spring
6. Pawl
7. Rope pulley
8. Rewind spring
9. Plate
10. Rope handle
11. Ignition coil/module
12. Screws
13. Ground wire
14. Wire to stop switch
15. Spark plug wire

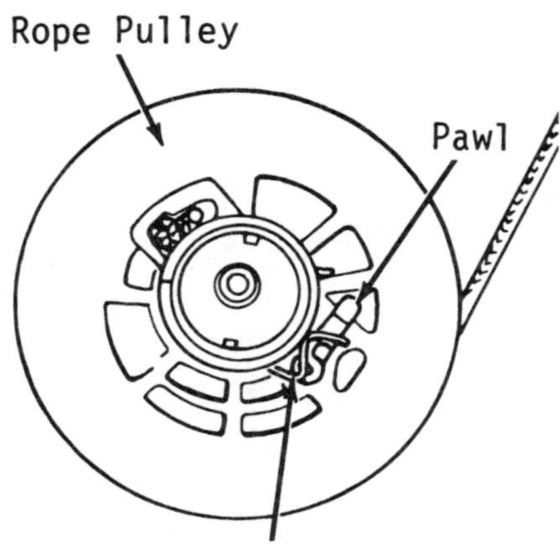

Fig. MK16—View showing proper engagement of the starter pawl and brake spring.

turns counterclockwise before inserting the rope through the guide hole in the housing and install the handle.

To check for spring preload, pull the rope out to its full extension and check that pulley can be turned an additional 1/2 turn without causing the spring to bind. Allow the rope to rewind and make sure the handle is pulled against the housing. If the spring binds, remove some spring preload and recheck. If the handle is not wound against the housing, increase the preload and recheck.

CHAIN BRAKE. The chain brake assembly is designed to stop the chain quickly should kickback occur. The chain brake is activated when the operator's hand strikes the hand guard (1—Fig. MK17). When the brake system is activated, spring (8) tightens the brake band (9) around the clutch drum. To release, pull the hand guard back until the mechanism is reset.

The chain brake must be released before the housing (10) can be removed. To disassemble, remove cover plate (3). Lift out brake band (9), spring (8), linkage (6) and lever (5).

Lubricate all of the pivot points with suitable low temperature grease when assembling. No adjustment of the mechanism is required.

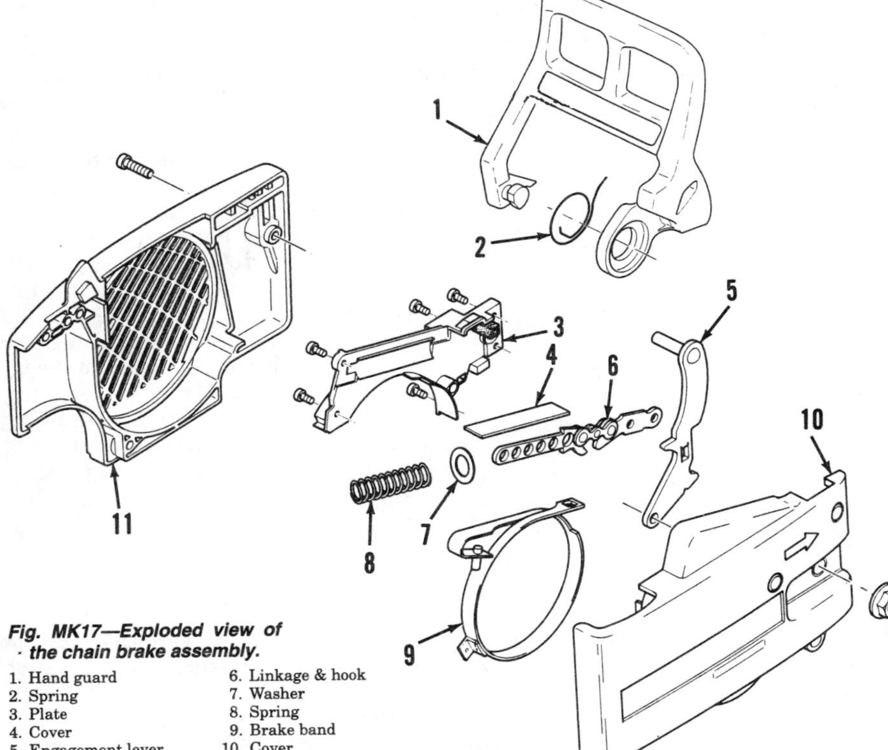

Fig. MK17—Exploded view of the chain brake assembly.

1. Hand guard
2. Spring
3. Plate
4. Cover
5. Engagement lever
6. Linkage & hook
7. Washer
8. Spring
9. Brake band
10. Cover

MAKITA

Model	Bore mm (in.)	Stroke mm (in.)	Displacement cc (cu. in.)	Drive Type
DCS430	40 (1.57)	34 (1.34)	43 (2.62)	Direct
DCS520i	44 (1.73)	34 (1.34)	52 (3.17)	Direct
DCS5200i	44 (1.73)	34 (1.34)	52 (3.17)	Direct

MAINTENANCE

SPARK PLUG. Recommended spark plug is Bosch WSR-6F or NGK BPMR-7A. Electrode gap should be 0.5 mm (0.020 in.) for all models. The spark plug should be tightened to the torque listed in the TIGHTENING TORQUE paragraph.

CARBURETOR. Walbro WT 76 carburetor is used on 430 models; Tillotson HU 83C or HU 83D carburetor is used on 520i and 5200i models. Refer to the appropriate Tillotson or Walbro section of the CARBURETOR SERVICE section in this manual for service and exploded views.

Refer to Fig. MK21 for the location of the carburetor adjustments. Initial setting of the low-speed mixture needle for all models is 1 turn open from lightly seated. Initial setting of the high-speed mixture needle for DCS 430 models is 1 turn open from lightly seated. Initial setting for DCS520i and DCS5200i models is 1-1/8 turn open from lightly seated.

To adjust the mixture needles, first remove and clean the air filter, then reinstall it. Start the engine and allow it to run until it reaches normal operating temperature. If necessary, turn each of the mixture needles clockwise until seated lightly, then back the needles out (counterclockwise) to the initial setting so the engine can be started.

Turn the idle speed stop screw so the engine idles at about 2,500 rpm. Adjust the low-speed mixture needle so the engine idles smoothly and accelerates without hesitation. Adjust the idle speed to just slower than clutch engagement speed, then recheck low-speed mixture adjustment.

Adjust the high-speed mixture needle to provide the best performance while operating at maximum speed under load. The high-speed mixture needle may be set slightly rich to improve performance under load. The engine may be damaged if the high-speed mixture is set too lean.

Final adjustment of the mixture needles should be within 1/4 turn of the initial settings. Large differences may indicate air leaks, plugged passages or other problems.

To remove carburetor, first remove filter cover (1—Fig. MK22) and air filter (2). Disconnect fuel line from the carburetor. Remove carburetor mounting screws. Lift out carburetor and disconnect choke lever (8) and throttle linkage (15). When installing carburetor, tighten the carburetor attaching screws to the torque listed in the TIGHTENING TORQUE paragraph.

IGNITION. All models are equipped with a breakerless electronic ignition system. All electronic circuitry is contained in a one-piece ignition module/coil located outside the flywheel. Ignition timing is fixed and not adjustable. The flywheel attaching nut should be tightened to the torque listed in TIGHTENING TORQUE paragraph.

Air gap between the legs of the module/coil and the flywheel magnets should be 0.2-0.3 mm (0.008-0.012 in.). When installing, set the air gap between the flywheel magnets and the legs of the ignition module as follows.

Install the ignition module, but tighten the two screws only enough to hold it in place away from the flywheel. Insert setting gauge (part No. 944 500 890) or brass/plastic shim stock of the proper thickness between the legs of the ignition module and the flywheel, then turn the flywheel until the flywheel magnets are near the module legs. Loosen the screws attaching the ignition module and press legs of the ignition module against the setting gauge. Tighten the two attaching screws to the torque listed in the TIGHTENING TORQUE paragraph.

Remove the setting gauge, then turn the flywheel and check that flywheel does not hit the legs of the coil.

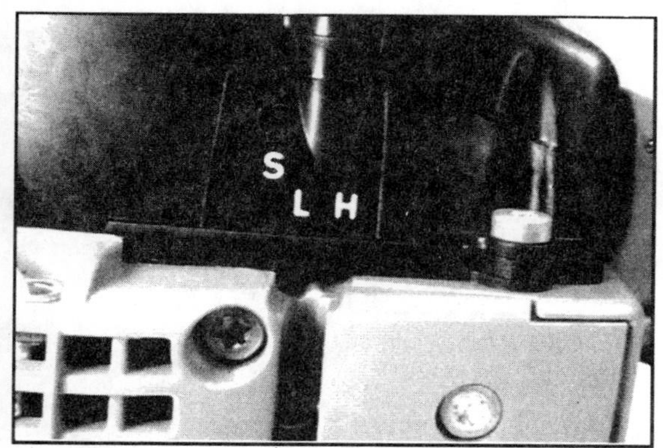

Fig. MK21—View showing location of the carburetor adjustment screws. The idle speed stop screw is located at "S," low-speed mixture needle at "L" and high-speed mixture needle at "H."

LUBRICATION. The engine is lubricated by mixing oil with the gasoline fuel. The manufacturer recommends mixing MAKITA two-stroke oil with regular grade gasoline at a ratio of 40:1 after break-in. When using regular two-stroke engine oil, mix at a ratio of 25:1. During the initial break-in the fuel to oil ratio should be 30:1 when using MAKITA oil or 20:1 when using other approved oil.

Use a separate container to mix gasoline and oil before filling the fuel tank. The manufacturer recommends not using fuel containing alcohol.

Fig. MK22—Exploded view of engine intake components.

1. Filter cover
2. Air filter element
3. Cylinder cover
4. Seal
5. Gasket
6. Filter lower housing
7. Carburetor heat plug
8. Choke lever
9. Seal
10. Intermediate flange
11. Gasket
12. Carburetor
13. Adjustment guide
14. Inlet elbow
15. Throttle link

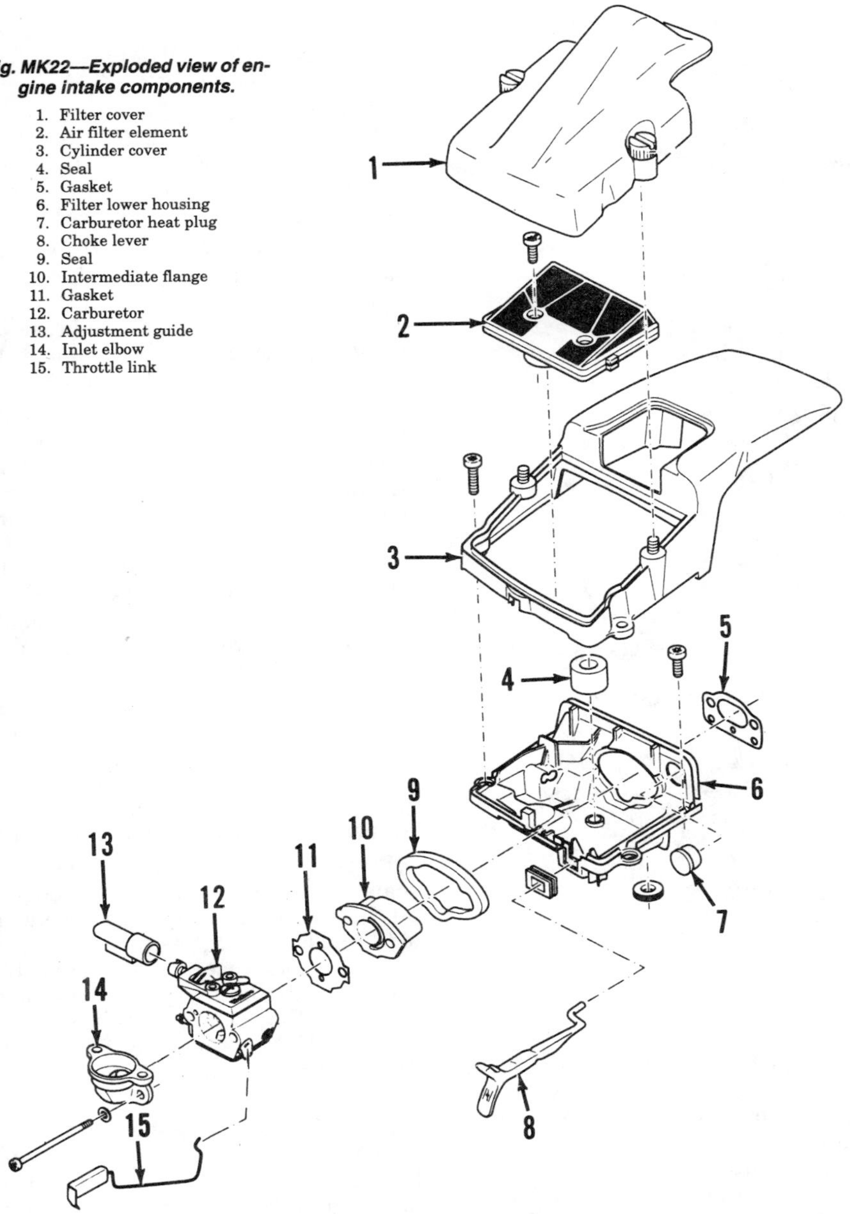

All saws are equipped with an automatic chain oiling system. The manufacturer recommends using MAKITA Saw Chain oil or other good quality oil designed for lubricating saw chain. Make sure the reservoir is filled at all times.

The volume of oil delivered by the pump is adjustable by turning screw (Fig. MK23). The screw is located under the saw on the right side.

Fig. MK23—The chain oil adjustment screw is located as shown. The chain and guide bar are removed for clarity. Turn the screw clockwise to reduce the amount of oil or counterclockwise to increase the amount of oil.

REPAIRS

TIGHTENING TORQUE. Recommended tightening torque values are as follows.

Carburetor attaching screws	5.0-5.5 N•m (44-48 in.-lb.)
Clutch hub	35.0-35.5 N•m (310-314 in.-lb.)
Crankcase	10-11 N•m (88.5-97 in.-lb.)
Cylinder	10-11 N•m (88.5-97 in.-lb.)
Flywheel	25-30 N•m (221-265 in.-lb.)
Ignition module/coil	6-7 N•m (53-62 in.-lb.)
Muffler	8.5-9.0 N•m (75-80 in.-lb.)
Spark plug	20-30 N•m (177-265 in.-lb.)
Tubular handle	2.7-3.0 N•m (23.9-26.5 in.-lb.)
Vibration isolator	1.8-2.2 N•m (15.9-19.5 in.-lb.)

PISTON, PIN, RINGS AND CYLINDER. Refer to Fig. MK24 for exploded view of typical engine. To remove cylinder, unbolt and remove air filter cover (1—Fig. MK22), cylinder cover (3), carburetor (12), intake flange (10), air filter bottom (6), muffler and top handle. Remove cylinder mounting screws and lift cylinder from crankcase and piston.

Models DCS 430 and DCS 431 are equipped with one piston ring and models DCS 520i and DCS5200i are equipped with two piston rings. Rings are pinned in the groove(s) of all models to prevent movement.

The piston pin (4—Fig. MK24) rides in a needle bearing (15) located in the small end of the connecting rod. The piston pin is retained in the piston by retainer rings (5) located in the piston at each end of the pin. Always install new retainer rings if they are removed and position the opening toward the bottom of the piston.

Inspect the cylinder bore for excessive wear or damage. Oversize parts are not available and the cylinder is available only with a matching piston.

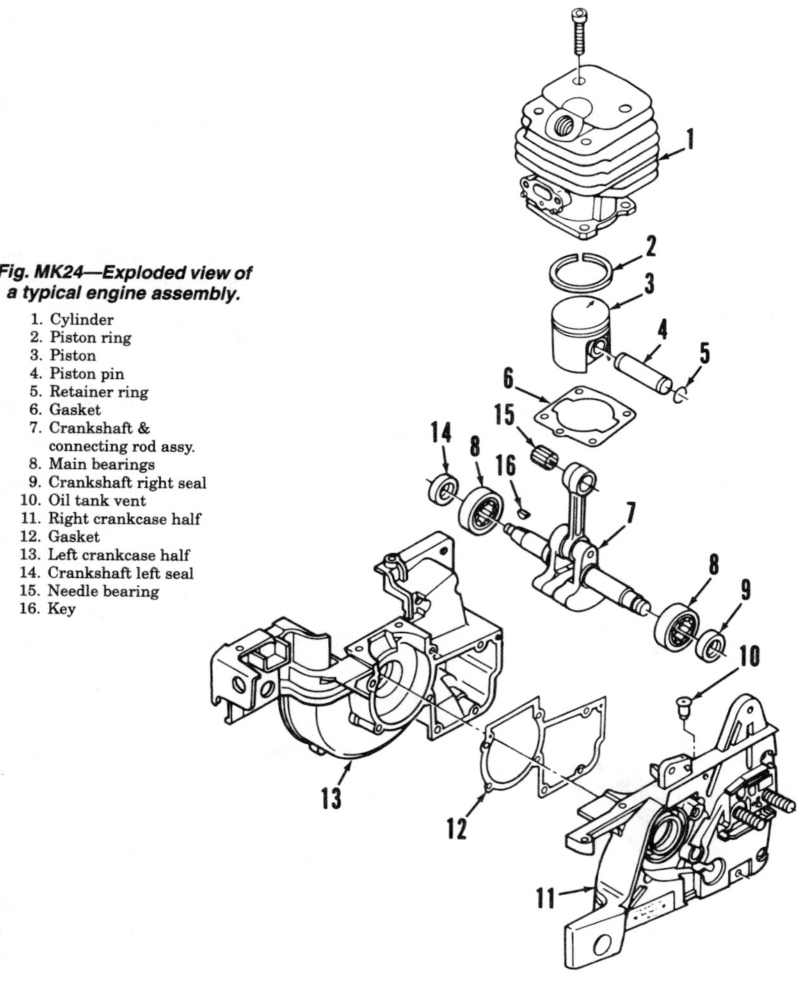

Fig. MK24—Exploded view of a typical engine assembly.

1. Cylinder
2. Piston ring
3. Piston
4. Piston pin
5. Retainer ring
6. Gasket
7. Crankshaft & connecting rod assy.
8. Main bearings
9. Crankshaft right seal
10. Oil tank vent
11. Right crankcase half
12. Gasket
13. Left crankcase half
14. Crankshaft left seal
15. Needle bearing
16. Key

Piston may be available separately, but the cylinder and piston are available as a matched set. Tops of the cylinder and piston for DCS 520i and DCS 5200i models are marked with "A, B," or "C" and both should have the same letter.

When assembling, make sure the arrow on the piston crown is visible and pointing toward the exhaust (muffler) side of the cylinder. A fork tool can be positioned between the bottom of the piston skirt and the crankcase to prevent movement of the piston when installing the cylinder.

Use a suitable ring compressor to compress the piston ring, making certain that the ring ends surround the locating pin. Lubricate cylinder with engine oil, then slide cylinder over the piston. Tighten the cylinder retaining screws to the torque listed in TIGHTENING TORQUE paragraph.

CRANKSHAFT, CONNECTING ROD AND CRANKCASE. The clutch, oil pump, pump drive worm, flywheel, cylinder, and piston must be removed before separating the crankcase halves.

Rotate the crankshaft in the crankcase main bearings and check for roughness before removing the crankshaft assembly. Tap the crankcase as necessary with a soft faced hammer to separate the crankcase halves.

The roller type main bearings (8—Fig. MK24) and shaft seals (9 and 14) are located in the case halves. Main bearings and shaft seals should be removed only if new parts will be installed in the case halves. Rotate the connecting rod around the crankpin while checking for roughness, excessive play or other damage. The crankshaft and connecting rod are a unit assembly and not available separately.

Do not remove the main bearings (8) from the crankcase unless it is necessary to install new bearings. Heat the case halves to approximately 100 degrees C (212 degrees F) before pressing the bearings from or into the case bores.

When assembling, lubricate the shaft seals and bearings with clean engine oil. Insert the crankshaft in the clutch side crankcase half, position a new gasket against the case, and then assemble the other case half. Tighten the screws attaching the crankcase halves to the torque listed in TIGHTENING TORQUE paragraph.

CLUTCH. The two-shoe centrifugal clutch uses a coil type garter spring (7—Fig. MK25). The clutch hub (6) is attached to the right end of the engine crankshaft with left-hand threads (turn clockwise to remove). A special tool should be used to grip the clutch hub while turning.

Remove spark plug and install an appropriate piston stopper in spark plug hole to prevent the crankshaft from turning. The clutch drum (3) can be withdrawn after the hub and shoes are removed. The original chain drive sprocket of some models may be integral with the clutch drum. A clutch drum with separate floating sprocket (8—Fig. MK25) is originally installed on most models and may be installed on other models.

Lightly lubricate the needle bearing located in the clutch drum before assembling. Tighten the clutch hub to the torque listed in TIGHTENING TORQUE paragraph.

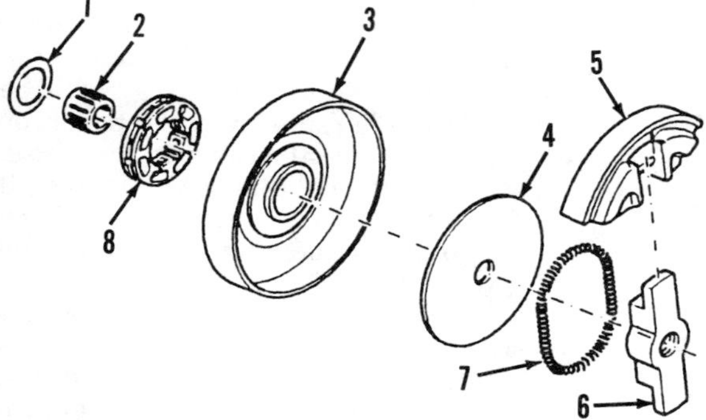

Fig. MK25—Exploded view of clutch typical of type used.

1. Stop disc
2. Needle bearing
3. Clutch drum
4. Special spacer
5. Clutch shoe
6. Clutch hub
7. Spring
8. Floating sprocket

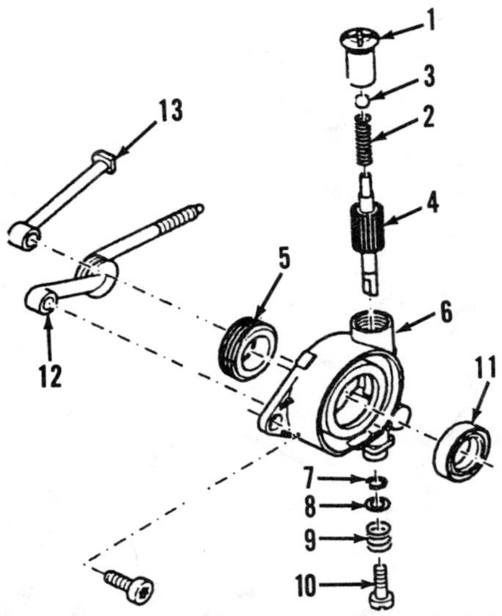

Fig. MK26—Exploded view of the automatic chain oil pump, typical of all models.

1. Plug
2. Spring
3. Ball
4. Plunger
5. Worm gear
6. Housing
7. "O" ring
8. Washer
9. Spring
10. Adjusting screw
11. Seal
12. Suction line to pump
13. Pressure line

OIL PUMP. All models are equipped with an automatic chain oil pump typical of the type shown in Fig. MK26. Oil is pumped by plunger (4), which is turned by worm gear (5). Pump output is adjusted by turning screw (10).

The oil pump can be unbolted and pulled from the engine after removing the clutch assembly. Oil suction and pressure lines can be inspected after the oil pump is removed. Install new hoses if cracked or leaking. Use suitable sealer on suction hose to prevent leakage. Special tool (part No. 957 433 000) should be used to pull the worm drive gear (5) from the crankshaft.

Inspect plunger (4), worm gear (5) and bore in pump housing (6) for wear of damage. If wear or damage is excessive, it is suggested that a new pump assembly and worm drive gear be installed.

To install the worm gear, screw the worm gear onto special tool (part No. 957 433 000), then heat the worm gear to approximately 100 degrees C (212 degrees F). Position the worm gear on the crankshaft until the tool is bottomed, allow the worm gear to cool, then remove the special tool leaving the worm on the crankshaft.

REWIND STARTER. Refer to Fig. MK27 for exploded view typical of the starter used. The starter assembly can be unbolted and removed from the engine.

If the rewind spring is under pressure, remove the assembly from the engine. Pull the rope out about 20 cm (8 in.), hold the pulley (5) and unwind the rope from the pulley. Allow the pulley to slowly unwind.

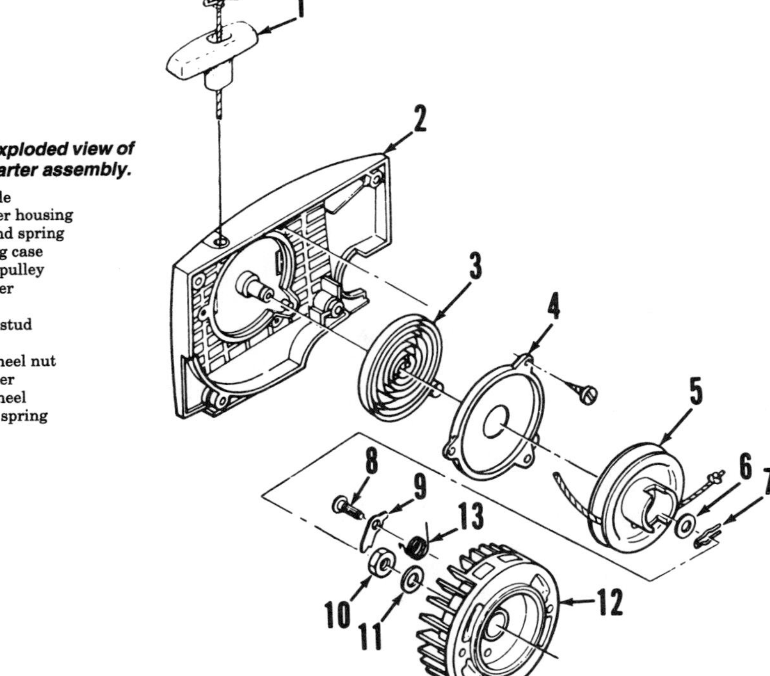

Fig. MK27—Exploded view of the rewind starter assembly.

1. Handle
2. Starter housing
3. Rewind spring
4. Spring case
5. Rope pulley
6. Washer
7. Clip
8. Pawl stud
9. Pawl
10. Flywheel nut
11. Washer
12. Flywheel
13. Pawl spring

Remove clip (7) and washer (6), then slide pulley (5) from the shaft. Make sure that rewind spring is completely unwound before removing the pulley.

If damaged, 98 cm of new 3.5 mm diameter rope should be attached to the pulley. Make sure the knot is properly nested in the pulley.

If not damaged, the rewind spring (3) should remain in spring case (4) after the case is detached from the housing. Inspect the spring to make sure that both ends are in good condition and the spring is not broken. If the spring is removed from the spring case, it should be wound into the case in a counterclockwise direction starting with the outer coil.

New spring and case are available as an assembly with the spring installed in the case. Attach the spring case to the housing with the spring installed.

Install the pulley (5) with rope attached. The pulley should engage the inner end of the spring (3). Install washer (6) and clip (7). Wind rope onto the pulley, preload the pulley approximately 2 turns, insert the end of the rope through guide in the housing, and then attach the handle (1).

Pull the rope out fully and check that pulley can be turned an additional 1/2 turn without causing the spring to bind. Allow the rope to rewind and make sure the handle is pulled against the housing. If the spring binds, remove some spring preload and recheck. If the handle is not pulled against the housing, increase the preload and recheck.

Inspect the condition of the pawl (9) and spring (13), then replace parts as necessary. The stud should be pressed into the flywheel after coating the surface of the stud and bore with locking agent (part No. 980 009 000 or equivalent).

CHAIN BRAKE. The chain brake assembly is designed to stop the chain quickly should kickback occur. The chain brake is activated when the operator's hand strikes the hand guard (1—Fig. MK28). When the brake system is activated, spring (17) draws the brake band (13) tight around the clutch drum. To release, pull the hand guard back until the mechanism is reset.

The chain brake must be released before the housing (6) can be removed. To disassemble, insert a screwdriver through slot in cover plate (16—Fig. MK28) and release chain brake. Remove retaining rings (10 and 18) and screws attaching cover plate to housing (6). Unhook brake spring (17) and withdraw brake band assembly (13).

Inspect and renew components as necessary. Lubricate all of the pivot

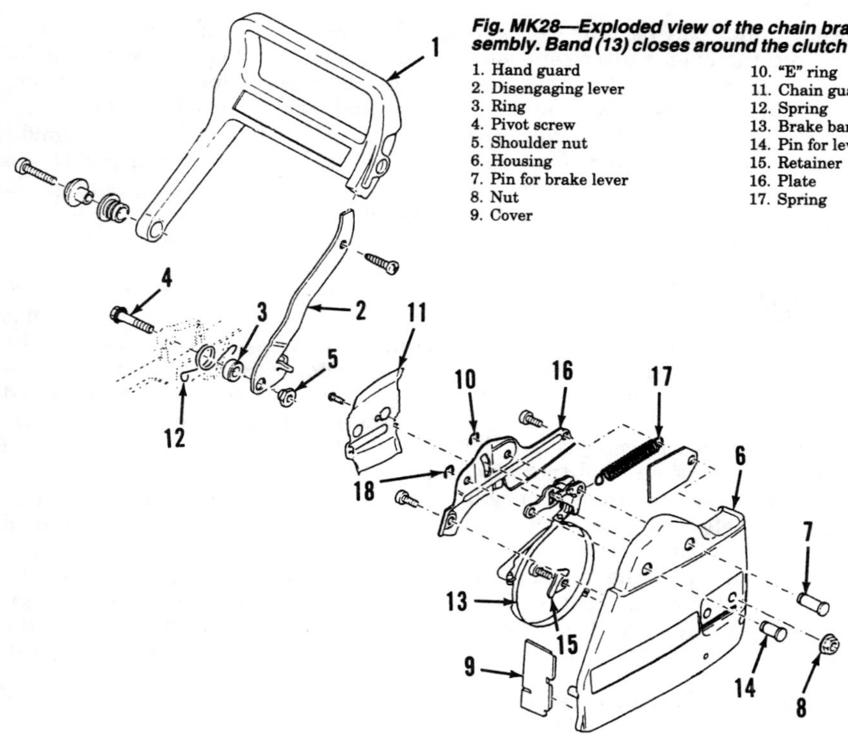

Fig. MK28—Exploded view of the chain brake assembly. Band (13) closes around the clutch drum.

1. Hand guard
2. Disengaging lever
3. Ring
4. Pivot screw
5. Shoulder nut
6. Housing
7. Pin for brake lever
8. Nut
9. Cover
10. "E" ring
11. Chain guard
12. Spring
13. Brake band assy.
14. Pin for lever
15. Retainer
16. Plate
17. Spring

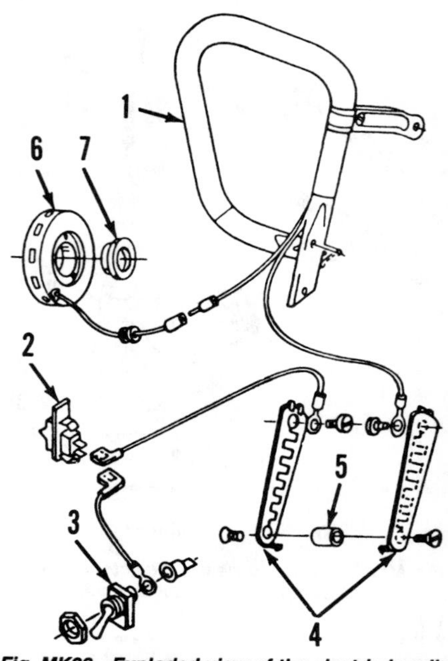

Fig. MK29—Exploded view of the electric handle heating system available on some models. Generator coil (6) is located behind the flywheel.

1. Front handle & heating attachment
2. Heater switch
3. Ignition switch
4. Rear grip heater elements
5. Connector
6. Generator
7. Centering guide

points with suitable low temperature grease when assembling. No adjustment of the mechanism is required.

HEATED HANDLES. Some models are equipped with electrically heated handles. A generator coil (6—Fig MK29), located behind the generator, supplies electrical current. Switch (2) completes the circuit to ground, allowing the current to heat the handle (1) and elements (4).

MAKITA

Model	Bore mm (in.)	Stroke mm (in.)	Displacement cc (cu. in.)	Drive Type
DCS6000i	46 (1.81)	36 (1.42)	60 (3.66)	Direct
DCS6800iFL	49 (1.93)	36 (1.42)	68 (4.15)	Direct
DCS6800iFW	49 (1.93)	36 (1.42)	68 (4.15)	Direct

MAINTENANCE

SPARK PLUG. Recommended spark plug is Bosch WSR-5F. Electrode gap should be 0.5 mm (0.020 in.). The spark plug should be tightened to the torque listed in the TIGHTENING TORQUE paragraph.

CARBURETOR. Tillotson HS-236 carburetor is used. Refer to the appropriate Tillotson section of the CARBURETOR SERVICE section in this manual for service and exploded views.

To remove carburetor, first remove air filter cover (1—Fig. MK30) and filter element (2). Remove carburetor mounting screws. Disconnect fuel line and throttle link. Remove intake elbow (14) and carburetor (12).

Refer to Fig. MK31 for the location of the carburetor adjustment screws. Initial setting of both the low-speed and high-speed mixture needles for all models is 1 turn open from lightly seated.

To adjust the mixture needles, first remove and clean the air filter, then reinstall it. Start the engine and allow it to run until it reaches normal operating temperature. If necessary, turn each of the mixture needles clockwise until seated lightly, then back the needles out (counterclockwise) to the initial setting so the engine can be started.

Turn the idle speed stop screw so the engine idles at about 2,400 rpm. Adjust the low-speed mixture needle so the engine idles smoothly and accelerates without hesitation. Adjust the idle speed to just slower than clutch engagement speed, then recheck low-speed mixture adjustment.

Adjust the high-speed mixture needle to provide the best performance while operating at maximum speed under load. Maximum no-load speed (with bar and chain installed) is 13,000 rpm for PS6000i models or 12,500 rpm for PS6800i models. The high-speed mixture needle may be set slightly rich to improve performance under load. The engine may be damaged if the high-speed mixture is set too lean.

Final adjustment of the mixture needles should be within 1/4 turn of the initial settings. Large differences may indicate air leaks, plugged passages or other problems. Make certain that hot air shutter (4—Fig. MK30) is closed during warm weather operation.

IGNITION. All models are equipped with a breakerless electronic ignition

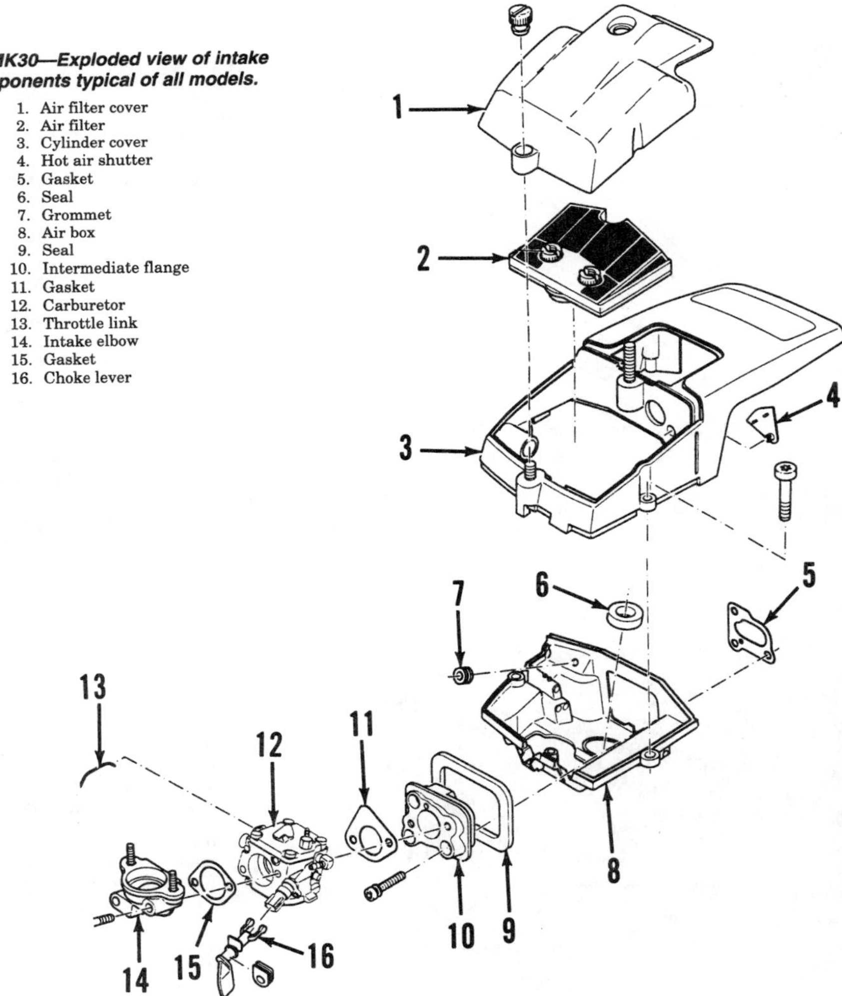

Fig. MK30—Exploded view of intake components typical of all models.

1. Air filter cover
2. Air filter
3. Cylinder cover
4. Hot air shutter
5. Gasket
6. Seal
7. Grommet
8. Air box
9. Seal
10. Intermediate flange
11. Gasket
12. Carburetor
13. Throttle link
14. Intake elbow
15. Gasket
16. Choke lever

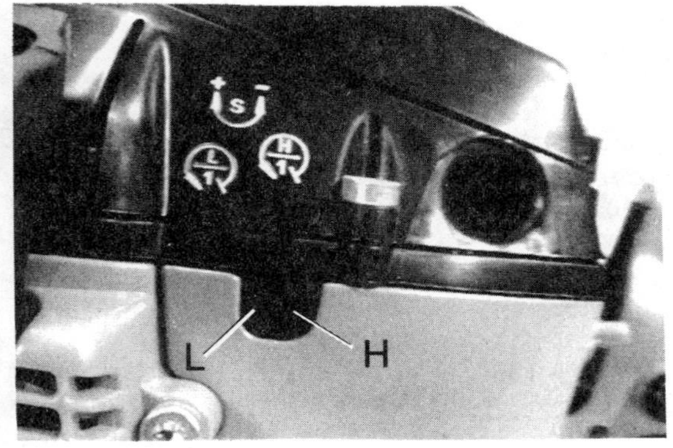

Fig. MK31—View showing location of the carburetor adjustment screws. The idle speed stop screw is located at "S," low-speed mixture needle at "L" and high-speed mixture needle at "H."

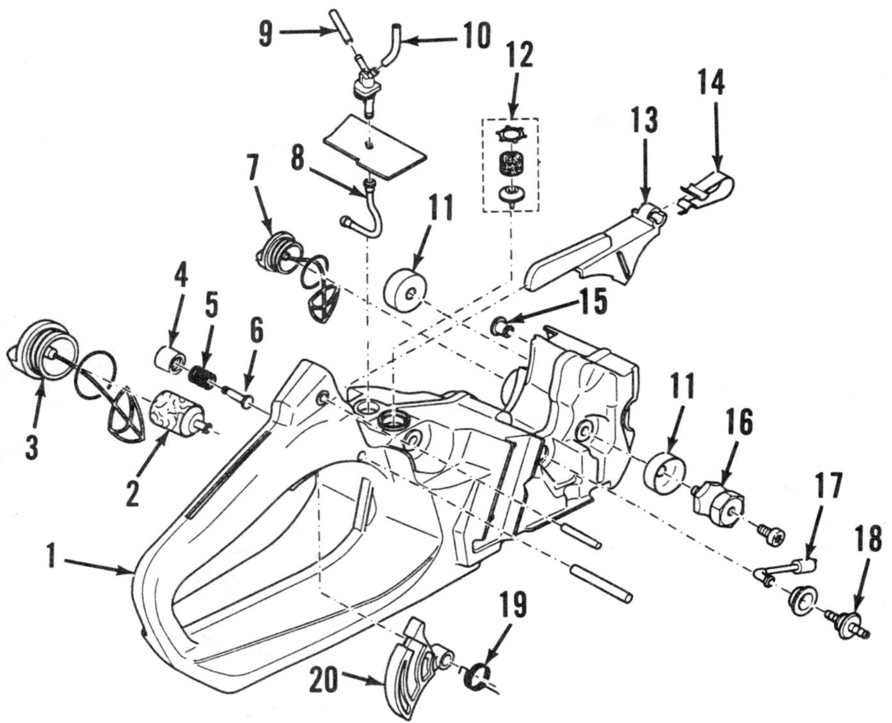

Fig. MK32—Exploded view of fuel tank/rear handle and related components.

1. Fuel tank/handle
2. Filter
3. Fuel tank cap
4. Half-throttle lock button
5. Spring
6. Stop pin
7. Oil tank cap
8. Fuel suction line
9. Vent line
10. Fuel supply line
11. Cup
12. Vent valve
13. Throttle latch
14. Spring
15. Vent valve
16. Vibration isolator
17. Oil suction line
18. Hose fitting
19. Return spring
20. Throttle trigger

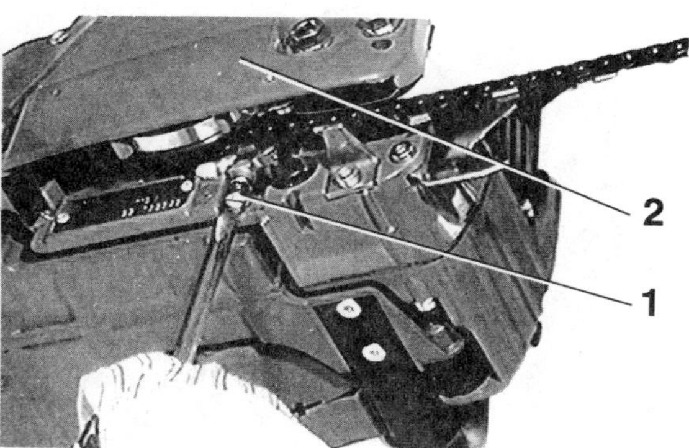

Fig. MK33—The chain oil adjustment screw (1) is located in the housing underneath the sprocket guard (2). Turn the screw clockwise to reduce the amount of oil or counterclockwise to increase the amount of oil.

system. All electronic circuitry is contained in a one-piece ignition module/coil located outside the flywheel. Ignition timing is fixed and not adjustable.

Air gap between the legs of the module/coil and the flywheel magnets should be 0.15 mm (0.006 in.). When installing, set the air gap between the flywheel magnets and the legs of the ignition module as follows.

Install the ignition module, but tighten the two screws only enough to hold it in place away from the flywheel. Insert setting gauge (part No. 944 500 890) or brass/plastic shim stock of the proper thickness between the legs of the ignition module and the flywheel, then turn the flywheel until the flywheel magnets are near the module legs. Loosen the screws attaching the ignition module and press legs of the ignition module against the setting gauge. Tighten the two attaching screws to the torque listed in the TIGHTENING TORQUE paragraph. Remove the setting gauge, then turn the flywheel and check that flywheel does not hit the legs of the coil.

LUBRICATION. The engine is lubricated by mixing oil with the gasoline fuel. The manufacturer recommends mixing MAKITA two-stroke oil with regular grade gasoline at a ratio of 40:1 after break-in. When using regular two-stroke engine oil, mix at a ratio of 25:1. During the initial break-in (first 10 hours) the fuel to oil ratio should be 30:1 when using MAKITA oil or 20:1 when using other approved oil. Use a separate container to mix gasoline and oil before filling the fuel tank.

A fuel filter (2—Fig. MK32) is located in the fuel tank. Filter should be inspected periodically for contamination and replaced as necessary. Filter can be pulled out through tank filler opening using a piece of wire bent at one end to form a hook.

All saws are equipped with an automatic chain oiling system. The manufacturer recommends using MAKITA Saw Chain oil or other good quality oil designed for lubricating saw chain. Make sure the reservoir is filled at all times.

The volume of oil delivered by the automatic oil pump is adjustable by turning screw (Fig. MK33) located under the saw on the right side. The engine must be stopped before turning the adjusting screw. Turn the screw clockwise to reduce the amount of oil or counterclockwise to increase the amount of oil.

REPAIRS

TIGHTENING TORQUE. Recommended tightening torque values are as follows.

Carburetor attaching screws	5.0-7.0 N•m (44-62 in.-lb.)
Clutch hub	52.5-57.5 N•m (460-509 in.-lb.)
Crankcase	10-11 N•m (88.5-97 in.-lb.)
Cylinder	11.5-12.5 N•m (102-110 in.-lb.)
Flywheel	27.5-30.0 N•m (243-265 in.-lb.)
Ignition module/coil	3.0-4.0 N•m (26.6-35 in.-lb.)
Intermediate flange (intake)	5.5-6.5 N•m (48.5-57.5 in.-lb.)
Muffler	8.0-9.0 N•m (71-79.7 in.-lb.)
Spark plug	20-30 N•m (177-265 in.-lb.)
Tubular handle	4.5-5.5 N•m (40-48.7 in.-lb.)
Vibration isolator	7.0-8.0 N•m (62-70.8 in.-lb.)

PISTON, PIN, RINGS AND CYLINDER. The cylinder can be removed after removal of the air box cover (1—Fig. MK30), air cleaner (2), carburetor (12), cylinder cover (3), intake manifold (10), air box (8) and muffler. Remove four screws attaching cylinder (1—Fig. MK34) to crankcase and withdraw cylinder from piston.

The piston pin (4—Fig. MK34) rides in a needle bearing (6) located in the small end of the connecting rod. The piston pin is retained in the piston by retainer rings (5) located in the piston at each end of the pin. Remove retaining ring and push pin from piston to separate piston from connecting rod. Always install new retaining rings if they are removed.

Inspect the cylinder bore for excessive wear or damage. Oversize parts are not available and the cylinder is available only with a matching piston. Pistons may be available separately. Tops of the cylinder and piston are marked with "A, B," or "C" and both should have the same letter.

The piston is equipped with two piston rings (2) that are prevented from rotating in their grooves by locating pins. When assembling, make sure the arrow on the piston crown is visible and pointing toward the exhaust (muffler) side of the cylinder. Make certain that piston pin retainer (5) is seated in the groove, and position the opening toward the bottom of the piston.

Slide a fork tool or a piece of wood between the bottom of the piston skirt and the crankcase to hold the piston up while installing the cylinder. Use a suitable ring compressor to compress the piston rings. Make certain that the ring ends surround the locating pins. Lubricate cylinder with engine oil and slide cylinder over the piston. Tighten the cylinder retaining screws to the torque listed in TIGHTENING TORQUE paragraph.

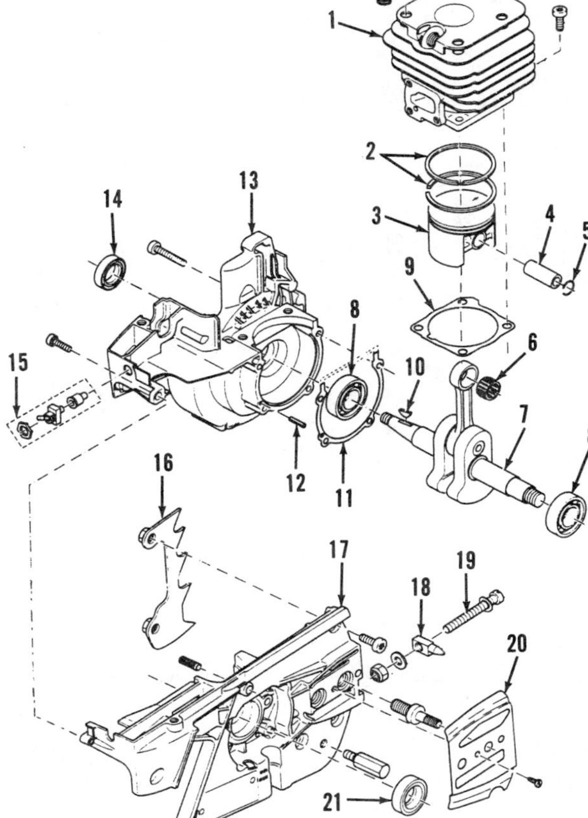

Fig. MK34—Exploded view of the engine assembly typical of all models.

1. Cylinder
2. Piston rings
3. Piston
4. Piston pin
5. Retaining ring
6. Needle bearing
7. Crankshaft & connecting rod
8. Ball bearings
9. Gasket
10. Wooodruff key
11. Gasket
12. Dowel
13. Crankcase left half
14. Seal
15. Engine stop switch
16. Spike bar
17. Crankcase right half
18. Nut w/pin
19. Chain adjusting screw
20. Guide plate
21. Seal

CRANKSHAFT, CONNECTING ROD AND CRANKCASE. To remove crankshaft and connecting rod assembly, remove the starter housing, flywheel and ignition coil/module from left side. Remove cylinder cover, carburetor, air box, cylinder and piston from the top. Remove bar and chain, chain brake assembly, clutch, oil pump and pump drive worm from right side. Remove fuel tank/rear handle (1—Fig. MK32) from crankcase.

Rotate the crankshaft in the crankcase main bearings and check for roughness before removing the crankshaft assembly. Tap the crankcase as necessary with a soft faced hammer to separate the crankcase halves (13 and 17—Fig. MK34).

The ball type main bearings (8—Fig. MK34) and shaft seals (14 and 21) are located in the case halves. Main bearings and shaft seals should be removed only if new parts will be installed in the case halves.

Rotate the connecting rod around the crankpin while checking for roughness, excessive play or other damage. The crankshaft and connecting rod are a unit assembly and not available separately.

If main bearings (8) are to be removed from the crankcase, heat the case halves to approximately 100 degrees C (212 degrees F) before pressing the bearings from or into the case bores.

When assembling, lubricate the shaft seals and bearings with clean engine oil. Insert the crankshaft in the clutch (right) side crankcase half, position a new gasket against the case, and assemble the other case half. Tighten the screws attaching the crankcase halves to the torque listed in TIGHTENING TORQUE paragraph.

CLUTCH. A two-shoe centrifugal clutch with a coil type garter spring (2—Fig. MK35) is used. The clutch hub (1) is attached to the right end of the engine crankshaft with left-hand threads (turn clockwise to remove).

To remove clutch, first remove sprocket guard and chain brake assembly. Remove bar and chain. Remove spark plug and install a suitable piston stop tool or length of rope in spark plug

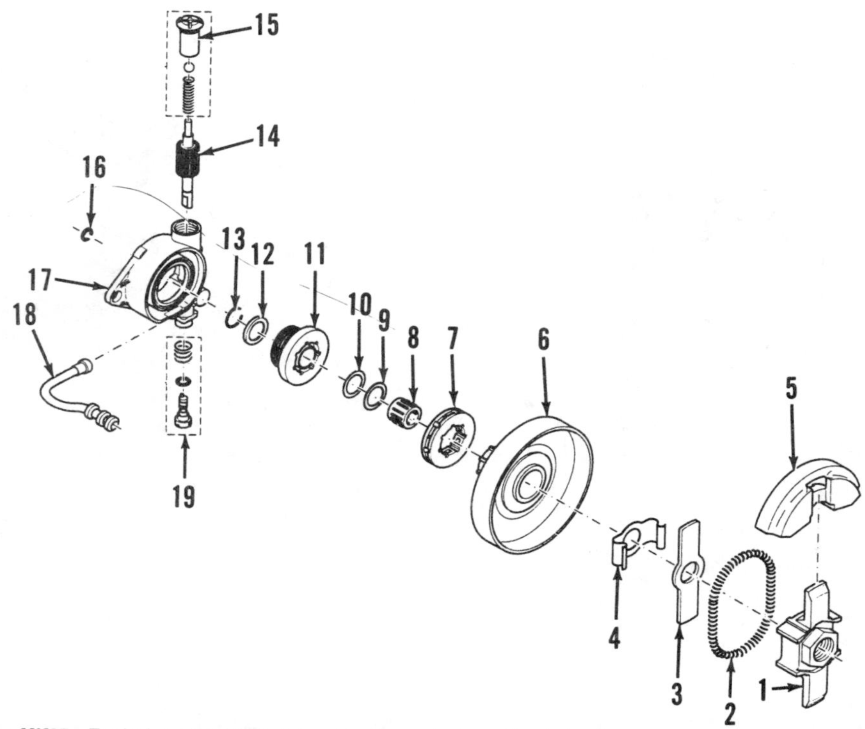

Fig. MK35—Exploded view of clutch assembly and automatic chain oil pump assembly typical of all models.

1. Clutch hub
2. Spring
3. Guide plate
4. Clamp
5. Clutch shoes
6. Clutch drum
7. Sprocket
8. Needle bearing
9. Spacer washer
10. Spacer washer
11. Worm gear
12. Stop ring
13. Spring clip
14. Oil pump plunger
15. Plug, ball & spring
16. "O" ring
17. Oil pump housing
18. Suction line
19. Adjusting screw

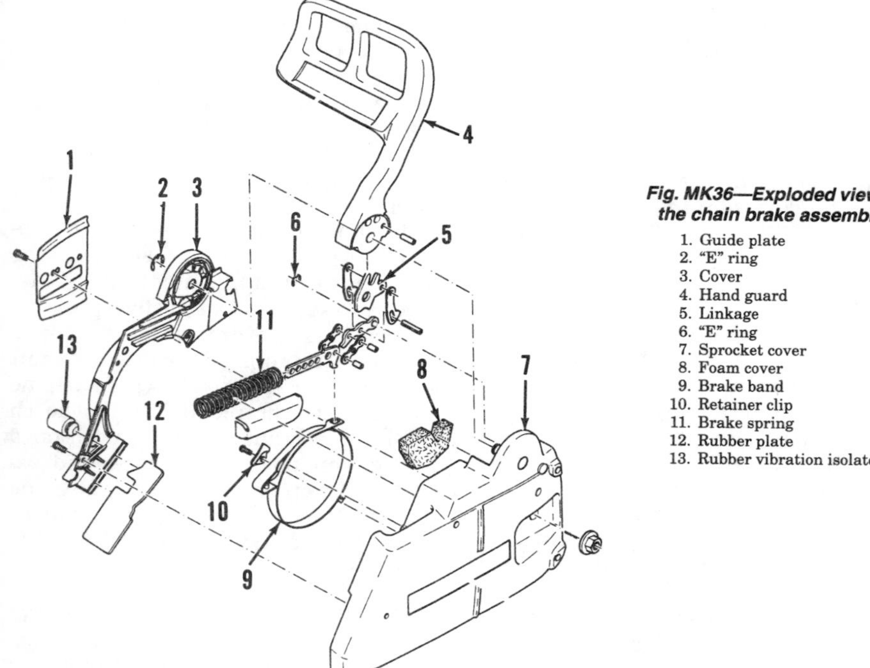

Fig. MK36—Exploded view of the chain brake assembly.

1. Guide plate
2. "E" ring
3. Cover
4. Hand guard
5. Linkage
6. "E" ring
7. Sprocket cover
8. Foam cover
9. Brake band
10. Retainer clip
11. Brake spring
12. Rubber plate
13. Rubber vibration isolator

hole to prevent the crankshaft from turning. The clutch hub can be turned using a 17 mm socket wrench. The clutch drum (6) can be withdrawn after the hub and shoes are removed. The chain drive floating sprocket (7) is splined to the clutch drum.

When assembling, install the smaller spacer (10) next to the oil pump, with the larger spacer (9) next to the clutch drum. Grease the needle bearing (8) lightly before assembling the bearing and drum. Assemble the clutch shoes (5), and spring (2) on the hub (1), making sure that the connection of the spring is centered in one of the shoes. Assemble thrust plate (3) and clamp (4). Install the clutch assembly, tightening the hub to the torque listed in TIGHTENING TORQUE paragraph.

OIL PUMP. All models are equipped with an automatic chain oil pump typical of the type shown in Fig. MK35. Oil is pumped by plunger (14), which is turned by worm gear (11). Pump output is adjusted by turning screw (19).

The oil pump can be unbolted and pulled from the engine after removing the clutch assembly. Oil suction and pressure lines can be inspected after the oil pump is removed. Install new hoses if cracked or leaking. Use suitable sealer on suction hose to prevent leakage.

Inspect plunger (14), worm gear (11) and bore in pump housing (17) for wear or damage. If wear or damage is excessive, it is suggested that a new pump assembly and worm drive gear be installed.

CHAIN BRAKE. The chain brake assembly is designed to stop the chain quickly should kickback occur. The chain brake is activated when the operator's hand strikes the hand guard (4—Fig. MK36). When the brake system is activated, spring (11) tightens the brake band (9) around the clutch drum. To release, pull the hand guard back until the mechanism is reset.

To remove the brake assembly, unbolt and remove sprocket guard (7) with chain brake components from the saw. Engage the chain brake by pushing hand guard (4) forward. Engaging the brake relaxes the spring (11). Remove cover plate (3). Separate hand guard with linkage, spring (11) and brake band (9) from sprocket guard.

Inspect parts and replace as necessary. No adjustment of the mechanism is required.

REWIND STARTER. Refer to Fig. MK37 for exploded view of typical starter. The starter can be removed as a unit by unbolting the housing (1).

To disassemble the starter, remove the rope handle and allow the rope to wind into the housing. Remove snap ring (7) and lift the rope pulley (6) from the housing. Be careful to prevent injury in case the spring (3) unwinds suddenly.

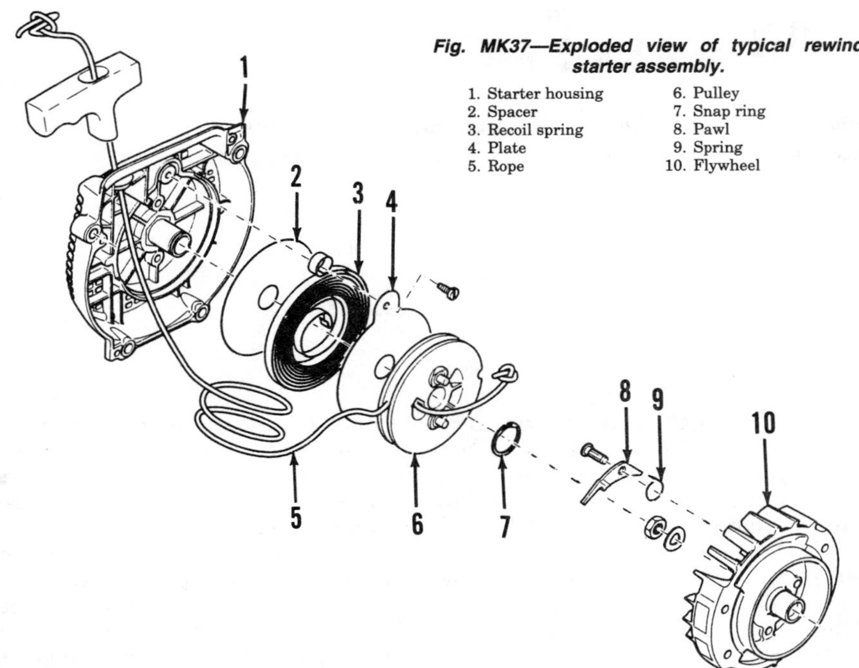

Fig. MK37—Exploded view of typical rewind starter assembly.

1. Starter housing
2. Spacer
3. Recoil spring
4. Plate
5. Rope
6. Pulley
7. Snap ring
8. Pawl
9. Spring
10. Flywheel

Clean and inspect parts for damage. The 4 mm diameter starter rope (5) should be 100 cm long. Replacement rewind spring (3) comes under tension in a wire retaining ring. Do not remove the retaining ring. Lightly lubricate the spring with grease.

To assemble, position spacer plate (2) in the housing cavity. If installing new rewind spring (3), push the spring with wire retainer into the housing. The wire retainer will slide off the spring as the spring is pushed into the housing. If installing original rewind spring, wind the spring into the housing in a clockwise direction beginning with the outside coil. Install the spacer plate (4) and secure with screw.

Wind the rope onto the pulley (6) in a clockwise direction as viewed from the flywheel side of pulley, then install over the post in housing. Preload the recoil spring by turning the pulley about 4 turns clockwise before passing the rope through the opening in the housing (1) and attaching the handle. Install snap ring (7) and check spring preload as follows.

Pull the rope out fully and check that pulley can be turned an additional 1/2 turn without causing the spring to bind. Allow the rope to rewind and make sure the handle is pulled against the housing. If the spring binds, remove some spring preload and recheck. If the handle is not wound against the housing, increase the preload and recheck.

Inspect the condition of the pawl (8—Fig. MK37) and spring (9) attached to the flywheel (10). The pawl stud should be pressed into the flywheel after coating the surface of the stud and bore with locking agent (part No. 980 009 000 or equivalent). Install a new flywheel if damaged.

MAKITA

Model	Bore mm (in.)	Stroke mm (in.)	Displacement cc (cu. in.)	Drive Type
DCS 9000FL, DCS 9000FW	52 (2.05)	42 (1.65)	90 (5.49)	Direct

MAINTENANCE

SPARK PLUG. Recommended spark plug is Bosch WSR-6F or NGK BPMR-7A. Electrode gap should be 0.5 mm (0.020 in.). The spark plug should be tightened to the torque listed in the TIGHTENING TORQUE paragraph.

CARBURETOR. Bing 49-B carburetor is used. Refer to the appropriate Bing section of the CARBURETOR SERVICE section for service and exploded views.

Initial setting of the low-speed and high-speed mixture needles is 1 turn open from lightly seated. To adjust the mixture needles, first remove and clean the air filter, then reinstall it. Start the engine and allow it to run until it reaches normal operating temperature. If necessary, turn each of the mixture needles (L and H—Fig. MK40) clockwise until seated lightly, then back the needles out (counterclockwise) to the initial setting so the engine can be started.

Turn the idle speed stop screw (S) so the engine idles at about 2,200 rpm. Adjust the low-speed mixture needle so the engine idles smoothly and accelerates without hesitation. Adjust the idle speed to just slower than clutch engagement speed, then recheck low-speed mixture adjustment.

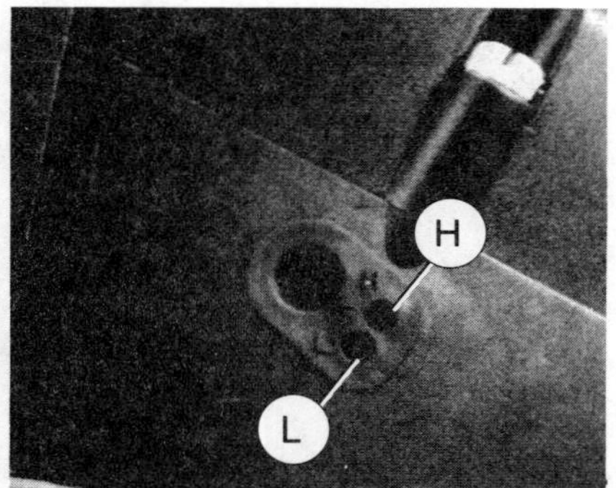

Fig. MK40—View showing location of the carburetor adjustment screws. The idle speed stop screw is located at "S," low-speed mixture needle at "L" and high-speed mixture needle at "H."

Adjust the high-speed mixture needle to provide the best performance while operating at maximum speed under load. Maximum no-load speed (with bar and chain installed) is 11,800 rpm. The high-speed mixture needle may be set slightly rich to improve performance under load. The engine may be damaged if the high-speed mixture is set too lean.

Final adjustment of the mixture needles should be within 1/4 turn of the initial settings. Large differences may indicate air leaks, plugged passages or other problems.

To remove carburetor, first remove air cleaner cover (1—Fig. MK41) and filter element (3). Unscrew stud nuts (4) and remove filter plate (5) and retainer plate (6). Disconnect fuel line,

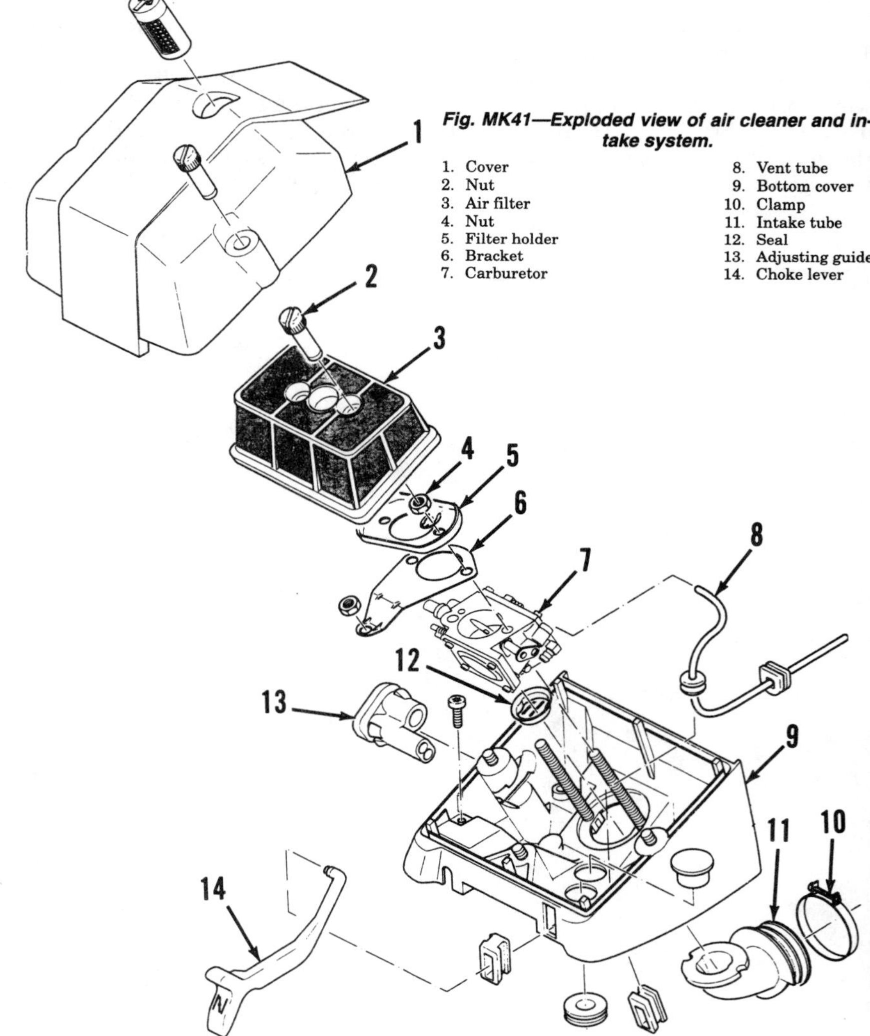

Fig. MK41—Exploded view of air cleaner and intake system.

1. Cover
2. Nut
3. Air filter
4. Nut
5. Filter holder
6. Bracket
7. Carburetor
8. Vent tube
9. Bottom cover
10. Clamp
11. Intake tube
12. Seal
13. Adjusting guide
14. Choke lever

Fig. MK42—The chain oil adjustment screw (1) is located underneath the saw. Turn the screw clockwise to reduce the amount of oil or counterclockwise to increase the amount of oil.

vent tube, choke lever and throttle cable. Remove the carburetor.

IGNITION. All models are equipped with a breakerless electronic ignition system. All electronic circuitry is contained in a one-piece ignition module/coil located outside the flywheel. Ignition timing is fixed and not adjustable. The ignition unit limits the engine speed to 11,800 rpm.

Air gap between the legs of the module/coil and the flywheel magnets should be 0.2 mm (0.008 in.). When installing, set the air gap between the flywheel magnets and the legs of the ignition module as follows.

Install the ignition module, but tighten the two screws only enough to hold it in place away from the flywheel. Insert setting gauge (part No. 944 500 890) or brass/plastic shim stock of the proper thickness between the legs of the ignition module and the flywheel, then turn the flywheel until the flywheel magnets are near the module legs. Loosen the screws attaching the ignition module and press legs of the ignition module against the setting gauge.

Tighten the two attaching screws to the torque listed in the TIGHTENING TORQUE paragraph. Remove the setting gauge, then turn the flywheel and check that flywheel does not hit the legs of the coil.

LUBRICATION. The engine is lubricated by mixing oil with the gasoline fuel. The manufacturer recommends mixing MAKITA two-stroke oil with regular grade gasoline at a ratio of 50:1 after break-in. When using regular two-stroke engine oil, mix at a ratio of 40:1. Always use a separate container to mix gasoline and oil before filling the fuel tank.

The saw is equipped with an automatic chain oiling system. An automatic oil pump supplies oil to the bar and chain. The manufacturer recommends using MAKITA Saw Chain oil or other good quality oil designed for lubricating saw chain. Make sure the reservoir is filled at all times.

The volume of oil delivered by the pump is adjustable by turning screw (Fig. MK42). The screw is located under the saw on the right side. Turn screw clockwise to decrease oil quantity or counterclockwise to increase oil flow.

REPAIRS

TIGHTENING TORQUE. Recommended tightening torque values are as follows.

Carburetor	6-7 N•m (53-62 in.-lb.)
Clutch hub	52.5-57.5 N•m (465-509 in.-lb.)
Crankcase	10-11 N•m (88.5-97 in.-lb.)
Cylinder	9-11 N•m (80-97 in.-lb.)
Flywheel	27.5-32.5 N•m (243-288 in.-lb.)
Ignition Module/coil	6-7 N•m (53-62 in.-lb.)
Intermediate flange (intake)	5.5-6.5 N•m (49-57.5 in.-lb.)
Muffler	8.0-12.0 N•m (71-106 in.-lb.)
Spark plug	24.5-25.5 N•m (217-226 in.-lb.)
Tubular handle	7-8 N•m (62-71 in.-lb.)
Vibration isolator	5-6 N•m (44-53 in.-lb.)

PISTON, PIN, RINGS AND CYLINDER. The cylinder can be removed after removal of the airbox cover (1—Fig. MK41, air cleaner (3), carburetor (7), bottom cover (9), cylinder cover, muffler, starter housing and sprocket guard. Remove four screws attaching cylinder to crankcase and withdraw cylinder from piston.

The piston pin is retained by wire retainer rings (9—Fig. MK43). Remove retaining rings and push pin (10) out of piston. Remove piston and needle bearing (8) from connecting rod. The piston is equipped with two piston rings (12) that are prevented from rotating in their grooves by locating pins.

The decompression valve (13) is installed in the cylinder to reduce engine compression during starting. The valve can be removed for cleaning, inspection and replacement.

Inspect the cylinder bore for excessive wear or damage. Oversize parts are not available. The piston is available separately, but the cylinder is only available with the proper piston. Tops of the cylinder and piston are marked with "A, B," or "C" and both should have the same letter.

When assembling, make sure the arrow on the piston crown is visible and pointing toward the exhaust (muffler) side of the cylinder. If retainer rings (9) are removed, always install new rings. Make certain that retaining rings are seated in the groove and position the opening toward the bottom of the piston.

Slide a fork tool or a piece of wood between the bottom of the piston skirt and the crankcase to hold the piston up while installing the cylinder. Use a suitable ring compressor to compress the piston rings, making certain that the ring end gap is aligned with the locating pin. Lubricate cylinder with engine oil and slide cylinder over the piston. Tighten the cylinder retaining screws to the torque listed in TIGHTENING TORQUE paragraph.

CRANKSHAFT, CONNECTING ROD AND CRANKCASE. The engine must be separated from the fuel tank/handle assembly (24—Fig. MK44) in order to service the crankshaft and connecting rod. The bar and chain, clutch, oil pump, pump drive worm, starter housing, flywheel, cylinder, and piston must be removed before separating the crankcase halves.

Rotate the crankshaft (7—Fig. MK43) in the main bearings (6) and check for roughness before removing the crankshaft assembly. Remove screws attaching crankcase halves together, then tap the crankcase as necessary with a soft faced hammer to separate the halves. DO NOT insert any type of pry bar between the crankcase halves as damage to the crankcase sealing surfaces could result.

The ball type main bearings (6) and shaft seals (2 and 21) are located in the case halves. Main bearings and shaft seals should be removed only if new parts will be installed in the case halves. Rotate the connecting rod around the crankpin while checking for roughness, excessive play or other damage. The crankshaft and connecting rod

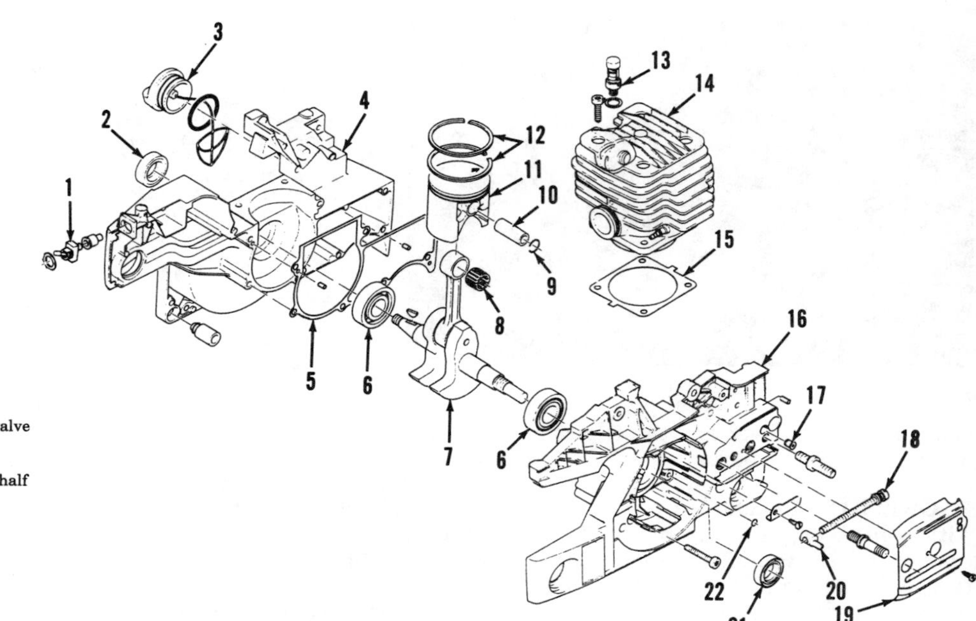

Fig. MK43—Exploded view of the cylinder, piston, cylinder and crankshaft assembly.

1. Stop switch
2. Seal
3. Oil tank cap
4. Crankcase left half
5. Gasket
6. Ball bearing
7. Crankshaft & connecting rod
8. Needle bearing
9. Retaining ring
10. Piston pin
11. Piston
12. Piston rings
13. Decompression valve
14. Cylinder
15. Base gasket
16. Crankcase right half
17. Oil tank vent
18. Chain adjuster
19. Guide plate
20. Adjuster nut
21. Seal
22. Seal ring

are a unit assembly and not available separately.

Do not remove the main bearings from the crankcase unless it is necessary to install new bearings. Heat the case halves to approximately 100 degrees C (212 degrees F) before pressing the bearings from or into the case bores. Install the main bearings before installing the seals. Special tools (part No. 944 603 360, 944 603 370 and 944 603 410 or equivalent) are required for installing new crankshaft seals.

When assembling, lubricate the shaft seals and bearings with clean engine oil. Insert the crankshaft through the clutch side crankcase half, position a new gasket against the case, and assemble the other case half. Tighten the screws attaching the crankcase halves to the torque listed in TIGHTENING TORQUE paragraph.

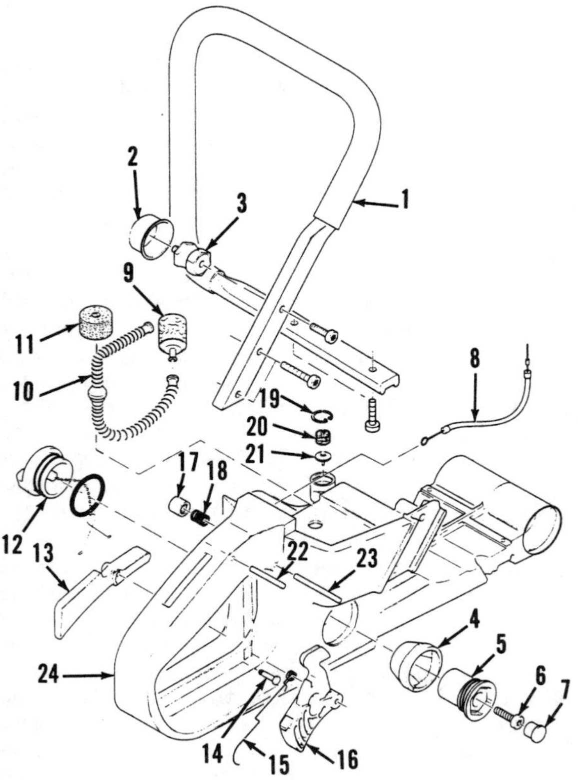

Fig. MK44—Exploded view of the fuel tank, handles and associated parts.

1. Tubular handle
2. Cup
3. Vibration isolator
4. Spacer (4 used)
5. Vibration isolator (4 used)
6. Screw
7. Plug
8. Throttle cable
9. Fuel filter
10. Fuel line
11. Seal
12. Cap
13. Throttle interlock
14. Pin
15. Return spring
16. Throttle trigger
17. Button
18. Spring
19. Snap ring
20. Filter
21. Air valve
22. Pin (3x28 mm)
23. Pin (3x45 mm)
24. Fuel tank & handle

CLUTCH. The three-shoe centrifugal clutch is shown in Fig. MK45. Remove sprocket guard (2) and bar and chain for access to the clutch.

The floating sprocket (9) and clutch drum (11) can be withdrawn after removing the "E" ring (6) and washers (7 and 8). The needle bearing (10) located in the clutch drum should be lubricated lightly before assembling.

The clutch hub (12) is attached to the right end of the engine crankshaft with left-hand threads (turn clockwise to remove). Special tool (part No. 944 603 420) should be used to grip the clutch hub while turning. Prevent the crankshaft from turning by using an appropriate piston stopper.

Clutch springs are available, but the shoes and hub are not available except as a complete clutch assembly. Tighten the clutch hub to the torque listed in TIGHTENING TORQUE paragraph.

OIL PUMP. The automatic chain oil pump is shown in Fig. MK45. Oil is pumped by plunger (32), which is turned by worm gear (23). Pump output is adjusted by turning screw (27). The oil pump can be unbolted and pulled from the engine after removing the chain brake assembly and clutch assembly.

Failure of the oil tank vent (17—Fig. MK43) or sealing ring (22) may cause oiling problems. The vent is removed by pushing it into the oil tank using a 4 mm diameter punch. Then, a 6 mm punch is used to press the new vent into

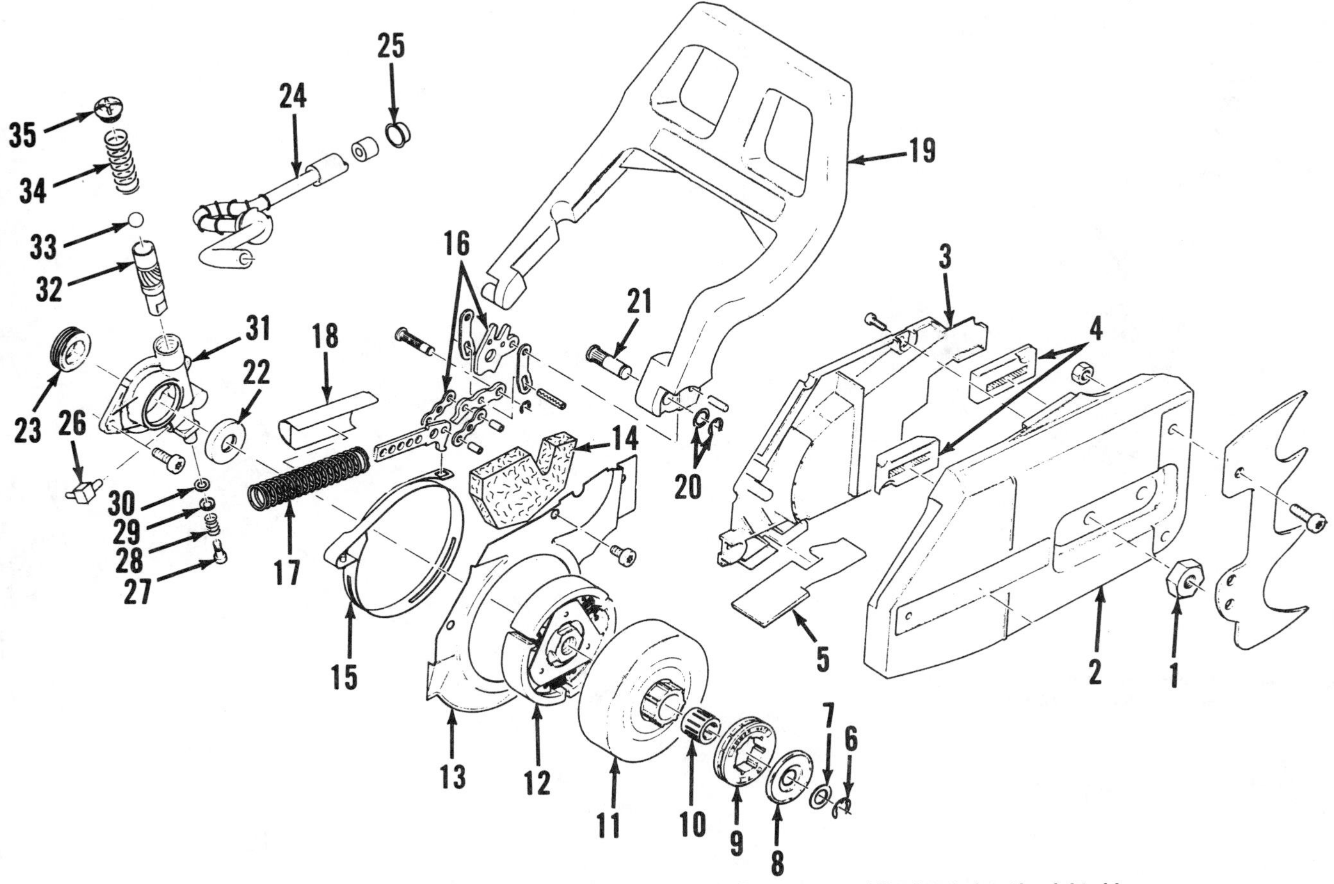

Fig. MK45—Exploded view of the clutch, chain brake and oil pump assemblies located on the right side.

1. Clamp nuts
2. Cover
3. Chip guide
4. Chain guide
5. Rubber plate
6. "E" ring
7. Washer
8. Washer
9. Sprocket
10. Needle bearing
11. Clutch drum
12. Clutch assembly
13. Plate
14. Foam
15. Brake band
16. Brake linkage
17. Brake spring
18. Spring guide
19. Hand guard
20. "E" ring & washer
21. Pin
22. Seal
23. Pump drive worm
24. Suction line
25. Filter screen
26. Elbow
27. Adjusting screw
28. Spring
29. Washer
30. Seal
31. Housing
32. Pump body
33. Ball
34. Spring
35. Plug

position. Lip of seal (22—Fig. MK45) should be toward clutch.

Use special tool (part No. 957 434 000 or equivalent) to remove and install the drive worm. To install the worm gear, screw the worm gear onto special tool, then heat the worm gear to approximately 100 degrees C (212 degrees F). Position the worm gear on the crankshaft until the tool is bottomed, allow the worm gear to cool, then remove the special tool leaving the worm on the crankshaft.

CHAIN BRAKE. The chain brake assembly is designed to stop the chain quickly should kickback occur. The chain brake is activated when the operator's hand strikes the hand guard (19—Fig. MK45). When the brake system is activated, spring (17) tightens the brake band (15) around the clutch drum (11). To release, pull the hand guard back until the mechanism is reset.

To remove the brake band (15), first remove the clutch drum (11) and clutch assembly (12). Engage the chain brake by pushing hand guard (19) forward. Engaging the brake after removing the clutch drum relaxes the spring (17) enough to remove the band. Install cover (part No. 944 603 390) over the spring to hold it in position, then unhook the ends of the chain brake and lift it out.

The spring (17) can be removed using pointed pliers after removing the temporarily installed cover. The brake linkage (16) can be disassembled and removed after removing "E" rings and pins.

Installation of the brake spring is easier using needle nose pliers (part No. 944 603 080 or equivalent) to compress the spring. Install the brake band by hooking the ends of the band over the mounting points. Install cover (part No. 944 603 390 or equivalent) before compressing the brake spring (releasing the brake band). The chain brake must be released before the clutch can be removed. No adjustment of the mechanism is required.

REWIND STARTER. Refer to Fig. MK46 for exploded view of the rewind starter. The starter assembly can be unbolted and removed from the engine.

If the recoil spring is under pressure, remove the starter from the engine. Pull the rope out about 20 cm (8 in.) and hold the pulley (5). Unwind the rope from the pulley, then allow the pulley to slowly unwind. Remove screw (7) and axle (6), then slide pulley (5) from the shaft. Make sure spring is completely unwound before removing the pulley.

If damaged, 100 cm of new 4 mm diameter rope should be attached to the pulley. Make sure the knot is properly nested in the pulley.

If not damaged, the rewind spring (3) can remain in spring case (4). Inspect the spring to make sure that both ends are in good condition and the spring is not broken. If the spring is removed, it

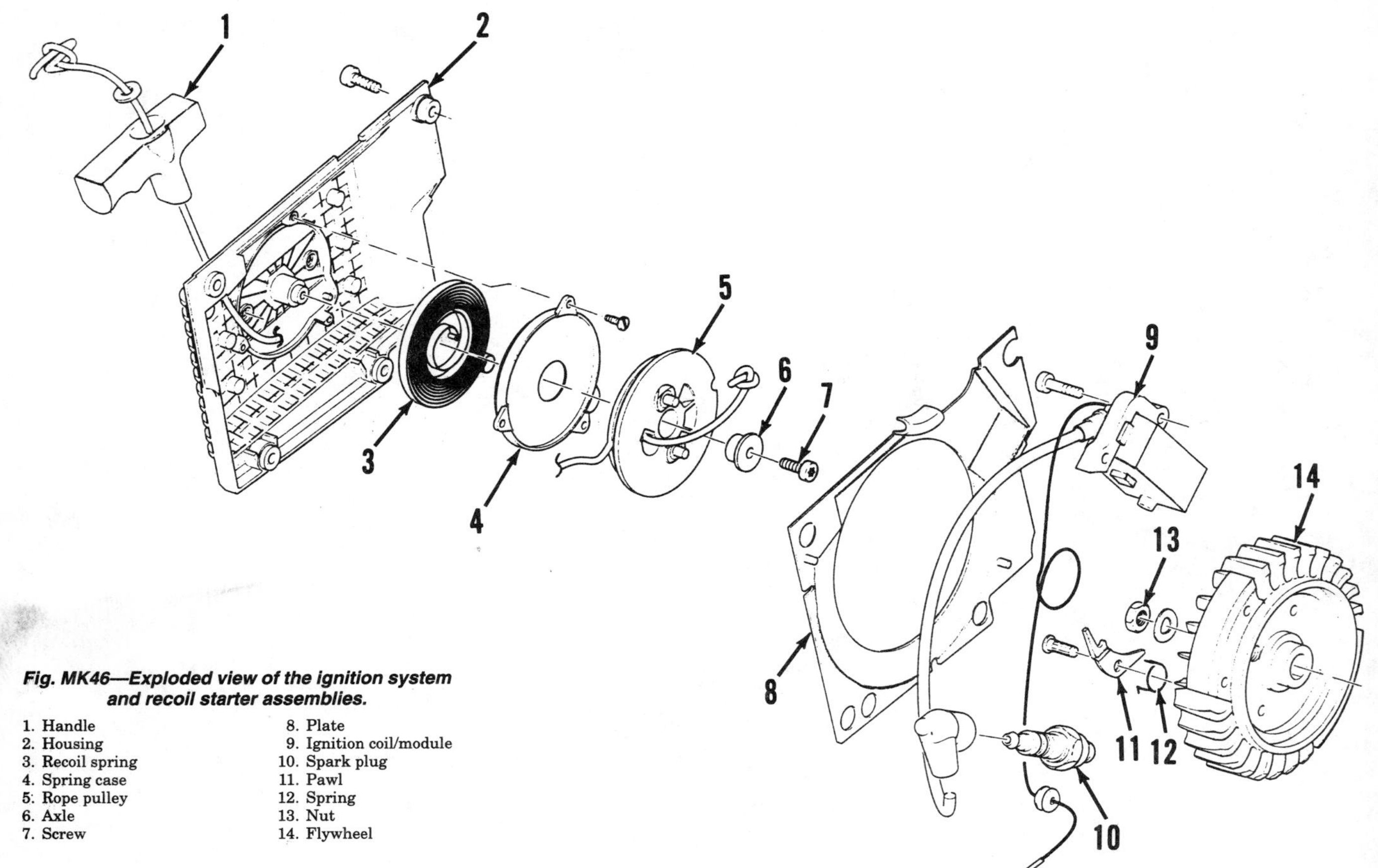

Fig. MK46—Exploded view of the ignition system and recoil starter assemblies.

1. Handle
2. Housing
3. Recoil spring
4. Spring case
5. Rope pulley
6. Axle
7. Screw
8. Plate
9. Ignition coil/module
10. Spark plug
11. Pawl
12. Spring
13. Nut
14. Flywheel

should be wound into the case in a counterclockwise direction starting with the outer coil. Attach the spring case (4) to the housing after the spring is installed.

Install the pulley (5) with rope attached. The pulley should engage the inner end of the spring (3). Install axle (6) and screw (7). Wind rope onto the pulley in a clockwise direction. Preload the pulley approximately 2 turns clockwise, insert the end of the rope through guide in the housing, and attach the handle (1).

Pull the rope out fully and check that pulley can be turned an additional 1/2 turn without causing the spring to bind. Allow the rope to rewind and make sure the handle is pulled against the housing. If the spring binds, remove some spring preload and recheck. If the handle is not wound against the housing, increase the preload and recheck.

Inspect the condition of the pawl (11) and spring (12) attached to the flywheel. The pawl stud should be pressed into the flywheel after coating the surface of the stud and bore with locking agent (part No. 980 009 000 or equivalent).

MASSEY-FERGUSON

Model	Bore mm (in.)	Stroke mm (in.)	Displacement cc (cu. in.)	Drive Type
MF190, 190A	34.9 (1.375)	32.5 (1.281)	31.1 (1.9)	Direct
MF370, 370A, 370AR	46 (1.8125)	36.5 (1.4375)	60.6 (3.7)	Direct

MAINTENANCE

SPARK PLUG. Recommended spark plug is a Champion DJ6J for Models MF190 and MF190A. Champion CJ6 is recommended for all other models. Spark plug electrode gap should be 0.025 inch (0.63 mm) for all models.

CARBURETOR. A Tillotson Model HS diaphragm type carburetor is used on Models MF190 and MF190A while a Walbro Model HDC diaphragm type carburetor is used on Models MF370, MF370A and MF370AR. Refer to Tillotson or Walbro sections of CARBURETOR SERVICE for carburetor overhaul and exploded views.

Initial adjustment of Tillotson carburetor is 1⅛ turns open for idle mixture screw and 1 turn open for high speed mixture screw. Initial adjustment of Walbro carburetor is 1 turn open for idle mixture screw and ¾-turn open for high speed mixture screw. Final adjustments should be made with engine warm. High speed mixture screw should be adjusted with engine under cutting load to obtain optimum performance. Do not adjust high speed mixture too lean as engine damage may result.

MAGNETO AND TIMING. A conventional flywheel magneto is used on all models. Ignition timing is fixed. Recommended breaker-point gap is 0.015 inch (0.38 mm) for all models. Incorrect breaker-point gap will affect ignition timing. Magneto air gap should be 0.008 inch (0.20 mm).

LUBRICATION. The engine is lubricated by mixing oil with fuel. A good quality oil designed for use in an air-cooled two-stroke engine should be mixed with regular gasoline at the ratio of 16:1. Fuel:oil ratio should be increased during break-in with ¾ pint (0.35 L) of oil added to one gallon (3.785 L) of gasoline. This break-in ratio should be used for the first four gallons (15.14 L) of fuel mixture.

Models MF190A, MF370A and MF370AR are equipped with an automatic chain oil pump. All models are equipped with a manual chain oil pump. Recommended chain oil is a good quality SAE 30 oil for summer use and SAE 20 for winter use. If saw is used in extremely cold weather, SAE 10 oil may be mixed with a small amount of kerosene.

REPAIRS

PISTON, PIN, RINGS AND CYLINDER. Before cylinder can be removed, crankcase end plate on Models MF190 and MF190A must be removed. Refer to CRANKCASE AND CRANKSHAFT section. Cylinder has chromed aluminum bore on all models with cylinder head integral with cylinder. Piston has two pinned piston rings. Piston pin is fully floating and retained by snap rings at each end. Piston pin on Models MF370, MF370A and MF370AR rides in a needle roller bearing in small end of connecting rod. Piston pin on Models MF190 and MF190A rides directly in small end of rod. Piston must be heated to remove and install piston pin.

Inspect chrome bore of cylinder for scoring, flaking, cracking or other signs of damage or excessive wear. Inspect piston pin, bearing and connecting rod small end. Install new piston pin bearing, on models so equipped, by pressing

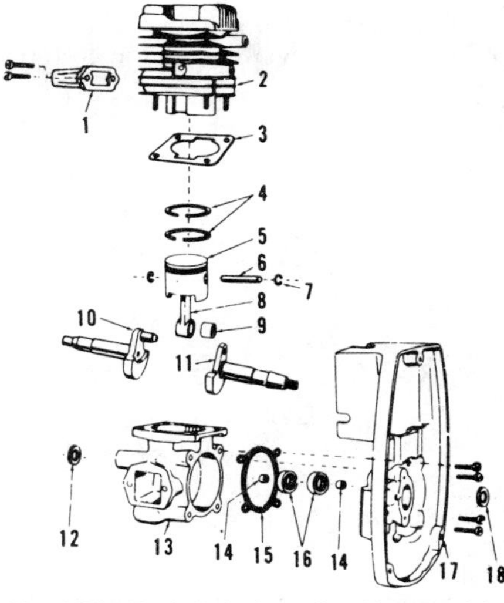

Fig. MF2—Exploded view of engine used on Models MF190 and MF190A.

1. Muffler
2. Cylinder
3. Gasket
4. Piston rings
5. Piston
6. Piston pin
7. Snap rings
8. Connecting rod
9. Needle bearing
10. Crankshaft (drive end)
11. Crankshaft (flywheel end)
12. Seal
13. Crankcase
14. Roller bearings (Torrington B86)
15. Gasket
16. Roller bearing (Torrington DD40798)
17. End plate
18. Seal

Fig. MF1—Exploded view of magneto assembly.

1. Condenser
2. Ignition coil
3. Stator plate & breaker points
4. Cover
5. Flywheel

on lettered side of bearing. Be sure rod is properly supported when pressing against bearing to prevent damage to lower portion of rod if rod is still attached to crankshaft. Piston, pin and connecting rod are available only as a unit assembly on Models MF190 and MF190A.

Heat piston before installing piston pin which must be installed with closed end of pin towards exhaust port. Install piston with "EXH" marking on piston crown toward exhaust port of cylinder. Be sure piston rings are properly aligned with locating pins in ring grooves when installing cylinder. Tighten cylinder base nuts to 30-40 in.-lbs. (3.4-4.5 N·m) on Models MF190 and MF190A and to 80-100 in.-lbs. (9.0-11.3 N·m) on Models MF370, MF370A and MF370AR.

CONNECTING ROD. Connecting rod on Models MF370, MF370A and MF370AR can be removed after removing piston and unscrewing rod cap screws. Be careful not to lose bearing rollers (14 – Fig. MF3) when removing rod and cap. To remove rod on Models MF190 and MF190A, crankshaft must be separated as outlined in CRANKCASE AND CRANKSHAFT section.

Thirty-one loose bearing rollers are used in crankpin bearing on Models MF370, MF370A and MF370AR while a needle roller bearing is used on crankpin of Models MF190 and MF190A. Piston pin on Models MF190 and MF190A rides directly in small end of connecting rod. Piston rod on Models MF370, MF370A and MF370AR is supported by a needle roller bearing in connecting rod. Install roller bearing by pressing on lettered side of bearing. Connecting rod, piston and piston pin on Models MF190 and MF190A are available only as a unit assembly.

Loose bearing rollers on Models MF370, MF370A and MF370AR can be held in place with heavy grease or wax on strip of new bearing rollers. Note match marks (M – Fig. MF4) on connecting rod and rod cap which must be aligned for installation. Install rod so match marks are toward flywheel end of crankshaft.

CRANKCASE AND CRANKSHAFT. Access to crankcase and crankshaft is possible after removing end plate (17 – Fig. MF2 or 18 – Fig. MF3). Flywheel end of crankshaft on all models is supported by a roller bearing. On Models MF190 and MF190A, two bearings (14 and 16 – Fig. MF2) are used. Drive end of crankshaft is supported by two roller bearings on Models MF190 and MF190A and by a ball bearing on Models MF370, MF370A and MF370AR. Heat should be applied to crankcase or end plate to remove roller bearings. Ball bearing (8 – Fig. MF3) is pressed on crankshaft and retained in crankcase by retainers (6). It may be necessary to apply heat to crankcase to remove bearing and crankshaft from crankcase.

Models MF190 and MF190A are equipped with a two-piece crankshaft (10 and 11 – Fig. MF2). End plate (17), crankshaft half (11) and cylinder must be removed before connecting rod (8) can be removed. Drive end of crankshaft (10) may be removed after connecting rod (8) is removed. Drive (10) and flywheel (11) ends are available separately.

Ball bearing (8 – Fig. MF3) on Models MF370, MF370A and MF370AR is pressed on crankshaft. Groove around outer race of bearing must be adjacent to crankpin. Heat crankcase (1) in bearing area and install crankshaft and bearing. Coat screw (7) threads with CV grade Loctite and install bearing retainers (6) and screws. Be sure screws do not contact crankshaft when shaft is turned.

REED VALVE. All models are equipped with a reed valve induction system. Refer to Figs. MF5 and MF6. Inspect reed petals for cracks or other damage. Inspect reed valve seats for pitting or other damage which may prevent petals from seating properly. Reed petals and seat are available only as a unit assembly.

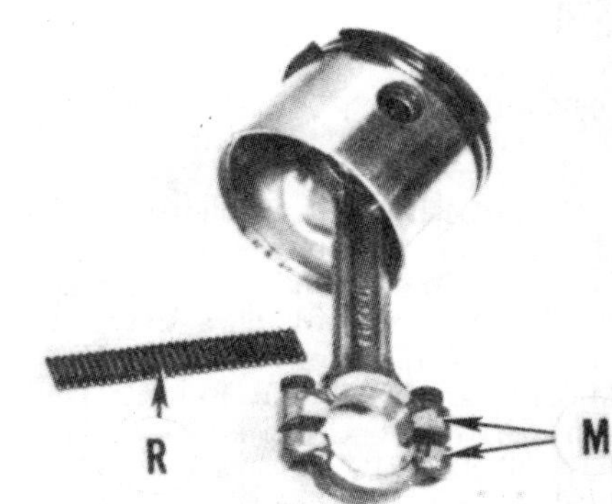

Fig. MF4 – On Models MF370, MF370A and MF370AR, be sure connecting rod match marks (M) are aligned. Rod bearing has 31 rollers (R).

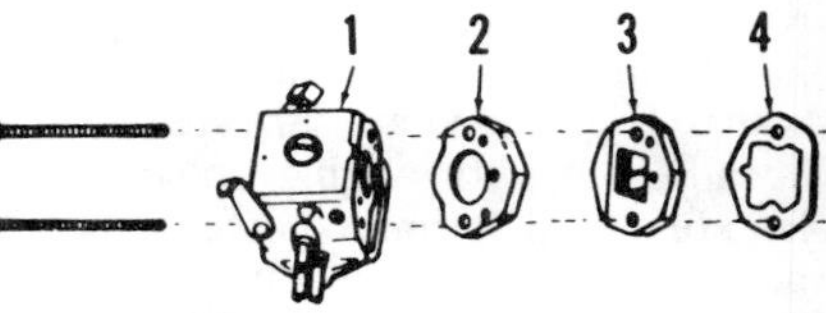

Fig. MF5 – View of induction system used on Models MF190 and MF190A.

1. Carburetor
2. Spacer
3. Reed valve assy.
4. Gasket

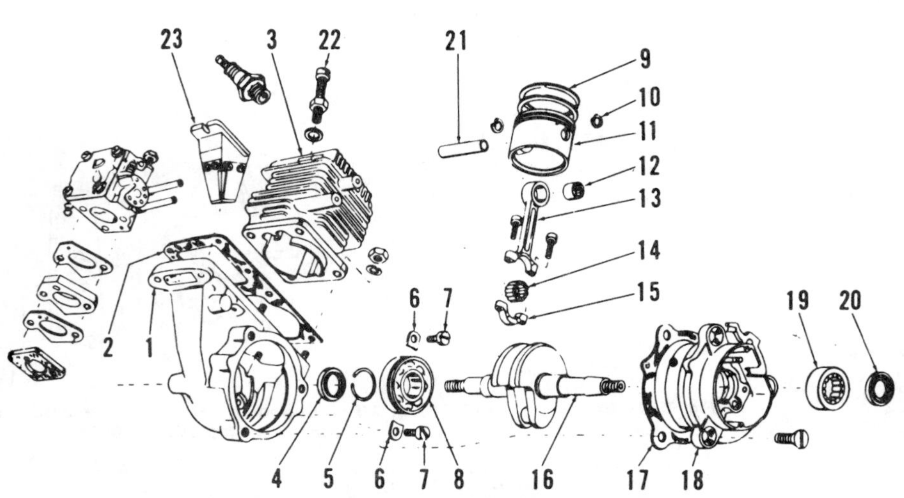

Fig. MF3 – Exploded view of engine used on Models MF370, MF370A and MF370AR.

1. Crankcase
2. Gasket
3. Cylinder
4. Seal
5. Retainer
6. Retainers
7. Screws
8. Ball bearing
9. Piston rings
10. Snap ring
11. Piston
12. Needle bearing
13. Connecting rod
14. Bearing rollers (31)
15. Rod cap
16. Crankshaft
17. Gasket
18. End plate
19. Roller bearing
20. Seal
21. Piston pin
22. Compression release
23. Reed valve

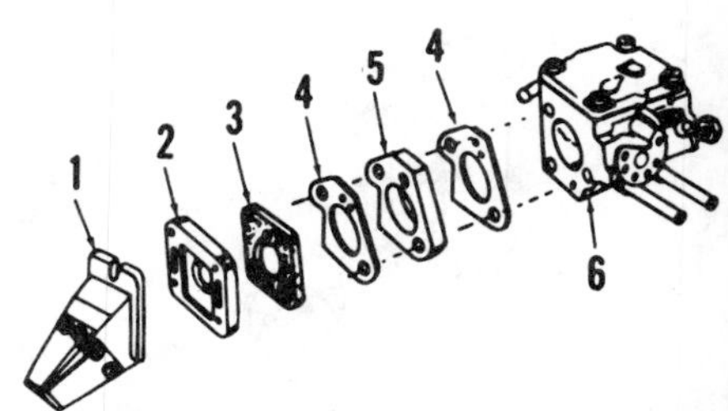

Fig. MF6 – View of induction system used on Models MF370, MF370A and MF370AR.

1. Reed valve assy.
2. Spacer
3. Cork gasket
4. Gasket
5. Heat insulator
6. Carburetor

REWIND STARTER. Refer to Fig. MF7 for exploded view of rewind starter used on all models. To disassemble starter, proceed as follows: Remove starter housing from end plate. Remove rope handle and allow rope to rewind into starter. Remove "E" ring (6) and remove rope pulley (8) being careful not to dislodge rewind spring (9). If necessary, remove rewind spring being careful as injury may result if spring is allowed to uncoil uncontrolled.

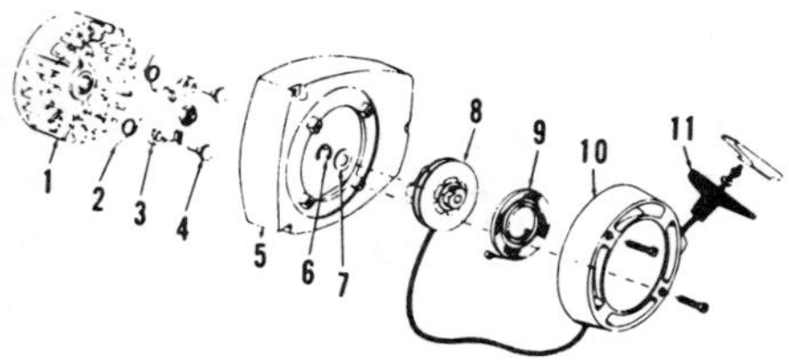

Rewind spring is wound in clockwise direction in housing. Rope is wound on pulley in clockwise direction when viewing pulley installed in housing. Place tension on rewind spring by turning pulley clockwise before passing rope through rope outlet. Pulley should be turned a sufficient number of turns to draw rope handle against housing when rope is released, but not so many turns that rewind spring is fully extended when rope is completely withdrawn.

Fig. MF7—Exploded view of rewind starter assembly.

1. Flywheel
2. Spring
3. Pawl
4. Pivot post
5. Fan shroud
6. "E" ring
7. Washer
8. Rope pulley
9. Rewind spring
10. Starter housing
11. Rope handle

McCULLOCH

Model	Bore	Stroke	Displ.	Drive Type
10-10 Auto	1.75 in. (44.4 mm)	1.375 in. (34.92 mm)	3.3 cu. in. (54.0 cc)	Direct
7-10 Auto	2.0 in. (50.8 mm)	1.375 in. (34.92 mm)	4.3 cu. in. (70.5 cc)	Direct
PM700	2.0 in. (50.8 mm)	1.375 in. (34.92 mm)	4.3 cu. in. (70.5 cc)	Direct
PM10-10S, PM55, PM555	1.812 in. (46.02 mm)	1.375 in. (34.92 mm)	3.5 cu. in. (57.4 cc)	Direct
PM60, SP60	1.875 in. (47.62 mm)	1.375 in. (34.92 mm)	3.8 cu. in. (62.3 cc)	Direct
PM800, PM805, PM850, SP80, SP81, Double Eagle 80	2.06 in. (52.3 mm)	1.5 in. (38.1 mm)	5.0 cu. in. (81.9 cc)	Direct

MAINTENANCE

SPARK PLUG. Recommended spark plug is AC CS45T for Models 10-10 Auto, PM10-10S, PM55 and PM555. Recommended spark plug is AC CS42T on all other models. Recommended spark plug electrode gap is 0.025 inch (0.63 mm). Note spark plug has a conical seat which does not require a gasket. Tighten spark plug to 144-180 in.-lbs. (16.3-20.3 N•m) torque.

CARBURETOR. A McCulloch "W" series, Tillotson HS, Walbro SDC or Zama carburetor may be used. Refer to Tillotson, Walbro or Zama carburetor section in CARBURETOR SERVICE section for service on those carburetors.

Initial adjustment of mixture needles on Tillotson, Walbro and Zama carburetors is one turn open for both low and high speed mixture needles. Make final adjustment on Tillotson, Walbro and Zama carburetors with engine warm and running. Adjust idle speed screw so engine idles just below clutch engagement speed. Adjust low speed mixture screw so engine will accelerate cleanly without hesitation. Adjust high speed mixture screw to obtain optimum performance under cutting load. Some chain saws with Tillotson or Walbro carburetors are equipped with a throttle latch to advance the throttle opening to a fast idle position for starting. Throttle opening is adjusted by turning adjusting screw (S – Fig. MC6-3) on bottom of trigger.

McCulloch series "W" carburetor was manufactured as two different models. Early model is shown in Fig. MC6-4 and later model is shown in Fig. MC6-5. On early models, fuel is metered by an adjustable needle valve attached to the throttle shaft. On later models, this only adjusts idle mixture. High speed operation on early models is controlled by an adjusting screw which determines throttle plate opening. Later models utilize a fuel needle for high speed adjustment. Both models use a primer plunger for choking operation. Choking on early models is accomplished by forcing fuel past needle valve into the carburetor bore. Later models force fuel from a chamber into the carburetor bore.

Be sure primer operates correctly as fuel leaking into bore will change fuel mixture. Primer "O" rings must be installed correctly to prevent leakage. Some plungers shown in Fig. MC6-4

Fig. MC6-1 – Air cleaner cover and filter element removed to show carburetor adjustment points of early McCulloch Models "W" series carburetor. Later models are similar except for high speed mixture screw.

1. High speed mixture screw
2. Idle speed screw
3. Idle speed mixture screw
4. Throttle butterfly

Fig. MC6-2 – Keep finger on throttle butterfly as shown when adjusting carburetor. Refer to text for procedure.

Fig. MC6-3 – Fast idle adjustment on some models is performed by turning adjusting screw (S) on bottom of trigger.

Illustrations courtesy McCulloch Corp.

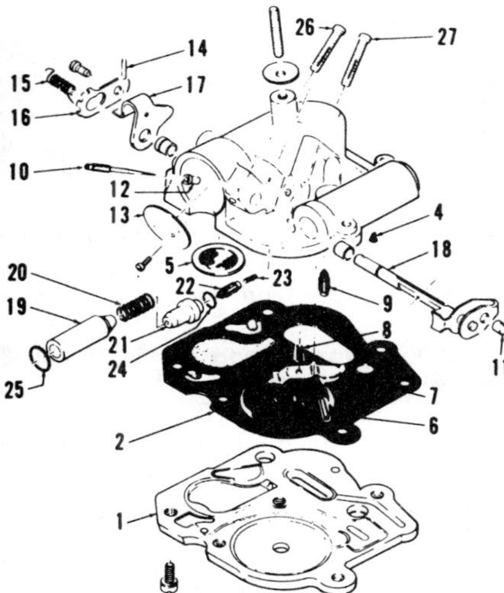

Fig. MC6-4—Exploded view of early McCulloch Model "W" series carburetor. Refer to Fig. MC6-1 for view of carburetor installed.

1. Base plate
2. Diaphragm
4. Check valve
5. Capillary seal
6. Inlet valve pin
7. Inlet lever
8. Spring
9. Inlet valve needle
10. Metering (low idle) mixture needle
11. Swivel
12. Air orifice
13. Throttle butterfly
14. Roll pin
15. Idle governor spring
16. Clip
17. Throttle lever
18. Throttle shaft
19. Primer plunger
20. Plunger spring
21. Seat
22. Primer needle
23. Needle spring
24. "O" ring
25. "O" ring
26. Idle speed screw
27. High speed mixture screw

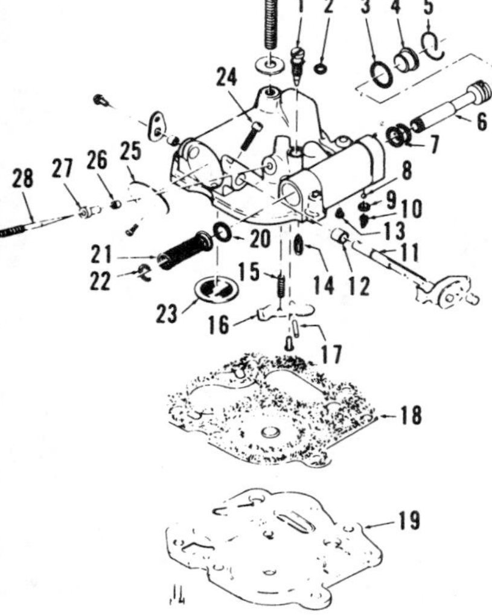

Fig. MC6-5—Exploded view of later McCulloch Model "W" series carburetor. Refer to Fig. MC6-4 for view of early model.

1. High speed mixture needle
2. "O" ring
3. "O" ring
4. Plug
5. Retainer
6. Primer plunger
7. "O" ring or "V" packing
8. Ball
9. Ball seat
10. Valve
11. Throttle shaft
12. Bushing
13. Valve
14. Fuel inlet valve
15. Spring
16. Inlet lever
17. Pin
18. Diaphragm
19. Base plate
20. "O" ring
21. Spring
22. Retaining ring
23. Seal
24. Idle speed screw
25. Throttle plate
26. Fuel orifice
27. Air orifice
28. Idle metering needle

have a cup to retain "O" ring (25). Install cup 5/64 inch (1.98 mm) from end of primer housing bore as shown in Fig. MC6-6. Two types of primer plungers have been used on the carburetor shown in Fig. MC6-5. The rear groove of the plunger is 0.090 inch (2.29 mm) or 0.120 inch (3.05 mm) wide as shown in Fig. MC6-7. An "O" ring is used in the narrow groove while "V" packing is used in the wide groove as a service replacement.

If carburetor has been disassembled, make a preliminary adjustment prior to starting engine and make final adjustment after engine has been started and brought to operating temperature.

To make the preliminary adjustment on "W" series carburetors, refer to Fig. MC6-1 and proceed as follows: Turn the idle speed screw (2) counterclockwise until throttle butterfly (4) is completely closed. Hold a finger against the closed butterfly as shown in Fig. MC6-2 and turn the idle mixture screw (3–Fig. MC6-1) clockwise until the butterfly starts to open, then turn the idle mixture needle three turns counterclockwise. Return to the idle speed screw (2) and while holding finger against butterfly (4), turn idle air screw clockwise until butterfly begins to open, then continue to turn the screw clockwise an additional ½ turn. Hold the throttle trigger in the wide open position, turn the high speed mixture screw (1) as required until throttle butterfly is in horizontal position. Now turn screw (1) clockwise until throttle butterfly (4) starts to close, then turn the high speed mixture screw two turns counterclockwise. On later models, initial adjustment of main fuel needle (1–Fig. MC6-5) is one turn. Do not attempt to adjust throttle plate opening.

With preliminary adjustment made as outlined, start engine and bring to operating temperature. Let engine run at idle rpm and if necessary, adjust idle speed screw until engine is operating just below chain creep speed. Now accelerate engine rapidly several times and check engine operation. If engine falters during acceleration, the mixture is too lean and idle mixture needle should be turned counterclockwise as necessary. If engine runs rough and smokes excessively during acceleration, the mixture is too rich and the idle mixture needle should be turned clockwise as necessary. Make this adjustment in small increments and check engine operation after each adjustment. If the idle mixture is changed it may also be necessary to readjust the idle speed screw to keep engine idle rpm below chain creep speed. Refer to Fig. MC6-8 and set the tension governor spring so engine idles smoothly in all positions. Reduce tension on spring if chain creeps.

With engine idle rpm and mixture adjusted, load engine (make a cut) and turn the high speed adjustment screw (1–Fig. MC6-1) on early models counter-

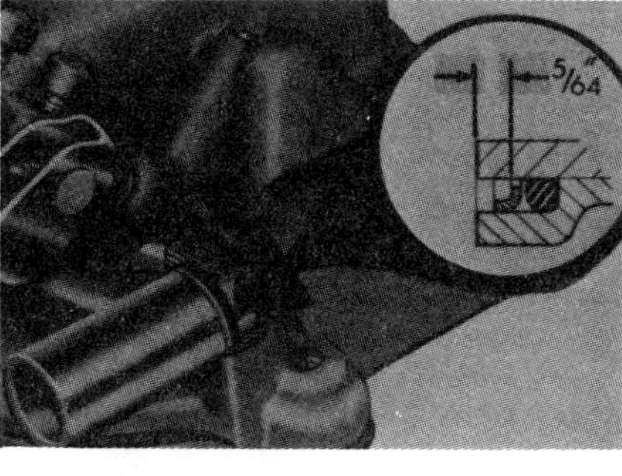

Fig. MC6-6—Some early McCulloch "W" series carburetors have a seal cup which must be installed 5/64 inch (1.98 mm) inside primer bore as shown above.

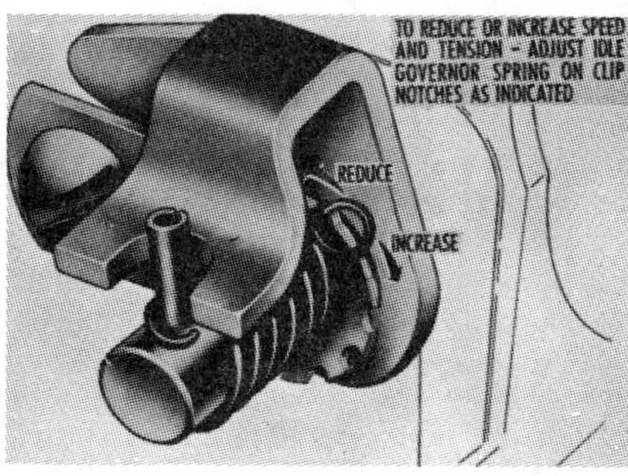

Fig. MC6-8—View showing installation of idle governor spring. Later McCulloch "W" series carburetors do not have governor spring. Adjust spring as shown so engine will idle smoothly in any position.

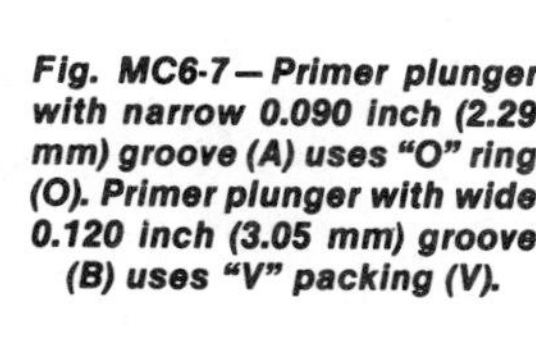

Fig. MC6-7—Primer plunger with narrow 0.090 inch (2.29 mm) groove (A) uses "O" ring (O). Primer plunger with wide 0.120 inch (3.05 mm) groove (B) uses "V" packing (V).

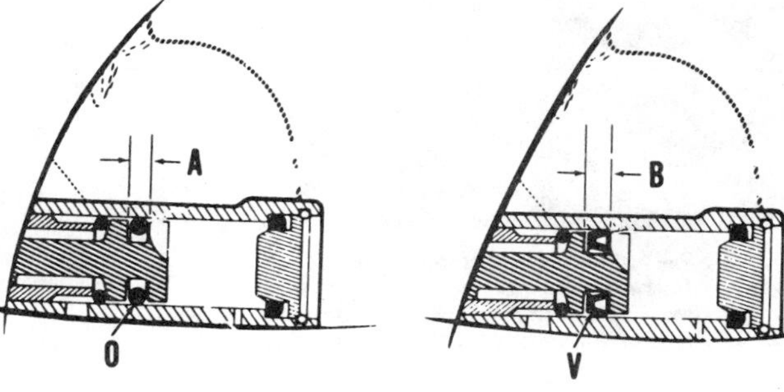

Illustrations courtesy McCulloch Corp.

clockwise in small increments until engine operation begins to roughen, then turn the screw clockwise just enough to eliminate the engine roughness. On later models of "W" carburetor, the high speed mixture screw is turned clockwise to lean fuel mixture.

IGNITION. Early models are equipped with a breaker-point type flywheel magneto ignition system while later models use an electronic ignition system.

On models equipped with breaker-points, breaker-point gap should be 0.019 inch (0.48 mm). Clearance between ignition coil legs and flywheel magnets should be 0.010-0.012 inch (0.25-0.30 mm) and can be adjusted after loosening coil mounting screws. Ignition timing is 26 degrees BTDC and is not adjustable, however, incorrect breaker-point gap will affect ignition timing.

Clearance between ignition coil module legs and flywheel magnets should be 0.011-0.015 inch (0.28-0.38 mm) on models equipped with electronic ignition. Ignition timing is 26 degrees BTDC but is not adjustable.

Note that two different electronic systems have been used on later models. Individual components should not be interchanged. The different systems may be identified by noting color of components which are all black on one of the ignition systems.

LUBRICATION. Engine is lubricated by a mixture of regular gasoline and oil. The gasoline and oil should be mixed in a separate container before being put in the engine fuel tank. If using McCulloch engine oil, use 3 ounces (88.7 mL) of oil for each gallon (3.7853 L) of gasoline (approx. 1:40). If McCulloch oil is not available, use 6 ounces (177.4 mL) of SAE 40 two-stroke oil for each gallon (3.7853 L) of gasoline (approx. 1:20).

Fill chain oiler tank each time fuel tank is filled. Use SAE 30 motor oil for temperatures above 40°F (4°C). When cutting wood with a high sap or pitch content the chain oil may be diluted up to 50 percent with kerosene, if necessary. Adjust oil pump output on models with automatic chain oiler as shown in Fig. MC6-9.

On gear drive models, use SAE 140 all-purpose gear oil in transmission. With bar pointed down and filler plug removed, oil should be level with bottom of filler hole.

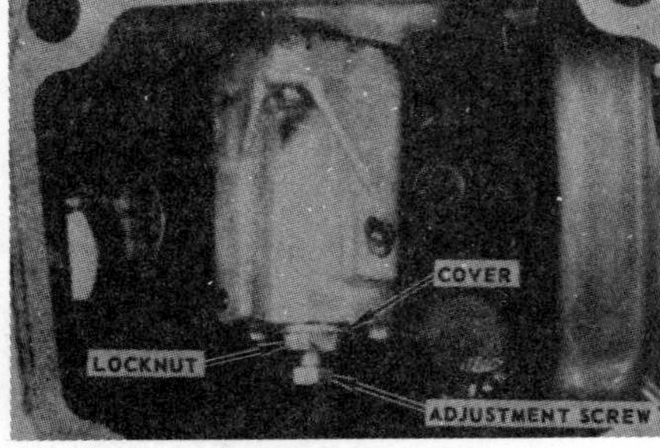

Fig. MC6-9 — Automatic oil pump output is adjusted by loosening locknut and turning adjustment screw. Locknut may be absent on later models. Adjustment should be made in small increments.

CARBON. If a noticeable lack of power or a decrease in the exhaust noise level is evident it is possible that the muffler and exhaust ports need cleaning. Use a wood scraper when cleaning exhaust ports to avoid damage to cylinder or piston.

REPAIRS

CONNECTING ROD. Removal of connecting rod requires separating cylinder and crankcase. To gain access to the cylinder and crankcase, remove clutch guard and starter assembly, clutch, fan housing, flywheel, ignition components, air cleaner cover and air cleaner screen, carburetor, spark arrester, cylinder shroud and fuel tank assembly.

With the above assemblies removed, drain chain oiler tank, if necessary, then remove the crankcase cover. Remove the four interior and four exterior cylinder retaining cap screws and separate crankcase from cylinder. Remove the rod cap screws and remove rod and piston from crankshaft. Do not lose any of the 22 loose rollers used in PM800, PM805, PM850, SP80, SP81 and Double Eagle 80 or 20 loose rollers used in all other models. Heat piston evenly to about 200°F (93.4°C), support piston boss on a 9/16 inch deep socket and using a driver smaller than piston pin, press piston pin from rod.

NOTE: Piston support tool is P/N63093 and driver is P/N63094.

Inspect connecting rod for worn or scored bearing surfaces, bends or twists. If any of these defects are found, renew rod.

To reassemble, heat piston pin end of rod to about 300°F (149°C) and reinstall by reversing removal procedure. Install rod in piston with pips on rod and cap aligned. Use grease to hold rollers in crankshaft end of rod. Tighten rod cap screws to 65-70 in.-lbs. (7.3-7.9 N·m) with oiled threads.

PISTON, PIN, RINGS AND CYLINDER. Later models are equipped with a chrome cylinder bore. On these models, except Double Eagle 80, standard size pistons and rings only are available. Cylinder bore and piston on Models PM800, PM850 and Double Eagle 80 are graded. "A," "B" or "C" according to size. Letter size should be the same on piston and cylinder to obtain desired clearance. If cylinder is unmarked, use a

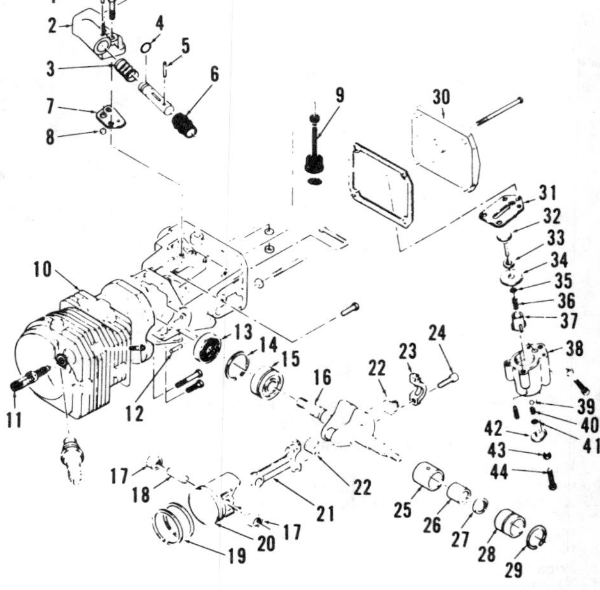

Fig. MC6-10 — Exploded view of typical engine assembly, and early type manual and automatic oil pumps. Later type manual and automatic oil pumps are shown in Fig. MC6-12A. Note that early models used insert (28) and snap ring (29) while late models use insert (25) and pin (12).

1. Roll pin
2. Manual oil pump housing
3. Spring
4. "O" ring
5. Roll pin
6. Boot
7. Gasket
8. Valve
9. Oil hose
10. Cylinder
11. Compression valve
12. Dowel pin
13. Oil seal
14. Snap ring
15. Ball bearing
16. Crankshaft
17. Needle bearing
18. Piston pin
19. Piston ring
20. Piston
21. Connecting rod
22. Roller bearing
23. Rod cap
24. Rod screws
25. Bearing insert
26. Roller bearing
27. Oil seal
28. Bearing insert
29. Snap ring
30. Oil tank cover
31. Gasket
32. Piston
33. Teflon washer
34. Piston ring
35. "O" ring
36. Spring
37. Adjustment sleeve
38. Automatic oil pump housing
39. Outlet ball valve
40. Spring
41. "O" ring
42. Valve cover
43. Locknut
44. Adjusting screw

Illustrations courtesy McCulloch Corp.

piston marked "B." Piston letter size is marked on crown while cylinder is marked adjacent to compression release valve. Oversize pistons and rings are available on models with a cast iron liner in the cylinder.

Models with cast iron liner should conform to the following specifications: Piston-to-wall clearance should be 0.003-0.005 inch (0.08-0.13 mm) measured at piston skirt. Cylinder taper or out-of-round should not exceed 0.005 inch (0.13 mm). Piston ring end gap should be 0.006-0.017 inch (0.16-0.43 mm) on unpinned rings and 0.051-0.066 inch (1.30-1.67 mm) on models with pinned piston rings. Maximum piston ring end gap should be 0.0055 inch (0.14 mm) on Model 10-10 Auto and 0.006 inch (0.15 mm) on Models 7-10 Auto and PM700. Minimum ring side gap is 0.003 inch (0.08 mm) for Models 10-10 Auto, 7-10 Auto and PM700. If cylinder is bored to an oversize, the tip of the compression release valve (DSP) must be cut one-half the amount of the oversize. For example, the compression release valve would be cut 0.010 inch (0.25 mm) if the cylinder is bored 0.020 inch (0.51 mm) oversize. Be sure valve does not protrude into cylinder and contact piston or piston rings.

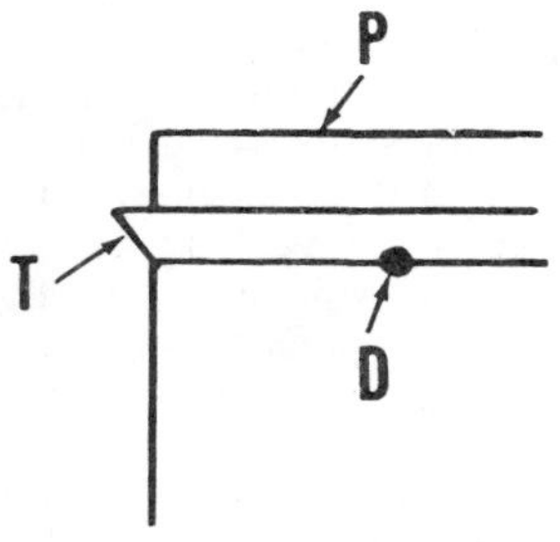

Fig. MC6-11 – Tapered piston rings on some models must be installed so taper (T) is toward top of piston (P). Locating dot (D) on ring will be toward bottom when installed correctly.

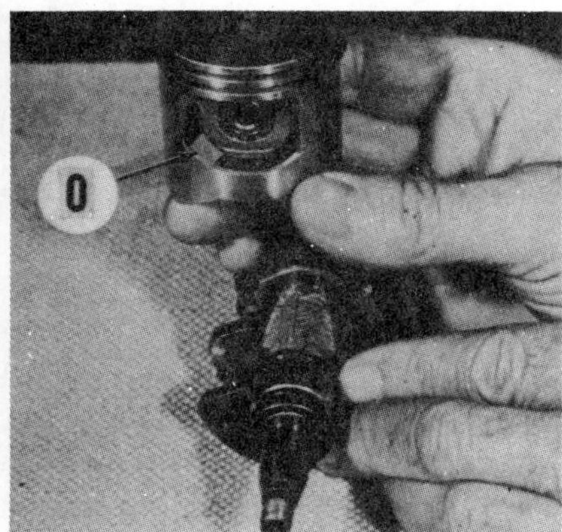

Fig. MC6-12 – Install piston so large offset (O) at piston pin boss is toward clutch.

Recommended piston-to-cylinder clearance is measured 3/8 inch (9.5 mm) from bottom of piston skirt. On models with chrome cylinder bore clearance should be 0.002-0.004 inch (0.06-0.10 mm) except for Models PM800 and PM850 which is 0.0024-0.0038 inch (0.061-0.096 mm) and Model Double Eagle 80 which is 0.009 inch (0.23 mm). Cylinder should be inspected and renewed if chrome has cracked, flaked or worn away and exposed soft base metal underneath. Pistons and rings are available in standard sizes only. Piston ring end gap should be 0.055-0.091 inch (1.40-2.31 mm) for Models PM555, PM700, PM800 and PM850. On Model Double Eagle 80, ring end gap should be 0.070 inch (1.78 mm). Piston rings used with chrome cylinder are tapered on some models and must be installed with taper pointing up as shown in Fig. MC6-11.

If needle bearings in piston require renewal, support piston on outer end of pin boss, place insert support or McCulloch special tool between piston bosses (in place of rod) and press top bearing out toward inside. Turn piston over and repeat operation on opposite bearing.

NOTE: Bearing enters hole in insert support as it is pressed out. Do not reuse any bearings that have been removed.

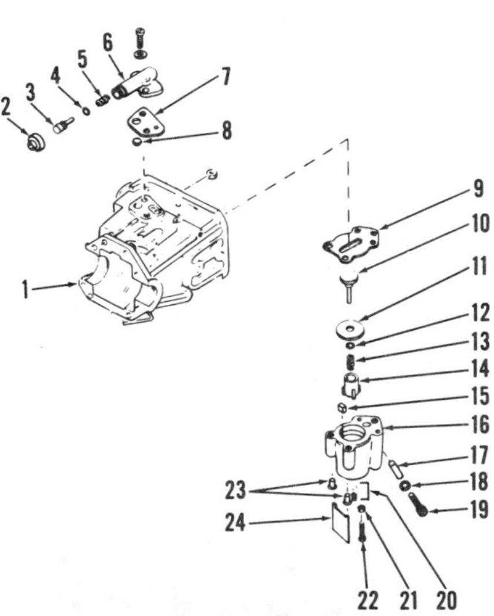

Fig. MC6-12A – Exploded view of later type manual and automatic chain oil pump. Locknut (21) may be absent on some models.

1. Crankcase
2. Boot
3. Plunger
4. "O" ring
5. Spring
6. Manual oil pump housing
7. Gasket
8. Valve
9. Gasket
10. Piston
11. Piston ring
12. "O" ring
13. Spring
14. Adjustment sleeve
15. Pad
16. Automatic oil pump housing
17. Sleeve
18. Washer
19. Cap screw
20. Ball valve & spring
21. Locknut
22. Adjusting screw
23. Eyelet
24. Spring clip

To install new bearings in piston, heat piston to about 200°F (93.4°C) and reverse procedure but use solid end of insert support and press bearing into piston until bearing butts against the insert support. This positions bearing inner end flush with inner ends of piston pin boss.

Pistons on all engines have piston pin offset in piston. Piston must be installed on connecting rod with large offset (O – Fig. MC6-12) toward clutch. The piston on most engines is also marked with "EX" and must be installed with "EX" side adjacent to exhaust port. Heat connecting rod eye to approximately 300°F (149°C) before installing piston and pressing in piston pin.

CRANKSHAFT. The crankshaft is supported by a ball bearing at flywheel end and a needle bearing at clutch end. Crankshaft should be discarded if it shows uneven or excessive wear, or any other signs of damage. When installing bearing on crankshaft, place shielded side of ball bearing next to counterweight of crankshaft and press bearing on shaft until it bottoms. When crankshaft and piston assembly is positioned in cylinder, be sure inner end of needle bearing is positioned 1/8 inch (3.17 mm) away from counterweight of crankshaft and that shaft seals are installed with lips facing inward. Tighten the four interior crankcase bolts to 55-60 in.-lbs. (6.3-6.8 N·m) and the four exterior crankcase bolts to 35-40 in.-lbs. (4.0-4.5 N·m) torque.

AUTOMATIC OILER. All models have an automatic chain oiler in addition to the manual chain oiler. The oil pump is operated by crankcase pulsations.

The oil pump is adjusted as shown in Fig. MC6-9. Chain oil is routed first through the manual oiler then through the automatic oiler before it exits at the bar pad. This allows the manual oiler to be used independently as well as providing priming for the automatic oiler. The oil pump is contained within the oil tank and may be removed after draining

Fig. MC6-13 – Flywheel may be locked in place on SP60, SP80, SP81, PM700 and PM850 Models by inserting 1/4 inch locking pin through base plate into notch in flywheel.

oil tank and removing tank cover. Oil pump should be cleaned and inspected for damage or excessive wear. Be sure all oil passages are open and clean and renew piston disc if warped or cracked. Before starting chain saw, prime automatic oil pump by operating manual oiler several times.

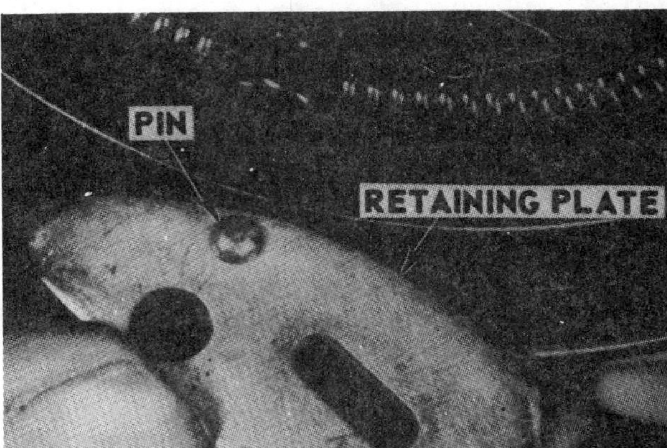

Fig. MC6-16—Install clutch spring (4—Fig. MC6-15) so spring ends will contact locating pin in clutch spring retaining plate.

CLUTCH. To remove clutch, remove clutch guard and starter assembly, bar, chain and fan (flywheel) housing. Lock flywheel by inserting a screwdriver between bossed portion of flywheel and leg of coil lamination (DO NOT use flywheel fin). Flywheel on SP60, SP80, SP81 and PM850 models is secured by inserting a ¼ inch (6.35 mm) locking pin through the base plate as shown in Fig. MC6-13 and rotating flywheel until pin engages notch in flywheel. Remove clutch retaining nut and pull clutch from crankshaft. Remove clutch drum and bearing, and shims. Refer to Figs. MC6-14 and MC6-15.

Inspect all parts for signs of excessive wear or other damage. Clutch shoes must be renewed as a unit. Clutch spring(s) should also be renewed. Renew clutch rotor if it allows excessive play of clutch shoes. Renew shims if grooved or damaged. Inspect sprocket and renew if excessively worn. Inspect starter pawls on models equipped with recoil starter on clutch side of saw. Pawls can be renewed by removing rivets and installing new pawls and rivets.

Note that one retaining plate of clutch assembly used on Model SP80 has a pin which prevents the clutch spring from rotating. The clutch spring must be installed so that the ends of the spring will be underneath retaining pin when the plate is installed on clutch shoe. Refer to Fig. MC6-16. The clutch drum on gear drive models is equipped with a seal which must be installed with lips of seal toward clutch bearing. Tighten clutch nut to 400-420 in.-lbs. (45.2-47.4 N·m) on Model SP80 and to 160-170 in.-lbs. (18.1-19.2 N·m) torque on all other models.

REWIND STARTER. Chain saw may be equipped with a rewind starter mounted on right or left side. Refer to Fig. MC6-18 for exploded view of recoil starter mounted on right side of chain saw. Rewind spring is wound in counterclockwise direction in housing and rope is wound in counterclockwise direction around rope pulley as viewed installed in housing. New rope length is 50 inches (127 cm). Early models have a hole in the rope pulley and a nail or other device can be inserted through the hole to hold the rewind spring on the rope pulley as shown in Fig. MC6-19. Note that the spring is wound clockwise if this method is used to install rewind spring.

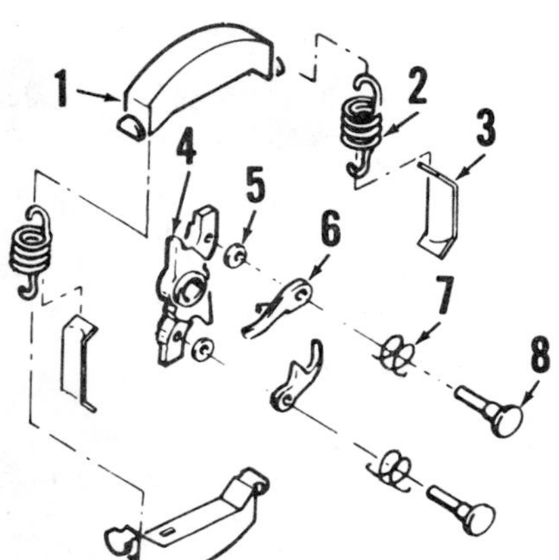

Fig. MC6-14—Exploded view of clutch used on all models except SP80.

1. Shoe
2. Spring
3. Retainer
4. Rotor
5. Washer
6. Pawl
7. Spring
8. Rivet

Fig. MC6-18—Exploded view of typical right hand rewind starter.

1. Snap ring
2. Dust shield
3. Thrust washer
4. Rope pulley
5. Rewind spring
6. Spring shield
7. Nylon bushing
8. Fan housing

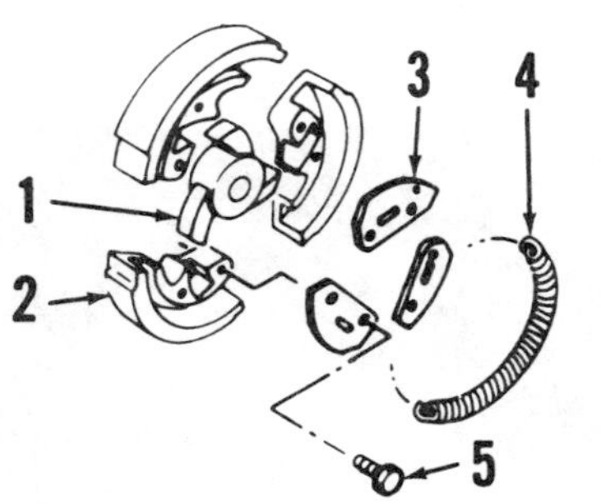

Fig. MC6-15—Exploded view of clutch shoe assembly used on Model SP80.

1. Rotor
2. Clutch shoes
3. Retainer plates
4. Clutch spring
5. Cap screw

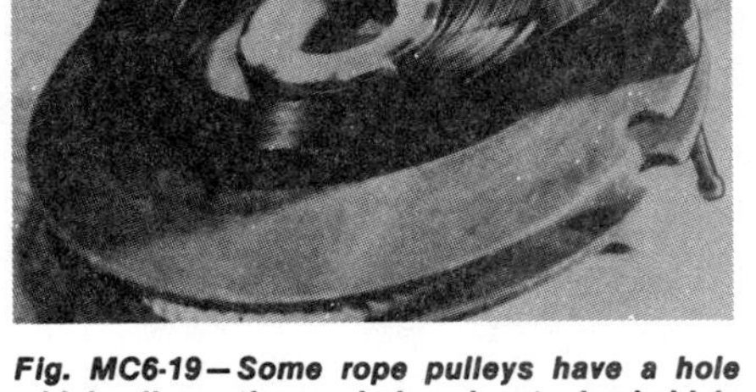

Fig. MC6-19—Some rope pulleys have a hole which allows the rewind spring to be held in position by inserting a nail or other device as shown.

Fig. MC6-20—Note difference between old (O) and new (N) style rewind springs and rope pulleys. Refer to text.

Illustrations courtesy McCulloch Corp

An early and late type of rewind spring and rope pulley have been used. Refer to Fig. MC6-20. Early and late spring and pulley should not be interchanged. Early type spring and pulley must be used in early starter housing. Later type spring and pulley can be used in early or later starter housing.

Place tension on rope by pulling rope handle then hold rope pulley so notch on outer edge of pulley aligns with rope outlet. Pull loose rope into housing and rotate rope pulley one or two turns in counterclockwise direction. Release rope and check starter operation.

Refer to Fig. MC6-21 for view of left hand starter found on saws manufactured in United States and some export models. Install rewind spring on fan housing in counterclockwise direction. Wind rope on rope pulley so it is wound in counterclockwise direction when viewed with pulley installed on housing. New rope length should be 42 inches (106.7 cm). Check operation of starter to be sure there is sufficient rewind spring tension to rewind rope, but rewind spring is bottomed when rope is pulled to its full length. Spring tension is altered by turning rope pulley while housing cover is removed.

Left-hand starter used on some saw models manufactured for export is shown in Fig. MC6-22. Rewind spring is wound in clockwise direction as viewed with pulley installed in housing. Place tension on rope by pulling rope handle and then hold rope pulley so notch on outer edge of pulley aligns with rope outlet. Pull loose rope into housing and rotate rope pulley one or two turns in clockwise direction. Release rope and check starter operation.

CHAIN BRAKE. Some later models are equipped with the chain brake mechanism shown in Fig. MC6-25. The chain brake stops chain motion when the operator's hand contacts brake lever (11) and steel strap (3) tightens around the clutch drum thereby stopping chain motion. Chain brake components must operate freely for the chain brake mechanism to be effective.

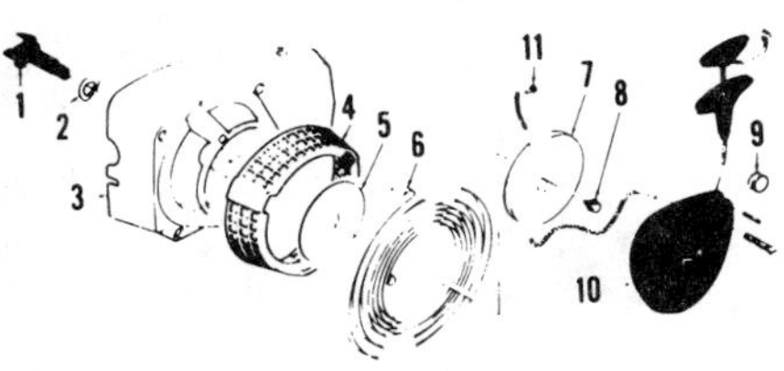

Fig. MC6-21 — Exploded view of left-hand rewind starter used on U.S. models and some export models.

1. Starter shaft
2. Wave washer
3. Fan housing
4. Sawdust guard
5. Spring shield
6. Rewind spring
7. Rope pulley
8. Cap screw
9. Rope roller
10. Cover
11. Rivet

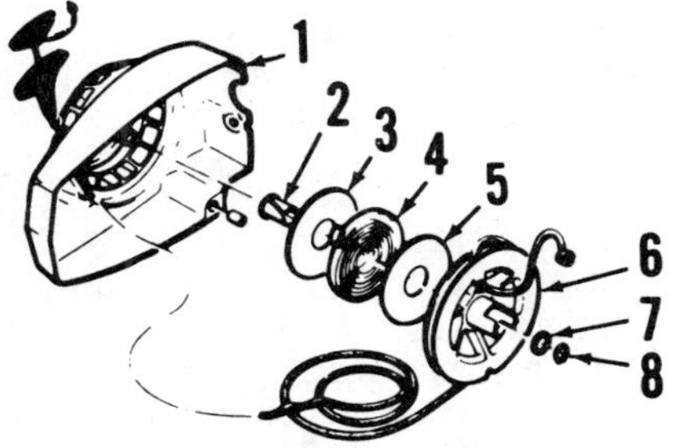

Fig. MC6-22 — Exploded view of left-hand rewind starter used on some export models.

1. Fan housing
2. Nylon bushing
3. Spring shield
4. Rewind spring
5. Dust shield
6. Rope pulley
7. Washer
8. Snap ring

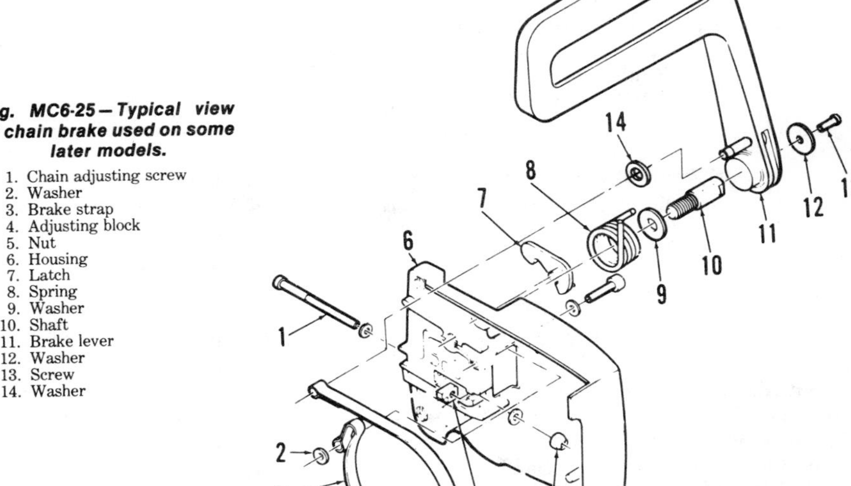

Fig. MC6-25 — Typical view of chain brake used on some later models.

1. Chain adjusting screw
2. Washer
3. Brake strap
4. Adjusting block
5. Nut
6. Housing
7. Latch
8. Spring
9. Washer
10. Shaft
11. Brake lever
12. Washer
13. Screw
14. Washer

McCULLOCH

Model	Bore	Stroke	Displ.	Drive Type
Mini-Mac 25, Mini-Mac 30	1.375 in. (34.9 mm)	1.200 in. (30.5 mm)	1.78 cu. in. (29.1 cc)	Direct
Mini-Mac 35	1.438 in. (36.5 mm)	1.200 in. (30.5 mm)	2.0 cu. in. (32.8 cc)	Direct
Power Mac 6	1.438 in. (36.5 mm)	1.200 in. (30.5 mm)	2.0 cu. in. (32.8 cc)	Direct
PM510, PM515, SP40	1.562 in. (39.7 mm)	1.200 in. (30.5 mm)	2.3 cu. in. (37.7 cc)	Direct
*PM310, PM320, PM330, PM340, PM355, PM365, PM375, Eager Beaver 2.1	1.496 in. (38 mm)	1.200 in. (30.5 mm)	2.1 cu. in. (34.4 cc)	Direct
Wildcat, MacCat	1.563 in. (39.7 mm)	1.200 in. (30.5 mm)	2.3 cu. in. (38 cc)	Direct
†Mac 110, Mac 120, Mac 130, Mac 140	1.375 in. (34.9 mm)	1.200 in. (30.5 mm)	1.78 cu. in. (29.1 cc)	Direct
Eager Beaver, PM155, PM165	1.438 in. (36.5 mm)	1.200 in. (30.5 mm)	2.0 cu. in. (32.9 cc)	Direct

***NOTE: Metric and American fasteners are used on 2.1 cu. in. (34.4 cc) saws. Be sure correct fastener is used.**
†Later Mac 110 and 120 models have a 1.430 inch (36.3 mm) bore and 2.0 cu. in. (32.8 cc) displacement.

MAINTENANCE

SPARK PLUG. Recommended spark plug is AC CS42T or equivalent for SP40 models. For all other models, recommended spark plug is AC CS45T, Champion RDJ6 or equivalent. On all models, spark plug electrode gap is 0.025 inch (0.63 mm). Note that spark plug has a tapered seat and does not require a gasket. Tighten spark plug to a torque of 105-120 in.-lbs. (11.9-13.5 N·m).

CARBURETOR. Models may be equipped with either a Tillotson, Walbro or Zama diaphragm type carburetor.

Tillotson HU carburetors are used on some PM310, PM320, PM330 and PM340 models.

Walbro WA carburetors are used on some PM310, PM320, PM330, PM340 and PM510 models. Walbro MDC carburetors are used on Eager Beaver, Power Mac 6, PM155, PM165, all Mini-Mac models and some Mac 110, 120, 130 and 140 models.

Zama C1 carburetors are used on all PM355, PM365, PM375, PM515 and SP40 models and some PM310, PM320, PM330, PM340, PM510 and Eager Beaver 2.1, Wildcat and MacCat models. Zama M1 carburetors are used on some Mac 110, 120, 130 and 140 models.

Refer to CARBURETOR SERVICE section for overhaul and exploded views of Tillotson, Walbro and Zama carburetors. On all models except Walbro MDC and Zama M1, initial adjustment of idle and high speed mixture needles (Fig. MC7-1) is one turn open from a lightly seated position.

On Walbro Model MDC, initial adjustment for idle and high speed mixture screws is ¾ turn open from a lightly seated position. On Zama Model M1, initial adjustment for idle and high speed mixture needles is 1¼ turns open.

On models equipped with Zama C1 carburetor, high speed mixture is not adjustable on some carburetors due to absence of high speed mixture needle.

On all types of carburetors, make final adjustment with engine warm and running. Make certain air filter is clean as a dirty filter can affect engine performance in the same manner as a carburetor that is not adjusted correctly.

Adjust idle speed screw so engine idles just below clutch engagement speed. Adjust idle speed mixture needle so engine will accelerate cleanly without hesitation. Adjust high speed mixture needle to obtain optimum performance under cutting load. Do not operate saw with high speed mixture needle set too lean (turned too far clockwise) as engine damage may occur due to lack of lubrication.

IGNITION. All 2.1 cu. in. (34.4 cc) models, Wildcat, MacCat and late Eager Beaver (2.0 cu. in. [32.8 cc]) saws are equipped with an electronic ignition. Refer to Fig. MC7-3. Ignition coil and electronic circuitry are contained in a

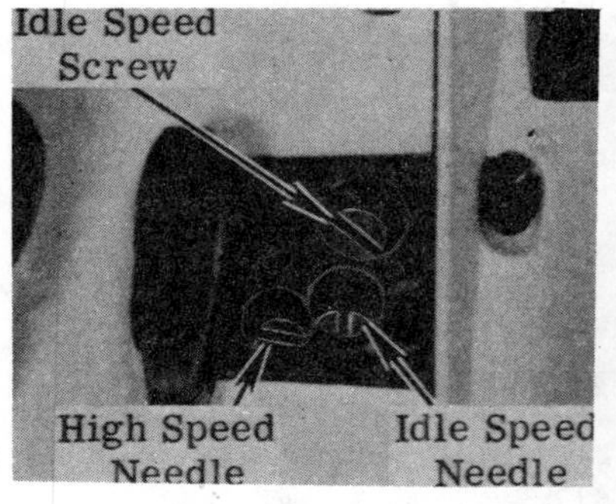

Fig. MC7-1—View showing location of carburetor adjustment screws on Mac 110, 120, 130, 140 and Power Mac 6 and all Mini-Mac models.

Illustrations courtesy McCulloch Corp.

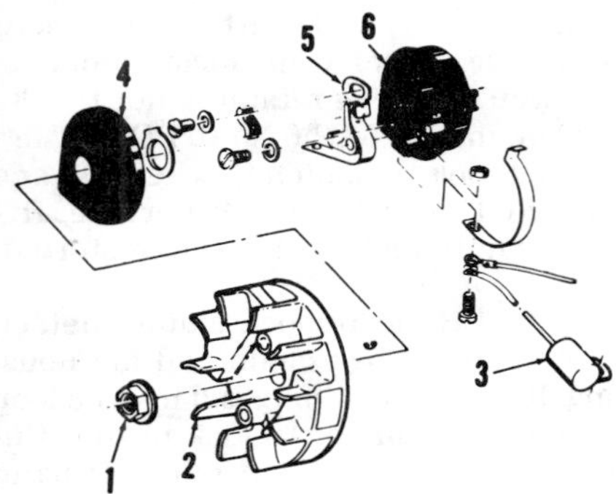

Fig. MC7-2—Exploded view of ignition system used on early models equipped with breaker-point ignition.

1. Flywheel nut
2. Flywheel
3. Condenser
4. Cover
5. Ignition breaker points
6. Breaker box

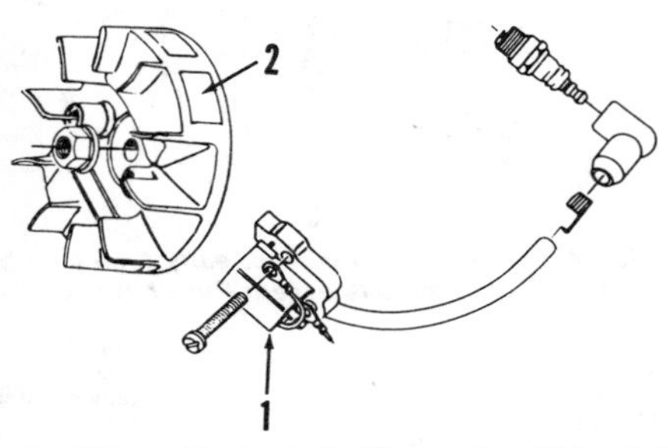

Fig. MC7-3—Electronic ignition system (1) is used on late models.

one-piece ignition module (1) which must be serviced as a unit assembly.

Air gap between flywheel magnets and laminated legs of module should be 0.012 inch (0.30 mm). Loosen ignition module mounting screws and move module to obtain desired air gap.

All other models are equipped with a conventional breaker-point flywheel magneto ignition system with the breaker points located in breaker-box (6—Fig. MC7-2) located behind the flywheel. Breaker-point gap should be 0.018 inch (0.46 mm). Clearance between laminated coil legs and flywheel magnets should be 0.010 inch (0.25 mm) and can be adjusted after loosening coil mounting screws.

LUBRICATION. The engine is lubricated with a mixture of regular gasoline and oil. Recommended fuel:oil ratio is 40:1 when using McCulloch oil. If McCulloch oil is not available, a good grade oil designed for use in air-cooled two-stroke engines should be mixed at a 20:1 ratio. Do not use oil designed for automotive use. Use a separate container to mix fuel and oil.

All models are equipped with a chain oiler system. Recommended oil is McCulloch Chain, Bar and Sprocket oil. Oil designed for automotive use may also be used. Select oil viscosity according to ambient temperature. Use SAE 10 oil when temperature is below 40°F (5°C) and SAE 30 oil when temperature is above 40°F (5°C).

On some models, automatic oil pump output can be adjusted by turning adjusting screw (A—Fig. MC7-4). Turn screw clockwise to decrease oil flow or counterclockwise to increase oil flow.

CARBON. If a noticeable lack of power or a decrease in the exhaust noise level is evident, it is possible that muffler and exhaust ports need cleaning. Use a wood scraper when cleaning exhaust ports to avoid damage to cylinder or piston.

REPAIRS

CRANKCASE PRESSURE TEST. An improperly sealed crankcase can cause the engine to be hard to start, run rough, have low power and overheat. Refer to ENGINE SERVICE section of this manual for crankcase pressure test procedure. If crankcase leakage is indicated, pressurize crankcase and use a soap and water solution to check gaskets, seals, pulse line and castings for leakage.

PISTON, RINGS AND CYLINDER. To remove piston it is necessary to separate crankcase and cylinder as outlined in CRANKSHAFT AND CRANKCASE section.

Piston pin (27—Fig. MC7-4) on Mini-Mac 25, 30 and 35 models, Power Mac 6 and some Mac 110, 120, 130 and 140 models is supported by two needle bearings that are a press fit in piston bore. Piston pin is a press fit in connecting rod and pin retaining rings (25) are not used. Use McCulloch or other suitable tools to support piston, then use a $^1/_4$ inch (6 mm) drift pin to press piston pin and one of the bearings out of piston. Remove piston from connecting rod and press out remaining bearing. Bearings must be renewed due to damage during removal. When assembling piston, pin and connecting rod, care should be taken not to damage bearings or piston. Heating piston with a heat lamp will ease removal and installation of bearings.

Piston pin on Models Eager Beaver, Eager Beaver 2.1, Wildcat, MacCat, PM155, PM165, PM310, PM320, PM330, PM340, PM355, PM365, PM375, PM510, PM515, SP40 and some Mac 110, 120, 130 and 140 models rides in a roller bearing (22) in the connecting rod and is retained in piston by retaining rings (25). Piston pin may be tapped out of piston after removing pin retainers. Be careful not to lose the loose bearing rollers in connecting rod. Install a new bearing (22) in connecting rod so bearing cage is centered in small end of rod.

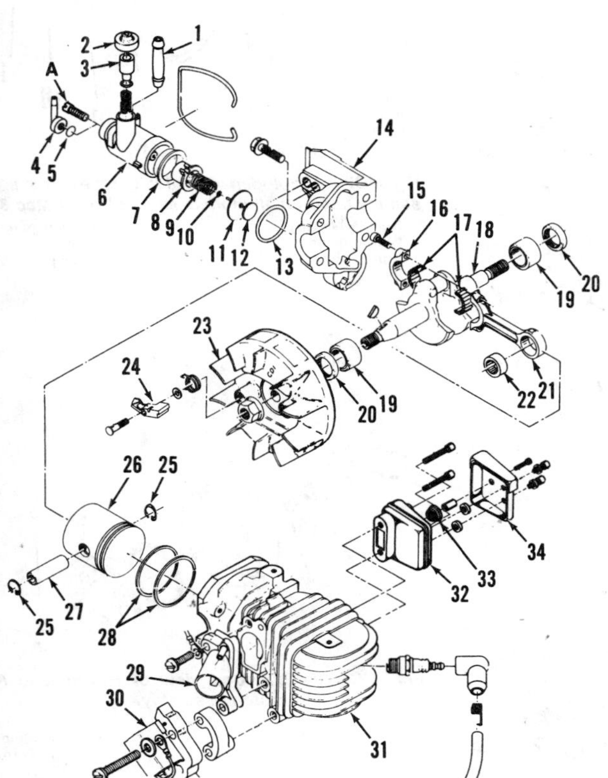

Fig. MC7-4—Exploded view of engine typical of all models except Power Mac 6. Piston pin (27) on Mini-Mac models and some Mac 110, 120, 130 and 140 models, is supported by two needle bearings (not shown) in piston instead of single roller bearing (22) in connecting rod.

1. Oil outlet
2. Cap
3. Pump plunger
4. Adjusting screw
5. Oil inlet
6. Oil pump body
7. Collar
8. Sleeve
9. Spring
10. "O" ring
11. Ring
12. Piston
13. "O" ring
14. Crankcase
15. Screw
16. Rod cap
17. Bearing rollers (20)
18. Crankshaft
19. Bearing
20. Seal
21. Connecting rod
22. Roller bearing
23. Flywheel
24. Starter pawl
25. Retaining ring
26. Piston
27. Piston pin
28. Piston rings
29. Intake manifold
30. Ignition module
31. Cylinder
32. Muffler
33. Spark arrestor screen
34. Muffler cover

Illustrations courtesy McCulloch Corp.

Piston on Model PM510 may be equipped with flat (F—Fig. MC7-6) or round (R) piston pin retainers. Be sure pin retainer matches retainer groove in piston pin bore.

Cylinder bore is chrome plated and no oversize piston or piston ring is available. If chrome plating is worn away or if cylinder bore is scuffed or scored, cylinder should be renewed. Ring end gap is 0.004-0.024 inch (0.10-0.61 mm) for 2.1 cu. in. (34.4 cc) models and 0.005-0.015 inch (0.13-0.38 mm) for all other models. Ring side clearance in piston ring groove is 0.0045-0.0070 inch (0.12-0.18 mm) for Models PM510, PM515 and SP40 and 0.0030-0.0045 inch (0.08-0.12 mm) for all other models. Renew piston if ring side clearance is excessive.

Position piston rings on piston so end gap is away from cylinder exhaust port. On models using retaining rings to secure piston pin in piston, assemble piston to connecting rod so closed end of pin will face the exhaust port.

CONNECTING ROD. Refer to PISTON section to remove piston from connecting rod. Unscrew rod cap screws to remove rod from crankshaft. Rod cap bearing has 20 needle rollers.

Inspect connecting rod for worn or damaged bearing surfaces. Connecting rod should not be bent or twisted. Inspect crankshaft crankpin for wear or scoring.

To reassemble, use grease to hold bearing rollers in place in connecting rod and cap and install connecting rod on crankshaft making sure pips on rod and cap shown in Fig. MC7-7 are aligned. Connecting rod and cap are fractured and serration must mate correctly. Tighten connecting rod cap screws to 35-40 in.-lbs. (3.9-4.5 N·m).

CRANKSHAFT AND CRANKCASE. Crankshaft is supported by two needle roller bearings. To remove crankshaft, first remove sprocket cover, bar and chain. Remove fan housing, fuel tank, air filter housing and carburetor. Disconnect oil line and remove oil tank assembly. Remove two bolts attaching engine to bottom shroud and withdraw engine. Remove spark plug and insert a knotted rope in spark plug hole to prevent crankshaft from rotating. Remove flywheel nut and tap flywheel counterbalance with plastic mallet to unseat flywheel from crankshaft taper. Remove clutch assembly (retaining nut has left-hand threads). Remove crankcase mounting screws and separate crankcase from cylinder. Remove crankshaft, connecting rod and piston as an assembly from cylinder. Separate piston and connecting rod from crankshaft.

Bearings on Power Mac 6 are retained by snap rings (5—Fig. MC7-5). Thrust washers (7) on Power Mac 6 must be installed with chamfer on inside. Install crankshaft bearings on all models with lettered end of bearing facing outward.

Crankcase and cylinder have mated surfaces and must not be interchanged. Use a suitable sealant on mating surfaces during reassembly. Tighten crankcase screws to 60-70 in.-lbs. (6.8-7.9 N·m).

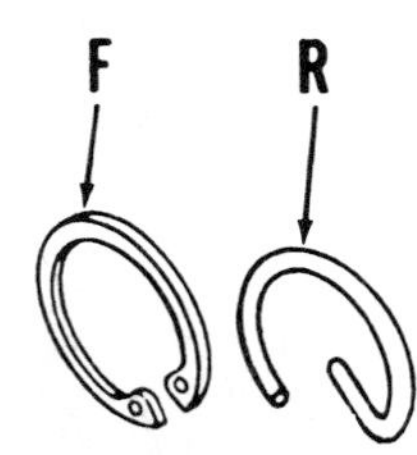

Fig. MC7-6—Model PM510 may be equipped with flat (F) or round (R) piston pin retainers. Be sure retainer matches groove in piston.

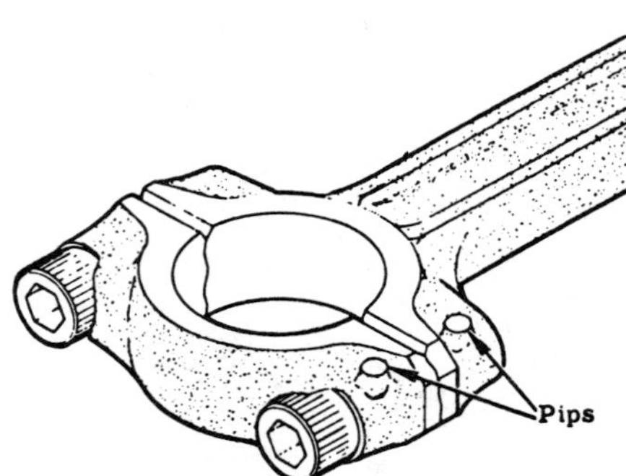

Fig. MC7-7—For correct connecting rod assembly, pips must be aligned as shown.

Make certain crankshaft rotates freely. If not, disassemble and locate problem. Tighten flywheel retaining nut to 190-200 in.-lbs. (21.5-22.6 N·m). DO NOT use impact tools to tighten flywheel nut and DO NOT over-torque, otherwise flywheel hub can be cracked or distorted.

CLUTCH. To remove clutch, detach clutch guard, bar, chain and fan housing. Remove spark plug and insert a loop of rope in cylinder to lock piston. Unscrew clutch retaining nut (left-hand threads) clockwise and remove clutch components from crankshaft. Refer to Figs. MC7-8, MC7-9 and MC7-10 for exploded views of clutch assemblies.

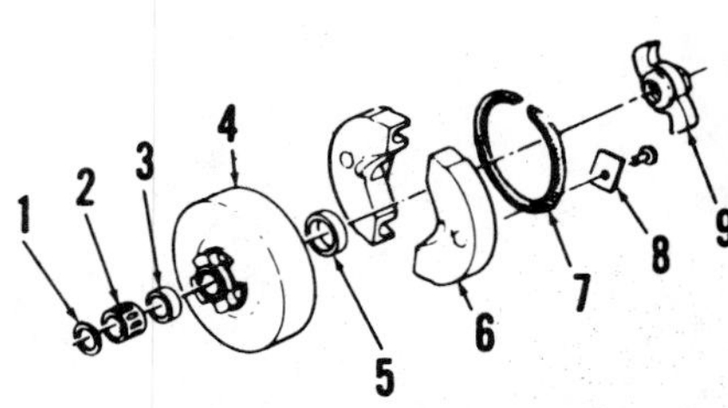

Fig. MC7-8—Exploded view of early type clutch used on all models except Power Mac 6.

1. Washer
2. Bearing
3. Spacer
4. Clutch drum
5. Spacer
6. Clutch shoes
7. Spring
8. Retainer plates
9. Rotor

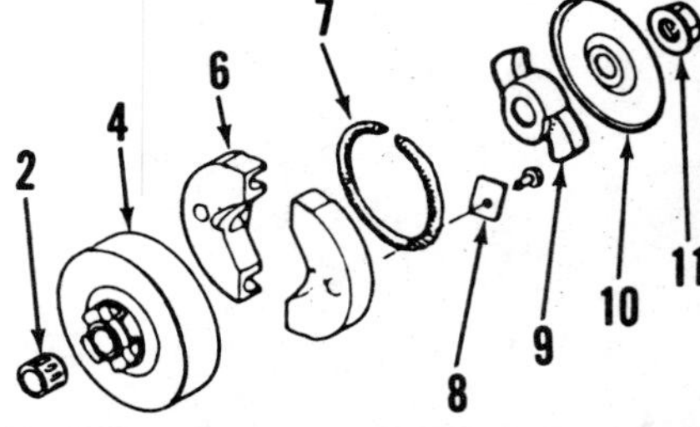

Fig. MC7-9—Exploded view of later type clutch assembly used on all models except Power Mac 6.

2. Needle bearing
4. Clutch drum
6. Clutch shoes
7. Spring
8. Retainer plates
9. Rotor
10. Cover plate
11. Nut

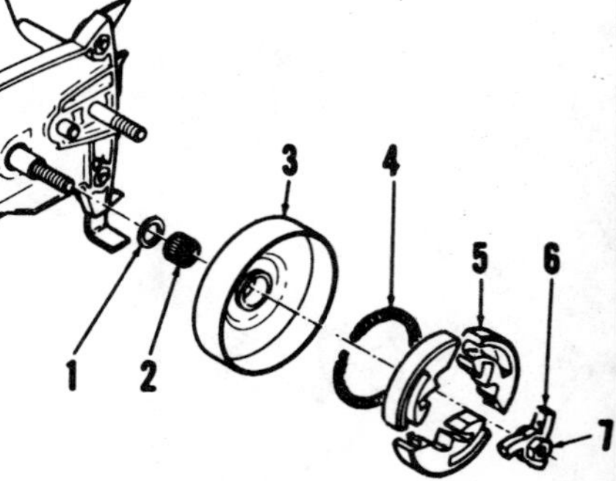

Fig. MC7-10—Exploded view of Power Mac 6 clutch assembly.

1. Washer
2. Bearing
3. Drum & sprocket
4. Garter spring
5. Shoe
6. Rotor
7. Nut

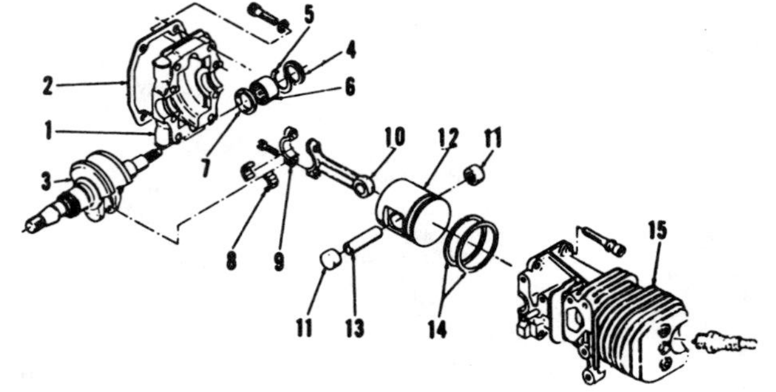

Fig. MC7-5—Exploded view of Power Mac 6 power head assembly.

1. Crankcase bottom
2. Gasket
3. Crankshaft
4. Oil seal
5. Snap ring
6. Needle bearing
7. Thrust washer
8. Bearing rollers (20)
9. Connecting rod cap
10. Connecting rod
11. Bearing
12. Piston
13. Piston pin
14. Piston rings
15. Cylinder

Illustrations courtesy McCulloch Corp.

If necessary to renew clutch shoes, renew complete set of shoes. Check sprocket for worn rails and pins. Inspect sprocket needle bearing for wear. Clutch spring on all models except Power Mac 6 is retained by retainer plates (8—Fig. MC7-8 or Fig. MC7-9). A flat retainer plate or a plate with a bent corner has been used. Plates with a bent corner should be used in place of the flat retainer plates. Install clutch spring in clutch shoes with spring ends located where one of the retainer plates is to be installed. Install retainer plate adjacent to clutch spring ends with bent corner of plate up. Install other retainer plate with bent corner down contacting spring.

Tighten clutch nut to 160 in.-lbs. (18.0 N·m). Nut has left-hand threads. Note that the use of an impact wrench to loosen or tighten clutch nut is not recommended.

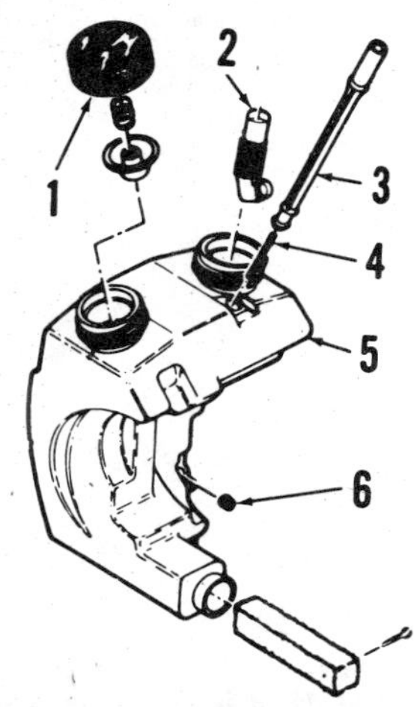

Fig. MC7-11—View of manual oil pump used on Eager Beaver, Mini-Mac 25, 30, 35, Mac 110, 120, 130, 140, PM155, PM165, MP510, PM515 and SP40.

1. Cap
2. Pump body
3. Pump piston
4. Spring
5. Fuel & oil tank
6. Check valve

MANUAL CHAIN OILER. Refer to Fig. MC7-11 for an exploded view of oil pump used on Eager Beaver, Mini-Mac 25, 30, 35, Mac 110, 120, 130, 140, PM155, PM165, PM510, PM515 and SP40 with manual chain oiler. Three check valves (6) have been used and are colored black, green or gray. Recommended check valve is colored gray. Check valve is not renewable on some models. Be sure oil connector and oil discharge line are properly connected to prevent oil leaks.

Refer to Figs. MC7-12 and MC7-13 for exploded views of manual oil pumps used on Power Mac 6. Note that type of pump shown in Fig. MC7-12 pumps oil using a diaphragm and spring while the manual oiler shown in Fig. MC7-13 uses a valve disc.

The manual oil pump used on Models PM310, PM320, PM330, PM340, PM355, PM365, PM375 and Eager Beaver 2.1 is integral with automatic oil pump. Pump plunger (12—Fig. MC7-15) is operated by a remote button and push rod.

AUTOMATIC CHAIN OILER. Refer to Fig. MC7-13 for an exploded view of automatic chain oiler used on Power Mac 6. Oil pump cylinder (1) is removed by turning it in counterclockwise direction. Oil tank (19) must be removed to remove piston assembly. Check condition of "O" rings and be sure oil suction and pressure passages are clear.

The automatic chain oiler used on Models PM155, PM165, PM510, PM515, SP40, Mini-Mac 25, 30, 35, Mac 110, 120, 130 and 140 is shown in Fig. MC7-14. Remove front cover and fuel tank for access to automatic oil pump. Some models are equipped with a washer to prevent movement of "O" ring (9). Washer must be sealed to crankcase (10) to prevent leakage. Later models have an "O" ring on the pump piston (7) and a piston ring with a smaller ID. These components should be installed in place of original components if low oil output occurs.

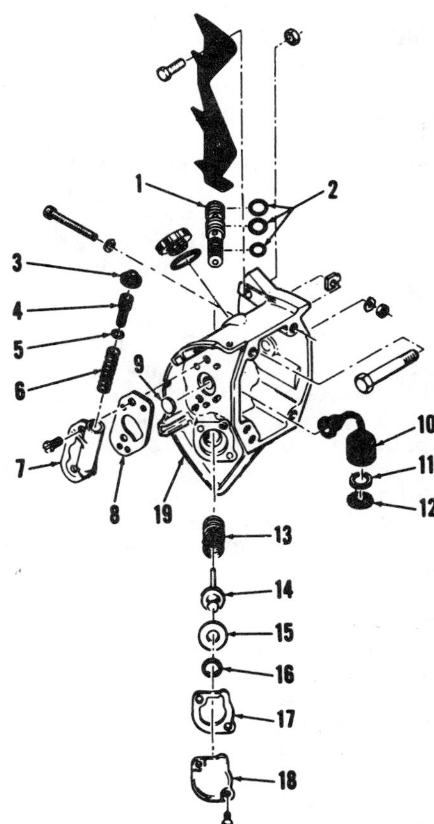

Fig. MC7-13—Exploded view of automatic oiler and manual oiler used on some Power Mac 6 saws. Note difference in size of "O" rings (2) used on cylinder (1).

1. Oil pump cylinder
2. "O" rings
3. Cap
4. Pump plunger
5. "O" ring
6. Spring
7. Pump body
8. Gasket
9. Valve
10. Oil hose
11. Weight
12. Screen
13. Spring
14. Oiler piston
15. Piston ring
16. "O" ring
17. Gasket
18. Cover
19. Oil tank

Fig. MC7-14—Exploded view of automatic oil pump used on Models PM155, PM165, PM510, PM515, SP40, Mini-Mac 25, 30, 35, Mac 110, 120, 130 and 140.

- A. Adjusting screw
1. Oil intake
2. Oil outlet
3. Oil pump body
4. Pump sleeve
5. Spring
6. Washer
7. Pump piston
8. Chain bar mounting bolt
9. "O" ring
10. Crankcase

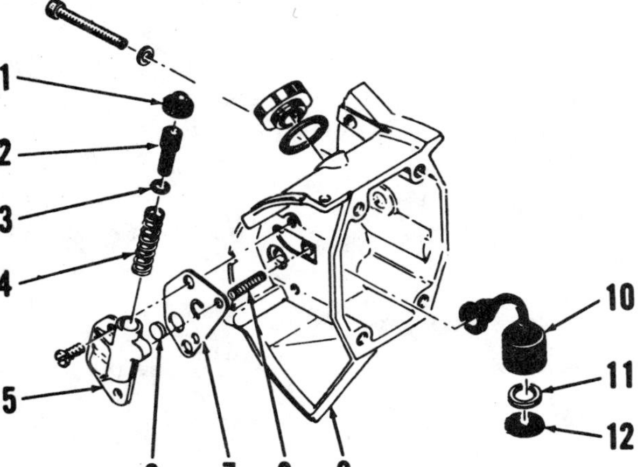

Fig. MC7-12—Exploded view of manual oiler assembly used on some Power Mac 6 saws.

1. Cap
2. Pump plunger
3. "O" ring
4. Spring
5. Pump body
6. Valve
7. Diaphragm
8. Spring
9. Oil tank
10. Oil hose
11. Weight
12. Screen

Models PM310, PM320, PM330, PM340, PM355, PM375, Eager Beaver 2.1, Wildcat and MacCat are equipped with automatic oil pump shown in Fig. MC7-15. Oil tank cap is vented and must be unobstructed for proper oil pump operation. The oil pump uses two check valves that must function correctly for pump to operate. Check valve (2) is accessible after removing oil inlet (1). There is also a check valve located in pump body, which is not available separately from body. Note bosses on pump body (3) when installing pump body on crankcase.

REWIND STARTER. To disassemble rewind starter, first remove starter housing (2—Fig. MC7-16) from saw. Remove rope handle and allow rope and pulley to slowly rewind. Remove starter cover (1) and pulley mounting screw (6) and remove rope pulley (4). Care should be taken when removing rewind spring (3) not to allow spring to unwind uncontrolled to prevent injury.

Rewind spring should be wound in housing in clockwise direction from outer end. Wind rope on pulley in clockwise direction viewed from flywheel side. To pre-tension rewind spring, complete starter assembly and pass rope through housing outlet and install rope handle. Pull a small amount of rope back through outlet and engage rope in notch of rope pulley. Rotate pulley one turn clockwise with rope in notch. Release rope from notch in pulley, pull rope handle and check rewind action. Repeat procedure as necessary until desired rewind action is obtained. Be sure excessive tension is not placed on spring, otherwise spring may break when rope is pulled to its full length. It should be possible to turn pulley at least an additional 1/2 turn clockwise with rope fully extended.

CHAIN BRAKE. Some models are equipped with a chain brake which stops chain motion when the operator's hand contacts chain brake lever (8—Figs. MC7-17 or MC7-18). To check for proper chain brake operation, place saw on flat surface and run at wide open throttle. Activate chain brake lever and chain should stop moving immediately. Pull brake lever rearward to disengage brake. No adjustment of chain brake is required. If brake fails to operate properly, disassemble and inspect for problem.

Two different chain brake assemblies have been used. Refer to Fig. MC7-17 and Fig. MC7-18. To disassemble either unit, remove brake housing (5) from saw. Remove brake lever (8) and carefully disengage spring (10). Remove brake band (2) from housing. Inspect all components for evidence of wear or damage and renew as necessary. Brake band (2) should be renewed if any point is worn to a thickness of 0.021 inch (0.5 mm) or less.

When reassembling, lubricate compression spring, pivot points and latch engaging surface with light coat of lithium base grease.

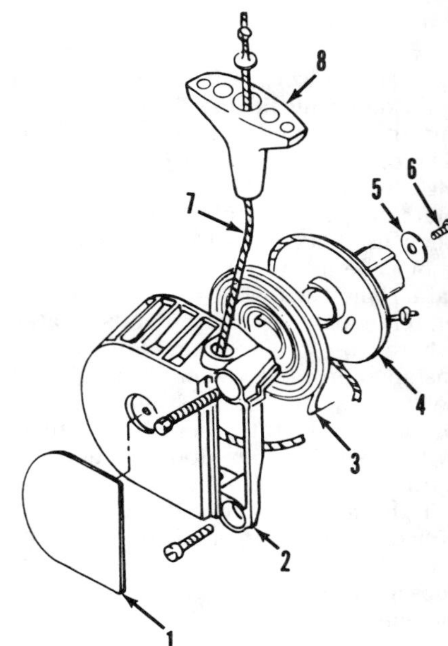

Fig. MC7-16—Exploded view of rewind starter typical of all models.

1. Cover
2. Housing
3. Rewind spring
4. Pulley
5. Washer
6. Screw
7. Rope
8. Handle

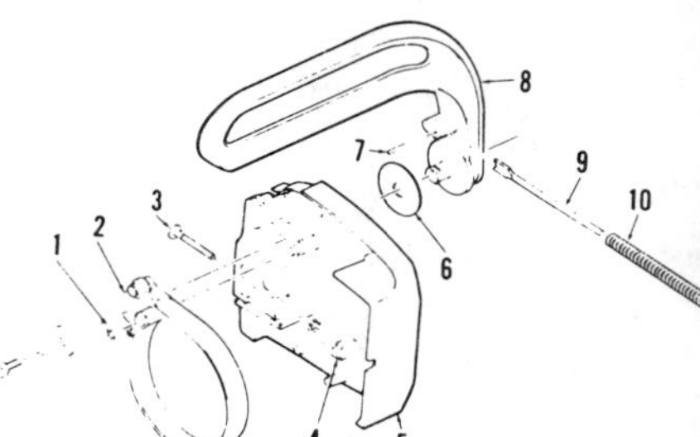

Fig. MC7-17—Exploded view of chain brake mechanism used on Model SP40 and later Mini-Mac 25 models.

1. Spring fastener
2. Brake strap
3. Chain adjusting screw
4. Adjusting nut
5. Clutch cover
6. Washer
7. Pin
8. Chain brake lever
9. Spring guide
10. Brake spring

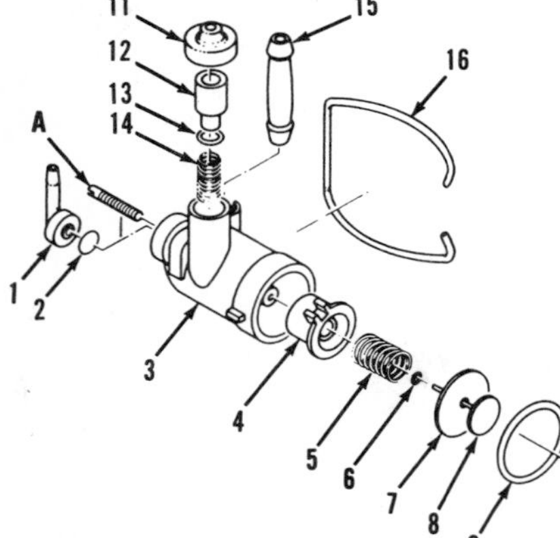

Fig. MC7-15—Exploded view of oil pump used on Models PM310, PM320, PM330, PM340, PM355, PM365, PM375, Eager Beaver 2.1, Wildcat and MacCat. Adjusting screw (A) is not used on some models.

1. Oil inlet
2. Check valve
3. Pump body
4. Sleeve
5. Spring
6. "O" ring
7. Washer
8. Piston
9. "O" ring
11. Cap
12. Plunger
13. "O" ring
14. Spring
15. Oil outlet
16. Retainer

Fig. MC7-18—Exploded view of chain brake mechanism used on Models Mac 110, 120, 130, 140, PM155, PM165, PM310, PM320, PM340, PM355, PM365, PM375, PM510, PM515, Eager Beaver, Eager Beaver 2.1, Wildcat and MacCat.

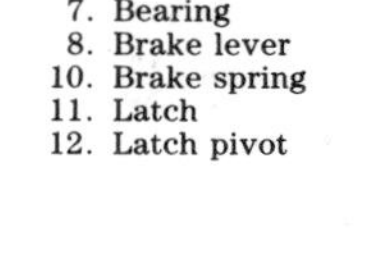

1. Brake lever pivot
2. Brake band
3. Chain adjuster screw
4. Adjuster nut
5. Brake housing
6. Roller pin
7. Bearing
8. Brake lever
10. Brake spring
11. Latch
12. Latch pivot

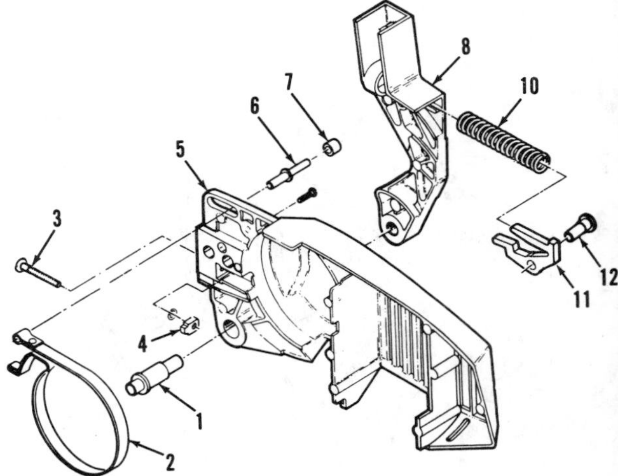

Illustrations courtesy McCulloch Corp.

McCULLOCH

Model	Bore	Stroke	Displ.	Drive Type
PM605	40 mm (1.57 in.)	35 mm (1.38 in.)	58 cc (3.5 cu. in.)	Direct
PM610, Super 610	47 mm (1.85 in.)	35 mm (1.38 in.)	60 cc (3.7 cu. in.)	Direct
PM650, PM655	47 mm (1.85 in.)	35 mm (1.38 in.)	60 cc (3.7 cu. in.)	Direct
Eager Beaver 3.7	47 mm (1.85 in.)	35 mm (1.38 in.)	60 cc (3.7 cu. in.)	Direct
TimberBear	46 mm (1.81 in.)	35 mm (1.38 in.)	55 cc (3.4 cu. in.)	Direct

NOTE: These McCulloch models are equipped with metric fasteners.

MAINTENANCE

SPARK PLUG. Recommended spark plug is AC CS45T, Champion RDJ6 or equivalent. Spark plug electrode gap is 0.025 inch (0.63 mm). Note that plug has a tapered seat and does not require a gasket. Tighten spark plug to 120 in.-lbs. (13.6 N·m).

Spark plug should be removed, cleaned and inspected periodically. The use of an abrasive type spark plug cleaning machine is not recommended.

CARBURETOR. Models PM650 and PM655 are equipped with a Walbro HDB diaphragm type carburetor. Model PM610 may be equipped with a Tillotson HK, Walbro HDB or Zama C2S diaphragm carburetor. Models Super 610, Eager Beaver 3.7 and PM605 are equipped with a Zama C2S diaphragm carburetor. TimberBear saw is equipped with Walbro HDB diaphragm carburetor. Refer to CARBURETOR SERVICE section for overhaul and exploded view of Tillotson, Walbro and Zama carburetors.

On all types of carburetor, initial adjustment of idle and high speed mixture needles (Fig. MC8-1) is one turn open from a lightly seated position. Make final adjustment with engine warm and running. Be sure air filter is clean before making final carburetor adjustment.

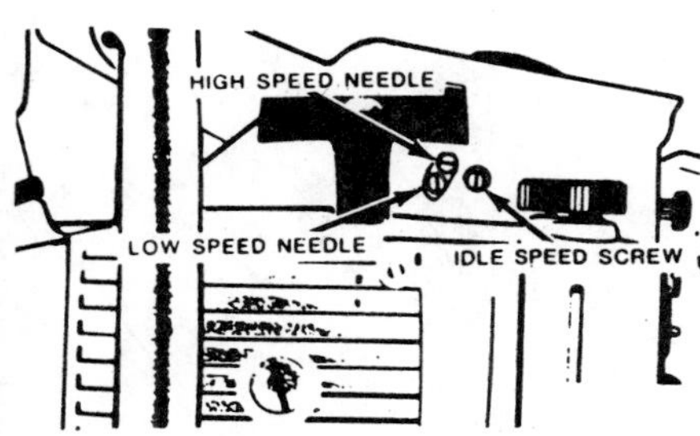

Fig. MC8-1—Drawing showing location of carburetor adjustment points typical of all saws.

Adjust idle speed screw so engine idles just below clutch engagement speed. Adjust idle mixture needle so engine will accelerate cleanly without hesitation. Adjust high speed mixture needle to obtain optimum performance under cutting load. Saw should never be operated with high speed mixture needle set less than one full turn out (clockwise) unless in high altitude area, as engine could be damaged from lack of lubrication.

IGNITION. All models are equipped with a capacitor discharge solid-state ignition system. Ignition components are contained in an ignition module located adjacent to flywheel. Ignition timing is 26 degrees BTDC and is not adjustable. Ignition module must be positioned so there is 0.011-0.015 inch (0.28-0.38 mm) gap between module laminated legs and flywheel magnets. Loosen module mounting screws and move module as necessary to obtain specified gap.

LUBRICATION. The engine is lubricated by mixing oil with fuel. Recommended fuel:oil ratio is 40:1 if using McCulloch oil, or 20:1 when using any other brand of oil designed for two-stroke air-cooled engine. If McCulloch oil is not used, the addition of a fuel stabilizer (such as STA-Bil Gas Stabilizer or equivalent) is recommended to minimize the formation of fuel gum deposits. The use of oil designed for automotive use is not recommended. Regular grade unleaded or leaded gasoline is recommended, but use only one type. Changing fuel types can cause engine damage. Use a separate container when mixing oil and fuel.

All models are equipped with a manual and automatic oil pump. Oil output of automatic oil pump may be adjusted by removing air filter cover and turning adjusting screw (Fig. MC8-2). McCulloch Chain, Bar and Sprocket Oil is recommended for use in all temperatures. The use of automotive type oil is also acceptable. Select oil viscosity according to ambient temperature. Use SAE 10 oil when temperature is below 40°F (5°C) and SAE 30 oil when temperature is above 40°F (5°C).

REPAIRS

CRANKCASE PRESSURE TEST. An improperly sealed crankcase can cause the engine to be hard to start, run rough, have low power and overheat. Refer to ENGINE SERVICE section of this manual for crankcase pressure test procedure. If crankcase leakage is indi-

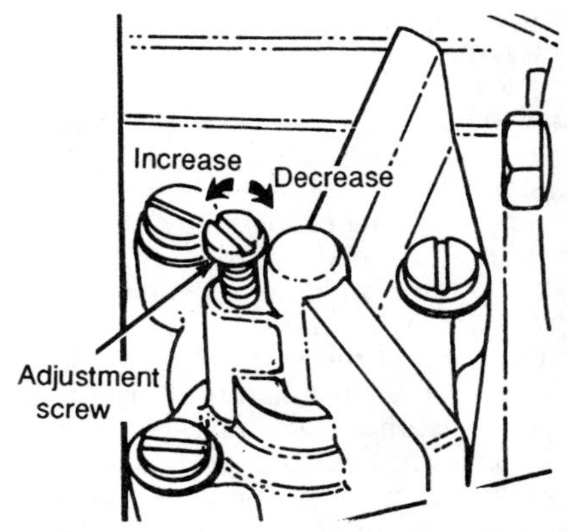

Fig. MC8-2—Access to automatic oil pump adjustment screw is obtained by removing air filter cover. Turn screw as indicated to increase or decrease oil flow.

cated, pressurize crankcase and use a soap and water solution to check gaskets, seals, pulse line and castings for leakage.

TIGHTENING TORQUES. Refer to the following table for tightening torque values:

Connecting rod	65-75 in.-lbs. (7.4-8.4 N·m)
Crankcase to cylinder	70-75 in.-lbs. (7.9-8.4 N·m)
Crankcase to oil tank	75-80 in.-lbs. (8.4-9.0 N·m)
Decompression valve	110-120 in.-lbs. (12.4-13.5 N·m)
Carburetor	25-40 in.-lbs. (2.8-4.5 N·m)
Flywheel nut	265-325 in.-lbs. (30.0-36.7 N·m)
Clutch nut	160-170 in.-lbs. (18.1-19.2 N·m)
Muffler	65-75 in.-lbs. (7.4-8.4 N·m)
Spark plug	120 in.-lbs. (13.5 N·m)
Air filter housing	35-40 in.-lbs. (4.0-4.5 N·m)
Ignition module	55-60 in.-lbs. (6.2-6.8 N·m)
Oil pump cover	7-10 in.-lbs. (0.8-1.1 N·m)
Oil pump housing	10-15 in.-lbs. (1.1-1.7 N·m)

PISTON, RINGS AND CYLINDER. To remove piston, it is necessary to separate crankcase and cylinder as outlined in CRANKSHAFT AND CRANKCASE section. Press piston pin (6—Fig. MC8-3) out of piston and connecting rod. Needle bearings (7) are a press fit in piston. Piston should be heated to aid in removing needle bearings.

The cylinder bore is chrome plated and should be inspected for flaking, cracking or excessive wear. Oversize piston and ring are not available. Note that Model PM610 saws built before February 1984 are equipped with a thicker piston ring than later models. Do not interchange piston rings.

The piston pin is a press fit in connecting rod small end. Piston pin rides in needle bearings that are a press fit in piston. The piston should be heated when removing or installing piston pin bearings. Special tools, part number 84223, are available to support and press in the bearings.

Connecting rod small end should be heated to ease installation of piston pin. Install piston so side marked with an "E" is toward exhaust port. A locating pin is present in piston ring groove to prevent piston ring rotation. Be sure ring end gap is positioned around locating pin when installing piston in cylinder.

CRANKSHAFT, CONNECTING ROD AND CRANKCASE. The crankcase (17—Fig. MC8-3) must be separated from the cylinder (1) to remove crankshaft assembly (16). For access to crankcase, remove chain brake, guide bar and chain, air filter cover, air filter, starter housing, oil pump and left side cover. Remove fuel tank, handle, air box and carburetor. Remove spark plug and install piston stop tool in spark plug hole. Remove clutch assembly (left-hand threads) and flywheel nut (right-hand threads). Detach bottom shroud, muffler, oil tank and kill switch plate. Remove crankcase mounting screws and separate crankcase, crankshaft assembly and cylinder.

The connecting rod rides on 20 loose bearing rollers (9). Inspect connecting rod and crankpin for excessive wear or damage. To assemble connecting rod on crankshaft, use grease to hold bearing rollers in place in rod and cap. Make sure dots on rod and cap are aligned. Rod and cap are fractured and serration must mate correctly. Tighten connecting rod screws to 65-75 in.-lbs. (7.4-8.4 N·m).

The crankshaft is supported by a ball bearing (14) on the flywheel end and a roller bearing (11) on the clutch end. To install bearings, heat bearings with a heat lamp, then press onto crankshaft until bottomed against crankshaft shoulder. Be sure bearing (14) is positioned with snap ring (15) nearer crankshaft counterweights. Install new seals (12 and 13) on crankshaft.

Lubricate piston, cylinder and crankshaft bearings with engine oil prior to assembly. Apply thin bead of R.T.V. sealant to mating surfaces of cylinder and crankcase. Be sure that snap ring (15) engages groove in crankcase and cylinder and that seals are located properly. Tighten crankcase screws to 70-75 in.-lbs. (7.9-8.5 N·m). Rotate crankshaft to make certain it turns freely. If not, disassemble and locate problem. Complete reassembly by reversing disassembly procedure.

CLUTCH. Refer to Fig. MC8-4 for an exploded view of clutch assembly. To remove clutch, first remove chain brake, guide bar and chain. Install piston lock tool in spark plug hole or use other suitable means to lock piston. Unscrew clutch mounting nut clockwise (left-hand threads). Remove and separate clutch components.

Clutch shoes (5), springs (7) and retainers (8) are renewed as pairs. Inspect clutch drum (4), needle bearing (3) and sprocket (2) for excessive wear and renew as necessary.

Lubricate needle bearing with grease. Install clutch assembly and tighten mounting nut to 160-170 in.-lbs. (18.1-19.2 N·m).

DECOMPRESSION VALVE. Models PM650 and PM655 are equipped with a decompression valve located in cylinder to aid engine starting. On Model PM650,

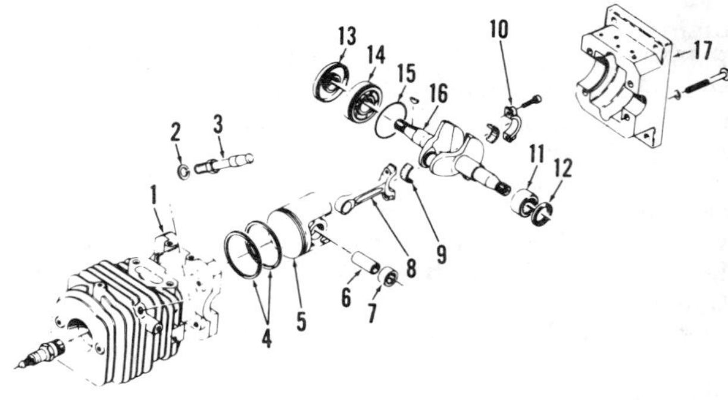

Fig. MC8-3—Exploded view of engine assembly.

1. Cylinder
2. Washer
3. Decompression valve
4. Piston rings
5. Piston
6. Piston pin
7. Needle bearing (2)
8. Connecting rod
9. Bearing rollers (20)
10. Rod cap
11. Needle bearing
12. Seal
13. Seal
14. Ball bearing
15. Snap ring
16. Crankshaft
17. Crankcase

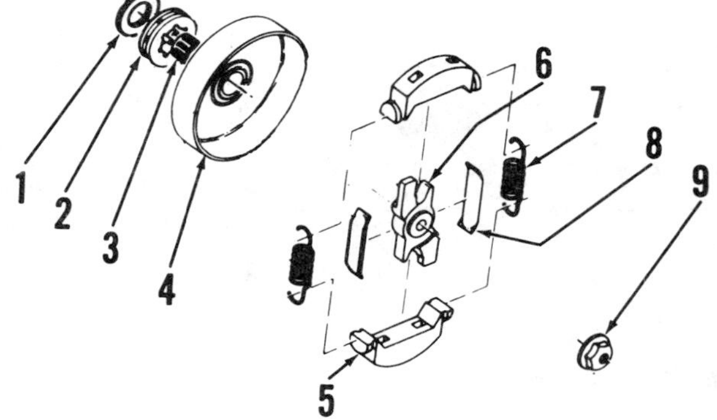

Fig. MC8-4—Exploded view of clutch typical of all models.

1. Shim
2. Sprocket
3. Roller bearing
4. Clutch drum
5. Clutch shoe
6. Hub
7. Spring
8. Retainer
9. Nut (L.H.)

Illustrations courtesy McCulloch Corp.

two different valves have been used that are identified by nut length on the valve. See Fig. MC8-5. Each valve must be installed with the proper thickness washer for correct fit in cylinder. Note that thin washer (T) must be installed on valve with long nut (L), and thick washer (W) must be used with valve having short nut (S).

OIL PUMP. All models are equipped with the oil pump shown in Fig. MC8-6. The automatic oil pump is operated by crankcase pulsations directed against diaphragm (10) that moves piston (9). The manual oil pump is operated by forcing push rod against pump plunger (2).

For access to oil pump, remove air filter cover. Remove oiler push rod retainer clip. Remove oil pump mounting screws and remove oil pump assembly from crankcase. Remove pump cover (11) and inspect components for wear or damage.

To adjust automatic oil pump output, turn adjusting screw (A) counterclockwise to increase oil flow or clockwise to decrease oil flow.

REWIND STARTER. Rewind starter components are contained in starter housing (1—Fig. MC8-7). To disassemble, remove starter housing, detach rope handle and allow rope to wind slowly onto pulley (3). Unscrew retaining nut (6) and remove rope pulley. Use caution when removing rewind spring (2) to prevent injury due to uncontrolled uncoiling of spring.

Note that some starters use a bolt and nut to retain rope pulley, and other starters are equipped with a screw that threads into starter post.

When reassembling, wrap rewind spring in housing in a clockwise direction from outer end. Wrap rope on pulley in a clockwise direction viewed from flywheel side of pulley. Tighten rope pulley retaining screw, if so equipped, to 25-30 in.-lbs. (2.8-3.4 N·m), or tighten nut to 35 in.-lbs. (3.9 N·m). Wind rope in clockwise direction on pulley. Turn pulley and rope one turn clockwise to place tension on rewind spring, then install rope handle and check for proper operation. If rope handle does not stand upright when rope is rewound, turn pulley another turn clockwise with rope fully extended.

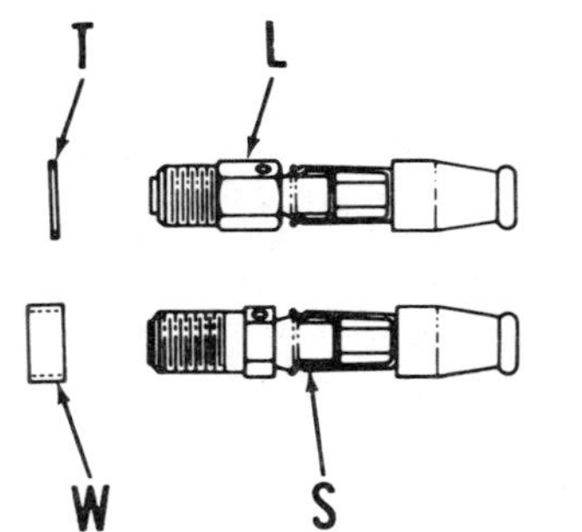

Fig. MC8-5—Thin washer (T) must be used with long-nut decompression valve (L), while thick washer (W) is used with short-nut valve (S).

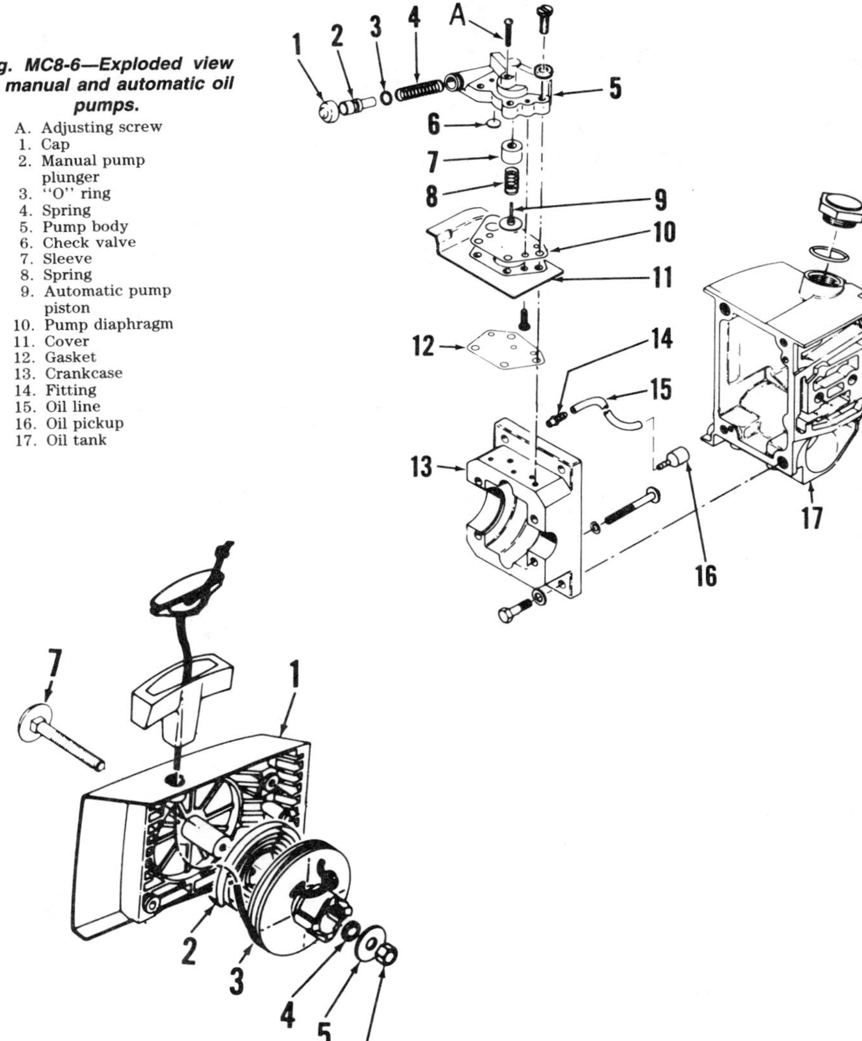

Fig. MC8-6—Exploded view of manual and automatic oil pumps.

A. Adjusting screw
1. Cap
2. Manual pump plunger
3. "O" ring
4. Spring
5. Pump body
6. Check valve
7. Sleeve
8. Spring
9. Automatic pump piston
10. Pump diaphragm
11. Cover
12. Gasket
13. Crankcase
14. Fitting
15. Oil line
16. Oil pickup
17. Oil tank

Fig. MC8-7—Exploded view of rewind starter. A screw is used in place of bolt (7) and nut (6) on some models. Refer to text.

1. Starter housing
2. Rewind spring
3. Rope pulley
4. Spacer
5. Washer
6. Nut
7. Bolt

Illustrations courtesy McCulloch Corp.

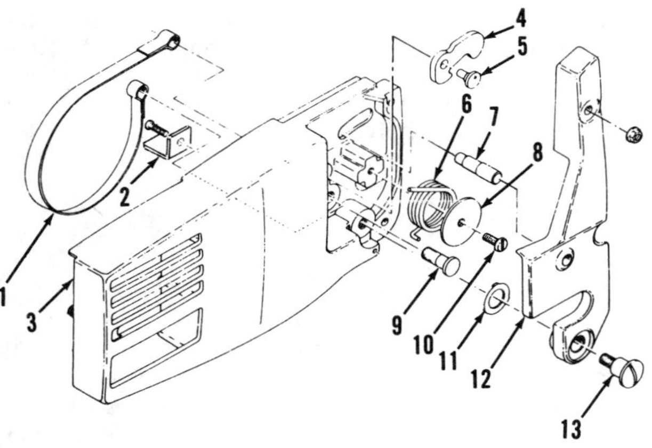

Fig. MC8-8—Exploded view of chain brake assembly used on some models.

1. Brake band
2. Chain stop
3. Brake housing
4. Latch
5. Pivot pin
6. Spring
7. Pin
8. Washer
9. Brake band pin
10. Screw
11. Special washer
12. Brake lever
13. Pivot bolt

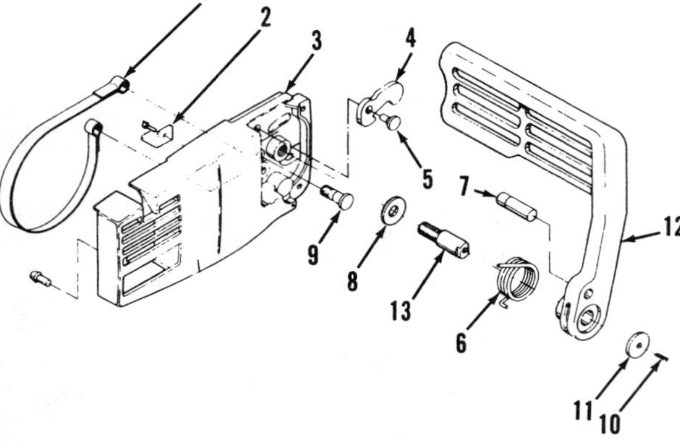

Fig. MC8-9—Exploded view of chain brake assembly used on some models.

1. Brake band
2. Chain stop
3. Brake housing
4. Latch
5. Pivot pin
6. Spring
7. Pin
8. Washer
9. Brake band pin
10. Screw
11. Washer
12. Brake lever
13. Pivot pin

CHAIN BRAKE. Some models are equipped with a chain brake system designed to stop chain movement should kickback occur. The chain brake is activated when operator's hand strikes chain brake lever (12—Fig. MC8-8 or Fig. MC8-9) that trips latch (4) and releases spring (6) to pull brake band (1) tight around clutch drum. Pull back chain brake lever to reset mechanism.

To check for proper chain brake operation, place saw on flat surface and run at one-half throttle. Activate chain brake lever and chain should stop moving immediately. No adjustment of chain brake is required. If brake fails to operate properly, disassemble and inspect for problem.

Two different chain brake assemblies have been used. Refer to Fig. MC8-8 and MC8-9. To disassemble either unit, remove brake housing (3) from saw. Remove brake lever (12) and carefully disengage spring (6). Remove brake band (1) from housing. Inspect all components for evidence of wear or damage and renew as necessary. Brake band (1) should be renewed if any point is worn to a thickness of 0.021 inch (0.5 mm) or less.

McCULLOCH

Model	Bore	Stroke	Displ.	Drive Type
PM1000	2.36 in. (60 mm)	1.42 in. (36 mm)	6.1 cu. in. (100 cc)	Direct

NOTE: This McCulloch model is equipped with metric fasteners.

MAINTENANCE

SPARK PLUG. Recommended spark plug is Bosch WS5F. Spark plug electrode gap should be 0.020 in. (0.5 mm).

CARBURETOR. A Tillotson HS diaphragm type carburetor is used. Refer to Tillotson section of CARBURETOR SERVICE section for service and exploded view of carburetor.

Initial adjustment of both low and high speed mixture screws is one turn open from a lightly seated position. Make final adjustment with engine warm and running. Adjust idle speed screw so engine idles just below clutch engagement speed. Adjust low speed mixture screw so engine will accelerate cleanly without hesitation. Adjust high speed mixture screw to obtain optimum performance under cutting load.

IGNITION. A breakerless capacitor discharge ignition system is used. Ignition timing is not adjustable. Air gap between ignition coil legs (2–Fig. MC9-1) and flywheel should be 0.014-0.018 inch (0.35-0.45 mm).

Fig. MC9-1 – Illustrated view of ignition components.

1. Flywheel
2. Ignition coil
3. High tension wire
4. Ignition module
5. Ground lead
6. Right rear handle support

LUBRICATION. Engine is lubricated by mixing engine oil with gasoline. Recommended oil is McCulloch two-stroke oil mixed at ratio as designated on oil container. If McCulloch oil is not available, a good quality oil designed for two-stroke air-cooled engines may be used when mixed at a 25:1 ratio. Use a separate container when mixing the oil and gas.

An adjustable automatic chain oil pump is used. Adjustment screw is located on bottom of saw. Rotating screw clockwise decreases oil output. Refer to OIL PUMP section. Chain oil should be clean SAE 30 oil if ambient temperature is above 40°F (4°C) or SAE 10 at lower temperatures.

CARBON. If a noticeable lack of power or a decrease in the exhaust noise level is evident it is possible that the muffler and exhaust ports need cleaning. Use a wood scraper when cleaning exhaust ports to avoid damage to cylinder or piston.

REPAIRS

PISTON, PIN, RINGS AND CYLINDER. The piston is accessible after removing the cylinder assembly. The aluminum alloy piston is fitted with two pinned rings. Reject piston pin and piston if there is any visible up and down play of pin in the piston bosses. Piston and pin are not available separately. Piston pin rides in needle roller bearing in small end of connecting rod. Inspect and renew bearing if excessive wear or damage is evident. Install piston so arrow on piston crown points toward exhaust port.

Cylinder bore is chrome plated and no piston or piston ring oversizes are available. Maximum allowable ring end gap is 0.031 inch (0.8 mm). Renew rings or cylinder as required when service limit is exceeded. Make certain ring end gap is around locating pins when installing cylinder.

CONNECTING ROD, CRANKSHAFT AND CRANKCASE. The connecting rod and crankshaft are available only as a unit assembly. Crankshaft is supported by ball bearings at both ends.

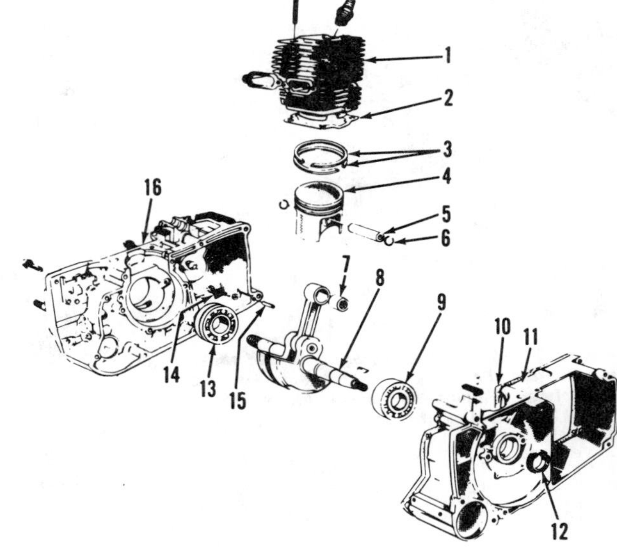

Fig. MC9-2 – Exploded view of engine. Right crankshaft seal is shown in Fig. MC9-4.

1. Cylinder
2. Gasket
3. Piston rings
4. Piston
5. Piston pin
6. Pin retainer
7. Needle bearing
8. Crankshaft & rod assy.
9. Main bearing
10. Gasket
11. Left crankcase half
12. Seal
13. Main bearing
14. Bearing retainer
15. Guide pin
16. Right crankcase half

Illustrations courtesy McCulloch Corp.

Clutch side main bearing is located by retainer (14 – Fig. MC9-2) while flywheel side main bearing is located by a shoulder in crankcase. Care should be taken not to damage mating surfaces of crankcase halves. Check rotation of connecting rod around crankpin and renew crankshaft unit if roughness or other damage is found.

When reassembling, be sure flywheel side main bearing is flush against its seat in left crankcase half and that retainer (14) engages groove in clutch side main bearing. Heat may be applied to crankcase bearing bores to ease reassembly. Make certain crankshaft is centered in crankcase and will rotate freely. Clutch side crankshaft seal should be installed flush with crankcase face. Flywheel side crankshaft seal should protrude 0.04 inch (1 mm) from crankcase face when installed.

CLUTCH. To remove clutch, detach clutch guard, bar and chain. The flywheel may be locked by inserting a suitable tool through hole in left crankcase half and into drilling in flywheel. Clutch hub (1 – Fig. MC9-3) has left-hand threads. Inspect clutch shoes and drum for excessive wear or damage due to overheating. Inspect clutch drum, bearing and crankshaft for damage. Tighten clutch hub to 29 ft.-lbs. (40 N•m) torque.

OIL PUMP. A manual and an automatic oil pump is used. The manual oil pump (8 – Fig. MC9-4) is attached to the right crankcase half behind the guide bar mounting studs. The manual pump may be removed for cleaning or renewal of components after removal of guide bar, chain and two retaining screws.

The automatic chain oil pump is located in right crankcase half and is driven by gear (13) on crankshaft. Oil pump operation is accomplished when plunger (7 – Fig. MC9-5) is rotated by gear (13) and reciprocates as the oblique end of plunger bears against adjuster ball (10) thereby pumping oil. Oil output is changed by turning adjuster (10).

Automatic oil pump may be withdrawn from crankcase for repair or renewal of individual components after removing retainer (1). Drive gear (13) may be pulled off crankshaft after removing clutch assembly (12 – Fig. MC9-4), seal (10) and spacer (9). Drive gear must be heated before installation on crankshaft to prevent crankshaft displacement.

REWIND STARTER. Rewind starter is shown in Fig. MC9-6. To disassemble starter, remove rope handle and allow rope to wind around rope pulley. Disengage pulley retaining clip (8) and carefully remove rope pulley. Rewind spring is now accessible and may be removed.

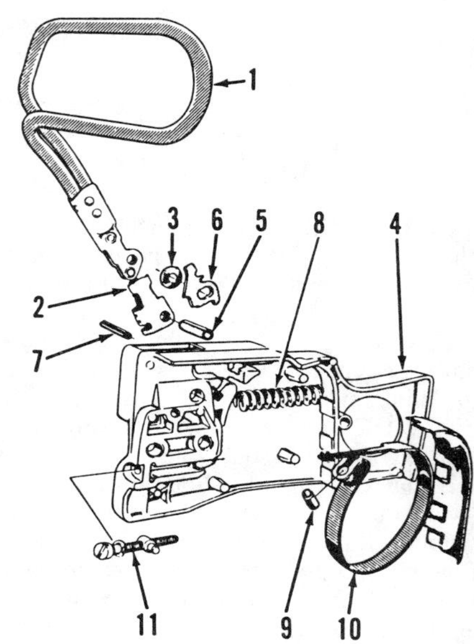

Fig. MC9-7 – Exploded view of chain brake assembly.

1. Chain brake lever
2. Sleeve
3. Washer
4. Housing
5. Pin
6. Trigger
7. Pin
8. Spring
9. Pin
10. Brake band
11. Chain tensioner

Fig. MC9-3 – Exploded view of clutch assembly.

1. Clutch hub
2. Clutch shoes
3. Garter spring
4. Clip
5. Sleeve
6. Drum
7. Needle bearing

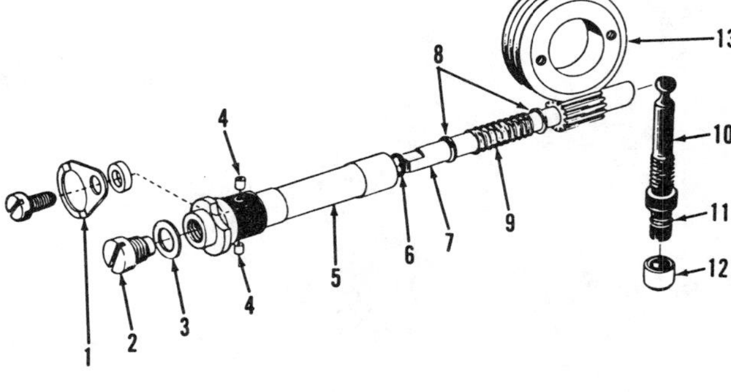

Fig. MC9-5 – Exploded view of automatic oil pump.

1. Pump retainer
2. Plug
3. Washer
4. Orifice
5. Pump housing
6. "O" ring
7. Plunger
8. "O" ring
9. Spring
10. Adjuster
11. "O" ring
12. Cap
13. Drive gear

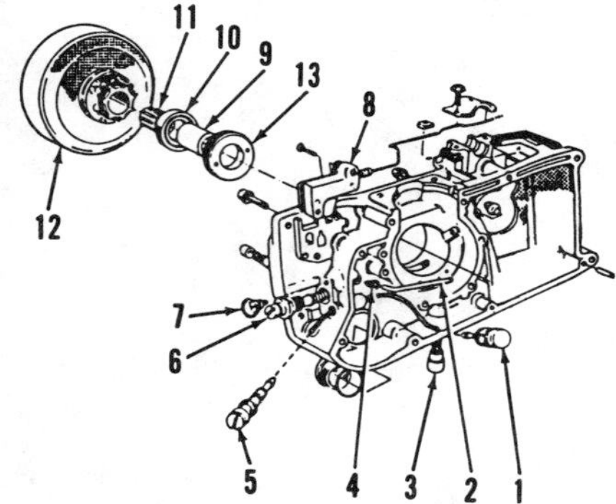

Fig. MC9-4 – View of right crankcase half showing location of automatic and manual oil pumps and related components. Refer to Fig. MC9-5 for exploded view of automatic oil pump.

1. Oil filter
2. Vent tube
3. Grommet
4. Oil pump adjuster
5. Oil pickup fitting
6. Automatic oil pump
7. Pump retainer
8. Manual oil pump
9. Spacer
10. Crankshaft seal
11. Needle bearing
12. Clutch assy.
13. Pump drive gear

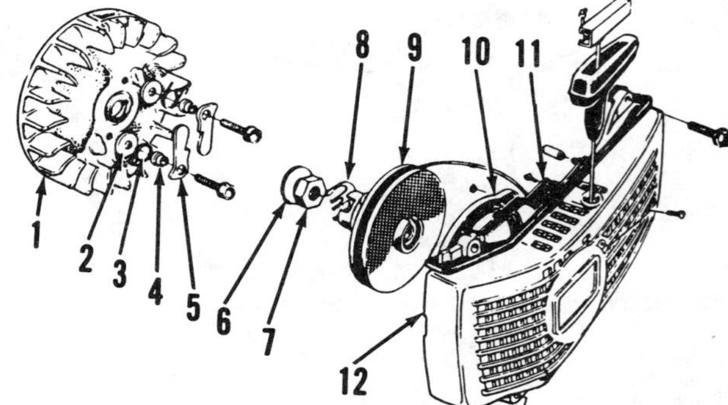

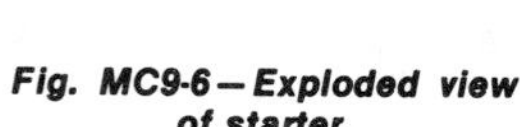

Fig. MC9-6 – Exploded view of starter.

1. Flywheel
2. Washer
3. Spring
4. Bushing
5. Pawl
6. Washer
7. Nut
8. Clip
9. Rope pulley
10. Rewind spring
11. Shield
12. Starter housing

Illustrations courtesy McCulloch Corp.

Install rewind spring in a clockwise direction viewed with spring installed in housing. Rope must be wrapped around rope pulley in a clockwise direction viewed with rope pulley in housing. Tension should be placed on starter rope by rotating rope pulley two turns clockwise.

CHAIN BRAKE. A chain brake system designed to stop chain movement should kickback occur is used. Refer to Fig. MC9-7 for an exploded view of chain brake. Chain brake is activated when the operator's hand strikes the chain brake lever thereby allowing trigger (6) to release spring (8). Spring then draws brake band tight around clutch drum to stop chain. Pull back chain brake lever to reset mechanism. No adjustment of brake mechanism is required.

Disassembly for repair or renewal of individual components is evident after inspection of unit and referral to the appropriate exploded view. It is recommended that a clutch drum be inserted in brake band and brake engaged, to facilitate removal of brake lever. When reassembling, make certain spring (8) is screwed completely on brake band and roll pins (5 and 7) are installed with split side towards front of saw.

McCULLOCH

Model	Bore	Stroke	Displ.	Drive Type
Double Eagle 50	1.72 in. (43.7 mm)	1.26 in. (32.0 mm)	3.1 cu. in. (50.0 cc)	Direct

MAINTENANCE

SPARK PLUG. Recommended spark plug is Champion DJ8J. Spark plug electrode gap should be 0.025 inch (0.63 mm).

CARBURETOR. A Walbro HDA diaphragm type carburetor is used. Refer to CARBURETOR SERVICE section for overhaul and exploded view of Walbro carburetors.

Initial adjustment of low and high speed mixtures is one turn open from a lightly seated position. Make final adjustment with engine warm and running. Adjust idle speed screw so engine idles just below clutch engagement speed. Adjust low speed mixture so engine will accelerate cleanly without hesitation. Adjust high speed mixture to obtain optimum full throttle performance under cutting load. Do not adjust high speed mixture too lean as engine damage could result. Remove top cover to gain access to adjustment screws.

IGNITION. An electronic ignition system is used. Ignition coil and ignition circuitry are an integral part of an one-piece ignition module which must be serviced as a unit assembly. Air gap between ignition module core legs and flywheel magnets should be 0.010-0.012 inch (0.25-0.30 mm). Ignition timing is not adjustable.

LUBRICATION. The engine is lubricated by mixing gasoline with oil. The recommended oil is McCulloch two-stroke engine oil mixed at 40:1 ratio. If McCulloch two-stroke engine oil is not available, a good quality oil designed for use in two-stroke air-cooled engines can be used mixed at a 20:1 ratio.

An automatic as well as manual chain oil pump is used. Automatic oiler (5 – Fig. MC10-1) is driven by worm gear (3) which is fitted on crankshaft (1). Note that right crankcase seal (6) is an integral part of oil pump. The automatic oil pump can be removed for inspection or repair after removing chain, guide bar and clutch assembly. The manual oil pump is a plunger type and is mounted to the left of trigger handle in saw body.

CARBON. If a noticeable lack of power or a decrease in the exhaust noise lever is evident, it is possible the muffler and exhaust ports are restricted with carbon. Use a wooden scraper when cleaning carbon deposits from exhaust ports to avoid damaging piston or cylinder.

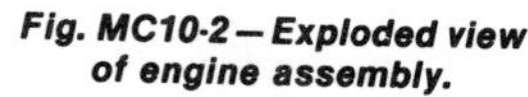

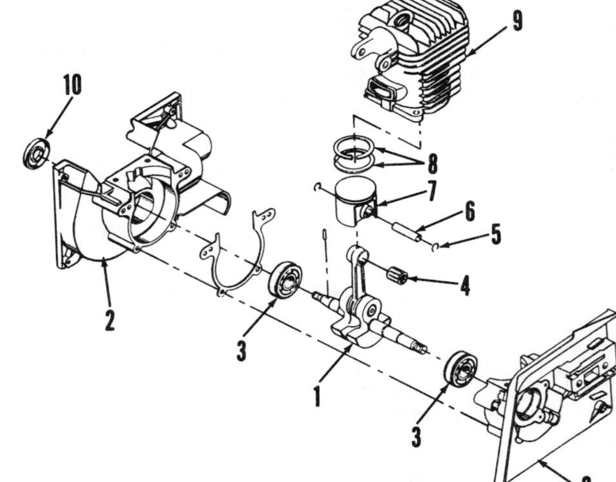

Fig. MC10-2 — Exploded view of engine assembly.

1. Crankshaft & connecting rod assy.
2. Crankcase halves
3. Ball bearings
4. Needle roller bearings
5. Piston pin retainer
6. Piston pin
7. Piston
8. Piston rings
9. Cylinder
10. Crankcase seal

REPAIRS

PISTON, PIN, RINGS AND CYLINDER. The piston is accessible after removal of cylinder (9 – Fig. MC10-2). The two piston rings (8) are pinned to prevent ring rotation. Piston pin (6) rides in needle roller bearing (4), in small end of connecting rod, and is retained in piston with two wire clips (5). Piston ring end gap should be 0.070 inch (1.78 mm). When installing piston, align "EX" on piston crown with exhaust port.

The cylinder bore is chrome plated and oversize pistons and cylinders are not available. Recommended piston-to-cylinder clearance is measured ⅜ inch (9.5 mm) from bottom of piston skirt. Clearance should be 0.004 inch (0.10 mm). Renew piston and cylinder assembly if flaking, cracking or other damage is noted in cylinder bore.

CONNECTING ROD, CRANKSHAFT AND CRANKCASE. The crankshaft is supported by two ball bearings (3 – Fig. MC10-2) located in crankcase halves (2). Use care not to damage mating surfaces when splitting crank-

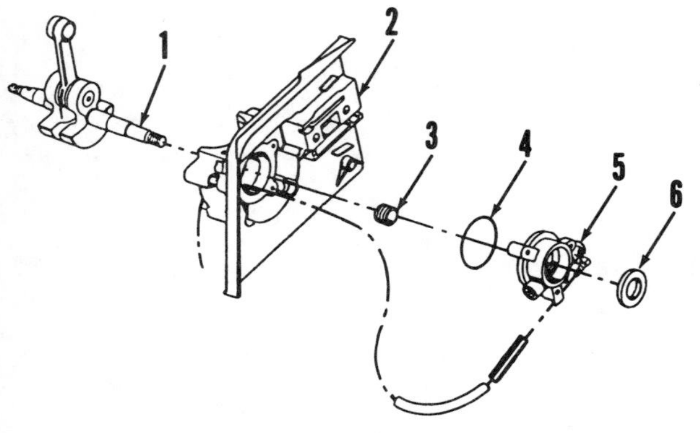

Fig. MC10-1 — Exploded view of automatic chain oil pump.

1. Crankshaft & connecting rod assy.
2. Right crankcase half
3. Worm gear
4. "O" ring
5. Oil pump assy.
6. Crankcase seal

Illustrations courtesy McCulloch Corp.

case. Crankshaft and connecting rod are a unit assembly. Rotate connecting rod around crankpin to check for roughness, excessive wear or other damage. Renew as necessary.

Heat may be applied to bearing bores in crankcase halves to ease reassembling. Make certain crankshaft is centered in crankcase and will rotate freely.

CLUTCH. A three-shoe centrifugal clutch is used. Clutch rotor (6–Fig. MC10-3) has left-hand threads. Inspect clutch shoes (5) and drum (3) for excessive wear or damage due to overheating. Clutch shoes should be renewed as a set.

Periodically inspect clutch bearing (2) and lubricate with a suitable high temperature grease. When installing clutch spring (7), locate spring ends at rivet (9) to prevent spring rotation.

REWIND STARTER. Rewind starter shown in Fig. MC10-4 is used. To disassemble starter, remove rope handle (2) and carefully allow rope pulley (5) to turn counterclockwise to relieve tension on rewind spring. Remove screw (12) and lift off washer (11), pawl plate (10), pawl plate springs (9), pawls (7) and pawl springs (6). Be careful and withdraw rope pulley (5) noting how pulley engages with rewind spring and housing assembly (4). Individual components can now be serviced.

Rope must be wrapped on pulley in a clockwise direction when reassembling. Turn rope pulley two turns clockwise before passing rope through rope guide to apply tension on rewind spring.

CHAIN BRAKE. A chain brake system designed to stop chain movement should kickback occur is used. The chain brake is activated when the operator's hand strikes chain brake lever (1–Fig. MC10-5), tripping latch (4), and releasing spring (8). The spring pulls brake band (11) tight around clutch drum, stopping chain movement. Pull back chain brake lever to reset mechanism.

Disassembly for repair or component replacement is evident after referral to exploded view and inspection of unit. No adjustment of chain brake system is required.

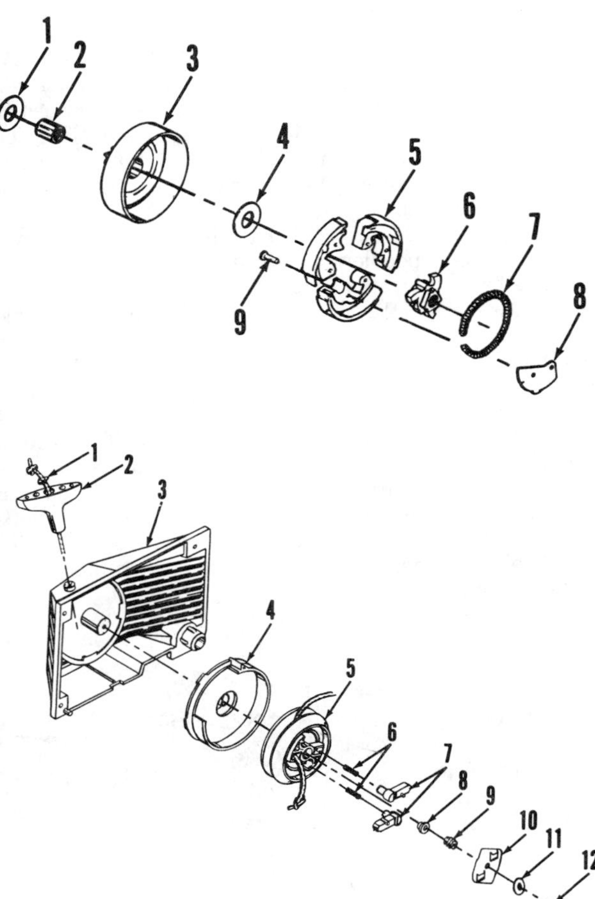

Fig. MC10-3 – Exploded view of clutch assembly.

1. Shim
2. Needle roller bearing
3. Drum & sprocket assy.
4. Shim
5. Shoes
6. Rotor
7. Spring
8. Shoe plate
9. Rivet

Fig. MC10-4 – Exploded view of rewind starter.

1. Washer
2. Rope handle
3. Housing
4. Rewind spring & housing assy.
5. Rope pulley
6. Pawl springs
7. Pawls
8. Pulley bushing
9. Pawl plate spring
10. Pawl plate
11. Washer
12. Screw

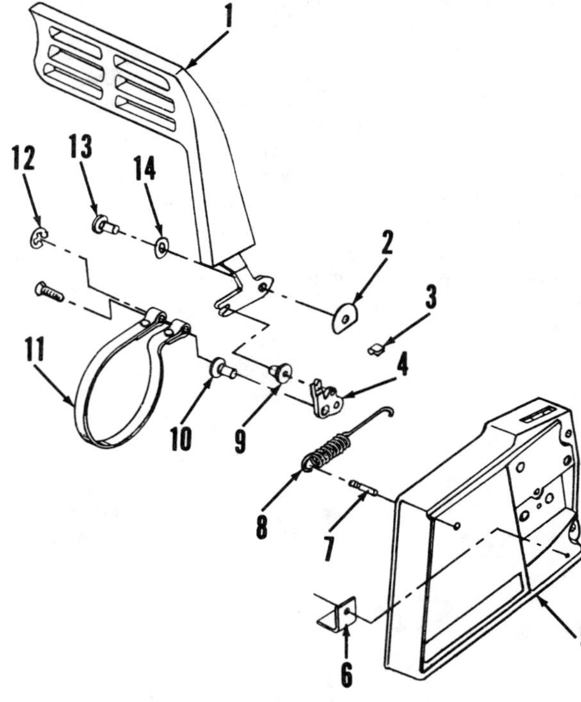

Fig. MC10-5 – Exploded view of chain brake system.

1. Chain brake lever
2. Washer
3. Clip
4. Latch
5. Housing
6. Chain stop
7. Pin
8. Spring
9. Latch slider
10. Pivot
11. Brake band
12. "E" clip
13. Pivot
14. Washer

Illustrations courtesy McCulloch Corp.

McCULLOCH

Model	Bore	Stroke	Displ.	Drive Type
PM380, PM380AS, Eager Beaver 2.3	1.575 in. (40 mm)	1.181 in. (30 mm)	2.3 cu. in. (37.7 cc)	Direct

MAINTENANCE

SPARK PLUG. Recommended spark plug is AC CS45T or Champion DJ8. Spark plug electrode gap should be 0.025 inch (0.63 mm).

CARBURETOR. All models are equipped with a Tillotson diaphragm type carburetor. Refer to CARBURETOR SERVICE section for overhaul and exploded views.

Initial adjustment for high and low mixture screws is one turn open from a lightly seated position. Make final adjustment with engine warm and running. Adjust idle speed screw so engine idles just below clutch engagement speed. Adjust low speed mixture screw so engine accelerates cleanly without hesitation. Adjust high speed mixture screw to obtain optimum full throttle performance under cutting load. Do not adjust high speed mixture too lean as engine damage could occur. Adjustment screws are accessible through opening in rewind starter housing (4–Fig. MC11-1).

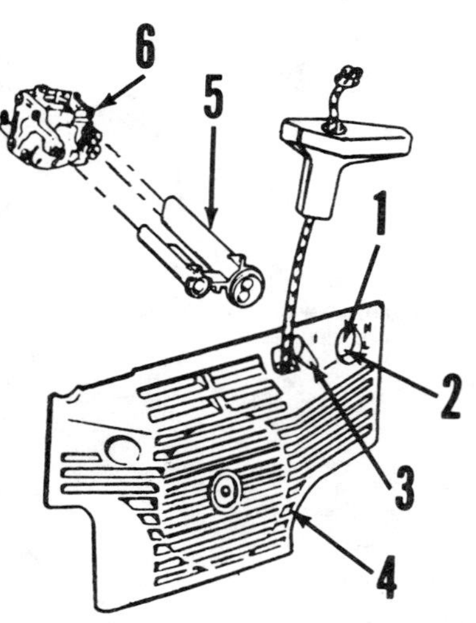

Fig. MC11-1 — View showing position of carburetor adjustment screws.

1. High speed mixture screw
2. Low speed mixture screw
3. Idle speed screw
4. Rewind starter housing
5. Guide tube
6. Carburetor

IGNITION. All models are equipped with a solid state electronic ignition system. Ignition coil and all ignition circuitry are contained in an one-piece ignition module. Ignition module is serviced as a unit assembly only. Ignition timing is fixed at 26 degrees BTDC and is not adjustable. Air gap between ignition module core legs and flywheel magnets should be 0.010-0.012 inch (0.25-0.30 mm).

LUBRICATION. The engine is lubricated by mixing oil with regular leaded gasoline. Recommended oil is McCulloch two-stroke engine oil mixed at a 40:1 ratio. If McCulloch two-stroke engine oil is not available, a good quality oil designed for use in two-stroke air-cooled engines can be used mixed at a 20:1 ratio.

All models are equipped with a manual and an adjustable automatic chain oil pump. Automatic oil pump is actuated by pulsations from the crankcase and output is adjusted by turning screw (4–Fig. MC11-2). Use SAE 30 oil for temperatures above 40°F (4°C) and SAE 10 for temperatures below 40°F (4°C).

CARBON. If noticeable lack of power or a decrease in exhaust noise level is evident, it is possible the muffler and exhaust ports are restricted with carbon. Use a wooden scraper to remove carbon deposits to avoid damaging cylinder or piston.

REPAIRS

PISTON, PIN, RINGS AND CYLINDER. The piston is fitted with two cast iron compression rings. Pins located in the piston ring grooves prevent ring rotation. When installing piston rings, make certain ring end gaps are around pins. Piston pin (7–Fig. MC11-3) rides on needle roller bearing (5) fitted in the connecting rod small end and is held in place by two retainers (6). To remove piston, remove the piston pin retainers and tap out piston pin using a suitable driver. When installing piston, align the "EX" stamped on piston crown with exhaust port.

Cylinder bore is chrome plated and should be inspected for flaking, cracking, scoring or other damage. Oversize piston and cylinder assemblies are not available.

CONNECTING ROD, CRANKSHAFT AND CRANKCASE. Crankshaft and connecting rod are serviced as a unit assembly. Rotate connecting rod around crankpin to check for roughness, excessive wear or other damage. Renew as necessary.

The crankshaft is supported by two needle roller bearings (3–Fig. MC11-3) located in crankcase halves.

When reassembling, apply a suitable sealer to crankcase mating surfaces. Make certain crankshaft is centered in crankcase and will turn freely.

CLUTCH. Refer to Fig. MC11-4 for a view identifying clutch assembly (7). Clutch shoes and rotor are serviced as a unit assembly only. Clutch rotor has left-hand threads. Clutch drum and sprocket assembly (8) is retained on crankshaft by

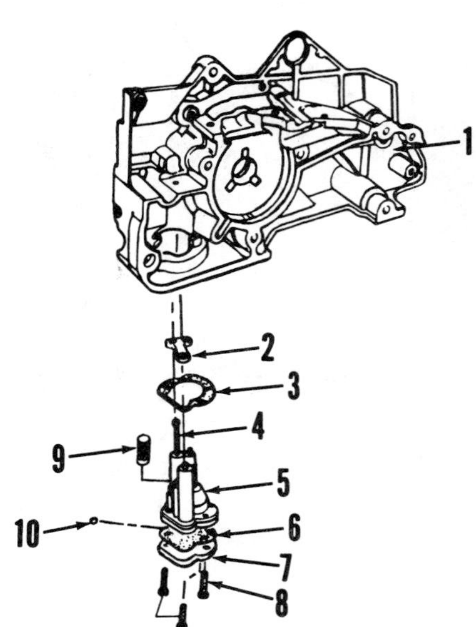

Fig. MC11-2 — Exploded view of automatic chain oil pump.

1. Right crankcase half
2. Gasket
3. Gasket
4. Adjusting screw
5. Pump body
6. Gasket
7. Cover
8. Screw
9. Filter screen
10. Check ball

Illustrations courtesy McCulloch Corp.

snap ring (10). Note shield (6) used to prevent dirt or sawdust from entering clutch assembly. Tighten clutch rotor and shoe assembly to 125-150 in.-lbs. (14.2-17.0 N•m).

AUTO SHARP. Model PM380AS is equipped with automatic chain sharpening system shown in Fig. MC11–5. Except for knob (1) and spring (2), the auto sharp attachment is serviced as a unit assembly.

REWIND STARTER. All models are equipped with the rewind starter shown in Fig. MC11-6. To disassemble, fully extend rope, then pull slack rope back through rope guide and carefully allow rope pulley (6) to unwind relieving tension on rewind spring (5). Remove nut (9) and washer (8) and lift off rope pulley noting how pulley engages rewind spring. All components can now be serviced.

When reassembling, install rewind spring (5) into starter housing (2) making certain hook in outer coil engages notch in housing. Wind rope in a clockwise direction on rope pulley as viewed from pulley side of starter. When installing rope pulley, engage dog on pulley with hook on inner coil of rewind spring. To apply tension on rewind spring, sufficiently extend starter rope to allow rope pulley to be turned one turn clockwise. Then, carefully allow rope pulley to rewind rope. If rope handle is not tight against housing, repeat procedure one additional turn clockwise.

CHAIN BRAKE. All models are equipped with a chain brake system designed to stop chain movement should kickback occur. Chain brake is activated when operator's hand strikes chain brake lever (1–Fig. MC11-4), tripping latch (4), releasing spring (3) and pulling brake band (11) tight around clutch drum (8). Disassembly for repair or component renewal is evident after referral to exploded view and inspection of unit. No adjustment of chain brake system is required.

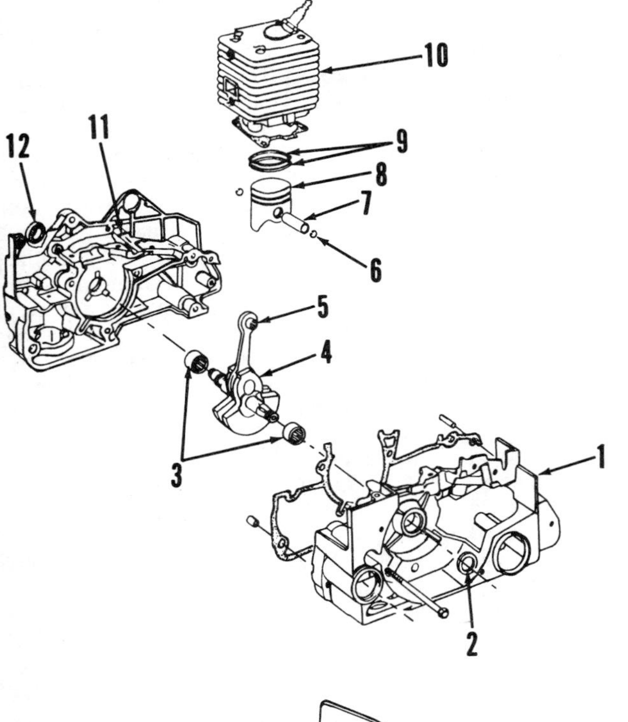

Fig. MC11-3—Exploded view of engine.

1. Left crankcase half
2. Crankcase seal
3. Needle roller bearings
4. Crankshaft & connecting rod assy.
5. Needle roller bearing
6. Retainer
7. Piston pin
8. Piston
9. Piston rings
10. Cylinder
11. Right crankcase half
12. Crankcase seal

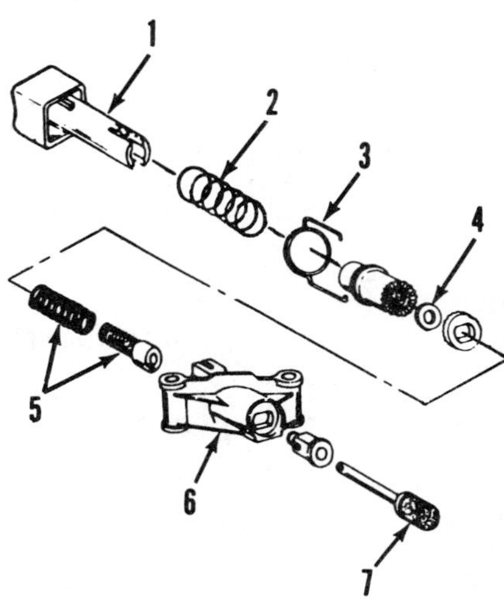

Fig. MC11-5—Exploded view of auto sharp assembly used on Model PM380AS.

1. Knob
2. Spring
3. Wire bail
4. Washer
5. Springs
6. Housing
7. Grinding wheel

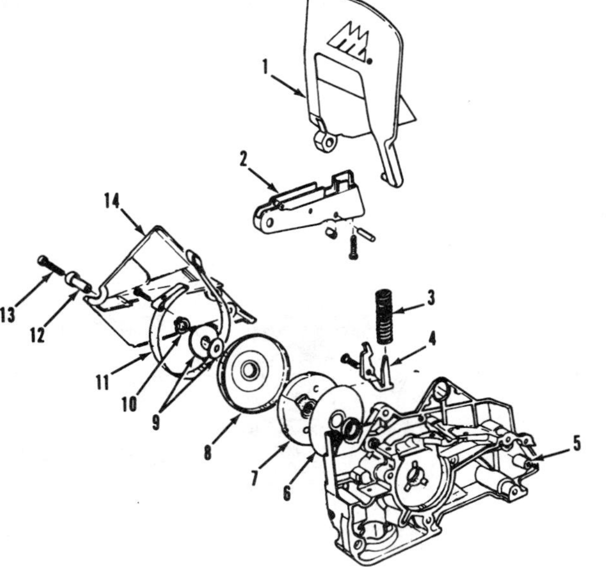

Fig. MC11-4—Exploded view of clutch and chain brake assembly.

1. Chain brake lever
2. Brake box
3. Brake spring
4. Latch
5. Right crankcase half
6. Shield
7. Clutch assy.
8. Clutch drum & sprocket assy.
9. Washers
10. Snap ring
11. Brake band
12. Brake bushing
13. Screw
14. Clutch cover

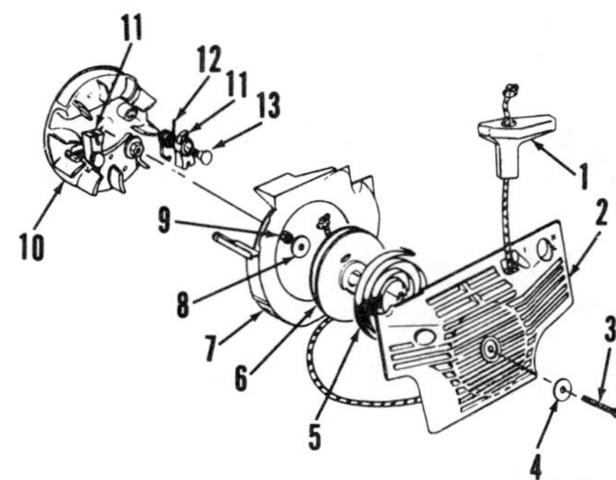

Fig. MC11-6—Exploded view of rewind spring starter.

1. Rope handle
2. Housing
3. Screw
4. Washer
5. Rewind spring
6. Rope pulley
7. Fan baffle
8. Washer
9. Nut
10. Flywheel
11. Pawl
12. Pawl spring
13. Pawl pin

McCULLOCH

Model	Bore	Stroke	Displ.	Drive Type
Titan 35	38 cc (1.496 in.)	30 cc (1.181 in.)	35 cc (2.1 cu. in.)	Direct
Titan 40	40 mm (1.575 in.)	30 mm (1.181 in.)	38 cc (2.3 cu. in.)	Direct

NOTE: These McCulloch models are equipped with metric fasteners.

MAINTENANCE

SPARK PLUG. Recommended spark plug is Champion RDJ8J or equivalent. Spark plug electrode gap is 0.63 mm (0.025 in.). Note that plug has a tapered seat and does not require a gasket. Tighten spark plug to 13.6 N·m (120 in.-lbs.).

Spark plug should be removed, cleaned and inspected periodically. The use of an abrasive type spark plug cleaning machine is not recommended.

CARBURETOR. Titan 35 saw may be equipped with either a Tillotson HU 57 or Walbro WT 113 diaphragm type carburetor. Titan 45 saw is equipped with a Tillotson HU 58 diaphragm carburetor. Refer to CARBURETOR SERVICE section for overhaul and exploded views of Tillotson and Walbro carburetors. See Fig. MC12-1 for exploded view of throttle controls.

On all types of carburetors, initial adjustment of both idle and high speed mixture needles is one turn open from a lightly seated position. Make final adjustment with engine warm and running. Be sure air filter is clean before making final carburetor adjustment.

Adjust idle speed screw (1—Fig. MC12-2) so engine idles just below clutch engagement speed. Adjust idle mixture needle (3) so engine will accelerate cleanly without hesitation. Adjust high speed mixture needle (2) to obtain optimum performance under cutting load. Saw should not be operated with high speed mixture needle set too lean (turned too far clockwise), as engine could be damaged from lack of lubrication. Engine speed at wide open throttle with no-load should be 10,500-11,000 rpm. Readjust idle speed screw, if necessary, so chain does not move when engine is idling.

IGNITION. All models are equipped with a capacitor discharge electronic ignition system. Ignition components are contained in an ignition module located adjacent to flywheel. Ignition timing is not adjustable. Ignition module must be positioned so there is 0.25-0.30 mm (0.010-0.012 in.) gap between module laminated legs and flywheel magnets. Loosen module mounting screws and move module as necessary to obtain specified gap.

LUBRICATION. The engine is lubricated by mixing oil with fuel. Recommended fuel:oil ratio is 40:1 if using McCulloch oil, or 20:1 when using any other brand of oil designed for two-stroke air-cooled engines. If McCulloch oil is not used, the addition of a fuel stabilizer (such as STA-BIL Gas Stabilizer or equivalent) is recommended to minimize the formation of fuel gum deposits. The use of oil designed for automotive use is not recommended. Regular grade unleaded or leaded gasoline is recommended, but use only one type. Changing fuel types can cause engine damage. Use a separate container when mixing oil and fuel.

All models are equipped with an automatic chain oiler system. Output of automatic oil pump is not adjustable. The chain oil reservoir will run out at about the same time as the fuel supply runs out. McCulloch Chain, Bar and Sprocket Oil is recommended for use in all temperatures. The use of automotive type oil is also acceptable. Select oil viscosity according to ambient temperature. Use SAE 10 oil when temperature is below 40°F (5°C) and SAE 30 oil when temperature is above 40°F (5°C).

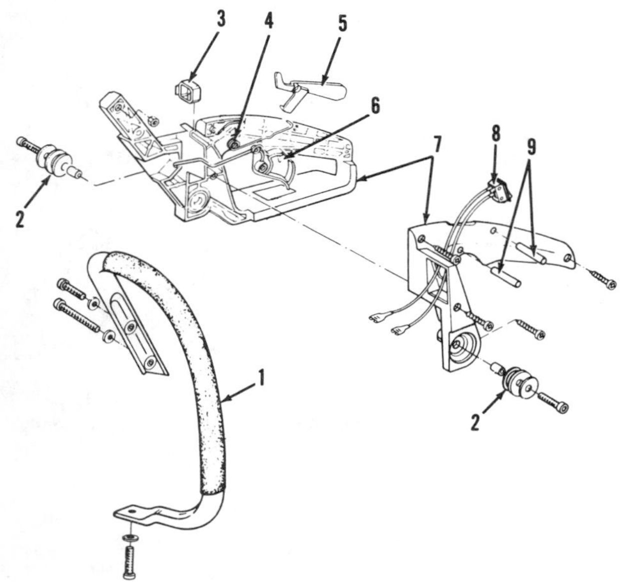

Fig. MC12-1—Exploded view of control handle assembly.

1. Front handle
2. Rubber mounts
3. Plug
4. Throttle return spring
5. Trigger
6. Throttle lever
7. Rear handle
8. Ignition switch
9. Pins

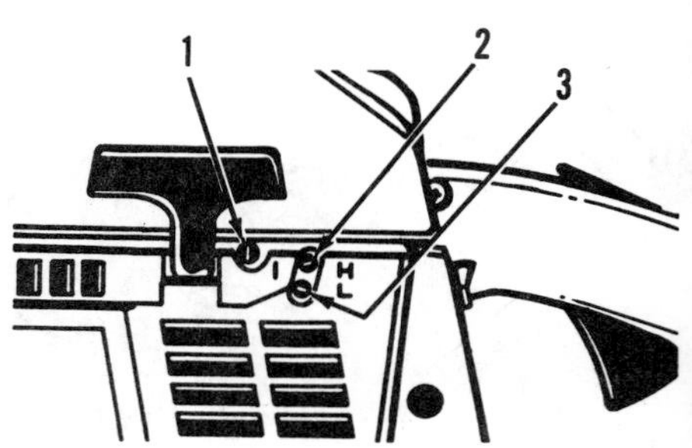

Fig. MC12-2—Drawing showing location of idle speed screw (1), high speed mixture needle (2) and low speed mixture needle (3).

Illustrations courtesy McCulloch Corp.

REPAIRS

CRANKCASE PRESSURE TEST. An improperly sealed crankcase can cause the engine to be hard to start, run rough, have low power and overheat. Refer to ENGINE SERVICE section of this manual for crankcase pressure test procedure. If crankcase leakage is indicated, pressurize crankcase and use a soap and water solution to check gaskets, seals, pulse line and castings for leakage.

TIGHTENING TORQUES. Refer to the following table for tightening torque values:

Crankcase to cylinder . . . . 8.0-9.0 N·m (71-80 in.-lbs.)
Crankcase halves . . . . 5.5-6.0 N·m (49-54 in.-lbs.)
Flywheel nut . . . . 24.0-25.0 N·m (210-220 in.-lbs.)
Clutch . . . . 18 N·m (161 in.-lbs.)
Muffler . . . . 4.0-5.0 N·m (36-45 in.-lbs.)
Spark plug . . . . 13.5 N·m (120 in.-lbs.)
Air filter housing . . . . 3.0-4.0 N·m (27-36 in.-lbs.)
Ignition module . . . . 4.0-5.0 N·m (36-45 in.-lbs.)
Oil pump . . . . 3.5-4.5 N·m (31-40 in.-lbs.)
Brake band screw . . . . 3.5-4.5 N·m (31-40 in.-lbs.)
Reed valve block . . . . 2.5-3.5 N·m (22-31 in.-lbs.)

PISTON, RINGS AND CYLINDER. To disassemble, remove engine cover. Unbolt and remove muffler assembly from cylinder. Remove spark plug. Remove cylinder mounting screws and withdraw cylinder from piston. Remove piston rings (3—Fig. MC12-3) from piston ring grooves. Piston (4) should only be removed if it is to be renewed. Remove piston pin retainers (6) and use special tool No. 236020 or similar piston pin removal tool to press piston pin (5) out of piston and connecting rod. Remove needle rollers (17) from small end of connecting rod. Bearing cage is a press fit in connecting rod. Use special tool No. 236026 or similar tool to remove and install bearing cage. Bearing cage should be centered in connecting rod bore.

The cylinder bore is chrome plated and should be inspected for flaking, scoring or excessive wear. Cylinder should be renewed if chrome plating is worn through.

Inspect piston for scoring or excessive wear. Piston skirt diameter wear limit is 37.85 mm (1.490 in.) for Titan 35 and 39.85 mm (1.568 in.) for Titan 40. Piston pin boss inside diameter wear limit is 9.0 mm (0.354 in.) for all models. Maximum allowable ring groove width is 1.60 mm (0.062 in.). Piston may be reused if piston skirt is discolored, but is not scored or excessively worn. Piston rings should be renewed. If piston is renewed, a new piston pin and new piston rings should also be installed.

Piston can be installed with either side facing the exhaust port. Heating piston with a heat lamp will ease installation of piston pin. Use grease to hold needle rollers in place in bearing cage when installing piston pin. Lubricate piston rings and cylinder bore with light coat of SAE 30 oil before installing cylinder.

CRANKSHAFT, CONNECTING ROD AND CRANKCASE. The crankcase halves (14 and 19—Fig. MC12-3) must be separated to remove crankshaft assembly (16). For access to crankcase, remove engine cover and spark plug. Insert a loop of rope in spark plug hole to lock piston. Remove chain brake, guide bar and chain, clutch (left-hand threads) and oil pump. Remove air filter housing, carburetor, muffler, front and rear handles, starter housing and flywheel. Unbolt and remove cylinder from crankcase. Remove crankcase mounting screws and separate crankcase halves and crankshaft. Remove oil seals (13 and 23), snap ring (22) and main bearings (15 and 30), being careful not to damage crankcase halves.

The crankshaft and connecting rod are a unit assembly. Check rotation of connecting rod around crankpin and renew crankshaft assembly if roughness, excessive play or other damage is noted.

The crankshaft is supported by a ball bearing (30) on the flywheel end and a roller bearing (15) on the clutch end. Renew bearings if roughness or other damage is indicated. New seals (13 and 23) can be installed after crankshaft is installed in crankcase. Lubricate crankshaft with oil prior to installing seals.

To install crankshaft assembly, reverse removal procedure. Be sure mating surfaces of crankcase halves are clean and free of burrs. Apply Loctite 242 to threads of crankcase mounting screws and tighten to 5.6-6.0 N·m (49-54 in.-lbs.). Rotate crankshaft to make certain it turns freely. If not, disassemble and locate problem.

CLUTCH. Refer to Fig. MC12-4 for an exploded view of clutch assembly. To re-

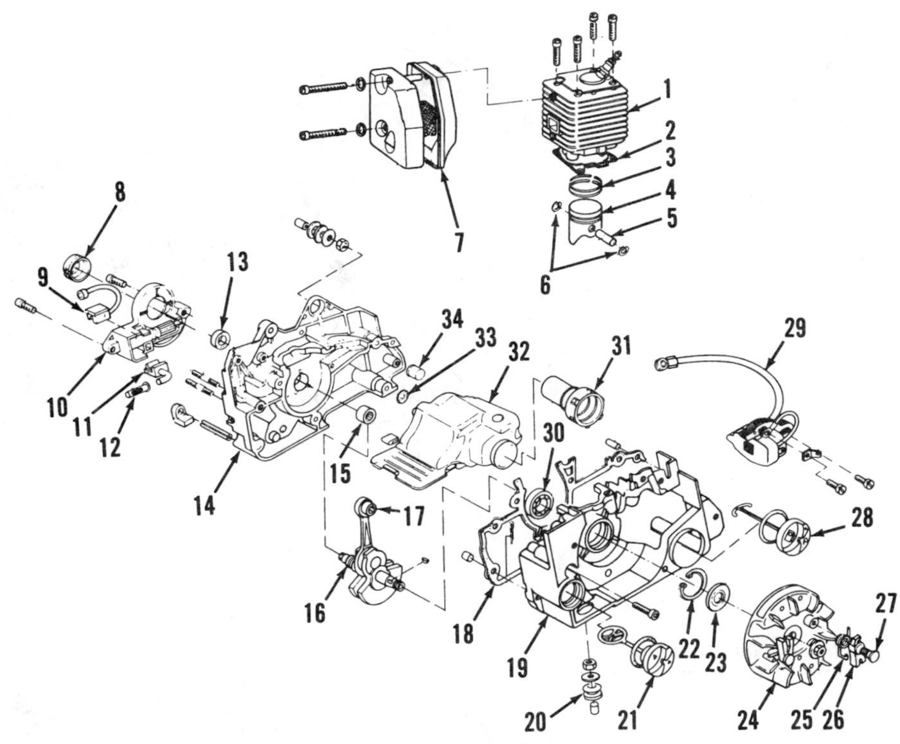

Fig. MC12-3—Exploded view of engine assembly typical of all models.

1. Cylinder
2. Gasket
3. Piston rings
4. Piston
5. Piston pin
6. Retaining rings
7. Muffler
8. Worm gear
9. Oil outlet tube
10. Oil pump
11. Oil inlet tube
12. Oil screen
13. Seal
14. Crankcase half
15. Roller bearing
16. Crankshaft & connecting rod assy.
17. Needle bearing
18. Gasket
19. Crankcase half
20. Rubber mount
21. Oil tank cap
22. Snap ring
23. Seal
24. Flywheel
25. Spring
26. Starter pawl
27. Pin
28. Fuel tank cap
29. Ignition module
30. Ball bearing
31. Filler tube
32. Fuel tank shield
33. Gasket
34. Support

Illustrations courtesy McCulloch Corp.

move clutch, first remove chain brake, guide bar and chain. Remove engine cover and remove spark plug. Insert loop of rope in spark plug hole or use other suitable means to lock piston. Remove "E" ring (12), washer (13) and drum (14). Unscrew clutch hub clockwise (left-hand threads). Remove and separate clutch components.

Clutch shoes (18), hub (19) and spring (20) are serviced as an assembly. Inspect clutch drum (14), needle bearing and sprocket for excessive wear and renew as necessary.

Lubricate clutch drum needle bearing with grease. Install clutch assembly and tighten to 18 N·m (161 in.-lbs.). Note that "E" ring (12) tends to get stretched out of shape during removal and should be renewed if it does not fit tightly.

CHAIN BRAKE. All models are equipped with a chain brake system designed to stop chain movement should kickback occur. The chain brake is activated when operator's hand strikes chain brake lever (1—Fig. MC12-4), which trips latch (6) and releases spring (5) to pull brake band (11) tight around clutch drum (14). Pull back chain brake lever to reset mechanism.

To check for proper chain brake operation, place saw on flat surface and run at one-half throttle. Activate chain brake lever and chain should stop moving immediately. No adjustment of chain brake is required. If brake fails to operate properly, disassemble and inspect for problem.

To disassemble chain brake, remove clutch cover, guide bar and chain and clutch assembly. Move brake lever (1—Fig. MC12-4) forward to engage brake and relieve brake spring tension. Remove brake lever pivot screw (7) and brake band retaining screw (10). Remove pivot pin (3) and roller (4) and separate brake band (11) from brake housing (2).

Inspect all components for evidence of wear or damage and renew as necessary. Brake band (11) should be renewed if worn to a thickness of 0.021 inch (0.5 mm) or less. To reassemble, reverse disassembly procedure.

OIL PUMP. All models are equipped with an automatic chain oil pump (10—Fig. MC12-3) located on clutch side of crankcase. The automatic oil pump is operated by a worm gear (8) on the crankshaft.

For access to oil pump, remove clutch cover, bar and chain, clutch assembly and chain brake. Remove oil pump mounting screws, disconnect oil outlet hose (9) and pry oil pump assembly from crankcase.

Thoroughly clean all components and inspect for wear or damage. Oil pump is serviced as a unit assembly.

Be sure to clean all silicone sealer residue from pump housing and crankcase. When installing oil pump, apply light coat of fuel resistant silicone sealer to outside edge of pump housing.

REWIND STARTER. Rewind starter components are contained in starter housing (4—Fig. MC12-5). To disassemble, remove starter housing, detach rope handle and allow rope to wind slowly onto pulley (2). Unscrew retaining screw (5) and remove rope pulley. Use caution when removing rewind spring (3) to prevent injury due to uncontrolled uncoiling of spring.

Starter rope length should be 85 cm (33.5 in.) and diameter should be 3 mm (0.125 in.). When reassembling, install rewind spring in housing so spring coils wrap in a clockwise direction from outer end as viewed from flywheel side of starter housing. Wrap rope on pulley in a clockwise direction viewed from flywheel side of pulley. Install rope pulley and secure with retaining screw and nut. Turn pulley and rope one turn clockwise to place tension on rewind spring, then install rope handle and check for proper operation. If rope handle does not stand upright when rope is rewound, turn pulley another turn clockwise. With rope fully extended, it should be possible to rotate rope pulley a minimum of 1/2 turn clockwise before rewind spring bottoms. Do not place more tension on rewind spring than is necessary to draw rope handle against housing.

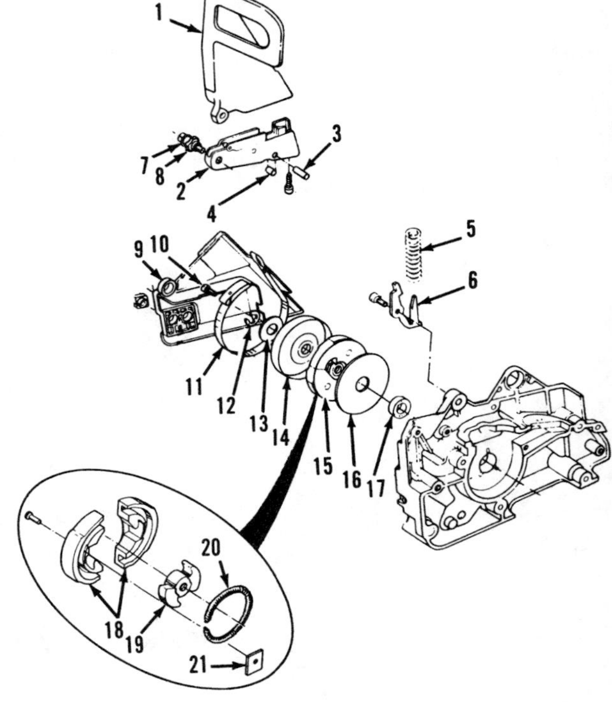

Fig. MC12-4—Exploded view of chain brake assembly and clutch assembly.

1. Chain brake lever
2. Brake housing
3. Pin
4. Roller
5. Brake spring
6. Latch
7. Pivot bolt
8. Wavy washer
9. Clutch cover
10. Screw
11. Brake band
12. "E" ring
13. Washer
14. Clutch drum
15. Clutch assy.
16. Dust shield
17. Seal
18. Clutch shoes
19. Hub
20. Spring
21. Retainer plate

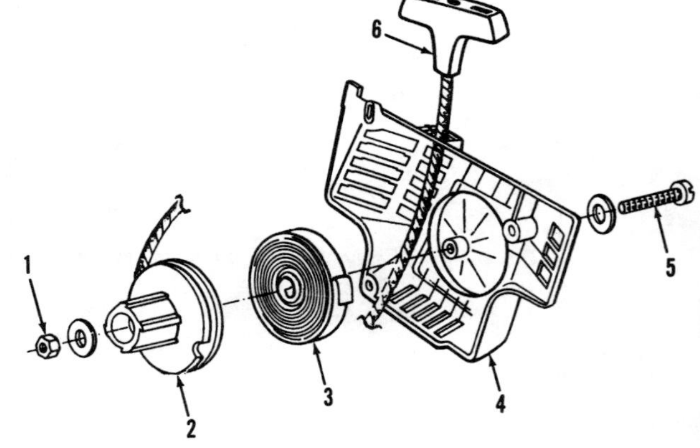

Fig. MC12-5—Exploded view of rewind starter assembly.

1. Nut
2. Rope pulley
3. Rewind spring
4. Starter housing
5. Bolt
6. Rope handle

Illustrations courtesy McCulloch Corp.

McCULLOCH

Model	Bore	Stroke	Displ.	Drive Type
Titan 50	45 mm (1.77 in.)	32 mm (1.26 in.)	51 cc (3.1 cu. in.)	Direct
Titan 57	47 mm (1.85 in.)	33 mm (1.30 in.)	57 cc (3.5 cu. in.)	Direct

MAINTENANCE

SPARK PLUG. Recommended spark plug is Champion DJ8J or equivalent. Spark plug electrode gap is 0.025 inch (0.63 mm). Note that spark plug has a tapered seat and does not require a gasket. Tighten spark plug to a torque of 108-135 in.-lbs. (12.2-15.2 N·m).

CARBURETOR. All models are equipped with a Walbro HDA diaphragm carburetor. Refer to CARBURETOR SERVICE section for overhaul and exploded view of carburetor.

Initial adjustment for both low speed and high speed mixture needles is one turn open from a lightly seated position. Make final adjustment with engine warm and running. Be sure air filter is clean before making final carburetor adjustment.

Adjust idle speed screw (1—Fig. MC13-1) so engine idles just below clutch engagement speed. Adjust idle mixture needle (2) so engine will accelerate cleanly without hesitation. Adjust high speed mixture needle (3) to obtain optimum performance under cutting load. Saw should not be operated with high speed mixture needle set too lean (turned too far clockwise), as engine could be damaged from lack of lubrication and overheating. Engine speed at wide-open throttle with no-load should be 11,000-11,500 rpm. Readjust idle speed screw, if necessary, so chain does not move when engine is idling.

The Titan 57 saw is equipped with a carburetor heater valve designed to heat the intake air to prevent icing of carburetor when operating in cold, damp conditions. To operate heater, remove engine cover (2—Fig. MC13-3) and close the flapper valve located in engine cover. This will allow carburetor to draw a mixture of outside air through lower duct in cover and warm air from the powerhead. Flap must be in "open" position when operating in warm weather to avoid engine overheating.

IGNITION. All models are equipped with a capacitor discharge electronic ignition system. Ignition components are contained in an ignition module located adjacent to flywheel. Ignition timing is not adjustable. Ignition module must be positioned so there is 0.010-0.012 inch (0.25-0.30 mm) gap between module laminated legs and flywheel magnets. Loosen module mounting screws and move module as necessary to obtain specified gap.

LUBRICATION. The engine is lubricated by mixing oil with fuel. Recommended fuel:oil ratio is 40:1 if using McCulloch oil, or 20:1 when using any other brand of oil designed for two-stroke air-cooled engines. If McCulloch oil is not used, the addition of a fuel stabilizer (such as STA-BIL Gas Stabilizer or equivalent) is recommended to minimize the formation of fuel gum deposits. The use of oil designed for automotive use is not recommended. Regular grade unleaded or leaded gasoline is recommended, but use only one type. Changing fuel types can cause engine damage. Use a separate container when mixing oil and fuel.

All models are equipped with an automatic chain oil pump and a manual oil pump. Oil output of automatic oil pump is adjustable. Pump adjusting screw is located between clutch assembly and crankcase (Fig. MC13-2) and is accessible through opening in bottom of saw. Adjustment screw is turned fully clockwise at the factory. Turning adjustment screw counterclockwise will decrease oil flow and turning screw clockwise will increase oil output.

McCulloch Chain, Bar and Sprocket Oil is recommended for use in all temperatures. The use of automotive type oil is also acceptable. Select oil viscosity according to ambient temperature. Use SAE 10 oil when temperature is below 40°F (5°C) and SAE 30 oil when temperature is above 40°F (5°C).

REPAIRS

CRANKCASE PRESSURE TEST. An improperly sealed crankcase can cause the engine to be hard to start, run rough, have low power and overheat. Refer to ENGINE SERVICE section of this manual for crankcase pressure test procedure. If crankcase leakage is indicated, pressurize crankcase and use a soap and water solution to check gaskets, seals, pulse line and castings for leakage.

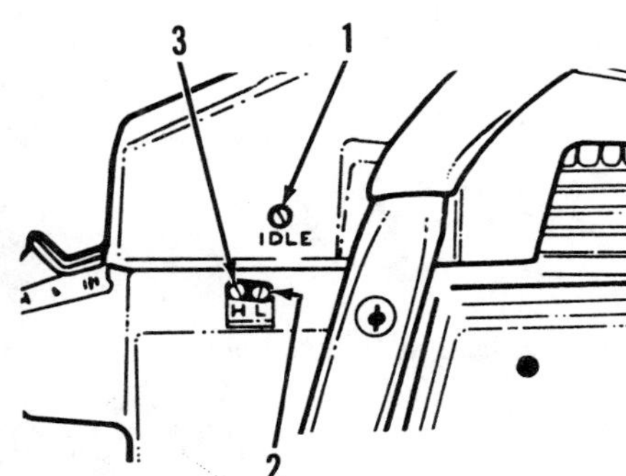

Fig. MC13-1—Drawing showing location of idle speed adjusting screw (1), low speed mixture needle (2) and high speed mixture needle (3).

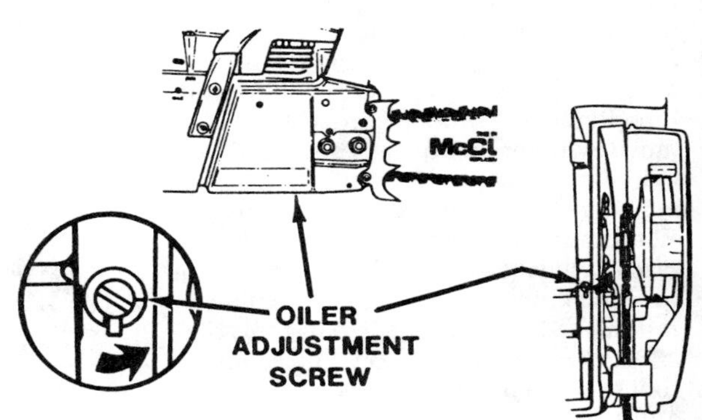

Fig. MC13-2—Automatic oil pump adjusting screw is located in bottom of saw. Turn screw clockwise to increase oil flow.

Illustrations courtesy McCulloch Corp.

TIGHTENING TORQUES. Refer to the following table for tightening torque values:

Crankcase halves	70 in.-lbs. (7.9 N·m)
Cylinder	90 in.-lbs. (10.1 N·m)
Oil pump	30 in.-lbs. (3.4 N·m)
Ignition module	35-45 in.-lbs. (4.0-5.0 N·m)
Air filter box	20 in.-lbs. (2.2 N·m)
Carburetor	45 in.-lbs. (5.0 N·m)
Clutch	150-168 in.-lbs. (17.0-19.0 N·m)
Flywheel	150-168 in.-lbs. (17.0-19.0 N·m)
Starter pawl plate	75 in.-lbs. (8.5 N·m)
Chain brake band	85-90 in.-lbs. (9.6-10.1 N·m)
Spark plug	108-135 in.-lbs. (12.2-15.2 N·m)

MAIN FRAME. The main frame (34—Fig. MC13-3) can be pivoted away from power head for access to all hoses and carburetor, or saw can be separated into two sections—main frame assembly and power head assembly.

To pivot main frame away from power head, remove air box cover (2) and air filter (3). Pry ignition switch/choke control assembly (19—Fig. MC13-4) out of control handle. Remove two air box retaining screws and pivot power head away from main frame. To separate main frame from power head, disconnect fuel line, oil lines and carburetor linkage. Remove two forward anti-vibration mounts (12) and separate main frame from power head.

PISTON, RINGS AND CYLINDER. To disassemble, remove engine cover and pivot main frame away from power head as outlined above. Remove starter housing (14—Fig. MC13-3) and air baffle (15). Unbolt and remove muffler assembly (18) from cylinder. Remove spark plug. Disconnect throttle rod, choke rod and fuel line. Remove carburetor mounting screws and anti-vibration mount screws, then remove carburetor (5) and air box (6). Pry rear mount assemblies (19, 20 and 21) off cylinder roll pin. Remove cylinder shroud (12). Remove cylinder mounting screws and tap cylinder with plastic mallet to break cylinder-to-crankcase gasket compound. Withdraw cylinder from piston. Remove piston rings (2—Fig. MC13-5) from piston ring grooves. Remove piston pin retainers (3) and use special tool No. 236020 or similar piston pin removal tool to press piston pin (5) out of piston and connecting rod.

The cylinder bore is chrome plated and should be inspected for flaking, scoring or excessive wear. Cylinder should be renewed if chrome plating is worn through.

Inspect piston for scoring or excessive wear. Piston skirt diameter wear limit is 1.761 inch (44.75 mm) for Titan 50 and 1.841 inch (46.79 mm) for Titan 57. Piston pin boss inside diameter wear limit is 0.3955 inch (10.05 mm) for all models. Maximum allowable ring groove width is 0.315 inch (0.80 mm) for all models. Piston may be reused if piston skirt is discolored, but is not scored or excessively worn. Piston rings should be renewed. If piston is renewed, a new piston pin and new piston rings should also be installed. Inspect needle bearing (6) in small end of connecting rod and renew if pitted, worn or damaged.

Piston must be installed so arrow on piston crown points toward exhaust port. Heating piston with a heat lamp will ease installation of piston pin. Install new piston pin retainers (3). Lubricate piston rings and cylinder bore with light coat of SAE 30 oil before installing cylinder. Apply Loctite Gasket Eliminator to cylinder mounting surface. If intake boot (9—Fig. MC13-3) was removed from cylinder shroud (12), reinstall boot using Loctite BlackMax adhe-

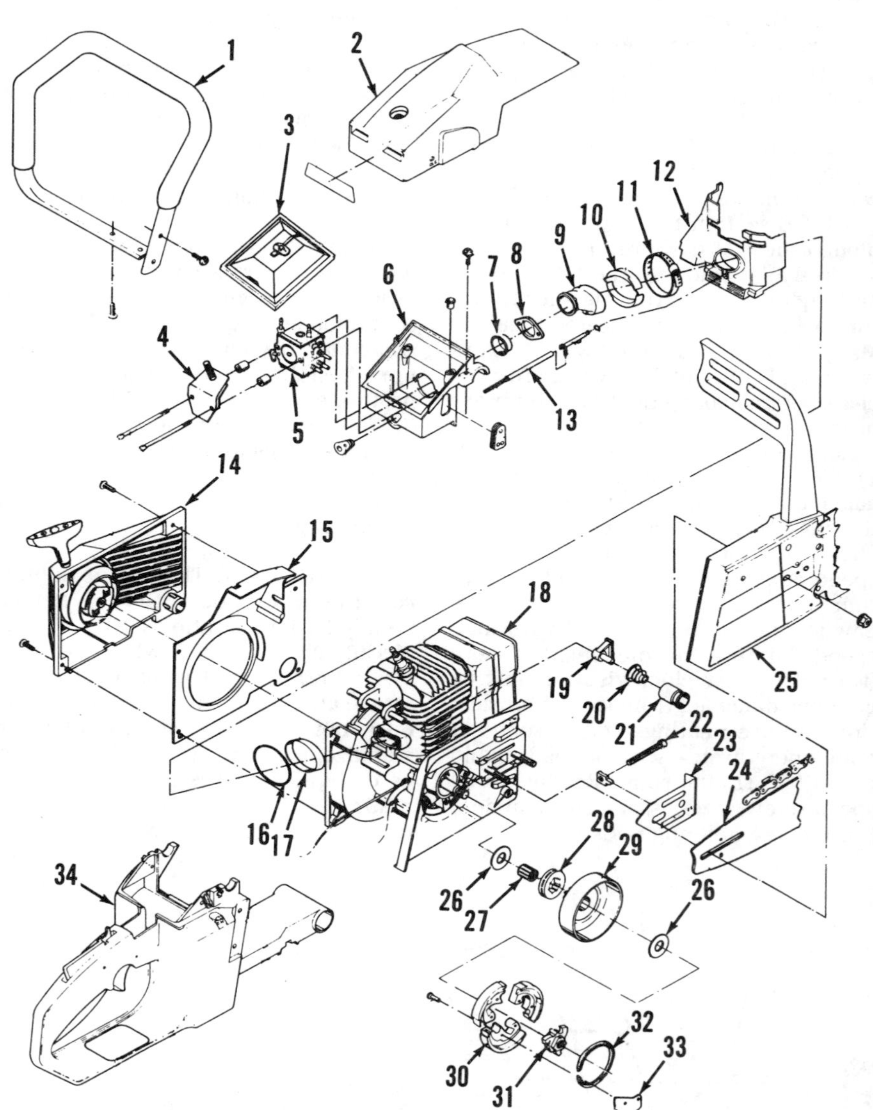

Fig. MC13-3—Exploded view of chain saw components typical of all models.

1. Front handle
2. Engine cover
3. Air filter
4. Shield
5. Carburetor
6. Air box
7. Sleeve
8. Flange
9. Intake boot
10. Spacer
11. Clamp
12. Cylinder shroud
13. Fuel line
14. Starter housing
15. Air baffle
16. "O" ring
17. Sleeve
18. Muffler
19. Mount retainer
20. Rear mount
21. Mount carrier
22. Bar adjustment screw
23. Bar plate
24. Bar
25. Chain brake assy.
26. Washer
27. Needle bearing
28. Sprocket
29. Clutch drum
30. Clutch shoes
31. Hub
32. Spring
33. Plate
34. Main frame assy.

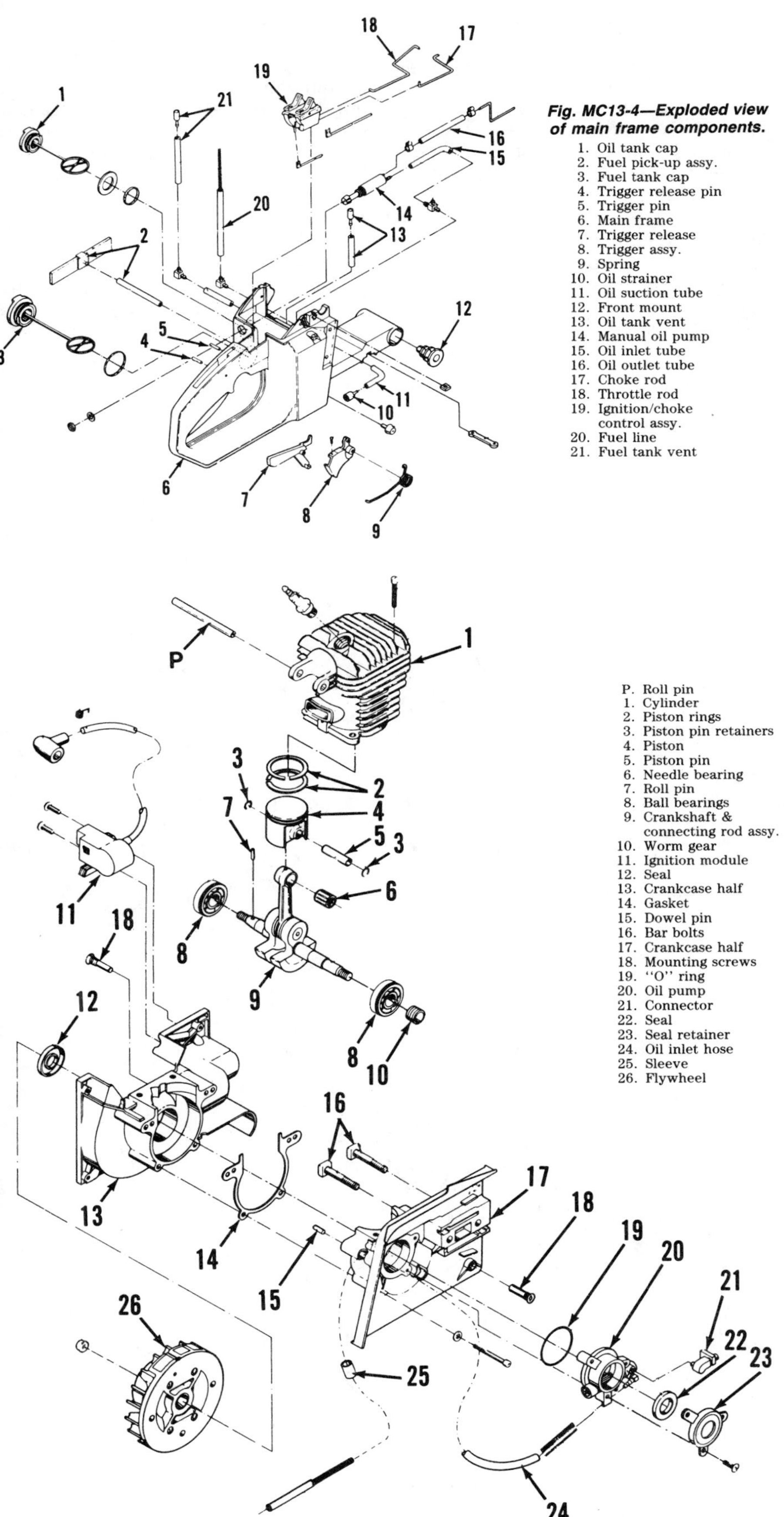

Fig. MC13-4—Exploded view of main frame components.

1. Oil tank cap
2. Fuel pick-up assy.
3. Fuel tank cap
4. Trigger release pin
5. Trigger pin
6. Main frame
7. Trigger release
8. Trigger assy.
9. Spring
10. Oil strainer
11. Oil suction tube
12. Front mount
13. Oil tank vent
14. Manual oil pump
15. Oil inlet tube
16. Oil outlet tube
17. Choke rod
18. Throttle rod
19. Ignition/choke control assy.
20. Fuel line
21. Fuel tank vent

P. Roll pin
1. Cylinder
2. Piston rings
3. Piston pin retainers
4. Piston
5. Piston pin
6. Needle bearing
7. Roll pin
8. Ball bearings
9. Crankshaft & connecting rod assy.
10. Worm gear
11. Ignition module
12. Seal
13. Crankcase half
14. Gasket
15. Dowel pin
16. Bar bolts
17. Crankcase half
18. Mounting screws
19. "O" ring
20. Oil pump
21. Connector
22. Seal
23. Seal retainer
24. Oil inlet hose
25. Sleeve
26. Flywheel

Fig. MC13-5—Exploded view of engine typical of all models.

sive or equivalent fuel resistant adhesive.

CRANKSHAFT, CONNECTING ROD AND CRANKCASE. The crankcase halves (13 and 17—Fig. MC13-5) must be separated to remove crankshaft assembly (9). For access to crankcase, power head must be separated from main frame as previously outlined. Remove spark plug and insert a loop of rope in spark plug hole to lock piston. Remove chain brake, guide bar and chain, clutch (left-hand threads) and oil pump. Remove starter housing, air baffle and flywheel. Unbolt and remove cylinder from crankcase. Remove crankcase mounting screws. Heat one of the crankcase halves in area of main bearing, then carefully tap end of crankshaft to separate crankcase halves. Heat the other crankcase half and tap crankshaft from case half. Use suitable puller to remove worm gear (10) and bearings (8) from crankshaft. Remove oil seals (12 and 22) from crankcase and oil pump housing.

The crankshaft and connecting rod are a unit assembly. Check rotation of connecting rod around crankpin and renew crankshaft assembly if roughness, excessive play or other damage is noted. Renew ball bearings (8) if roughness or other damage is indicated. Press bearings and worm gear onto crankshaft until they are seated against shoulders of crankshaft. New seals (12 and 22) can be installed after crankshaft is installed in crankcase. Lubricate crankshaft with oil prior to installing seals.

Heat crankcase halves in area of main bearings prior to installing crankshaft assembly. Assemble crankcase using new gasket (14). Tighten crankcase mounting screws before crankcase halves cool to 70 in.-lbs. (7.9 N·m), then retorque screws after case cools. Rotate crankshaft to make certain it turns freely. If not, disassemble and locate problem.

CLUTCH. Refer to Fig. MC13-3 for an exploded view of clutch assembly. To remove clutch, first remove chain brake (25), guide bar (24) and chain. Remove engine cover (2) and remove spark plug. Insert a knotted rope in spark plug hole to lock piston. Unscrew clutch hub (31) clockwise (left-hand threads). Remove and separate clutch components.

Clutch shoes (30), hub (31), spring (32) and plate (33) are serviced as an assembly. Inspect clutch drum (29), needle bearing (27) and sprocket (28) for excessive wear and renew as necessary.

Lubricate clutch drum needle bearing (27) with grease. Install clutch assembly and tighten to 150-168 in.-lbs. (17.0-19.0 N·m).

OIL PUMP. All models are equipped with a manual oil pump (14—Fig. MC13-4) located in main frame and an automatic chain oil pump (20—Fig. MC13-5) located on clutch side of crankcase. The automatic oil pump is operated by a worm gear (10) on the crankshaft.

For access to automatic oil pump, remove chain brake assembly, bar and chain and clutch assembly. Remove oil pump mounting screws, disconnect oil hose (24) and remove oil pump assembly from crankcase. To remove manual oil pump, pivot main frame away from power head. Disconnect oil lines (15 and 16—Fig. MC13-4), remove pump retaining nut and remove pump from main frame.

Thoroughly clean all components and inspect for wear or damage. Both the automatic oil pump and manual oil pump are serviced as unit assemblies.

An adjusting screw is located in bottom of automatic oil pump. Turn screw clockwise to increase oil output or counterclockwise to decrease oil flow.

CHAIN BRAKE. All models are equipped with a chain brake system designed to stop chain movement should kickback occur. The chain brake is activated when operator's hand strikes chain brake lever (2—Fig. MC13-6), which trips latch (5) and releases spring (12) to pull brake band (11) tight around clutch drum. Pull back chain brake lever to reset mechanism.

To check for proper chain brake operation, place saw on flat surface and run at full throttle. Push chain brake lever forward to activate brake. The chain should stop moving immediately. No adjustment of chain brake is required. If brake fails to operate properly, disassemble and inspect for problem.

To disassemble chain brake, move brake lever (2—Fig. MC13-6) forward to engage brake and relieve brake spring tension. To remove brake band (11), rotate guide plate (8) and remove "E" ring (9) and retaining screw (10). Disconnect brake spring (12). Drive out pins (6 and 7) to remove brake lever (2) and latch (5).

Inspect all components for evidence of wear or damage and renew as necessary. Brake band (11) should be renewed if worn to a thickness of 0.021 inch (0.5 mm) or less. To reassemble, reverse disassembly procedure.

REWIND STARTER. Rewind starter components are contained in starter housing (2—Fig. MC13-7). To disassemble, remove starter housing, detach rope handle (1) and allow rope to wind slowly onto pulley (4). Unscrew retaining screw (12) and remove pawl plate (10), spring (9), bushing (8) and pawls (7). Note the plate position in relation to starter pawls (7) so plate can be reinstalled in same position. Lift out rope pulley (4). Rewind spring is contained within housing (3). If spring is to be removed, use caution to prevent spring from uncoiling uncontrolled. Rewind spring and housing are available only as an assembly.

Inspect all parts for wear or damage and renew as necessary. Rope length should be 46-48 inches (117-122 cm).

If rewind spring should become disengaged from housing, it may be rewound by hand in clockwise direction from outer end. Wrap rope on pulley in a clockwise direction viewed from flywheel side of pulley. Tighten rope pulley retaining screw to 50 in.-lbs. (5.6 N·m). To put tension on rewind spring, pull a loop of rope back through starter housing opening and turn pulley and rope two turns clockwise. Release rope and check starter operation. Rope handle should retract snugly against starter housing. Be sure spring does not bottom out when rope is fully extended. It must be possible to rotate pulley at least 1/2 turn clockwise before rewind spring bottoms.

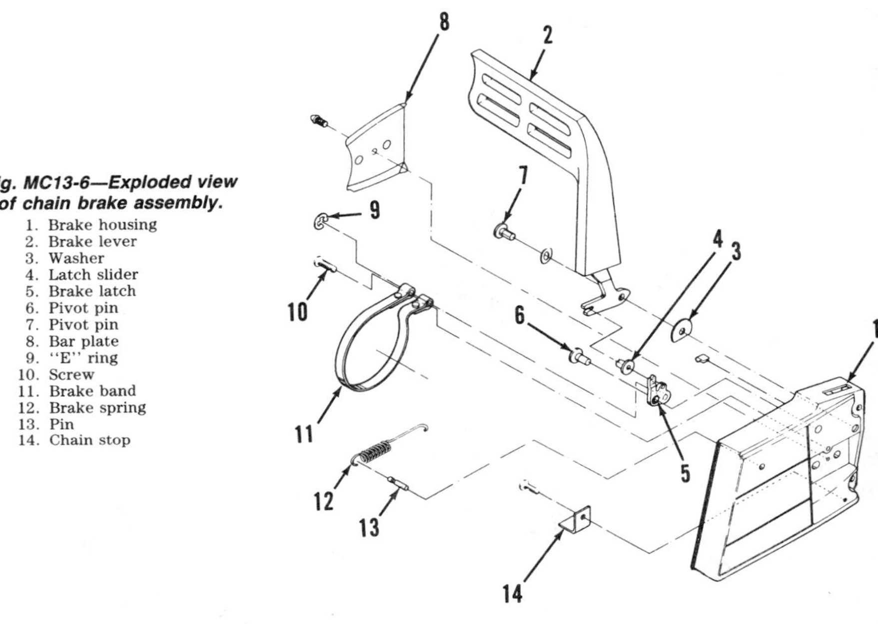

Fig. MC13-6—Exploded view of chain brake assembly.

1. Brake housing
2. Brake lever
3. Washer
4. Latch slider
5. Brake latch
6. Pivot pin
7. Pivot pin
8. Bar plate
9. "E" ring
10. Screw
11. Brake band
12. Brake spring
13. Pin
14. Chain stop

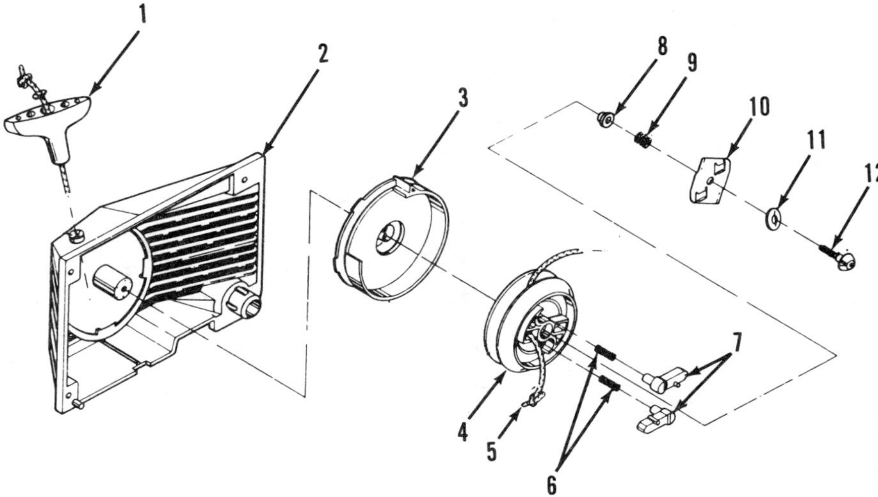

Fig. MC13-7—Exploded view of rewind starter assembly.

1. Rope handle
2. Starter housing
3. Spring/housing assy.
4. Rope pulley
5. Rope
6. Springs
7. Pawls
8. Bushing
9. Spring
10. Pawl plate
11. Washer
12. Screw

McCULLOCH

Model	Bore	Stroke	Displ.	Drive Type
Eager Beaver 2116, Silver Eagle 2116	38 mm (1.5 in.)	30 mm (1.2 in.)	35 cc (2.1 cu. in.)	Direct
Eager Beaver 2316, Eager Beaver 2318 Super, Silver Eagle 2318	40 cc (1.6 in.)	30 mm (1.2 in.)	38 cc (2.3 cu. in.)	Direct
Pro Mac 3205	36 mm (1.4 in.)	30 mm (1.2 in.)	32 cc (2.0 cu. in.)	Direct
Mac 3516, Pro Mac 3505, MacCat Super 16	38 mm (1.5 in.)	30 mm (1.2 in.)	35 cc (2.1 cu. in.)	Direct
Mac 3818, Pro Mac 3805, MacCat Super 18	40 cc (1.6 in.)	30 mm (1.2 in.)	38 cc (2.3 cu. in.)	Direct

MAINTENANCE

SPARK PLUG. Recommended spark plug is Champion DJ7Y or equivalent for all models. Spark plug electrode gap is 0.025 in. (0.6 mm) for all models. Note that spark plug has a tapered seat and does not require a gasket. Tighten spark plug to 150 in.-lbs. (17 N•m).

CARBURETOR. A Zama C1Q-M28 diaphragm type carburetor is used on 32 cc and 35 cc models. A Zama C1Q-M33 diaphragm type carburetor is used on 38 cc models. Refer to CARBURETOR SERVICE section for overhaul procedures and exploded views of Zama carburetors.

Initial adjustment for both the low-speed and high-speed mixture screws is one turn open from a lightly seated position. Make final adjustment with engine warm and running. Make certain that the air cleaner is clean.

Adjust idle speed screw so engine idles just below clutch engagement speed. Adjust low-speed mixture screw to obtain highest possible engine speed, then turn screw out (counterclockwise) 1/8 to 1/4 turn. Engine should accelerate cleanly without hesitation. If engine stumbles or seems sluggish when accelerating, adjust low-speed mixture screw until engine accelerates cleanly. Readjust idle speed screw if necessary to obtain recommended idle speed of 2800-3300 rpm. Chain must not move when engine is idling.

High-speed mixture screw should be adjusted to obtain optimum performance with saw under cutting load. Do not adjust high-speed mixture screw too lean (turned too far clockwise) as maximum permissible engine speed may be exceeded and engine may be damaged from lack of lubrication and overheating. Maximum no-load speed (with bar and chain installed) must not exceed 11,000 rpm.

To remove carburetor (4—Fig. MC100), remove the air filter cover (1) and filter element. Remove the two screws securing the filter base (3) and carburetor. Remove the filter base and carburetor, and disconnect fuel line and throttle link. Tighten carburetor mounting screws to 30-40 in.-lbs. (3.4-4.5 N•m).

IGNITION. All engines are equipped with an electronic ignition system. The ignition coil and electronic circuitry are contained in a one-piece ignition module (10—Fig. MC100), which is serviced as a unit assembly.

Air gap between the flywheel magnets and the laminated legs of the module should be 0.010-0.015 in. (0.25-0.38 mm). Loosen ignition module mounting screws and move module to obtain desired air gap. If air gap is excessive, engine may be hard to start or may not start.

LUBRICATION. The engine is lubricated by oil mixed with the gasoline fuel. Recommended fuel:oil ratio is 40:1 when using McCulloch 2-cycle oil. If McCulloch oil is not used, a good grade oil designed for use in air-cooled, two-stroke engines should be mixed at a 20:1 ratio. Do not use oil designed for automotive use. Use a separate container to mix the fuel and oil.

All models are equipped with an automatic chain oiling system. Recommended oil is McCulloch Chain, Bar and Sprocket oil. Oil designed for automotive use may also be used. Select oil viscosity according to ambient temperature.

REPAIRS

CRANKCASE PRESSURE TEST. An improperly sealed crankcase can cause the engine to be hard to start, run rough, have low power and overheat. Refer to ENGINE SERVICE section of this manual for crankcase pressure test procedure. If crankcase leakage is indicated, pressurize the crankcase and use a solution of soap and water to check gasket, seals, pulse line and castings for leakage.

PISTON, RINGS AND CYLINDER. To remove the piston, it is necessary to remove the powerhead (1—Fig. MC101) and separate the cylinder from the crankcase as follows: Unbolt and re-

Illustrations courtesy McCulloch Corp.

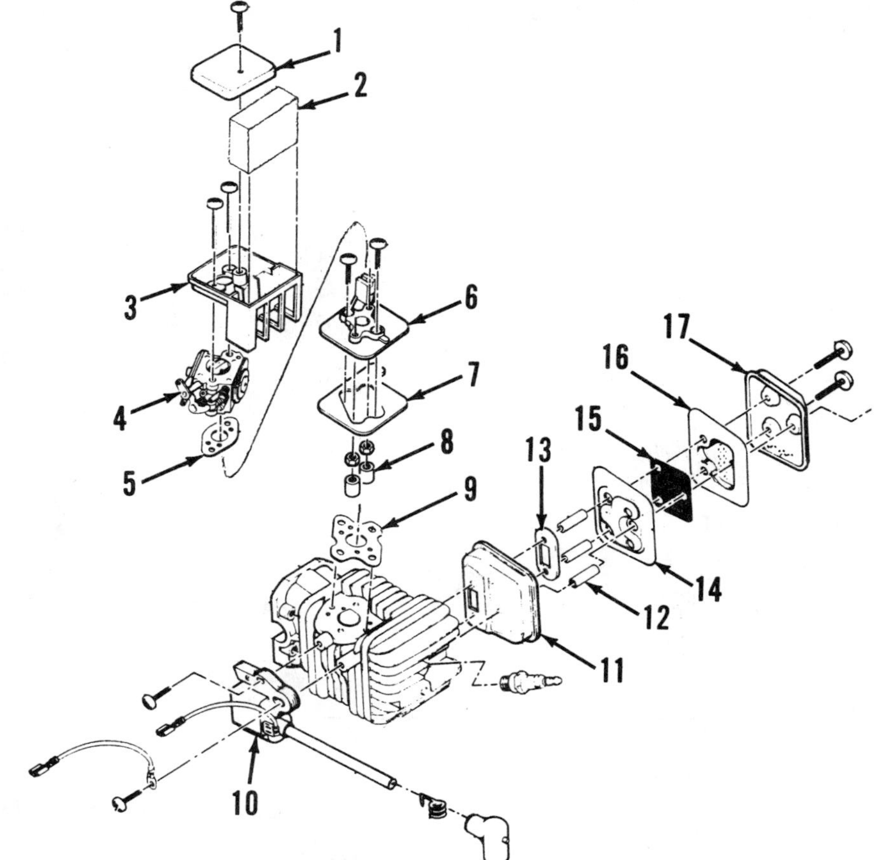

Fig. MC100—Exploded view of intake and exhaust components.

1. Shield
2. Air filter element
3. Filter housing
4. Carburetor
5. Gasket
6. Insulator
7. Seal
8. Spacer
9. Gasket
10. Ignition module
11. Muffler body
12. Spacers
13. Reinforcing plate
14. Baffle
15. Spark arrestor screen
16. Baffle
17. Muffler cover

move chain brake housing (8—Fig. MC101), bar and chain. Remove the air filter cover (7), rear handle (9 and 22), fan housing (28), fuel tank (4) and oil tank (17). Remove the ignition module, air filter assembly, carburetor and muffler.

Remove spark plug and install a suitable piston stop tool or insert the end of a rope in spark plug hole to prevent the crankshaft from rotating. Note that flywheel retaining nut has right-hand threads (turn counterclockwise to remove) and clutch retaining nut has left-hand threads (turn clockwise to remove). Remove the flywheel nut and tap flywheel counterbalance with a plastic mallet to unseat the flywheel (18—Fig. MC102) from crankshaft taper. Remove the air shroud (19) and oil pump (15). Remove clutch retaining nut (33) and withdraw the clutch assembly.

Remove screws attaching the crankcase (27) to the cylinder (1), and separate the crankcase from the cylinder. Care should be taken not to damage the mating surfaces of the crankcase and cylinder. Remove the crankshaft (7), connecting rod (8) and piston (3) as an assembly from the cylinder. Remove retaining rings (5) and push piston pin (4) from the piston. Be careful not to apply side thrust to the connecting rod when removing the piston pin.

Cylinder bore is chrome plated and no oversize piston or piston ring is available. If chrome plating is worn away or if cylinder bore is scuffed or scored, cylinder should be renewed.

Apply a thin coat of sealant to mating surface of crankcase and cylinder when assembling. Tighten the crankcase screws to 60-70 in.-lbs. (6.8-7.9 N•m).

CONNECTING ROD. Refer to PISTON section to remove connecting rod (8—Fig. MC102) from engine. Remove rod cap to separate connecting rod from crankshaft. Rod cap needle bearings will be loose when rod cap is removed.

Inspect connecting rod for worn or damaged bearing surfaces. Connecting rod should not be bent or twisted. Inspect crankshaft crankpin for wear or scoring.

To reassemble, use grease to hold bearing rollers in place in connecting rod and cap. Install connecting rod on crankshaft making sure that match marks on rod and cap are aligned. Connecting rod and cap are fractured and serration must mate correctly. Tighten connecting rod cap screws to 35-40 in.-lbs. (4.0-4.5 N•m).

CRANKSHAFT AND CRANKCASE. Crankshaft (7—Fig. MC102) is supported in two caged needle roller bearings (10). Refer to PISTON section to remove crankshaft from engine. Remove the connecting rod cap and separate the connecting rod and piston from crankshaft.

Inspect crankshaft and bearings for wear or damage. Note that crankcase and cylinder have mated surfaces and must be renewed as an assembly. Apply a thin coat of sealer to mating surfaces of crankcase and cylinder during assembly. Tighten crankcase screws to 60-70 in.-lbs. (6.8-7.9 N•m). Make certain that the crankshaft rotates freely. If not, disassemble and locate problem. Tighten flywheel retaining nut to 180 in.-lbs. (20.3 N•m). Do not use impact tools to tighten flywheel nut and do not over-torque, otherwise flywheel hub can be cracked and distorted.

CLUTCH. To remove the clutch, detach chain brake housing (8—Fig. MC101), bar and chain. Remove the spark plug and install a suitable piston stop tool or insert the end of a rope in spark plug hole to prevent the crankshaft from rotating. Clutch retaining nut (33—Fig. MC102) has left-hand threads (turn clockwise to remove). Remove retaining nut, dust cover (32) clutch assembly (31), clutch drum (30) and needle bearing (29).

Inspect all parts for signs of overheating and excessive wear. If necessary to renew clutch shoes, renew as complete set. Check sprocket for worn rails and pins. Inspect the sprocket needle bearing for wear.

Tighten clutch retaining nut to 180 in.-lbs. (20.3 N•m). Nut has left-hand threads. The use of an impact wrench to loosen or tighten clutch nut is not recommended.

AUTOMATIC CHAIN OILER. The automatic chain oil pump is shown in Fig. MC102. Remove the fan housing,

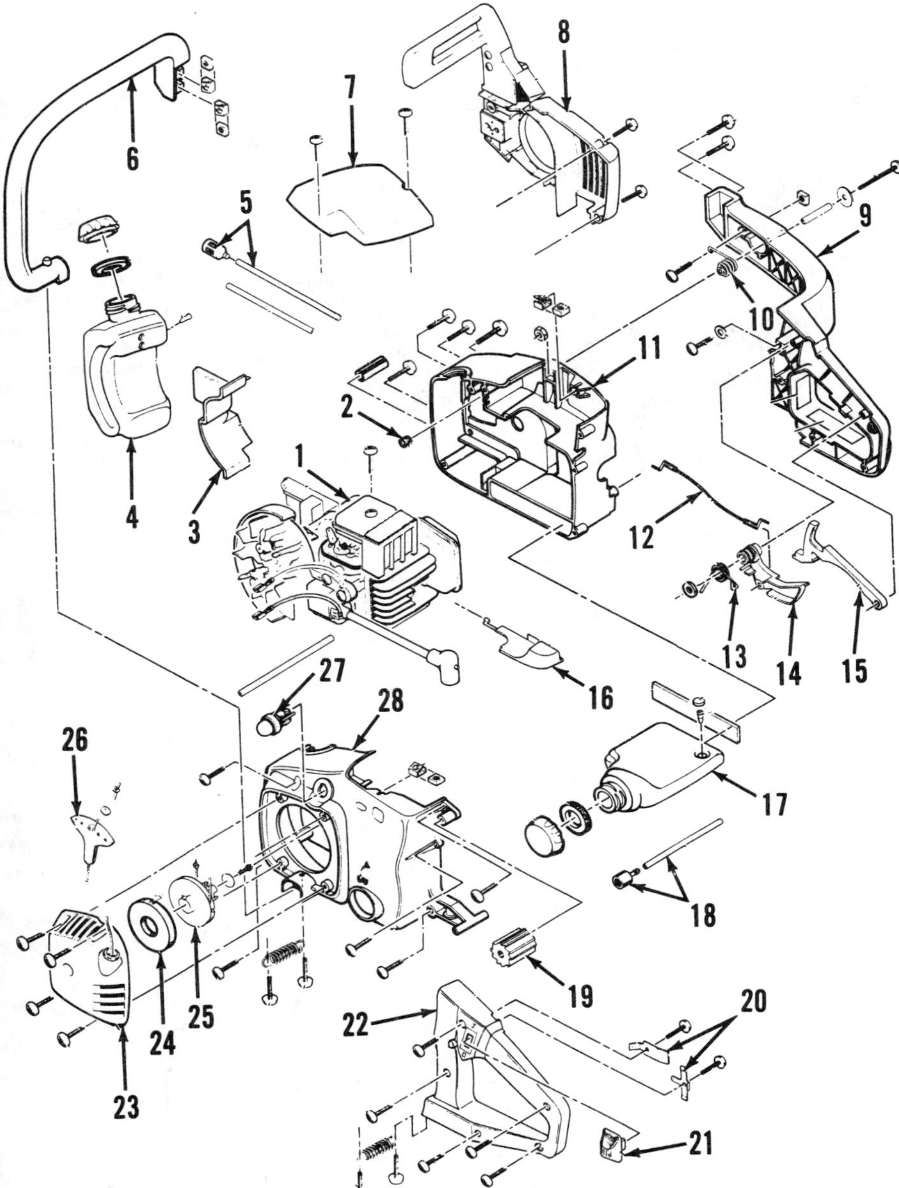

Fig. MC101—Exploded view of saw components typical of all models.

1. Powerhead
2. Vent filter
3. Shield
4. Fuel tank
5. Fuel pick-up hose & screen
6. Front handle
7. Air filter cover
8. Chain brake housing
9. Rear handle half
10. Spring
11. Housing, R.H.
12. Throttle cable
13. Return spring
14. Throttle trigger
15. Throttle latch
16. Choke rod
17. Oil tank
18. Oil pick-up hose and screen
19. Vibration isolator
20. Ignition ground contacts
21. Stop switch
22. Rear handle half
23. Starter housing
24. Rewind spring & case
25. Rope pulley
26. Rope handle
27. Fuel primer bulb
28. Fan housing

flywheel and air shroud for access to the oil pump. A plunger gear repair kit is available for the pump. Oil pump output is not adjustable.

CHAIN BRAKE. All models are equipped with a chain brake that stops the chain motion when the operator's hand contacts the chain hand guard (1—Fig. MC103). To check for proper chain brake operation, place saw on flat surface and run at wide-open throttle. Activate chain hand guard and chain should stop moving immediately. Pull hand guard rearward to disengage brake. No adjustment of chain brake is required. If brake fails to operate properly, disassemble and inspect for problem.

To disassemble chain brake, unbolt and remove brake housing (8—Fig. MC103) from saw. Engage the brake to relieve spring tension. Remove brake actuating lever (5) and carefully disengage spring (6). Remove brake band (9) from housing.

Inspect all components for evidence of wear or damage and renew as necessary. Brake band should be renewed if any point is worn to a thickness of 0.020 inch (0.5 mm) or less.

When reassembling, lubricate pivot points and latch engaging surface with light coat of multipurpose grease.

REWIND STARTER. To disassemble rewind starter, remove starter housing (2—Fig. MC104) from fan housing. Remove rope handle (1) and allow rope and pulley to slowly rewind. Remove pulley retaining screw (5) and withdraw rope pulley (4). Care should be taken when removing rewind spring (3) not to allow spring to unwind uncontrolled.

Inspect starter pawls (16—Fig. MC102) and springs (17) for wear or damage and renew as necessary.

Rewind spring is contained in a case (3—Fig. MC104). If spring becomes disengaged from the case, it should be wound into the case in a clockwise di-

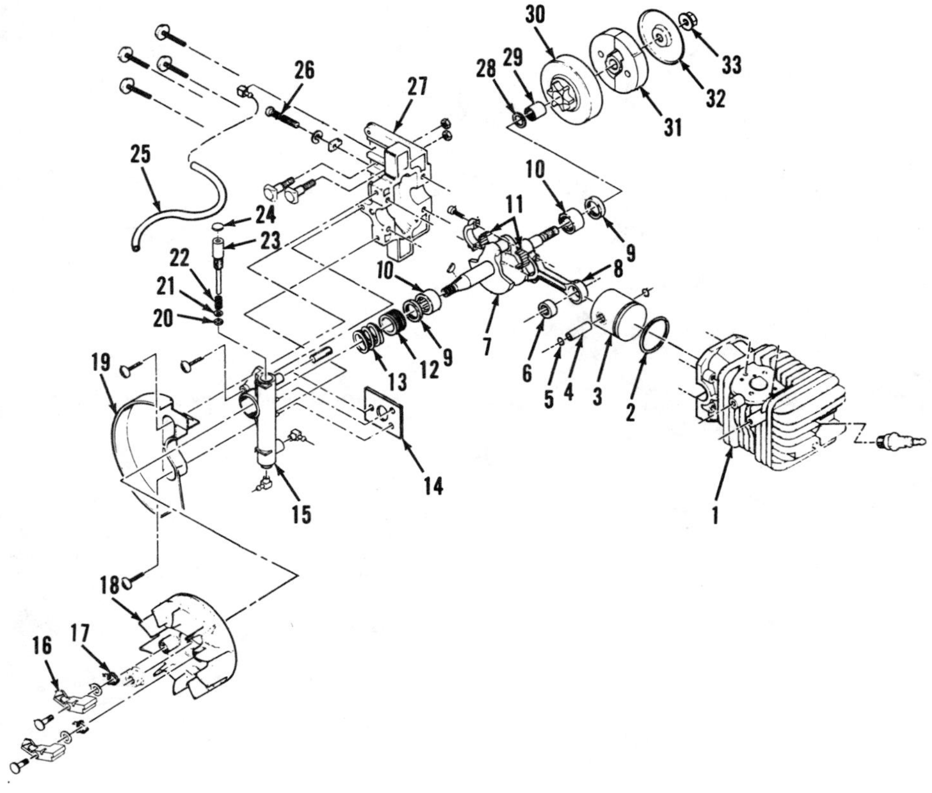

Fig. MC102—Exploded view of powerhead typical of all models.

1. Cylinder
2. Piston ring
3. Piston
4. Piston pin
5. Snap ring
6. Needle bearing
7. Crankshaft
8. Connecting rod
9. Seal
10. Main bearing
11. Needle rollers
12. Worm gear
13. Spring
14. Seal
15. Oil pump housing
16. Starter pawl
17. Spring
18. Flywheel
19. Air shroud
20. "O" ring
21. Washer
22. Spring
23. Oil pump plunger
24. Plug
25. Oil hose
26. Adjusting screw
27. Crankcase
28. Washer
29. Needle bearing
30. Clutch drum
31. Clutch hub & shoes
32. Dust cover
33. Nut

rection from outer end. Starter rope length is 50 inches (127 cm). Wind rope on pulley in clockwise direction viewed from flywheel side.

To pre-tension rewind spring, complete starter assembly and pass rope through housing outlet. Install rope handle, then pull a loop of rope back through the outlet and engage rope in notch of rope pulley. Rotate pulley one turn clockwise with rope in notch. Release rope from notch in pulley. Rope should be held snugly against the starter housing.

Pull rope handle and check rewind operation. With starter rope fully extended, it should be possible to turn pulley at least an additional 1/2 turn clockwise. Be sure excessive tension is not placed on rewind spring, otherwise spring may break when rope is pulled to its full length. Repeat spring pretension procedure until desired rewind action is obtained.

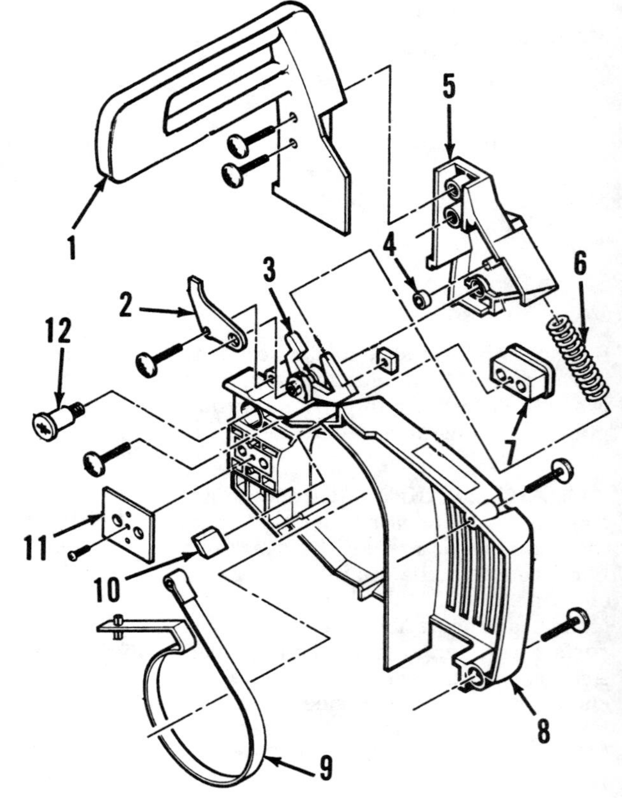

Fig. MC103—Exploded view of chain brake assembly.

1. Hand guard
2. Brake stop
3. Brake latch
4. Roller
5. Actuating lever
6. Brake spring
7. Bar pad spacer
8. Brake housing
9. Brake band
10. Foam seal
11. Shield
12. Shoulder bolt

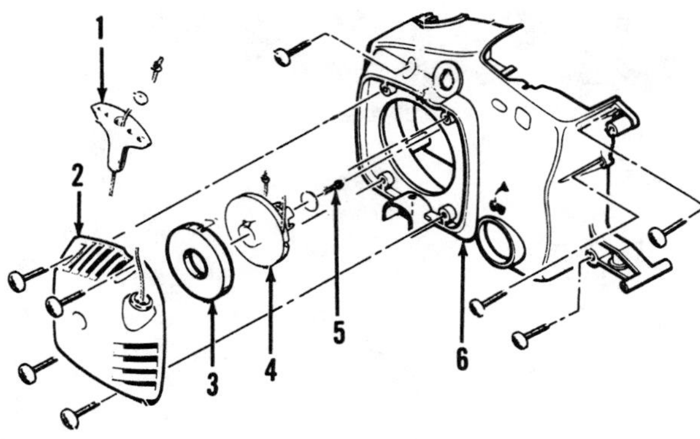

Fig. MC104—Exploded view of rewind starter.

1. Rope handle
2. Starter housing
3. Rewind spring & case
4. Rope pulley
5. Screw
6. Fan housing

Illustrations courtesy McCulloch Corp.

McCULLOCH

Model	Bore	Stroke	Displ.	Drive Type	
Mac 4600, Pro-Mac 4700		43 mm	32 mm	46 cc	Direct
	(1.69 in.)	(1.26 in.)	(2.8 cu. in.)		
Mac 4900, Pro-Mac 5000		44 mm	32 mm	49 cc	Direct
	(1.74 in.)	(1.26 in.)	(3.0 cu. in.)		
Silver Eagle 2818	43 mm	32 mm	46 cc	Direct	
	(1.69 in.)	(1.26 in.)	2.8 cu. in.)		
Silver Eagle 3020	44 mm	32 mm	49 cc	Direct	
	(1.74 in.)	(1.26 in.)	(3.0 cu. in.)		

MAINTENANCE

SPARK PLUG. Recommended spark plug is Champion DJ8J or RDJ8J for all models. Spark plug electrode gap is 0.025 in. (0.6 mm) for all models. Tighten spark plug to 110-120 in.-lbs. (12.5-13.5 N•m).

CARBURETOR. A Walbro WT diaphragm type carburetor is used on all models. Refer to CARBURETOR SERVICE section for overhaul procedures and exploded views of Walbro carburetors.

Initial adjustment for both the low-speed and high-speed mixture screws is 1-1/4 turns open from a lightly seated position. Make final adjustment with engine warm and running. Make certain that the air cleaner is clean.

Adjust idle speed screw (8—Fig. MC120) so engine idles just below clutch engagement speed. Adjust low-speed mixture screw (6) to obtain highest possible engine speed, then turn screw out (counterclockwise) 1/8 to 1/4 turn. Engine should accelerate cleanly without hesitation. If engine stumbles or seems sluggish when accelerating, adjust low-speed mixture screw until engine accelerates cleanly. Readjust idle speed screw if necessary to obtain recommended idle speed of 2800-3300 rpm. Chain must not move when engine is idling.

High-speed mixture screw (5) should be adjusted to obtain optimum performance with saw under cutting load. Do not adjust high-speed mixture screw too lean (turned too far clockwise) as maximum permissible engine speed may be exceeded and engine may be damaged from lack of lubrication and overheating. Maximum no-load speed (with bar and chain installed) must not exceed 11,500 rpm.

To remove carburetor (4—Fig. MC120), remove the air filter cover, filter element and engine top cover. Remove the two screws securing the

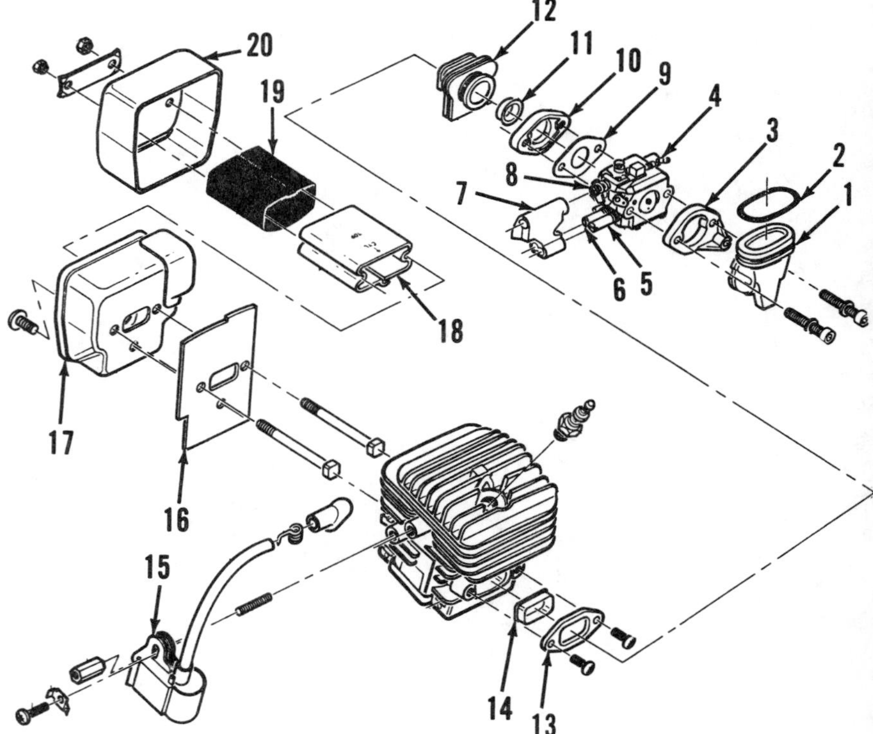

Fig. MC120—Exploded view of intake and exhaust components typical of all models.

1. Intake boot
2. Garter spring
3. Carburetor bracket
4. Carburetor
5. High-speed mixture screw
6. Low-speed mixture screw
7. Adjustment boot
8. Idle speed screw
9. Gasket
10. Carburetor flange
11. Sleeve
12. Boot
13. Flange
14. Boot
15. Ignition module
16. Gasket
17. Muffler body
18. Baffle
19. Spark arrestor screen
20. Muffler body

Illustrations courtesy McCulloch Corp.

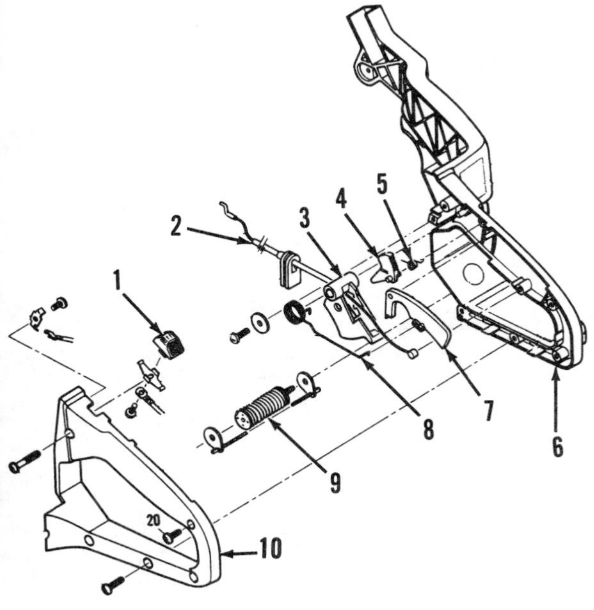

Fig. MC121—Exploded view of rear handle and throttle controls.

1. Stop switch
2. Throttle cable
3. Throttle trigger
4. High idle latch
5. Spring
6. Rear handle frame
7. Release trigger
8. Trigger spring
9. Vibration isolator
10. Rear handle cover

intake boot (1) and carburetor. Disconnect the fuel hose, pulse hose, choke link and throttle cable (2—Fig. MC121). Remove the carburetor.

When installing carburetor, tighten the carburetor mounting screws to 25-30 in.-lbs. (2.8-3.4 N•m).

IGNITION. All engines are equipped with an electronic ignition system. The ignition coil and electronic circuitry are contained in a one-piece ignition module (15—Fig. MC120), which is serviced as a unit assembly.

Air gap between the flywheel magnets and the laminated legs of the module should be 0.012-0.016 in. (0.3-0.4 mm). Loosen ignition module mounting screws and move module to obtain desired air gap. If the air gap is excessive, the engine may be hard to start or may not start.

LUBRICATION. The engine is lubricated by oil mixed with the gasoline fuel. Recommended fuel:oil ratio is 40:1 when using McCulloch 2-cycle oil. If McCulloch oil is not used, a good grade oil designed for use in air-cooled, two-stroke engines should be mixed at a 20:1 ratio. Do not use oil designed for automotive use. Use a separate container to mix the fuel and oil.

All models are equipped with an automatic chain oiling system. Recommended oil is McCulloch Chain, Bar and Sprocket oil. Oil designed for automotive use may also be used. Select oil viscosity according to ambient temperature. Oil pump output can be adjusted by turning the adjuster screw located on underside of the saw.

REPAIRS

CRANKCASE PRESSURE TEST. An improperly sealed crankcase can cause the engine to be hard to start, run rough, have low power and overheat. Refer to ENGINE SERVICE section of this manual for crankcase pressure test procedure. If crankcase leakage is indicated, pressurize the crankcase and use a solution of soap and water to check gasket, seals, pulse line and castings for leakage.

TIGHTENING TORQUE. Refer to the following table for tightening torque values.

Carburetor boot flange	45-50 in.-lbs. (5.1-5.6 N•m)
Carburetor mounting screws	25-30 in.-lbs. (2.8-3.4 N•m)
Crankcase to cylinder	70-80 in.-lbs. (7.9-9.0 N•m)
Crankcase to saw housing	55-60 in.-lbs. (6.2-6.8 N•m)
Flywheel nut	175-185 in.-lbs. (19.8-20.9 N•m)
Muffler	50-55 in.-lbs. (5.7-6.2 N•m)
Spark plug	110-120 in.-lbs. (12.5-13.5 N•m)

PISTON, RINGS AND CYLINDER. To remove the piston, it is necessary to remove the powerhead (20—Fig. MC122) and separate the cylinder from the crankcase as follows: Unbolt and remove chain brake housing (19), bar and chain. Remove the air filter cover (22), air filter (21) and engine cover (23). Remove starter housing (1), front handle (2) and rear handle (10). Remove the ignition module, carburetor and muffler.

Remove the spark plug and install a suitable piston stop tool or insert the end of a rope in spark plug hole to prevent the crankshaft from rotating. Note that the nut (1—Fig. MC123) retaining the flywheel has right-hand threads (turn counterclockwise to remove) and the clutch hub (28) has left-hand threads (turn clockwise to remove). Remove the clutch assembly, dust cover (25) and oil pump assembly (19). If service to the crankshaft or main bearings is required, remove the flywheel nut (1) and tap the flywheel with a plastic mallet to unseat the flywheel from the crankshaft taper. Remove the cap screws (8—Fig. MC122) attaching the powerhead to the saw housing and withdraw the powerhead.

Remove screws attaching the cylinder (14—Fig. MC123) to the crankcase halves (5 and 9), and separate the cylinder from the crankcase. Care should be taken not to damage the mating surfaces of the crankcase and cylinder. Remove the retaining rings (10) and push the piston pin (11) from the piston. Be careful not to apply side thrust to the connecting rod when removing the piston pin.

Cylinder bore is chrome plated and no oversize piston or piston ring is available. If chrome plating is worn away or if cylinder bore is scuffed or scored, cylinder should be renewed.

To reassemble, reverse the disassembly procedure while noting the following special instructions: Lubricate needle bearing (8) and piston pin (11), before inserting the piston pin . Always install NEW retaining rings (10) and be sure end gap is down toward the crankshaft. Lubricate piston and cylinder bore with oil, compress the piston ring, and slide the piston into the cylinder.

CONNECTING ROD, CRANKSHAFT AND CRANKCASE. The connecting rod and crankshaft (6—Fig. MC123) are available as a unit assembly. The crankshaft is supported by ball bearings (4) at both ends. A needle bearing (8) is located in small end of connecting rod.

To remove connecting rod and crankshaft, refer to PISTON section to remove cylinder and piston. Separate the crankcase halves (5 and 9) and withdraw the crankshaft. Care should be taken not to damage the mating sur-

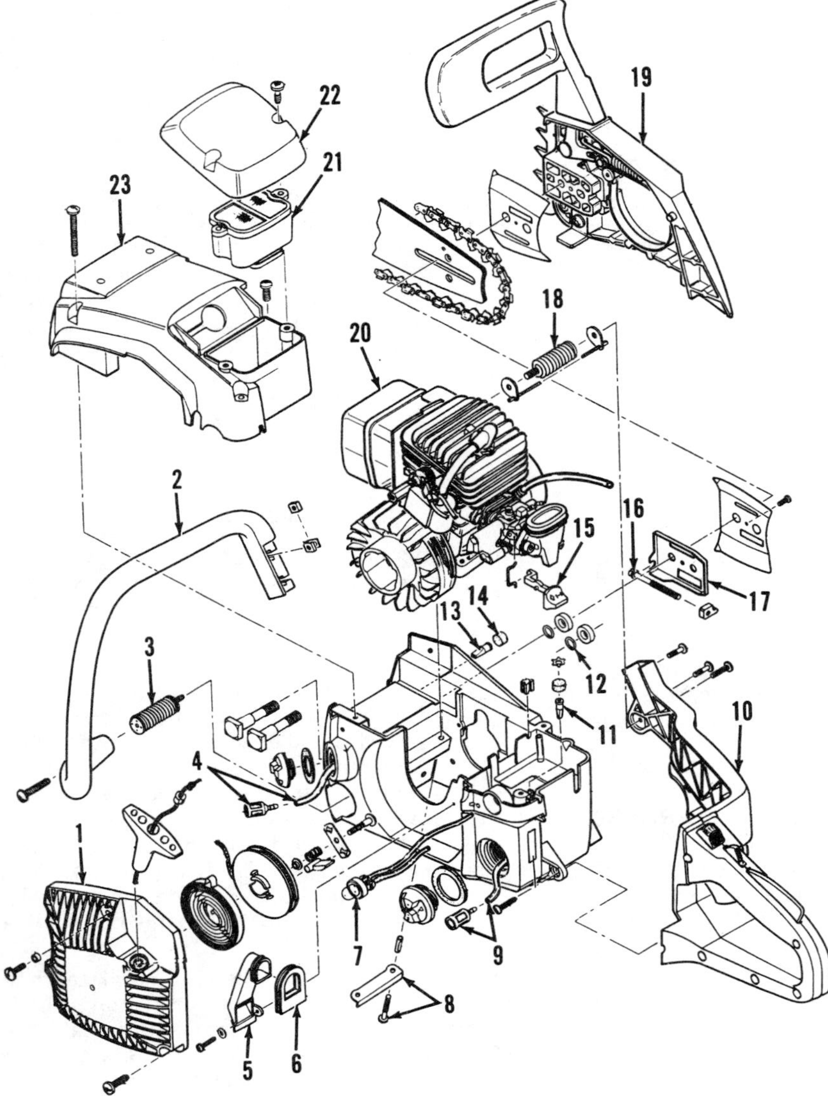

Fig. MC122—Exploded view of saw components typical of all models.

1. Starter housing
2. Front handle
3. Vibration isolator
4. Oil pick-up screen & hose
5. Precleaner tube
6. Boot
7. Primer bulb
8. Crankcase mounting screw & plate
9. Fuel pick-up screen & hose
10. Rear handle frame
11. Duckbill valve
12. "O" ring
13. Duckbill valve
14. Foam filter
15. Choke lever
16. Chain adjuster
17. Bar plate
18. Vibration isolator
19. Chain brake housin
20. Powerhead
21. Air filter element
22. Filter cover
23. Engine cover

faces of the crankcase halves. Remove the oil seals (3) and main bearings (4).

Check rotation of connecting rod around crankpin and renew crankshaft assembly if roughness or other damage is found. Renew main bearings (4) if roughness or other damage is indicated. Install new seals during assembly.

CLUTCH. To remove the clutch, detach chain brake housing (19—Fig. MC122), bar and chain.. Remove the spark plug and install a suitable piston stop tool or insert the end of a rope in spark plug hole to prevent the crankshaft from rotating. Clutch hub (28—Fig. MC123) has left-hand threads (turn clockwise to remove). Unscrew clutch hub and remove clutch drum (27) and needle bearing (26).

Inspect all parts for signs of overheating and excessive wear. If necessary to renew clutch shoes, renew as complete set.

When installing clutch drum (27), make certain that oil pump worm gear (18) engages notches in the drum.

AUTOMATIC CHAIN OILER. All models are equipped with an automatic chain oiling system. The oil pump is driven by a worm gear (18—Fig. MC123) that engages the clutch drum (27). The pump is actuated only when the clutch is engaged and the chain is rotating.

To remove the oil pump, first remove the spark plug and install a suitable piston stop tool or insert the end of a rope in spark plug hole to prevent the crankshaft from turning. Remove chain brake housing, bar and chain. Remove the clutch assembly as outlined previously in CLUTCH section. Remove dust cover (25) and felt washer (24). Remove oil pump mounting screws, disconnect oil line and withdraw oil pump assembly.

Remove adjuster (21), seal (23) and pump plunger (22). Thoroughly clean all components and inspect for wear or damage and renew as needed.

Oil pump output can be adjusted by turning the adjuster screw (21).

CHAIN BRAKE. All models are equipped with a chain brake that stops the chain motion when the operator's hand contacts the chain hand guard (1—Fig. MC124). To check for proper chain brake operation, place saw on flat surface and run at wide-open throttle. Activate chain hand guard and chain should stop moving immediately. Pull hand guard rearward to disengage brake. No adjustment of chain brake is required. If brake fails to operate properly, disassemble and inspect for problem.

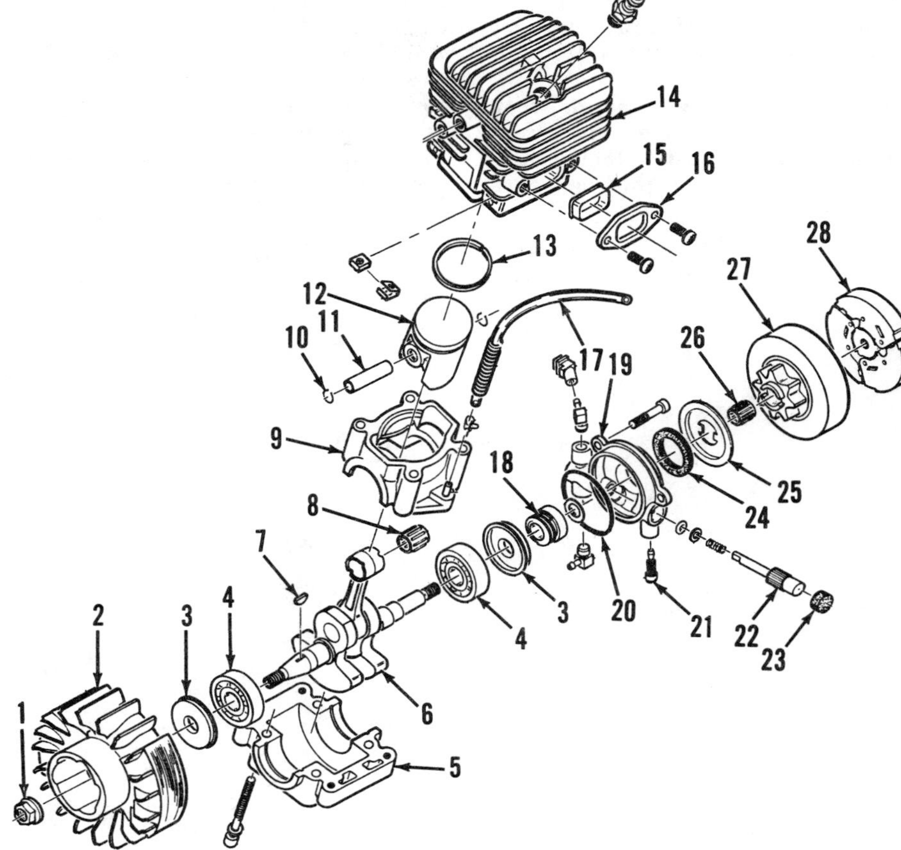

Fig. MC123—Exploded view of engine, oil pump and clutch components.

1. Nut
2. Flywheel
3. Seals
4. Bearings
5. Crankcase lower half
6. Crankshaft & connecting rod assy.
7. Woodruff key
8. Needle bearing
9. Crankcase upper half
10. Retaining ring (2)
11. Piston pin
12. Piston
13. Piston ring
14. Cylinder
15. Intake boot
16. Flange
17. Pulse hose
18. Worm gear
19. Oil pump housing
20. "O" ring
21. Adjuster screw
22. Oil pump plunger
23. Felt seal
24. Felt washer
25. Dust cover
26. Needle bearing
27. Clutch drum
28. Clutch shoes & hub

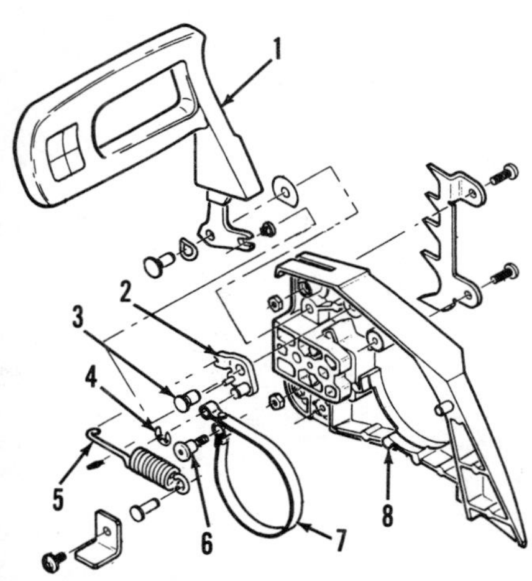

Fig. MC124—Exploded view of chain brake assembly.

1. Hand guard
2. Latch
3. Latch pivot
4. E-ring
5. Brake spring
6. Shoulder bolt
7. Brake band
8. Chain brake housing

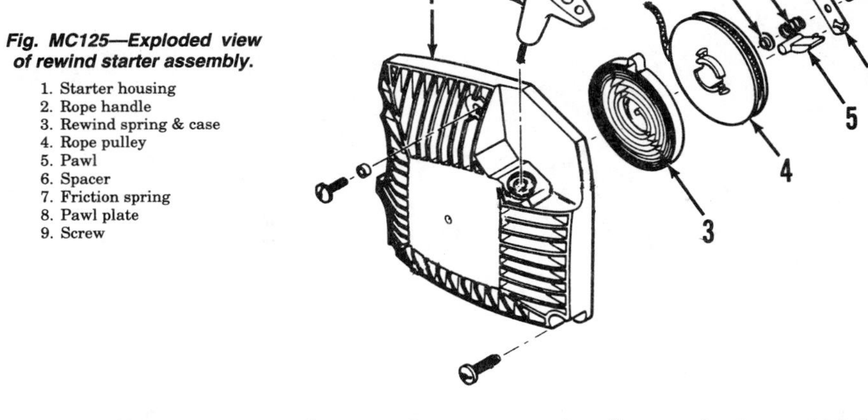

Fig. MC125—Exploded view of rewind starter assembly.

1. Starter housing
2. Rope handle
3. Rewind spring & case
4. Rope pulley
5. Pawl
6. Spacer
7. Friction spring
8. Pawl plate
9. Screw

To disassemble chain brake, unbolt and remove chain brake housing (8—Fig. MC124) from saw. Engage the brake to relieve spring tension. Carefully disengage the brake spring (5). Remove E-ring (4) and shoulder bolt (6), and withdraw brake band (7) from housing. Remove hand guard (1) and latch (2).

Clean all components and inspect for evidence of wear or damage and renew as necessary. Brake band should be renewed if any point is worn to a thickness of 0.020 inch (0.5 mm) or less.

When reassembling, lubricate pivot points and latch engaging surface with light coat of multipurpose grease.

REWIND STARTER. To disassemble rewind starter, unbolt and remove starter housing (1—Fig. MC125) from saw. Remove rope handle (2) and allow rope and pulley to slowly rewind. Remove pulley retaining screw (9) and pawl plate (6). Withdraw rope pulley (4), using care that rewind spring (3) is not allowed to unwind uncontrolled to prevent injury.

Inspect starter pawl (5) and spring (8) for wear or damage and renew as necessary.

Rewind spring is contained in a case (3). If spring becomes disengaged from the case, it should be wound into the case in a counterclockwise direction

Illustrations courtesy McCulloch Corp.

from outer end. Starter rope length is 41 inches (104 cm). Wind rope on pulley in clockwise direction viewed from flywheel side.

To pre-tension rewind spring, complete starter assembly and pass rope through housing outlet. Install rope handle, then pull a loop of rope back through the outlet and engage rope in notch of rope pulley. Rotate pulley one turn clockwise with rope in notch. Release rope from notch in pulley. Rope should be held snugly against the starter housing.

Pull rope handle and check rewind operation. With starter rope fully extended, it should be possible to turn pulley at least an additional 1/2 turn clockwise. Be sure excessive tension is not placed on rewind spring, otherwise spring may break when rope is pulled to its full length. Repeat spring pretension procedure until desired rewind action is obtained.

Illustrations courtesy McCulloch Corp.

McCULLOCH

Model	Bore	Stroke	Displ.	Drive Type
Eager Beaver 2010, Mac 3210	36 mm (1.4 in.)	30 mm (1.2 in.)	32 cc (2.1 cu. in.)	Direct
Silver Eagle 2012	36 mm (1.4 in.)	30 mm (1.2 in.)	32 cc (2.1 cu. in.)	Direct
Eager Beaver 2014, Mac 3214, Silver Eagle 2014	36 mm (1.4 in.)	30 mm (1.2 in.)	32 cc (2.1 cu. in.)	Direct
Eager Beaver 2016, Mac 3216, Silver Eagle 2016	36 mm (1.4 in.)	30 mm (1.2 in.)	32 cc (2.1 cu. in.)	Direct

MAINTENANCE

SPARK PLUG. Recommended spark plug is Champion DJ7Y or equivalent for all models. Spark plug electrode gap is 0.025 in. (0.6 mm) for all models. Note that spark plug has a tapered seat and does not require a gasket. Tighten spark plug to 150 in.-lbs. (17 N•m).

CARBURETOR. A Zama C1Q-M27 diaphragm type carburetor is used on all models. Refer to CARBURETOR SERVICE section for overhaul procedures and exploded views of Zama carburetors.

Initial adjustment for both the low-speed and high-speed mixture screws is one turn open from a lightly seated position. Make final adjustment with engine warm and running. Make certain that the air cleaner is clean.

Adjust idle speed screw so engine idles just below clutch engagement speed. Adjust low-speed mixture screw to obtain highest possible engine speed, then turn screw out (counterclockwise) 1/8 to 1/4 turn. Engine should accelerate cleanly without hesitation. If engine stumbles or seems sluggish when accelerating, adjust low-speed mixture screw until engine accelerates cleanly. Readjust idle speed screw if necessary to obtain recommended idle speed of 2800-3300 rpm. Chain must not move when engine is idling.

High-speed mixture screw should be adjusted to obtain optimum performance with saw under cutting load. Do not adjust high-speed mixture screw too lean (turned too far clockwise) as maximum permissible engine speed may be exceeded and engine may be damaged from lack of lubrication and overheating. Maximum no-load speed (with bar and chain installed) must not exceed 11,000 rpm.

To remove carburetor (4—Fig. MC130), remove the air filter cover (1) and filter element. Remove the two screws securing the filter base (3) and carburetor. Remove the filter base and carburetor, and disconnect fuel line and throttle link. Tighten carburetor mounting screws to 30-40 in.-lbs. (3.4-4.5 N•m).

IGNITION. All engines are equipped with an electronic ignition system. The ignition coil and electronic circuitry are contained in a one-piece ignition module (10—Fig. MC130), which is serviced as a unit assembly.

Air gap between the flywheel magnets and the laminated legs of the module should be 0.010-0.015 in. (0.25-0.38 mm). Loosen ignition module mounting screws and move module to obtain desired air gap. If air gap is excessive, engine may be hard to start or may not start.

LUBRICATION. The engine is lubricated by oil mixed with the gasoline fuel. Recommended fuel:oil ratio is 40:1 when using McCulloch 2-cycle oil. If McCulloch oil is not used, a good grade oil designed for use in air-cooled, two-stroke engines should be mixed at a 20:1 ratio. Do not use oil designed for automotive use. Use a separate container to mix the fuel and oil.

All models are equipped with an automatic chain oiling system. Recommended oil is McCulloch Chain, Bar and Sprocket oil. Oil designed for automotive use may also be used. Select oil viscosity according to ambient temperature.

REPAIRS

CRANKCASE PRESSURE TEST. An improperly sealed crankcase can cause the engine to be hard to start, run rough, have low power and overheat. Refer to ENGINE SERVICE section of this manual for crankcase pressure test procedure. If crankcase leakage is indicated, pressurize the crankcase and use a solution of soap and water to check gasket, seals, pulse line and castings for leakage.

PISTON, RINGS AND CYLINDER. To remove the piston, it is necessary to remove the powerhead (12—Fig. MC131) and separate the cylinder from the crankcase as follows: Unbolt and remove chain brake housing (13—Fig. MC131), bar and chain. Remove the air filter cover (10), fan housing (24), fuel tank (7) and oil tank (20). Remove the ignition module, air filter assembly, carburetor and muffler.

Remove spark plug and install a suitable piston stop tool or insert the end of a rope in spark plug hole to prevent the crankshaft from rotating. Note that fly-

Illustrations courtesy McCulloch Corp.

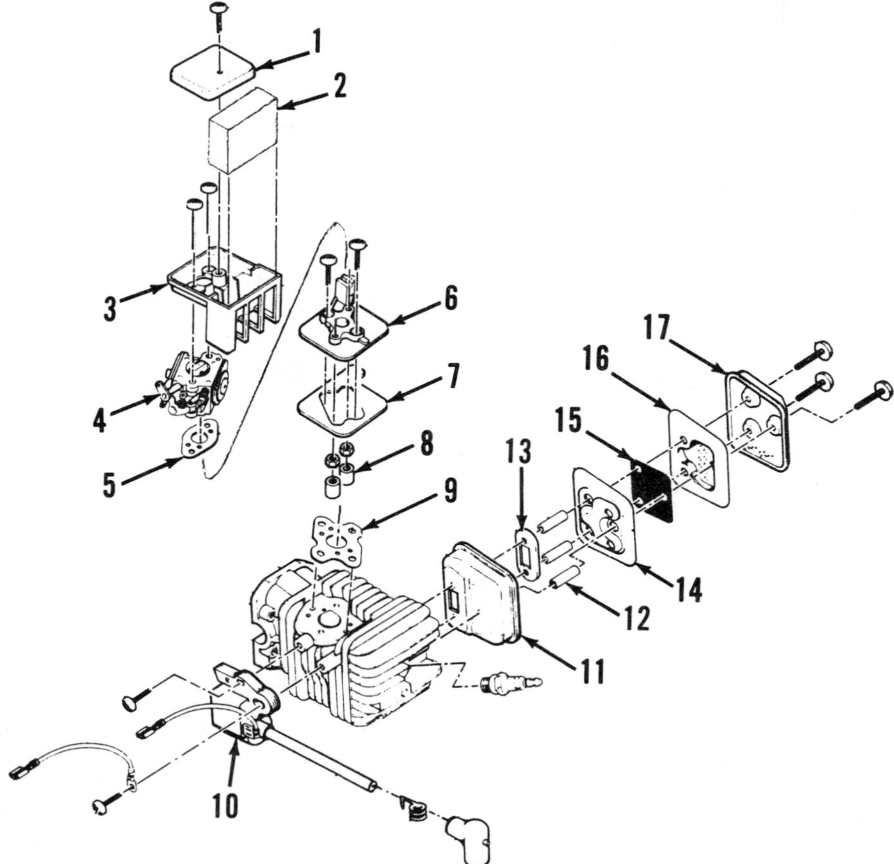

Fig. MC130—Exploded view of intake and exhaust components.

1. Shield
2. Air filter element
3. Filter housing
4. Carburetor
5. Gasket
6. Insulator
7. Seal
8. Spacer
9. Gasket
10. Ignition module
11. Muffler body
12. Spacers
13. Reinforcing plate
14. Baffle
15. Spark arrestor screen
16. Baffle
17. Muffler cover

wheel retaining nut has right-hand threads (turn counterclockwise to remove) and clutch retaining nut has left-hand threads (turn clockwise to remove). Remove the flywheel nut and tap flywheel counterbalance with a plastic mallet to unseat the flywheel (18—Fig. MC132) from crankshaft taper. Remove the air shroud (19) and oil pump (15). Remove clutch retaining nut (33) and withdraw the clutch assembly.

Remove screws attaching the crankcase (27) to the cylinder (1), and separate the crankcase from the cylinder. Care should be taken not to damage the mating surfaces of the crankcase and cylinder. Remove the crankshaft (7), connecting rod (8) and piston (3) as an assembly from the cylinder. Remove retaining rings (5) and push piston pin (4) from the piston. Be careful not to apply side thrust to the connecting rod when removing the piston pin.

Cylinder bore is chrome plated and no oversize piston or piston ring is available. If chrome plating is worn away or if cylinder bore is scuffed or scored, cylinder should be renewed.

Apply a thin coat of sealant to mating surface of crankcase and cylinder when assembling. Tighten the crankcase screws to 60-70 in.-lbs. (6.8-7.9 N•m).

CONNECTING ROD. Refer to PISTON section to remove connecting rod (8—Fig. MC132) from engine. Remove rod cap to separate connecting rod from crankshaft. Rod cap needle bearings will be loose when rod cap is removed.

Inspect connecting rod for worn or damaged bearing surfaces. Connecting rod should not be bent or twisted. Inspect crankshaft crankpin for wear or scoring.

To reassemble, use grease to hold bearing rollers in place in connecting rod and cap. Install connecting rod on crankshaft making sure that match marks on rod and cap are aligned. Connecting rod and cap are fractured and serration must mate correctly. Tighten connecting rod cap screws to 35-40 in.-lbs. (4.0-4.5 N•m).

CRANKSHAFT AND CRANKCASE. Crankshaft (7—Fig. MC132) is supported in two caged needle roller bearings (10). Refer to PISTON section to remove crankshaft from engine. Remove the connecting rod cap and separate the connecting rod and piston from crankshaft.

Inspect crankshaft and bearings for wear or damage. Note that crankcase and cylinder have mated surfaces and must be renewed as an assembly. Apply a thin coat of sealer to mating surfaces of crankcase and cylinder during assembly. Tighten crankcase screws to 60-70 in.-lbs. (6.8-7.9 N•m). Make certain that the crankshaft rotates freely. If not, disassemble and locate problem. Tighten flywheel retaining nut to 180 in.-lbs. (20.3 N•m). Do not use impact tools to tighten flywheel nut and do not over-torque, otherwise flywheel hub can be cracked and distorted.

CLUTCH. To remove the clutch, detach chain brake housing (13—Fig. MC131), bar and chain. Remove the spark plug and install a suitable piston stop tool or insert the end of a rope in spark plug hole to prevent the crankshaft from rotating. Clutch retaining nut (33—Fig. MC132) has left-hand threads (turn clockwise to remove). Remove retaining nut, dust cover (32) clutch assembly (31), clutch drum (30) and needle bearing (29).

Inspect all parts for signs of overheating and excessive wear. If necessary to renew clutch shoes, renew as complete set. Check sprocket for worn rails and pins. Inspect the sprocket needle bearing for wear.

Tighten clutch retaining nut to 180 in.-lbs. (20.3 N•m). Nut has left-hand threads. The use of an impact wrench to loosen or tighten clutch nut is not recommended.

AUTOMATIC CHAIN OILER. The automatic chain oil pump is shown in Fig. MC132. Remove the fan housing, flywheel and air shroud for access to the oil pump. A plunger gear repair kit is available for the pump. Oil pump output is not adjustable.

CHAIN BRAKE. All models are equipped with a chain brake that stops the chain motion when the operator's hand contacts the chain hand guard (1—Fig. MC133). To check for proper

Illustrations courtesy McCulloch Corp.

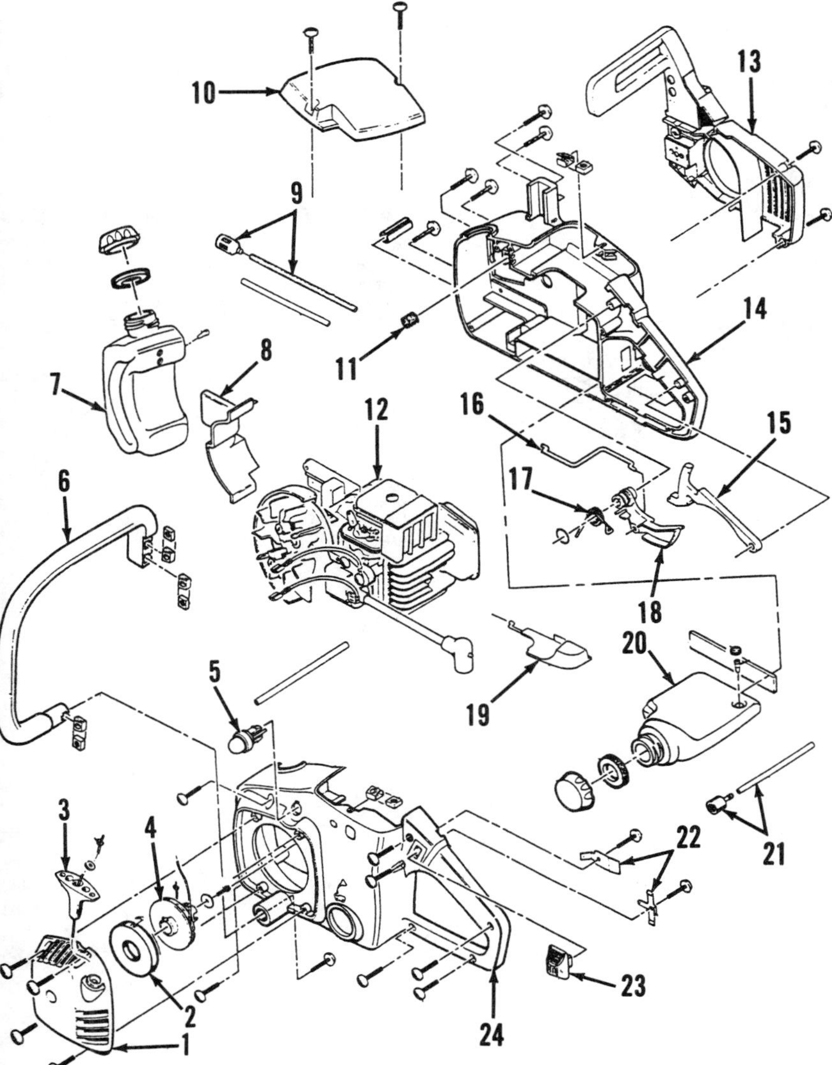

Fig. MC131—Exploded view of saw components typical of all models.

1. Starter housing
2. Rewind spring
3. Rope handle
4. Rope pulley
5. Fuel primer bulb
6. Front handle
7. Fuel tank
8. Heat shield
9. Fuel hose & screen
10. Air filter cover
11. Foam filter
12. Powerhead
13. Chain brake assy.
14. Engine housing
15. Throttle latch
16. Throttle rod
17. Return spring
18. Throttle trigger
19. Choke rod
20. Oil tank
21. Oil pickup hose & screen
22. Stop switch contacts
23. Stop switch button
24. Fan housing

chain brake operation, place saw on flat surface and run at wide-open throttle. Activate chain hand guard and chain should stop moving immediately. Pull hand guard rearward to disengage brake. No adjustment of chain brake is required. If brake fails to operate properly, disassemble and inspect for problem.

To disassemble chain brake, unbolt and remove brake housing (8—Fig. MC133) from saw. Engage the brake to relieve spring tension. Remove brake actuating lever (5) and carefully disengage spring (6). Remove brake band (9) from housing.

Inspect all components for evidence of wear or damage and renew as necessary. Brake band should be renewed if any point is worn to a thickness of 0.020 inch (0.5 mm) or less.

When reassembling, lubricate pivot points and latch engaging surface with light coat of multipurpose grease.

REWIND STARTER. To disassemble rewind starter, remove starter housing (2—Fig. MC134) from fan housing. Remove rope handle (1) and allow rope and pulley to slowly rewind. Remove pulley retaining screw (5) and withdraw rope pulley (4). Care should be taken when removing rewind spring (3) not to allow spring to unwind uncontrolled.

Inspect starter pawls (16—Fig. MC132) and springs (17) for wear or damage and renew as necessary.

Rewind spring is contained in a case (3—Fig. MC134). If spring becomes disengaged from the case, it should be wound into the case in a clockwise direction from outer end. Starter rope length is 50 inches (127 cm). Wind rope on pulley in clockwise direction viewed from flywheel side.

To pre-tension rewind spring, complete starter assembly and pass rope through housing outlet. Install rope handle, then pull a loop of rope back through the outlet and engage rope in notch of rope pulley. Rotate pulley one turn clockwise with rope in notch. Release rope from notch in pulley. Rope should be held snugly against the starter housing.

Pull rope handle and check rewind operation. With starter rope fully extended, it should be possible to turn pulley at least an additional 1/2 turn clockwise. Be sure excessive tension is not placed on rewind spring, otherwise spring may break when rope is pulled to its full length. Repeat spring pretension procedure until desired rewind action is obtained.

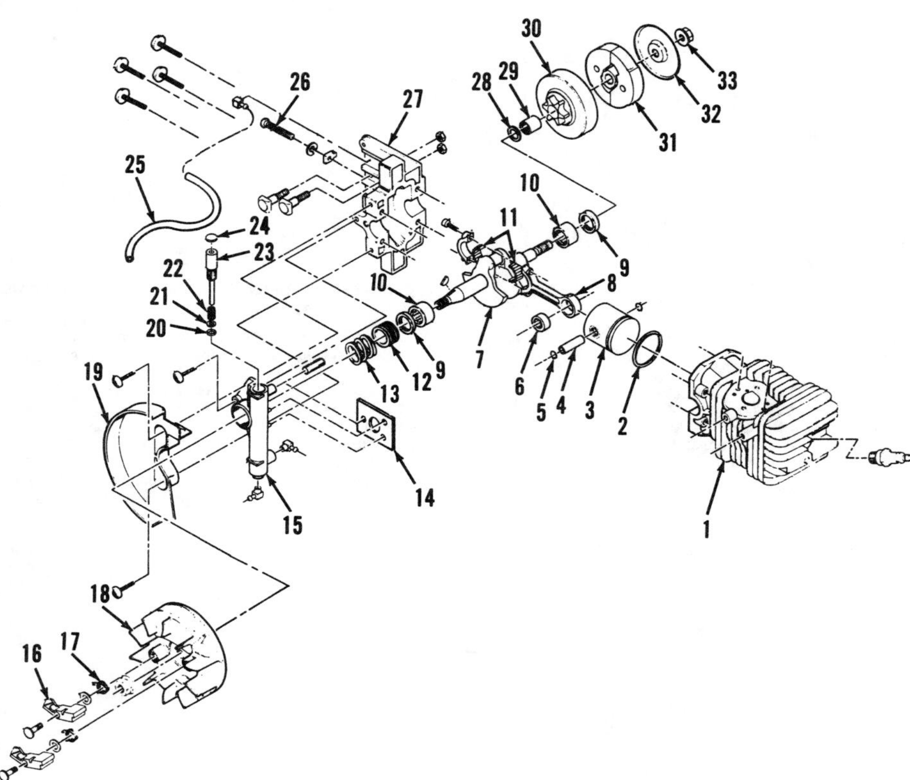

Fig. MC132—Exploded view of powerhead typical of all models.

1. Cylinder
2. Piston ring
3. Piston
4. Piston pin
5. Snap ring
6. Needle bearing
7. Crankshaft
8. Connecting rod
9. Seal
10. Main bearing
11. Needle rollers
12. Worm gear
13. Spring
14. Seal
15. Oil pump housing
16. Starter pawl
17. Spring
18. Flywheel
19. Air shroud
20. "O" ring
21. Washer
22. Spring
23. Oil pump plunger
24. Plug
25. Oil hose
26. Adjusting screw
27. Crankcase
28. Washer
29. Needle bearing
30. Clutch drum
31. Clutch hub & shoes
32. Dust cover
33. Nut

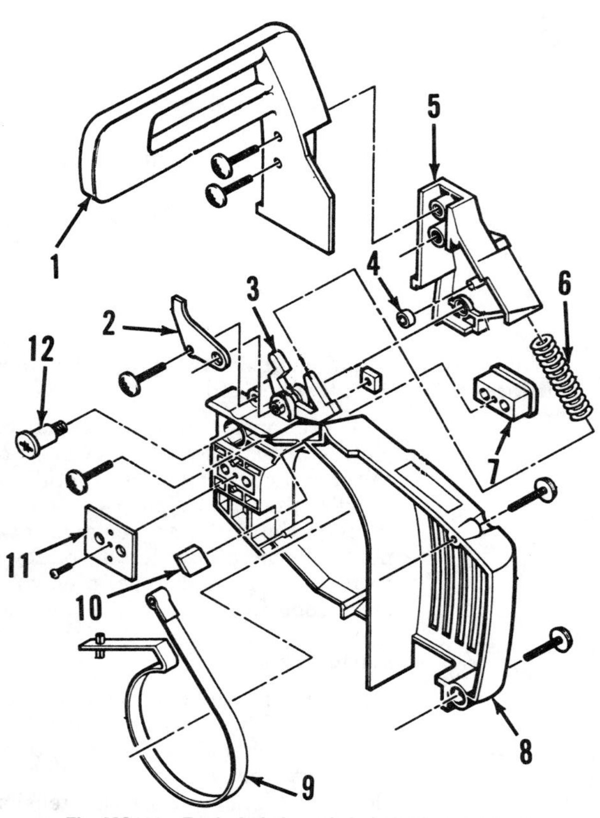

Fig. MC133—Exploded view of chain brake assembly.

1. Hand guard
2. Brake stop
3. Brake latch
4. Roller
5. Actuating lever
6. Brake spring
7. Bar pad spacer
8. Brake housing
9. Brake band
10. Foam seal
11. Shield
12. Shoulder bolt

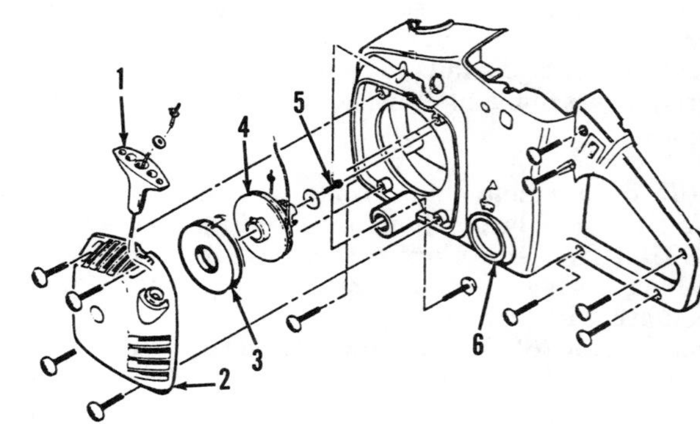

Fig. MC134—Exploded view of rewind starter.

1. Rope handle
2. Starter housing
3. Rewind spring & case
4. Rope pulley
5. Screw
6. Fan housing

Illustrations courtesy McCulloch Corp.

OLYMPYK

Model	Bore mm (in.)	Stroke mm (in.)	Displacement cc (cu. in.)	Drive Type
234, 234 AV	38 (1.5)	30 (1.18)	34 (2.1)	Direct
240, 241, 244, 244 AV, 244 F	40 (1.57)	30 (1.18)	38 (2.3)	Direct

MAINTENANCE

SPARK PLUG. Recommended spark plug for all models is Bosch WS7F. Spark plug electrode gap should be 0.63 mm (0.025 in.).

CARBURETOR. Tillotson HU and Walbro WA diaphragm type carburetors have been used. Refer to Tillotson and Walbro sections of CARBURETOR SERVICE section for service procedures and exploded views.

Initial adjustment for low and high speed mixture screws is one turn open from a lightly seated position. Final adjustment should be made with engine running at normal operating temperature. Adjust low speed mixture so engine will accelerate cleanly without hesitation. Adjust high speed mixture to obtain optimum full throttle performance under cutting load. Do not adjust high speed mixture too lean as overheating and engine damage could result. Adjust idle speed to just below clutch engagement speed.

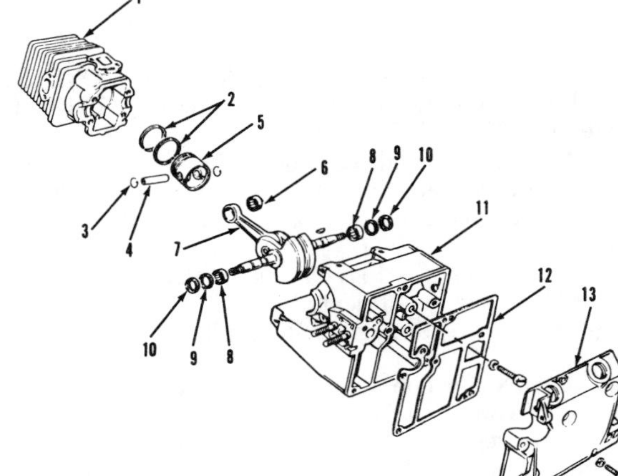

Fig. OL2—Exploded view of engine assembly.

1. Cylinder
2. Piston rings
3. Retainer
4. Piston pin
5. Piston
6. Needle bearing
7. Crankshaft & connecting rod assy.
8. Main bearing
9. Thrust washer
10. Seal
11. Crankcase
12. Gasket
13. Cover

IGNITION. Early Model 240 is equipped with a conventional flywheel magneto ignition system with breaker points located behind the flywheel. Breaker-point gap should be 0.40 mm (0.016 in.). Breaker-point gap is adjusted by rotating stator plate. Breaker-point gap must be correctly adjusted as point gap affects ignition timing. Air gap between ignition coil legs and flywheel magnets should be 0.30 mm (0.012 in.).

Later Model 240 and all other models are equipped with a breakerless electronic ignition system. Ignition coil and all electronic circuitry are contained in an one-piece ignition module (2–Fig. OL1) located outside of flywheel (1). Except for faulty wiring and wiring connections, repair of ignition system malfunctions is accomplished by component renewal. Use a process of elimination to trouble-shoot ignition module. Module to flywheel air gap shoud be 0.30 mm (0.012 in.). Ignition timing is fixed and not adjustable. Models 244 built before serial number 040440001 are equipped with a Phelon ignition system. Models 244 built after serial number 040440000 are equipped with a Selettra ignition system. The two ignition systems are interchangeable if entire system (module and flywheel) is exchanged.

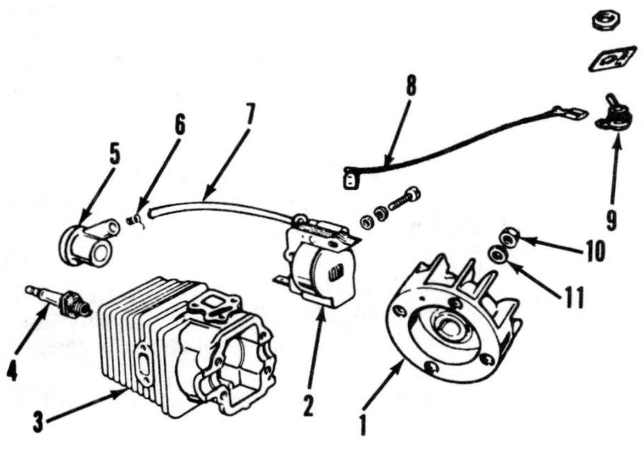

Fig. OL1—Exploded view of electronic ignition system.

1. Flywheel
2. Ignition module
3. Cylinder
4. Spark plug
5. Boot
6. Spring connector
7. High tension lead
8. Primary lead
9. Ignition switch
10. Nut
11. Washer

LUBRICATION. The engine is lubricated by mixing oil with the fuel. The recommended oil is BIA certified two-stroke air-cooled engine oil. Fuel:oil ratio should be 40:1 when using a recommended oil. If BIA certified two-stroke air-cooled oil is not available, use a good quality oil designed for use in air-cooled two-stroke engines mixed at a 20:1 ratio. Use a separate container when mixing fuel and oil.

Illustrations courtesy Olympyk, Oleo-Mac s.p.a.

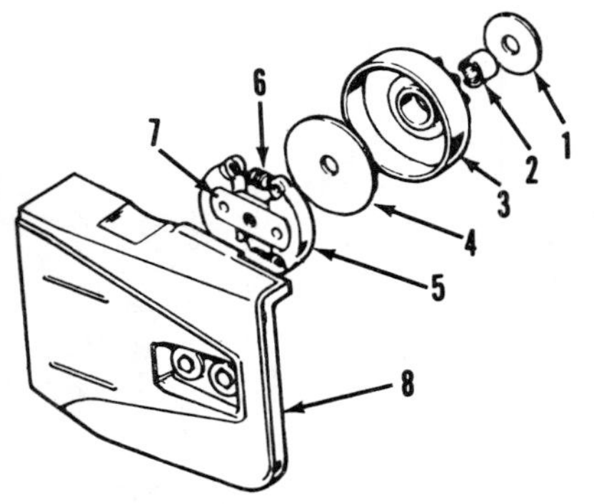

Fig. OL3—Exploded view of centrifugal clutch assembly.

1. Washer
2. Needle bearing
3. Drum
4. Washer
5. Shoe
6. Spring
7. Hub
8. Cover

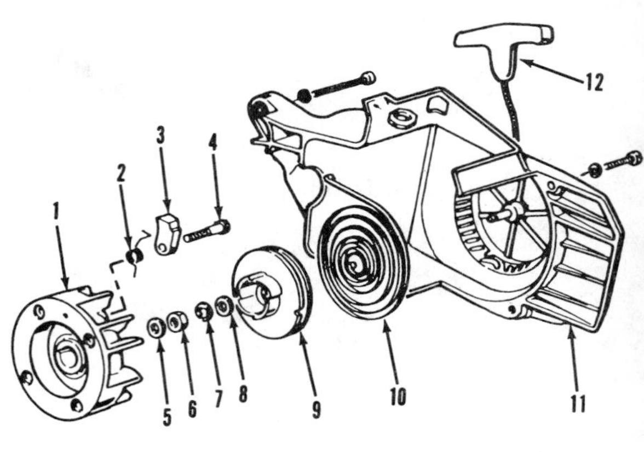

Fig. OL5—Exploded view of rewind starter. Two pawls (3), springs (2) and bolts (4) are used.

1. Flywheel
2. Spring
3. Pawl
4. Bolt
5. Washer
6. Nut
7. Snap ring
8. Washer
9. Rope pulley
10. Rewind spring
11. Starter housing
12. Rope handle

All models are equipped with adjustable automatic chain oil pumps. Refer to OIL PUMP in REPAIRS section for service and exploded views. Manufacturer recommends using oil specifically designed for saw chain lubrication.

Needle bearing (2–Fig. OL3) in clutch drum (3) should be lubricated with SAE 20 or SAE 30 oil at regular intervals.

CARBON. Carbon deposits should be removed from muffler and exhaust ports at regular intervals. Position piston at top dead center to prevent loosened carbon from entering cylinder. Use a wooden scraper to remove carbon. Use caution not to scratch piston or cylinder.

REPAIRS

CYLINDER, PISTON, PIN AND RINGS. Cylinder bore is chrome plated and should be renewed if cracking, flaking, scoring or other damage is noted. Cylinder (1–Fig. OL2) and crankcase (11) are a unit assembly and are not available separately.

Piston (5) and cylinder (1) are graded "A," "B," "C" or "D" during production with "A" being the largest size. Piston grade mark is stamped on piston crown while cylinder grade mark is stamped on cylinder head. Piston and cylinder marks should match although one size larger piston can be installed in a used cylinder, if matched piston is not available. For instance, piston marked "A" can be installed in a used cylinder marked "B."

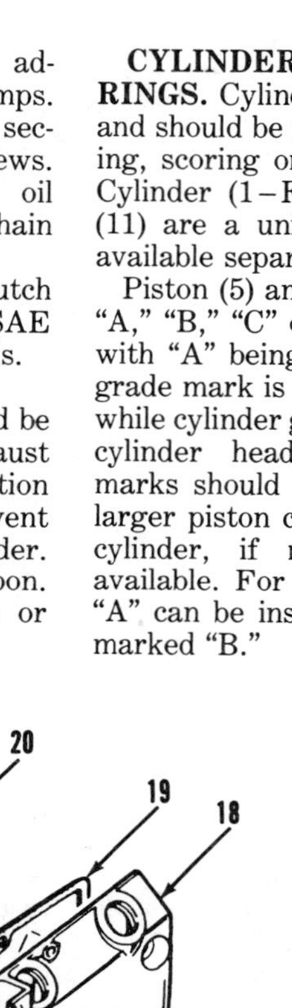

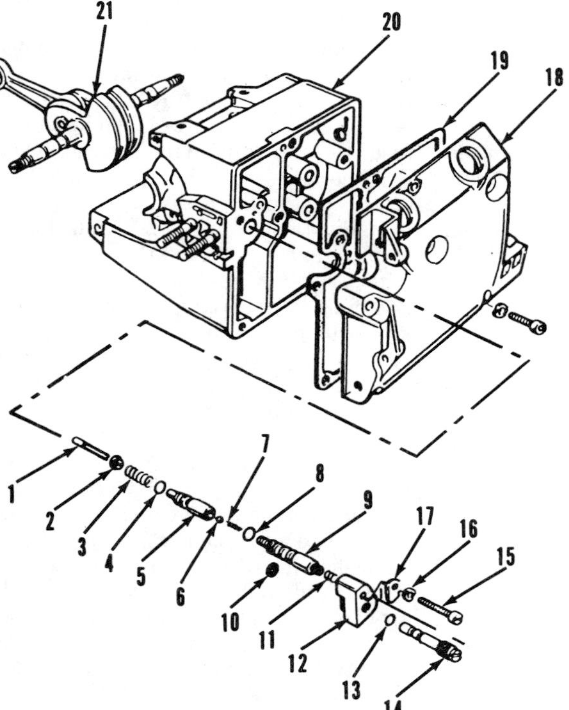

Fig. OL4—Exploded view of automatic oil pump and crankcase.

1. Plunger
2. Spring seat
3. Spring
4. "O" ring
5. Pump body
6. Check ball
7. Spring
8. "O" ring
9. Pump body
10. "O" ring
11. Spring
12. Pump fixture
13. "O" ring
14. Adjusting screw
15. Screw
16. Washer
17. Retainer
18. Cover
19. Gasket
20. Crankcase
21. Crankshaft

Piston (5) is equipped with two piston rings (2). Locating pins are present in ring grooves to prevent ring rotation. Make certain ring end gaps are properly positioned around locating pins when installing cylinder. Piston pin (4) rides in needle bearing (6) and is held in place with two wire retainers (3). Inspect piston, pin and needle bearing for excessive wear or damage and renew as required. Install piston in cylinder with arrow on piston crown facing toward exhaust port.

CRANKSHAFT, CONNECTING ROD AND CRANKCASE. Crankshaft assembly is loose in crankcase when cylinder is removed. Crankshaft and connecting rod are a unit assembly. Check rotation of connecting rod around crankpin and renew crankshaft assembly if roughness, excessive play or other damage is noted.

Crankshaft is supported at both ends with needle type main bearings (8–Fig. OL2). Note location of thrust washers (9). Make certain thrust washers are properly located in grooves of crankcase and cylinder when reassembling. Use a suitable sealant on mating surfaces of crankcase and cylinder base.

CLUTCH. All models are equipped with the centrifugal clutch shown in Fig. OL3. Clutch hub (7) has left-hand threads. Inspect clutch shoes (5), drum (3), needle bearing (2) and needle bearing wear surface on crankshaft for excessive wear or damage due to overheating.

OIL PUMP. All models are equipped with the adjustable automatic oil pump shown in Fig. OL4. Oil is pumped by plunger (1) which is driven by a cam ground on engine crankshaft (21). Pump output is regulated by rotating adjusting screw (14). Clockwise rotation decreases output.

Pump assembly can be withdrawn for inspection or repair after removing screw (15). Inspect all components for excessive wear or damage and renew as required. Check ball (6) must seat properly in pump body (5) for correct pump operation. Prime pump with clean oil prior to reassembly.

REWIND STARTER. To disassemble starter, pull out rope approximately 30 cm (12 in.) and hold rope pulley (9–Fig. OL5) from turning. Grasp rope and place into notch in rope pulley. Carefully allow pulley to unwind, relieving tension on rewind spring (10). Pry off snap ring (7) and remove rope pulley (9) being careful not to dislodge rewind spring (10). If rewind spring must be removed, use caution not to allow spring to uncoil uncontrolled.

During reassembly, lightly lubricate rewind spring and wind into starter housing in a clockwise direction starting with outer coil. Wind rope onto rope pulley in a clockwise direction as viewed from flywheel side of pulley. Preload rewind spring by placing rope into notch in rope pulley and rotating pulley in clockwise direction. Holding pulley firmly, allow tension on rewind spring to retract rope into starter housing. Spring tension is correct if rope handle is snug against housing with rope retracted and with rope fully extended, rope pulley will rotate one turn further.

CHAIN BRAKE. Some models are equipped with a chain brake system designed to quickly stop chain movement should kickback occur. Chain brake is activated when operator's hand strikes chain brake lever (1–Fig. OL6), tripping latch (4) to allow spring (6) to pull brake band (8) tight around clutch drum. Pull back chain brake lever to reset mechanism.

Disassembly for inspection or repair is evident after referral to exploded view and inspection of unit. Lubricate pivot points with a suitable grease. Do not lubricate brake band or outer diameter of clutch drum. No adjustment of chain brake system is required.

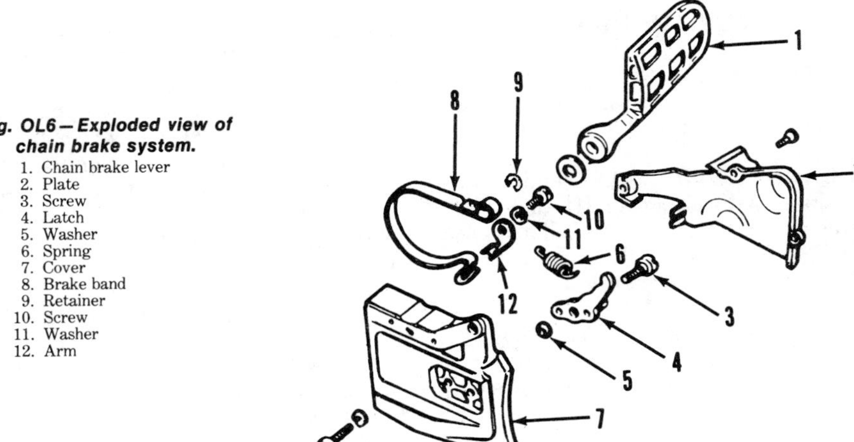

Fig. OL6—Exploded view of chain brake system.
1. Chain brake lever
2. Plate
3. Screw
4. Latch
5. Washer
6. Spring
7. Cover
8. Brake band
9. Retainer
10. Screw
11. Washer
12. Arm

Illustrations courtesy Olympyk, Oleo-Mac s.p.a.

OLYMPYK

Model	Bore mm (in.)	Stroke mm (in.)	Displacement cc (cu. in.)	Drive Type
945, 945AV, 945 F, 946	44 (1.73)	30 (1.18)	46 (2.8)	Direct
950, 950AV, 950 DF, 950 F	45 (1.77)	31 (1.22)	50 (3.0)	Direct

MAINTENANCE

SPARK PLUG. Recommended spark plug is Bosch WS7F. Spark plug electrode gap should be 0.5 mm (0.020 in.).

CARBURETOR. All models are equipped with a Tillotson HK diaphragm type carburetor. Refer to Tillotson secton of CARBURETOR SERVICE section for service procedures and exploded views.

Initial adjustment for both low and high speed mixture screws is one turn open from a lightly seated position. Make final adjustment with engine running at operating temperature. Adjust low speed mixture so engine will accelerate cleanly without hesitation. Adjust high speed mixture to obtain optimum full throttle performance under cutting load. Adjust idle speed to just below clutch engagement speed.

IGNITION. All models are equipped with a breakerless electronic ignition system. Ignition coil and all electronic circuitry are contained in an one-piece ignition module (2–Fig. OL15). Except for faulty wiring and wiring connections, repair of ignition system malfunctions is accomplished by component renewal. Use a process of elimination to trouble-shoot ignition module. Ignition timing is not adjustable. Air gap between ignition module core laminations and flywheel magnets should be 0.35 mm (0.014 in.). Flywheel nut (9) should be tightened to 9.8 N·m (7 ft.-lbs.).

LUBRICATION. The engine is lubricated by mixing oil with the fuel. The recommended oil is BIA certified two-stroke air-cooled oil. Fuel:oil mixture should be a 40:1 ratio when using a recommended oil. If BIA certified two-stroke air-cooled oil is not available, use a good quality oil designed for use in two-stroke air-cooled engines mixed at a 20:1 ratio. Use a separate container when mixing fuel and oil.

All models are equipped with adjustable automatic chain oil pump assemblies. Refer to OIL PUMP in REPAIRS section for service, adjustment procedures and exploded views. Use clean SAE 30 or SAE 40 automotive oil for saw chain lubrication. During cold weather operation, chain oil may be diluted up to 50 percent with kerosene.

CARBON. Carbon deposits should be removed from muffler and exhaust ports at regular intervals. Use a wooden scraper to remove carbon to prevent damaging piston or cylinder. Position piston at top dead center to prevent loosened carbon from entering cylinder.

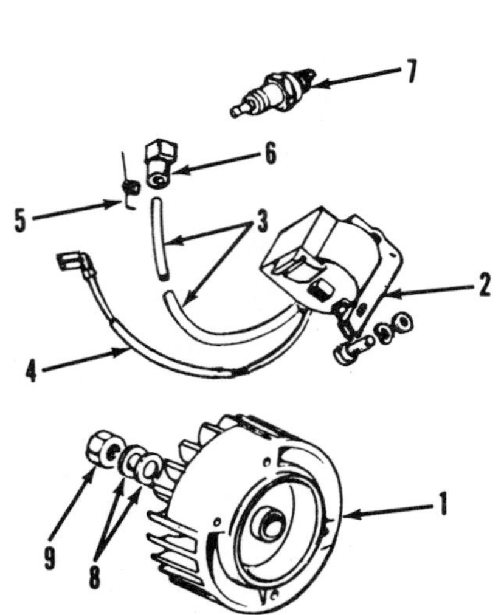

Fig. OL15 – Exploded view of ignition system used on all models.

1. Flywheel
2. Ignition module
3. High tension lead
4. Primary lead
5. Connector
6. Boot
7. Spark plug
8. Washers
9. Nut

Fig. OL16 – Exploded view of engine assembly.

1. Cylinder
2. Gasket
3. Piston rings
4. Piston pin
5. Retainer
6. Needle bearing
7. Crankshaft & connecting rod assy.
8. Right crankcase half
9. Seal
10. Main bearing
11. Main bearing
12. Seal
13. Gasket
14. Left crankcase half

Illustrations courtesy Olympyk, Oleo-Mac s.p.a.

REPAIRS

CYLINDER, PISTON, PIN AND RINGS. Cylinder bore is chrome plated and should be renewed if cracking, flaking, scoring or other damage is noted in cylinder bore. Inspect piston and renew if excessively worn or damaged. Piston and cylinder are marked "A," "B," "C" or "D" during production to obtain the desired piston-to-cylinder clearance with "A" being the largest size. Piston and cylinder grade marks should match although one size larger piston may be installed in a used cylinder. For instance, a piston marked "A" may be installed in a used cylinder marked "B." Piston is marked on piston crown while cylinder is marked adjacent to spark plug hole as shown in Fig. OL17. Piston is equipped with two piston rings. Locating pins are present in ring grooves to prevent ring rotation. Make certain ring end gaps are properly positioned around locating pins when installing cylinder. Piston pin rides in a needle roller bearing in connecting rod small end and is held in place with two wire retainers. Check needle bearing for excessive wear or discoloration due to overheating. Check fit of piston pin in piston and renew pin and piston as required. Piston pin, pin retainers and piston rings are available separately, but piston is only available as an assembly with piston rings, pin and retainers. Install piston in cylinder with arrow on piston crown toward exhaust port. Apply Loctite 242 or a suitable equivalent on threads of cylinder screws and tighten to 11.8 N·m (9 ft.-lbs.).

CRANKSHAFT, CONNECTING ROD AND CRANKCASE. Crankcase halves must be split to remove crankshaft. Take care not to damage crankcase mating surfaces. Heat may be applied to crankcase to ease removal and installation of main bearings and crankshaft. Crankshaft and connecting rod are only available as a unit assembly. Check rotation of connecting rod around crankpin and renew crankshaft assembly if roughness, excessive play or other damage is noted. Use a suitable sealant on crankcase gasket upon reassembly.

CLUTCH. All models are equipped with the three-shoe centrifugal clutch shown in Fig. OL18. Clutch hub (2) has left-hand threads. Inspect shoes (1), drum (5) and needle bearing for wear or damage due to overheating. Tighten clutch hub to 19.6 N·m (14 ft.-lbs.).

OIL PUMP. All models are equipped with an adjustable automatic chain oil pump. Oil is pumped by plunger (10 – Fig. OL19) which is driven by a cam ground on engine crankshaft. Oil pump output is regulated by rotating adjusting screw (2) located at front of engine next to guide bar. Clockwise rotation decreases oil output.

Inspect plunger (10) and pump body (7) for excessive wear or damage. Inspect "O" rings for hardening or cracking. Check ball (6) must seat properly in pump body (7) for correct pump operation. Nut (1) should be tightened in pump body (7) to 20 N·m (15 ft.-lbs.). Tighten pump assembly in crankcase to 10 N·m (7 ft.-lbs.).

REWIND STARTER. All models are equipped with the rewind starter shown in Fig. OL20. To disassemble starter, pull out rope approximately 30 cm (12 in.) and hold rope pulley from turning. Place rope into notch (N) in rope pulley (10) and carefully allow pulley to unwind, relieving tension on rewind spring (11). Remove screw (5) and lift out rope

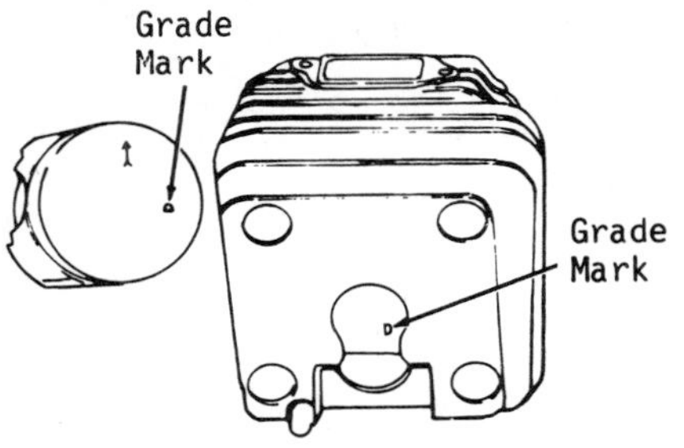

Fig. OL17 — View showing location of piston and cylinder grade marks. Grade "D" is shown.

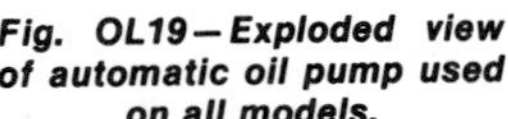

Fig. OL19 — Exploded view of automatic oil pump used on all models.

1. Nut
2. Adjusting screw
3. Spring
4. "O" ring
5. Spring
6. Check ball
7. Pump body
8. "O" rings
9. Spring
10. Plunger
11. "O" rings

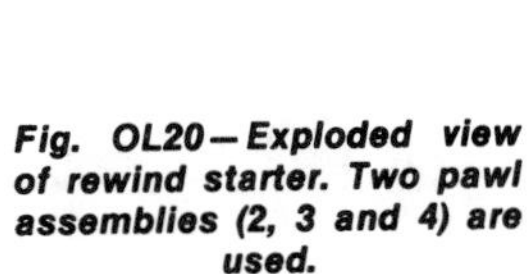

Fig. OL20 — Exploded view of rewind starter. Two pawl assemblies (2, 3 and 4) are used.

1. Flywheel
2. Spring
3. Pawl
4. Bolt
5. Screw
6. Washer
7. Washer
8. Washers
9. Nut
10. Rope pulley
11. Rewind spring
12. Plate
13. Starter housing
14. Rope handle
N. Notch

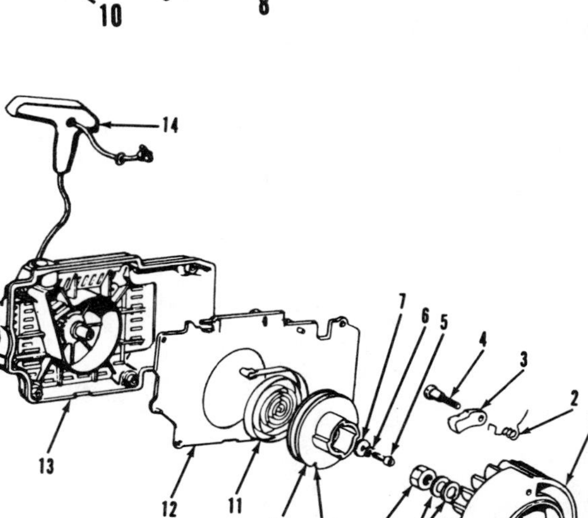

Fig. OL18 — Exploded view of clutch assembly.

1. Shoe
2. Hub
3. Spring
4. Washer
5. Drum
6. Sprocket
7. Washer
8. Needle bearing
9. Washer

pulley being careful not to dislodge rewind spring. If rewind spring must be removed, use caution not to allow spring to uncoil uncontrolled.

Wind rewind spring into starter housing (13) in a clockwise direction starting from outer coil. New rope should be 96 cm (38 in.) long and 3 mm (1/8 in.) in diameter. Wind rope onto pulley in a clockwise direction as viewed from flywheel side of pulley. Lightly grease pulley shaft in starter housing before installing pulley. Apply Loctite 242 or a suitable equivalent onto threads of screw (5). To preload rewind spring, place rope into notch (N) and rotate pulley clockwise. Tension on rewind spring is correct if rope handle is snug against starter housing with rope retracted and with rope fully extended, rope pulley will rotate one additional turn clockwise. If rewind spring tension is not correct, repeat above procedure and either add more tension or remove tension as needed.

When installing rewind starter assembly onto saw, slowly pull out rope to engage pawls (3) with rope pulley. Tighten starter housing screws to 2 N·m (18 in.-lbs.).

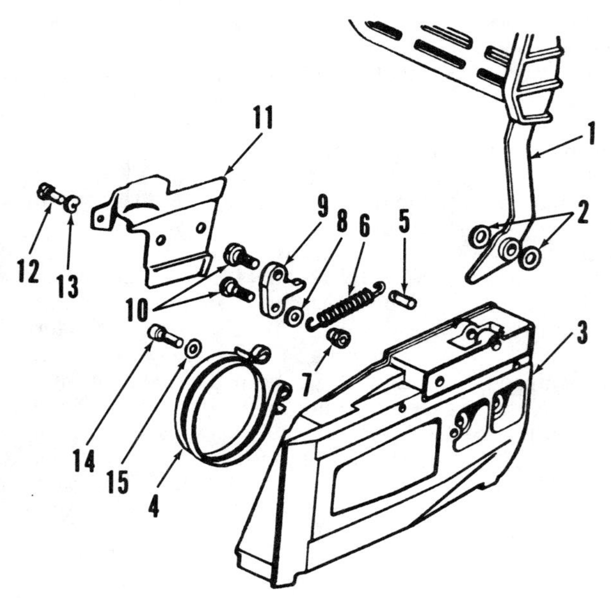

Fig. OL21—Exploded view of chain brake system used on so equipped models.

1. Lever
2. Washers
3. Housing
4. Brake band
5. Pin
6. Spring
7. Spacer
8. Washer
9. Arm
10. Screws
11. Chain guide
12. Screw
13. Washer
14. Screw
15. Washer

CHAIN BRAKE. Some models are equipped with a chain brake system designed to quickly stop chain movement should kickback occur. Chain brake is activated when operator's hand strikes chain brake lever (1 – Fig. OL21). Forward movement of chain brake lever disengages arm (9), allowing spring (6) to draw band (4) tight around clutch drum. Pull back chain brake lever to reset mechanism.

Disassembly is evident after referral to exploded view and inspection of unit. Chain brake should be in the activated position when removing spring (6). Renew brake band (4) if band is worn beyond 3/4 of its original thickness at the most worn area. Chain brake should be kept clean and free of sawdust and dirt accumulation. Lightly lubricate pivot points being careful not to allow grease to get on working surface of brake band or clutch drum. No adjustment of chain brake system is required.

Illustrations courtesy Olympyk, Oleo-Mac s.p.a.

OLYMPYK

Model	Bore mm (in.)	Stroke mm (in.)	Displacement cc (cu. in.)	Drive Type
251, 251B, 252	44 (1.73)	32 (1.26)	49 (3.0)	Direct
251	46 (1.81)	32 (1.26)	54 (3.3)	Direct
252 Super	46 (1.81)	32 (1.26)	54 (3.3)	Direct
254, 254 AV	46 (1.81)	32 (1.26)	54 (3.3)	Direct
261	47 (1.85)	35 (1.38)	61 (3.7)	Direct
264, 264 AV, 264 F	47 (1.85)	35 (1.38)	61 (3.7)	Direct
271	49 (1.93)	35 (1.38)	67 (4.1)	Direct
272, 272AV, 272 F	49 (1.93)	35 (1.38)	67 (4.1)	Direct
284, 284AV	52 (2.05)	38 (1.5)	80.7 (4.9)	Direct
284 F	52 (2.05)	38 (1.5)	80.7 (4.9)	Direct
355, 355AV, 355 DF	46 (1.81)	32 (1.26)	54 (3.3)	Direct
Super 481, S481	52 (2.05)	38 (1.5)	80.7 (4.9)	Direct
482 AV, 482 MP	52 (2.05)	38 (1.5)	80.7 (4.9)	Direct

MAINTENANCE

SPARK PLUG. Recommended spark plug for all models is Bosch WS7F or Champion CJ7Y. Spark plug electrode gap should be 0.5 mm (0.020 in.). Tighten spark plug to 29 N·m (22 ft.-lbs.).

CARBURETOR. All models except Model 264F are equipped with a Tillotson HS diaphragm type carburetor. Model 264F is equipped with a Walbro WJ diaphragm type carburetor. Refer to Tillotson or Walbro section of CARBURETOR SERVICE section for service procedure and exploded view of carburetors.

Initial adjustment of low speed mixture needle (L—Fig. OL30) is 1½ turns open from a lightly seated position. Initial adjustment of high speed mixture needle (H) is one turn open from a lightly seated position on all models except 264F. On Model 264F, high speed mixture needle should be 1½ turns open. Final adjustment should be made with engine warm and running. Make certain that engine air filter is clean before adjusting carburetor.

Adjust low speed mixture needle so engine will accelerate cleanly without hesitation. Adjust high speed mixture needle to obtain optimum full throttle performance under cutting load. Do not operate saw with high speed setting too lean (turned too far clockwise) as engine seizure could result from lack of lubrication and overheating. Adjust low idle speed screw (T) so engine idles just below clutch engagement speed.

IGNITION. Models 251, 261, 271, 481 Super, 482AV, 482MP and early 272 are equipped with a conventional breaker-point ignition system. Two types of breaker-point ignition systems are used. Models 261, 271, 481 Super, 482AV, 482MP and early 272 are equipped with a CEV ignition system (Fig. OL31) and Model 251 is equipped with a Selettra ignition system (Fig. OL32).

Engine flywheel must be removed to service breaker-point ignition components. Use Olympyk tool 60.00301 or equivalent puller to remove flywheel. Do not strike flywheel or flywheel magnets with a hammer. It may be necessary to remove one starter pawl if pawl hinders usage of flywheel puller.

NOTE: Flywheel used with breaker-point ignition systems has a "P" stamped on outer face of flywheel.

Breaker-point gap should be 0.45 mm (0.017 in.) on all models. On Model 251, air gap between flywheel magnets (7—Fig. OL32) and ignition coil (1) should be 0.35 mm (0.014 in.). There is no air gap adjustment on models equipped with CEV breaker-point ignition system.

Use Olympyk timing tool 60.00302 or a suitable dial indicator assembly to check ignition timing. Olympyk timing tool 60.00302 is equipped with an angle adapter used to hold dial indicator plunger at correct angle in spark plug hole. If angle adapter is used, set timing so breaker points just start to open

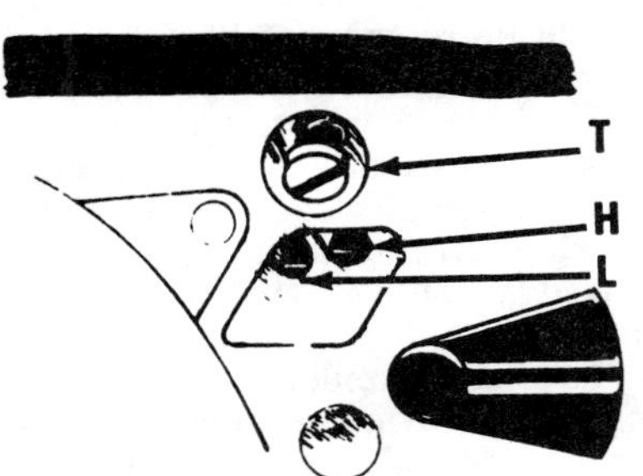

Fig. OL30—Drawing showing carburetor idle speed adjusting screw (T), low speed mixture needle (L) and high speed mixture needle (H).

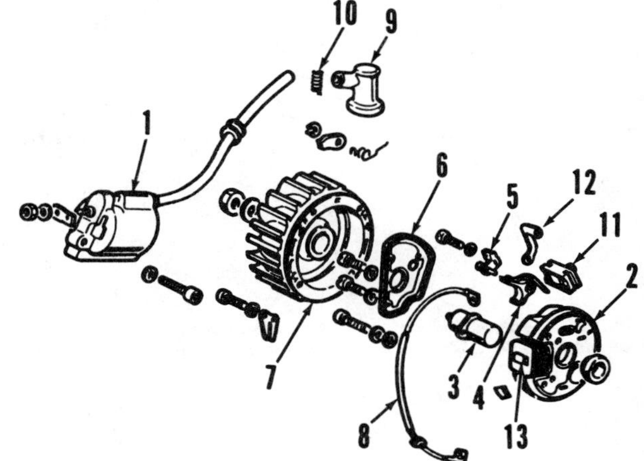

Fig. OL31—Exploded view of CEV breaker-point ignition system used on Models 261, 481 Super, 482AV, 482MP and early 272.

1. Ignition coil
2. Stator plate
3. Condenser
4. Moveable breaker-point
5. Fixed breaker-point
6. Cover
7. Flywheel
8. Primary lead
9. Boot
10. Connector
11. Insulator
12. Strap
13. Charge coil

Illustrations courtesy Olympyk, Oleo-Mac s.p.a.

at 2.2 mm (0.087 in.) BTDC for Model 251 and 2.6 mm (0.102 in.) BTDC for all other models. If angle adapter is not available, position dial indicator so plunger projects directly into spark plug hole and set timing so breaker points just start to open at 2.7 mm (0.106 in.) BTDC on Model 251 and 2.9 mm (0.114 in.) BTDC on all other models. Rotate stator plate to adjust ignition timing.

Models 251B, 251 Super, 252, 254, 254AV, 264, 264F, 264AV, 0272AV, 284, 284F, 284AV, 355, 355AV and later 272 are equipped with a breakerless capacitor discharge ignition system. Olympyk module and coil tester 60.00893 may be used to test ignition module. If tester is not available, trouble-shoot by substituting a known good ignition unit and check for spark.

Air gap between ignition module and flywheel magnets should be 0.35 mm (0.014 in.). Loosen ignition module mounting screws and move module to adjust air gap. Use Loctite 242 on threads of module mounting screws. Ignition timing is not adjustable. If flywheel requires removal, use Olympyk tool 60.00301 or a suitable equivalent puller to remove flywheel. Do not strike flywheel with a hammer. It may be necessary to remove one starter pawl if pawl hinders usage of flywheel puller.

NOTE: Flywheel used with capacitor discharge ignition systems has an "E" stamped on outer face of flywheel.

LUBRICATION. The engine is lubricated by mixing oil with the fuel. The recommended oil is high grade oil certified for use in two-stroke air-cooled engines. Fuel:oil mixture ratio should be 40:1 when using recommended oil. The use of automotive type oil is not recommended. Use a separate container when mixing fuel and oil.

An adjustable automatic chain oil pump is used on all models. Model 482MP is equipped with a manual pump in addition to the automatic oil pump. Refer to OIL PUMP in REPAIRS section for service procedures. It is recommended that a good quality oil designed for lubrication of bar and chain be used. Oil pump output is adjusted by turning adjuster (14—Fig. OL37 or 21—Fig. OL38). Clockwise rotation of adjuster reduces oil flow.

CARBON. Carbon deposits should be cleaned from muffler and exhaust port at regular intervals. Position piston at top dead center to prevent loosened carbon from entering cylinder. Use a wooden scraper when removing carbon to prevent damage to piston or cylinder.

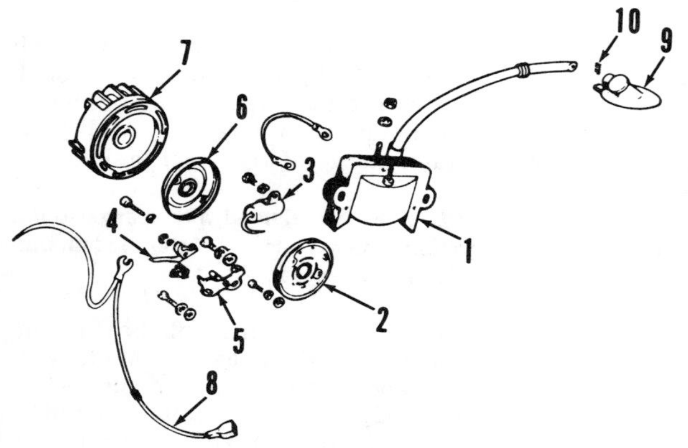

Fig. OL32—Exploded view of Selettra breaker-point ignition system used on Model 251.

1. Ignition coil
2. Stator plate
3. Condenser
4. Moveable breaker-point
5. Fixed breaker-point
6. Cover
7. Flywheel
8. Primary lead
9. Boot
10. Connector

REPAIRS

CRANKCASE PRESSURE TEST. An improperly sealed crankcase can cause the engine to be hard to start, run rough, have low power and overheat. Refer to ENGINE SERVICE section of this manual for crankcase pressure test procedure. If crankcase leakage is indicated, pressurize crankcase and use a soap and water solution to check gaskets, seals, pulse line and castings for leakage.

CYLINDER, PISTON, PIN AND RINGS. To disassemble, remove engine cover and air filter. Remove front handle, muffler and carburetor. Remove cylinder mounting screws and pull cylinder (1—Fig. OL33) off piston (4). Remove piston rings (3) and piston pin retainers (6). Use Olympyk tool 60.00366 or suitable equivalent piston pin removal tool to press piston pin out of piston. Press piston pin from flywheel side of engine toward clutch side.

Cylinder bore is chrome plated and should be renewed if bore is cracked, scored or if plating is worn through. Inspect piston skirt for scuffing, scratches or excessive wear and renew as necessary. It is recommended that piston rings (3) and pin retainers (6) be renewed whenever they are removed from piston.

Piston and cylinder are graded according to size during production to obtain desired piston-to-cylinder clearance. Piston and cylinder grade marks are "A," "B," "C" and "D" with "A" being the largest size. Piston grade mark

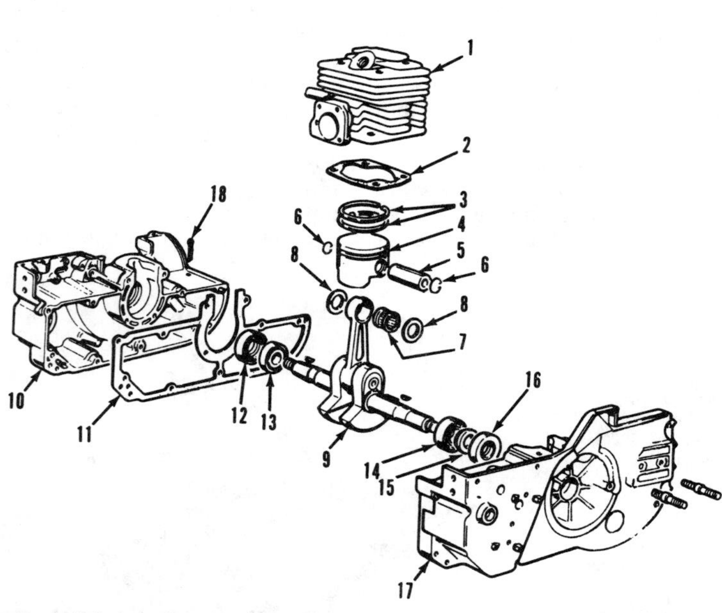

Fig. OL33—Exploded view of engine assembly typical of all models. Thrust washers (8) are absent on Models 264, 264F and 264AV. Models 481 Super, 482AV and 482MP use a worm gear in place of cam (15).

1. Cylinder
2. Gasket
3. Piston rings
4. Piston
5. Piston pin
6. Retainer
7. Needle bearing
8. Thrust washer
9. Crankshaft & connecting rod assy.
10. Left crankcase half
11. Gasket
12. Seal
13. Main bearing
14. Main bearing
15. Cam
16. Seal
17. Right crankcase half
18. Oil tank vent

Illustrations courtesy Olympyk, Oleo-Mac s.p.a.

is stamped on piston crown and cylinder grade mark is stamped on cylinder head. Piston and cylinder marks should match although one size smaller piston may be used if matched piston is not available.

Assemble piston to connecting rod with arrow on piston crown pointing toward exhaust port. Press pin into piston from flywheel side. It is recommended that a dummy pin be used to align piston with needle bearing (7) and thrust washers (8) during assembly.

Locating pins are present in piston ring grooves to prevent ring rotation. Make certain ring end gaps are properly positioned around locating pins when installing cylinder. Lubricate piston rings and cylinder bore with engine oil prior to assembly. Tighten cylinder screws to 10.8 N·m (95 in.-lbs.).

CRANKCASE, CRANKSHAFT AND CONNECTING ROD. Crankcase must be split on all models to remove crankshaft. For access to crankcase halves (10 and 17—Fig. OL33), remove engine cover, starter housing, chain brake, bar and chain. Remove spark plug and install a piston stop tool in spark plug hole or use other suitable means to prevent crankshaft from rotating. Remove flywheel nut (right-hand threads) and use a suitable puller to remove flywheel. Remove clutch assembly as outlined in CLUTCH section. Remove cylinder and piston as outlined above. Remove right side crankcase seal (16—Fig. OL33) and cam (15) or worm gear (if so equipped) prior to separating crankcase halves. Remove screws retaining crankcase halves and use Olympyk tool 11283 or a suitable equivalent to separate crankcase halves. Use caution not to damage crankcase mating surfaces. Once crankcase is split, tap or press crankshaft assembly (9) out of crankcase.

Crankshaft and connecting rod are available as a unit assembly only. Check rotation of connecting rod around crankpin and renew crankshaft assembly if roughness, excessive play or other damage is noted. Crankshaft is supported at both ends with ball type main bearings (13 and 14—Fig. OL33). Use proper size driver to remove and install main bearings in crankcase halves. If main bearings remain on crankshaft during disassembly, use a suitable jaw-type puller to remove bearings from crankshaft. Install main bearings in crankcase halves prior to installing crankshaft.

NOTE: A new design crankshaft assembly with larger counterweights is used on 251 Super models starting with serial number 520200800 and 254 and 254AV models starting with serial number 540200800. Old design and new design crankshaft assemblies are not interchangeable.

Tighten crankcase screws in a criss-cross pattern in small increments until a final torque of 10 N·m (89 in.-lbs.) is obtained. Make certain that crankshaft rotates freely. If not, disassemble and check for problem. Install new crankshaft seals (12 and 16). Refer to OIL PUMP for installation of oil pump drive cam (or worm gear).

CLUTCH. Models 264, 264F and 264AV are equipped with the three-shoe centrifugal clutch shown in Fig. OL35. All other models are equipped with the three-shoe clutch assembly shown in Fig. OL34.

On Models 264, 264F and 264AV, clutch hub (3—Fig. OL35) is threaded and screws onto crankshaft. Hub and clutch retaining nut (9) both have left-hand threads (turn clockwise to remove). On all other models, clutch retaining nut (9—Fig. OL34) has left-hand threads and clutch hub (3—Fig. OL34) is a press fit on crankshaft with a Woodruff key. Clutch hub has three threaded holes to accommodate Olympyk puller 60.00301 or other suitable bolt type puller.

Clutch shoes (2—Figs. OL34 and OL35) should be renewed as a set to prevent an unbalanced condition. Springs (1—Fig. OL34) should also be renewed as a set. Needle bearing (6—Figs. OL34 and OL35) should be lubricated with high temperature grease. Tighten clutch nut (9) to 19.6 N·m (173 in.-lbs.).

MANUAL OIL PUMP. Fig. OL36 shows an exploded view of the manual oil pump used on Model 482MP. Install check valves (8) with line in valve (see inset) facing opposite of oil flow direction. Copper suction line (11) should be positioned under copper discharge line (10) when clamping lines to crankcase. Be sure suction hose (12) is connected to lower port of pump body (7). Prime pump and hose and line assemblies with clean oil during reassembly.

AUTOMATIC OIL PUMP. Models 481 Super, 482AV and 482MP are equipped with the gear type automatic oil pump shown in Fig. OL37. All other models are equipped with the piston type automatic oil pump shown in Fig. OL38.

On gear type pump (Fig. OL37), worm gear (1) on engine crankshaft rotates plunger (3). Oil is pumped by the plunger as it reciprocates in pump body (5) due to cam pin (6) riding in oblique groove in plunger.

To disassemble pump, remove plug (16) with Olympyk tool 82.00584. Using a suitable hooked tool, withdraw pump assembly from crankcase. Remove cam pin (6) and snap ring (12) to remove plunger (3). Inspect "O" rings, plunger and pump body for excessive wear or damage. Worm gear (1) and plunger (3) must be renewed as a set. Use Olympyk tool 82.00910 to pull worm gear from crankshaft. Some worm gears have threaded holes to accommodate a bolt-type puller.

NOTE: Oil pump assembly must be removed from crankcase prior to worm gear removal or installation.

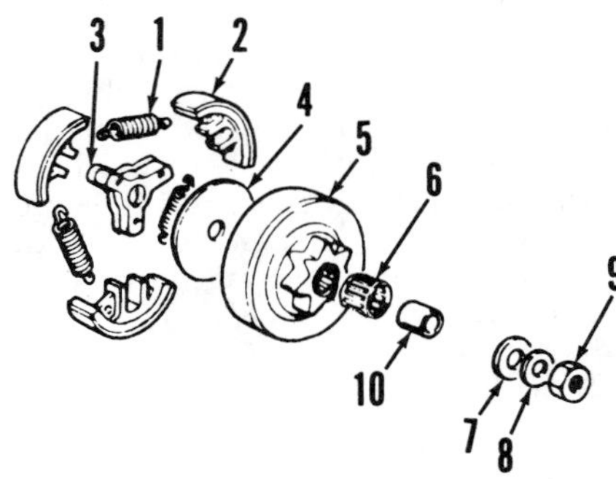

Fig. OL34—Exploded view of clutch assembly used on all models except 264, 264F and 264AV.

1. Spring
2. Shoe
3. Hub
4. Washer
5. Drum
6. Needle bearing
7. Washer
8. Washer
9. Nut
10. Bushing

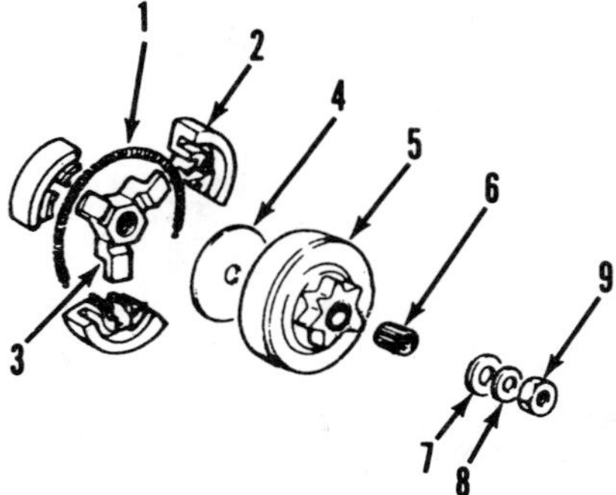

Fig. OL35—Exploded view of clutch assembly used on Models 264, 264F and 264AV. Refer to Fig. OL34 for component identification.

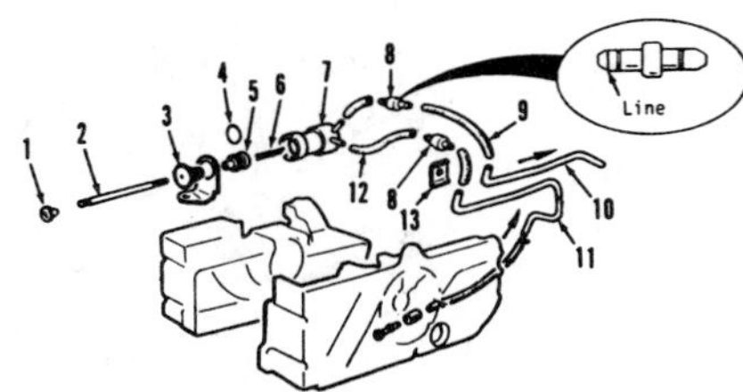

Fig. OL36—Exploded view of manual oil pump used on Model 482MP.

1. Button
2. Rod
3. Nut
4. "O" ring
5. Piston
6. Spring
7. Pump body
8. Check valve
9. Discharge hose
10. Discharge line
11. Suction line
12. Suction hose
13. Bracket

Install worm gear with Olympyk tool 60.00576 or a suitable equivalent driver. Make certain worm gear is a tight fit on crankshaft. Prime pump with clean oil before installation into crankcase. Pump output is adjusted by rotating adjuster (14). Clockwise rotation decreases pump output.

Refer to Fig. OL38 for an exploded view of piston type oil pump. Oil is pumped by piston (9), which is driven by the cam (3) on engine crankshaft. Oil is drawn into the pump through hole in pump body (14). Pressurized oil forces check ball (15) off seat and oil is discharged through valve body (17). Two discharge ports are present in valve body. Port in center of valve body carries oil to guide bar and chain. Port located at end of valve body (toward adjusting screw) returns excess discharge oil back to the oil tank. Make sure both ports are open during service. Ports are located under "O" rings (13).

To disassemble pump, remove plug (22) with Olympyk tool 60.00542 or suitable equivalent. Remove adjusting screw (21). Thread tool 60.00542 into valve body (17) and withdraw pump assembly. Remainder of disassembly is accomplished by unscrewing valve body from pump body (14).

Check ball must seat properly in pump body for correct pump operation. Use caution not to nick, scratch or damage valve body or pump body during service. Prime pump with clean oil before reassembly into crankcase. Adjust pump output by rotating screw (21). Do not loosen plug (22) when adjusting output. Clockwise rotation decreases output.

Use Olympyk tool 60.00420 or a suitable jaw-type puller to pull cam (3) from crankshaft. Position jaws of puller at right angles to lobe of cam. Use Olympyk tool 60.00576 or suitable driver to install cam on crankshaft. Install cam with lobe facing away from crankshaft counterweights. Make certain cam is a tight fit on crankshaft.

On all models, oil filter and pickup assembly can be serviced by removing cover (8) and withdrawing gaskets (5 and 7) and filter (6). Gaskets (5 and 7) should be renewed when reassembling filter and pickup assembly.

REWIND STARTER. Models 261, 271, 481 Super, 482AV, 482MP and early 272 are equipped with the rewind starter shown in Fig. OL39. Models 284, 284F, 284AV, 272AV and late 272 are similar except a baffle plate mounts on starter housing. On Models 261, 271, 481 Super, 482AV, 482MP and early 272, ignition coil is mounted on starter housing. Disconnect coil primary lead at ignition switch prior to removing starter housing.

Models 264, 264F and 264AV are equipped with the rewind starter shown in Fig. OL40. All other models are equipped with the rewind starter shown in Fig. OL41. On Models 355 and 355AV, washer (12—Fig. OL41) is not used.

On all models, tension on rewind spring must be relieved before disassembling starter. Pull out rope approximately 30 cm (12 in.) and hold rope pulley firmly to keep from turning. Place rope into notch in outer circumference of pulley and allow pulley to slowly unwind to relieve rewind spring tension. Remove screw (7—Figs. OL39, OL40 and OL41) and lift out rope pulley being careful not to dislodge rewind spring (11). If rewind spring must be removed, use caution not to allow spring to uncoil uncontrolled.

Rope should be 100 cm (39 in.) long and 3.5 mm (1/8 in.) in diameter on Models 251, 251B, 251 Super, 252, 254, 254AV, 355 and 355AV. On all other

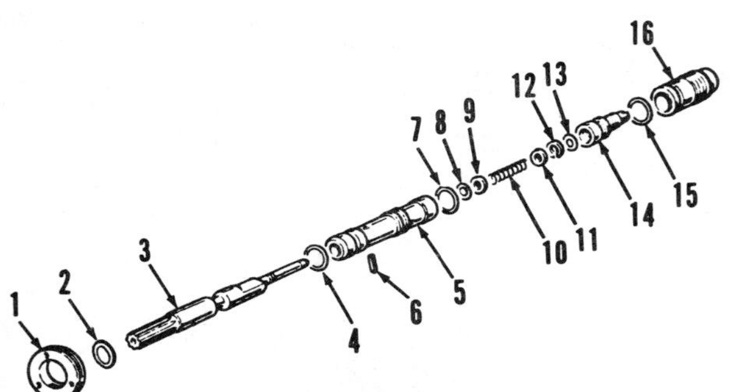

Fig. OL37—Exploded view of gear plunger type oil pump used on Models 481 Super, 482AV and 482MP.

1. Worm gear
2. "O" ring
3. Plunger
4. "O" ring
5. Pump body
6. Cam pin
7. "O" ring
8. "O" ring
9. Washer
10. Spring
11. Washer
12. Snap ring
13. Washer
14. Adjuster
15. "O" ring
16. Plug

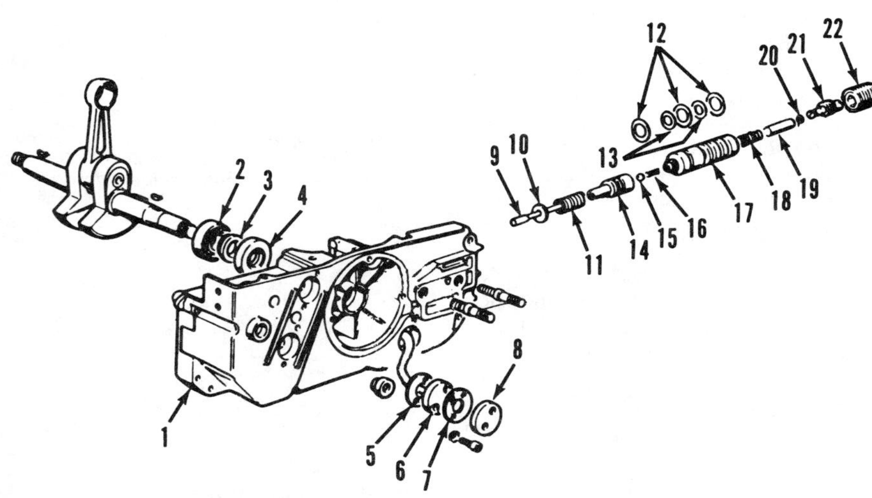

Fig. OL38—Exploded view of piston type oil pump used on all models except 481 Super, 482AV and 482MP. Oil filter and pickup assembly (5, 6, 7 and 8) is typical of all models.

1. Right crankcase half
2. Main bearing
3. Cam
4. Seal
5. Gasket
6. Oil filter
7. Gasket
8. Cover
9. Piston
10. Washer
11. Spring
12. "O" rings
13. "O" rings
14. Pump body
15. Check ball
16. Spring
17. Valve body
18. Spring
19. Oil flow valve
20. "O" ring
21. Adjusting screw
22. Plug

Fig. OL39—Exploded view of rewind starter used on Models 261, 271, 481 Super, 482AV and 482MP. Models 272, 272AV, 284, 284F and 284AV are similar except a baffle within the starter housing is used.

1. Flywheel
2. Pawl spring
3. Pawl
4. Retainer
5. Washer
6. Nut
7. Screw
8. Washer
9. Bushing
10. Rope pulley
11. Rewind spring
12. Washer
14. Housing
15. Rope handle

Illustrations courtesy Olympyk, Oleo-Mac s.p.a.

models, rope should be 120 cm (47 in.) long and 4 mm (5/32 in.) in diameter.

Install rewind spring into housing in a clockwise direction starting with outer coil. Wind rope onto rope pulley in a clockwise direction as viewed from flywheel side of pulley. When installing rope pulley into housing, make certain pulley properly engages rewind spring. Apply Loctite 242 or a suitable equivalent onto threads of screw (7—Figs. OL39, OL40 and OL41). Tighten screw to 10 N·m (89 in.-lbs.).

To preload rewind spring, fully extend rope and place rope into notch in outer circumference of rope pulley. Rotate pulley five turns clockwise on Models 251, 251B, 251 Super, 252, 254, 254F, 254AV, 355 and 355AV. On all other models, rotate rope pulley seven turns clockwise. Then on all models, disengage rope from notch in pulley and allow rope to slowly wind onto pulley. With rope fully retracted, rope handle should be snug against starter housing. With rope fully extended, rope pulley should rotate at least one turn further against spring tension.

When installing starter assembly onto engine, pull out rope approximately 30 cm (12 in.) and slowly allow rope to rewind as starter is installed on engine to engage starter pawls.

CHAIN BRAKE. Some models are equipped with a chain brake system designed to quickly stop chain movement should kickback occur. Chain brake is activated when operator's hand strikes chain brake lever (1—Figs. OL42 and OL43). On Models 272, 272AV, 284, 284F and 284AV, arm (13—Fig. OL43) disengages lever (12) allowing spring (2) to draw brake band (3) tight around clutch drum. On all other models, actuation lever (11—Fig. OL42) disengages pawl (8) from arm (7) allowing spring (2) to draw brake band (3) tight around clutch drum. Pull back chain brake lever to reset mechanism.

Disassembly is evident after inspection of unit and referral to appropriate exploded view. Renew any component found to be excessively worn or damaged in any way. No adjustment of chain brake system is required.

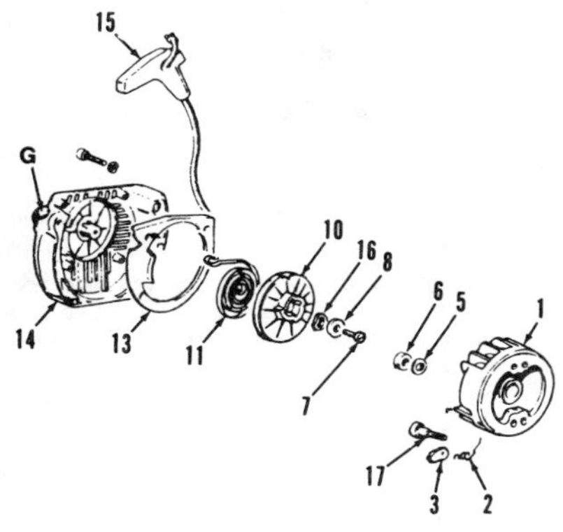

Fig. OL40—Exploded view of rewind starter used on Models 264, 264F and 264AV.

1. Flywheel
2. Pawl spring
3. Pawl
5. Washer
6. Nut
7. Screw
8. Washer
10. Rope pulley
11. Rewind spring
13. Baffle
14. Housing
15. Rope handle
16. Washer
17. Bolt

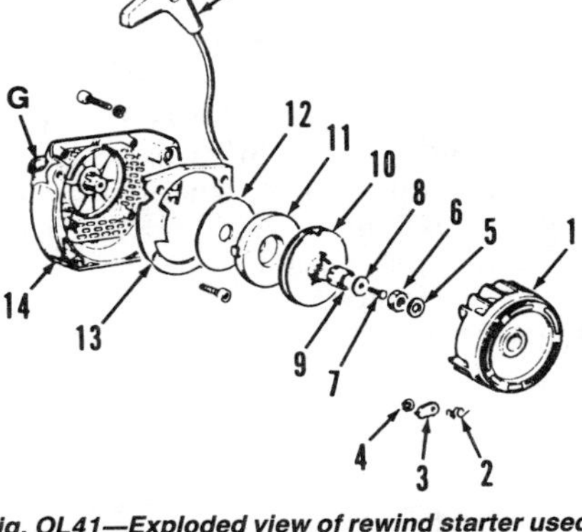

Fig. OL41—Exploded view of rewind starter used on Models 251, 251B, 251 Super, 252, 254, 254AV, 355 and 355AV. Washer (12) is absent on Models 355 and 355AV.

1. Flywheel
2. Pawl spring
3. Pawl
4. Retainer
5. Washer
6. Nut
7. Screw
8. Washer
9. Bushing
10. Rope pulley
11. Rewind spring
12. Washer
13. Baffle
14. Housing
15. Rope handle

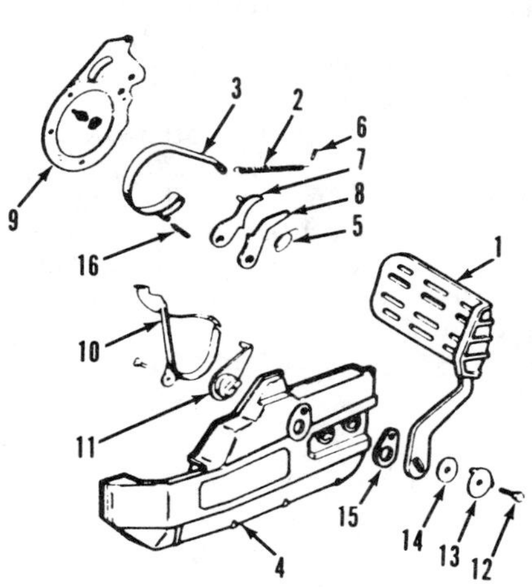

Fig. OL42—Exploded view of chain brake system used on some models.

1. Lever
2. Spring
3. Brake band
4. Cover
5. Spring
6. Pin
7. Arm
8. Pawl
9. Cover
10. Cover
11. Actuation lever
12. Screw
13. Washer
14. Washer
15. Washer
16. Pin

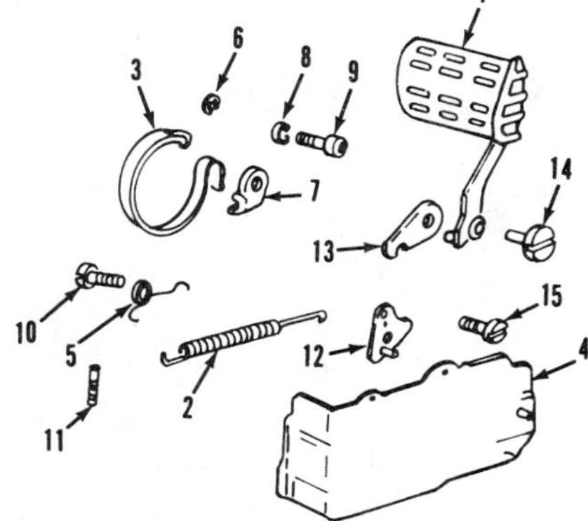

Fig. OL43—Exploded view of chain brake system used on some models.

1. Lever
2. Spring
3. Brake band
4. Cover
5. Spring
6. "E" ring
7. Latch
8. Washer
9. Screw
10. Screw
11. Pin
12. Lever
13. Arm
14. Screw
15. Screw

Illustrations courtesy Olympyk, Oleo-Mac s.p.a.

OLYMPYK

Model	Bore mm (in.)	Stroke mm (in.)	Displacement cc (cu. in.)	Drive Type
935 DF, 935 F	38 (1.5)	30 (1.18)	34 (2.1)	Direct

MAINTENANCE

SPARK PLUG. Recommended spark plug for all models is Bosch WS7F or Champion CJ7Y. Spark plug electrode gap should be 0.5 mm (0.020 in.). Tighten spark plug to 29 N·m (22 ft.-lbs.).

CARBURETOR. A Walbro WT diaphragm type carburetor is used. Refer to Walbro section of CARBURETOR SERVICE section for service procedures and exploded view of carburetor.

Initial adjustment for both low speed mixture needle (L—Fig. OL50) and high speed mixture needle (H) is 1¼ turns open from a lightly seated position. Final adjustment should be made with engine running at normal operating temperature. Make certain air filter is clean before adjusting carburetor.

Adjust low speed mixture needle so engine will accelerate cleanly without hesitation. Adjust high speed mixture needle to obtain optimum full throttle performance under cutting load. Do not operate saw with high speed setting too lean (turned too far clockwise) as engine seizure could result from lack of lubrication and overheating. Adjust low idle speed screw (T) so engine idles just below clutch engagement speed.

IGNITION. An electronic ignition system is used on Model 935DF. The ignition module (4—Fig. OL51) is mounted outside the flywheel. Air gap between ignition module and flywheel magnets should be 0.35 mm (0.014 in.). Loosen ignition module mounting screws and move module to adjust air gap. Ignition timing is not adjustable. Olympyk module and coil tester 60.00893 may be used to test ignition module. If tester is not available, trouble-shoot ignition module

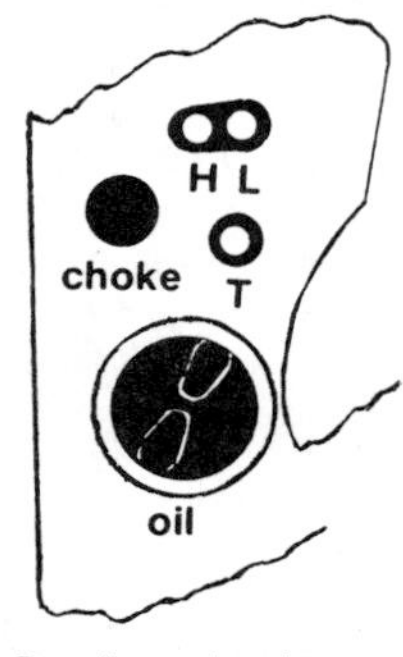

Fig. OL50—Drawing showing carburetor idle speed adjusting screw (T), low speed mixture needle (L) and high speed mixture needle (H). Refer to text for adjustment procedure.

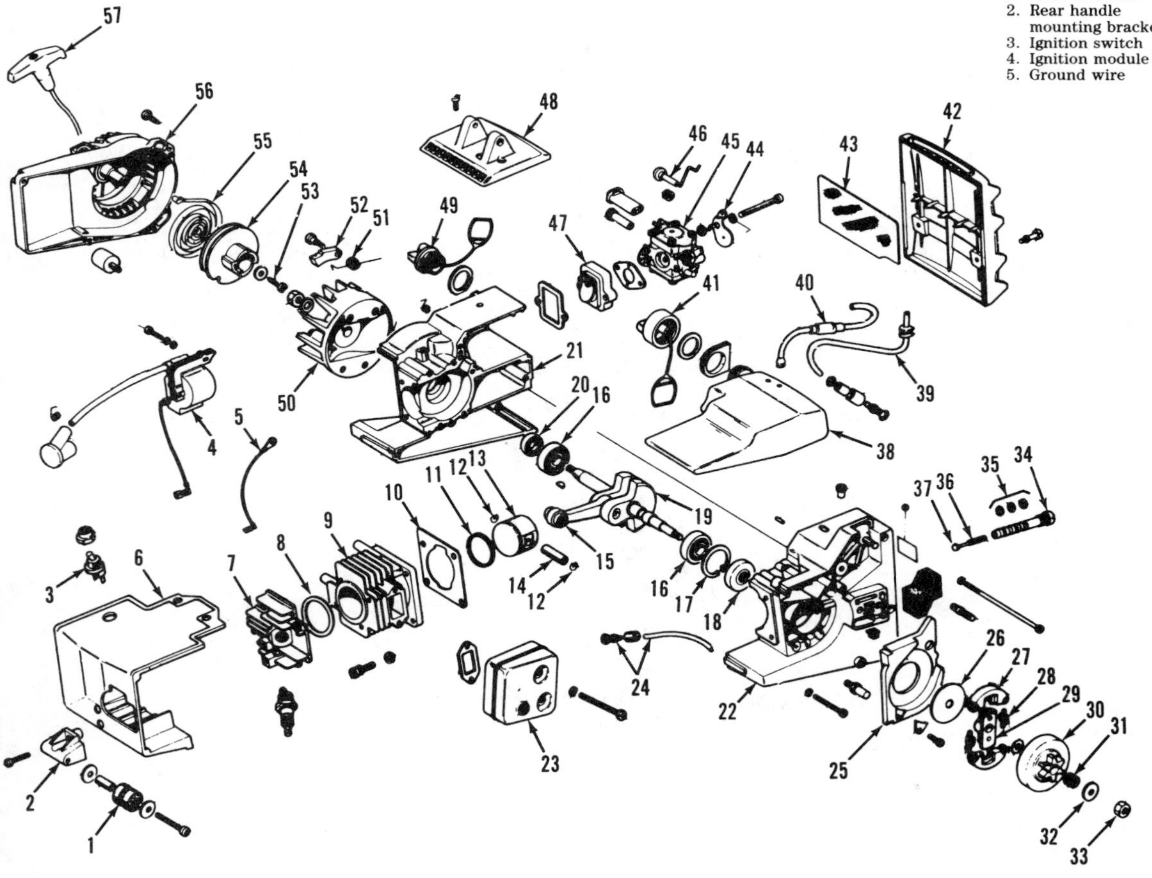

1. Rubber mount
2. Rear handle mounting bracket
3. Ignition switch
4. Ignition module
5. Ground wire
6. Cylinder cover
7. Cylinder head
8. Gasket
9. Cylinder
10. Gasket
11. Piston ring
12. Retaining rings
13. Piston
14. Piston pin
15. Needle bearing
16. Ball bearings
17. Snap ring
18. Seal
19. Crankshaft & connecting rod assy.
20. Seal
21. Crankcase half
22. Crankcase half
23. Muffler
24. Oil pickup tube & strainer screen
25. Plate
26. Washer
27. Clutch shoe
28. Spring
29. Hub
30. Clutch drum
31. Needle bearing
32. Washer
33. Nut
34. Oil pump body
35. "O" rings
36. Spring
37. Plunger
38. Fuel tank
39. Fuel line
40. Vent tube
41. Fuel tank cap
42. Air filter cover
43. Air filter
44. Choke plate
45. Carburetor
46. Choke knob
47. Reed valve plate
48. Handle top mounting plate
49. Oil tank cap
50. Flywheel
51. Spring
52. Starter pawl
53. Screw
54. Pulley
55. Rewind spring
56. Starter housing
57. Rope handle

Fig. OL51—Exploded view of Model 935DF chain saw.

Illustrations courtesy Olympyk, Oleo-Mac s.p.a.

by substituting a known good unit and check for spark.

LUBRICATION. The engine is lubricated by mixing oil with the fuel. Use only high quality oil certified for two-stroke air-cooled engines. Specified fuel:oil mixture ratio is 40:1. The use of automotive type oil is not recommended. Use a separate container when mixing fuel and oil.

An adjustable automatic chain oil pump is used on all models. Refer to OIL PUMP in REPAIRS section for service procedures. It is recommended that a good quality bar and chain oil be used. Oil pump output is adjusted by turning pump adjuster located at front of saw below the chain adjuster screw.

CARBON. Carbon deposits should be removed from muffler and exhaust ports at regular intervals. Position piston at top dead center to prevent loosened carbon from entering cylinder. Use a wooden scraper when removing carbon to prevent damage to piston or cylinder.

REPAIRS

CRANKCASE PRESSURE TEST. An improperly sealed crankcase can cause the engine to be hard to start, run rough, have low power and overheat. Refer to ENGINE SERVICE section of this manual for crankcase pressure test procedure. If crankcase leakage is indicated, pressurize crankcase and use a soap and water solution to check gaskets, seals, pulse line and castings for leakage.

CYLINDER, PISTON, PIN AND RINGS. To disassemble, remove starter housing (56—Fig. OL51), ignition module (4), muffler cover, muffler (23), rear handle assembly and cylinder cover (6). Remove cylinder mounting screws and withdraw cylinder head (7) and cylinder (9) from crankcase. Remove piston ring (11) and piston pin retainers (12). Use suitable pin removal tool to press piston pin (14) out of piston (13).

Cylinder bore is chrome plated and should be renewed if bore is cracked, scored or if plating is worn through. Inspect piston skirt for scuffing, scratches or excessive wear and renew as necessary. It is recommended that piston ring (11) and pin retainers (12) be renewed whenever they are removed from piston. Check fit of piston pin in piston and renew pin and piston as required. Piston pin, pin retainers and piston rings are available separately, but piston is available only as an assembly with piston rings, pin and retainers. Inspect needle bearing (15) in small end of connecting rod for excessive wear or discoloration due to overheating and renew as necessary.

Assemble piston to connecting rod with arrow on piston crown pointing toward exhaust port. It is recommended that a dummy pin be used to align piston with needle bearing (15) during assembly.

Locating pin is present in piston ring groove to prevent ring rotation. Make certain ring end gap is properly positioned around locating pin when installing cylinder. Lubricate piston ring and cylinder bore with engine oil prior to assembly.

CRANKCASE, CRANKSHAFT AND CONNECTING ROD. Crankcase must be split to remove crankshaft. For access to crankcase halves (21 and 22—Fig. OL51), remove starter housing, chain brake assembly, bar and chain. Remove front and rear handles, handle top mounting plate (48), cylinder cover (6) and ignition module (4). Remove air filter cover (42), carburetor (45), reed plate (47) and fuel tank (38). Remove spark plug and install a piston stop tool in spark plug hole or use other suitable means to prevent crankshaft from rotating. Remove flywheel nut (right-hand threads) and use a suitable puller to remove flywheel (50). Remove clutch retaining nut (left-hand threads), clutch drum (30), clutch hub (29), washer (26) and plate (25). Remove cylinder and piston as outlined above. Remove screws retaining crankcase halves and carefully separate crankcase halves. Use caution not to damage crankcase mating surfaces. Once crankcase is split, tap or press crankshaft assembly (19) out of crankcase. Remove seals (18 and 20) and ball bearings (16) from crankcase halves.

Crankshaft and connecting rod are available as a unit assembly only. Check rotation of connecting rod around crankpin and renew crankshaft assembly if roughness, excessive play or other damage is noted. Crankshaft is supported at both ends with ball type main bearings (16—Fig. OL51). Use proper size driver to remove and install main bearings in crankcase halves. If main bearings remain on crankshaft during disassembly, use a suitable jaw-type puller to remove bearings from crankshaft. Install main bearings in crankcase halves prior to installing crankshaft.

Tighten crankcase screws in a crisscross pattern. Make certain that crankshaft rotates freely. If not, disassemble and check for problem. Install new crankshaft seals (18 and 20). Complete reassembly by reversing disassembly procedure.

CLUTCH. A two-shoe centrifugal clutch is used as shown in Fig. OL51. Note that clutch retaining nut (33) has left-hand threads (turn clockwise to remove).

Inspect clutch shoes (27), drum (30) and needle bearing (31) for wear or damage. Clutch shoes should be renewed in complete sets to prevent an unbalanced condition. Needle bearing should be lubricated with high temperature grease.

OIL PUMP. An adjustable automatic chain oil pump is used. Oil pump is located in front side of crankcase and driven by a cam on crankshaft. Oil pump output is regulated by rotating pump body (34—Fig. OL51).

Inspect plunger (37) and pump body (34) for excessive wear or damage and renew as necessary.

REWIND STARTER. All models are equipped with the rewind starter shown in Fig. OL51. To disassemble starter, remove starter housing (56). Pull out rope approximately 30 cm (12 in.) and hold rope pulley from turning. Place rope into notch in rope pulley (54) and allow pulley to slowly unwind to relieve tension on rewind spring (55). Remove screw (53) and lift out rope pulley being careful not to dislodge rewind spring. If rewind spring must be removed, use caution not to allow spring to uncoil uncontrolled.

Wind rewind spring into housing in a clockwise direction starting from outer coil. Wind rope onto pulley in a clockwise direction as viewed from flywheel side of pulley. Lightly grease pulley shaft in starter housing before installing pulley. Apply Loctite 242 to threads of screw (53). To preload rewind spring, place rope in notch in pulley and rotate pulley clockwise. Tension on rewind spring is correct if rope handle is snug against starter housing with rope retracted, and with rope fully extended, rope pulley will rotate one additional turn clockwise. If rewind spring tension is not correct, repeat above procedure and either add more tension or remove tension as needed.

When installing rewind starter assembly onto saw, slowly pull out rope to engage pawls (52) with rope pulley.

CHAIN BRAKE. All models are equipped with a chain brake system designed to quickly stop chain movement should kickback occur. Chain brake is activated when operator's hand strikes chain brake lever (1—Fig. OL52). Forward movement of chain brake lever disengages trigger mechanism, allowing spring (5) to draw band (7) tight around clutch drum. Pull back chain brake le-

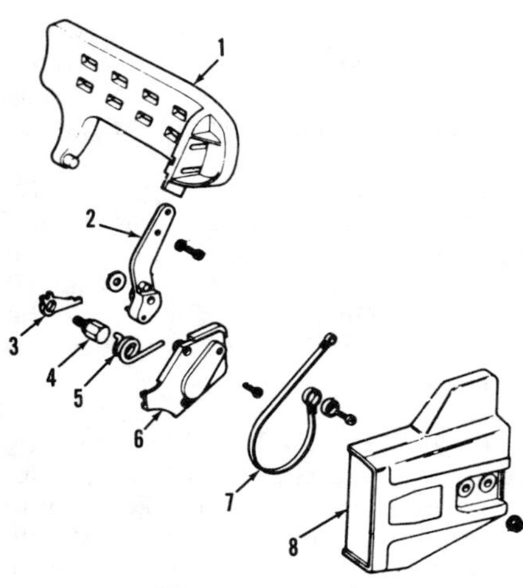

Fig. OL52—Exploded view of chain brake assembly.

1. Brake lever
2. Brake arm
3. Trigger
4. Pivot bolt
5. Brake spring
6. Brake housing
7. Brake band
8. Clutch cover

ver to reset mechanism. Chain brake should be kept clean and free of sawdust and dirt accumulation.

Disassembly is evident after removing chain brake unit from saw and referral to exploded view and inspection of unit. Chain brake should be in activated (engaged) position when removing spring (5). Renew all worn parts. Lightly lubricate pivot points being careful not to allow grease to get on working surface of brake band or clutch drum. No adjustment of chain brake system is required.

Illustrations courtesy Olympyk, Oleo-Mac s.p.a.

OLYMPYK

Model	Bore mm (in.)	Stroke mm (in.)	Displacement cc (cu. in.)	Drive Type
941, 942	...	...	42 (2.5)	Direct
946	...	...	46 (2.8)	Direct
951	...	...	50 (3.0)	Direct

MAINTENANCE

SPARK PLUG. Recommended spark plug for all models is Bosch WS7F or Champion CJ7Y. Spark plug electrode gap should be 0.5 mm (0.020 in.). Tighten spark plug to 29 N·m (22 ft.-lbs.).

CARBURETOR. A Walbro WT diaphragm type carburetor is used on all models. Refer to Walbro section of CARBURETOR SERVICE section for service procedures and exploded view of carburetor.

Initial adjustment for both low speed mixture needle and high speed mixture needle is 1$^1/_8$ turns open from a lightly seated position. Final adjustment should be made with engine running at normal operating temperature. Make certain air filter is clean before adjusting carburetor.

Adjust low speed mixture needle so engine will accelerate cleanly without hesitation. Adjust high speed mixture needle to obtain optimum full throttle performance under cutting load. Do not operate saw with high speed setting too lean (turned too far clockwise) as engine seizure could result from lack of lubrication and overheating. Adjust low idle speed screw so engine idles just below clutch engagement speed.

IGNITION. All models are equipped with a Selettra electronic ignition system. The ignition module is mounted outside the flywheel. Air gap between ignition module and flywheel should be 0.35 mm (0.014 in.). Loosen ignition module mounting screws and move module to adjust air gap. Ignition timing is not adjustable. Olympyk module and coil tester 60.00893 may be used to test ignition module. If tester is not available, trouble-shoot ignition module by substituting a known good unit and check for spark.

LUBRICATION. The engine is lubricated by mixing oil with the fuel. Use only high quality oil certified for two-stroke air-cooled engines. Specified fuel:oil mixture ratio is 25:1. The use of automotive type oil is not recommended. Use a separate container when mixing fuel and oil.

An adjustable automatic chain oil pump is used on all models. Refer to OIL PUMP in REPAIRS section for service procedures. It is recommended that a good quality oil designed for lubrication of bar and chain be used. Oil pump output is adjusted by turning adjuster (8—Fig. OL62). Adjuster is accessible from lower side of chain cover. Clockwise rotation of adjuster increases oil flow.

CARBON. Carbon deposits should be removed from muffler and exhaust ports at regular intervals. Position piston at top dead center to prevent loosened carbon from entering cylinder. Use a wooden scraper when removing carbon to prevent damage to piston or cylinder.

REPAIRS

CRANKCASE PRESSURE TEST. An improperly sealed crankcase can cause the engine to be hard to start, run rough, have low power and overheat. Refer to ENGINE SERVICE section of this manual for crankcase pressure test procedure. If crankcase leakage is indicated, pressurize crankcase and use a soap and water solution to check gaskets, seals, pulse line and castings for leakage.

CYLINDER, PISTON, PIN AND RINGS. Cylinder and piston can be removed from engine without separating power head from saw frame. Remove air filter cover, engine cover, starter housing and ignition module. Remove muffler and intake manifold (5—Fig. OL60)

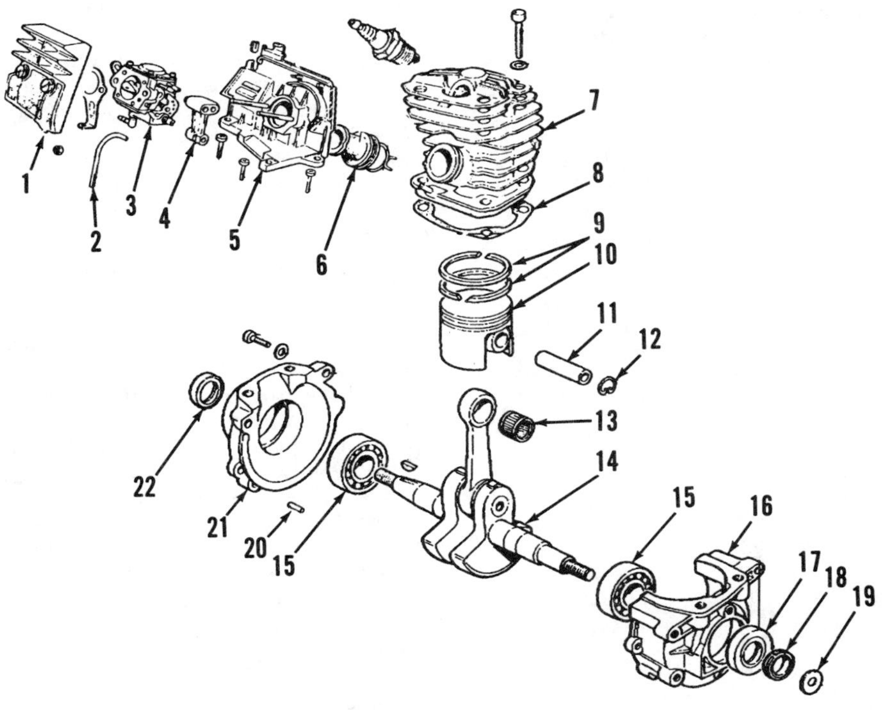

Fig. OL60—Exploded view of engine assembly typical of all models.

1. Air filter
2. Fuel line
3. Carburetor
4. Adjusting screw guide
5. Intake manifold
6. Intake boot
7. Cylinder
8. Gasket
9. Piston rings
10. Piston
11. Piston pin
12. Retaining rings
13. Needle bearing
14. Crankshaft & connecting rod assy.
15. Ball bearings
16. Crankcase half
17. Seal
18. Worm gear
19. Washer
20. Dowel pin
21. Crankcase half
22. Seal

Illustrations courtesy Olympyk, Oleo-Mac s.p.a.

with carburetor (3). Remove cylinder mounting screws and withdraw cylinder (7) from piston. Remove piston rings (9) and piston pin retainers (12). Use suitable pin removal tool to press piston pin (11) out of piston.

Cylinder bore is chrome plated and should be renewed if bore is cracked, scored or if plating is worn through. Inspect piston skirt for scuffing, scratches or excessive wear and renew as necessary. It is recommended that piston rings (9) and pin retainers (12) be renewed whenever they are removed from piston. Check fit of piston pin in piston and renew pin and piston as required. Piston pin, pin retainers and piston rings are available separately, but piston is only available as an assembly with piston rings, pin and retainers. Inspect needle bearing (13) in small end of connecting rod for excessive wear or discoloration due to overheating and renew as necessary.

Assemble piston to connecting rod with arrow on piston crown pointing toward exhaust port. It is recommended that a dummy pin be used to align piston with needle bearing (13) during assembly.

Locating pins are present in piston ring grooves to prevent ring rotation. Make certain ring end gaps are properly positioned around locating pins when installing cylinder. Lubricate piston rings and cylinder bore with engine oil prior to assembly.

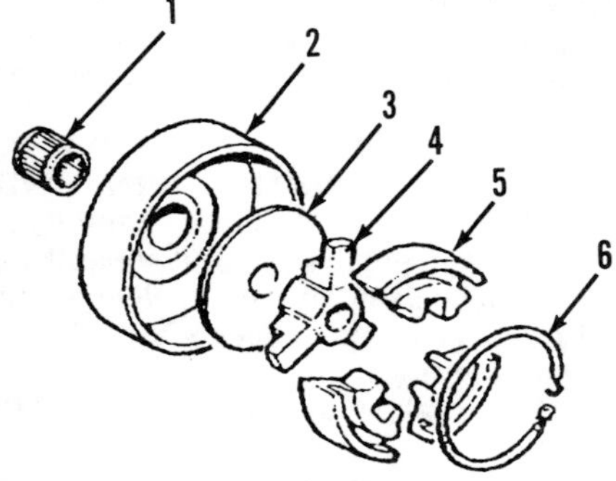

Fig. OL61—Exploded view of clutch assembly used on all models.

1. Needle bearing
2. Clutch drum
3. Washer
4. Hub
5. Clutch shoes
6. Spring

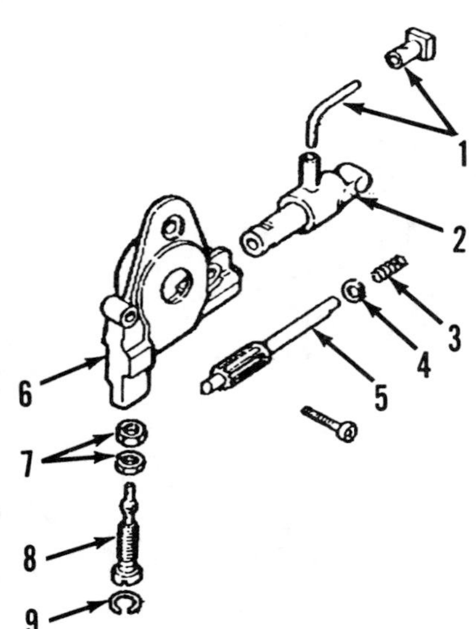

Fig. OL62—Exploded view of automatic chain oil pump.

1. Oil outlet
2. Pump body
3. Spring
4. Washer
5. Plunger
6. Pump housing
7. Nuts
8. Adjuster
9. Ring

CRANKCASE, CRANKSHAFT AND CONNECTING ROD. Crankcase must be split on all models to remove crankshaft. For access to crankcase halves (16 and 21—Fig. OL60), remove engine cover, starter housing, chain brake, bar and chain. Remove spark plug and install a piston stop tool in spark plug hole or use other suitable means to prevent crankshaft from rotating. Remove flywheel nut (right-hand threads) and use a suitable puller to remove flywheel. Remove clutch assembly (clutch hub has left-hand threads) and oil pump. Remove cylinder and piston as outlined above. Remove power head mounting screws and remove power head from saw frame. Remove worm gear (18) from crankshaft prior to separating crankcase halves. Remove screws retaining crankcase halves and carefully separate crankcase halves. Use caution not to damage crankcase mating surfaces. Once crankcase is split, tap or press crankshaft assembly (14) out of crankcase.

Crankshaft and connecting rod are available as a unit assembly only. Check rotation of connecting rod around crankpin and renew crankshaft assembly if roughness, excessive play or other damage is noted. Crankshaft is supported at both ends with ball type main bearings (15—Fig. OL60). Use proper size driver to remove and install main bearings in crankcase halves. If main bearings remain on crankshaft during disassembly, use a suitable jaw-type puller to remove bearings from crankshaft. Install main bearings in crankcase halves prior to installing crankshaft.

Tighten crankcase screws in a crisscross pattern. Make certain that crankshaft rotates freely. If not, disassemble and check for problem. Install new crankshaft seals (17 and 22). Complete reassembly by reversing disassembly procedure.

CLUTCH. All models are equipped with the three-shoe centrifugal clutch shown in Fig. OL61. Clutch hub (4) screws onto crankshaft (left-hand threads).

Inspect clutch shoes (5), drum (2) and needle bearing (1) for wear or damage. Clutch shoes should be renewed in complete sets to prevent an unbalanced condition. Needle bearing should be lubricated with high temperature grease.

OIL PUMP. All models are equipped with an adjustable automatic chain oil pump. Oil pump is mounted on clutch side of crankcase and driven by a worm gear on crankshaft. Oil pump output is regulated by rotating adjuster (8—Fig. OL62) located at bottom of chain cover. Clockwise rotation increases oil output.

Inspect plunger (5) and pump body (2) for excessive wear or damage. A filter screen is located in the oil tank and is accessible from bottom of oil tank.

REWIND STARTER. All models are equipped with the rewind starter shown in Fig. OL63. To disassemble starter, remove starter housing (2). Pull out rope approximately 30 cm (12 in.) and hold rope pulley from turning. Place rope into notch in rope pulley (4) and allow pulley to slowly unwind to relieve tension on rewind spring (3). Remove screw (6) and lift out rope pulley being careful not to dislodge rewind spring. If rewind spring must be removed, use caution not to allow spring to uncoil uncontrolled.

Wind rewind spring into housing in a clockwise direction starting from outer coil. Wind rope onto pulley in a clockwise direction as viewed from flywheel side of pulley. Lightly grease pulley shaft in starter housing before installing pulley. Apply Loctite 242 to threads of screw (6). To preload rewind spring, place rope in notch in pulley and rotate pulley clockwise. Tension on rewind spring is correct if rope handle is snug against starter housing with rope retracted, and with rope fully extended, rope pulley will rotate one additional turn clockwise. If rewind spring tension is not correct, repeat above procedure and either add more tension or remove tension as needed.

When installing rewind starter assembly onto saw, slowly pull out rope to engage pawls (8) with rope pulley.

CHAIN BRAKE. All models are equipped with a chain brake system designed to quickly stop chain movement should kickback occur. Chain brake is activated when operator's hand strikes chain brake lever (1—Fig. OL64). Forward movement of chain brake lever disengages trigger mechanism (8), allowing spring (7) to draw band (9) tight around clutch drum. Pull back chain brake lever to reset mechanism. Chain

Illustrations courtesy Olympyk, Oleo-Mac s.p.a.

brake should be kept clean and free of sawdust and dirt accumulation.

Disassembly is evident after removing chain brake unit from saw and referral to exploded view and inspection of unit. Chain brake should be in activated (engaged) position when removing spring (7). Renew all worn parts. Lightly lubricate pivot points being careful not to allow grease to get on working surface of brake band or clutch drum. No adjustment of chain brake mechanism is required.

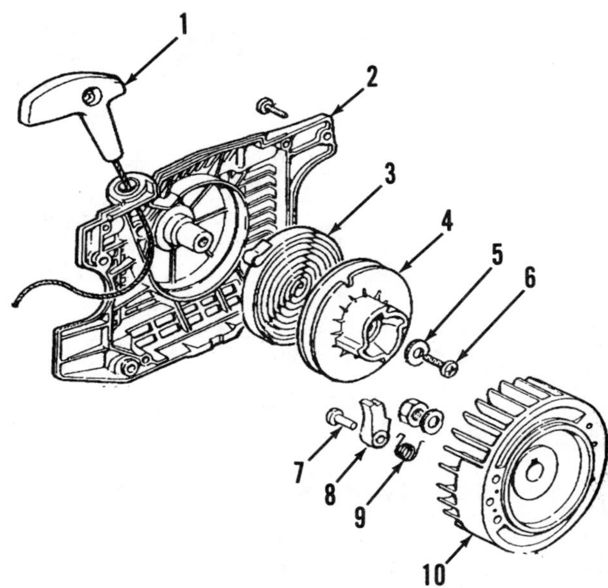

Fig. OL63—Exploded view of rewind starter. Two pawl assemblies (7, 8 and 9) are used.

1. Rope handle
2. Starter housing
3. Spring
4. Rope pulley
5. Washer
6. Screw
7. Pin
8. Starter pawl
9. Spring
10. Flywheel

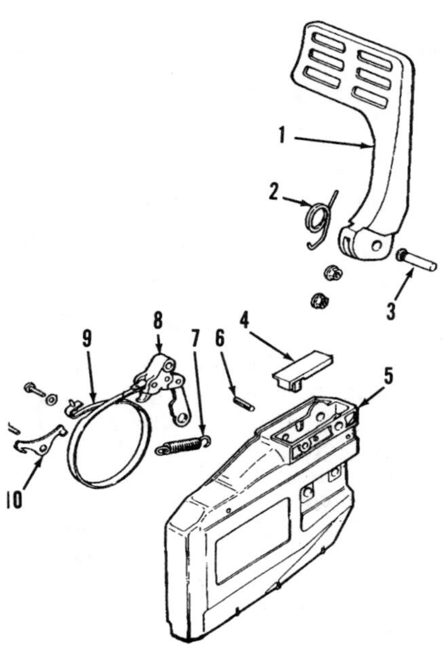

Fig. OL64—Exploded view of chain brake assembly.

1. Brake lever
2. Spring
3. Pin
4. Cover
5. Brake housing
6. Pin
7. Brake spring
8. Brake mechanism
9. Brake band
10. Trigger

PIONEER/PARTNER

Model	Bore mm (in.)	Stroke mm (in.)	Displacement cc (cu. in.)	Drive Type
330, 350, 360	36.5 (1.4375)	32.5 (1.28)	34 (2.1)	Direct

MAINTENANCE

SPARK PLUG. Recommended spark plug is Champion CJ6 or RCJ6 with an electrode gap of 0.025 inch (0.63 mm) on Models 330 and 350. Recommended spark plug is Champion RCJ7Y with an electrode gap of 0.024 inch (0.60 mm) on Model 360.

CARBURETOR. A Walbro WT diaphragm type carburetor is used on all models. Refer to CARBURETOR SERVICE section for service on Walbro carburetor.

On Models 330 and 350, initial setting of both high and low speed mixture screws is 1⅛ turns open from a lightly seated position. On Model 360, initial setting of both high and low speed mixture screws is one turn open from a lightly seated position. Make final adjustment with engine warm and running. Adjust idle speed screw so engine idles just below clutch engagement speed. Adjust low speed mixture screw so engine will accelerate cleanly without hesitation. Adjust high speed mixture screw to obtain optimum performance under cutting load. High speed mixture must not be adjusted too lean as engine may be damaged.

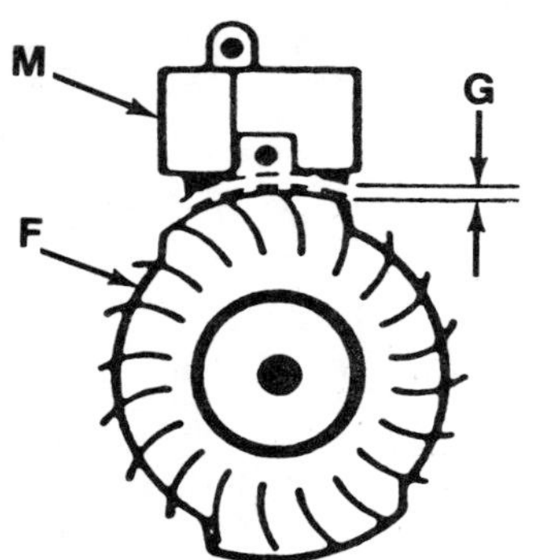

Fig. PP1-Air gap (G) between flywheel (F) magnets and module/ignition coil assembly (M) should be 0.015 inch (0.38 mm) on Models 330 and 350 and 0.012 inch (0.30 mm) on Model 360.

IGNITION. All models are equipped with a Phelon type capacitor discharge ignition (CDI) system. Air gap (G – Fig. PP1) between flywheel magnets and module/ignition coil assembly should be 0.015 inch (0.38 mm) on Models 330 and 350 and 0.012 inch (0.30 mm) on Model 360.

LUBRICATION. Engine is lubricated by mixing engine oil with fuel. Recommended oil is Beaird-Poulan engine oil approved for a fuel-to-oil mixture ratio of 40:1. If recommended oil is not available, a good quality oil designed for two-stroke air-cooled engines may be used when mixed at a 24:1 ratio. Use a separate container when mixing the oil and gas.

The oil reservoir should be filled with Pioneer/Partner Chain Oil or, if not available, use a good quality SAE 10 to SAE 30 motor oil depending upon ambient temperature.

Early Model 330 is equipped with a manual oil pump and an automatic oiling system. Late Model 330 and Models 350 and 360 are equipped with a positive displacement oil pump assembly located behind flywheel.

CARBON. Carbon should be removed from exhaust system and cylinder periodically. Loose carbon should not be allowed to enter cylinder and care should be taken not to damage cylinder or piston.

REPAIRS

CYLINDER, PISTON, PIN AND RINGS. Cylinder (15 – Fig. PP2) is also upper crankcase half. Crankshaft is loose in crankcase when cylinder is removed. Care must be taken not to nick or scratch crankcase mating surfaces during disassembly.

Cylinder head is integral with cylinder and cylinder must be removed to remove piston. Piston is equipped with a single piston ring and floating type piston pin (11). On Models 330 and 350, piston may need to be heated to remove or install piston pin. Needle bearings (12) are used in connecting rod small end on Model 360. On all models, piston and connecting rod are available as a unit assembly only. Piston and ring are available in standard size only. Cylinder bore is chrome plated and should be inspected to determine if chrome is scored, peeling or excessively worn. Renew cylinder and piston if damaged or excessively worn. If either half of crankcase requires renewal, then both halves must be renewed as they are a matched set.

Refer to CRANKSHAFT AND SEALS for proper assembly of crankcase and cylinder.

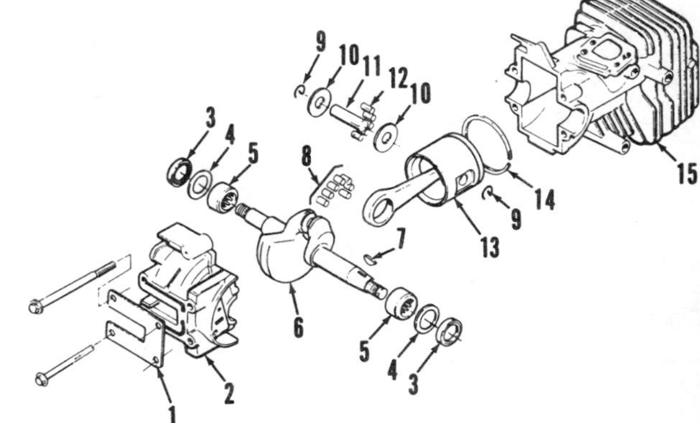

Fig. PP2 – Exploded view of engine assembly. Roller bearings (12) and thrust washers (10) are not used on Models 330 and 350.

1. Plate
2. Lower crankcase half
3. Seal
4. Retaining ring
5. Needle bearing
6. Crankshaft
7. Key
8. Roller bearings
9. Retaining clip
10. Thrust washer
11. Piston pin
12. Needle bearings
13. Piston & connecting rod assy.
14. Piston ring
15. Cylinder & upper crankcase half

CONNECTING ROD. To remove connecting rod, remove cylinder (15–Fig. PP2). Note that cylinder is also upper crankcase half and crankshaft assembly is loose when cylinder is removed. Connecting rod (13) is one-piece and supported on crankpin by 11 loose bearing rollers (8). Be careful not to lose loose rollers that may fall out during disassembly. Rollers can be removed by sliding rod off rollers. To install rod bearing, hold rollers in place with heavy grease or petroleum jelly and position rod over rollers. Be sure rollers do not fall out during assembly of crankcase.

CRANKSHAFT AND SEALS. Crankshaft is supported by needle roller bearings (5–Fig. PP2) at both ends. Crankshaft assembly can be removed after removing flywheel, oil pump (Late Model 330 and Models 350 and 360), clutch and cylinder. Care should be taken when removing cylinder as crankshaft will be loose in crankcase and connecting rod may slide off bearing rollers allowing them to fall into crankcase.

Before reassembling crankcases, apply a light coat of a form-in-place gasket compound on crankcase mating surface. Be sure mating surfaces are not damaged during assembly. Retaining rings (4) must fit in ring grooves (G–Fig. PP3) of lower crankcase and upper crankcase halves.

CLUTCH. A two-shoe centrifugal type clutch is used on all models. Clutch hub has left-hand threads. Clutch needle bearing (6–Fig. PP4) should be inspected for excessive wear or damage. Inspect clutch shoes and drum for signs of excessive heat.

OIL PUMP. Early Model 330 is equipped with a manual oil pump and automatic oiling system. Refer to Fig.

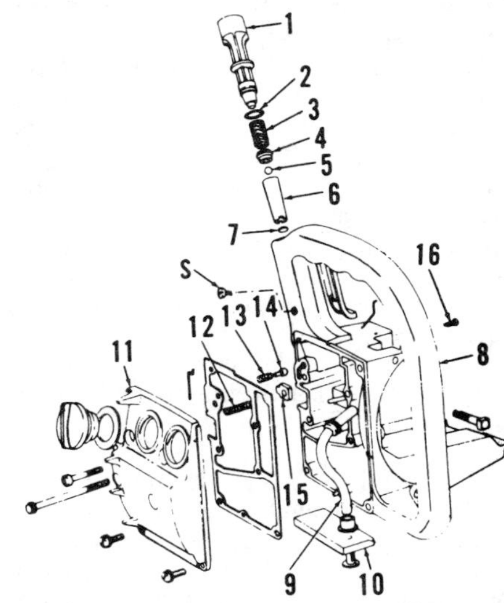

Fig. PP5—Exploded view of manual pump and front housing on early Model 330.

1. Piston
2. "O" ring
3. Spring
4. Spring seat
5. Ball
6. Pump body
7. Screen
8. Front housing
9. Fuel hose
10. Filter
11. Front cover
12. Spring
13. Spring
14. Oil outlet valve
15. Nut
16. Pressure check valve

Fig. PP3—Be sure retaining rings (R) are seated in grooves (G) of upper and lower crankcase halves.

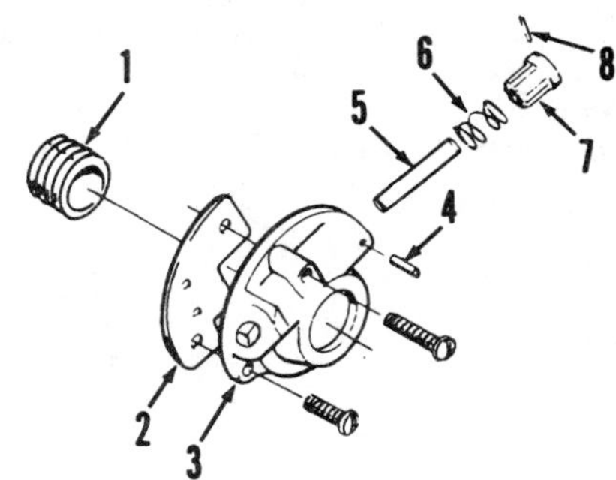

Fig. PP6—Exploded view of positive displacement oil pump assembly used on later Model 330 and Models 350 and 360.

1. Worm gear
2. Gasket
3. Housing
4. Roll pin
5. Plunger
6. Spring
7. Gear
8. Pin

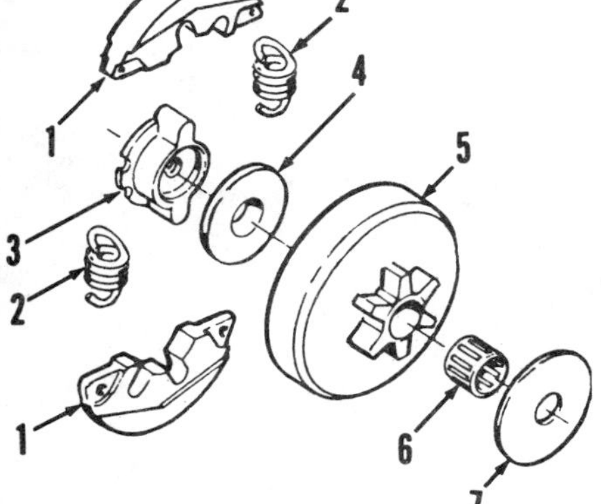

Fig. PP4—Exploded view of clutch assembly.

1. Shoe half
2. Spring
3. Hub
4. Washer
5. Drum
6. Needle bearing
7. Washer

Fig. PP7—Exploded view of rewind starter, flywheel and associated parts used on Models 330 and 350. Components on Model 360 are similar except for starter housing (11).

1. Flywheel
2. Spring
3. Pawl
4. Pivot pin
5. Washer
6. Nut
7. Screw
8. Washer
9. Rope pulley
10. Rewind spring
11. Starter housing
12. Rope
13. Handle

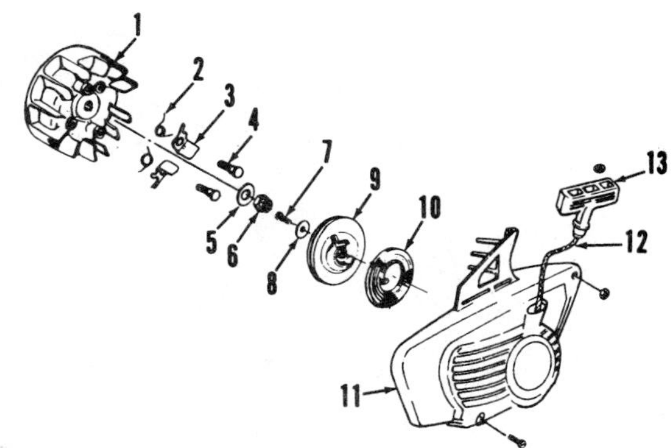

PP5 for exploded view of manual oil pump. Automatic oiling is accomplished by crankcase pulsations which pressurize oil tank and force oil to bar. One-way valve (16) prevents oil from entering crankcase.

Later Model 330 and Models 350 and 360 are equipped with a positive displacement oil pump assembly located behind flywheel. Oil pump assembly is driven by a worm gear on crankshaft. Remove oil pump plunger retaining roll pin (4–Fig. PP6) and withdraw plunger (5), gear (7) and spring (6) to service. Use suitable tools to pry worm gear (1) off crankshaft. Renew any component that is excessively worn or damaged. Plunger (5) is renewable only with complete oil pump assembly.

REWIND STARTER. Refer to Fig. PP7 for exploded view of pawl type starter typical of the type used on all models. Care should be exercised when removing rewind spring (10) to prevent spring from uncoiling uncontrolled.

Rewind spring (10) should be wound in clockwise direction into housing. Wind starter rope in clockwise direction around rope pulley (9) as viewed in starter housing (11).

CHAIN BRAKE. All models are equipped with a chain brake designed to stop the saw chain quickly should kickback occur. It is necessary to unlock chain brake before removing or installing side cover (5–Fig. PP8 or Fig. PP9). Sawdust and debris should be cleaned from around the brake mechanism as needed to ensure proper operation of chain brake.

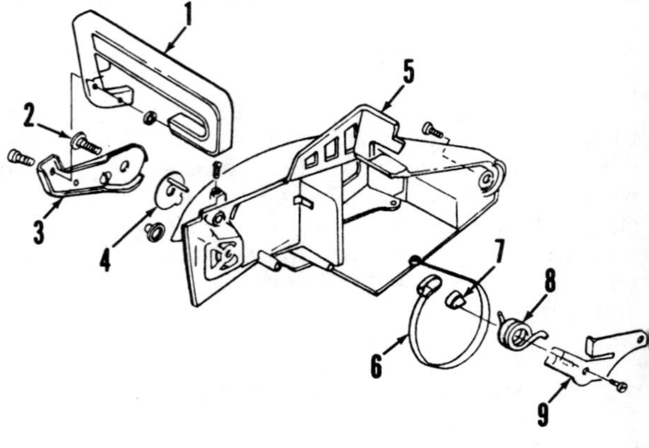

Fig. PP8—Exploded view of chain brake assembly used on Models 330 and 350.

1. Guard
2. Pivot pin
3. Trip lever
4. Stop plate
5. Side cover
6. Brake band
7. Clip
8. Spring
9. Detent cover

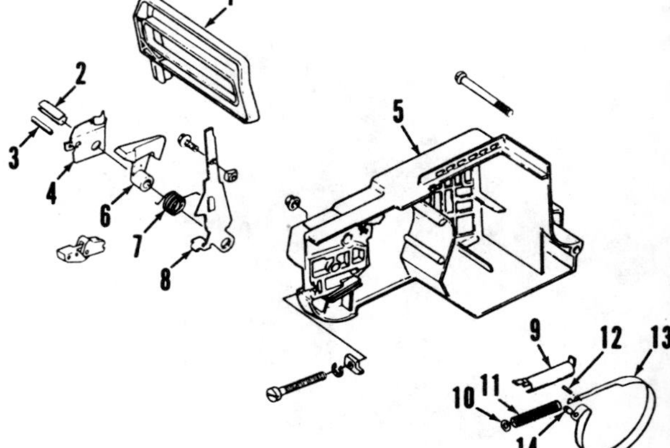

Fig. PP9—Exploded view of chain brake assembly used on Model 360.

1. Guard
2. Roll pin
3. Roll pin
4. Detent cover
5. Side cover
6. Inertia weight
7. Spring
8. Lever
9. Cover
10. Washer
11. Spring
12. Roll pin
13. Brake band
14. Pin

PIONEER/PARTNER

Model	Bore mm (in.)	Stroke mm (in.)	Displacement cc (cu. in.)	Drive Type
P39	47.6 (1.875)	36.5 (1.437)	65 (3.97)	Direct
P42, P42W	47.6 (1.875)	36.5 (1.437)	65 (3.97)	Direct
P45, P45W	50 (1.97)	36.5 (1.437)	72 (4.38)	Direct
P52, P52W	52.4 (2.062)	38.1 (1.5)	82 (5.0)	Direct
P62, P62W, P65, P65W	57.1 (2.25)	38.1 (1.5)	98 (6.0)	Direct

MAINTENANCE

SPARK PLUG. Recommended spark plug is a Champion KCJ7Y with an electrode gap of 0.025 inch (0.63 mm) on all models.

CARBURETOR. A Walbro WJ diaphragm type carburetor is used on all models. Refer to Walbro section of CARBURETOR SERVICE for service and exploded view of carburetor.

Initial adjustment for both low speed and high speed mixture screws is one turn open from a lightly seated position. Make final adjustment with engine warm and running. Adjust idle speed screw so engine idles just below clutch engagement speed. Adjust low speed mixture screw so engine will accelerate cleanly without hesitation. Adjust high speed mixture screw to obtain optimum performance under cutting load.

IGNITION. All models are equipped with a Phelon breakerless capacitor discharge ignition system. Ignition timing is not adjustable. Air gap between coil legs and flywheel should be 0.25-0.38 mm (0.010-0.015 in.).

LUBRICATION. Engine is lubricated by mixing engine oil with gasoline. Recommended oil is Beaird-Poulan engine oil approved for a fuel-to-oil mixture ratio of 40:1. If recommended oil is not available, a good quality oil designed for two-stroke air-cooled engines may be used when mixed at a 24:1 ratio. Use a separate container when mixing the oil and gas.

All models are equipped with an automatic chain oil pump. Models P62 and P65 are also equipped with a manual oil pump. Oil output is adjustable by turning adjusting screw on bottom of saw. Refer to AUTOMATIC CHAIN OILER under REPAIRS section. Chain oil should be Pioneer/Partner Chain Oil or, if not available, use a good quality SAE 10 to SAE 30 motor oil depending upon ambient temperature.

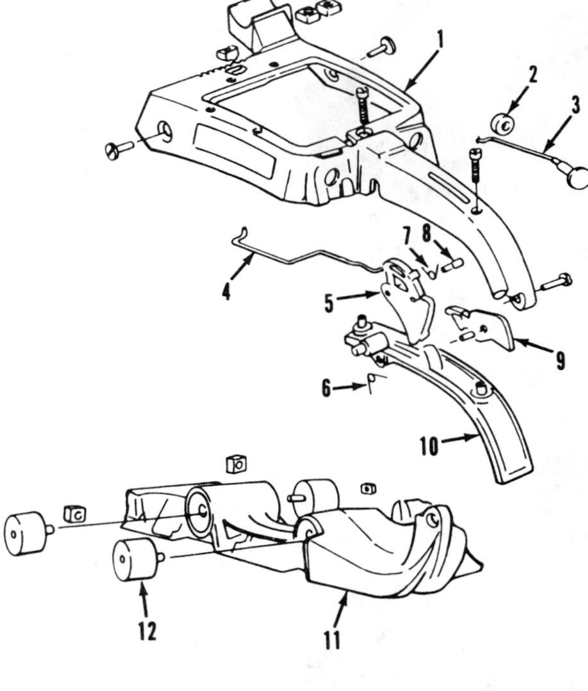

Fig. PP10 — Exploded view of rear handle assembly.

1. Rear handle
2. Grommet
3. Choke linkage & knob
4. Throttle linkage
5. Throttle control
6. Return spring
7. Return spring
8. Pin
9. Throttle lock
10. Rear handle cover
11. Base
12. Isolation mounts

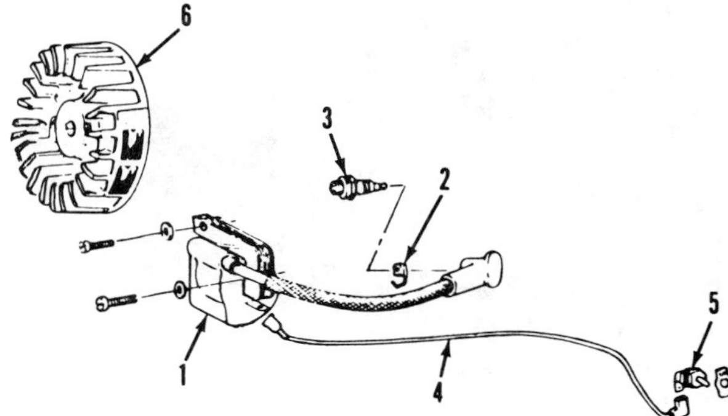

PP11 — Exploded view of Phelon CD ignition system.

1. Ignition module/coil assy.
2. Terminal end
3. Spark plug
4. Lead
5. Run-stop switch
6. Flywheel

CARBON. Carbon should be cleaned from muffler and exhaust ports at regular intervals. When scraping carbon, be careful not to damage the chamfered edges of the exhaust ports.

REPAIRS

PISTON, PIN, RINGS AND CYLINDER. Compression pressure should be 155 psi (1069 kPa) on P62 and P65 models and 150 psi (1035 kPa) on all other models when checked with a gage while rotating crankshaft with rewind starter. Rewind starter and handle assembly must be removed before removing the cylinder. The cylinder and head is one-piece and is attached to crankcase with four screws. Cylinder bore is chrome plated and should be renewed if the plating is worn away exposing the soft base metal. The aluminum alloy piston is fitted with two piston rings. Piston should be heated to 300° F (149° C) before removing the piston pin. Use care to prevent bending the connecting rod even after the piston is heated. The piston pin is equipped with a caged needle bearing (8 – Fig. PP12). Pins located in the piston ring grooves must be positioned toward flywheel, away from cylinder exhaust port.

NOTE: Incorrect installation of piston will cause extensive damage to the piston and cylinder. Use Pioneer/Partner piston pin remover/installer tool 475420 when servicing piston pin. The ends of the piston pin retaining clips must engage notch in piston.

Tighten cylinder mounting screws to 90-100 in.-lbs. (10.2-11.3 N·m) using a criss-cross pattern.

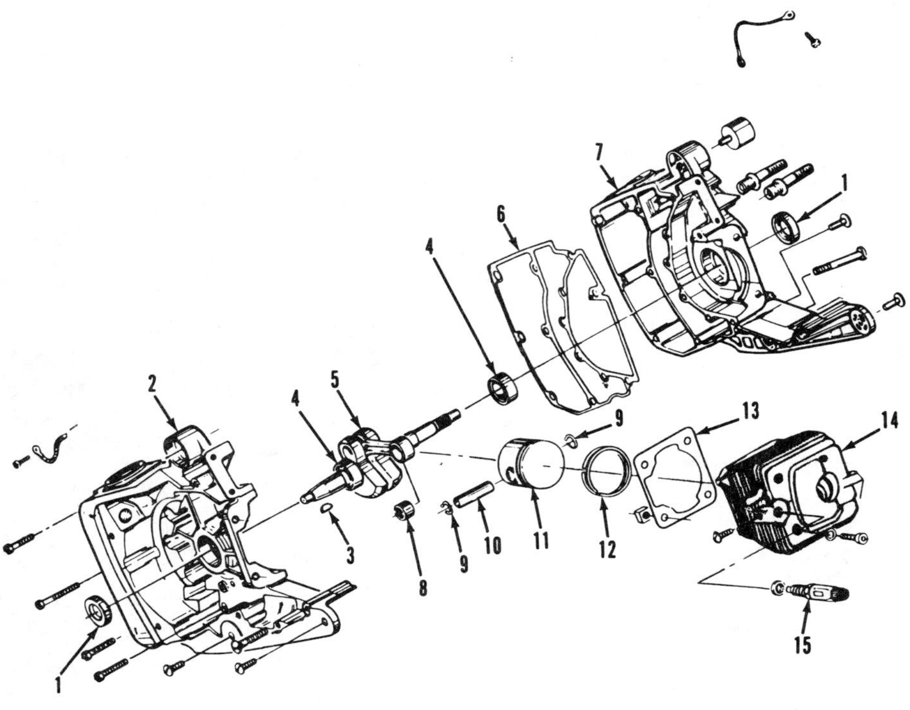

Fig. PP12 – Exploded view of engine assembly.

1. Seal
2. Crankcase half
3. Key
4. Ball bearing
5. Crankshaft & connecting rod assy.
6. Gasket
7. Crankcase half
8. Needle bearing
9. Retainer clip
10. Piston pin
11. Piston
12. Piston rings
13. Gasket
14. Cylinder
15. Decompression valve

Fig. PP13 – View of crankcase halves separated. Compartment (C) is crankcase, (O) is oil reservoir and (G) is the fuel tank. Be sure to clean gasket surfaces thoroughly and install new gasket before assembling.

CRANKSHAFT AND CONNECTING ROD. The crankshaft, crankpin and connecting rod are pressed together and are available only as a complete assembly. Crankshaft can be easily damaged by incorrect service procedures. Dropping the crankshaft or pounding on the ends can easily knock the crankshaft out of alignment. Crankshaft seals can be removed and installed without separating the crankcase halves. Use a small screwdriver between shaft and seal to remove and Pioneer/Partner tool 427407 to install drive side seal and Pioneer/Partner tool 429445 to install flywheel side seal.

To separate the crankcase halves, remove air filter assembly, handle bar, rewind starter, handle assembly, carburetor, reed valve, flywheel, ignition module/coil assembly, saw chain, guide bar, clutch, chain oiler pump, pump worm, cylinder and piston. Remove the screws attaching crankcase halves together. Use Pioneer/Partner flywheel and crankcase puller 475501 and carefully separate crankcase halves.

NOTE: Main bearings are a press fit on crankshaft. Bearings can be removed from crankshaft using Pioneer/Partner bearing puller 471015.

If main bearings remain in crankcase halves during separation, heat main bearing area of crankcase halves to approximately 200° F (93° C) and use Pioneer/Partner main bearing driver 470335 to drive bearings from each crankcase half.

Gasket surface between the two crankcase halves must be completely clean and free from nicks and burrs. The crankcase forms three different compartments when the halves are joined together: Engine crankcase (C – Fig. PP13), Fuel tank (G) and Chain oil reservoir (O).

When assembling, heat main bearing area of crankcase halves to approximately 200° F (93° C) prior to installing crankshaft assembly. The two screws (B – Fig. PP14) should be 2¼ inches (57.1 mm) long, screw (C) should be 2½ inches (63.5 mm) long and the remaining eleven screws (A) should be 1¼ inches (31.7 mm) long.

REED VALVE. The reed valve assembly (Fig. PP15) can be removed after removing air filter assembly and carburetor. Renew reed petal (3) if cracked or worn and be sure reed petal is centered over opening of reed plate (4). Use new gaskets (1 and 5) during installation.

CLUTCH. The clutch can be disassembled after removing side cover, saw chain, guide bar and nut (8 – Fig. PP16). Clutch hub (6) should slide easily off crankshaft splines. Inspect the crankshaft, needle bearing (3) and drum (4) for wear and evidence of overheating. Inspect clutch shoes (5), hub (6), garter spring (7), drum (4) and floating sprocket (2) for damage.

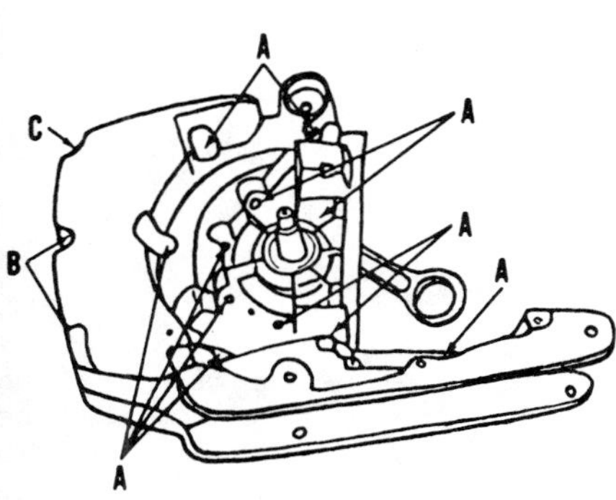

Fig. PP14 – Screws (A) should be 1¼ inches (31.7 mm) long, screws (B) should be 2¼ inches (57.1 mm) long and screw (C) should be 2½ inches (63.5 mm) long. Fuel pickup line should be withdrawn to facilitate removal and installation of one screw.

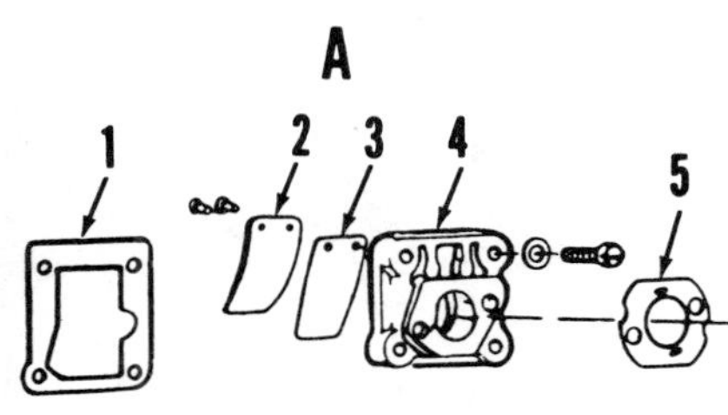

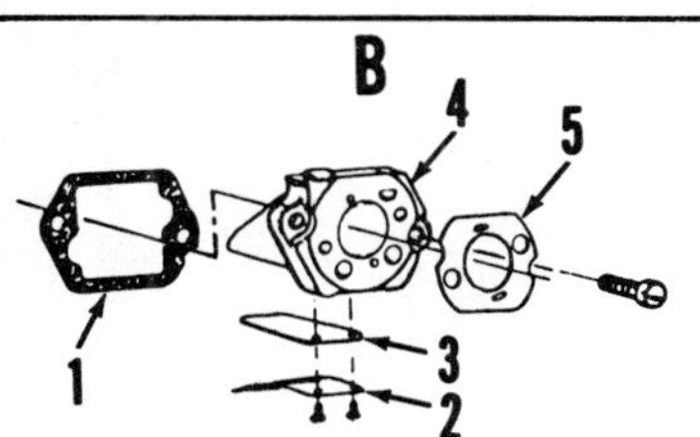

Fig. PP15 – Exploded view of reed valve assembly. Components shown in view "A" are used on P39, P42 and P45 models. Components shown in view "B" are used on P52, P62 and P65 models.

1. Gasket
2. Reed stopper
3. Reed petal
4. Reed plate
5. Gasket

Washer (1) should be installed next to crankcase. Lubricate needle bearing (3) with a small amount of general purpose automotive grease before installing. Floating sprocket (2) should be installed with open side away from clutch drum (4). Install hub (6) with hex nut side facing toward outside (side cover). Pioneer/Partner tool 475212 is available to facilitate assembly of clutch shoes (5) and garter spring (7) around hub (6). Lubricate crankshaft threads and install hub and clutch shoe assembly, then install nut (8) and tighten to 30-35 ft.-lbs. (40.8-47.6 N·m).

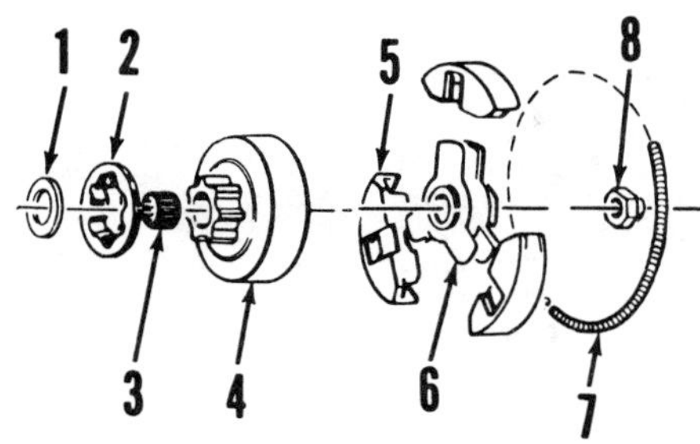

Fig. PP16 – Exploded view of clutch assembly.

1. Washer
2. Floating sprocket
3. Needle bearing
4. Drum
5. Shoe
6. Hub
7. Garter spring
8. Nut

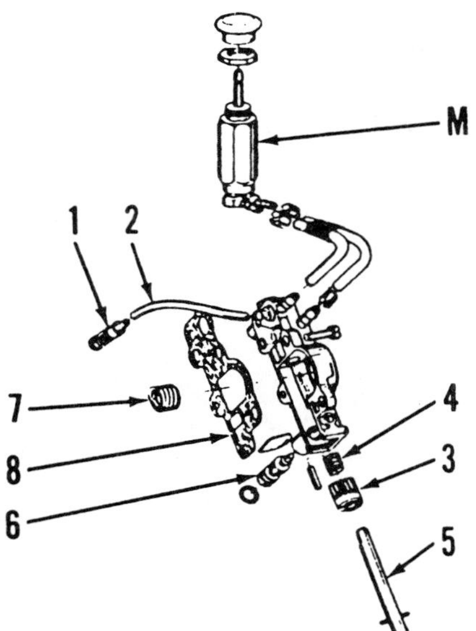

Fig. PP17 – Exploded view of automatic oil pump assembly. Models P62 and P65 are also equipped with manual pump (M).

1. Oil pickup
2. Hose
3. Driven gear
4. Spring
5. Shaft
6. Adjuster screw
7. Worm gear
8. Gasket

OIL PUMP. All models are equipped with an automatic oil pump assembly. Models P62 and P65 are also equipped with manual pump (M – Fig. PP17).

Turning adjuster screw (6) will change the volume of oil that is pumped to the bar and chain. Adjuster can be turned only approximately one turn, but the volume is increased from 8 to 17 mL (0.27 to 0.57 oz.) per minute within this adjusting range. Turning counterclockwise will increase the volume delivered. The oil adjustment screw should be set wide open when first operating the saw to ensure that the bar and chain will receive an adequate supply of oil during initial operation. After initial operation, the setting can be decreased at the discretion of the operator to meet various cutting conditions such as temperature, oil viscosity, type of work and size of wood.

Worm gear (7) on the crankshaft rotates and turns pump shaft and gear (3). End of pump shaft (5) is machined on an angle to provide a cam surface which rides against surface of adjuster screw (6). As the pump shaft turns, the cam surface pushes the shaft in and out of pump body. The in and out movement pumps oil to the chain. A flat on the pump shaft acts as a valve to open the intake port on the outward stroke and the outlet port on the inward stroke. A small amount of grease should be used to lubricate the pump gears. Pioneer/Partner puller 474329 is available for pulling the worm gear from crankshaft.

Fig. PP18 – Exploded view of rewind starter. Starter housing (1) shown is used on Models P42, P52, P62 and P65. Two pivots (16), pawls (17), springs (18) and washers (19) are used.

1. Starter housing
2. Shield
3. Handle
4. Starter rope
5. Baffle plate
6. Ferrule
7. Bushing
8. Rewind spring
9. Pulley
10. Washer
11. Lockwasher
12. Screw
13. Nut
14. Washer
15. Flywheel
16. Pivot
17. Pawl
18. Spring
19. Washer

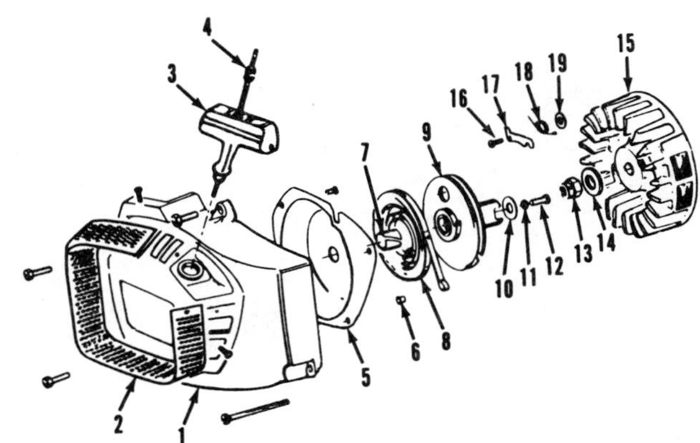

When installing pump, be sure that pickup (1) is directed toward bottom of the tank while saw is held in an upright position.

REWIND STARTER. Starter pawls (17–Fig. PP18) are located on flywheel (15) and engage a notch in pulley (9) for starting. All models are equipped with two sets of pawls (17). Starter must be disassembled to renew rope (4) or rewind spring (8). The 5/32 inch (3.97 mm) diameter nylon cord should be 41 inches (104.1 cm) long. Clean and apply automotive grease on rewind spring (8). Rewind spring should be preloaded three turns during reassembly.

CHAIN BRAKE. All models are equipped with a chain brake designed to stop the saw chain quickly should kickback occur. It is necessary to unlock chain brake before removing or installing side cover (8–Fig. PP19). Sawdust and debris should be cleaned from around the brake mechanisim as needed to ensure proper operation of chain brake.

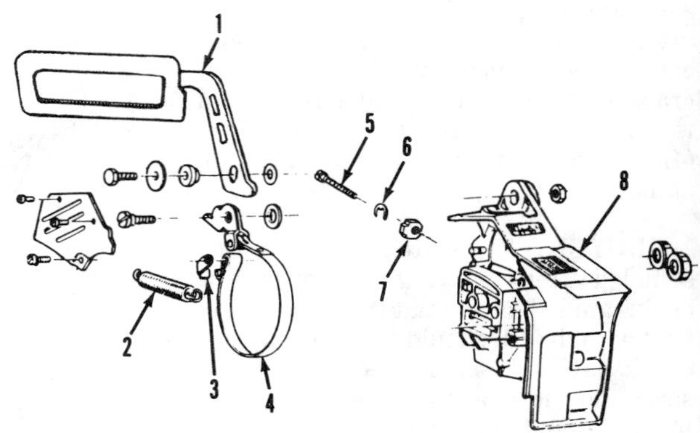

Fig. PP19 – Exploded view of chain brake typical of type used on Models P42, P45, P52, P62 and P65. Chain brake assembly used on P39 models is similar. On P39 models, make sure spring (2) is installed completlely on brake band (4) end.

1. Brake lever
2. Spring
3. Retainer
4. Brake band & cam assy.
5. Tension adjusting screw
6. "E" clip
7. Tensioner plate
8. Side cover

PIONEER/PARTNER

Model	Bore mm (in.)	Stroke mm (in.)	Displacement cc (cu. in.)	Drive Type
500	44 (1.73)	32 (1.26)	49 (3.0)	Direct
5000, Plus, H Plus	44 (1.73)	32 (1.26)	49 (3.0)	Direct

MAINTENANCE

SPARK PLUG. Recommended spark plug is Champion DJ6Y for all models. Electrode gap should be 0.5 mm (0.020 in.).

CARBURETOR. A Walbro WA diaphragm type carburetor is used on all models. Refer to Walbro section of CARBURETOR SERVICE for service and exploded views of carburetor.

Initial adjustment for both low speed and high speed mixture screws is one turn open from a lightly seated position. Make final adjustment with engine warm and running. Adjust idle speed screw so engine idles just below clutch engagement speed. Adjust low speed mixture screw so engine will accelerate cleanly without hesitation. Adjust high speed mixture screw to obtain optimum performance under cutting load.

IGNITION. All models are equipped with a breakerless capacitor discharge ignition system. Ignition timing is not adjustable. Air gap between coil legs and flywheel should be 0.25-0.30 mm (0.009-0.012 in.).

Fig. PP20 — Exploded view of throttle control and handle assemblies used on 5000 and 5000H plus models. Side protector (8) is not used on 500 models.

1. Vibration-damper
2. Rear handle
3. Vibration-damper
4. Throttle lock
5. Throttle control
6. Throttle linkage
7. Rear handle cover
8. Side protector
9. Safety strap
10. Connector plug
11. Cap screw
12. Coil spring
13. Housing
14. Washer
15. Front handle

LUBRICATION. Engine is lubricated by mixing engine oil with regular leaded gasoline. Recommended oil is Beaird-Poulan engine oil approved for a fuel-to-oil mixture ratio of 40:1. If recommended oil is not available, a good quality oil designed for two-stroke air-cooled engines may be used when mixed at a 24:1 ratio. Use a separate container when mixing the oil and gas.

All models are equipped with an automatic chain oil pump. Oil output on all models is adjusted by turning screw located behind guide bar. Refer to AUTOMATIC CHAIN OILER under REPAIRS section.

REPAIRS

PISTON, PIN, RINGS AND CYLINDER. The piston is accessible after removing the cylinder assembly. Piston is fitted with one piston ring on all models. A locating pin is present in piston ring groove to prevent piston ring rotation. Oversize pistons and rings are not available. Reject piston pin and piston if there is any visible radial play of pin in the piston bosses. All models have needle type piston pin bearings. Install piston so arrow on piston crown points toward exhaust port.

Inspect cylinder bore for excessive wear or damage to bore surface. Cylinder should be renewed if new piston ring end gap in cylinder exceeds 0.8 mm (0.031 in.).

CRANKSHAFT, CONNECTING ROD AND CRANKCASE. Crankshaft and connecting rod are a unit assembly. When separating crankcase halves first remove cylinder, then withdraw oil pump drive gear from crankshaft using Pioneer/Partner special tool 505 381816. Remove crankcase retaining cap screws and press crankshaft out of left crankcase half using Pioneer/Partner special tool 505 381811. Crankshaft may be driven out of right crankcase half using a suitable plastic mallet. Main bearings (11 – Fig. PP21) can be pulled from crankshaft by using a bearing puller. Heat main bearing in oil to install on crankshaft. Heat crankcase halves on an electric hot plate prior to assembling crankcase. Oil pump drive gear (4 – Fig. PP24) should be positioned on crankshaft so outer gear face is 1 mm (0.04 in.) below flush of gear mounting land (L).

Fig. PP21 — Exploded view of engine used on all models.

1. Intake manifold
2. Exhaust gasket
3. Cylinder
4. Gasket
5. Piston
6. Piston rings
7. Piston pin
8. Lock ring
9. Needle bearing
10. Crankshaft & rod assy.
11. Main bearings
12. Right crankcase half
13. Seal
14. Left crankcase half
15. Seal
16. Pin
17. Gasket
18. Fuel tank vent
19. Stop switch
20. Fuel cap
21. Fuel filter
22. Oil cap

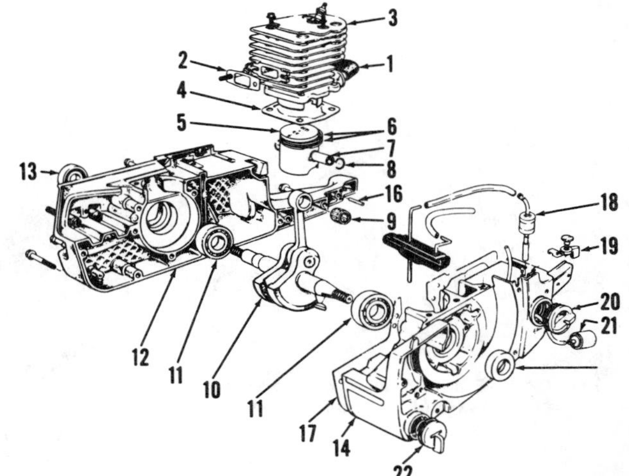

CLUTCH. All models are equipped with a two-shoe centrifugal clutch. Clutch hub has left-hand threads. Inspect clutch shoes and drum for excessive wear or damage due to overheating. Inspect clutch drum, bearing and crankshaft for damage. Clutch hub (1 – Fig. PP22) and clutch shoes (2) are available as an assembly. Clutch drum (5) is available with needle bearing (6). Spring (3), washer (4), needle bearing (6), rim sprocket (7) and washer (8) are available individually.

AUTOMATIC CHAIN OILER. All models are equipped with an automatic chain oiler pump which is driven by gear (4 – Fig. PP23) on crankshaft. Oil pump output on all models can be adjusted between 4-9 mL (0.14-0.30 oz.) per minute by turning screw (S) in end of pump housing (7). Rotating screw counterclockwise provides maximum output.

Access to oil pump components is obtained after removing chain, guide bar, clutch and oil pump cover plate (1). When reassembling, make certain notch in pump housing (7 – Fig. PP24) engages locating lug in crankcase and that pin (2) is inserted in oil tank vent passage.

REWIND STARTER. All models are equipped with the rewind starter shown in Fig. PP25. To disassemble rewind starter, first remove starter housing from saw. Pull starter rope and hold rope pulley with notch in pulley adjacent to rope outlet. Pull rope back through outlet so it engages notch in pulley and allow pulley to completely unwind. Unscrew pulley retaining cap screw (1) and remove rope pulley. If rewind spring requires removal, unsnap tabs securing spring retainer (3) to starter housing (5) and withdraw from housing. Care should be taken not to allow spring to uncoil from retainer.

Reassembly is the reverse of disassembly while noting the following: Wrap starter rope around rope pulley in a clockwise direction as viewed with pulley in starter housing. Turn rope pulley two turns clockwise before passing rope through rope outlet to place tension on rewind spring. Spring tension is correct if rope pulley can be rotated approximately ½ turn further when rope is at its greatest length.

When installing starter assembly on saw, make sure starter pulley properly engages pawls on flywheel before tightening retaining cap screws.

CHAIN BRAKE. All models are equipped with a chain brake system designed to stop chain movement should kickback occur.

The chain brake is activated when the operator's hand strikes the chain brake lever thereby forcing actuating plate (3 – Fig. PP26) off of pin in housing releasing spring (7). Spring then draws brake band tight around clutch drum to stop chain. Pull back chain brake lever to reset mechanism. No adjustment of brake mechanism is required.

If brake requires disassembly for repair or renewal of individual components, it is recommended that a clutch drum be inserted in brake band and brake engaged, to facilitate removal of brake lever. When reassembling, make certain spring (7) is screwed completely on brake band and roll pins (4 and 6) are installed with split side toward front of saw.

HANDLE HEATER. Model 5000H plus is equipped with the front and rear handle heating system shown in Fig. PP27. Valve (2) is attached to the muf-

Fig. PP22 – Exploded view of two-shoe type clutch assembly used on all models.

1. Hub
2. Shoe
3. Spring
4. Washer
5. Drum
6. Needle bearing
7. Rim sprocket
8. Washer

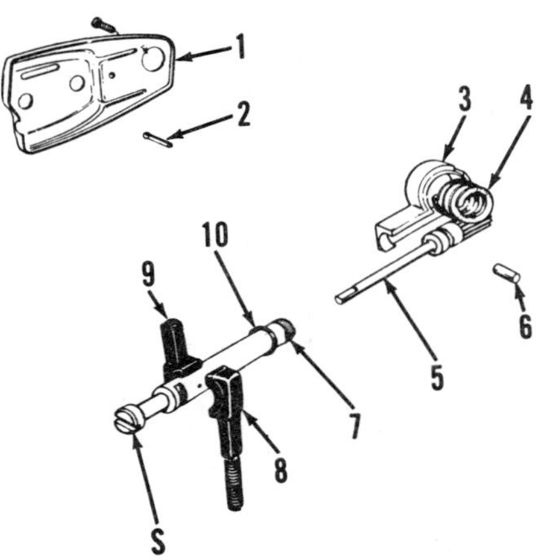

Fig. PP23 – Exploded view of adjustable chain oil pump used on all models.

S. Adjusting screw
1. Cover plate
2. Oil tank vent pin
3. Gear protector
4. Drive gear
5. Plunger
6. Pin
7. Pump housing
8. Inlet tube
9. Outlet tube
10. "O" ring

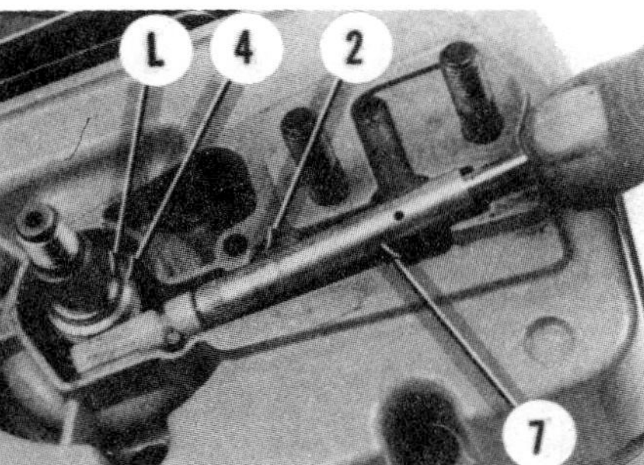

Fig. PP24 – Install oil pump components as outlined in text. Refer to Fig. PP23 for parts identification.

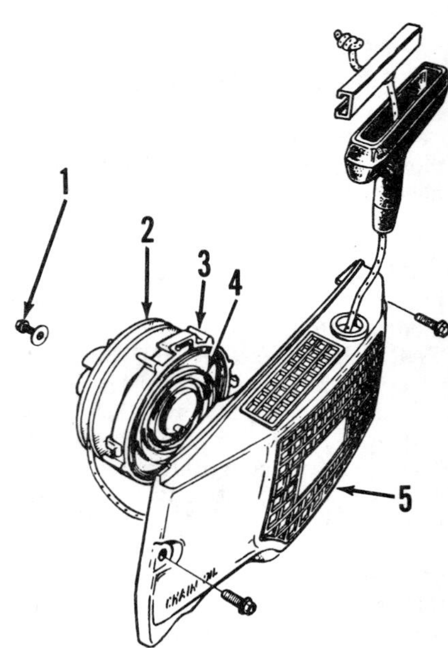

Fig. PP25 – Exploded view of rewind starter.

1. Cap screw
2. Rope pulley
3. Rewind spring retainer
4. Rewind spring
5. Starter housing

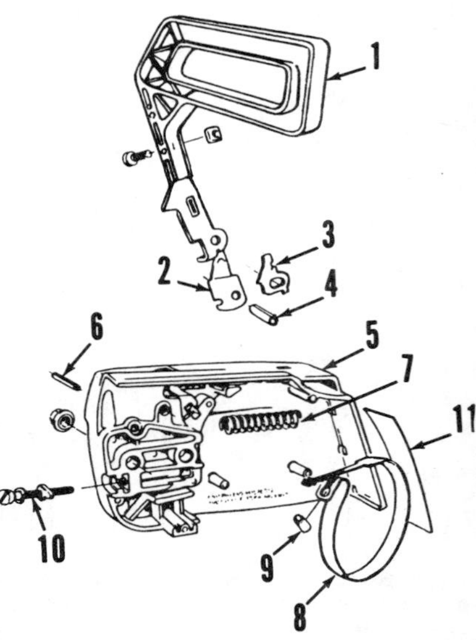

Fig. PP26 – Exploded view of chain brake used on all models.

1. Chain brake lever
2. Sleeve
3. Actuating plate
4. Pin
5. Housing
6. Pin
7. Spring
8. Brake band
9. Pin
10. Chain tensioner
11. Chain guard

fler allowing a small quantity of heated exhaust gas produced by the engine to flow through hoses (6 and 8) and enter chambers in front and rear handles. Front handle temperature is controlled by adjusting screw (3) while rear handle temperature is controlled by adjusting screw (4). Turning adjusting screws completely in shuts off heat.

Heating system should be periodically disassembled and carbon deposits removed. Inspect and renew hoses (6 and 8) if hoses are restricted due to carbon build up or show signs of cracking.

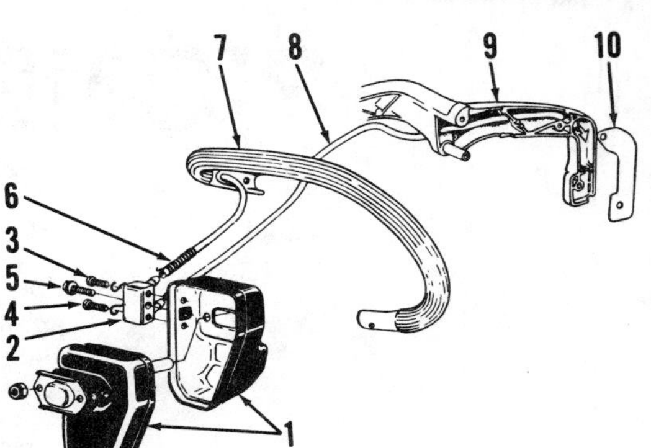

Fig. PP27—Exploded view of handle heating system used on 5000H plus models.

1. Muffler
2. Valve
3. Front handle temp. adjuster
4. Rear handle temp. adjuster
5. Cap screw
6. Hose
7. Front handle
8. Hose
9. Rear handle
10. Gasket

PIONEER/PARTNER

Model	Bore	Stroke	Displ.	Drive Type
550	44 mm (1.73 in.)	36 mm (1.42 in.)	55 cc (3.36 cu. in.)	Direct
7000 plus	50 mm (1.968 in.)	36 mm (1.42 in.)	70 cc (4.27 cu. in.)	Direct

MAINTENANCE

SPARK PLUG. Recommended spark plug is Champion CJ6 or Bosch WS5E for both models with an electrode gap of 0.5 mm (0.020 in.).

CARBURETOR. A Walbro WJ or WS diaphragm type carburetor is used on both models. Refer to Walbro section of CARBURETOR SERVICE for service and exploded views of carburetors.

Initial adjustment for both low speed and high speed mixture screws is one turn open from a lightly seated position. Make final adjustment with engine warm and running. Adjust idle speed screw so engine idles just below clutch engagement speed. Adjust low speed mixture screw so engine will accelerate cleanly without hesitation. Adjust high speed mixture screw to obtain optimum performance under cutting load.

IGNITION. Both models are equipped with an Electrolux "EM" breakerless capacitor discharge ignition system. Ignition timing is not adjustable. Air gap between coil legs and flywheel should be 0.35-0.45 mm (0.014-0.018 in.).

LUBRICATION. Engine is lubricated by mixing engine oil with gasoline. Recommended oil is Beaird-Poulan engine oil approved for a fuel-to-oil mixture ratio of 40:1. If recommended oil is not available, a good quality oil designed for two-stroke air-cooled engines may be used when mixed at a 24:1 ratio. Use a separate container when mixing the oil and gas.

Both models are equipped with an automatic chain oil pump. Oil output is adjustable by turning adjusting screw on bottom of saw. Refer to AUTOMATIC CHAIN OILER under REPAIRS section. Chain oil should be Pioneer/Partner Chain Oil or, if not available, use a good quality SAE 10 or SAE 30 motor oil depending upon ambient temperature.

CARBON. Carbon should be cleaned from muffler and exhaust ports at regular intervals. When scraping carbon, be careful not to damage the chamfered edges of the exhaust ports.

REPAIRS

PISTON, PIN, RING AND CYLINDER. The piston is accessible after removing the cylinder assembly. The aluminum alloy piston is fitted with one pinned piston ring. Reject piston pin and piston if there is any visible radial play of pin in the piston bosses. Piston and pin are not available separately. A needle type piston pin bearing is used.

Cylinder bore is Nickel-Sil impregnated. Inspect cylinder bore for excessive wear or damage to bore surface. Pistons and cylinders are graded with a letter to designate size. Letter size is located on piston crown and top of cylinder. Letters on piston and cylinder should be the same to obtain desired piston-to-cylinder clearance. For instance, a piston with letter grade "B" should be used in a cylinder with letter grade "B." Install piston so arrow on piston crown points toward exhaust port.

CONNECTING ROD AND CRANKSHAFT. Crankshaft and connecting rod assembly (8 – Fig. PP31) is available only as a complete unit. Main bearings (10) are ball bearings. Outer races of the ball type main bearings are shrink fit in crankcase half and if bearings fall from their bores by their own weight, bearings and crankcase halves should be renewed.

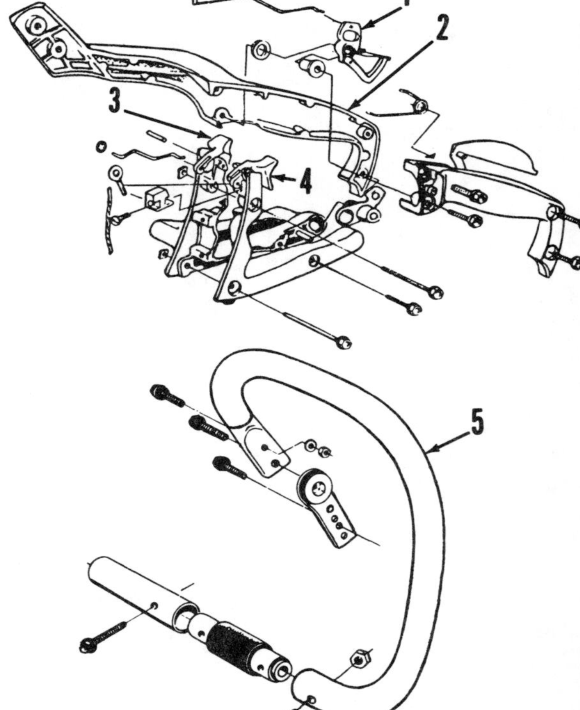

Fig. PP30 – Exploded view of handle assembly.
1. Throttle control
2. Rear handle
3. Choke button
4. Stop button
5. Front handle

To renew main bearings, first remove cylinder. Remove screws retaining crankcase halves together. Use Pioneer/ Partner puller tool 505 381811 or a suitable equivalent and extract magneto side crankcase half from crankshaft and clutch side crankcase half. Remove crankshaft assembly from clutch side crankcase half by tapping on opposite end of crankshaft using a soft-faced mallet. Press ball bearings (10) off crankshaft ends using suitable tools. The manufacturer recommends renewing ball bearings (10) and seals (12 and 15) any time crankcase halves are split.

With ball bearings (10) installed on crankshaft assembly, heat bearing bores in crankcase halves to approximately 150° C (302° F) to install crankshaft assembly. Make sure a new gasket (16) is positioned between halves. Tighten crankcase halves retaining screws to 10 N•m (88 in.-lbs.). Make certain crankshaft is centered in crankcase and will rotate freely. Clutch side crankshaft seal should be installed flush with crankcase face. Flywheel side crankshaft seal should protrude 1 mm (0.04 in.) from crankcase face when installed.

CLUTCH. A two-shoe centrifugal type clutch is used. Clutch hub (1 – Fig. PP32) has left-hand threads. Clutch needle bearing (5) should be inspected for excessive wear or damage. Inspect clutch shoes and drum for signs of excessive heat.

AUTOMATIC CHAIN OILER. The chain oiler pump is located in the left (magneto side) crankcase half and is driven by gear (14 – Fig. PP33) on crankshaft flywheel side. Oil pump operation is accomplished when plunger (4) is rotated by gear (14) and reciprocates as the oblique end of plunger bears against adjuster (7) ball thereby pumping oil. Oil output can be adjusted between 5-15 mL (0.17-0.51 oz.) per minute by rotating adjuster (7). Drive gear (14) can be pulled off crankshaft after removing flywheel and seal (15 – Fig. PP31). Drive gear (14 – Fig. PP33) must be heated before installation on crankshaft to prevent crankshaft displacement.

REWIND STARTER. All models are equipped with the rewind starter shown in Fig. PP34. To disassemble starter, remove rope handle (12) and allow rope (9) to wind around rope pulley (8). Disengage pulley retaining clip (7) and carefully remove rope pulley (8). Rewind spring (10) is now accessible and may be removed.

Install rewind spring (10) in a clockwise direction viewed with spring installed in housing (11). Rope (9) must be wrapped around rope pulley (8) in a clockwise direction viewed with rope pulley in housing (11). Tension should be placed on starter rope (9) by rotating rope pulley (8) two turns clockwise.

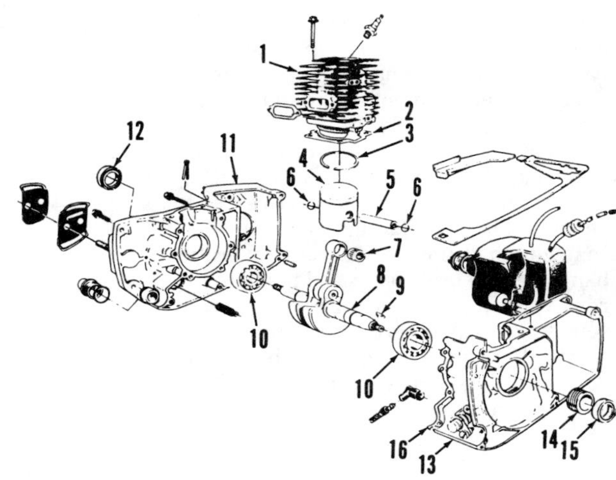

Fig. PP31 – Exploded view of engine assembly.

1. Cylinder
2. Gasket
3. Piston ring
4. Piston
5. Piston pin
6. Retainer clip
7. Needle bearing
8. Crankshaft & connecting rod assy.
9. Key
10. Bearing
11. Crankcase half
12. Seal
13. Crankcase half
14. Oil pump drive gear
15. Seal
16. Gasket

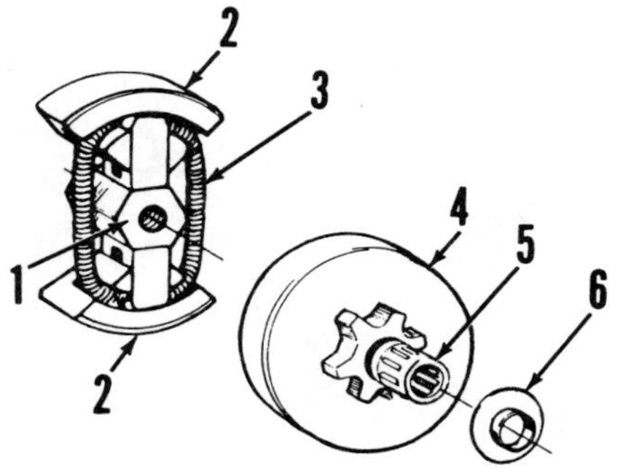

Fig. PP32 – Exploded view of two-shoe centrifugal clutch assembly.

1. Hub
2. Shoe
3. Garter spring
4. Drum
5. Needle bearing
6. Washer

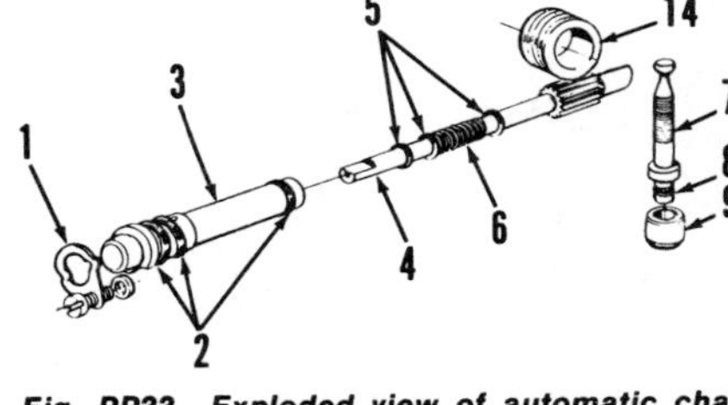

Fig. PP33 – Exploded view of automatic chain oiler.

1. Retainer
2. "O" rings
3. Housing
4. Plunger
5. "O" rings
6. Spring
7. Adjuster
8. "O" ring
9. Cap
14. Drive gear

Fig. PP34 – Exploded view of rewind starter.

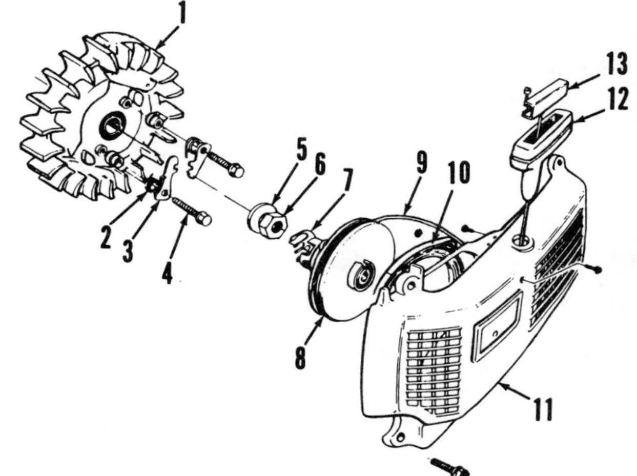

1. Flywheel
2. Spring
3. Pawl
4. Screw
5. Washer
6. Nut
7. Clip
8. Rope pulley
9. Rope
10. Rewind spring
11. Housing
12. Handle
13. Anchor

CHAIN BRAKE. Both models are equipped with a chain brake system designed to stop chain movement should kickback occur. Chain brake is activated when the operator's hand strikes chain brake guard (1–Fig. PP35) thereby allowing trigger (5) to release spring (9). Spring then draws brake band (10) tight around clutch drum to stop chain. Pull back chain brake guard to reset mechanism. No adjustment of brake mechanism is required.

Disassembly for repair or renewal of individual components is evident after inspection of unit and referral to exploded view. The manufacturer recommends that clutch drum be inserted in brake band (10) and brake engaged to facilitate removal of brake lever (2). When reassembling, make certain spring (9) is screwed completely on brake band and roll pins (6 and 7) are installed with split side toward front of saw.

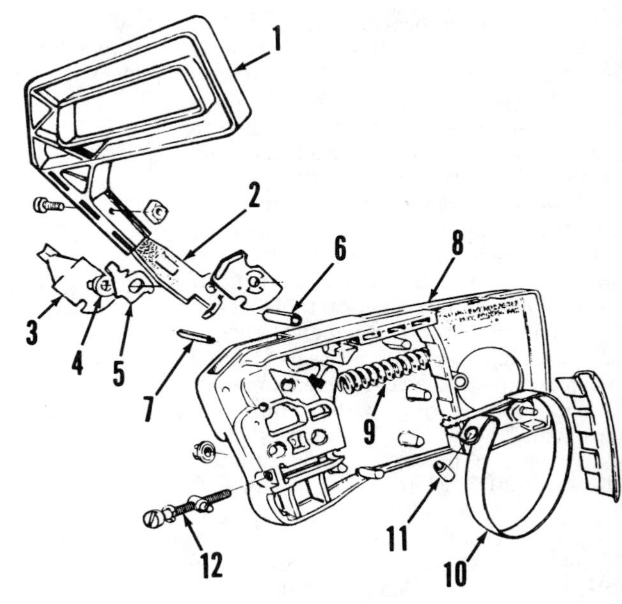

Fig. PP35 — Exploded view of chain brake assembly.

1. Guard
2. Lever
3. Detent cover
4. Washer
5. Trigger
6. Pin
7. Pin
8. Side cover
9. Spring
10. Brake band
11. Pin
12. Chain tensioner

PIONEER/PARTNER

Model	Bore	Stroke	Displ.	Drive Type
400	40 mm (1.57 in.)	32 mm (1.26 in.)	40 cc (2.4 cu. in.)	Direct
450	42 mm (1.65 in.)	32 mm (1.26 in.)	44 cc (2.7 cu. in.)	Direct

MAINTENANCE

SPARK PLUG. Recommended spark plug for both models is Champion RC-J7Y with an electrode gap of 0.5 mm (0.020 in.).

CARBURETOR. A Walbro WT carburetor is used on both models. Refer to Walbro section of CARBURETOR SERVICE for service and exploded view of carburetor.

Initial adjustment for low speed and high speed mixture screws is one turn open from a lightly seated position. Make final adjustment with engine warm and running. Adjust idle speed screw so engine idles just below clutch engagement speed. Adjust low speed mixture screw so engine will accelerate cleanly without hesitation. Adjust high speed mixture screw to obtain optimum performance under cutting load. Do not adjust high speed mixture screw too lean as overheating and engine damage could result.

IGNITION. Both models are equipped with Electrolux breakerless ignition system shown in Fig. PP41. Ignition timing is not adjustable. Air gap between ignition module core and flywheel magnets should be 0.3 mm (0.012 in.). Adjust air gap by loosening ignition module retaining screws and repositioning module.

LUBRICATION. Engine is lubricated by mixing engine oil with fuel. Recommended oil is Beaird-Poulan engine oil approved for a fuel-to-oil mixture ratio of 40:1. If recommended oil is not available, a good quality oil designed for two-stroke air-cooled engines may be used when mixed at a 24:1 ratio. Use a separate container when mixing the oil and gasoline.

Both models are equipped with an automatic chain oil pump. The oil reservoir should be filled with Pioneer/Partner Chain Oil or, if not available, use a good quality SAE 10 to SAE 30 motor oil depending upon ambient temperature. Oil pump output is not adjustable.

REPAIRS

CYLINDER, PISTON, RING AND PIN. Cylinder has a chrome plated bore which should be inspected for flaking, cracking or other damage to chromed surface. Inspect piston and discard if excessive wear or damage is evident. New cylinders are available only with fitted pistons. Piston is renewable only in standard size and as an assembly with piston ring, piston pin, needle roller bearing and retaining clips.

The piston is fitted with a single piston ring. A locating pin is present in piston ring groove to prevent piston ring rotation. Be sure ring end gap is around locating pin when installing cylinder.

The piston pin is retained by wire retainers and rides in a needle roller bearing in small end of connecting rod. Be sure piston is properly supported when removing piston pin to prevent damage. Arrow on piston crown must point toward exhaust port when installing piston.

CRANKSHAFT, CONNECTING ROD AND CRANKCASE. Crankshaft and connecting rod are a unit assembly. Crankshaft main roller bearings (9–Fig. PP42) are supported in interlocking bearing carriers (7). Separate bearing carriers (7) and withdraw from crankshaft ends to service roller bearings (9) and seals (8). Make sure seals (8) are installed in bearing carriers with seal lip facing toward crankshaft assembly. Grease seal lips prior to assembling bearing carriers (7) onto crankshaft. Check rotation of connecting rod around crankpin and renew crankshaft unit if roughness or other damage is noted.

When installing crankshaft assembly, make sure mating surfaces of bearing carriers (7), lower crankcase (12) and cylinder (1) are clean and dry. Place a thin bead of a suitable form-in-place gasket compound onto sealing areas of lower crankcase (12) and cylinder (1).

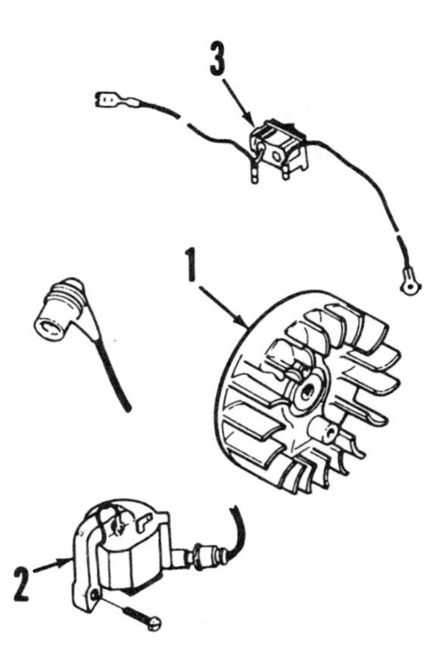

Fig. PP41 — Exploded view of ignition system.
1. Flywheel
2. Ignition module
3. Ignition switch

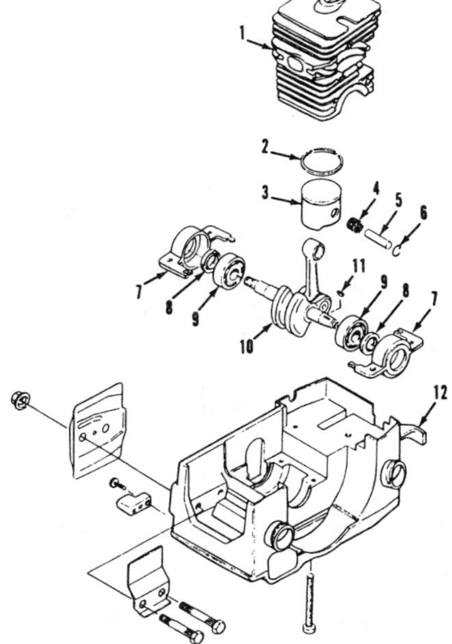

Fig. PP42 — Exploded view of engine assembly.
1. Cylinder
2. Piston ring
3. Piston
4. Needle roller bearing
5. Piston pin
6. Retainer
7. Bearing carriers
8. Seals
9. Roller bearings
10. Crankshaft & rod assy.
11. Key
12. Lower crankcase & saw body

Lubricate piston and crankshaft assembly with engine oil and wipe off excess oil. Correctly install piston into cylinder bore and position bearing carriers (7) into crankcase area of cylinder (1). Position insulation block on cylinder, then correctly install cylinder with crankshaft assembly onto lower crankcase (12). Tighten the four mounting screws in a criss-cross pattern to 11 N•m (97 in.-lbs.). Make sure crankshaft rotates freely.

CLUTCH. Both models are equipped with two-shoe centrifugal clutch shown in Fig. PP43. Clutch hub (1) has left-hand threads. Inspect clutch shoes (2) and clutch drum (5) for excessive wear or damage due to overheating. Inspect clutch drum, needle bearing (6) and crankshaft end for damage. Clutch hub (1) and clutch shoes (2) are available as an assembly. Clutch drum (5) is available with needle bearing (6). Spring (3), needle bearing (6), washer (4) and washer (7) are available individually.

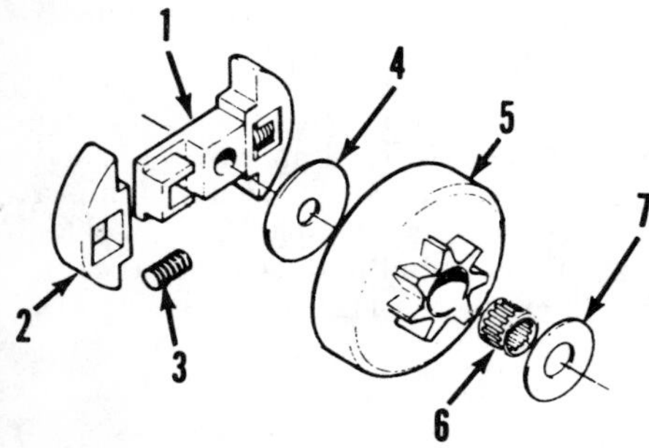

Fig. PP43—Exploded view of clutch assembly.

1. Hub
2. Shoe
3. Spring
4. Washer
5. Drum
6. Needle bearing
7. Washer

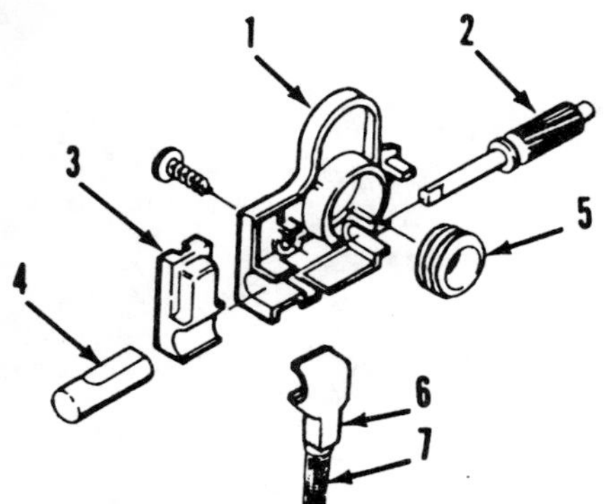

Fig. PP44—Exploded view of automatic oil pump assembly.

1. Pump housing
2. Plunger
3. Pressure pipe
4. Plunger housing
5. Worm gear
6. Suction pipe
7. Strainer

OIL PUMP. Both models are equipped with an automatic chain oiler pump which is driven by worm gear (5–Fig. PP44) on crankshaft. Oil pump output is not adjustable.

Access to oil pump components is obtained after removing chain, guide bar and clutch. Oil pump suction pipe (6) and strainer (7) may be withdrawn from oil tank using a suitable screwdriver.

REWIND STARTER. To disassemble rewind starter, remove starter housing from saw. Pull starter rope (12–Fig. PP45) out 15-20 cm (6-8 in.) and hold rope pulley (8). Pull rope back through outlet so rope engages an ear on pulley (8) and allow pulley to completely unwind. Unscrew pulley retaining screw (6) and remove rope pulley. If rewind spring (9) requires removal, care should be taken not to allow spring to uncoil from retainer.

Reassembly is the reverse of disassembly while noting the following: Wrap starter rope (12) around rope pulley (8) in a clockwise direction as viewed with pulley in starter housing (10). Turn rope pulley two turns clockwise before passing rope through rope outlet to place tension on rewind spring or reverse the procedure used to relieve spring tension outlined in the previous paragraph. Spring tension is correct if rope pulley (8) can be rotated approximately ½ turn further when rope is at extended length.

Fig. PP45—Exploded view of rewind starter assembly.

1. Flywheel
2. Nut
3. Spring
4. Pawl
5. Retainer
6. Screw
7. Washer
8. Rope pulley
9. Rewind spring
10. Starter housing
11. Handle
12. Starter rope
13. Rope guide

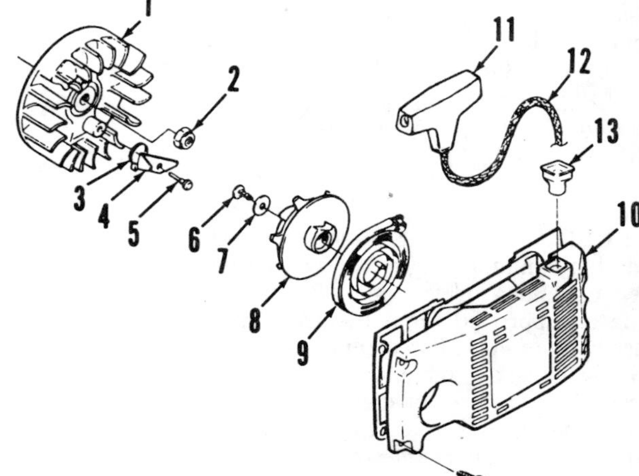

When installing starter assembly on saw, make sure starter pulley properly engages pawls (4) on flywheel before tightening retaining cap screws.

CHAIN BRAKE. Both models are equipped with a chain brake system designed to stop movement of chain should kickback occur. Refer to Fig. PP46 for exploded view of chain brake system used. It is necessary to unlock chain brake before removing or installing side cover (5). Sawdust and debris should be cleaned from around the brake mechanism as needed to ensure proper operation of chain brake.

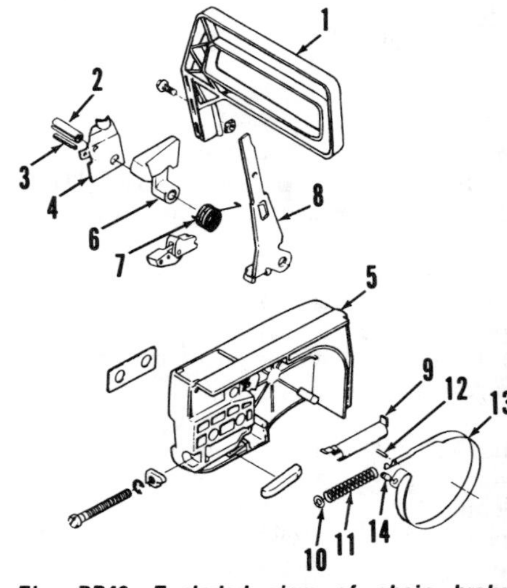

Fig. PP46—Exploded view of chain brake assembly.

1. Guard
2. Roll pin
3. Roll pin
4. Detent cover
5. Side cover
6. Inertia weight
7. Spring
8. Lever
9. Cover
10. Washer
11. Spring
12. Roll pin
13. Brake band
14. Pin

POULAN

Model	Bore mm (in.)	Stroke mm (in.)	Displacement cc (cu. in.)	Drive Type
S25, S25AV, S25CVA, S25D and S25DA	...	...	38 (2.3)	Direct

MAINTENANCE

SPARK PLUG. Recommended spark plug is Champion CJ8. Spark plug electrode gap should be 0.025 inch (0.63 mm).

CARBURETOR. Most models are equipped with a Tillotson Model HU diaphragm carburetor. Some models are equipped with a Walbro WA diaphragm carburetor. Refer to Tillotson or Walbro section of CARBURETOR SERVICE section for operation and overhaul of carburetor.

Initial setting of idle mixture screw and high speed mixture screw is one turn open. Adjust idle speed screw until engine will idle just below clutch engagement speed. Adjust idle mixture screw so engine will accelerate without hesitation. High speed mixture screw should be adjusted to obtain optimum performance with engine under cutting load. Be sure mixture settings are not too lean as engine damage will result.

IGNITION. Conventional flywheel magneto ignition system with breaker points located behind the flywheel is used on early models and a breakerless capacitor discharge ignition system is used on later models.

On models with breaker points, breaker-point gap should be 0.017 inch (0.43 mm). Ignition timing is fixed but incorrect breaker-point gap will affect timing. Magneto air gap should be 0.010-0.014 inch (0.25-0.35 mm). Magneto air gap is adjusted by loosening screws (2–Fig. PN1) and placing 0.012 inch (0.30 mm) shim stock between lamination legs and flywheel magnets. Move coil assembly until lamination legs contact shim stock and tighten screws (2). Recheck air gap.

On breakerless models, ignition components are mounted outside the flywheel making it unnecessary to remove the flywheel for most ignition service. The only adjustment of the unit is the air gap between the ignition module core and the flywheel magnets. Air gap should be 0.008-0.014 inch (0.20-0.35 mm). Air gap adjustment is similar to the procedures previously outlined for breaker point models.

On all models, flywheel nut should be tightened to 13-15 ft.-lbs. (17.6-20.3 N•m).

Fig. PN1 – View of flywheel and coil assembly. Note that washer (3) must have outer diameter contacting flywheel.

LUBRICATION. Engines on all models are lubricated by mixing oil with fuel. Recommended oil is Poulan/Weed Eater engine oil available in blends approved for 16:1 and 32:1 fuel mixtures. When using a recommended oil, follow mixing instructions on oil container. If a recommended oil is not available, a good quality oil designed for use in air-cooled two-stroke engines may be used when mixed at a 16:1 ratio. Use a separate container when mixing oil and gasoline.

Model S25D is equipped with a manual chain oil pump. All other models are equipped with manual and automatic chain oil pumps. Automatic pump output is not adjustable. A good quality SAE 30 oil should be used when ambient temperature is 40° F (4.4° C) or above or SAE 10 when ambient temperature is below 40° F (4.4° C).

CARBON. Carbon deposits should be removed from muffler and exhaust ports at regular intervals. Be careful not to damage engine cylinder, piston or ex-

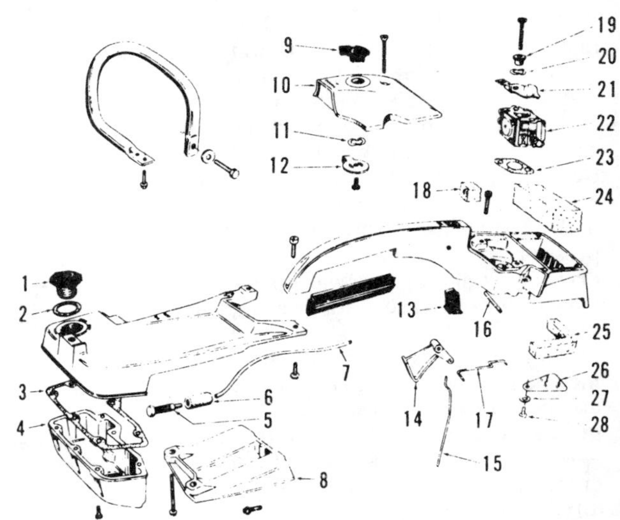

Fig. PN2 – Exploded view of handle and gas tank assemblies.

1. Fuel cap
2. Gasket
3. Gasket
4. Fuel tank
5. Fuel pickup weight
6. Filter
7. Fuel line
8. Cylinder shroud
9. Choke knob
10. Cover
11. Wave washer
12. Choke lever
13. Manual oil pump button
14. Trigger
15. Oil pump rod
16. Trigger pin
17. Throttle link
18. Throttle link boot
19. Spacer
20. Wave washer
21. Choke shutter
22. Carburetor
23. Gasket
24. Air filter
25. Dust seal
26. Reed valve petal
27. Washer
28. Screw

haust port when scraping carbon. Do not allow loosened carbon to enter cylinder.

REPAIRS

CYLINDER. Cylinder has a chrome-plated bore that should be inspected and renewed if chrome is scored, cracked or excessively worn.

PISTON, PIN AND RINGS. Piston should be heated to approximately 200° F (93.4° C) to aid in piston pin removal and installation. Closed end of piston pin must be toward exhaust port of cylinder. Snap ring on exhaust side of piston is sunk in retaining groove and will require use of a sharp hook type tool for removal. It may be necessary to drill a 1/8 inch hole (3.175 mm) hole into groove to gain access to snap ring. Manufacturer recommends discarding piston if a hole must be drilled to remove snap ring.

Piston is equipped with two piston rings. Piston rings are retained by a pin in each ring groove. Be sure piston rings are correctly aligned with pins and do not overlap pins when cylinder is installed. Install piston with ring locating pins on magneto side of engine. Piston and rings are available in standard sizes only.

CONNECTING ROD, CRANKSHAFT AND CRANKCASE. Crankcase halves (1 and 20 – Fig. PN3) must be separated to remove crankshaft and to remove connecting rod from crankshaft. Be careful during disassembly not to nick or damage mating surfaces.

Unscrew connecting rod screws and remove rod and cap being careful not to lose loose bearing rollers (11). There are 28 bearing rollers in connecting rod bearing. Connecting rod small end bearing must be pressed out of rod. Be sure rod is properly supported when removing or installing bearing. Use heavy grease to hold bearing rollers (11) in rod and cap when installing connecting rod on crankshaft. Match marks on sides of rod and cap must be aligned during installation. Tighten connecting rod screws to 55-60 in.-lbs. (6.2-6.8 N·m). Crankshaft is supported by a needle roller bearing (17) in each crankcase half. Crankcase bearings must be pressed out of crankcase using a suitable driver. Install bearings by pressing bearings into crankcase until bearings are 1/32 inch (0.794 mm) below inner surface of crankcase. Thrust washers (6) may be installed with either side up and are held in place with a light coat of grease. Use a suitable seal protector when passing crankshaft end through crankcase seals. Be sure thrust washers (6) do not dislodge during assembly. Tighten crankcase screws to 55-60 in.-lbs. (6.2-6.8 N·m).

CLUTCH. Refer to Fig. PN4 for exploded view of clutch assembly. Clutch hub has left-hand threads. Inspect clutch drum (6) and clutch shoes (5) for excessive wear or overheating and renew if required. Press clutch bushing (7) out of clutch drum and inspect bushing for roughness and wear.

REED VALVE. All models are equipped with a single reed valve petal (26 – Fig. PN2) beneath the carburetor. Reed valve is retained by screw (28) and washer (27). Sharp edge of washer (27) must be against reed petal. Tighten screw to 8-12 in.-lbs. (0.9-1.3 N·m). Reed petal should not stand open more than 0.010 inch (0.25 mm) from seat. Inspect reed petal for cracks and seat for burrs.

AUTOMATIC CHAIN OILER. Models S25DA and S25CVA are equipped with automatic chain oil pump shown in Fig. PN3. Crankcase pulsations pass through impulse hole (1 – Fig. PN5) and actuate diaphragm and piston (31 – Fig. PN3), which forces chain oil out discharge line (28). Inspect pump components for wear or damage which may cause pump malfunction. Diaphragm piston (31) should move freely in hole of pump housing (27) for a stroke of approximately 1/4 inch (6.35 mm). Piston hole may be cleaned using a 0.063 inch drill bit in a hand drill. Do not use an electric drill. Do not insert drill bit more than 9/16 inch (14.3 mm) into hole. Be sure hole in diaphragm (31) for impulse passage in housing is aligned with passage as shown in Fig. PN5 during assembly.

REWIND STARTER. Refer to Fig. PN6 for exploded view of rewind starter used on all models. To disassemble starter, remove starter housing (17). Remove rope handle and allow rope to wind into rope pulley (15). Unscrew retaining screw (13) and remove rope pulley (15) being careful not to dislodge rewind spring (16). Rewind spring (16)

Fig. PN3 – Exploded view of engine. Automatic oil pump shown is not used on Model S25D.

1. Crankcase half
2. Gasket
3. Cylinder
4. Gasket
5. Crankshaft
6. Thrust washer
7. Washer
8. Nut
9. Rod cap
10. Connecting rod
11. Bearing rollers (28)
12. Piston
13. Bearing
14. Piston pin
15. Snap ring
16. Piston rings
17. Bearing
18. Seal
19. Gasket
20. Crankcase half
21. Intake oil line & valve
22. Cap
23. Manual pump plunger
24. "O" ring
25. Spring
26. Gasket
27. Pump housing
28. Exhaust oil line
29. Gasket
30. Spring
31. Diaphragm & piston
32. Cover

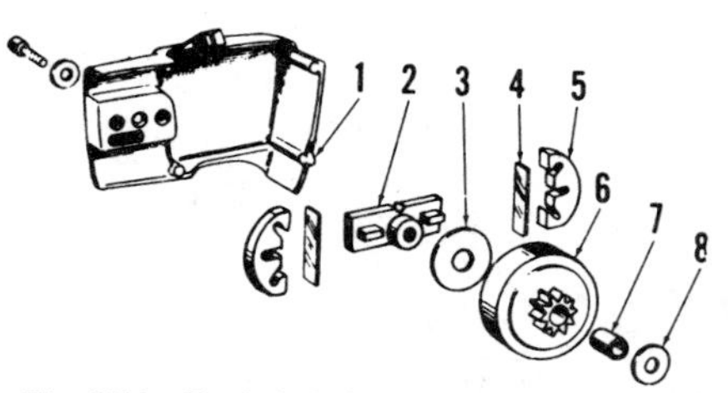

Fig. PN4 – Exploded view of clutch assembly.

1. Housing
2. Hub
3. Disc
4. Spring
5. Shoe
6. Drum
7. Bushing
8. Washer

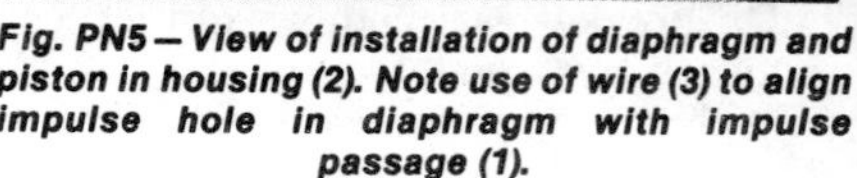

Fig. PN5 – View of installation of diaphragm and piston in housing (2). Note use of wire (3) to align impulse hole in diaphragm with impulse passage (1).

can now be removed if necessary, but precaution should be taken not to allow spring to uncoil uncontrolled.

Rewind spring is wound in clockwise direction in housing. Wind rope on rope pulley (15) in clockwise direction when viewing pulley as installed in housing. Turn pulley (15) 1½-2 turns before passing rope through rope outlet in housing (17).

CHAIN BRAKE. Some models may be equipped with a chain brake system designed to stop chain movement should kickback occur. Chain brake is activated when operator's hand strikes chain brake lever (1–Fig. PN7) releasing spring (5) and drawing brake band (6) tight around clutch drum (8). Pull back chain brake lever to reset mechanism.

Disassembly for repair and component renewal is evident after referral to exploded view and inspection of unit. No adjustment of chain brake system is required.

Fig. PN6—Exploded view of ignition and rewind starter assemblies.

9. Base plate
10. Breaker-point assy.
11. Cover
12. Flywheel
13. Screw
14. Washer
15. Rope pulley
16. Rewind spring
17. Starter housing
18. Ignition coil
19. High tension wire

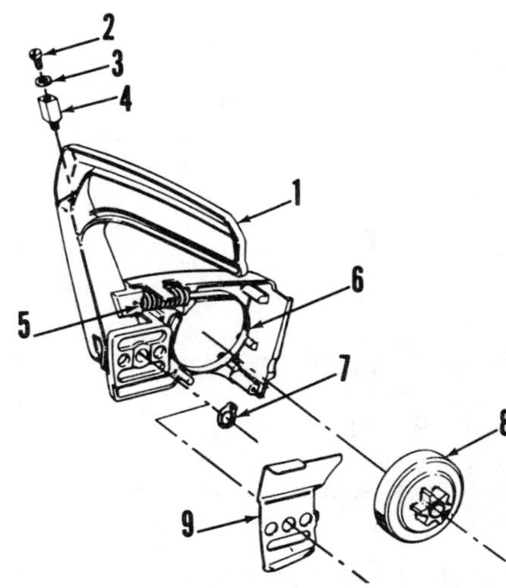

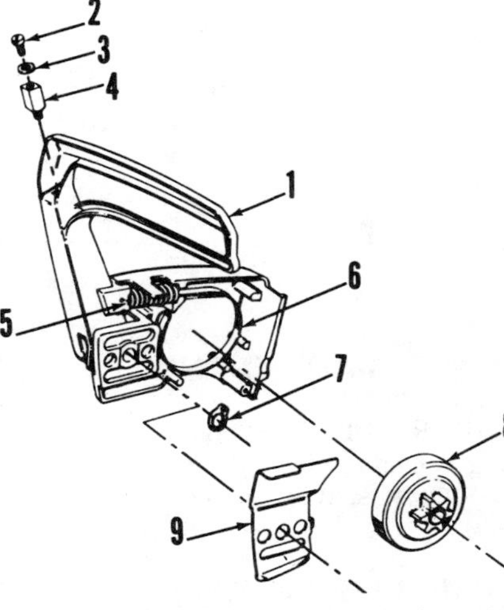

Fig. PN7—Exploded view of chain brake system used on some models.

1. Chain brake lever
2. Screw
3. Washer
4. Anchor
5. Spring
6. Brake band
7. Snap ring
8. Clutch drum
9. Chain guard

POULAN

Model	Bore mm (in.)	Stroke mm (in.)	Displacement cc (cu. in.)	Drive Type
20, 20D	34.92 (1.375)	31.75 (1.25)	30.48 (1.86)	Direct

MAINTENANCE

SPARK PLUG. Recommended spark plug is Champion CJ8. Spark plug electrode gap should be 0.025 inch (0.63 mm).

CARBURETOR. Models 20 and 20D are equipped with a Tillotson Model HU diaphragm carburetor. Refer to Tillotson section of CARBURETOR SERVICE for exploded view and service of carburetor.

Initial adjustment of idle mixture screw is one turn open. Carburetor has a fixed main fuel jet so high speed fuel mixture is not adjustable. Adjust idle mixture screw so engine will accelerate without hesitation. Adjust idle speed screw so engine idles just below clutch engagement speed.

MAGNETO AND TIMING. A flywheel magneto is used on all models. The ignition coil is located adjacent to the flywheel while the breaker-points are located on the right crankcase half.

Breaker-point gap should be 0.020-0.022 inch (0.51-0.56 mm) for new points and 0.017 inch (0.43 mm) for used points. Ignition timing is not adjustable and breaker-point gap must be set correctly or ignition timing will be affected. Air gap between coil legs and flywheel should be 0.010 inch (0.25 mm).

LUBRICATION. The engine is lubricated by mixing oil with the fuel. Recommended oil is Beaird-Poulan engine oil available in blends approved for 16:1 and 32:1 fuel mixture ratios. Follow manufacturers mixing instructions on oil container when using a recommended oil. If Beaird-Poulan engine oil is not available, a good quality oil designed for use in air-cooled two-stroke engines may be used when mixed at a 16:1 ratio. Use a separate container when mixing fuel and oil. Regular gasoline is recommended.

Both models are equipped with manual and automatic chain oil pumps. The manual oil pump is operated by pushing plunger (18–Fig. PN10). The automatic oil pump is operated by crankcase pulsations through impulse line (10). Check valve (11) in end of impulse line (10) prevents entrance of oil into crankcase. Check valve must be located in slot just forward of filler hole in upper part of oil tank to prevent immersion of check valve in oil. Automatic oil pump (14) is available only as a unit assembly.

REPAIRS

CYLINDER, PISTON PIN AND RINGS. Cylinder can be removed after detaching fan housing, flywheel, carburetor, front handle, chain bar and muffler. Care must be used when handling piston and rod assembly to prevent rod from slipping off bearing rollers (12–Fig. PN11) as rollers may fall into crankcase.

Cylinder has a chrome plated bore which should be inspected for flaking, scoring or other damage. Be sure piston is properly supported when removing piston pin to prevent damage to connecting rod. Piston pin rides directly in connecting rod. Check fit by inserting piston pin in small end of connecting rod and renew pin and rod if excessively worn. Tighten cylinder base nuts evenly to 100-110 in.-lbs. (11.3-12.4 N·m).

Fig. PN10—Exploded view of right crankcase half.

1. Right crankcase half
2. Ignition breaker-points
3. Seal
4. Breaker-point cover
5. Spacer
6. Clutch drum
7. Bushing
8. Washer
9. Clutch assy.
10. Impulse line
11. Check valve
12. Gasket
13. "O" ring
14. Automatic oil pump
15. Filter
16. Gasket
17. Cover
18. Manual oil pump plunger
19. Spring
20. Washer
21. "O" rings

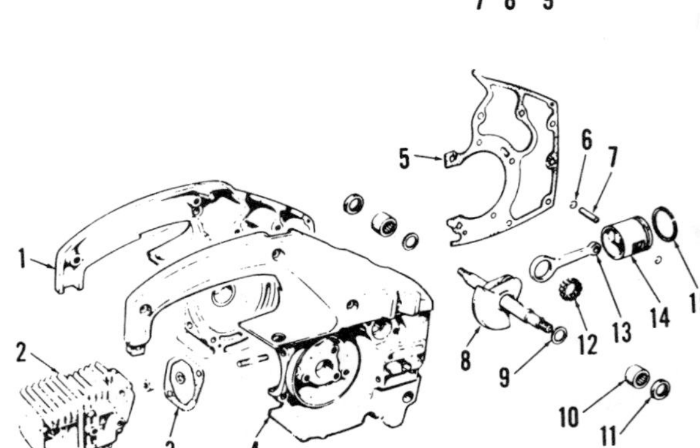

Fig. PN11—Exploded view of engine.

1. Left crankcase half
2. Cylinder
3. Gasket
4. Right crankcase half
5. Gasket
6. Pin retainer
7. Piston pin
8. Crankshaft
9. Washer
10. Needle roller bearing
11. Seal
12. Bearing rollers (12)
13. Connecting rod
14. Piston
15. Piston ring

CONNECTING ROD, CRANKSHAFT AND CRANKCASE. Connecting rod is one-piece and rides on 12 loose bearing rollers (12–Fig. PN11). Be careful not to lose any loose bearing rollers during disassembly. Bearing rollers can be removed after rod is slid off rollers. Bearing rollers may be held in place with petroleum jelly or heavy grease when installing connecting rod.

The crankshaft is supported by a needle roller bearing at each end. Install bearings so end of bearing is 0.6225-0.6265 inch (15.811-15.913 mm) from machined gasket surface. Washers (9–Fig. PN11) must be installed with beveled edge nearest crankpin. Ignition coil-to-breaker point wire must be routed through crankcase halves and trigger assembly installed before crankcase halves are mated. Be sure crankcase impulse line and fuel pickup lines are properly located and not pinched. Be sure a fiber washer (2–Fig. PN12) is installed on long crankcase screw. Absence of washer will result in oil leakage. Tighten crankcase screws to 30-35 in.-lbs. (3.4-3.9 N•m).

CLUTCH. Clutch hub has left-hand threads. Clutch hub, shoes and spring are available only as a unit assembly. Clutch drum (6–Fig. PN10) and bushing (7) are available separately.

REWIND STARTER. The rewind starter is located on the left end of the crankshaft. Starter pawls are located on back side of flywheel (3–Fig. PN13). Starter pawls are not available without renewing flywheel. Flywheel and starter pawls must be serviced as a unit assembly. Rope pulley (6) rides on needle roller bearing (5). Care should be used if rewind spring is removed to prevent spring from uncoiling uncontrolled. Install rewind spring (7) into rope pulley so outer end of spring is pointing in a clockwise direction. Wind rope around rope pulley in counterclockwise direction as viewed from flywheel side of pulley. Lubricate rope pulley bearing. Apply tension on rewind spring by turning rope pulley three turns clockwise before passing rope through rope outlet. Be sure spacer (4) is installed or starter pawls will rub against rope pulley. Align dot on flywheel shown in Fig. PN14 with keyway in crankshaft when installing flywheel. This will align key in crankshaft with corresponding slot in flywheel. Tighten flywheel nut to 8-10 ft.-lbs. (0.9-1.1 N•m).

Fig. PN12—Long crankcase screw must be installed with fiber washer (2) to prevent oil leakage.

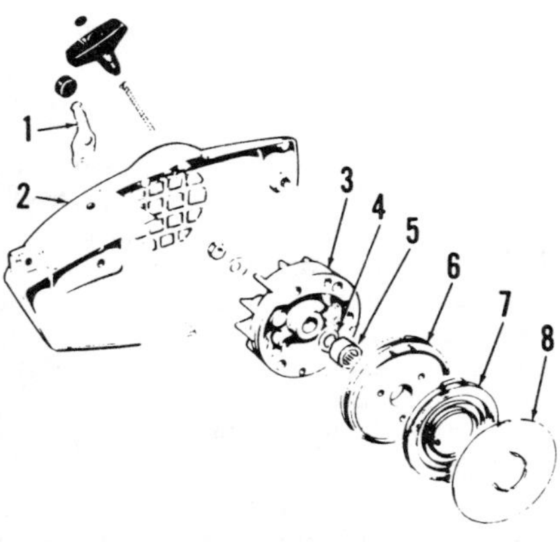

Fig. PN13—Exploded view of rewind starter.

1. Choke plate
2. Left side cover
3. Flywheel
4. Spacer
5. Needle roller bearing
6. Rope pulley
7. Rewind spring
8. Spring plate

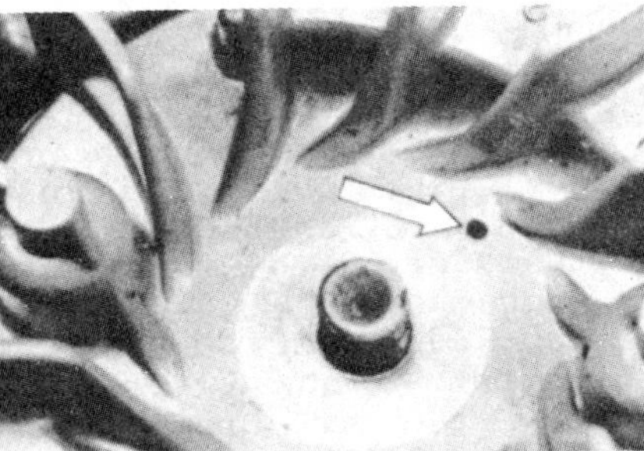

Fig. PN14—Align dot on flywheel with crankshaft keyway to assist in mating key with flywheel slot.

POULAN

Model	Bore mm (in.)	Stroke mm (in.)	Displacement cc (cu. in.)	Drive Type
M25, M25D, MS25D, MS25CVA, MS25PS	34.9 (1.375)	31.7 (1.25)	30.4 (1.8)	Direct
180	34.9 (1.375)	31.7 (1.25)	30.4 (1.8)	Direct
200, 205, 225, 235, 236	...	...	37.7 (2.3)	Direct
2000, 2100	...	...	32.7 (2.0)	Direct
2300, 2300AV, 2300CVA, 2350CVA, 2400	...	...	37.7 (2.3)	Direct

MAINTENANCE

SPARK PLUG. Recommended spark plug is Champion CJ8. Spark plug electrode gap should be 0.025 inch (0.63 mm).

CARBURETOR. All models are equipped with either a Walbro WA or WT diaphragm carburetor. Refer to Walbro section of CARBURETOR SERVICE section for exploded view and service of carburetor.

Initial adjustment of idle and high speed mixture screws is one turn open from a lightly seated position. Adjust idle mixture screw so engine will accelerate without hesitation. Adjust high speed mixture screw to obtain optimum full throttle performance under cutting load. Do not operate saw with high speed mixture setting too lean (needle turned too far clockwise) as engine damage could result from lack of lubrication and overheating. Adjust idle speed screw so engine idles just below clutch engagement speed.

IGNITION. A conventional flywheel magneto ignition system with breaker points located behind the flywheel is used on early models. A breakerless capacitor discharge ignition system is used on later models.

On models with breaker points, flywheel must be removed to service breaker points. Breaker point gap should be 0.014-0.016 inch (0.36-0.41 mm). Ignition timing is not adjustable. Breaker point gap must be set correctly or ignition timing will be affected. Air gap between coil legs and flywheel should be 0.008-0.014 inch (0.20-0.36 mm).

On models with electronic ignition system, ignition components are mounted outside the flywheel making it unnecessary to remove the flywheel for most ignition service. The only adjustment of the unit is the air gap between the ignition module core and flywheel magnets. Air gap should be 0.008-0.014 inch (0.20-0.36 mm). Loosen ignition module mounting screws and move module as necessary to obtain specified air gap.

On all models, flywheel nut should be tightened to 13-15 ft.-lbs. (18-20 N·m).

LUBRICATION. The engine is lubricated by mixing oil with the fuel. Recommended oil is Poulan/Weed Eater Engine Oil, which is available in blends approved for 16:1 and 32:1 fuel mixture ratios. Follow manufacturer's mixing instructions on oil container when using recommended oil. If Poulan/Weed Eater oil is not available, a good quality oil designed for use in air-cooled two-stroke engines may be used when mixed at a 16:1 ratio. The use of automotive type oil is not recommended. Also, the use of gasoline containing alcohol is not recommended. Use a separate container when mixing oil and fuel.

An automatic, nonadjustable oiler provides oil for chain lubrication. Crankcase pulsations pressurize the oil tank to force oil through oil pump body and oil line to oil port on bar pad. Be sure end of oil line does not extend beyond oil port opening or oil flow will be reduced. A check valve, located behind the clutch, allows crankcase pressure to enter oil tank and blocks chain saw oil entry into crankcase.

REPAIRS

CRANKCASE PRESSURE TEST. An improperly sealed crankcase can cause the engine to be hard to start, run rough, have low power and overheat. Refer to ENGINE SERVICE section of this manual for crankcase pressure test procedure. If crankcase leakage is indicated, pressurize crankcase and use a soap and water solution to check gaskets, seals, pulse line and castings for leakage.

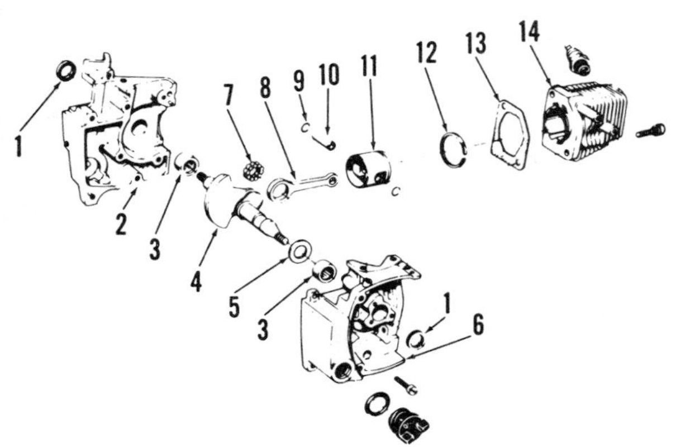

Fig. PN16—Exploded view of engine used on Models M25, M25D, MS25D, MS25CVA, 1800 and early Model 2000.

1. Seals
2. Crankcase half (R.H.)
3. Bearings
4. Crankshaft
5. Thrust washer
6. Crankcase half (L.H.)
7. Bearing rollers (12)
8. Connecting rod
9. Pin retainer
10. Piston pin
11. Piston
12. Piston ring
13. Gasket
14. Cylinder

CYLINDER, PISTON, PIN AND RING. To disassemble, disconnect fuel line from handle fuel fitting. Remove clutch cover, fan housing, fuel tank and handle/carburetor housing. Remove ignition coil and muffler. Remove cylinder mounting screws and slide cylinder off piston. Remove piston pin retainer (9—Figs. PN16 or PN17) from flywheel side of piston, then push pin (10) out of piston and connecting rod. Heat may be applied to piston crown to ease piston pin removal and installation. Be sure piston and connecting rod are properly supported when removing piston pin to avoid bending connecting rod.

Piston pin rides directly in connecting rod on Models M25, M25D, MS25CVA, 1800 and early Model 2000. Check fit by inserting piston pin in small end of connecting rod. Renew piston pin and connecting rod if excessive play is evident. Piston pin on all other models and later Model 2000 rides in 21 loose needle bearings (16—Fig. PN17).

A locating pin is present in piston ring groove to prevent ring rotation. Install piston with locating pin facing flywheel side of crankshaft. On models equipped with needle bearings in connecting rod, use grease to hold needle bearings in place. Apply heat to piston crown and install piston pin from flywheel side of piston until pin bottoms against retaining ring. Be sure closed end of piston pin is toward clutch side of crankshaft. Make certain piston pin retaining rings are seated in piston grooves. Lubricate connecting rod, piston ring and cylinder bore with oil. Apply Loctite 242 to threads of cylinder mounting screws and tighten to 100-110 in.-lbs. (11.3-12.4 N·m) on Models M25, M25D, MS25D, MS25CVA, 1800 and early 2000 (without needle bearing in small end of connecting rod). On all other models, tighten cylinder head screws to 85-95 in.-lbs. (9.6-10.7 N·m).

CONNECTING ROD, CRANKSHAFT AND CRANKCASE. Connecting rod (8—Figs. PN16 or PN17) is one-piece and rides on 12 loose bearing rollers (7). Crankshaft (4) is supported by a needle roller bearing (3) at each end. Crankcase halves must be split for access to crankshaft and connecting rod.

To split crankcase, first remove clutch cover, bar and chain, fan housing, fuel tank and carburetor housing and handle assembly. Remove spark plug and install piston stop tool in spark plug hole or use other suitable means to prevent crankshaft from rotating. Remove clutch assembly and flywheel. Note that clutch hub has left-hand threads (turn clockwise to remove) and flywheel nut has right-hand threads (turn counterclockwise to remove). Remove contact points and points box on models so equipped. Remove cylinder and piston as previously outlined. Remove crankcase screws and separate crankcase halves being careful not to damage crankcase mating surfaces. Remove crankshaft and connecting rod. Drive seals (1) and bearings (3) out of crankcase.

To reassemble, reverse the disassembly procedure while noting the following special instructions: Use Poulan tool 31064 to install bearings (3) in crankcase halves. Seals (1) should be driven in flush with outer face of castings. Apply small amount of grease to connecting rod bearing rollers (7) to hold them in place when installing connecting rod. Apply thin bead of sealant (Poulan number 30054) to mating surfaces of crankcase halves. Apply Loctite 242 to threads of crankcase screws and tighten to 45-50 in.-lbs. (5.1-5.6 N·m). Tighten flywheel nut to 13-15 ft.-lbs. (18-20 N·m).

CLUTCH. Remove clutch cover, bar and chain for access to clutch. Clutch hub (1—Fig. PN18) has left-hand threads (turn clockwise to remove). Clutch hub, shoes and spring are available only as a unit assembly. Clutch drum (3) and needle bearing (4) are available separately.

REWIND STARTER. Refer to Fig. PN19 for exploded view of starter assembly. To disassemble starter, extend rope and hold rope pulley (3) from turning. Pull rope back through starter housing (5) and allow pulley to slowly unwind to relieve tension on rewind spring (4). Remove screw (1) and lift off rope pulley. Use caution if removing rewind spring. Do not allow rewind spring to uncoil uncontrolled.

Rope is wound on pulley in a clockwise direction as viewed from flywheel side of side cover. Lightly lubricate pulley shaft with silicon grease. To apply tension to rewind spring, pull rope out about 12 inches (30 cm) and turn pulley three turns clockwise.

REED VALVE. A single petal reed valve (1—Fig. PN20) is located under the carburetor and attached to the underside of the handle assembly. Maximum gap between tip of reed petal and seating surface is 0.010 inch (0.25 mm). Re-

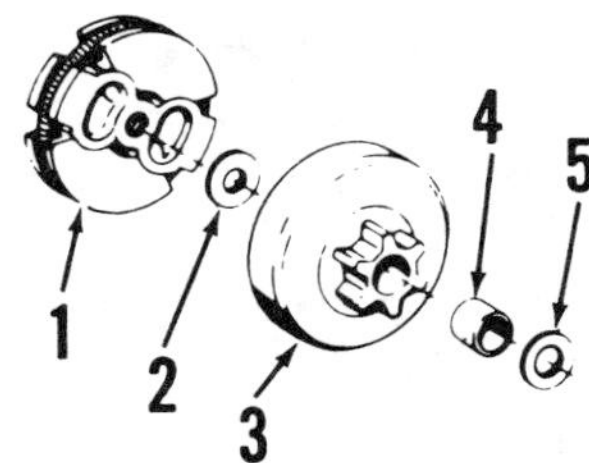

Fig. PN18—Exploded view of clutch. Note hub, shoes and spring are available only as an assembly (1).

1. Hub & shoe assy.
2. Washer
3. Clutch drum
4. Bushing
5. Spacer

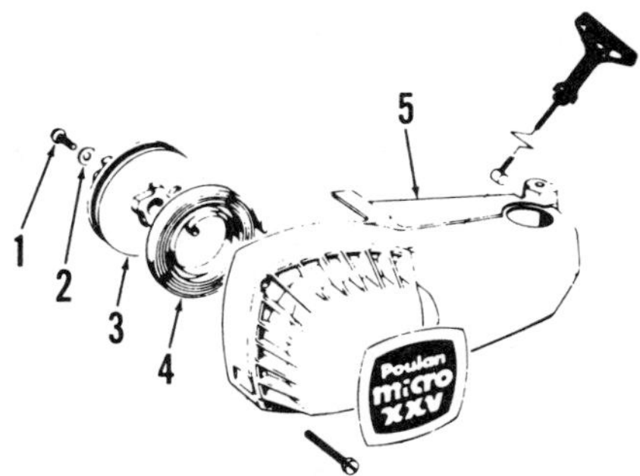

Fig. PN19—Exploded view of rewind starter. Models 2300, 2300AV and 2300CVA are equipped with a fan baffle located between rewind spring (4) and housing (5).

1. Screw
2. Washer
3. Rope pulley
4. Rewind spring
5. Starter/fan housing

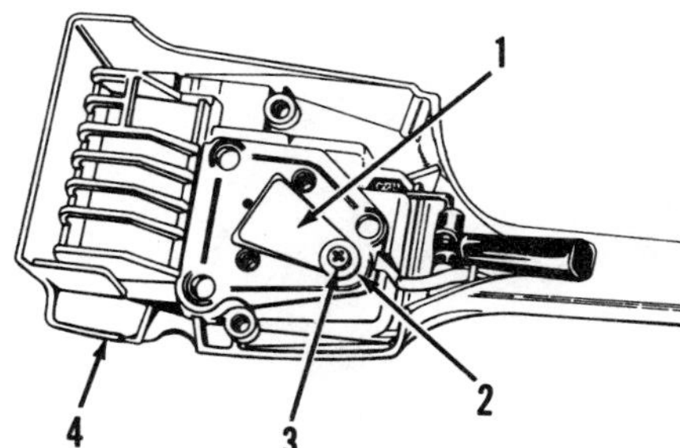

Fig. PN20—Reed valve is mounted on underside of carburetor housing/handle assembly.

1. Reed petal
2. Reed stop washer
3. Screw
4. Carburetor housing/handle assy.

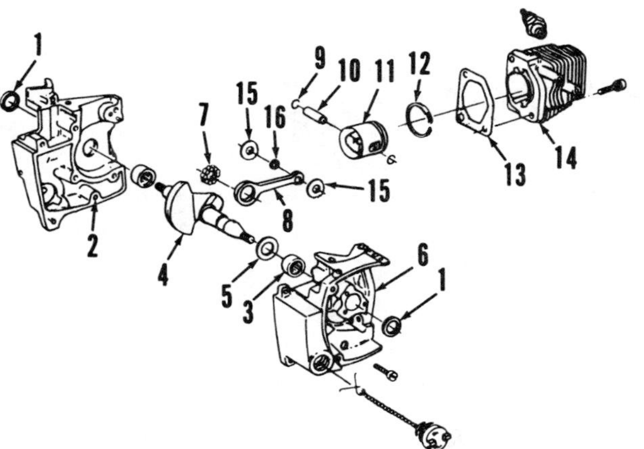

Fig. PN17—Exploded view of engine assembly used on Models 180, 200, 205, 225, 235, 2300, 2300AV, 2300CVA, 2350CVA and late Model 2000.

1. Seals
2. Crankcase half (R.H.)
3. Bearings
4. Crankshaft
5. Thrust washer
6. Crankcase half (L.H.)
7. Bearing rollers (12)
8. Connecting rod
9. Pin retainer
10. Piston pin
11. Piston
12. Piston ring
13. Gasket
14. Cylinder
15. Washers
16. Needle roller bearing

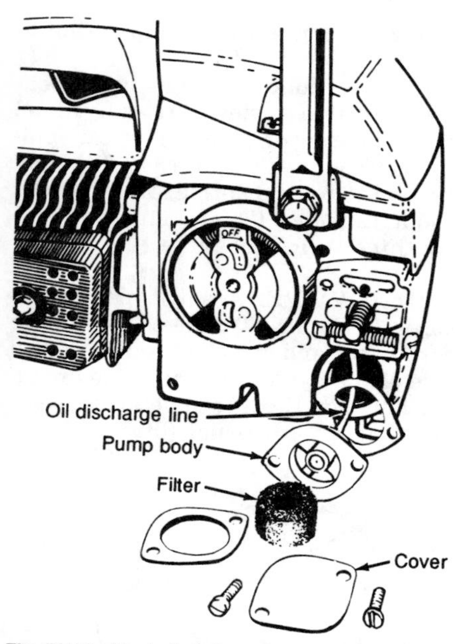

Fig. PN21—Exploded view of automatic oil pump assembly. Oil system check valve is located in crankcase behind the clutch. Oil pump is actuated by pressure pulses from crankcase.

new reed if bent, broken or otherwise damaged. Inspect reed petal seat and renew carburetor housing/handle assembly if seat is damaged or warped. Washer (2) under reed retaining screw (3) serves as a reed stop and should be installed with sharp side against reed petal. Tighten reed petal screw to 8-10 in.-lbs. (0.9-1.1 N·m).

AUTOMATIC OIL PUMP. The chain oil tank is pressurized by pulses from the crankcase through a check valve. Automatic oil system is not adjustable. Oil pump components (Fig. PN21) may be serviced after removing clutch cover, bar and chain. Clutch assembly must be removed for access to check valve.

To renew oil discharge line without separating crankcase halves, cut a piece of plastic tubing (part number 8133) 6 inches (15 cm) long with a taper cut on one end. Feed a piece of wire through hole on bar pad and out through oil pump hole. Attach end of wire (1—Fig. PN22) to tapered end of tubing (2), then pull wire and tubing back through oil pump hole and out bar pad hole (3). Remove the wire and cut tapered end of tubing square, then pull tubing back through hole in bar pad until end of tubing is flush with outer surface of casting. Make certain end of tubing does not extend outside casting, otherwise oil discharge hole could be blocked. Attach oil pump body to other end of tubing and install oil pump assembly making sure open side of pump body faces downward.

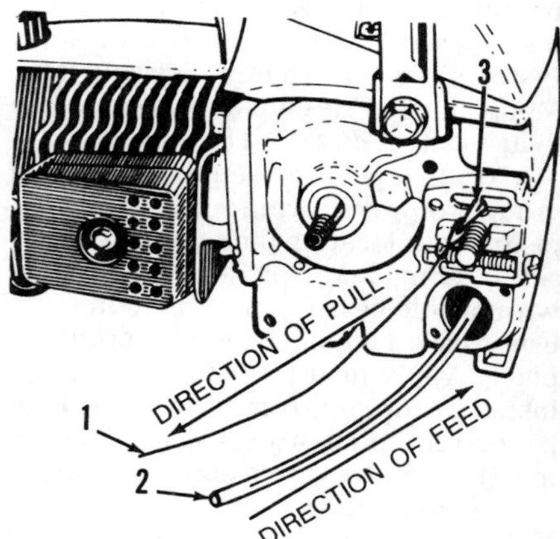

Fig. PN22—Oil discharge tube (2) can be renewed without splitting crankcase halves. Refer to text for details.

POULAN

Model	Bore mm (in.)	Stroke mm (in.)	Displacement cc (cu. in.)	Drive Type
245A, SA	50.92 (2.005)	36.5 (1.437)	73.7 (4.5)	Direct
252A	50.92 (2.005)	36.5 (1.437)	73.7 (4.5)	Gear
306, 306A, 306SA	45.41 (1.788)	36.5 (1.437)	59 (3.6)	Direct
361	45.41 (1.788)	36.5 (1.437)	59 (3.6)	Direct

MAINTENANCE

SPARK PLUG. Recommended spark plug for all models is Poulan spark plug 3014 or Champion CJ8. Spark plug electrode gap should be 0.025 inch (0.63 mm).

CARBURETOR. All models are equipped with a Tillotson Model HS diaphragm carburetor. Initial idle and high speed mixture settings are one turn open. Adjust idle speed screw so engine idles at engine speed just below clutch engagement speed. Adjust idle mixture screw so engine will accelerate without hesitation. Adjust high speed mixture screw to give optimum performance under cutting load. It may be necessary to readjust idle mixture screw after adjusting high speed screw. Be sure mixture settings are not too lean as engine damage may result.

Refer to Tillotson section of CARBURETOR SERVICE section for carburetor operation and overhaul.

IGNITION. A conventional flywheel magneto ignition system (Fig. PN30) with breaker points located behind the flywheel is used on all models except later production 245A, 245S, 306A and 306SA models, which are equipped with a breakerless capacitor discharge ignition system.

On breaker-point models, breaker point gap should be 0.015 inch (0.38 mm) on Model 361 and 0.017 inch (0.43 mm) on all other models. Magneto air gap should be 0.012 inch (0.30 mm) and may be adjusted by loosening coil mounting screws.

On breakerless models, ignition components are mounted outside the flywheel making it unnecessary to remove the flywheel for most ignition service. The only adjustment of the unit is the air gap between the ignition module core and the flywheel magnets. Air gap should be 0.008-0.014 inch (0.20-0.35 mm).

Fig. PN30—View of Model 361 magneto.

1. Flywheel
2. Breaker points
3. Condenser
4. Stator
5. Ignition coil

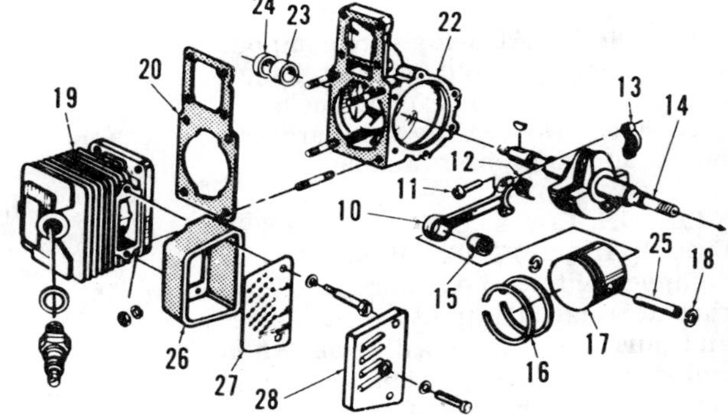

Fig. PN31—Exploded view of engine used on Model 361. Refer also to Fig. PN33. Refer to Fig. PN32 for parts identification except: 26. Muffler, 27. Muffler baffle and 28. Cover.

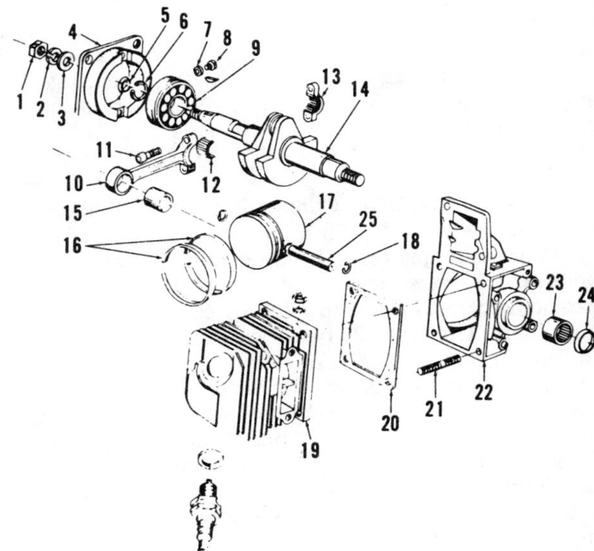

Fig. PN32—Exploded view of engine used on Models 245A, 245SA, 252A, 306, 306A and 306SA. Carrier (4) is a partial view showing rear of side cover (15—Fig. PN38).

1. Nut
2. Lockwasher
3. Washer
4. Bearing carrier
5. Seal
6. Snap ring
7. Washer
8. Cap screw
9. Bearing
10. Connecting rod
11. Socket head screw
12. Bearing rollers
13. Rod cap
14. Crankshaft
15. Bearing
16. Piston rings
17. Piston
18. Snap ring
19. Cylinder
20. Gasket
21. Stud
22. Crankcase
23. Bearing
24. Seal
25. Piston pin

LUBRICATION. All engines are lubricated by mixing oil with fuel. Recommended oil is Poulan/Weed Eater engine oil available in blends approved for 16:1 and 32:1 fuel ratios. Follow manufacturer's mixing instructions on oil container when using a recommended oil. If Poulan/Weed Eater engine oil is not available, a good quality oil designed for use in air-cooled two-stroke engines may be used when mixed at a 16:1 ratio. Use a separate container when mixing oil and fuel.

All models are equipped with a manual chain oiler. All models except 306 and 361 are equipped with an automatic chain oiler. Fill oiler reservoir with a good quality SAE 30 oil if ambient temperature is above 40°F (4.4°C) or SAE 10 if temperature is 40°F (4.4°C) or below.

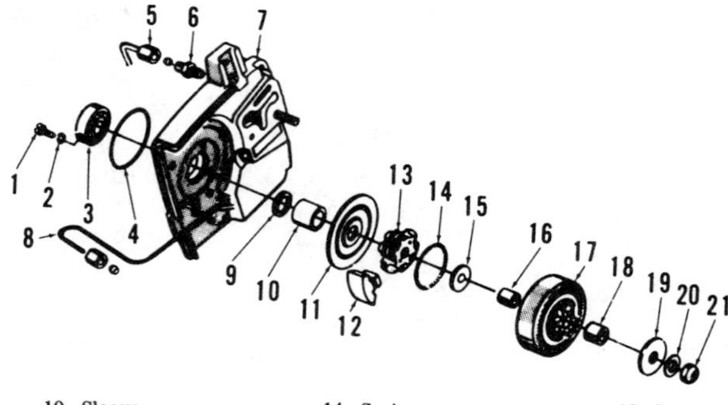

Fig. PN33—Exploded view of clutch and bearing housing carrier used on Model 361.

1. Cap screw
2. Washer
3. Bearing
4. "O" ring
5. Oil line
6. Oil fitting
7. Bearing housing carrier
8. Oil line
9. Seal
10. Sleeve
11. Clutch cover
12. Clutch shoe
13. Clutch hub
14. Spring
15. Thrust washer
16. Bearing race
17. Clutch drum
18. Bearing
19. Washer
20. Washer
21. Nut

Fig. PN34—Exploded view of Models 245A, 245SA, 306A and 306SA manual and automatic oil pump and clutch assemblies.

1. Plunger
2. Plunger rod
3. Spring
4. Manual oil pump housing
5. Intake valve
6. Spring
7. Oil pump button
8. Oil tank
9. Gasket
10. Gasket
11. Oil outlet valve
12. Washer
13. Spring
14. Piston
15. Lever
16. Quad ring
17. Disc
18. Cam
19. Gear
20. Auto. oil pump cover
21. Seal
22. Thrust washer
23. Bearing
24. Bearing race
25. Clutch drum
26. Clutch shoe
27. Thrust washer
28. Clutch hub
29. Clutch spring
30. Retaining ring
31. Spirolox

CARBON. Carbon deposits should be removed from muffler and exhaust ports at regular intervals. When scraping carbon, be careful not to damage engine cylinder or piston. Do not allow loosened carbon to enter cylinder.

REPAIRS

CYLINDER. All models are equipped with a chrome plated cylinder. Renew cylinder if cylinder is scored, cracked or excessively worn. Only standard size piston and rings are available.

PISTON, PIN AND RINGS. Refer to Figs. PN31 and PN32. All models are equipped with two piston rings. Piston rings are retained by pins in ring grooves and must be aligned with pins when cylinder is installed. Install piston so ring locating pins are on magneto side of engine. Piston wrist pin has one closed end, which must be toward exhaust port. Heat piston to approximately 200°F (93.4°C) to aid in pin installation. Piston pin snap rings should be installed so sharp edge is out.

Pistons and rings are available in standard size only. Manufacturer does not specify piston or piston ring clearances.

CONNECTING ROD. Connecting rod may be removed after removing cylinder and piston. Unscrew connecting rod screws and remove rod and cap being careful not to lose loose bearing rollers. There are 25 bearing rollers in connecting rod on Model 361. All other models are equipped with 28 bearing rollers. Connecting rod small end bearing must be pressed out of rod. Be sure rod is properly supported when removing or installing bearing.

Use heavy grease to hold roller bearings in rod and cap. Match marks on sides of rod and cap must be aligned during installation.

CRANKSHAFT AND CRANKCASE. Crankshaft is supported in antifriction bearings at both ends. Flywheel end of crankshaft on Model 361 is supported by needle roller bearing (23—Fig. PN31) in the crankcase and ball bearing (9—Fig. PN32) contained in side cover (4) is used to support flywheel end of crankshaft on all other models. Clutch end of crankshaft on Model 361 is supported by ball bearing (3—Fig. PN33) in bearing carrier (7) and needle roller bearing (23—Fig. PN32) in crankcase (22) supports clutch end of crankshaft on all other models.

Fuel, oil, ignition, starter and clutch assemblies must be removed from engine to remove crankshaft. Remove cylinder, piston and connecting rod. On all models except 361, remove bearing carrier (4—Fig. PN32), bearing (9) and crankshaft (14) from crankcase. Unscrew retaining cap screws (8) and separate bearing (9) and crankshaft from bearing carrier (4). Remove snap ring (6) and pull bearing (9) off crankshaft. To remove crankshaft from Model 361, unscrew bearing carrier (7—Fig. PN33) screws and remove bearing carrier and crankshaft from crankcase. Remove crankshaft from bearing (3). Unscrew two retaining screws (1) and separate bearing from carrier (7). To reassemble, reverse disassembly procedure. Install ball bearing with groove in outer race adjacent to crankshaft counterweight. Bearing carrier (4—Fig. PN32) and bearing carrier (7—Fig. PN33) must be heated to 200°F (93.4°C) before installing bearing.

CLUTCH. Clutch hub is equipped with left-hand threads. Clutch hub bearing is available for all models. Refer to Figs. PN33, PN34 or PN35 for exploded view of clutch.

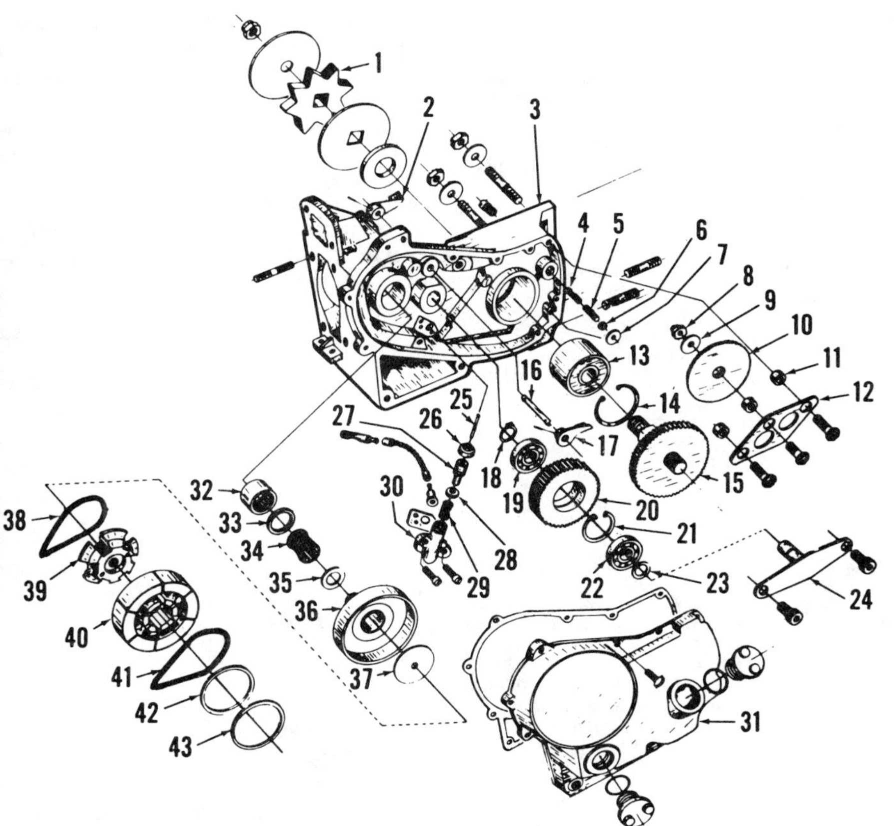

Fig. PN35—Exploded view of Model 252A gear transmission.

1. Sprocket
2. Manual oil pump lever
3. Crankcase
4. Spring
5. Auto. oil pump piston
6. Quad ring
7. Washer
8. Nut
9. Washer
10. Auto. oil pump cam & gear
11. Spacer
12. Plate
13. Bearing
14. Snap ring
15. Chain drive gear
16. Shaft
17. Manual oil pump lever
18. Snap ring
19. Bearing
20. Idler gear
21. Snap ring
22. Bearing
23. Spacer
24. Idler gear plate
25. Plunger rod
26. Cap
27. Plunger
28. Quad ring
29. Spring
30. Manual oil pump housing
31. Cover
32. Bearing
33. Seal
34. Clutch bearing
35. Thrust washer
36. Clutch drum
37. Thrust washer
38. Spring
39. Clutch hub
40. Clutch shoe
41. Spring
42. Retaining ring
43. Spirolox

TRANSMISSION. Gear transmission on Model 252A may be disassembled after removing gearcase cover. Remove clutch assembly and disassemble transmission. Note that bearings (19 and 22—Fig. PN35) are separated by a snap ring (21) and cannot be driven out of idler gear (20) simultaneously. Automatic oil pump drive gear must be adjusted to mesh with chain drive gear (15). Pump drive gear plate (12) has an adjusting slot to adjust gear mesh so gears turn freely without binding.

REED VALVE. All models are equipped with reed valve induction (Fig. PN36) with four reed petals on a pyramid reed block. Inspect reed block (3) for nicks, chips or burrs. Be sure reed petal (4) lays flat against seat.

AUTOMATIC CHAIN OIL PUMP. The following models are equipped with an automatic oil pump: 245A, 245SA, 252A, 306A and 306SA.

Oil pump on Model 252A is driven by a cam on gear (10—Fig. PN35). Pump drive gear plate (12) has an adjusting slot to adjust gear mesh so pump gear and chain drive gear will turn freely.

Oil pump on remainder of automatic chain oiler models is driven by cam (18—Fig. PN34) on engine crankshaft. Inspect bronze gear (19) and renew if gear teeth are broken or excessively worn. If button on lever (15) is worn, renew lever. Pack oil pump cavity with a suitable grease before reassembly. Install seal (21) in cover and carefully install cam (18) in seal with step of cam toward seal until seal seats against shoulder of cam. Be careful not to damage seal. Install pump lever (15) in cover and gear (19) on cam (18). Place disc (17) in housing and install washer (12), spring (13), piston (14) and quad ring (16). Install cover (20) and pump components in cover on crankshaft.

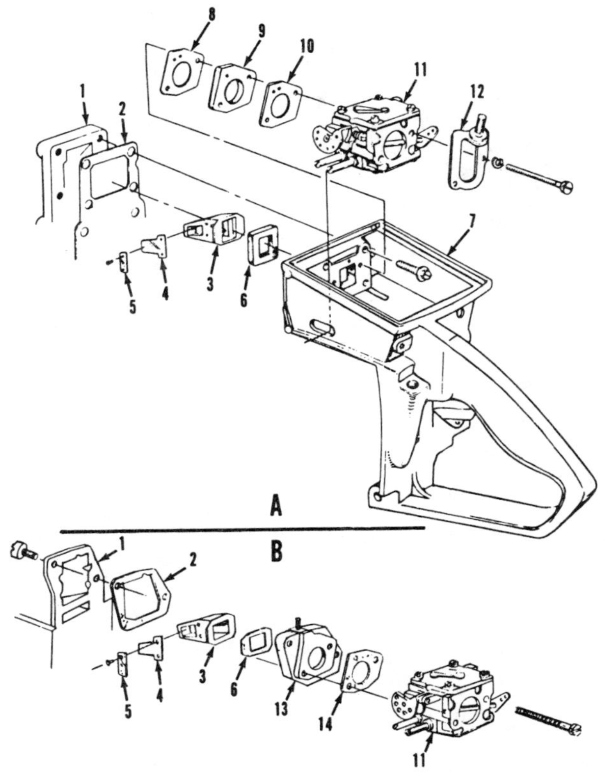

Fig. PN36—View "A" identifies location of reed valve components on Model 361 and view "B" identifies location of reed valve components on all other models.

1. Crankcase
2. Gasket
3. Reed block
4. Petal
5. Stopper
6. Gasket
7. Rear handle assy.
8. Gasket
9. Spacer
10. Gasket
11. Carburetor
12. Bracket
13. Adapter
14. Gasket

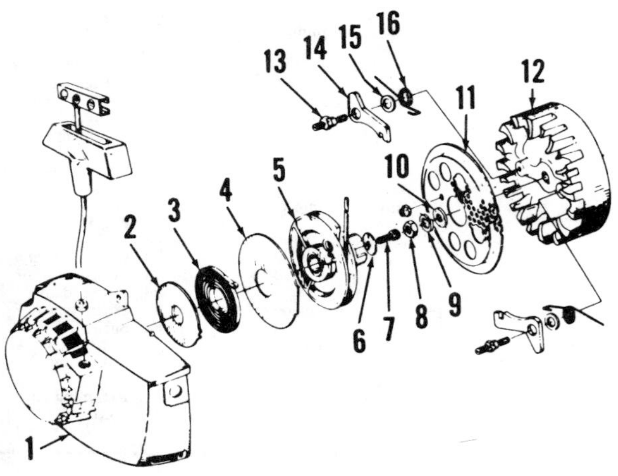

Fig. PN37—Exploded view of rewind starter used on Model 361.

1. Starter housing
2. Spring plate
3. Rewind spring
4. Spring cover
5. Rope pulley
6. Washer
7. Screw
8. Flywheel nut
9. Lockwasher
10. Washer
11. Flywheel cover
12. Flywheel
13. Stud
14. Starter pawl
15. Washer
16. Spring

REWIND STARTER. Refer to Figs. PN37 and PN38 for exploded views of rewind starters. Rewind spring should be wound in clockwise direction when viewed installed in housing. Starter rope should be wound on rope pulley in clockwise direction when viewed installed in starter housing. Turn rope pulley sufficient turns to place tension on rewind spring before passing rope through outlet so rope will rewind into housing.

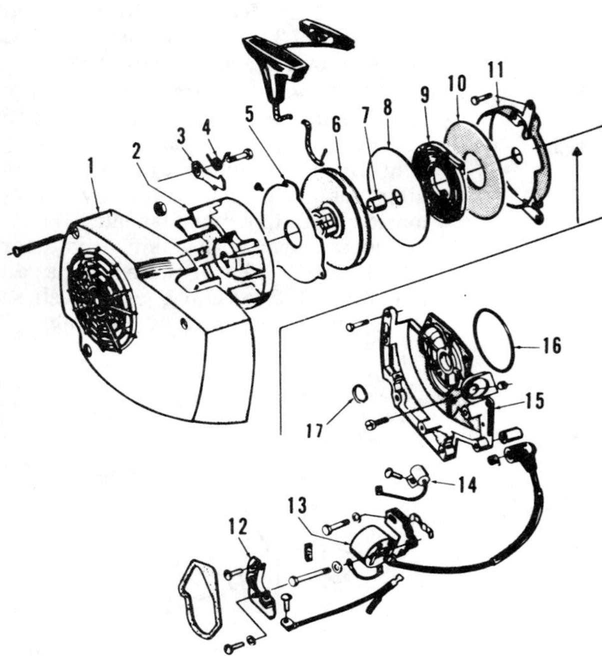

Fig. PN38—Exploded view of rewind starter and ignition assembly used on all models except Model 361. Later 245A, 245SA, 306A and 306SA models have breakerless ignition.

1. Fan housing
2. Flywheel
3. Starter pawl
4. Spring
5. Plate
6. Rope pulley
7. Bearing
8. Spring plate
9. Rewind spring
10. Spring plate
11. Starter housing
12. Breaker points
13. Coil & armature
14. Condenser
15. Side cover
16. "O" ring
17. Seal

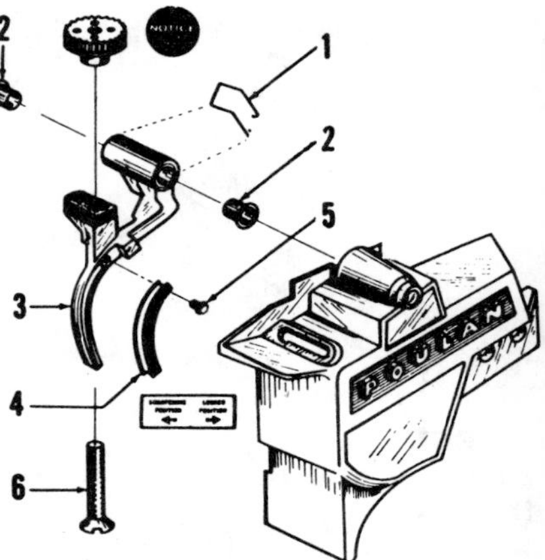

Fig. PN39—Exploded view of chain sharpener offered on some models.

1. Spring
2. Nylon bearing
3. Arm
4. Sharpening stone
5. Lock screw
6. Adjusting screw

POULAN

Models	Bore	Stroke	Displ.	Drive Type
4200, 4400, 6900	1.845 in. (46.86 mm)	1.5626 in. (39.69 mm)	4.2 cu. in. (68.8 cc)	Direct
4900, 7700	1.957 in. (49.70 mm)	1.5626 in. (39.69 mm)	4.7 cu. in. (77.0 cc)	Direct
5200, 5400, 8500	2.066 in. (52.48 mm)	1.5626 in. (39.69 mm)	5.2 cu. in. (85.2 cc)	Direct

MAINTENANCE

SPARK PLUG. Recommended spark plug for Models 6900, 7700 and 8500 is Champion CJ6. Recommended spark plug for all other models is Champion CJ8. Spark plug electrode gap should be 0.025 inch (0.63 mm).

CARBURETOR. Listed models are equipped with a Tillotson Model HS diaphragm carburetor. Refer to CARBURETOR SERVICE section for exploded view and service of carburetor.

Initial adjustment of idle and high speed mixture screws is one turn open. Make final adjustments with engine warm and running. Adjust idle mixture screw so engine will accelerate without stumbling. Adjust high speed mixture screw to obtain optimum performance with engine under cutting load. High speed mixture screw should not be adjusted less than 7/8 turn open to prevent engine from running too lean, as engine damage could result. Adjust idle speed screw so engine idles just below clutch engagement speed.

IGNITION. All models are equipped with a solid state capacitor discharge ignition system. Ignition timing is not adjustable. Air gap between ignition module (IM—Fig. PN50) and flywheel should be 0.012-0.015 inch (0.30-0.38 mm). Loosen module mounting screws and move module to obtain desired air gap.

If ignition is malfunctioning, use the following procedure to locate faulty component: Check spark plug. Disconnect ignition switch wire and check ignition switch operation. Be sure ground strap (G—Fig. PN51) between handle and right crankcase half is properly connected. If engine does not stop when ignition switch is in "OFF" position, but ignition switch operates properly, check for short to ground in module to ignition switch lead. To check the ignition module, disconnect transformer lead from module and replace it with a lead from a continuity test light. Connect remaining lead of test light to a cylinder fin. Note if test light is on, reverse test light leads and again note if test light is on. A dim light should appear with test light leads connected one way but not when the leads are reversed. If a dim light is not present with either connection, renew the module. Repeat the test light connection that resulted in a dim light from the test light and carefully install the starter housing. Be sure leads do not contact housing (test light will glow brightly if leads contact housing). Pull starter rope. Test light should flash brightly on and off, if not, renew module. If module operation is satisfactory, inspect wire between module and transformer. The ignition coil may be checked using a suitable coil tester.

LUBRICATION. The engine is lubricated by mixing oil with the fuel. Recommended oil is Beaird-Poulan engine oil available in blends approved for 16:1 and 32:1 fuel ratios. Follow manufacturer's mixing instructions on oil container when using a recommended oil. If Beaird-Poulan engine oil is not available, a good quality oil designed for use in air-cooled two-stroke engines may be used when mixed at a 16:1 ratio.

Fig. PN51—Ground strap (G) must be connected as shown for proper operation of ignition system.

Fig. PN50—View of ignition module (IM) and transformer (T).

Fig. PN52—View showing location of oil pump adjusting screw (S).

Use a separate container when mixing oil and fuel.

All models are equipped with an automatic chain oil pump. Oil output is adjusted by turning screw (S—Fig. PN52). Turn screw counterclockwise to increase oil output. Use clean automotive oil only for chain oil. SAE 30 oil is recommended for warm weather operation while SAE 10 is recommended for cold weather operation.

REPAIRS

CYLINDER, PISTON, PIN AND RINGS. All models are equipped with a cylinder which has a chrome plated bore. Inspect cylinder bore for excessive wear or damage to chrome surface. The piston is equipped with two piston rings. Piston and rings are available in standard size only. Piston ring grooves have a locating pin in each groove to prevent piston ring rotation. Be sure ring end gap is properly aligned with locating pin when installing cylinder.

The connecting rod is aligned by two thrust washers (10—Fig. PN53) which are each 0.032 inch (0.81 mm) thick. The piston must be installed with "EXH" on piston crown toward exhaust port. See Fig. PN54. Heat may be applied to piston crown to ease removal and installation of piston pin.

CRANKSHAFT, CONNECTING ROD AND CRANKCASE. Crankshaft is supported at both ends by a ball bearing. Crankshaft and connecting rod are a unit assembly and are not available separately. Heat crankcase halves to remove or install main bearings. Tighten crankcase screws to 55-60 in.-lbs. (6.2-6.8 N·m).

CLUTCH. All models are equipped with the three shoe clutch shown in Fig. PN55. Clutch hub (19) has left-hand threads. Inspect clutch shoes and drum for excessive wear or damage due to excessive slippage. Inspect bearing (16) inner race (15) and clutch drum for wear and damage.

AUTOMATIC OIL PUMP. Refer to Fig. PN55 for an exploded view of automatic chain oil pump. Oil pump may be disassembled after removing roll pin (11). Manufacturer recommends renewing both gears if either gear requires renewal. Note that worm gear (2) is driven by crankshaft only if clutch hub is sufficiently tight to hold worm gear against shoulder on crankshaft.

REED VALVE. All models are equipped with a reed valve induction system. Reed valve is accessible after removing carburetor. Check gap between end of each reed valve petal and petal seat. If gap exceeds 0.010 inch (0.25 mm), renew reed petal. Renew any petal which is cracked, bent, rusted or will not seal against seat.

REWIND STARTER. Refer to Fig. PN56 for an exploded view of rewind starter. To disassemble starter, remove rope handle and allow rope to wind into starter. Unscrew socket head screw (7) and remove rope pulley (9) being careful not to dislodge rewind spring (11). Care should be used if rewind spring is removed to prevent spring from uncoiling uncontrolled. Install rewind spring in starter housing with spring coils in a clockwise direction from outer end. Rope length should be 45 inches (114 cm). Wind rope around rope pulley in clockwise direction as viewed with pulley in starter housing. Place tension on rewind spring by turn-

Fig. PN54—Piston must be installed with arrow and "EXH" toward exhaust port.

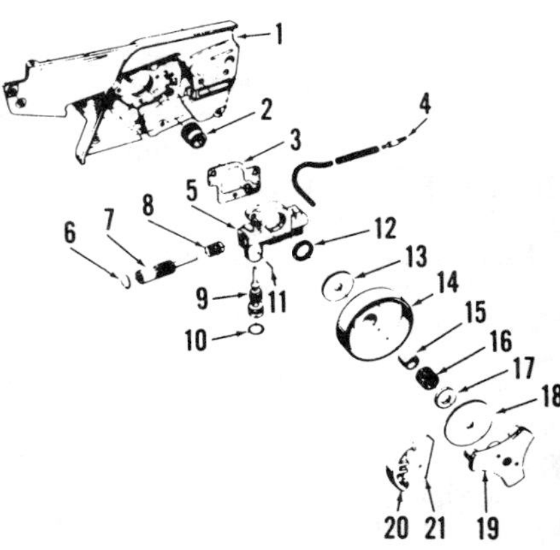

Fig. PN55—Exploded view of oil pump and clutch assemblies.

1. Right crankcase half
2. Oil pump worm gear
3. Gasket
4. Oil pickup
5. Oil pump housing
6. Plug
7. Plunger
8. Spring
9. Adjuster
10. "O ring
11. Pin
12. Seal
13. Washer
14. Clutch drum
15. Inner race
16. Bearing
17. Washer
18. Washer
19. Clutch hub
20. Clutch shoe
21. Spring

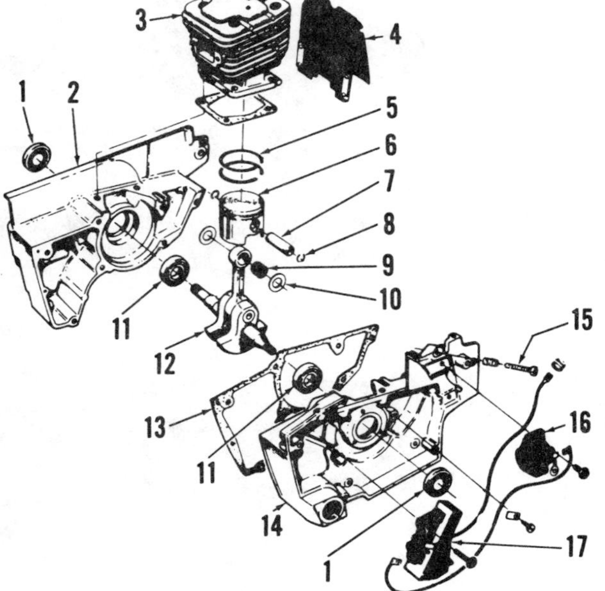

Fig. PN53—Exploded view of engine and ignition components.

1. Oil seal
2. Right crankcase half
3. Cylinder
4. Air baffle
5. Piston rings
6. Piston
7. Piston pin
8. Piston retainer
9. Roller bearing
10. Thrust washer
11. Bearing
12. Crankshaft & rod assy.
13. Gasket
14. Left crankcase half
15. Idle speed screw
16. Transformer
17. Ignition module

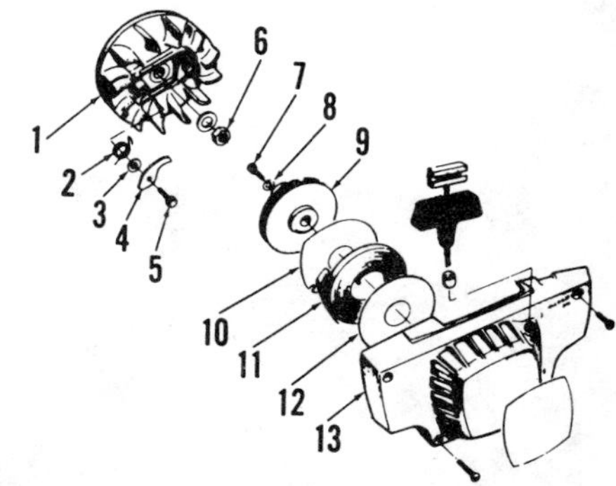

Fig. PN56—Exploded view of rewind starter used on all models.

1. Flywheel
2. Spring
3. Washer
4. Pawl
5. Screw
6. Nut
7. Screw
8. Washer
9. Rope pulley
10. Washer
11. Rewind spring
12. Washer
13. Starter housing

ing rope pulley three turns clockwise before passing rope through rope outlet.

CHAIN BRAKE. Some models are equipped with a chain brake system designed to stop chain movement should kickback occur. Chain brake is activated when operator's hand strikes chain brake lever (1—Fig. PN57) releasing latch (4) allowing spring (6) to draw brake band (9) tight around clutch drum. Pull back chain brake lever to reset mechanism.

Disassembly for repair and component renewal is evident after referral to exploded view and inspection of unit. To adjust brake, rotate screw (14) in ½ turn increments until chain brake engages with minimal effort but will not engage itself from vibration of engine running under cutting load.

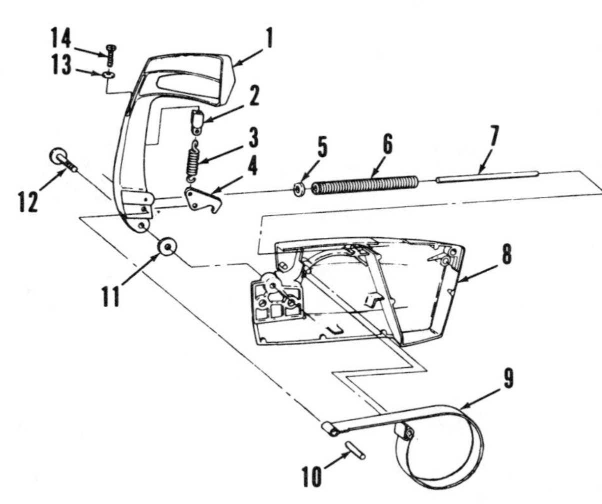

Fig. PN57—Exploded view of chain brake system used on some models.

1. Chain brake lever
2. Anchor
3. Spring
4. Latch
5. Washer
6. Spring
7. Guide rod
8. Chain guard
9. Brake band
10. Pin
11. Washer
12. Screw
13. Washer
14. Adjusting screw

POULAN

Model	Bore mm (in.)	Stroke mm (in.)	Displacement cc (cu. in.)	Drive Type
5500	52 (2.047)	42 (1.654)	89 (5.4)	Direct
6000, S6000	55 (2.165)	42 (1.654)	100 (6.1)	Direct

MAINTENANCE

SPARK PLUG. Recommended spark plug is Champion CJ4. Spark plug electrode gap should be 0.025 inch (0.63 mm).

CARBURETOR. All models are equipped with a Tillotson Model HS diaphragm carburetor. Refer to CARBURETOR SERVICE section for overhaul and exploded view of carburetor.

Initial setting of idle and high speed mixture screws is one turn open. Make final adjustments with engine warm and running. Adjust idle mixture screw so engine will accelerate without stumbling. Adjust high speed mixture screw to obtain optimum engine performance with engine under cutting load. Adjust idle speed screw so engine idles just below clutch engagement speed.

IGNITION. Model 5500 is equipped with a flywheel magneto ignition system while all other models are equipped with a capacitor discharge solid state ignition system. Ignition timing marks are located on fan as shown in Fig. PN60. Fan and flywheel may be separated and should be marked before disassembly so timing marks on fan will correspond with piston position for correct ignition timing. Spark should occur when mark (EL) on fan is aligned with mark shown in Fig. PN60. Ignition timing is adjusted by loosening stator plate mounting screws and moving stator plate. Initial ignition timing setting is provided by aligning crankcase mark with mark on stator. See Fig. PN61. Breaker-point gap is 0.012-0.016 inch (0.30-0.40 mm) on Model 5500. Air gap between coil legs and flywheel on Model 5500 is 0.0010-0.0015 inch (0.020-0.038 mm).

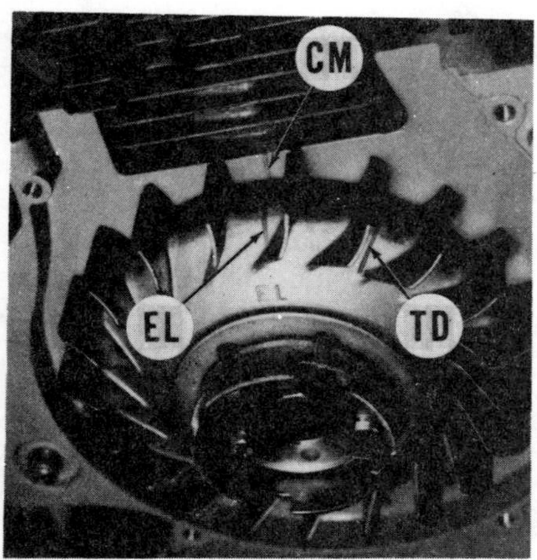

Fig. PN60—View of ignition marks: CM—crankcase mark; EL—flywheel timing mark; TD—top dead center.

LUBRICATION. The engine is lubricated by mixing oil with the fuel. Recommended oil is Beaird-Poulan engine oil available in blends approved for 16:1 and 32:1 fuel ratios. Follow manufacturer's mixing instructions on oil container when using a recommended oil. If Beaird-Poulan engine oil is not available, a good quality oil designed for use in air-cooled two-stroke engines may be used when mixed at a 16:1 ratio. Use a separate container when mixing fuel and oil.

Fig. PN61—Arrow shows alignment of stator plate mark and crankcase mark.

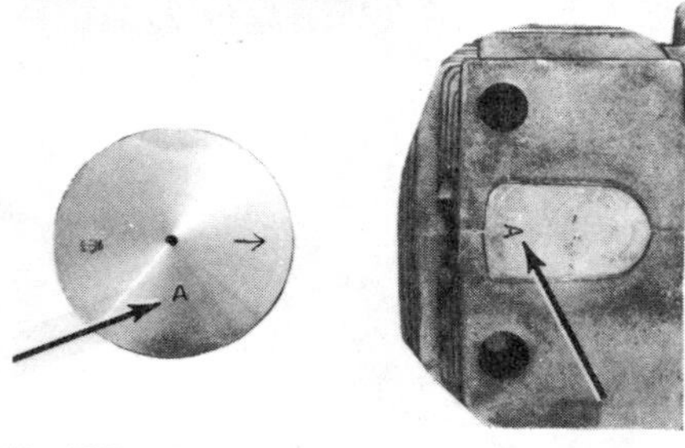

Fig. PN62—View showing location of piston and cylinder grade letters. Note that arrow on piston crown must point toward exhaust port.

All models are equipped with an automatic chain oil pump. Oil pump output is adjusted by turning adjusting screw adjacent to bar spike on Models 5500 and 6000 or adjacent to clutch on Model S6000. Turning screw clockwise will decrease oil output while turning screw counterclockwise will increase oil output.

REPAIRS

PISTON, PIN, RINGS AND CYLINDERS. The cylinder may be removed after removal of airbox cover, air cleaner, carburetor, cylinder shroud and muffler. The cylinder is chrome plated and should be inspected for excessive wear or damage to chrome plating.

Piston pin is retained by wire retainers and rides in a roller bearing in the small end of the connecting rod. The piston is equipped with two piston rings which are retained in position by locating pins in the ring grooves. The piston must be installed with the arrow on the piston crown pointing toward the exhaust port. See Fig. PN62. Some pistons have a letter "A" stamped near the arrow which must not be confused with letter stamped on piston crown to indicate piston size.

Cylinder and piston are marked "A," "B" or "C" during production to obtain desired piston-to-cylinder clearance. Cylinder and piston must have same letter marking to obtain proper clearance. Cylinders are stamped on top of cylinder or on cylinder flange. Pistons are stamped on piston crown but letter indicating piston size should not be confused with letter "A" which is stamped on some piston crowns to indicate which side of piston must be installed adjacent to exhaust port.

CONNECTING ROD, CRANKSHAFT AND CRANKCASE. Crankcase halves must be split on all models to remove crankshaft assembly. The crankshaft is supported at both ends by ball bearings.

Connecting rod and crankshaft are a pressed together assembly which should be disassembled only by a shop with the tools and experience necessary to assemble and realign crankshaft. Connecting rod, bearing and crankpin are available as a unit assembly.

On Models 5500 and 6000, the automatic oil pump is driven by worm (2—Fig. PN64) located between main bearing and oil seal. On these models, worm should be pressed on crankshaft prior to installing crankshaft assembly in crankcase. Heat worm gear to 210°F (99°C) to ease reassembly of worm to crankshaft.

CLUTCH. Four- and six-shoe clutches have been used. The clutch on all models is retained by a nut with left-hand threads. A puller should be used to remove clutch hub from crankshaft. Models 5500 and 6000 are equipped with two springs (15—Fig. PN64) which should be renewed in pairs.

Tighten clutch nut to 22 ft-lbs. (30 N·m) on Models 5500 and 6000 or to 19 ft.-lbs. (26 N·m) on S6000 models.

CHAIN OILER. All models are equipped with an automatic chain oil pump. The oil pump on Model S6000 is contained in a removable oil pump housing (8—Fig. PN65) with plunger (7) driven by worm (3) located outside the right crankcase oil seal. The oil pump on all other models is contained in the right crankcase half. The oil pump plunger (5—Fig. PN64) is driven by worm (2) which is located between main bearing and oil seal (11).

To disassemble oil pump on Models 5500 and 6000, remove chain, bar and clutch. Remove snap ring (8) and unscrew adjusting screw (7). Remove cam screw (CS—Fig. PN66) and withdraw oil pump components. When reassembling, be sure cam screw (CS) is correctly meshed with groove in plunger (5—Fig. PN64).

Worm gear (2—Fig. PN64 or 3—Fig. PN65) may be extracted without removing crankshaft by using a suitable puller. Mark position of worm gear on Models 5500 and 6000 prior to removal. On S6000 models, install seal (14—Fig. PN65) so seal lip will be toward clutch.

REWIND STARTER. Refer to Fig. PN67 for exploded view of rewind starter. To disassemble starter, remove starter housing from saw, remove rope

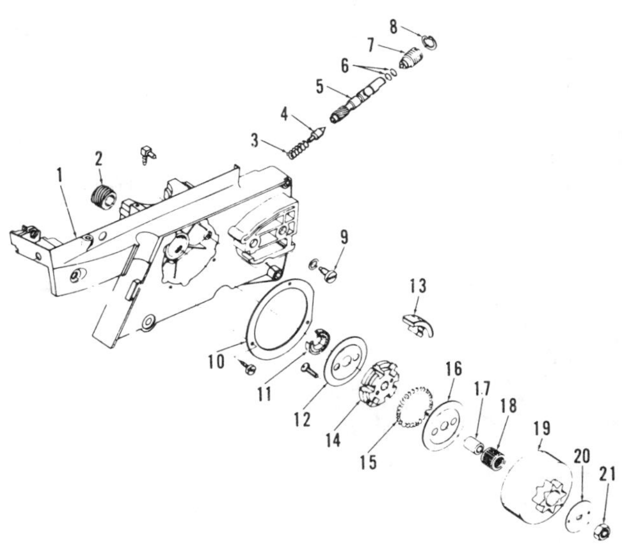

Fig. PN64—Exploded view of Model 5500 and 6000 oil pump and clutch assemblies. Two garter springs (15) are used. Oil pump worm gear (2) is pressed on crankshaft.

1. Right crankcase half
2. Oil pump worm gear
3. Spring
4. Thrust pin
5. Oil pump plunger
6. "O" rings
7. Adjusting screw
8. Snap ring
9. Cam screw
10. Cover plate
11. Seal
12. Guide plate
13. Clutch shoe
14. Clutch hub
15. Garter spring
16. Guide plate
17. Inner bearing race
18. Needle bearing
19. Clutch drum
20. Washer
21. Nut

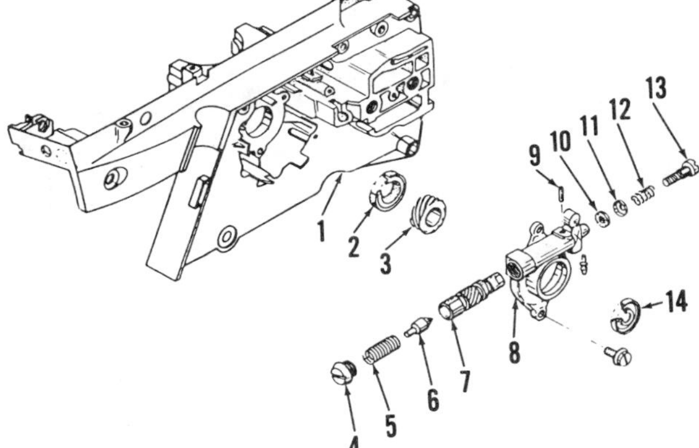

Fig. PN65—Exploded view of oil pump used on S6000 models.

1. Right crankcase half
2. Oil seal
3. Worm
4. Plug
5. Spring
6. Thrust pin
7. Plunger
8. Pump housing
9. Pin
10. Rubber washer
11. Spring seat
12. Spring
13. Adjusting screw
14. Seal

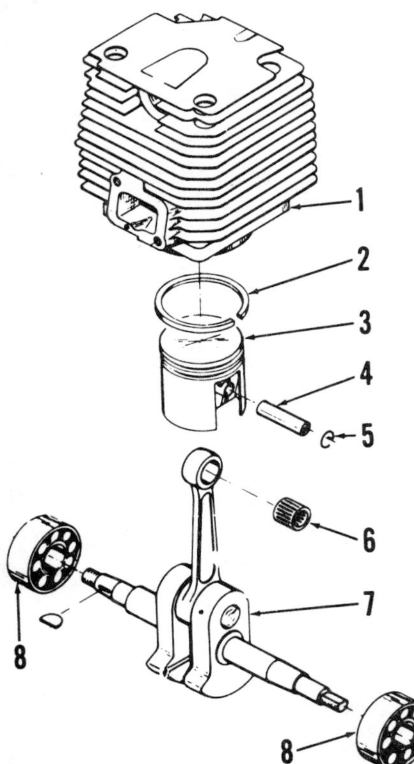

Fig. PN63—Exploded view of engine. Piston is equipped with two piston rings.

1. Cylinder
2. Piston rings
3. Piston
4. Piston pin
5. Pin retainer
6. Needle bearing
7. Crankshaft & rod assy.
8. Ball bearing

Fig. PN66—View showing location of cam screw (CS) which must be unscrewed before oil pump plunger (5—Fig. PN64) can be withdrawn.

handle and allow rope to wind into starter. Remove snap rings and pawl springs (8) and withdraw rope pulley being careful not to dislodge rewind spring. If necessary to remove rewind spring, precautions should be taken to prevent spring from uncoiling uncontrolled.

Install rewind spring in starter housing in clockwise direction from outer end. Wind rope around rope pulley in clockwise direction as viewed with pulley in starter housing. Pawl springs (8) must be positioned against spring spacer (7) as shown in Fig. PN68. To place tension on starter rope, rotate rope pulley clockwise six turns before passing rope through outlet. Check operation of rewind starter. Rope handle should rest snugly against starter housing with rope released. It should be possible to turn rope pulley ¼ turn clockwise with rope fully extended. Readjust spring tension if rope handle is loose against starter housing or rewind spring is coil bound with rope fully extended.

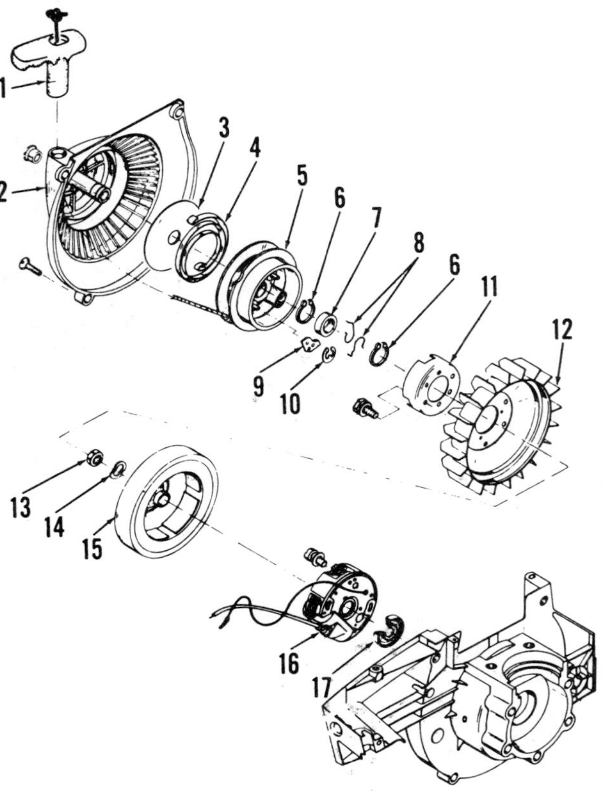

Fig. PN67—Exploded view of rewind starter and ignition assemblies. Refer to Fig. PN68 for installation of pawl springs (8).

1. Rope handle
2. Starter housing
3. Spacer
4. Rewind spring
5. Rope pulley
6. Snap ring
7. Spacer
8. Pawl springs
9. Pawl
10. "E" ring
11. Starter cup
12. Fan
13. Nut
14. Spring washer
15. Flywheel
16. Stator plate
17. Seal

Fig. PN68—View showing installation of spring spacer (7), pawl springs (8) and pawls (9).

POULAN

Model	Bore mm (in.)	Stroke mm (in.)	Displacement cc (cu. in.)	Drive Type
375	...	...	61 (3.7)	Direct
385, 395	...	...	64 (3.9)	Direct
3400	...	...	56 (3.4)	Direct
3700	...	...	61 (3.7)	Direct
3800	...	...	61 (3.7)	Direct
4000	...	...	64 (3.9)	Direct

MAINTENANCE

SPARK PLUG. Recommended spark plug is Champion CJ8Y or RCJ8Y. Spark plug electrode gap should be 0.025 inch (0.63 mm). Tighten spark plug to 18-22 ft.-lbs. (25-30 N·m).

CARBURETOR. All models are equipped with either a Walbro HDB-8 or Zama C1 diaphragm carburetor (17—Fig. PN70). Refer to Walbro or Zama section of CARBURETOR SERVICE section for exploded view and service of carburetor.

Initial adjustment of idle and high-speed mixture needles is one turn open from a lightly seated position. Make final adjustment with engine running at operating temperature. Adjust idle mixture needle so engine will accelerate without hesitation. Adjust high-speed mixture needle to obtain optimum full throttle performance under cutting load. Do not operate saw with high speed mixture setting too lean (needle turned too far clockwise) as engine damage could result from lack of lubrication and overheating. Adjust idle speed screw so engine idles just below clutch engagement speed.

IGNITION. All models are equipped with electronic capacitor discharge ignition system. The only adjustment of the unit is the air gap between the ignition module core (2—Fig. PN71) and flywheel magnets. Air gap should be 0.010-0.014 inch (0.25-0.35 mm). Loosen ignition module mounting screws and move module as necessary to obtain specified air gap.

On all models, flywheel nut should be tightened to 13-15 ft.-lbs. (18-20 N·m).

LUBRICATION. The engine is lubricated by mixing oil with the fuel. Recommended oil is Poulan/Weed Eater Engine Oil, which is available in blends approved for 16:1 and 32:1 fuel mixture ratios. Follow manufacturer's mixing instructions on oil container when using recommended oil. If Poulan/Weed Eater oil is not available, a good quality oil designed for use in air-cooled two-stroke engines may be used when mixed at a 16:1 ratio. The use of automotive type oil is not recommended. Also, the use of gasoline containing alcohol is not recommended. Use a separate container when mixing oil and fuel.

Saw chain is lubricated by oil from the automatic and manual chain oil pump shown in Fig. PN74. Oil pump used on early 3400 models is equipped with an oil output adjustment screw. Adjustment screw is accessible from underside of saw and should be set two turns open from seated position. Later 3400 models and all 375, 3700, 3800 and 4000 models have nonadjustable oil pumps. It is recommended that a good quality chain and bar oil be used. Clean automotive oil may also be used. SAE 30 oil is recommended for warm weather operation while SAE 10 oil is recommended for cold weather operation.

REPAIRS

CRANKCASE PRESSURE TEST. An improperly sealed crankcase can cause the engine to be hard to start, run rough, have low power and overheat. Refer to ENGINE SERVICE section of this manual for crankcase pressure test procedure. If crankcase leakage is indicated, pressurize crankcase and use a soap and water solution to check gaskets, seals, pulse line and castings for leakage.

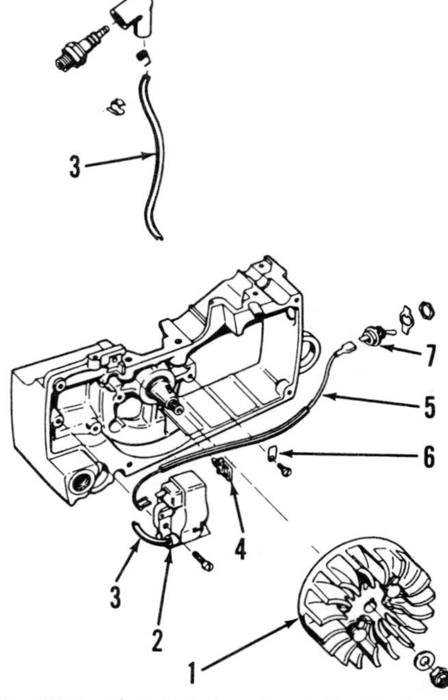

Fig. PN71—Exploded view of capacitor discharge ignition components used on all models.

1. Flywheel
2. Ignition module
3. High tension lead
4. Lead retainer
5. Ground wire
6. Wire retainer
7. Stop switch

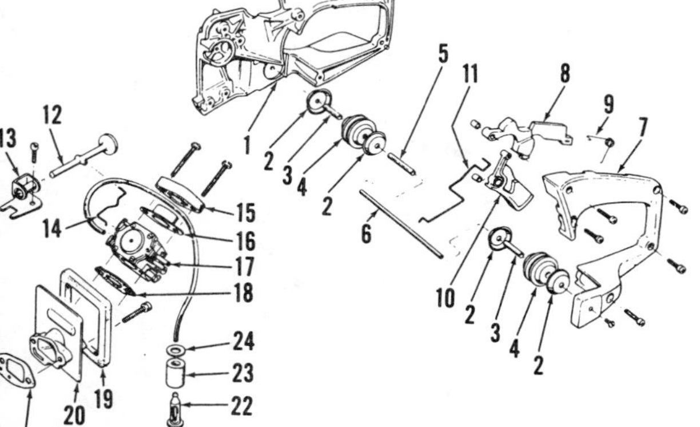

Fig. PN70—Exploded view of rear handle assembly and related components.

1. Right handle half
2. Cup
3. Spacer
4. Isolator
5. Center spacer
6. Shaft
7. Left handle half
8. Throttle lock
9. Spring
10. Throttle trigger
11. Throttle linkage
12. Choke button
13. Choke bracket
14. Choke linkage
15. Seal
16. Seal adapter
17. Carburetor
18. Gasket
19. Intake manifold
20. Intake manifold
21. Gasket
22. Fuel pickup
28. Fuel filter
24. Washer

CYLINDER, PISTON, PIN AND RINGS. To service cylinder and piston, remove air filter cover, cylinder shield, choke assembly, carburetor and muffler. Remove cylinder mounting screws and slide cylinder (1—Fig. PN72) off piston (4). Remove piston rings (3) and use suitable piston pin removal tool, such as Poulan tool 31069, to press piston pin out of piston.

All models are equipped with a cylinder that has a chrome plated bore except later Model 3400 that is equipped with a silicon impregnated cylinder bore. Inspect cylinder bore for excessive wear or damage to chrome surface and renew as necessary. The piston is equipped with two piston rings. Piston and rings are available in standard size only. Piston ring grooves have a locating pin in each groove to prevent piston ring rotation. When installing piston, be sure piston ring locating pins are toward inlet port (rear of engine).

Lubricate piston rings and cylinder bore with oil before installing cylinder. Make certain ring end gaps are properly aligned with locating pins in ring grooves. Tighten cylinder mounting screws to 90-100 in.-lbs. (10.2-11.3 N·m).

CRANKSHAFT, CONNECTING ROD AND CRANKCASE. Crankshaft (6—Fig. PN72) is supported at both ends by a roller bearing (9). Crankcase halves (10 and 11) must be split to remove crankshaft assembly. To separate crankcase, remove air filter cover, cylinder shield, choke assembly, fan housing, fuel tank, clutch cover, bar and chain. Remove spark plug and install piston stop tool in spark plug hole or use other suitable means to prevent crankshaft from rotating. Remove flywheel nut (right-hand threads) and clutch assembly (left-hand threads). Remove oil pump, cylinder and front and rear handle. Remove crankcase screws and separate crankcase halves being careful not to damage crankcase mating surfaces.

The crankshaft and connecting rod are a unit assembly and are not available separately. Check rotation of connecting rod around crankpin and renew crankshaft assembly if roughness or other damage is found. Check main bearing contact surfaces on crankshaft for damage or excessive wear. If main bearings (9) require renewal, remove seals (12) and drive out main bearings toward center of crankcase.

Install new main bearings in bearing bores from inside of crankcase using support tool 31033 and bearing locating tool 31074. Numbered face of bearings should face up. Install crankshaft seals with open side toward main bearings. Drive seals into crankcase bores until flush to 0.015 inch (0.38 mm) below outer surface of casting boss. Thrust washers (8) should be placed on crankshaft with stepped side toward main bearings. Apply thin bead of part number 30054 sealant to left crankcase half (11) mating surface, then assemble crankshaft and crankcase halves being careful not to damage crankshaft seals. Apply Loctite 242 to threads of crankcase screws and tighten to 45-50 in.-lbs. (5.1-5.6 N·m). Complete reassembly by reversing disassembly procedure. Tighten flywheel nut to 15-20 ft.-lbs. (20-27 N·m).

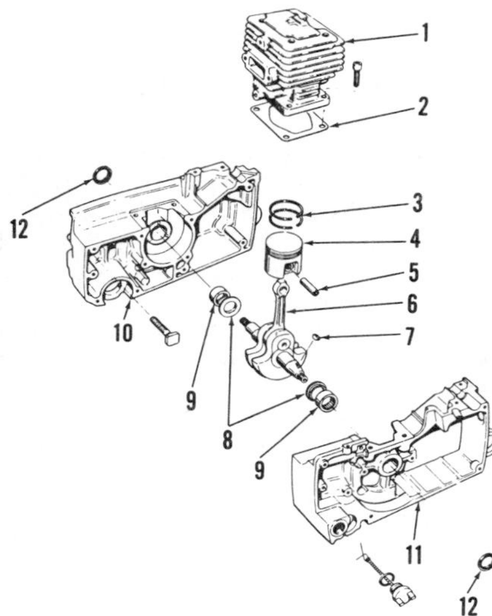

Fig. PN72—Exploded view of engine assembly.

1. Cylinder
2. Gasket
3. Piston rings
4. Piston
5. Piston pin
6. Crankshaft & connecting rod assy.
7. Woodruff key
8. Thrust washers
9. Main bearings
10. Right crankcase half
11. Left crankcase half
12. Crankshaft seals

CLUTCH. All models are equipped with the three-shoe clutch shown in Fig. PN73. Clutch hub (1) has left-hand threads. Note arrow on hub indicating direction of rotation (clockwise) to remove.

Inspect clutch shoes (2) and drum (5) for excessive wear or damage due to excessive slippage. Inspect bearing (6) and contact surface on crankshaft for wear and damage.

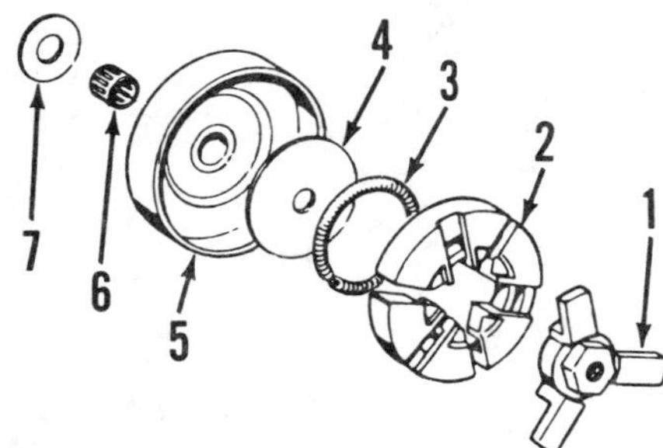

Fig. PN73—Exploded view of clutch assembly used on all models.

1. Clutch hub
2. Clutch shoes
3. Spring
4. Plate
5. Clutch drum
6. Needle bearing
7. Thrust washer

CHAIN OILER PUMP. Refer to Fig. PN74 for an exploded view of manual and automatic oil pump assembly used on all models. Oil pump may be removed for disassembly and repair after removing clutch assembly and oil pump cover plate (17).

Inspect and renew any questionable components. Oil pump used on early 3400 models is equipped with an adjustment screw to regulate oil output. Adjustment screw is accessible from under saw and should be set two turns open from seated position. Lubricate pump internal components with SAE 30 oil during reassembly.

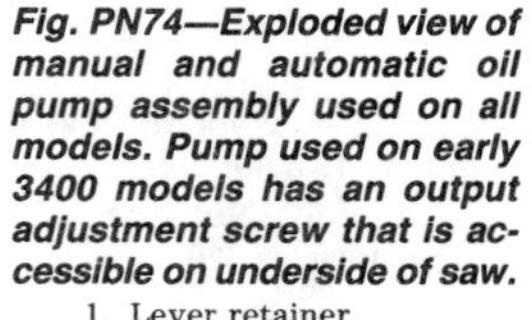
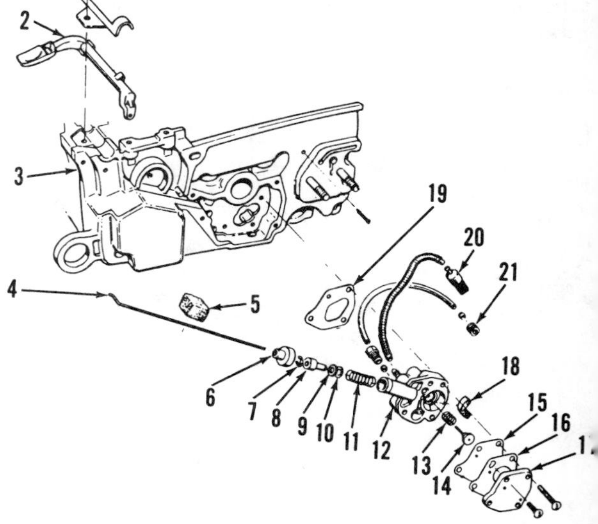

Fig. PN74—Exploded view of manual and automatic oil pump assembly used on all models. Pump used on early 3400 models has an output adjustment screw that is accessible on underside of saw.

1. Lever retainer
2. Manual pump lever
3. Right crankcase half
4. Manual pump rod
5. Boot
6. Cap
7. Snap ring
8. Pump piston
9. Quad ring
10. Washer
11. Spring
14. Pintle
15. Diaphragm
16. Gasket
17. Cover
18. Filter
19. Gasket
20. Oil pickup
21. Oil outlet

REWIND STARTER. Refer to Fig. PN75 for an exploded view of rewind starter. To disassemble starter, first remove starter housing from saw. Remove air baffle (5), then pull starter rope and hold rope pulley (6) with notch in pulley adjacent to rope outlet. Pull rope back through outlet so it engages notch in pulley and allow pulley to slowly unwind. Unscrew pulley retaining screw (4) and remove rope pulley. If rewind spring requires removal, remove shield (7) and carefully withdraw rewind spring from starter housing. Care should be taken to prevent spring from uncoiling uncontrolled.

Reassembly is the reverse of disassembly while noting the following: Install rewind spring in starter housing with spring coils wound in a clockwise direction from outer end. Rope length should be 48 inches (122 cm). Wrap starter rope around rope pulley in clockwise direction as viewed with pulley in starter housing. Place tension on rewind spring by turning rope pulley two turns clockwise before passing rope through rope outlet. Rope handle will be snug against starter housing if rewind spring preload is correct.

CHAIN BRAKE. Some models are equipped with a chain brake system designed to stop chain movement should kickback occur. Chain brake is activated when operator's hand strikes chain brake lever (1—Fig. PN76), tripping latch (2) and allowing spring (3) to draw brake band (6) tight around clutch drum. Pull back chain brake lever to reset mechanism.

Disassembly for repair and component renewal is evident after referral to exploded view and inspection of unit.

To adjust chain brake, rotate adjustment screw (11) in 1/2 turn increments until chain brake engages with minimal effort but will not activate itself due to engine vibration.

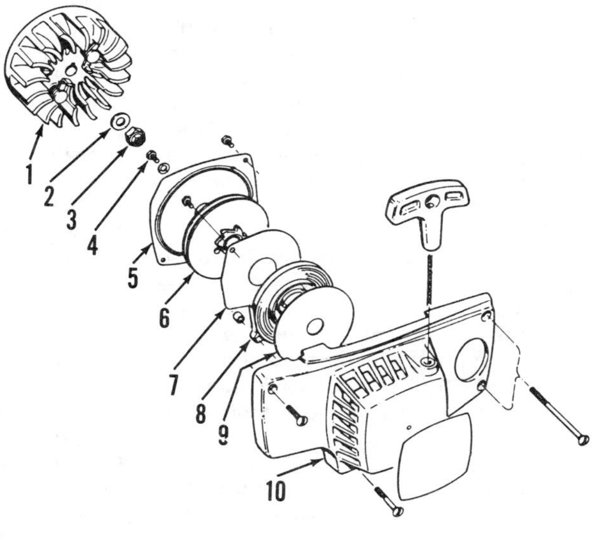

Fig. PN75—Exploded view of rewind starter used on all models.

1. Flywheel
2. Washer
3. Nut
4. Cap screw
5. Air baffle
6. Rope pulley
7. Spring shield
8. Rewind spring
9. Washer
10. Starter housing

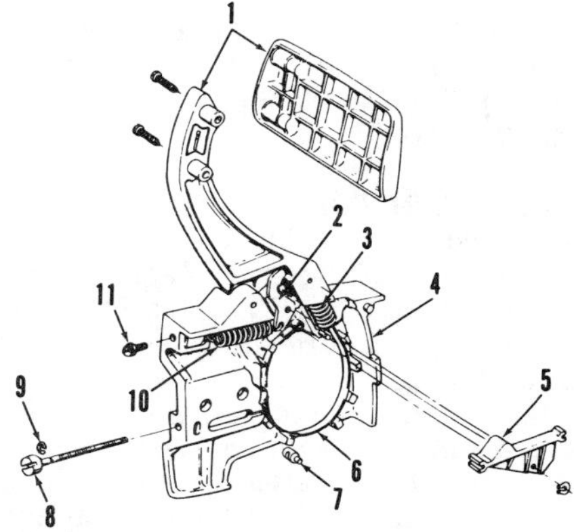

Fig. PN76—Exploded view of chain brake system used on some models.

1. Chain brake lever
2. Latch
3. Spring
4. Housing
5. Guard
6. Brake band
7. Bar adjusting screw anchor
8. Bar adjusting screw
9. "E" ring
10. Spring
11. Adjusting screw

POULAN

Model	Bore mm (in.)	Stroke mm (in.)	Displacement cc (cu. in.)	Drive Type
285	...	...	46 (2.8)	Direct
305	...	...	49 (3.0)	Direct
335, 336	...	...	54 (3.3)	Direct
365	...	...	60 (3.7)	Direct
2700, 2750, 2800, 2900	...	...	46 (2.8)	Direct
3000, 3100			49 (3.0)	Direct
3300, 3350	...	...	54 (3.3)	Direct
3500,3600			60 (3.7)	Direct

MAINTENANCE

SPARK PLUG. Recommended spark plug is Champion CJ4. Spark plug electrode gap should be 0.025 inch (0.63 mm). Tighten spark plug to 18-22 ft.-lbs. (25-30 N·m).

CARBURETOR. All models are equipped with a Walbro HDA diaphragm type carburetor. Refer to Walbro section of CARBURETOR SERVICE section for overhaul procedure and exploded view of carburetor.

Initial adjustment of high- and low-speed mixture needles is one turn open from a lightly seated position. Make final adjustment with engine running at operating temperature. Adjust low-speed mixture needle (Fig. PN85) so engine will accelerate without hesitation. Adjust high-speed mixture needle to obtain optimum full throttle performance under cutting load. Do not operate saw with high speed mixture setting too lean (needle turned too far clockwise) as engine damage could result from lack of lubrication and overheating. Adjust idle speed screw so engine idles just below clutch engagement speed.

IDLE SPEED SCREW
LOW SPEED SCREW
HIGH SPEED SCREW

Fig. PN85—Drawing showing carburetor adjustment points. Refer to text for adjustment procedure.

IGNITION. All models are equipped with a breakerless capacitor discharge ignition system. Ignition timing is not adjustable. Air gap between ignition module and flywheel magnets should be 0.012 inch (0.30 mm). Loosen module mounting screws and move module to obtain desired air gap.

LUBRICATION. Engine is lubricated by mixing oil with fuel. Recommended oil is Poulan/Weed Eater Engine Oil available in blends approved for 16:1 and 32:1 fuel ratios. Follow manufacturer's mixing instructions when using recommended oil. If Poulan/Weed Eater Engine Oil is not available, a good quality oil designed for use in air-cooled two-stroke engines may be used when mixed at a 16:1 ratio. The use of automotive type oil is not recommended. Use a separate container when mixing the fuel and oil.

All models are equipped with an adjustable automatic chain oil pump. Oil designed for chain and bar lubrication may be used in all temperatures. Clean automotive type oil may also be used. SAE 30 oil is recommended for use in warm weather and SAE 10 oil may be used for cold weather operation.

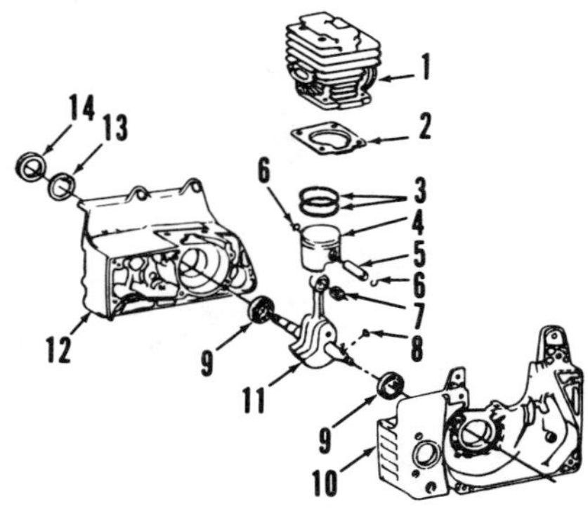

Fig. PN86—Exploded view of engine assembly.

1. Cylinder
2. Gasket
3. Piston rings
4. Piston
5. Piston pin
6. Retainer clip
7. Needle roller bearing
8. Woodruff key
9. Ball bearing
10. Left crankcase half
11. Crankshaft & connecting rod assy.
12. Right crankcase half
13. Snap ring
14. Seal

REPAIRS

CRANKCASE PRESSURE TEST. An improperly sealed crankcase can cause the engine to be hard to start, run rough, have low power and overheat. Refer to ENGINE SERVICE section of this manual for crankcase pressure test procedure. If crankcase leakage is indicated, pressurize crankcase and use a soap and water solution to check gaskets, seals, pulse line and castings for leakage.

CYLINDER, PISTON, PIN AND RINGS. To disassemble cylinder (1—Fig. PN86) and piston (4), remove carburetor cover, cylinder cover and starter housing.

NOTE: Do not mix chrome-colored fan housing screws with black-colored cylinder shroud screws. If screws are interchanged you may strip the threads in crankcase.

Disconnect carburetor adapter from cylinder. Remove muffler cover and muffler. Remove cylinder mounting screws and slide cylinder off piston. Support connecting rod with support tool 31048. Remove piston pin retainers (6), apply heat to piston crown and push piston pin (5) out of piston.

Inspect piston skirt and cylinder bore for scoring, scratches and excessive wear. Piston and rings are available in standard size only. Piston rings (3) and pin retainer clips (6) are available separately. Piston is available only as a kit with piston rings, pin and retainer clips.

Locating pins are present in piston ring grooves to prevent piston ring rotation. Make certain ring end gaps are properly aligned with locating pins when installing cylinder. Install piston with arrow on piston crown facing exhaust side of cylinder. Insert an alignment tool through piston and connecting rod bearing. Apply heat to top of piston to aid piston pin installation. Pin should be a hand push fit when piston is heated. Do not drive pin in as piston and connecting rod could be damaged. Install new piston pin retainer clips. Lubricate rings and cylinder bore with engine oil prior to assembly. Compress piston rings and install cylinder using a new gasket (2). Apply Loctite 242 to cylinder mounting screws and tighten to 90-100 in.-lbs. (10.2-11.3 N·m). Complete reassembly by reversing disassembly procedure.

CRANKSHAFT, CONNECTING ROD AND CRANKCASE. Crankshaft (11—Fig. PN86) is supported by ball bearing (9) on both ends. Crankcase halves (10 and 12) must be split to remove crankshaft assembly. To split crankcase, remove starter housing, ignition module, cylinder cover, clutch cover and bar and chain. Remove spark plug and install piston stop tool in spark plug hole or use some other means of preventing crankshaft rotation. Remove flywheel nut (right-hand threads) and clutch assembly (left-hand threads). Tap counterweight side of flywheel with a soft mallet to remove from crankshaft. Unbolt and remove oil pump assembly. A special tool 31115 is available for removing oil pump worm gear from crankshaft. Remove cylinder and piston as previously outlined. Remove crankcase mounting screws and separate crankcase halves being careful not to damage crankcase mating surfaces. Remove crankshaft assembly. Remove seal (14) and snap ring (13) from crankcase half (12). The seal for other side of crankshaft is located in oil pump housing. Drive or press main bearings (9) toward inside to remove from crankcase halves.

Crankshaft and connecting rod are a unit assembly and are not available separately. Check rotation of connecting rod around crankpin and renew if roughness, excessive play or other damage is found. Crankcase halves are available only as a matched set.

Install new main bearings in bearing bores from inside of crankcase using support tool 31118 and bearing locating tool 31119. Numbered face of bearings should face inside of crankcase. Install crankshaft seals with open side toward main bearings. Apply thin bead of part number 30054 sealant to left crankcase half (12) mating surface, then assemble crankshaft and crankcase halves being careful not to damage crankshaft seals. Apply Loctite 242 to threads of crankcase screws and tighten evenly to 40-50 in.-lbs. (4.5-5.6 N·m). Complete reassembly by reversing disassembly procedure. Tighten flywheel nut to 15-20 ft.-lbs. (20-27 N·m). Tighten clutch hub to 25-30 ft.-lbs. (34-40 N·m).

CLUTCH. All models are equipped with the two-shoe centrifugal clutch shown in Fig. PN87. When removing clutch assembly, note that clutch hub has left-hand threads (turn clockwise to remove).

Inspect clutch shoes (1), drum (3) and sprocket (5) for excessive wear or damage due to overheating. Clutch shoes, spring and hub are available as a unit assembly only. Inspect bearing (4) for damage or discoloration. Inspect bearing contact surface on crankshaft for excessive wear or other damage.

Lubricate bearing with high temperature grease when reasssembling. Tighten clutch hub to 25-30 ft.-lbs. (34-40 N·m).

AUTOMATIC OIL PUMP. Refer to Fig. PN87 for view of automatic oil pump used on all models. Remove guide bar, chain and clutch assembly to gain access to oil pump. Plunger (14) is actuated by spur gear (13) that is driven by worm gear (17) on crankshaft.

All pump components should be inspected and renewed if excessive wear or damage is found. Crankshaft seal (16) for clutch side of engine is located in pump housing. When installing pump assembly, tighten pump mounting screws to 40-50 in.-lbs. (4.5-5.6 N·m).

Pump output is adjusted by rotating adjusting screw (10) located in bottom of saw. Turning the screw clockwise reduces flow of oil. Remove pin (9) to remove adjusting screw for inspection or renewal.

REWIND STARTER. Refer to Fig. PN88 for exploded view of rewind starter. To disassemble starter, remove starter housing from engine. Remove rope handle (13) and allow rope pulley (9) to unwind slowly to relieve tension on rewind spring (10). Remove screw (4), wave washer (5), cam (6), retainer (7) and starter pawls (8). Remove rope pulley using caution not to dislodge rewind spring (10). Note how pulley engages rewind spring. If rewind spring must be removed, do not allow spring to uncoil uncontrolled.

Reassembly is the reverse of disassembly while noting the following: Make certain hook on outer coil of rewind spring properly engages starter housing (12). Wind rope in a clockwise direction on rope pulley as viewed from flywheel side of pulley. Rotate rope pulley approximately two turns clockwise to preload rewind spring before passing rope through rope guide in starter housing. Rope handle will be snug against starter housing if rewind spring preload is correct.

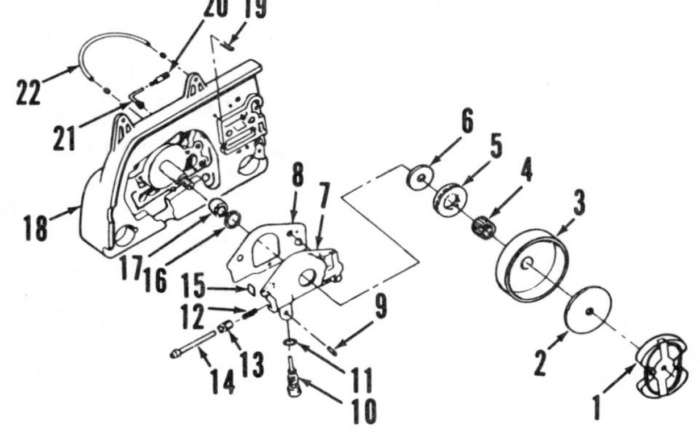

Fig. PN87—Exploded view of clutch and automatic oil pump assemblies. Sprocket (5) is absent on Models 285, 2700, 2800 and 3000.

1. Clutch shoes & hub assy.
2. Plate
3. Clutch drum
4. Needle bearing
5. Sprocket
6. Thrust washer
7. Oil pump housing
8. Gasket
9. Pin
10. Adjusting screw
11. "O" ring
12. Spring
13. Spur gear
14. Plunger
15. Plug
16. Seal
17. Worm gear
18. Right crankcase half
19. Oil tank vent wire
20. Oil filter & pickup assy.
21. Oil suction line
22. Oil discharge line

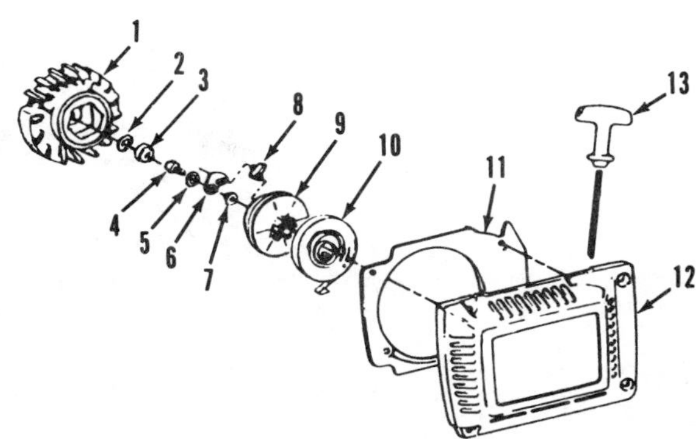

Fig. PN88—Exploded view of rewind starter assembly.

1. Flywheel
2. Washer
3. Nut
4. Screw
5. Wave washer
6. Cam
7. Retainer
8. Pawl
9. Rope pulley
10. Rewind spring
11. Baffle
12. Starter housing
13. Rope handle

POULAN

Model	Bore mm (in.)	Stroke mm (in.)	Displacement cc (cu. in.)	Drive Type
255	...	...	40 (2.44)	Direct
295	...	...	46 (2.8)	Direct
2500, 2600	...	...	40 (2.44)	Direct

MAINTENANCE

SPARK PLUG. Recommended spark plug is Champion CJ7Y. Spark plug electrode gap should be 0.025 inch (0.63 mm).

CARBURETOR. All models are equipped with a Walbro WT diaphragm carburetor. Refer to Walbro section of CARBURETOR SERVICE section for exploded view and service of carburetor.

Initial adjustment of idle and high-speed mixture needles is one turn open from a lightly seated position. Adjust idle mixture needle so engine will accelerate without hesitation. Adjust high-speed mixture needle to obtain optimum full throttle performance under cutting load. Do not operate saw with high speed mixture setting too lean (needle turned too far clockwise) as engine damage could result from lack of lubrication and overheating. Adjust idle speed screw so engine idles just below clutch engagement speed.

IGNITION. A breakerless capacitor discharge ignition system is used on all models. Ignition components are mounted outside the flywheel making it unnecessary to remove the flywheel for most ignition service. The only adjustment of the unit is the air gap between the ignition module core and flywheel magnets. Air gap should be 0.008-0.014 inch (0.20-0.36 mm). Loosen ignition module mounting screws and move module as necessary to obtain specified air gap.

LUBRICATION. The engine is lubricated by mixing oil with the fuel. Recommended oil is Poulan/Weed Eater Engine Oil, which is available in blends approved for 16:1 and 32:1 fuel mixture ratios. Follow manufacturer's mixing instructions on oil container when using recommended oil. If Poulan/Weed Eater oil is not available, a good quality oil designed for use in air-cooled two-stroke engines may be used when mixed at a 16:1 ratio. The use of automotive type oil is not recommended. Also, the use of gasoline containing alcohol is not recommended. Use a separate container when mixing oil and fuel.

An automatic nonadjustable oil pump is used to provide oil for lubrication of chain. It is recommended that a good quality chain and bar oil be used. Clean automotive oil may also be used. SAE 30 oil is recommended for warm weather operation while SAE 10 oil is recommended for cold weather operation.

REPAIRS

CRANKCASE PRESSURE TEST. An improperly sealed crankcase can cause the engine to be hard to start, run rough, have low power and overheat. Refer to ENGINE SERVICE section of this manual for crankcase pressure test procedure. If crankcase leakage is indicated, pressurize crankcase and use a soap and water solution to check gaskets, seals, pulse line and castings for leakage.

CYLINDER, PISTON, PIN AND RING. To service cylinder and piston, remove cylinder cover (1—Fig. PN100), air filter cover (15) and starter housing. Remove clutch cover, guide bar and chain. Disconnect fuel line and throttle linkage and remove carburetor (17), carburetor adapter (19), turbo air cleaner (23 and 24), ignition module (3) and muffler (4). Remove spark plug and install piston stop tool in spark plug hole or use other suitable means to lock piston and crankshaft. Remove flywheel, clutch assembly and oil pump. Remove power head mounting screws and separate power head from saw frame. Remove cylinder mounting screws and slide cylinder (8) off piston (7). Remove piston ring (5) and use suitable piston pin removal tool, such as Poulan tool 31069, to press piston pin (9) out of piston.

Inspect cylinder bore for scratches or other damage and renew as necessary. The piston is equipped with one piston ring. Piston and ring are available in standard size only. Piston has a locating pin in ring groove to prevent piston ring rotation. Make certain ring end gap is

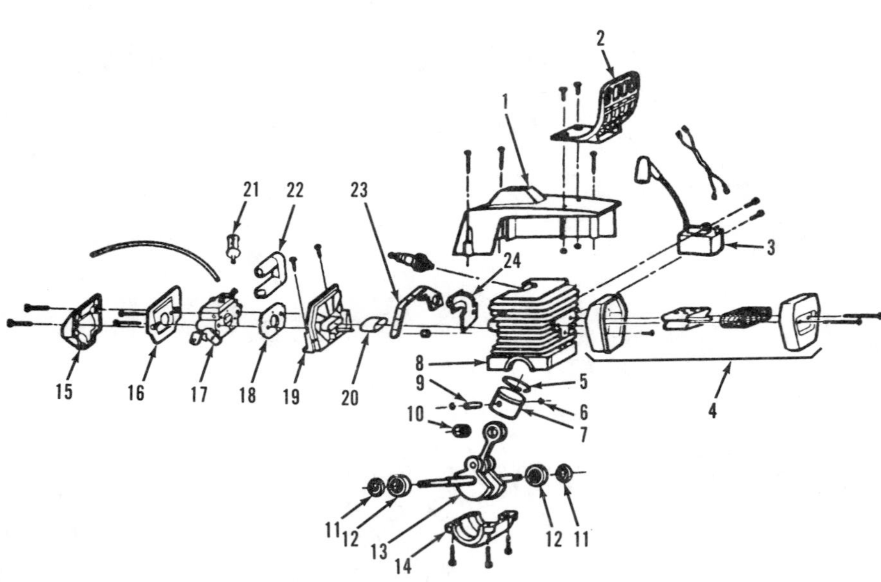

Fig. PN100—Exploded view of engine assembly.

1. Cylinder cover
2. Hand guard
3. Ignition module
4. Muffler assy.
5. Piston ring
6. Retaining ring
7. Piston
8. Cylinder
9. Piston pin
10. Bearing
11. Seals
12. Bearings
13. Crankshaft & connecting rod assy.
14. Crankcase
15. Air cleaner cover
16. Air filter
17. Carburetor
18. Gasket
19. Carburetor adapter
20. Intake sleeve
21. Fuel filter
22. Grommet
23. Seal
24. Turbo air cleaner

aligned with locating pin when installing cylinder. Install piston with arrow on piston crown facing exhaust side of cylinder. Insert an alignment tool through piston and connecting rod bearing. Apply heat to top of piston to aid piston pin installation. Pin should be a hand push fit when piston is heated. Do not drive pin in as piston and connecting rod could be damaged. Install new piston pin retainer clips (6). Lubricate piston and cylinder bore with engine oil prior to assembly.

CRANKSHAFT, CONNECTING ROD AND CRANKCASE. Crankshaft (13—Fig. PN100) is supported at both ends by a roller bearing (12). Power head must be removed from saw frame as outlined above in CYLINDER, PISTON, PIN AND RING section to remove crankshaft assembly.

The crankshaft and connecting rod are a unit assembly and are not available separately. Check rotation of connecting rod around crankpin and renew crankshaft assembly if roughness or other damage is found. Check main bearing contact surfaces on crankshaft for damage or excessive wear. Apply thin bead of sealant to crankcase mating surface, then assemble crankshaft, bearings (12) and seals (11) in cylinder and crankcase. Complete reassembly by reversing disassembly procedure.

CLUTCH. All models are equipped with the two-shoe clutch shown in Fig. PN101. Clutch is accessible after removing clutch cover (1), guide bar and chain. Clutch hub (2) has left-hand threads (turn clockwise to remove).

Inspect clutch shoes (2) and drum (4) for excessive wear or damage due to excessive slippage. Inspect bearing (5) and contact surface on crankshaft for wear and damage. Renew parts as necessary.

CHAIN OILER PUMP. A nonadjustable automatic oil pump assembly (7—Fig. PN101) is used on all models. Oil pump is driven by a worm (8) on crankshaft. Oil pump may be removed for disassembly and repair after removing clutch assembly. Inspect and renew any questionable components. Lubricate pump internal components with SAE 30 oil during reassembly.

REWIND STARTER. Refer to Fig. PN102 for an exploded view of rewind starter. To disassemble starter, first remove starter housing (2) from saw. Pull starter rope and hold rope pulley (4) with notch in pulley adjacent to rope outlet. Pull rope back through outlet so it engages notch in pulley and allow pulley to slowly unwind. Unscrew pulley retaining screw (5) and remove rope pulley. If rewind spring (3) requires removal, remove carefully to prevent spring from uncoiling uncontrolled.

Reassembly is the reverse of disassembly while noting the following: Wrap starter rope around rope pulley in clockwise direction as viewed with pulley in starter housing. To place tension on rewind spring, lift a loop of rope from pulley and place into notch in pulley. While holding rope in notch, turn rope pulley two turns clockwise. Rope handle will be snug against starter housing if rewind spring preload is correct.

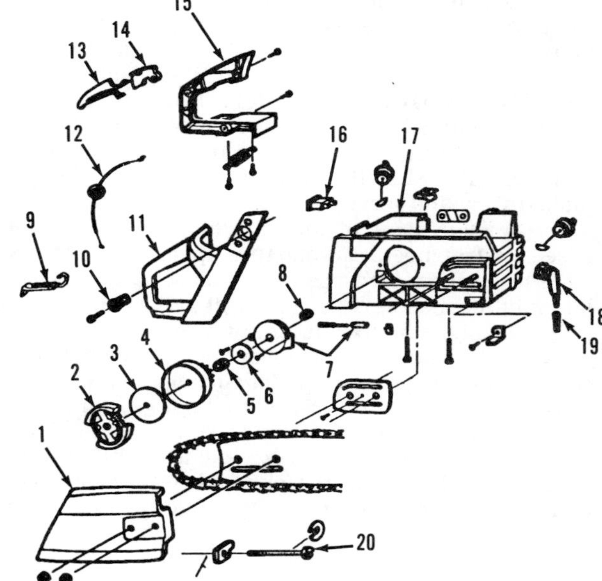

Fig. PN101—Exploded view of control handle, clutch assembly and oil pump.

1. Clutch cover
2. Clutch assy.
3. Washer
4. Clutch drum
5. Needle bearing
6. Thrust washer
7. Oil pump assy.
8. Worm
9. Choke lever
10. Vibration isolator
11. Rear handle
12. Throttle cable
13. Throttle lockout
14. Throttle trigger
15. Handle cover
16. Ignition switch
17. Saw frame
18. Oil pick-up
19. Oil screen
20. Chain adjusting screw

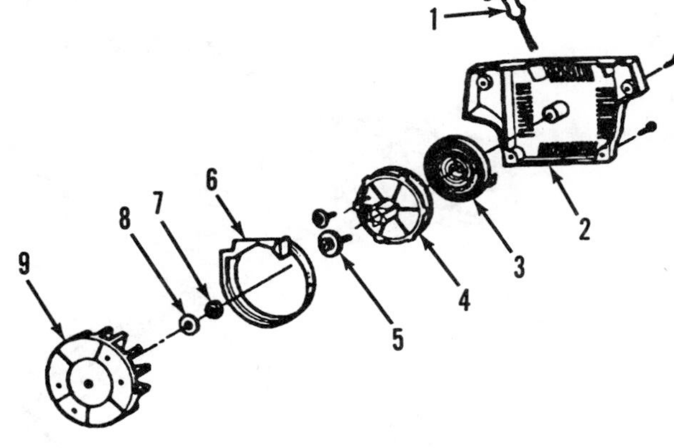

Fig. PN102—Exploded view of rewind starter assembly.

1. Rope handle
2. Starter housing
3. Rewind spring
4. Rope pulley
5. Screw
6. Air baffle
7. Nut
8. Washer
9. Flywheel

POULAN

Model	Bore mm (in.)	Stroke mm (in.)	Displacement cc (cu. in.)	Drive Type
325	...	...	53 (3.23)	Direct

MAINTENANCE

SPARK PLUG. Recommended spark plug is Champion DJ8J. Spark plug electrode gap should be 0.025 inch (0.63 mm).

CARBURETOR. All models are equipped with a Walbro WT diaphragm carburetor. Refer to Walbro section of CARBURETOR SERVICE section for exploded view and service of carburetor.

Initial adjustment of idle and high-speed mixture needles is one turn open from a lightly seated position. Adjust idle mixture needle so engine will accelerate without hesitation. Adjust high-speed mixture needle to obtain optimum full throttle performance under cutting load. Do not operate saw with high speed mixture setting too lean (needle turned too far clockwise) as engine damage could result from lack of lubrication and overheating. Adjust idle speed screw so engine idles just below clutch engagement speed.

IGNITION. A breakerless capacitor discharge ignition system is used on all models. Ignition module is mounted outside the flywheel and is serviced as a unit. The only adjustment of the unit is the air gap between the ignition module core and flywheel magnets. Air gap should be 0.25-0.30 mm (0.009-0.012 in.). Loosen ignition module mounting screws and move module as necessary to obtain specified air gap.

LUBRICATION. The engine is lubricated by mixing oil with the fuel. Recommended oil is Poulan/Weed Eater Engine Oil, which is available in blends approved for 16:1 and 32:1 fuel mixture ratios. Follow manufacturer's mixing instructions on oil container when using recommended oil. If Poulan/Weed Eater oil is not available, a good quality oil designed for use in air-cooled two-stroke engines may be used when mixed at a 16:1 ratio. The use of automotive type oil is not recommended. Also, the use of gasoline containing alcohol is not recommended. Use a separate container when mixing oil and fuel.

An automatic chain oil pump is used to provide oil for lubrication of chain. Oil output is adjusted by turning screw located behind guide bar. It is recommended that a good quality chain and bar oil be used. Clean automotive oil may also be used. SAE 30 oil is recommended for warm weather operation and SAE 10 oil is recommended for cold weather operation.

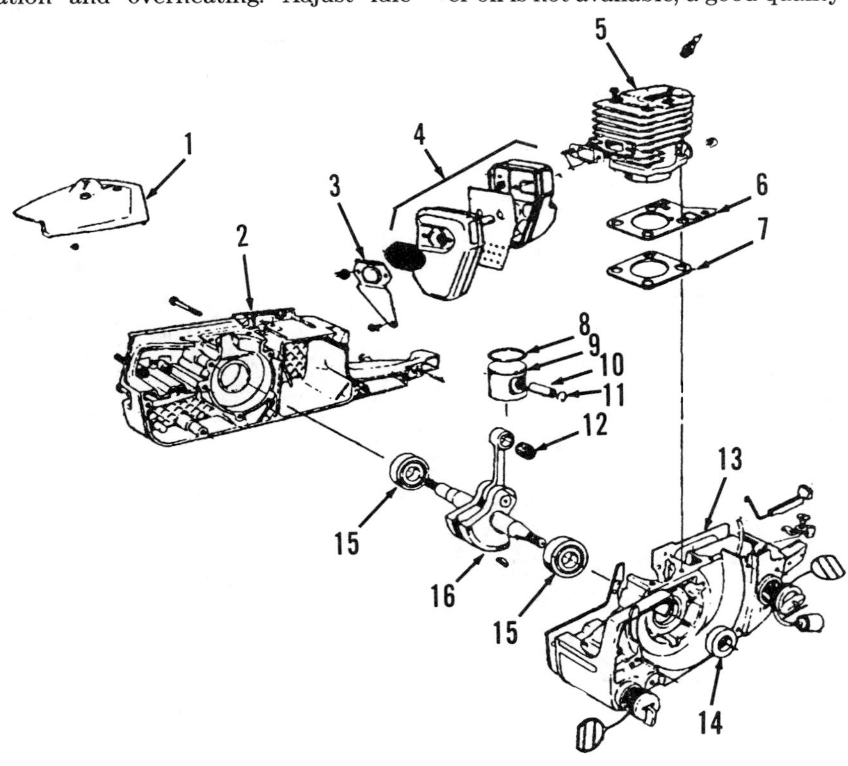

Fig. PN110—Exploded view of engine assembly.

1. Cylinder cover
2. Crankcase half
3. Muffler bracket
4. Muffler assy.
5. Cylinder
6. Insulator
7. Gasket
8. Piston ring
9. Piston
10. Piston pin
11. Retaining ring
12. Needle bearing
13. Crankcase half
14. Seal
15. Bearings
16. Crankshaft & connecting rod assy.

REPAIRS

CRANKCASE PRESSURE TEST. An improperly sealed crankcase can cause the engine to be hard to start, run rough, have low power and overheat. Refer to ENGINE SERVICE section of this manual for crankcase pressure test procedure. If crankcase leakage is indicated, pressurize crankcase and use a soap and water solution to check gaskets, seals, pulse line and castings for leakage.

CYLINDER, PISTON, PIN AND RING. Cylinder may be removed after removing cylinder cover, muffler, carburetor and carburetor adapter plate. Remove cylinder mounting screws and slide cylinder (5—Fig. PN110) off piston (9). Remove piston ring (8) and piston pin retainers (11). Heat piston to aid removal of piston pin (10), push pin out of piston and separate piston from connecting rod.

Inspect cylinder bore and piston for cracking, flaking, excessive wear or other damage. Piston is available only as a kit with piston ring, pin and retaining rings.

Piston must be installed on connecting rod with arrow on piston crown pointing toward exhaust ports. Lubricate piston and cylinder bore with engine oil prior to reassembly. The piston is fitted with a locating pin in piston ring groove to prevent ring rotation. Make certain ring end gap is positioned around locating pin when installing cylinder.

CONNECTING ROD, CRANKSHAFT AND CRANKCASE. To remove crankshaft, first drain fuel tank and oil tank. Remove cylinder cover, starter housing, clutch cover, guide bar and chain. Remove spark plug and install piston stop tool in spark plug hole or use other suitable means to lock piston. Remove flywheel retaining nut (right-hand threads) and pull flywheel off crankshaft. Remove clutch hub (left-hand threads), clutch drum, oil pump assembly and oil pump worm gear. Remove cylinder and piston. Remove crankcase mounting bolts and separate crankcase halves (2 and 13—Fig. PN110) and crankshaft assembly (16) being careful not to damage crankcase mating surfaces.

Crankshaft and connecting rod are a unit assembly and are not available separately. Check rotation of connecting rod around crankpin and renew if roughness, excessive play or other damage is found.

To reassemble crankcase, press main bearings (15) onto crankshaft. Heat area around main bearing bore of crankcase halves and assemble crankshaft and crankcase assemblies. Make certain that crankshaft turns freely in crankcase.

CLUTCH. A two-shoe centrifugal clutch is used. Remove clutch cover (3—Fig. PN111) and guide bar and chain (1) for access to clutch. Clutch hub has left-hand threads (turn clockwise to remove).

Clutch shoes (4) and drum (6) should be inspected for excessive wear or damage due to overheating. Needle roller bearing (7) should be inspected for damage or discoloration and lubricated with high temperature grease before reassembling.

AUTOMATIC OIL PUMP. The automatic chain oil pump is driven by worm gear (17—Fig. PN111) on the crankshaft. Oil pump output is adjusted by rotating adjusting screw (13). Rotating screw counterclockwise increases pump output.

Remove clutch assembly for access to oil pump. Inspect plunger (16), pump body and worm for excessive wear. Check oil inlet screen (15) for plugging and clean or renew as necessary. When installing oil pump, make certain notch in pump housing engages boss in crankcase casting.

REWIND STARTER. To disassemble rewind starter, remove starter housing (8—Fig. PN112). Pull out approximately 30 cm (12 in.) of rope and align notch in rope pulley (5) with rope guide. Insert rope into notch in pulley and allow pulley to slowly unwind, releasing tension on rewind spring. Remove pulley retaining screw and withdraw rope pulley using care not to disturb rewind spring. If rewind spring (6) must be removed, depress tabs which secure rewind spring cover to starter housing (8) and remove spring taking care not to allow spring to unwind uncontrolled.

To reassemble starter, lightly oil rewind spring and install into starter housing. Wind approximately five revolutions of rope onto rope pulley in a clockwise direction as viewed from flywheel side of pulley. Install rope pulley into starter housing and tighten retaining screw securely. Pull out short length of rope and position rope into notch of pulley. Turn rope pulley clockwise two turns to preload rewind spring. Rope pulley should be able to rotate an additional half turn with rope fully extended. Do not place more tension on rewind spring than is necessary to draw rope handle snugly up against housing.

CHAIN BRAKE. Some saws may be equipped with a chain brake system designed to stop chain movement should kickback occur. The chain brake is activated when the operator's hand strikes the chain brake lever (1—Fig. PN113), tripping actuating plate (4) and allowing spring (7) to draw brake band (8) tight around clutch drum. Pull back chain brake lever to reset mechanism.

Remove brake housing (6) for access to brake components. Inspect parts for excessive wear and renew as necessary. No adjustment of brake mechanism is required.

When reassembling, make certain spring (7) is screwed completely onto brake band (8) and roll pins (3 and 5) are installed with split sides facing forward.

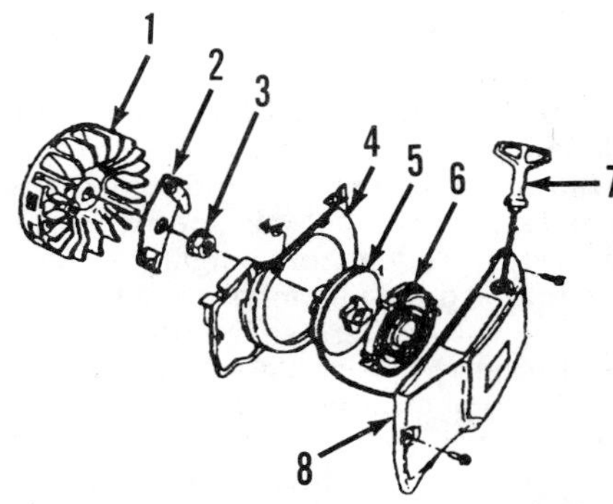

Fig. PN112—Exploded view of rewind starter assembly.

1. Flywheel
2. Pawl plate
3. Nut
4. Air baffle
5. Rope pulley
6. Rewind spring
7. Rope handle
8. Starter housing

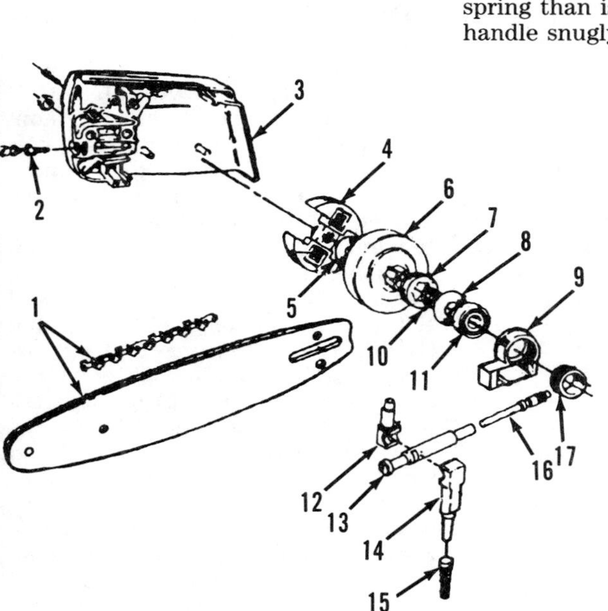

Fig. PN111—Exploded view of clutch assembly and automatic chain oil pump assembly.

1. Guide bar & chain
2. Chain adjusting screw
3. Clutch cover
4. Clutch assy.
5. Washer
6. Clutch drum
7. Sprocket
8. Washer
9. Oil pump housing
10. Bearing
11. Seal
12. Oil outlet
13. Adjusting screw
14. Oil inlet
15. Screen
16. Pump plunger
17. Worm

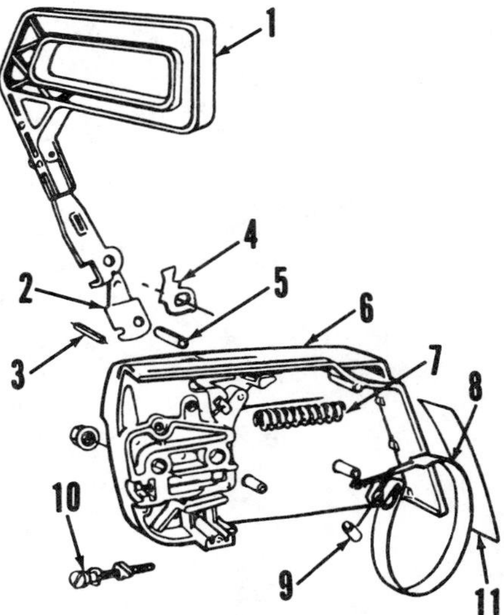

Fig. PN113—Exploded view of optional chain brake mechanism used on some saws.

1. Chain brake lever
2. Sleeve
3. Roll pin
4. Actuating plate
5. Roll pin
6. Brake housing
7. Spring
8. Brake band
9. Pin
10. Chain adjuster assy.
11. Chain guard

POULAN

Model	Bore mm (in.)	Stroke mm (in.)	Displacement cc (cu. in.)	Drive Type
405	47.6 (1.875)	36.5 (1.437)	65 (4.0)	Direct
455	50 (1.97)	36.5 (1.437)	72 (4.4)	Direct
655	57.1 (2.25)	38.1 (1.5)	98 (6.0)	Direct

MAINTENANCE

SPARK PLUG. Recommended spark plug is Champion CJ7Y. Spark plug electrode gap should be 0.63 mm (0.025 in).

CARBURETOR. All models are equipped with a Walbro WJ diaphragm carburetor. Refer to Walbro section of CARBURETOR SERVICE section for exploded view and service of carburetor.

Initial adjustment of idle and high-speed mixture needles is approximately $1^1/_2$ turns open from a lightly seated position. Adjust idle mixture needle so engine will accelerate cleanly without hesitation. Adjust high-speed mixture needle to obtain optimum full throttle performance under cutting load. Do not operate saw with high speed mixture setting too lean (needle turned too far clockwise) as engine damage could result from lack of lubrication and overheating. Adjust idle speed screw so engine idles just below clutch engagement speed.

IGNITION. A breakerless capacitor discharge ignition system is used on all models. Ignition module is mounted outside the flywheel making it unnecessary to remove the flywheel for most ignition service. The ignition module is serviced as a unit assembly. The only adjustment of the unit is the air gap between the ignition module core and flywheel magnets. Air gap should be 0.25-0.38 mm (0.010-0.015 in). Loosen ignition module mounting screws and move module as necessary to obtain specified air gap.

LUBRICATION. The engine is lubricated by mixing oil with the fuel. Recommended oil is Poulan/Weed Eater Engine Oil, which is available in blends approved for 16:1 and 32:1 fuel mixture ratios. Follow manufacturer's mixing instructions on oil container when using recommended oil. If Poulan/Weed Eater oil is not available, a good quality oil designed for use in air-cooled two-stroke engines may be used when mixed at a 16:1 ratio. The use of automotive type oil is not recommended. Also, the use of gasoline containing alcohol is not recommended. Use a separate container when mixing oil and fuel.

An automatic chain oil pump is used to provide oil for lubrication of chain on all models. Model 655 is also equipped with a manual oil pump. On all models, output of automatic oil pump is adjustable. Oil pump adjustment screw is accessible from underside of saw. It is recommended that a good quality chain and bar oil be used. Clean automotive oil may also be used. SAE 30 oil is recommended for warm weather operation while SAE 10 oil is recommended for cold weather operation.

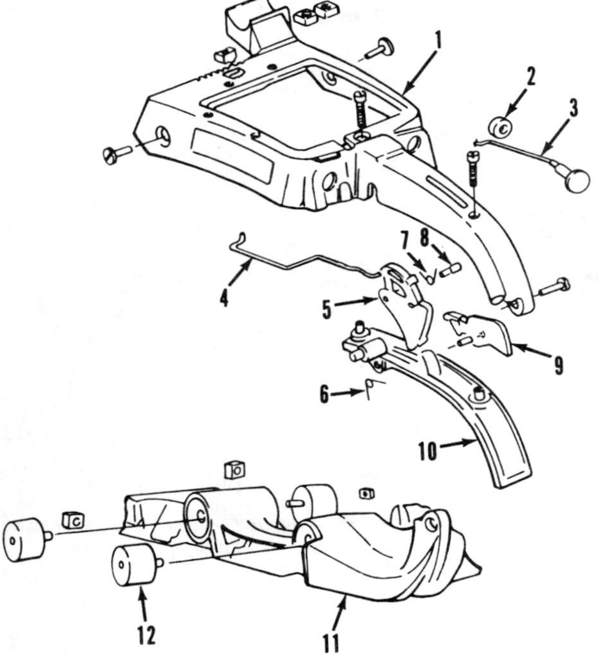

Fig. PN120—Exploded view of rear handle assembly.

1. Rear handle
2. Grommet
3. Choke linkage
4. Throttle linkage
5. Throttle control
6. Return spring
7. Return spring
8. Pin
9. Throttle lock
10. Rear handle cover
11. Base
12. Isolation mounts

REPAIRS

CRANKCASE PRESSURE TEST. An improperly sealed crankcase can cause the engine to be hard to start, run rough, have low power and overheat. Refer to ENGINE SERVICE section of this manual for crankcase pressure test procedure. If crankcase leakage is indicated, pressurize crankcase and use a soap and water solution to check gaskets, seals, pulse line and castings for leakage.

CYLINDER, PISTON, PIN AND RINGS. To service cylinder and piston, remove guide bar and chain, air filter assembly, starter housing and cylinder shroud. Remove ignition module. Disconnect throttle and choke linkage and fuel line. Remove carburetor, rear handle frame (1—Fig. PN120) and muffler. Remove cylinder mounting screws and slide cylinder (14—Fig. PN121) off piston (11). Remove piston rings (12) and piston pin retainers (9). Heat piston to ease removal of piston pin (10) and separate piston from connecting rod.

Cylinder bore is chrome plated and should be renewed if plating is worn away exposing the base metal. The piston is equipped with two piston rings. Piston ring grooves have a locating pin in each groove to prevent piston ring rotation. Piston must be installed with locating pin positioned toward flywheel, away from cylinder exhaust port.

Lubricate piston rings and cylinder bore with oil before installing cylinder. Make certain ring end gaps are aligned with locating pins in ring grooves.

CRANKSHAFT, CONNECTING ROD AND CRANKCASE. Crankshaft (5—Fig. PN121) is supported at both ends by bearings (4). Crankcase halves (2 and 7) must be split to remove crankshaft assembly. To separate crankcase, first drain oil tank and fuel tank. Remove air filter assembly, starter housing and cylinder shield, clutch cover, guide bar and chain. Remove carburetor, reed valve, ignition module, rear handle top frame (1—Fig. PN120) and bottom frame (11). Remove spark plug and install piston stop tool in spark plug hole or use other suitable means to prevent crankshaft from rotating. Remove flywheel nut (right-hand threads) and pull flywheel off crankshaft. Remove clutch assembly (left-hand threads) and oil pump assembly. Remove cylinder and piston. Remove crankcase screws and use suitable crankcase puller tool to separate crankcase halves being careful not to damage crankcase mating surfaces.

If main bearings remain in crankcase halves during separation, heat main bearing area of crankcase halves to approximately 100°C (212°F) and drive bearings from each crankcase half.

Gasket surface between the two crankcase halves must be completely clean and free from nicks and burrs. The crankcase forms three different compartments when the halves are joined together: engine crankcase, fuel tank and chain oil tank.

The crankshaft and connecting rod are a unit assembly and are not available separately. Check rotation of connecting rod around crankpin and renew crankshaft assembly if roughness or other damage is found. Check main bearing contact surfaces on crankshaft for damage or excessive wear.

When assembling, heat main bearing area of crankcase halves to approximately 100°C (212°F) prior to installing crankshaft assembly. Refer to Fig. PN122 and note length and position of crankcase screws.

CLUTCH. All models are equipped with the three-shoe clutch shown in Fig. PN123. The clutch can be disassembled after removing clutch cover, guide bar and chain. Clutch retaining nut (8) has left-hand threads (turn clockwise to remove).

Inspect clutch shoes (5) and drum (4) for excessive wear or damage due to excessive slippage. Inspect bearing (3) and contact surface on crankshaft and clutch drum for wear and damage.

When reassembling, washer (1) should be installed next to crankcase. Lubricate needle bearing (3) with small amount of multipurpose grease. Floating sprocket (2) should be installed with open side away from clutch drum (4).

CHAIN OILER PUMP. All models are equipped with an automatic oil pump assembly. Model 655 is also equipped with manual oil pump (M—Fig. PN124). Oil pump may be removed for disassembly and repair after removing clutch assembly and oil pump cover plate. Inspect and renew any questionable components.

Lubricate pump internal components with SAE 30 oil during reassembly. When installing pump, be sure that pickup (1) is directed toward bottom of the tank while saw is held in an upright position.

Turning adjuster screw (6) will change the volume of oil that is pumped to the bar and chain. Adjuster can only be turned approximately one turn. Turning adjuster counterclockwise will increase the volume of oil delivered. The oil adjustment screw should be set wide open when first operating the saw to ensure that the bar and chain will receive an adequate supply of oil during initial operation, then setting can be

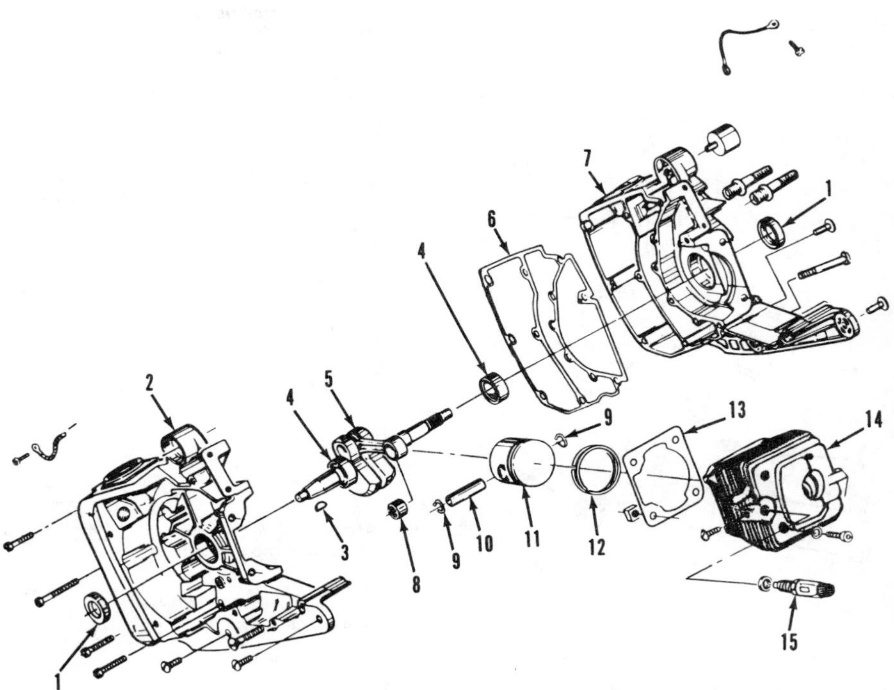

Fig. PN121—Exploded view of engine assembly. On Model 655, thrust washers (not shown) are located on either side of piston pin bearing (8).

1. Seal
2. Crankcase half
3. Key
4. Ball bearing
5. Crankshaft & connecting rod assy.
6. Gasket
7. Crankcase half
8. Needle bearing
9. Retainer clip
10. Piston pin
11. Piston
12. Piston rings
13. Gasket
14. Cylinder
15. Decompression valve

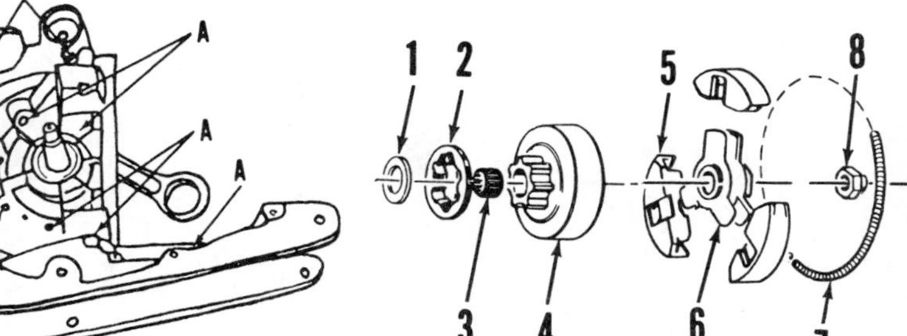

Fig. PN122—Crankcase screws (A) should be 32 mm (1¼ in.) long, screws (B) should be 57 mm (2¼ in.) long and screw (C) should be 63.5 mm (2½ in.) long.

Fig. PN123—Exploded view of clutch assembly.

1. Washer
2. Sprocket
3. Needle bearing
4. Drum
5. Clutch shoe
6. Hub
7. Garter spring
8. Nut

decreased as desired to meet various cutting conditions.

REWIND STARTER. Refer to Fig. PN125 for an exploded view of rewind starter. To disassemble starter, first remove starter housing (1) from saw. Remove air baffle (5), then pull starter rope and hold rope pulley (9) with notch in pulley adjacent to rope outlet. Pull rope back through outlet so it engages notch in pulley and allow pulley to slowly unwind. Unscrew pulley retaining screw (12) and remove rope pulley. If rewind spring (8) requires removal, care should be taken to prevent spring from uncoiling uncontrolled.

Reassembly is the reverse of disassembly while noting the following: Install rewind spring in starter housing with spring coils wound in a clockwise direction from outer end. Wrap starter rope around rope pulley in clockwise direction as viewed with pulley in starter housing. Place tension on rewind spring by turning rope pulley two turns clockwise before passing rope through rope outlet. Rope handle will be snug against starter housing if rewind spring preload is correct.

CHAIN BRAKE. All models are equipped with a chain brake system designed to stop chain movement should kickback occur. Chain brake is activated when operator's hand strikes chain brake lever (1—Fig. PN126), tripping brake band latch and allowing spring (2) to draw brake band (4) tight around clutch drum. Pull back chain brake lever to reset mechanism.

Disassembly for repair and component renewal is evident after referral to exploded view and inspection of unit. Renew worn or damaged parts as necessary. No adjustment of chain brake mechanism is required.

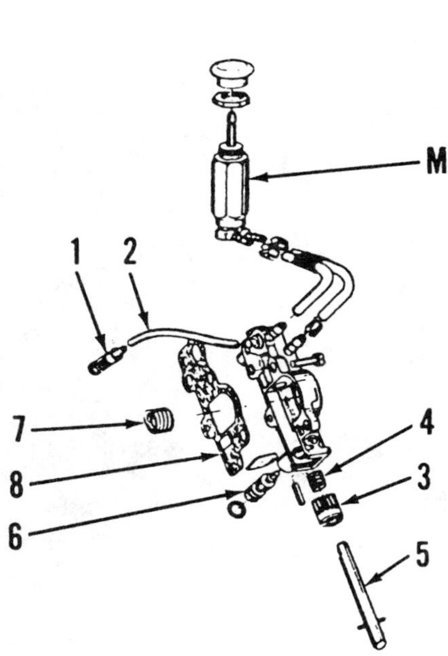

Fig. PN124—Exploded view of automatic oil pump assembly typical of all models. Model 655 is also equipped with manual pump (M).

1. Oil pickup
2. Hose
3. Driven gear
4. Spring
5. Shaft
6. Adjuster screw
7. Worm gear
8. Gasket

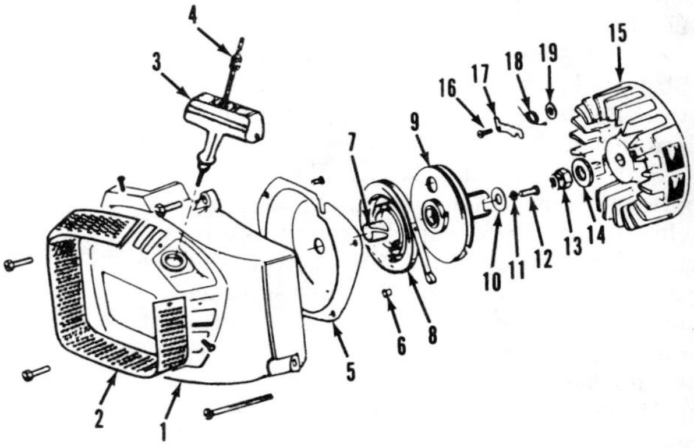

Fig. PN125—Exploded view of rewind starter used on Model 655. Starter used on Models 405 and 455 is similar except starter housing (1) includes a cylinder shroud.

1. Starter housing
2. Shield
3. Handle
4. Starter rope
5. Baffle plate
6. Ferrule
7. Bushing
8. Rewind spring
9. Pulley
10. Washer
11. Lockwasher
12. Screw
13. Nut
14. Washer
15. Flywheel
16. Pivot
17. Pawl
18. Spring
19. Washer

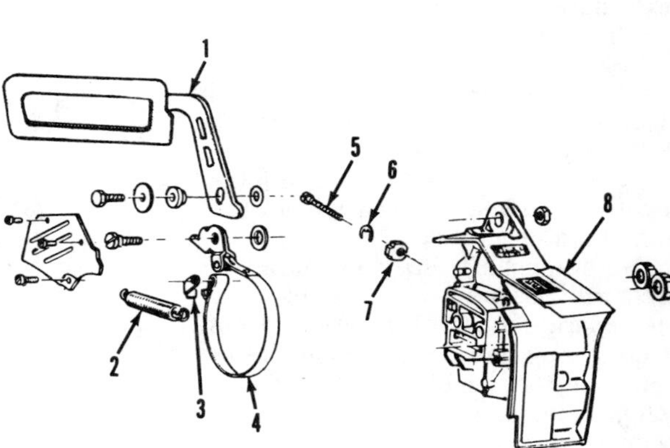

Fig. PN126—Exploded view of chain brake mechanism.

1. Brake lever
2. Spring
3. Retainer
4. Brake band & cam assy.
5. Chain tension adjusting screw
6. "E" clip
7. Plate
8. Side cover

POULAN

Model	Bore mm (in.)	Stroke mm (in.)	Displacement cc (cu. in.)	Drive Type
415	...	...	65 (4.0)	Direct
475	...	...	77 (4.7)	Direct

MAINTENANCE

SPARK PLUG. Recommended spark plug is CJ7Y. Spark plug electrode gap should be 0.63 mm (0.025 in).

CARBURETOR. All models are equipped with a Walbro WJ diaphragm carburetor. Refer to Walbro section of CARBURETOR SERVICE section for exploded view and service of carburetor.

Initial adjustment of idle and high-speed mixture needles is approximately $1^{1}/_{2}$ turns open from a lightly seated position. Adjust idle mixture needle so engine will accelerate smoothly without hesitation. Adjust high-speed mixture needle to obtain optimum full throttle performance under cutting load. Do not operate saw with high speed mixture setting too lean (needle turned too far clockwise) as engine damage could result from lack of lubrication and overheating. Adjust idle speed screw so engine idles just below clutch engagement speed.

IGNITION. A breakerless capacitor discharge ignition system is used on all models. Ignition module is mounted outside the flywheel making it unnecessary to remove the flywheel for most ignition service. Ignition module is serviced as a unit assembly. The only adjustment of the unit is the air gap between the ignition module core and flywheel magnets. Air gap should be 0.20-0.36 mm (0.008-0.014 in). Loosen ignition module mounting screws and move module as necessary to obtain specified air gap.

LUBRICATION. The engine is lubricated by mixing oil with the fuel. Recommended oil is Poulan/Weed Eater Engine Oil, which is available in blends approved for 16:1 and 32:1 fuel mixture ratios. Follow manufacturer's mixing instructions on oil container when using recommended oil. If Poulan/Weed Eater oil is not available, a good quality oil designed for use in air-cooled two-stroke engines may be used when mixed at a 16:1 ratio. The use of automotive type oil is not recommended. Also, the use of gasoline containing alcohol is not recommended. Use a separate container when mixing oil and fuel.

An automatic oil pump is used to provide oil for lubrication of chain. Oil pump output is adjusted by rotating adjusting screw located on bottom of saw. It is recommended that a good quality chain and bar oil be used. Clean automotive oil may also be used. SAE 30 oil is recommended for warm weather operation while SAE 10 oil is recommended for cold weather operation.

REPAIRS

CRANKCASE PRESSURE TEST. An improperly sealed crankcase can cause the engine to be hard to start, run rough, have low power and overheat. Refer to ENGINE SERVICE section of this manual for crankcase pressure test procedure. If crankcase leakage is indicated, pressurize crankcase and use a soap and water solution to check gaskets, seals, pulse line and castings for leakage.

CYLINDER, PISTON, PIN AND RING. To disassemble, remove cylinder cover, muffler and intake manifold tube. Remove cylinder mounting screws and slide cylinder (15—Fig. PN130) off piston (12). Remove piston ring (13) and piston pin retainers (10). Heat piston to aid removal of piston pin (11), push pin out of piston and separate piston from connecting rod.

Inspect cylinder bore and piston for cracking, flaking, excessive wear or other damage. When reassembling, lubricate piston and cylinder bore with engine oil prior to reassembly. The piston is fitted with a locating pin in piston ring groove to prevent ring rotation. Make certain ring end gap is positioned around locating pin when installing cylinder.

CONNECTING ROD, CRANKSHAFT AND CRANKCASE. To remove crankshaft, first drain fuel tank and oil tank. Remove cylinder cover, starter housing, clutch cover, guide bar and chain. Disconnect intake manifold tube from cylinder. Remove vibration isolator mounts and separate fuel tank and rear handle assembly from crankcase. Remove spark plug and install piston stop tool in spark plug hole or use other suitable means to lock piston. Remove flywheel retaining

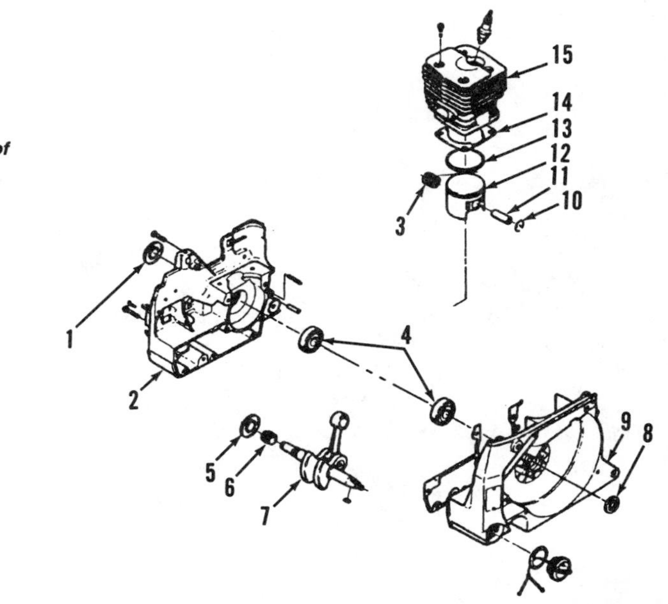

Fig. PN130—Exploded view of engine assembly.

1. Seal
2. Crankcase half
3. Needle bearing
4. Main bearings
5. Shim washer
6. Oil pump drive worm
7. Crankshaft & connecting rod assy.
8. Seal
9. Crankcase half
10. Retainer ring
11. Piston pin
12. Piston
13. Piston ring
14. Gasket
15. Cylinder

nut (right-hand threads) and pull flywheel off crankshaft. Remove clutch assembly (left-hand threads), oil pump assembly and oil pump worm gear. Remove cylinder and piston. Remove crankcase mounting bolts and separate crankcase halves (2 and 9—Fig. PN130) and crankshaft assembly (7) being careful not to damage crankcase mating surfaces.

Crankshaft and connecting rod are a unit assembly and are not available separately. Check rotation of connecting rod around crankpin and renew if roughness, excessive play or other damage is found.

To reassemble crankcase, press main bearings (4) onto crankshaft. Heat area around main bearing bore of crankcase halves and assemble crankshaft and crankcase assemblies. Make certain that crankshaft turns freely in crankcase.

CLUTCH. A three-shoe centrifugal clutch is used (Fig. PN131). Remove clutch cover and guide bar and chain for access to clutch. Clutch hub has left-hand threads (turn clockwise to remove).

Clutch shoes (6) and drum (5) should be inspected for excessive wear or damage due to overheating. Needle roller bearing (3) should be inspected for damage or discoloration and lubricated with high temperature grease before reassembling.

AUTOMATIC OIL PUMP. The automatic chain oil pump is driven by worm gear on the crankshaft. Oil pump output is adjusted by rotating adjusting screw (9—Fig. PN131) located in bottom of saw.

Remove clutch assembly for access to oil pump. Inspect plunger (13), pump body and worm for excessive wear. Check oil inlet screen (8) for plugging and clean or renew as necessary.

REWIND STARTER. To disassemble rewind starter, remove starter housing (3—Fig. PN132). Pull out approximately 30 cm (12 in.) of rope and align notch in rope pulley (7) with rope guide. Insert rope into notch in pulley and allow pulley to slowly unwind, releasing tension on rewind spring. Remove pulley retaining screw and withdraw rope pulley. If rewind spring (4) must be removed, use care to prevent spring from uncoiling uncontrolled.

To reassemble starter, lightly oil rewind spring and install into starter housing. Wind rope onto rope pulley in a clockwise direction as viewed from flywheel side of pulley. Install rope pulley into starter housing and tighten retaining screw securely. Pull out short length of rope and position rope into notch of pulley. Turn rope pulley clockwise two turns to preload rewind spring. Rope pulley should be able to rotate an additional half turn with rope fully extended. Do not place more tension on rewind spring than is necessary to draw rope handle snugly up against housing.

CHAIN BRAKE. All saws are equipped with a chain brake system designed to stop chain movement should kickback occur. The chain brake is activated when the operator's hand strikes the chain brake lever (1—Fig. PN133), tripping actuating arm (2) and allowing spring (5) to draw brake band (4) tight around clutch drum. Pull back chain brake lever to reset mechanism.

Remove clutch cover, guide bar and chain for access to brake components. Inspect parts for excessive wear and renew as necessary. No adjustment of brake mechanism is required.

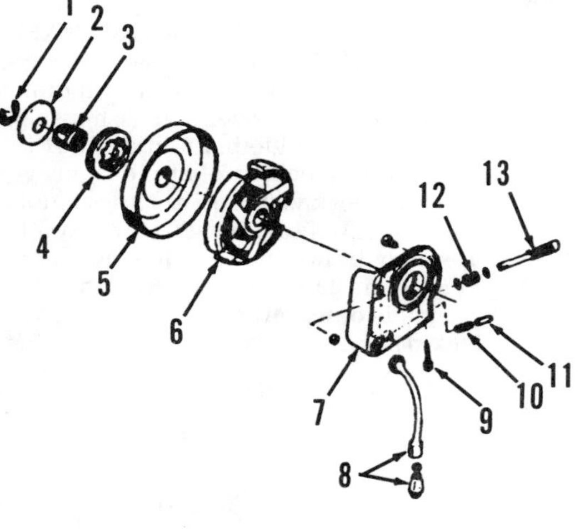

Fig. PN131—Exploded view of clutch assembly and automatic chain oil pump.

1. "E" ring
2. Cup washer
3. Needle bearing
4. Sprocket
5. Clutch drum
6. Clutch assembly
7. Oil pump housing
8. Oil pickup tube & strainer
9. Adjusting screw
10. Spring
11. Pin
12. Spring
13. Pump plunger

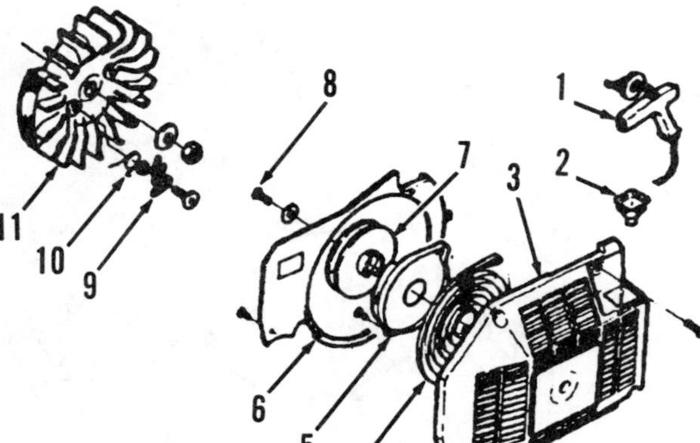

Fig. PN132—Exploded view of rewind starter assembly.

1. Rope handle
2. Rope guide
3. Starter housing
4. Rewind spring
5. Spring case
6. Air baffle
7. Rope pulley
8. Screw
9. Pawl
10. Spring
11. Flywheel

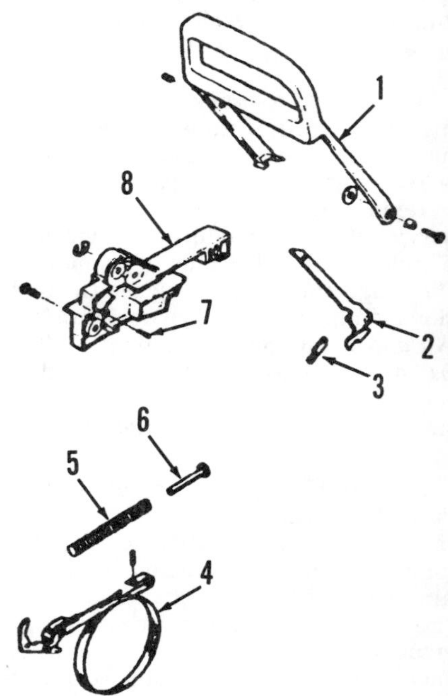

Fig. PN133—Exploded view of chain brake assembly.

1. Brake lever
2. Actuating arm
3. Block & spring
4. Brake band
5. Brake spring
6. Pin
7. Pin
8. Brake housing

PROKUT

Model	Bore mm (in.)	Stroke mm (in.)	Displacement cc (cu. in.)	Drive Type
55	44 (1.73)	36 (1.42)	55 (3.4)	Direct
65	47 (1.85)	37.3 (1.47)	65 (4.0)	Direct

MAINTENANCE

SPARK PLUG. Recommended spark plug for both models is Champion CJ7Y. Electrode gap should be 0.5 mm (0.020 in.).

CARBURETOR. Both models are equipped with a Tillotson HK diaphragm carburetor. Refer to Tillotson section of CARBURETOR SERVICE section for service procedure and exploded view.

Initial adjustment of low speed mixture screw is 1-1/2 turns open on Model 55 and 1-3/8 turns open on Model 65. Initial adjustment of high speed mixture screw is ¾ turn open for both models.

Final adjustment should be made with engine running at operating temperature. Adjust idle speed to just below clutch engagement speed. Adjust low speed mixture screw so engine will accelerate cleanly without hesitation. Adjust high speed mixture screw to obtain maximum no-load speed of 12,000 rpm for Model 55 and 11,600 rpm for Model 65.

IGNITION. Model 55 manufactured prior to 1985 and Model 65 manufactured prior to 1984 are equipped with a breaker-point ignition system. Breaker-point gap should be 0.45-0.50 mm (0.018-0.020 in.). Air gap between ignition coil legs and flywheel magnets should be 0.45 mm (0.018 in.). Loosen coil attaching screws and move coil to adjust air gap. Use a suitable thread locking solution on coil attaching screws. Ignition timing is not adjustable, however, breaker-point gap will affect timing. Be sure breaker-point gap is adjusted correctly as a gap too wide will advance timing and a gap too close will retard timing.

Model 55 manufactured after 1984 and Model 65 manufactured after 1983 are equipped with a breakerless electronic ignition system. Some models are equipped with a standard ignition coil with an electronic module located behind flywheel. On other models, ignition coil and all electronic circuitry are contained in a one-piece ignition module/coil (2—Fig. PK35). Air gap between ignition module/coil and flywheel magnets should be 0.35-0.40 mm (0.014-0.016 in.). Use a suitable thread locking solution on module/coil attaching screws.

On both models, use ProKut 4180140 to remove flywheel. If ProKut tool 4180140 is not available, remove starter pawl assemblies (6, 7, 8 and 9) to accommodate a bolt-type puller. Use a suitable thread locking solution on pawl bolts (6) upon reassembly. Tighten flywheel nut (10) to 34.8 N·m (26 ft.-lbs.).

LUBRICATION. The engine is lubricated by mixing oil with the fuel. Use a good quality oil designed for use in air-cooled two-stroke engines. Fuel:oil mixture should be a 16:1 ratio. Use a separate container when mixing fuel and oil.

Both models are equipped with an automatic chain oil pump. Oil pump is driven by a worm gear coupled to clutch drum. Pump output is not adjustable. Refer to OIL PUMP under REPAIRS section for service and exploded view. Use clean automotive oil for saw chain lubrication.

REPAIRS

CYLINDER, PISTON, PIN AND RINGS. Cylinder bore is chrome plated and should be renewed if cracking, scoring or other damage is noted in cylinder bore.

Piston and cylinder are marked during production to obtain desired piston-to-cylinder clearance of 0.02 mm (0.0008 in.). Original equipment piston and cylinder are marked "A." Factory renewal piston and cylinder assemblies are marked "B." Piston or cylinder marked "C" is 0.127 mm (0.005 in.) oversize. Piston or cylinder marked "D" is 0.127 mm (0.005 in.) undersize. Piston and cylinder markings should match, however, a new piston marked "B" can be installed into a used cylinder marked "A."

NOTE: Do not install a new piston marked "B" or "C" into a new cylinder marked "A."

Piston is equipped with two piston rings. Maximum piston ring end gap should not exceed 1.0 mm (0.039 in.). Locating pins are present in ring grooves to prevent ring rotation. Make certain ring end gaps are properly positioned around locating pins when installing cylinder.

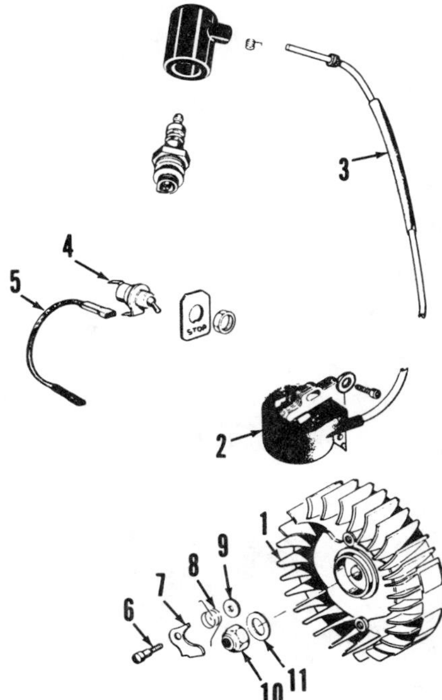

Fig. PK35—Exploded view of breakerless electronic ignition system typical of type used. Refer to text.

1. Flywheel
2. Ignition module/coil
3. High tension lead
4. Ignition switch
5. Primary lead
6. Pawl bolt
7. Pawl
8. Spring
9. Washer
10. Nut
11. Washer

Piston pin (7—Fig. PK36) rides in needle bearing (6) and is retained with two snap rings (5). Use ProKut tool 4180010 or a suitable equivalent to press out pin. Piston may be heated to approximately 110°-120° C (230°-248° F) to ease piston pin installation.

NOTE: Use electric oven or hot oil bath to heat piston. Do not use an open flame.

Install piston into cylinder with arrow on piston crown facing toward exhaust port.

CRANKSHAFT, CONNECTING ROD AND CRANKCASE. Crankshaft and connecting rod (8—Fig. PK36) are available as a unit assembly only. Check

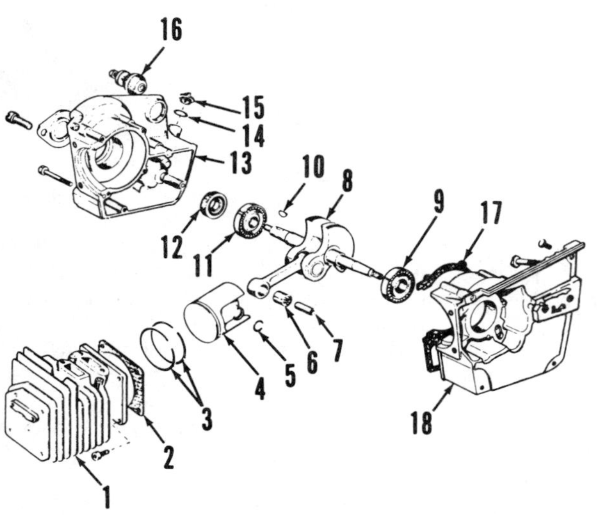

Fig. PK36—Exploded view of typical engine assembly.

1. Cylinder
2. Gasket
3. Piston rings
4. Piston
5. Retainer
6. Needle bearing
7. Piston pin
8. Crankshaft & connecting rod assy.
9. Right main bearing
10. Woodruff key
11. Left main bearing
12. Seal
13. Left crankcase half
14. Seal
15. Oil cap
16. Vibration isolator
17. Gasket
18. Right crankcase half

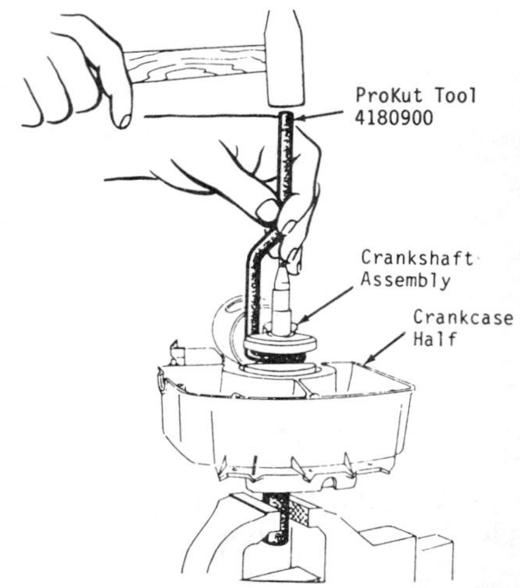

Fig. PK37—View showing installation of crankshaft and connecting rod assembly into crankcase using ProKut tool 4180900. Main bearing (9—Fig. PK36) is pressed into crankcase half prior to installation of crankshaft assembly.

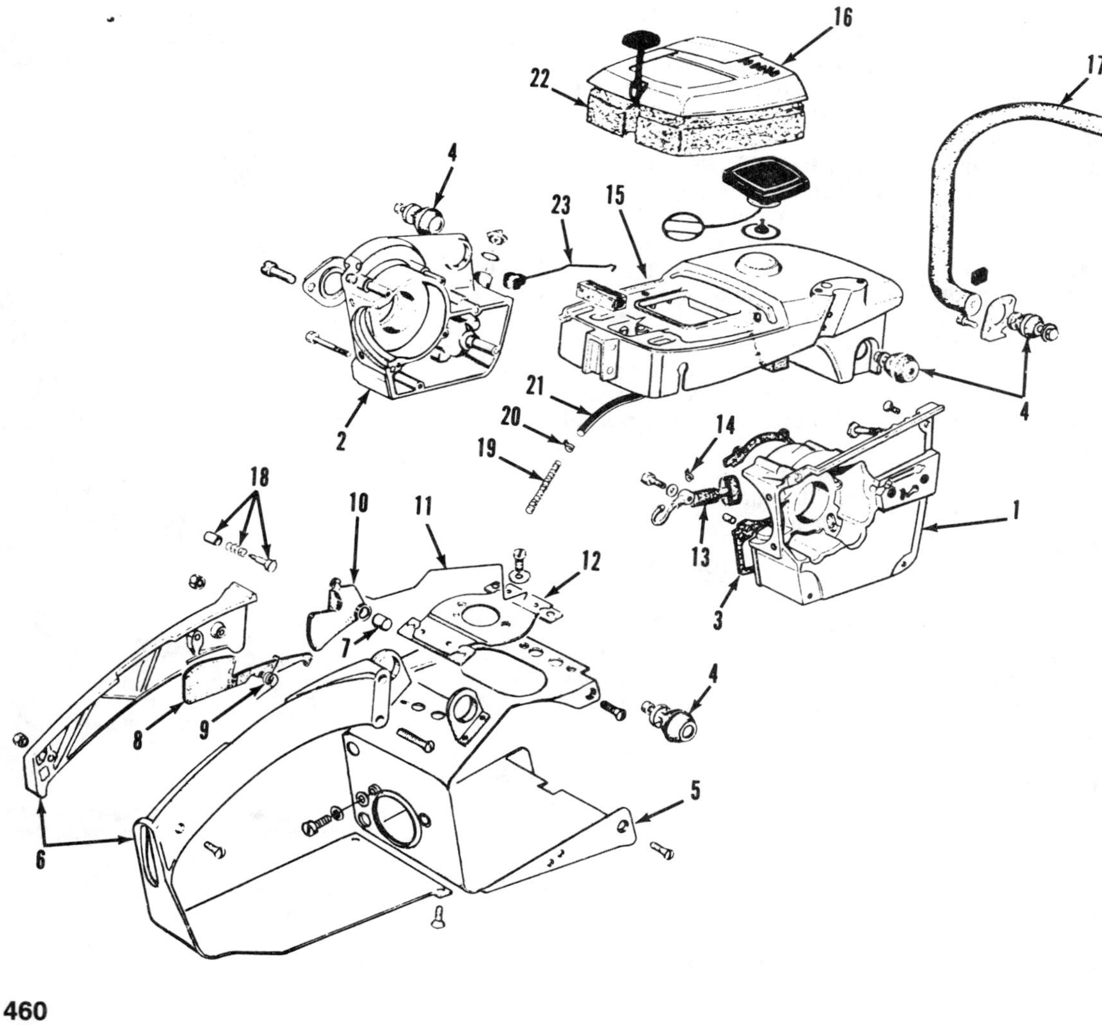

Fig. PK38—Exploded view of rear grip and front handle assemblies, crankcase, fuel tank assembly and related components.

1. Right crankcase half
2. Left crankcase half
3. Gasket
4. Vibration isolator
5. Cylinder cover
6. Rear grip assy.
7. Bushing
8. Saftey lever
9. Spring
10. Trigger
11. Throttle rod
12. Carburetor support
13. Oil pickup assy.
14. Clamp
15. Fuel tank assy.
16. Air filter cover
17. Front handle assy.
18. Trigger lock assy.
19. Spring
20. Clamp
21. Fuel hose
22. Air filter
23. Choke rod

rotation of connecting rod around crankpin and renew crankshaft assembly if roughness, excessive play or other damage is noted. Check crankshaft runout by supporting crankshaft assembly between two counterpoints such as a lathe. Make certain no damage exists to centering holes at each end of crankshaft. Maximum allowable runout is 0.08 mm (0.0031 in.).

NOTE: Crankshaft runout can be checked while still assembled in crankcase. Remove clutch and flywheel and mount dial indicators on both sides of crankshaft as close to main bearings as possible. Measure runout while rotating crankshaft. Renew crankshaft assembly if runout exceeds 0.07 mm (0.0027 in.) when measured in this manner.

Crankshaft is supported at both ends with ball-type main bearings (9 and 11). Main bearings locate in crankcase halves (13 and 18). Use the proper size drivers to remove and install main bearings. Use ProKut tool 4180900 to install crankshaft assembly into main bearing. Refer to Fig. PK37. Do not use gasket sealer on crankcase gasket (17—Fig. PK36). Tighten crankcase screws using a crisscross pattern to 6.4 N·m (57 in.-lbs.).

CLUTCH. Refer to Fig. PK39 for an exploded view of clutch assembly used on both models. Clutch hub (4) has left-hand threads. Inspect shoes (5), drum (3) and needle bearing (2) for excessive wear or damage due to overheating. Shoes (5) are available only as a complete set. Tighten clutch hub (4) to 41.2 N·m (31 ft.-lbs.).

OIL PUMP. Both models are equipped with the automatic oil pump shown in Fig. PK40. Oil is pumped by plunger (6) which is rotated by worm gear (1). Drive lugs (L) on worm gear (1) engage clutch drum, therefore oil is pumped only when saw chain is rotating.

To disassemble pump, remove cam bolt (5), plug (8) and bushing (7). Plunger (6) can now be removed for inspection or renewal. Carefully inspect seal (2) and seal surface on worm gear (1). Note that slight wear on seal or worm gear may allow pump to draw air causing pump malfunction. It is recommended to renew seal (2) any time pump is disassembled.

REWIND STARTER. All models are equipped with the rewind starter shown in Fig. PK41. To disassemble starter, remove starter housing (5) from saw. Remove rope handle (4) and carefully allow rope to wind into starter, relieving tension on rewind spring (2). Starter drive (6) is a press fit in rope pulley (3). Remove rope and tap drive (6) out of pulley (3) toward flywheel side of housing (5) using a proper size punch and hammer.

Rewind spring (2) is retained in a plastic case. Install spring with open side of case toward starter cover (1). Install starter drive (6) with hole in drive aligned with hole in rope pulley. Wind rope onto rope pulley in a clockwise direction as viewed from flywheel side of pulley.

Rotate starter cover (1) clockwise before installing cover screws to engage rope pulley and preload rewind spring. Preload spring only enough to pull rope handle snug against housing. Rope pulley should be able to rotate an additional ½ turn clockwise with rope fully extended to prevent rewind spring breakage.

Refer to Fig. PK35 for view of starter pawls. Use a suitable thread locking solution on pawl bolts (6).

CHAIN BRAKE. Some models are equipped with a chain brake system designed to stop chain movement should kickback occur. Chain brake is activated when operator's hand strikes hand guard (12—Fig. PK39), tripping lever (16) and allowing spring (15) to draw brake band (14) tight around clutch drum (3). Pull back hand guard to reset mechanism.

Disassembly is evident after inspection of unit and referral to exploded view. Renew any component excessively worn or damaged. Chain brake should be clean and free of sawdust and dirt accumulation. No adjustment of chain brake is required.

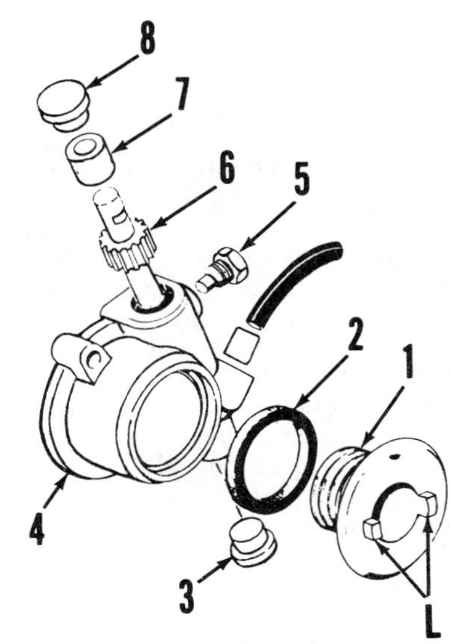

Fig. PK40—Exploded view of automatic oil pump assembly.

1. Worm gear
2. Seal
3. Plug
4. Housing
5. Cam bolt
6. Plunger
7. Bushing
8. Plug
L. Drive lugs

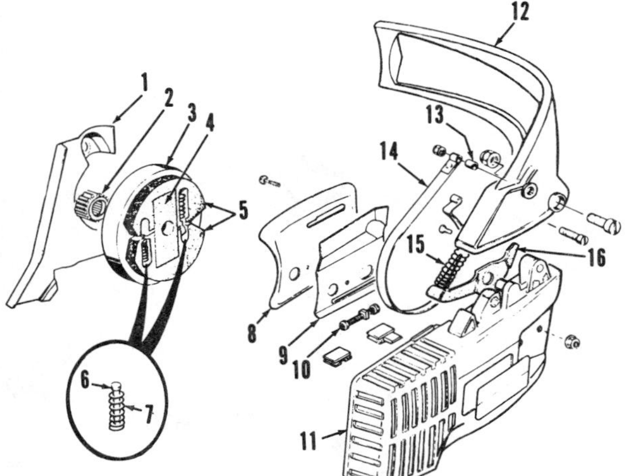

Fig. PK39—Exploded view of clutch and chain brake. Chain brake is optional on both models.

1. Plate
2. Needle bearing
3. Drum
4. Hub
5. Shoes
6. Spring guide
7. Spring
8. Inner guide plate
9. Outer guide plate
10. Bar adjusting screw
11. Cover
12. Hand guard
13. Spacer
14. Brake band
15. Spring
16. Lever

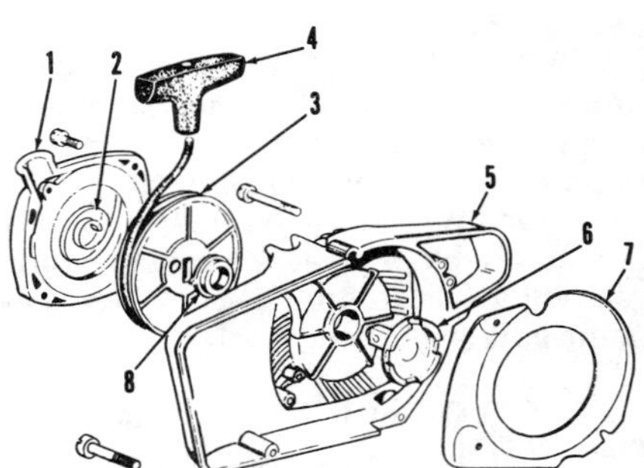

Fig. PK41—Exploded view of rewind starter assembly.

1. Starter cover
2. Rewind spring
3. Rope pulley
4. Rope handle
5. Housing
6. Starter drive
7. Baffle
8. Bushing

PROKUT

Model	Bore mm (in.)	Stroke mm (in.)	Displacement cc (cu. in.)	Drive Type
70	51 (2.0)	34.5 (1.36)	70 (4.3)	Direct
120	58 (2.28)	45.5 (1.79)	120 (7.3)	Direct

MAINTENANCE

SPARK PLUG. Recommended spark plug for both models is Champion CJ7Y. Electrode gap should be 0.5 mm (0.020 in.).

CARBURETOR. All models are equipped with a Tillotson HS diaphragm carburetor. Refer to Tillotson section of CARBURETOR SERVICE section for service and exploded views.

Initial adjustment of low speed mixture screw is 1-7/8 turns open on Model 120 and 1-3/4 turns open on Model 70. Initial adjustment of high speed mixture screw is 7/8 turn open on Model 120 and ¾ turn open on Model 70. Final adjustment should be made with engine running at operating temperature. Adjust idle speed to just below clutch engagement speed. Adjust low speed mixture screw so engine will accelerate cleanly without hesitation. Adjust high speed mixture screw to obtain maximum speed of 10,300 rpm on Model 120 and 10,500 rpm on Model 70.

IGNITION. Model 70 manufactured prior to 1984 is equipped with a breaker-point ignition system. Model 120 and Model 70, manufactured after 1983, are equipped with a breakerless electronic ignition system.

BREAKER-POINT IGNITION. Breaker-point gap should be 0.45-0.50 mm (0.018-0.020 in.). Air gap between ignition coil lamination and flywheel magnets should be 0.45 mm (0.018 in.). Use a suitable thread locking solution on coil attaching screws. Ignition timing is not adjustable, however, breaker-point gap will affect timing. Be sure breaker-point gap is adjusted correctly.

ELECTRONIC IGNITION. Refer to Fig. PK51 for exploded view of electronic ignition system used on so equipped Model 70. Note that coil (8) is located outside of flywheel (1) while ignition module (13) is located behind flywheel (1). Model 120 is equipped with the electronic ignition system shown in Fig. PK52. Ignition coil and all electronic circuitry are contained in a one-piece ignition module (13).

Except for faulty wiring or wiring connections, repair of ignition system malfunctions is accomplished by component renewal.

On Model 120, air gap between ignition module and flywheel magnets should be 0.65 mm (0.026 in.). Air gap between ignition coil and flywheel magnets on all other models should be 0.40 mm (0.016 in.). Use a suitable thread locking solution on module (or coil) attaching screws. Ignition timing is not adjustable on all models.

Starter pawl assemblies (2, 3, 4 and 7—Fig. PK51) can be removed to accommodate a suitable bolt-type puller to remove flywheel on all models. Use a suitable thread locking solution on bolts (2) when reassembling pawls. Tighten flywheel to 39.2 N·m (29 ft.-lbs.) on Model 120 and 28.4 N·m (21 ft.-lbs.) on Model 70.

LUBRICATION. The engine is lubricated by mixing oil with the fuel. Use a good quality oil designed for use in air-cooled two-stroke engines. Fuel:oil mixture should be a 16:1 ratio. Use a separate container when mixing fuel and oil.

Models 70 and 120 are equipped with an automatic chain oil pump. Automatic oil pump output is only adjustable on Model 120. Refer to OIL PUMP under REPAIRS section for service and exploded views of manual and automatic oil pump assemblies. Use clean automotive oil for saw chain lubrication.

REPAIRS

CYLINDER, PISTON, PIN AND RINGS. Cylinder bore is chrome plated and should be renewed if cracking, scor-

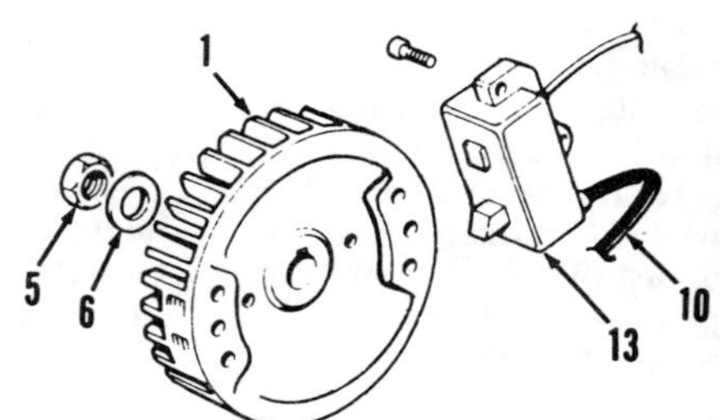

Fig. PK52—Exploded view of electronic ignition system used on Model 120. Refer to Fig. PK51 for component identification.

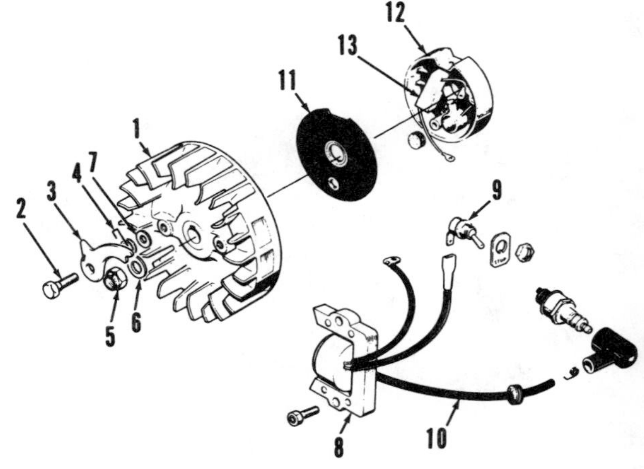

Fig. PK51—Exploded view of electronic ignition system used on Model 70 manufactured after 1983. Note two pawl assemblies (2, 3, 4 and 7) are used.

1. Flywheel
2. Bolt
3. Pawl
4. Spring
5. Nut
6. Washer
7. Washer
8. Ignition coil
9. Ignition switch
10. High tension lead
11. Cover
12. Module case
13. Module

ing or other damage is noted in cylinder bore. Note that cylinder used on Model 120 is equipped with decompression valve (28—Fig. PK54) to ease starting.

Piston and cylinder are marked during production to obtain desired piston-to-cylinder clearance of 0.02 mm (0.0008 in.). Original equipment piston and cylinder are marked "A." Factory renewal piston and cylinder assemblies are marked "B." Piston or cylinder marked "C" is 0.127 mm (0.005 in.) oversize. Piston or cylinder marked "D" is 0.127 mm (0.005 in.) undersize. Piston and cylinder markings should match, however, a new piston marked "B" can be installed into a used cylinder marked "A."

NOTE: Do not install a new piston marked "B" or "C" into a new cylinder marked "A."

Piston is equipped with two piston rings. Piston should be inspected and renewed if cracking or scoring is noted. Maximum allowable piston ring end gap is 1.0 mm (0.039 in.). Locating pins are present in ring grooves to prevent ring rotation. Be certain ring end gaps are properly positioned around locating pins when installing cylinder. Tighten cylinder screws to 11.8 N·m (9 ft.-lbs.) on all models.

On Model 70, piston pin (8—Fig. PK53) is a press fit in connecting rod small end.

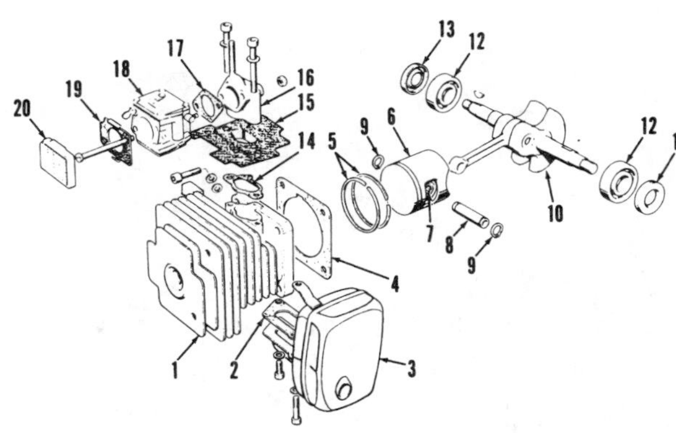

Fig. PK53—Exploded view of engine assembly, carburetor and related components used on Model 70. Two needle bearings (7) are used. Refer to text.

1. Cylinder
2. Gasket
3. Muffler
4. Gasket
5. Piston rings
6. Piston
7. Needle bearing
8. Piston pin
9. Snap ring
10. Crankshaft & connecting rod assy.
11. Seal
12. Main bearing
13. Seal
14. Gasket
15. Gasket
16. Intake manifold
17. Gasket
18. Carburetor
19. Plate
20. Screen

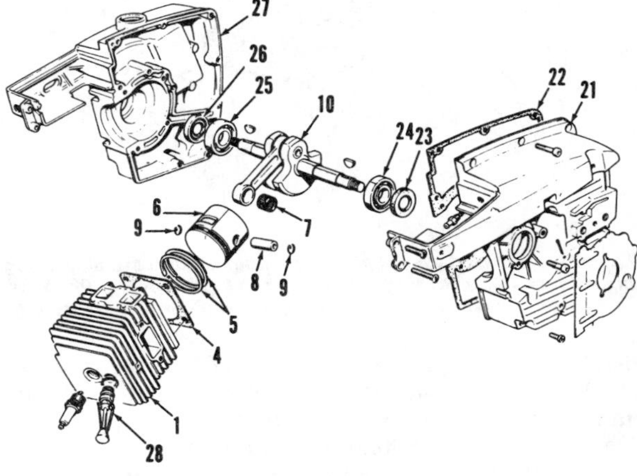

Fig. PK54—Exploded view of engine assembly used on Model 120.

1. Cylinder
4. Gasket
5. Piston rings
6. Piston
7. Needle bearing
8. Piston pin
9. Wire clip
10. Crankshaft & connecting rod assy.
21. Right crankcase half
22. Gasket
23. Seal
24. Main bearing
25. Main bearing
26. Seal
27. Left crankcase half
28. Decompression valve

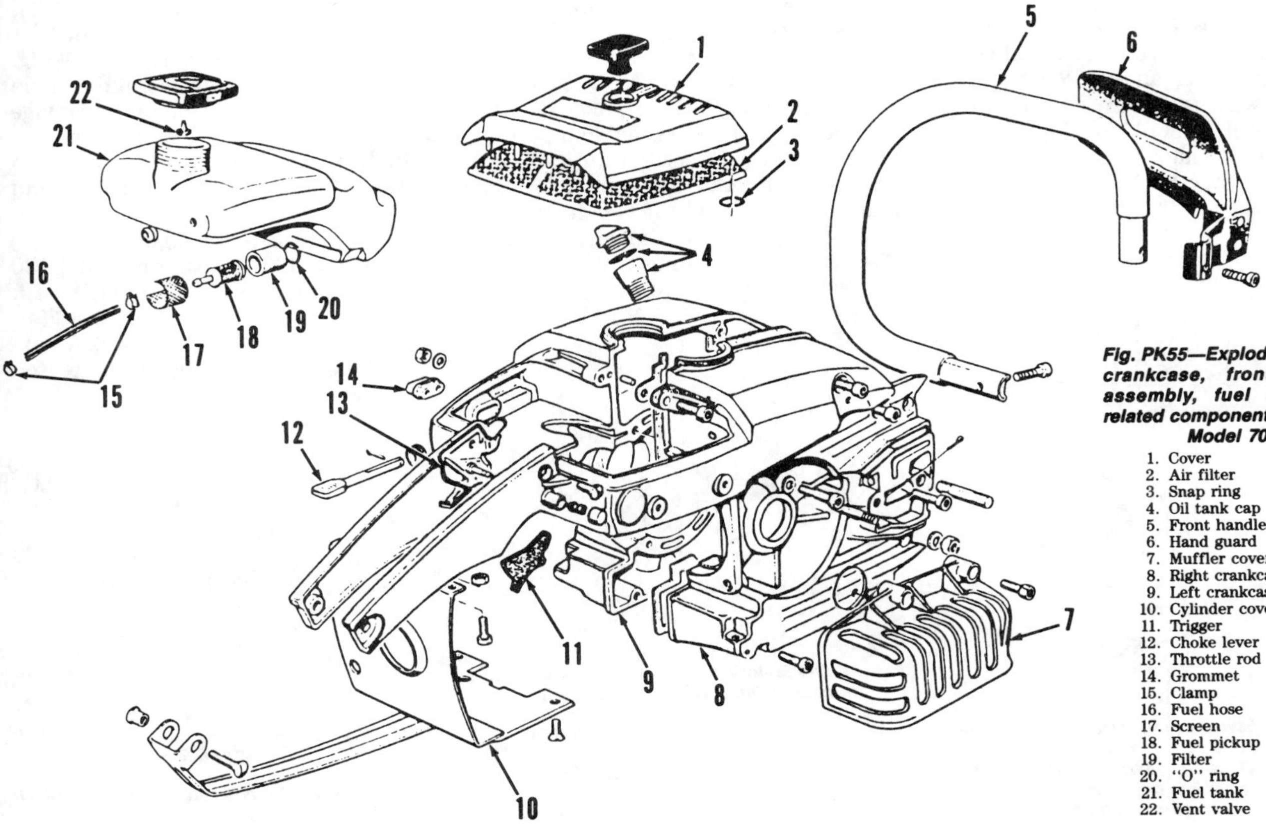

Fig. PK55—Exploded view of crankcase, front handle assembly, fuel tank and related components used on Model 70.

1. Cover
2. Air filter
3. Snap ring
4. Oil tank cap assy.
5. Front handle
6. Hand guard
7. Muffler cover
8. Right crankcase half
9. Left crankcase half
10. Cylinder cover
11. Trigger
12. Choke lever
13. Throttle rod
14. Grommet
15. Clamp
16. Fuel hose
17. Screen
18. Fuel pickup
19. Filter
20. "O" ring
21. Fuel tank
22. Vent valve

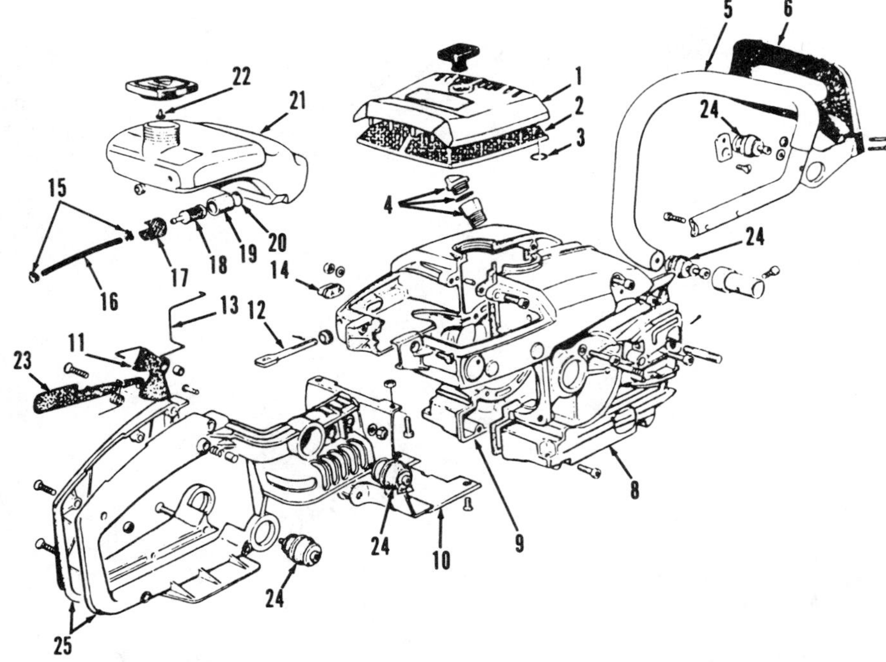

Fig. PK56—Exploded view of crankcase, front handle assembly, rear grip assembly, fuel tank and related components similar to Model 120. Refer to legend in Fig. PK55 for component identification except, safety lever (23), vibration isolator (24) and rear grip assembly (25).

Piston pin rides in needle bearings (7) installed in each side of piston. Piston pin is retained with two snap rings (9). Use ProKut tool 4180020 or a suitable equivalent press to remove and install piston. Be sure piston is properly supported to prevent damage to piston.

On Model 120, piston pin (8—Fig. PK54) is a press fit in piston and rides in one needle bearing (7) installed in connecting rod small end. Piston pin is retained with two wire clips (9). Use ProKut tool 4180010 or a suitable equivalent to remove and install piston pin. Piston may be heated to approximately 110°-120° C (230°-248° F) to ease installation of piston pin.

NOTE: Use an oven or a hot oil bath to heat piston. Do not use an open flame.

On all models, install piston into cylinder with arrow on piston crown facing toward exhaust port.

CRANKSHAFT, CONNECTING ROD AND CRANKCASE. Crankshaft and connecting rod are available as a unit assembly only. Check rotation of connecting rod around crankpin and renew crankshaft assembly if roughness, excessive play or other damage is noted. Check crankshaft runout by supporting crankshaft between two counterpoints such as a lathe. Make certain no damage is present in centering holes at each end of crankshaft. Renew crankshaft assembly if runout exceeds 0.08 mm (0.0031 in.).

NOTE: Crankshaft runout can be checked while still assembled in crankcase. Remove clutch and flywheel and mount dial indicators on each side of crankshaft as close to main bearings as possible. Measure runout while rotating crankshaft. Renew crankshaft assembly if runout exceeds 0.07 mm (0.0027 in.) when measured in this manner.

Crankshaft is supported with ball-type main bearings (12—Fig. PK53) or (24 and 25—Fig. PK54) at both ends. Main bearings are a press fit into crankcase halves. Use the proper size drivers to remove and install main bearings. Use ProKut tool 4180900 or a suitable equivalent to install crankshaft assembly into crankcase. Refer to Fig. PK57. Do not use gasket sealer on crankcase gasket. Tighten crankcase screws using a crisscross pattern to 7.8 N·m (69 in.-lbs.) on Model 120 and 7.3 N·m (65 in.-lbs.) on Model 70.

ProKut Tool 4180900

Crankshaft Assembly

Crankcase Half

Fig. PK57—View showing installation procedure of crankshaft and connecting rod assembly into crankcase half using ProKut tool 4180900. Main bearing is pressed into crankcase half prior to installation of crankshaft assembly.

CLUTCH. Late Model 70 is equipped with the clutch assembly shown in Fig. PK58. Late Model 120 is equipped with the clutch assembly shown in Fig. PK60. Refer to Fig. PK59 for view of shoes (4), hub (5) and spring (3) used on all early models. Note that hub (5—Figs. PK58, PK59 and PK60) is keyed to crankshaft on all models. Inspect shoes (4—Fig. PK58 or PK60), drum (7) and needle bearing (9) for excessive wear or damage due to overheating. Use ProKut tool 4180110 or a suitable bolt-type puller to remove clutch. Nut (12) has right-hand threads. Clutch shoes (4) are available only as a complete set. Tighten nut (12) to 45.1 N·m (33 ft.-lbs.) on Model 120 and 35.3 N·m (26 ft.-lbs.) on Model 70.

OIL PUMP. Refer to Fig. PK62 for exploded view of automatic oil pump used

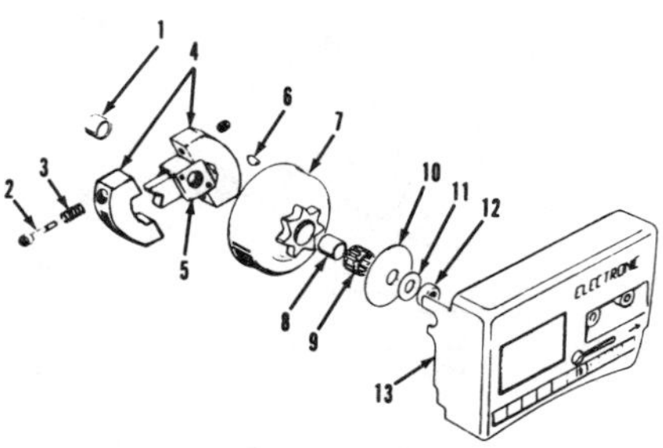

Fig. PK58—Exploded view of new design centrifugal clutch used on late Model 70.

1. Bushing
2. Screw
3. Spring
4. Shoes
5. Hub
6. Woodruff key
7. Drum
8. Bushing
9. Needle bearing
10. Washer
11. Washer
12. Nut
13. Cover

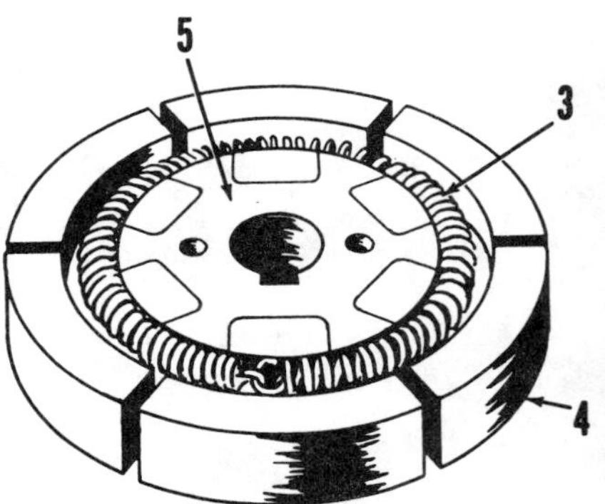

Fig. PK59—View showing clutch shoes (4), hub (5) and spring (3) used on all early models.

on Model 70. Oil is pumped by piston (5) which is rotated by drive plate (10). Drive plate is cycled up and down by plunger (15) which rides on cam of engine crankshaft. Piston (5) rotates one notch with each down stroke of drive plate (10). Spring (12) forces piston brake (13) against piston (5), preventing piston (5) from backing up during drive plate (10) return stroke.

Plunger (15) is 31 mm (1.22 in.) long when new. Renew plunger if worn shorter than 30.3 mm (1.193 in.). Renew drive plate (10) if wear at piston contact area exceeds 1.5 mm (0.059 in.) when compared with a new drive plate. Reservoir (R) should be filled with high temperature lithium base grease and capped with felt plug (20). Pump output is not adjustable.

Refer to Fig. PK63 for exploded view of adjustable automatic oil pump used on Model 120. Oil is pumped by piston (5) which is rotated by worm gear (23) mounted on engine crankshaft. Pump output is regulated by turning adjusting lever (28). Renew piston and worm gear if excessive wear or damage is noted. Closely inspect seal (30) and seal surface on worm gear (23). Note that slight wear on seal or worm gear may allow pump to draw air causing pump malfunction. It is recommended to renew seal (30) any time pump is disassembled.

REWIND STARTER. To disassemble starter, remove rope handle (10—Fig. PK64) and carefully allow rope to wind into housing, relieving tension on rewind spring (5). Remove screw (9) and rope pulley (6) using caution not to dislodge rewind spring (5). If rewind spring (5) must be removed, use caution not to allow spring to uncoil uncontrolled.

Install rewind spring (5) into housing (2) in a clockwise direction starting with outer coil. Install rope onto rope pulley (6) in a clockwise direction as viewed from flywheel side of pulley. Rotate pulley (6) clockwise to apply tension on rewind spring. Apply only enough tension on rewind spring (5) to pull rope handle snug against housing. Rope pulley should be able to rotate an additional ½ turn with rope completely extended.

Refer to Fig. PK51 for exploded view of starter pawl assemblies. Use a suitable thread locking solution on pawl bolts (2).

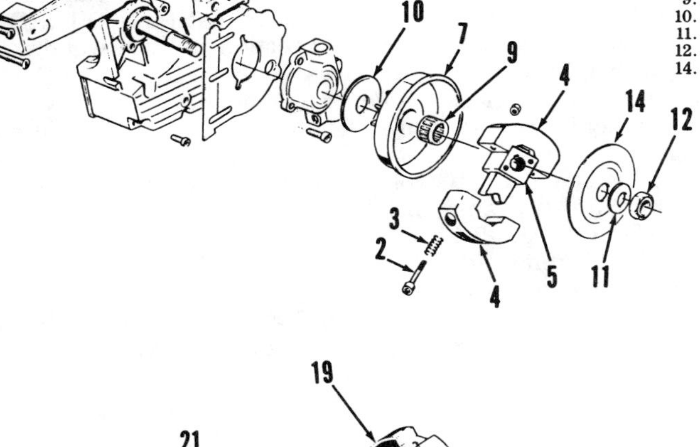

Fig. PK60—Exploded view of centrifugal clutch used on late Model 120.

2. Screw
3. Spring
4. Shoes
5. Hub
7. Drum
9. Needle bearing
10. Washer
11. Washer
12. Nut
14. Washer

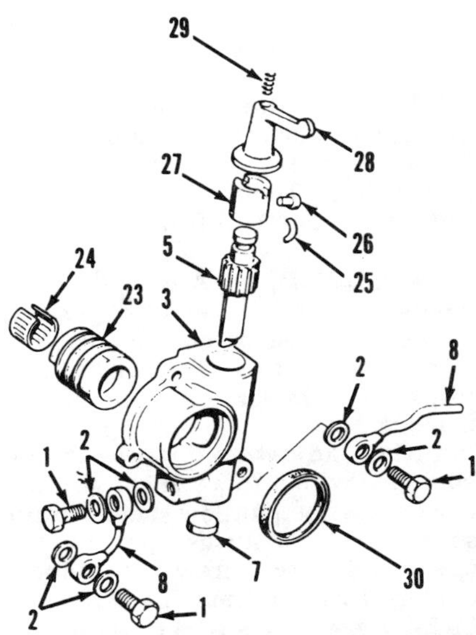

Fig. PK63—Exploded view of adjustable automatic oil pump used on Model 120.

1. Banjo bolt
2. Washers
3. Pump body
5. Piston
7. Plug
8. Tube
23. Worm gear
24. Collar
25. Pin
26. Pin
27. Bushing
28. Adjusting lever
29. Spring
30. Seal

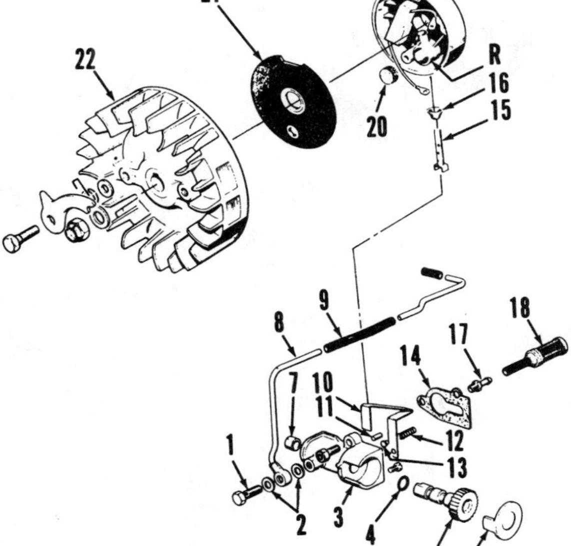

Fig. PK62—Exploded view of automatic oil pump used on Model 70.

1. Banjo bolt
2. Washers
3. Pump body
4. "O" ring
5. Piston
6. Cover
7. Plug
8. Tube
9. Hose
10. Drive plate
11. Pin
12. Spring
13. Piston brake
14. Gasket
15. Plunger
16. Seal
17. Fitting
18. Oil pickup
19. Module case
20. Felt plug
21. Cover
22. Flywheel
R. Reservoir

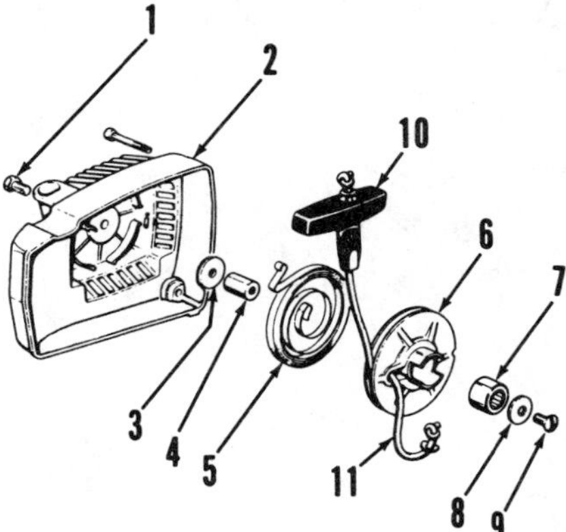

Fig. PK64—Exploded view of rewind starter used on Model 70. Model 120 is similar except, washer (11) is not used and shaft (4) is part of housing (2).

1. Bolt
2. Housing
3. Washer
4. Shaft
5. Rewind spring
6. Rope pulley
7. Needle bearing
8. Washer
9. Screw
10. Rope handle
11. Rope

REDMAX

Model	Bore mm (in.)	Stroke mm (in.)	Displacement cc (cu. in.)	Drive Type
G300T, G300TS, G300AV, G300AVS	36 (1.42)	28 (1.1)	28.5 (1.74)	Direct

MAINTENANCE

SPARK PLUG. Recommended spark plug for all models is Champion CJ8Y. Recommended electrode gap is 0.6 mm (0.024 in.). Tighten spark plug to 14.7-17.6 N·m (11-13 ft.-lbs.).

CARBURETOR. All models are equipped with a Zama Z1 or Z1A diaphragm type carburetor. Refer to Zama section of CARBURETOR SERVICE section for service procedure and exploded view.

Initial adjustment for models equipped with a Zama Z1 carburetor is 1-1/8 turns open for low speed mixture screw and 1-3/8 turns open for high speed mixture screw. On models equipped with a Zama Z1A carburetor, initial adjustment is 1-1/4 turns open for low and high speed mixture screws.

Final adjustment should be made with engine running at operating temperature. Adjust low speed mixture so engine wilil accelerate cleanly without hesitation. Adjust high speed mixture to obtain optimum full throttle performance under cutting load. Adjust idle speed so engine operates at 2,700-3,100 rpm or just below clutch engagement speed.

IGNITION. All models are equipped with an electronic capacitor discharge ignition system. Ignition coil and all electronic circuitry are contained in a one-piece ignition module (3—Fig. R10) located outside of flywheel. Except for faulty wiring or connections, repair of ignition system malfunction is accomplished by component renewal. Ignition timing is not adjustable. Air gap between ignition module (3) and flywheel magnets (2) should be 0.3-0.4 mm (0.012-0.016 in.). If removed, tighten flywheel nut to 14.7-16.7 N·m (11-12 ft.-lbs.).

LUBRICATION. The engine is lubricated by mixing oil with the fuel. Recommended oil is RedMax two-stroke engine oil. Fuel and oil mixture should be a 40:1 ratio when using the recommended oil. If RedMax two-stroke engine oil is not available, a good quality oil designed for use in air-cooled two-stroke engines may be used when mixed at a 25:1 ratio.

All models are equipped with an automatic chain oil pump. Pump output is not adjustable. Refer to OIL PUMP in REPAIRS section for service and exploded views.

RedMax genuine chain oil is recommended for saw chain lubrication. If RedMax genuine chain oil is not available, clean SAE 10W-30 automotive oil may be used.

REPAIRS

CYLINDER, PISTON, PIN AND RING. Refer to Fig. R11 for exploded

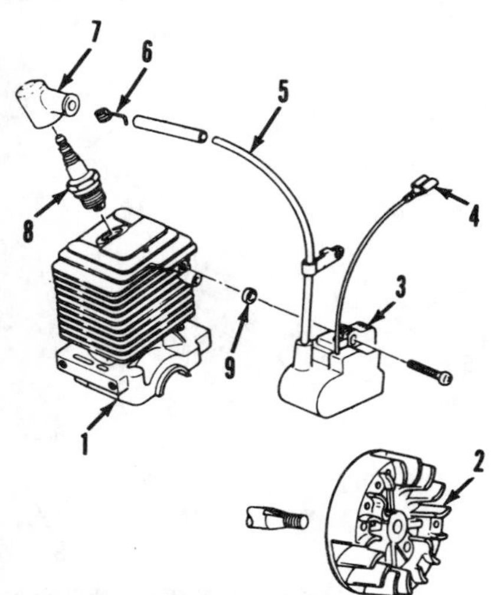

Fig. R10—Exploded view of ignition system used on all models.

1. Cylinder
2. Flywheel
3. Ignition module
4. Primary ignition wire
5. High tension lead
6. Spring connector
7. Boot
8. Spark plug

Fig. R11—Exploded view of engine assembly, engine case and related components.

1. Cylinder
2. Piston ring
3. Piston
4. Piston pin
5. Clip
6. Washer
7. Needle bearing
8. Crankshaft & connecting rod assy.
9. Main bearing
10. Seal
11. Snap ring
12. Seal
13. Crankcase
14. Screw
15. Carburetor
16. Gasket
17. Reed valve assy.
18. Gasket
19. Seal
20. Engine case
21. Screw
22. Spacer

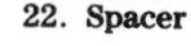

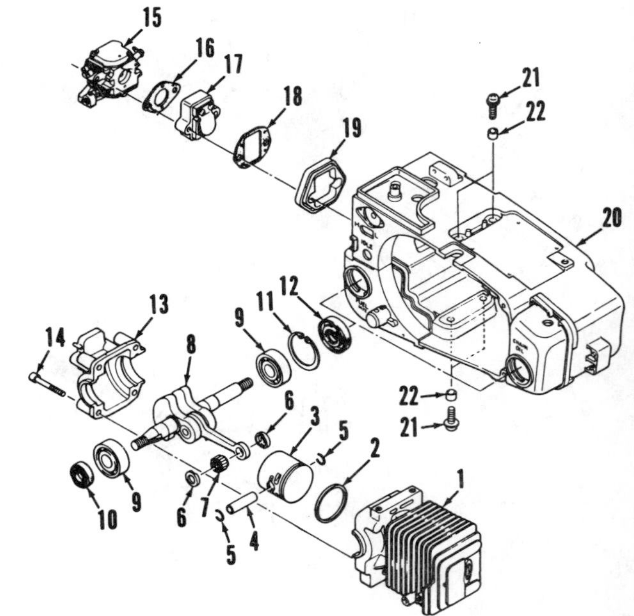

Illustrations courtesy RedMax, Div. of Komatsu Zenoah America, Inc.

view of engine assembly. After removing mounting screws, tap cylinder (1) and crankcase (13) with a soft-faced mallet to split crankcase from cylinder. Take care not to damage mating surfaces. Note that cylinder is also part of engine crankcase. Inspect cylinder bore and renew cylinder if cracking, flaking or other damage is noted in cylinder bore plating. Maximum cylinder bore diameter is 36.05 mm (1.419 in.). Piston is equipped with one piston ring (2). Minimum piston diameter is 35.7 mm (1.40) and maximum ring end gap is 0.7 mm (0.027 in.). Piston pin (4) is supported in connecting rod small end by needle bearing (7) and is retained in piston pin bore with two wire clips (5). Note location of washers (6). Closed end of piston pin (4) must be installed facing exhaust port. Piston may be installed in either direction.

CRANKSHAFT AND CONNECTING ROD. Crankshaft is loose in crankcase with cylinder removed. Crankshaft and connecting rod (8—Fig. R11) are a unit assembly and supported at both ends with ball type main bearings (9). Rotate connecting rod around crankpin and renew assembly if roughness, excessive play or other damage is noted.

Check crankshaft runout by supporting crankshaft at points (A—Fig. R-12) and measuring at points (B). Maximum crankshaft runout should not exceed 0.07 mm (0.0027 in.).

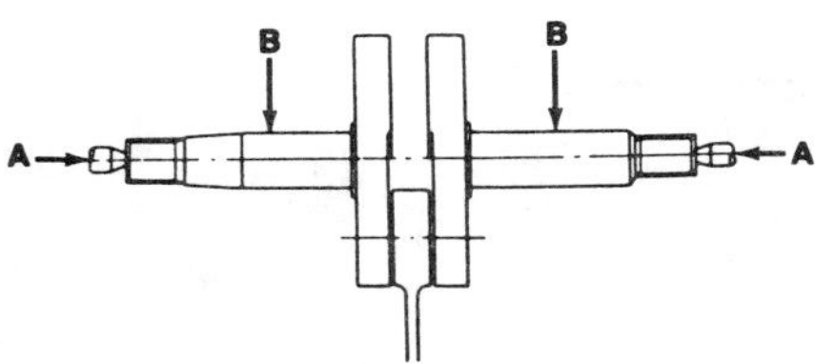

Fig. R12—Measure crankshaft runout by supporting crankshaft at points (A). Runout measured at points (B) should not exceed 0.07 mm (0.0027 in).

Fig. R13—View of reed valve assembly. Refer to text for service procedures.

Main bearings (9—Fig. R11) and seals (10 and 12) should be installed on crankshaft when reassembling cylinder and crankcase. Clutch side seal (12) should be against snap ring (11). Starter side seal (10) should be installed with outer face of seal flush with outer surface of cylinder and crankcase. Use a suitable form-in-place gasket compound on mating surfaces of cylinder and crankcase. Tighten crankcase screws (14) to 4.9-7.8 N·m (43-69 in.-lbs).

Install engine assembly into engine case (20). Use a suitable thread locking solution on screws (21) and tighten screws to 2.9-3.9 N·m (26-35 in.-lbs.).

REED VALVE. The reed valve assembly (17—Fig. R11) should be inspected whenever the carburetor is removed. Reed petal (P—Fig. R13) should seat very lightly against insulator block (B) throughout its entire length with the least possible tension. Tip of reed petal must not stand open more than 0.7 mm (0.027 in). Reed stop (S) opening should be 5.3-5.7 mm (0.209-0.224 in.). Adjust reed stop opening by bending reed stop (S).

CLUTCH. All models are equipped with the two-shoe centrifugal clutch shown in Fig. R14. Use RedMax tool 3330-97110 to remove and install clutch. Clutch hub (3) has left-hand threads. Shoes (1) should be renewed in sets to prevent an unbalanced condition. Clutch springs (2) should be renewed if stretched, broken or damaged or if clutch engagement speed is below 4,200 rpm. Springs should be renewed in pairs. Install shoes with recess in shoes facing outward. Make certain oil pump drive plate (7) properly engages clutch drum (5) and notches in oil pump worm gear (1—Fig. R15 or R16). Tighten clutch hub to 21.6-25.5 N·m (16-19 ft.-lbs.).

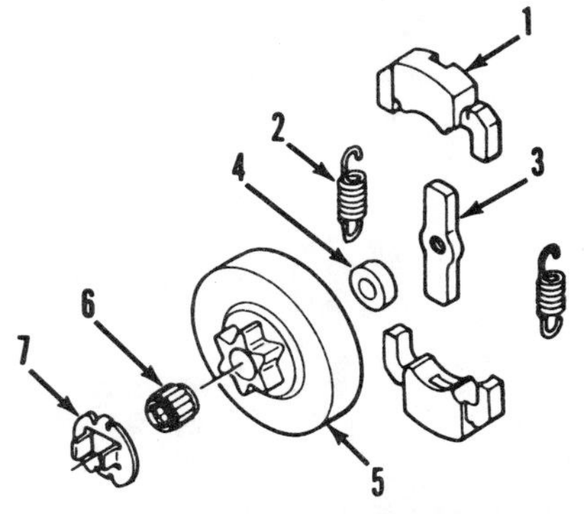

Fig. R14—Exploded view of clutch assembly used on all models.

1. Shoe
2. Spring
3. Hub
4. Spacer
5. Drum
6. Needle bearing
7. Oil pump plate

OIL PUMP. All models are equipped with a nonadjustable automatic chain oil pump. Refer to Fig. R15 or R16 for views of pump. Oil pump (2—Fig. R15) is a unit assembly and cannot be disassembled. Oil pump drive plate (7—Fig. R14) is driven by clutch drum (5) and engages worm gear (1—Fig. R15 and R16). Worm gear (1) rotates plunger (4—Fig. R16). Oil is pumped by plunger (4) as it reciprocates due to cam pin (3) riding in oblique groove in end of plunger.

Apply a suitable grease on worm gear prior to reassembly. Prime oil pump by

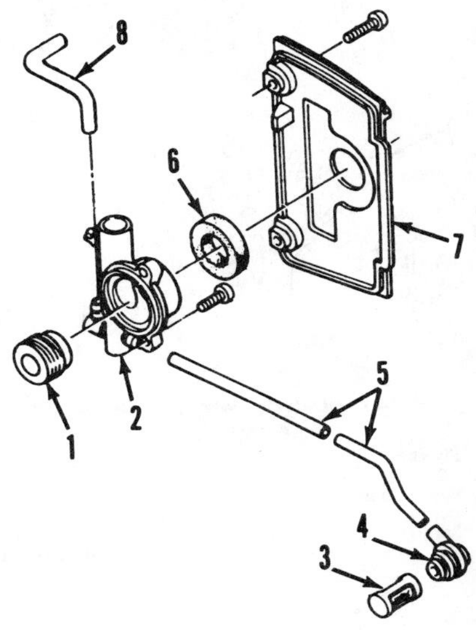

Fig. R15—Exploded view of automatic oil pump.

1. Worm gear
2. Pump assy.
3. Filter
4. Grommet
5. Suction line
6. Seal
7. Cover
8. Discharge

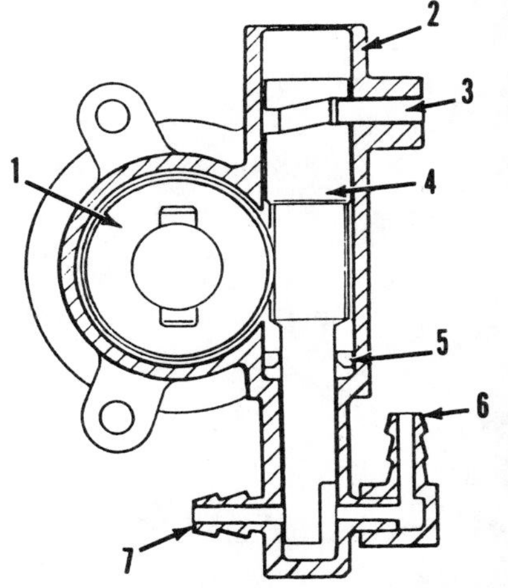

Fig. R16—Cross-sectional view of automatic oil pump.

1. Worm gear
2. Housing
3. Cam pin
4. Plunger
5. Seal
6. Discharge
7. Inlet port

adding clean oil to inlet port (7) before attaching suction line to suction port. Be certain oil pump drive plate properly engages worm gear before installing clutch.

REWIND STARTER. All models are equipped with the rewind starter shown in Fig. R17. To disassemble starter, remove starter housing (11), rope handle (3) and slowly allow rope to wind into starter housing, relieving tension on rewind spring (10). Remove screw (7) and lift out rope pulley (9) being careful not to dislodge rewind spring (10). If rewind spring must be removed, use caution not to allow spring to uncoil uncontrolled. Flywheel (1) must be removed to disassemble pawl assembly (4 and 5). Note location of "E" ring on back side of flywheel. Renew any components found to be excessively worn or damaged. Tighten flywheel nut to 14.7-16.7 N·m (11-12 ft.-lbs.).

Lightly lubricate rewind spring (10) and bore of rope pulley (9) with a suitable low temperature grease prior to installing rewind spring into starter housing. Install rope pulley with rope attached into housing. Run rope through rope guide (12) and install handle (3). Place rope into notch in rope pulley and rotate pulley five turns clockwise to preload rewind spring. Carefully allow rewind rope onto pulley. If rewind tension is correct, rope pulley will be able to rotate at least one turn further with rope fully extended and rope handle will be held against housing by spring tension in released position.

CHAIN BRAKE. Models G300TS and G300AVS are equipped with a chain brake system designed to quickly stop chain movement should kickback occur. Chain brake is activated when operator's hand strikes hand guard (1—Fig. R18), lifting latch (3) thereby allowing spring (4) to draw brake band (6) tight around drum. Pull back hand guard to reset mechanism.

Disassembly for inspection or repair is evident after referral to exploded view and inspection of unit. Renew any component found to be excessively worn or damaged. Chain brake mechanism should be clean and free of sawdust and dirt accumulation. Lightly lubricate all moving parts and pivot points. No adjustment of chain brake system is required.

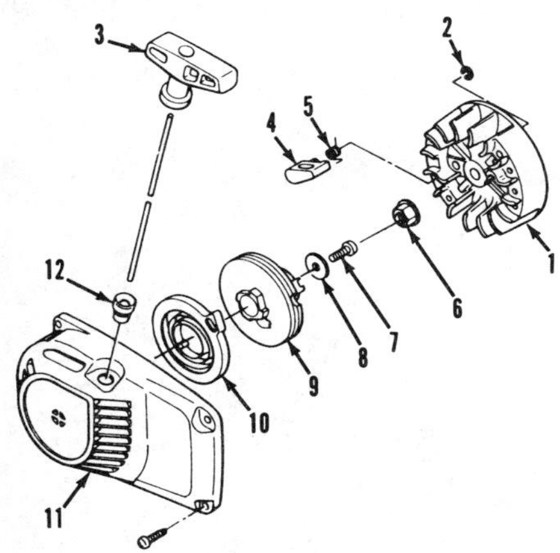

Fig. R17—Exploded view of rewind starter assembly.

1. Flywheel
2. "E" ring
3. Rope handle
4. Pawl
5. Spring
6. Nut
7. Screw
8. Washer
9. Rope pulley
10. Rewind spring & case assy.
11. Starter housing
12. Rope guide

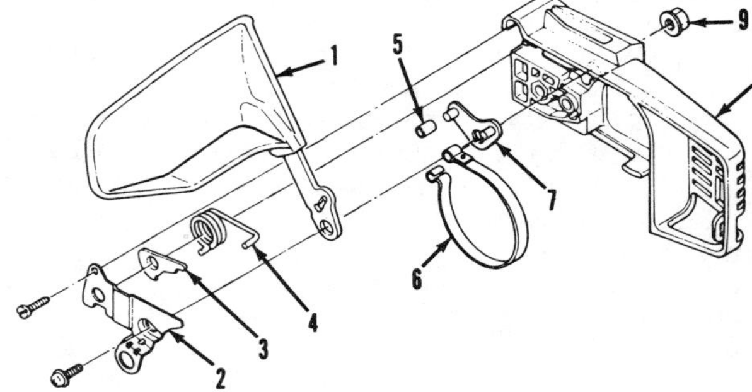

Fig. R18—Exploded view of chain brake system used on Models G3300TS and G300AVS.

1. Hand guard & lever assy.
2. Bracket
3. Latch
4. Spring
5. Roller
6. Brake band
7. Lever
8. Cover
9. Nut

REDMAX

Model	Bore mm (in.)	Stroke mm (in.)	Displacement cc (cu. in.)	Drive Type
G561AV, G561AVS, G561AVSH	44 (1.73)	35 (1.38)	53.2 (3.25)	Direct
G621, G621AV, G621AVS, G621AVSH	47.5 (1.87)	35 (1.38)	62 (3.78)	Direct

MAINTENANCE

SPARK PLUG. Recommended spark plug for all models is Champion CJ7Y or RCJ7Y. Spark plug electrode gap should be 0.60-0.70 mm (0.024-0.027 in.)

CARBURETOR. All models are equipped with a Walbro HDA diaphragm type carburetor. Refer to Walbro section of CARBURETOR SERVICE section for service procedure and exploded view.

Initial adjustment of the low speed mixture screw is 1-1/4 to 1-1/2 turns open from a lightly seated position. Initial adjustment of the high speed mixture screw is 1-1/4 to 1-3/4 turns open from a lightly seated position.

Make final adjustment with engine running at operating temperature. Adjust low speed mixture screw to obtain maximum idle speed. Once maximum idle speed is obtained, open low speed mixture screw an additional ¼ turn. Adjust idle speed screw so engine operates at 2,400-2,600 rpm. Repeat this procedure until best possible idling condition is achieved. A tachometer should be used to make final adjustment of high speed mixture to prevent exceeding maximum allowable speed. Adjust high speed mixture to obtain clean acceleration and optimum full throttle performance under cutting load. Maximum allowable no-load speed is 12,000 rpm for Models G561AV, G561AVS and G561AVSH and 12,500 rpm for all other models. If necessary, readjust idle speed to 2,400-2,600 rpm.

IGNITION. All models are equipped with a breakerless electronic ignition system. Refer to Fig. R28. Except for faulty wiring and connections, repair of ignition system malfunction is accomplished by component renewal.

Ignition module can be checked with an ohmmeter. Module primary resistance should be approximately 0.72-0.98 ohm. Coil secondary resistance should be approximately 5,490-6,710 ohms. Ignition timing is not adjustable. Air gap between module lamination and flywheel magnets should be 0.4-0.5 mm (0.016-0.020 in). Flywheel nut should be tightened to 14.7-19.6 N·m (11-14 ft.-lbs.).

LUBRICATION. The engine is lubricated by mixing oil with the fuel. Recommended oil is RedMax two-stroke engine oil mixed at a 40:1 ratio. If RedMax two-stroke engine oil is not available, a good quality oil designed for use in air-cooled two-stroke engines may be used when mixed at a 25:1 ratio. Use a separate container when mixing oil and fuel.

All models are equipped with the automatic chain oil pump shown in Fig. R29. Oil pump output is adjusted by rotating adjusting shaft (8). Clockwise rotation of shaft decreases pump output.

RedMax genuine chain oil is recommended for saw chain lubrication. If RedMax genuine chain oil or suitable equivalent is not available, clean SAE 10W-30 automotive oil may be used.

REPAIRS

CYLINDER, PISTON, PIN AND RINGS. Cylinder (1—Fig. R30) bore is chrome plated and should be renewed if cracking, flaking or other damage to cylinder bore is noted. Oversize piston and rings are not available. Piston (4) is equipped with two piston rings (3). Maximum ring end gap is 0.6 mm (0.024 in.) on 561 series engines and 0.7 mm (0.028 in.) on 621 series engines. Maximum allowable piston ring side clearance is 0.13 mm (0.005 in.) for all models. Locating pins are present in ring grooves to prevent ring rotation. Make certain ring end gaps are properly positioned around locating pins before installing cylinder. Piston pin (5) rides in needle bearing (7) and is retained in position with two wire clips (6). Once removed, wire clips should not be reused. New wire clips should be installed with end gaps facing upward. It should be possible to push out piston pin (5) by hand. If pin is stuck, tap out with a suitable hammer and driver while properly supporting piston to prevent damage to connecting rod. Install piston with arrow on piston crown toward exhaust port. Note location of thrust washers (8) when installing piston. Tighten cylinder screws to 6.9-8.8 N·m (61-78 in.-lbs.).

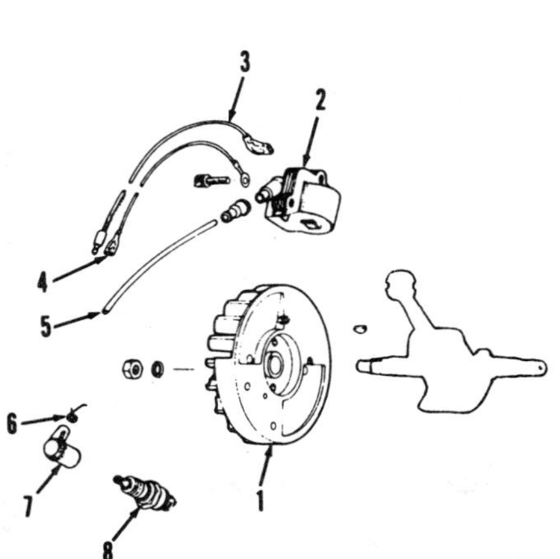

Fig. R28—Exploded view of ignition system used on all models.

1. Flywheel
2. Ignition module
3. Primary lead
4. Ground lead
5. High tension lead
6. Connector
7. Boot
8. Spark plug

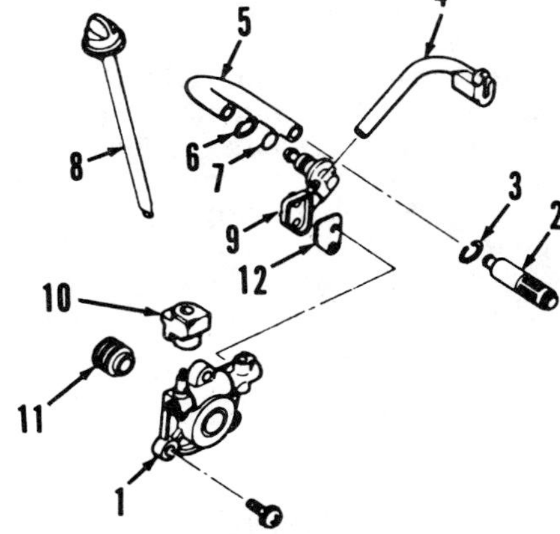

Fig. R29—Exploded view of automatic oil pump used on all models.

1. Pump assy.
2. Pickup filter
3. Clip
4. Discharge hose
5. Suction hose
6. Clip
7. "O" ring
8. Adjusting shaft
9. Connector
10. Grommet
11. Worm gear
12. Gasket

Illustrations courtesy RedMax, Div. of Komatsu Zenoah America, Inc.

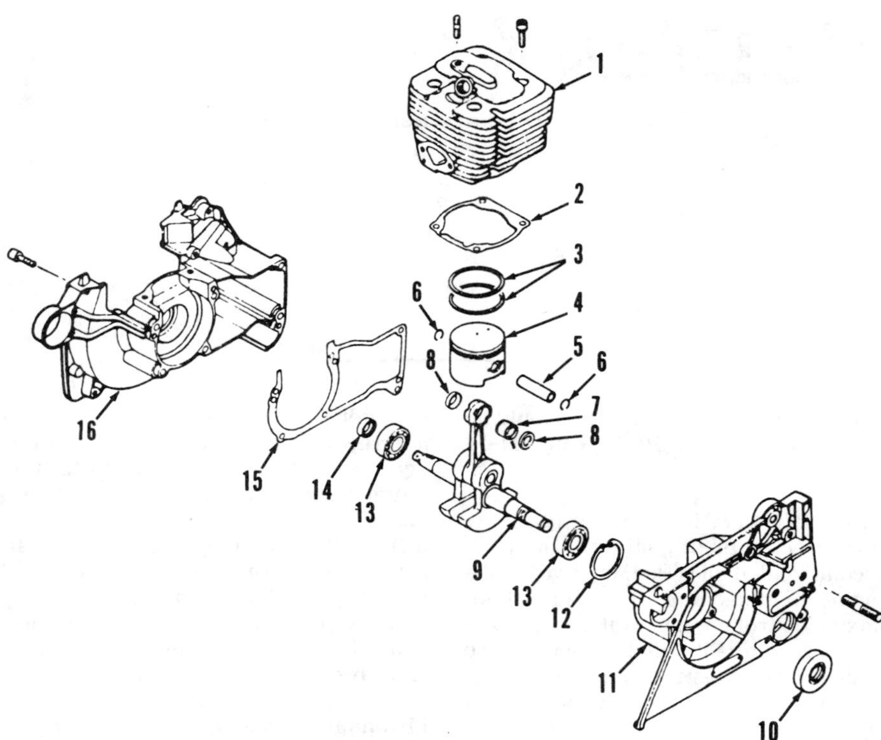

Fig. R30—Exploded view of engine assembly.

1. Cylinder
2. Gasket
3. Piston rings
4. Piston
5. Piston pin
6. Wire clip
7. Needle bearing
8. Thrust washer
9. Crankshaft & connecting rod assy.
10. Seal
11. Right crankcase half
12. Snap ring
13. Main bearing
14. Seal
15. Gasket
16. Left crankcase half

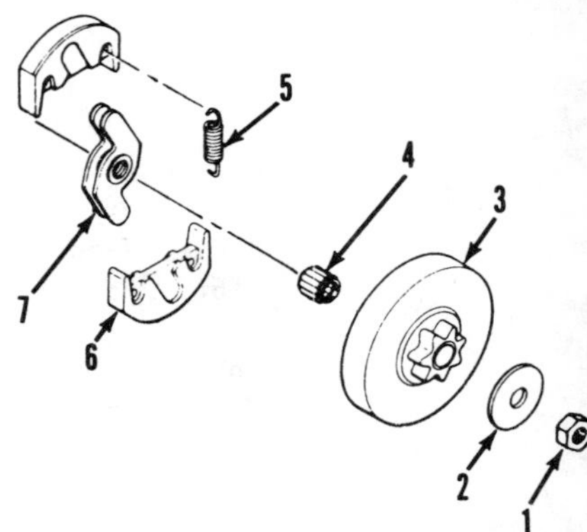

Fig. R34—Exploded view of two-shoe clutch assembly used on models so equipped.

1. Nut
2. Washer
3. Drum
4. Needle bearing
5. Spring
6. Shoe
7. Hub

CRANKSHAFT, CONNECTING ROD AND CRANKCASE. Crankcase halves (11 and 16—Fig. R30) must be split to remove crankshaft (9). Use a soft-faced mallet to tap crankcase halves apart. Do not damage crankcase mating surfaces. Crankshaft and connecting rod are a unit assembly and are not available separately. Rotate connecting rod around crankpin and renew assembly if roughness, excessive play or other damage is noted. Crankshaft is supported at both ends with ball type main bearings (13).

Check crankshaft runout by supporting crankshaft at points (A—Fig. R31) and measuring at points (B). Maximum allowable runout is 0.1 mm (0.004 in.).

Use a press and the proper size drivers and supports when removing and installing main bearings (13—Fig. R30) and seals (10 and 14). Install left side main bearing 14.8-15.0 mm (0.583-0.591 in.) below crankcase mating surface. Refer to Fig. R32. Install right side main bearing 4.5-5.5 mm (0.178-0.216 in.) from outer surface of bearing bore. Refer to Fig. R33. Install left side crankcase seal (14—Fig. R30) 3.5 mm (0.138 in.) below outer surface of crankcase bore. Press right side crankcase seal (10) into bearing bore until it contacts snap ring (12). Make certain oil suction hose is properly installed before reassembling crankcase. Tighten crankcase screws to 6.9-9.3 N·m (61-82 in.-lbs). Make certain crankshaft is centered in crankcase and rotates freely.

CLUTCH. A two-shoe (Fig. R34) and a three-shoe (Fig. R35) clutch have been used. Clutch nut and hub have left-hand threads on all models. Shoes and hub are a unit assembly on all models and are not available separately. Clutch drum rides on a needle roller bearing. Shoes, drum and needle bearing should be inspected for excessive wear or damage due to overheating. Renew excessively worn or damaged components. Tighten clutch hub to 24.5-29.4 N·m (18-22 ft.-lbs.) on all models. Tighten clutch nut to 14.7-19.6 N·m (11-14 ft.-lbs.) on all

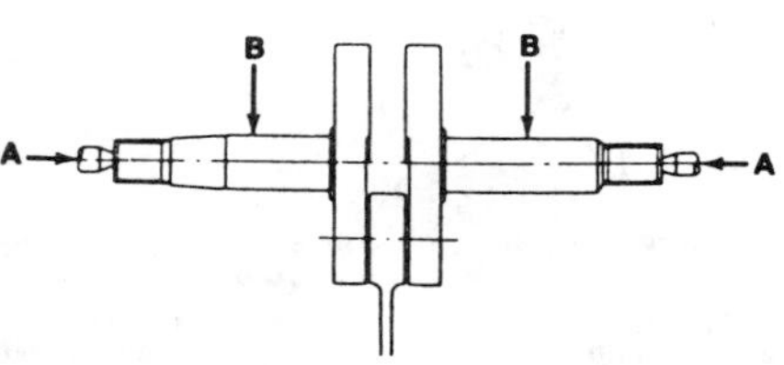

Fig. R31—Measure crankshaft runout by supporting crankshaft at points (A). Runout measured at points (B) should not exceed 0.1 mm (0.004 in.).

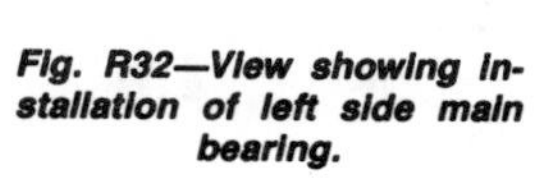

Fig. R32—View showing installation of left side main bearing.

Crankcase Mating Surface
Driver
Left Crankcase Half
14.8 - 15.0 mm (0.583 - 0.591 in.)
Main Bearing
Seal
Support

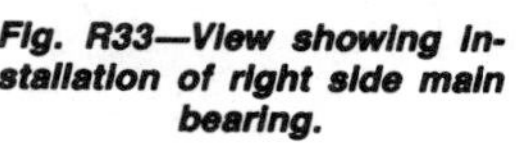

Fig. R33—View showing installation of right side main bearing.

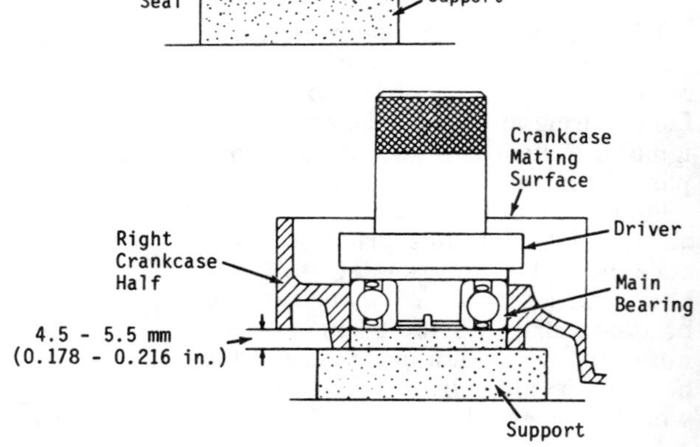

models. Use RedMax tool 3356-96210 to remove and install two-shoe clutch assemblies and RedMax tool 2616-96210 to remove and install three-shoe clutch assemblies.

OIL PUMP. All models are equipped with an adjustable automatic chain oil pump. Oil pump output is adjusted by rotating adjusting shaft (8—Fig. R29). Pump is driven by worm gear (11) located on engine crankshaft. Inspect pump plunger and worm gear for excessive wear or damage. Pump plunger is not available separately from pump body. Inspect suction and discharge hoses and renew if cracking or other damage is noted. Apply a suitable grease on pump plunger upon reassembly. Oil tank vent valve is located behind ignition module and is retained in tank with a snap ring.

REWIND STARTER. All models are equipped with the rewind starter shown in Fig. R36. To disassemble starter, remove rope handle (14) and carefully allow rope to wind into starter housing (12) relieving tension on rewind spring (11). Remove screw (7) and lift out rope pulley (9) noting how pulley engages inner coil of rewind spring. If rewind spring must be removed, use caution not to allow spring to uncoil uncontrolled. Renew any component found to be excessively worn or damaged.

Lightly lubricate rewind spring and rope pulley shaft in starter housing with a suitable low temperature grease. Wind rewind spring into spring case (10) in a counterclockwise direction starting with outer coil as viewed from spring side of case. Assemble rope pulley to rewind spring case making certain hook on inner coil of rewind spring properly engages slot in rope pulley. Install rope pulley with rewind spring and case into starter housing and install washer (8) and screw (7). Make sure pulley turns freely. Pass rope through rope guide (13). Place rope into notch in outer edge of rope pulley and rotate pulley clockwise until spring is coil bound. Back off pulley one-full turn and carefully allow pulley to rewind rope onto pulley. If spring tension is correct, rope pulley should be able to rotate 1-1/2 to 2 turns clockwise with rope fully extended.

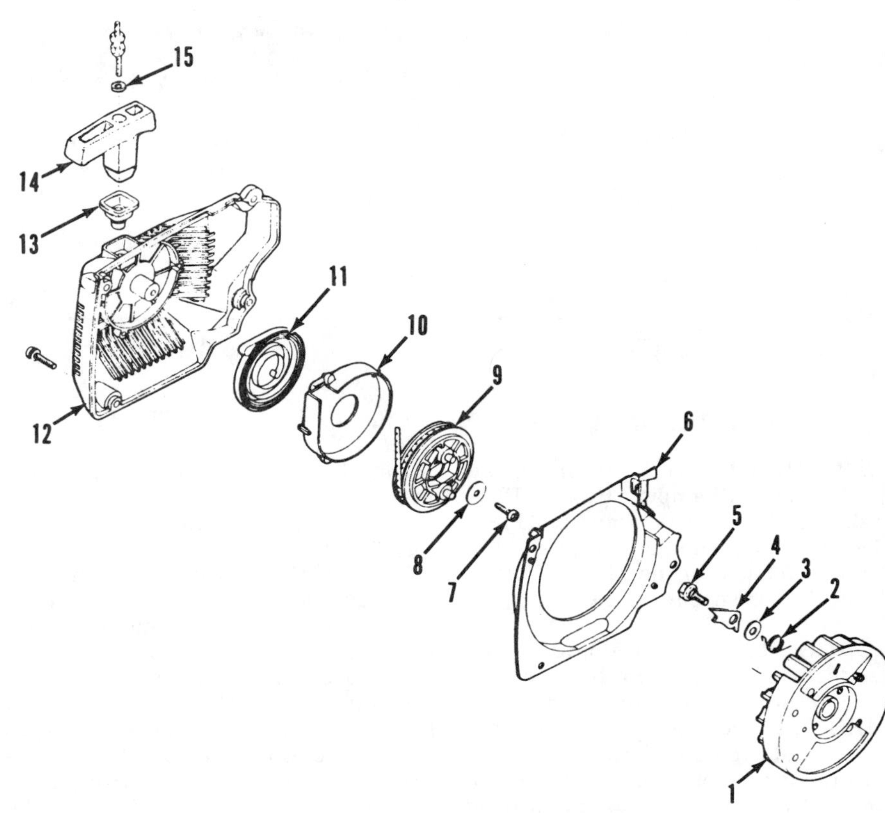

Fig. R36—Exploded view of rewind starter.

1. Flywheel
2. Spring
3. Washer
4. Pawl
5. Pivot screw
6. Cover
7. Screw
8. Washer
9. Rope pulley
10. Rewind spring case
11. Rewind spring
12. Starter housing
13. Rope guide
14. Rope handle
15. Washer

CHAIN BRAKE. Models G561AVS, G561AVSH, G621AVS and G621AVSH are equipped with a chain brake system designed to quickly stop chain movement should kickback occur. Chain brake is activated when operator's hand strikes hand guard (1—Fig. R37). Forward movement of brake lever (5) causes stopper (4) to disengage arm (11) allowing spring (10) to draw brake band (9) tight around clutch drum. Pull back hand guard to reset mechanism.

Disassembly for inspection or repair is evident after referral to exploded view and inspection of unit. Renew any component found to be excessively worn or damaged. Lightly lubricate pivot points with a suitable grease. No adjustment of chain brake system is required.

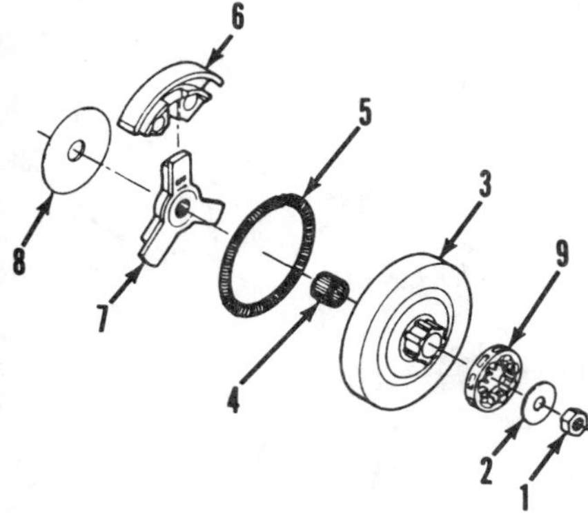

Fig. R35—Exploded view of three-shoe clutch assembly used on models so equipped. Refer to Fig. R34 for component identification except washer (8) and sprocket (9).

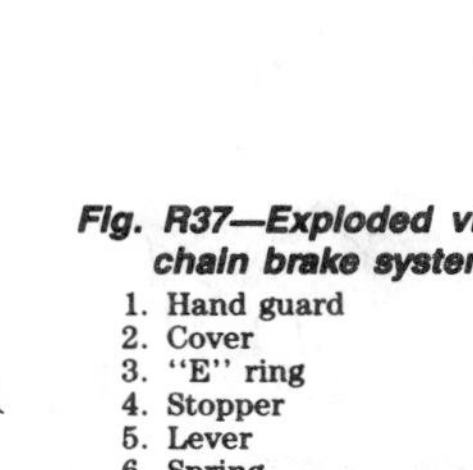

Fig. R37—Exploded view of chain brake system.

1. Hand guard
2. Cover
3. "E" ring
4. Stopper
5. Lever
6. Spring
7. Pin
8. Roller
9. Brake band
10. Spring
11. Arm
12. "E" ring
13. Shoulder screw

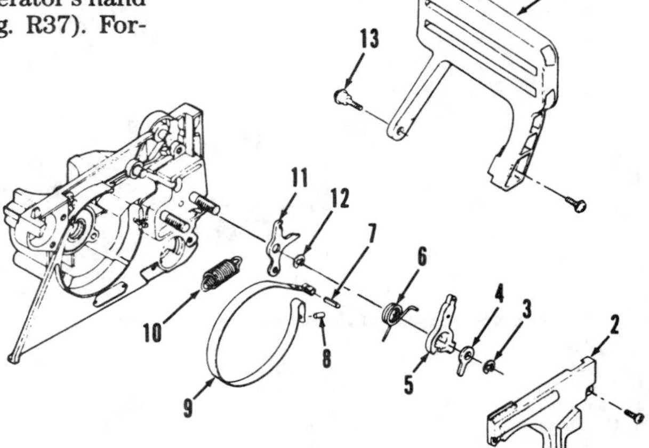

Illustrations courtesy RedMax, Div. of Komatsu Zenoah America, Inc.

REDMAX

Model	Bore mm (in.)	Stroke mm (in.)	Displacement cc (cu. in.)	Drive Type
G310TS	37 (1.46)	28 (1.1)	30.1 (1.84)	Direct

MAINTENANCE

SPARK PLUG. Recommended spark plug is Champion RCJ8Y. Electrode gap should be 0.6 mm (0.023 in.). The spark plug should be tightened to the torque listed in the TIGHTENING TORQUE paragraph.

CARBURETOR. A Walbro WT carburetor is used. Refer to the appropriate Walbro section of the CARBURETOR SERVICE section for service and exploded views.

To remove carburetor (5—Fig. R40), remove front cover (1). Remove screws (2), disconnect fuel line and throttle link. Withdraw carburetor. Tighten the carburetor attaching screws to the torque listed in the TIGHTENING TORQUE paragraph.

Initial settings of the low-speed and high-speed mixture needles are approximately 1-1/4 turns open from lightly seated.

To adjust the mixture screws, first remove and clean the air filter, then reinstall it. Start the engine and allow it to run until it reaches normal operating temperature. If necessary, turn each of the mixture needles clockwise until seated lightly, then back the needles out (counterclockwise) to the initial setting so the engine can be started.

Turn the idle speed stop screw so the engine idles at about 2,900 rpm. Adjust the low-speed mixture needle so the engine idles smoothly and accelerates without hesitation. Adjust the idle speed to just slower than clutch engagement speed, then recheck low-speed mixture adjustment.

Adjust the high-speed mixture needle to provide the best performance while operating at maximum speed under load. Without load, engine speed should be 10,500-12,000 rpm. The high-speed mixture screw may be set slightly rich to improve performance under load. The engine may be damaged if the high-speed screw is set too lean.

IGNITION. All models are equipped with a breakerless electronic ignition system. All electronic circuitry is contained in a one-piece ignition module/coil (1—Fig. R41) located outside the flywheel. Ignition timing is fixed and not adjustable. The flywheel attaching nut should be tightened to the torque listed in TIGHTENING TORQUE paragraph.

Air gap between the legs of the module/coil and the flywheel magnets should be 0.3-0.4 mm (0.0118-0.0157 in.). When installing, set the air gap between the flywheel magnets and the legs of the ignition module as follows. Install the ignition module, but tighten the two screws only enough to hold it in place away from the flywheel. Insert setting gauge (part No. 3330-97310) or

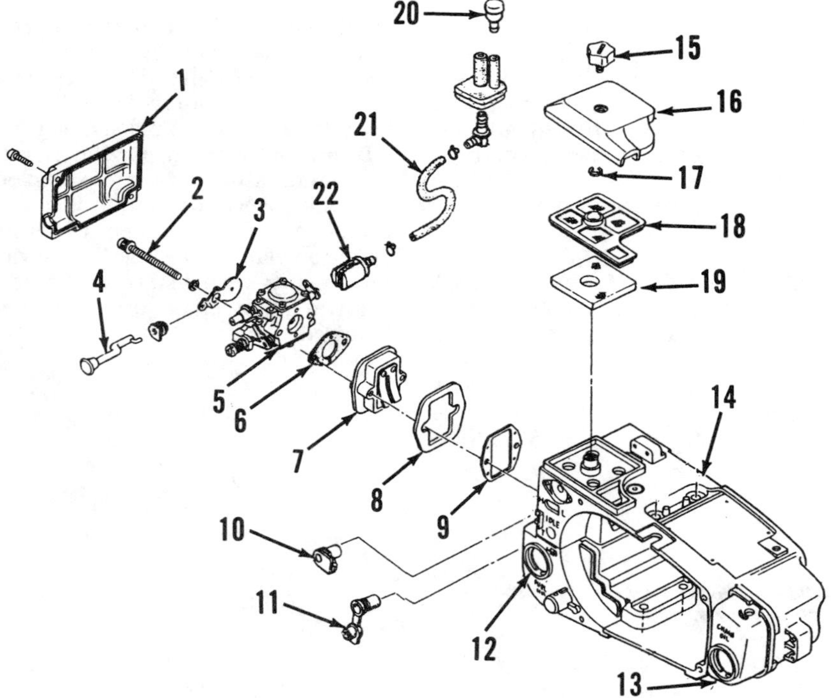

Fig. R40—Exploded view of engine case, carburetor and air cleaner components.

1. Carburetor cover
2. Screw
3. Choke shutter
4. Choke rod
5. Carburetor
6. Gasket
7. Reed valve assy.
8. Seal
9. Gasket
10. Grommet
11. Grommet
12. Fuel tank
13. Oil tank
14. Engine case
15. Knob
16. Air cleaner cover
17. Snap ring
18. Air cleaner holder
19. Air cleaner element
20. Breather
21. Fuel hose
22. Filter

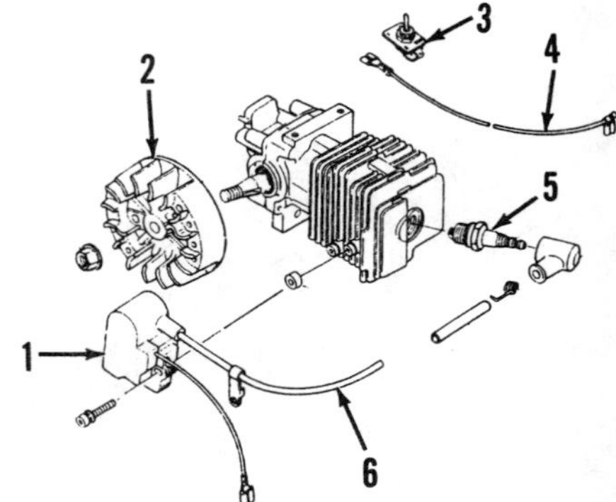

Fig. R41—Exploded view of ignition system.

1. Ignition module
2. Flywheel
3. Stop switch
4. Primary ignition wire
5. Spark plug
6. High tension wire

brass/plastic shim stock of the proper thickness between the legs of the ignition module and the flywheel, then turn the flywheel until the flywheel magnets are near the module legs. Loosen the screws attaching the ignition module and press legs of the ignition module against the setting gauge. Tighten the two attaching screws to the torque listed in the TIGHTENING TORQUE paragraph. Before final tightening, the threads should be coated with Three Bond #1342 or equivalent thread locking compound. Remove the setting gauge, then turn the flywheel and check that flywheel does not hit the legs of the coil.

LUBRICATION. The engine is lubricated by mixing oil with the gasoline fuel. The manufacturer recommends mixing RedMax two-stroke oil with regular grade gasoline at a ratio of 40:1 after break-in. When using regular two-stroke engine oil, mix at a ratio of 25:1. During the initial break-in (first 10 hours) the fuel to oil ratio may be increased to 20:1 to provide initial lubrication. Always use a separate container to mix gasoline and oil before filling the fuel tank. The manufacturer recommends not using fuel containing alcohol.

The saw is equipped with an automatic chain oiling system. The manufacturer recommends using good quality oil designed for lubricating saw chain; however, multi-grade 10W-30 engine oil may be used. Make sure the reservoir is filled at all times. The volume of oil delivered by the pump is not adjustable.

REPAIRS

CRANKCASE PRESSURE TEST. An improperly sealed crankcase can cause the engine to be hard to start, run rough, have low power and overheat. Refer to ENGINE SERVICE section of this manual for crankcase pressure test procedure. If crankcase leakage is indicated, pressurize the crankcase and use a solution of soap and water to check gasket, seals, pulse line and castings for leakage.

TIGHTENING TORQUE. Recommended tightening torque values are as follows.

Carburetor
- Attaching screws . . . . 4.9-7.8 N•m (43.4-69.5 in.-lb.)
- Cover . . . . 0.7-1.5 N•m (6.1-13 in.-lb.)

Chain brake
- Front guard . . . . 2.9-3.9 N•m (26-34.7 in.-lb.)
- Spring cover. . . . . 0.98-1.96 N•m (8.6-17.4 in.-lb.)

Chain catcher . . . . 1.96-2.9 N•m (17.4-26 in.-lb.)

Clutch hub . . . . 23.5 N•m (17.36 ft.-lb.)

Crankcase. . . . . 4.9-7.8 N•m (43.4-69.5 in.-lb.)

Engine mounting screws . 4.9-7.8 N•m (43.4-69.5 in.-lb.)

Flywheel nut . . . . 14.7-18.6 N•m (10.85-13.7 ft.-lb.)

Ignition
- Module/coil*. . . . . 2.9-4.9 N•m (26-43.4 in.-lb.)

Muffler* . . . . 3.9-4.9 N•m (34.7-43.4 in.-lb.)

Oil pump
- Cover. . . . . 0.7-1.5 N•m (6.1-13.1 in.-lb.)
- Mounting screws . . . . . 0.98-1.96 N•m (17.4-26 in.-lb.)

Spark plug . . . . 14.7-17.6 N•m (10.85-13.02 ft.-lb.)

Starter
- Inner cover. . . . . 0.7-1.5 N•m (6.1-13 in.-lb.)
- Housing . . . . 0.7-1.5 N•m (6.1-13 in.-lb.)
- Pulley retainer . . . . 2-2.9 N.m (17.4-26 in.-lb.)

Handles
- Rear/top . . . . 2.9-3.9 N•m (26-34.7 in.-lb.)
- Throttle cover . . . . 0.7-1.5 N•m (6.1-13 in.-lb.)
- Tubular . . . . 1.96-2.9 N•m (17.4-26 in.-lb.)

Vibration isolator . . . . . 0.69-1.47 N•m (6.1-13 in.-lb.)

* Coat threads of indicated screws with Three Bond #1342 or equivalent thread locking compound before tightening.

PISTON, PIN, RINGS, CYLINDER AND CRANKSAHFT. To disassemble, the engine must be removed from the engine case. Remove guide bar and chain, chain brake assembly and starter housing. Remove carburetor cover (1—Fig. R40), carburetor (5) and reed valve (7). Remove muffler guard and muffler. Remove stop switch from engine housing and disconnect electrical leads. Remove ignition module/coil assembly (1—Fig. R41). Remove spark plug, then install piston stop tool in spark plug hole or insert end of a rope in the cylinder through the spark plug hole to act as a piston stop. Remove the flywheel retaining nut (right-hand threads) and use a suitable puller to remove the flywheel (2). Unscrew clutch hub (left-hand threads) using special wrench (part No. 2670-96210) or equivalent, then remove the clutch assembly. Remove tubular handle (2—Fig. R42) and top handle (9). Unbolt and remove the oil pump cover and oil pump. Remove cover (1—Fig. R43) and the four engine mounting screws (2), then withdraw the engine from engine case (3).

Remove crankcase mounting screws (9—Fig. R43) and separate crankcase (8) from cylinder (17). Withdraw crankshaft, connecting rod and piston from cylinder. Care should be taken not to scratch or nick mating surfaces of cylinder and crankcase. Remove piston ring (16) from piston. Remove retaining rings (12) and push piston pin (13) from the piston, while catching the thrust washers (12). Separate piston (15) and

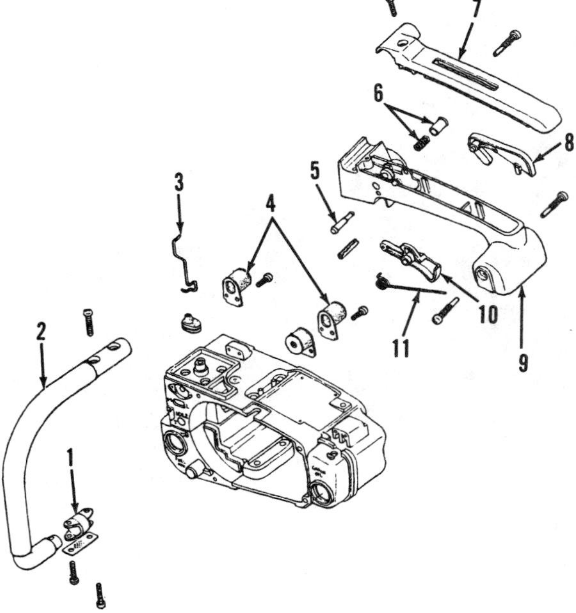

Fig. R42—Exploded view of the engine case and handles.

1. Vibration isolator
2. Tubular handle
3. Throttle rod
4. Vibration isolators
5. Pin
6. Spring & knob
7. Handle cover
8. Throttle trigger
9. Top handle
10. Throttle lever
11. Return spring

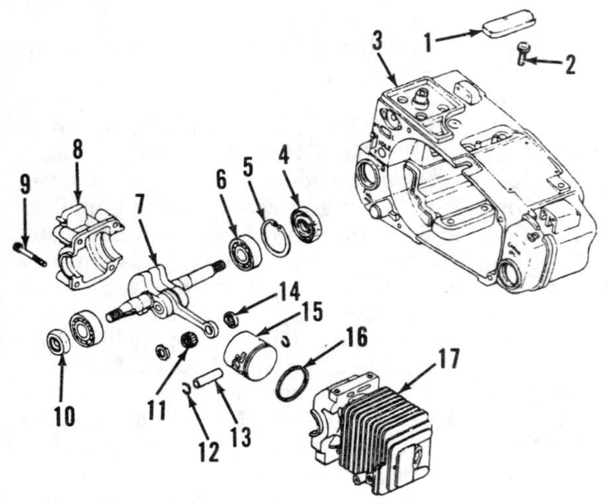

Fig. R43—Exploded view of the engine assembly.

1. Cap
2. Engine retaining screws
3. Engine case
4. Seal
5. Snap ring
6. Bearing
7. Crankshaft & connecting rod
8. Crankcase
9. Screw
10. Seal
11. Needle bearing
12. Retaining ring
13. Piston pin
14. Thrust washer
15. Piston
16. Piston ring
17. Cylinder

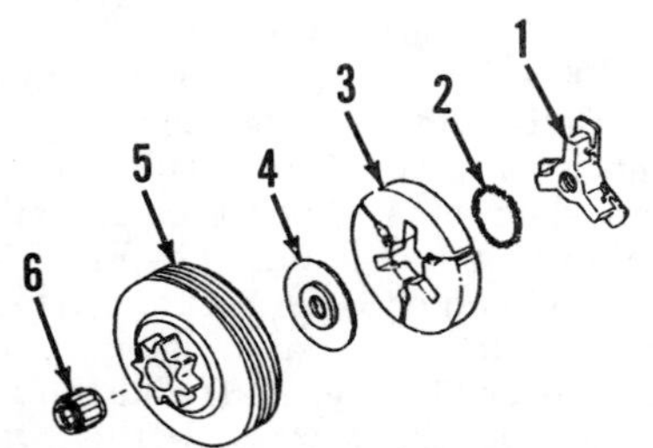

Fig. R44—Exploded view of the three-shoe clutch assembly.

1. Hub
2. Spring
3. Shoes
4. Plate
5. Clutch drum
6. Needle bearing

needle bearing (11) from connecting rod.

Note the following wear limits and renew parts as necessary. Piston skirt OD - 36.86 mm (1.451 in.), piston pin hole – 9.05 mm (0.356 in.), side clearance between ring and ring groove – 0.10 mm (0.0039 in.), piston ring end gap – 0.6 mm (0.0236 in.), connecting rod small end ID – 12.05 mm (0.474 in.).

Renew cylinder if plating is peeling or worn, exposing the aluminum bore.

Do not remove the crankshaft main ball bearings (6) unless new bearings are available for installation. Carefully support the crankshaft while removing and installing the main bearings. The crankshaft and connecting rod are available only as a complete assembly.

To reassemble, reverse the disassembly procedure while noting the following special instructions: Install piston on connecting rod so arrow in top of piston points toward the output (saw chain) end of crankshaft. Lubricate needle bearing (11) and piston pin (13), then position thrust washers (14) on either side of connecting rod before inserting the piston pin. Always install NEW retaining rings (12) and be sure end gap of retaining rings is down toward the crankshaft. Lubricate lip of seals (4 and 10) with grease before installation. Make certain that piston ring end gap indexes with locating pin in piston ring groove.

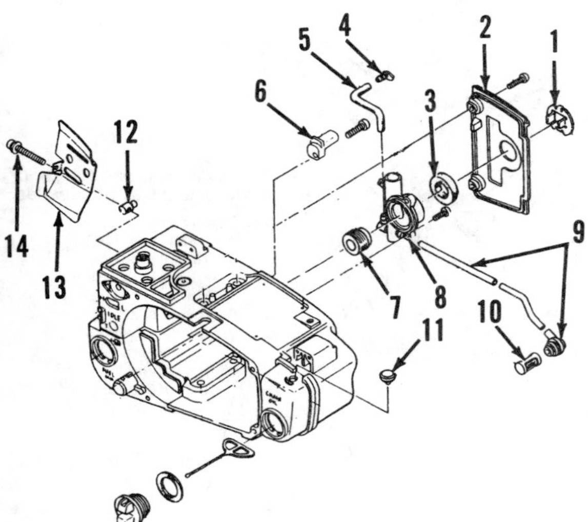

Fig. R45—Exploded view of the oil pump assembly.

1. Drive plate
2. Cover
3. Seal
4. Oil pipe
5. Delivery tube
6. Chain catcher
7. Oil pump gear
8. Oil pump assy.
9. Oil inlet tube
10. Filter
11. Breather
12. Chain tension nut
13. Guide plate
14. Chain tension screw

Lubricate piston and cylinder bore with oil, compress the piston ring and slide piston into cylinder. Apply light coat of RTV silicone sealant to crankcase mating surface then assemble crankcase (8) to cylinder (17). Be sure crankshaft seals (4 and 10) are flush with outer surface of cylinder and crankcase. Gently tap on both ends of crankshaft to center all components, then tighten crankcase screws (9) to specified torque.

REED VALVE. The reed valve assembly (7—Fig. R40) should be inspected whenever the carburetor is removed. Reed petals should seat very lightly against the reed plate throughout their entire length with the least possible tension. Install new reed assembly if reed standout exceeds 0.7 mm (0.0276 in.). Clearance between the reed valve and reed stop should be 5.5-6.5 mm (0.217-0.256 in.).

CLUTCH. The three-shoe clutch should engage at 3,800-4,400 rpm. To remove the clutch, remove chain brake assembly, guide bar and chain. Remove spark plug, then use a suitable piston stop to prevent the crankshaft from turning.

NOTE: If a special piston stop is not available, insert the end of a rope in the cylinder through the spark plug hole to act as a piston stop.

Unscrew clutch hub (left-hand threads) using special wrench (part No. 2670-96210) or equivalent, then remove the clutch assembly (Fig. R44).

Inspect the clutch shoes (3) and if necessary, install three new shoes as a set to prevent unbalanced condition. Special tools (part No. 2670-96240) are available for spreading the shoes after the spring (2) is installed so the hub (1) can be inserted. Grease the needle bearing before installing. Be sure the oil pump drive plate (1—Fig. R45) correctly engages both the clutch drum (5—Fig. R44) and oil pump gear (7—Fig. R45). Tighten the clutch hub to the torque listed in TIGHTENING TORQUE paragraphs.

OIL PUMP. The non-adjustable oil pump is shown in Fig. R45. The pump is available only as an assembly and must not be disassembled. The oil pump drive plate (1) is driven by the clutch drum (5—Fig. R44) and drives oil pump gear (7—Fig. R45) only when the clutch and chain are engaged.

To remove oil pump, remove chain brake assembly, bar and chain, and

Illustrations courtesy RedMax, Div. of Komatsu Zenoah America, Inc.

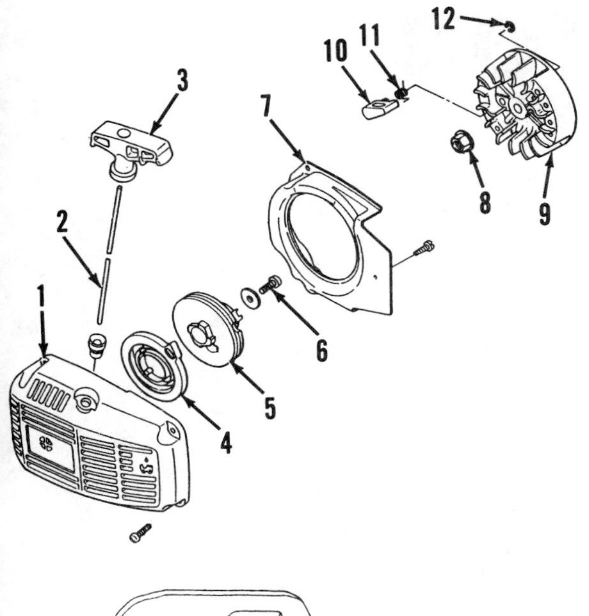

Fig. R46—Exploded view of rewind starter.

1. Starter housing
2. Rope
3. Handle
4. Rewind spring & case
5. Rope pulley
6. Screw
7. Cover
8. Nut
9. Flywheel
10. Pawl
11. Spring
12. Snap ring

Fig. R47—Exploded view of chain brake assembly.

1. Hand guard & lever
2. Return spring
3. Return spring
4. Spacer
5. Weight
6. Arm
7. Brake spring
8. Pin
9. Spring cover
10. Brake band
11. Pin
12. Spring
13. Chain cover
14. Brake lever assy.

clutch assembly. Remove drive plate (1—Fig. R45) and pump cover (2). Disconnect oil hoses, remove pump mounting screw and withdraw pump assembly (8).

Apply lithium base grease to the worm drive gear (7) while assembling. Prime oil pump by adding clean oil to the inlet port before attaching the inlet hose (9) to the pump. Be especially careful to be sure that the drive plate (1) correctly engages the drive gear and the clutch drum when assembling.

REWIND STARTER. To disassemble the rewind starter (Fig. R46), first unbolt and remove the starter housing (1). If rope is not broken, pull the rope handle from the housing, remove the handle (3) and allow the rope to slowly rewind into the housing until spring tension is relieved. Remove the cover (7), then the screw (6). Lift the pulley (5) from the housing, being careful not to dislodge the spring (4). If the rewind spring must be removed, be careful not to allow the spring to uncoil uncontrolled. The flywheel (9) must be removed to remove snap ring (12) before removing the pawl (10) and spring (11).

Inspect all components and renew any that are damaged, or worn excessively. Tighten the flywheel retaining nut (8) to the torque listed in the TIGHTENING TORQUE paragraph.

Lubricate the rewind spring lightly before winding it into the spring case. Attach a rope of the proper diameter and length to the pulley (5) using a double knot. Pass the rope through the starter housing (1) and rope guide, then attach the handle (3). Wind the rope onto the pulley and form a loop in the rope at the notch in pulley. Install the pulley, engaging the pulley with the inner end of the rewind spring. Install the washer and screw (6), tightening the screw to the torque listed in the TIGHTENING TORQUE paragraph. Hold the loop of rope at the pulley notch and wind the pulley to preload the rewind spring about 5 turns.

Release the loop of rope from the pulley and check for proper preload. Pull the rope completely from the housing and check that pulley can be turned an additional 1/2 turn before spring binds. If the spring binds before the rope can be pulled completely from the housing, pull a loop into the notch in the pulley and allow the spring to unwind a turn or two, then recheck. Release the rope and make sure the handle is pulled against the housing. If the rope does not rewind completely pull a loop into the notch in the pulley and preload the spring another turn or two, then recheck.

CHAIN BRAKE. The chain brake system (Fig. R47) is designed to stop chain movement should kickback occur. The chain brake is activated when operator's hand strikes hand guard (1). When activated (engaged), the brake band (10) is drawn around clutch drum by spring (7).

To disassemble chain brake, remove the guide bar, chain and chain cover (13). Remove screws attaching the spring cover (9). Push hand guard (1) forward, then remove the screw attaching hand guard (1). Carefully disengage brake spring (7) from cover and remove brake band (10).

Renew any component found that is excessively worn or damaged. Lubricate all pivot points, especially the lever assembly (14), with lithium base grease.

When properly assembled, the chain brake should stop saw chain instantly when engaged. Brake band should not contact clutch drum when disengaged. The brake is not adjustable.

REMINGTON

Model	Bore mm (in.)	Stroke mm (in.)	Displacement cc (cu. in.)	Drive Type
Mighty Mite 100, 200, 300	36.5 (1.437)	30.5 (1.2)	31.1 (1.9)	Direct
Mighty Might 400, 500, 600	39.7 (1.562)	30.5 (1.2)	37.7 (2.3)	Direct
812, 814, 816	36.5 (1.437)	30.5 (1.2)	31.1 (1.9)	Direct
816 AV, 840 AV, 850 AV, A860 AV	39.7 (1.562)	30.5 (1.2)	37.7 (2.3)	Direct
Yardmaster	36.5 (1.437)	30.5 (1.2)	31.1 (1.9)	Direct

MAINTENANCE

SPARK PLUG. Recommended spark plug for all models is Champion CJ7Y. Spark plug electrode gap should be 0.025 inch (0.63 mm).

CARBURETOR. All models are equipped with a Walbro WA diaphragm carburetor. Refer to CARBURETOR SERVICE section for carburetor servicing.

High speed mixture is not adjustable. Initial setting of idle mixture screw is 1¼ turns open. Adjust idle speed screw so engine idles just below clutch engagement speed.

If intake spacer between carburetor and cylinder is removed, be sure to install spacer so larger opening is nearest cylinder.

IGNITION. Models 812, 814, 816, 816AV, 840AV, 850AV, 860AV and all other later production models, are equipped with a breakerless capacitor discharge ignition system. Ignition timing is not adjustable.

All other models are equipped with a conventional flywheel magneto ignition system having breaker points located under the flywheel. Breaker-point gap should be 0.015 inch (0.38 mm). Breaker points, condenser, felt wiper, breaker box and cover are available only as a unit assembly.

On all models, air gap between coil legs and flywheel magnets should be 0.010 inch (0.25 mm).

LUBRICATION. The engine is lubricated by mixing oil with the fuel. The oil should be a good quality SAE 30 oil designed for use in chain saw or air-cooled two-stroke engines. Fuel: oil ratio is 16:1 for all engines.

An automatic nonadjustable oil pump is used on all models. Recommended chain oil is SAE 20 for warm climate or SAE 10 for winter usage.

REPAIRS

CYLINDER, PISTON, PIN AND RINGS. To remove cylinder, remove air filter and unscrew seven screws securing housing halves. Separate halves sufficiently to disconnect ignition switch wires then remove left housing half. Remove flywheel and ignition coil and disconnect oil line from housing. Detach throttle and oil control linkage and remove chain brake handle. Unscrew two nuts securing right housing half to engine and remove housing half. Partially disassemble chain brake for access to adjacent cylinder screw. Unscrew cylinder screws and carefully remove cylinder.

NOTE: Piston aligns connecting rod on rod bearing rollers. Excessive piston movement during or after cylinder removal may allow connecting rod bearing rollers to fall off crankpin.

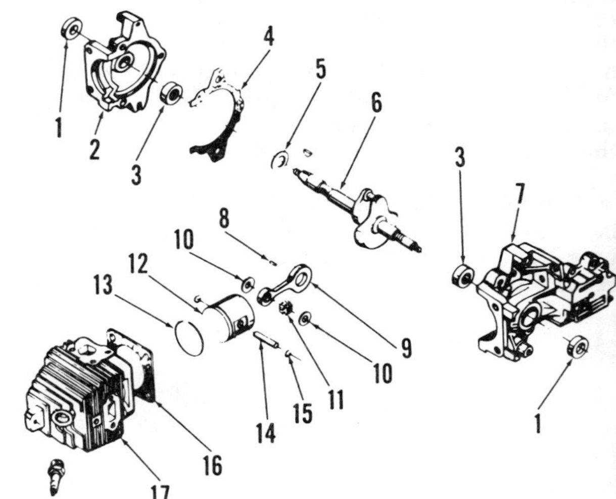

Fig. RE10—Exploded view of engine.
1. Seal
2. Crankcase half (L.H.)
3. Bearing
4. Gasket
5. Thrust washer
6. Crankshaft
7. Crankcase half (R.H.)
8. Bearing rollers (12)
9. Connecting rod
10. Thrust washers
11. Bearing rollers (18)
12. Piston
13. Piston ring
14. Piston pin
15. Pin retainers
16. Gasket
17. Cylinder

Reverse disassembly to install cylinder and refer to CHAIN BRAKE section for adjustment.

Cylinder is chrome plated and oversize pistons and rings are not available. Inspect cylinder bore for scoring or excessive wear which may expose soft base metal underneath chrome.

Eighteen loose roller bearings are used in small end of connecting rod. Hold bearing rollers in place with grease and place a thrust washer on each side of rod before installing piston. Install piston so "EXH' on piston crown is toward exhaust port and with closed end of piston pin toward exhaust port. Tighten cylinder mounting screws to 90-115 in.-lbs (10.2-13.0 N•m).

CONNECTING ROD, CRANKSHAFT AND CRANKCASE. The connecting rod is one-piece type which may be removed from crankshaft after crankcase halves are separated.

Inspect all components for damage and excessive wear. Check crankshaft runout and renew if bent. Note thrust washer (5–Fig. RE10) between crankshaft arm and main bearing. When installing connecting rod, hold 12 bearing rollers on crankpin with grease then direct connecting rod over flywheel end of crankshaft and onto bearing rollers. Install crankshaft seals with numbered or lettered side toward crankshaft end. Tighten crankcase screws to 110-135 in.-lbs (12.4-15.2 N•m).

If removed, install antivibration shock mounts on crankcase with stud end marked "-" threaded into crankcase.

CLUTCH. All models are equipped with a two-shoe centrifugal type clutch. The clutch hub has left-hand threads. Clutch bearing (6–Fig. RE11) should be inspected and renewed if damaged. Inspect shoes and drum for signs of excessive heat.

OIL PUMP. An automatic oil pump is used on all models. Crankcase pulsations are used to pressurize oil tank. Oil flow is regulated by throttle. On early models, the oil outlet tube is pinched by a rod mechanism connected to the throttle while on later models the throttle operates a shut-off valve.

A one-way valve (6–Fig. RE12) attached to the oil tank prevents oil from entering engine crankcase. Valve can be checked by pressurizing oil tank to 5 psi (34.5 kPa) with throttle closed. If tank will not hold pressure, be sure oil outlet tube is closed before suspecting one-way valve.

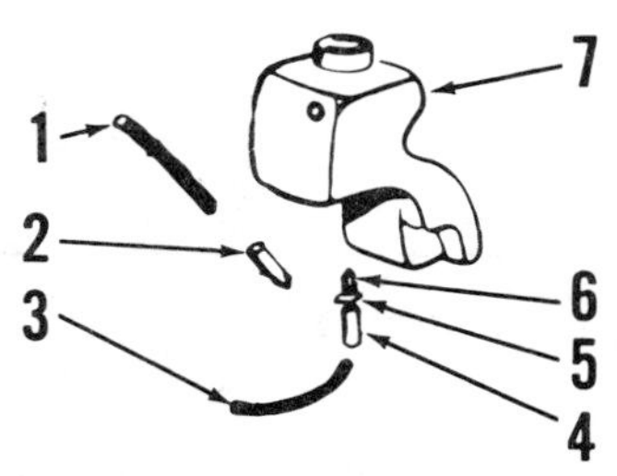

Fig. RE12—Exploded view of oil tank assembly.
1. Oil line
2. Oil pickup
3. Crankcase pressure line
4. Fitting
5. "O" ring
6. Valve
7. Oil tank

REWIND STARTER. Refer to Fig. RE13 for an exploded view of rewind starter. To disassemble starter, remove air filter and unscrew seven screws securing housing halves. Separate halves sufficiently to disconnect ignition switch wires then remove left housing half. Remove rope handle and allow rope to wind into starter. Unscrew rope pulley retaining screw (5) and carefully remove rope pulley (4). If rewind spring (2) must be removed, care should be used to prevent personal injury due to uncontrolled uncoiling of spring.

Install rewind spring (2) with coils wrapped in clockwise direction from outer spring end. Wrap rope around rope pulley in clockwise direction as viewed with pulley installed in left housing half. Rewind spring should be preloaded by turning rope pulley three turns clockwise before passing rope through rope outlet in housing.

CHAIN BRAKE. Some models are equipped with the chain brake shown in Fig. RE14. To adjust chain brake, pull chain brake to rearmost position (toward engine) and check chain for ease of movement. If chain does not move freely, turn brake rod end (R–Fig. RE14) counterclockwise so clutch drum can rotate freely. Make sure chain tension is adjusted correctly. Turn brake rod end (R) clockwise so it is difficult to pull chain around bar then turn brake rod end counterclockwise to point just after chain will move freely around bar.

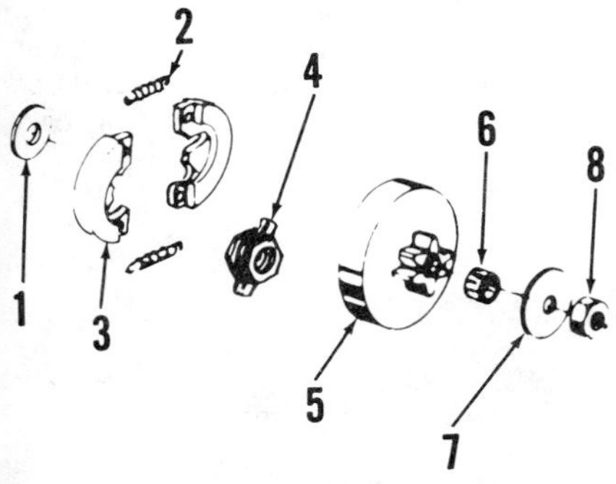

Fig. RE11—Exploded view of clutch. Clutch hub (4) has left-hand threads.
1. Washer
2. Springs
3. Clutch shoes
4. Hub
5. Clutch drum
6. Bearing
7. Washer
8. Nut

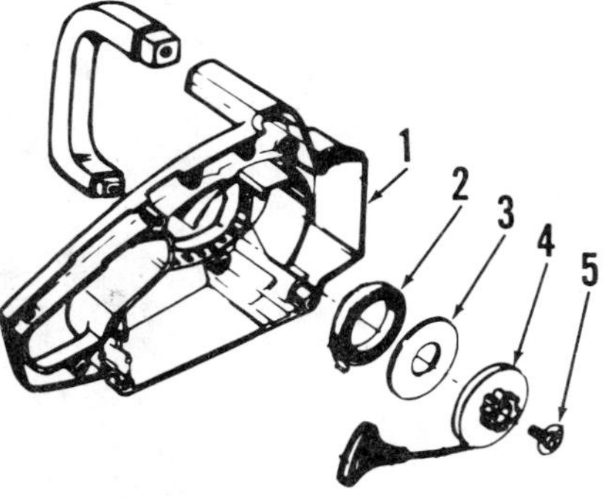

Fig. RE13—Exploded view of rewind starter.
1. Housing half
2. Rewind spring
3. Spring cover
4. Rope pulley
5. Screw

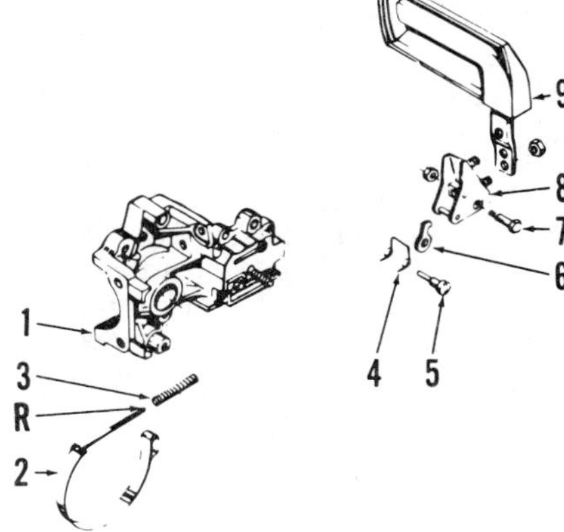

Fig. RE14—View of chain brake assembly.
1. Crankcase half (R.H.)
2. Brake band & rod
3. Spring
4. Spring
5. Pivot pin
6. Latch
7. Shoulder bolt
8. Actuator
9. Chain brake arm

REMINGTON

Model	Bore mm (in.)	Stroke mm (in.)	Displacement cc (cu. in.)	Drive Type
Mighty Mite Auto, Bantam, Deluxe, Electric Start	38.1 (1.5)	30.5 (1.2)	34.4 (2.1)	Direct
SL-4A	46.0 (1.81)	35.1 (1.38)	59 (3.6)	Direct
SL-7A	57.1 (2.25)	36.6 (1.44)	93.4 (5.7)	Direct
SL-9, SL9A	42.9 (1.69)	31.7 (1.25)	45.9 (2.8)	Direct
SL-11, SL-11A	48.5 (1.91)	35.1 (1.38)	65.5 (4.0)	Direct
SL-14A, SL-16A	42.9 (1.69	31.7 (1.25)	45.9 (2.8)	Direct
SL-55A	52.3 (2.06)	38.1 (1.5)	81.9 (5.0)	Direct

MAINTENANCE

SPARK PLUG. Recommended spark plug for all models is Champion CJ6. Spark plug electrode gap should be 0.025 inch (0.63 mm).

CARBURETOR. All models are equipped with a Tillotson Model HS or HU diaphragm carburetor. Initial adjustment of idle and high-speed adjusting screws is one turn open. High speed adjusting screw should be adjusted so optimum performance is obtained when saw is under cutting load. High speed screw should not be adjusted too lean as engine may be damaged.

Refer to Tillotson section of CARBURETOR SERVICE section for carburetor operation and overhaul.

MAGNETO AND TIMING. A flywheel magneto is used on all models. Ignition timing is fixed at 30 degrees BTDC and is nonadjustable. Breaker point gap should be 0.015 inch (0.38 mm). Be sure breaker-point gap is correct as incorrect gap setting will affect ignition timing.

Air gap setting on all Mighty Mite models should be 0.010 inch (0.25 mm). To adjust air gap, loosen coil lamination mounting screws and insert 0.010 inch (0.25 mm) thick shim or feeler gage between lamination and flywheel. Tighten mounting screws when correct gap is obtained.

LUBRICATION. The engine is lubricated by mixing oil with the fuel. The oil should be a good quality SAE 30 oil designed for use in chain saw or air-cooled two-stroke engines. Fuel: oil ratio is 16:1 for all engines.

A manual chain oiler is used on all models. An automatic chain oiler is also used on Models SL-4A, SL-7A, SL-9A, SL-11A, SL-14A, SL-16A, Mighty Mite Auto, Mighty Mite Deluxe and Mighty Mite Electric Start. Fill chain oiler tank with equal parts of SAE 30 oil and kerosene. Output of automatic oil pump is adjusted by turning adjusting screw located near trigger or near front handle. Turning screw clockwise decreases oil flow while turning the screw counterclockwise will increase oil flow. Oil pump screen or filter on automatic oil pump models should be removed and cleaned periodically.

CARBON. Carbon deposits should be removed from muffler and exhaust ports at regular intervals. Be careful not to damage cylinder when scraping carbon. Do not allow loosened carbon into cylinder.

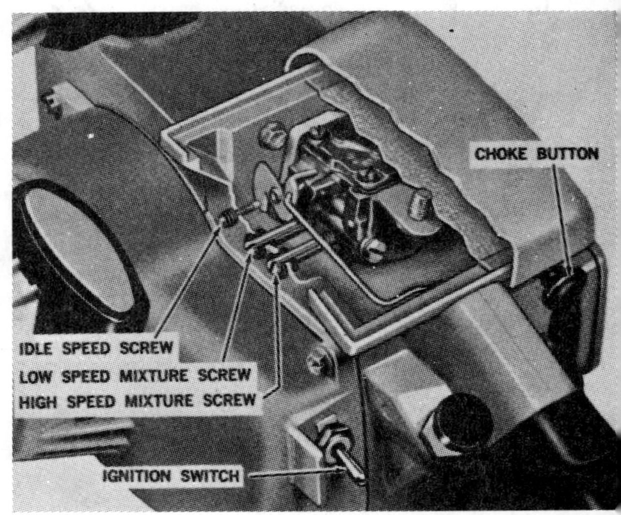

Fig. RE30—View showing location of carburetor adjusting screws on most models except Mighty Mite models.

REPAIRS

CYLINDER, PISTON, PIN AND RINGS. To remove cylinder on all Mighty Mite models, remove chain guard, starter housing and carburetor cover. Disconnect choke linkage and compression release rod, if so equipped. Remove carburetor and disconnect throttle linkage and fuel line. Remove rear handle assembly, unscrew cylinder base screws and remove cylinder. Remove muffler from cylinder.

To remove cylinder on all other models, remove starter housing, flywheel and stator. Remove carburetor, disconnect oil lines and detach rear handle cover. Remove compression release rod on models so equipped and remove rear handle assembly. Unscrew cylinder base nuts and remove cylinder.

Cylinder is chrome plated and oversize pistons and rings are not available. Inspect cylinder bore for scoring or excessive wear which may expose soft base metal underneath chrome.

Piston rings on all models except late Mighty Mite models are pinned to prevent rotation. Late Mighty Mite models are equipped with a single piston ring which is not pinned. Pinned and unpinned rings may not be interchanged. Piston rings on all models must be installed with inner bevel toward top of piston. Pistons with two rings are marked "EXH" on piston crown and must be installed with "EXH" toward exhaust port of cylinder. Insert piston pin with solid end of pin toward exhaust port on all models except Mighty Mite models. Model SL-7A has spacers between connecting rod and piston. Install spacers with recess toward piston pin bearing. Place piston pin snap rings in piston with sharp edge out and gap toward piston skirt. Tighten cylinder base nuts to 60 in.-lbs. (6.8 N•m).

CONNECTING ROD. To remove connecting rod, remove cylinder and piston as previously outlined. Unscrew connecting rod screws and remove rod being careful not to lose loose bearing rollers. Models SL-7A, SL-55A and all Mighty Mite models have 24 bearing rollers. Models SL-9, SL-9A, SL-14A and SL-16A have 26 bearing rollers, and all other models have 28 bearing rollers.

The connecting rod is fractured and has match marks on one side of rod and cap. Be sure rod and cap are correctly meshed and match marks are aligned during assembly. Tighten connecting rod screws to 35 in.-lbs. (3.9 N•m) on Mighty Mite models and to 50 in.-lbs. (5.6 N•m) on all other models.

CRANKSHAFT AND CRANKCASE. To remove crankshaft on Mighty Mite models, remove clutch and flywheel. Remove rear handle. Remove connecting rod as previously outlined. Remove crankcase cover (1 – Fig. RE33). Crankshaft may now be removed.

To remove crankshaft on all other models, remove clutch and rear handle. Remove connecting rod as previously outlined. Remove right crankcase cover and remove crankshaft. On Models SL-4A, SL-7A, SL-11 and SL11A, crankcase may be separated from fuel tank. On Models SL-55A, SL-9, SL-9A, SL-14A and SL-16A, crankcase is integral with fuel tank.

Inspect bearings and seals for damage or excessive wear. Crankshaft bearings should be installed so numbered side of bearing is inward. Press on inward side of bearing so bearing is flush with recessed shoulder. Seals should be flush with surface.

AUTOMATIC CHAIN OILER. All models except Mighty Mite Bantam, SL-9 and SL-11 are equipped with an automatic chain oiling system. The oil tank is pressurized by crankcase or cylinder pressure to force oil to chain. Check valve operation should be checked if excessive oil smoke is produced by the engine. Check valve on Mighty Mite Auto, Mighty Mite Deluxe and Mighty Mite Electric Start models is located in oil tank cavity shown in Fig. RE32. Check valve on all other models with automatic chain oiler is located in oil line fitting in oil tank. All models with

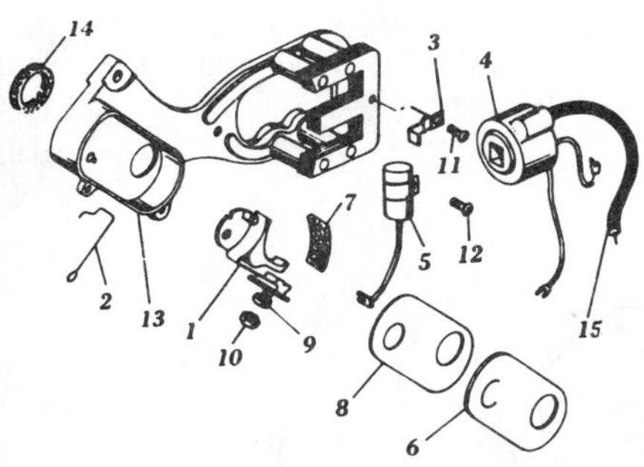

Fig. RE31 — Exploded view of typical magneto assembly used on all models except Mighty Mite models.

1. Breaker points
2. Clamp
3. Coil clip
4. Coil
5. Condenser
6. Cover
13. Core & stator
14. Felt washer

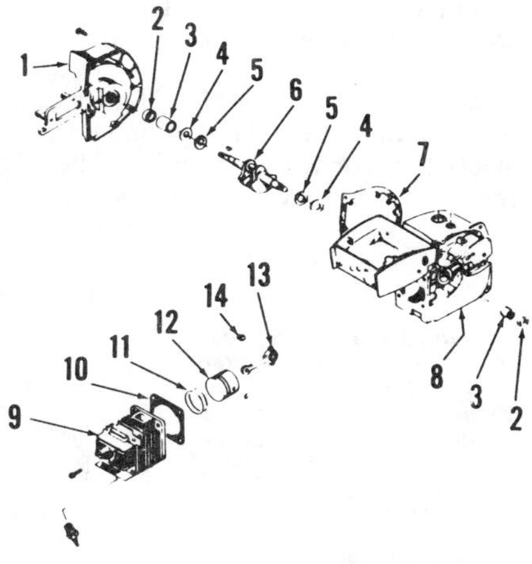

Fig. RE33 — Exploded view of engine used on Mighty Mite series models.

1. Crankcase cover
2. Seal
3. Bearing
4. Thrust washer
5. Thrust bearing
6. Crankshaft
7. Gasket
8. Crankcase & frame
9. Cylinder
10. Gasket
11. Piston rings
12. Piston
13. Connecting rod & cap
14. Bearing

Fig. RE32 — View showing location of check valve (C) in oil tank of Mighty Mite Auto, Mighty Mite Deluxe and Mighty Mite Electric Start models.

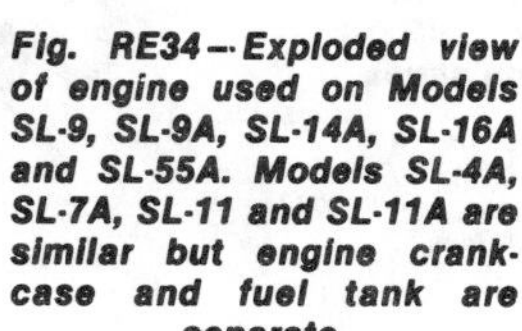

Fig. RE34 — Exploded view of engine used on Models SL-9, SL-9A, SL-14A, SL-16A and SL-55A. Models SL-4A, SL-7A, SL-11 and SL-11A are similar but engine crankcase and fuel tank are separate.

1. Cylinder
2. Piston rings
3. Piston
4. Snap ring
5. Piston pin
6. Bearing
7. Connecting rod & cap
8. Bearing
9. Screw
10. Gasket
11. Seal
12. Bearing
13. Crankcase & fuel tank
14. Thrust washer
15. Thrust bearing
16. Crankshaft
17. "O" ring
18. Crankcase cover

automatic oiler except Mighty Mite Auto, Mighty Mite Deluxe and Mighty Mite Electric Start are equipped with a shut-off valve to stop oil flow when engine is stopped or at slow idle. Oil shut-off valve on Model SL-55A is built into manual oil pump body and is actuated by the throttle trigger. Shut-off valve on other models so equipped is located adjacent to manual oil pump and is controlled by a link from the throttle trigger.

CLUTCH. An inboard type clutch is used on Model SL-7A and all Mighty Mite models. All other models have clutch drum mounted outside of clutch hub. Clutch hub is screwed on crankshaft with left-hand threads. Models with clutch drum mounted outboard have a right hand threaded nut to retain drum. Tighten clutch nut to 175 in.-lbs. (19.8 N•m) on Models SL-4A, SL-11, SL-11A and SL-55A. Tighten clutch nut on Models SL-9, SL-9A, SL-14A and SL-16A to 100 in.-lbs. (11.3 N•m).

REED VALVES. All models except Mighty Mite models are equipped with reed valve induction. Reed valve petals should be inspected for warpage, cracks or nicks. Reed valve seat should also be inspected for damage. Reed petals are available separately from reed valve housing.

REWIND STARTER. Refer to Fig. RE38 for exploded view of typical rewind starter used on all models except Mighty Mite Electric Start. To disassemble starter, remove starter housing from saw. Remove rope handle and allow rope to rewind into starter. Unscrew retaining screw on Mighty Mite Auto or "E" ring (11) on all other models. Remove friction shoe assembly. Remove rope pulley being careful not to disturb rewind spring. If necessary to remove rewind spring, be careful not to allow spring to uncoil uncontrolled.

Edges of friction shoes (9) should be sharp. Renew friction shoes if excessively worn. Renew fiber washers (8 and 10) if glazed or oil soaked. To reassemble starter, reverse disassembly procedure. Install rewind spring so that windings are in clockwise direction. Wrap rope around pulley and install pulley being sure inner hook of rewind spring engages pulley. Place tension on rewind spring by turning pulley three turns before passing rope through hole in housing. Be sure that friction shoe assembly is installed correctly. If properly installed, sharp ends of friction shoes will extend when rope is pulled.

ELECTRIC START. Mighty Mite Electric Start model is equipped with an electric motor to start engine. The electric motor is driven by an external 12 volt battery which may be recharged. Starter mechanism is gear driven by electric motor as shown in Fig. RE39.

Wires for electric starter should be connected as follows: One white lead of battery connector (6) should be connected to rear pole of switch (4) while other white lead should be connected to positive "+" terminal of starter motor. A black wire should be connected between negative "-" terminal of starter motor and middle pole of switch (4). A green wire should be connected to middle pole of switch (4) and grounded to starter housing (5). A blue wire should be connected to the front pole of switch (4) and the ignition coil primary wire.

Battery should be discarded if minimum voltage level of 12.8 volts is not attained after 48 hours of charging. The battery charger may be checked by connecting a voltmeter to battery connector of charger–exposed pin is negative. With battery charger plugged into a 110 volt circuit, battery charger output should be in excess of 12.5 volts. If battery and charger operate satisfactorily, remove starter cover and note if starter motor will turn freely. If starter motor is not binding, connect battery to starter housing plug and using a voltmeter and appropriate voltage checks, determine if starter switch, starter motor or wiring is defective.

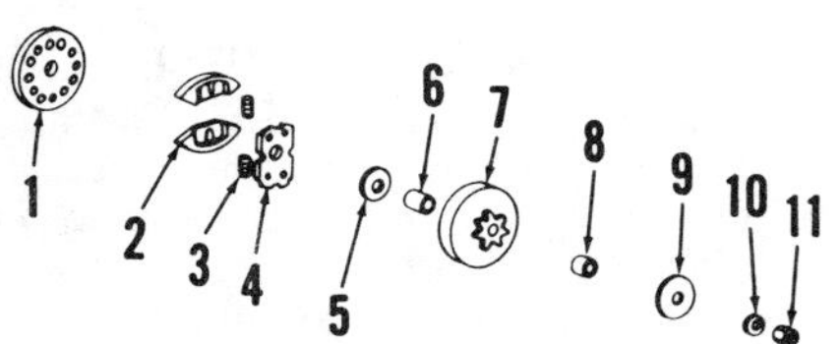

Fig. RE35 – Exploded view of typical clutch used on all models except SL-4A, SL-11, SL-11A and SL-55A. Clutch drum is mounted inboard on all Mighty Mite models.

1. Cover
2. Clutch shoe
3. Spring
4. Clutch hub
5. Thrust washer
6. Sprocket race
7. Clutch drum
8. Bearing
9. Washer
10. Washer
11. Nut (L.H.)

Fig. RE38 – Exploded view of rewind starter. Starter used on Mighty Mite Auto, Mighty Mite Deluxe uses a retaining screw in place of "E" ring (11).

1. Rope bushing
2. Starter housing
3. Spring shield
4. Rewind spring
5. Dust shield
6. Rope pulley
7. Brake spring
8. Fiber washer
9. Friction shoe assy.
10. Fiber washer
11. "E" ring

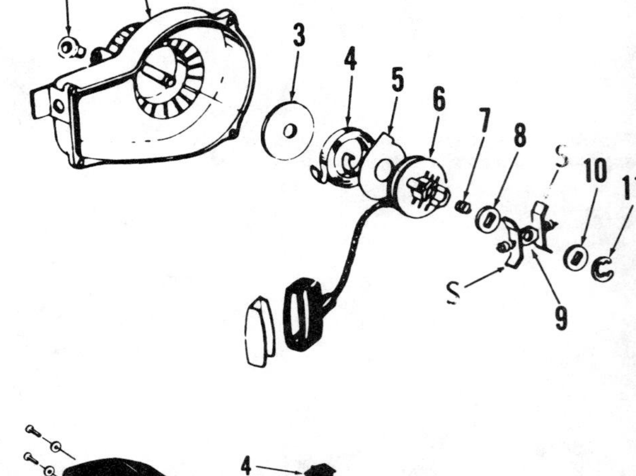

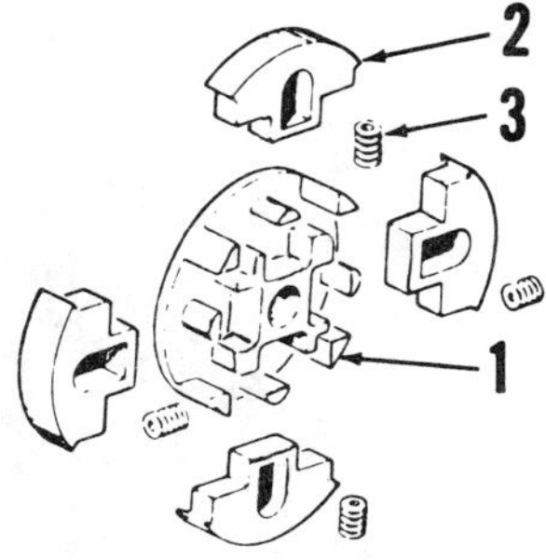

Fig. RE37 – Exploded view of clutch hub (1), shoes (2) and springs (3) used on Models SL-4A, SL-11 and SL-11A.

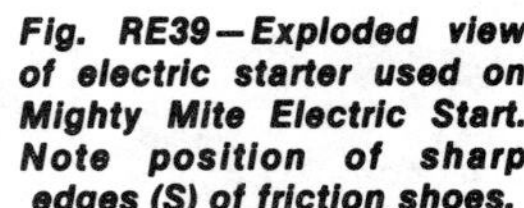

Fig. RE39 – Exploded view of electric starter used on Mighty Mite Electric Start. Note position of sharp edges (S) of friction shoes.

1. Cover
2. Starter motor
3. Pinion gear
4. Starter switch
5. Starter housing
6. Battery connector
7. Idler gear
8. Starter gear
9. Drive washer
10. Spring
11. Fiber washer
12. Friction shoe assy.
13. Fiber washer
14. Washer
15. SEMS screw

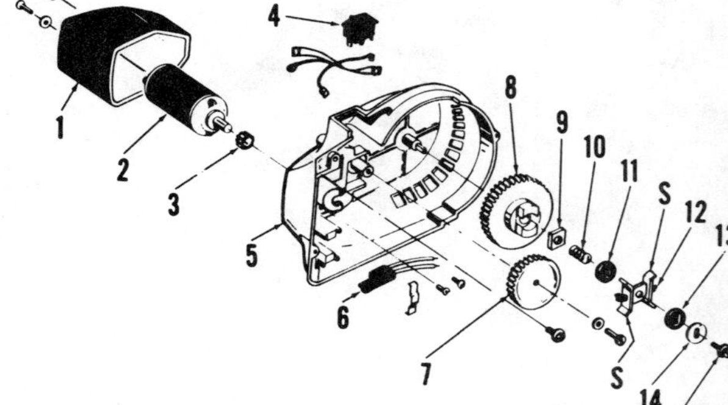

ROPER

Model	Bore mm (in.)	Stroke mm (in.)	Displacement cc (cu. in.)	Drive Type
C110, C121	34.9 (1.375)	32.5 (1.28)	31.1 (1.9)	Direct
C332, C343, C354	46 (1.8125)	36.5 (1.4375)	60.6 (3.7)	Direct

MAINTENANCE

SPARK PLUG. Recommended spark plug is a Champion DJ6J for Models C110 and C121. Champion CJ6 is recommended for all other models. Spark plug electrode gap should be 0.025 inch (0.63 mm) for all models.

CARBURETOR. A Tillotson Model HS diagphragm type carburetor is used on Models C110 and C121 while a Walbro Model HDC diaphragm type carburetor is used on Models C332, C343 and C354. Refer to Tillotson or Walbro sections of CARBURETOR SERVICE section for carburetor overhaul and exploded views.

Initial adjustment of Tillotson carburetor is 1⅛ turns open for idle mixture screw and one turn open for high speed mixture screw. Initial adjustment of Walbro carburtor is one turn open for idle mixture screw and ¾-turn open for high speed mixture screw. Final adjustments should be made with engine warm. High speed mixture screw should be adjusted with engine under cutting load to obtain optimum performance. Do not adjust high speed mixture too lean as engine damage may result.

MAGNETO AND TIMING. A conventional flywheel magneto is used on all models. Ignition timing is fixed. Recommended breaker-point gap is 0.015 inch (0.38 mm) for all models. Incorrect breaker-point gap will affect ignition timing. Magneto air gap should be 0.005-0.010 inch (0.13-0.25 mm).

LUBRICATION. The engine is lubricated by mixing oil with fuel. A good quality oil designed for use in an air-cooled two-stroke engine should be mixed with regular gasoline at the ratio of 16:1. Fuel:oil ratio should be increased during break-in with ¾-pint (0.35 L) of oil added to one gallon (3.785 L) of gasoline. This break-in ratio should be used for the first gallon (3.785 L) of fuel mixture.

Models C121, C343 and C354 are equipped with an automatic chain oil pump. All models are equipped with a manual chain oil pump. Recommended chain oil is a good quality SAE 30 oil for summer use and SAE 20 for winter use. If saw is used in extremely cold weather, SAE 10 oil may be mixed with a small amount of kerosene.

REPAIRS

PISTON, PIN, RINGS, AND CYLINDER. Before cylinder can be removed, crankcase end plate must be removed. Refer to CRANKCASE AND CRANKSHAFT section. Cylinder has chromed aluminum bore on all models with cylinder head integral with cylinder. Piston has two pinned piston rings. Piston pin is fully floating and retained by snap rings at each end. Piston pin on Models C332, C343 and C354 rides in a needle roller bearing in small end of connecting rod. Piston pin on other models rides directly in small end of rod. Piston must be heated to remove and install piston pin.

Inspect chrome bore of cylinder for scoring, flaking, cracking or other signs of damage or excessive wear. Inspect piston pin, bearing and connecting rod small end. Install new piston pin bearing, on models so equipped, by pressing on lettered side of bearing. Be sure rod is properly supported when pressing against bearing to prevent damage to lower portion of rod if rod is still attached to crankshaft. Piston, pin and connecting rod are available only as a unit assembly on Models C110 and C121.

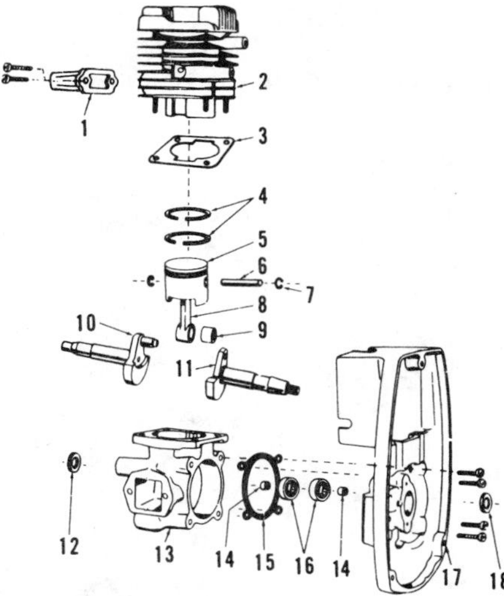

Fig. RP2—Exploded view of engine used on Models C110 and C121.

1. Muffler
2. Cylinder
3. Gasket
4. Piston rings
5. Piston
6. Piston pin
7. Snap rings
8. Connecting rod
9. Needle bearing
10. Crankshaft (drive end)
11. Crankshaft (flywheel end)
12. Seal
13. Crankcase
14. Roller bearings (Torrington B86)
15. Gasket
16. Roller bearings (Torrington DD40798)
17. End plate
18. Seal

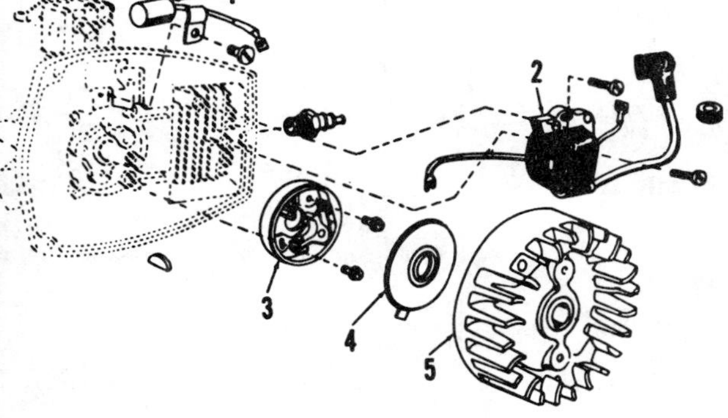

Fig. RP1—Exploded view of magneto assembly.

1. Condenser
2. Ignition coil
3. Stator plate & breaker points
4. Cover
5. Flywheel

Heat piston before installing piston pin which must be installed with closed end of pin toward exhaust port. Install piston with "EXH" marking on piston crown toward exhaust port of cylinder. Be sure piston rings are properly aligned with locating pins in ring grooves when installing cylinder. Tighten cylinder base nuts on Models C110 and C121 to 30-40 in.-lbs. (3.4-4.5 N•m) and to 80-100 in.-lbs. (9.0-11.3 N•m) on all other models.

CONNECTING ROD. Connecting rod on Models C332, C343 and C354 can be removed after removing piston and unscrewing rod cap screws. Be careful not to lose bearing rollers (14–Fig. RP3) when removing rod and cap. To remove rod on Models C110 and C121, crankshaft must be separated as outlined in CRANKCASE AND CRANKSHAFT section.

Thirty-one loose bearing rollers are used in crankpin bearing on Models C332, C343 and C354 while a cartridge roller bearing is used on Models C110 and C121. Piston pin rides directly in small end of connecting rod Models C110 and C121. Piston pin is supported by a needle roller bearing in connecting rod on Models C332, C343 and C354. Install roller bearing by pressing on lettered side of bearing. Connecting rod, piston and piston pin are available only as a unit assembly on Models C110 and C121.

On Models C332, C343 and C354, loose bearing rollers can be held in place with heavy grease or wax on strip of new bearing rollers. Note match marks on connecting rod and rod cap which must be aligned for installation.

CRANKCASE AND CRANKSHAFT. Access to crankcase and crankshaft is possible after removing end plate (17–Fig. RP2 or 18–Fig. RP3). Flywheel end of crankshaft on all models is supported by a roller bearing. Two bearings (14 and 16–Fig. RP2) are used on Models C110 and C121. Drive end of crankshaft is supported by two roller bearings on Models C110 and C121 and by a ball bearing on Models C332, C343 and C354. Heat should be applied to crankcase or end plate to remove roller bearings. Ball bearing (8–Fig. RP3) is pressed on crankshaft and retained in crankcase by retainers (6). It may be necessary to apply heat to crankcase to remove bearing and crankshaft from crankcase.

Models C110 and C121 are equipped with a two-piece crankshaft (10 and 11–Fig. RP2). End plate (17), crankshaft half (11) and cylinder must be removed before connecting rod (8) can be removed. Drive end of crankshaft (10) may be removed after connecting rod (8) is removed. Drive (10) and flywheel (11) ends are available separately.

Ball bearing (8–Fig. RP3) on Models C332, C343 and C354 is pressed on crankshaft. Groove around outer race of bearing must be adjacent to crankpin. Heat crankcase (1) in bearing area and install crankshaft and bearing. Coat screw (7) threads with Loctite 222 or 242 and install bearing retainers (6) and screws. Be sure screws do not contact crankshaft when shaft is turned.

REED VALVE. All models are equipped with a reed valve induction system. Refer to Figs. RP4 and RP5. Inspect reed petals for cracks or other damage. Inspect reed valve seats for pitting o other damage which may prevent petal from seating properly. Reed petals an seat are available only as a uni assembly.

REWIND STARTER. Refer to Fig RP6 for exploded view of rewind starte used on all models. To disassembl starter, proceed as follows: Remov starter housing from end plate Remov rope handle and allow rope to rewind in to starter. Remove "E' ring (6) an remove rope pulley (8) being careful no to dislodge rewind spring (9). I necessary, remove rewind spring being careful as injury may result if spring i allowed to uncoil uncontrolled.

Rewind spring is wound in clockwis direction in housing. Rope is wound o pulley in clockwise direction when view ing pulley installed in housing. Place ten sion on rewind spring by turning pulle clockwise before passing rope throug rope outlet. Pulley should be turned sufficient number of turns to draw rop handle against housing when rope i released, but not so many turns that re wind spring is fully extended when rop is completely withdrawn.

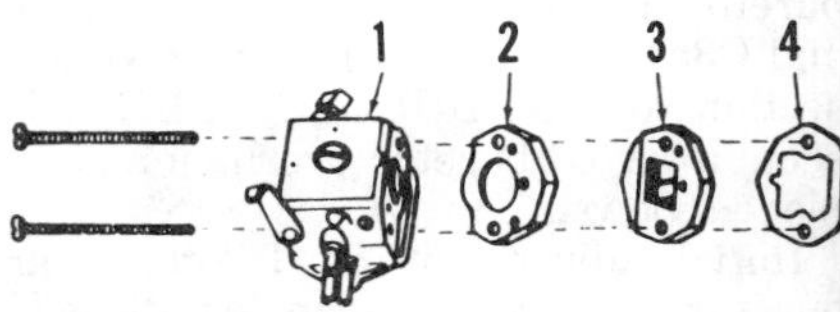

Fig. RP4–View of induction system used o Models C110 and C121.

1. Carburetor
2. Spacer
3. Reed valve ass
4. Gasket

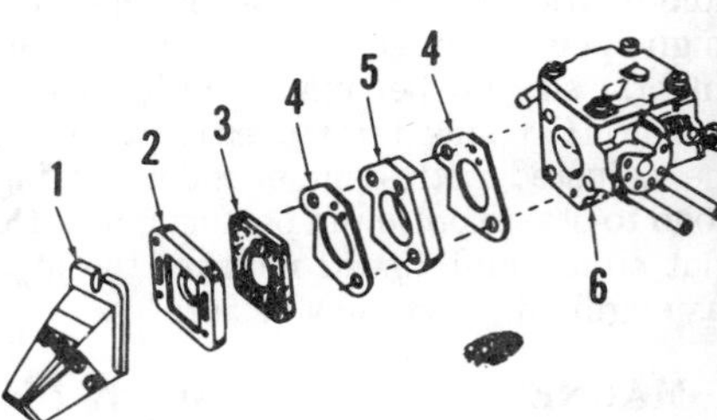

Fig. RP5–View of induction system used o Models C332, C343 and C354.

1. Reed valve assy.
2. Spacer
3. Cork gasket
4. Gasket
5. Heat insulato
6. Carburetor

Fig. RP3–Exploded view of engine used on Models C332, C343 and C354.

1. Crankcase
2. Gasket
3. Cylinder
4. Seal
5. Retainer
6. Retainers
7. Screws
8. Ball bearing
9. Piston rings
10. Snap ring
11. Piston
12. Needle bearing
13. Connecting rod
14. Bearing rollers (31)
15. Rod cap
16. Crankshaft
17. Gasket
18. End plate
19. Roller bearing
20. Seal
21. Piston pin
22. Compression release
23. Reed valve

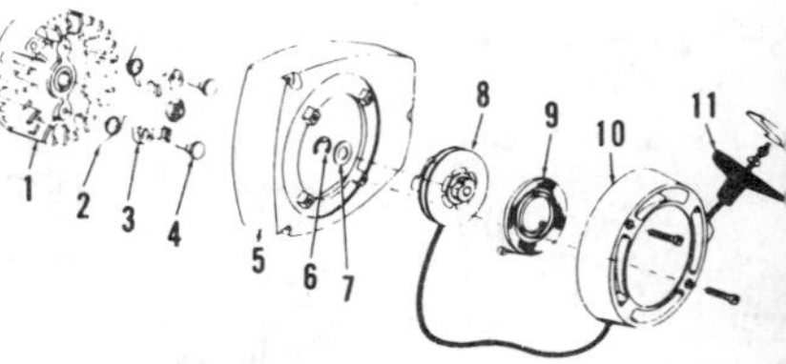

Fig. RP6–Exploded view of rewind starte assembly.

1. Flywheel
2. Spring
3. Pawl
4. Pivot post
5. Fan shroud
6. "E" ring
7. Washer
8. Rope pulley
9. Rewind spring
10. Starter housin
11. Rope handle

ROPER

Model	Bore mm (in.)	Stroke mm (in.)	Displacement cc (cu. in.)	Drive Type
C611, C625, C636	39.7 (1.562)	33.3 (1.312)	41 (2.5)	Direct

MAINTENANCE

SPARK PLUG. Recomended spark plug is Champion DJ6J. Spark plug electrode gap should be 0.025 inch (0.63 mm).

CARBURETOR. A Tillotson HK diaphragm carburetor is used on all models. Refer to CARBURETOR SERVICE section for overhaul procedures.

Initial setting of idle and high speed mixture screws is one turn open. Adjust idle mixture screw so engine will accelerate without hesitation. Adjust high speed mixture screw to obtain optimum performance with saw under cutting load.

MAGNETO AND TIMING. A breaker-point type flywheel magneto is used on all models. Ignition timing is fixed. Recommended breaker-point gap is 0.015 inch (0.38 mm) for all models. Incorrect breaker-point gap will affect ignition timing. Magneto air gap should be 0.008 inch (0.20 mm). Tighten flywheel nut to 130-150 in.-lbs. (14.7-16.9 N·m).

LUBRICATION. The engine is lubricated by mixing oil with the fuel. A good quality oil designed for use in air-cooled two-stroke engines should be mixed with regular gasoline at a ratio of 16:1. Fuel:oil ratio should be increased during break-in with ¾-pint (0.35 L) of oil added to one gallon (3.785 L) of gasoline. This break-in ratio should be used for the first gallon (3.785 L) of fuel mixture.

All models are equipped with an automatic chain oil pump while Model C636 is also equipped with a manual oil pump. Recommended chain oil is a good quality SAE 30 oil for summer use and SAE 20 for winter use. If saw is used in extremely cold weather, SAE 10 oil may be mixed with a small amount of kerosene.

REPAIRS

CYLINDER, PISTON, PIN AND RINGS. Cylinder (23 – Fig. RP10) on all models is also upper crankcase half. Crankshaft is loose in crankcase when cylinder is removed. Care must be taken not to nick or scratch crankcase mating surfaces during disassembly.

Cylinder head is integral with cylinder and cylinder must be removed to remove piston. Piston is equipped with two piston rings and a floating type piston pin. It may be necessary to heat piston to remove or install piston pin. Piston, pin and rings are available in standard size only. Cylinder bore is chrome and should be inspected to determine if chrome is scored, peeling or excessively worn. Renew cylinder and piston if damaged or excessively worn.

Refer to CRANKSHAFT section for proper assembly of crankcase and cylinder.

CONNECTING ROD, CRANKSHAFT AND CRANKCASE. The connecting rod is supported on crankshaft by 26 bearing rollers. Tighten connecting rod screws to 45-55 in.-lbs. (5.1-6.2 N·m).

Two needle roller bearings (12 – Fig. RP10) support crankshaft. Inspect crankshaft and renew if worn, bent or damaged. Crankcase and cylinder mating surfaces must be free of nicks and gouges or other damage which will prevent crankcase sealing.

Before reassembling crankcase and cylinder, apply a light coat of non-hardening sealant to crankcase and cylinder mating surfaces. Be sure retaining rings (11) mesh with grooves in crankcase and cylinder. Tighten crankcase screws to 60-75 in.-lbs. (6.8-8.5 N·m).

CLUTCH. All models are equipped with a two-shoe centrifugal clutch. Clutch hub (1 – Fig. RP10) has left-hand threads. Clutch shoes and hub are available only as a unit assembly. Clutch drum (5) is supported by bearings (4 and 7).

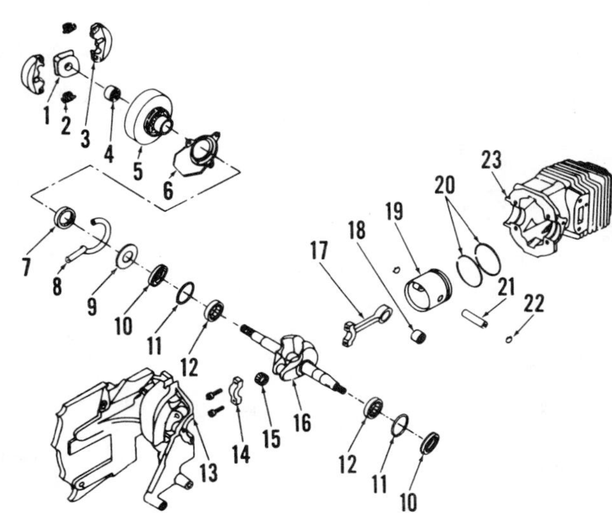

Fig. RP10 — Exploded view of engine and clutch.

1. Clutch hub
2. Springs
3. Shoes
4. Bearing
5. Clutch drum
6. Cover
7. Bearing
8. Oil outlet line
9. Washer
10. Seal
11. Retainer ring
12. Bearing
13. Crankcase
14. Rod cap
15. Bearing rollers (26)
16. Crankshaft
17. Conecting rod
18. Bearing
19. Piston
20. Piston rings
21. Piston pin
22. Pin retainer
23. Cylinder

OIL PUMP. All models are equipped with an automatic chain oil pump. Crankcase pulsations pressurize the oil tank through a check valve to force oil to the chain. Note that oil outlet line (8–Fig. RP10) is routed around crankshaft. Be sure check valve in oil tank operates correctly or oil may enter crankcase.

REWIND STARTER. Refer to Fig. RP11 for an exploded view of rewind starter. To disassemble starter, detach starter housing from saw, remove rope handle and allow rope to rewind into housing. Remove "E" ring (1) and washer (2) then carefully remove rope pulley (3) being careful not to dislodge rewind spring (4). If spring must be removed, care must be taken not to allow spring to uncoil uncontrolled.

Install spring so coils are wrapped in a clockwise direction from outer end. Wind rope on pulley in a clockwise direction as viewed with pulley installed in housing. Turn rope pulley two turns clockwise before passing rope through rope outlet so spring is preloaded.

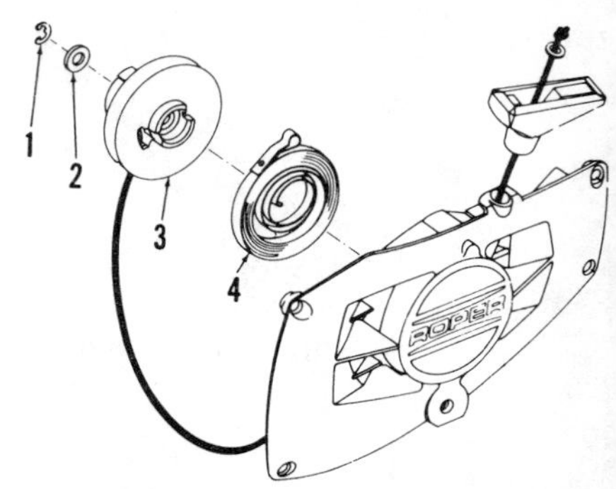

Fig. RP11 – Exploded view of rewind starter.

1. "E" ring
2. Washer
3. Rope pulley
4. Rewind spring

SHINDAIWA

Model	Bore mm (in.)	Stroke mm (in.)	Displacement cc (cu. in.)	Drive Type
345	34 (1.34)	33 (1.3)	30 (1.8)	Direct
350	37 (1.45)	33 (1.3)	35.5 (2.2)	Direct
415, 416	39 (1.54)	33 (1.3)	39.4 (2.4)	Direct
450, 451	41 (1.62)	33 (1.3)	43.6 (2.7)	Direct
500	43 (1.69)	33 (1.3)	47.9 (2.9)	Direct

MAINTENANCE

SPARK PLUG. Recommended spark plug is Champion CJ8Y for all models. Spark plug electrode gap should be 0.6 mm (0.024 in.).

CARBURETOR. A Walbro WA diaphragm type carburetor is used on all models. Refer to Walbro section of CARBURETOR SERVICE section for service procedures and exploded view of carburetor.

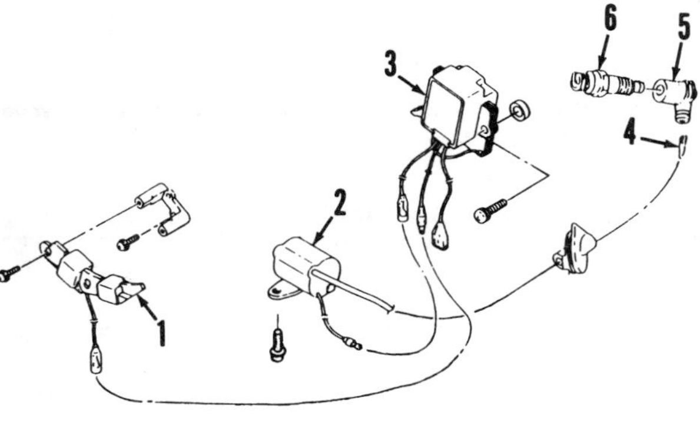

Fig. SW11—Exploded view of breakerless electronic ignition components used on Model 345.

1. Pulser coil
2. Ignition coil
3. Exciter/module coil
4. Terminal
5. Spark plug boot
6. Spark plug

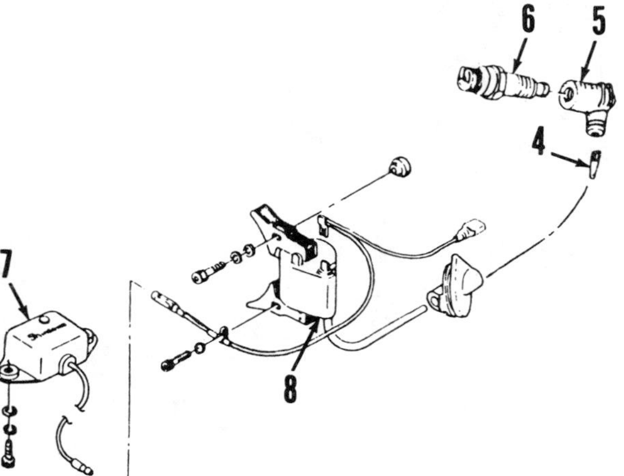

Fig. SW12—Exploded view of brearkerless electronic ignition components used on Models 350, 415, 416, 450, 451 and 500.

4. Terminal
5. Spark plug boot
6. Spark plug
7. Module assy.
8. Ignition coil

Initial adjustment for both low speed and high speed mixture screws is 1¼ turns open from a lightly seated position. Be sure that air filter is clean before performing final adjustment of carburetor.

Make final adjustment with engine warm and running. Adjust idle speed screw so engine idles just below clutch engagement speed (approximately 2800 rpm). Adjust low speed mixture screw so engine will accelerate cleanly without hesitation. Readjust idle speed screw, if necessary, so chain does not move when engine is at idle speed. Adjust high speed mixture screw to obtain optimum performance under cutting load. Do not turn high speed mixture screw to less than one turn open. Operating saw with high speed mixture too lean may cause engine damage due to lack of lubrication and overheating.

IGNITION. All models are equipped with a breakerless electronic ignition system. Ignition timing is not adjustable. There is no periodic maintenance required for the electronic ignition system.

On Model 345, air gap between pulser coil (1—Fig. SW11) legs and flywheel magnets and between exciter/module coil (3) legs and flywheel magnets should be 0.30-0.35 mm (0.012-0.014 in.). On all other models, air gap between ignition coil (8—Fig. SW12) legs and flywheel magnets should be 0.30-0.35 mm (0.012-0.014 in.).

LUBRICATION. The engine is lubricated by mixing oil with gasoline. Recommended oil is Shindaiwa Premium 2-Cycle Oil mixed at a ratio of 40:1. If Shindaiwa Premium 2-Cycle Oil is not available, a good quality oil designed for air-cooled two-stroke engines may be used when mixed at a 25:1 ratio. Use a separate container when mixing the oil and gasoline.

All models are equipped with an automatic chain oiler system. The automatic oil pump operates only when the chain is operating. Recommended chain oil is Shindaiwa Bar and Chain Oil. Oil output on all models is adjusted by turning oil pump adjuster shaft, which is accessible through opening in top of saw.

REPAIRS

CRANKCASE PRESSURE TEST. An improperly sealed crankcase can cause the engine to be hard to start, run rough, have low power and overheat. Refer to ENGINE SERVICE section of this manual for crankcase pressure test procedure. If crankcase leakage is indicated, pressurize crankcase and use a soap and water solution to check gaskets, seals, pulse line and castings for leakage.

CYLINDER, PISTON, PIN AND RINGS. To disassemble, remove clutch cover, guide bar and chain, front handle and starter housing. Remove muffler, carburetor and rear handle assembly (2—Fig. SW13). Remove spark plug and install a piston stop tool or insert end of a rope in spark plug hole to lock piston and crankshaft. Unscrew clutch hub (left-hand threads) and remove clutch assembly from crankshaft. Remove oil pump assembly. Remove flywheel mounting nut (right-hand threads), then use suitable puller to remove flywheel. Remove ignition unit, fuel tank and oil tank. Remove engine cover mounting screws and separate engine from cover (1—Fig. SW14). Remove screws attaching crankcase (1—Fig. SW15) to cylinder (20) and tap crankcase gently to separate crankcase from cylinder. Pull piston out of cylinder. Remove piston rings (16) from piston. Pry piston pin retainer clips (13) out of piston, then tap piston pin out of piston and connecting rod. Be careful not to apply side thrust to connecting rod when removing piston pin. Remove piston, thrust washers (11) and needle bearing (12) from connecting rod.

Cylinder bore is chrome plated and cannot be honed or bored. Cylinder should be renewed if cracking, flaking or other damage to cylinder bore is noted. Renew cylinder if out-of-round more than 0.03 mm (0.001 in.) or if cylinder wall taper exceeds 0.05 mm (0.002 in.). Cylinder and crankcase must be renewed as an assembly.

Recommended piston-to-cylinder clearance is 0.025-0.061 mm (0.0010-0.0024 in.) with a maximum limit of 0.18 mm (0.007 in.).

Piston pin standard diameter is 10 mm (0.3937 in.) and wear limit is 9.98 mm (0.3929 in.). Piston pin boss standard inner diameter is 9.99-10.0 mm (0.3937-0.3940 in.) and wear limit is 10.1 mm (0.3976 in.).

When reassembling, install piston on connecting rod so arrow mark on piston crown points toward exhaust port side of engine. Install piston pin with closed end toward exhaust port. Once removed, piston pin clips (13) should not be reused. Install new piston pin clips, positioning open end of clip 90 degrees from horizontal slot in piston pin hole. Locating pins are present in ring grooves to prevent ring rotation. Make certain that ring end gaps are properly positioned around locating pins before installing piston in cylinder. Lubricate piston, cylinder and connecting rod bearings before installation. Apply thin even coat of form-in-place gasket compound to mating surfaces of cylinder and crankcase halves. Apply thread locking compound to crankcase mounting screws, then tighten screws in several steps to final torque of 6.9-7.9 N·m (61-70 in.-lbs.). Complete reassembly by reversing disassembly procedure. Tight-

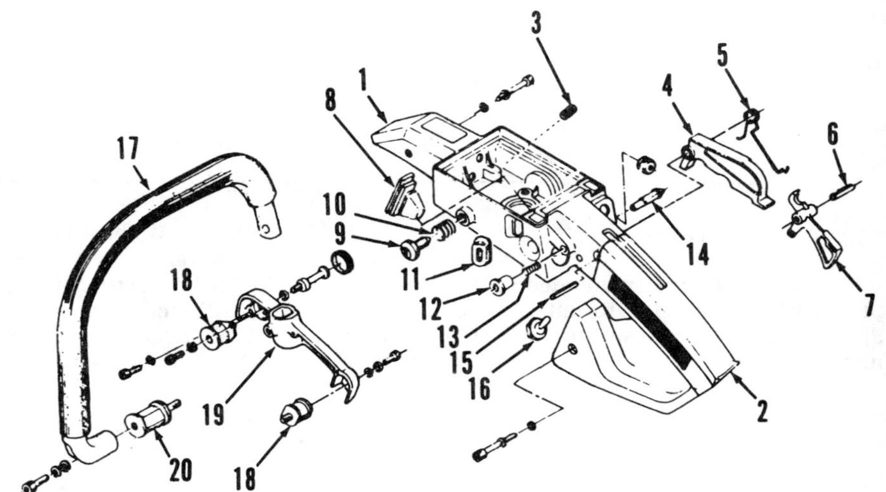

Fig. SW13—Exploded view of throttle trigger assembly, front and rear handle assemblies and associated parts.

1. Rear handle
2. Handle grip
3. Spring
4. Lock lever
5. Spring
6. Spring pin
7. Trigger
8. Grommet
9. Adjuster screw
10. Spring
11. Grommet
12. Stop knob
13. Spring
14. Stopper
15. Spring pin
16. Run/stop switch
17. Front handle
18. Vibration damper
19. Bracket
20. Vibration damper

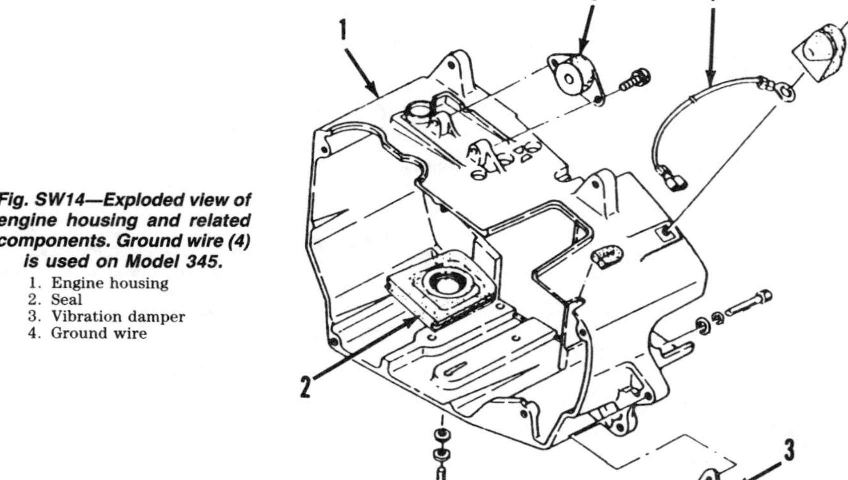

Fig. SW14—Exploded view of engine housing and related components. Ground wire (4) is used on Model 345.

1. Engine housing
2. Seal
3. Vibration damper
4. Ground wire

Illustrations courtesy Shindaiwa, Inc.

en flywheel retaining nut to 11.8-13.8 N·m (104-122 in.-lbs.) and clutch hub to 1.9-2.4 N·m (17-22 in.-lbs.).

CRANKSHAFT AND CONNECTING ROD. To remove crankshaft assembly (10—Fig. SW15), follow disassembly procedure outlined in CYLINDER, PISTON, PIN AND RINGS section. Crankshaft and connecting rod are a unit assembly and should not be disassembled.

Rotate connecting rod around crankpin and renew assembly if roughness, excessive play or other damage is noted. Maximum crankshaft runout measured on main bearing journals and supported between lathe centers is 0.07 mm (0.0027 in.). Standard inside diameter of connecting rod small end is 14 mm (0.5512 in.) and wear limit is 14.04 mm (0.5528 in.).

Assemble thrust washers (8—Fig. SW15), side plates (7) and roller bearings (6). Note that beveled side of thrust washer must face crankshaft counterweight and oil hole in needle bearing must point toward cylinder. Lubricate lip of new seals (5) and install on crankshaft with lip facing inward. Install crankshaft and piston in cylinder and measure side clearance between crankshaft and side plate. Recommended side clearance is 0.07-0.24 mm (0.003-0.009 in.). Renew side plates and/or thrust washers as necessary if clearance is excessive. Side plates are available in two different thicknesses to provide means of adjusting side clearance. Apply a thin even coat of suitable form-in-place gasket compound to mating surfaces of cylinder and crankcase halves. Apply thread locking compound to crankcase mounting screws, then tighten screws in several steps to final torque of 6.9-7.9 N·m (61-70 in.-lbs.). Make sure that crankshaft turns smoothly after crankcase screws are tightened.

CLUTCH. A centrifugal type clutch is used on all models. Remove chain brake housing, guide bar and chain for access to clutch. Remove starter housing and use suitable tool to hold flywheel from turning. Unscrew clutch hub (8—Fig. SW16) from crankshaft (left-hand threads) and remove clutch assembly.

Inspect clutch drum needle bearing (1) for roughness or wear and renew as necessary. Inspect clutch shoes (6) and drum (4) for signs of excessive heat. Sprocket (3) should be renewed if teeth are worn in excess of 25 mm (0.010 in.). If sprocket is badly worn, inspect chain for excessive wear also. Do not install a new chain over a worn sprocket.

Apply grease to drive flanges of hub (8) and to needle bearing (1) prior to installation. Install clutch assembly on crankshaft and tighten clutch hub to 1.9-2.4 N·m (17-22 in.-lbs.).

AUTOMATIC CHAIN OILER. All models are equipped with an automatic chain oiler system. An automatic oil pump is driven by clutch drum via gears (11 and 12—Fig. SW17) to provide oil to the system whenever clutch and chain are operating.

Oil pump assembly (9) is not serviceable and must be renewed as an assembly if faulty. Initial setting of oil pump output is the midrange position between minimum and maximum output. To adjust, rotate adjuster shaft (8) clockwise to decrease oil pump output or counterclockwise to increase oil pump output.

REWIND STARTER. Refer to Fig. SW18 for exploded view of rewind starter used on Model 345. Refer to Fig. SW19 for exploded view of rewind starter used on Models 415 and 450. Refer to Fig. SW20 for exploded view of rewind starter used on Models 350 and 416. Refer to Fig. SW21 for exploded view of rewind starter used on Models 451 and 500.

To disassemble starter on all models, first unbolt and remove starter housing from engine. Remove rope handle and allow rope to wind onto pulley while keeping some tension on pulley until spring tension is relieved. Unscrew pulley mounting screw and remove pulley, being careful not to dislodge rewind spring. If necessary to remove rewind

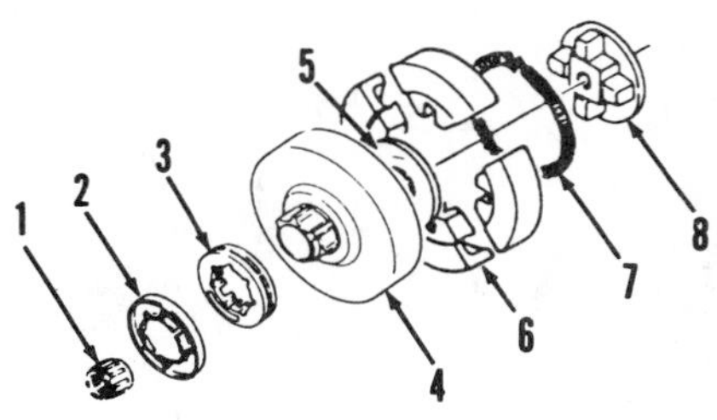

Fig. SW16—Exploded view of centrifugal clutch assembly typical of all models.

1. Needle bearing
2. Cover
3. Floating sprocket
4. Clutch drum
5. Washer
6. Clutch shoes
7. Spring
8. Hub

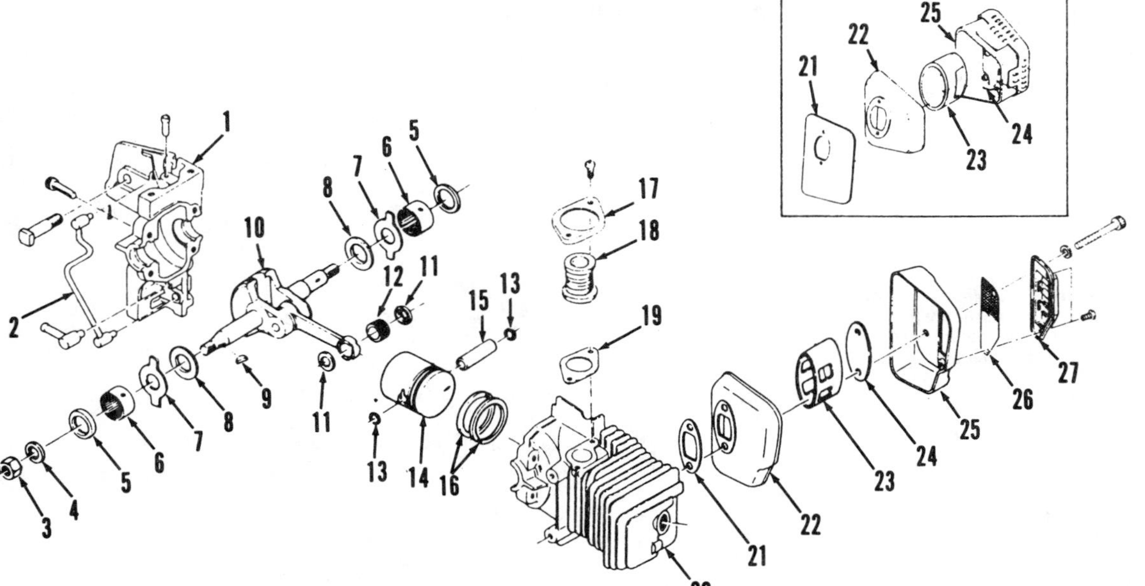

1. Lower crankcase half
2. Oil tube
3. Flywheel nut
4. Lockwasher
5. Oil seal
6. Roller bearing
7. Side plate
8. Thrust washer
9. Key
10. Crankshaft & connecting rod assy.
11. Thrust washer
12. Needle bearing
13. Retainer clip
14. Piston
15. Piston pin
16. Piston rings
17. Plate
18. Boot
19. Gasket
20. Cylinder & upper crankcase half
21. Gasket
22. Muffler half
23. Baffle
24. Plate
25. Muffler half
26. Spark arrestor
27. Cover

Fig. SW15—Exploded view of engine assembly typical of all models. Inset shows muffler assembly used on Model 350. Gasket (19) and side plates (7) are not used on Model 345.

spring, care should be used not to allow spring to uncoil uncontrolled.

Apply a light coat of multipurpose grease to both sides of rewind spring. Install rewind spring in starter housing with coils wrapped in clockwise direction from outer end of spring. Wind rope around pulley in a clockwise direction as viewed from flywheel side of pulley. Turn pulley approximately three turns clockwise to preload rewind spring before passing rope through starter housing. Attach rope handle and check starter operation. It should be possible to pull rope to its full extension and still turn rope pulley approximately 1/2 turn clockwise. If rewind spring binds before rope is fully extended, reduce tension on rope by pulling rope up into notch in rope pulley and allowing pulley to unwind one turn. Recheck starter operation.

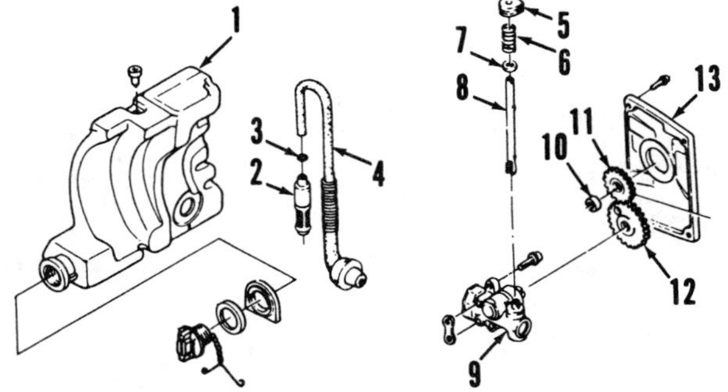

Fig. SW17—Exploded view of automatic chain oiler system. A dust plate is used between oil pump assembly (9) and gears (11 and 12) on Models 350, 415, 416, 450, 451 and 500.

1. Oil tank
2. Strainer
3. Retainer
4. Pickup hose
5. Grommet
6. Spring
7. Washer
8. Adjuster shaft
9. Oil pump assy.
10. Collar
11. Drive gear
12. Oil pump input gear
13. Cover

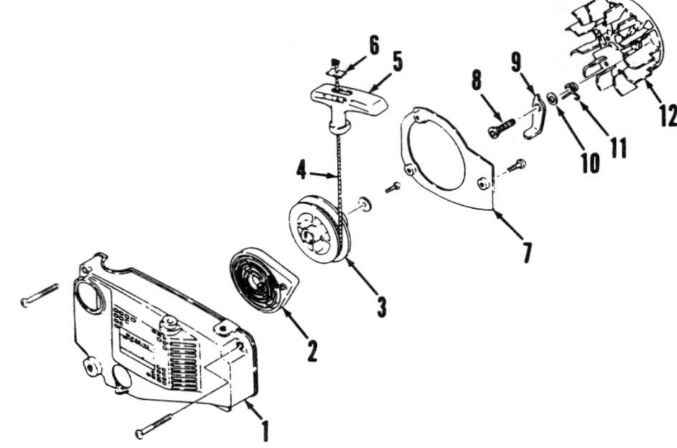

Fig. SW18—Exploded view of rewind starter assembly used on Model 345.

1. Starter housing
2. Rewind spring
3. Rope pulley
4. Rope
5. Handle
6. Anchor
7. Baffle
8. Pivot screw
9. Pawl
10. Washer
11. Return spring
12. Flywheel

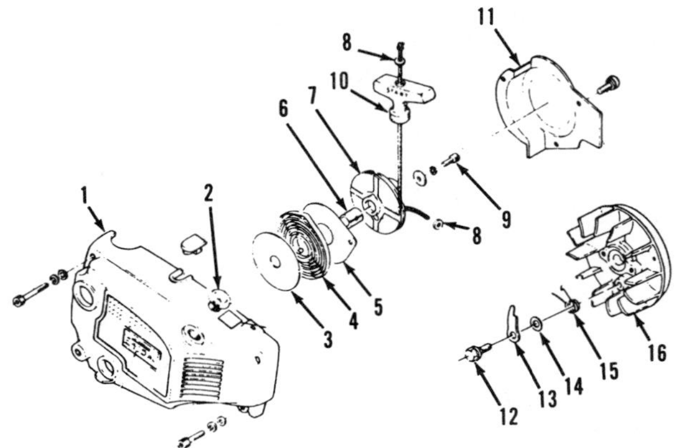

Fig. SW19—Exploded view of rewind starter assembly used on Models 415 and 450.

1. Starter housing
2. Rope guide
3. Plate
4. Rewind spring
5. Plate
6. Bushing
7. Pulley
8. Anchor
9. Screw
10. Rope handle
11. Air baffle
12. Pivot screw
13. Pawl
14. Washer
15. Return spring
16. Flywheel

Illustrations courtesy Shindaiwa, Inc.

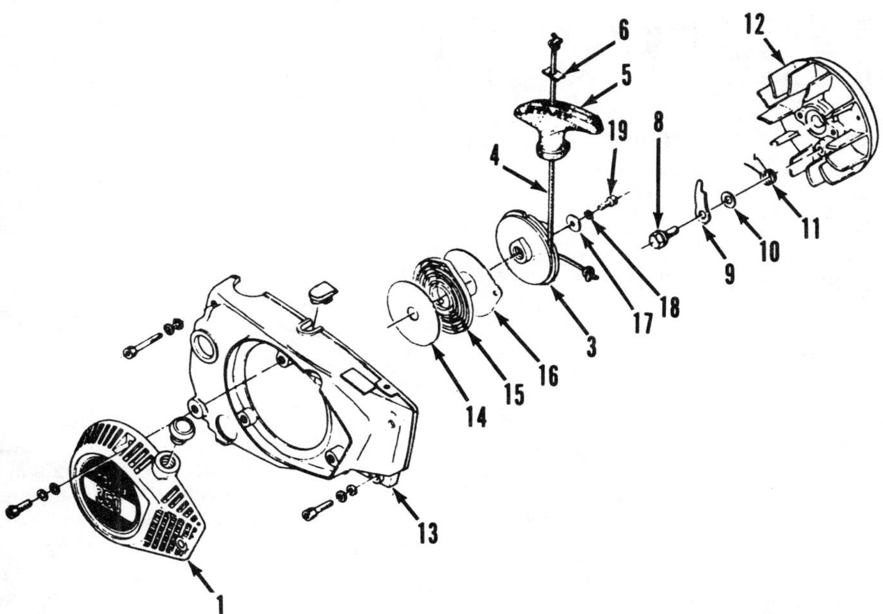

Fig. SW20—Exploded view of rewind starter assembly used on Models 350 and 416.

1. Starter housing
3. Rope pulley
4. Rope
5. Handle
6. Anchor
8. Pivot screw
9. Pawl
10. Washer
11. Return spring
12. Flywheel
13. Side cover
14. Plate
15. Rewind spring
16. Plate
17. Flat washer
18. Lockwasher
19. Screw

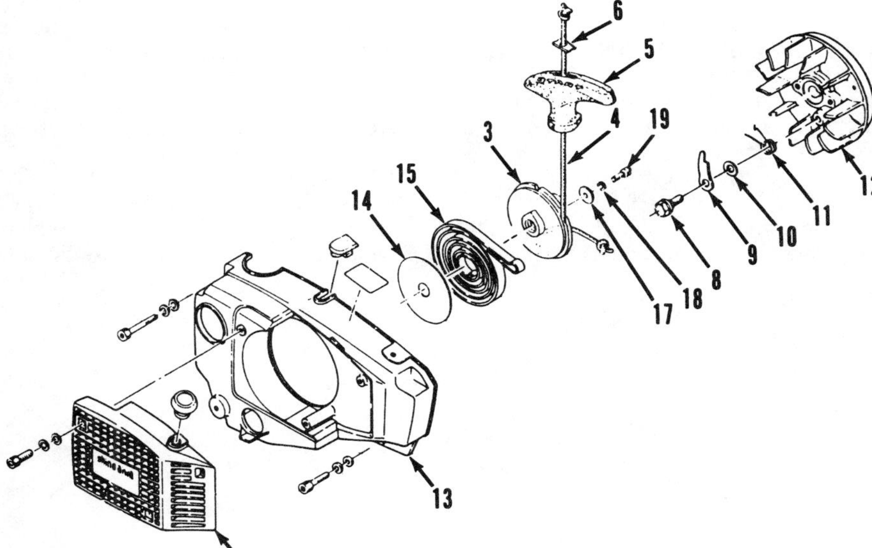

Fig. SW21—Exploded view of rewind starter assembly used on Models 451 and 500. Refer to legend in Fig. SW20 for identification of components.

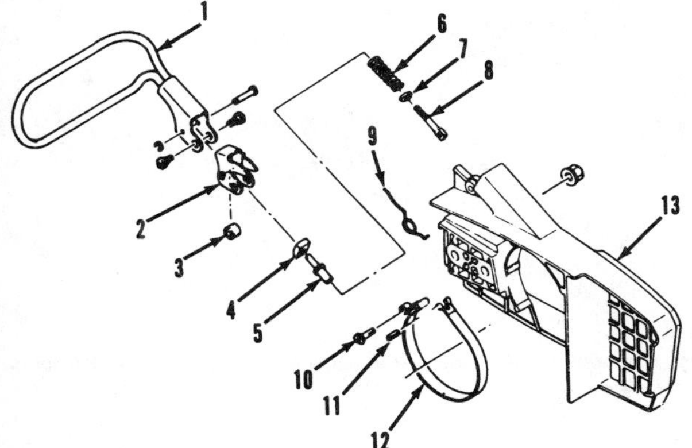

Fig. SW22—Exploded view of chain brake assembly.

1. Lever
2. Latch
3. Spacer
4. Cover
5. Adjuster
6. Spring
7. Washer
8. Adjustment rod
9. Spring
10. Pivot screw
11. Pin
12. Brake band
13. Housing

CHAIN BRAKE. All models are equipped with a chain brake designed to stop the saw chain quickly should kickback occur. Chain brake is activated when operator's hand strikes lever (1—Fig. SW22), releasing latch (2) thereby allowing spring (6) to draw brake band (12) tight around clutch drum. Pull back lever (1) to reset mechanism.

Disassembly for inspection or repair is evident after referral to exploded view and inspection of unit. Renew any component found to be excessively worn or damaged. Chain brake mechanism should be clean and free of sawdust and dirt accumulation. Lightly lubricate all moving parts and pivot points.

To adjust chain brake, first remove spark plug boot from spark plug and properly ground plug wire terminal end. Place chain brake lever (1) in released (vertical) position. Use a screwdriver to rotate adjuster (5) clockwise until saw chain cannot be rotated around guide bar by hand pressure. Then, rotate adjuster counterclockwise until brake band does not contact clutch drum. Normal adjustment is 2-4 turns counterclockwise from clutch locked position. Make sure brake band does not drag on outside of clutch drum with brake lever in the released position. With brake lever in applied position, saw chain should not be free to rotate around guide bar.

SHINDAIWA

Model	Bore mm (in.)	Stroke mm (in.)	Displacement cc (cu. in.)	Drive Type
575	45 (1.77)	36 (1.42)	57.3 (3.5)	Direct
680, 695	49 (1.93)	36 (1.42)	67.9 (4.1)	Direct

MAINTENANCE

SPARK PLUG. Recommended spark plug is Champion CJ8Y for both models. Electrode gap should be 0.6 mm (0.024 in.).

CARBURETOR. A Walbro HDA diaphragm type carburetor is used on both models. Refer to Walbro section of CARBURETOR SERVICE for service and exploded views of carburetor.

Initial adjustment for both low speed and high speed mixture screws is 1¼ turns open from a lightly seated position. Make final adjustment with engine warm and running. Adjust idle speed screw so engine idles just below clutch engagement speed (approximately 2800 rpm). Adjust low speed mixture screw so engine will accelerate cleanly without hesitation. Adjust high speed mixture screw to obtain optimum performance under cutting load. During first 10 hours of operation, the manufacturer recommends rotating mixture screws an additional ⅛ turn toward rich setting.

IGNITION. Both models are equipped with a breakerless electronic ignition system. Ignition timing is not adjustable. Air gap between pulser coil (1–Fig. SW26) legs and flywheel and exciter/module coil (3) legs and flywheel should be 0.5 mm (0.020 in.). Tighten flywheel retaining nut to 11.9-13.5 N•m (105-120 in.-lbs.).

LUBRICATION. Engine is lubricated by mixing engine oil with premium grade unleaded gasoline. Recommended oil is Shindaiwa Premium 2-Cycle Oil mixed at a ratio of 40:1. If Shindaiwa Premium 2-Cycle Oil is not available, a good quality oil designed for air-cooled two-stroke engines may be used when mixed at a 25:1 ratio. Use a separate container when mixing the oil and gas.

Both models are equipped with an automatic chain oil pump. Recommended chain oil is Shindaiwa Bar and Chain Oil or a good quality bar and chain oil. Oil output on both models is adjusted by turning oil pump adjuster shaft. Access hole is located in bottom of right crankcase half. Refer to AUTOMATIC CHAIN OILER under REPAIRS section.

CARBON. Carbon should be cleaned from muffler and exhaust ports at regular intervals. When scraping carbon, be careful not to damage the chamfered edges of the exhaust ports.

REPAIRS

CYLINDER, PISTON, PIN AND RINGS. Cylinder (15–Fig. SW27) bore is chrome plated and should be renewed if cracking, flaking or other damage to cylinder bore is noted. Recommended piston-to-cylinder clearance is 0.074-0.102 mm (0.0029-0.0040 in.) with a maximum limit of 0.18 mm (0.0071 in.). Oversize piston and rings are not available. Piston (11) is equipped with two piston rings (13). Locating pins are present in ring grooves to prevent ring rotation. Make certain ring end gaps are properly positioned around locating pins before installing cylinder. Piston pin (12) rides in needle bearing (8) and is retained in position with two wire retainer clips (10). Once removed, wire clips should not be reused. Install piston on connecting rod so arrow on piston crown points toward exhaust port. On Model 575, note location of thrust washers (7 and 9) when installing piston. Tighten screws securing cylinder (15) to crankcase to 6.9-7.9 N•m) (61-70 in.-lbs.) after first applying a suitable thread fastening solution on threads of screws.

CRANKSHAFT AND CONNECTING ROD. Cylinder (15–Fig. SW27) must be removed and crankcase halves (1 and 16) must be split to remove

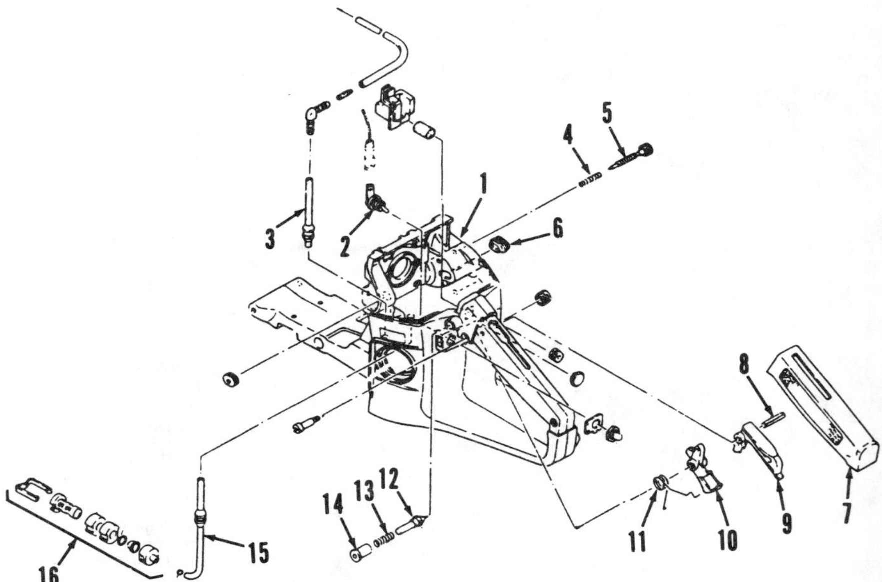

Fig. SW25—Exploded view of trigger assembly, rear handle assembly and associated components.

1. Rear handle
2. Run/stop switch
3. Vent tube
4. Spring
5. Adjuster screw
6. Grommet
7. Handle grip
8. Spring pin
9. Lock lever
10. Trigger
11. Spring
12. Stopper
13. Spring
14. Stop knob
15. Fuel pickup hose
16. Fuel strainer assy.

crankshaft and connecting rod assembly. Crankshaft and connecting rod (6) are a unit assembly and supported at both ends with ball type main bearings (4). Rotate connecting rod around crankpin and renew assembly if roughness, excessive play or other damage is noted. Renew ball bearings (4) if roughness, excessive play or other damage is noted. Maximum crankshaft runout measured on main bearing journals and supported between lathe centers is 0.068 mm (0.0027 in.).

New seals (3) should be installed into crankcase halves and gaskets (2 and 14) renewed during reassembly. After reassembly, slowly rotate crankshaft assembly to be sure crankshaft assembly and piston rotate freely without binding otherwise damage to engine could result. Tighten screws securing crankcase halves (1 and 16) to 6.9-7.9 N•m (61-70 in.-lbs.) after first applying a suitable thread fastening solution on threads of screws.

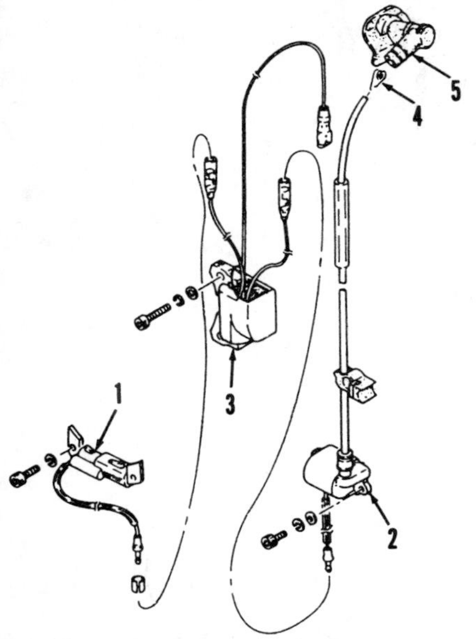

CLUTCH. A three-shoe centrifugal type clutch is used on both models. Clutch hub has left-hand threads. Clutch needle bearing (4 – Fig. SW28) should be inspected for excessive wear or damage. Inspect clutch shoes and drum for signs of excessive heat.

AUTOMATIC CHAIN OILER. All models are equipped with an automatic chain oil pump assembly. Oil pump assembly is driven by clutch drum via gear (5 – Fig. SW29). Oil pump assembly (2) is not serviceable and renewable only as a complete assembly.

Initial setting of oil pump output is ⅔ open position between minimum and maximum output. To adjust, use a suitable tool and rotate adjuster shaft (3) clockwise to decrease oil pump output and counterclockwise to increase oil pump output.

Fig. SW26 – Exploded view of breakerless electronic ignition components.

1. Pulser coil
2. Ignition coil
3. Exciter/module coil
4. Terminal
5. Spark plug boot

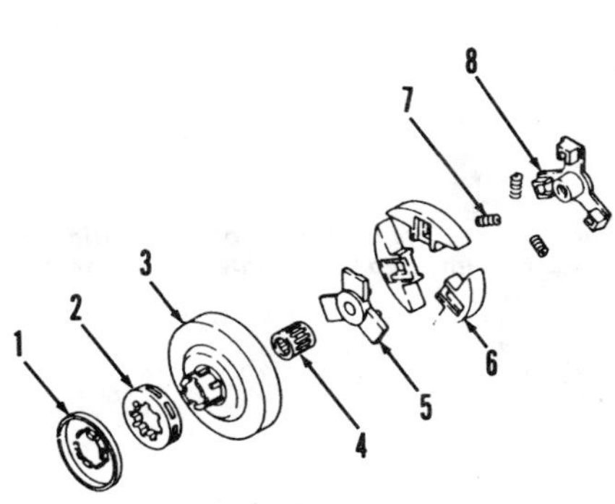

Fig. SW28 – Exploded view of three-shoe clutch assembly.

1. Cover
2. Floating sprocket
3. Drum
4. Needle bearing
5. Outer hub
6. Shoe
7. Spring
8. Inner hub

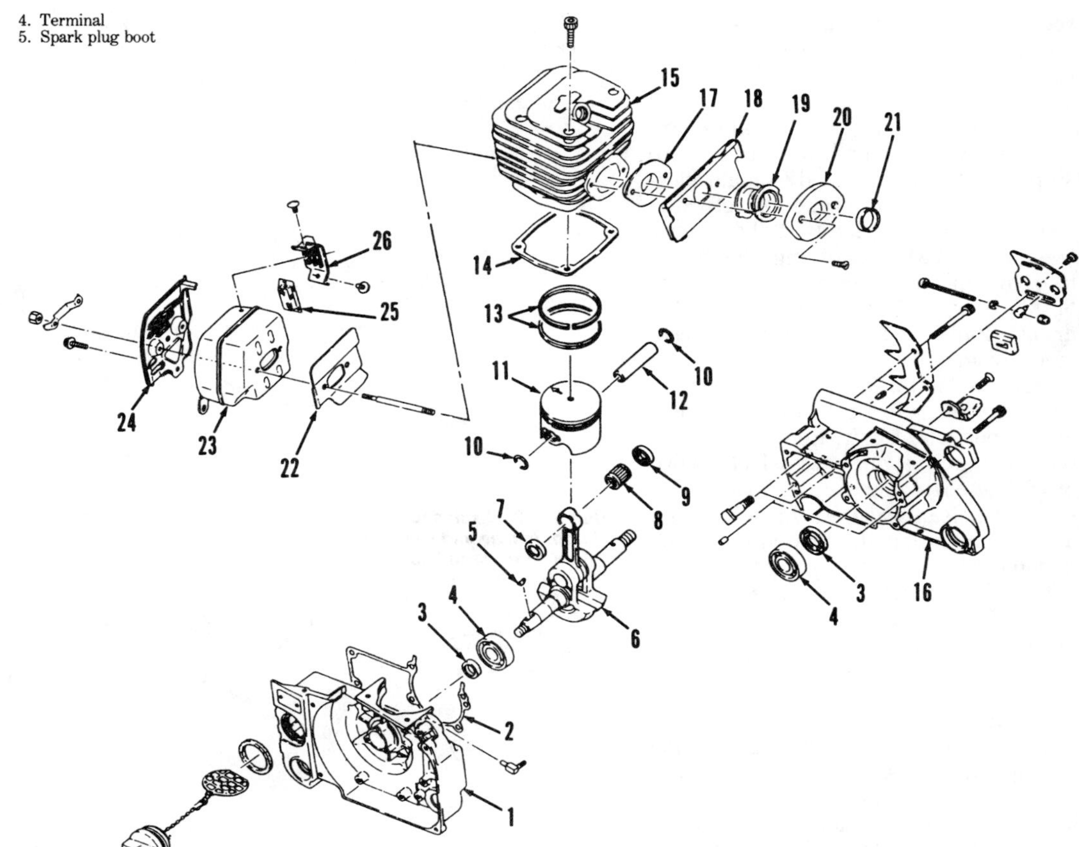

Fig. SW27 – Exploded view of engine, intake and muffler assemblies. Model 695 does not use thrust washers (7 and 9). Adapter plate (17) is not used on Model 575.

1. Crankcase half
2. Gasket
3. Seal
4. Bearing
5. Key
6. Crankshaft & connecting rod assy.
7. Thrust washer
8. Needle bearing
9. Thrust washer
10. Retainer clip
11. Piston
12. Piston pin
13. Piston rings
14. Gasket
15. Cylinder
16. Crankcase half
17. Adapter plate
18. Gasket
19. Boot
20. Plate
21. Sleeve
22. Gasket
23. Muffler assy.
24. Guard
25. Spark arrestor
26. Cover

Illustrations courtesy Shindaiwa, Inc.

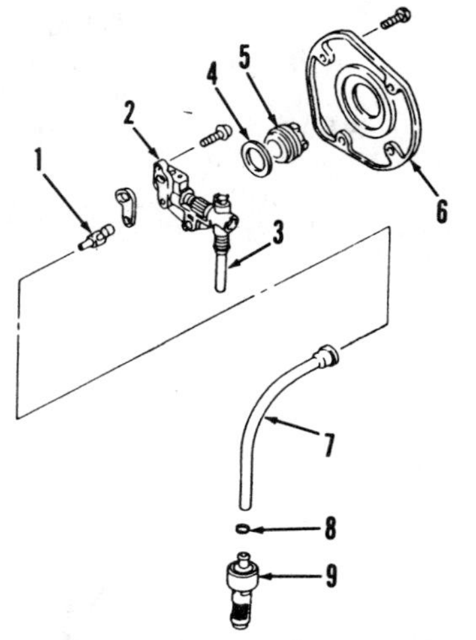

Fig. SW29—Exploded view of automatic oil pump assembly and associated components.

1. Fitting
2. Oil pump assy.
3. Adjuster shaft
4. Thrust washer
5. Drive gear
6. Cover
7. Pickup hose
8. Retainer
9. Strainer

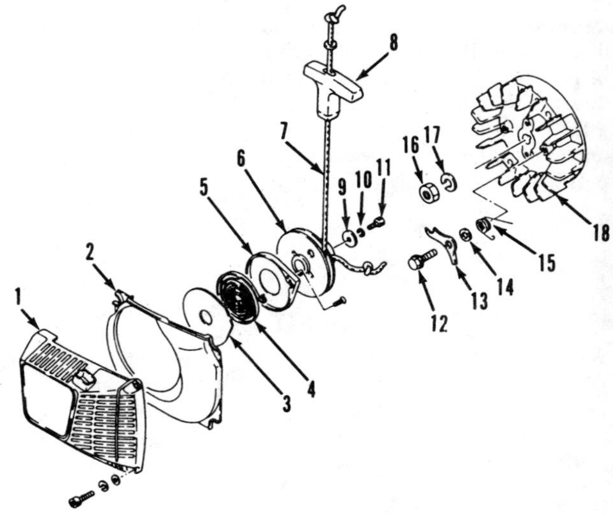

Fig. SW30—Exploded view of rewind starter assembly.

1. Housing
2. Baffle
3. Plate
4. Rewind spring
5. Cassette
6. Rope pulley
7. Rope
8. Handle
9. Flat washer
10. Lockwasher
11. Screw
12. Pivot screw
13. Pawl
14. Washer
15. Return spring
16. Nut
17. Lockwasher
18. Flywheel

REWIND STARTER. Refer to Fig. SW30 for exploded view of pawl type starter used on both models. Care should be exercised when removing rewind spring (4) to prevent spring from uncoiling uncontrolled.

During reassembly, do not apply anymore tension on rewind spring than required to properly draw rope handle up against starter housing in relaxed position.

CHAIN BRAKE. All models are equipped with a chain brake designed to stop the saw chain quickly should kickback occur. Chain brake is activated when operator's hand strikes lever (1–Fig. SW31), releasing latch (2) thereby allowing spring (6) to draw brake band (12) tight around clutch drum. Pull back lever (1) to reset mechanism.

Disassembly for inspection or repair is evident after referral to exploded view and inspection of unit. Renew any component found to be excessively worn or damaged. Chain brake mechanism should be clean and free of sawdust and dirt accumulation. Lightly lubricate all moving parts and pivot points.

To adjust chain brake, first remove spark plug boot from spark plug and properly ground terminal end. Place chain brake lever (1) in released position. Use a suitable size screwdriver and rotate adjuster (5) clockwise until saw chain cannot be rotated around guide bar by hand pressure. Then rotate adjuster (5) counterclockwise noting when brake band (12) does not contact outside surface of clutch drum. Normal adjust-

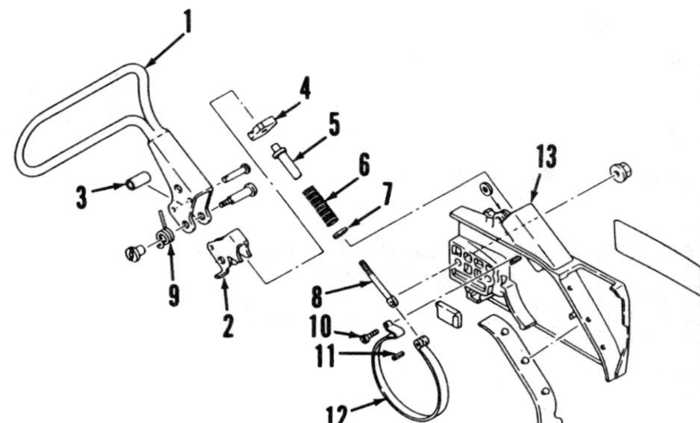

Fig. SW31—Exploded view of chain brake assembly.

1. Lever
2. Latch
3. Spacer
4. Cover
5. Adjuster
6. Spring
7. Washer
8. Adjustment rod
9. Spring
10. Pivot screw
11. Pin
12. Brake band
13. Housing

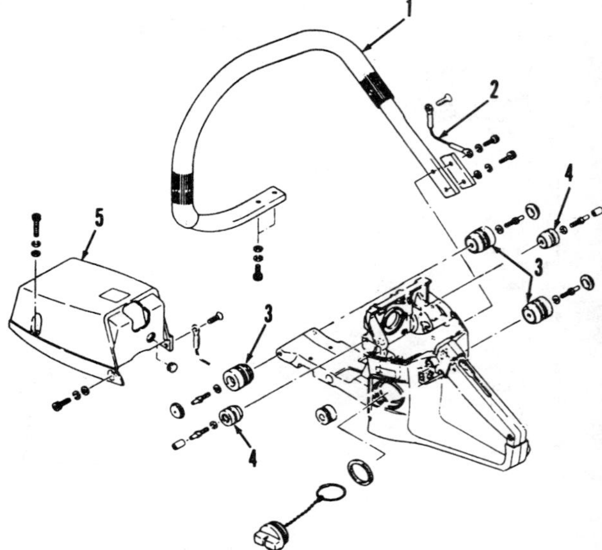

Fig. SW32—Exploded view of front handle and vibration damper assemblies.

1. Front handle
2. Ground wire
3. Vibration damper
4. Vibration damper
4. Cylinder cover

Illustrations courtesy Shindaiwa, Inc.

ment is 2-4 turns counterclockwise from saw chain bound position. Make sure brake band does not drag on outside of clutch drum with brake lever in released position. With brake lever in applied position, saw chain should not be free to rotate around guide bar.

HANDLE HEATER. Some 695 models are equipped with the handle heating system shown in Fig. SW33. Generating coil (2) located behind flywheel (18) produces an electric current which flows through on/off switch (3) and then to heating elements in rear handle (4) and front handle (1).

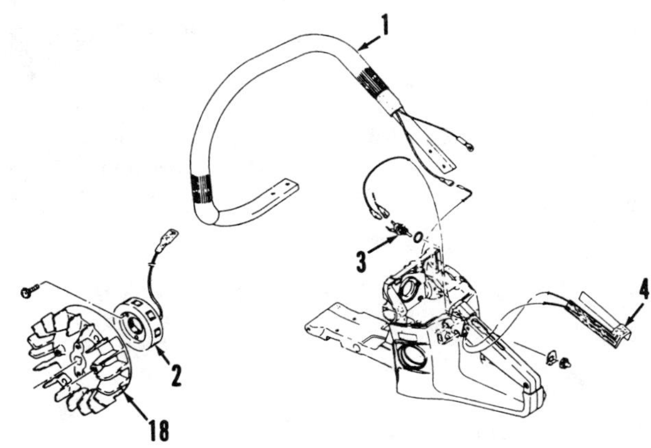

Fig. SW33—Exploded view of handle heating assembly on so equipped 695 models.
1. Front handle heating element
2. Generating coil
3. On/off switch
4. Rear handle heating element
18. Flywheel

Illustrations courtesy Shindaiwa, Inc.

SHINDAIWA

Model	Bore mm (in.)	Stroke mm (in.)	Displacement cc (cu. in.)	Drive Type
300, 300S	36 (1.42)	28 (1.1)	28.5 (1.74)	Direct
360	40 (1.575)	28 (1.10)	35.2 (2.15)	Direct
377	40 (1.575)	30 (1.18)	37.7 (2.30)	Direct

MAINTENANCE

SPARK PLUG. Recommended spark plug is Champion CJ8Y or NGK BPM6A for Model 300. Recommended spark plug for other models is Champion CJ6Y or NGK BPM7A. Spark plug electrode gap should be 0.6 mm (0.024 in.) for all models. The spark plug should be tightened to the torque listed in the TIGHTENING TORQUE paragraph.

CARBURETOR. A Walbro WYM-1 diaphragm type carburetor is used on Model 300 and Walbro WYM-1A is used on Model 300S. Model 360 is equipped with a Walbro WT-89 and Model 377 is equipped with a Walbro WT-229 diaphragm type carburetor. Refer to the appropriate Walbro section of CARBURETOR SERVICE for service procedures and exploded views of carburetors. Tighten the carburetor attaching screws to the torque listed in the TIGHTENING TORQUE paragraph.

For Models 300 and 300S, initial adjustment for the low-speed mixture needle (Fig. SW40) is 12-13 turns IN (clockwise) from a fully unscrewed position. High-speed mixture is determined by a fixed main jet and is not adjustable.

For Models 360 and 377, initial adjustment for both low-speed and high-speed mixture needles is 1-1/4 turns OUT from a lightly seated position. Ends of low-speed mixture needle (L—Fig. SW41), high-speed mixture needle (H) and idle speed stop screw (I) for Models 360 and 377 are accessible as shown.

To adjust the mixture screws, first remove and clean the air filter, then reinstall it. Start the engine and allow it to run until it reaches normal operating temperature. Turn the idle speed stop screw so the engine idles at about 3,000 rpm. Adjust the low-speed mixture needle so the engine idles smoothly and accelerates without hesitation. Adjust the idle speed to just slower than clutch engagement speed, then recheck low-speed mixture adjustment.

Fig. SW40—Low-speed mixture needle (2) is located in throttle barrel (3) and covered by a plug (1) on Models 300 and 300S.

Fig. SW41—View showing location of carburetor adjustment screws for Models 360 and 377.

Briefly operate engine at full throttle with no load. Turn the high-speed mixture needle (if so equipped) clockwise then counterclockwise to find the lean and rich drop-off points at full throttle. Adjust high-speed mixture screw to the midway point between the lean and rich drop-off points. Maximum speed at full throttle with no load is 13,500 rpm for Models 300, 300S and 377; or 13,000 rpm for Model 360. High-speed mixture setting is correct when the engine just begins to "stutter or four-cycle" at full throttle with no load. This indicates a slightly rich mixture that will provide the best performance under load. The engine may be damaged if the high-speed screw is set too lean.

Final adjustment of the mixture needles should be within 1/4 turn of the initial settings. Large differences may indicate air leaks, plugged passages or other problems.

IGNITION. All models are equipped with a breakerless electronic ignition system. All electronic circuitry is contained in a one-piece ignition module/coil located outside the flywheel. Ignition timing is fixed and not adjustable and no periodic maintenance is required. The flywheel retaining nut should be tightened to the torque listed in TIGHTENING TORQUE paragraph.

Air gap between the legs of the module/coil and the flywheel magnets should be 45-50 mm (0.018-0.020 in.). To set the air gap, insert setting gauge (part No. 22154-96210) or brass/plastic shim stock of the proper thickness between the legs of the ignition module

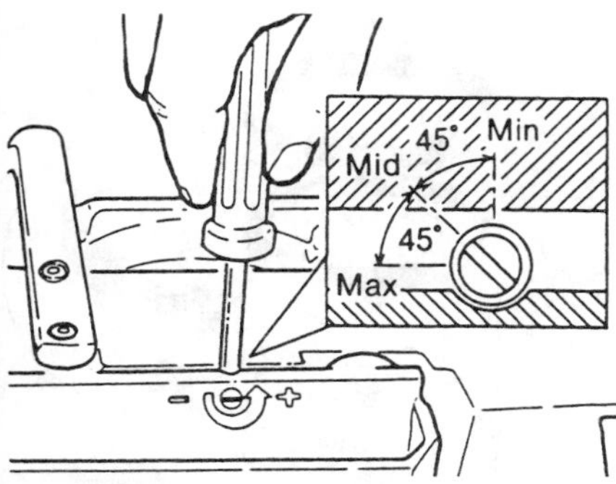

Fig. SW42—Automatic chain oiler can be adjusted by turning adjuster counterclockwise to increase oil output or clockwise to decrease output.

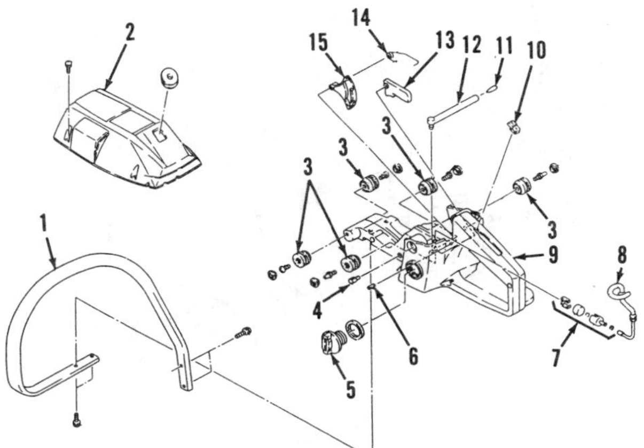

Fig. SW43—Exploded view of throttle trigger assembly, rear handle and related components.

1. Front handle
2. Cylinder cover
3. Vibration dampers
4. Support
5. Fuel cap
6. Pin
7. Fuel filter assy.
8. Fuel line
9. Rear handle assy.
10. Stop
11. Element
12. Vent tube
13. Lock lever
14. Spring
15. Throttle lever

and the flywheel. Turn the flywheel until the flywheel magnets are near the module legs. Loosen the screws attaching the ignition module and press legs of the ignition module against the setting gauge. Tighten the two attaching screws to the torque listed in the TIGHTENING TORQUE paragraph. Remove the setting gauge, then turn the flywheel and check that flywheel does not hit the legs of the coil.

LUBRICATION. Engine is lubricated by oil mixed with the gasoline. Recommended oil is Shindaiwa Premium 2-Cycle Oil mixed at a ratio of 40:1. If Shindaiwa Premium 2-Cycle Oil is not available, a good quality oil designed for air-cooled two-stroke engines may be used when mixed at a 25:1 ratio. Use a separate container when mixing the oil and gasoline.

All models are equipped with an automatic guide bar and chain oiling system. The automatic oil pump is actuated by the clutch and operates only when the clutch and chain are moving. Recommended chain oil is Shindaiwa Bar and Chain Oil or an equivalent good quality bar and chain oil. Oil output can be adjusted by turning oil pump adjuster shaft (Fig. SW42). Turn counterclockwise to increase oil flow or clockwise to decrease oil flow.

CARBON. Carbon deposits should be cleaned from muffler and exhaust ports at regular intervals. When scraping carbon, be careful not to damage the chamfered edges of the exhaust ports.

REPAIRS

CRANKCASE PRESSURE TEST. An improperly sealed crankcase can cause the engine to be hard to start, run rough, have low power and overheat. Refer to ENGINE SERVICE section of this manual for crankcase pressure test procedure. If crankcase leakage is indicated, pressurize crankcase and use a soap and water solution to check gaskets, seals, pulse line and castings for leakage.

TIGHTENING TORQUE. Recommended tightening torque values are as follows.

Carburetor
- 4 mm. . . . . 2-3 N·m (17-25 in.-lb.)
- 5 mm. . . . . 3-4 N·m (25-35 in.-lb.)

Crankcase. . 6.9-7.8 N·m (61-70 in.-lb.)
Cylinder. . . 6.9-7.8 N·m (61-70 in.-lb.)
Flywheel. . . . . 11.8-13.7 N·m (104-122 in.-lb.)

Front handle
- 5 mm. . . . . 2.9-3.9 N·m (25-35 in.-lb.)
- 5.5 mm . . . 2.9-4.9 N·m (25-44 in.-lb.)

Ignition
- Module/coil 3.9-4.3 N·m (35-44 in.-lb.)

Muffler. . . . 6.9-7.8 N·m (61-70 in.-lb.)
Oil pump. . . 2.0-2.2 N·m (17-22 in.-lb.)
Spark plug. . . . . 16.7-18.6 N·m (148-165 in.-lb.)

Other nuts
- 5 mm. . . . . 2.5-3.4 N·m (23-30 in.-lb.)
- 8 mm. . 10.2-12.0 N·m (90-106 in.-lb.)

Other Phillips head screws
- 4 mm. . . . . 1.5-2.5 N·m (13-22 in.-lb.)
- 5 mm. . . . . 2.9-3.9 N·m (25-35 in.-lb.)
- 6 mm. . . . . 3.9-5.9 N·m (35-52 in.-lb.)

Other socket head screws. . . . .
- 4 mm. . . . . 2.9-4.4 N·m (25-39 in.-lb.)
- 5 mm. . . . . 4.9-6.9 N·m (43-61 in.-lb.)
- 6 mm. . . 8.8-11.8 N·m (79-104 in.-lb.)

CYLINDER, PISTON, PIN AND RINGS. To disassemble, remove chain brake cover, guide bar and chain, front handle (1—Fig. SW43) and starter housing. Remove cylinder cover (2), air filter cover, filter element, filter base and carburetor (25—Fig. SW44). Remove muffler (21).

Remove cylinder mounting screws and withdraw cylinder (17—Fig. SW44) from crankcase. Remove piston ring (15) from piston. Pry piston pin retainer clips (12) out of piston (13), then push piston pin (14) out of piston and connecting rod. If pin removal is difficult, use a suitable piston pin removal tool (such as part No. 72282-96300) to push the pin from the piston. Be careful not to apply side thrust to connecting rod when removing piston pin. DO NOT attempt to drive the pin from an unsupported piston as damage to the piston and possibly the connecting rod can result. Remove piston, thrust washers (10) and needle bearing (11) from connecting rod.

Cylinder bore is chrome plated and cannot be honed or bored. Cylinder should be renewed if cracking, flaking or other damage to cylinder bore is noted. Renew cylinder if out-of-round more than 0.03 mm (0.001 in.) or if cylinder wall taper exceeds 0.05 mm (0.002 in.). Inspect piston for scuffing, scoring or other damage and renew as necessary.

Standard piston ring end gap is 0.1-0.3 mm (0.004-0.012 in.) and wear limit is 0.7 mm (0.027 in.). Standard piston ring-to-ring groove side clearance is 0.04-0.09 mm (0.0015-0.0035 in.) and wear limit is 0.09 mm (0.0079 in.).

When reassembling, install piston on connecting rod so arrow mark on piston crown points toward exhaust port side of engine (Fig. SW45). Once removed, piston pin retaining rings should not be reused. Install retaining rings with open end facing either down or up as shown in Fig. SW46. Locating pins (Fig. SW47) are present in ring grooves to prevent ring rotation. Make certain that ring end gaps are properly positioned around locating pins before installing piston in cylinder.

Lubricate piston, cylinder and connecting rod bearings before installation. A slotted scrap of wood can be used to stabilize the piston during installation of cylinder (Fig. SW48). Align cylinder exhaust port with the arrow on piston crown. Compress the piston rings and slide the cylinder over the piston. Do not rotate the cylinder on the piston as the piston rings may disen-

Illustrations courtesy Shindaiwa, Inc.

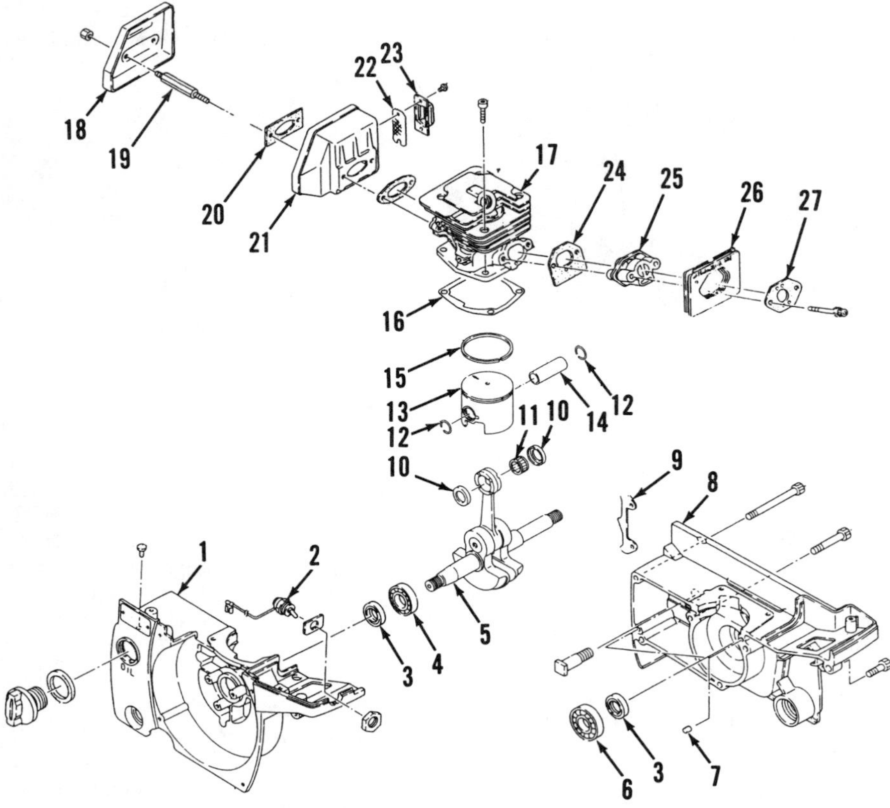

Fig. SW44—Exploded view of engine typical of all models.

1. Crankcase half
2. Stop switch
3. Oil seal
4. Ball bearing
5. Crankshaft & connecting rod assy.
6. Ball bearing
7. Dowel pin
8. Crankcase half
9. Gasket
10. Thrust washers
11. Needle bearing
12. Retaining rings
13. Piston
14. Piston pin
15. Piston ring
16. Gasket
17. Cylinder
18. Cover
19. Stud
20. Muffler
21. Gasket
22. Spark arrestor
23. Cover
24. Gasket
25. Insulator
26. Seal
27. Gasket

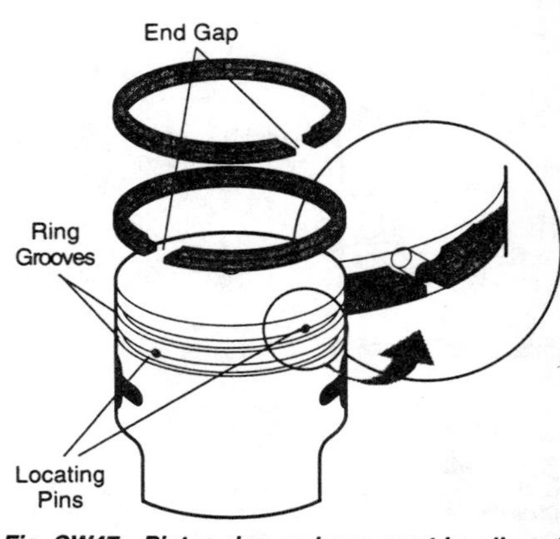

Fig. SW47—Piston ring end gap must be aligned with locating pin in ring groove.

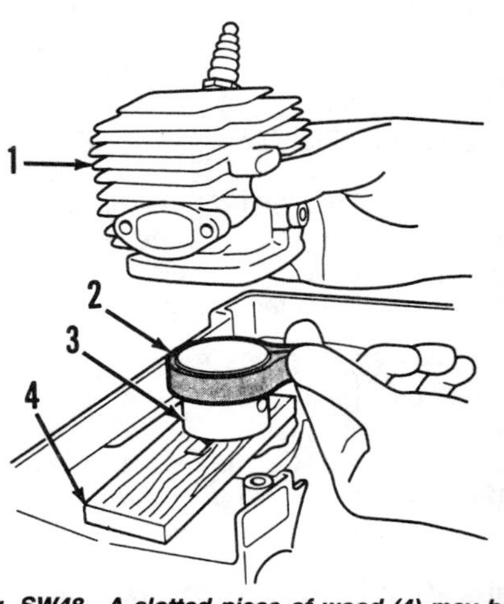

Fig. SW48—A slotted piece of wood (4) may be used to stabilize the piston (3) when installing the cylinder (1).

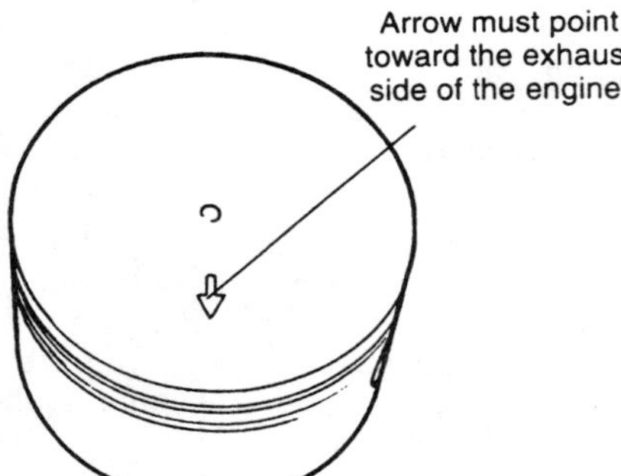

Fig. SW45—Install piston so arrow on piston crown points toward exhaust side of engine.

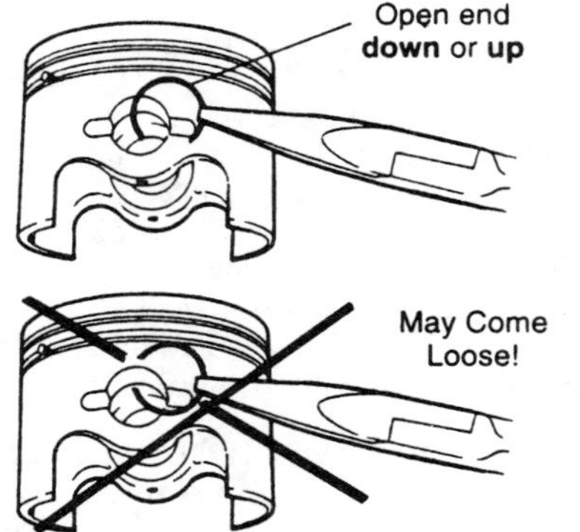

Fig. SW46—Install piston pin retaining rings with open end facing either up or down (upper illustration).

gage from the locating pins, resulting in damage to cylinder and ring.

Apply ThreeBond 1360 or equivalent thread locking compound to threads of cylinder base mounting screws. Tighten each screw finger tight, then center the cylinder in the crankcase by slowly rotating the crankshaft while checking for binding between the piston and cylinder. When cylinder is properly centered, tighten cylinder base screws to torque specified in TIGHTENING TORQUE paragraph.

CRANKSHAFT AND CONNECTING ROD. To disassemble, remove clutch cover and chain brake, guide bar and chain, cylinder cover (2—Fig. SW43), front handle (1) and starter housing. Remove muffler, carburetor and rear handle assembly (9). Remove spark plug and install a piston stop tool or insert end of a rope in spark plug hole to lock piston and crankshaft. Unscrew clutch hub (left-hand threads) and remove clutch assembly from crankshaft. Remove oil pump assembly. Remove flywheel mounting nut (right-hand threads), then use suitable puller to remove flywheel. Remove ignition unit. Remove screws attaching the cylinder, then withdraw cylinder from crankcase. Remove piston from connecting rod. Remove screws attaching the crankcase halves (1 and 8—Fig. SW44) together. Hold one crankcase half and tap end of crankshaft with a soft hammer to separate the crankshaft from crankcase. Remove oil seals (3) from crankcase halves.

Inspect main bearings (7) for damage or roughness. If bearing renewal is necessary, tap bearings from the crankcase bores using a suitable bearing driver. Bearing removal and installation can be made easier by using a heat gun to heat the crankcase bearing bore to not more than 100 degrees C (210 degrees F).

Illustrations courtesy Shindaiwa, Inc.

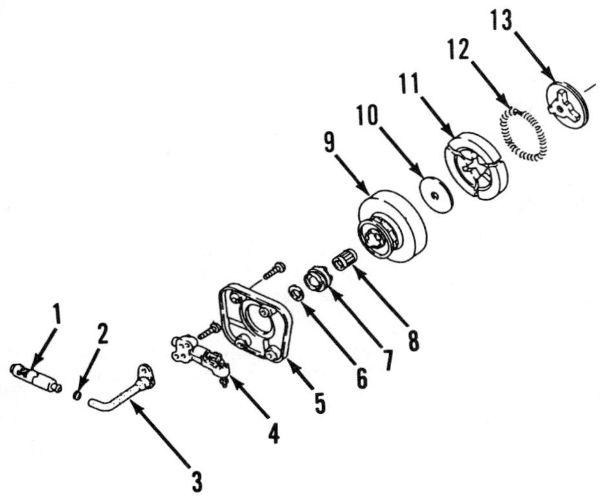

Fig. SW49—Exploded view of centrifugal clutch assembly.

1. Oil filter
2. Clip
3. Oil tube
4. Oil pump assy.
5. Cover
6. Thrust plate
7. Drive gear
8. Needle bearing
9. Clutch drum & sprocket assy.
10. Washer
11. Clutch shoes
12. Spring
13. Hub

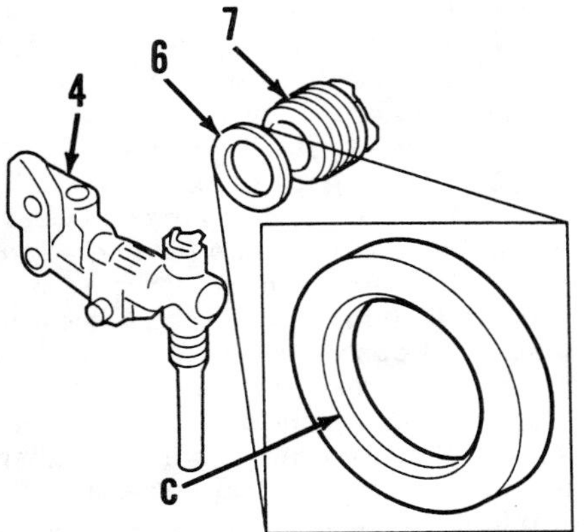

Fig. SW50—Chamfered side of thrust plate (C) must face the oil pump.

Crankshaft and connecting rod (5) are a unit assembly and should not be disassembled. Rotate connecting rod around crankpin and renew assembly if roughness, excessive play or other damage is noted. Renew crankshaft if runout exceeds 0.07 mm (0.0027 in.). Renew ball bearings (4 and 6) and needle bearing (11) if roughness or other damage is noted.

New seals (3) should be installed in crankcase halves during assembly. After assembling crankshaft assembly in crankcase, rotate crankshaft to be sure crankshaft rotates freely. Tighten crankcase screws to the torque listed in the TIGHTENING TORQUES paragraph.

CLUTCH. A centrifugal type clutch is used on all models. Remove chain brake housing, guide bar and chain for access to clutch. Remove spark plug and insert a suitable piston stop tool or the end of a starter rope in spark plug hole to prevent crankshaft from turning. Note that clutch hub (13—Fig. SW49) has left-hand threads (turn clockwise to remove). Unscrew clutch hub and remove clutch assembly.

Inspect clutch drum needle bearing (8) for roughness or wear and renew as necessary. Inspect clutch shoes (11) and drum (9) for signs of excessive heat. Clutch drum should be renewed if sprocket teeth are worn in excess of 25 mm (0.010 in.). If sprocket is badly worn, inspect chain for excessive wear also. Do not install a new chain over a worn sprocket.

Apply a light film of grease to drive flanges of hub (13), clutch bearing (8), oil pump gear (7) and thrust plate (6) prior to installation. Note that thrust plate has a chamfered bore and must be installed with chamfer (C—Fig. SW50) toward the oil pump.

AUTOMATIC CHAIN OILER. All models are equipped with an automatic chain oiling system. An automatic oil pump (4—Fig. SW49), driven by clutch drum via gear (7), provides oil for the system whenever clutch and chain are operating. Oil pump output is adjusted by turning the oil pump adjuster counterclockwise to increase oil output or clockwise to decrease output (Fig. SW42).

Remove chain brake housing, guide bar and chain, and clutch assembly for access to oil pump. Remove oil pump gear (7—Fig. SW49), thrust plate (6), dust cover (5) and oil pump (4). Oil filter (1) can be removed through oil tank filler opening for cleaning, inspection or renewal.

Oil pump components are not serviced separately. Pump must renewed as an assembly if faulty.

Apply a light film of grease to oil pump gear (7) and thrust plate (6) prior to installation. Note that thrust plate has a chamfered bore and must be installed with chamfer (C—Fig. SW50) toward the oil pump.

REWIND STARTER. Refer to Fig. SW51 for an exploded view of rewind starter assembly used on all models. To disassemble, remove starter housing (1) from engine. Remove rope handle (4) and allow rope to wind slowly onto pulley (6) until spring tension is relieved. The pulley retaining screw threads are coated with thread locking compound. To ease removal of screw, use a heat gun to heat starter housing threads to approximately 100 degrees C (212 degrees F). Unscrew pulley mounting screw (11) and remove ratchet assembly (7-10) and pulley (6), being careful not to dislodge rewind spring (2). If necessary to remove rewind spring, care should be used not to allow spring to uncoil uncontrolled.

Starter rope diameter is 3.8 mm (0.150 in.) and length is 700 mm (27.5 in.).

Apply a light coat of multipurpose grease to both sides of rewind spring. Install rewind spring in starter housing with coils wrapped in clockwise direc-

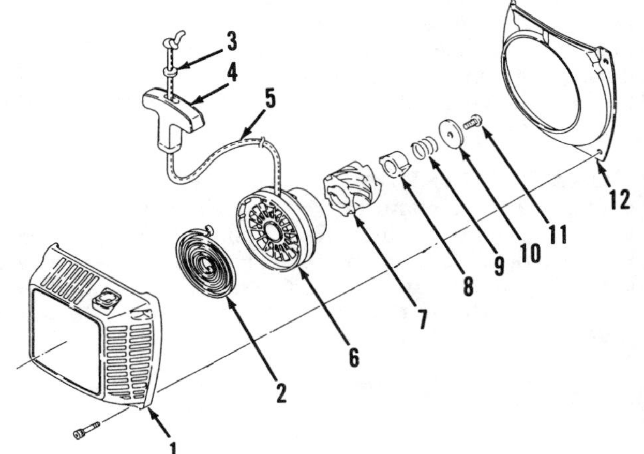

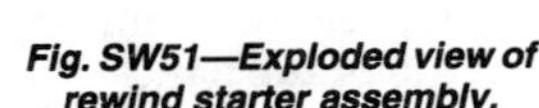
Fig. SW51—Exploded view of rewind starter assembly.

1. Starter housing
2. Rewind spring
3. Rope stop
4. Rope handle
5. Rope
6. Pulley
7. Ratchet
8. Guide
9. Spring
10. Washer
11. Screw
12. Air deflector

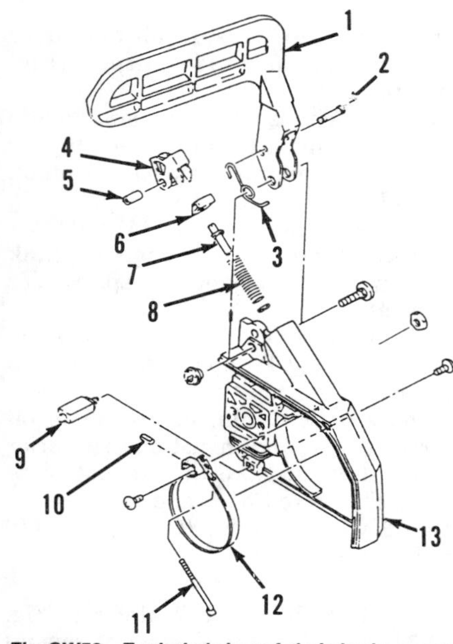

Fig. SW52—Exploded view of chain brake assembly typical of 300, 300S and 360 models.

1. Hand guard lever
2. Stop pin
3. Lever spring
4. Inner lever
5. Pin
6. Block
7. Adjuster
8. Brake spring
9. Chain protector
10. Pin
11. Adjuster rod
12. Brake band
13. Clutch cover

tion from outer end of spring. Wind rope around pulley in a counterclockwise direction as viewed from flywheel side of pulley. Install pulley and ratchet assembly.

NOTE: Threads of pulley retaining screw (11) are coated with a thread locking compound. It is recommended that retaining screw be renewed whenever it is removed for starter repair.

Turn pulley two to three turns clockwise to preload rewind spring before passing rope through starter housing. Attach rope handle and check starter operation. It should be possible to pull rope to its full extension and still turn rope pulley approximately 1/2 turn. If rewind spring binds before rope is fully extended, reduce tension on rope by pulling rope up into notch in rope pulley and allowing pulley to unwind one turn. Recheck starter operation.

CHAIN BRAKE. All models are equipped with a chain brake designed to stop the saw chain quickly should kickback occur. The chain brake is activated when operator's hand strikes hand guard lever (1—Fig. SW52 or SW53), releasing latch (4) thereby allowing spring (8) to draw the brake band (12) tight around clutch drum. Pull back hand guard (1) to reset mechanism.

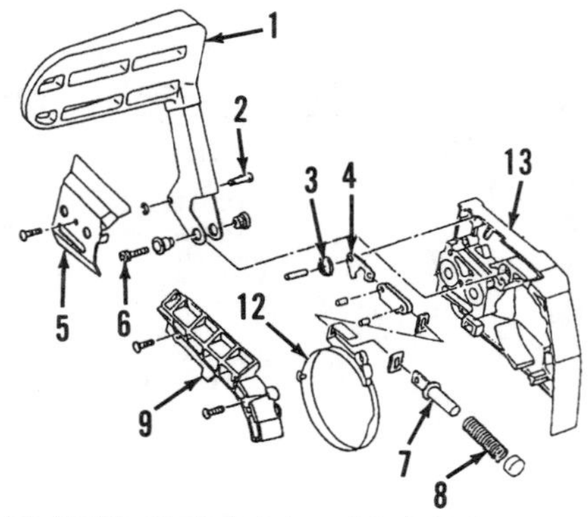

Fig. SW53—Exploded view of chain brake assembly typical of 377 model saw.

1. Hand guard lever
2. Stop pin
3. Return spring
4. Inner lever
5. Guide plate
6. Pivot
7. Rod
8. Brake spring
9. Cover plate
12. Brake band
13. Clutch cover

Models 300, 300S and 360. To disassemble chain brake, pull hand guard (1—Fig. SW52) rearward to disengage brake. Remove bar retaining nuts and withdraw clutch cover (13) and brake assembly from saw. Remove hand lever retaining nut and spring (3), then push lever forward to actuate the brake. Remove hand lever and inner lever (4). Loosen adjuster screw (7) and remove block (6), adjuster screw (7) and spring (8). Remove band retaining screw and withdraw brake band (12).

Renew any component that is excessively worn or damaged. Chain brake mechanism should be clean and free of sawdust and dirt accumulation. Assembly of chain brake is the reverse of disassembly. Lightly lubricate all moving parts and pivot points with grease.

To adjust chain brake, first disconnect spark plug boot and properly ground terminal end. Place chain brake lever (1) in released (vertical) position. Use a screwdriver to turn adjusting screw (Fig. SW54) clockwise until chain cannot be moved by hand pressure. Then, turn adjusting screw counterclockwise noting when brake band does not contact clutch drum. Normal adjustment is 2-4 turns counterclockwise from the chain locked position.

Make sure brake band does not drag on outside of clutch drum with brake lever in released position. With brake lever in applied position, it should not be possible to rotate chain around guide bar.

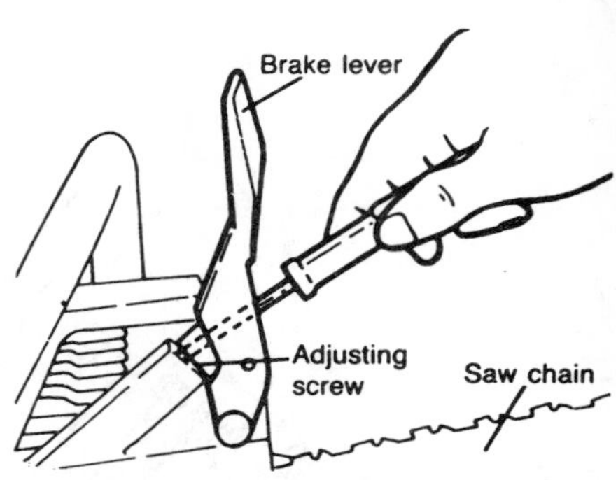

Fig. SW54—Chain brake is adjustable on 300, 300S and 360 model saws. Refer to text.

Model 377. To disassemble chain brake, pull hand guard (1—Fig. SW53) rearward to disengage brake. Remove bar retaining nuts. Disengage brake lever support arm from left side of saw. Depress top of clutch cover (13—Fig. SW53) to disengage cover locking tab, then withdraw cover and brake assembly. Remove guide plate (5) and cover plate (9). Remove hand lever return spring (3), temporarily reinstall cover plate, and push hand lever forward to actuate the brake. Remove cover plate, stop pin (2), pivot bolt (6) and hand lever (1). Remove brake band (12), inner lever (4) and spring (8) as an assembly.

Renew any component that is excessively worn or damaged. Chain brake mechanism should be clean and free of sawdust and dirt accumulation. Lightly lubricate all moving parts and pivot points prior to reassembly.

Lightly lubricate all moving parts and pivot points with grease. Install brake band and coil spring asssembly. Temporarily install hand lever (1—Fig. SW53) and cover plate (9) without the return spring (3). Pull back on hand lever until lever clicks into the disengaged position. Remove the cover plate being careful not to engage brake. Install lever return spring (3), cover plate (9) and guide (5).

The chain brake is not adjustable. To check brake operation, hold saw with tip of bar about 50 cm (20 in.) above a block of wood. Release the front handle, allowing the saw to quickly rotate so bar tip strikes the wooden block. The chain brake must engage when bar tip strikes the wooden block. If brake fails to operate properly, disassemble and inspect for worn, damaged or improperly assembled parts.

SHINDAIWA

Model	Bore mm (in.)	Stroke mm (in.)	Displacement cc (cu. in.)	Drive Type
488	43 (1.69)	33 (1.3)	47.9 (2.9)	Direct
577	45 (1.77)	36 (1.41)	57.3 (3.5)	Direct
757	51 (2.01)	36 (1.41)	73.5 (4.5)	Direct

MAINTENANCE

SPARK PLUG. Recommended spark plug is Champion CJ6Y or NGK type BPM7A. Spark plug electrode gap should be 0.6 mm (0.024 in.). The spark plug should be tightened to the torque listed in the TIGHTENING TORQUE paragraph.

CARBURETOR. Carburetor used for Model 488 is Walbro HDA-79A; Walbro HDA-132 for Model 577; and Walbro HDA-123 for Model 757. Refer to Walbro section in CARBURETOR SERVICE section for service procedures and exploded view of carburetor.

Initial adjustments for both low- and high-speed mixture needles are 1-1/4 turns open from a lightly seated position for all models. Make sure engine air cleaner is clean before performing final adjustment of carburetor.

Make final carburetor adjustment with engine warm and running. Adjust idle speed screw (I—Fig. SW61) so engine idles just below clutch engagement speed (approximately 2,800 rpm for 488 and 577 models or 2,500 for 757 model). Adjust low-speed mixture needle (L) to obtain highest idle speed. Engine should accelerate cleanly without hesitation. If engine stumbles or seems sluggish when accelerating, adjust idle mixture needle until engine accelerates without hesitation. Readjust idle speed screw so engine idles just under clutch engagement speed.

Operate engine at full throttle with no load and turn high-speed mixture needle (H) clockwise until engine speed increases and four-stroking sound stops. Then, turn high-speed needle counterclockwise until four-stroking sound just returns. Maximum rpm without load should be approximately 13,500 rpm for 488 model, 12,000 rpm for 577 model or 13,000 rpm for 757 model. Do not operate saw with high speed mixture too lean as engine damage may result from lack of lubrication and overheating.

Final adjustment of the mixture needles should be within 1/4 turn of the initial settings. Large differences may indicate air leaks, plugged passages or other problems.

To remove carburetor (5—Fig. SW62), remove filter cover (1) and filter element (2). Disconnect the fuel line and impulse tube. Remove carburetor mounting screws, disconnect throttle and choke rods, and remove carburetor. When installing carburetor, tighten the carburetor attaching screws to the torque listed in the TIGHTENING TORQUE paragraph.

IGNITION. Engine is equipped with a breakerless electronic ignition system (Fig. SW63). Ignition timing is fixed and not adjustable. There is no periodic maintenance required for the electronic ignition system. The flywheel attaching nut should be tightened to the torque listed in TIGHTENING TORQUE paragraph.

Air gap between the legs of the ignition charging coil and flywheel magnets should be 0.35 mm (0.014 in.) for 488 model. Air gap between legs of the charging coil and flywheel magnets for other models should be 0.50-0.55 mm (0.020-0.022 in.).

When installing, set the air gap between the flywheel magnets and the coil legs. Install the ignition charging coil, but tighten the retaining screws only enough to hold it in place away from the flywheel. Insert setting gauge or brass/plastic shim stock of the proper thickness between the legs of the ignition charging coil and the flywheel. Setting gauge part No. 22160-96210 may be used for Model 488 or part No.

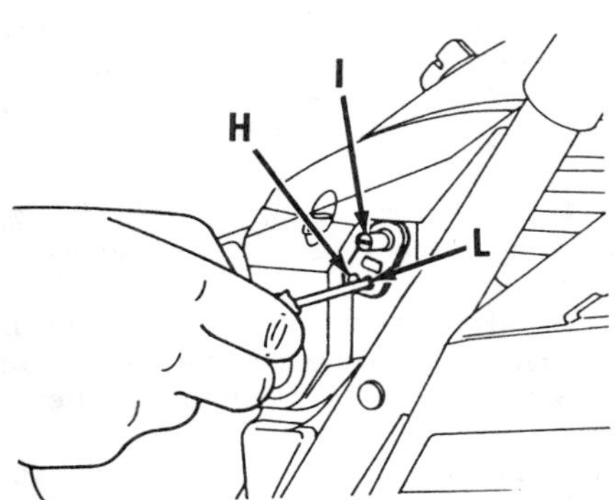

Fig. SW61—View of carburetor adjustment points. Refer to text for adjustment procedure.

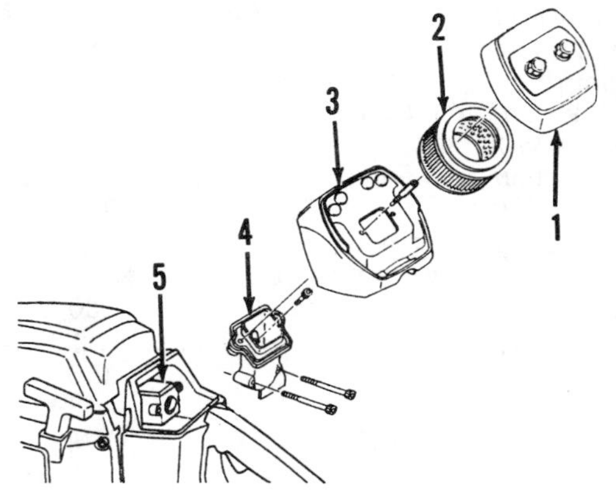

Fig. SW62—Exploded view of air cleaner assembly for 757 model. Other models are similar.

1. Filter cover
2. Filter element
3. Filter base
4. Elbow
5. Carburetor

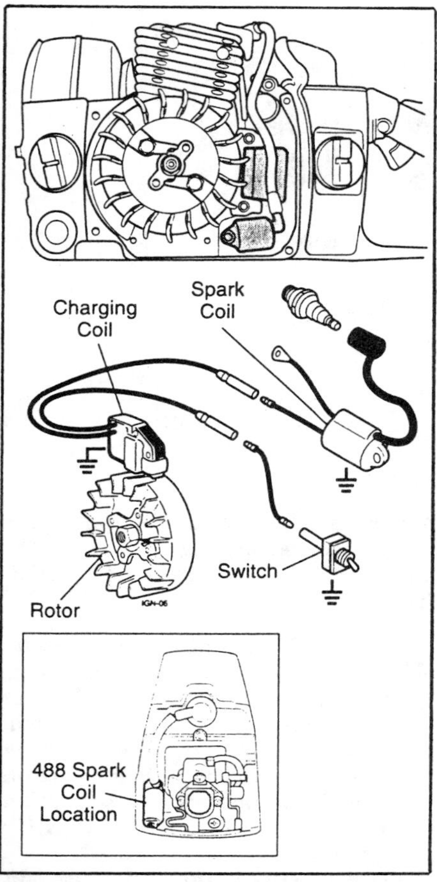

Fig. SW63—A two-piece electronic ignition system is used on all models.

22160-96210 for Models 577 and 757. Turn the flywheel until the flywheel magnets are near the coil's legs. Loosen the screws attaching the ignition charging coil and press legs of the ignition module against the setting gauge. Tighten the two attaching screws to the torque listed in the TIGHTENING TORQUE paragraph. Remove the setting gauge, then turn the flywheel and check that flywheel does not hit the legs of the coil.

LUBRICATION. Engine is lubricated by engine oil mixed with the gasoline. Recommended oil is Shindaiwa Premium 2-Cycle Oil mixed at a ratio of 40:1. If Shindaiwa Premium 2-Cycle Oil is not available, a good quality oil designed for air-cooled two-stroke engines may be used when mixed at a 25:1 ratio. Use a separate container when mixing the oil and gasoline.

All models are equipped with an automatic guide bar and chain oiling system. The automatic oil pump is actuated by the clutch and operates only when the clutch and chain are moving. Recommended chain oil is Shindaiwa Bar and Chain Oil or an equivalent good quality bar and chain oil. Oil output on all models is adjusted by turning oil pump adjuster shaft, accessible from lower side of sprocket cover. Turn counterclockwise to increase oil flow or clockwise to decrease oil flow.

CARBON. Carbon deposits should be cleaned from muffler and exhaust ports at regular intervals. When scraping carbon, be careful not to damage the chamfered edges of the exhaust ports.

REPAIRS

CRANKCASE PRESSURE TEST. An improperly sealed crankcase can cause the engine to be hard to start, run rough, have low power and overheat. Refer to ENGINE SERVICE section of this manual for crankcase pressure test procedure. If crankcase leakage is indicated, pressurize crankcase and use a soap and water solution to check gaskets, seals, pulse line and castings for leakage.

TIGHTENING TORQUE. Recommended tightening torque values are as follows.

Carburetor
- 4 mm . . . . 2-3 N•m (17-25 in.-lb.)
- 5 mm . . . . 3-4 N•m (25-35 in.-lb.)

Crankcase
- Model 488 . . . . 6.9-7.8 N•m (61-70 in.-lb.)
- Model 577 . . . . 7.8-8.8 N•m (70-80 in.-lb.)
- Model 757 . . . . 6.9-7.8 N•m (61-70 in.-lb.)

Cylinder to crankcase
- Model 488 . . . . 6.9-7.8 N•m (61-70 in.-lb.)
- Model 577 . . . . 7.8-8.8 N•m (70-80 in.-lb.)
- Model 757. . . . . 8.8-11.8 N•m (79-104 in.-lb.)

Flywheel
- Model 488. . . . . 11.8-13.7 N•m (104-122 in.-lb.)
- Models 577 & 757 . . . . 22.6-23.5 N•m (200-208 in.-lb.)

Front handle
- 5 mm . . . . 2.9-3.9 N•m (25-35 in.-lb.)
- 5.5 mm. . . . . 2.9-4.9 N•m (25-44 in.-lb.)

Ignition
- Charging coil . . . . 2.5-4.3 N•m (30-40 in.-lb.)
- Spark coil. . . . . 2.9-3.4 N•m (26-30 in.-lb.)

Muffler
- Model 488 . . . . 6.9-7.8 N•m (61-70 in.-lb.)
- Model 577 . . . . 7.8-8.8 N•m (70-79 in.-lb.)
- Model 757 (5 mm) . . . . . . 7.8-8.8 N•m (70-79 in.-lb.)
- 6 mm . . . . 11.8 N•m (105 in.-lb.)

Oil pump . . . . 2.0-2.2 N•m (17-22 in.-lb.)

Spark plug. . . . . 16.7-18.6 N•m (148-165 in.-lb.)

Other nuts
- 5 mm . . . . 2.5-3.4 N•m (23-30 in.-lb.)
- 8 mm . . . . 10.2-12.0 N•m (90-106 in.-lb.)

Other Phillips head screws
- 4 mm . . . . 1.5-2.5 N•m (13-22 in.-lb.)
- 5 mm . . . . 2.9-3.9 N•m (25-35 in.-lb.)
- 6 mm . . . . 3.9-5.9 N•m (35-52 in.-lb.)

Other socket head screws
- 4 mm . . . . 2.9-4.4 N•m (25-39 in.-lb.)
- 5 mm . . . . 4.9-6.9 N•m (43-61 in.-lb.)
- 6 mm . . . . 8.8-11.8 N•m (79-104 in.-lb.)

CYLINDER, PISTON, PIN AND RINGS. To disassemble, remove chain brake cover, guide bar and chain, front handle and starter housing. Remove cylinder cover, air cleaner, carburetor and muffler. Remove cylinder mounting screws and withdraw cylinder (25—Fig. SW64) from crankcase. Remove piston rings (19) from piston. Pry piston pin retainer clips (16) out of piston (17). It is recommended that a suitable piston pin removal tool be used to press the piston pin (18) from the piston and connecting rod. Do not attempt to drive the pin from an unsupported piston, as damage to piston and connecting rod can result. Be careful not to apply side thrust to connecting rod when removing piston pin. Remove piston, thrust washers (14) and needle bearing (15) from connecting rod.

Cylinder bore is chrome plated and cannot be honed or bored. Cylinder should be renewed if cracking, flaking or other damage to cylinder bore is noted. Renew cylinder if out-of-round more than 0.03 mm (0.001 in.) or if cylinder wall taper exceeds 0.05 mm (0.002 in.). Inspect piston for scuffing, scoring or other damage and renew as necessary.

When reassembling, install piston on connecting rod so arrow mark on piston crown points toward exhaust port side of engine (Fig. SW65). Be sure that thrust washers (14—Fig. SW64) are positioned on each side of needle bearing (15) on Models 488 and 577. Once re-

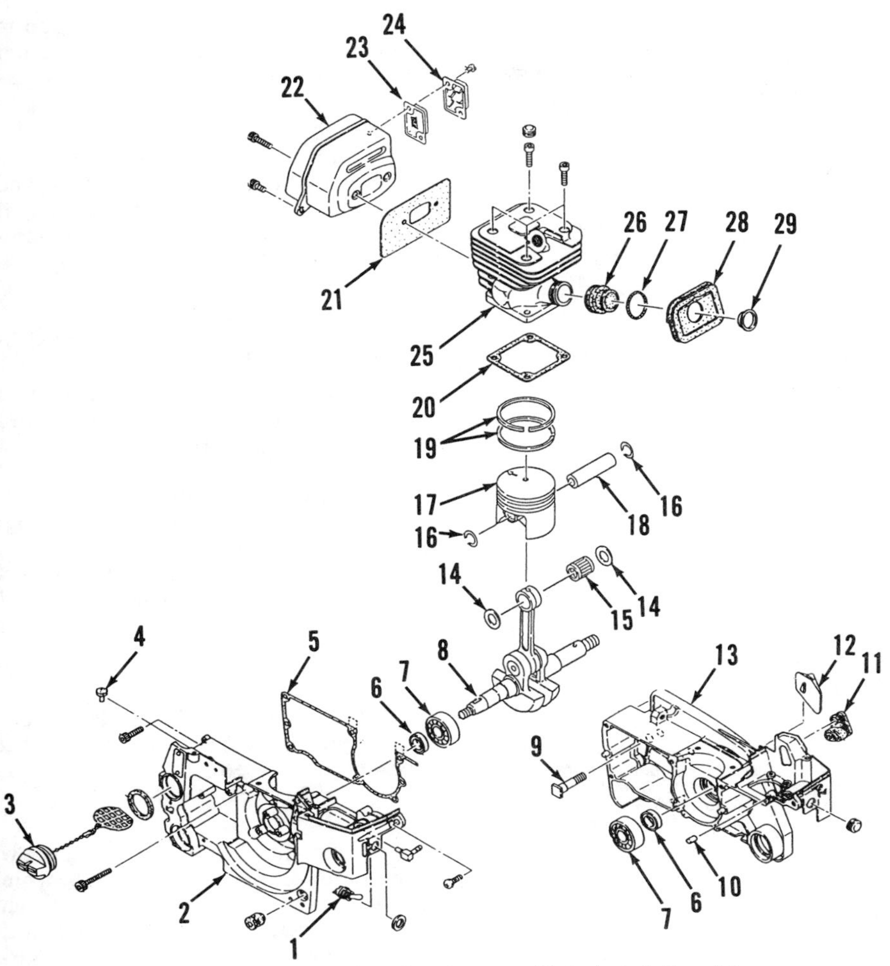
Fig. SW64—Exploded view of engine assembly typical of all models.

1. Stop switch
2. Crankcase half
3. Oil tank cap
4. Oil tank vent
5. Gasket
6. Oil seal
7. Ball bearing
8. Crankshaft assy.
9. Guide bar bolt
10. Dowel pin
11. Carburetor grommet
12. Stop plate
13. Crankcase half
14. Thrust washers
15. Needle bearing
16. Retaining ring
17. Piston
18. Piston pin
19. Piston rings
20. Gasket
21. Gasket
22. Muffler
23. Spark arrestor
24. Cover
25. Cylinder
26. Intake boot
27. Spring
28. Seal
29. Sleeve

moved, piston pin retainer clips (16) should not be reused. Install new retainer clips with their open end facing either toward the top or the bottom of the piston (Fig. SW66). Be sure each retaining clip is seated firmly in its groove.

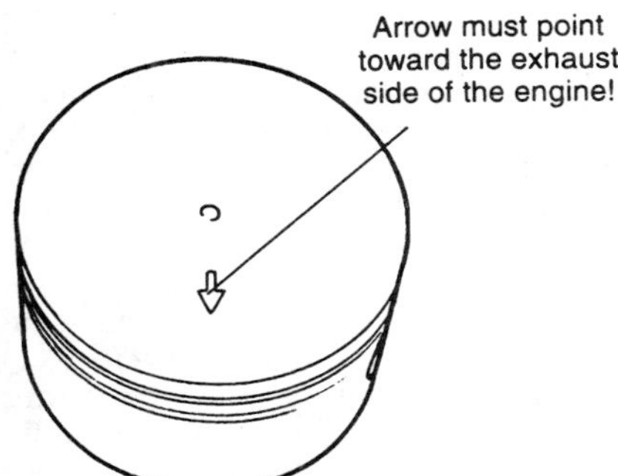

Fig. SW65—Install piston so arrow on piston crown points toward exhaust side of engine.

Locating pins are present in ring grooves to prevent ring rotation. Make certain that ring end gaps are properly positioned around locating pins before installing piston in cylinder (Fig. SW67).

Lubricate piston, cylinder and connecting rod bearings before installation. A slotted scrap of wood can be used to stabilize the piston during installation of cylinder (Fig. SW68). Align cylinder exhaust port with the arrow on piston crown. Compress the piston rings and slide the cylinder over the piston. Do not rotate the cylinder on the piston as the piston rings may disengage from the locating pins, resulting in damage to cylinder and rings.

On Models 488 and 577, apply ThreeBond 1360 or equivalent thread locking compound to threads of cylinder base mounting screws. On Model 757, install four new precoated cylinder base mounting screws. Tighten each screw finger tight, then center the cylinder in the crankcase by slowly rotating the crankshaft while checking for binding between the piston and cylin-

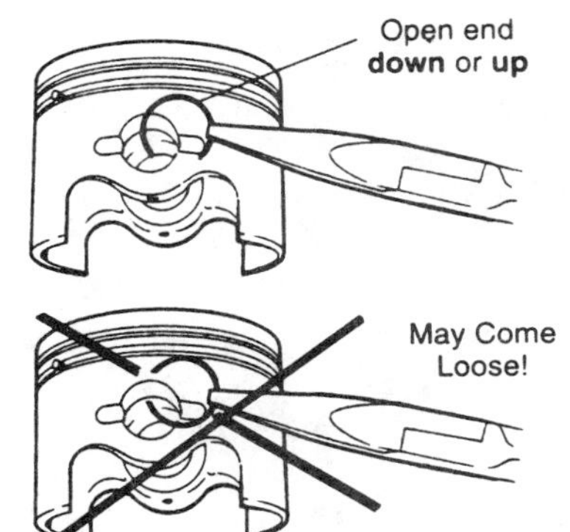

Fig. SW66—Install piston pin retaining rings with open end facing either up or down (upper illustration).

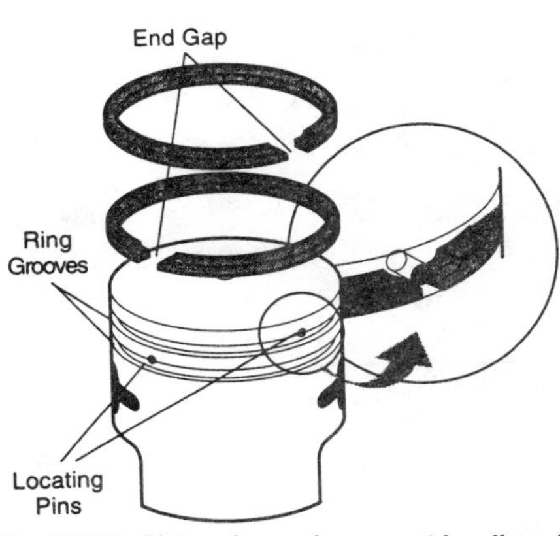

Fig. SW67—Piston ring end gap must be aligned with locating pin in ring groove.

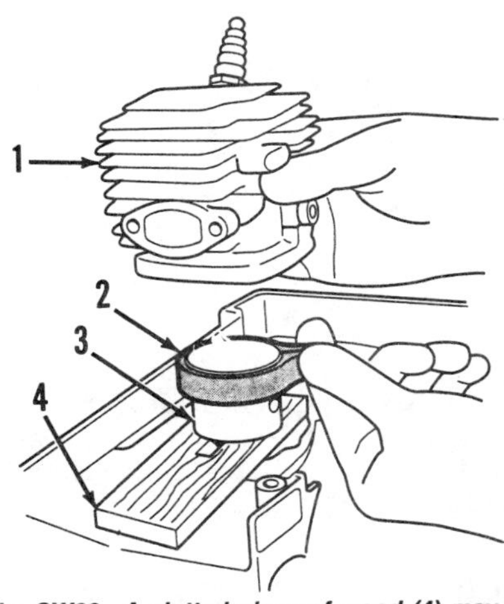
Fig. SW68—A slotted piece of wood (4) may be used to stabilize the piston (3) when installing the cylinder (1).

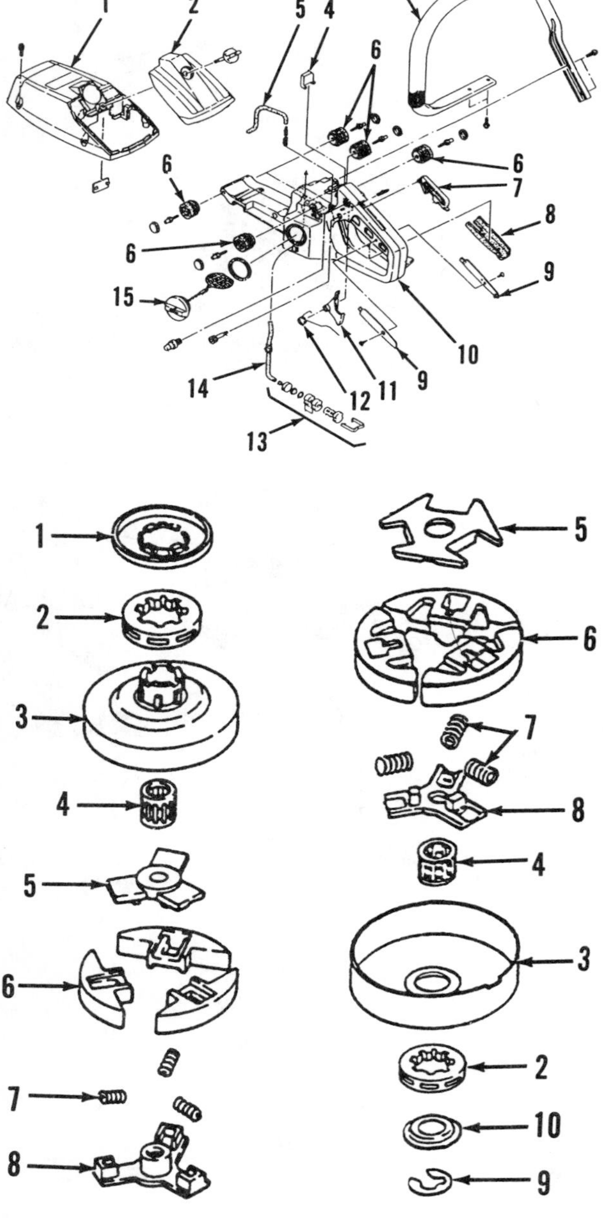

Fig. SW69—Exploded view of rear handle and associated components typical of all models.

1. Cylinder cover
2. Air cleaner cover
3. Front handle
4. Stop
5. Vent tube
6. Vibration damper
7. Lock lever
8. Handle grip
9. Side plate
10. Rear handle assy.
11. Throttle lever
12. Lever spring
13. Fuel filter assy.
14. Fuel line
15. Fuel tank cap

Fig. SW70—Exploded view of centrifugal clutch assemblies. Clutch shown in left illustration is used on 488 and 577 models. Clutch shown in right illustration is used on 757 models.

1. Dirt shield
2. Sprocket
3. Clutch drum
4. Bearing
5. Inner hub
6. Clutch shoes
7. Springs
8. Outer hub
9. E-ring
10. Washer

der. When cylinder is properly centered, tighten cylinder base screws to torque specified in TIGHTENING TORQUE paragraph.

CRANKSHAFT AND CONNECTING ROD. To disassemble, remove clutch cover and chain brake, guide bar and chain, cylinder cover (1—Fig. SW69), front handle (3) and starter housing. Remove muffler, carburetor and rear handle assembly (10). Remove spark plug and install a piston stop tool or insert the end of a rope in spark plug hole to lock piston and crankshaft. Unscrew clutch hub (left-hand threads) and remove clutch assembly from crankshaft. Remove oil pump assembly. Remove flywheel mounting nut (right-hand threads), then use suitable puller to remove flywheel. Remove ignition unit.

Remove screws attaching the cylinder then withdraw cylinder from crankcase. Remove piston from connecting rod. Remove screws attaching crankcase halves together. Hold one crankcase half and tap end of crankshaft with a soft hammer to separate crankshaft from crankcase. Remove oil seals (6—Fig. SW64).

Inspect main bearings (7) for damage or roughness. If bearing renewal is necessary, tap bearings from the crankcase bores using a suitable bearing driver. Bearing removal and installation can be made easier by using a heat gun to heat the crankcase bearing bore to not more than 100 degrees C (210 degrees F).

Crankshaft and connecting rod (8) are a unit assembly and should not be disassembled. Rotate connecting rod around crankpin and renew assembly if roughness, excessive play or other damage is noted. Renew ball bearings (7) and needle bearing (15) if roughness or other damage is noted.

New seals (6) should be installed in crankcase halves during assembly. After installing crankshaft assembly in crankcase, rotate crankshaft to be sure crankshaft rotates freely.

CLUTCH. A centrifugal type clutch is used. Remove chain brake housing, guide bar and chain for access to clutch. Remove spark plug, then install a suitable piston stop tool or insert the end of a rope in the spark plug hole to prevent the crankshaft from turning.

NOTE: Clutch hubs for all models are attached to the crankshaft with left-hand threads. Rotate hub CLOCKWISE to remove.

On 488 and 577 models, unscrew clutch hub (5 and 8—Fig. SW70) from crankshaft using proper hub wrench (part No. 22155-91580) or equivalent. Remove clutch shoe assembly (6), bearing (4), drum (3), sprocket (2) and cover (1).

On 757 models, remove the retaining E-ring (9—Fig. SW70), then remove washer (10), sprocket (11), drum (12) and bearing (13).

NOTE: On Model 757, the crankshaft nut forms the slot for the E-ring (9). It is NOT necessary to remove the nut in order to remove the clutch assembly.

Use a hub wrench (part No. 22169-96580) or equivalent and turn the clutch hubs (5 and 8—Fig. SW70) clockwise to unscrew the clutch hubs from the crankshaft.

On all models, inspect clutch drum needle bearing (4—Fig. SW70) for roughness or wear and renew as necessary. Inspect clutch shoes (6) and drum (3) for signs of excessive heat. Clutch shoes should be renewed if worn in excess of 25 mm (0.010 in.) when compared to a new shoe. Sprocket (2) should be renewed if sprocket teeth are excessively worn. If sprocket is badly worn, inspect chain for excessive wear also. Do not install a new chain over a worn sprocket.

Illustrations courtesy Shindaiwa, Inc.

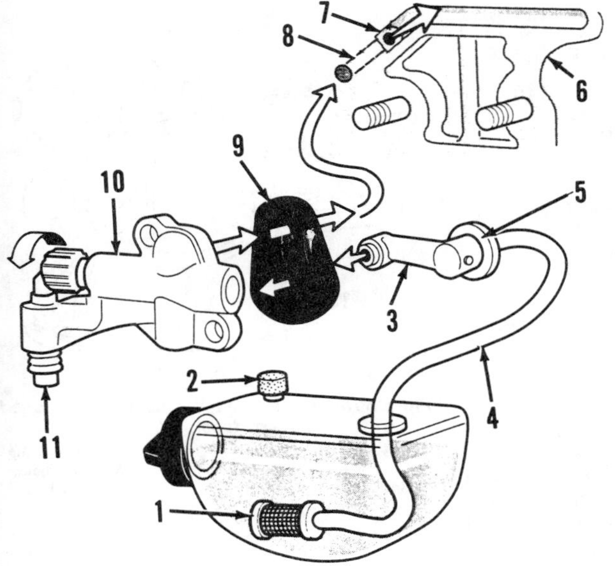

Fig. SW71—Drawing of automatic chain oiling system typical of all models.

1. Oil filter
2. Tank vent
3. Elbow
4. Suction tube
5. Grommet
6. Bar pad
7. Oil discharge port
8. Crankcase oil passage
9. Pump grommet
10. Oil pump assy.
11. Adjuster shaft

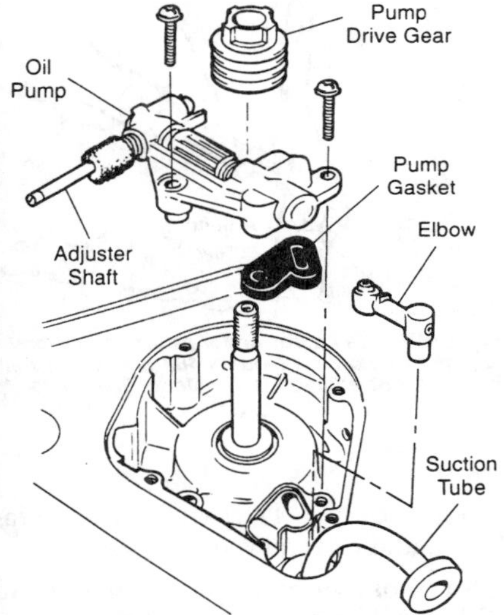

Fig. SW72—Exploded view of automatic bar and chain oiling components.

On all models, apply grease to needle bearing (4) prior to installation.

On all models except 757, make sure the notches in the inner edge of the clutch drum (3—Fig. SW70) correctly engage the tangs of the oil pump drive gear.

On 757 models, the oil pump drive gear is driven by a notch in the outer edge of the clutch drum (3—Fig. SW70). On late model saws, the width of the notch and the mating tang of the oil pump drive gear has been increased from 7 mm (0.275 in.) to 9 mm (0.354 in.) to provide a more durable drive. To upgrade an early drive gear, the gear and clutch drum must be replaced as a matched set. Make sure that notch in the drum correctly engages the pump drive gear when assembling the drum, sprocket and cup washer before installing E-ring (9).

AUTOMATIC CHAIN OILER. All models are equipped with an automatic chain oiling system, which incorporates a pump similar to that shown in Fig. SW71. The clutch drum drives the oil pump gear of all models. The pump provides oil for the system whenever the clutch is engaged and the chain is moving. Oil output is adjusted by turning the pump adjuster (11) counterclockwise to increase the oil flow or clockwise to decrease oil flow.

To check oil pump output, operate the saw with the bar and chain removed and observe oil flow. If no oil appears or if the oil flow is erratic, check the following:

If bubbles appear at the discharge port, check for an air leak in the suction tube (4—Fig. SW71) or elbow (3). If there is no oil flow or irregular flow, check for wrong type or weight oil, plugged oil filter (1) or tank vent (2), collapsed suction tube (4), damaged oil pump drive, or worn oil pump (10).

The oil filter can be removed through the oil tank filler opening. Inspect, clean or renew filter as necessary.

To remove oil pump, first remove clutch cover, bar and chain. Remove clutch assembly as previously outlined. Remove oil pump dust cover. Remove pump mounting screws and remove pump assembly.

Oil pump components are not serviced separately. Pump must be renewed as an assembly if faulty.

REWIND STARTER. Refer to Fig. SW73 for an exploded view of typical rewind starter assembly. To disassemble, remove starter housing (1) from engine. Remove retainer (7) and rope handle (6) and allow rope to wind slowly onto pulley (4) until spring tension is relieved. Note that pulley retaining screw threads have been coated with a thread locking compound and may be difficult to remove. Heat may be applied to the starter housing with a heat gun to make screw removal easier. Unscrew pulley retaining screw (9) and remove pulley (4), being careful not to dislodge rewind spring (2). If necessary to remove rewind spring, care should be used not to allow spring to uncoil uncontrolled. Inspect pawls (10) and return springs (12) for wear or damage and renew as necessary.

When replacing the rewind rope, make certain that the correct length and diameter rope is installed. Specified rope length is 700 mm (27.5 in.) for

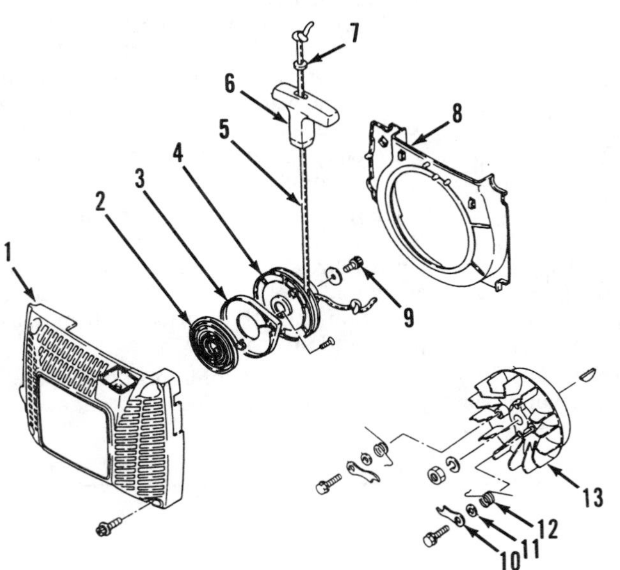

Fig. SW73—Exploded view of typical rewind starter assembly.

1. Starter housing
2. Rewind spring
3. Case
4. Rope pulley
5. Rope
6. Rope handle
7. Retainer
8. Air deflector
9. Screw
10. Pawl
11. Washer
12. Spring
13. Flywheel

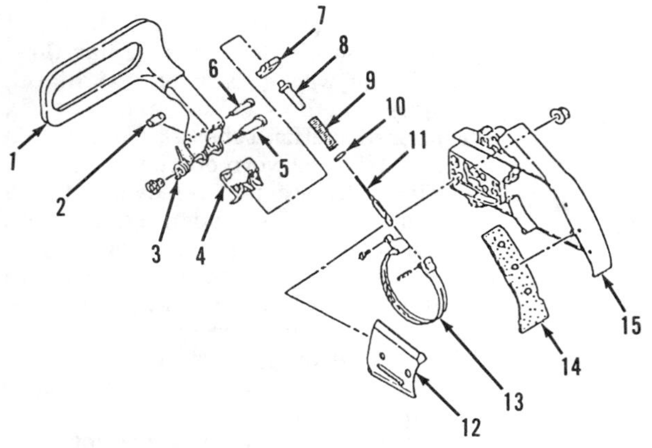

Fig. SW74—Exploded view of chain brake assembly used on Models 488 and 577.

1. Lever
2. Bushing
3. Lever spring
4. Inner lever
5. Pivot bolt
6. Stop pin
7. Block
8. Adjusting screw
9. Brake spring
10. Washer
11. Adjusting rod
12. Guide plate
13. Brake band
14. Protector
15. Clutch cover

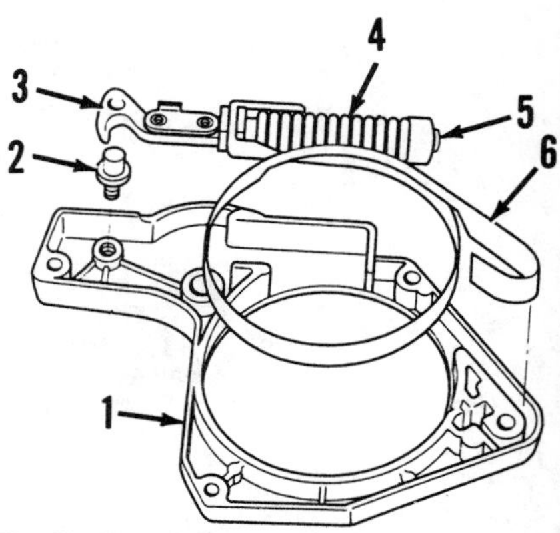

Fig. SW75—A cassette type chain brake is used on Model 757.

1. Cassette body
2. Lever pivot bolt
3. Brake inner lever
4. Brake spring
5. Spring holder
6. Brake band

Model 488 or 950 mm (37.4 in.) for Models 577 and 757. Specified rope diameter is 3.8 mm (0.150 in.) for Model 488 or (0.157 in.) for models 577 and 757.

Apply a light coat of multipurpose grease to both sides of rewind spring. The cassette type rewind spring is wound in the cassette in a counterclockwise direction from outer end of spring. Install the assembled spring cassette face down in the starter housing. Wind rope around pulley in a counterclockwise direction as viewed from rewind spring side of pulley. Turn pulley approximately three turns clockwise to preload rewind spring before passing rope through starter housing. Apply suitable thread locking compound to threads of pulley retaining screw (9—Fig. SW73) during final assembly.

Attach rope handle and check starter operation. It should be possible to pull rope to its full extension and still turn rope pulley approximately 1/2 turn. If rewind spring binds before rope is fully extended, reduce tension on rope by pulling rope up into notch in rope pulley and allowing pulley to unwind one turn. Recheck starter operation.

CHAIN BRAKE. All models are equipped with a chain brake designed to stop the saw chain quickly should kickback occur. The chain brake is activated when operator's hand strikes lever (1—Fig. SW74), releasing latch (4) allowing spring (9) to draw brake band (13) tight around clutch drum. Pull back lever (1) to reset mechanism.

To disassemble brake for inspection or repair on 488 or 577 models, remove clutch cover (15—Fig. SW74) and clean saw dust and dirt from brake assembly. Loosen but do not remove lever pivot bolt nut. Use pliers to release tension on lever spring (3), then remove lever nut and spring. Temporarily reinstall pivot bolt nut and push brake lever forward to activate brake mechanism (relieve spring tension). Remove brake lever (1) and inner lever (4). Loosen adjuster screw (8) and remove block (7), screw and spring (9). Remove brake band retaining screw and withdraw brake band (13). Assembly is the reverse of disassembly.

A modular cassette type chain brake is used on Model 757 saw. To remove brake for inspection or repair, pull handle rearward to disengage brake. Remove brake hand lever, clutch cover and chain guide plate. Remove five brake cassette mounting screws (one screw is located above the rear bar bolt). Use a screwdriver to pry the brake assembly from the saw.

To disassemble 757 brake, install a 5 mm x 30 mm Allen screw through the rear of the cassette case and into the end of spring holder (5—Fig. SW75). Tighten the Allen screw to reduce brake spring tension. Remove snap ring from brake pivot pin and remove brake lever. Remove inner lever pivot bolt (2). Remove Allen screw from end of cassette, then separate brake band (6), inner lever and spring assembly from cassette body (1). Assembly is the reverse of disassembly.

On all models, renew any component that is excessively worn or damaged. Chain brake mechanism should be clean and free of sawdust and dirt accumulation. Lightly lubricate all moving parts and pivot points.

The 757 model chain brake is not adjustable. If brake does not engage or disengage properly, chain brake assembly should be renewed.

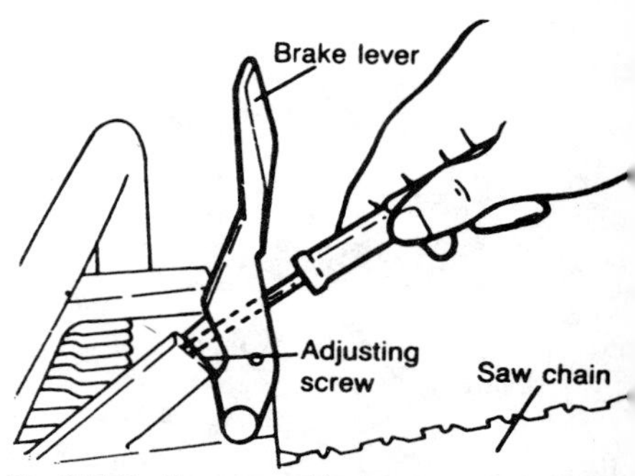

Fig. SW76—Use screwdriver to turn chain brake adjusting screw on Models 488 and 577. Chain brake is not adjustable on Model 757. Refer to text.

To adjust the chain brake for 488 and 577 models, first disconnect spark plug boot and properly ground terminal end. Place chain brake lever (1—Fig. SW74) in released (vertical) position. Use a screwdriver to turn adjusting screw (Fig. SW76) clockwise until chain cannot be moved by hand pressure. Then, turn adjusting screw counterclockwise noting when brake band does not contact clutch drum. Normal adjustment is 2-4 turns counterclockwise from the chain locked position.

Make sure brake band does not drag on outside of clutch drum with brake lever in released position. With brake lever in applied position, it should not be possible to rotate chain around guide bar.

SHINDAIWA

Model	Bore mm (in.)	Stroke mm (in.)	Displacement cc (cu. in.)	Drive Type
357	37 (1.46)	33 (1.30)	35.5 (2.17)	Direct

MAINTENANCE

SPARK PLUG. Recommended spark plug is Champion CJ6Y or NGK type BMP7A. Spark plug electrode gap should be 0.6 mm (0.024 in.). The spark plug should be tightened to the torque listed in the TIGHTENING TORQUE paragraph.

CARBURETOR. A Walbro WT-301B diaphragm type carburetor is used. Refer to the appropriate Walbro section of CARBURETOR SERVICE for service procedures and exploded view of carburetor. Tighten the carburetor attaching screws to the torque listed in the TIGHTENING TORQUE paragraph.

Initial adjustments for both low-speed and high-speed mixture needles are 1-1/4 turns open from a lightly seated position. Ends of low-speed mixture needle (1—Fig. SW90), high-speed mixture needle (2) and idle speed stop screw (4) are accessible as shown.

To adjust the mixture screws, first remove and clean the air filter, then reinstall it. Start the engine and allow it to run until it reaches normal operating temperature. If necessary, turn each of the mixture needles clockwise until seated lightly, then back the needles out (counterclockwise) to the initial setting so the engine can be started. Turn the idle speed stop screw so the engine idles at about 2,800 rpm.

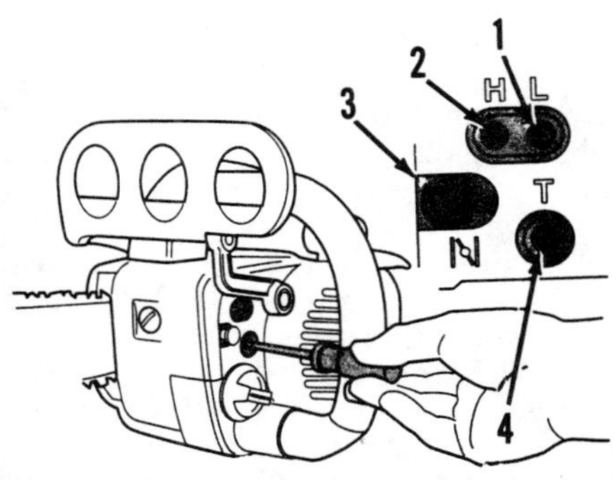

Fig. SW90—View of carburetor adjustment points. Refer to text for adjustment procedure.

Adjust the low-speed mixture needle so the engine idles smoothly and accelerates without hesitation. If the saw hesitates on acceleration, enrich the low-speed mixture slightly by turning the low-speed adjusting screw counterclockwise. Adjust the idle speed to just slower than clutch engagement speed, then recheck low-speed mixture adjustment.

Adjust the high-speed mixture needle to provide the best performance while operating at maximum speed under load. Engine no-load speed (with bar and chain installed) must not exceed 11,500 rpm. The high-speed mixture screw may be set slightly rich to improve performance under load. The engine may be damaged if the high-speed screw is set too lean.

Final adjustment of the mixture needles should be within 1/4 turn of the initial settings. Large differences may indicate air leaks, plugged passages or other problems.

IGNITION. A breakerless electronic ignition system is used. All electronic circuitry is contained in a one-piece ignition module/coil located outside the flywheel. Ignition timing is fixed and not adjustable and no periodic maintenance is required. The flywheel attaching nut should be tightened to the torque listed in TIGHTENING TORQUE paragraph.

Air gap between the legs of the module/coil and the flywheel magnets should be 35 mm (0.014 in.). To set the air gap, insert setting gauge (part No. 22154-96210) or brass/plastic shim stock of the proper thickness between the legs of the ignition module and the flywheel. Turn the flywheel until the flywheel magnets are near the module legs. Loosen the screws attaching the ignition module and press legs of the ignition module against the flywheel magnets. Tighten the two attaching screws to the torque listed in the TIGHTENING TORQUE paragraph. Remove the setting gauge, then turn the flywheel and check that flywheel does not hit the legs of the coil.

LUBRICATION. Engine oil mixed with gasoline provides lubrication for the engine. Recommended oil is Shindaiwa Premium 2-Cycle Oil mixed at a ratio of 40:1. If Shindaiwa Premium 2-Cycle Oil is not available, a good quality oil designed for air-cooled two-stroke engines may be used when mixed at a 25:1 ratio. Use a separate container when mixing the oil and gasoline.

All models are equipped with an automatic guide bar and chain oiling system. The automatic oil pump is actuated by the clutch and operates only when the clutch and chain are moving. Recommended chain oil is Shindaiwa Bar and Chain Oil or an equivalent good quality bar and chain oil. Oil output is not adjustable.

CARBON. Carbon deposits should be cleaned from muffler and exhaust ports at regular intervals. When scraping carbon, be careful not to damage the chamfered edges of the exhaust ports.

REPAIRS

CRANKCASE PRESSURE TEST. An improperly sealed crankcase can cause the engine to be hard to start, run rough, have low power and overheat. Refer to ENGINE SERVICE section of this manual for crankcase pressure test procedure. If crankcase leakage is indicated, pressurize crankcase and use a soap and water solution to check gaskets, seals, pulse line and castings for leakage.

TIGHTENING TORQUE. Recommended tightening torque values are as follows.

Carburetor
- 4 mm . . . . 2-3 N•m (17-25 in.-lb.)
- 5 mm . . . . 3-4 N•m (25-35 in.-lb.)

Crankcase . . . . 5.9-7.8 N•m (52-69 in.-lb.)

Illustrations courtesy Shindaiwa, Inc.

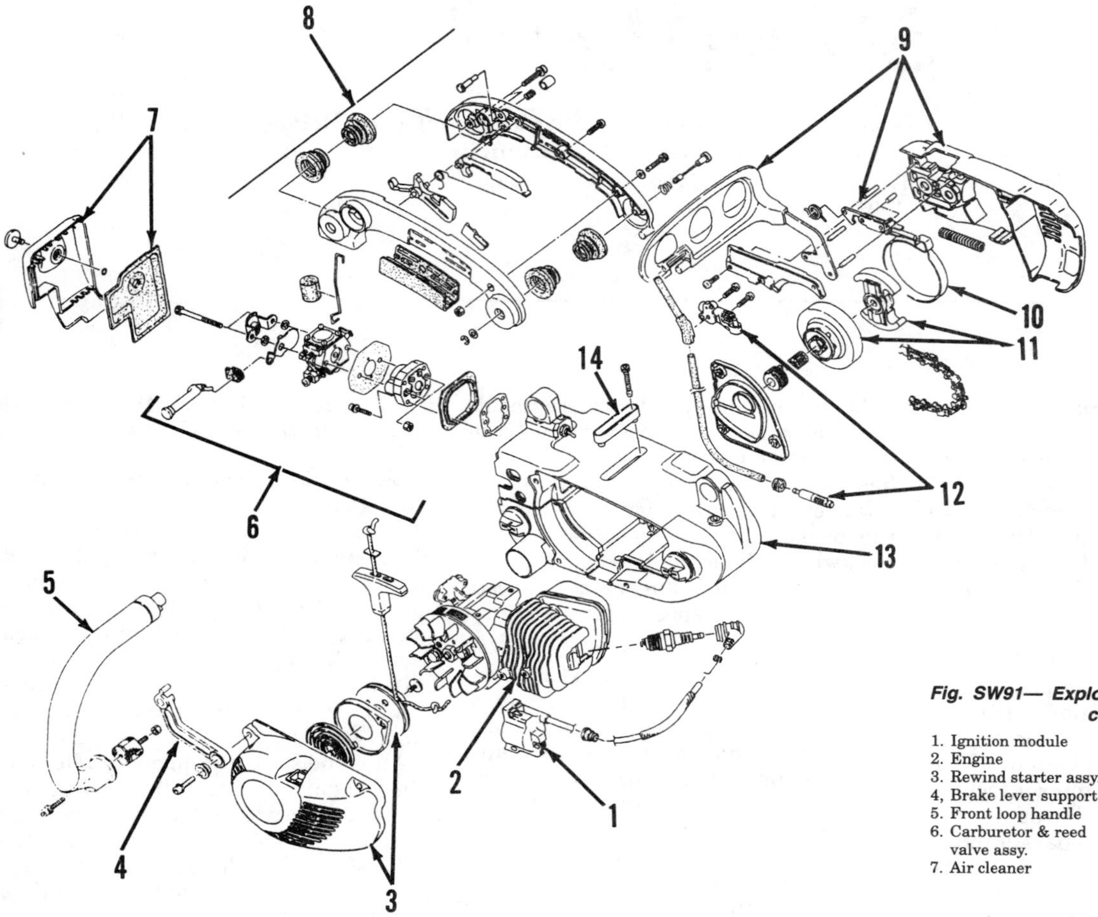

Fig. SW91— Exploded view of Model 357 saw components.

1. Ignition module
2. Engine
3. Rewind starter assy.
4. Brake lever support
5. Front loop handle
6. Carburetor & reed valve assy.
7. Air cleaner
8. Handle and throttle assy.
9. Clutch cover & chain brake assy.
10. Brake band
11. Clutch assy.
12. Oil pump & lines
13. Saw case
14. Insert (2 used)

Front handle
- 5 mm .... 2.9-3.9 N·m (25-35 in.-lb.)
- 5.5 mm .... 2.9-4.9 N·m (25-44 in.-lb.)

Flywheel .... 11.8-13.7 N·m (104-122 in.-lb.)

Ignition Module/coil .... 3.9-4.3 N·m (35-44 in.-lb.)

Muffler .... 6.9-7.8 N·m (61-70 in.-lb.)

Oil pump .... 2.0-2.2 N·m (17-22 in.-lb.)

Spark plug .... 16.7-18.6 N·m (148-165 in.-lb.)

Other nuts
- 5 mm .... 2.5-3.4 N·m (23-30 in.-lb.)
- 8 mm .... 10.2-12.0 N·m (90-106 in.-lb.)

Other Phillips head screws
- 4 mm .... 1.5-2.5 N·m (13-22 in.-lb.)
- 5 mm .... 2.9-3.9 N·m (25-35 in.-lb.)
- 6 mm .... 3.9-5.9 N·m (35-52 in.-lb.)

Other socket head screws
- 4 mm .... 2.9-4.4 N·m (25-39 in.-lb.)

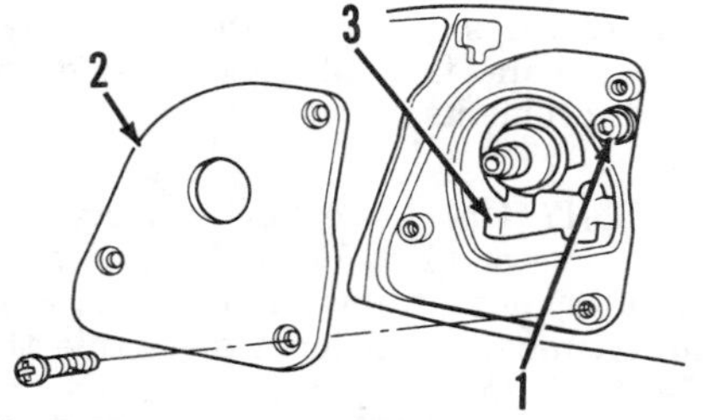

Fig. SW962—The fifth screw (1) that attaches the engine to the case is located behind the oil pump cover (2).

- 5 mm .... 4.9-6.9 N·m (43-61 in.-lb.)
- 6 mm .... 8.8-11.8 N·m (79-104 in.-lb.)

PISTON, PIN, RINGS, CYLINDER AND CRANKSAHFT. Refer to Fig. SW91 for exploded view of the handles, engine case, carburetor and related parts.

To disassemble, the engine must be removed from the engine case. Remove guide bar and chain, starter assembly (3—Fig. SW91) and front handle (5). Remove stop switch from engine housing and disconnect electrical leads. Remove ignition module/coil assembly (1). Remove chain brake assembly (9), air cleaner (7), carburetor and reed valve assembly (6). Remove spark plug, then insert end of a rope in the cylinder through the spark plug hole to act as a piston stop. Remove the flywheel retaining nut (right-hand threads) and use a suitable puller (part No. 22150-96101 or equivalent) to remove the flywheel. Unscrew clutch hub (left-hand threads), then remove the clutch assembly (11). Unbolt and remove the oil pump cover and the oil pump (12).

Remove the five screws attaching the engine in the case. Note that two screws are located in each of the inserts (14) located at the top and bottom of saw case (13). A fifth screw (1—Fig. SW92) and flat washer are located above the oil pump on the right-hand side of the saw. Withdraw engine (2—Fig. SW91) from the saw case.

To disassemble the engine, remove crankcase screws (14—Fig. SW93) and separate crankcase (13) from cylinder (1). Withdraw crankshaft, connecting rod and piston from cylinder. Care should be taken not to scratch or nick mating surfaces of cylinder and crankcase. Remove piston ring (2) from pis-

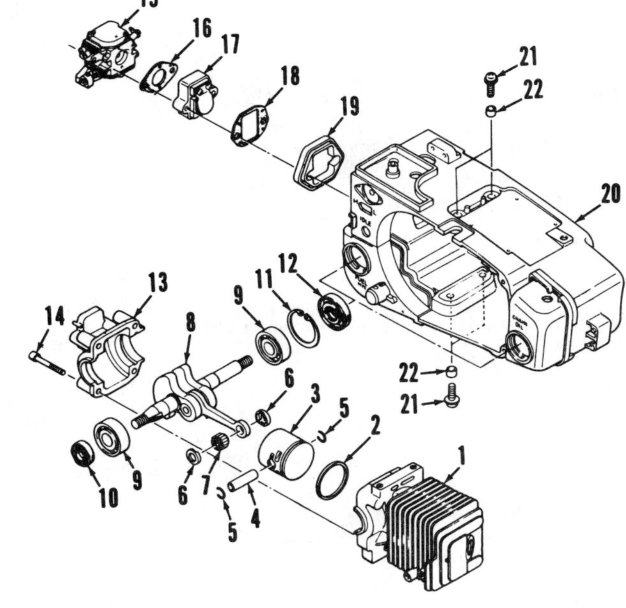

Fig. SW93—Exploded view of the engine assembly.

1. Cylinder
2. Piston ring
3. Piston
4. Piston pin
5. Retainer clips
6. Washers
7. Needle bearing
8. Crankshaft and connecting rod assy.
9. Main bearing
10. Seal
11. Snap ring
12. Main bearing
13. Crankcase half
14. Screw

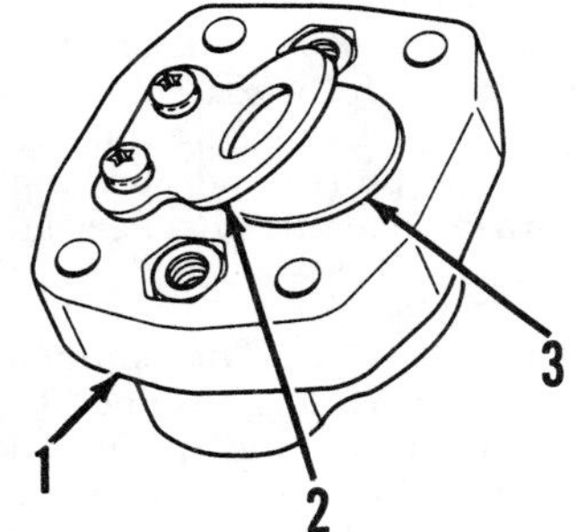

Fig. SW94—View of the reed valve block (1), reed stop plate (2) and reed (3). Do not disassemble the unit.

ton. Remove retaining rings (5) and push piston pin (4) from the piston, while catching the thrust washers (6). Separate piston (3) and needle bearing (7) from connecting rod.

Do not remove the crankshaft main ball bearings (9) unless new bearings are available for installation. Carefully support the crankshaft while removing and installing the main bearings. The crankshaft and connecting rod are available only as a complete assembly.

To reassemble, reverse the disassembly procedure while noting the following special instructions: Install piston on connecting rod so arrow on top of piston points toward the output (saw chain) end of crankshaft. Lubricate needle bearing (7) and piston pin, then position thrust washers (6) on either side of connecting rod before inserting the piston pin (4). Always install NEW retaining rings (5) and be sure end gap is down toward the crankshaft. Lubricate lip of crankshaft seals (10 and 12) with grease before installation. Make certain that piston ring end gap indexes with locating pin in piston ring groove. Lubricate piston and cylinder bore with oil, compress the piston ring and slide piston into cylinder.

Apply light coat of RTV silicone sealant to crankcase mating surface then assemble crankcase (13) to cylinder (1). Be sure crankshaft seals (10 and 12) are flush with outer surface of cylinder and crankcase. Gently tap on both ends of crankshaft to center all components then tighten crankcase screws (14) to the torque specified in the TIGHTENING TORQUE paragraph.

REED VALVE. The reed valve assembly (Fig. SW94) should be cleaned and inspected whenever the carburetor is removed.

Reed petal (3) should seat very lightly against the insulator throughout its entire length with the least possible tension. Install new reed assembly if reed standout is excessive or if any cracks are found. The reed valve should not be disassembled.

CLUTCH. The two-shoe centrifugal type clutch should engage at 3,800 rpm.

To remove the clutch, remove clutch cover (7—Fig. SW95) and chain brake

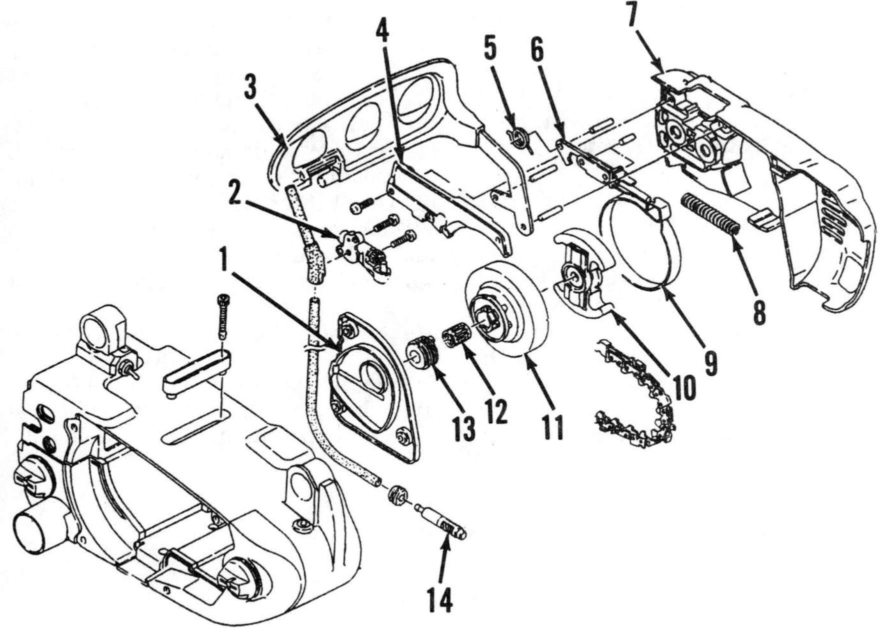

Fig. SW95—Exploded view of chain brake assembly, clutch assembly and chain oil pump.

1. Oil pump cover
2. Oil pump
3. Hand guard
4. Brake cover
5. Spring
6. Brake linkage
7. Clutch cover/brake housing
8. Brake spring
9. Brake band
10. Clutch hub & shoes
11. Clutch drum & sprocket
12. Needle bearing
13. Worm gear
14. Oil pick-up screen

Illustrations courtesy Shindaiwa, Inc.

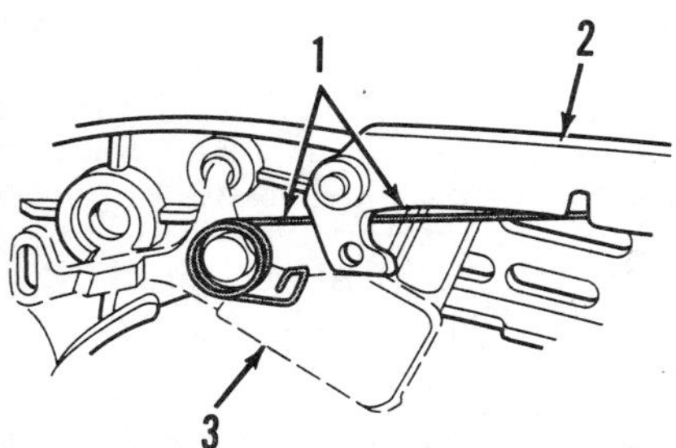

Fig. SW96—Assemble the throttle lock spring (1), throttle lock (2) and throttle lever (3) as shown.

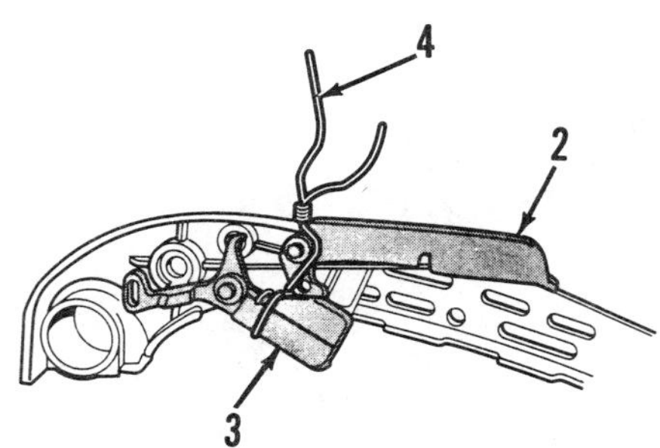

Fig. SW97—Use a length of soft wire (4) to hold the throttle lever (3) and lock (2) in position while installing the handle assembling on the saw.

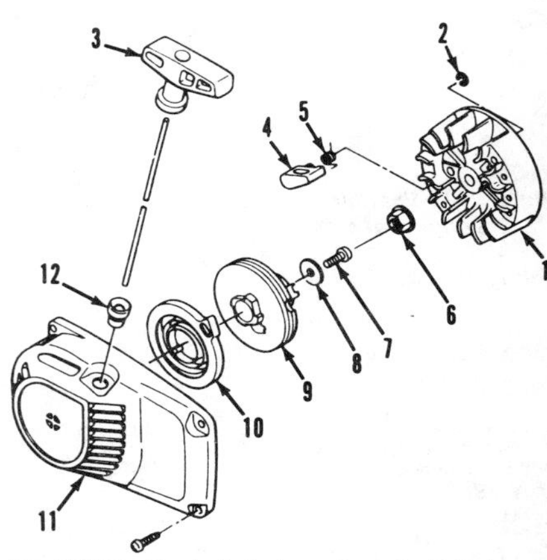

Fig. SW98—Exploded view of rewind starter assembly.

1. Flywheel
2. "E" ring
3. Rope handle
4. Pawl
5. Spring
6. Nut
7. Screw
8. Washer
9. Rope pulley
10. Rewind spring and case
11. Starter housing
12. Rope guide

assembly, guide bar, and chain. Remove spark plug, then use a suitable piston stop to prevent the crankshaft from turning. Turn clutch hub (10) clockwise (left-hand threads) to remove hub and clutch shoes from crankshaft. Remove clutch drum (11) and bearing (12).

Inspect clutch drum needle bearing for roughness or wear and renew as necessary. Inspect clutch shoes and drum for signs of excessive heat. Clutch drum should be renewed if sprocket teeth are worn in excess of 25 mm (0.010 in.). If sprocket is badly worn, inspect chain for excessive wear also. Do not install a new chain over a worn sprocket.

Apply grease to drive flanges of hub and to needle bearing prior to installation.

AUTOMATIC CHAIN OILER. All models are equipped with an automatic bar and chain oiling system. An automatic oil pump (2—Fig. SW95), driven by clutch drum via worm gear (13), provides oil for the system whenever clutch and chain are operating.

Oil pump components are not serviced separately. Pump must renewed as an assembly if faulty. Periodically inspect oil pick-up screen (14) and tube for contamination and clean as necessary.

THROTTLE TRIGGER AND HANDLE. If the handle and throttle are disassembled, assemble the throttle return spring as shown in Fig. SW96. Use a short piece of soft wire to hold the throttle lever, lockout lever and spring in place as show in Fig. SW97 while assembling the handle halves. Be sure screws are installed in their original locations and refer to TIGHTENING TORQUE paragraph.

REWIND STARTER. Refer to Fig. SW98 for an exploded view of rewind starter assembly typical of the type used. To disassemble, remove the screws attaching the starter housing (11) to saw case. If rope is not broken, remove rope handle (3) and allow rope to wind slowly onto pulley (9) until spring tension is relieved. Unscrew pulley mounting screw (7) and remove pulley, being careful not to dislodge rewind spring (10). If necessary to remove rewind spring, care should be used not to allow spring to uncoil uncontrolled.

The flywheel must be removed to remove the starter pawl (4). The "E" ring (2) is located on the back of the flywheel.

Install any components that are worn or damaged. If a new rope is installed, be sure the diameter and length are the same as originally installed.

If removed, apply a light coat of multipurpose grease to both sides of rewind spring. Wind the spring in its case in a counterclockwise direction from outer end of spring. Install the spring and its case in the starter housing (11). Attach the rope to the pulley then install the pulley and retaining screw (7) with washer (8). Feed the end of the rope through the starter housing and guide (12) then install handle (3).

Position a loop in the rope between the pulley and the inside of the starter housing and rotate the starter pulley five turns clockwise. This will preload the rewind spring five turns. Pull the rope handle (3) to remove the slack (loop) from the rope then carefully allow the rope to wind around pulley.

Check starter operation. It should be possible to pull rope to its full extension and still turn rope pulley approximately 1/2 turn. If rewind spring binds before rope is fully extended, reduce tension on rope by pulling rope up into notch in rope pulley and allowing pulley to unwind one turn. Recheck starter operation.

CHAIN BRAKE. The chain brake system (Fig. SW95) is designed to stop chain movement should kickback occur. The chain brake is activated when operator's hand strikes the hand guard (3). When activated (engaged), the brake band (9) is drawn around the clutch drum (11) by spring pressure and immediately stops clutch and chain movement.

Remove clutch cover (7) for access to chain brake components. Remove brake cover (4) and carefully remove brake spring (8) and brake band (9).

Renew any component that is excessively worn or damaged. Lubricate all pivot points, especially the lever assembly with lithium base grease.

When properly assembled, the chain brake should stop saw chain instantly when engaged. Brake band should not contact clutch drum when disengaged. Make sure brake band does not drag on outside of clutch drum with brake lever in released position. With brake lever in applied position, it should not be possible to rotate chain around guide bar.

SOLO

Model	Bore mm (in.)	Stroke mm (in.)	Displacement cc (cu. in.)	Drive Type
635	54 (2.126)	40 (1.575)	92 (5.6)	Direct
642	58 (2.283)	40 (1.575)	106 (6.47)	Direct

MAINTENANCE

SPARK PLUG. A Bosch W175 spark plug is recommended. Recommended equivalent is Champion J8J. Set electrode gap to 0.6 mm (0.025 in.).

CARBURETOR. A Tillotson diaphragm carburetor with integral fuel pump is used on both models. Early Model 635 uses an HL-239A while Model 642 and late Model 635 use a Model HL-296A.

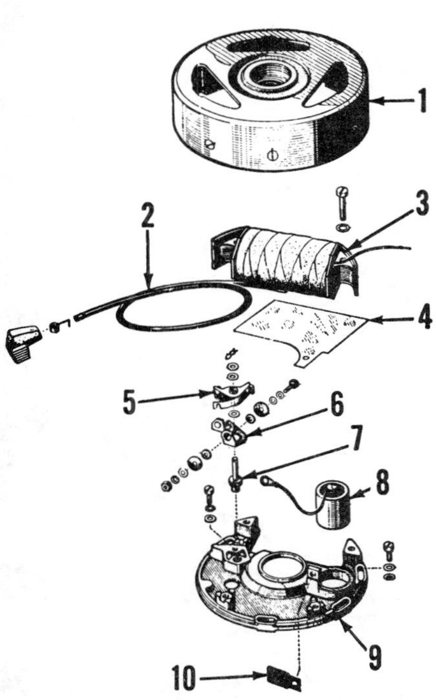

Fig. SO1—Exploded view of Bosch magneto used on Model 635 chain saws. Model 642 is similar.

1. Rotor
2. High tension wire
3. Ignition coil
4. Insulating guard
5. Breaker point-lever
6. Breaker point base
7. Pivot bolt
8. Condenser
9. Stator plate
10. Cam wiper

Refer to Tillotson section of CARBURETOR SERVICE for carburetor service and exploded views. Initial setting of idle mixture screw is 3/4 turn open while high speed mixture screw is 1½ turns open. Make final adjustment with engine warm and running. Set the fuel needle for smoothest idle operation and adjust idle speed stop screw so that engine idles at just below clutch engagement speed. Open main fuel needle until engine four-cycles (fires only on every other stroke) then, turn needle in slowly until engine two-strokes (fires on every stroke) at operating speed.

MAGNETO AND TIMING. Refer to Fig. SO1 for exploded view of Bosch flywheel-type magneto. Breaker-point gap should be 0.5 mm (0.020 in.).

To check or adjust timing remove blower fan so that flywheel openings are exposed. If Solo timing gage (Part No. 00 80 162) is available, screw gage finger tight into spark plug hole. Turn engines so that timing gage indicates piston is at top dead center. Breaker point gap should then be 0.25-0.3 mm (0.010-0.012 in.). If not, check maximum breaker point opening to be sure that point gap is properly adjusted to 0.5 mm (0.020 in.). If gap is correct and point opening with piston at TDC is not 0.25-0.3 mm (0.010-0.012 in.), adjust stator position in slotted mounting holes to obtain correct measurement. Then, turn engine clockwise so that timing gage indicator falls 3 marks; breaker points should then be just starting to open. (Three marks on timing gage equals approximately 2.5 mm piston travel BTDC or 0.1 inch BTDC).

LUBRICATION. Engine is lubricated by mixing oil with fuel. During the first 20 hours of operation (break-in period), mix one part oil with 20 parts gasoline; thereafter, mix one part oil with 25 parts gasoline. Use a good grade of oil designed for use in air-cooled, two-stroke engines and regular grade gasoline.

Both models are equipped with automatic chain oilers depicted in Fig. SO2. Exploded views are shown in Fig. SO3. Chain oilers used on Models 635 and 642 are pump driven by a cam or crankshaft end. All oil chain reservoirs should be filled with SAE 30 oil.

Both models are equipped with a manual chain oiler system. It is possible to unclog the automatic system by operating the manual system.

Needle roller bearing in clutch drum should be removed, cleaned and lubricated with Lubriplate or similar grease occasionally.

REPAIRS

CONNECTING ROD. The connecting rod is of one-piece construction and is serviced only as an assembly with the

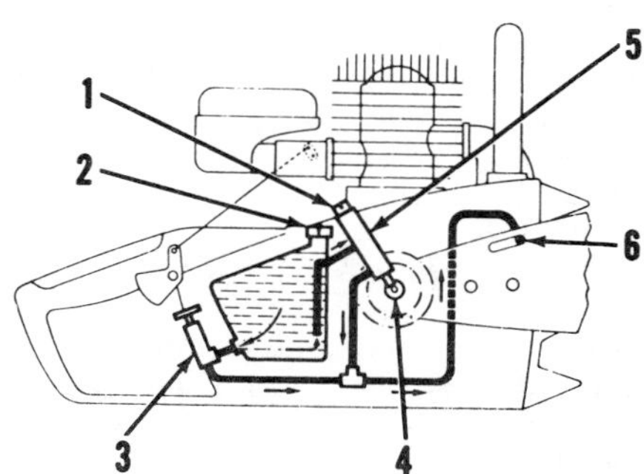

Fig. SO2—Schematic view of automatic chain oiler used on Models 635 and 642. The oil pump (5) is driven by a cam on the crankshaft end (4) thus forcing oil to the chain (6). A manual pump (3) will also force oil to the chain. To vary amount of oil going to chain from automatic pump (5), turn outer control screw (1).

Illustrations courtesy Solo Inc.

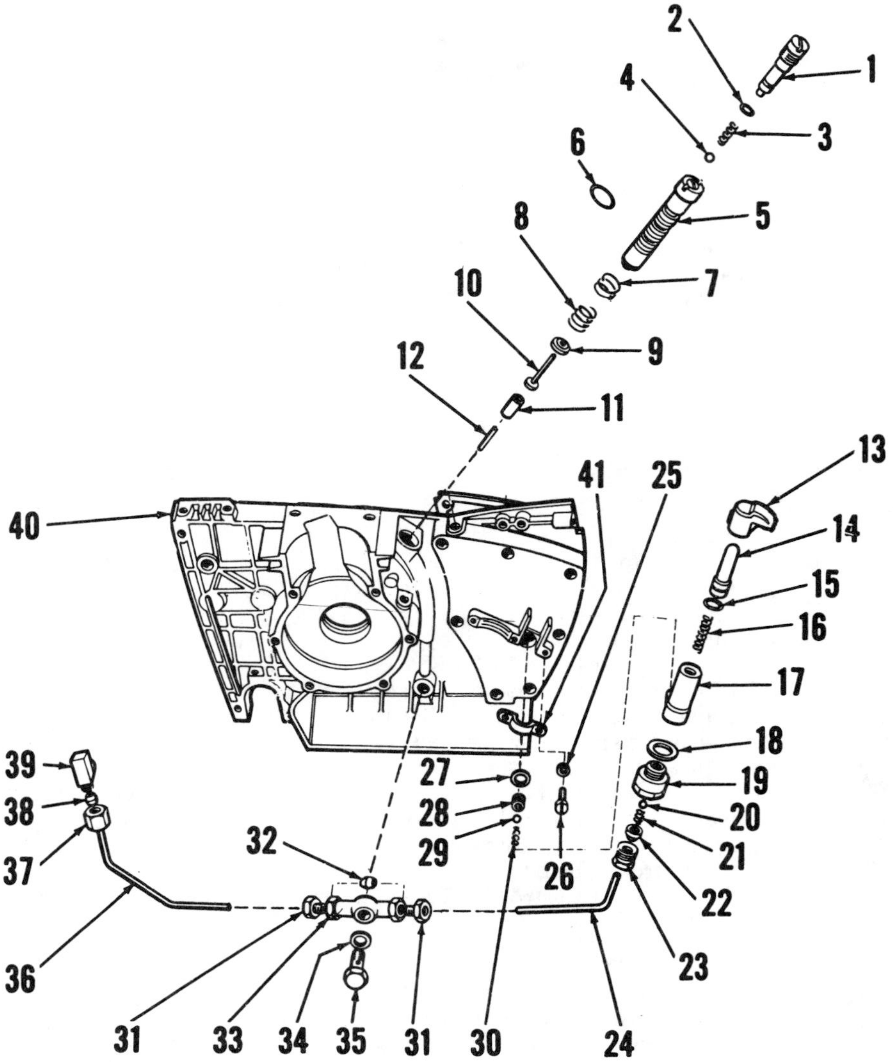

1. Threaded plug
2. "O" ring
3. Spring
4. Check ball
5. Pump housing
6. "O" ring
7. Check spring
8. Piston spring
9. Spring retainer
10. Pump piston
11. Bushing
12. Plunger
13. Manual pump control
14. Piston
15. "O" ring
16. Spring
17. Pump housing
18. Gasket
19. Valve
20. Check ball
21. Valve spring
22. Cone ring
23. Nipple
24. Oil pipe
25. Washer
26. Screw
27. Gasket
28. Stud
29. Check ball
30. Spring
31. Flanged nut
32. Ferrule
33. Tee
34. Gasket
35. Screw
36. Oil pipe
37. Flanged nut
38. Flanged ring
39. Elbow
40. Crankcase half

Fig. SO3—Exploded view of automatic chain oil pump assembly as used on Models 635 and 642. Refer to Fig. SO2 for schematic view. Be sure to install "O" rings (6) in original position when reassembling.

crankshaft. If crankpin bearing is rough, burned or excessively worn, renew the crankshaft and connecting rod assembly.

Connecting rod upper end is fitted with a needle bearing. Use drivers of proper size and adequately support connecting rod when removing and installing bearing.

PISTON, PIN AND RINGS. Piston, pin and rings are available in standard size only. Piston and piston pin are available only as a fitted assembly. The two compression rings are available separately.

To remove piston from rod and crankshaft assembly, remove the pin retaining rings, support piston and tap or press the pin from piston and connecting rod.

When installing piston, arrow on piston crown should point towards exhaust port.

CRANKSHAFT AND MAIN BEARINGS. The crankshaft is supported by two ball bearing type mains. The main bearings can be renewed after removing the cylinder and separating the split type crankcase. Crankcase halves should be heated in oven or under heat lamp to about 250° F (121° C) to remove bearing or to install crankshaft and bearing assembly in crankcase.

As with all two-stroke engines, maintenance of crankshaft oil seals is to utmost importance. When installing seals or crankshaft assembly, be careful

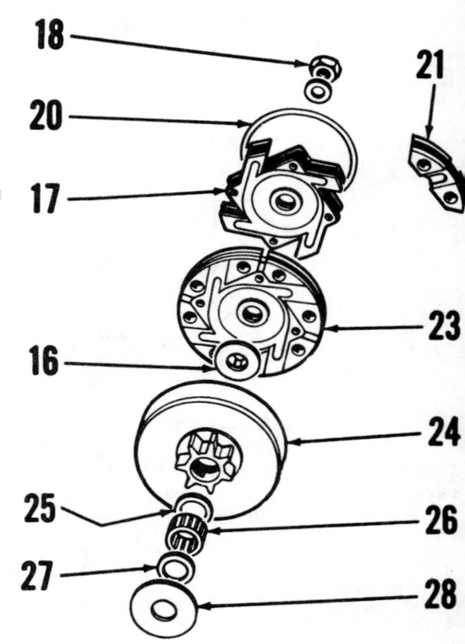

Fig. SO4—Exploded view of Model 635 and 642 clutch assembly. Refer to Fig. SO5 for parts identification.

not to damage seal lips. Tape threads, shoulders and keyways on crankshaft or use seal protectors.

CLUTCH. The clutch rotor and clutch retaining nut are threaded to the crankshaft with left-hand threads.

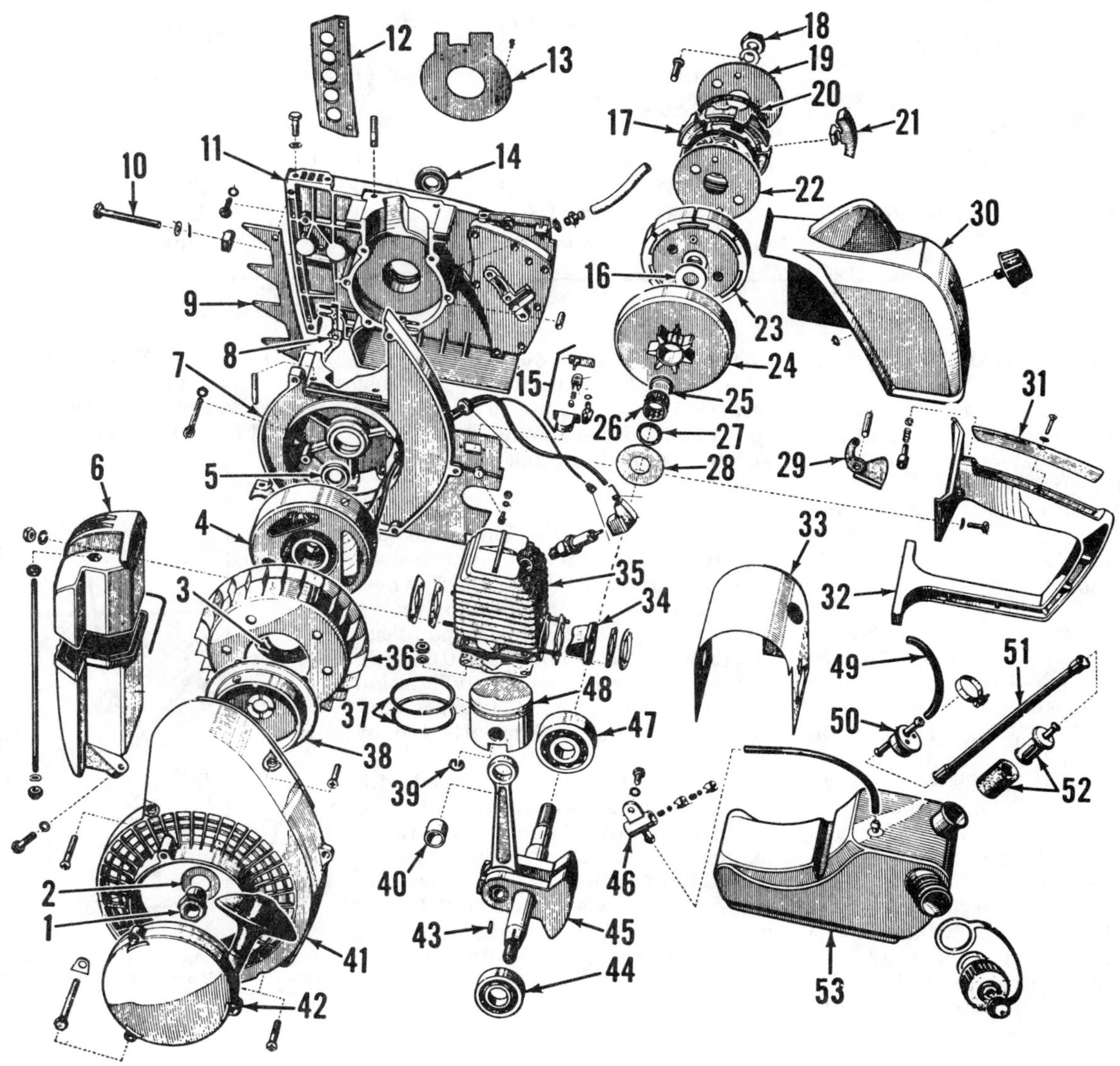

Fig. SO5—Exploded view of early 635 powerhead. Model 642 and later 635 are similar. Refer to Fig. SO1 for exploded view of magneto (4). Clutch assembly for 635 and 642 is shown in Fig. SO4.

1. Flywheel nut
2. Washer
3. Spacer
4. Magneto assy.
5. Oil seal
6. Muffler assy.
7. Crankcase half
8. Gasket
9. Spike
10. Adjusting screw
11. Crankcase half
12. Bumper plate
13. Cover
14. Oil seal
15. Ignition switch
16. Washer
17. Clutch rotor
18. Clutch nut
19. Disc
20. Clutch springs
21. Clutch shoes
22. Disc
23. Clutch assembly
24. Clutch assembly & sprocket assy.
25. Felt ring
26. Needle bearing
27. Felt ring
28. Washer
29. Throttle trigger
30. Cover
31. Insert
32. Handle
33. Shield
34. Carburetor port
35. Cylinder
36. Blower fan
37. Piston rings
38. Starter cup
39. Snap rings
40. Bushing
41. Blower housing
42. Starter assy.
43. Key
44. Ball bearing
45. Crankshaft & rod assy.
46. Breather valve
47. Ball bearing
48. Piston & pin assy.
49. Fuel line
50. Hose connector
51. Hose
52. Fuel pickup
53. Fuel tank

Illustrations courtesy Solo Inc.

SOLO

Model	Bore mm (in.)	Stroke mm (in.)	Displacement cc (cu. in.)	Drive Type
600, 600K, 605AV, 605AVK	38 (1.496)	28 (1.102)	32 (1.95)	Direct
606AV, 606AVK	42 (1.653)	28 (1.102)	38 (2.32)	Direct
631, 631K, 632, 632AVK	38 (1.496)	28 (1.102)	32 (1.95)	Direct
634	38 (1.496)	30 (1.18)	34 (2.1)	Direct
638, 638AVK	42 (1.653)	28 (1.102)	38 (2.32)	Direct
641	42 (1.653)	30 (1.18)	41.5 (2.53)	Direct

MAINTENANCE

SPARK PLUG. Recommended spark plug is Bosch WSR6F, Champion RCJ6Y or equivalent for Models 634 and 641. On all other models, recommended spark plug is Bosch WKA 175T6, Champion RCJ6 or equivalent. Spark plug electrode gap should be 0.5 mm (0.020 in.) on all models.

CARBURETOR. Models 600, 605 and 606 are equipped with a Walbro HDC 29 diaphragm type carburetor. Models 631K, 632AVK and 638AVK are equipped with a Walbro HDC 10 diaphragm carburetor. Models 634 and 641 are equipped with a Bing 48C 104B diaphragm carburetor. Some models may also be equipped with a Tillotson HK55-96A carburetor. Refer to Bing, Tillotson or Walbro section of CARBURETOR SERVICE section for service procedures and exploded views of carburetors.

For initial carburetor adjustment, turn both mixture screws (2 and 3—Fig. SO10) in until lightly seated. Then, turn high speed mixture screw counterclockwise about one turn and idle mixture screw about 3/4 turn on Models 600, 605 and 606. On Models 631K, 632AVK and 638AVK, back out high speed mixture screw 5/8 turn and low speed mixture screw 1 1/8 turns. On Models 634 and 641, back out both mixture screws 1 turn.

Make final carburetor adjustments with engine running at operating temperature. Adjust idle mixture screw (2) to obtain maximum idle speed, then turn screw counterclockwise (open) about 1/8 turn. Accelerate engine to full speed several times. If engine stumbles or seems sluggish when accelerating, adjust idle mixture screw until engine accelerates without hesitation. Adjust idle speed screw (1) so engine idles just under clutch engagement speed. Operate engine at full throttle with no load and turn high speed mixture needle (3) clockwise until engine speed increases and four-stroking sound stops. Then, turn high speed needle counterclockwise until four-stroking sound just returns. Do not operate saw with high speed mixture too lean as engine damage may result from lack of lubrication and overheating.

IGNITION. A flywheel magneto ignition system with breaker points is used on some early model saws. The flywheel must be removed for access to breaker points (7—Fig. SO12). Breaker point gap should be 0.35-0.45 mm (0.014-0.017 in.). Air gap between flywheel and ignition coil should be 0.25 mm (0.010 in.). Timing is fixed, but will be affected by breaker point setting.

Later model saws are equipped with an electronic ignition system built into the ignition coil. There is no periodic maintenance required on this system. The coil-to-flywheel air gap on electronic ignition models should be 0.25-0.30 mm (0.009-0.011 in.). Timing is not adjustable on electronic ignition models.

LUBRICATION. The engine is lubricated by mixing oil with gasoline. Recommended oil is Castrol Super TT or Castrol TTS mixed at a 40:1 ratio. If Cas-

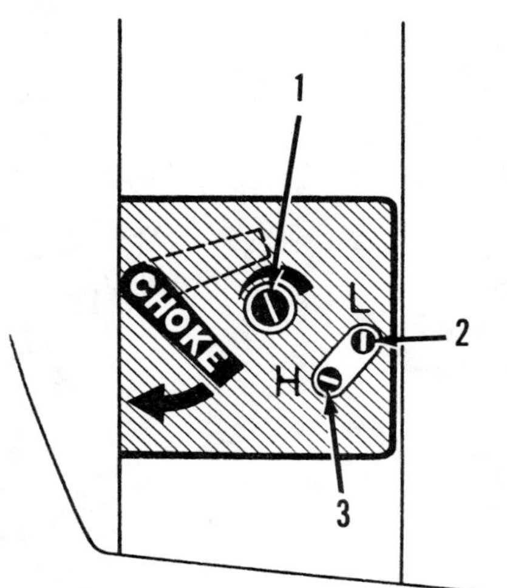

Fig. SO10—View of idle speed screw (1), idle mixture screw (2) and high speed mixture screw (3).

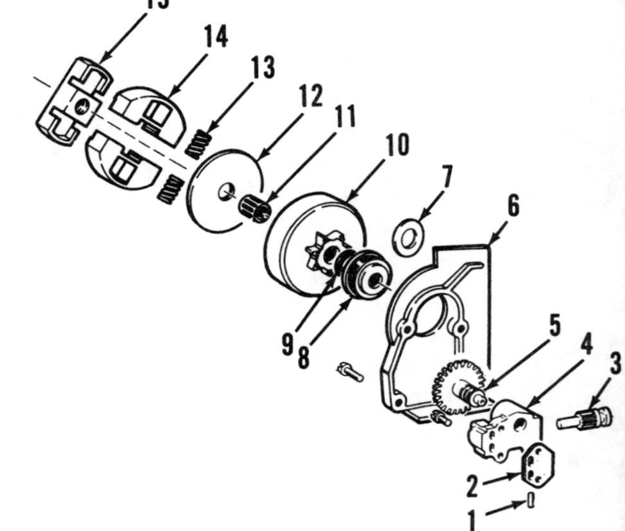

Fig. SO11—Exploded view of clutch and oil pump assembly.

1. Roller
2. Gasket
3. Piston
4. Oil pump body
5. Worm & gear
6. Cover plate
7. Washer
8. Drive gear
9. Washer
10. Clutch drum & sprocket
11. Needle bearing
12. Plate
13. Springs
14. Clutch shoes
15. Clutch hub

Illustrations courtesy Solo, Inc.

trol Super TT or Castrol TTS oil is not available, use a good quality oil designed for use in air-cooled two-stroke engines mixed according to the oil manufacturer's instructions, but no higher than a ratio of 40:1.

All models are equipped with a nonadjustable automatic chain oiler system. Refer to Fig. SO11 for an exploded view of oil pump.

The needle roller bearing (11—Fig. SO11) in the clutch drum should be removed occasionally, cleaned and lubricated with Lubriplate or a similar high-temperature grease.

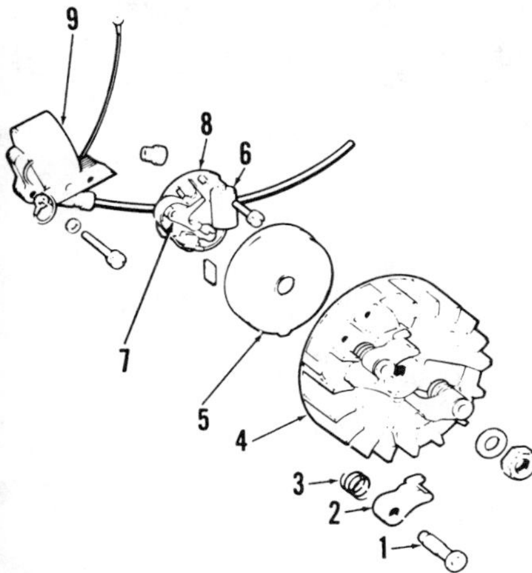

Fig. SO12—Exploded view of breaker point type ignition system used on early models.

1. Stud
2. Starter pawl
3. Spring
4. Flywheel
5. Ignition box
6. Condenser
7. Breaker points
8. Breaker plate
9. Ignition coil

REPAIRS

CRANKCASE PRESSURE TEST. An improperly sealed crankcase can cause the engine to be hard to start, run rough, have low power and overheat. Refer to ENGINE SERVICE section of this manual for crankcase pressure test procedure. If crankcase leakage is indicated, pressurize crankcase and use a soap and water solution to check gaskets, seals, pulse line and castings for leakage.

CONNECTING ROD, CRANKSHAFT AND CRANKCASE. The crankshaft (10—Fig. SO13) is supported by a ball bearing at both ends. Crankshaft and connecting rod are serviced as an assembly.

To remove crankshaft, remove guide bar, chain, starter housing (15—Fig. SO14), chain brake assembly, fuel/oil tanks and handle assembly (18), side covers (6 and 12) and rear handle assembly (17 and 18). Remove spark plug and install piston stop tool or end of a rope in spark plug hole to lock piston and crankshaft. Unscrew clutch hub (left-hand threads) and flywheel nut (right-hand threads). Remove clutch assembly, oil pump assembly, flywheel, ignition system, muffler and carburetor. Remove crankcase mounting screws and separate crankcase (6—Fig. SO13) from cylinder (20). Withdraw crankshaft, connecting rod and piston from cylinder. Remove piston pin retainers (11), push out piston pin (12) and separate piston (13) from connecting rod.

Check crankshaft, connecting rod and bearings for wear or damage and renew as necessary. Install new oil seals (7).

To install crankshaft, reverse removal procedure. Be sure that "A" mark on piston crown faces exhaust port side of engine. Apply gasket sealing compound to crankcase mating surface and tighten mounting screws evenly.

PISTON, PIN, RINGS AND CYLINDER. Some models are equipped with an aluminum cylinder with an iron sleeve. Other models have an aluminum cylinder with a chrome bore. Pistons and cylinders are graded according to size and are identified with a letter stamped on top of cylinder and piston. Piston and cylinder letter sizes must be the same for proper fit of piston in cylinder. A new piston can be used in a used cylinder. However, if cylinder must be renewed, a new piston and the other crankcase half must also be replaced.

Install piston with arrow mark on piston crown pointing toward exhaust port side of engine.

CLUTCH. The clutch hub (15—Fig. SO11) is threaded on the crankshaft with left-hand threads. Clutch drum (10) rides on a bearing (11) and drives oil pump drive gear (8), which, in turn, drives pump worm gear (5).

To remove clutch assembly, remove chain guard, guide bar and chain. Remove spark plug and install piston stop tool or end of a rope in spark plug hole to lock piston and crankshaft. Unscrew clutch hub from crankshaft. Remove clutch shoes (14), clutch plate (12) and clutch drum (10).

The needle bearing should be cleaned and lubricated with Lubriplate or similar high-temperature grease. Renew chain sprocket if teeth are worn in excess of 1 mm (0.040 in.). If sprocket is worn excessively, check chain drive links for wear also. Do not install a new chain over a worn sprocket.

REWIND STARTER. To disassemble starter, remove rope handle and allow rope to rewind into starter. Remove "E" ring or clip (9—Fig SO14) and remove rope pulley (13) while being careful not to dislodge rewind spring (14). If rewind spring must be removed, care should be used not to allow spring to uncoil uncontrolled.

New rope length should be 900 mm (35.5 in.). Install rewind spring in housing in a clockwise direction from outer spring end. To place tension on rewind spring, install rope pulley and pawl assembly with rope unwound. Pass rope through outlet in starter housing and attach handle. Rotate rope pulley in a clockwise direction without winding

Fig. SO13—Exploded view of typical engine.

1. Oil hose
2. Strainer
3. Impulse nipple
4. Nipple
5. Gasket
6. Crankcase
7. Seal
8. Washer
9. Needle bearing
10. Crankshaft
11. Pin retainers
12. Piston pin
13. Piston
14. Piston ring
15. Muffler
16. Adapter
17. Carburetor
18. Gaskets
19. Intake manifold
20. Cylinder
21. Needle bearing
22. Key
23. Fuel pickup
24. Filter

rope on pulley until rewind spring is tight. Allow pulley to unwind one full turn, then allow rope to wind on pulley as pulley is slowly released. Rope handle should fit snugly against rope outlet.

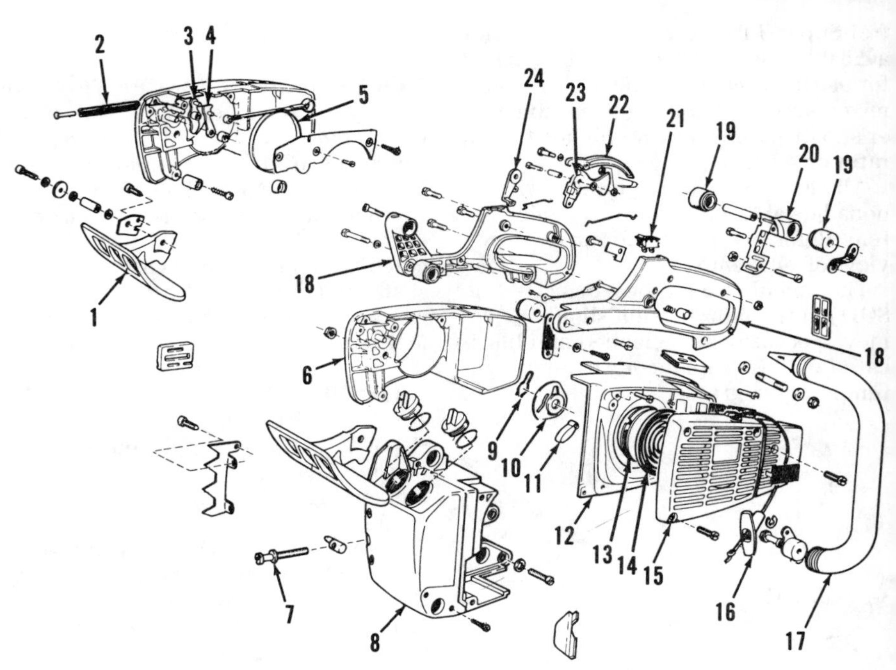

Fig. SO14—Exploded view of starter, chain brake and engine covers typical of all models.

1. Chain brake handle
2. Spring
3. Cam
4. Brake lever
5. Chain brake band
6. Side cover
7. Chain tension screw
8. Fuel/oil tank
9. Retainer clip
10. Plate
11. Starter pawl
12. Side cover
13. Rope pulley
14. Rewind spring
15. Starter housing
16. Rope handle
17. Handle bar
18. Handle assy.
19. Cushions
20. Flange
21. Stop switch
22. Lever
23. Throttle trigger
24. Lever

SOLO

Model	Bore mm (in.)	Stroke mm (in.)	Displacement cc (cu. in.)	Drive Type
616AV, 616AVK	45* (1.77)	32 (1.26)	52* (3.17)	Direct

* Early 616 models may have 42 mm (1.654 in.) bore and 45 cc (2.75 cu. in.) displacement.

MAINTENANCE

SPARK PLUG. Recommended spark plug for this model is Bosch WKA 175 T6 or Champion RCJ6. Electrode gap should be 0.5 mm (0.020 inch).

CARBURETOR. Model 616 is equipped with a Walbro HDC 29 diaphragm carburetor. Refer to Walbro section of CARBURETOR SERVICE section for service and exploded views.

For initial carburetor adjustment, back idle speed adjusting screw out until throttle valve is completely closed then turn screw back in until it contacts idle stop plus ½ turn additional. Turn both fuel adjusting needles, shown in Fig. SO20, in until lightly seated, then back main fuel needle out about one turn and back idle mixture screw out about ¾ turn. Start engine, readjust idle speed and fuel needles so that engine idles at just below clutch engagement speed. With engine running at full throttle, readjust main fuel needle so that engine will run at highest obtainable speed under cutting load.

IGNITION. A conventional flywheel magneto ignition system is used. Breaker point gap should be 0.35-0.45 mm (0.014-0.017 inch). Air gap between flywheel and ignition coil legs should be 0.25 mm (0.010 inch). Timing is fixed but will be affected by breaker points setting.

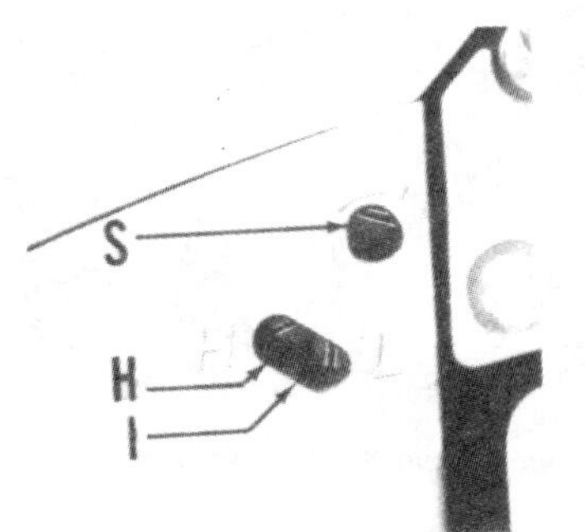

Fig. SO20—View of idle speed screw (S) high speed mixture screw (H) and idle mixture screw (I).

LUBRICATION. Engine is lubricated by mixing oil with fuel. During the first 20 hours of operation (break-in period), mix one part oil with 20 parts gasoline; thereafter, mix one part oil with 25 parts gasoline. Use a good grade of oil designed for use in air-cooled, two-stroke engines and regular grade gasoline.

Model 616 is equipped with the automatic adjustable chain oiler shown in Fig. SO21. The gear-driven, piston-type pump flow can be adjusted with the screw below the chain tightening screw. Turn screw toward "+" to increase and counterclockwise toward "−" to reduce oil flow. To shut off oil flow completely (as when using other attachments), turn adjusting screw to neutral position (Fig. SO22). Reduce oil flow only when using a very short bar or if a lightweight oil must be used on a hot day.

Needle roller bearing in clutch drum should be removed, cleaned and relubricated with Lubriplate or similar grease occasionally.

REPAIRS

CONNECTING ROD. The connecting rod is one-piece construction and is serviced only as an assembly with the crankshaft. If crankpin bearing is rough, burned or excessively worn, renew the crankshaft and connecting rod assembly.

The upper end of the connecting rod is fitted with a needle bearing. Use drivers of proper size and adequately support rod when installing or removing bearing.

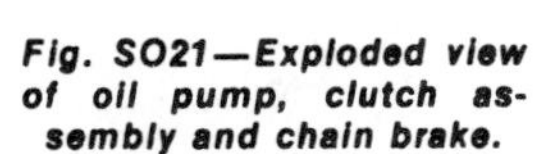

Fig. SO21—Exploded view of oil pump, clutch assembly and chain brake.

1. Plate
2. Adjuster shaft
3. Spacer
4. Oil adjuster
5. "O" ring
6. Piston
7. Ball
8. Spring
9. Oil strainer
10. Hose
11. Housing
12. Worm & gear
13. Needle bearing
14. Felt ring
15. Pump cover
16. Bushing
17. Sprocket
18. Oil pump drive gear
19. Washer
20. Clutch drum
21. Clutch assy.
22. Guide shoe
23. Lever
24. Pin
25. Brake band
26. Spacer
27. Spring seat
28. Lever
29. Springs
30. Hand guard
31. Bucking spikes

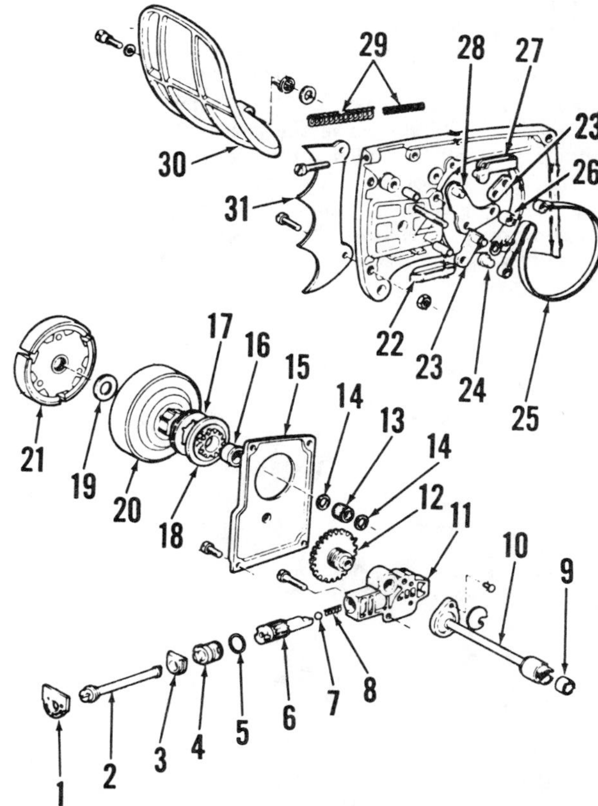

Illustrations courtesy Solo Inc.

PISTON, PIN, RINGS AND CYLINDER. Model 616 is equipped with a chromed bore aluminum cylinder. Pistons and cylinders are graded with a letter stamped on the top of the cylinder and top of piston. Piston and cylinder should be marked with some letter grade for proper fit. Install pistons with arrow on piston crown towards exhaust port.

CRANKSHAFT AND CRANKCASE. Crankshaft is supported on two roller bearings. It may be necessary to heat crankcase around bearings to facilitate removal of crankshaft and bearings from crankcase halves. For ease of installation of crankshaft assembly, apply heat around main bearing bores.

CLUTCH. The clutch drum is retained by an "E" ring. Clutch hub has left hand threads. Clutch hub, shoes and springs are available only as a unit assembly.

REWIND STARTER. To disassemble starter, remove rope handle and allow rope to rewind into starter. Detach "E" ring (16—Fig. SO24) and remove rope pulley (17) being careful not to dislodge rewind spring. If rewind spring (19) must be removed, care should be used not to allow spring to uncoil uncontrolled.

Install rewind spring so coils are wrapped in clockwise direction from outer spring end. To place tension in rewind spring, install rope pulley and pawl assembly with rope unwound, pass rope through outlet in starter housing and attach handle. Turn rope pulley in a clockwise direction without winding rope on pulley until rewind spring is coil bound. Allow pulley to unwind 1/4-1/2 turn and then allow rope to wind on pulley. Rope handle should fit snugly against rope outlet.

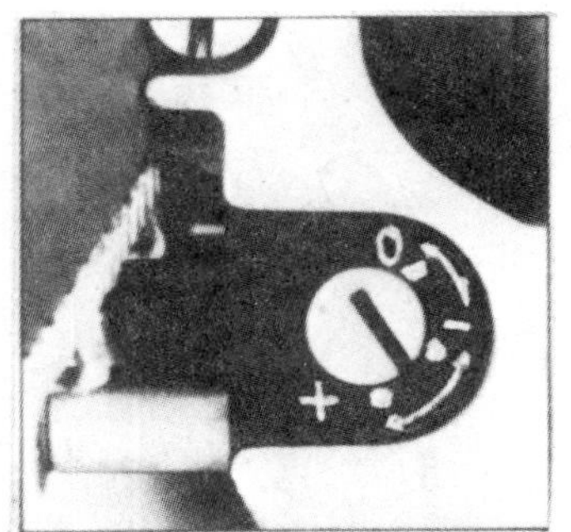

Fig. SO22—Chain oil adjustment screw. Refer to text for adjustments.

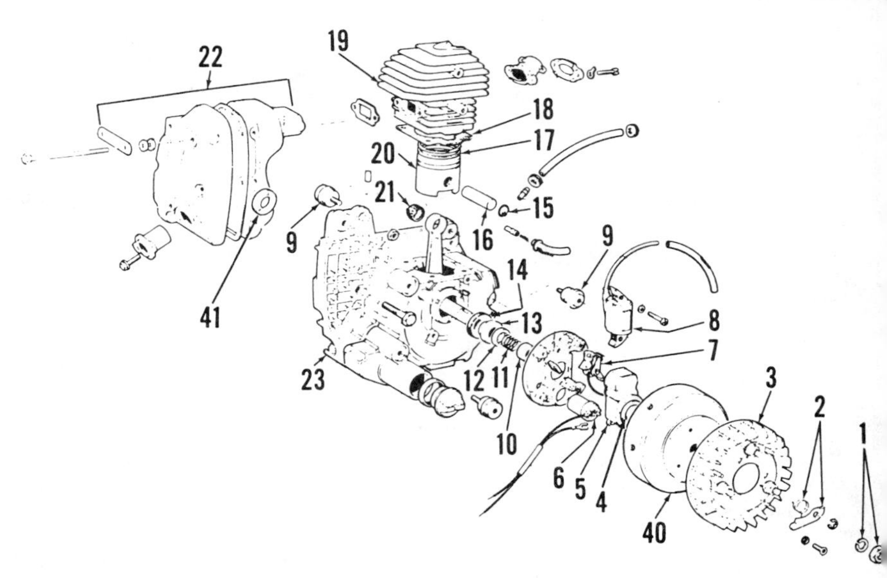

Fig. SO23—Exploded view of engine used on Model 616.

1. Nut & lockwasher
2. Spring & pawl
3. Fan
4. Felt ring
5. Breaker box
6. Condenser
7. Breaker points
8. Ignition coil
9. Motor mount
10. Cam
11. Spring
12. Felt ring
13. Spacer
14. Seal
15. Pin retainer
16. Piston pin
17. Piston rings
18. Gasket
19. Cylinder
20. Piston
21. Needle bearing
22. Muffler assembly
23. Crankcase and crankshaft assy.
40. Flywheel
41. Seal

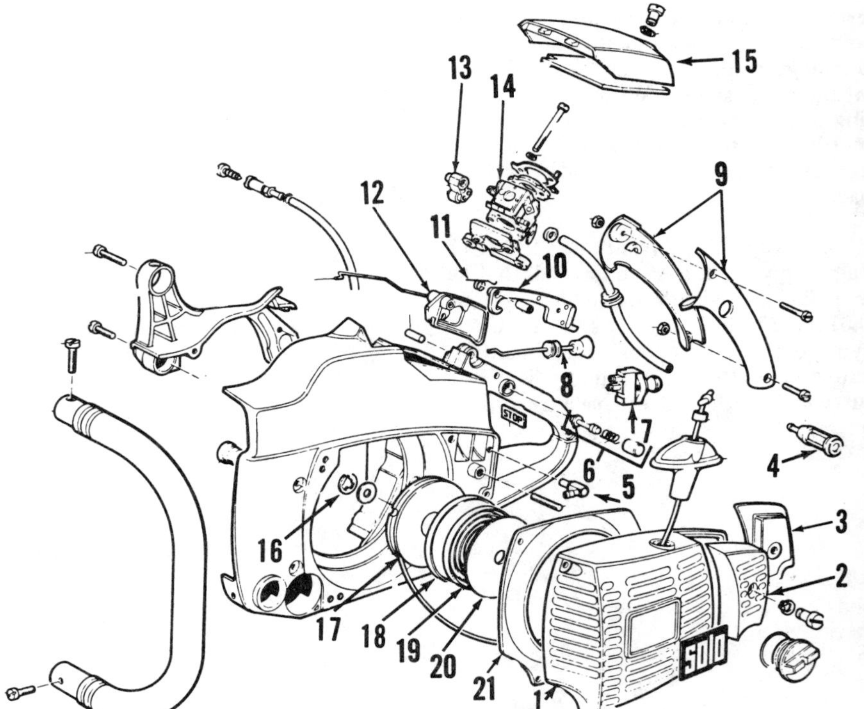

Fig. SO24—Exploded view of starter assembly and throttle assembly.

1. Starter housing
2. Cover
3. Filter
4. Fuel pick-up
5. Nipple
6. Retainer button, pin & spring
7. Stop button
8. Choke link
9. Handle grips
10. Lever
11. Spring
12. Throttle
13. Spacer
14. Carburetor
15. Air filter and cover
16. "E" ring
17. Rope pulley
18. Spring cove
19. Spring
20. Washer
21. Plate

Illustrations courtesy Solo In

SOLO

Model	Bore mm (in.)	Stroke mm (in.)	Displacement cc (cu. in.)	Drive Type
610AV, 610AVK	40 (1.57)	28 (1.102)	35 (2.1)	Direct
615	42 (1.653)	32 (1.26)	44 (2.7)	Direct
620, 620AV	44 (1.73)	34 (1.34)	52 (3.1)	Direct
650, 650AV	48 (1.89)	34 (1.34)	62 (3.7)	Direct
655, 655AV	48 (1.89)	38 (1.5)	70 (4.2)	Direct
660	52 (2.05)	38 (1.5)	81 (5.0)	Direct

MAINTENANCE

SPARK PLUG. Recommended spark plug for all models is Bosch WKA175T6 or equivalent. Electrode gap should be 0.5 mm (0.020 inch).

CARBURETOR. Models 610 and 615 are equipped with a Tillotson Model HU diaphragm carburetor while all other models are equipped with a Tillotson Model HS diaphragm carburetor. Refer to Tillotson section of CARBURETOR SERVICE section for service and exploded views.

Initial setting of idle mixture screws is ¾ turns open on all models. Initial setting of high speed mixture screw is 1 turn open on Models 610 and 615 and 1¼ turns open on all other models. Idle mixture screw should be adjusted so that engine will accelerate cleanly without stumbling. High speed mixture screw should be adjusted to provide optimum performance with saw under a cutting load. Adjust idle speed screw so that engine idles just below clutch engagement speed.

IGNITION. Early models are equipped with a conventional flywheel magneto ignition system while later models are equipped with an electronic breakerless ignition system.

Breaker-point gap on models so equipped should be 0.35-0.45 mm (0.014-0.017 in.) Air gap between flywheel and ignition coil legs should be 0.25 mm (0.010 in.). Ignition timing is fixed but will be affected by ignition breaker point setting.

LUBRICATION. Oil is mixed with the fuel to lubricate engine. Recommended fuel:oil ratio is 20:1 during the first 20 hours of operation (break-in period) and 25:1 thereafter. Oil should be designed for air-cooled two-stroke engines.

All models are equipped with a gear driven piston type automatic chain oil pump. Oil pump output is adjustable by moving lever on side of clutch cover on Models 610 and 615 or by turning adjusting screw on top of clutch cover on all other models. Chain oil should be

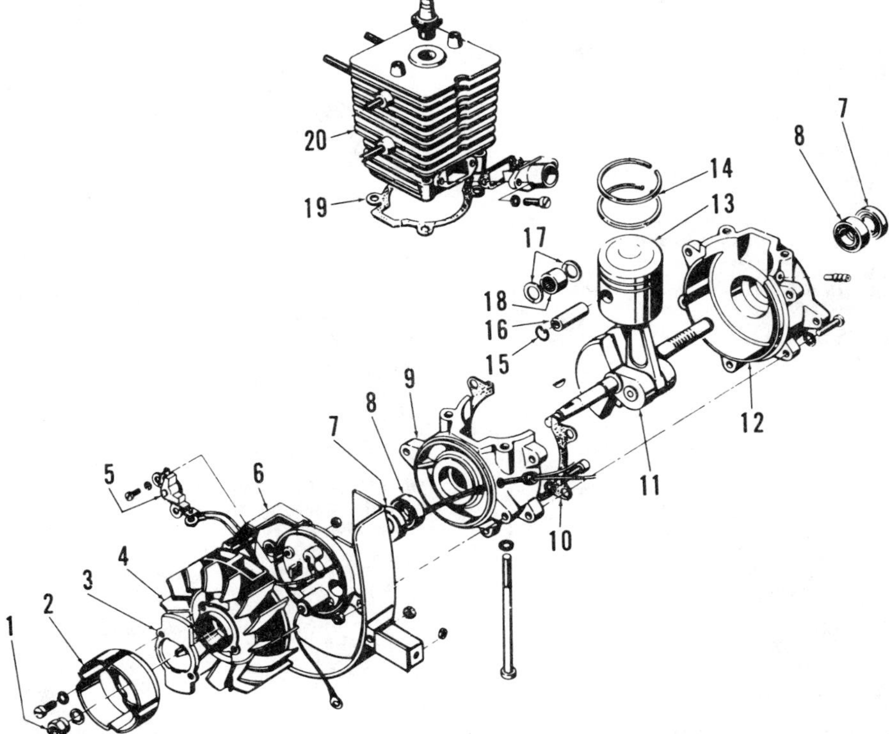

Fig. SO30—Exploded view of engine used on Models 610 and 615.

1. Nut
2. Starter cup
3. Spacer
4. Flywheel
5. Breaker points
6. Air shroud
7. Seal
8. Bearing
9. Left crankcase half
10. Gasket
11. Crankshaft assy.
12. Right crankcase half
13. Piston
14. Piston rings
15. Pin retainer
16. Piston pin
17. Thrust washers
18. Needle bearing
19. Gasket
20. Cylinder

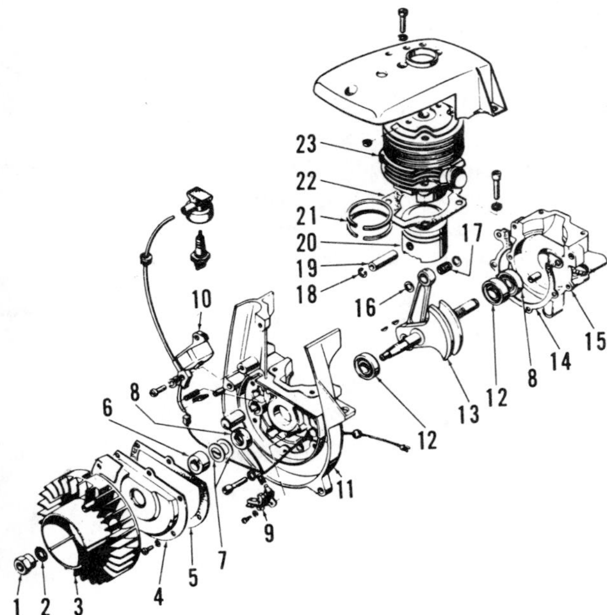

Fig. SO31—Exploded view of engine used on Models 620, 650, 655 and 660. Later models are equipped with electronic ignition in place of breaker points (9).

1. Nut
2. Washer
3. Flywheel
4. Breaker point cover
5. Gasket
6. Breaker point cam
7. Spring discs
8. Seal
9. Breaker points
10. Ignition coil
11. Left crankcase half
12. Bearing
13. Crankshaft assy.
14. Gasket
15. Right crankcase half
16. Thrust washers
17. Needle bearing
18. Pin retainer
19. Piston pin
20. Piston
21. Piston rings
22. Gasket
23. Cylinder

clean and the viscosity determined by ambient temperature.

REPAIRS

PISTON, PIN, RINGS AND CYLINDER. Models 610 and 620 are equipped with aluminum clyinders which have a steel sleeve. All other models are equipped with chromed bore aluminum cylinders. Pistons and cylinders on all models are graded with a letter stamped on the top of the cylinder the top of the piston. Letters on cylinders stamped "A, N or U" must use pistons stamped with the same letter. Cylinders stamped "B" may use pistons stamped "B or A"; cylinders stamped "C" may use pistons stamped "A, B or C"; cylinders stamped "D" may use pistons stamped "B, C or D"; cylinders stamped "E" may use pistons stamped "C, D or E". **Install pistons with arrow** on piston crown towards exhaust port.

CRANKSHAFT, CONNECTING ROD AND CRANKCASE. Crankshaft is supported on two ball bearings. It may be necessary to heat crankcase around bearings to facilitate removal of crankshaft and bearings from crankcase halves. Crankshaft and connecting rod are available only as a unit assembly and should not be disassembled. Apply heat around main bearing bores if crankcase halves to ease installation of crankshaft assembly.

CLUTCH. The clutch drum on all models is retained by an "E" ring (11–Fig. SO32 or 9–Fig. SO33). Clutch hub has left-hand threads. Clutch hub, **shoes and springs on Models 620, 650,** 655 and 660 are available only as a unit assembly.

REWIND STARTER. Refer to Fig. SO34 or Fig. SO35 for an exploded view of rewind starter. To disassemble starter, remove rope handle and allow rope to rewind into starter. Remove spring clip and remove rope pulley and pawl assembly being careful not to dislodge rewind spring. If rewind spring must be removed, care should be used not to allow spring to uncoil uncontrolled. Rewind spring on Models 610 and 615 is located in starter housing while rewind spring on all other models is located in left side of rope pulley (6–Fig. SO35).

Rope length should be 85 cm (33½ in.) on Models 610 and 615 or 95 cm (37½ in.) on all other models. Install rewind spring in a clockwise direction

Fig. SO32—Exploded view of clutch used on Models 610 and 615.

1. Washer
2. Clutch shoe
3. Clutch hub
4. Spring
5. Washer
6. Felt seal
7. Needle bearing
8. Clutch drum
9. Felt seal
10. Washer
11. "E" ring

Fig. SO34—Exploded view of rewind starter used on Models 610 and 615.

1. Starter housing
2. Spring cup
3. Rewind spring
4. Rope pulley
5. Pawl
6. Slotted washers
7. Serrated washer
8. Spring clip

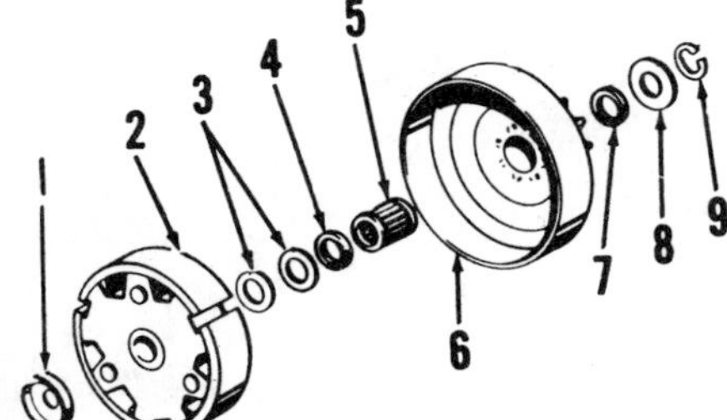

Fig. SO33—Exploded view of clutch used on Models 620, 650, 655 and 650. Clutch hub, shoes and springs are available only as a unit.

1. Cup washer
2. Clutch assy.
3. Washers
4. Felt seal
5. Needle bearing
6. Clutch drum
7. Felt seal
8. Washer
9. "E" ring

Fig. SO35—Exploded view of starter used on Models 620, 650, 655 and 660.

1. Starter housing
2. Felt seal
3. Spring cup
4. Rewind spring
5. Plate
6. Left pulley half
7. Rope
8. Right pulley half
9. Pawl
10. Felt seal
11. Slotted washer
12. Pawl hub
13. Washer
14. Serrated washer
15. Spring clip

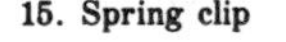

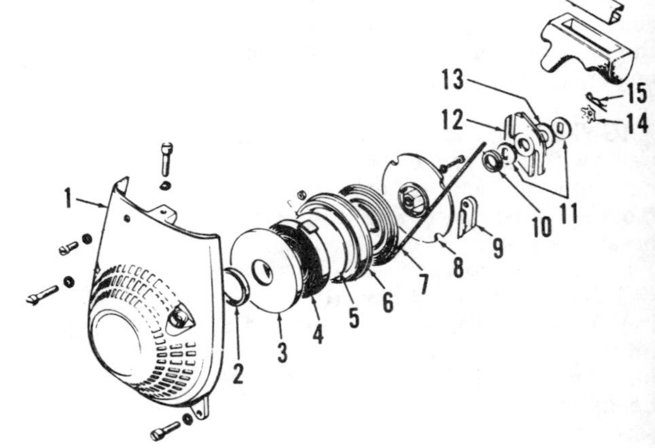

Illustrations courtesy Solo Inc.

in starter housing of Models 610 and 615 and in a counter-clockwise direction in left rope pulley half on all other models. To place tension in rewind spring, install rope pulley and pawl assembly with rope unwound, pass rope through outlet in starter housing and attach handle. Wind rope pulley in a clockwise direction without winding rope on pulley until rewind spring is coil bound. Allow pulley to unwind 1/4-1/2 turns and then allow rope to wind on pulley. Rope handle should fit snugly against rope outlet.

OIL PUMP. All models are equipped with an automatic oil pump driven by the chain sprocket. Refer to Fig. SO36 or Fig. SO37 for an exploded view of oil pump.

Oil pump used on Models 610 and 615 is driven by a series of gears. Steel gears were used on early models while later models are equipped with plastic gears. Steel and plastic gears may not be interchanged unless the whole set of gears is replaced. Drive gear (16—Fig. SO36) screws into pump driver (5) on later models with plastic gears, but is pressed into driver on early models with steel gears.

Oil pump adjuster (11) must be installed with high point towards idler gear (18). Oil pump flow may also be adjusted by turning screw in oil tank cover (1) adjacent to "MAX" letters on cover.

Models 620, 650, 655 and 660 are equipped with a worm drive reciprocating-type pump. Loctite should be applied to screw (1—Fig. SO37) threads.

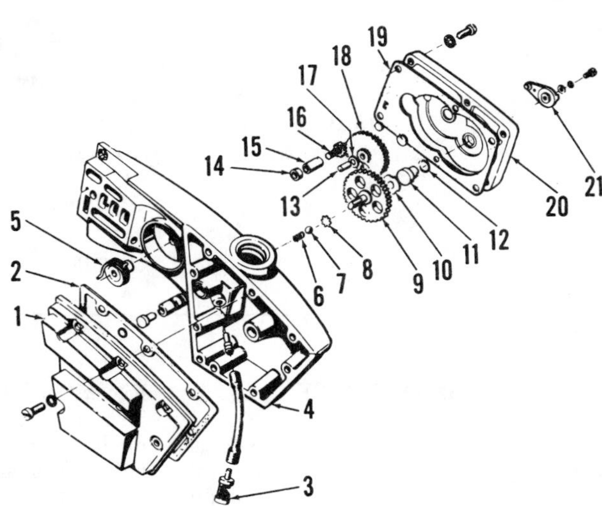

Fig. SO36—Exploded view of oil pump assembly used on Models 610 and 615.

1. Oil tank cover
2. Gasket
3. Oil pick-up
4. Oil tank housing
5. Pump driver
6. Spring
7. Check ball
8. Washer
9. Pump gear
10. Disc
11. Adjuster
12. "O" ring
13. Pin
14. Seal
15. Bushing
16. Pump drive gear
17. Washer
18. Idler gear
19. Gasket
20. Pump cover
21. Adjusting lever

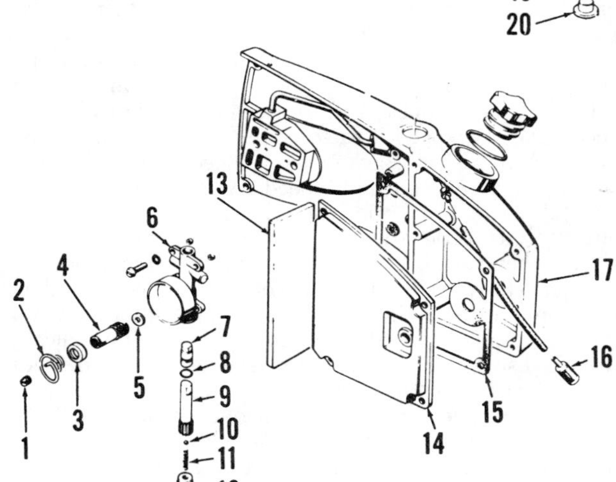

Fig. SO37—Exploded view of oil pump used on Models 620, 650, 655 and 660.

1. Set screw
2. Drive spring
3. Gasket
4. Worm
5. Washer
6. Oil pump housing
7. Beveled plug
8. "O" ring
9. Plunger
10. Ball
11. Spring
12. Plug
13. Plate
14. Oil tank cover
15. Gasket
16. Oil pick-up
17. Cover
18. Retainer
19. Washer
20. Adjuster

SOLO

Model	Bore mm (in.)	Stroke mm (in.)	Displacement cc (cu. in.)	Drive Type
647	42 (1.653)	34 (1.34)	47 (2.9)	Direct
654	45 (1.77)	34 (1.34)	54 (3.3)	Direct

MAINTENANCE

SPARK PLUG. Recommended spark plug is Bosch WSR6F or Champion RCJ64. Electrode gap should be 0.5 mm (0.020 in.).

CARBURETOR. Models 647 and 654 are equipped with either a Tillotson HU or a Walbro WT diaphragm carburetor. Refer to Tillotson or Walbro section of CARBURETOR SERVICE section for service and exploded views.

For initial adjustment, turn high speed and low speed mixture screws in until lightly seated. Back out low speed screw 1¼ turns and high speed screw one full turn. Rotate idle speed screw out until throttle valve is completely closed, then turn back in until screw tip contacts stop plus ½ turn. Make final adjustments with engine warm and running. Adjust low speed screw to obtain the highest possible rpm. Readjust idle speed screw to obtain 2,700-2,800 rpm. Adjust high speed screw so engine operation is 12,000 rpm at full throttle with no load applied. Refer to Fig. SO47 for view locating adjustment screws.

IGNITION. All models are equipped with electronic ignition system shown in Fig. SO48. Ignition timing is not adjustable. Air gap between ignition module core legs (2) and flywheel magnets (1) should be set at 0.2-0.3 mm (0.08-0.12 in.).

LUBRICATION. Engine is lubricated by mixing oil with gasoline. Recommended oil is Castrol Super TT or Castrol TTS mixed at a 40:1 ratio during break-in period and normal operation. If Castrol Super TT or Castrol TTS is not available, use a good quality oil designed for use in air-cooled two-stroke engines mixed at a 20:1 ratio during break-in period and a 25:1 ratio for normal operation.

Models 647 and 654 are equipped with an adjustable, automatic, gear driven oil pump. Refer to Fig. SO49. Clean automotive oil may be used with viscosity determined by ambient conditions.

Periodically the needle roller bearing in clutch drum should be removed, cleaned and lubricated with MOBILTEM 78 or an equivalent high temperature grease.

REPAIRS

PISTON, PIN, RINGS, AND CYLINDER. Model 647 is equipped with an aluminum cylinder with a steel sleeve. There are two sizes of pistons and cylinders available. The standard size will have a "N" stamped on cylinder head while the piston will be unmarked. Oversize piston and cylinder will have a "U" stamped on the cylinder head and piston crown. Only piston and cylinder which corresponds should be used together.

The cylinder wall on Model 654 is Nikasil impregnated. Three sizes of pistons and cylinders are available. The pistons and cylinders are identified with the markings "A," "B" or "C" stamped on the cylinder head and piston crown with "A" being the smallest and "C" being the largest. On new assemblies, a piston marked "A" can be used in a cylinder marked "A" or "B." A piston marked "B" can be used in a cylinder marked "B" or "C."

Piston marked "C" can only be used in a cylinder marked "C." When installing a used cylinder, a piston marked "A" can

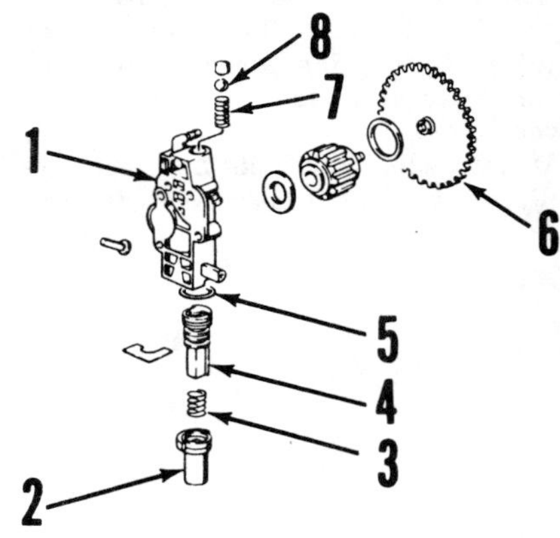

Fig. SO49—Exploded view of oil pump assembly.

1. Pump body
2. Adjuster
3. Spring
4. Intermediate adjuster
5. "O" ring
6. Driven gear
7. Spring
8. Check ball

Fig. SO47—Idle speed screw is accessible through opening (S). High speed mixture screw and low speed mixture screw are accessible through opening (M). "L" and "H" on side cover identify location of screws.

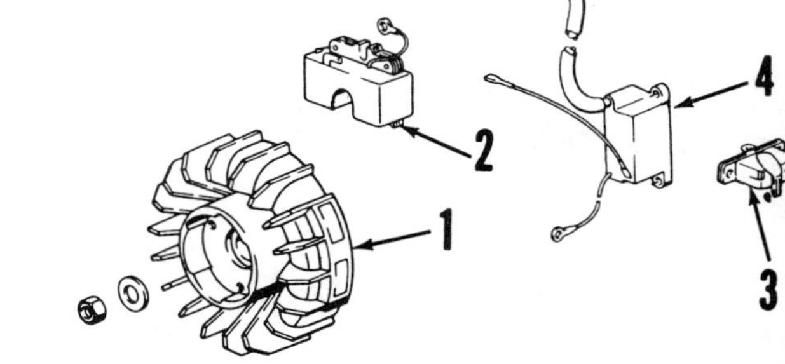

Fig. SO48—Exploded view of electronic ignition system.

1. Flywheel
2. Ignition module
3. Ignition switch
4. Ignition coil

Illustrations courtesy Solo Inc.

be used in a cylinder marked "A" or "B." A piston marked "B" can be used in a cylinder marked "A," "B" or "C." Pistons marked "C" can be used in a cylinder marked "B" or "C." Locating pins are used in piston ring grooves to prevent piston ring rotation. Be sure ring end gaps are around locating pins when installing cylinder. Install piston with arrow on piston crown pointing toward exhaust port. Refer to Fig. SO50 for exploded view of engine assembly.

CRANKSHAFT, CONNECTING ROD AND CRANKCASE. Crankshaft is supported by two ball bearings pressed on the crankshaft. Ball bearings (10 – Fig. SO50) must be removed using a jaw type bearing puller. Once a bearing has been removed, the bearing should be discarded and a new one installed. Crankshaft and connecting rod are available as a unit assembly only and should not be disassembled.

CLUTCH. All models are equipped with a three-shoe centrifugal clutch. Clutch hub is threaded with left-hand threads. Clutch drum rides on needle roller bearing (6 – Fig. SO51) and drives oil pump. Clutch hub, shoes and spring are available as a unit assembly only.

REWIND STARTER. To disassemble starter, extend rope until one full turn is unwound. Pull slack rope back through rope guide and carefully let pulley (4 – Fig. SO52) unwind, unloading tension on rewind spring (2). After removing spring clip (6), starter pawl (7), washer (5) and rope pulley (4) can be lifted off starter assembly. If rewind spring (2) is to be removed, care should be taken not to let rewind spring unwind uncontrolled. Install rewind spring (2) into spring cup (3) in a clockwise direction starting with outer coil. Install rewind spring and spring cup into starter housing making sure hook in outer coil engages notch in starter housing.

Starter rope length should be 90 cm (35.4 in.). To install starter rope, wind four turns of rope onto rope pulley and lay pulley on spring cup making sure hook on inner spring coil engages notch in pulley. Install starter pawl (7), washer (5) and spring clip (6). Insert rope into notch on pulley and rotate a pulley approximately 1½ turns in a clockwise direction to apply tension on rewind spring. Carefully let pulley rewind to retract rope. Rope tension is correct if rope pulley is able to tighten one full turn after rope is fully extended.

OIL PUMP. Models 647 and 654 are equipped with an adjustable, automatic, piston type pump. The oil pump is driven by a drive gear on chain sprocket (9 – Fig. SO51).

CHAIN BRAKE. Models 647 and 654 are equipped with a chain brake system designed to stop chain movement should kickback occur. The chain brake is activated when the operator's hand strikes chain brake lever (1 – Fig. SO53) tripping lock lever (4) and releasing spring (5) and plunger (2) pulling brake band (8) tight around clutch drum. Pull back chain brake lever to reset mechanism.

If disassembly is required, chain brake must be in off position before chain guard can be removed. Inspect lock lever and plunger for excessive wear

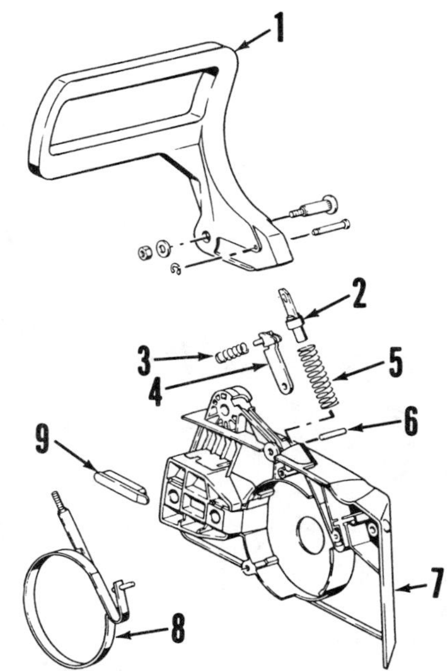

Fig. SO53 — Exploded view of chain brake system.

1. Chain brake lever
2. Plunger
3. Spring
4. Lock lever
5. Spring
6. Pin
7. Chain guard
8. Brake band
9. Guide shoe

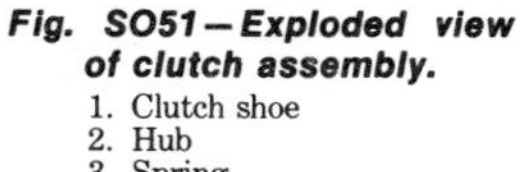

Fig. SO51 — Exploded view of clutch assembly.

1. Clutch shoe
2. Hub
3. Spring
4. Washer
5. Felt ring
6. Needle roller bearing
7. Clutch drum
8. Washer
9. Oil pump drive gear
10. Washer

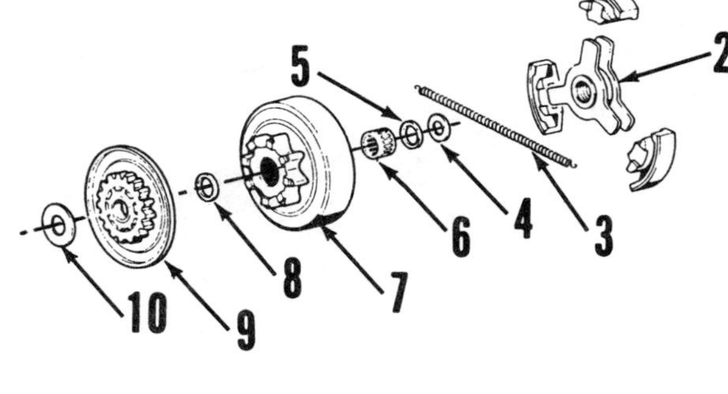

Fig. SO50 — Exploded view of engine assembly.

1. Cylinder
2. Muffler
3. Gasket
4. Cover
5. Piston ring
6. Piston
7. Crankshaft & connecting rod assy.
8. Crankshaft seal
9. Washer
10. Ball bearing
11. Crankcase half
12. Needle roller bearing
13. Piston pin
14. Pin retainer

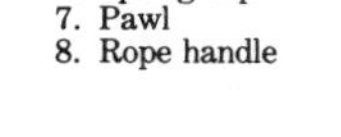

Fig. SO52 — Exploded view of starter assembly.

1. Starter housing
2. Rewind spring
3. Spring cup
4. Rope pulley
5. Washer
6. Spring clip
7. Pawl
8. Rope handle

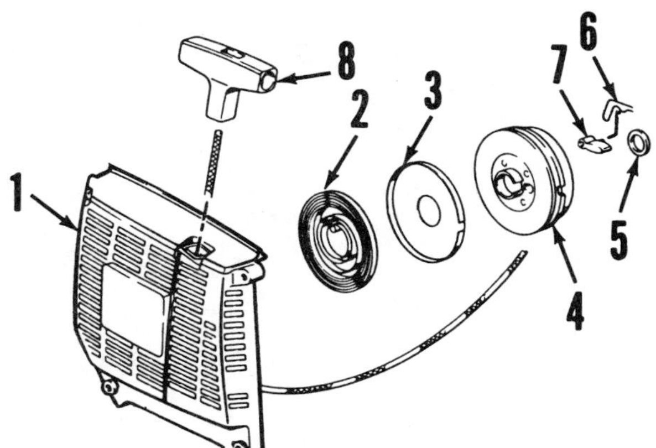

Illustrations courtesy Solo Inc.

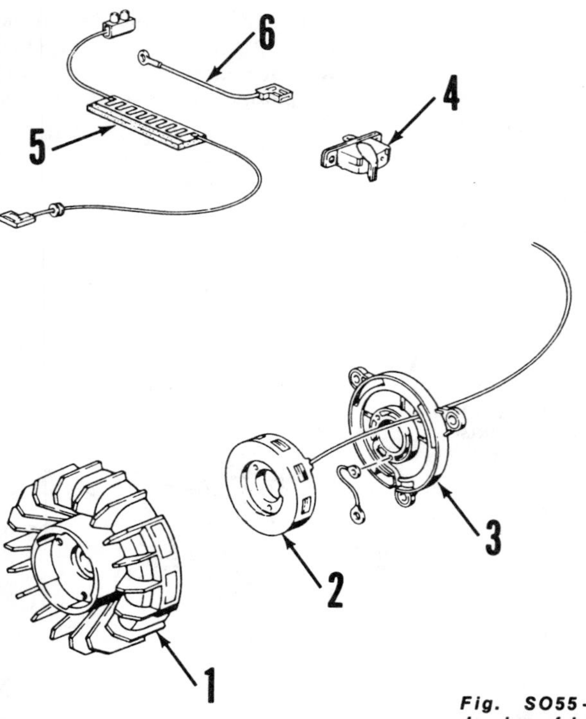

Fig. SO54—Exploded view of handle heating system on models so equipped.

1. Flywheel
2. Generator
3. Generator seat
4. Switch
5. Heating element
6. Lead

and renew if necessary. To remove plunger (2), trip lock lever (4) with a screwdriver. Use caution when releasing spring as spring is under high load. When reassembling plunger (2), screw plunger into connector 7-9 full turns. The brake band must come in contact with the retaining edges of spring seat. If not, screw plunger in or out to adjust.

To test chain brake adjustment, position assembly in a soft-jawed vise so handle is parallel with top of vise jaws. The chain brake should engage when a weight of 4.4 kg (9.7 lbs.) is suspended from the chain brake lever. If engagement is above or below this specification, inspect for worn lock lever and plunger or weak or broken spring. Renew components as necessary.

HEATED HANDLE. Some models are equipped with a front and rear handle heating system. Generating coil (2–Fig. SO54) located under the flywheel provides an electrical current to heating coils (5) in front and rear handles. The heating coils are wired in series. Switch (4) opens or closes a common ground. Refer to Fig. SO55 for schematic drawing.

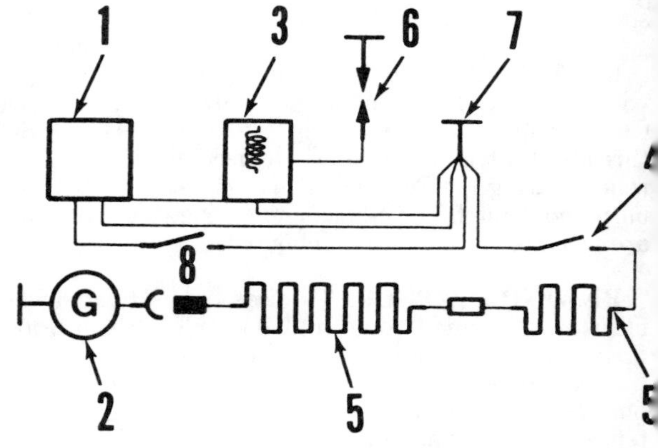

Fig. SO55—Schematic drawing of ignition system and handle heating system on models so equipped.

1. Ignition module
2. Generator
3. Ignition coil
4. Heater switch
5. Heating elements
6. Spark plug
7. Ground connection
8. Ignition switch

SOLO

Model	Bore mm (in.)	Stroke mm (in.)	Displacement cc (cu. in.)	Drive Type
603, 603W	56 (2.2)	42 (1.653)	103 (6.3)	Direct
644	42 (1.653)	32 (1.26)	44.3 (2.7)	Direct
651	45 (1.77)	32 (1.26)	51 (3.1)	Direct
662	46 (1.81)	38 (1.5)	63 (3.84)	Direct
667, 667W	48 (1.89)	38 (1.5)	69 (4.2)	Direct
670, 670W	48 (1.89)	38 (1.5)	69 (4.2)	Direct
680, 680W	52 (2.05)	38 (1.5)	81 (5.0)	Direct
690	54 (2.125)	40 (1.575)	91 (5.6)	Direct

MAINTENANCE

SPARK PLUG. Recommended spark plug is Bosch WSR6F or Champion RCJ6Y. Spark plug electrode gap should be 0.5 mm (0.020 in.) for all models.

CARBURETOR. Model 644 is equipped with either a Walbro HDA or Zama C3A diaphragm type carburetor. Model 651 is equipped with a Walbro HDA diaphragm type carburetor. All other models are equipped with either a Walbro WJ3 or a Tillotson diaphragm type carburetor. Refer to CARBURETOR SERVICE section for service procedures and exploded views.

For initial carburetor adjustment, screw in the low-speed and high-speed mixture screws (Fig. SO65) until lightly seated. Then, turn both mixture screws out 1 to 1-1/4 turns. Final adjustment should be made with engine running at operating temperature.

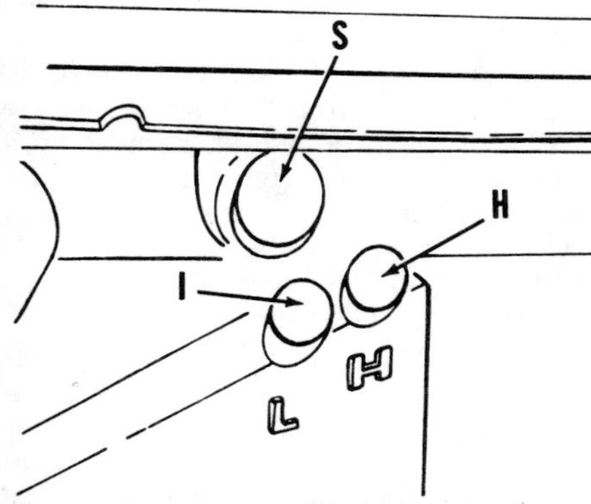

Fig. SO65—View identifying location of idle speed screw (S), low-speed mixture screw (I) and high-speed mixture screw (H).

Turn idle speed screw (S) until engine idles just below clutch engagement speed. Adjust low speed mixture screw (I) to obtain highest possible rpm, then turn screw out slightly until rpm begins to drop. Accelerate engine several times. If engine seems sluggish or stumbles, adjust idle mixture screw until engine accelerates without stumbling. Readjust idle speed screw as necessary so chain does not move when engine is idling.

Operate engine at full throttle with no load (bar and chain installed). Turn high-speed mixture screw (H) clockwise until maximum engine speed is obtained and four-stroking sound stops. Then, turn high-speed mixture screw counterclockwise until four-stroking sound just returns. The following specified maximum no-load engine rpm (with bar and chain installed) must not be exceeded: 11,500 rpm for Model 603; 13,500 rpm for Models 644 and 651; 12,000 rpm for Models 662, 667, 670, 680 and 690. Do not operate saw with high-speed mixture too lean as engine damage may result from lack of lubrication and overheating.

IGNITION. All models are equipped with an electronic ignition system. Ignition timing is not adjustable. No periodic maintenance is required on the ignition system. Refer to Fig. SO66 for exploded view of ignition system components typical of all models.

Air gap between the ignition coil lamination and flywheel magnets should be 0.2-0.3 mm (0.008-0.012 in.). Loosen ignition module mounting screws and move module as necessary to obtain correct air gap.

LUBRICATION. The engine is lubricated by oil mixed with the gasoline fuel. The recommended oil is Solo Superior 2-cycle oil or Castrol Super TT 2-cycle oil mixed at a 40:1 ratio. If recommended oil is not available, a good quality oil designed for use in

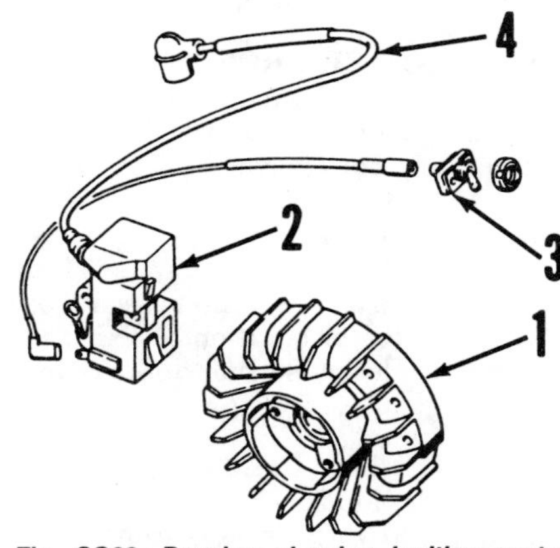

Fig. SO66—Drawing showing ignition system components typical of all models.

1. Flywheel
2. Ignition coil
3. Ignition switch
4. Spark plug lead

Illustrations courtesy Solo Inc.

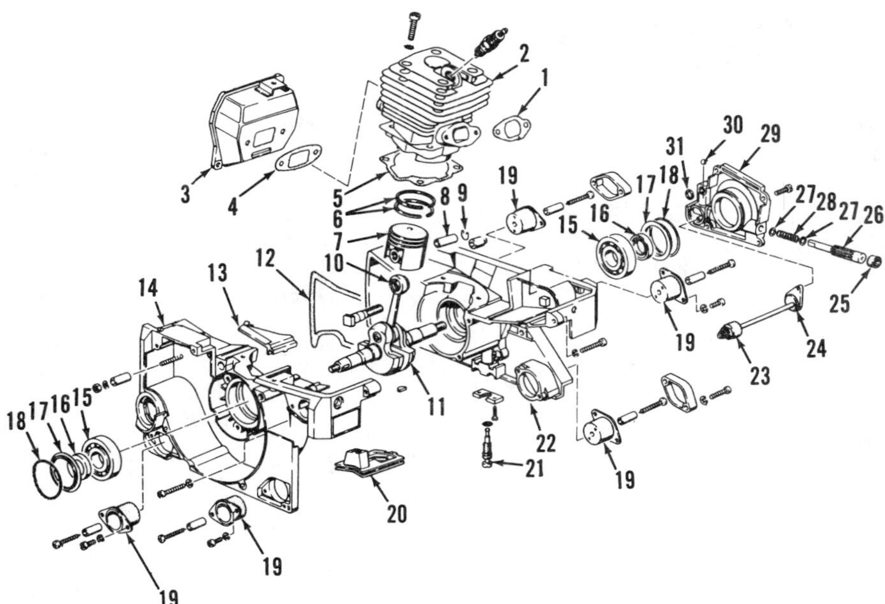

Fig. SO67—Exploded view of engine assembly typical of Models 670, 680 and 603. Other models are similar.

1. Intake gasket
2. Cylinder
3. Muffler
4. Exhaust gasket
5. Cylinder gasket
6. Piston rings
7. Piston
8. Piston pin
9. Retaining ring
10. Needle bearing
11. Crankshaft assy.
12. Gasket
13. Air guide
14. Crankcase half
15. Ball bearings
16. Seals
17. Support washer
18. "O" ring
19. Vibration cushions
20. Seal plate
21. Oil adjusting screw
22. Crankcase half
23. Strainer
24. Oil pick-up tube
25. Plug
26. Piston
27. Washers
28. Spring
29. Oil pump housing
30. Ball
31. "O" ring

air-cooled, two-stroke engines may be used mixed at a 25:1 ratio.

All models are equipped with an automatic guide bar and chain oiling system. A piston type pump is used to supply oil to the oiling system. The oil pump is driven by a worm gear located inside the clutch drum. The oil pump is actuated only when the clutch and chain are rotating.

It is recommended that oil designed for bar and chain lubrication be used. Oil pump output is adjustable by turning the adjuster screw (21—Fig. SO67) located on bottom of saw on clutch side.

REPAIRS

CRANKCASE PRESSURE TEST. An improperly sealed crankcase can cause the engine to be hard to start, run rough, have low power and overheat. Refer to ENGINE SERVICE section of this manual for crankcase pressure test procedure. If crankcase leakage is indicated, pressurize the crankcase and use a soap and water solution to check the gaskets, seals, pulse line and castings for leakage.

CYLINDER, PISTON, RINGS AND PIN. Models 644, 651 and 667 are equipped with an aluminum cylinder with Nikasil impregnated cylinder walls. Model 662 is equipped with an aluminum cylinder with a steel sleeve.

Models 662 and 667 have two sizes of pistons and cylinder assemblies available. Standard size assemblies will have a "N" stamped on the cylinder head, but the piston will be unmarked. Oversize assemblies will have a "U" stamped on the cylinder head and the piston crown. Only the piston and cylinder that correspond should be used together.

Models 603, 670 and 680 are equipped with Nikasil impregnated cylinder walls. Three sizes of piston and cylinder assemblies are available. Size designations are identified by letters "A, B or C," which will be stamped on cylinder and piston crown.

When using new piston and cylinder, piston marked "A" or "B" can be used in cylinder marked "A" or "B." Piston "B" can be used in cylinder marked "B" or "C." Piston marked "C" can be used only in cylinders marked "C."

When installing a new piston in a used cylinder, piston marked "A" can be used in cylinder marked "A" or "B." Piston marked "B" can be used in cylinder marked "A," "B" or "C." Piston marked "C" can be used in cylinder marked "B" or "C."

To remove cylinder and piston, remove top cover, starter housing and air guide. Unbolt and remove air cleaner, carburetor and muffler. Remove four screws attaching cylinder to crankcase, then withdraw the cylinder (2—Fig. SO67) from the piston (7). Remove piston pin retaining rings (9) and push piston pin (8) out of piston. Be careful not to apply side force to connecting rod when removing the piston pin. Remove piston and needle bearing from connecting rod.

When reassembling, note that retaining rings (9—Fig. SO67) should be renewed if removed from piston. Install retaining rings with open end facing either towards the top or bottom of the piston. Install piston on connecting rod so arrow on piston crown points toward the exhaust port.

Locating pins are present in the piston ring grooves to prevent ring rotation. Make certain that ring end gaps are properly positioned around the locating pins before installing the cylinder.

Lubricate the piston, rings and cylinder bore with engine oil. Position a new gasket (5) on the crankcase. Align the exhaust port with the arrow on top of piston, then slide the cylinder over the piston while compressing the piston rings. The piston may be rocked back and forth while fitting it over the piston rings. But, do not rotate the cylinder, as the piston rings may become disengaged from the locating pins, resulting in damage to the rings, piston and cylinder.

CRANKSHAFT, CONNECTING ROD AND CRANKCASE. To remove crankshaft assembly (11—Fig. SO67), the crankcase halves (14 and 22) must be separated. Remove top cover, starter housing, air guide, chain guard and chain brake assembly, chain, and guide bar. Unbolt and remove muffler, air filter assembly, carburetor, intake manifold, rear handle with throttle control, front handle bar, anti-vibration cushions and main housing and fuel tank assembly.

Remove spark plug and install piston stop tool or insert the end of a rope into spark plug hole to lock the piston and crankshaft. Remove flywheel nut (right-hand threads). Use Solo tool 00 80 460 or other suitable puller to remove flywheel from crankshaft. Remove ignition coil. Remove clutch drum, then unscrew clutch hub from crankshaft. Note that clutch hub has left-hand threads (turn clockwise to remove). Unbolt and remove chain oil pump.

Remove cylinder and piston as previously outlined. Remove screws attaching crankcase halves, then use a puller to separate crankcase halves from crankshaft assembly. If main bearings (15) remain on the crankshaft, use a puller to remove them. If main bearings remain in crankcase halves, use suitable driver to press bearings out of crankcase. Main bearings should be renewed whenever they are removed from crankshaft or crankcase.

Crankshaft and connecting rod are a unit assembly and should not be disassembled. Check rotation of connecting rod on crankpin. If roughness is noted, renew crankshaft and connecting rod assembly. The upper end of connecting rod is equipped with a renewable needle bearing (10).

To install main bearings on crankshaft, heat bearings to approximately 120 degrees C (250 degrees F) using either an oven or hot oil bath. Do not use an open flame to heat bearings. The crankcase halves will require heating to approximately 180 degres C (350 degrees F). Be sure to remove all plastic and rubber parts before heating crankcase halves.

To insure proper alignment of crankshaft during assembly, attach special tool 00 80 462 or suitable equivalent in bearing opening on flywheel side of crankcase. Assemble crankshaft, bearings and crankcase halves and tighten mounting screws evenly to 6 N•m (52 in.-lbs.). Make certain that crankshaft turns freely and that the counterweights do not contact crankcase. Complete installation by reversing the removal procedure.

CLUTCH. All models are equipped with a three-shoe centrifugal clutch similar to clutch shown in Fig. SO68. The clutch drum (7) rides on needle roller bearing (6). The clutch hub drives the worm gear (8), which in turn drives the chain oil pump.

Clutch hub (1) is threaded on crankshaft with left-hand threads (turn clockwise to remove). Use special Solo tool 00 80 456 or insert the end of a rope in spark plug hole to prevent crankshaft from turning while removing the clutch hub. Inspect clutch drum (7) and shoes (2) for excessive wear or evidence of overheating and renew as necessary.

When assembling clutch, be sure that spring (3) end hooks are positioned in the open area between two clutch shoes (2). Lubricate needle bearing with high temperature grease. Tighten clutch hub to 40 N•m (30 ft.-lbs.).

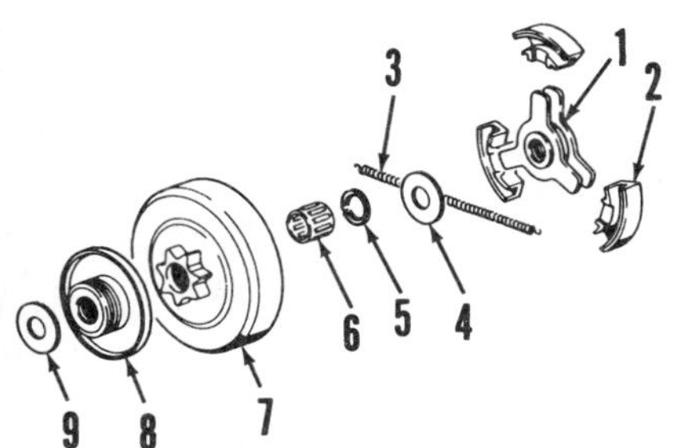

Fig. SO68—Exploded view of typical clutch assembly. Some models may differ slightly. Worm gear (8) drives the chain oil pump.

1. Clutch hub
2. Clutch shoes
3. Spring
4. Washer
5. Gasket
6. Needle bearing
7. Clutch drum
8. Worm gear
9. Washer

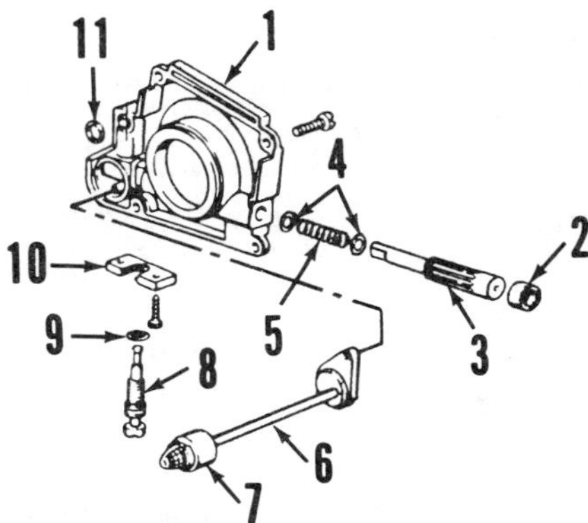

Fig. SO69—Exploded view of automatic chain oil pump assembly.

1. Pump housing
2. Plug
3. Piston
4. Washers
5. Spring
6. Oil pick-up tube
7. Oil strainer
8. Adjuster
9. "O" ring
10. Adjuster check plate
11. "O" ring

OIL PUMP. All models are equipped with a piston type, automatic oil pump. A worm gear (8–Fig. SO68), which is driven by clutch drum (7), drives the oil pump. Therefore, oil is delivered only when the clutch is engaged and the chain is revolving.

Oil pump output is adjustable. The adjuster (8—Fig. SO69) is located on the bottom of the saw on the clutch side.

The oil pump is accessible after removing the clutch assembly as previously outlined. Remove oil flow adjuster (8), then unbolt and remove the oil pump housing (1). Remove piston (3) from housing and check for wear, scoring or other damage. Oil pump components are available separately.

CHAIN BRAKE. All models are equipped with a chain brake system designed to stop chain movement should saw kickback occur. The chain brake is activated when the operator's hand strikes the chain hand guard (1—Fig. SO70). Forward movement of the hand guard trips the lock lever (4), which releases the spring (5) and plunger, allowing the brake band (10) to be pulled tightly around the clutch drum. Pull hand guard rearward to reset the brake mechanism.

To disassemble the chain brake, first pull the hand guard rearward to disengage the brake. Remove the chain guard (9—Fig. SO70) and brake assembly. Push hand guard or trip the lock lever (4) with a screwdriver to engage the brake and relieve spring tension. Remove the brake cover (11) and hand guard. Carefully pry brake band (10), spring (5) and plunger (2) from chain guard. Inspect all parts for wear or damage and renew as necessary.

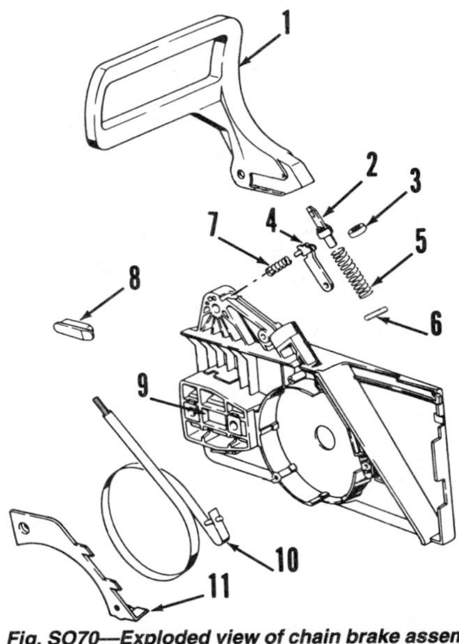

Fig. SO70—Exploded view of chain brake assembly typical of all models.

1. Hand guard
2. Plunger
3. Spacer
4. Lock lever
5. Spring
6. Pin
7. Spring
8. Guide shoe
9. Chain guard
10. Brake band
11. Chain brake cover

When reassembling, screw plunger (2) into brake band connector five full turns. Make sure that beveled edge of plunger is facing opposite of lock lever (4). The brake band must come in contact with retaining edges of spring seat. If not, adjust by changing depth of plunger.

To test chain brake assembly, position assembly in a soft-jawed vise so that handle is parallel with top of vise jaws. The chain brake should engage when a weight of 4 kg (8.8 lbs.) is suspended from the chain hand guard (1). If above or below this specification, check for excessive wear on lock lever and plunger. Also check for weak or broken springs. Renew components as necessary.

REWIND STARTER. To disassemble starter, unbolt and remove starter housing from saw. Remove rope handle and allow rope pulley (4—Fig. SO71) to turn slowly counterclockwise to release spring tension. Remove spring clip (8), pawl plate (7) and rope pulley (4). If rewind spring (2) must be removed, care should be used not to allow the spring to uncoil uncontrolled.

A new replacement rewind spring will come pre-wound in a new cup (3). Lightly lubricate the rewind spring and

Illustrations courtesy Solo Inc.

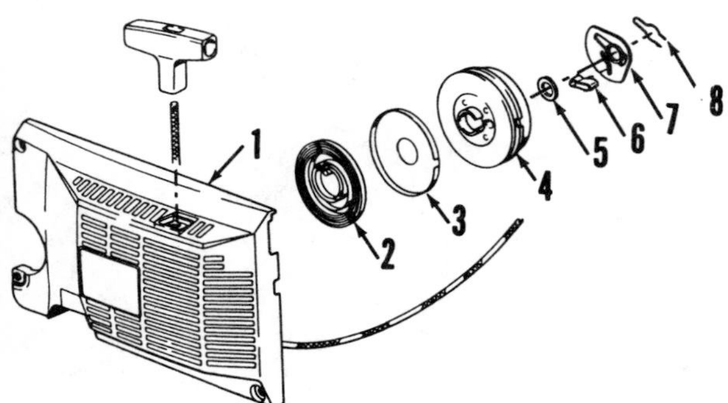

Fig. SO71—Exploded view of starter assembly typical of all models.

1. Starter housing
2. Rewind spring
3. Spring cup
4. Rope pulley
5. Washer
6. Starter pawl
7. Plate
8. Spring clip

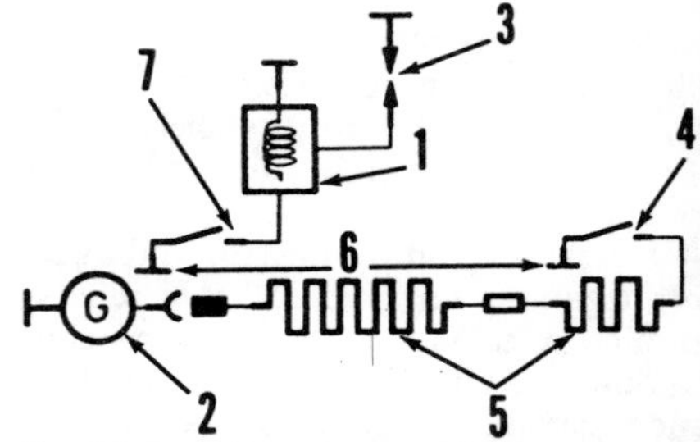

Fig. SO73—Schematic drawing of ignition system and handle heating system on models so equipped.

1. Ignition module
2. Generator
3. Spark plug
4. Heater switch
5. Heating coils
6. Ground connection
7. Stop switch

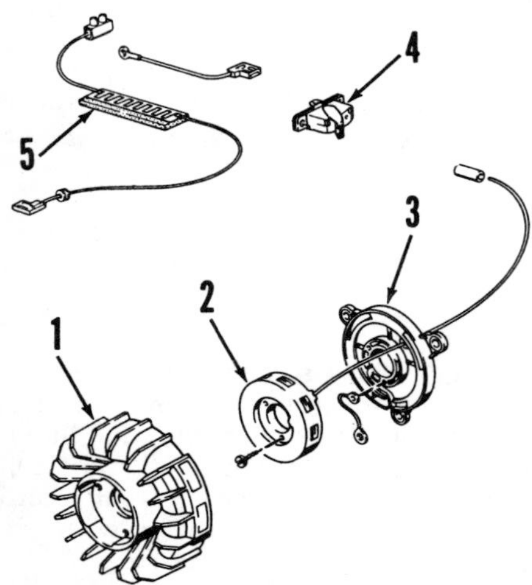

Fig. SO72—Exploded view of handle heating system used on some models.

1. Flywheel
2. Generator
3. Generator seat
4. Switch
5. Heating coil

starter shaft with oil, then place spring into starter housing. Make sure that hook in outer coil engages notch in starter housing. If the rewind spring becomes disengaged from the case, wind spring in the case in a counterclockwise direction working from the outside towards the inside.

New starter rope should be 110 cm (43 in.) long and 4.0 mm (5/32 in.) in diameter. Wind rope approximately five turns on pulley in a clockwise direction (as viewed from flywheel side of pulley). Place pulley onto spring case making sure that the hook on the inside coil engages the notch in pulley hub. Install thrust washer (5) pawl holder (7) and spring clip (8).

Insert rope into recess in pulley and preload spring by turning pulley approximately two turns clockwise. Thread the rope through opening in starter housing and attach rope handle.

Rewind spring tension is correct if rope handle is pulled snugly against starter housing with rope fully retracted and if pulley will rotate at least an additional half turn with rope fully extended. If rewind spring binds before the rope is fully extended, reduce tension on rope by pulling rope up into notch in rope pulley and allowing pulley to unwind partially. Recheck starter operation.

HEATED HANDLES. Some models may be equipped with front and rear handle heating system. A generating coil (2—Fig. SO72) located behind the flywheel provides an electrical current to the heating coils (5) enclosed in the front and rear handles. The heating coils are wired in series. Switch (4) opens or closes a common ground.

Refer to Fig. SO73 for a schematic drawing of the heating electrical system. If heater malfunction occurs, use an ohmmeter to check generating coil, heating elements and connecting wires for open or short circuits.

Illustrations courtesy Solo Inc.

SOLO

Model	Bore	Stroke	Displ.	Drive Type
639	39 mm	32 mm	39 cc	Direct
645	42 mm	32 mm	45 cc	Direct

MAINTENANCE

SPARK PLUG. Recommended spark plug is Bosch WSR6F or Champion RCJ-6Y. Electrode gap should be 0.5 mm (0.020 in.).

CARBURETOR. Both models are equipped with a Walbro HDA127 carburetor. Refer to Walbro section of CARBURETOR SERVICE section for service procedures and exploded views.

Initial adjustment (turns open from a lightly seated position) for the low-speed mixture screw (4—Fig. SO80) and high-speed mixture screw (5) is 1-1/4 turns. Make final adjustment with engine warm and running.

Adjust idle speed screw (6) so engine idles just below clutch engagement speed (approximately 2800 rpm).

Adjust low-speed mixture screw to obtain maximum engine rpm, then turn screw out (counterclockwise) 1/8 to 1/4 turn. Engine should accelerate cleanly without hesitation. If engine stumbles or seems sluggish when accelerating, adjust low-speed mixture screw until engine accelerates cleanly. Readjust idle speed screw if necessary. Chain must not move when engine is idling.

High-speed mixture screw should be adjusted to obtain optimum performance with saw under cutting load. Do not adjust high-speed mixture screw too lean (turned too far clockwise) as maximum permissible engine speed may be exceeded and engine may be damaged from lack of lubrication and overheating. Maximum no-load speed (with bar and chain installed) must not exceed 11,600 rpm.

To remove carburetor, remove engine cover. Remove air filter housing mounting screws and filter housing (15—Fig. SO80). Disconnect fuel hose and throttle rod, then withdraw carburetor. Refer to Fig. SO81 for illustration of fuel tank throttle control linkage.

IGNITION. All models are equipped with a breakerless electronic ignition system. Ignition timing is not adjustable. Air gap between ignition coil assembly and flywheel magnets should be 0.20-0.30 mm (0.008-0.012 in.). To adjust, loosen module mounting screws and move module as necessary.

LUBRICATION. The engine is lubricated by oil mixed with the gasoline fuel. The recommended oil is Solo Superior 2-cycle oil mixed at a 40:1 ratio. If Solo Superior oil is not available, a good quality oil designed for use in air-cooled, two-stroke engines may be used mixed at a ratio of 25:1.

All models are equipped with an automatic bar and chain oiling system. A piston type oil pump is used to supply the lubricating oil. The pump is driven by the clutch and is operational only when the clutch is engaged and the chain is moving. Oil output is adjustable by turning the adjuster screw located on bottom of saw on clutch side. Turning the adjuster counterclockwise increases the oil pump output.

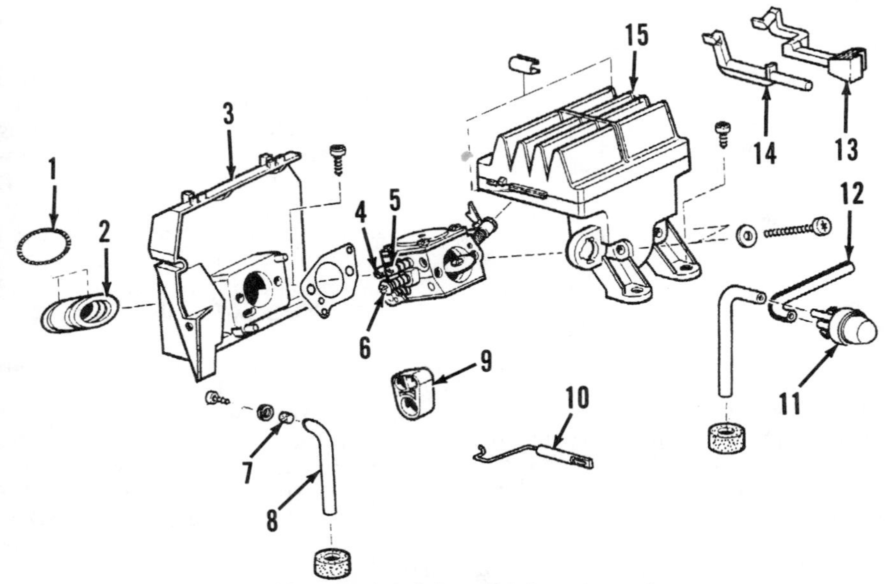

Fig. SO80—Exploded view of intake components.

1. Retaining ring
2. Intake hose
3. Intake manifold
4. Low-speed mixture screw
5. High-speed mixture screw
6. Idle speed screw
7. Filter
8. Vent tube
9. Adjustment screw guide
10. Throttle link
11. Primer bulb
12. Fuel line
13. Choke lever
14. Fast idle lever
15. Air filter housing

REPAIRS

CRANKCASE PRESSURE TEST. An improperly sealed crankcase can cause the engine to be hard to start, run rough, have low power and overheat. Refer to ENGINE SERVICE section of this manual for crankcase pressure test procedure. If crankcase leakage is indicated, pressurize the crankcase and use a soap and water solution to check the gaskets, seals, pulse line and castings for leakage.

CYLINDER, PISTON, RINGS AND PIN. To remove cylinder and piston, remove engine cover and starter housing. Unbolt and remove the ignition module, air filter housing, carburetor and muffler. Remove cylinder mounting screws (15—Fig. SO82) and withdraw cylinder (2). Remove retaining ring (8) and push piston pin (7) out of piston (5). Be careful not to apply side force to connecting rod when removing the piston pin. Separate the piston and needle bearing (9) from the connecting rod.

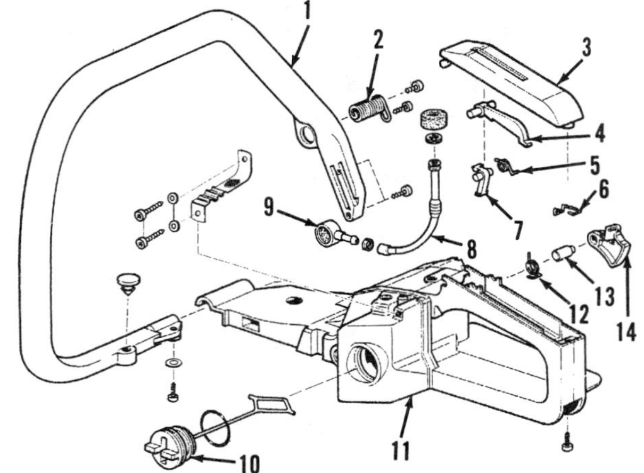

Fig. SO81—Exploded view of rear handle and throttle controls.

1. Handle bar
2. Vibration damper
3. Handle cap
4. Safety lever
5. Spring
6. Throttle link
7. Lock lever
8. Fuel suction hose
9. Filter
10. Fuel tank cap
11. Fuel tank/handle assy.
12. Return spring
13. Pin
14. Throttle lever

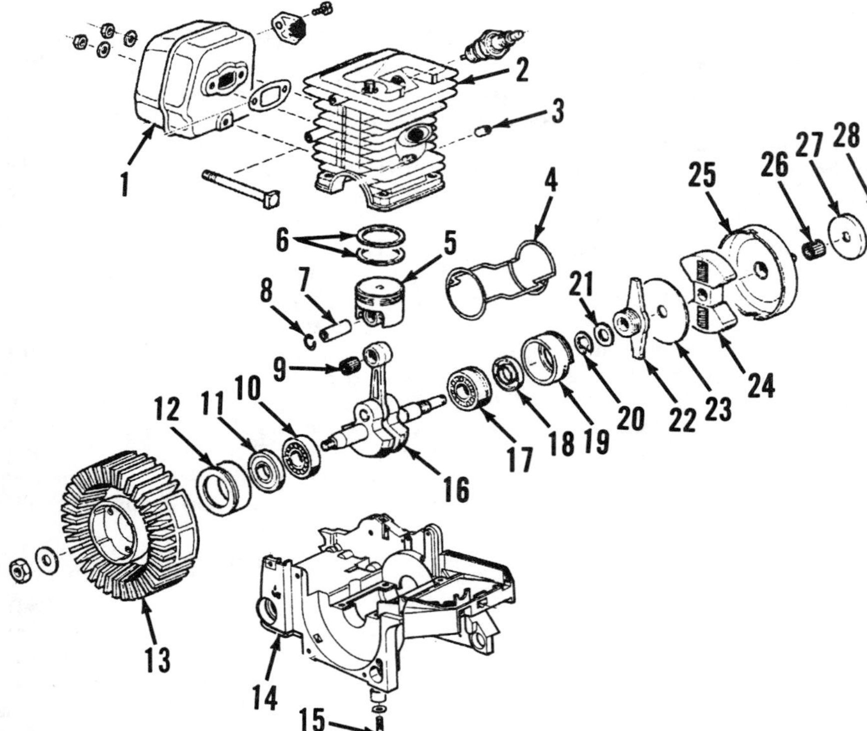

Fig. SO82—Exploded view of engine and clutch components typical of all models.

1. Muffler
2. Cylinder
3. Impulse tube
4. Gasket
5. Piston
6. Piston rings
7. Piston pin
8. Retaining ring (2)
9. Needle bearing
10. Main bearing
11. Seal
12. Bearing sleeve
13. Flywheel
14. Crankcase/engine housing
15. Cap screw (4)
16. Crankshaft & connecting rod assy.
17. Main bearing
18. Seal
19. Bearing sleeve
20. Snap ring
21. Thrust washer
22. Worm gear
23. Dust shield
24. Clutch hub & shoes
25. Clutch drum
26. Needle bearing
27. Washer
28. Snap ring

Inspect piston and cylinder bore for scratches, scoring or other damage and renew as needed.

When reassembling, note that wire retaining rings (8—Fig. SO82) should be renewed if removed from piston. Install retaining rings with open end facing either towards the top or bottom of the piston. Install piston on connecting rod so arrow on piston crown points toward the exhaust port.

Locating pins are present in the piston ring grooves to prevent ring rotation. Make certain that ring end gaps are properly positioned around the locating pins before installing the cylinder.

Lubricate piston and cylinder bore with engine oil. Align the exhaust port with the arrow on top of piston, then slide cylinder over the piston. Do not rotate the cylinder when installing as the piston rings may become disengaged from the locating pins, resulting in damage to the rings, piston and cylinder. Make certain that impulse tube (3) and intake hose (2—Fig. SO80) are properly connected to the intake manifold (3).

CRANKSHAFT AND CONNECTING ROD. To remove crankshaft and connecting rod (16—Fig. SO82), remove top handle bar, engine cover, starter housing, chain guard, bar and chain. Remove chain brake assembly. Unbolt and remove air filter housing, carburetor, intake manifold and muffler. Remove spark plug and install a suitable piston stop tool or insert the end of a rope in spark plug hole to prevent the crankshaft from rotating. Remove flywheel nut (right-hand threads) and pull flywheel from crankshaft using a suitable puller. Remove ignition module. Remove snap ring (28—Fig. SO82), dust cover (27) and clutch drum (25). Note that clutch hub (24) has left-hand threads (turn clockwise to remove). Unscrew clutch hub and remove dust shield (23), oil pump drive worm (22), thrust washer (21) and snap ring (20). Unbolt and remove the oil pump assembly. Remove the four cylinder mounting cap screws (15—Fig. SO82) and withdraw cylinder and crankshaft as an assembly from crankcase/engine housing (14).

Separate cylinder and piston from crankshaft and connecting rod. Remove bearing sleeves (12 and 19) and seals (11 and 18). Check main bearings (10 and 17) for roughness, excessive play or other damage. Main bearings should be renewed if removed from the crankshaft.

Crankshaft and connecting rod are a unit assembly and should not be disassembled. Check rotation of connecting rod on crankpin. If roughness or excessive play is noted, renew crankshaft and connecting rod assembly. The upper end of connecting rod is equipped with a needle bearing (9).

Reassemble using new seals (11 and 18—Fig. SO82) and gasket (4).

CLUTCH. A two-shoe centrifugal clutch is used on all models. To remove the clutch, remove chain guard, bar and chain. Remove the engine cover. Remove the spark plug and install a suitable piston stop tool or insert the end of a rope in spark plug hole to prevent crankshaft from rotating. Remove snap ring (28—Fig. SO82), washer (27), clutch drum (25) and needle bearing (26). Clutch hub (24) has left-hand threads (turn clockwise to remove). Unscrew clutch hub from crankshaft.

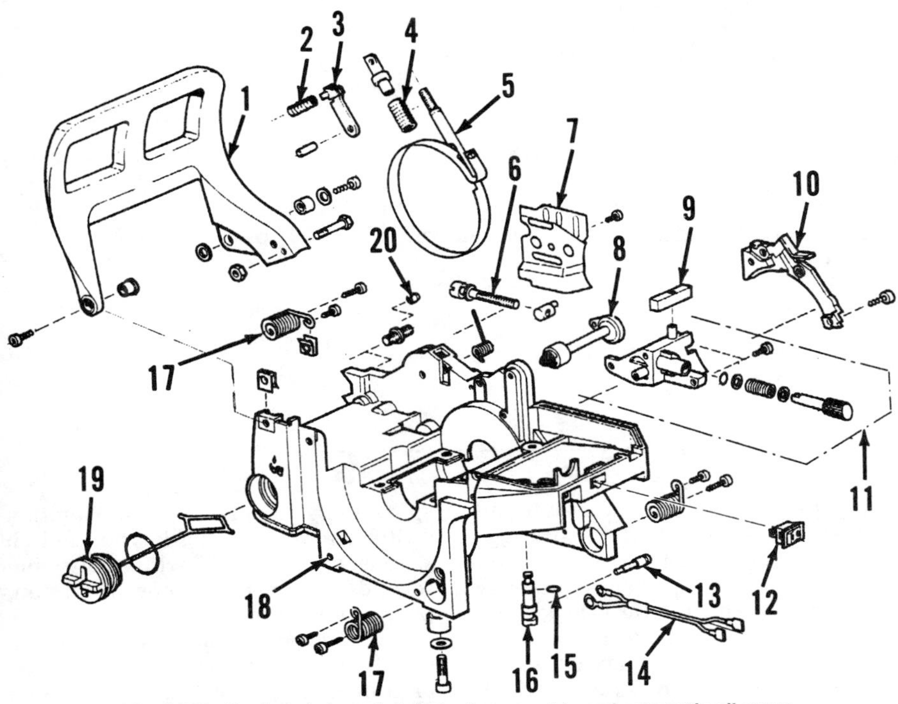

Fig. SO83—Exploded view of chain brake assembly and automatic oil pump.

1. Hand guard
2. Spring
3. Lock release lever
4. Brake spring
5. Brake band
6. Chain adjuster
7. Bar guide
8. Oil suction hose
9. Seal
10. Brake cover
11. Oil pump assy.
12. Stop switch
13. Bolt
14. Stop switch wires
15. "O" ring
16. Oil pump adjuster
17. Vibration isolator
18. Crankcase/engine housing
19. Oil tank cap

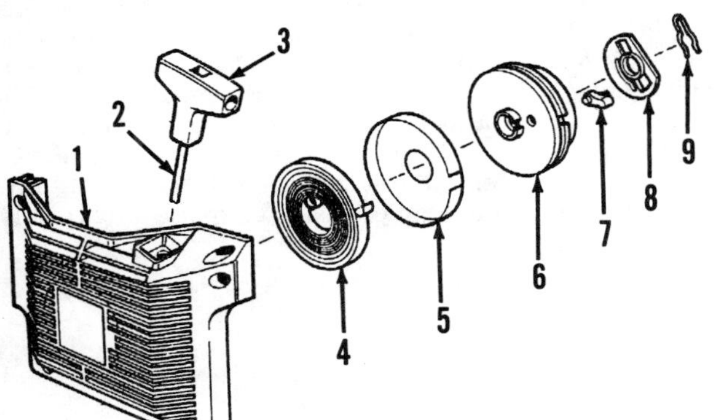

Fig. SO84—Exploded view of rewind starter typical of all models.

1. Starter housing
2. Rope
3. Rope handle
4. Rewind spring
5. Spring case
6. Rope pulley
7. Pawl
8. Pawl guide
9. Spring clip

Check needle bearing for excessive wear or damage. Inspect clutch shoes and drum for signs of wear or excessive heat. Clutch shoes are available as an assembly with clutch hub (24).

OIL PUMP. All models are equipped with an automatic oil pump that provides lubricant to the bar and chain. The oil pump is driven by the chain clutch. The pump is in operation only when the clutch and chain are in motion.

The oil pump (11—Fig. SO83) is accessible after removing the clutch assembly as previously outlined. Remove oil flow adjuster screw (16), then unbolt and remove oil pump housing. Remove piston from housing and check for wear, scoring or other damage. Oil pump components are available separately.

Oil pump output is adjustable. Turning the adjuster screw (16—Fig. SO83) counterclockwise increases the oil flow.

CHAIN BRAKE. All models are equipped with a chain brake system designed to stop chain movement should kickback occur. The chain brake is activated when the operator's hand strikes the hand guard (1—Fig. SO83). This trips the lock release lever (3) allowing the brake spring to draw the brake band (5) tightly around the clutch drum. Pull the hand guard rearward to release the brake.

To inspect and service the chain brake, remove the clutch cover, bar and chain, chain guard (7—Fig. SO83) and clutch drum. Push the hand guard forward to engage the brake and relieve spring tension. Remove the brake cover (10), then separate brake band (5), hand guard (1) and linkage from the saw as necessary.

Inspect all parts and renew any component found to be worn or damaged. Individual parts are available for service. When reassembling, lubricate all moving parts and pivot points. No adjustment of the brake system is required.

REWIND STARTER. To disassemble starter, first unbolt and remove starter housing (1—Fig. SO84). If rope is not broken, pull rope out one full turn of rope pulley. Remove rope handle (3) and allow pulley to unwind slowly to release rewind spring tension. Remove spring clip (9), pawl guide (8) and rope pulley (6). If rewind spring (4) must be removed, care should be used not to allow the spring to uncoil uncontrolled.

If rewind spring is to be renewed, the new spring will come pre-wound in a new case (5). Lightly lubricate rewind spring and starter shaft with oil, then place spring into starter housing. Make certain that the hook in outer coil engages the notch in the starter housing. If spring becomes disengaged from the case, wind spring in the case in a counterclockwise direction working from the outside towards the inside.

New starter rope should be 900 mm (35 in.) long and 3.5 mm (9/64 in.) in diameter. Wind rope on pulley in a clockwise direction (as viewed from flywheel side of pulley). Place pulley onto spring case making sure that the hook on the inside coil engages the notch in pulley hub. Install pawl holder (8) and spring clip (9).

Insert rope into recess in pulley and preload spring by turning pulley approximately two turns clockwise. Thread the rope through opening in starter housing and attach rope handle.

Rewind spring tension is correct if rope handle is pulled snugly against starter housing with rope fully retracted and if pulley will rotate at least an additional half turn with rope fully extended. If rewind spring binds before the rope is fully extended, reduce tension on rope by pulling rope up into notch in rope pulley and allowing pulley to partially unwind. Recheck starter operation.

STIHL

Model	Bore mm (in.)	Stroke mm (in.)	Displacement cc (cu. in.)	Drive Type
015, 015AV, 015AVE, 015L, 015LE	38 (1.496)	28 (1.102)	32 (1.95)	Direct

MAINTENANCE

SPARK PLUG. Recommended spark plug is Bosch WSR6F or Champion RCJ6Y. Electrode gap should be 0.5 mm (0.020 in.). Tighten spark plug to 25 N·m (18 ft.-lbs.).

CARBURETOR. A Walbro HDC diaphragm carburetor is used on all models. Refer to Walbro section of CARBURETOR SERVICE section for repair procedure and an exploded view of carburetor.

Initial adjustment of low speed mixture screw (L—Fig. ST1) and high speed mixture screw (H) is $^3/_4$ turn open from a lightly seated position. Final adjustment should be made with engine warm and running. Make certain engine air filter is clean before adjusting carburetor.

Adjust low speed mixture screw to obtain highest idle speed, then turn screw counterclockwise approximately $^1/_8$ turn. Engine should accelerate smoothly without hesitation. If engine stumbles or seems sluggish when accelerating, adjust low speed mixture screw until engine accelerates without hesitation. Adjust idle speed screw (LA) so engine idles just below clutch engagement speed. Adjust high speed mixture screw to obtain optimum full throttle performance under cutting load. Do not operate saw with high speed mixture setting too lean (needle turned too far clockwise) as engine damage could result from lack of lubrication and overheating.

IGNITION. Models 015, 015AV and 015L are equipped with a conventional breaker point controlled flywheel magneto ignition system (Fig. ST2). Models 015VE and 015LE are equipped with a breakerless transistor ignition system (Fig. ST3).

Trouble-shooting a faulty ignition system is similar for either type system. Check for fouled, worn or damaged spark plug. Check for faulty ignition switch (there is no spark when switch wire is grounded). Check primary and secondary wires for poor insulation, poor connections or broken wires. Check for poor ground connections. Check for burned, pitted or worn breaker contact points on magneto ignition system. On all ignition systems, ignition coil may be tested with an ignition coil tester or an ohmmeter may be used to measure resistance of primary and secondary windings. To test primary winding, remove flywheel and disconnect primary lead from contact set or trigger plate. Connect one lead of tester to primary wire and the other test lead to ground. Resistance should be 0.8-1.3 ohms for magneto ignition system and 1.5-1.9 ohms for transistor ignition system. To test secondary winding, connect one lead of tester to spark plug termi-

Fig. ST1—View showing carburetor adjustment points: idle speed screw (LA), low speed mixture screw (L) and high speed mixture screw (H).

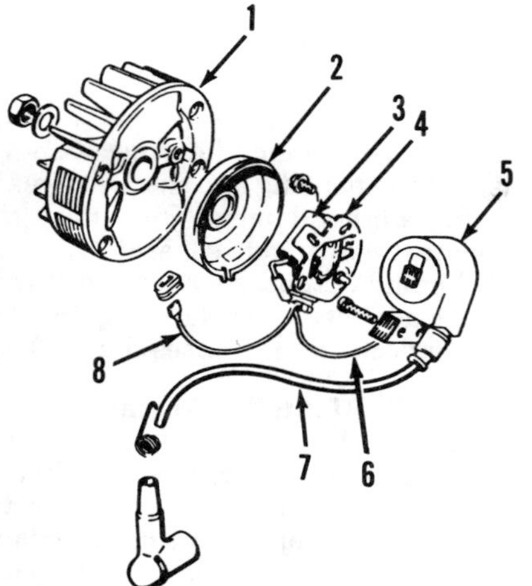

Fig. ST2—Exploded view of magneto ignition system used on Models 015, 015AV and 015L.

1. Flywheel
2. Cover
3. Condenser
4. Breaker-point assy.
5. Ignition coil
6. Primary wire
7. High tension wire
8. Ignition switch wire

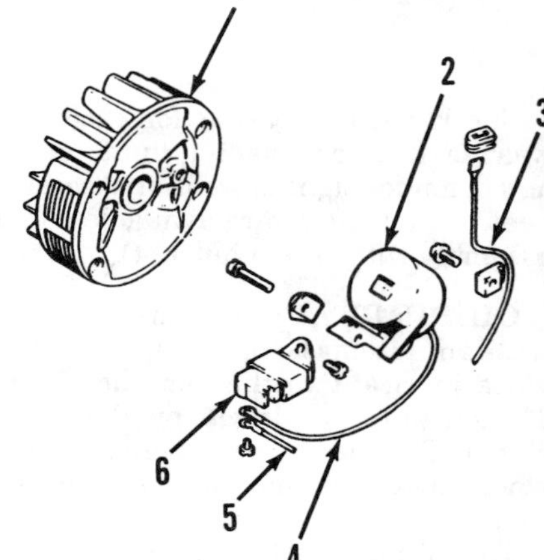

Fig. ST3—Exploded view of transistor ignition system used on Models 015AVE and 015LE.

1. Flywheel
2. Ignition coil
3. Ground wire
4. Primary wire
5. Ignition switch wire
6. Electronic trigger assy.

Illustrations courtesy Stihl Inc.

nal of high tension wire and other test lead to ground. Resistance should be 6500-9000 ohms for all models. Renew coil assembly if readings vary greatly from specifications. To check electronic trigger switch (6—Fig. ST3), install a known good switch and check for spark.

Refer to the appropriate following paragraphs for service.

Flywheel Magneto Ignition. Flywheel must be removed to service breaker points. Ignition breaker point gap should be 0.35-0.40 mm (0.014-0.016 in.). Ignition timing is not adjustable except by adjusting breaker point gap. Ignition timing should occur at 2.3 mm (0.090 in.) BTDC. Air gap between magneto coil legs and flywheel magnets should be 0.2-0.3 mm (0.008-0.012 in.). To adjust air gap, loosen coil mounting screws and move coil as necessary. Magneto edge gap (E—Fig. ST4) should be 3.0-7.3 mm (0.12-0.29 in.). Magneto edge gap should be measured at the point when breaker contact points just begin to open. Magneto edge gap may be adjusted slightly by adjusting breaker point gap and by loosening flywheel nut and rotating flywheel on crankshaft as there is a small clearance between flywheel groove and crankshaft key.

Transistor Ignition. Models 015VE and 015LE are equipped with a Bosch breakerless transistor ignition (Fig. ST3). The transistor circuit is designed to take the place of breaker points in a conventional ignition system. The system is triggered magnetically by a magnet in the flywheel (1). The ignition coil (2) is mounted outside the flywheel and the electronic trigger plate (6) is mounted behind the flywheel.

Because the electronic trigger plate is not subject to any mechanical wear, ignition timing will remain constant as long as trigger plate is operating properly. To check ignition timing, install Stihl timing tool 0000 850 4000 on chain bar studs. Using a piston locating tool, set piston at 2.2 mm (0.087 in.) BTDC. At this point, scribe a line on clutch hub in line with arrow of timing tool. Reinstall spark plug and connect timing light to spark plug wire. Start engine and set engine speed at 6000 rpm. When timing light is directed at the clutch, scribe mark on hub should appear to be in alignment with arrow of timing tool if timing is correct. Ignition timing may be adjusted slightly by loosening flywheel nut and rotating flywheel on crankshaft as there is a small clearance between flywheel groove and crankshaft key.

Recommended air gap between ignition coil armature legs and flywheel magnet is 0.2-0.3 mm (0.008-0.012 in.). Loosen ignition coil mounting screws and move ignition coil to adjust air gap.

LUBRICATION. The engine is lubricated by mixing oil with the fuel. Fuel:oil ratio is 40:1 when using Stihl two-stroke engine oil. If Stihl two-stroke engine oil is not available, a good quality oil designed for two-stroke air-cooled engines may be used when mixed at a 25:1 ratio. Use a separate container when mixing the oil and gasoline.

All models are equipped with an automatic chain oiler system. Manufacturer recommends using oil designed specifically for saw chain lubrication. If necessary, clean automotive oil may be used to lubricate saw chain. Use SAE 30 oil in warm weather and SAE 10 oil in cold weather.

REPAIR

CRANKCASE PRESSURE TEST. An improperly sealed crankcase can cause the engine to be hard to start, run rough, have low power and overheat. Refer to ENGINE SERVICE section of this manual for crankcase pressure test procedure. If crankcase leakage is indicated, pressurize crankcase and use a soap and water solution to check gaskets, seals, pulse line and castings for leakage.

CYLINDER, PISTON PIN AND RINGS. To disassemble, first drain oil and fuel tanks. Remove clutch cover, bar and chain. Remove air filter cover, air filter, choke lever, handle housing and fan housing. Remove spark plug and install a piston stop tool in spark plug hole or use some other means to prevent crankshaft from rotating. Unscrew clutch hub (left-hand threads) and remove clutch assembly, oil pump cover and oil pump assembly. Remove flywheel nut (right-hand threads) and use suitable puller to remove flywheel from crankshaft. Remove carburetor and muffler. On models equipped with breaker points, remove breaker box dust cover and contact point set. On all models, remove four screws from bottom of crankcase and pull cylinder (1—Fig. ST5) off lower part of crankcase (15). Remove piston pin retainer clips (4) and push piston pin (3) out of piston (5).

Cylinder and front crankcase are one-piece and matched to lower crankcase half. Therefore, replacement cylinders are supplied only with other half of crankcase. Piston, piston ring, piston pin and pin retainers are available separately. Inspect all parts for damage or excessive wear and renew as necessary.

Piston must be installed with "A" arrow (Fig. ST6) pointing toward exhaust port (clutch end of crankshaft). Install piston pin with closed end toward "A" arrow side of piston and secure with new retainer clips. A locating pin is positioned in piston ring groove to prevent ring rotation. Be sure piston ring end gap is properly positioned around pin when installing cylinder. Lubricate pis-

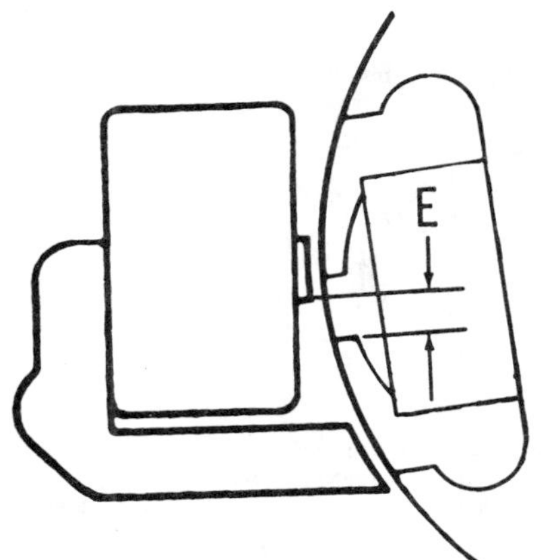

Fig. ST4—Magneto coil edge gap (E) on Models 015, 015AV and 015L should be 3.0-7.3 mm (0.12-0.29 in.).

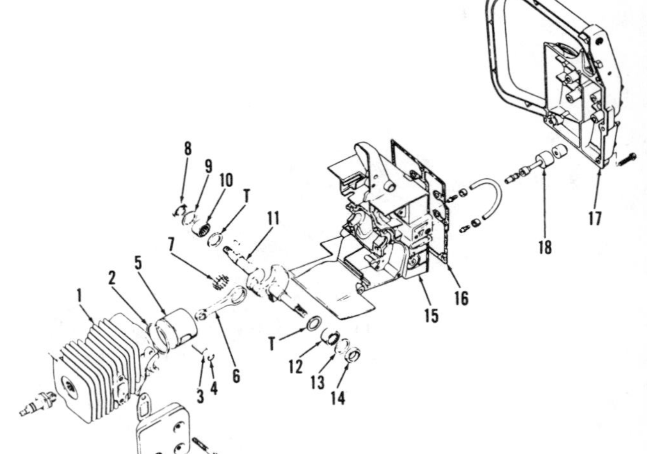

Fig. ST5—Exploded view of engine used on all models. Thrust washers (T) are used on models produced after 1978.

1. Cylinder
2. Piston ring
3. Piston pin
4. Pin retainer
5. Piston
6. Connecting rod
7. Bearing rollers (12)
8. Oil seal
9. Retaining ring
10. Needle bearing
11. Crankshaft
12. Needle bearing
13. Retaining ring
14. Oil seal
15. Crankcase
16. Gasket
17. Handle assy.
18. Oil pickup

Illustrations courtesy Stihl Inc.

ton ring and cylinder bore with oil prior to reassembly. Apply a light coat of nonhardening sealant to mating surface of crankcase halves, then place crankcase on cylinder and tighten mounting screws to 7.0 N·m (62 in.-lbs.). Complete reassembly by reversing disassembly procedure.

CRANKSHAFT, CONNECTING ROD AND SEALS. The crankshaft rides on needle bearings (10 and 12—Fig. ST5) held between the cylinder (1) and lower crankcase (15). The connecting rod (6) is one-piece and supported on crankpin by 12 loose bearing rollers (7). Refer to CYLINDER, PISTON, PIN AND RINGS section for removal of crankshaft and connecting rod. When removing connecting rod from crankshaft, be careful not to lose the bearing rollers, which may fall out during disassembly.

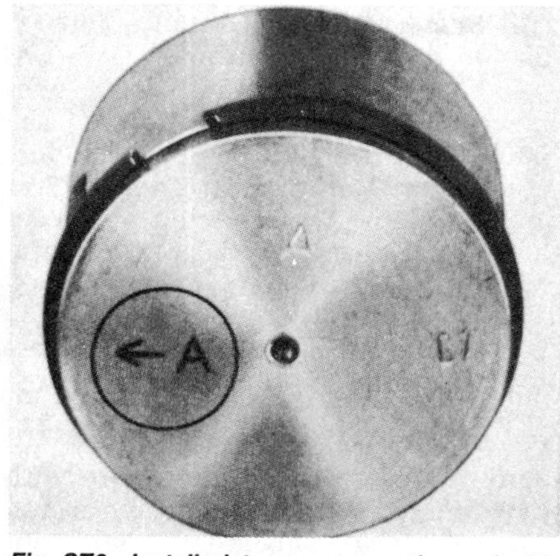

Fig. ST6—Install piston on connecting rod with "A" arrow on piston crown pointing toward exhaust port in cylinder.

Inspect connecting rod, crankshaft and bearings for excessive wear or damage. Renew oil seals (8 and 14).

When reassembling, use grease to hold bearing rollers (7) in place on crankshaft, then slip connecting rod over the bearing rollers. Assemble thrust washers, needle bearings and retaining rings on crankshaft.

NOTE: Large diameter needle bearing (10), retaining ring (9) and seal (8) on later models must be installed on flywheel end of crankshaft, and smaller diameter bearing (12), retaining ring (13) and seal (14) must be installed on clutch end. Bearings, retaining rings and seals on early models have the same outer diameter and may be installed on either end of crankshaft.

Install piston and crankshaft assembly in cylinder making sure clutch end of crankshaft is toward exhaust port. Apply a light coat of nonhardening sealant to mating surface of crankcase halves. Assemble crankcase half (15) to cylinder half making certain retaining rings (9 and 13) fit in ring grooves of crankcase and cylinder. Tighten crankcase mounting screws to 7.0 N·m (62 in.-lbs.). Install new oil seals (8 and 14) with seal lips facing inward.

CLUTCH. Models without chain brake are equipped with the two-shoe centrifugal type clutch shown in Fig. ST7. Models with chain brake are equipped with the three-shoe type clutch shown in Fig. ST8.

To remove clutch assembly, first remove spark plug and install piston stop tool in spark plug hole or use other suitable means to prevent crankshaft rotation. Remove clutch cover, bar and chain. On both types of clutch, clutch hub has left-hand threads (turn clockwise to remove).

Inspect clutch shoes, drum and needle bearing for wear or signs of damage due to excessive heat and renew as necessary. Lubricate needle bearing with grease when reassembling.

On models without chain brake, be sure rear guide washer (11—Fig. ST7) is installed with raised inner diameter facing away from clutch drum. Tighten clutch hub to 25 N·m (18 ft.-lbs.).

On models with chain brake, flanged edge of rear guide washer (16—Fig. ST8) should face the crankcase. One side of threaded hole in clutch hub (13) is counterbored to a depth of approximately 2 mm (0.080 in.) and this side must face the crankcase. Tighten clutch hub to 25 N·m (18 ft.-lbs.). Install front guide washer (12) so raised inner diameter faces clutch hub. Tighten locking nut (11) to 30 N·m (22 ft.-lbs.).

OIL PUMP. All models are equipped with a plunger type automatic chain oil pump. Oil pump is driven by the clutch through gear (8—Fig. ST7) that engages with the clutch drum. The oil pump operates only when clutch drum is turning. A worm attached to driven gear (6) turns pump plunger (3). The plunger reciprocates in pump housing as the cam groove in end of plunger rides against pin (4).

Remove chain bar, clutch and cover plate (7) for access to oil pump. Pin (4) must be removed before plunger (3) can be withdrawn from pump housing (2). Use a magnet to remove pin, then withdraw pump plunger out of housing. Renew any worn or damaged parts.

Coat helical end and teeth of plunger with grease before reassembling. Be sure spacer washer (5) is installed on worm gear bearing shaft before installing spur gear (6).

CHAIN BRAKE. Some models may be equipped with a chain brake system de-

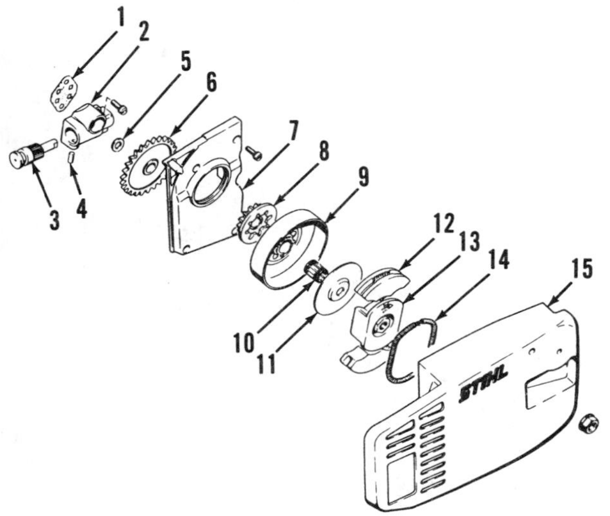

Fig. ST7—Exploded view of clutch assembly and chain oiler pump.

1. Gasket
2. Oil pump housing
3. Pump plunger
4. Pin
5. Washer
6. Driven gear & worm
7. Cover
8. Drive gear
9. Clutch drum
10. Needle bearing
11. Plate
12. Clutch shoe
13. Clutch hub
14. Spring
15. Housing

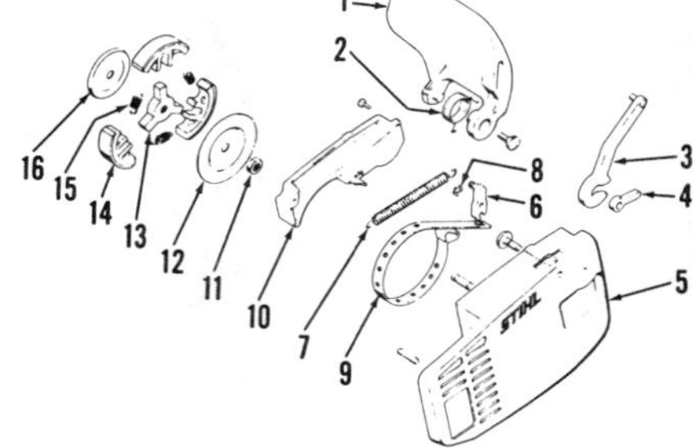

Fig. ST8—Exploded view of chain brake and clutch assembly used on some models.

1. Hand guard
2. Spring
3. Brake lever
4. Actuating lever
5. Housing
6. Pivot
7. Spring
8. "E" ring
9. Brake band
10. Shield
11. Nut
12. Washer
13. Clutch hub
14. Clutch shoe
15. Clutch spring
16. Washer

signed to stop chain movement should kickback occur. The chain brake is activated when the operator's hand strikes hand guard (1—Fig. ST8), thereby allowing brake lever (3) to release spring (7) that draws brake band (9) tight around clutch drum to stop chain. Pull back hand guard to reset brake mechanism. No adjustment of chain brake is required.

To disassemble, remove cover (10) and detach brake spring (7). Remove "E" ring (8) and lift out pivot lever (6) and brake band (9). To remove brake lever (3) and actuating lever (4), drive out lever pivot pin toward inside of housing (5).

Lubricate all pivot points before reassembly. Reassembly is reverse of disassembly.

REWIND STARTER. Two types of rewind starter assemblies are used. On Models 015AV and 015AVE equipped with anti-vibration handle, starter assembly shown in Fig. ST9 is used. On all other models, starter assembly shown in Fig. ST10 is used.

Models With Anti-Vibration Handle. To service starter on models with anti-vibration handle, remove mounting screw from lower end of handlebar and swing handlebar to the side to provide access to starter cover (1—Fig. ST9). Remove cover mounting screws and pry cover out of fan shroud (7). Remove "E" ring (10) and withdraw rope pulley (9) from cover (1). Lift rewind spring assembly (3) from cover being careful not to allow spring to unwind uncontrolled.

To reassemble, lubricate rewind spring with a few drops of oil. Install spring and housing in starter cover making sure spring outer loop engages lug on cover. If spring becomes disengaged from spring housing during installation, wind spring in housing in a counterclockwise direction, starting with outer end and working inward. Rope length should be 960 mm (38 in.) long and 3.5 mm (1/8 in.) in diameter. Lubricate starter cover pivot shaft with oil, then install rope pulley, bushing and "E" ring. Insert end of rope through starter housing and install rope handle. Wind rope on pulley in clockwise direction as viewed from flywheel side of pulley. To preload rewind spring, turn pulley three turns clockwise, then position starter cover in shroud. Pull out starter rope until resistance is felt, then release rope so flywheel pawls can engage rope pulley. Rope handle (4) should rest snugly against shroud when spring is correctly tensioned.

Models Without Anti-Vibration Handle. To service starter used on models without anti-vibration handle, remove choke lever, spark plug, air filter cover and air filter. Unbolt and remove starter housing/fan shroud (2—Fig. ST10) from engine. If rope is not broken, remove rope handle (1) and allow rope pulley to slowly unwind to relieve tension on rewind spring. Remove "E" ring (7) and lift rope pulley (6) upward only far enough so that a screwdriver or other suitable tool can be inserted through rope guide bore in housing and pushed between pulley and rewind spring (4) to ensure spring does not become disengaged as pulley is removed. Remove rope pulley being careful not to allow rewind spring (4) to unwind uncontrolled. If it is necessary to remove rewind spring, carefully grasp spring with large pliers and remove from housing or position starter housing on a flat surface with spring side facing downward and tap on housing to dislodge spring from housing.

A new rewind spring comes ready to install with a wire strap holding it in the coiled position. The wire strap is pushed off spring as it is installed. Spring must be wound in clockwise direction in housing, starting with outer end. Be sure outer loop of spring engages lug on starter housing. Rope length should be 960 mm (38 in.) long and 3.5 mm (1/8 in.) in diameter. Wind rope on pulley in clockwise direction as viewed from flywheel side of pulley. Insert end of rope through starter housing and install rope handle. Lubricate starter pivot shaft with oil, then install rope pulley, bushing and "E" ring. Be sure inner loop of rewind spring engages gap in rib of pulley. To preload rewind spring, pull rope about 40 cm (16 in.) out of housing and hold pulley in this position. Pull loop of rope through notch in pulley, then rotate pulley three turns clockwise. While holding pulley, pull rope back through notch in pulley and out opening in housing. Release pulley slowly and allow rope to wind onto pulley. Rope handle (1) should rest snugly against shroud when spring is correctly tensioned.

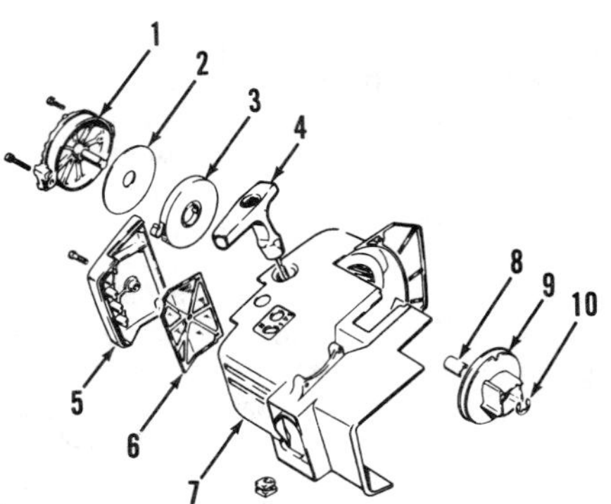

Fig. ST9—Exploded view of rewind starter assembly used on Models 015AV and 015AVE.

1. Starter cover
2. Washer
3. Rewind spring
4. Rope handle
5. Air filter cover
6. Air filter
7. Shroud
8. Bushing
9. Rope pulley
10. "E" ring

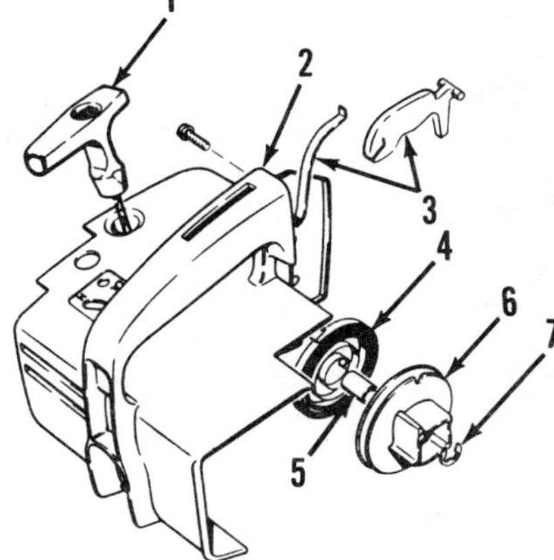

Fig. ST10—Exploded view of rewind starter assembly used on Models 015, 015L and 015LE.

1. Rope handle
2. Starter housing
3. Trigger interlock
4. Rewind spring
5. Bushing
6. Rope pulley
7. "E" ring

Illustrations courtesy Stihl Inc.

STIHL

Model	Bore mm (in.)	Stroke mm (in.)	Displacement cc (cu. in.)	Drive Type
020, 020AV, 020AVPE	38 (1.496)	28 (1.102)	32 (1.95)	Direct
020AVS, 020AVSE, 020AVSEQ	40 (1.57)	28 (1.102)	35.2 (2.15)	Direct
040, 041, 041AV, 041AVE, 041AVQ, 041FB, 041AVFB, 041AVEFB	44 (1.73)	40 (1.57)	61 (3.72)	Direct
041G	44 (1.73)	40 (1.57)	61 (3.72)	Gear
041S, 041AVSE	48 (1.89)	40 (1.57)	72 (4.4)	Direct
050AV, 051AV, 051AVE, 051AVEQ	52 (2.05)	42 (1.65)	89 (5.42)	Direct
075 AVE, 076 AVE, 076AVEQ	58 (2.28)	42 (1.65)	111 (6.77)	Direct

MAINTENANCE

SPARK PLUG. Recommended spark plug is Bosch WSR6F, Champion RCJ6Y or NGK BPMR-7A. Spark plug electrode gap should be 0.5 mm (0.020 in.) for all models. Tighten spark plug to 25 N·m (18 ft.-lbs.).

CARBURETOR. Saws may be equipped with Tillotson Series HU or HS or Walbro Series WA, WS or WT diaphragm carburetor. Carburetor model designation is stamped on carburetor.

Fig. ST11—View of carburetor adjustment points typical of all models. High speed mixture needle (1) and low speed mixture needle (2) may be positioned differently on some models. Refer to text for adjustment procedure.

Refer to the appropriate section of CARBURETOR SERVICE section for carburetor overhaul procedure and exploded views.

Initial adjustment of carburetor low speed and high speed mixture screws is one turn open from a lightly seated position. Make final adjustments with engine warm and running. Make certain engine air filter is clean before adjusting carburetor.

Adjust idle speed screw (3—Fig. ST11) so engine idles just below clutch engagement speed. Adjust low speed mixture screw (2) to obtain highest idle speed, then turn screw counterclockwise approximately 1/8 turn. Engine should accelerate smoothly without hesitation. If engine stumbles or seems sluggish when accelerating, adjust low speed mixture screw until engine accelerates without hesitation. Adjust high speed mixture screw (1) to obtain optimum performance under cutting load. Do not adjust high speed mixture screw too lean (turned too far clockwise) as engine may be damaged from lack of lubrication and overheating.

IGNITION. Models 020AV, 040, 041, 041FB, 041AV, 041AVFBQ, 050AV and 051AV are equipped with a conventional breaker point controlled flywheel magneto ignition system. Models 041AVEQ, 041AVE Super and 041G are equipped with a breakerless capacitor discharge ignition system. Models 020AVEP, 020AVSEQ, 051AVEQ, 075AVE, 076AVE and 076AVEQ are equipped with a breakerless transistor ignition system.

Breaker Point Ignition. Flywheel must be removed for access to breaker points. Breaker point gap on all models so equipped should be 0.35-0.40 mm (0.014-0.016 in.). Ignition timing should occur as follows: 2.0-2.2 mm (0.080-0.087 in.) BTDC on Model 020AV; 2.4-2.6 mm (0.095-0.102 in.) BTDC on Models 040, 041, 041FB, 041AV and 041AVFBQ; 2.3-2.7 mm (0.090-0.106 in.) BTDC on Models 050AV and 051AV to serial number 2981245 and 1.9-2.1 mm (0.075-0.083 in.) after serial number 2981245. Loosen magneto base plate screws and rotate magneto base plate to adjust ignition timing.

Ignition edge gap should be checked whenever ignition timing is adjusted. Edge gap should also be checked if engine is difficult to start or misfires at full throttle. To check edge gap, rotate flywheel counterclockwise until breaker points just start to open. On Models 040, 041, 041FB, 041AV and 041AVFBQ, edge gap is measured from trailing edge of flywheel magnet and adjacent edge of ignition coil leg as shown in Fig. ST12. Edge gap should be 6-9 mm (0.24-0.35 in.). On all other models, edge gap is measured from trailing edge of flywheel magnet and adjacent edge of ignition coil center leg as shown in Fig. ST13.

Illustrations courtesy Stihl Inc.

Edge gap should be 4-6 mm (0.16-0.24 in.) on Model 020AV. On 050AV and 051AV models to serial number 2981245, edge gap should be 9-13 mm (0.35-0.51 in.) and 12-16 mm (0.47-0.63 in.) after serial number 2981245. On all models, adjust edge gap by changing breaker point gap.

Air gap between flywheel magnets and ignition coil should be 0.20-0.30 mm (0.008-0.012 in.) on Models 020AV, 040, 041, 041FB, 041AV and 041AVFBQ and 0.15-0.30 mm (0.006-0.012 in.) on all other models. Loosen ignition coil mounting screws and move coil assembly to adjust air gap.

Capacitor Discharge Ignition. Early Models 041AVE and 041G are equipped with Bosch capacitor discharge ignition systems shown in Fig. ST14. Later model Bosch capacitor discharge ignition is identical in function, but all components are sealed in stator plate casting and are not individually serviceable. If malfunction occurs, entire stator assembly must be renewed. Models after serial number 9158250 are equipped with SEM capacitor discharge ignition. Operation of SEM and Bosch ignitions are basically the same and are interchangeable if entire ignition systems are exchanged. SEM ignition can be identified by a removable ignition coil. On all models, flywheel must be removed for access to ignition components.

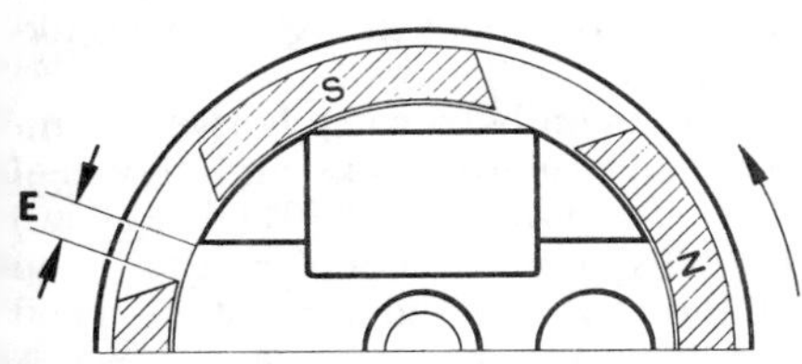

Fig. ST12—On Models 040, 041, 041FB, 041AV and 041AVFBQ, magneto edge gap (E) is measured between trailing edge of flywheel north pole shoe and adjacent edge of ignition coil leg. Refer to text for specifications.

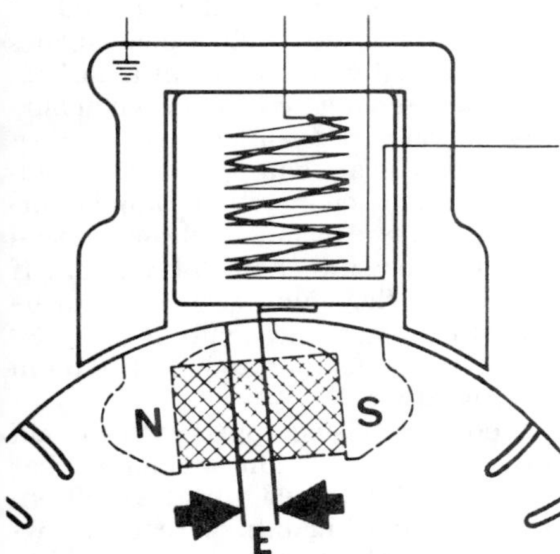

Fig. ST13—On all other breaker-point ignition models, magneto edge gap (E) is measured between trailing edge of flywheel north pole shoe and adjacent edge of ignition coil center leg. Refer to text for specifications.

To properly time early model Bosch ignition, trigger coil (IC—Fig. ST14) must be in correct relationship with flywheel magnet. Ignition timing should be 1.9 mm (0.075 in.) BTDC for Models 041AVE and 041G. To check ignition timing, install a timing gage in spark plug hole and rotate crankshaft until piston is at ignition position as specified above. Note if flywheel mark (F—Fig. ST15) is aligned with mark (C) on crankcase. Remove flywheel and note if mark on stator plate is aligned with crankcase mark (Fig. ST16). If either of these marks is not aligned, ignition must be adjusted.

To adjust ignition, rotate flywheel until piston is at correct ignition timing position as indicated above. Make a mark on crankcase adjacent to mark on flywheel. Remove flywheel, loosen stator plate mounting screws (S—Fig. ST14) and rotate stator plate until mark on plate is aligned with previously made mark on crankcase. Retighten stator plate mounting screws. A timing light may also be used to check ignition timing as follows: Remove spark plug, install timing gage and rotate crankshaft until correct piston position for ignition is indicated. Make two aligned marks on rotating screen and starter housing cover. Install spark plug and connect timing light. Using a tachometer, run engine at 6000 rpm and check alignment of previously made marks with timing light. Loosen stator plate mounting screws and turn plate to adjust timing as required. Recheck timing with light.

If early model Bosch ignition is defective, check for faulty spark plug, high tension lead, ignition switch and all terminals and ground connections. An ohmmeter may be used to check for a faulty ignition coil (IC—Fig. ST14). Connect one test lead to high tension lead and other test lead to ground. Ohmmeter reading should be 1000-3000 ohms. To check primary windings, disconnect yellow wire at terminal "B" on stator plate and connect one lead of ohmmeter to yellow wire and other test lead to ground. Ohmmeter reading should be less than one ohm. To check charging coil (CC), disconnect coil wire from terminal "C" on stator plate. Connect one lead of ohmmeter to coil wire and other lead to ground. Note ohmmeter reading, then reverse lead connections of ohmmeter and again note ohmmeter reading. One reading should be at least ten times larger or smaller than the other reading. Capacitor capacitance should be 0.6-0.9 mfd. Capacitor and stator plate must be renewed as an assembly. Air gap between ignition coil and flywheel magnets on early Bosch ignition should be 0.25-0.35 mm (0.010-0.014 in.). Individual compo-

Fig. ST14—View of Bosch capacitor discharge ignition found on early Models 041AVE and 041G. Trigger module (T) contains diodes and thyristor. All components are sealed in stator plate casting on later models.

CA. Capacitor
CC. Charging coil
IC. Ignition coil
S. Stator mounting screws
T. Trigger module

Fig. ST15—Flywheel mark (F) and crankcase mark (C) should be aligned for correct ignition timing on early models with earlier style Bosch capacitor discharge ignition. Most models with breaker-point ignition have similar marks.

Fig. ST16—View of stator plate and crankcase timing marks (T) on early Bosch capacitor discharge models.

nents cannot be tested on later Bosch ignition. Complete stator plate assembly must be renewed if malfunction is noted.

To test ignition coil primary winding on SEM ignition, disconnect primary wire and connect ohmmeter to primary connection and ground. Reading should be 0.4-0.5 ohm. To test secondary winding, connect ohmmeter to spark plug end of high tension lead and ground. Reading should be 2700-3300 ohms. Renew ignition coil if correct readings are not obtained. Air gap between ignition coil and flywheel magnets should be 0.2-0.3 mm (0.008-0.011 in.).

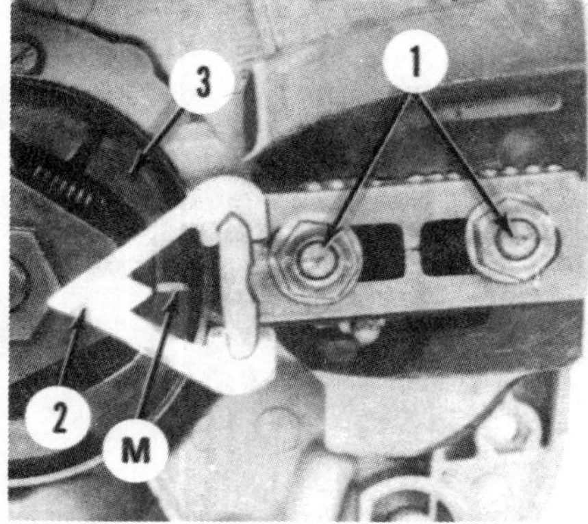

Fig. ST17—View showing reference mark (M), guide bar studs (1), special tool 0000 850 4000 (2) and clutch shoe. Refer to text for ignition timing instructions.

To check ignition timing on later Bosch and SEM ignitions, remove spark plug and install dial indicator into spark plug hole. Remove saw chain and guide bar and install special tool number 0000 850 4000 on guide bar studs with pointer toward clutch as shown in Fig. ST17. Rotate flywheel clockwise and make a reference mark (M) on clutch shoe (3) opposite of pointer (2) when piston is at 1.9 mm (0.075 in.) BTDC on models up to serial number 2783541 and 2.5 mm (0.098 in.) BTDC on models after serial number 2783541. Replace spark plug and connect a suitable power timing light. Using a tachometer, check ignition timing at 6000 rpm. When timing light is directed at the clutch, scribe mark on hub should appear to be in alignment with arrow of timing tool if timing is correct. If reference marks do not align, adjust by rotating stator plate. Recheck timing after adjusting plate.

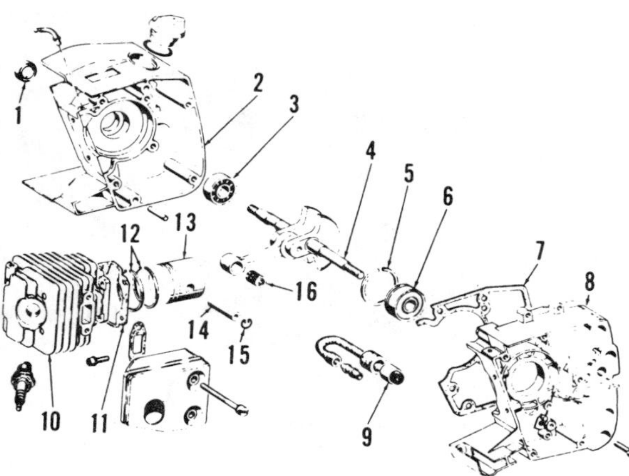

Fig. ST18—Exploded view of engine typical of Models 020AV, 020AVPE and 020AVSEQ.

1. Seal
2. Crankcase half
3. Bearing
4. Crankshaft & connecting rod assy.
5. Snap ring
6. Bearing
7. Gasket
8. Crankcase half
9. Oil pickup
10. Cylinder
11. Gasket
12. Piston rings
13. Piston
14. Piston pin
15. Pin retainer
16. Roller bearing

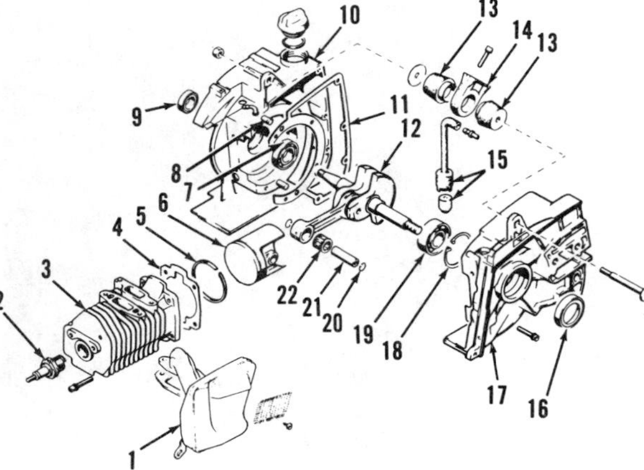

Fig. ST19—Exploded view of engine typical of Models 041AVQ, 041AVEQ and 041AVFB. Models 041, 041AV, 041AVE, 041AVE Super and 041G are similar.

1. Muffler
2. Spark plug
3. Cylinder
4. Gasket
5. Piston ring
6. Piston
7. Bearing
8. Dowel pin
9. Seal
10. Crankcase half
11. Gasket
12. Crankshaft & connecting rod assy.
13. Rubber mounts
14. Support
15. Oil pickup tube & strainer
16. Seal
17. Crankcase half
18. Snap ring
19. Bearing
20. Retaining ring
21. Piston pin
22. Needle bearing

Transistor Ignition. Models 020AVPE 020AVSEQ, 051AVEQ, 075AVE, 076AVE and 076AVEQ are equipped with a Bosch breakerless transistor ignition. The transistor circuit is designed to take the place of breaker points in a conventional ignition system. The transistor ignition system is triggered magnetically by a magnet in the flywheel. The ignition coil is mounted outside the flywheel and the electronic trigger unit is mounted behind the flywheel.

Because the electronic trigger plate is not subject to any mechanical wear, ignition timing will remain constant as long as trigger plate is operating properly. To check ignition timing, install Stihl timing tool 0000 850 4000 on chain bar studs as shown in Fig. ST17. Using a piston locating tool, set piston at 2.3 mm (0.090 in.) BTDC on Model 020AVPE and 2.5 mm (0.098 in.) on all other models. At this point, scribe a line (M) on clutch hub in line with arrow of timing tool (2). Reinstall spark plug and connect timing light to spark plug wire. Start engine and set engine speed at 6000 rpm. When timing light is directed at the clutch, scribe mark on hub should appear to be in alignment with arrow of timing tool if timing is correct. Ignition timing may be adjusted slightly by loosening flywheel nut and rotating flywheel on crankshaft as there is a small clearance between flywheel groove and crankshaft key.

Recommended air gap between ignition coil armature legs and flywheel magnets is 0.15-0.25 mm (0.006-0.010 in.) on all models. Loosen ignition coil mounting screws and move ignition coil to adjust air gap.

LUBRICATION. The engine is lubricated by mixing oil with the fuel. Fuel:oil ratio is 40:1 when using Stihl two-stroke engine oil. If Stihl two-stroke oil is not available, a good quality oil designed for two-stroke air-cooled engines may be used when mixed at a 25:1 ratio. Use a separate container when mixing the oil and gasoline.

All models are equipped with an automatic chain oiler system. Manufacturer recommends using oil designed specifically for saw chain lubrication. If necessary, clean automotive oil may be used to lubricate saw chain. Use SAE 30 oil in warm weather and SAE 10 oil in cold weather.

Model 041G is equipped with a chain drive gear reduction assembly that should be lubricated with SAE 30 oil. Fill drive housing until oil reaches lower edge of fill plug hole.

CARBON. The muffler assembly should be removed from the engine and the carbon scraped from the exhaust ports and muffler periodically. Be careful not to damage piston or exhaust ports when scraping carbon.

REPAIRS

CRANKCASE PRESSURE TEST. An improperly sealed crankcase can cause the engine to be hard to start, run rough, have low power and overheat. Refer to ENGINE SERVICE section of this manual for crankcase pressure test procedure. If crankcase leakage is indicated, pressurize crankcase and use a soap and water solution to check gaskets, seals, pulse line and castings for leakage.

CYLINDER, PISTON, RINGS AND PIN. Refer to appropriate Fig. ST18, ST19 or ST20 for exploded view of engine components. To disassemble, remove fan housing, sprocket cover, bar and chain. Remove air filter housing, handle bar and frame, carburetor, cylinder shroud and muffler. Remove cylinder mounting screws and slide cylinder off piston. Remove piston pin retainer rings. Support piston and connecting rod to prevent side force being applied to connecting rod and push piston pin out of piston. If pin is stuck, tap it out lightly with hammer and drift.

The aluminum alloy piston may be equipped with either one or two piston rings. The floating piston pin is retained in the piston with a snap ring at each end. The pin bore of the piston is unbushed. The connecting rod has a caged needle roller piston pin bearing. An oversize piston pin is not available.

Cylinder is available only with a fitted piston. Piston and cylinder on early Models 040, 041, 041AV, 041AVE, 041AVE Super and 041G and on Model 050AV prior to 1971, are grouped into different size ranges. Each group is marked with letters "A" to "E." Letter "A" denotes smallest size and letter "E" the largest size. On later models, the cylinders are still coded "A" to "E," but pistons are available only in "B" and "C" codes. The "B" code piston is used in "A," "B" and "C" cylinders and the "C" code piston is used in "D" and "E" cylinders. The revised cylinder-piston groups are interchangeable with the early pistons and cylinders. In other words, a new "B" piston may be used in early "A," "B" or "C" cylinder and a new "C" piston may be used in early "D" or "E" cylinder. The code letter is stamped on the top of the piston on all models, at the bottom of the cylinder on early models, and at the top of the cylinder on later models.

The piston and cylinder matching code has been simplified on later Model 050AV and Models 051AV, 051AVE, 051AVEQ, 075AVE and 076AVE. New cylinder and piston assemblies are coded "A," "B" and "C." The cylinder is available only with a matched piston. New pistons for installation in used cylinders are available in code "B" only and may be used with any cylinder.

Cylinder bore on all models except some 075AVE and 076AVE models is chrome plated. Cylinders that do not have chrome plated bores are identified by the letters "SIL" on cylinder base. Pistons for use with "SIL" cylinders are identified by a circle around the cylinder matching code letter stamped in the piston crown. Do not interchange pistons used with chrome bore cylinders with pistons used in "SIL" cylinders.

Installation of piston and cylinder will be simplified by the use of a wood block that will fit between piston skirt and crankcase, supporting the piston as shown in Fig. ST21. A notch should be cut in the wood block so it will fit around the connecting rod. To reinstall piston on connecting rod, first install one snap ring in piston. Lubricate the piston pin needle bearing with engine oil and slide bearing into pin bore of connecting rod. Install piston on rod so arrow (2—Fig. ST21) on piston crown points toward exhaust port. Use an assembly drift to align piston pin bore and connecting rod bearing bore, then push piston pin in far enough to install second snap ring. Locating pins are present in piston ring grooves to prevent ring rotation. Make certain ring end gaps are properly positioned around locating pins when installing cylinder. Install a new cylinder gasket. Lubricate piston rings and cylinder bore with engine oil. Use suitable ring compressor to compress piston rings and push cylinder down over piston. Remove ring compressor and wooden support. Tighten cylinder mounting screws in a diagonal pattern to 8 N·m (70 in.-lbs.).

CONNECTING ROD, CRANKSHAFT AND CRANKCASE. Refer to Figs. ST18, ST19 and ST20 for an exploded view of engine. The connecting rod and crankshaft are a unit assembly and must be removed and serviced as a unit.

Crankcase must be split to remove connecting rod and crankshaft. Remove fan housing, sprocket cover, bar and chain. Remove air filter housing, handle bar and frame, carburetor, cylinder shroud and muffler. Remove spark plug and install a piston stop tool in spark plug hole or use other suitable means to prevent crankshaft from rotating. Remove clutch retaining nut and clutch assembly. Note that both nut and clutch hub have left-hand threads (turn clock-

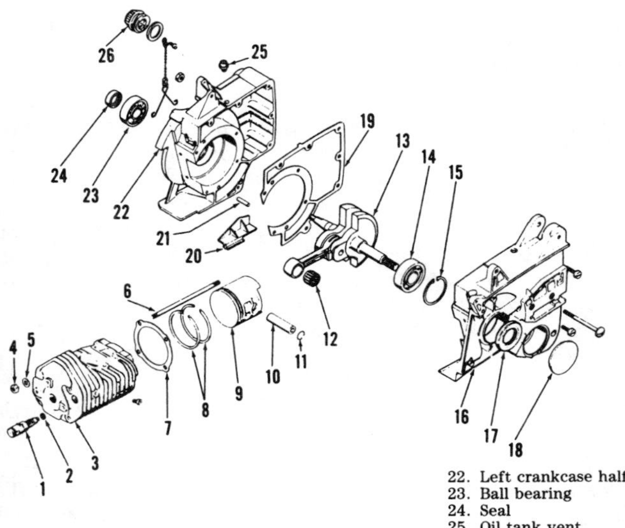

Fig. ST20—Exploded view of engine assembly used on 050AV, 051AV, 051AVE, 051AVEQ, 075AVE and 076AVE models. Decompression valve (1) is optional on some models.

1. Decompression valve
2. Seal
3. Cylinder
4. Nut
5. Washer
6. Stud
7. Gasket
8. Piston rings
9. Piston
10. Piston pin
11. Pin retainer
12. Needle bearing
13. Crankshaft & connecting rod assy.
14. Ball bearing
15. Snap ring
16. Right crankcase half
17. Seal
18. Cover
19. Gasket
20. Insert
21. Dowel pin
22. Left crankcase half
23. Ball bearing
24. Seal
25. Oil tank vent
26. Oil tank cap

Fig. ST21—To facilitate removal and installation of piston, a wooden block (1) may be fabricated and installed between piston and crankcase as shown. When installing piston, be sure arrow and "A" (2) point toward cylinder exhaust port. Piston size code letter (3) is stamped on piston crown.

Illustrations courtesy Stihl Inc.

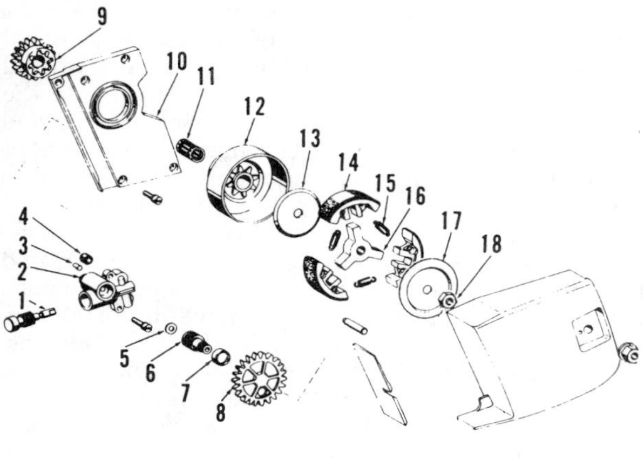

Fig. ST22—Exploded view of Model 020AV and 020AVPE automatic oil pump and clutch assembly. Refer to Fig. ST23 for view of clutch used on models with chain brake.

1. Plunger
2. Body
3. Pin
4. Seal
5. Washer
6. Worm gear
7. Seal
8. Driven gear
9. Drive gear
10. Cover
11. Clutch bearing
12. Clutch drum
13. Washer
14. Clutch shoe
15. Spring
16. Clutch hub
17. Washer
18. Nut

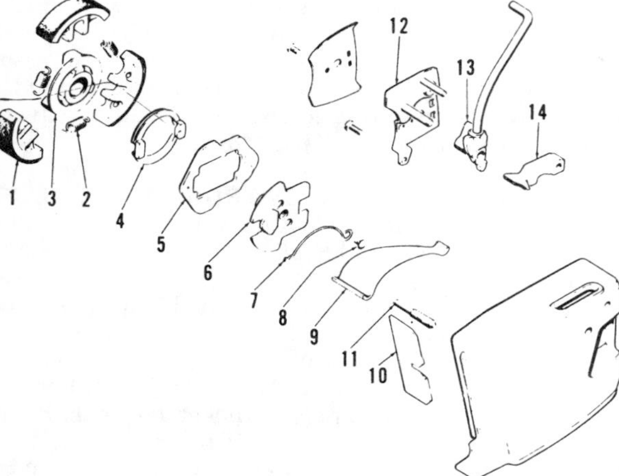

Fig. ST23—Exploded view of clutch and chain brake used on some 020AV and 020AVPE models.

1. Clutch shoe
2. Clutch spring
3. Clutch hub
4. Locking slider
5. Retainer
6. Clutch nut plate
7. Spring
8. Pin
9. Brake spring
10. Cover
11. Pin
12. Brake plate
13. Brake rod
14. Brake shoe

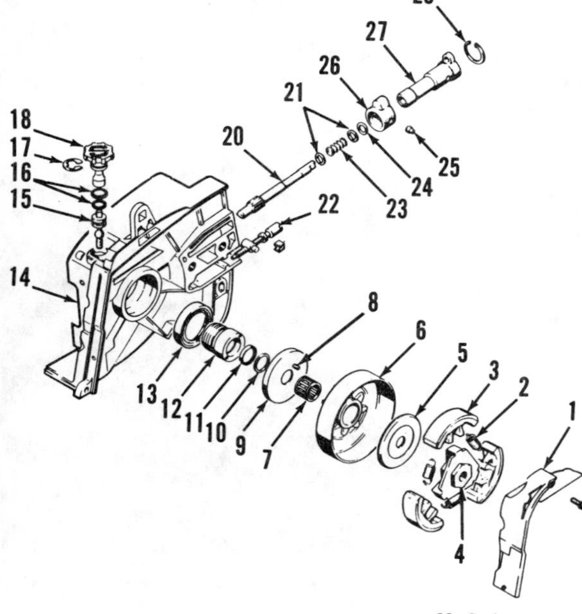

Fig. ST24—Exploded view of clutch assembly and automatic chain oiler pump used on Models 040, 041, 041AV, 041AVE, 041AVEQ, 041G, 050AV, 051AV and early 051AVE and 051AVEQ. Oil pump operates only when clutch is engaged and rotating. Oil output is adjusted by turning control knob (18) except on Models 050AV, 051AV and 051AVE. Output is adjusted on Models 050AV, 051AVE and 051AVEQ by moving lever under hand grip frame on exhaust side of saw.

1. Guard
2. Spring
3. Clutch shoe
4. Clutch hub
5. Washer
6. Clutch drum
7. Needle bearing
8. Pump drive pin
9. Plate
10. Ring
11. Seal
12. Worm gear
13. Seal
14. Crankcase half
15. Control bolt
16. "O" rings
17. "E" ring
18. Oil control knob
20. Pump plunger
21. Washers
22. Chain adjusting screw
23. Spring
24. "O" ring
25. Bushing
26. Rubber ring
27. Pump housing
28. Snap ring

wise to remove). Remove flywheel nut (right-hand threads) and use suitable puller to remove flywheel. Remove ignition components, oil pump, oil pump worm, cylinder and piston. Remove screws holding crankcase halves together, drive the two locating dowel pins into ignition side crankcase half and separate crankcase. It may be necessary to tap clutch end of crankshaft with a soft hammer if halves do not separate easily.

Crankshaft and connecting rod unit assembly should not be disassembled. Connecting rod big end rides on a roller bearing and should be inspected for excessive wear and damage. Check rotation of connecting rod on crankpin. If roughness is noted, renew crankshaft and connecting rod assembly. The upper end of connecting rod is equipped with a needle bearing. Inspect main bearings and crankshaft journals for wear or damage and renew as necessary. Oil seals should be renewed. Crankcase halves are available only as matched unit.

When reassembling, heat crankcase halves on a hot plate to approximately 175°C (350°F) to ease installation of main bearings in crankcase bores. Main bearing inner races should also be heated to ease assembly of crankshaft into main bearings. Assemble crankshaft and crankcase halves using a new bearing. Drive alignment pins into clutch side half of crankcase, then tighten crankcase screws evenly. Assembly of remaining parts is reverse of disassembly procedure.

CLUTCH. All models are equipped with a three-shoe centrifugal type clutch. Refer to Figs. ST22, ST23, ST24 and ST25 for exploded views of clutch assemblies used. A locking bolt should be screwed into the spark plug hole or some other suitable means used to prevent crankshaft rotation when removing clutch nut and/or hub. Clutch nut and hub have left-hand threads (turn clockwise to remove).

Check clutch shoes, drum and needle bearing for wear and damage and renew as necessary. Clutch shoes should be renewed as a unit to prevent unbalanced clutch operation.

Make certain drive plate (9—Fig. ST24) properly engages oil pump worm gear (12) on models so equipped before installing clutch. On all models, install clutch retaining washers so inner face of washers is against clutch hub.

GEAR TRANSMISSION. Model 041G is equipped with a gear reduction chain drive transmission. Refer to Fig. ST26 for exploded view of gear transmission. Disassembly is evident with inspection of unit. A suitable puller should be used to remove chain sprocket (3) and gear (10) from shaft (9).

Inspect components for excessive wear or damage. Refill drive housing with SAE 30 oil until oil level reaches lower edge of oil fill hole.

OIL PUMP. All models are equipped with an automatic chain oiler system. The oil pump used on all models except Models 020AV, 020AVPE and 020AVSEQ is driven by a cover plate (9—Fig. ST24 and 27—Fig. ST27) that engages clutch drum on one side and the oil pump worm gear (12—Fig. ST24 and 25—Fig. ST25) on the other side. Oil pump used on Models 020AV, 020AVPE and 020AVSEQ is driven by a spur gear (9—Fig. ST22) that engages clutch drum.

If oiler system fails to work properly, drain oil tank and inspect first for plugged or broken oil pickup tube and strainer. To check pump drive components, remove sprocket cover, bar and chain and clutch assembly.

On Models 020AV, 020AVPE and 020AVSEQ, remove cover plate (10—Fig. ST22) and check for worn or damaged spur gears (8 and 9). Remove oil pump mounting screw and withdraw pump assembly (2). Pin (3) must be removed before pump plunger (1) can be removed from pump housing.

On all other models, check for worn or damaged pins in drive plate. Check lugs on pump worm gear for wear. To remove worm gear, rotate drive plate counterclockwise and remove from crankshaft. To remove oil pump assembly, remove snap ring (28—Fig. ST24 or 36—Fig. ST27). Thread a M5 screw into end of pump body (27 or 35) and pry against head of screw to remove pump assembly from crankcase. Remove bushing (25 or 35) and separate pump components for inspection.

CHAIN BRAKE. Some models are equipped with a chain brake system designed to stop chain movement should kickback occur. Refer to Figs. ST23, ST25 and ST28 for exploded views of chain brake systems used. On all models, brake is activated when operator's hand strikes hand guard, pushing hand guard and brake rod forward. Forward movement of brake rod activates brake mechanism and allows brake spring to force brake shoe tight against clutch drum. To reset brake mechanism, pull back hand guard.

On models equipped with chain brake shown in Fig. ST23, retainer (5) and locking slider (4) disengage clutch at the same time brake is applied, allowing engine to continue running freely.

On models equipped with chain brake shown in Fig. ST25, drive plate (7) engages dogs on clutch hub carrier (3). Spring plate (6) holds drive plate against release plate (22) causing inner teeth of drive plate to engage clutch hub (9). When chain brake is activated, actuating lever (14) releases cam (17) allowing spring (18) to draw brake band (20) tight around clutch drum. At the same time, release plate (22) pushes drive plate (7) into flat spring plate (6), disengaging hub (9) allowing engine to continue to run freely.

Chain brake must be in disengaged position before chain cover can be removed. Inspect all parts for excessive wear and renew as necessary. Models 041, 041AV and 041AVE use coil springs instead of flat brake springs (9—Fig. ST23). When reassembling coil springs, install large diameter spring to the front directly above brake shoe lining. Install small diameter spring toward rear of brake shoe. On models equipped with chain brake shown in Fig. ST23, make certain retainer (5) and locking slider (4) will move easily and clutch rotates freely with locking slider (4) disengaged. On

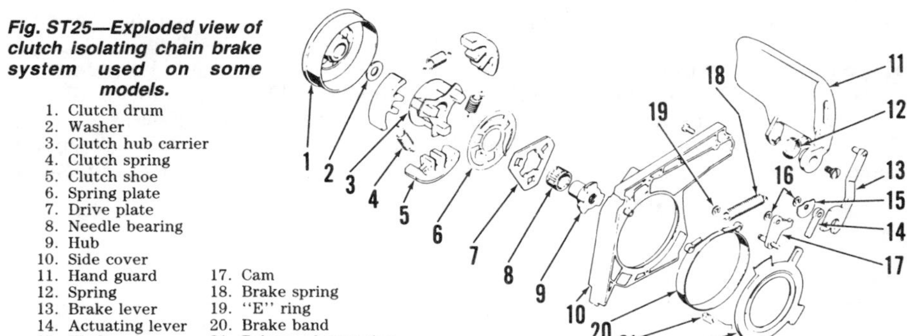

Fig. ST25—Exploded view of clutch isolating chain brake system used on some models.

1. Clutch drum
2. Washer
3. Clutch hub carrier
4. Clutch spring
5. Clutch shoe
6. Spring plate
7. Drive plate
8. Needle bearing
9. Hub
10. Side cover
11. Hand guard
12. Spring
13. Brake lever
14. Actuating lever
15. Washer
16. "E" ring
17. Cam
18. Brake spring
19. "E" ring
20. Brake band
21. Release plate spring
22. Release plate

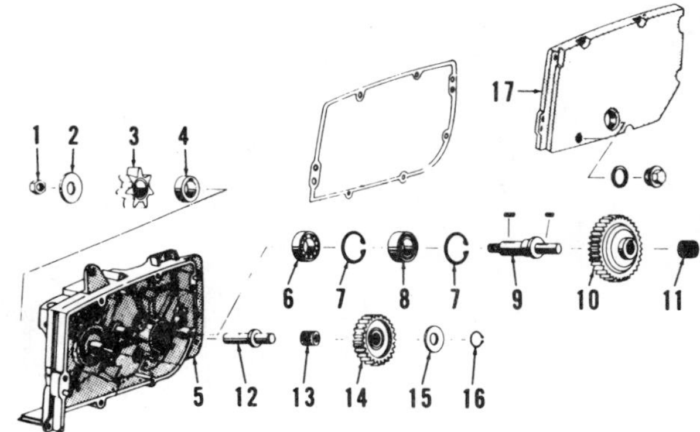

Fig. ST26—Exploded view of reduction gear transmission used on Model 041G.

1. Nut
2. Washer
3. Sprocket
4. Spacer
5. Gearcase
6. Bearing
7. Snap ring
8. Seal
9. Shaft
10. Gear
11. Bearing
12. Shaft
13. Bearing
14. Gear
15. Washer
16. Snap ring
17. Cover

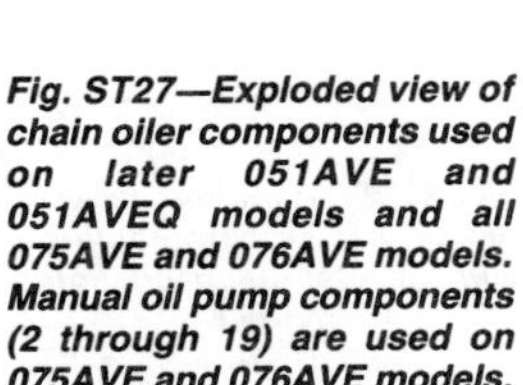

Fig. ST27—Exploded view of chain oiler components used on later 051AVE and 051AVEQ models and all 075AVE and 076AVE models. Manual oil pump components (2 through 19) are used on 075AVE and 076AVE models.

1. Right crankcase half
2. Button
3. "O" ring
4. Cap
5. "O" ring
6. Snap ring
7. Seal
8. "O" ring
9. Pump piston
10. Spring retainer
11. Spring
12. Washer
13. "O" ring
14. Bushing
15. Rod
16. Housing
17. Check ball
18. Spring
19. Seals
20. Oil pump pickup
21. Hose
22. Oil control lever
23. "O" ring
24. "O" ring
25. Worm gear
26. Seal
27. Plate
28. Cover
29. Pump piston
30. Spring
31. Washer
32. "O" ring
33. Seal
34. Pump housing
35. Bushing
36. Snap ring
37. Plug
38. Cap screw

models equipped with chain brake shown in Fig. ST25, make certain spring tabs on spring plate (6) are facing outward when reassembling.

On models equipped with chain brake similar to type shown in Fig. ST28, brake components can be removed after first removing sprocket cover (7) and brake cover (2).

On all models, lightly lubricate moving parts with grease. No adjustment of chain brake system is required.

REWIND STARTER. Several different friction shoe type and pawl type rewind starters have been used. Refer to Fig. ST29 for an exploded view of typical friction shoe type starter used on some models and to Figs. ST31 and ST32 for typical pawl type starters used on some models.

On models equipped with starter shown in Fig. ST29, unbolt and remove fan housing (1). Pull starter rope out of housing about 30 cm (12 in.), then pull loop of rope back through rope guide opening and unwind rope from pulley two turns while holding pulley. Allow pulley to slowly unwind to release rewind spring tension. Remove ''E'' ring (24) while holding thrust washer (23) down to prevent rewind spring from flying out. Carefully remove components from starter housing. If rewind spring (12) is to be removed, use care to prevent spring from unwinding uncontrolled.

New rope length should be 100 cm (39 in.) long and 4.5 mm ($^{3}/_{16}$ in.) in diameter. The leading edges (E—Fig. ST30) of friction shoes (17) must be sharp for proper starter operation. If leading edge is blunt from wear, shoes may be turned 180 degrees one time. Shoes should be renewed if both edges of shoe are blunt.

When reassembling, be sure rewind spring is wound in housing in clockwise direction starting with outer coil. Be sure that friction washers (18 and 20—Fig. ST29) are positioned on each side of brake lever (19) and that lugs of brake lever point in clockwise direction as shown in Fig. ST30. Wind rope on pulley in clockwise direction as viewed from flywheel side of pulley. Turn pulley one turn clockwise to preload rewind spring, then pull rope through opening in fan housing and install rope handle. When rope is properly tensioned, rope handle should fit snugly against fan housing. When starter rope is fully extended, it should be possible to rotate rope pulley at least another half turn clockwise.

On models equipped with starter shown in Fig. ST31, starter can be disassembled without removing fan housing (10) from engine. Remove starter cover mounting screws and pry starter cover (1) out of fan housing. Remove ''E'' ring (9) and withdraw rope pulley (7) from cover. Lift rewind spring assembly (3) from cover being careful not to allow spring to unwind uncontrolled.

To reassemble, lubricate rewind spring with a few drops of oil. Install spring and housing in starter cover making sure spring outer loop engages lug on cover. If spring becomes disengaged from spring housing during installation, wind spring in housing in a counterclockwise direction, starting with outer end and working inward. Rope length should be 96 cm (38 in.) long and 3.5 mm ($^{1}/_{8}$ in.) in diameter. Lubricate starter cover pivot shaft with oil, then install rope pulley, bushing and ''E'' ring. Insert end of rope through starter hous-

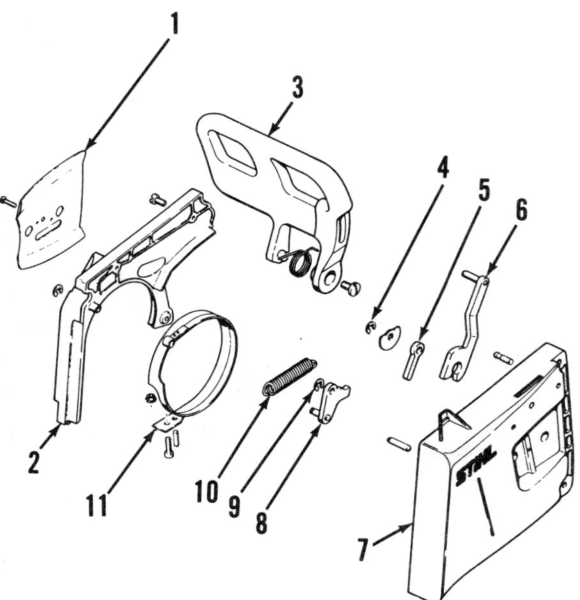

Fig. ST28—Exploded view of chain brake assembly typical of models not equipped with clutch isolating system.

1. Side plate
2. Brake cover
3. Hand guard
4. ''E'' ring
5. Actuating lever
6. Brake lever
7. Sprocket cover
8. Cam
9. ''E'' ring
10. Brake spring
11. Brake band

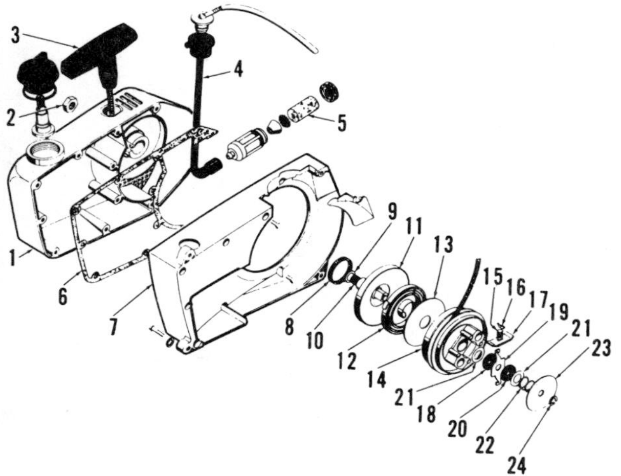

Fig. ST29—Exploded view of typical friction shoe type rewind starter used on some models.

1. Starter housing/fuel tank
2. Nut
3. Rope handle
4. Fuel pickup
5. Filter
6. Gasket
7. Fan cover
8. Felt ring
9. Spring washer
10. Pulley shaft
11. Cover
12. Rewind spring
13. Washer
14. Rope pulley
15. Spring
16. Spring retainer
17. Friction shoe
18. Slotted washer
19. Brake lever
20. Slotted washer
21. Washer
22. Spring
23. Washer
24. ''E'' ring

Fig. ST30—View of starter friction shoe assembly showing correct installation of brake lever (19). Leading edges (E) of friction shoes (17) must be sharp for proper starter operation.

ing and install rope handle. Wind rope on pulley in clockwise direction as viewed from flywheel side of pulley. To preload rewind spring, turn pulley three turns clockwise, then position starter cover in shroud. Pull out starter rope until resistance is felt, then release rope so flywheel pawls can engage rope pulley. Rope handle (5) should rest snugly against shroud when spring is correctly tensioned. With rope fully extended, it should be possible to turn pulley a minimum of $^1/_2$ turn further clockwise.

On models equipped with starter of the type shown in Fig. ST32, starter/fan housing (1) must be removed to service starter. On some models, fan housing and starter housing are two separate parts and fan housing should be separated from starter housing for better access to starter components. Remove rope handle (9) and allow rope pulley (11) to slowly unwind to relieve tension on rewind spring. Remove retainer clip (14) and withdraw rope pulley and pawl (12). If necessary, lift rewind spring (10) from housing being careful not to allow spring to unwind uncontrolled.

Rewind spring should be wound in clockwise direction in housing starting with outer coil. Starter rope length should be 100 cm (39 in.) long and 4.5 mm ($^3/_{16}$ in.) in diameter. Wind rope on pulley in clockwise direction as viewed from flywheel side of pulley. To preload rewind spring, pull rope out of housing about 30 cm (12 in.). While holding rope pulley from turning, wind two turns of rope on pulley, then release pulley. Spring tension is correct if rope handle is pulled snugly against starter housing. With rope fully extended, it should be possible to rotate pulley a minimum of $^1/_2$ turn further clockwise.

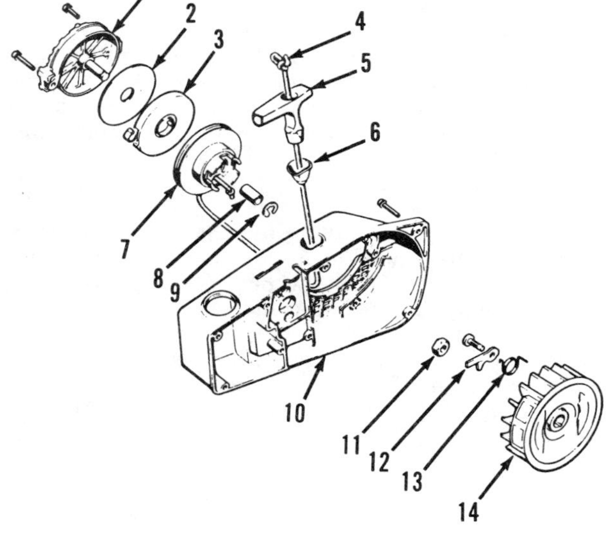

Fig. ST31—Exploded view of pawl type rewind starter used on some models.

1. Starter housing
2. Washer
3. Rewind spring assy.
4. Rope
5. Rope handle
6. Rope guide
7. Rope pulley
8. Bushing
9. "E" ring
10. Fan housing
11. Screw
12. Pawl
13. Spring
14. Flywheel

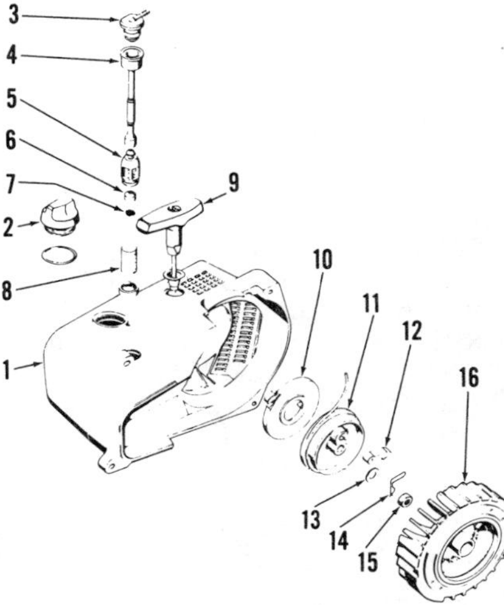

Fig. ST32—Exploded view of pawl type rewind starter used on some models. Starter housing (1) and fan housing are two separate parts on some models.

1. Starter/fan housing
2. Fuel tank cap
3. Connector
4. Hose
5. Pickup body
6. Insert
7. Strainer
8. Filter
9. Rope handle
10. Rewind spring
11. Rope pulley
12. Pawl
13. Washer
14. Spring clip
15. Nut
16. Flywheel

Illustrations courtesy Stihl Inc.

STIHL

Model	Bore mm (in.)	Stroke mm (in.)	Displacement cc (cu. in.)	Drive Type
08S, 08SO, 08SQ, 08SEQ	47 (1.85)	32 (1.26)	56 (3.39)	Direct
S-10	47 (1.85)	32 (1.26)	56 (3.39)	Direct
070, 070AV	58 (2.28)	40 (1.57)	106 (6.47)	Direct
090G	58 (2.28)	40 (1.57)	106 (6.47)	Gear
090, 090AV, 090R	66 (2.6)	40 (1.57)	137 (8.36)	Direct

MAINTENANCE

SPARK PLUG. Recommended spark plug for Model S-10 is Bosch WS7E. Recommended spark plug for all other models is Bosch WSR6F, Champion RCJ6Y or NGK BPMR7A. Spark plug electrode gap should be 0.5 mm (0.020 in.) for all models. Tighten spark plug to 24 N·m (18 ft.-lbs.).

CARBURETOR. All models are equipped with a Zama LA or LB or a Tillotson HL or HS diaphragm type carburetor. Refer to Zama or Tillotson section of CARBURETOR SERVICE for carburetor overhaul procedure and exploded views.

Carburetor model designation is stamped on carburetor. Initial adjustment of low speed mixture screw and high speed mixture screw is 1 turn open from a lightly seated position. Make final adjustment with engine warm and running. Be sure engine air filter is clean before adjusting carburetor.

Turn low speed mixture screw (1—Fig. ST40) until maximum idle speed is reached, then turn needle $^1/_8$ turn counterclockwise. Engine should accelerate cleanly without hesitation. If engine stumbles or seems sluggish when accelerating, adjust idle mixture screw until engine accelerates without hesitation. Adjust idle speed screw (3) so engine idles without stalling and chain does not rotate. Adjust high speed mixture screw (2) to obtain optimum performance with saw operating under cutting load. Do not adjust high speed mixture screw too lean (turned too far clockwise) as engine may be damaged from lack of lubrication and overheating.

GOVERNOR. Some models are equipped with an air vane type engine governor. The governor linkage is attached to the carburetor choke shaft lever. Thus, maximum speed is controlled by the air vane governor closing the choke disc.

Maximum governed speed is adjustable by changing the position of spring (6—Fig. ST41) in the notched speed control plate (8), which changes tension of the governor spring. The adjusting plate is mounted to the engine behind the starter/fan housing. After maximum speed is adjusted at the factory, position of spring is secured by a lead seal. If necessary to readjust governor, new position of governor spring should be sealed or wired securely. Maximum no-load governed speed on Models 070,

Fig. ST40—View of carburetor used on Model 08S showing adjustment points. Other models are similar.

1. Low speed mixture screw
2. High speed mixture screw
3. Idle speed adjusting screw

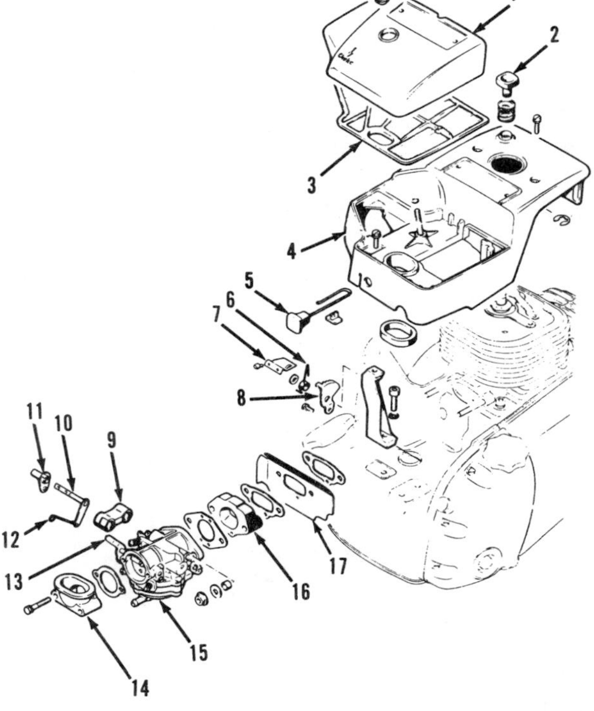

Fig. ST41—Exploded view of governor linkage used on Model 070. Other models are similar.

1. Air filter cover
2. Compression release button
3. Air filter
4. Air filter housing/cylinder shroud
5. Choke rod
6. Governor spring
7. Governor air vane
8. Notched speed control plate
9. Grommet
10. Governor shaft
11. Retainer
12. Governor link
13. Choke shaft
14. Intake elbow
15. Carburetor
16. Adapter
17. Heat shield

070AV, 090, 090AV, 090G and 090R should be 7500 rpm. On Models 08S and 08SQ, maximum no-load governed speed should be 8000 rpm.

IGNITION. All models are equipped with a conventional breaker point controlled flywheel magneto ignition system. Flywheel must be removed for access to ignition components.

Ignition breaker point gap should be set at 0.35-0.45 mm (0.014-0.016 in.). To check ignition timing, remove spark plug and position a dial indicator through spark plug hole so indicator contacts piston crown. Ignition timing is also indicated by timing marks on flywheel and crankcase on Models 08S, 08SQ and S-10. Ignition timing should occur as follows: 2.0 mm (0.080 in.) BTDC on Models 08S, 08SQ and S-10; and 3.0 mm (0.120 in.) BTDC on all other models. Ignition timing may be adjusted a small amount on Models 08S, 08SQ and S-10 by changing breaker point gap. Ignition timing on all other models may be adjusted by loosening ignition stator plate mounting screws and rotating plate as required.

LUBRICATION. The engine is lubricated by mixing oil with the fuel. Fuel:oil ratio is 40:1 when using Stihl two-stroke engine oil. If Stihl two-stroke oil is not available, a good quality oil designed for two-stroke air-cooled engines may be used when mixed at a 25:1 ratio. Use a separate container when mixing the oil and gasoline.

All models are equipped with an automatic chain oiler system. Manufacturer recommends using oil designed specifically for saw chain lubrication. If necessary, clean automotive oil may be used to lubricate saw chain. Use SAE 30 oil in warm weather and SAE 10 oil in cold weather.

Model 090G is equipped with a chain drive gear reduction transmission that should be lubricated with SAE 30 oil. Fill drive housing until oil reaches lower edge of fill plug hole.

CARBON. The muffler should be removed from the engine and the carbon scraped from the exhaust ports and muffler periodically.

REPAIRS

CRANKCASE PRESSURE TEST. An improperly sealed crankcase can cause the engine to be hard to start, run rough, have low power and overheat. Refer to ENGINE SERVICE section of this manual for crankcase pressure test procedure. If crankcase leakage is indicated, pressurize crankcase and use a soap and water solution to check gaskets, seals, pulse line and castings for leakage.

TIGHTENING TORQUES. The following torque values should be observed:

Clutch nut—
070, 070AV, 090,
090AV, 090G . . . . 44 N·m (32 ft.-lbs.)
Other models . . . . 30 N·m (22 ft.-lbs.)
Flywheel nut—
070, 070AV, 090,
090AV, 090G . . . . 34 N·m (25 ft.-lbs.)
Other models . . . . 30 N·m (22 ft.-lbs.)
Cylinder screws . . . . 9.8 N·m (87 in.-lbs.)
Connecting rod cap screws—
Early 070, 070AV,
090AV, 090G, 090R . . . . 9.8 N·m (87 in.-lbs.)

PISTON, RINGS, PIN AND CYLINDER. To remove cylinder and piston, first remove chain sprocket cover and fan housing on Models 08S, 08SQ and S-10. On all other models, remove filter cover, air filter and cylinder shroud. On all models, disconnect governor linkage and remove carburetor and muffler. Remove cylinder mounting screws and pull cylinder off piston. Remove piston pin retaining rings and push piston pin out of piston. Remove thrust washers (if used) and needle bearing from small end of connecting rod.

Cylinder bore is chrome plated and cylinder must be renewed if bore is deeply scratched, scored or if plating is worn through. Cylinder is available only with a fitted piston. Piston and cylinder are grouped into different size ranges and each group is marked with letter "A" to "E" on some models or "A" to "F" on other models. Letter "A" denotes smallest size with "E" or "F" being largest. The code letter stamped on the top of the piston and on either the top or bottom of the cylinder must be the same for proper fit of new piston in new cylinder. However, a new piston may be installed in a worn cylinder if clearance is satisfactory.

To reinstall piston on connecting rod, install one snap ring in piston. Lubricate piston pin needle bearing with engine oil and slide bearing into pin bore of connecting rod. Install piston on rod so arrow on piston crown points toward exhaust port of cylinder. Push piston pin into piston far enough to install second snap ring.

Locating pins are present in piston ring grooves to prevent ring rotation. Make certain ring end gaps are positioned around locating pins when installing cylinder. Lubricate piston rings and cylinder bore with engine oil. Use a suitable ring compressor to compress piston rings, then push cylinder down over piston. Tighten cylinder retaining screws in a crosswise pattern to torque of 9.8 N·m (87 in.-lbs.). Complete installation by reversing removal procedure.

CRANKSHAFT, CONNECTING ROD AND CRANKCASE. All models are equipped with a two-piece crankcase that must be separated to remove crankshaft and connecting rod. On early 070, 070AV, 090, 090AV, 090G and 090R models, connecting rod is a two-piece component (Fig. ST43). On all other models, connecting rod and crankshaft are a unit assembly and must be removed and serviced as a unit (Figs. ST42 and ST44).

To disassemble, proceed as follows: On Models 070, 070AV, 090, 090AV, 090G and 090R, remove air filter cover, air filter and cylinder shroud. On all models, remove fan housing, sprocket cover, bar and chain. Remove spark plug and install piston stop tool in spark plug hole or use other suitable means to prevent crankshaft from turning. Remove flywheel nut (right-hand threads) and use suitable puller to remove flywheel. Remove ignition stator plate. Remove clutch retaining nut (left-hand threads) and remove clutch assembly. A puller may be required to remove clutch rotor from crankshaft. Remove cylinder and piston as previously outlined. Remove screws or stud nuts retaining crankcase halves and drive out dowel pins. Separate crankcase halves being careful not to damage mating surfaces. Remove crankshaft from crankcase halves. On models with two-piece connecting rod, remove rod cap, connecting rod and roller bearings from crankshaft.

Inspect all parts for excessive wear or damage. Check rotation of connecting rod on crankpin. If roughness is noted, renew crankshaft and connecting rod assembly. The upper end of connecting rod is equipped with a needle bearing. Inspect main bearings and crankshaft journals for wear or damage and renew as necessary. Oil seals should be renewed. Crankcase halves are available only as matched unit. Crankcase halves should be heated to 100°C (212°F) prior to removing and installing main bearings.

On models with two-piece connecting rod, color coding is used to match connecting rod to crankshaft. Colors (red or green) must match on connecting rod and crankshaft for proper clearance. Rod and crankshaft dimensions are as follows:

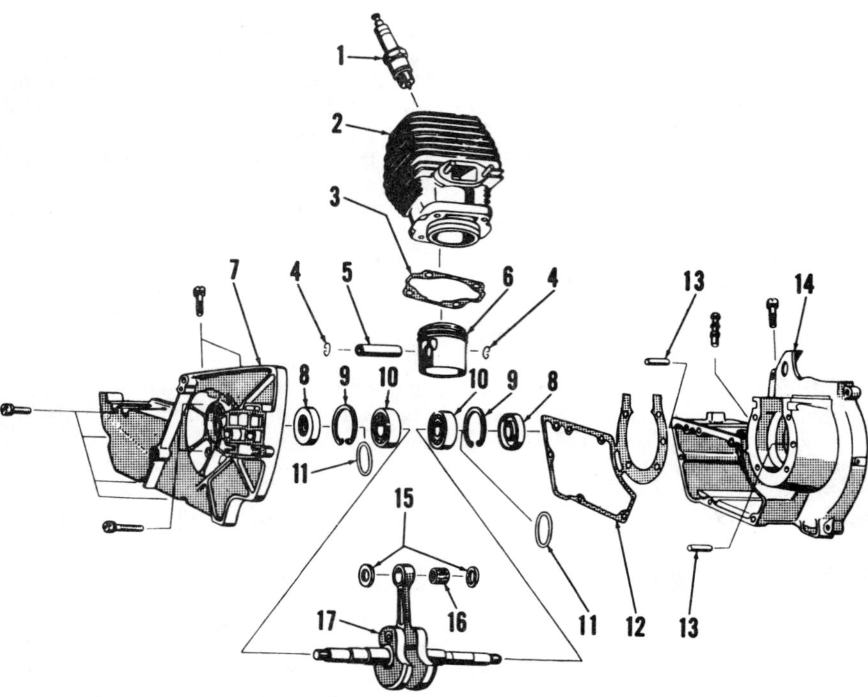

Fig. ST42—View of engine used on Models 08S, 08SQ and S-10. Shims (11) are used on S-10 models to control crankshaft end play. Washers (15) are absent on later Models 08S and 08SQ.

1. Spark plug
2. Cylinder
3. Gasket
4. Snap ring
5. Piston pin
6. Piston
7. Crankcase half
8. Seal
9. Snap ring
10. Ball bearing
11. Shim
12. Gasket
13. Dowel pin
14. Crankcase half
15. Washers
16. Bearing
17. Crankshaft & connecting rod assy.

Fig. ST43—Exploded view of early Model 090 engine. Early Models 070, 07AV, 090AV, 090G and 090R are similar.

1. Spark plug
2. Cylinder
3. Gasket
4. Retainer
5. Flat spring
6. Retainer
7. Valve
8. Insert
9. Rivet
10. Washer
11. Snap ring
12. Seal
13. Crankcase half
14. Snap ring
15. Washer
16. Roller bearing
17. Washer
18. Bearing
19. Connecting rod
20. Bearing
21. Crankshaft
22. Connecting rod cap
23. Check plate
24. Gasket
25. Crankcase half
26. Plug
27. Piston
28. Piston pin

Crankpin OD	Rod Bore
Green	
17.996-18.000 mm (0.7085-0.7087 in.)	24.010-24.014 mm (0.9453-0.9454 in.)
Red	
18.001-18.005 mm (0.7087-0.7088 in.)	24.015-24.019 mm (0.9455-0.9456 in.)

Use grease to hold bearing rollers in place when installing two-piece connecting rod. Tighten rod cap screws to 9.8 N·m (87 in.-lbs.).

Models 08S, 08SQ and S-10 are equipped with ball type main bearings which locate in crankcase with snap rings (9—Fig. ST42). Do not obstruct main bearing oil hole in crankcase when installing snap rings. Crankshaft end play is controlled by shims (11) on S-10 models. Desired end play is 0.20 mm (0.008 in.). When reassembling crankcase halves, tighten crankcase screws to 4.9 N·m (43 in.-lbs.).

Models 070, 070AV, 090, 090AV, 090G and 090R are equipped with roller type main bearings at each end of crankshaft. On some models, crankshaft end play is controlled by plastic check plates (23—Fig. ST43 and 12—Fig. ST44) which locate between shoulder on crankshaft (21) and roller bearings (16). Desired end play is 0.20-0.30 mm (0.008-0.016 in.). When reassembling crankcase halves, tighten stud nuts to 6.9 N·m (61 in.-lbs.).

CLUTCH. All models are equipped with a three- or six-shoe centrifugal type clutch. Refer to Figs. ST45, ST46 and ST47 for exploded views of clutch assemblies used.

To remove clutch assembly, first remove chain sprocket cover, bar and chain. Remove spark plug and install piston stop tool in spark plug hole to prevent crankshaft rotation. On some models, a crankshaft locking bolt is installed in place of plug (26—Fig. ST43) to prevent crankshaft from rotating. Note that clutch retaining nut has left-hand threads (turn clockwise to remove). A puller may be required to remove clutch rotor from crankshaft.

On Models 08S, 08SQ and S-10, clutch nut holds pin (1—Fig. ST45) that drives automatic chain oil pump contained in chain cover (17—Fig. ST49). Be sure pin is not damaged and meshes correctly with pump.

Clutch shoes and springs must be renewed in complete sets. Inspect clutch drum, needle bearing and chain drive sprocket for excessive wear and renew as necessary.

To install clutch, reverse removal procedure. Lubricate needle bearing with grease. On Models 070, 070AV, 090, 090AV, 090G and 090R, sleeve (4—Fig. ST46 and ST47) swells when clutch retaining nut is tightened to ensure tight

Illustrations courtesy Stihl Inc.

it of rotor (5) on crankshaft. Be certain leeve is clean and dry when installing. 'ighten clutch retaining nut to 30 N·m 22 ft.-lbs.) on Models 08S, 08SQ and S-0 and 44 N·m (32 ft.-lbs.) on all other nodels.

GEAR TRANSMISSION. Model 090G equipped with a gear reduction chain rive transmission. Chain drive sprocket 3—Fig. ST48) is a press fit on drive shaft 8). After removing retaining nut (1), procket may be removed using suitable uller. To disassemble transmission, rain oil from gear case and remove ransmission cover. Remove clutch assembly from crankshaft. Remove retaining bracket (13), spur gear (12) and needle bearing (11) from idler shaft (10). emove drive sprocket (3) as outlined bove and key (7) from drive shaft (8), nen withdraw spur gear (9) and shaft. Jse puller to remove spur gear from rive shaft if renewal is required. Remove snap ring (6) and bearing (5) from ear case.

Inspect components for excessive vear or damage. Reassembly is reverse f disassembly procedure. Refill gear ase with SAE 30 oil until oil level eaches lower edge of oil fill hole.

OIL PUMP. All models are equipped vith an automatic chain oiler system. Refer to Fig. ST49 and Fig. ST50 for exploded view of oil pumps.

Oil pump used on Models 08S, 08SQ and S-10 is actuated by pin (1—Fig. ST45) in clutch retaining nut. Drain oil tank and remove chain sprocket cover (17—Fig. ST49) for access to oil pump. To disassemble, pry out rubber plug (13) and use magnet to remove roller pin (3). Remove plunger (12) from pump housing (11). Tap worm gear (9) and seal (6) out of housing. Inspect all parts and renew as necessary. Lubricate all parts with oil during assembly. Oil pump output is not adjustable.

Oil pump used on Models 070, 070AV, 090, 090AV, 090G and 090R is actuated by crankcase pulsations against diaphragm (10—Fig. ST50) which causes pump plunger (13) to rotate. A pin (11) extends into groove in plunger and causes plunger to move back and forth in pump housing (6) as plunger rotates. On some models, pump output is adjustable by turning adjustment screw located on inner side of crankcase housing (1). Drain and remove oil tank (9) for access to oil pump. Unbolt and remove oil pump assembly from crankcase. Remove pin (11), then pull pump plunger (13) out of pump housing (6). Remove diaphragm (10) with pump rod. Remove snap ring (19) and separate washer (18), roller retainers (16), washers (17) and rollers (15) from plunger. Remove check valves (2) and manual pump piston (4).

Inspect all parts for wear or damage. If rollers (15) are scratched, oil output

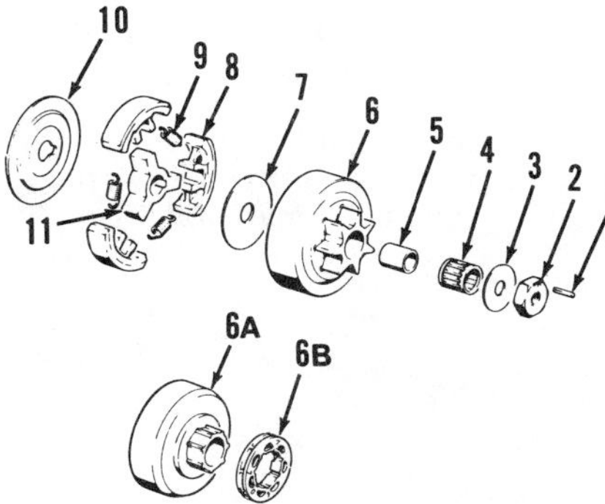

Fig. ST45—Exploded view of clutch assembly used on Models 08S, 08SQ and S-10. Pin (1) drives automatic chain oil pump. Clutch drum (6A) and sprocket (6B) are separate components on some models.

1. Pin
2. Nut
3. Washer
4. Needle bearing
5. Bearing race
6. Clutch drum
7. Washer
8. Clutch shoe
9. Spring
10. Washer
11. Rotor

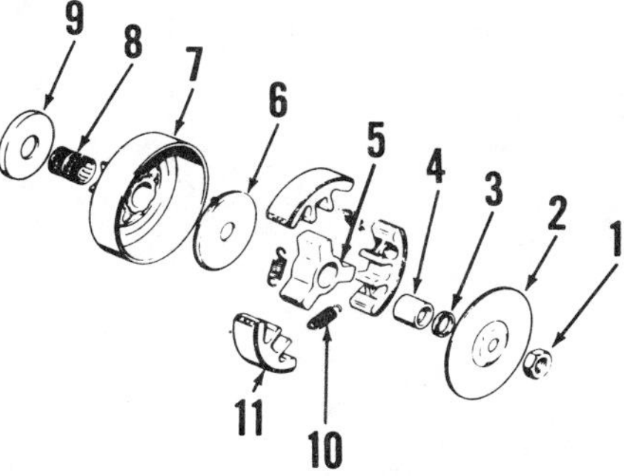

Fig. ST46—Exploded view of clutch used on Models 070 and 070AV.

1. Nut
2. Washer
3. Washer
4. Adapter sleeve
5. Rotor
6. Retainer
7. Clutch drum
8. Bearing
9. Plate
10. Springs
11. Clutch shoes

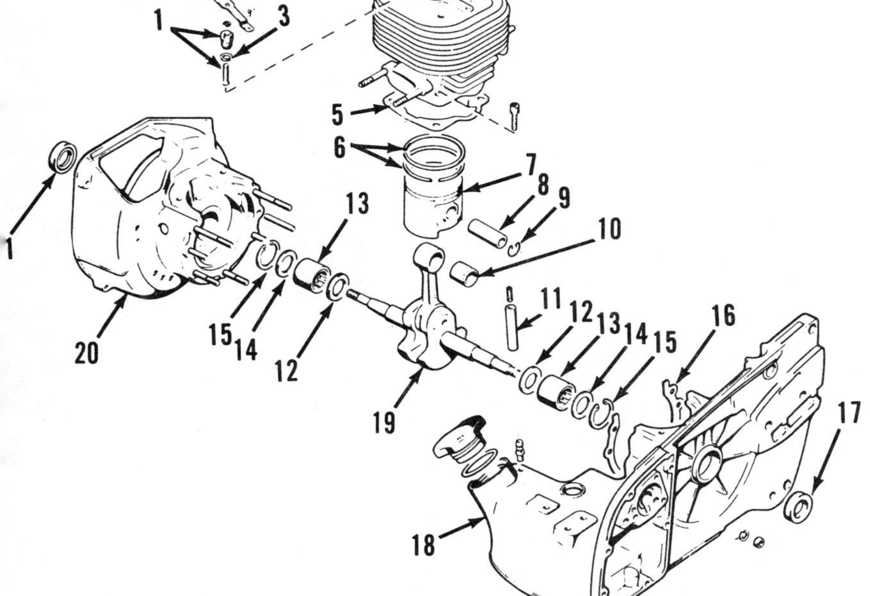

Fig. ST44—Exploded view of engine used on later 070, 070AV, 090, 090AV and 090G models.

Compression release valve
Flat spring
Seal ring
Cylinder
Gasket
6. Piston rings
7. Piston
8. Piston pin
9. Retaining ring
10. Needle bearing
11. Fuel tank vent
12. Check plates
13. Needle bearings
14. Thrust washers
15. Snap rings
16. Gasket
17. Seal
18. Crankcase half
19. Crankshaft & connecting rod assy.
20. Crankcase half
21. Seal

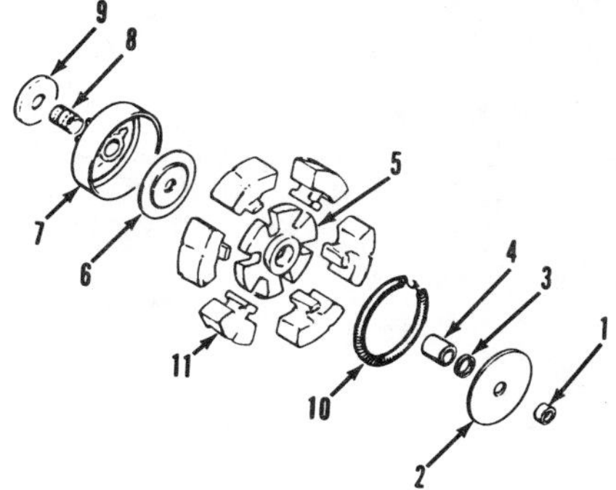

Fig. ST47—Exploded view of clutch assembly used on 090, 090AV, 090G and 090R models.

1. Nut
2. Washer
3. Spacer
4. Sleeve
5. Rotor
6. Washer
7. Clutch drum
8. Needle roller bearing
9. Plate
10. Spring
11. Clutch shoe

may be erratic. Polish out scratches with an oil stone or renew rollers as necessary. Renew all "O" rings. Make certain oil pickup line and strainer (7) are not plugged.

To reassemble, reverse disassembly procedure. When installing diaphragm (10), be sure that seal ring (12) is positioned on diaphragm rod and that rod properly engages roller retainers (16). When installing oil tank cover (9), make certain that manual pump rod (8) is correctly aligned with pump piston (4).

REWIND STARTER. Either a friction shoe type rewind starter as shown in Fig. ST51 or a pawl type rewind starter as shown in Fig. ST53 may be used.

On models equipped with friction shoe-type starter, unbolt and remove fan housing (3—Fig. ST51). Pull starter rope out of housing about 30 cm (12 in.), then pull loop of rope back through rope guide opening and unwind rope from pulley two turns while holding pulley. Allow pulley to slowly unwind to release rewind spring tension. Remove "E" ring (16) while holding thrust washer (15) down to prevent rewind spring from flying out. Carefully remove components from starter housing. If rewind spring (4) is to be removed, use care to prevent spring from unwinding uncontrolled.

New rope length should be 100 cm (39 in.) long and 4.5 mm ($^{3}/_{16}$ in.) in diameter. The leading edges (E—Fig. ST52) of friction shoes must be sharp to ensure proper starter operation. If leading edge is blunt from wear, shoes should be renewed.

When reassembling, be sure rewind spring is wound in housing in clockwise direction starting with outer coil. Be sure that friction washers (9—Fig. ST51) are positioned on each side of brake lever (13) and that lugs of brake lever point in clockwise direction as shown in Fig. ST52. Wind rope on pulley in clockwise direction as viewed from flywheel side of pulley. Turn pulley two turns clockwise to preload rewind spring, then pull rope through opening in fan housing and install rope handle. When rope is properly tensioned, rope handle should fit snugly against fan housing. When starter rope is fully extended, it should be possible to rotate rope pulley at least another half turn clockwise.

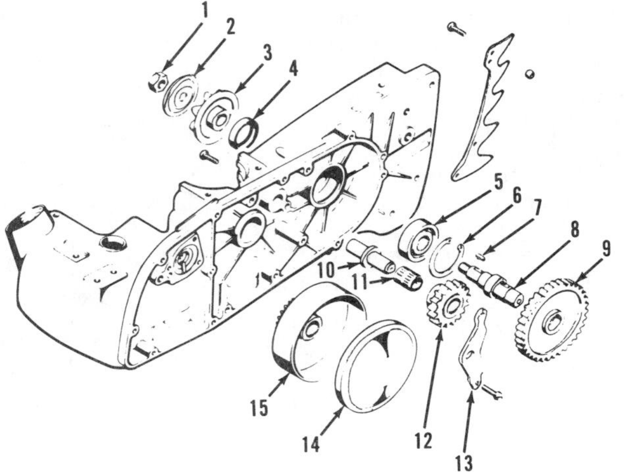

Fig. ST48—Exploded view of reduction gear chain drive transmission used on Model 090G.

1. Nut
2. Washer
3. Chain sprocket
4. Oil seal
5. Bearing
6. Snap ring
7. Key
8. Drive shaft
9. Spur gear
10. Idler shaft
11. Needle bearing
12. Idler gear
13. Retainer bracket
14. Cover
15. Clutch drum

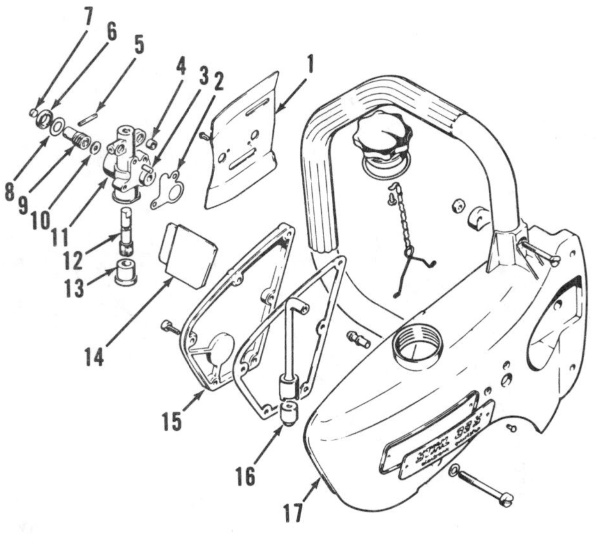

Fig. ST49—Exploded view of automatic chain oiler pump used on Models 08S, 08SQ and S-10. Pump output is not adjustable.

1. Guide plate
2. Gasket
3. Roller
4. Packing ring
5. Pin
6. Seal
7. Seal
8. Washer
9. Worm gear
10. Washer
11. Pump housing
12. Pump plunger
13. Plug
14. Dust guard plate
15. Oil tank cover
16. Oil pickup body
17. Sprocket cover/oil tank

Illustrations courtesy Stihl Inc

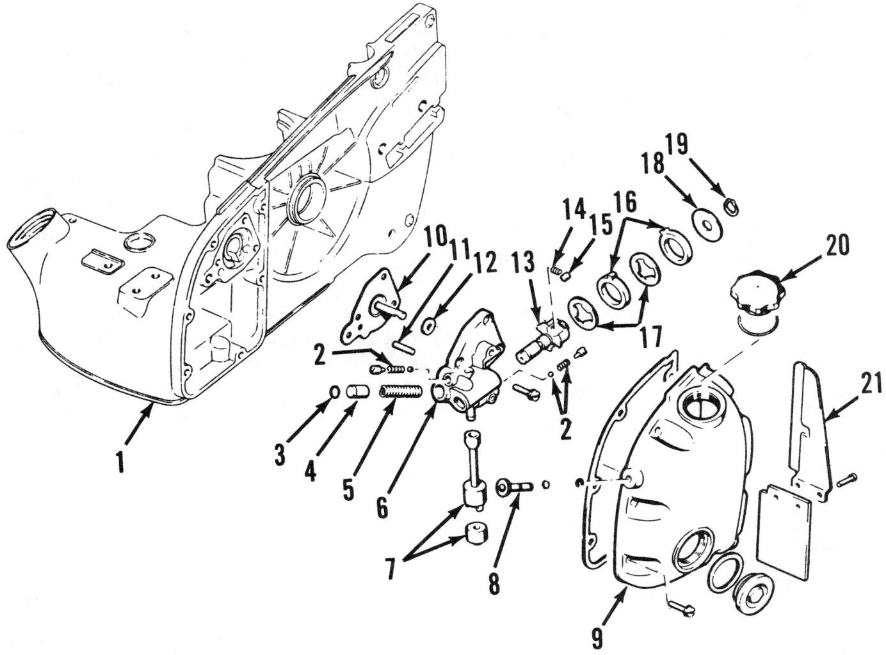

Fig. ST50—Exploded view of automatic chain oiler pump used on Models 070, 070AV, 090, 090AV, 090G and 090R.

1. Crankcase half
2. Check valves
3. "O" ring
4. Manual pump piston
5. Spring
6. Pump housing
7. Oil pickup tube
8. Manual pump button
9. Oil tank cover
10. Diaphragm
11. Pin
12. Sealing ring
13. Pump plunger
14. Spring
15. Roller
16. Roller retainers
17. Washers
18. Washer
19. Snap ring
20. Oil tank cap
21. Saw dust guard

Fig. ST51—Exploded view of typical friction shoe type starter used on some models.

1. Rope handle
2. Guide bushing
3. Starter housing
4. Rewind spring
5. Washer
6. Bushing
7. Rope pulley
8. Washer
9. Friction washers
10. Spring retainer
11. Spring
12. Friction shoe plate
13. Brake lever
14. Spring
15. Thrust washer
16. "E" ring

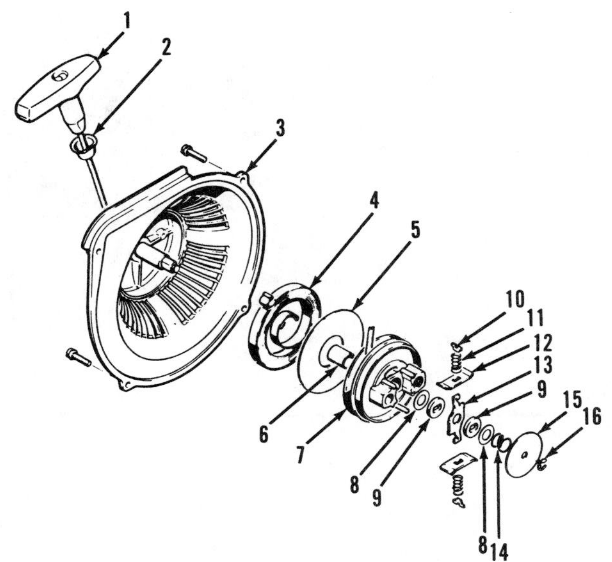

Fig. ST52—Leading edges (E) of friction shoe plates must be sharp or shoes may not properly engage starter drum.

Illustrations courtesy Stihl Inc.

On models equipped with pawl-type starter, fan housing (3—Fig. ST53) must be removed to service starter. Remove rope handle (1) and allow rope pulley (6) to slowly unwind to relieve tension on rewind spring. Remove retainer clip (9) and withdraw rope pulley and pawls (8). If necessary, lift rewind spring (5) from housing being careful not to allow spring to unwind uncontrolled.

Rewind spring should be wound in counterclockwise direction in the spring housing starting with outer coil. Starter rope length should be 100 cm (39 in.) long and 4.5 mm ($^3/_{16}$ in.) in diameter. Wind rope on pulley in clockwise direction as viewed from flywheel side of pulley. To preload rewind spring, pull rope out of housing about 30 cm (12 in.). While holding rope pulley from turning, wind two turns of rope on pulley, then release pulley. Spring tension is correct if rope handle is pulled snugly against starter housing. With rope fully extended, it should be possible to rotate pulley at least another half turn clockwise.

CHAIN BRAKE. Model 08SQ is equipped with a chain brake system designed to stop chain movement should kickback occur. Chain brake is activated when the operator's hand strikes hand guard (1—Fig. ST54), thereby allowing cam (7) to release brake spring (14). Spring then draws brake band tight around clutch drum to stop chain. Pull back hand guard to reset mechanism. No adjustment of brake mechanism is required.

To disassemble brake unit, remove chain sprocket guard, bar and chain. Unbolt and remove brake cover (9—Fig. ST54). Disconnect brake spring (14). Remove brake anchor screw (13) and brake band. Remove "E" ring (8), brake actuating cam (7) and levers (3 and 4) as necessary.

Renew components as required. Reassembly is reverse of disassembly procedure. No adjustment of brake mechanism is required.

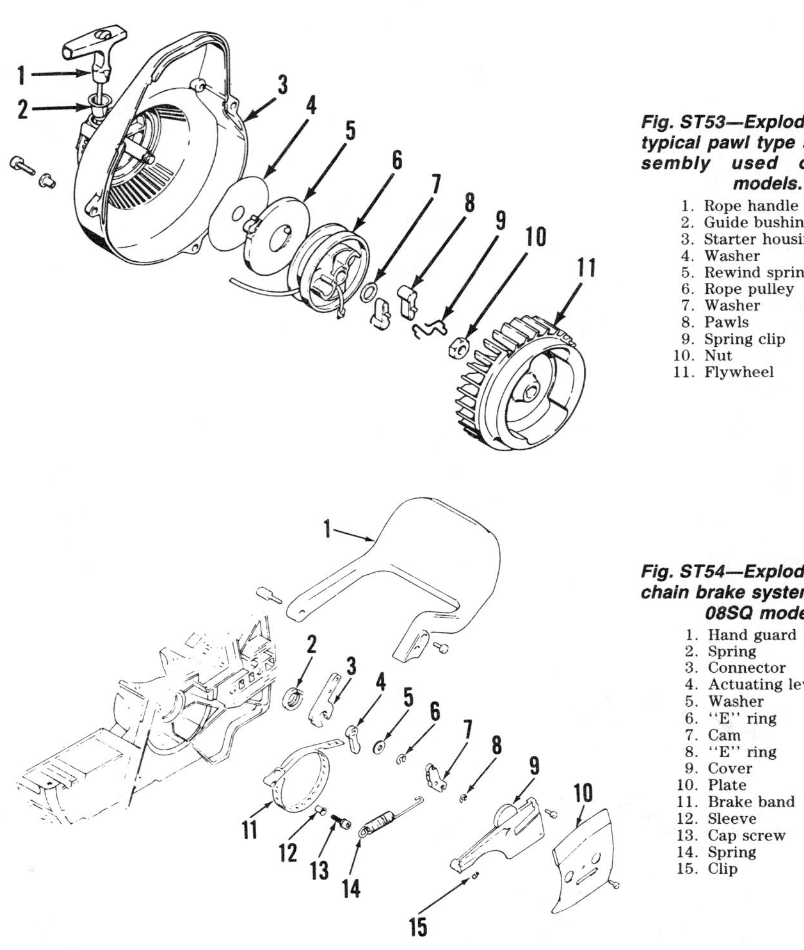

Fig. ST53—Exploded view of typical pawl type starter assembly used on some models.

1. Rope handle
2. Guide bushing
3. Starter housing
4. Washer
5. Rewind spring
6. Rope pulley
7. Washer
8. Pawls
9. Spring clip
10. Nut
11. Flywheel

Fig. ST54—Exploded view of chain brake system used on 08SQ models.

1. Hand guard
2. Spring
3. Connector
4. Actuating lever
5. Washer
6. "E" ring
7. Cam
8. "E" ring
9. Cover
10. Plate
11. Brake band
12. Sleeve
13. Cap screw
14. Spring
15. Clip

Illustrations courtesy Stihl Inc

STIHL

Model	Bore mm (in.)	Stroke mm (in.)	Displacement cc (cu. in.)	Drive Type
028AV, 028AVE, 028WB, 028WBE	42* (1.65)	31 (1.22)	43* (2.62)	Direct
028AVEQ, 028AVEQWB	44 (1.73)	31 (1.22)	47 (2.87)	Direct
028AVS, 028AVSEQ, 028AVSEQWB	46 (1.81)	31 (1.22)	51.4 (3.14)	Direct
038AV, 038AVE, 038AVEFB, 038FB	48 (1.89)	34 (1.34)	61 (3.72)	Direct
038S, 038AVSE, 038AVSEQ, 038SP	50 (1.97)	34 (1.34)	67 (4.09)	Direct
038AVSEQFB, 038AVSEQSP	50 (1.97)	34 (1.34)	67 (4.09)	Direct
038M, 038AVMEQ, 038MAG, 038AVMERQZ	52 (2.05)	34 (1.34)	72.2 (4.4)	Direct
042AVE	49 (1.93)	36 (1.42)	68 (4.15)	Direct
048AVE, 048AVSEQ	52 (2.05)	36 (1.42)	76 (4.64)	Direct

* Some 028 models may have 44 mm (1.73 in.) bore and 47 cc (2.87 cu. in.) displacement.

MAINTENANCE

SPARK PLUG. Recommended spark plug is Bosch WSR6F or NGK BPMR7A. Spark plug electrode gap should be 0.5 mm (0.02 in.).

CARBURETOR. Series 028 saws may be equipped with either a Tillotson HU or a Walbro WT diaphragm carburetor. Series 038 saws may be equipped with either a Tillotson HK or a Bing diaphragm carburetor. Model 042AVE and 048 series saws are equipped with a Walbro WS diaphragm carburetor. Refer to CARBURETOR SERVICE section for carburetor overhaul.

Initial setting of low and high speed mixture screws for all models is one turn open from a lightly seated position. Make final adjustments with engine warm and running. Adjust idle speed screw so engine idles just below clutch engagement speed. Adjust low speed mixture screw to obtain highest idle speed, then turn screw counterclockwise approximately $^1/_8$ turn. Engine should accelerate smoothly without hesitation. If engine stumbles or seems sluggish when accelerating, adjust low speed mixture screw until engine accelerates without hesitation. Adjust high speed mixture screw to obtain optimum performance with saw under cutting load. Do not adjust high speed mixture screw too lean (turned too far clockwise) as engine may be damaged from lack of lubrication and overheating.

IGNITION. Breaker Point Ignition. Models 028AV, 028WB and 038AV are equipped with breaker points, while all other models use a breakerless transistor ignition system.

Flywheel must be removed to service breaker points (5—Fig. ST60). Breaker point gap should be 0.35-0.40 mm (0.014-0.016 in.) on Models 028AV, 028WB and 038AV. Air gap between flywheel magnets and coil legs should be 0.20-0.30 mm (0.008-0.012 in.). Air gap can be adjusted by loosening coil mounting screws and repositioning coil as necessary. Ignition timing should be 2.1-2.3 mm (0.083-0.090 in.) BTDC on 028AV and 028WB models and 2.3-2.7 mm (0.090-0.106 in.) BTDC on Model 038AV. Timing marks are located on flywheel and crankcase. Vary breaker point gap to adjust timing. Edge gap (E—Fig. ST61) between trailing edge of flywheel north magnet and upper edge of ignition coil center leg should be 4-8 mm (0.157-0.315 in.) at point of ignition. Edge gap should be correct if ignition timing is properly timed. Edge gap may be adjusted by adjusting breaker point gap.

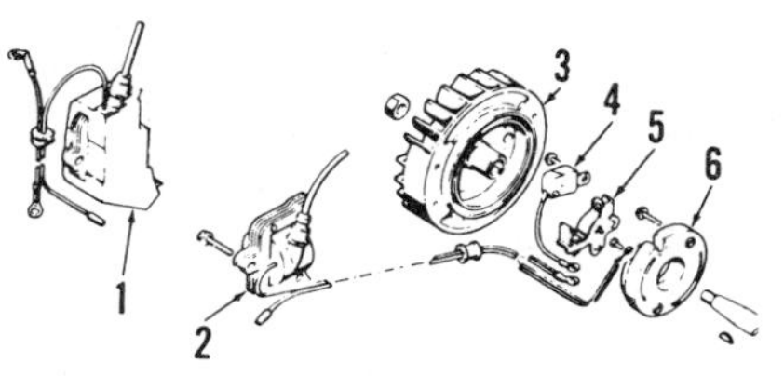

Fig. ST60—Components (2, 3, 4 and 5) are used on models with breaker point ignition. Components (2, 3 and 6) are used on models with Bosch electronic ignition. Components (1 and 3) are used on Models with SEM electronic ignition system.

1. SEM ignition module
2. Ignition coil
3. Flywheel
4. Condenser
5. Breaker points
6. Bosch ignition module

Breakerless Ignition (All Models Except 028AV, 028WB and 038AV). Models 042AVE, 048AVE, 048AVES AND 048AVSEQ are equipped with a SEM breakerless transistor ignition system while Models 028AVE, 028AVEQ, 028WBE, 028AVSEQ, 038AVE, 038AVEQ, 038AVSE and 038AVMEQ may be equipped with either a Bosch or SEM breakerless transistor ignition sys-

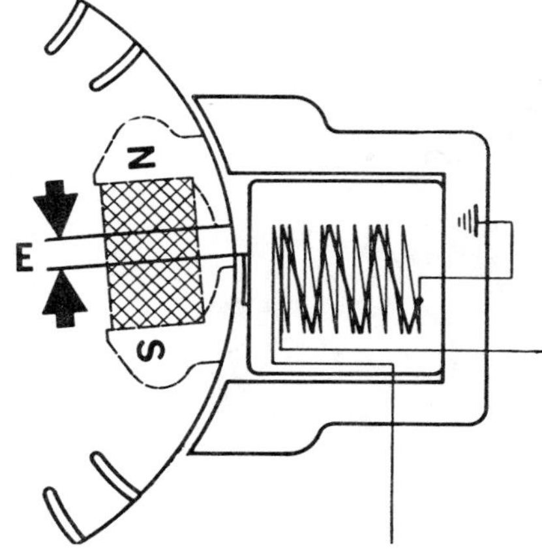

Fig. ST61—Edge gap (E) between trailing edge of magnet north pole shoe and adjacent edge of ignition coil center leg should be 4-8 mm (0.157-0.315 in.) on models with breaker-point ignition.

tem. The Bosch system is identified by the ignition module (6—Fig. ST60) located behind the flywheel and an external ignition coil (2) while the SEM ignition module and ignition coil are a one-piece externally mounted unit (1).

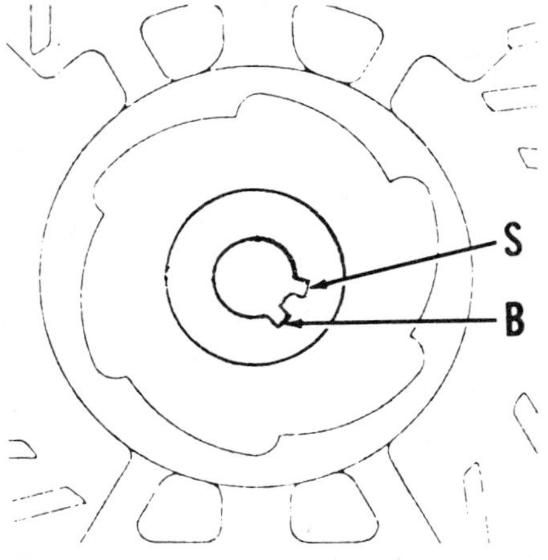

Fig. ST62—View showing location of replacement flywheel keyways for Bosch (B) or SEM (S) ignition system. See text.

NOTE: Replacement flywheel for some models has two keyways for use with Bosch or SEM ignition systems. When viewed from finned side of flywheel, keyway (S—Fig. ST62) should mate with crankshaft key on SEM equipped models and keyway (B) should be used on Bosch equipped models.

Air gap between flywheel magnets and coil legs on models with electronic ignition should be 0.20-0.30 mm (0.008-0.012 in.). Ignition timing is not adjustable, but timing may be checked to ensure proper ignition module operation. A timing light is required to check ignition timing on transistor ignition. Ignition should occur at 2.5 mm (0.098 in.) BTDC on 028 series saws, 042AVE models and 048 series saws. On 038 series saws, ignition should occur at 2.9 mm (0.114 in.) BTDC. To check timing, use a dial indicator to locate piston at specified timing point and scribe timing marks on flywheel and armature leg. A specially modified fan housing with a hole cut in lower right half of the housing must be used for this test procedure so that timing marks can be seen. Install modified fan housing and spark plug, then check timing with engine running at 8000 rpm. Timing marks should appear to be aligned if ignition module is functioning properly.

Bosch ignition coil can be tested using an ohmmeter to measure resistance of coil windings. Primary resistance should be 0.7 ohm. Secondary resistance should be 7700-10,300 ohms. Renew coil if readings are not within specified limits.

LUBRICATION. The engine is lubricated by mixing oil with the fuel. Recommended oil is Stihl two-stroke engine oil. Recommended fuel:oil ratio is 40:1 when using Stihl two-stroke engine oil. If Stihl two-stroke engine oil is not available, a good quality oil designed for use in air-cooled two-stroke engines may be used when mixed at a 25:1 ratio. Use a separate container when mixing oil and gasoline.

All models are equipped with an automatic chain oiler system. Manufacturer recommends using saw chain lubricating oil, or clean automotive type oil may be used as an alternative. Automatic oil pump output on 028 series saws is not adjustable. Oil pump output on all other models is adjusted by turning screw located on underside of saw.

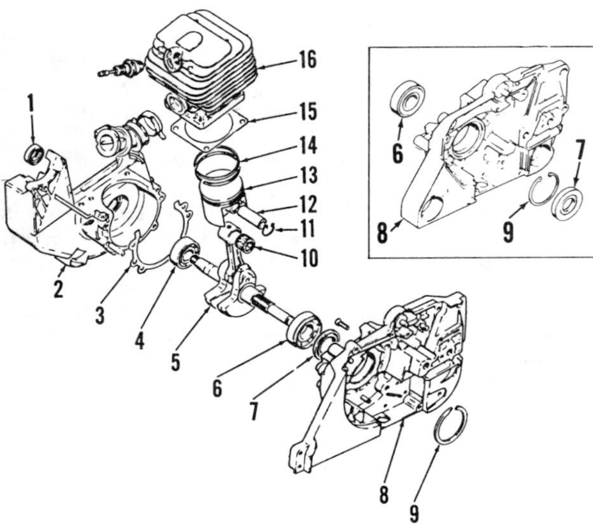

Fig. ST63—Exploded view of Model 042AVE engine. Other models are similar. Right main bearing, snap ring and seal used on 038 series saws are shown in inset. Refer to text.

1. Oil seal
2. Crankcase half
3. Gasket
4. Bearing
5. Crankshaft & connecting rod assy.
6. Bearing
7. Oil seal
8. Crankcase half
9. Snap ring
10. Needle bearing
11. Pin retainer
12. Piston pin
13. Piston
14. Piston rings
15. Gasket
16. Cylinder

Fig. ST64—Exploded view of clutch used on early 028 series saws without a chain brake.

1. Plate
2. Spring
3. Clutch shoe
4. Hub
5. Clutch drum
6. Oil pump drive gear
7. Bearing
8. Side cover
9. Bearing
10. Sprocket
11. Washer
12. "E" ring

REPAIRS

CRANKCASE PRESSURE TEST. An improperly sealed crankcase can cause the engine to be hard to start, run rough, have low power and overheat. Refer to ENGINE SERVICE section of this manual for crankcase pressure test procedure. If crankcase leakage is indicated, pressurize crankcase and use a soap and water solution to check gaskets, seals, pulse line and castings for leakage.

TIGHTENING TORQUES. Refer to the following table of torque values when tightening fasteners.

Flywheel nut (all models) .... 30 N·m (22 ft.-lbs.)

Clutch hub or hub carrier—
028AV, 028AVE, 028AVEQ, 028AVSEQ, 028WB, 028WBE .... 50 N·m (37 ft.-lbs.)

All other models .... 60 N·m (44 ft.-lbs.)

Cylinder—
028AV, 028AVE, 028AVEQ, 028WB, 028WBE, 028AVSEQ, 038AV, 038AVE, 038AVSE, 038AVMEQ .... 8 N·m (70 in.-lbs.)

Illustrations courtesy Stihl Inc.

042AVE, 048AVE, 048AVES,
048AVSEQ . . . . 10 N·m (89 in.-lbs.)
Crankcase—
028AV, 028AVE, 028AVEQ, 028AVSEQ, 028WB, 028WBE . . . . 8 N·m (70 in.-lbs.)
All other models . . . . 5 N·m (44 in.-lbs.)

PISTON, PIN, RINGS AND CYLINDER. To disassemble, remove air filter cover, cylinder shroud, muffler and carburetor. Remove cylinder mounting screws and pull cylinder (16—Fig. ST63) off the piston (13). Extract snap rings (11) and push piston pin (12) out of piston. If pin is stuck, it may be necessary to tap it out using a brass drift and hammer. Be careful not to apply side pressure to connecting rod when removing piston pin.

The cylinder is available only with a fitted piston. However, a new piston marked "B" is available and may be used with any used cylinder.

All models are equipped with two piston rings. On all models, a locating pin is present in piston ring grooves to prevent ring rotation. Be sure piston ring end gaps are properly positioned around locating pin when installing cylinder. Install piston so arrow and "A" mark on piston crown point toward cylinder exhaust port. Lubricate piston rings and cylinder bore with engine oil, then install cylinder using a new gasket (15). Tighten cylinder screws evenly to specified torque.

CONNECTING ROD, CRANKSHAFT AND CRANKCASE. All models are equipped with a connecting rod, bearing and crankshaft (5—Fig. ST63) which are pressed together and available only as a unit assembly. The crankshaft is supported by a ball bearing at each end. Crankcase halves (2 and 8) must be split to remove crankshaft assembly. To split crankcase, remove fan housing, flywheel, generator, sprocket guard, bar and chain, chain brake assembly, and clutch assembly. Remove cylinder and piston as outlined above. Unbolt and remove tank housing and handlebar. Remove crankcase mounting screws and drive the two crankcase dowel pins into ignition side crankcase half. Tap end of crankshaft with a soft hammer to split crankcase and remove crankshaft from main bearings.

Heat crankcase halves to approximately 175°C (300°F) prior to installing main bearings (4 and 6). Install bearings so outer race bottoms against snap ring (9) or bearing seat shoulder. On all models except 038 series saws, note that oil seal recess of clutch side main bearing (6) should face outward. Clutch side oil seal (7) seats in outer flange of main bearing. On 038 series saws, crankshaft seal (7) shown in inset of Fig. ST62 is positioned on the outside of snap ring (9) and seats in right crankcase half (8).

On all models, heat inner races of ball bearings with a soldering iron to ease installation of crankshaft. Tighten crankcase screws in a diagonal pattern to specified torque and drive locating dowel pins into clutch side crankcase half.

CLUTCH. Early 028 series saws without chain brake are equipped with the clutch shown in Fig. ST64. Install plate (1) so concave side is toward clutch hub (4). Clutch hub has left-hand threads and should be tightened to 37 ft.-lbs. (50 N·m). Install oil pump drive gear (6) so gear teeth are toward clutch drum.

Early 028 series saws with chain brake and 042AVE models with chain brake use the clutch shown in Fig. ST65. Hub carrier (11) has left-hand threads and screws onto crankshaft. Special socket 1118 893 1300 for early 028 series saws or special socket 1117 893 1300 may be used to remove or install hub carrier. Carrier teeth engage teeth of drive plate (12) which has slots to accept clutch hub (17) dogs. Spring plate (14) is located between drive plate (12) and clutch hub and must be installed so spring leaves extend toward drive plate (12) as shown in Fig. ST66. Clutch hub (17—Fig. ST65) is retained by snap ring (19) and supported by needle bearing (13) which rides on carrier (11). Clutch drum (20) is supported on crankshaft by needle bearing (21). The automatic oil pump is driven by drive gear (26) which is mounted on clutch drum (20) with gear teeth toward drum.

Most later 028 series saws and 038 series saws are equipped with clutch assembly shown in Fig. ST67. Clutch hub (17) has left-hand threads. Clutch drum (20) is supported by needle bearing (21). The automatic oil pump is driven by

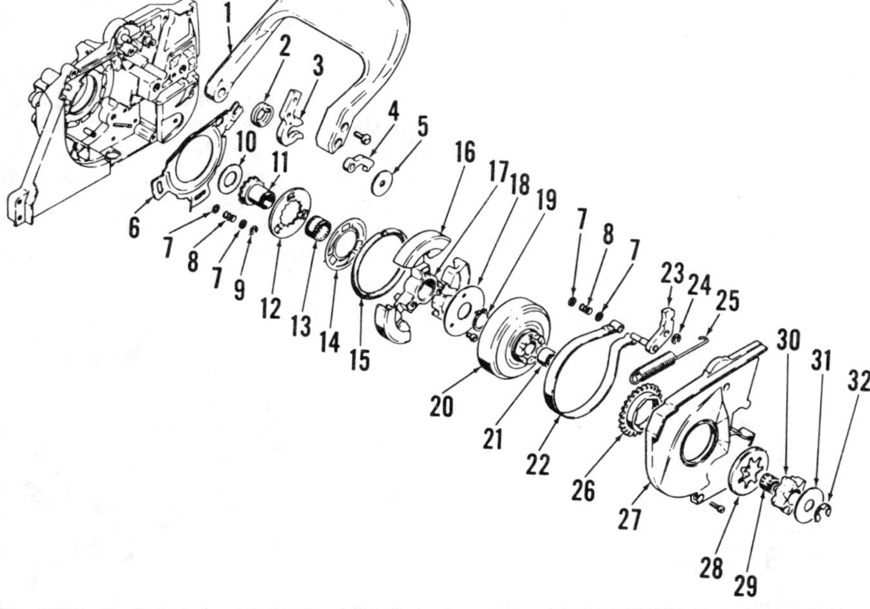

Fig. ST65—Exploded view of clutch and chain brake used on Model 042AVE. Early 028 series saws with chain brake are similar.

1. Brake lever
2. Spring
3. Brake arm
4. Latch
5. Washer
6. Plate
7. Washer
8. Spring
9. "E" ring
10. Washer
11. Hub carrier
12. Drive plate
13. Needle bearing
14. Spring plate
15. Spring
16. Clutch shoe
17. Hub
18. Plate
19. Snap ring
20. Clutch drum
21. Needle bearing
22. Brake band
23. Brake band lever
24. "E" ring
25. Brake spring
26. Oil pump drive gear
27. Side cover
28. Sprocket washer
29. Needle bearing
30. Sprocket
31. Washer
32. "E" ring

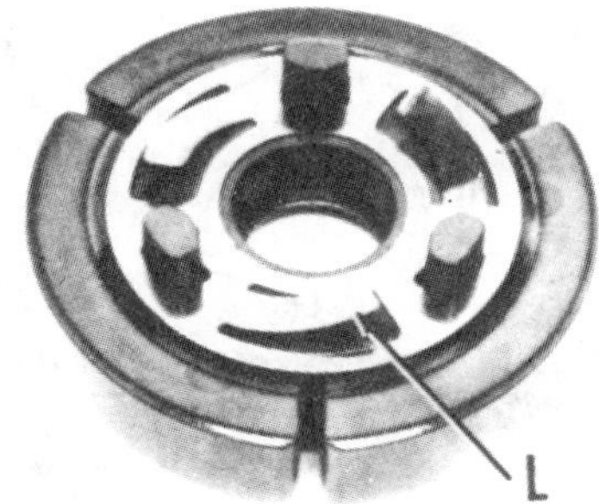

Fig. ST66—Install spring plate on clutch hub so spring leaves (L) extend toward drive plate (12—Fig. ST65).

drive gear (26) which is mounted on clutch drum (20) with gear teeth toward the drum. Washer (33) and snap ring (34) retain oil pump drive gear in position.

All other models, with or without chain brake systems, are equipped with a clutch assembly typical of the type shown in Fig. ST68. Clutch hub (17) has left-hand threads. Plate (18) is absent on 028 series and 038 series saws.

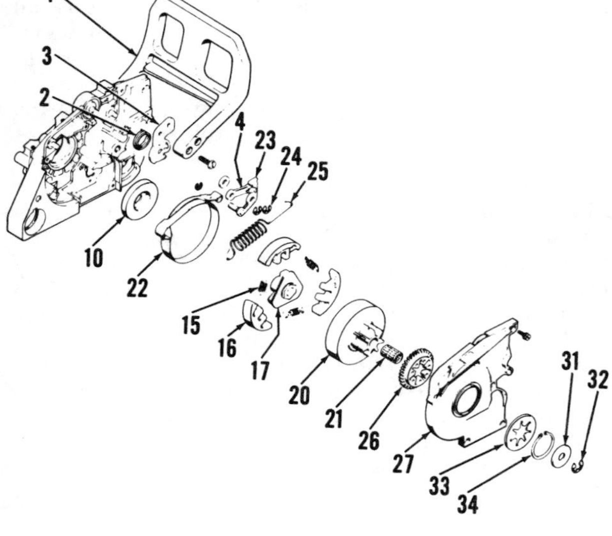

Fig. ST67—Exploded view of clutch assembly used on most later 028 series saws and 038 series saws. Refer to Fig. ST65 for parts identification except for washer (33) and snap ring (34). Chain brake system is used on 028AVEQ and 038AVEQ models.

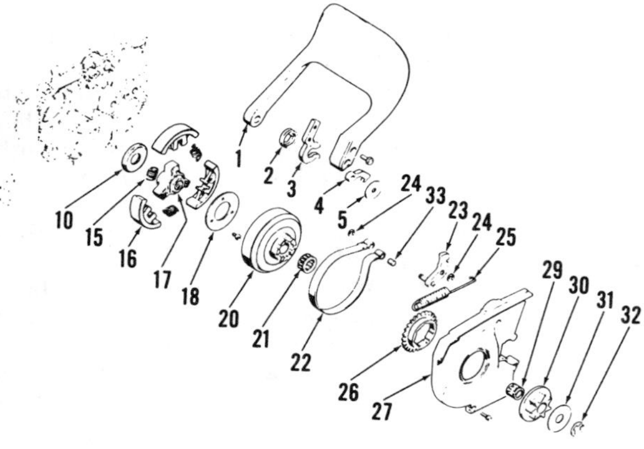

Fig. ST68—Exploded view of clutch and chain brake used on 048 series saws and some 028 and 038 series saws. Refer to Fig. ST65 for parts identification.

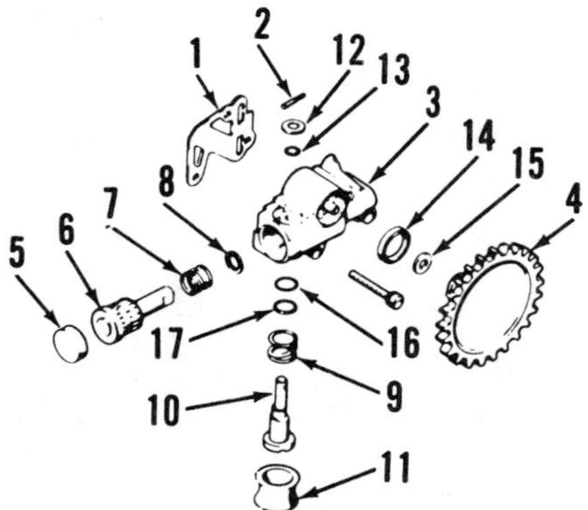

Fig. ST69—Exploded view of Model 042AVE and 038 and 048 series automatic oil pumps.

1. Gasket
2. Adapter pin
3. Pump body
4. Oil pump driven gear
5. Plug
6. Plunger
7. Spring
8. Washer
9. Spring
10. Adjuster
11. Boot
12. Spring washer
13. "O" ring
14. Seal
15. Washer
16. "O" ring
17. Washer

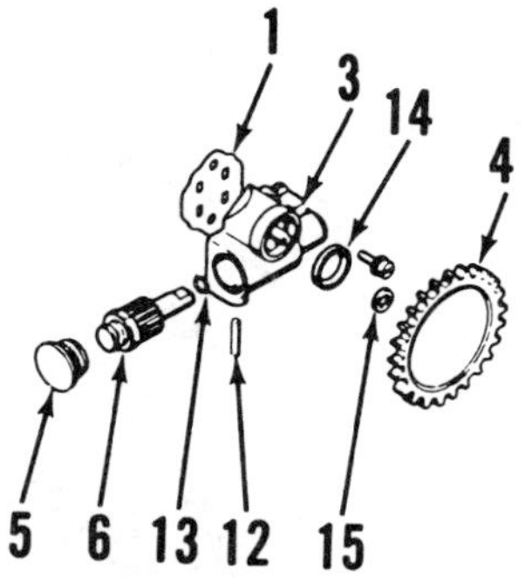

Fig. ST70—Exploded view of typical oil pump used on 028 series saws. "O" ring (13) and seal (14) are absent on some pumps. When disassembling, use a magnet to remove pin (12) prior to removing plunger (6).

1. Gasket
3. Pump body
4. Oil pump driven gear
5. Plug
6. Plunger
12. Pin
13. "O" ring
14. Seal
15. Washer

CHAIN BRAKE. Early 028 series saws and Model 042AVE are equipped with chain brake system shown in Fig. ST65 while remaining models may be equipped with chain brake systems shown in Figs. ST67 or ST68.

On all models, chain brake is activated when operator's hand strikes brake lever (1) causing latch (4) to disengage brake band lever (23) which releases brake spring (25). The brake spring then pulls brake band (22) around clutch drum to stop chain movement. No adjustment of chain brake mechanism is required.

If chain brake fails to operate correctly, remove side cover (27) and inspect components for wear or damage. Renew faulty parts as necessary.

OIL PUMP. All models are equipped with the gear driven chain oil pump shown in Fig. ST69 or ST70. The oil pump drive gear is mounted on the clutch drum and meshes with driven gear (4). A worm on driven gear backside rotates oil plunger (6). Oil plunger reciprocates in pump body due to cam on plunger riding against adjuster (10—Fig. ST69) or pin (12—Fig. ST70) on nonadjustable pumps.

Oil tank vent is located in oil tank of Model 042AVE and 048 series saws while vent on 028 and 038 series saws is located adjacent to bar studs. Tank vent (V—Fig. ST71) on models so equipped may be pried out for inspection or renewal. Press or drive vent into bore so annular groove is flush with top edge of bore.

REWIND STARTER. All models except early 042AVE models are equipped with the pawl type starter shown in Fig. ST72. To disassemble starter, detach starter housing, remove rope handle and allow rope to wind slowly onto rope pulley. Remove retaining clip (7) and remove rope pulley (3). Care should be

Fig. ST71—View of oil tank vent (V) used on 028 and 038 series saws. Vent may be pried from bore as shown. Vent must be open for proper operation of chain oiler system.

Illustrations courtesy Stihl Inc.

used when removing rewind spring (2) and case as uncontrolled uncoiling of spring may be harmful.

Rope length should be 100 cm (40 in.) and 4.5 mm (3/16 in.) in diameter. Wind rope around rope pulley in a clockwise direction as viewed from flywheel side of pulley. Note that clip (7) retains pulley and pawl (6). Turn rope pulley three turns clockwise when preloading rewind spring. Rewind spring tension is correct if rope handle is pulled snugly against housing with rope fully retracted and if pulley will rotate at least an additional half turn with rope fully extended.

Early Model 042AVE is equipped with the friction shoe type starter shown in Fig. ST73. To disassemble starter, detach starter housing, remove rope handle and allow rope to slowly wind onto rope pulley. Remove "E" ring (13) while holding thrust washer (12) down to prevent rewind spring from flying out. Carefully remove friction shoe assembly and rope pulley from starter housing. If rewind spring (2) is to be removed, use care to prevent spring from unwinding uncontrolled.

The leading edges (E—Fig. ST73A) of friction shoes must be sharp to ensure proper starter operation. If leading edge is blunt from wear, shoes should be renewed. New rope length should be 115 cm (45 in.) long and 4.5 mm (3/16 in.) in diameter.

When reassembling, be sure rewind spring is wound in spring case (2) in counterclockwise direction starting with outer coil. Be sure that friction washers (6—Fig. ST73) are positioned on each side of brake lever (10) and that lugs of brake lever point in clockwise direction as shown in Fig. ST73A. Wind rope on pulley in clockwise direction as viewed from flywheel side of pulley. Turn pulley two turns clockwise to preload rewind spring, then pull rope through opening in fan housing and install rope handle. When rope is properly tensioned, rope handle should fit snugly against fan housing. When starter rope is fully extended, it should be possible to rotate rope pulley at least another half turn clockwise.

HANDLE HEATER. Some models are equipped with an electric handle heating system. An electric current generated by a coil module located under the flywheel passes through a switch and then to heating elements in the handlebar and rear grip.

To check system, remove carburetor cover and rear grip insert. Use an ohmmeter to perform the following checks: Disconnect wire from switch and connect ohmmeter leads to switch terminal 1 and to ground. Continuity should be indicated when switch is in "heat" position. To perform remaining checks, disconnect generator wire (G—Fig. ST74) from terminal (T1). Connect ohmmeter leads to terminals (T1 and T2). Ohmmeter should read approximately 1 ohm. If ohmmeter reads infinity, heating element in rear grip is faulty and must be renewed. If ohmmeter reads zero ohms, insulation of rear grip heating element is damaged and must be repaired. Connect ohmmeter leads to terminal (T2) and to ground. Ohmmeter reading should be approximately 2 ohms. If ohmmeter reads infinity, handlebar heating element is faulty and handlebar must be renewed as heating element is not available separately. If ohmmeter reads zero ohms, insulation is damaged and must be repaired. Connect ohmmeter leads to generator lead (G) and to ground. Ohmmeter should read approximately 0.6 ohms. If ohmmeter reads infinity, generator must be renewed. If ohmmeter reads zero, insulation is damaged and must be repaired.

When installing generator, be sure generator is centered on crankshaft and coils do not contact flywheel.

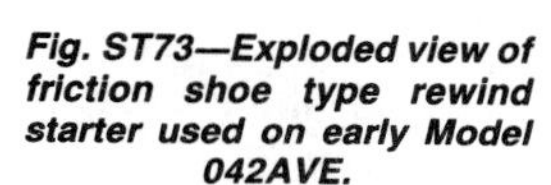

Fig. ST73—Exploded view of friction shoe type rewind starter used on early Model 042AVE.

1. Starter housing
2. Rewind spring & case
3. Rope pulley
4. Pin
5. Washer
6. Slotted washer
7. Retainer
8. Spring
9. Friction shoe plate
10. Brake lever
11. Spring
12. Thrust washer
13. "E" ring
14. Starter cup
15. Flywheel

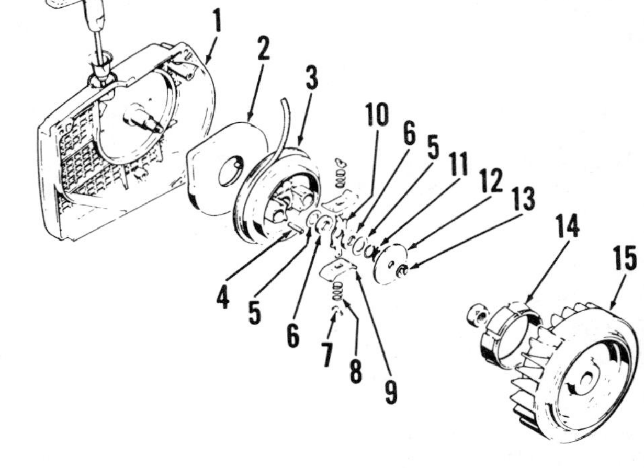

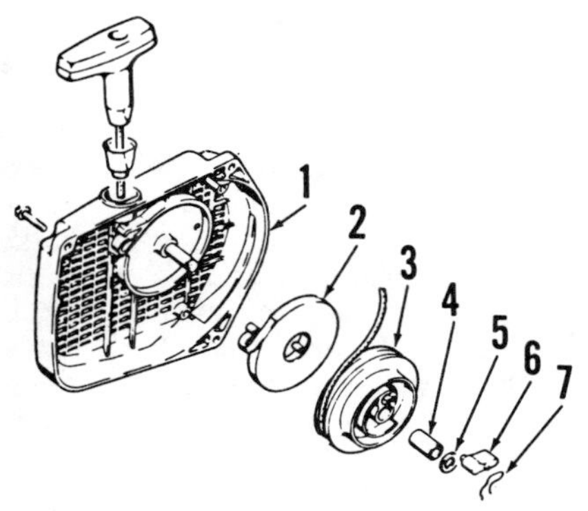

Fig. ST72—Exploded view of typical pawl type rewind starter used on all models except early 042AVE models which use starter shown in Fig. ST73.

1. Starter housing
2. Rewind spring & case
3. Rope pulley
4. Bushing
5. Washer
6. Pawl
7. Spring clip

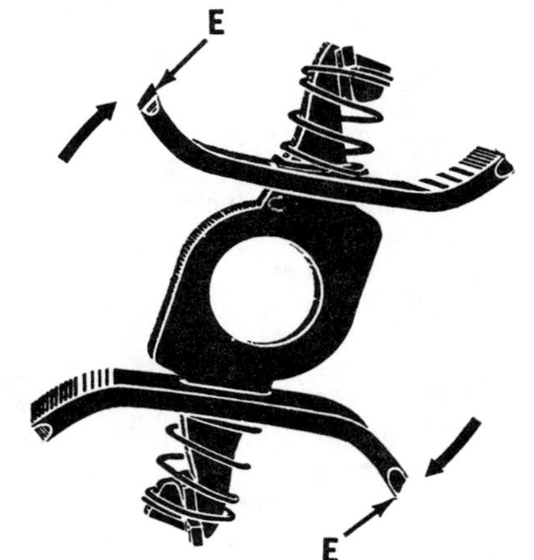

Fig. ST73A—Leading edges (E) of friction shoe plates must be sharp or shoes may not properly engage starter drum.

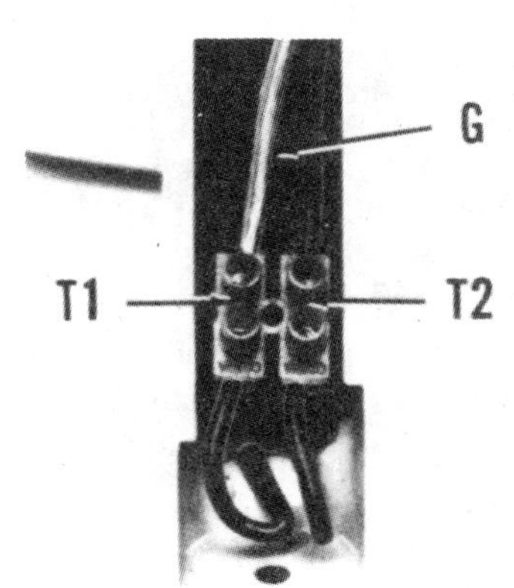

Fig. ST74—View showing location of heater wire terminals in rear grip.

STIHL

Model	Bore mm (in.)	Stroke mm (in.)	Displacement cc (cu. in.)	Drive Type
030AV	42 (1.65)	32 (1.26)	45 (2.7)	Direct
031AV, 031AVE	44 (1.73)	32 (1.26)	48 (3.2)	Direct
032AV, 032AVE	45 (1.77)	32 (1.26)	51 (3.11)	Direct
045AV, 045AVE	50 (1.97)	38 (1.5)	75 (4.58)	Direct
045AVSE	54 (2.13)	38 (1.5)	87 (5.3)	Direct
056AVE	52 (2.05)	38 (1.5)	81 (4.94)	Direct
056AVS, 056AVSE, 056AVSEQ	54 (2.13)	38 (1.5)	87 (5.3)	Direct
056M, 056MR, 056AVME, 056AVMEQ	56 (2.2)	38 (1.5)	93.4 (5.7)	Direct

MAINTENANCE

SPARK PLUG. Recommended spark plug is Bosch WSR6F. Spark plug electrode gap should be 0.020 inch (0.5 mm).

CARBURETOR. All models are equipped with either a Walbro WA, Walbro WJ, Tillotson HS or Tillotson HU diaphragm type carburetor. Carburetor model numbers are stamped on carburetor for identification purposes. Refer to Tillotson or Walbro sections of CARBURETOR SERVICE for carburetor overhaul and exploded views.

On all models, initial adjustment of mixture screws from a lightly seated position should be 1-1¼ turns open for idle speed mixture screw and 1¼-1½ turns open for high speed mixture screw. Make final adjustment with engine warm and running. Adjust idle speed screw just below clutch engagement speed. Adjust idle mixture screw so engine will accelerate cleanly without hesitation. Adjust high speed mixture screw to obtain optimum engine performance with engine under cutting load. Do not adjust high speed mixture too lean as engine damage could result.

IGNITION. Models 030AV, 031AV, 032AV and 045AV are equipped with a conventional flywheel magneto ignition system. Models 031AVE and 032AVE are equipped with a breakerless transistor ignition system while all other models are equipped with a breakerless capacitor discharge ignition system.

Flywheel-Magneto Ignition. Ignition breaker-point gap on models so equipped should be set at 0.014-0.016 inch (0.35-0.40 mm). Ignition timing is adjusted by loosening stator mounting screws and rotating stator plate. On models not equipped with a stator plate, vary breaker-point gap to adjust timing. Ignition timing should occur 0.08-0.09 inch (2.0-2.3 mm) BTDC on Models 030AV and 031AV; 0.083-0.090 inch (2.1-2.3 mm) BTDC on Model 032AV; and 0.098-0.106 in. (2.5-2.7 mm) on 045AV models.

Air gap between ignition coil and flywheel magnets should be 0.008-0.012 inch (0.2-0.3 mm) on all models. Loosen ignition coil attaching screws and move coil to adjust air gap.

Edge gap is the distance between the trailing edge of the north (N) flywheel magnet and the adjacent edge of the center ignition coil leg. Edge gap on Models 030AV and 031AV should be 0.14-0.15 inch (3.5-3.7 mm); 0.18-0.33 inch (4.7-8.5 mm) on Model 032AV and 0.24-0.35 inch (6.0-9.0 mm) on Model 045AV. To check edge gap, rotate flywheel in a counterclockwise direction and measure edge gap at the instant breaker-points begin to open. Vary breaker-point gap and ignition timing to adjust edge gap.

Capacitor Discharge Ignition. Models 045AVE, 045AVSE, 056AVE, 056AVSE, 056AVSEQ, 056AVME and 056AVMEQ are equipped with a capacitor discharge ignition system. Ignition must be serviced as a unit assembly as individual components are not available separately.

To properly time ignition, trigger coil must be in correct relationship with flywheel magnet. Ignition timing should be 0.098-0.106 inch (2.5-2.7 mm) BTDC for all models. To check ignition timing, install a timing gage in spark plug hole and rotate engine until piston is at ignition position as indicated above. Note if mark on flywheel is aligned with mark on crankcase. Remove flywheel and note if mark on stator plate is aligned with crankcase mark. If either of these marks is not aligned, ignition must be adjusted.

To adjust ignition, rotate engine with flywheel installed until correct piston position is indicated by timing gage. Make a mark on crankcase adjacent to mark on flywheel. Remove flywheel, loosen stator plate mounting screws and rotate stator plate until mark on plate is aligned with previously made mark on crankcase. Retighten stator plate mounting screws. A timing light may also be used to check ignition timing as follows: Remove spark plug, install timing gage and rotate engine until correct piston position for ignition is indicated. Remove guide bar and install special tool 0000 850 4000 on guide bar studs. Make a reference mark opposite of arrow on tool 0000 850 4000 on clutch plate or clutch shoe on earlier models. Recheck piston position to be sure marks are correct. Install spark plug and connect timing light. Using a tachometer, run engine at 6000 rpm and check alignment of previously made reference mark and arrow on special tool 0000 850 4000 with timing light. Loosen stator plate mounting screws and adjust timing as required. Recheck timing with light.

Transistor Ignition. Models 031AVE and 032AVE are equipped with a Bosch

Illustrations courtesy Stihl Inc.

breakerless transistor ignition. The transistor circuit is designed to take the place of breaker-points in a conventional ignition system. The transistor ignition system is triggered magnetically by a magnet in the flywheel.

To check ignition timing, install Stihl timing tool 0000 850 4000 on chain bar studs. Using either a piston locating tool or a timing light note whether mark on clutch hub is aligned with pointer on timing tool. Ignition timing should be 0.078-0.090 inch (2.0-2.3 mm) BTDC on Model 031AVE and 0.106 inch (2.7 mm) BTDC on Model 032AVE. Ignition timing may be adjusted slightly by loosening flywheel nut and rotating flywheel on crankshaft as there is a small clearance between flywheel groove and crankshaft key.

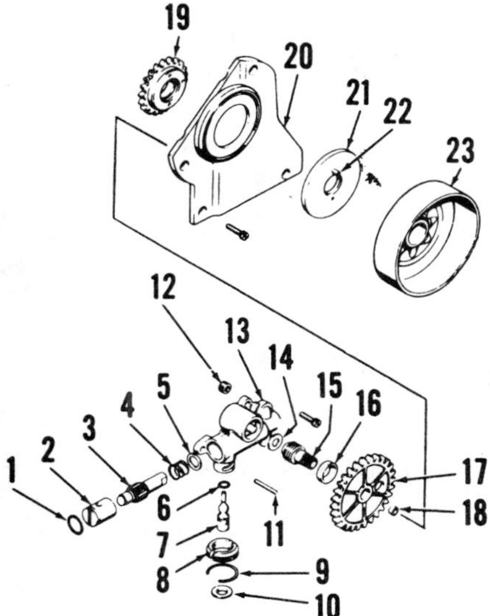

Fig. ST75 — Exploded view of automatic oil pump assembly used on early Models 030AV, 031AV, 031AVE, 032AV and 032AVE.

1. "O" ring
2. Bushing
3. Plunger
4. Spring
5. Washer
6. "O" ring
7. Adjusting screw
8. Segments
9. Retainer
10. Dirt seal
11. Pin
12. Seal
13. Pump body
14. Washer
15. Worm gear
16. Seal
17. Gear
18. Plug
19. Gear
20. Cover
21. Drive plate
22. Drive pin
23. Clutch drum

Recommended air gap between coil armature legs and flywheel is 0.008-0.012 inch (0.2-0.3 mm). Loosen ignition coil mounting screws and move ignition coil to adjust air gap.

Tighten flywheel nut on all models to 22 ft.-lbs. (30 N•m).

LUBRICATION. The engine is lubricated by mixing oil with the fuel. Fuel:oil ratio is 40:1 when using STIHL two-stroke engine oil. If STIHL two-stroke engine oil is not available, a good quality oil designed for two-stroke air-cooled engines may be used when mixed at a 25:1 ratio. Use a separate container when mixing the oil and gasoline.

Fill chain oiler tank with SAE 30 non-detergent motor oil. All models are equipped with an automatic chain oiler system. Early Models 030AV, 031AV, 031AVE, 032AV and 032AVE are equipped with plunger type pump shown in Fig. ST75 while all other models are equipped with plunger type pump shown in Fig. ST76. On all models, oil pump output is determined by adjusting screw (7). Turning adjusting screw changes stroke of plunger (3). Slot of adjusting screw (7) is found on bottom of saw and may be turned ¼ turn.

CARBON. The muffler assembly should be removed from the engine and the carbon scraped from the exhaust ports and muffler periodically.

REPAIRS

PISTON, PIN, RINGS, AND CYLINDER. The aluminum alloy piston is equipped with two piston rings. The floating piston pin is retained in the piston with a snap ring at each end. The piston pin is supported in the connecting rod small end by a caged needle roller bearing. An oversize piston pin is not available.

Cylinder and cylinder head are cast in one piece. The cylinder bore is chrome plated. The cylinder is available only with a fitted piston. On 030AV, 031AV, 031AVE, 032AV and 032AVE models, piston and cylinder are grouped into different sizes. Each group size is marked with a code letter "A" to "E." Letter "A" denotes smallest size with "E" being largest. The code letter is stamped on the top of the piston and the bottom of the cylinder on early models, and at the top of the cylinder on later models. On early models, the code letter of the piston and the cylinder must be the same for proper fit of a new piston in a new cylinder. On later models, the piston and cylinder grouping system has been simplified. Pistons are marked either "B" or "C" with a "B" piston fitting "A," "B" or "C" cylinders and a "C" piston fitting "D" or "E" cylinders.

To reinstall piston on connecting rod, proceed as follows: Install one snap ring in piston. Lubricate the piston pin needle bearing with motor oil and slide bearing into pin bore of connecting rod. Install piston on rod so arrow on piston crown points toward exhaust port. Push piston pin in far enough to install second snap ring.

After piston and rod assembly is attached to crankshaft, install cylinder as follows: Turn crankshaft to top dead center and support piston with a wood block that will fit between piston skirt

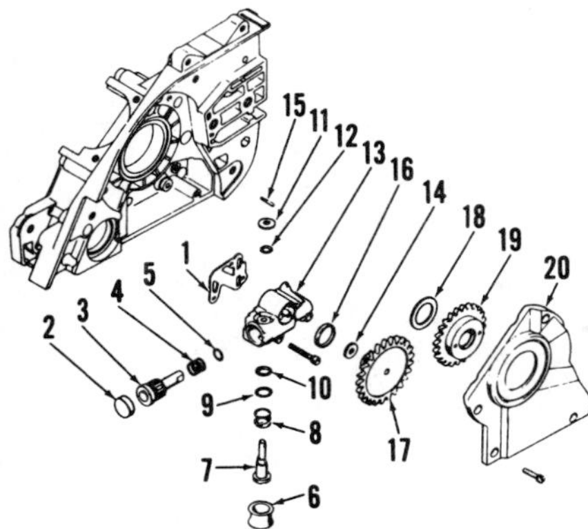

Fig. ST76 — Exploded view of automatic oil pump assembly used on later 030AV, 031AV and 031 AVE models and Models 032AVE, 032AVE, 045AV, 045AVE, 045AVSE, 056AVE, 056AVSE, 056AVSEQ, 056AVME and 056AVMEQ.

1. Gasket
2. Plug
3. Plunger
4. Spring
5. Washer
6. Grommet
7. Adjusting screw
8. Spring
9. Washer
10. "O" ring
11. Special washer
12. "O" ring
13. Pump body
14. Washer
15. Stepped pin
16. Seal
17. Gear
18. Washer
19. Gear
20. Cover

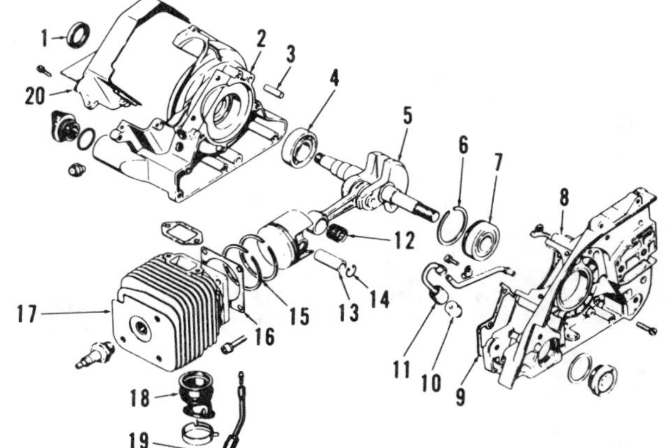

Fig. ST77 — Exploded view of engine used on Models 045AV 045AVE, and 045AVSE. Other models are similar.

1. Seal
2. Crankcase half
3. Dowel pin
4. Ball bearing
5. Crankshaft & rod assy.
6. Snap ring
7. Ball bearing
8. Crankcase half
9. Gasket
10. Oil pickup
11. Oil hose
12. Roller bearing
13. Piston pin
14. Pin retainer
15. Piston rings
16. Gasket
17. Cylinder
18. Intake manifold
19. Crankcase pulse hose
20. Fan cover

Illustrations courtesy Stihl Inc.

and crankcase when cylinder gasket is in place. A notch should be cut in the wood block so it will fit around connecting rod. Locating pins are present in piston ring grooves to prevent ring rotation. Make certain ring end gaps are properly positioned around locating pins when installing cylinder. Two sizes of piston rings are used on 045 and 056 series saws. Be certain to install the thicker ring in the second (bottom) piston ring groove. Lubricate piston and rings with motor oil and compress rings with a ring compressor that can be removed after cylinder is pushed down over piston. Tighten cylinder screws to 71 in.-lbs. (8 N•m) on Models 030AV, 031AV, 031AVE, 032AV and 032AVE. On 045 and 056 series saws, tighten cylinder screws to 64 in.-lbs. (7.2 N•m).

CONNECTING ROD, CRANKSHAFT AND CRANKCASE. All models are equipped with a connecting rod, bearing and crankshaft which are pressed together and available only as a unit assembly. The crankshaft is supported by a ball bearing at each end. Flywheel side main bearing (4–Fig. ST77) is held in position by a shoulder in crankcase half (2) while snap ring (6) retains clutch side main bearing (7). On early 031AV and 031AVE models and all 030AV, 045AV, 045AVE, 045AVSE, 056AVE, 056AVSE, 056AVSEQ, 056AVME and 056AVMEQ models, snap ring (6) is installed in groove on main bearing (7). On all other models, snap ring is installed in crankcase half (8). Heat crankcase halves prior to installation of bearings. Heat bearing inner races with a soldering gun prior to installing crankshaft. Tighten crankcase screws using a diagonal pattern.

CLUTCH. Fig. ST78 is an exploded view of clutch assembly typical of all models except for models equipped with an isolating clutch chain brake system which uses clutch assembly shown in Fig. ST79.

On models equipped with clutch shown in Fig. ST78, clutch hub (8) and nut (10) have left hand threads. Install clutch retaining washers so face of inner diameter is against clutch hub. On some later models, washer (9) is absent and nut (10) is incorporated with clutch hub (8). Clutch shoes and springs should be renewed as a unit to prevent unbalanced clutch operation. When installing clutch on models equipped with nut (10), clutch hub (8) should be tightened to 36 ft.-lbs. (49 N•m) and nut (10) should be tightened to 25 ft.-lbs. (34 N•m). On models with integral nut and hub assembly, hub and nut assembly should be tightened to 29 ft.-lbs. (40 N•m).

On models equipped with clutch shown in Fig. ST79, clutch components are retained by drive plate (6). Drive plate has left hand threads. Use Stihl tool 1113 890 3600 or equivalent to remove or install drive plate. Drive plate should be tightened to 29 ft.-lbs. (40 N•m).

REWIND STARTER. Two types of rewind starters may be used. Friction shoe type starter used on early 045AV, 045AVE and 045AVSE models is shown in Fig. ST81. Pawl type starter used on

Fig. ST78—Exploded view of clutch used on most early models. Washer (9) and nut (10) are absent on all later models except 045 series. Refer to text.

1. Drive pin
2. Drive plate
3. Bearing
4. Clutch drum
5. Washer
6. Shoe
7. Spring
8. Clutch hub
9. Washer
10. Nut

Fig. ST81—Exploded view of friction shoe type starter used on early Models 045AV, 045AVE and 045AVSE. Refer to Fig. ST84 for assembly of friction shoe plates (10) and brake lever (9).

1. Handle
2. Starter rope
3. Housing
4. Fan cover
5. Rewind spring
6. Rope pulley
7. Washer
8. Slotted washer
9. Brake lever
10. Friction shoe
11. Spring
12. Spring retainer
13. Slotted washer
14. Washer
15. Spring
16. Washer
17. "E" ring

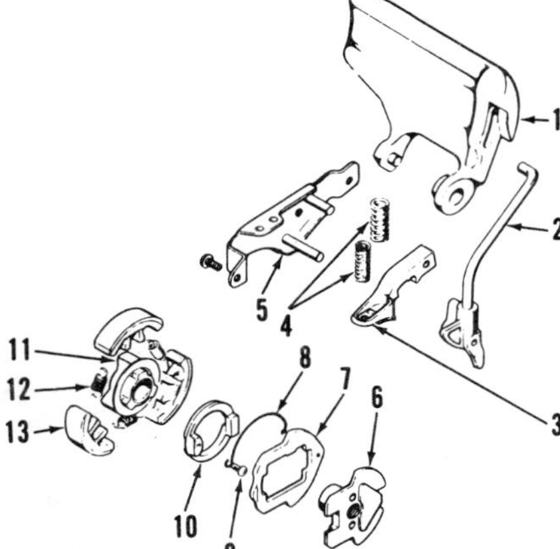

Fig. ST79—Exploded view of isolating clutch chain brake assembly used on some models.

1. Hand guard
2. Brake rod
3. Brake shoe
4. Brake spring
5. Plate
6. Drive plate
7. Retainer
8. Wire spring
9. Pin
10. Locking slider
11. Clutch hub
12. Clutch spring
13. Clutch shoe

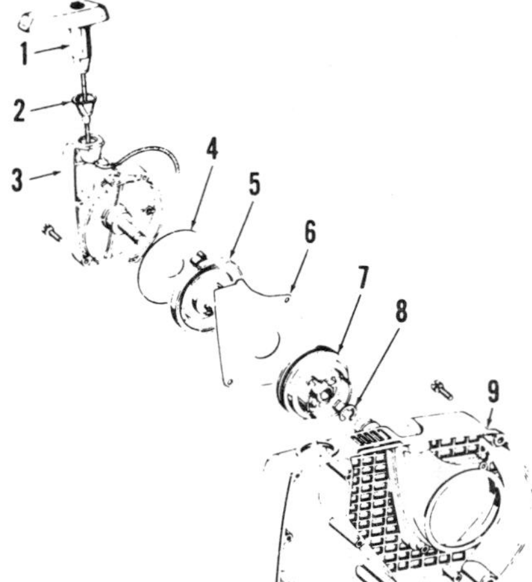

Fig. ST82—Exploded view of pawl type rewind starter used on Models 030AV, 031AV and 031AVE. Pawls on flywheel are not shown.

1. Rope handle
2. Bushing
3. Housing
4. Washer
5. Rewind spring
6. Cover
7. Rope pulley
8. "E" ring
9. Fan housing

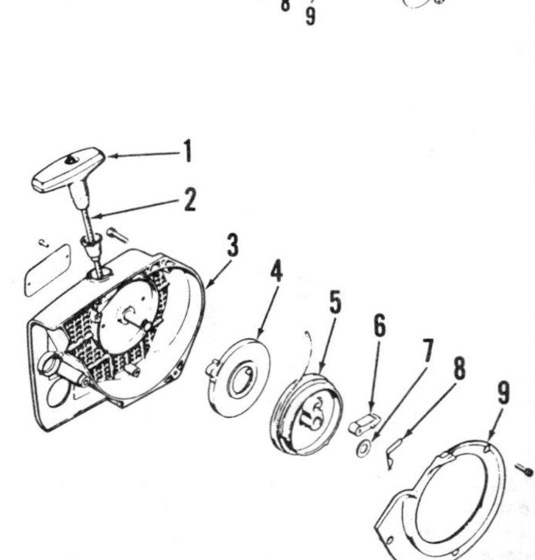

Fig. ST83—Exploded view of pawl type rewind starter used on Models 032AV, 032AVE, 056AVE, 056AVSE, 056AVSEQ, 056AVME, 056AVMEQ and later 045AV, 045AVE and 045AVSE models.

1. Rope handle
2. Starter rope
3. Housing
4. Rewind spring
5. Rope pulley
6. Pawl
7. Washer
8. Spring clip
9. Fan cover

Illustrations courtesy Stihl Inc.

030AV, 031AV and 031AVE models is shown in Fig. ST82 while pawl type starter used on 032AV, 032AVE, 056 AVE, 056AVSE, 056AVSEQ, 056 AVME, 056AVMEQ and later 045AV, 045AVE and 045AVSE models is shown in Fig. ST83.

On early Models 045AV, 045AVE and 045AVSE, assemble starter shoes on brake lever as shown in Fig. ST84. Be sure assembly is installed as shown in exploded views and leading edges of friction shoes are sharp or shoes may not properly engage drum.

To place tension on rope of Models 030AV, 031AV and 031AVE, assemble starter components but do not install starter on saw. Pull starter rope and hold rope pulley to prevent spring from rewinding rope on pulley. Pull rope back through rope outlet and wrap two additional turns of rope on pulley without moving pulley. Release pulley and allow rope to rewind. Rope handle should be pulled against housing and rope pulley should be able to rotate ½ turn further when rope is pulled to greatest length.

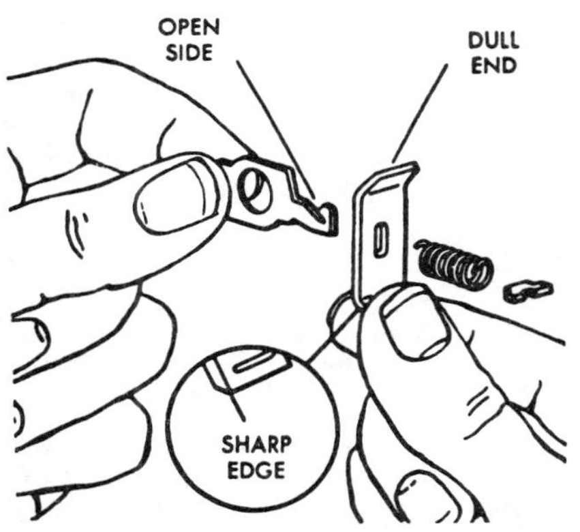

Fig. ST84 – Drawing showing proper method of assembly of friction shoe plates and starter brake lever.

To place tension on rope of all other models, proceed as follows: Pull rope out of handle until notch in pulley is adjacent to rope outlet and hold pulley to prevent rope from rewinding. Pull rope back through outlet and place into notch in pulley. On pawl type starter assemblies shown in Fig. ST83, turn rope pulley three turns clockwise and release rope back through notch. On friction shoe type starter assemblies shown in Fig. ST81, turn rope pulley seven turns clockwise. Check starter operation. Rope handle should be held against housing by spring tension and rope pulley should be able to rotate ½ turn further when rope is extended to greatest length.

CHAIN BRAKE. Some models are equipped with a chain brake system designed to stop chain movement should kickback occur.

On models equipped with the chain brake and isolating clutch system shown in Fig. ST79, brake is activated when operator's hand strikes hand guard (1). Forward movement of hand guard (1) and brake rod (2) releases brake shoe (3) and allows springs (4) to push brake shoe tight against clutch drum. At the same instant, retainer (7) and locking slider (10) disengage drive plate (6) and clutch hub (11) allowing engine to continue running unhindered. To reset brake mechanism, return engine to idle speed and pull back hand guard.

Disassembly for repair and component renewal is evident after inspection of unit and referral to Fig. ST79 noting that large diameter spring (4) should be assembled directly over brake shoe lining and smaller diameter spring to rear of brake shoe. Lubricate moving parts and pivot points with Molykote or suitable equivalent. No adjustment of brake system is required.

Models equipped with the chain brake system shown in Fig. ST85 use a brake band (10) instead of brake shoe (3 – Fig. ST79). Forward movement of hand guard (2 – Fig. ST85) and brake rod (3) release actuating lever (4) and cam (6) allowing spring (9) to draw brake band (10) tight around clutch drum. Pull back hand guard to reset mechanism.

Disassembly for repair or component renewal is evident after inspection of unit and referral to Fig. ST85. Lubricate moving parts and pivot points with Molykote or suitable equivalent. No adjustment of chain brake system is required.

Both chain brake systems should be kept clean and free from dirt and sawdust accumulation which could hinder proper operation. Renew any components found to be excessively worn or damaged.

HEATED HANDLES. Some 031AV and 031AVE models are equipped with a handle heating system which utilizes heat from engine exhaust gases. Hot exhaust from muffler enter valve (4 – Fig. ST86) and are routed to front handle and rear grip through heat tubes. Exhaust gases are then vented to the atmosphere. Rotate valve (3) to regulate heat.

Some models are equipped with an electrical handle heating system. A generator located under the flywheel creates an alternating current which passes through a switch and to heating elements in front handle and rear grip.

Check heating elements, switch and generator with an ohmmeter. Rear heating element should have a resistance of approximately one ohm. Front heating element should have a resistance of approximately two ohms and generator approximately 0.6 ohm.

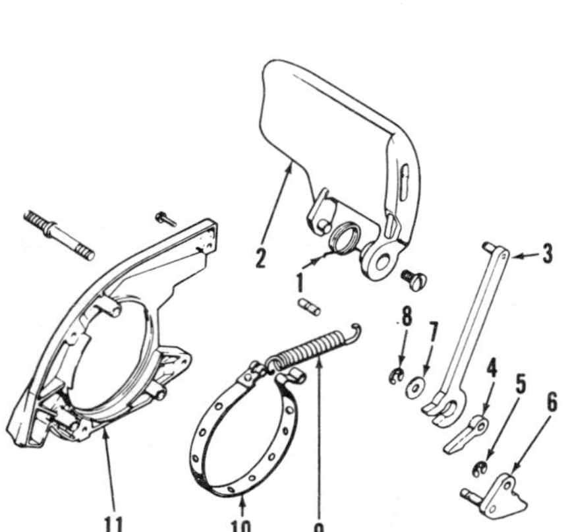

Fig. ST85 – Exploded view of band type chain brake system used on some 032AV and 032AVE models and on some 045 and 056 series saws.

1. Spring
2. Hand guard
3. Brake rod
4. Actuating lever
5. "E" ring
6. Cam
7. Washer
8. "E" ring
9. Spring
10. Brake band
11. Cover

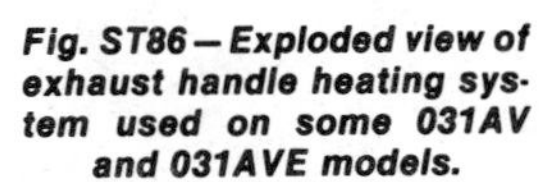
Fig. ST86 – Exploded view of exhaust handle heating system used on some 031AV and 031AVE models.

1. Heat tube
2. Hose
3. Adjusting valve
4. Valve body
5. Clamp
6. Wire clip

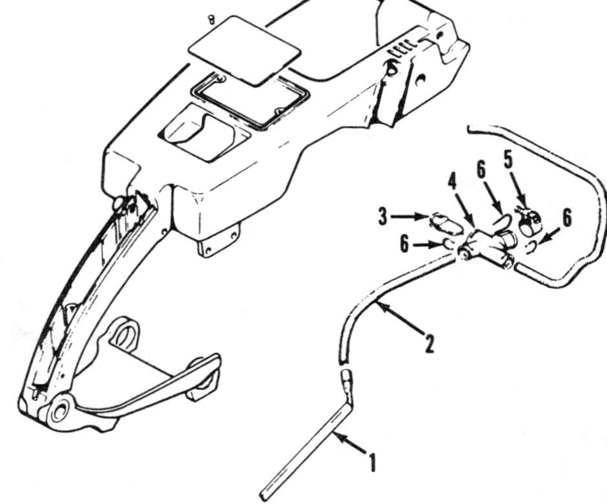

Illustrations courtesy Stihl Inc.

STIHL

Model	Bore mm (in.)	Stroke mm (in.)	Displacement cc (cu. in.)	Drive Type
009, 009E, 009EQ, 009EQZ	36 (1.42)	36 (1.42)	37 (2.26)	Direct
009 L, 009LEQ, 009LES	38 (1.496)	36 (1.42)	41 (2.5)	Direct
010 AV, 010 AVE	36 (1.42)	36(1.42)	37 (2.26)	Direct
011AV, 011AVE, 011AVEQ, 011AVT, 011AVTEQ, 011T	38 (1.496)	36 (1.42)	41 (2.5)	Direct
012AVE, 012AVP, 012AVEQ, 012AVTEQ	40 (1.57)	36 (1.42)	45 (2.74)	Direct

MAINTENANCE

SPARK PLUG. Recommended spark plug is Bosch WSR6F or equivalent. Spark plug electrode gap should be 0.020 inch (0.5 mm).

CARBURETOR. A Walbro WA or WT diaphragm type carburetor or Zama C1S diaphragm type carburetor is used on all models. Refer to Walbro or Zama sections of CARBURETOR SERVICE section for repair and an exploded view of carburetor.

Initial adjustment of idle and high speed mixture screw is 1 turn open from a lightly seated position. Make final adjustments with engine warm and running. Adjust idle speed screw just below clutch engagement speed. Adjust idle mixture screw so engine will accelerate cleanly without hesitation. Adjust high speed mixture screw to obtain optimum performance under cutting load. Do not adjust high speed mixture needle too lean as engine may be damaged.

IGNITION. Models 009, 010AV and 011AV are equipped with a conventional flywheel magneto ignition system. All other models are equipped with a breakerless capacitor discharge ignition system.

Flywheel-Magneto Ignition. Ignition breaker-point gap on models so equipped should be 0.012-0.016 inch (0.3-0.4 mm). Ignition should occur at 0.071-0.083 inch (1.8-2.1 mm) BTDC. Ignition timing is adjusted by varying breaker-point gap. Some models have timing marks located on flywheel and crankcase as shown in Fig. ST87. A dial indicator should be used to check timing.

Recommended air gap between ignition coil and flywheel magnets should be 0.008 inch (0.2 mm). Loosen ignition coil mounting screws and move coil to adjust air gap.

Magneto edge gap should be 0.020 inch (0.5 mm) at ignition. As proper edge gap is preferred over breaker-point gap and ignition timing, vary breaker-point gap if edge gap should require adjustment.

Capacitor-Discharge Ignition. Models 009E, 009EQ, 009LES, 010AVE, 011AVE, 011AVEQ, 011AVTEQ, 012AVE, 012AVEQ and 012AVTEQ are equipped with a breakerless capacitor discharge ignition system. All electronic components are contained in a one-piece ignition module and must be serviced as unit assembly. Air gap between ignition module and flywheel magnets should be 0.006-0.008 inch (0.15-0.20 mm). Loosen ignition module mounting screws and move module to adjust air gap. Ignition timing should be 0.071-0.087 inch (1.8-2.2 mm) BTDC. Ignition timing is not adjustable but should be checked periodically to ensure proper ignition module operation.

LUBRICATION. The engine is lubricated by mixing oil with the fuel. Fuel:oil ratio is 40:1 when using STIHL two-stroke engine oil. If STIHL two-stroke engine oil is not available, a good quality oil designed for two-stroke air-cooled engines may be used when mixed at a 25:1 ratio. Use a separate container when mixing the oil and gasoline.

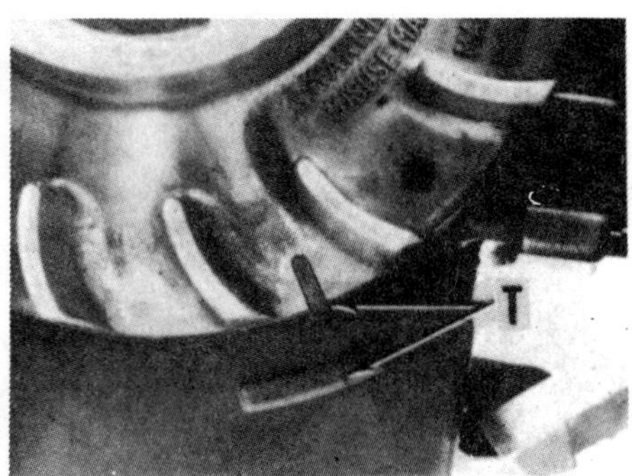

Fig. ST87 — Timing marks (T) on models so equipped, may be used to check ignition timing. Refer to text.

All models are equipped with an automatic chain oiler system. Manufacturer recommends the use of approved oils designed specifically for saw chain lubrication. If necessary, clean automotive oil may be used to lubricate saw chain. Chain oil may be diluted with kerosene during cold weather. Oil:kerosene mixture ratio should not exceed 4 parts oil to 1 part kerosene.

REPAIRS

CYLINDER, PISTON, PIN AND RINGS. Cylinder head is integral with cylinder. Cylinder can be removed after detaching fan housing, muffler, front handle and rear handle. Care must be taken when handling piston and rod assembly to prevent rod from slipping off bearing rollers (8 – Fig. ST88) as rollers

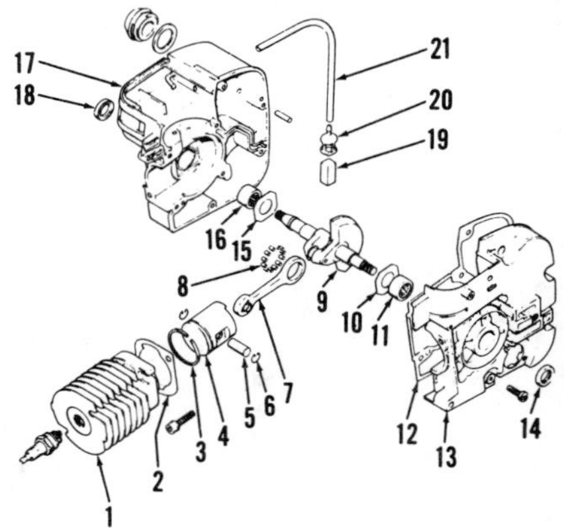

Fig. ST88 — Exploded view of engine assembly typical of all models.

1. Cylinder
2. Gasket
3. Piston ring
4. Piston
5. Piston pin
6. Pin retainer
7. Connecting rod
8. Needle rollers
9. Crankshaft
10. Thrust washer
11. Needle bearing
12. Gasket
13. Right crankcase half
14. Seal
15. Thrust washer
16. Needle bearing
17. Left crankcase half
18. Seal
19. Fuel filter
20. Fuel pickup
21. Hose

may fall into crankcase. Cylinder has a chrome bore which should be inspected for flaking, scoring, or other damage.

The aluminum alloy piston is equipped with one piston ring. The piston pin is retained by wire retainers and rides in a needle roller bearing in the connecting rod small end. Be sure piston is properly supported when removing piston pin to prevent damage to connecting rod. Piston must be installed with arrow on piston crown facing toward exhaust port in cylinder. Piston pin must move freely in piston upon reassembly. Piston and piston pin are available in standard sizes only. Tighten cylinder screws in two steps, initially to 53-62 in.-lbs. (6-7 N·m) and then to a final torque of 84-106 in.-lbs. (9.5-12 N·m).

CONNECTING ROD, CRANKSHAFT AND CRANKCASE. Connecting rod is one-piece and rides on 12 loose bearing rollers (8 – Fig. ST88). Be careful not to lose any loose bearing rollers during disassembly. Bearing rollers can be removed after rod is slid off rollers. Bearing rollers may be held in place with petroleum jelly or heavy grease when installing connecting rod. Manufacturer recommends using special clamping tool 1120 893 9100 to secure connecting rod in place during disassembly and reassembly.

The crankshaft is supported by a needle roller bearing (11 and 16) in each crankcase half. Crankcase bearings must be renewed using Stihl press arbor 1120 893 7200 or equivalent. When installed, bearings should not interfere with installation of crankshaft seals (14 and 18) and thrust washers (10 and 15). Install crankshaft seals, with seal lip toward bearing, flush with crankcase surface. Insert thrust washers into recesses in crankcase halves. Use a suitable seal protector when passing crankshaft end through crankcase seals. Be sure thrust washers (10 and 15) do not dislodge during assembly. Tighten crankcase screws to 44 in.-lbs. (5 N·m).

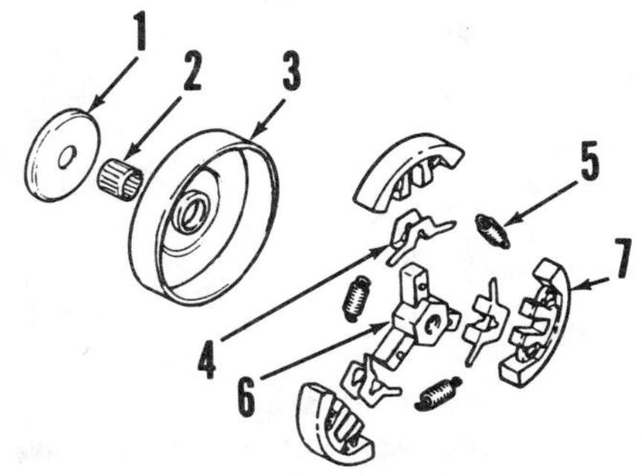

Fig. ST91 – Exploded view of three-shoe type clutch assembly used on 012 series saws.

1. Washer
2. Needle bearing
3. Clutch drum
4. Retainer
5. Spring
6. Clutch hub
7. Clutch shoe

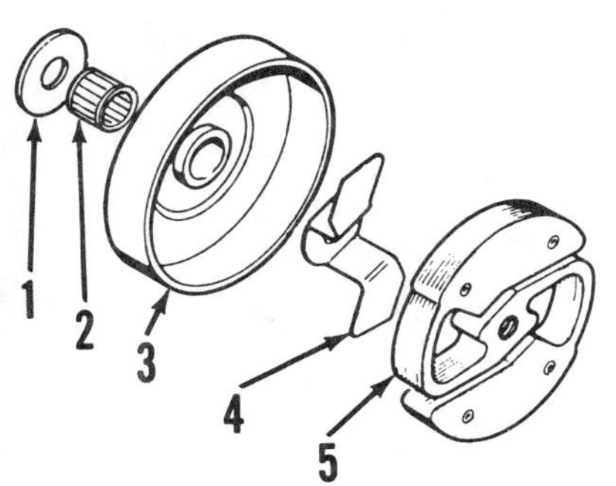

Fig. ST89 – Exploded view of clutch assembly used on all models except Models 012AVE, 012AVEQ and 012AVTEQ.

1. Washer
2. Needle bearing
3. Clutch drum
4. Retainer
5. Hub & shoe assy.

Fig. ST90 – View showing correct installation of retainer (4) and clutch and shoe assembly (5) for clutch assembly shown in Fig. ST89.

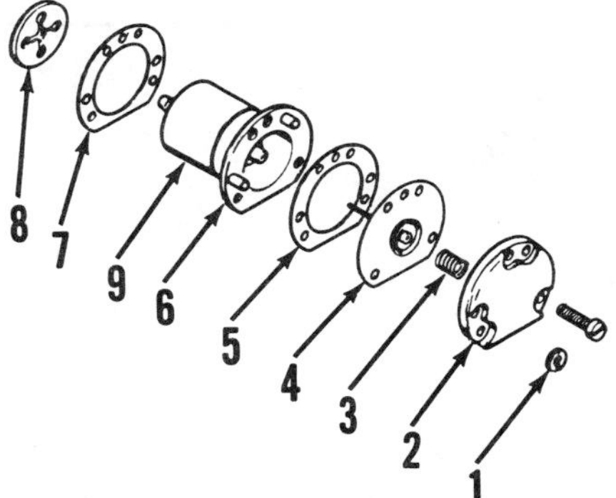

Fig. ST92 – Exploded view of automatic chain oiler pump.

1. "C" ring
2. Cover
3. Spring
4. Diaphragm & plunger
5. Gasket
6. Body
7. Gasket
8. Filter retainer
9. Oil filter

CLUTCH. All models except 012 series saws are equipped with the one-piece "S" configuration clutch shown in Fig. ST89. Clutch hub (5) has left hand threads and must be installed with retainer (4) positioned as shown in Fig. ST90. Clean and inspect clutch hub, drum and bearing for damage or excessive wear. Inspect crankshaft for wear or damage caused by clutch bearing. Clutch hub should be tightened to 22 ft.-lbs. (30 N·m).

Models 012AVE, 012AVEQ and 012AVTEQ are equipped with the three-shoe centrifugal clutch shown in Fig. ST91. Clutch hub (6) has left hand threads. Clutch drum rides on needle bearing (2). Inspect needle bearing for excessive wear or other damage and lubricate periodically with a suitable high temperature grease. Clutch shoes (7) and springs (5) should be renewed as complete sets only.

OIL PUMP. All models are equipped with a diaphragm type automatic chain oiler pump. Crankcase pulses move diaphragm and plunger (4 – Fig. ST92) to force oil out oil outlet. Oil tank vent, located below oil outlet, should be cleaned regularly to prevent oil flow restriction. Oil pump should be occasionally disassembled and cleaned with a suitable solvent to remove oil deposits and foreign material which may prohibit pump operation. Inspect and renew diaphragm (4), gaskets (5) and filter (9) if signs of deterioration or cracking are evident.

Fig. ST93 – Exploded view of rewind starter and breaker-point ignition used on 010AV models. Rewind starter on all other models is similar.

1. Starter housing
2. Rope handle
3. Rewind spring
4. Rope pulley
5. Pawl
6. Washer
7. Grooved spacer
8. Clip
9. Screw
10. Fan cover
11. Nut
12. Washer
13. Flywheel
14. Woodruff key
15. Ignition coil
16. Breaker plate
17. Contact spring
18. Cable clamp

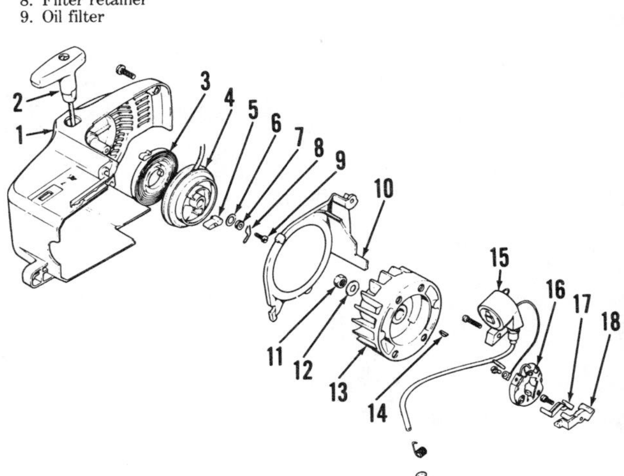

Illustrations courtesy Stihl Inc.

REWIND STARTER. All models are equipped with a pawl type rewind starter typical of the type shown in Fig. ST93. To disassemble starter, detach starter housing, remove rope handle and allow rope to wind onto rope pulley. Remove retaining clip (8) and remove rope pulley. Care should be used when removing rewind spring as uncontrolled uncoiling of spring may be harmful. Rope length should be 37¾ inches (96 cm). Wind rope around rope pulley in a clockwise direction as viewed with pulley installed in housing. Note that clip (8) retains pulley and pawl (5). Turn rope pulley two turns clockwise when preloading rewind spring. Rope handle should be pulled against housing with rope retracted and rope pulley should be able to rotate ½ turn further with rope fully extended.

CHAIN BRAKE. Some models may be equipped with a chain brake system designed to stop chain movement should kickback occur. The chain brake is activated when the operator's hand strikes hand guard (1–Figs. ST94 and ST95) thereby allowing brake lever (3) to release spring (6). Spring then draws brake band (8) tight around clutch drum to stop chain. Pull back hand guard to reset mechanism. No adjustment of brake mechanism is required.

Disassembly for repair or renewal of individual components is evident after inspection of unit and referral to Fig. ST94 or Fig. ST95.

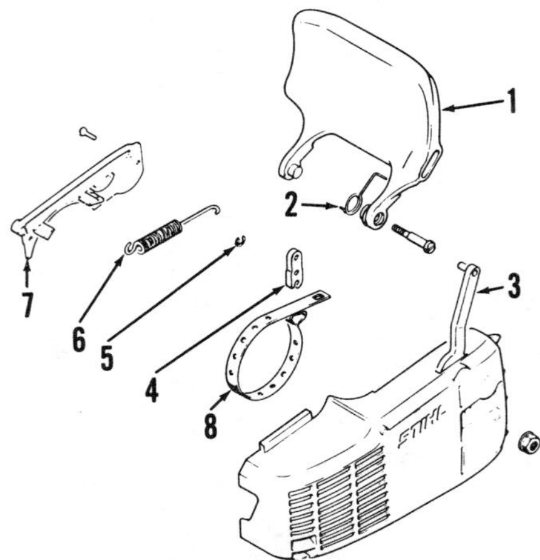

Fig. ST94 — Exploded view of optional chain brake assembly used on earlier models.

1. Hand guard
2. Spring
3. Brake lever
4. Pivot
5. "E" ring
6. Spring
7. Shield
8. Brake band

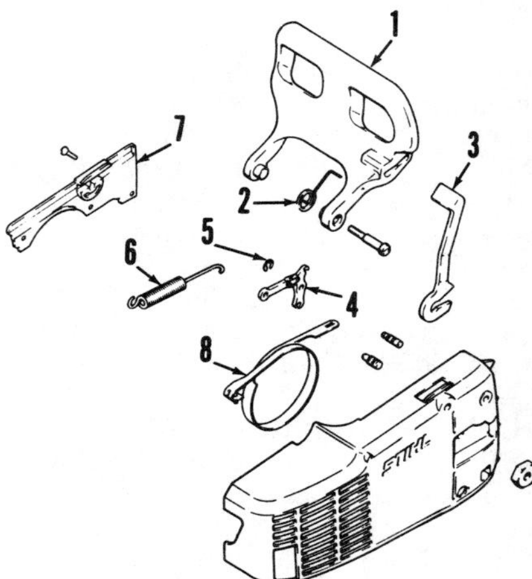

Fig. ST95 — Exploded view of chain brake system used on some later models. Refer to Fig. ST94 for component identification.

Illustrations courtesy Stihl Inc.

STIHL

Model	Bore mm (in.)	Stroke mm (in.)	Displacement cc (cu. in.)	Drive Type
024AVE, 024AVEQ, 024AVEQW	42 (1.65)	30 (1.18)	41.6 (2.54)	Direct
024AVSE, 024AVSEQ, 024AVSEQW	42 (1.65)	32 (1.26)	44.3 (2.7)	Direct
026AVEQZ	44 (1.73)	32 (1.26)	48.7 (2.97)	Direct
044AVEQZ	50 (1.97)	36 (1.41)	70.7 (4.3)	Direct
084AVE, 084AVEQ, 084AVREQ	60 (2.36)	43 (1.69)	121.6 (7.4)	Direct
088	60 (2.35)	43 (1.69)	121.6 (7.42)	Direct

MAINTENANCE

SPARK PLUG. Recommended spark plug is Bosch WSR6F or NGK BPMR7A. Recommended spark plug electrode gap is 0.50 mm (0.020 in.). Tighten spark plug to 25 N•m (18 ft.-lb.).

CARBURETOR. All models are equipped with an all position diaphragm type carburetor. Series 024 saws are equipped with a Tillotson HU or a Walbro WT carburetor. Model 026AVEQZ saw is equipped with a Walbro WT carburetor. Model 044AVEQZ saw is equipped with a Zama C3M carburetor. Series 084 saws are equipped with Tillotson HT carburetors.

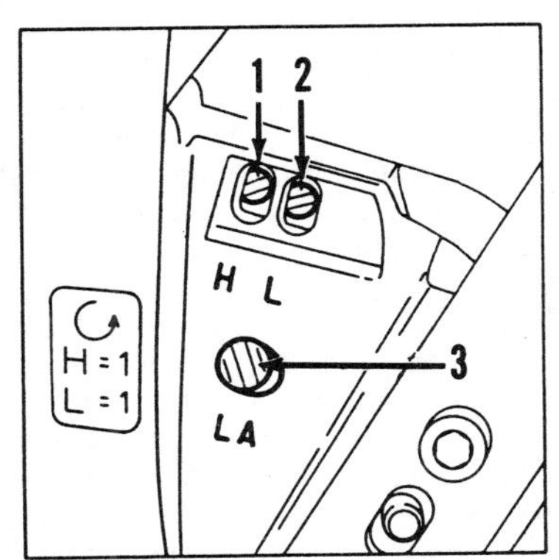

Fig. ST100—Drawing showing carburetor high-speed mixture screw (1), low-speed mixture screw (2) and idle speed screw (3). Some carburetors are not equipped with a high-speed adjusting screw.

The following carburetor removal instructions apply to most models. First remove air cleaner cover, air filter element and filter base. Remove handle molding and disconnect throttle rod and choke rod. Disconnect fuel hose and impulse hose. Unscrew carburetor stud nuts (if used) and remove the carburetor. Refer to Tillotson, Walbro or Zama section of CARBURETOR SERVICE section for carburetor overhaul procedure and exploded views.

Initial adjustment on all models except 084AVE and 084AVEQ models equipped with Tillotson HT-2 carburetor is one turn open from a lightly seated position for both the low-speed and high-speed mixture needles (Fig. ST100). On 084AVE and 084AVEQ models equipped with a Tillotson HT-2 carburetor, initial adjustment of low-speed mixture needle is 1-1/4 turns open. High-speed mixture is fixed and high-speed screw should be turned down completely and left in that position.

On all models, final adjustment of carburetor should be made with engine running at operating temperature. Be sure engine air filter is clean before adjusting carburetor. Adjust low-speed mixture needle (2) to obtain highest idle speed, then turn screw counterclockwise approximately 1/8 turn. Engine should accelerate smoothly without hesitation. If engine stumbles or seems sluggish when accelerating, adjust low-speed mixture needle until engine accelerates without hesitation. Adjust idle speed screw (3) so clutch does not engage (chain stops) when engine is idling.

High-speed mixture needle (if so equipped) should be adjusted to obtain optimum performance with saw under cutting load. Do not adjust high-speed mixture needle too lean (turned too far clockwise) as maximum permissible engine speed will be exceeded and engine may be damaged from lack of lubrication and overheating. Maximum no-load speed with chain and bar installed must not exceed 13,000 rpm for 024 series and Model 026AVEQZ; 14,000 rpm for Model 044AVEQZ; 10,500 rpm for 084; and 12,000 rpm for 088 series saws. If an accurate tachometer is not available, do not vary high-speed mixture from initial setting.

IGNITION. All models are equipped with a breakerless transistor controlled ignition system. Except for faulty wiring connections, repair of ignition system malfunction is accomplished by component renewal. Note that high tension lead is threaded into ignition coil and may be renewed separately from coil.

Saws may be equipped with a one-piece ignition module shown in Fig. ST101 or a two-piece system shown in Fig. ST102 which consists of an ignition coil (3) and a trigger mechanism (4). Air

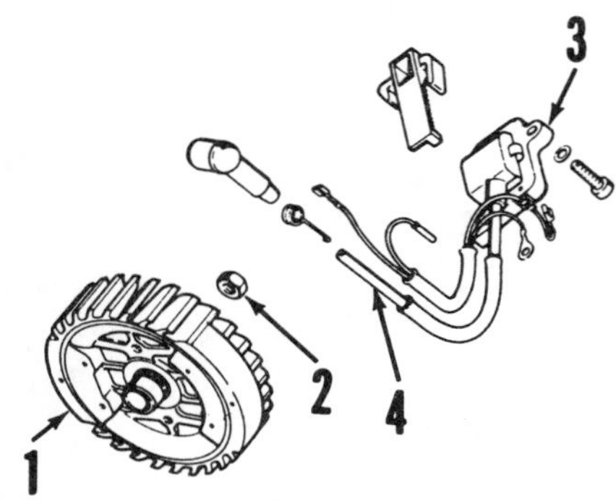

Fig. ST101—Exploded view of one-piece electronic ignition system used on some models.

1. Flywheel
2. Nut
3. Ignition module
4. High tension lead

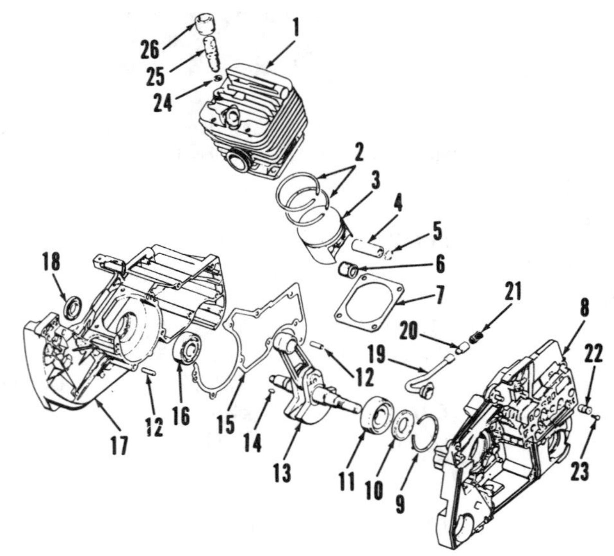

Fig. ST103—Exploded view of engine assembly typical of all models. Snap ring (9) and decompression valve assembly (24, 25 and 26) are used on 084 series saws only.

1. Cylinder
2. Piston rings
3. Piston
4. Piston pin
5. Pin retainer
6. Needle bearing
7. Gasket
8. Right crankcase half
9. Snap ring
10. Oil seal
11. Main bearing
12. Dowel pin
13. Crankshaft & connecting rod assy.
14. Key
15. Gasket
16. Main bearing
17. Left crankcase half
18. Oil seal
19. Oil hose
20. Oil pickup
21. Oil strainer
22. Oil tank vent
23. Split pin
24. Seal
25. Decompression valve
26. Grommet

Fig. ST102—Exploded view of two-piece electronic ignition system used on some models.

1. Flywheel
2. Nut
3. Ignition coil
4. Trigger module
5. High tension lead

gap between ignition module or ignition coil and flywheel magnets should be 0.2-0.3 mm (0.008-0.012 in.) on all models. Loosen module or coil mounting screws and move unit as necessary to obtain desired air gap.

Ignition timing is not adjustable but may be checked with a power timing light to ensure proper ignition module or trigger module operation. Ignition timing should be as follows: 2.1 mm (0.083 in.) BTDC for 024AVE, 024AVEQ and 024AVEQW models; 2.3 mm (0.090 in.) BTDC for 024AVSE, 024AVSEQ, A024AVSEQW and 026AVEQZ; 2.6 mm (0.100 in.) for Model 044AVEQZ; 2.8 mm (0.110 in.) for 084 series; and 2.3-3.3 mm (0.91-0.130 in.) for 088 series saws.

To check timing, use a dial indicator to locate piston at specified timing point and scribe timing marks on flywheel and ignition coil. A specially modified fan housing with a hole cut in lower right half of the housing must be used for this test procedure so that timing marks can be seen. Install modified fan housing and spark plug, then check timing with engine running at 8000 rpm. Timing marks should appear to be aligned if ignition module is functioning properly.

Models with separate ignition coil can be accurately tested using an ignition coil tester. An ohmmeter may also be used to test ignition coil by measuring resistance of coil windings. To check primary resistance, connect ohmmeter leads to connector sleeve on "On-Off" switch wire and to engine ground. With "On-Off" switch in "On" position, resistance should be 0.7-1.0 ohm. To check secondary resistance, connect ohmmeter leads to spark plug terminal and to engine ground. Resistance should be 7,700-10,300 ohms. Renew coil unit if readings vary greatly from specified limits.

LUBRICATION. The engine is lubricated by oil mixed with the gasoline fuel. The manufacturer recommends mixing STIHL 50:1 two-stroke oil with regular grade gasoline at the ratio recommended on the package. When using regular two-stroke engine oil, mix at a ratio of 25:1. Always use a separate container to mix gasoline and oil before filling the fuel tank. The manufacturer recommends using gasoline with octane of 87 or higher.

All models are equipped with an automatic chain oil pump. Oil pump output is adjustable on all models except 024 series and Model 026AVEQZ. Refer to OIL PUMP under REPAIRS section for service and adjustment procedures.

Manufacturer recommends the use of oil designed specifically for saw chain lubrication. If approved oil is not available, clean automotive oil may be used with viscosity chosen according to ambient temperature.

REPAIRS

CRANKCASE PRESSURE TEST. An improperly sealed crankcase can cause the engine to be hard to start, run rough, have low power and overheat. Refer to ENGINE SERVICE section of this manual for crankcase pressure test procedure. If crankcase leakage is indicated, pressurize crankcase and use a soap and water solution to check gaskets, seals, pulse line and castings for leakage.

CYLINDER, PISTON, PIN AND RINGS. To disassemble, remove sprocket cover, bar and chain. Drain the fuel and oil tanks. Remove carburetor box cover and cylinder shroud. Unbolt and remove muffler assembly and carburetor. Pull intake sleeve out of manifold. Remove cylinder mounting screws and slide cylinder off piston.

To separate piston (3—Fig. ST103) from connecting rod, remove piston pin retainers (5) and push piston pin (4) out of piston (3) and connecting rod. If piston pin is stuck, tap pin out using a brass drift. Be sure to support piston and connecting rod so side forces are not applied to connecting rod when removing piston pin.

Inspect piston and cylinder bore for deep scratches, scoring or excessive

Illustrations courtesy Stihl Inc.

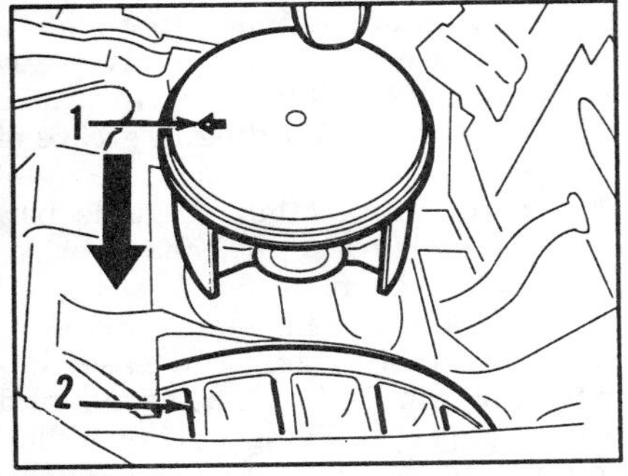

Fig. ST104—Install piston so arrow mark on piston crown points toward exhaust port of cylinder.

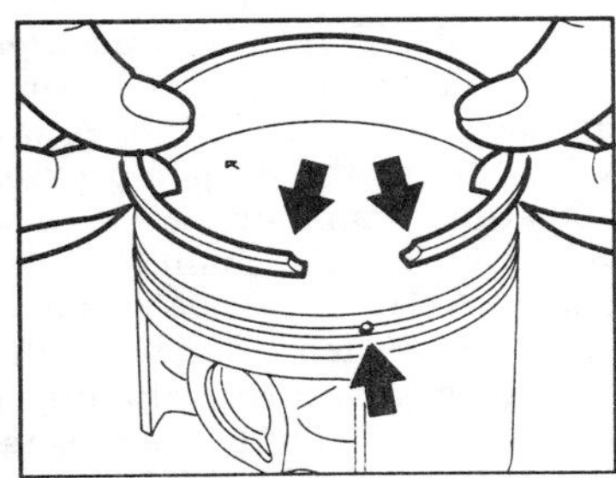
Fig. ST105—Install piston rings so that radii at ring ends face upward and end gap is positioned around locating pin in ring groove.

wear. New cylinder is available only with a new fitted piston. If only the piston requires renewal, piston marked "B" on piston crown may be used in all "broken in" cylinders.

To reassemble, install piston with arrow and "A" markings on piston crown pointing toward exhaust port (Fig. ST104). Piston pin must slide easily into piston bore. When installing hookless wire piston pin retainers (5–Fig. ST103), it is recommended that Stihl tool 5910 890 8200 be used for 024 series and Model 026AVEQZ; Stihl tool 5910 890 2210 for Model 044AVEQZ; Stihl tool 5910 890 2213 for 084 series; and Stihl tool 5910 890 2212 for 088 series. Pin retainers must be installed with end gap facing either top or bottom of piston.

Piston is equipped with locating pins in ring grooves to prevent piston ring rotation. Install rings in grooves so that the radii at the ring ends face upward and the ring end gap is positioned around locating pins (Fig. ST105) before installing cylinder.

Lubricate piston rings and cylinder bore with engine oil. Support piston with a wooden block that will fit between piston skirt and top of crankcase. A notch should be cut in wooden block so block will fit around connecting rod.

If removed, install intake manifold tube (1—Fig. ST106) on cylinder so tube points upward. Secure tube with

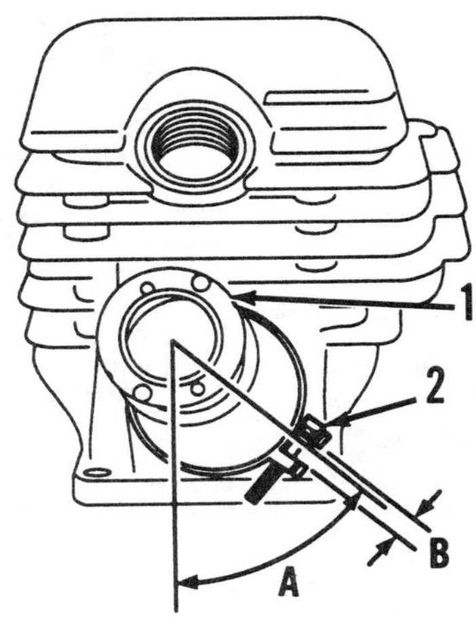

Fig. ST106—Install manifold (1) so that it points upward. Hose clamp (2) should be positioned so that ends point down and to the right at an angle of approximately 45 degrees (A).

the hose clamp (2). Note that ends of hose clamp must point downward and to the right at an angle of approximately 45 degrees (A). Tighten the hose clamp until there is a gap (B) of about 6.5 mm (1/4 in.) between the ends of hose clamp.

Compress the rings and slide the cylinder over piston. Do not rotate the cylinder as the rings may disengage from the locating pins, resulting in damage to the cylinder and rings. Tighten cylinder screws evenly in a diagonal pattern to the following torque: 10 N•m (88 in.-lb.) for 024 and 026 series; 10.5 N•m (93 in.-lb.) for 044 series; and 15 N•m (133 in.-lb.) for 084 and 088 series saws.

To fit the manifold tube (1—Fig. ST106) in the tank housing intake opening, wrap a piece of string around the back of the manifold flange. Pass the ends of the string through the intake opening. Guide the manifold downward into the intake opening while pulling the ends of the string outward, and pull the manifold flange through the opening.

CRANKCASE, CRANKSHAFT AND CONNECTING ROD. All models are equipped with a two-piece split type crankcase that is available as a complete crankcase assembly only. The crankshaft and connecting rod are a unit assembly and are not available separately. Crankcase must be split to remove crankshaft.

To split crankcase, drain oil and fuel tanks. Remove fan housing, sprocket guard, bar and chain. Remove chain brake assembly, clutch assembly, oil pump, flywheel, ignition coil, trigger module (if used) and generator (if used). Remove muffler, carburetor, cylinder and piston as outlined above. Unbolt and remove tank housing and handlebar. Remove crankcase mounting screws and drive the two crankcase dowel pins into ignition side crankcase half. Tap end of crankshaft with a soft hammer to split crankcase and remove crankshaft from main bearings.

Rotate connecting rod around crankpin and renew entire assembly if roughness or other damage is noted. Inspect crankshaft main bearings (11 and 16—Fig. ST103) for roughness and renew as required.

Heat crankcase halves to approximately 120 degrees C (250 degrees F) to ease installation of main bearings. Inner races of main bearings should also be heated with a soldering iron prior to installing crankshaft. On 084 and 088 models, clutch side main bearing locates against snap ring (9) in right crankcase half (8). On all other models, main bearings locate against shoulder in crankcase halves.

Assemble crankshaft and crankcase halves, drive dowel pins into clutch side crankcase half and tighten crankcase screws evenly to torque of 8 N•m (70 in.-lb.) for 024 series and Model 026AVEQZ; 9 N•m (80 in.-lb.) for Model 044AVEQZ and 084 series; and 11.5 N•m (102 in.-lb.) for 088 series saws.

Seals (10 and 18) may be installed after crankshaft is assembled in crankcase. An assembly sleeve should be installed on clutch side of crankshaft to protect seal lip from sharp edges. Lubricate seal lip with grease. Press oil seals into crankcase with sealing lip facing inward. Clutch side crankcase seal (10) seats into outer flange of main bearing (11). Install seal with outer face of seal flush with bearing outer race. Install flywheel side crankcase seal (18) flush with outer face of crankcase. Assembly of remaining parts is reverse of disassembly procedure.

CLUTCH. All models are equipped with a three-shoe centrifugal clutch. Refer to Figs. ST107, ST108 and ST109. Clutch hub (8) has left-hand threads (turn clockwise to remove) on all models.

When servicing clutch, note color of clutch springs. Springs with yellow marking should be replaced with new design springs having white color code. Clutch springs and the clutch shoes must be renewed in sets. Inspect clutch drum (4) and needle bearing (3) for excessive wear, damage or discoloration due to overheating. Lubricate bearing with suitable high temperature grease.

On Model 044AVEQZ, be sure cover washer (9—Fig. ST108) is installed with raised center facing outward. Tighten clutch hub to 70 N•m (51 ft.-lb.) for 084 series saws; 80 N•m (59 ft.-lb.)

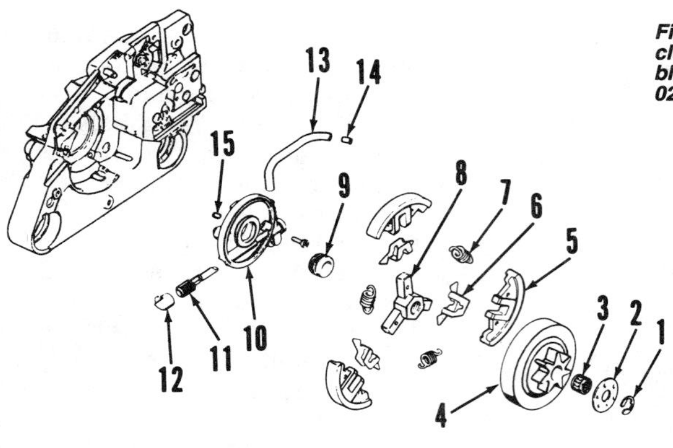

Fig. ST107—Exploded view of clutch and oil pump assemblies used on Model 026AVEQZ and 024 series saws.

1. "E" clip
2. Thrust washer
3. Needle bearing
4. Clutch drum
5. Clutch shoe
6. Retainer
7. Spring
8. Clutch hub
9. Worm gear
10. Oil pump body
11. Plunger
12. Plug
13. Oil hose
14. Sleeve
15. Cam pin

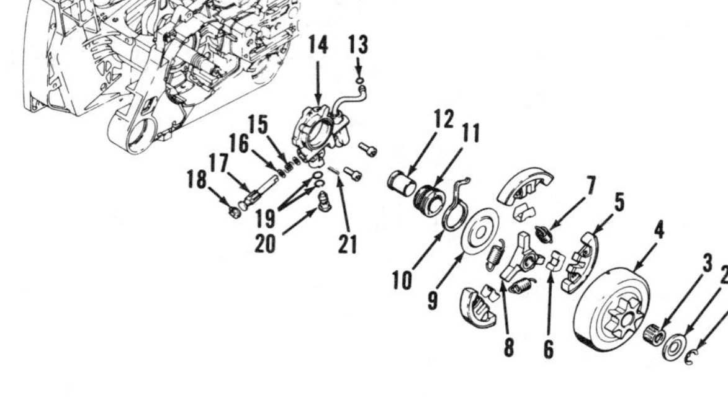

Fig. ST108—Exploded view of clutch and oil pump assemblies used on Model 044AVEQZ.

1. "E" ring
2. Thrust washer
3. Needle bearing
4. Clutch drum
5. Clutch shoe
6. Retainer
7. Spring
8. Clutch hub
9. Cover washer
10. Drive spring
11. Worm gear
12. Sleeve
13. "O" ring
14. Pump housing
15. Spring
16. Washers
17. Plunger
18. Plug
19. "O" rings
20. Adjusting screw
21. Pin

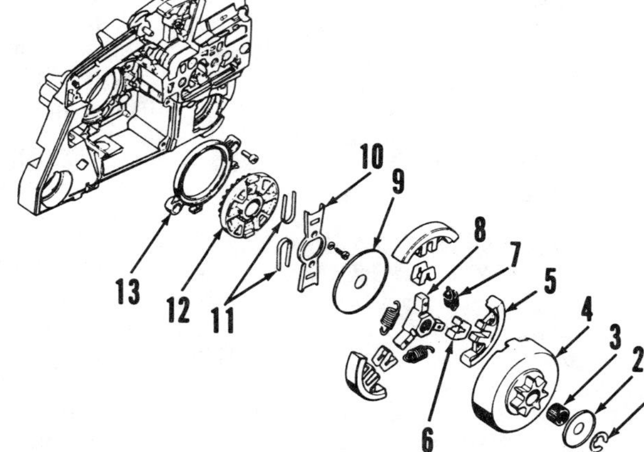

Fig. ST109—Exploded view of clutch assembly used on 084 series saws.

1. "E" clip
2. Thrust washer
3. Needle bearing
4. Clutch drum
5. Clutch shoe
6. Retainer
7. Spring
8. Clutch hub
9. Washer
10. Oil pump drive plate
11. Springs
12. Oil pump drive gear
13. Cover

for 088 series; and 50 N•m (37 ft.-lb.) on all other saws.

The clutch drum (4—Fig. ST109) of 084 and 088 series saws must properly engage oil pump drive plate (10). Using a small screwdriver or similar tool, rotate oil pump drive plate to a horizontal position and center notch in drive plate with cutout in crankcase to ease installation of clutch drum. Align mark on outer face of clutch drum with lower edge of crankcase cutout. Rotate clutch drum to be certain clutch drum and oil pump drive plate are properly engaged.

OIL PUMP. Model 026AVEQZ and 024 series saws are equipped with the automatic chain oil pump shown in Fig. ST107. Oil pump output is not adjustable. Pump plunger (11) is driven by worm gear (9). Plunger reciprocates due to cam pin (15) riding in groove of plunger.

Remove sprocket guard, guide bar, chain, clutch assembly, chain brake band and cover plate for access to oil pump. Drain oil tank and remove oil pump assembly from crankcase. Remove cam pin (15) with a magnet and pry out plug (12). Plunger (11) can then be removed from pump housing (10).

Apply grease on all moving parts upon reassembly. Make certain cam pin properly engages groove in plunger and does not extend beyond pump body.

Model 044AVEQZ is equipped with the adjustable automatic chain oil pump shown in Fig. ST108. A worm gear (11) drives the oil pump plunger (17) creating a pumping action to supply oil to the bar and chain. The worm gear is driven by the drive spring (10) that engages a notch in the clutch drum (4). The worm gear turns only when the clutch is engaged and the chain is moving.

Remove sprocket guard, guide bar, chain, brake band and clutch assembly for access to oil pump. Turn worm gear (11) and drive spring (10) clockwise and pull them off crankshaft. Drain oil tank and unbolt and remove oil pump from crankcase.

To disassemble pump, remove adjusting screw (20) and drive out pin (21). Pry out plug (18) and withdraw plunger (17). Renew any components with excessive wear or damage. Renew all "O" rings.

Apply grease to all moving parts upon reassembly. Be sure drive spring is properly installed on worm gear. Oil pump output is adjusted by rotating adjusting screw (20).

Series 084 are equipped with the adjustable automatic oil pump shown in Fig. ST110. Series 088 saws are similar. Clutch drum rotates the oil pump drive gear which meshes with oil pump driven gear (2). The driven gear is pressed on the worm gear (4) which rotates the plunger (13). Oil pump output is adjusted by rotating the adjusting pin (22) or by moving a lever attached to cable (17). The cable actuates the adjusting slide (14).

To remove the oil pump, drain the oil tank. Remove carburetor cover, sprocket cover, side cover, guide bar and chain. Turn clutch drum to align mark on face of drum with edge of crankcase cutout. Remove pump cover (1—Fig. ST110). Disconnect oil hose (26). Disconnect cable (17) from adjuster lever and tie a wire to end of cable to prevent it from being pulled out

Illustrations courtesy Stihl Inc.

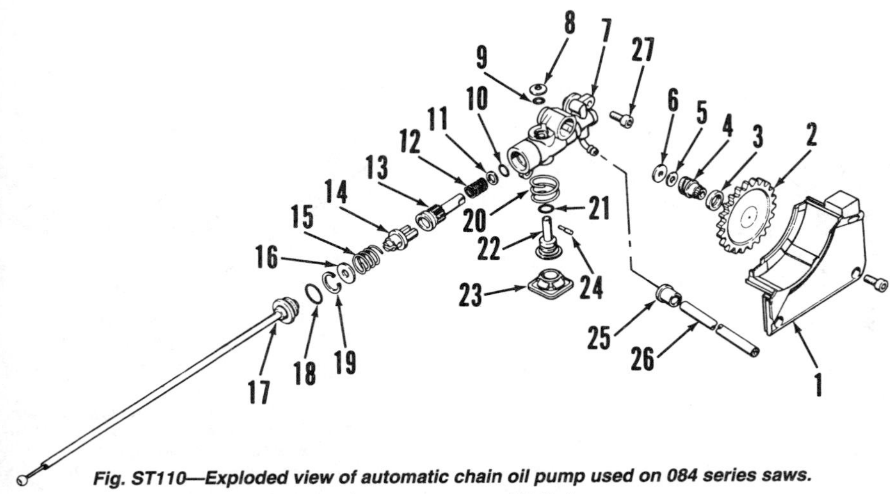

Fig. ST110—Exploded view of automatic chain oil pump used on 084 series saws.

1. Cover
2. Driven gear
3. Oil seal
4. Worm gear
5. Washer
6. Washer
7. Pump body
8. Spring washer
9. "O" ring
10. "O" ring
11. Washer
12. Spring
13. Plunger
14. Adjusting slide
15. Spring
16. Washer
17. Adjusting cable
18. "O" ring
19. Snap ring
20. Spring
21. "O" ring
22. Adjusting pin
23. Grommet
24. Pin
25. Retainer
26. Oil hose
27. Screw

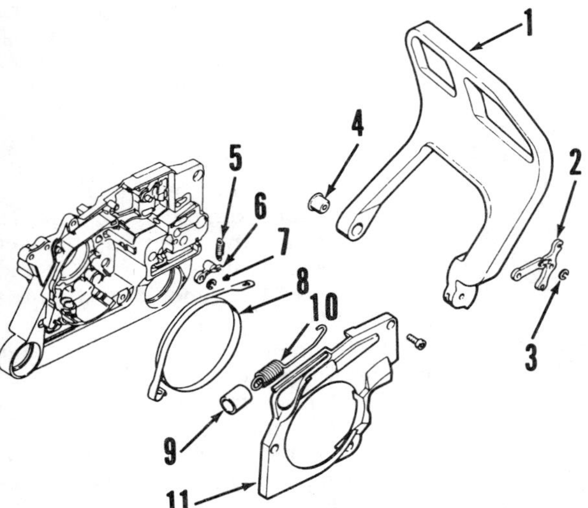

Fig. ST111—Exploded view of chain brake system components typical of all models.

1. Chain brake lever
2. Lever assy.
3. "E" ring
4. Bushing
5. Spring
6. Latch
7. "E" ring
8. Brake band
9. Sleeve
10. Spring
11. Cover

completely when oil pump is removed. Remove oil pump mounting screws and carefully pull oil pump out of crankcase as far as possible while holding adjuster cable in place. Pry cable plug out of pump housing, remove snap ring (19) and pull out cable with washer (16), spring (15) and adjusting slide (14). Remove pin (24) and withdraw adjusting pin (22). Plunger (13) can now be removed from housing. Pry driven gear (2) off worm gear (4). Clamp worm gear in vise and pry pump housing (7) away from worm.

Any excessively worn or damaged components should be renewed. Reassembly is reverse of disassembly. Worm gear seal (3) should always be renewed if worm gear is removed from housing.

NOTE: Before installing worm gear (4—Fig. ST110) and seal (3), fill pump body with clean oil to prime pump. If it becomes necessary to prime pump after pump is assembled, pry back plug at adjusting cable (17) and inject clean oil through small hole in driven gear (2) until oil flows from pump body at plug of adjusting cable.

Apply a suitable sealant on threads of pump housing front mounting screw. Be sure oil hose is properly secured on pump nipple by retainer (25).

On all models, oil tank vent (22—Fig. ST103) is located in oil tank and may be removed for inspection or renewal. Insert a long punch inside oil tank and drive out vent from inside. When installing vent, press into oil tank until outer face of vent is about 1 mm (0.040 in.) below surface of crankcase.

CHAIN BRAKE. Some models are equipped with a chain brake system designed to stop chain movement should kickback occur. Chain brake is activated when operator's hand strikes chain brake lever (1—Fig. ST111), tripping latch (6) thereby allowing spring (10) to draw brake band (8) tight around clutch drum. Pull back chain brake lever to reset mechanism. No adjustment of chain brake system is required.

To disassemble, remove sprocket cover, bar and chain. Engage chain brake, then remove brake cover (11—Fig. ST111) and disconnect brake spring (10). Remove brake band mounting screw and pry brake band (8) from crankcase.

Renew any component found to be excessively worn or damaged. Lubricate all pivot points with Molykote or similar lubricant.

REWIND STARTER. Model 044AVEQZ and 084 series saws are equipped with the rewind starter shown in Fig. ST112. All other models are similar except a single pawl (2) is used and cover (6) is absent.

To disassemble, remove starter housing (7) from engine. Pull rope out about 30 cm (12 in.). While holding rope pulley (4), unwind three or four turns of rope from pulley. Then, allow pulley to slowly unwind to relieve tension on rewind spring. Pry off wire clip (1) and remove rope pulley using caution not to dislodge rewind spring (5). If rewind spring must be removed, be careful not to allow spring to uncoil uncontrolled.

When installing rewind spring, be sure hook on outer coil of spring engages lug of starter housing. Rope length should be 100 cm (40 in.) long and 4.5 mm (3/16 in.) in diameter. Apply light coat of grease to starter housing post (12) before installing rope pulley. Thread end of rope through rope guide in starter housing, then position pulley on starter housing post and rotate pulley to engage inner end of rewind spring in pulley. Install rope handle (10).

To preload rewind spring, wind rope on pulley in a clockwise direction as viewed from flywheel side of pulley until rope handle is about 20 cm (8 in.) from starter housing. Make a loop in the rope between pulley and housing and grip loop of rope close to pulley. Use loop of rope to rotate pulley three turns clockwise. Allow pulley to slowly rewind to take up slack in rope. With rope

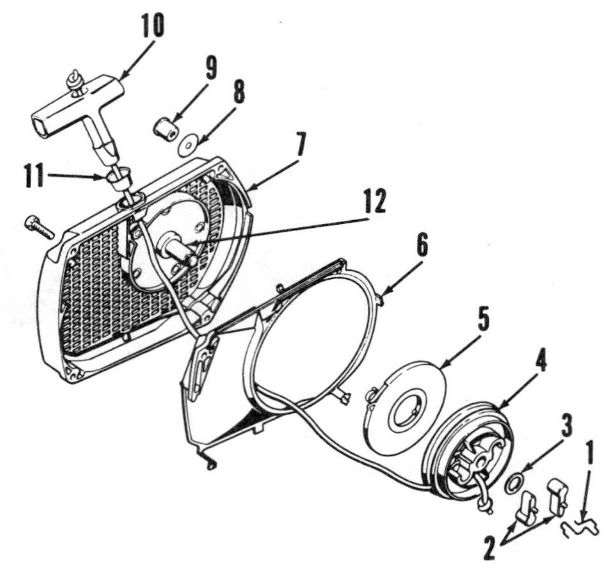

Fig. ST112—Exploded view of rewind starter used on Model 044AVEQZ and 084 series saws. Starter used on other models is similar except only one pawl (2) is used and cover (6) is absent.

1. Wire clip
2. Pawls
3. Washer
4. Rope pulley
5. Rewind spring & case
6. Cover
7. Starter housing
8. Washer
9. Sleeve
10. Rope handle
11. Rope guide
12. Shaft

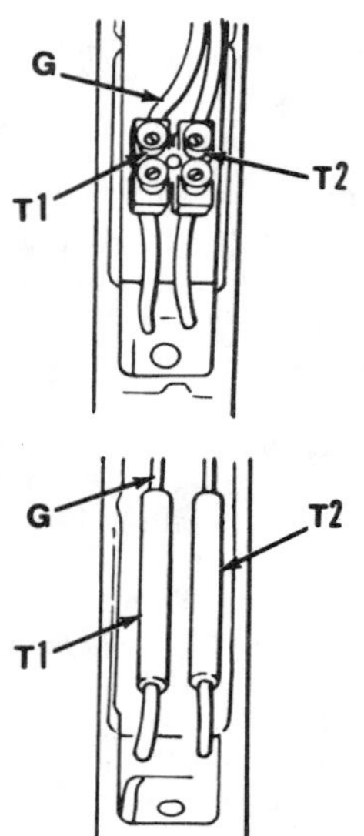

Fig. ST113—Drawing showing location of heater wire terminals in rear grip used on 024 series saws. Both styles of connectors have been used. Refer to text.

fully retracted, rope handle should be snug against housing. With rope fully extended, rope pulley should be able to rotate at least an additional half turn clockwise.

HANDLE HEATER. Some models are equipped with an electric handle heating system. A generator located behind the flywheel supplies an electrical current to a switch and heating elements in front handle and rear grip.

To test handle heating system on 024 series saws, remove carburetor cover and rear grip insert. Disconnect wire from heater switch and connect ohmmeter between switch and ground. Reading should be zero ohms with switch in the "ON" position. To perform the remaining checks, disconnect the generator wire (G—Fig. ST113) from terminal (T1). Connect ohmmeter leads to terminals (T1 and T2) to test heating element in rear grip. Reading should be approximately one ohm. Connect ohmmeter leads between terminal (T2) and ground to test heating element in front handle. Reading should be approximately two ohms. Connect ohmmeter leads between generator lead (G) and ground to check generator coil. Reading should be approximately 0.6 ohm.

On all tests, if reading is zero ohms, check for damaged insulation causing a short in circuit being tested. An infinite reading indicates an open circuit and component being tested should be renewed.

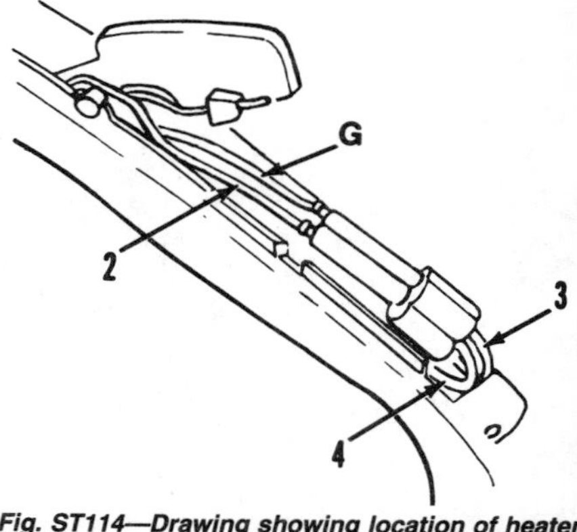

Fig. ST114—Drawing showing location of heater wires in rear grip on Model 044AVEQZ and 084 series saws. Refer to text.

To check handle heating system on Models 044AVEQZ, 084AVE, 084AVEQ and 084AVREQ, remove air filter and rear handle molding. Disconnect wire (G—Fig. ST114) from generator to rear handle heating element wire (3). Set heater switch to "I" position and connect ohmmeter leads to generator wire and to heating element wire to test resistance of all components in heating system. Reading should be about 2.5 ohms. If reading is significantly higher or lower, check each individual component separately to determine fault.

To test heating element in rear grip, disconnect wires (3 and 4) and connect ohmmeter between wires. Reading should be approximately 0.25 ohm. To test front heating element, connect ohmmeter leads between wire (2) and ground. Resistance should be approximately 1.6-2.2 ohms.

To test generator, connect ohmmeter between generator wire (G) and ground. Resistance should be approximately 0.6 ohm for generator. On all tests, a zero reading indicates damaged insulation causing a short circuit. Insulation may be repaired. An infinite reading indicates an open circuit and component should be renewed.

Element in rear handle may be renewed separately from handle. Front element is available only as an assembly with front handlebar. Flywheel must be removed for access to generator.

STIHL

Model	Bore mm (in.)	Stroke mm (in.)	Displacement cc (cu. in.)	Drive Type
017	37 (1.46)	28 (1.10)	30.1 1.84)	Direct
021, 021WB	40 (1.57)	28 (1.102)	35.2 (2.15)	Direct
023, 023WB	40 (1.57)	32 (1.26)	40.2 (4.45)	Direct
025, 025WB	42 (1.65)	32 (1.26)	44.3 (2.7)	Direct
029, 029FB	45 (1.77)	34 (1.34)	54.1 (3.14)	Direct
039	49 (1.93)	34 (1.34)	64.1 (3.9)	Direct

MAINTENANCE

SPARK PLUG. Recommended spark plug for all models except 017 is Bosch WSR6F or NGK BPMR7A. Recommended spark plug for 017 model is Champion RCJ6Y. For all models, the electrode gap should be 0.50 mm (0.020 in.). The spark plug should be tightened to the torque listed in the TIGHTENING TORQUE paragraph.

CARBURETOR. All models are equipped with an all position diaphragm type carburetor. Refer to the appropriate section of the CARBURETOR SERVICE section for service and exploded views of the carburetor used. The automatic choke system used on 029 and 039 models should be checked for proper operation if saw is difficult to start. Do not attempt to remove the choke mechanism from 029 or 039 models.

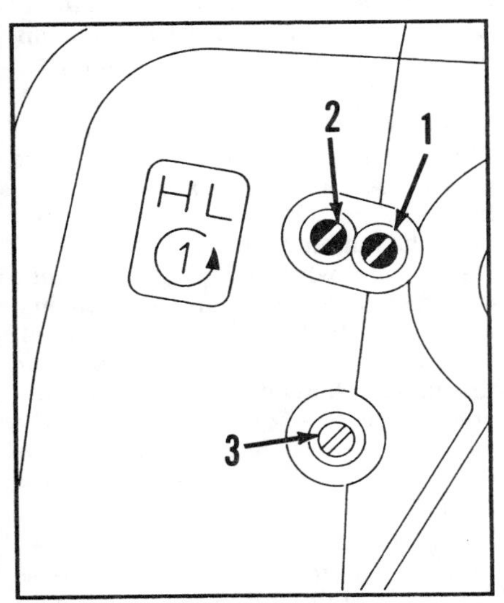

Fig. ST190—Initial setting for low-speed and high-speed mixture screws (1 and 2) is one turn open from lightly seated position.

To remove carburetor, remove air cleaner cover, air filter element and filter housing if used. Remove flange nuts (Models 017, 021, 023 and 025) from carburetor mounting studs. Disconnect throttle rod and fuel hose. Pull the carburetor off the mounting studs. On all models, tighten the carburetor attaching screws to the torque listed in the TIGHTENING TORQUE paragraph.

Initial adjustment of carburetor on all models is one turn open from a lightly seated position for both low-speed and high-speed mixture needles (Fig. ST190). The carburetor used on Model 017 has a fixed high-speed jet and is not adjustable.

On all models, final adjustment of carburetor should be made with engine running at operating temperature. Be sure engine air filter is clean before adjusting carburetor.

Adjust low-speed mixture needle (1—Fig. ST190) to obtain highest idle speed, then turn screw counterclockwise approximately 1/8 turn. Engine should accelerate smoothly without hesitation. If engine stumbles or seems sluggish when accelerating, adjust low-speed mixture needle until engine accelerates without hesitation. Adjust idle speed screw (3) so engine idles just below clutch engagement speed.

High-speed mixture needle (2—Fig. ST190) should be adjusted to obtain optimum performance with saw under cutting load. Do not adjust high-speed mixture needle too lean (turned too far clockwise) as maximum permissible engine speed may be exceeded and engine can be damaged from lack of lubrication and overheating. Maximum no-load speed with chain and bar installed must not exceed 11,500 rpm for Model 021; 12,500 rpm for Models 023 and 025; 13,000 rpm for Models 029 and 039. If an accurate tachometer is not available, do not change high-speed mixture from initial setting.

IGNITION. All models are equipped with a breakerless transistor controlled ignition system. Except for faulty wiring connections, repair of ignition system malfunction is accomplished by component renewal.

Air gap between the legs of the ignition module (1—Fig. ST191) and flywheel magnets should be 0.15-0.30 mm (0.006-0.012 in.) for 017, 029 and 039 models. Air gap for all other models should be 0.2-0.4 mm (0.008-0.016 in.). When installing, set the air gap between the flywheel magnets and the legs of the ignition module as follows.

Install the ignition module, but tighten the two screws only enough to hold it in place away from the flywheel. Insert setting gauge (part No. 1111 890 6400) or brass/plastic shim stock of the proper thickness between the legs of the ignition module and the flywheel, then turn the flywheel until the flywheel magnets are near the module legs. Loosen the screws attaching the ignition module and press legs of the ignition module against the setting

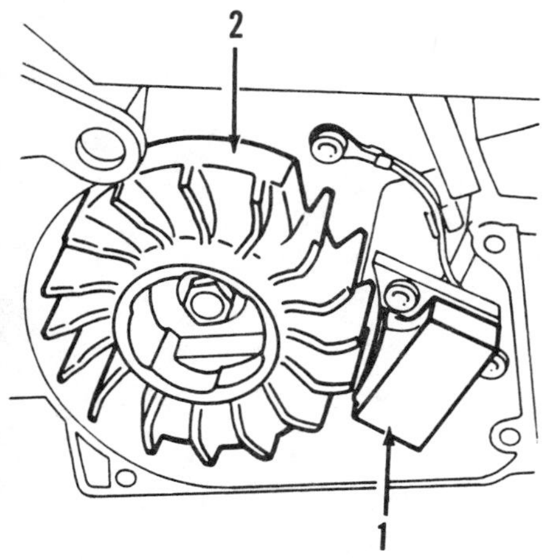

Fig. ST191—Air gap between ignition module (1) and flywheel magnets (2) is adjustable. Refer to text.

gauge. Tighten the two attaching screws to the torque listed in the TIGHTENING TORQUE paragraph. Remove the setting gauge, then turn the flywheel and check that flywheel does not hit the legs of the coil.

Ignition timing is not adjustable, and since there is no mechanical wear in the ignition system, the timing cannot get out of adjustment unless there is an internal fault in the ignition module. Specified ignition timing at 8,000 rpm is 1.0-1.6 mm (0.04-0.063 in.) BTDC for Model 017; 1.6-2.2 mm (0.063-086 in.) BTDC for Model 021; 1.9-2.5 mm (0.075-098 in.) BTDC for Models 023 and 025; 2.0-2.8 mm (0.08-0.10 in.) for 029 and 039 models.

LUBRICATION. The engine is lubricated by oil mixed with the gasoline fuel. The manufacturer recommends mixing STIHL 50:1 two-stroke oil with regular grade gasoline at the ratio recommended on the package. When using regular two-stroke engine oil, mix at a ratio of 25:1. Always use a separate container to mix gasoline and oil before filling the fuel tank. The manufacturer recommends using gasoline with octane of 87 or higher.

All models are equipped with automatic bar and chain oiling system. The oil pump output is adjustable for Models 029 and 039, but is not adjustable for other models. Refer to OIL PUMP under REPAIRS section for service procedures.

The manufacturer recommends using good quality oil designed for lubricating saw chain. If saw chain oil is not available, clean automotive oil may be used with viscosity chosen according to ambient temperature. Make sure the reservoir is filled at all times.

REPAIRS

CRANKCASE PRESSURE TEST. An improperly sealed crankcase can cause the engine to be hard to start, run rough, have low power and overheat. Refer to ENGINE SERVICE section of this manual for crankcase pressure test procedure. If crankcase leakage is indicated, pressurize crankcase and use a soap and water solution to check gaskets, seals, pulse line and castings for leakage.

TIGHTENING TORQUE. Recommended tightening torque values are as follows.

Guide bar
Attachment . . . . 16 N·m (142 in.-lb.)
Stud/collar screw . . . . 32 N·m (264 in.-lb.)
Carburetor . . . . 3.5 N·m (31 in.-lb.)
Clutch hub . . . . 50 N·m (444 in.-lb.)
Crankcase to cylinder . . . . 8 N·m (84 in.-lb.)
Engine to housing
Model 017 . . . . 9.5 N·m (71 in.-lb.)
Models 029 & 039 . . . . 11 N·m (97 in.-lb.)
Fan housing/starter housing
Model 017 . . . . 4.5 N·m (40 in.-lb.)
Models 029 & 039 . . . . 3.5 N·m (31 in.-lb.)
Flywheel . . . . 27.5 N·m (244 in.-lb.)
Hand guard(left)
Model 017 . . . . 1.7 N·m (16 in.-lb.)
Models 029 & 039 . . . . 3.5 N·m (31 in.-lb.)
Handle (front) . . . . 3.5 N·m (31 in.-lb.)
Ignition module/coil . . . . . 4.8-5.0 N·m (42-44 in.-lb.)
Muffler
Model 017 . . . . 7 N·m (62 in.-lb.)
Models 029 & 039 . . . . 9.0 N·m (79 in.-lb.)
Spark plug . . . . 25 N·m (222 in.-lb.)

REMOVE ENGINE. The following description is specifically for 029 and 039 models, but is similar for other models. Remove the plugs covering the mounting screws attaching the front handle assembly, then remove the attaching screws (Fig. ST192) and handle. Remove air filter cover, air filter and filter housing. Remove the carburetor assembly. Slide washer (1—Fig. ST193) from the carburetor mounting

Fig. ST192—Front handle mounting screws.

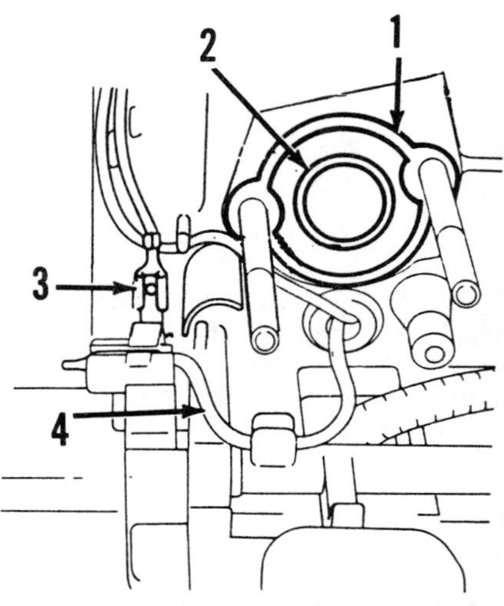

Fig. ST193—Drawing showing intake manifold and stop switch wires.

1. Washer
2. Sleeve
3. Ground wire
4. Short circuit wire

studs and withdraw the sleeve (2) from the intake manifold. Detach ground wire (3) and pull short circuit wire connector (4) from the engine stop switch shaft.

Remove the plugs from the center of the vibration isolators on the hand guard. Use a screwdriver or similar tool to push the vibration isolator buffer from the engine housing. Pull the handle forward while pushing the intake manifold through the handle housing. Release the grommet (5—Fig. ST194) for the engine stop switch wires from the handle housing. Remove the impulse hose (6—Fig. ST194) from the handle housing. Remove the handle while pulling the stop switch wires from the housing.

Remove the spark plug, flywheel, clutch, oil pump and muffler. Release the spark plug lead from the cylinder cover. Remove cover mounting screws, then lift the cover from the engine. A

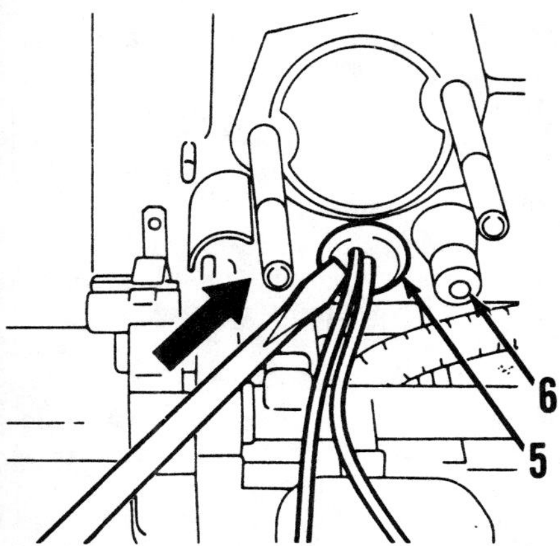

Fig. ST194—Push grommet (5) and impulse hose (6) from handle housing when removing handle from saw.

Fig. ST196—Exploded view of engine assembly typical of all models. Connecting rod (6) and crankshaft (15) are available separately on Model 021. Crankshaft and connecting rod unit assembly (16) is used on Models 023 and 025.

1. Cylinder
2. Piston rings
3. Piston
4. Piston pin
5. Retaining rings
6. Connecting rod
7. Needle bearing
8. Bearing rollers
9. Ball bearings
10. Seals
11. Snap ring
12. Engine housing
13. Crankcase cover
14. Segment
15. Crankshaft
16. Crankshaft & connecting rod assy.

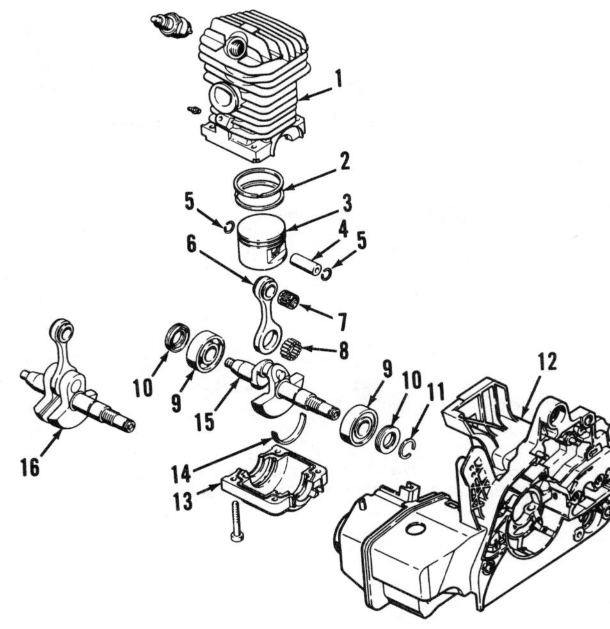

ground wire may be attached to the cylinder cover. Unbolt and remove the cylinder cover. Detach the ground wire from the cylinder. Remove the guide bar collar stud located nearest the crankshaft. The collar stud is installed with thread locking compound and it may be necessary to apply heat before the stud can be removed. Remove the four engine attaching screws from under the saw then lift the engine from the housing.

When installing the engine, reverse the removal procedure. Tighten screws to the torque listed in the TIGHTENING TORQUE paragraph.

CYLINDER, PISTON, PIN AND RINGS. Engine must be removed from saw to service cylinder, piston, pin and rings. To disassemble, remove fan housing, carburetor cover (1—Fig. ST195), air filter housing (2), carburetor (5) and muffler. Remove sprocket cover, bar and chain.

Remove spark plug and install a suitable piston stop tool or insert the end of a rope in the spark plug hole to prevent the crankshaft from turning. Remove flywheel retaining nut (right-hand threads) and pull flywheel off crankshaft. Remove clutch assembly. Note that clutch hub has left-hand threads (turn clockwise to remove). Remove oil pump worm and drive spring. Remove front handle assembly. Remove oil pump connector and oil pump from bottom of engine housing.

Disconnect ground wires from cylinder. Remove four engine mounting screws from bottom of engine housing, then slide engine sideways out of engine housing (12—Fig. ST196). Remove baffle plate and intake manifold tube from cylinder. Separate crankcase cover (13) from cylinder (1). Withdraw crankshaft and connecting rod with piston from cylinder. Remove snap rings (5) and push out piston pin (4) to separate piston (3) from connecting rod.

Inspect piston and cylinder bore for scratches, scoring or other damage and renew as necessary. Piston, pin and rings are available separately, but cylinder is available only with matching piston.

When assembling piston on connecting rod, be sure arrow mark on piston crown is positioned in relation to crankshaft as shown in Fig. ST197. Piston pin retaining rings (5—Fig. ST196) must be installed with end gap facing either top or bottom of piston.

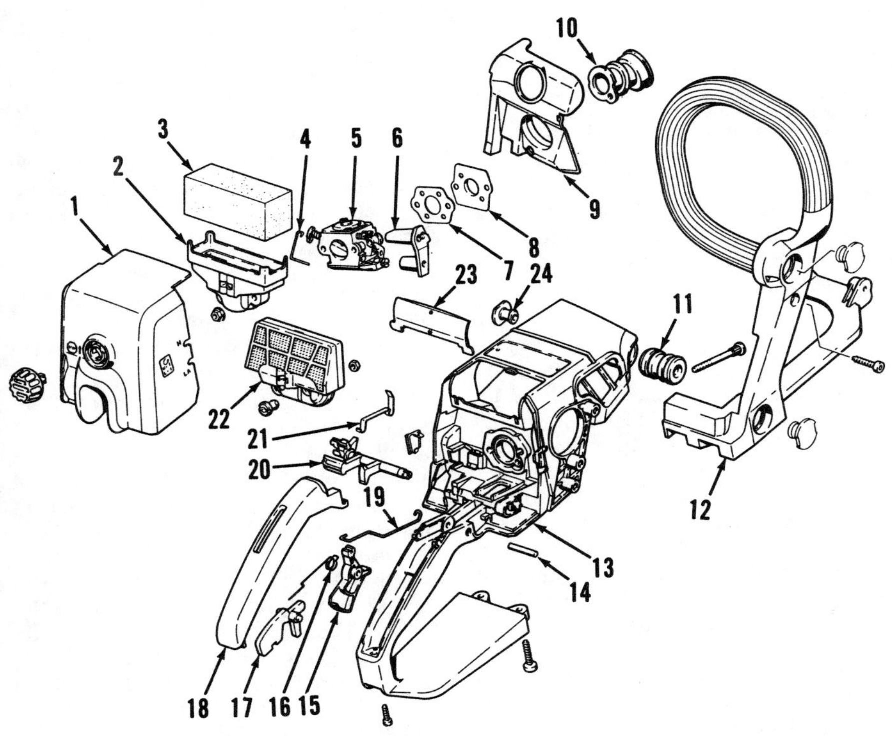

Fig. ST195—Exploded view of handle housing and air filter assembly typical of all models.

1. Carburetor cover
2. Air filter housing (standard)
3. Air filter
4. Choke lever
5. Carburetor
6. Grommet
7. Gasket
8. Shim
9. Baffle plate
10. Intake tube
11. Anti-vibration rubber mount
12. Front handle
13. Handle housing
14. Pin
15. Throttle trigger
16. Torsion spring
17. Throttle lock
18. Handle cover
19. Throttle rod
20. Switch
21. Contact spring
22. Air filter (optional)

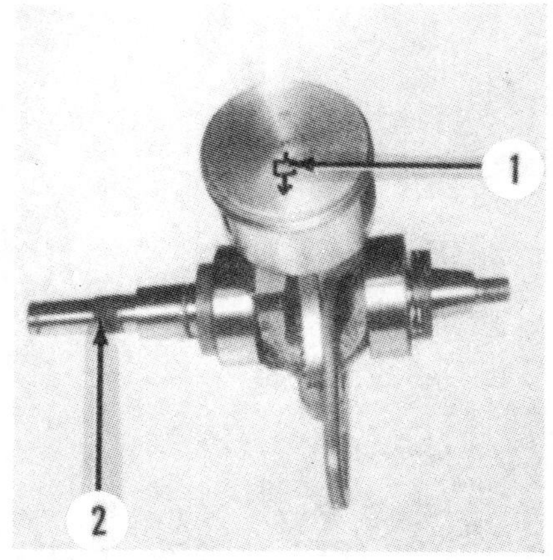

Fig. ST197—Piston must be installed on connecting rod so arrow mark (1) on piston crown is positioned in relation to clutch side of crankshaft (2) as shown.

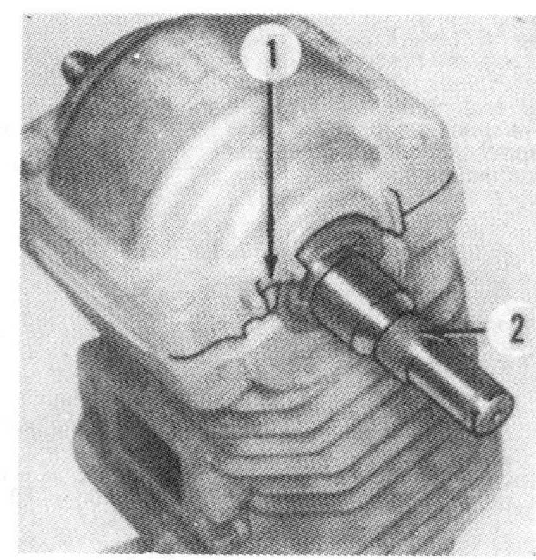

Fig. ST199—When installing crankcase cover, make certain oil pump seat (1) is positioned on clutch side of crankshaft (2) as shown.

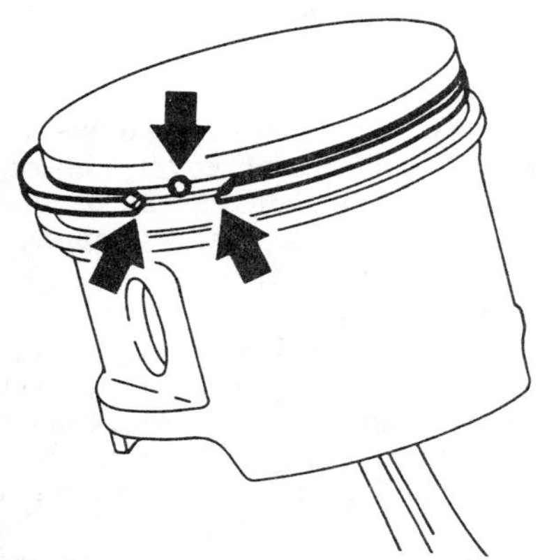
Fig. ST198—Install piston rings with radii at ring ends facing upward and end gap positioned around locating pin.

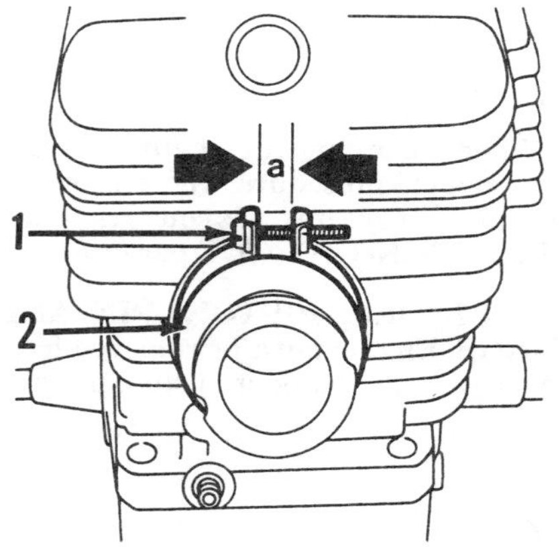

Fig. ST200—Install intake manifold (2) so straight faces of manifold and intake port are aligned. Tighten clamp (1) until gap (a) is about 8 mm (5/16 in.).

Piston is equipped with locating pins in ring grooves to prevent piston ring rotation. Be certain that ring end gap is positioned around locating pin and that the radii at the ring ends face upward as shown in Fig. ST198 before installing cylinder.

Lubricate piston rings and cylinder bore with engine oil. Compress the rings, align the cylinder exhaust port with the arrow mark on piston crown, and slide the cylinder over the piston. Do not rotate the cylinder as the rings may disengage from the locating pins, resulting in damage to the cylinder and rings.

Apply thin bead of sealant to mating surface of crankcase cover (13—Fig. ST196). Assemble crankcase cover to cylinder so seat for oil pump is positioned on clutch side of engine as shown in Fig. ST199. Install intake manifold tube (2—Fig. ST200) on cylinder so that straight faces of manifold and intake port are aligned. Manifold clamp (1) should be installed with gap at top. Tighten clamp until gap between ends is about 8 mm (5/16 in.) wide. Remainder of assembly is reverse of disassembly procedure.

CONNECTING ROD AND CRANKSHAFT. The crankshaft is supported by ball bearings (9—Fig. ST196) at both ends. Connecting rod is supported on crankpin by roller bearings. On Models 017 and 021 the connecting rod (6), roller bearings (8) and crankshaft (15) may be renewed separately. On Models 023, 025, 029 and 039 the connecting rod, roller bearings and crankshaft (16) are a unit assembly and are not available separately. On all models, engine must be removed from engine housing and disassembled as previously outlined in CYLINDER, PISTON, PIN AND RINGS section to service connecting rod and crankshaft.

On Models 017 and 021, connecting rod can be separated from crankshaft after first pulling ball bearing off flywheel side of crankshaft. Note that connecting rod bearing rollers are loose and will fall out as connecting rod is removed. Bearing rollers must be renewed as a complete set. When reassembling, use grease to hold roller bearings in place.

On Models 023, 025, 029 and 039, rotate connecting rod around crankpin and renew assembly if roughness, excessive play or other damage is noted.

Ball bearings (9) should be heated to approximately 50 degrees C (120 degrees F) before pressing them onto crankshaft. Closed side of bearings must face outward. Be sure bearings bottom against crankshaft shoulders.

Coat the lips of oil seals (10) with grease and apply thin bead of sealant to outer diameter of seals prior to installation. Install crankshaft, connecting rod and piston in cylinder with arrow mark (1—Fig. ST197) on piston crown pointing toward exhaust port. Apply sealant to mating surface of crankcase cover. Install crankcase cover so oil pump seat is positioned on clutch side of engine as shown in Fig. ST199.

CLUTCH. All models are equipped with a three-shoe centrifugal type clutch shown in Fig. ST201. To gain access to clutch assembly, remove sprocket cover, bar and chain. Remove "E" ring (1), washer (2), clutch drum (3) and needle bearing (4). Remove spark plug and install piston stop tool or insert the end of a rope in spark plug hole to prevent crankshaft from rotating. Note that clutch hub (8) has left-hand threads and must be turned clockwise to remove it from crankshaft. Disengage clutch springs (7) and separate shoes (5) and retainers (6) from hub.

Inspect all parts for evidence of excessive wear or damage due to overheating. Clutch shoes, retainers and springs must be renewed in sets to prevent unbalanced operation.

When reassembling, note that a series number is stamped on one side of clutch shoes (5). Retainers (6) must be installed on shoes with narrow side of retainer positioned on same side as series number, and series number must face outward when shoes are installed on clutch hub. Tighten clutch hub to the torque listed in the TIGHTENING TORQUE paragraph. Lubricate needle bearing (4) with high temperature grease prior to installation. Be sure oil pump drive spring (9) engages notch in clutch drum (3).

OIL PUMP (Except 029 and 039). All models except 029 and 039 are equipped with a nonadjustable automatic chain oil pump. The oil pump

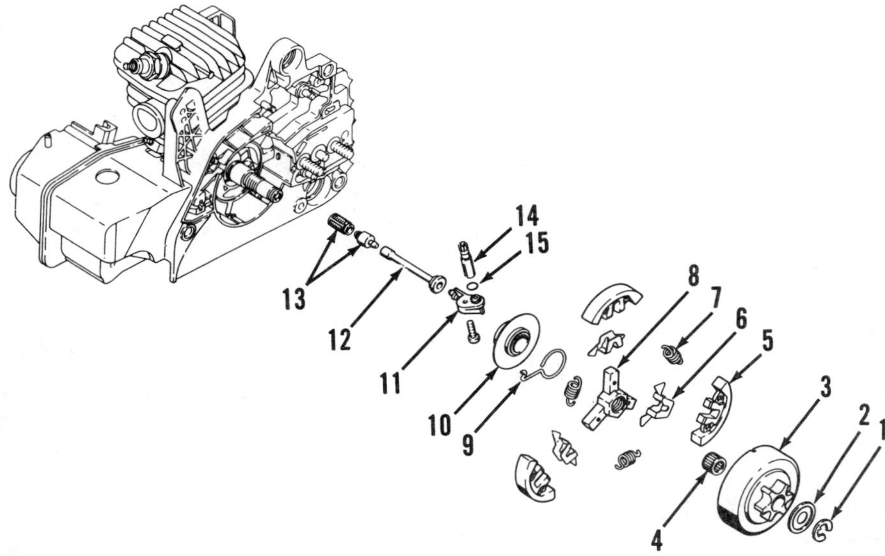

Fig. ST201—Exploded view of clutch assembly typical of all models. The automatic chain oil pump components shown are typical of all models except 029 and 039. On some models, clutch drum (3) and chain sprocket are two separate components.

1. "E" ring
2. Washer
3. Clutch drum & sprocket
4. Needle bearing
5. Clutch shoe
6. Retainer
7. Spring
8. Hub
9. Drive spring
10. Pump drive worm
11. Oil pump connector
12. Oil inlet hose
13. Oil strainer
14. Oil pump
15. "O" ring

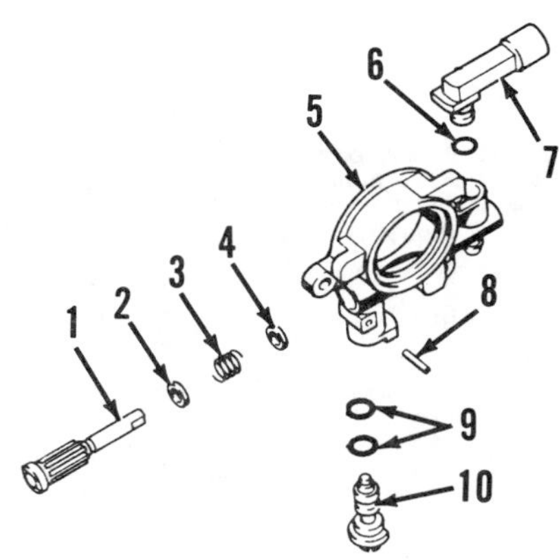

Fig. ST203—Exploded view of oil pump used on 029 and 039 models.

1. Pump piston
2. Washer
3. Spring
4. Washer
5. Pump housing
6. O-ring
7. Connector
8. Spring pin
9. O-rings
10. Adjustment screw

(14—Fig. ST201) is located in bottom of engine housing.

To remove oil pump, first drain the oil tank. Remove oil pump connector retaining screw and pull connector (11) out of oil pump and oil intake hose (12). Stihl special tool 1123 890 2200 is recommended for use in removing and installing pump. If tool is not available, note installed height of pump before it is removed so it can be reinstalled to the same depth. Thread special tool fork head or bolt into end of oil pump and pull pump out bottom of engine housing. Pump drive spring (9) and worm (10) can be removed from crankshaft after removing clutch assembly.

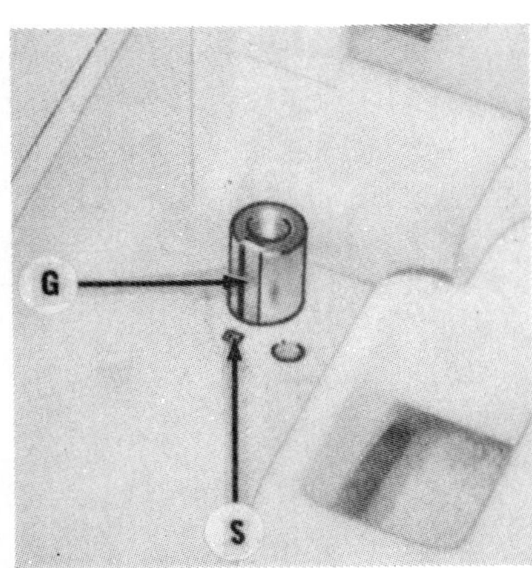

Fig. ST202—Install oil pump so groove (G) in pump body is aligned with square mark (S) on engine housing of models except 029 and 039.

When installing oil pump, position pump so groove (G—Fig. ST202) in pump is aligned with square mark (S) on housing. Push pump into housing to same depth as noted prior to removal. If using special tool 1123 890 2200, pump will be installed to correct depth when tool fork head bottoms against engine housing.

Oil tank vent valve is located in oil tank wall adjacent to bar studs. Vent must be open for proper operation of oil pump. Vent may be removed for inspection by driving it inward into oil tank and then removing it through oil tank filler opening. Press vent into housing bore until outer face of valve is about 1 mm (0.040 in.) below outer surface of housing.

OIL PUMP (Models 029 and 039). Models 029 and 039 are equipped with an adjustable automatic chain oil pump. The volume of oil delivered by the pump can be changed by turning the adjustment screw (10—Fig. ST203). The screw is located under the saw on the right side.

The oil pump is located behind the clutch assembly. The spring wire shown in Fig. ST204 drives the oil pump gear. The spring wire engages a notch in the clutch drum and turns only when the clutch is engaged and the chain is moving. To remove the oil pump, first remove the clutch, then withdraw the worm drive gear. Detach the connector hoses from the pump. Remove the attaching screws, then lift the pump from the engine. When assembling, coat all parts and sealing joints with grease. Make sure the drive spring wire (Fig. ST204) correctly engages the clutch drum.

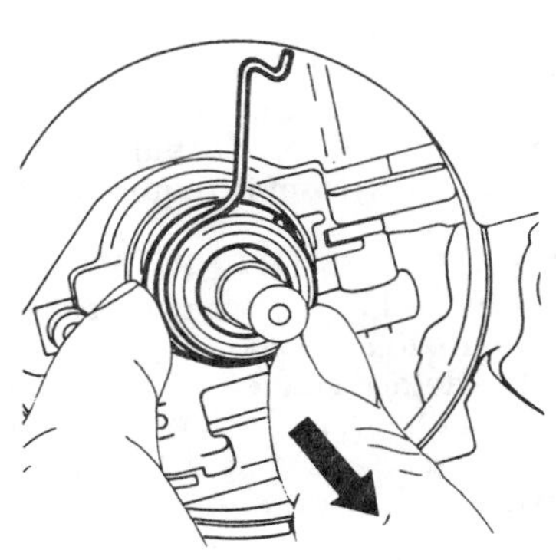

Fig. ST204—A spring wire that engages a notch in the clutch hub drives the oil pump drive gear of 029 and 039 models.

CHAIN BRAKE. All models are equipped with a chain brake designed to stop chain movement should kickback occur. Forward movement of hand guard (1—Fig. ST205) actuates brake lever bellcrank (2). The bellcrank trips the brake cam (8) thereby allowing brake spring (6) to draw brake band (7) tight around clutch drum. Pull hand guard rearward to reset mechanism.

To disassemble brake, remove sprocket guard, guide bar and chain, and clutch drum. Disengage brake and remove brake cover (5). Carefully disconnect brake spring (6), then pry brake band (7) out of engine housing.

To remove brake linkage, remove hand guard retaining screw and remove "E" clip from bellcrank (2). Pry hand guard (1), strap (3) and bellcrank off their pivot pins. Pull cam lever (8)

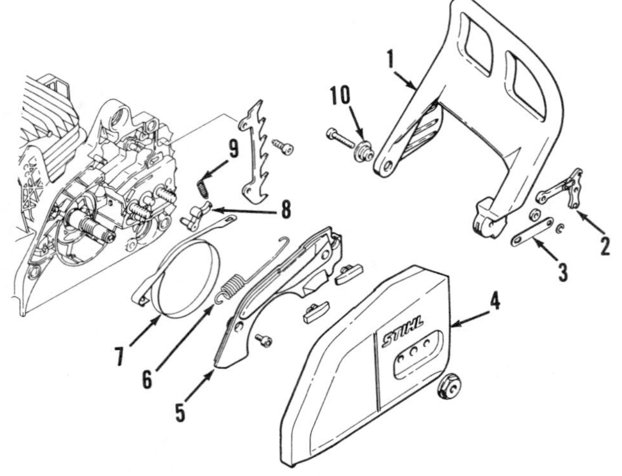

Fig. ST205—Exploded view of chain brake components typical of type used on all models.

1. Hand guard
2. Bellcrank
3. Strap
4. Sprocket cover
5. Brake cover
6. Brake spring
7. Brake band
8. Cam lever
9. Spring
10. Bushing

out of housing and disconnect spring (9).

Inspect all parts for wear or damage and renew as necessary. Lubricate pivot points with light coat of grease. Assembly of brake is reverse of disassembly procedure. No adjustment of chain brake system is required.

REWIND STARTER. All models are equipped with the pawl type starter shown in Fig. ST206. To disassemble starter, detach starter housing, remove rope handle (1) and allow rope to wind slowly onto rope pulley (5) to relieve tension on rewind spring. Remove retaining clip (8) and remove washer (10), pawl (7) and rope pulley (5). Care should be used when removing rewind spring (4) and case as uncontrolled uncoiling of spring may be harmful.

If rewind spring is removed from its case, assemble spring in case in counterclockwise direction starting from the outside and working inward.

If renewing starter rope, new rope length should be 96 cm (38 in.) and 3 mm (1/8 in.) in diameter. Wind rope around rope pulley in a clockwise direction as viewed from flywheel side of pulley.

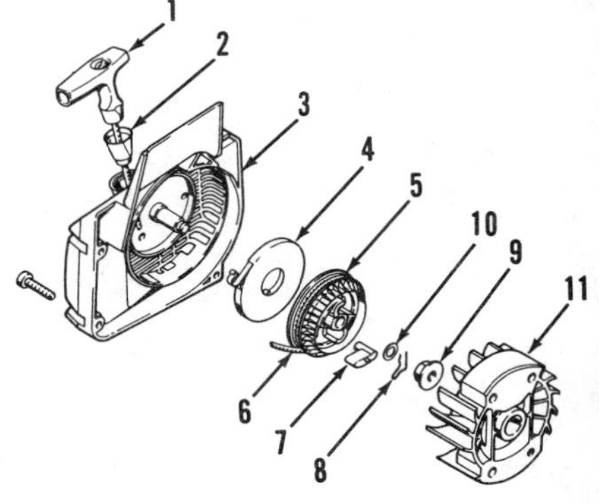

Fig. ST206—Exploded view of rewind starter assembly typical of type used on all models.

1. Rope handle
2. Rope guide
3. Starter housing
4. Rewind spring
5. Rope pulley
6. Rope
7. Pawl
8. Retainer clip
9. Nut
10. Washer
11. Flywheel

Apply light coat of grease to starter housing post before installing rope pulley. Note that clip (8) retains pulley (5) and pawl (7). Be sure the clip engages pawl guide peg.

Turn rope pulley two turns clockwise to preload rewind spring. Rewind spring tension is correct if rope handle is pulled snugly against housing with rope fully retracted and if pulley will rotate at least an additional half turn with rope fully extended.

STIHL

Model	Bore mm (in.)	Stroke mm (in.)	Displacement cc (cu. in.)	Drive Type
034, 034AVE, 034AVEQ, 034AVEQWB	46 (1.81)	34 (1.34)	56.5 (3.45)	Direct
034S, 034AVSEQ, 034AVSEQW	48 (1.89)	34 (1.34)	61.5 (3.75)	Direct
036AVSEQ	48 (1.89)	34 (1.34)	61.5 (3.75)	Direct
064, 064AVE, 064AVEQ, 064AVREQ	52 (2.05)	40 (1.57)	85 (5.19)	Direct
066, 066M, 066AVEQ, 066AVREQ	54 (2.12)	40 (1.57)	91.6 (5.59)	Direct

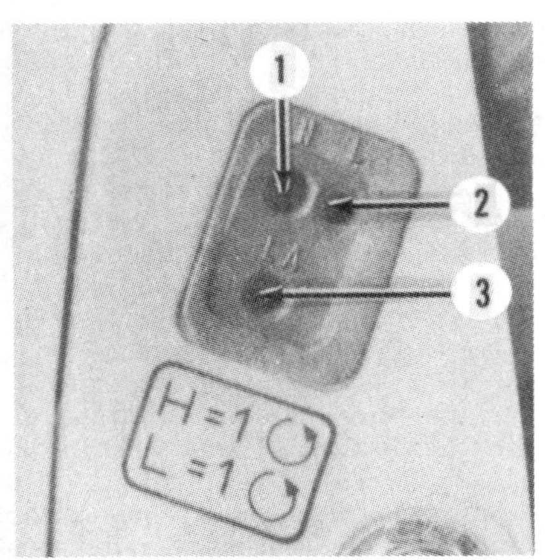

Fig. ST130—View of carburetor adjustment points typical of all models. Initial adjustment of high speed mixture screw (1) and low speed mixture screw (2) is one turn open from a lightly seated position.

Fig. ST131—Electronic ignition module (1) is located outside the flywheel (2) on all models. Some early models used a two-piece ignition system consisting of a trigger module and coil.

MAINTENANCE

SPARK PLUG. Recommended spark plug is Bosch WSR6F or NGK BPMR7A. Recommended spark plug electrode gap is 0.50 mm (0.020 in.). Tighten spark plug to 25 N·m (18 ft.-lbs.).

CARBURETOR. All models are equipped with an all-position diaphragm type carburetor. Series 034 saws are equipped with either a Tillotson HK or a Zama C3A carburetor. Series 036 saws are equipped with a Zama C3A carburetor. Series 064 saws are equipped with either a Walbro WJ or a Bing 49A carburetor. Model 066 Magnum saw is equipped with Walbro WJ carburetor. Refer to Bing, Walbro or Zama sections of CARBURETOR SERVICE section for carburetor overhaul procedure and exploded views.

Initial carburetor adjustment on all models is one turn open from a lightly seated position for both low and high speed mixture screws. On all models, final adjustment of carburetor should be made with engine running at operating temperature. Be sure engine air filter is clean before adjusting carburetor.

Adjust low speed mixture screw (2—Fig. ST130) to obtain highest idle speed, then turn screw counterclockwise approximately $^1/_8$ turn. Engine should accelerate smoothly without hesitation. If engine stumbles or seems sluggish when accelerating, adjust low speed mixture screw until engine accelerates without hesitation. Adjust idle speed screw (3) so engine idles just below clutch engagement speed. High speed mixture screw (1) should be adjusted to obtain optimum performance with saw under cutting load. Do not adjust high speed mixture screw too lean (turned too far clockwise) as maximum permissible engine speed will be exceeded and engine may be damaged from lack of lubrication and overheating. Maximum no-load speed with chain and bar installed must not exceed 13,000 rpm on 034 and 036 series saws or 12,000 rpm on 064 and 066 series saws. If an accurate tachometer is not available, do not vary high speed mixture from initial setting.

IGNITION. All models are equipped with a breakerless transistor controlled ignition system. Except for faulty wiring connections, repair of ignition system malfunction is accomplished by component renewal. Note that high tension lead is threaded into the ignition coil and may be renewed separately from coil.

All models are equipped with a one-piece ignition module shown in Fig. ST131 except for some early production saws that were equipped with a two-piece system, which consists of an ignition coil and a trigger mechanism. If early two-piece unit is faulty, it is recommended that a one-piece unit be used to replace it. Air gap between ignition module (1—Fig. ST131) or ignition coil and flywheel magnets (2) should be 0.2-0.3 mm (0.008-0.012 in.) on all models. Loosen module or coil mounting screws and move unit as necessary to obtain desired air gap. Apply Loctite 242 to threads of mounting screws and tighten to 9 N·m (80 in.-lbs.).

Ignition timing is not adjustable, and because there is no mechanical wear in the ignition system, the timing cannot get out of adjustment unless there is an internal fault in the ignition module.

An ohmmeter may be used to test ignition coil windings for open or short circuits by measuring resistance of coil windings. To check primary resistance, connect ohmmeter leads to connector sleeve on ''On-Off'' switch wire and to engine ground. Resistance should be 0.7-1.0 ohm. To check secondary resistance, connect ohmmeter leads to spark plug terminal and to engine ground. Resistance should be 7700-10,300 ohms. Renew coil unit if readings vary greatly from specified limits.

LUBRICATION. The engine is lubricated by mixing oil with the fuel. Recommended oil is Stihl two-stroke engine oil mixed at a fuel:oil ratio of 50:1. If Stihl two-stroke engine oil is not available, a good quality oil designed for use in air-cooled two-stroke engines may be used when mixed at a 25:1 ratio. Use a separate container when mixing oil and gasoline.

All models are equipped with an adjustable automatic chain oil pump. To adjust oil pump output, turn adjusting screw located in bottom of oil pump housing. Refer to OIL PUMP under REPAIRS section for service procedures.

Manufacturer recommends using oil designed specifically for saw chain lubrication. If an approved oil is not available, clean automotive oil may be used with viscosity chosen according to ambient temperature.

REPAIRS

CRANKCASE PRESSURE TEST. An improperly sealed crankcase can cause the engine to be hard to start, run rough, have low power and overheat. Refer to ENGINE SERVICE section of this manual for crankcase pressure test procedure. If crankcase leakage is indicated, pressurize crankcase and use a soap and water solution to check gaskets, seals, pulse line and castings for leakage.

CYLINDER, PISTON, PIN AND RINGS. To disassemble, remove sprocket cover, bar and chain. Drain fuel and oil tanks. Remove carburetor box cover and cylinder shroud. Unbolt and remove muffler assembly and carburetor. Remove cylinder mounting screws and pull cylinder off piston while pushing intake tube through hole in tank housing. To separate piston (4—Fig. ST132) from connecting rod, remove piston pin retainers (6) and push piston pin (5) out of piston (4) and connecting rod. If piston pin is stuck, tap pin out using a brass drift. Be sure to support piston and connecting rod so side forces are not applied to connecting rod when removing piston pin.

Inspect piston and cylinder bore for deep scratches, scoring or excessive wear. New cylinder is available only with a new fitted piston. If only the piston requires renewal, piston marked ''B'' on piston crown may be used in all ''broken in'' cylinders.

To reassemble, install piston with arrow mark on piston crown pointing toward exhaust port. Piston pin must slide easily into piston bore. Be sure that piston pin retainers (6) are seated properly in piston boss grooves and that retainer end gap faces either top or bottom of piston. Piston is equipped with locating pins in ring grooves to prevent piston ring rotation. Be certain ring end gap is properly positioned around locating pins before installing cylinder. Lubricate piston rings and cylinder bore with engine oil. Support piston with a wooden block that will fit between piston skirt and top of crankcase. Cut a notch in wooden block so block will fit around connecting rod. If removed, install intake manifold tube on cylinder so tube points upward. Compress piston rings and slide cylinder over piston. Tighten cylinder screws in diagonal pattern to 10 N·m (88 in.-lbs.).

CRANKCASE, CRANKSHAFT AND CONNECTING ROD. All models are equipped with a two-piece split type crankcase that is available as a complete crankcase assembly only. The crankshaft and connecting rod are a unit assembly and are not available separately. Crankcase must be split to remove crankshaft.

To split crankcase, drain oil and fuel tanks. Remove fan housing, sprocket guard, bar and chain. Remove chain brake assembly, clutch assembly, oil pump, flywheel, ignition coil, trigger module (if used) and generator (if used). Remove muffler, carburetor, cylinder and piston as previously outlined. Unbolt and remove tank housing and handlebar. Remove crankcase mounting screws and drive the two crankcase dowel pins into ignition side crankcase half. Tap end of crankshaft with a soft hammer to split crankcase and remove crankshaft from main bearings.

Rotate connecting rod around crankpin and renew entire assembly if roughness or other damage is noted. Inspect crankshaft main bearings (12 and 14—Fig. ST132) for roughness and renew as required.

Heat crankcase halves to approximately 120°C (250°F) to ease installation of main bearings. Inner races of main bearings should also be heated with a soldering iron prior to installing crankshaft. On all models, main bearings locate against shoulder in crankcase halves. Oil seals (9 and 15) should not be installed until after crankshaft and crankcase halves have been assembled. Assemble crankshaft and crankcase halves, drive dowel pins into clutch side crankcase half and tighten crankcase screws evenly to torque of 9 N·m (80 in.-lbs.). An assembly sleeve should be installed on crankshaft to protect seal lips from sharp edges. Lubricate seal lip with grease. Press oil seals into crankcase with sealing lip facing inward. Clutch side crankcase seal (15) seats into outer flange of main bearing (14). Install seal so outer face of seal is flush with bearing outer race. Install flywheel side crankcase seal (9) flush with outer face of crankcase. Assembly of remaining

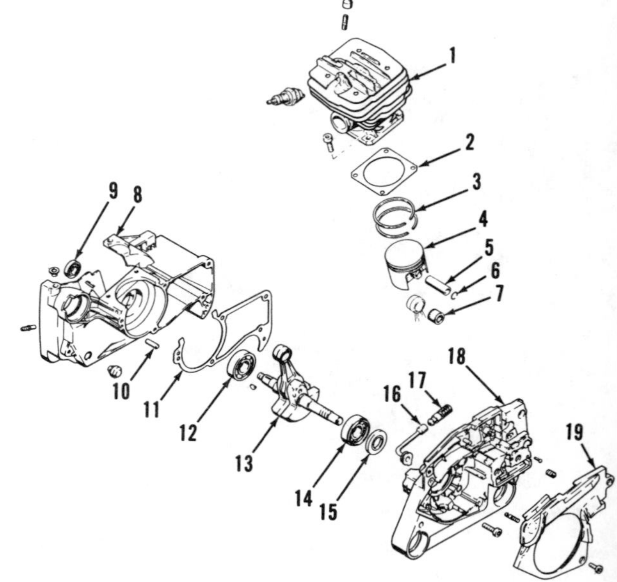

Fig. ST132—Exploded view of engine typical of all models.

1. Cylinder
2. Gasket
3. Piston rings
4. Piston
5. Piston pin
6. Pin retainer
7. Needle bearing
8. Crankcase half
9. Oil seal
10. Dowel pin
11. Gasket
12. Ball bearing
13. Crankshaft & connecting rod assy.
14. Ball bearing
15. Oil seal
16. Oil pickup tube
17. Oil strainer
18. Crankcase half
19. Cover

Illustrations courtesy Stihl Inc.

parts is reverse of disassembly procedure.

CLUTCH. All models are equipped with three-shoe centrifugal type clutch shown in Fig. ST133. To gain access to clutch assembly, remove sprocket cover, bar and chain. Remove "E" ring (1), washer (2), clutch drum (4) and needle bearing (3). Remove spark plug and install piston stop tool in spark plug hole or use other suitable means to prevent crankshaft from rotating. Note that clutch hub (6) has left-hand threads and must be turned clockwise to remove it from crankshaft. Disengage clutch springs (8) and separate shoes (5) and retainers (7) from hub.

Inspect all parts for evidence of excessive wear or damage due to overheating. Clutch shoes, retainers and springs must be renewed in sets to prevent unbalanced operation.

When reassembling, note that a series number is stamped on one side of clutch shoes (5). Retainers (7) must be installed on shoes with narrow side of retainer positioned on same side as series number, and series number must face outward when shoes are installed on clutch hub. Tighten clutch hub to 50 N·m (37 ft.-lbs.). Lubricate needle bearing (3) with high temperature grease prior to installation. Be sure oil pump drive spring (10) engages notch in clutch drum (4).

OIL PUMP. All models are equipped with an adjustable automatic chain oil pump. The oil pump (12—Fig. ST133) is located in the crankcase behind the clutch. To remove oil pump, first drain the oil tank and remove clutch assembly. Remove side plate, cover plate and chain brake band. Remove oil pump mounting screws and withdraw pump assembly from crankshaft.

To disassemble pump, unscrew adjusting screw (17) noting that screw has left-hand threads. Remove worm (11) and drive spring (10). Remove pin (18), pry out plug (14) and pull plunger (15) from pump housing.

Clean all components and inspect for excessive wear or damage. When reassembling pump, coat plunger (15) and worm (11) with grease. Make certain drive spring (10) is properly installed on worm gear (11). Be sure that drive spring properly engages notch in clutch drum.

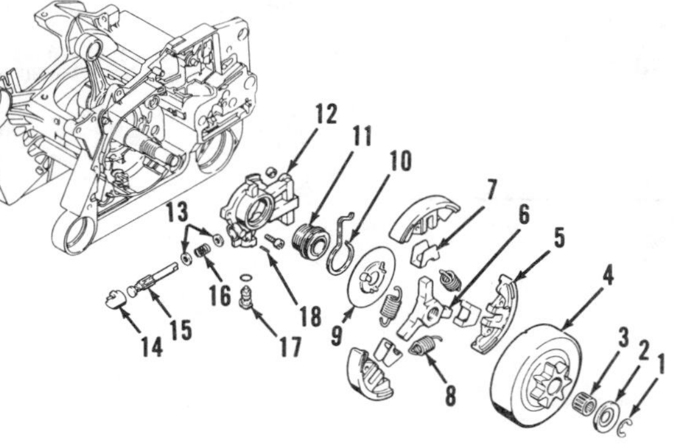

Fig. ST133—Exploded view of centrifugal clutch and oil pump components typical of all models.

1. "E" ring
2. Washer
2. Needle bearing
4. Clutch drum
5. Clutch shoe
6. Hub
7. Retainer
8. Spring
9. Cover washer
10. Drive spring
11. Pump worm gear
12. Pump housing
13. Washers
14. Plug
15. Plunger
16. Spring
17. Adjusting screw
18. Pin

Fig. ST134—Exploded view of chain brake assembly typical of all models.

1. Hand guard
2. Bellcrank
3. "E" ring
4. Bushing
5. Spring
6. Cam lever
7. "E" ring
8. Brake band
9. Sleeve
10. Brake spring
11. Cover

Oil pump output is adjusted by rotating adjusting screw (17).

On all models, oil tank vent is located in oil tank wall adjacent to bar studs. Vent must be open for proper operation of oil pump. To remove vent, drain oil tank and insert a long punch inside oil tank and drive out vent from inside. Press vent into housing bore until outer face of valve is about 1 mm (0.040 in.) below outer surface of housing.

CHAIN BRAKE. All models are equipped with a chain brake designed to stop chain movement should kickback occur. Forward movement of hand guard (1—Fig. ST134) actuates brake lever bellcrank (2) which trips brake cam (6) thereby allowing brake spring (10) to draw brake band (8) tight around clutch drum. Pull back hand guard to reset mechanism.

To disassemble brake, remove sprocket guard, guide bar and chain, and clutch drum. Disengage brake and remove brake cover (11). Carefully disconnect brake spring (10), then pry brake band (8) out of engine housing. To remove brake linkage, remove hand guard retaining screw and remove "E" clip (3) from bellcrank (2). Pry hand guard and bellcrank off their pivot pins. Pull cam lever (6) out of housing and disconnect spring (5).

Inspect all parts for wear or damage and renew as necessary. Lubricate pivot points with light coat of grease. Assembly of brake is reverse of disassembly procedure. No adjustment of chain brake system is required.

REWIND STARTER. All models are equipped with a pawl type starter similar to starter shown in Fig. ST135. To disassemble starter, detach starter housing (3), remove rope handle (1) and allow rope to wind slowly onto rope pulley (7) to relieve tension on rewind spring. Remove retaining clip (10) and withdraw pawls (9), washer (8) and rope pulley (7). Care should be used when removing rewind spring (6) and case as uncontrolled uncoiling of spring may be harmful.

Rope length should be 96 cm (38 in.) and 3 mm (1/8 in.) in diameter for 034 and 036 series saws. Rope length should be 100 cm (40 in.) and 4.5 mm (3/16 in.) in diameter on 064 and 066 series saws. On all models, wind rope around rope pulley in a clockwise direction as viewed from flywheel side of pulley. Apply light coat of grease to starter housing post (4) before installing rope pulley. Note that clip (10) retains pulley (7) and pawls (9). Be sure the clip engages pawl guide pegs. Turn rope pulley two turns clockwise to preload rewind spring. Rewind spring tension is correct if rope handle is pulled snugly against housing with rope fully retracted and if pulley will rotate at least an additional half turn with rope fully extended.

HANDLE HEATER. Some models are equipped with an electric handle heating system. A generator located behind the flywheel supplies an electrical current to a switch and heating elements in front handle and rear grip.

To check handle heating system, remove air filter and rear handle molding. Disconnect wire (G—Fig. ST136) from generator to rear handle heating element wire (3). Set heater switch to "I" position and connect ohmmeter leads to generator wire and to heating element wire to test resistance of all components in heating system. Reading should be about 2.5 ohms. If reading is significantly higher or lower, check each individual component separately to determine fault. To test heating element in rear grip, disconnect wires (3 and 4) and connect ohmmeter between wires. Reading should be approximately 0.25 ohm. To test front heating element, connect ohmmeter leads between wire (2) and ground. Resistance should be approximately 1.6-2.2 ohms. To test generator, connect ohmmeter between generator wire (G) and ground. Resistance should be approximately 0.6 ohm for generator. On all tests, a zero reading indicates damaged insulation causing a short circuit. Insulation may be repaired. An infinite reading indicates an open circuit and component should be renewed.

Element in rear handle may be renewed separately from handle. Front element is available only as an assembly with front handlebar. Flywheel must be removed for access to generator.

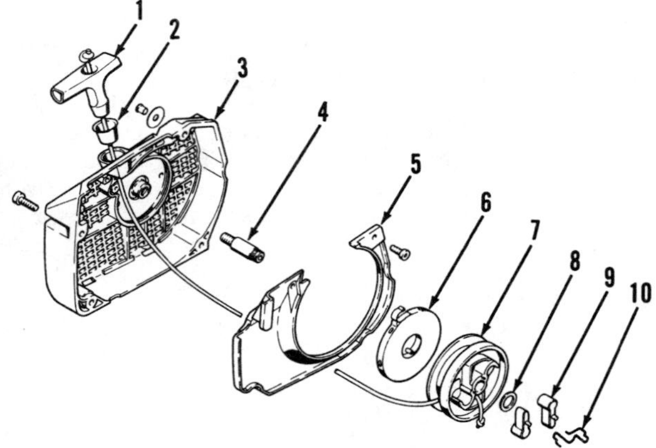

Fig. ST135—Exploded view of rewind starter assembly typical of 064 and 066 series saws. Other models are similar except that pivot shaft (4) is not available separately from housing (3) and shroud (5) is absent.

1. Rope handle
2. Guide bushing
3. Starter housing
4. Pivot shaft
5. Shroud
6. Rewind spring & case
7. Rope pulley
8. Washer
9. Pawls
10. Retainer clip

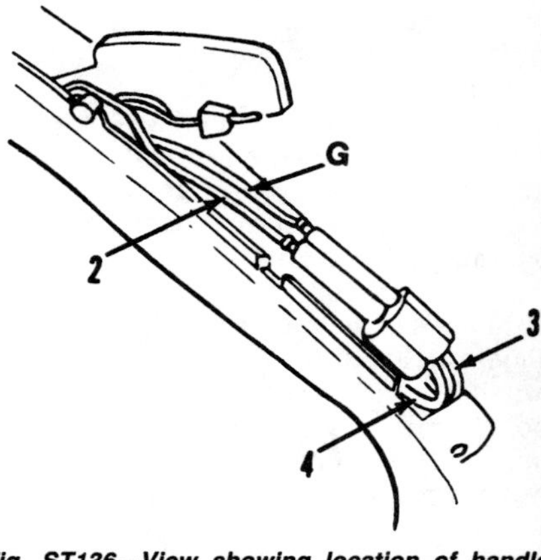

Fig. ST136—View showing location of handle heater wires in rear grip.

G. Generator wire
2. Wire to front handle element
3 & 4. Wires to rear handle element

STIHL

Model	Bore mm (in.)	Stroke mm (in.)	Displacement cc (cu. in.)	Drive Type
019T	40 (1.57)	28 (1.10)	35.2 (2.15)	Direct

MAINTENANCE

SPARK PLUG. Recommended spark plug is Champion RCJ6Y or NGK BPMR7A. Electrode gap should be 0.5 mm (0.020 in.). The spark plug should be tightened to the torque listed in the TIGHTENING TORQUE paragraph.

CARBURETOR. Refer to the appropriate section of the CARBURETOR SERVICE section for service and exploded views of the carburetor used. The engine must be removed from the saw housing in order to remove the carburetor. Disconnect fuel hose from carburetor and remove the fuel tank. Remove two screws attaching intake casing and carburetor to engine. Remove the intake casing and disconnect choke rod at the same time. Remove carburetor from the intake casing. Tighten the carburetor attaching screws to the torque listed in the TIGHTENING TORQUE paragraph.

Initial setting of both the low-speed and high-speed mixture needles is 1 turn open from lightly seated. Refer to Fig. ST140. To adjust the mixture needles, first remove and clean the air filter, then reinstall it. Start the engine and allow it to run until it reaches normal operating temperature. If necessary, turn each of the mixture needles clockwise until seated lightly, then back the needles out (counterclockwise) to the initial setting so the engine can be started.

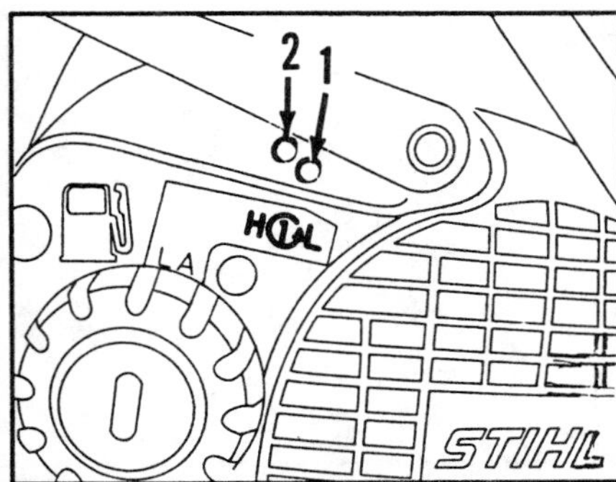

Fig. ST140—The carburetor mixture screws (1 and 2) are located as shown.

Turn the idle speed stop screw so the engine idles at about 2,800 rpm. Adjust the low-speed mixture needle (1—Fig. ST140) so the engine idles smoothly and accelerates without hesitation. Adjust the idle speed to just slower than clutch engagement speed, then recheck low-speed mixture adjustment.

Adjust the high-speed mixture needle (2) to provide the best performance while operating at maximum speed under load. The high-speed mixture needle may be set slightly rich to improve performance under load. Maximum engine speed with the bar and chain installed, but without load is 12,000 rpm. The engine may be damaged if the high-speed needle is set too lean. Large differences in needle settings from the initial setting may indicate air leaks, plugged passages or other problems.

IGNITION. A breakerless electronic ignition system is used, and all electronic circuitry is contained in a one-piece ignition module/coil located outside the flywheel. Ignition timing should occur when the piston is 1.6-2.3 mm (0.63-0.091 in.) BTDC at 8,000 rpm; however, timing is fixed and not adjustable. The flywheel attaching nut should be tightened to the torque listed in TIGHTENING TORQUE paragraph.

Air gap between the legs of the module/coil and the flywheel magnets should be 0.25 mm (0.010 in.). When installing, set the air gap between the flywheel magnets and the legs of the ignition module as follows. Install the ignition module, but tighten the two screws only enough to hold it in place away from the flywheel. Insert setting gauge (part No. 1111 890 6400) or brass/plastic shim stock of the proper thickness between the legs of the ignition module and the flywheel, then turn the flywheel until the flywheel magnets are near the module legs. Loosen the screws attaching the ignition module and press legs of the ignition module against the setting gauge. Tighten the two attaching screws to the torque listed in the TIGHTENING TORQUE paragraph. Remove the setting gauge, then turn the flywheel and check that flywheel does not hit the legs of the coil.

LUBRICATION. The engine is lubricated by oil mixed with the gasoline fuel. The manufacturer recommends mixing STIHL 50:1 two-stroke oil with regular grade gasoline at the ratio recommended on the package. When using regular two-stroke engine oil, mix at a ratio of 25:1. Always use a separate container to mix gasoline and oil before filling the fuel tank. The manufacturer recommends using gasoline with octane of 87 or higher.

The saw is equipped with an automatic chain oiling system. The manufacturer recommends using good quality oil designed for lubricating saw chain. Make sure the reservoir is filled at all times. The volume of oil delivered by the oil pump is not adjustable.

REPAIRS

CRANKCASE PRESSURE TEST. An improperly sealed crankcase can cause the engine to be hard to start, run rough, have low power and overheat. Refer to ENGINE SERVICE section of this manual for crankcase pressure test procedure. If crankcase leakage is indicated, pressurize the crankcase and use a solution of soap and water to check gasket, seals, pulse line and castings for leakage.

TIGHTENING TORQUE. Recommended tightening torque values are as follows.

Bar (stud to case) . . . . 16 N·m (142 in.-lb.)

Carburetor
Spacer flange to crankcase . . . 8 N·m (71 in.-lb.)

Intake housing
attaching screws. . . . . 5 N·m (44 in.-lb.)

Clutch hub . . . . 50 N·m (444 in.-lb.)

Crankcase to cylinder	8 N·m (71 in.-lb.)
Engine to housing	8 N·m (71 in.-lb.)
Fan housing/starter housing	4.0 N·m (36 in.-lb.)
Flywheel	28 N·m (336 in.-lb.)
Hand guard(left)	1.7 N·m (16 in.-lb.)
Ignition module/coil	4.5 N·m (40 in.-lb.)
Muffler	7 N·m (62 in.-lb.)
Reed block to spacer	2 N·m (18 in.-lb.)
Spark plug	25 N·m (222 in.-lb.)
Handle molding/front handle	3.5 N·m (31 in.-lb.)

REMOVE ENGINE. Remove the spark plug and install a suitable piston stop tool or insert the end of a rope in spark plug hole to prevent the crankshaft from turning. Remove the bar, saw chain, clutch assembly (left-hand thread) and the oil pump worm with drive spring (1—Fig. ST141). Disassemble the top handle and remove the throttle trigger. Detach the wires (2 and 3—Fig. ST142). Remove the intake pipe with grommet (4—Fig. ST143) from the intake case and engine housing. Remove the throttle cable (5—Fig. ST144) from the grommet, then pull the cable out of the handle. Remove the four screws attaching the engine to the top and bottom side of the engine housing, then pull the engine sideways from the grommets in the housing (Fig. ST144).

Before installing the engine, be sure the grommets are in place and in good condition. Tighten the engine mounting screws to the torque listed in the TIGHTENING TORQUE paragraph. Be sure that seals on the intake pipe are in good condition and properly positioned for sealing.

PISTON, PIN, RINGS AND CYLINDER. The engine must be removed from saw to service cylinder, piston, pin and rings. To disassemble, unbolt and remove the ignition coil/module. Install a suitable piston stop tool or insert the end of a rope in spark plug hole to prevent the crankshaft from turning. Remove flywheel retaining nut and pull flywheel from the crankshaft. Remove the air baffle. Remove muffler and carburetor. Unbolt and remove the reed valve and spacer flange (1—Fig. ST145) from the crankcase (2). Remove the four attaching screws, then separate the crankcase from the cylinder. Hold the crankshaft in the crankcase and withdraw the cylinder from the piston. Remove snap rings then push piston pin from the piston to separate the piston from the connecting rod. Inspect piston and cylinder bore for scratches, scoring or other damage and renew as necessary. Piston, pin and rings are available separately, but cylinder is available only with matching piston. When assembling piston on connecting rod, be sure arrow mark on piston crown is pointing toward the longer (clutch/drive) end of the crankshaft (Fig. ST146). Piston pin retaining rings must be installed with their end gap toward the bottom of piston (toward crankshaft). Install piston ring in the groove with radii at ring ends facing upward (Fig. ST147). Piston is equipped with a locating pin in ring groove to prevent piston ring rotation. Be certain ring end gap is positioned around locating pin before installing cylinder.

Lubricate piston rings and cylinder bore with engine oil. Coat the lips of crankshaft seals with grease and apply thin bead of sealant to outer diameter before positioning on the shaft. Install piston in cylinder so arrow on piston crown points toward exhaust port. The long end of the crankshaft must be on

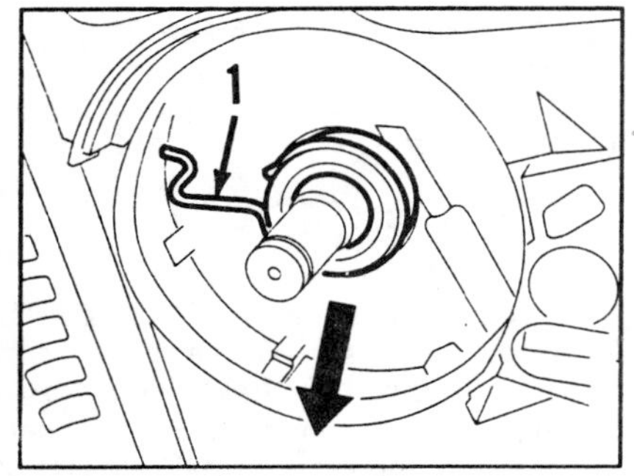

Fig. ST141—The oil pump worm drive gear is driven by spring (1) as shown.

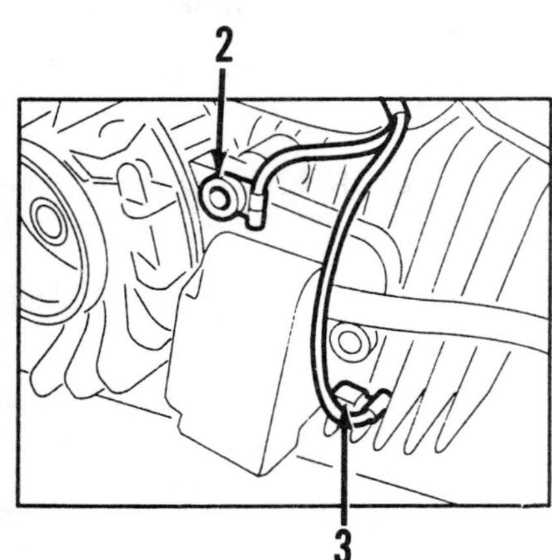

Fig. ST142—View of screw (2) and wire (3) that must be detached before removing the engine.

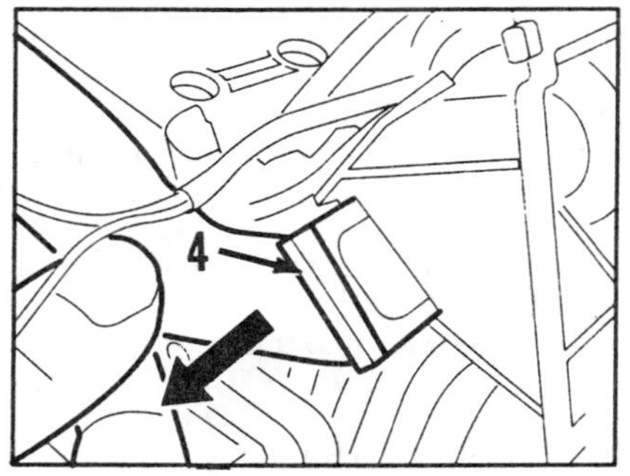

Fig. ST143—When removing the intake pipe (4), first pull it from the casting, then pull the pipe and grommet from the engine housing.

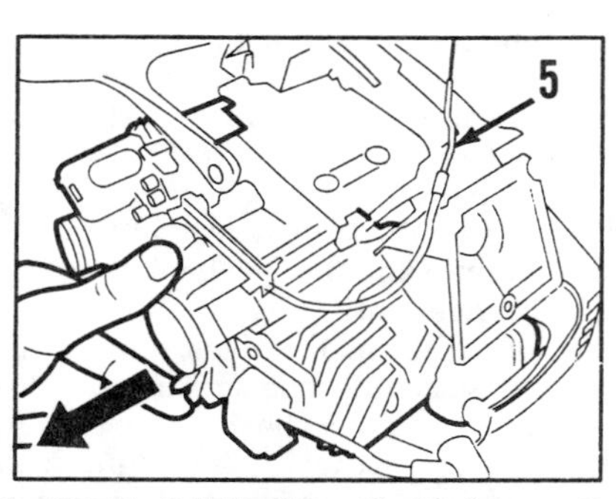

Fig. ST144—Pull throttle cable (5) down, out of the handle as shown before removing the engine.

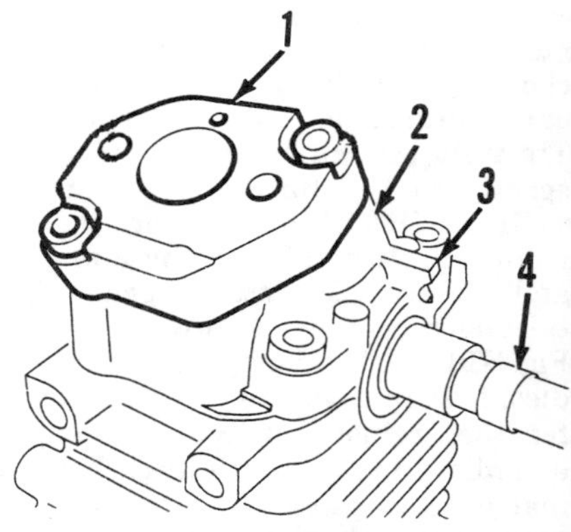

Fig. ST145—The seat (3) for the oil pump must be on same side as crankshaft output (4) and cylinder exhaust port.

1. Spacer flange
2. Crankcase cover
3. Oil pump seat
4. Crankshaft drive end

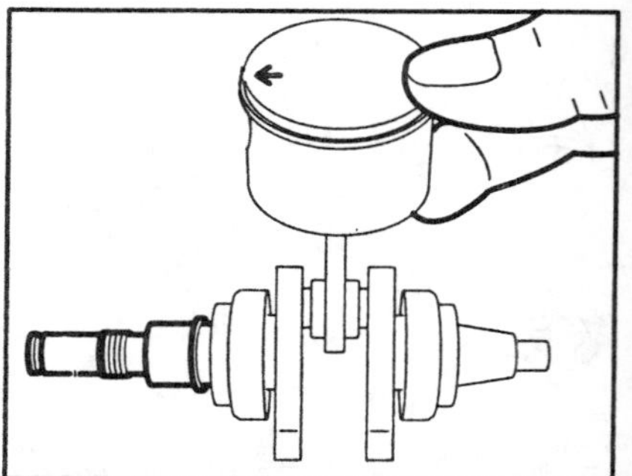

Fig. ST146—The arrow on the piston should point toward the longer drive end of the crankshaft. The cylinder exhaust port should be on the same side.

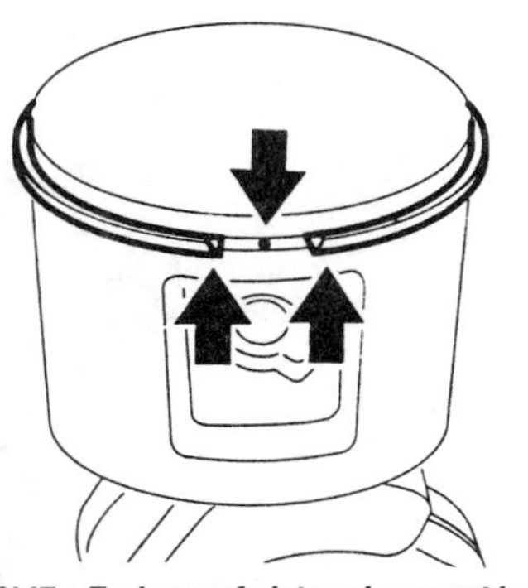

Fig. ST147—End gap of piston ring must be positioned around the locating pin in ring groove.

same side as the exhaust port in cylinder. Apply thin bead of sealant to mating surface of crankcase cover. Assemble crankcase against the cylinder so seat (3—Fig. ST145) for oil pump is positioned on clutch side of engine. Tighten screws to the torque listed in TIGHTENING TORQUE paragraph.

CRANKSHAFT, CONNECTING ROD AND CRANKCASE. The crankshaft is supported by ball bearings at both ends. Connecting rod is supported on crankpin by roller bearings. The connecting rod, roller bearings and crankshaft are a unit assembly and are not available separately. The engine must be removed from engine housing and disassembled as previously outlined to service connecting rod and crankshaft. Rotate connecting rod around crankpin and renew assembly if roughness, excessive play or other damage is noted. Ball type main bearings should not be removed unless new bearing will be installed. Be sure the crankshaft is properly supported before removing or installing the bearings. Heat the bearings to approximately 50 degrees C (120 degrees F) before pressing them onto the crankshaft. Closed side of bearings must face outward. Be sure bearings bottom against crankshaft shoulders.

Coat the lips of crankshaft seals with grease and apply thin bead of sealant to outer diameter before positioning on the shaft.

Install crankshaft, connecting rod and piston in cylinder with arrow mark on piston crown pointing toward the cylinder's exhaust port. Apply sealant to mating surface of crankcase. Install crankcase with the oil pump seat positioned on clutch side of engine as shown in Fig. ST145.

CLUTCH. The three-shoe centrifugal type clutch is shown in Fig. ST148. To gain access to clutch assembly, remove sprocket cover, bar and chain. Remove "E" ring (1), washer (2), clutch drum (3) and needle bearing (4). Remove spark plug and install suitable piston stop tool or insert the end of a rope in spark plug hole to prevent crankshaft from rotating. Note that clutch hub (8) has left-hand threads and must be turned clockwise to remove it from crankshaft. Disengage clutch springs (7) and separate shoes (5) and retainers (6) from hub. Inspect all parts for evidence of excessive wear or damage due to overheating. Clutch shoes, retainers and springs must be renewed in sets to prevent unbalanced operation.

When reassembling, note that a number is stamped on one side of clutch shoes (5). Retainers (6) must be installed on shoes with narrow side of retainer positioned on same side as series number, and series number must face outward when shoes are installed on clutch hub. Tighten clutch hub to the torque listed in TIGHTENING TORQUE paragraph. Lubricate needle bearing (4) with high temperature grease prior to installation. Be sure oil pump drive spring (9) engages notch in clutch drum (3).

OIL PUMP. To remove the oil pump, it is first necessary to remove the engine from the engine housing. Pull the oil tank and push the suction hose from its seat at the same time. The suction hose can be removed from the tank if necessary. Check the condition of the oil pick up screen in the tank. The hose should be removed from the tank before installing the tank.

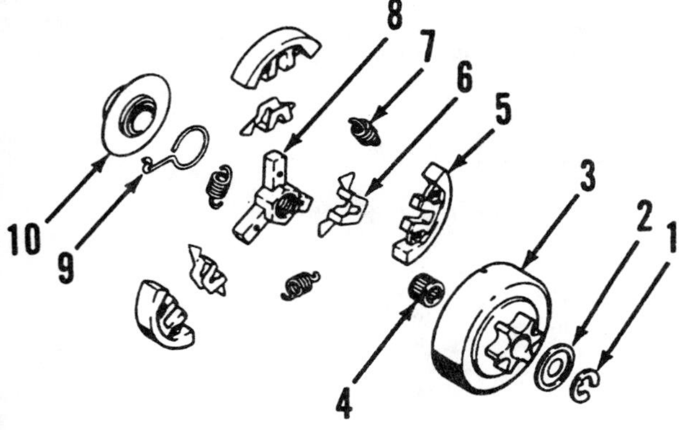

Fig. ST148—Exploded view of the clutch assembly.

1. "E" ring
2. Washer
3. Clutch drum and sprocket
4. Needle bearing
5. Clutch shoe
6. Retainer
7. Spring
8. Hub
9. Drive spring
10. Pump drive worm

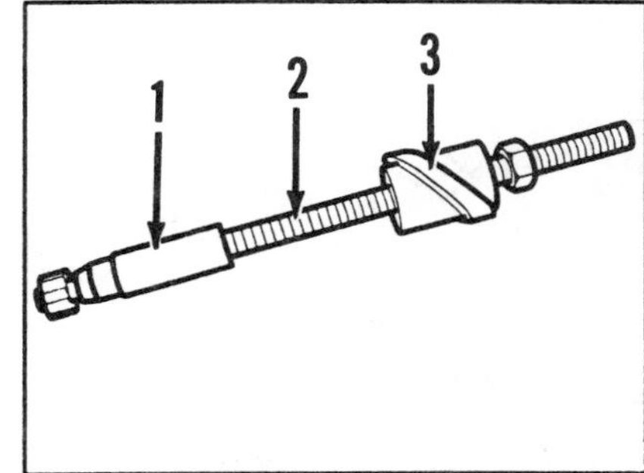

Fig. ST149—View of the oil pump (1), threaded rod (2) and thrust piece (3). Refer to text for removing the oil pump.

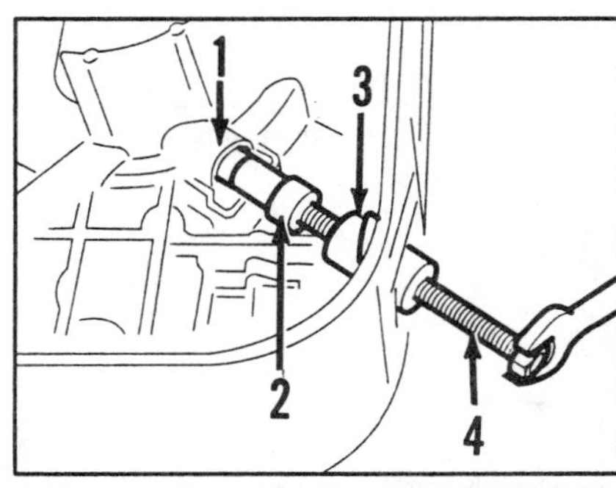

Fig. ST150—Arbor, threaded rod and thrust piece are used to install oil pump. Refer to text for tool numbers.

1. Engine housing
2. Arbor
3. Thrust piece
4. Threaded rod

Remove the pump from its bore in the engine housing using the special threaded rod (part No. 1132 893 8200), thrust piece (part No. 1132 893 8700) or equivalent outside the housing, and an M5 nut to pull the pump from its bore in housing. See Fig. ST149.

Use the special arbor (part No. 1132 893 7200), thrust piece (part No. 1132 893 8700) inside the housing, and special screw (part No. 9008 319 1450) or equivalent to push the pump into position. See Fig. ST150. The arbor should be tight against housing.

Remove the installation tools and install the oil tank. Attach the oil supply hose before installing the tank, then pull the hose while pressing the tank into position.

REWIND STARTER. Remove the air filter. Remove the filler caps from the oil tank and fuel tank then drain both tanks. Remove the two screws attaching the handle and the four screws attaching the starter housing. Pull the hand guard off the boss on the starter housing and remove the starter housing. To relieve tension on rewind

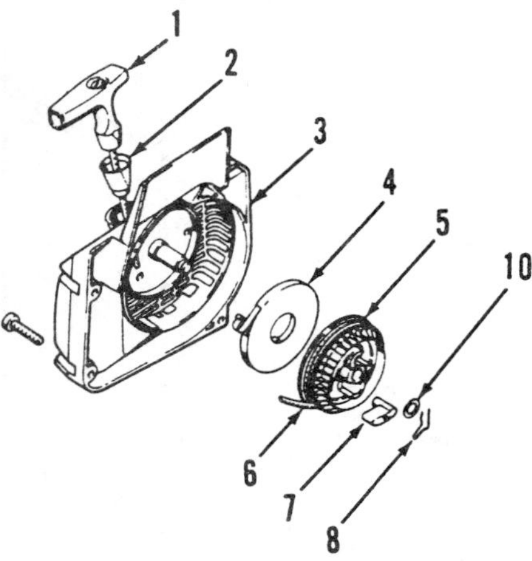

Fig. ST151—Exploded view of rewind starter typical of the type used. The fan housing is shaped differently than shown.

1. Rope handle
2. Rope guide
3. Starter housing
4. Rewind spring
5. Rope pulley
6. Rope
7. Pawl
8. Retainer clip
10. Nut

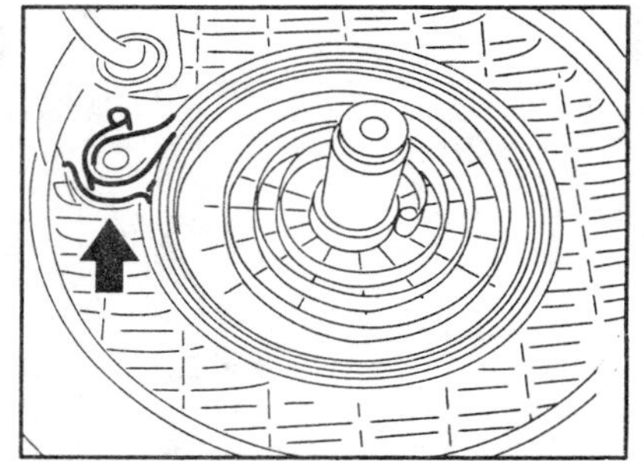

Fig. ST152—Rewind spring is wound in clockwise direction in starter housing.

spring, remove rope handle (1—Fig. ST151) and allow rope to wind slowly onto rope pulley (5). Remove retaining clip (8) and remove washer (10), pawl (7) and rope pulley (5). Care should be used when removing rewind spring (4) and case as uncontrolled uncoiling of spring may be harmful.

Replacement rewind spring is held together with a wire retainer. The retainer slips off as the spring is installed into the starter housing. If rewind spring becomes disengaged from the starter housing, position spring anchor loop over the lug in the starter housing (Fig. ST152) and wind spring in a clockwise direction, starting outside and working inwards. Rope length should be 96 cm (38 in.) and 3 mm (1/8 in.) in diameter. Wind rope around pulley in a clockwise direction as viewed from flywheel side of pulley. Apply light coat of grease to starter housing post before installing rope pulley. Note that clip (8—Fig. ST151) retains pulley (5) and pawl (7). Be sure the clip engages pawl guide peg.

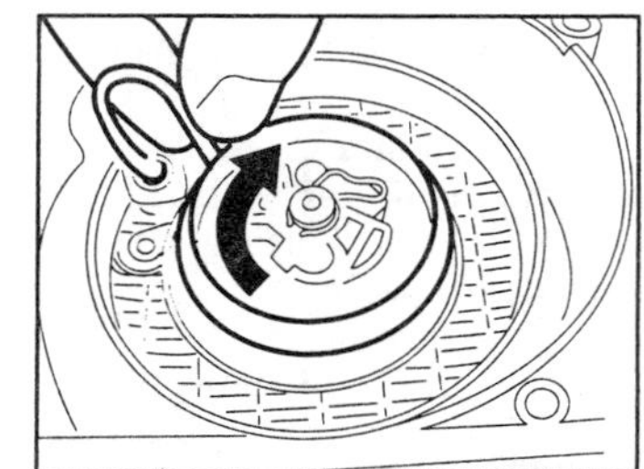

Fig. ST153—Rewind spring preload can be increased by forming a loop in the rope as shown and winding the pulley clockwise.

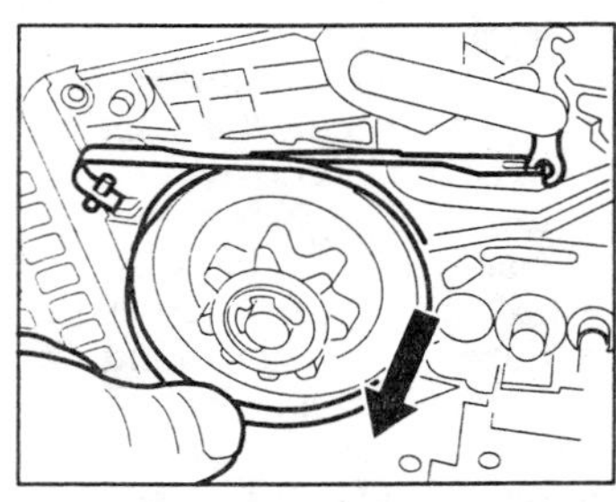

Fig. ST154—View showing brake band removal.

Form a loop in the rope as shown in Fig. ST153 and wind the pulley an additional two turns clockwise to preload rewind spring. Rewind spring tension is correct if rope handle is pulled snugly against housing with rope fully retracted and if pulley will rotate at least an additional half turn with rope fully extended.

CHAIN BRAKE. The chain brake is designed to stop the chain very quickly should kickback occur. Forward movement of the hand guard actuates the brake allowing a spring to draw the brake band tight around the clutch drum. Pull the hand guard back to reset the brake mechanism.

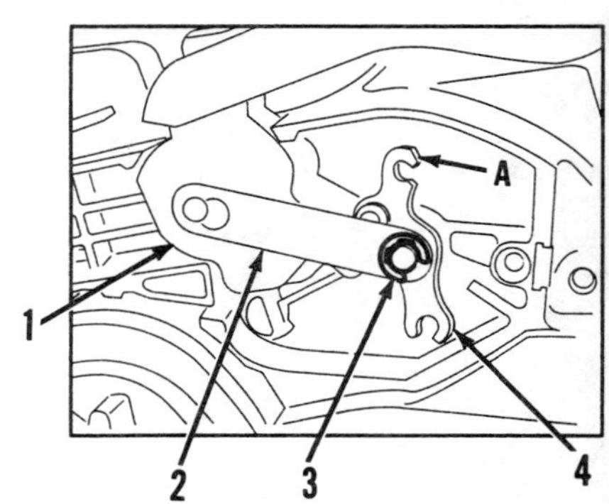

Fig. ST155—View of brake linkage. Short arm (A) of bellcrank should be up as shown when installing in hand guard.

1. Hand guard
2. Link
3. "E" ring
4. Bellcrank

To disassemble, remove the chain sprocket cover. Push the hand guard forward to relieve tension on brake spring. Remove the brake cover. Carefully disconnect brake spring, then pry brake band from the housing (Fig. ST154).

To remove brake linkage, remove hand guard retaining screw. Remove "E" clip (3—Fig. ST155) from bellcrank and slide link (2) from the pivot pin. Remove the washer from the pivot pin. Carefully ease the hand guard (1) with bellcrank (4) from the pivot pins. The bellcrank can be pulled from the hand guard.

Inspect all parts for wear or damage and renew as necessary. Lubricate pivot points with light coat of grease.

The short arm (A—Fig. ST155) of the bellcrank must be up toward the top of the hand guard when installing the bellcrank into the end of the hand guard. Assembly of brake is reverse of disassembly procedure. Note that the brake spring attaches to short arm of bellcrank and the brake band attaches to long arm. No adjustment of chain brake system is required.

STIHL

Model	Bore	Stroke	Displacement	Drive Type
046, 046M	52 cc (2.05 in.)	36 cc (1.42 in.)	76.5 cc (4.67 cu. in.)	Direct

MAINTENANCE

SPARK PLUG. Recommended spark plug is Bosch WSR6F or NGK BPMR7A. Spark plug electrode gap should be 0.5 mm (0.02 in.). Tighten spark plug to 25 N•m (220 in.-lb.)

CARBURETOR. An all position diaphragm type carburetor is used. Refer to the appropriate section of the CARBURETOR SERVICE section for service procedures and exploded views of the carburetor used.

To remove carburetor, first drain the fuel from the tank. Remove air filter cover, air baffle and air filter. Remove stud nuts retaining air filter base and remove the filter base. Pull the grommet off the carburetor adjusting screws. Disconnect throttle rod from the throttle trigger and the throttle shaft. Remove the baffle plate with the throttle rod. Withdraw carburetor from mounting studs.

When installing carburetor, make certain that the sleeve and washer are in position on the intake manifold. Tighten the carburetor attaching screws to the torque listed in the TIGHTENING TORQUE paragraph.

Initial adjustment of carburetor on all models is one turn open from a lightly seated position for both low-speed and high-speed mixture needles.

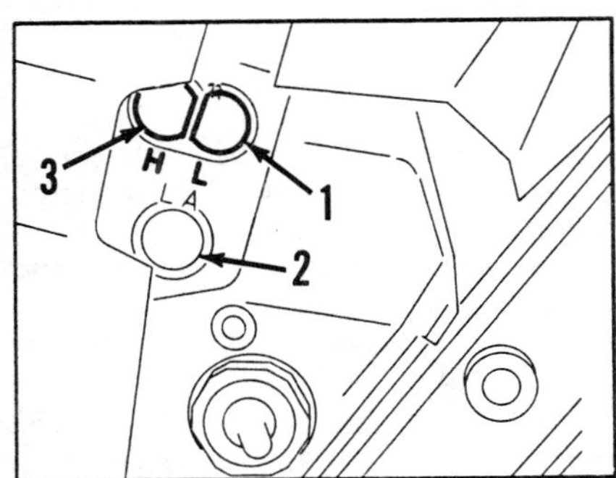

Fig. ST170—View of carburetor adjustment points.

1. Low-speed mixture needle
2. Idle speed stop screw
3. High-speed mixture needle

Final adjustment of carburetor should be made with engine running at operating temperature. Be sure engine air filter is clean before adjusting carburetor.

Adjust low-speed mixture needle (1—Fig. ST170) to obtain highest idle speed, then turn screw counterclockwise approximately 1/8 turn. Engine should accelerate smoothly without hesitation. If engine stumbles or seems sluggish when accelerating, adjust low-speed mixture needle until engine accelerates without hesitation. Adjust idle speed screw (2) so engine idles just below clutch engagement speed.

High-speed mixture needle (3) should be adjusted to obtain optimum performance with saw under cutting load. Do not adjust high-speed mixture needle too lean (turned too far clockwise) as maximum permissible engine speed may be exceeded and engine can be damaged from lack of lubrication and overheating. Maximum no-load speed with chain and bar installed must not exceed 13,500 rpm. If an accurate tachometer is not available, do not change high-speed mixture from initial setting.

IGNITION. A breakerless electronic ignition system is used. All electronic circuitry is contained in a one-piece ignition module/coil located outside the flywheel. Ignition timing is fixed and not adjustable. The flywheel attaching nut should be tightened to the torque listed in TIGHTENING TORQUE paragraph.

Air gap between the legs of the module/coil and the flywheel magnets should be 0.15-0.30 mm (0.006-0.012 in.). When installing, set the air gap between the flywheel magnets and the legs of the ignition module as follows. Install the ignition module, but tighten the attaching screws only enough to hold it in place away from the flywheel. Insert setting gauge (part No. 1111 890 6400) or brass/plastic shim stock of the proper thickness between the legs of the ignition module and the flywheel. Turn the flywheel until the flywheel magnets are near the module legs (the two raised portions of the flywheel will be aligned with the ignition module). Loosen the screws attaching the ignition module and press legs of the ignition module against the setting gauge. Tighten the attaching screws to the torque listed in the TIGHTENING TORQUE paragraph. Remove the setting gauge, then turn the flywheel and check that flywheel does not hit the legs of the coil.

LUBRICATION. The engine is lubricated by oil mixed with the gasoline fuel. The manufacturer recommends mixing STIHL 50:1 two-stroke oil with regular grade gasoline at the ratio recommended on the package. When using regular two-stroke engine oil, mix at a ratio of 25:1. Always use a separate container to mix gasoline and oil before filling the fuel tank. The manufacturer recommends using gasoline with octane of 87 or higher.

The saw is equipped with an automatic bar and chain oiling system. An oil pump that is driven by the clutch delivers lubricating oil only when the clutch is engaged and the chain is moving. The output of the pump can be adjusted by turning the adjusting screw located on underside of saw.

Refer to OIL PUMP under REPAIRS section for service procedures.

The manufacturer recommends using good quality oil designed for lubricating saw chain. If an approved oil is not available, clean automotive oil may be used with viscosity chosen according to ambient temperature. Make sure the reservoir is filled at all times.

REPAIRS

CRANKCASE PRESSURE TEST. An improperly sealed crankcase can cause the engine to be hard to start, run rough, have low power and overheat. Refer to ENGINE SERVICE section of this manual for crankcase pressure test procedure. If crankcase leakage is indicated, pressurize crankcase and use a soap and water solution to check gaskets, seals, pulse line and castings for leakage.

TIGHTENING TORQUE. Refer to the following table of torque values when tightening fasteners.

Brake band screw	3 N•m (26 in.-lb.)
Brake hand guard	3 N•m (26 in.-lb.)
Carburetor	6 N•m (53 in.-lb.)
Chain catcher	6 N•m (53 in.-lb.)
Clutch hub or hub carrier	50 N•m (37 ft.-lbs.)
Crankcase	11.5 N•m (138 in.-lb.)
Cylinder	15 N•m (132 in.-lb.)
Decompression valve	14 N•m (124 in.-lb.)
Flywheel nut	32.5 N•m (288 in.-lb.)
Generator	3.5 N•m (31 in.-lb.)
Ignition coil/module	7 N•m (62 in.-lb.)
Muffler/crankcase	15 N•m (132 in.-lb.)
Muffler/cylinder	11.5 N•m (138 in.-lb.)
Muffler (top)	6.5 N•m (53 in.-lb.)
Oil pump	3.5 N•m (31 in.-lb.)
Starter/fan housing	7 N•m (62 in.-lb.)
Tank housing	5.5 N•m (48 in.-lb.)

PISTON, PIN, RINGS AND CYLINDER. To disassemble, remove air filter cover, cylinder shroud, muffler and carburetor. Remove the washer and sleeve from the intake manifold. Remove cylinder mounting screws. Pull cylinder (1—Fig. ST171) off the piston (3) while pushing the intake manifold through the tank housing.

Extract retaining rings (5) and push piston pin (4) out of piston (3). If pin is stuck, it may be necessary to tap it out using a brass drift and hammer. Be careful not to apply side pressure to connecting rod when removing piston pin. Heating the piston will make pin removal easier.

Inspect piston and cylinder bore for scratches, scoring or other damage and renew as necessary. Piston, pin and rings are available separately, but cylinder is available only with a matching piston. To reassemble, install piston with arrow on piston crown pointing toward exhaust port (note the alignment of arrow in relation to the flywheel in Fig. ST172). Piston pin must slide into piston bore without excessive force. Heating the piston to approximately 60 degrees C 140 degrees F will make piston pin installation easier. A tool (No. 5910 890 2212) is available for installing the wire ring type piston pin retainers. Install the piston pin retainers with end gap facing either top or bottom of piston.

Install a new cylinder gasket with the raised center facing the crankcase.

A wooden block similar to the one shown in Fig. ST172 can be used to support the piston and connecting rod during assembly. A notch should be cut in the wooden block so block will fit around the connecting rod. Note that a locating pin is located in each piston ring groove to prevent ring from rotating. Be sure that the piston ring end gaps are properly positioned around locating pin and the radii at the ring ends face upward as shown in Fig. ST173.

Install the intake manifold with the clamp positioned as shown in Fig. ST174. Tighten hose clamp until gap (b) between ends is about 5-6 mm (0.20-0.24 in.). Lubricate piston rings and cylinder bore with engine oil. Align

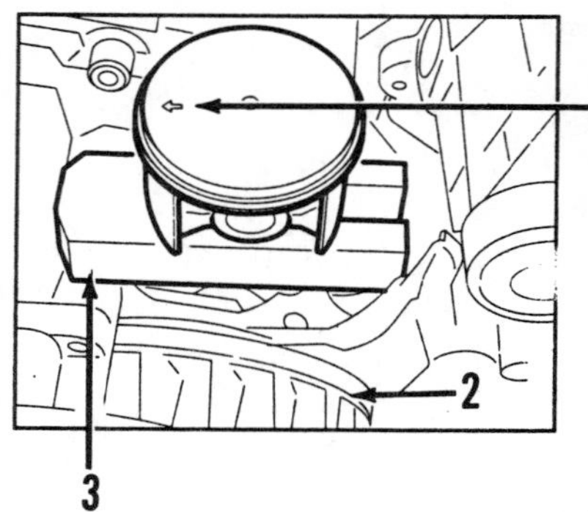

Fig. ST172—Arrow (1) on piston crown must point toward exhaust port. A notched piece of wood (3) can be used to support piston and connecting rod during assembly.

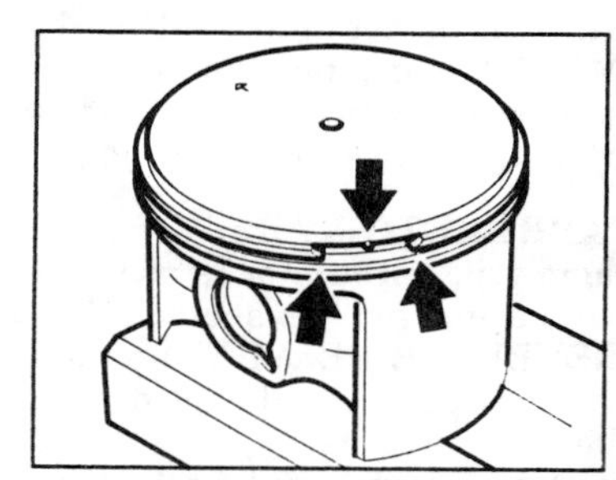
Fig. ST173—Piston ring is installed with radii at ends of ring facing up and end gap positioned around locating pin in ring groove.

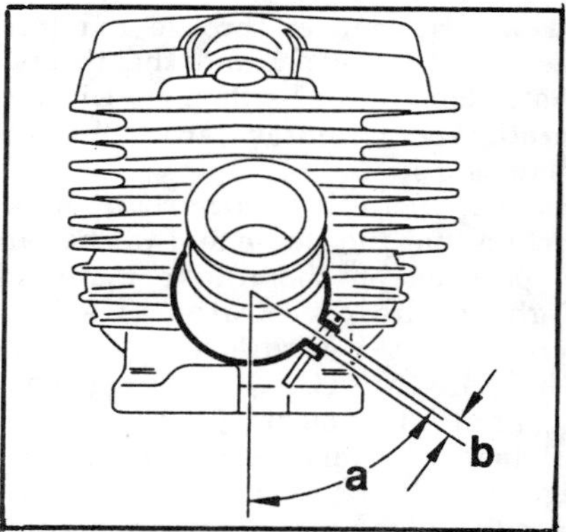

Fig. ST174—The clamp for the intake manifold should be installed at 45 degree angle (a). The gap (b) should be about 5-6 mm (0.020-0.024 in.) when clamp is tight. Do not overtighten.

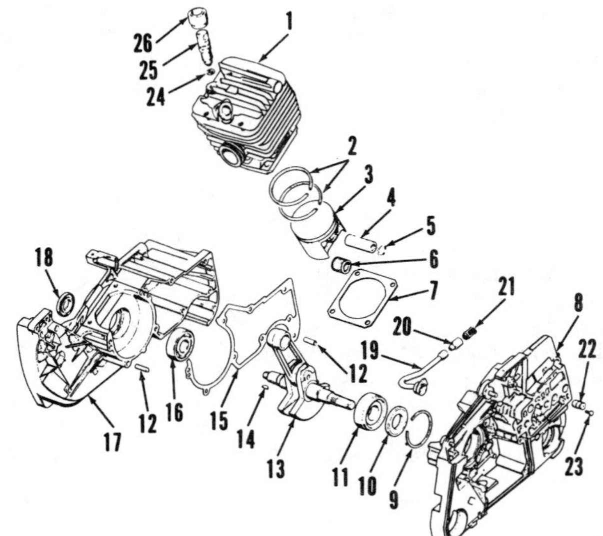

Fig. ST171—Exploded view of an engine typical of that used. Some differences may be noted.

1. Cylinder
2. Piston rings
3. Piston
4. Piston pin
5. Pin retainer
6. Needle bearing
7. Gasket
8. Crankcase half
9. Snap ring
10. Oil seal
11. Main bearing
12. Dowel pin
13. Crankshaft & connecting rod assy.
14. Key
15. Gasket
16. Main bearing
17. Crankcase half
18. Oil seal
19. Oil hose
20. Oil pickup
21. Oil strainer
22. Oil tank vent
23. Split pin
24. Seal
25. Decompression valve
26. Grommet

Illustrations courtesy Stihl Inc.

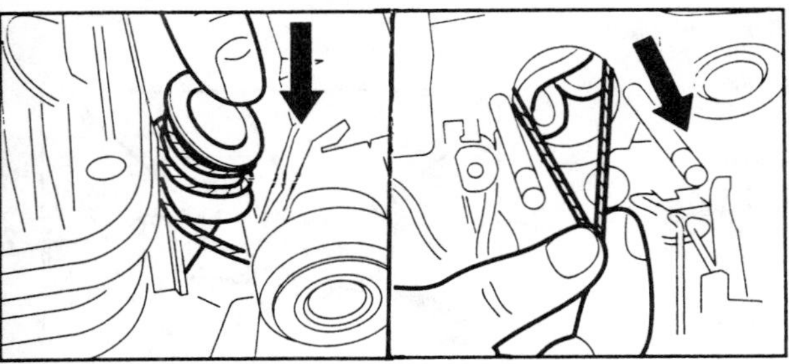

Fig. ST175—A string can be used to facilitate installing the manifold through the hole in the tank housing. Refer to text.

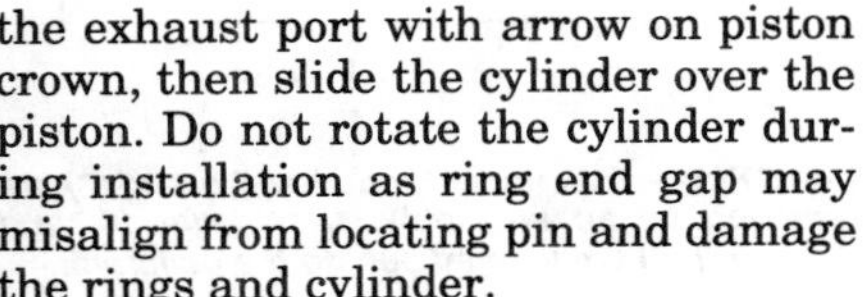

the exhaust port with arrow on piston crown, then slide the cylinder over the piston. Do not rotate the cylinder during installation as ring end gap may misalign from locating pin and damage the rings and cylinder.

The intake manifold can be pulled through the hole in the tank housing by first wrapping a string around the manifold flange (Fig. ST175). Push the manifold down while installing the cylinder and insert the ends of the string through the hole in the tank housing. Pull the string to pull the manifold through the hole in the tank housing (Fig. ST175).

Tighten cylinder screws evenly to the torque specified in TIGHTENING TORQUE paragraph.

CONNECTING ROD, CRANKSHAFT AND CRANKCASE. The connecting rod, bearing and crankshaft (13—Fig. ST171) are pressed together and available only as a unit assembly. Special tools are required to safely separate the crankcase halves and to remove the crankshaft. If the special tools are not available, the crankshaft assembly and the crankcase halves can be easily damaged. The crankshaft is supported by a ball bearing (11 and 16) at each end. Crankcase halves (8 and 17) must be split to remove crankshaft assembly.

To split crankcase, remove spark plug and install a suitable piston stop tool or insert the end of a rope in spark plug hole to prevent the crankshaft from rotating. Remove fan housing, flywheel, ignition module and generator if so equipped. Remove sprocket guard, bar and chain, chain brake assembly, clutch assembly, oil pump worm with drive spring and oil pump assembly. Remove cylinder and piston as outlined above.

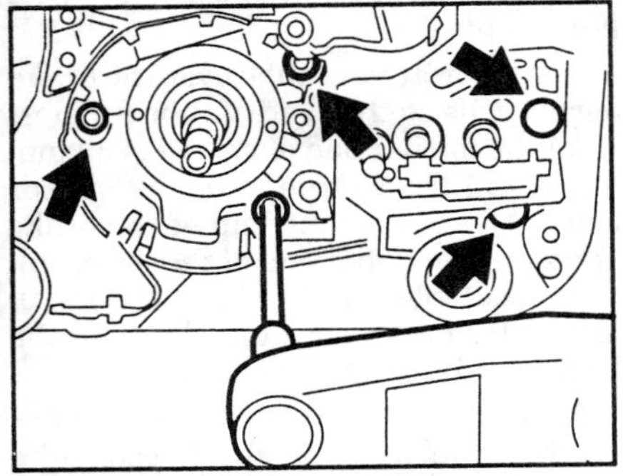

Fig. ST176—Five screws attach crankcase halves together.

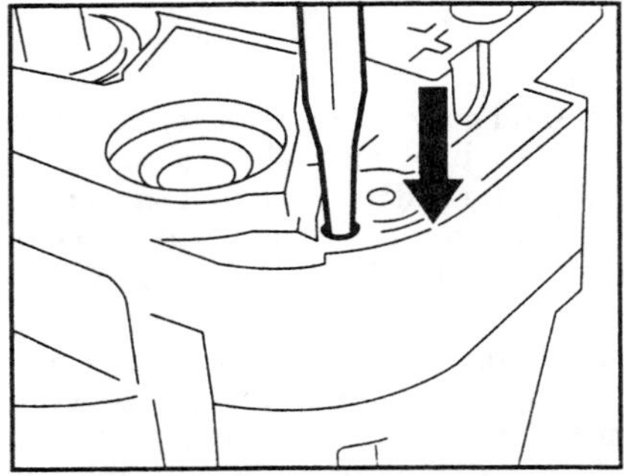

Fig. ST177—Drive dowel pin from crankcase half with a punch before attempting to separate the halves.

Remove the attaching screws and the front handle. Remove plugs covering the vibration damper screws, then remove the screws attaching the vibration dampers. Unbolt and remove chain catcher and bar spike. Separate the tank housing from the engine while pushing the manifold flange out of the tank housing and withdrawing the wiring harness. Remove five screws (Fig. ST176) attaching the crankcase halves together. Use a 5 mm (3/16 in.) punch (Fig. ST177) to drive the crankcase dowel pin from the crankcase halves. Remove retaining ring from crankshaft stub.

Attach the splitter tool as shown in Fig. ST178 and withdraw the chain side crankcase. Position the special tool (Fig. ST179) on flywheel side of crankcase so that the number "12" on the plate is at the bottom of the crankcase. Insert three M5-72 screws in plate holes marked "12" and tighten against the plate. Turn the forcing screw counterclockwise to push the crankshaft out of main bearing. The main ball bearings should remain in the crankcase halves.

Heat crankcase halves to approximately 300 degrees F (175 degrees C) prior to removing and installing main bearings (11 and 16—Fig. ST171). Install bearings so outer race bottoms against bearing seat shoulder. Install the clutch side main bearing with stepped side down (outward). Install flywheel side main bearing with closed side of bearing up (toward inside). Lubricate lip of seals (10 and 18) with grease before installing with lips toward inside.

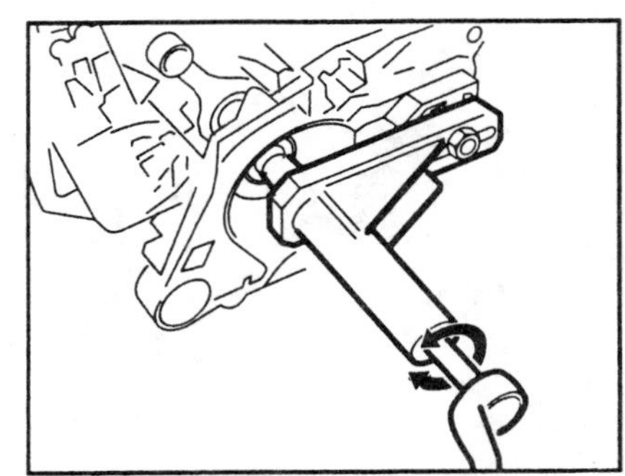

Fig. ST178—View of special tool No. AS 5910 007 2205 attached for removing the chain side crankcase half. Turn spindle of tool clockwise to press crankshaft from main bearing.

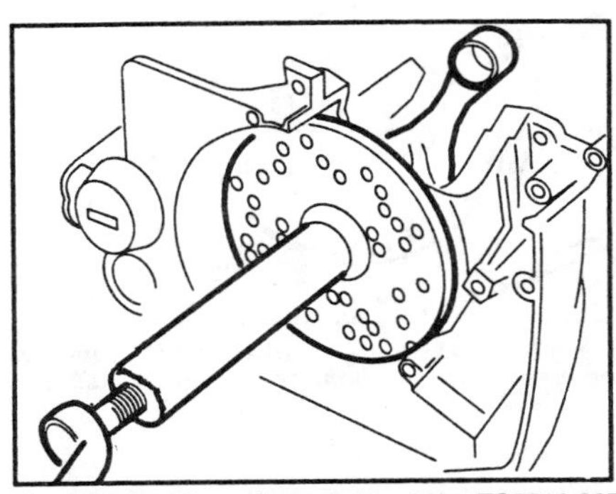

Fig. ST179—View of special tool No. ZS5910 007 2220 attached for pressing the crankshaft from the flywheel side crankcase half.

Be sure that old gasket is removed completely from both crankcase halves, then install a new gasket to one of the crankcase halves. Use special tool ZS 5910 007 2220 and threaded sleeve 5910 893 2420 to pull the crankshaft into the main bearings while assembling the crankcase halves over the crankshaft. Drive locating pin (Fig. ST177) into crankcase half. Tighten crankcase screws (Fig. ST176) in a diagonal pattern to the torque listed in the TIGHTENING TORQUE paragraph. Trim away excess gasket material before installing the piston and cylinder.

CLUTCH. To remove the clutch assembly, remove the two nuts attaching the chain sprocket cover to the right side of the saw and withdraw the cover. Make sure the chain brake is disengaged by pulling the hand guard rearward toward the front handle. Remove the E-ring (1—Fig. ST180) and washer

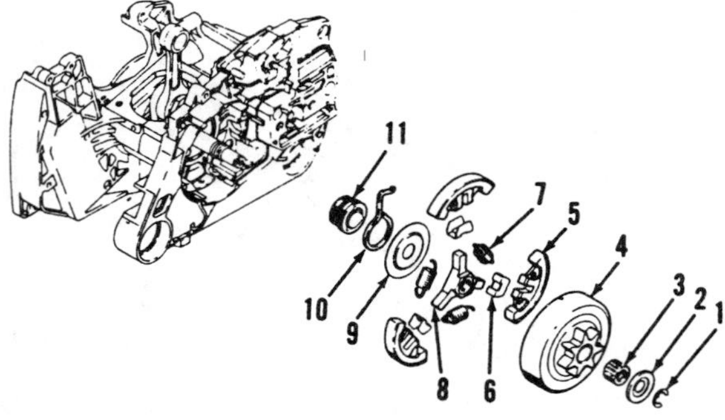

Fig. ST180—Exploded view of clutch assembly typical of the type used.

1. E-ring
2. Washer
3. Needle bearing
4. Clutch drum
5. Clutch shoe (3)
6. Retainer
7. Spring
8. Clutch hub
9. Cover washer
10. Drive spring
11. Worm gear

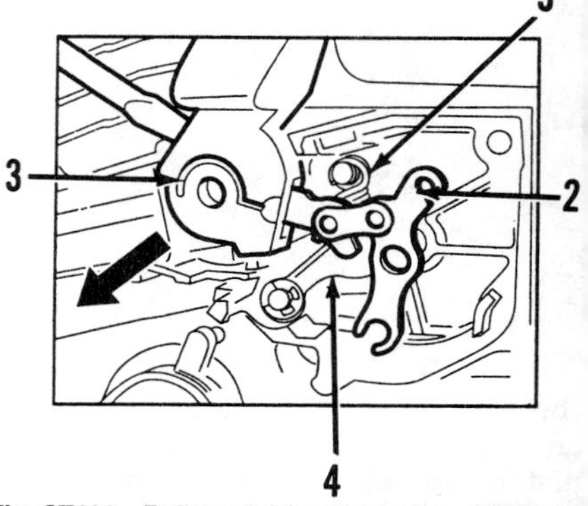

Fig. ST182—Bellcrank (2) and hand guard (3) are removed as an assembly. Cam lever (4) and spring (5) are located behind the bellcrank.

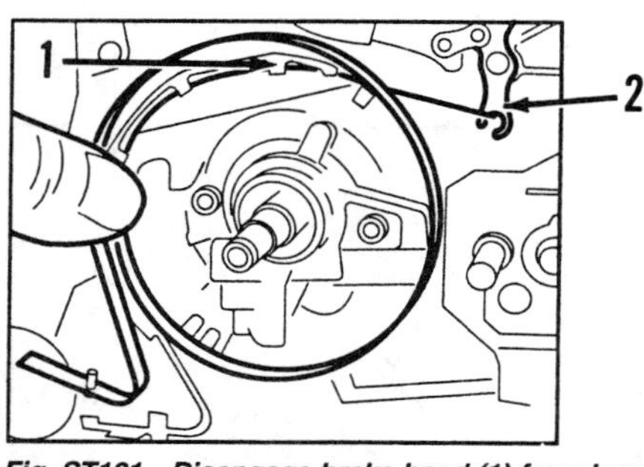

Fig. ST181—Disengage brake band (1) from lugs on crankcase, and unhook band from bellcrank (2).

(2) from the end of the crankshaft. If a rim sprocket is used, it can be removed without removing the clutch drum. Pull the clutch drum (4) and needle bearing (3) from the end of the crankshaft. Inspect the outside rim of the clutch drum for excessive wear or severe scoring. Inspect the clutch engagement surface inside the drum and the bearing surface. Brake and clutch surfaces can be cleaned using #120 emery cloth. Install a new clutch drum if any thickness is less than 80% of a new drum or if bearing surface is damaged. Wash all parts before assembly.

To remove clutch assembly, remove the spark plug and insert locking tool (part No. 0000 893 5903) or the end of a rope into the spark plug hole to prevent the crankshaft from turning. Make sure the decompression valve is closed to prevent damage to the valve. The crankshaft and hub have left-hand threads. Unscrew the clutch hub (8) from the crankshaft by turning in a clockwise direction. A cover washer is located behind the clutch. Disassemble the clutch and install new parts as necessary.

Install the inner washer (9—Fig. ST180) with the word "TOP" toward the outside. Install the assembled clutch, tightening the hub to the torque listed in the TIGHTENING TORQUE paragraph.

CHAIN BRAKE. The chain brake is activated when operator's hand strikes the hand guard. The brake spring pulls the brake band around the clutch drum to stop the clutch drum and saw chain. No adjustment of chain brake mechanism is required.

Check operation by pushing the hand guard forward engaging the brake, starting the saw and attempt to operate the engine at full speed for a short time. The chain should not move. Stop the saw, pull the hand guard back to release the brake, start the saw and run the engine fast enough to engage the clutch. With the clutch engaged and the engine still operating at high speed, engage the brake by pushing the hand guard forward and make sure the saw chain stops very quickly. If chain brake fails to completely stop the saw chain, remove sprocket cover and inspect components for wear or damage.

To remove the chain brake, first remove the clutch assembly. Remove screws attaching the top engine covers and remove both covers. Use a screwdriver to pry the bar side plate off the collar studs. Remove the two screws attaching brake cover and remove the cover.

Push hand guard forward to engage the brake and relieve spring tension. Use a screwdriver to pry the rear of the brake spring from the rear stud, then unhook the spring from the bellcrank at the front. The spring coils should be closed tightly when the spring is relaxed.

Remove the screw attaching the brake band at the lower rear then pull the brake band from the housing as shown in Fig. ST181. Inspect the brake band. Install a new band if less than 0.6 mm (0.024 in.) thick or otherwise damaged. Small imperfections can be removed using # 120 emery cloth.

To remove the linkage, remove the pivot screw from the left side of the hand guard. Remove the E-ring from the bellcrank pivot pin then carefully remove the hand guard (3—Fig. ST182) and bellcrank assembly (2) as shown. The bellcrank can be withdrawn from the hand guard. Remove E-ring from cam lever pivot pin. Unhook spring and remove cam lever (4).

Fig. ST183—Be sure that the cam lever is properly located against face of the hand guard as shown.

When assembling, insert the bellcrank in the hand guard with the short arm up as shown in Fig. ST182. Use pliers to hold the cam lever (4) down against its spring while installing the hand guard (3) and bellcrank (2). The cam lever must be properly positioned against the surface of the hand guard bearing boss as shown in Fig. ST183. Install the E-ring attaching the bellcrank.

Attach the brake band to the lower end of the bellcrank (2) and insert the band into the housing (Fig. ST181). Apply Loctite to threads of brake band attaching screw and tighten to the torque listed in the TIGHTENING TORQUE paragraph.

Install protective tube over the brake spring coils so that end of tube furthest from the anchor end of spring is 32 mm (1-1/4 in.) from the end of the anchor loop. Attach the long end of the brake spring to the upper end of the bellcrank then use tool (part No. 1117 890 0900) or similar brake spring tool to slip the looped end over the anchor pin.

Push the side plate over the collar studs. Use a properly fitted tube around the studs and a light hammer to seat the side plate tightly against the

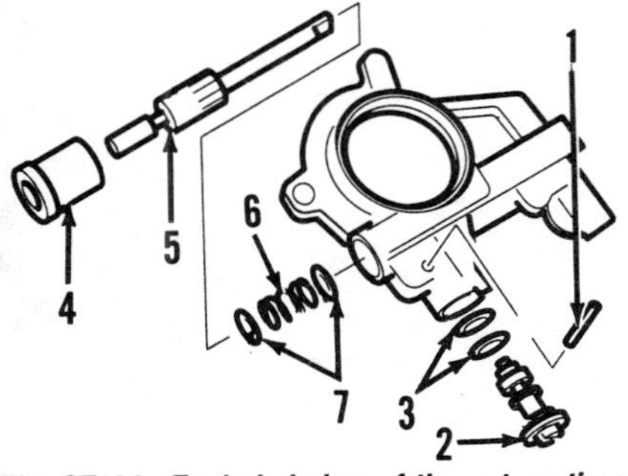

Fig. ST184—Exploded view of the automatic oil pump.

1. Spring pin
2. Adjuster screw
3. O-rings
4. Plug
5. Pump plunger
6. Spring
7. Washers

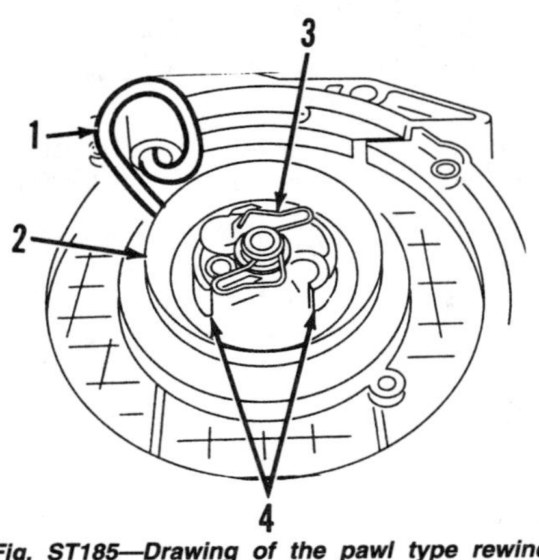

Fig. ST185—Drawing of the pawl type rewind starter used.

1. Rope
2. Rope pulley
3. Wire retaining clip
4. Pawls

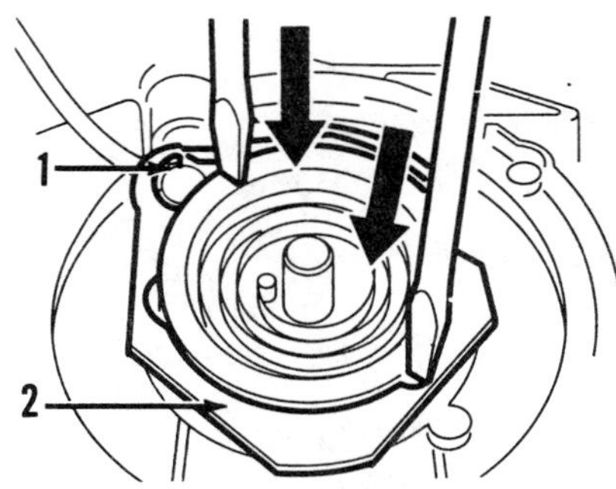

Fig. ST186—Rewind spring (1) is wound in clockwise direction in the starter housing. Replacement spring comes with a retainer (2) to hold it in correct position for assembly. Retainer slips off as spring is pushed into housing.

crankcase. Remainder of assembly is reverse of disassembly.

OIL PUMP. The gear driven oil pump automatically delivers oil stored in the oil tank to the saw chain. The oil pump worm gear (11—Fig. ST180) is driven from the clutch drum by spring wire (10). The worm gear meshes with driven gear of plunger (5—Fig. ST184). The pump is accessible after removing the clutch assembly.

To disassemble, drive out spring pin (1—Fig. ST184). Remove adjusting screw (2). Pry the plug (4) out of housing and withdraw pump plunger (5), spring (6) and washers.

Inspect parts for wear or damage and renew as needed. Install new "O" rings (3) when assembling. Lubricate pump plunger (5) and worm gear with grease before installing. Be sure to install a new sealing ring between the pump and crankcase.

REWIND STARTER. To disassemble starter, detach starter housing, remove rope handle and allow rope to wind slowly onto rope pulley. Pry off wire retaining clip (3—Fig. ST185) and remove rope pulley (2). Care should be used when removing rewind spring as uncontrolled uncoiling of spring may be harmful.

Replacement rewind spring (1—Fig. ST186) comes ready for installation in a retainer (2). The retainer slips off as the spring is installed into the starter housing. If rewind spring becomes disengaged from the starter housing, position spring anchor loop over the lug in the starter housing (Fig. ST186) and wind spring in a clockwise direction, starting outside and working inwards. Check the rope originally installed and install rope that is the same diameter and length. Wind rope around rope pulley in a clockwise direction as viewed from flywheel side of pulley. Note that clip (3—Fig. ST185) retains pulley (2) and pawls (4). Turn rope pulley three turns clockwise to preload the rewind spring. Rewind spring tension is correct if rope handle is pulled snugly against housing with rope fully retracted and if pulley will rotate at least an additional half turn with rope fully extended.

HANDLE HEATER. Some models are equipped with an electric handle heating system. An electric current generated by a coil module located behind the flywheel passes through a switch and then to heating elements in the handlebar and rear grip.

To check system, remove carburetor cover and rear grip insert. Use an ohmmeter to check continuity of the switch. Disconnect wire from switch and connect ohmmeter leads to switch terminal and to engine ground. Continuity should be indicated when switch is in "heat" position.

Use ohmmeter to check resistance of the generating coil. Disconnect wire (G—Fig. ST187) from generator to rear handle element wire (3). Connect ohmmeter leads to generator wire and to ground. Resistance of the generator should be approximately 1.2 ohms. Infinite resistance indicates a broken wire, while zero resistance indicates a short or damaged insulation.

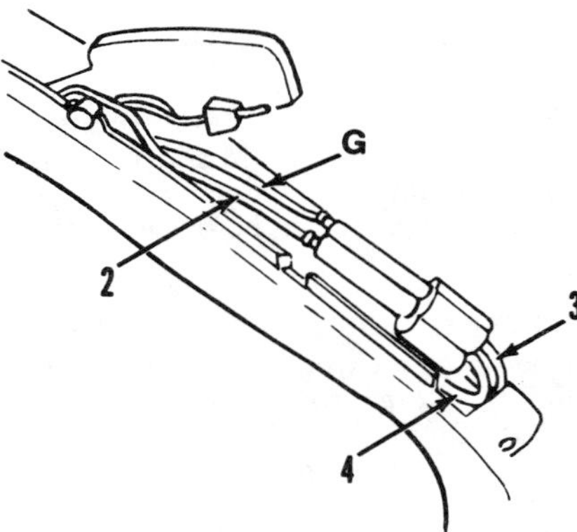

Fig. ST187—Drawing showing location of heater wires in rear grip on Model 044AVEQZ and 084 series saws. Refer to text.

Use ohmmeter to check resistance of each heating element. To check rear heating element, disconnect wires (3 and 4) and connect ohmmeter leads between the two wires (3 and 4). Resistance of the rear handle element should be 0.9-1.1 ohms. To check resistance of front handle element, connect ohmmeter between wire (2) and ground. Resistance of the front handle element should be 6.3-7.7 ohms. If ohmmeter reads infinity, heating element is faulty. The handlebar heating element is not available separately. If ohmmeter reads zero ohms, insulation is damaged and may be repaired.

When installing generator, be sure generator is centered on crankshaft and coils do not contact flywheel.

Illustrations courtesy Stihl Inc.

TANAKA

Model	Bore mm (in.)	Stroke mm (in.)	Displacement cc (cu. in.)	Drive Type
ECS-290, 300	35 (1.38)	30 (1.18)	29 (1.8)	Direct
ECS-320, 330	37 (1.46)	30 (1.18)	32.3 (2.0)	Direct
ECS-3301, 3351	37 (1.46)	30 (1.18)	32.3 (2.0)	Direct

MAINTENANCE

SPARK PLUG. Recommended spark plug is NGK BMR6A or Champion CJ8 for all models. Spark plug electrode gap should be 0.6 mm (0.024 in.).

CARBURETOR. A Walbro WT diaphragm type carburetor is used on all models. Refer to Walbro section of CARBURETOR SERVICE for service procedures and exploded view of carburetor.

Initial adjustment for both low-speed and high-speed mixture screws is one turn open from a lightly seated position on Models ECS-290 and ECS-300. On other models, initial adjustment of low-speed mixture screw (L—Fig. TK1) is 1-1/4 turns out from a lightly seated position and initial adjustment of high-speed mixture screw (H) is 1-3/8 turns out. Be sure engine air filter is clean before adjusting carburetor.

Make final carburetor adjustments with engine warm and running. Adjust idle speed screw so engine idles just below clutch engagement speed (approximately 2800 rpm). Adjust low speed mixture screw (L) to obtain highest idle speed, then turn screw counterclockwise about 1/8 turn. Engine should accelerate cleanly without hesitation. If engine stumbles or seems sluggish when accelerating, adjust idle mixture screw until engine accelerates without hesitation. Readjust idle speed screw so engine idles just under clutch engagement speed.

Operate engine at full throttle with no load and turn high-speed mixture screw (H) clockwise until engine speed increases and four-stroking sound stops. Then, turn high-speed needle counterclockwise until four-stroking sound just returns. Do not operate saw with high-speed mixture too lean as engine damage may result from lack of lubrication and overheating.

To remove carburetor (12—Fig. TK2), remove front cover (8) and air filter element (9). Remove carburetor mounting screws. Disconnect choke lever, throttle rod and fuel hose. Remove the carburetor.

IGNITION. All models are equipped with a breakerless electronic ignition system. No periodic maintenance is required. Ignition timing is not adjustable.

Air gap between ignition module/coil assembly (17—Fig. TK3) and flywheel magnets should be 0.35 mm (0.014 in.). To adjust, loosen module mounting screws and move module as necessary.

LUBRICATION. Engine is lubricated by oil mixed with leaded or unleaded gasoline having an octane rating of at least 87. Recommended oil is Tanaka Two-Stroke Oil mixed at a ratio of 50:1. If Tanaka Two-Stroke Oil is not available, a good quality oil designed for air-cooled two-stroke engines may be used. When using oil other than Tanaka Two-Stroke Oil, follow the oil manufacturer's recommended mixing ratio. If a recommended mixing ratio is not designated, mix at 25:1. Use a separate container when mixing the oil and gasoline.

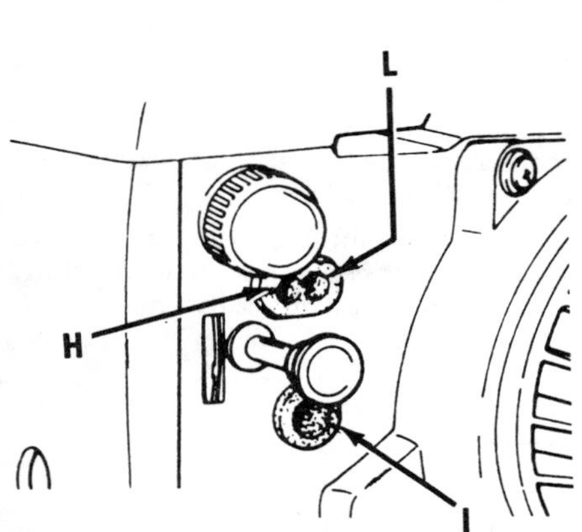

Fig. TK1—View of carburetor adjustment points typical of all models.

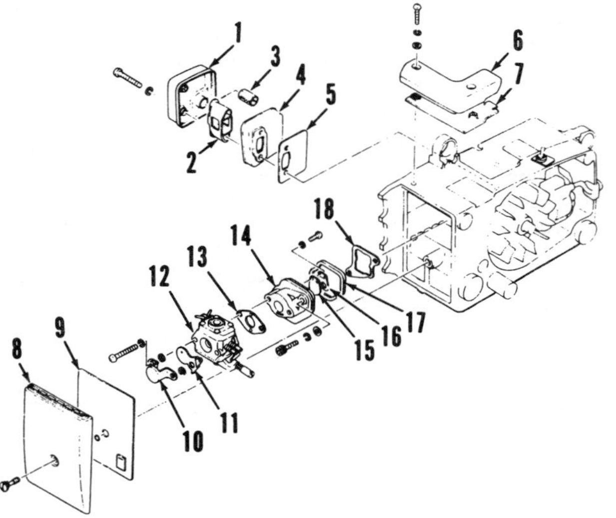

Fig. TK2—Exploded view of intake and muffler components.

1. Muffler half
2. Baffle
3. Spark arrestor
4. Muffler half
5. Gasket
6. Upper cover
7. Lower cover
8. Front cover
9. Air cleaner element
10. Redirection bracket
11. Choke valve
12. Carburetor assy.
13. Gasket
14. Intake manifold
15. Reed petal
16. Reed stop
17. Insulator rubber
18. Gasket

Illustrations courtesy Tanaka Kogyo (USA) Co.

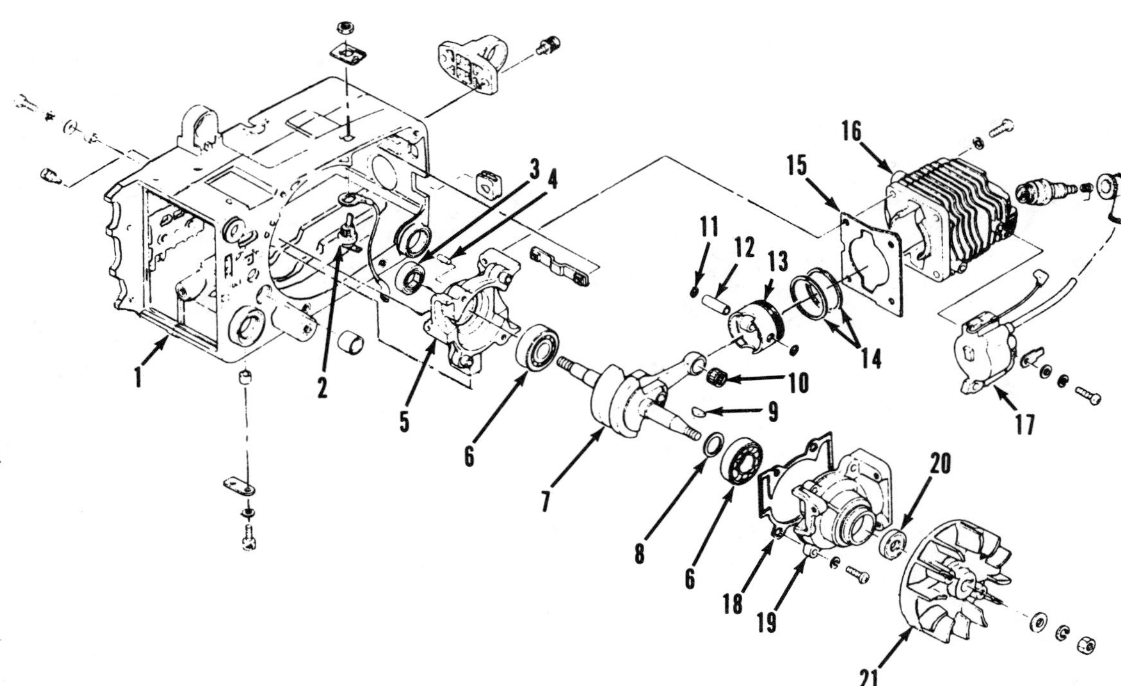

Fig. TK3—Exploded view of engine assembly typical of all models.

1. Engine case
2. Stop switch
3. Seal
4. Dowel pin
5. Crankcase half
6. Bearing
7. Crankshaft & connecting rod assy.
8. Shim
9. Key
10. Needle bearing
11. Retainer clip
12. Piston pin
13. Piston
14. Piston rings
15. Gasket
16. Cylinder
17. Ignition module/coil assy.
18. Gasket
19. Crankcase half
20. Seal
21. Flywheel

All models are equipped with an automatic chain oiling system. A good quality chain oil should be used. Oil output on all models is adjusted by turning oil pump adjuster (2—Fig. TK4). Turn adjusting screw clockwise to increase oil output or counterclockwise to decrease oil output.

CARBON. Carbon should be cleaned from muffler and exhaust ports at regular intervals. When scraping carbon, be careful not to damage the chamfered edges of the exhaust ports.

REPAIRS

CYLINDER, PISTON, PIN AND RINGS. To disassemble, remove side cover, guide bar and chain, front handle and starter housing. Remove muffler (1 through 5—Fig. TK2), air cleaner assembly (6 through 9), carburetor (10 through 12) and intake manifold assembly (13 through 18). Remove spark plug and install piston stop tool or insert the end of a rope in spark plug hole to prevent crankshaft from turning. Unscrew clutch hub (left-hand threads) from crankshaft and remove clutch assembly and oil pump assembly. Remove flywheel mounting nut and remove flywheel (21—Fig. TK3) using a suitable puller. Remove ignition coil (17). Remove engine assembly from engine case (1).

Remove cylinder mounting screws and withdraw cylinder (16) from crankcase. Remove piston rings (14) from piston. Pry piston pin retainer clips (11) out of piston (13), then tap piston pin (12) out of piston and connecting rod. Be careful not to apply side thrust to connecting rod when removing piston pin. Remove piston and needle bearing (10) from connecting rod.

Cylinder bore is chrome plated and cannot be honed or bored. Cylinder should be renewed if cracking, flaking or other damage to cylinder bore is noted. Renew cylinder if bore is out-of-

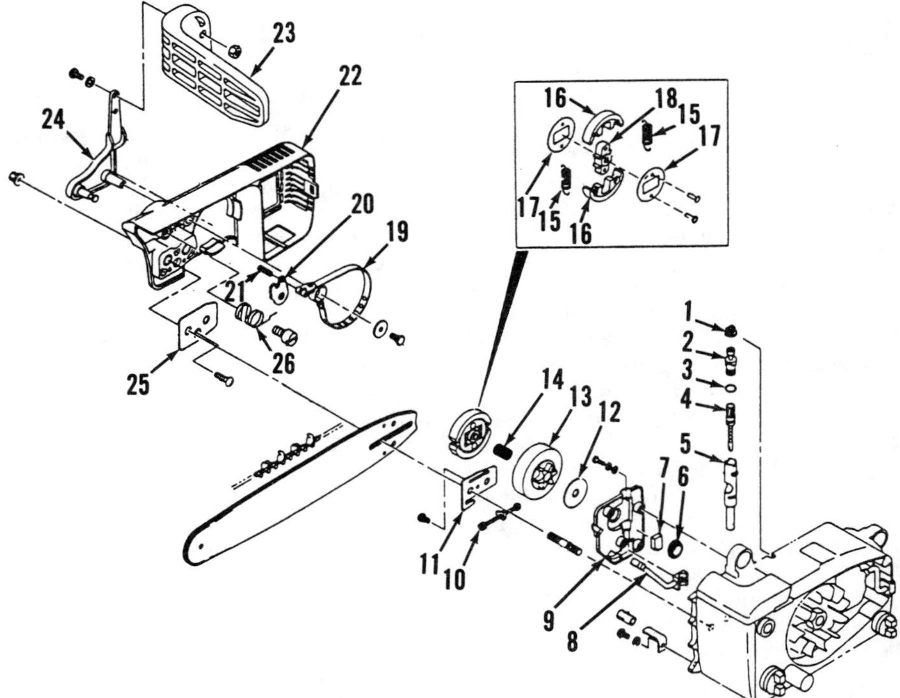

Fig. TK4—Exploded view of clutch and oil pump assemblies. Chain brake is not used on all models.

1. Grommet
2. Oil flow adjuster
3. "O" ring
4. Plunger
5. Pump body
6. Worm gear
7. Air vent sponge
8. Oil pipe
9. Cover
10. Chain adjuster bolt
11. Plate
12. Washer
13. Clutch drum
14. Needle bearing
15. Springs
16. Clutch shoes
17. Plates
18. Clutch hub
19. Chain brake band
20. Brake arm
21. Spring pin
22. Side cover
23. Chain brake handle
24. Chain brake lever
25. Plate
26. Spring

Illustrations courtesy Tanaka Kogyo (USA) Co.

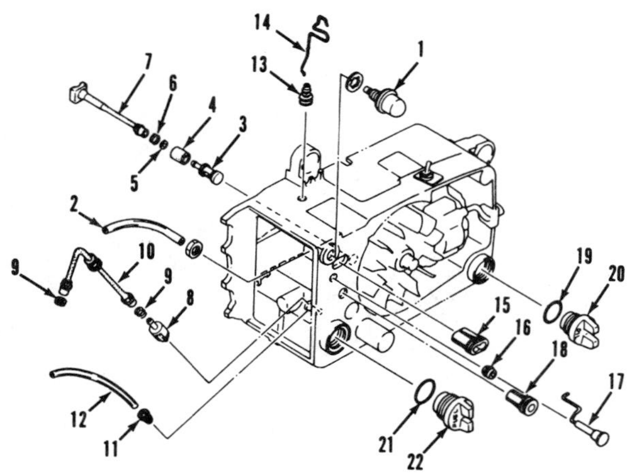

Fig. TK5—Exploded view of fuel system components and oil system components typical of all models.

1. Priming pump
2. Hose
3. Oil filter body
4. Oil filter
5. Washer
6. Clip
7. Oil pump suction hose
8. Fuel filter
9. Clip
10. Carburetor supply hose
11. Fitting
12. Return hose
13. Boot
14. Throttle link
15. Carburetor mixture screws grommet
16. Choke knob grommet
17. Choke knob
18. Idle speed screw grommet

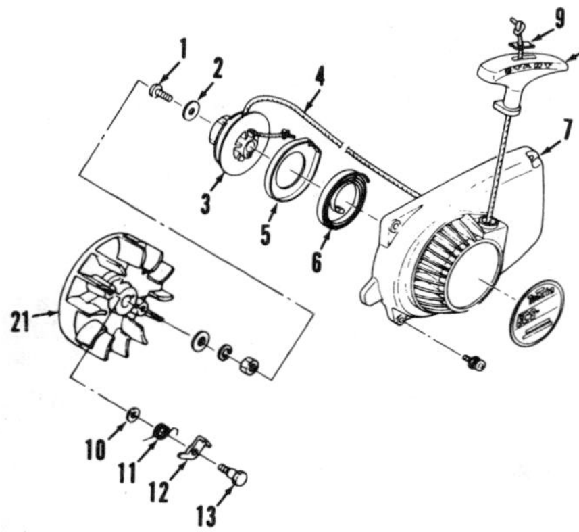

Fig. TK6—Exploded view of rewind starter assembly.

1. Screw
2. Washer
3. Rope pulley
4. Rope
5. Rewind spring case
6. Rewind spring
7. Housing
8. Handle
9. Arbor
10. Washer
11. Spring
12. Pawl
13. Pivot screw
21. Flywheel

round more than 0.03 mm (0.001 in.) or if cylinder wall taper exceeds 0.10 mm (0.004 in.). Inspect piston for scuffing, scoring or other damage and renew as necessary. Piston ring end gap should be 0.1-0.3 mm (0.004-0.012 in.).

When reassembling, install piston on connecting rod so arrow mark on piston crown points toward exhaust port side of engine. Once removed, piston pin clips (11) should not be reused. Locating pins are present in ring grooves to prevent ring rotation. Make certain that ring end gaps are properly positioned around locating pins before installing piston in cylinder. Lubricate piston, cylinder and connecting rod bearings before installation.

CRANKSHAFT AND CONNECTING ROD. To disassemble, remove cylinder and piston as outlined above. Remove crankcase mounting bolts and separate crankcase halves (5 and 19—Fig. TK3).

Crankshaft and connecting rod (7) are a unit assembly and should not be disassembled. Rotate connecting rod around crankpin and renew assembly if roughness, excessive play or other damage is noted. Renew ball bearings (6) and needle bearing (10) if roughness or other damage is noted.

New seals (3 and 20) should be installed in crankcase halves during assembly. After installing crankshaft assembly in crankcase, rotate crankshaft to be sure crankshaft rotates freely. Recommended crankshaft end play is 0.3 mm (0.012 in.). Adjust thickness of shim (8) to obtain correct end play.

CLUTCH. A centrifugal type clutch is used on all models. Remove side cover (22—Fig. TK4), guide bar and chain for access to clutch. Remove starter housing and use suitable tool to hold flywheel from turning. Unscrew clutch hub (18) from crankshaft (left-hand threads) and remove clutch assembly.

Inspect clutch drum needle bearing (14) for roughness or wear and renew as necessary. Inspect clutch shoes (16) and drum (13) for signs of excessive heat. Clutch drum should be renewed if sprocket teeth are worn in excess of 25 mm (0.010 in.). If sprocket is badly worn, inspect chain for excessive wear also. Do not install a new chain over a worn sprocket.

Apply grease to needle bearing (14) prior to installation.

AUTOMATIC CHAIN OILER. All models are equipped with an automatic chain oiling system. Oil pump plunger (4—Fig. TK4) is driven by worm gear (6) mounted on crankshaft end.

To remove oil pump, remove side cover (22), bar and chain, clutch assembly and pump cover (9) for access to the pump. Oil pump plunger (4) and body (5) are not serviced separately. Pump must renewed as an assembly if faulty.

To adjust oil pump output, rotate adjuster (2) clockwise to increase oil flow and counterclockwise to decrease oil flow.

CHAIN BRAKE. Some models are equipped with a chain brake system designed to stop chain movement should kickback occur. Chain brake is activated when operator's hand strikes chain brake handle (23—Fig. TK4), tripping brake arm (20) thereby allowing spring (26) to draw brake band (19) around clutch drum (13). Pull chain brake handle rearward to reset mechanism.

Remove side cover (22) for access to chain brake components. Inspect brake band (19) and linkage for wear or damage and renew as necessary. Lubricate all pivot points with Molykote or suitable equivalent. No adjustment of chain brake system is required.

REWIND STARTER. Refer to Fig. TK6 for exploded view of rewind starter assembly. To disassemble, remove starter housing (7) from engine. Remove retainer (9) and rope handle (8) and allow rope to wind slowly onto pulley (3) until spring tension is relieved. Unscrew pulley mounting screw (1) and remove pulley, being careful not to dislodge rewind spring (6). If necessary to remove rewind spring, care should be used not to allow spring to uncoil uncontrolled.

Apply a light coat of multipurpose grease to both sides of rewind spring. Install rewind spring in starter housing with coils wrapped in a clockwise direction from outer end of spring. Wind rope around pulley in a clockwise direction as viewed from flywheel side of pulley. Turn pulley approximately three turns clockwise to preload rewind spring before passing rope through starter housing. Attach rope handle and check starter operation.

Rewind spring tension is correct if rope handle is pulled snugly against housing with rope fully retracted and if pulley will rotate at least an additional half turn with rope fully extended. If rewind spring binds before rope is fully extended, reduce tension on rope by pulling rope up into notch in rope pulley and allowing pulley to unwind one turn. Recheck starter operation.

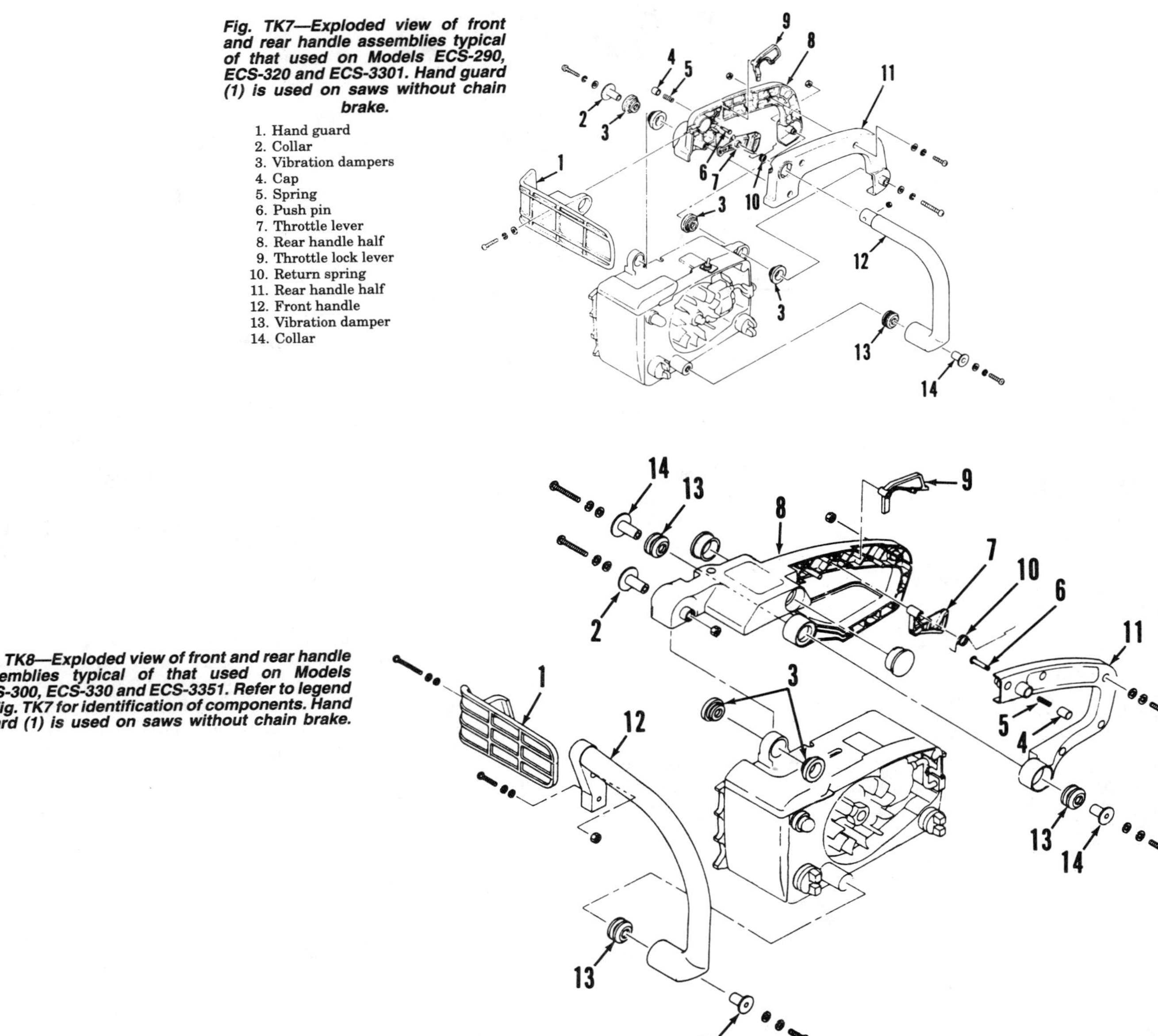

Fig. TK7—Exploded view of front and rear handle assemblies typical of that used on Models ECS-290, ECS-320 and ECS-3301. Hand guard (1) is used on saws without chain brake.

1. Hand guard
2. Collar
3. Vibration dampers
4. Cap
5. Spring
6. Push pin
7. Throttle lever
8. Rear handle half
9. Throttle lock lever
10. Return spring
11. Rear handle half
12. Front handle
13. Vibration damper
14. Collar

Fig. TK8—Exploded view of front and rear handle assemblies typical of that used on Models ECS-300, ECS-330 and ECS-3351. Refer to legend in Fig. TK7 for identification of components. Hand guard (1) is used on saws without chain brake.

Illustrations courtesy Tanaka Kogyo (USA) Co.

TANAKA

Model	Bore mm (in.)	Stroke mm (in.)	Displacement cc (cu. in.)	Drive Type
ECS-350, 351, 355, 356	38 (1.5)	30 (1.18)	34 (2.1)	Direct
ECS-370	38 (1.5)	32 (1.26)	36 (2.2)	Direct

MAINTENANCE

SPARK PLUG. Recommended spark plug is NGK BM7A for Model 370 and NGK BM6A of all other models. Electrode gap should be 0.6 mm (0.024 in.).

CARBURETOR. A Walbro WA diaphragm type carburetor is used on all models. Refer to Walbro section of CARBURETOR SERVICE for service and exploded views of carburetor.

Initial adjustment for both low speed and high speed mixture screws is one turn open from a lightly seated position. Make final adjustment with engine warm and running. Adjust idle speed screw so engine idles just below clutch engagement speed (approximately 2800 rpm). Adjust low speed mixture screw so engine will accelerate cleanly without hesitation. Adjust high speed mixture screw to obtain maximum no-load speed of 11,800 rpm.

IGNITION. Early models ECS-350 and ECS-351 are equipped with a breaker-point ignition system. All other models are equipped with a breakerless electronic ignition system. On breaker-point ignition models, breaker-points (32 – Fig. TK11) should just start to open when "M" mark on flywheel surface aligns with raised mark (approximately 10 o'clock position) on crankcase surface. Breaker-point gap should be 0.35 mm (0.014 in.). Make sure breaker-point gap is properly adjusted as ignition timing will be affected.

On all models with a breakerless electronic ignition system, ignition timing is not adjustable. Air gap between ignition coil assembly (28) legs and flywheel (27) should be 0.35 mm (0.014 in.).

LUBRICATION. Engine is lubricated by mixing engine oil with leaded or unleaded gasoline having an octane rating of at least 87. Recommended oil is Tanaka Two-Stroke Oil mixed at a ratio of 50:1. If Tanaka Two-Stroke Oil is not available, a good quality oil designed for air-cooled two-stroke engines and for mixture ratios between 25:1-to-50:1 may be used when mixed as outlined by oil manufacturer. Use a separate container when mixing the oil and gasoline.

All models are equipped with an automatic chain oil pump. Recommended chain oil is SAE 30 oil. Oil output on all models, except early Model ECS-350, is adjusted by turning oil pump output adjuster (1 – Fig. TK11). Refer to AUTOMATIC CHAIN OILER under REPAIRS section.

CARBON. Carbon should be cleaned from muffler and exhaust ports at regular intervals. When scraping carbon, be careful not to damage the chamfered edges of the exhaust ports.

REPAIRS

CYLINDER, PISTON, PIN AND RINGS. Cylinder (18 – Fig. TK11) bore is chrome plated and should be renewed if cracking, flaking or other damage to cylinder bore is noted. Oversize piston and rings are not available. Cylinder (18) should be renewed if bore is out-of-round or tapered 0.10 mm (0.004 in.) beyond standard bore dimension. Piston (15) is equipped with two piston rings (16). Piston ring end gap should be

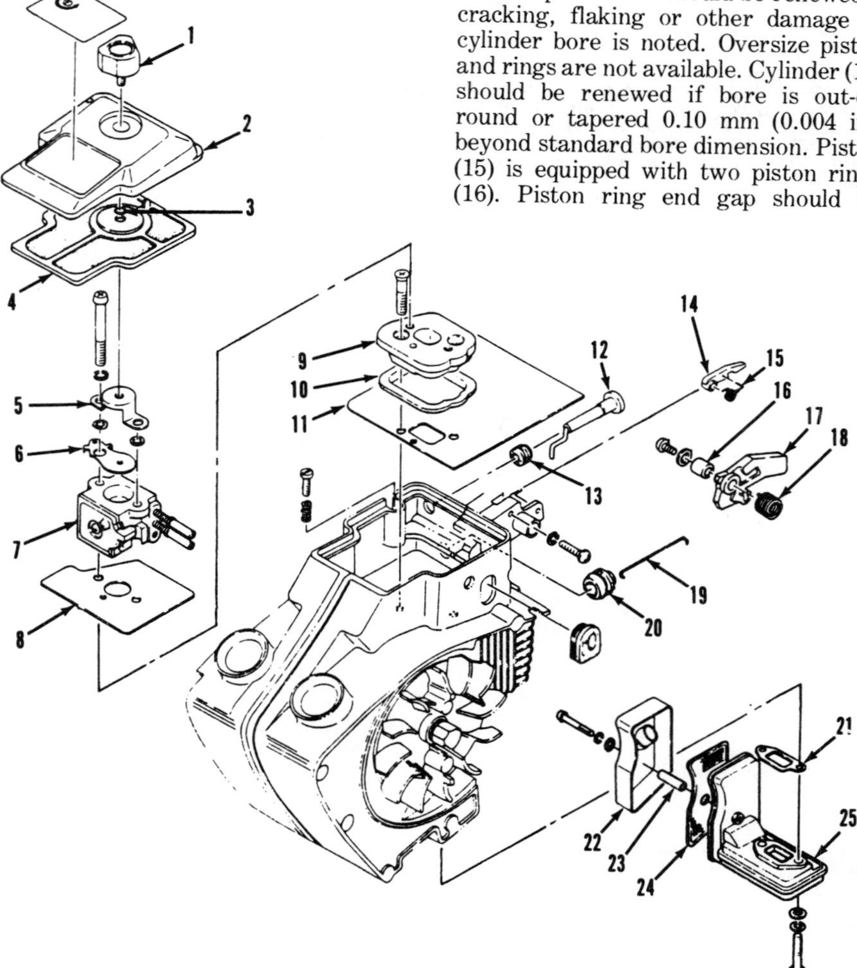

Fig. TK10 — Exploded view of intake and muffler components.

1. Knob
2. Upper cover
3. "O" ring
4. Air cleaner element
5. Redirection bracket
6. Choke valve
7. Carburetor assy.
8. Gasket
9. Insulator block
10. Insulator block rubber
11. Heat shield
12. Choke knob
13. Grommet
14. Throttle lock
15. Spring
16. Spacer
17. Throttle lever
18. Spring
19. Throttle link
20. Grommet
21. Gasket
22. Muffler half
23. Spacer
24. Spark arrestor
25. Muffler half

Illustrations courtesy Tanaka Kogyo (USA) Co.

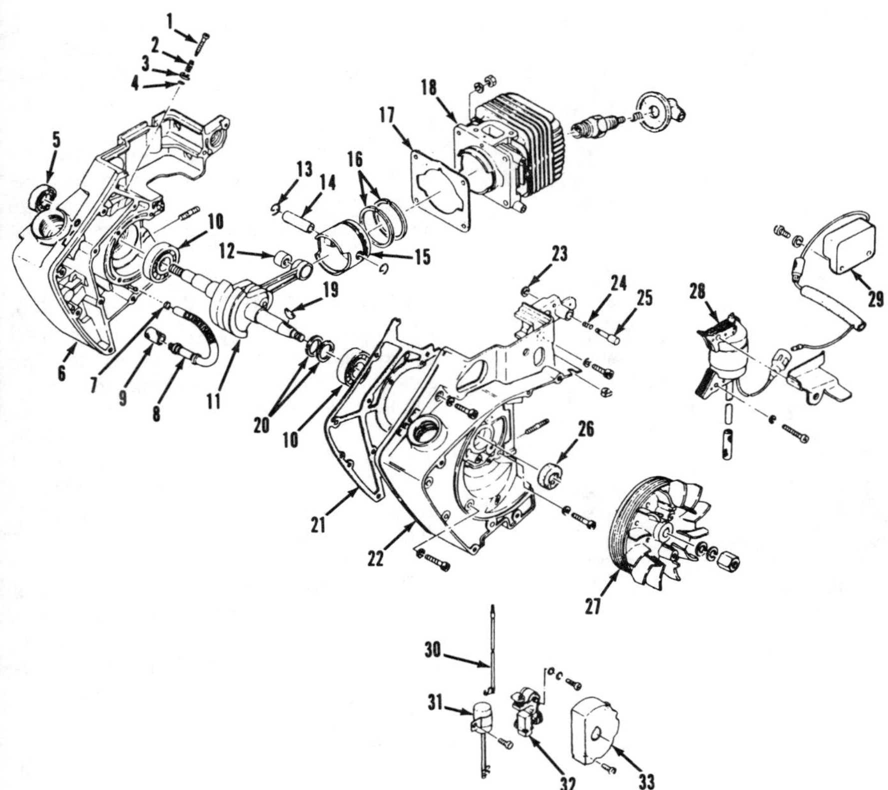

Fig. TK11—Exploded view of engine assembly and related components. Oil pump output is nonadjustable on Model ECS-350. Magneto breaker-point ignition is used on early ECS-350 and early ESC-351 models.

1. Oil pump adjuster
2. Spring
3. Washer
4. "O" ring
5. Seal
6. Crankcase half
7. Retainer
8. Oil pump suction hose
9. Strainer
10. Bearing
11. Crankshaft & connecting rod assy.
12. Needle bearing
13. Retainer clip
14. Piston pin
15. Piston
16. Piston rings
17. Gasket
18. Cylinder
19. Key
20. Shim or shims
21. Gasket
22. Crankcase half
23. Clip
24. Spring
25. Push pin
26. Seal
27. Flywheel
28. Ignition coil
29. Ignition module
30. Primary lead
31. Condenser
32. Breaker-point assy.
33. Cover

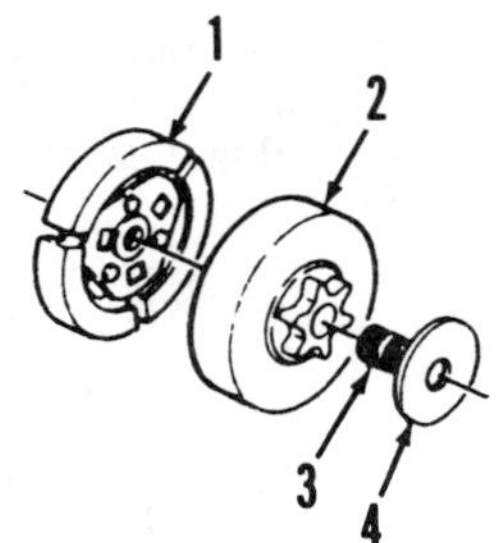

Fig. TK12—Exploded view of three-shoe clutch assembly.

1. Hub & shoe assy.
2. Drum
3. Needle bearing
4. Washer

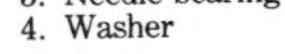

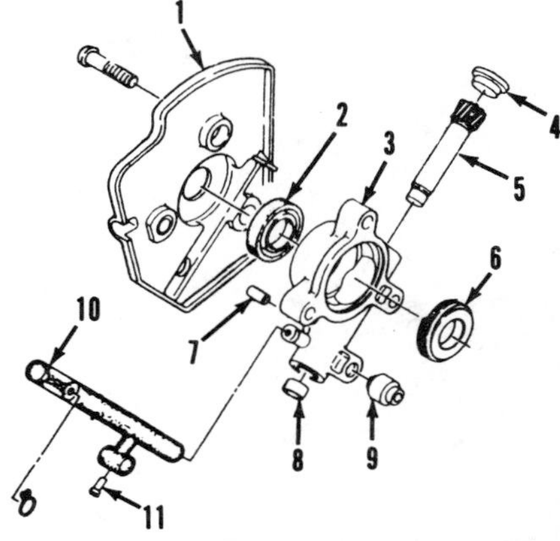

Fig. TK13—Exploded view of automatic oil pump assembly.

1. Cover
2. Seal
3. Body
4. Grommet
5. Plunger
6. Worm gear
7. Pin
8. Grommet
9. Air pipe
10. Discharge hose
11. Jet

0.1-0.3 mm (0.004-0.012 in.). Locating pins are present in ring grooves to prevent ring rotation. Make certain ring end gaps are properly positioned around locating pins before installing cylinder. Piston pin (14) rides in needle bearing (12) and is retained in position with two wire retainer clips (13). Once removed, wire clips should not be reused. Install piston on connecting rod so arrow on piston crown points toward exhaust port.

CRANKSHAFT AND CONNECTING ROD. Crankcase halves must be split to remove crankshaft assembly. Crankshaft and connecting rod (11–Fig. TK11) are a unit assembly and supported at both ends with roller type main bearings (10). Rotate connecting rod around crankpin and renew assembly if roughness, excessive play or other damage is noted.

New seals (5 and 26) should be installed in crankcase halves prior to installing crankshaft assembly. Recommended crankshaft end play is 0.3 mm (0.012 in.). Adjust thickness of shim or shims (20) to obtain correct end play. Shim or shims (20) are available in thicknesses of 0.05, 0.10, 0.15 and 0.20 mm.

CLUTCH. A three-shoe centrifugal type clutch is used on all models. Clutch hub has left hand threads. Clutch needle bearing (3–Fig. TK12) should be inspected for excessive wear or damage. Inspect clutch shoes and drum for signs of excessive heat. Clutch assembly (1) is only renewable as a complete unit.

AUTOMATIC CHAIN OILER. All models are equipped with an automatic chain oil pump assembly. Oil pump plunger (5–Fig. TK13) is driven by worm gear (6) mounted on crankshaft end. On all models, except early Model

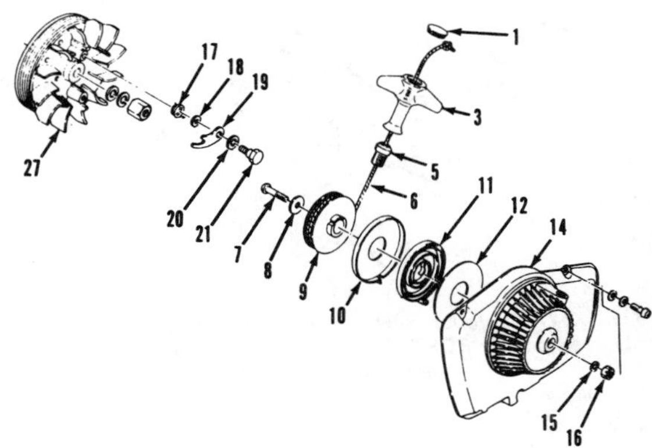

Fig. TK14—Exploded view of early style rewind starter assembly.

1. Cap
3. Handle
5. Guide
6. Rope
7. Screw
8. Washer
9. Rope pulley
10. Case
11. Rewind spring
12. Washer
14. Housing
15. Washer
16. Castle nut
17. Return spring
18. Washer
19. Pawl
20. Washer
21. Pivot screw
27. Flywheel

Illustrations courtesy Tanaka Kogyo (USA) Co.

ECS-350, rotate oil pump output adjuster (1–Fig. TK11) clockwise to increase oil flow and counterclockwise to decrease oil flow.

REWIND STARTER. Refer to Fig. TK14 for exploded view of early style pawl type starter used on all models so equipped. Refer to Fig. TK15 for exploded view of late style pawl type starter used on all models so equipped. Care should be exercised when removing rewind spring (11) to prevent spring from uncoiling uncontrolled.

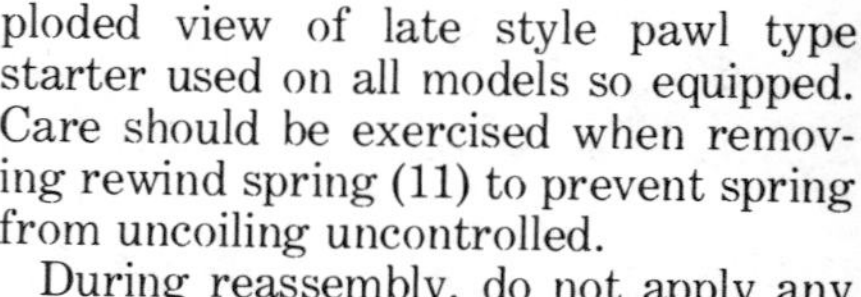

During reassembly, do not apply any more tension on rewind spring than required to properly draw rope handle up against starter housing in relaxed position.

Fig. TK15 – Exploded view of late style rewind starter assembly.

1. Cap
2. Anchor
3. Handle
4. Clip
5. Guide
6. Rope
7. Screw
8. Washer
9. Rope pulley
10. Case
11. Rewind spring
12. Washer
13. Baffle
14. Housing
15. Washer
16. Castle nut
17. Return spring
18. Washer
19. Pawl
20. Washer
21. Pivot screw
27. Flywheel

CHAIN BRAKE. Models ECS-355, ECS-356 and ECS-370 are equipped with a chain brake designed to stop the saw chain quickly should kickback occur. Chain brake is activated when operator's hand strikes hand guard (1–Fig. TK16 or Fig. TK17), releasing brake band lever (6) thereby allowing spring (5) to draw brake band (8) tight around clutch drum. Pull back hand guard (1) to reset mechanism.

Disassembly for inspection or repair is evident after referral to appropriate exploded view and inspection of unit. Renew any component found to be excessively worn or damaged. Chain brake mechanism should be clean and free of sawdust and dirt accumulation. Lightly lubricate all moving parts and pivot points. No adjustment of brake system is required.

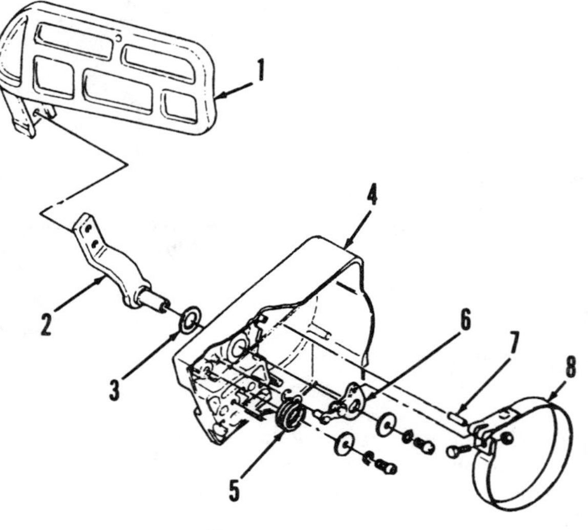

Fig. TK16 – Exploded view of chain brake assembly used on early ECS-355, ECS-356 and ECS-370 models.

1. Hand guard
2. Lever
3. Washer
4. Side case
5. Spring
6. Brake band lever
7. Pin
8. Brake band

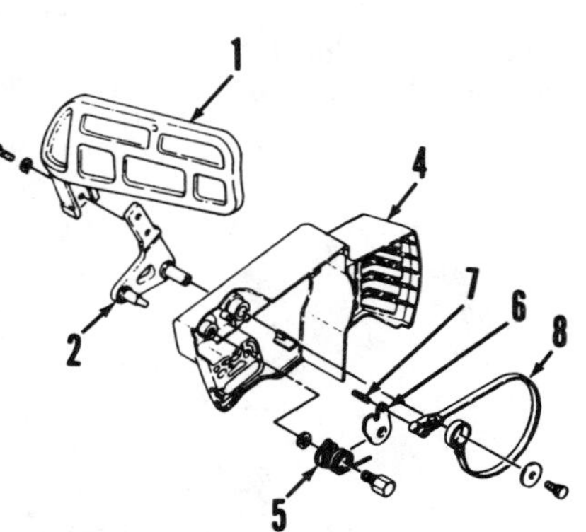

Fig. TK17 – Exploded view of chain brake assembly used on late ECS-355, ECS-356 and ESC-370 models.

1. Hand guard
2. Lever
4. Side case
5. Spring
6. Brake band lever
7. Pin
8. Brake band

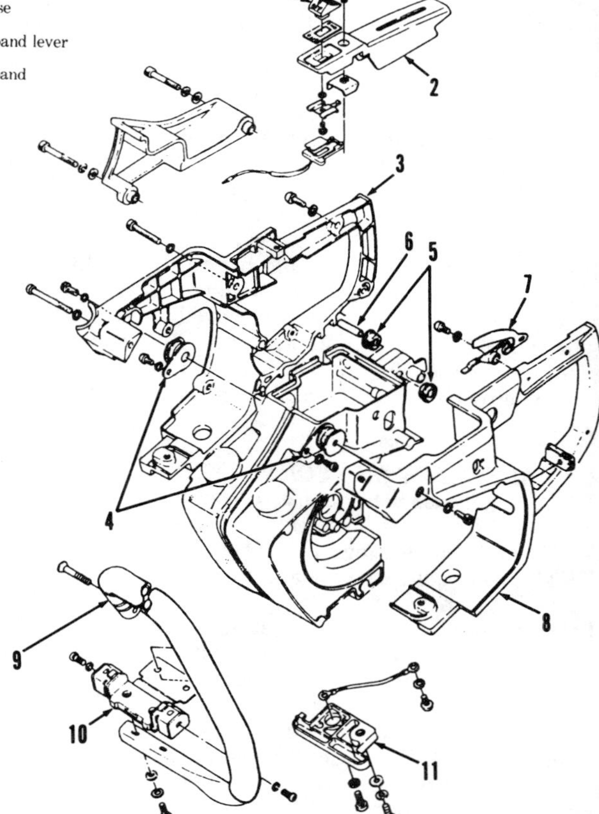

Fig. TK18 – Exploded view of front and rear handle assemblies.

1. Run/stop switch
2. Handle grip
3. Right handle half
4. Vibration dampers
5. Vibration dampers
6. Collar
7. Safety lever
8. Left handle half
9. Front handle
10. Front handle vibration damper
11. Cover

Illustrations courtesy Tanaka Kogyo (USA) Co.

TANAKA

Model	Bore mm (in.)	Stroke mm (in.)	Displacement cc (cu. in.)	Drive Type
ECS-415	40 (1.6)	32 (1.26)	40 (2.4)	Direct

MAINTENANCE

SPARK PLUG. Recommended spark plug is NGK BPM7A. Electrode gap should be 0.6 mm (0.024 in.).

CARBURETOR. A Walbro WT diaphragm type carburetor is used. Refer to Walbro section of CARBURETOR SERVICE for service and exploded views of carburetor.

Initial adjustment for both low speed and high speed mixture screws is one turn open from a lightly seated position. Make final adjustment with engine warm and running. Adjust idle speed screw so engine idles just below clutch engagement speed (approximately 2800 rpm). Adjust low speed mixture screw so engine will accelerate cleanly without hesitation. Adjust high speed mixture screw to obtain maximum no-load speed of 11,800 rpm.

IGNITION. A breakerless electronic ignition system is used. Ignition timing is not adjustable. Air gap between ignition coil assembly (21–Fig. TK21) legs and flywheel (20) should be 0.35 mm (0.014 in.).

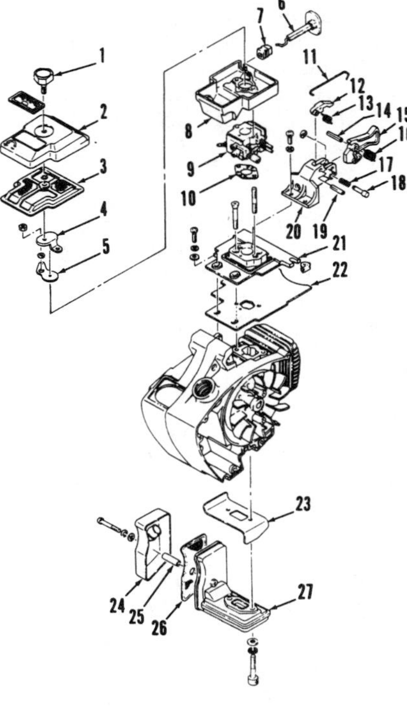

Fig. TK20—Exploded view of intake and muffler components.

1. Knob
2. Upper cover
3. Air cleaner element
4. Redirection bracket
5. Choke valve
6. Chock knob
7. Grommet
8. Lower cover
9. Carburetor assy.
10. Gasket
11. Link
12. Throttle lock lever
13. Spring
14. Spring pin
15. Throttle lever
16. Spring
17. Spring
18. Push pin
19. Spring pin
20. Bracket
21. Insulator block
22. Heat shield
23. Gasket
24. Muffler half
25. Spacer
26. Spark arrestor
27. Muffler half

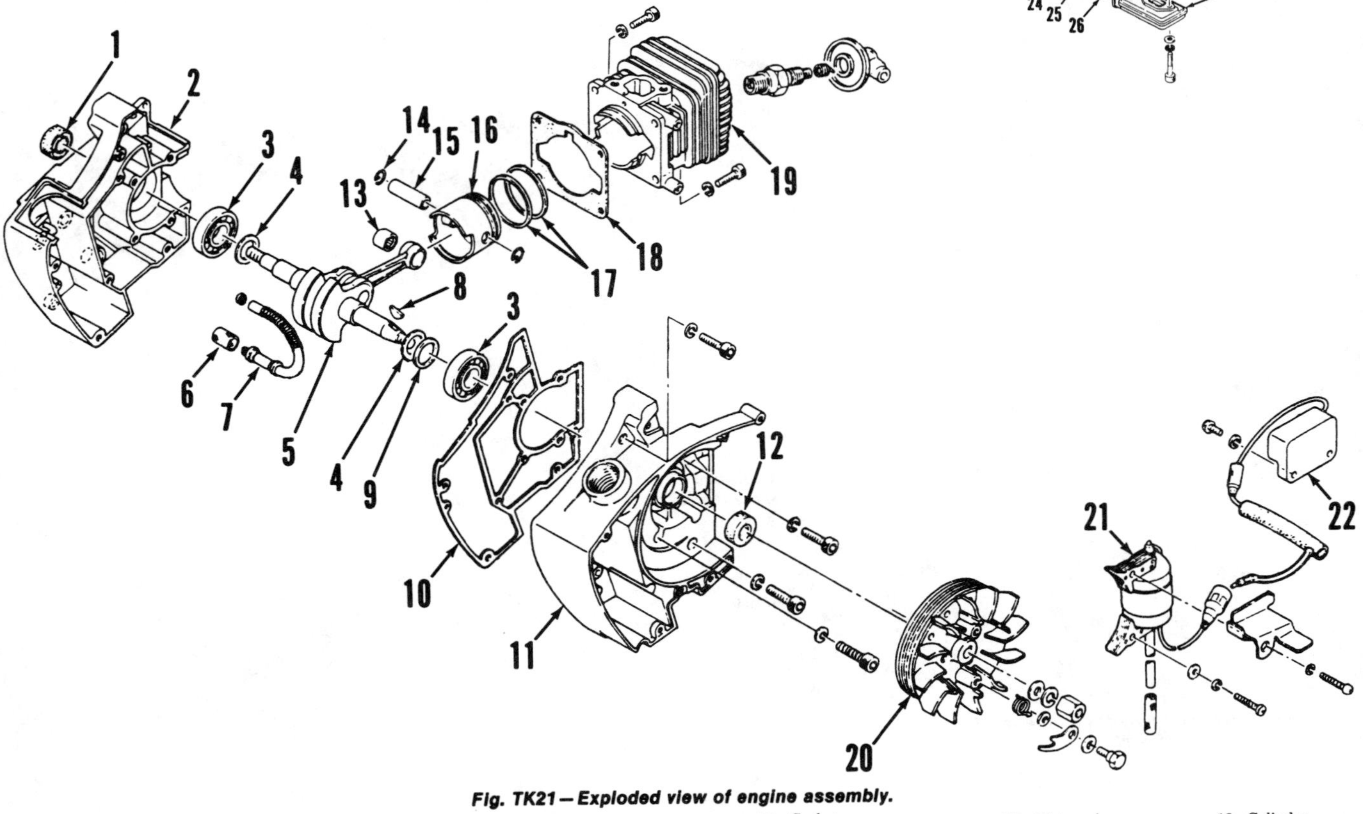

Fig. TK21—Exploded view of engine assembly.

1. Seal
2. Crankcase half
3. Bearing
4. Thrust washer
5. Crankshaft & connecting rod assy.
6. Strainer
7. Oil pump suction hose
8. Key
9. Shim
10. Gasket
11. [not listed]
12. Seal
13. Needle bearing
14. Retainer
15. Piston pin
16. Piston
17. Piston rings
18. Gasket
19. Cylinder
20. Flywheel
21. Ignition coil
22. Ignition module

Illustrations courtesy Tanaka Kogyo (USA) Co.

LUBRICATION. Engine is lubricated by mixing engine oil with leaded or unleaded gasoline having an octane rating of at least 87. Recommended oil is Tanaka Two-Stroke Oil mixed at a ratio of 50:1. If Tanaka Two-Stroke Oil is not available, a good quality oil designed for air-cooled two-stroke engines and for mixture ratios between 25:1-to-50:1 may be used when mixed as outlined by oil manufacturer. Use a separate container when mixing the oil and gasoline.

An automatic chain oil pump is used. Recommended chain oil is SAE 30 oil. Oil output is adjusted by turning oil pump adjuster (2–Fig. TK23). Refer to AUTOMATIC CHAIN OILER under REPAIRS section.

CARBON. Carbon should be cleaned from muffler and exhaust ports at regular intervals. When scraping carbon, be careful not to damage the chamfered edges of the exhaust ports.

REPAIRS

CYLINDER, PISTON, PIN AND RINGS. Cylinder (19–Fig. TK21) bore is chrome plated and should be renewed if cracking, flaking or other damage to cylinder bore is noted. Oversize piston and rings are not available. Cylinder (19) should be renewed if bore is out-of-round or tapered 0.10 mm (0.004 in.) beyond standard bore dimension. Piston (16) is equipped with two piston rings (17). Piston ring end gap should be 0.1-0.3 mm (0.004-0.012 in.). Locating pins are present in ring grooves to prevent ring rotation. Make certain ring end gaps are properly positioned around locating pins before installing cylinder. Piston pin (15) rides in needle bearing (13) and is retained in position with two wire retainer clips (14). Once removed, wire clips should not be reused. Install piston on connecting rod so arrow on piston crown points toward exhaust port.

CRANKSHAFT AND CONNECTING ROD. Crankcase halves must be split to remove crankshaft assembly. Crankshaft and connecting rod (5–Fig. TK21) are a unit assembly and supported at both ends with roller type main bearings (3). Rotate connecting rod around crank pin and renew assembly if roughness, excessive play or other damage is noted.

New seals (1 and 12) should be installed in crankcase halves prior to installing crankshaft assembly. Recommended crankshaft end play is 0.3 mm (0.012 in.). Adjust thickness of shim (9) to obtain correct end play. Shim (9) is available in thicknesses of 0.05, 0.10, 0.15 and 0.20 mm.

CLUTCH. A three-shoe centrifugal type clutch is used. Clutch hub has left hand threads. Clutch needle bearing (3–Fig. TK22) should be inspected for excessive wear or damage. Inspect clutch shoes and drum for signs of excessive heat. Clutch assembly (1) is only renewable as a complete unit.

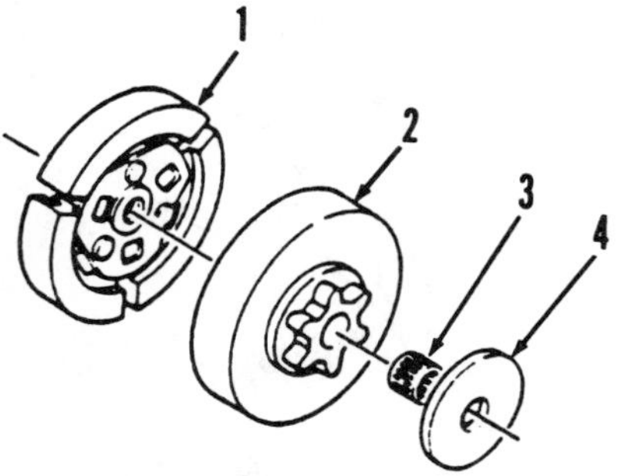

Fig. TK22—Exploded view of three-shoe clutch assembly.

1. Hub & shoe assy.
2. Drum
3. Needle bearing
4. Washer

Fig. TK24—Exploded view of rewind starter assembly.

1. Handle
2. Guide
3. Clip
4. Rope
5. Screw
6. Washer
7. Rope pulley
8. Rewind spring case
9. Rewind spring
10. Washer
11. Baffle
12. Housing
13. Toothed lockwasher
14. Castle nut
15. Return spring
16. Washer
17. Pawl
18. Washer
19. Pivot screw
20. Flywheel

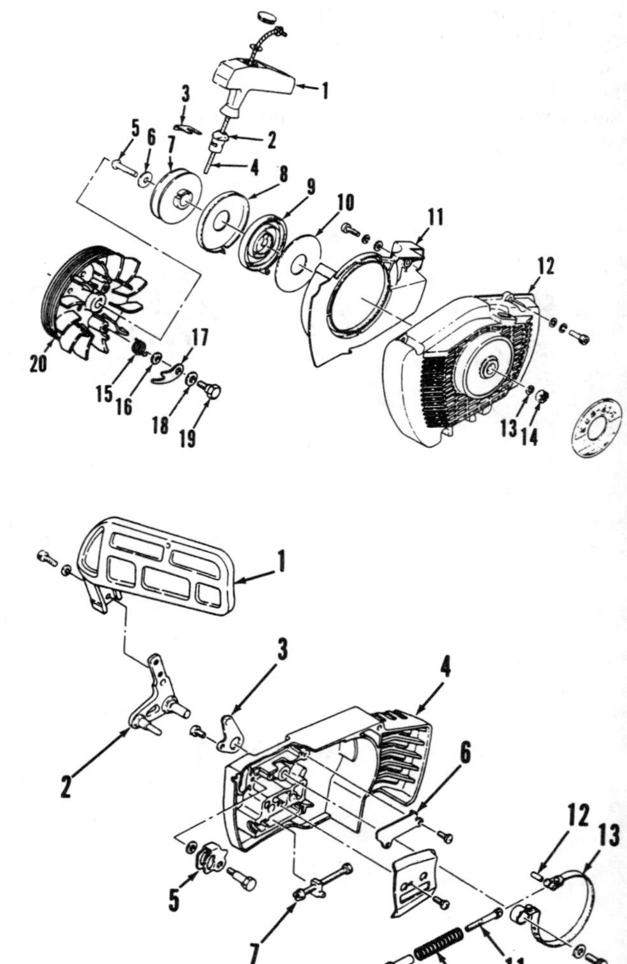

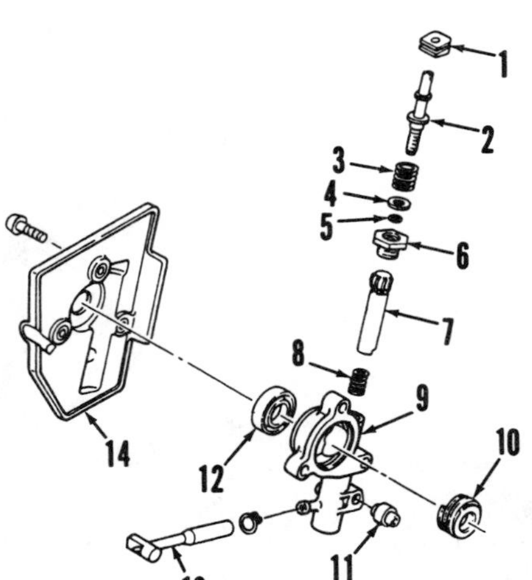

Fig. TK23—Expoded view of automatic oil pump assembly.

1. Grommet
2. Output adjuster
3. Spring
4. Washer
5. "O" ring
6. Cap
7. Plunger
8. Spring
9. Body
10. Worm gear
11. Air pipe
12. Seal
13. Discharge hose
14. Cover

Fig. TK25—Exploded view of chain brake assembly.

1. Hand guard
2. Lever
3. Detent
4. Side case
5. Arm
6. Spring holder
7. Saw chain tension adjuster
8. Lockplate
9. Adjuster
10. Spring
11. Rod
12. Pin
13. Brake band

AUTOMATIC CHAIN OILER. An automatic chain oil pump assembly is used. Oil pump plunger (7–Fig. TK23) is driven by worm gear (10) mounted on crankshaft end. Rotate oil pump output adjuster (2) counterclockwise to increase oil flow and clockwise to decrease oil flow.

REWIND STARTER. Refer to Fig. TK24 for exploded view of pawl type starter. Care should be exercised when removing rewind spring (9) to prevent spring from uncoiling uncontrolled.

During reassembly, do not apply any more tension on rewind spring than required to properly draw rope handle up against starter housing in relaxed position.

CHAIN BRAKE. A chain brake designed to stop the saw chain quickly should kickback occur is used. Chain brake is activated when operator's hand strikes hand guard (1–Fig. TK25), releasing arm (5) thereby allowing spring (10) to draw brake band (13) tight around clutch drum. Pull back hand guard (1) to reset mechanism.

Disassembly for inspection or repair is evident after referral to appropriate exploded view and inspection of unit. Renew any component found to be excessively worn or damaged. Chain brake mechanism should be clean and free of sawdust and dirt accumulation. Lightly lubricate all moving parts and pivot points.

To adjust chain brake, first remove spark plug boot from spark plug and properly ground terminal end. Place chain brake lever (2) in released position. Use a suitable sized screwdriver and rotate adjuster (9) clockwise until saw chain cannot be rotated around guide bar by hand pressure. Then rotate adjuster (9) counterclockwise noting when brake band (13) does not contact outside surface of clutch drum. Make sure brake band does not drag on outside of clutch drum with brake lever in released position. With brake lever in applied position, saw chain should not be free to rotate around guide bar.

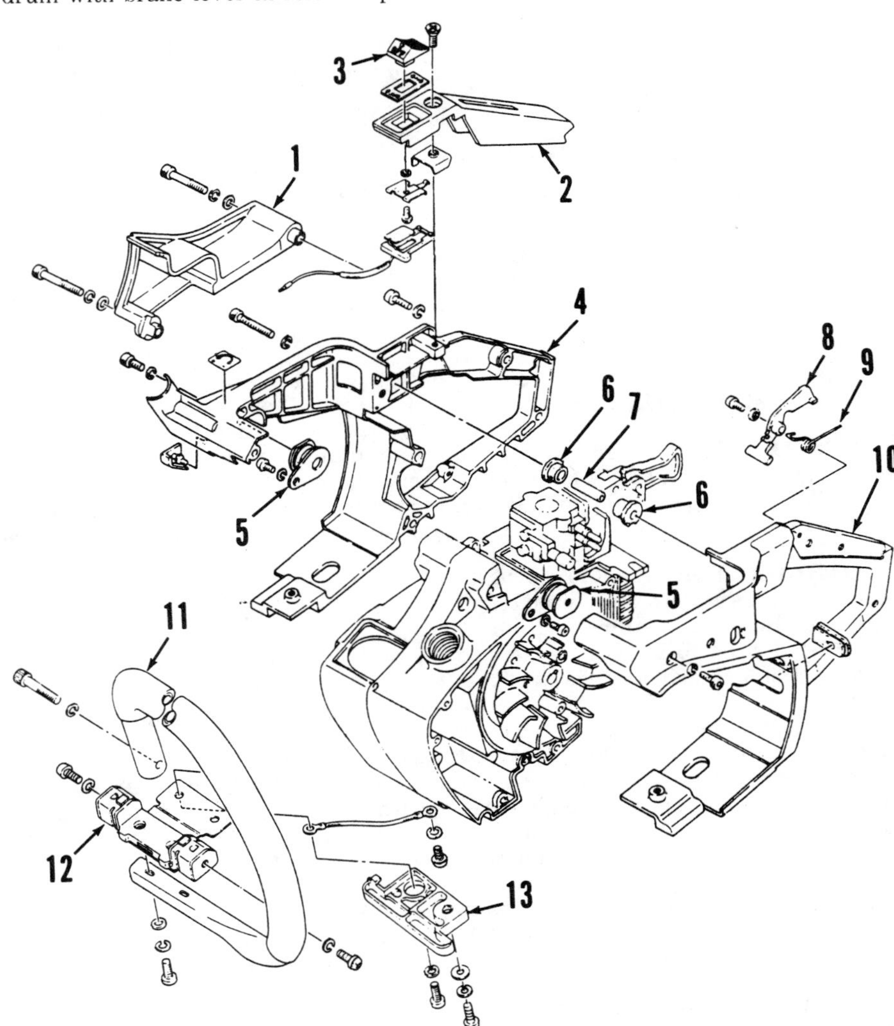

Fig. TK26 – Exploded view of front and rear handle assemblies.

1. Guard
2. Handle grip
3. Run/stop switch
4. Rear handle half
5. Vibration damper
6. Damper
7. Collar
8. Safety lever
9. Spring
10. Rear handle half
11. Front handle
12. Front handle vibration damper
13. Cover

TANAKA

Model	Bore mm (in.)	Stroke mm (in.)	Displacement cc (cu. in.)	Drive Type
ECS-506	41 (1.6)	38 (1.5)	50 (3.1)	Direct
ECS-650, ESC-655	46 (1.8)	38 (1.5)	63 (3.8)	Direct

MAINTENANCE

SPARK PLUG. Recommended spark plug is NGK BPM7A for all models. Electrode gap should be 0.6 mm (0.024 in.).

CARBURETOR. A Walbro HDA diaphragm type carburetor is used on all models. Refer to Walbro section of CARBURETOR SERVICE for service information and exploded views of carburetor.

Initial adjustment (turns open from a lightly seated position) for low-speed mixture screw (1—Fig. TK30) is 1-1/4 turns and 1-3/8 turns for high-speed mixture screw (2). Make final adjustment with engine warm and running.

Adjust idle speed screw (3) so engine idles just below clutch engagement speed (approximately 2800 rpm). Adjust low-speed mixture screw (2) to obtain maximum engine rpm, then turn screw out (counterclockwise) 1/8 to 1/4 turn. Engine should accelerate cleanly without hesitation. If engine stumbles or seems sluggish when accelerating, adjust low-speed mixture screw until engine accelerates cleanly. Readjust idle speed screw if necessary. Chain must not move when engine is idling.

High-speed mixture screw (3) should be adjusted to obtain optimum performance with saw under cutting load. Do not adjust high-speed mixture screw too lean (turned too far clockwise) as maximum permissible engine speed may be exceeded and engine may be damaged from lack of lubrication and overheating. Maximum no-load speed (with bar and chain installed) must not exceed 11,800 rpm.

To remove carburetor, remove air cleaner cover (2—Fig. TK31). Remove lower cover mounting screws and remove lower cover (9). Disconnect fuel hose and throttle rod, then withdraw carburetor (10).

IGNITION. All models are equipped with a breakerless electronic ignition system. Ignition timing is not adjustable. Air gap between ignition coil assembly and flywheel magnets should be 0.35 mm (0.014 in.). To adjust, loosen module mounting screws and move module as necessary.

LUBRICATION. The engine is lubricated by oil mixed with unleaded gasoline. Recommended oil is Tanaka Two-Stroke Oil mixed at the ratio specified on the oil container. If Tanaka Two-Stroke Oil is not available, a good quality oil designed for air-cooled two-stroke engines may be used mixed as recommended by the oil manufacturer. Manufacturer recommends NOT using gasohol or gasoline containing alcohol. Use a separate container when mixing the oil and gasoline.

All models are equipped with an automatic bar and chain oiling system. Use a good quality bar oil and fill the oil reservoir each time the gas tank is filled. Oil output is adjusted by turning the oil pump adjuster (1—Fig. TK32). Oil flow is adjusted at the factory for

Fig. TK30—View of carburetor adjustment points. Refer to text for carburetor adjustment procedure.

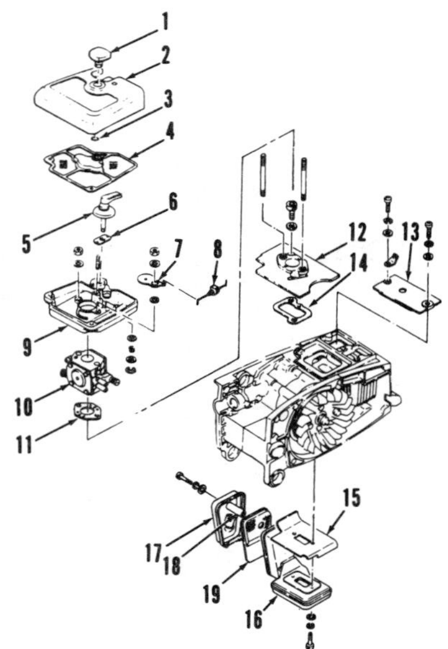

Fig. TK31—Exploded view of intake and muffler assemblies.

1. Knob
2. Upper cover
3. "O" ring
4. Air cleaner element
5. Choke knob
6. Choke actuating bracket
7. Choke valve
8. Choke link
9. Lower cover
10. Carburetor assy.
11. Gasket
12. Insulator block
13. Plate
14. Gasket
15. Bracket
16. Muffler half
17. Muffler half
18. Spacer
19. Spark arrestor

Fig. TK32—Bar and chain lubricating oil pump is adjusted by turning oil pump adjuster (1). Turn adjuster counterclockwise to reduce oil flow.

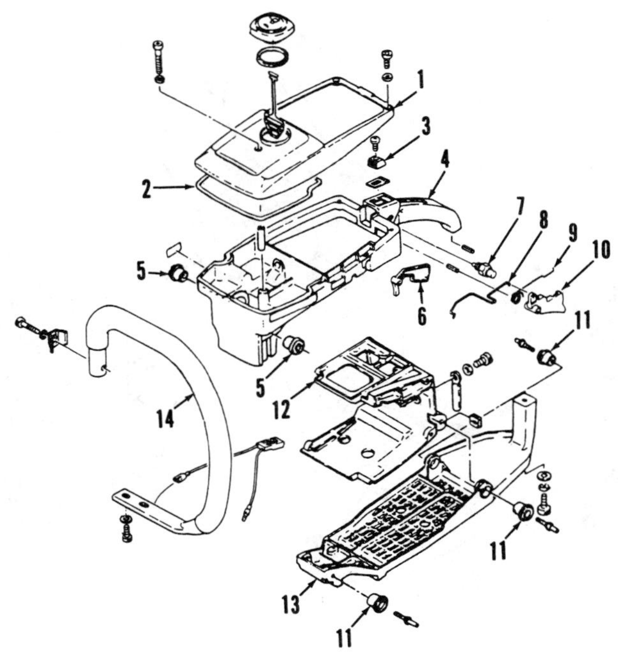

Fig. TK33—Exploded view of front and rear handle assemblies.

1. Fuel tank cover
2. Gasket
3. Stop switch
4. Fuel tank & rear handle
5. Vibration damper
6. Safety lever
7. Push pin
8. Throttle link
9. Spring
10. Throttle lever
11. Vibration damper
12. Cylinder cover
13. Engine lower brace
14. Front handle

maximum flow. Turning the adjusting screw counterclockwise will reduce the oil flow.

CARBON. Carbon should be cleaned from the muffler and exhaust ports at regular intervals. When scraping carbon, be careful not to damage the chamfered edges of the exhaust ports.

REPAIRS

CYLINDER, PISTON, PIN AND RINGS. To remove cylinder and piston, first remove air cleaner cover (2—Fig. TK31), lower cover (9) and carburetor (10). Remove muffler and heat shield (15-19). Remove fuel tank cover (1—Fig. TK33), fuel tank and rear handle (4), engine brace (13) and cylinder cover (12). Remove cylinder mounting screws and pull the cylinder (14—Fig. TK34) off the piston.

To remove piston (11), disengage retainer clips (9) from piston and push piston pin (10) from piston. Be careful not to apply side force to connecting rod when removing the piston pin.

The cylinder bore is chrome plated and should be renewed if cracking, flaking or other damage to bore is noted. Cylinder should be renewed if bore is out-of-round or tapered 0.10 mm (0.004 in.) or more.

Piston is equipped with two piston rings (12). Piston ring end gap should be 0.1-0.3 mm (0.004-0.012 in.). Piston pin rides in a needle bearing (8).

When reassembling, note that wire retaining clips (9) should be renewed if removed from piston. Install retaining clips with open end facing either towards the top or bottom of the piston. Install piston on connecting rod so arrow on piston crown points toward the exhaust port.

Locating pins are present in piston ring grooves to prevent ring rotation. Make certain that ring end gaps are properly positioned around locating pins before installing the cylinder.

Lubricate piston and cylinder bore with engine oil. Align the exhaust port with the arrow on top of piston, then slide cylinder over the piston. Do not rotate cylinder when installing as piston rings may become disengaged from locating pins resulting in damage to the rings, piston and cylinder.

CRANKSHAFT AND CONNECTING ROD. Crankcase halves must be split to remove crankshaft assembly. Remove clutch cover with brake assembly, bar and chain. Remove starter housing. Remove spark plug and install a suitable piston stop tool or insert the end of a rope into spark plug hole to prevent crankshaft from rotating. Remove clutch assembly. Clutch hub has left-hand threads (turn clockwise to remove). Remove oil pump cover and worm gear. Remove ignition module (19—Fig. TK34) and coil (21). Remove flywheel nut and pull flywheel (20) off crankshaft. Remove carburetor, muffler, fuel tank and handle, cylinder cover and cylinder as outlined above. Remove screws attaching crankcase halves (2 and 17). Separate crankcase halves using care not to damage the crankcase sealing surfaces.

Crankshaft and connecting rod (6—Fig. TK34) are a unit assembly and must not be separated. Rotate connecting rod around crankshaft and renew assembly if roughness, excessive play or other damage is noted. Main bearings (3) should be renewed if they are removed.

New seals (1 and 18) should be installed in crankcase halves prior to installing the crankshaft assembly. Recommended crankshaft end play is 0.3 mm (0.012 in.). Install shims (15) as needed to obtain correct end play.

CLUTCH. A three-shoe centrifugal type clutch is used on all models (Fig. TK35). To remove the clutch, remove clutch cover (3) with the chain brake as-

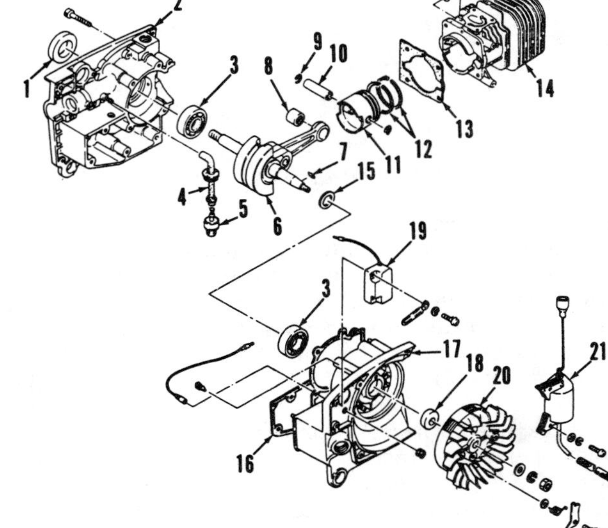

Fig. TK34—Exploded view of engine assembly.

1. Seal
2. Crankcase half
3. Bearing
4. Oil pump suction hose
5. Oil strainer
6. Crankshaft & connecting rod assy.
7. Key
8. Needle bearing
9. Retainer clip
10. Piston pin
11. Piston
12. Piston rings
13. Gasket
14. Cylinder
15. Shim
16. Gasket
17. Crankcase half
18. Seal
19. Ignition module
20. Flywheel
21. Ignition coil

Illustrations courtesy Tanaka Kogyo (USA) Inc.

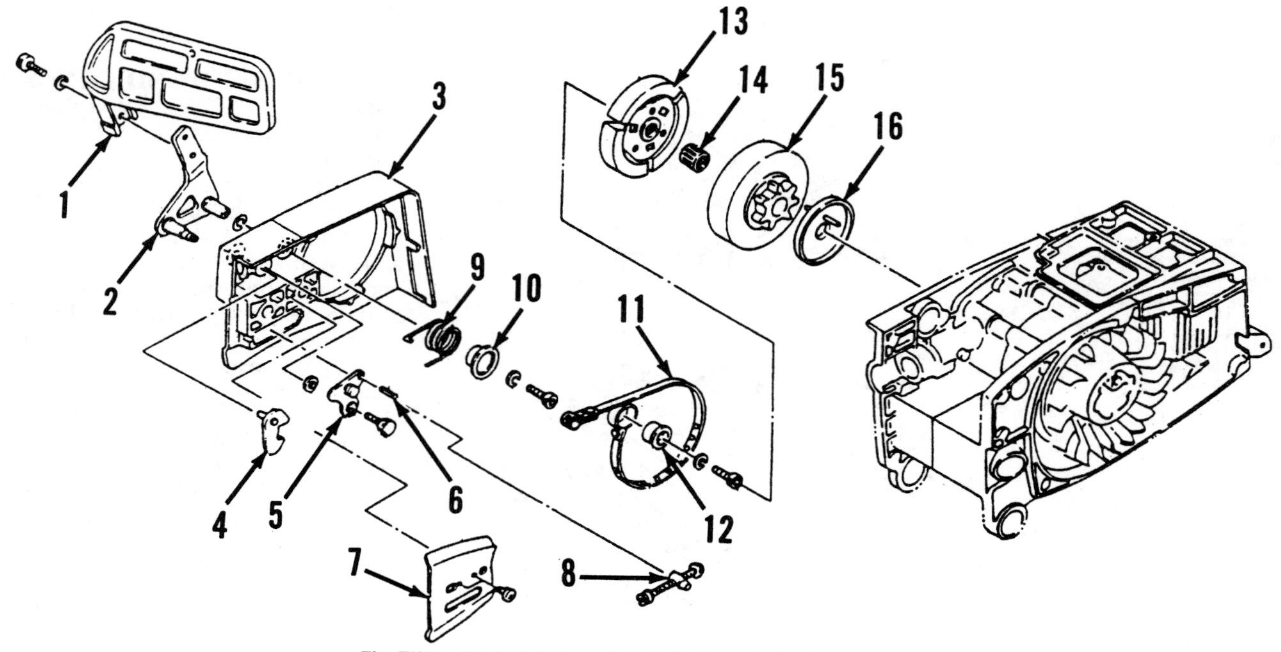

Fig. TK35—Exploded view of chain brake and clutch assemblies.

1. Hand guard
2. Brake lever
3. Clutch cover
4. Brake reset lever
5. Brake arm
6. Pin
7. Guide plate
8. Chain adjuster
9. Brake spring
10. Washer
11. Brake band
12. Band anchor
13. Clutch hub & shoes assy.
14. Needle bearing
15. Clutch drum
16. Sprocket washer

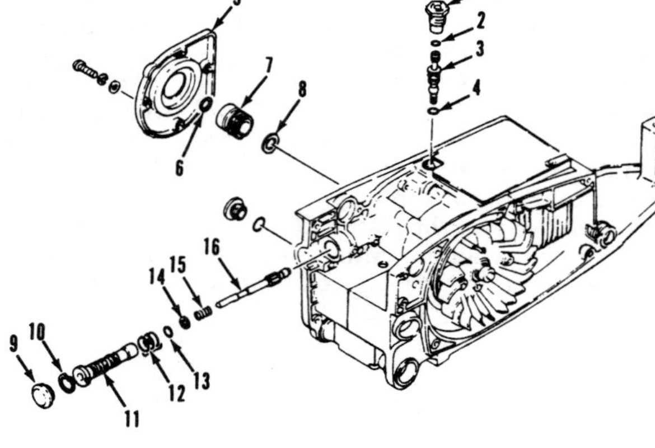

Fig. TK36—Exploded view of automatic oil pump assembly.

1. Cap
2. "O" ring
3. Adjuster screw
4. "O" ring
5. Cover
6. Seal
7. Worm gear
8. Thrust washer
9. Cap
10. Snap ring
11. Plunger body
12. "O" ring
13. "O" ring
14. Washer
15. Spring
16. Plunger

sembly. Remove the spark plug and install a suitable piston stop tool or insert the end of a rope in the spark plug hole to prevent the crankshaft from rotating. Unscrew the clutch hub (13) from crankshaft. Note that clutch hub has left-hand threads (turn clockwise to remove). Remove needle bearing (14) and clutch drum (15).

Check needle bearing for excessive wear or damage. Inspect clutch shoes and drum for signs of wear or excessive heat. Clutch shoes are available as an assembly with the hub (13).

When reassembling, make certain that the sprocket washer (16) properly engages the oil pump worm gear.

AUTOMATIC CHAIN OILER. All models are equipped with an automatic bar and chain oiling system (Fig. TK36). The automatic chain oil pump is driven by the clutch drum. Oil pump is operational only when the clutch is engaged and the chain is moving. Oil pump output is adjusted by turning adjuster (3) clockwise to increase oil flow or counterclockwise to decrease the flow.

To remove the oil pump, remove clutch cover (3–Fig. TK35) and thoroughly clean the saw. Remove clutch assembly, cover (5–Fig. TK36), and worm gear (7). Remove cap (9) and retaining ring (10), then withdraw oil pump components (11-16). Remove cap (1) and adjuster (3).

Inspect oil pump for wear or damage and renew components as necessary.

Install new "O" rings when reassembling. Make certain that thrust washer (8) is in place and that sprocket washer (16—Fig. TK35) engages the oil pump worm gear (7—Fig. TK36).

CHAIN BRAKE. All models are equipped with a chain brake designed to stop the saw chain quickly should kickback occur. Chain brake is activated when operator's hand strikes the hand guard (1—Fig. TK35). This releases the arm (5) thereby allowing the spring (9) to draw the brake band (11) tightly around the clutch drum (15). Pull the hand guard rearward to reset brake mechanism.

To service the chain brake, remove clutch cover (3) with brake assembly. Activate the brake to relieve spring tension. To disassemble, remove brake arm (5), brake band anchor bolt and spring anchor bolt.

Renew any component found to be worn or damaged. When reassembling, lightly lubricate all moving parts and

Illustrations courtesy Tanaka Kogyo (USA) Inc.

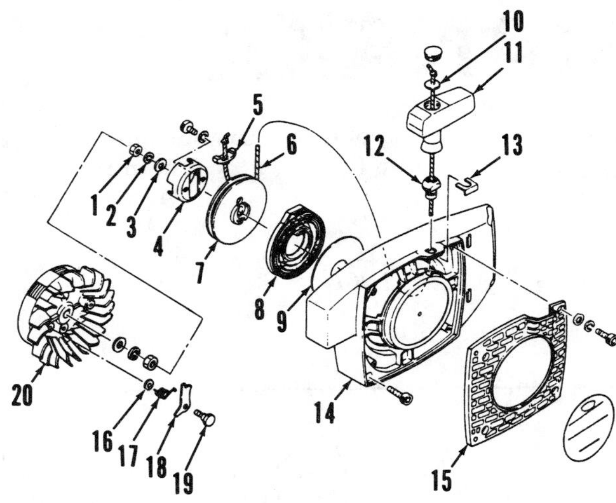

Fig. TK37—Exploded view of rewind starter assembly used on early models.

1. Nut
2. Washer
3. Washer
4. Cup
5. Anchor
6. Rope
7. Rope pulley
8. Rewind spring & case
9. Plate
10. Anchor
11. Handle
12. Guide
13. Clip
14. Housing
15. Cover
16. Washer
17. Return spring
18. Pawl
19. Pivot screw
20. Flywheel

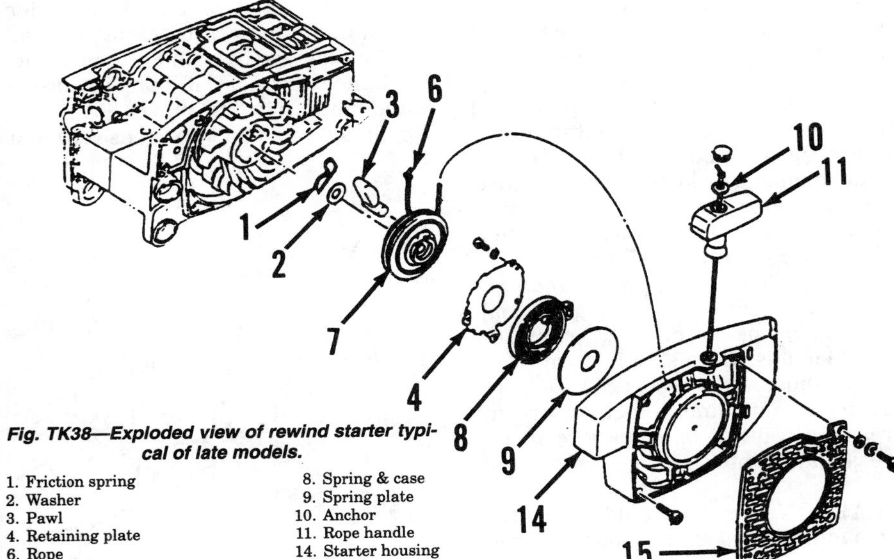

Fig. TK38—Exploded view of rewind starter typical of late models.

1. Friction spring
2. Washer
3. Pawl
4. Retaining plate
6. Rope
7. Pulley
8. Spring & case
9. Spring plate
10. Anchor
11. Rope handle
14. Starter housing
15. Cover

pivot points. No adjustment of brake system is required.

REWIND STARTER. Rewind starter used on some early models is illustrated in Fig. TK37. Fig. TK38 illustrates the starter used on later models.

To service either starter, first remove starter housing (14) from saw. If rope is intact, remove rope handle (11) and allow starter pulley to slowly unwind to relieve spring tension.

On early models, remove nut (1—Fig. TK37), starter cup (4) and rope pulley (7). Carefully remove rewind spring and case (8).

On late models, remove friction spring (1—Fig. TK38), washer (2), pawl (3) and rope pulley (7). Unbolt and remove retainer plate (4), recoil spring (8) and spring plate (9).

If the rewind spring becomes disengaged from its case, wind spring in the case in a counterclockwise direction working from the outside towards the inside. Wind rope onto pulley in a clockwise direction (viewed from flywheel side). To preload the rewind spring, turn rope pulley approximately two turns clockwise before passing rope through starter housing. Attach the rope handle and check starter operation.

Rewind spring tension is correct if rope handle is pulled snugly against housing with rope fully retracted and if pulley will rotate at least an additional half turn with rope fully extended. If the rewind spring binds before rope is fully extended, reduce tension on rope by the pulling rope up into notch in rope pulley and allowing pulley to partially unwind. Recheck starter operation.

TANAKA

Model	Bore mm (in.)	Stroke mm (in.)	Displacement cc (cu. in.)	Drive Type
ECS-3500, 3500B	38 (1.5)	30 (1.18)	34 (2.1)	Direct
ECS-4000, 4000B	39.8 (1.57)	32 (1.26)	40 (2.4)	Direct

MAINTENANCE

SPARK PLUG. Recommended spark plug is NGK BPM6A or equivalent for all models. Spark plug electrode gap should be 0.6 mm (0.024 in.).

CARBURETOR. A Walbro WT diaphragm type carburetor is used on all models. Refer to Walbro section of CARBURETOR SERVICE for service procedures and exploded view of carburetor.

Initial adjustment for both low speed and high speed mixture screws is one turn open from a lightly seated position on all models. Be sure engine air filter is clean before adjusting carburetor.

Make final carburetor adjustments with engine warm and running. Adjust idle speed screw (1—Fig. TK50) so engine idles just below clutch engagement speed (approximately 2800 rpm). Adjust low speed mixture screw (3) to obtain highest idle speed, then turn screw counterclockwise about 1/8 turn. Engine should accelerate cleanly without hesitation. If engine stumbles or seems sluggish when accelerating, adjust idle mixture screw until engine accelerates without hesitation. Readjust idle speed screw so engine idles just under clutch engagement speed. Operate engine at full throttle with no load and turn high speed mixture screw (2) clockwise until engine speed increases and four-stroking sound stops. Then, turn high speed needle counterclockwise until four-stroking sound just returns. Do not operate saw with high speed mixture too lean as engine damage may result from lack of lubrication and overheating.

IGNITION. All models are equipped with a breakerless electronic ignition system. No periodic maintenance is required. Ignition timing is not adjustable.

Air gap between ignition module/coil assembly and flywheel magnets should be 0.35 mm (0.014 in.). To adjust, loosen module mounting screws and move module as necessary.

LUBRICATION. Engine is lubricated by mixing engine oil with leaded or unleaded gasoline having an octane rating of at least 87. Recommended oil is Tanaka Two-Stroke Oil mixed at a ratio of 50:1. If Tanaka Two-Stroke Oil is not available, a good quality oil designed for air-cooled two-stroke engines that is made to be mixed at a ratio between 25:1 and 50:1 may be used. When using oil other than Tanaka Two-Stroke Oil, follow the oil manufacturer's recommended mixing ratio. If a recommended mixing ratio is not designated, mix at 25:1. Use a separate container when mixing the oil and gasoline.

All models are equipped with an automatic chain oiler system. A good quality chain oil should be used. Oil output on all models is adjusted by turning oil pump adjuster (S—Fig. TK51). Turn adjusting screw counterclockwise to increase oil output or clockwise to decrease oil output.

CARBON. Carbon should be cleaned from muffler and exhaust ports at regular intervals. When scraping carbon, be careful not to damage the chamfered edges of the exhaust ports.

REPAIRS

CYLINDER, PISTON, PIN AND RINGS. To disassemble, remove side cover, guide bar and chain, front handle and starter housing. Remove muffler (Fig. TK52) and air cleaner assembly and carburetor. Unbolt and remove fuel tank and rear handle assembly (5—Fig. TK53), engine base (19), cylinder cover (8—Fig. TK52) and intake manifold assembly. Remove flywheel mounting nut and use suitable puller to remove flywheel (12—Fig. TK54) from crankshaft. Remove ignition coil (20). Remove cylinder mounting screws and withdraw cylinder (19) from crankcase. Remove piston rings (17) from piston (14). Pry piston pin retainer clips (13) out of piston, then tap piston pin (16) out of piston and connecting rod. Be careful not to apply side thrust to connecting rod when removing piston pin. Remove piston and needle bearing (15) from connecting rod.

Cylinder bore is chrome plated and cannot be honed or bored. Cylinder should be renewed if cracking, flaking or other damage to cylinder bore is noted. Renew cylinder if bore is out-of-round more than 0.03 mm (0.001 in.) or if cylinder wall taper exceeds 0.10 mm

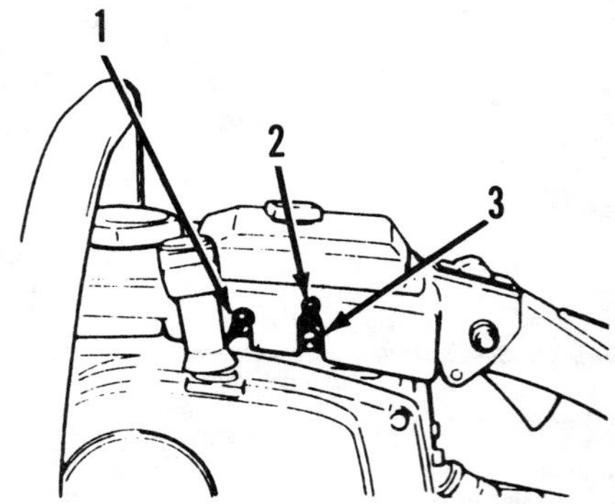

Fig. TK50—View showing location of carburetor idle adjusting screw (1), high speed mixture adjustment screw (2) and low speed mixture adjustment screw (3).

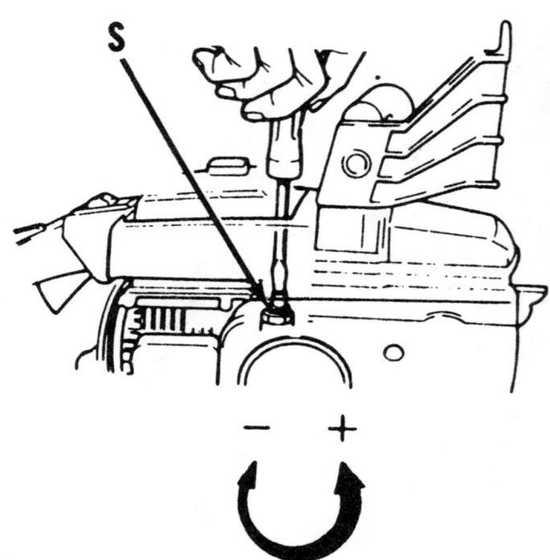

Fig. TK51—To adjust automatic chain oiler output, turn adjusting screw (S) counterclockwise to increase oil flow or clockwise to decrease oil flow.

Illustrations courtesy Tanaka Kogyo (USA) Co.

(0.004 in.). Inspect piston for scuffing, scoring or other damage and renew as necessary. Piston ring end gap should be 0.1-0.3 mm (0.004-0.012 in.).

When reassembling, install piston on connecting rod so arrow mark on piston crown points toward exhaust port side of engine. Once removed, piston pin clips (13—Fig. TK54) should not be reused. Locating pins are present in ring grooves to prevent ring rotation. Make certain that ring end gaps are positioned around locating pins before installing piston in cylinder. Lubricate piston, cylinder and connecting rod bearings before installation.

CRANKSHAFT AND CONNECTING ROD. To disassemble, remove clutch assembly and oil pump from engine. Remove cylinder and piston as previously outlined. Remove crankcase mounting bolts and separate crankcase halves (4 and 10—Fig. TK54).

Crankshaft and connecting rod (7) are a unit assembly and should not be disassembled. Rotate connecting rod around crankpin and renew assembly if roughness, excessive play or other damage is noted. Renew ball bearings (5) and needle bearing (15) if roughness or other damage is noted.

New seals (2 and 11) should be installed in crankcase halves during assembly. After installing crankshaft assembly in crankcase, rotate crankshaft to be sure crankshaft rotates freely. Recommended crankshaft end play is 0.3 mm (0.012 in.). Adjust thickness of shim (8) to obtain correct end play.

CLUTCH. A centrifugal type clutch is used on all models. Remove side cover (1—Fig. TK55), guide bar (5) and chain for access to clutch. Remove starter housing and use suitable tool to hold flywheel from turning. Unscrew clutch hub from crankshaft (left-hand threads) and remove clutch assembly (11).

Inspect clutch drum needle bearing (12) for roughness or wear and renew as necessary. Inspect clutch shoes and drum (13) for signs of excessive heat. Clutch drum should be renewed if sprocket teeth are worn in excess of 25 mm (0.010 in.). If sprocket is badly worn, inspect chain for excessive wear also. Do not install a new chain over a worn sprocket.

Apply grease to needle bearing (12) prior to installation.

AUTOMATIC CHAIN OILER. All models are equipped with an automatic chain oiler system. Oil pump plunger is driven by worm gear (22—Fig. TK55) mounted on crankshaft end.

Oil pump plunger and body (21) are not serviced separately. Pump must be renewed as an assembly if faulty. To adjust oil pump output, rotate adjuster (16) clockwise to decrease oil flow and counterclockwise to increase oil flow.

CHAIN BRAKE. All models are equipped with a chain brake system designed to stop chain movement should kickback occur. Chain brake is activated when operator's hand strikes chain brake handle (3—Fig. TK55), tripping brake arm (9) thereby allowing spring (8) to draw brake band (10) around clutch drum (13). Pull back chain brake handle to reset mechanism.

Disassembly is evident after inspection of unit and referral to exploded view (Fig. TK55). No adjustment of chain brake system is required. Renew any component found to be excessively worn or damaged. Lubricate all pivot points with Molykote or suitable equivalent.

REWIND STARTER. Refer to Fig. TK56 for exploded view of rewind starter assembly. To disassemble, remove starter housing (10) from engine. Remove retainer (12) and rope handle (11) and allow rope to wind slowly onto pulley (8) until spring tension is relieved. Unscrew pulley mounting screw (6) and remove pulley, being careful not to dislodge rewind spring (9). If necessary to remove rewind spring, care should be used not to allow spring to uncoil uncontrolled.

Apply a light coat of multipurpose grease to both sides of rewind spring. Install rewind spring in starter housing with coils wrapped in a clockwise direction from outer end of spring. Wind rope around pulley in a clockwise direction as viewed from flywheel side of pulley. Turn pulley approximately three turns clockwise to preload rewind spring before passing rope through starter housing. Attach rope handle and check start-

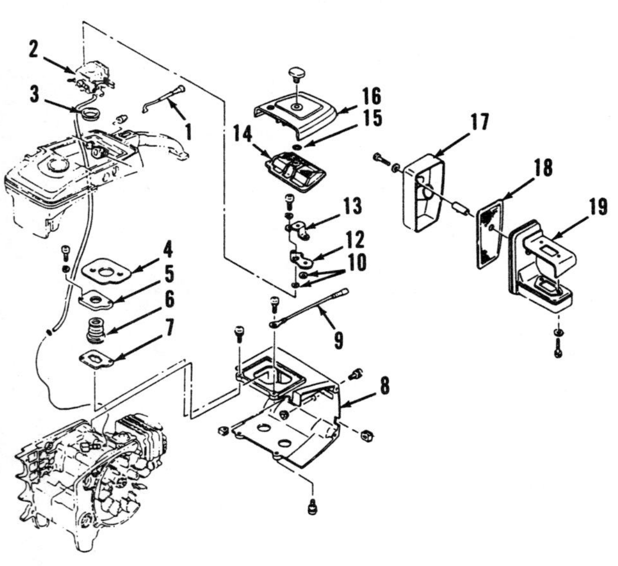

Fig. TK52—Exploded view of intake and exhaust components.

1. Choke button
2. Carburetor
3. Manifold spacer
4. Air deflector
5. Manifold flange
6. Intake manifold
7. Gasket
8. Cylinder cover
9. Ground wire
10. Shims
12. Choke valve
13. Blow-back check valve
14. Air cleaner element
15. "O" ring
16. Cover
17. Muffler body
18. Spark arrestor
19. Muffler assy.

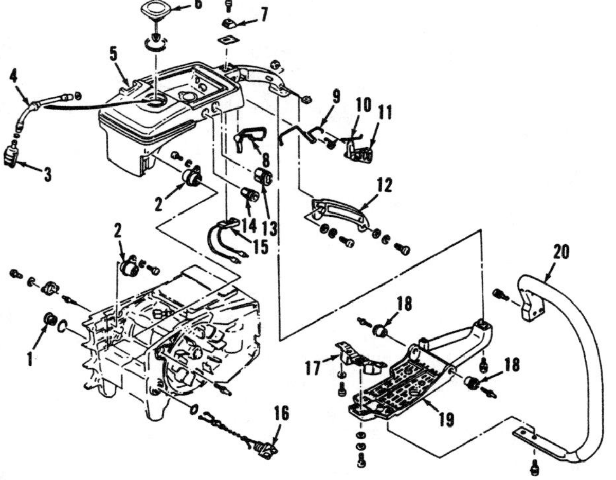

Fig. TK53—Exploded view of front and rear handle assemblies.

1. Oil level cap
2. Vibration dampers
3. Fuel filter
4. Fuel line
5. Fuel tank & rear handle assy.
6. Fuel tank cap
7. Stop button
8. Safety lever
9. Throttle rod
10. Throttle lever spring
11. Throttle lever
12. Rear handle
13. Carburetor adjuster grommet
14. Grommet
15. Stop switch
16. Oil tank cap
17. Vibration damper
18. Vibration damper
19. Engine base
20. Front handle

Illustrations courtesy Tanaka Kogyo (USA) Co.

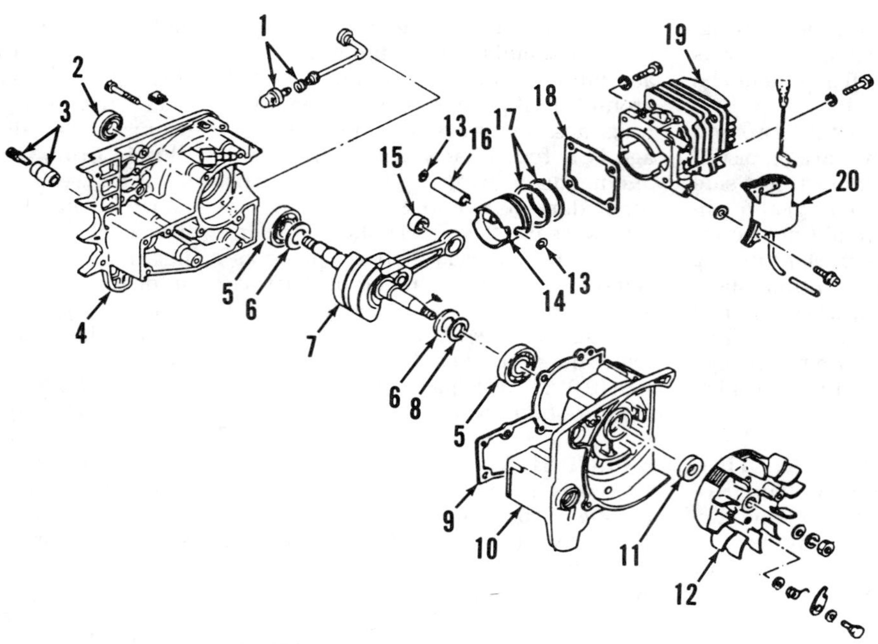

Fig. TK54—Exploded view of engine assembly.

1. Oil line & filter
2. Oil seal
3. Air vent valve
4. Crankcase half
5. Bearing
6. Washers
7. Crankshaft & connecting rod assy.
8. Shim washer
9. Gasket
10. Crankcase half
11. Oil seal
12. Flywheel
13. Retaining clip
14. Piston
15. Needle bearing
16. Piston pin
17. Piston rings
18. Gasket
19. Cylinder
20. Ignition module/coil

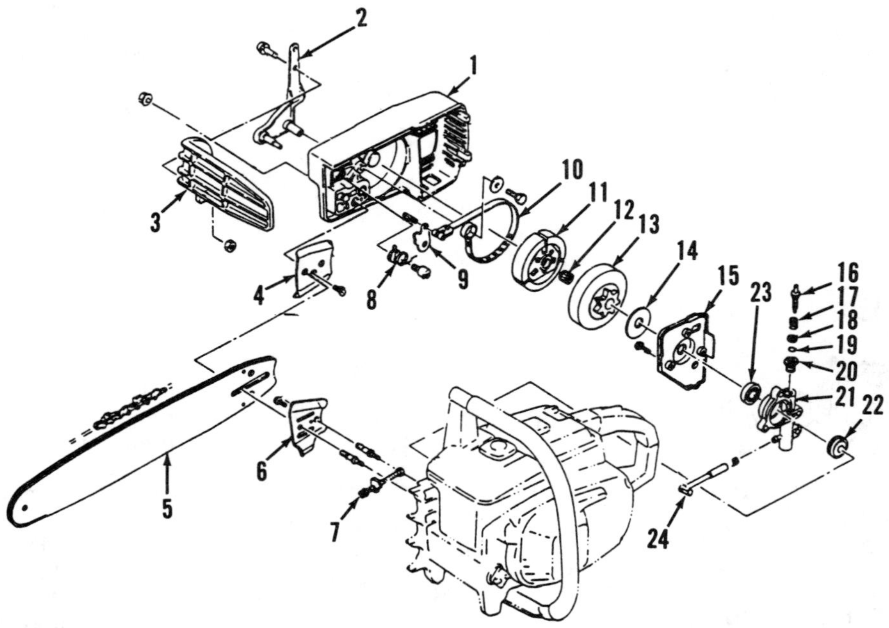

Fig. TK55—Exploded view of chain brake, clutch assembly and automatic oil pump assembly.

1. Side cover
2. Chain brake lever
3. Brake handle
4. Guide plate
5. Guide bar
6. Guide plate
7. Chain adjusting bolt
8. Spring
9. Brake arm
10. Brake band
11. Clutch assy.
12. Needle bearing
13. Clutch drum
14. Washer
15. Oil pump cover
16. Adjuster
17. Spring
18. Washer
19. "O" ring
20. Cap
21. Oil pump body
22. Worm gear
23. Oil seal
24. Oil line

Illustrations courtesy Tanaka Kogyo (USA) Co.

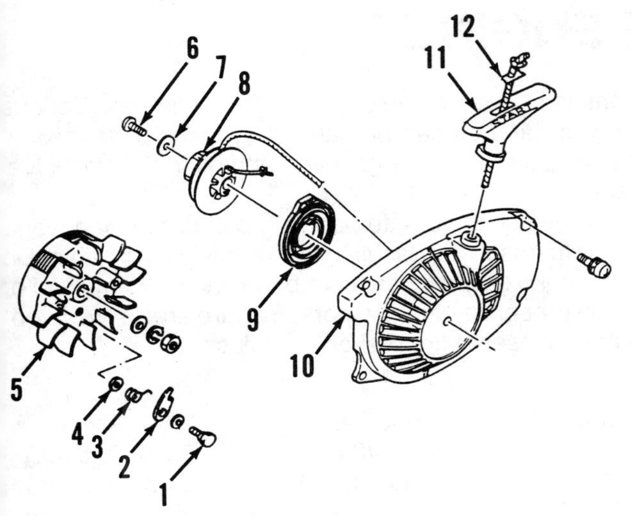

Fig. TK56—Exploded view of rewind starter assembly.

1. Screw
2. Pawl
3. Spring
4. Washer
5. Flywheel
6. Screw
7. Washer
8. Rope pulley
9. Rewind spring
10. Starter housing
11. Rope handle
12. Retainer

er operation. Rewind spring tension is correct if rope handle is pulled snugly against housing with rope fully retracted and if pulley will rotate at least an additional half turn with rope fully extended. If rewind spring binds before rope is fully extended, reduce tension on rope by pulling rope up into notch in rope pulley and allowing pulley to unwind one turn. Recheck starter operation.

Illustrations courtesy Tanaka Kogyo (USA) Co.

TWO-STROKE ENGINES

MIXING GASOLINE AND OIL

Most two-stroke engines are lubricated by oil mixed with the gasoline. The manufacturers carefully determine which type of oil and how much oil should be mixed with the gasoline to provide the most desirable operation, then list these mixing instructions. Often, two or more gasoline-to-oil ratios will be listed depending upon type of oil or severity of service.

You should always follow the manufacturer's recommended mixing instructions, because mixing the wrong amount of oil or using the wrong type of oil can cause extensive engine damage. Too much oil can cause lower power, spark plug fouling and excessive carbon buildup. Not enough oil will cause inadequate lubrication and will probably result in scuffing, seizure or other forms of engine damage.

Use only the gasoline type and octane rating recommended by manufacturer. Never use gasoline that has been stored for a long period of time.

Accurate measurement of gasoline and oil is necessary to assure correct lubrication. Proper quantities of gasoline and oil for some of the more common mixture ratios are shown in the accompanying chart.

When mixing, use a separate, approved, safety container that is large enough to hold the desired amount of fuel with additional space for mixing. Pour about half the required amount of gasoline into container, add the required amount of oil, then shake vigorously until completely mixed. Pour remaining amount of gasoline into container, then complete mixing by shaking. Serious engine damage can be caused by incomplete mixing. Never attempt to mix gasoline and oil in the unit's fuel tank.

Always observe safe handling practices when working with gasoline. Gasoline is extremely flammable. Do not smoke or allow sparks or open flame around fuel or in the presence of fuel vapors. Be sure area is well-ventilated. Observe fire prevention rules.

Ratio	Gasoline	Oil
14:1	0.9 Gal. (3.4 L)	8 oz. (235 mL)
16:1	1.0 Gal. (3.8 L)	8 oz. (235 mL)
20:1	1.25 Gal. (4.7 L)	8 oz. (235 mL)
25:1	1.5 Gal. (5.7 L)	8 oz. (235 mL)
30:1	1.9 Gal. (7.2 L)	8 oz. (235 mL)
32:1	2.0 Gal. (7.6 L)	8 oz. (235 mL)
40:1	2.5 Gal. (9.4 L)	8 oz. (235 mL)
50:1	3.1 Gal. (11.7 L)	8 oz. (235 mL)

Ratio	Gasoline	Oil
14:1	1 Gal. (3.8 L)	9.1 oz. (270 mL)
16:1	1 Gal. (3.8 L)	8.0 oz. (235 mL)
20:1	1 Gal. (3.8 L)	6.4 oz. (190 mL)
25:1	1 Gal. (3.8 L)	5.1 oz. (150 mL)
30:1	1 Gal. (3.8 L)	4.2 oz. (125 mL)
32:1	1 Gal. (3.8 L)	4.0 oz. (120 mL)
40:1	1 Gal. (3.8 L)	3.2 oz. (95 mL)
50:1	1 Gal. (3.8 L)	2.5 oz. (75 mL)

METRIC CONVERSION

Square centimeters	x .155	= Square inches	
Square centimeters	= 6.4515	x Square inches	
Square meters	x 10.7641	= Square feet	
Square meters	= .0929	x Square feet	
Cubic centimeters	x .061025	= Cubic inches	
Cubic centimeters	= 16.387	x Cubic inches	
Cubic meters	x 35.3156	= Cubic feet	
Cubic meters	= .0283	x Cubic feet	
Cubic meters	x 1.308	= Cubic yards	
Cubic meters	= .765	x Cubic yards	
Liters	x 61.023	= Cubic inches	
Liters	= .0164	x Cubic inches	
Liters	x .2642	= U.S. gallons	
Liters	= 3.7854	x U.S. gallons	
Grams	x 15.4324	= Grains	
Grams	= .0648	x Grains	
Grams	x .03527	= Ounces avoirdupois	
Grams	= 28.3495	x Ounces avoirdupois	
Kilograms	x 2.2046	= Pounds	
Kilograms	= .4536	x Pounds	
Kilograms per square centimeter	x 14.2231	= Pounds per square inch	
Kilograms per square centimeter	= .0703	x Pounds per square inch	
Kilograms per cubic meter	x .06243	= Pounds per cubic foot	
Kilograms per cubic meter	= 16.0189	x Pounds per cubic foot	
Metric tons (1000 kilograms)	x 1.1023	= Tons (2000 pounds)	
Metric tons (1000 kilograms)	= .9072	x Tons (2000 pounds)	
Kilowatts	= .746	x Horsepower	
Kilowatts	x 1.3405	= Horsepower	
Millimeters	x .03937	= Inches	
Millimeters	= 25.4	x Inches	
Meters	x 3.2809	= Feet	
Meters	= .3048	x Feet	
Kilometers	x .62138	= Miles	
Kilometers	= 1.6093	x Miles	

METRIC CONVERSION

MM.	INCHES			MM.	INCHES			MM.	INCHES			MM.	INCHES			MM.	INCHES			MM.	INCHES		
1	0.0394	1/32	+	51	2.0079	2.0	+	101	3.9764	3 31/32	+	151	5.9449	5 15/16	+	201	7.9134	7 29/32	+	251	9.8819	9 7/8	+
2	0.0787	3/32	−	52	2.0472	2 1/16	−	102	4.0157	4 1/32	−	152	5.9842	5 31/32	+	202	7.9527	7 15/16	+	252	9.9212	9 29/32	+
3	0.1181	1/8	−	53	2.0866	2 3/32	−	103	4.0551	4 1/16	−	153	6.0236	6 1/32	−	203	7.9921	8.0	−	253	9.9606	9 31/32	−
4	0.1575	5/32	+	54	2.1260	2 1/8	+	104	4.0945	4 3/32	+	154	6.0630	6 1/16	+	204	8.0315	8 1/32	+	254	10.0000	10.0	
5	0.1969	3/16	+	55	2.1654	2 5/32	+	105	4.1339	4 1/8	+	155	6.1024	6 3/32	+	205	8.0709	8 1/16	+	255	10.0393	10 1/32	+
6	0.2362	1/4	−	56	2.2047	2 7/32	−	106	4.1732	4 3/16	−	156	6.1417	6 5/32	−	206	8.1102	8 1/8	−	256	10.0787	10 3/32	−
7	0.2756	9/32	−	57	2.2441	2 1/4	−	107	4.2126	4 7/32	−	157	6.1811	6 3/16	−	207	8.1496	8 5/32	−	257	10.1181	10 1/8	−
8	0.3150	5/16	+	58	2.2835	2 9/32	+	108	4.2520	4 1/4	+	158	6.2205	6 7/32	+	208	8.1890	8 3/16	+	258	10.1575	10 5/32	+
9	0.3543	11/32	+	59	2.3228	2 5/16	+	109	4.2913	4 9/32	+	159	6.2598	6 1/4	+	209	8.2283	8 7/32	+	259	10.1968	10 3/16	+
10	0.3937	13/32	−	60	2.3622	2 3/8	−	110	4.3307	4 11/32	−	160	6.2992	6 5/16	−	210	8.2677	8 9/32	−	260	10.2362	10 1/4	−
11	0.4331	7/16	−	61	2.4016	2 13/32	−	111	4.3701	4 3/8	−	161	6.3386	6 11/32	−	211	8.3071	8 5/16	−	261	10.2756	10 9/32	−
12	0.4724	15/32	+	62	2.4409	2 7/16	+	112	4.4094	4 13/32	+	162	6.3779	6 3/8	+	212	8.3464	8 11/32	+	262	10.3149	10 5/16	+
13	0.5118	1/2	+	63	2.4803	2 15/32	+	113	4.4488	4 7/16	+	163	6.4173	6 13/32	+	213	8.3858	8 3/8	+	263	10.3543	10 11/32	+
14	0.5512	9/16	−	64	2.5197	2 17/32	−	114	4.4882	4 1/2	−	164	6.4567	6 15/32	−	214	8.4252	8 7/16	−	264	10.3937	10 13/32	−
15	0.5906	19/32	−	65	2.5591	2 9/16	−	115	4.5276	4 17/32	−	165	6.4961	6 1/2	−	215	8.4646	8 15/32	−	265	10.4330	10 7/16	−
16	0.6299	5/8	+	66	2.5984	2 19/32	+	116	4.5669	4 9/16	+	166	6.5354	6 17/32	+	216	8.5039	8 1/2	+	266	10.4724	10 15/32	+
17	0.6693	21/32	+	67	2.6378	2 5/8	+	117	4.6063	4 19/32	+	167	6.5748	6 9/16	+	217	8.5433	8 17/32	+	267	10.5118	10 1/2	+
18	0.7087	23/32	−	68	2.6772	2 11/16	−	118	4.6457	4 21/32	−	168	6.6142	6 5/8	−	218	8.5827	8 19/32	−	268	10.5512	10 9/16	−
19	0.7480	3/4	−	69	2.7165	2 23/32	−	119	4.6850	4 11/16	−	169	6.6535	6 21/32	−	219	8.6220	8 5/8	−	269	10.5905	10 19/32	−
20	0.7874	25/32	+	70	2.7559	2 3/4	+	120	4.7244	4 23/32	+	170	6.6929	6 11/16	+	220	8.6614	8 21/32	+	270	10.6299	10 5/8	+
21	0.8268	13/16	+	71	2.7953	2 25/32	+	121	4.7638	4 3/4	+	171	6.7323	6 23/32	+	221	8.7008	8 11/16	+	271	10.6693	10 21/32	+
22	0.8661	7/8	−	72	2.8346	2 27/32	−	122	4.8031	4 13/16	−	172	6.7716	6 25/32	−	222	8.7401	8 3/4	−	272	10.7086	10 23/32	−
23	0.9055	29/32	−	73	2.8740	2 7/8	−	123	4.8425	4 27/32	−	173	6.8110	6 13/16	−	223	8.7795	8 25/32	−	273	10.7480	10 3/4	−
24	0.9449	15/16	+	74	2.9134	2 29/32	+	124	4.8819	4 7/8	+	174	6.8504	6 27/32	+	224	8.8189	8 13/16	+	274	10.7874	10 25/32	+
25	0.9843	31/32	+	75	2.9528	2 15/16	+	125	4.9213	4 29/32	+	175	6.8898	6 7/8	+	225	8.8583	8 27/32	+	275	10.8268	10 13/16	+
26	1.0236	1 1/32	−	76	2.9921	3.0	−	126	4.9606	4 31/32	−	176	6.9291	6 15/16	−	226	8.8976	8 29/32	−	276	10.8661	10 7/8	−
27	1.0630	1 1/16	+	77	3.0315	3 1/32	+	127	5.0000	5.0		177	6.9685	6 31/32	−	227	8.9370	8 15/16	−	277	10.9055	10 29/32	−
28	1.1024	1 3/32	+	78	3.0709	3 1/16	+	128	5.0394	5 1/32	+	178	7.0079	7.0	+	228	8.9764	8 31/32	+	278	10.9449	10 15/16	+
29	1.1417	1 5/32	−	79	3.1102	3 1/8	−	129	5.0787	5 3/32	−	179	7.0472	7 1/16	−	229	9.0157	9 1/32	−	279	10.9842	10 31/32	+
30	1.1811	1 3/16	−	80	3.1496	3 5/32	−	130	5.1181	5 1/8	−	180	7.0866	7 3/32	−	230	9.0551	9 1/16	−	280	11.0236	11 1/32	−
31	1.2205	1 7/32	+	81	3.1890	3 3/16	+	131	5.1575	5 5/32	+	181	7.1260	7 1/8	+	231	9.0945	9 3/32	+	281	11.0630	11 1/16	+
32	1.2598	1 1/4	+	82	3.2283	3 7/32	+	132	5.1968	5 3/16	+	182	7.1653	7 5/32	+	232	9.1338	9 1/8	+	282	11.1023	11 3/32	+
33	1.2992	1 5/16	−	83	3.2677	3 9/32	−	133	5.2362	5 1/4	−	183	7.2047	7 7/32	−	233	9.1732	9 3/16	−	283	11.1417	11 5/32	−
34	1.3386	1 11/32	−	84	3.3071	3 5/16	−	134	5.2756	5 9/32	−	184	7.2441	7 1/4	−	234	9.2126	9 7/32	−	284	11.1811	11 3/16	−
35	1.3780	1 3/8	+	85	3.3465	3 11/32	+	135	5.3150	5 5/16	+	185	7.2835	7 9/32	+	235	9.2520	9 1/4	+	285	11.2204	11 7/32	+
36	1.4173	1 13/32	+	86	3.3858	3 3/8	+	136	5.3543	5 11/32	+	186	7.3228	7 5/16	+	236	9.2913	9 9/32	+	286	11.2598	11 1/4	+
37	1.4567	1 15/32	−	87	3.4252	3 7/16	−	137	5.3937	5 13/32	−	187	7.3622	7 3/8	−	237	9.3307	9 11/32	−	287	11.2992	11 5/16	−
38	1.4961	1 1/2	−	88	3.4646	3 15/32	−	138	5.4331	5 7/16	−	188	7.4016	7 13/32	−	238	9.3701	9 3/8	−	288	11.3386	11 11/32	−
39	1.5354	1 17/32	+	89	3.5039	3 1/2	+	139	5.4724	5 15/32	+	189	7.4409	7 7/16	+	239	9.4094	9 13/32	+	289	11.3779	11 3/8	+
40	1.5748	1 9/16	+	90	3.5433	3 17/32	+	140	5.5118	5 1/2	+	190	7.4803	7 15/32	+	240	9.4488	9 7/16	+	290	11.4173	11 13/32	+
41	1.6142	1 5/8	−	91	3.5827	3 19/32	−	141	5.5512	5 9/16	−	191	7.5197	7 17/32	−	241	9.4882	9 1/2	−	291	11.4567	11 15/32	−
42	1.6535	1 21/32	−	92	3.6220	3 5/8	−	142	5.5905	5 19/32	−	192	7.5590	7 9/16	−	242	9.5275	9 17/32	−	292	11.4960	11 1/2	−
43	1.6929	1 11/16	+	93	3.6614	3 21/32	+	143	5.6299	5 5/8	+	193	7.5984	7 19/32	+	243	9.5669	9 9/16	+	293	11.5354	11 17/32	+
44	1.7323	1 23/32	+	94	3.7008	3 11/16	+	144	5.6693	5 21/32	+	194	7.6378	7 5/8	+	244	9.6063	9 19/32	+	294	11.5748	11 9/16	+
45	1.7717	1 25/32	−	95	3.7402	3 3/4	−	145	5.7087	5 23/32	−	195	7.6772	7 11/16	−	245	9.6457	9 21/32	−	295	11.6142	11 5/8	−
46	1.8110	1 13/16	−	96	3.7795	3 25/32	−	146	5.7480	5 3/4	−	196	7.7165	7 23/32	−	246	9.6850	9 11/16	−	296	11.6535	11 21/32	−
47	1.8504	1 27/32	+	97	3.8189	3 13/16	+	147	5.7874	5 25/32	+	197	7.7559	7 3/4	+	247	9.7244	9 23/32	+	297	11.6929	11 11/16	+
48	1.8898	1 7/8	+	98	3.8583	3 27/32	+	148	5.8268	5 13/16	+	198	7.7953	7 25/32	+	248	9.7638	9 3/4	+	298	11.7323	11 23/32	+
49	1.9291	1 15/16	−	99	3.8976	3 29/32	−	149	5.8661	5 7/8	−	199	7.8346	7 27/32	−	249	9.8031	9 13/16	−	299	11.7716	11 25/32	−
50	1.9685	1 31/32	−	100	3.9370	3 15/16	−	150	5.9055	5 29/32	−	200	7.8740	7 7/8	−	250	9.8425	9 27/32	−	300	11.8110	11 13/16	−

NOTE: The + or − sign indicates that the decimal equivalent is larger or smaller than the fractional equivalent.

OBSOLETE PARTS BUYERS' GUIDE

The following is a listing of sources offering old and obsolete parts and accessories for chain saws that are no longer available from the usual sources. The sources' addresses and phone numbers are listed in the SOURCE DIRECTORY. A cross-reference by parts makes and brands is listed in the CROSS-REFERENCE DIRECTORY.

These listings were compiled by *Power Equipment Trade* magazine, a publication of Hatton-Brown Publishers, Inc., P.O. Box 2268, Montgomery, AL 36102. The listings were provided courtesy of *Power Equipment Trade* magazine to Intertec Publishing for reprint in this service manual.

The listings are free, and the information came directly from those listed. If you, or someone you know is not included in the listings as a source and should be, please notify Intertec Publishing and/or *Power Equipment Trade* magazine so that the master list may be updated.

This obsolete parts source directory is provided solely for the convenience of users of this service manual. Intertec Publishing or *Power Equipment Trade* magazine does not recommend, endorse, or verify the accuracy of any of the listings, and has no responsibility connected with transactions or negotiations between parties using this directory.

SOURCE DIRECTORY

ARNOLD'S LAWN & GARDEN EQUIPMENT
7010 Blue Pkwy.
Kansas City, MO 64129
(816) 923-6440 Fax: (816) 924-2275
John Deere, Stihl.

BEAVER CREEK TRACTOR SERVICE
381 Carlson Road
Elgin, OK 73538
(580) 365-4805
David Bradley, Husqvarna, Poulan, Sears, Stihl.

BOB'S LAWNMOWER ENGINE SERVICE
7632 State Hwy. 7
Maryland, NY 12116
(607) 638-9297
Green Machine, McCulloch.

BROWNELL LANDCLEARING
83 Dover Point Road
Dover, NH 03820
(603) 742-3723
Homelite, McCulloch, Mall, Strunk, Lombard.

CARTWRIGHT MAC'S
211 S. St. Francis
Wichita, KS 67202
(316) 267-1401
Echo, Homelite, Pioneer, Shindaiwa.

CLOONAN'S AIR COOLED ENGINES
RD No. 2, Hall Road
Oswego, NY 13126
(315) 343-3104
Homelite, Mall, Clinton, Jonsered, Partner.

COMPTON MACHINE & REPAIR
801 W. 13th Street
Lamar, MO 64759
(417) 682-5163
Pioneer.

GABHART SAW SERVICE
Rt. 3A, Box 115
Springfield, KY 40069
(606) 262-5654
Mall, Remington.

GIZMO'S SMALL ENGINE SALES & SERVICE
21307 W. Main Street
Greenleaf, ID 83626
(208) 459-4867
Poulan, Shindaiwa, TML.

GUIHO SAW SALES
950 Riverside Drive
Timmins, Ont., Can. P4N 3W3
(705) 264-4119
Husqvarna, Stihl.

HALVORSON SERVICE
70 Himango Road
Esko, MN 55733
(218) 879-4947
Jonsered.

HOLZHAUER, JAMES
Rt. 2, Box 34
Sorento, IL 62086
(618) 664-4339
Mall, Homelite.

JACOBS EQUIPMENT
Box 37
Elcho, WI 54428
(715) 275-3530
Alpina, Castor.

JONES & IRELAND REPAIR
15 Kings Hwy, N.
Westport, CT 06880
(203) 227-2431
Homelite, McCulloch.

MEARL'S CHAIN SAW SHOP
1107 2nd St., Box 324
Britton, SC 57430
(605) 448-2563
McCulloch, Wizz, Wright, Tecumseh.

MIDWEST SPRAY INC.
4515 Reading Road
Cincinnati, OH 45229
(513) 242-4500
Lombard, Dynamark, Timbercut.

PARRISH IMPLEMENT
913 E. Liberty 51
Box 4128
Louisville, KY 40204
(502) 584-6346
Wright, Poulan.

RED FOX PARTS & EQUIPMENT
Rt. 30
Schoharie, NY 12157
(518) 295-8900
Lombard, Pioneer, Stihl, Remington.

RITE WAY
714 N. Ardmore Ave.
Villa Park, IL 60181
(708) 834-4321
Partner, search service for any parts.

RON'S SAW SALES
RR1, Box 122A
Lake Norden, SD 57248
(605) 882-1234
Stihl.

WALTER A. SMITH INC.
Box 8, Rt. 611
Riegeisville, PA 18077
(215) 749-2151
Echo, Homelite, McCulloch, Stihl.

SWISHER REPAIR
Rt. 150, Box 489
Avis, PA 17721
(717) 769-7276
Homelite, Jonsered.

TAIT DISTRIBUTORS
14136-128 Avenue
Edmonton, Alb., Can. T5L 3H5
(403) 451-4321
McCulloch.

VISSER RADIATOR SERVICE
2940 T Ave.
Herington, KS 67440
(785) 258-2800
Homelite.

WALLENBERG SALES CORP.
8311 Secura Wy.
Santa Fe Springs, CA 90670
(213) 698-2543, (800) 225-4756
in CA (800) 523-3907
McCulloch, Partner.

WESTERN WHOLESALE
1200 N. Bluegum Street
Anaheim, CA 92806
(714) 632-9130
Clinton, O & R, Reo, Hahn, Pincore

WHITE ENGINE SERVICE
351 Wilson Rd.
Willshire, OH 45898
(419) 495-2569
Echo.

WILSON'S SAW SHOP
RR 2, Box 449
Osgood, IN 47037
(812) 852-4421
Homelite, Pioneer, Clinton, Power Products, Wright.

ZIP POWER PARTS
2008 E. 33rd Street
Box 10308
Erie, PA 16514
(800) 824-8521
and P.O. Box 5877
London, Ont., Can. N5Y 3G2
Bars and Sprockets.

CROSS-REFERENCE DIRECTORY

This directory lists the chain saw manufacturers in alphabetical order. Following the manufacturer's name is a list of parts sources. Refer to theSource Directory to find the sources' addresses and phone numbers.

ALPINA/CASTOR: Jacobs.

BARS/CHAIN/SPROCKETS: Gabhart, Holzhauer, Wilson's, Zip.

CLINTON: Cloonan's, Western, Wilson's.

DAVID BRADLEY: Beaver Creek.

DYNAMARK: Midwest.

ECHO: Cartwright's, Walter A. Smith, White Engine.

GREEN MACHINE: Bob's Lawn mower.

HAHN: Western Wholesale.

HOMELITE: Brownell, Cartwright's, Hozhauer, Jones & Ireland, Walter A. Smith, Swisher, Visser, Wilson's

HUSQVARNA: Beaver Creek, Guiho.

JOHN DEERE: Arnold's.

JONSERED: Guiho, Halvorson, Swisher.

LOMBARD: Brownell, Gabhart, Holzhauer.

McCULLOCH: Bob's, Brownell, Guiho, Jones & Ireland, Mearl's, Walter A. Smith, Tait, Wallenberg.

O&R (OHLSSON & RICE): Western Wholesale.

PARTNER: Rite Way, Wallenberg.

PARTS SEARCH SERVICE: Rite Way.

PIONEER: Cartwright, Compton, John Wheeler, Red Fox, Wilson's.

POULAN: Beaver Creek, Gizmo's.

REMINGTON: Gabhart, Red Fox, White.

SEARS: Beaver Creek.

SHINDAIWA: Cartwright's, Gizmo's.

STIHL: Arnold's, Beaver Creek, Guiho, Red Fox, Ron's, Walter A. Smith.

STRUNK: Brownell.

TECUMSEH/POWER PRODUCTS: Mearl's, Wilson's.

TIMBERKUT: Midwest.

WIZZ: Mearl's.

WRIGHT: Mearl's, Parrish, Wilson's.

NOTES

NOTES

NOTES

Genuine John Deere Service Literature

For ordering information, call John Deere at 1-800-522-7448.
All major credit cards accepted.

PARTS CATALOG

The parts catalog lists service parts available for your machine with exploded view illustrations to help you identify the correct parts. It is also useful in assembling and disassembling.

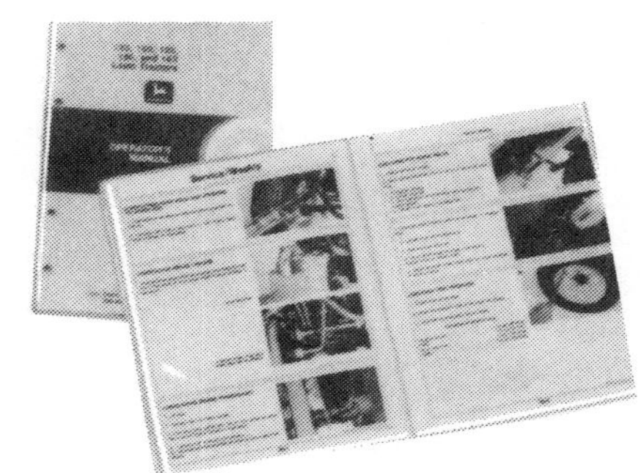

OPERATOR'S MANUAL

The operator's manual provides safety, operating, maintenance, and service information about John Deere machines.

The operator's manual and safety signs on your machine may also be available in other languages.

TECHNICAL AND SERVICE MANUALS

Technical and service manuals are service guides for your machine. Included in the manual are specifications, diagnosis, and adjustments. Also illustrations of assembly and disassembly procedures, hydraulic oil flows, and wiring diagrams.

Component technical manuals are required for some products. These supplemental manuals cover specific components.

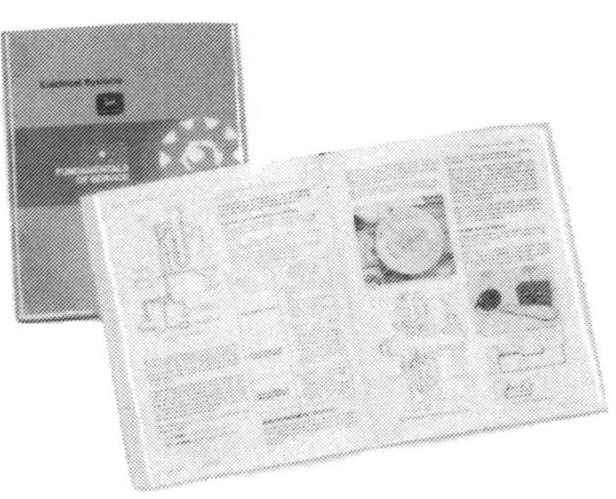

FUNDAMENTALS OF SERVICE MANUALS

These basic manuals cover most makes and types of machines. FOS manuals tell you how to SERVICE machine systems. Each manual starts with basic theory and is fully illustrated with colorful diagrams and photographs. Both the "whys" and "hows" of adjustments and repairs are covered in this reference library.